Koren Talmud Bavli

EIRUVIN · PART ONE

Shefa

KOREN

תלמוד בבלי

KOREN TALMUD BAVLI

DAF YOMI SIZE

עירובין א

EIRUVIN · PART ONE

COMMENTARY BY

Rabbi Adin Even-Israel
(Steinsaltz)

EDITOR-IN-CHIEF

Rabbi Dr Tzvi Hersh Weinreb

EXECUTIVE EDITOR

Rabbi Joshua Schreier

•

SHEFA FOUNDATION
KOREN PUBLISHERS JERUSALEM

Supported by the Matanel Foundation

Koren Talmud Bavli
Volume 4: Tractate Eiruvin, Part One
Daf Yomi Size

ISBN 978 965 301 611 8

First Hebrew/English Edition, 2012

Koren Publishers Jerusalem Ltd.
PO Box 4044, Jerusalem 91040, ISRAEL
PO Box 8531, New Milford, CT 06776, USA
www.korenpub.com

Shefa Foundation

Shefa Foundation is the parent organization of institutions established by Rabbi Adin Even-Israel (Steinsaltz)

PO Box 45187, Jerusalem 91450 ISRAEL
Telephone: +972 2 646 0900, Fax +972 2 624 9454
www.hashefa.co.il

Hardcover design by Ben Gasner

Shefa

Managing Editor
Rabbi Jason Rappoport

Senior Content Editor
Rabbi Dr. Shalom Z. Berger

Editors
Rabbi Joshua Amaru, *Coordinating Editor*
Rabbi David Jay Derovan
Rabbi Dov Karoll
Rabbi Adin Krohn
Sally Mayer
Rabbi Avishai Magence, *Content Curator*
Rabbi Jonathan Mishkin
Gavriel Reiss
Shira Shmidman
Rabbi Michael Siev
Avi Steinhart
Rabbi David Strauss
Rabbi Abe Y. Weschler

Copy Editors
Aliza Israel, *Coordinator*
Bracha Hermon
Ita Olesker
Shira Finson
Debbie Ismailoff
Ilana Sobel

Language Consultants
Dr. Stephanie E. Binder, *Greek & Latin*
Yaakov Hoffman, *Arabic*
Dr. Shai Secunda, *Persian*

KOREN

Design & Typesetting
Raphaël Freeman, *Design & Typography*
Dena Landowne Bailey, *Typesetting*
Tani Bayer, *Jacket Design*

Images
Rabbi Eliahu Misgav, *Illustration*
Yehudit Cohen, *Image Acquisition*

Digital Edition
Raphaël Freeman, *Team Leader*
Eliyahu Skoczylas, *Senior Architect*
Tani Bayer, *User Interface Design*
Dena Landowne Bailey, *Concept*
Rabbi Hanan Benayahu, *Concept*
Laura Messinger, *Commercial Liaison*

Contents

For the vocalized Vilna Shas layout, please open as a Hebrew book.

Haskama

Rabbi Moshe Feinstein

RABBI MOSES FEINSTEIN
455 F. D. R. DRIVE
New York, N. Y. 10002
ORegon 7-1222

משה פיינשטיין
ר"ם תפארת ירושלים
בנוא יארק

בע"ה

הנה ראיתי הפירוש החשוב של הרב הגאון מוהר"ר עדין שטיינזלץ
שליט"א מעיה"ק ירושלים, על מסכתות ביצה ור"ה. באמת כבר ידוע
לי פירושו של הרה"ג הנ"ל על מסכתות מתלמוד בבלי, וכבר כתבתי
מכתב הסכמה עליהם. ובאתי בזה רק להדגיש מחדש איך שהפירושים
של הרה"ג הנ"ל, שכולל פירוש חדש על הגמרא עצמו וגם פירוש שיש
בו סיכום להלכה מהנידונים שבגמרא, נוסף לעוד כמה חלקים, הם
באמת עבודה גדולה, שיכולים להיות לתועלת לא רק לאלו שכבר
מורגלים בלמוד הגמרא, ורוצים להעמק יותר, אלא גם לאלו שמתחילים
ללמוד, להדריכם בדרכי התורה איך להבין ולהעמיק בים התלמוד.

והריני מברך להרה"ג הנ"ל שיצליחהו השי"ת בספריו אלו ושיזכה
לחבר עוד ספרים, להגדיל תורה ולהאדירה, לתפארת השם ותורתו.

ועל זה באתי על החתום לכבוד התורה ביום ז' לחודש אייר תשמ"ג.

משה פיינשטיין

משה פיינשטיין

...These new commentaries – which include a new interpretation of the Talmud, a halakhic summary of the debated issues, and various other sections – are a truly outstanding work; they can be of great benefit not only to those familiar with talmudic study who seek to deepen their understanding, but also to those who are just beginning to learn, guiding them through the pathways of the Torah and teaching them how to delve into the sea of the Talmud.

I would like to offer my blessing to this learned scholar. May the Holy One grant him success with these volumes and may he merit to write many more, to enhance the greatness of Torah, and bring glory to God and His word...

Rabbi Moshe Feinstein
New York, 7 Adar 5743

ר׳ משה פיינשטיין שליט״א
הנה ראיתי את מסכת אחת מהש״ס שנקד אותה וגם צייר צורות הצמחים וכדומה מדברים שלא ידוע לכמה אנשים הרה״ג ר׳ עדין שטייגזלץ מירושלים שליט״א וגם הוסיף שם בגליון פירושים והידושים וניכר שהוא ת״ח וראויין לעיין בהם ת״ח ובני הישיבה וטוב גם לקנותם בבתי כנסיות ובבתי מדרשות שיש שיהיו להם לתועלת. — ועל זה באתי עה״ח ג׳ אדר ב׳ תש״ל.
נאם משה פיינשטיין
ר״מ תפארת ירושלים, ניו־יורק, ארה״ב

I have seen one tractate from the Talmud to which the great scholar Rabbi Adin Steinsaltz שליט״א has added *nikkud* (vowels) and illustrations to explain that which is unknown to many people; he has also added interpretations and innovations, and is evidently a *talmid hakham*. *Talmidei hakhamim* and yeshiva students ought to study these volumes, and synagogues and *batei midrash* would do well to purchase them, as they may find them useful.

Rabbi Moshe Feinstein
New York, Adar 5730

 THIS HASKAMA REFERS TO THE ORIGINAL HEBREW EDITION OF THE STEINSALTZ TALMUD, UPON WHICH THIS VOLUME IS BASED

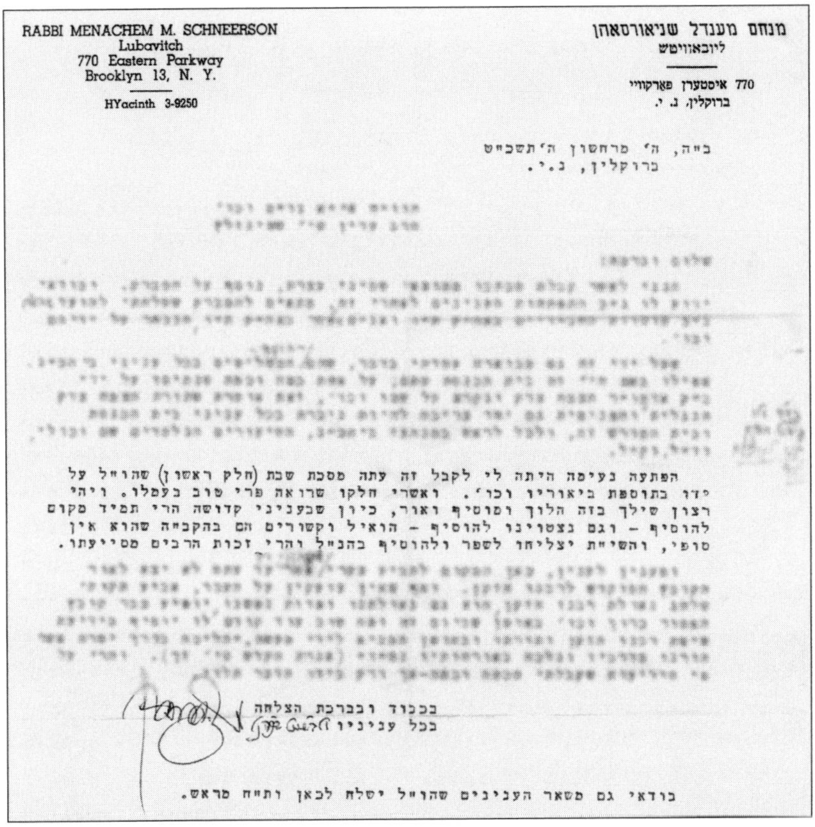

RABBI MENACHEM M. SCHNEERSON
Lubavitch
770 Eastern Parkway
Brooklyn 13, N. Y.

HYacinth 3-9250

מנחם מענדל שניאורסאהן
ליובאוויטש

770 איסטערן פארקוויי
ברוקלין, נ. י.

ב״ה, ה׳ מרחשון ה׳תשכ״ט
ברוקלין, נ.י.

הפתעה נעימה היתה לי לקבל זה עתה מסכת שבת (חלק ראשון) שהו״ל על ידו בתוספת ביאוריו וכו׳. ואשרי חלקו שרואה פרי טוב בעמלו. ויהי רצון שילך בזה הלוך ומוסיף ואור, כיון שבעניני קדושה הרי תמיד מקום להוסיף – וגם נצטוינו להוסיף – הואיל וקשורים הם בהקב״ה שהוא אין סופי, והשי״ת יצליחו לשפר ולהוסיף בהנ״ל והרי זכות הרבים מסייעתו.

בכבוד וברכת הצלחה
בכל עניניו

בודאי גם משאר העניינים שהו״ל ישלח לכאן ותי״ח מראש.

…I have just had the pleasant surprise of receiving tractate *Shabbat* (part one), which has been published by [Rabbi Steinsaltz] along with his explanations, etc. Happy is the man who sees good fruits from his labors. May he continue in this path and increase light, for in the matters of holiness there is always room to add – and we have been commanded to add – for they are linked to the Holy One, Blessed be He, Who is infinite. And may the Holy One grant him success to improve and enhance this work, since the greater good strengthens his hand…

Rabbi Menachem Mendel Schneerson
The Lubavitcher Rebbe
Brooklyn, 5 Marḥeshvan, 5729

Haskama
Rabbi Menachem Mendel Schneerson

Haskama

Rabbi Moshe Zvi Neria

י״ג כסלו של הרב משה צבי נריה

ב"ה

"ושמעו ביום ההוא החרשים דברי ספר"

(ישעי׳ כט׳ יח׳)

תרגום ספרי קדמונים לשפת דורות אחרונים – היא משימתם של חכמי דור ודור. ובישראל שמצוות "ושננתם לבניך" מקיפה את כל חלקי האומה, ודאי שהיתה זאת המשימה בכל עידן ועידן.

בכל דור כך, ובדורנו אשר רבים בו הקרובים שנתרחקו וחוזרים ומתקרבים – לא כל שכן. כי רבים היום האומרים "מי ישקנו מים מבאר" התלמוד, ומועטים הם הדולים ומשקים.

ראוי אפוא להערכה מיוחדת נסיונו המבורך של הצעיר המופלא, הרב עדין שטינזלץ, לפרש פרקי-תלמוד בהסברה מורחבת-תמציתית, אשר נוסף על הפרוש המלולי והעניני הוא מעלה גם את ההגיון של הדברים ומתרגמת אותם לשפת-המושגים של בן-דורנו.

דומה שכל הנגשים אל חומר למודי מתוך רצון להבינו – התלמיד החרוץ והמבוגר המשכיל – לא יתקלו בשום קושי בבואם ללמוד סוגיא תלמודית לפי פרוש זה. ולא עוד אלא שיש לקוות כי ההסברה הגיונית תעמידם מיד על טוב-הטעם [redacted] של דף-הגמרא, והם ימשכו יותר ויותר אל הלמוד העיוני הזה אשר טובי המוחות בישראל לנו בעומקו, ואשר ממנו פינה, ממנו יתד לבנין חיינו.

נועם ד׳ על המפרש הנמרץ להמשיך במפעלו, וברוכים כל העוזרים להוצאתו לאור-עולם.

ביקר אורייתא

(חתימה)

The translation of the books of our past into the language of the present – this was the task of the sages of every generation. And in Israel, where the command to "teach them repeatedly to your children" applies to all parts of the nation, it was certainly the task of every era. This is true for every generation, and in our time – when many of those who have strayed far are once again drawing near – all the more so. For many today say, "Who will let us drink from the well" of Talmud, and few are those who offer up the waters to drink.

We must, therefore, particularly commend the blessed endeavor of Rabbi Adin Steinsaltz to explain the chapters of the Talmud in this extensive yet succinct commentary, which, in addition to its literal interpretation of the text, also explicates the latter's underlying logic and translates it into the language of our generation.

It appears that all those who seek to study Talmud – the diligent student and the learned adult – will have no difficulty understanding when using this commentary. Moreover, we may hope that the logical explanation will reveal to them the beauty of the talmudic page, and they will be drawn deeper and deeper into the intellectual pursuit which has engaged the best Jewish minds, and which serves as the cornerstone of our very lives…

Rabbi Moshe Zvi Neria

ב"ה

MORDECHAI ELIAHU

FORMER CHIEF RABBI OF ISRAEL & RICHON LEZION

מרדכי אליהו

הראשון לציון והרב הראשי לישראל לשעבר

ז' בתשרי תשנ"ד
נד.5-137

מכתב ברכה

הגמרא בעירובין כ"א: אומרת: דרש רבא מאי דכתיב ויותר שהיה קהלת חכם, עוד לימד דעת את העם - ואזן וחקר תקן משלים הרבה". לימד דעת את העם - קבע כיצד לקרוא פסוק וסימנים בין תיבות המקרא וממשיכה הגמרא ואומרת: אמר עולא אמר ר' אליעזר בתחילה היתה תורה דומה לכפיפה שאין לה אזנים עד שבא שלמה ועשה לה אזנים". וכדברי רש"י שם: "וע"י כך אוחזין ישראל במצוות שנתרחקו מן העבירה כדרך שנוח לאחוז בכלי שיש לו בית יד וכו' (ערובין כ"א, י').

דברים מעין אלו אפשר לאמר על האי גברא יקירא, על איש מורם מעם, משכמו ומעלה בתורה ובמידות. ויותר ממה שעשה בתורה שבע"פ עושה בתורה שבכתב - מלמד דעת את העם. ולא זו בלבד אלא גם עושה אזנים לתורה, היא תורת התלמוד שהוא חתום וסתום בפני רבים. ורק מעט מזער מבני עליה שהם מועטים ומי שלומד בישיבה יכל כיום ללמוד בש"ס ולהבין מה שלפניו, ואף שיש לנו פירוש רש"י, עדין לא הכל ממשמשין בו. עד שקם הרב הגדול מעוז ומגדול הרה"ג ר' **עדין שטיינזלץ** שליט"א ועשה אזנים לתורה, שאפשר לאחוז גמרא ביד וללמוד, ואפי' לפשוטי העם ועשה פרושים ושם אותם בצד הארון, פרושים נאים בשפה ברורה ונעימה דבר דבור על אופניו. ועם הסברים וציורים להבין ולהשכיל, כדי שמי שרוצה לקרבה אל מלאכת ה' ללמוד יכל לעשות זאת.

ועיני ראו ולא זר שבשיעורי תורה בגמרא הרבה באים עם גמרות בידם ואלה שבאים עם "פירוש הרב שטיינזלץ לתלמוד הבבלי" הם מוכנים ומבינים טוב יותר. כי כבר יש להם הקדמה מפרושיו ומבאוריו.
ואמינא לפועלו יישר ומן שמיא זכו ליה ללמד דעת את העם .

ויהי רצון שחפץ בידו יצלח, וכל אשר יפנה ישכיל ויצליח, ויזכה להגדיל תורה ולהאדירה, ויוסיף לנו עוד גמרות מבוארות כהנה וכהנה עד לסיומו , "וישראל עושה חיל".

ובזכות לימוד תורה ואני זאת בריתי וכו', ובא לציון גואל, בב"א.

מרדכי אליהו
ראשון לציון הרב הראשי לישראל לשעבר

Haskama
Rabbi Mordechai Eliyahu

The Talmud in *Eruvin* 21b states: "Rava continued to interpret verses homiletically. What is the meaning of the verse: 'And besides being wise, Kohelet also taught the people knowledge; and he weighed, and sought out, and set in order many proverbs'? (Ecclesiastes 12:9). He explains: He taught the people knowledge; he taught it with the accentuation marks in the Torah, and explained each matter by means of another matter similar to it. And he weighed [*izen*], and sought out, and set in order many proverbs; Ulla said that Rabbi Eliezer said: At first the Torah was like a basket without handles [*oznayim*] until Solomon came and made handles for it." And as Rashi there explains: "And thus were Israel able to grasp the mitzvot and distance themselves from transgressions – just as a vessel with handles is easily held, etc."

Such things may be said of this beloved and eminent man, a great sage of Torah and of virtue. And far more than he has done with the Oral Torah, he does with the Written Torah – teaching the people knowledge. And beyond that, he also affixes handles to the Torah, i.e., to the Talmud, which is obscure and difficult for many. Only the intellectual elite, which are a precious few, and those who study in yeshiva, can today learn the Talmud and understand what it says – and even though we have Rashi, still not everyone uses him. But now the great scholar Rabbi Adin Steinsaltz שליט״א has come and affixed handles to the Torah, allowing the Talmud to be held and studied, even by simple men. And he has composed a commentary alongside the text, a fine commentary in clear, comprehensible language, "a word fitly spoken" with explanations and illustrations, so that all those who seek to study the work of God can do so.

Rabbi Mordechai Eliyahu
Former Chief Rabbi of Israel, 7 Tishrei, 5754

Message from Rabbi Adin Even-Israel (Steinsaltz)

The Talmud is the cornerstone of Jewish culture. True, our culture originated in the Bible and has branched out in directions besides the Talmud, yet the latter's influence on Jewish culture is fundamental. Perhaps because it was composed not by a single individual, but rather by hundreds and thousands of Sages in *batei midrash* in an ongoing, millennium-long process, the Talmud expresses not only the deepest themes and values of the Jewish people, but also of the Jewish spirit. As the basic study text for young and old, laymen and learned, the Talmud may be said to embody the historical trajectory of the Jewish soul. It is, therefore, best studied interactively, its subject matter coming together with the student's questions, perplexities, and innovations to form a single intricate weave. In the entire scope of Jewish culture, there is not one area that does not draw from or converse with the Talmud. The study of Talmud is thus the gate through which a Jew enters his life's path.

The *Koren Talmud Bavli* seeks to render the Talmud accessible to the millions of Jews whose mother tongue is English, allowing them to study it, approach it, and perhaps even become one with it.

This project has been carried out and assisted by several people, all of whom have worked tirelessly to turn this vision into an actual set of books to be studied. It is a joyful duty to thank the many partners in this enterprise for their various contributions. Thanks to Koren Publishers Jerusalem, both for the publication of this set and for the design of its very complex graphic layout. Thanks of a different sort are owed to the Shefa Foundation and its director, Rabbi Menachem Even-Israel, for their determination and persistence in setting this goal and reaching it. Many thanks to the translators, editors, and proofreaders for their hard and meticulous work. Thanks to the individuals and organizations that supported this project, chief among them the Matanel Foundation. And thanks in advance to all those who will invest their time, hearts, and minds in studying these volumes – to learn, to teach, and to practice.

Rabbi Adin Even-Israel (Steinsaltz)
Jerusalem 5772

Introduction by the Editor-in-Chief

The vastly expanded audience of Talmud study in our generation is a phenomenon of historical proportions. The reasons for this phenomenon are many, and include the availability of a wide array of translations, commentaries, and study aids.

One outstanding example of such a work is the translation of the Talmud into modern Hebrew by Rabbi Adin Even-Israel (Steinsaltz). The product of a lifetime of intense intellectual labor, this translation stands out in its uniqueness.

But what can the interested student do if he or she does not comprehend the Hebrew, even in its modern form? Where is the English speaker who wishes to access this instructive material to turn?

The *Koren Talmud Bavli* that you hold in your hand is designed to be the answer to those questions.

This work is the joint effort of Rabbi Steinsaltz himself, his closest advisory staff, and Koren Publishers Jerusalem. It is my privilege to have been designated Editor-in-Chief of this important project, and to have worked in close collaboration with a team of translators and proofreaders, artists and graphic designers, scholars and editors.

Together we are presenting to the English-speaking world a translation that has all the merits of the original Hebrew work by Rabbi Steinsaltz, and provides assistance for the beginner of any age who seeks to obtain the necessary skills to become an adept talmudist.

This is the fourth volume of the project, tractate *Eiruvin*, part I. It includes the entire original text, in the traditional configuration and pagination of the famed Vilna edition of the Talmud. This enables the student to follow the core text with the commentaries of Rashi, *Tosafot*, and the customary marginalia. It also provides a clear English translation in contemporary idiom, faithfully based upon the modern Hebrew edition.

At least equal to the linguistic virtues of this edition are the qualities of its graphic design. Rather than intimidate students by confronting them with a page-size block of text, we have divided the page into smaller thematic units. Thus, readers can focus their attention and absorb each discrete discussion before proceeding to the next unit. The design of each page allows for sufficient white space to ease the visual task of reading. The illustrations, one of the most innovative features of the Hebrew edition, have been substantially enhanced and reproduced in color.

The end result is a literary and artistic masterpiece. This has been achieved through the dedicated work of a large team of translators, headed by Rabbi Joshua Schreier, and through the unparalleled creative efforts of Raphaël Freeman and his gifted staff.

The group of individuals who surround Rabbi Steinsaltz and support his work deserve our thanks as well. I have come to appreciate their energy, initiative, and persistence. And I thank the indefatigable Rabbi Menachem Even-Israel, whom I cannot praise highly enough. The quality of his guidance and good counsel is surpassed only by his commitment to the dissemination and perpetuation of his father's precious teachings.

Finally, in humility, awe, and great respect, I acknowledge Rabbi Adin Even-Israel (Steinsaltz). I thank him for the inspirational opportunity he has granted me to work with one of the outstanding sages of our time.

Rabbi Tzvi Hersh Weinreb
Jerusalem 5772

Preface by the Executive Editor

Tractate *Eiruvin* is regarded as one of the most difficult tractates to comprehend both conceptually and technically. The discussions of the joining of courtyards and Shabbat limits, as well as the merging of alleyways, provide myriad challenges to beginners and accomplished scholars alike.

In the middle of the first chapter (13b), a roadmap to successful Torah study is provided in this famous talmudic passage: "Rabbi Abba said that Shmuel said: For three years Beit Shammai and Beit Hillel disagreed. These said: The *halakha* is in accordance with our opinion, and these said: The *halakha* is in accordance with our opinion. Ultimately, a Divine Voice emerged and proclaimed: Both these and those are the words of the living God. However, the *halakha* is in accordance with the opinion of Beit Hillel."

The message is clear. There is room for more than one legitimate opinion in the study of God's Torah.

The Gemara continues and asks: Since both these and those are the words of the living God, why were Beit Hillel privileged to have the *halakha* established in accordance with their opinion? If both are legitimate, why is the opinion of Beit Hillel preferred?

Surprisingly, the answer has little to do with scholarship. The reason is that they were agreeable and forbearing, showing restraint when affronted, and when they taught the *halakha* they would teach both their own statements and the statements of Beit Shammai. Moreover, when they formulated their teachings, in deference to Beit Shammai, when citing a dispute they prioritized the statements of Beit Shammai over their own statements.

Beit Hillel serve as paradigmatic role models for all those studying Torah. One who seeks preeminence must combine excellence in scholarship together with exemplary personal conduct. It is only the fulfillment of mitzvot between man and his Maker in tandem with mitzvot between man and his fellow man that is the hallmark of a true Torah scholar.

The *Koren Talmud Bavli* seeks to follow in the footsteps of Beit Hillel.

Its user-friendly layout, together with its accessible translation, takes the Steinsaltz commentary on the Talmud one step further. It opens the doors to even more students who might have previously felt excluded from the exciting give and take of the study hall, enabling them to take their place as full-fledged participants in the world of Talmud study.

My involvement in the production of the *Koren Talmud Bavli* has been both a privilege and a pleasure. The Shefa Foundation, headed by Rabbi Menachem Even-Israel and devoted to the dissemination of the wide-ranging, monumental works of Rabbi Adin Even-Israel (Steinsaltz), constitutes the Steinsaltz side of this partnership; Koren Publishers Jerusalem, headed by Matthew Miller, with the day-to-day management in the able hands of Raphaël Freeman, constitutes the publishing side of this partnership. The combination of the inspiration, which is the hallmark of Shefa, with the creativity and professionalism for which Koren is renowned and which I experience on a daily basis, has lent the *Koren Talmud Bavli* its outstanding quality in terms of both content and form.

I would like to express my appreciation for Rabbi Dr. Tzvi Hersh Weinreb, the Editor-in-Chief, whose insight and guidance have been invaluable. The contribution of my friend and colleague, Rabbi Dr. Shalom Z. Berger, the Senior Content Editor, cannot be overstated; his title does not begin to convey the excellent direction he has provided in all aspects of this project. The erudite and articulate men and women who serve as translators, editors and proofreaders have ensured that this project adheres to the highest standards.

There are several others whose contributions to this project cannot be overlooked. On the Steinsaltz side: Meir HaNegbi, Yacov Elbert, Tsipora Ifrah, and Oria Tubul. On the Koren side, my colleagues at Koren: Rabbi David Fuchs, Rabbi Hanan Benayahu, Efrat Gross, Rachel Hanstater Meghnagi, Eliyahu Misgav, Rabbi Yinon Chen, and Rabbi Carmiel Cohen. Their assistance in all matters, large and small, is appreciated.

At the risk of being repetitious, I would like to thank Rabbi Dr. Berger for introducing me to the world of Steinsaltz. Finally, I would like to thank Rabbi Menachem Even-Israel, with whom it continues to be a pleasure to move forward in this great enterprise.

Rabbi Joshua Schreier
Jerusalem 5772

Introduction by the Publisher

The Talmud has sustained and inspired Jews for thousands of years. Throughout Jewish history, an elite cadre of scholars has absorbed its learning and passed it on to succeeding generations. The Talmud has been the fundamental text of our people.

Beginning in the 1960s, Rabbi Adin Even-Israel (Steinsaltz) שליט״א created a revolution in the history of Talmud study. His translation of the Talmud, first into modern Hebrew and then into other languages, as well the practical learning aids he added to the text, have enabled millions of people around the world to access and master the complexity and context of the world of Talmud.

It is thus a privilege to present the *Koren Talmud Bavli*, an English translation of the talmudic text with the brilliant elucidation of Rabbi Steinsaltz. The depth and breadth of his knowledge are unique in our time. His rootedness in the tradition and his reach into the world beyond it are inspirational.

Working with Rabbi Steinsaltz on this remarkable project has been not only an honor, but a great pleasure. Never shy to express an opinion, with wisdom and humor, Rabbi Steinsaltz sparkles in conversation, demonstrating his knowledge (both sacred and worldly), sharing his wide-ranging interests, and, above all, radiating his passion. I am grateful for the unique opportunity to work closely with him, and I wish him many more years of writing and teaching.

Our intentions in publishing this new edition of the Talmud are threefold. First, we seek to fully clarify the talmudic page to the reader – textually, intellectually, and graphically. Second, we seek to utilize today's most sophisticated technologies, both in print and electronic formats, to provide the reader with a comprehensive set of study tools. And third, we seek to help readers advance in their process of Talmud study.

To achieve these goals, the *Koren Talmud Bavli* is unique in a number of ways:

- The classic *tzurat hadaf* of Vilna, used by scholars since the 1800s, has been reset for great clarity, and opens from the Hebrew "front" of the book. Full *nikkud* has been added to both the talmudic text and Rashi's commentary, allowing for a more fluent reading with the correct pronunciation; the commentaries of *Tosafot* have been punctuated. Upon the advice of many English-speaking teachers of Talmud, we have separated these core pages from the translation, thereby enabling the advanced student to approach the text without the distraction of the translation. This also reduces the number of volumes in the set. At bottom of each *daf*, there is a reference to the corresponding English pages. In addition, the Vilna edition was read against other manuscripts and older print editions, so that texts which had been removed by non-Jewish censors have been restored to their rightful place.
- The English translation, which starts on the English "front" of the book, reproduces the *menukad* Talmud text alongside the English translation (in bold) and commentary and explanation (in a lighter font). The Hebrew and Aramaic text is presented in logical paragraphs. This allows for a fluent reading of the text for the non-Hebrew or non-Aramaic reader. It also allows for the Hebrew reader to refer easily to the text alongside. Where the original text features dialogue or poetry, the English text is laid out in a manner appropriate to the genre. Each page refers to the relevant *daf*.

- Critical contextual tools surround the text and translation: personality notes, providing short biographies of the Sages; language notes, explaining foreign terms borrowed from Greek, Latin, Persian, or Arabic; and background notes, giving information essential to the understanding of the text, including history, geography, botany, archeology, zoology, astronomy, and aspects of daily life in the talmudic era.
- Halakhic summaries provide references to the authoritative legal decisions made over the centuries by the rabbis. They explain the reasons behind each halakhic decision as well as the ruling's close connection to the Talmud and its various interpreters.
- Photographs, drawings, and other illustrations have been added throughout the text – in full color in the Standard and Electronic editions, and in black and white in the Daf Yomi edition – to visually elucidate the text.

This is not an exhaustive list of features of this edition, it merely presents an overview for the English-speaking reader who may not be familiar with the "total approach" to Talmud pioneered by Rabbi Steinsaltz.

Several professionals have helped bring this vast collaborative project to fruition. My many colleagues are noted on the Acknowledgements page, and the leadership of this project has been exceptional.

RABBI MENACHEM EVEN-ISRAEL, DIRECTOR OF THE SHEFA FOUNDATION, was the driving force behind this enterprise. With enthusiasm and energy, he formed the happy alliance with Koren and established close relationships among all involved in the work.

RABBI DR. TZVI HERSH WEINREB שליט״א, EDITOR-IN-CHIEF, brought to this project his profound knowledge of Torah, intellectual literacy of Talmud, and erudition of Western literature. It is to him that the text owes its very high standard, both in form and content, and the logical manner in which the beauty of the Talmud is presented.

RABBI JOSHUA SCHREIER, EXECUTIVE EDITOR, assembled an outstanding group of scholars, translators, editors, and proofreaders, whose standards and discipline enabled this project to proceed in a timely and highly professional manner.

RABBI MEIR HANEGBI, EDITOR OF THE HEBREW EDITION OF THE STEINSALTZ TALMUD, lent his invaluable assistance throughout the work process, supervising the reproduction of the Vilna pages.

RAPHAËL FREEMAN, EXECUTIVE EDITOR OF KOREN, created this Talmud's unique typographic design which, true to the Koren approach, is both elegant and user-friendly.

It has been an enriching experience for all of us at Koren Publishers Jerusalem to work with the Shefa Foundation and the Steinsaltz Center to develop and produce the *Koren Talmud Bavli*. We pray that this publication will be a source of great learning and, ultimately, greater *Avodat Hashem* for all Jews.

Matthew Miller, Publisher
Koren Publishers Jerusalem
Jerusalem 5772

Introduction to **Eiruvin**

See that God has given you the Shabbat, therefore He has given you on the sixth day the bread of two days; remain every man in his place, let no man go out of his place on the seventh day.

(Exodus 16:29)

If you turn away your foot because of the Shabbat, from pursuing your business on My holy day; and call the Shabbat a delight, and the holy of God honorable; and shall honor it by not doing your usual ways, nor pursuing your business, nor speaking of it; then you shall delight yourself in God, and I will make you ride upon the high places of the earth, and I will feed you with the heritage of Jacob your father; for the mouth of God has spoken it.

(Isaiah 58:13–14)

Neither carry forth a burden out of your houses on the Shabbat day, nor do any work; but make the Shabbat day holy, as I commanded your fathers.

(Jeremiah 17:22)

Tractate *Eiruvin,* in its entirety, is an elaboration and conclusion of the subject matter discussed in tractate *Shabbat,* as it focuses on one aspect of the *halakhot* of Shabbat that was not comprehensively elucidated. Tractate Shabbat opened with a discussion of the prohibited labor of carrying out on Shabbat. Tractate *Eiruvin* analyzes the details of the rabbinic laws that apply to this act. This prohibited labor is unique in that it is not an inherently creative act; rather, it is merely the act of transferring an object from one domain to another.

In essence, the labor of carrying out highlights the significance of Shabbat as a day of rest; not only a day during which specific activities are prohibited, but also a day on which a premium is placed on quiet, rest, and a sense of relaxation. Shabbat demands that one take a break from the everyday hustle-and-bustle of moving and carrying from the public to the private domain and vice versa. Similarly, the public thoroughfare calms down from its weekday business and trade. This is accomplished by the creation of domains that are unique to Shabbat. That is, they do not correspond to the domains in force with regard to the rules of commerce, nor those of ritual purity. Transference between different domains is forbidden, as is carrying in the public domain.

The laws of Shabbat recognize four basic domains:

- A private domain
- A public domain
- A *karmelit,* which is an intermediate domain, neither public nor private
- An exempt domain, which is not really a domain at all

In effect, there are only three domains on Shabbat: the private and the public, both of which are domains by Torah law, and the *karmelit,* which is a domain by rabbinic law. All other areas fall into the category of exempt domain.

The private domain is an area of four handbreadths by four handbreadths; a handbreadth is the distance from the tip of the thumb to the tip of the little finger, or slightly more. A private domain is separated from the area around it by walls that are at least ten handbreadths high. In terms of the *halakhot* of Shabbat, an area is a private domain even if it is open to the public and available for use.

The public domain is a thoroughfare at least sixteen cubits wide; a cubit is the distance from the elbow to the end of the index finger. According to some opinions, for an area to be defined as a public domain it must also be frequented by more than 600,000 people daily. The *halakhot* of the public domain apply only up to a height of ten handbreadths.

According to Torah law, these are the two primary domains. The Sages added a third, the *karmelit,* whose legal status by rabbinic law is that of a public domain. The *karmelit* is at least four handbreadths by four handbreadths and not surrounded by walls. Examples of this domain are fields, lakes, etc.

An exempt domain is an area of less than four handbreadths by four handbreadths. In addition, the airspace above ten handbreadths in a public domain or a *karmelit* is an exempt domain, where the *halakhot* of carrying do not apply.

For many years, these domains constituted the only restrictions with regard to carrying out and movement on Shabbat. After the Jewish people settled and began to develop their land, the rabbinic leadership grew concerned that in the course of mundane living in towns and villages, Shabbat was not accorded its due. In particular, the distinctions between the domains of Shabbat were obfuscated; their theoretical parameters did not correspond to the actual utilization of those areas, and the domains and their *halakhot* were interchanged. After all, a private domain full of people and activity could appear, at least superficially, indistinguishable from a public domain. Moreover, people were able to engage in most of their typical weekday activities without actually violating any of the Torah prohibitions. Consequently, the idea of Shabbat as a day of rest was not realized.

Already in the First Temple era, the rabbinic Sages began to issue decrees intended to raise the general level of consciousness concerning Shabbat observance. These decrees fall into the category of *shevut,* prohibitions by rabbinic law designed to enhance the character of Shabbat as a day of rest. Such decrees severely limited the permitted uses of the private domains and placed renewed emphasis on the plain meaning of the passage in Exodus that is the source for all of the Shabbat domains: "Let no man go out of his place on the seventh day." The Sages' decrees limited the designation of private domains to those places that actually belong to an individual and his family. Private domains utilized by more than one individual, e.g., a courtyard shared by several households, as well as the alleyways and paths into which courtyards open, were rendered public domains by rabbinic law.

The decrees issued by the Sages are the starting point for tractate *Eiruvin*. The tractate attempts to arrive at practical solutions for the problems created by these restrictions. The objective is not to abrogate the decrees, but rather to discover alternative methods to underscore the differences between the public and private domains. Similarly, the tractate attempts to discover how one could go beyond the Shabbat limits while maintaining the framework that requires limiting travel on Shabbat. The myriad ordinances that constitute the bulk of tractate *Eiruvin* work within the framework of the established principles of the *halakhot* of Shabbat. Within the halakhic framework, there is extensive use of a series of abstract concepts, e.g., domain, limit, partition, and space. Although these principles are often the basis for stringencies and restrictions, they can also serve as the basis for far-reaching leniencies. The two primary concepts analyzed in the framework of tractate *Eiruvin* are the essence of a partition and the essence of a residence.

The partition is a fundamental component of domains, alleyways, courtyards, houses, and more. Clearly a solid wall with no openings is a partition; however, in most cases the demarcation is less clear cut. At times, the wall is not sturdy enough to serve as a partition. At times, there are windows, doorways, and other spaces in the wall. At times, the wall does not cover the entire opening. It was therefore necessary to create broader criteria that apply to all forms of partitions, despite their quantitative and qualitative differences: Concepts like *lavud*, which determines that objects less than three handbreadths apart are considered joined; *gode*, through which an incomplete partition can be extended upward or downward; *ḥavot*, through which a cross beam is lowered, and others that broaden the parameters of the concept of partition to include incomplete partitions, e.g., cross beam, side post, form of a doorway, and upright boards.

In a similar vein, it must be established what is considered one's fixed residence. Here too, there are clear-cut examples with regard to which there is no uncertainty. One who eats and sleeps and remains in a house that is his alone, certainly has a residence that is exclusively his. However, since reality is a bit more complex, as in practice most people do not live alone and do not spend all their lives in one place. Therefore, it was necessary to create a broader abstract definition of the concept of fixed residence and establish when it is that several people have the legal status of one person, where family relations and dependence unify them, and to what degree must one be tied to or be present at a certain place in order to be considered a resident. Once these definitions are determined, the simplistic distinction between resident and guest is no longer necessarily significant. The concept of one's residence can, on the one hand, be restricted to the individual alone, while on the other hand it can be expanded to include others. Based on the expansive interpretation of the concept of residence, the possibility of establishing the joining of the courtyards, the merging of the alleyways, and the joining of the Shabbat boundaries becomes feasible.

While some of these solutions might appear to be a disingenuous attempt to circumvent the fundamental *halakha*, in fact, life in accordance with halakhic principles requires their formulation and definition in an abstract and expansive manner. Especially in the case of *eiruv*, where the original prohibitions are rabbinic in nature, there is room for far-reaching leniency in implementing these halakhic principles.

Eiruvin is divided into ten chapters, the first four of which are included in the present volume:

Chapter One of *Eiruvin* deals with an alleyway that is open to the public domain on one side, and into which several courtyards open. In order for all residents of the houses in those courtyards to carry in the alleyway, there are two requirements:

Every household must contribute to a jointly owned food item. All the residents of the courtyard assume the legal status of one extended household. This is in fact the *eiruv* for which this tractate is named.

A physical change must be made in the alleyway to symbolically demarcate it from the public domain. This may be accomplished with the addition of a side post positioned near the entrance or a cross beam over the entranceway, which will facilitate awareness that one is leaving a private domain and entering a public domain.

Chapter Two discusses the special ordinances of upright boards and the *halakhot* of those parts of the private domain that are not used as residences.

Chapter Three discusses the food items which may be used in establishing an *eiruv*. The chapter continues with a discussion of the *halakhot* of the joining of Shabbat boundaries and the uncertainties that arise with regard to the effectiveness of joining boundaries in different cases.

Chapter Four continues the discussion of the joining of Shabbat boundaries. It treats the establishment of limits for one who goes beyond his designated limit, or for one who has no residence and seeks to acquire one for the purposes of joining the boundaries.

The *halakhot* in this tractate are not merely theoretical. Hundreds of *eiruvin* have been established in cities and towns throughout the United States and around the world based on real-world application of the principles found in this tractate.

Introduction to **Perek I**

This chapter deals primarily with the modifications undertaken in order to render alleyways fit for one to carry within them on Shabbat. More specifically, it discusses the *halakhot* governing alleyways that open into the public domain on one side and are closed on the other three sides by virtue of the partitions of the courtyards and houses located there. Consequently, the public cannot pass through this closed alleyway. An open alleyway, on the other hand, is a small and narrow passageway that is so seldom used that it cannot be considered a public domain, yet, being that it is open on opposite ends, it serves as a passageway from one public domain to another.

In order to establish an *eiruv* in an alleyway enabling the residents of the alleyway to carry objects there on Shabbat, two actions must be taken: First, every household must contribute to a jointly owned food item. All the residents of the courtyard then assume the legal status of one extended household and it is permitted for them to carry there on Shabbat. This action, the merging of alleyways, is elucidated in later chapters of this tractate. The second action involves modification of the alleyway itself. The purpose of this modification is to clearly demarcate the alleyway as distinct from the public domain. Accordingly, a symbolic fourth partition is placed at the point where the alleyway and the public domain intersect. There are three types of symbolic partitions; they are a cross beam, a side post, and the form of a doorway. A crossbeam is placed over the entrance to the alleyway. A side post is placed adjacent to the wall on the side of the entrance to the alleyway. The form of a doorway consisting of two doorposts and a lintel is considered an effective symbolic partition even in open-ended alleyways. These partitions accentuate the fact that the alleyway is closed to the public.

These methods were universally accepted by the Sages. However, the details of these *halakhot* require elaboration. The focus of this chapter is, then, to elucidate in detail the *halakhot* of side posts, cross beams, and forms of doorways, how they are created, their dimensions, and the extent of their legal effect. These clarifications are tied to a more fundamental analysis of the essence of all these partitions: Are they merely symbolic partitions serving as conspicuous markers, or are they actual partitions that meet the minimal requirements of the *halakha*? This leads to another question: What is the legal status of the alleyway in terms of *halakha* in general, and in terms of the *halakhot* of Shabbat in particular? Clarification of these issues from several perspectives constitutes the primary focus this chapter.

מתני׳ מָבוֹי שֶׁהוּא גָּבוֹהַּ לְמַעְלָה מֵעֶשְׂרִים אַמָּה – יְמַעֵט. רַבִּי יְהוּדָה אוֹמֵר: אֵינוֹ צָרִיךְ.

MISHNA If an alleyway is enclosed on three sides with courtyards opening into it from three sides, and the fourth side opens into a public domain, it is prohibited by rabbinic law to carry objects in it on Shabbat. However, carrying in an alleyway under those circumstances is permitted if a cross beam is placed horizontally over the entrance to the alleyway. The mishna teaches that if the cross beam spans the entrance to **an alleyway** at a **height above twenty cubits, one must diminish** the height of the cross beam so that it is less than twenty cubits.[H] **Rabbi Yehuda says: He need not** diminish it, since the cross beam enables one to carry in the alleyway even at that height.[N]

וְהָרָחָב מֵעֶשֶׂר אַמּוֹת – יְמַעֵט. וְאִם יֵשׁ לוֹ צוּרַת הַפֶּתַח, אַף עַל פִּי שֶׁהוּא רָחָב מֵעֶשֶׂר אַמּוֹת – אֵין צָרִיךְ לְמַעֵט.

If the entrance to the alleyway is **wider than ten cubits, one must diminish** its width. **However, if** the entrance to the alleyway **has the form of a doorway,**[B] i.e., two vertical posts on the two sides, and a horizontal beam spanning the space between them, **even if it is wider than ten cubits, he need not diminish** it, as it is then regarded as an entrance, rather than a breach, even if it is very wide.

גמ׳ תְּנַן הָתָם: סוּכָּה שֶׁהִיא גְּבוֹהָה לְמַעְלָה מֵעֶשְׂרִים אַמָּה – פְּסוּלָה, וְרַבִּי יְהוּדָה מַכְשִׁיר. מַאי שְׁנָא גַּבֵּי סוּכָּה דְּתָנֵי ״פְּסוּלָה״ וְגַבֵּי מָבוֹי תָּנֵי תַּקַּנְתָּא?

GEMARA **We learned** in a mishna **there,** in tractate *Sukka*: **A *sukka* that is more than twenty cubits high is unfit,**[H] **and Rabbi Yehuda deems it fit.** The *halakhot* are similar in substance but differ in formulation, and accordingly the Gemara asks: **What is the difference** that **with regard to a *sukka*** the mishna **teaches** that it is **unfit, whereas with regard to an alleyway, it teaches** the method of **rectification,** that one must diminish the height of the cross beam?

סוּכָּה דְּאוֹרַיְיתָא – תָּנֵי פְּסוּלָה, מָבוֹי דְּרַבָּנַן – תָּנֵי תַּקַּנְתָּא.

The Gemara answers: With regard to ***sukka,*** since it is a mitzva **by Torah law,** the mishna **teaches** that it is **unfit,** as if it is not constructed in the proper manner, no mitzva is fulfilled. Whereas with regard to **an alleyway,** where the entire prohibition of carrying is only **by rabbinic law,**[N] the mishna **teaches** the method of **rectification,** as the cross beam comes only to rectify a rabbinic prohibition, but does not involve a mitzva by Torah law.

וְאִיבָּעֵית אֵימָא: דְּאוֹרַיְיתָא נַמִי תָּנֵי תַּקַּנְתָּא, אֶלָּא: סוּכָּה דִּנְפִישִׁין מִילֵּיהּ – פָּסֵיק וְתָנֵי ״פְּסוּלָה״, מָבוֹי דְּלָא נְפִישֵׁי מִילֵּיהּ – תָּנֵי תַּקַּנְתָּא.

The Gemara suggests an alternative explanation: **And if you wish, say** instead that **even** with regard to matters prohibited **by Torah law,** it would have been appropriate for the mishna to teach a method of **rectification. However,** with regard to ***sukka,*** **whose matters are numerous, it categorically teaches** that it is **unfit.** Merely diminishing the height of a *sukka* is insufficient to render it fit; it must also satisfy requirements governing its size, its walls, and its roofing. Teaching the remedy for each disqualification would have required lengthy elaboration. With regard to **an alleyway,** however, **whose matters are not numerous,** the mishna **teaches** the method of **rectification.** Once the height is diminished, it is permitted to carry in the alleyway.

HALAKHA

An alleyway that is higher than twenty cubits – מָבוֹי הַגָּבוֹהַּ מֵעֶשְׂרִים: A cross beam spanning the entrance of an alleyway does not render the alleyway fit for carrying within it on Shabbat if it is more than twenty cubits above the ground. However, a side post renders the alleyway fit for carrying within it, in accordance with the unattributed mishna (*Shulḥan Arukh, Oraḥ Ḥayyim* 363:26).

A *sukka* that is higher than twenty cubits – סוּכָּה הַגְּבוֹהָה מֵעֶשְׂרִים: A *sukka* that is more than twenty cubits high is unfit, in accordance with the mishna in tractate *Sukka* (*Shulḥan Arukh, Oraḥ Ḥayyim* 633:1).

BACKGROUND

The form of a doorway – צוּרַת הַפֶּתַח:

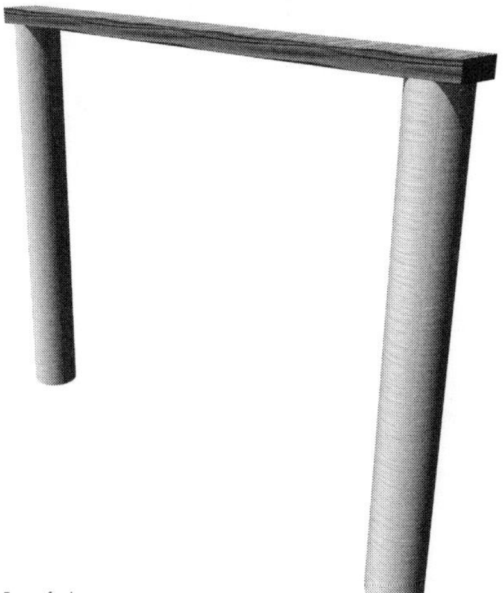

Form of a doorway

NOTES

Opinions of Rabbi Yehuda and the Rabbis – שִׁיטַת רַבִּי יְהוּדָה וְהַחֲכָמִים: According to the Gemara's conclusion, this dispute is not about the interpretation of biblical verses. Rather, Rabbi Yehuda derived his position from palace doorways, which are exceedingly high and wide. However, in the Jerusalem Talmud, as well as in the commentaries of Rabbi Yehonatan, the *Me'iri*, and Rabbi Ovadia Bartenura, the dispute is a fundamental one with regard to the function and significance of the cross beam. According to the Rabbis, the cross beam merely serves as a conspicuous sign. When it is higher than twenty cubits it is not conspicuous. Rabbi Yehuda maintains that the legal status of a cross beam is that of an actual wall, in accordance with the principle: The edge of a ceiling extends downward and seals the space. Therefore, it is effective even above twenty cubits.

An alleyway by rabbinic law – מָבוֹי דְּרַבָּנַן: Although the Gemara later attributes the institution of *eiruv* to King Solomon, nevertheless, since the *halakha* is not explicitly written in the Torah, it is classified as rabbinic, similar to other later ordinances, including those mentioned in the Prophets (Rav Nissim Gaon).

אָמַר רַב יְהוּדָה אָמַר רַב: חֲכָמִים לֹא לְמָדוּהָ אֶלָּא מִפִּתְחוֹ שֶׁל הֵיכָל, וְרַבִּי יְהוּדָה לֹא לְמָדָהּ אֶלָּא מִפִּתְחוֹ שֶׁל אוּלָם.

Rav Yehuda said that **Rav said: The Rabbis only derived** this *halakha*, that an opening more than twenty cubits high is not considered an entrance, **from the doorway of the Sanctuary,** the inner sanctum of the Temple. **And Rabbi Yehuda only derived** his opinion, that even an opening more than twenty cubits high is considered an entrance, **from the doorway of the Entrance Hall** leading into the Sanctuary.[B]

דִּתְנַן: פִּתְחוֹ שֶׁל הֵיכָל גׇּבְהוֹ עֶשְׂרִים אַמָּה וְרׇחְבּוֹ עֶשֶׂר אַמּוֹת, וְשֶׁל אוּלָם גׇּבְהוֹ אַרְבָּעִים אַמָּה וְרׇחְבּוֹ עֶשְׂרִים אַמּוֹת.

As we learned in a mishna: **The doorway of the Sanctuary is twenty cubits high and ten cubits wide, and that of the Entrance Hall is forty cubits high and twenty cubits wide.**[H]

וּשְׁנֵיהֶן מִקְרָא אֶחָד דָּרְשׁוּ: "וּשְׁחָטוֹ פֶּתַח אֹהֶל מוֹעֵד". דְּרַבָּנַן סָבְרִי: קְדוּשַּׁת הֵיכָל לְחוּד, וּקְדוּשַּׁת אוּלָם לְחוּד. וְכִי כְּתִיב: "פֶּתַח אֹהֶל מוֹעֵד" – אַהֵיכָל כְּתִיב.

The Gemara explains the basis of this tannaitic dispute. **Both of them,** the Rabbis and Rabbi Yehuda, **interpreted the same verse homiletically:** "And he shall lay his hand upon the head of his offering **and slaughter it at the doorway of the Tent of Meeting,** and Aaron's sons, the priests, shall sprinkle the blood on the altar round about" (Leviticus 3:2). **As the Rabbis hold** that **the sanctity of the Sanctuary is discrete and the sanctity of the Entrance Hall is discrete,** i.e., the Sanctuary and the Entrance Hall have distinct levels of sanctity.[N] **And** since the essence of the Temple is the Sanctuary and not the Entrance Hall, and since the Sanctuary in the Temple parallels the Tent of Meeting in the Tabernacle, **when** the verse **speaks of the doorway of the Tent of Meeting, it is referring to** the doorway of **the Sanctuary.** Therefore, the term doorway applies to an opening similar to the doorway of the Sanctuary, which is twenty cubits high. There is no source indicating that an opening with larger dimensions is also considered a doorway.

וְרַבִּי יְהוּדָה סָבַר: הֵיכָל וְאוּלָם קְדוּשָּׁה אַחַת הִיא, וְכִי כְּתִיב: "פֶּתַח אֹהֶל מוֹעֵד" – אַתַּרְוַיְיהוּ הוּא דִּכְתִיב.

And Rabbi Yehuda holds that **the Sanctuary and the Entrance Hall are one,** equal, **sanctity, and** therefore, **when it is written: "The doorway of the Tent of Meeting," it is referring to both of them,** and accordingly, the term doorway applies to a larger entrance as well.

וְאִיבָּעֵית אֵימָא: לְרַבִּי יְהוּדָה נַמִי קְדוּשַּׁת אוּלָם לְחוּד, וּקְדוּשַּׁת הֵיכָל לְחוּד. וְהָכָא הַיְינוּ טַעְמָא דְּרַבִּי יְהוּדָה – דִּכְתִיב: "אֶל פֶּתַח אוּלָם הַבַּיִת".

The Gemara suggests an alternative understanding of the dispute. **And if you wish, say** instead that **even according to Rabbi Yehuda, the sanctity of the Sanctuary is discrete and the sanctity of the Entrance Hall is discrete. And here, this is the reasoning of Rabbi Yehuda:** By fusing together language from different verses, the result is **as it is written: To the doorway of the Entrance Hall of the House.**[N] Therefore, even the doorway of the Entrance Hall is referred to in the Torah as a doorway, and the same is true of any opening with comparable dimensions.

וְרַבָּנַן אִי הֲוָה כְּתַב: "אֶל פֶּתַח אוּלָם" – כִּדְקָאָמְרַתְּ, הָשְׁתָּא דִּכְתִיב: "אֶל פֶּתַח אוּלָם הַבַּיִת" – הַבַּיִת הַפָּתוּחַ לָאוּלָם.

And the Rabbis say: **Had** the verse **written: "To the doorway of the Entrance Hall,"** it would be interpreted **as you said.** However, **now that it is written: "To the doorway of the Entrance Hall of the House,"** it is to be understood: To the doorway of **the House that opens into the Entrance Hall,** i.e., the Sanctuary, and consequently, the definition of doorway is derived from the dimensions of the doorway of the Sanctuary.

BACKGROUND

Entrance Hall and Sanctuary – אוּלָם וְהֵיכָל: The diagram shows the basic floor plan of the Sanctuary. One entered the building from the east, climbing the stairs into the Entrance Hall. A doorway led to the Sanctuary, where the golden incense altar, the candelabrum, and the table with the showbread stood. A lavishly embroidered curtain divided the Sanctuary from the Holy of Holies at the west end of the building.

The diagram does not depict the rows of chambers that were situated along the outside walls of the Sanctuary and the Holy of Holies. The Temple building overlooked the Priests' Courtyard, the Israelites' Courtyard, and the Women's Courtyard, not pictured.

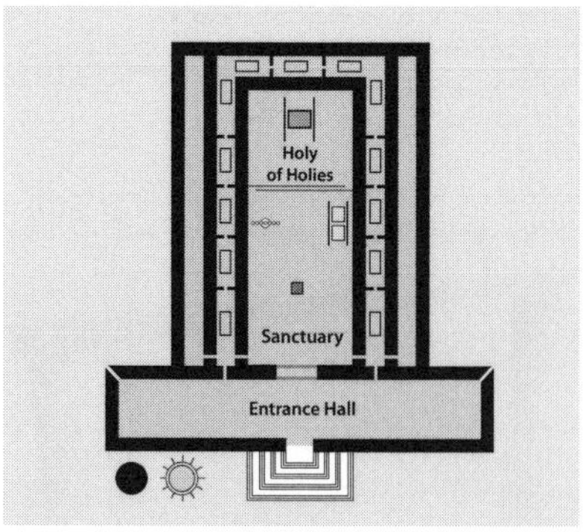

Diagram of Entrance Hall and Sanctuary

HALAKHA

The doorway of the Sanctuary and the Entrance Hall – פֶּתַח הֵיכָל וְאוּלָם: The doorway of the Sanctuary in the Temple was twenty cubits high and ten cubits wide, while the doorway of the Entrance Hall was forty cubits high and twenty cubits wide, as detailed in tractate *Middot* (Rambam *Sefer Avoda, Hilkhot Beit HaBeḥira* 4:7).

NOTES

Sanctity of the Sanctuary and the Entrance Hall – קְדוּשַּׁת הֵיכָל וְאוּלָם: The Rabbis and Rabbi Yehuda dispute the precise relationship between the Tent of Meeting in the desert Tabernacle and the corresponding sections of the Temple in Jerusalem. The Tent in the Tabernacle consisted of only two rooms, the Holy, i.e., the Sanctuary, and the Holy of Holies, while in the Temple the Entrance Hall was appended to the Sanctuary. Therefore, the Sages disagreed whether or not the sanctity of Entrance Hall was equivalent to that of the Sanctuary, in which case anything stated with regard to the Tent of Meeting applied there as well.

The doorway of the Entrance Hall of the House – פֶּתַח אוּלָם הַבַּיִת: *Tosafot* point out that no such verse exists in the Bible. Indeed, inaccurate quotations of verses are quite common in the Talmud. At times a verse is cited in abridged form, or two verses are united. This particular instance can be explained in several ways. One opinion is that the verse "And behold, at the doorway of the Sanctuary of the Lord, between the Entrance Hall and the altar, were about twenty-five men, with their backs to the Sanctuary of God" (Ezekiel 8:16) indicates that the Sanctuary is also called an Entrance Hall.

וְהָא כִּי כְּתִיב הַאי בְּמִשְׁכָּן כְּתִיב!

The Gemara raises a difficulty with the very basis of this explanation: **But when this is written:** "The doorway of the Tent of Meeting," **isn't it written with regard to the Tabernacle** in the wilderness? How can the status in the permanent Sanctuary, i.e., the Temple in Jerusalem, be derived from matters stated with regard to the Tabernacle?

אַשְׁכַּחַן מִשְׁכָּן דְּאִיקְּרִי מִקְדָּשׁ, וּמִקְדָּשׁ דְּאִיקְּרִי מִשְׁכָּן. דְּאִי לָא תֵּימָא הָכִי – הָא דְּאָמַר רַב יְהוּדָה אָמַר שְׁמוּאֵל: שְׁלָמִים שֶׁשְּׁחָטָן קוֹדֶם פְּתִיחַת דַּלְתוֹת הַהֵיכָל – פְּסוּלִין, שֶׁנֶּאֱמַר: "וּשְׁחָטוֹ פֶּתַח אֹהֶל מוֹעֵד" בִּזְמַן שֶׁפְּתוּחִין, וְלֹא בִּזְמַן שֶׁהֵן נְעוּלִים. וְהָא כִּי כְּתִיב הַהִיא בְּמִשְׁכָּן כְּתִיב! אֶלָּא: אַשְׁכַּחַן מִקְדָּשׁ דְּאִיקְּרִי מִשְׁכָּן, וּמִשְׁכָּן דְּאִיקְּרִי מִקְדָּשׁ.

The Gemara answers: **We find that the Tabernacle is called Temple, and that the Temple is called Tabernacle;** therefore, the *halakhot* that govern one can be derived from the other. **As if you do not say so,** that the Tabernacle and the Temple are one with regard to their *halakhot*, **that which Rav Yehuda said** that **Shmuel said: Peace-offerings that were slaughtered** in the Temple **prior to the opening of the doors of the Sanctuary**[H] in the morning **are disqualified** would be difficult. That *halakha* is derived **as it is stated: "And he shall slaughter it at the doorway [*petaḥ*] of the Tent of Meeting,"** from which it is derived: **When** the doors to the Tent of Meeting **are open [*petuḥin*], and not when they are closed. But when this is written:** The doorway of the Tent of Meeting, **isn't it written with regard to the Tabernacle? Rather,** for halakhic purposes, **we find the Temple called Tabernacle, and the Tabernacle called Temple.**

בִּשְׁלָמָא מִקְדָּשׁ דְּאִיקְּרִי מִשְׁכָּן – דִּכְתִיב: "וְנָתַתִּי (אֶת) מִשְׁכָּנִי בְּתוֹכְכֶם". אֶלָּא מִשְׁכָּן דְּאִיקְּרִי מִקְדָּשׁ מְנָלַן? אִילֵימָא מִדִּכְתִיב: "וְנָסְעוּ הַקְּהָתִים נֹשְׂאֵי הַמִּקְדָּשׁ וְהֵקִימוּ אֶת הַמִּשְׁכָּן עַד בֹּאָם"

The Gemara questions its previous conclusion: **Granted, the Temple is called Tabernacle, as it is written: "And I will set My Tabernacle among you"** (Leviticus 26:11), and the reference is to the permanent Sanctuary, i.e., the Temple, as the verse is referring to that which will transpire after the Jewish people settle in their land. **However,** the fact that **the Tabernacle is called Temple, from where do we** derive it? The Gemara answers: **If you say** that it is derived **from that which is written: "And the Kehatites, the bearers of the Temple, set forward, that they may set up the Tabernacle before they came"** (Numbers 10:21),

Perek **I**
Daf **2** Amud **b**

– הַהוּא בָּאָרוֹן כְּתִיב. אֶלָּא מֵהָכָא: "וְעָשׂוּ לִי מִקְדָּשׁ וְשָׁכַנְתִּי בְּתוֹכָם".

that instance of the term Temple **is** not written with regard to the Tabernacle; rather, it is **written with regard to the ark** and the other sacred objects in the Tabernacle, as the sons of Kehat carried only the sacred vessels and not the Tabernacle itself. **Rather,** it is derived **from here: "And let them make Me a Temple that I may dwell among them"** (Exodus 25:8), where the reference is to the Tabernacle.

בֵּין לְרַבָּנַן וּבֵין לְרַבִּי יְהוּדָה לֵילְפוּ מִפֶּתַח שַׁעַר הֶחָצֵר, דִּכְתִיב: "אוֹרֶךְ הֶחָצֵר מֵאָה בָאַמָּה וְרֹחַב חֲמִשִּׁים בַּחֲמִשִּׁים וְקוֹמָה חָמֵשׁ אַמּוֹת" וּכְתִיב: "וַחֲמֵשׁ עֶשְׂרֵה אַמָּה קְלָעִים לַכָּתֵף" וּכְתִיב: "וְלַכָּתֵף הַשֵּׁנִית מִזֶּה וּמִזֶּה לְשַׁעַר הֶחָצֵר קְלָעִים חֲמֵשׁ עֶשְׂרֵה אַמָּה", מַה לְּהַלָּן – חָמֵשׁ בְּרוֹחַב עֶשְׂרִים, אַף כָּאן חָמֵשׁ בְּרוֹחַב עֶשְׂרִים!

The Gemara asks: **Both according to** the opinion of **the Rabbis and according to** the opinion of **Rabbi Yehuda, let them derive** the maximum width of a doorway **from the doorway of the gate of the courtyard** of the Tabernacle. **As it is written: "The length of the courtyard shall be one hundred cubits and the breadth fifty everywhere, and the height five cubits"** (Exodus 27:18). **And it is written: "The hangings on one side of the gate shall be fifteen cubits;** their pillars three and their sockets three" (Exodus 27:14). **And it is written: "And for the other side of the court gate, on this hand and on that hand, were hangings of fifteen cubits;** their pillars three and their sockets three" (Exodus 38:15). If the hangings on both sides of the gate covered thirty of the courtyard's total width of fifty cubits, apparently, the gate of the courtyard was twenty cubits wide and five cubits high. Therefore, **just as there,** with regard to the Tabernacle, an entrance **five** cubits high **by twenty** cubits **wide** is considered a doorway, **so too here,** with regard to the *halakhot* of *eiruv*, an entrance **five** cubits high **by twenty** cubits **wide** should be considered a doorway.

"פֶּתַח שַׁעַר הֶחָצֵר" – אִיקְּרִי, פֶּתַח סְתָמָא – לָא אִיקְּרִי.

The Gemara rejects this assertion: There is no proof from there, as that entrance **is called the doorway of the gate of the courtyard,**[N] but **it is not called a doorway, unmodified.** Consequently, the dimensions of a doorway mentioned without qualification cannot be derived from that doorway.

HALAKHA

Peace-offerings that were slaughtered prior to the opening of the doors of the Sanctuary – שְׁלָמִים שֶׁשְּׁחָטָן קוֹדֶם פְּתִיחַת דַּלְתוֹת הַהֵיכָל: Peace-offerings that were slaughtered prior to the opening of the Sanctuary doors are disqualified, and the same is true if the animal was slaughtered after the doors were open if the Sanctuary doors were temporarily closed, in accordance with the opinion of Shmuel (Rambam *Sefer Avoda, Hilkhot Ma'aseh HaKorbanot* 5:5).

NOTES

The doorway of the gate of the courtyard – פֶּתַח שַׁעַר הֶחָצֵר: The main focus of the question is the width rather than the height of the gate. The Gemara's statement: Just as there, five cubits high by twenty cubits wide, serves to reinforce the question. If at a height of five cubits it is considered an entrance if it is twenty cubits wide, all the more so would it be considered an entrance if it is twenty cubits high (Rabbi Yitzḥak ben Avraham of Saens, quoted by the Rashba).

וְאִיבָּעֵית אֵימָא: כִּי כְּתִיב: ״קְלָעִים חֲמֵשׁ עֶשְׂרֵה אַמָּה לַכָּתֵף״ – בְּגוֹבְהָהּ הוּא דִּכְתִיב.

The Gemara offers an alternative answer: **And if you wish, say** instead that **when it is written: "The hangings on one side of the gate shall be fifteen cubits,"** it is referring **to the height** of the hangings.[N] The width of the hangings, however, is not specified in the Torah at all, and therefore the width of the doorway of the gate of the courtyard is unknown.

גּוֹבְהָהּ?! וְהָא כְּתִיב: ״וְקוֹמָה חָמֵשׁ אַמּוֹת״! הַהוּא מִשְּׂפַת מִזְבֵּחַ וּלְמַעְלָה.

The Gemara raises an objection: Could it be that the **height** of the hangings was fifteen cubits? **Isn't it written** explicitly in the verse: **"And the height five cubits"?** The Gemara answers: The verse is stating that the height of the hangings was five cubits, measured **from the edge of the altar and above.** The altar itself was ten cubits high, while the hangings of the courtyard were fifteen cubits high, five cubits higher than the altar.

וְרַבִּי יְהוּדָה מִפִּתְחוֹ שֶׁל אוּלָם גָּמַר? וְהָא תְּנַן ״וְהָרָחָב מֵעֶשֶׂר אַמּוֹת יְמַעֵט״ וְלָא פָּלֵיג רַבִּי יְהוּדָה!

The Gemara asks: **Did Rabbi Yehuda** actually **derive** his opinion **from the doorway of the Entrance Hall? But didn't we learn** in the mishna that if the entrance to an alleyway is **wider than ten cubits, one must diminish** its width? **And Rabbi Yehuda does not dispute** this ruling. Wasn't the doorway of the Entrance Hall wider than ten cubits?

אָמַר אַבַּיֵי: פָּלֵיג בְּבָרַיְיתָא, דְּתַנְיָא: וְהָרָחָב מֵעֶשֶׂר אַמּוֹת יְמַעֵט, רַבִּי יְהוּדָה אוֹמֵר: אֵינוֹ צָרִיךְ לְמַעֵט.

Abaye said: In fact, Rabbi Yehuda **disagrees** with the unattributed opinion of the first *tanna* **in a *baraita*. As it was taught** in a *baraita*: If the entrance to an alleyway is **wider than ten cubits, he must diminish** its width; **Rabbi Yehuda** disagrees and **says: He need not diminish it.**

וְלִיפְלוֹג בְּמַתְנִיתִין! פָּלֵיג בְּגוֹבְהָהּ, וְהוּא הַדִּין לְרָחְבָּהּ.

The Gemara asks further: If so, **let him disagree in the mishna.** Why is Rabbi Yehuda's dispute cited only in the *baraita*, and not in the mishna? The Gemara answers: Rabbi Yehuda **disagrees** in the mishna **with regard to** an entrance's **height, but the same applies to its width.** His statement: He need not reduce it, is referring both to the entrance's height and to its width.

וְאַכַּתִּי, רַבִּי יְהוּדָה מִפִּתְחוֹ שֶׁל אוּלָם גָּמַר? וְהָתַנְיָא: מָבוֹי שֶׁהוּא גָּבוֹהַּ מֵעֶשְׂרִים אַמָּה – יְמַעֵט, וְרַבִּי יְהוּדָה מַכְשִׁיר עַד אַרְבָּעִים וַחֲמִשִּׁים אַמָּה. וְתָנֵי בַּר קַפָּרָא: עַד מֵאָה.

The Gemara poses a question: **And still,** is it possible that **Rabbi Yehuda derived** his opinion **from the doorway of the Entrance Hall? Wasn't it taught** in a *baraita*: With regard to a cross beam spanning the entrance to **an alleyway that is higher than twenty cubits, one must diminish** its height; **and Rabbi Yehuda deems it fit up to forty and fifty cubits. And** in a different *baraita*, **bar Kappara taught** the opinion of Rabbi Yehuda: It is fit **up to a hundred** cubits.

בִּשְׁלָמָא לְבַר קַפָּרָא – גּוּזְמָא, אֶלָּא לְרַב יְהוּדָה מַאי גּוּזְמָא? בִּשְׁלָמָא לְרַבִּי יְהוּדָה, אַרְבָּעִים – גָּמַר מִפִּתְחוֹ שֶׁל אוּלָם, אֶלָּא חֲמִשִּׁים מְנָא לֵיהּ?

The Gemara clarifies its question: **Granted, according to bar Kappara,** the phrase: Up to a hundred, can be understood as **an exaggeration,**[N] not as an exact number. All that Rabbi Yehuda meant to say is that it is permitted to carry in the alleyway even if the cross beam is significantly higher than twenty cubits. **However, according to** the opinion of **Rav Yehuda** in the name of Rav, **what exaggeration** is there? He certainly meant precisely what he said. **Granted,** with regard to **forty** cubits, **Rabbi Yehuda derived** it **from the doorway of the Entrance Hall. However,** with regard to **fifty** cubits, **from where does he derive** it? Apparently, Rabbi Yehuda did not derive the dimensions of an entrance from the doorway of the Entrance Hall. He derived them from a different source.

אָמַר רַב חִסְדָּא: הָא מַתְנִיתָא אַטְעִיתֵיהּ לְרַב, דְּתַנְיָא: מָבוֹי שֶׁהוּא גָּבוֹהַּ מֵעֶשְׂרִים אַמָּה, יוֹתֵר מִפִּתְחוֹ שֶׁל הֵיכָל יְמַעֵט. הוּא סָבַר: מִדְּרַבָּנַן מִפִּתְחוֹ שֶׁל הֵיכָל גָּמְרִי, רַבִּי יְהוּדָה – מִפִּתְחוֹ שֶׁל אוּלָם גָּמַר. וְלָא הִיא, רַבִּי יְהוּדָה מִפִּתְחָא דְּמַלְכִין גָּמַר.

Rav Ḥisda said: It was **this *baraita*** that **misled Rav** and led him to explain that Rabbi Yehuda derived the measurements of an entrance from the doorway of the Entrance Hall. **As it was taught** in a *baraita*: With regard to a cross beam spanning the entrance to **an alleyway that is higher than twenty cubits, higher than the doorway of the Sanctuary, one must diminish** its height. Rav **maintains: From** the fact **that the Rabbis derived** the dimensions of an entrance **from the doorway of the Sanctuary, Rabbi Yehuda** must have **derived** those dimensions **from the doorway of the Entrance Hall. But that is not so.** Rather, **Rabbi Yehuda derived** the dimensions of an entrance **from the entrance of kings,**[N] whose regular practice was to erect their entrances exceedingly high and wide.

NOTES

Fifteen cubits is referring to the height of the hangings – חֲמֵשׁ עֶשְׂרֵה אַמָּה בְּגוֹבְהָהּ: Many difficulties were raised and resolutions offered with regard to this issue. One explanation, based on the version of the Gemara that reads: From the edge of the cloth partitions upward, is that the hangings at the entrance to the courtyard were five cubits higher than the other cloth partitions surrounding the desert Tabernacle, i.e., fifteen cubits high (see Ritva).

An exaggeration – גּוּזְמָא: This term appears in several places in the Talmud. Its basic meaning is that in certain circumstances a Sage was imprecise in his formulation. He did not intend to deviate from the truth. Rather, it was to express the general idea, without concern for its exact parameters. There are also formulaic numbers employed in exaggeration, e.g., thirteen, sixty, one hundred, and others (*Tosafot*); however, the numbers forty and fifty were never employed by the Sages as exaggerations. Therefore, they must be precise.

Entrances of kings – פִּתְחֵי מְלָכִים: This can be somewhat proven from the Bible. The doorway of both King Solomon and King Ahasuerus is referred to as an entrance [*petaḥ*], and Rabbi Yehuda received a tradition that they were very high (*Ge'on Ya'akov*).

וְרַבָּנַן, אִי מִפִּתְחוֹ שֶׁל הֵיכָל גָּמְרִי – לִיבְעוּ דְּלָתוֹת כְּהֵיכָל, אַלְמָה תְּנַן: הֶכְשֵׁר מָבוֹי, בֵּית שַׁמַּאי אוֹמְרִים: לֶחִי וְקוֹרָה וּבֵית הִלֵּל אוֹמְרִים: לֶחִי אוֹ קוֹרָה!

The Gemara asks: **And,** according to **the Rabbis, if they derived** their opinion **from the doorway of the Sanctuary, let them require doors** in order to render an alleyway fit for one to carry within it, **just as** there were doors in **the Sanctuary. Why** then **did we learn** in the mishna: With regard to the method of **rendering an alleyway fit** for carrying within it, **Beit Shammai say:** Both **a side post** placed adjacent to one of the sides of the alleyway's entrance **and a** cross **beam** over the entrance to the alleyway are required. **And Beit Hillel say:** Either **a side post or a** cross **beam** is sufficient. However, not even according to the more stringent opinion of Beit Shammai are doors required.

דַּלְתוֹת הֵיכָל לִצְנִיעוּת בְּעָלְמָא הוּא דַּעֲבִידָן.

The Gemara answers: **The Sanctuary doors were made solely for** the purpose of **privacy,** but served no practical function. The doorway of the Sanctuary did not require doors to be considered an entrance. It was a full-fledged entrance even without them.

אֶלָּא מֵעַתָּה, לָא תֵּיהֲנֵי לֵיהּ צוּרַת הַפֶּתַח, דְּהָא הֵיכָל צוּרַת הַפֶּתַח הֲוָיָא לוֹ, אֲפִילּוּ הָכִי עֶשֶׂר אַמּוֹת הוּא דְּרָוֵיהּ. אַלְמָה תְּנַן: אִם יֵשׁ לוֹ צוּרַת הַפֶּתַח, אַף עַל פִּי שֶׁרָחָב מֵעֶשֶׂר אַמּוֹת – אֵינוֹ צָרִיךְ לְמַעֵט!

The Gemara raises another question: **But if so,** that the Rabbis derive their opinion from the entrance to the Sanctuary, **the form of a doorway,** i.e., two vertical posts on the two sides, with a horizontal cross beam spanning the space between them, **should not be effective** if the alleyway is more than ten cubits wide, **as the Sanctuary had the form of a doorway, and even so, it was** no more than **ten cubits wide. Why** then **did we learn** in the mishna: If the entrance **has the form of a doorway,** then **even if it is wider than ten cubits, he need not diminish** its width?

מִידֵּי הוּא טַעְמָא אֶלָּא לְרַב – הָא מַתְנֵי לֵיהּ רַב יְהוּדָה לְחִיָּיא בַּר רַב קַמֵּיהּ דְּרַב: אֵינוֹ צָרִיךְ לְמַעֵט. וְאָמַר לֵיהּ: אַתְנְיֵיהּ "צָרִיךְ לְמַעֵט".

The Gemara answers: **As that is the reason only according to Rav,** who holds that the Rabbis derive their opinion from the doorway of the Sanctuary. **Didn't Rav Yehuda teach** this mishna to **Ḥiyya bar Rav before Rav,** saying that if the entrance had the form of a doorway **he need not diminish it, and Rav said to him** to **teach** a different version: **He must diminish it.** Apparently, according to Rav himself, the form of a doorway does not render it permitted to carry within the alleyway if its entrance is wider than the doorway of the Sanctuary, and therefore the question about the form of a doorway poses no difficulty to his opinion.

אֶלָּא מֵעַתָּה

The Gemara raises an additional difficulty: **However, if** that is **so,**

Perek **I**
Daf **3** Amud **a**

לָא תֵּיהֲנֵי לֵיהּ אֲמַלְתְּרָא, דְּהָא הֵיכָל אֲמַלְתְּרָא הֲוָיָא לֵיהּ, וַאֲפִילּוּ הָכִי עֶשְׂרִים אַמָּה הוּא דְּגָבוֹהַּ. דִּתְנַן: חָמֵשׁ אֲמַלְתְּרָאוֹת שֶׁל מֵילָה הָיוּ עַל גַּבָּיו, זוֹ לְמַעְלָה מִזּוֹ, וְזוֹ לְמַעְלָה מִזּוֹ.

a molded or protruding **cornice** [*amaltera*][L] crowning the entrance **should not be effective** in rendering an alleyway fit to carry within it if it is higher than twenty cubits, **as the Sanctuary had a cornice, and even so** it was **twenty cubits high,** and no more. **As we learned** in a mishna: **Over it were five oak cornices,**[B] **one** protruding **above the other.**[H]

וְהַאי מַאי תְּיוּבְתָּא, דִּילְמָא כִּי תַּנְיָא הַהִיא דַּאֲמַלְתְּרָאוֹת – בְּאוּלָם תַּנְיָא?

The Gemara attempts to dismiss this difficulty: **And,** with regard to **that** mishna, **what is the refutation? Perhaps when that** mishna **with regard to cornices was taught, it was taught with regard to the Entrance Hall,**[N] whose height was forty cubits, and not with regard to the Sanctuary.

LANGUAGE

Cornice [*amaltera*] – אֲמַלְתְּרָא: From the Greek μέλαθρον, *melathron*, meaning a cross beam for strengthening the roof. It can also mean cage.

BACKGROUND

The cornices in the Entrance Hall – אֲמַלְתְּרָאוֹת בָּאוּלָם:

Doorway of the Entrance Hall, twenty cubits wide and forty cubits high, with the five cornices above it

HALAKHA

Cornices in the Temple – אֲמַלְתְּרָאוֹת שֶׁבַּמִּקְדָּשׁ: Over the doorway of the Entrance Hall of the Temple building, there were five oak cornices, each protruding above the other, with a layer of stone separating them. Each cornice was two cubits longer than the one below it (Rambam *Sefer Avoda*, *Hilkhot Beit HaBeḥira* 4:8).

NOTES

Perhaps when that mishna with regard to cornices was taught, it was taught with regard to the Entrance Hall – דִּילְמָא כִּי תַּנְיָא הַהִיא דַּאֲמַלְתְּרָאוֹת בְּאוּלָם תַּנְיָא: The word perhaps is problematic in this context. According to the commentaries, it should not be understood as expressing uncertainty, but rather as a matter received through tradition. The proof is that there is a mishna concerning cornices and the Entrance Hall which appears in tractate *Middot* (Ritva).

HALAKHA

Cornices with regard to *eiruv* – אֲמַלְתְּרָאוֹת לְעִנְיַן עֵירוּבִין: The cornice that allows one to carry within an alleyway even if the cross beam spanning its entrance is higher than twenty cubits is decorative metalwork in the alleyway or on the cross beam. The *halakha* is in accordance with this opinion, because even those who expressed a differing opinion agreed that this is effective (Vilna Gaon; *Shulḥan Arukh, Oraḥ Ḥayyim* 363:26).

וְהַאי מַאי קוּשְׁיָא?! דִּילְמָא תַּבְנִית הֵיכָל כְּתַבְנִית אוּלָם?

The Gemara responds: **And what is the difficulty** with **that? Perhaps the design of the Sanctuary was like the design of the Entrance Hall.** Just as there were cornices in one doorway, there were cornices in the other.

אַלְמָה אָמַר רַבִּי אִילְעָא אָמַר רַב: רָחְבָּהּ אַרְבָּעָה אַף עַל פִּי שֶׁאֵינָהּ בְּרִיאָה, וְאִם יֵשׁ לָהּ אֲמַלְתְּרָא – אֲפִילּוּ גְּבוֹהָה יוֹתֵר מֵעֶשְׂרִים אַמָּה אֵינוֹ צָרִיךְ לְמַעֵט.

The Gemara returns to its question with regard to a cornice: **Why** then **did Rabbi Ile'a say** that **Rav** himself **said:** If the **width** of a cross beam is **four** handbreadths, **even if it is not sturdy,** it renders the alleyway fit for carrying within it. **And if it has a cornice, even if it is higher than twenty cubits, one need not diminish** its height.[H]

אָמַר רַב יוֹסֵף: אֲמַלְתְּרָא מַתְנִיתָא הִיא, מַאן קָתָנֵי לַהּ?

Rav Yosef said: This *halakha* with regard to a **cornice** was not actually stated by Rav, but rather it **is a *baraita*. Who,** in fact, **teaches** that *baraita*? Perhaps it is not an authoritative *baraita*, and Rav does not have to accept what it says.

אָמַר אַבַּיֵי: וְהָא חָמָא בְּרֵיהּ דְּרַבָּה בַּר אֲבוּהּ קָתָנֵי לַהּ. וְתֶיהֱוֵי אֲמַלְתְּרָא מַתְנִיתָא, וְתִיקְשֵׁי לְרַב!

Abaye said: Isn't it Ḥama, son of Rabba bar Avuh, who teaches it? And therefore, even if the *halakha* with regard to a **cornice will be a *baraita*, it** nevertheless **poses a difficulty to Rav.**

אָמַר לָךְ רַב: דַּל אֲנָא מֵהָכָא, מַתְנְיָיתָא מִי לָא קַשְׁיָין אַהֲדָדֵי? אֶלָּא מַאי אִית לָךְ לְמֵימַר – תַּנָּאֵי הִיא, לְדִידִי נַמִי – תַּנָּאֵי הִיא.

Rav could have **said to you:** Even if you **eliminate me** and my explanation **from** the discussion **here, don't the** two ***baraitot*** themselves, the *baraita* that states that the Rabbis derive the dimensions of an entrance from the doorway of the Sanctuary and the *baraita* that states that in the case of a cornice, even if it is higher than twenty cubits, it need not be lowered, **contradict each other? Rather, what have you to say** to reconcile the contradiction? The matter is the subject of a dispute between ***tanna'im*; so too, according to my** opinion, it **is** the subject of a dispute between ***tanna'im*.**

רַב נַחְמָן בַּר יִצְחָק אָמַר: בְּלֹא רַב מַתְנְיָיתָא אַהֲדָדֵי לָא קַשְׁיָין; לְרַבָּנַן, קוֹרָה טַעְמָא מַאי – מִשּׁוּם הֶיכֵּרָא. וְהַאי דְּקָתָנֵי "יָתֵר מִפִּתְחוֹ שֶׁל הֵיכָל" – סִימָנָא בְּעָלְמָא.

Rav Naḥman bar Yitzḥak said: Without Rav, the *baraitot* do not contradict each other, as **according to the Rabbis, what is the reason** that **a** cross **beam** renders an alleyway fit for carrying? Because it serves **as a conspicuous marker** between the alleyway and the public domain. Ordinarily a cross beam more than twenty cubits high is not noticeable; however, a cornice attracts attention even at that height. **And that which is taught** in the other *baraita* with regard to the height of a beam at the entrance to an alleyway: **Greater than the entrance of the Sanctuary,** is **merely a mnemonic** device. No actual *halakhot* are derived from the entrance of the Sanctuary.

וְרַב נַחְמָן בַּר יִצְחָק, הָנִיחָא אִי לָא סְבִירָא לֵיהּ הָא דְּרַבָּה, אֶלָּא אִי סְבִירָא לֵיהּ הָא דְּרַבָּה, דְּאָמַר רַבָּה: כְּתִיב: "לְמַעַן יֵדְעוּ דוֹרוֹתֵיכֶם כִּי בַסֻּכּוֹת הוֹשַׁבְתִּי" עַד עֶשְׂרִים אַמָּה אָדָם יוֹדֵעַ שֶׁדָּר בַּסּוּכָּה, לְמַעְלָה מֵעֶשְׂרִים אַמָּה – אֵין אָדָם יוֹדֵעַ, מִשּׁוּם דְּלָא שָׁלְטָא בֵּיהּ עֵינָא.

The Gemara notes: **And** that the explanation of **Rav Naḥman bar Yitzḥak works out well if he does not hold this** opinion **of Rabba; however, if he holds this** opinion **of Rabba,** it is difficult. As **Rabba said** with regard to the fitness of a *sukka* whose roofing is higher than twenty cubits that **it is written: "In order that your generations should know that I made** the children of Israel **dwell in booths** when I brought them out of the land of Egypt; I am the Lord your God" (Leviticus 23:43). When the roofing of a *sukka* is **up to twenty cubits** high, **a person is aware that he is dwelling in a *sukka*;** however, when the roofing of the *sukka* is **above twenty cubits, a person is not aware** that he is dwelling in a *sukka*, **because the eye does not discern** the *sukka* roofing. One does not usually raise his head to look that high, and consequently, he sees the walls and does not notice the defining feature of the *sukka*, its roofing.

אַלְמָא: גַּבֵּי סוּכָּה נַמִי בְּהֶיכֵּרָא פְּלִיגִי, אִיפְּלוּגֵי בְּתַרְתֵּי לָמָּה לִי?

The Gemara explains the difficulty: **Apparently, with regard to *sukka* as well,** the Rabbis and Rabbi Yehuda **disagree** whether or not an item more than twenty cubits high is **conspicuous.** According to Rav Naḥman bar Yitzḥak, **why do I** need them to **disagree** about the same point **in two cases,** that of *sukka* and that of an alleyway? That the dispute between the Rabbis and Rabbi Yehuda with regard to *sukka* revolves around this issue indicates that their dispute with regard to an alleyway revolves around a different point, as asserted by Rav.

צְרִיכָא, דְּאִי אַשְׁמְעִינַן גַּבֵּי סוּכָּה – בְּהָא קָאָמַר רַבִּי יְהוּדָה, כֵּיוָן דְּלִישִׁיבָה עֲבִידָא – שָׁלְטָא בֵּיהּ עֵינָא. אֲבָל מָבוֹי, דִּלְהִילּוּךְ עֲבִיד – אֵימָא מוֹדֶה לְהוּ לְרַבָּנַן. וְאִי אַשְׁמְעִינַן בְּהָא – בְּהָא קָאָמְרִי רַבָּנַן, אֲבָל בְּהַךְ – אֵימָא מוֹדוּ לֵיהּ לְרַבִּי יְהוּדָה, צְרִיכָא.

The Gemara answers: It is **necessary** to teach both disputes, **as had** the mishna **taught us** only **with regard to** ***sukka***, one might have thought that only **in this** case does **Rabbi Yehuda say** that an object is conspicuous even above twenty cubits; **since a** ***sukka*** **is designed for** extended **dwelling, the eye** undoubtedly **discerns** the roofing at some point. **However,** in the case of **an alleyway,** which **is designed for walking, say** that **he concedes to** the **Rabbis** that a person walking in an alleyway does not notice objects at so significant a height. **And had** the mishna **taught us** only **with regard to that** case of an alleyway, one might have thought that only **in that** case do **the Rabbis say** that people do not notice objects at so significant a height; **however, in that** case of *sukka*, **say** that **they concede to Rabbi Yehuda,** for the above-stated reason. Therefore, it is **necessary** to teach both disputes.

מַאי אַמַלְתְּרָא? רַב חָמָא בְּרֵיהּ דְּרַבָּה בַּר אֲבוּהּ אָמַר: קִינֵּי. כִּי אֲתָא רַב דִּימִי אֲמַר, אָמְרִי בְּמַעַרְבָא: פַּסְקֵי דְּאַרְזָא.

The Gemara seeks to arrive at a precise definition of *amaltera*, translated above as cornice. **What is an** ***amaltera*****?**[N] **Rav Ḥama, son of Rabba bar Avuh, said:** It refers to decorative wood carvings in the shape of **birds' nests. When Rav Dimi came** from Eretz Yisrael to Babylonia, **he said** that **they say in the West,**[N] Eretz Yisrael, it is referring to **cedar poles.**[N]

מַאן דְּאָמַר פַּסְקֵי דְּאַרְזָא – כׇּל שֶׁכֵּן קִינֵּי, מַאן דְּאָמַר קִינֵּי אֲבָל פַּסְקֵי דְּאַרְזָא לָא.

The Gemara explains: **The one who said** that *amaltera* refers to **cedar poles** would **all the more so** permit use of carvings of **birds' nests,** as a cross beam engraved with images attracts attention and is noticeable even at a great height. However, **the one who said** that *amaltera* refers to carvings of **birds' nests** would say that the *halakha* with regard to a cornice applies only to them, **but not to cedar poles.**

וּמַאן דְּאָמַר פַּסְקֵי דְּאַרְזָא מַאי טַעְמָא – מִשּׁוּם דְּנָפֵישׁ מַשְׁכֵיהּ, וְהָא סוּכָּה דְּנָפֵישׁ מַשְׁכֵיהּ, וְקָאָמְרִי רַבָּנַן דְּלָא!

The Gemara clarifies the opinion of **the one who said cedar poles. What is the reason** for his opinion? He holds that **since its length is great,** a cedar pole attracts attention. **But isn't the length of a** ***sukka*** **great** as well, **and** nevertheless, **the Rabbis say that** a *sukka* higher than twenty cubits is **not** fit?

אֶלָּא: כֵּיוָן דְּקָא חֲשִׁיב – אִית לֵיהּ קָלָא.

Rather, the reason is as follows: **Since** a cedar pole **is of significant** value, **it** generates **publicity.** People passing through an alleyway stop and stare at a cross beam of that kind, even when it is higher than twenty cubits, leading others publicity to do so as well.

מִקְצָת קוֹרָה בְּתוֹךְ עֶשְׂרִים וּמִקְצָת קוֹרָה לְמַעְלָה מֵעֶשְׂרִים, מִקְצָת סְכָךְ בְּתוֹךְ עֶשְׂרִים וּמִקְצָת סְכָךְ לְמַעְלָה מֵעֶשְׂרִים, אָמַר רַבָּה: בְּמָבוֹי – כָּשֵׁר, בַּסּוּכָּה – פָּסוּל.

The Gemara raises a question: If **part of the** cross **beam** of an alleyway is **within twenty** cubits of the ground, **and part of the** cross **beam** is **above twenty** cubits,[NH] and similarly, if **part of the roofing** of a *sukka*[N] is **within twenty** cubits, **and part of the** roofing is **above twenty** cubits,[H] what is its legal status? **Rabba said: In the case of an alleyway, it is fit;** in the case of a ***sukka*****, it is unfit.**

מַאי שְׁנָא בְּמָבוֹי דְּכָשֵׁר – דְּאָמְרִינַן קְלוֹשׁ, סוּכָּה נַמִי לֵימָא קְלוֹשׁ!

The Gemara asks: **What is different in** the case of **an alleyway** that the ruling is **that it is fit?** It is because **we say: Thin** the part of the cross beam that is beyond twenty cubits, i.e., consider it as if it were not there. If so, in the case of ***sukka*** **too, say: Thin** the roofing that is beyond twenty cubits.

אִי קָלְשַׁתְּ הָוְיָא לָהּ חַמָּתָהּ מְרוּבָּה מִצִּילָּתָהּ.

The Gemara answers: **If you thin** the roofing beyond twenty cubits, **it will result in** a *sukka* **whose sun is more than its shade.** Were the section of the roofing above twenty cubits removed, the roofing that remained would not provide sufficient shade for the *sukka*.

הָכָא נַמִי, אִי קָלְשַׁתְּ – הָוְיָא לָהּ קוֹרָה הַנִּיטֶּלֶת בָּרוּחַ. אֶלָּא: עַל כׇּרְחָךְ נַעֲשׂוּ כְּשַׁפּוּדִין שֶׁל מַתֶּכֶת, הָכָא נַמִי: עַל כׇּרְחָךְ נַעֲשֵׂית צִילָּתָהּ מְרוּבָּה מֵחַמָּתָהּ!

The Gemara rejects this argument: **Here too,** in the case of a cross beam, **if you thin** the section above twenty cubits, **it would become** a weak and unstable cross **beam that is removed by the wind,** which does not render the alleyway fit for carrying within it. **Rather, perforce,** the status of the remaining parts of those cross beams **becomes like** that of **metal skewers** [***shefudin***],[L] which, although they are thin, are not removed by the wind. **Here too,** in the case of a *sukka*, **perforce,** even after the upper roofing is removed, the status of the *sukka* **becomes like** that of a *sukka* **whose shade is more than its sun.**

NOTES

What is an ***amaltera*** **– מַאי אַמַלְתְּרָא:** Most commentaries agree that this question refers to an *amaltera* in the context of the *halakhot* of *eiruvin*, and not to an *amaltera* of the Temple (Ra'avad and others). Some explain that it refers to an *amaltera* of the Temple as well. Although it is explicitly stated that the latter was made from oak wood, perhaps the Sages considered oak a member of the cedar family (Ritva, in the name of *Tosafot*).

The West – מַעַרְבָא: In the Babylonian Talmud, Eretz Yisrael is called the West, as it is southwest of Babylonia. Later, the customs in Eretz Yisrael were referred to as western, as opposed to the eastern customs of Babylonia.

Birds' nests [*kinnei*] and cedar poles – קִינֵּי וּפַסְקֵי דְּאַרְזָא: Some commentaries explain that *kinnei* are small, decorative openings in the walls beneath the cross beam in which birds occasionally nest. Cedar poles are four handbreadths wide, and the statement: It is of great length, refers to their width, in accordance with the earlier statement of Rav. Other authorities explain cedar poles as poles sunk into the wall that protrude from the sides of the entrance beneath the cross beam and create the impression of lowering the cross beam (*Arukh*).

The height of the cross beam – גּוֹבַהּ הַקּוֹרָה: The conclusion in the Jerusalem Talmud is that everyone agrees that the entire cross beam must be no more than twenty cubits off the ground, lest one raise it above twenty cubits and render the alleyway unfit for carrying within it.

Roofing of a ***sukka*** **– סְכָךְ:** A *sukka* must have a minimum length and breadth of seven handbreadths and a minimum height of ten handbreadths. The maximum permitted height is twenty cubits. It must have at least three walls, one of which need only be a handbreadth. The *sukka* must be roofed with material that grows in the ground but is no longer attached, e.g., branches or leaves, and which is not susceptible to ritual impurity.

HALAKHA

If part of the cross beam is within twenty cubits, and part of the cross beam is above twenty cubits – מִקְצָת קוֹרָה בְּתוֹךְ עֶשְׂרִים וּמִקְצָת קוֹרָה לְמַעְלָה מֵעֶשְׂרִים: If part of a cross beam is less than twenty cubits off the ground, then even if part of it is above twenty cubits, the cross beam renders the alleyway fit for carrying within it, since the space between the cross beam and the ground is less than twenty cubits. The *halakha* is in accordance with the opinion of Rava, since he is a greater authority than Rabba bar Rav Ulla, and because Rav Pappa cited support for his view in the *Tosefta* (*Shulḥan Arukh, Oraḥ Ḥayyim* 363:26).

If part of the roofing is within twenty cubits, and part of the roofing is above twenty cubits – מִקְצָת סְכָךְ בְּתוֹךְ עֶשְׂרִים וּמִקְצָת סְכָךְ לְמַעְלָה מֵעֶשְׂרִים: If the roofing of a *sukka* extended above twenty cubits, but the bottom of the roofing was twenty cubits or less off the ground, the *sukka* is fit, in accordance with the opinion of Rava (*Shulḥan Arukh, Oraḥ Ḥayyim* 633:1).

LANGUAGE

Skewer [*shefud*] – שַׁפּוּד: From the Greek σποδός, *spodos*, meaning ashes. In Hebrew the word means metal skewer, especially one on which meat is roasted.

אָמַר רָבָא מִפַּרְזַקְיָא: סוּכָּה דִּלְיָחִיד הִיא – לָא מִדְכַּר, מָבוֹי דִּלְרַבִּים – מִדְכְּרִי אַהֲדָדֵי.

The Gemara explains Rabba's distinction differently. **Rava from Parzakya said: A *sukka*, which is** generally erected **for an individual,** if the portion of the roofing below twenty were removed and only the portion above twenty remained, **he** would **not be reminded** to lower the remaining roofing and would dwell in a *sukka* that is unfit. **An alleyway,** in contrast, **which is** used by **many** people, if the section of the cross beam below twenty cubits were removed, **they** would **remind each other** to remedy the situation.

רָבִינָא אָמַר: סוּכָּה דְּאוֹרַיְיתָא – אַחְמִירוּ בָּהּ רַבָּנַן, מָבוֹי דְּרַבָּנַן – לָא אַחְמִירוּ בֵּיהּ רַבָּנַן.

Ravina said a different explanation: **With regard to a *sukka*,** since its mitzva **is by Torah law, the Sages were stringent.** However, **with regard to an alleyway,** since the entire requirement to place a cross beam across the entrance in order to permit carrying in an alleyway **is** only **by rabbinic law, the Sages were not stringent.**

רַב אַדָּא בַּר מַתָּנָה מַתְנֵי לְהָא שְׁמַעְתָּא דְּרַבָּה אִיפְּכָא; אָמַר רַבָּה: בְּמָבוֹי – פָּסוּל, בַּסּוּכָּה – כְּשֵׁירָה.

The Gemara cites a different version of Rabba's distinction: **Rav Adda bar Mattana taught this *halakha* of Rabba** in the **opposite** manner. **Rabba said: In** the case of **an alleyway, it is unfit;** **in** the case of **a *sukka*, it is fit.** As a result, all the previous explanations must be reversed.

מַאי שְׁנָא סוּכָּה דִּכְשֵׁירָה – דְּאָמְרִינַן קְלוֹשׁ, בְּמָבוֹי נַמִי – לֵימָא קְלוֹשׁ!

The Gemara asks: **What is different in** the case of **a *sukka*** that **it is fit?** Because **we say: Thin** the roofing that is beyond twenty cubits. If so, then **in** the case of **a** cross **beam as well, let us say: Thin** the part of the cross beam that is beyond twenty cubits.

אִי קָלְשַׁתְּ הָוֵי לָהּ קוֹרָה הַנִּיטֶּלֶת בָּרוּחַ. הָכָא נַמִי אִי קָלְשַׁתְּ – הָוְיָא לָהּ חַמָּתָהּ מְרוּבָּה מִצִּילָּתָהּ! אֶלָּא עַל כָּרְחָךְ נַעֲשֵׂית צִילָּתָהּ מְרוּבָּה מֵחַמָּתָהּ, הָכָא נַמִי: עַל כָּרְחָךְ נַעֲשׂוּ כִּשְׁפוּדִין שֶׁל מַתֶּכֶת!

The Gemara answers: **If you thin** the part beyond twenty cubits, **it will become a** weak and unstable cross **beam that moves in the wind.** The Gemara rejects this argument: **Here too,** in the case of a *sukka*, **if you thin** the upper section of the roofing, **it would become a** *sukka* **whose sun is more than its shade. Rather, perforce,** even after the upper roofing is removed, the status of the *sukka* **becomes like** that of a *sukka* **whose shade is more than its sun; here too,** in the case of an alleyway, **perforce,** the status of the remaining parts of those cross beams **becomes like** that of **metal skewers,** which, although they are thin, do not move in the wind.

אָמַר רָבָא מִפַּרְזַקְיָא: סוּכָּה דִּלְיָחִיד הִיא – רָמֵי אַנַּפְשֵׁיהּ וּמִדְכַּר, מָבוֹי דִּלְרַבִּים הִיא – סָמְכִי אַהֲדָדֵי, וְלָא מִדְכְּרִי. דְּאָמְרִי אֱינָשֵׁי: קִדְרָא דְּבֵי שׁוּתָּפֵי לָא חֲמִימָא וְלָא קְרִירָא.

The Gemara offers a different explanation of Rabba's distinction: **Rava from Parzakya said:** In the case of **a *sukka*, which is** generally erected **for an individual, he casts** responsibility **upon himself and is reminded** to make certain that the roofing is fit. In the case of **an alleyway, which is** used by **many** people, **they** are likely to **rely upon each other and are not reminded** to check the height of the cross beam. **As people say: A pot** belonging to **partners is neither hot nor cold.** When responsibility falls upon more than one person, each relies on the other, and ultimately the task is not completed.

רָבִינָא אָמַר: סוּכָּה דְּאוֹרַיְיתָא – לָא בָּעֵי חִיזּוּק, מָבוֹי דְּרַבָּנַן – בָּעֵי חִיזּוּק.

Ravina offered a different explanation and **said:** The mitzva of ***sukka*,** which **is by Torah law, does not require reinforcement** by the Sages, and consequently, they were lenient in that case. However, since the entire requirement to place a cross beam across the entrance to **an alleyway is by rabbinic law,** it **requires reinforcement,** and therefore the Sages were stringent.

מַאי הָוֵי עֲלַהּ? רַבָּה בַּר רַב עוּלָּא אָמַר: זֶה וָזֶה פָּסוּל. רָבָא אָמַר: זֶה וָזֶה כָּשֵׁר.

Since there are two contradictory versions of Rabba's statement, the Gemara inquires: **What** practical conclusion **was** reached **about this** problem, if part of the roofing of the *sukka* or the cross beam was above twenty cubits? **Rabba bar Rav Ulla said:** In that case, both **this,** an alleyway, **and that,** a *sukka*, **are unfit.** **Rava said:** Both **this and that are fit,**

חֲלַל סוּכָּה תְּנַן, חֲלַל מָבוֹי תְּנַן.

as that which **we learned** in the mishna, with regard to the unfitness of a *sukka* higher than twenty cubits, is referring to the interior **space of the *sukka*;** and that which **we learned** in the mishna, that a cross beam spanning an alleyway that is more than twenty cubits must be lowered, is referring to the **space** at the entrance **of the alleyway** beneath the cross beam.

אֲמַר לֵיהּ רַב פָּפָּא לְרָבָא: תַּנְיָא דִּמְסַיַּיע לָךְ, מָבוֹי שֶׁהוּא גָּבוֹהַּ מֵעֶשְׂרִים אַמָּה יוֹתֵר מִפִּתְחוֹ שֶׁל הֵיכָל – יְמַעֵט. וְהֵיכָל גּוּפוֹ – חֲלָלוֹ עֶשְׂרִים.

Rav Pappa said to Rava: A *baraita* **was taught that supports your** opinion: If the cross beam spanning the entrance of **an alleyway is higher than twenty cubits** off the ground, **greater than the entrance of the Sanctuary, one must diminish its** height. **And the space of the** entrance of the **Sanctuary itself was twenty** cubits high, and its roof was higher than twenty cubits. Apparently, the twenty cubits mentioned with regard to a *sukka* and an alleyway refers to the space beneath the roofing and the cross beam.

אֵיתִיבֵיהּ רַב שִׁימִי בַּר רַב אַשִׁי לְרַב פָּפָּא: כֵּיצַד הָיָה עוֹשֶׂה – מַנִּיחַ קוֹרָה מִשְּׂפַת עֶשְׂרִים וּלְמַטָּה.

Rav Shimi bar Rav Ashi raised an objection to Rav Pappa from the *Tosefta*: **How** precisely **would he do it? He places the** cross **beam from the edge of twenty** cubits **and below.**[N] Apparently, the entire cross beam must be within twenty cubits of the ground, and if any part of it rises above twenty it is unfit.

אֵימָא "וּלְמַעְלָה". וְהָא "לְמַטָּה" קָתָנֵי!

Rav Pappa replied: Emend the *Tosefta* and **say:** From the edge of twenty cubits **and above.** Rav Shimi retorted: **But isn't it taught:** And **below?** What justification is there to completely reverse the meaning of the *Tosefta*?

הָא קָא מַשְׁמַע לָן: דִּלְמַטָּה כִּלְמַעְלָה, מָה לְמַעְלָה – חֲלָלָהּ עֶשְׂרִים, אַף לְמַטָּה – חֲלָלָהּ עֲשָׂרָה.

Rava explained that there is no need to emend the language of the *baraita*, but merely to reinterpret it. The *baraita* **is teaching us the following:** The *halakha* **below is like** the *halakha* **above. Just as above,** with regard to the maximum height of the cross beam, it is the **space** beneath the cross beam that may not be more than **twenty** cubits, **so too below,** with regard to the minimum height of the cross beam, it is the **space** beneath the cross beam that may not be less than **ten** handbreadths. However, a cross beam placed within ten handbreadths of the ground is unfit and does not render it permitted to carry within the alleyway.

אָמַר אַבַּיֵי מִשְּׁמֵיהּ דְּרַב נַחְמָן: אַמַּת סוּכָּה וְאַמַּת מָבוֹי – בְּאַמָּה בַּת חֲמִשָּׁה. אַמַּת כִּלְאַיִם – בְּאַמָּה בַּת שִׁשָּׁה.

The Gemara considers the measure of the cubit mentioned in the mishna and elsewhere. **Abaye said in the name of Rav Naḥman: The cubit** mentioned with regard to the *halakhot* **of *sukka* and the cubit** mentioned in connection with the *halakhot* **of an alleyway** is a small **cubit** consisting **of five** handbreadths. In contrast, **the cubit of** a forbidden mixture of **diverse kinds** of seeds **is a** large **cubit** consisting **of six** handbreadths.[N] Apparently, Rav Naḥman rules stringently in all cases.

"אַמַּת מָבוֹי – בְּאַמָּה בַּת חֲמִשָּׁה". לְמַאי הִלְכְתָא – לְגוֹבְהוֹ וּלְפִירְצַת מָבוֹי,

The Gemara elaborates: **The cubit of an alleyway is a cubit** consisting **of five** handbreadths. **With regard to what *halakha*** does this ruling apply? It applies **to** the issue of the height of the cross beam spanning an alleyway that may not be more than twenty cubits high, **and to the breach of an alleyway** that may not be more than ten cubits wide.

NOTES

From the edge of twenty cubits and below – מִשְּׂפַת עֶשְׂרִים וּלְמַטָּה: Rav Pappa explains the ruling of the *baraita* as follows: He places the cross beam on the edge of twenty and above, and does likewise below. The term below is an abridged formulation of a second *halakha*. Just as above, when the cross beam is at its maximum height, it must be positioned so that there is an interior space of no more than twenty cubits, the same applies below. When the cross beam is set at its lowest position, there must be an interior space of no less than ten cubits.

Large and small cubits – אַמּוֹת גְּדוֹלוֹת וּקְטַנּוֹת: Since the measure of a cubit was originally based on the length of the forearm, i.e., the distance between the elbow and the tip of the middle finger, there was no single fixed measure. Not only were there cubits of five or six handbreadths, but there was even a distinction among cubits of six handbreadths, as explained below, between those measured with expansive handbreadths and those measured with depressed ones. In the Temple, cubits slightly larger than six handbreadths were used.

וְהָא אִיכָּא מֶשֶׁךְ מָבוֹי בְּאַרְבַּע אַמּוֹת דִּלְקוּלָּא!

The Gemara poses a question: **But isn't there** also the issue of **the** minimal **length of an alleyway?** For carrying in an alleyway to be rendered permissible by means of a side post or a cross beam, it must be at least **four cubits** long. In that case, measuring the alleyway with small cubits will lead **to a leniency.**

כְּמַאן דְּאָמַר בְּאַרְבָּעָה טְפָחִים.

The Gemara resolves this difficulty: Rav Naḥman holds **in accordance with the one who said** that the length of an alleyway need only be **four handbreadths.** However, a cubit mentioned in the context of an alleyway is always a small cubit, which is a stringency.

וְאִיבָּעֵית אֵימָא: בְּאַרְבַּע אַמּוֹת, וְרוֹב אַמּוֹת קָאָמַר.

The Gemara proposes an alternative solution: **And if you wish, say** instead that actually Rav Naḥman holds in accordance with the opinion that the length of an alleyway must be **four cubits,** and in that case, the alleyway is measured with large cubits of six handbreadths as a stringency. When he is saying that the cubit of an alleyway is a cubit of five handbreadths, **he is speaking of most,** but not all, **cubits** mentioned in the context of an alleyway.

״אַמַּת סוּכָּה בְּאַמָּה בַּת חֲמִשָּׁה״ לְמַאי הִלְכְתָא – לְגוֹבְהָהּ וּלְדוֹפֶן עֲקוּמָּה.

Rav Naḥman said that **the cubit of a *sukka*** is a small **cubit** consisting **of five** handbreadths. The Gemara asks: **With regard to what *halakha*** does this ruling apply? It applies **to the** *halakha* governing **its height,** i.e., that a *sukka* may not be more than twenty cubits high, **and to the** *halakha* of **a curved wall.**[B] A *sukka* is considered valid if there are up to four cubits of invalid roofing, provided that this roofing is adjacent to one of the walls of the *sukka*. In that case, the invalid roofing is considered an extension of the wall, i.e., the wall is considered to be curved, and consequently, the entire *sukka* is valid. With regard to both *halakhot*, the ruling is stringent and distance is measured with small cubits.

וְהָא אִיכָּא מֶשֶׁךְ סוּכָּה בְּאַרְבַּע אַמּוֹת, דִּלְקוּלָּא. דְּתַנְיָא, רַבִּי אוֹמֵר: אוֹמֵר אֲנִי, כׇּל סוּכָּה שֶׁאֵין בָּהּ אַרְבַּע אַמּוֹת עַל אַרְבַּע אַמּוֹת – פְּסוּלָה!

The Gemara asks: **But isn't there** also the *halakha* of **the** minimal **length of a *sukka*,** which must be at least **four cubits** long? If it is measured with small cubits, **that** will lead **to a leniency. As it was taught** in a *baraita*: **Rabbi** Yehuda HaNasi **says: I say, any *sukka* that does not** have **in it** an area of at least **four cubits by four cubits is invalid.**

כְּרַבָּנַן, דְּאָמְרִי: ״אֲפִילּוּ אֵינָהּ מַחֲזֶקֶת אֶלָּא רֹאשׁוֹ וְרוּבּוֹ וְשׁוּלְחָנוֹ״.

The Gemara resolves this difficulty: Rav Naḥman holds **in accordance with** the opinion of **the Rabbis, who say:** A *sukka* is valid **even if it holds only one's head, most of his** body, **and his table.**

וְאִיבָּעֵית אֵימָא: לְעוֹלָם רַבִּי הִיא, וְרוֹב אַמּוֹת קָאָמַר.

The Gemara suggests another solution: **And if you wish, say** instead: **Actually,** Rav Naḥman's statement holds true even if **it is** in accordance with the opinion of **Rabbi** Yehuda HaNasi that a *sukka* must be at least four cubits long. Indeed, the *sukka* is measured with large cubits consisting of six handbreadths, which is a stringency. **And** when he says that the cubit of a *sukka* is a cubit of five handbreadths, **he is speaking of most,** but not all, **cubits** mentioned with regard to *sukka*.

״אַמַּת כִּלְאַיִם בְּאַמָּה בַּת שִׁשָּׁה״. לְמַאי הִילְכְתָא – לְקׇרַחַת הַכֶּרֶם וְלִמְחוֹל הַכֶּרֶם.

The Gemara continues: As stated above, Rav Naḥman said that **the cubit of a** forbidden mixture of **diverse kinds** of seeds **is a cubit** consisting **of six handbreadths.** The Gemara asks: **With regard to what *halakha*** does this ruling apply? It applies **to the** *halakha* of **a clearing in a vineyard and to** the *halakha* of **the perimeter of a vineyard.**[N]

דִּתְנַן: קׇרַחַת הַכֶּרֶם, בֵּית שַׁמַּאי אוֹמְרִים: עֶשְׂרִים וְאַרְבַּע אַמּוֹת, וּבֵית הִלֵּל אוֹמְרִים: שֵׁשׁ עֶשְׂרֵה אַמּוֹת. וּמְחוֹל הַכֶּרֶם, בֵּית שַׁמַּאי אוֹמְרִים: שֵׁשׁ עֶשְׂרֵה אַמּוֹת, וּבֵית הִלֵּל אוֹמְרִים: שְׁתֵּים עֶשְׂרֵה אַמּוֹת.

As we learned in a mishna in tractate *Kilayim*: With regard to **a clearing in a vineyard,**[H] **Beit Shammai say:** Its measure is **twenty-four cubits, and Beit Hillel say: Sixteen cubits.** With regard to **the perimeter of a vineyard,**[H] **Beit Shammai say: Sixteen cubits, and Beit Hillel say: Twelve cubits.**

HALAKHA

A clearing in a vineyard – קׇרַחַת הַכֶּרֶם: One may sow foreign seeds in the middle of a vineyard *ab initio* only if there is an area of sixteen by sixteen cubits clear of vines, in accordance with the opinion of Beit Hillel. If he distanced the seeds from the vines more than four cubits on either side, neither the vines nor the other crops are prohibited after the fact (*Shulḥan Arukh, Yoreh De'a* 296:42).

The perimeter of a vineyard – מְחוֹל הַכֶּרֶם: One may sow foreign seeds between the vineyard and the fence *ab initio* only if there is an empty space of twelve cubits, in accordance with the opinion of Beit Hillel. Even if one distanced the other seeds four cubits from the vines, neither the vines nor the other crops are prohibited after the fact (*Shulḥan Arukh, Yoreh De'a* 296:43).

BACKGROUND

Curved wall – דּוֹפֶן עֲקוּמָּה: If part of the roof of a *sukka*, adjacent to one of its walls, is made of common roofing material, unfit for use in a *sukka*, then this part of the roof is considered an extension of the *sukka* wall. It is as if the wall is curved at the top. If it is four cubits wide, it invalidates the *sukka*.

Portion of the *sukka* roof made of common roofing material

NOTES

Diverse kinds in a vineyard – כִּלְאֵי הַכֶּרֶם: The Torah prohibits planting or maintaining foreign crops in a vineyard. The relevant *halakhot* are elucidated in tractate *Kilayim* in the mishna and Jerusalem Talmud. Some of the fundamental *halakhot* of diverse kinds in a vineyard are: The prohibition only applies in a vineyard. Therefore, in the case of a lone vine or vines not planted in the form of a vineyard, one need only distance foreign crops six handbreadths from the vines. Since cultivation of a vineyard begins with plowing, which was performed with oxen, one must leave four cubits on either side of the vines as the work area of the vineyard. Similarly, one may not sow in the four cubits adjacent to the fence of the vineyard, because people would walk there.

The dispute between Beit Shammai and Beit Hillel with regard to a clearing in a vineyard and the perimeter is based on a different *halakha*. If a person sows seeds in a vineyard, even if the seeds are distanced four cubits from the vines, the sown area is negated relative to the vines, and the sowing is prohibited. It is permitted only if the sown area is large enough to be considered a separate field. According to Beit Hillel, the minimum size of a field is four by four cubits, while Beit Shammai maintain that the minimum size is eight by eight cubits.

אֵיזוֹ הִיא קָרַחַת הַכֶּרֶם – כֶּרֶם שֶׁחָרֵב אֶמְצָעִיתוֹ, אֵין שָׁם שֵׁשׁ עֶשְׂרֵה אַמּוֹת – לֹא יָבִיא זֶרַע לְשָׁם, הָיוּ שָׁם שֵׁשׁ עֶשְׂרֵה אַמָּה – נוֹתֵן לוֹ כְּדֵי עֲבוֹדָתוֹ וְזוֹרֵעַ אֶת הַמּוֹתָר.

The mishna explains: **What is a clearing in a vineyard?** It is referring to **a vineyard whose middle** section **was laid bare** of vines. If **there are not sixteen cubits** across in the clearing, **one may not bring** foreign **seeds** and sow them **there,** due to the Torah prohibition against sowing other crops in a vineyard (Deuteronomy 22:9). If **there were sixteen cubits** across in the clearing, **one provides** the vineyard with **its** requisite **work area,** i.e., four cubits along either side of the vines are left unsown to facilitate cultivation of the vines, **and he sows the rest** of the cleared area with foreign crops.

וְאֵיזֶהוּ מְחוֹל הַכֶּרֶם – בֵּין כֶּרֶם לַגָּדֵר; אֵין שָׁם שְׁתֵּים עֶשְׂרֵה אַמָּה – לֹא יָבִיא זֶרַע לְשָׁם, הָיוּ שָׁם שְׁתֵּים עֶשְׂרֵה אַמָּה – נוֹתֵן לוֹ כְּדֵי עֲבוֹדָתוֹ וְזוֹרֵעַ אֶת הַשְּׁאָר.

The mishna continues: **What is the perimeter of a vineyard?**[B] It is the vacant area **between the vineyard and the fence** surrounding it. If **there are not twelve cubits** in that area, **one may not bring** foreign **seeds** and sow them **there.** If **there were twelve cubits** in that area, **he provides** the vineyard, with **its** requisite **work area,** four cubits, **and he sows the rest.**

וְהָא אִיכָּא רְצוּפִים בְּאַרְבַּע אַמּוֹת דִּלְקוּלָּא, דִּתְנַן: כֶּרֶם הַנָּטוּעַ עַל פָּחוֹת מֵאַרְבַּע אַמּוֹת, רַבִּי שִׁמְעוֹן אוֹמֵר: אֵינוֹ כֶּרֶם, וַחֲכָמִים אוֹמְרִים: כֶּרֶם, וְרוֹאִין אֶת הָאֶמְצָעִיִּים כְּאִילּוּ אֵינָם!

The Gemara raises a difficulty: **But isn't there** also the *halakha* of vines that planted **consecutively, within four cubits** of each other, with regard to **which** measuring the distance with large cubits would lead **to a leniency? As we learned** in a mishna: With regard to **a vineyard that was planted** in consecutive rows **with less than four cubits** between them, **Rabbi Shimon says:** Since the rows are planted so closely together, **it is not** considered **a vineyard,** and if one plants other crops there he is not liable. **And the Rabbis say:** It is **a vineyard, and one regards the middle** vines, those planted between two appropriately spaced rows, **as if they are not** there.[H] One who plants other crops there is indeed liable. According to Rabbi Shimon's opinion, measuring the distance between the rows with large cubits leads to leniency.

כְּרַבָּנַן, דְּאָמְרִי הָוֵי כֶּרֶם. וְאִיבָּעֵית אֵימָא: לְעוֹלָם רַבִּי שִׁמְעוֹן, וְרוֹב אַמּוֹת קָאָמַר.

The Gemara resolves the difficulty: Rav Naḥman made his statement **in accordance with** the opinion of **the Rabbis, who say** that a densely planted vineyard **is a vineyard. And if you wish, say** instead: **Actually,** Rav Naḥman's statement holds true even if **it is** in accordance with the opinion of **Rabbi Shimon,** that a densely planted vineyard is not a vineyard, and the distance between the rows is measured with small cubits consisting of five handbreadths as a stringency. When he says that the cubit of diverse kinds of seeds is a cubit consisting of six handbreadths, **he is speaking of most,** but not all, **cubits** mentioned with regard to a forbidden mixture of diverse kinds of seeds.

וְרָבָא מִשְּׁמֵיהּ דְּרַב נַחְמָן אָמַר: כׇּל אַמּוֹת בְּאַמָּה בַּת שִׁשָּׁה, אֶלָּא הַלָּלוּ שׂוֹחֲקוֹת וְהַלָּלוּ עֲצֵבוֹת.

The above was based on the ruling of Rav Naḥman according to Abaye. **But Rava said in the name of Rav Naḥman:**[N] **All cubits** mentioned in measurements by the Sages consisted of a large **cubit of six** handbreadths.[H] **However, these,** the cubits mentioned with regard to diverse kinds of seeds, **are** measured with **expansive** handbreadths, with the fingers spread apart, **whereas those,** the cubits mentioned with regard to an alleyway and a *sukka,* **are** measured with **compressed** handbreadths, with the fingers held together.[N]

מֵיתִיבִי: כׇּל אַמּוֹת שֶׁאָמְרוּ חֲכָמִים בְּאַמָּה בַּת שִׁשָּׁה, וּבִלְבַד

The Gemara raises an objection from a *baraita*: **All cubits that were mentioned by the Sages are cubits of six** handbreadths, **provided**

BACKGROUND

Perimeter of a vineyard – מְחוֹל הַכֶּרֶם:

Sketch of the vacant area between the vineyard and the fence surrounding it

HALAKHA

A densely planted vineyard – כֶּרֶם רָצוּף: If the rows of vines in a vineyard were planted close together, less than four cubits apart, it is still considered a vineyard. If one sows foreign seeds there, the vines and other crops are prohibited, in accordance with the opinion of the Rabbis (*Shulḥan Arukh, Yoreh De'a* 296:33).

The measure of a cubit – שִׁיעוּר הָאַמָּה: All cubits mentioned in the measurements of the Sages are cubits of six handbreadths, in accordance with the opinion of Rava, which is supported by a *baraita* (*Shulḥan Arukh, Oraḥ Ḥayyim* 349:1, 396:1 and *Yoreh De'a* 296:68).

NOTES

The measure of cubits according to Rava – שִׁיעוּר אַמּוֹת לְשִׁיטַת רָבָא: Some commentaries explain that all the objections and resolutions recorded above with regard to expansive and depressed cubits in the context of Abaye's opinion also apply to expansive and depressed cubits in the discussion of Rava's opinion. The larger or smaller measures are applied based on the stringency entailed (Rambam; Rosh; Rabbi Zeraḥya HaLevi). Other authorities maintain that since the difference is slight, no distinction is made. Rather, the cubits of an alleyway and a *sukka* are always measured with five-cubit handbreadths, while those of diverse kinds are always measured with six-cubit handbreadths (Rashba).

Expansive [*sokhakot*] and depressed [*atzevot*] handbreadths – שׂוֹחֲקוֹת וַעֲצֵבוֹת: The *Arukh* explains that the larger cubits are measured with handbreadths in which the fingers of the hand are slightly apart. They are called laughing [*sokhakot*], because one who laughs separates his lips. The smaller cubits are called sad [*atzevot*], as one who is sad tightens the lips. The commentaries state that the difference between an expansive and a depressed cubit is roughly half a fingerbreadth (Rambam; Rabbi Zeraḥya HaLevi; see also Rav Nissim Gaon).

HALAKHA

The cubit of the base of the altar and the cubit of the surrounding ledge – אַמָּה יְסוֹד וְאַמָּה סוֹבֵב: The height of the base of the altar and width of the surrounding ledge of the altar are measured in cubits of five handbreadths, as stated by the Gemara (Rambam *Sefer Avoda, Hilkhot Beit HaBeḥira* 2:6).

NOTES

The measures of the altar – מִדּוֹת הַמִּזְבֵּחַ: The measurements of the future Temple that appear in the book of Ezekiel are not clearly defined. Therefore, the Sages interpreted them homiletically in various ways. The verse quoted in this context evidently refers to two different sized cubits, the regular cubit and the cubit of "a cubit and a handbreadth." See the two versions of Rashi's commentary that offer two different explanations of the text. Nevertheless, both explanations lead to the same conclusion.

BACKGROUND

The altar – הַמִּזְבֵּחַ: The height of the altar, including its horns, was ten cubits. However, these cubits were not uniform in length. Rather, some were longer and others were shorter. Consequently, the height of the altar totaled fifty-eight handbreadths, and not sixty. The altar had five cubits of five handbreadths: The cubit of the height of the base, the cubit of the width of the foundation, the cubit of the width of the surrounding ledge, the cubit of the height of the horns, and the cubit of the width of the horns.

Altar in the Second Temple

שֶׁלֹּא יְהוּ מְכוּוָּנוֹת. בִּשְׁלָמָא לְרָבָא – כִּי הֵיכִי דְּלִיהֱוְיָין הַלָּלוּ שׁוֹחֲקוֹת וְהַלָּלוּ עֲצֵבוֹת. אֶלָּא לְאַבָּיֵי קַשְׁיָא!

that they are not precisely a cubit. **Granted, according to Rava,** the *baraita* means: **So that these,** the cubits of diverse kinds of seeds, **should be** measured with **expansive** handbreadths, **and those,** the cubits of *sukka*, should be measured with **depressed** handbreadths. **However, according to Abaye,** it is **difficult.**

אָמַר לָךְ אַבָּיֵי: אֵימָא: "אַמַּת כִּלְאַיִם בְּאַמָּה בַּת שִׁשָּׁה".

The Gemara answers: **Abaye** could have **said to you:** Emend the *baraita* and **say: The cubit of diverse kinds** of seeds mentioned by the Sages **is** measured **with a cubit of six** handbreadths, not the other cubits.

וְהָא מִדְּקָתָנֵי סֵיפָא " רַבָּן שִׁמְעוֹן בֶּן גַּמְלִיאֵל אוֹמֵר: כׇּל אַמּוֹת שֶׁאָמְרוּ חֲכָמִים בְּכִלְאַיִם בְּאַמָּה בַּת שִׁשָּׁה, וּבִלְבַד שֶׁלֹּא יְהוּ מְצוּמְצָמוֹת" מִכְּלָל דְּתַנָּא קַמָּא כׇּל אַמּוֹת קָאָמַר!

The Gemara raises a difficulty. **However, from** the fact **that it is taught** in **the latter clause** of the *baraita* that **Rabban Shimon ben Gamliel says: All the cubits that the Sages mentioned with regard to diverse kinds** of seeds are measured **with cubits of six** handbreadths, **provided that they are not** measured with **exact** handbreadths? This proves **by inference** that **the** anonymous **first *tanna* is speaking of all cubits,** and not only those in the case of diverse kinds of seeds.

אָמַר לָךְ אַבָּיֵי: וְלָאו מִי אִיכָּא רַבָּן שִׁמְעוֹן בֶּן גַּמְלִיאֵל דְּקָאֵי כְּוָותִי? אֲנָא דְּאָמְרִי כְּרַבָּן שִׁמְעוֹן בֶּן גַּמְלִיאֵל.

The Gemara answers that **Abaye** could have **said to you: Isn't there Rabban Shimon ben Gamliel, who holds in accordance with my** opinion? **I stated** my opinion **in accordance with** the opinion of **Rabban Shimon ben Gamliel.**

לְאַבָּיֵי וַדַּאי תַּנָּאֵי הִיא. לְרָבָא מִי לֵימָא תַּנָּאֵי הִיא?

The Gemara comments: **According to Abaye,** the issue of large and small cubits **is certainly** subject to a dispute between ***tanna'im***, as his ruling can only be in accordance with the opinion of Rabban Shimon ben Gamliel. **According to Rava,** however, **must it be said** that **this is** subject to a dispute between ***tanna'im*?**

אָמַר לָךְ רָבָא: רַבָּן שִׁמְעוֹן בֶּן גַּמְלִיאֵל הָא אֲתָא לְאַשְׁמוֹעִינַן: אַמַּת כִּלְאַיִם לֹא יְצַמְצֵם.

The Gemara answers: This is not necessarily the case, as **Rava** could have **said to you: Rabban Shimon ben Gamliel** does not dispute the basic teaching of the anonymous first *tanna* that all the cubits mentioned by the Sages are cubits of six handbreadths. Rather, he **came to teach us this: One** should **not reduce the cubit of diverse kinds** of seeds, i.e., one should not measure it with depressed handbreadths.

וְלֵימָא "אַמַּת כִּלְאַיִם לֹא יְצַמְצֵם", בְּאַמָּה בַּת שִׁשָּׁה לְמַעוּטֵי מַאי? לָאו לְמַעוּטֵי אַמַּת סוּכָּה וְאַמַּת מָבוֹי?!

The Gemara raises an objection. **And** if that is the case, **let him say: One must not reduce the cubit of diverse kinds** of seeds. **What does** the phrase: **A cubit** consisting **of six** handbreadths come **to exclude? Does it not** come **to exclude the cubit of a *sukka* and the cubit of an alleyway,** which are measured with cubits of five handbreadths?

לֹא, לְמַעוּטֵי אַמָּה יְסוֹד וְאַמָּה סוֹבֵב.

The Gemara rejects this argument. **No,** Rabban Shimon ben Gamliel's formulation comes **to exclude the cubit of the base** of the altar, which is the bottom level of the altar, one cubit high with a ledge one cubit wide, **and the cubit of the surrounding ledge**[H] of the altar, which is five cubits above the base, six cubits above the ground, and one cubit wide. Everyone agrees that those cubits are small cubits of five handbreadths.

דִּכְתִיב: "וְאֵלֶּה מִדּוֹת הַמִּזְבֵּחַ בָּאַמּוֹת אַמָּה אַמָּה וָטֹפַח וְחֵיק הָאַמָּה וְאַמָּה רֹחַב וּגְבוּלָהּ אֶל שְׂפָתָהּ סָבִיב זֶרֶת הָאֶחָד וְזֶה גַּב הַמִּזְבֵּחַ". "חֵיק הָאַמָּה" – זֶה יְסוֹד, "וְאַמָּה רֹחַב" – זֶה סוֹבֵב, "וּגְבוּלָהּ אֶל שְׂפָתָהּ סָבִיב" – אֵלּוּ הַקְּרָנוֹת, "וְזֶה גַּב הַמִּזְבֵּחַ" – זֶה מִזְבַּח הַזָּהָב.

As it is written: "And these are the measures of the altar[N] **by cubits; the cubit is a cubit and a handbreadth, the bottom shall be a cubit, and the breadth a cubit, and its border by its edge round about shall be a span: And this shall be the higher part of the altar"** (Ezekiel 43:13). And the Sages explained this verse as follows: **"The bottom shall be a cubit," this is the base** of the altar; **"and the breadth a cubit," this is the surrounding ledge** of the altar; **"and its border by its edge round about," these are the horns** of the altar, i.e., extensions of the corners of the altar; **"and this shall be the higher part of the altar,"** this refers to **the golden altar** that stood inside the Sanctuary and was also measured by small cubits.[B]

אָמַר רַבִּי חִיָּיא בַּר אַשִׁי אָמַר רַב: שִׁיעוּרִין חֲצִיצִין וּמְחִיצִין הֲלָכָה לְמֹשֶׁה מִסִּינַי.

Since the Gemara discussed measurements, it proceeds to cite that which **Rabbi Ḥiyya bar Ashi said** that **Rav said: The measures** relating to mitzvot in the Torah, and the *halakhot* governing **interpositions** that invalidate ritual immersions, and the *halakhot* of **partitions are** all ***halakhot*** transmitted **to Moses from Sinai.** These *halakhot* have no basis in the Written Torah, but according to tradition they were orally transmitted by God to Moses together with the Written Torah.

שִׁיעוּרִין? דְּאוֹרַיְיתָא הוּא! דִּכְתִיב: "אֶרֶץ חִטָּה וּשְׂעֹרָה וגו'" וְאָמַר רַב חָנָן: כָּל הַפָּסוּק הַזֶּה לְשִׁיעוּרִין נֶאֱמַר.

The Gemara questions this assertion: Are **measures**[H] a *halakha* transmitted to Moses from Sinai? **They are** written **in the Torah,**[N] **as it is written: "A land of wheat, and barley,** and vines, and figs, and pomegranates, a land of olive oil and honey" (Deuteronomy 8:8), **and Rav Ḥanan said: This entire verse was stated for** the purpose of teaching **measures** with regard to different *halakhot* in the Torah.

חִטָּה – לִכְדִתְנַן: הַנִּכְנָס לְבַיִת הַמְנוּגָּע, וְכֵלָיו עַל כְּתֵיפָיו, וְסַנְדָּלָיו וְטַבְּעוֹתָיו בְּיָדָיו – הוּא וְהֵם טְמֵאִין מִיָּד. הָיָה לָבוּשׁ כֵּלָיו, וְסַנְדָּלָיו בְּרַגְלָיו, וְטַבְּעוֹתָיו בְּאֶצְבְּעוֹתָיו – הוּא טָמֵא מִיָּד, וְהֵן טְהוֹרִין עַד שֶׁיִּשְׁהֶא בִּכְדֵי אֲכִילַת פְּרָס, פַּת חִיטִּין וְלֹא פַּת שְׂעוֹרִין, מֵיסֵב וְאוֹכֵל בְּלִיפְתָּן.

Wheat was mentioned as the basis for calculating the time required for one to become ritually impure when entering a house afflicted with leprosy, **as that which we learned** in a mishna: **One who enters a house afflicted with leprosy**[N] of the house[H] (see Leviticus 14), **and his clothes** are draped **over his shoulders, and his sandals and his rings are in his hands,** both **he and they,** the clothes, sandals, and rings, **immediately** become **ritually impure.** However, if **he was dressed in his clothes, and his sandals were on his feet, and his rings were on his fingers, he immediately** becomes **ritually impure, but they,** the clothes, sandals, and rings, **remain pure until he stays** in the house **long enough to eat half a loaf** of bread. This calculation is based on **wheat bread,** which takes less time to eat, **and not** on **barley bread,** and it relates to one who is **reclining and eating** it together **with relish,** which hastens the eating. This is a Torah measurement connected specifically to wheat.

שְׂעוֹרָה – דִּתְנַן: עֶצֶם כִּשְׂעוֹרָה מְטַמֵּא בְּמַגָּע וּבְמַשָּׂא, וְאֵינוֹ מְטַמֵּא בְּאֹהֶל.

Barley is also used as a basis for measurements, **as we learned** in a mishna: **A bone** from a corpse the size **of a** grain of **barley**[H] **imparts** ritual **impurity through contact and by being carried,** but **it does not impart impurity** by means **of a tent,** i.e., if the bone was inside a house, it does not render all the articles in the house ritually impure.

גֶּפֶן – כְּדֵי רְבִיעִית יַיִן לְנָזִיר.

The halakhic measure determined by a **vine is the quantity of a quarter-*log* of wine for a nazirite.**[HN] A nazirite, who is prohibited to drink wine, is liable to be flogged if he drinks that measure.

HALAKHA

Measures – שִׁיעוּרִין: The measures relating to various Torah prohibitions are *halakhot* transmitted to Moses from Sinai. According to Torah law, one is liable for punishment only if one transgresses with the prohibited measure. If one intentionally transgresses with less than the requisite measure, one is punished with lashes administered by rabbinic decree (Rambam *Sefer Kedusha, Hilkhot Ma'akhalot Assurot* 14:2).

The impurity of a plagued house – טוּמְאַת בֵּית הַמְנוּגָּע: One who enters a house that is plagued with leprosy [*tzara'at*] and who is dressed in the usual manner contracts ritual impurity immediately. However, his clothes contract impurity only if he remains in the house for the duration of time required to eat half a loaf of bread. This is the normal time necessary to eat three egg-bulks of wheat bread with a relish. If his clothes or jewelry were in his hands, they too contract impurity immediately upon entry (Rambam *Sefer Tahara, Hilkhot Tumat Tzara'at* 16:7).

A bone the size of a grain of barley – עֶצֶם כִּשְׂעוֹרָה: A bone from a corpse imparts ritual impurity through contact or by being carried if it is the size of a barleycorn or larger. It does not impart impurity via a tent, in accordance with the mishna cited here (Rambam *Sefer Tahara, Hilkhot Tumat Met* 3:2).

Wine for a nazirite – יַיִן לְנָזִיר: A nazirite who drinks a quarter-*log* of wine or wine products is punished with lashes (Rambam *Sefer Hafla'a, Hilkhot Nezirut* 5:2).

NOTES

Measures…are written in the Torah – שִׁיעוּרִין דְּאוֹרַיְיתָא: Rav Ḥanan understands that the verse speaks in praise of the fruit of Eretz Yisrael, such that even the measures for various Torah laws are determined by its fruit (Rashi).

One who enters a house afflicted with leprosy – הַנִּכְנָס לְבַיִת הַמְנוּגָּע: A house plagued with leprosy [*tzara'at*] is in a certain sense treated like a house containing a corpse: Anything inside it and anyone who enters in it contracts impurity. However, two verses refer to this situation: "One who enters the house shall be impure until the evening" (Leviticus 14:46), and: "One who eats in the house shall wash his clothes" (Leviticus 14:47). The first verse refers to the impurity of the person himself or to that of anything brought into the house, while the second verse, which speaks of washing clothes, deals with the clothing worn by a person who enters the house. The clothing contracts impurity only if it remains in the house for the duration of "eating," which, according to rabbinic tradition, is the time required to eat half a loaf of bread.

A quarter-*log* of wine for a nazirite – רְבִיעִית יַיִן לְנָזִיר: *Tosafot* point out that Rashi's explanation, which states that if a nazirite drinks this measure of wine he is liable for flogging, requires elaboration. This is based on the fact that the word vines indicates more than simply the prohibition against a nazirite drinking wine. Rather, one should explain as follows: A quarter-*log* is a measurement of volume. Indeed, all measures of a quarter-*log*, whether for wine or water, are equal. However, the volume of solid food is determined, according to *halakha*, by measuring the amount of liquid displaced by the food when it is inserted into a liquid. Consequently, when measuring foods prohibited to a nazirite, e.g., grapes and grape products, to which the measure of a quarter-*log* applies, there will be a slight difference between measuring with water and measuring with wine, because the viscosity of wine and that of water are different. Therefore, the amount of liquid displaced will be different (*Ge'on Ya'akov*).

HALAKHA

A dried fig-bulk with regard to carrying out on Shabbat – כִּגְרוֹגֶרֶת לְהוֹצָאַת שַׁבָּת: One who carries food fit for humans from one domain to another is liable if he carried at least a dried fig-bulk of food (Rambam *Sefer Zemanim, Hilkhot Shabbat* 18:1).

Vessels belonging to homeowners – כְּלֵי בַעֲלֵי בָתִּים: Bone or wood vessels that have a hole through which a medium-sized pomegranate can pass are no longer susceptible to ritual impurity (Rambam *Sefer Tahara, Hilkhot Kelim* 6:2).

Eating on Yom Kippur – אֲכִילָה בְּיוֹם כִּיפּוּר: One is liable for eating on Yom Kippur only if he eats an amount of food equal in size to a large date (*Shulḥan Arukh, Oraḥ Ḥayyim* 612:1).

Interpositions in immersions – חֲצִיצָה בִּטְבִילָה: When one immerses in a ritual bath [*mikve*] to purify himself, he must immerse his entire body at the same time. In addition, there must be nothing that interposes between his body and the water (*Shulḥan Arukh, Yoreh De'a* 198:1).

The measure of a ritual bath – שִׁיעוּר מִקְוֶה: To be suitable for purification, a ritual bath must measure a cubit in width, by a cubit in depth, by three cubits in height. The volume of a ritual bath of that size is forty *se'a*. A ritual bath is measured using large cubits of six handbreadths and half a finger each, as the cubits for a ritual bath must be expansive cubits (Rashba). The dimensions of the ritual bath need not be in exactly this ratio. However, the ritual bath must contain forty *se'a* and it must be possible to immerse one's entire body in it at one time (*Shulḥan Arukh, Yoreh De'a* 201:1).

Interpositions with regard to hair – חֲצִיצָה בְּשֵׂיעָר: If the person immersing is bothered by single, knotted hair when immersing, or if most people are bothered by this (*Shakh*), it constitutes an interposition. Two hairs or more that were knotted together are not an interposition. If one is not particular about a knotted hair, the immersion is not invalidated, unless most of the hair was individually knotted. This is in accordance with the ruling of the *ge'onim*, based on the opinion of Rabbi Yoḥanan in tractate *Nidda*, that two hairs knotted together do not constitute an interposition (*Shulḥan Arukh, Yoreh De'a* 198:5).

NOTES

Honey…a large date-bulk – דְּבַשׁ כְּכוֹתֶבֶת הַגַּסָּה: In the Bible, the term honey does not refer exclusively to bees' honey. Rather, all kinds of sweet things are called honey, especially dates (Rashi). The use of a large date as a minimal measure of eating on Yom Kippur stems from the fact that there is no explicit prohibition against eating on Yom Kippur. Fasting is merely part of the affliction to be endured on that day, and the Sages had a tradition that as long as a person has not eaten an amount of food equivalent to the size of a large date, the person's mind is not settled and he is still considered afflicted.

A single hair tied in a knot constitutes an interposition – נִימָא אַחַת קְשׁוּרָה חוֹצֶצֶת: The authorities disagree as to whether hair has its own special law concerning interpositions or whether it is considered part of the body. Even according to the first opinion, a single hair in a knot invalidates an immersion only if most of the hairs on one's head are knotted in this manner (*ge'onim*). Other commentaries state that even if most of the hairs are knotted in a manner that interposes, it still does not invalidate the immersion according to Torah law, unless, when considered together with the head, most of the body is covered by interposing matter.

תְּאֵנָה – כִּגְרוֹגֶרֶת לְהוֹצָאַת שַׁבָּת,

Fig alludes to the measure of **a dried fig-bulk with regard to** the *halakhot* of **carrying out** on **Shabbat.**[H] One is liable for carrying food fit for human consumption on Shabbat, provided that he carries a dried fig-bulk of that food.

רִמּוֹן – כִּדְתְנַן: כֹּל כְּלֵי בַעֲלֵי בָתִּים שִׁיעוּרָן כָּרִימּוֹנִים.

Pomegranate teaches the measure, **as that which we learned** in a mishna: **All** ritually impure wooden **vessels belonging to** ordinary **homeowners**[H] become pure through being broken, as broken vessels cannot contract or maintain ritual impurity, and they are considered broken if they have holes **the size of pomegranates.**

אֶרֶץ זֵית שֶׁמֶן (וּדְבָשׁ)" אֶרֶץ שֶׁכָּל שִׁיעוּרֶיהָ כַּזֵּיתִים. "כָּל שִׁיעוּרֶיהָ" סָלְקָא דַּעְתָּךְ?! וְהָאִיכָּא הָנֵי דַּאֲמַרַן! אֶלָּא אֵימָא: אֶרֶץ שֶׁרוֹב שִׁיעוּרֶיהָ כַּזֵּיתִים.

The Sages interpreted: **A land of olive oil and honey,** as: **A land, all of whose measures are olive-bulks.** The Gemara poses a question: **Does it enter your mind** that it is a land **all of whose measures** are olives-bulks? **Yet aren't there those** measures **that we** just **mentioned** above, which are not olive-bulks? **Rather, say: A land, most of whose measures are olive-bulks,** as most measures, e.g., those relating to forbidden foods and to impurity imparted by a corpse in a tent and by contact with an animal carcass, are olive-bulks.

דְּבַשׁ – כְּכוֹתֶבֶת הַגַּסָּה לְיוֹם הַכִּיפּוּרִים.

Honey, i.e., dates from which date honey is extracted, also determines a measure, as with regard **to** eating on **Yom Kippur,** one is liable only if he eats **a large date-bulk**[N] of food.[H] Clearly, the measurements pertaining to mitzvot are explicitly written in the Torah and were not transmitted to Moses from Sinai.

וְתִיסְבְּרָא, שִׁיעוּרִין מִיכְתַּב כְּתִיבִי?! אֶלָּא: הִלְכְתָא נִינְהוּ, וְאַסְמְכִינְהוּ רַבָּנַן אַקְּרָאֵי.

The Gemara refutes this argument: **And can you hold** that all these **measures are** explicitly **written** in the Torah with regard to each of the *halakhot* mentioned above? **Rather, they are** ***halakhot*** that were transmitted to Moses from Sinai, **and the Sages based them on verses** in the Torah.

חֲצִיצִין – דְּאוֹרַיְיתָא נִינְהוּ! דִּכְתִיב: "וְרָחַץ אֶת כָּל בְּשָׂרוֹ (בַּמַּיִם)" – שֶׁלֹּא יְהֵא דָּבָר חוֹצֵץ בֵּין בְּשָׂרוֹ לַמַּיִם. 'בַּמַּיִם' – בְּמֵי מִקְוֶה, כָּל בְּשָׂרוֹ – מַיִם שֶׁכָּל גּוּפוֹ עוֹלֶה בָּהֶן. וְכַמָּה הֵן – אַמָּה עַל אַמָּה בְּרוּם שָׁלֹשׁ אַמּוֹת. וְשִׁיעֲרוּ חֲכָמִים מֵי מִקְוֶה אַרְבָּעִים סְאָה.

Rabbi Ḥiyya bar Ashi said above that Rav said that the laws governing **interpositions** that invalidate ritual immersion are *halakhot* transmitted to Moses from Sinai. The Gemara challenges this assertion: These, too, **are** written **in the Torah, as it is written: "And he shall bathe all his flesh in the water"** (Leviticus 15:16), and the Sages derived **that nothing should intervene between his flesh and the water.**[H] The definite article in the phrase **"in the water"** indicates that this bathing is performed in water mentioned elsewhere, i.e., specifically **in the water of a ritual bath,** and not in just any water. And the phrase **"all his flesh"** indicates that it must be in **water into which all of his body can enter,** i.e., in which a person can immerse his entire body at once. **And how much** water **is that?** It is **a cubit by a cubit by the height of three cubits. And the Sages calculated** the volume of a ritual bath of this size and determined that **the waters of a ritual bath** measure **forty *se'a*.**[H] As this is derived from the Written Torah, what need is there for a *halakha* transmitted to Moses from Sinai?

כִּי אִיצְטְרִיךְ הִילְכְתָא – לְשַׂעֲרוֹ, וְכִדְרַבָּה בַּר רַב הוּנָא. דְּאָמַר רַבָּה בַּר רַב הוּנָא: נִימָא אַחַת קְשׁוּרָה – חוֹצֶצֶת, שָׁלֹשׁ – אֵינָן חוֹצְצוֹת, שְׁתַּיִם – אֵינִי יוֹדֵעַ.

The Gemara answers: The ***halakha*** transmitted to Moses from Sinai **is needed** with regard **to his hair,** that it too must be accessible to the water without interposition. **And this is in accordance with** the opinion of **Rabba bar Rav Huna, as Rabba bar Rav Huna said: A single hair tied** in a knot **constitutes an interposition**[N] and invalidates the immersion. **Three** hairs tied together in a knot **do not constitute an interposition,** because three hairs cannot be tied so tightly that water cannot penetrate them. With regard to **two** hairs tied together in a knot, **I do not know** the *halakha*. This *halakha* with regard to hair is a *halakha* transmitted to Moses from Sinai.[H]

שַׂעֲרוֹ נַמִּי דְּאוֹרַיְיתָא הוּא, דְּתַנְיָא: "וְרָחַץ אֶת כָּל בְּשָׂרוֹ" – אֶת הַטָּפֵל לִבְשָׂרוֹ, וְזֶהוּ שֵׂעָר!

The Gemara raises a difficulty: The *halakha* with regard to **his hair is also** written **in the Torah, as it was taught** in a *baraita*: **And he shall bathe all [*et kol*] his flesh.** The superfluous word *et* comes to amplify and include **that which is subordinate to his flesh, and that is hair.**

כִּי אֲתַאי הִילְכְתָא – לְרוּבּוֹ וּלְמִיעוּטוֹ, וּלְמַקְפִּיד וּלְשֶׁאֵין מַקְפִּיד, וְכִדְרַבִּי יִצְחָק.

The Gemara answers: The *halakha* transmitted to Moses from Sinai **comes** to teach the details of interpositions on the body **with regard to its majority and its minority, and with regard to one who is particular and one who is not particular, in accordance with** the opinion of **Rabbi Yitzḥak.**

דְּאָמַר רַבִּי יִצְחָק: דְּבַר תּוֹרָה, רוּבּוֹ וּמַקְפִּיד עָלָיו – חוֹצֵץ, וְשֶׁאֵינוֹ מַקְפִּיד עָלָיו – אֵינוֹ חוֹצֵץ. וְגָזְרוּ עַל רוּבּוֹ שֶׁאֵינוֹ מַקְפִּיד מִשּׁוּם רוּבּוֹ הַמַּקְפִּיד, וְעַל מִיעוּטוֹ הַמַּקְפִּיד מִשּׁוּם רוּבּוֹ הַמַּקְפִּיד.

As Rabbi Yitzḥak said: By Torah law, if there is an interposition between a person and the water, and it covers **the majority of his** body, **and he is particular** and wants the interposing substance removed, only then **is it** considered **an interposition** that invalidates immersion in a ritual bath. **However, if he is not particular about** that substance, **it is not** considered **an interposition.** The Sages, however, **issued a decree** prohibiting substances covering **the majority** of one's body with regard to which **he is not particular, due to** substances covering **the majority** of one's body with regard to which **he is particular. And,** they issued a decree prohibiting substances covering **the minority** of **his** body with regard to which **one is particular, due to** substances covering **the majority** of **his** body with regard to which **one is particular.**

וְלִיגְזוֹר נַמִי עַל מִיעוּטוֹ שֶׁאֵינוֹ מַקְפִּיד מִשּׁוּם מִיעוּטוֹ הַמַּקְפִּיד, אִי נַמִי מִשּׁוּם רוּבּוֹ שֶׁאֵינוֹ מַקְפִּיד!

The Gemara raises a question: Then **let us also issue a decree** deeming substances covering **the minority** of **one's** body with regard to which **he is not particular** an interposition **due to** substances covering **the minority** of **his** body with regard to which **one is particular, or alternatively, due to** substances covering **the majority** of **his** body with regard to which **he is not particular.**[H]

הִיא גּוּפָהּ גְּזֵירָה, וַאֲנַן נֵיקוּם וְנִיגְזוֹר גְּזֵירָה לִגְזֵירָה?!

The Gemara answers: We do not issue that decree, because the *halakha* that deems both an interposition covering the minority of his body about which one is particular and an interposition covering the majority of his body about which one is not particular **an interposition is itself a decree. Shall we** then **rise up and issue** one **decree to** prevent violation of another **decree?** In any case, these details with regard to interpositions are neither written nor alluded to in the Torah; rather, they are *halakhot* transmitted to Moses from Sinai.

׳מְחִיצוֹת׳ – דְּאוֹרַיְיתָא נִינְהוּ,

Rabbi Ḥiyya bar Ashi said that Rav said that the *halakhot* of **partitions** were transmitted to Moses from Sinai. The Gemara challenges this assertion as well: **They are** written **in the Torah,** as the fundamental principle that a partition ten handbreadths high establishes a separate domain is derived from the Torah.

דְּאָמַר מָר: אָרוֹן תִּשְׁעָה. וְכַפּוֹרֶת טֶפַח – הֲרֵי כָּאן עֲשָׂרָה!

As the Master said: The Holy **Ark** in the Tabernacle was **nine** handbreadths high, as the verse states that its height was a cubit and a half. A cubit contains six handbreadths, so its height totaled nine handbreadths. **And the cover** atop the Ark was one **handbreadth, which** total **ten.** There is a tradition that the Divine Presence does not descend into the domain of this world, which is derived from the verse that states that the Divine Presence would reveal itself from above the cover of the Ark. Apparently, a partition of ten handbreadths creates a separate domain.

לָא צְרִיכָא, לְרַבִּי יְהוּדָה, דְּאָמַר: אַמַּת בִּנְיָן בְּאַמָּה בַּת שִׁשָּׁה, אַמַּת כֵּלִים בְּאַמָּה בַּת חֲמִשָּׁה.

The Gemara answers: The *halakha* transmitted to Moses from Sinai **is necessary only** according to the opinion of **Rabbi Yehuda, who said: The cubit** mentioned with regard to **the building** of the Tabernacle and the Temple **was a** large **cubit of six** handbreadths, whereas **the cubit** mentioned with regard to the sacred **vessels was a cubit of five** handbreadths. According to this opinion, the Ark, which was a cubit and a half, and its cover, which was a handbreadth, measured eight and a half handbreadths. Therefore, nothing can be derived with regard to a partition of ten handbreadths.

וּלְרַבִּי מֵאִיר, דְּאָמַר: כָּל הָאַמּוֹת הָיוּ בְּבֵינוֹנִית, מַאי אִיכָּא לְמֵימַר?

The Gemara poses a question. **And according to** the opinion of **Rabbi Meir, who said: All the cubits were medium** ones, regular cubits of six handbreadths; **what can be said?** Apparently, according to his opinion, the laws governing partitions are explicitly stated in the Torah.

HALAKHA

Interposition and particularity – חֲצִיצָה וְהַקְפָּדָה: Anything of any size that intervenes between one's body and the water of a ritual bath constitutes an interposition if most people are particular about it and will remove it from their bodies. If only the person immersing is always particular about this kind of interposition, then it constitutes an interposition for that person (Rambam; *Darkhei Moshe*; *Bah*). Any substance that covers most of the body constitutes an interposition even if people are usually not particular about it. One should not immerse with a foreign substance on one's body, *ab initio*, for the purpose of becoming pure, e.g., in the case of a menstruating woman, even if the substance is not considered an interposition (Rema; *Shulḥan Arukh*, *Yoreh De'a* 198:1).

לְרַבִּי מֵאִיר, כִּי אֲתָאי הִילְכְתָא – לְגוּד וּלְלָבוּד וּלְדוֹפֶן עֲקוּמָּה.

The Gemara answers: **According to** the opinion of **Rabbi Meir,** the *halakha* with regard to a partition of ten handbreadths is indeed written in the Torah. However, the ***halakha*** transmitted to Moses from Sinai **comes** to teach other *halakhot* concerning partitions, e.g., the *halakhot* of **extending [*gode*],** according to which an existing partition is extended upward or downward to complete the requisite measure; **and** the *halakhot* of **joining [*lavud*],** according to which two solid surfaces are joined if they are separated by a gap of less than three handbreadths; **and** the *halakhot* of **the curved wall** of a *sukka*. A *sukka* is valid even if there are up to four cubits of invalid roofing, provided that this roofing is adjacent to one of the walls of the *sukka*. In that case, the invalid roofing is considered a bent extension of the wall. These concepts are certainly not written in the Torah.

הָיָה גָּבוֹהַּ מֵעֶשְׂרִים אַמָּה וּבָא לְמַעֲטוֹ כַּמָּה מְמַעֵט. ״כַּמָּה מְמַעֵט״?! כַּמָּה דְּצָרִיךְ לֵיהּ!

The Gemara returns to the laws of alleyways: If the cross beam spanning the entrance to an alleyway **was higher than twenty cubits** from the ground **and one comes to diminish its** height, **how much must he diminish** it? The Gemara is surprised by the question: **How much must he diminish** it? **The amount that he needs** in order to render its height less than twenty cubits.[H]

אֶלָּא: רָחְבּוֹ בְּכַמָּה? רַב יוֹסֵף אָמַר: טֶפַח. אַבַּיֵי אָמַר: אַרְבָּעָה.

Rather, the space between the cross beam and the ground must, of course, be reduced to twenty cubits. However, when one raises the alleyway, **how much** must **the width** of the raised section be in order to render the alleyway fit for carrying within it? **Rav Yosef said:** One **handbreadth. Abaye said: Four** handbreadths.[N]

לֵימָא בְּהָא קָא מִיפַּלְגִי, דְּמַאן דְּאָמַר: טֶפַח, קָסָבַר: מוּתָּר לְהִשְׁתַּמֵּשׁ תַּחַת הַקּוֹרָה.

The Gemara suggests: **Let us say** that these *amora'im* **disagree about this: The one who said** one **handbreadth holds** that **one is permitted to utilize** the area **beneath the** cross **beam** spanning the entrance to the alleyway, as he maintains that the cross beam serves as a partition, and the alleyway is considered as if it were sealed by a partition descending from the outer edge of the cross beam that faces the public domain. Since the area beneath the cross beam is part of the alleyway and is less than twenty cubits, there is a conspicuous demarcation for one standing in the alleyway.

HALAKHA

Diminishing the height of a cross beam – מִיעוּט בְּקוֹרָה: If a cross beam across the entrance to an alleyway is more than twenty cubits off the ground, the alleyway can be rendered fit for carrying within it by raising a portion of the ground under the cross beam. The width of the raised section must be at least a handbreadth. This ruling is in accordance with Rav Yosef's opinion, since he was Abaye's teacher and the Gemara's discussion agrees with his position, as explained by the Rambam, the Rosh, Rabbeinu Yehonatan, and others (*Shulḥan Arukh, Oraḥ Ḥayyim* 363:26).

NOTES

Diminishing the height of the alleyway – מִיעוּט מָבוֹי: There are several variant texts as well as several interpretative approaches with regard to this issue. According to one variant text, the Sage who says: One handbreadth, rules that it is prohibited to utilize the area under the cross beam. Therefore, it is enough to raise an area the width of a handbreadth, since that handbreadth will not itself be used. The Sage who says: Four handbreadths, holds that one is permitted to utilize the area under the cross beam. Consequently, four handbreadths are required so the boundary of the alleyway is clearly recognizable (Ra'avad; *Sefer Haltim*).

Other commentaries follow the Rif's explanation, according to which diminishing the height of the alleyway is accomplished by adding another cross beam under the existing one, so that the space between the cross beam and the ground will be less than twenty cubits. According to this approach, the argument revolves around the question of how large the second cross beam must be in order to supersede the first beam. Nevertheless, according to this explanation, the logic of the Gemara's discussion is difficult to understand. In addition, it is explicitly stated in the Jerusalem Talmud that the dispute relates to a raised section built underneath the cross beam.

Perek **I**
Daf **5** Amud **a**

וּמַאן דְּאָמַר אַרְבָּעָה קָסָבַר: אָסוּר לְהִשְׁתַּמֵּשׁ תַּחַת הַקּוֹרָה.

And the one who said four handbreadths **holds** that the alleyway is considered as if it were sealed from the inside edge of the cross beam, and consequently it is prohibited **to utilize** the area **beneath the** cross **beam.** As the area beneath the cross beam is not part of the alleyway, a significant demarcation, i.e., one of four handbreadths, is required within the alleyway itself.

לָא, דְּכוּלֵּי עָלְמָא קָסָבְרִי: מוּתָּר לְהִשְׁתַּמֵּשׁ תַּחַת הַקּוֹרָה, וּבְהָא קָא מִיפַּלְגִי: מָר סָבַר: קוֹרָה מִשּׁוּם הֶיכֵּר, וּמָר סָבַר: קוֹרָה מִשּׁוּם מְחִיצָּה.

The Gemara rejects this explanation: **No, everyone agrees that it is permitted to utilize** the area **beneath the** cross **beam,**[H] **and they disagree with regard to this:** This **Master,** Rav Yosef, **holds** that **a** cross **beam** functions in an alleyway **as a conspicuous marker**[H] that demarcates the alleyway from the public domain, and consequently a mere handbreadth is sufficient, as even a handbreadth is sufficiently conspicuous. **And** this **Master,** Abaye, **holds** that **a** cross **beam** serves **as a partition,** and a partition is not effective for an area of less than four handbreadths. The principle that an outer edge descends and seals the alleyway does not apply if the beam is higher than twenty cubits. In order for it to be considered a partition, there must be at least four handbreadths that are less than twenty cubits beneath the cross beam.

HALAKHA

Utilizing the area beneath the cross beam – שִׁימּוּשׁ תַּחַת הַקּוֹרָה: One is permitted to make use of an alleyway, including the area under the cross beam itself (*Shulḥan Arukh, Oraḥ Ḥayyim* 365:4).

A cross beam as a conspicuous marker – קוֹרָה מִשּׁוּם הֶיכֵּר: A cross beam across the entrance to an alleyway is not considered a partition, but only a conspicuous marker (Rambam *Sefer Zemanim, Hilkhot Shabbat* 17:9, 15).

וְאִיבָּעֵית אֵימָא: דְּכוּלֵּי עָלְמָא קוֹרָה – מִשּׁוּם הֶיכֵּר, וְהָכָא בְּהֶיכֵּר שֶׁל מַטָּה וּבְהֶיכֵּר שֶׁל מַעְלָה קָא מִיפַּלְגִי; דְּמָר סָבַר: אָמְרִינַן "הֶיכֵּר שֶׁל מַטָּה כְּהֶיכֵּר שֶׁל מַעְלָה", וּמָר סָבַר: לָא אָמְרִינַן "הֶיכֵּר שֶׁל מַטָּה כְּהֶיכֵּר שֶׁל מַעְלָה".

The Gemara proposes an alternative explanation: **And if you wish, say** instead **that everyone agrees** that a cross **beam** serves **as a conspicuous marker, and here they disagree with regard to** the relationship between **a conspicuous marker below,** i.e., the raised area of the alleyway, **and a conspicuous marker above,** i.e., the cross beam. This **Master,** Rav Yosef, **holds** that **we say** that the *halakha* that governs **the conspicuous marker below is like** the *halakha* that applies to **the conspicuous marker above,** and one handbreadth suffices.[H] **And** this **Master,** Abaye, **holds** that **we do not say** that the *halakha* that governs **the conspicuous marker below is like** the *halakha* that applies to **the conspicuous marker above.** The lower sign must be more prominent and extend four handbreadths.

וְאִיבָּעֵית אֵימָא: דְּכוּלֵּי עָלְמָא אָמְרִינַן "הֶיכֵּר שֶׁל מַטָּה כְּהֶיכֵּר שֶׁל מַעְלָה" וְהָכָא בִּגְזֵירָה שֶׁמָּא יִפְחוֹת קָמִיפַּלְגִי.

The Gemara proposes yet another explanation of the amoraic dispute: **And if you wish, say** instead **that everyone agrees** that **we say** that fundamentally, the *halakha* that governs **the conspicuous marker below is like** the *halakha* that applies to the **conspicuous marker above,** and even a handbreadth should suffice. **But here they disagree whether** the Sages **decreed** that four handbreadths are necessary, **lest** people treading upon it will erode and **diminish** the raised area.[N] Rav Yosef is not concerned that it will be diminished and therefore holds that a raised area of a handbreadth is sufficient, whereas Abaye is concerned that the raised area of a handbreadth will erode to less than a handbreadth, rendering it inconspicuous, and the alleyway will come to be utilized in a prohibited manner.

"הָיָה פָּחוֹת מֵעֲשָׂרָה טְפָחִים וְחָקַק בּוֹ לְהַשְׁלִימוֹ לַעֲשָׂרָה". כַּמָּה חוֹקֵק? כַּמָּה חוֹקֵק?! כַּמָּה דִּצְרִיךְ לֵיהּ! אֶלָּא: מִשְׁכּוֹ בְּכַמָּה? רַב יוֹסֵף אָמַר: בְּאַרְבָּעָה, אַבַּיֵי אָמַר: בְּאַרְבַּע אַמּוֹת.

The Gemara considers a new case: If the cross beam spanning the entrance to an alleyway **was less than ten handbreadths** above the ground, **and one hollowed out** the ground under the cross beam in order **to complete** the distance from the ground to the cross beam **to ten, how much must he hollow out?** The Gemara is surprised by the question: **How much must he hollow out? However much is necessary for it** to increase the height to at least ten handbreadths. **Rather,** the question is as follows: **How far must** the hollowed-out area **extend**[N] into the alleyway in order to render it permitted to carry throughout the alleyway? **Rav Yosef said: Four** handbreadths. **Abaye said: Four cubits.**[H]

לֵימָא בִּדְרַבִּי אַמִּי וְרַבִּי אַסִּי קָמִיפַּלְגִי; דְּאִיתְּמַר: מָבוֹי שֶׁנִּפְרַץ מִצִּידּוֹ כְּלַפֵּי רֹאשׁוֹ, אִיתְּמַר מִשְּׁמֵיהּ דְּרַבִּי אַמִּי וְרַבִּי אַסִּי: אִם יֵשׁ שָׁם פַּס אַרְבָּעָה – מַתִּיר בְּפִירְצָה עַד עֶשֶׂר.

The Gemara suggests: **Let us say that** these *amora'im* **disagree with regard to** the ruling of **Rabbi Ami and Rabbi Asi. As it was stated** with regard to the following question: If **the side wall of an alleyway was breached**[H] **toward its entrance,**[B] i.e., close to where the alleyway opens into the public domain, what is the *halakha*? **It was stated in the name of Rabbi Ami and Rabbi Asi: If** an upright **board four** handbreadths long remains of the original wall or is set up where the original wall had ended, the cross beam or side post at the entrance to the alleyway **renders it permitted** to carry in the alleyway even if there is **a breach of up to ten** cubits long.

NOTES

Decreed lest people…erode and diminish – גְּזֵירָה שֶׁמָּא יִפְחוֹת: According to all of these explanations, Abaye's opinion should be explained as follows: Since one handbreadth is insufficient for some reason, e.g., a decree lest the raised area become worn down, therefore, some other significant measure is required, and that is four handbreadths (Rashba).

How far must the hollowed-out area extend – מִשְׁכּוֹ בְּכַמָּה: In the Jerusalem Talmud, other Sages dispute this same issue as follows: The one who rules that the width of the hollowed-out area must extend four cubits argues that this is the measure of an alleyway. The one who maintains that four handbreadths are sufficient argues that this defines an area as a place.

The authorities disagree with regard to the width of the area that must be dug. The Rif states that four cubits are required, because his text reads: Four cubits by four cubits. Based on a different textual reading, the *Baḥ* claims that a width of four handbreadths is sufficient. The Rosh requires that the entire length of the alleyway must be hollowed out. In the Jerusalem Talmud, another opinion is offered in this matter: It is enough if one hollows out three handbreadths into the alleyway, so long as one digs adjacent to its walls.

BACKGROUND

If the side wall of an alleyway was breached toward its entrance – מָבוֹי שֶׁנִּפְרַץ מִצִּידּוֹ כְּלַפֵּי רֹאשׁוֹ: This describes an alleyway, the side wall of which was breached close to its entrance, with an upright board of wall four handbreadths in length remaining adjacent to the entrance. This is in accordance with the explanation that its head, i.e., the entrance, is the side facing the public domain.

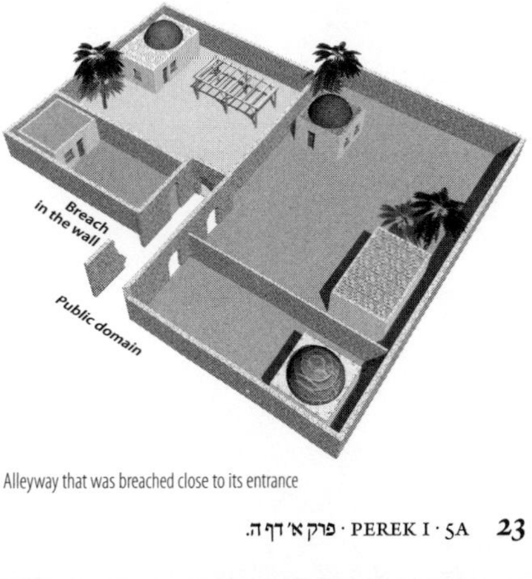

Alleyway that was breached close to its entrance

HALAKHA

A conspicuous marker above and a conspicuous marker below – הֶיכֵּר שֶׁל מַעְלָה וְהֶיכֵּר שֶׁל מַטָּה: When the ground is raised in order to diminish the height of a cross beam to less than twenty cubits, a raised area one handbreadth wide suffices, in accordance with the opinion of Rav Yosef. However, care must be taken that it not be worn down by people walking over it (*Magen Avraham*; *Shulḥan Arukh, Oraḥ Ḥayyim* 363:26).

The length of the hollowed-out area in an alleyway – מֶשֶׁךְ מָבוֹי חָקוּק: When hollowing out an alleyway to complete its height to ten handbreadths, the hollowed-out area must extend four cubits into the alleyway. This ruling is in accordance with the view of Abaye, because the talmudic discussion appears to endorse his opinion, both in this context (*Hagahot Maimoniyot*) and elsewhere (Vilna Gaon). The width of the hollowed-out section is a matter of dispute between the early commentaries. Some say that a width of four handbreadths is sufficient (*Korban Netanel*), but most authorities maintain that it must extend the entire width of the alleyway (Rosh), so long as its width is not greater than its length (*Baḥ*; *Shulḥan Arukh, Oraḥ Ḥayyim* 363:26).

If the side wall of an alleyway was breached – מָבוֹי שֶׁנִּפְרַץ מִצִּידּוֹ: If the side wall of an alleyway was breached close to where the alleyway opens onto the public domain, so long as there remains an upright board four handbreadths long adjacent to the entrance, one may carry in the alleyway provided that the breach is less than ten cubits. However, if there is no such upright board or if it is less than four handbreadths long, one may carry only if the breach is less than three handbreadths wide (*Shulḥan Arukh, Oraḥ Ḥayyim* 365:1).

וְאִם לָאו, פָּחוֹת מִשְּׁלֹשָׁה – מַתִּיר, שְׁלֹשָׁה – אֵינוֹ מַתִּיר. לְרַב יוֹסֵף – אִית לֵיהּ דְּרַבִּי אַמִי, לְאַבַּיֵּי – לֵית לֵיהּ דְּרַבִּי אַמִי.

And if there is **no** upright board there, the following distinction applies: If the breach is **less than three** handbreadths, the cross beam or side post **renders it permitted** to carry in the alleyway, based on the principle of *lavud*. If the breach is **three** or more handbreadths, the cross beam or side post **does not render it permitted** to carry. The Gemara proposes that **Rav Yosef,** who says that the hollowed-out area need only extend four handbreadths, **adopts** the opinion **of Rabbi Ami,** whereas **Abaye,** who requires a hollowed-out area of four cubits, **does not adopt** the opinion **of Rabbi Ami.**

אָמַר לָךְ אַבַּיֵּי: הָתָם – סוֹף מָבוֹי, הָכָא – תְּחִלַּת מָבוֹי, אִי אִיכָּא אַרְבַּע אַמּוֹת – אִין, אִי לָא – לָא.

The Gemara rejects this argument: **Abaye** could have **said to you** that the two cases are not comparable: **There,** in Rav Ami's case, we are dealing with **the final** stage **of an alleyway,** i.e., an alleyway that had at first been properly structured, and only later did it become breached. **Here,** we are dealing with **the initial** stage **of an alleyway,** i.e., an alleyway that from the very outset did not fulfill the necessary conditions. In this case: **If there are four cubits** in the hollowed-out area, **yes,** it is considered an alleyway, and **if not, no,** it is not considered an alleyway.

אָמַר אַבַּיֵּי: מְנָא אָמִינָא לָהּ – דְּתַנְיָא: אֵין מָבוֹי נִיתָּר בַּלֶּחִי וְקוֹרָה עַד שֶׁיְּהוּ בָּתִּים וַחֲצֵרוֹת פְּתוּחִין לְתוֹכוֹ.

Abaye said: From where do I say that a length of at least four cubits is required? **As it was taught** in a *baraita*: **An alleyway is permitted by means of a side post or** cross **beam only if it has** both **houses** opening into courtyards **and courtyards opening into it,**[H] as only in that case can it be called an alleyway.

וְאִי בְּאַרְבָּעָה, הֵיכִי מַשְׁכַּחַתְּ לֵיהּ?

And if the entire length of the alleyway is only **four** handbreadths, as is indicated by Rav Yosef's opinion, **how can you find this** case? Under what circumstances is it possible for such a short alleyway to have courtyards opening into it? Even if there are only two such courtyards, the entrance to each is at least four handbreadths wide.

וְכִי תֵּימָא: דְּפָתַח לָהּ בַּדּוֹפֶן הָאֶמְצָעִי – וְהָאָמַר רַב נַחְמָן נְקִיטִינַן, אֵיזֶהוּ מָבוֹי שֶׁנִּיתָּר בַּלֶּחִי וְקוֹרָה – כֹּל שֶׁאׇרְכּוֹ יָתֵר עַל רׇחְבּוֹ, וּבָתִּים וַחֲצֵרוֹת פְּתוּחִין לְתוֹכוֹ.

And if you say that the alleyway **opens** into the courtyards **through** its **middle wall,** i.e., the alleyway is only four handbreadths long but is wide enough to have two entrances opening into two courtyards, this is difficult. **Didn't Rav Naḥman say** that **we hold** on the authority of tradition: **Which is an alleyway that is permitted by a side post or** a cross **beam? Any** alleyway **whose length is greater than its width**[N] **and has houses and courtyards opening into it.** Accordingly, if the alleyway is only four handbreadths long, its width must be even less than that. Consequently, argues Abaye, a length of at least four cubits is required.

וְרַב יוֹסֵף? דְּפָתַח לֵיהּ בְּקֶרֶן זָוִית.

And Rav Yosef, how would he respond to this? Rav Yosef explains that the *baraita* is dealing with a case **where** the courtyards **open** into the alleyway **at its corners.** In this way it is possible to have two openings, each of which is at least four handbreadths wide, although the length of the alleyway itself is no greater than four handbreadths,[B] as the four handbreadths of the openings to the courtyards are divided between the width and the length of the alleyway.

אָמַר אַבַּיֵּי: מְנָא אָמִינָא לָהּ – דְּאָמַר רָמִי בַּר חָמָא אָמַר רַב הוּנָא: לֶחִי הַבּוֹלֵט מִדּוֹפְנוֹ שֶׁל מָבוֹי, פָּחוֹת מֵאַרְבַּע אַמּוֹת – נִידּוֹן מִשּׁוּם לֶחִי, וְאֵינוֹ צָרִיךְ לֶחִי אַחֵר לְהַתִּירוֹ. אַרְבַּע אַמּוֹת – נִידּוֹן מִשּׁוּם מָבוֹי, וְצָרִיךְ לֶחִי אַחֵר לְהַתִּירוֹ.

Abaye further **said: From where do I say** that a length of at least four cubits is required? **As Rami bar Ḥama said** that **Rav Huna said:** With regard to **a side post that protrudes from the wall** on the side **of an alleyway** into the opening of the alleyway, if its protrusion was **less than four cubits, it is deemed a side post** that renders it permitted to carry in the alleyway, **and no other side post is required to render it permitted** to carry in it. However, if it protruded **four cubits,** that section **is deemed an alleyway,** as though there were an additional alleyway within an alleyway, **and another side post is required to render it permitted** to carry there. This shows that anything less than four cubits does not have the status of an alleyway, which supports the position of Abaye.

וְרַב יוֹסֵף: לְאַפּוֹקֵי מִתּוֹרַת לֶחִי – עַד דְּאִיכָּא אַרְבַּע אַמּוֹת, לְמֶיהֱוֵי מָבוֹי – אֲפִילּוּ בְּאַרְבָּעָה טְפָחִים נַמִי הָוֵי מָבוֹי.

The Gemara asks: **And Rav Yosef,** how would he respond to this? Rav Yosef distinguishes between the cases: With regard **to removing its status as a side post,** this status remains **until there are four cubits** in the length of the side post. However, **in order to be** deemed **an** independent **alleyway, even with** a wall of **four handbreadths it is also** considered **an alleyway.**

HALAKHA

Houses and courtyards opening into it – בָּתִּים וַחֲצֵרוֹת לְתוֹכוֹ: The Sages permitted one to carry in an alleyway with a conspicuous marker of a side post or a cross beam, if at least two courtyards open into the alleyway and each courtyard contains at least two houses (Rashi; Rosh; *Shulḥan Arukh, Oraḥ Ḥayyim* 363:26).

NOTES

Whose length is greater than its width – אׇרְכּוֹ יָתֵר עַל רׇחְבּוֹ: This statement demonstrates that the length of an alleyway is not necessarily its longest side. If that were the case, the idea of an alleyway whose width is greater than its length would be meaningless. Rather, the length of an alleyway refers to the direction of the alleyway that extends from the opening onto the public domain, while the other dimension is called the width of the alleyway.

BACKGROUND

An alleyway of four handbreadths – מָבוֹי בֵּן אַרְבָּעָה טְפָחִים: The area of the alleyway is four handbreadths by four handbreadths. The entrances to the two adjacent courtyards are on either side of the alleyway. The diagram below differs slightly from the diagram found in Rashi in order to present the measurements more precisely (*Tosafot*).

Small alleyway, the length and width of which are four handbreadths

גּוּפָא, אָמַר רָמִי בַּר חָמָא, אָמַר רַב הוּנָא: לֶחִי הַבּוֹלֵט מִדָּפְנוֹ שֶׁל מָבוֹי,

The Gemara examines Rami bar Ḥama's statement cited in the course of the previous discussion. As to the matter **itself: Rami bar Ḥama said** that **Rav Huna said:** With regard to **a side post that protrudes from the wall** on the side **of an alleyway** into the entrance of the alleyway,

פָּחוֹת מֵאַרְבַּע אַמּוֹת – נִידּוֹן מִשּׁוּם לֶחִי, וְאֵין צָרִיךְ לֶחִי אַחֵר לְהַתִּירוֹ. אַרְבַּע אַמּוֹת – נִידּוֹן מִשּׁוּם מָבוֹי, וְצָרִיךְ לֶחִי אַחֵר לְהַתִּירוֹ.

if its protrusion is **less than four cubits, it is deemed a side post** that renders it permitted to carry in the alleyway, **and no other side post is required to render it permitted.** However, if it protrudes **four cubits,** that section **is deemed an alleyway, and another side post is required to render it permitted to** carry in it.[NHB]

אוֹתוֹ לֶחִי הֵיכָן מַעֲמִידוֹ? אִי דְּמוֹקֵי לֵיהּ בַּהֲדֵיהּ – אוֹסְפֵי הוּא דְּקָא מוֹסִיף עֲלֵיהּ!

The Gemara poses a question: **That side post,** which is added in order to permit carrying within the alleyway that was formed by the four-cubit side post, **where does one position it** such that one may carry within the alleyway? The Gemara clarifies its difficulty: **If one positions it alongside** the first side post as an addition to it, it looks as if **he is** merely **extending** the original side post, and it is not noticeable that an extra side post is present.

אָמַר רַב פַּפָּא: דְּמוֹקֵי לֵיהּ לְאִידָּךְ גִּיסָא. רַב הוּנָא בְּרֵיהּ דְּרַב יְהוֹשֻׁעַ אָמַר: אֲפִילּוּ תֵּימָא דְּמוֹקֵי לָהּ בַּהֲדֵיהּ. דְּמְטַפֵּי בֵּיהּ, אוֹ דִּמְבַצֵּר בֵּיהּ.

Rav Pappa said: He should position it, the extra side post, **on the other side** of the alleyway, near the opposite wall. **Rav Huna, son of Rav Yehoshua, said: Even if you say that he positions it alongside** the first side post, it is valid, so long as **he adds to it or diminishes from it** in thickness or height, so that it will be noticeable that it is a side post of its own.[H]

אָמַר רַב הוּנָא בְּרֵיהּ דְּרַב יְהוֹשֻׁעַ: לָא אֲמַרַן אֶלָּא בְּמָבוֹי שְׁמוֹנָה, אֲבָל בְּמָבוֹי שִׁבְעָה – נִיתָּר בְּעוֹמֵד מְרוּבֶּה עַל הַפָּרוּץ.

The Gemara limits the application of Rami bar Ḥama's ruling: **Rav Huna, son of Rav Yehoshua, said: We stated** this halakha with regard to a side post protruding four cubits into the alleyway **only in** the case of **an alleyway** that is at least **eight** cubits wide. **However, in** the case of **an alleyway** that is only **seven** cubits wide, it is **permitted** to carry within the alleyway without an additional side post, not because the original side post functions as a side post but rather because it sufficiently seals off the entrance to the alleyway such that the **standing** segment **is greater than the breached** segment. The alleyway is now closed off from all four sides, and the remaining opening to the public domain is regarded as an entrance, as most of that side is closed and only a small part of it is open.

וְקַל וָחוֹמֶר מֵחָצֵר. וּמָה חָצֵר שֶׁאֵינָהּ נִיתֶּרֶת בְּלֶחִי וְקוֹרָה – נִיתֶּרֶת בְּעוֹמֵד מְרוּבֶּה עַל הַפָּרוּץ, מָבוֹי שֶׁנִּיתָּר בְּלֶחִי וְקוֹרָה – אֵינוֹ דִּין שֶׁנִּיתָּר בְּעוֹמֵד מְרוּבֶּה עַל הַפָּרוּץ?

And this is derived by means of **an *a fortiori* inference from a courtyard: Just as** in **a courtyard, which is not** rendered a **permitted** domain **by** means of **a side post or a** cross **beam,** but actual partitions are required, it **is** nevertheless rendered a **permitted** domain even if there are gaps in the partitions, as long **as the standing** segment **is greater than the breached** segment in **an alleyway,** with regard to which the Sages were lenient, **as it is** rendered a **permitted** domain **by** means of **a side post or a** cross **beam, is it not right** that it **is** rendered a **permitted** domain **when the standing** segment of the partition is **greater than the breached** segment?

מָה לְחָצֵר שֶׁכֵּן פִּרְצָתָהּ בְּעֶשֶׂר, תֹּאמַר בְּמָבוֹי שֶׁפִּרְצָתוֹ בְּאַרְבַּע!

The Gemara refutes this *a fortiori* inference that was based on the fact that the legal status of a courtyard is more lenient than that of an alleyway, as it is in fact more stringent than that of an alleyway in at least one respect. With regard to **what** is true **of a courtyard, that** as long as **its breach is** less than **ten** cubits it remains a permitted domain, can **you say** the same **of an alleyway,** which is more stringent, as in a case where **its breach is** only **four** handbreadths it is not permitted to carry in the alleyway? Therefore, the *halakha* of an alleyway cannot be derived from the *halakha* of a courtyard.

NOTES

A side post that protrudes into an alleyway – לֶחִי הַבּוֹלֵט לְמָבוֹי: A majority of the commentaries hold that this side post was not originally placed for the purpose of rendering the alleyway fit for carrying. Rather, it served the needs of the alleyway, e.g., it was one of the beams supporting the walls of the alleyway or the adjacent houses (Rosh). Many commentaries tried to explain the Gemara's words in this context as referring to a side post that does not protrude into the width of the alleyway, but extends lengthwise into the alleyway (*Me'iri*). Other authorities state that the protruding side post is located not at the entrance to the alleyway, but in its middle, thereby dividing the alleyway into two: The section from the entrance to the side post and the section from the side post to the end of the alleyway. The ensuing debate is whether a protruding side post of this kind is sufficient to render it permitted to carry in both sections of the alleyway (Ra'avad; see Rabbeinu Yehonatan).

HALAKHA

A side post along the width of an alleyway – לֶחִי בְּרוֹחַב מָבוֹי: If a side post greater than four cubits is found in an alleyway, and it was not placed there to render it permitted to carry in the alleyway or is not relied upon for that halakhic purpose (*Beit Yosef*), then a second side post must be added to permit use of the alleyway. This ruling is in accordance with the view of Rav Huna (*Shulḥan Arukh, Oraḥ Ḥayyim* 363:12).

Placing the side post – תִּיקּוּן הַלֶּחִי: If an additional side post is required for an alleyway, it should be placed on the opposite side of the alleyway from the first side post, in accordance with Rav Pappa's opinion. Alternatively, it can also be placed alongside the first side post, if one alters its width or height such that it is evident that it serves as a halakhic side post, in accordance with the opinion of Rav Huna, son of Rav Yehoshua (*Shulḥan Arukh, Oraḥ Ḥayyim* 363:12).

BACKGROUND

A side post that protrudes into an alleyway – לֶחִי הַבּוֹלֵט לְמָבוֹי:

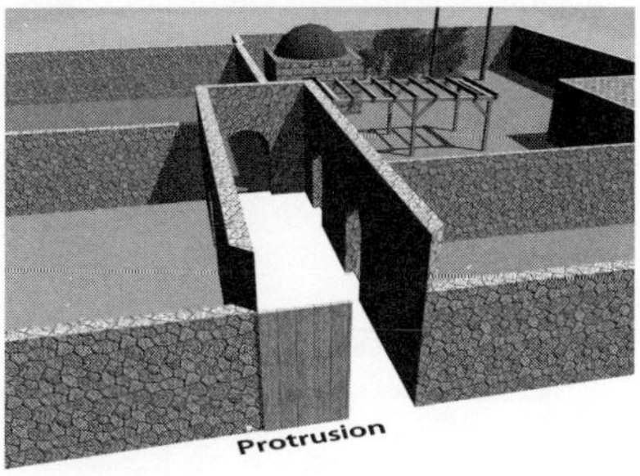

Alleyway with side post

קָסָבַר רַב הוּנָא בְּרֵיהּ דְּרַב יְהוֹשֻׁעַ: מָבוֹי נַמִי, פִּרְצָתוֹ בְּעֶשֶׂר. לְמַאן קָאָמְרִינַן – לְרַב הוּנָא, וְהָא רַב הוּנָא פִּרְצָתוֹ בְּאַרְבַּע סְבִירָא לֵיהּ!

The Gemara answers: **Rav Huna, son of Rav Yehoshua, holds** that **the breach of an alleyway** is **also ten** cubits. The Gemara raises a difficulty: But **in accordance with whose** opinion **did we state** this *a fortiori* inference? It is **in accordance with** the opinion of **Rav Huna. But doesn't Rav Huna** himself **hold that the breach** of an alleyway is **four** handbreadths.

רַב הוּנָא בְּרֵיהּ דְּרַב יְהוֹשֻׁעַ טַעְמָא דְּנַפְשֵׁיהּ קָאָמַר.

The Gemara answers: **Rav Huna, son of Rav Yehoshua,** did not come to explain Rav Huna's position. Rather, he **stated his own view,** and he does not accept Rav Huna's opinion with regard to the law of a breach in an alleyway.

רַב אַשִׁי אָמַר: אֲפִילּוּ תֵּימָא בְּמָבוֹי שְׁמוֹנָה נַמִי לֹא צָרִיךְ לֶחִי. מַה נַּפְשָׁךְ, אִי עוֹמֵד נָפֵישׁ – נִיתָּר בְּעוֹמֵד מְרוּבֶּה עַל הַפָּרוּץ, וְאִי פָּרוּץ נָפֵישׁ – נִידּוֹן מִשּׁוּם לֶחִי

Rav Ashi went further than Rav Huna, son of Rav Yehoshua, and **said: Even if you say** that the law with regard to a side post protruding four cubits into the alleyway applies **in** the case of **an alleyway** that is exactly **eight** cubits wide,[H] in that it **too does not require an** additional **side post. Whichever** way **you** look at it, you are forced to arrive at this conclusion: **If** you say that the **standing** segment **is greater,** then the alleyway **is permitted,** because its **standing** segment **is greater than the breached** segment; **and if** you say that the **breached** segment **is greater,** then the protrusion is **deemed a side post,** as its width must be less than four cubits.

מַאי אָמְרַתְּ – דְּשָׁווּ תַּרְוַויְיהוּ כִּי הֲדָדֵי, הֲוָה לֵיהּ סְפֵק דִּבְרֵיהֶן, וּסְפֵק דִּבְרֵיהֶן לְהָקֵל.

What might **you say** that would require an additional side post? Would you suggest that there is yet another possibility, **that the two are** exactly **equal,** the standing portion and the breach?[N] **This is an uncertainty** with regard to **rabbinic law,** as carrying in an alleyway is forbidden only by rabbinic law, **and** the principle is that where there is **an uncertainty** with regard to **a rabbinic law,** one may assume the **lenient** position, as opposed to an uncertainty arising with respect to a Torah law, where one assumes the stringent position.

אָמַר רַב חָנִין בַּר רָבָא, אָמַר רַב: מָבוֹי שֶׁנִּפְרַץ

The Gemara considers a new case: **Rav Ḥanin bar Rava said** that **Rav said:** With regard to **an alleyway that was breached,**

HALAKHA

An alleyway that is eight – מָבוֹי שְׁמוֹנָה: The laws mentioned above with regard to a side post only apply to an alleyway that is wider than eight cubits. However, if the alleyway is exactly eight cubits wide or less, it is permitted to use a side post of four cubits, in accordance with the opinion of Rav Ashi, which is the later opinion (*Shulḥan Arukh*, *Oraḥ Ḥayyim* 363:12).

NOTES

The standing segment is equal to the breached segment – עוֹמֵד כְּפָרוּץ: The discussion of the case where the standing portion of the wall and the breach are exactly equal is connected to a more general question raised in the Talmud: Is precision possible? Can two things be exactly equal to one another in length? *Tosafot* and other commentaries discuss at length the issue of whether it is possible for man-made things to be fashioned precisely or whether this is impossible. If this is in fact impossible, then since the two portions cannot be equal, carrying within the alleyway should be permitted in either case. It has been suggested that Rav Ashi made his comment only in accordance with the opinion of Rav Huna, son of Rav Yehoshua, who holds that when the breached segment is equal to the standing segment, the wall is considered breached. However, according to those who disagree, his statement was unnecessary. The Rashba is uncertain whether it may be inferred from this discussion that a side post that protrudes past the midline of an alleyway always renders it permitted to carry in the alleyway, even in cases where the width of the alleyway greatly exceeds eight handbreadths. The Rambam maintains, based on Rav Ashi's statement, that an alleyway of this kind is permitted, whatever its width.

מִצִּידּוֹ – בְּעֶשֶׂר, מֵרֹאשׁוֹ – בְּאַרְבָּעָה.

if it was breached **from its side,**[H] the side wall of the alleyway, carrying within the alleyway is prohibited if the breach is **ten** cubits wide. But if it was breached **from its front,**[N] the wall that faces the public domain, carrying within the alleyway is prohibited even if the breach is only **four** handbreadths wide.

מַאי שְׁנָא מִצִּידּוֹ בְּעֶשֶׂר – דְּאָמַר פִּתְחָא הוּא, מֵרֹאשׁוֹ נַמִי – נֵימָא פִּתְחָא הוּא!

The Gemara poses a question: **What is the difference** such that carrying is prohibited due to a breach **from the side** only if the breach is **ten** cubits? This is **because** you **say** that up to ten cubits **it is** deemed **an entrance.** If the breach is **in the front, let us also say it is an entrance,** and carrying should be permitted if the breach is less than ten cubits.

אָמַר רַב הוּנָא בְּרֵיהּ דְּרַב יְהוֹשֻׁעַ: כְּגוֹן שֶׁנִּפְרַץ בְּקֶרֶן זָוִית, דְּפִתְחָא בְּקֶרֶן זָוִית לָא עָבְדִי אֱינָשֵׁי.

Rav Huna, son of Rav Yehoshua, said: We are dealing with **a case where the breach is in a corner.**[B] Since **people do not make an entrance in a corner,** a breach of this kind cannot be viewed as an entrance, and if the breach is larger than four handbreadths it must be sealed.

HALAKHA

An alleyway that was breached from its side – מָבוֹי שֶׁנִּפְרַץ מִצִּידּוֹ: It is prohibited to carry in an alleyway that was breached from the side, or one that was breached directly from the front and not at the corner (*Magen Avraham*), if the breach is ten cubits wide. This rule applies only if people do not regularly cross through the breach. However, if people regularly cross through it, it is prohibited to carry in the alleyway until the breach is repaired, even if the breach is only four handbreadths wide (Rema). This ruling is in accordance with the opinion of Rav Ḥanin bar Rava, either because the Talmud itself does not issue a final ruling and the *halakha* is lenient in matters of rabbinic law (Rosh), or because Rav Huna, son of Rav Yehoshua, who is a later authority, agrees with him (Vilna Gaon; *Shulḥan Arukh*, *Oraḥ Ḥayyim* 365:2).

BACKGROUND

The breach is in a corner – נִפְרַץ בְּקֶרֶן זָוִית: This phrase refers to an alleyway where part of the opening facing the public domain had been closed off. If the corner of these two adjoining walls is breached, then the Gemara terms this a breach in a corner.

NOTES

Breached from its front – נִפְרַץ מֵרֹאשׁוֹ: Various opinions were offered with regard to the phrase: Breached from its front. Some commentaries explained this as a case where the side wall of the alleyway was breached at the end that opens out into the public domain. Therefore, there was nothing left of the entrance to the alleyway (cited by the *Me'iri*). Other authorities taught that the above phrase means that the end wall of the alleyway was breached (Rema). Rabbeinu Ḥananel interpreted the phrase in the latter manner as well, and even had a variant reading that supports this interpretation. The *Me'iri* also preferred this opinion, and the wording of the Jerusalem Talmud supports it as well.

וְרַב הוּנָא אָמַר: אֶחָד זֶה וְאֶחָד זֶה בְּאַרְבָּעָה. וְכֵן אָמַר לֵיהּ רַב הוּנָא לְרַב חָנָן בַּר רָבָא: לָא תִּפְלוֹג עֲלַאי, דְּרַב אִיקְּלַע לְדַמְחַרְיָא וַעֲבַד עוּבְדָא כְּוָותִי. אָמַר לֵיהּ: רַב בִּקְעָה מָצָא, וְגָדַר בָּהּ גָּדֵר.

Rav Huna disagreed with Rav Ḥanin bar Rava and **said:** There is no distinction between the side and the front, for in **both this** case **and that,** a breach of up to **four** handbreadths is allowed. **And so Rav Huna said to Rav Ḥanan bar Rava: Do not dispute me, as Rav** himself **arrived at** a place called **Damḥarya and performed an action,** i.e., issued a practical ruling, **in accordance with my** opinion. Rav Ḥanan bar Rava **said** in response **to him:** No proof can be brought from that incident, for in that case **Rav found an** unguarded **valley**[N] **and fenced it in,** i.e., , Rav saw the need to add a safeguard and was therefore stringent in this case. His ruling, however, was not generally applied.

אָמַר רַב נַחְמָן בַּר יִצְחָק: כְּוָותֵיהּ דְּרַב הוּנָא מִסְתַּבְּרָא. דְּאִיתְּמַר: מָבוֹי עָקוּם, רַב אָמַר: תּוֹרָתוֹ כִּמְפוּלָּשׁ, וּשְׁמוּאֵל אָמַר: תּוֹרָתוֹ כְּסָתוּם.

Rav Naḥman bar Yitzḥak said: Rav Huna's opinion stands to reason, as it was stated that the *amora'im* disagree about the following issue: With regard to **a crooked,** L-shaped **alleyway**[HBN] that opens onto the public domain at both ends, **Rav said: Its law is like** that of an alleyway that is **open** on two opposite sides, and it must be treated in a manner suitable for such an alleyway, i.e., an opening in the form of a doorway must be constructed at both ends, or else such an opening must be constructed at the point where the two arms of the alleyway meet and a side post or a cross beam must be placed at each end. **And Shmuel said: Its law is like** that of an alleyway that is **closed** on one side, and all that is necessary is a side post or a cross beam at each end.[N]

בְּמַאי עָסְקִינַן? אִילֵימָא בְּיוֹתֵר מֵעֶשֶׂר – בְּהָא לֵימָא שְׁמוּאֵל תּוֹרָתוֹ כְּסָתוּם?!

The Gemara clarifies the particular circumstances of the case: **With what are we dealing? If you say** that the width of the alleyway at the point of the turn is **more than ten** cubits wide, **in this** case, **would Shmuel say that its law is like** that of an alleyway that is **closed** on one side? With an opening of that size, it must be considered like an alleyway that is open on both ends.

אֶלָּא לָאו – בְּעֶשֶׂר, וְקָאָמַר רַב: תּוֹרָתוֹ כִּמְפוּלָּשׁ. אַלְמָא: פִּירְצַת מָבוֹי מִצִּידּוֹ בְּאַרְבָּעָה.

Rather, are we not dealing with a case where the width of the alleyway at the point of the turn is **ten** cubits or less, **and Rav** nonetheless **said** that **the law** of such an alleyway **is like that of** an alleyway that is **open** on both ends. **Apparently, a breach in the side** wall **of an alleyway** renders it prohibited to carry even if it is only **four** handbreadths wide, in accordance with the opinion of Rav Huna.

וְרַב חָנָן בַּר רָבָא – שָׁאנֵי הָתָם, דְּקָא בָּקְעִי בָּהּ רַבִּים.

And Rav Ḥanan bar Rava argues that the cases cannot be compared: **It is different there,** in the case of the L-shaped alleyway, **for many people cross through** the opening from one arm to the other. Since in practice the alleyway is open to regular traffic, the ruling is stringent even with regard to a small breach.

מִכְּלָל דְּרַב הוּנָא סָבַר אַף עַל גַּב דְּלָא בָּקְעִי בָּהּ רַבִּים? מַאי שְׁנָא מִדְּרַבִּי אַמִי וְרַבִּי אַסִי?

The Gemara asks: Can it be **inferred** from this **that Rav Huna holds** that **even if many people** do **not cross through** the opening, a breach of four handbreadths still prohibits carrying? **What is the difference** between this case and the case of the ruling of **Rabbi Ami and Rabbi Asi** cited earlier, that an upright board of four handbreadths suffices in order to allow a breach of up to ten cubits?

NOTES

Rav found an unguarded valley – רַב בִּקְעָה מָצָא: That is to say, the residents of that community were ignorant of Torah and did not know enough to be meticulous in their observance. Therefore, they are compared to an unguarded valley that is open to all.

A crooked alleyway – מָבוֹי עָקוּם: Most commentaries and halakhic authorities understood the law of a crooked alleyway according to Rashi's interpretation: The Gemara's discussion concerns an L-shaped alleyway that opens into two different public domains. Nevertheless, other explanations have been suggested. Some commentaries explain that it refers to an alleyway shaped like the letter U, with a middle segment and two ends that open into the same public domain. An alternative opinion is that it is shaped like the letter V with only one turn, in which both ends opening into the same public domain. Still other authorities state that it refers to an alleyway open on only one end to the public domain, but out of its side there is another, smaller alleyway that opens into a different public domain (*Me'iri*).

The law of a crooked alleyway – דִּין מָבוֹי עָקוּם: The dispute between Rav and Shmuel also appears in the Jerusalem Talmud, where Rabbi Yoḥanan's opinion aligns with that of Rav, while Reish Lakish's opinion aligns with that of Shmuel. The wording of the Jerusalem Talmud suggests that according to Reish Lakish, the inhabitants of each of the two segments of the alleyway can only carry in their own section, from the entrance to the point where the alleyway turns. Therefore, the inhabitants of the two sections are considered residents of two adjacent alleyways. Rabbi Yoḥanan maintains that since the inhabitants of the two sections of the alleyway share a common area, they are all prohibited from carrying until the middle section of the alleyway is set up in the required manner.

HALAKHA

A crooked, L-shaped alleyway – מָבוֹי עָקוּם: An L-shaped alleyway is treated like an alleyway that is open at both ends. Therefore, it requires an opening in the form of a doorway at the point of the turn, as well as a side post or a cross beam at its entrances. Alternatively, it requires a side post or cross beam at the point of turn, as well as an opening in the form of a doorway at its entrances. This ruling is in accordance with the opinion of Rav, because his opinion, as opposed to that of Shmuel, is accepted in matters of ritual law (*Shulḥan Arukh, Oraḥ Ḥayyim* 364:3).

BACKGROUND

A crooked alleyway – מָבוֹי עָקוּם:

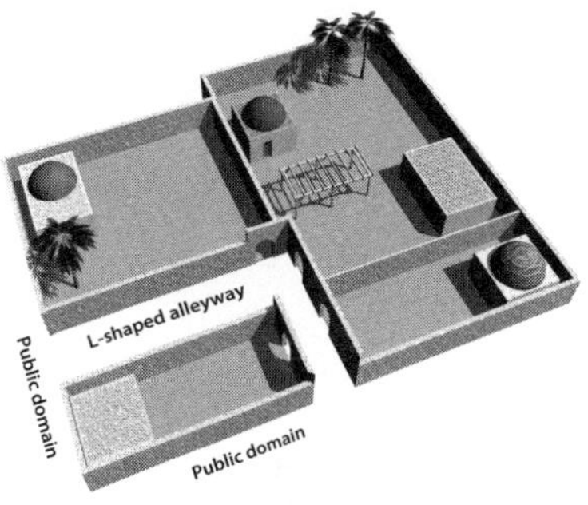

L-shaped alleyway, with its two ends opening into different public domains

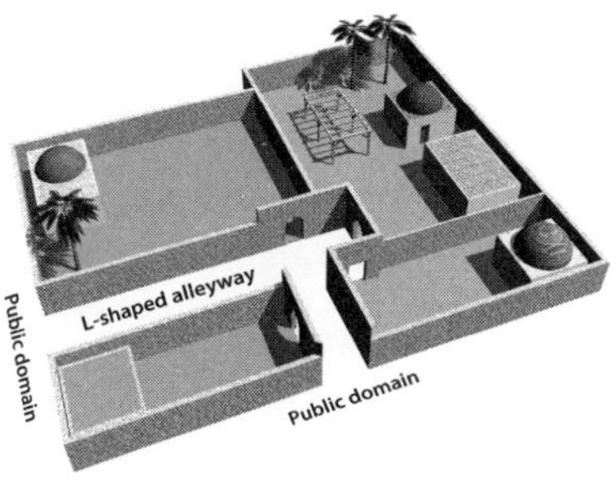

Crooked alleyway, formed by a closed alleyway with a another alleyway which opens to the public domain on its side (*Me'iri*)

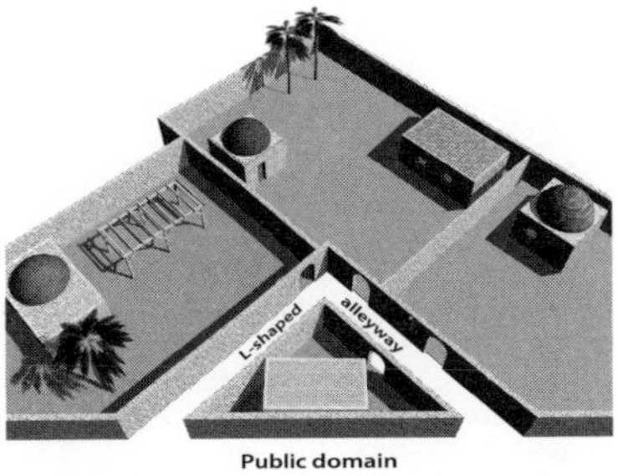

Crooked, V-shaped alleyway that makes one turn, with both ends facing the same public domain (*Me'iri*)

התם – דאיכא גידודי, הכא – דליכא גידודי.

The Gemara answers: **There, there are remnants of a wall** that render it difficult to pass through the breach, and therefore that breach does not annul the partitions. However, **here, there are no remnants of a wall.**

תנו רבנן: כיצד מערבין דרך רשות הרבים – עושה צורת הפתח מכאן, ולחי וקורה מכאן. חנניה אומר; בית שמאי אומרים: עושה דלת מכאן ודלת מכאן, וכשהוא יוצא ונכנס – נועל. בית הלל אומרים: עושה דלת מכאן, ולחי וקורה מכאן.

The Sages taught in a *baraita*: **How does one render a public thoroughfare fit** for carrying **by** means of **an** ***eiruv*****? He constructs an** opening in the **form of a doorway from here,** on one side of the thoroughfare, **and a side post or a** cross **beam from here,** on the other side. **Ḥananya** disagrees and **says:** This is the subject of an early dispute between *tanna'im*, for **Beit Shammai say: He constructs a door from here,** on one side, **and a door from here,** on the other side, **and when he exits and enters, he must lock** the door. It is not sufficient to construct a symbolic door; rather, there must be a door that actually closes. And **Beit Hillel say: He constructs a door from here,** on one side, **and a side post or a** cross **beam from here,** on the other side.

ורשות הרבים מי מיערבא? והתניא: יתר על כן אמר רבי יהודה:

The Gemara raises a fundamental question: **Can a public domain be rendered fit** for carrying **by** means of an ***eiruv*****? Wasn't it taught** in a *baraita*: **Furthermore, Rabbi Yehuda said:**

Perek **I**
Daf **6** Amud **b**

מי שהיו לו שני בתים משני צידי רשות הרבים – עושה לחי מכאן ולחי מכאן, או קורה מכאן וקורה מכאן – ונושא ונותן באמצע. אמרו לו: אין מערבין רשות הרבים בכך.

One who has two houses opposite each other **on the two sides of the public domain,** and he wishes to carry from one house to the other on Shabbat via the public domain, **he may place a side post from here,** on one side of one of the houses, **and** an additional **side post from here,** on the other side. **Alternatively,** he may place **a** cross **beam from here,** from one end of one house, **and** an additional cross **beam from here,** from the other side of the house, **and** then **he may carry** objects **and place** them in the area **between** them, for in this manner he turns the middle area into a private domain. The Rabbis **said to him: One cannot render a public domain fit** for carrying **by** means of **an** ***eiruv*****[N] in this manner.** Apparently, there is no way to establish an absolute public domain fit for carrying by means of an *eiruv*.

וכי תימא: בכך הוא דלא מיערבא, הא בדלתות מיערבא. והאמר רבה בר בר חנה, אמר רבי יוחנן: ירושלים, אילמלא דלתותיה ננעלות בלילה חייבין עליה משום רשות הרבים!

The Gemara questions its previous conclusion: **And if you say** that it is only **in this manner,** by way of a side post or a cross beam, **that** a public domain **cannot be rendered fit** for carrying, **but by** means of **doors** it can be **rendered fit for carrying. But** this is not true, as **didn't Rabba bar bar Ḥana say** that **Rabbi Yoḥanan** said: With regard to **Jerusalem, were it not for** the fact that **its doors are locked at night, one would be liable for** carrying in **it** on Shabbat, **because** its thoroughfares are regarded **as a public domain?**[H] This shows that the presence of a door is not sufficient to render it permitted to carry in a public domain; rather, the door must actually be locked.

ואמר עולא: הני אבולי דמחוזא, אילמלא דלתותיהן ננעלות – חייבין עליהן משום רשות הרבים!

And similarly, **Ulla stated:** With regard to **the** city **entrances** [*abbulei*][L] **of Meḥoza,** which meet the criteria for a public domain, **were it not for the fact that their doors are locked, one** would be **liable for** carrying in **them, because** they are regarded as **a public domain.** Apparently, without the actual locking of doors it is impossible to establish a public domain fit for carrying by means of the symbolic partitions of a side post or a cross beam. If so, how can the Sages in the *baraita* argue about how to establish a public domain fit for carrying?

NOTES

One cannot render a public domain fit for carrying by means of an ***eiruv*** **– אין מערבין רשות הרבים:** Some of the *ge'onim* understand that even according to the Gemara's conclusion, there is no way whatsoever to establish a public domain fit for carrying. Rabbi Yoḥanan's statement does not mean that Jerusalem became a private domain through the locking of its doors. Rather, due to its doors, it was no longer considered a full-fledged public domain (*Me'iri*),

HALAKHA

Locked doors – דלתות נעולות: A public domain can be rendered fit for carrying only via doors that are locked at night, in accordance with the opinion of Rabbi Yoḥanan (*Shulḥan Arukh, Oraḥ Ḥayyim* 364:2).

LANGUAGE

City entrances [*abbulei*] – אבולי: Rav Binyamin Mosafya and others explain that this term comes from the Greek ἔμβολος, *embolos*, meaning a portico or a stopper. It is likely, however, that its root is the Syrian *abula*, and it is possibly related to the Hebrew *uval*, meaning stream (see Daniel 8:2).

אָמַר רַב יְהוּדָה, הָכִי קָאָמַר: כֵּיצַד מְעָרְבִין מְבוֹאוֹת הַמְפוּלָּשִׁין לִרְשׁוּת הָרַבִּים – עוֹשֶׂה צוּרַת הַפֶּתַח מִכָּאן, וְלֶחִי וְקוֹרָה מִכָּאן.	Rather, **Rav Yehuda said:** The wording of the *baraita* must be emended so that **this is what it says: How does one render alleyways that** are not themselves public domains but are **open**[HB] on two opposite sides **into the public domain fit** for carrying **by** means of **an** ***eiruv***?[N] **He constructs an opening** in the **form of a doorway from here,** on one side of the alleyway, **and a side post or a** cross **beam from here,** on the other side.
אִיתְּמַר, רַב אָמַר: הִילְכְתָא כְּתַנָּא קַמָּא, וּשְׁמוּאֵל אָמַר: הֲלָכָה כַּחֲנַנְיָה.	**It was stated** that the *amora'im* differed on how the *halakha* is to be decided with regard to this issue. **Rav said:** The ***halakha*** **is in accordance with** the opinion of **the** anonymous **first** ***tanna*** of the *baraita,* and it is sufficient to have the form of a doorway on one side and a side post or cross beam on the other side in order to render it permitted to carry in an alleyway that is open on two opposite sides to the public domain. **And Shmuel says:** The ***halakha*** **is in accordance with** the opinion of **Ḥananya,** following the position of Beit Hillel, who also require a door on one side.
אִיבַּעְיָא לְהוּ: לַחֲנַנְיָה אַלִּיבָּא דְּבֵית הִלֵּל, צָרִיךְ לִנְעוֹל אוֹ אֵין צָרִיךְ לִנְעוֹל: תָּא שְׁמַע, דְּאָמַר רַב יְהוּדָה, אָמַר שְׁמוּאֵל: אֵינוֹ צָרִיךְ לִנְעוֹל. וְכֵן אָמַר רַב מַתָּנָה, אָמַר שְׁמוּאֵל: אֵינוֹ צָרִיךְ לִנְעוֹל. אִיכָּא דְּאָמְרִי, אָמַר רַב מַתָּנָה: בְּדִידִי הֲוָה עוּבְדָּא, וְאָמַר לִי שְׁמוּאֵל: אֵין צָרִיךְ לִנְעוֹל.	**A dilemma was raised before** the Sages concerning the position of Beit Hillel: According **to Ḥananya, in accordance with** the opinion **of Beit Hillel, must** this door **be locked or need it not be locked? Come** and **hear** a proof from that **which Rav Yehuda said** that **Shmuel said,** who, as mentioned earlier, rules in accordance with Beit Hillel: The door **need not be locked. And similarly, Rav Mattana said** that **Shmuel said:** The door **need not be locked. Some say** that **Rav Mattana said: A case** involving this very issue **happened to me, and Shmuel said to me:** The door **need not be locked.**

HALAKHA

Alleyways that are open – מְבוֹאוֹת הַמְפוּלָּשִׁין: It is permitted to carry in an alleyway that is open at two opposite sides into the public domain or into a *karmelit* if an entrance in the form of a doorway is constructed at one end, and a side post or a cross beam is placed at the other end. This ruling is in accordance with the view of Rav, as his opinion is accepted in matters of ritual law (*Shulḥan Arukh, Oraḥ Ḥayyim* 364:1).

BACKGROUND

Alleyways that are open – מְבוֹאוֹת הַמְפוּלָּשִׁין: According to *Tosafot*, an open alleyway is considered a full-fledged public domain, because the length of the public domain runs through the alleyway. Alternatively an open alleyway may not be considered a public domain, in the case where the public domain does not pass through the alleyway. Rather, two public domains pass by the alleyway's entrances.

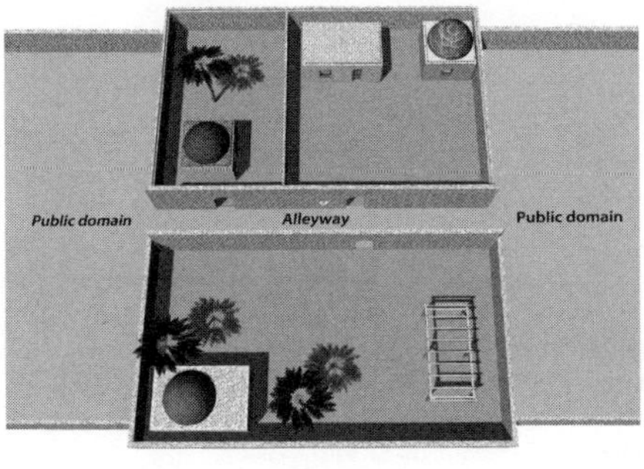

Open alleyway with a public domain passing through it

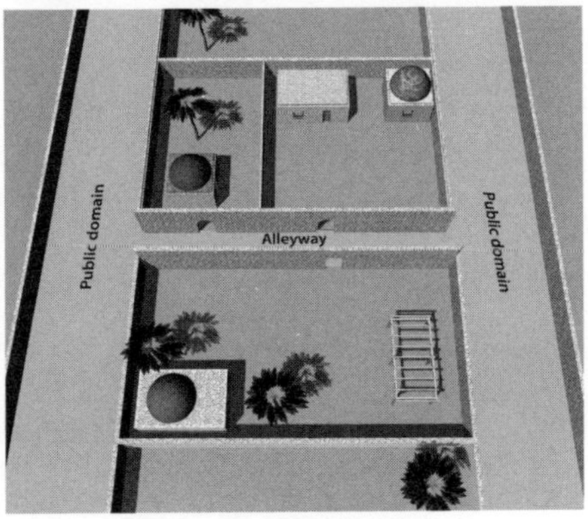

Open alleyway with public domains passing by its entrances

NOTES

Open alleyways – מְבוֹאוֹת מְפוּלָּשִׁין: According to Rashi, since an alleyway does not have the requisite width of a public domain, i.e., a minimum of sixteen cubits, it is always considered an alleyway, even if the public regularly passes through it. *Tosafot* differentiate between various types of alleyways, because they do not accept Rashi's position on this matter.

בָּעוּ מִינֵּיהּ מֵרַב עָנָן: צָרִיךְ לִנְעוֹל, אוֹ אֵין צָרִיךְ לִנְעוֹל? אֲמַר לְהוּ: תָּא חֲזִי הָנֵי אַבּוּלֵי דִּנְהַרְדְּעָא, דְּטִימָן עַד פַּלְגַּיְיהוּ בְּעַפְרָא, וְעָיֵיל וְנָפֵיק מָר שְׁמוּאֵל, וְלָא אֲמַר לְהוּ וְלָא מִידֵּי.

They raised a dilemma before Rav Anan with regard to this issue: **Need** the door **be locked or need** it **not be locked? He said to them: Come** and **see these** city **entrances of Neharde'a** that open on two opposite sides into the public domain, the gateways of **which were filled up halfway with earth,** so that the doors themselves could not possibly be locked. **Mar Shmuel** regularly **goes in and out** through them, **but has never said anything to** the people of Neharde'a about them. This shows that it is not necessary for the doors to be locked.

אָמַר רַב כָּהֲנָא: הָנָךְ מְגוּפוֹת הֲוַאי.

Rav Kahana rejected this proof and **said: Those** doors in Neharde'a **were** partially **blocked,** and therefore there was no need to lock them, but in general, the door of an alleyway that opens on both sides into the public domain must be locked.

כִּי אֲתָא רַב נַחְמָן, אֲמַר: פַּנְיוּהּ לְעַפְרַיְיהוּ. לֵימָא קָסָבַר רַב נַחְמָן ״צָרִיךְ לִנְעוֹל״? לֹא, כֵּיוָן דִּרְאוּיוֹת לִנְעוֹל, אַף עַל פִּי שֶׁאֵין נִנְעָלוֹת.

The Gemara relates that **when Rav Naḥman came** to Neharde'a, **he said: Clear away the earth,** so that the doors can be locked. The Gemara attempts to understand Rav Naḥman's instruction: **Let us say that Rav Naḥman holds** that the door of an alleyway that is open on two opposite sides **must be locked.** The Gemara explains: **No,** this is not proof. In order for carrying to be permitted in such an alleyway, it is enough that the doors **be fit to be locked,**[H] **even if they are not** actually **locked.**

הַהוּא מָבוֹי עָקוּם דַּהֲוָה בִּנְהַרְדְּעָא, רָמֵי עֲלֵיהּ חוּמְרֵיהּ דְּרַב וְחוּמְרֵיהּ דִּשְׁמוּאֵל, וְאַצְרְכוּהוּ דְּלָתוֹת. חוּמְרֵיהּ דְּרַב – דְּאָמַר ״תּוֹרָתוֹ כִּמְפוּלָּשׁ״. וְהָאָמַר רַב הֲלָכָה כְּתַנָּא קַמָּא!

The Gemara describes **a certain crooked,** L-shaped **alleyway that was in Neharde'a,**[NB] **upon which they imposed the stringency of Rav and the stringency of Shmuel,**[N] **and required it** to have **doors.** The Gemara attempts to understand this ruling: **The stringency of Rav,** namely, that **which he said,** that an L-shaped alleyway **is regarded like** an alleyway that is **open** on two opposite sides. **But** this is difficult, for **didn't Rav say** that **the law follows the** anonymous **first** ***tanna*** of the *baraita*, who says that even an open alleyway itself does not require doors, and that an opening in the form of a doorway suffices?

כִּשְׁמוּאֵל, דְּאָמַר: הֲלָכָה כַּחֲנַנְיָה. וְהָאָמַר שְׁמוּאֵל: תּוֹרָתוֹ כִּסְתוּם! כְּרַב, דְּאָמַר: תּוֹרָתוֹ כִּמְפוּלָּשׁ.

The Gemara answers: They required doors **in accordance with** the opinion of **Shmuel, who said** that **the** ***halakha*** **is in accordance with** the opinion of **Ḥananya. But** this too is difficult, for if the doors were required in accordance with Shmuel's opinion, **didn't Shmuel say** that an L-shaped alleyway **is regarded like** an alleyway that is **closed** on one side, which does not need any doors at all? The Gemara explains: The doors were required **in accordance with** the opinion of **Rav, who said** that an L-shaped alleyway **is regarded like** an alleyway that is **open** on two opposite sides. Therefore, they adopted the stringencies of both Rav and Shmuel: Rav's stringency that an L-shaped alleyway is deemed an open alleyway, and Shmuel's stringency that an open alleyway requires a door.

HALAKHA

Doors that are fit to be locked – דְּלָתוֹת הָרְאוּיוֹת לִנְעוֹל: Some authorities state that the doors of a city that is considered public domain need not be locked, so long as it is possible to lock the doors, as in that case it is considered as if they are actually locked. This is in accordance with the Gemara's understanding of Rav Naḥman's position (*Shulḥan Arukh, Oraḥ Ḥayyim* 364:2).

BACKGROUND

The alleyway in Neharde'a – הַמָּבוֹי בִּנְהַרְדְּעָא: According to Rashi, the two ends of the alleyway of Neharde'a did not open into two different public domains, in contrast to other crooked alleyways. Rather, the alleyway was shaped like the letter U, with both ends opening into the same public domain.

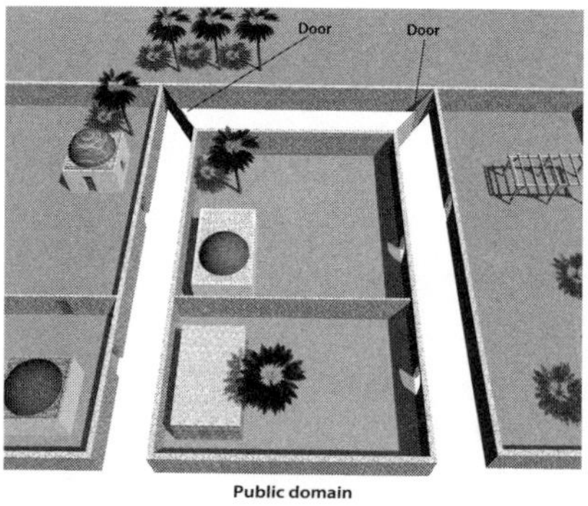

Alleyway with both ends opening into the same public domain

According to *Tosafot*, the alleyway in Neharde'a was both an open and a crooked alleyway

Alleyway in Neharde'a according to *Tosafot*

NOTES

A crooked alleyway that was in Neharde'a – מָבוֹי עָקוּם דַּהֲוָה בִּנְהַרְדְּעָא: According to Rashi, this crooked alleyway was in the shape of the letter U, with both its ends facing the same public domain. Rashi found it necessary to explain it in this manner because the Gemara states that doors were required, implying two doors. *Tosafot* disagree and say that an alleyway of this kind would be considered closed even according to Rav. Rather, the alleyway in Neharde'a actually required only one door, in accordance with Rabbeinu Ḥananel's text of the Gemara. Therefore, *Tosafot* suggest a crooked alleyway of a different shape, i.e., one that is also an open alleyway, with regard to which all agree that two doors are required (see illustrations in the Background notes).

In accordance with Rav and Shmuel – כְּרַב וּשְׁמוּאֵל: Rif explains that the inhabitants of Neharde'a ruled in accordance with Rav, as the law follows him. However, since Neharde'a was Shmuel's place of residence, they did not want to dismiss his words entirely, so they acted stringently in accordance with his opinion as well.

וּמִי עָבְדִינַן כִּתְרֵי חוּמְרֵי? וְהָא תַּנְיָא: לְעוֹלָם הֲלָכָה כְּבֵית הִלֵּל, וְהָרוֹצֶה לַעֲשׂוֹת כְּדִבְרֵי בֵית שַׁמַּאי – עוֹשֶׂה, כְּדִבְרֵי בֵית הִלֵּל – עוֹשֶׂה, מִקּוּלֵּי בֵית שַׁמַּאי וּמִקּוּלֵּי בֵית הִלֵּל – רָשָׁע, מֵחוּמְרֵי בֵית שַׁמַּאי וּמֵחוּמְרֵי בֵית הִלֵּל – עָלָיו הַכָּתוּב אוֹמֵר: ״הַכְּסִיל בַּחֹשֶׁךְ הוֹלֵךְ״, אֶלָּא, אִי כְּבֵית שַׁמַּאי – כְּקוּלֵּיהוֹן וּכְחוּמְרֵיהוֹן, אִי כְּבֵית הִלֵּל – כְּקוּלֵּיהוֹן וּכְחוּמְרֵיהוֹן.

The Gemara poses a question: **But do we adopt the** respective **stringencies of two** authorities who disagree on a series of issues? **Wasn't it taught** in a *baraita*: The *halakha* **is always in accordance with** the opinion of **Beit Hillel, but one who wishes to act in accordance with the opinion of Beit Shammai may do so,** and one who wishes to act **in accordance with the opinion of Beit Hillel may do so.** If he wishes to adopt both **the leniencies of Beit Shammai and** also **the leniencies of Beit Hillel,** he is **a wicked person.** And if he wishes to adopt both **the stringencies of Beit Shammai and** also **the stringencies of Beit Hillel, with regard to him the verse states: "The fool walks in darkness"** (Ecclesiastes 2:14).[N] **Rather,** he should act **either in accordance with Beit Shammai,** following both **their leniencies and their stringencies, or in accordance with Beit Hillel,** following both **their leniencies and their stringencies.**

הָא גּוּפָא קַשְׁיָא: אָמְרַתְּ ״לְעוֹלָם הֲלָכָה כְּבֵית הִלֵּל״, וַהֲדַר אָמְרַתְּ: ״הָרוֹצֶה לַעֲשׂוֹת כְּדִבְרֵי בֵית שַׁמַּאי עוֹשֶׂה״!

The Gemara first raises a problem concerning the wording of the *baraita*: The *baraita* **is itself difficult** to understand, because it contains an internal contradiction between its clauses: **You** first **said** that the ***halakha* is always in accordance with** the opinion of **Beit Hillel, and then you reversed** that and **said** that **one who wishes to act in accordance with the view of Beit Shammai may do so.**

לָא קַשְׁיָא; כָּאן – קוֹדֶם בַּת קוֹל, כָּאן – לְאַחַר בַּת קוֹל.

The Gemara answers: This is **not difficult. Here,** the *baraita's* statement that a person may act as he wishes was made **before the Divine Voice** emerged and announced that the *halakha* is always in accordance with Beit Hillel; and **here,** the statement that the *halakha* is always in accordance with Beit Hillel was made **after the Divine Voice** issued this ruling.

וְאִיבָּעֵית אֵימָא: הָא וְהָא לְאַחַר בַּת קוֹל,

And if you wish, say a different answer: Both **this** statement **and that** statement were made **after the Divine Voice** announced that the *halakha* is in accordance with Beit Hillel,

NOTES

The fool walks in darkness – הַכְּסִיל בַּחֹשֶׁךְ הוֹלֵךְ: In tractate *Rosh HaShana*, *Tosafot* explain that this phrase refers not only to one who is uncertain about the law and is stringent due to the uncertainty, but also to one who is knowledgeable about the law yet wishes to add stringencies.

Perek **I**
Daf **7** Amud **a**

וְרַבִּי יְהוֹשֻׁעַ הִיא, דְּלָא מַשְׁגַּח בְּבַת קוֹל.

and the latter statement **is** in accordance with the opinion of **Rabbi Yehoshua, who does not pay attention to a Divine Voice**[N] that attempts to intervene in matters of *halakha*, for according to him, the dispute between Beit Shammai and Beit Hillel has not yet been decided.

וְאִיבָּעֵית אֵימָא, הָכִי קָאָמַר: כָּל הֵיכָא דְּמַשְׁכַּחַתְּ תְּרֵי תַּנָּאֵי וּתְרֵי אֲמוֹרָאֵי דִּפְלִיגִי אַהֲדָדֵי כְּעֵין מַחֲלוֹקֶת בֵּית שַׁמַּאי וּבֵית הִלֵּל – לָא לֶיעֱבַד כִּי קוּלֵּיהּ דְּמָר וְכִי קוּלֵּיהּ דְּמָר, וְלָא כְּחוּמְרֵיהּ דְּמָר וְכִי חוּמְרֵיהּ דְּמָר. אֶלָּא: אוֹ כִּי קוּלֵּיהּ דְּמָר וּכְחוּמְרֵיהּ עָבֵיד, אוֹ כְּקוּלֵּיהּ דְּמָר וּכְחוּמְרֵיהּ עָבֵיד.

The Gemara suggests yet another resolution: **And if you wish, say** instead that **this is** what the *baraita* **is saying: Wherever you find two *tanna'im* or two *amora'im* who disagree with each other in the manner of the disputes between Beit Shammai and Beit Hillel, one should not act either in accordance with the leniency of the** one **Master and in accordance with the leniency of** the other **Master,** nor should one act **in accordance with the stringency of** the one **Master and in accordance with the stringency of** the other **Master. Rather, one should act either in accordance with** both **the leniencies and the stringencies of** the one **Master, or in accordance with** both **the leniencies and the stringencies** of the other **Master.**

מִכָּל מָקוֹם קַשְׁיָא!

All of this is suggested to explain the wording of the *baraita*. **In any case, it is difficult** to explain the law with regard to the alleyway in Neharde'a, concerning which they simultaneously adopted the stringencies of both Rav and Shmuel.

אָמַר רַב נַחְמָן בַּר יִצְחָק: כּוּלֵּיהּ כְּרַב עֲבַדוּהַ, דְּאָמַר רַב הוּנָא, אָמַר רַב: ״הֲלָכָה וְאֵין מוֹרִין כֵּן״.

Rav Naḥman bar Yitzḥak said: In fact, **they acted entirely in accordance with** the opinion of **Rav,** and the reason that they required doors and did not rely on the opening in the form of a doorway alone is due to that which **Rav Huna said** that **Rav said:** This is the ***halakha*; however,** a public **ruling is not issued to that effect *ab initio*.** Although Rav maintains that an opening in the form of a doorway is sufficient in an open alleyway, a public ruling is not issued to that effect; rather, the ruling is stringent, in accordance with Ḥananya's position, and requires doors.

NOTES

Who does not pay attention to a Divine Voice – דְּלָא מַשְׁגַּח בְּבַת קוֹל: As related in tractate *Bava Metzia*, even when a Divine Voice announced that the *halakha* was in accordance with the opinion of Rabbi Eliezer, Rabbi Yehoshua refused to listen to it. Furthermore, he declared that the Torah is not in Heaven and that halakhic decisions reside in the hands of an earthly court.

וּלְרַב אַדָּא בַּר אַהֲבָה אָמַר רַב, דְּאָמַר: ״הֲלָכָה וּמוֹרִין כֵּן״, מַאי אִיכָּא לְמֵימַר?

The Gemara asks: **And according to** the statement of **Rav Adda bar Ahava** that **Rav said, as** Rav Adda bar Ahava **said** that Rav said with regard to the same issue: This is the ***halakha*** **and a** public **ruling is issued to that effect, what can be said?** Why did the residents of Neharde'a adopt the stringencies of the two authorities?

אָמַר רַב שֵׁיזְבִי: כִּי לָא עָבְדִינַן כְּחוּמְרֵי דְּבֵי תְּרֵי – הֵיכָא דְּסָתְרִי אַהֲדָדֵי,

Rav Sheizvi said: The principle of dictating **when we do not act in accordance with the stringencies of two** authorities applies only in a case **where** the two stringencies **contradict one another.** In these types of cases, following both stringencies would result in an internal contradiction.

כְּגוֹן שִׁדְרָה וְגוּלְגּוֹלֶת. דִּתְנַן: הַשִּׁדְרָה וְהַגּוּלְגּוֹלֶת שֶׁחָסְרוּ, וְכַמָּה חֶסְרוֹן בַּשִּׁדְרָה? בֵּית שַׁמַּאי אוֹמְרִים שְׁתֵּי חוּלְיוֹת, וּבֵית הִלֵּל אוֹמְרִים: חוּלְיָא אַחַת, וּבַגּוּלְגּוֹלֶת, בֵּית שַׁמַּאי אוֹמְרִים: כִּמְלֹא מַקְדֵּחַ, וּבֵית הִלֵּל אוֹמְרִים: כְּדֵי שֶׁיִּנָּטֵל מִן הַחַי וְיָמוּת.

The Gemara illustrates this principle with **an example** from the laws governing **the spine and skull. As we learned** in a mishna: **The spine and the skull** of a corpse that are **incomplete** do not impart ritual impurity[H] via a tent as a corpse would; rather, they impart impurity only through contact or if they are carried as individual bones.[N] This basic law was unanimously accepted, but the details were the subject of dispute: **How much** is considered **a deficiency in the spine** for this purpose? **Beit Shammai say:** If it is missing **two vertebrae, and Beit Hillel say:** Even if it is missing only **one vertebra. And** similarly, they argued over the deficiency **in the skull: Beit Shammai say:** It must be missing piece the **size of a drill hole, and Beit Hillel say:** It must be missing an amount that, **when removed from a living** person, would cause him **to die,** which is a larger amount.

וְאָמַר רַב יְהוּדָה, אָמַר שְׁמוּאֵל: וְכֵן לְעִנְיַן טְרֵיפָה.

And Rav Yehuda said that **Shmuel said:** Beit Shammai and Beit Hillel argued **likewise with respect to a** ***tereifa*****,** a kosher animal suffering from a wound or illness that will cause it to die within twelve months, and which is prohibited to be eaten even after the required ritual slaughter. Beit Shammai say that an animal is regarded as a *tereifa* if it is missing two vertebrae, while Beit Hillel hold that it is a *tereifa* if it lacks even one.[H] In such a situation, a person must not be stringent with regard to the *halakhot* of *tereifa* in accordance with the view of Beit Hillel, and at the same time be stringent with regard to the *halakhot* of ritual impurity of a corpse in accordance with the view of Beit Shammai, for the two disputes relate to the same issue, and one must not act in accordance with two contradictory opinions.

אֲבָל הֵיכָא דְּלָא סָתְרִי אַהֲדָדֵי – עָבְדִינַן.

Rav Sheizvi continues: **However, in a case where** the two stringencies **do not contradict one another, we may** indeed **act** in accordance with the stringencies of two authorities. Therefore, the stringencies adopted in the case of the alleyway in Neharde'a were legitimate, for the two stringencies related to two separate issues: Rav's stringency was that an L-shaped alleyway is regarded like an open alleyway, and Shmuel's stringency was that an open alleyway requires a door.

וְהֵיכָא דְּסָתְרִי אַהֲדָדֵי לָא עָבְדִינַן?! מְתִיב רַב מְשַׁרְשְׁיָא: מַעֲשֶׂה בְּרַבִּי עֲקִיבָא שֶׁלִּיקֵּט אֶתְרוֹג בְּאֶחָד בִּשְׁבָט, וְנָהַג בּוֹ שְׁנֵי עִישּׂוּרִין, אֶחָד כְּדִבְרֵי בֵּית שַׁמַּאי וְאֶחָד כְּדִבְרֵי בֵּית הִלֵּל!

The Gemara challenges Rav Sheizvi's assertion: Is it true that **we do not act** in accordance with the stringencies of two authorities in a case **where** the two stringencies **contradict one another? Rav Mesharshiya raised an objection** from a *baraita*: There was **an incident involving Rabbi Akiva, who gathered** the fruit of **a citron** tree **on the first of** the month of **Shevat and applied** the laws of **two tithes**[N] **to it.** After *teruma* and the first tithe have been separated, an additional tithe is separated from what is left. During the first, second, fourth, and fifth years of the Sabbatical cycle, second tithe is set aside to be taken to Jerusalem and eaten there by its owner, while during the third and sixth years, poor man's tithe is set aside to be distributed to the needy. When tithing the fruit picked on the first of Shevat, Rabbi Akiva set aside both additional tithes, second tithe and poor man's tithe: He set aside **one in accordance with the statement of Beit Shammai,** who say that the new year for trees begins on the first of Shevat, and as that day belongs to the new year, a tithe must be set aside in accordance with the law of that year; and he set aside **one in accordance with the statement of Beit Hillel,** that the new year for trees is the fifteenth of Shevat, and any fruit picked prior to that date must be tithed in accordance with the law of the previous year. Apparently, Rabbi Akiva adopted for himself two contradictory stringencies.

HALAKHA

An incomplete spine with regard to impurity – שִׁדְרָה שֶׁחָסְרָה לְעִנְיַן טוּמְאָה: If the spine of a corpse is missing one vertebra, or if a skull is missing a piece the size of a large coin [*sela*], they no longer impart ritual impurity via a tent. Rather, they impart impurity like ordinary bones, in accordance with the opinion of Beit Hillel (Rambam *Sefer Taharot, Hilkhot Tumat Met* 2:8).

An incomplete spine in a sick animal [*tereifa*] – שִׁדְרָה שֶׁחָסְרָה בִּטְרֵפוֹת: If the spine of a large animal is missing one vertebra while the rest of the spinal cord is intact, or if its skull is missing a piece the size of a large coin [*sela*], the animal is considered a sick animal [*tereifa*] and is unfit to eat (*Shulḥan Arukh, Yoreh De'a* 30:2, 54:4).

NOTES

An incomplete spine or skull – חֶסְרוֹן בְּשִׁדְרָה וּבְגוּלְגּוֹלֶת: A corpse imparts ritual impurity through contact, by being carried, and via a tent over a corpse. However, not all parts of a corpse impart impurity in every one of these three ways. A single bone from a dead body does not impart ritual impurity via a tent over the corpse. On the other hand, bones that constitute a significant part of a corpse, e.g., a majority of the bone count or a majority of the frame, do impart ritual impurity in this manner. As such, a spine and a skull impart ritual impurity via a tent, provided the spine and skull are whole. If they are missing a portion that would cause death in a living person, then the spine or skull no longer fulfills its function. Their importance is annulled and therefore they do not transmit impurity via a tent.

Two tithes – שְׁנֵי עִישּׂוּרִין: The *Me'iri* quotes the early commentaries, who ask how it is possible to be stringent based on an uncertainty and separate two tithes without creating a series of other problems, such as separating too much or too little. In the Jerusalem Talmud it is explained that Rabbi Akiva first separated the second tithe conditionally, then redeemed it and gave it to the poor. If the tithe was indeed the second tithe, then he had separated and redeemed it properly. If it was not the second tithe, then all he had accomplished was to give charity to the poor. He then took the money upon which he redeemed the second tithe to Jerusalem and used it to buy food, in accordance with the law of second tithe.

רַבִּי עֲקִיבָא גְּמָרֵיהּ אִיסְתַּפֵּיק לֵיהּ, וְלָא יָדַע אִי בֵּית הִלֵּל בְּחַד בִּשְׁבָט אָמוּר, אִי בַּחֲמֵיסַר בִּשְׁבָט אָמוּר, וַעֲבַד הָכָא לְחוּמְרָא וְהָכָא לְחוּמְרָא.

The Gemara answers: **Rabbi Akiva** did not act in this way in order to be stringent in accordance with both opinions, but because **he was in doubt with regard to his tradition and did not know whether Beit Hillel said** the New Year for trees falls **on the first of Shevat or on the fifteenth of Shevat, and** therefore **he acted stringently here and stringently there.**

יְתֵיב רַב יוֹסֵף קַמֵּיהּ דְּרַב הוּנָא, וְיָתֵיב וְקָאָמַר: אָמַר רַב יְהוּדָה, אָמַר רַב: מַחְלוֹקֶת בִּסְרַטְיָא מִכָּאן וּסְרַטְיָא מִכָּאן וּפְלַטְיָא מִכָּאן וּפְלַטְיָא מִכָּאן.

The Gemara resumes its discussion of alleyways that are open on two opposite sides. **Rav Yosef sat before Rav Huna, and he sat and said: Rav Yehuda said** that **Rav said: The dispute** between the anonymous first *tanna* of the *baraita* and Ḥananya refers **to** a case where there is **a main street** [*seratya*][NL] **from here,** on one side of the alleyway, **and a main street from here,** on the other side. **Alternatively,** it refers to a case where there is **a plaza** [*pelatya*][L] **from here,** on one side of the alleyway, **and a plaza from here,** on the other side.

אֲבָל סְרַטְיָא מִכָּאן וּבִקְעָה מִכָּאן, אוֹ בִּקְעָה מִכָּאן וּבִקְעָה מִכָּאן – עוֹשֶׂה צוּרַת הַפֶּתַח מִכָּאן, וְלֶחִי וְקוֹרָה מִכָּאן.

But if there is **a main street from here,** on one side, **and a valley from here,** on the other side, a valley being a *karmelit*, which is neither a public domain nor a private domain, in which carrying is prohibited on Shabbat by rabbinic decree, **or** if there is **a valley from here,** on one side, **and a valley from here,** on the other side, **one constructs** an opening in the **form of a doorway from here,** on one side of the alleyway, **and** places **a side post or a** cross **beam from here,** on the other side. One is thereby permitted to carry in the alleyway even according to the opinion of Ḥananya.[H]

הַשְׁתָּא סְרַטְיָא מִכָּאן וּבִקְעָה מִכָּאן עוֹשֶׂה לוֹ צוּרַת הַפֶּתַח מִכָּאן, וְלֶחִי וְקוֹרָה מִכָּאן, בִּקְעָה מִכָּאן וּבִקְעָה מִכָּאן מִיבַּעְיָא?!

The Gemara raises a question about this ruling: **Now,** if you say that where there is **a main street from here,** on one side of the alleyway, **and a valley from here,** on the other side, it is sufficient to **construct** an opening in **the form of a doorway from here,** on one side, **and a side post or a** cross **beam from here,** on the other side, **was it necessary** to state that these are sufficient if there is **a valley from here,** on one side of the alleyway, **and a valley from here,** on the other side?

הָכִי קָאָמַר: סְרַטְיָא מִכָּאן וּבִקְעָה מִכָּאן – נַעֲשָׂה כְּבִקְעָה מִכָּאן וּבִקְעָה מִכָּאן.

The Gemara answers: **This is** what **he** intended **to say:** If there is **a main street from here,** on one side, **and a valley from here,** on the other side, **it is considered as if there were a valley from here,** on one side, **and a valley from here,** on the other side.

וּמְסַיֵּים בָּהּ מִשְּׁמֵיהּ דְּרַב יְהוּדָה: אִם הָיָה מָבוֹי כָּלֶה לִרְחָבָה – אֵין צָרִיךְ כְּלוּם.

The Gemara continues: **And** when Rav Yosef reported this ruling, **he concluded** with a statement **in the name** of **Rav Yehuda** himself, without attributing it to one of Rav Yehuda's teachers: **If the alleyway terminated in a backyard,**[B] i.e., a closed-off area behind a group of houses, then even if there is a breach in the wall between the yard and the public domain beyond it, **nothing is needed** on this side of the alleyway, as it is considered closed.

אֲמַר לֵיהּ אַבָּיֵי לְרַב יוֹסֵף: הָא דְּרַב יְהוּדָה – דִּשְׁמוּאֵל הִיא.

Abaye said to Rav Yosef: This ruling **of Rav Yehuda is** a ruling **of** his teacher **Shmuel,** and not of his other teacher, Rav.

NOTES

The dispute refers to a case where there is a main street, etc. – מַחְלוֹקֶת בִּסְרַטְיָא וכו׳: One might ask: What innovative idea was Rav teaching with this statement? He already stated that an opening in the form of a doorway is sufficient to render it permitted to carry even in an alleyway that is open on two opposite sides. One answer is that he is in fact expressing a new idea. Previously, Rav ruled with regard to an alleyway open at both ends: This is the *halakha*, but a public ruling is not issued to that effect. However, in the case of an alleyway that terminates in an open valley, even Rav agrees that this is the *halakha*, and a public ruling is issued to that effect (Rashba).

LANGUAGE

Main street [*seratya*] – סְרַטְיָא: From the Greek στρατός, *stratos*, army, strata in Latin, meaning a street or a public road.

Plaza [*pelatya*] – פְּלַטְיָא: From the Greek πλατεῖα, *plateia*, meaning plaza, large street, or city square.

HALAKHA

An open alleyway – מָבוֹי מְפוּלָּשׁ: If an alleyway is open on two opposite ends, whether they both open into a public domain or whether one side opens to a public domain and the other to a *karmelit*, or even if both sides open to a *karmelit* (Rema; *Beit Yosef*, based on Rambam), it is permitted to carry in the alleyway if an opening in the form of a doorway is constructed at one end and a side post or a cross beam is placed at the other end (*Shulḥan Arukh, Oraḥ Ḥayyim* 364:1).

BACKGROUND

If the alleyway terminated in a backyard – מָבוֹי כָּלֶה בִּרְחָבָה: The image shows an alleyway that is open to a public domain at one end and terminates in a yard behind two houses. Each house has a front courtyard as well, where most domestic functions are performed, although the backyard is also utilized. The backyard itself opens on its other side into the public domain.

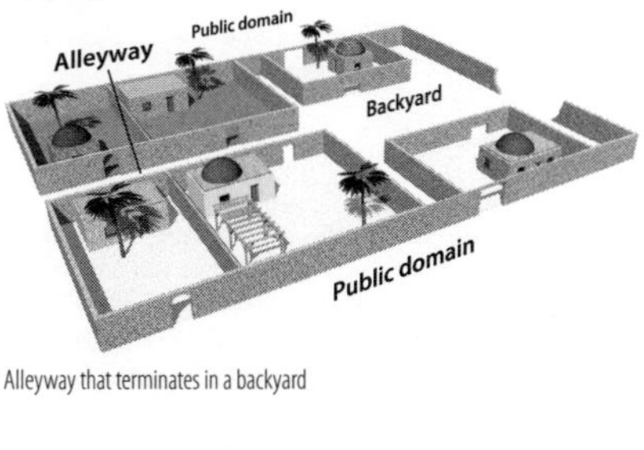

Alleyway that terminates in a backyard

דְּאִי דְּרַב – קַשְׁיָא דְּרַב אַדְּרַב בִּתְרָתֵי. דְּאָמַר רַב יִרְמְיָה בַּר אַבָּא, אָמַר רַב: מָבוֹי שֶׁנִּפְרַץ בִּמְלוֹאוֹ לֶחָצֵר, וְנִפְרְצָה חָצֵר כְּנֶגְדּוֹ – חָצֵר מוּתֶּרֶת וּמָבוֹי אָסוּר. וְאַמַּאי? לֶיהֱוֵי כְּמָבוֹי שֶׁכָּלֶה לִרְחָבָה!

For if it is a ruling **of Rav,** the apparent contradiction between one statement **of Rav** and another statement **of Rav** poses **a difficulty in two** ways.[N] The first is with regard to the fact that this alleyway opens into the public domain on two opposite sides, and the second is based on that **which Rav Yirmeya bar Abba said** that **Rav said:** If **an alleyway was breached along the entire** length[B] of its back wall **into a courtyard, and** likewise **the courtyard was breached opposite it** into the public domain, it is **permitted** to carry in **the courtyard, and** it is **prohibited** to carry in **the alleyway,**[H] since this alleyway is now open on two opposite sides to the public domain. **Why** should this be the ruling? In this case, **let it be like an alleyway that terminates in a backyard,** where Rav Yehuda ruled that nothing further is needed to permit carrying.

אֲמַר לֵיהּ: אֲנָא לָא יָדַעְנָא; עוּבְדָּא הֲוָה בְּדוּרָא דְּרַעֲוָתָא מָבוֹי שֶׁכָּלֶה לִרְחָבָה הֲוָה, וַאֲתָא לְקַמֵּיהּ דְּרַב יְהוּדָה וְלָא אַצְרְכֵיהּ וְלָא מִידֵּי. וְאִי קַשְׁיָא מִשְּׁמֵיהּ דְּרַב – תֶּיהֱוֵי מִשְּׁמֵיהּ דִּשְׁמוּאֵל, וְלָא קַשְׁיָא מִידֵּי.

Rav Yosef **said to** Abaye: **I do not know** in accordance with which of his teachers Rav Yehuda issued this ruling. All I know is that there was **an incident in a shepherds' village** where **an alleyway terminated in a backyard, and** the matter **came before Rav Yehuda** for a ruling, **and he did not require anything** to render it permitted to carry in the alleyway. **And if,** as you say, **it is difficult** if we say that he issued his ruling **in the name of Rav, let it be** suggested that he issued it **in the name of** his other teacher, **Shmuel, and** then **there will be no difficulty.**

הַשְׁתָּא דַּאֲמַר לֵיהּ רַב שֵׁשֶׁת לְרַב שְׁמוּאֵל בַּר אַבָּא, וְאָמְרִי לֵיהּ לְרַב יוֹסֵף בַּר אַבָּא: אַסְבְּרָא לָךְ, כָּאן – שֶׁעֵירְבוּ, כָּאן – שֶׁלֹּא עֵירְבוּ.

The Gemara comments: **Now that Rav Sheshet said to Rav Shmuel bar Abba,**[N] **and some say** that he said **to Rav Yosef bar Abba: I will explain to you** Rav's statement with regard to an alleyway that was breached along the entire length of its back wall into a courtyard. One must make a distinction based on the nature of the case: **Here** it is referring to a case **where** the residents of the courtyard **established an** ***eiruv*** together.[N] In that case, Rav permits carrying in the alleyway and is not concerned with the breach into the courtyard, as the courtyard and the alleyway are treated as a single domain. **There** it is referring to a case **where** the residents **did not establish an** ***eiruv*** together.[N] In that case, Rav prohibits carrying in the alleyway, because the alleyway now has new residents, i.e., the residents of the courtyard, who did not participate in the *eiruv*, and they prevent the residents of the alleyway from carrying.

דְּרַב אַדְּרַב נַמִי לָא קַשְׁיָא, כָּאן – שֶׁעֵירְבוּ בְּנֵי חָצֵר עִם בְּנֵי מָבוֹי, כָּאן – שֶׁלֹּא עֵירְבוּ.

Consequently, it can be said that Rav Yehuda's statement with regard to an alleyway that terminates in a backyard is in accordance with the opinion of Rav, as the apparent contradiction between one statement **of Rav** and another statement **of Rav also** poses **no difficulty. Here,** where Rav Yehuda permits carrying in an alleyway that terminates in a backyard, he is referring to a case **where the residents of the courtyard and the residents of the alleyway established a joint** ***eiruv,*** whereas **here,** where Rav prohibits carrying in an alleyway that was breached along the entire length of its back wall into a courtyard, he is referring to a case **where** the residents of the courtyard and the residents of the alleyway **did not establish a joint** ***eiruv.***

NOTES

A difficulty in two ways – קַשְׁיָא...בִּתְרָתֵי: There is a variant text that does not include the phrase: In two. This version of the text is more suitable to the discussion, as the Gemara doesn't explicate two difficulties but only one, and this is not in keeping with the style of the Gemara. Some commentaries explain the version that reads in two, not as a reference to two difficulties, but to two aspects of the case that are difficult. The question is whether it is prohibited due to the fact that it is an open alleyway or due to the fact that it opens into a domain that prohibits carrying within it (*Korban Netanel*).

Now that Rav Sheshet said to Rav Shmuel bar Abba – הַשְׁתָּא דַּאֲמַר לֵיהּ רַב שֵׁשֶׁת לְרַב שְׁמוּאֵל בַּר אַבָּא: According to one opinion in *Tosafot*, Rav Sheshet's distinction does not refer to the statement of Rav Yirmeya bar Abba, but to that of Rav Yosef. Therefore, the distinction would be between a case where the breached alleyway opens into a backyard that is joined by an *eiruv*, and a case where the backyard is not joined by an *eiruv* (Ritva).

Here, where the residents established an *eiruv* together – כָּאן שֶׁעֵירְבוּ: Some commentaries offer an explanation that is directly opposed to that of Rashi: If the residents join the courtyard and the alleyway with an *eiruv*, the two areas are considered a single domain because the residents may carry within the alleyway. However, if it is an open alleyway, it is open to a public domain on two opposite sides, and it is prohibited to carry within it. If the residents of the courtyard did not establish an *eiruv* with the residents of the alleyway, the residents of the courtyard are forbidden to carry within the alleyway, because the two areas are considered separate domains. Consequently, carrying in the alleyway is not prohibited on their account (Rabbi Zeraḥya HaLevi).

There, where the residents did not establish an *eiruv* together – כָּאן שֶׁלֹּא עֵירְבוּ: According to Rashi, the owners of the backyard are always considered people who established an *eiruv*, for the yard itself has no residents. Consequently, the backyard does not render prohibited carrying within the alleyway due to its residents. However, according to the Ra'avad, as well as one opinion in *Tosafot*, the discussion refers to a backyard that has residents, and it is only permitted if the residents that use the backyard establish an *eiruv* with the residents of the alleyway.

HALAKHA

An alleyway that was breached into a courtyard – מָבוֹי שֶׁנִּפְרַץ לֶחָצֵר: When an alleyway is breached along the entire length of its back wall, where it opens into a courtyard, and the facing wall of the courtyard is breached into the public domain, the residents of the alleyway are permitted to carry within the alleyway, so long as they established an *eiruv* together with the residents of the courtyard. If they failed to do so, carrying is permitted in the courtyard but prohibited in the alleyway, in accordance with the opinion of Rav, as explained by Rav Sheshet (*Shulḥan Arukh, Oraḥ Hayyim* 365:3).

BACKGROUND

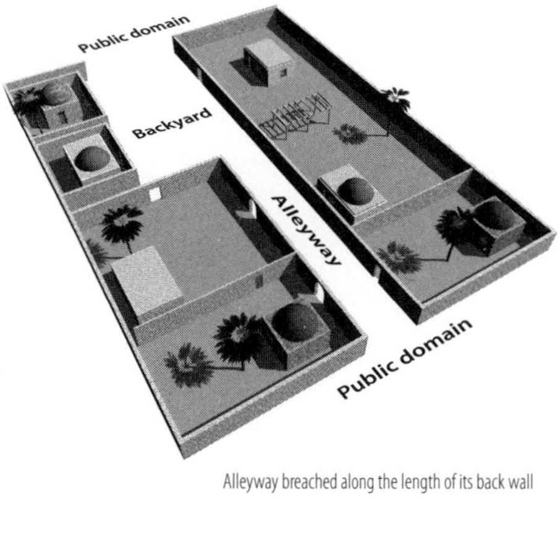

Alleyway breached along the length of its back wall

If an alleyway was breached along the entire length – מָבוֹי שֶׁנִּפְרַץ בִּמְלוֹאוֹ: The discussion concerns an alleyway that was breached along the entire length of its back wall, where it opened into a courtyard, and the courtyard was breached on the facing side into the public domain.

וּלְמַאי דִּסְלֵיק אַדַּעְתִּין מֵעִיקָּרָא, בֵּין שֶׁעֵירְבוּ וּבֵין שֶׁלֹּא עֵירְבוּ פְּלִיגִי; בְּעֵירְבוּ בְּמַאי פְּלִיגִי, בְּשֶׁלֹּא עֵירְבוּ בְּמַאי פְּלִיגִי?

And with regard **to what first entered our minds,** that Rav and Shmuel **disagree both** in the case **where** the residents of the alleyway and the residents of the yard **established an *eiruv*** together, **as well as** in the case **where they did not establish an *eiruv*** together, explanation is necessary. The Gemara seeks to explicate **on what** point **they disagree in** the case **where they established a** joint ***eiruv*,** and **on what** point **they disagree** in the case **where they did not establish a** joint ***eiruv*.** That is to say, what is the crux of the argument in these two cases?

בְּשֶׁלֹּא עֵירְבוּ פְּלִיגִי בְּ״נִרְאֶה מִבַּחוּץ וְשָׁוֶה מִבִּפְנִים״.

The Gemara explains: In the case **where they did not establish** a joint *eiruv*, Rav and Shmuel **disagree concerning** the *halakha* governing an alleyway that **appears** closed **from the outside.** Outside the alleyway there is a wider courtyard, so that from the perspective of those standing in the courtyard, the breach at the end of the alleyway seems like an entrance, and the alleyway appears to be closed, **but** appears to be **even from the inside.** From the perspective of those inside the alleyway, the breach is even with the walls of the alleyway, so that the breach does not look like an entrance, and the alleyway appears to be open. The dispute revolves around the question of whether an alleyway of this kind is considered open or closed. According to the authority who says that it is considered a closed alleyway, one is permitted to carry within an alleyway that terminates in a backyard in this manner.

בְּעֵירְבוּ – קָמִיפַּלְגִי בִּדְרַב יוֹסֵף, דְּאָמַר רַב יוֹסֵף: לֹא שָׁנוּ אֶלָּא שֶׁכָּלָה לְאֶמְצַע רְחָבָה. אֲבָל כָּלָה לְצִידֵּי רְחָבָה – אָסוּר.

And in the case **where they established a** joint ***eiruv*, they disagree about** the principle stated by **Rav Yosef. For Rav Yosef said:** The allowance to carry in an alleyway that terminates in a backyard **was only taught** in a case **where** the alleyway **terminates in the middle of the backyard,**[N] so that when viewed from the yard, the alleyway appears to be closed. **But** if it **terminates on** one of **the sides of the backyard,**[B] so that the alleyway and yard appear continuous, carrying in the alleyway **is prohibited.**[H]

אָמַר רַבָּה: הָא דְּאָמְרַתְּ ״לְאֶמְצַע רְחָבָה מוּתָּר״, לָא אֲמַרַן אֶלָּא זֶה שֶׁלֹּא כְּנֶגֶד זֶה, אֲבָל זֶה כְּנֶגֶד זֶה – אָסוּר.

Rabba took the discussion one step further and **said: That which you say:** Where the alleyway terminates **in the middle of the backyard,** carrying **is permitted,** this **was only stated** with regard to a case where the breach in the back wall of the alleyway into the yard and the breach in the facing wall of the yard into the public domain **are not opposite one another. But** if the two breaches **are opposite one another,**[B] carrying within the alleyway **is prohibited.**[H]

NOTES

Where the alleyway terminates in the middle of the backyard – אֶלָּא שֶׁכָּלָה לְאֶמְצַע רְחָבָה: According to one opinion in *Tosafot*, the Sages do not dispute Rav Yosef's ruling itself. Rather, the dispute concerns the very *halakha* with regard to an alleyway that terminates in the middle of a backyard, whether or not it is considered an alleyway that is open on two opposite sides (Ritva).

HALAKHA

An alleyway that terminates in a backyard – מָבוֹי הַכָּלֶה לִרְחָבָה: This refers to an alleyway that opens into a backyard that was either surrounded by a fence for the purpose of residence, or whose size is no greater than two *beit se'a* (*Tosafot*; Rosh). Alternatively, the case involves an alleyway that terminates in a courtyard. If the alleyway is breached in the middle of the wall of the yard, from the perspective of one standing in the yard, it appears that these are two separate domains. Consequently, as long as the residents of the yard established an *eiruv* with the other residents whose yards are connected to the alleyway, nothing further is required to permit carrying in both areas. However, if the alleyway ends in one of the sides of the yard, such that the wall of the backyard is a continuation of the wall of the alleyway, it is all considered one long, open alleyway. Therefore, it is forbidden to carry in it or to establish an *eiruv* in it until it is corrected according to the requirements of an open alleyway (*Shulḥan Arukh, Oraḥ Ḥayyim* 365:3).

If the two breaches are opposite one another – פִּרוּץ זֶה כְּנֶגֶד זֶה: It is permitted to carry in an alleyway that ends in the middle of a wall of a yard, when the opening of the yard into the public domain does not line up with the breach of the alleyway into the yard. If, however, the two breaches are opposite one another, it is forbidden to carry, in accordance with the statement of Rabba (*Shulḥan Arukh, Oraḥ Ḥayyim* 365:3).

BACKGROUND

Terminates on one of the sides of the backyard – כָּלָה לְצִידֵּי רְחָבָה: This refers to an alleyway that ends on one of the sides of a yard, so that the wall of the alleyway and the wall of the backyard are continous.

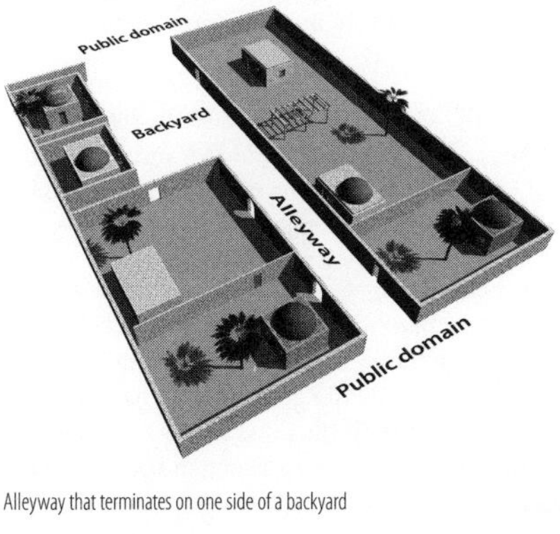

Alleyway that terminates on one side of a backyard

Opposite one another – זֶה כְּנֶגֶד זֶה: An alleyway that ends in a backyard, such that the breach of the yard that opens into the public domain is directly across from the breach of the alleyway into the yard, forms an alleyway that is open on two opposite sides to a public domain.

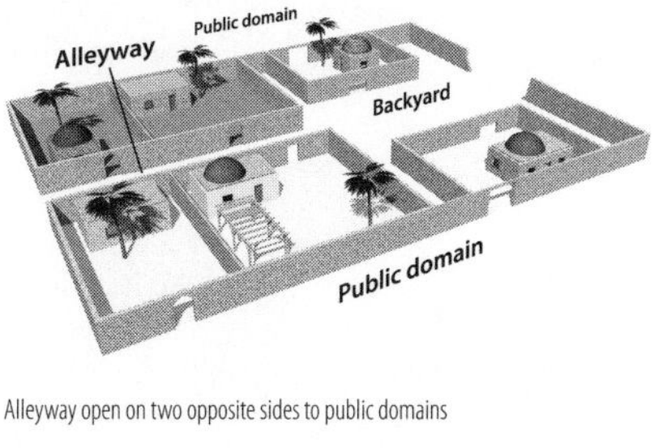

Alleyway open on two opposite sides to public domains

אָמַר רַב מְשַׁרְשְׁיָא: הָא דְּאָמְרַתְּ ״זֶה שֶׁלֹּא כְּנֶגֶד זֶה מוּתָּר״, לָא אֲמַרַן אֶלָּא רְחָבָה דְּרַבִּים, אֲבָל רְחָבָה דְּיָחִיד – זִימְנִין דְּמִימְלַךְ עֲלַהּ וּבָנֵי לַהּ בָּתִּים, וְהָוֵי לַהּ כְּמָבוֹי שֶׁכָּלָה לַהּ לְצִידֵּי רְחָבָה – וְאָסוּר.

Rav Mesharshiya continued this line of thought and **said: That which you say:** If the two breaches **are not opposite one another,** carrying within the alleyway **is permitted,** this **was only stated** with regard to the case where **the backyard** belongs to **many** people. **But** if **the yard** belongs to a single **individual,**[H] **he might sometime change his mind about it and build houses** in that part of the yard that is wider than the alleyway, **and** then the alleyway **will become like an alleyway that terminates on** one of **the sides of the backyard,** which is **prohibited.** If the owner of the yard closes off one side of the yard with houses, the alleyway will no longer terminate in the middle of the yard, but on one of its sides, in which case carrying will be forbidden. Consequently, although the houses have not yet been built, adjustments must be made in the alleyway to permit carrying, so that no problems should arise in the future.

וּמְנָא תֵּימְרָא דְּשָׁנֵי לָן בֵּין רְחָבָה דְּרַבִּים לִרְחָבָה דְּיָחִיד – דְּאָמַר רָבִין בַּר רַב אַדָּא, אָמַר רַבִּי יִצְחָק: מַעֲשֶׂה בְּמָבוֹי אֶחָד שֶׁצִּידּוֹ אֶחָד כָּלֶה לַיָּם וְצִידּוֹ אֶחָד כָּלֶה לָאַשְׁפָּה, וּבָא מַעֲשֶׂה לִפְנֵי רַבִּי וְלֹא אָמַר בָּהּ לֹא הֶיתֵּר וְלֹא אִיסּוּר.

Rav Mesharshiya adds: **And from where do you say that we distinguish between a backyard** that belongs to **many** people **and a backyard** that belongs to a single **individual? As Ravin bar Rav Adda said that Rabbi Yitzḥak said:** There was **an incident involving a certain alleyway,** where **one of its sides terminated in the sea**[NN] **and one of its sides terminated in a refuse heap,**[H] resulting in an alleyway closed on both sides. **And the incident came before Rabbi** Yehuda HaNasi, so that he may rule on whether these partitions are sufficient or whether some additional construction is necessary, **and he did not say** anything **about it, neither permission nor prohibition.**

אִיסּוּר לֹא אָמַר בָּהּ – דְּהָא קָיְימִי מְחִיצוֹת, הֶיתֵּר לֹא אָמַר בָּהּ – חָיְישִׁינַן: שֶׁמָּא תִּינָּטֵל אַשְׁפָּה, וְיַעֲלֶה הַיָּם שִׂרְטוֹן.

The Gemara clarifies: Rabbi Yehuda HaNasi **did not state** a ruling indicating **a prohibition** to carry **in** the alleyway, **for partitions,** i.e., the sea and the refuse heap, indeed **stand,** and the alleyway is closed off on both sides. However, **he** also **did not state** a ruling granting **permission** to carry **in** the alleyway, **for we are concerned that perhaps the refuse heap will be removed** from its present spot, leaving one side of the alleyway open. **And,** alternatively, perhaps **the sea will raise up sand,** and the sandbank will intervene between the end of the alleyway and the sea, so that the sea can no longer be considered a partition for the alleyway.

וּמִי חָיְישִׁינַן שֶׁמָּא תִּינָּטֵל אַשְׁפָּה? וְהָתְנַן: אַשְׁפָּה בִּרְשׁוּת הָרַבִּים גְּבוֹהַּ עֲשָׂרָה טְפָחִים, חַלּוֹן שֶׁעַל גַּבָּהּ זוֹרְקִין לָהּ בְּשַׁבָּת,

The Gemara continues: **Are we** really **concerned that perhaps the refuse heap will be removed? But didn't we learn** in a mishna: **A refuse heap in the public domain** that is **ten handbreadths high,** so that it has the status of a private domain, and there is **a window above** the pile of refuse, i.e., the window is in a house adjacent to the refuse heap, **we may throw** refuse from the window **onto** the heap **on Shabbat.** Carrying on Shabbat from one private domain, i.e., the house, to another, i.e., the refuse heap, is permitted. We are not concerned that someone might remove some of the refuse, thus lowering the heap until it is no longer a private domain, such that throwing refuse upon it is prohibited. This seems to present a contradiction, for in some cases we are concerned that the refuse heap might be removed, but in other cases we are not.

אַלְמָא: שָׁנֵי בֵּין אַשְׁפָּה דְּרַבִּים לְאַשְׁפָּה דְּיָחִיד.

Apparently, we **distinguish between a public refuse heap and a private refuse heap,** such that in the case of a private refuse heap we cannot assume that it will remain in place permanently, as it is likely to be emptied at some point.

הָכָא נַמִי, שָׁנֵי בֵּין רְחָבָה דְּרַבִּים לִרְחָבָה דְּיָחִיד.

Here, too, we **distinguish between a backyard** belonging to **many** people, where buildings are not likely to be added, **and a backyard** belonging to **a** single **individual,** where he might consider making changes and add buildings.

וְרַבָּנַן מַאי?

The case involving an alleyway opening on one side to the sea and on the other side to a refuse heap was brought before Rabbi Yehuda HaNasi, who did not rule on the matter. The Gemara inquires: **And the Rabbis** of Rabbi Yehuda HaNasi's generation, **what** was their opinion with regard to this case? The fact that we are told that Rabbi Yehuda HaNasi did not want to issue a ruling indicates that his colleagues disagreed with him.

HALAKHA

A backyard of an individual – רְחָבָה שֶׁל יָחִיד: Permission to carry in an alleyway that opens into a yard is limited to a yard where many people reside. However, if the yard belongs to an individual, carrying in the alleyway is prohibited, in accordance with the statement of Rav Mesharshiya (*Shulḥan Arukh*, *Oraḥ Ḥayyim* 365:3).

A refuse heap and the sea – אַשְׁפָּה וְיָם: A public refuse heap is not considered likely to be cleared away, and one can assume that it will remain as is. In addition, there is no concern that the sea might raise up sand and change the shape of the beach. Rema cites opinions that express concern for shifting sandbanks (Rosh; *Tur*). The basis of this dispute is whether the Gemara reads: We are concerned, or: We are not concerned (Vilna Gaon; *Shulḥan Arukh*, *Oraḥ Ḥayyim* 365:29).

NOTES

One of its sides terminated in the sea – צִידּוֹ אֶחָד כָּלֶה לַיָּם: There is a variant reading: One of its sides is the sea, which is probably the reading of Rashi's text as well. According to this reading, the alleyway, in this context, has two walls running lengthwise that are not actual walls. There is the seashore on one side and a refuse heap on the other, and the two ends of the alleyway are properly closed or have an opening in the form of a doorway. According to our reading, only the entrances to the alleyway face the sea and the refuse dump, but not its lengthwise walls (Rabbeinu Ḥananel; see Ritva).

Terminated in the sea – כָּלֶה לַיָּם: The seashore does not render the sea a private domain as it does an alleyway. Rather, the sea has the status of a *karmelit*, because the seashores are very long. Consequently, the sea is comparable to an enclosure [*karpef*] that was not surrounded by a fence for the purpose of residence. However, with regard to a specific segment of the alleyway, the sea bank is sufficient to render the alleyway closed (*Ge'on Ya'akov*).

אָמַר רַב יוֹסֵף בַּר אַבְדִּימִי, תָּנָא: וַחֲכָמִים אוֹסְרִין. אָמַר רַב נַחְמָן: הֲלָכָה כְּדִבְרֵי חֲכָמִים. אִיכָּא דְּאָמְרִי, אָמַר רַב יוֹסֵף בַּר אַבְדִּימִי, תָּנָא: וַחֲכָמִים מַתִּירִין. אָמַר רַב נַחְמָן: אֵין הֲלָכָה כְּדִבְרֵי חֲכָמִים.

Rav Yosef bar Avdimi said: It was taught in a *baraita*: **And the Rabbis prohibit** carrying in such an alleyway. **Rav Naḥman said: The *halakha* is in accordance with the statement of** the **Rabbis. There are some who state** a different version of the previous statements as follows: **Rav Yosef bar Avdimi said: It was taught** in a *baraita*: **And the Rabbis permit** carrying in such an alleyway. **Rav Naḥman said: The *halakha* is not in accordance with the opinion of** the **Rabbis.**

מָרֵימָר פָּסֵיק לָהּ לְסוּרָא בְּאוּזְלֵי, אֲמַר: חָיְישִׁינַן שֶׁמָּא יַעֲלֶה הַיָּם שִׂרְטוֹן.

The Gemara relates: **Mareimar would block off** the ends of the alleyways of **Sura**, which opened to a river, **with nets**[N] to serve as partitions. **He said:** Just as **we are concerned that perhaps the sea will raise up sand,** so too, we are concerned that the river will raise up sand, and hence we cannot rely on its banks to serve as partitions.

הַהוּא מָבוֹי עָקוּם דַּהֲוָה בְּסוּרָא, כַּרוּךְ בּוּדְיָא, אוֹתִיבוּ בֵּיהּ בְּעַקְמוּמִיתֵיהּ. אֲמַר רַב חִסְדָּא: הָא לָא כְּרַב וְלָא כִּשְׁמוּאֵל. לְרַב דְּאָמַר ״תּוֹרָתוֹ כִּמְפוּלָּשׁ״ – צוּרַת הַפֶּתַח בָּעֵי, לִשְׁמוּאֵל דְּאָמַר ״תּוֹרָתוֹ כְּסָתוּם״ – הָנֵי מִילֵּי לֶחִי מְעַלְּיָא, אֲבָל הַאי כֵּיוָן דְּנָשֵׁיב בֵּיהּ זִיקָא וְשָׁדֵי לֵיהּ – לָאו כְּלוּם הוּא.

The Gemara further relates: With regard to **a certain crooked** L-shaped **alleyway that was in Sura,** the residents of the place **rolled up a mat** and **placed it at the turn** to serve as a side post to permit carrying within it. **Rav Ḥisda said: This** was done **neither in accordance with** the opinion of **Rav nor in accordance with** that of **Shmuel.** The Gemara explains: **According to Rav,** who **said** that **the *halakha*** of a crooked L-shaped alleyway **is like that of an** alleyway that is **open** on two opposite sides, it **requires** an opening in **the form of a doorway.** And even **according to Shmuel,** who **said** that **its *halakha* is like that of an** alleyway that is **closed** at one side, so that carrying is permitted by means of a side post, **this applies only** to a case where **a proper side post** was erected. **But** with regard to **this** mat, **once the wind blows upon it, it throws it over; it is** regarded as **nothing** and is totally ineffective.

וְאִי נָעֵיץ בֵּיהּ סִיכְּתָא וְחַבְרֵיהּ – חַבְרֵיהּ.

The Gemara comments: **But if a peg was inserted** into the mat, **and** thus the mat was properly **attached** to the wall, it is considered **attached** and serves as an effective side post.

גּוּפָא, אָמַר רַב יִרְמְיָה בַּר אַבָּא, אָמַר רַב: מָבוֹי שֶׁנִּפְרַץ בִּמְלוֹאוֹ לֶחָצֵר, וְנִפְרְצָה חָצֵר כְּנֶגְדּוֹ – חָצֵר מוּתֶּרֶת, וּמָבוֹי אָסוּר.

The Gemara examines Rav Yirmeya bar Abba's statement cited in the course of the previous discussion. **As to the matter itself, Rav Yirmeya bar Abba said that Rav said: An alleyway that was breached along the entire** length of its back wall **into a courtyard, and** likewise **the courtyard was breached on its opposite side** into the public domain, **the courtyard is permitted** for carrying, **and the alleyway is prohibited** for carrying.

אֲמַר לֵיהּ רַבָּה בַּר עוּלָּא לְרַב בֵּיבַי בַּר אַבַּיֵי: רַבִּי, לָא מִשְׁנָתֵנוּ הִיא זוֹ? ״חָצֵר קְטַנָּה שֶׁנִּפְרְצָה לִגְדוֹלָה – גְּדוֹלָה מוּתֶּרֶת וּקְטַנָּה אֲסוּרָה, מִפְּנֵי שֶׁהִיא כְּפִתְחָהּ שֶׁל גְּדוֹלָה״.

Rabba bar Ulla said to Rav Beivai bar Abaye: My Master, is this case **not** the same as **our Mishna? A smaller courtyard that was breached** along the entire length of one of its walls **into a larger** courtyard,[B] the **larger one is permitted** for carrying, **and the smaller one is prohibited, because** the breach **is** regarded **as the entrance to the larger** courtyard. With regard to the larger courtyard, the breach running the entire length of the smaller courtyard is considered like an entrance in one of its walls, for the breach is surrounded on both sides by the remaining portions of the wall of the larger courtyard, and therefore carrying is permitted. With regard to the smaller courtyard, however, one wall is missing in its entirety, and therefore carrying is forbidden. This seems to be exactly the same as the case of an alleyway that was breached along the entire length of its back wall into a courtyard.

אֲמַר לֵיהּ: אִי מֵהָתָם הֲוָה אָמֵינָא: הָנֵי מִילֵּי – הֵיכָא דְּלָא קָא דָּרְסִי בָּהּ רַבִּים, אֲבָל הֵיכָא דְּקָא דָּרְסִי בָּהּ רַבִּים – אֵימָא אֲפִילּוּ חָצֵר נָמֵי.

He, Rav Beivai bar Abaye, **said to him,** Rabba bar Ulla: **If** this was learned **from there** alone, **I would have said** that we must distinguish between the cases: The Mishna's ruling **only applies in a place where many people do not tread.** The breach between the smaller and larger courtyard will not cause more people to pass through the larger courtyard, and therefore it remains a unit of its own. **But in a place where many people tread,** i.e., in the case where a courtyard is breached on one side into an alleyway and on the other side into the public domain, you might **say** that carrying is prohibited **even** in the **courtyard as well,** owing to the people passing through it from the alleyway to the public domain.

NOTES

Would block off the ends of the alleyways of Sura with nets – פָּסֵיק לָהּ לְסוּרָא בְּאוּזְלֵי: Rabbeinu Ḥananel and other commentaries had a variant text that stated, Mareimar said: We are not concerned that the sea will raise up sand. According to this reading, Mareimar relied on the rivulets and creeks of the river, into which nets were cast, to serve as partitions for the ends of alleyways, and he did not require anything else of them. The Rambam also ruled in accordance with this reading.

BACKGROUND

A smaller courtyard that was breached into a larger courtyard – חָצֵר קְטַנָּה שֶׁנִּפְרְצָה לִגְדוֹלָה: From the perspective of those in the larger courtyard, it is clear that the smaller courtyard is a separate unit. However, from the perspective of those in the smaller courtyard, the entire fence appears to be breached and no partition remains between it and the larger courtyard.

Small courtyard breached into a larger courtyard

NOTES

A public domain with regard to ritual impurity – רְשׁוּת הָרַבִּים לְטוּמְאָה: As is derived from the verses, in cases of uncertainty with regard to the ritual purity of a person or object, if the item was found in a private domain, it is considered impure based on the uncertainty. However, if it is found in a public domain, it is considered pure based on the uncertainty. For the purpose of the *halakhot* of ritual impurity, a public domain is not defined by partitions or by ownership. Instead, its status is determined by the number of people who regularly pass through it.

HALAKHA

A courtyard through which many people cross – חָצֵר שֶׁהָרַבִּים בּוֹקְעִים בָּהּ: With regard to the *halakhot* of Shabbat, a courtyard that is properly enclosed by partitions is treated like a private domain, even if many people pass through it, as stated by the *Tosefta* (*Shulḥan Arukh*, *Oraḥ Ḥayyim* 365:3). With regard to the *halakhot* of ritual impurity, however, a courtyard of this kind has the status of a public domain, and in cases of uncertainty, the person or article is considered pure (Rambam *Sefer Tahara*, *Hilkhot She'ar Avot HaTumot* 20:3).

וְהָא נַמִי תָּנֵינָא: חָצֵר שֶׁהָרַבִּים נִכְנָסִין לָהּ בָּזוֹ וְיוֹצְאִין לָהּ בָּזוֹ – רְשׁוּת הָרַבִּים לְטוּמְאָה, וּרְשׁוּת הַיָּחִיד לַשַּׁבָּת.

The Gemara raises a difficulty: **But didn't we** already **learn this as well,** that the mere fact that many people tread through a courtyard does not forbid carrying, for we learned in the Tosefta: **A courtyard** that was properly surrounded by partitions, **into** which **many people enter on this** side **and exit on that** side, is considered **a public domain** with regard to the *halakhot* of **ritual impurity,**[N] so that in cases of doubt, we say that the person or article is pure, **but** it is still **a private domain** with regard to the *halakhot* of **Shabbat.**[H] Therefore, we see that with regard to Shabbat, the sole criterion is the existence of partitions, and the fact that many people pass through the courtyard does not impair its status as a private domain.

אִי מֵהָתָם הֲוָה אָמֵינָא: הָנֵי מִילֵּי – זֶה שֶׁלֹּא כְּנֶגֶד זֶה,

The Gemara refutes this argument: **If** this was derived **there** alone, **I would have said** that this **only applies** in a case where the two breaches are **not opposite one another,**

Perek **I**
Daf **8** Amud **b**

אֲבָל זֶה כְּנֶגֶד זֶה – אֵימָא לָא.

but if the two breaches **are opposite one another,** you might **say** that it is **not** considered a private domain even with regard to Shabbat. Rav therefore teaches us that even if the breaches of the courtyard line up with each other, carrying is nonetheless permitted therein.

וּלְרַבָּה דְּאָמַר ״זֶה כְּנֶגֶד זֶה אָסוּר״ הָא דְּרַב בְּמַאי מוֹקֵי לַהּ? בְּזֶה שֶׁלֹּא כְּנֶגֶד זֶה. תַּרְתֵּי לָמָּה לִי?

The Gemara raises a difficulty: **And according to Rabba, who said** that where the alleyway terminates in a backyard and the breaches **are one opposite another,** carrying **is prohibited, how does** he **construe Rav's** case? Rav's ruling must refer to a case where the breaches **are not one opposite another,** and if so, **why do I** need **two** rulings?[N] The essence of this *halakha*, that the yard is deemed a private domain with regard to Shabbat, was already stated in the *Tosefta*, so why did Rav need to teach another *halakha* with regard to the very same issue?

אִי מֵהָתָם הֲוָה אָמֵינָא: הָנֵי מִילֵּי – לִזְרוֹק, אֲבָל לְטַלְטֵל – אֵימָא לָא, קָא מַשְׁמַע לַן.

The Gemara explains that there is a novelty in Rav's teaching: **If** one learned the *halakha* **from there,** the *Tosefta*, alone, **I would have said** that this ruling that the courtyard is a private domain with regard to Shabbat **only applies** to the issue **of throwing,** i.e., that one who throws from the public domain into this courtyard is liable, since it is considered a private domain according to Torah law. **But** to allow **carrying** in it like a proper private domain, you might **say no,** that the Sages forbade carrying in it, owing to the many people passing through it. Rav therefore **teaches us** that we are not concerned about this, and that carrying in the yard is permitted, even by rabbinic law.

NOTES

Why do I need two rulings – תַּרְתֵּי לָמָּה לִי: There are those who asked: This difficulty is usually raised only with regard to the repetition of tannaitic statements, but not with regard to the words of a *baraita* and the statement of an *amora*. Why then is it raised here (Rashba)? The answer given is that the difficulty is raised with regard to two *halakhot* of Rav on the very same topic, where the second doesn't appear to add anything to the first (*Tosafot*, cited by Rashba). An alternative interpretation is that the question is directed not at the repetitive nature of Rav's statement, but at the fact that he deviates from the wording of the *baraita*. Had Rav wanted to state the *halakha* mentioned in the *baraita*, why didn't he cite it directly?

אִיתְּמַר, מָבוֹי הֶעָשׂוּי כַּנָּדָל, אָמַר אַבַּיֵי: עוֹשֶׂה צוּרַת הַפֶּתַח לְגָדוֹל, וְהָנָךְ כּוּלְּהוּ מִישְׁתָּרוּ בְּלֶחִי וְקוֹרָה.

It was stated that the *amora'im* disagree about the following matter: With regard to **an alleyway** that is **shaped like a centipede,**[NBH] i.e., a long alleyway that opens to the public domain but with a series of small alleyways branching off of it on both of its sides, all of which also open to the public domain,[B] **Abaye said:** An opening in **the form of a doorway is made for the large** alleyway, **and all the** small alleyways **are permitted by** means of **a side post or a** cross **beam.**

אָמַר לֵיהּ רָבָא: כְּמַאן – כִּשְׁמוּאֵל, דְּאָמַר: ״תּוֹרָתוֹ כְּסָתוּם״ לָמָּה לֵיהּ צוּרַת הַפֶּתַח? וְעוֹד; הָא הַהוּא מָבוֹי עָקוּם דַּהֲוָה בִּנְהַרְדְּעָא, וְחָשׁוּ לָהּ לְדְרַב!

Rava said to him: According to whom do you state this *halakha*? Apparently according to the opinion of **Shmuel, who said that the** *halakha* **of** a crooked L-shaped alleyway **is like** that of an alleyway that is **closed** at one side. For in this case of an alleyway that is shaped like a centipede, when each of the smaller alleyways connects to the larger alleyway, it forms a crooked L-shaped alleyway. However, if the *halakha* is indeed in accordance with the opinion of Shmuel, **why is the form of a doorway** needed **for it?** According to Shmuel, an alleyway of this kind only requires a side post or a cross beam at each end in order to permit carrying within it. **And furthermore,** with regard to **the crooked,** L-shaped **alleyway in Neharde'a,** which was Shmuel's place of residence, **didn't they take into consideration** the position **of Rav?** This indicates that the *halakha* in practice follows Rav as opposed to Shmuel.

אֶלָּא אָמַר רָבָא: עוֹשֶׂה צוּרַת הַפֶּתַח לְכוּלְּהוּ לְהַאי גִּיסָּא, וְאִידָּךְ גִּיסָּא מִישְׁתָּרוּ בְּלֶחִי וְקוֹרָה.

Rather, Rava said: An alleyway made like a centipede can be rendered fit for one to carry within it as follows: An opening in **the form of a doorway is made for all of** the small alleyways **on this** one of their **sides, and the other side is permitted by** means of **a side post or a** cross **beam.**

אָמַר רַב כָּהֲנָא בַּר תַּחֲלִיפָא מִשְּׁמֵיהּ דְּרַב כָּהֲנָא בַּר מִנְיוּמִי מִשְּׁמֵיהּ דְּרַב כָּהֲנָא בַּר מַלְכִּיוּ מִשְּׁמֵיהּ דְּרַב כָּהֲנָא רַבֵּיהּ דְּרַב, וְאָמְרִי לָהּ רַב כָּהֲנָא בַּר מַלְכִּיוּ הַיְינוּ רַב כָּהֲנָא רַבֵּיהּ דְּרַב: מָבוֹי שֶׁצִּידּוֹ אֶחָד אָרוֹךְ וְצִידּוֹ אֶחָד קָצָר, פָּחוֹת מֵאַרְבַּע אַמּוֹת – מַנִּיחַ אֶת הַקּוֹרָה בַּאֲלַכְסוֹן, אַרְבַּע אַמּוֹת – אֵינוֹ מַנִּיחַ אֶת הַקּוֹרָה אֶלָּא כְּנֶגֶד הַקָּצָר. רָבָא אָמַר: אֶחָד זֶה וְאֶחָד זֶה – אֵינוֹ מַנִּיחַ אֶת הַקּוֹרָה אֶלָּא כְּנֶגֶד הַקָּצָר.

The Gemara considers a new case: **Rav Kahana bar Taḥalifa said in the name of Rav Kahana bar Minyumi,** who said **in the name of Rav Kahana bar Malkiyu,** who said **in the name of Rav Kahana, the teacher of Rav; and some say** that **Rav Kahana bar Malkiyu is Rav Kahana, the teacher of Rav:** With regard to **an alleyway that** opens into the public domain, **its one side** being **long**[H] **and its other side** being **short,** i.e., one side juts out into the public domain more than the other, the *halakha* is as follows: If the difference in length between the two sides is **less than four cubits, the** cross **beam is placed diagonally**[B] across the opening between the ends of the two walls of the alleyway. If, however, the difference is **four cubits** or more, **the** cross **beam is placed** straight **across** the alleyway at the end **of the short** side, i.e., at the end of the short side straight across toward the corresponding spot on the longer wall such that the beam is perpendicular to both walls, and no use may be made of the portion of the alleyway that lies beyond the cross beam. **Rava** disagreed and **said:** In **both this** case **and** in **that** case, **the** cross **beam is placed** straight **across** the alleyway at the end **of the short** side.

NOTES

An alleyway that is shaped like a centipede – מָבוֹי הֶעָשׂוּי כַּנָּדָל: Ritva and other commentaries interpret Rashi as understanding that all of the small alleyways are located on one side of the large alleyway. The majority of commentaries, however, explain that it is shaped like an actual centipede, with small alleyways situated across from one another along the main alleyway. There is also a dispute with regard to the large alleyway. Some hold that the main alleyway is closed on one side (Rashi, *Me'iri*, and others), while others hold that it opens into the public domain at both ends (Rabbeinu Yonatan, Ri'az, and others).

BACKGROUND

Centipede [*nadal*] – **נָדָל:** These creatures are arthropods belonging to the Chilopoda class. All of them possess elongated bodies, with a pair of legs attached to each body segment, although the number of pairs of legs varies from one species to another. The poisonous centipede, *Scolopendra*, possesses twenty-one pairs of legs. It has a pair of poisonous claws near its head, used to deliver venom into its prey. Its bite is painful, although not usually dangerous to humans. It is likely that these and similar species are what the Torah refers to as multi-legged creatures (see Rashi on Leviticus 11:42).

Centipede of the genus *Scolopendra*

An alleyway shaped like a centipede – מָבוֹי הֶעָשׂוּי כַּנָּדָל: A centipede alleyway is a large, closed alleyway that has smaller alleyways extending from its two sides, each one opening to the public domain, apparently in accordance with the opinion of Rashi. See *Tosafot*, whose opinion differs somewhat.

The cross beam is placed diagonally – הַקּוֹרָה בַּאֲלַכְסוֹן: An alleyway where the wall on one side opening into the public domain is longer than the other, so the entrance is not perpendicular with the street of the public domain.

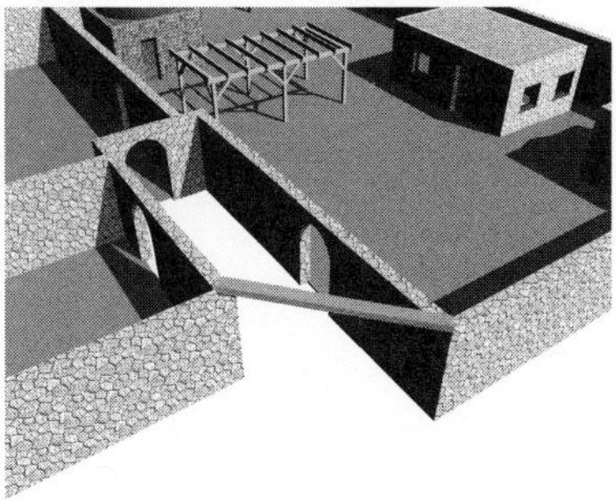

Cross beam placed on a diagonal from the end of the short wall to the end of the long wall

HALAKHA

An alleyway that is shaped like a centipede – מָבוֹי הֶעָשׂוּי כַּנָּדָל: This applies when a large alleyway has a series of smaller alleyways extending from both sides, all of which open into the public domain, even if the small alleyways are not positioned one across from the other (Rambam). An opening in the form of a doorway must be made on the side where each of the small alleyways open into the large alleyway, and a side post or a cross beam must be placed on the side that opens into the public domain in order to permit carrying within each of them, in accordance with Rava's conclusion (*Shulḥan Arukh, Oraḥ Ḥayyim* 364:5).

An alleyway that opens into the public domain, its one side being long – מָבוֹי שֶׁצִּידּוֹ אֶחָד אָרוֹךְ: If the entrance to an alleyway from the public domain has one wall that is longer than the other, the cross beam must be placed across the entrance perpendicularly toward the corresponding spot on the longer wall. Similarly, when using a side post, it must be positioned directly across from the end of the short wall (*Magen Avraham*). However, if a cross beam is placed on a diagonal inside the alleyway within the area of the short wall, it is permitted to utilize the area of the alleyway up to where the cross beam meets the short wall (Rosh; *Shulḥan Arukh, Oraḥ Ḥayyim* 363:30).

וְאֵימָא טַעְמָא דִּידִי, וְאֵימָא טַעְמָא דִּידְהוּ. אֵימָא טַעְמָא דִּידִי: קוֹרָה טַעְמָא מַאי – מִשּׁוּם הֶיכֵּר, וּבַאֲלַכְסוֹן לָא הָוֵי הֶיכֵּר;

Rava added: **I will state my reason, and I will state their reason. I will state my reason: What is the reason for** a cross **beam?** To function **as a conspicuous marker** that separates the alleyway from the public domain, so that the residents of the alleyway should know the boundary within which carrying is permitted, **and** when placed **diagonally,** the cross beam **is not** sufficiently **conspicuous.** Those who see people carrying in the section extending past the short side will think that one is generally permitted to carry in a public domain.

וְאֵימָא טַעְמָא דִּידְהוּ: קוֹרָה מִשּׁוּם מַאי – מִשּׁוּם מְחִיצָה, וּבַאֲלַכְסוֹן נַמִּי הָוֵי מְחִיצָה.

I will state their reason as well: **What is the reason for** a cross **beam? To** function **as a partition,** that is to say, the cross beam is considered as though it descended to the ground, creating a fourth wall for the alleyway. Hence, **even** when placed **diagonally, it is** considered **a partition.**[B]

אָמַר רַב כָּהֲנָא: הוֹאִיל וּשְׁמַעְתְּתָא דְּכָהֲנֵי הִיא – אֵימָא בָּהּ מִילְּתָא: הָא דְּאָמְרַתְּ מַנִּיחַ הַקּוֹרָה בַּאֲלַכְסוֹן – לָא אֲמַרַן אֶלָּא שֶׁאֵין בַּאֲלַכְסוֹנוֹ יוֹתֵר מֵעֶשֶׂר, אֲבָל יֵשׁ בַּאֲלַכְסוֹנוֹ יוֹתֵר מֵעֶשֶׂר – דִּבְרֵי הַכֹּל אֵינוֹ מַנִּיחַ אֶלָּא כְּנֶגֶד הַקָּצָר.

Rav Kahana said: Since this involves ***halakhot*** **of** Sages named **Kahana,**[P] I too **will say something** with regard **to it: That which you said,** that **the** cross **beam is placed diagonally** across the alleyway, this **was only said** in a case **where the diagonal is no more than ten** cubits. **But if the diagonal is more than ten** cubits, then even if the width of the alleyway itself is less than ten cubits, **all agree that** the cross beam **must be placed** straight **across** the alleyway at the end of **the short** side,[B] for an entrance wider than ten cubits cannot be permitted by a cross beam, and here the entire length under the cross beam is considered an entrance.

אִיבַּעְיָא לְהוּ: מַהוּ לְהִשְׁתַּמֵּשׁ תַּחַת הַקּוֹרָה? רַב וְרַבִּי חִיָּיא וְרַבִּי יוֹחָנָן אָמְרוּ: מוּתָּר לְהִשְׁתַּמֵּשׁ תַּחַת הַקּוֹרָה. שְׁמוּאֵל וְרַבִּי שִׁמְעוֹן בַּר רַבִּי וְרַבִּי שִׁמְעוֹן בֶּן לָקִישׁ אָמְרוּ: אָסוּר לְהִשְׁתַּמֵּשׁ תַּחַת הַקּוֹרָה.

A dilemma was raised before the Sages: **What is** the *halakha* with regard to **utilizing** and carrying in the area **beneath the** cross **beam** spanning the opening of an alleyway, which the beam permits carrying? Opinions differ on the matter. **Rav, Rabbi Ḥiyya, and Rabbi Yoḥanan said: It is permitted to utilize** the area **beneath the** cross **beam.**[H] **Shmuel, Rabbi Shimon bar Rabbi, and Rabbi Shimon ben Lakish said: It is prohibited to utilize** the area **beneath the** cross **beam.**

לֵימָא בְּהָא קָמִיפַּלְגִי, דְּמָר סָבַר: קוֹרָה מִשּׁוּם הֶיכֵּר, וּמָר סָבַר קוֹרָה מִשּׁוּם מְחִיצָה.

The Gemara suggests a way to understand this dispute: **Shall we say** that these *amora'im* **argue over the following** issue, **that Master,** representing those who permit it, **holds:** A cross **beam serves** in an alleyway **as a conspicuous marker** that separates it from the public domain, **and Master,** representing those who prohibit it, **holds:** A cross **beam serves as a partition.**

לֹא, דְּכוּלֵּי עָלְמָא – קוֹרָה מִשּׁוּם הֶיכֵּר, וְהָכָא בְּהָא קָמִיפַּלְגִי; דְּמָר סָבַר: הֶיכֵּירָא מִלְּגָיו, וּמָר סָבַר: הֶיכֵּירָא מִלְּבַר.

The Gemara rejects this argument: **No, everyone** might **agree** that a cross **beam serves as a conspicuous marker, but here they argue over the following: Master,** representing those who forbid it, **holds** that **the conspicuous marker** is intended for those situated **inside** the alleyway, and hence the area outside the inner edge of the cross beam may not be used; **and Master,** representing those who permit it, **holds** that **the conspicuous marker** is intended for those **outside** in the public domain, and it is therefore permitted to carry up to the outer edge of the cross beam.

BACKGROUND

Diagonal cross beam – קוֹרָה בַּאֲלַכְסוֹן:

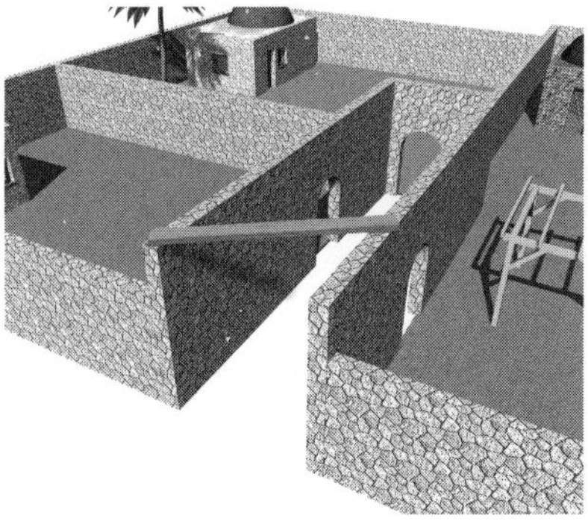

Cross beam positioned diagonally across the entrance to an alleyway that has walls of equal length

Placed straight across the alleyway at the end of the short side – מַנִּיחַ אֶלָּא כְּנֶגֶד הַקָּצָר: In a case where one side of an alleyway is longer than the other, there are two ways to position a cross beam at its entrance. In certain cases, the Rabbis permitted positioning a cross beam diagonally at the entrance. The more accepted method, however, is to position the cross beam across from the shorter side, and to make use of the alleyway only up to the cross beam.

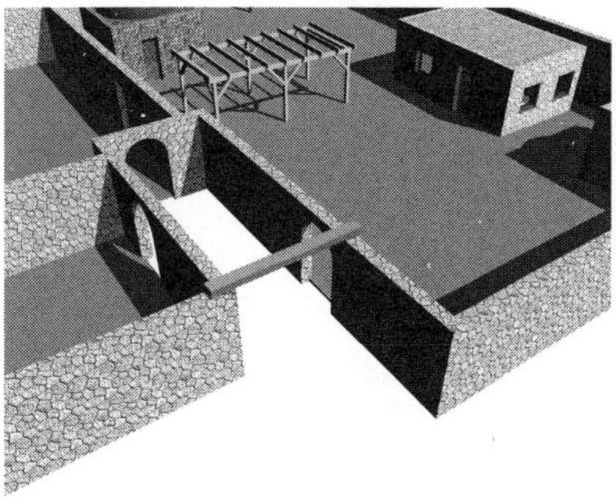

Cross beam positioned across from the shorter side of an alleyway

HALAKHA

Utilizing the space beneath the cross beam – שִׁימּוּשׁ תַּחַת הַקּוֹרָה: It is permitted to utilize the space beneath the cross beam, in accordance with the opinion of Rav and Rabbi Yoḥanan, since the *halakha* generally follows them when they disagree with other Sages (*Shulḥan Arukh, Oraḥ Ḥayyim* 365:4).

PERSONALITIES

Halakhot of Sages named Kahana – שְׁמַעְתְּתָא דְּכָהֲנֵי: Sages named Kahana happened to hand down these *halakhot*, each in the name of the other. In addition to these Sages, who lived in several different generations, there were other Sages called simply Rabbi Kahana, but their similarity in name and chronological proximity make it hard to distinguish between them in a consistent manner.

One source identifies Rav Kahana bar Malkiyu as Rav's teacher, while in a different source, the Jerusalem Talmud, he handed down a teaching in the name of Rav. Neither Rav Kahana bar Taḥalifa nor Rav Kahana bar Minyumi are mentioned often. There were several Sages that appear as Rav Kahana without mention of their fathers. One was a student-colleague of Rav, called simply Kahana in the Jerusalem Talmud, who was among the first generation of *amora'im*. Another was a student of Rav Yehuda, which places him in the third generation of *amora'im*. A third was a student of Rava, from the fifth generation of *amora'im*. This Rav Kahana was Rav Ashi's teacher, and he is presumably the one mentioned in connection with the *halakha* cited in this context. Yet another Rav Kahana was a friend and contemporary of Rav Ashi. Some commentaries hold that there was another Sage named Rav Kahana who was a student of Rav from the second generation of *amora'im*.

וְאִיבָּעֵית אֵימָא: דְּכוּלֵּי עָלְמָא ״מִשּׁוּם מְחִיצָּה״, וְהָכָא בְּהָא קָמִיפַּלְגִי: דְּמָר סָבַר: חוּדוֹ הַפְּנִימִי יוֹרֵד וְסוֹתֵם, וּמָר סָבַר: חוּדוֹ הַחִיצוֹן יוֹרֵד וְסוֹתֵם.

The Gemara proposes an alternative explanation: **And if you wish,** you can **say that everyone** agrees that a cross beam permits carrying **as a partition, and here they argue over the following** issue: **As one Sage holds that the inner edge** of the cross beam **descends** to the ground **and seals off** the alleyway, and therefore under the cross beam is not within the closed-off area; **and the other Sage holds that the** cross **beam's outer edge descends** to the ground **and seals off** the alleyway, and therefore it is permitted to carry even in the area beneath the cross beam. Consequently, there is no need to connect the dispute with regard to utilizing the area beneath the cross beam to the dispute with regard to the nature of the cross beam.

אָמַר רַב חִסְדָּא: הַכֹּל מוֹדִים בְּבֵין לְחָיַיִם שֶׁאָסוּר.

Rav Ḥisda **said: All concede** that utilizing the area **between the side posts** placed at the entrance to an alleyway to permit carrying **is prohibited,** for a side post functions as a partition, and therefore one may only use the space up to its inner edge, but no further.

בְּעָא מִינֵּיהּ רָמִי בַּר חָמָא מֵרַב חִסְדָּא: נָעַץ שְׁתֵּי יְתֵידוֹת בִּשְׁנֵי כּוֹתְלֵי מָבוֹי מִבַּחוּץ, וְהִנִּיחַ קוֹרָה עַל גַּבֵּיהֶן מַהוּ?

Rami bar Ḥama raised a dilemma before Rav Ḥisda: What is the *halakha* in a case where a person **inserted two pegs in the two alleyway walls,** one in each wall, **on the outside** of the entrance facing the public domain, **and he placed a** cross **beam on top of** the pegs,[B] such that the beam is attached to the front of the alleyway walls instead of on top of them? Does this cross beam permit carrying within the alleyway?[NH]

אֲמַר לֵיהּ: לְדִבְרֵי הַמַּתִּיר – אָסוּר, לְדִבְרֵי הָאוֹסֵר – מוּתָּר.

Rav Ḥisda **said to him: According to the statement of** the one **who permits** utilizing the area beneath the cross beam, carrying within the alleyway **is prohibited,** for he holds that the cross beam's outer edge is the critical one, and here this outer edge is positioned outside the alleyway and therefore cannot permit it. Whereas **according to the statement of** the authority **who prohibits** utilizing the area beneath the cross beam, carrying in the alleyway **is permitted,** for the cross beam's inner edge is attached to the entrance of the alleyway.

רָבָא אָמַר: לְדִבְרֵי הָאוֹסֵר, נַמִי אָסוּר. בָּעֵינַן קוֹרָה עַל גַּבֵּי מָבוֹי, וְלֵיכָּא.

Rava, however, disagreed and **said: Even according to the opinion of** the one **who prohibits** utilizing the area beneath the cross beam, carrying in the alleyway **is prohibited, for we require** that **the** cross **beam** that permits the alleyway be placed **on top of** the walls of **the alleyway, and** it **is not.** A cross beam that merely touches the alleyway from the outside does not permit it.

אֵיתִיבֵיהּ רַב אַדָּא בַּר מַתָּנָה לְרָבָא: הָיְתָה קוֹרָתוֹ

Rav Adda bar Mattana raised an objection to Rava from a *baraita*: **If the** cross **beam** being used to render an alleyway permitted for carrying **is**

BACKGROUND

Cross beam attached to an alleyway – קוֹרָה הַצְּמוּדָה לַמָּבוֹי: The cross beam rests on pegs and is attached to the alleyway walls on the outside.

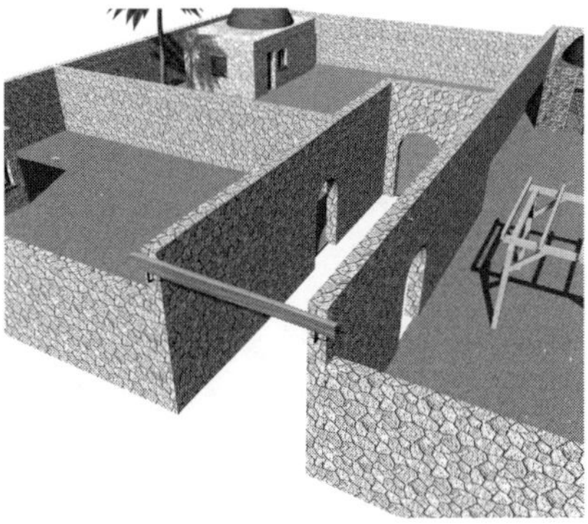

Cross beam attached with pegs to alleyway walls

HALAKHA

A cross beam outside the alleyway – קוֹרָה מִחוּץ לַמָּבוֹי: A cross beam that protrudes beyond the alleyway walls is invalid, in accordance with the opinion of Rava. He is the later authority, and Rabbi Ashi appears to agree with him as well (*Shulḥan Arukh, Oraḥ Ḥayyim* 363:14).

NOTES

A cross beam outside the alleyway – קוֹרָה מִחוּץ לַמָּבוֹי: The commentaries ask: Why isn't the cross beam considered to be part of the alleyway walls, according to the principle of joined sections [*lavud*]? They explain that applying the principle of joined sections assumes the cross beam does not exist, but rather is negated along its entire width to become part of the alleyway's walls. Indeed, a nonexistent cross beam cannot serve as a partition. It is logical that these two formalistic principles, joined sections [*lavud*] and the principle that a partition extends downward [*gode aḥit meḥitzta*], cannot be applied simultaneously in a case such as this one, as they contradict each other (Rashba).

מְשׁוּכָה אוֹ תְּלוּיָה; פָּחוֹת מִשְּׁלֹשָׁה – אֵין צָרִיךְ לְהָבִיא קוֹרָה אַחֶרֶת, שְׁלֹשָׁה – צָרִיךְ לְהָבִיא קוֹרָה אַחֶרֶת. רַבָּן שִׁמְעוֹן בֶּן גַּמְלִיאֵל אוֹמֵר: פָּחוֹת מֵאַרְבָּעָה – אֵין צָרִיךְ לְהָבִיא קוֹרָה אַחֶרֶת, אַרְבָּעָה – צָרִיךְ לְהָבִיא קוֹרָה אַחֶרֶת.

drawn away from the alleyway walls[B] **or suspended**[N] in the air,[B] the following distinction applies: If the cross beam is **less than three** handbreadths from the walls, **one is not required to bring a different** cross **beam,** for it is considered attached to the walls based on the principle of *lavud,* which views two solid surfaces as connected if the gap between them is less than three handbreadths wide. However, if the distance is **three** or more handbreadths from the walls, **he is required to bring a different** cross **beam** in order to permit carrying in the alleyway. **Rabban Shimon ben Gamliel,** who holds that the principle of *lavud* applies to a gap of up to four handbreadths wide, **says:** If the cross beam is **less than four** handbreadths from the wall, **one is not required to bring a different** cross **beam;** but if the distance is **four** handbreadths from the wall, **he is required to bring a different** cross **beam.**

מַאי לָאו – מְשׁוּכָה מִבַּחוּץ, וּתְלוּיָה מִבִּפְנִים!

The Gemara wishes to clarify the *baraita*: **What, is it not** that when the *baraita* speaks of a cross beam that is **drawn away** from the alleyway walls, it is referring to a cross beam that is distanced from the alleyway walls and situated **on the outside** in the public domain, similar to the case of the cross beam resting on pegs mentioned above? **And** when it speaks of a cross beam that is **suspended,** isn't it referring to a cross beam that is distanced from the alleyway walls and placed **on the inside** in the alleyway? This interpretation contradicts Rava's statement above that disqualifies such a cross beam.

לֹא, אִידִי וְאִידִי מִבִּפְנִים; מְשׁוּכָה – מֵרוּחַ אַחַת, וּתְלוּיָה – מִשְׁתֵּי רוּחוֹת.

The Gemara rejects this interpretation: **No,** both **this,** the cross beam that is drawn away, **and that,** the crossbeam that is suspended, are located **on the inside** of the alleyway. The difference between them is that the cross beam that is **drawn away** is distanced from the wall **from one direction,** while a **suspended** cross beam does not lie on the alleyway walls at all, but is distanced from them **from both directions.**

מַהוּ דְּתֵימָא: מֵרוּחַ אַחַת אָמְרִינַן לָבוּד, מִשְׁתֵּי רוּחוֹת לָא אָמְרִינַן לָבוּד, קָא מַשְׁמַע לָן.

Lest you say that if the cross beam is distanced from the wall **from one direction, we say** that the principle of ***lavud*** applies, and it is as if the cross beam is joined to the wall; but if it is distanced from the wall **from two directions, we do not say** that the principle of ***lavud*** applies. The *baraita,* therefore, comes and **teaches us** that there is no difference in this regard.

רַב אַשִׁי אָמַר: מְשׁוּכָה וְהִיא תְּלוּיָה. וְהֵיכִי דָּמֵי – כְּגוֹן שֶׁנָּעַץ שְׁתֵּי יְתֵידוֹת עֲקוּמוֹת עַל שְׁנֵי כּוֹתְלֵי מָבוֹי, שֶׁאֵין בְּגוֹבְהָן שְׁלֹשָׁה, וְאֵין בְּעַקְמוּמִיתָן שְׁלֹשָׁה. מַהוּ דְּתֵימָא: אוֹ ״לָבוּד״ אָמְרִינַן אוֹ ״חָבוּט״ אָמְרִינַן, לָבוּד וְחָבוּט לָא אָמְרִינַן, קָא מַשְׁמַע לָן.

Rav Ashi said: The *baraita* refers to a cross beam that is **drawn away** from the walls **and** also **suspended** in the air.[B] **And what are the circumstances** where this would be the case? **For example, where he inserted two bent pegs on** the tops of **the two alleyway walls,** and **the height** of the pegs from the top of the walls **is less than three** handbreadths, **and their bend** inward **is less than three handbreadths,** and a cross beam rests on top of them. **Lest you say** that **we either say *lavud,*** i.e., we consider the cross beam to be virtually extended and thus connected to the wall, **or we say *ḥavut,*** pressed down, that we consider the cross beam to be pressed down vertically; but **we do not say** both ***lavud* and *ḥavut.***[NH] The *baraita* therefore **teaches us** that even in that case we say that any item adjacent to another with a gap of less than three handbreadths between them is considered connected to it, whether to the side or below, and even in both directions at once.

BACKGROUND

Cross beam drawn away from one direction – קוֹרָה מְשׁוּכָה מֵרוּחַ אַחַת:

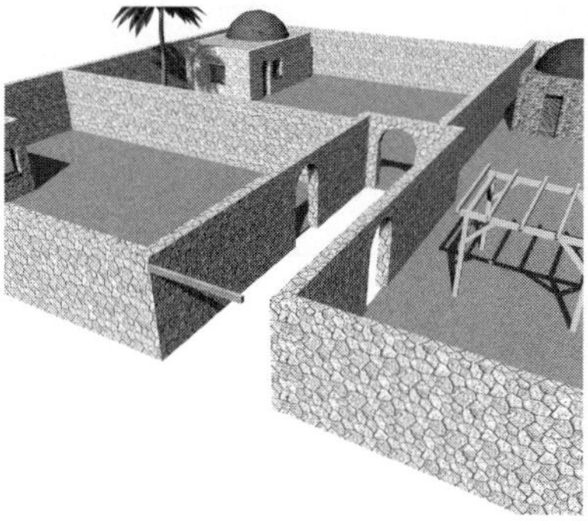

Cross beam that is attached to one wall of an alleyway but does not reach the other wall

Cross beam suspended in the air – קוֹרָה תְּלוּיָה מִשְׁתֵּי רוּחוֹת:

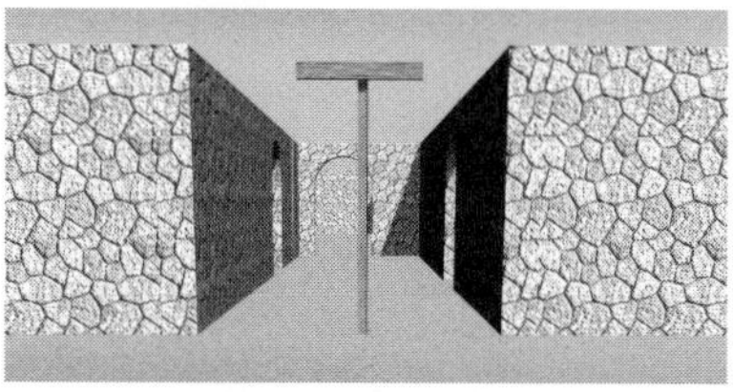

Cross beam not attached to the alleyway walls but distanced from them on both sides

Cross beam suspended and drawn away – קוֹרָה תְּלוּיָה וּמְשׁוּכָה:

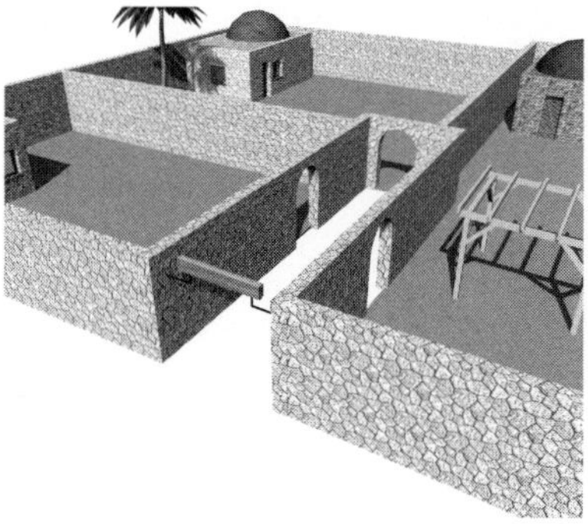

Cross beam suspended in the air above the entrance to the alleyway and distanced from the two alleyway walls

HALAKHA

Joined [*lavud*] and pressed down [*ḥavut*] – לָבוּד וְחָבוּט: A cross beam that is distanced from and above the walls of the alleyway by less than three handbreadths is valid, because we say that the cross beam is both joined [*lavud*] and pressed down [*ḥavut*], in accordance with the statement of the Gemara (*Shulḥan Arukh, Oraḥ Ḥayyim* 363:25).

NOTES

Drawn away or suspended – מְשׁוּכָה אוֹ תְּלוּיָה: Apparently, if it is permitted to carry in an alleyway where the cross beam is suspended in the air, it is certainly permitted to carry in an alleyway where the cross beam is drawn away. Why, then, are both *halakhot* needed? Had it only stated the *halakha* with regard to a cross beam that is suspended, the implication would have been that a cross beam that is drawn away is permitted, even if it is more than three handbreadths from the wall (Rav Ya'akov Emden).

Pressed down [*ḥavut*] – חָבוּט: The principle of *ḥavut* usually refers to something that is placed high up off the ground. The object is considered as though it were thrown to the ground. *Tosafot* ask: Why isn't a cross beam higher than three handbreadths from the alleyway walls also permitted due to *ḥavut*? Ritva answers that since the principle of joining [*lavud*] is applied, the principle of being pressed down [*ḥavut*] cannot be applied as well. It is illogical to consider the cross beam as though it were pressed down from above to below, and then to extend the imaginary cross beam to the sides as well.

תָּנֵי רַבִּי זַכַּאי קַמֵּיהּ דְּרַבִּי יוֹחָנָן: בֵּין לְחָיַיִם וְתַחַת הַקּוֹרָה – נִידּוֹן כְּכַרְמְלִית. אֲמַר לֵיהּ: פּוּק תְּנֵי לְבָרָא.

Rabbi Zakkai taught the following *baraita* **before Rabbi Yoḥanan:** The area **between the side posts and beneath the** cross **beam** has the **legal status** of a ***karmelit,*** and it is forbidden to carry in it. Rabbi Yoḥanan **said to him: Exit** and **teach** this *halakha* **outside,**[N] i.e., this *baraita* is not in accordance with the accepted *halakha,* and therefore it should not be made part of the regular learning in the study hall.

אֲמַר אַבַּיֵי: מִסְתַּבְּרָא מִילְּתֵיהּ דְּרַבִּי יוֹחָנָן תַּחַת הַקּוֹרָה, אֲבָל בֵּין לְחָיַיִן – אָסוּר. וְרָבָא אֲמַר: בֵּין לְחָיַיִם נַמִי מוּתָּר.

The Gemara records a dispute with regard to the scope of Rabbi Yoḥanan's statement: **Abaye said: Rabbi Yoḥanan's statement is reasonable** with regard to the area **beneath the** cross **beam,** as only the area beneath the cross beam should be considered a private domain, **but between the side posts,** carrying **is** indeed **prohibited,** in accordance with the opinion of Rabbi Zakkai. **And Rava said:** The entire statement of Rabbi Zakkai is to be rejected, as Rabbi Yoḥanan asserted, and **even** in the area **between the side posts**[H] carrying **is permitted.**

אֲמַר רָבָא: מְנָא אָמִינָא לַהּ – דְּכִי אֲתָא רַב דִּימִי אָמַר רַבִּי יוֹחָנָן: מָקוֹם שֶׁאֵין בּוֹ אַרְבָּעָה עַל אַרְבָּעָה – מוּתָּר לִבְנֵי רְשׁוּת הָרַבִּים וְלִבְנֵי רְשׁוּת הַיָּחִיד לְכַתֵּף עָלָיו, וּבִלְבַד שֶׁלֹּא יַחֲלִיפוּ.

Rava said: From where do I know to **say this,** that carrying is permitted even between the side posts? **For when Rav Dimi came** from Eretz Yisrael to Babylonia, he said that **Rabbi Yoḥanan said: A place that has** an area of **less than four by four** handbreadths and is located between a public and private domain but belongs to neither has the status of an exempt domain with regard to carrying on Shabbat. Therefore, **it is permitted for** both **the people in the public domain** as well as **the people in the private domain to** use it for **loading** their burdens **onto their shoulders, so long as they do not exchange** objects with one another. Therefore, a place having an area of less than four handbreadths is not considered a *karmelit,* but rather an exempt domain, where carrying is permitted. Consequently, the area between the side posts should likewise be considered an exempt domain, and carrying should be permitted within it.

וְאַבַּיֵי – הָתָם בְּגָבוֹהַּ שְׁלֹשָׁה.

And Abaye said that this offers no proof, as **there,** with regard to Rav Dimi's statement, the area being discussed **is** at least **three** handbreadths **high,** setting it apart from the other domains. It is therefore considered a domain in its own right, and has the *halakha* of an exempt domain.

אֲמַר אַבַּיֵי: מְנָא אָמִינָא לַהּ – דְּאָמַר רַב חָמָא בַּר גּוּרְיָא, אָמַר רַב: תּוֹךְ הַפֶּתַח צָרִיךְ לֶחִי אַחֵר לְהַתִּירוֹ.

The Gemara considers the position of Abaye: **Abaye said: From where do I** know to **say this,** that the area between the side posts has the *halakha* of a *karmelit*? **For Rav Ḥama bar Guria said that Rav said:** The area **within the opening,** i.e., the doorway between two entrance posts that serve as side posts to permit carrying in the alleyway, **requires another side post** in order **to permit** carrying there, for the entrance posts alone do not suffice. This demonstrates that it is forbidden to carry in the space between the side posts without another side post.

וְכִי תֵּימָא דְּאִית בֵּיהּ אַרְבָּעָה עַל אַרְבָּעָה. וְהָאָמַר רַב חָנִין בַּר רָבָא אָמַר רַב: תּוֹךְ הַפֶּתַח, אַף עַל פִּי שֶׁאֵין בּוֹ אַרְבָּעָה עַל אַרְבָּעָה – צָרִיךְ לֶחִי אַחֵר לְהַתִּירוֹ.

And if you say that this is a case where the doorway **has** an area **four by four** handbreadths, and therefore an additional side post is required to permit carrying there, this is not a valid argument. **For didn't Rav Ḥanin bar Rava say that Rav said:** The area **within the opening** itself, **even if it does not have** an area of **four by four** handbreadths, **requires an additional side post** in order **to permit** carrying within it. This indicates that the area between the side posts is not to be used.

וְרָבָא – הָתָם דְּפָתוּחַ לְכַרְמְלִית,

And Rava replies that a distinction must be made between the cases: **There,** the case of Rav's ruling refers to a scenario where the alleyway's entrance **opens to a *karmelit,***[H] and thus the space between the entrance posts is also viewed as a *karmelit,* and an additional side post is required.

אֲבָל לִרְשׁוּת הָרַבִּים מַאי – שָׁרֵי? יַצִּיבָא בְּאַרְעָא וְגִיּוֹרָא בִּשְׁמֵי שְׁמַיָּא!

The Gemara poses a question: **But** if the entrance opens **to a public domain, what** would be the *halakha*? Would it be **permitted** to carry there even without an additional side post? If so, it follows that the *halakha* of a *karmelit* is more stringent than that of a public domain. However, this seems untenable, for carrying in a *karmelit* is prohibited only by rabbinic decree, owing to the similarity between a *karmelit* and the public domain. This is similar to a situation where **a permanent resident is** down **on the ground,**[N] **while a stranger is** raised up **to the highest heaven,** the very opposite of the appropriate state of affairs.

NOTES

Exit and teach outside – פּוּק תְּנֵי לְבָרָא: This expression indicates that a certain source taught by the person who would recite the *mishnayot* in the *beit midrash* has been totally rejected and should not be taught in the study hall. The practical implication is that one who seeks to clarify this *baraita* should do so outside the study hall's walls. Indeed, the Gemara reports instances of Sages leaving the study hall to clarify for themselves ideas that were not taught there. The meaning of the expression in this context is that this *baraita* has no place within the framework of accepted *halakha.*

A permanent resident is on the ground – יַצִּיבָא בְּאַרְעָא: This expression is a translation, worded slightly differently, of a verse found in portions of rebuke in the book of Deuteronomy: "The stranger that is in your midst shall rise above you higher and higher, and you shall come down lower and lower" (Deuteronomy 28:43). Its meaning expresses astonishment and even bitterness over a state of affairs that seems to be the opposite of the proper order.

HALAKHA

Between the side posts – בֵּין לְחָיַיִם: It is permitted to carry between the side posts in an alleyway. This is in accordance with the opinion of Rava, whose opinion is followed when he disagrees with Abaye, and because his opinion accords with Rabbi Yoḥanan's statement (*Shulḥan Arukh, Oraḥ Ḥayyim* 365:4).

An entrance that opens to a *karmelit* – פֶּתַח הַפָּתוּחַ לְכַרְמְלִית: It is prohibited to use the space under a cross beam when the entrance opens to a *karmelit* as opposed to a public domain, because of the principle: It has found its own type and been awakened. This is in accordance with the statement of Rava. However, if the cross beam is four handbreadths wide and strong, it is considered like a roof. Thus, its outer edge closes off the alleyway, and it is permitted to use the space underneath it even if the alleyway opens to a *karmelit* (*Magen Avraham*; *Taz*; *Shulḥan Arukh, Oraḥ Ḥayyim* 365:4).

אִין, מָצָא מִין אֶת מִינוֹ וְנֵיעוֹר.

The Gemara comments: **Yes,** it is possible that this is the ruling, for we can say that **it has found its own type and been awakened.**[N] In other words, as the area within the entranceway is not a defined domain, it doesn't have the status of an independent domain. Therefore, when it opens into a *karmelit*, to which it is similar, its status is negated, and it joins with the *karmelit* to form a single unit. However, when it opens into a public domain, it cannot join with it because it is not similar to a public domain, which has a totally different set of laws; and therefore it is considered part of the alleyway, and it is permitted to carry within it.

אָמַר לֵיהּ רַב הוּנָא בְּרֵיהּ דְּרַב יְהוֹשֻׁעַ לְרָבָא: וְאַתְּ לָא תִּסְבְּרָא דְּבֵין לְחָיַיִן אָסוּר? וְהָאָמַר רַבָּה בַּר בַּר חָנָה, אָמַר רַבִּי יוֹחָנָן: מָבוֹי שֶׁרְצָפוֹ בִּלְחָיַיִן פָּחוֹת פָּחוֹת מֵאַרְבָּעָה – בָּאנוּ לְמַחֲלוֹקֶת רַבָּן שִׁמְעוֹן בֶּן גַּמְלִיאֵל וְרַבָּנָן.

Rav Huna, the son of Rav Yehoshua, said to Rava: And you do not hold that in the area **between the side posts** carrying **is prohibited? But didn't Rabba bar bar Ḥana say that Rabbi Yoḥanan said:** If **an alleyway was lined with side posts,**[B] **each** one set more than three but **less than four** handbreadths apart from its neighbor, **we have arrived** in this matter **at the dispute** between **Rabban Shimon ben Gamliel and the Rabbis** with regard to the measure of *lavud*.

לְרַבָּן שִׁמְעוֹן בֶּן גַּמְלִיאֵל דְּאָמַר אָמְרִינַן לָבוּד – מִשְׁתַּמֵּשׁ עַד חוּדוֹ הַפְּנִימִי שֶׁל לֶחִי הַפְּנִימִי, לְרַבָּנַן דְּאָמְרִי לָא אָמְרִינַן לָבוּד – מִשְׁתַּמֵּשׁ עַד חוּדוֹ הַפְּנִימִי שֶׁל חִיצוֹן. אֲבָל בֵּין לְחָיַיִן – דְּכוּלֵּי עָלְמָא אָסוּר!

How so? According **to Rabban Shimon ben Gamliel,** who **said** that if the gap between two items is less than four handbreadths, **we say** that the principle of ***lavud*** applies; all the side posts are considered a single side post. **He may** therefore only **utilize** the alleyway **up to the inner edge of the innermost side post,** but no more. However, according to **the Rabbis,** who **say** that **we do not say** the principle of *lavud* applies unless the gap is less than three handbreadths, he **may utilize** the alleyway **up to the inner edge of the outermost** side post. This discussion demonstrates that the argument revolves around the question as to which side post establishes the permitted area. **But** with regard to the area **between the side posts, all agree** that carrying **is prohibited.**

וְרָבָא – הָתָם נַמִי דְּפָתוּחַ לְכַרְמְלִית.

And Rava answers that **there too,** it refers to a case where the alleyway's entrance **opens to a *karmelit*.**

אֲבָל לִרְשׁוּת הָרַבִּים מַאי – שָׁרֵי? יַצִּיבָא בְּאַרְעָא וְגִיּוֹרָא בִּשְׁמֵי שְׁמַיָּא! אִין, מָצָא מִין אֶת מִינוֹ וְנֵיעוֹר.

The Gemara raises a difficulty: **But** if the entrance opens **to a public domain, what** is its legal status – would carrying be **permitted?** If so, the *halakha* of a *karmelit* is more severe than that of a public domain. Once again, this can be likened to a situation where **a permanent resident** is down **on the ground, while a stranger** is raised up **to the highest heaven.** The Gemara answers: **Yes,** indeed, this is the ruling, but one should not be perplexed, as we have explained: **it has found its own type and been awakened.**

Perek **I**
Daf **9** Amud **b**

רַב אַשִׁי אָמַר: כְּגוֹן שֶׁרְצָפוֹ בִּלְחָיַיִם פָּחוֹת פָּחוֹת מֵאַרְבָּעָה, בְּמֶשֶׁךְ אַרְבַּע אַמּוֹת.

The Gemara provides an alternative explanation of Rabbi Yoḥanan's statement. **Rav Ashi said:** According to Rabbi Yoḥanan, carrying in the area between the side posts is actually permitted. The dispute between Rabban Shimon ben Gamliel and the Rabbis concerning the principle of *lavud* is in a case **where** there was an alleyway **that one lined with side posts, each** positioned **less than four** handbreadths from the next, and the side posts extend **for a length of four cubits.**

לְרַבָּן שִׁמְעוֹן בֶּן גַּמְלִיאֵל דְּאָמַר "אָמְרִינַן לָבוּד" – הָוֵה לֵיהּ מָבוֹי, וְצָרִיךְ לֶחִי אַחֵר לְהַתִּירוֹ. וּלְרַבָּנַן דְּאָמְרִי לָא אָמְרִינַן לָבוּד – לֹא צָרִיךְ לֶחִי אַחֵר לְהַתִּירוֹ.

According to Rabban Shimon ben Gamliel, who said that for a gap of up to four handbreadths **we say** that the principle of ***lavud*** applies, all the side posts are considered a single side post, and since the side post in that case is four cubits long, **it is** considered a separate **alleyway;** therefore, it **requires an additional side post to permit** carrying in it. **And according to the Rabbis, who say** that **we do not say** that the principle of ***lavud*** applies unless the gap is less than three handbreadths, this area **does not require an additional side post to permit** carrying within it.

NOTES

It has found its own type and been awakened [*nei'or*] – מָצָא מִין אֶת מִינוֹ וְנֵיעוֹר: This expression appears in other halakhic contexts as well, particularly with regard to the *halakhot* of mixtures. Some commentaries explain the word *nei'or* to mean shaken [*nin'ar*], i.e., once it found its own type, it leaves its previous place and cleaves to the similar type. Nevertheless, apparently *nei'or* is related to the verse "like a man who awakens [*yei'or*] from his sleep" (Zechariah 4:1). In other words, the prohibition, which was lying in a concealed, dormant state, reawakens after finding its own type (Rashi).

BACKGROUND

An alleyway was lined with side posts – מָבוֹי שֶׁרְצָפוֹ בִּלְחָיַיִן:

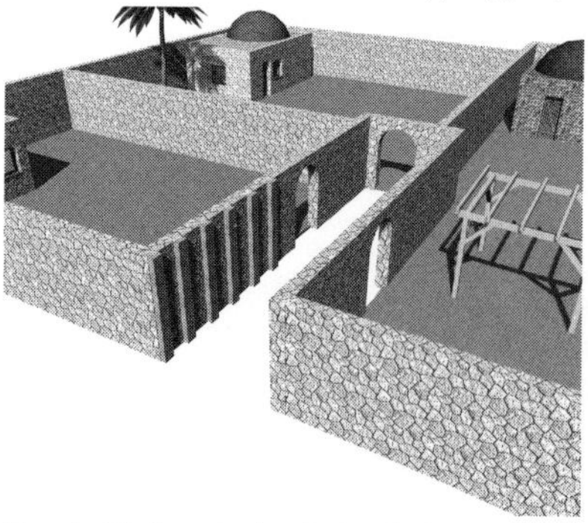

Alleyway in which side posts have been placed one after the other

וּלְרַבָּן שִׁמְעוֹן בֶּן גַּמְלִיאֵל, לֶהֱוֵי כְּנִרְאֶה מִבַּחוּץ וְשָׁוֶה מִבִּפְנִים!

The Gemara asks: **And** even **according to** the opinion of **Rabban Shimon ben Gamliel,** why is another side post required? **Let it** have the same legal status **as** a side post that is **visible from the outside,** protruding from the wall of the alleyway, **but** appears to be **even** with the wall **from the inside.** Since it is evident from the outside that it is a side post and not part of the building, carrying is permitted there.

מִידֵּי הוּא טַעְמָא אֶלָּא לְרַבִּי יוֹחָנָן, הָא כִּי אֲתָא רָבִין אָמַר רַבִּי יוֹחָנָן: נִרְאֶה מִבַּחוּץ וְשָׁוֶה מִבִּפְנִים – אֵינוֹ נִידּוֹן מִשּׁוּם לֶחִי.

The Gemara answers: As Rav Ashi's **reason is only according to** the opinion of **Rabbi Yoḥanan, when Ravin came** from Eretz Yisrael to Babylonia, **didn't** he say that **Rabbi Yoḥanan said:** If a side post is **visible from the outside,** protruding from the wall of the alleyway, **but** it appears to be **even** with the wall **from the inside, it is not considered** to have the legal status **of a side post?**

אִיתְּמַר; נִרְאֶה מִבִּפְנִים וְשָׁוֶה מִבַּחוּץ – נִידּוֹן מִשּׁוּם לֶחִי. נִרְאֶה מִבַּחוּץ וְשָׁוֶה מִבִּפְנִים, רַבִּי חִיָּיא וְרַבִּי שִׁמְעוֹן בְּרַבִּי. חַד אָמַר: נִידּוֹן מִשּׁוּם לֶחִי, וְחַד אָמַר: אֵינוֹ נִידּוֹן מִשּׁוּם לֶחִי.

An amoraic dispute **was stated:** If a side post is **visible from the inside,** protruding from the wall of the alleyway, **but** it appears to be **even** with the wall **from the outside,**[BH] **it is considered a side post.**[B] However, if a side post is **visible from the outside** protruding from the wall, **but** it appears to be **even** with the wall **from the inside,** there is a disagreement between **Rabbi Ḥiyya and Rabbi Shimon, son of Rabbi** Yehuda HaNasi, with regard to its status. **One said: It is considered** to have the legal status **of a side post. And** the other **one said: It is not considered** to have the legal status **of a side post.**

תִּסְתַּיֵּים דְּרַבִּי חִיָּיא הוּא דְּאָמַר ״נִידּוֹן מִשּׁוּם לֶחִי״, דְּתָנֵי רַבִּי חִיָּיא: כּוֹתֶל שֶׁצִּידּוֹ אֶחָד כָּנוּס מֵחֲבֵירוֹ, בֵּין שֶׁנִּרְאֶה מִבַּחוּץ וְשָׁוֶה מִבִּפְנִים, וּבֵין שֶׁנִּרְאֶה מִבִּפְנִים וְשָׁוֶה מִבַּחוּץ – נִידּוֹן מִשּׁוּם לֶחִי, תִּסְתַּיֵּים.

The Gemara clarifies: **Conclude that Rabbi Ḥiyya** is the one **who said** that **it is considered** to have the legal status **of a side post, as Rabbi Ḥiyya taught:** In the case of **a wall** at the entrance to an alleyway **whose one side is more recessed than the other, whether** the recess **is visible from outside** the alleyway **but** appears to be **even from the inside, or** the recess **is visible from the inside but** appears to be **even from the outside,** it **is considered** to have the legal status **of a side post.** The Gemara states: Indeed, **conclude** that Rabbi Ḥiyya is the one who said it has the legal status of a side post.

וְרַבִּי יוֹחָנָן מִי לָא שְׁמִיעַ לֵיהּ הָא?! אֶלָּא: שְׁמִיעַ לֵיהּ, וְלָא סְבַר לַהּ, רַבִּי חִיָּיא נָמֵי, לָא סְבַר לַהּ!

The Gemara rejects this conclusion: **And Rabbi Yoḥanan,** who explicitly said that a side post of that kind is not considered a side post, **did he not hear this** *halakha*? The *Tosefta* was widely known. **Rather, he heard it, but he does not hold** in accordance **with it.** Perhaps, then, **Rabbi Ḥiyya also does not hold** in accordance with **it.**

הָאי מַאי?! בִּשְׁלָמָא רַבִּי יוֹחָנָן לָא סָבַר לַהּ – מִשּׁוּם הָכִי לָא תָּנֵי לַהּ, אֶלָּא רַבִּי חִיָּיא – אִי אִיתָא דְּלָא סָבַר לַהּ, לָמָּה לֵיהּ לְמִיתְנְיָא?

The Gemara answers: **What is this** comparison? **Granted, Rabbi Yoḥanan does not hold** in accordance with **that** *halakha.* **That is why he did not teach it. But Rabbi Ḥiyya, if it is** true **that he does not hold** in accordance with **it, why would he teach it?**

אָמַר רַבָּה בַּר רַב הוּנָא: נִרְאֶה מִבַּחוּץ וְשָׁוֶה מִבִּפְנִים – נִידּוֹן מִשּׁוּם לֶחִי. אָמַר רַבָּה: וּמוֹתְבִינַן אַשְׁמַעְתִּין ״חָצֵר קְטַנָּה שֶׁנִּפְרְצָה לִגְדוֹלָה – גְּדוֹלָה מוּתֶּרֶת וּקְטַנָּה אֲסוּרָה, מִפְּנֵי שֶׁהִיא כְּפִתְחָהּ שֶׁל גְּדוֹלָה״. וְאִם אִיתָא, קְטַנָּה נָמֵי תִּשְׁתְּרֵי בְּנִרְאֶה מִבַּחוּץ וְשָׁוֶה מִבִּפְנִים!

Rabba bar Rav Huna said: If a side post is **visible from the outside,** protruding from the wall of the alleyway, **but** appears to be **even** with the wall **from the inside, it is considered** to have the legal status **of a side post. Rabba said: And we raise an objection to our** own ***halakha*** from a mishna: With regard to **a small courtyard that was breached** along the entire length of one of its walls so that it opens **into a large** courtyard, in **the large one** it **is permitted** to carry **and** in **the small one** it is **prohibited** to carry. This is **because** the breach **is considered an entrance of the large** courtyard. The wall of the smaller courtyard was breached along its entire length, therefore there is no visible partition from inside the smaller courtyard. However, the partition is noticeable from the outside, i.e., in the large courtyard, since the breach is flanked on both sides by the remaining segments of the wall of the large courtyard. **And if it is so,** that a partition that is visible from the outside is considered a partition, carrying in **the small** courtyard **should also be permitted** in this case, as the wall **is visible from the outside but** appears to be **even from the inside.**

BACKGROUND

A side post that is not conspicuous – לֶחִי שֶׁאֵינוֹ נִיכָּר: This side post, which is positioned within the alleyway, is visible to those inside the alleyway; however, to people on the outside it appears as a continuation of the alleyway wall.

Side post visible only from the inside of the alleyway

A side post that is visible from the inside and from the outside – לֶחִי הַנִּרְאֶה מִבִּפְנִים וּמִבַּחוּץ: According to Rashi, this is the side post that is visible both from within the alleyway and by those standing outside it.

Side post visible from both sides

HALAKHA

Visible from the inside but appears to be even from the outside – נִרְאֶה מִבִּפְנִים וְשָׁוֶה מִבַּחוּץ: A side post [*leḥi*] that can be seen only from the inside but looks even from the outside is considered a side post, and all agree that it renders the alleyway fit for one to carry within it (*Shulḥan Arukh, Oraḥ Ḥayyim* 363:9).

NOTES

Where the walls of the small courtyard protrude into the large one – בִּנְכְנָסִין כּוֹתְלֵי קְטַנָּה לִגְדוֹלָה: The *ge'onim*, who might have had a variant reading of this text, explain that this is a case where the walls of the smaller courtyard protrude three handbreadths into the larger one, and the principle of *lavud* should be applied to the length of the walls rather than to their width.

אָמַר רַבִּי זֵירָא: בִּנְכְנָסִין כּוֹתְלֵי קְטַנָּה לִגְדוֹלָה.

Rabbi Zeira said: This mishna is referring to a case **where the walls of the small** courtyard **protrude**[B] **into the large one,**[N] i.e., the breached wall of the small courtyard is not in line with the wall of the large one. Therefore, even when viewed from the outside there are no walls visible, and that is why carrying is prohibited there.

וְלֵימָא ״לָבוּד״ וְתִשְׁתְּרֵי!

The Gemara asks: **And let us say** that the principle of ***lavud***[B] applies, **and** then carrying **will be permitted** even in the small courtyard. The ends of the breached wall should be considered attached to the side walls of the large courtyard, rendering the wall of the large courtyard visible. Then it will be permitted to carry in the small courtyard based on the principle governing side posts visible from the outside.

וְכִי תֵּימָא דְּמַפְלְגִי טוּבָא – וְהָא תָּנֵי רַב אַדָּא בַּר אֲבִימִי קַמֵּיהּ דְּרַבִּי חֲנִינָא: קְטַנָּה בְּעֶשֶׂר, גְּדוֹלָה בְּאַחַת עֶשְׂרֵה!

And if you say that the walls of the smaller courtyard **are too separate** from the walls of the larger courtyard, such that the distance between the walls is too great for the principle of *lavud* to apply, **didn't Rav Adda bar Avimi teach before Rabbi Ḥanina: The small** courtyard of which they speak is referring even **to one ten cubits** wide; the **large** one is referring even **to one eleven** cubits wide? Apparently, this *halakha* applies even when the difference in width between the courtyards is a single cubit, which is six handbreadths. Assuming the small courtyard is located equidistant from the ends of the large courtyard, only three handbreadths separate it on each side from the wall of the large one. Therefore, the principle of *lavud* applies.

אָמַר רָבִינָא: בְּמוּפְלָגִין מִכּוֹתֶל זֶה בִּשְׁנַיִם, וּמִכּוֹתֶל זֶה בְּאַרְבָּעָה.

Ravina said: It is a case **where** the walls of the smaller courtyard **are separated from this wall** of the larger courtyard **by two** handbreadths **and from this wall** of the larger courtyard on the other side **by four** handbreadths. Since there is a distance of more than three handbreadths, the principle of *lavud* does not apply.

וְלֵימָא לָבוּד מֵרוּחַ אַחַת, וְתִשְׁתְּרֵי!

The Gemara asks: **And let us say** that the principle of ***lavud*** applies **from one direction,** then carrying **will be permitted** even in the small courtyard.

BACKGROUND

Where the walls of the small courtyard protrude – בִּנְכְנָסִין כּוֹתְלֵי קְטַנָּה: In the image below, there is a small courtyard adjacent to a large one. The wall between them has been breached and the walls of the small courtyard protrude into the large one. Therefore, when viewed from inside the small courtyard, it appears to be entirely open into the large one.

Adjacent courtyards with protruding walls

And let us say the principle of *lavud* applies – וְלֵימָא לָבוּד: If the principle of *lavud* is applied and the walls of the smaller courtyard attach to the adjacent, parallel walls of the larger courtyard, then the walls of the smaller courtyard no longer protrude into the larger one, and it is considered like the typical case of a small courtyard that opens into a large one.

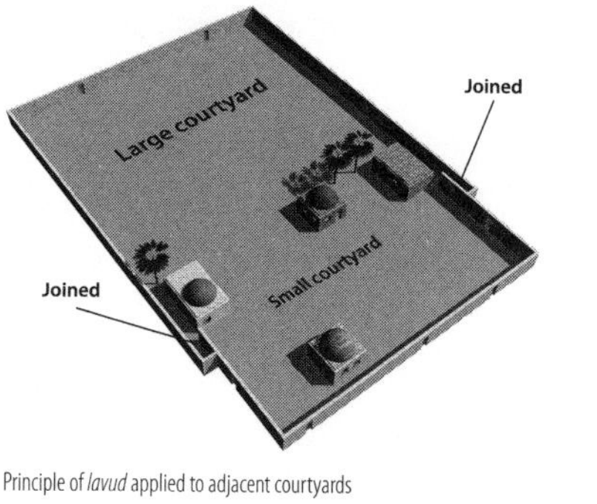

Principle of *lavud* applied to adjacent courtyards

רַבִּי הִיא, דְּאָמַר: בָּעֵינַן שְׁנֵי פַּסִּין. דְּתַנְיָא: חָצֵר נִיתֶּרֶת בְּפַס אֶחָד, רַבִּי אוֹמֵר: בִּשְׁנֵי פַּסִּין.

The Gemara answers: This mishna **is** in accordance with the opinion of **Rabbi** Yehuda HaNasi, **who said** that in order to permit carrying in a courtyard that was breached, **we require two** upright **boards,** one on either side of the breach. **As it was taught** in a *baraita*: If **a courtyard** was breached and opens into the public domain, and the width of the breach does not exceed ten cubits, it **becomes permitted** to carry there, even **with** only **one** upright **board** remaining on one side of the breach. **Rabbi** Yehuda HaNasi **says:** It is permitted only **with two** upright **boards** remaining, one on each side of the breach.

הַאי מַאי?! אִי אָמְרַתְּ בִּשְׁלָמָא ״נִרְאֶה מִבַּחוּץ וְשָׁוֶה מִבִּפְנִים – אֵינוֹ נִידּוֹן מִשּׁוּם לֶחִי״, וְרַבִּי סָבַר לָהּ כְּרַבִּי יוֹסֵי, וּדְרַבִּי זֵירָא וּדְרָבִינָא לֵיתָא – מִשּׁוּם הָכִי: קְטַנָּה בְּעֶשֶׂר, וּגְדוֹלָה בְּאַחַת עֶשְׂרֵה, מִשּׁוּם דְּרַבִּי סָבַר לָהּ כְּרַבִּי יוֹסֵי.

The Gemara rejects this entire explanation: **What is this** comparison? **Granted, if you say** that the legal status of a side post that is **visible from the outside but** appears to be **even** with the wall **from the inside is not considered** like that of **a side post; and** that **Rabbi** Yehuda HaNasi **holds in accordance with** the opinion of **Rabbi Yosei** that a side post or an upright board in a courtyard must be at least three handbreadths wide; **and that** the explanations of the mishna offered earlier by **Rabbi Zeira and Ravina are not** accepted; **that is why** there is significance to the fact that the **small** courtyard is **ten** cubits wide and the **large one is eleven** cubits wide. It is **due to** the fact that **Rabbi** Yehuda HaNasi **holds in accordance with** the opinion of **Rabbi Yosei.** Since Rabbi Yosei holds that a side post must be three handbreadths wide, we require that the two upright boards together measure six handbreadths, i.e., one cubit, which is the minimal difference in size between the two courtyards.

אֶלָּא אִי אָמְרַתְּ ״נִרְאֶה מִבַּחוּץ וְשָׁוֶה מִבִּפְנִים – נִידּוֹן מִשּׁוּם לֶחִי״, וּדְרַבִּי זֵירָא וּדְרָבִינָא אִיתָא, וְרַבִּי לָא סָבַר לָהּ כְּרַבִּי יוֹסֵי – גְּדוֹלָה בְּאַחַת עֶשְׂרֵה לָמָּה לִי?

However, if you say that the legal status of a side post that is **visible from the outside but** appears to be **even** with the wall **from the inside is considered** like that of **a side post; and** that **Rabbi Zeira's and Ravina's** explanations **are** accepted as *halakha*; and that **Rabbi** Yehuda HaNasi **does not hold in accordance with** the opinion **Rabbi Yosei, why do I** need to explain that the **large** courtyard measures **eleven** cubits?

מִמָּה נַפְשָׁךְ: אִי לְמִשְׁרְיֵיהּ לִגְדוֹלָה קָאָתֵי – בְּעֶשֶׂר וּשְׁנֵי טְפָחִים סַגְיָא. וְאִי לְמֵיסְרָהּ לִקְטַנָּה קָאָתֵי – לְאַשְׁמוּעִינַן דְּמַפְלְגִי טוּבָא!

Whichever way you look at it, there is a difficulty: **If** the *baraita* **is coming to permit** one to carry in **the large** courtyard, then a width **of ten** cubits **and two handbreadths suffices.** These two handbreadths can be considered the upright boards that render the courtyard fit for one to carry within it. **And if it is coming to** teach a novel *halakha* according to Rabbi Yehuda HaNasi and **prohibit** one to carry in **the small** courtyard, **it should teach us** a case where the walls of the two courtyards are much **farther removed** from each other, rather than a case where they are only one cubit apart. Therefore, the second explanation cannot be accepted.

אֶלָּא לָאו שְׁמַע מִינַּהּ: נִרְאֶה מִבַּחוּץ וְשָׁוֶה מִבִּפְנִים – אֵינוֹ נִידּוֹן מִשּׁוּם לֶחִי, שְׁמַע מִינַּהּ.

Rather, can we not conclude from the *baraita* that a side post that is **visible from the outside but** appears to be **even** with the wall **from the inside is not considered** to have the legal status of **a side post?** The Gemara concludes: Indeed, **conclude from this.**

אָמַר רַב יוֹסֵף: לָא שְׁמִיעַ לִי הָא שְׁמַעְתְּתָא.

Rav Yosef said: I did not hear this *halakha* of Rabba bar Rav Huna from my teachers. Rav Yosef had become ill and forgotten his learning, which is why he could not recall the *halakha* that a side post that is visible from the outside is considered to have the legal status of a side post.

אָמַר לֵיהּ אַבַּיֵי: אַתְּ אָמְרַתְּ נִיהֲלַן, וְאַהָא אָמְרַתְּ נִיהֲלַן; דְּאָמַר רָמִי בַּר אַבָּא, אָמַר רַב הוּנָא: לֶחִי הַמּוּשָׁךְ עִם דׇּפְנוֹ שֶׁל מָבוֹי, פָּחוֹת מֵאַרְבַּע אַמּוֹת – נִידּוֹן מִשּׁוּם לֶחִי וּמִשְׁתַּמֵּשׁ עִם חוּדּוֹ הַפְּנִימִי, אַרְבַּע אַמּוֹת – נִידּוֹן מִשּׁוּם מָבוֹי, וְאָסוּר לְהִשְׁתַּמֵּשׁ בְּכוּלּוֹ.

His student **Abaye said to him: You** yourself **told us** this *halakha*, **and** it was **with regard to this** that **you told** it **to us. As Rami bar Abba said** that **Rav Huna said:** With regard to **a side post that extends along the wall of an alleyway** and beyond,[NB] in which case it appears from the inside to be a continuation of the wall but due to its narrow width it is clearly visible as a side post from the outside, if that side post is **less than four cubits** long **it is considered** to have the legal status **of a side post. And one may use** the alleyway **up to the inner edge** of the side post. However, if the side post itself extends **four cubits,** the alleyway has no side post and **it is considered to** have the legal status **of an alleyway, and it is prohibited to utilize the entire** alleyway.

NOTES

A side post that extends along the wall of an alleyway and beyond – לֶחִי הַמּוּשָׁךְ עִם דׇּפְנוֹ שֶׁל מָבוֹי: The Gemara indicates that the side post continues beyond the walls of the alleyway into the public domain. If so, this case does not prove anything with regard to carrying between side posts, as perhaps carrying next to this side post is prohibited due to the fact that there is only one partition outside the alleyway. The Rashba explains that it is referring to a case where the opposite alleyway wall also extends outward, so that the protruding side post serves as a second partition.

BACKGROUND

A side post that extends along the wall of an alleyway – לֶחִי הַמּוּשָׁךְ עִם דׇּפְנוֹ שֶׁל מָבוֹי: The side post, i.e., the thin board alongside the wall, extends along the wall of the alleyway, and continues beyond it. The illustration is in accordance with the Rashba's explanation of this case.

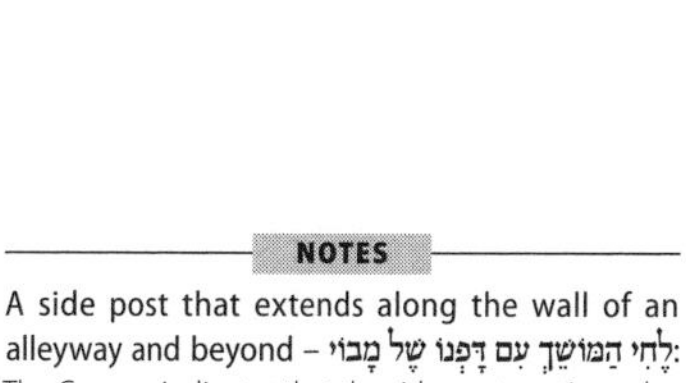

Side post that extends beyond the alleyway wall

וְאַתְּ אָמְרַתְּ לָן עֲלַהּ: שְׁמַע מִינָּהּ תְּלָת; שְׁמַע מִינָּהּ: בֵּין לְחָיַיִן אָסוּר, וּשְׁמַע מִינָּהּ: מֶשֶׁךְ מָבוֹי בְּאַרְבַּע, וּשְׁמַע מִינָּהּ: נִרְאֶה מִבַּחוּץ וְשָׁוֶה מִבִּפְנִים – נִידּוֹן מִשּׁוּם לֶחִי.

And you said to us about this: Learn from this statement **three** *halakhot* with regard to *eiruvin*. **Learn from it** that in the area **between the side posts it is prohibited** to carry, as Rav Huna rules that one may use the alleyway only up to the inner edge of the side post. **And learn from it** that the minimal **length of an alleyway is four** cubits. **And learn from it** that a side post that is **visible from the outside but** appears to be **even** with the wall of the alleyway **from the inside is considered** to have the legal status **of a side post.**

וְהִלְכְתָא: נִרְאֶה מִבַּחוּץ וְשָׁוֶה מִבִּפְנִים – נִידּוֹן מִשּׁוּם לֶחִי. תְּיוּבְתָּא וְהִלְכְתָא?!

The Gemara concludes: **The *halakha*** is that a side post that is **visible from the outside but** appears to be **even** with the wall **from the inside is considered** to have the legal status **of a side post.** The Gemara asks: It is possible that there is **a conclusive refutation** of this opinion, **and** it is also **the *halakha*?** This opinion was refuted earlier. Can the *halakha* then be decided in accordance with it?

אִין מִשּׁוּם דְּתָנֵי רַבִּי חִיָּיא כְּוָותֵיהּ.

The Gemara answers: **Yes,** it can **because Rabbi Ḥiyya taught** a *baraita*[N] **in accordance with it.** Although the deductive analysis of the statements of other *tanna'im* led to different conclusions, the *halakha* relies on Rabbi Ḥiyya's explicit statement.

״וְהָרָחָב מֵעֶשֶׂר יְמַעֵט״. אָמַר אַבַּיֵי, תָּנָא: וְהָרָחָב מֵעֶשֶׂר יְמַעֵט, רַבִּי יְהוּדָה אוֹמֵר: אֵינוֹ צָרִיךְ לְמַעֵט. וְעַד כַּמָּה?

The opening mishna states: If the entrance to an alleyway is **wider than ten** cubits, **one must diminish** its width. **Abaye said** that a Sage **taught** in the *Tosefta*: If the entrance to an alleyway **is wider than ten** cubits,[H] **one must diminish** its width. **Rabbi Yehuda says: He need not diminish it.** The question arises: **Until what** width does Rabbi Yehuda still permit carrying in the alleyway?

סָבַר רַב אַחַי קַמֵּיהּ דְּרַב יוֹסֵף לְמֵימַר: עַד שְׁלֹשׁ עֶשְׂרֵה אַמָּה וּשְׁלִישׁ. וְקַל וָחוֹמֶר מִפַּסֵּי בִירָאוֹת,

Initially, **Rav Aḥai thought to say before Rav Yosef: Up to thirteen and a third cubits. And** he derived this figure through **an *a fortiori*** argument **from** upright **boards surrounding a well.** Rabbi Yehuda maintains that if one placed upright boards up to thirteen and a third cubits apart from one another, he may consider the partitioned area around the well as a private domain and therefore carry within it.

וּמַה פַּסֵּי בִירָאוֹת שֶׁהִתַּרְתָּה בָּהֶן פָּרוּץ מְרוּבֶּה עַל הָעוֹמֵד – לֹא הִתַּרְתָּה בָּהֶן יוֹתֵר מִשְּׁלֹשׁ עֶשְׂרֵה אַמָּה וּשְׁלִישׁ, מָבוֹי שֶׁלֹּא הִתַּרְתָּה בּוֹ פָּרוּץ מְרוּבֶּה עַל הָעוֹמֵד – אֵינוֹ דִּין שֶׁלֹּא תַּתִּיר בּוֹ יוֹתֵר מִשְּׁלֹשׁ עֶשְׂרֵה אַמָּה וּשְׁלִישׁ!

Rav Aḥai explains: **Just as** in the case of upright **boards surrounding a well,**[B] **where you permitted** carrying, even though the boards form a partition where the **breached** segment **is greater than the standing** segment, **you did not permit** carrying **within them** if the gap between the boards is **more than thirteen and a third cubits** wide; in the case of **an alleyway, where you did not permit** carrying if the **breached** segment of its walls **is greater than the standing** segment, **is it not right that you will not permit** carrying **within it** if there is a gap **more than thirteen and a third cubits** wide?

וְהִיא הַנּוֹתֶנֶת, פַּסֵּי בִירָאוֹת שֶׁהִתַּרְתָּה בָּהֶן פָּרוּץ מְרוּבֶּה עַל הָעוֹמֵד – לֹא תַּתִּיר בָּהֶן יוֹתֵר מִשְּׁלֹשׁ עֶשְׂרֵה אַמָּה וּשְׁלִישׁ, מָבוֹי שֶׁלֹּא הִתַּרְתָּה בּוֹ פָּרוּץ מְרוּבֶּה עַל הָעוֹמֵד – תַּתִּיר בּוֹ יוֹתֵר מִשְּׁלֹשׁ עֶשְׂרֵה אַמּוֹת וּשְׁלִישׁ!

But that reasoning **provides** support for a contrary conclusion as well. Just as in the case of upright **boards surrounding a well, where you permitted** carrying **within them,** even though the boards form a partition where the **breached** segment **is greater than the standing** segment, **you will not** extend the leniency and **permit** carrying **within them,** when the gap between the boards is **more than thirteen and a third cubits;** in **an alleyway, where you** were stringent and **did not permit** carrying when the **breached** segment **is greater than the standing** segment, in a case where most of the walls are standing, **you will** certainly **permit** carrying, even when the gap is **more than thirteen and a third cubits.**

אִי נַמִי לְאִידָּךְ גִּיסָא: פַּסֵּי בִירָאוֹת דְּאַקִּילַתְּ בְּהוּ חַד קוּלָּא – אַקִּיל בְּהוּ קוּלָּא אַחֲרִינָא, מָבוֹי כְּלָל כְּלָל לֹא.

Alternatively, one may argue **to the contrary.** One should be more stringent in the case of an alleyway. In the case of upright **boards surrounding a well, with regard to which you were lenient** and issued **one leniency, be lenient and** issue **another leniency** and maintain that a gap of up to thirteen and a third cubits still be considered an entrance. However, in the case of **an alleyway,** you should **not** be lenient **at all.**[N] Therefore, there is no way to determine Rabbi Yehuda's opinion with regard to the width of an alleyway entrance.

NOTES

Because Rabbi Ḥiyya taught a *baraita* – מִשּׁוּם דְּתָנֵי רַבִּי חִיָּיא: In the Jerusalem Talmud it is stated that this *baraita* concerning a smaller and larger courtyard is not found in the authoritative collections of *baraitot*. Therefore, unlike the other *mishnayot* that came from the study hall of Rabbi Ḥiyya and Rabbi Oshaya, one should not learn or teach from it.

Not at all – כְּלָל כְּלָל לֹא: The Rashba asks: Clearly, holds that the width of an alleyway permitted by Rabbi Yehuda is greater that the width permitted by the Rabbis, so how is it possible to say that he added nothing at all? Apparently, one cannot derive anything from the case of upright boards surrounding a well. In fact, Rabbi Yehuda may have added a great amount, as according to several opinions he derived his *halakha* from the entrance of the Temple or from palace entrances, which are twenty or more cubits wide (Rabbi Eliezer Meir Horowitz).

HALAKHA

An alleyway that is wider than ten – מָבוֹי הָרָחָב מֵעֶשֶׂר: If the entrance to an alleyway is wider than ten cubits, a cross beam cannot be used to permit carrying in the alleyway, unless its width is diminished to ten cubits or less. This *halakha* is in accordance with the unattributed mishna (*Shulḥan Arukh, Oraḥ Ḥayyim* 363:26).

BACKGROUND

Upright boards surrounding a well – פַּסֵּי בִירָאוֹת: See the detailed description and illustrations of upright boards at the beginning of Chapter Two.

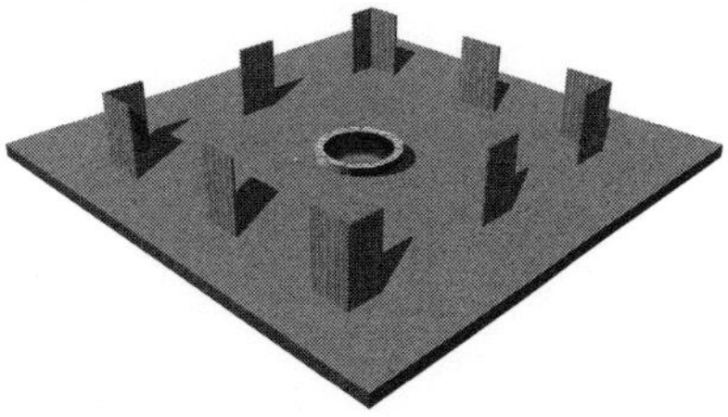

Upright boards surrounding a well

תָּנֵי לֵוִי: מָבוֹי שֶׁהוּא רָחָב עֶשְׂרִים אַמָּה, נוֹעֵץ קָנֶה בְּאֶמְצָעִיתוֹ, וְדַיּוֹ. הוּא תָּנֵי לַהּ וְהוּא אָמַר לַהּ: דְּאֵין הֲלָכָה כְּאוֹתָהּ מִשְׁנָה. אִיכָּא דְּאָמְרִי, אָמַר שְׁמוּאֵל מִשְּׁמֵיהּ דְּלֵוִי: אֵין הֲלָכָה כְּאוֹתָהּ מִשְׁנָה.

Levi taught a *baraita* with regard to reducing the width of an alleyway in order to render it fit for one to carry within it. **If an alleyway is twenty cubits wide, one may stick a reed in** the **center** of its entrance[N] **and** that is **sufficient** to create two separate alleyways, each ten cubits wide. **He taught** this *baraita*, **and he said** about **it that the** ***halakha*** **is not in accordance with that teaching,** as the insertion of a reed is not effective in reducing the width. **Some say** that **Shmuel said in the name of Levi: The** ***halakha*** **is not in accordance with that teaching.**

אֶלָּא הֵיכִי עָבֵיד? אָמַר שְׁמוּאֵל מִשְּׁמֵיהּ דְּלֵוִי:

The Gemara asks: **Rather, how should one act** in order to render an alleyway of that sort fit for one to carry within it? **Shmuel said in the name of Levi:**

NOTES

One may stick a reed in the center – נוֹעֵץ קָנֶה בְּאֶמְצָעִיתוֹ: According to the Jerusalem Talmud, the cross beam is invalid only if it rests solely on the reed inserted in the center. However, if it rests on the alleyway's two walls as well, it is valid. However, the Babylonian Talmud did not accept this assumption.

Perek **I**
Daf **10** Amud **b**

עוֹשֶׂה פַּס גָּבוֹהַּ עֲשָׂרָה בְּמֶשֶׁךְ אַרְבַּע אַמּוֹת, וּמַעֲמִידוֹ לְאָרְכּוֹ שֶׁל מָבוֹי.

One prepares a board ten handbreadths **high with a length of four cubits and stands it lengthwise** down the middle **of the alleyway,** and thereby forms two small alleyways at the entrance to the alleyway, neither of which is more than ten cubits wide.[H]

אִי נַמִּי כִּדְרַב יְהוּדָה, דְּאָמַר רַב יְהוּדָה: מָבוֹי שֶׁהוּא רָחָב חֲמֵשׁ עֶשְׂרֵה אַמָּה – מַרְחִיק שְׁתֵּי אַמּוֹת וְעוֹשֶׂה פַּס שָׁלֹשׁ אַמּוֹת.

Alternatively, one can act **in accordance with** the opinion of **Rav Yehuda,** as **Rav Yehuda said: If an alleyway is fifteen cubits wide,** how does one reduce its width? **He distances** himself **two cubits** from one of the walls of the alleyway **and prepares a board three cubits** wide,[B] thereby leaving an opening of only ten cubits.[H]

וְאַמַּאי? יַעֲשֶׂה פַּס אַמָּה וּמֶחֱצָה, וְיַרְחִיק שְׁתֵּי אַמּוֹת, וְיַעֲשֶׂה פַּס אַמָּה וּמֶחֱצָה. שְׁמַע מִינָּהּ: עוֹמֵד מְרוּבֶּה עַל הַפָּרוּץ מִשְׁתֵּי רוּחוֹת – לָא הָוֵי עוֹמֵד!

The Gemara asks: **And why** must one reduce the width in this manner? **One** could also **prepare a board a cubit and a half**[B] wide, **and distance** himself **two cubits, and** then **prepare** another board **a cubit and a half** wide, leaving the alleyway with an opening of only ten cubits. Apparently, one may **conclude from** the fact that Rav Yehuda did not suggest **this** possibility that if the **standing** segment of a wall is **greater than the breached** segment only when one combines the standing segments **from two directions,** i.e., both sides of the breach, it **is not considered** as though the **standing** segment were greater.

לְעוֹלָם אֵימָא לָךְ ״הָוֵי עוֹמֵד״, וְשָׁאנֵי הָכָא – דְּאָתֵי אֲוֵירָא דְּהַאי גִּיסָּא וַאֲוֵירָא דְּהַאי גִּיסָּא וּמְבַטֵּל לֵיהּ.

The Gemara rejects this: **Actually, I would say to you** that ordinarily **it is considered** as **standing** even when one must combine the standing segments on the two sides of the breach. **However, it is different here, as the air,** i.e., the one and a half cubit opening, **of this one side** of the far board **and the air,** i.e., the ten cubit opening, **of this** other **side** of the board **come** together **and negate it.** Therefore, in this case, the board that is farther from the wall cannot serve to close off the alleyway.

BACKGROUND

Board three cubits wide – פַּס שָׁלֹשׁ: The image depicts an alleyway fifteen cubits wide in which a board of three cubits has been set up across its entrance, in accordance with the opinion of Rav Yehuda.

Board placed across alleyway's entrance

Board a cubit and a half – פַּס אַמָּה וּמֶחֱצָה: This image is an etching of a different construction that can be used to diminish the width of an alleyway, namely, using two boards, each a cubit and a half in width, as stated by the Gemara.

Two boards placed across alleyway's entrance

HALAKHA

Diminishing the entrance of a wide alleyway – הַמְעָטַת מָבוֹי רָחָב: If the entrance to an alleyway is twenty cubits wide, a low, thin board at least ten handbreadths high and four cubits wide should be positioned down the middle of the alleyway, forming two alleyways. A cross beam that reaches from one wall of the original alleyway to the other wall should be placed at the entrance to these two alleyways. Care should be taken that the cross beam is positioned above the board or within three handbreadths of it (Rashba; Rosh). The two new alleyways must each meet all the conditions of an alleyway in which carrying is permitted. The section of the alleyway from the board to the back wall is considered an L-shaped alleyway (*Beit Yosef*). Some commentaries state that it does not have the *halakha* of an L-shaped alleyway unless the distance between the board to the back wall is greater than ten cubits (Rema, based on the Rosh; Rabbeinu Yeruḥam and others; *Shulḥan Arukh, Oraḥ Ḥayyim* 363:33).

Diminishing the entrance of a wide alleyway – הַמְעָטַת מָבוֹי רָחָב: Rav Yehuda proposed an alternate method to diminish the entrance to the alleyway, positioning a thin board across the alleyway entrance. There are several ways to accomplish this. If the alleyway is twenty cubits wide, one can prepare a thin board three cubits wide at a distance of two cubits from each of the alleyway's walls.

Another method involves preparing a thin board that is a cubit and a half wide at a distance of one cubit from the alleyway wall. Then, another thin board, a cubit and a half wide, is prepared a cubit away from the first thin board. A matching set of thin boards is then prepared on the other side of the alleyway's entrance.

Yet another method is to prepare a thin board, two cubits and four handbreadths wide, at a distance of two cubits and two handbreadths from the alleyway wall and to do the same on the other side (*Maggid Mishne* in the name of the Rashba).

All these methods are accepted in the Gemara. The basic principle of these constructions is that the width of the thin board should be greater than the space between it and the wall, in keeping with the principle that the standing segment must be greater than the breached segment from one direction (*Shulḥan Arukh, Oraḥ Ḥayyim* 363:34).

וְיַעֲשֶׂה פַּס אַמָּה, וְיַרְחִיק אַמָּה, וְיַעֲשֶׂה פַּס אַמָּה וְיַרְחִיק אַמָּה וְיַעֲשֶׂה פַּס אַמָּה, שְׁמַע מִינַּהּ: עוֹמֵד כְּפָרוּץ – אָסוּר!

The Gemara suggests: **And one** could instead **prepare a board** one **cubit** wide **and distance** himself one **cubit, and prepare** another **board of a cubit and distance** himself one **cubit, and prepare** a third **board** of one **cubit,** thus ensuring that the open space is not greater than the standing segment on both sides. Apparently, since Rav Yehuda did not suggest this possibility, one may **conclude from this** that if the **standing** segment of a wall **is equal to the breached** segment, carrying in the alleyway **is prohibited.**

לְעוֹלָם אֵימָא לָךְ ״מוּתָּר״, וְשָׁאנֵי הָכָא – דְּאָתְיָא אֲוִירָא דְּהַאי גִּיסָא וּדְהַאי גִּיסָא וּמְבַטֵּל לֵיהּ.

The Gemara rejects this assumption: **Actually, I would say to you** that ordinarily carrying **is permitted** in that case. **But here it is different, since the air,** the opening, **on this side** of the board **and the air,** the opening, **on that side** of the board **come** together **and negate** the effectiveness of the board.

וְיַרְחִיק אַמָּה, וְיַעֲשֶׂה פַּס אַמָּה וּמֶחֱצָה וְיַרְחִיק אַמָּה וְיַעֲשֶׂה פַּס אַמָּה וּמֶחֱצָה!

The Gemara suggests: **And** one could **distance** himself **one cubit** from the wall, **and prepare a board of a cubit and a half, and distance** himself another **cubit, and prepare** another **board of a cubit and a half.** In this manner, one could diminish the width of the entrance of the alleyway to ten cubits.

אִין הָכִי נַמִּי, וְכוּלֵּי הַאי לָא אַטְרְחוּהּ רַבָּנַן.

The Gemara answers: **Yes, it is indeed so;** this would work equally as well. **But the Sages did not burden him this much,** requiring him to prepare two boards where one suffices.

וְלֵיחוּשׁ דִּלְמָא שָׁבֵיק פִּיתְחָא רַבָּה, וְעָיֵיל בְּפִיתְחָא זוּטָא! אָמַר רַב אַדָּא בַּר מַתָּנָה: חֲזָקָה, אֵין אָדָם מַנִּיחַ פֶּתַח גָּדוֹל וְנִכְנָס בְּפֶתַח קָטָן.

The Gemara raises a new issue: **But let us be concerned lest one abandon** use of **the larger entrance,**[N] which is ten cubits wide, **and** begin to **enter** the alleyway **through the smaller entrance,** which has a width of two cubits. This would negate the larger opening's status as an entrance and render the alleyway unfit for one to carry within it, as it would no longer have an entrance with a side post. **Rav Adda bar Mattana said:** The **presumption** is that **a person does not abandon a larger entrance and enter** instead **through a smaller entrance.**[H]

וּמַאי שְׁנָא מִדְּרַבִּי אַמִי וּדְרַבִּי אַסִי?

The Gemara raises a difficulty: **And** in **what** way is this **different** from the opinion **of Rabbi Ami**[N] **and Rabbi Asi,** who maintain that in the case of an alleyway that is breached on its side wall close to its entrance, if the breach is large enough for one to enter through it, carrying in the alleyway is prohibited? There, too, such a breach should not be problematic, as a person does not abandon a larger entrance to enter through a smaller one.

הָתָם קָא מְמַעֵט בְּהִילּוּכָא, הָכָא לָא קָא מְמַעֵט בְּהִילּוּכָא.

The Gemara answers: **There,** in the case of Rabbi Ami and Rabbi Asi, the smaller entrance **reduces** his **walking** distance. If one approaches the alleyway from the side, the smaller entrance provides a shortcut, and therefore one might enter through it as well. However, **here,** in the case of the two entrances one two cubits and one ten cubits, **it does not reduce** his **walking** distance, as both openings are situated at the front of the alleyway.

תְּנַן הָתָם: עוֹר הָעַסְלָא וְחָלָל שֶׁלּוֹ – מִצְטָרְפִין בְּטֶפַח.

The Gemara returns to the issue of the standing segment that is greater than the breached segment. **We learned** in the *Tosefta* **there,** in tractate *Kelim*: **The leather** covering **of a stool** [*asla*][NL] **and its hole join** together **to** complete **a handbreadth** with regard to ritual impurity imparted by a tent over a corpse. Any person, vessel, or food that is beneath a covering that is at least a handbreadth in size together with a portion of a corpse of at least an olive-bulk becomes ritually impure with impurity imparted by a corpse. The *baraita* teaches that the leather covering of a stool and its hole combine to complete the measure of a handbreadth.

מַאי ״עוֹר הָעַסְלָא״? אָמַר רַבָּה בַּר בַּר חָנָה, אָמַר רַבִּי יוֹחָנָן: עוֹר כִּיסּוּי שֶׁל בֵּית הַכִּסֵּא.

The Gemara asks: **What is the leather** covering **of a stool** referred to in the *Tosefta*? **Rabba bar bar Ḥana said** that **Rav Yoḥanan said: The leather covering of a bathroom.**

NOTES

Lest one abandon the larger entrance – שָׁבֵיק פִּיתְחָא רַבָּה: The Ra'avad states that this concern applies only in a case where the cross beam does not span the entire width of the alleyway. However, if the cross beam spans the breached section as well, it makes no difference through which entrance one passes.

In what way is this different from the opinion of Rabbi Ami – מַאי שְׁנָא מִדְּרַבִּי אַמִי: Many commentaries explain that this question does not refer to the statement of Rabbi Ami and Rabbi Asi concerning an alleyway that is breached on its side wall close to its entrance. Rather, it is referring to their statement permitting a large breach at the side of an alleyway of up to ten cubits, without concern as to how many people might pass through this breach (Rashba).

The leather covering of a stool – עוֹר הָעַסְלָא: Some commentaries explain that this case involves the ritual impurity of the leather itself, contracted when a *zav* sat on the stool, as a certain minimum measure. The question, then, is whether or not the hole combines with the leather to complete the minimal measurement for these purposes (Ra'avad; Rav Shimshon of Saens).

HALAKHA

Large and small entrances – פֶּתַח קָטָן וְגָדוֹל: When diminishing a wide alleyway by placing thin boards across its entrance, one must be careful not to make a habit of passing through the small entrance between the wall and the board. If one does so, carrying in the alleyway can be permitted only by means of the form of a doorway, as is implied by the statements of the Gemara (*Shulḥan Arukh, Oraḥ Ḥayyim* 363:34).

LANGUAGE

Stool [*asla*] – עַסְלָא: This word also appears in its more common form, *asla*, with the first letter an *alef* rather than an *ayin*. It originates from the Latin sella, seat, or the Greek σέλλα, *sella*, or σελλίον, *sellion*, meaning chair. In its original form, and especially in our sources, it refers to a toilet seat.

וְכַמָּה? כִּי אֲתָא רַב דִּימִי, אֲמַר: אֶצְבָּעַיִים מִכָּאן וְאֶצְבָּעַיִים מִכָּאן, וְאֶצְבָּעַיִים רֶיוַח בְּאֶמְצַע. כִּי אֲתָא רָבִין, אֲמַר: אֶצְבַּע וּמֶחֱצָה מִכָּאן, וְאֶצְבַּע וּמֶחֱצָה מִכָּאן, וְאֶצְבַּע רֶיוַח בְּאֶמְצַע.

The Gemara asks: **And how large** can the hole be and still combine with the leather covering to complete the handbreadth? **When Rav Dimi came** from Eretz Yisrael to Babylonia, **he said: Two fingers** of leather **from here,** on one side, **and two fingers** of leather **from here,** on the other side, **and a space of two fingers** for the hole **in the middle.** However, **when Ravin came** from Eretz Yisrael to Babylonia, **he said: A finger and a half** of leather **from here, and a finger and a half** on the leather **from here, and a space of** a single **finger** for the hole **in the middle.**

אֲמַר לֵיהּ אַבָּיֵי לְרַב דִּימִי: מִי פְּלִיגִיתוּ? אֲמַר לֵיהּ: לָא, הָא – בְּרַבְרְבָתָא, הָא – בְּזוּטַרְתָּא, וְלָא פְּלִיגִין.

Abaye said to Rav Dimi: Do the two of **you,** yourself and Ravin, **disagree** in principle? Rav Dimi **said to him: No,** rather **this,** Ravin's statement, **is referring to the large** finger, i.e., the thumb, and **this,** my own statement, **is referring to the small** finger, the pinkie, **and we do not disagree.**[N] Both were describing one handbreadth, which equals the width of four thumbs or six pinkies.

אֲמַר לֵיהּ: לָאֵיי, פְּלִיגִיתוּ, וּבְעוֹמֵד מְרוּבֶּה עַל הַפָּרוּץ מִשְּׁתֵּי רוּחוֹת פְּלִיגִיתוּ; לְדִידָךְ – הָוֵי עוֹמֵד, מִשְּׁתֵּי רוּחוֹת, לְרָבִין, מֵרוּחַ אַחַת – הָוֵי עוֹמֵד, מִשְּׁתֵּי רוּחוֹת – לָא הָוֵי עוֹמֵד.

Abaye **said to him:** This is **not so** [*la'ei*].[L] **You disagree, and you disagree with regard to** the *halakha* in a case where the **standing** segment of a wall is **greater than the breached** segment only when one combines the standing segments **from two directions,** i.e., both sides of the breached segment. **According to you,** this wall **is considered as standing,** even when one must combine the standing segments **from two directions. According to Ravin,** if the standing segment **on one side** of the breach is greater, the wall **is considered as standing;** however, if the standing segment is greater only after combining the standing segments **from the two directions,** it **is not considered as standing.**

דְּאִי סָלְקָא דַּעְתָּךְ לָא פְּלִיגִיתוּ – לְרָבִין הָכִי אִיבָּעֵי לֵיהּ לְמֵימַר: אֶצְבַּע וּשְׁלִישׁ מִכָּאן, וְאֶצְבַּע וּשְׁלִישׁ מִכָּאן, וְאֶצְבַּע וּשְׁלִישׁ רֶיוַח בְּאֶמְצַע.

Abaye continues: **For if it should enter your mind** to say that **you do not disagree,** but simply refer to the same measures by different names, **to** express his opinion, **Ravin should have said as follows: A finger and a third** of leather **from here, and a finger and a third** of leather **from here, and** a space of **a finger and a third** for the hole **in the middle.** In this case, there would still be a handbreadth in total, but each side of leather alone would not be larger than the space in the middle. The fact that Ravin presented a case where the hole in the middle is smaller than the width of the leather on either side indicates that his dispute with Rav Dimi is a fundamental one.

וְאֶלָּא מַאי – פְּלִיגִינַן, לְדִידִי הָכִי אִיבָּעֵי לִי לְמֵימַר: אֶצְבַּע וּשְׁנֵי שְׁלִישִׁים מִכָּאן, וְאֶצְבַּע וּשְׁנֵי שְׁלִישִׁים מִכָּאן, וְאֶצְבָּעַיִים וּשְׁנֵי שְׁלִישִׁים רֶיוַח בְּאֶמְצַע!

Rav Dimi responds: **Rather, what** do you wish to say, that **we disagree?** If so, **to** express the opinion attributed to **me, I should have said as follows: A finger and two thirds** of leather **from here, and a finger and two thirds** of leather **from here, and a space of two fingers and two thirds in the middle.** This would provide a more striking case where, despite the fact that the breach is much greater than the standing segments on either of its sides, the two standing segments combine together so that the standing segments are considered greater than the breached segment.

אֶלָּא אִי אִיכָּא לְמֵימַר דִּפְלִיגִינַן – בְּפָרוּץ כְּעוֹמֵד פְּלִיגִינַן.

Rather, if there is room **to say that we disagree,** our dispute relates to a different point, and **we argue** in the case where **the breached** segment **is** exactly **equal to the standing** segment on each side. According to Ravin, it is considered breached; while according to Rav Dimi, it is considered standing.

״אִם יֵשׁ לוֹ צוּרַת הַפֶּתַח אַף עַל פִּי שֶׁרָחָב מֵעֶשֶׂר אֵינוֹ צָרִיךְ לְמַעֵט״. אַשְׁכַּחַן צוּרַת הַפֶּתַח דְּמַהַנְיָא בְּרָחְבּוֹ, וְאַמַּלְתְּרָא דְּמַהַנְיָא בְּגָבְהוֹ.

The Gemara returns to the mishna: **If** the entrance to the alleyway **has** an opening in the **form of a doorway,** then, **even if it is wider than ten** cubits, **one need not diminish** its width. The Gemara comments: **We find** that an opening in the **form of a doorway**[H] **is effective** to permit carrying in an alleyway **with** regard to **its width,** i.e., when its entrance is more than ten cubits wide, **and** that **a cornice is effective with** regard to **its height,** i.e., when it is more than twenty cubits high.

NOTES

Do you disagree…and we do not disagree – מִי פְּלִיגִיתוּ...וְלָא פְּלִיגִין: The two rulings with regard to the measure of a stool were cited separately, and it was unclear even to those who transmitted them how to reconcile them. Did they reflect a difference of opinion due to a retraction on Rabbi Yoḥanan's part or because one of them erred in transmission of the tradition? Are they both expressing the same idea but in two different ways? Did Rabbi Yoḥanan himself repeat the same idea twice in different words, but with identical meaning? Consequently, Abaye, who commented only on what he heard from Rav Dimi, and Rav Dimi himself could not disagree definitively over the meaning of Rav Dimi's words.

LANGUAGE

Not so [*la'ei*] **– לָאֵיי:** The root of the word and its meaning have not been sufficiently clarified. According to Rashi, it means in truth or indeed. Some maintain that the word is a shortened form of the Hebrew expression *lo hi* or the Aramaic phrase *la hei*, both meaning not so. The *Arukh* claims that it is a compound of two words: The Aramaic *la* and the Greek **υἱός**, *huios*, meaning son. The word *la'ei* then means: No, my son.

HALAKHA

The form of a doorway – צוּרַת הַפֶּתַח: If the entrance to an alleyway has a doorframe, it is unnecessary to diminish the width of the entrance, even if it is greater than ten cubits, as stated by the mishna (*Shulḥan Arukh*, *Oraḥ Ḥayyim* 362:10).

NOTES

A cornice with regard to the alleyway's width – אֲמַלְתְּרָא בְּרָחְבּוֹ: The question appears to be related to the basic reason for the leniency in the case of a cornice. If the cornice is effective because its ornamentation causes it to stand out and attract people's attention even when the cross beam is much higher than twenty cubits, that would not be relevant to the case of an alleyway whose entrance is more than ten cubits wide. If, however, the cornice is effective due to its importance and its ability to turn an opening into an entrance, then the leniency should apply to a wide alleyway just as it applies to a high alleyway (*Ge'on Ya'akov*).

HALAKHA

A cornice with regard to the alleyway's width – אֲמַלְתְּרָא בְּמָבוֹי רָחָב: If an alleyway is more than ten cubits wide, a cornice does not render carrying in the alleyway permitted. This issue was not resolved in the Gemara. Although the *halakha* is lenient in cases of uncertainty involving a rabbinic prohibition such as this, the *halakha* is stringent in this case, because the rationale to prohibit is convincing (*Beit Yosef*; *Tur*, *Oraḥ Ḥayyim* 363).

Form of a doorway – צוּרַת הַפֶּתַח: The form of a doorway renders it permitted for one to carry even where the breach is greater than the standing segment of the walls, and even where the opening is more than ten cubits. This is in accordance with the Gemara's conclusion, as even Rabbi Yoḥanan accepts this *halakha* (*Shulḥan Arukh*, *Oraḥ Ḥayyim* 362:10).

אִיפְּכָא מַאי?

The Gemara asks: **What is** the *halakha* in **the opposite** situation? Does an opening in the form of a doorway also serve to permit carrying in an alleyway that is more than twenty cubits high?

תָּא שְׁמַע, דְּתַנְיָא: מָבוֹי שֶׁהוּא גָּבוֹהַּ מֵעֶשְׂרִים אַמָּה – יְמַעֵט וְאִם יֵשׁ לוֹ צוּרַת הַפֶּתַח – אֵינוֹ צָרִיךְ לְמַעֵט.

The Gemara answers: **Come** and **hear** the answer to this question, **as it was taught** in a *baraita*: If the cross beam placed over the entrance to **an alleyway is higher than twenty cubits, one must diminish** its height, **but if** the entrance **has an opening in the form of a doorway, he need not diminish it.**

אֲמַלְתְּרָא בְּרָחְבּוֹ מַאי? תָּא שְׁמַע, דְּתַנְיָא: מָבוֹי שֶׁהוּא גָּבוֹהַּ מֵעֶשְׂרִים אַמָּה – יְמַעֵט וְהָרָחָב מֵעֶשֶׂר – יְמַעֵט, וְאִם יֵשׁ לוֹ צוּרַת הַפֶּתַח – אֵינוֹ צָרִיךְ לְמַעֵט, וְאִם יֵשׁ לוֹ אֲמַלְתְּרָא – אֵינוֹ צָרִיךְ לְמַעֵט.

The Gemara asks: **What is** the effect of **a cornice with** regard to the need to diminish the alleyway's **width?**[N] Does the cornice render the alleyway fit for one to carry within it, even if the entrance is more than ten cubits wide? The Gemara answers: **Come** and **hear** an answer **as it was taught** in a *baraita*: If the cross beam placed over the entrance to **an alleyway is higher than twenty cubits, one must diminish** its height, **and** if the alleyway is **wider than ten** cubits, **one must diminish** its width. **However, if** the entrance to the alleyway **has an opening in the form of a doorway, he need not diminish it, and,** similarly, **if it has a cornice, he need not diminish it.**[H]

מַאי לָאו אַסֵּיפָא? לָא, אַרֵישָׁא.

The Gemara explains the proof it wishes to adduce from this *baraita*: **What, is** this statement with regard to the cornice **not** referring **to the latter** clause, i.e., the case of an alleyway that is wider than ten cubits, proving that a cornice can render an alleyway otherwise too wide fit for one to carry within it? The Gemara refutes this argument: **No,** this statement is referring **to the first** clause of the *baraita*, that a cornice is effective for an alleyway more than twenty cubits high, but it tells us nothing about one that is more than ten cubits wide.

מַתְנֵי לֵיהּ רַב יְהוּדָה לְחִיָּיא בַּר רַב קַמֵּיהּ דְּרַב: ״אֵינוֹ צָרִיךְ לְמַעֵט״. אֲמַר לֵיהּ: אַתְנְיֵיהּ: ״צָרִיךְ לְמַעֵט״.

With regard to the same issue, **Rav Yehuda would teach** the *baraita* to **Ḥiyya bar Rav before Rav** as follows: If the entrance to an alleyway that is wider than ten cubits has an opening in the form of a doorway, **he need not diminish** its width. **Rav said to him: Teach him** that the correct version of the *baraita* is: **He must diminish** its width.

אָמַר רַב יוֹסֵף, מִדִּבְרֵי רַבֵּינוּ נִלְמַד: חָצֵר שֶׁרוּבָּהּ פְּתָחִים וְחַלּוֹנוֹת – אֵינָהּ נִיתֶּרֶת בְּצוּרַת הַפֶּתַח.

Rav Yosef said: From the statement of our teacher, Rav, who said that the entrance to an alleyway must be diminished even if it has an opening in the form of a doorway, **we will learn** that with regard to **a courtyard,** the walls of **which are mostly entrances and windows, it is not permitted** to carry within it even **by** having an opening in **the form of a doorway.** Even if the entrances have an opening in the form of a doorway, this does not render a mostly breached courtyard wall into a closed wall.[H]

מַאי טַעְמָא – הוֹאִיל וְיוֹתֵר מֵעֶשֶׂר אוֹסֵר בְּמָבוֹי, וּפָרוּץ מְרוּבֶּה עַל הָעוֹמֵד אוֹסֵר בֶּחָצֵר, מַה יּוֹתֵר מֵעֶשֶׂר הָאוֹסֵר בְּמָבוֹי – אֵינוֹ נִיתָּר בְּצוּרַת הַפֶּתַח, אַף פָּרוּץ מְרוּבֶּה עַל הָעוֹמֵד, הָאוֹסֵר בֶּחָצֵר – אֵינוֹ נִיתָּר בְּצוּרַת הַפֶּתַח.

What is the reason? Since an opening of **more than ten** cubits **renders it prohibited** for one to carry **in an alleyway, and** likewise when the **breached** segment of a wall that **is greater than its standing** segment **renders it prohibited** for one to carry **in a courtyard,** the following claim can be made: **Just as,** according to Rav, in the case of an opening **more than ten** cubits wide **that renders it prohibited** for one to carry **in an alleyway,** carrying in the alleyway **is not permitted by the form of a doorway** in the opening, **so too** a case where **breached** segment of a wall **is greater than its standing** segment **that renders it prohibited** for one to carry **in a courtyard,** carrying in the courtyard **is not permitted by the form of a doorway** in the opening.

מַה לְּיוֹתֵר מֵעֶשֶׂר הָאוֹסֵר בְּמָבוֹי – שֶׁכֵּן לֹא הִתַּרְתָּ בּוֹ אֵצֶל פַּסֵּי בִירָאוֹת לְרַבִּי מֵאִיר, תֹּאמַר בְּפָרוּץ מְרוּבֶּה עַל הָעוֹמֵד הָאוֹסֵר בֶּחָצֵר – שֶׁכֵּן הִתַּרְתָּ אֵצֶל פַּסֵּי בִירָאוֹת לְדִבְרֵי הַכֹּל.

The Gemara rejects this argument: **What** is the basis for comparison to an opening that is **more than ten** cubits wide **that renders it prohibited** for one to carry **in an alleyway?** It is not permitted by having an opening in the form of a doorway **because you did not permit** an opening of that size **with regard** to the case of upright **boards surrounding a well, in accordance with** the opinion of **Rabbi Meir.** Can **you say** the same **in** a case where the **breached** segment of a wall is **greater than the standing** segment **that renders it prohibited** for one to carry **in a courtyard,** that carrying in the courtyard will not be permitted by the form of a doorway? That situation is clearly not as severe a problem, **as you permitted** carrying **with regard to** upright **boards surrounding a well according to everyone.** Consequently, no comparison can be made between the case of an opening wider than ten cubits in an alleyway and a partition in which the breached segment is greater than the standing segment in a courtyard.

לֵימָא מְסַיַּיע לֵיהּ: דְּפָנוֹת הַלָּלוּ שֶׁרוּבָּן פְּתָחִים וְחַלּוֹנוֹת – מוּתָּר, וּבִלְבַד שֶׁיְּהֵא עוֹמֵד מְרוּבֶּה עַל הַפָּרוּץ.

The Gemara suggests: **Let us say** that the following *baraita* **supports** this opinion that the form of a doorway is ineffective in a case where the breached segments of a wall are greater than its standing segments: With regard to the area enclosed by **these walls that most of them** consist of **entrances and windows,** it is **permitted** to carry on Shabbat therein, **provided that the standing** segments **are greater than the breached** segments.

״שֶׁרוּבָּן״ סָלְקָא דַּעְתָּךְ?! אֶלָּא אֵימָא: שֶׁרִיבָּה בָּהֶן פְּתָחִים וְחַלּוֹנוֹת, וּבִלְבַד שֶׁיְּהֵא עוֹמֵד מְרוּבֶּה עַל הַפָּרוּץ.

The Gemara first analyzes the wording of the *baraita*: The Gemara analyzes the formulation of the *baraita*: **Can it enter your mind that** the *baraita* is referring to a case **where most of** the walls are entrances and windows? If so, the standing segments are not greater than the breached segments. **Rather,** emend the *baraita*: Carrying in the area enclosed by these walls **to which he added** many **entrances and windows is permitted, provided that the standing** segments **are greater than the breached** segments. Apparently, if the breached segments are greater than the standing segments, carrying is not permitted even if the breaches are in the form of doorways.

אָמַר רַב כָּהֲנָא: כִּי תַּנְיָא הַהִיא – בְּפִיתְחֵי שִׁימָאֵי.

Rav Kahana said that his is not an absolute proof: **When this** *baraita* **was taught,** it was taught **with regard to broken entrances** [*pitḥei shima'ei*][NLB] that lack the proper form of doorways.

מַאי פִּיתְחֵי שִׁימָאֵי? פְּלִיגִי בָּהּ רַב רְחוּמֵי וְרַב יוֹסֵף; חַד אָמַר: דְּלֵית לְהוּ שַׁקְפֵי, וְחַד אָמַר: דְּלֵית לְהוּ תִּיקְרָה.

The Gemara asks: **What are broken entrances? Rav Reḥumei and Rav Yosef disagreed** on the matter. **One said that they do not have** proper **doorposts, and** the other **one said that they do not have lintels** above the openings.

וְאַף רַבִּי יוֹחָנָן סָבַר לָהּ לְהָא דְּרַב. דְּאָמַר רָבִין בַּר רַב אַדָּא, אָמַר רַבִּי יִצְחָק: מַעֲשֶׂה בְּאָדָם אֶחָד מִבִּקְעַת בֵּית חוֹרְתָן שֶׁנָּעַץ אַרְבָּעָה קוּנְדֵּיסִין בְּאַרְבַּע פִּינּוֹת הַשָּׂדֶה, וּמָתַח זְמוֹרָה עֲלֵיהֶם, וּבָא מַעֲשֶׂה לִפְנֵי חֲכָמִים, וְהִתִּירוּ לוֹ לְעִנְיַן כִּלְאַיִם.

The Gemara comments: **And even Rabbi Yoḥanan holds that** opinion **of Rav,** that an opening in the form of a doorway does not permit carrying if the opening is more than ten cubits wide. **As Ravin bar Rav Adda said** that **Rabbi Yitzḥak said:** There was **an incident involving a person from the valley of Beit Ḥortan who stuck four poles** [*kunddeisin*][L] into the ground **in the four corners**[N] **of his field, and stretched a vine over them,**[B] creating the form of a doorway on each side. He intended to seal the area so that he would be permitted to plant a vineyard in close proximity without creating a forbidden mixture of diverse kinds in a vineyard. **And the case came before the Sages, and they permitted him** to consider it sealed **with regard to diverse kinds.**

וְאָמַר רֵישׁ לָקִישׁ: כְּדֶרֶךְ שֶׁהִתִּירוּ לוֹ לְעִנְיַן כִּלְאַיִם – כָּךְ הִתִּירוּ לוֹ לְעִנְיַן שַׁבָּת. רַבִּי יוֹחָנָן אָמַר: לְכִלְאַיִם – הִתִּירוּ לוֹ, לְעִנְיַן שַׁבָּת – לֹא הִתִּירוּ לוֹ.

And Reish Lakish said: Just as they permitted him to consider it sealed **with regard to diverse kinds, so too they permitted him** to consider it sealed **with regard to Shabbat,** i.e., they permitted carrying within this area. **Rabbi Yoḥanan said: With regard to diverse kinds, they permitted him** to consider it sealed, however, **with regard to Shabbat, they did not permit him** to do so.

NOTES

Broken entrances – פִּיתְחֵי שִׁימָאֵי: The *Arukh* explains that a construction without a roof is referring to the common practice of building a small roof over a gate for protection against heat and cold. In the case of broken entrances, this roof was not in place. Some *ge'onim* have a variant reading: Does not have *shakfei*, to mean that broken entrances are missing a lintel [*mashkof*] above the opening. Other commentaries understand that *shakfei* is referring to that part of the doorpost into which the hinge of the door is inserted.

Poles in the four corners – קוּנְדֵּיסִין בְּאַרְבַּע פִּינּוֹת: Rabbeinu Ḥananel explains that reeds stood between the side posts, each one less than three handbreadths apart from the next. The reeds serve as a partition, in part because the vines keep them from falling over. Rashba and other commentaries understand that this explanation is supported in the Jerusalem Talmud.

LANGUAGE

Broken entrances [*pitḥei shima'ei*] – פִּיתְחֵי שִׁימָאֵי: Rashi tries to find a Hebrew source and root for the term *shima'ei*. *Tosafot* cite Rabbeinu Ḥananel's interpretation that it means the entrance to Eretz Yisrael. Rabbeinu Ḥananel's statement is based not only on the expression the land of the sons of Shem, but also on the Arabic شام, *shām*, which is the traditional name for Syria and Eretz Yisrael, as stated in the *Arukh*.

Poles [*kunddeisin*] – קוּנְדֵּיסִין: From the Greek word κοντός, *kontos*, contus in Latin, meaning a side post or a sharp-edged pole.

BACKGROUND

Broken entrances – פִּיתְחֵי שִׁימָאֵי:

Opening that is lacking doorposts and is merely a breach in the wall

Poles and vines – קוּנְדֵּיסִין וּזְמוֹרוֹת:

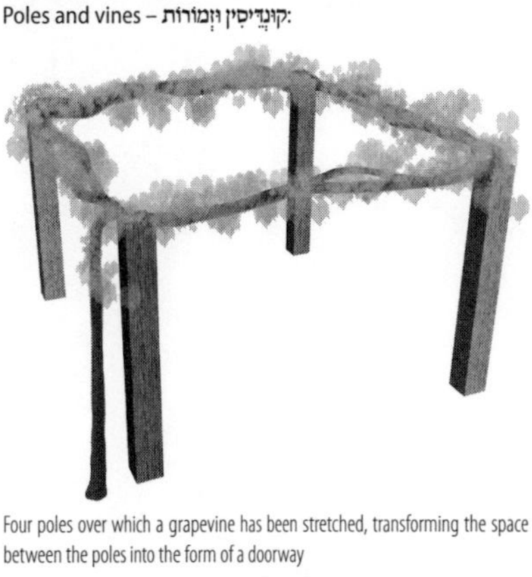

Four poles over which a grapevine has been stretched, transforming the space between the poles into the form of a doorway

NOTES

The form of a doorway from the side – **צוּרַת הַפֶּתַח מִן הַצַּד**: Some *ge'onim*, as well as Rabbeinu Ḥananel and Rif, explain this in a completely different manner: The person constructed a doorframe properly, but instead of placing it in the center of the breach, he positioned it near the wall or in a corner.

HALAKHA

The form of a doorway from the side – **צוּרַת הַפֶּתַח מִן הַצַּד**: The form of a doorway that is constructed so that the horizontal cross beam is on the side, rather than on top, of the two vertical posts is not considered the form of a doorway with regard to the *halakhot* of Shabbat. This principle is in accordance with the opinion of Rav Ḥisda (*Shulḥan Arukh*, *Oraḥ Ḥayyim* 362:11).

בְּמַאי עָסְקִינַן? אִילֵימָא מִן הַצַּד – וְהָאָמַר רַב חִסְדָּא: צוּרַת הַפֶּתַח שֶׁעֲשָׂאָהּ מִן הַצַּד – לֹא עָשָׂה וְלֹא כְלוּם.

The Gemara clarifies: **With what** case **are we dealing** here? **If you say** that he draped the vines on the posts **from the side,** rather than on top of them, **didn't Rav Ḥisda say** with regard to Shabbat: If **one constructed** an opening in **the form of a doorway from the side,**[NH] **he has done nothing?**

אֶלָּא עַל גַּבָּן; וּבְמַאי? אִילֵימָא בְּעֶשֶׂר – בְּהָא לֵימָא רַבִּי יוֹחָנָן "בְּשַׁבָּת לָא"?!

Rather, it must be that he set the vines **on top of** the posts. **And in what** circumstances did Rabbi Yoḥanan and Reish Lakish disagree? **If you say** that the posts were set at a distance **of ten** cubits from each other, **would Rabbi Yoḥanan say in that** case that **with regard to Shabbat,** they did **not** permit him to consider the area sealed? Everyone agrees that the form of a doorway is effective for an entrance that is only ten cubits wide.

אֶלָּא לָאו – בְּיָתֵר מֵעֶשֶׂר!

Rather, isn't it referring to a case **where** the posts were **more than ten** cubits apart? Apparently, Rabbi Yoḥanan agrees with Rav, that an opening in the form of a doorway does not permit carrying if the original opening is wider than ten cubits.

לֹא, לְעוֹלָם בְּעֶשֶׂר וּמִן הַצַּד, וּבִדְרַב חִסְדָּא קָא מִיפַּלְגִי.

The Gemara refutes this proof: **No, actually** it is referring to a case **where** the posts were **ten** cubits apart, **and** the person attached the vines to the posts **from the side. And** Reish Lakish and Rabbi Yoḥanan **disagree with regard to** the opinion of **Rav Ḥisda.** Reish Lakish maintains that the form of a doorway is effective even when the horizontal cross beam is attached to the vertical posts from the side, and Rabbi Yoḥanan agrees with Rav Ḥisda that a form of a doorway is ineffective for the purpose of carrying on Shabbat when constructed in such a manner.

וְרָמֵי דְּרַבִּי יוֹחָנָן אַדְּרַבִּי יוֹחָנָן, וְרָמֵי דְּרֵישׁ לָקִישׁ אַדְּרֵישׁ לָקִישׁ. דְּאָמַר רֵישׁ לָקִישׁ מִשּׁוּם רַבִּי יְהוּדָה בְּרַבִּי חֲנִינָא:

The Gemara comments: **But** it is possible to **raise a contradiction** between this statement **of Rabbi Yoḥanan and** another statement **of Rabbi Yoḥanan; and** it is possible to **raise a contradiction** between this statement **of Reish Lakish and** another statement **of Reish Lakish. As Reish Lakish said in the name of Rabbi Yehuda, son of Rabbi Ḥanina:**

Perek **I**
Daf **11** Amud **b**

פֵּיאָה מוּתֶּרֶת לְעִנְיַן כִּלְאַיִם, אֲבָל לֹא לְשַׁבָּת. וְרַבִּי יוֹחָנָן אָמַר: כִּמְחִיצוֹת לְשַׁבָּת – דְּלָא, כָּךְ מְחִיצוֹת לְכִלְאַיִם – דְּלָא.

A braid of vines plaited around poles to form a partition **is permitted with regard to diverse kinds,** i.e., it is considered a partition that renders planting grapevines in close proximity to other crops permitted, **but not with regard to Shabbat. And Rabbi Yoḥanan said: Just as** such a braid is **not** considered a **partition with regard to Shabbat, so** too it is **not** considered **a partition with regard to diverse kinds.** Their opinions in the dispute here apparently contradict their opinions in the dispute cited above.

בִּשְׁלָמָא דְּרֵישׁ לָקִישׁ אַדְּרֵישׁ לָקִישׁ לָא קַשְׁיָא, הָא – דִּידֵיהּ, הָא – דְּרַבֵּיהּ. אֶלָּא דְּרַבִּי יוֹחָנָן אַדְּרַבִּי יוֹחָנָן קַשְׁיָא!

Granted, the apparent contradiction between one statement **of Reish Lakish** and the other statement **of Reish Lakish** poses **no difficulty, as this** statement, according to which such a braid of vines is an effective partition even with regard to Shabbat, reflects **his** own opinion; **that** statement, according to which it is an effective partition only with regard to diverse kinds, reflects the opinion **of his teacher,** Rabbi Yehuda, son of Rabbi Ḥanina. **However,** the apparent contradiction between one statement **of Rabbi Yoḥanan and** the other statement **of Rabbi Yoḥanan,** poses **a difficulty.**

אִי אָמְרַתְּ בִּשְׁלָמָא: הָתָם – עַל גַּבָּן, הָכָא – מִן הַצַּד, שַׁפִּיר. אֶלָּא אִי אָמְרַתְּ אִידִי וְאִידִי מִן הַצַּד, מַאי אִיכָּא לְמֵימַר?

Granted, if you say that **there,** where Rabbi Yoḥanan ruled that a braid of vines is an effective partition with regard to diverse kinds, it is referring to a case where the vines were placed **on top of** the posts, while **here,** where he rules that it is ineffective even with regard to diverse kinds, it is referring to a case where they were attached to the posts **from the side,** it works out **well. However, if you say** that both **this and that** are cases where the vines were attached **from the side, what is there to say?**

לְעוֹלָם אִידִי וְאִידִי מִן הַצַּד, הָתָם – בְּעֶשֶׂר, הָכָא – בְּיוֹתֵר מֵעֶשֶׂר.

The Gemara answers: **Actually,** both **this and that** are cases where the vines were attached to the side posts **from the side. There,** where Rabbi Yoḥanan ruled that the braid is an effective partition with regard to diverse kinds, it is referring to a case **where** the poles were only **ten** cubits apart; **here,** where he rules that it is ineffective even with regard to diverse kinds, it is referring to a case **where** the poles were **more than ten** cubits apart.

וּמְנָא תֵּימְרָא דְּשָׁנֵי לַן בֵּין עֶשֶׂר לְיוֹתֵר מֵעֶשֶׂר – דְּאָמַר לֵיהּ רַבִּי יוֹחָנָן לְרֵישׁ לָקִישׁ: לֹא כָּךְ הָיָה הַמַּעֲשֶׂה שֶׁהָלַךְ רַבִּי יְהוֹשֻׁעַ אֵצֶל רַבִּי יוֹחָנָן בֶּן נוּרִי לִלְמוֹד תּוֹרָה, אַף עַל פִּי שֶׁבָּקִי בְּהִלְכוֹת כִּלְאַיִם, וּמְצָאוֹ שֶׁיּוֹשֵׁב בֵּין הָאִילָנוֹת וּמָתַח זְמוֹרָה מֵאִילָן לְאִילָן. וְאָמַר לוֹ: רַבִּי, אִי גְּפָנִים כָּאן מַהוּ לִזְרוֹעַ כָּאן? אָמַר לוֹ: בְּעֶשֶׂר – מוּתָּר, בְּיוֹתֵר מֵעֶשֶׂר – אָסוּר.

And from where do you say that we distinguish between an opening of **ten** cubits **and** an opening of **more than ten** cubits? **As Rabbi Yoḥanan said to Reish Lakish: That is not** the way that **the incident** transpired. **As Rabbi Yehoshua went to Rabbi Yoḥanan ben Nuri to study Torah, even though** Rabbi Yehoshua himself was an **expert**[N] **in the *halakhot* of diverse kinds and found him sitting among the trees, and** Rabbi Yehoshua **stretched a vine from one tree to another and said to him: Rabbi, if there are grapevines here,** in the enclosed area, **what** is the *halakha* with regard to **sowing** diverse kinds of seeds **here,** on the other side of the partition? Rabbi Yoḥanan ben Nuri **said to him:** In a case **where** the trees are only **ten** cubits apart, it is **permitted;** however, **where** they are **more than ten** cubits apart, it is **prohibited.**

בְּמַאי עָסְקִינַן? אִילֵימָא עַל גַּבָּן – יוֹתֵר מֵעֶשֶׂר אָסוּר – וְהָתַנְיָא: הָיוּ שָׁם קָנִין הַדּוּקְרָנִין, וְעָשָׂה לָהֶן פֵּיאָה מִלְמַעְלָה, אֲפִילּוּ בְּיוֹתֵר מֵעֶשֶׂר – מוּתָּר!

The Gemara clarifies the case: **With what are we dealing** here? **If you say** that the vines were placed **on top of** the trees, when they are **more than ten** cubits apart **is it prohibited? But wasn't it taught** in a *baraita* with regard to diverse kinds: **If there were forked reeds there and he plaited a braid** of vines **above them,** then **even** if the reeds were set **more than ten** cubits apart, **it is permitted?** With regard to diverse kinds, the form of a doorway when properly constructed is certainly effective.

אֶלָּא לָאו מִן הַצַּד, וְקָאָמַר לֵיהּ: בְּעֶשֶׂר – מוּתָּר, יוֹתֵר מֵעֶשֶׂר – אָסוּר. שְׁמַע מִינַּהּ.

Rather, is it **not** referring to a case where he attached the vines to the trees **from the side, and he is saying to him: In** a case where the trees are only **ten** cubits apart, it is **permitted;** however, **in** a case where the trees are **more than ten** cubits apart, **it is prohibited?** The Gemara concludes: Indeed, **learn from it** that there is a distinction between poles that are ten cubits apart and poles that are more than ten cubits apart, and that this distinction resolves the contradiction between the two statements of Rabbi Yoḥanan.

גּוּפָא, אָמַר רַב חִסְדָּא: צוּרַת הַפֶּתַח שֶׁעֲשָׂאָהּ מִן הַצַּד – לֹא עָשָׂה וְלֹא כְּלוּם.

The Gemara now examines **the matter itself** with regard to Rav Ḥisda's statement cited above. **Rav Ḥisda said:** If **one prepared** an opening in **the form of a doorway from the side,**[B] placing the horizontal cross beam to the sides, rather than on top, of the vertical posts, **he has not done anything.**

וְאָמַר רַב חִסְדָּא: צוּרַת הַפֶּתַח שֶׁאָמְרוּ – צְרִיכָה שֶׁתְּהֵא בְּרִיאָה כְּדֵי לְהַעֲמִיד בָּהּ דֶּלֶת, וַאֲפִילּוּ דֶּלֶת שֶׁל קַשִּׁין.

And Rav Ḥisda also **said: The** opening in the **form of a doorway of which** the Sages **spoke must be strong enough to mount a door in it, and even** if it is merely a flimsy **door of straw.**[H]

אָמַר רֵישׁ לָקִישׁ מִשּׁוּם רַבִּי יַנַּאי: צוּרַת הַפֶּתַח צְרִיכָה הֶיכֵּר צִיר. מַאי "הֶיכֵּר צִיר"? אָמַר רַב אָוְיָא: אַבְקָתָא.

Reish Lakish said in the name of Rabbi Yannai: The opening in the **form of a doorway requires a mark** in the doorpost **for hinges.** The Gemara asks: **What is an mark for hinges? Rav Avya said: Loops** [*avkata*][N] into which the hinge is inserted, so that it will be possible to mount a door in the doorway.

אַשְׁכַּחִינְהוּ רַב אַחָא בְּרֵיהּ דְּרַב אָוְיָא לְתַלְמִידֵי דְּרַב אַשִׁי, אֲמַר לְהוּ: אֲמַר מָר מִידֵּי בְּצוּרַת הַפֶּתַח? אָמְרוּ לֵיהּ: לֹא אָמַר וְלֹא כְּלוּם.

The Gemara relates that **Rav Aḥa, the son of Rav Avya,** once **found the students of Rav Ashi and said to them: Did the Master,** Rav Ashi, **say anything with regard to** an opening in **the form of a doorway? They said to him: He said nothing,**[N] implying that an indication for hinges is unnecessary.

תָּנָא: צוּרַת הַפֶּתַח שֶׁאָמְרוּ – קָנֶה מִכָּאן וְקָנֶה מִכָּאן וְקָנֶה עַל גַּבֵּיהֶן. צְרִיכִין לִיגַּע אוֹ אֵין צְרִיכִין לִיגַּע? רַב נַחְמָן אָמַר: אֵין צְרִיכִין לִיגַּע. וְרַב שֵׁשֶׁת אָמַר: צְרִיכִין לִיגַּע.

A Sage **taught** a *baraita*: **The form of a doorway of which they spoke** consists of **a reed from here,** on one side, **and a reed from there,** on the opposite side, **and a reed on top of them.** The Gemara asks: **Need** the lower reeds reach high enough **to touch** the upper reed, **or do they not need to touch it?**[H] **Rav Naḥman said: They do not need to touch it; and Rav Sheshet said: They need to touch it.**

NOTES

Even though Rabbi Yehoshua was an expert – אַף עַל פִּי שֶׁבָּקִי: Although Rabbi Yehoshua was an expert in the *halakhot* of forbidden mixtures of diverse kinds [*kilayim*], nevertheless, he went to study with Rabbi Yoḥanan ben Nuri, because the latter had an accepted tradition with regard to these *halakhot* (*Me'iri*).

Loops [*avkata*] – אַבְקָתָא: Some commentaries explain that the term *avkata* is referring to holes in the threshold and in the lintel into which the hinge of the door is inserted (Rashi and others). Other authorities explain that *avkata* is referring to metal hardware that is attached to the doorpost, into which the hinge of the door is placed (*ge'onim*).

He said nothing – לֹא אָמַר וְלֹא כְּלוּם: The Rosh explains that he asked them whether they had heard anything new with regard to this issue in Rav Ashi's study hall. Since they had nothing new to report, it was Rav Aḥa who said to them that a Sage taught the following *baraita*: The opening in the form of a doorway of which they spoke, etc.

BACKGROUND

Opening in the form of a doorway from the side – צוּרַת הַפֶּתַח מִן הַצַּד: When the horizontal cross beam does not rest on the vertical posts of a doorframe, it does not permit carrying on Shabbat.

Form of a doorway with cross beam attached to sides of vertical posts

HALAKHA

The strength of the form of a doorway – חוֹזֶק צוּרַת הַפֶּתַח: A halakhic form of a doorway must be sturdy enough to support an actual door, even if it is made only out of straw. This requirement applies only to the doorposts (Jerusalem Talmud; *Shulḥan Arukh, Oraḥ Ḥayyim* 362:11).

The lintel of an opening in the form of a doorframe – מַשְׁקוֹף צוּרַת הַפֶּתַח: The horizontal cross beam that serves as the lintel of the doorframe need not touch the vertical posts. Even if it is several cubits higher than them, it is permitted, as long as the cross beam is positioned directly above them. The *halakha* is in accordance with the opinion of Rabbi Naḥman, since the *baraita* concerning an arched gateway supports his opinion (*Shulḥan Arukh, Oraḥ Ḥayyim* 362:11).

NOTES

Rav Gadda and the members of the Exilarch's court – רַב גַּדָּא וְאִינְשֵׁי רֹאשׁ הַגּוֹלָה: Apparently, the members of the Exilarch's court thought at first that Rav Gadda had acted on his own initiative, and they believed that he had no authority to act contrary to the opinion of Rabbi Naḥman, who was one of the leading authorities of the generation. However, when they realized that he was carrying out the orders of Rav Sheshet, they released him from jail (Rav Ya'akov Emden).

BACKGROUND

Arched gateway – שַׁעַר הֶעָשׂוּי כְּכִיפָּה:

Arched gateway that can be hollowed out along the dotted line to complete the necessary size of the opening

Arched gateway that cannot be hollowed out to complete the necessary size of the opening

אֲזַל רַב נַחְמָן וַעֲבַד עוּבְדָּא בֵּי רֵישׁ גָּלוּתָא כִּשְׁמַעְתֵּיהּ, אָמַר לֵיהּ רַב שֵׁשֶׁת לְשַׁמָּעֵיהּ רַב גַּדָּא: זִיל, שְׁלוֹף שְׁדֵינְהוּ. אֲזַל, שָׁלַף שַׁדִּינְהוּ. אַשְׁכַּחוּהוּ דְּבֵי רֵישׁ גָּלוּתָא, חֲבָשׁוּהוּ. אֲזַל רַב שֵׁשֶׁת קָם אַבָּבָא, אָמַר לֵיהּ: גַּדָּא, פּוּק תָּא! נְפַק וַאֲתָא.

The Gemara relates that **Rav Naḥman went** ahead **and performed an action in the house of the Exilarch in accordance with** his own **opinion.** He constructed an opening in the form of a doorway such that the upper reed was not in contact with the lower reeds. **Rav Sheshet said to his attendant, Rav Gadda: Go, remove** those reeds and **throw them** away. The attendant **went, removed** the reeds, and **threw them** away. Members **of the Exilarch's court found him**[N] and **imprisoned him** for destroying the form of a doorway that permitted them to carry. **Rav Sheshet went** and **stood at the door** of the prison, and **called** out **to him: Gadda, go out** and **come** to me. The Exilarch's men released him, and **he went out and came** to Rav Sheshet.

אַשְׁכְּחֵיהּ רַב שֵׁשֶׁת לְרַבָּה בַּר שְׁמוּאֵל, אֲמַר לֵיהּ: תָּנֵי מָר מִידֵּי בְּצוּרַת הַפֶּתַח? אָמַר לֵיהּ: אִין, תָּנֵינָא; כִּיפָּה, רַבִּי מֵאִיר מְחַיֵּיב בִּמְזוּזָה וַחֲכָמִים פּוֹטְרִין. וְשָׁוִין שֶׁאִם יֵשׁ בְּרַגְלֶיהָ עֲשָׂרָה שֶׁהִיא חַיֶּיבֶת.

The Gemara relates that **Rav Sheshet** once **found Rabba bar Shmuel** and **said to him: Did the Master teach anything with regard to** the *halakhot* of **the form of a doorway? He said to him: Yes, we learned** in a *baraita*: With regard to **an arched gateway, Rabbi Meir deems** the owner **obligated to** affix a *mezuza*, **and the Rabbis deem** him **exempt. However, they** both **agree that if its supports,** the vertical sides of the gate before it arches, **are ten** handbreadths high, **that** the gate **requires** a *mezuza*.

אָמַר אַבַּיֵי: הַכֹּל מוֹדִים אִם גְּבוֹהָה עֲשָׂרָה וְאֵין בְּרַגְלֶיהָ שְׁלֹשָׁה, אִי נַמִּי: יֵשׁ בְּרַגְלֶיהָ שְׁלֹשָׁה וְאֵין גְּבוֹהָה עֲשָׂרָה – וְלֹא כְלוּם.

In order to explain the dispute, **Abaye said: Everyone agrees that if** the entire arch **is ten** handbreadths **high, but its supports are less than three** handbreadths high, or, **alternatively,** if **its supports are three** handbreadths high but the entire arch **is less than ten** handbreadths **high,** the arch requires **no** *mezuza* **at all.** Both of these gateways lack the requisite parameters of the form of a doorway to require a *mezuza*.

כִּי פְּלִיגִי – בְּיֵשׁ בְּרַגְלֶיהָ שְׁלֹשָׁה וּגְבוֹהָה עֲשָׂרָה וְאֵין רָחְבָּהּ אַרְבָּעָה, וְיֵשׁ בָּהּ לָחוֹק לְהַשְׁלִימָהּ לְאַרְבָּעָה.

Where they disagree is in a case where **the supports are three** handbreadths high **and** the entire arch is **ten** handbreadths **high,** and at the height of ten handbreadths the arch **is less than four** handbreadths **wide; however, there is** room **to carve out** the area **to complete it to four** handbreadths, so that the opening of the arch measures four handbreadths wide and ten handbreadths high.[B]

רַבִּי מֵאִיר סָבַר: חוֹקְקִין לְהַשְׁלִים, וְרַבָּנַן סָבְרִי: אֵין חוֹקְקִין לְהַשְׁלִים.

Abaye explains the dispute: **Rabbi Meir holds** that **one carves** out the area **to complete** the four handbreadths, i.e., the arch is considered as though it has already been carved out, and the opening has the necessary dimensions. **And the Rabbis hold** that **one does not carve out** the arch **to complete** the four handbreadths. Since the opening is not actually four handbreadths wide at a height of ten handbreadths, no *mezuza* need be affixed. Rabba bar Shmuel indicates that everyone agrees that the lintel need not touch the doorposts of the entrance; if the arch's opening were four handbreadths wide at a height of ten handbreadths, it would require a *mezuza* even though the ceiling is separated by the arch and does not touch the doorposts directly. So too, with regard to the form of a doorway, the upper reed need not touch the lower reeds, contrary to the opinion of Rav Sheshet.

אֲמַר לֵיהּ: אִי מַשְׁכַּחַתְּ לְהוּ – לָא תֵּימָא לְהוּ לְבֵי רֵישׁ גָּלוּתָא וְלָא מִידֵּי מֵהָא מַתְנִיתָא דְּכִיפָּה.

Rav Sheshet **said to** Rabba bar Shmuel: **If you find them, do not say to** the members of **the Exilarch's household anything with regard to this *baraita*** **of an arched gateway,** as it is proof against my opinion.

מתני׳ הֶכְשֵׁר מָבוֹי; בֵּית שַׁמַּאי אוֹמְרִים: לֶחִי וְקוֹרָה, וּבֵית הִלֵּל אוֹמְרִים: אוֹ לֶחִי אוֹ קוֹרָה. רַבִּי אֱלִיעֶזֶר אוֹמֵר: לְחָיַיִן.

MISHNA There is a basic dispute with regard to the method of **rendering an alleyway fit** for one to carry within it on Shabbat. **Beit Shammai say:** Both a **side post and a** cross **beam** are required. **Beit Hillel say: Either a side post or a** cross **beam. Rabbi Eliezer says:** Two **side posts** are required, one on each side of the alleyway.

מִשּׁוּם רַבִּי יִשְׁמָעֵאל אָמַר תַּלְמִיד אֶחָד לִפְנֵי רַבִּי עֲקִיבָא: לֹא נֶחְלְקוּ בֵּית שַׁמַּאי וּבֵית הִלֵּל עַל מָבוֹי שֶׁהוּא פָּחוֹת מֵאַרְבַּע אַמּוֹת שֶׁהוּא נִיתָּר אוֹ בַּלֶּחִי אוֹ בַּקּוֹרָה, עַל מַה נֶּחְלְקוּ – עַל רָחָב מֵאַרְבַּע אַמּוֹת וְעַד עֶשֶׂר, שֶׁבֵּית שַׁמַּאי אוֹמְרִים לֶחִי וְקוֹרָה, וּבֵית הִלֵּל אוֹמְרִים: אוֹ לֶחִי אוֹ קוֹרָה. אָמַר רַבִּי עֲקִיבָא: עַל זֶה וְעַל זֶה נֶחְלְקוּ.

In the name of Rabbi Yishmael, one student said before Rabbi Akiva: Beit Shammai and Beit Hillel did not disagree about an alleyway that is less than four cubits wide, as they both agree **that** carrying **is rendered permitted by either a side post or a cross beam. With regard to what did they disagree? It is with regard to** an alleyway that is **wider than four cubits, and up to ten** cubits wide; **as Beit Shammai say:** It requires both **a side post and a** cross **beam. And Beit Hillel say:** It requires **either a side post or a** cross **beam. Rabbi Akiva said** to the disciple: It is not so, as **they disagree** both **about this** case, i.e., an alleyway that is less than four cubits wide, **and about that** case, i.e., an alleyway that is between four and ten cubits wide.

גמ׳ כְּמַאן? דְּלָא כַּחֲנַנְיָה וְלָא כְּתַנָּא קַמָּא!

GEMARA Before clarifying the various opinions in the mishna, the Gemara seeks to determine: **In accordance with whose** opinion was this mishna taught? Apparently, it is **neither in accordance with** the opinion of **Ḥananya, nor in accordance with** the unattributed opinion of **the first *tanna*** of the *baraita*, who disagree about an alleyway that is open to a public domain on two opposite sides. The dispute is whether the form of a doorway on one end and a side post and a cross beam on the other end suffice to render it permitted for one to carry within it, or whether actual doors are required, at least on one end. However, they both agree that a side post and a cross beam alone are not effective. Since at this point the Gemara assumes that the dispute in the mishna between Beit Shammai and Beit Hillel applies to all alleyways, whether closed on one side or open on two opposite sides to the public domain, these opinions reflect an entirely different position.

אָמַר רַב יְהוּדָה, הָכִי קָאָמַר: ״הֶכְשֵׁר מָבוֹי סָתוּם כֵּיצַד? בֵּית שַׁמַּאי אוֹמְרִים: לֶחִי וְקוֹרָה, וּבֵית הִלֵּל אוֹמְרִים: אוֹ לֶחִי אוֹ קוֹרָה״.

Rav Yehuda said that **this is what** the mishna **is saying: How is a closed alleyway rendered fit** for one to carry within it on Shabbat? **Beit Shammai say:** It requires both **a side post and a** cross **beam. And Beit Hillel say: Either a side post or a** cross **beam.**

״בֵּית שַׁמַּאי אוֹמְרִים: לֶחִי וְקוֹרָה״, לְמֵימְרָא דְּקָא סָבְרִי בֵּית שַׁמַּאי אַרְבַּע מְחִיצוֹת דְּאוֹרַיְיתָא?

The Gemara discusses the basis of each opinion. **Beit Shammai say:** It requires both **a side post and a** cross **beam. Is that to say** that **Beit Shammai hold** that in order for an area to be considered a private domain, **four partitions are** required **by Torah law?** Since a side post with a cross beam qualifies as a partition, the fact that they do not permit carrying within an alleyway without a side post indicates that they maintain that a private domain requires four partitions.

לֹא, לִזְרוֹק – מִשָּׁלֹשׁ הוּא דְּמִיחַיַּיב, לְטַלְטֵל – עַד דְּאִיכָּא אַרְבַּע.

The Gemara rejects this argument: **No,** there is no proof, as one cannot conclude the parameters for a private domain based on the number of walls required to permit carrying. As with regard to the Torah prohibition **to throw** an object into a private domain from the public domain, **once** an enclosed area has **three** partitions, **one is liable** by Torah law. However, to permit one **to carry** an object within a private domain, the Rabbis decreed that it is not permitted **until there are** partitions on all **four** sides.

״בֵּית הִלֵּל אוֹמְרִים אוֹ לֶחִי אוֹ קוֹרָה״, לֵימָא קָא סָבְרִי בֵּית הִלֵּל שָׁלֹשׁ מְחִיצוֹת דְּאוֹרַיְיתָא?

The Gemara attempts to draw an inference from that which **Beit Hillel say: Either a side post or a** cross **beam** is required. **Is that to say** that **Beit Hillel hold that** at least **three partitions** are required **by Torah law,** and that an area with fewer is not considered a private domain?

לֹא, לִזְרוֹק – מִשְּׁתַּיִם הוּא דְּמִיחַיַּיב, לְטַלְטֵל – עַד דְּאִיכָּא שָׁלֹשׁ.

The Gemara rejects this argument as well: **No** proof can be cited from here. With regard to the Torah prohibition **to throw** an object into a private domain from the public domain, **once** an enclosed area has merely **two** partitions, **one is liable** by Torah law. However, to permit one **to carry** an object within a private domain, the Rabbis decreed that it is not permitted **until there are** partitions on **three** sides. A cross beam and a side post do not function as partitions but merely as conspicuous markers, so that one does not mistakenly carry outside the alleyway.

״רַבִּי אֱלִיעֶזֶר אוֹמֵר: לְחָיַיִן״. אִיבַּעְיָא לְהוּ: רַבִּי אֱלִיעֶזֶר לְחָיַיִן וְקוֹרָה קָאָמַר, אוֹ דִּילְמָא לְחָיַיִן בְּלֹא קוֹרָה קָאָמַר?

We learned in the mishna that **Rabbi Eliezer says:** Two **side posts** are required. A **dilemma was raised** before the Sages: Did **Rabbi Eliezer** intend to **say** that two **side posts and a** cross **beam** are required, adding a stringency to Beit Shammai's opinion, that in addition to the cross beam not one, but two side posts are required? **Or perhaps he** intended to **say** that two **side posts without a** cross **beam** are required.

תָּא שְׁמַע: מַעֲשֶׂה בְּרַבִּי אֱלִיעֶזֶר שֶׁהָלַךְ אֵצֶל רַבִּי יוֹסֵי בֶּן פְּרִידָא תַּלְמִידוֹ

Come and hear a resolution to this dilemma from that which was related in the *Tosefta*. There was **an incident involving Rabbi Eliezer, who went to Rabbi Yosei ben Perida, his disciple,**

Perek **I**
Daf **12** Amud **a**

לְאוֹבְלִין וּמְצָאוֹ שֶׁיּוֹשֵׁב בְּמָבוֹי שֶׁאֵין לוֹ אֶלָּא לֶחִי אֶחָד. אָמַר לוֹ: בְּנִי, עֲשֵׂה לֶחִי אַחֵר. אָמַר לוֹ: וְכִי לְסוֹתְמוֹ אֲנִי צָרִיךְ?! אָמַר לוֹ: יִסָּתֵם, וּמַה בְּכָךְ.

at the town of **Ovelin, and found him dwelling in an alleyway that had only one side post.**[N] **He said to him: My son, set up another side post.** Rabbi Yosei **said to him: Am I required to close it up?**[N] Rabbi Eliezer **said to him: Let it be closed up; what does it matter?**

אָמַר רַבָּן שִׁמְעוֹן בֶּן גַּמְלִיאֵל: לֹא נֶחְלְקוּ בֵּית שַׁמַּאי וּבֵית הִלֵּל עַל מָבוֹי שֶׁהוּא פָּחוֹת מֵאַרְבַּע אַמּוֹת שֶׁאֵינוֹ צָרִיךְ כְּלוּם, עַל מַה נֶּחְלְקוּ – עַל רָחָב מֵאַרְבַּע אַמּוֹת וְעַד עֶשֶׂר; שֶׁבֵּית שַׁמַּאי אוֹמְרִים: לֶחִי וְקוֹרָה, וּבֵית הִלֵּל אוֹמְרִים: אוֹ לֶחִי אוֹ קוֹרָה.

We learned in that same *Tosefta*: **Rabban Shimon ben Gamliel said: Beit Shammai and Beit Hillel did not disagree about an alleyway** whose width **is less than four cubits,** as they both agree **that** this alleyway **does not require anything** to render it permitted for one to carry within it.[H] **About what did they disagree? About** an alleyway that is **wider than four cubits, and up to ten** cubits; **as Beit Shammai say:** It is permitted to carry within it only if there is both **a side post and a cross beam, and Beit Hillel say:** It requires **either a side post or a cross beam.**

קָתָנֵי מִיהַת: "וְכִי לְסוֹתְמוֹ אֲנִי צָרִיךְ", אִי אָמְרַתְּ בִּשְׁלָמָא לְחָיַיִן וְקוֹרָה – מִשּׁוּם הָכִי אָמַר: "וְכִי לְסוֹתְמוֹ אֲנִי צָרִיךְ", אֶלָּא אִי אָמְרַתְּ לְחָיַיִן בְּלֹא קוֹרָה – מַאי "לְסוֹתְמוֹ"?

The Gemara explains the proof from this *Tosefta*. **In any case, it teaches:** Rabbi Yosei ben Perida said to Rabbi Eliezer: **Am I required to seal it? Granted, if you say** that Rabbi Eliezer requires two **side posts and a cross beam,**[B] **for that** reason the disciple **said: Am I required to seal it? However, if you say** that he requires **side posts without a cross beam, what** is the meaning **of to seal it?** The entrance to the alleyway remains open from above.

הָכִי קָאָמַר: וְכִי לְסוֹתְמוֹ בִּלְחָיַיִן אֲנִי צָרִיךְ.

The Gemara rejects this argument: No absolute proof can be cited from here, as perhaps **this is what he is saying: Am I required to seal it with side posts?**

אָמַר מָר, אָמַר רַבָּן שִׁמְעוֹן בֶּן גַּמְלִיאֵל: לֹא נֶחְלְקוּ בֵּית שַׁמַּאי וּבֵית הִלֵּל עַל מָבוֹי שֶׁפָּחוֹת מֵאַרְבַּע אַמּוֹת שֶׁאֵינוֹ צָרִיךְ כְּלוּם. וְהָא אֲנַן תְּנַן, מִשּׁוּם רַבִּי יִשְׁמָעֵאל אָמַר תַּלְמִיד אֶחָד לִפְנֵי רַבִּי עֲקִיבָא: לֹא נֶחְלְקוּ בֵּית שַׁמַּאי וּבֵית הִלֵּל עַל מָבוֹי שֶׁהוּא פָּחוֹת מֵאַרְבַּע אַמּוֹת, שֶׁהוּא נִיתָּר אוֹ בְּלֶחִי אוֹ בְקוֹרָה!

The Master said in the *Tosefta*: **Rabban Shimon ben Gamliel said** that **Beit Shammai and Beit Hillel do not disagree about an alleyway** whose width **is less than four cubits,** as they both agree **that it does not require anything** to render it permitted to carry within it. **But didn't we learn** in the mishna: **A certain disciple said before Rabbi Akiva in the name of Rabbi Yishmael: Beit Shammai and Beit Hillel did not disagree about an alleyway** whose width **is less than four cubits,** as they both agree **that** carrying in an alleyway of that sort **is permitted by either a side post or a cross beam.** How could Rabban Shimon ben Gamliel have said that according to Beit Shammai and Beit Hillel even that minimal action is unnecessary?

אָמַר רַב אַשִׁי, הָכִי קָאָמַר: אֵינוֹ צָרִיךְ לֶחִי וְקוֹרָה כְּבֵית שַׁמַּאי, וְלֹא לְחָיַיִן כְּרַבִּי אֱלִיעֶזֶר, אֶלָּא אוֹ לֶחִי אוֹ קוֹרָה כְּבֵית הִלֵּל.

Rav Ashi said: This is what Rabban Shimon ben Gamliel **is saying. It neither requires** both **a side post and a** cross **beam, in accordance with** the opinion of **Beit Shammai, nor** does it require two **side posts, in accordance with** the opinion of **Rabbi Eliezer; rather,** it requires **either a side post or a** cross **beam, in accordance with** the statement of **Beit Hillel** with regard to a large alleyway. When it said that Rabban Shimon ben Gamliel does not require anything, it meant anything more than that required by Beit Hillel.

NOTES

Rabbi Eliezer's disciple – תַּלְמִידוֹ שֶׁל רַבִּי אֱלִיעֶזֶר: Rashba asks: According to which opinion in the mishna did that disciple act: The opinion of Beit Shammai or of Beit Hillel? The Rashba explains that had the student acted in accordance with the opinion of Beit Hillel, he would have said so to his teacher. Rather, he acted according to the opinion of Beit Shammai, with whom Rabbi Eliezer concurs. However, the disciple understood that Rabbi Eliezer's opinion states that if a cross beam is present, two side posts are no longer required. Consequently, his teacher informed him that a cross beam has no effect whatsoever; everything depends on the side posts.

Am I required to close it up – וְכִי לְסוֹתְמוֹ אֲנִי צָרִיךְ: In the Jerusalem Talmud, this dialogue serves as proof that Rabbi Eliezer rules that a side post must be at least three handbreadths wide, which is why the addition of another side post considerably narrows the width of the alleyway, giving it the appearance of being sealed. However, this is not the approach of the Babylonian Talmud. The Rashba explains that this is a case of a very narrow alleyway. Therefore, even a side post of minimal width is significant in sealing the entrance. Yet other commentaries explain this question as an indication that if two side posts and a cross beam are required, people would think that carrying in an alleyway is permitted only if there are four complete walls. Rabbi Eliezer, responded that this indeed is the case. An alleyway must be closed on all four sides.

BACKGROUND

Side posts and a cross beam – לְחָיַיִן וְקוֹרָה: The illustration shows an alleyway that has two side posts, one on each side, and a cross beam above, so that the entrance to the alleyway appears closed.

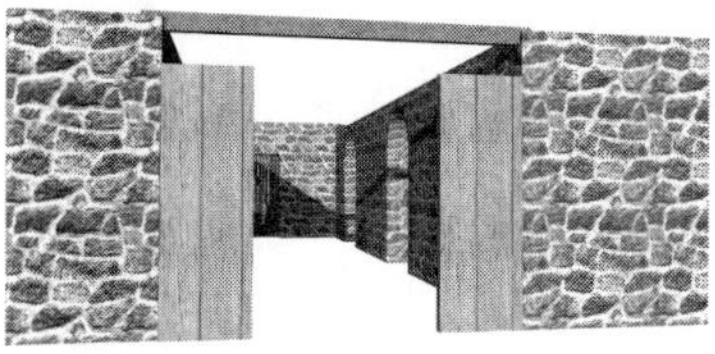

Entrance to an alleyway with side posts and cross beam

HALAKHA

An alleyway whose width is less than four cubits – מָבוֹי פָּחוֹת מֵאַרְבַּע: An alleyway less than three handbreadths wide requires nothing added to permit carrying. Some authorities rule that even if it is less than four handbreadths wide, it does not require any additions to permit carrying within it.

The first opinion is that of the Rambam, who ruled according to the Gemara's second answer explains that Rabbi Aḥlei's statement is the subject of a dispute between the *tanna'im*, and the *halakha* follows Shmuel's statement rather than that of Rav Aḥlei (Vilna Gaon). The second opinion is that of the Rashba and the Rosh, who maintain that an entrance must be at least four handbreadths wide, and that an individual opinion cited is the Gemara is insufficient proof with regard to this issue (*Maggid Mishne*; *Shulḥan Arukh, Oraḥ Ḥayyim* 363:28).

וְכַמָּה? אָמַר רַב אַחְלַי, וְאִיתֵימָא רַב יְחִיאֵל: עַד אַרְבָּעָה.

The Gemara asks: **And how** narrow must an alleyway be so that it would not require even a side post, according to all opinions? **Rav Aḥlei said, and some say** it was **Rav Yeḥiel** who said: **Up to** a width of **four** handbreadths, the alleyway requires nothing in order to render it permitted for one to carry within it.

אָמַר רַב שֵׁשֶׁת, אָמַר רַב יִרְמְיָה בַּר אַבָּא, אָמַר רַב: מוֹדִים חֲכָמִים לְרַבִּי אֱלִיעֶזֶר בְּפַסֵּי חָצֵר. וְרַב נַחְמָן אָמַר: הֲלָכָה כְּרַבִּי אֱלִיעֶזֶר בְּפַסֵּי חָצֵר.

Rav Sheshet said that **Rav Yirmeya bar Abba said** that **Rav said: The Rabbis concede to Rabbi Eliezer with regard to the** upright **boards of a courtyard.**[H] That is to say, the Rabbis disagree with Rabbi Eliezer only about the number of side posts needed to permit carrying within an alleyway. However, they agree that if a courtyard was breached into the public domain, it can be considered closed only if upright boards of wall, similar to side posts, remain on both sides of the breach. **But Rav Naḥman said: The *halakha* is in accordance with** the opinion of **Rabbi Eliezer with regard to the** upright **boards of** wall that are required in **a courtyard.**[N]

אָמַר רַב נַחְמָן בַּר יִצְחָק: מַאן מוֹדִים – רַבִּי. הֲלָכָה מִכְּלָל דִּפְלִיגִי, [מַאן פָּלֵיג עֲלֵיהּ –] רַבָּנַן. דְּתַנְיָא: חָצֵר נִיתֶּרֶת בְּפַס אֶחָד. רַבִּי אוֹמֵר: בִּשְׁנֵי פַסִּין.

Rav Naḥman bar Yitzḥak said: Who are the Rabbis to whom Rav referred when he stated that they **concede** to Rabbi Eliezer? He was referring to **Rabbi** Yehuda HaNasi. Furthermore, as Rav Naḥman said that the ***halakha*** is in accordance with the opinion of Rabbi Eliezer, one can learn **by inference that** the Sages **dispute** this issue as well. **Who** are the ones who **disagree with** Rabbi Yehuda HaNasi? It is **the Rabbis, as it was taught** in a *baraita*: In **a courtyard** that was breached into the public domain, with the width of the breach not exceeding ten cubits, it **is permitted** to carry if **one** upright **board** remains on one side of the breach. **Rabbi** Yehuda HaNasi **says:** It is permitted only if there remain **two** upright **boards,** one on each side of the breach.

אָמַר רַבִּי אַסִי, אָמַר רַבִּי יוֹחָנָן: חָצֵר צְרִיכָה שְׁנֵי פַסִּין. אֲמַר לֵיהּ רַבִּי זֵירָא לְרַבִּי אַסִי: מִי אָמַר רַבִּי יוֹחָנָן הָכִי? וְהָא אַתְּ הוּא דְּאָמְרַתְּ מִשְּׁמֵיהּ דְּרַבִּי יוֹחָנָן: פַּסֵּי חָצֵר צְרִיכִין שֶׁיְּהֵא בָּהֶן אַרְבָּעָה! וְכִי תֵּימָא אַרְבָּעָה מִכָּאן וְאַרְבָּעָה מִכָּאן –

Rabbi Asi said that **Rabbi Yoḥanan said: A courtyard** that was breached **requires two** upright **boards** of wall on either side of the breach, in accordance with the opinion of Rabbi Yehuda HaNasi. **Rabbi Zeira said to Rabbi Asi: Did Rabbi Yoḥanan** really **say that? But weren't you the one who said in the name of Rabbi Yoḥanan: The** upright **boards in a courtyard must be four** handbreadths wide? This indicates that only one board is necessary. **And if you say** that Rabbi Yoḥanan requires one upright **four** handbreadths board **from here,** one side of the breach, **and** one upright **four** handbreadths board **from there,** the other side of the breach, this is difficult.

וְהָתָנֵי רַב אַדָּא בַּר אֲבִימִי קַמֵּיהּ דְּרַבִּי חֲנִינָא, וְאָמְרִי לַהּ קַמֵּיהּ דְּרַבִּי חֲנִינָא בַּר פַּפִּי: קְטַנָּה – בְּעֶשֶׂר, וּגְדוֹלָה – בְּאַחַת עֶשְׂרֵה!

But didn't Rav Adda bar Avimi teach the following *baraita* **before Rabbi Ḥanina, and some say** it was **before Rabbi Ḥanina bar Pappi,** with regard to the *halakha* governing a small courtyard that was breached along its entire length into a large courtyard. The *baraita* teaches that the residents of the large courtyard may use their courtyard even if the **small** courtyard has a width of **ten** cubits, **and the large** one has a width of **eleven** cubits. In this case, the difference between the length of the smaller courtyard and that of the larger courtyard is only one cubit, i.e., six handbreadths. Therefore, there cannot be upright boards of four handbreadths on each side, as together they would amount to more than a cubit.

כִּי סְלֵיק רַבִּי זֵירָא מִיַּמֵּי, פְּרַשָׁהּ: בְּרוּחַ אַחַת – בְּאַרְבָּעָה, מִשְּׁתֵּי רוּחוֹת – מַשֶּׁהוּ לְכָאן וּמַשֶּׁהוּ לְכָאן.

The Gemara resolves this difficulty: **When Rabbi Zeira ascended from** his **sea** travels,[N] **he explained** the contradiction between the statements of Rav Yoḥanan in the following manner: If there is a upright board **in** only **one direction,** it must be **four** handbreadths, however, if there are upright boards **from two directions,** it suffices if there is **any amount here,** on one side, **and any amount there,** on the other side.

וְהָדְתָנֵי אַדָּא בַּר אֲבִימִי – רַבִּי הִיא, וְסָבַר לַהּ כְּרַבִּי יוֹסֵי.

And that which Adda bar Avimi taught with regard to the difference in size between the two courtyards is not universally accepted, as according to Rabbi Zeira it is sufficient if one courtyard is four handbreadths larger than the other. Rather, **it is** in accordance with the view of **Rabbi** Yehuda HaNasi, who requires two upright boards of wall in a breached courtyard. And furthermore, Rabbi Yehuda HaNasi **holds in accordance with** the opinion of **Rabbi Yosei,** who says that a side post must be at least three handbreadths wide. Consequently, the two upright boards together must be at least six handbreadths, which is why the minimum difference between the smaller and the larger courtyards is a cubit.

HALAKHA

The upright boards of a courtyard – פַּסֵּי חָצֵר: If an entire wall of a courtyard was breached and the breach was less than ten cubits wide, the courtyard can be rendered fit for one to carry within it by means of a board four handbreadths wide on one side of the breach, or by means of two boards of minimal width on both sides of the breach. This *halakha* is in accordance with the opinion of Rabbi Zeira, Rav Pappa, and Rav Huna, son of Rav Yehoshua. The same applies if a section of the wall remains. Carrying is permitted in the courtyard if there is a wall four handbreadths wide on one side, or a wall one handbreadth wide on each side. The *Beit Yosef* rules that the walls on either side can be less than one handbreadth wide (Rabbeinu Yehonatan; *Shulḥan Arukh, Oraḥ Ḥayyim* 363:2).

NOTES

The *halakha* is in accordance with Rabbi Eliezer with regard to the upright boards in a courtyard – הֲלָכָה כְּרַבִּי אֱלִיעֶזֶר בְּפַסֵּי חָצֵר: *Tosafot* ask: Why did Rabbi Naḥman state that the *halakha* follows Rabbi Eliezer, rather than stating that the *halakha* follows Rabbi Yehuda HaNasi? Some commentaries explain that Rabbi Yehuda HaNasi agrees with Rabbi Yosei and maintains that a side post must be three handbreadths wide. Therefore, the Gemara emphasizes that the *halakha* follows Rabbi Eliezer, who requires only two upright boards of minimal length (*Tosafot Yeshanim*).

When Rabbi Zeira ascended from his sea travels [*yamei*] – כִּי סְלֵיק רַבִּי זֵירָא מִיַּמֵּי: The Ritva explains the term *yamei* not as the plural of sea [*yam*] but the name of a particular place.

NOTES

I do not know – אֲנָא לָא יָדַעְנָא: The phrase means: I do not know how to resolve the contradiction, but I do know that Rav Yehuda permitted it, in accordance with the lenient opinion (*Me'iri*).

HALAKHA

Suspended partition – מְחִיצָה תְּלוּיָה: A suspended partition is not considered a proper partition. However, it does permit carrying in a courtyard when it is suspended over water that entered the courtyard because the Sages were lenient with regard to water, as stated by Rav (*Shulḥan Arukh, Oraḥ Ḥayyim* 355:3).

אָמַר רַב יוֹסֵף, אָמַר רַב יְהוּדָה, אָמַר שְׁמוּאֵל: חָצֵר נִיתֶּרֶת בְּפַס אֶחָד. אָמַר לֵיהּ אַבַּיֵי לְרַב יוֹסֵף: מִי אָמַר שְׁמוּאֵל הָכִי? וְהָא אֲמַר לֵיהּ שְׁמוּאֵל לְרַב חֲנַנְיָה בַּר שֵׁילָא: אַתְּ לָא תַּעֲבֵיד עוּבְדָא אֶלָּא אוֹ בְּרוֹב דּוֹפֶן אוֹ בִּשְׁנֵי פַּסִּין!

Rav Yosef said that Rav Yehuda said that Shmuel said: A breached **courtyard is permitted** if **one** upright **board** of wall remains on one side of the breach. **Abaye said to Rav Yosef: Did Shmuel** really **say this? But didn't Shmuel say to Rav Ḥananya bar Sheila: You must not perform an action,** i.e., issue a ruling to permit carrying in a breached courtyard, **unless** there remains standing **either the majority of the wall or two** upright **boards** on either side of the breach.

אֲמַר לֵיהּ: וַאֲנָא לָא יָדַעְנָא, דְּעוּבְדָא הֲוָה בְּדוּרָה דְּרַעֲוָתָא, לְשׁוֹן יָם הַנִּכְנָס לְחָצֵר הֲוָה, וַאֲתָא לְקַמֵּיהּ דְּרַב יְהוּדָה וְלָא אַצְרְכֵיהּ אֶלָּא פַּס אֶחָד.

Rav Yosef **said to** Abaye: **I do not know** how to resolve this contradiction.[N] All I know is that **there was an incident in a shepherds' village** with regard to **a narrow inlet of the sea that penetrated a courtyard,** breaching one of its walls in its entirety, **and** the matter **came before Rav Yehuda, and he required only one** upright **board** of wall to remain in order to permit it.

אֲמַר לֵיהּ: לְשׁוֹן יָם קָאָמְרַתְּ – קַל הוּא שֶׁהֵקֵלּוּ חֲכָמִים בְּמַיִם.

Abaye **said to** Rav Yosef: **You speak of a narrow in inlet of the sea,** but an inlet is different and nothing can be derived from that case, for we know that **this is a leniency in which the Sages lessened** the requirements **in** cases involving **water.** In these cases, the Sages did not require properly constructed partitions, but were satisfied with inferior ones.

כְּדִבְעָא מִינֵּיהּ רַבִּי טַבְלָא מֵרַב: מְחִיצָה תְּלוּיָה, מַהוּ שֶׁתַּתִּיר בְּחוּרְבָּה? אֲמַר לֵיהּ: אֵין מְחִיצָה תְּלוּיָה מַתֶּרֶת אֶלָּא בְּמַיִם, קַל הוּא שֶׁהֵקֵלּוּ חֲכָמִים בְּמַיִם,

The Gemara supports the assertion that the Sages were more lax with regard to water from the following **dilemma** that **Rabbi Tavla raised before Rav: Does a suspended partition permit** carrying **in a ruin?** Do we say that the remnants of the walls that are suspended in the air are considered as if they descend to the ground, closing off the area so that it is regarded as a private domain? Rav **said to him: A suspended partition**[H] of this kind **permits** carrying **only** in the case of **water; this is a leniency in which the Sages lessened** the requirements **in** cases involving **water.**

מִכָּל מָקוֹם קַשְׁיָא!

The Gemara continues: **In any case, it is difficult.** The contradiction between the conflicting statements of Shmuel remains unresolved.

כִּי אָתוּ רַב פַּפָּא וְרַב הוּנָא בְּרֵיהּ דְּרַב יְהוֹשֻׁעַ מִבֵּי רַב, פֵּירְשׁוּהָ: מֵרוּחַ אַחַת – בְּאַרְבָּעָה, מִשְּׁתֵּי רוּחוֹת – מַשֶּׁהוּ לְכָאן וּמַשֶּׁהוּ לְכָאן.

The Gemara resolves the difficulty: **When Rav Pappa and Rav Huna, son of Rav Yehoshua, came from the house of their teacher, they explained** the contradiction in the following manner: If there is an upright board **from** only **one direction,** it must be **of four** handbreadths; but if there are upright boards **from two directions,** i.e., both sides of he breach, it suffices if there is **a bit here,** on one side, **and bit here,** on the other side.

אָמַר רַב פַּפָּא: אִי קַשְׁיָא לִי – הָא קַשְׁיָא לִי; דַּאֲמַר לֵיהּ שְׁמוּאֵל לְרַב חֲנַנְיָה בַּר שֵׁילָא: אַתְּ לָא תַּעֲבֵיד עוּבְדָא אֶלָּא אוֹ בְּרוֹב דּוֹפֶן אוֹ בִּשְׁנֵי פַּסִּין.

Rav Pappa said: If this issue **is difficult for me** to understand, **this is my difficulty: For Shmuel said to Rav Ḥananya bar Sheila: You must not perform an action,** i.e., issue a ruling to permit carrying in a breached courtyard, **unless** there remains standing **either most of the wall or two** upright **boards** on either side of the breach.

לָמָּה לִי רוֹב דּוֹפֶן? בְּפַס אַרְבָּעָה סַגִּי! וְכִי תֵּימָא מַאי בְּרוֹב דּוֹפֶן – בְּדוֹפֶן שִׁבְעָה, דְּבְאַרְבָּעָה הֲוָה לֵיהּ רוֹב דּוֹפֶן. לָמָּה לִי אַרְבָּעָה? בִּשְׁלֹשָׁה וּמַשֶּׁהוּ סַגִּי! דְּהָא אָמַר רַב אַחְלַי, וְאִיתֵּימָא רַב יְחִיאֵל: עַד אַרְבָּעָה!

The Gemara asks: **Why do I need most of the wall?** An upright **board of four** handbreadths **should suffice.** The Gemara further explains the difficulty: **And if you say, what is** the meaning of **most of the wall** mentioned here? It is referring to the special case where the **wall** is **seven** handbreadths wide, so that **four** handbreadths **constitutes most of the wall,** this too is difficult. Even if the wall is seven handbreadths wide, **why do I** require an upright board of **four** handbreadths to seal? **Three** handbreadths **and any amount should suffice, as Rav Aḥlei, and some say** it was **Rav Yeḥiel who said:** A narrow alleyway **up to four** handbreadths wide requires nothing at all. Here too, after sealing up slightly more than three handbreadths, the remaining gap that remains is less than four handbreadths, so nothing further should be required.

אִיבָּעֵית אֵימָא: כָּאן – בְּחָצֵר, כָּאן בְּמָבוֹי. וְאִיבָּעֵית אֵימָא: דְּרַב אַחְלַי גּוּפֵיהּ תַּנָּאֵי הִיא.

The Gemara answers: **If you wish, say** that **here,** the statement of Shmuel is referring **to a courtyard,** where even a breach of less than four handbreadths requires action. **There,** the statement of Rav Aḥlei, is referring **to an alleyway. And if you wish, say** that the statement of **Rav Aḥlei is itself** subject to a dispute between the ***tanna'im.***

תָּנוּ רַבָּנַן: לָשׁוֹן יָם הַנִּכְנָס לֶחָצֵר – אֵין מְמַלְּאִין הֵימֶנּוּ בְּשַׁבָּת אֶלָּא אִם כֵּן יֵשׁ לוֹ מְחִיצָה גָּבוֹהַּ עֲשָׂרָה טְפָחִים. בַּמֶּה דְּבָרִים אֲמוּרִים – שֶׁפִּירְצָתוֹ בְּיוֹתֵר מֵעֲשָׂרָה, אֲבָל עֲשָׂרָה – אֵין צָרִיךְ כְּלוּם.

The Sages taught the following *baraita*: With regard to **a narrow inlet of the sea that enters into a courtyard,**[BHN] partially breaching one of its walls, **one may not fill** water **from it on Shabbat.** The inlet is a *karmelit*, from which it is prohibited to carry into a private domain, e.g. a courtyard. This is the *halakha* **unless there is a partition ten handbreadths high** at one side of the wall's breach, which would incorporate the inlet as part of the courtyard. **In what** case **is this statement said? Where the breach** through which the water enters **is more than ten** cubits wide; **but** if it is only **ten** cubits wide, **nothing is required."**

מְמַלֵּא הוּא דְּלָא מְמַלְּאִינַן, הָא טַלְטוּלֵי – מְטַלְטְלִינַן. וְהָא נִפְרְצָה חָצֵר בִּמְלוֹאָהּ לְמָקוֹם הָאָסוּר לָהּ!

The Gemara asks: The *baraita* indicates that **one may not fill** water from the inlet because that would involve carrying from a *karmelit* into a private domain, **but** in the courtyard itself **one may** indeed **carry. But isn't the courtyard breached along its entirety,** i.e., more than ten cubits, **into a place that is prohibited to it?** Since it is prohibited to carry to or from the inlet, it should also be prohibited to carry within the courtyard itself.

NOTES

A narrow inlet of the sea that enters into a courtyard – לָשׁוֹן יָם הַנִּכְנָס לֶחָצֵר: Some commentaries explain that when the *baraita* says that "*it* has a partition," the reference is to the inlet, namely, that inlet itself was separated from the courtyard by ten handbreadths. This could occur, for example, if the sea formed a deep trench in the ground which it filled with water (see Rashba and *Me'iri*).

BACKGROUND

A narrow inlet in a courtyard – לְשׁוֹן הַיָּם בֶּחָצֵר: This illustration depicts a case where the wall of the courtyard remains mostly intact. In that case it is permitted to carry in the courtyard itself, as well as from the inlet to the courtyard.

Wall of a courtyard breached by an inlet

HALAKHA

A narrow inlet of the sea that enters into a courtyard – לָשׁוֹן יָם הַנִּכְנָס לֶחָצֵר: If the sea breaches part of a courtyard wall and penetrates into a courtyard, one is permitted to draw water and carry in the courtyard, so long as the breach is less than ten cubits wide. However, if the wall is fully breached or if the breach is more than ten cubits wide, then one is permitted to draw water in the courtyard only when there are remnants of the wall ten handbreadths high, even though the remnants are covered by water. Still, one may not carry the water from the courtyard into the house unless a proper partition is constructed, in accordance with the *baraita* (*Shulḥan Arukh*, *Oraḥ Ḥayyim* 356:2).

Perek **I**
Daf **12** Amud **b**

הָכָא בְּמַאי עָסְקִינַן דְּאִית לֵיהּ גִּידוּדֵי.

The Gemara answers: **With what are we dealing here** in this *baraita*? It is a case **where** the wall has not been fully breached, but rather **remnants**[N] **of the wall** remain on each side (Rabbeinu Ḥananel; Rif).

אָמַר רַב יְהוּדָה: מָבוֹי שֶׁלֹּא נִשְׁתַּתְּפוּ בּוֹ, הִכְשִׁירוּ בְּלֶחִי – הַזּוֹרֵק לְתוֹכוֹ חַיָּיב, הִכְשִׁירוּ בְּקוֹרָה – הַזּוֹרֵק לְתוֹכוֹ פָּטוּר.

Rav Yehuda said: If several courtyards open onto a common alleyway, the residents of the houses in the courtyards are prohibited to carry in the alleyway, unless the alleyway is rendered fit for one to carry within it by placing a side post or a cross beam at its entrance, and by the inhabitants of each courtyard placing food in a common area for the duration of Shabbat, symbolically converting the entire alleyway into a single household. It is prohibited to carry in **an alleyway** that the residents **did not merge.** Nevertheless, if the alleyway **was rendered fit by** means of **a side post** placed at its entrance, **one who throws** an object **into it** from the public domain **is liable;** the side post functions as a partition, and the alleyway is deemed a full-fledged private domain. If, however, the alleyway **was rendered fit by** means of a cross **beam, one who throws** an object **into it** from the public domain **is exempt;** the cross beam functions only as a conspicuous marker. It is not considered a partition that renders the alleyway a private domain.[H]

NOTES

Remnants – גִּידוּדֵי: Various explanations have been offered with regard to these remnants (see Rashi and *Tosafot*). Some commentaries explain that these are large stones protruding from the water, such that there is no breach of more than ten cubits between the protrusions. Although below, in the water itself, the space between them is greater than ten cubits (Rabbeinu Yehonatan). Other commentaries teach that these remnants served as an additional partition between the water and the courtyard, and the distance from sea floor to the top of the partition was ten handbreadths (see *Tosafot*; Rashba).

HALAKHA

Throwing into an alleyway – זְרִיקָה לְתוֹךְ מָבוֹי: If an alleyway is closed on one side and rendered fit for one to carry within it by a cross beam, one who throws an object from the public domain into the alleyway is exempt, even though it is a private domain in the sense that it is permitted to carry in the alleyway. However, if the alleyway was rendered fit by a side post, the one who throws an object into it is liable. This ruling is in accordance with the explanation of the Gemara that maintains that a side post functions as a partition, while a cross beam functions as a conspicuous marker. According to the Rambam's variant reading, a private domain requires four partitions by Torah law. The Ra'avad, on the other hand, rules that three partitions suffice. Therefore, the Gemara is referring to an open alleyway, as explained by Rashi (*Maggid Mishne*; Rambam *Sefer Zemanim*, *Hilkhot Shabbat* 17:9).

מַתְקִיף לָהּ רַב שֵׁשֶׁת: טַעְמָא דְּלֹא נִשְׁתַּתְּפוּ בּוֹ, הָא נִשְׁתַּתְּפוּ בּוֹ – אֲפִילּוּ הִכְשִׁירוּ בְּקוֹרָה נַמִי חַיָּיב. וְכִי כִּכָּר זוֹ עָשָׂה אוֹתוֹ רְשׁוּת הַיָּחִיד אוֹ רְשׁוּת הָרַבִּים?

Rav Sheshet strongly objects to this due to the following: **The reason** that one is exempt in the latter case is due to the fact the residents of the alleyway **did not merge.** By inference, **if they did** in fact **merge, one would be liable even if** the alleyway **was rendered fit by** way of a cross **beam.** This, however, is difficult. One can ask: **Does this loaf,** through which the residents joined together to form a single household, **render** the alleyway **a private domain or a public domain?**

וְהָתַנְיָא: חֲצֵירוֹת שֶׁל רַבִּים וּמְבוֹאוֹת שֶׁאֵינָן מְפוּלָּשִׁין, בֵּין עֵירְבוּ וּבֵין לֹא עֵירְבוּ – הַזּוֹרֵק לְתוֹכָן חַיָּיב!

But wasn't it taught in a *baraita*: **Courtyards** shared **by many and alleyways that are not open** on two opposite sides, **whether** the residents **established an *eiruv* or did not establish an *eiruv*, one who throws** an object **into them** from the public domain **is liable.** This seems to contrary to Rav Yehuda's statement.

אֶלָּא אִי אִיתְּמַר – הָכִי אִיתְּמַר, אָמַר רַב יְהוּדָה: מָבוֹי שֶׁאֵינוֹ רָאוּי לְשִׁיתּוּף, הִכְשִׁירוּ בְּלֶחִי – הַזּוֹרֵק לְתוֹכוֹ חַיָּיב. הִכְשִׁירוּ בְּקוֹרָה – הַזּוֹרֵק לְתוֹכוֹ פָּטוּר.

Rather, if it was stated, it was stated as follows. Rav Yehuda said: In the case of **an alleyway that is not fit for merging,** i.e., an alleyway that is open on two opposite sides, if the alleyway **was rendered fit** for one to carry within it **by** means of **a side post, one who throws** an object **into it** from the public domain **is liable.** In that case, the side post is considered a third partition, and since the alleyway is closed on three sides it is deemed a private domain. If, however, the alleyway **was rendered fit** for one to carry within in **by** means of a cross **beam, one who throws** an object **into it is exempt.**

אַלְמָא קָסָבַר: לֶחִי מִשּׁוּם מְחִיצָה, וְקוֹרָה מִשּׁוּם הֶיכֵּר. וְכֵן אָמַר רַבָּה: לֶחִי מִשּׁוּם מְחִיצָה וְקוֹרָה מִשּׁוּם הֶיכֵּר. וְרָבָא אָמַר: אֶחָד זֶה וְאֶחָד זֶה מִשּׁוּם הֶיכֵּר.

Apparently, Rav Yehuda **holds** that **a side post** functions **as a partition, whereas a** cross **beam** functions **as a conspicuous marker** but is not considered a partition. **And, so too, Rabba said: A side post** functions **as a partition, whereas** a cross **beam** functions **as a conspicuous marker. But Rava said: Both this,** the side post, **and that,** the cross beam, function **as a conspicuous marker.**

אֵיתִיבֵיהּ רַבִּי יַעֲקֹב בַּר אַבָּא לְרָבָא: הַזּוֹרֵק לְמָבוֹי, יֵשׁ לוֹ לֶחִי – חַיָּיב, אֵין לוֹ לֶחִי – פָּטוּר!

Rabbi Ya'akov bar Abba raised an objection to Rava from the following *baraita*: **One who throws** an object from the public domain **into an alleyway, if** the alleyway **has a side post, he is liable; if it does not have a side post he is exempt.** This shows that a side post is considered a proper partition.

הָכִי קָאָמַר: אֵינוֹ צָרִיךְ אֶלָּא לֶחִי, הַזּוֹרֵק לְתוֹכוֹ – חַיָּיב, לֶחִי וְדָבָר אַחֵר – הַזּוֹרֵק לְתוֹכוֹ פָּטוּר.

Rava replied: **This is what** the *baraita* **is saying:** If the alleyway is closed on one side such that **it requires only a side post** in order to permit carrying within in, **one who throws** an object **into it** from the public domain **is liable** because the alleyway already has three partitions and is therefore a proper private domain according to Torah law. However, if the alleyway requires **a side post and something else** in order to permit carrying within it, **one who throws** an object **into it** from the public domain **is exempt** because the alleyway has only two partitions and is therefore not considered a private domain.

אֵיתִיבֵיהּ: יָתֵר עַל כֵּן אָמַר רַבִּי יְהוּדָה: מִי שֶׁיֵּשׁ לוֹ שְׁנֵי בָתִּים בִּשְׁנֵי צִידֵּי רְשׁוּת הָרַבִּים עוֹשֶׂה לֶחִי מִכָּאן וְלֶחִי מִכָּאן, אוֹ קוֹרָה מִכָּאן וְקוֹרָה מִכָּאן, וְנוֹשֵׂא וְנוֹתֵן בָּאֶמְצַע.

He raised an additional **objection**[N] to Rava from the following *baraita*. **Furthermore, Rabbi Yehuda said:** The *halakha* is as follows with regard to **one who has two houses** opposite each other **on two sides of the public domain,** if he chooses, **he may** create a private domain for himself in the area of the public domain. He may **place a** ten-handbreadth high **side post from here,** perpendicular to the public domain. This creates a symbolic wall which, in the *halakhot* of alleyways, has the legal status of a wall. **And,** he may place **an** additional **post from here,** on the other side, and that has the same legal status as if he closed the public domain on all of its sides. **Or,** he can implement a different solution appropriate for alleyways by placing **a beam** extending **from here,** from one end of one house, to the end of the house opposite it. This creates a symbolic partition across the width of the street. **And,** he may place **a beam** extending **from here,** from the other side of the house. According to Rabbi Yehuda, in that way, one is permitted to **carry** objects **and place** them **in** the area **between** the symbolic partitions, as he would in a private domain.

NOTES

He raised an objection – אֵיתִיבֵיהּ: The commentaries point out that the objection cannot be based solely on the statement of Rabbi Yehuda. If that were case, Rava could have replied that he agrees with the opinion of the anonymous *tanna* of the *baraita*, which is the accepted *halakha*. Rather, the question arises from the wording of his disputants, which indicates that they do not disagree with Rabbi Yehuda's basic approach with regard to a side post and a cross beam. Instead, they indicate that in a place used as a public thoroughfare, the passersby nullify status of a private domain that was established by the partitions (Ritva; see Rashi and *Tosafot*). Rabbi Akiva Eiger points out that Rabbi Yehuda's statement appears to offer proof that even a cross beam is considered a partition. He explains that, at the very least, all seem to agree that a side post functions as a partition, as stated by Rav Yehuda.

אָמְרוּ לוֹ: אֵין מְעָרְבִין רְשׁוּת הָרַבִּים בְּכָךְ!

The Rabbis **said to him: One may not place an *eiruv* in the public domain in that** way. One who seeks to transform a public domain into a private domain must place actual partitions. Apparently, according to Rabbi Yehuda, the side posts function as partitions in the public domain, creating a private domain between the two houses. It follows from this that a side post is in fact deemed a proper partition, contrary to Rava's statement.

הָתָם קָסָבַר רַבִּי יְהוּדָה: שְׁתֵּי מְחִיצוֹת דְּאוֹרַיְיתָא.

The Gemara answers: This is not the reason behind Rabbi Yehuda's statement. Rather, **there Rabbi Yehuda holds** that **by Torah law two partitions** suffice to constitute a private domain, and he requires side posts only as a conspicuous marker. Therefore, Rava's position cannot be disproved from this source either.

אָמַר רַב יְהוּדָה, אָמַר רַב: מָבוֹי שֶׁאׇרְכּוֹ כְּרׇחְבּוֹ אֵינוֹ נִיתָּר בְּלֶחִי מַשֶּׁהוּ. אָמַר רַב חִיָּיא בַּר אַשִׁי, אָמַר רַב: מָבוֹי שֶׁאׇרְכּוֹ כְּרׇחְבּוֹ אֵינוֹ נִיתָּר בְּקוֹרָה טֶפַח.

Rav Yehuda said that Rav said: Unlike other alleyways, carrying within **an alleyway whose length is equal to its width is not permitted by** means of **a side post of minimal** width. Like a courtyard, carrying within it is permitted only by means of an upright board four handbreadths wide. **Rav Ḥiyya bar Ashi said in the name of Rav:** Carrying within **an alleyway whose length is equal to its width is not permitted by** a cross **beam** with the width **of a handbreadth.**

אָמַר רַבִּי זֵירָא: כַּמָּה מְכֻוּוֹנֶן שְׁמַעְתָּא דְּסָבֵי; כֵּיוָן דְּאׇרְכּוֹ כְּרׇחְבּוֹ – הָוֵה לֵיהּ חָצֵר, וְחָצֵר אֵינָהּ נִיתֶּרֶת בְּלֶחִי וְקוֹרָה אֶלָּא בְּפַס אַרְבָּעָה.

Rabbi Zeira said: How precise are the traditions of the Elders. He explains: **Since the length** of the alleyway **is equal to its width, it is** regarded like **a courtyard, and** carrying within **a courtyard is not permitted by** means of **a side post or** a cross **beam, but** only **by** means of **an** upright **board of four** handbreadths.

אָמַר רַבִּי זֵירָא: אִי קַשְׁיָא לִי – הָא קַשְׁיָא לִי, לֶיהֱוֵי הַאי לֶחִי כְּפַס מַשֶּׁהוּ וְנִשְׁתְּרֵי!

Rabbi Zeira said: Nonetheless, **if** this issue **is difficult for me** to understand, **this is my difficulty: Let this side post be** considered **like** an upright **board of minimal** width **and permit** carrying within the alleyway, just as an upright board permits carrying in a breached courtyard.

אִישְׁתַּמִּיטְתֵּיהּ הָא דְּאָמַר רַבִּי אַסִּי אָמַר רַבִּי יוֹחָנָן: פַּסֵּי חָצֵר צְרִיכִין שֶׁיְּהֵא בָּהֶן אַרְבָּעָה

The Gemara explains that this is incorrect, as **that which Rabbi Asi said** that **Rabbi Yoḥanan said escaped** Rabbi Zeira's **attention: The** upright **boards of a courtyard must be four** handbreadths wide, whereas a side post may be of minimal size.

אָמַר רַב נַחְמָן: נְקִטִינַן, אֵיזֶהוּ מָבוֹי שֶׁנִּיתָּר בְּלֶחִי וְקוֹרָה – כֹּל שֶׁאׇרְכּוֹ יָתֵר עַל רׇחְבּוֹ, וּבָתִּים וַחֲצֵרוֹת פְּתוּחִים לְתוֹכוֹ. וְאֵיזוֹ הִיא חָצֵר שֶׁאֵינָהּ נִיתֶּרֶת בְּלֶחִי וְקוֹרָה אֶלָּא בְּפַס אַרְבָּעָה – כֹּל שֶׁמְּרוּבַּעַת.

Rav Naḥman said: We have a tradition that states: **What is the** type of **alleyway** in **which** carrying **is permitted**[H] **by** means of **a side post or** a cross **beam? Any** alleyway **whose length is greater than its width and has houses and courtyards opening into it. And what is the** type of **courtyard** in **which** carrying **is not permitted by** means of **a side post or** a cross **beam, but by** an upright **board of four** handbreadths? **Any** courtyard **that is square.**

מְרוּבַּעַת – אִין, עֲגוּלָּה – לָא?! הָכִי קָאָמַר: אִי אֲרִיכָה יָתֵר עַל רְחָבָה – הָוֵה לֵיהּ מָבוֹי, וּמָבוֹי בְּלֶחִי וְקוֹרָה סַגִּיא, וְאִי לָא – הָוְיָא לַהּ חָצֵר.

The Gemara wonders: If it is **square,** then **yes,** is it considered a courtyard? If it is **round, no,** is it not considered a courtyard? The Gemara makes a correction: **This is** what **it is saying: If its length is greater than its width,**[N] **it is** considered **an alleyway, and** for **an alleyway a side post or** a cross **beam suffices; but if** its length is **not** greater than its width, i.e., it is square, **it is** considered **a courtyard.**

וְכַמָּה? סָבַר שְׁמוּאֵל לְמֵימַר: עַד דְּאִיכָּא פִּי שְׁנַיִם בְּרׇחְבָּהּ. אֲמַר לֵיהּ רַב, הָכִי אָמַר חֲבִיבִי: אֲפִילּוּ מַשֶּׁהוּ.

The Gemara asks: **And** by **how much** must its length exceed its width so that it can be considered an alleyway? **Shmuel thought** at first **to say:** It is not considered an alleyway **unless** its length is **double its width,** until **Rav said to him: My uncle [*ḥavivi*],**[L] Rav Ḥiyya, **said this: Even** if its length is greater than its width by only **a minimal amount,** the *halakhot* of an alleyway apply to it.

מִשּׁוּם רַבִּי יִשְׁמָעֵאל אָמַר תַּלְמִיד אֶחָד כו׳״.

We learned in the mishna: **A certain disciple said** before Rabbi Akiva **in the name of Rabbi Yishmael, etc.**

LANGUAGE

My uncle [*ḥavivi*] – חֲבִיבִי: The primary meaning of *ḥaviv* is beloved. It took on the secondary meaning of uncle, since it became synonymous with the word *dod*, which also has two meanings, beloved and uncle. The Palestinian Targum of the Torah translates *dod* and *doda*, uncle and aunt respectively, as *ḥavivei* and *ḥavivatei*.

HALAKHA

The alleyway which is permitted – אֵיזֶהוּ מָבוֹי שֶׁנִּיתָּר: In the case of an alleyway whose length is greater than its width and that has houses and courtyards opening into it, carrying within it can be permitted only by means of a side post or a cross beam. This *halakha* is in accordance with the statement of Rav Naḥman (*Shulḥan Arukh*, *Oraḥ Ḥayyim* 363:26).

NOTES

A courtyard whose length is greater than its width – חָצֵר שֶׁאֲרֻכָּה יָתֵר עַל רְחָבָה: The text of the Ra'avad reads: If its length is greater than its width. In his version of the text, the sentence is formulated in the masculine. Thus, it is referring to an alleyway rather than a courtyard. Similarly, according to the majority of the halakhic authorities, even though a square alleyway is treated like a courtyard, a courtyard cannot be considered an alleyway.

NOTES

And the *halakha* is in accordance with the opinion of that disciple – וְהֲלָכָה כְּאוֹתוֹ תַּלְמִיד: Some explain that Rabbi Akiva intended to say that although he knows that there is no such tradition and Rabbi Yishmael certainly did not make that statement, nevertheless, that student's opinion seems logical (*Ge'on Ya'akov*).

Destroying the whole world in its entirety – מַחֲרִיב אֶת כָּל הָעוֹלָם כּוּלּוֹ: See Rashi and *Tosafot*, who offer various examples demonstrating that the meaning of a verse can change with the addition or omission of a single letter. The examples illustrate that minor changes can possibly destroy the entire world, e.g., when they lead to readings that involve heresy, sacrilege, or blasphemy.

LANGUAGE

Copper sulfate [*kankantom*] – קַנְקַנְתּוֹם: From the Greek χάλκανθος, *chalkanthos*, meaning copper sulfate.

Scribe [*lavlar*] – לַבְלָר: From the Latin librarius, meaning scribe or one whose profession is copying books.

BACKGROUND

The preparation of ink – עֲשִׂיַּית דְּיוֹ: In the talmudic period, ink was primarily a combination of soot and oil. Various substances were added to it before it was mixed with water. On most parchment, this ink was erasable and could be blotted out with water. To overcome this problem, they would occasionally utilize substances, e.g., copper sulfate, that would render the ink more permanent and prevent its erasure.

HALAKHA

Writing a Torah scroll with copper sulfate – כְּתִיבַת תּוֹרָה בְּקַנְקַנְתּוֹם: A Torah scroll is written with ink made from the soot of burnt oils and gall water *ab initio*. However, ink with copper sulfate is acceptable after the fact (*Shulḥan Arukh*, *Yoreh De'a* 271:6).

״רַבִּי עֲקִיבָא אוֹמֵר: עַל זֶה וְעַל זֶה נֶחְלְקוּ כו׳״.

The mishna relates that a student recited a *halakha* before Rabbi Akiva, and he did not accept the student's version of the dispute between Beit Shammai and Beit Hillel, as **Rabbi Akiva said: They disagree about this,** an alleyway less than four cubits wide, **and about that,** an alleyway more than four cubits wide.

רַבִּי עֲקִיבָא הַיְינוּ תַּנָּא קַמָּא! אִיכָּא בֵּינַיְיהוּ דְּרַב אַחְלָי וְאִיתֵימָא רַב יְחִיאֵל, וְלָא מְסַיְּימִי.

The Gemara asks: In that case, the opinion of **Rabbi Akiva** is identical with the opinion **first *tanna*** of the mishna, as he too holds that Beit Shammai and Beit Hillel disagree in all cases, irrespective of the width of the alleyway. The Gemara answers: **There is** a practical difference **between them** with regard to the *halakha* stated by **Rav Aḥlai, and some say** it was **Rav Yeḥiel,** that an alleyway less than four handbreadths wide requires no corrective action. However, their respective opinions **are not defined;** which *tanna* accepts the view of Rav Aḥlai and which *tanna* rejects it cannot be determined.

תַּנְיָא, אָמַר רַבִּי עֲקִיבָא: לֹא אָמַר רַבִּי יִשְׁמָעֵאל דָּבָר זֶה, אֶלָּא אוֹתוֹ תַּלְמִיד אָמַר דָּבָר זֶה – וַהֲלָכָה כְּאוֹתוֹ תַּלְמִיד.

It was taught in a *baraita* that **Rabbi Akiva said: Rabbi Yishmael did not state this matter,** as it is unlikely that Rabbi Yishmael would err in this manner; **rather,** it was **that disciple who stated that matter** on his own, **and the *halakha* is in accordance with** the opinion of **that disciple.**[N]

הָא גּוּפָהּ קַשְׁיָא: אָמְרַתְּ ״לֹא אָמַר רַבִּי יִשְׁמָעֵאל דָּבָר זֶה״ – אַלְמָא לֵית הִלְכְתָא כְּוָותֵיהּ, וַהֲדַר אָמְרַתְּ ״הֲלָכָה כְּאוֹתוֹ תַּלְמִיד״!

With regard to that *baraita* the Gemara asks: **This** *baraita* **itself is difficult. You stated** initially that **Rabbi Yishmael did not state this matter; apparently the *halakha* is not in accordance with** the opinion of the disciple. **And then you said: The *halakha* is in accordance with** the opinion of **that disciple.**

אָמַר רַב יְהוּדָה, אָמַר שְׁמוּאֵל: לֹא אֲמָרָהּ רַבִּי עֲקִיבָא אֶלָּא לְחַדֵּד בָּהּ הַתַּלְמִידִים.

Rav Yehuda said that **Shmuel said: Rabbi Akiva said** that the *halakha* is in accordance with that disciple **only to sharpen** the minds of **his students with** his statement. Seeking to encourage his students to suggest novel opinions, he praised that disciple before them but did not actually rule in accordance with the disciple's opinion.

וְרַב נַחְמָן בַּר יִצְחָק אָמַר: נִרְאִין אִיתְּמַר.

And Rav Naḥman bar Yitzḥak said, in another attempt to resolve the contradiction: The statement of the disciple **appears** to be reasonable **was stated.** Although Rabbi Yishmael himself did not make that statement, the statement of the disciple is reasonable.

אָמַר רַבִּי יְהוֹשֻׁעַ בֶּן לֵוִי: כָּל מָקוֹם שֶׁאַתָּה מוֹצֵא מִשּׁוּם רַבִּי יִשְׁמָעֵאל אָמַר תַּלְמִיד אֶחָד לִפְנֵי רַבִּי עֲקִיבָא – אֵינוֹ אֶלָּא רַבִּי מֵאִיר, שֶׁשִּׁימֵּשׁ אֶת רַבִּי יִשְׁמָעֵאל וְאֶת רַבִּי עֲקִיבָא.

Rabbi Yehoshua ben Levi said: Anywhere that you find a statement introduced with: **A certain disciple said before Rabbi Akiva in the name of Rabbi Yishmael, it is none other than Rabbi Meir,** who was the student **who served** both **Rabbi Yishmael and Rabbi Akiva.**

דְּתַנְיָא, אָמַר רַבִּי מֵאִיר: כְּשֶׁהָיִיתִי אֵצֶל רַבִּי יִשְׁמָעֵאל הָיִיתִי מַטִּיל קַנְקַנְתּוֹם לְתוֹךְ הַדְּיוֹ וְלֹא אָמַר לִי דָּבָר. כְּשֶׁבָּאתִי אֵצֶל רַבִּי עֲקִיבָא, אֲסָרָהּ עָלַי.

As it was taught in a *baraita* that **Rabbi Meir said: When I was** a student **with Rabbi Yishmael, I used to put copper sulfate** [***kankantom***][L] **into the ink**[B] with which I wrote Torah scrolls,[H] **and he did not say anything to me. When I came** to study **with Rabbi Akiva, he prohibited me** from doing so.

אִינִי?! וְהָאָמַר רַב יְהוּדָה, אָמַר שְׁמוּאֵל מִשּׁוּם רַבִּי מֵאִיר: כְּשֶׁהָיִיתִי לוֹמֵד אֵצֶל רַבִּי עֲקִיבָא הָיִיתִי מַטִּיל קַנְקַנְתּוֹם לְתוֹךְ הַדְּיוֹ וְלֹא אָמַר לִי דָּבָר. וּכְשֶׁבָּאתִי אֵצֶל רַבִּי יִשְׁמָעֵאל, אָמַר לִי: בְּנִי, מַה מְּלַאכְתְּךָ? אָמַרְתִּי לוֹ: לַבְלָר אֲנִי. אָמַר לִי: בְּנִי, הֱוֵי זָהִיר בִּמְלַאכְתְּךָ, שֶׁמְּלַאכְתְּךָ מְלֶאכֶת שָׁמַיִם הִיא, שֶׁמָּא אַתָּה מְחַסֵּר אוֹת אַחַת אוֹ מְיַיתֵּר אוֹת אַחַת – נִמְצֵאתָ מַחֲרִיב אֶת כָּל הָעוֹלָם כּוּלּוֹ.

The Gemara challenges this statement: **Is that so? Didn't Rav Yehuda say** that **Shmuel said in the name of Rabbi Meir: When I studied with Rabbi Akiva** as his disciple, **I used to put copper sulfate into the ink, and he did not say anything to me. But when I came** to study **with Rabbi Yishmael, he said to me: My son, what is your vocation? I replied: I am a scribe** [*lavlar*][L] who writes Torah scrolls. **He said to me: My son, be careful in your vocation, as your vocation is heavenly service,** and care must be taken **lest you omit a single letter or add a single letter** out of place, **and you will end up destroying the whole world in its entirety.**[N] Addition or omission of a single letter can change the meaning from truth [*emet*] to death [*met*].

אָמַרְתִּי לוֹ: דָּבָר אֶחָד יֵשׁ לִי וְ׳קַנְקַנְתּוֹם׳ שְׁמוֹ, שֶׁאֲנִי מַטִּיל לְתוֹךְ הַדְּיוֹ. אָמַר לִי: וְכִי מַטִּילִין קַנְקַנְתּוֹם לְתוֹךְ הַדְּיוֹ? וַהֲלֹא אָמְרָה תּוֹרָה ״וְכָתַב״ ״וּמָחָה״ – כְּתָב שֶׁיָּכוֹל לִמָּחוֹת.

I said to him: I have one substance called copper sulfate, which I place into the ink, and therefore I am not concerned. **He said to me: May one place copper sulfate into the ink? Didn't the Torah state** with regard to *sota*: "And the priest **shall write** these curses in a book, **and he shall blot them out** into the water of bitterness" (Numbers 5:23)? The Torah requires **writing that can be blotted out.**

מַאי קָאָמַר לֵיהּ, וּמַאי קָא מְהַדַּר לֵיהּ?

The Gemara clarifies elements of the conversation: **What is** Rabbi Yishmael **saying to** Rabbi Meir, **and what is he answering him?** Rabbi Meir's response with regard to copper sulfate does not seem to address Rabbi Yishmael's comments with regard to omissions and additions.

הָכִי קָאָמַר לֵיהּ: לָא מִיבַּעְיָא בַּחֲסֵירוֹת וּבִיתֵירוֹת [דְּלָא טָעֵינָא] דִּבְקִי אֲנָא, אֶלָּא אֲפִילּוּ מֵיחַשׁ לִזְבוּב נַמִי, דִּילְמָא אָתֵי וְיָתֵיב אַתָּגֵיהּ דְּדל״ת וּמָחֵיק לֵיהּ וּמְשַׁוֵּי לֵיהּ רי״ש, דָּבָר אֶחָד יֵשׁ לִי וְקַנְקַנְתּוֹם שְׁמוֹ שֶׁאֲנִי מַטִּיל לְתוֹךְ הַדְּיוֹ.

The Gemara explains that **this is** what Rabbi Meir **is saying to** Rabbi Yishmael: **There is no need** to mention **defective and plene** words, **as I am an expert; however, even with regard to the concern that a fly might come and land on the crown of** the letter ***dalet* and blot it out and render it a *reish*,**[N] thereby changing the meaning of the word, I am not concerned, as **I have a substance called copper sulfate that I place into the ink** so that it will not be erased.

קַשְׁיָא שִׁימּוּשׁ אַשִּׁימּוּשׁ, קַשְׁיָא אֲסָרָהּ אַאֲסָרָהּ!

Nevertheless, **there is a difficulty between service and service,** as one source states that Rabbi Meir initially served Rabbi Akiva, whereas the other source states that he served Rabbi Yishmael first. **There is a difficulty between** the words **he prohibited it** in the *baraita*, which is referring to Rabbi Akiva, **and he prohibited it** in the statement of Rav Yehuda, which is referring to Rabbi Yishmael.

בִּשְׁלָמָא שִׁימּוּשׁ אַשִּׁימּוּשׁ לָא קַשְׁיָא; מֵעִיקָּרָא אֲתָא לְקַמֵּיהּ דְּרַבִּי עֲקִיבָא, וּמִדְּלָא מָצֵי לְמֵיקַם אַלִּיבֵּיהּ – אֲתָא לְקַמֵּיהּ דְּרַבִּי יִשְׁמָעֵאל וּגְמַר גְּמָרָא, וַהֲדַר אֲתָא לְקַמֵּיהּ דְּרַבִּי עֲקִיבָא וּסְבַר סְבָרָא.

The Gemara comments: **Granted, there is no difficulty between** the accounts in the two sources with regard to **service and service,** as it can be suggested as follows: Rabbi Meir **initially came** to study **before Rabbi Akiva, and since he was unable to comprehend** the teachings **in accordance with his** opinion, **he came before Rabbi Yishmael and studied the tradition, and again came before Rabbi Akiva and studied logical** analysis. After studying the basic principles from Rabbi Yishmael, he was able to understand the more complex teachings of Rabbi Akiva.

אֶלָּא אֲסָרָהּ אַאֲסָרָהּ קַשְׁיָא! קַשְׁיָא.

Having reconciled the first difficulty, the Gemara continues: **However, the difficulty with regard to** whether Rabbi Akiva **prohibited** copper sulfate or Rabbi Yishmael **prohibited** it remains **difficult.** The Gemara notes: It indeed remains **difficult;** no answer was found.

תַּנְיָא רַבִּי יְהוּדָה אוֹמֵר, רַבִּי מֵאִיר הָיָה אוֹמֵר: לַכֹּל מַטִּילִין קַנְקַנְתּוֹם לְתוֹךְ הַדְּיוֹ, חוּץ מִפָּרָשַׁת סוֹטָה. וְרַבִּי יַעֲקֹב אוֹמֵר מִשְּׁמוֹ: חוּץ מִפָּרָשַׁת סוֹטָה שֶׁבַּמִּקְדָּשׁ.

The Gemara continues the discussion of copper sulfate. **It was taught** in a *baraita*: **Rabbi Yehuda says** that **Rabbi Meir would say: One may place copper sulfate into the ink** that is to be used **for all** sacred writings, **except for** the writing of **the** Torah **passage** with regard to a ***sota*,** as it must be possible to erase that writing.[N] **Rabbi Ya'akov says in his name: Except for** the writing of **the** Torah **passage** with regard to **a *sota*** used **in the Temple**[H] in the ordeal to determine the guilt or innocence of the wife suspected of adultery.

מַאי בֵּינַיְיהוּ? אָמַר רַב יִרְמְיָה: לְמִחוֹק לָהּ מִן הַתּוֹרָה אִיכָּא בֵּינַיְיהוּ.

The Gemara asks: **What is** the difference **between their** opinions, i.e., what is their point of dispute? The Gemara answers: **Rav Yirmeya said:** The difference **between their** opinions **is** whether it is permissible **to erase** the passage of a *sota* **from a Torah** scroll. The *tanna'im* of the *baraita* disagree whether or not a section taken from a Torah scroll may be used for this purpose, or whether a special scroll must be written for use in the ordeal of the *sota*.

וְהָנֵי תַּנָּאֵי כִּי הָנֵי תַּנָּאֵי; דְּתַנְיָא: אֵין מְגִילָּתָהּ כְּשֵׁירָה לְהַשְׁקוֹת בָּהּ סוֹטָה אַחֶרֶת. רַבִּי אַחַי בַּר יֹאשִׁיָּה אָמַר: מְגִילָּתָהּ כְּשֵׁירָה לְהַשְׁקוֹת בָּהּ סוֹטָה אַחֶרֶת.

And those *tanna'im* disagree in the same dispute **as these *tanna'im*, as it was taught** in a *baraita*: A scroll that was written for one woman suspected of infidelity but was not used, **her scroll is not fit** to prepare the water **to give to another *sota* to drink.** However, **Rabbi Aḥai bar Yoshiya said: Her scroll is fit** to be used to prepare the water **to give another *sota* to drink.** The legal status of a Torah scroll, which is not written for a particular *sota*, should be the same.

NOTES

Dalet and reish – דל״ת וְרי״ש: This example also alludes to a specific instance, namely, the phrase: "The Lord is One [*eḥad*]" (Deuteronomy 6:4). If the crown of the letter *dalet* is erased, the letter becomes a *reish*, and the phrase becomes: God is other [*aḥer*], which is blasphemous.

Erasing the Torah passage with regard to a *sota* – מְחִיַּית פָּרָשַׁת סוֹטָה: The *halakhot* of *sota* are detailed in the Torah (Numbers 5) and in tractate *Sota*. The relevant details in this context are elements in the ordeal to which the *sota* is subjected. The curses stated in the Torah with regard to a *sota* were written on a scroll, which was then immersed in water until the writing dissolved, after which the woman drank from the water. The dispute between the Sages here relates to the question which of these actions, the writing or the erasing of the scroll in water, must be performed specifically in the name of the particular woman undergoing the ordeal.

HALAKHA

The Torah passage with regard to a *sota* used in the Temple – פָּרָשַׁת סוֹטָה שֶׁבַּמִּקְדָּשׁ: The scroll used in the ordeal of a *sota* in the Temple may not be written in ink with copper sulfate, since in that case the writing would not be erasable (Rambam *Sefer Nashim*, *Hilkhot Sota* 3:8).

אָמַר רַב פַּפָּא: דִּילְמָא לֹא הִיא; עַד כָּאן לָא קָאָמַר תַּנָּא קַמָּא הָתָם – אֶלָּא כֵּיוָן דְּאִינְתִּיק לְשׁוּם רָחֵל, תּוּ לָא הָדְרָא מִינְתְּקָא לְשׁוּם לֵאָה. אֲבָל גַּבֵּי תּוֹרָה דִּסְתָמָא מִיכְּתְבָא – הָכִי נַמִּי דְּמָחֲקִינַן.

Rav Pappa said: Perhaps that is not the case, as the two circumstances are not comparable. **The first *tanna*** of the *baraita* **stated** his opinion that one woman's scroll may not be used for another woman **only there; since it had** originally **been designated in the name of** one woman, e.g., **Rachel, it cannot then be designated in the name of** another woman, e.g., **Leah.**[H] **However, in the case of a Torah** scroll, **which is written with no particular** person in mind, he **too** may say that **we** may **erase** it to be used for another woman, and it is not disqualified because it was not written in her name.

אָמַר רַב נַחְמָן בַּר יִצְחָק: דִּילְמָא לֹא הִיא; עַד כָּאן לָא קָאָמַר רַבִּי אַחַי בַּר יֹאשִׁיָּה הָתָם – אֶלָּא דְּאִיכְּתִיב מִיהַת לְשׁוּם סוֹטָה בָּעוֹלָם, אֲבָל גַּבֵּי תּוֹרָה דִּלְהִתְלַמֵּד כְּתִיבָא – הָכִי נַמִּי דְּלָא מָחֲקִינַן.

Furthermore, **Rav Naḥman bar Yitzḥak said** in another attempt to resolve the matter: **Perhaps it is not so,** as an additional distinction exists between the two cases: **Rabbi Aḥai bar Yoshiya stated** his opinion that the first woman's scroll may be used for another woman **only there because at least,** in that case, **it was written for** a particular ***sota* in the world. However, in the case of a Torah** scroll, **which was written for study,** he **too** would agree that **we do not erase** it.

וְלֵית לֵיהּ לְרַבִּי אַחַי בַּר יֹאשִׁיָּה הָא דִּתְנַן: כָּתַב [גֵּט] לְגָרֵשׁ אֶת אִשְׁתּוֹ,

The Gemara asks: **And does Rabbi Aḥai bar Yoshiya not hold** in accordance with **that which we learned** in a mishna: **If one wrote a bill of divorce to divorce his wife,**

וְנִמְלַךְ, וּמְצָאוֹ בֶּן עִירוֹ וְאָמַר: שִׁמְךָ כְּשִׁמִי וְשֵׁם אִשְׁתְּךָ כְּשֵׁם אִשְׁתִּי – פָּסוּל לְגָרֵשׁ בּוֹ!

but later **reconsidered** and did not divorce her, **and a resident of his city found him and said: Your name is** the same **as my name, and your wife's name is** the same **as my wife's name,** and we reside in the same town; give me the bill of divorce, and I will use it to divorce my wife, then this document **is invalid to divorce with it?** Apparently, a man may not divorce his wife with a bill of divorce written for another woman, and the same should apply to the scroll of a *sota*.

הָכִי הָשְׁתָּא?! הָתָם "וְכָתַב לָהּ" כְּתִיב – בָּעֵינַן כְּתִיבָה לִשְׁמָהּ, הָכָא "וְעָשָׂה לָהּ" כְּתִיב – בָּעֵינַן עֲשִׂיָּה לִשְׁמָהּ, עֲשִׂיָּה דִּידָהּ מְחִיקָה הִיא.

The Gemara rejects this argument: **How can you compare** the two cases? **There,** with regard to a bill of divorce, **it is written: "And he shall write for her"** (Deuteronomy 24:1), and therefore **we require writing** it **in her name,** specifically for her;[H] whereas **here,** with regard to a *sota*, **it is written: "And he shall perform with her** all this ritual" (Numbers 5:30), and therefore **we require performance in her name.** In **her** case, the **performance is erasure;** however, writing of the scroll need not be performed specifically for her.

אָמַר רַבִּי אַחָא בַּר חֲנִינָא: גָּלוּי וְיָדוּעַ לִפְנֵי מִי שֶׁאָמַר וְהָיָה הָעוֹלָם שֶׁאֵין בְּדוֹרוֹ שֶׁל רַבִּי מֵאִיר כְּמוֹתוֹ, וּמִפְּנֵי מָה לֹא קָבְעוּ הֲלָכָה כְּמוֹתוֹ – שֶׁלֹּא יָכְלוּ חֲבֵירָיו לַעֲמוֹד עַל סוֹף דַּעְתּוֹ. שֶׁהוּא אוֹמֵר עַל טָמֵא טָהוֹר וּמַרְאֶה לוֹ פָּנִים, עַל טָהוֹר טָמֵא וּמַרְאֶה לוֹ פָּנִים.

On the topic of Rabbi Meir and his Torah study, the Gemara cites an additional statement. **Rabbi Aḥa bar Ḥanina said: It is revealed and known before the One Who spoke and the world came into being that in the generation of Rabbi Meir**[P] **there was no** one of the Sages who is **his equal. Why** then **didn't** the Sages **establish the *halakha* in accordance with his** opinion? It is **because his colleagues were unable to ascertain the profundity of his opinion.** He was so brilliant that he could present a cogent argument for any position, even if it was not consistent with the prevalent *halakha*. **As he** would **state with regard to** a ritually **impure** item that it is **pure, and display justification** for that ruling, and likewise he would state **with regard to** a ritually **pure** item that it is **impure, and display justification** for that ruling. The Sages were unable to distinguish between the statements that were *halakha* and those that were not.

HALAKHA

Writing the *sota's* scroll in her name – פָּרָשַׁת סוֹטָה לִשְׁמָהּ: A *sota's* scroll must be written in her name. If it was not written or erased in her name, it is invalid. This ruling is in accordance with the conclusion of the Gemara's discussion in tractate *Sota* (Rambam *Sefer Nashim, Hilkhot Sota* 3:8).

PERSONALITIES

Rabbi Meir – רַבִּי מֵאִיר: One of the greatest *tanna'im* of the generation that preceded the redaction of the Mishna. There is no clear information available concerning Rabbi Meir's parents, though it is told that he descended from a family of converts from the house of the Roman emperors.

His exceptional brilliance in Torah study was evident from a very early age, and he was a student of the two greatest scholars of the generation, Rabbi Yishmael and Rabbi Akiva. He was also the lone Sage who continued to study with Elisha ben Avuya, despite the latter's estrangement from Judaism. His primary teacher was Rabbi Akiva, who ordained him at a very young age, which is the reason that he was ordained a second time by Rabbi Yehuda ben Bava.

In recognition of his outstanding scholarship, Rabbi Meir was officially appointed *ḥakham*, literally, wise man, the third level below *nasi*, head of the Sanhedrin. The halakhic discussions between him and his colleagues Rabbi Yehuda, Rabbi Yosei, Rabbi Shimon, and Rabbi Elazar form one of the most important foundations of the Mishna.

Rabbi Meir's greatest undertaking appears to have been a structured, oral redaction of the Oral Law, including establishing specific formats for the *halakhot*. Apparently, Rabbi Yehuda HaNasi followed in Rabbi Meir's footsteps and incorporated his work in the Mishna. Consequently, it is a well-known principle that the author of an unattributed statement in the Mishna is Rabbi Meir, as the assumption is that this was one of the *mishnayot* he formulated.

Due to his involvement in the attempt to depose Rabban Shimon ben Gamliel, the head of the Sanhedrin, he was punished by the latter, and for a long period his teachings were not cited in his name but were introduced with the words: Others say.

His private life was full of suffering. His two sons died during his lifetime, and his extraordinary wife Beruria also died in painful circumstances. Nevertheless, it is known that a daughter of his survived. He was eventually forced into exile to Asia Minor, where he died, with the order that his coffin be transferred to Eretz Yisrael and that he be temporarily interred on the shore of the sea whose waves reach the Holy Land.

Rabbi Meir was famous in his lifetime, not only for his sharp intellect, which exceeded that of all his peers, but also for his personal attributes, his efforts as a peacemaker, and his willingness to relinquish personal honor for the good of others. He was known as a magnificent public speaker. It is said that following his death, those who composed parables ceased. Several of his animal parables were repeated for many generations. He was also renowned as a miracle worker, and for many years a charity fund named after him, Rabbi Meir the Miracle Worker [*Ba'al HaNes*] served as the main source of funding for the Jews in Eretz Yisrael.

HALAKHA

Writing a bill of divorce in her name – כְּתִיבַת גֵּט לִשְׁמָהּ: A bill of divorce that was written in the name of one woman cannot be used in the divorce proceedings of another woman. This restriction applies even if the names of the women, their husbands, and their places of residence are the same, because a bill of divorce must be written in the name of a particular woman (*Shulḥan Arukh, Even HaEzer* 131:2).

תָּנָא: לֹא רַבִּי מֵאִיר שְׁמוֹ, אֶלָּא רַבִּי נְהוֹרַאי שְׁמוֹ. וְלָמָּה נִקְרָא שְׁמוֹ רַבִּי מֵאִיר – שֶׁהוּא מֵאִיר עֵינֵי חֲכָמִים בַּהֲלָכָה. וְלֹא נְהוֹרַאי שְׁמוֹ, אֶלָּא רַבִּי נְחֶמְיָה שְׁמוֹ, וְאָמְרִי לָהּ: רַבִּי אֶלְעָזָר בֶּן עֲרָךְ שְׁמוֹ. וְלָמָּה נִקְרָא שְׁמוֹ נְהוֹרַאי – שֶׁמַּנְהִיר עֵינֵי חֲכָמִים בַּהֲלָכָה.

It was taught in a *baraita*: **Rabbi Meir was not his name; rather, Rabbi Nehorai was his name. And why was he called** by the **name Rabbi Meir?** It was **because he illuminates [*meir*] the eyes of the Sages in** matters of **the *halakha*. And Rabbi Nehorai was not the name** of the *tanna* known by that name; **rather, Rabbi Neḥemya was his name, and some say: Rabbi Elazar ben Arakh was his name. And why was he called** by the **name Rabbi Nehorai?** It is **because he enlightens [*manhir*] the eyes of the Sages in** matters of **the *halakha*.**

אָמַר רַבִּי: הַאי דְּמִחַדַּדְנָא מֵחַבְרַאי – דַּחֲזִיתֵיהּ לְרַבִּי מֵאִיר מֵאֲחוֹרֵיהּ. וְאִילּוּ חֲזֵיתֵיהּ מִקַּמֵּיהּ – הֲוָה מְחַדַּדְנָא טְפֵי. דִּכְתִיב: ״וְהָיוּ עֵינֶיךָ רוֹאוֹת אֶת מוֹרֶיךָ״.

The Gemara relates that **Rabbi** Yehuda HaNasi **said:** The fact **that I am** more **incisive than my colleagues is** due to the fact **that I saw Rabbi Meir from behind,** i.e., I sat behind him when I was his student. **Had I seen him from the front,**[H] **I would be** even more **incisive, as it is written: "And your eyes shall see your teacher"** (Isaiah 30:20). Seeing the face of one's teacher increases one's understanding and sharpens one's mind.

אָמַר רַבִּי אַבָּהוּ, אָמַר רַבִּי יוֹחָנָן: תַּלְמִיד הָיָה לוֹ לְרַבִּי מֵאִיר וְסוּמָכוֹס שְׁמוֹ, שֶׁהָיָה אוֹמֵר עַל כָּל דָּבָר וְדָבָר שֶׁל טוּמְאָה אַרְבָּעִים וּשְׁמוֹנָה טַעֲמֵי טוּמְאָה, וְעַל כָּל דָּבָר וְדָבָר שֶׁל טָהֳרָה אַרְבָּעִים וּשְׁמוֹנָה טַעֲמֵי טָהֳרָה.

And the Gemara stated that **Rabbi Abbahu said** that **Rabbi Yoḥanan said: Rabbi Meir had a disciple, and his name was Sumakhus, who would state with regard to each and every matter of ritual impurity forty-eight reasons** in support of the ruling of **impurity, and with regard to each and every matter of ritual purity forty-eight reasons** in support of the ruling of **purity.**

תָּנָא: תַּלְמִיד וָתִיק הָיָה בְּיַבְנֶה שֶׁהָיָה מְטַהֵר אֶת הַשֶּׁרֶץ בְּמֵאָה וַחֲמִשִּׁים טְעָמִים.

It was taught in a *baraita*: **There was a distinguished disciple at Yavne who could** with his incisive intellect **purify the creeping animal,**[N] explicitly deemed ritually impure by the Torah, adducing **one hundred and fifty reasons** in support of his argument.

אָמַר רָבִינָא: אֲנִי אָדוּן וַאֲטַהֲרֶנּוּ; וּמָה נָּחָשׁ שֶׁמֵּמִית וּמַרְבֶּה טוּמְאָה – טָהוֹר, שֶׁרֶץ שֶׁאֵין מֵמִית וּמַרְבֶּה טוּמְאָה לֹא כָּל שֶׁכֵּן?

Ravina said: I too **will deliberate and purify it** employing the following reasoning: **And just as a snake that kills** people and animals **and** thereby **increases ritual impurity** in the world, as a corpse imparts impurity through contact, through being carried, and by means of a tent, **is ritually pure** and transmits no impurity, **a creeping animal that does not kill and** does not **increase impurity** in the world, **all the more so** should it be pure.

וְלֹא הִיא, מַעֲשֵׂה קוֹץ בְּעָלְמָא קָעָבֵיד.

The Gemara rejects this: **And it is not so;** that is not a valid *a fortiori* argument, as it can be refuted. A snake **is performing a mere act of a thorn.** A thorn causes injury and even death; nevertheless, it is not ritually impure. The same applies to a snake, and therefore this *a fortiori* argument is rejected.

אָמַר רַבִּי אַבָּא, אָמַר שְׁמוּאֵל: שָׁלֹשׁ שָׁנִים נֶחְלְקוּ בֵּית שַׁמַּאי וּבֵית הִלֵּל, הַלָּלוּ אוֹמְרִים הֲלָכָה כְּמוֹתֵנוּ וְהַלָּלוּ אוֹמְרִים הֲלָכָה כְּמוֹתֵנוּ. יָצְאָה בַּת קוֹל וְאָמְרָה: אֵלּוּ וָאֵלּוּ דִּבְרֵי אֱלֹהִים חַיִּים הֵן, וַהֲלָכָה כְּבֵית הִלֵּל.

Rabbi Abba said that **Shmuel said: For three years Beit Shammai and Beit Hillel disagreed. These said: The *halakha* is in accordance with our** opinion, **and these said: The *halakha* is in accordance with our** opinion. Ultimately, **a Divine Voice emerged and proclaimed:** Both **these and those are the words of the living God.**[N] **However, the *halakha* is in accordance with** the opinion of **Beit Hillel.**

וְכִי מֵאַחַר שֶׁאֵלּוּ וָאֵלּוּ דִּבְרֵי אֱלֹהִים חַיִּים, מִפְּנֵי מָה זָכוּ בֵּית הִלֵּל לִקְבּוֹעַ הֲלָכָה כְּמוֹתָן – מִפְּנֵי שֶׁנּוֹחִין וַעֲלוּבִין הָיוּ וְשׁוֹנִין דִּבְרֵיהֶן וְדִבְרֵי בֵּית שַׁמַּאי. וְלֹא עוֹד אֶלָּא שֶׁמַּקְדִּימִין דִּבְרֵי בֵּית שַׁמַּאי לְדִבְרֵיהֶן.

The Gemara asks: **Since both these and those are the words of the living God, why were Beit Hillel privileged to** have **the *halakha* established in accordance with their** opinion? The reason is **that they were agreeable and forbearing,**[N] showing restraint when affronted, and when they taught the *halakha* they would **teach** both **their** own **statements and the statements of Beit Shammai. Moreover,** when they formulated their teachings and cited a dispute, **they prioritized the statements of Beit Shammai to their** own **statements,** in deference to Beit Shammai.

HALAKHA

Had I seen him from the front – אִילּוּ חֲזֵיתֵיהּ מִקַּמֵּיהּ: Students must sit before their teacher so that they can all see him (*Shulḥan Arukh, Yoreh De'a* 246:9).

NOTES

Purify the creeping animal – מְטַהֵר אֶת הַשֶּׁרֶץ: See *Tosafot's* comments on this statement. The plain sense of this idea is that excessive brilliance of this type, a trait listed among the qualities required of the Sages of the Sanhedrin, is a crucial characteristic of great Sages, enabling them to arrive at innovative conclusions. However, it is precisely for this reason that outstanding scholars were regarded with a certain measure of suspicion. Others were unable to discern whether or not they were utilizing their great talents to prove ideas that they themselves did not consider correct.

Both these and those are the words of the living God – אֵלּוּ וָאֵלּוּ דִּבְרֵי אֱלֹהִים חַיִּים: Some commentaries refer to a midrash that appears in the Jerusalem Talmud to resolve the difficulties raised by this statement: When God gave the Torah to Moses, He gave it to him with forty-nine rationales for purity and forty-nine rationales for impurity, meaning that the Torah itself, from the moment it was given, could be interpreted in either direction. Although the decisions with regard to the disputes were determined by the Sages throughout the generations, all the divergent opinions have their place in the Torah as it was given, and therefore: Both these and those are the words of the living God (Rabbeinu Nissim Gaon; Ritva).

Agreeable and forbearing – נוֹחִין וַעֲלוּבִין: The early commentaries note that the fact that the Sages of Beit Hillel were easygoing and forbearing cannot serve as a rationale to rule in accordance with their opinion. In fact, the scholars of Beit Hillel comprised the majority of the Sages; and while the members of Beit Shammai were more brilliant than their colleagues in Beit Hillel, the *halakha* was decided in accordance with the majority opinion, as dictated by the Torah. It has also been suggested that since the scholars of Beit Hillel were easygoing and forbearing, they would closely analyze the rulings of Beit Shammai, who did not do the same with the rulings of Beit Hillel. Therefore, wherever the members of Beit Hillel disagreed, it is reasonable to assume that they had solid grounds for doing so.

כְּאוֹתָהּ שֶׁשָּׁנִינוּ: "מִי שֶׁהָיָה רֹאשׁוֹ וְרוּבּוֹ בַּסּוּכָּה וְשֻׁלְחָנוֹ בְּתוֹךְ הַבַּיִת בֵּית שַׁמַּאי פּוֹסְלִין וּבֵית הִלֵּל מַכְשִׁירִין. אָמְרוּ בֵּית הִלֵּל לְבֵית שַׁמַּאי: לֹא כָּךְ הָיָה מַעֲשֶׂה שֶׁהָלְכוּ זִקְנֵי בֵּית שַׁמַּאי וְזִקְנֵי בֵּית הִלֵּל לְבַקֵּר אֶת רַבִּי יוֹחָנָן בֶּן הַחוֹרָנִית, וּמְצָאוּהוּ יוֹשֵׁב רֹאשׁוֹ וְרוּבּוֹ בַּסּוּכָּה וְשֻׁלְחָנוֹ בְּתוֹךְ הַבַּיִת. אָמְרוּ לָהֶן בֵּית שַׁמַּאי: אִי מִשָּׁם רְאָיָה?! אַף הֵן אָמְרוּ לוֹ: אִם כָּךְ הָיִיתָ נוֹהֵג לֹא קִיַּימְתָּ מִצְוַת סוּכָּה מִיָּמֶיךָ".

As in the mishna **that we learned:** In the case of **one whose head and most of his body were in the** ***sukka*****,**[H] **but his table was in the house, Beit Shammai deem** this *sukka* **invalid; and Beit Hillel deem it valid. Beit Hillel said to Beit Shammai: Wasn't there an incident in which the Elders of Beit Shammai and the Elders of Beit Hillel went to visit Rabbi Yoḥanan ben HaḤoranit, and they found him sitting** with **his head and most of his body in the** ***sukka*****, but his table was in the house? Beit Shammai said to them: From there** do you seek to adduce **a proof? Those visitors, too, said to him: If that was** the manner in which **you were accustomed** to perform the mitzva, **you have never fulfilled the mitzva of** ***sukka*** **in all your days.** It is apparent from the phrasing of the mishna that when the Sages of Beit Hillel related that the Elders of Beit Shammai and the Elders of Beit Hillel visited Rabbi Yoḥanan ben HaḤoranit, they mentioned the Elders of Beit Shammai before their own Elders.

לְלַמֶּדְךָ, שֶׁכָּל הַמַּשְׁפִּיל עַצְמוֹ – הַקָּדוֹשׁ בָּרוּךְ הוּא מַגְבִּיהוֹ, וְכָל הַמַּגְבִּיהַּ עַצְמוֹ – הַקָּדוֹשׁ בָּרוּךְ הוּא מַשְׁפִּילוֹ. כָּל הַמְחַזֵּר עַל הַגְּדוּלָּה – גְּדוּלָּה בּוֹרַחַת מִמֶּנּוּ, וְכָל הַבּוֹרֵחַ מִן הַגְּדוּלָּה – גְּדוּלָּה מְחַזֶּרֶת אַחֲרָיו. וְכָל הַדּוֹחֵק אֶת הַשָּׁעָה – שָׁעָה דּוֹחַקְתּוֹ, וְכָל הַנִּדְחֶה מִפְּנֵי שָׁעָה – שָׁעָה עוֹמֶדֶת לוֹ.

This is **to teach you that anyone who humbles himself, the Holy One, Blessed be He, exalts him, and anyone who exalts himself, the Holy One, Blessed be He, humbles him. Anyone who seeks greatness, greatness flees from him, and,** conversely, **anyone who flees from greatness, greatness seeks him. And anyone who** attempts to **force the moment** and expends great effort to achieve an objective precisely when he desires to do so, **the moment forces him** too, and he is unsuccessful. **And** conversely, **anyone who** is patient and **yields to the moment, the moment stands** by **his** side, and he will ultimately be successful.

תָּנוּ רַבָּנַן: שְׁתֵּי שָׁנִים וּמֶחֱצָה נֶחְלְקוּ בֵּית שַׁמַּאי וּבֵית הִלֵּל, הַלָּלוּ אוֹמְרִים: נוֹחַ לוֹ לְאָדָם שֶׁלֹּא נִבְרָא יוֹתֵר מִשֶּׁנִּבְרָא, וְהַלָּלוּ אוֹמְרִים: נוֹחַ לוֹ לְאָדָם שֶׁנִּבְרָא יוֹתֵר מִשֶּׁלֹּא נִבְרָא. נִמְנוּ וְגָמְרוּ: נוֹחַ לוֹ לְאָדָם שֶׁלֹּא נִבְרָא יוֹתֵר מִשֶּׁנִּבְרָא, עַכְשָׁיו שֶׁנִּבְרָא – יְפַשְׁפֵּשׁ בְּמַעֲשָׂיו. וְאָמְרִי לַהּ: יְמַשְׁמֵשׁ בְּמַעֲשָׂיו.

The Sages taught the following *baraita*: **For two and a half years, Beit Shammai and Beit Hillel disagreed. These say: It would have been preferable had man not been created than to have been created. And those said: It is preferable for man to have been created than had he not been created.** Ultimately, **they were counted and concluded:**[N] **It would have been preferable had man not been created than to have been created.** However, **now that he has been created, he should examine his actions** that he has performed and seek to correct them. **And some say: He should scrutinize his** planned **actions**[N] and evaluate whether or not and in what manner those actions should be performed, so that he will not sin.

מתני׳ הַקּוֹרָה שֶׁאָמְרוּ – רְחָבָה כְּדֵי לְקַבֵּל אָרִיחַ. וְאָרִיחַ חֲצִי לְבֵנָה שֶׁל שְׁלֹשָׁה טְפָחִים. דַּיָּיה לַקּוֹרָה שֶׁתְּהֵא רְחָבָה טֶפַח כְּדֵי לְקַבֵּל אָרִיחַ לְרׇחְבּוֹ.

MISHNA **The** cross **beam, which the Sages stated** may be used to render an alleyway fit for one to carry within it, must be **wide enough to receive** and hold **a small brick.**[NH] **And this small brick is half a large brick,** which measures **three handbreadths,**[B] i.e., a handbreadth and a half. **It is sufficient that the** cross **beam will be a handbreadth in width,** not a handbreadth and a half, **enough to hold a small brick across its width.**

רְחָבָה כְּדֵי לְקַבֵּל אָרִיחַ, וּבְרִיאָה כְּדֵי לְקַבֵּל אָרִיחַ. רַבִּי יְהוּדָה אוֹמֵר: רְחָבָה אַף עַל פִּי שֶׁאֵין בְּרִיאָה. הָיְתָה שֶׁל קַשׁ וְשֶׁל קָנִים – רוֹאִין אוֹתָהּ כְּאִילּוּ הִיא שֶׁל מַתֶּכֶת.

And the cross beam must be **wide enough to hold a small brick** and also **sturdy enough to hold a small brick**[H] and not collapse. **Rabbi Yehuda says:** If it is wide enough to hold the brick, **even though it is not sturdy** enough to actually support it, it is sufficient. Therefore, even if the cross beam **is made of straw or reeds, one considers it as though it were** made **of metal.**

עֲקוּמָּה – רוֹאִין אוֹתָהּ כְּאִילּוּ הִיא פְּשׁוּטָה, עֲגוּלָּה – רוֹאִין אוֹתָהּ כְּאִילּוּ הִיא מְרוּבַּעַת. כָּל שֶׁיֵּשׁ בְּהֶיקֵּיפוֹ שְׁלֹשָׁה טְפָחִים – יֵשׁ בּוֹ רוֹחַב טֶפַח.

If the cross beam is **curved,** so that a small brick cannot rest on it, **one considers it as though it were straight;**[N] if it is **round, one considers it as though it were square.** The following principle was stated with regard to a round cross beam: **Any** beam **with a circumference of three handbreadths is a handbreadth in width,** i.e., in diameter.

HALAKHA

Whose head and most of his body were in the ***sukka*** **– רֹאשׁוֹ וְרוּבּוֹ בַּסּוּכָּה:** If one sits with his head and most of his body in the *sukka*, but his table is inside the house, it is as though he were not sitting in the *sukka*, in accordance with the opinion of Beit Shammai, with whom Beit Hillel ultimately agreed on this matter (*Shulḥan Arukh, Oraḥ Ḥayyim* 634:4).

The width of the cross beam – רוֹחַב הַקּוֹרָה: A cross beam must be at least a handbreadth wide to render an alleyway fit for one to carry within it on Shabbat (*Shulḥan Arukh, Oraḥ Ḥayyim* 363:17).

The sturdiness of the cross beam – חוֹזֶק הַקּוֹרָה: A cross beam must be sturdy enough to support a small brick. In the Jerusalem Talmud, the criterion is that it be sturdy enough to support bricks lined up along its entire length, up to three handbreadths away from the two sides of the alleyway (*Magen Avraham*, based on *Beit Yosef*; *Shulḥan Arukh, Oraḥ Ḥayyim* 363:17).

BACKGROUND

A small brick and a large brick – אָרִיחַ וּלְבֵנָה: A large brick is usually a square of three by three handbreadths. A small brick, which is half a brick, is a rectangle three handbreadths long and one and a half handbreadths wide.

Large brick and small brick

NOTES

They were counted and concluded – נִמְנוּ וְגָמְרוּ: Some commentaries explain that the question was whether or not the potential positive actions of a person are greater than his opportunities for failure. Ultimately, they counted the mitzvot and concluded that there are more negative precepts than positive precepts, which means that the danger of transgressing negative commandments is greater than the possibility of fulfilling positive ones. Due to this danger, it would have been preferable had a person not been created (Maharsha).

Examine and scrutinize – יְפַשְׁפֵּשׁ וִימַשְׁמֵשׁ: Some explain that a person should examine the actions that he has already performed and scrutinize the actions that he plans to undertake (Ritva). Others suggest that one should examine the totality of one's actions and scrutinize each individual action (*Mesillat Yesharim*).

Enough to receive a small brick – כְּדֵי לְקַבֵּל אָרִיחַ: In the Jerusalem Talmud, it is explained that the cross beam must be sturdy enough to bear a complete row of bricks along its entire length, with the bricks laid out lengthwise or widthwise. The rationale is that otherwise the cross beam would look as though it were a small wooden plank not placed permanently in that spot.

Curved…as though it were straight – עֲקוּמָּה...כְּאִילּוּ הִיא פְּשׁוּטָה: It is said in the Jerusalem Talmud that the entire latter section of the mishna is stated in accordance with the opinion of Rabbi Yehuda. According to most commentaries, that is not the understanding in the Babylonian Talmud, although some commentaries, including Rabbeinu Yehonatan, dispute this.

גמ׳ טֶפַח?! טֶפַח וּמֶחֱצָה בָּעֵי!

GEMARA The Gemara questions the statement in the mishna with regard to the minimum width of the cross beam: **A handbreadth? A handbreadth and a half is required,** as a small brick is a handbreadth and a half wide.

כֵּיוָן דְּרָחָב לְקַבֵּל טֶפַח, אִידָּךְ חֲצִי טֶפַח מְלַבֵּין לֵיהּ בְּטִינָא, מַשֶּׁהוּ מֵהַאי גִּיסָא וּמַשֶּׁהוּ מֵהַאי גִּיסָא, וְקָיְימָא.

The Gemara answers: **Since** the cross beam **is wide enough to receive** and hold **a handbreadth, one can affix the remaining half handbreadth with plaster,** a small **amount on this side and** a small **amount on** that **side, and** the brick will **stand** in place.

אָמַר רַבָּה בַּר רַב הוּנָא: קוֹרָה שֶׁאָמְרוּ – צְרִיכָה שֶׁתְּהֵא בְּרִיאָה כְּדֵי לְקַבֵּל אָרִיחַ, וּמַעֲמִידֵי קוֹרָה אֵינָן צְרִיכִין שֶׁיִּהְיוּ בְּרִיאִין כְּדֵי לְקַבֵּל קוֹרָה וְאָרִיחַ. וְרַב חִסְדָּא אָמַר: אֶחָד זֶה וְאֶחָד זֶה צְרִיכִין שֶׁיִּהְיוּ בְּרִיאִין כְּדֵי לְקַבֵּל קוֹרָה וְאָרִיחַ.

Rabba bar Rav Huna said: The cross **beam of which** the Sages **spoke must be sturdy enough to receive** and hold **a small brick; however, the supports of the** cross **beam**[NH] **need not be sturdy** enough **to receive** and hold **a** cross **beam and a small brick.** Criteria were established for the cross beam itself, which renders the alleyway fit for one to carry within it; criteria were not established for its supports. **Rav Ḥisda** disagreed and **said: Both this,** the beam, **and that,** its supports, **must be sturdy** enough **to hold** a cross **beam and a small brick.**

אָמַר רַב שֵׁשֶׁת: הִנִּיחַ קוֹרָה עַל גַּבֵּי מָבוֹי, וּפֵרֵס עָלֶיהָ מַחֲצֶלֶת, וְהִגְבִּיהָהּ מִן הַקַּרְקַע שְׁלֹשָׁה – קוֹרָה אֵין כָּאן, מְחִיצָה אֵין כָּאן. קוֹרָה אֵין כָּאן – דְּהָא מִיכַּסְיָא, מְחִיצָה אֵין כָּאן – דַּהֲוְיָא לַהּ מְחִיצָה שֶׁהַגְּדָיִים בּוֹקְעִין בָּהּ.

Rav Sheshet said: If one placed a cross **beam over** the entrance **of an alleyway, and draped a mat over it, and raised** the lower end of the mat **three** handbreadths **from the ground,**[H] **there is neither** a cross **beam here,**[N] **nor is there a partition here** to render the alleyway fit for one to carry within it. **There is neither** a cross **beam here, as it is obscured** and therefore inconspicuous. **Nor is there a partition here, as it is a partition** that is more than three handbreadths off the ground **through which goats can pass,** and therefore it does not have the legal status of a partition.

תָּנוּ רַבָּנַן: קוֹרָה הַיּוֹצְאָה מִכּוֹתֶל זֶה וְאֵינָהּ נוֹגַעַת בְּכוֹתֶל זֶה, וְכֵן שְׁתֵּי קוֹרוֹת אַחַת יוֹצְאָה מִכּוֹתֶל זֶה וְאַחַת יוֹצְאָה מִכּוֹתֶל זֶה וְאֵינָן נוֹגְעוֹת זוֹ בָּזוֹ. פָּחוֹת מִשְּׁלֹשָׁה – אֵין צָרִיךְ לְהָבִיא קוֹרָה אַחֶרֶת, שְׁלֹשָׁה – צָרִיךְ לְהָבִיא קוֹרָה אַחֶרֶת.

Our Sages taught in the *Tosefta*: **If a** cross **beam projects from this wall** of an alleyway **but does not touch that wall** opposite, **and similarly,** if there are **two** cross **beams,**[B] **one projecting from this wall and one projecting from that wall** opposite, **and they do not touch one another,**[H] if there is a gap of **less than three** handbreadths between the beam and the wall, or between the two beams respectively, **one need not bring another** cross **beam** to render the alleyway fit for one to carry within it, as they are considered joined based on the principle of *lavud*. However, if there is a gap of **three** handbreadths, **one must bring another** cross **beam.**

רַבָּן שִׁמְעוֹן בֶּן גַּמְלִיאֵל אוֹמֵר: פָּחוֹת מֵאַרְבַּע – אֵין צָרִיךְ לְהָבִיא קוֹרָה אַחֶרֶת, אַרְבַּע – צָרִיךְ לְהָבִיא קוֹרָה אַחֶרֶת.

Rabban Shimon ben Gamliel says: If the gap is **less than four** handbreadths, **one need not bring another** cross **beam.** However, if it is **four** handbreadths, **he must bring another** cross **beam,** as in his opinion the principle of *lavud* applies to a gap up to four handbreadths wide.

וְכֵן שְׁתֵּי קוֹרוֹת הַמַּתְאִימוֹת, לֹא בָּזוֹ כְּדֵי לְקַבֵּל אָרִיחַ וְלֹא בָּזוֹ כְּדֵי לְקַבֵּל אָרִיחַ, אִם מְקַבְּלוֹת אָרִיחַ לְרָחְבּוֹ טֶפַח – אֵין צָרִיךְ לְהָבִיא קוֹרָה אַחֶרֶת, וְאִם לָאו – צָרִיךְ לְהָבִיא קוֹרָה אַחֶרֶת.

And similarly, if **two matching,** extremely narrow cross **beams**[NH] are placed alongside each other, even though **there is not** sufficient width **in this beam to receive a small brick, and there is not** sufficient width **in that** beam, **if the two beams together can receive a small brick along its handbreadth width, one need not bring another** cross **beam** to render the alleyway fit for one to carry within it; **but if not, one is required to bring another** cross **beam.**

HALAKHA

The supports of the cross beam – מַעֲמִידֵי קוֹרָה: Some hold that the supports of the cross beam must be sturdy enough to support the cross beam and a small brick on top of it. They rule in accordance with the opinion of Rav Ḥisda because he was a greater authority than Rabba bar Rav Huna (Vilna Gaon; Rabbeinu Ḥananel; Rambam; *Maggid Mishne*; *Or Zarua*; *Roke'aḥ*). Other authorities rule that the supports of the cross beam need be sturdy enough only to support the weight of the cross beam alone, in accordance with the opinion of Rabba bar Rav Huna, because in disputes relating to rabbinic law the ruling is lenient (Rosh; *Mordekhai*; Rema; and others). In practice, some authorities ruled leniently (*Shulḥan Arukh HaRav*), while others ruled stringently *ab initio* because the majority of authorities ruled stringently (*Mishna Berura*; *Shulḥan Arukh*, *Oraḥ Ḥayyim* 363:18).

A cross beam covered by a mat – קוֹרָה הַמְכוּסָּה בְּמַחֲצֶלֶת: A cross beam covered by a mat that does not reach within three handbreadths of the ground does not render an alleyway fit for one to carry within it, in accordance with the opinion of Rav Sheshet (*Shulḥan Arukh*, *Oraḥ Ḥayyim* 363:24).

Adjacent cross beams that do not touch one another – קוֹרוֹת סְמוּכוֹת: If a cross beam projects from one wall and reaches within three handbreadths of the opposite wall, or if two cross beams project from two opposite walls and reach within three handbreadths of each other, they render an alleyway fit for one to carry within it. Based on the principle of *lavud*, it is as though they were a single cross beam (*Shulḥan Arukh*, *Oraḥ Ḥayyim* 363:21).

Matching, extremely narrow cross beams – קוֹרוֹת הַמַּתְאִימוֹת: If two narrow cross beams are placed parallel to each other within three handbreadths of each other, and neither is wide enough to hold a small brick, they are considered as one cross beam and render the alleyway fit for one to carry within it, based on the principle of *lavud* (Rambam). Others say that they must be within one handbreadth of each other, as the Gemara requires that they must actually be capable of supporting a small brick (*Tosafot*; *Tur*; *Hagahot Maimoniyot*; Rabbeinu Yehonatan). *Shulḥan Arukh HaRav* rules stringently (*Shulḥan Arukh*, *Oraḥ Ḥayyim* 363:22).

BACKGROUND

Two cross beams – שְׁתֵּי קוֹרוֹת: The illustration below shows two cross beams projecting from two alleyway walls, but not touching each other. Each of these cross beams also serves as an example of a cross beam that projects from one wall but does not reach the opposite wall.

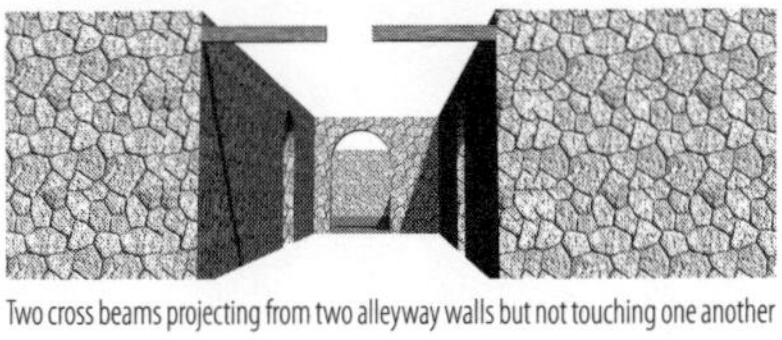

Two cross beams projecting from two alleyway walls but not touching one another

NOTES

The supports of the cross beam – מַעֲמִידֵי קוֹרָה: Rabbeinu Ḥananel explains that the supports of the cross beam are the alleyway walls upon which the cross beam rests.

There is neither a cross beam here – קוֹרָה אֵין כָּאן: The question is raised, Why isn't the mat an extension of the cross beam? A thick cross beam also renders the alleyway fit for one to carry within it. Some answer that since the mat is not sturdy enough to support a small brick, it cannot serve as a cross beam (Rashba).

Two matching, extremely narrow cross beams – שְׁתֵּי קוֹרוֹת הַמַּתְאִימוֹת: The early commentaries disagree with regard to this case. Some (Rambam and other authorities) explain that the situation involves two cross beams, each of which measures half a handbreadth or more; together they are minimally a handbreadth wide. If the two parallel cross beams are less than three handbreadths apart, then the principle of *lavud* applies, and they are considered a single cross beam. Others hold that if the cross beams are close enough that a small brick can be placed across them, they render the alleyway fit for one to carry within it, even if the two cross beams together are less than a handbreadth wide (Ra'avad; Ritva; *Tosafot*). This approach maintains that, according to the principle of *lavud*, the space between the two cross beams is considered as though it were filled.

HALAKHA

One above and one below – אַחַת לְמַעְלָה וְאַחַת לְמַטָּה: If two cross beams that are narrower than required are set one above the other and they are within three handbreadths of each other, they constitute a valid cross beam, provided that neither of them is above twenty cubits or below ten handbreadths (*Tur*, citing Rambam). The *halakha* is in accordance with the opinion of Rabbi Yosei, son of Rabbi Yehuda, whose opinion is cited elsewhere in the Gemara (Vilna Gaon; *Shulḥan Arukh*, *Oraḥ Ḥayyim* 363:26).

Four handbreadths wide – רוֹחַב אַרְבָּעָה: A cross beam that is four handbreadths wide renders an alleyway fit for one to carry within it, even if it is not sturdy enough to hold a small brick. This ruling is in accordance with the opinion of Rav (*Shulḥan Arukh*, *Oraḥ Ḥayyim* 363:17).

רַבָּן שִׁמְעוֹן בֶּן גַּמְלִיאֵל אוֹמֵר: אִם מְקַבֶּלֶת אָרִיחַ לְאׇרְכּוֹ שְׁלֹשָׁה – אֵין צָרִיךְ לְהָבִיא קוֹרָה אַחֶרֶת, וְאִם לָאו – צָרִיךְ לְהָבִיא קוֹרָה אַחֶרֶת.

Rabban Shimon ben Gamliel says: If the two cross beams can **receive a small brick along its length,** which is **three** handbreadths, **one need not bring another** cross **beam, but if not, one must bring another** cross **beam.**

הָיוּ אַחַת לְמַעְלָה וְאַחַת לְמַטָּה, רַבִּי יוֹסֵי בְּרַבִּי יְהוּדָה אוֹמֵר: רוֹאִין אֶת הָעֶלְיוֹנָה כְּאִילּוּ הִיא לְמַטָּה, וְאֶת הַתַּחְתּוֹנָה כְּאִילּוּ הִיא לְמַעְלָה, וּבִלְבַד שֶׁלֹּא תְּהֵא עֶלְיוֹנָה לְמַעְלָה מֵעֶשְׂרִים אַמָּה וְתַחְתּוֹנָה לְמַטָּה מֵעֲשָׂרָה.

If these two narrow cross beams **are** placed **one above and one below,**[H] **Rabbi Yosei, son of Rabbi Yehuda, says: One considers the upper** one **as though it were below, and the lower one as though it were above,** i.e., close together. If the two together are fit to hold a small brick, they render the alleyway fit for one to carry within it, although they are not actually close to each other, **provided that the upper** cross **beam is not above twenty cubits and the lower** one is not **below ten** handbreadths, between which a cross beam renders an alleyway fit for one to carry within it.

אָמַר אַבַּיֵי: רַבִּי יוֹסֵי בְּרַבִּי יְהוּדָה סָבַר לָהּ כַּאֲבוּהּ בַּחֲדָא, וּפָלֵיג עֲלֵיהּ בַּחֲדָא. סָבַר לָהּ כַּאֲבוּהּ בַּחֲדָא – דְּאִית לֵיהּ רוֹאִין,

Abaye said: Rabbi Yosei, son of Rabbi Yehuda, holds in accordance with the opinion of **his father with regard to one** matter, **and disagrees with his** opinion **with regard to one** matter. **He holds in accordance with** the opinion of **his father in one** matter, **as he is** of the opinion that the principle: **One considers,** applies. Just as Rabbi Yehuda stated in the mishna that the cross beam is considered as though it were sturdy even though it is not, his son, Rabbi Yosei, holds that one considers two cross beams placed apart as though they were adjacent.

וּפָלֵיג עֲלֵיהּ בַּחֲדָא – דְּאִילּוּ רַבִּי יְהוּדָה סָבַר: לְמַעְלָה מֵעֶשְׂרִים, וְרַבִּי יוֹסֵי בְּרַבִּי יְהוּדָה סָבַר: בְּתוֹךְ עֶשְׂרִים – אִין, לְמַעְלָה מֵעֶשְׂרִים – לָא.

And Rabbi Yosei **disagrees with his** father's opinion **with regard to one** matter. **While Rabbi Yehuda holds** that a cross beam renders an alleyway fit for one to carry within it even if it is **higher than twenty** cubits, **Rabbi Yosei, son of Rabbi Yehuda, holds: Within twenty cubits, yes,** it renders the alleyway fit for one to carry within it; **above twenty,** it does **not.**

״רַבִּי יְהוּדָה אוֹמֵר: רְחָבָה אַף עַל פִּי שֶׁאֵינָהּ בְּרִיאָה״. מַתְנֵי לֵיהּ רַב יְהוּדָה לְחִיָּיא בַּר רַב קַמֵּיהּ דְּרַב: רְחָבָה אַף עַל פִּי שֶׁאֵינָהּ בְּרִיאָה. אֲמַר לֵיהּ: אַתְנְיֵיהּ רְחָבָה וּבְרִיאָה.

It was stated in the mishna that **Rabbi Yehuda says:** It suffices if the cross beam is **wide** enough to hold a small brick, **even though it is not sturdy** enough to actually support it. **Rav Yehuda taught** this clause of the mishna **to Ḥiyya bar Rav in the presence of Rav:** It suffices if the cross beam is **wide** enough to hold a small brick, **even though it is not sturdy** enough to actually support it. Rav **said to him: Teach** it to **him** as follows: **Wide** enough **and sturdy** enough to hold a small brick.

וְהָאָמַר רַבִּי אֶילְעַאי, אָמַר רַב: רְחָבָה אַרְבָּעָה אַף עַל פִּי שֶׁאֵינָהּ בְּרִיאָה! רְחָבָה אַרְבָּעָה שָׁאנֵי.

The Gemara challenges this statement: **Didn't Rabbi Elai say** that **Rav said:** A cross beam that is **four** handbreadths **wide**[H] renders an alleyway fit for one to carry within it **even if it is not sturdy** enough to hold a small brick? The Gemara answers: A cross beam that is **four handbreadths wide is different,** as a beam of that width is considered a roof and not a beam. It is considered as though the edge of the roof descended and constituted an actual partition, not merely a conspicuous distinction.

״הָיְתָה שֶׁל קַשׁ כו׳״. מַאי קָא מַשְׁמַע לָן – דְּאָמְרִינַן רוֹאִין, הַיְינוּ הַךְ!

It was stated in the mishna: Even **if** the cross beam **is** made **of straw** or reeds, one considers it as though it were made of metal. The Gemara asks: **What is** the mishna **teaching us?** If it is teaching **that we say one considers** the cross beam as though it were fit to bear a brick, then **this** clause **is the same as the** previous clause in the mishna: Wide enough even though it is not sturdy enough.

מַהוּ דְּתֵימָא: בְּמִינָהּ – אָמְרִינַן, שֶׁלֹּא בְּמִינָהּ – לָא אָמְרִינַן, קָא מַשְׁמַע לָן.

The Gemara answers: There is a novel point here, **lest you say** that with regard to a cross beam made of material that other beams **of its own kind** are sturdy, e.g., wood, **we say** that even the flimsiest of cross beams is considered sturdy. However, with regard to a cross beam made of material that only beams **not of its own kind** are sturdy, e.g., straw, which can never support a brick, **we do not say** that one considers the cross beam as if it were made of metal. Therefore, the mishna **teaches us** that there is no difference between the cases.

״עֲקוּמָּה רוֹאִין אוֹתָהּ כְּאִילּוּ הִיא פְּשׁוּטָה״. פְּשִׁיטָא! קָא מַשְׁמַע לָן כִּדְרַבִּי זֵירָא; דְּאָמַר רַבִּי זֵירָא: הִיא בְּתוֹךְ הַמָּבוֹי וְעַקְמוּמִיתָהּ חוּץ לְמָבוֹי, הִיא בְּתוֹךְ עֶשְׂרִים וְעַקְמוּמִיתָהּ לְמַעְלָה מֵעֶשְׂרִים, הִיא לְמַעְלָה מֵעֲשָׂרָה וְעַקְמוּמִיתָהּ לְמַטָּה מֵעֲשָׂרָה, רוֹאִין, כׇּל שֶׁאִילּוּ יִנָּטֵל עַקְמוּמִיתָהּ וְאֵין בֵּין זֶה לָזֶה שְׁלֹשָׁה – אֵין צָרִיךְ לְהָבִיא קוֹרָה אַחֶרֶת, וְאִם לָאו – צָרִיךְ לְהָבִיא קוֹרָה אַחֶרֶת.

It was taught in the mishna: If the cross beam is **curved,**[HB] **one considers it as though it were straight.** The Gemara challenges: That is **obvious.** The Gemara answers that this is **in accordance with** the opinion of **Rabbi Zeira, as Rabbi Zeira said:** If the cross beam **is inside the alleyway, and its curved** section **is outside the alleyway;** or **it is within twenty** cubits of the ground, **and its curved** section **is above twenty** cubits; or **it is above ten** handbreadths, **and its curved** section **is below ten** handbreadths, meaning that the curved part of the beam is outside the area where a cross beam is effective, **one considers** the situation: In **any** case **where, were the curved** section outside the area where a cross beam is effective **removed, there would not be** a gap of **three** handbreadths **between this** effective part of the cross beam **and that** effective part of the cross beam, **one need not bring another** cross **beam. And if not,** if the gap would be greater, **he must bring another** cross **beam.**

הָא נַמִּי פְּשִׁיטָא! הִיא בְּתוֹךְ מָבוֹי וְעַקְמוּמִיתָהּ חוּץ לְמָבוֹי אִיצְטְרִיכָא לֵיהּ, מַהוּ דְּתֵימָא: לֵיחוּשׁ דִּילְמָא אָתֵי לְאַמְשׁוֹכֵי בַּתְרָהּ, קָא מַשְׁמַע לָן.

The Gemara comments: **That too is obvious,** as the curved portion of the cross beam is considered as though it were straight. The Gemara explains: In a case where the cross beam **is inside the alleyway and its curved** portion **is outside the alleyway, it was necessary for him** to teach the *halakha.* **Lest you say: Let us be concerned that he** will **come to be drawn after it** and carry in the area where the curvature extends beyond the alleyway, Rabbi Zeira **teaches us** that this is not a concern.

״עֲגוּלָּה רוֹאִין אוֹתָהּ כְּאִילּוּ הִיא מְרוּבַּעַת״. הָא תּוּ לָמָּה לִי? סֵיפָא אִיצְטְרִיכָא לֵיהּ: כׇּל שֶׁיֵּשׁ בְּהֶיקֵּפוֹ שְׁלֹשָׁה טְפָחִים יֵשׁ בּוֹ רֹחַב טֶפַח.

The mishna continues: If the cross beam is **round,**[H] **one considers it as though it were square.** The Gemara asks: **Why do I need this** clause **as well?** Similar cases were already taught in the mishna. The Gemara answers: **It was necessary** to teach **the last clause** of this section, i.e., the principle that **any circle with a circumference of three handbreadths is a handbreadth in diameter.**[N]

מְנָא הָנֵי מִילֵּי? אָמַר רַבִּי יוֹחָנָן, אָמַר קְרָא: ״וַיַּעַשׂ אֶת הַיָּם מוּצָק עֶשֶׂר בָּאַמָּה מִשְּׂפָתוֹ עַד שְׂפָתוֹ עָגֹל סָבִיב וְחָמֵשׁ בָּאַמָּה קוֹמָתוֹ וְקָו שְׁלֹשִׁים בָּאַמָּה יָסוֹב אוֹתוֹ סָבִיב״.

The Gemara asks: **From where are these matters,** this ratio between circumference and diameter, derived? **Rabbi Yoḥanan said** that **the verse said** with regard to King Solomon: **"And he made a molten sea, ten cubits from the one brim to the other: It was round all about, and its height was five cubits; and a line of thirty cubits did circle it round about"** (I Kings 7:23).[B]

וְהָא אִיכָּא שְׂפָתוֹ!

The Gemara asks: **But isn't there its brim** that must be taken into account? The diameter of the sea was measured from the inside, and if its circumference was measured from the outside, this ratio is no longer accurate.

אָמַר רַב פַּפָּא: שְׂפָתוֹ שְׂפַת פֶּרַח שׁוֹשָׁן כְּתִיב בֵּיהּ, דִּכְתִיב: ״וְעׇבְיוֹ טֶפַח וּשְׂפָתוֹ כְּמַעֲשֵׂה כוֹס פֶּרַח שׁוֹשָׁן אַלְפַּיִם בַּת יָכִיל״.

Rav Pappa said: With regard to its brim, it is written that **the brim** is as **the petals of a lily,** as stated in the verse: **"And it was a handbreadth thick; and its brim was wrought as the brim of a cup, as the petals of a lily; it contained two thousand *bat*"**[B] (I Kings 7:26). The brim was very thin.

וְהָאִיכָּא מַשֶּׁהוּ! כִּי קָא חָשֵׁיב – מִגַּוָּאי קָא חָשֵׁיב.

The Gemara asks: **But** nevertheless, **isn't there** the minimal **amount** of the thickness of the brim? The Gemara answers: **When one calculates** the circumference, **he calculates from the inside.**[N]

תַּנְיָא רַבִּי חִיָּיא: יָם שֶׁעָשָׂה שְׁלֹמֹה הָיָה מַחֲזִיק מֵאָה וַחֲמִשִּׁים מִקְוֶה טׇהֳרָה. מִכְּדִי, מִקְוֶה כַּמָּה הָוֵי – אַרְבָּעִים סְאָה, כִּדְתַנְיָא: ״וְרָחַץ אֶת בְּשָׂרוֹ

Rabbi Ḥiyya taught in a *baraita*: **The sea that Solomon fashioned contained** a volume of **one hundred and fifty baths of ritual purification.** The Gemara asks: **After all,** with regard to **a ritual bath, how much is** its volume? It is **forty *se'a*, as it was taught** in a *baraita*: **And he shall bathe his flesh**

NOTES

The diameter of a circle – קוֹטְרוֹ שֶׁל עִיגּוּל: *Tosafot* note that this calculation is imprecise, as the ratio between a circle's circumference and its diameter is greater than three to one. In practice, the difference here is so small, i.e., less than one-twentieth of a handbreadth, that the Sages did not take it into consideration (*Ḥeshek Shlomo*). As for the principle itself, Rambam writes that since this ratio is clearly a number that fundamentally cannot be defined by means of other numbers, the Sages accepted the simplest approximation of three to one because they could not arrive at a true and definitive number for the ratio (Rambam's Commentary on the Mishna).

He calculates from the inside – מִגַּוָּאי קָא חָשֵׁיב: Since it must have been obvious when measuring the laver that its circumference was nearly a cubit and a half longer (see *Ge'on Ya'akov*) than three times its diameter, some commentaries explain that the diameter was measured from the outside, while the circumference was measured from the inside. Calculated in this manner, the inner circumference was in fact only slightly more than thirty cubits.

HALAKHA

Curved cross beam – קוֹרָה עֲקוּמָּה: If cross beam is curved, and the curved section is located above, below, or outside the area where a cross beam is valid, the cross beam is considered as though the curved part were removed. If the remaining sections are close enough for the principle of *lavud* to apply, the cross beam is considered valid, in accordance with the opinion of Rabbi Zeira (*Shulḥan Arukh, Oraḥ Ḥayyim* 363:20).

Round cross beam – קוֹרָה עֲגוּלָּה: A round cross beam is valid, provided that its circumference is at least three handbreadths (*Shulḥan Arukh, Oraḥ Ḥayyim* 363:24).

BACKGROUND

Curved cross beam – קוֹרָה עֲקוּמָּה: If a cross beam is curved outward, the Gemara states that the section protruding outside the alleyway is disregarded and considered completely missing. The halakhic validity of the cross beam depends on the length of the gap, represented in the sketch below with a broken line. If it is longer than three handbreadths the cross beam is invalid; if it is less than three handbreadths, the cross beam is valid.

Cross beam curved outward

Solomon's Sea – יָם שֶׁל שְׁלֹמֹה: The sea, according to the plain sense of the verses, was a huge half-sphere made of copper, with a diameter of ten cubits and a circumference of approximately thirty cubits. It held the water used for washing the priests' hands and feet. The laver rested on twelve statues resembling cattle, which were arranged three on each side.

Depiction of Solomon's Sea

***Bat* – בַּת:** The liquid equivalent of an *eipha*, it is one-tenth of a *kor*, ranging from approximately 25–43 ℓ.

NOTES

Three lower cubits were square – **שָׁלֹשׁ אַמּוֹת תַּחְתּוֹנוֹת מְרוּבָּעוֹת**: In the Jerusalem Talmud, the conclusion is the same, based on the fact that Solomon's Sea is described in the verses as both square and round. Since the verse states that the rim of the laver was round, the implication is that below its rim it was square (*Ge'on Ya'akov*).

BACKGROUND

Square and round – **מְרוּבָּעוֹת וַעֲגוּלוֹת**:

Model of Solomon's Sea according to Rami bar Yeḥezkel

בַּמַּיִם״ – בְּמֵי מִקְוֶה. ״כָּל בְּשָׂרוֹ״ – מַיִם שֶׁכָּל גּוּפוֹ עוֹלֶה בָּהֶן. וְכַמָּה הֵן – אַמָּה עַל אַמָּה בְּרוּם שָׁלֹשׁ אַמּוֹת. וְשִׁיעֲרוּ חֲכָמִים מֵי מִקְוֶה אַרְבָּעִים סְאָה.

in water; specifically **in the water of a ritual bath.** The expression **"all his flesh"** (Leviticus 15:16) teaches that one must immerse in **water that his whole body can enter** at once. **And how much is that? A cubit by a cubit by the height of three cubits. And the Sages calculated** that the volume of **water** necessary for **a ritual bath** of this size **is forty *se'a*.**

כַּמָּה הָווּ לְהוּ חֲמֵשׁ מְאָה גַּרְמִידֵי, לִתְלָת מְאָה מְאָה, לִמְאָה וַחֲמְשִׁין חַמְשִׁין, בְּאַרְבַּע מְאָה וַחֲמְשִׁין סַגְיָא!

The Gemara now calculates **how many** ritual baths should have been contained in Solomon's Sea. The volume of the sea was **five hundred** cubic **cubits,** as it was ten cubits in length, ten cubits in width, and five cubits in height. The minimum volume of a ritual bath is three cubic cubits. Therefore, **three hundred** cubic cubits is the volume of **a hundred** ritual baths, and **one hundred and fifty** cubic cubits is the volume of another **fifty** ritual baths. Consequently, **four hundred and fifty** cubic cubits **are enough** to contain a hundred and fifty ritual baths; but the volume of the sea was five hundred.

הָנֵי מִילֵּי בְּרִיבּוּעָא, יָם שֶׁעָשָׂה שְׁלֹמֹה עָגוֹל הָיָה.

The Gemara answers that there is an error in the calculation: **These** calculations with regard to the volume of the sea would **apply to a square,** but the **sea fashioned by Solomon was round,** and its volume was therefore smaller.

מִכְּדֵי, כַּמָּה מְרוּבָּע יָתֵר עַל הָעִגּוּל – רְבִיעַ; לְאַרְבַּע מְאָה – מְאָה, לִמְאָה – עֶשְׂרִים וַחֲמִשָּׁה, הָנֵי מֵאָה וְעֶשְׂרִים וַחֲמִשָּׁה הָווּ לְהוּ!

The Gemara continues to ask: **Now, how much larger is a square** of ten-by-ten cubits **than a circle** with a diameter of ten cubits? **A quarter.** Consequently, **four hundred** cubic cubits of our original calculation must be reduced to three hundred, which is the volume of **one hundred** ritual baths; and the remaining **hundred** cubits must be reduced to seventy-five, which is the volume of **twenty-five** ritual baths. According to this calculation, Solomon's Sea was the size of only **one hundred and twenty-five** ritual baths, not one hundred and fifty as stated above.

תָּנֵי רָמִי בַּר יְחֶזְקֵאל: יָם שֶׁעָשָׂה שְׁלֹמֹה שָׁלֹשׁ אַמּוֹת תַּחְתּוֹנוֹת מְרוּבָּעוֹת וּשְׁתַּיִם עֶלְיוֹנוֹת עֲגוּלוֹת.

In answer to this question, **Rami bar Yeḥezkel taught** as follows: In the **sea that Solomon fashioned,** the **three lower cubits were square**[N] **and the upper two were round.**[B] Consequently, the three lower cubits of the sea contained the volume of a hundred ritual baths, and its upper three cubits contained the volume of fifty ritual baths, for a total of one hundred and fifty ritual baths.

נְהִי דְּאִיפְּכָא לָא מָצֵית אָמְרַתְּ, דְּ״שְׂפָתוֹ עָגוֹל״ כְּתִיב, אֶלָּא אֵימָא חֲדָא!

The Gemara comments: **Although you cannot say the opposite,** that the bottom of the sea was round, **as it is written** in the verse that **its brim was round;** you can, **however,** say that only **one** cubit on top was round.

לָא סָלְקָא דַּעֲתָךְ, דִּכְתִיב: ״אַלְפַּיִם בַּת יָכִיל״, בַּת כַּמָּה הָוְיָא – שָׁלֹשׁ סְאִין, דִּכְתִיב: ״מַעְשַׂר הַבַּת מִן הַכּוֹר״. דַּהֲוָה לְהוּ שִׁיתָּא אַלְפֵי גְּרִיוֵי.

The Gemara rejects this possibility: **This cannot enter your mind, as it is written** with regard to the sea: "And it was a handbreadth thick, and its brim was wrought like the brim of a cup, like the petals of a lily; **it contained two thousand *bat*"** (I Kings 7:26). **How much is** the measure of **a *bat*? Three *se'a*,** as the verse states: "Concerning the ordinance of oil, the *bat* of oil, you shall offer **the tenth part of a *bat* out of the *kor*,** which is a *ḥomer* of ten *bat*, for ten *bat* are a *ḥomer*" (Ezekiel 45:14). This proves that the *bat* is a tenth of a *kor*, or three *se'a*, as a *kor* is thirty *se'a*. Consequently, the sea, which contained two thousand *bat*, **contained six thousand *se'a*,** the volume of exactly one hundred and fifty ritual baths.

וְהָא כְּתִיב: ״מַחֲזִיק בַּתִּים שְׁלֹשֶׁת אֲלָפִים״! הַהוּא לְגוּדְשָׁא.

The Gemara asks: **Isn't it written** elsewhere with regard to Solomon's Sea: **"It received** and held **three thousand *bat*"** (II Chronicles 4:5)? The Gemara answers: **That** is referring **to the heaped measure** of dry goods that the sea could hold, as dry goods can be heaped above the brim.

אָמַר אַבַּיֵי, שְׁמַע מִינַּהּ: הַאי גּוּדְשָׁה תִּלְתָּא הָוֵי. וּתְנַן נַמִּי: שִׁידָּה תֵּיבָה וּמִגְדָּל, כַּוֶּורֶת הַקַּשׁ, וְכַוֶּורֶת הַקָּנִים, וּבוֹר סְפִינָה אֲלֶכְּסַנְדְּרִית, אַף עַל פִּי שֶׁיֵּשׁ לָהֶן שׁוּלַיִם וְהֵן מַחֲזִיקוֹת אַרְבָּעִים סְאָה בַּלַּח, שֶׁהֵן כּוֹרַיִים בַּיָּבֵשׁ – טְהוֹרִין.

Abaye said: Learn from it that **the surplus** of dry goods in a vessel relative to liquids **is one-third** of the contents of the vessel. **We also learned** the same thing in the following mishna: **A carriage, a box, and a cupboard, a round straw barrel, and a round barrel** made of **reeds, and the cistern of an Alexandrian ship,** which is a large vessel placed on a boat and filled with potable water, **although** these vessels **have bottoms,** i.e., they are receptacles, since they **have a capacity of forty** ***se'a*** **of liquid, which is the** equivalent of **two** ***kor*** of **dry** goods, they are **ritually pure.**[H] Even if they come into contact with a source of ritual impurity, they do not become impure. Beyond a certain size, containers are no longer considered vessels and, consequently, cannot become ritually impure. This mishna states clearly that a vessel that holds forty *se'a* of liquids can hold two *kor*, or sixty *se'a*, of dry goods.

מתני׳ לְחָיַיִן שֶׁאָמְרוּ – גׇּבְהָן עֲשָׂרָה טְפָחִים, וְרׇחְבָּן וְעׇבְיָין כׇּל שֶׁהוּא. רַבִּי יוֹסֵי אוֹמֵר: רׇחְבָּן שְׁלֹשָׁה טְפָחִים.

MISHNA **The side posts** the Sages **spoke** of with regard to rendering an alleyway fit for one to carry within it, **their height** must be at least **ten handbreadths, and their width and thickness** may be **any amount.**[H] **Rabbi Yosei says: Their width** must be at least **three handbreadths.**

גמ׳ ״לְחָיַיִן שֶׁאָמְרוּ כו׳״. לֵימָא תְּנַן סְתָמָא כְּרַבִּי אֱלִיעֶזֶר, דְּאָמַר לְחָיַיִן בָּעֵינַן!

GEMARA We learned in the mishna: **The side posts** the Sages **spoke** of, **etc.** The Gemara asks: **Shall we say the mishna taught an unattributed ruling in accordance with** the opinion of **Rabbi Eliezer, who said** that in order to permit carrying in an alleyway, **we require** two **side posts?**

לָא, מַאי לְחָיַיִן – לְחָיַיִן דְּעָלְמָא. אִי הָכִי קוֹרָה נַמִּי נִיתְנֵי קוֹרוֹת, וּמַאי קוֹרוֹת – קוֹרוֹת דְּעָלְמָא!

The Gemara responds: **No; what** is meant by the plural term **side posts? Side posts in general,** and not those required by a single alleyway. The Gemara asks: **If so, let** the previous mishna **also teach** the *halakha* of a cross **beam** with the plural term cross **beams, and** we would say: **What** is meant by the plural term cross **beams?** Cross beams **in general.**

הָכִי קָאָמַר: אוֹתָן לְחָיַיִן שֶׁנֶּחְלְקוּ בָּהֶן רַבִּי אֱלִיעֶזֶר וַחֲכָמִים – גׇּבְהָן עֲשָׂרָה טְפָחִים, וְרׇחְבָּן וְעׇבְיָין כׇּל שֶׁהוּא. וְכַמָּה כׇּל שֶׁהוּא? תָּנֵי רַבִּי חִיָּיא: אֲפִילּוּ כְּחוּט הַסַּרְבָּל.

The Gemara answers that **this is what** the mishna **is saying: Those side posts that Rabbi Eliezer and the Sages disagreed about,** of which Rabbi Eliezer required two and the Sages sufficed with one, **their height** must be at least **ten handbreadths, and their width and thickness** may be **any amount.** The Gemara asks: **And how much is any amount?**[N] **Rabbi Ḥiyya taught: Even as** small as **the string** used to tie **a coat.**[N]

תָּנָא: עָשָׂה לֶחִי לַחֲצִי מָבוֹי – אֵין לוֹ אֶלָּא חֲצִי מָבוֹי. פְּשִׁיטָא! אֶלָּא אֵימָא: יֵשׁ לוֹ חֲצִי מָבוֹי. הָא נַמִּי פְּשִׁיטָא! מַהוּ דְּתֵימָא: לֵיחוּשׁ דִּילְמָא אָתֵי לְאִישְׁתַּמּוֹשֵׁי בְּכוּלֵּיהּ, קָא מַשְׁמַע לַן.

It was taught in a *Tosefta*: With regard to **one who erected a side post for half an alleyway,**[H] i.e., he put it up halfway down the alleyway rather than at its entrance, **he has** the right to carry **only** in the inner **half of the alleyway,** but not in the outer half. The Gemara asks: **That is obvious;** what novel element was introduced here? **Rather, say: He** may carry in the inner **half of the alleyway** even though there is no side post at the entrance to the alleyway. The Gemara asks: **That too is obvious.** The Gemara explains that nonetheless there is a novelty here: **Lest you say** that **we should be concerned that** if it is permitted to carry in the inner half **one might come to use the entire** alleyway, the *Tosefta* **teaches** that carrying in the inner half is permitted.

אָמַר רָבָא: עָשָׂה לֶחִי לַמָּבוֹי וְהִגְבִּיהוֹ מִן הַקַּרְקַע שְׁלֹשָׁה, אוֹ שֶׁהִפְלִיגוֹ מִן הַכּוֹתֶל שְׁלֹשָׁה – לֹא עָשָׂה וְלֹא כְּלוּם. אֲפִילּוּ לְרַבָּן שִׁמְעוֹן בֶּן גַּמְלִיאֵל דְּאָמַר אָמְרִינַן לָבוּד – הָנֵי מִילֵּי לְמַעְלָה; אֲבָל לְמַטָּה, כֵּיוָן דְּהָוְיָא מְחִיצָה שֶׁהַגְּדָיִין בּוֹקְעִין בָּהּ – לָא קָאָמַר.

Rava said: With regard to **one who erected a side post in an alleyway and raised it three** handbreadths **from the ground,**[H] **or distanced it three** handbreadths **from the wall, he has not done anything,** as it is not a valid side post. **Even according to** the opinion of **Rabban Shimon ben Gamliel, who said: We say** that objects separated by a gap of up to four handbreadths are considered **connected, that applies only above,** e.g., to a cross beam that does not reach the wall of the alleyway; **but below, since it is a partition through which goats can pass,** as a goat can pass through an opening three handbreadths high, even **he did not say** that they are considered connected.[B]

״רַבִּי יוֹסֵי אוֹמֵר רׇחְבָּן שְׁלֹשָׁה טְפָחִים״. אָמַר רַב יוֹסֵף, אָמַר רַב יְהוּדָה, אָמַר שְׁמוּאֵל: אֵין הֲלָכָה כְּרַבִּי יוֹסֵי לֹא בְּהִילְמֵי וְלֹא בִּלְחָיַיִן.

We learned in the mishna that **Rabbi Yosei says: The width** of the side posts must be at least **three handbreadths. Rav Yosef said** that **Rav Yehuda said** that **Shmuel said: The** ***halakha*** **is not in accordance with** the opinion of **Rabbi Yosei, not with regard to** preparing salt **brine** [*hilmei*][L] on Shabbat, **and not with regard to side posts.**

HALAKHA

Vessels that do not contract impurity – כֵּלִים שֶׁאֵין נִטְמָאִים: Vessels that are generally made to remain in a particular place and which hold forty *se'a* are not susceptible to ritual impurity (Rambam *Sefer Tahara, Hilkhot Kelim* 3:2).

The measurements of a side post – שִׁיעוּרֵי לֶחִי: It is permitted to carry in an alleyway when a single side post is placed at one side of the entrance. It must be at least ten handbreadths high, but may be of minimal width and thickness, as stated by the unattributed mishna and in accordance with the prevalent custom reported in the Gemara (*Shulḥan Arukh, Oraḥ Ḥayyim* 363:3).

One who erected a side post for half an alleyway – עָשָׂה לֶחִי לַחֲצִי מָבוֹי: If one erected a side post halfway down an alleyway, carrying is permitted in the inner half of the alleyway, as stated in the *Tosefta*. However, if the outer half of the alleyway also has the requisite measurements of an alleyway and it has a side post at its entrance, then carrying is forbidden in the alleyway unless the residents of the two halves merge the two sections of the alleyway together [*shituf mevuot*] (*Shulḥan Arukh, Oraḥ Ḥayyim* 363:31).

Raised it three handbreadths from the ground – הִגְבִּיהוֹ מִן הַקַּרְקַע שְׁלֹשָׁה: If one placed the side post three handbreadths from the wall or raised it three handbreadths from the ground, it is invalid, as stated by Rava (*Shulḥan Arukh, Oraḥ Ḥayyim* 363:10).

NOTES

How much is any amount – כַּמָּה כׇּל שֶׁהוּא: This question seems to be superfluous. Nevertheless, several talmudic sources indicate that at times, even when a *halakha* requires any amount of a particular item, there is a specific minimum measurement that is required. Consequently, the question is very pertinent (Rashba).

As small as the string used to tie a coat – כְּחוּט הַסַּרְבָּל: Some commentaries explain that this refers to the thick thread with which a coat is sewn (Rav Hai Gaon).

BACKGROUND

A side post that is not in its place – לֶחִי שֶׁאֵינוֹ בִּמְקוֹמוֹ: The illustration below features two side posts, neither of which is valid, due to improper placement. The side post adjacent to the wall is invalid because it is raised from the ground by more than the permitted three handbreadths. The other side post, which is placed on the ground, is invalid because it is not positioned within three handbreadths of the alleyway wall.

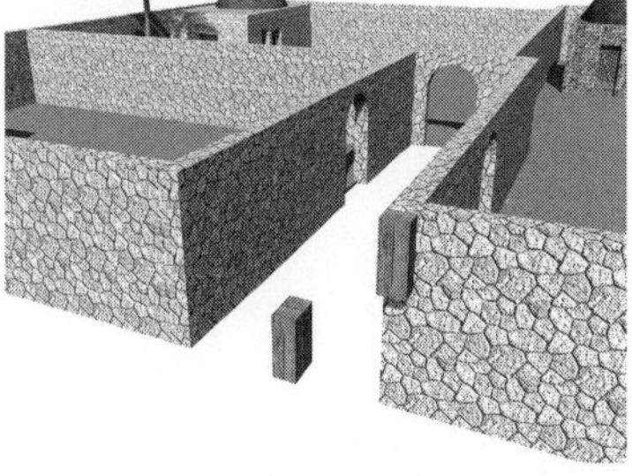

Two non-valid side posts

LANGUAGE

Brine [*hilmei*] – הִילְמֵי: From the Greek ἅλμη, *almè*, meaning concentrated salt water or brine.

NOTES

With regard to side posts you did not tell us this – בְּלְחָיַין לָא אָמְרַתְּ לָן: Rav Yosef suffered from an illness later in life that caused him to forget much of his learning. Consequently, his students would sometimes remind him of what he had taught them before his illness.

Rabbi Yosei's reasoning is with him – רַבִּי יוֹסֵי נִימּוּקוֹ עִמּוֹ: The halakhic authorities disagree whether the principle: Rabbi Yosei, his reasoning is with him, is limited to ruling in accordance with Rabbi Yosei when he disagrees with a single opposing Sage, or whether it applies even when a majority of the Sages disagree with him. Some authorities prove from this context that the *halakha* is in accordance with the opinion of Rabbi Yosei even against a majority (see *Yad Malakhi* and *Maharitz Ḥayyot*). Others state that usually the halakha is in accordance with the Sages when they argue with Rabbi Yosei, yet it could have been argued that in these specific cases the halakha is in accordance with Rabbi Yosei, as his reasoning is exceptionally logical here. Nonetheless, the halakha is in accordance with the view of the majority (Ritva).

LANGUAGE

Reasoning [*nimmuk*] – נִימּוּק: Probably related to the Greek **νομικός**, *nomikos*, meaning connected to the law or having knowledge of the statutes and law. Consequently, the statement that Rabbi Yosei's *nimmuk* is with him means that his opinion is based upon sound legal reasoning.

HALAKHA

One who drinks water to quench his thirst – הַשּׁוֹתֶה מַיִם לִצְמָאוֹ: One who drinks water to quench his thirst recites the following blessing beforehand: By Whose word all things came to be. Afterward he recites the blessing: Who creates the many forms of life, as this is the prevalent custom (*Shulḥan Arukh, Oraḥ Ḥayyim* 204:7).

אֲמַר לֵיהּ רַב הוּנָא בַּר חִינָּנָא: בְּהִילְמֵי אָמְרַתְּ לָן, בִּלְחָיַין לָא אָמְרַתְּ לָן. מַאי שְׁנָא בְּהִילְמֵי – דִּפְלִיגִי רַבָּנַן עֲלֵיהּ, לְחָיַין נַמִי פְּלִיגִי רַבָּנַן עֲלֵיהּ! אֲמַר לֵיהּ: שָׁאנֵי לְחָיַין, מִשּׁוּם דְּקָאֵי רַבִּי כְּוָותֵיהּ.

Rav Huna bar Ḥinana said to him: With regard to brine you told us that the *halakha* is not in accordance with the opinion of Rabbi Yosei, but **with regard to side posts you did not tell us** this;[N] perhaps you have forgotten that the *halakha* is in accordance with his view in that case. Rav Yosef asked: **What is different about brine,** with regard to which **the Sages disagree with** Rabbi Yosei? In the case of **side posts also the Sages disagree with him,** and therefore the *halakha* should not be in accordance with his view in either case. Rav Huna bar Ḥinana **said to him: Side posts are different, as Rabbi** Yehuda HaNasi **holds in accordance with** the opinion of Rabbi Yosei, and therefore the *halakha* may be decided in accordance with their jointly held position.

רַב רַחוּמֵי מַתְנֵי הָכִי, אֲמַר רַב יְהוּדָה בְּרֵיהּ דְּרַב שְׁמוּאֵל [בַּר שֵׁילַת] מִשְּׁמֵיהּ דְּרַב: אֵין הֲלָכָה כְּרַבִּי יוֹסֵי לֹא בְּהִילְמֵי וְלֹא בִּלְחָיַין. אֲמַר לֵיהּ: אָמְרַתְּ? אֲמַר לְהוּ: לָא. אֲמַר רָבָא: הָאֱלֹהִים! אֲמָרָהּ, וּגְמִירְנָא לָהּ מִינֵּיהּ. וּמַאי טַעְמָא קָא הֲדַר בֵּיהּ – מִשּׁוּם דְּרַבִּי יוֹסֵי נִימּוּקוֹ עִמּוֹ.

The Gemara reports that **Rav Raḥumei taught this** version of the previous discussion: **Rav Yehuda, the son of Rav Shmuel bar Sheilat, said in the name of Rav: The *halakha* is not in accordance with** the opinion of **Rabbi Yosei, not with regard to brine and not with regard to side posts.** At some later point, someone **said to him: Did you** really **say this? He said to them: No. Rava said,** reinforcing his words with an oath: **By God! He did** in fact **say this, and I learned it from him,** but he later retracted this ruling. **And what is the reason he retracted it? Due to** the well-known principle that **Rabbi Yosei's reasoning [*nimmuko*]**[L] **is with him,**[N] and the *halakha* follows his opinion even against the majority view.

אֲמַר לֵיהּ רָבָא בַּר רַב חָנָן לְאַבַּיֵי: הִילְכְתָא מַאי? אֲמַר לֵיהּ: פּוּק חֲזֵי מַאי עַמָּא דְּבַר.

Rava bar Rav Ḥanan said to Abaye: What is the accepted ***halakha*** with regard to the width of a side post? **He said to him: Go out** and observe **what the people are doing;** it is common practice to rely on a side post of minimal width.

אִיכָּא דְּמַתְנִי לָהּ אַהָא; הַשּׁוֹתֶה מַיִם לִצְמָאוֹ אוֹמֵר: "שֶׁהַכֹּל נִהְיֶה בִּדְבָרוֹ", רַבִּי טַרְפוֹן אוֹמֵר: "בּוֹרֵא נְפָשׁוֹת רַבּוֹת וְחֶסְרוֹנָן עַל כָּל מַה שֶּׁבָּרָאתָ". אֲמַר לֵיהּ רַב חָנָן לְאַבַּיֵי: הִלְכְתָא מַאי? אֲמַר לֵיהּ: פּוּק חֲזֵי מַאי עַמָּא דְּבַר.

The Gemara notes that **there are** those **who taught** that **this** answer was given **with regard to this** discussion: **One who drinks water** to quench **his thirst**[H] **recites** the following blessing prior to drinking: **By Whose word all things came to be. Rabbi Tarfon** disagrees and **says** he recites the blessing: **Who creates the many forms of life and their needs, for all that You have created. Rav Ḥanan said to Abaye: What is the *halakha*? He said to him: Go out** and observe **what the people are doing;** the customary practice is to say: By Whose word all things came to be.

Perek **I**
Daf **15** Amud **a**

HALAKHA

A side post that stands by itself – לֶחִי הָעוֹמֵד מֵאֵלָיו: A side post renders permitted carrying in an alleyway even if it was not originally erected for that purpose, provided that one resolved to rely on it prior to the beginning of Shabbat. This principle is in accordance with the opinion of Abaye. One is not required to explicitly state that he is relying on the side post. Rather, if it was in place on Friday, it is assumed that the person relies on it (Rema), unless he explicitly states that he is not relying on it (*Magen Avraham, Shulḥan Arukh HaRav; Shulḥan Arukh, Oraḥ Ḥayyim* 363:11).

NOTES

They relied on it from yesterday – סָמְכִינַן עֲלֵיהּ מֵאֶתְמוֹל: All the Sages, including Abaye, agree that a side post must be relied upon from the previous day, because a side post is not a real partition. However, a full-fledged partition functions as a wall according to Torah law in every regard, irrespective of whether or not someone relied upon it from the previous day (see *Me'iri*).

אִיתְּמַר: לֶחִי הָעוֹמֵד מֵאֵלָיו, אַבַּיֵי אָמַר: הָוֵי לֶחִי. רָבָא אָמַר: לָא הָוֵי לֶחִי.

It was stated that the *amora'im* disagreed about **a side post that stands by itself,**[H] i.e., a side post at the entrance to an alleyway that was not put there for the express purpose of permitting one to carry on Shabbat. **Abaye said: It is a valid side post. Rava said: It is not a valid side post.**

הֵיכָא דְּלָא סָמְכִינַן עֲלֵיהּ מֵאֶתְמוֹל – כּוּלֵּי עָלְמָא לָא פְּלִיגִי דְּלָא הָוֵי לֶחִי. כִּי פְּלִיגִי – הֵיכָא דְּסָמְכִינַן עֲלֵיהּ מֵאֶתְמוֹל. אַבַּיֵי אָמַר: הָוֵי לֶחִי, דְּהָא סָמְכִינַן עֲלֵיהּ מֵאֶתְמוֹל. רָבָא אָמַר: לָא הָוֵי לֶחִי, כֵּיוָן דְּמֵעִיקָּרָא לָאו אַדַּעְתֵּיהּ דְּהָכִי עֲבִידִי – לָא הָוֵי לֶחִי.

The Gemara first narrows the scope of the dispute: In a place **where** the inhabitants of the alleyway **did not rely on it from yesterday,** e.g., the alleyway had another side post that fell down on Shabbat, **all agree that it is not a valid side post. Where they disagree** is in a case **where they relied on it from yesterday.**[N] **Abaye said: It is a valid side post, as they relied on it from yesterday. Rava said: It is not a valid side post; since it was not originally erected for this purpose, it is not** considered **a valid side post.**

קָא סָלְקָא דַּעְתָּךְ כִּי הֵיכִי דִּפְלִיגִי בְּלֶחִי פְּלִיגִי נַמִי בִּמְחִיצָּה.

The Gemara comments: It might **enter your mind** to say that **just as they disagree with regard to a side post, they also disagree with regard to** whether **a partition** that was not erected to serve that function is considered a valid partition.

תָּא שְׁמַע: הָעוֹשֶׂה סוּכָּתוֹ בֵּין הָאִילָנוֹת, וְאִילָנוֹת דְּפָנוֹת לָהּ – כְּשֵׁירָה! הָכָא בְּמַאי עָסְקִינַן – שֶׁנְּטָעָן מִתְּחִילָּה לְכָךְ. אִי הָכִי, פְּשִׁיטָא! מַהוּ דְּתֵימָא: לִיגְזוֹר דִּילְמָא אָתֵי לְאִישְׁתַּמּוֹשֵׁי בְּאִילָן, קָא מַשְׁמַע לַן.

Come and **hear** a proof based upon what we learned in the following mishna: With regard to **one who makes his *sukka* among the trees, and the trees serve as its walls,**[H] **it is** a **valid** *sukka*. This proves that the trees function as partitions even though they were not erected for this purpose. The Gemara responds: **With what are we dealing here,** in this mishna? To a case **where he planted** the trees **from the outset for this** purpose. The Gemara asks: **If so,** it is **obvious** that the trees constitute valid walls. The Gemara answers: **Lest you say** the Sages **should issue** a decree to prohibit using a *sukka* with trees as its walls, due to a concern that **perhaps one will come to use the tree** on the Festival and detach a branch or leaf in the process, the mishna therefore **teaches us** that no such decree was made and the *sukka* is permitted.

תָּא שְׁמַע: הָיָה שָׁם אִילָן אוֹ גָּדֵר אוֹ חִיצַת הַקָּנִים – נִידּוֹן מִשּׁוּם דְּיוֹמֵד.

The Gemara tries to present another proof. **Come** and **hear** a proof from a *baraita*: If **there was a tree there, or a fence, or a barrier of reeds** that are interconnected and form a hedge, **it is judged** to be a valid **double post,** i.e., it qualifies as a partition suitable to enclose a public well, as will be explained below. This indicates that a partition not constructed to serve as a partition is nonetheless valid.

הָכָא נַמִי בְּמַאי עָסְקִינַן – שֶׁעֲשָׂאָן מִתְּחִילָּה לְכָךְ. אִי הָכִי מַאי קָא מַשְׁמַע לַן? [קָא מַשְׁמַע לַן:] חִיצַת הַקָּנִים קָנֶה קָנֶה פָּחוֹת מִשְּׁלֹשָׁה טְפָחִים, כְּדִבְעָא מִינֵּיהּ אַבַּיֵּי מֵרַבָּה.

The Gemara rejects this proof: **Here, too, with what are we dealing?** With a case **where one constructed them from the outset for this** purpose. The Gemara asks: **If so, what does it teach us;** is it not obvious that it is a valid double post? The Gemara answers: **It teaches us** that **a barrier of reeds** is a valid partition if the distance between **one reed and the next is less than three handbreadths, as Abaye raised** this **dilemma to Rabba,** and the *baraita* teaches that it is valid.

תָּא שְׁמַע: אִילָן הַמֵּסִיךְ עַל הָאָרֶץ, אִם אֵין נוֹפוֹ גָּבוֹהַּ מִן הָאָרֶץ שְׁלֹשָׁה טְפָחִים – מְטַלְטְלִין תַּחְתָּיו. הָכָא נַמִי בְּמַאי עָסְקִינַן – שֶׁנְּטָעוֹ מִתְּחִילָּה לְכָךְ.

The Gemara suggests another proof. **Come** and **hear** a proof from the following mishna: With regard to **a tree** whose branches **hang over** from a height of greater than ten handbreadths and reach almost to **the ground, if** the ends of **its branches are not higher than three handbreadths from the ground, one may carry under it;** the branches constitute partitions all around, and it is therefore permissible to carry in the enclosed area. The Gemara responds: **Here, too, with what are we dealing?** With a case **where he planted** the tree **from the outset for this** purpose.

אִי הָכִי לִיטַלְטֵל בְּכוּלּוֹ, אַלְמָה אָמַר רַב הוּנָא בְּרֵיהּ דְּרַב יְהוֹשֻׁעַ: אֵין מְטַלְטְלִין בּוֹ אֶלָּא בֵּית סָאתַיִם!

The Gemara asks: **If so, it should** be permitted to **carry in all of it** no matter how large the area. **Why,** then, **did Rav Huna, the son of Rav Yehoshua, say: One may only carry** under the tree if its branches enclose an area no larger than **two *beit se'a*,** i.e., five thousand square cubits? If the area is larger, it is not considered a courtyard, and carrying there is prohibited. This indicates that the branches are not considered full-fledged partitions.

מִשּׁוּם דְּהָוֵי דִּירָה שֶׁתַּשְׁמִישָׁהּ לָאֲוִיר, וְכׇל דִּירָה שֶׁתַּשְׁמִישָׁהּ לָאֲוִיר אֵין מְטַלְטְלִין בָּהּ אֶלָּא בֵּית סָאתַיִם.

The Gemara answers: The reason that carrying is permitted only if the enclosed area is less than this size is **because it is a dwelling whose use is for** the open **air** beyond it, i.e., it is used by guards who are watching the fields beyond it, rather than as an independent dwelling place, **and the** *halakha* with regard to **any dwelling whose use is for** the open **air** beyond it is that **one may carry in it only if** its area is no larger than **two *beit se'a*.**

תָּא שְׁמַע: שָׁבַת בְּתֵל שֶׁהוּא גָּבוֹהַּ עֲשָׂרָה, וְהוּא מֵאַרְבַּע אַמּוֹת וְעַד בֵּית סָאתַיִם. וְכֵן בְּנֶקַע שֶׁהוּא עָמוֹק עֲשָׂרָה, וְהוּא מֵאַרְבַּע אַמּוֹת וְעַד בֵּית סָאתַיִם, וְקָמָה קְצוּרָה וְשִׁיבּוֹלוֹת מַקִּיפוֹת אוֹתָהּ – מְהַלֵּךְ אֶת כּוּלָּהּ וְחוּצָה לָהּ אַלְפַּיִם אַמָּה.

The Gemara suggests another proof. **Come** and **hear** that which was taught in the following *baraita*: With regard to **one** who **established his Shabbat** abode **on a mound that was ten** handbreadths **high and** its area was anywhere **from four cubits to** the **two *beit se'a*; and similarly,** one who established his Shabbat abode **in a** natural **cavity**[H] of a rock **that is ten** handbreadths **deep and** its area was anywhere **from four cubits to two *beit se'a*;** and similarly, one who established his Shabbat abode in a field of **reaped grain, and** rows of **stalks** ten handbreadths high that have not been reaped **surround it,** serving as a partition enclosing the reaped area, **he may walk in the entire** enclosed area, **and outside it** an additional **two thousand cubits.** This indicates that a partition not specifically constructed to serve as a partition is nonetheless valid.

HALAKHA

Trees serving as the walls of a *sukka* – אִילָנוֹת כִּדְפָנוֹת לְסוּכָּה: A *sukka* whose walls are formed by trees is a valid *sukka* (*Shulḥan Arukh, Oraḥ Ḥayyim* 630:10).

One who established his Shabbat abode on a mound or in a cavity – שָׁבַת בְּתֵל אוֹ בְּנֶקַע: If one established his Shabbat abode in a place that is surrounded by walls that were not constructed for the purpose of creating a dwelling place, and the enclosed area is less than two *beit se'a*, the enclosed area is comparable to one's private domain. One may walk on Shabbat throughout the area and another two thousand cubits beyond its walls (*Shulḥan Arukh, Oraḥ Ḥayyim* 396:2).

NOTES

A mound and a cavity – תֵּל וְנֶקַע: The primary proof is from the choice of words. The words mound [*tel*] and cavity [*neka*], refer exclusively to places not fashioned by human hands, as a man-made valley is called a ditch or something similar (see Rashi in tractate *Sukka*).

Rav and Rav Huna – רַב וְרַב הוּנָא: A similar story is recounted in the Jerusalem Talmud, or perhaps it is a different version of the incident recounted here: Rav pulled down the side post of a certain alleyway because it was not constructed in accordance with the *halakha*, and he did not want to rely on the palm tree that was situated at the entrance to the alleyway because they had not relied on it from the previous day.

HALAKHA

A partition that stands by itself – מְחִיצָה הָעוֹמֶדֶת מֵאֵלֶיהָ: A partition that was not originally constructed to serve as a partition is nonetheless valid (*Shulḥan Arukh, Oraḥ Ḥayyim* 362:50).

וְכִי תֵּימָא, הָכָא נַמִי שֶׁעָשָׂה מִתְּחִילָּה לְכָךְ – בִּשְׁלָמָא קָמָה, לְחַיֵּי. אֶלָּא תֵּל וָנֶקַע מַאי אִיכָּא לְמֵימַר?

And if you say that **here, too,** it is a case **where he made it from the outset for this** purpose, there is a difficulty. **Granted,** in the case of the **grain,** this answer is **all right; but** with regard to **a mound and a cavity, what can be said?**[N] They were there from time immemorial and were not constructed to serve as partitions.

אֶלָּא: בִּמְחִיצוֹת כּוּלֵּי עָלְמָא לָא פְּלִיגִי דְּהָוְיָא מְחִיצָה, כִּי פְּלִיגִי בְּלֶחִי. אַבַּיֵי לְטַעְמֵיהּ, דְּאָמַר: לֶחִי מִשּׁוּם מְחִיצָה, וּמְחִיצָה הָעֲשׂוּיָה מֵאֵלֶיהָ הָוְיָא מְחִיצָה. וְרָבָא לְטַעְמֵיהּ, דְּאָמַר: לֶחִי מִשּׁוּם הֶיכֵּר. אִי עֲבִידָא בְּיָדַיִם – הָוְיָא הֶיכֵּר, וְאִי לָא – לָא הָוֵי הֶיכֵּר.

Rather, the Gemara rejects its previous argument and explains: **With regard to partitions, all agree that** a partition that stands by itself **is a partition,**[H] despite the fact that it was not erected for that purpose. **Where they disagree** is **with regard to a side post. Abaye follows his** usual line of **reasoning, as he said** that **a side post** serves **as a partition, and a partition that stands by itself is** a valid **partition. And Rava follows his** usual line of **reasoning, as he said** that **a side post** serves **as a conspicuous marker.** Therefore, **if it was made with** a person's **hands** for that purpose, **it is** considered **a conspicuous marker; and if not, it is not** considered **a conspicuous marker.**

תָּא שְׁמַע: אַבְנֵי גָּדֵר הַיּוֹצְאוֹת מִן הַגָּדֵר, מוּבְדָּלוֹת זוֹ מִזּוֹ פָּחוֹת מִשְּׁלֹשָׁה – אֵין צָרִיךְ לֶחִי אַחֵר, שְׁלֹשָׁה – צָרִיךְ לֶחִי אַחֵר.

The Gemara now attempts to prove which side is correct according to this version of the dispute. **Come** and **hear** a proof from the *Tosefta*: With regard to **stones of a wall that protrude from the wall** and are **separated from each other** by **less than three** handbreadths, **there is no need for another side post** in order to permit carrying in the alleyway; the protruding stones join together to form a side post. However, if they are separated by **three** handbreadths, **there is a need for another side post.** This indicates that a side post is valid even if it was not erected for that purpose.

הָכָא נַמִי, שֶׁבְּנָאָן מִתְּחִילָּה לְכָךְ. אִי הָכִי, פְּשִׁיטָא! מַהוּ דְּתֵימָא לְמֵיסַר בִּנְיָינָא הוּא דַּעֲבִידָא, קָא מַשְׁמַע לָן.

The Gemara rejects this proof: **Here, too,** we are dealing with a case **where one built them from the outset for this** purpose. The Gemara comments: **If so, it is obvious** that the side post is valid. The Gemara explains: **Lest you say** that it was only **in order to connect the building** to another building that **he built** the wall with protruding stones, **it teaches us** that it is a valid side post. We are not concerned that onlookers might assume that the wall was not originally built as a side post.

תָּא שְׁמַע, דְּתָנֵי רַבִּי חִיָּיא: כּוֹתֶל שֶׁצִּידּוֹ אֶחָד כָּנוּס מֵחֲבֵירוֹ, בֵּין שֶׁנִּרְאֶה מִבַּחוּץ וְשָׁוֶה מִבִּפְנִים, וּבֵין שֶׁנִּרְאֶה מִבִּפְנִים וְשָׁוֶה מִבַּחוּץ – נִדּוֹן מִשּׁוּם לֶחִי.

The Gemara suggests another proof: **Come** and **hear** the following *Tosefta* **taught by Rabbi Ḥiyya: A wall, one side of which is more recessed than the other, whether** the indentation **is visible from the outside and** the wall looks **even from the inside, or** it **is visible from the inside and** the wall looks **even from the outside, it is considered a side post.** This indicates that a side post is valid even if it was not erected for that purpose.

הָכָא נַמִי שֶׁעֲשָׂאוֹ מִתְּחִילָּה לְכָךְ. אִי הָכִי מַאי קָא מַשְׁמַע לָן? הָא קָא מַשְׁמַע לָן: נִרְאֶה מִבַּחוּץ וְשָׁוֶה מִבִּפְנִים – נִדּוֹן מִשּׁוּם לֶחִי.

The Gemara answers: **Here, too,** it is a case **where one fashioned it from the outset for this** purpose, to serve as a side post. The Gemara asks: **If so, what does it teach us?** The Gemara answers: **This teaches us** that a side post that **is visible from the outside and** looks **even** with the wall **from the inside is considered a side post,** although this view is not universally accepted.

תָּא שְׁמַע: דְּרַב הֲוָה יָתֵיב בְּהַהוּא מְבוֹאָה, הֲוָה יָתֵיב רַב הוּנָא קַמֵּיהּ. אֲמַר לֵיהּ לְשַׁמָּעֵיהּ: זִיל אַיְיתִי לִי כּוּזָא דְּמַיָּא. עַד דַּאֲתָא נְפַל לֶחְיָא. אַחְוֵי לֵיהּ בִּידֵיהּ, קָם אַדּוּכְתֵּיהּ. אֲמַר לֵיהּ רַב הוּנָא: לָא סָבַר לָהּ מָר לִסְמוֹךְ אַדִּיקְלָא? אֲמַר: דָּמֵי הַאי מֵרַבָּנַן כְּמַאן דְּלָא פְּרִישֵׁי אֱינָשֵׁי שְׁמַעְתָּא. מִי סָמְכִינַן עֲלֵיהּ מֵאֶתְמוֹל?

The Gemara suggests another proof: **Come** and **hear** the following story: **Rav was sitting in a certain alleyway,** and **Rav Huna was sitting before him.**[N] **He said to his attendant: Go, bring me a** small **pitcher of water. By the time he came** back with the water, **the side post** at the entrance to the alleyway **had fallen.** Rav **signaled to him with his hand** that he should stop, and the attendant **stood in his place. Rav Huna said to** Rav: **Doesn't the Master hold** that it is permissible **to rely on the palm tree** located at the entrance to this alleyway as a side post? Rav **said: This scholar,** Rav Huna, **is comparable to one who does not know the teachings** of the Sages. **Did we rely on** the palm tree **from yesterday?** Since we did not, carrying in the alleyway is not permitted.

טַעְמָא – דְּלָא סָמְכִינַן, הָא סָמְכִינַן – הָוֵי לֶחִי!

Based on Rav's response, the Gemara argues as follows: **The reason** that the palm tree could not serve as a side post is **because we did not rely** on the palm tree from yesterday. This indicates that **had we relied** on it, **it would be a** valid **side post,** thus proving that a side post that was not erected for that purpose is nonetheless valid, in accordance with the opinion of Abaye.

לֵימָא אַבַּיֵי וְרָבָא בִּדְלָא סָמְכִינַן עֲלֵיהּ פְּלִיגִי, הָא סָמְכִינַן עֲלֵיהּ – הָוֵה לְחִי? לָא סָלְקָא דַּעְתָּךְ, דְּהַהוּא בַּרְקָא דַּהֲוָה בֵּי בַּר חָבוּ, דְּהָווּ פְּלִיגִי בָּהּ אַבַּיֵי וְרָבָא כּוּלֵּי שְׁנַיְיהוּ.

The Gemara suggests: **Shall we say that Abaye and Rava disagree** only in a case **where they did not rely on it** before Shabbat, but in a case **where they did rely on it,** all agree **it is** a valid **side post?** The Gemara answers: This **should not enter your mind, as there was a certain balcony** [*barka*][L] **that was in the house of Bar Ḥavu that Abaye and Rava disagreed about their entire lives.** The residents of the alleyway began relying on a pillar upon which the balcony rested as their side post. Since Abaye and Rava disagreed about this case, it is clear that their disagreement applies even when the residents had relied on the item as a side post from before Shabbat.

מתני׳ בַּכֹּל עוֹשִׂין לְחָיַין, אֲפִילּוּ בְּדָבָר שֶׁיֵּשׁ בּוֹ רוּחַ חַיִּים, וְרַבִּי מֵאִיר אוֹסֵר. וּמְטַמֵּא מִשּׁוּם גּוֹלֵל,

MISHNA One may construct side posts from anything, even a living creature,[N] provided that it was properly attached to the entrance of the alleyway,[H] **and Rabbi Meir prohibits** using a living creature as a side post. The mishna continues with a similar dispute: Even a living creature **imparts ritual impurity** if it used as the **covering of a grave.**[NH]

LANGUAGE

Balcony [*barka*] – בַּרְקָא: The plural form of the biblical word *yatzi'a*, i.e., a second story (*Arukh*). Some authorities claim that this word originates from the Middle Persian word vārag, which can mean an enclosure.

NOTES

A living creature – דָּבָר שֶׁיֵּשׁ בּוֹ רוּחַ חַיִּים: The rationale of those who prohibit utilizing an animal is either because it might die and then shrink at the time of death to less than the required height, or because a partition of this kind, which is maintained by the spirit, i.e., whose entire essence is the life it contains, is not considered a partition. Opinions cited in the Jerusalem Talmud differentiate between a side post and a partition, and hold that a living creature is valid for only one of these two functions; some say as a side post, while others say as a partition.

Covering of a grave – גּוֹלֵל: The nature of this item is subject to dispute. The *ge'onim*, Rashi, Rambam, and other commentaries explain that a *golel* is the gravestone placed over a grave. Rabbeinu Ḥananel and other authorities state that *golel* refers to the heavy stone placed over the corpse in order to cover the open coffin.

HALAKHA

A side post from a living creature – לֶחִי מִבַּעַל חַיִּים: A side post can be fashioned from anything, including a living creature. However, if it is an animal, it must be securely tied in place so that it cannot run away or crouch down below the required height. Even a person who is tied up can serve as a side post (*Shulḥan Arukh*, *Oraḥ Ḥayyim* 363:3, in the comment of the Rema).

The impurity of the covering of a grave – טוּמְאַת גּוֹלֵל: Anything can become ritually impure as the covering of a grave. If an animal is tied in place over a grave, it transmits seven-day impurity to whoever touches it as long as it is tied there (Rambam *Sefer Tahara*, *Hilkhot Tumat Met* 6:4).

Perek **I**
Daf **15** Amud **b**

וְרַבִּי מֵאִיר מְטַהֵר. וְכוֹתְבִין עָלָיו גִּיטֵּי נָשִׁים, וְרַבִּי יוֹסֵי הַגְּלִילִי פּוֹסֵל.

But Rabbi Meir deems it pure. Likewise, **one may write women's bills of divorce on** anything, even a living creature.[H] **But Rabbi Yosei HaGelili invalidates** a bill of divorce written on a living creature.

גמ׳ תַּנְיָא, רַבִּי מֵאִיר אוֹמֵר: כׇּל דָּבָר שֶׁיֵּשׁ בּוֹ רוּחַ חַיִּים אֵין עוֹשִׂין אוֹתוֹ לֹא דּוֹפֶן לַסּוּכָּה, וְלֹא לֶחִי לַמָּבוֹי, לֹא פַּסִּין לַבִּירָאוֹת, וְלֹא גּוֹלֵל לַקֶּבֶר. מִשּׁוּם רַבִּי יוֹסֵי הַגְּלִילִי אָמְרוּ: אַף אֵין כּוֹתְבִין עָלָיו גִּיטֵּי נָשִׁים.

GEMARA It was taught in a *baraita* that **Rabbi Meir says: An animate object may neither be used as a wall for a *sukka*, nor as a side post for an alleyway, nor as** one of the upright **boards** surrounding **a well, nor as the covering of a grave. They said in the name of Rabbi Yosei HaGelili: Nor may one write women's bills of divorce on it.**

מַאי טַעְמָא דְּרַבִּי יוֹסֵי הַגְּלִילִי? דְּתַנְיָא: ״סֵפֶר״, אֵין לִי אֶלָּא סֵפֶר, מִנַּיִין לְרַבּוֹת כׇּל דָּבָר – תַּלְמוּד לוֹמַר ״וְכָתַב לָהּ״ מִכׇּל מָקוֹם. אִם כֵּן מַה תַּלְמוּד לוֹמַר ״סֵפֶר״ – לוֹמַר לְךָ: מַה סֵּפֶר דָּבָר שֶׁאֵין בּוֹ רוּחַ חַיִּים וְאֵינוֹ אוֹכֶל, אַף כׇּל דָּבָר שֶׁאֵין בּוֹ רוּחַ חַיִּים וְאֵינוֹ אוֹכֶל.

The Gemara asks: **What is the reason for Rabbi Yosei HaGelili's opinion? As it was taught** in a *baraita* with regard to the verse: "When a man takes a wife, and marries her, then it comes to pass if she finds no favor in his eyes, because he has found some unseemly thing in her; that he write her **a scroll** of severance and give it in her hand, and send her out of his house" (Deuteronomy 24:1): From the word scroll, **I have** derived that **only a scroll** is valid. **From where** is it derived **to include all objects** as valid materials upon which a bill of divorce may be written? **The Torah states: "That he write her," in any case,** i.e., any surface upon which the formula can be written. **If so, why does the verse state "scroll"? To tell you** that a bill of divorce must be written on a surface like a scroll: **Just as a scroll is neither alive nor food, so too,** a bill of divorce may be written on **any object that is neither alive nor food.** That is why Rabbi Yosei HaGelili invalidates a bill of divorce written on a living being.

HALAKHA

On what may a bill of divorce be written – עַל מָה נִכְתָּב גֵּט: A bill of divorce may be written on any surface, even on an animal. It must then be legally transferred to the woman. This *halakha* is in accordance with the ruling in the unattributed mishna (*Shulḥan Arukh*, *Even HaEzer* 124:2).

וְרַבָּנַן: מִי כְּתִיב "בַּסֵּפֶר"? "סֵפֶר" כְּתִיב – לִסְפִירוּת דְּבָרִים בְּעָלְמָא הוּא דַּאֲתָא.

The Gemara asks: **And** how do **the Rabbis,** who disagree and say that a bill of divorce may be written even on a living creature or on food, interpret the verse? They contend: **Is** the verse **written:** "Let him write for her **in the scroll** [***basefer***]," indicating the only type of surface on which the bill of divorce may be written? No, **scroll** [***sefer***] **is written, which comes to** teach that **a mere account of the matters** [***sefirot devarim***] is required. In other words, *sefer* is referring not to the surface on which a bill of divorce must be written, but rather to the essence of the bill of divorce. The verse teaches that the bill of divorce must contain particular content.

ורבנן, האי "וכתב לה" מאי דרשי ביה? ההוא מבעי ליה: בכתיבה מתגרשת, ואינה מתגרשת בכסף. סלקא דעתך אמינא: הואיל ואיתקש יציאה להויה, מה הויה בכסף אף יציאה בכסף – קא משמע לן.

The Gemara continues: **And what do the Rabbis derive** from **the** phrase **"that he write her"?** The Gemara answers: **That** phrase **is required** to teach the principle that a woman **is divorced** only **by means of writing,** i.e., a bill of divorce, **and she is not divorced by means of money.**[H] **It might have entered your mind to say: Since** in the verse, **leaving** marriage, i.e., divorce, **is juxtaposed to becoming** married, i.e., betrothal, then, **just as becoming** married **is** effected **with money, so** too, **leaving** marriage may be effected **with money.** Therefore, the Torah **teaches us:** "That he write for her"; divorce can be effected only with a written bill of divorce.

ורבי יוסי הגלילי, האי סברא מנא ליה? נפקא ליה מ"ספר כריתות" – ספר כורתה ואין דבר אחר כורתה.

The Gemara asks: **And Rabbi Yosei HaGelili, from where does he** derive **this reasoning,** that a woman cannot be divorced with money? The Gemara answers: **He derives it from** the phrase: **A scroll of severance,** which teaches that **a scroll,** i.e., a written document, **severs her** from her husband **and nothing else severs her** from him.

ורבנן, האי "ספר כריתות" מיבעי ליה לדבר הכורת בינו לבינה. לכדתניא: הרי זה גיטך על מנת שלא תשתי יין, על מנת שלא תלכי לבית אביך לעולם – אין זה כריתות. כל שלשים יום – הרי זה כריתות.

The Gemara continues: **And the Rabbis** explain that **this** phrase: **A scroll of severance,**[N] **is required** to teach that a bill of divorce must be **a matter that severs** all connection **between him and her.**[N] **As it was taught** in a *baraita*: If a man says to his wife: **This is your bill of divorce, on condition that you will** never **drink wine,** or **on condition that you will never go to your father's house, that is not severance;** the bill of divorce is not valid. If a bill of divorce imposes a condition upon the woman that permanently binds her to her husband, her relationship with her husband has not been completely severed, which is a prerequisite for divorce. If, however, he imposes a condition **for the duration of thirty days,** or any other limited period of time, **that is severance,** and the bill of divorce is valid, as the relationship will be completely terminated at the end of the thirty-day period.[H]

ורבי יוסי הגלילי נפקא ליה מ"כרת" "כריתות".

And Rabbi Yosei HaGelili derives that a condition without a termination point invalidates the divorce **from** the fact that instead of using the term ***karet,*** the verse uses the more expanded term ***keritut.*** Inasmuch as both terms denote severance, using the longer term teaches us two things: Divorce can be effected only by means of writing and not through money, and divorce requires total severance.

ורבנן, "כרת" "כריתות" לא דרשי.

And as for **the Rabbis, they do not derive** anything from the expansion of ***karet*** to ***keritut.***

מתני׳ שיירא שחנתה בבקעה והקיפוה כלי בהמה – מטלטלין בתוכה, ובלבד שיהא גדר גבוה עשרה טפחים, ולא יהו פירצות יתרות על הבנין.

MISHNA If **a caravan camped in a valley,** i.e., an open space not enclosed by walls, **and** the travelers **enclosed** their camp **with** partitions made of the **animals' equipment,** e.g., saddles and the like, **one may carry inside** the enclosed area, **provided that** the resultant partition **will be a fence ten handbreadths high, and** that **there will not be breaches** in the partition **greater** than **the built** segment.

כל פירצה שהיא כעשר אמות – מותרת, מפני שהיא כפתח, יתר מכאן – אסור.

Any breach that is approximately ten cubits wide **is permitted** and does not invalidate the partition **because it is** considered **like an entrance.**[H] However, if one of the breaches is **greater than** ten cubits, **it is prohibited** to carry anywhere in the enclosed area.

גמ׳ איתמר: פרוץ כעומד, רב פפא אמר: מותר. רב הונא בריה דרב יהושע אמר: אסור.

GEMARA **It is stated** that the *amora'im* disagree about the case where the **breached** segment of the partition **equals the standing** portion. **Rav Pappa said: It is permitted** to carry within that enclosure. **Rav Huna, son of Rav Yehoshua, said: It is prohibited.**

HALAKHA

With what means can a woman be divorced – במה מתגרשת: A woman may be divorced only by means of a bill of divorce, not through the transfer of money or by any other means (Rambam *Sefer Nashim, Hilkhot Geirushin* 1:1).

Conditions in a bill of divorce – תנאי בגט: A bill of divorce that contains a condition that binds the woman to her husband indefinitely is not valid. One should refrain from attaching a condition that is limited in time if it difficult for her to fulfill it, as it is likely that this will cause the bill of divorce to be invalidated retroactively, which would lead to extreme halakhic difficulties (*Shulḥan Arukh, Even HaEzer* 143:20–21).

The size of a breach – גודל פירצה: A gap in a partition up to ten cubits wide is considered an entrance. If the breach is greater, it is not considered an entrance, and the partition is halakhically disqualified (*Shulḥan Arukh, Oraḥ Ḥayyim* 362:9).

NOTES

A matter that severs all connection between him and her – דבר הכורת בינו לבינה: The addendum of a condition to a bill of divorce does not in itself invalidate it, even if the condition will be in effect for many years. Some authorities maintain that even a condition that is in effect for a lifetime does not invalidate the bill of divorce. If a woman wants the divorce to take effect, she must fulfill any valid condition stipulated in the bill of divorce. However, if the content of the bill of divorce clearly indicates that the husband is not releasing the woman from all of her obligations to him, the bill of divorce in invalid since it does not result in severance.

Scroll [*sefer*] of severance – ספר כריתות: Some commentaries interpret this phrase as requiring the husband to clearly tell his wife that he is separating from her, since the Hebrew *sefer*, a book or scroll, is etymologically related to the verb *sapper*, tell. Therefore, in the case of a bill of divorce that includes an indefinite condition, when receiving the bill of divorce, there is no way for the wife to be certain whether or not she will be effectively divorced, If she fails to fulfill the condition, the bill of divorce will be invalidated. Consequently, a bill of divorce of this kind does not include an account [*sippur*] of severance (Rabbi Elazar Moshe Horowitz).

רַב פָּפָּא אָמַר: מוּתָּר, הָכִי אַגְמְרֵיהּ רַחֲמָנָא לְמֹשֶׁה: לֹא תִּפְרוֹץ רוּבָּהּ. רַב הוּנָא בְּרֵיהּ דְּרַב יְהוֹשֻׁעַ אָמַר: אָסוּר, הָכִי אַגְמְרֵיהּ רַחֲמָנָא לְמֹשֶׁה: גְּדוֹר רוּבָּהּ.

The Gemara explains: **Rav Pappa said: It is permitted. This is what the Merciful One taught Moses:**[N] **Do not breach the majority** of the partition; as long as the greater part is not breached, it is considered a partition. **Rav Huna, son of Rav Yehoshua, said: It is prohibited. This is what the Merciful One taught Moses: Circumscribe the greater** part; if the greater part is not enclosed, it is not a partition.

תְּנַן: וְלֹא יְהוּ פִּירְצוֹת יְתֵרוֹת עַל הַבִּנְיָן, הָא כַּבִּנְיָן – מוּתָּר!

We learned in the mishna: **And there will not be breaches** in the partition **greater** than **the built** segment. Only then would carrying be permitted in the enclosed area. By inference, **if** the breaches **equal the built** segment, **it is permitted.** This presents a difficulty for Rav Huna, son of Rav Yehoshua.

לָא תֵּימָא הָא כַּבִּנְיָן מוּתָּר, אֶלָּא אֵימָא: אִם בִּנְיָן יָתֵר עַל הַפִּירְצָה – מוּתָּר.

The Gemara responds: **Do not say:** By inference if they **equal the built** segment, **it is permitted; rather, say: If the built** segment **is greater than the breach, it is permitted** to carry in the enclosed area.

אֲבָל כַּבִּנְיָן מַאי? אָסוּר? אִי הָכִי, לִיתְנֵי: ״לֹא יְהוּ פִּירְצוֹת כַּבִּנְיָן״! קַשְׁיָא.

The Gemara continues: **However,** according to that way of understanding the mishna, if the breach **equals the built** segment, **what** is the *halakha*? Is carrying **prohibited? If so, let** the mishna **teach** that carrying is permitted, provided that the **breaches do not equal the built** segment. It can be inferred from this that if the breaches are greater than the built segment, it is certainly prohibited. The Gemara concludes: Indeed, this poses **a difficulty** to the opinion of Rav Huna, son of Rav Yehoshua.

תָּא שְׁמַע: הַמְקָרֶה סוּכָּתוֹ בְּשַׁפּוּדִין אוֹ בַּאֲרוּכוֹת הַמִּטָּה, אִם יֵשׁ רֶיוַח בֵּינֵיהֶן כְּמוֹתָן – כְּשֵׁירָה!

The Gemara cites a proof to support Rav Pappa's opinion. **Come** and **hear** that which the mishna taught about the *halakhot* of *sukka*: With regard to **one who roofed his *sukka* with** metal **skewers**[H] **or with bed posts,** both of which are unfit for *sukka* roofing because they are susceptible to ritual impurity, **if there is space between them, equal to their** width, filled with materials valid for *sukka* roofing, the *sukka* **is valid.**[N] Apparently, with regard to roofing, if the valid materials equal the invalid, the *sukka* is valid. Similarly, if the built segment of an enclosure equals the breached segment, it is a valid enclosure for the purpose of carrying on Shabbat. This supports Rav Pappa's opinion against that of Rav Huna, son of Rav Yehoshua.

הָכָא בְּמַאי עָסְקִינַן – כְּשֶׁנִּכְנָס וְיוֹצֵא.

The Gemara contests this conclusion. **With what are we dealing here?** It is with a case **where** the skewers can be **inserted and extracted** easily. In other words, the case of the mishna in *Sukka* is not one where there are equal amounts of valid and invalid roofing. It is referring to a case where there is additional space between the skewers, which allows for their easy insertion and removal. Consequently, the space filled by the valid roofing is greater than that filled by the skewers.

וְהָא אֶפְשָׁר לְצַמְצֵם!

The Gemara asks: **Isn't it possible to be precise?** Couldn't the mishna in *Sukka* be understood as describing a case where the gaps between the skewers equal the width of the skewers? That understanding supports the opinion of Rav Pappa, who maintains that when the valid segment precisely equals the invalid segment, the whole is valid.

אָמַר רַבִּי אַמִי: בְּמַעְדִּיף.

Rabbi Ami said: This mishna is referring to a case **where one adds** roofing, so that the area of the valid roofing is greater than that of the skewers.

רָבָא אָמַר: אִם הָיוּ נְתוּנִין עֵרֶב – נוֹתְנוֹ שְׁתִי, שְׁתִי – נוֹתְנוֹ עֵרֶב.

Rava said: This is referring to a case where **if** the skewers **were placed crosswise** to the *sukka*, **he should place** the valid roofing **lengthwise,** and similarly, if the skewers were placed **lengthwise, he should place** the valid roofing **crosswise,** ensuring that there is more valid than invalid roofing.

תָּא שְׁמַע: שַׁיָּירָא שֶׁחָנְתָה בְּבִקְעָה וְהִקִּיפוּהָ בִּגְמַלִּין, בְּאוּכָּפוֹת,

The Gemara seeks to adduce a proof in support of the opinion of Rav Huna, son of Rav Yehoshua: **Come** and **hear** that which was taught in a *baraita*: If **a caravan camped in a field, and** the travelers **surrounded** their camp **with camels** that were made to crouch down, or **with** their **saddles,**

NOTES

The Merciful One taught Moses – אַגְמְרֵיהּ רַחֲמָנָא לְמֹשֶׁה: Some commentaries were troubled by this passage, which implies that an enclosure whose combined breaches are wider than its combined standing portions is invalid either by Torah law or on the basis of a *halakha* transmitted to Moses from Sinai (Rashba; Ritva). Given the *halakha* of boards surrounding a well, it is unlikely that the invalidation of a partition whose breached segments are greater than its standing segments is Torah law (see the mishna on 17b, p. 95, and the Gemara on 10a, p. 48). The Ra'avad explains that the phrase: The Merciful One taught Moses, should not be taken literally. He maintains that the disqualification of a partition is only by rabbinic decree, even in a case where the breached segments are greater than the standing segments of the partition.

A *sukka* and a partition – סוּכָּה וּמְחִיצָה: How can the law of the walls of a courtyard be compared to the laws of the roofing of a *sukka*? Since these laws are not derived from the same source, perhaps their requirements are completely different. The Ritva answers that initially the Gemara entertained the possibility that there is an abstract, general question with regard to objects consisting of both valid and invalid components. When the valid component is greater than the invalid, or vice versa, the legal status of the object is determined by the majority. The question here is with regard to the status of an item that is composed of exactly half valid and half invalid components. Ultimately, the Gemara concludes that there is no overriding principle in this matter. In some *halakhot*, the legal status of half is like that of the majority. In others, the legal status of half is like that of the minority and does not determine the object's status.

HALAKHA

A *sukka* roofed with skewers – סוּכָּה הַמְקוֹרָה בְּשַׁפּוּדִין: If one roofed his *sukka* with skewers that are less than four handbreadths wide, and the gaps between the skewers are exactly equal to the width of the skewers, the *sukka* is invalid, since it is impossible to make certain that the precise amount of requisite roofing is in place. However, if one widened the gaps between the skewers even minimally, or if one positioned the roofing material across rather than parallel to the skewers, the *sukka* is valid, in accordance with the ruling of Rabbi Ami and Rava (*Shulḥan Arukh*, *Oraḥ Ḥayyim* 631:8).

בעביטין, בשליפין, בקנים, בקולחות – מטלטלין בתוכה, ובלבד שלא יהא בין גמל לגמל כמלא גמל, ובין אוכף לאוכף כמלא אוכף, ובין עביט לעביט כמלא עביט.

or with saddle **cushions** [*avitin*],[N] or **with wheat sheaves,** or **with boards,** or **with stalks** [*kolaḥot*],[N] **one may carry within** the enclosed area, **provided that there is no camel-length** gap **between one camel and another, or a saddle-length** gap **between one saddle and another, or a cushion-length** gap **between one cushion and another.** Apparently, from this *baraita* it can be understood that if the breach is equal to the standing segment, it is not a valid enclosure.

הכא נמי, כשנכנס ויוצא.

The Gemara rejects this conclusion. **Here, too,** it is referring to gaps through which the various objects can easily **be inserted and extracted,** so that the breached segment is in fact slightly greater than that of the standing segment.

תא שמע: נמצאת אתה אומר שלש מדות במחיצות: כל שהוא פחות משלשה – צריך שלא יהא בין זה לזה שלשה, כדי שלא יזדקר הגדי בבת ראש.

The Gemara cites yet another proof: **Come** and **hear** that which was taught in the *Tosefta* in tractate *Kilayim*: **Ultimately, you say that there are three measures for partitions.**[N] These partitions form a barrier that demarcates between vines and seeds. They are needed to render permitted the sowing of a field with diverse kinds of seeds. In the case of **any** partition consisting of boards that are each **less than three** handbreadths wide,[H] **it is necessary that there will not be** a gap of **three** handbreadths **between this** board **and that, so that a goat would not** be able to **leap**[N] **headlong** through it unimpeded. If the gap is wider than three handbreadths, i.e., wide enough that a goat can leap through it, the boards are not considered joined and it is not considered a partition.

כל שהוא שלשה ומשלשה עד ארבעה – צריך שלא יהא בין זה לזה כמלואו, כדי שלא יהא פרוץ כעומד. ואם היה פרוץ מרובה על העומד – אף כנגד העומד אסור.

In the case of **any** partition that consists of boards that are **three** handbreadths wide, **as well as** boards **from three to four** handbreadths wide,[H] the gap between the boards may be greater than three handbreadths. Nonetheless, **it is necessary that there will not be** a gap equal to **the full width** of a board **between one** board **and the next, so that the breached** segment **will not equal the standing** segment. **And if the breached** segment **is greater than the standing** segment, **it is prohibited** to sow another species, **even** in the area **opposite the standing** segment, as the breached segment invalidates the entire partition.

כל שהוא ארבעה ומארבעה עד עשר אמות – צריך שלא יהא בין זה לזה כמלואו, שלא יהא פרוץ כעומד. ואם היה פרוץ כעומד – כנגד העומד מותר, כנגד הפרוץ אסור. ואם היה עומד מרובה על הפרוץ – אף כנגד הפרוץ מותר.

With regard to **any** partition that consists of boards that are **four** handbreadths wide, **as well as** boards **from four** handbreadths **to ten cubits** wide, **it is necessary that there not be** a gap **the full** width of a board **between one** board **and the next, so that the breached** segment **will not equal the standing** segment. **And if the breached** segment **equals the standing** segment, then in the area **opposite the standing** segment, **it is permitted** to sow other species, as there is a partition there; however, in the area **facing the breached** segment **it is prohibited. And if the** sum of the **standing** segments **is greater than the** sum of **the breached** segments, sowing other species **is permitted, even** in the area **opposite the breached** part.

נפרצה ביותר מעשר – אסור. היו שם קנים הדוקרנים ועושה להן פיאה מלמעלה – אפילו ביותר מעשר מותר.

However, if, the partition was **breached more than ten** cubits, sowing diverse kinds **is prohibited,** as a breach of more than ten cubits invalidates the entire partition. **But if there were pronged stakes stuck** in the ground **there, and one made them a braid** [*pe'a*] of straw **above them**[N] in the form of a doorway, **even if** the stakes were set **more than ten** cubits apart, sowing **is permitted.** The form of a doorway renders the partition valid, even if there is a breach wider than ten cubits.

קתני מיהת רישא משלשה עד ארבעה, ובלבד שלא יהא בין זה לזה כמלואו, תיובתא דרב פפא!

The Gemara explains how the passage from the *Tosefta* of tractate *Kilayim* supports the opinion of Rav Huna, son of Rav Yehoshua, contrary to that of Rav Pappa. **In any case, the first clause** of the *Tosefta* **teaches** that if each of the boards that make up the partition is **from three to four** handbreadths wide, sowing other species is permitted, **provided that there is not** a gap **the full** width of a board **between one** board **and the next.** This is **a conclusive refutation** of the opinion of **Rav Pappa,** who permits carrying when the breach equals the standing segment of the partition.

NOTES

Cushions [*avitin*] – **עביטין:** The Ra'avad understands that in this context the word *avitin* refers to a kind of bucket. This is its meaning in other contexts in the Talmud.

Stalks [*kolaḥot*] – **קולחות:** The *Arukh* explains that *kolaḥot* are dry vegetable stalks.

Three measures for partitions – **שלש מדות במחיצות:** A lengthy discussion of this *baraita* found in the Jerusalem Talmud concludes that the rules for partitions detailed in this *baraita* apply only to the *halakhot* of forbidden diverse kinds and not to the *halakhot* of partitions pertaining to carrying on Shabbat. On Shabbat, the partition must be complete so as to create an enclosed domain. With respect to diverse kinds, the main function of the partition is to create a conspicuous demarcation between the grape vines and the other crops. Consequently, with respect to diverse kinds, in the case of a ten-cubit-long fence that has a breach of more than ten cubits, the fence is still a partition in that it prevents the crops opposite the standing segment from becoming forbidden. In contrast, with respect to Shabbat, a partition with a breach that is greater than ten cubits does not count as a partition at all, even if the standing segment is greater than the breached segment (see Rashba and Ritva).

So that a goat would not be able to leap – **שלא יזדקר הגדי:** Rashba explains that the strict standard that no gap be wide enough for a goat to jump through, i.e., wider than three handbreadths, is due to the fact that a partition consisting of boards that are each less than three handbreadths wide is regarded as an inferior partition. A partition composed of boards more than three but less than four handbreadths wide is valid, even if it has gaps wider than three handbreadths, as long as none of the gaps is wider than its adjacent standing segments. However, that partition is regarded as inferior compared to one made up of components that are more than four handbreadths wide. When the standing components are wider than four handbreadths, the individual components are still regarded as significant and protect the crops facing them from becoming forbidden due to diverse kinds, even when the partition as a whole is invalid, either because of a ten-cubit gap or because of the sum of the gaps is greater than the sum of the standing segments.

A braid [*pe'a*] **above them** – **פאה מלמעלה:** The *Arukh* explains that anything that surrounds another object without affording it protection is called a *pe'a*.

HALAKHA

A partition of less than three handbreadths – **מחיצה פחות משלשה:** In the case of a partition made of boards less than three handbreadths wide, in order for it to be a valid partition, there may not be a gap of three handbreadths between any two boards (*Shulḥan Arukh, Yoreh De'a* 296:45).

A partition from three to four handbreadths – **מחיצה משלשה עד ארבעה טפחים:** In the case of a partition made of boards, each of which is between three and four handbreadths wide, there may not be a gap the width of a board between any two boards (*Shulḥan Arukh, Yoreh De'a* 296:40).

אָמַר לְךָ רַב פַּפָּא: מַאי מְלוֹאוֹ – נִכְנָס וְיוֹצֵא.

Rav Pappa could have **said to you: What** does the *baraita* mean by a gap **the full** width of a board? It means a gap through which the board could easily be **inserted and extracted,** which is a gap slightly wider than the board itself.

הָכִי נַמִי מִסְתַּבְּרָא, מִדְּקָתָנֵי: אִם הָיָה פָּרוּץ מְרוּבֶּה עַל הָעוֹמֵד – אַף כְּנֶגֶד הָעוֹמֵד אָסוּר. הָא כְּעוֹמֵד – מוּתָּר. שְׁמַע מִינַּהּ.

The Gemara comments: **So too, it stands to reason, from** the fact that the *Tosefta* **teaches** later: **If the breached** segment **is greater than the standing** segment, **it is prohibited** to sow another species, **even** in the area **opposite the standing** portion. By inference, **if** the breached segment **equals the standing** segment, sowing other species **is** in fact **permitted.** The Gemara concludes: Indeed, **learn from here** proof for the opinion of Rav Pappa.

לֵימָא תֶּיהֱוֵי תְּיוּבְתֵּיהּ דְּרַב הוּנָא בְּרֵיהּ דְּרַב יְהוֹשֻׁעַ אָמַר לְךָ: וְלִיטַעְמִיךְ, אֵימָא סֵיפָא: אִם הָיָה עוֹמֵד מְרוּבֶּה עַל הַפָּרוּץ – אַף כְּנֶגֶד הַפָּרוּץ מוּתָּר. הָא כְּפָרוּץ – אָסוּר.

The Gemara asks: **Let us say that this** conclusion **is a conclusive refutation** of the opinion of **Rav Huna, son of Rav Yehoshua.** The Gemara rejects this: Rav Huna, son of Rav Yehoshua, could have **said to you: And according to your reasoning, say the latter clause** of the *Tosefta* as follows: **If the sum of the standing** segment **is greater than the sum of the breached** segment, sowing other species **is permitted even** in the area **opposite the breached** segment. This clause indicates that if the breached segment **equals the standing** segment, sowing other species **is prohibited.**

סֵיפָא קַשְׁיָא לְרַב פַּפָּא, רֵישָׁא קַשְׁיָא לְרַב הוּנָא בְּרֵיהּ דְּרַב יְהוֹשֻׁעַ.

The Gemara points out that that analysis of the *baraita* leads to the conclusion that **the latter clause poses a difficulty for Rav Pappa's opinion; the first clause poses a difficulty for** the opinion of **Rav Huna, son of Rav Yehoshua.**

סֵיפָא לְרַב פַּפָּא לָא קַשְׁיָא – אַיְּידֵי דִּתְנָא רֵישָׁא ״פָּרוּץ מְרוּבֶּה עַל הָעוֹמֵד״ תְּנָא סֵיפָא ״עוֹמֵד מְרוּבֶּה עַל הַפָּרוּץ״.

The Gemara answers: **The latter clause poses no difficulty to Rav Pappa. Since the first clause taught** the expression: If **the** sum of **the breached** segment **is greater than the** sum of the **standing** segment, **the latter clause** of the *baraita* **taught** the parallel expression: If **the** sum of the **standing** segment **is greater than** the sum of **the breached** segment, even though the latter formulation is imprecise, as the same *halakha* applies even if the two are equal.

רֵישָׁא לְרַב הוּנָא בְּרֵיהּ דְּרַב יְהוֹשֻׁעַ לָא קַשְׁיָא, אַיְּידֵי דְּבָעֵי לְמִיתְנֵי סֵיפָא ״עוֹמֵד מְרוּבֶּה עַל הַפָּרוּץ״ תְּנָא רֵישָׁא ״פָּרוּץ מְרוּבֶּה עַל הָעוֹמֵד״.

Similarly, the Gemara explains that **the first clause does not pose a difficulty to Rav Huna, son of Rav Yehoshua. Since** the *baraita* **sought to teach** the expression **in the latter clause:** If the sum of **the standing** segments **is greater than the** sum of the **breached** segments, in **the first clause taught** the parallel expression : If the sum of **the breached** segments **is greater than** the sum of **the standing** segments, even though this formulation is imprecise, as the same *halakha* applies even if the two are equal.

בִּשְׁלָמָא לְרַב פַּפָּא – מִשּׁוּם הָכִי לָא עָרֵיב לְהוּ וְתָנֵי לְהוּ,

The Gemara continues: **Granted, according to Rav Pappa,** who permits carrying in the case where the breaches equal the standing segments, the *baraita* makes sense, as **for that** reason the *tanna* **did not combine** the case of boards less than three handbreadths wide with the case of boards three handbreadths wide **and teach them** in a single clause. According to Rav Pappa, there is a significant difference between the two situations. In a case where the boards are less than three handbreadths wide, the partition is invalid if there is a gap of three handbreadths between one bar and the next. However, if the boards are precisely three handbreadths wide, the partition is valid unless there is a gap of more than three handbreadths between them.

אֶלָּא לְרַב הוּנָא בְּרֵיהּ דְּרַב יְהוֹשֻׁעַ לִיעָרְבִינְהוּ וְלִיתְנִינְהוּ: כֹּל שֶׁהוּא פָּחוֹת מִשְּׁלֹשָׁה וּשְׁלֹשָׁה – צָרִיךְ שֶׁלֹּא יְהֵא בֵּין זֶה לָזֶה שְׁלֹשָׁה!

However, according to Rav Huna, son of Rav Yehoshua, who considers a partition invalid when its breached segments are equal to its standing segments, the *baraita* **should have combined** the case of boards less than three handbreadths wide with the case of boards exactly three handbreadths wide **and taught them** in the following single clause: **Any** partition made of boards **less than three** handbreadths wide **or** exactly **three** handbreadths wide, **it is necessary that there not be** a gap of **three** handbreadths **between one** board **and another.** According to Rav Huna, son of Rav Yehoshua, if a partition with boards three handbreadths wide is to be valid, the gap must be less than three handbreadths.

מִשּׁוּם דְּלָא דָּמֵי פְּסוּלָא דְרֵישָׁא לִפְסוּלָא דְסֵיפָא; פְּסוּלָא דְרֵישָׁא – כְּדֵי שֶׁלֹּא יְזַדֵּקֵר הַגְּדִי בְּבַת אַחַת, פְּסוּלָא דְסֵיפָא – שֶׁלֹּא יְהֵא פָּרוּץ כְּעוֹמֵד.

The Gemara explains why the two cases were not combined according to Rav Huna, son of Rav Yehoshua. It is **because the disqualification in the first clause is not similar to the disqualification in the latter clause.** The reason for **the disqualification in the first clause** is because a valid partition must be constructed **so that a goat would not** be able **to jump** through the gap **in one** leap; the reason for **the disqualification in the latter clause,** where the boards are three handbreadths wide, is **so that the breached** segments **will equal the** combined **standing** segments. In practice, just as in the case of boards less than three handbreadths wide, the gap must be less than three handbreadths, so too, in the case of boards three handbreadths wide, the gap must also be less than three handbreadths. However, in terms of underlying reasoning, the case of boards three handbreadths wide must be categorized in the second grouping in the *Tosefta,* not the first. Therefore, no proof can be cited from here, neither in support of the opinion of Rav Pappa nor in support of the opinion of Rav Huna, son of Rav Yehoshua.

פָּחוֹת מִשְּׁלֹשָׁה מַנִּי – רַבָּנַן הִיא, דְּאָמְרִי: פָּחוֹת מִשְּׁלֹשָׁה אָמְרִינַן לָבוּד, שְׁלֹשָׁה לָא אָמְרִינַן לָבוּד.

The Gemara briefly discusses the ruling cited in the *Tosefta* that a breach of **less than three** handbreadths does not invalidate a partition. In accordance with **whose** opinion is that ruling? It is in accordance with the opinion of **the Rabbis,** who **say:** In the case of a gap **less than three** handbreadths, **we say,** i.e., we apply, the principle of ***lavud,*** and the partitions are considered joined; however, if the gap is **three** handbreadths, **we do not say *lavud.***

אֵימָא סֵיפָא: כֹּל שֶׁהוּא שְׁלֹשָׁה וּמִשְּׁלֹשָׁה וְעַד אַרְבָּעָה –

Say the latter clause with regard to a partition of boards as follows: In the case of any partition whose boards are **three** handbreadths wide, **and** any partition whose boards are **from three to four** handbreadths wide,

אֲתָאן לְרַבָּן שִׁמְעוֹן בֶּן גַּמְלִיאֵל, דְּאָמַר: פָּחוֹת מֵאַרְבָּעָה לָבוּד! דְּאִי רַבָּנַן – מִשְּׁלֹשָׁה וְעַד אַרְבָּעָה?! שְׁלֹשָׁה וְאַרְבָּעָה חַד הוּא!

we have arrived at the opinion of **Rabban Shimon ben Gamliel,**[N] **who said:** Concerning any gap **less than four** handbreadths wide, the principle of ***lavud*** is applied. **As had** it been taught in accordance with the opinion of **the Rabbis,** why does the *baraita* list **from three to four** handbreadths as a separate category? In the case of both **three and four** handbreadths, the *halakha* **is one** and the same: The principle of *lavud* does not apply from three handbreadths upward.

אָמַר אַבָּיֵי: מִדְּרֵישָׁא רַבָּנַן סֵיפָא נַמִי רַבָּנַן, וּמוֹדוּ רַבָּנַן דְּכָל לְמִישְׁרָא כְּנֶגְדּוֹ, אִי אִיכָּא מָקוֹם אַרְבָּעָה – חֲשִׁיב, וְאִי לָא – לָא חֲשִׁיב.

Abaye said: From the fact **that the first clause is** in accordance with the opinion of **the Rabbis, the latter clause** must **also be** in accordance with the opinion of **the Rabbis. And the Rabbis concede that** with regard to **any case** where the *halakha* **permits** sowing other species in the area **opposite** the standing portion, **if there is an area of four** handbreadths, **it is** considered **a significant** partition, which permits sowing; **and if not, it is not** considered **a significant** partition and does not permit sowing. Accordingly, there is a difference between a fence of three handbreadths and one of four handbreadths, as even the Rabbis concede that a fence of four handbreadths is more significant.

רָבָא אָמַר: מִדְּסֵיפָא רַבָּן שִׁמְעוֹן בֶּן גַּמְלִיאֵל רֵישָׁא נַמִי רַבָּן שִׁמְעוֹן בֶּן גַּמְלִיאֵל, וְכִי אָמַר רַבָּן שִׁמְעוֹן בֶּן גַּמְלִיאֵל אָמְרִינַן לָבוּד – הָנֵי מִילֵּי לְמַעְלָה, אֲבָל לְמַטָּה הָוֵה לֵיהּ כִּמְחִיצָה שֶׁהַגְּדָיִים בּוֹקְעִין בָּהּ – לָא אָמְרִינַן לָבוּד.

Rava said: From the fact **that the latter clause is** in accordance with the opinion of **Rabban Shimon ben Gamliel, the first clause** must **also be** in accordance with the opinion of **Rabban Shimon ben Gamliel. And when Rabban Shimon ben Gamliel said** that **we say** the principle of ***lavud*** in the case of a gap up to four handbreadths wide, **this applies above,** off the ground, e.g., in the case of a cross beam suspended at a distance from the wall. **However, below,** near the ground, **it is like a partition through which goats can pass,** and therefore he too agrees that **we do not say** the principle of ***lavud*** in that case.

NOTES

Rabban Shimon ben Gamliel's opinion – שִׁיטַת רַבָּן שִׁמְעוֹן בֶּן גַּמְלִיאֵל: The early commentaries noted that this statement does not resolve all the difficulties, as a distinction between three and four handbreadths remains, while according to Rabban Shimon ben Gamliel the measure of three handbreadths has no significance whatsoever. The Ra'avad answers that this statement accepts Rabban Shimon ben Gamliel's opinion with regard to the definition of an important place while adopting the opinion of the Rabbis with regard to the principle of *lavud* (see Rashba and Ritva).

תָּא שְׁמַע: דְּפָנוֹת הַלָּלוּ שֶׁרוּבָּן פְּתָחִים וְחַלּוֹנוֹת – מוּתָּר, וּבִלְבַד שֶׁיְּהֵא עוֹמֵד מְרוּבֶּה עַל הַפָּרוּץ.

The Gemara returns to the dispute with regard to a breach equal to the standing segments of a partition and cites another proof. **Come and hear** that which was taught in the following *baraita*: With regard to an area enclosed by **these walls,** in a case **where most of them** consist of **entrance and windows,** it is **permitted** to carry on Shabbat within the area, **provided that the standing** segments **are greater than the breached** segments.

שֶׁרוּבָּן סָלְקָא דַּעְתָּךְ?! אֶלָּא: שֶׁרִיבָּה בָּהֶן פְּתָחִים וְחַלּוֹנוֹת מוּתָּר, וּבִלְבַד שֶׁיְּהֵא עוֹמֵד מְרוּבֶּה עַל הַפָּרוּץ.

The Gemara analyzes the formulation of the *baraita*: **Can it enter your mind that** the *baraita* is referring to a case where **most of** the walls are entrances and windows? If so, the standing segments are certainly not greater than the breached segments. **Rather,** emend the *baraita* as follows: Carrying in the area enclosed by these walls, **to which one added** many **entrances and windows, is permitted, provided that the standing** segments **are greater than the breached** segments.

הָא כְּפָרוּץ – אָסוּר! תְּיוּבְתָּא דְּרַב פַּפָּא – תְּיוּבְתָּא. וְהִילְכְתָא כְּוָותֵיהּ דְּרַב פַּפָּא.

The Gemara draws an inference: **If** the standing segments **equal the breached** segments,[H] carrying **is prohibited** in that enclosure. This is **a conclusive refutation** of the opinion **of Rav Pappa.** The Gemara concludes: Indeed, it is **a conclusive refutation.** Nevertheless, **the *halakha* is in accordance with** the opinion of **Rav Pappa.**

תְּיוּבְתָּא וְהִילְכְתָא?! אִין, מִשּׁוּם דְּדַיְיקָא מַתְנִיתִין כְּוָותֵיהּ, דִּתְנַן: לֹא יְהוּ פְּרָצוֹת יְתֵירוֹת עַל הַבִּנְיָן. הָא כַּבִּנְיָן – מוּתָּר.

The Gemara wonders: **A conclusive refutation and the *halakha*?** The Gemara answers: **Yes,** that is the case, **because the precise reading of the mishna is in accordance with** the opinion of Rav Pappa. **As we learned** in the mishna the following phrase: Provided… **there will not be breaches** in the partition **greater** than **the built** segment. This is clearly indicating that if the breached segments are **equal to the built** segments, carrying **is permitted,** as maintained by Rav Pappa.

מתני׳ מַקִּיפִין שְׁלֹשָׁה חֲבָלִים זֶה לְמַעְלָה מִזֶּה וְזֶה לְמַעְלָה מִזֶּה, וּבִלְבַד שֶׁלֹּא יְהוּ בֵּין חֶבֶל לַחֲבֵירוֹ שְׁלֹשָׁה טְפָחִים.

MISHNA If a caravan is camped in a field, and the travelers seek to construct partitions to render the area fit for one to carry within it on Shabbat, **one surrounds** the area with **three ropes, one above another, and** a third **one above** the **other** two. One is permitted to carry within the circumscribed area **provided that there will not be** a gap of **three handbreadths between** one **rope and the next.**[H]

שִׁיעוּר חֲבָלִים וְעוֹבְיָין – יָתֵר עַל טֶפַח, כְּדֵי שֶׁיְּהֵא הַכֹּל עֲשָׂרָה טְפָחִים.

The measure of the ropes and their combined **thickness** must be **greater than a handbreadth, so that the entire** partition, consisting of three ropes and the empty spaces between them, **will be ten handbreadths** high.

מַקִּיפִין בְּקָנִים, וּבִלְבַד שֶׁלֹּא יְהֵא בֵּין קָנֶה לַחֲבֵירוֹ שְׁלֹשָׁה טְפָחִים.

Alternatively, **one** may **surround** the area **with boards** that stand upright, **provided that there will not be** a gap of **three handbreadths between one board and the next.**

בְּשַׁיָּירָא דִּבְּרוּ, דִּבְרֵי רַבִּי יְהוּדָה. וַחֲכָמִים אוֹמְרִים: לֹא דִּבְּרוּ בְּשַׁיָּירָא, אֶלָּא בַּהוֹוֶה.

When the Sages issued this ruling, **they spoke** exclusively **of a caravan;** this is **the statement of Rabbi Yehuda,** who maintains that a partition of this kind, which consists of only horizontal or vertical elements, is permitted exclusively in exigent circumstances. Otherwise, full-fledged partitions are required. **However, the Rabbis say: They spoke of a caravan** in the mishna **only** because they spoke **in the present,**[N] citing the most typical case. Those traveling in caravans were typically unable to erect full-fledged partitions, so they would surround their camps with ropes or boards. However, the *halakha* in the mishna applies in all cases.

כָּל מְחִיצָה שֶׁאֵינָהּ שֶׁל שְׁתִי וְשֶׁל עֵרֶב – אֵינָהּ מְחִיצָה, דִּבְרֵי רַבִּי יוֹסֵי בְּרַבִּי יְהוּדָה. וַחֲכָמִים אוֹמְרִים: אֶחָד מִשְּׁנֵי דְּבָרִים.

The mishna cites an additional dispute: **Any partition that is not** constructed **of** both **warp and woof,** i.e., vertical and horizontal elements, **is not a partition;** this is **the statement of Rabbi Yosei, son of Rabbi Yehuda.** He holds that the vertical boards and the horizontal ropes are not considered a partition, even in the exigent circumstances of a caravan. **However, the Rabbis say: One of the two elements,** either vertical or horizontal, is sufficient.

גמ׳ אָמַר רַב הַמְנוּנָא, אָמַר רַב: הֲרֵי אָמְרוּ עוֹמֵד מְרוּבֶּה עַל הַפָּרוּץ בִּשְׁתִי – הָוֵי עוֹמֵד. בָּעֵי רַב הַמְנוּנָא: בְּעֵרֶב מַאי?

GEMARA **Rav Hamnuna said** that **Rav said:** It was concluded in the previous mishna that the Rabbis **said** that **in** the case of a partition that consists only of **warp,** i.e., vertical, elements, if **the standing** segment of the partition **is greater than the breached** segment, the fence **is** considered **standing. Rav Hamnuna raised a dilemma: What is** the *halakha* in the case of a partition that consists only of **woof,** i.e., horizontal, elements? Is it also considered standing if the standing segment is greater than the breached segment, or not?

HALAKHA

The breach is equal to the standing segments – פָּרוּץ כְּעוֹמֵד: A partition whose breached segments equal its standing segments permits one to carry within the enclosure, in accordance with the opinion of Rav Pappa and the Gemara's conclusion (*Shulḥan Arukh, Oraḥ Ḥayyim* 362:9).

A partition of ropes – מְחִיצַת חֲבָלִים: A partition may be made from ropes that are strung less than three handbreadths apart from each other. A partition of this kind is effective in all places, not only in the case of a caravan. This *halakha* is in accordance with the opinion of the Rabbis (*Shulḥan Arukh, Oraḥ Ḥayyim* 362:8).

NOTES

They spoke in the present – דִּבְּרוּ בַּהוֹוֶה: In certain cases, the Sages of the Mishna disagreed about correct interpretation of earlier *mishnayot*. In this context, the *halakha* governing a caravan was familiar to Rabbi Yehuda and the Rabbis, who disputed its understanding. Does this *halakha* apply exclusively to a particular set of circumstances? Or, was this *halakha* merely couched in typical circumstances and its application is universal? If the latter option is correct, then the earlier mishna spoke of a caravan merely as a typical example from which no halakhic conclusions may be drawn.

BACKGROUND

A breach at the bottom – פְּרוּץ מִלְּמַטָּה: The image shows a partition formed by ropes extending horizontally. The distance from the bottom rope to the ground is slightly less than four handbreadths.

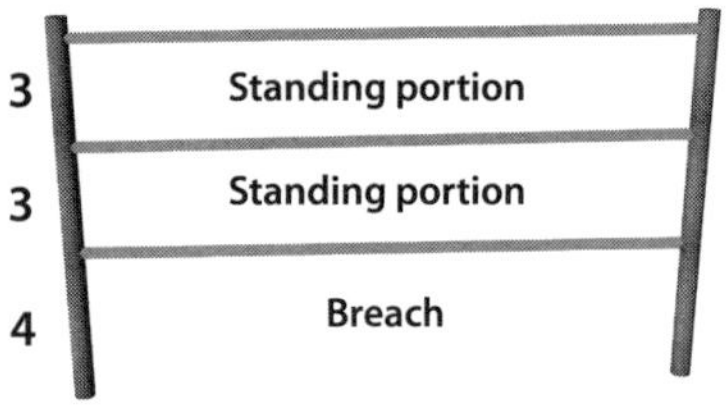

Partition of ropes with breach at the bottom

A breach at the top – פְּרוּץ מִלְמַעְלָה: The image illustrates a partition of ropes in which the breached segment, a space of slightly less than four handbreadths, is positioned at the top.

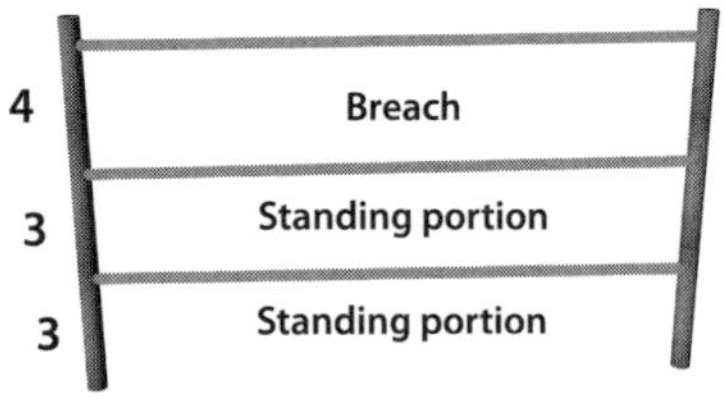

Partition of ropes with breach at the top

A breach in the middle – פְּרוּץ בָּאֶמְצַע: The image illustrates a partition of ropes in which the breached segment, a space of slightly less than four handbreadths, is situated in the middle, between the two spaces that are both less than three handbreadths in height.

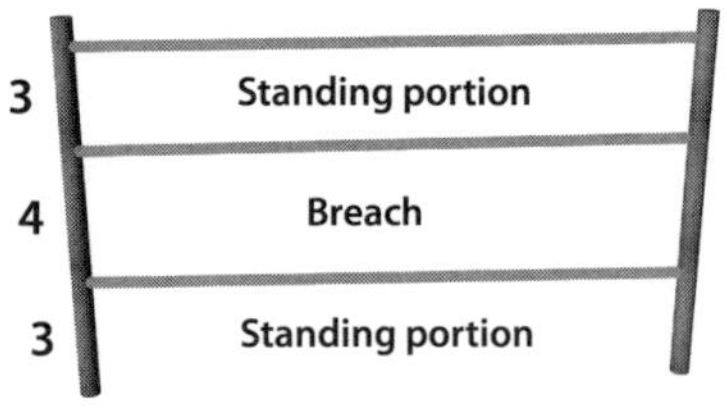

Partition of ropes with breach in the middle

A mat with a hole carved out of it – מַחֲצֶלֶת חֲקוּקָה: Below is an image of a mat slightly wider than seven handbreadths. A hole of three handbreadths is carved out of it, and it is suspended so the top of the mat is ten handbreadths from the ground.

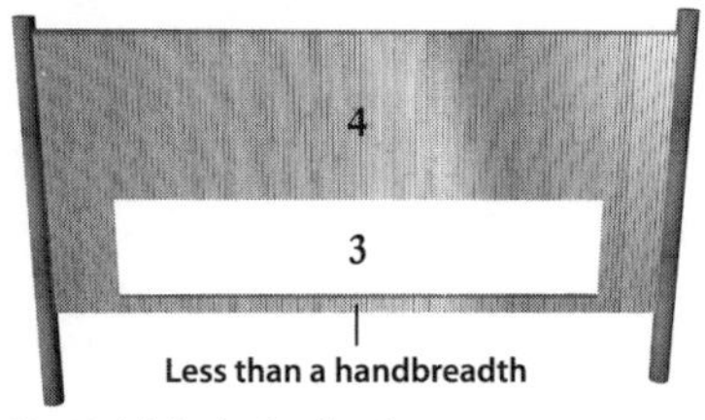

Mat with a hole three handbreadths wide

אָמַר אַבַּיֵי, תָּא שְׁמַע: שִׁיעוּר חֲבָלִים וְעוֹבְיָין יָתֵר עַל טֶפַח, שֶׁיְּהוּ הַכֹּל עֲשָׂרָה טְפָחִים. וְאִי אִיתָא – לָמָּה לִי יָתֵר עַל טֶפַח?

Abaye said: Come and **hear** a resolution to this dilemma from the mishna: **The measure of the ropes and their** combined **thickness** must be **greater than a handbreadth, so that the entire** partition **will be ten handbreadths** high. **And if it is** so that, in a case where the standing segment is greater than the breached segment, the partition is considered standing even in the case of a fence that consists of horizontal elements, **why do I need** ropes with a combined thickness of **greater than a handbreadth?**

לִיעֲבִיד פָּחוֹת מִשְּׁלֹשָׁה וְחֶבֶל מַשֶּׁהוּ, פָּחוֹת מִשְּׁלֹשָׁה וְחֶבֶל מַשֶּׁהוּ, פָּחוֹת מֵאַרְבָּעָה וְחֶבֶל מַשֶּׁהוּ!

Instead, **let one leave** a space slightly **less than three** handbreadths, **and** place **a rope of any size,** leave another space slightly **less than three** handbreadths, **and** place another **rope of any size,** leave a third space slightly **less than four** handbreadths, **and** place a third **rope** of **any size.** The ropes between which there is a space less than three handbreadths should be considered joined, based on the principle of *lavud*. The entire partition should be considered standing because the standing segment, measuring six handbreadths, is greater than the breached segment, which measures four handbreadths.

וְתִיסְבְּרָא, הַאי פָּחוֹת מֵאַרְבָּעָה הֵיכָא מוֹקִים לֵיהּ? אִי מוֹקִים לֵיהּ תַּתַּאי – הֲוָה לֵיהּ כִּמְחִיצָּה שֶׁהַגְּדָיִים בּוֹקְעִין בָּהּ,

The Gemara presents a difficulty: **And** how can **you understand** that this would be effective? **Where does he position** the space of slightly **less than four** handbreadths? **If he positions it at the bottom,**[B] its legal status **is like** that of **a partition through which goats pass,** which is not a valid partition.

אִי מוֹקִים לֵיהּ עִילַּאי – אָתֵי אֲוִירָא דְּהַאי גִּיסָא וּדְהַאי גִּיסָא וּמְבַטֵּל לֵיהּ.

If he positions it at the top,[B] then **the air on this side, above** the uppermost rope, **and on that side,** below that rope, **come and negate it.** As there are more than three handbreadths between them the upper and lower ropes, they are not joined together based on the principle of *lavud*. The four handbreadths below the uppermost rope and the airspace above it combine to negate the connection.

אִי מוֹקִים לֵיהּ בְּמִיצְעֵי – הֲוָה לֵיהּ עוֹמֵד מְרוּבֶּה עַל הַפָּרוּץ מִשְּׁתֵּי רוּחוֹת. שָׁמְעַתְּ מִינָּהּ: עוֹמֵד מְרוּבֶּה עַל הַפָּרוּץ מִשְּׁתֵּי רוּחוֹת הָוֵי עוֹמֵד!

If he positions it in the middle,[B] then **the standing** segment of the partition **is greater than the breached** segment, provided that the standing portions **on the two sides** of the breach are combined.[N] However, if each side is considered separately, the breach is greater than the standing portion. If it is nevertheless deemed a partition, **conclude from it** that even if **the standing segment is greater than the breached** segment only when the standing segments **on the two sides** of the breach are combined, the partition is considered **standing.** However, that circumstance was raised as a dilemma and remained unresolved.

אֶלָּא רַב הַמְנוּנָא הָכִי קָא מִיבַּעְיָא לֵיהּ: כְּגוֹן דְּאַיְיתֵי מַחֲצֶלֶת דְּהָוֵי שִׁבְעָה וּמַשֶּׁהוּ, וְחָקַק בָּהּ שְׁלֹשָׁה וּשְׁבַק בָּהּ אַרְבָּעָה וּמַשֶּׁהוּ, וְאוֹקְמֵיהּ בְּפָחוֹת מִשְּׁלֹשָׁה.

Rather, Rav Hamnuna raised the following dilemma: What is the *halakha* in a case **where one brought a mat that is seven** handbreadths **and any** additional amount, **and carved in it** a hole **three** handbreadths wide, **and left four** handbreadths above the hole **and any** additional amount below it, **and positioned** the mat **less than three** handbreadths off the ground?[B]

רַב אַשִׁי אָמַר: מְחִיצָּה תְּלוּיָה אִיבַּעְיָא לֵיהּ, כְּדִבְעָא מִינֵּיהּ רַבִּי טַבְלָא מֵרַב: מְחִיצָּה תְּלוּיָה מַהוּ שֶׁתַּתִּיר בְּחוּרְבָּה? אָמַר לֵיהּ: אֵין מְחִיצָּה תְּלוּיָה מַתֶּרֶת אֶלָּא בַּמַּיִם, קַל הוּא שֶׁהֵקֵלּוּ חֲכָמִים בַּמַּיִם.

Rav Ashi said: The dilemma he raised is with regard to the legal status of a ten-handbreadth **partition suspended** off the ground. That dilemma is **similar to that which Rabbi Tavla raised** as **a dilemma before Rav: Does a suspended partition** act as if it were a partition that reaches the ground and **render it permitted** for one to carry **in a ruin?** Rav **said to him: A suspended partition renders it permitted** for one to carry **only** when it is suspended over **water,** as there is a **leniency** introduced **by the Sages with regard to water.**

NOTES

The standing segment is greater than the breached segment on the two sides – עוֹמֵד מְרוּבֶּה מִשְּׁתֵּי רוּחוֹת: Some commentaries explain that the uncertainty with regard to cases where the standing segments of the partition on the two sides of the breach are greater than the breached segments pertains exclusively when the standing segments themselves are greater only due to the principle of *lavud*, e.g., in the case of ropes surrounding the camp. There is no uncertainty in cases where the standing segments are actually greater than the breached segments.

״מַקִּיפִין בְּקָנִים וכו׳״: בְּשַׁיָּירָא – אִין, בְּיָחִיד – לָא. וְהָתַנְיָא, רַבִּי יְהוּדָה אוֹמֵר: כׇּל מְחִיצּוֹת שַׁבָּת לֹא הִתִּירוּ לְיָחִיד יוֹתֵר מִבֵּית סָאתַיִם!

We learned in the mishna: **One** may **surround** the area **with boards** that stand upright, provided there will not be a gap of three handbreadths between one board and the next. Rabbi Yehuda said that this leniency, which allows the establishment of a partition consisting exclusively of horizontal or vertical elements, was stated only with regard to a caravan. The Gemara infers: **With regard to a caravan, yes,** it is permitted; **with regard to an individual, no,** it is not permitted. **Wasn't it taught** in a *baraita*: **Rabbi Yehuda says:** With regard to **all** unsteady **partitions of Shabbat,** e.g., those consisting exclusively of horizontal or vertical elements, the Sages **did not permit** their use **for an individual** if the space that they enclose is **greater than two *beit se'a*?**[N] This indicates that, for an area of up to two *beit se'a*, Rabbi Yehuda permits these partitions even for an individual.

כִּדְאָמַר רַב נַחְמָן, וְאִיתֵּימָא רַב בֵּיבָי בַּר אַבַּיֵּי: לֹא נִצְרְכָא אֶלָּא לִיתֵּן לָהֶן כׇּל צׇרְכָּן, הָכָא נַמִּי: לִיתֵּן לָהֶן כׇּל צׇרְכָּן.

The Gemara answers: Rabbi Yehuda's statement in the mishna can be understood **in accordance with that which Rav Naḥman, and some say** it was **Rav Beivai bar Abaye, said** with regard to a different statement: This *halakha* **was necessary only** in order **to provide** those traveling in the caravan with space to satisfy **all their needs. Here, too,** in the mishna, Rabbi Yehuda's statement can be understood as coming **to provide** those traveling in the caravan with space to satisfy **all their needs.** In other words, Rabbi Yehuda does not dispute the fundamental effectiveness of a partition of this kind, even for an individual. When he says that the *halakha* applies solely to a caravan, he means that it applies only in the case of a caravan, regardless of the size of the area in question. However, in the case of an individual, a partition of that kind is effective only if it encloses an area up to two *beit se'a*.

הֵיכָא אִיתְּמַר דְּרַב נַחְמָן וְאִיתֵּימָא רַב בֵּיבָי בַּר אַבַּיֵּי – אַהָא דִּתְנַן: כׇּל מְחִיצָּה שֶׁאֵינָהּ שֶׁל שְׁתִי וָעֵרֶב – אֵינָהּ מְחִיצָּה, דִּבְרֵי רַבִּי יוֹסֵי בְּרַבִּי יְהוּדָה.

The Gemara asks: **Where was** this statement **of Rav Naḥman, and some say** of **Rav Beivai bar Abaye, stated?** It was stated with regard **to this** ruling at the end of the mishna: **Any partition that is not** made of both **vertical and horizontal** elements **is not a partition;** this is the statement of **Rabbi Yosei, son of Rabbi Yehuda.**

וּמִי אָמַר רַבִּי יוֹסֵי בְּרַבִּי יְהוּדָה הָכִי? וְהָתַנְיָא: אֶחָד יָחִיד וְאֶחָד שַׁיָּירָא לַחֲבָלִים, וּמַה בֵּין יָחִיד לְשַׁיָּירָא? יָחִיד – נוֹתְנִין לוֹ בֵּית סָאתַיִם, שְׁנַיִם – נוֹתְנִין לָהֶם בֵּית סָאתַיִם, שְׁלֹשָׁה – נַעֲשׂוּ שַׁיָּירָא, וְנוֹתְנִין לָהֶן בֵּית שֵׁשׁ, דִּבְרֵי רַבִּי יוֹסֵי בְּרַבִּי יְהוּדָה.

The Gemara asks: **Did Rabbi Yosei, son of Rabbi Yehuda,** actually **say this? Wasn't it taught** in a *baraita*: For **both an individual and a caravan,** partitions made of **ropes** are effective? **And what,** then, **is the difference between an individual and a caravan?** With regard to an **individual,** the *halakha* **provides him** with an area of **two *beit se'a*,** in which he may carry by virtue of partitions of this kind. With regard to **two** individuals as well, the *halakha* **provides them** with an area of **two *beit se'a*. Three** individuals **assume the** legal **status of a caravan,**[N] **and** the *halakha* **provides** each of **them** with an area of two *beit se'a*, for a total of **six *beit se'a*.** This is **the statement of Rabbi Yosei, son of Rabbi Yehuda.**

וַחֲכָמִים אוֹמְרִים: אֶחָד יָחִיד וְאֶחָד שַׁיָּירָא נוֹתְנִין לָהֶן כׇּל צׇרְכָּן, וּבִלְבַד שֶׁלֹּא יְהֵא בֵּית סָאתַיִם פָּנוּי.

And the Rabbis say: With regard to **both an individual and** those traveling in **a caravan, one provides them** with space to satisfy **all their needs, provided that there will not be an unoccupied space of two *beit se'a*.** They may not enclose an area that is two *beit se'a* larger than the space that they require. Apparently, Rabbi Yosei, son of Rabbi Yehuda, relies on the ruling that ropes render an area fit for one to carry within it, even for an individual.

אָמַר רַב נַחְמָן, וְאִיתֵּימָא רַב בֵּיבָי בַּר אַבַּיֵּי: לֹא נִצְרְכָא אֶלָּא לִיתֵּן לָהֶן כׇּל צׇרְכָּן.

Rav Naḥman, and some say it was **Rav Beivai bar Abaye, said:** The opinion of Rabbi Yosei, son of Rabbi Yehuda, in the mishna **was necessary only to provide them** with the space to satisfy **all their needs** in the case of a properly constructed partition consisting of both horizontal and vertical elements. A partition consisting of exclusively horizontal or vertical elements renders an area of six *beit se'a* fit for one to carry within it, only in the case of a caravan.

דָּרַשׁ רַב נַחְמָן מִשּׁוּם רַבֵּינוּ שְׁמוּאֵל: יָחִיד נוֹתְנִין לוֹ בֵּית סָאתַיִם, שְׁנַיִם נוֹתְנִין לְהוּ בֵּית סָאתַיִם, שְׁלֹשָׁה – נַעֲשׂוּ שַׁיָּירָא, וְנוֹתְנִין לָהֶן בֵּית שֵׁשׁ.

Rav Naḥman taught in the name of Rabbeinu Shmuel: With regard to an **individual,** the *halakha* **provides him** with an area of **two *beit se'a*.** With regard to **two** individuals, the *halakha* **provides them** with an area **of two *beit se'a*** as well. **Three** individuals **assume the** legal **status of a caravan, and** the *halakha* **provides** each of **them** with an area of two *beit se'a*, for a total of **six *beit se'a*.**

שָׁבְקַתְּ רַבָּנַן וַעֲבַדְתְּ כְּרַבִּי יוֹסֵי בְּרַבִּי יְהוּדָה?!

Rav Naḥman was asked: **Did you abandon** the majority opinion of **the Rabbis and act in accordance with** the individual opinion of **Rabbi Yosei, son of Rabbi Yehuda?**

NOTES

Two *beit se'a* – בֵּית סָאתַיִם: The area required to grow two measures of grain is equal to the size of the courtyard of the Tabernacle. This was the measure determined for a courtyard because the *halakhot* of carrying objects on Shabbat from one domain to another were derived from the Jewish people's journeys in the wilderness. From there it was also derived that the area of a courtyard is two *se'a* (Rif; Rabbeinu Ḥananel).

Three assume the status of a caravan – שְׁלֹשָׁה נַעֲשׂוּ שַׁיָּירָא: In the Jerusalem Talmud, it is stated that a gentile is not counted as one of the three people for the purpose of this *halakha*. The Rambam, based on an unresolved dilemma raised in the Jerusalem Talmud, rules that a minor cannot be counted for this purpose either.

הֲדַר אוֹקִים רַב נַחְמָן אָמוֹרָא עֲלֵיהּ וְדָרַשׁ: דְּבָרִים שֶׁאָמַרְתִּי לִפְנֵיכֶם טָעוּת הֵן בְּיָדִי, בְּרַם כָּךְ אָמְרוּ: יָחִיד – נוֹתְנִין לוֹ בֵּית סָאתַיִם, שְׁנַיִם – נוֹתְנִין לָהֶן בֵּית סָאתַיִם, שְׁלֹשָׁה – נַעֲשׂוּ שַׁיָּירָא, וְנוֹתְנִין לָהֶן כׇּל צׇרְכָּן.

Rav Naḥman then placed a speaker standing **over him, and taught: The matters that I stated before you are an error on my part. Indeed, this** is what the Rabbis **said:** With regard to an **individual,** the *halakha* **provides him** with an area of **two** *beit se'a*. With regard to **two** individuals, the *halakha* **provides them** with an area of **two** *beit se'a* as well. **Three** individuals **assume the** legal **status of a caravan, and** the *halakha* **provides them** with space to satisfy **all their needs.**[H]

HALAKHA

The measure of the enclosure of a field – שִׁיעוּר הֶיקֵּף בִּבְקָעָה: If one or two people seek to enclose an area for themselves with ropes for Shabbat, they may enclose only an area of two *beit se'a*. If a group of three people seek to do so, they may enclose enough space to satisfy all their needs. However, if the enclosed area is six *beit se'a* and it includes a vacant area of two *beit se'a*, it is prohibited to carry in the entire area, in accordance with the conclusion of Rav Naḥman (*Shulḥan Arukh, Oraḥ Ḥayyim* 362:1).

Perek **I**
Daf **17** Amud **a**

רֵישָׁא רַבִּי יוֹסֵי בְּרַבִּי יְהוּדָה וְסֵיפָא רַבָּנַן!

The Gemara asks: Is that to say that **the first clause** of Rav Naḥman's ruling **is** in accordance with the opinion of **Rabbi Yosei, son of Rabbi Yehuda, and the latter clause is** in accordance with the opinion of **the Rabbis?**

אִין, מִשּׁוּם דְּקָאֵי אֲבוּהּ בְּשִׁיטָתֵיהּ.

The Gemara answers: **Yes, because his father,** Rabbi Yehuda, **holds in accordance with his opinion**[N] with regard to areas enclosed for the sake of an individual. This being the case, their opinion on this matter is that of the many.

אָמַר רַב גִּידֵּל, אָמַר רַב: שְׁלֹשָׁה, בְּחָמֵשׁ – אֲסוּרִין, בְּשֶׁבַע – מוּתָּרִין. אָמְרוּ לֵיהּ: אָמַר רַב הָכִי? אָמַר לְהוּ: אוֹרַיְיתָא נְבִיאֵי וּכְתִיבֵי, דַּאֲמַר רַב הָכִי.

Rav Giddel said that **Rav said:** At times, for **three** people it is **prohibited** to carry even **in** an area of **five** *beit se'a*;[H] at times, it is **permitted** for them to carry even **in** an area of **seven** *beit se'a*. These statements appear irreconcilable, and his colleagues **said to him: Did Rav** actually **say that? He said to them:** I swear by **the Torah, the Prophets, and the Writings, that Rav said so.**

אֲמַר רַב אַשִׁי: מַאי קַשְׁיָא? דִּילְמָא הָכִי קָאָמַר: הוּצְרְכוּ לְשֵׁשׁ וְהִקִּיפוּ בְּשֶׁבַע – אֲפִילּוּ בְּשֶׁבַע מוּתָּרִין, לֹא הוּצְרְכוּ אֶלָּא לְחָמֵשׁ וְהִקִּיפוּ בְּשֶׁבַע – אֲפִילּוּ בְּחָמֵשׁ אֲסוּרִין.

Rav Ashi said: What is the difficulty here? **Perhaps this is what he is saying:** If **they needed six** *beit se'a*, **and they enclosed seven, they are permitted** to carry **even in** all **seven,** as one empty *beit se'a* does not render it prohibited for one to carry in the rest of the area. If, however, **they needed only five** *beit se'a*, **and they enclosed seven,** carrying **even in five is prohibited,** as there is an unoccupied space of two *beit se'a*.

וְאֶלָּא הָא דְּקָתָנֵי ״וּבִלְבַד שֶׁלֹּא יְהֵא בֵּית סָאתַיִם פָּנוּי״, מַאי לָאו פָּנוּי מֵאָדָם? לֹא, פָּנוּי מִכֵּלִים.

The Gemara asks: **However,** with regard to **that which** the *baraita* **is teaching,** that the partition renders the area fit for one to carry within it **provided that there will not be an unoccupied space of two** *beit se'a*, **what, is it not** in fact referring to **space unoccupied by people?** In other words, isn't the *baraita* teaching that the enclosed area may not be two *beit se'a* larger than a measure of two *beit se'a* per person? Accordingly, if three people enclosed an area of seven *beit se'a*, it should always be permitted for them to carry there, as they are entitled to six *beit se'a* and only one *beit se'a* is unoccupied. The Gemara answers: **No,** it means **unoccupied by utensils.** Although they would be entitled to six *beit se'a* if needed, since they need only five in practice and a space of two *beit se'a* remains unoccupied, the effectiveness of the partitions is negated and carrying therein is prohibited.

אִיתְּמַר: שְׁלֹשָׁה וָמֵת אֶחָד מֵהֶן, שְׁנַיִם וְנִתּוֹסְפוּ עֲלֵיהֶן. רַב הוּנָא וְרַבִּי יִצְחָק, חַד אָמַר: שַׁבָּת גּוֹרֶמֶת, וְחַד אָמַר: דִּיוּרִין גּוֹרְמִין.

It is stated: If there were **three** people in a caravan **and one of them died** on Shabbat, or if there were **two** people, **and** others **were added to them** on Shabbat, **Rav Huna and Rabbi Yitzḥak** disagree with regard to the area in which they are permitted to carry on Shabbat. **One said: Shabbat determines** the status of the area.[H] The *halakha* is determined in accordance with the prevailing situation at the onset of Shabbat. **And one said** that **the residents,** i.e., the actual number of people present at any given moment, **determine** the status.

NOTES

Because his father holds in accordance with his opinion – מִשּׁוּם דְּקָאֵי אֲבוּהּ בְּשִׁיטָתֵיהּ: It is clear that the final conclusion is that the *halakha* is in accordance with the opinion of Rabbi Yehuda. Nevertheless, the statement of Rabbi Yosei, son of Rabbi Yehuda, was cited because it is clearer.

HALAKHA

For three people it is prohibited to carry even in an area of five ***beit se'a*** – שְׁלֹשָׁה, בְּחָמֵשׁ אֲסוּרִין: If three people made an enclosure consisting of only horizontal or only vertical partitions, and the enclosed area is less than six *beit se'a*, they are all permitted to carry in the entire area. However, if they enclosed an area greater than six *beit se'a*, and this enclosure includes an unoccupied, unused area of two *beit se'a*, it is prohibited to carry in the entire enclosure (*Beit Yosef*). This *halakha* is derived from the statement of Rav Giddel, as explained by Rav Ashi. According to this approach, the Rabbis are not more stringent than Rabbi Yosei, son of Rabbi Yehuda, as an enclosed area of up to six *beit se'a* is permitted in any case. The *Taz*, in accordance with the opinions of the Rashba, the Ritva, and Rabbeinu Ḥananel, disagrees. He maintains that if the enclosed area is less than six *beit se'a*, and it includes an area of two *beit se'a* that the people in the enclosure do not require, it is prohibited to carry there. The *Shulḥan Arukh HaRav* cites both opinions and rules leniently, since carrying in the enclosure is prohibited by rabbinic law (*Shulḥan Arukh, Oraḥ Ḥayyim* 362:1).

Shabbat determines – שַׁבָּת גּוֹרֶמֶת: With regard to the *halakhot* of *eiruv*, the *halakha* is determined by the situation at the onset of Shabbat, in accordance with the opinion of Rav Huna, as Rav Yehuda agrees with his opinion (*Maggid Mishne*; *Shulḥan Arukh, Oraḥ Ḥayyim* 362:2).

תִּסְתַּיֵּים דְּרַב הוּנָא הוּא דְּאָמַר שַׁבָּת גּוֹרֶמֶת. דְּאָמַר רַבָּה: בְּעַאי מֵרַב הוּנָא, וּבְעַאי מֵרַב יְהוּדָה: עֵירֵב דֶּרֶךְ הַפֶּתַח וְנִסְתַּם הַפֶּתַח, דֶּרֶךְ הַחַלּוֹן וְנִסְתַּם הַחַלּוֹן, מַהוּ? וְאָמַר לִי: שַׁבָּת הוֹאִיל וְהוּתְּרָה – הוּתְּרָה. תִּסְתַּיֵּים.

The Gemara comments: **Conclude that it is Rav Huna who said that Shabbat determines** the status, as **Rabba said: I raised a dilemma before Rav Huna, and I raised a dilemma before Rav Yehuda** with regard to the following case: If one **established an** *eiruv* to join one courtyard to another **via a certain opening and that opening was sealed** on Shabbat, or if one established an *eiruv* **via** a certain **window and that window was sealed** on Shabbat,[N] **what is the** *halakha*? Can one continue to rely on this *eiruv* and carry from one courtyard to the other via other entrances? **And he said to me: Since** it was **permitted** to carry from courtyard to courtyard at the onset of **Shabbat, it was permitted** and remains so[H] until Shabbat's conclusion. The Gemara comments: Indeed, **conclude** that it is Rav Huna who maintains the determining factor is Shabbat, not the residents.

לֵימָא רַב הוּנָא וְרַבִּי יִצְחָק בִּפְלוּגְתָּא דְּרַבִּי יוֹסֵי וְרַבִּי יְהוּדָה קָמִיפַּלְגִי. דִּתְנַן: חָצֵר שֶׁנִּפְרְצָה מִשְּׁתֵּי רוּחוֹתֶיהָ, וְכֵן בַּיִת שֶׁנִּפְרַץ מִשְּׁתֵּי רוּחוֹתָיו, וְכֵן מָבוֹי שֶׁנִּיטְּלוּ קוֹרוֹתָיו אוֹ לְחָיָיו – מוּתָּרִין לְאוֹתָהּ שַׁבָּת וַאֲסוּרִין לֶעָתִיד לָבֹא, דִּבְרֵי רַבִּי יְהוּדָה.

The Gemara asks: **Let us say that Rav Huna and Rabbi Yitzḥak are disagreeing in the** earlier **dispute of** the *tanna'im* **Rabbi Yosei and Rabbi Yehuda. As we learned** in a mishna: If during Shabbat a **courtyard was breached from two of its sides, or** if **a house was breached from two of its sides, or** if **an alleyway's** cross **beams or side posts were removed,** it is **permitted** to carry within them **on that Shabbat, but** it is **prohibited** to do so **in the future;** this is **the statement of Rabbi Yehuda.**

רַבִּי יוֹסֵי אוֹמֵר: אִם מוּתָּרִין לְאוֹתָהּ שַׁבָּת – מוּתָּרִין לֶעָתִיד לָבֹא, וְאִם אֲסוּרִין לֶעָתִיד לָבֹא – אֲסוּרִין לְאוֹתָהּ שַׁבָּת.

Rabbi Yosei says: If it is **permitted** to carry there **on that Shabbat,** it is also **permitted** to do so **in the future. However, if** it is **prohibited** to carry there **in the future,** it is also **prohibited** to do so **on that Shabbat.** Since it is prohibited to carry there in the future, it is also prohibited to carry there on that Shabbat. This opinion disputes the principle that since it is permitted at the onset of Shabbat it remains permitted.

לֵימָא רַב הוּנָא דְּאָמַר כְּרַבִּי יְהוּדָה, וְרַבִּי יִצְחָק דְּאָמַר כְּרַבִּי יוֹסֵי?

Let us say that it is **Rav Huna who stated** his opinion **in accordance with** the opinion of **Rabbi Yehuda,** and he held that the situation at the onset of Shabbat determines the halakhic status. **And** it is **Rabbi Yitzḥak who stated** his opinion **in accordance with** the opinion of **Rabbi Yosei.**

אָמַר לָךְ רַב הוּנָא: אֲנָא דַּאֲמַרִי אֲפִילּוּ לְרַבִּי יוֹסֵי, עַד כָּאן לָא קָאָמַר רַבִּי יוֹסֵי הָתָם – אֶלָּא דְּלֵיתַנְהוּ לִמְחִיצוֹת, הָכָא – אִיתַנְהוּ לִמְחִיצוֹת.

The Gemara rejects this explanation. **Rav Huna** could have **said to you:** It is **I who stated** my opinion **even in accordance with** the opinion of **Rabbi Yosei. Rabbi Yosei stated** his opinion **only there,** in a case **where there are no** longer **partitions** intact; however, **here there are partitions** intact. Since the status of the area is dependent upon the existence of partitions, he would also agree that carrying is permitted in this case.

וְרַבִּי יִצְחָק אָמַר: אֲנָא דַּאֲמַרִי אֲפִילּוּ לְרַבִּי יְהוּדָה, עַד כָּאן לָא קָאָמַר רַבִּי יְהוּדָה הָתָם אֶלָּא דְּאִיתַנְהוּ לְדִיּוּרִין, הָכָא לֵיתַנְהוּ לְדִיּוּרִין.

And Rabbi Yitzḥak could have **said** to you: It is **I who stated** my opinion **even in accordance with** the opinion of **Rabbi Yehuda. Rabbi Yehuda stated** his opinion **only there,** in a case **where there are residents.** However, **here, there are no** remaining **residents** that are alive, so he too would prohibit carrying.

״וַחֲכָמִים אוֹמְרִים אֶחָד מִשְּׁנֵי דְבָרִים״. הַיְינוּ תַּנָּא קַמָּא!

We learned in the mishna: **However, the Rabbis say: One of the two elements,** either vertical or horizontal, is sufficient. The Gemara asks: **This is** identical to the opinion of **the first** *tanna* of the mishna. What did the Rabbis add?

אִיכָּא בֵּינַיְיהוּ יָחִיד בַּיִּישּׁוּב.

The Gemara answers: **There is** a practical halakhic difference **between them** with regard to **an individual** in **a settlement.** The first *tanna* does not allow one to rely on a partition of this type *ab initio*, whereas the Rabbis permit doing so in all cases.

מתני׳ אַרְבָּעָה דְּבָרִים פָּטְרוּ בְּמַחֲנֶה: מְבִיאִין עֵצִים מִכָּל מָקוֹם, וּפְטוּרִין מֵרְחִיצַת יָדַיִם, וּמִדְּמַאי, וּמִלְּעָרֵב.

MISHNA The Sages **exempted** a soldier **in** a military **camp**[NH] in **four matters: One may bring wood** for kindling **from any place** with no concern that he is stealing wood from its owners; **and one is exempt from** ritual **washing** of the **hands** before eating; **and** one is exempt **from** the separation of tithes from **doubtfully tithed produce** [*demai*], i.e., produce purchased from an *am ha'aretz*, one who is not diligent in separating tithes; **and** one is exempt **from establishing an** ***eiruv.***

NOTES

An *eiruv* that broke on Shabbat – עֵירוּב שֶׁנִּתְקַלְקֵל בְּשַׁבָּת: The *halakha* is in accordance with the opinion of Rav Huna with regard to enclosed fields and in accordance with Rabbi Yosei's opinion with regard to an alleyway that was breached on Shabbat. Apparently, Rav Huna's answer is not merely a refutation. Rather, he maintains that the principle that stipulates that if carrying was permitted at the beginning of Shabbat it remains permitted throughout applies only if the partitions are still extant. If, however, the partitions are removed, it is no longer permitted to carry within the area previously enclosed by them.

Camp – מַחֲנֶה: In the Jerusalem Talmud, there is a discussion with regard to what constitutes a camp. The conclusion is that the presence of at least ten people is necessary to meet the halakhic criterion of a camp. In addition, the leniencies of a military camp apply only to those engaged in an optional war. However, additional activities are permitted for those engaged in a mandatory war.

HALAKHA

Since it was permitted at the onset of Shabbat, it was permitted and remains so – שַׁבָּת הוֹאִיל וְהוּתְּרָה הוּתְּרָה: If two courtyards were joined with an *eiruv* via a certain opening, and that opening was sealed on Shabbat, the residents of the two courtyards may still carry there. Some commentaries, including Rashi, state that the residents are permitted to carry from one courtyard to the other through openings in the wall. Other authorities, including the Rambam, rule that under these circumstances, the residents of each courtyard are permitted to carry only within their respective courtyards (*Shulḥan Arukh, Oraḥ Ḥayyim* 374:1).

Matters that the Sages exempted in a camp – דְּבָרִים שֶׁפָּטְרוּ בְּמַחֲנֶה: The soldiers in a military camp who are going off to war or returning from battle (Rambam based on the Jerusalem Talmud) are exempt from tithing *demai*, from ritual hand washing, and from joining courtyards. They are also permitted to take wood for their own needs, even if it is dry and detached, as per the mishna and the explanation in the Gemara (Rambam *Sefer Shofetim, Hilkhot Melakhim* 6:13).

גמ׳ תָּנוּ רַבָּנַן: מַחֲנֶה הַיּוֹצֵאת לְמִלְחֶמֶת הָרְשׁוּת – מוּתָּרִין בְּגֶזֶל עֵצִים יְבֵשִׁים. רַבִּי יְהוּדָה בֶּן תֵּימָא אוֹמֵר: אַף חוֹנִין בְּכׇל מָקוֹם, וּבִמְקוֹם שֶׁנֶּהֶרְגוּ שָׁם נִקְבָּרִין.

GEMARA **The Sages taught** in a *Tosefta*: With regard to a military **camp that goes out to** wage **an optional war,**[N] **it is permitted** for the soldiers **to steal dry wood. Rabbi Yehuda ben Teima says: They may also encamp in any location,**[H] even if they damage the field in which they are encamped. **And in the place where they were killed, there they are buried**[NH] and the owner of the site cannot object, as moving the corpse for burial elsewhere dishonors the dead.

״מוּתָּרִין בְּגֶזֶל עֵצִים יְבֵשִׁים״. הַאי תַּקַּנְתָּא דִיהוֹשֻׁעַ הֲוָה, דְּאָמַר מָר: עֲשָׂרָה תְּנָאִים הִתְנָה יְהוֹשֻׁעַ: שֶׁיְּהוּ מַרְעִין בְּחוֹרָשִׁין וּמְלַקְּטִין עֵצִים מִשְּׂדוֹתֵיהֶן!

The Gemara analyzes this *Tosefta*. What is the novelty in the following statement: **They are permitted to steal dry wood? This was an ordinance** enacted **by Joshua,** as **the Master said** in a *baraita*: There is a tradition that **Joshua stipulated ten conditions**[H] with the Jewish people as they entered Eretz Yisrael, among them **that** one **may graze** his animals **in woods** belonging to others without objection, and one may **gather wood** for his own use **from their fields.**

הָתָם בְּהִיזְמֵי וְהִיגֵי, הָכָא בִּשְׁאָר עֵצִים.

The Gemara answers: **There,** Joshua's ordinance permitted gathering various types of **shrubs** [***hizmei***][B] **and thorns** [***higei***],[B] with regard to which people are not particular; **here,** the ordinance in the mishna pertaining to a military camp is referring to **other** types of **wood.**

אִי נַמִי: הָתָם בִּמְחוּבָּרִין, הָכָא בִּתְלוּשִׁין.

Alternatively: There, Joshua's ordinance referred **to** gathering thorns still **attached** to the ground, as removing those thorns benefits the field's owner. **Here,** however, the mishna is referring **to** gathering thorns that are already **detached.**

אִי נַמִי: הָתָם בְּלַחִין, הָכָא בִּיבֵשִׁים.

Alternatively: There, Joshua's ordinance referred **to** gathering **moist** thorns. Owners are not particular about them because they are not immediately suitable for kindling. **Here,** the mishna is referring even **to dry** thorns.

״רַבִּי יְהוּדָה בֶּן תֵּימָא אוֹמֵר: אַף חוֹנִין בְּכׇל מָקוֹם וּבִמְקוֹם שֶׁנֶּהֶרְגִים שָׁם נִקְבָּרִים״. פְּשִׁיטָא, מֵת מִצְוָה הוּא, וּמֵת מִצְוָה קוֹנֶה מְקוֹמוֹ!

It was taught in the *Tosefta* that **Rabbi Yehuda ben Teima says: They may also encamp in any place, and in the place where they were killed, there they are buried.** The Gemara raises a difficulty: This is **obvious,** as a the body of a dead soldier **is** considered to be **a corpse with no one to bury it** [***met mitzva***],[NH] and the principle is that **a *met mitzva* acquires its place.** In other words, the body must be interred where it is found, and the owner of the field cannot prevent burial.

לָא צְרִיכָא, אַף עַל גַּב

The Gemara answers: **No,** this ostensibly obvious statement is indeed **necessary** to teach that this principle applies in the case of a military camp, **even though**

NOTES

A camp that goes out to wage an optional war – מַחֲנֶה הַיּוֹצֵאת לְמִלְחֶמֶת הָרְשׁוּת: Rav Hai Gaon explains that as long as the Jewish people were involved in their wars of conquest, the Sages did not institute the laws of *eiruv* for the entire Jewish people. Support for his argument can be found in the mishna that states that they were not particular about rabbinic prohibitions of this kind in a military camp (*Ḥeshek Shlomo*).

And in the place where they were killed, there they are buried – בִּמְקוֹם שֶׁנֶּהֶרְגִים שָׁם נִקְבָּרִים: The rationale for this *halakha* is that since everyone is preoccupied with the fighting, if they do not bury the fallen soldiers immediately, in the place where they fell, they will not do so at all. Consequently, there is concern that the corpses will suffer the indignity of not being buried (see the parallel discussion in the Jerusalem Talmud).

A corpse with no one to bury it [*met mitzva*] – מֵת מִצְוָה: It is an important mitzva to tend to a corpse, so that it not be left unburied in an undignified state. This mitzva, based on the ideal of human dignity, is so significant that even a High Priest and a nazirite, for whom it is prohibited to become ritually impure, are obligated to become ritually impure for a *met mitzva*.

HALAKHA

They may also encamp in any location – חוֹנִים בְּכׇל מָקוֹם: Soldiers heading off to war may encamp in any place, in accordance with the opinion Rabbi Yehuda ben Teima. His opinion is the accepted *halakha* because the Gemara conducts a discussion of his opinion (Rambam *Sefer Shofetim*, *Hilkhot Melakhim* 6:12).

Where they were killed, there they are buried – בִּמְקוֹם שֶׁנֶּהֶרְגִים שָׁם נִקְבָּרִים: Soldiers are buried in the place where they were killed. The owner of the field may not object, since they are considered a *met mitzva* (Rambam *Sefer Shofetim*, *Hilkhot Melakhim* 6:12).

The conditions of Joshua – מִתְנָאֵי יְהוֹשֻׁעַ: One of the ten conditions stipulated by Joshua is that one is permitted to graze one's animals in woods belonging to others. Sheep are allowed only to graze where the trees are large. However, if the trees are small, it is prohibited to graze them there without the owner's permission. It is also permitted to gather thorny shrubs from fields, provided they are moist and attached (Rambam *Sefer Nezikim*, *Hilkhot Nizkei Mamon* 5:3).

A corpse with no one to bury it [*met mitzva*] – מֵת מִצְוָה: If a corpse is found along a road or in a city of gentiles with no one to bury it, it is prohibited for the person who found it to leave the place until the corpse is buried in the place where it was found. The person may only leave if he is in a place where if one calls other people will come and tend to every aspect of the burial (*Shulḥan Arukh*, *Yoreh De'a* 374:3).

BACKGROUND

Shrubs [*hizmei*] – הִיזְמֵי: The common *hizmei*, *Alhagi maurorum* Medik, is a spiny shrub with smooth leaves. It typically grows to a height is around 30 cm, although it can reach 1 m. It is commonly found in fields and salt flats.

Alhagi maurorum Medik

Thorns [*higei*] – הִיגֵי: *Higei* refers to what is probably the thorny rest-harrow, *Ononis spinosa* L., from the Papilionaceae family. The *higei* is a thorny shrub that grows to a height of up to 75 cm, with trifoliolate leaves and thorny side branches. The *higei* grows in fields and wadis.

Ononis spinosa L.

דְּאִית לֵיהּ קוֹבְרִין, דְּתַנְיָא: אֵיזֶהוּ מֵת מִצְוָה – כֹּל שֶׁאֵין לוֹ קוֹבְרִין, קוֹרֵא וַאֲחֵרִים עוֹנִין אוֹתוֹ – אֵין זֶה מֵת מִצְוָה.

there are people available **to bury it. As it was taught** in a *baraita*: **Which is** the corpse that is considered **a** ***met mitzva*? Any** corpse **that has no one** available **to bury it.** If, however, the deceased has friends or relatives to tend to his burial, his corpse is not considered a *met mitzva*. Likewise, if the body is in a place where if **one calls out, others** can **answer him,**[N] **this is not a** ***met mitzva*.** The *Tosefta* teaches a novel ruling applicable to the case of a military camp: A solider is buried where he was killed, even if the conditions for *met mitzva* are not met there.

וּמֵת מִצְוָה קָנָה מְקוֹמוֹ? וְהָתַנְיָא: הַמּוֹצֵא מֵת מוּטָל בְּסִרְטְיָא – מְפַנֵּיהוּ לִימִין אִסְרַטְיָא אוֹ לִשְׂמֹאל אִסְרַטְיָא.

With regard to the *halakha* itself, the Gemara asks: **And does a** ***met mitzva*** actually **acquire its place? Wasn't it taught** in a *baraita*: **One who finds a corpse laid out on a main street evacuates it** for burial either **to the right of the street or to the left of the street,** but it may not be buried under the main street itself?

שְׂדֵה בּוּר וּשְׂדֵה נִיר – מְפַנֵּיהוּ לִשְׂדֵה בּוּר, שְׂדֵה נִיר וּשְׂדֵה זֶרַע – מְפַנֵּיהוּ לִשְׂדֵה נִיר, הָיוּ שְׁתֵּיהֶן נִירוֹת, שְׁתֵּיהֶן זְרוּעוֹת, שְׁתֵּיהֶן בּוּרוֹת – מְפַנֵּהוּ לְכָל רוּחַ שֶׁיִּרְצֶה.

If one can move the corpse either to **an uncultivated field or** to **a plowed field, he evacuates it to the uncultivated field.** If the choice is between **a plowed field and a sown field, he evacuates it to the plowed field.** If **both** fields **are plowed,** or if **both are sown,** or if **both are uncultivated, he evacuates it to any side that he wishes** to move it. Apparently, a *met mitzva* is not necessarily buried where it is found. It may be moved elsewhere.

אָמַר רַב בֵּיבַי: הָכָא בְּמֵת מוּטָל עַל הַמֵּיצַר עָסְקִינַן, מִתּוֹךְ שֶׁנִּיתְּנָה רְשׁוּת לְפַנּוֹתוֹ מִן הַמֵּיצַר – מְפַנֵּיהוּ לְכָל רוּחַ שֶׁיִּרְצֶה.

Rav Beivai said: Here we are dealing with a corpse laid out across on the side of a public path,[H] and it stretches across the path and reaches the other side. Were the corpse buried there, it would prohibit passage by priests. **Since permission was** already **granted to evacuate it from the side** of a public path, **one may evacuate it to any side he wishes.** If, however, the corpse was in a field, moving it would be prohibited.

״וּפְטוּרִין מֵרְחִיצַת יָדַיִם״. אָמַר אַבָּיֵי: לֹא שָׁנוּ אֶלָּא מַיִם רִאשׁוֹנִים, אֲבָל מַיִם אַחֲרוֹנִים – חוֹבָה.

We learned in the mishna that in a military camp **one is exempt from** ritual **washing of the hands.**[H] **Abaye said: They taught** this exemption **only** with regard to **first waters,** i.e., hand-washing before eating. **However, final waters,** i.e., hand-washing after eating and before reciting Grace after Meals, **is an obligation** even in a military camp.

אָמַר רַב חִיָּיא בַּר אַשִׁי: מִפְּנֵי מָה אָמְרוּ מַיִם אַחֲרוֹנִים חוֹבָה – מִפְּנֵי שֶׁמֶּלַח סְדוֹמִית יֵשׁ, שֶׁמְּסַמֵּא אֶת הָעֵינַיִם.

Rav Ḥiyya bar Ashi said: For what reason **did** the Sages **say that the final waters are an obligation?** It is **due to** the fact **that there is the presence of Sodomite salt,**[B] **which blinds the eyes** even in a small amount. Since Sodomite salt could remain on one's hands, one must wash them after eating. This obligation is binding even in a camp because soldiers are also obligated to maintain their health.

אָמַר אַבָּיֵי: וּמִשְׁתַּכְּחָא כְּקוֹרְטָא בְּכוֹרָא. אֲמַר לֵיהּ רַב אַחָא בְּרֵיהּ דְּרָבָא לְרַב אַשִׁי: כָּיֵיל מִילְחָא מַאי? אֲמַר לֵיהּ: [הָא] לָא מִיבַּעְיָא.

Abaye said: And this type of dangerous salt **is present** in the proportion of a single **grain [*korta*]**[L] **in an entire** ***kor*** of innocuous salt. **Rav Aḥa, son of Rava, said to Rav Ashi: If one measured salt** and came into contact with Sodomite salt not during mealtime, **what** is the *halakha*? Is there an obligation to wash his hands afterward? **He said to him: It was unnecessary** to say **this,** as he is certainly obligated to do so.

NOTES

If one calls out others can answer – קוֹרֵא וַאֲחֵרִים עוֹנִין אוֹתוֹ: Some explain this to mean that were the deceased still alive and called out, others would answer (*Tosafot, Yevamot* 43b). Rabbi Nissim Gaon explains that it means that if the one who finds the corpse can call out and others would answer, it is not a *met mitzva*. Consequently, in this circumstance a priest would be prohibited to become ritually impure to tend to burial.

BACKGROUND

Sodomite salt – מֶלַח סְדוֹמִית: The salt mentioned in this context is probably magnesium chloride (MgC), which is found in extremely high concentrates in the Dead Sea. Magnesium chloride can easily become intermingled with regular salt, which is extracted in great quantities along the shores of the Dead Sea. Since magnesium chloride is poisonous, there is a danger that its introduction into the eye by unwashed hands could lead to an eye infection.

Salt crystal formation at the Dead Sea

LANGUAGE

Grain [*korta*] – קוֹרְטָא: From the Arabic root قرط, *qrt'*, meaning to dice into little pieces. *Korta* is a small piece or a crumb.

HALAKHA

A corpse laid out across on the side of a public path – מֵת מוּטָל עַל הַמֵּיצַר: If a corpse, with no one available to bury it, is located between two fields in a place where it cannot be buried, then it should be laid to rest in the place that causes the least damage to the owner of the field. If the two fields are equal in terms of potential damage, one should bury the corpse in the closer field. If both fields are equally close, one may bury it in either field, as stated in the *baraita* (*Shulḥan Arukh, Yoreh De'a* 364:3).

One is exempt from washing of the hands – פְּטוּרִין מֵרְחִיצַת יָדַיִם: Soldiers in a military camp are exempt from washing their hands before a meal. This *halakha* applies to other cases of imminent danger as well (*Shulḥan Arukh, Oraḥ Ḥayyim* 158:8). However, they must wash their hands after a meal, due to the danger of Sodomite salt (Rambam *Sefer Shofetim, Hilkhot Melakhim* 6:13).

LANGUAGE

Quartered soldiers [*akhsanya*] – אַכְסַנְיָא: From the Greek ξένια, *xenia*, meaning hospitality shown to a guest or to strangers, i.e., a place set aside for guests. Some authorities read the word as *afsanya*, from the Greek ὀψωνία, *opsonia*, meaning supply of food for the military.

HALAKHA

One may feed doubtfully tithed produce [*demai*] – מַאֲכִילִין דְּמַאי: One may feed poor people and soldiers *demai*, and there is no need to separate the tithe. However, they must be informed of the matter, so they can separate the tithe if they wish. In addition, it is permitted to feed guests *demai*, if they are passing from place to place and will not be spending the night where they are eating (Radbaz; Rambam *Sefer Zera'im*, *Hilkhot Ma'aserot* 10:11 and *Sefer Shofetim*, *Hilkhot Melakhim* 6:13).

***Eiruvin* in a camp – עֵירוּבִין בְּמַחֲנֶה:** Soldiers at war are exempt from the joining of courtyards [*eiruv ḥatzerot*], as stated in the mishna. However, they are required to join Shabbat boundaries [*eiruv teḥumin*]. Some commentaries conclude from here that the members of a caravan who enclosed their tents with a partition are also exempt from a joining of courtyards (Rambam *Sefer Shofetim*, *Hilkhot Melakhim* 6:13; *Shulḥan Arukh*, *Oraḥ Ḥayyim* 366:2).

One is flogged by Torah law if there is no joining of Shabbat boundaries – לוֹקִין עַל עֵירוּבֵי תְחוּמִין: According to the Rambam and the *ge'onim*, the Shabbat limits determined by Torah law is twelve *mil*, and one who ventures beyond it on Shabbat is punishable by lashes. Other authorities argue that this is only the opinion of Rabbi Akiva. Consequently, there is no Torah restriction of Shabbat limits (Rabbi Zeraḥya HaLevi; Ramban; Rashba; Rosh; Rambam *Sefer Zemanim*, *Hilkhot Shabbat* 27:1).

NOTES

Joining of Shabbat boundaries – עֵירוּבֵי תְחוּמִין: The commentaries and especially the halakhic authorities discuss this passage at length, as it apparently contradicts the accepted conclusion drawn from other contexts that the restrictions with regard to Shabbat boundaries are not by Torah law. Some commentaries understand the Gemara here in terms of Rabbi Akiva's opinion. He maintains that overstepping the Shabbat boundary is indeed prohibited by Torah law, but the limit by Torah law is twelve *mil* from the edge of town. Other authorities hold that Rav Ḥiyya's opinion is that there is a Torah prohibition against overstepping a limit of even two thousand or four thousand cubits.

"וּמִדְּמַאי". דִּתְנַן: מַאֲכִילִין אֶת הָעֲנִיִּים דְּמַאי וְאֶת אַכְסַנְיָא דְּמַאי. אָמַר רַב הוּנָא: תָּנָא, בֵּית שַׁמַּאי אוֹמְרִים: אֵין מַאֲכִילִין אֶת הָעֲנִיִּים דְּמַאי וְאֶת אַכְסַנְיָא דְּמַאי. וּבֵית הִלֵּל אוֹמְרִים: מַאֲכִילִין אֶת הָעֲנִיִּים דְּמַאי וְאֶת אַכְסַנְיָא דְּמַאי.

The mishna continues: **And** in a military camp, one is exempt **from** the separation of tithes from **doubtfully tithed produce** [*demai*]. **As we learned** in a mishna: **One may feed the poor *demai*, and** one may also feed **quartered soldiers** [*akhsanya*][L] ***demai*.**[H] **Rav Huna said:** A *tanna* **taught** in a *baraita*: **Beit Shammai say** that **one may neither feed the poor *demai*, nor** may one feed **quartered soldiers *demai*. And Beit Hillel say** that **one may feed the poor *demai*, and** one may also feed **quartered soldiers *demai*.**

"וּמִלְּעָרֵב". אָמְרִי דְּבֵי רַבִּי יַנַּאי: לֹא שָׁנוּ אֶלָּא עֵירוּבֵי חֲצֵירוֹת, אֲבָל עֵירוּבֵי תְחוּמִין – חַיָּיבִין.

We learned in the mishna: **And** in a military camp, one is exempt **from establishing an *eiruv*.** The Sages of **the school of Rabbi Yannai said: They taught** that this exemption applies **only** with regard to **the joining of** houses in **courtyards. However,** even those in a military encampment **are obligated** to establish an *eiruv* if they desire to effect **a joining of Shabbat boundaries,**[N] whereby one extends the Shabbat limits beyond which one may not walk on Shabbat.[H]

דְּתָנֵי רַבִּי חִיָּיא: לוֹקִין עַל עֵירוּבֵי תְחוּמִין דְּבַר תּוֹרָה.

As Rabbi Ḥiyya taught a *baraita*: **One is flogged by Torah law for** going beyond the Shabbat limit if there is no **joining of Shabbat boundaries.**[H] The Torah states: "No man shall go out [*al yetze*] of his place on the seventh day" (Exodus 16:29). Since this is a Torah prohibition, leniency is possible only in life-threatening circumstances.

מַתְקִיף לַהּ רַבִּי יוֹנָתָן: וְכִי לוֹקִין עַל לָאו שֶׁבְּ"אַל"? מַתְקִיף רַב אַחָא בַּר יַעֲקֹב: אֶלָּא מֵעַתָּה דִּכְתִיב: "אַל תִּפְנוּ אֶל הָאוֹבוֹת וְאֶל הַיִּדְּעוֹנִים" הָכִי נַמִי דְּלָא לָקֵי?

Rabbi Yonatan strongly objects: Is one flogged for violating a **prohibition that is** expressed in the Torah with the negative ***al***, rather than the negative *lo*? **Rav Aḥa bar Ya'akov strongly objects** to the question: **If** what you say is **so,** with regard to **that which is written: "Turn you not [*al*] unto the ghosts, nor unto familiar spirits"** (Leviticus 19:31), is the *halakha* there **too that one is not flogged?**

רַבִּי יוֹנָתָן הָכִי קַשְׁיָא לֵיהּ: לָאו שֶׁנִּיתַּן לְאַזְהָרַת מִיתַת בֵּית דִּין, וְכָל לָאו שֶׁנִּיתַּן לְאַזְהָרַת מִיתַת בֵּית דִּין אֵין לוֹקִין עָלָיו.

Rather, **this is the difficulty for Rabbi Yonatan:** The prohibition against overstepping the Shabbat limits is **a prohibition that was given** primarily **as a warning of court-imposed capital punishment,** i.e., a prohibition which, under certain conditions, is punishable by the death and not merely by lashes, as is the case with most prohibitions. In fact, the prohibition against carrying objects out to the public domain is derived from that same verse, and one who violates that prohibition is liable for execution by the court. **And** this principle applies: **Any prohibition that was given** primarily **as a warning of court-imposed capital punishment one is not flogged,** even if the death penalty does not apply in that particular case.

אָמַר רַב אָשֵׁי: מִי כְּתִיב "אַל יוֹצִיא"? "אַל יֵצֵא" כְּתִיב.

Rav Ashi said: Is it written in the Torah: **No man shall carry out [*yotzi*],** indicating a prohibition against carrying objects from one domain to another on Shabbat? **"No man shall go out [*yetze*]" is written.** Indeed, according to its plain meaning, the verse deals exclusively with the prohibition of going beyond the Shabbat limits and not with the prohibition of carrying out. Everyone agrees that there is no death penalty administered by the court in overstepping the Shabbat limit.

הדרן עלך מבוי

Summary of **Perek I**

Most of the *halakhot* related to rendering an alleyway fit for one to carry within it on Shabbat were summarized in this chapter. It is apparent that the accepted halakhic opinion is that an area surrounded by partitions on three of its four sides is a private domain, and therefore an alleyway that is not open-ended is in fact a private domain. However, the Sages instituted a rabbinic ordinance to prevent violation of the *halakhot* of Shabbat, mandating creation of a divider at the point where the alleyway and the public domain intersect, in order to demarcate between them and prevent one from unintentionally carrying objects out from the alleyway into the public domain.

This can be accomplished by means of a cross beam, which, based on the halakhic determination in this chapter, serves merely as a conspicuous marker. A cross beam renders the alleyway fit for one to carry within it only when placed no higher than twenty cubits and no lower than ten handbreadths. Alternatively, this can be accomplished by means of a side post, whose legal status is that of a fourth partition. The result is that an alleyway with a side post is considered closed on four sides. In practice, it was determined that the side post must be attached to the wall of the alleyway and adjacent to the opening of the alleyway *ab initio*. It must be ten handbreadths high and can be of any width, and it must be clear that it is indeed serving as a side post. The Sages deliberated over the question: What form must a side post take in order to make it clear that it is serving that purpose?

An even more efficacious method of rendering the fourth side of the alleyway closed from a halakhic perspective is the creation of the form of a doorway. The form of a doorway is effective even in cases where cross beams and side posts are ineffective due to the fact that the openings are higher or wider than the dimensions dictated by *halakha*. The form of a doorway serves as an actual partition in every sense, and effectively renders even open alleyways permitted for one to carry within them. Although most Sages did not accept the opinion that two parallel partitions alone are sufficient to create a private domain, an open-ended alleyway is not considered a full-fledged public domain either. It is therefore sufficient to close the side where an open-ended alleyway and the public domain intersect with the form of a doorway. Indeed, it was mentioned incidentally in this chapter that it is possible to transform the public domain into a private domain by erecting doors on both open sides and partially close them.

This chapter also included a discussion with regard to the *halakhot* of establishing an *eiruv* for those in transit in a caravan. Here, the Sages allowed them to erect partitions that would not be considered actual partitions in other circumstances. Similarly, the Sages said that a military encampment at a time of war is exempt from all the *halakhot* of *eiruv*, as these *halakhot* were instituted only for those living at home in peace.

Introduction to **Perek II**

This chapter deals primarily with two somewhat interrelated topics: The laws of upright boards surrounding a well and the matter of an enclosure [*karpef*] that is for storage and not for residence.

Continuing the discussion of the special leniencies cited in the first chapter with regard to establishing an *eiruv* for those in transit in a caravan, this chapter discusses the halakhic ruling with regard to the establishment of upright boards around a well. This involves a well that is ten cubits deep, which is a private domain that is located in the public domain. The well is surrounded with a virtual partition comprised of two boards forming a right angle at each corner of the well, with additional individual boards situated between the corners if a larger partition is necessary. The Sages declared that a partition of this sort renders the area surrounding the well a private domain, enabling one to draw water from the well on Shabbat and to give his animals water to drink.

In the course of the discussion of the halakhic validity of upright boards surrounding a well and their utilization, a related problem arises: Under what circumstances and to what extent is it permitted to move objects in areas that are not the residence of an individual, although they are surrounded by a partition that would accord them the legal status of objects in a private domain? The dilemma is: Are enclosures or yards considered private domains in every sense? Or, although it is prohibited to carry objects between them and the public domain, perhaps since those areas were not designated as residences, they are not full-fledged private domains to the extent that it is permitted to carry there? Although, by Torah law, partitions create a private domain, the Sages prohibited carrying within private domains that are similar to public domains. Therefore, here too the question arises: At which point do these enclosures cease to be full-fledged private domains and assume the legal status of an intermediate domain [*karmelit*], in which carrying is prohibited by rabbinic law? Clarification of the details and parameters of these fundamental issues constitute the primary focus of this chapter.

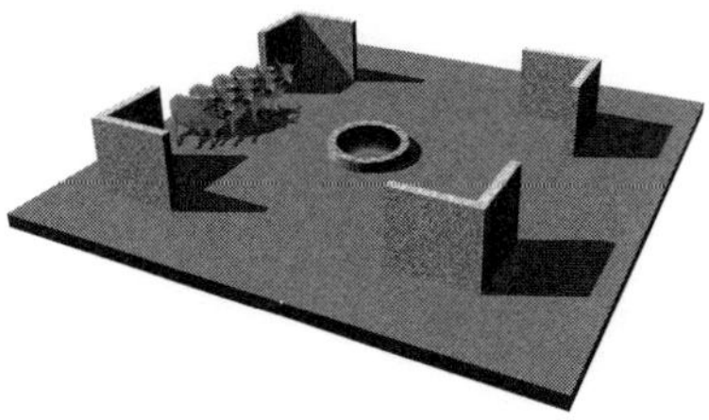

Sketch of a well surrounded by upright boards. The cows adjoined to one another entering the space between the posts determine, according to Rabbi Meir, the permitted distance between the posts.

מתני׳ עוֹשִׂין פַּסִּין לַבִּירָאוֹת,

MISHNA **One may arrange** upright **boards [*passin*]**[L] **around a well**[HN] in the public domain in order to permit drawing water from the well on Shabbat. A well is usually at least four handbreadths wide and ten handbreadths deep. Therefore, it is considered a private domain, and it is prohibited to draw water from it on Shabbat, as that would constitute a violation of the prohibition to carry from a private domain into a public one. The Sages therefore instituted that a virtual partition may be built in the area surrounding the well, so that the enclosed area could be considered a private domain, thus permitting use of the well and carrying of the water within the partitioned area.

אַרְבָּעָה דְּיוֹמָדִין נִרְאִין כִּשְׁמוֹנָה, דִּבְרֵי רַבִּי יְהוּדָה. רַבִּי מֵאִיר אוֹמֵר: שְׁמוֹנָה נִרְאִין כִּשְׁנֵים עָשָׂר, אַרְבָּעָה דְּיוֹמְדִים וְאַרְבָּעָה פְּשׁוּטִין.

In this specific instance, the Sages demonstrated special leniency and did not require a proper partition to enclose the entire area. For this purpose, it suffices if there are **four double posts [*deyomadin*] that look like eight** single posts, i.e., four corner pieces, each comprised of two posts joined together at right angles; this is **the statement of Rabbi Yehuda. Rabbi Meir says:** There must be **eight** posts that **look like twelve.**[B] How so? There must be **four double posts,** one in each corner, with **four plain** posts, one between each pair of double posts.

גּוֹבְהָן עֲשָׂרָה טְפָחִים וְרוֹחְבָּן שִׁשָּׁה, וְעוֹבְיָים כׇּל שֶׁהוּא. וּבֵינֵיהֶן כִּמְלֹא שְׁתֵּי רְבָקוֹת שֶׁל שָׁלֹשׁ שָׁלֹשׁ בָּקָר, דִּבְרֵי רַבִּי מֵאִיר.

The height of the double posts must be at least **ten handbreadths, their width** must be **six** handbreadths, **and their thickness** may be even **a minimal amount. And between them,** i.e., between the posts, there may be a gap **the size of two teams [*revakot*]**[NB] **of three oxen each;** this is **the statement of Rabbi Meir.**

רַבִּי יְהוּדָה אוֹמֵר: שֶׁל אַרְבַּע. קְשׁוּרוֹת וְלֹא מוּתָּרוֹת, אַחַת נִכְנֶסֶת וְאַחַת יוֹצֵאת.

Rabbi Yehuda disagrees and **says:** There may be a slightly larger gap, the size of two teams **of four** oxen each, and this gap is measured with the cows being **tied** together **and not untied,** and with the minimal space necessary for **one** team to be **entering** while the other **one is leaving.**

מוּתָּר לְהַקְרִיב לַבְּאֵר וּבִלְבַד שֶׁתְּהֵא פָּרָה רֹאשָׁהּ וְרוּבָּהּ בִּפְנִים וְשׁוֹתָה.

It is permitted to bring the posts **closer to the well, provided that** the enclosed area is large enough for **a cow to** stand with **its head and the majority of its** body **inside** the partitioned space while **it drinks.**

מוּתָּר **It is permitted**

LANGUAGE

Upright boards [*passin*] – פַּסִּין: Rabbi Binyamin Mosafya has suggested that the source for this word is the Greek letter φ, *phi*, because its shape served as a model for upright boards inserted in the ground to form a partition, principally for animals.

HALAKHA

Upright boards around a well – פַּסִּין לַבִּירָאוֹת: One may erect four L-shaped units of upright boards around a well with each unit creating a corner. The distance between the posts must be large enough to allow two teams of cattle, with four oxen in each team, to enter the well area. This law is in accordance with Rabbi Yehuda, as the rule is to follow Rabbi Yehuda when he disagrees with Rabbi Meir (Rambam *Sefer Zemanim*, *Hilkhot Shabbat* 17:27).

BACKGROUND

Eight that look like twelve – שְׁמוֹנָה נִרְאִין כִּשְׁנֵים עָשָׂר:

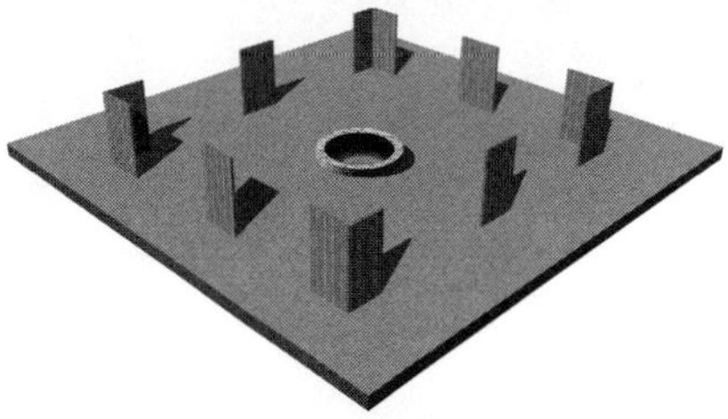

Posts surrounding a well, according to the opinion of Rabbi Meir

Team – רְבָקָה: Most commentaries explain that a *revaka* is a type of yoke or harness that binds several oxen together. Other commentaries understand the word *revaka* to mean a trough or a similar place where a number of oxen feed (see the *Arukh*; Rav Natan Av HaYeshiva).

NOTES

Upright boards [*passin*] around a well – פַּסִּין לַבִּירָאוֹת: *Tosafot* and other early commentaries ask: Why do they constitute a halakhically valid partition? They are mostly open and therefore should not create a partition. Their basic answer is that the leniency with regard to wells is a law that was transmitted to Moses from Sinai (see Ritva). Some answer that each side of the structure is considered individually. This way, each side seems to be an opening between two walls that has a side post [*leḥi*] on each side and is therefore considered enclosed. When viewing all four sides in this manner, it is as though the well were surrounded by partitions on all sides (*Ḥakham Tzvi*).

Two teams – שְׁתֵּי רְבָקוֹת: In talmudic times, it was customary during the week to have a team of four oxen plow a field and then take them to the well to drink while still harnessed together. Consequently, the gap between the upright boards must be wide enough to accommodate one team of oxen entering the well area while another team of oxen exits, without knocking down the boards (Rabbeinu Yehonatan).

NOTES

Pen [*dir*] – **דִּיר**: A *dir* is an enclosure for sheep, although apparently the shepherd also resided there (Rashi; Rabbeinu Yehonatan). Other commentaries teach that a sheep pen is considered to be an area surrounded by a fence for the purpose of residence, even if it houses only animals and no humans (*Or Hadash*). This opinion is rejected in the *Noda Bihuda*.

Stable [*sahar*] – **סַהַר**: The *Arukh* explains that the term *sahar* is based on the root *saḥar*, which means to go around, i.e., something that is surrounded by a fence for the purpose of residence.

BACKGROUND

Increases the upright boards – **יִרְבֶּה בְּפַסִּין**:

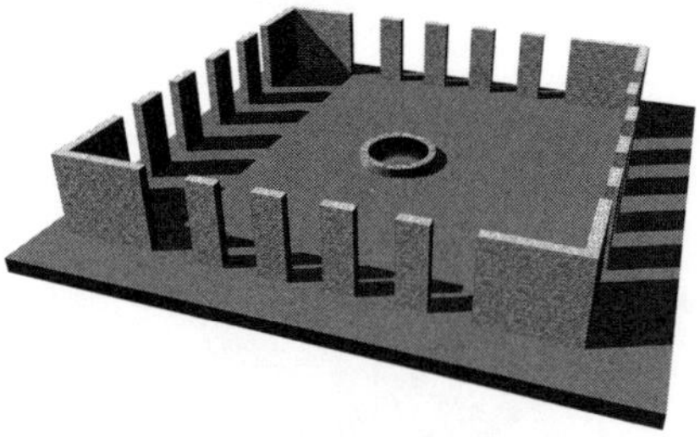

Upright boards added around a well in order to enclose a larger area

לְהַרְחִיק כָּל שֶׁהוּא, וּבִלְבַד שֶׁיַּרְבֶּה בְּפַסִּין. רַבִּי יְהוּדָה אוֹמֵר: עַד בֵּית סָאתַיִם.

to distance the boards from the well and expand the enclosed area by **any amount,** i.e., as much as one wishes, **provided that he increases the** number of upright **boards** between the double posts. **Rabbi Yehuda says:** The partitioned area may be expanded **up to** an area of **two *beit se'a*,** which is an area of five thousand square cubits.

אָמְרוּ לוֹ: לֹא אָמְרוּ בֵּית סָאתַיִם אֶלָּא לַגִּנָּה וְלַקַּרְפֵּף, אֲבָל אִם הָיָה דִּיר אוֹ סַהַר אוֹ מוּקְצֶה אוֹ חָצֵר – אֲפִילּוּ בֵּית חֲמֵשֶׁת כּוֹרִין אֲפִילּוּ בֵּית עֲשָׂרָה כּוֹרִין – מוּתָּר. וּמוּתָּר לְהַרְחִיק כָּל שֶׁהוּא, וּבִלְבַד שֶׁיַּרְבֶּה בְּפַסִּין:

The Rabbis **said to him: They only spoke of** an area of **two *beit se'a* with regard to a garden or an enclosure** used for storing wood, scrap, and the like [***karpef***]**. But if it was a pen** [***dir***],[N] **or a stable** [***sahar***],[N] **or a backyard, or a courtyard** in front of the house, **even** if it had an area of **five *beit kor*** or **even ten *beit kor*, it is permitted. And it is permitted to distance** the boards and expand the enclosed area **by any amount, provided that one increases the** upright **boards** between the double posts.[B]

גמ׳ לֵימָא מַתְנִיתִין דְּלָא כַּחֲנַנְיָא, דְּתַנְיָא: עוֹשִׂין פַּסִּין לַבּוֹר וַחֲבָלִין לַשַּׁיָּרָא. וַחֲנַנְיָא אוֹמֵר: חֲבָלִין לַבּוֹר, אֲבָל לֹא פַּסִּין.

GEMARA The Gemara suggests: **Let us say that the mishna is not in accordance with** the opinion of **Ḥananya, as it was taught** in a *baraita*: **One may arrange** upright **boards around a** water **cistern and ropes around a caravan. Ḥananya** disagrees and **says:** One may set up **ropes for a cistern, but not** upright **boards.**

אֲפִילּוּ תֵּימָא חֲנַנְיָא, בּוֹר לְחוּד בְּאֵר לְחוּד.

The Gemara rejects this suggestion: **Even if you say** that the mishna was taught in accordance with the opinion of **Ḥananya, a cistern** of collected rain water has a **discrete** law, as the water will eventually be consumed and the upright boards will become unnecessary; and **a well** of spring **water** has a **discrete** law, as the water is constantly renewed and the upright boards will remain useful.

אִיכָּא דְּאָמְרִי: מִדְּלָא קָתָנֵי חֲנַנְיָא אוֹמֵר עוֹשִׂין חֲבָלִין לַבּוֹר וּפַסִּין לַבְּאֵר – מִכְּלָל דְּלַחֲנַנְיָא לָא שְׁנָא בּוֹר וְלָא שְׁנָא בְּאֵר, חֲבָלִין – אִין, פַּסִּין – לָא. לֵימָא מַתְנִיתִין דְּלָא כַּחֲנַנְיָא!

Some say a different version of the previous passage: **From** the fact **that** the *baraita* **does not teach: Ḥananya says: One may set up ropes around** a water **cistern and boards around a well, by inference, according to** the opinion of **Ḥananya, there is no difference between a cistern and a well.** In both cases, **ropes** are **indeed** permitted, whereas upright **boards are not. Let us say the mishna is not in accordance with** the opinion of **Ḥananya.**

אֲפִילּוּ תֵּימָא חֲנַנְיָא, לְמַאי דְּקָאָמַר תַּנָּא קַמָּא קָא מְהַדַּר לֵיהּ.

The Gemara rejects this argument: **Even if you say** that the mishna was taught in accordance with the opinion of **Ḥananya,** he was only replying **to that which the first *tanna* had said;** since the first *tanna* had spoken only of a cistern, there was no need for Ḥananya to fully clarify his own position and distinguish between a cistern and a well.

לֵימָא מַתְנִיתִין דְּלָא כְּרַבִּי עֲקִיבָא, דִּתְנַן: אֶחָד בְּאֵר הָרַבִּים וּבוֹר הָרַבִּים וּבְאֵר הַיָּחִיד – עוֹשִׂין לָהֶן פַּסִּין, אֲבָל בּוֹר הַיָּחִיד עוֹשִׂין לוֹ מְחִיצָה גָּבוֹהַּ עֲשָׂרָה טְפָחִים, דִּבְרֵי רַבִּי עֲקִיבָא.

The Gemara further suggests: **Let us say the mishna is not in accordance with** the opinion of **Rabbi Akiva. As we learned** in a mishna: In **each of** the cases of **a public well, a public cistern, and a private well, one may arrange** upright **boards for them, but** in the case of **a private cistern, one must establish** a proper **partition for it ten handbreadths high;** this is **the statement of Rabbi Akiva.**

וְאִילּוּ הָכָא קָתָנֵי לַבֵּירָאוֹת, לַבֵּירָאוֹת – אִין, לַבּוֹרוֹת – לָא.

Whereas here in the mishna **it teaches:** One may arrange upright boards **for a well,** from which one may infer that **for a well, yes,** it is permitted to use posts, but **for a cistern, no,** it is not permitted. This is opposed to Rabbi Akiva's opinion, which maintains that posts may be arranged for a public cistern.

אֲפִילּוּ תֵּימָא רַבִּי עֲקִיבָא, בְּאֵר מַיִם חַיִּים דִּפְסִיקָא לֵיהּ – לָא שְׁנָא דְּרַבִּים וְלָא שְׁנָא דְּיָחִיד, קָתָנֵי, בּוֹר מְכוּנָּסִין, דְּלָא פְּסִיקָא לֵיהּ – לָא קָתָנֵי.

The Gemara rejects this argument as well: **Even if you say** that the mishna is in accordance with the opinion of **Rabbi Akiva,** the *tanna* of the mishna **teaches** the case of **a well of spring water, which he** can teach in **a distinct** manner because **there is no difference** whether it belongs to **the public and there is no difference** whether it belongs **to an individual,** as it is always permitted. However, **he did not teach** the case of **a cistern** containing **collected** rain water, **which he** could **not** teach in a **distinct** manner because there is a difference between a public cistern and a private one. However, it cannot be proven from here that he disagrees with Rabbi Akiva.

לֵימָא מַתְנִיתִין דְּלָא כְּרַבִּי יְהוּדָה בֶּן בָּבָא, דִּתְנַן רַבִּי יְהוּדָה בֶּן בָּבָא אוֹמֵר: אֵין עוֹשִׂין פַּסִּין אֶלָּא לִבְאֵר הָרַבִּים בִּלְבַד. וְאִילּוּ הָכָא קָתָנֵי לַבֵּירָאוֹת, לָא שְׁנָא דְּרַבִּים וְלָא שְׁנָא דְּיָחִיד!

The Gemara further suggests: **Let us say the mishna is not in accordance with** the opinion of **Rabbi Yehuda ben Bava, as we learned** in a mishna: **Rabbi Yehuda ben Bava says: One may only arrange** upright **boards for a public well, whereas here** the mishna **states: For wells.** The plural term implies that **there is no difference** if the well belongs to **the public, and there is no difference** if the well belongs **to an individual.**

אֲפִילּוּ תֵּימָא רַבִּי יְהוּדָה בֶּן בָּבָא, מַאי בֵּירָאוֹת – בֵּירָאוֹת דְּעָלְמָא.

The Gemara also rejects this line of reasoning: **Even if you say** that the mishna is in accordance with **Rabbi Yehuda ben Bava,** to **what** is the mishna referring when it says **wells?** It is referring to **wells in general,** but the *tanna* means to include only public wells.

מַאי דְּיוֹמָדִין? אָמַר רַבִּי יִרְמְיָה בֶּן אֶלְעָזָר: דְּיוֹ עַמּוּדִין.

The mishna had mentioned double posts [*deyomadin*]: The Gemara asks: **What are** ***deyomadin*****?**[L] **Rabbi Yirmeya ben Elazar said: Two [*deyo*] posts [*amudin*],** which are put together to create a single corner piece.

ד״יו לְמ״נוּדֶּה שֶׁבַ״ח זוּנ״ית נִתְקַ״לְקֵל בְּמִידָ״ה שְׁלֹשָׁ״ה סִימָן.

Having cited Rabbi Yirmeya ben Elazar's statement with reference to the prefix *deyo,* the Gemara cites other statements of his. **Two, to** one who was **ostracized, praise, nourishment, ruin, attribute, three,** are **mnemonics**[N] for the following statements by Rabbi Yirmeya ben Elazar.

תְּנַן הָתָם, רַבִּי יְהוּדָה אוֹמֵר: כׇּל הַשִּׁיתִּין פְּטוּרִין חוּץ מִן הַדְּיוּפְרָא. מַאי דְּיוּפְרָא? אָמַר עוּלָּא: אִילָן הָעוֹשֶׂה דְּיוֹ פֵּירוֹת בְּשָׁנָה.

We learned there in a mishna: **Rabbi Yehuda says: All inferior figs are exempt**[N] from being tithed, even if they are of doubtfully tithed produce [*demai*], as even if the seller is an *am ha'aretz,* he must certainly have already separated tithes from them, since the loss incurred by tithing is negligible, **except for** ***deyufra*****.** The Gemara asks: **What is** ***deyufra*****?**[L] **Ulla said: A tree that yields two [*deyo*]** harvests **of fruit [*peirot*] each year.**[B]

אָמַר רַבִּי יִרְמְיָה בֶּן אֶלְעָזָר: דְּיוֹ פַּרְצוּף פָּנִים הָיָה לוֹ לְאָדָם הָרִאשׁוֹן, שֶׁנֶּאֱמַר: ״אָחוֹר וָקֶדֶם צַרְתָּנִי״. כְּתִיב: ״וַיִּבֶן ה׳ אֱלֹהִים אֶת הַצֵּלָע וגו׳״, רַב וּשְׁמוּאֵל; חַד אָמַר: פַּרְצוּף, וְחַד אָמַר: זָנָב.

Rabbi Yirmeya ben Elazar also **said: Adam** was first created with **two [*deyo*] faces,** one male and the other female. **As it is stated: "You have formed me behind and before,** and laid Your hand upon me" (Psalms 139:5). Similarly, **it is written: "And the *tzela,* which** the Lord, God, had taken from the man, **He made** a woman, and brought her unto the man" (Genesis 2:22). **Rav and Shmuel** disagree over the meaning of the word *tzela*: **One said:** It means a female **face,** from which God created Eve; **and one said:** Adam was created with **a tail [*zanav*],**[N] which God removed from him and from which He created Eve.

בִּשְׁלָמָא לְמַאן דְּאָמַר פַּרְצוּף – הַיְינוּ דִּכְתִיב: ״אָחוֹר וָקֶדֶם צַרְתָּנִי״, אֶלָּא לְמַאן דְּאָמַר זָנָב – מַאי ״אָחוֹר וָקֶדֶם צַרְתָּנִי״?

The Gemara asks: **Granted, according to the one who says** that *tzela* means **face;** it is understandable **that it is written: "You have formed me [*tzartani*] behind and before."**[N] **However, according to the one who says** that *tzela* means **tail, what is** meant by the verse: **"You have formed me [*tzartani*] behind and before"?**

כִּדְרַבִּי אַמִּי, דְּאָמַר רַבִּי אַמִּי: אָחוֹר לְמַעֲשֵׂה בְרֵאשִׁית, וָקֶדֶם לְפוּרְעָנוּת.

The Gemara answers that this verse is to be understood as bearing a moral message, **in accordance with** the opinion of **Rabbi Ami, as Rabbi Ami said: Behind** means Adam was created at the end of **the act of creation; and before** means that he was first **for punishment.**

LANGUAGE

Deyomadin **– דְּיוֹמָדִין:** Rabbi Yirmeya teaches that this word is a Greek-Hebrew amalgam. It begins with the ancient Greek prefix **δύο**, *duo*, meaning two, and ends with the Hebrew word *amud*, meaning a post. Other authorities say that the whole word *deyomad* comes from the Greek **δίδυμον**, *didumon*, meaning double or paired.

Deyufra **– דְּיוּפְרָא:** From the Greek **δίφορος**, *diforos*, meaning twice-bearing, i.e., a tree that bears fruit twice in one year.

NOTES

Two, to one who was ostracized, etc. – ד״יו למ״נודה: This mnemonic refers to the topics discussed by Rabbi Yirmeya ben Elazar in the following pages: Two faces; Adam who was ostracized; a small part of a one's praise; a dove and its nourishment; a house in which words of Torah are heard; two letters; Babylonia was cursed; the character of the Holy One, Blessed be He; and three entrances to Gehenna.

Inferior figs are exempt – הַשִּׁיתִּין פְּטוּרִין: The rationale for the obligation to separate the tithes from doubtfully tithed produce [*demai*] is the concern that in an effort to save money, the original owner of the produce might not have separated tithes in the proper manner. However, there is no such concern in the case of inferior fruit. Since inferior figs have so little value, their owner would separate tithes from them even if he is an *am ha'aretz*.

Tail [*zanav*] – זָנָב: The word *zanav* appears here and in several other places in the Talmud. It refers to an appendage that is unlike the object to which it is attached, in appearance or size (*Arukh*). Some explain *zanav* as a limb of secondary importance, as a tail is to a body (Rashba).

You have formed me [*tzartani*] behind and before – אָחוֹר וָקֶדֶם צַרְתָּנִי: Apparently, Rabbi Ami explains that the word *tzartani* is related to the word affliction, *tzara*, i.e., last in creation, but first for affliction (Ritva).

BACKGROUND

Inferior figs of a ***deyufra*** **– שִׁיתִּין דְּיוּפְרָא:** The fig tree does not bear all its fruit at once. Rather, the ripening of its fruit takes several weeks. The main season for the ripening of figs is the summer. Indeed, the Hebrew word for summer, *kayitz*, is named for the harvesting [*ketzitza*] of figs. Nevertheless, the fig tree occasionally produces fruit in the winter as well, although these figs are generally inedible. There are, however, certain strains of fig trees whose inferior figs are also fit to be eaten, and these are termed *deyufra*.

Fig tree producing fruit in winter

בִּשְׁלָמָא אָחוֹר לְמַעֲשֵׂה בְרֵאשִׁית – דְּלָא אִיבְּרִי עַד מַעֲלֵי שַׁבְּתָא, אֶלָּא וָקֶדֶם לְפוּרְעָנוּת מַאי הִיא? אִילֵימָא מִשּׁוּם קְלָלָה – הָא בַּתְּחִילָּה נִתְקַלֵּל נָחָשׁ, וּלְבַסּוֹף נִתְקַלְּלָה חַוָּה, וּלְבַסּוֹף נִתְקַלֵּל אָדָם!

The Gemara asks: **Granted,** it is understandable that Adam was **behind,** or last, **in the act of creation,** meaning that **he was not created until** the sixth day, **Shabbat eve. However, before,** or first, **for punishment, what** does **this** mean? **If you say** that he was punished first **because of the curse** pronounced in the wake of the sin involving the Tree of Knowledge, there is a difficulty. **Wasn't the snake was cursed first, and afterward Eve was cursed,** and only **at the end was Adam cursed?**

אֶלָּא לַמַּבּוּל, דִּכְתִיב: ״וַיִּמַח אֶת כָּל הַיְקוּם אֲשֶׁר עַל פְּנֵי הָאֲדָמָה מֵאָדָם וְעַד בְּהֵמָה וגו׳״.

Rather, this refers **to** the punishment of the **Flood, as it is written:** "**And He blotted out every living substance which was upon the face of the ground, both man and cattle,** creeping things and fowl of the heaven" (Genesis 7:23). This indicates that the punishment began with man.

בִּשְׁלָמָא לְמַאן דְּאָמַר פַּרְצוּף – הַיְינוּ דִּכְתִיב: ״וַיִּיצֶר״ תְּרֵין יוּדִי״ן. אֶלָּא לְמַאן דְּאָמַר זָנָב – מַאי ״וַיִּיצֶר״?

The Gemara asks: **Granted, according to the one who said** that Eve was originally **a face** or side of Adam; it is understandable **that it is written:** "Then the Lord God **formed** [*vayyitzer*] man" (Genesis 2:7). *Vayyitzer* is written with **a double** ***yod***, one for Adam and one for Eve. **However, according to the one who said** that Eve was created from **a tail, what is** conveyed by spelling ***vayyitzer*** with a double *yod*?

כִּדְרַבִּי שִׁמְעוֹן בֶּן פָּזִי, דְּאָמַר רַבִּי שִׁמְעוֹן בֶּן פָּזִי: אוֹי לִי מִיִּצְרִי אוֹי לִי מִיּוֹצְרִי.

The Gemara responds: This is interpreted homiletically, **in accordance with** the opinion of **Rabbi Shimon ben Pazi, as Rabbi Shimon ben Pazi said:** This comes to emphasize that which one says to himself in every circumstance: **Woe unto me from my** evil **inclination** [*yetzer*] if I perform the will of my Maker, **and woe to me from my Maker** [*Yotzri*] if I perform the will of my inclination.

בִּשְׁלָמָא לְמַאן דְּאָמַר פַּרְצוּף – הַיְינוּ דִּכְתִיב: ״זָכָר וּנְקֵבָה בְּרָאָם״, אֶלָּא לְמַאן דְּאָמַר זָנָב – מַאי ״זָכָר וּנְקֵבָה בְּרָאָם״?

The Gemara asks: **Granted, according to the one who said** that Eve was **a face,** it is understanable **that it is written: "Male and female, He created them,** and blessed them, and called their name Man in the day when they were created" (Genesis 5:2), which indicates that from the very beginning of their creation, He fashioned two faces, one for the male and the other for the female. **However, according to the one who said** that Eve was created from **a tail, what is** the meaning of the verse: "**Male and female, He created them**"?

לִכְדְרַבִּי אַבָּהוּ, דְּרַבִּי אַבָּהוּ רָמֵי, כְּתִיב: ״זָכָר וּנְקֵבָה בְּרָאָם״, וּכְתִיב: ״(כִּי) בְּצֶלֶם אֱלֹהִים בָּרָא אוֹתוֹ״ – בַּתְּחִלָּה עָלְתָה בְּמַחֲשָׁבָה לִבְרֹאות שְׁנַיִם, וּלְבַסּוֹף לֹא נִבְרָא אֶלָּא אֶחָד.

The Gemara answers: It can be explained **in accordance with** the opinion of **Rabbi Abbahu, as Rabbi Abbahu raised a contradiction** between the verses: On the one hand **it is written: "Male and female, He created them,"** in the plural, **and** on the other hand **it is written:** "So God created man in His own image, **for in the image of God He created him**" (Genesis 1:27), in the singular. **At first, the thought entered** God's mind **to create two, and ultimately, only one was** actually **created.**

בִּשְׁלָמָא לְמַאן דְּאָמַר פַּרְצוּף – הַיְינוּ דִּכְתִיב: ״וַיִּסְגּוֹר בָּשָׂר תַּחְתֶּנָּה״. אֶלָּא לְמַאן דְּאָמַר זָנָב – מַאי ״וַיִּסְגּוֹר בָּשָׂר תַּחְתֶּנָּה״?

The Gemara asks: **Granted, according to the one who said** that Eve was **a face,** it is understandable **that it is written:** "And He took one of his sides **and closed up the flesh in its place**" (Genesis 2:21). **However, according to the one who said** that Eve was created from **a tail, what is** meant by the verse: "**And He closed up the flesh in its place**"?

אָמַר רַב זְבִיד, וְאִיתֵימָא רַבִּי יִרְמְיָה, וְאִיתֵימָא רַב נַחְמָן בַּר יִצְחָק: לֹא נִצְרְכָה אֶלָּא לִמְקוֹם חֲתָךְ.

Rav Zevid said, and some say it was **Rabbi Yirmeya, and some say** it was **Rav Naḥman bar Yitzḥak: It was necessary** to say that the fleshed closed up **only with regard to the place of the incision.**

בִּשְׁלָמָא לְמַאן דְּאָמַר זָנָב – הַיְינוּ דִּכְתִיב: ״וַיִּבֶן״, אֶלָּא לְמַאן דְּאָמַר פַּרְצוּף – מַאי ״וַיִּבֶן״?

The Gemara challenges the other opinion: **Granted, according to the one who said** that Eve was created from **a tail;** it is understandable **that it is written: "And** the Lord God **built** the *tzela*" (Genesis 2:22), as it was a completely new building. **However, according to the one who said** that Eve was a complete **face** or side, **what is** the meaning of: **"And He built"?** What needed to be built?

לִכְדְרַבִּי שִׁמְעוֹן בֶּן מְנַסְיָא, דְּדָרֵישׁ רַבִּי שִׁמְעוֹן בֶּן מְנַסְיָא: ״וַיִּבֶן ה׳ אֱלֹהִים אֶת הַצֵּלָע״ – מְלַמֵּד שֶׁקִּילְּעָהּ הַקָּדוֹשׁ בָּרוּךְ הוּא לְחַוָּה וֶהֱבִיאָהּ לְאָדָם הָרִאשׁוֹן, שֶׁכֵּן בִּכְרַכֵּי הַיָּם קוֹרִין לְקִלְעִיתָא בְּנָיְיתָא.

The Gemara responds: This must be interpreted homiletically, **in accordance with** the opinion of **Rabbi Shimon ben Menasya, as Rabbi Shimon ben Menasya interpreted homiletically** the verse: **"And the Lord God built the** ***tzela***." This verse **teaches that the Holy One, Blessed be He, braided for Eve** her hair, **and** then **brought her to Adam, as in the coastal towns, they call braiding** hair **building.**

דָּבָר אַחֵר: ״וַיִּבֶן ה׳ אֱלֹהִים״, אָמַר רַב חִסְדָּא, וְאָמְרִי לָהּ בְּמַתְנִיתָא תָּנָא: מְלַמֵּד שֶׁבְּנָאָהּ הַקָּדוֹשׁ בָּרוּךְ הוּא לְחַוָּה כְּבִנְיַין

Alternatively, the verse: **"And the Lord God built,"** can be understood as a description of Eve's basic shape, as **Rav Ḥisda said, and some say it is taught in a** ***baraita***: This verse **teaches that the Holy One, Blessed be He, built Eve like the structure**

אוֹצָר, מָה אוֹצָר זֶה רָחָב מִלְּמַטָּה וְקָצָר מִלְּמַעְלָה כְּדֵי לְקַבֵּל אֶת הַפֵּירוֹת – אַף הָאִשָּׁה רְחָבָה מִלְּמַטָּה וּקְצָרָה מִלְּמַעְלָה כְּדֵי לְקַבֵּל אֶת הַוָּלָד.

of a storehouse. Just as a storehouse is built **wide on the bottom and narrow on top, in order to hold produce** without collapsing, **so too a woman** is created **wide on the bottom and narrow on top, in order to hold the fetus.**

"וַיְבִאֶהָ אֶל הָאָדָם" – מְלַמֵּד שֶׁעָשָׂה הַקָּדוֹשׁ בָּרוּךְ הוּא שׁוֹשְׁבִינוּת לְאָדָם הָרִאשׁוֹן, מִכָּאן לְגָדוֹל שֶׁיַּעֲשֶׂה שׁוֹשְׁבִינוּת לְקָטָן וְאַל יֵרַע לוֹ.

The Gemara cites an exposition of the end of the previously cited verse: **"And brought her unto the man"** (Genesis 2:22). This verse **teaches that the Holy One, Blessed be He, was Adam the first** man's **best man,** attending to all his wedding needs and bringing his wife to him. **From here** we learn **that a greater individual should serve as a best man for a lesser individual and should not feel bad** about it as something beneath his dignity.

וּלְמַאן דְּאָמַר פַּרְצוּף – הֵי מִינַּיְיהוּ סַגִּי בְּרֵישָׁא? אָמַר רַב נַחְמָן בַּר יִצְחָק: מִסְתַּבְּרָא דְּזָכָר סַגִּי בְּרֵישָׁא. דְּתַנְיָא: לֹא יְהַלֵּךְ אָדָם אֲחוֹרֵי אִשָּׁה בַּדֶּרֶךְ, וַאֲפִילּוּ הִיא אִשְׁתּוֹ. נִזְדַּמְּנָה עַל הַגֶּשֶׁר – יְסַלְּקֶנָּה לַצְּדָדִין. וְכָל הָעוֹבֵר אֲחוֹרֵי אִשָּׁה בַּנָּהָר – אֵין לוֹ חֵלֶק לָעוֹלָם הַבָּא.

The Gemara asks: **And according to the one who says** that Eve was **a face** or side of Adam, **which one of them walked in front? Rav Naḥman bar Yitzḥak said: It is reasonable** to say **that the male walked in front,** as this is proper behavior, **as it was taught** in a *baraita*: **A man should not walk behind a woman**[H] **on a path, even if she is his wife. If she happens** upon him **on a bridge, he should** walk quickly in order to catch up to her and consequently **move her to** his **side,** so that she will not walk before him. **And anyone who walks behind a woman**[N] **in a river,** where she has to lift up her skirt in order to cross, **has no share in the World-to-Come.**

תָּנוּ רַבָּנַן: הַמַּרְצֶה מָעוֹת לְאִשָּׁה מִיָּדוֹ לְיָדָהּ אוֹ מִיָּדָהּ לְיָדוֹ בִּשְׁבִיל שֶׁיִּסְתַּכֵּל בָּהּ, אֲפִילּוּ דּוֹמֶה לְמֹשֶׁה רַבֵּינוּ שֶׁקִּיבֵּל תּוֹרָה מֵהַר סִינַי – לֹא יִנָּקֶה מִדִּינָהּ שֶׁל גֵּיהִנָּם. וְעָלָיו הַכָּתוּב אוֹמֵר: "יָד לְיָד לֹא יִנָּקֶה רָע" – לֹא יִנָּקֶה מִדִּינָהּ שֶׁל גֵּיהִנָּם.

The Sages taught: With regard to **one who counts out money for a woman from his hand into her hand or from her hand into his hand, in order to look upon her, even if** in other matters **he is like Moses our teacher, who received the Torah from Mount Sinai, he will not be absolved from the punishment of Gehenna. The verse says about him: "Hand to hand, the evil man shall not go unpunished"** (Proverbs 11:21).[N] One who hands money from his hand to her hand, even if he received the Torah from God's hand to his own, like Moses, **he will not be absolved from the punishment of Gehenna,** which is called evil.

אָמַר רַב נַחְמָן: מָנוֹחַ עַם הָאָרֶץ הָיָה, שֶׁנֶּאֱמַר: "וַיָּקָם וַיֵּלֶךְ מָנוֹחַ אַחֲרֵי אִשְׁתּוֹ".

Rav Naḥman said: From the following verse, it is known that Samson's father, **Manoah, was an ignoramus, as it is stated: "And Manoah arose, and went after his wife"** (Judges 13:11), which shows that he was unfamiliar with the principle that one must not walk behind a woman.

מַתְקִיף לַהּ רַב נַחְמָן בַּר יִצְחָק: אֶלָּא מֵעַתָּה, גַּבֵּי אֶלְקָנָה דִּכְתִיב: "וַיֵּלֶךְ אֶלְקָנָה אַחֲרֵי אִשְׁתּוֹ" הָכִי נַמִי? וְגַבֵּי אֱלִישָׁע דִּכְתִיב: "וַיָּקָם וַיֵּלֶךְ אַחֲרֶיהָ" הָכִי נַמִי?

Rav Naḥman bar Yitzḥak strongly objects to this: If that is so, if the verse relating to Manoah is understood literally, what will one say about the verse **with regard to Elkana,** the father of the prophet Samuel, **as it is written: "And Elkana walked after his wife."**[N] Does **this** verse mean that Elkana was **also** an ignorant person? **And** what of the verse **with regard to** the prophet **Elisha, as it is written:** "And the mother of the child said: As the Lord lives, and as your soul lives, I will not leave you; **and he arose and followed her"** (II Kings 4:30). Does **this** verse mean that Elisha was **also** an uneducated person?

אֶלָּא: אַחֲרֵי דְּבָרֶיהָ וַעֲצָתָהּ, הָכָא נַמִי: אַחֲרֵי דְּבָרֶיהָ וַעֲצָתָהּ.

Rather, certainly each of these verses means that **he followed her words and advice.** If so, **here too,** the verse concerning Manoah may be similarly interpreted. He did not literally walk behind his wife, but rather **he followed** her **words and advice.**

אָמַר רַב אַשִׁי: וּלְמַאי דְּאָמַר רַב נַחְמָן, מָנוֹחַ עַם הָאָרֶץ הָיָה, אֲפִילּוּ בֵּי רַב נַמִי לֹא קָרָא. דִּכְתִיב: "וַתָּקָם רִבְקָה וְנַעֲרוֹתֶיהָ וַתִּרְכַּבְנָה עַל הַגְּמַלִּים וַתֵּלַכְנָה אַחֲרֵי הָאִישׁ" – וְלֹא לִפְנֵי הָאִישׁ.

Rav Ashi said: And according to what Rav Naḥman said, that **Manoah was an ignoramus, he did not even read** the basic Torah stories that children learn **in school. As it is written: "Rebecca arose, and her damsels, and they rode upon the camels, and followed the man"** (Genesis 24:61); they followed him and did **not** walk **before the man.**

HALAKHA

A man should not walk behind a woman – לֹא יְהַלֵּךְ אָדָם אֲחוֹרֵי אִשָּׁה: A man should not walk close behind a woman. If he finds himself in that situation, he should speed up and pass her (*Shulḥan Arukh, Even HaEzer* 21:1).

NOTES

Anyone who walks behind a woman – הָעוֹבֵר אֲחוֹרֵי אִשָּׁה: Rashi explains that the prohibition against walking behind a woman in a river only refers to a married woman. *Tosafot* explain that the severe punishment specified in the Gemara is for one who makes a habit of violating this prohibition because ultimately it will lead to adultery. The rationale for this prohibition is that by looking at a woman from behind, a man cannot avoid sinful thoughts. The prohibition is extended to a man's own wife. Not everybody would know she is his wife, and so he might be suspected of wrongdoing (see *Me'iri*).

Hand to hand, the evil man shall not go unpunished – יָד לְיָד לֹא יִנָּקֶה רָע: The phrase hand to hand, is given a double meaning: The first is one who gives from his hand to her hand or the reverse. The second meaning is the explanation that even if one received the Torah from God's hand to his hand like Moses our master, he still will not be absolved.

And Elkana walked after his wife – וַיֵּלֶךְ אֶלְקָנָה אַחֲרֵי אִשְׁתּוֹ: Many have noted that there is no such verse in the Bible. Some commentaries state that there is a similar expression in the verse: "And Elkana went to Rama, to his house" (I Samuel 2:11). They explain that his house refers to his wife, and that he walked to Rama behind his wife (Maharshal).

HALAKHA

Behind a synagogue – אֲחוֹרֵי בֵּית הַכְּנֶסֶת: It is prohibited to walk past the entrance of a synagogue while the congregation is praying. If one is carrying a load or wearing phylacteries, if there is another synagogue in the city, if the synagogue has an additional entrance on another side of the building, or if one is riding an animal (*Beit Yosef*), he is permitted to do so (*Shulḥan Arukh, Oraḥ Ḥayyim* 90:8).

NOTES

Bore spirits, demons, and female demons – הוֹלִיד רוּחִין וְשֵׁידִים וְלִילִין: Rav Hai Gaon teaches: As explained in the Gemara, semen released by a man even accidentally, such as by a nocturnal emission or through illness, is used by various spirits to form different creatures in a process resembling conception and birth. These creatures are not people but rather destructive angels of various types.

Belts [*zarzei*] of fig leaves – זַרְזֵי תְאֵנִים: The *ge'onim* explain that the word *zarzei* means straps, similar to those used to tie a saddle to a donkey.

It is enough for the world to use only two letters – דַּיּוֹ לָעוֹלָם שֶׁיִּשְׁתַּמֵּשׁ בִּשְׁתֵּי אוֹתִיּוֹת: Rav Hai Gaon teaches that during the Temple period, the priests in the Temple would pronounce the Tetragrammaton, that name of God that consists of four letters. After the destruction of the Temple, it became prohibited to pronounce this name, so that nowadays only the first half of the name may be uttered.

אָמַר רַבִּי יוֹחָנָן: אַחֲרֵי אֲרִי וְלֹא אַחֲרֵי אִשָּׁה, אַחֲרֵי אִשָּׁה וְלֹא אַחֲרֵי עֲבוֹדָה זָרָה, אֲחוֹרֵי עֲבוֹדָה זָרָה וְלֹא אֲחוֹרֵי בֵּית הַכְּנֶסֶת בְּשָׁעָה שֶׁמִּתְפַּלְּלִין.

On this topic, **Rabbi Yoḥanan said:** It is preferable to walk **behind a lion, and not behind a woman.** And it is preferable to walk **behind a woman and not behind idolatry.** When a procession honoring idolatry is passing in the street, it is better to walk behind a woman than appear to be accompanying the idolatry. It is preferable to walk **behind idolatry and not behind a synagogue at a time of prayer.**[H] By walking behind a synagogue at a time of prayer and not entering, one appears as though he were denying the God to Whom the congregation is directing its prayers.

וְאָמַר רַבִּי יִרְמְיָה בֶּן אֶלְעָזָר: כָּל אוֹתָן הַשָּׁנִים שֶׁהָיָה אָדָם הָרִאשׁוֹן בְּנִידּוּי הוֹלִיד רוּחִין וְשֵׁידִין וְלִילִין, שֶׁנֶּאֱמַר: "וַיְחִי אָדָם שְׁלֹשִׁים וּמְאַת שָׁנָה וַיּוֹלֶד בִּדְמוּתוֹ כְּצַלְמוֹ", מִכְּלָל דְּעַד הָאִידָּנָא לָאו כְּצַלְמוֹ אוֹלִיד.

Having cited an aggadic statement of Rabbi Yirmeya ben Elazar, the Gemara cites other statements of his: **Rabbi Yirmeya ben Elazar said: All those years during which Adam was ostracized** for the sin involving the Tree of Knowledge, **he bore spirits, demons, and female demons,**[N] **as it is stated: "And Adam lived a hundred and thirty years, and begot a son in his own likeness, after his image,** and called his name Seth" (Genesis 5:3). **By inference, until now,** the age of one hundred thirty, **he did not bear after his image,** but rather bore other creatures.

מֵיתִיבִי, הָיָה רַבִּי מֵאִיר אוֹמֵר: אָדָם הָרִאשׁוֹן חָסִיד גָּדוֹל הָיָה, כֵּיוָן שֶׁרָאָה שֶׁנִּקְנְסָה מִיתָה עַל יָדוֹ יָשַׁב בְּתַעֲנִית מֵאָה שְׁלֹשִׁים שָׁנָה, וּפֵירֵשׁ מִן הָאִשָּׁה מֵאָה שְׁלֹשִׁים שָׁנָה, וְהֶעֱלָה זַרְזֵי תְאֵנִים עַל בְּשָׂרוֹ מֵאָה שְׁלֹשִׁים שָׁנָה?!

The Gemara raises **an objection** from a *baraita*: **Rabbi Meir would say: Adam the first** man **was very pious. When he saw that death was imposed as a punishment because of him, he observed a fast for a hundred thirty years, and he separated from** his **wife for a hundred thirty years, and wore belts [*zarzei*] of fig** leaves[N] **on his body** as his only garment for **a hundred thirty years.** If so, how did he father demons into the world?

כִּי קָאָמְרִינַן הַהוּא – בְּשִׁכְבַת זֶרַע דְּחֲזָא לְאוֹנְסֵיהּ.

The Gemara answers: **When** Rabbi Yirmeya **made his statement,** he meant that those destructive creatures were formed **from the semen that** Adam **accidentally emitted,** which brought the destructive creatures into being.

וְאָמַר רַבִּי יִרְמְיָה בֶּן אֶלְעָזָר: מִקְצָת שִׁבְחוֹ שֶׁל אָדָם אוֹמְרִים בְּפָנָיו, וְכוּלּוֹ שֶׁלֹּא בְּפָנָיו. מִקְצָת שִׁבְחוֹ בְּפָנָיו – דִּכְתִיב: "כִּי אוֹתְךָ רָאִיתִי צַדִּיק לְפָנַי בַּדּוֹר הַזֶּה",

And Rabbi Yirmeya ben Elazar further **said:** Only **some of a person's praise should be said in his presence, and all of it** may be said **not in his presence.** Only **some of his praise should be said in his presence, as it is written:** "And the Lord said to Noah, come, you and all your house into the ark, **for you have I seen righteous before Me in this generation"** (Genesis 7:1).

כּוּלּוֹ שֶׁלֹּא בְּפָנָיו – דִּכְתִיב: "נֹחַ אִישׁ צַדִּיק תָּמִים הָיָה בְּדוֹרוֹתָיו".

And all of it may be said **not in his presence, as it is written:** "These are the generations of Noah; **Noah was a righteous man, and perfect in his generations,** and Noah walked with God" (Genesis 6:9). When not referring to him in his presence, God refers to Noah as a righteous and perfect man.

וְאָמַר רַבִּי יִרְמְיָה בֶּן אֶלְעָזָר: מַאי דִּכְתִיב: "וְהִנֵּה עֲלֵה זַיִת טָרָף בְּפִיהָ" – אָמְרָה יוֹנָה לִפְנֵי הַקָּדוֹשׁ בָּרוּךְ הוּא: רִבּוֹנוֹ שֶׁל עוֹלָם, יִהְיוּ מְזוֹנוֹתַי מְרוֹרִין כַּזַּיִת וּמְסוּרִין בְּיָדְךָ, וְאַל יִהְיוּ מְתוּקִין כִּדְבַשׁ וּתְלוּיִין בְּיַד בָּשָׂר וָדָם. כְּתִיב הָכָא "טָרָף" וּכְתִיב הָתָם "הַטְרִיפֵנִי לֶחֶם חוּקִּי".

And Rabbi Yirmeya ben Elazar also **said: What is** the meaning of that **which is written:** "And the dove came in to him in the evening, **and lo, in her mouth was an olive leaf, plucked off [*taraf*];** so Noah knew that the waters were abated from off the earth" (Genesis 8:11)? **The dove said before the Holy One, Blessed be He: Master of the Universe, let my food be bitter as an olive but given into Your hand, and let it not be sweet as honey but dependent upon flesh and blood.** He adds this explanation: **Here it is written:** ***Taraf.*** **And there it is written:** "Remove far from me falsehood and lies; give me neither poverty nor riches; **feed me [*hatrifeni*] my allotted portion"** (Proverbs 30:8).

וְאָמַר רַבִּי יִרְמְיָה בֶּן אֶלְעָזָר: כָּל בַּיִת שֶׁנִּשְׁמָעִין בּוֹ דִּבְרֵי תוֹרָה בַּלַּיְלָה – שׁוּב אֵינוֹ נֶחֱרָב, שֶׁנֶּאֱמַר: "וְלֹא אָמַר אַיֵּה אֱלוֹהַּ עוֹשָׂי נוֹתֵן זְמִירוֹת בַּלָּיְלָה".

And Rabbi Yirmeya ben Elazar also **said: Any house in which the words of Torah are heard at night will never be destroyed, as it is stated: "But none says: Where is God my Maker, Who gives songs in the night"** (Job 35:10). The verse implies that one who sings songs of Torah in his house at night will not need to lament the destruction of his home.

וְאָמַר רַבִּי יִרְמְיָה בֶּן אֶלְעָזָר: מִיּוֹם שֶׁחָרַב בֵּית הַמִּקְדָּשׁ דַּיּוֹ לָעוֹלָם שֶׁיִּשְׁתַּמֵּשׁ בִּשְׁתֵּי אוֹתִיּוֹת, שֶׁנֶּאֱמַר: "כֹּל הַנְּשָׁמָה תְּהַלֵּל יָהּ הַלְלוּיָהּ".

And Rabbi Yirmeya ben Elazar further **said: From the day that the Temple was destroyed, it is enough for the world to use** in its praise of God, or in greeting one another with the name of God, only **two letters** of the Tetragrammaton,[N] namely *yod* and *heh*, **as it is stated: "Let everything that has breath praise the Lord [*Yah*].** ***Halleluya*"** (Psalms 150:6), without mentioning the full name of God, comprised of four letters.

וְאָמַר רַבִּי יִרְמְיָה בֶּן אֶלְעָזָר: נִתְקַלְּלָה בָּבֶל – נִתְקַלְּלוּ שְׁכֵינֶיהָ, נִתְקַלְּלָה שׁוֹמְרוֹן – נִתְבָּרְכוּ שְׁכֵינֶיהָ. נִתְקַלְּלָה בָּבֶל נִתְקַלְּלוּ שְׁכֵינֶיהָ – דִּכְתִיב: ״וְשַׂמְתִּיהָ לְמוֹרַשׁ קִיפּוֹד וְאַגְמֵי מָיִם״. נִתְקַלְּלָה שׁוֹמְרוֹן נִתְבָּרְכוּ שְׁכֵינֶיהָ – דִּכְתִיב: ״וְשַׂמְתִּי שׁוֹמְרוֹן לְעִי הַשָּׂדֶה

And Rabbi Yirmeya ben Elazar also **said:** When **Babylonia was cursed, its neighbors were cursed** along with it. When **Samaria was cursed, its neighbors were blessed.** He explains: When **Babylonia was cursed, its neighbors were cursed, as it is written: "I will also make it a possession for wild birds, and pools of water"** (Isaiah 14:23), and the arrival of predatory animals brings harm to the surrounding neighbors as well. When **Samaria was cursed, its neighbors were blessed, as it is written: "Therefore I will turn Samaria into a heap of rubble in the field**

Perek **II**
Daf **19** Amud **a**

לְמַטָּעֵי כָרֶם״.

for planting vines" (Micah 1:6), which benefits all the surrounding inhabitants.

וְאָמַר רַבִּי יִרְמְיָה בֶּן אֶלְעָזָר: בֹּא וּרְאֵה שֶׁלֹּא כְּמִדַּת הַקָּדוֹשׁ בָּרוּךְ הוּא מִדַּת בָּשָׂר וָדָם; מִדַּת בָּשָׂר וָדָם, מִתְחַיֵּיב אָדָם הֲרִיגָה לַמַּלְכוּת – מַטִּילִין לוֹ חַכָּה לְתוֹךְ פִּיו כְּדֵי שֶׁלֹּא יְקַלֵּל אֶת הַמֶּלֶךְ,

And Rabbi Yirmeya ben Elazar also **said: Come and see that the attribute of flesh and blood is unlike the attribute of the Holy One, Blessed be He.** For **the attribute of flesh and blood** is to **place an** iron or wooden **hook in the mouth** of **a person who was sentenced to death by the government, so that he should not** be able to **curse the king** when he is taken away for execution.

מִדַּת הַקָּדוֹשׁ בָּרוּךְ הוּא אָדָם מִתְחַיֵּיב הֲרִיגָה לַמָּקוֹם – שׁוֹתֵק, שֶׁנֶּאֱמַר: ״לְךָ דֻמִיָּה תְהִלָּה״. וְלֹא עוֹד אֶלָּא שֶׁמְּשַׁבֵּחַ, שֶׁנֶּאֱמַר ״תְּהִלָּה״. וְלֹא עוֹד אֶלָּא שֶׁדּוֹמֶה לוֹ כְּאִילּוּ מַקְרִיב קָרְבָּן, שֶׁנֶּאֱמַר: ״וּלְךָ יְשֻׁלַּם נֶדֶר״.

But **the attribute of the Holy One, Blessed be He**[N] is that **one is** willingly **silent** when he **is sentenced to death by the Omnipresent, as it is stated: "For You silence is praise,** O God in Zion, and to You shall the vow be performed" (Psalms 65:2). **And what is more, he praises** God for his sufferings, **as it is stated: "Praise." And what is more, it appears to him as though he were offering a sacrifice**[N] in atonement for his sin, **as it is stated: "And to You shall the vow be performed."**

הַיְינוּ דְּאָמַר רַבִּי יְהוֹשֻׁעַ בֶּן לֵוִי: מַאי דִּכְתִיב: ״עֹבְרֵי בְּעֵמֶק הַבָּכָא מַעְיָן יְשִׁיתוּהוּ גַּם בְּרָכוֹת יַעְטֶה מוֹרֶה״;

And this is what **Rabbi Yehoshua ben Levi said: What is** the meaning of that **which is written: "Those who pass through the valley of weeping turn it into a water spring; moreover, the early rain covers it with blessings"** (Psalms 84:7)?

״עֹבְרֵי״ – אֵלּוּ בְּנֵי אָדָם שֶׁעוֹבְרִין עַל רְצוֹנוֹ שֶׁל הַקָּדוֹשׁ בָּרוּךְ הוּא, ״עֵמֶק״ – שֶׁמַּעֲמִיקִין לָהֶם גֵּיהִנָּם, ״הַבָּכָא״ – שֶׁבּוֹכִין וּמוֹרִידִין דְּמָעוֹת כְּמַעְיָין שֶׁל שִׁיתִין, ״גַּם בְּרָכוֹת יַעְטֶה מוֹרֶה״ – שֶׁמַּצְדִּיקִין עֲלֵיהֶם אֶת הַדִּין, וְאוֹמְרִים לְפָנָיו: רִבּוֹנוֹ שֶׁל עוֹלָם, יָפֶה דַּנְתָּ, יָפֶה זִכִּיתָ, יָפֶה חִיַּיבְתָּ, וְיָפֶה תִּקַּנְתָּ גֵּיהִנָּם לָרְשָׁעִים, גַּן עֵדֶן לַצַּדִּיקִים.

"Those who pass through [*overei*]," **these are people who transgress** [*overin*] **the will of the Holy One, Blessed be He. "Valley** [*emek*]" indicates that their punishment is that **Gehenna is deepened** [*ma'amikin*] **for them. "Of weeping** [*bakha*]" and "turn it into a water spring [*ma'ayan yeshituhu*]," indicates that **they weep** [*bokhin*] **and make tears flow like a spring** [*ma'ayan*] **of the foundations** [*shitin*], meaning like a spring that descends to the foundations of the earth. **"Moreover, the early rain covers it with blessings,"** indicates that **they accept** the justice of God's **judgment, and say before Him: Master of the Universe, You have judged properly, You have acquitted properly, You have condemned properly, and it is befitting that You have prepared Gehenna for the wicked and the Garden of Eden for the righteous.**

אִינִי?! וְהָאָמַר רַבִּי שִׁמְעוֹן בֶּן לָקִישׁ: רְשָׁעִים אֲפִילּוּ עַל פִּתְחוֹ שֶׁל גֵּיהִנָּם אֵינָם חוֹזְרִין בִּתְשׁוּבָה, שֶׁנֶּאֱמַר: ״וְיָצְאוּ וְרָאוּ בְּפִגְרֵי הָאֲנָשִׁים הַפֹּשְׁעִים בִּי וגו׳״, ״שֶׁפָּשְׁעוּ״ לֹא נֶאֱמַר, אֶלָּא ״הַפּוֹשְׁעִים״ – שֶׁפּוֹשְׁעִים וְהוֹלְכִין לְעוֹלָם!

The Gemara raises a difficulty: **Is that so? Didn't Rabbi Shimon ben Lakish say: The wicked do not repent, even at the entrance to Gehenna,**[N] **as it is stated: "And they shall go forth, and look upon the carcasses of the men who rebel against Me;** for their worm shall not die, neither shall their fire be quenched; and they shall be an abhorrence to all flesh" (Isaiah 66:24)? The verse **does not say: Who rebelled, but** rather: **"Who rebel,"** in the present tense, meaning **they continue rebelling forever.**

לָא קַשְׁיָא; הָא – בְּפוֹשְׁעֵי יִשְׂרָאֵל, הָא – בְּפוֹשְׁעֵי אוּמּוֹת הָעוֹלָם.

The Gemara answers: This is **not difficult; here,** i.e., where it is said that they accept God's judgment, it is referring **to the sinners of the Jewish people; there,** i.e., where it is said that they do not recant, it is referring **to the rebels among the nations of the world.**

NOTES

The attribute of the Holy One, Blessed be He – מִדַּת הַקָּדוֹשׁ בָּרוּךְ הוּא: There are two reasons for the distinction between the human and divine attributes: One may think that a judgment of a human king is unfair, but he will know that God's judgment is always fair. Furthermore, when one is about to die, he is no longer afraid of a human king and feels free to curse him, since the king cannot punish him after death. However, God can punish a person even after his death (Ritva; Maharsha).

As though he were offering a sacrifice – כְּאִילּוּ מַקְרִיב קָרְבָּן: When one offers a sacrifice, it is as though he were sacrificing himself to atone for his sins. Therefore, when one is punished and sentenced to Gehenna, it is considered as though he were offering a sacrifice (Maharsha).

Even at the entrance to Gehenna – אֲפִילּוּ עַל פִּתְחוֹ שֶׁל גֵּיהִנָּם: Since the verse indicates that it is possible to go out and see the carcasses, it implies that they are not actually in Gehenna but only at its entrance. Nevertheless, they continue to sin.

הָכִי נַמִּי מִסְתַּבְּרָא, דְּאִם כֵּן קַשְׁיָא דְּרֵישׁ לָקִישׁ אַדְּרֵישׁ לָקִישׁ. דְּאָמַר רֵישׁ לָקִישׁ: פּוֹשְׁעֵי יִשְׂרָאֵל אֵין אוּר גֵּיהִנָּם שׁוֹלֶטֶת בָּהֶן, קַל וָחוֹמֶר מִמִּזְבַּח הַזָּהָב:

So too, it is reasonable to say this, for **if** you do not say **so,** there would be **a contradiction** between one statement **of Reish Lakish and** another statement **of Reish Lakish. As Reish Lakish said:** With regard to **the sinners of the Jewish people, the fire of Gehenna has no power over them,** as may be learned by ***a fortiori*** reasoning **from the golden altar.**

מַה מִּזְבַּח הַזָּהָב שֶׁאֵין עָלָיו אֶלָּא כְּעוֹבִי דִּינָר זָהָב עָמַד כַּמָּה שָׁנִים וְלֹא שָׁלְטָה בּוֹ הָאוּר, פּוֹשְׁעֵי יִשְׂרָאֵל שֶׁמְּלֵיאִין מִצְוֹת כָּרִמּוֹן, שֶׁנֶּאֱמַר: ״כְּפֶלַח הָרִמּוֹן רַקָּתֵךְ״, וְאָמַר רַבִּי שִׁמְעוֹן בֶּן לָקִישׁ אַל תִּיקְרֵי ״רַקָּתֵךְ״ אֶלָּא ״רֵיקָתֵיךְ״, שֶׁאֲפִילּוּ רֵיקָנִין שֶׁבָּךְ מְלֵיאִין מִצְוֹת כָּרִמּוֹן – עַל אַחַת כַּמָּה וְכַמָּה.

If the golden altar in the Temple, **which was only covered by** gold **the thickness of a golden dinar, stood for many years and the fire did not burn it,** for its gold did not melt, so too **the sinners of the Jewish people, who are filled with good deeds like a pomegranate, as it is stated: "Your temples [*rakatekh*] are like a split pomegranate** behind your veil" (Song of Songs 6:7), will not be affected by the fire of Gehenna. **And Rabbi Shimon ben Lakish said** about this: **Do not read: Your temples [*rakatekh*],** but rather: **Your empty ones [*reikateikh*],** meaning that **even the sinners among you are full of mitzvot like a pomegranate; how much more so** should the fire of Gehenna have no power over them.

אֶלָּא הָא דִּכְתִיב: ״עוֹבְרֵי בְּעֵמֶק הַבָּכָא״ – הַהוּא דִּמְחַיְּיבֵי הַהִיא שַׁעְתָּא בַּגֵּיהִנָּם, וְאָתֵי אַבְרָהָם אָבִינוּ וּמַסֵּיק לְהוּ וּמְקַבֵּל לְהוּ, בַּר מִיִּשְׂרָאֵל שֶׁבָּא עַל הַגּוֹיָה דְּמָשְׁכָה עׇרְלָתוֹ וְלָא מְבַשְׁקַר לֵיהּ.

However, that which is written: "Those who pass through the valley of weeping" (Psalms 84:7), which implies that the sinners nonetheless descend to Gehenna, should be explained as follows: **There** it speaks of **those who are liable at that time** for punishment **in Gehenna, but our father Abraham comes and raises them up and receives them.** He does not leave the circumcised behind and allow them to enter Gehenna, **except for a Jew who had relations with a gentile woman,**[N] in punishment for which **his foreskin is drawn, and** our father Abraham **does not recognize him** as one of his descendants.

מַתְקִיף לַהּ רַב כָּהֲנָא: הַשְׁתָּא דְּאָמְרַתְּ ״הַפּוֹשְׁעִים״ דְּפָשְׁעִי וְאָזְלִי, אֶלָּא מֵעַתָּה דִּכְתִיב: ״הַמּוֹצִיא וְהַמַּעֲלֶה״ דְּמַסֵּיק וּדְמַפֵּיק הוּא?! אֶלָּא דְּאַסֵּיק וְאַפֵּיק, הָכִי נַמִּי דְּפָשְׁעִי הוּא.

Rav Kahana strongly objected to this: Now that **you have said** that the words **those who rebel** are referring to **those who go on rebelling, if so,** in those verses in which **it is written of** Him: **"He Who brings out"** (see Exodus 6:7) **and "He Who raises up"** Israel from Egypt (see Leviticus 11:45), do these expressions mean: **He Who** is currently **raising** them **up and bringing** them **out? Rather,** you must understand these terms to mean: **He Who** already **raised** them **up and brought** them **out; here too** then, the phrase those who rebel means **those who** already **rebelled.**

וְאָמַר רַבִּי יִרְמְיָה (בַּר) אֶלְעָזָר: שְׁלֹשָׁה פְּתָחִים יֵשׁ לַגֵּיהִנָּם, אֶחָד בַּמִּדְבָּר, וְאֶחָד בַּיָּם, וְאֶחָד בִּירוּשָׁלַיִם. בַּמִּדְבָּר, דִּכְתִיב: ״וַיֵּרְדוּ הֵם וְכׇל אֲשֶׁר לָהֶם חַיִּים שְׁאֹלָה״.

And Rabbi Yirmeya ben Elazar also **said: There are three entrances to Gehenna,**[N] **one in the wilderness, one in the sea, and one in Jerusalem.** There is one entrance **in the wilderness, as it is written** with regard to Korah and his company: **"And they, and all that appertained to them, went down alive into the pit [*She'ol*],** and the earth closed upon them, and they perished from among the congregation" (Numbers 16:33).

בַּיָּם, דִּכְתִיב: ״מִבֶּטֶן שְׁאוֹל שִׁוַּעְתִּי שָׁמַעְתָּ קוֹלִי״.

In the sea there is a second entrance to Gehenna, **as it is written** about Jonah in the fish's belly: **"Out of the belly of the netherworld [*She'ol*] I cried, and You did hear my voice"** (Jonah 2:3).

בִּירוּשָׁלַיִם, דִּכְתִיב: ״נְאֻם ה׳ אֲשֶׁר אוּר לוֹ בְּצִיּוֹן וְתַנּוּר לוֹ בִּירוּשָׁלָיִם״. וְתָנָא דְּבֵי רַבִּי יִשְׁמָעֵאל: ״אֲשֶׁר אוּר לוֹ בְּצִיּוֹן״ – זוֹ גֵּיהִנָּם, ״וְתַנּוּר לוֹ בִּירוּשָׁלָיִם״ – זוֹ פִּתְחָהּ שֶׁל גֵּיהִנָּם.

And there is a third entrance to Gehenna **in Jerusalem, as it is written: "Says the Lord, Whose fire is in Zion, and Whose furnace is in Jerusalem"** (Isaiah 31:9). **And** it was **taught** in the **school of Rabbi Yishmael: "Whose fire is in Zion," this is Gehenna; and "Whose furnace is in Jerusalem," this is an entrance to Gehenna.**

וְתוּ לֵיכָּא? וְהָאָמַר רַבִּי מָרְיוֹן, אָמַר רַבִּי יְהוֹשֻׁעַ בֶּן לֵוִי, וְאָמְרִי לַהּ תָּנָא רַבָּה בַּר מָרְיוֹן בִּדְבֵי רַבִּי יוֹחָנָן בֶּן זַכַּאי: שְׁתֵּי תְמָרוֹת יֵשׁ בְּגֵי בֶן הִנּוֹם וְעוֹלֶה עָשָׁן מִבֵּינֵיהֶן, וְזוֹ הִיא שֶׁשָּׁנִינוּ צִינֵּי הַר הַבַּרְזֶל כְּשֵׁירוֹת, וְזוֹ הִיא פִּתְחָהּ שֶׁל גֵּיהִנָּם! דִּילְמָא הַיְינוּ דִּירוּשָׁלַיִם.

The Gemara asks: **Are there no more** entrances? **Didn't Rabbi Maryon say in the name of Rabbi Yehoshua ben Levi, and some say** it was **Rabba bar Maryon** who **taught in** the name of **the school of Rabbi Yoḥanan ben Zakkai: There are two date trees in the valley of ben Hinnom, and smoke rises from between them,** and with regard to **this** statement about date trees that differ from other palms **we learned: The palms of Har HaBarzel are fit** for the mitzva of palm branches [*lulav*], **and this is the entrance to Gehenna.** The Gemara answers: This is not difficult, for **perhaps this is the** entrance **in Jerusalem.**

NOTES

Except for a Jew who had relations with a gentile woman – בַּר מִיִּשְׂרָאֵל שֶׁבָּא עַל הַגּוֹיָה: The rationale for this is that the merit of our father Abraham protects those who guard the covenant of circumcision, as Abraham was the first to accept upon himself the fulfillment of this covenant. However, a man who sins by engaging in sexual relations with a gentile woman and one who draws his foreskin in an attempt to disguise that he is circumcised deny the covenant of our father Abraham, and so this merit no longer protects them.

Three entrances to Gehenna – שְׁלֹשָׁה פְּתָחִים יֵשׁ לַגֵּיהִנָּם: Some commentaries explain these entrances symbolically. The entrance in the wilderness is referring to the sin of dispute, symbolized by Korah and his company. The entrance in the sea represents the unwillingness to reprove sinners, symbolized by Jonah son of Amittai. The entrance in Jerusalem symbolizes the sins of the people of the city involving pride and corrupt standards of behavior (*Naḥalat Ya'akov*).

אָמַר רַבִּי יְהוֹשֻׁעַ בֶּן לֵוִי: שִׁבְעָה שֵׁמוֹת יֵשׁ לַגֵּיהִנָּם, וְאֵלּוּ הֵן: שְׁאוֹל וַאֲבַדּוֹן, וּבְאֵר שַׁחַת, וּבוֹר שָׁאוֹן, וְטִיט הַיָּוֵן, וְצַלְמָוֶת, וְאֶרֶץ הַתַּחְתִּית.

Rabbi Yehoshua ben Levi said: Gehenna has seven names,[N] **and they are as follows: She'ol, Avadon, Be'er Shaḥat, Bor Shaon, Tit HaYaven, Tzalmavet, and Eretz HaTaḥtit.**

שְׁאוֹל – דִּכְתִיב: "מִבֶּטֶן שְׁאוֹל שִׁוַּעְתִּי שָׁמַעְתָּ קוֹלִי". אֲבַדּוֹן – דִּכְתִיב: "הַיְסוּפַּר בַּקֶּבֶר חַסְדֶּךָ אֱמוּנָתְךָ בָּאֲבַדּוֹן". בְּאֵר שַׁחַת – דִּכְתִיב: "כִּי לֹא תַעֲזוֹב נַפְשִׁי לִשְׁאוֹל לֹא תִתֵּן חֲסִידְךָ לִרְאוֹת שָׁחַת". וּבוֹר שָׁאוֹן וְטִיט הַיָּוֵן – דִּכְתִיב: "וַיַּעֲלֵנִי מִבּוֹר שָׁאוֹן מִטִּיט הַיָּוֵן". וְצַלְמָוֶת – דִּכְתִיב: "יוֹשְׁבֵי חוֹשֶׁךְ וְצַלְמָוֶת". וְאֶרֶץ הַתַּחְתִּית – גְּמָרָא הוּא.

She'ol, as it is written: "Out of the belly of the netherworld [*she'ol*] **I cried and You did hear my voice"** (Jonah 2:3). **Avadon, as it is written: "Shall Your steadfast love be reported in the grave or Your faithfulness in destruction** [*avadon*]**?"** (Psalms 88:12). **Be'er Shaḥat, as it is written: "For You will not abandon my soul to the netherworld; nor will You suffer Your pious one to see the pit** [*shaḥat*]**"** (Psalms 16:10). **And Bor Shaon and Tit HaYaven, as it is written: "He brought me up also out of the gruesome pit** [*bor shaon*]**, out of the miry clay** [*tit hayaven*]**"** (Psalms 40:3). **And Tzalmavet, as it is written: "Such as sat in darkness and in the shadow of death** [*tzalmavet*]**,** bound in affliction and iron" (Psalms 107:10). **And** with regard to **Eretz Taḥtit,** i.e., the underworld, **it is** known by **tradition** that this is its name.

וְתוּ לֵיכָּא? וְהָאִיכָּא גֵּיהִנָּם! גֵּיא שֶׁעֲמוּקָּה (כְּגֵיהִנָּם) שֶׁהַכֹּל יוֹרֵד לָהּ עַל עִסְקֵי הִנָּם.

The Gemara poses a question: **Are there no more** names? **Isn't there** the name **Gehenna?** The Gemara answers that this is not a name rather a description: **A valley that is as deep as the valley** [*gei*] of ben **Hinnom.** An alternative explanation is: **Into which all descend for vain** [*hinnam*] and wasteful **acts,**[N] understanding the word *hinnam* as if it were written *ḥinnam*, meaning for naught.

וְהָאִיכָּא "תָּפְתֶּה", דִּכְתִיב: "כִּי עָרוּךְ מֵאֶתְמוּל תָּפְתֶּה"! הַהוּא – שֶׁכָּל הַמִּתְפַּתֶּה בְּיִצְרוֹ יִפּוֹל שָׁם.

The Gemara asks: **Isn't there** also the name **Tofte, as it is written: "For its hearth** [*tofte*] **is ordained of old"** (Isaiah 30:33). The Gemara answers: **That** name too is a description, meaning **that anyone who allows himself to be seduced** [*mitpateh*] **by his** evil **inclination will fall there.**

גַּן עֵדֶן, אָמַר רֵישׁ לָקִישׁ: אִם בְּאֶרֶץ יִשְׂרָאֵל הוּא – בֵּית שְׁאָן פִּתְחוֹ, וְאִם בַּעֲרַבְיָא – בֵּית גֶּרֶם פִּתְחוֹ, וְאִם בֵּין הַנְּהָרוֹת הוּא – דּוּמַסְקַנִין פִּתְחוֹ. בְּבָבֶל, אַבַּיֵי מִשְׁתַּבַּח בְּפֵירֵי דְּמֵעֲבַר יְמִינָא, רָבָא מִשְׁתַּבַּח בְּפֵירֵי דְּהַרְפַּנְיָא.

Having discussed the entrances to Gehenna, the Gemara also mentions the entrance to **the Garden of Eden. Reish Lakish said: If it is in Eretz Yisrael, its entrance is Beit She'an, and if** it is **in Arabia, its entrance is Beit Garem, and if** it is **between the rivers** of Babylonia, **its entrance is Dumsekanin,** for all these places feature a great abundance of vegetation and fertile land. The Gemara relates that **Abaye** would **praise the fruits of the right bank** of the Euphrates River, **and Rava** would **praise the fruits of Harpanya.**

"וּבֵינֵיהֶן כִּמְלוֹא שְׁתֵּי וְכוּ'". פְּשִׁיטָא, כֵּיוָן דְּתָנָא לֵיהּ דִּקְשׁוּרוֹת הָווּ אֲנַן יָדְעִינַן דְּלָא הָווּ מוּתָּרוֹת!

The Gemara goes back to the mishna in which we learned: **And between them,** i.e., between the upright boards and the double posts, there may be a gap **the size of two teams** of four oxen each, as measured when tied together and not when they are untied. The Gemara asks: This is **obvious; since the** ***tanna*** **taught** that **they are tied, we know that they are not untied.**

מַהוּ דְּתֵימָא: קְשׁוּרוֹת כְּעֵין קְשׁוּרוֹת, אֲבָל מַמָּשׁ לֹא, קָא מַשְׁמַע לָן "וְלֹא מוּתָּרוֹת".

The Gemara answers: This is specified, **lest you say** that **tied** means **similar to tied,** i.e., close to each other, **but not** necessarily that they are **actually** tied. Therefore, the mishna **teaches us** that it is not enough that they be close; rather, they must be actually tied **and not untied.**

"אַחַת נִכְנֶסֶת וְאַחַת יוֹצֵאת". תָּנָא: רְבָקָה נִכְנֶסֶת וּרְבָקָה יוֹצֵאת. תָּנוּ רַבָּנַן: כַּמָּה רֹאשָׁהּ וְרוּבָּהּ שֶׁל פָּרָה – שְׁתֵּי אַמּוֹת. וְכַמָּה עוֹבְיָהּ שֶׁל פָּרָה – אַמָּה וּשְׁנֵי שְׁלִישֵׁי אַמָּה,

The mishna continued: There must be sufficient space left so that **one can enter and another can leave.** A *Tosefta* **was taught** that explains the mishna: Enough space so that **one team can enter and** another **team can leave. Our Sages taught** in a *baraita*: **How much is** the length of **the head and most of the body of a cow? Two cubits. And how much is the thickness of a cow? A cubit and two-thirds of a cubit,**

NOTES

Gehenna has seven names – שִׁבְעָה שֵׁמוֹת יֵשׁ לַגֵּיהִנָּם: Apparently, these seven names refer to the seven levels of Gehenna, one below the other, while the words Gehenna and Tofteh are general names for Hell (Maharsha; *Ge'on Ya'akov*).

Gehenna…for vain [*hinnam*] acts – גֵּיהִנָּם...עַל עִסְקֵי הִנָּם: According to the first explanation, Gehenna is as deep as the valley of ben Hinnom in relation to its surroundings. According to the second explanation, people go down to Gehenna because of matters of *hinnam*, which apparently refers to forbidden sexual relations (Maharsha).

HALAKHA

More than thirteen – יְתֵירוֹת עַל שָׁלֹשׁ עֶשְׂרֵה: The gaps between the upright boards and double posts around a well must not be greater than thirteen and a third cubits (Rambam *Sefer Zemanim*, *Hilkhot Shabbat* 17:27).

שֶׁהֵן כְּעֶשֶׂר, דִּבְרֵי רַבִּי מֵאִיר. רַבִּי יְהוּדָה אוֹמֵר: כִּשְׁלֹשׁ עֶשְׂרֵה אַמָּה וּכְאַרְבַּע עֶשְׂרֵה אַמָּה.

so that the total width of six oxen **is approximately ten** cubits; this is **the statement of Rabbi Meir. Rabbi Yehuda said** the following, in accordance with his own opinion that the gap may be the size of two teams of four oxen each: The total width is **approximately thirteen cubits or approximately fourteen cubits.**

״כְּעֶשֶׂר״? הָא עֶשֶׂר הָוְיָין! מִשּׁוּם דְּבָעֵי לְמִיתְנָא סֵיפָא ״כִּשְׁלֹשׁ עֶשְׂרֵה״,

The Gemara asks: Why does the *tanna* of the *baraita* say: **Approximately ten** cubits in Rabbi Meir's statement? **Isn't it** exactly **ten** cubits? The Gemara answers: **Since he wanted to teach: Approximately thirteen, in the last clause,** i.e., Rabbi Yehuda's statement, he therefore also taught: Approximately ten, in the first clause.

כִּשְׁלֹשׁ עֶשְׂרֵה טְפֵי הָוְיָין, מִשּׁוּם דְּבָעֵי לְמִתְנֵי ״כְּאַרְבַּע עֶשְׂרֵה״ – וּכְאַרְבַּע עֶשְׂרֵה הָא לָא הָוְיָא! אָמַר רַב פַּפָּא: יְתֵירוֹת עַל שָׁלֹשׁ עֶשְׂרֵה, וְאֵינָן מַגִּיעוֹת לְאַרְבַּע עֶשְׂרֵה.

The Gemara asks: But how could he say: **Approximately thirteen,** when **it is more?** The Gemara answers: **Since he wanted to teach: Approximately fourteen,** he therefore also teaches: Approximately thirteen. The Gemara continues this line of questioning: **But they are not approximately fourteen,** but rather are less. **Rav Pappa said:** It is a third of a cubit **more than thirteen**[H] cubits, **and** it does **not reach fourteen** cubits.

אָמַר רַב פַּפָּא: בְּבוֹר שְׁמוֹנֶה דְּכוּלֵּי עָלְמָא לָא פְּלִיגִי דְּלָא בָּעֵינַן פְּשׁוּטִין,

Rav Pappa said: With regard to a water **cistern** whose own width is **eight** cubits,[B] **everyone agrees,** both Rabbi Yehuda and Rabbi Meir, **that there is no need** to position **upright** boards between the double posts. In such a case, the width of the enclosed area, which is the width of the cistern together with the space required for the cows, i.e., two cubits on each side, is twelve cubits. Since the width of each double post is one cubit, the gap between the double posts is ten cubits, and a gap of this size is permitted even according to Rabbi Meir.

בְּבוֹר שְׁתֵּים עֶשְׂרֵה, דְּכוּלֵּי עָלְמָא לָא פְּלִיגִי דְּבָעֵינַן פְּשׁוּטִין.

With regard to a cistern whose width is **twelve** cubits,[B] **everyone agrees that there is a need for upright** posts. In this case, even if only two cubits are added on each side for the cows, the enclosed area will be sixteen cubits, and the gap between the double posts will be fourteen cubits, which must be closed off even according to Rabbi Yehuda.

כִּי פְּלִיגִי – מִשְּׁמוֹנֶה עַד שְׁתֵּים עֶשְׂרֵה. לְרַבִּי מֵאִיר בָּעֵינַן פְּשׁוּטִין, לְרַבִּי יְהוּדָה לָא בָּעֵינַן פְּשׁוּטִין.

Where they disagree is in the case of a cistern whose width is **between eight** and **twelve** cubits. **According to** the opinion of **Rabbi Meir, one must** add **upright** posts, whereas **according to** the opinion of **Rabbi Yehuda, one need not** add **upright** posts.

וְרַב פַּפָּא מַאי קָא מַשְׁמַע לָן? תָּנֵינָא!

The Gemara asks: **And what is Rav Pappa teaching us? We** already **learned** in the *baraita* that according to Rabbi Meir the gap may not be more than ten cubits, whereas according to Rabbi Yehuda it may be up to thirteen and a third cubits.

BACKGROUND

A cistern whose own width is eight cubits – בּוֹר שְׁמוֹנֶה: The width of the cistern in this illustration is eight cubits. If the upright boards are two cubits from the well, as they should be, the resulting gap between the double posts measures ten cubits. Therefore, there is no need to add to the number of boards.

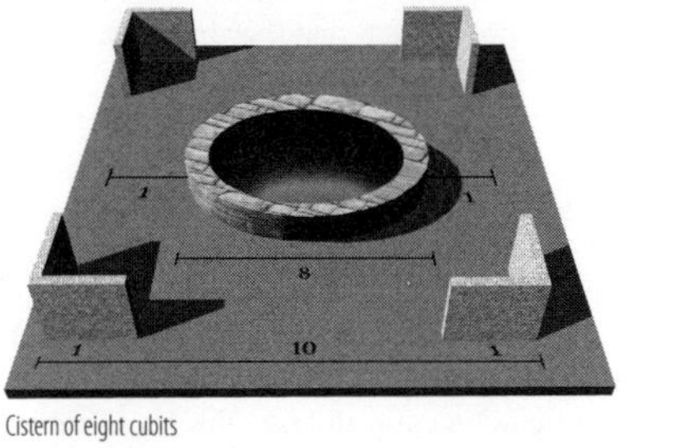

Cistern of eight cubits

A cistern whose width is twelve cubits – בּוֹר שְׁתֵּים עֶשְׂרֵה: When the double posts are two cubits from the cistern, the gap between the posts becomes fourteen cubits. This is more than the amount permitted even by Rabbi Yehuda, who requires the addition of upright boards between the double posts in this case.

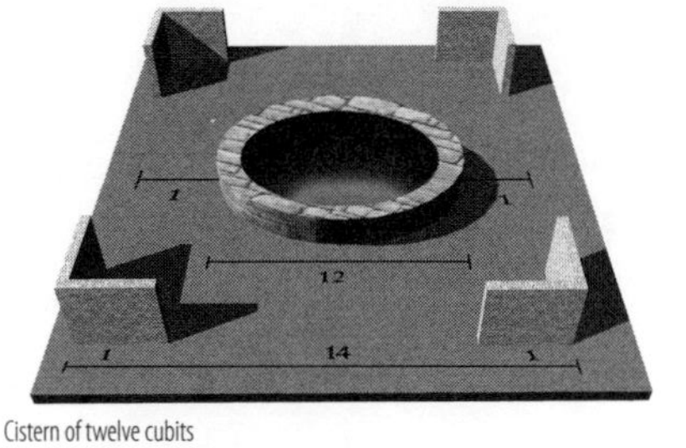

Cistern of twelve cubits

רַב פַּפָּא בָּרַיְיתָא לָא שְׁמִיעַ לֵיהּ, וְקָא מַשְׁמַע לָן כְּבָרַיְיתָא.

The Gemara answers: Indeed, for us nothing new is being taught here; however, **Rav Pappa did not hear** this ***baraita*,**[N] **and he taught us** on his own **as** was taught in the ***baraita*.**

ארי״ך יות״ר בת״ל חיצ״ת חצ״ר שיבש״ה סִימָן. בְּעָא מִינֵּיהּ אַבַּיֵי מֵרַבָּה: הֶאֱרִיךְ בְּדְיוֹמָדִין כְּשִׁיעוּר פְּשׁוּטִין, לְרַבִּי מֵאִיר מַהוּ?

Extended, more, in a mound, a barrier of, a courtyard, that dried up;[N] this is a **mnemonic** containing key words in a series of issues raised by Abaye before Rabba. **Abaye raised a dilemma before Rabba:** If the gaps between the double posts were more than ten cubits, and **one extended the double posts,** that is, he widened each arm of the corner pieces, adding **the measure of an upright** board, i.e., another cubit, on each side, so that the gaps were no longer more than ten cubits, **what** is the law **according to** the opinion of **Rabbi Meir?** Do we say that this suffices and it is no longer necessary to arrange upright boards between the two double posts, or must upright boards be positioned in the gaps?

אָמַר לֵיהּ: תְּנֵיתוּהָ, וּבִלְבַד שֶׁיַּרְבֶּה בְּפַסִּין. מַאי לָאו דְּמַאֲרִיךְ בִּדְיוֹמָדִין? לָא, דְּמַפֵּישׁ וְעָבֵיד פְּשׁוּטִין.

Rabba said **to him: We** already **learned it** in the mishna: **Provided that he increases the boards. Does** this **not** mean **that he extends the double posts,** increasing them in width? Abaye refutes this: **No,** perhaps it means **that he makes more upright** boards,[H] increasing them in number.

אִי הָכִי, הַאי ״וּבִלְבַד שֶׁיַּרְבֶּה בְּפַסִּין״, ״עַד שֶׁיַּרְבֶּה פַּסִּין״ מִיבָּעֵי לֵיהּ! תְּנֵי: עַד שֶׁיַּרְבֶּה פַּסִּין.

Rabba said to him: **If so, this** wording: **Provided that he increases the boards,** is imprecise, for it implies that one increases the boards themselves, and instead **it should have** stated: **Provided that he increases the** number of upright **boards.** Abaye answered: There is no need to be particular about this. **Teach: Provided that he increases** the number of upright **boards.**[N]

אִיכָּא דְּאָמְרִי, אָמַר לֵיהּ: תְּנֵיתוּהָ, וּבִלְבַד שֶׁיַּרְבֶּה בְּפַסִּין, מַאי לָאו דְּמַפֵּישׁ וְעָבֵיד פְּשׁוּטִין? לָא, דְּמַאֲרִיךְ בִּדְיוֹמָדִין.

The Gemara cites an alternative version of the previous discussion: **There are** some **who say** that Rabba **said to** Abaye as follows: **We** already **learned it: Provided that he increases the boards. Does** this **not** mean **that he makes more upright** boards, increasing them in number? Abaye refutes this: **No,** perhaps it means **that he extends the double posts,** increasing them in width.

הָכִי נַמִי מִסְתַּבְּרָא, מִדְּקָתָנֵי ״וּבִלְבַד שֶׁיַּרְבֶּה בְּפַסִּין״ – שְׁמַע מִינָּהּ.

The Gemara comments: **So too, it is reasonable** to say this, **from the fact that** the mishna **teaches: Provided that he increases the** upright **boards,** which implies that he extends the width of the boards themselves, in accordance with the second version. The Gemara concludes: Indeed, **learn from this** that this is the correct understanding.

בְּעָא מִינֵּיהּ אַבַּיֵי מֵרַבָּה: יוֹתֵר מִשְּׁלֹשׁ עֶשְׂרֵה אַמָּה וּשְׁלִישׁ לְרַבִּי יְהוּדָה מַהוּ? פְּשׁוּטִין עָבֵיד אוֹ בִּדְיוֹמָדִין מַאֲרִיךְ?

Abaye raised another **dilemma before Rabba:** If the gaps are **more than thirteen and a third cubits, what** is the law **according to** the opinion of **Rabbi Yehuda? Does he bring upright** boards and position them between the double posts, **or does he extend the double posts,** increasing them in width?

אָמַר לֵיהּ: תְּנֵיתוּהָ, כַּמָּה הֵן מְקוֹרָבִין – כְּדֵי רֹאשָׁהּ וְרוּבָּהּ שֶׁל פָּרָה, וְכַמָּה מְרוּחָקִין – אֲפִילוּ כּוֹר וַאֲפִילוּ כּוֹרַיִים,

Rabba **said to him: We** already **learned** the law in a similar case, for it was taught in a *baraita*: **How close** may the double posts be to the well? They can be **as** close as the length of **the head and most** of the body **of a cow. And how far** may they be from the well? If one wishes, the enclosed area may be expanded **even** to the area of **a *kor* and even** to **two *kor*,** provided that one increases the number of upright boards adequately to keep the gaps under the allowable limit.

רַבִּי יְהוּדָה אוֹמֵר: בֵּית סָאתַיִם – מוּתָּר, יוֹתֵר מִבֵּית סָאתַיִם – אָסוּר. אָמְרוּ לוֹ לְרַבִּי יְהוּדָה: אִי אַתָּה מוֹדֶה בְּדִיר וְסַהַר וּמוּקְצֶה וְחָצֵר אֲפִילוּ בַּת חֲמֵשֶׁת כּוֹרִים וַאֲפִילוּ בַּת עֲשָׂרָה כּוֹרִים שֶׁמּוּתָּר?

The *baraita* continues: **Rabbi Yehuda says:** Up to an area of **two *beit se'a*, it is permitted** to enclose the area in this manner; but expanding the enclosed area so it is **more than** an area of **two *beit se'a* is prohibited.** The other Rabbis **said to Rabbi Yehuda: Do you not agree with regard to a pen, and stable, and a backyard, and a courtyard that even** an area **of five *beit kor* and even of ten *beit kor* is permitted** for use?

אָמַר לָהֶן: זוֹ מְחִיצָה, וְאֵלּוּ פַּסִּין.

The *baraita* continues: Rabbi Yehuda **said to them:** There is a significant difference between these cases, for **this** one, i.e., the wall surrounding the courtyard and the like, **is a** proper **partition, whereas these are** merely upright **boards.**

NOTES

Rav Pappa did not hear of this *baraita* – בָּרַיְיתָא לָא שְׁמִיעַ לֵיהּ: This answer could be acceptable because it would not be surprising or insulting that an *amora* would not be familiar with a particular *baraita*. During the period of the Gemara, the *baraitot* were not anthologized. Consequently, sometimes only a few individual Sages had access to a specific tradition. In this case, however, Rabbi Pappa had earlier resolved the difficulty the *baraita* presented. How, then, could he not have heard of the *baraita*? *Tosafot* answer that he learned of it at some later point, and only then did he correct its wording. Other commentaries explain that this correction was not made by Rabbi Pappa himself but was inferred from his words (Ra'avad; see Rashba).

Extended, more, etc. – ארי״ך יות״ר וכו׳: This mnemonic is a list of dilemmas posed by Abaye to Rabba. The last refers to the question on 20a, p. 107 with regard to a well that dried up on Shabbat. This mnemonic does not appear in all versions of the text, and it also does not include all of the dilemmas.

Teach: Provided that he increases the number of upright boards – תְּנֵי עַד שֶׁיַּרְבֶּה פַּסִּין: This does not mean that the wording of the mishna should actually be emended. Rather, it indicates that this phrase alone is not enough to decide the issue, since it can be understood to mean that one should add boards, as opposed to increasing the width of the existing boards (*Ge'on Ya'akov*).

HALAKHA

He makes more upright boards – מַפֵּישׁ וְעָבֵיד פְּשׁוּטִין: If the gap between the double posts is greater than the permitted amount, one must erect upright boards in the middle of the gap. Although Abaye refuted Rabba's proof, the rule is still in accordance with Rabba's conclusion (*Maggid Mishne*; Rambam *Sefer Zemanim*, *Hilkhot Shabbat* 17:29).

וְאִם אִיתָא – זוֹ מְחִיצָה וְזוֹ הִיא מְחִיצָה מִיבְּעֵי לֵיהּ!

The Gemara asks with regard to Rabba's statement: **And if it is so** that one extend the double posts, this means that he makes a proper partition of increasingly wider double posts in the area surrounding the well, this is equivalent to the partitions of a courtyard, **he,** Rabbi Yehuda, **should have** said: **This is a partition and that is a partition.**

הָכִי קָאָמַר: זוֹ תּוֹרַת מְחִיצָה עָלֶיהָ, וּפִרְצוֹתֶיהָ בְּעֶשֶׂר, וְאֵלּוּ תּוֹרַת פַּסִּין עֲלֵיהֶן, וּפִרְצוֹתֵיהֶן בִּשְׁלֹשׁ עֶשְׂרֵה אַמָּה וּשְׁלִישׁ.

The Gemara answers: No proof can be brought from here, for Rabbi Yehuda **is saying as follows: This** one, the walls of a courtyard, are governed by **the laws of a partition, and** therefore **its breaches** must not be more than **ten** cubits. **Whereas these,** which surround the well, are governed by **the laws of** upright **boards, and their breaches** may be up to **thirteen and a third cubits.** Consequently, only an area of two *beit se'a* can be enclosed in this manner. Therefore, no proof can be brought from this *baraita* to Abaye's dilemma.

בְּעָא מִינֵּיהּ אַבַּיֵי מֵרַבָּה: תֵּל הַמִּתְלַקֵּט עֲשָׂרָה מִתּוֹךְ אַרְבַּע נִידּוֹן מִשּׁוּם דְּיוֹמֵד, אוֹ אֵינוֹ נִידּוֹן מִשּׁוּם דְּיוֹמֵד?

Abaye raised another **dilemma before Rabba: Can a mound that rises** to a height of **ten** handbreadths **within** an area of **four** cubits **serve as a double post or can it not serve as a double post?**[N]

אֲמַר לֵיהּ: תְּנֵיתוּהָ, רַבִּי שִׁמְעוֹן בֶּן אֶלְעָזָר אוֹמֵר: הָיְתָה שָׁם אֶבֶן מְרוּבַּעַת, רוֹאִין, כֹּל שֶׁאִילּוּ תֵּחָלֵק וְיֵשׁ בָּהּ אַמָּה לְכָאן וְאַמָּה לְכָאן – נִידּוֹן מִשּׁוּם דְּיוֹמֵד, וְאִם לָאו – אֵינוֹ נִידּוֹן מִשּׁוּם דְּיוֹמֵד.

Rabba **said to him: We** already **learned this** in the following *baraita*: **Rabbi Shimon ben Elazar says:** If **a square stone**[B] **was present, we see** the stone as if it were altered: **Wherever it can be divided** in such a way that **there would remain a cubit here** in one direction **and a cubit there** at a right angle to it, **it can serve as a double post; but if not, it cannot serve as a double post.**

רַבִּי יִשְׁמָעֵאל בְּנוֹ שֶׁל רַבִּי יוֹחָנָן בֶּן בְּרוֹקָה אוֹמֵר: הָיְתָה שָׁם אֶבֶן עֲגוּלָּה, רוֹאִין, כֹּל שֶׁאִילּוּ תֵּחָקֵק וְתֵחָלֵק וְיֵשׁ בָּהּ אַמָּה לְכָאן וְאַמָּה לְכָאן – נִידּוֹן מִשּׁוּם דְּיוֹמֵד, וְאִם לָאו – אֵינוֹ נִידּוֹן מִשּׁוּם דְּיוֹמֵד.

Rabbi Yishmael, son of Rabbi Yoḥanan ben Beroka, says: If **a round stone**[B] **was present, we see** the stone as if it were altered: **Wherever it could be chiseled** down into a square, **and** then **divided** in such a way that **there would remain a cubit here** in one direction **and a cubit there** at a right angle to it, **it can serve as a double post; but if not, it cannot serve as a double post.** In any case, it is learned from these two statements that anything can serve as a double post if it is of the requisite size and shape.

בְּמַאי קָא מִיפַּלְגִי? מָר סָבַר: חַד רוֹאִין אָמְרִינַן, תְּרֵי רוֹאִין – לָא אָמְרִינַן. וּמָר סָבַר: אֲפִילּוּ תְּרֵי רוֹאִין נַמִי אָמְרִינַן.

With regard to the *baraita* itself, the Gemara asks: **With regard to what do** these two *tanna'im* **disagree?** The Gemara explains that one **Sage,** Rabbi Shimon ben Elazar, **holds** that **we say: We see, once.** However, **we do not say: We see, twice.** That is to say, while the stone can be considered as if it were divided, it cannot also be considered as though it were chiseled down into a square. **And** the other **Sage,** Rabbi Yishmael, son of Rabbi Yoḥanan ben Beroka, **holds** that **we even say: We see,**[N] **twice.** Since a mound is similar to a round stone, it can therefore serve as a double post.

בְּעָא מִינֵּיהּ אַבַּיֵי מֵרַבָּה: חֵיצַת הַקָּנִים, קָנֶה קָנֶה פָּחוֹת מִשְּׁלֹשָׁה נִידּוֹן מִשּׁוּם דְּיוֹמֵד אוֹ לָאו?

Abaye raised another **dilemma before Rabba:** With regard to **a barrier of reeds** in the shape of a double post, where **each reed is less than three** handbreadths apart from the next, so that they are considered connected by the principle of *lavud*, **can it serve as a double post**[H] **or not?**

אֲמַר לֵיהּ: תְּנֵיתוּהָ, הָיָה שָׁם אִילָן אוֹ גָּדֵר אוֹ חֵיצַת הַקָּנִים – נִידּוֹן מִשּׁוּם דְּיוֹמֵד. מַאי לָאו קָנֶה קָנֶה פָּחוֹת מִשְּׁלֹשָׁה!

Rabba **said to him: We** already **learned this** law in a *baraita* that states: If **a tree, or a fence, or a barrier of reeds was present, it serves as a double post. Does** this **not** refer to a barrier of reeds where **each reed is less than three** handbreadths from the next?

לָא, גּוּדְרִיתָא דְּקָנֵי. אִי הָכִי הַיְינוּ אִילָן!

The Gemara refutes this: **No,** it may perhaps refer to **a thicket of reeds**[N] planted close together, forming a kind of post. The Gemara raises a difficulty: **If so, it is** equivalent to **a tree,** and the *tanna* would not repeat the same case twice.

וְאֶלָּא מַאי – קָנֶה קָנֶה פָּחוֹת מִשְּׁלֹשָׁה, הַיְינוּ גָּדֵר! אֶלָּא מַאי אִית לָךְ לְמֵימַר – תְּרֵי גַּוְונֵי גָּדֵר, הָכָא נַמִי: תְּרֵי גַּוְונֵי אִילָן.

The Gemara rejects this argument: **What, then?** Would you say that the *baraita* is referring to a barrier of reeds where **each reed is less than three** handbreadths apart? If so, **it is a fence. Rather, what must you say** is that the *baraita* **teaches two types of fence; here too,** then, you can say that it teaches **two types of tree,** and therefore no proof can be brought from this *baraita*.

NOTES

Double post – דְּיוֹמֵד: The Jerusalem Talmud discusses these issues and resolves all the dilemmas raised by Abaye by saying that in all these cases the object in question can serve as a double post. In addition, it is stated there that even a hole hollowed out of the ground has the status of a double post, if it is ten handbreadths deep and six handbreadths long and wide.

We see – רוֹאִין: According to the conclusion, it is obvious to Rabba that we say: We see, even twice, because the tree has the status of a double post even though it is round. Rabba did not cite a proof from the tree because he wanted to cite the *baraita* that explicitly deals with this issue.

Thicket of reeds – גּוּדְרִיתָא דְּקָנֵי: Some commentaries explain that this refers to a bundle of detached reeds placed at the corner of the well area to serve as a double post (Rambam; *Or Zarua*).

BACKGROUND

Square stone – אֶבֶן מְרוּבַּעַת:

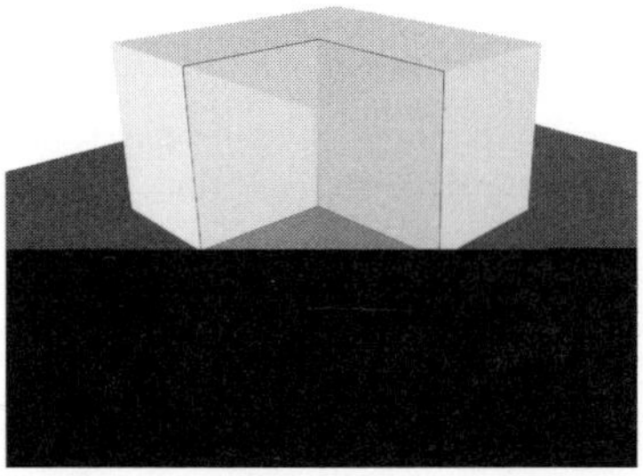

Diagram of a square stone divided so that part of it has the shape of a double post, demonstrating that a square stone can be viewed as if it were altered in such a way that it has the shape of a double post

Round stone – אֶבֶן עֲגוּלָּה:

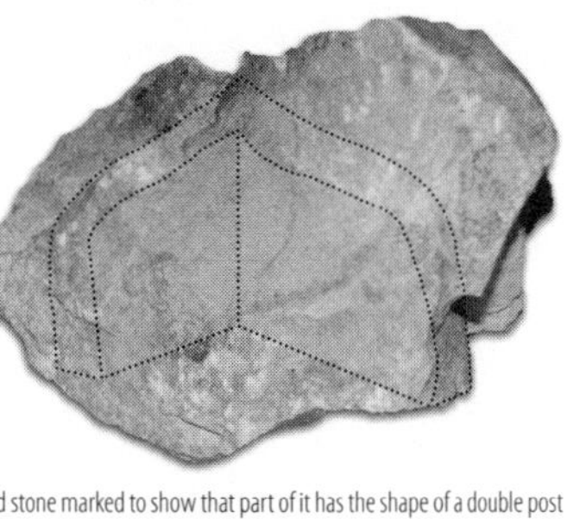

Round stone marked to show that part of it has the shape of a double post

HALAKHA

From what may a double post be made – מִמָּה עוֹשִׂים דְּיוֹמֵד: Various items can be considered to be a double post, such as a large stone, a tree, a bundle of reeds, a mound that rises to ten handbreadths with a diameter of four cubits, or five reeds separated by less than three handbreadths. In each case, we examine the item or the collection of items. If it is possible to divide it up in such a manner that it retains a cubit for each side, it has the status of a double post. Abaye refuted Rabba's proof, but did not prove that Rabba's opinion itself is incorrect. Therefore, Rabba's conclusion is accepted (*Maggid Mishne*; Rambam *Sefer Zemanim*, *Hilkhot Shabbat* 17:28).

איכא דאמרי: גודריתא דקני קא מיבעיא ליה, גודריתא דקני מאי? אמר ליה: תניתוה, היה שם גדר או אילן או חיצת הקנים – נידון משום דיומד, מאי לאו גודריתא דקני?

The Gemara cites an alternative version of the previous discussion: **There are** some **who say** that the question was posed differently, and the **dilemma** Abaye **raised before** Rabba was about whether or not a dense **thicket of reeds** can serve as a double post. Rabba **said to him: We** already **learned this** law in the following *baraita*: If **a tree, or a fence, or a barrier of reeds was present, it can serve as a double post. Does** this **not** refer to **a thicket of reeds?**

לא, קנה קנה פחות משלשה. אי הכי, היינו גדר!

The Gemara refutes this: **No,** it may perhaps refer to a barrier of reeds where **each reed is less than three** handbreadths apart from the next. The Gemara raises a difficulty: **If so, it is** exactly **a fence.**

ואלא מאי – גודריתא דקני, היינו אילן! אלא מאי אית לך למימר –

The Gemara rejects this argument: **What, then?** Would you say that the *baraita* refers to **a thicket of reeds?** If so, **this is a tree. Rather, what must you say is**

Perek **II**
Daf **20** Amud **a**

תרי גווני אילן, הכא נמי – תרי גווני גדר.

that the *baraita* teaches **two types of tree; here too,** then, you can say that it teaches **two types of fence,** and therefore no proof can be brought from this *baraita*.

בעא מיניה אביי מרבה: חצר שראשה נכנס לבין הפסין, מהו לטלטל מתוכה לבין הפסין, ומבין הפסין לתוכה? אמר ליה: מותר.

And Abaye further **inquired of Rabba:** With regard to **a courtyard,** the open **end of which interposed between the boards** surrounding a well,[B] **what is** the law **with regard to carrying from inside** the courtyard **to** the area **between the** upright **boards, and from** the area **between the boards into** the courtyard? Rabba **said to him: It is permitted.**

שתים מאי? אמר ליה: אסור.

Abaye then asked him: And if **two** adjacent courtyards interposed between the boards surrounding a well, **what** is the law? Is it permitted to carry from inside them to the area between the boards, and vice versa? Rabba **said to him** in response: **It is prohibited.**

אמר רב הונא: שתים אסורין, ואפילו עירבו, גזירה שמא יאמרו "עירוב מועיל לבין הפסין". רבא אמר: עירבו מותר.

Rav Huna said: In the case of **two** courtyards, it **is prohibited** to carry, **even if** the residents of the two courtyards **made an** ***eiruv*** together. This is because of **a decree lest they** come to **say** that **an** ***eiruv*** **is effective for** the area **between the** upright **boards. Rava,** however, disagreed and **said: If they made an** ***eiruv*** together,[N] **it is permitted** to carry between the courtyards and the area between the boards, and vice versa; with the preparation of the *eiruv*, the two courtyards are regarded as one.

אמר ליה אביי לרבא, תניא דמסייע לך: חצר שראשה אחד נכנס לבין הפסין – מותר לטלטל מתוכה לבין הפסין, ומבין הפסין לתוכה, אבל שתים – אסור. במה דברים אמורים – שלא עירבו, אבל עירבו – מותרין.

Abaye said to Rava: What **was taught** in a *baraita* **supports your** opinion, for the *baraita* states: In the case of **a courtyard, one end of which interposes between the** upright **boards**[NH] surrounding a well, **it is permitted to carry from inside** the courtyard **to** the area **between the** upright **boards, and from** the area **between the** upright **boards into** the courtyard, **but** if there were **two** adjacent courtyards, **this is prohibited. With regard to which case was this statement made?** The statement applies **where** the residents of the two courtyards **did not make an** ***eiruv*** together; **but if they made an** ***eiruv*** together, it **is permitted** to carry between the courtyards and the area between the boards, and vice versa.

HALAKHA

A courtyard, one end of which interposes between the boards – חצר שראשה אחד נכנס לבין הפסין: If a courtyard interposes into the area between the upright boards surrounding a well, one may carry from the courtyard into the area between the upright boards and from the area between the upright boards into the courtyard. However, if there are two courtyards it is prohibited, unless the residents established a joining of courtyards [*eiruv*]. This ruling is in accordance with Rava, since a straightforward reading of the *baraita* supports him (*Maggid Mishne*; Rambam *Sefer Zemanim*, *Hilkhot Shabbat* 17:34).

BACKGROUND

Courtyards and upright boards around a well – חצרות ופסי בירות: The image below illustrates a case in which there are two courtyards that interpose into the area between the upright boards surrounding a well, and the wall between the courtyards is breached. In this way, the courtyards become joined.

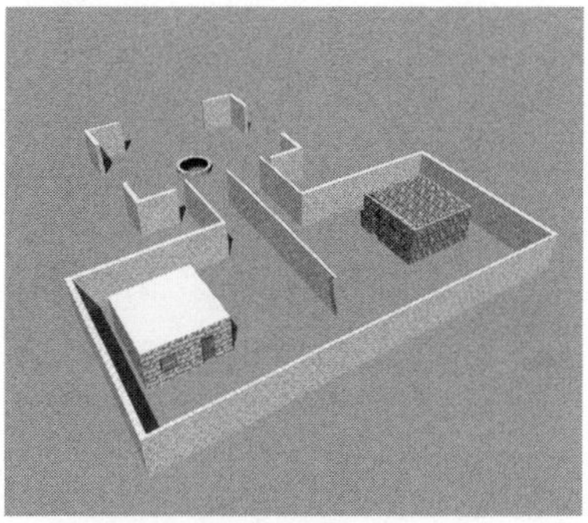

Courtyards with a breached wall between them

NOTES

If they made a joint *eiruv* – עירבו: The Ra'avad explains that the question refers to two courtyards where the joining of courtyards [*eiruv*] was accomplished in the manner of joint alleyways [*shitufei mevo'ot*], through the open space between the boards. This practice was prohibited because it looks like courtyards merging into a breached alleyway. The phrase: Later became joined, which appears a few lines later in the Gemara, means that a proper joining of courtyards [*eiruv*] was later made between the two courtyards through a different entrance directly connecting them.

A courtyard, one end of which interposes between the upright boards – חצר שראשה אחד נכנס לבין הפסין: In the Jerusalem Talmud, a different opinion is cited: One is permitted to carry from the courtyard to the area between the upright boards, but it is prohibited to carry from the area between the upright boards to the courtyard. The Ritva explains the rationale of the permission to carry inside the area surrounded by the upright boards without having to establish a joining of courtyards [*eiruv*]. Since the area between the boards is not a place of actual human residence, there is no need to establish an *eiruv* between the courtyard and the area between the upright boards.

לֵימָא תֶּיהֱוֵי תְּיוּבְתָּא דְּרַב הוּנָא! אָמַר לָךְ רַב הוּנָא: הָתָם דְּהָדְרָן וְעָרְבָן.

The Gemara asks: **Shall we say that this is a refutation** of the opinion **of Rav Huna,** for the *baraita* explicitly contradicts his opinion? The Gemara rejects this argument: **Rav Huna** could have **said to you: There,** the *baraita* is dealing with a case where the two courtyards **later became joined** by means of the wall that separated them being breached, and it is clear to all that it is a single courtyard, so that there is no concern that people will say that an *eiruv* is effective for the area between the boards.

בְּעָא מִינֵּיהּ אַבַּיֵי מֵרַבָּה: יָבְשׁוּ מַיִם בַּשַּׁבָּת מַהוּ? אֲמַר לֵיהּ: כְּלוּם נַעֲשֵׂית מְחִיצָּה אֶלָּא בִּשְׁבִיל מַיִם, מַיִם אֵין כָּאן – מְחִיצָּה אֵין כָּאן.

Abaye asked Rabba yet another question: If **the water** in the cistern **dried up on Shabbat, what is** the law? Is it still permitted to carry between the boards? Rabba **said to him:** The boards **are considered** a valid **partition only on account of the water;** since **there is no** longer any **water here, there is** also **no** longer a valid **partition here.**

בָּעֵי רָבִין: יָבְשׁוּ מַיִם בַּשַּׁבָּת וּבָאוּ בַּשַּׁבָּת מַהוּ? אֲמַר לֵיהּ אַבַּיֵי: יָבְשׁוּ בַּשַּׁבָּת לָא תִּיבָּעֵי לָךְ. דְּבָעֵי מִינֵּיהּ דְּמָר וּפָשֵׁיט לִי דַּאֲסִיר.

Ravin raised a dilemma: If the water in the well **dried up on Shabbat, and** then **on** the same **Shabbat** it rained and other water **came**[N] in its place, **what is** the law? Is the original allowance to carry restored? **Abaye said to him:** The case where the water **dried up on Shabbat**[H] **should not be a dilemma for you, for I** already **raised this dilemma before my Master,** Rabba, **and he resolved for me that it is prohibited to** carry in the enclosed area.

בָּאוּ נַמִי לָא תִּיבָּעֵי לָךְ, דַּהֲוָה לֵיהּ מְחִיצָּה הָעֲשׂוּיָה בַּשַּׁבָּת, וְתַנְיָא: כָּל מְחִיצָּה הָעֲשׂוּיָה בַּשַּׁבָּת, בֵּין בְּשׁוֹגֵג בֵּין בְּמֵזִיד, בֵּין בְּאוֹנֶס בֵּין בְּרָצוֹן – שְׁמָהּ מְחִיצָּה.

The case where other water **came** on Shabbat[H] **should also not be a dilemma for you, for** this **is** a case of **a partition erected on Shabbat, and it was** already **taught** in a *baraita*: **Any partition erected on Shabbat,**[H] **whether** it was erected **unwittingly, or whether intentionally, whether by unavoidable accident, or whether willingly, it is called** a valid **partition.** The fact that it was erected in a prohibited manner, in violation of prohibitions related to building, does not negate its effectiveness.

וְלָאו אִיתְּמַר עֲלָהּ, אָמַר רַב נַחְמָן: לֹא שָׁנוּ אֶלָּא לִזְרוֹק, אֲבָל לְטַלְטֵל – לֹא!

Ravin raised a difficulty: **Was it not stated with regard** to this *halakha* that **Rav Naḥman said: They only taught** that such a partition is called a partition as a stringency; it is prohibited by Torah law **to throw** objects from an area enclosed by such a partition into the public domain and vice versa, **but to carry in it** as a full-fledged private domain is **not** permitted by the Sages?

כִּי אִיתְּמַר דְּרַב נַחְמָן – אַמֵּזִיד אִיתְּמַר.

The Gemara refutes this objection: **Rav Naḥman's statement applies** only in a case where the partition was erected **intentionally.** Since the partition was erected intentionally on Shabbat, the Sages imposed a penalty that it is prohibited to carry within the enclosed area. However, in the case of a partition that was erected unwittingly or that arose by itself, no such penalty was imposed, and it is permitted to carry there.

אָמַר רַבִּי אֶלְעָזָר: הַזּוֹרֵק לְבֵין פַּסֵּי הַבֵּירָאוֹת – חַיָּיב. פְּשִׁיטָא! אִי לָאו מְחִיצָּה הִיא הֵיכִי מִשְׁתְּרֵי לֵיהּ לְמַלְאוֹת?!

Rabbi Elazar said: One who throws an object from the public domain **into** the area **between the** upright **boards**[H] **surrounding a well is liable.** The Gemara asks: This is **obvious,** for **were it not** a valid **partition, how could he be permitted to draw** water from the well? This shows that it is a full-fledged private domain.

לָא צְרִיכָא, דַּעֲבַד כְּעֵין פַּסֵּי בֵּירָאוֹת בִּרְשׁוּת הָרַבִּים, וְזָרַק לְתוֹכָהּ – חַיָּיב.

The Gemara answers: Rabbi Elazar's ruling **is only necessary** to teach that in the case **where one arrange** an enclosure **similar to the** upright **boards surrounding a well in the public domain,** in a place where there was no well, **and threw** an object **into it** from the public domain, **he is liable.**

הָא נַמִי פְּשִׁיטָא! אִי לָאו דִּבְעָלְמָא מְחִיצָּה הִיא – גַּבֵּי בּוֹר הֵיכִי מִשְׁתְּרֵי לֵיהּ לְטַלְטוֹלֵי? לָא צְרִיכָא, אַף עַל גַּב דְּקָא בָּקְעִי בָּהּ רַבִּים.

The Gemara raises a difficulty: **Isn't this obvious as well?** As, **were it not** regarded as **a partition in general, how could he be permitted to carry in** the case of **a cistern?** The Gemara explains: **It is only necessary** to teach you that **even though** such a partition does not bar entry and **many** people **pass through it,** it is nonetheless considered a partition in regard to Shabbat.

וּמַאי קָא מַשְׁמַע לָן – דְּלָא אָתוּ רַבִּים וּמְבַטְּלִי מְחִיצָּתָא, הָא אָמַר רַבִּי אֶלְעָזָר חֲדָא זִימְנָא!

The Gemara asks: **And what is he teaching us** by this statement, **that the** passage of **many** people **does not come and negate the** effectiveness of **a partition? But Rabbi Elazar stated** this idea **once** before.

NOTES

Other water came on Shabbat – בָּאוּ מַיִם בַּשַּׁבָּת: According to the Rambam, the *Me'iri*, and the Ritva, even if there was no water whatsoever at the onset of Shabbat, and the well filled with water on Shabbat itself, it is permitted to carry between the upright boards.

HALAKHA

Water dried up on Shabbat – יָבְשׁוּ מַיִם בַּשַּׁבָּת: If the water in a well dries up on Shabbat, it becomes prohibited to carry in the area between the upright boards surrounding the well, in accordance with Rabba (Rambam *Sefer Zemanim, Hilkhot Shabbat* 17:34).

Other water came on Shabbat – בָּאוּ מַיִם בַּשַּׁבָּת: If a cistern filled with water on Shabbat, one may carry in the area between the boards, even if the cistern was dry when Shabbat began (Rambam *Sefer Zemanim, Hilkhot Shabbat* 17:34).

A partition erected on Shabbat – מְחִיצָּה הָעֲשׂוּיָה בַּשַּׁבָּת: It is permitted to carry in an area surrounded by a partition that was unwittingly erected on Shabbat. If the partition was intentionally erected on Shabbat, it is indeed considered a partition, but only for matters of halakhic stringency. Consequently, it is prohibited to carry from an area enclosed by such a partition into the public domain and vice versa, and the Sages prohibited carrying within the area as well. This rule is in accordance with Rav Naḥman's understanding of the *baraita* (*Shulḥan Arukh, Oraḥ Ḥayyim* 362:3).

One who throws into the area between the boards – הַזּוֹרֵק לְבֵין פַּסֵּי הַבֵּירָאוֹת: One may not throw an object from the public domain into the area between upright boards, even if there is no well and many people pass through there, in accordance with the opinion of Rabbi Elazar (Rambam *Sefer Zemanim, Hilkhot Shabbat* 17:33).

דִּתְנַן, רַבִּי יְהוּדָה אוֹמֵר: אִם הָיְתָה דֶּרֶךְ רְשׁוּת הָרַבִּים מַפְסַקְתָּן, יְסַלְּקֶנָּה לַצְּדָדִין, וַחֲכָמִים אוֹמְרִים: אֵינוֹ צָרִיךְ. רַבִּי יוֹחָנָן וְרַבִּי אֶלְעָזָר דְּאָמְרִי תַּרְוַיְיהוּ: כָּאן הוֹדִיעֲךָ כֹּחָן שֶׁל מְחִיצּוֹת.

As we learned in a mishna: **Rabbi Yehuda says** the following with regard to the upright boards surrounding a well: **If the path of the public domain** passes through the area of the wells and the posts and **obstructs them, he** must **divert it to the sides,** or else the partition is invalid. **And the Rabbis say: He need not** divert the path of the public domain, for even if many people pass through there, the partition is valid. With regard to this mishna, **Rabbi Yoḥanan and Rabbi Elazar both said: Here,** the Rabbis **informed you of the strength of partitions.** Therefore, we see that Rabbi Elazar already expressed his opinion that the validity of a partition is not canceled by the passage of many people through it.

אִי מֵהָתָם – הֲוָה אָמִינָא: כָּאן – וְלָא סְבִירָא לֵיהּ, קָא מַשְׁמַע לַן: כָּאן – וּסְבִירָא לֵיהּ.

The Gemara answers: **If** it was derived **from there** alone, **I would have said** that what Rabbi Elazar meant is that **here** the Rabbis informed you of the strength of partitions, **but he,** Rabbi Elazar, **does not agree** with them. **He** therefore **teaches us** in his present ruling that what he meant is that **here** they informed you of this law **and he agrees** with them.

וְלֵימָא הָא וְלָא בָּעֵי הַךְ! חֲדָא מִכְּלָל חֲבֵירְתָּהּ אִיתְּמַר.

The Gemara asks: If so, **let** Rabbi Elazar **say this** ruling that one who throws an object into the area enclosed by upright boards is liable, **and he would not have need to** make his **other** comment that here the Rabbis informed you of the strength of partitions. The Gemara answers: Rabbi Elazar did not in fact make two statements, but rather **one was stated by inference from the other.**[N] He only made one of these statements explicitly; the other was reported by his students in his name based on an inference from what he had said.

"מוּתָּר לְהַקְרִיב לַבְּאֵר וכו'". תְּנַן הָתָם: לֹא יַעֲמוֹד אָדָם בִּרְשׁוּת הָרַבִּים וְיִשְׁתֶּה בִּרְשׁוּת הַיָּחִיד, בִּרְשׁוּת הַיָּחִיד וְיִשְׁתֶּה בִּרְשׁוּת הָרַבִּים, אֶלָּא אִם כֵּן מַכְנִיס רֹאשׁוֹ וְרוּבּוֹ לַמָּקוֹם שֶׁהוּא שׁוֹתֶה.

We learned in the mishna: **It is permitted to bring** the upright boards **closer to the well,** provided that the enclosed area is large enough for a cow to stand in and drink, with its head and most of its body inside the partitioned space. Similarly, **we learned there** in a mishna: **A person may not stand in a public domain and drink in the private domain,** and likewise he may not stand **in the private domain and drink in a public domain, unless he brings his head and most of his** body **into the place where he is drinking.**

NOTES

One was stated by inference from the other – חֲדָא מִכְּלָל חֲבֵירְתָּהּ אִיתְּמַר: There are different opinions as to which statement was made by Rabbi Elazar himself and which statement was inferred from his words. Some commentaries indicate that Rabbi Elazar explicitly stated the law concerning one who throws an object from the public domain into the area between the upright boards surrounding a well. His students inferred from it the case of a public thoroughfare passing through the boards (Rashba). Other commentaries teach that the statement: Here the Sages informed you, was Rabbi Elazar's original ruling, from which his students inferred the law governing the case of one who throws an object into the area between the upright boards surrounding a well (Maharshal). However Rabbi Elazar's opinion is understood, it seems that Rabbi Yoḥanan, cited along with Rabbi Elazar on the statement: Here the Rabbis taught about the strength of partitions, does not agree with the Rabbis. Elsewhere, he maintains that an inferior partition through which many people pass is an invalid partition (*Me'iri*).

Perek **II**
Daf **20** Amud **b**

וְכֵן בַּגַּת.

And the law is **likewise in a winepress** with respect to tithes. As long as one's head and most of his body is in the winepress, he may drink from the wine without first separating tithes because drinking wine in a winepress is considered incidental drinking, which does not require tithing. The activity of harvesting and ingathering grapes is not considered completed as long as the grapes are in the winepress, since the grapes are still intended for making wine. Consequently, at this stage one may consume the produce in a casual, incidental manner. Once the work has been completed, however, one must tithe the produce before consuming any of it.

גַּבֵּי אָדָם הָא אָמַר דְּבָעֵי רֹאשׁוֹ וְרוּבּוֹ; גַּבֵּי פָּרָה, מִי בָּעֵינַן לַהּ רֹאשָׁהּ וְרוּבָּהּ אוֹ לָא?

The Gemara clarifies several laws related to this issue: **With regard to a person, it was said** in connection to these laws **that it is necessary** that **his head and most of his** body be inside the domain from which he is drinking. However, a question may be raised **with regard to a cow** standing in a public domain and drinking from a private domain, or vice versa: **Is it necessary** that **its head and most of its** body[N] be inside the domain from which it is drinking, **or not?**

כָּל הֵיכָא דְּקָא נָקֵיט מָנָא וְלָא נָקֵיט לַהּ – לָא תִּיבָּעֵי לָךְ דְּבָעֵי רֹאשָׁהּ וְרוּבָּהּ מִלְּגָיו. כִּי תִּיבָּעֵי לָךְ – הֵיכָא דְּנָקֵיט מָנָא וְנָקֵיט לַהּ, מַאי?

The Gemara clarifies: **Wherever** one **holds the bucket** from which the cow is drinking **but does not hold** the animal, there **should not be a dilemma for you,** for **it is** certainly **necessary** for **its head and most of its** body to be **inside,** as the cow might move backward and pull the bucket with it, causing him to carry it from one domain to the other. **Where there should be a dilemma for you is where he holds the bucket and** also **holds** the animal. **What** is the law in such a case?

NOTES

Its head and most of its body – רֹאשׁוֹ וְרוּבּוֹ: Rashi explains that the Gemara's concern is that one might carry the bucket from one domain to the other while the animal drinks. However, it is explained in the Jerusalem Talmud that the concern is that the water passes from one domain to another inside the body of the person or animal.

אֲמַר לֵיהּ: תְּנֵיתוּהָ, וּבִלְבַד שֶׁתְּהֵא הַפָּרָה רֹאשָׁהּ וְרוּבָּהּ מִבִּפְנִים וְשׁוֹתָה. מַאי לָאו דְּנָקֵיט לָהּ וְנָקֵיט מָנָא! לָא, דְּנָקֵיט מָנָא וְלָא נָקֵיט לָהּ.

He said to him: We already **learned** a resolution to this dilemma, for we have learned in the mishna: It is permitted to bring the upright boards closer to the well, **provided that** the enclosed area is large enough for **a cow** to stand in, with **its head and most of its** body **inside** the partitioned space **and drink. Does this not** refer even to a case **where** one **holds** the cow **and** also **holds the bucket?** The Gemara rejects this argument: **No,** this may refer exclusively to the case **where he holds the bucket but does not hold** the animal.

וְכִי נָקֵיט מָנָא וְלָא נָקֵיט לָהּ מִי שָׁרֵי? וְהָתַנְיָא: לֹא יְמַלֵּא אָדָם מַיִם וְיִתֵּן בַּשַּׁבָּת לִפְנֵי בְּהֶמְתּוֹ, אֲבָל מְמַלֵּא הוּא וְשׁוֹפֵךְ, וְהִיא שׁוֹתָה מֵאֵילֶיהָ!

The Gemara raises a difficulty: **And where he holds the bucket but does not hold** the animal, **is it permitted** to give his animal to drink in such a fashion? **Wasn't it taught** in the following *baraita*: **A person may not fill** a bucket with **water and hold** it **before his animal on Shabbat; but he may fill** it **and pour** it **out** into a trough, **and it,** i.e., the animal, **drinks of its own accord?** Consequently, we see that it is prohibited to give an animal to drink from a bucket if he does not hold the animal.

הָא אִתְּמַר עֲלָהּ, אָמַר אַבַּיֵי: הָכָא בְּאֵבוּס הָעוֹמֵד בִּרְשׁוּת הָרַבִּים, גָּבוֹהַּ עֲשָׂרָה טְפָחִים וְרוֹחַב אַרְבָּעָה וְרֹאשׁוֹ אֶחָד נִכְנָס לְבֵין הַפַּסִּין,

The Gemara refutes this: **Wasn't it stated with regard to this** *baraita* that **Abaye said: Here** we are dealing with a cow standing inside a house with windows open to the public domain, eating from **a manger** or trough **that stands in the public domain** that is **ten handbreadths high and four** handbreadths **wide,** i.e., it constitutes a private domain, **and one end** of this manger **interposes into** the area **between the** upright **boards** surrounding a well?[N]

גְּזֵירָה דִּילְמָא חָזֵי לֵיהּ לְאֵבוּס דְּמִקַּלְקַל וְאָתֵי לְתַקּוֹנֵיהּ וּדְרָא לֵיהּ לְדַוְולָא בַּהֲדֵיהּ, וְקָא מַפֵּיק מֵרְשׁוּת הַיָּחִיד לִרְשׁוּת הָרַבִּים.

In such a case, it is prohibited to fill a bucket with water in the area enclosed by the upright boards and hold it before his animal, unless the animal is within the enclosed area. This is a rabbinical **decree, lest one see that the manger was damaged** on the side in the public domain **and go to fix it, and he might take the bucket with him,** thereby **carrying** it **from the private domain to the public domain.** Rather, he must pour out the water into the manger, so that it reaches the animal on its own.

וְכִי הַאי גַּוְונָא מִי מִיחַיַּיב? וְהָאָמַר רַב סַפְרָא, אָמַר רַבִּי אַמִי, אָמַר רַבִּי יוֹחָנָן: הַמְפַנֶּה חֲפָצָיו מִזָּוִית לְזָוִית וְנִמְלַךְ עֲלֵיהֶן וְהוֹצִיאָן – פָּטוּר, שֶׁלֹּא הָיְתָה עֲקִירָה מִשָּׁעָה רִאשׁוֹנָה לְכָךְ!

The Gemara asks: Even if he carried the bucket into the public domain, **would he be liable in such a case? Didn't Rav Safra say** that **Rabbi Ami said** that **Rabbi Yoḥanan said:** With regard to **one who transfers objects from corner to corner** in a house, **and changed his mind about them** while carrying them **and carried them out**[H] to the public domain, **he is exempt because the lifting at the first moment was not for that** purpose of carrying out to a different domain; when he picked them up, he intended merely to move them around his house. Here too, then, one should not be liable, since when he picked up the bucket he did not intend from the outset to carry it into the public domain; accordingly, there is no room for such a decree.

אֶלָּא זִמְנִין דְּמִתַּקֵּן לֵיהּ וַהֲדַר מְעַיֵּיל לֵיהּ, וְקָא מְעַיֵּיל מֵרְשׁוּת הָרַבִּים לִרְשׁוּת הַיָּחִיד.

Rather, say that the decree is due to a different concern, that **at times one would fix** the manger **and** then **bring** the bucket **back in again,** thereby **carrying from the public domain into the private domain.** In this case one picks up the bucket from the outset with the intention of carrying it from a public domain into a private domain.

אִיכָּא דְּאָמְרִי: גַּבֵּי אָדָם – הָא קָאָמְרִינַן דְּסַגִּי לֵיהּ בְּרֹאשׁוֹ וְרוּבּוֹ. גַּבֵּי פָּרָה מִי סַגִּי לָהּ בְּרֹאשָׁהּ וְרוּבָּהּ, אוֹ לָא?

Some say a different version of the previous discussion. **With regard to a person, we said that it is sufficient** if **his head and most of his** body are inside the domain from which he is drinking. But a question may be raised **with regard to a cow** standing in a public domain and drinking from a private domain, or vice versa: **Is it sufficient** if **its head and most of its** body are inside the domain from which it is drinking, **or not?** Perhaps all of the cow must be in that domain.

הֵיכָא דְּנָקֵיט מָנָא וְנָקֵיט לָהּ – לָא תִּיבָּעֵי לָךְ דְּסַגִּי לָהּ בְּרֹאשָׁהּ וְרוּבָּהּ, אֶלָּא כִּי תִּיבָּעֵי לָךְ דְּנָקֵיט מָנָא וְלָא נָקֵיט לָהּ, מַאי?

The Gemara clarifies the question. The case **where** one **holds the bucket** from which the cow is drinking **and** also **holds** the animal **should not be a dilemma for you,** as **it is** certainly **enough** if **its head and most of its** body are in the domain. **Rather,** the case **where** there **should be a dilemma for you is where he holds the bucket but does not hold** the animal. **What** is the *halakha* in such a case?

NOTES

A manger that interposes into the area between the upright boards – אֵבוּס בֵּין הַפַּסִּים: Rashi explains that the animal is standing in a private domain, while the feeding trough is located partly in the public domain and partly in the area between the upright boards surrounding a well. Most commentaries, however, maintain that this is a case where an animal is standing in the public domain and eating from a manger, one end of which interposes into the area between the upright boards surrounding a well (see *Tosafot*; Rashba; Ritva).

HALAKHA

One who changed his mind and carried out – נִמְלַךְ לְהוֹצִיא: If one picks up an object in a private domain intending to put it down somewhere else in that domain, but then decides to carry it out to the public domain, he is exempt from liability according to Torah law, because the initial lifting up of the object was not done for this purpose, as stated by Rabbi Yoḥanan. However, this is prohibited by rabbinic decree (Rambam *Sefer Zemanim*, *Hilkhot Shabbat* 13:12).

אֲמַר לֵיהּ: תְּנֵיתוּהָ, וּבִלְבַד שֶׁתְּהֵא פָּרָה רֹאשָׁהּ וְרוּבָּהּ מִבִּפְנִים וְשׁוֹתָה. מַאי לָאו דְּנָקֵיט מָנָא וְלָא נָקֵיט לָהּ! לָא, דְּנָקֵיט מָנָא וְנָקֵיט לָהּ.

He said to him: We already **learned** a resolution to this dilemma in the mishna: It is permitted to bring the upright boards closer to the well, **provided that** the enclosed area is large enough for **a cow** to stand in, with **its head and most of** its body **inside** the partitioned space, **and drink. Doesn't this** refer even to a case **where** one **holds the bucket but does not hold** the animal? The Gemara rejects this argument: **No,** this may refer only to the case **where he holds the bucket and** also **holds** the animal.

וְהָכִי נַמִי מִסְתַּבְּרָא, דְּאִי נָקֵיט מָנָא וְלָא נָקֵיט לָהּ מִי שָׁרֵי?! וְהָתַנְיָא: לֹא יְמַלֵּא אָדָם מַיִם וְיִתֵּן לִפְנֵי בְהֶמְתּוֹ, אֲבָל מְמַלֵּא וְשׁוֹפֵךְ וְהִיא שׁוֹתָה מֵאֵילֶיהָ!

The Gemara comments: **So too, it is reasonable** to say this, **for if one holds the bucket but does not hold** the animal, **is it** in fact **permitted** to give his animal to drink in such a fashion? **Wasn't it taught** in a *baraita*: **A person may not fill** a bucket with **water and hold** it **before his animal** on Shabbat. **But he may fill** it **and pour** it **out** into a trough, **and** the animal **drinks of its own accord.**

הָא אִיתְּמַר עֲלַהּ, אָמַר אַבַּיֵי: הָכָא בְּאֵבוּס הָעוֹמֵד בִּרְשׁוּת הָרַבִּים גָּבוֹהַּ עֲשָׂרָה טְפָחִים וְרוֹחַב אַרְבָּעָה, וְרֹאשׁוֹ נִכְנָס לְבֵין הַפַּסִּין, דִּזְמְנִין דְּחָזֵי לֵיהּ לְאֵבוּס דְּמִקַּלְקַל וְאָתֵי לְתַקּוֹנֵיהּ, וְדָרֵי לֵיהּ לְדַוְולָא בַּהֲדֵיהּ וְקָא מַפֵּיק מֵרְשׁוּת הַיָּחִיד לִרְשׁוּת הָרַבִּים.

The Gemara refutes this argument: **Wasn't it stated with regard to this** *baraita* that **Abaye said: Here,** we are dealing with **a manger that stands in the public domain,** and it is **ten handbreadths high and four** handbreadths **wide,** i.e., it constitutes a private domain, **and one end** of the manger **interposes into** the area **between the** upright **boards** surrounding a well, and the animal is standing at the other end in the public domain. In such a case, it is prohibited to fill a bucket with water in the area enclosed by the boards and hold it before his animal, unless the animal is within the enclosed area. This is a rabbinical decree, lest **at times one see that the manger was damaged** on the side in the public domain **and go to fix it and take the bucket with him,** thereby **carrying** it **from the private domain into the public domain.**

וְכִי הַאי גַּוְונָא מִי מִיחַיַּיב? וְהָאָמַר רַב סַפְרָא, אָמַר רַבִּי אַמִי, אָמַר רַבִּי יוֹחָנָן: הַמְפַנֶּה חֲפָצָיו מִזָּוִית לְזָוִית וְנִמְלַךְ עֲלֵיהֶן וְהוֹצִיאָן – פָּטוּר, שֶׁלֹּא הָיְתָה עֲקִירָה מִשָּׁעָה רִאשׁוֹנָה לְכָךְ!

The Gemara asks: **But would he be liable in such a case? Didn't Rav Safra say** that **Rabbi Ami said** that **Rabbi Yoḥanan said:** With regard to **one who transfers objects from corner to corner** in a house, **and changed his mind about them** while carrying them **and took them out** to the public domain, **he is exempt because the lifting at the first moment was not for that** purpose of carrying out to a different domain; when he picked them up, he intended merely to move them around his house. Here too, then, he should not be liable, since when he picked up the bucket he did not intend from the outset to carry it into the public domain; accordingly, there is no room for such a decree.

אֶלָּא, זִמְנִין דִּמְתַקֵּן לֵיהּ וַהֲדַר מְעַיֵּיל לֵיהּ, וְקָא מְעַיֵּיל לֵיהּ מֵרְשׁוּת הָרַבִּים לִרְשׁוּת הַיָּחִיד.

Rather, we must say that the decree is due to a different concern, that **at times one would fix** the manger **and** then **bring** the bucket **back in again, carrying from the public domain into the private domain.** In this case, he picks up the bucket with the intention of carrying it from a public domain into a private domain. In any case, no proof can be brought from this source.

תָּא שְׁמַע: גָּמָל שֶׁרֹאשׁוֹ וְרוּבּוֹ מִבִּפְנִים – אוֹבְסִין אוֹתוֹ מִבִּפְנִים. וְהָא אִיבּוּס כְּמַאן דְּנָקֵיט מָנָא וְנָקֵיט לָהּ דָּמְיָא, וְקָא בָּעֵינַן רֹאשָׁהּ וְרוּבָּהּ!

The Gemara cites a different proof. **Come and hear** the following *baraita*: **A camel whose head and most of its** body **are inside** a private domain **may be force-fed from inside** the private domain. **Now, force-feeding is like** the case where **he holds the bucket and** also **holds** the animal, as one cannot force-feed an animal without holding it by its neck, **and** nonetheless **we require** that **its head and most of its** body be inside the domain where it is eating.

אָמַר רַב אַחָא בַּר רַב הוּנָא, אָמַר רַב שֵׁשֶׁת: שָׁאנֵי גָּמָל הוֹאִיל וְצַוָּארוֹ אָרוֹךְ.

Rav Aḥa bar Rav Huna said that **Rav Sheshet said: A camel is different, as since its neck is long,** its head and most of its body must be inside; otherwise it could stretch its neck into the public domain, and the one feeding it might come to carry the bucket from the private domain into the public domain.[H] In the case of other animals, however, there is no reason for such stringency.

תָּא שְׁמַע: בְּהֵמָה שֶׁרֹאשָׁהּ וְרוּבָּהּ בִּפְנִים – אוֹבְסִין אוֹתָהּ מִבִּפְנִים. וְהָא אִבּוּס כְּמַאן דְּנָקֵיט מָנָא וְנָקֵיט לָהּ וְקָא בָּעֵינַן רֹאשׁוֹ וְרוּבּוֹ! מַאי בְּהֵמָה נַמִי דְּקָתָנֵי – גָּמָל.

The Gemara attempts to cite yet another proof. **Come** and **hear** the following *baraita*: **An animal whose head and most of its** body **were inside** a private domain **may be force-fed from inside** the private domain. **Now,** as stated above, **force-feeding is like** the case where **he holds the bucket and** also **holds** the animal, **and** nonetheless **we require** that **its head and most of its** body be inside the domain where it is eating. The Gemara refutes this argument: **What is this animal that is taught** in this *baraita*? It is **also a camel.**[N]

HALAKHA

Feeding an animal between two domains – הַאֲכָלַת בְּהֵמָה בֵּין שְׁתֵּי רְשׁוּיוֹת: If an animal is standing with its head and most of its body in a private domain, one is permitted to feed it, even if the entire animal cannot enter the private domain. The *halakha* follows this opinion because according to the first version it is obvious, and according to the second version the issue remains an unresolved problem. The *halakha* is decided according to the straightforward conclusion (*Maggid Mishne*; Rambam *Sefer Zemanim, Hilkhot Shabbat* 17:29).

NOTES

An animal and a camel – בְּהֵמָה וְגָמָל: The distance between the upright boards and the well is equal to the head and most of the body of a cow. In the Jerusalem Talmud it is stated that this distance is based on the size of a cow even for all other animals, from a small kid, whose entire body fits into the area, to a camel, most of whose body cannot fit into that space.

The author of *Ge'on Ya'akov* points out that the *halakha* should differentiate between a camel and other animals. Even though the laws are equated in this context, it is only for the purpose of refuting the absolute proof. The legal distinction, however, is reasonable and the law governing a camel is different.

NOTES

Were these two *baraitot* taught next to each other – מִידֵּי גַּבֵּי הֲדָדֵי תַּנְיָא: Rashi teaches that since the different *baraitot* were taught in different schools, such as the school of Rabbi Ḥiyya, the school of Rabbi Oshaya, and numerous others, it is impossible to prove the meaning of one *baraita* from the style of another *baraita* that was taught in a different school.

To Festival pilgrims – לְעוֹלֵי רְגָלִים: In the Jerusalem Talmud, a dispute among the *amora'im* is cited on this issue. Some Sages rule that the permission to carry in the area surrounded by upright boards around a well applies only to Festival pilgrims. Other Sages state that the permission is granted because of the Festival pilgrims, but that it applies to everyone. Yet other Sages teach that the allowance applies only during the period of Festival pilgrimage. It has been suggested that the rationale for the use of upright boards surrounding a well, which constitute an inferior partition, applies only for the purpose of a mitzva. Since Festival pilgrims bring many animals with them for their sacrifices, they require a large quantity of water. In Eretz Yisrael during the periods of pilgrimages, water was generally found only in cisterns and wells (Rabbeinu Yehonatan).

HALAKHA

The permission of upright boards surrounding a well – הֶיתֵּר פַּסֵּי בֵירָאוֹת: The permission to carry where upright boards surround a well was initially instituted so that Festival pilgrims could give their animals water to drink, rather than so that people could drink (Rambam *Sefer Zemanim*, *Hilkhot Shabbat* 17:30).

וְהָתַנְיָא בְּהֵמָה וְהָתַנְיָא גָּמָל!

The Gemara objects: **Wasn't it taught** as **animal** in one *baraita*, **and wasn't it taught** as **camel** in the other *baraita*? The implication is that this law applies not only to camels, but to other animals as well.

מִידֵּי גַּבֵּי הֲדָדֵי תַּנְיָא?! תַּנְיָא נַמִי הָכִי: רַבִּי אֱלִיעֶזֶר אוֹסֵר בְּגָמָל, הוֹאִיל וְצַוָּארוֹ אָרוֹךְ.

The Gemara answers: **Were** these two *baraitot* **taught next to each other?**[N] Had both of these *baraitot* been taught together, we would indeed expect the *tanna* not to teach the same law using different formulations. However, since these two *baraitot* come from different sources, it is possible that one of the *tanna'im* referred to a camel with the generic term animal, and hence no proof can be brought from here. **This** same idea that a camel is different **was also taught** in another *baraita*: **Rabbi Eliezer prohibits** this **in the case of a camel, since its neck is long.**

אָמַר רַבִּי יִצְחָק בַּר אַדָּא: לֹא הוּתְּרוּ פַּסֵּי בֵירָאוֹת אֶלָּא לְעוֹלֵי רְגָלִים בִּלְבַד. וְהָתַנְיָא: לֹא הוּתְּרוּ פַּסֵּי בֵירָאוֹת אֶלָּא לְגַבֵּי בְּהֵמָה בִּלְבַד! מַאי בְּהֵמָה – בֶּהֱמַת עוֹלֵי רְגָלִים, אֲבָל אָדָם

Rabbi Yitzḥak bar Adda said: Upright **boards surrounding wells were only permitted to Festival pilgrims.**[N] The Gemara raises a difficulty: **Wasn't it taught** in a *baraita* that **boards surrounding wells were permitted only for cattle?**[H] The Gemara answers: **What is** the **cattle** mentioned here? It means **the cattle of festival pilgrims. However, a person**

Perek **II**
Daf **21** Amud **a**

NOTES

Must climb up and climb down – מְטַפֵּס וְעוֹלֶה מְטַפֵּס וְיוֹרֵד: The author of *Ge'on Ya'akov* amends this phrase so that it reads logically: Must climb down and climb up. However, *Tosafot* (*Pesaḥim* 2a) teach that it is the way of the Gemara to mention ascending and entering first, even if this does not correspond to reality. Some commentators explain that the Gemara uses this phrasing to teach that one can do it several times (Rav Ya'akov Emden).

We require something that is fit for humans – בְּעֵינַן מִידֵּי דַּחֲזֵי לְאָדָם: The question is asked: If the permission to utilize upright boards surrounding a well is intended for animals alone, why must the water be suitable for humans? The answer is that in fact this permission occasionally applies to humans as well, as in the case of wide cisterns. While people can sometimes descend into a cistern to drink, animals cannot do so and must drink from a bucket or manger. Consequently, it is required to make use of such boards for their benefit. Nevertheless, the primary concern is for humans.

HALAKHA

Who is permitted to use the upright boards surrounding a well – לְמִי הוּתְּרוּ פַּסֵּי בֵירָאוֹת: One is not permitted to rely on the upright boards surrounding a well for his own needs. Rather, he must descend into the well or cistern and drink, or erect a proper partition around it. However, if one cannot descend into the cistern, he is also permitted to draw from it for his own use (Rambam *Sefer Zemanim*, *Hilkhot Shabbat* 17:30).

מְטַפֵּס וְעוֹלֶה מְטַפֵּס וְיוֹרֵד.

must climb up and **climb down**[N] into the well, and drink there.

אִינִי?! וְהָאָמַר רַב יִצְחָק, אָמַר רַב יְהוּדָה, אָמַר שְׁמוּאֵל: לֹא הוּתְּרוּ פַּסֵּי בֵירָאוֹת אֶלָּא לִבְאֵר מַיִם חַיִּים בִּלְבַד. וְאִי לִבְהֵמָה – מָה לִי חַיִּים מָה לִי מְכוּנָּסִין? בְּעֵינַן מִידֵּי דַּחֲזֵי לְאָדָם.

The Gemara raises a difficulty: **Is that so?** Is the allowance of upright boards for animals alone? **Didn't Rav Yitzḥak say** that **Rav Yehuda said** that **Shmuel said:** Upright **boards surrounding wells were permitted only** where the **wells** contain potable, running **spring water? If** the allowance is only **for animals, what is** the difference **to me** if it is **spring** water **and what is** the difference **to me** if it is **collected** water? Granted, collected water is inferior to spring water, but it is still suitable for animals to drink. The Gemara answers: **We require something that is fit for humans.**[N]

גּוּפָא: לֹא הוּתְּרוּ פַּסֵּי בֵירָאוֹת אֶלָּא לִבְהֵמָה בִּלְבַד, אֲבָל אָדָם מְטַפֵּס וְעוֹלֶה מְטַפֵּס וְיוֹרֵד, וְאִם הָיוּ רְחָבִין – אֲפִילּוּ לְאָדָם נַמִי. וְלֹא יְמַלֵּא אָדָם מַיִם וְיִתֵּן לִפְנֵי בְהֶמְתּוֹ, אֲבָל מְמַלֵּא הוּא וְשׁוֹפֵךְ לִפְנֵי בְהֵמָה וְשׁוֹתָה מֵאֵילֶיהָ.

The Gemara examines the *baraita* cited in the course of the previous discussion. Returning to **the matter itself,** the statement quoted above: Upright **boards surrounding wells were permitted only for cattle, but a person must climb up** and **climb down** into the well and drink there. **But if** the wells **were** too **wide** for him to climb, **they are** permitted **for a person as well.**[H] **A person may not fill** a bucket with **water and hold it before his animal on Shabbat, but he may fill** it **and pour** it **out** into a trough, **and** the animal **drinks of its own accord.**

מַתְקִיף לַהּ רַב עָנָן: אִם כֵּן מָה הוֹעִילוּ פַּסֵּי בֵירָאוֹת? מָה הוֹעִילוּ?! לְמַלְאוֹת מֵהֶן!

Rav Anan strongly objects to this explanation: **If so, what purpose do the boards surrounding a well serve?** The Gemara immediately expresses its surprise: How can he ask **what purpose do they serve?** They allow people **to draw** water **from** the wells, which would otherwise be prohibited.

אֶלָּא: מָה הוֹעִיל רֹאשָׁהּ וְרוּבָּהּ שֶׁל פָּרָה?

Rather, Rav Anan's question should be understood as follows: **What purpose is served** in requiring that the enclosed area be large enough for **the cow's head and most of its** body, if in any case the cow may not be given to drink straight from the bucket?

אָמַר אַבַּיֵי: הָכָא בְּמַאי עָסְקִינַן – בְּאֵיבוּס הָעוֹמֵד בִּרְשׁוּת הָרַבִּים, גָּבוֹהַּ עֲשָׂרָה וְרוֹחַב אַרְבָּעָה וְרֹאשׁוֹ נִכְנָס לְבֵין הַפַּסִּין וכו׳.

Abaye said: In fact, it is permitted to give the animal to drink in any manner in the area enclosed by the boards surrounding the well. **With what are we dealing here?** We are dealing with a special case, **with a manger** or trough **that stands in the public domain,** and is **ten** handbreadths **high and four** handbreadths **wide,** i.e., it constitutes a private domain, **and one end of it interposes into** the area **between the** upright **boards** surrounding a well.[H] In such a case, the Sages prohibited one to fill a bucket with water in the area enclosed by the upright boards and hold it before his animal; they were concerned that the manger might become damaged, and one might come to carry the bucket from the private domain into the public domain or vice versa while fixing the damaged manger.

אָמַר רַב יִרְמְיָה בַּר אַבָּא, אָמַר רַב: אֵין בּוּרְגָּנִין בְּבָבֶל וְלֹא פַּסֵּי בֵירָאוֹת בְּחוּץ לָאָרֶץ.

It is prohibited to walk more than two thousand cubits from a city on Shabbat. However, if there are small watchmen's huts [*burganin*] outside the city that are relatively close together, they are considered part of the city, and consequently the two thousand cubit limit is measured from the last such hut. **Rav Yirmeya bar Abba said** that **Rav said:** The law with regard to these **huts** [***burganin***][LB] **does not apply in Babylonia, nor does** the allowance with regard to upright **boards surrounding a well apply outside of Eretz** Yisrael.[N]

בּוּרְגָּנִין בְּבָבֶל לֹא – דִּשְׁכִיחִי בִּידְקֵי, פַּסֵּי בֵירָאוֹת בְּחוּץ לָאָרֶץ לֹא – דְּלָא שְׁכִיחִי מְתִיבָתָא. אֲבָל אִיפְּכָא עָבְדִינַן.

The Gemara explains: The law with regard to **huts does not** apply **in Babylonia because floods are common** there; and since the huts are liable to be swept away by the floodwaters, they are not regarded as dwellings. The allowance with regard to upright **boards surrounding a well does not** apply **outside of Eretz** Yisrael, **because *yeshivot* are not common** there, and the allowance was only granted to those traveling for the sake of a mitzva such as Torah study. **But we do** say **the opposite,** i.e., we apply the law of huts outside of Eretz Yisrael and we apply the allowance of upright boards surrounding a well in Babylonia.

אִיכָּא דְּאָמְרִי, אָמַר רַב יִרְמְיָה בַּר אַבָּא, אָמַר רַב: אֵין בּוּרְגָּנִין וּפַסֵּי בֵירָאוֹת, לֹא בְּבָבֶל וְלֹא בְּחוּץ לָאָרֶץ, בּוּרְגָּנִין בְּבָבֶל לֹא – דִּשְׁכִיחִי בִּידְקֵי, בְּחוּץ לָאָרֶץ נַמִי לֹא – דִּשְׁכִיחִי גַּנָּבֵי.

The Gemara cites an alternative version of the previous discussion. **Some say** that **Rav Yirmeya bar Abba said** that **Rav said:** The laws with regard to **huts and** upright **boards surrounding a well** apply **neither in Babylonia** specifically, **nor outside of Eretz** Yisrael generally. The Gemara explains: The law with regard to **huts does not apply in Babylonia, because floods are common** there. It **also does not** apply **outside of Eretz** Yisrael, **because thieves** who steal from such huts **are common** there; therefore, people do not regard the huts as dwellings.[H]

פַּסֵּי בֵירָאוֹת בְּבָבֶל לֹא – דִּשְׁכִיחִי מַיָּא, בְּחוּץ לָאָרֶץ נַמִי לֹא – דְּלָא שְׁכִיחִי מְתִיבָתָא.

The allowance with regard to upright **boards surrounding a well** does **not** apply **in Babylonia, because water is common** there. Babylonia has many rivers and canals, and therefore wells are not essential there. **Outside of Eretz** Yisrael in general it **also does not** apply, **because *yeshivot* are not common** there.

אֲמַר לֵיהּ רַב חִסְדָּא לְמָרֵי בְּרֵיהּ דְּרַב הוּנָא בְּרֵיהּ דְּרַב יִרְמְיָה בַּר אַבָּא: אָמְרִי אָתֵיתוּ מִבַּרְנִשׁ לְבֵי כְּנִישְׁתָּא דְּדָנִיֵּאל דַּהֲוָה תְּלָתָא פַּרְסֵי בְּשַׁבְּתָא, אַמַּאי סָמְכִיתוּ – אַבּוּרְגָּנִין, הָא אֲמַר אֲבוּהּ דַּאֲבוּהּ מִשְּׁמֵיהּ דְּרַב אֵין בּוּרְגָּנִין בְּבָבֶל!

Rav Ḥisda said to Marei, son of Rav Huna, son of Rav Yirmeya bar Abba: People say that **you walk from** the city of **Barnish to Daniel's synagogue, which is** a distance of **three parasangs** [***parsei***],[LB] **on Shabbat. Upon what do you rely?** Do you rely **on the huts** located at the city's outskirts that extend the Shabbat boundary toward the synagogue? **Didn't your father's father say in the name of Rav:** The law of **huts does not** apply **in Babylonia?**

LANGUAGE

Huts [*burganin*] – **בּוּרְגָּנִין:** Possibly from the German *burg*, meaning a fortress or small settlement; some say it derives from Greek. The word was used by Roman soldiers stationed as guards at various spots along the German border. From there it spread to other parts of the Roman Empire and to the language of the Sages.

Parasang [*parsa*] – **פַּרְסָה:** Probably from the Greek παρασαγγης, *parasangès*, which was borrowed from early Iranian languages..

BACKGROUND

Huts [*burganin*] – **בּוּרְגָּנִין:** These huts were small watchmen's booths. Some of the huts were no more than temporary, flimsy booths, whereas others were well-built and served almost as military fortresses. Watchmen living in these huts were entrusted with guarding fields and delivering messages to military authorities.

Burgan

Three parasangs [*parsei*] – **תְּלָתָא פַּרְסֵי:** A *parsa* is a distance of four *mil*. Converted into modern measurements, three *parsa* is approximately 11,480–14,000 meters or 7–8.5 miles.

NOTES

Babylonia and outside of Eretz Yisrael – בָּבֶל וְחוּץ לָאָרֶץ: This halakhic statement, like many other sources, demonstrates that the Sages placed Babylonia in an intermediate level of sanctity and importance between Eretz Yisrael and other countries. Babylonia's large Jewish population, its many towns and villages where the majority of the inhabitants were Jews, and its Torah learning and Torah academies, were some of the factors that raised Babylonia to a level above all other countries outside of Eretz Yisrael.

HALAKHA

A manger…one end of it interposes into the area between the upright boards surrounding a well – אֵיבוּס...וְרֹאשׁוֹ נִכְנָס לְבֵין הַפַּסִּים: This is referring to the case of a feeding trough located in the public domain, with one end extending into the area between the upright boards surrounding a well. The manger is ten handbreadths tall and four handbreadths wide, the size of a private domain. It is prohibited to fill the trough for his animal with water from the well, even inside the area enclosed by the upright boards, because he might fix the trough if he notices it is broken and thereby end up carrying from one domain to another, as stated by Abaye (Rambam *Sefer Zemanim, Hilkhot Shabbat* 17:32).

Huts – בּוּרְגָּנִין: Watchmen's huts, which are permanent dwellings located on the outskirts of a town, are regarded as part of the town with regard to measuring the Shabbat boundary. However, in a locale where thieves or floods are common, they are not taken into account, because they are not used as permanent dwellings (*Beit Yosef; Tur; Shulḥan Arukh, Oraḥ Ḥayyim* 398:6).

Ruins of towns – מְתָוָּתָא: This term connotes ruined houses. If they still have two walls and a roof or three walls even without a roof, they are regarded as part of the town with regard to measuring the Shabbat boundary (*Tur; Shulḥan Arukh, Oraḥ Ḥayyim* 398:6).

HALAKHA

Ruins of towns – מְתָווֹתָא: This term connotes ruined houses. If they still have two walls and a roof or three walls even without a roof, they are regarded as part of the town with regard to measuring the Shabbat boundary (*Tur*; *Shulḥan Arukh*, *Oraḥ Ḥayyim* 398:6).

NOTES

This was stated by David but he did not explain it – אֲמָרוֹ דָּוִד וְלֹא פֵּירְשׁוֹ: The author of the *Ge'on Ya'akov* explains that Mari bar Mar states that a teaching can sometimes remain unclear for many generations, until a later generation successfully clarifies it.

Its measure is longer than the earth – אֲרוּכָּה מֵאֶרֶץ מִדָּה: The point of this midrash is to teach the greatness of the Torah, which extends so far that the entire world and all its problems constitute only a tiny part of it. The various aspects of the Torah accented by the different prophets have been explained in many ways. One approach is that it refers to the four facets by which the Torah is expounded: The simple meaning, the homiletic interpretation, through creation and nature, and the hidden aspects (Maharsha).

The punishment of the righteous – פּוּרְעָנוּתָן שֶׁל צַדִּיקִים: Another version reads: The punishment of the wicked. This latter reading is probably based on the fact that the verse: "It is a lamentation and they shall make lament with it," refers to the downfall of Pharaoh, which implies that it is dealing with the downfall of the wicked. The explanation of the verse according to the standard reading indeed presents difficulties (see Rabbi Yoshiya Pinto).

A flying [*afa*] scroll – מְגִילָּה עָפָה: Most commentaries explain that the word *afa* is from the Aramaic *ayef*, meaning double. Thus, an *afa* scroll is a double scroll (*ge'onim* and others).

נְפַק וְאַחֲוֵי לֵיהּ הָנְהוּ מְתָווֹתָא, דְּמִבְלְעָן בְּשִׁבְעִים אַמָּה וְשִׁירַיִים.

Marei then **went out and showed** Rav Ḥisda **certain** ruins of **towns**[H] **that were subsumed within** a distance of **seventy cubits and a remainder,** two-thirds of a cubit, of each other. He relied upon the ruins, rather than upon the huts, to be permitted to walk the entire distance from Barnish to Daniel's synagogue.

אָמַר רַב חִסְדָּא, דָּרֵישׁ מָרִי בַּר מָר: מַאי דִּכְתִיב: ״לְכׇל תִּכְלָה רָאִיתִי קֵץ רְחָבָה מִצְוָתְךָ מְאֹד״, דָּבָר זֶה אֲמָרוֹ דָּוִד וְלֹא פֵּירְשׁוֹ, אֲמָרוֹ אִיּוֹב וְלֹא פֵּירְשׁוֹ, אֲמָרוֹ יְחֶזְקֵאל וְלֹא פֵּירְשׁוֹ, עַד שֶׁבָּא זְכַרְיָה בֶּן עִדּוֹ וּפֵירְשׁוֹ.

Rav Ḥisda said: Mari bar Mar interpreted homiletically: What is the meaning of that **which is written: "I have seen a limit to every purpose; but Your commandment is exceedingly broad"** (Psalms 119:96)? **This** idea with regard to the breadth of the Torah **was stated by David, but he did not explain it;**[N] it **was stated by Job, but he** too **did not explain it;** it was **stated by Ezekiel, but he** also **did not explain it, until Zechariah,** son of Berechiah, **son of Iddo, came and explained it.**

אֲמָרוֹ דָּוִד וְלֹא פֵּירְשׁוֹ, דִּכְתִיב: ״לְכׇל תִּכְלָה רָאִיתִי קֵץ רְחָבָה מִצְוָתְךָ מְאֹד״, אֲמָרוֹ אִיּוֹב וְלֹא פֵּירְשׁוֹ – דִּכְתִיב: ״אֲרוּכָּה מֵאֶרֶץ מִדָּה וּרְחָבָה מִנִּי יָם״,

Rav Ḥisda explains: This idea was **stated by David, but he did not explain it, as it is written: "I have seen a limit to every purpose; but Your commandment is exceedingly broad,"** i.e., he stated that the Torah is exceedingly broad, but he did not explain how broad. And likewise this idea was **stated by Job, but he** too **did not explain it, as it is written: "Its measure is longer than the earth**[N] **and broader than the sea"** (Job 11:9).

אֲמָרוֹ יְחֶזְקֵאל וְלֹא פֵּירְשׁוֹ – דִּכְתִיב: ״וַיִּפְרֹשׂ אוֹתָהּ לְפָנַי וְהִיא כְתוּבָה פָּנִים וְאָחוֹר וְכָתוּב אֵלֶיהָ קִינִים וָהֶגֶה וָהִי״.

And similarly, it was **stated by Ezekiel, but he** also **did not explain it, as it is written: "And He spread it,"** the scroll, **"before me, and it was written inside and outside; and in it was written lamentations, and melody [*hegeh*], and woe [*vahi*]"** (Ezekiel 2:10).

״קִינִים״ – זוֹ פּוּרְעָנוּתָן שֶׁל צַדִּיקִים בָּעוֹלָם הַזֶּה, וְכֵן הוּא אוֹמֵר: ״קִינָה הִיא וְקוֹנְנוּהָ״. ״וָהֶגֶה״ – זוֹ מַתַּן שְׂכָרָן שֶׁל צַדִּיקִים לֶעָתִיד לָבֹא, וְכֵן הוּא אוֹמֵר: ״עֲלֵי הִגָּיוֹן בְּכִנּוֹר״. ״וָהִי״ – זוֹ הִיא פּוּרְעָנוּתָן שֶׁל רְשָׁעִים לֶעָתִיד לָבֹא, וְכֵן הוּא אוֹמֵר: ״הֹוָה עַל הֹוָה תָּבֹא״.

The Gemara explains: **"Lamentations," this** refers to **the punishment of the righteous**[N] **in this world, and so it is stated: "It is a lamentation and they shall make lament with it"** (Ezekiel 32:16). **"And melody [*hegeh*]," this** refers to **the reward of the righteous in the World-to-Come, and** the proof that this word is an expression of joy is the verse that **states:** "Upon an instrument of ten strings, and upon the harp, **to the melody [*higayon*] of a lyre"** (Psalms 92:4). **And "woe [*vahi*]," this is the punishment of the wicked in the World-to-Come, and so it states: "Calamity [*hova*] shall follow upon calamity"** (Ezekiel 7:26).

עַד שֶׁבָּא זְכַרְיָה בֶּן עִדּוֹ וּפֵירְשׁוֹ, דִּכְתִיב: ״וַיֹּאמֶר אֵלַי מָה אַתָּה רוֹאֶה וָאוֹמַר אֲנִי רוֹאֶה מְגִילָּה עָפָה אׇרְכָּהּ עֶשְׂרִים בָּאַמָּה וְרׇחְבָּהּ עֶשֶׂר בָּאַמָּה״. וְכִי פָּשְׁטַתְּ לַהּ הָוְיָא לַהּ עֶשְׂרִין בְּעֶשְׂרִין, וּכְתִיב: ״הִיא כְתוּבָה פָּנִים וְאָחוֹר״. וְכִי קָלְפַתְּ לַהּ כַּמָּה הָוְיָא לַהּ – אַרְבְּעִין בְּעֶשְׂרִין,

But nonetheless, Ezekiel did not explain the extent of the Torah, **until Zechariah,** son of Berechiah, **son of Iddo, came and explained it, as it is written: "And he said to me: What do you see? And I said: I see a flying [*afa*] scroll;**[N] **the length of it is twenty cubits, and the breadth of it is ten cubits"** (Zechariah 5:2). Since the scroll was flying, the implication is that it had two equal sides, **so that when you open it, it is twenty by twenty** cubits. **And it is written: "And it was written inside and outside,"** i.e., on both sides. **And when you peel them apart** and separate the two sides, **how much is it?** Its entire area **amounts to forty by twenty** cubits, or eight hundred of God's cubits.

וּכְתִיב: ״מִי מָדַד בְּשׇׁעֳלוֹ מַיִם וְשָׁמַיִם בַּזֶּרֶת תִּכֵּן וגו׳״. נִמְצָא כׇּל הָעוֹלָם כּוּלּוֹ אֶחָד מִשְּׁלֹשֶׁת אֲלָפִים וּמָאתַיִם בַּתּוֹרָה.

In order to determine the measure of God's cubit, the Gemara cites a verse that describes the size of the span between God's thumb and little finger, in a manner of speaking. **And it is written: "Who has measured the waters in the hollow of His hand, and meted out heaven with the span,** and comprehended the dust of the earth in a measure" (Isaiah 40:12). If the entire world measures one square span, which is a quarter of one square cubit, **we find** according to this calculation that **the entire world is one** part **in three thousand and two hundred of the Torah.**

וְאָמַר רַב חִסְדָּא, דָּרֵישׁ מָרִי בַּר מָר: מַאי דִּכְתִיב: ״וְהִנֵּה שְׁנֵי דּוּדָאֵי תְאֵנִים מוּעָדִים לִפְנֵי הֵיכַל ה׳ הַדּוּד הָאֶחָד תְּאֵנִים טֹבוֹת מְאֹד כִּתְאֵנֵי

And Rav Ḥisda further **said: Mari bar Mar interpreted homiletically: What is** the meaning of that **which is written:** "The Lord showed me, **and behold two baskets of figs were set before the temple of the Lord,** after Nebuchadrezzar king of Babylon had carried away captive Jeconiah, son of Jehoiakim, the king of Judah, and the princes of Judah with the craftsmen and the smiths, from Jerusalem, and had brought them to Babylon. **One basket [*dud*] had very good figs, like the figs**

הַבַּכּוּרוֹת וְהַדּוּד הָאֶחָד תְּאֵנִים רָעוֹת מְאֹד אֲשֶׁר לֹא תֵאָכַלְנָה מֵרוֹעַ״.

that are first ripe, and the other basket [*dud*] had very bad figs, so bad they could not be eaten" (Jeremiah 24:1–2).

תְּאֵנִים הַטּוֹבוֹת – אֵלּוּ צַדִּיקִים גְּמוּרִים, תְּאֵנִים הָרָעוֹת – אֵלּוּ רְשָׁעִים גְּמוּרִים. וְשֶׁמָּא תֹּאמַר אָבַד סִבְרָם וּבָטַל סִיכּוּיָם – תַּלְמוּד לוֹמַר: ״הַדּוּדָאִים נָתְנוּ רֵיחַ״, אֵלּוּ וָאֵלּוּ עֲתִידִין שֶׁיִּתְּנוּ רֵיחַ.

Good figs, these are the **full-fledged righteous** people; **bad figs, these are** the **full-fledged wicked** people. **And lest you say that** the hope of the wicked **is lost and their prospect is void, the verse states,** interpreting the word *duda'im* homiletically: **"The baskets [*duda'im*] yield a fragrance"** (Song of Songs 7:14), meaning that **both of them,** the righteous and the wicked, **will eventually yield a fragrance.**

דָּרַשׁ רָבָא: מַאי דִּכְתִיב: ״הַדּוּדָאִים נָתְנוּ רֵיחַ״ – אֵלּוּ בַּחוּרֵי יִשְׂרָאֵל שֶׁלֹּא טָעֲמוּ טַעַם חֵטְא.

Rava interpreted the verse cited above **homiletically** as follows: **What is** the meaning of that **which is written:** "The mandrakes [*duda'im*] yield a fragrance, and at our doors are all manner of choice fruits, new and old, which I have laid up for you, O my beloved" (Song of Songs 7:14)? **"The mandrakes [*duda'im*] yield a fragrance,"**[N] **these are the young men of Israel who have never tasted the taste of sin.**

״וְעַל פְּתָחֵינוּ כָּל מְגָדִים״ – אֵלּוּ בְּנוֹת יִשְׂרָאֵל שֶׁמַּגִּידוֹת פִּתְחֵיהֶן לְבַעֲלֵיהֶן. לָשׁוֹן אַחֵר: שֶׁאוֹגְדוֹת פִּתְחֵיהֶן לְבַעֲלֵיהֶן.

"And at our doors [*petaḥeinu*] are all manner of choice fruits [*megadim*]," these are the daughters of Israel who inform [*maggidot*] their husbands about their passageway [*pit'ḥeihen*], i.e., they tell them when they are menstruating. **Another version** of this interpretation is: **They bind [*ogedot*] their passageway** and save it **for their husbands,** and do not have relations with others.

״חֲדָשִׁים גַּם יְשָׁנִים דּוֹדִי צָפַנְתִּי לָךְ״, אָמְרָה כְּנֶסֶת יִשְׂרָאֵל לִפְנֵי הַקָּדוֹשׁ בָּרוּךְ הוּא: רִבּוֹנוֹ שֶׁל עוֹלָם, הַרְבֵּה גְּזֵירוֹת גָּזַרְתִּי עַל עַצְמִי יוֹתֵר מִמַּה שֶּׁגָּזַרְתָּ עָלַי – וְקִיַּימְתִּים.

"New and old, which I have laid up for you, O my beloved," the Congregation of Israel said before the Holy One, Blessed be He, and continued: **Master of the Universe, I have decreed many decrees upon myself** through the enactments and ordinances of the Sages, **more than what You decreed upon me** in the Torah, **and I have fulfilled them.** These are the new laws which were added to the old ones stated in the Torah.

אֲמַר לֵיהּ רַב חִסְדָּא לְהַהוּא מִדְּרַבָּנַן דַּהֲוָה קָא מְסַדֵּר אַגַּדְתָּא קַמֵּיהּ: מִי שְׁמִיעַ לָךְ ״חֲדָשִׁים גַּם יְשָׁנִים״ מַהוּ? אֲמַר לֵיהּ: אֵלּוּ מִצְוֹת קַלּוֹת וְאֵלּוּ מִצְוֹת חֲמוּרוֹת.

It was related that **Rav Ḥisda said to one of the Sages who would arrange the** traditions of the *aggada* **before him: Did you hear what** the meaning of: **New and old** is? **He said to him: These,** the new, **are the** more **lenient mitzvot, and these,** the old, **are the** more **stringent mitzvot.**

אֲמַר לֵיהּ: וְכִי תּוֹרָה פְּעָמִים פְּעָמִים נִיתְּנָה? אֶלָּא הַלָּלוּ מִדִּבְרֵי תוֹרָה, וְהַלָּלוּ מִדִּבְרֵי סוֹפְרִים.

Rav Ḥisda **said to him:** This cannot be so, **for was the Torah given on two** separate **occasions,** i.e., were the more lenient and more stringent mitzvot given separately? **Rather, these,** the old, **are** mitzvot **from the Torah, and these,** the new, **are from the Sages.**

דָּרַשׁ רָבָא: מַאי דִּכְתִיב: ״וְיוֹתֵר מֵהֵמָּה בְּנִי הִזָּהֵר עֲשׂוֹת סְפָרִים הַרְבֵּה וגו׳״ – בְּנִי! הִזָּהֵר בְּדִבְרֵי סוֹפְרִים יוֹתֵר מִדִּבְרֵי תוֹרָה. שֶׁדִּבְרֵי תוֹרָה יֵשׁ בָּהֶן עֲשֵׂה וְלֹא תַעֲשֶׂה, וְדִבְרֵי סוֹפְרִים – כָּל הָעוֹבֵר עַל דִּבְרֵי סוֹפְרִים חַיָּיב מִיתָה.

Rava expounded another verse in similar fashion: **What is** the meaning of that **which is written: "And more than these,**[N] **my son, be careful: of making many books [*sefarim*]** there is no end; and much study is a weariness of the flesh" (Ecclesiastes 12:12)? **My son, be careful** to fulfill **the words of the Sages [*soferim*]** even **more than the words of the Torah. For the words of the Torah include positive and negative** commandments, and even with regard to the negative commandments, the violation of many of them is punishable only by lashes. **Whereas** with respect to **the words of the Sages, anyone who transgresses the words of the Sages is liable to** receive the **death** penalty,[N] as it is stated: "And whoever breaches through a hedge, a snake shall bite him" (Ecclesiastes 10:8), taking hedges to refer metaphorically to decrees.

שֶׁמָּא תֹּאמַר אִם יֵשׁ בָּהֶן מַמָּשׁ מִפְּנֵי מָה לֹא נִכְתְּבוּ – אָמַר קְרָא ״עֲשׂוֹת סְפָרִים הַרְבֵּה אֵין קֵץ״.

Lest you say: If the words of the Sages **are of substance** and have such great importance, **why were they not written** in the Torah, therefore, **the verse states: "Of making many books there is no end,"** meaning that it is impossible to fully commit the Oral Torah to writing, as it is boundless.

NOTES

The mandrakes [*duda'im*] yield a fragrance – הַדּוּדָאִים נָתְנוּ רֵיחַ: This second interpretation of the verse refers to the usual sense of the word *duda'im*, as a fragrant plant (Maharsha).

And more than these – וְיוֹתֵר מֵהֵמָּה: Maharsha explains that this hints at the Torah itself, as is written a few verses earlier: "Words of truth written in proper form" (Ecclesiastes 12:10).

Anyone who transgresses the words of the Sages – כָּל הָעוֹבֵר עַל דִּבְרֵי סוֹפְרִים: Some commentaries find support for this statement from the law of a rebellious elder. If a scholar refuses to accept one of the mitzvot of the Torah, he is not punished as a rebellious elder, but rather in accordance with the transgression. However, a scholar who rules against the laws of the Sages of his generation or the words of the earlier Sages, is a rebellious Elder and liable to the death penalty (Rav Tzvi Hirsch Ḥayyot).

HALAKHA

King Solomon instituted the ordinance of *eiruv* – שְׁלֹמֹה תִּיקֵּן עֵירוּבִין: King Solomon and his court instituted the rabbinic decree that one may not carry on Shabbat from one private domain into another private domain until an *eiruv* has been established between them (Rambam *Sefer Zemanim, Hilkhot Eiruvin* 1:2).

״וְלַהַג הַרְבֵּה יְגִיעַת בָּשָׂר״. אָמַר רַב פַּפָּא בְּרֵיהּ דְּרַב אַחָא בַּר אַדָּא מִשְּׁמֵיהּ דְּרַב אַחָא בַּר עוּלָּא: מְלַמֵּד שֶׁכָּל הַמַּלְעִיג עַל דִּבְרֵי חֲכָמִים נִידּוֹן בְּצוֹאָה רוֹתַחַת.

What is the meaning of the words: **"And much study [*lahag*] is a weariness of the flesh"?**[N] **Rav Pappa, son of Rav Aḥa bar Adda, said in the name of Rav Aḥa bar Ulla: This teaches that whoever mocks [*malig*] the words of the Sages will be sentenced to boiling excrement,** which results from the weariness of the flesh of man.

מַתְקִיף לָהּ רָבָא: מִי כְּתִיב ״לַעַג״? ״לַהַג״ כְּתִיב! אֶלָּא: כָּל הַהוֹגֶה בָּהֶן טוֹעֵם טַעַם בָּשָׂר.

Rava strongly objects to this explanation: **Is it written: Mock [*la'ag*]? "*Lahag*" is** the word that is **written. Rather,** the verse must be understood in the opposite manner: **Whoever meditates [*hogeh*] upon them,** the words of the Sages, **experiences** enjoyment as if it had **the taste of meat.**

תָּנוּ רַבָּנַן: מַעֲשֶׂה בְּרַבִּי עֲקִיבָא שֶׁהָיָה חָבוּשׁ בְּבֵית הָאֲסוּרִין וְהָיָה רַבִּי יְהוֹשֻׁעַ הַגַּרְסִי מְשָׁרְתוֹ. בְּכָל יוֹם וָיוֹם הָיוּ מַכְנִיסִין לוֹ מַיִם בְּמִדָּה. יוֹם אֶחָד מְצָאוֹ שׁוֹמֵר בֵּית הָאֲסוּרִין, אָמַר לוֹ: הַיּוֹם מֵימֶךָ מְרוּבִּין, שֶׁמָּא לַחְתּוֹר בֵּית הָאֲסוּרִין אַתָּה צָרִיךְ! שָׁפַךְ חֶצְיָין, וְנָתַן לוֹ חֶצְיָין.

Concerning the significance of observing the words of the Sages, the Gemara relates: **The Sages taught** in a *baraita*: **It once happened that Rabbi Akiva was incarcerated in a prison, and Rabbi Yehoshua HaGarsi would** come to the prison to **attend to his** needs. **Every day** his disciples **would bring him water in a measured** quantity. **One day the prison guard met** Rabbi Yehoshua HaGarsi and **said to him:** The amount of **your water today is more** than usual; **perhaps you need** it **in order to** soften the walls and thus **undermine the prison. He** then **poured out half** the water, **and gave him** the other **half** to take in to Rabbi Akiva.

כְּשֶׁבָּא אֵצֶל רַבִּי עֲקִיבָא, אָמַר לוֹ: יְהוֹשֻׁעַ, אֵין אַתָּה יוֹדֵעַ שֶׁזָּקֵן אֲנִי וְחַיַּי תְּלוּיִין בְּחַיֶּיךָ?

When Rabbi Yehoshua **came to Rabbi Akiva,** and the latter saw the small amount of water he had brought, **he said to him: Yehoshua, do you not know that I am old, and my life depends on your life?** No one else brings me water, so if you bring me less than I need, my life is endangered.

סָח לוֹ כָּל אוֹתוֹ הַמְּאוֹרָע. אָמַר לוֹ: תֵּן לִי מַיִם שֶׁאֶטּוֹל יָדַי. אָמַר לוֹ: לִשְׁתּוֹת אֵין מַגִּיעִין, לִיטּוֹל יָדֶיךָ מַגִּיעִין?! אָמַר לוֹ: מָה אֶעֱשֶׂה שֶׁחַיָּיבִים עֲלֵיהֶן מִיתָה, מוּטָב אָמוּת מִיתַת עַצְמִי וְלֹא אֶעֱבוֹר עַל דַּעַת חֲבֵירַי.

After Rabbi Yehoshua **related to him the entire incident,** Rabbi Akiva **said to him: Give me water so that I may wash my hands.** Rabbi Yehoshua **said to him:** The water that I brought **will not suffice for drinking;** how **will it suffice for washing your hands? He said to him: What can I do;** for transgressing the words of the Sages and eating without first washing hands **one is liable to** receive the **death** penalty. And if so, it is **better that I should die my own death** by thirst, **rather than transgress the opinion of my colleagues** who enacted that one must wash hands before eating.

אָמְרוּ: לֹא טָעַם כְּלוּם עַד שֶׁהֵבִיא לוֹ מַיִם וְנָטַל יָדָיו. כְּשֶׁשָּׁמְעוּ חֲכָמִים בַּדָּבָר, אָמְרוּ: מַה בְּזִקְנוּתוֹ כָּךְ – בְּיַלְדוּתוֹ עַל אַחַת כַּמָּה וְכַמָּה. וּמַה בְּבֵית הָאֲסוּרִין כָּךְ – שֶׁלֹּא בְּבֵית הָאֲסוּרִין עַל אַחַת כַּמָּה וְכַמָּה.

They said that **he would not taste anything until** Rabbi Yehoshua **brought him water and he washed his hands. When the Sages heard about this, they said: If in his old age** and weakened state he is still **so** meticulous in his observance of the mitzvot, **how much more so** must he have been **in his youth.** And **if in prison** he is **so** scrupulous in his behavior, **how much more so** must he have been **when not in prison.**

אָמַר רַב יְהוּדָה, אָמַר שְׁמוּאֵל: בְּשָׁעָה שֶׁתִּיקֵּן שְׁלֹמֹה עֵירוּבִין וּנְטִילַת יָדַיִם, יָצְתָה בַּת קוֹל וְאָמְרָה: ״בְּנִי אִם חָכָם לִבֶּךָ יִשְׂמַח לִבִּי גַם אָנִי״, וְאוֹמֵר: ״חֲכַם בְּנִי וְשַׂמַּח לִבִּי וְאָשִׁיבָה חֹרְפִי דָבָר״.

Rav Yehuda said that **Shmuel said: At the time that** King **Solomon instituted** the ordinances of ***eiruv*** of courtyards[H] **and** of **washing hands**[N] to purify them from their impurity, which are added safeguards to the words of the Torah, **a Divine Voice emerged and said** in his praise: **"My son, if your heart is wise, My heart will be glad, even Mine"** (Proverbs 23:15). **And it states** with regard to him: **"My son, be wise and make My heart glad, that I may respond to he who taunts Me"** (Proverbs 27:11).

דָּרַשׁ רָבָא: מַאי דִּכְתִיב: ״לְכָה דוֹדִי נֵצֵא הַשָּׂדֶה נָלִינָה בַּכְּפָרִים נַשְׁכִּימָה לַכְּרָמִים נִרְאֶה אִם פָּרְחָה הַגֶּפֶן פִּתַּח הַסְּמָדַר הֵנֵצוּ הָרִמּוֹנִים שָׁם אֶתֵּן אֶת דֹּדַי לָךְ״.

The Gemara cites additional teachings that **Rava interpreted homiletically: What is** the meaning of that **which is written: "Come, my beloved, let us go forth into the field; let us lodge in the villages. Let us get up early to the vineyards; let us see if the vine has flowered, if the grape blossoms have opened, if the pomegranates are in flower; there will I give you my loves"** (Song of Songs 7:12–13)?

NOTES

And much study is a weariness of the flesh – לַהַג הַרְבֵּה יְגִיעַת בָּשָׂר: The Rambam states as follows in his Commentary on the Mishna: The Sages state that whoever mocks the words of the Sages will be sentenced to boiling excrement. There is no greater boiling excrement than the foolishness that induced him to mock the words of the Sages. You will find that the only person who dismisses their words is one who seeks after his lusts, and prefers his sensory pleasures, which do not incline his heart to anything enlightened.

The ordinances of *eiruv* of courtyards and of washing hands – תַּקָּנַת עֵירוּבִין וּנְטִילַת יָדַיִם: In the *Sefer Mitzvot Gadol*, based on Rav Hai Gaon, it is explained that the period of King Solomon was the first appropriate time for instituting these decrees. The rationale is based on the Gemara at the end of Chapter One, where it is taught that neither the joining of courtyards [*eiruvin*] nor the washing of hands need be observed at a time of war. Until King Solomon's days there were constant wars, and as a man of peace he was the first who could establish these institutions and safeguards.

״לְכָה דוֹדִי נֵצֵא הַשָּׂדֶה״ – אָמְרָה כְּנֶסֶת יִשְׂרָאֵל לִפְנֵי הַקָּדוֹשׁ בָּרוּךְ הוּא: רִבּוֹנוֹ שֶׁל עוֹלָם, אַל תְּדִינֵנִי כְּיוֹשְׁבֵי כְּרַכִּים שֶׁיֵּשׁ בָּהֶן גָּזֵל וַעֲרָיוֹת וּשְׁבוּעַת שָׁוְא וּשְׁבוּעַת שֶׁקֶר. ״נֵצֵא הַשָּׂדֶה״ – בֹּא וְאַרְאֲךָ תַּלְמִידֵי חֲכָמִים שֶׁעוֹסְקִין בַּתּוֹרָה מִתּוֹךְ הַדְּחָק.

With regard to the words: **"Come, my beloved, let us go forth into the field," the Congregation of Israel said before the Holy One, Blessed be He: Master of the Universe, do not judge me like those who reside in large cities where there is robbery and licentiousness, and vain oaths and false oaths,** but rather: **"Let us go forth into the field," come and I will show You Torah scholars who** work the land but nonetheless **engage in Torah** study, **in** poverty and in **distress.**

״נָלִינָה בַּכְּפָרִים״ אַל תִּקְרֵי ״בַּכְּפָרִים״ אֶלָּא ״בַּכּוֹפְרִים״ – בֹּא וְאַרְאֲךָ אוֹתָם שֶׁהִשְׁפַּעְתָּ לָהֶן טוֹבָה וְהֵן כָּפְרוּ בְּךָ.

With regard to the words, **"Let us lodge in the villages," do not read** the phrase as: **In the villages [*bakefarim*], but rather** as: **By the deniers [*bakoferim*],** meaning, **come and I will show You** the nations of the world, **whom You showered with good, but** yet **they have denied You.**

״נַשְׁכִּימָה לַכְּרָמִים״ – אֵלּוּ בָּתֵּי כְּנֵסִיּוֹת וּבָתֵּי מִדְרָשׁוֹת. ״נִרְאֶה אִם פָּרְחָה הַגֶּפֶן״ – אֵלּוּ בַּעֲלֵי מִקְרָא. ״פִּתַּח הַסְּמָדַר״ – אֵלּוּ בַּעֲלֵי מִשְׁנָה. ״הֵנֵצוּ הָרִמּוֹנִים״ – אֵלּוּ בַּעֲלֵי גְּמָרָא. ״שָׁם אֶתֵּן אֶת דּוֹדַי לָךְ״ – אַרְאֲךָ כְּבוֹדִי וְגוֹדְלִי, שֶׁבַח בָּנַי וּבְנוֹתַי.

"Let us get up early to the vineyards," these are the synagogues and houses of study. "Let us see if the vine has flowered," these are the masters of Bible, who are proficient in the first stage of Torah study. **"If the grape blossoms have opened," these are the masters of Mishna. "If the pomegranates are in flower," these are the masters of Gemara. "There will I give you my loves,"** means **I will show You my glory and my greatness, the praise of my sons and daughters,** how they adhere to sanctity.

אָמַר רַב הַמְנוּנָא: מַאי דִּכְתִיב: ״וַיְדַבֵּר שְׁלֹשֶׁת אֲלָפִים מָשָׁל וַיְהִי שִׁירוֹ חֲמִשָּׁה וָאָלֶף״ – מְלַמֵּד שֶׁאָמַר שְׁלֹמֹה עַל כָּל דָּבָר וְדָבָר שֶׁל תּוֹרָה שְׁלֹשֶׁת אֲלָפִים מָשָׁל, עַל כָּל דָּבָר וְדָבָר שֶׁל סוֹפְרִים חֲמִשָּׁה וָאֶלֶף טְעָמִים.

The Gemara expounds further concerning King Solomon. **Rav Hamnuna said: What is** the meaning of that **which is written: "And he spoke three thousand proverbs, and his poems were a thousand and five"** (I Kings 5:12)? This **teaches that Solomon pronounced three thousand proverbs for each and every word of the Torah,** and **one thousand and five reasons for each and every word of the Scribes.**

דָּרַשׁ רָבָא: מַאי דִּכְתִיב: ״וְיוֹתֵר שֶׁהָיָה קֹהֶלֶת חָכָם עוֹד לִימַּד דַּעַת אֶת הָעָם [וְ]אִיזֵּן וְחִקֵּר תִּיקֵּן מְשָׁלִים הַרְבֵּה״. ״לִימַּד דַּעַת אֶת הָעָם״ – דְּאַגְמְרֵיהּ בְּסִימָנֵי טְעָמִים, וְאַסְבְּרָהּ בְּמַאי דְּדָמֵי לֵיהּ.

Rava also **taught: What is** the meaning of that **which is written: "And besides being wise, Koheleth also taught the people knowledge; and he weighed, and sought out, and set in order many proverbs"** (Ecclesiastes 12:9). Rava interpreted homiletically: **He taught the people knowledge,** meaning **he taught it with the accentuation marks** in the Torah, **and** he **explained** each matter **by means of** something **similar to it.**

״[וְ]אִיזֵּן וְחִקֵּר תִּיקֵּן מְשָׁלִים הַרְבֵּה״ – אָמַר עוּלָּא, אָמַר רַבִּי אֱלִיעֶזֶר: בַּתְּחִילָּה הָיְתָה תּוֹרָה דּוֹמָה לִכְפִיפָה שֶׁאֵין לָהּ אׇזְנַיִם, עַד שֶׁבָּא שְׁלֹמֹה וְעָשָׂה לָהּ אׇזְנַיִם.

With regard to: **"And he weighed [*izzen*], and sought out,**[N] **and set in order many proverbs," Ulla said** that **Rabbi Eliezer said: At first the Torah was like a basket without handles [*oznayim*], until Solomon came and made handles for it.** By means of his explanations and proverbs he enabled each person to understand and take hold of the Torah, fulfill its mitzvot, and distance himself from transgressions.

״קְוּוּצּוֹתָיו תַּלְתַּלִּים״. אָמַר רַב חִסְדָּא, אָמַר מָר עוּקְבָא: מְלַמֵּד שֶׁיֵּשׁ לִדְרוֹשׁ עַל כָּל קוֹץ וָקוֹץ תִּילֵּי תִּילִּים שֶׁל הֲלָכוֹת.

With regard to the verse, "His head is as the most fine gold, **his locks [*kevutzotav*] are wavy [*taltalim*],** and black as a raven" (Song of Songs 5:11), **Rav Ḥisda said** that **Mar Ukva said:** This **teaches that it is possible to expound from each and every stroke [*kotz*]** of the letters in the Torah **mounds upon mounds [*tilei tilim*] of laws.**

״שְׁחוֹרוֹת כָּעוֹרֵב״ – בְּמִי אַתָּה מוֹצְאָן – בְּמִי

Black [*sheḥorot*] as a raven [*orev*] means: **In whom do you find** the words of Torah? **In him**

NOTES

And he weighed and sought out – אִיזֵּן וְחִקֵּר: Rashi explains (*Yevamot* 21a) that before the time of King Solomon the Torah was difficult to understand, due to a lack of suitable explanations. King Solomon provided the Torah with handles, in a manner of speaking, by means of his proverbs and explanations, so that everyone could understand it.

שֶׁמַּשְׁכִּים וּמַעֲרִיב עֲלֵיהֶן לְבֵית הַמִּדְרָשׁ. רַבָּה אָמַר: בְּמִי שֶׁמַּשְׁחִיר פָּנָיו עֲלֵיהֶן כְּעוֹרֵב.

who, for the Torah's sake, gets up early in the morning [*shaḥar*] **and stays late** in the evening [*erev*] **in the study hall. Rabba said: In him who, for** the Torah's **sake, blackens his face like a raven,** i.e., who fasts and deprives himself for the sake of Torah study.

רָבָא אָמַר: בְּמִי שֶׁמֵּשִׂים עַצְמוֹ אַכְזָרִי עַל בָּנָיו וְעַל בְּנֵי בֵיתוֹ כְּעוֹרֵב. כִּי הָא דְּרַב אַדָּא בַּר מַתְנָא הֲוָה קָאָזֵיל לְבֵי רַב, אֲמַרָה לֵיהּ דְּבֵיתְהוּ: יָנוֹקֵי דִּידָךְ מַאי אַעֲבֵיד לְהוּ? אֲמַר לָהּ: מִי שְׁלִימוּ קוּרְמֵי בְּאַגְמָא?

Rava said: In him who makes himself cruel to his sons and other **members of his household like a raven** for the sake of Torah. This **was the case with Rav Adda bar Mattana,** who **was** about to **go to the study hall** to learn Torah, and **his wife said to him: What shall I do for your children?** How shall I feed them in your absence? **He said to her: Are all the rushes** [*kurmei*][B] **in the marsh** already **gone?** If there is no other bread, let them eat food prepared from rushes.

"וּמְשַׁלֵּם לְשׂוֹנְאָיו אֶל פָּנָיו לְהַאֲבִידוֹ", אָמַר רַבִּי יְהוֹשֻׁעַ בֶּן לֵוִי: אִילְמָלֵא מִקְרָא כָּתוּב אִי אֶפְשָׁר לְאוֹמְרוֹ, כִּבְיָכוֹל כְּאָדָם שֶׁנּוֹשֵׂא מַשּׂוֹי עַל פָּנָיו וּמְבַקֵּשׁ לְהַשְׁלִיכוֹ מִמֶּנּוּ.

The Gemara proceeds to interpret a different verse homiletically: **"And He repays them that hate Him to His face to destroy them;** He will not be slack to him that hates Him, He will repay him to his face" (Deuteronomy 7:10). **Rabbi Yehoshua ben Levi said: Were the verse not written** in this manner, **it** would **be impossible to utter it,** in deference to God, for it could be understood, **as it were,**[N] **like a person who bears a burden on his face, and wishes to throw it off.** Written slightly differently, the verse could have been understood as implying that God is unable, as it were, to bear the situation, but must punish the wicked immediately.

"לֹא יְאַחֵר לְשׂוֹנְאוֹ", אָמַר רַבִּי אִילָא: לְשׂוֹנְאָיו הוּא דְּלֹא יְאַחֵר, אֲבָל יְאַחֵר לְצַדִּיקִים גְּמוּרִים.

With regard to the words **"He shall not be slack to him that hates Him," Rabbi Ila said: He will not be slack** in bringing punishment **to him that hates Him, but He will be slack** in rewarding **those who are absolutely righteous,** as the reward of the righteous does not arrive immediately, but only in the World-to-Come.

וְהַיְינוּ דְּאָמַר רַבִּי יְהוֹשֻׁעַ בֶּן לֵוִי: מַאי דִּכְתִיב: "אֲשֶׁר אָנֹכִי מְצַוְּךָ הַיּוֹם לַעֲשׂוֹתָם", הַיּוֹם לַעֲשׂוֹתָם – וְלֹא לְמָחָר לַעֲשׂוֹתָם, הַיּוֹם לַעֲשׂוֹתָם – לְמָחָר לְקַבֵּל שְׂכָרָם.

And that is **what Rabbi Yehoshua ben Levi said: What is** the meaning of that **which is written:** "And you shall keep the commandments, and the statutes, and the judgments **which I command you today to do them"** (Deuteronomy 7:11)? It means: **Today** is the time **to do them,** in this world, **and tomorrow** is **not** the time **to do them,** as there is no obligation or opportunity to fulfill mitzvot in the World-to-Come. Furthermore, it means: **Today** is the time **to do them,** but only **tomorrow,** in the ultimate future, is the time **to receive reward for** doing **them.**

אָמַר רַבִּי חַגַּי, וְאִיתֵּימָא רַבִּי שְׁמוּאֵל בַּר נַחְמָנִי: מַאי דִּכְתִיב: "אֶרֶךְ אַפַּיִם" אֶרֶךְ אַף מִבָּעֵי לֵיהּ!

In a similar vein, **Rabbi Ḥaggai said, and some say** it was **Rabbi Shmuel bar Naḥmani: What is** the meaning of that **which is written:** "And the Lord passed by before him, and proclaimed: The Lord, the Lord, merciful and gracious, **long-suffering** [*erekh appayim*], and abundant in love and truth" (Exodus 34:6)? Why does it say *"erekh appayim,"* using a plural form? **It should have** said ***erekh af,*** using the singular form.

אֶלָּא: אֶרֶךְ אַפַּיִם לַצַּדִּיקִים, אֶרֶךְ אַפַּיִם לָרְשָׁעִים.

What this means is that God is long-suffering in two ways: He is **long-suffering toward the righteous,** i.e., He delays payment of their reward; and He is also **long-suffering toward the wicked,** i.e., He does not punish them immediately.

"רַבִּי יְהוּדָה אוֹמֵר: עַד בֵּית סָאתַיִם וְכוּ'". אִיבַּעְיָא לְהוּ: בּוֹר וּפַסִּין קָאָמַר אוֹ דִּילְמָא בּוֹר וְלֹא פַּסִּין קָאָמַר?

The mishna stated that **Rabbi Yehuda says:** The area may be expanded **up to** an area of **two** ***beit se'a,*** an area of five thousand square cubits. **A dilemma was raised before** the Sages in clarification of this statement: **Did he speak** of the area of **the cistern** itself **and** that enclosed by **the** upright **boards,** that the total area enclosed by the upright boards may be expanded up to, but may not exceed, an area of two *beit se'a*? **Or perhaps he spoke** of the area of **the cistern without** that enclosed by **the** upright **boards,** that the cistern itself may be expanded up to an area of two *beit se'a*? In that case, the total area enclosed by the boards could exceed an area of two *beit se'a*.

BACKGROUND

Rushes [*kurmei*] – קוּרְמֵי: The identity of the *kurmei* mentioned here is unclear. However, one explanation is that it refers to the *Glyceria fluitans* plant, a perennial that grows in marshy areas. It can grow up to a meter in height, and the length of its leaves can reach 10 cm. The stalk of this plant is juicy and is even suitable for human consumption, although it is generally utilized only as quality animal fodder. Its seeds are used to make porridge. For many years the seeds were a valuable commodity.

Rushes

NOTES

As it were [*kivyakhol*] – כִּבְיָכוֹל: Rashi offers a variety of meanings for this common expression in the different places it is used in the Gemara. In one instance he explains that it means that we are forced to say it in this way, as if were possible to express this statement. Elsewhere he explains this word by stating: It is stated with regard to the Holy One, Blessed be He, in the way it would be stated with regard to a person, as if it were possible to say such a thing. The word has also been expounded homiletically as follows: The Torah, which was given using the twenty-two [*kaf-bet*] letters of the Hebrew alphabet, can [*yakhol*] say such a thing, but we mortals may not say it (*Hilkhot Olam* by Rabbi Yosef Karo).

אָדָם נוֹתֵן עֵינָיו בְּבוֹרוֹ, וְלָא גָּזְרִינַן דִּילְמָא אָתֵי לְטַלְטוּלֵי יוֹתֵר מִבֵּית סָאתַיִם בְּקַרְפֵּף.

The underlying rationale of each side of this dilemma is as follows: Does one **fix his eyes on his cistern,** keeping in mind that the partition is made because of it, **and** therefore, since the area of the cistern is not greater than an area of two *beit se'a*, **we do not decree lest he come to carry** also **in an enclosure** [*karpef*], an enclosed storage space behind the house that was not originally surrounded by a fence for the purpose of residence, even when it is **more than** an area of **two *beit se'a*?**

אוֹ דִּילְמָא: אָדָם נוֹתֵן עֵינָיו בִּמְחִיצָתוֹ, וְגָזְרִינַן דִּילְמָא אָתֵי לְאִיחַלּוּפֵי יוֹתֵר מִבֵּית סָאתַיִם בְּקַרְפֵּף!

Or perhaps a person fixes his eyes on his partition, and does not pay attention to the cistern, but only to the area enclosed by the partition. **And** in this case **we** do **decree, lest he come to confuse** this case **with** that of a ***karpef*** that is **larger than** an area of **two *beit se'a*,** and come to carry there, because of the similarity between them.

תָּא שְׁמַע: כַּמָּה הֵן מְקוֹרָבִין – כְּדֵי רֹאשָׁהּ וְרוּבָּהּ שֶׁל פָּרָה. וְכַמָּה הֵן מְרוּחָקִין – אֲפִילּוּ כּוֹר, אֲפִילּוּ כּוֹרַיִים. רַבִּי יְהוּדָה אוֹמֵר: בֵּית סָאתַיִם – מוּתָּר, יָתֵר מִבֵּית סָאתַיִם – אָסוּר.

In order to resolve this question, the Gemara cites a proof: **Come** and **hear** what was taught in a *baraita*: **How close** may the boards be to the well? They may be **as** close as the length of **the head and most** of the body **of a cow. And how far may they be** from the well? The enclosed area may be expanded **even** to the area of **a *beit kor*** **and even two *beit kor*,** provided that one adds more upright boards or increases their size so as to reduce the size of the gaps between them. **Rabbi Yehuda says:** Up to an area of **two *beit se'a*, it is permitted** to enclose the area in this manner; **more than** an area of **two *beit se'a*, it is prohibited.**

אָמְרוּ לְרַבִּי יְהוּדָה: אִי אַתָּה מוֹדֶה בְּדִיר וְסַהַר מוּקְצֶה וְחָצֵר אֲפִילּוּ בֵּית חֲמֵשֶׁת כּוֹרִים וּבֵית עֲשֶׂרֶת כּוֹרִים שֶׁמּוּתָּר?

The other Rabbis **said to Rabbi Yehuda: Do you not concede with regard to a pen, a stable, a backyard, and a courtyard, that even** one the size **of five *beit kor*** and even **of ten *beit kor* is permitted** for use?

אָמַר לָהֶם: זוֹ מְחִיצָה, וְאֵלּוּ פַּסִּין.

Rabbi Yehuda **said to them:** A distinction can be made between the cases, for **this,** the wall surrounding the pen, the stable or the yard, is a proper **partition,** and hence it is permitted to carry in them even if they are more than an area of two *beit se'a*. However, **these are** only upright **boards,** and they only allow one to carry if the area they enclose is not more than an area of two *beit se'a*.

רַבִּי שִׁמְעוֹן בֶּן אֶלְעָזָר אוֹמֵר: בּוֹר בֵּית סָאתַיִם אַבֵּית סָאתַיִם – מוּתָּר, וְלֹא אָמְרוּ לְהַרְחִיק אֶלָּא כְּדֵי רֹאשָׁהּ וְרוּבָּהּ שֶׁל פָּרָה.

Rabbi Shimon ben Elazar says: A cistern the length of **two *beit se'a*** by the width of **two *beit se'a***[N] **is permitted, and they only said to distance** the upright boards from the cistern **as** much as the length of **the head and most** of the body **of a cow.**

הָא מִדְּקָאָמַר רַבִּי שִׁמְעוֹן בֶּן אֶלְעָזָר בּוֹר וְלֹא פַּסִּין – מִכְּלָל דְּרַבִּי יְהוּדָה בּוֹר וּפַסִּין קָאָמַר! וְלֹא הִיא, רַבִּי יְהוּדָה בּוֹר בְּלֹא פַּסִּין קָאָמַר.

The Gemara tries to draw an inference from this *baraita*: **From the** fact **that Rabbi Shimon ben Elazar spoke** only **of the cistern** itself **and not** of the upright **boards,** we can **infer** that **Rabbi Yehuda spoke of** both **the cistern** itself **and** the area enclosed by **the** upright **boards.** The Gemara rejects this argument: It is **not so.** When **Rabbi Yehuda** said that the area may be expanded up to an area of two *beit se'a*, **he was,** in fact, **speaking of** the area of **the cistern without** that which is enclosed by **the** upright **boards.**

אִי הָכִי, הַיְינוּ דְּרַבִּי שִׁמְעוֹן בֶּן אֶלְעָזָר! אִיכָּא בֵּינַיְיהוּ אָרִיךְ וְקַטִּין.

The Gemara asks: **If so, that is** exactly what **Rabbi Shimon ben Elazar** said. The Gemara answers: **There is** a practical halakhic difference **between them** in a case where the enclosed area is **long and narrow.** Rabbi Yehuda permits using it, whereas Rabbi Shimon ben Elazar requires that the area be square.

כְּלָל אָמַר רַבִּי שִׁמְעוֹן בֶּן אֶלְעָזָר: כָּל אֲוִיר שֶׁתַּשְׁמִישׁוֹ לְדִירָה, כְּגוֹן דִּיר וְסַהַר מוּקְצֶה וְחָצֵר, אֲפִילּוּ בֵּית חֲמֵשֶׁת כּוֹרִים וּבֵית עֲשֶׂרֶת כּוֹרִים – מוּתָּר.

The Gemara adds: **Rabbi Shimon ben Elazar stated a principle:** With regard to **any** enclosed **space that is used as a dwelling,**[H] **such as a pen, a stable, a backyard, or a courtyard,** even if it lacks a roof and **even** if the structure has the area of **five *beit kor*** **and** even **ten *beit kor*, it is permitted** to carry in it.

וְכָל דִּירָה שֶׁתַּשְׁמִישָׁהּ לַאֲוִיר, כְּגוֹן בּוּרְגָּנִין שֶׁבַּשָּׂדוֹת, בֵּית סָאתַיִם – מוּתָּר, יָתֵר מִבֵּית סָאתַיִם – אָסוּר.

And with regard to **any dwelling that is used for the space** outside it, i.e., whose partitions were arranged not so that it could be lived in, but for the sake of the field or yard outside, **such as field huts,** if its area was **two *beit se'a*, it is permitted** to carry in it; but if its area was **more than two *beit se'a*, it is prohibited** to do so.

NOTES

An area of two *beit se'a* by two *beit se'a* – בֵּית סָאתַיִם אַבֵּית סָאתַיִם: The Ra'avad explains that Rabbi Shimon ben Elazar maintains that the area between the boards surrounding a well can be an area of four *beit se'a*, but most commentaries reject this explanation. Nevertheless, even according to the interpretation that the reference in this context is to a square with an area of two *beit se'a*, it should be noted that the terminology is imprecise.

HALAKHA

An enclosed space that is used as a dwelling – אֲוִיר שֶׁתַּשְׁמִישׁוֹ לְדִירָה: If an area was not initially surrounded by a fence for the purpose of residence, and its area is greater than two *beit se'a*, it is prohibited to carry in it. However, if it was initially enclosed for the purpose of residence, then one is permitted to carry in it, even if its area is larger than two *beit se'a* (*Shulḥan Arukh, Oraḥ Ḥayyim* 358:1).

מתני׳ רַבִּי יְהוּדָה אוֹמֵר: אִם הָיָה דֶּרֶךְ רְשׁוּת הָרַבִּים מַפְסַקְתָּן – יְסַלְּקֶנָּה לַצְּדָדִין. וַחֲכָמִים אוֹמְרִים: אֵינוֹ צָרִיךְ.

MISHNA **Rabbi Yehuda says: If the path of the public domain passes through** the area of the upright boards surrounding a well[HB] **and obstructs it, one must divert** the path **to the sides,** so that the public will circumvent the enclosed area; otherwise, the partition is invalid and the enclosed area cannot be regarded as a private domain. **And the Rabbis say: One need not** divert the path of the public domain, for the partition is valid even if many people pass through it.

גמ׳ רַבִּי יוֹחָנָן וְרַבִּי אֶלְעָזָר דְּאָמְרִי תַּרְוַיְיהוּ: כָּאן הוֹדִיעֲךָ כּוֹחָן שֶׁל מְחִיצוֹת.

GEMARA **Rabbi Yoḥanan and Rabbi Elazar both said: Here,** the Rabbis **informed you of the strength of partitions;** although a path of the public domain passes through the partitions and the partitions do not constitute effective barriers, they are still strong enough to allow one to carry.

כָּאן וּסְבִירָא לֵיהּ! וְהָאָמַר רַבָּה בַּר בַּר חָנָה, אָמַר רַבִּי יוֹחָנָן: יְרוּשָׁלַיִם אִילְמָלֵא דַּלְתוֹתֶיהָ נִנְעָלוֹת בַּלַּיְלָה חַיָּיבִין עָלֶיהָ מִשּׁוּם רְשׁוּת הָרַבִּים!

The Gemara wishes to clarify the meaning of Rabbi Yoḥanan's statement: Did he mean **here** that the Rabbis expressed this idea, **and he agrees** with them that a public thoroughfare does not invalidate a partition? **Didn't Rabba bar bar Ḥana say** that **Rabbi Yoḥanan said:** With regard to **Jerusalem,** even though it is walled, **were it not for the fact that its doors are locked at night, one would be liable for** carrying in **it** on Shabbat **because** its thoroughfares are regarded **as the public domain?**[N] Apparently, Rabbi Yoḥanan maintains that a partition is not strong enough to overcome the passage of many people.

אֶלָּא: כָּאן וְלָא סְבִירָא לֵיהּ.

Rather, Rabbi Yoḥanan's statement must be understood as follows: **Here,** the Rabbis expressed this idea, although **he does not agree** with them.

וְרָמֵי דְּרַבִּי יְהוּדָה אַדְּרַבִּי יְהוּדָה, וְרָמֵי דְּרַבָּנַן אַדְּרַבָּנַן.

The Gemara **raised a contradiction between** this statement of **Rabbi Yehuda** and another statement of **Rabbi Yehuda, and raised a contradiction** between this statement of **the Rabbis** and another statement of **the Rabbis.**

דְּתַנְיָא: יָתֵר עַל כֵּן אָמַר רַבִּי יְהוּדָה: מִי שֶׁהָיוּ לוֹ שְׁנֵי בָתִּים מִשְּׁנֵי צִידֵּי רְשׁוּת הָרַבִּים – עוֹשֶׂה לוֹ לֶחִי מִכָּאן וְלֶחִי מִכָּאן, אוֹ קוֹרָה מִכָּאן וְקוֹרָה מִכָּאן, וְנוֹשֵׂא וְנוֹתֵן בָּאֶמְצַע. אָמְרוּ לוֹ: אֵין מְעָרְבִין רְשׁוּת הָרַבִּים בְּכָךְ.

The other statements are **as it was taught** in the *Tosefta*: **Furthermore, Rabbi Yehuda said: If one had two houses on the two sides of the public domain,** and he wishes to carry from one house to the other on Shabbat via the public domain, **he may place a side post from here,** perpendicular to the public domain, **and** an additional **side post from here,** on the other side of the public domain, **or** he may place a cross **beam from here,** from one end of one house to the end of the house opposite it, **and** another cross **beam from here,** from the other side of the house, **and carry** objects **and place** them **in** the area **between them** because the two added partitions turn the area in the middle into a private domain. The Rabbis **said to him: One cannot make the public domain fit** for carrying **by** means of **an *eiruv* in this manner,** i.e., by means of a side post alone, when many people continue to walk through the public thoroughfare in the middle.

קַשְׁיָא דְּרַבִּי יְהוּדָה אַדְּרַבִּי יְהוּדָה, קַשְׁיָא דְּרַבָּנַן אַדְּרַבָּנַן!

Consequently, there is **a contradiction between** one statement of **Rabbi Yehuda and** the other statement of **Rabbi Yehuda,**[N] and there is also **a contradiction between** one statement of **the Rabbis and** the other statement of **the Rabbis.**

דְּרַבִּי יְהוּדָה אַדְּרַבִּי יְהוּדָה לָא קַשְׁיָא, הָתָם: דְּאִיכָּא שְׁתֵּי מְחִיצוֹת מְעַלְּיָיתָא, הָכָא – לֵיכָּא שְׁתֵּי מְחִיצוֹת מְעַלְּיָיתָא.

The Gemara answers: Between one statement of **Rabbi Yehuda and** the other statement of **Rabbi Yehuda** there is **no contradiction,** because one can differentiate between them. **There,** in the case of the two houses, **there are two proper partitions,** for the houses are real partitions, and two partitions suffice to establish a separate domain. However, **here,** in the case of the upright boards, **there are not two proper partitions,** for the upright boards are not real partitions.

דְּרַבָּנַן אַדְּרַבָּנַן [נַמִי] לָא קַשְׁיָא: הָכָא – אִיכָּא שֵׁם אַרְבַּע מְחִיצוֹת, הָתָם – לֵיכָּא שֵׁם אַרְבַּע מְחִיצוֹת.

Between one statement of **the Rabbis** and the other statement of **the Rabbis** there is **also no contradiction,** as **here,** with regard to the upright boards, **there is a nominal** set **of four partitions;**[N] on all four sides side there are at least two cubits of some form of partition, so the cistern is regarded as enclosed by four partitions. However, **there,** with regard to the two houses, **there is not a nominal** set **of four partitions.**

HALAKHA

A path of the public domain passing through the upright boards surrounding a well – דֶּרֶךְ הָרַבִּים בֵּין הַפַּסִּין: If a path of the public domain passes through the upright boards surrounding a well, it is not necessary to divert the path to one of the sides, as the partition is valid even if many people pass through it, in accordance with the opinion of the Rabbis (Rambam *Sefer Zemanim*, *Hilkhot Shabbat* 17:33).

BACKGROUND

A path of the public domain passing between the upright boards surrounding a well – דֶּרֶךְ בְּתוֹךְ הַפַּסִּים: If a path passes between the upright boards surrounding a well, Rabbi Yehuda rules that it should be diverted to one of the sides, as illustrated below along the shaded path.

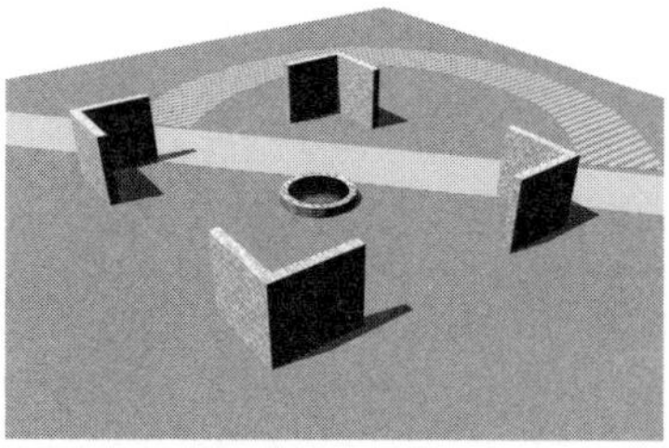

Diversion of a public domain path

NOTES

Jerusalem and its partitions – יְרוּשָׁלַיִם וּמְחִיצוֹתֶיהָ: Because the public passes through Jerusalem from every direction, it is as though the city has no walls around it; it is considered as not having even two proper partitions (*Tosafot*; Rabbi Zeraḥya HaLevi).

The contradiction between statements of Rabbi Yehuda – הַסְּתִירָה בְּדִבְרֵי רַבִּי יְהוּדָה: In the Jerusalem Talmud there are Sages who state that the positions must be reversed in the *Tosefta*. Other Sages explain that Rabbi Yehuda's permission in the case of two proper partitions applies only to a *karmelit*, but not to a full-fledged public domain.

A nominal set of four partitions – שֵׁם אַרְבַּע מְחִיצוֹת: The question arises: If a side post has the status of a partition, then two proper partitions and two side posts would also constitute four partitions. One answer is that these Sages are of the opinion that a side post is merely to provide a conspicuous distinction and does not have the status of a partition at all (Rashba).

אָמַר רַבִּי יִצְחָק בַּר יוֹסֵף אָמַר רַבִּי יוֹחָנָן: אֶרֶץ יִשְׂרָאֵל אֵין חַיָּיבִין עָלֶיהָ מִשּׁוּם רְשׁוּת הָרַבִּים. יְתֵיב רַב דִּימִי וְקָאָמַר לֵיהּ לְהָא שְׁמַעְתָּא. אָמַר לֵיהּ אַבַּיֵי לְרַב דִּימִי: מַאי טַעְמָא?

Rabbi Yitzḥak bar Yosef said that **Rabbi Yoḥanan said:** In **Eretz Yisrael one is not liable for** carrying in **the public domain. Rav Dimi sat and recited this** ***halakha*****. Abaye said to Rav Dimi: What is the reason** underlying this ruling?

Perek **II**
Daf **22** Amud **b**

אִילֵימָא מִשּׁוּם דְּמַקִּיף לָהּ סוּלָּמָא דְּצוֹר מֵהַךְ גִּיסָא וּמַחְתְּנָא דְּגָדֵר מֵהַךְ גִּיסָא – בָּבֶל נַמִי מַקִּיף לָהּ פְּרָת מֵהַךְ גִּיסָא וְדִיגְלַת מֵהַאי גִּיסָא. דְּכוּלָּא עָלְמָא נַמִי מַקִּיף אוֹקְיָינוֹס! דִּילְמָא מַעֲלוֹת וּמוֹרָדוֹת קָאָמְרַתְּ?!

If you say this law **because** Eretz Yisrael **is surrounded by the Ladder of Tyre**[B] **on one side and the slope of Gader**[B] **on the other side,** each formation being over ten handbreadths high and constituting a valid partition, then **Babylonia,** which **is also surrounded by** the **Euphrates** River **on one side and** the **Tigris** River **on the other side,** should not be considered a public domain either. Moreover, **the entire world is also surrounded by the ocean,** and therefore there should be no public domain anywhere in the world.[N] Rather, **perhaps you spoke of the ascents and descents** of Eretz Yisrael,[H] which are not easy to traverse and hence should not have the status of a public domain?

אָמַר לֵיהּ: קַרְקַפְנָא חֲזֵיתֵיהּ לְרֵישָׁךְ בֵּי עַמּוּדֵי כִּי אָמַר רַבִּי יוֹחָנָן לְהָא שְׁמַעְתָּא.

Rav Dimi **said to him:** Man of great **skull,** i.e., man of distinction, I **saw your head**[N] **between the pillars** of the study hall **when Rabbi Yoḥanan taught this** ***halakha*****,** meaning you grasped the meaning as though you actually were present in the study hall and heard the statement from Rabbi Yoḥanan himself.

אִיתְּמַר נַמִי, כִּי אֲתָא רָבִין אָמַר רַבִּי יוֹחָנָן, וְאָמְרִי לָהּ אָמַר רַבִּי אַבָּהוּ, אָמַר רַבִּי יוֹחָנָן: מַעֲלוֹת וּמוֹרָדוֹת שֶׁבְּאֶרֶץ יִשְׂרָאֵל אֵין חַיָּיבִין עֲלֵיהֶן מִשּׁוּם רְשׁוּת הָרַבִּים, לְפִי שֶׁאֵינָן כְּדִגְלֵי מִדְבָּר.

It was also stated that **when Ravin came** from Eretz Yisrael he **said** that **Rabbi Yoḥanan said, and some say** it was **Rabbi Abbahu** who **said** that **Rabbi Yoḥanan said:** In the case of **the ascents and descents of Eretz Yisrael, one is not liable for** carrying in **the public domain, because they are not like the banners in the desert.** To be regarded as a public domain, a place must be similar to the area in which the banners of the tribes of Israel passed in the desert, i.e., it must be level and suitable for the passage of large numbers of people.

בְּעָא מִינֵּיהּ רַחֲבָה מֵרָבָא: תֵּל הַמִּתְלַקֵּט עֲשָׂרָה מִתּוֹךְ אַרְבַּע, וְרַבִּים בּוֹקְעִין בּוֹ, חַיָּיבִין עָלָיו רְשׁוּת הָרַבִּים אוֹ אֵין חַיָּיבִין עָלָיו?

Raḥava raised a dilemma before Rava: In the case of **a mound that rises to** a height of **ten** handbreadths **within four** cubits, thereby fulfilling the conditions that create a private domain, **but many people traverse it, is one liable for** carrying in **the public domain or is one not liable?**

אַלִּיבָּא דְּרַבָּנַן לָא תִּיבָּעֵי לָךְ, הַשְׁתָּא וּמַה הָתָם דְּנִיחָא תַּשְׁמִישְׁתֵּיהּ, אָמְרִי רַבָּנַן לָא אָתוּ רַבִּים וּמְבַטְּלִי לָהּ מְחִיצָּתָא, הָכָא דְּלָא נִיחָא תַּשְׁמִישְׁתֵּיהּ – לֹא כׇּל שֶׁכֵּן.

The Gemara explains: **According to** the opinion of **the Rabbis,** this **should not be a dilemma for you. Just as there,** with regard to the upright boards surrounding a well, **where the use** of the public domain **is convenient, the Rabbis say** that **the public does not come and invalidate the partition; here, where its use is inconvenient** due to the slope, **all the more so** should the mound be considered partitioned off as a private domain, and the passage of the public should not invalidate it.

BACKGROUND

The Ladder of Tyre – סוּלָּמָא דְּצוֹר: Nowadays the Ladder of Tyre is called Rosh HaNikra, a series of steep cliffs along the seacoast in the northern part of Eretz Yisrael. The boulders of the Ladder of Tyre form a kind of wall located on one side of the country.

Portion of Rosh HaNikra known as the Foot of the Elephant

The slope of Gader – מַחְתְּנָא דְּגָדֵר: The slope of Gader refers to the steep slope from the heights on the eastern side of the Jordan River and the Gilead region toward the Sea of Galilee. The marked difference in height, together with the steepness of the slope, creates the impression of a huge wall of rock situated on the eastern side of the Sea of Galilee and the Jordan River. This forms a second partition to the east of Eretz Yisrael.

View of the Sea of Galilee facing east

NOTES

The natural boundaries of the world – מְחִיצוֹת הָעוֹלָם: In the Jerusalem Talmud Reish Lakish is quoted as arguing that because of the natural boundaries of the world, such as the mountains and rivers, there are currently no public domains. Only in the future will there be public domains, when "every valley shall be raised up, and every mountain and hill shall be made low" (Isaiah 40:4).

The question discussed in this context can also be approached from a different angle: Why shouldn't the mountains or rivers, in fact, serve as partitions, since in various cases the seashore or the banks of a river do have the status of partitions? The Ritva suggests that mountains and rivers are ineffective as partitions in Shabbat law if they are so far away that one does not think of himself as placed within their perimeter.

I saw your head – חֲזֵיתֵיהּ לְרֵישָׁךְ: Some commentaries (see *Tosafot*) explain that Abaye's head, meaning his teacher, Rabba, was present when Rabbi Yoḥanan made this statement. Some commentaries ask, based on this understanding, why Abaye is asking Rav Dimi about this matter when he could cite his explanation from Rabba in the name of Rabbi Yoḥanan (Rashba).

HALAKHA

The ascents and descents of Eretz Yisrael – מַעֲלוֹת וּמוֹרָדוֹת שֶׁבְּאֶרֶץ יִשְׂרָאֵל: Any area that the masses cannot easily traverse is not a public domain. Rather, it is a *karmelit*, in accordance with Rabbi Yoḥanan's statement with regard to the ascents and descents of Eretz Yisrael (*Shulḥan Arukh, Oraḥ Ḥayyim* 345:14).

כִּי תִּיבָּעֵי לָךְ אַלִּיבָּא דְּרַבִּי יְהוּדָה, מַאי? הָתָם הוּא דְּנִיחָא תַּשְׁמִישְׁתֵּיהּ, הָכָא הוּא דְּלָא נִיחָא תַּשְׁמִישְׁתֵּיהּ – לָא אָתוּ רַבִּים וּמְבַטְּלִי מְחִיצְתָּא, אוֹ דִּילְמָא לָא שְׁנָא? אֲמַר לֵיהּ: חַיָּיבִין.

Where there should be a dilemma for you is **according to** the opinion of **Rabbi Yehuda. What is** the *halakha*? Does he maintain his position only **there, because the use** of the public domain **is convenient,** whereas **here, where its use is inconvenient,** he too would agree that **the public does not come and invalidate the partition? Or perhaps there is no difference?** Rava **said to** Raḥava: In such a case, **one is liable** for carrying in a public domain.

וַאֲפִילּוּ עוֹלִין לוֹ בְּחֶבֶל?! אֲמַר לֵיהּ: אִין. וַאֲפִילּוּ בְּמַעֲלוֹת בֵּית מֵרוֹן?! אֲמַר לֵיהּ: אִין.

Raḥava asked him: **And** do you issue this ruling **even** in the case of a slope that is so steep that in order to climb it **one must ascend it by means of a rope? He said to him: Yes.** He asked him further: **And even in** the case of **the ascents of Beit Meron,** which are exceedingly steep? **He said to him: Yes.**

אֵיתִיבֵיהּ: חָצֵר שֶׁהָרַבִּים נִכְנָסִין לָהּ בָּזוֹ וְיוֹצְאִין בָּזוֹ – רְשׁוּת הָרַבִּים לְטוּמְאָה וּרְשׁוּת הַיָּחִיד לְשַׁבָּת.

Raḥava **raised an objection** to Rava's opinion from the *Tosefta*: **A courtyard** that was properly surrounded by partitions, **into which many people enter on this** side **and exit on that** other side, is treated like **the public domain** with regard to **ritual impurity,** so that in cases of doubt, the person is considered ritually pure, as uncertainty concerning ritual impurity only renders a person impure in an area defined as a private domain; however, it is still treated like **the private domain** with regard to **Shabbat.**

מַנִּי? אִילֵימָא רַבָּנַן – הָשְׁתָּא וּמָה הָתָם דְּנִיחָא תַּשְׁמִישְׁתֵּיהּ אָמְרִי רַבָּנַן לָא אָתוּ רַבִּים וּמְבַטְּלִי מְחִיצְתָּא, הָכָא דְּלָא נִיחָא תַּשְׁמִישְׁתֵּיהּ – לֹא כׇּל שֶׁכֵּן!

He proceeds to clarify the *Tosefta*: **Who** is the author of this statement? **If you say** it was **the Rabbis,** there is a difficulty: **Just as there,** with regard to the upright boards surrounding a well, **where the use** of the public domain **is convenient, the Rabbis say that the public does not come and invalidate the partition; here,** in the case of the courtyard, **where its use** as a path for a public domain **is inconvenient, all the more so** should they say that the passage of many people does not invalidate the partition and therefore there would be no need to discuss this case.

אֶלָּא לָאו – רַבִּי יְהוּדָה הִיא!

Rather, is it not in accordance with the opinion of **Rabbi Yehuda?** This indicates that even Rabbi Yehuda differentiates between different paths in the public domain.

לֹא, לְעוֹלָם רַבָּנַן, וּרְשׁוּת הָרַבִּים לְטוּמְאָה אִיצְטְרִיכָא לֵיהּ.

Rava replied: **No; actually,** you can explain that this *Tosefta* was taught in accordance with the opinion of **the Rabbis.** As to the question raised with regard to the novelty of this case according to their approach, **it was necessary for them** to teach us that such a courtyard is treated like **the public domain** with regard **to ritual impurity,** even though it is considered a private domain with respect to Shabbat.

תָּא שְׁמַע: מְבוֹאוֹת הַמְפוּלָּשׁוֹת בְּבוֹרוֹת בְּשִׁיחִין וּבִמְעָרוֹת רְשׁוּת הַיָּחִיד לְשַׁבָּת, וּרְשׁוּת הָרַבִּים לְטוּמְאָה.

Raḥava attempts to cite a proof again, this time from a mishna: **Come** and **hear** the following teaching: **Alleyways that open in cisterns, ditches or caves** constitute **the private domain** with regard **to Shabbat and the public domain** with regard **to ritual impurity.**

בְּבוֹרוֹת סָלְקָא דַּעְתָּךְ?! אֶלָּא: לְבוֹרוֹת. רְשׁוּת הַיָּחִיד לְשַׁבָּת וּרְשׁוּת הָרַבִּים לְטוּמְאָה.

The Gemara first clarifies the wording of the mishna: **Should it enter your mind** to say that the correct reading is **in cisterns** [*baborot*]; is it possible to speak of alleyways that open inside cisterns? **Rather,** it should be corrected as follows: Alleyways that open out **into cisterns** [*laborot*] constitute **the private domain** with regard **to Shabbat and the public domain** with regard **to ritual impurity.**

מַנִּי? אִילֵימָא רַבָּנַן – הָשְׁתָּא וּמָה הָתָם דְּנִיחָא תַּשְׁמִישְׁתֵּיהּ – אָמְרִי לָא אָתוּ רַבִּים וּמְבַטְּלִי לַהּ, הָכָא דְּלָא נִיחָא תַּשְׁמִישְׁתֵּיהּ לֹא כׇּל שֶׁכֵּן? אֶלָּא לָאו רַבִּי יְהוּדָה הִיא!

Raḥava proceeds to clarify the matter: **Who** is the author of this mishna? **Now, if you say** it is **the Rabbis,** there is a difficulty: **Just as there,** with regard to the upright boards surrounding a well, **where the use** of the public thoroughfare **is convenient,** the Rabbis **say** that **the public does not come and invalidate** the partition; **here,** in the case of an alleyway, **where its use** as a public thoroughfare **is inconvenient, all the more so** should they say that the passage of many people does not invalidate the partition, and so there was no need to discuss this case. **Rather, isn't it** in accordance with the opinion of **Rabbi Yehuda?**

לא, לעולם רבנן, ורשות הרבים לטומאה איצטריכא ליה.

Rava refutes this argument: **No; actually,** you can explain that this mishna was taught in accordance with the opinion of **the Rabbis.** It does present a novel teaching, as **it was necessary for them** to teach us that such an alleyway has the status of **the public domain** with regard **to ritual impurity.** Although it is not a convenient place to cross, it is considered a public domain with respect to impurity, since many people are found there.

תא שמע: שבילי בית גילגול וכיוצא בהן רשות היחיד לשבת, ורשות הרבים לטומאה.

Once again Raḥava attempts to cite a proof from a mishna: **Come** and **hear** the following teaching: **The paths of Beit Gilgul,**[NB] which are difficult to traverse, **and similar ones** have the status of **the private domain** with regard **to Shabbat, and** that of **the public domain** with regard **to ritual impurity.**

ואיזהו שבילי בית גילגול? אמרי דבי רבי ינאי: כל שאין העבד יכול ליטול סאה של חיטין וירוץ לפני סרדיוט.

The Gemara asks: **And what** paths **are like the paths of Beit Gilgul? The school of Rabbi Yannai say:** This is **any** path in which **a slave** [*eved*] **is unable**[N] **to take up a** ***se'a*** **of wheat** by hand **and run before an officer** [*sardeyot*],[L] despite his fear of him.

מני? אילימא רבנן – השתא ומה התם דניחא תשמישתא אמרי רבנן לא אתו רבים ומבטלי לה מחיצתא, הכא דלא ניחא תשמישתא לא כל שכן? אלא לאו רבי יהודה היא!

RaḥavaHe proceeds to clarify the issue: **Who** is the author of this mishna? **Now, if you say** it is **the Rabbis,** there is a difficulty: **Just as there,** with regard to the upright boards surrounding a well, **where the use** of the public thoroughfare **is convenient, the Rabbis say** that **the public does not come and invalidate the partition; here,** in the case of the paths of Beit Gilgul, **where their use** as a public pathway **is inconvenient, all the more so** should they say that the passage of many people does not invalidate the partitions. **Rather, is it not** in accordance with the opinion of **Rabbi Yehuda?**

אמר ליה: שבילי בית גילגול קאמרת – יהושע אוהב ישראל היה, עמד ותיקן להם דרכים וסרטיא, כל היכא דניחא תשמישתא – מסרה לרבים, כל היכא דלא ניחא תשמישתא – מסרה ליחיד:

Rava **said to him: Did you say the paths of Beit Gilgul? Joshua,** who conquered the land and divided it among the tribes, **was a lover of Israel. He rose up and established roads and highways for them; any place that was convenient to use he handed over to the public,** and **any place that was inconvenient to use he handed over to an individual.**[N] Therefore, the roads of Eretz Yisrael, which like the paths of Beit Gilgul are not easy to use, have the status of a private domain. However, there is no general rule in other places that roads that are difficult to traverse do not have the status of a public domain.

מתני׳ אחד בור הרבים ובאר הרבים ובאר היחיד עושין להן פסין,

MISHNA In the case of **a public cistern** containing collected water, **as well as a public well** containing spring water, **and** even **a private well, one may arrange** upright **boards around them** in order to allow one to carry in the enclosed area, as delineated above.

אבל לבור היחיד עושין לו מחיצה גבוה עשרה טפחים, דברי רבי עקיבא.

But in the case of **a private cistern,** there are two deficiencies: It belongs to an individual, and it does not contain spring water. Consequently, it is impossible to permit drawing from it on Shabbat by means of boards set up in the corners; rather, **one must construct for it a** proper **partition ten handbreadths high;** this is **the statement of Rabbi Akiva.**

רבי יהודה בן בבא אומר: אין עושין פסין אלא לבאר הרבים בלבד, ולשאר עושין חגורה גבוה עשרה טפחים.

Rabbi Yehuda ben Bava says: One may arrange upright **boards only for a public well.**[H] **But for the others,** that is, a public cistern or a private well, **one must set up a belt,**[H] i.e., a partition consisting of ropes, **ten handbreadths high.** Such an arrangement creates a proper partition based on the principle of *lavud*, namely, that solid surfaces with gaps between them smaller than three handbreadths are considered joined.

NOTES

Beit Gilgul – בית גילגול: Most commentaries explain that Beit Gilgul refers to a very steep place. Other commentaries state that it is a mountain that cannot be climbed by a straight path, but only via paths that wind around the mountain (Rav Ya'akov Emden). A variant reading of Beit Gilgul as Beit Gadgad explicitly indicates that it is a place containing partitions, inclines [*gedudim*] and descents (Rabbeinu Ḥananel).

In which a slave [*eved*] is unable – שאין העבד יכול: The *ge'onim* had a different reading: In which one passing by [*over*] is unable, meaning that none of the passersby can run along this path.

He handed over to an individual – מסרה ליחיד: The individual who was granted control of such a path could block the path and construct partitions on each side. Consequently, even if such a place is not currently enclosed by partitions, it is not considered a public domain; rather, it has the status of a *karmelit* (see Rashba).

BACKGROUND

Beit Gilgul – בית גילגול: Beit Gilgul may refer to a place in the Judean mountains called Beit HaGilgal in the Bible (see Nehemiah 12:29). According to the descriptions of the place in the Books of the Maccabees and in Josephus, it appears that the settlement was built on a rocky cliff and was accessible only by means of a narrow and very steep path. It is likely that this name was applied to any steep and difficult path.

LANGUAGE

Officer [*sardeyot*] – סרדיוט: From the Greek στρατιώτης, *stratyotes*, meaning a military man or an officer.

HALAKHA

The permissibility of upright boards surrounding a well – היתר פסי בירות: The permission to utilize upright boards surrounding a well applies only to a public well of spring water, as the Gemara stated that the *halakha* is in accordance with the opinion of Rabbi Yehuda ben Bava (Rambam *Sefer Zemanim*, *Hilkhot Shabbat* 17:30).

Belt – חגורה: On Shabbat, water may not be drawn from cisterns and wells unless some form of proper partition is constructed around them, as they are not included in the permission to use upright boards. An example of a proper partition is a series of ropes rising to ten handbreadths high and separated from one another by less than three handbreadths. This is in accordance with the opinion of Rabbi Yehuda ben Bava (Rambam *Sefer Zemanim*, *Hilkhot Shabbat* 17:31).

גמ׳ אָמַר רַב יוֹסֵף, אָמַר רַב יְהוּדָה, אָמַר שְׁמוּאֵל: הֲלָכָה כְּרַבִּי יְהוּדָה בֶּן בָּבָא. וְאָמַר רַב יוֹסֵף, אָמַר רַב יְהוּדָה, אָמַר שְׁמוּאֵל: לֹא הוּתְּרוּ פַּסֵּי בֵירָאוֹת אֶלָּא לִבְאֵר מַיִם חַיִּים בִּלְבַד.

GEMARA **Rav Yosef said** that **Rav Yehuda said** that **Shmuel said:** The ***halakha* is in accordance with** the opinion of **Rabbi Yehuda ben Bava. And Rav Yosef** also **said** that **Rav Yehuda said** that **Shmuel said:** Upright **boards** surrounding a **well were permitted only in** the case of **a well** containing potable, running **spring water.**

וּצְרִיכָא, דְּאִי אַשְׁמְעִינַן הֲלָכָה כְּרַבִּי יְהוּדָה בֶּן בָּבָא – הֲוָה אָמִינָא דְּרַבִּים, וַאֲפִילּוּ מְכוּנָּסִין.

The Gemara comments: **And it was necessary** to cite both of these statements, even though their content appears to be the same. **As had** he **taught us** only that the ***halakha* is in accordance with** the opinion of **Rabbi Yehuda ben Bava** that upright boards may only be set arranged for a well, **I would have said** that with regard to water belonging to **the public,** upright boards are permitted not only in the case of spring water, but **even** in the case of water **collected** in a cistern.

וְהַאי דְּקָתָנֵי בְּאֵר הָרַבִּים – לְאַפּוֹקֵי מִדְּרַבִּי עֲקִיבָא. קָא מַשְׁמַע לָן דְּלֹא הוּתְּרוּ פַּסֵּי בֵירָאוֹת אֶלָּא לִבְאֵר מַיִם חַיִּים.

And that which was taught: One may only arrange boards for **a public well,** that was **to exclude** the opinion **of Rabbi Akiva** that upright boards may be arranged even for a private well, but not to allow us to infer that boards may not be arranged for a public cistern filled with collected water. Therefore, Shmuel **teaches us** that **boards** surrounding a **well were permitted only** in the case of **a well of spring water.**

וְאִי אַשְׁמְעִינַן בְּאֵר מַיִם חַיִּים – הֲוָה אָמִינָא: לָא שְׁנָא דְּרַבִּים וְלָא שְׁנָא דְּיָחִיד, קָא מַשְׁמַע לָן: הֲלָכָה כְּרַבִּי יְהוּדָה בֶּן בָּבָא.

And in the opposite direction, **had** he **taught us** that upright boards may only be arranged for **a well** containing potable, running **spring water, I would have said** that **there is no difference** whether it is a **public** well **and there is no difference** whether it is a **private** well. Shmuel therefore **teaches us** that the ***halakha* is in accordance with** the opinion of **Rabbi Yehuda ben Bava,** who says that upright boards may be arranged only for a public well, but not for one that belongs to an individual.

מתני׳ וְעוֹד אָמַר רַבִּי יְהוּדָה בֶּן בָּבָא: הַגִּינָּה וְהַקַּרְפֵּף שֶׁהֵן שִׁבְעִים אַמָּה וְשִׁירַיִים עַל שִׁבְעִים אַמָּה וְשִׁירַיִים, הַמּוּקָּפוֹת גָּדֵר גָּבוֹהַּ עֲשָׂרָה טְפָחִים – מְטַלְטְלִין בְּתוֹכָהּ, וּבִלְבַד שֶׁיְּהֵא בָּהּ שׁוֹמֵירָה אוֹ בֵּית דִּירָה, אוֹ שֶׁתְּהֵא סְמוּכָה לָעִיר.

MISHNA **And furthermore, Rabbi Yehuda ben Bava said:** With regard to **a garden or a** *karpef*, an enclosed courtyard used for storage, **that is** not more than **seventy cubits and a remainder,** a little more, as will be explained below, **by seventy cubits and a remainder, and is surrounded by a wall ten handbreadths high, one may carry inside it,** as it constitutes a proper private domain. This is **provided that it contains a watchman's booth or a dwelling place, or it is near the town**[N] in which its owner lives, so that he uses it and it is treated like a dwelling.

רַבִּי יְהוּדָה אוֹמֵר: אֲפִילּוּ אֵין בָּהּ אֶלָּא בּוֹר וְשִׁיחַ וּמְעָרָה מְטַלְטְלִין בְּתוֹכָהּ. רַבִּי עֲקִיבָא אוֹמֵר: אֲפִילּוּ אֵין בָּהּ אַחַת מִכָּל אֵלּוּ מְטַלְטְלִין בְּתוֹכָהּ, וּבִלְבַד שֶׁיְּהֵא בָּהּ שִׁבְעִים אַמָּה וְשִׁירַיִים עַל שִׁבְעִים אַמָּה וְשִׁירַיִים.

Rabbi Yehuda says: This is not necessary, for **even if it contains only a** water **cistern, an** elongated water **ditch, or a cave,** i.e., a covered pit containing water, **one may carry inside it,** as the water bestows upon it the status of a dwelling. **Rabbi Akiva says: Even if it has none of these**[N] **one may carry inside it, provided that it measures** not more than **seventy cubits and a remainder by seventy cubits and a remainder.**[H]

רַבִּי אֱלִיעֶזֶר אוֹמֵר: אִם הָיְתָה אׇרְכָּהּ יָתֵר עַל רׇחְבָּהּ אֲפִילּוּ אַמָּה אַחַת – אֵין מְטַלְטְלִין בְּתוֹכָהּ. רַבִּי יוֹסֵי אוֹמֵר: אֲפִילּוּ אׇרְכָּהּ פִּי שְׁנַיִם בְּרׇחְבָּהּ מְטַלְטְלִין בְּתוֹכָהּ.

Rabbi Eliezer says: If its length is greater than its breadth, even by one cubit, one may not carry inside it, even though its total area does not exceed an area of two *beit se'a*, because in an area that was enclosed not for the purpose of residence, carrying is only permitted if the area is perfectly square. **Rabbi Yosei says: Even if its length is double its breadth, one may carry inside it,** and there is no need to be particular about a square shape.

אָמַר רַבִּי אֶלְעַאי, שָׁמַעְתִּי מֵרַבִּי אֱלְעָזָר: וַאֲפִילּוּ הִיא כְּבֵית כּוֹר.

Rabbi Elai said: I heard from Rabbi Eliezer[N] that one is permitted to carry in a garden or *karpef*, **even** if the garden **is** an area of a ***beit kor***, i.e., thirty times larger than the area of a *beit se'a*.

NOTES

Near the town – סְמוּכָה לָעִיר: According to most commentaries, near means within two thousand cubits, the Shabbat limit, although some commentaries rule that it must be within a little more than seventy cubits (*Me'iri*). The rationale is that if the enclosed area is close to a place of residence, it resembles a garden and a courtyard near a person's residence, which grants it the status of an area enclosed for the purpose of residence.

Even if it has none – אֲפִילּוּ אֵין בָּהּ אַחַת: Many old texts have the following version: Even if it only has one of these. This version is problematic, because it implies that a cistern or something similar is required, which is the opinion of Rabbi Yehuda ben Bava. The explanation given for this is that Rabbi Akiva means that any one of the conditions stipulated by Rabbi Yehuda ben Bava is required: The size of the area, or that it be enclosed for the sake of dwelling, or that it contain a residential house or something similar (Rashba).

I heard from Rabbi Eliezer – שָׁמַעְתִּי מֵרַבִּי אֱלִיעֶזֶר: In the standard Vilna edition of the Talmud, the mishna quotes Rabbi Elai saying that he heard the statement from Rabbi Elazar. The Gemara below (26b) refers to the *tanna* from whom Rabbi Elai heard the statement as Rabbi Eliezer. This version of the mishna, Rabbi Eliezer, is found in virtually all other editions of the Talmud. In an attempt to preserve both traditions, the Hebrew mishna reflects the version that appears in the Vilna edition and its translation reflects the version that appears in the Gemara and the other editions.

HALAKHA

An area enclosed not for the purpose of residence – מְחִיצָה שֶׁאֵין בָּהּ בֵּית דִּירָה: It is permitted to carry in an enclosed area, even if it was not enclosed for the purpose of residence, provided it is not larger that the area of two *beit se'a*, or about five thousand square cubits, even if its shape is not square. This is in accordance with the opinions of Rabbi Akiva and Rabbi Yosei, as the Gemara states that the *halakha* follows their opinions (*Shulḥan Arukh, Oraḥ Ḥayyim* 358:1).

וְכֵן שָׁמַעְתִּי מִמֶּנּוּ: אַנְשֵׁי חָצֵר שֶׁשָּׁכַח אֶחָד מֵהֶן וְלֹא עֵירֵב – בֵּיתוֹ אָסוּר מִלְּהַכְנִיס וּלְהוֹצִיא לוֹ, אֲבָל לָהֶם מוּתָּר.

Incidentally, he adds: **And I also heard from him** another *halakha*: If **one of the residents of a courtyard forgot and did not join in an *eiruv*** with the other residents when they established an *eiruv*, and on Shabbat he ceded ownership of his part in the courtyard to the other residents, then it **is prohibited for him,** the one who forgot to establish an *eiruv*, **to bring in** objects **or take** them **out** from **his house** to the courtyard; **however, it is permitted to them,** the other residents, to bring objects from their houses to that person's house via the courtyard, and vice versa. We do not say that the failure of one resident to join in the *eiruv* nullifies the validity of the *eiruv* for the entire courtyard.

וְכֵן שָׁמַעְתִּי מִמֶּנּוּ שֶׁיּוֹצְאִין בְּעַרְקַבְלִין בְּפֶסַח, וְחָזַרְתִּי עַל כָּל תַּלְמִידָיו וּבִקַּשְׁתִּי לִי חָבֵר וְלֹא מָצָאתִי.

And I also heard from him another *halakha,* **that one may fulfill his obligation** to eat bitter herbs **on Passover with *arkablin,*** a certain bitter herb. With regard to all three rulings, **I circulated among all** of Rabbi Eliezer's **disciples, seeking a colleague**[N] who had also heard these matters from him, **but I could not find** one.

גמ׳ מַאי תַּנָּא דְּקָתָנֵי ״וְעוֹד״?

GEMARA The Gemara first analyzes the wording of this mishna: **What was taught** previously, **that** the *tanna* **teaches** in this mishna: **And furthermore**[N] Rabbi Yehuda ben Bava said, which implies a continuation of the previous mishna?

אִילֵימָא מִשּׁוּם דְּתָנָא לֵיהּ חֲדָא לְחוּמְרָא וְקָתָנֵי אַחֲרִיתִי מִשּׁוּם הָכִי קָתָנֵי ״וְעוֹד״ – וְהָא רַבִּי יְהוּדָה דְּתָנָא לֵיהּ חֲדָא לְחוּמְרָא וְקָתָנֵי אַחֲרִיתִי, וְלָא קָתָנֵי ״וְעוֹד״!

If you say that **because he** first **taught one stringency** concerning the upright boards surrounding a well, **and** then **he teaches another** stringency[N] about an enclosure, and **for that reason** the *tanna* of the mishna **teaches: And furthermore,** then there is a difficulty. **Didn't Rabbi Yehuda** also **teach one stringency and** then **teach another** stringency, **and** yet the *tanna* of the mishna **does not teach: And furthermore** Rabbi Yehuda said?

הָתָם אַפְסְקוּהּ רַבָּנַן, הָכָא לָא אַפְסְקוּהּ רַבָּנַן.

The Gemara answers that the cases are different: **There, the Rabbis interrupted** Rabbi Yehuda's statements in order to disagree with him, and hence it is not possible to say: And furthermore Rabbi Yehuda said. **Here,** however, **the Rabbis did not interrupt him,** as the two statements of Rabbi Yehuda ben Bava immediately follow one another.

וְכָל הֵיכָא דְּאַפְסְקוּהּ רַבָּנַן לָא קָתָנֵי ״וְעוֹד״? וְהָא רַבִּי אֱלִיעֶזֶר דְּסוּכָּה, דְּאַפְסְקוּהּ רַבָּנַן וְקָתָנֵי ״וְעוֹד״!

The Gemara raises a difficulty: Does this mean that **wherever the** disputing **Rabbis interrupt** their colleague, the *tanna* **teaches: And furthermore? But** with regard to **Rabbi Eliezer** in a mishna **in** tractate ***Sukka*** (27a), **where the Rabbis interrupted his** statements, nonetheless the *tanna* **teaches: And furthermore.**

הָתָם בְּמִילְּתֵיהּ הוּא דְּאַפְסְקוּהּ, הָכָא בְּמִילְּתָא אַחֲרִיתִי אַפְסְקוּהּ.

The Gemara answers: It is not the same; **there, they interrupted** Rabbi Eliezer **with** a ruling with regard to **his** own **topic; here,** however, **they interrupted** Rabbi Yehuda with a ruling with regard to **an** altogether **different matter.** Consequently, his first statement had already been forgotten, and it is not the Mishna's style to join together statements where the sequential link between them has already been severed.

״רַבִּי עֲקִיבָא אוֹמֵר: אֲפִילּוּ אֵין בָּהּ אֶחָד מִכָּל אֵלּוּ מְטַלְטְלִין בְּתוֹכָהּ״.

We learned in the mishna: **Rabbi Akiva said: Even** if the courtyard **has none of these** elements that indicate dwelling stipulated by the other Rabbis, **one may carry inside it,** provided that it measures no more than seventy cubits and a remainder by seventy cubits and a remainder.

NOTES

Seeking a colleague – בִּקַּשְׁתִּי לִי חָבֵר: Rabbi Elai, who was Rabbi Eliezer's preeminent student, heard him teach these three laws, but he could not find among the other students a single person who could also recall hearing even one of them. Consequently, he was worried that he might be mistaken. However, elsewhere it is related (*Pesaḥim* 39a) that Rabbi Elai heard one of his master's colleagues teaching one of these laws in his master's name.

What was taught, that he teaches: And furthermore – מַאי תַּנָּא דְּקָתָנֵי ״וְעוֹד״: It is unusual to say: And furthermore, unless one is dealing with the same issue, whereas in this context the words of Rabbi Yehuda ben Bava are not a continuation of his statement with regard to upright boards surrounding a well. Therefore, the Gemara questions the use of the phrase: And furthermore (Ritva).

Teaches a stringency – תָּנָא לְחוּמְרָא: The common denominator among Rabbi Yehuda ben Bava's statements is that his approach is the most stringent of all the opinions taught concerning the law of upright boards surrounding a well and of enclosed areas.

רַבִּי עֲקִיבָא הַיְינוּ תַּנָּא קַמָּא!

The Gemara asks: But the view of **Rabbi Akiva is** the same as that of **the first *tanna*,** i.e., Rabbi Yehuda ben Bava, who maintains that in the case of a garden that was not enclosed for the purpose of residence, one is only permitted to carry if the area of the enclosed area is no more than two *beit se'a*. Rabbi Akiva disagrees only about whether we require a watchman's booth or a dwelling place as well, but the two agree with regard to the size of the garden. Therefore, Rabbi Akiva's stipulation: Provided that it measures not more than seventy cubits and a remainder by seventy cubits and a remainder, is superfluous.

אִיכָּא בֵּינַיְיהוּ דָּבָר מוּעָט. דְּתַנְיָא, רַבִּי יְהוּדָה אוֹמֵר: דָּבָר מוּעָט יֵשׁ עַל שִׁבְעִים אַמָּה וְשִׁירַיִם, וְלֹא נָתְנוּ חֲכָמִים בּוֹ שִׁיעוּר.

The Gemara answers: **There is** a practical difference **between them** with regard to **a tiny amount.** And what is this tiny amount? It is **as it was taught** in a *baraita*: **Rabbi Yehuda says:** It is by **a tiny amount**[N] that one of the sides of a square measuring two *beit se'a* **exceeds seventy cubits and a remainder, but the Sages did not give its** exact **measurement,** owing to its small size and because it is impossible to be absolutely precise about the matter.

וְכַמָּה שִׁיעוּר סָאתַיִם – כַּחֲצַר הַמִּשְׁכָּן.

And what is the **measure** of the area of **two *beit se'a*?**[H] It is as large **as the courtyard of the Tabernacle,**[B] which was fifty cubits by one hundred cubits. The first *tanna* and Rabbi Akiva dispute this issue: The first *tanna* maintains that the garden may have an area as large as two *beit se'a*, whereas Rabbi Akiva says that it must not exceed seventy and two-thirds cubits squared.

מְנָא הָנֵי מִילֵּי?

The Gemara asks: **From where are these matters derived?** The matters referred to are that we must square the courtyard of the Tabernacle in order to reach the size of garden or similar enclosure in which one is permitted to carry on Shabbat.

אָמַר רַב יְהוּדָה: דְּאָמַר קְרָא: "אֹרֶךְ הֶחָצֵר מֵאָה בָאַמָּה וְרֹחַב חֲמִשִּׁים בַּחֲמִשִּׁים", אָמְרָה תּוֹרָה: טוֹל חֲמִשִּׁים וְסַבֵּב חֲמִשִּׁים.

The Gemara answers: **Rav Yehuda said:** This is learned from **the** verse that **stated: "The length of the courtyard shall be a hundred cubits, and the breadth fifty by fifty,** and the height, five cubits of fine twined linen, and their sockets of brass" (Exodus 27:18). **The Torah said: Take** a square of **fifty** cubits by fifty cubits, **and surround** it with the remaining **fifty** cubits[NB] until they form a square, each side of which measures seventy cubits and a remainder.

NOTES

A tiny amount – דָּבָר מוּעָט: In the Jerusalem Talmud, the Sages explain that the measure of seventy cubits and a remainder is actually seventy and two-thirds cubits. The area of a square with each side measuring seventy and two-thirds cubits is slightly less than two *beit se'a* of grain, which is five thousand cubits. A more precise measure for the side of the square is 70.71 cubits, which yields an area exact to a tenth of a square cubit. Since the absolutely precise measure of the side of the square is the square root of five thousand, an irrational number, it is impossible to establish it exactly (see Rambam's Commentary on the Mishna). Rabbi Yehuda ben Bava maintains that we must try to get as close as possible to the correct size, whereas Rabbi Akiva teaches for the purpose of this law that the looser approximation determined by the Sages, seventy cubits and a remainder, is adequate. There is no need to be more exact with regard to something that can never be precisely measured.

Take fifty and surround it with fifty – טוֹל חֲמִשִּׁים וְסַבֵּב חֲמִשִּׁים: Rashi explains that the phrase: Surround it with fifty, refers to a method of finding the square root of a number. Since the various methods of finding the square root of a number were highly complicated, it was generally accomplished by cutting strips and moving them around until the required size was reached.

HALAKHA

The measure of the area of two *beit se'a* – שִׁיעוּר סָאתַיִם: The measure of two *beit se'a*, utilized in various areas of *halakha*, is equal to the area of the courtyard of the Tabernacle, five thousand square cubits (Rambam *Sefer Zemanim, Hilkhot Shabbat* 6:4).

BACKGROUND

The Tabernacle – הַמִּשְׁכָּן: As stated in the book of Exodus, the length of the Tabernacle courtyard was one hundred cubits, and its width was fifty cubits. The Tabernacle itself was located fifty cubits from the entrance to the courtyard, which left an area of fifty cubits by fifty cubits for the courtyard itself. The Tabernacle's own measurements were thirty cubits length by ten cubits width. The area of the courtyard of the Tabernacle, which was determined as two *beit se'a*, was used as the basis for a number of measurements related to the *halakhot* of Shabbat.

Illustration of the Tabernacle and its courtyard

Take fifty and surround it with fifty – טוֹל חֲמִשִּׁים וְסַבֵּב חֲמִשִּׁים: The courtyard of the Tabernacle was one hundred cubits by fifty cubits. To find the square root of its area, the Sages divided it into different units. In the illustration, the white area represents fifty by fifty cubits. This is what the Gemara terms: Take fifty. The other section, which also represents fifty by fifty cubits, features various markings that indicate how it is cut into strips and made to surround the first square (see Rashi's commentary).

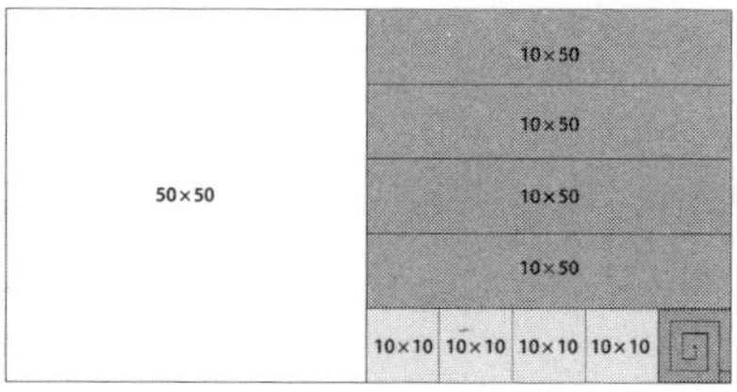

Area of the Tabernacle courtyard divided into strips

The interpretation in the Jerusalem Talmud of the words: Take fifty and surround it with fifty, begins with a square seventy cubits by seventy cubits, and adds to it strips of a third of a cubit on all four sides, filling in the corners. This yields a calculation within two-ninths of a square cubit of the precise measurement.

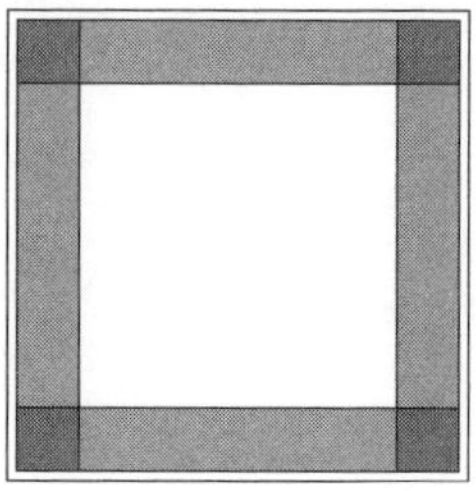

Strips all around and in corners

Corners filled in

פְּשָׁטֵיהּ דִּקְרָא בְּמַאי כְּתִיב? אָמַר אַבָּיֵי: הַעֲמֵד מִשְׁכָּן עַל שְׂפַת חֲמִשִּׁים, כְּדֵי שֶׁיְּהֵא חֲמִשִּׁים אַמָּה לְפָנָיו, וְעֶשְׂרִים אַמָּה לְכָל רוּחַ וְרוּחַ.

The Gemara asks: But **to what does the plain meaning of the verse refer?** The plain sense of the text cannot be coming to teach us the laws of carrying. **Abaye said** that it means as follows: The Tabernacle was thirty cubits long and ten cubits wide. The courtyard was a hundred cubits long and fifty cubits wide. **Position the Tabernacle** in the middle of the courtyard **at the edge of fifty** cubits, **so that there is** a space of **fifty cubits in front of it, and** a space of **twenty cubits in every direction,** on each of the two sides and behind it.

״רַבִּי אֱלִיעֶזֶר אוֹמֵר: אִם הָיְתָה אׇרְכָּהּ כו׳״. וְהָתַנְיָא, רַבִּי אֱלִיעֶזֶר אוֹמֵר: אִם הָיְתָה אׇרְכָּהּ יָתֵר עַל פִּי שְׁנַיִם בְּרׇחְבָּהּ אֲפִילּוּ אַמָּה אַחַת אֵין מְטַלְטְלִין בְּתוֹכָהּ!

We learned in the mishna that **Rabbi Eliezer says: If its length is** greater than its breadth, even by one cubit, one may not carry inside it. The Gemara asks: **Wasn't it taught** in a *baraita* that **Rabbi Eliezer says: If its length is more than double its breadth, even by one cubit, one may not carry inside it?**

אָמַר רַב בֵּיבָי בַּר אַבָּיֵי: כִּי תְּנַן נַמִּי מַתְנִיתִין, [יָתֵר עַל] פִּי שְׁנַיִם בְּרׇחְבָּהּ תְּנַן. אִי הָכִי הַיְינוּ רַבִּי יוֹסֵי!

Rav Beivai bar Abaye said: When we learned this **in the mishna,** we **also** learned that it refers to a case where the length of the enclosure is **more than double its breadth.** The Gemara raises a difficulty: **If so, this is** the same as the opinion of **Rabbi Yosei,** who stated that one is permitted to carry in the garden or *karpef* even if its length is double its width.

אִיכָּא בֵּינַיְיהוּ רִיבּוּעָא דְּרִיבְּעוּהָ רַבָּנַן.

The Gemara answers: **There is** a difference **between them** with regard to **the square that the Sages squared it,**[NB] because the Sages calculated squares with the diagonal. According to the opinion of Rabbi Eliezer, if the diagonal is more than double the breadth, even though the length may not be more than double the breadth, it is prohibited to carry within the enclosure. According to Rabbi Yosei, however, it is permitted (Rabbeinu Ḥananel).

״רַבִּי יוֹסֵי אוֹמֵר כו׳״. אִיתְּמַר, אָמַר רַב יוֹסֵף, אָמַר רַב יְהוּדָה, אָמַר שְׁמוּאֵל: הֲלָכָה כְּרַבִּי יוֹסֵי. וְרַב בֵּיבָי אָמַר רַב יְהוּדָה, אָמַר שְׁמוּאֵל: הֲלָכָה כְּרַבִּי עֲקִיבָא.

We learned in the mishna that **Rabbi Yosei says:** Even if its length is double its breadth, one may carry inside it. **It was stated** that the *amora'im* disagreed on the following matter: **Rav Yosef said** that **Rav Yehuda said** that **Shmuel said:** The ***halakha* is in accordance with** the opinion of **Rabbi Yosei. And Rav Beivai said** that **Rav Yehuda said** that **Shmuel said:** The ***halakha* is in accordance with** the opinion of **Rabbi Akiva.**

וְתַרְוַיְיהוּ לְקוּלָּא. וּצְרִיכָא, דְּאִי אַשְׁמְעִינַן הֲלָכָה כְּרַבִּי יוֹסֵי – הֲוָה אָמִינָא עַד דְּאִיכָּא שׁוֹמֵירָה אוֹ בֵּית דִּירָה, קָא מַשְׁמַע לָן הֲלָכָה כְּרַבִּי עֲקִיבָא.

The Gemara explains that **both** rulings **are** stated **leniently, and** that both were **necessary. As had** the Gemara **taught** only that the ***halakha* is in accordance with** the opinion of **Rabbi Yosei, I would have said** that one is not permitted to carry **unless** the place **contains a watchman's booth or a dwelling place,** for Rabbi Yosei did not specify that these are not required. Therefore, the Gemara **teaches us** that the ***halakha* is in accordance with Rabbi Akiva,** who is particular only about the courtyard's size, but not that it be enclosed for the purpose of residence.

וְאִי אַשְׁמְעִינַן הֲלָכָה כְּרַבִּי עֲקִיבָא – הֲוָה אָמִינָא דַּאֲרִיךְ וּקְטִין לָא, קָא מַשְׁמַע לָן הֲלָכָה כְּרַבִּי יוֹסֵי.

And, on the other hand, **had** the Gemara **taught** only that the ***halakha* is in accordance with** the opinion of **Rabbi Akiva, I would have said** that if the courtyard is **long and narrow,** one is **not** permitted to carry. Therefore, the Gemara **teaches** that the ***halakha* is in accordance with** the opinion of **Rabbi Yosei,** who clearly states that the courtyard need not be square.

קַרְפֵּף שֶׁהוּא יוֹתֵר מִבֵּית סָאתַיִם שֶׁהוּקַּף לְדִירָה, נִזְרַע רוּבּוֹ – הֲרֵי הוּא כְּגִינָּה, וְאָסוּר.

The Sages taught: Within **a *karpef* that is greater than two *beit se'a,*** but **which was enclosed** from the outset **for the purpose of residence,** carrying is permitted regardless of its size; however, if subsequently **the greater part of it was sown** with seed crops, **it is** considered **like a garden,** which is not a place of dwelling, **and it is prohibited** to carry anything within it.

נִטַּע רוּבּוֹ – הֲרֵי הוּא כְּחָצֵר, וּמוּתָּר.

However, if **the greater part of it was planted** with trees, **it is** considered **like a courtyard,** which is a place of dwelling, **and** one **is permitted** to carry. The reason for this distinction is that the presence of trees does not nullify the status of the *karpef* as a place of residence, because people normally plant trees even in their courtyards. However, people ordinarily plant seed crops only in gardens at some distance from their houses, in places they do not use for dwelling; therefore, the presence of seed crops does nullify the residential status of the *karpef.*

NOTES

The square that the Sages squared it – רִיבּוּעָא דְּרִיבְּעוּהָ רַבָּנַן: Rashi explains that there is no halakhic dispute here. Rather, the Sages are discussing theoretical question of whether or not the shape must be a square or a rectangle, *ab initio*. One explanation (Rabbeinu Ḥananel and the *ge'onim*) is that the disagreement involves a rhombus-shaped field where each side is of equal length while one diagonal is twice the length of the other (*Korban Netanel*).

BACKGROUND

The square that the Sages squared it – רִיבּוּעָא דְּרִיבְּעוּהָ רַבָּנַן: In this rectangle the length (a–d) is less than twice the width (a–b), but the diagonal (a–c) is more than twice the width. According to Rabbi Eliezer it is prohibited to carry in an enclosed area with such dimensions.

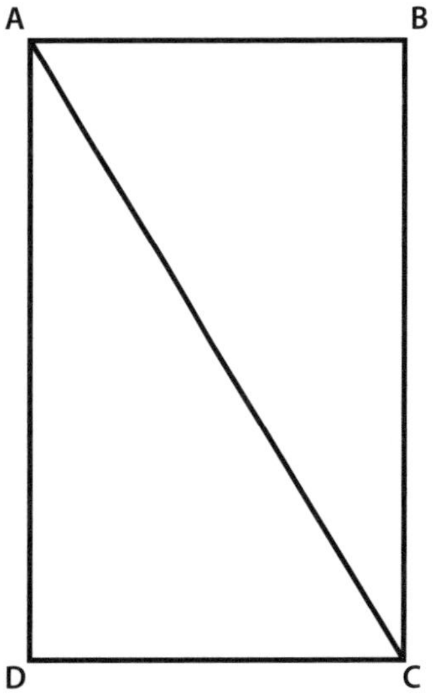

Long rectangular enclosure

NOTES

The domain of utensils that began Shabbat – רְשׁוּת לְכֵלִים שֶׁשָּׁבְתוּ: The common feature of a roof, a courtyard, and an enclosed area [*karpef*] is that none of them is an actual place of human residence, and the law that applies to them resembles that of a *karmelit*. According to Rabbi Shimon, since none of these areas is a place of permanent residence, they are not divided into separate domains, as are houses and courtyards. Consequently, it is unnecessary to make a joining of courtyards [*eiruv*] in order to carry from one to another. However, it is prohibited to carry utensils that were in the house into an enclosed area, because they are certainly two separate domains.

״נִזְרַע רוּבּוֹ״, אָמַר רַב הוּנָא בְּרֵיהּ דְּרַב יְהוֹשֻׁעַ: לָא אֲמַרַן אֶלָּא יוֹתֵר מִבֵּית סָאתַיִם, אֲבָל בֵּית סָאתַיִם – מוּתָּר.

It was stated above that if **the greater part of** the *karpef* **was sown** with seed crops, it is prohibited to carry in it. **Rav Huna, son of Rav Yehoshua, said: We only said** this in a case where the sown section is **greater than two *beit se'a*, but** if it is no more than **two *beit se'a*,** it is **permitted.**

כְּמַאן – כְּרַבִּי שִׁמְעוֹן; דִּתְנַן, רַבִּי שִׁמְעוֹן אוֹמֵר: אֶחָד גַּגּוֹת וְאֶחָד חֲצֵירוֹת וְאֶחָד קַרְפֵּיפוֹת רְשׁוּת אַחַת הֵן לְכֵלִים שֶׁשָּׁבְתוּ בְּתוֹכָן, וְלֹא לְכֵלִים שֶׁשָּׁבְתוּ בְּתוֹךְ הַבַּיִת.

The Gemara comments: **In accordance with whose** opinion was this stated? It was stated **in accordance with** the opinion of **Rabbi Shimon, as we learned** in a mishna: **Rabbi Shimon says: Roofs, courtyards, and *karpeifot* are all one domain with regard to utensils that began Shabbat**[N] **in them,** even if the utensils belong to different people. Since these are not proper dwelling places, setting an *eiruv* is unnecessary, and objects may be carried from place to place within them. But they are **not** one domain **with regard to utensils that began Shabbat in the house** and that were later taken outside. This shows that the unsown part of a *karpef* and the sown part, which has the status of a garden, are considered a single domain, in which one is permitted to carry, as the garden section does not prohibit the *karpef* section.

לְרַבִּי שִׁמְעוֹן נַמִי, כֵּיוָן דְּנִזְרַע רוּבּוֹ – הָוֵי הַהוּא מִעוּטָא

The Gemara rejects this argument: **Even according to** the opinion of **Rabbi Shimon, since the greater part of** the *karpef* **is sown, the minor** part

Perek **II**
Daf **24** Amud **a**

HALAKHA

The greater part of the *karpef* was sown – נִזְרַע רוּבּוֹ: If most of the enclosed area [*karpef*] is sown, it is prohibited to carry in it, even if the enclosure is no larger than two *beit se'a* of grain. Some commentaries rule that it is prohibited to carry even if the enclosure is smaller than two *beit se'a* (Rema; Vilna Gaon; *Shulḥan Arukh, Oraḥ Ḥayyim* 358:9).

A minor part of the *karpef* was sown – נִזְרַע מִיעוּטוֹ: If less than half of the enclosed area [*karpef*] is sown, and the sown area is the size of two *beit se'a*, then it is permitted to carry. It is prohibited to carry if the sown area is greater than two *beit se'a*, since the *halakha* follows the second version in the Gemara (*Maggid Mishne*). Furthermore, Rabbi Shimon's opinion is accepted as the *halakha* (*Taz*; *Shulḥan Arukh*, *Oraḥ Ḥayyim* 358:9).

Planted in rows – עֲשׂוּיִין אִצְטַבְלָאוֹת: The presence of trees in an enclosure does not render it prohibited to carry, even if they were not arranged in rows. The *halakha* is in accordance with the opinion of Rav Naḥman both because he was a preeminent authority and because the Gemara reports an actual case that was ruled in accordance with his opinion (*Shulḥan Arukh*, *Oraḥ Ḥayyim* 358:9).

NOTES

Rows – אִצְטַבְלָאוֹת: Some commentaries explain that it is inconvenient to walk through the garden if the trees are not arranged in rows, and that this impairs the ability of the *karpef* to serve as a residence (*Arukh*).

LANGUAGE

Rows [*itztablaot*] – אִצְטַבְלָאוֹת: From the Latin stabulum, meaning a horse stable. The Talmud uses the word to connote stables, and by extension, to describe other items arranged in rows like horses in a stable.

בָּטֵיל לֵיהּ לְגַבֵּי רוּבָּה, וַהֲוָה לֵיהּ קַרְפֵּף יוֹתֵר מִבֵּית סָאתַיִם – וְאָסוּר.

is nullified relative **to the greater part,** and it is as though the *karpef* were entirely sown. **And** therefore, **it is** regarded as **a *karpef* greater than two *beit se'a*,** in which it is **prohibited** to carry.

אֶלָּא, אִי אִיתְּמַר הָכִי אִיתְּמַר: הָא מִיעוּטָא שָׁרֵי. אָמַר רַב הוּנָא בְּרֵיהּ דְּרַב יְהוֹשֻׁעַ: לָא אֲמַרַן אֶלָּא דְּלָא הָוֵי בֵּית סָאתַיִם, אֲבָל בֵּית סָאתַיִם – אָסוּר.

Rather, if this was stated, this is what was stated by Rav Huna, son of Rav Yehoshua: If the greater part of the *karpef* was sown,[H] it is prohibited to carry within it. It follows that if only a **minor** part of the *karpef* was sown,[H] it is **permitted** to carry within it. **Rav Huna, son of Rav Yehoshua, said: We said** that it is permitted to carry **only** if the sown section **is not** as large as **two *beit se'a*, however,** if it is at least **two *beit se'a*,** it **is prohibited** to carry anywhere in the *karpef*, even though most of it is not sown.

כְּמַאן – כְּרַבָּנַן.

The Gemara asks: **According to whose** opinion was this stated? It is **according to** the opinion of **the Rabbis,** who disagree with Rabbi Shimon and say that a *karpef* and a courtyard are regarded as separate domains, so that it is prohibited to carry from one to the other.

וְרַב יִרְמְיָה מִדִּיפְתִּי מַתְנֵי לְקוּלָּא: הָא מִיעוּטָא – שָׁרֵי. אָמַר רַב הוּנָא בְּרֵיהּ דְּרַב יְהוֹשֻׁעַ: לָא אֲמַרַן אֶלָּא בֵּית סָאתַיִם, אֲבָל יוֹתֵר מִבֵּית סָאתַיִם – אָסוּר, כְּמַאן – כְּרַבִּי שִׁמְעוֹן.

And Rav Yirmeya from Difti would teach this matter **as a leniency,** as follows: It was stated that if the greater part of the *karpef* was sown, it is prohibited to carry within it. From here it follows that if only a **minor** part was sown, it **is permitted** to carry within it. **Rav Huna, son of Rav Yehoshua said: We only said** that it is permitted to carry if the sown section is not more than **two *beit se'a*, but** if it is **more than two *beit se'a*,** it **is prohibited** to carry. **According to whose** opinion was this stated? It was **according to** the opinion of **Rabbi Shimon.**

״נִטַּע רוּבּוֹ – הֲרֵי הוּא כְּחָצֵר, וּמוּתָּר״. אָמַר רַב יְהוּדָה, אָמַר אֲבִימִי: וְהוּא שֶׁעֲשׂוּיִין אִצְטַבְלָאוֹת. וְרַב נַחְמָן אָמַר: אַף עַל פִּי שֶׁאֵין עֲשׂוּיִין אִצְטַבְלָאוֹת.

It was stated earlier that if **the greater part of** the *karpef* **was planted** with trees, **it is** considered **like a courtyard, and** it is **permitted** to carry. **Rav Yehuda said** that **Avimi said: This is** only if the trees **were planted in rows** [***itztablaot***],[HNL] the customary manner of planting ornamental trees in a courtyard. But if they were arranged differently it is considered an orchard, which is not made for dwelling, and where it is prohibited to carry. **But Rav Naḥman said:** This applies **even if they were not planted in rows,** as people commonly plant trees in any arrangement in the courtyards of their houses.

מָר יְהוּדָה אִקְלַע לְבֵי רַב הוּנָא בַּר יְהוּדָה, חַזְנְהוּ לְהָנְהוּ דְּלָא עֲבִידִי אִצְטַבְלָאוֹת, וְקָא מְטַלְטְלֵי בְּגַוַּויְהוּ. אֲמַר לֵיהּ: לָא סָבַר לַהּ מָר לְהָא דַּאֲבִימִי? אֲמַר לֵיהּ: אֲנָא כְּרַב נַחְמָן סְבִירָא לִי.

Mar Yehuda happened to come **to the house of Rav Huna bar Yehuda,** where **he saw certain** trees **that were not planted in rows, and** people **were** nevertheless **carrying among them.** Mar Yehuda **said to** Rav Huna: **Doesn't the Master hold** in accordance **with this** opinion **of Avimi?** Rav Huna **said to him: I hold like** the opinion of **Rav Naḥman,** that it is permitted to carry even if the trees are not planted in rows.

אָמַר רַב נַחְמָן, אָמַר שְׁמוּאֵל: קַרְפֵּף יוֹתֵר מִבֵּית סָאתַיִם שֶׁלֹּא הוּקַּף לְדִירָה, כֵּיצַד הוּא עוֹשֶׂה? פּוֹרֵץ בּוֹ פִּירְצָה יוֹתֵר מֵעֶשֶׂר, וְגוֹדְרוֹ וּמַעֲמִידוֹ עַל עֶשֶׂר, וּמוּתָּר.

Rav Naḥman said that **Shmuel said:** With regard to **a *karpef* that is greater than two *beit se'a*,** and **which was not enclosed** from the outset **for** the purpose of **residence, what should one do** if he wishes to carry within it? **He should make a breach** in the fence **larger than ten** cubits, which nullifies the partition, **and** then **fence it off and reduce** the opening **to** only **ten** cubits, which thereby creates an entrance. He **is** then **permitted** to carry in the *karpef*, because it is now regarded as having been enclosed for the purpose of residence.[H]

אִיבַּעְיָא לְהוּ: פָּרַץ אַמָּה וְגָדַר אַמָּה [וּפָרַץ אַמָּה וּגְדָרָהּ] עַד שֶׁהִשְׁלִימוֹ לְיוֹתֵר מֵעֶשֶׂר, מַהוּ?

The Gemara **raises a dilemma:** If he did not make the breach at once, but rather **he breached one cubit and fenced off** that same **cubit, and** then **breached** another **cubit and fenced it off, until he completed** the breaching and fencing off of **more than ten** cubits, **what is** the law?

אֲמַר לֵיהּ: לָאו הַיְינוּ דִּתְנַן: כׇּל כְּלֵי בַעֲלֵי בָתִּים שִׁיעוּרָן כְּרִמּוֹנִים.

He said to him: Is this not as we learned in a mishna: **All** ritually impure wooden **utensils belonging to** ordinary **homeowners** become ritually pure through breaking the utensil, if they have holes **the size of pomegranates.**[H]

וּבָעֵי חִזְקִיָּה: נִיקַּב כְּמוֹצִיא זַיִת וּסְתָמוֹ, וְחָזַר וְנִיקַּב כְּמוֹצִיא זַיִת וּסְתָמוֹ עַד שֶׁהִשְׁלִימוֹ לְמוֹצִיא רִמּוֹן, מַהוּ?

And Ḥizkiya raised a dilemma: If a utensil **was perforated** with a hole large enough **for an olive to emerge, and he sealed it, and then it was perforated again** with a hole large enough **for an olive to emerge, and he sealed it** again, and this went on **until** the holes together **completed** a space large enough for **a pomegranate to emerge, what** is the *halakha*? In other words, is the ruling that because the sum of all the holes is the size of a pomegranate the utensil is pure, or is the ruling that it remains ritually impure because each hole was filled before the next hole was formed?

וַאֲמַר לֵיהּ רַבִּי יוֹחָנָן: רַבִּי, שָׁנִיתָה לָנוּ: סַנְדָּל שֶׁנִּפְסְקָה אַחַת מֵאׇזְנָיו וְתִיקְּנָהּ – טָמֵא מִדְרָס,

Rabbi Yoḥanan his student **said to him: Master, you taught us** that with regard to a **sandal**[B] **that** became ritually impure by impurity imparted by the treading of a *zav*, and **one of its ears,** i.e., straps, **broke and he repaired it,** it remains **ritually impure** with impurity imparted by **treading** [*midras*][N] and can still render people and utensils ritually impure. If one of a sandal's straps is torn, it can still be used as a sandal, and therefore it does not lose its status as a utensil.

נִפְסְקָה שְׁנִיָּה וְתִיקְּנָהּ – טָהוֹר בָּהּ מִן הַמִּדְרָס, אֲבָל טָמֵא מַגַּע מִדְרָס.

If the second **ear** broke and he repaired it, it is **ritually pure** in the sense that it no longer renders other objects ritually impure as would a vessel that became a primary source of ritual impurity **by means of** impurity imparted by **treading.**[H] **However,** the sandal itself is **ritually impure**[N] due to **contact** with an object that became ritually impure with impurity imparted by **treading,** i.e., the sandal before its second strap ripped. Therefore, it can transmit ritual impurity to food and liquids.

וְאָמַרְתָּ עֲלָהּ מַאי שְׁנָא רִאשׁוֹנָה – דְּהָא קַיְימָא שְׁנִיָּה, שְׁנִיָּה נָמֵי הָא קַיְימָא רִאשׁוֹנָה!

And you said about this *halakha*: **What is different** in a case where **the first** ear breaks, that the sandal remains impure? It is **because** the **second** one is **intact.** However, when the **second** ear breaks, the **first** ear is **intact;** so how does the sandal lose its utensil status?

NOTES

Ritual impurity imparted by treading [*midras*] and ritual impurity from contact with a ritually impure object by treading – מִדְרָס וּמַגַּע מִדְרָס: A utensil contracts ritual impurity imparted by treading [*midras*] when a *zav*, or a *zava*, or a woman after childbirth, or a menstruating woman sits or treads upon it. This is a stringent form of ritual impurity, as an object with this type of impurity defiles other objects that come into contact with it.

The impurity of a sandal – טוּמְאַת הַסַּנְדָּל: See Rashi and *Tosafot* for explanations of the sandal's impurity due to contact with an object that became ritually impure with impurity imparted by treading [*midras*]. Apparently, there is reason to question the source of this impurity. Most commentaries agree that a ripped sandal strap loses its ritual impurity imparted by treading, but contracts a lower level of impurity when it is reattached to the sandal, from contact with an object with impurity imparted by treading. This impurity subsequently spreads throughout the entire sandal, but it is irrelevant because the sandal still has a more severe level of impurity, namely, the ritual impurity imparted by treading. However, when the impurity imparted by treading is removed, the lower level impurity, the impurity of contact with an object with impurity imparted by treading, still remains (Rashba). See *Tosafot* for a clarification of some of the difficulties with this explanation.

HALAKHA

Rendering a *karpef* fit for carrying within it – תִּיקּוּן קַרְפֵּף: If a *karpef* had been enclosed initially not for the purpose of residence, and now one wishes to utilize it for dwelling, he must make a breach in the wall larger than ten cubits wide, and then rebuild the fence to reduce the opening to only ten cubits. This breach is effective even if it was made in stages, in accordance with the conclusion of the Gemara (*Shulḥan Arukh, Oraḥ Ḥayyim* 358:2).

Homeowners' utensils – כְּלֵי בַּעֲלֵי בָתִּים: A ritually impure wooden utensil that belongs to an individual becomes ritually pure if it is broken, with a hole no smaller than the size of a pomegranate. If one makes a hole the size of an olive in the wooden utensil and then seals it, and once again makes a hole the size of an olive and seals it, and continues to make holes and to seal them until the sum of all the holes is the size of a pomegranate, the utensil becomes ritually pure. This is in accordance with the conclusion of the Gemara (Rambam *Sefer Tahara, Hilkhot Kelim* 6:2).

The purification of a sandal – טָהֳרַת סַנְדָּל: A sandal retains ritual impurity imparted by treading [*midras*] if one of the straps rips. If the sandal is fixed and then the second strap rips, the sandal is still impure due to contact with an object that became ritually impure with impurity imparted by treading. However, if the second strap rips before the first one is fixed, the sandal becomes pure (Rambam *Sefer Tahara, Hilkhot Kelim* 7:12).

BACKGROUND

A sandal – סַנְדָּל: The strap [*ozen*] of the sandal probably refers to the strap that holds the foot tightly to the sole of the sandal.

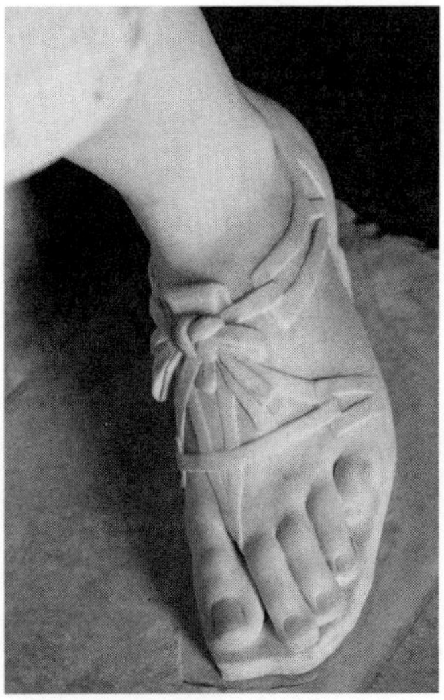

Detail of statue with sandal from the talmudic period

וְאָמְרַתְּ לַן עֲלַהּ: פָּנִים חֲדָשׁוֹת בָּאוּ לְכָאן. הָכָא נַמִי פָּנִים חֲדָשׁוֹת בָּאוּ לְכָאן.

And then **you said to us** with regard to **this** that the reason it is no longer a utensil is because **a new entity has arrived here.** The legal status of the sandal with the two repaired ears is not that of the original sandal; it is a new sandal. **Here, too,** with regard to a utensil that was perforated several times, where the sum of all the holes adds up to the size of a pomegranate, let us say that **a new entity has arrived here,** as the entire area of the hole is completely new, and the utensil is no longer the same utensil that had been ritually impure.

קָרֵי עֲלֵיהּ: לֵית דֵּין בַּר אֱינָשׁ! אִיכָּא דְּאָמְרִי: כְּגוֹן דֵּין בַּר נָשׁ!

Ḥizkiya was so impressed by Rabbi Yoḥanan's comment that **he exclaimed about him: This is not a human being;** rather, he is an angel, as he is capable of resolving a problem that I struggle with, from something that I myself taught. **Some say** that he said: **This is an** ideal **human being.** This parallel analysis teaches that if one breached one cubit and fenced it off, breached another cubit and fenced it off, and continued this way until he breached and fenced off more than ten cubits, then this is effective, and he need not breach more than ten meters at once.

אָמַר רַב כָּהֲנָא: רְחָבָה שֶׁאֲחוֹרֵי הַבָּתִּים, אֵין מְטַלְטְלִין בּוֹ אֶלָּא בְּאַרְבַּע אַמּוֹת.

Rav Kahana said: A fenced-in **yard** located **behind** a group of **houses,**[H] which is used to store objects not in regular use and which measures more than two *beit se'a*, is not treated as a full-fledged private domain. Therefore, **inside it, one may carry** objects a distance of **only four cubits.**

וְאָמַר רַב נַחְמָן: אִם פָּתַח לוֹ פֶּתַח – מוּתָּר לְטַלְטֵל בְּכוּלּוֹ, פֶּתַח מַתִּירוֹ. וְלָא אֲמַרַן אֶלָּא שֶׁפָּתַח וּלְבַסּוֹף הוּקַּף, אֲבָל הוּקַּף וּלְבַסּוֹף פָּתַח – לֹא.

Rav Naḥman said: If one opened an entrance to it from the house, **it is permitted to carry throughout the entire** area, because **the entrance permits it,** allowing it to be considered as part of the house. **And we stated** this allowance **only where he opened** the entrance **and afterward fenced in** the area; **but if he** first **fenced it in and** only **afterward opened** the entrance, he may **not** carry throughout the yard.

פָּתַח וּלְבַסּוֹף הוּקַּף, פְּשִׁיטָא! לָא צְרִיכָא, דְּאִית בֵּיהּ בֵּי דָּרֵי. מַהוּ דְּתֵימָא: אַדַּעְתָּא דְּבֵי דָּרֵי עַבְדֵּיהּ, קָא מַשְׁמַע לַן.

The Gemara raises a difficulty: If he first **opened** the entrance **and afterward fenced in** the area, it is **obvious** that it is permitted to carry throughout the yard, because it is clear that the area was enclosed for the entrance, i.e., in order to use it from the house. The Gemara answers: This ruling **is necessary only** in the case **where there is a threshing floor** in the yard. This is because **you might have said** that **he made** the entrance **with the threshing floor in mind,**[N] and not so that he would be able to use the entire yard. **He** therefore comes and **teaches us** that the entrance renders it permitted to carry in the yard in all cases.

קַרְפֵּף יוֹתֵר מִבֵּית סָאתַיִם שֶׁהוּקַּף לְדִירָה וְנִתְמַלֵּא מַיִם, סְבוּר רַבָּנַן לְמֵימַר כִּזְרָעִים דָּמוּ – וַאֲסִיר.

The Gemara considers a new case: With regard to a ***karpef*** measuring **more than two *beit se'a*, which had been enclosed for** the purpose of **residence but became filled with water,** by floods or any other cause, **the Rabbis thought to say** that the water **is** considered **like seeds.** This means that the *karpef* is regarded as if it were sown with seeds, so that it **is prohibited** to carry. It is no longer considered as having been enclosed for the purpose of dwelling, since it is not normal to live in a place filled with water.

אָמַר לְהוּ רַב אַבָּא אֲבוּהּ דְּרַב בְּרֵיהּ דְּרַב מְשַׁרְשְׁיָא: הָכִי אָמְרִינַן מִשְּׁמֵיהּ דְּרָבָא: מַיִם כִּנְטָעִים דָּמוּ – וְשָׁרֵי.

Rav Abba, father of Rav, son of Rav Mesharshiya, said: We say in the name of Rava as follows: Water is considered **like planted** trees,[H] so that one **is permitted** to carry. A courtyard filled with water is still suitable for dwelling, since the water benefits the residents of the courtyard.

HALAKHA

A yard behind houses – רְחָבָה שֶׁאֲחוֹרֵי הַבָּתִּים: It is prohibited to carry in an enclosed area behind a house if it is larger than two *beit se'a*. However, if it has an entrance from the house, it has the status of a courtyard and one is permitted to carry in it (*Shulḥan Arukh, Oraḥ Ḥayyim* 359:1).

Water is like planted trees – מַיִם כִּנְטָעִים: If a *karpef* larger than two *beit se'a* was enclosed for the purpose of residence and was then flooded with water, it is permitted to carry in it, since the same law applies to water as to planted trees. This ruling is in accordance with the opinion of Rava (*Shulḥan Arukh, Oraḥ Ḥayyim* 358:11).

NOTES

He made it with the threshing floor in mind – אַדַּעְתָּא דְּבֵי דָּרֵי עַבְדֵּיהּ: The uncertainty centers on whether the new enclosure was made for the sake of the yard itself or for the sake of the threshing floor. The assumption is that an enclosure for the sake of a threshing floor is not an enclosure constructed for the purpose of residence. According to a variant version that reads: He opened it with the threshing floor in mind, a novel approach is required, namely, that the opening of an entrance in a yard of that kind serves to change its purpose (see Rashba).

אָמַר אַמֵימָר: וְהוּא דְּחָזְיָין לְתַשְׁמִישְׁתָּא, אֲבָל לָא חָזְיָין לְתַשְׁמִישְׁתָּא – לָא.

Ameimar said: This ruling **applies only if** the water **is fit for** its regular **use,**[N] i.e., for drinking, because in that case it provides for the needs of residence. **However,** if the water **is not fit for use,** then it is **not** considered like planted trees. Therefore, the *karpef* is no longer considered enclosed for the purpose of residence, and it is prohibited to carry in the *karpef.*

אָמַר רַב אַשִׁי: וּדְחָזְיָין לְתַשְׁמִישְׁתָּא נָמֵי לָא אֲמַרַן אֶלָּא שֶׁאֵין בְּעוּמְקוֹ יוֹתֵר מִבֵּית סָאתַיִם, אֲבָל אִם יֵשׁ בְּעוּמְקוֹ יוֹתֵר מִבֵּית סָאתַיִם – אָסוּר.

Rav Ashi said: And even where the water **is fit for use, this** ruling **applies only if** the water **is not** ten handbreadths **deep** over an area **greater than two** ***beit se'a;*** **but if** the water is ten handbreadths **deep** over an area **greater** than **two** ***beit se'a,*** it **is prohibited** to carry in it, as in such a case the *karpef* is no longer considered enclosed for the sake of dwelling.[H]

וְלָאו מִילְּתָא הִיא, מִידֵּי דַּהֲוָה אַכְּרְיָא דְּפֵירֵי.

The Gemara comments: **And it is not so, just as** it is **in** the case of **a pile of fruit,** as even if the pile of fruit is very large, the *karpef* does not lose its status as having been enclosed for the purpose of residence.

הַהִיא רַחְבָה דַּהֲוַאי בְּפוּם נַהֲרָא דְּחַד גִּיסָּא הֲוָה פְּתִיחַ לְמָתָא, וְחַד גִּיסָּא הֲוָה פְּתִיחַ לִשְׁבִיל שֶׁל כְּרָמִים, וּשְׁבִיל שֶׁל כְּרָמִים הֲוָה סָלֵיק לְגוּדָּא דְּנַהֲרָא.

The Gemara relates: **There was a certain yard in** the town of **Pum Nahara** that was larger than two *beit se'a* and that had not been enclosed for the purpose of residence. **One of its sides opened to** an alleyway in **the town, and the other opened to** a walled **path**[HB] **between the vineyards, and that vineyard path led to the bank of a river** ten handbreadths high, which is considered a partition.

אָמַר אַבָּיֵי: הֵיכִי נַעֲבֵיד? לַעֲבֵיד לֵיהּ מְחִיצָה אַגּוּדָּא דְּנַהֲרָא – אֵין עוֹשִׂין מְחִיצָה עַל גַּבֵּי מְחִיצָה.

Abaye said: What shall we do to permit carrying in the yard, which is a *karmelit,* without having to make a breach in one of its walls wider than ten cubits and then fence it up again? **Shall we construct a partition for it on the river bank,** so that the vineyard path is surrounded by partitions on all sides? This is not a viable solution, as **one cannot construct an** effective **partition on top of another** partition that already exists, and the river bank is considered a partition relative to the river.

וְלַעֲבֵיד לֵיהּ צוּרַת הַפֶּתַח אַפּוּמָּא דִּשְׁבִיל שֶׁל כְּרָמִים – אָתוּ גַּמְלֵי שָׁדְיָין לֵיהּ.

Shall we arrange a doorframe at the mouth of the vineyard path? That is also not an effective solution in this case, for **the camels** that walk down this path in order to drink water from the river **will come**[N] **and knock it over.**

אֶלָּא אָמַר אַבָּיֵי: לַיעֲבֵיד לֶחִי אַפִּיתְחָא דִּשְׁבִיל שֶׁל כְּרָמִים, דְּמִגּוֹ דִּמְהַנְּיָא לִשְׁבִיל שֶׁל כְּרָמִים – מְהַנֵּי נָמֵי לְרַחְבָה.

Rather, Abaye said: We should arrange a side post at the opening of the vineyard path to the yard, **since as it is effective**[N] **for the vineyard path,** to allow one to carry on the path, as it is no longer breached into a *karmelit,* **it is also effective for the yard,** and the side post will be considered an additional partition that renders it permitted to carry in the yard.

אֲמַר לֵיהּ רָבָא: יֹאמְרוּ לֶחִי מוֹעִיל לִשְׁבִיל שֶׁל כְּרָמִים דְּעָלְמָא!

Rava said to him: If so, people **will say** that **a side post is effective** in permitting one to carry in **a vineyard path generally,**[N] and this will cause the public to err, as vineyard paths are usually open at both ends and do not lead to a river or the like.

HALAKHA

Water in a ***karpef*** **– מַיִם בְּקַרְפֵּף:** The presence of potable water in a *karpef* does not negate the permission to carry in it, even if the water is more than ten handbreadths deep and extends over two *beit se'a,* as Rav Ashi's opinion was rejected. If the water is not potable, and it is also more than ten handbreadths deep, it is considered like sown seeds. Consequently, the *karpef* is not regarded as an enclosure that was enclosed for the purpose of residence (*Shulḥan Arukh, Oraḥ Ḥayyim* 358:11).

A yard open to a path – רַחֲבָה הַפְּתוּחָה לִשְׁבִיל: If a yard is open on one side to a town and on the other side to a path that reaches the river bank, one may arrange a side post at the entrance facing the town to allow him to carry throughout the yard, in accordance with Rava (Rambam *Sefer Zemanim, Hilkhot Shabbat* 16:11).

BACKGROUND

A yard and a path – רַחֲבָה וּשְׁבִיל:

Yard behind a house opening on one side to a vineyard path that reaches the river, and opening on the other side to the street that leads into town

NOTES

Is fit for use – וְהוּא דְּחָזְיָין לְתַשְׁמִישְׁתָּא: The presence of potable water facilitates dwelling in the *karpef,* just as planting trees in it facilitates living there. However, water that is not potable, but only for watering plants and the like, is considered like sown seeds. Even though it has some use, it does not facilitate living in the enclosure.

Camels will come – אָתוּ גַּמְלֵי: Some commentaries state that these camels are not going to the river bank, as explained by Rashi and *Tosafot,* since if they were, why would one build a partition on the bank of the river itself? Rather, the camels are brought to work in the vineyard or to carry out its produce (Ritva).

Since as it is effective – דְּמִגּוֹ דִּמְהַנְּיָא: The concept of *miggo* applies in many areas of *halakha* and its application here is typical. The assumption is that a partition is either effective in all cases or ineffective in all cases. Therefore, since the side post is an effective partition in an alleyway, it should be equally effective as a partition for a yard, even though a side post is not generally halakhically effective with regard to a yard.

People will say a side post is effective for a vineyard path – יֹאמְרוּ לֶחִי מוֹעִיל לִשְׁבִיל שֶׁל כְּרָמִים: See Rashi and *Tosafot.* Rashba explains that although some residents did indeed use this path, it was called a vineyard path because only a few residents used it and because the path continued beyond their houses. Consequently, people might mistakenly say that a side post is effective for a vineyard path, even if there are no residents at all. This is incorrect, since a side post is halakhically effective only in an alleyway that has residents.

אֶלָּא אָמַר רָבָא: עָבְדִינַן לֵיהּ לֶחִי לְפִיתְחָא דְּמָתָא, דְּמִגּוֹ דִּמְהַנֵּי לֵיהּ לֶחִי לְמָתָא – מְהַנֵּי נַמִי לְרַחֲבָה.

Rather, Rava said: They should arrange a side post at the opening of the yard **to the town, as since the side post is effective** and is considered a partition **for the town, it is also effective for the yard,** to permit one to carry within it.

הִלְכָּךְ, טִלְטוּלֵי בְּמָתָא גּוּפָהּ – שָׁרֵי, טִלְטוּלֵי בְּרַחֲבָה גּוּפָהּ – שָׁרֵי, מִמָּתָא לְרַחֲבָה וּמֵרַחֲבָה לְמָתָא – פְּלִיגִי בַּהּ רַב אַחָא וְרָבִינָא, חַד אָסַר וְחַד שָׁרֵי.

Therefore, in summary, **it is permitted to carry within the town itself** and **to carry within the yard itself.** However, with regard to carrying **from the town to the yard or from the yard to the town, Rav Aḥa and Ravina disagree: One prohibits** doing so **and the other permits** it.

Perek **II**
Daf **25** Amud **a**

מַאן דְּשָׁרֵי – דְּהָא לֵיכָּא דִּיּוּרִין, וּמַאן דְּאָסַר – זִימְנִין דַּהֲוֵי בַּהּ דִּיּוּרִין, וְאָתֵי לְטַלְטוּלֵי.

The Sage **who permits** doing so holds that it is permitted since in the yard itself **there are no residents,** and a place without residents cannot prohibit carrying in another, adjacent domain. **And the** Sage **who prohibits** doing so holds that it is prohibited because **sometimes there are residents in it**[N] who can prohibit carrying in the other domain, **and** people **might** unwittingly **come to carry** from the yard to the town in their usual manner, even though it is prohibited.

קַרְפֵּף יוֹתֵר מִבֵּית סָאתַיִם שֶׁלֹּא הוּקַּף לְדִירָה וּבָא לְמַעֲטוֹ, מִיעֲטוֹ בְּאִילָנוֹת – לָא הָוֵי מִיעוּט,

With regard to a ***karpef*** that measures **more than two *beit se'a*** and **that had not been fenced in** from the outset **for** the purpose of **residence, and one came to reduce its** size,[N] if **he reduced it by** planting **trees**[H] in a section of the space, **it is not a** valid **reduction,** because trees are commonly found in a *karpef* designed for dwelling; therefore, they are not considered something out of the ordinary that would reduce its size.

בָּנָה בּוֹ עַמּוּד גָּבוֹהַּ עֲשָׂרָה וְרָחָב אַרְבָּעָה – הָוֵי מִיעוּט. פָּחוֹת מִשְּׁלֹשָׁה – לָא הָוֵי מִיעוּט. מִשְּׁלֹשָׁה וְעַד אַרְבָּעָה, רַבָּה אָמַר: הָוֵי מִיעוּט, וְרָבָא אָמַר: לָא הָוֵי מִיעוּט.

But **if he built up a column ten** handbreadths **high and four** handbreadths **wide, it is an** effective **reduction,**[H] i.e., if the *karpef* is thereby reduced to the area of two *beit se'a,* one is permitted to carry within it. However, if the column is **less than three** handbreadths wide, **it is not an** effective **reduction.** And if it is **between three to four** handbreadths wide, there is a dispute between *amora'im.* **Rabba said: It constitutes an** effective **reduction, and Rava said: It does not constitute an** effective **reduction.**

רַבָּה אָמַר: הָוֵי מִיעוּט – דְּהָא נָפֵיק לֵיהּ מִתּוֹרַת לָבוּד. רָבָא אָמַר: לָא הָוֵי מִיעוּט – כֵּיוָן דְּלָא הָוֵי מָקוֹם אַרְבָּעָה – לָא חֲשִׁיב.

The Gemara explains the two opinions. **Rabba said** that **it constitutes an** effective **reduction because** it is large enough **to be excluded from the principle of *lavud*,** namely, that solid surfaces with gaps between them less than three handbreadths are considered joined. Since the column stands independently, it reduces the size of the *karpef.* **Rava said** that **it does constitute a** valid **reduction because as it is not a place** of at least **four** handbreadths, **it is not significant.** An area of less than four handbreadths is not considered independent.

הִרְחִיק מִן הַכּוֹתֶל אַרְבָּעָה וְעָשָׂה מְחִיצָה – הוֹעִיל, פָּחוֹת מִשְּׁלֹשָׁה – לֹא הוֹעִיל. מִשְּׁלֹשָׁה וְעַד אַרְבָּעָה, רַבָּה אָמַר: הוֹעִיל, רָבָא אָמַר: אֵינוֹ מוֹעִיל.

It was further stated: **If one distanced** himself **four** handbreadths **from the wall**[H] of the *karpef* **and erected an** additional **partition** for the sake of dwelling, **it is effective** in permitting one to carry in the fenced-off inner area. But if the distance is **less than three** handbreadths, **it is not effective,** as the new wall is considered attached to the first by means of the principle of *lavud,* and it is like one partition built on top of another. And if the distance is **between three to four** handbreadths, that is the topic of the dispute among the *amora'im,* in which **Rabba said: It is effective,** and **Rava said: It is not effective.**

רַבָּה אָמַר: הוֹעִיל – דְּהָא נָפֵיק לֵיהּ מִתּוֹרַת לָבוּד. רָבָא אָמַר: אֵינוֹ מוֹעִיל – כֵּיוָן דְּלָא הָוֵי מָקוֹם אַרְבָּעָה – לָא חֲשִׁיב.

The Gemara explains the two opinions. **Rabba said: It is effective, as it** is far enough away **to be removed from the principle of *lavud*.** **Rava** disagreed and **said: It is not effective, because as it is not a place of** at least **four** handbreadths, **it is not significant.**

NOTES

Sometimes there are residents in it – **זִימְנִין דַּהֲוֵי בַּהּ דִּיּוּרִין**: Even though the Sages did not generally institute such decrees in the laws of *eiruvin*, this context is different. Even when residents are present, the residents of the yard will think that it is permitted to carry in the yard, because they may carry from the yard into the alleyway. Consequently, they will not realize that it is prohibited to carry in the yard itself, even for those who carry from the yard into the alleyway, because it was not enclosed for the purpose of residence (Rabbi Eliezer Meir Horowitz).

Reducing the size of a *karpef* – **מִיעוּט הֶיקֵף בְּקַרְפֵּף**: The disputes concerning the reduction of the size of an enclosure can be understood in several ways. The early commentaries disagree with regard to the law and the correct reading of the text. One approach is to explain that the construction of new partitions around the enclosure is to define it as fenced in for the purpose of residence, which would permit one to carry in the entire area. Alternatively, the discussion can also be understood as relating to partitions built to reduce the area of the enclosure to less than two *beit se'a*. The disagreements among the commentaries focus particularly on the correct textual version and contextual understandings of the statement of Rabbi Simi, or, according to variant readings, of Rabba bar Sheila (see *Maggid Mishne*; *Me'iri*; Ritva).

HALAKHA

Reduction by planting trees – **מִיעוּט בְּאִילָנוֹת**: If an enclosure that is larger than two *beit se'a* and that was not initially fenced in for the purpose of residence is planted with trees, the space taken up by the trees does not reduce the area of the enclosure, even if each tree is the size of an independent domain (*Shulḥan Arukh, Oraḥ Ḥayyim* 358:4).

Reduction by a column – **מִיעוּט בְּעַמּוּד**: If the area of a *karpef* is reduced by means of a column ten handbreadths high, the reduction is effective, provided that the column is more than three handbreadths wide. This is in accordance with Rabba's opinion, since the *halakha* follows the lenient opinion with respect to *eiruvin* (*Shulḥan Arukh, Oraḥ Ḥayyim* 358:5).

If one distanced himself…from the wall – **הִרְחִיק מִן הַכּוֹתֶל**: If one distances himself at least three handbreadths from the wall of a *karpef* and erects an additional partition, it is effective, in accordance with Rabba's lenient opinion and based on the first version of the dispute cited in the Gemara (*Shulḥan Arukh, Oraḥ Ḥayyim* 358:6).

רַב שִׁימִי מַתְנֵי לְקוּלָּא: טָח בּוֹ טִיט וְיָכוֹל לַעֲמוֹד בִּפְנֵי עַצְמוֹ – הָוֵי מִיעוּט. אֵינוֹ יָכוֹל לַעֲמוֹד בִּפְנֵי עַצְמוֹ, רַבָּה אָמַר: הָוֵי מִיעוּט, רָבָא אָמַר: לָא הָוֵי מִיעוּט.

Rav Simi would teach a more **lenient** version of the dispute between Rabba and Rava. **If one plastered** the walls of a *karpef* larger than two *beit se'a* **with plaster,**[H] **and** the plaster **can stand on its own,** all agree that **it is an** effective **reduction,** as it is considered as if he has made a new partition. But if the plaster **cannot stand on its own,** and it only stays in place because it is attached to the existing wall, there is an amoraic dispute in which **Rabba said: It is an** effective **reduction,** and **Rava said: It is not an** effective **reduction.**

רַבָּה אָמַר: הָוֵי מִיעוּט – הָשְׁתָּא מִיהָא קָאֵי. רָבָא אָמַר: לָא הָוֵי מִיעוּט – כֵּיוָן דְּלָא יָכוֹל לְמֵיקַם בִּפְנֵי עַצְמוֹ – לָאו כְּלוּם הוּא.

The Gemara explains the two opinions. **Rabba says: It is an** effective **reduction,** because for **now, in any case, it stands. Rava says: It is not an** effective **reduction, because as it cannot stand on its own, it is nothing,** i.e., it is insignificant.

הִרְחִיק מִן הַתֵּל אַרְבָּעָה וְעָשָׂה מְחִיצָה – הוֹעִיל.

If one distanced himself **four** handbreadths **from a mound** ten handbreadths high that stands in a *karpef* larger than two *beit se'a,* **and** he **erected a partition** for the sake of dwelling, **it is effective** to permit one to carry.

פָּחוֹת מִשְּׁלֹשָׁה אוֹ עַל שְׂפַת הַתֵּל, רַב חִסְדָּא וְרַב הַמְנוּנָא; חַד אָמַר: הוֹעִיל, וְחַד אָמַר: לֹא הוֹעִיל.

But if he erected the partition **less than three** handbreadths from the mound **or on the edge of the mound** itself, so that it is like a partition built on top of another partition, this is a dispute between **Rav Ḥisda and Rav Hamnuna. One** of them **said: It is effective,** and **the other one said: It is not effective.**

תִּסְתַּיֵּים דְּרַב חִסְדָּא אָמַר הוֹעִיל. דְּאִתְּמַר: הָעוֹשֶׂה מְחִיצָה עַל גַּבֵּי מְחִיצָה, אָמַר רַב חִסְדָּא: בְּשַׁבָּת – הוֹעִיל,

The Gemara seeks to clarify which of the Sages held which opinion. **Conclude that** it was **Rav Ḥisda** who **said it is effective, for it was stated** that the *amora'im* disagreed about the following: If **one erected a partition on top of an** existing **partition, Rav Ḥisda said:** With regard to the *halakhot* of **Shabbat,** e.g., if the first partition was not erected for the purpose of residence, the second partition **is effective.**

בְּנִכְסֵי הַגֵּר – לֹא קָנָה.

However, **with regard to the property of a convert,**[N] **he does not acquire** it. The property of a convert who dies without heirs is regarded as ownerless unless he had transferred it to someone as a gift during his lifetime. Whoever first implements a valid mode of acquisition upon such property acquires it. For example, one may acquire property by performing an act of taking possession, such as construction of a partition around it. But if one erects a partition around the property of a deceased convert on top of an existing partition,[H] he does not acquire the property in this manner.

וְרַב שֵׁשֶׁת אָמַר: אַף בְּשַׁבָּת נַמִי לֹא הוֹעִיל, תִּסְתַּיֵּים.

And Rav Sheshet said: Even with regard to Shabbat it is not effective. The Gemara comments: Indeed, **conclude** that it is Rav Ḥisda who maintains that one partition built on top of another is effective for Shabbat.[H]

אָמַר רַב חִסְדָּא: וּמוֹדֶה לִי רַב שֵׁשֶׁת שֶׁאִם עָשָׂה מְחִיצָה עַל הַתֵּל שֶׁהוֹעִיל.

Rav Ḥisda said: Rav Sheshet agrees with me that if one erected a partition on the mound,[N] rather than merely adjacent to it, **that it is effective** to permit one to carry on the mound itself, even though, according to him, it is prohibited to carry in the rest of the *karpef.*

מַאי טַעְמָא – הוֹאִיל וּבַאֲוִיר מְחִיצוֹת הָעֶלְיוֹנוֹת הוּא דָּר.

What is the reason for this? **Since he dwells in the space** between **the upper partitions,** he utilizes these new partitions and they serve a function. Although in relation to one positioned below the mound these are partitions built on top of the pre-existing partitions of the mound, and therefore they do not allow him to carry in the *karpef,* they are nonetheless effective in allowing him to carry on the mound itself.

בָּעֵי רַבָּה בַּר בַּר חָנָה: נִבְלְעוּ מְחִיצוֹת הַתַּחְתּוֹנוֹת וְהָעֶלְיוֹנוֹת קַיָּימוֹת, מַהוּ?

Rabba bar bar Ḥana raised a dilemma: If the lower partitions were swallowed up, e.g., if they sank in boggy ground, and **the upper** partitions that he had erected still **stand, what is** the law?

לְמַאי? אִי לְנִכְסֵי הַגֵּר – הַיְינוּ דְּיִרְמְיָה בִּירָאָה, דְּאָמַר יִרְמְיָה בִּירָאָה, אָמַר רַב יְהוּדָה: הַאי מַאן דִּשְׁדָא לִיפְתָּא אַפִּילָא דְּאַרְעָא דְּגֵר, וַאֲתָא יִשְׂרָאֵל אַחֲרִינָא וּרְפַק בָּהּ פּוּרְתָּא – בַּתְרָא קָנֵי, קַמָּא לָא קָנֵי.

The Gemara asks: **With regard to what** issue was this dilemma raised? **If** it was raised **with regard to** acquiring **the property of a convert, this** is precisely the same as the ruling cited by **Yirmeya Bira'a,** as **Yirmeya Bira'a said** that **Rav Yehuda said:** If **one sowed turnip** seeds **in cracks** which he found **in land** that had belonged to **a convert, and another Jew came** and **plowed** the ground **a little, the latter one,** the one who plowed, **acquires** the property, and **the first one does not acquire** it.

HALAKHA

If one plastered the walls with plaster – **טָח בּוֹ טִיט:** If one plasters the walls of an enclosure and the plaster can stand on its own, the action serves to reduce the size of the enclosure. However, if the plaster cannot stand on its own, the action does not reduce the size of the enclosure, in accordance with Rava's opinion and as explained by the Ra'avad and Rabbi Zeraḥya HaLevi. The apparent contradiction between this ruling and the prior one has been noted by the *Baḥ* and the *Perisha* (*Shulḥan Arukh, Oraḥ Ḥayyim* 358:7).

A partition on top of an existing partition – **מְחִיצָה עַל גַּבֵּי מְחִיצָה:** A partition erected on top of another partition does not suffice for the acquisition of the property of a deceased convert (*Shulḥan Arukh, Ḥoshen Mishpat* 275:23).

A partition on top of an existing partition with regard to Shabbat – **מְחִיצָה עַל גַּבֵּי מְחִיצָה בְּשַׁבָּת:** A partition erected on top of another partition is not halakhically effective with regard to Shabbat, since the *halakha* is in accordance with the opinion of Rav Sheshet, who was considered a greater authority than Rav Ḥisda. However, if it was erected on top of a mound, the partition is effective, as in that case even Rav Sheshet agrees (*Shulḥan Arukh, Oraḥ Ḥayyim* 358:8).

NOTES

The property of a convert – **נִכְסֵי הַגֵּר:** A Jew by birth always has heirs. Even if one does not have sons or close relatives, his ancestry is traced in search of relatives, if necessary all the way back to the patriarch Jacob. However, a convert's familial connections are severed by the conversion. Therefore, if no children were born to the convert after his conversion, he has no legal heirs, and at his death his property is regarded as ownerless.

A partition on the mound – **מְחִיצָה עַל הַתֵּל:** Several explanations have been offered concerning the nature of this mound. Rashi teaches that the mound was one of the partitions of the *karpef*. The Ritva understands that the enclosure was surrounded on all sides by a mound. Other commentaries explain that the enclosure was surrounded by a ditch ten handbreadths deep, and that consequently, the construction of a partition on top of this ditch is considered the addition of a partition on top of a pre-existing partition (see *Me'iri*).

BACKGROUND

A roofed *karpef* – קַרְפֵּף מְקוֹרֶה:

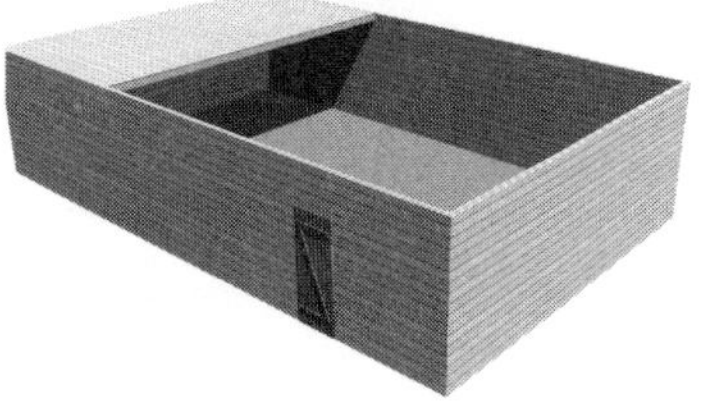

Enclosure with a third of its area covered with a roof

NOTES

Its covered space renders it in excess [*meyatero*] – אֲוִיר קֵירוּוָיו מְיַיתְּרוֹ: Some commentaries have an alternate version: Its covered space permits it [*matiro*]. In this version, this sentence expresses the view that the covered space reduces the size of the enclosure such that one is permitted to carry in it, rather than the view that it is prohibited to carry in the enclosure. Interestingly, the slight linguistic adjustment here leads to a reversal in the descriptions of the opinions of Rava and Rabbi Zeira.

מַאי טַעְמָא? בְּעִידָּנָא דִּשְׁדָא – לָא קָא שְׁבַח, כִּי קָא שְׁבְחָא מִמֵּילָא קָא מַשְׁבְּחָא.

What is the reason that the first one who sowed the seeds does not acquire the property? **At the time that he sowed,** the land **was not improved** by his sowing. **When it did improve,** with the growth of the turnips, **it improved on its own.**[H] That is to say, the act of sowing alone is not a sufficiently noticeable action that changes and improves the property at the time. Although the sowing later proves to have been beneficial, this is seen as an improvement of the land that comes on its own. Therefore, an action that will only provide benefit in the future cannot serve as an act of acquisition.

וְאֶלָּא לְעִנְיַן שַׁבָּת – הָוֵי מְחִיצָה הַנַּעֲשָׂה בַּשַּׁבָּת,

Rather, you must say that the dilemma was raised **with respect to Shabbat,** in which case it is **a partition that was made on Shabbat;** beforehand it was not a valid partition, and the upper ones acquired the status of a partition only after the lower partitions sank into the ground.

וְתַנְיָא: כׇּל מְחִיצָה הַנַּעֲשָׂה בַּשַּׁבָּת, בֵּין בְּשׁוֹגֵג בֵּין בְּמֵזִיד – שְׁמָהּ מְחִיצָה.

And it was already **taught** in a *baraita*: **Any partition made on Shabbat, whether unwittingly or intentionally, is called a** valid **partition.**[H] Consequently, the upper partitions should be regarded as valid partitions that allow one to carry in the *karpef*.

לָאו אִיתְּמַר עֲלַהּ, אָמַר רַב נַחְמָן: לֹא שָׁנוּ אֶלָּא לִזְרוֹק, אֲבָל לְטַלְטֵל – אָסוּר.

The Gemara raises a difficulty: **Wasn't it stated about this** law that **Rav Naḥman said: They taught** that such a partition is called a partition **only** as a stringency, in that it is prohibited **to throw** from an area enclosed by such a partition into the public domain and vice versa; **but to carry** within it as a full-fledged private domain **is prohibited.** This implies that these are not proper partitions.

כִּי אִיתְּמַר דְּרַב נַחְמָן – אַמֵּזִיד אִיתְּמַר.

The Gemara refutes this objection: **When** that statement of **Rav Naḥman was stated, it was stated** with regard to a case where one erected the partition **intentionally.** Since one intentionally violated Shabbat when he erected the partition, the Sages imposed a penalty that he is prohibited to carry within the enclosed area. But if the partition was made unwittingly or came about by itself, no such penalty was imposed, and one is permitted to carry.

הַהִיא אִיתְּתָא דַּעֲבְדָה מְחִיצָה עַל גַּבֵּי מְחִיצָה בְּנִכְסֵי הַגֵּר, אֲתָא הַהוּא גַּבְרָא רְפַק בָּהּ פּוּרְתָּא. אֲתָא לְקַמֵּיהּ דְּרַב נַחְמָן, אוֹקְמָהּ בִּידֵיהּ. אֲתַת אִיהִי וְקָא צָווְחָא קַמֵּיהּ. אֲמַר לָהּ: מַאי אִיעֲבִיד לָךְ דְּלָא מַחְזַקְתְּ כְּדְמַחְזְקִי אֱינָשֵׁי?

The Gemara cites a related incident: **A certain woman erected a partition on top of** another **partition in the property of a** deceased **convert. A certain man** then **came** and **plowed** the ground **a little.** The man **came before Rav Naḥman, who established the** property **in his possession.** The woman then **came and cried out before** Rav Naḥman. **He said to her: What can I do for you, as** you **did not take possession** of the property **in the manner that people take possession.**

קַרְפֵּף בֵּית שָׁלֹשׁ, וְקֵירָה בּוֹ בֵּית סְאָה; רָבָא אָמַר: אֲוִיר קֵירוּוָיו מְיַיתְּרוֹ, וְרַבִּי זֵירָא אָמַר: אֵין אֲוִיר קֵירוּוָיו מְיַיתְּרוֹ.

With regard to **a *karpef*** the size of **three *beit se'a*, and one roofed** one ***beit se'a* of it,**[HB] the *amora'im* disputed whether or not the area of *karpef* is two *beit se'a*, in which case it is permitted to carry there, or three *beit se'a*, in which case it would be prohibited. **Rava said: Its roofed space renders it in excess**[N] of two *beit se'a*, meaning that the roofed area is not considered separate from the rest, and so it is prohibited to carry in the *karpef*. **And Rabbi Zeira said: Its roofed space does not render it in excess** of two *beit se'a*, and it is permitted to carry there.

HALAKHA

Taking possession on its own – חֲזָקָה מִמֵּילָא: The property of a deceased convert can be acquired only by an action that produces an immediate improvement upon or change in the property. Therefore, actions such as sowing or building one partition on top of another are not effective, as they bring about improvement only at some later point (*Shulḥan Arukh*, *Ḥoshen Mishpat* 275:22).

A partition that formed on its own – מְחִיצָה מִמֵּילָא: A partition that was formed on its own on Shabbat is a valid partition and allows one to carry. An example would be if a lower partition sank into the ground, leaving the upper partition above ground (*Shulḥan Arukh*, *Oraḥ Ḥayyim* 358:8).

A *karpef* covered with a roof – קַרְפֵּף שֶׁקֵּירָה בּוֹ: If an enclosure is larger than three *beit se'a*, and the owner roofs one *beit se'a*, then one is permitted to carry throughout the *karpef*, in accordance with the opinion of Rabba according to the variant reading of the Rambam and the Rosh that it is Rabba who maintains the lenient position, because the *halakha* follows the lenient opinion with regard to the *halakhot* of eiruv (*Shulḥan Arukh*, *Oraḥ Ḥayyim* 358:12).

לֵימָא רָבָא וְרַבִּי זֵירָא בִּפְלוּגְתָּא דְּרַב וּשְׁמוּאֵל קָא מִיפַּלְגִי? דְּאִיתְּמַר, אַכְסַדְרָה בְּבִקְעָה, רַב אָמַר: מוּתָּר לְטַלְטֵל בְּכוּלָּהּ, וּשְׁמוּאֵל אָמַר: אֵין מְטַלְטְלִין אֶלָּא בְּאַרְבַּע אַמּוֹת.

The Gemara comments: **Let us say** that **Rava and Rabbi Zeira dispute the** same point that was the subject of **dispute between Rav and Shmuel.** These *amora'im* disagreed about the following, **as it was stated:** With regard to **an enclosed veranda** [***akhsadra***],[LB] which is a roofed structure without walls or with incomplete walls, **in a field**[H] that has the status of a *karmelit*, **Rav said: One is permitted to carry in the entire** enclosed veranda, as it is considered a private domain. **And Shmuel said: One may carry only** a distance of **four cubits.**

רַב אָמַר: מוּתָּר לְטַלְטֵל בְּכוּלָּהּ – אָמְרִינַן: פִּי תִקְרָה יוֹרֵד וְסוֹתֵם. וּשְׁמוּאֵל אָמַר: אֵין מְטַלְטְלִין אֶלָּא בְּאַרְבַּע אַמּוֹת – לָא אָמְרִינַן פִּי תִקְרָה יוֹרֵד וְסוֹתֵם.

The Gemara explains the two opinions: **Rav said: One is permitted to carry in the entire** enclosed veranda, since **we say** that **the edge of the roof descends** to the ground **and closes up** the enclosed veranda on all sides; consequently, it is considered a separate private domain. **And Shmuel said: One may carry only** a distance of **four cubits,** as **we do not say** that **the edge of the roof descends and closes up** the enclosed veranda.

LANGUAGE

Enclosed veranda [*akhsadra*] – אַכְסַדְרָה: From the Greek ἐξέδρα, *exedra*, meaning an entrance room or a kind of open porch.

HALAKHA

An enclosed veranda in a field – אַכְסַדְרָא בְּבִקְעָה: An enclosed veranda in a field that has the status of a *karmelit* is regarded as a private domain in which one is permitted to carry, since the edge of the roof is regarded as though it descends to the ground and encloses the veranda on all sides. This is in accordance with the opinion of Rav, as the *halakha* is ruled according to his opinion in disputes with Shmuel over ritual law (Rambam *Sefer Zemanim*, *Hilkhot Shabbat* 17:35).

BACKGROUND

Enclosed veranda [*akhsadra*] – אַכְסַדְרָה: According to Rashi, an *akhsadra* is a roof resting on pillars. According to Rav, the outer edge of the roof is regarded as descending to the ground and sealing off the veranda on all sides.

Roof resting on pillars

Perek **II**
Daf **25** Amud **b**

אִי דַּעֲבִידָא כִּי אַכְסַדְרָה – הָכִי נַמִי. הָכָא בְּמַאי עָסְקִינַן – דַּעֲבָדָה כִּי אוּרְזִילָא.

The Gemara rejects this argument: **If** the roof in the covered section of the *karpef* **were made like an enclosed veranda** whose roof is level, **indeed,** both Rava and Rabbi Zeira would agree that the edge of the roof descends to the ground and closes up the area. **With what are we dealing here?** We are dealing with a case where the roof **is made like a hammock,** i.e., slanted, and therefore one cannot say that the edge of the roof descends to the ground and encloses the area.

אָמַר רַבִּי זֵירָא: וּמוֹדֵינָא בְּקַרְפֵּף שֶׁנִּפְרַץ בִּמְלוֹאוֹ לֶחָצֵר, שֶׁאָסוּר. מַאי טַעְמָא – הוֹאִיל וַאֲוִיר חָצֵר מְיַיתְּרוֹ.

Rabbi Zeira said: I agree with Rava **with regard to a *karpef* that is fully breached into a courtyard,**[H] meaning the entire wall between them is breached, **that** it is **prohibited** to carry in it. **What is the reason** for this? **Because the** additional **space of the courtyard** joins to the *karpef* and **renders it in excess** of two *beit se'a*. Consequently, it is prohibited to carry in it.

מַתְקִיף לָהּ רַב יוֹסֵף: וְכִי אֲוִיר הַמּוּתָּר לוֹ אוֹסְרוֹ?!

Rav Yosef strongly objects to this explanation: **Does a space in which it is permitted to** carry,[N] the courtyard, **render** the *karpef*, **prohibited?** Given that it had been permitted beforehand to carry from the courtyard to the *karpef*, why say that now that the partition between them is breached, the additional space, which was itself permitted, should render it prohibited to carry in the *karpef*?

HALAKHA

A *karpef* that is fully breached into a courtyard – קַרְפֵּף שֶׁנִּפְרַץ בִּמְלוֹאוֹ לֶחָצֵר: If the entire wall of an enclosure that separates it from a courtyard is breached, and the enclosure is exactly the area of two *beit se'a*, it is prohibited to carry in the enclosure because the width of the walls counts toward the area of two *se'a*. In addition, if the courtyard is not wider than the enclosure and nothing remains of the wall separating it from the enclosure, then it is prohibited to carry in the courtyard as well (*Magen Avraham*; *Shulḥan Arukh*, *Oraḥ Ḥayyim* 358:13).

NOTES

Does a space in which it is permitted – וְכִי אֲוִיר הַמּוּתָּר: Rav Yosef thought that the rationale for Rabbi Zeira's opinion is that it is prohibited to carry from the courtyard into the enclosure, based on the following principle: If it is prohibited to carry between two domains, then the removal of the partition separating the two domains creates a prohibition to carry within each domain. Consequently, he was surprised when Rabbi Shimon taught that this case is prohibited, since the airspace of the courtyard does not render it prohibited to carry in the enclosure.

אָמַר לֵיהּ אַבַּיֵי: כְּמַאן – כְּרַבִּי שִׁמְעוֹן, לְרַבִּי שִׁמְעוֹן נַמִי, הָא אִיכָּא אֲוִיר מְקוֹם מְחִיצוֹת!

Abaye said to him: In accordance with whose opinion do you say this? Apparently, it is **in accordance with** the opinion of **Rabbi Shimon,** who holds that one is permitted to carry from a courtyard to a *karpef.* But **even according to Rabbi Shimon, there is the space where the walls** that are now breached had once stood. This space had not been fit for carrying from the outset, even according to Rabbi Shimon; therefore, if the *karpef* had been at first exactly the area of two *beit se'a,* it would be prohibited to carry in the entire *karpef* due to the additional space of the fallen walls.

דְּאָמַר רַב חִסְדָּא: קַרְפֵּף שֶׁנִּפְרַץ בִּמְלוֹאוֹ לֶחָצֵר – חָצֵר מוּתֶּרֶת וְקַרְפֵּף אָסוּר.

This is **as Rav Ḥisda said** with regard to **a *karpef* that is fully breached into a courtyard:** In **the courtyard** one is **permitted** to carry **and** in **the *karpef*** he is **prohibited** to carry.

חָצֵר מַאי טַעְמָא – דְּאִית לֵיהּ גִּיפּוּפֵי, וְהָא זִמְנִין דְּמַשְׁכַּחַתְּ לָהּ אִיפְּכָא!

The Gemara asks: As for the **courtyard, what is the reason** that this is permitted? Is it **because it has the remnants** of the original walls on either side of the breach, which allow the breach to be treated like an entrance? **But at times you find** just **the opposite;** if the courtyard was narrower than the *karpef* and the partition between them was fully breached, it is the *karpef* that retains the remnants of the original walls on either side of the breach, while the courtyard is breached in its entirety.

אֶלָּא: מִשּׁוּם דְּאָמְרִינַן זֶה – אֲוִיר מְחִיצוֹת מְיַיתְּרוֹ, וְזֶה – אֵין אֲוִיר מְחִיצוֹת מְיַיתְּרוֹ.

Rather, it is **because we say** that with regard to **this** one, the *karpef,* which was not enclosed for the purpose of residence and where one is permitted to carry only if it is no more than two *beit se'a,* **the space of the** fallen **walls renders it in excess** of two *beit se'a.* However, with regard to **that** one, the courtyard, which was enclosed for the purpose of residence and where there is no size limit above which it is prohibited to carry, **the space of the** fallen **walls does not render it in excess of** any limit.

הַהוּא בּוּסְתָּנָא דַּהֲוָה סְמִיךְ לְגוּדָּא דְּאַפַּדְנָא, נְפַל אַשִּׁיתָא בָּרַיְיתָא דְּאַפַּדְנָא. סָבַר רַב בֵּיבָי לְמֵימַר: לִיסְמוֹךְ אַגּוּדָּא גַּוָּויָאתָא.

The Gemara cites a related incident: **A certain orchard** [*bustana*][L] **was adjacent to the wall of a mansion** [*apadna*].[LB] The orchard was larger than two *beit se'a* and was enclosed for the purpose of residence by a wall, part of which was the wall of the mansion. One day **the outer wall of the mansion,** which also served as a wall for the orchard, **collapsed. Rav Beivai thought to say** that **we can rely upon** one of **the** mansion's **inner walls** to serve as a partition for the orchard and thereby permit one to carry there in the future as well.

אֲמַר לֵיהּ רַב פַּפִּי: מִשּׁוּם דַּאֲתוּ מִמּוּלָאֵי אָמְרִיתוּ מִילֵּי מוּלַיְיאָתָא?! הָנָךְ מְחִיצוֹת, לְגַוַּאי – עֲבִידָן, לְבַרַּאי – לָא עֲבִידָן.

Rav Pappi said to him: Because you come from truncated [*mula'ei*] **people,**[N] as Rav Beivai's family traced their lineage to the house of Eli, all of whose descendants were destined to be short-lived (see I Samuel 2:31), **you speak truncated** [*mulayata*] **matters,** as the inner wall cannot be relied upon at all. That is because **these walls were made for the inside** of the mansion, and **they were not made for the outside;** that is, they were not designed from the outset to serve as partitions for the orchard.

הַהִיא אַבְוַורְנְקָא דַּהֲוָה לֵיהּ לְרֵישׁ גָּלוּתָא בְּבוּסְתָּנֵיהּ, אֲמַר לֵיהּ לְרַב הוּנָא בַּר חִינָּנָא: לִיעֲבִיד מָר תַּקַּנְתָּא, דִּלְמָחָר נֵיכוֹל נַהֲמָא הָתָם.

The Gemara relates: **The Exilarch had a** banqueting **pavilion** [*abvarneka*][LBN] **in his orchard** that was larger than two *beit se'a* and that had not been enclosed from the outset for the purpose of residence. The Exilarch **said to Rav Huna bar Ḥinnana: Let the Master make** some **arrangement so that tomorrow,** on Shabbat, **we may eat bread there,** i.e., so that we may be permitted to carry food and utensils from the house to the pavilion via the orchard.

אֲזַל עֲבַד קָנֶה קָנֶה פָּחוֹת מִשְּׁלֹשָׁה. אֲזַל רָבָא

Rav Huna bar Ḥinnana **went and erected** a fence of **reeds,** each reed separated from the next by **less than three** handbreadths. That is to say, he erected two such partitions[H] between the house and the pavilion with a passageway between them, through which the Exilarch and his men could carry whatever they needed, as the partitions were constructed in the proper manner for the purpose of residence. **Rava,** however, **went**

LANGUAGE

Orchard [*bustana*] – **בּוּסְתָּנָא**: From the Persian bōstān, meaning garden.

Mansion [*apadna*] – **אַפַּדְנָא**: From the Old Persian apadāna, meaning palace or audience hall. The word was borrowed into Aramaic at a relatively early stage and appears in the book of Daniel with the meaning of palace or splendid house.

Pavilion [*abvarneka*] – **אַבְוַורְנְקָא**: Probably originally *akhvarnka*, this word was borrowed from Iranian and is apparently related to the Middle Persian xwarnaq, meaning a sumptuous building. The *ge'onim* describe the structure as a small pavilion built inside a garden.

BACKGROUND

An orchard and a mansion – **בּוּסְתָּן וְאַרְמוֹן**: If the outer wall of the mansion were to collapse, the orchard would still be fenced off by one of the inner walls of the mansion. Rabbi Beivai suggested relying on this wall as a partition.

Orchard adjacent to mansion

An orchard and a pavilion – **בּוּסְתָּן וְאַבְוַורְנְקָא**: The path from the orchard to the pavilion [*abvarneka*] was enclosed by partitions made of reeds.

Path from orchard to pavilion

NOTES

You come from truncated [*mula'ei*] people – **דַּאֲתוּ מִמּוּלָאֵי**: Various explanations have been offered for this expression. Elsewhere, Rashi explains that *mula'ei* is related to *umlalim*, miserable ones. He further suggests that *mula'ei* means blemished ones [*ba'alei mumim*] or hunchbacks. Some commentaries explain that the descendants of Eli were called *mula'ei* because they came from a place called Mamla (*Tosafot*; Rashbam). The *ge'onim* explain that this is an expression referring to a great person who makes grand and clever statements.

A banqueting pavilion – **אַבְוַורְנְקָא**: Various explanations of the context and content of this incident are offered by the early commentaries, including two versions cited by Rashi. The translation above is based on the mainstream view among the early commentaries and is the second explanation cited by Rashi from the *ge'onim*. According to Rashi's first explanation, the case is one of a very large tree which provides shade over an area greater than two *beit se'a*; the question becomes what type of enclosure is necessary to render it permitted to carry under the tree. Rabbeinu Ḥananel also basically accepts Rashi's first explanation.

Within the framework of Rashi's first explanation, most commentaries explain that the partition of reeds was not made to serve as a path. Rather, either Rav Huna bar Ḥinnana constructed it so that part of the orchard would be enclosed for the purpose of residence, or he intended to utilize the reed partition to reduce the area of the orchard to less than two *beit se'a* (see Rabbeinu Ḥananel; Rashba; *Me'iri*).

HALAKHA

Two partitions – **שְׁתֵּי מְחִיצוֹת**: This is referring to a case in which an enclosure larger than the area necessary to grow two measures of grain was not initially enclosed for the purpose of residence, and one wall of the enclosure was breached to a length of more than ten cubits before being closed off by a partition. If this latter partition falls as well, then once again it is prohibited to carry within the enclosure, even if there is another partition present (*Shulḥan Arukh*, *Oraḥ Ḥayyim* 358:14).

שַׁלְפִינְהוּ. אֲזַל רַב פַּפָּא וְרַב הוּנָא בְּרֵיהּ דְּרַב יְהוֹשֻׁעַ נַקְטִינְהוּ מִבַּתְרֵיהּ.

and **removed** the reeds, as he maintained that they were unnecessary; he regarded the entire orchard as having been enclosed for the purpose of residence, owing to the banqueting pavilion. **Rav Pappa and Rav Huna, son of Rav Yehoshua, went after him and collected** the reeds, so as to prevent Rav Huna bar Ḥinnana from restoring the partitions, as they were Rava's students and wanted to enforce his ruling.

לְמָחָר אֵיתִיבֵיהּ רָבִינָא לְרָבָא: עִיר חֲדָשָׁה מוֹדְדִין לָהּ מִיְּשִׁיבָתָהּ, וִישָׁנָה מֵחוֹמָתָהּ.

On the following day, on Shabbat, **Ravina raised an objection**[N] **to Rava's** opinion from a *baraita* which states: In the case of **a new town, we measure** the Shabbat limit **from its settled** area, from where it is actually inhabited; **and** in the case of **an old** town, we measure the Shabbat limit **from its wall,** even if it is not inhabited up to its wall.[H]

אֵיזוֹ הִיא חֲדָשָׁה וְאֵיזוֹ הִיא יְשָׁנָה? חֲדָשָׁה – שֶׁהוּקְּפָה וּלְבַסּוֹף יָשְׁבָה, יְשָׁנָה – יָשְׁבָה וּלְבַסּוֹף הוּקְּפָה. וְהַאי נַמִי, כְּהוּקְּפָה וּלְבַסּוֹף יָשְׁבָה דָּמֵי.

What is a new town, **and what is an old** town? **A new** town is one **that was** first **surrounded** by a wall, **and** only **afterward settled,** meaning that the town's residents arrived after the wall had already been erected; **an old** town is one **that was** first **settled, and** only **afterward surrounded** by a wall. Ravina raised his objection: **And this** orchard **should also be considered like** a town **that was** first **surrounded** by a wall **and** only **afterward settled,** as it had not been enclosed from the outset for the purpose of residence. Even if a dwelling was later erected there, this should not turn it into a place that had been enclosed for the purpose of residence.

אֲמַר לֵיהּ רַב פַּפָּא לְרָבָא: וְהָאָמַר רַב אַסִי: מְחִיצוֹת אַדְרִיכָלִין לֹא שְׁמָהּ מְחִיצָה. אַלְמָא: כֵּיוָן דִּלְצְנִיעוּתָא עֲבִידָא לָהּ – לָא הָוְיָא מְחִיצָה. הָכָא נַמִי, כֵּיוָן דִּלְצְנִיעוּתָא עֲבִידָא – לָא הָוְיָא מְחִיצָה.

Seeing that an additional objection could be raised against his teacher's position, **Rav Pappa said to Rava: Didn't Rav Asi say** that **the** temporary **screens** erected by **architects**[H] to serve as protection against the sun and the like **are not deemed** valid **partitions? Apparently, since it was erected** only **for privacy,** and not for the purpose of permanent dwelling, **it is not considered** a valid **partition. Here too,** then, with regard to the fence around the orchard, **since it was erected** only **for privacy, it should not be considered** a valid **partition.**

וְאָמַר רַב הוּנָא בְּרֵיהּ דְּרַב יְהוֹשֻׁעַ לְרָבָא, וְהָאָמַר רַב הוּנָא: מְחִיצָה הָעֲשׂוּיָה לְנַחַת – לֹא שְׁמָהּ מְחִיצָה,

And **Rav Huna, son of Rav Yehoshua, said to Rava: Didn't Rav Huna say** that **a partition made for resting** objects[N] alongside it and thereby providing them with protection **is not considered** a valid **partition?**

דְּהָא רַבָּה בַּר אֲבוּהּ מְעָרֵב לָהּ לְכוּלַּהּ מְחוֹזָא עַרְסָיָיתָא עַרְסָיָיתָא מִשּׁוּם פִּירָא דְּבֵי תוֹרֵי; וְהָא פִּירָא דְּבֵי תוֹרֵי כִּמְחִיצָה הָעֲשׂוּיָה לְנַחַת דָּמְיָא!

This is **as Rabba bar Avuh** did, when he **constructed an** *eiruv* separately for each **row of houses in the whole** town **of Meḥoza, due to the ditches** from which **the cattle** would feed that separated the rows of houses from one another.[B] **Shouldn't** such **cattle ditches**[N] **be considered like a partition made for resting** objects alongside it? Such a partition is invalid. All these proofs indicate that Rava was wrong to remove the reed fences erected by Rav Huna bar Ḥinnana, for those fences were indeed necessary.

קָרֵי עֲלַיְיהוּ רֵישׁ גָּלוּתָא: ״חֲכָמִים הֵמָּה לְהָרַע וּלְהֵיטִיב לֹא יָדָעוּ״.

With regard to the resolution of this incident, **the Exilarch recited** the following **verse about** these Rabbis: **"They are wise to do evil, but to do good they have no knowledge"** (Jeremiah 4:22), as on Friday they ruined the arrangement that Rav Huna bar Ḥinnana had made to permit carrying from the house to the pavilion, and the next day all they could do was prove that they had acted improperly the day before and that it was prohibited to carry in the orchard.

אָמַר רַבִּי אֶלְעַאי: שָׁמַעְתִּי מֵרַבִּי אֱלִיעֶזֶר וַאֲפִילּוּ בֵּית כּוֹר״. מַתְנִיתִין דְּלָא כַּחֲנַנְיָה. דְּתַנְיָא, חֲנַנְיָה אוֹמֵר: וַאֲפִילּוּ הִיא אַרְבָּעִים סְאָה כְּאִסְטְרַטְיָא שֶׁל מֶלֶךְ.

We learned in the mishna: **Rabbi Elai said: I heard from Rabbi Eliezer** that one is permitted to carry in a garden or *karpef*, **even** if the garden **is the size of a** *beit kor,* thirty times larger than a *beit se'a*. The Gemara notes that all agree that what the mishna taught was **not in accordance with** the opinion of **Ḥananya, as it was taught** in a *baraita* that **Ḥananya says:** One is permitted to carry **even if it** is the size of of **forty** *beit se'a,* **like the court of a king.**

NOTES

Ravina raised an objection – אֵיתִיבֵיהּ רָבִינָא: According to Rabbeinu Ḥananel's reading of the text, Ravina's argument constitutes an objection against Rava, rather than support, as claimed by Rashi in his first explanation. Rav Pappa and Rav Huna, son of Rabbi Yehoshua, attempt to answer the objection.

A partition made for resting [*naḥat*] – מְחִיצָה הָעֲשׂוּיָה לְנַחַת: Some commentaries explain that a partition made for resting is referring to a partition on which people generally walk; its status as a partition is then nullified (Ra'avad). Other authorities read: A partition that is not made for *naḥat*, and state that it is referring to a partition that was intended to be moved, rather than one made to be fixed in one spot (Rambam and others).

Cattle ditches – פִּירָא דְּבֵי תוֹרֵי: The *Arukh* explains that this is a pit in which oxen rest. According to the explanation that a partition made for *naḥat* is referring to a partition on which people walk, the reference in this context is to a pit that does not have real partitions. Rather, it is partitioned off by being lower than its surroundings. However, the people tending the animals continually walk on this partition and trample it down (see *Me'iri*).

HALAKHA

New and old towns – עִיר חֲדָשָׁה וִישָׁנָה: In the case of a new town, one that was first surrounded by a wall and only afterward settled, the Shabbat limit is measured from its settled area, rather than from its wall. However, in the case of an old town, which was first settled and only afterward surrounded by a wall, the limit is measured from the wall, as stated in the *baraita* (*Shulḥan Arukh, Oraḥ Ḥayyim* 398:11).

Screens of architects – מְחִיצוֹת אַדְרִיכָלִין: A partition that was constructed for a purpose other than to establish an enclosure for residence, such as a partition erected by a builder to rest objects against it, serves as a partition to permit one to carry, but does not render a place enclosed for the purpose of residence (based on the Rosh; *Shulḥan Arukh, Oraḥ Ḥayyim* 362:1).

BACKGROUND

The *eiruv* of Meḥoza – עֵירוּב מְחוֹזָא: Rows of houses separated by cattle ditches require a separate joining of courtyards [*eiruv*] for each row.

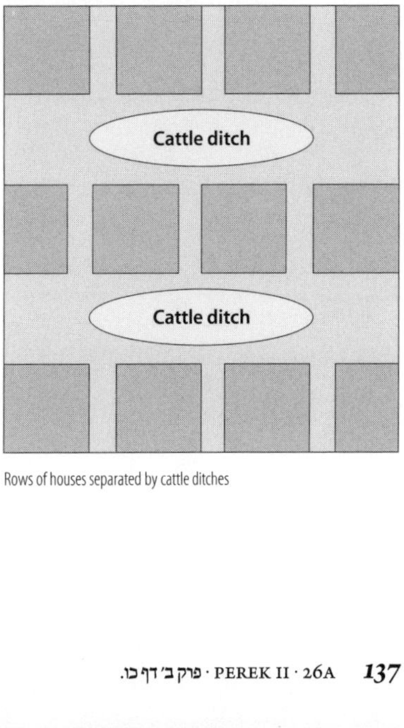

Rows of houses separated by cattle ditches

אָמַר רַבִּי יוֹחָנָן: וּשְׁנֵיהֶם מִקְרָא אֶחָד דָּרְשׁוּ, שֶׁנֶּאֱמַר: "וַיְהִי יְשַׁעְיָהוּ לֹא יָצָא אֶל חָצֵר הַתִּיכוֹנָה", כְּתִיב "הָעִיר" וְקָרֵינַן "חָצֵר" מִכָּאן לְאִסְטְרַטְיָא שֶׁל מֶלֶךְ, שֶׁהָיוּ כַּעֲיָירוֹת בֵּינוֹנִיּוֹת.

Rabbi Yoḥanan said: Both Rabbi Elai and Ḥananya **derived** their opinion **from the same verse,**[N] **as it is stated: "And it came to pass, before Isaiah was gone out into the middle courtyard,** that the word of the Lord came to him, saying" (II Kings 20:4). In the biblical text, **it is written: "The city [*ha'ir*]," and we read** it as: "The middle **courtyard [*ḥatzer*],"**[N] as there is a difference in this verse between the written word and how it is spoken. **From here** it is derived that **royal courts were** as large **as intermediate**-sized **cities.** Consequently, there is no contradiction, as the central courtyard of the royal palace was itself like a small town.

בְּמַאי קָמִיפַּלְגִי? מָר סָבַר: עֲיָירוֹת בֵּינוֹנִיּוֹת הָוְיָין בֵּית כּוֹר, וּמָר סָבַר אַרְבָּעִים סְאָה הָוְיָין.

The Gemara explains: **With regard to what** principle **do** Rabbi Elai and Ḥananya **disagree? One Sage,** Rabbi Elai, **maintains: Intermediate**-sized **towns are** the size of a field that had an area of **a *beit kor*; and one Sage,** Ḥananya, **maintains: They are** the size of **forty *se'a*.**

וִישַׁעְיָהוּ מַאי בָּעֵי הָתָם? אָמַר רַבָּה בַּר בַּר חָנָה, אָמַר רַבִּי יוֹחָנָן: מְלַמֵּד שֶׁחָלָה חִזְקִיָּה, וְהָלַךְ יְשַׁעְיָהוּ וְהוֹשִׁיב יְשִׁיבָה עַל פִּתְחוֹ.

The Gemara asks about the Biblical narrative cited above: **What did Isaiah need** to do **there** in the middle court, i.e., why was he there? The Gemara answers: **Rabba bar bar Ḥana said** that **Rabbi Yoḥanan said: This teaches that Hezekiah took ill, and Isaiah went and established a** Torah **academy at his door,** so that Torah scholars would sit and occupy themselves with Torah outside his room, the merit of which would help Hezekiah survive.

מִכָּאן לְתַלְמִיד חָכָם שֶׁחָלָה שֶׁמּוֹשִׁיבִין יְשִׁיבָה עַל פִּתְחוֹ. וְלָאו מִילְּתָא הִיא, דִּילְמָא אָתֵי לְאִיגְרוּיֵי בֵּיהּ שָׂטָן.

Based on this, it is derived, **with regard to a Torah scholar who took ill, that one establishes an academy at** the **entrance** to **his** home. The Gemara comments: **This,** however, **is not a** proper **course** of action, as **perhaps they will come to provoke Satan against him.**[N] Challenging Satan might worsen the health of a sick person rather than improve it.

"וְכֵן שָׁמַעְתִּי הֵימֶנּוּ: אַנְשֵׁי חָצֵר שֶׁשָּׁכַח אֶחָד וְלֹא עֵירֵב – בֵּיתוֹ אָסוּר".

The mishna cites another statement made by Rabbi Elai in the name of Rabbi Eliezer: **And I also heard from him** another *halakha*: If **one of the residents of a courtyard forgot and did not join in an *eiruv*** with the other residents, and on Shabbat he ceded ownership of his share in the courtyard to the other residents, it **is prohibited** for him, the one who forgot to establish an *eiruv*, to bring in objects or take them out from **his house** to the courtyard; but it is permitted to the other residents to bring objects from their houses to that other person's house via the courtyard, and vice versa.

וְהָתְנַן: בֵּיתוֹ אָסוּר לְהוֹצִיא וּלְהַכְנִיס לוֹ וְלָהֶן!

The Gemara raises an objection: **Didn't we learn** in a mishna: It **is prohibited** for the one who forgot to establish an *eiruv* to bring in objects or take them out from **his house** to the courtyard, **and for** the other residents who did make an *eiruv*, **to take out** objects from the house to the courtyard **or to bring** them into the house from the courtyard.

אָמַר רַב הוּנָא בְּרֵיהּ דְּרַב יְהוֹשֻׁעַ, אָמַר רַב שֵׁשֶׁת: לָא קַשְׁיָא;

Rav Huna, son of Rav Yehoshua, said that **Rav Sheshet said:** This is **not difficult.**

NOTES

Both derived their opinion from the same verse – וּשְׁנֵיהֶם מִקְרָא אֶחָד דָּרְשׁוּ: Both Sages agree that a large courtyard can be the size of a medium-sized town. This idea is based on the substitution of the word courtyard for the word town. They teach that both descriptions are correct: Utilized as a courtyard and the size of a town.

It is written...but we read – כְּתִיב וְקָרֵינַן: In the method applied in this context, which is also utilized by the Radak in his commentary on the Bible, there is no contradiction between how the word is written and how it is read. In addition, the way the word is read does not come to correct the way it is written; both the written version and the way the word is read teach a particular idea, and each teaches something about the other.

They might come to provoke Satan against him – אָתֵי לְאִיגְרוּיֵי בֵּיהּ שָׂטָן: According to a number of commentators, including Rashi, it is inappropriate to establish a Torah academy near the residence of a sick person, because in the course of their studies, Torah scholars engage in heated arguments about the meaning of the Torah. Consequently, there is a concern that Satan, who is most active in times of danger, will provoke the scholars and will cause them to come to erroneous conclusions as a result of their arguments, even though they are for the sake of Heaven (Rabbi Yoshiya Pinto).

הָא – רַבִּי אֱלִיעֶזֶר, וְהָא – רַבָּנַן.

This, the mishna here, is in accordance with the opinion of **Rabbi Eliezer, while that,** the other mishna, is in accordance with the opinion of **the Rabbis.**

כְּשֶׁתִּימְצֵי לוֹמַר, לְדִבְרֵי רַבִּי אֱלִיעֶזֶר הַמְבַטֵּל רְשׁוּת חֲצֵירוֹ – רְשׁוּת בֵּיתוֹ בִּיטֵּל. לְרַבָּנַן, הַמְבַטֵּל רְשׁוּת חֲצֵירוֹ – רְשׁוּת בֵּיתוֹ לֹא בִּיטֵּל.

Rav Sheshet adds: **When you examine** the matter closely,[N] you will find that **according to the statement of Rabbi Eliezer, one who renounces** his **authority over his** share in the **courtyard**[NH] to the other residents of the courtyard also **renounces** his **authority over his** own **house.** However, **according to** the opinion of **the Rabbis, one who renounces** his **authority over his** share in the **courtyard** to the other residents **does not renounce** his **authority over his** own **house** to them.

פְּשִׁיטָא!

The Gemara expresses surprise at this comment: But it is **obvious** that this is the point over which the *tanna'im* disagree.

אָמַר רַחֲבָה: אֲנָא וְרַב הוּנָא בַּר חִינָּנָא תַּרְגִּימְנָא: לֹא נִצְרְכָא אֶלָּא לַחֲמִשָּׁה שֶׁשְּׁרוּיִן בְּחָצֵר אֶחָד, וְשָׁכַח אֶחָד מֵהֶן וְלֹא עֵירַב.

The Gemara answers: **Raḥava said:** Both **Rav Huna bar Ḥinnana and I explained:** Rav Sheshet's explanation **was necessary only with regard to** the case of **five** people **who lived in the same courtyard, one of whom forgot to join in an** *eiruv* with the others.

לְדִבְרֵי רַבִּי אֱלִיעֶזֶר, כְּשֶׁהוּא מְבַטֵּל רְשׁוּתוֹ – אֵין צָרִיךְ לְבַטֵּל לְכָל אֶחָד וְאֶחָד.

According to the statement of Rabbi Eliezer, when he renounces his authority, he need not renounce it to each and every one of the residents, as we already know that Rabbi Eliezer holds that one who renounces authority does so in a generous manner,[N] renouncing authority not only of his share in the courtyard, but also of his own house. Consequently, if he is required to renounce authority to many people, we assume that he does so even if this is not explicitly stated.

לְרַבָּנַן, כְּשֶׁהוּא מְבַטֵּל רְשׁוּתוֹ – צָרִיךְ לְבַטֵּל לְכָל אֶחָד וְאֶחָד.

In contrast, **according to** the opinion of **the Rabbis, when he renounces his authority,** it does not suffice that he renounces it in favor of one person; rather, **he must** explicitly **renounce it to each and every one,** as we cannot presume that he renounces authority in a generous manner.[H]

כְּמַאן אָזְלָא הָא דְּתַנְיָא: חֲמִשָּׁה שֶׁשְּׁרוּיִן בְּחָצֵר אֶחָד וְשָׁכַח אֶחָד מֵהֶן וְלֹא עֵירַב, כְּשֶׁהוּא מְבַטֵּל רְשׁוּתוֹ – אֵין צָרִיךְ לְבַטֵּל רְשׁוּת לְכָל אֶחָד וְאֶחָד. כְּמַאן – כְּרַבִּי אֱלִיעֶזֶר.

The Gemara continues: **In accordance with which** *tanna* is the ruling **that was taught** in the following *baraita*? **If five** people **lived in the same courtyard, and one of them forgot and did not join in an** *eiruv* with the other residents, **when he renounces his authority, he need not renounce his authority to each and every one** of the residents. The Gemara asks: **In accordance with whose** opinion is it? It is **in accordance with Rabbi Eliezer,** as explained above.

רַב כָּהֲנָא מַתְנֵי הָכִי. רַב טַבְיוֹמֵי מַתְנֵי הָכִי: כְּמַאן אָזְלָא הָא דְּתַנְיָא חֲמִשָּׁה שֶׁשְּׁרוּיִם בְּחָצֵר אֶחָד וְשָׁכַח אֶחָד מֵהֶן וְלֹא עֵירַב, כְּשֶׁהוּא מְבַטֵּל רְשׁוּתוֹ – אֵינוֹ צָרִיךְ לְבַטֵּל רְשׁוּת לְכָל אֶחָד וְאֶחָד. כְּמַאן? אָמַר רַב הוּנָא בַּר יְהוּדָה, אָמַר רַב שֵׁשֶׁת: כְּמַאן – כְּרַבִּי אֱלִיעֶזֶר.

Rav Kahana taught the passage **this way,** as cited above, that it was Raḥava and Rav Huna bar Ḥinnana who applied Rav Sheshet's explanation to the case of the five people living in the same courtyard. **Rav Tavyomei,** on the other hand, **taught** it **as follows,** that it was Rav Sheshet himself who applied it to that case: **In accordance with which** *tanna* is the ruling **that was taught** in the following *baraita*? If **five** people **lived in the same courtyard, and one of them forgot and did not join in an** *eiruv* with the other residents, **when he renounces his authority, he need not renounce his authority to each and every one** of the residents. This statement is **in accordance with whose** opinion? **Rav Huna bar Yehuda said** that **Rav Sheshet said: In accordance with whom? In accordance with Rabbi Eliezer.**

אָמַר לֵיהּ רַב פָּפָּא לְאַבָּיֵי: לְרַבִּי אֱלִיעֶזֶר, אִי אָמַר "לָא מְבַטֵּילְנָא", וּלְרַבָּנַן אִי אָמַר "מְבַטֵּילְנָא", מַאי?

Rav Pappa said to Abaye: According to the opinion of **Rabbi Eliezer,** which presumes that one renounces his authority over his house as well, **if** one who forgot to join in an *eiruv* with the other residents of the courtyard explicitly **stated: I am not renouncing** authority of my house, **and** likewise, **according to** the opinion of **the Rabbis, if he** explicitly **stated: I am renouncing** authority of my house, **what is** the *halakha* in such cases?

NOTES

When you examine [*keshetimtzei lomar*] – כְּשֶׁתִּימְצֵי לוֹמַר: This is a talmudic expression meaning: If you examine the matter and investigate its roots. It is generally used when the Gemara seeks to clarify the basis of a dispute or to present a certain opinion in a more complete and inclusive manner.

Some commentaries explain the expression *keshetimtzei lomar* literally, based on the word *metzia*, which means a found object: If you examine and investigate, you will find a clear result (Rashi). Other authorities explain the phrase as meaning, If you exhaust [*keshetematzeh*] the issue to its depths, you will arrive at the following conclusion (*Shita Mekubbetzet*).

Renouncing authority over one's share in a courtyard – בִּיטּוּל רְשׁוּת חֲצֵירוֹ: In the Jerusalem Talmud the converse is stated: According to the Rabbis, one who renounces authority over his own house does not cede ownership of his share in the courtyard. Due to that resident's share in the courtyard, all are prohibited to carry from his house to the courtyard.

Renouncing authority in a generous manner – בִּיטּוּל בְּעַיִן יָפָה: According to Raḥava's explanation, the dispute between Rabbi Eliezer and the Rabbis is based on the question of whether one who renounces authority does so entirely willingly and includes everyone, or whether, as the Rabbis assume, one does not renounce more than the absolute minimum and consequently must demonstrate his intention if he wishes to renounce more. Rav Pappa subsequently raises the question of whether the dispute is in fact based on the manner of renouncing authority, or if it is based on other matters.

HALAKHA

One who renounces authority over his share in the courtyard – הַמְבַטֵּל רְשׁוּת: One who renounces authority over his part in a courtyard does not renounce authority over his own house, in accordance with the opinion of the Rabbis (*Shulḥan Arukh, Oraḥ Ḥayyim* 380:1).

Renouncing authority to many people – בִּיטּוּל רְשׁוּת לְרַבִּים: If one resides with several people in the same courtyard, but did not participate in the joining of courtyards [*eiruv*] with them and consequently needs to renounce his authority over his share in the courtyard, he must renounce it to each and every one of them. According to Rambam, one must say to each of the neighbors that he is renouncing his authority to that neighbor. Other authorities rule that it is sufficient for him to say: I renounce my authority to all of you (*Tur*; *Maggid Mishne*). Some later commentaries teach that the Rambam does not dispute this, and that his ruling should not be read that narrowly (*Arukh HaShulḥan*). The *Shulḥan Arukh HaRav* rules in accordance with the latter approach (*Shulḥan Arukh, Oraḥ Ḥayyim* 380:1).

טַעְמָא דְּרַבִּי אֱלִיעֶזֶר – מִשּׁוּם דְּקָסָבַר: הַמְבַטֵּל רְשׁוּת חֲצֵירוֹ – רְשׁוּת בֵּיתוֹ בִּיטֵּל, וְהַאי אֲמַר ״אֲנָא לָא מְבַטֵּילְנָא״.

The Gemara clarifies: Is **Rabbi Eliezer's reason because he maintains** in general that **one who renounces authority over his** share in a courtyard to the other residents presumably also **renounces** to them **authority over his** own **house, but** that since **this** person explicitly **stated: I am not renouncing** authority of my house, he therefore maintains his authority?

אוֹ דִּילְמָא: טַעְמָא דְּרַבִּי אֱלִיעֶזֶר מִשּׁוּם דְּבַיִת בְּלָא חָצֵר לָא עָבְידִי אֱינָשֵׁי דְּדָיְירֵי וְכִי קָאָמַר לָא מְבַטֵּילְנָא – לָאו כָּל כְּמִינֵּיהּ, אַף עַל גַּב דַּאֲמַר דָּיֵירְנָא, לָאו כְּלוּם קָאָמַר.

Or perhaps Rabbi Eliezer's reason is **because people do not** generally **live** in **a house without a courtyard,** and therefore anyone who renounces authority over his share in a courtyard automatically renounces authority over his own house regardless of what he says. Therefore, **when he says: I am not renouncing** authority over my house, it is **not in his power** to do so, **as even though he says:** I will continue **to live** in and retain authority over my house, **he has said nothing.**

וּלְרַבָּנַן, אִי אֲמַר ״מְבַטֵּילְנָא״ מַאי? טַעְמָא דְּרַבָּנַן מִשּׁוּם דְּקָסָבְרִי הַמְבַטֵּל רְשׁוּת חֲצֵירוֹ רְשׁוּת בֵּיתוֹ לֹא בִּיטֵּל – וְהַאי אֲמַר ״מְבַטֵּילְנָא״.

And the question likewise arises **according to** the opinion of **the Rabbis. If** one explicitly **stated: I am renouncing** authority of my house as well, **what** is the *halakha*? Is **the reason** for the opinion of **the Rabbis because they maintain** that **one who renounces authority over his** share in a **courtyard** to the other residents presumably **does not renounce authority over his** own **house** to them, **but** since **this** person explicitly **stated: I am renouncing** authority over my house, the other residents should be permitted to carry?

אוֹ דִּילְמָא: טַעְמָא דְּרַבָּנַן מִשּׁוּם דְּלָא עָבֵיד אִינִישׁ דִּמְסַלֵּק נַפְשֵׁיהּ לְגַמְרֵי מִבַּיִת וְחָצֵר, וְהָוֵי כִּי אוֹרֵחַ לְגַבַּיְיהוּ. וְהַאי כִּי אֲמַר מְבַטֵּילְנָא – לָאו כָּל כְּמִינֵּיהּ קָאָמַר.

Or perhaps the for the opinion of **the Rabbis** is **because one does not usually remove himself entirely from a house and courtyard, making himself like a guest among** his neighbors. **And** therefore, **when he states: I am renouncing** authority over my house, it is **not in his power** to do so, and his statement is disregarded.

אָמַר לֵיהּ: בֵּין לְרַבָּנַן בֵּין לְרַבִּי אֱלִיעֶזֶר, כֵּיוָן דְּגַלֵּי דַּעְתֵּיהּ – גַּלֵּי.

Abaye **said to** Rav Pappa in answer to his question: **Both according to the Rabbis and according to Rabbi Eliezer, once one has revealed his wishes, he has revealed** them,[H] and everything follows his express wishes.

״וְכֵן שָׁמַעְתִּי מִמֶּנּוּ שֶׁיּוֹצְאִים בְּעַרְקַבְלִין בְּפֶסַח״. מַאי עַרְקַבְלִין? אָמַר רֵישׁ לָקִישׁ: אַצְוָותָא חֲרוּזְיָאתָא.

The mishna records yet another teaching handed down by Rabbi Elai: **And I also heard from** Rabbi Eliezer another *halakha*, **that one may fulfill his obligation** to eat bitter herbs **on Passover with** ***arkablin***,[B] a certain bitter herb. The Gemara asks: **What is** ***arkablin***? **Reish Lakish said:** It is ***Atzvata ḥaruziyata***,[B] a type of fiber that wraps itself around a date palm.

הדרן עלך עושין פסין

HALAKHA

Once one reveals his wishes, he has revealed them – **כֵּיוָן דְּגַלֵּי דַּעְתֵּיהּ גַּלֵּי**: If one explicitly says that he is renouncing authority over his own house as well, it is considered renounced (*Shulḥan Arukh, Oraḥ Ḥayyim* 380:2).

BACKGROUND

Arkablin – **עַרְקַבְלִין**: A wide range of identities have been suggested for the plant called *arkablin* or *akrablin*. Indeed, it is doubtful whether all of the references to it in the Talmud are referring to the same plant. One proposed identity is a plant from the family of the scorpion's tail, Heliotropium. These are annual or perennial plants, whose flowers have the appearance of a scorpion's tail.

These plants grow wild in various parts of Eretz Yisrael. Some species are cultivated for decorative purposes, due to their shape and scent. The leaves of several similar species were used for the extraction of various medicines, and they are also apparently mentioned in the Talmud.

Hairy scorpion's tail

Atzvata ḥaruziyata – **אַצְוָותָא חֲרוּזְיָאתָא**: One tradition with regard to *atzvata ḥaruziyata* identifies the *arkablin* with a prickly climber, a species of spurge, possibly *Euphorbia officinalis*.

Summary of **Perek II**

In the course of the deliberation in the Mishna and Gemara in this chapter with regard to upright boards surrounding a well, one got a sense of the complexity of this leniency. On the one hand, there was a tendency to restrict the application of the *halakhot* of these upright boards. On the other hand, there was an effort to expand the scope of their validity and applicability. In practice, the leniency that allows placing upright boards around wells is in effect only in the specific circumstance of wells containing spring water. Similarly, the time and place where this leniency is in effect is limited to wells containing spring water located on roads used by pilgrims on their ascent to Jerusalem for the three Festivals. At the same time, the Sages determined that all of the *halakhot* that apply to partitions, including all fundamental leniencies, may be applied to upright boards surrounding a well. Indeed, any partition suitable for use in any other circumstances may be used to surround a well.

The other topic discussed in this chapter involves enclosures, gardens, or yards. From the perspective of their partitions, their status should be that of a private domain. However, they are not enclosed for residential purposes. The deliberations here, for all intents and purposes, revolved around a single fundamental principle: A comparison between an ordinary courtyard and the courtyard of the Tabernacle. Just as the construction of and service in the Tabernacle serve as a paradigm for many of the *halakhot* of Shabbat, the courtyard of the Tabernacle serves as the prototype from which the measures of all courtyards in the *halakhot* of Shabbat are ascertained. Through their deliberations, the Sages determined which enclosures or yards are deemed similar to the courtyard of the Tabernacle, in which it is permitted to carry as in a full-fledged private domain, and which are those that exceed two *beit se'a*, which was the area of the Tabernacle, and thus assume a distinct legal status. Although they are considered private domains by Torah law, the Sages prohibited carrying within them just as they prohibited carrying in courtyards and alleyways without an *eiruv*.

This chapter also addressed additional topics. One was the concept of renunciation of rights, which can be effected by a resident of a courtyard who failed to contribute his part to the food designated for the joining of the courtyards before Shabbat. The manner in which renunciation of rights is accomplished, as well as its effect, were discussed in this chapter.

Introduction to **Perek III**

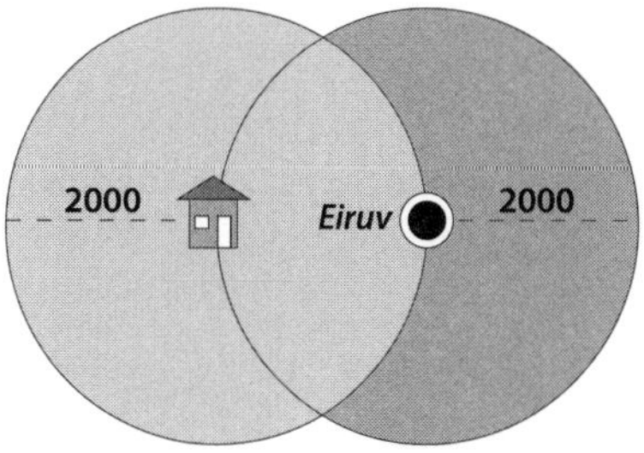

A joining of the Shabbat boundaries: The sketch depicts a person's home and the Shabbat limit that surrounds it. If he places his *eiruv* in the designated location at the edge of the boundary, that becomes his residence for Shabbat, and he may proceed two thousand cubits from that point. In this way, he is permitted to return home on Friday night and in the morning travel to the edge of the area extended by the *eiruv*.

Two topics are discussed in this chapter. One is placement of the *eiruv*, food for one meal, which is an inseparable component of the establishment of any *eiruv*, whether joining of courtyards, merging of alleyways, or joining of Shabbat boundaries. The necessity of contributing food to the *eiruv* is due to the fact that the place where one's food is located is considered his residence. Consequently, inclusion of several people in a common meal creates a form of common ownership of the residence, the precise nature of which is discussed in the Gemara. Placement of one's food in a specific location is, in a sense, tantamount to moving his residence to that location. The Gemara discusses several issues, among them, the types of food that may constitute a meal for the purpose of *eiruv*. Are there foods that are not suited for an *eiruv*? In addition, must all those who placed the *eiruv* have access to the food in order for the *eiruv* to be effective?

Since the issue of the food suitable for placement in an *eiruv* applies both to *halakhot* of joining of the courtyards and joining of Shabbat boundaries, the Gemara in Chapter Three proceeds to discuss the latter subject: The *halakhot* of joining Shabbat boundaries. The *halakha* – some say by Torah law while others say by rabbinic law – is that one may not travel more than two thousand cubits outside his place on Shabbat. However, in certain cases the Sages permitted establishing a joining of Shabbat boundaries that allows one to travel a longer distance. This is accomplished by placing food sufficient for two meals in a specific location that is not his place of residence; that location, for all intents and purposes, becomes his residence, and he may travel two thousand cubits from that location.

There are many details involved in this universally accepted *halakha*, and in this chapter the Gemara elucidates how and when one places the food for the *eiruv*, as well as in what cases the *eiruv* is in effect and when it is invalidated due either to an inappropriate location or a problem with the food item itself. Similarly, the Gemara discusses whether the placement of the *eiruv* is an irreversible and unequivocal decision to reside at that location, or whether it is possible to place the *eiruv* conditionally and to decide in the course of Shabbat when and in which direction the *eiruv* takes effect. These questions with regard to the *halakhot* of a joining of Shabbat boundaries are elucidated in this chapter and in those that follow.

מתני׳ בְּכֹּל מְעָרְבִין וּמִשְׁתַּתְּפִין – חוּץ מִן הַמַּיִם וּמִן הַמֶּלַח.

MISHNA **One may establish a joining** of houses in courtyards [*eiruv ḥatzerot*] in order to permit carrying on Shabbat in a courtyard shared by two or more houses, and one may establish a joining of Shabbat borders [*eiruv teḥumin*] in order to extend the distance one is permitted to walk on Shabbat; **and** similarly, **one may merge** courtyards in order to permit carrying in an alleyway shared by two or more courtyards. This may be done **with all** kinds of food[H] **except for water and salt,**[N] as they are not considered foods and therefore may not be used for these purposes.

וְהַכֹּל נִיקָּח בְּכֶסֶף מַעֲשֵׂר – חוּץ מִן הַמַּיִם וּמִן הַמֶּלַח. הַנּוֹדֵר מִן הַמָּזוֹן – מוּתָּר בַּמֶּלַח וּבַמַּיִם.

The mishna continues with two similar principles: **All** types of food **may be bought with** second-**tithe money,** which must be taken to Jerusalem and used to purchase food (Deuteronomy 14:26), **except for water and salt.** Similarly, **one who vows that nourishment** is prohibited to him **is permitted** to eat **water and salt,** as they are not considered sources of nourishment.

מְעָרְבִין לְנָזִיר בַּיַּיִן, וּלְיִשְׂרָאֵל בִּתְרוּמָה. סוּמְכוֹס אוֹמֵר: בְּחוּלִּין.

It was further stated with regard to the laws of joining courtyards that **one may establish an *eiruv teḥumin* for a nazirite with wine,** even though he is prohibited to drink it, because it is permitted to others. **And** similarly, one may establish an *eiruv teḥumin* **for an Israelite with *teruma*,** even though he may not eat it, because it is permitted to a priest. The food used for an *eiruv teḥumin* must be fit for human consumption, but it is not essential that it be fit for the consumption of the one for whom it is being used. **Summakhos,** however, **says:** One may only establish an *eiruv teḥumin* for an Israelite **with unconsecrated** food.

וּלְכֹהֵן בְּבֵית הַפְּרָס, רַבִּי יְהוּדָה אוֹמֵר: אֲפִילּוּ בֵּין הַקְּבָרוֹת,

It was additionally stated that one may establish an *eiruv teḥumin* **for a priest in a *beit haperas*,**[NL] a field containing a grave that was plowed over. There is doubt as to the location of bone fragments in the entire area. A priest is prohibited to come into contact with a corpse, and therefore may not enter a *beit haperas*. **Rabbi Yehuda says:** An *eiruv teḥumin* may be established for a priest **even between the graves** in a graveyard, an area which the priest may not enter by Torah law,

HALAKHA

One may establish a joining of houses and one may merge courtyards with all kinds of food – בְּכֹּל מְעָרְבִין וּמִשְׁתַּתְּפִין: One may establish an *eiruv* with all types of food except for water and salt. One may not create an *eiruv* even with both water and salt, unless they are mixed together (*Shulḥan Arukh, Oraḥ Ḥayyim* 386:5).

NOTES

One may establish a joining of houses…with all kinds of food except for water and salt – בְּכֹּל מְעָרְבִין...חוּץ מִן הַמַּיִם וּמִן הַמֶּלַח: Two reasons are suggested in the Jerusalem Talmud for why one may not establish a joining of courtyards [*eiruv*] with water or salt: First, water and salt are not nourishing. Second, they serve as symbols and reminders of a curse. Water represents the generation of the Flood, and salt is a reminder of the destruction of Sodom (see Genesis 19).

***Beit haperas* – בֵּית הַפְּרָס:** All agree that a *beit haperas* is an area in which there is doubt concerning the location of a grave. However, the Sages of the Talmud disagreed about the specific circumstance: Some Sages held that it was known that there was a grave in the *beit haperas*, but the people forgot its exact location. Other Sages maintained that the phrase is referring to a field in which a grave was plowed over, and it is therefore likely that bones are scattered over a wide area. There are also other explanations. Nevertheless, all agree that the ritual impurity of a *beit haperas* is rabbinic in origin and not a Torah law.

LANGUAGE

***Beit haperas* – בֵּית הַפְּרָס:** Various explanations have been suggested for this phrase. Some authorities explain that it comes from the word *perisa*, meaning spread out or widening, because the ritual impurity is spread throughout the field (Rambam's Commentary on the Mishna). Rashi teaches that the impurity in the field is *perusa*, meaning broken. *Tosafot* explain that the word is referring to footsteps, *parsot*, because people refrain from treading there.

Other commentaries explain that this term is related to the Latin word forum, meaning plaza or in this context a plaza in front of a cemetery, or to the Greek equivalent **φόρος**, *foros* (Rabbi Binyamin Musafya).

מִפְּנֵי שֶׁיָּכוֹל לָחוֹץ וְלֵילֵךְ וְלֶאֱכוֹל.

since he can interpose between himself and the graves **and go and eat** the food that comprises the *eiruv* without contracting ritual impurity.

גמ׳ אָמַר רַבִּי יוֹחָנָן: אֵין לְמֵידִין מִן הַכְּלָלוֹת וַאֲפִילּוּ בְּמָקוֹם שֶׁנֶּאֱמַר בּוֹ חוּץ.

GEMARA **Rabbi Yoḥanan said: One may not learn from general statements,**[N] i.e., when a general statement is made in a mishna using the word all, it is not to be understood as an all-inclusive, general statement without exceptions. This is true **even in a place where it says** the word **except.** Even in that case, there may be other exceptions to the rule that are not listed.

מִדְּקָאָמַר: ״אֲפִילּוּ בְּמָקוֹם שֶׁנֶּאֱמַר בּוֹ חוּץ״, מִכְּלָל דְּלָאו הָכָא קָאֵי, הֵיכָא קָאֵי?

The Gemara notes: **From** the fact that Rabbi Yoḥanan **said: Even in a place where it says except,** this proves **by inference that he was not relating to** the general statement made **here** in the mishna, which uses the word except. **To which** mishna, then, **was he relating** when he formulated his principle?

NOTES

One may not learn from general statements – אֵין לְמֵידִין מִן הַכְּלָלוֹת: Some say that this only applies to tannaitic statements, since the *tanna'im* speak in a terse style and occasionally fail to fully explain themselves. However, this principle is not applicable to the statements of *amora'im* (see Rabbeinu Yehonatan). The Rashba, the Ritva, and other commentaries explained that this principle includes amoraic statements as well. In terms of determining the practical *halakha*, some authorities state that this principle is not to be taken literally. Rather, if there is a proof from a mishna or a *baraita* that indicates a ruling contrary to the general statement, the general statement is not considered to contradict it. However, in the absence of any proof to the contrary, one may in fact learn from general statements (Ramban). Others dispute this qualification (*Tosafot*; see *Yad Malakhi*).

HALAKHA

Anything that is carried upon a *zav* – כֹּל שֶׁנִּישָּׂא עַל גַּבֵּי הַזָּב: Anything that a *zav* carries is ritually impure (Rambam *Sefer Tahara, Hilkhot Metamei Mishkav UMoshav* 6:6).

Anything on which a *zav* is carried – כֹּל שֶׁהַזָּב נִישָּׂא עָלָיו: Anything on which a *zav* is carried is ritually pure, provided that he does not touch it, e.g., if there is something intervening between the *zav* and the object utilized to carry him, and that the object is not designed for reclining or sitting (Rambam *Sefer Tahara, Hilkhot Metamei Mishkav UMoshav* 6:6).

A human being who carries a *zav* – אָדָם הַנּוֹשֵׂא אֶת הַזָּב: One who carries a *zav* contracts ritual impurity, even if he does not have physical contact with the *zav* (Rambam *Sefer Tahara, Hilkhot Metamei Mishkav UMoshav* 6:6).

The impurity of a saddle – טוּמְאַת אוּכָּף: A saddle is susceptible to the ritual impurity contracted when a *zav* rides on something meant for riding (Rambam *Sefer Tahara, Hilkhot Kelim* 25:20).

An *eiruv* of truffles and mushrooms – עֵירוּב בִּכְמֵיהִין וּפִטְרִיּוֹת: Truffles and mushrooms may not be used for an *eiruv*. Some say that if they are cooked, they may be used (Vilna Gaon; *Shulḥan Arukh, Oraḥ Ḥayyim* 386:5).

BACKGROUND

A saddle and a pommel – אוּכָּף וְתָפוּס:

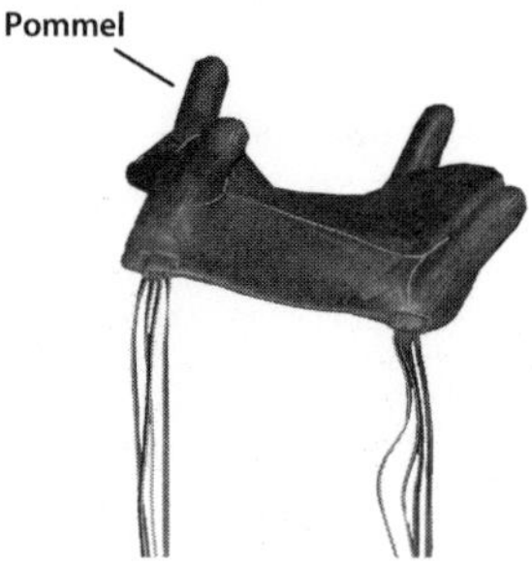

Construction of a Roman saddle with pommels

הָתָם קָאֵי: כָּל מִצְוַת עֲשֵׂה שֶׁהַזְּמַן גְּרָמָא אֲנָשִׁים חַיָּיבִין וְנָשִׁים פְּטוּרוֹת, וְשֶׁלֹּא הַזְּמַן גְּרָמָא – אֶחָד נָשִׁים וְאֶחָד אֲנָשִׁים חַיָּיבִין.

The Gemara answers: **He was relating** to a mishna found **there:** With regard to **all time-bound, positive commandments,** i.e., mitzvot that can only be performed at a certain time of the day, or during the day rather than at night, or on certain days of the year, **men are obligated** to perform them **and women are exempt.** But positive commandments **that are not time-bound, both women and men are obligated** to perform.

וּכְלָלָא הוּא דְּכָל מִצְוַת עֲשֵׂה שֶׁהַזְּמַן גְּרָמָא נָשִׁים פְּטוּרוֹת?! הֲרֵי מַצָּה שִׂמְחָה וְהַקְהֵל, דְּמִצְוַת עֲשֵׂה שֶׁהַזְּמַן גְּרָמָא הוּא – וְנָשִׁים חַיָּיבוֹת.

Is it a general **principle** that **women are exempt from all time-bound, positive commandments** without exception? But **there is** the commandment to eat ***matza*** on Passover, the commandment of **rejoicing** on a Festival, and the commandment of **assembly** in the Temple courtyard once every seven years during the festival of *Sukkot* following the Sabbatical Year, all of which **are time-bound, positive commandments, and** nevertheless, **women are obligated** to perform them.

וְכָל מִצְוַת עֲשֵׂה שֶׁלֹּא הַזְּמַן גְּרָמָא נָשִׁים חַיָּיבוֹת? הֲרֵי תַּלְמוּד תּוֹרָה, פְּרִיָּה וּרְבִיָּה, וּפִדְיוֹן הַבֵּן, דְּמִצְוַת עֲשֵׂה שֶׁלֹּא הַזְּמַן גְּרָמָא – וְנָשִׁים פְּטוּרוֹת! אֶלָּא אָמַר רַבִּי יוֹחָנָן: אֵין לְמֵידִין מִן הַכְּלָלוֹת, וַאֲפִילּוּ בְּמָקוֹם שֶׁנֶּאֱמַר בּוֹ חוּץ.

Similarly, **are women obligated in all positive commandments that are not time-bound?** But **there is** the commandment of **Torah study,** the commandment to **be fruitful and multiply,** and the commandment of **redemption of the firstborn,** all of which are **positive commandments that are not time-bound, and** nevertheless, **women are exempt** from them. **Rather, Rabbi Yoḥanan said: One may not learn from general statements, even in a place where it says except,** because it is always possible that there other exceptions to the rule.

אָמַר אַבַּיֵי, וְאִיתֵּימָא רַבִּי יִרְמְיָה: אַף אֲנַן נַמִי תָּנֵינָא; עוֹד כְּלָל אַחֵר אָמְרוּ: כֹּל שֶׁנִּישָּׂא עַל גַּבֵּי הַזָּב – טָמֵא, וְכֹל שֶׁהַזָּב נִישָּׂא עָלָיו – טָהוֹר, חוּץ מִן הָרָאוּי לְמִשְׁכָּב וּמוֹשָׁב וְהָאָדָם. וְתוּ לֵיכָּא?! וְהָא אִיכָּא מֶרְכָּב!

Abaye said, and some say it was **Rabbi Yirmeya** who said: **We, too, have also learned** a proof for Rabbi Yoḥanan's principle from a mishna: **They stated** yet **another** general **principle: Anything** that is **carried upon a *zav***[H] is ritually **impure. And anything on which a *zav* is carried**[H] is ritually **pure, except for** an object **suitable for lying or sitting upon and a human being,**[H] which become defiled if a *zav* is borne on them. The following objection may be raised: **And is there nothing else? But there is** an object upon which a person **rides**[N] that becomes impure, as explained in the Torah itself.

מֶרְכָּב הֵיכִי דָּמֵי? אִי דְּיָתֵיב עֲלֵיהּ – הַיְינוּ מוֹשָׁב! אֲנַן הָכִי קָאָמְרִינַן: הָא אִיכָּא גַּבָּא דְּאוּכְּפָא, דְּתַנְיָא: הָאוּכָּף טָמֵא מוֹשָׁב, וְהַתָּפוּס טָמֵא מֶרְכָּב. אֶלָּא שְׁמַע מִינָּהּ: אֵין לְמֵידִין מִן הַכְּלָלוֹת, וַאֲפִילּוּ בְּמָקוֹם שֶׁנֶּאֱמַר בּוֹ חוּץ.

The Gemara first asks: **What are the circumstances** of an object upon which **one rides? If he sat upon it, it is a seat.** If not, how does it become defiled? What is there that is suitable for riding upon but does not fall into the category of something upon which one lies or sits? The Gemara answers: **We say as follows: There is the upper part of a saddle,** which becomes ritually impure as a riding accessory and not as a regular seat. **As it was taught** in the *Tosefta*: **A saddle** upon which a *zav* sat **is impure**[H] as **a seat** of a *zav*, **and the pommel,**[BN] which is attached to the front of the saddle and used by the rider to maintain his position or to assist in mounting, **is impure** as **a riding** accessory. Therefore, we see that the general statement found in the mishna omits that which is suitable for riding upon. **Rather, conclude from this** that **one may not learn from general statements, even in a place where it says except.**

אָמַר רָבִינָא, וְאִיתֵּימָא רַב נַחְמָן: אַף אֲנַן נַמִי תָּנֵינָא: בַּכֹּל מְעָרְבִין וּמִשְׁתַּתְּפִין, חוּץ מִן הַמַּיִם וְהַמֶּלַח. וְתוּ לֵיכָּא?! וְהָא אִיכָּא כְּמֵיהִין וּפִטְרִיּוֹת! אֶלָּא שְׁמַע מִינָּהּ: אֵין לְמֵידִין מִן הַכְּלָלוֹת, וַאֲפִילּוּ בְּמָקוֹם שֶׁנֶּאֱמַר בּוֹ חוּץ.

Ravina said, and some say it was **Rav Naḥman** who said: **We, too, have also learned** a proof for Rabbi Yoḥanan's principle from the mishna, which states: **One may establish an *eiruv* and merge** alleyways **with all** kinds of food, **except for water and salt. And is there nothing else? But there are truffles and mushrooms,** which also may not be used for an *eiruv*[H] because they are not regarded as food. **Rather, conclude from this** that **one may not learn from general statements, even in a place where it says except.**

NOTES

The riding seat of a *zav* – מֶרְכַּב הַזָּב: Rabbeinu Ḥananel had a variant text that was slightly different from ours and which is preferred by the Rashba and some other commentaries. According to his version, the Gemara asks: But is there a riding seat? The Gemara then states: What is a riding seat? It is a saddle. Therefore, when he sits on it, it is a seat. The Gemara responds: But even according to your approach, the Torah mentions both something upon which one rides and something upon which one sits, implying that both terms can apply to the same object, such as the saddle and the grip, which is connected to it.

A saddle and a pommel – אוּכָּף וְתָפוּס: *Tosafot* ask: How is it possible for one utensil to be defiled by two separate kinds of ritual impurity? They answer that a saddle and a pommel are two utensils: A saddle is used for sitting, even if it is not on an animal, while a pommel is only used when riding (Ritva).

"הַכֹּל נִיקָּח בְּכֶסֶף מַעֲשֵׂר כּוּ". רַבִּי אֱלִיעֶזֶר וְרַבִּי יוֹסֵי בַּר חֲנִינָא, חַד מַתְנֵי אַעֵירוּב וְחַד מַתְנֵי אַמַּעֲשֵׂר.

We learned in the mishna: **All** types of food **may be bought with** second-**tithe money,** except for water and salt. **Rabbi Eliezer and Rabbi Yosei bar Ḥanina** both had the same tradition, but **one teaches it with regard to *eiruv*, and one teaches** it **with regard to** the second **tithe.**

חַד מַתְנֵי אַעֵירוּב: לֹא שָׁנוּ אֶלָּא מַיִם בִּפְנֵי עַצְמוֹ וּמֶלַח בִּפְנֵי עַצְמוֹ, דְּאֵין מְעָרְבִין – אֲבָל בְּמַיִם וּמֶלַח מְעָרְבִין.

The Gemara elaborates: **One teaches** this *halakha* **with regard to** the issue of *eiruv*, as follows: **They only taught** that **one may not establish an *eiruv*** with water or salt in the case of **water by itself or salt by itself. But** with **water and salt** together, **one may** indeed **establish an *eiruv*.**[H]

וְחַד מַתְנֵי אַמַּעֲשֵׂר: לֹא שָׁנוּ אֶלָּא מַיִם בִּפְנֵי עַצְמוֹ וּמֶלַח בִּפְנֵי עַצְמוֹ דְּאֵין נִיקָּחִין, אֲבָל מַיִם וּמֶלַח – נִיקָּחִין בְּכֶסֶף מַעֲשֵׂר.

And the other **one teaches** this *halakha* **with regard to** the issue of the second **tithe: They only taught** that water or salt **may not be bought** with second-tithe money in the case of **water by itself or salt by itself. But water and salt** mixed together **may** indeed **be bought with** second-**tithe** money.[H]

מַאן דְּמַתְנֵי אַמַּעֲשֵׂר – כׇּל שֶׁכֵּן אַעֵירוּב, וּמַאן דְּמַתְנֵי אַעֵירוּב – אֲבָל אַמַּעֲשֵׂר לֹא. מַאי טַעְמָא – פֵּירָא בָּעֵינַן.

The Gemara comments: **The one who teaches** this law **with regard to** the second **tithe, all the more so** would he apply it **to an *eiruv*,** i.e., he would certainly maintain that water and salt together are suitable to be used for an *eiruv*. However, according to **the one who teaches** this law **with regard to an *eiruv*,** it applies only to an *eiruv*; **but with regard to** the second tithe, **no,** it does not apply. **What is the reason** for this distinction? For the second tithe, **we require produce,** as stated in the Torah, and even when water and salt are mixed together they do not have the status of produce.

כִּי אֲתָא רַבִּי יִצְחָק, מַתְנֵי אַמַּעֲשֵׂר. מֵיתִיבִי, הֵעִיד רַבִּי יְהוּדָה בֶּן גָּדִישׁ לִפְנֵי רַבִּי אֱלִיעֶזֶר: שֶׁל בֵּית אַבָּא הָיוּ לוֹקְחִין צִיר בְּכֶסֶף מַעֲשֵׂר. אָמַר לוֹ: שֶׁמָּא לֹא שָׁמַעְתָּ אֶלָּא כְּשֶׁקִּרְבֵי דָּגִים מְעוֹרָבִין בָּהֶן. וַאֲפִילּוּ רַבִּי יְהוּדָה בֶּן גָּדִישׁ לָא קָאָמַר אֶלָּא בְּצִיר, דְּשׁוּמְנָא דְּפֵירָא הִיא, אֲבָל מַיִם וּמֶלַח – לֹא!

When Rabbi Yitzḥak came from Eretz Yisrael to Babylonia, **he taught** this law **with regard to** the second **tithe.** The Gemara **raises an objection** from the following *baraita*: **Rabbi Yehuda ben Gadish testified before Rabbi Eliezer: In Father's house they would buy** fish **brine with** second-**tithe money. He said to him: Perhaps you only heard** this in a case **where the fish's innards were mixed with** the brine. Since this mixture contains a small portion of the fish, the brine becomes significant enough to be purchased with second-tithe money. **And even Rabbi Yehuda ben Gadish only said** his statement **with regard to brine, which is the fat of produce,** i.e., because a certain amount of fish fat, which itself may be purchased with second-tithe money, is mixed in with the brine; **but** a mixture of **water and salt** alone may **not** be bought with it.

אָמַר רַב יוֹסֵף:

In response to this difficulty, **Rav Yosef said:**

HALAKHA

An *eiruv* of water and salt – עֵירוּב בְּמַיִם וּמֶלַח: Water and salt may not be used for an *eiruv*. However, when they are mixed together they may be used for an *eiruv*. Some authorities state that this only applies if oil was added to the mixture (*Tosafot*; *Hagahot Asheri*; *Shulḥan Arukh*, *Oraḥ Ḥayyim* 386:5).

Water and salt with regard to the second tithe – מַיִם וּמֶלַח לְמַעֲשֵׂר שֵׁנִי: Water and salt may not be purchased with second-tithe money, unless they were mixed together and some oil was added (Rambam *Sefer Zera'im*, *Hilkhot Ma'aser Sheni* 7:4).

Perek **III**
Daf **27** Amud **b**

לֹא נִצְרְכָה אֶלָּא שֶׁנָּתַן לְתוֹכָן שֶׁמֶן.

Rabbi Yitzḥak's ruling that water and salt mixed together may be bought with second-tithe money **was only necessary** in a case **where one added oil to them.**[NH] But a mixture of water and salt alone may not be purchased with second-tithe money.

אָמַר לֵיהּ אַבָּיֵי: וְתִיפּוֹק לֵיהּ מִשּׁוּם שֶׁמֶן! לָא צְרִיכָא שֶׁנָּתַן דְּמֵי מַיִם וּמֶלַח בְּהַבְלָעָה.

Abaye said to Rav Yosef: If so, **let him derive** that the mixture may be bought with second-tithe money **because of the oil** alone. The Gemara refutes this argument: **No, it was necessary** for a case in which **one paid the value of the water and salt by including** it in the payment for the oil. Although ostensibly the money that he paid was for the oil, he added to the price of the oil in order to include payment for the water and salt that were mixed with it.

NOTES

One added oil to them – שֶׁנָּתַן לְתוֹכָן שֶׁמֶן: The commentaries disagree with regard to this issue. Most authorities rule that the addition of oil is necessary only to allow one to purchase salt and water with second-tithe money (Rif; Rambam). However, *Tosafot*, the Ritva, and other commentaries maintain that the addition of oil to the mixture of water and salt is required in order to use them for an *eiruv* as well.

HALAKHA

Water, salt, and oil – מַיִם מֶלַח וְשֶׁמֶן: Water and salt may not be purchased with second-tithe money, unless oil was added to the mixture and payment for the water and salt was combined with the payment for the oil (Rambam *Sefer Zera'im*, *Hilkhot Ma'aser Sheni* 7:10).

וּבְהַבְלָעָה מִי שָׁרֵי? אִין, וְהָתַנְיָא, בֶּן בַּג בַּג אוֹמֵר: ״בַּבָּקָר״ – מְלַמֵּד שֶׁלּוֹקְחִין בָּקָר עַל גַּב עוֹרוֹ, ״וּבַצֹּאן״ – מְלַמֵּד שֶׁלּוֹקְחִין צֹאן עַל גַּב גִּיזָּתָהּ, ״וּבַיַּיִן״ – מְלַמֵּד שֶׁלּוֹקְחִין יַיִן עַל גַּב קַנְקַנּוֹ, ״וּבַשֵּׁכָר״ – מְלַמֵּד שֶׁלּוֹקְחִין תֶּמֶד מִשֶּׁהֶחֱמִיץ.

The Gemara asks: **But** if something may not be bought with second-tithe money, **is one permitted** to buy it **by including** it in the payment for something which may be bought with second-tithe money? The Gemara answers: **Yes, and so it was taught** in the following *baraita*: **Ben Bag Bag**[P] **says** in exposition of the verse: "And you shall bestow that money on all that your heart desires, on oxen, on sheep, on wine, on strong drink, on whatever your soul requests" (Deuteronomy 14:26): **"On oxen" teaches that one may buy an ox** and include in its price payment for **its hide.**[H] Although the hide cannot be eaten, it may be bought together with the ox, and it does not acquire the sanctity of the second tithe. **"On sheep" teaches that one may buy a sheep** and include in its price payment for **its fleece,** which is used for purposes other than eating. **"On wine" teaches that one may buy wine** and include in its price payment for **its jug. "On strong drink" teaches that** one is permitted to buy not only actual wine, but **one may buy** even **mead,** water in which grape seeds are soaked, **once it has fermented** and acquired the flavor of wine.

אָמַר רַבִּי יוֹחָנָן: מַאן דִּמְתַרְגֵּם לִי ״בַּבָּקָר״ אַלִּיבָּא דְּבֶן בַּג בַּג – מוֹבִילְנָא מָאנֵיהּ אַבַּתְרֵיהּ לְבֵי מַסּוּתָא.

Having cited ben Bag Bag's exposition of the verse, the Gemara continues: **Rabbi Yoḥanan said: Whoever interprets** the words **"on oxen" for me in accordance with** the opinion of **ben Bag Bag, I will carry his clothes after him**[N] **into the bathhouse,** i.e., I will honor him to such an extent that I will be prepared to treat him as a servant treats his master.

מַאי טַעְמָא? כּוּלְּהוּ צְרִיכִי, לְבַר מִ״בַּבָּקָר״ דְּלָא צָרִיךְ. מַאי צְרִיכִי? דְּאִי כְּתַב רַחֲמָנָא ״בַּבָּקָר״, הֲוָה אָמִינָא: בָּקָר הוּא דְּמִזְדַּבַּן עַל גַּב עוֹרוֹ, מִשּׁוּם דְּגוּפֵיהּ הוּא, אֲבָל צֹאן עַל גַּב גִּיזָּתָהּ דְּלָאו גּוּפֵיהּ הוּא – אֵימָא לָא.

What is the reason for Rabbi Yoḥanan's difficulty? **All** parts of the verse cited above **are necessary, except for** the expression **"on oxen," which is not necessary.** The Gemara clarifies: For **what** purpose are all the other words **necessary? As, if the Torah had written** only **"on oxen," I might have said** that **it is** only an **ox that may be bought** together **with its hide** with second-tithe money **because** the hide **is** an inseparable part of **its body,** and therefore it is not considered an independent entity from its flesh. **But** as for buying a **sheep** together **with its fleece, which is not** an inseparable part of **its body** because the fleece can be removed from the sheep while it is alive, you might **say no,** second-tithe money may not be spent in this manner. It was therefore necessary to state "on sheep."

וְאִי כְּתַב רַחֲמָנָא ״בַּצֹּאן״ עַל גַּב גִּיזָּתָהּ – הֲוָה אָמִינָא: מִשּׁוּם דִּמְחוּבָּר בָּהּ, אֲבָל יַיִן עַל גַּב קַנְקַנּוֹ – אֵימָא לָא.

And if the Torah had also **written** "**on sheep,**" teaching that one may buy even a sheep with second-tithe money together **with its fleece, I might have said** that it is only a sheep that may be bought together with its fleece **because** the fleece **is attached to it,** and therefore it is considered part of the animal. **But** as for buying **wine** together **with its jug,** you might **say no,** second-tithe money may not be spent this way. It was therefore necessary to state "on wine."

וְאִי כְּתַב רַחֲמָנָא ״בַּיַּיִן״ הֲוָה אָמִינָא: מִשּׁוּם דְּהַיְינוּ נְטִירוּתֵיהּ, אֲבָל תֶּמֶד מִשֶּׁהֶחֱמִיץ דְּקִיוְהָא בְּעָלְמָא הוּא – אֵימָא לָא, כְּתַב רַחֲמָנָא ״שֵׁכָר״.

And if the Torah had also **written "on wine,"** indicating that one may even buy wine together with its jug with second-tithe money, **I might** still **have said** that this is **because** the jug **is** needed for the wine's **preservation,** as there is no way to carry wine without some sort of container. **But** as for **mead**[N] **that has fermented,**[H] **which is mere acidity,** you might **say no,** it should not be included among the items that may be bought with second-tithe money. Therefore, **the Torah wrote:** "On **strong drink.**"

וְאִי כְּתַב רַחֲמָנָא ״בַּשֵּׁכָר״ – הֲוָה אָמִינָא: מַאי שֵׁכָר – דְּבֵילָה קְעִילִית, דְּפֵירָא הוּא, אֲבָל יַיִן עַל גַּב קַנְקַנּוֹ – אֵימָא לָא.

The necessity of each word much be proven in the opposite order as well. **And if the Torah had** only **written "on strong drink," I might have said: What is** meant by **strong drink? Dried figs from** the town of **Ke'ila, which are** choice and juicy figs that can have an intoxicating effect. They are therefore considered **produce** and not merely mead. **But** as for buying **wine** together **with its jug,** you might **say no,** this may not be done with second-tithe money, and therefore it was necessary to state "on wine."

וְאִי כְּתַב רַחֲמָנָא יַיִן עַל גַּב קַנְקַנּוֹ – דְּהַיְינוּ נְטִירוּתֵיהּ, אֲבָל צֹאן עַל גַּב גִּיזָּתָהּ – אֵימָא לָא, כְּתַב רַחֲמָנָא ״צֹאן״ דַּאֲפִילּוּ עַל גַּב גִּיזָּתָהּ.

And if the Torah had also **written** "on wine," indicating that one may buy even **wine** together **with its jug** with second-tithe money, I might have said that this is because the jug **is** needed for the wine's **preservation. But** as for buying a **sheep** together **with its fleece,** you might **say no,** this may not be done with second-tithe money. Therefore, **the Torah stated** "on **sheep,**" to teach **that** a sheep may be bought with second-tithe money **even** together **with its fleece.**

PERSONALITIES

Ben Bag Bag – בֶּן בַּג בַּג: The full name of this Sage was Rabbi Yoḥanan ben Bag Bag. He was one of the Sages of the Mishna from the generation of the destruction of the Second Temple. However, some commentaries state that he was a contemporary of Hillel and Shammai. Although only a few statements of Rabbi Yoḥanan ben Bag Bag are recorded in the Talmud and midrash, it appears that he was highly regarded by the Sages of his generation. Indeed, Rabbi Yehuda ben Beteira wrote to him: I know that you are expert in the chambers of Torah.

Some commentaries say that he was a son of converts and that ben Bag Bag was a nickname. *Tosafot* claim that the nickname refers to the patriarch Avraham, to whose name the letter *heh* was added. The numerical value of *bag* [*bet* and *gimmel*] is five, corresponding to the numerical value of the letter *heh*. Other authorities explain that the word *bag* is an acronym for son of a convert [*ben ger*] and son of a female convert [*ben giyoret*].

HALAKHA

An ox with its hide – בָּקָר עַל גַּבֵּי עוֹרוֹ: One may utilize second-tithe money to purchase an ox hide along with an ox or to acquire a jug along with wine, provided that the payment for the hide or jug is included in the payment for the ox or wine. However, it is prohibited to make such purchases from a merchant. Since the merchant knows the price of the hide or jug, the payment for these objects cannot be considered to have been absorbed in the other payments (Jerusalem Talmud; Rambam *Sefer Zera'im*, *Hilkhot Ma'aser Sheni* 8:1).

Mead that has fermented – תֶּמֶד מִשֶּׁהֶחֱמִיץ: Mead that has fermented may be purchased with second-tithe money (Rambam *Sefer Zera'im*, *Hilkhot Ma'aser Sheni* 7:6).

NOTES

I will carry his clothes after him – מוֹבִילְנָא מָאנֵיהּ אַבַּתְרֵיהּ: This expression, used by Rabbi Yoḥanan on several occasions, conveys extreme deference. Bringing clothes to the bathhouse for the master was a task only performed by a Canaanite slave, not by a student for his teacher or even by a Jewish servant for his master.

Mead – תֶּמֶד: Some commentaries explain that mead is water poured over wine sediment. The water absorbs the some of the taste of the wine and becomes similar to wine (see *Me'iri*).

"בַּבָּקָר" לָמָּה לִי? וְכִי תֵּימָא: אִי לָא כָּתַב רַחֲמָנָא "בַּבָּקָר" הֲוָה אָמִינָא: צֹאן עַל גַּב עוֹרָהּ – אִין, עַל גַּב גִּיזָּתָהּ – לָא, כָּתַב רַחֲמָנָא "בַּבָּקָר" לְאַתּוֹיֵי עוֹרוֹ. אִיַּיתַּר לֵיהּ "צֹאן" לְאַתּוֹיֵי גִּיזָּתָהּ.

If so, **why do I** need the words **"on oxen"?** If one may purchase a sheep together with its fleece with second-tithe money, it should certainly be permitted to buy an ox together with its hide. **And if you say** that **if the Torah had not written "on oxen," I might have said** that **a sheep** together **with its hide, yes,** it may be bought with second-tithe money, but together **with its fleece, no,** it may not be bought; therefore, **the Torah wrote "on oxen," to include its hide,** and so "on **sheep" remains** available for interpretation **to include its fleece,** i.e., that a sheep may be bought even together with its fleece. Therefore, the words "on oxen" are necessary, for without them I would have understood "on sheep" differently.

אִי לָא כָּתַב רַחֲמָנָא "בָּקָר" – לָא הֲוָה אָמִינָא צֹאן עַל גַּב עוֹרָהּ אִין עַל גַּב גִּיזָּתָהּ לָא. דְּאִם כֵּן – לִכְתּוֹב רַחֲמָנָא "בָּקָר" דְּמִמֵּילָא אִיַּיתַּר לֵיהּ צֹאן!

This argument can, however, be refuted: Even **if the Torah had not written "on oxen," I would not have said** that a **sheep** together **with its hide, yes,** it may be bought with second-tithe money, but together **with its fleece, no,** it may not. For **if** it were **so, the Torah should have written** "on oxen," **in which case** the words "on **sheep" would remain** available for interpretation. "On sheep" can be explained in two ways, both in reference to its hide as well as in reference to its fleece. Had the Torah wanted to teach only that an animal may be bought together with its hide but not with its fleece, it would have written "on oxen" only, which would have left no room for error, as oxen do not have fleece.

וְכֵיוָן דְּכָתַב רַחֲמָנָא "צֹאן", דַּאֲפִילּוּ עַל גַּב גִּיזָּתָהּ – "בַּבָּקָר" לָמָּה לִי? הַשְׁתָּא צֹאן עַל גַּב גִּיזָּתָהּ מִיזְדַּבְנָא, בָּקָר עַל גַּב עוֹרוֹ מִיבַּעְיָא?! הַיְינוּ דְּקָאָמַר רַבִּי יוֹחָנָן: מַאן דִּמְתַרְגֵּם לִי בַּבָּקָר אַלִּיבָּא דְּבֶן בַּג בַּג, מוֹבִילְנָא מָאנֵיהּ לְבֵי מַסּוּתָא.

And since the Torah writes "on **sheep,"** teaching that a sheep may be bought with second-tithe money **even** together **with its fleece, why do I need** the words **"on oxen"?** These words are **now** entirely superfluous. If a **sheep may be bought** together **with its fleece, is it necessary** to state that an **ox** may be bought together **with its hide? This is what Rabbi Yoḥanan** meant when he **said: Whoever interprets** the words **"on oxen" for me in accordance with** the opinion of **ben Bag Bag, I will carry his clothes after him into the bathhouse.**

בְּמַאי קָא מִיפַּלְגִי רַבִּי יְהוּדָה בֶּן גָּדִישׁ וְרַבִּי אֱלִיעֶזֶר וְהָנֵי תַּנָּאֵי דִּלְקַמָּן? רַבִּי יְהוּדָה בֶּן גָּדִישׁ וְרַבִּי אֱלִיעֶזֶר דָּרְשִׁי רִבּוּיֵי וּמִיעוּטֵי, וְהָנֵי תַּנָּאֵי דָּרְשִׁי כְּלָלֵי וּפְרָטֵי.

The Gemara now returns to the tannaitic disagreement pertaining to buying fish brine with second-tithe money: **With regard to what** principle **do Rabbi Yehuda ben Gadish, and Rabbi Eliezer, and these** ***tanna'im*** whose views will be cited **below, disagree?** The Gemara explains: **Rabbi Yehuda ben Gadish and Rabbi Eliezer expound** the verse based on the principle of **amplifications and restrictions, and these** ***tanna'im*** **expound** it based on the principle of **generalizations and details,**[N] which is a different approach to biblical exegesis.

רַבִּי יְהוּדָה בֶּן גָּדִישׁ וְרַבִּי אֱלִיעֶזֶר דָּרְשִׁי רִיבּוּיֵי וּמִיעוּטֵי: "וְנָתַתָּה הַכֶּסֶף בְּכֹל אֲשֶׁר תְּאַוֶּה נַפְשְׁךָ" – רִיבָּה, "בַּבָּקָר וּבַצֹּאן וּבַיַּיִן וּבַשֵּׁכָר" – מִיעֵט, "וּבְכֹל אֲשֶׁר תִּשְׁאָלְךָ נַפְשֶׁךָ" – חָזַר וְרִיבָּה. רִיבָּה וּמִיעֵט וְרִיבָּה – רִיבָּה הַכֹּל. מַאי רַבֵּי – רַבֵּי כָּל מִילֵּי, וּמַאי מִיעֵט – לְרַבִּי אֱלִיעֶזֶר מִיעֵט צִיר, לְרַבִּי יְהוּדָה בֶּן גָּדִישׁ מִיעֵט מַיִם וּמֶלַח.

Rabbi Yehuda ben Gadish and Rabbi Eliezer expound the verse based on the principle of **amplifications and restrictions.** When the verse states: **"And you shall bestow the money on all that your heart desires"** (Deuteronomy 14:26), **it has amplified.** When it then states: **"On oxen, on sheep, on wine, and on strong drink," it has restricted** its discussion to certain specific items. When it concludes with the phrase: **"On whatever your soul requests," it has once again amplified.** According to this exegetical approach, we conclude that since **it amplified and restricted and** once again **amplified, it has amplified** the general category to include **everything. What has it amplified** the category to include? **It has amplified** the category to include **everything. And what has it restricted** from inclusion in the category? Only one thing: **According to Rabbi Eliezer, it restricted brine** from inclusion because brine is not at all similar to the items listed in the verse; **according to Rabbi Yehuda ben Gadish, it restricted water and salt.**

NOTES

Amplification and restriction, and generalization and detail – רִבּוּי וּמִיעוּט וּכְלָל וּפְרָט: Amplification and restriction and generalization and detail are two exegetical approaches to biblical verses. They are attributed to Rabbi Akiva and Rabbi Yishmael, respectively. Nevertheless, all of the Sages would generally use both of these methods except for certain circumstances in which each would insist on using his own specific approach.

Both methods are applied to biblical verses in which there is a general statement followed by specific examples of the same law. Depending on the presentation, there may be an amplification and restriction or a generalization and detail; a restriction and amplification or a detail and generalization; or an amplification and restriction and amplification or a generalization and detail and generalization.

The principle of generalization and detail views the example mentioned in the verse as providing detail through an explanation and definition of the general rule. Consequently, the detail always limits the scope of the generalization, while the generalization is almost always an expansion of the specific example cited.

On the other hand, the method of amplification and restriction assumes that the specific case mentioned in the verse is not meant as an example but as a defining feature that limits the generalization by indicating what is not included in the amplification. When an amplification is followed by a restriction, and these two expressions are followed by another amplification, the only items excluded from the generalization are those that totally differ from the restriction. Therefore, this method of exegesis tends to be more inclusive than the principle of a generalization and detail and generalization, in which the final generalization expands the detail to include items similar to it.

NOTES

Fish are regarded as having grown from the ground – דָּגִים כְּגִידּוּלֵי קַרְקַע: As explained here, the category of things that have grown from the ground includes anything that receives sustenance from the ground. Therefore, even fish can be considered to have grown from the ground, as they are indirectly nourished by it.

HALAKHA

What may be bought with second-tithe money – מָה נִלְקָח בְּכֶסֶף מַעֲשֵׂר: One may utilize second-tithe money to purchase food fit for human consumption, which includes produce and anything else that grows from the ground. This ruling is in accordance with the Rambam's interpretation of the mishna (Radbaz; Rambam *Sefer Zera'im*, *Hilkhot Ma'aser Sheni* 7:3).

וְהָנֵי תַּנָּאֵי דָּרְשִׁי כְּלָלֵי וּפְרָטֵי, דְּתַנְיָא: "וְנָתַתָּה הַכֶּסֶף בְּכֹל אֲשֶׁר תְּאַוֶּה נַפְשְׁךָ" – כְּלָל, "בַּבָּקָר וּבַצֹּאן וּבַיַּיִן וּבַשֵּׁכָר" – פְּרָט, "וּבְכֹל אֲשֶׁר תִּשְׁאָלְךָ נַפְשְׁךָ" – חָזַר וְכָלַל. כְּלָל וּפְרָט וּכְלָל – אִי אַתָּה דָן אֶלָּא כְּעֵין הַפְּרָט; וּמָה הַפְּרָט מְפוֹרָשׁ – פְּרִי מִפְּרִי וְגִידּוּלֵי קַרְקַע, אַף כֹּל – פְּרִי מִפְּרִי וְגִידּוּלֵי קַרְקַע.

And these other ***tanna'im* expound** the verse according to the principle of **generalizations and details, as it was taught** in a *baraita*: The phrase: **"And you shall bestow the money on all that your heart desires"** is **a generalization,** as no particular type of food is specified. The phrase: **"On cattle, on sheep, on wine, and on strong drink"** is **a detail,** as specific types of food are mentioned. When the verse concludes: **"On whatever your soul requests," it has generalized again,** as no specific type of food is mentioned. Since the verse is formulated as **a generalization, and a detail, and a generalization, you may deduce** that the verse is referring **only** to items **similar to the detail. Just as** the items mentioned in **the detail** are clearly **defined as the produce of produce,** i.e., not only the produce itself but also things that come from it, such as the calf that comes from a cow or grapes from a seed, **and** they are also things **grown from the ground,** as all of these items grow from the ground or receive their main sustenance from it, **so** it includes **all** things that are **the produce of produce and are grown from the ground.**

וְתַנְיָא אִידָךְ: מָה הַפְּרָט מְפוֹרָשׁ – וְלַד וְלָדוֹת הָאָרֶץ, אַף כֹּל – וְלַד וְלָדוֹת הָאָרֶץ.

And it was taught in the other *baraita*: **Just as** the items mentioned in **the detail** are clearly **defined as the offspring of the offspring of the earth,** i.e., things that come from items that came from the ground, **so** it includes **all** things that are **the offspring of the offspring of the earth.**

מַאי בֵּינַיְיהוּ? אָמַר אַבָּיֵי: דָּגִים אִיכָּא בֵּינַיְיהוּ, לְמַאן דְּאָמַר: פְּרִי מִפְּרִי וְגִידּוּלֵי קַרְקַע – הָנֵי דָּגִים גִּידּוּלֵי קַרְקַע נִינְהוּ. לְמַאן דְּאָמַר וְלַד וְלָדוֹת הָאָרֶץ – דָּגִים מִמַּיָּא אִיבְּרוּ.

The Gemara asks: **What is** the practical difference **between** these two *baraitot*? **Abaye said: There is** a practical difference **between them** with regard to **fish. According to the one who said** that we apply the law to that which is **the produce of produce and grown from the ground, fish are** regarded as having **grown from the ground.**[N] However, **according to the one who said** we apply it to that which is **the offspring of the offspring of the earth, fish were created from water.** Therefore, they are not of the offspring of the earth, and consequently they are not included among the items that may be purchased with second-tithe money.[H]

וּמִי אָמַר אַבָּיֵי דָּגִים גִּידּוּלֵי קַרְקַע נִינְהוּ? וְהָאָמַר אַבָּיֵי:

The Gemara asks: **Did Abaye say** that **fish are** regarded as having been **grown from the ground? Didn't Abaye say the following?**

Perek **III**
Daf **28** Amud **a**

HALAKHA

If one ate a *putita* – אָכַל פּוּטִיתָא: If one ate a water insect known as a *putita*, one is liable to receive four sets of lashes. According to the Rambam, the reason for this is that one has violated several different types of prohibitions. Most authorities concur with the Rambam's conclusion, but explain it differently (see *Maggid Mishne*; Rambam *Sefer Kedusha*, *Hilkhot Ma'akhalot Assurot* 2:23).

אָכַל פּוּטִיתָא – לוֹקֶה אַרְבַּע, נְמָלָה – לוֹקֶה חָמֵשׁ, צִירְעָה – לוֹקֶה שֵׁשׁ. וְאִם אִיתָא, פּוּטִיתָא נַמִי לִילְקֵי מִשּׁוּם: "הַשֶּׁרֶץ הַשּׁוֹרֵץ עַל הָאָרֶץ"!

If **one ate a *putita*,**[H] a certain water insect, **he is given four** sets of **lashes,**[N] as he has transgressed four separate negative Torah commandments, two that relate to creeping animals in general and two that relate to water insects in particular. If he ate **an ant, he is given five** sets of **lashes** for violating the two general prohibitions and another three negative commandments stated with regard to insects that creep upon the earth. If he ate **a hornet, he is given six** sets of **lashes,** for in addition to the prohibitions applying to an ant, he has transgressed a prohibition stated with regard to flying insects. **And if it is** correct that something that lives in water is considered as growing from the ground, one who eats **a *putita* should also be given lashes for** violating the following prohibition: "And **every creeping thing that creeps upon the earth** is a detestable thing; it shall not be eaten" (Leviticus 11:41). Rather, fish must certainly not be considered as growing from the ground, and therefore this explanation is to be rejected.

NOTES

If one ate a *putita*, he is given four sets of lashes – אָכַל פּוּטִיתָא לוֹקֶה אַרְבַּע: The *Arukh* provides the mnemonic *talas*, representing the four prohibitions one violates in this case: The first is a prohibition against non-kosher seafood: "Of their flesh you shall not eat [*tokheilu*]" (Leviticus 11:11). The second and third prohibitions, which pertain to creeping animals in general, are derived from the phrases: "You shall not [*al*] make your souls abominable," and "And you shall not [*lo*] make yourselves unclean with them" (Leviticus 11:43). The fourth prohibition is derived from the additional verse that references non-kosher fish: "That does not have fins [*senappir*]" (Leviticus 11:10).

According to Abaye, if one violates numerous prohibitions at one time while eating, even if the prohibitions are included in a single category, he is liable to receive a separate set of lashes for each time the Torah expresses the prohibition. This is the opinion of the Ra'avad and the Ramban, and it is also implied by Rashi and the *ge'onim*. However, the Rambam maintains that one is not punished with multiple sets of lashes unless he has transgressed multiple prohibitions of different types. One who eats a *putita* receives distinct sets of lashes because it falls under the separate categories of a creeping land animal, a water insect, and a flying insect.

אֶלָּא אָמַר רָבִינָא: עוֹפוֹת אִיכָּא בֵּינַיְיהוּ. לְמַאן דְּאָמַר פְּרִי מִפְּרִי וְגִידּוּלֵי קַרְקַע – הָנֵי נַמִי גִּידּוּלֵי קַרְקַע נִינְהוּ. לְמַאן דְּאָמַר וְלַד וְלָדוֹת הָאָרֶץ – הָנֵי עוֹפוֹת מִן הָרְקָק נִבְרְאוּ.

Rather, Ravina said: **There is** a practical difference **between** the two *baraitot* with regard to **fowl. According to the one who said** that one may use second-tithe money only to purchase food which is **the produce of produce and grown from the ground,**[N] **these** fowl **are also** regarded as having **grown from the ground.** However, **according to the one who said** that we apply it to that which is **the offspring of the offspring of the earth, these fowl were created from mud**[N] and not from the ground, and consequently they are not included among the items that may be bought with second-tithe money.[H]

מַאן דִּמְרַבֵּי עוֹפוֹת מַאי טַעְמֵיהּ, וּמַאן דִּמְמַעֵיט עוֹפוֹת מַאי טַעְמֵיהּ?

These two distinct opinions are both based upon the exegetical principle of a generalization and a detail. The Gemara now asks: **What is the reason of the one who includes fowl, and what is the reason of the one who excludes fowl?**

מַאן דִּמְרַבֵּי עוֹפוֹת קָסָבַר: כְּלָלָא בַּתְרָא דַּוְקָא, פְּרָט וּכְלָל נַעֲשָׂה כְּלָל מוּסָף עַל הַפְּרָט, וְאִיתְרַבּוּ לְהוּ כָּל מִילֵּי. וְאַהֲנֵי כְּלָלָא קַמָּא לְמַעוּטֵי כָּל דְּלָא דָּמֵי לֵיהּ מִשְּׁנֵי צְדָדִין.

The Gemara explains: **The one who includes fowl holds** that when there is a generalization, a detail, and another generalization, **the latter generalization is primary.** Therefore, the rule is similar to that governing **a detail** followed by **a generalization,** which maintains that **the generalization is considered an addition to the detail, and all** other **items are included.** However, **the first generalization is effective in excluding anything that is not similar to** it **in two respects,** as it is nonetheless a case of a generalization, a detail, and a generalization. Therefore, he excludes anything that does not grow from the ground and is not the produce of produce.

וּמַאן דִּמְמַעֵט עוֹפוֹת קָסָבַר: כְּלָלָא קַמָּא דַּווְקָא, כְּלָל וּפְרָט – וְאֵין בִּכְלָל אֶלָּא מַה שֶּׁבִּפְרָט, הָנֵי – אִין, מִידֵּי אַחֲרִינָא – לָא. וְאַהֲנֵי כְּלָלָא בַּתְרָא לְרַבּוּיֵי כָּל דְּדָמֵי לֵיהּ מִשְּׁלֹשָׁה צְדָדִין.

And the one who excludes fowl holds that **the first generalization is primary.** Therefore, a generalization, detail, and generalization[N] is similar to a single **generalization** that is followed by **a detail,** with regard to which we maintain that **the generalization only includes that which is** spelled out **in the detail.** Therefore, with regard to **these** items mentioned in the verse, **yes,** one may purchase them with second-tithe money. With regard to **something else, no,** one may not. However, **the latter generalization is effective to include anything that is similar to it in three respects,** namely, it is the produce of produce, grows from the ground, and is offspring of the offspring of the earth, to the exclusion of fowl.

אָמַר רַב יְהוּדָה מִשְּׁמֵיהּ דְּרַב שְׁמוּאֵל בַּר שֵׁילַת מִשְּׁמֵיהּ דְּרַב: מְעָרְבִין בְּפַעֲפּוּעִין וּבַחֲלַגְלוֹגוֹת וּבַגּוּדְגְּדָנִיּוֹת, אֲבָל לֹא בְּחָזִיז, וְלֹא בְּכַפְנִיּוֹת.

Rav Yehuda said in the name of Rav Shmuel bar Sheilat, who said **in the name of Rav: One may establish an** ***eiruv*** with cheap and unimportant produce such as **cress, purslane,**[B] **and sweet clover,**[B] **but** one may **not** establish an *eiruv* **with green grain**[B] **or with unripe dates.**[H]

BACKGROUND

Purslane [*ḥalaglogot*] – חֲלַגְלוֹגוֹת: The word *ḥalaglogot* probably refers to a special, wide-leaved strain of the plant nowadays known as common purslane, *Portulaca oleracea*.

It is an annual plant that sprawls along the ground with fleshy, highly intertwined leaves and branches. It grows wild, mainly in the summer, in well-irrigated places. It is common in all areas of Eretz Yisrael, as well as in neighboring countries.

Purslane is gathered as food and can be eaten raw or pickled. Occasionally, it is even cultivated for this purpose.

Purslane plant

Sweet clover [*gudgedaniyyot*] – גּוּדְגְּדָנִיּוֹת: This plant is a species of sweet clover, *Melilotus alba*. Most early commentaries explained that this plant is a type of honey *Melilotus*, an annual or perennial plant from the legume family, which grows very tall in the wild. These plants have clover leaves, and their fruit grows in the form of pods that contain one or two seeds. This plant is usually used as animal fodder, although its seeds are also fit for human consumption. In the past, it was used for medicinal purposes as well.

Sweet clover

Green grain [*ḥaziz*] – חָזִיז: *Ḥaziz* is a general term for the green parts of various types of grains that are mainly fed to animals as fodder.

NOTES

The produce of produce and grown from the ground – פְּרִי מִפְּרִי וְגִידּוּלֵי קַרְקַע: The Jerusalem Talmud offers a slightly different version of this disagreement, according to which Rabbi Yishmael requires that an item be the offspring of offspring of the earth. Rabbi Akiva derives that something purchased with second-tithe money must be produce, the produce of produce, or that which facilitates the production of produce. According to Rabbi Yishmael, fowl, grasshoppers, truffles, and mushrooms are excluded from this category.

Fowl were created from mud – עוֹפוֹת מִן הָרְקָק נִבְרְאוּ: This idea is derived from a comparison of the two verses that relate to the creation of fowl in Genesis. The first is: "And God said: Let the waters swarm with moving creatures that have life, and let birds fly above the earth in the open firmament of heaven" (Genesis 1:20). The second is: "And out of the ground the Lord God formed every beast of the field and every bird of the heaven" (Genesis 2:19). By combining the two verses, the Sages expounded that fowl were created from a mixture of water and earth, i.e., from mud (*Ḥullin* 27b).

The nature of a generalization, detail, and generalization – טִיבוֹ שֶׁל כְּלָל וּפְרָט וּכְלָל: Both approaches that are explained in this context in the Gemara agree that the exegetical method of a generalization, a detail, and a generalization is not an independent method of derivation and exposition. Rather, it is a compound method that elaborates upon a more basic exegetical principle. The Sages disagreed whether it is as an elaboration of the principle of a generalization followed by a detail, or that of a detail followed by a generalization. Indeed, the list of seven methods by which the Torah is expounded according to the approach of Hillel the Elder does not include that of a generalization, a detail, and a generalization, even though it includes the method of a generalization and a detail, as well as that of a detail and a generalization.

HALAKHA

Fowl bought with second-tithe money – עוֹפוֹת בְּכַסְפֵּי מַעֲשֵׂר: Second-tithe money may be used for the purchase of poultry (Rambam *Sefer Zera'im*, *Hilkhot Ma'aser Sheni* 7:12).

An *eiruv* of unripe dates and sweet clover – עֵירוּב בְּכַפְנִיּוֹת וּבְגוּדְגְּדָנִיּוֹת: It is prohibited to establish an *eiruv* with unripe dates, in accordance with the view of Rav. In addition, one may not utilize sweet clover that hardened into seed. This ruling appears to follow the second approach in the Gemara, since no distinction is made between one who has many children and one who has only a few children (*Shulḥan Arukh*, *Oraḥ Ḥayyim* 386:5).

וּבְגוּדְגְּדָנִיּוֹת מִי מְעָרְבִין? וְהָתַנְיָא: גּוּדְגְּדָנִיּוֹת, מְרוּבֵּי בָנִים – יֹאכְלוּ, חֲשׂוּכֵי בָנִים – לֹא יֹאכְלוּ, וְאִם הוּקְשׁוּ לְזֶרַע – אַף מְרוּבֵּי בָנִים לֹא יֹאכְלוּ!

The Gemara asks: **But may one establish an *eiruv* with sweet clover? Wasn't it taught** in a *baraita* with regard to **sweet clover** that **those who have many children may eat** it, but **those without children may not eat** it, as it is harmful to one's reproductive capacity; **and if it was hardened into seed,** i.e., if it became very hard and already fit to be planted, **even those who have many children may not eat** it? Therefore, we see that it is prohibited to eat sweet clover. How can it possibly be used to establish an *eiruv*?

תַּרְגְּמָא אַשֶּׁלֹּא הוּקְשׁוּ לְזֶרַע, וּמְרוּבֵּי בָנִים.

The Gemara answers: **Interpret** Rav's statement as referring to sweet clover **that was not** yet **hardened into seed, and** its use for establishing an *eiruv* is limited to **those who have many children** and are therefore permitted to eat it.

וְאִיבָּעֵית אֵימָא: לְעוֹלָם לַחֲשׂוּכֵי בָנִים – דְּהָא חֲזוּ לִמְרוּבֵּי בָנִים. מִי לָא תְּנַן: מְעָרְבִין לְנָזִיר בְּיַיִן וּלְיִשְׂרָאֵל בִּתְרוּמָה. אַלְמָא: אַף עַל גַּב דְּלָא חֲזֵי לְהַאי – חֲזֵי לְהַאי. הָכָא נָמֵי: אַף עַל גַּב דְּלָא חֲזֵי לְהַאי – חֲזֵי לְהַאי.

And if you wish, you can **say** instead that **actually,** sweet clover is fit for an *eiruv* even **for those without children because it is fit** to be eaten by **those who have many children.** The food used for an *eiruv* must be edible, but it does not need to be edible for the particular person using it as his *eiruv*. **Didn't we learn** in the mishna: **One may establish an *eiruv* for a nazirite with wine, and for an Israelite with *teruma*? Apparently,** these items may be used as an *eiruv* **even though** they **are not fit for this** person, because they are **fit for that** other person. **Here too, even though** the sweet clover **is not fit for this** person, it may be used because **it is fit for that** other person.

וְאִיבָּעֵית אֵימָא: כִּי קָאָמַר רַב – בְּהִנְדְּקוּקֵי מָדַאי.

And if you wish, you can **say** instead: **When Rav said** that sweet clover may be used for an *eiruv*, he was referring to **Median clover,** which is of superior quality and is not harmful.

וּבְחָזִיז לָא?! וְהָאָמַר רַב יְהוּדָה, אָמַר רַב: כְּשׁוּת וְחָזִיז מְעָרְבִין בָּהֶן, וּמְבָרְכִין עֲלֵיהֶן "בּוֹרֵא פְּרִי הָאֲדָמָה"!

The Gemara considers the continuation of Rav's statement: **And** may one **not** establish an *eiruv* **with green grain? Didn't Rav Yehuda say that Rav said:** In the case of **dodder and green grain, one may establish an *eiruv* with them;** and when eating **them one recites the blessing: Who creates the fruit of the ground?**

לָא קַשְׁיָא; הָא – מִקַּמֵּי דַּאֲתָא רַב לְבָבֶל, הָא – לְבָתַר דַּאֲתָא רַב לְבָבֶל.

The Gemara answers: This is **not difficult. This** first statement, according to which green grain may not be used for an *eiruv*, was made **before Rav came to Babylonia. That** second statement was made **after Rav came to Babylonia** and saw that people there ate green grain, at which point he ruled that it is fit to be used for an *eiruv*.

וּבָבֶל הָוְיָא רוּבָּא דְּעָלְמָא?! וְהָתַנְיָא: הַפּוֹל וְהַשְּׂעוֹרָה וְהַתִּילְתָּן שֶׁזְּרָעָן לְיָרָק – בָּטְלָה דַּעְתּוֹ אֵצֶל כָּל אָדָם, לְפִיכָךְ: זַרְעָן חַיָּיב וְיַרְקָן פָּטוּר. הַשַּׁחֲלַיִם וְהַגַּרְגִּיר שֶׁזְּרָעָן לְיָרָק – מִתְעַשְּׂרִין יָרָק וָזֶרַע, זְרָעָן לְזֶרַע – מִתְעַשְּׂרִין זֶרַע וְיָרָק.

The Gemara asks: **Is Babylonia the majority of the world?**[N] Laws are established according to the custom prevalent in most of the world. **Wasn't it taught** in a *baraita*: In the case of **beans, barley,**[H] **and fenugreek**[H] **that** one **planted** in order to use **as an herb,** e.g., as animal fodder, **his opinion is rendered irrelevant by the opinions of all other people?** Since most people do not act this way, we do not consider this particular person's intention to be significant. **Therefore, one is obligated to tithe their seeds, and their herbs are exempt.** When one harvests these plants in their green state, before their seeds have matured, they are regarded as not having fully ripened. However, in the case of **cress and arugula,**[H] which are commonly eaten both in their green state and as seeds, if **one planted them** in order to use them **as herbs, they are tithed** both **as herbs and as seeds;** if **one planted them for** their **seeds, they are tithed as seeds and as herbs,** no matter how they are eaten. In any case, the first part of the *baraita* teaches that the law is determined in accordance with the common custom of most of the world and not with the practice in one particular place.

כִּי קָאָמַר רַב –

The Gemara answers: **When Rav said** that green grain may be used for an *eiruv*,

HALAKHA

Tithes from beans and barley – מַעֲשֵׂר פּוֹל וּשְׂעוֹרָה: If one planted beans, barley, or other types of grain and legumes with the intention to use them as herbs, one should not separate tithes from their green parts but from their seeds (Rambam *Sefer Zera'im*, *Hilkhot Terumot* 2:7).

Fenugreek – מַעֲשֵׂר תִּילְתָּן: According to the Rambam, if fenugreek was planted for its seeds, its branches are exempt from tithes. If it was planted for its green parts, tithes must be separated from its berries, but the rest of the green parts are exempt. Apparently, the Rambam did not rule in accordance with the *baraita* here, but in accordance with the mishna in tractate *Ma'asrot* (Maharam; Radbaz; Rambam *Sefer Zera'im*, *Hilkhot Terumot* 2:8).

Tithes from cress and arugula – מַעֲשֵׂר שַׁחֲלַיִים וְגַרְגִּיר: Cress and arugula, whether planted for seed or as herbs, are tithed in their green state and as seeds. The tithes are separated from the herbs when they are picked and from the seeds when they have fully ripened (Rambam *Sefer Zera'im*, *Hilkhot Terumot* 2:5).

NOTES

The majority of the world – רוּבָּא דְּעָלְמָא: *Tosafot* ask why the Gemara does not say that Babylonia is a particular place and the prevalent custom of a particular locale is not rendered irrelevant by the customs of other places. The Ritva explains that certainly the unique customs of an individual are considered irrelevant; however, with regard to the customs of a locale, there are three possible scenarios: If it is an unusual and strange custom, it is irrelevant even in that locale. If the custom is somewhat reasonable but is not practiced in most places, the custom is deemed significant in places where the majority of the population observes it, but not elsewhere. If the custom is one that is proper and worthy, but it is not prevalent in other places because of a lack of materials or due to other external circumstances, the custom is deemed significant for anyone who observes it in any location.

בְּדִגִּנוּנִיָּיתָא.

he was referring **to the garden variety,** which is commonly eaten.

זֶרַע גַּרְגִּיר לְמַאי חָזֵי? אָמַר רַבִּי יוֹחָנָן: שֶׁכֵּן רִאשׁוֹנִים שֶׁלֹּא הָיָה לָהֶן פִּלְפְּלִין, שׁוֹחֲקִין אוֹתוֹ וּמַטְבִּילִין בּוֹ אֶת הַצָּלִי.

Having mentioned **arugula**[B] **seeds,** the Gemara asks: **For what are they suitable?** Generally, only the plant's leaves are eaten. **Rabbi Yoḥanan said: The earlier** generations, **who had no pepper, would crush** these seeds **and dip** their **roasted meat in them.** Therefore, arugula seeds are also eaten, even though this is not their typical use.

רַבִּי זֵירָא כִּי הֲוָה חָלִישׁ מִגִּרְסֵיהּ הֲוָה אָזֵיל וְיָתֵיב אַפִּיתְחָא דְּרַב יְהוּדָה בַּר אַמֵּי, אָמַר: כִּי נָפְקִי וְעָיְילִי רַבָּנַן – אֵיקוּם מִקַּמַּיְיהוּ וְאֶקַבֵּל בְּהוּ אַגְרָא.

The Gemara relates that **when Rabbi Zeira was exhausted from his studies, he would go and sit at the entrance** to the academy **of Rav Yehuda bar Ami,** and **say: When the Sages go in and out, I shall stand up before them and receive reward for** honoring **them,**[N] as it is a mitzva to honor Torah scholars. Too tired to engage in actual Torah study, he sought a way to rest while fulfilling a different mitzva at the same time.

נְפַק אָתָא יָנוּקָא דְּבֵי רַב, אָמַר לֵיהּ: מַאי אַגְמְרָךְ רַבָּךְ? אָמַר לֵיהּ: כְּשׁוּת – "בּוֹרֵא פְּרִי הָאֲדָמָה", חָזִיז – "שֶׁהַכֹּל נִהְיָה בִּדְבָרוֹ". אָמַר לֵיהּ: אַדְּרַבָּה, אִיפְּכָא מִסְתַּבְּרָא: הַאי – מֵאַרְעָא קָא מִרְבֵי, וְהַאי – מֵאַוִּירָא קָא מִרְבֵי.

Once, a young **school child was leaving** the study hall. Rabbi Zeira **said to him: What did your teacher teach you** today? **He said to him:** The proper blessing for **dodder**[B] is: **Who creates the fruit of the ground;** the proper blessing for **green grain**[H] is: **By Whose word all things came to be.** Rabbi Zeira **said to him: On the contrary, the opposite is** more **reasonable,** as **this,** the green grain, **derives nourishment from the ground, whereas that,** the dodder, **derives nourishment from the air,** and it is fitting to recite a blessing over each item in accordance with its source of nourishment.

וְהִלְכְתָא כְּיָנוּקָא דְּבֵי רַב. מַאי טַעְמָא? הַאי – גְּמַר פֵּירֵי, וְהַאי – לָאו גְּמַר פֵּירֵי. וּמַאי דְּקָאָמְרַתְּ הַאי מֵאַרְעָא קָא רָבֵי וְהַאי מֵאַוִּירָא קָא רָבֵי – לָא הִיא. כְּשׁוּת נַמִי מֵאַרְעָא קָא רָבֵי, דְּהָא קָא חָזֵינַן דְּקָטְלִינַן לַהּ לְהִיזְמָתָא וּמַיְיתָא כְּשׁוּתָא.

The Gemara concludes: **The *halakha* is in accordance with** the young **school child. What is the reason** for this? **This,** the dodder, is **fully ripened produce, and that,** green grain, is **not fully ripened produce.** If produce is not fully ripened one can only recite the blessing: By Whose word all things came to be. **And that which you said: This,** the green grain, **derives nourishment from the ground, whereas that,** the dodder, **derives nourishment from the air, this is not so. Dodder also derives nourishment from the ground, for we see that when the** prickly **shrub is cut off, the dodder** attached to it **dies.** This shows that dodder also derives its nourishment from the ground, albeit indirectly.

BACKGROUND

Arugula [*gargir*] – **גַּרְגִּיר:** A reference to what is currently known as arugula, *Eruca sativa* L., an annual plant that grows to a height of 15–60 cm. Arugula flowers have a yellowish color and purple veins. Its leaves are eaten raw as part of a salad. For many generations, the fruit of the arugula was used as a pepper substitute. The plant is cultivated, but it can also be found on roadsides in all areas of Eretz Yisrael, except the Negev.

Flower of the arugula plant

Dodder – **כְּשׁוּת:** Dodder is from the Convolvulaceae family of the *Cuscuta* genus. The dodder is a parasitic plant that wraps itself around various other plants and absorbs its nourishment from them. The dodder has thin stems but lacks leaves, and it absorbs its nourishment by means of root-like, sucking branches, which penetrate the dodder's host plant. This explains why the dodder will also die if its host plant is uprooted. Dodder can be found throughout Eretz Yisrael. It mainly uses annual weeds and small bushes as hosts.

Dodder plant

NOTES

Receive reward for honoring them – אֲקַבֵּל בְּהוּ אַגְרָא: It is a mitzva to honor Torah scholars. Therefore, one who stands in honor of a Torah scholar fulfills the Torah's positive mitzva, "And you shall honor the face of the Elder" (Leviticus 19:32). The Sages explain that term Elder is referring to one who has acquired wisdom, i.e., a Torah scholar.

HALAKHA

The blessing for green grain – בִּרְכַּת חָזִיז: The blessing: By Whose word all things came to be, is recited over green grain that did not grow in a garden (*Shulḥan Arukh, Oraḥ Ḥayyim* 204:1).

וּבְכַפְנִיּוֹת אֵין מְעָרְבִין? וְהָתַנְיָא: קוֹר נִיקָּח בְּכֶסֶף מַעֲשֵׂר, וְאֵין מְטַמֵּא טוּמְאַת אוֹכָלִין. וְכַפְנִיּוֹת נִקָּחוֹת בְּכֶסֶף מַעֲשֵׂר, וּמְטַמְּאוֹת טוּמְאַת אוֹכָלִים.

The Gemara now considers the next part of Rav's statement: **And is it correct that one may not establish an *eiruv* with unripe dates?**[B] **Wasn't it taught** in a *baraita*: **Heart of palm,**[B] the soft, edible inner core of a palm tree, **may be bought with** second-**tithe money;**[H] **but it does not contract the** ritual **impurity of foods,**[H] as it is not actually a food, but rather a part of the tree itself. **And unripe dates may be bought with** second-**tithe money, and** they even **contract the** ritual **impurity of foods.**[HN]

רַבִּי יְהוּדָה אוֹמֵר: קוֹר הֲרֵי הוּא כָּעֵץ לְכָל דְּבָרָיו, אֶלָּא שֶׁנִּיקָּח בְּכֶסֶף מַעֲשֵׂר. וְכַפְנִיּוֹת – הֲרֵי הֵן כַּפְּרִי לְכָל דִּבְרֵיהֶם, אֶלָּא שֶׁפְּטוּרוֹת מִן הַמַּעֲשֵׂר.

Rabbi Yehuda says this somewhat differently: **Heart of palm is like a tree in all its** legal **aspects, except that it may be bought with** second-**tithe money,** as it is edible. **And unripe dates are like fruit in all regards,** as they are actual fruit, **except** with respect to one characteristic, which is **that they are exempt from tithes**[HN] because they are not yet fully ripened.

הָתָם בְּדְנִיסְחָנֵי.

The Gemara answers: **There,** the *baraita* is referring to the **fruit** of palms that **never** fully **ripen**. They are therefore regarded as full-fledged fruit even in their unripe state. Rav, however, was referring to the fruit of palms, which eventually ripen. Their unripe state is merely a transitional stage in their development.

אִי הָכִי, בְּהָא לֵימָא רַבִּי יְהוּדָה פְּטוּרוֹת מִן הַמַּעֲשֵׂר? וְהָתַנְיָא: אָמַר רַבִּי יְהוּדָה: לֹא הוּזְכְּרוּ פַּגֵּי בֵּיתְיוֹנִי אֶלָּא לְעִנְיַן מַעֲשֵׂר בִּלְבַד; פַּגֵּי בֵּיתְיוֹנִי וְאָהִינֵי דְטוֹבִינָא חַיָּיבִין בְּמַעֲשֵׂר.

The Gemara asks: **If so, would Rabbi Yehuda say with regard to this** that **they are exempt from tithes? Wasn't it taught** in a *baraita* that **Rabbi Yehuda said: The unripe figs of** the place called **Beityoni**[B] **were only mentioned with regard to tithes,** as it was stated: In the case of **the unripe figs of Beityoni, and the unripe dates of** the place called **Tuvina, one is obligated to tithe them** even though they never ripen, since they are considered full-fledged fruit in all respects?

אֶלָּא לְעוֹלָם לָאו בְּנִיסְחָנֵי, וּלְעִנְיַן טוּמְאַת אוֹכָלִין שָׁאנֵי. כִּדְאָמַר רַבִּי יוֹחָנָן: הוֹאִיל וְרָאוּי לְמַתְּקָן עַל יְדֵי הָאוּר. הָכָא נַמִי: הוֹאִיל וְיָכוֹל לְמַתְּקָן עַל יְדֵי הָאוּר.

Rather, say as follows: **Actually,** the *baraita* **is not referring to** the **fruit** of palms that **never** fully **ripen,** but rather to the fruit of palms that eventually ripen. However, the *halakha* **pertaining to the** ritual **impurity of foods is different,** and an item's status as a food with regard to the impurity of foods cannot be brought as proof of its status as a food with regard to an *eiruv*. **As Rabbi Yoḥanan said** elsewhere: **Since they are fit to be sweetened through** cooking with **fire,** they are regarded as food for the purpose of tithes; **here too,** we can say: **Since they are fit to be sweetened through** cooking with **fire,** unripe dates are fit to contract the impurity of foods. However, with regard to an *eiruv*, we require food that is ready for consumption, and something that can be prepared to become food is not sufficient.

BACKGROUND

Unripe dates [*kafniyot*] – **כַּפְנִיּוֹת:** The word *kayfniyot* probably refers to the date flowers located on the panicle, which is made up of thin, close-knit branches. While the plant is young, they are juicy and edible. Typically, the male flowers of the palm tree are eaten, since removing them does not damage the date crop. It is possible that the term *kafniyot* also includes the spathe, the leaf wrapped around the inflorescence, which was occasionally ground and used for making flour.

Date inflorescence wrapped in spathe

Flower panicle of the date

Heart of palm – **קוֹר:** The heart of palm refers to the top of the stem of the palm. The inner section of the trunk top is white and tasty and is considered a delicacy. It was rarely eaten because a date tree is ruined when its upper section is cut off, as it can no longer renew itself. Consequently, only the hearts of palm of trees that were slated to be chopped down in any event were eaten. In talmudic times, heart of palm was eaten both boiled and fried.

Beityoni – **בֵּיתְיוֹנִי:** Beityoni refers to the settlement known as Beit Hini, a small town a few kilometers from Jerusalem.

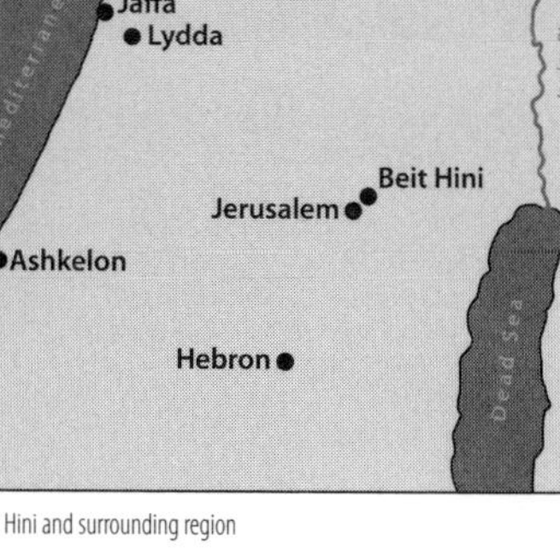

Beit Hini and surrounding region

HALAKHA

Heart of palm may be bought with second-tithe money – **קוֹר נִלְקָח בְּכֶסֶף מַעֲשֵׂר:** Second-tithe money may be used to purchase heart of palm (Rambam *Sefer Zera'im, Hilkhot Ma'aser Sheni* 7:8).

Heart of palm does not contract ritual impurity – **אֵינוֹ מְטַמֵּא:** Heart of palm does not contract the ritual impurity of foods, as stated in the mishna and the *baraitot*. However, if it was boiled or fried, it does contract the ritual impurity of foods, in accordance with the view of Rava (Rambam *Sefer Tahara, Hilkhot Tumat Okhalin* 1:10).

Unripe dates with regard to ritual impurity – **כַּפְנִיּוֹת לְעִנְיַן טוּמְאָה:** Unripe dates contract the ritual impurity of foods (Rambam *Sefer Tahara, Hilkhot Tumat Okhalin* 1:13).

Unripe dates with regard to tithes – **כַּפְנִיּוֹת לְעִנְיַן מַעֲשֵׂר:** Unripe dates are exempt from tithes because they are not considered full-grown fruit (Rambam *Sefer Zera'im, Hilkhot Ma'aser Sheni* 2:5).

NOTES

The impurity of foods – **טוּמְאַת אוֹכָלִים:** The impurity of foods refers to ritual impurity that can be contracted by food items, which, in general, are more susceptible to impurity than other substances. The definition of food for these purposes is a broad one. Still, anything that is unfit for human consumption or which people do not typically eat does not contract impurity.

Obligation to tithe – **חִיּוּב בְּמַעֲשֵׂר:** The obligation to separate tithes applies only to ripe produce. One who eats unripe produce, even if it is already fit for human consumption, is not obligated to separate the tithes because it is considered casual eating rather than a set meal. The main obligation applies once the produce has reached its completed state and, if possible, when the entire crop has been harvested together. Consequently, unripe fruit or small almonds are exempt from tithes, as one is obligated to separate tithes only from produce in its completed state, which requires no further work.

וְהֵיכָא אִתְּמַר דְּרַבִּי יוֹחָנָן – אַהָא: דְּתַנְיָא, שְׁקֵדִים הַמָּרִים, קְטַנִּים – חַיָּיבִין, גְּדוֹלִים – פְּטוּרִין. מְתוּקִים, גְּדוֹלִים – חַיָּיבִין, קְטַנִּים – פְּטוּרִין. רַבִּי שִׁמְעוֹן בְּרַבִּי יוֹסֵי אוֹמֵר מִשּׁוּם אָבִיו: זֶה וָזֶה לִפְטוֹר, וְאָמְרִי לָהּ: זֶה וָזֶה לְחִיּוּב. אָמַר רַבִּי אִילְעָא: הוֹרָה רַבִּי חֲנִינָא בְּצִיפּוֹרִי כְּדִבְרֵי הָאוֹמֵר זֶה וָזֶה לִפְטוֹר.

The Gemara asks: **Where was** this comment of **Rabbi Yoḥanan** originally **stated?** The Gemara answers: It was stated **on this** ruling, **which was taught** in a *baraita*: One is **obligated** to tithe **bitter almonds**[H] while they are still **small** and green, as they are fit to be eaten while still undeveloped. When they are **large,** however, one is **exempt** from tithing them, as they are no longer edible. One is **obligated to** tithe **sweet, large** almonds, whereas one is **exempt from** tithing **small ones,** as they have not yet fully ripened. **Rabbi Shimon, son of Rabbi Yosei, said in the name of his father:** One is **exempt from** tithing **both this and that,** large and small bitter almonds. **And some say** that he said in the name of his father: One is **obligated to** tithe **both this and that. Rabbi Ila said: Rabbi Ḥanina ruled in Tzippori in accordance with the one who said:** One is **exempt from** tithing **both this and that.**

וּלְמַאן דְּאָמַר זֶה וָזֶה לְחִיּוּב, לְמַאי חֲזֵי? אָמַר רַבִּי יוֹחָנָן: הוֹאִיל וְרָאוּי לְמַתְּקָן עַל יְדֵי הָאוּר.

The Gemara asks: **According to** the view of **the one who said** one is **obligated** to tithe **both this and that, for what are** large, bitter almonds **suitable? Rabbi Yoḥanan said: Since** these almonds **are fit to be sweetened** and made edible **through** cooking with **fire,** they are regarded as food for the purpose of tithes.

אָמַר מָר, רַבִּי יְהוּדָה אוֹמֵר: קוֹר הֲרֵי הוּא כָּעֵץ לְכָל דְּבָרָיו, אֶלָּא שֶׁנִּיקָּח בְּכֶסֶף מַעֲשֵׂר. הַיְינוּ תַּנָּא קַמָּא!

The Gemara further examines the *baraita* cited earlier. **The Master said** that **Rabbi Yehuda says: Heart of palm is like a tree in all its** legal **aspects, except that it may be bought with** second-**tithe money.** The Gemara asks: Rabbi Yehuda's opinion **is** identical to that of **the first *tanna*.**

אָמַר אַבָּיֵי: שְׁלָקוֹ וְטִגְּנוֹ אִיכָּא בֵּינַיְיהוּ.

Abaye said: There is a practical difference **between them** in a case where **one boiled or fried** the heart of palm. According to Rabbi Yehuda, it does not contract the ritual impurity of foods even if it was boiled or fried, whereas the first *tanna* holds that in that case it does contract impurity.

מַתְקִיף לָהּ רָבָא: מִי אִיכָּא לְמַאן דְּאָמַר שְׁלָקוֹ וְטִגְּנוֹ לֹא? וְהָתַנְיָא: הָעוֹר וְהַשִּׁלְיָא אֵין מְטַמְּאִין טוּמְאַת אוֹכָלִין, עוֹר שֶׁשְּׁלָקוֹ, וְשִׁלְיָא שֶׁחִישֵּׁב עָלֶיהָ מְטַמְּאִין טוּמְאַת אוֹכָלִין!

Rava strongly objects to this: Is there really **anyone who said** that even if **one boiled or fried it,** it does **not** contract the ritual impurity of foods? **Wasn't it taught** in a *baraita*: **The hide and the placenta** of an animal, which people do not typically eat, **do not contract the** ritual **impurity of foods;** however, **a hide that one boiled**[H] until it became edible **and a placenta that one intended** to eat **do contract the impurity of foods?** This indicates that even something not originally fit to be eaten contracts the impurity of foods once it has been boiled or fried, and the same should apply to heart of palm according to all opinions.

אֶלָּא אָמַר רָבָא: אִיכָּא בֵּינַיְיהוּ בְּרָכָה. דְּאִתְּמַר: קוֹר, רַב יְהוּדָה אָמַר: "בּוֹרֵא פְּרִי הָאֲדָמָה", וּשְׁמוּאֵל אָמַר: "שֶׁהַכֹּל נִהְיָה בִּדְבָרוֹ".

Rather, Rava said: There is a practical difference **between them** with regard to **the blessing** that must be recited prior to eating, **for it was stated** that the *amora'im* disagreed about the blessing recited over heart of palm:[N] **Rav Yehuda said** the appropriate blessing is: **Who creates the fruit of the ground. And Shmuel said** the appropriate blessing is: **By Whose word all things came to be.**

רַב יְהוּדָה אָמַר "בּוֹרֵא פְּרִי הָאֲדָמָה" – אוּכְלָא הוּא. וּשְׁמוּאֵל אָמַר "שֶׁהַכֹּל נִהְיָה בִּדְבָרוֹ" – כֵּיוָן שֶׁסּוֹפוֹ לְהַקְשׁוֹת לָא מְבָרְכִינַן עִילָּוֵיהּ "בּוֹרֵא פְּרִי הָאֲדָמָה".

The Gemara explains the two opinions: **Rav Yehuda said** the appropriate blessing is: **Who creates the fruit of the ground, as it is food.** Since heart of palm is edible it is called a fruit, and we recite a blessing over it in the manner of all fruits. **And Shmuel said** the appropriate blessing is: **By Whose word all things came to be. Since it will eventually harden** and become like an inedible tree, **we do not recite over it the blessing: Who creates the fruit of the ground,** as it will eventually lose the status of a fruit.

אָמַר לֵיהּ שְׁמוּאֵל לְרַב יְהוּדָה: שִׁינָּנָא, כְּוָותִיךְ מִסְתַּבְּרָא, דְּהָא צְנוֹן שֶׁסּוֹפוֹ לְהַקְשׁוֹת וּמְבָרְכִינַן עֲלֵיהּ "בּוֹרֵא פְּרִי הָאֲדָמָה".

Shmuel said to Rav Yehuda: *Shinnana*,[B] **your opinion is reasonable, as a radish will eventually harden, and yet we recite over it the blessing: Who creates the fruit of the ground.**[H]

HALAKHA

Bitter almonds – שְׁקֵדִים הַמָּרִים: Bitter almonds, whether large or small, are exempt from tithes. This ruling is in accordance with Rabbi Ḥanina, who issued a practical ruling to this effect, and the implied ruling in the Jerusalem Talmud (Rambam *Sefer Zera'im, Hilkhot Ma'aser Sheni* 1:9).

Hide that one boiled, etc. – עוֹר שֶׁשְּׁלָקוֹ וכו׳: A hide that was boiled until it became edible and a placenta that one intends to eat contract the ritual impurity of foods (Rambam *Sefer Tahara, Hilkhot Tumat Okhalin* 2:15).

The blessing over a radish – בִּרְכַּת הַצְּנוֹן: The blessing recited over a radish is: Who creates the fruit of the ground (*Shulḥan Arukh, Oraḥ Ḥayyim* 203:8).

NOTES

The blessing over heart of palm – בְּרָכָה עַל אֲכִילַת קוֹר: The blessing: Who creates fruit of the tree, cannot be recited over heart of the palm, since this blessing only applies to the main fruit of the palm, i.e., the dates. The *amora'im* disagree about whether heart of the palm can be categorized as a fruit that requires the blessing: Who creates fruit of the ground, or whether, since it is part of the trunk of the palm tree and only eaten infrequently, the blessing that must be recited is: By Whose word all things came to be.

BACKGROUND

Shinnana – שִׁינָּנָא: According to Rashi and others, *shinnana* means sharp or witty. Shmuel used this term to show the degree to which he respected his most prominent student, Rav Yehuda. However, the *ge'onim* explain that according to oral tradition, *shinnana* means big-toothed, and it was a nickname for Rav Yehuda based on his appearance.

BACKGROUND

Glasswort [*kalya*] – קליא: The identification of this plant is not clear, but it appears to refer to the so-called common glasswort, *Salicornia europaea*, a fleshy, annual plant with straight, segmented, and leafless stalks. The plant reaches a height of 10–40 cm, and it grows wild in marshes. The ashes of this plant contain a considerable amount of potassium, which was used in the manufacture of soap and as a detergent for washing clothes. The plant itself is edible.

Glasswort plant

ולא היא, צנון – נטעי אינשי אדעתא דפוגלא, דיקלא – לא נטעי אינשי אדעתא דקורא. ואף על גב דקלסיה שמואל לרב יהודה, הלכתא כוותיה דשמואל.

The Gemara comments: **But it is not so,** because **people plant radish with the intention** of eating it while it is **soft; but people do not plant palm trees with the intention** of eating **heart of palm.** Therefore, heart of palm is not considered the fruit of the palm, but rather food extracted from it, over which only the following blessing should be recited: By Whose word all things came to be.[H] **And** the Gemara concludes: **Even though Shmuel praised Rav Yehuda, the *halakha* is in accordance with** the opinion of **Shmuel.**

גופא, אמר רב יהודה, אמר רב: כשות וחזיז מערבין בהן, ומברכין עליהם "בורא פרי האדמה". כשות בכמה? כדאמר רב יחיאל: כמלא היד, הכא נמי – כמלא היד.

The Gemara now examines **the matter itself** cited in the previous discussion in the name of Rav. **Rav Yehuda said that Rav said** with regard to **dodder and green grain: One may establish an *eiruv* with them, and** when eating **them one recites the blessing: Who creates the fruit of the ground.** The Gemara asks: **How much dodder** must be used to establish an *eiruv*? The Gemara answers: **As Rav Yeḥiel said** with regard to a similar issue: **A handful. Here, too,** the measure is **a handful.**

חזיז בכמה? אמר רבה בר טוביה בר יצחק, אמר רב: כמלא אוזילתא דאיכרי.

Similarly, **how much green grain** is needed to establish an *eiruv*?[H] **Rabba bar Toviya bar Yitzḥak said that Rav said: A full farmers' bundle.**

אמר רב חלקיה בר טוביה: מערבין בקליא. בקליא סלקא דעתך?! אלא: בירקא דקליא. וכמה? אמר רב יחיאל: כמלא היד.

Rav Ḥilkiya bar Toviya said: One may establish an *eiruv* with glasswort.[B] The Gemara expresses astonishment: **Does it enter your mind** that one may establish an *eiruv* **with glasswort?** People do not eat glasswort. **Rather,** one may establish an *eiruv* **with the herb from** whose ashes **glasswort** is prepared, as it is fit for human consumption before it is burnt. **And how much** of it is needed to establish an *eiruv*? **Rav Yeḥiel said: A handful.**

רבי ירמיה נפק לקירייתא, בעו מיניה: מהו לערב בפולין לחין. לא הוה בידיה. כי אתא לבי מדרשא אמרו ליה, הכי אמר רבי ינאי: מערבין בפולין לחין. וכמה? אמר רב יחיאל: כמלא היד.

The Gemara relates that **Rabbi Yirmeya** once **went out to** visit certain **villages,** and the villagers **asked him: What is** the *halakha* with regard **to establishing an *eiruv* with moist beans? He did not have** an answer for them. **When he came to the study hall, they said to him: This is what Rabbi Yannai said: One may establish an *eiruv* with moist beans.**[H] **And how much** is needed for that purpose? **Rav Yeḥiel said: A handful.**

אמר רב המנונא: מערבין בתרדין חיין. איני?! והאמר רב חסדא: סילקא חייא קטיל גברא חייא!

Rav Hamnuna said: One may also **establish an *eiruv* with raw beets.**[H] The Gemara raises a difficulty: **Is that so? Didn't Rav Ḥisda say: Raw beet kills a healthy person,** which indicates that beets are unhealthy and should therefore be unfit for establishing an *eiruv*?

HALAKHA

The blessing over heart of palm – ברכת קור: The blessing recited over heart of palm is: By Whose word all things came to be, in accordance with the view of Shmuel (*Shulḥan Arukh, Oraḥ Ḥayyim* 204:1). However, nowadays, when palm trees are cultivated specifically for hearts of palm, many authorities rule that the proper blessing is: Who creates the fruit of the ground.

The measures for dodder and green grain – שיעור כשות וחזיז: An *eiruv* may be established with two quarter-*log* of green grain, and it may be established with a handful of dodder (Rambam *Sefer Zemanim, Hilkhot Eiruvin* 1:11).

An *eiruv* of moist beans – עירוב בפולין לחין: An *eiruv* may be established with a handful of moist beans (*Shulḥan Arukh, Oraḥ Ḥayyim* 386:7).

An *eiruv* of raw beets – עירוב בתרד חי: An *eiruv* may be established with a liter of beets, whether raw or cooked. The same applies to all vegetables (Rambam *Sefer Zemanim, Hilkhot Eiruvin* 1:11; *Shulḥan Arukh, Oraḥ Ḥayyim* 386:7).

הַהוּא בְּבַשִּׁיל וְלָא בַּשִּׁיל.

The Gemara answers: **That is** referring **to** a beet **that was** only **partially cooked,**[H] which is dangerous.

אִיכָּא דְּאָמְרִי, אָמַר רַב הַמְנוּנָא: אֵין מְעָרְבִין בִּתְרָדִין חַיִּין, דַּאֲמַר רַב חִסְדָּא: סִילְקָא חַיָּיא קָטֵיל גַּבְרָא חַיָּיא. וְהָא קָא חָזֵינַן דְּקָא אָכְלִי וְלָא מָיְיתִי! הָתָם בְּבַשִּׁיל וְלָא בַּשִּׁיל.

There are some **who say** that **Rav Hamnuna said: One may not establish an** ***eiruv*** **with raw beets,**[B] as **Rav Ḥisda said: Raw beet kills a healthy person.** The Gemara asks: **Don't we** see people **eating it and they do not die?** The Gemara answers: **There,** it is referring **to** a beet **that was** only **partially cooked,** which is dangerous.

אָמַר רַב חִסְדָּא: תַּבְשִׁיל שֶׁל תְּרָדִין יָפֶה לַלֵּב וְטוֹב לָעֵינַיִם, וְכׇל שֶׁכֵּן לִבְנֵי מֵעַיִים. אָמַר אַבָּיֵי: וְהוּא דְּיָתֵיב אַבֵּי תְפֵי וְעָבֵיד תּוּךְ תּוּךְ.

Rav Ḥisda said: A cooked dish of beets is beneficial for the heart, good for the eyes, and all the more so beneficial **for the intestines. Abaye said: That is** specifically when the dish **sits on the stove and makes a** ***tukh tukh*** sound, i.e., it is cooked thoroughly enough to produce a boiling sound.

אָמַר רָבָא: הֲרֵינִי כְּבֶן עַזַּאי בְּשׁוּקֵי טְבֶרְיָא. אֲמַר לֵיהּ הַהוּא מֵרַבָּנַן לְרָבָא: תַּפּוּחִים בְּכַמָּה? אֲמַר לֵיהּ: וְכִי מְעָרְבִין בְּתַפּוּחִים?

Rava once **said** when he was in an especially good mood: **Behold, I am like** the intellectually sharp **ben Azzai,** who would regularly expound **in the markets of Tiberias.** I, too, am ready to answer any question posed to me. **One of the Sages said to Rava: How many apples** are needed to establish an *eiruv*? Rava **said to him: Does one establish an** ***eiruv*** **with apples?**[N]

וְלָא?! וְהָתְנַן: כׇּל הָאוֹכָלִין מִצְטָרְפִין לִפְסוֹל אֶת הַגְּוִיָּה בַּחֲצִי פְרָס, וּבִמְזוֹן שְׁתֵּי סְעוּדוֹת לְעֵירוּב, וְכַבֵּיצָה לְטַמֵּא טוּמְאַת אוֹכָלִים!

The other Sage responded: **And is it not** permissible to establish an *eiruv* with them? **Didn't we learn** in a mishna: **All foods combine to disqualify the body**[HN] of a priest who eats **half of a half-loaf** of ritually impure food, **and** to complete the measure of **food** required for **two meals for** the purpose of **an** ***eiruv,***[H] **and** to complete the measure of **an egg-bulk** required for a food to be able **to contract the** ritual **impurity of foods?**[H] An apple is a kind of food, so it should be included in the items that may be used to establish an *eiruv*.

וְהַאי מַאי תְּיוּבְתָּא? אִילֵּימָא מִשּׁוּם דְּקָתָנֵי ״כׇּל הָאוֹכָלִין״ וְהָנֵי בְּנֵי אֲכִילָה נִינְהוּ – וְהָאָמַר רַבִּי יוֹחָנָן: אֵין לְמֵדִין מִן הַכְּלָלוֹת וַאֲפִילּוּ בְּמָקוֹם שֶׁנֶּאֱמַר בּוֹ חוּץ!

The Gemara asks: **And what is the refutation? If you say** it is **because it was taught** using the term **all foods, and these** apples **are fit for eating,** how can an objection be raised from such a general term? **Didn't Rabbi Yoḥanan** already **say: One may not learn from general statements** using the word all, **even in a place where it says except,** since no rule exhausts all cases?

אֶלָּא מִשּׁוּם דְּקָתָנֵי: ״וּבִמְזוֹן שְׁתֵּי סְעוּדוֹת לְעֵירוּב וְכַבֵּיצָה לְטַמֵּא טוּמְאַת אוֹכָלִין״, וְהָנֵי נַמִי בְּנֵי טַמּוּיֵי טוּמְאַת אוֹכָלִין נִינְהוּ.

Rather, it is **because it taught: And** all foods combine to complete the measure of **food** required for **two meals for** the purpose of **an** ***eiruv,*** **and** to complete the measure of **an egg-bulk to contract the** ritual **impurity of foods; and these** apples **are also susceptible to the** ritual **impurity of foods.** Therefore, there is clear proof that the mishna is referring to apples as well.

וְכַמָּה? אָמַר רַב נַחְמָן: תַּפּוּחִים בְּקַב.

Having established that an *eiruv* may be established with apples, the Gemara returns to the question raised above: **How many** apples are needed to establish an *eiruv*? **Rav Naḥman said:** The minimum measure of **apples** that must be used for an *eiruv* is **a** ***kav.***[H]

HALAKHA

Partially cooked – בְּשִׁיל וְלָא בְּשִׁיל: An *eiruv* may not be made from beets or other vegetables (Rambam) that were only partially cooked (Rambam *Sefer Zemanim, Hilkhot Eiruvin* 1:11; *Shulḥan Arukh, Oraḥ Ḥayyim* 386:5).

The disqualification of a priest's body – פְּסוּל גְּוִיָּה: All ritually impure foods combine to complete the measure of half a half-loaf, in order to disqualify one who eats them by imparting a lenient form of ritual impurity. This is true even if one does not actually come into contact with the food (Rambam *Sefer Tahara, Hilkhot Tumat Okhalin* 4:3).

Food for two meals for an ***eiruv*** **– מְזוֹן שְׁתֵּי סְעוּדוֹת לְעֵירוּב:** Most foods count toward the required measure of two meals' worth of food necessary in order to establish an *eiruv*. Even different types of food can be combined, in accordance with the view of Rabba (*Shulḥan Arukh, Oraḥ Ḥayyim* 386:4).

The measure of an egg-bulk to contract the impurity of foods – כַּבֵּיצָה לְטַמֵּא: All types of food combine to complete the measure of an egg-bulk necessary to contract the ritual impurity of foods (Rambam *Sefer Tahara, Hilkhot Tumat Okhalin* 4:3).

The minimum amount of apples for an ***eiruv*** **– שִׁיעוּר תַּפּוּחִים לְעֵירוּב:** A *kav* of wild apples may be used for an *eiruv*. Many commentaries maintain that this is the measure for all types of apples (*Mishna Berura*; *Shulḥan Arukh, Oraḥ Ḥayyim* 386:7).

BACKGROUND

Beets [*teradin*] – תְּרָדִין: The beet mentioned in this context is generally called *silka* in the Talmud. It is referring to *Beta vulgaris cicla*. This plant is an annual garden vegetable from the *Chenopodiaceae* family. Its large, fleshy leaves grow up to 15–30 cm long and are edible when cooked. Their taste is similar to that of spinach. Nowadays, the leaves are also used as bird food.

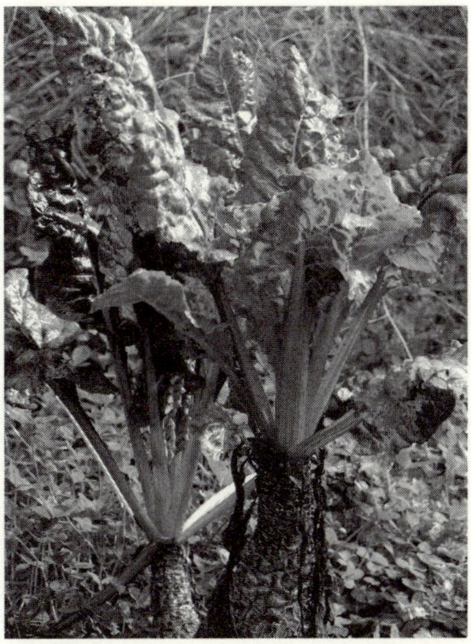

Beta vulgaris cicla

NOTES

Does one establish an ***eiruv*** **with apples – וְכִי מְעָרְבִין בְּתַפּוּחִים:** Rava's response seems quite surprising. Why would apples specifically be disqualified from use for an *eiruv*? Some commentaries explain that the reference here is to wild apples, which are of inferior quality and are eaten only when absolutely necessary. However, there is another answer: Apples are not generally eaten as a meal or even as a side dish, but rather as dessert. Consequently, the question arises as to whether or not they may be used for an *eiruv*, which is comprised of food for two meals (Rashba).

To disqualify the body – לִפְסוֹל אֶת הַגְּוִיָּה: According to Torah law, ritually impure foods do not defile one who touches them, since a person can only contract impurity from a primary source of ritual impurity. The Sages, however, decreed that anyone who eats a certain amount of ritually impure foods is disqualified from eating *teruma*. Strictly speaking, the term impure [*tamei*] refers to something impure that can impart impurity to something else, whereas something that has been defiled but cannot defile others is termed disqualified [*pasul*]. Accordingly, one who eats ritually impure food is disqualified from eating *teruma* and other consecrated foods.

מֵיתִיבִי, רַבִּי שִׁמְעוֹן בֶּן אֶלְעָזָר אוֹמֵר: עוּכְלָא תַּבְלִין, וְלִיטְרָא יָרָק, וַעֲשָׂרָה אֱגוֹזִין, וַחֲמִשָּׁה אֲפַרְסְקִין, וּשְׁנֵי רִמּוֹנִים, וְאֶתְרוֹג אֶחָד. וַאֲמַר גּוּרְסַק בַּר דָּרֵי מִשְּׁמֵיהּ דְּרַב מְנַשְּׁיָא בַּר שְׁגוּבְלֵי מִשְּׁמֵיהּ דְּרַב: וְכֵן לָעֵירוּב. וְהָנֵי נַמִּי לֶיהֱווּ כִּי אֲפַרְסְקִין?

The Gemara **raises an objection** from a *baraita*: **Rabbi Shimon ben Elazar says:** When distributing poor man's tithe, one must give each individual poor person at least **an *ukla*,**[B] an eighth of a *log*, **of spices, a liter of vegetables, ten nuts, five peaches,**[H] **two pomegranates,** or **one citron,** as these are worthy amounts for distribution. **And Gursak bar Darei said in the name of Rav Menashya bar Sheguvlei,** who said **in the name of Rav: And similarly,** this is the *halakha* **with regard to an *eiruv*.** Now, it can be asked: **These** apples **should also be like peaches,** as they are similar in size, and it should be enough to use five apples for an *eiruv*.

הָנֵי חֲשִׁיבִי וְהָנֵי לָא חֲשִׁיבִי.

The Gemara answers that there is a distinction between them: **These** peaches **are important,** and therefore five of them are a significant amount, **but these** apples **are not important,** and therefore one must use the larger measure of a *kav*.

אָמַר רַב יוֹסֵף: שָׁרֵא לֵיהּ מָרֵיהּ לְרַב מְנַשְּׁיָא בַּר שְׁגוּבְלֵי, אֲנָא אֲמַרִיתָא נִיהֲלֵיהּ אַמַּתְנִיתִין וְהוּא אֲמָרָהּ אַבָּרַיְיתָא. דִּתְנַן: אֵין פּוֹחֲתִין לֶעָנִי בַּגּוֹרֶן מֵחֲצִי קַב חִטִּין וְקַב שְׂעוֹרִין. רַבִּי מֵאִיר אוֹמֵר: חֲצִי קַב שְׂעוֹרִין, וְקַב וָחֵצִי כּוּסְמִין, וְקַב גְּרוֹגָרוֹת, אוֹ מָנֶה דְּבֵילָה. רַבִּי עֲקִיבָא אוֹמֵר: פְּרָס. וַחֲצִי לוֹג יַיִן, רַבִּי עֲקִיבָא אוֹמֵר: רְבִיעִית. וּרְבִיעִית שֶׁמֶן, רַבִּי עֲקִיבָא אוֹמֵר: שְׁמִינִית. וּשְׁאָר כָּל הַפֵּירוֹת, אָמַר אַבָּא שָׁאוּל: כְּדֵי שֶׁיִּמְכְּרֵם וְיִקַּח בָּהֶן מְזוֹן שְׁתֵּי סְעוּדוֹת. וְאָמַר רַב: וְכֵן לָעֵירוּב.

Rav Yosef said: May his Master, God, **forgive**[N] **Rav Menashya bar Sheguvlei,** for he erred and caused others to err. **I stated before him** a ruling in the name of Rav **concerning a mishna, and he stated it concerning the *baraita*,** which led to the error. **As we learned** in a mishna: **One may not give a pauper** receiving poor man's tithe **at the threshing floor less than half a *kav* of wheat or** less than **a *kav* of barley.**[H] **Rabbi Meir says:** He must be given at least **half a *kav* of barley.** Similarly, he must be given no less than **a *kav* and a half of spelt, a *kav* of dried figs, or a *maneh* of pressed figs. Rabbi Akiva says:** Not a *maneh*, but **half** a *maneh*. He must be given at least **half a *log* of wine. Rabbi Akiva says:** Half that amount, **a quarter** *log*. **And** similarly, he must be given **a quarter *log* of oil. Rabbi Akiva says:** Half that amount, **an eighth** of a *log*. **And** with regard to **all other fruit, Abba Shaul said:** He must be given **enough to sell them and buy food** that suffices **for two meals with** the proceeds of **their** sale. **And** with regard to this mishna, **Rav said: And similarly,** this is the *halakha* **with regard to an *eiruv*.**[H]

וּמַאי אוּלְמֵיהּ דְּהַאי מֵהַךְ? אִילֵימָא מִשּׁוּם דְּקָא תָּנֵי בְּהַךְ תַּבְלִין, וְתַבְלִין לָאו בְּנֵי אֲכִילָה נִינְהוּ – אַטּוּ הָכָא מִי לָא קָתָנֵי חִטִּין וּשְׂעוֹרִין, וְלָאו בְּנֵי אֲכִילָה נִינְהוּ.

The Gemara poses a question with regard to Rav Yosef's harsh reaction to Rav Menashya bar Sheguvlei's statement: **What is the strength of this over that?** The mishna and *baraita* seem to share the same content, so why should Rav's ruling be more applicable to one than the other? **If you say** it is **because** the *halakha* with regard to **spices** was also **taught in this** *baraita*, **and spices are not fit for eating** on their own but only when added as a flavoring to other foods, and therefore Rav could not have been referring to the *baraita* when he said that the same law applies to an *eiruv*; **wasn't** the *halakha* with regard to **wheat and barley taught here** in the mishna, **and they** too **are not** immediately **fit for eating** until they are processed further.

אֶלָּא מִשּׁוּם דְּקָתָנֵי חֲצִי לוֹג יַיִן. וְאָמַר רַב: מְעָרְבִין בִּשְׁתֵּי רְבִיעִיּוֹת שֶׁל יַיִן. מִדְּבָעֵינַן כּוּלֵּי הַאי – שְׁמַע מִינָּהּ כִּי אָמַר רַב וְכֵן לָעֵירוּב – אַהָא מַתְנִיתִין קָאָמַר, שְׁמַע מִינָּהּ.

Rather, it is **because it was taught** in the mishna that one must give **half a *log* of wine. And Rav said: One may establish an *eiruv* with two-quarters** of a *log* **of wine,** which is equal to half a *log*. **Since we require so much** wine, **learn from here** that **when Rav said: And similarly,** this is the *halakha* **with regard to an *eiruv*, he said it about this mishna** and the measures mentioned therein. The Gemara concludes: Indeed, **conclude from this** that this is the proper understanding of Rav's statement.

אָמַר מָר: וּבִמְזוֹן שְׁתֵּי סְעוּדוֹת לָעֵירוּב. סָבַר רַב יוֹסֵף לְמֵימַר: עַד דְּאִיכָּא סְעוּדָה מֵהַאי וּסְעוּדָה מֵהַאי. אָמַר לֵיהּ רַבָּה: אֲפִילּוּ לְמֶחֱצָה לִשְׁלִישׁ וְלִרְבִיעַ.

The Gemara further examines the mishna cited earlier. **The Master said: And** all foods combine to complete the measure of **food** required **for two meals for** the purpose of **an *eiruv*. Rav Yosef thought to say** that an *eiruv* may not be established **unless there is** a complete **meal of this** kind of food **and** a complete **meal of that** kind of food, meaning that an *eiruv* may only be established if each meal consists of a single type of food. **Rabba said to him:** An *eiruv* may be established with the amount of food required for two meals **even** if each type of food made up only **half, a third, or a quarter** of a meal.

BACKGROUND

Ukla – עוּכְלָא: The Babylonian Talmud (*Bava Batra* 90a) states than an *ukla* is one-twentieth of a *kav*. Some commentaries determine that the measure of an *ukla* is an eighth of a liter. The two measures are not very different in size.

HALAKHA

Five peaches, etc. – חֲמִשָּׁה אֲפַרְסְקִין וכו׳: A minimum of five peaches or two pomegranates must be used in order to establish an *eiruv*, in accordance with the *baraita*, as explained by Rav Menashya (*Shulḥan Arukh, Oraḥ Ḥayyim* 386:7).

The measure of poor man's tithe – שִׁיעוּר מַעֲשַׂר עָנִי: When distributing poor man's tithe, one may not give a pauper less than half a *kav* of wheat, a *kav* of barley, a *kav* of spelt (Rambam), a *kav* of dried figs, half a *log* of wine or a quarter *log* of oil. All other foods must be given in quantities equivalent in value to two meals (Rambam *Sefer Zera'im, Hilkhot Mattenot Aniyyim* 6:8).

And similarly, this is the *halakha* with regard to an *eiruv* – וְכֵן לָעֵירוּב: The minimum measure of regular wine needed for an *eiruv* is two-quarters of a *log*, while the measure of cooked wine is an amount sufficient to accompany two meals (*Maggid Mishne*; *Magen Avraham*; *Shulḥan Arukh, Oraḥ Ḥayyim* 386:6).

NOTES

May his Master forgive him – שָׁרֵא לֵיהּ מָרֵיהּ: Some commentators explain that Rav Yosef only reacted strongly toward Rav Menashya because he altered the presentation of Rav's statement, but as far as the *halakha* is concerned, there is no difference whether the statement was made with regard to the mishna or the *baraita*. Others, however, hold that according to Rav Yosef, Rav's statement is referring only to the mishna and should not be applied to the items listed in the *baraita*. *Tosafot* and several other commentators infer from the phrase: What is the strength of this over that, that even Rav Yosef did not hear the statement directly in Rav's name, and therefore he had to prove his claim, and he could not merely assert that he had heard that version in the original (see Rashba and Ritva).

גּוּפָא, אָמַר רַב: מְעָרְבִין בִּשְׁתֵּי רְבִיעִיּוֹת שֶׁל יַיִן. וּמִי בָּעֵינַן כּוּלֵּי הַאי? וְהָתַנְיָא, רַבִּי שִׁמְעוֹן בֶּן אֶלְעָזָר אוֹמֵר: יַיִן – כְּדֵי לֶאֱכוֹל בּוֹ, חוֹמֶץ – כְּדֵי לִטְבּוֹל בּוֹ, זֵיתִים וּבְצָלִים – כְּדֵי לֶאֱכוֹל בָּהֶן שְׁתֵּי סְעוּדוֹת.

The Gemara now examines Rav's statement **itself,** which was cited in the course of the previous discussion. **Rav said: One may establish an *eiruv* with two-quarters** of a *log* **of wine.** The following question may be raised: **Do we** really **need so much? Wasn't it taught** in a *baraita* that **Rabbi Shimon ben Elazar says:** The minimal amount of **wine** required for an *eiruv* is **enough to eat** bread **with it,** i.e., enough to soak the bread in to enable one to eat it? Additionally, the minimal amount of **vinegar** that may be used to establish an *eiruv* is **enough to dip** the food **in it,** and the minimal amount of **olives and onions** is **enough to eat them** together with the bread. All of these quantities are calculated on the basis of **two meals.** This *baraita* clearly indicates that an *eiruv* may be established with much less than two-quarters of a *log* of wine.

הָתָם בְּחַמְרָא מְבַשְּׁלָא.

The Gemara answers: **There,** the *baraita* is referring **to cooked wine,** which is very strong, and therefore even a small amount suffices.

אָמַר מָר: חוֹמֶץ כְּדֵי לִטְבּוֹל בּוֹ. אָמַר רַב גִּידֵּל, אָמַר רַב: כְּדֵי לִטְבּוֹל בּוֹ מְזוֹן שְׁתֵּי סְעוּדוֹת שֶׁל יָרָק. אִיכָּא דְּאָמְרִי, אָמַר רַב גִּידֵּל אָמַר רַב: יָרָק הַנֶּאֱכָל בִּשְׁתֵּי סְעוּדוֹת.

The Master said in the *baraita* that the minimal amount of **vinegar** that may be used for an *eiruv*[H] **is enough to dip** food **in it. Rav Giddel said that Rav said: Enough to dip in it the food of two meals** consisting **of vegetables. Some say** that **Rav Giddel said that Rav said:** Enough to dip in it the **vegetables that are eaten in two** ordinary **meals,** which is less than the amount consumed in two meals consisting entirely of vegetables.

אָמַר מָר: זֵיתִים וּבְצָלִים, כְּדֵי לֶאֱכוֹל בָּהֶן מְזוֹן שְׁתֵּי סְעוּדוֹת. וּבִבְצָלִים מִי מְעָרְבִין? וְהָתַנְיָא, אָמַר רַבִּי שִׁמְעוֹן בֶּן אֶלְעָזָר: פַּעַם אַחַת שָׁבַת רַבִּי מֵאִיר בְּעַרְדִּיסְקָא, וּבָא אָדָם אֶחָד לְפָנָיו. אָמַר לוֹ: רַבִּי, עֵירַבְתִּי בִּבְצָלִים לְטִיבְעִין. וְהוֹשִׁיבוֹ רַבִּי מֵאִיר בְּאַרְבַּע אַמּוֹת שֶׁלּוֹ.

The Master also **said** that the minimum measure of **olives and onions** that may be used for an *eiruv* is enough **to eat them** with **the food of two meals.** The Gemara asks: **May one establish an *eiruv* with onions? Wasn't it taught** in a *baraita* that **Rabbi Shimon ben Elazar said: Rabbi Meir once spent Shabbat in** the town of **Ardiska,**[B] **and a certain person came before him** and **said to him: Rabbi, I made an *eiruv*** of Shabbat borders [*eiruv teḥumin*] **with onions,** so that I might walk to the town of **Tiv'in.** Ardiska was located between the man's *eiruv* and his destination of Tiv'in, which was beyond his Shabbat limit as measured from his hometown. **And Rabbi Meir made him remain within his four cubits.** He forbade him to leave his four cubits, as he held that an *eiruv* made with onions is not an *eiruv,* and therefore the person had left his Shabbat limit without an *eiruv teḥumin.*

לָא קַשְׁיָא; הָא – בְּעָלִים, הָא – בְּאִימְּהוֹת. דְּתַנְיָא: אָכַל בָּצָל וְהִשְׁכִּים וָמֵת – אֵין אוֹמְרִין מִמָּה מֵּת. וְאָמַר שְׁמוּאֵל: לֹא שָׁנוּ אֶלָּא בְּעָלִים, אֲבָל בְּאִימְּהוֹת – לֵית לָן בַּהּ. וּבְעָלִין נָמֵי לָא אֲמַרַן, אֶלָּא

The Gemara answers: This is **not difficult. This** ruling, which states that onions may not be used for an *eiruv,* is referring **to** onion **leaves,** which are harmful; whereas **that** ruling, which states that onions may be used for an *eiruv,* is referring **to** onion **bulbs,** which are edible. **As it was taught** in a *baraita*: If one **ate an onion and died early** the next morning, **we need not ask from what he died,** as his death was certainly caused by the onion. **And Shmuel said: They only taught** this **with regard to the leaves; but with regard to** onion **bulbs, we have no** problem **with it. And even with regard to the leaves, we only stated** this concern

Perek **III**
Daf **29** Amud **b**

דְּלָא אַבְצִיל זִירְתָא, אֲבָל אַבְצִיל זִירְתָא – לֵית לָן בַּהּ.

in a case where the bulb **has not grown** to the size of **a span,** the distance between the thumb and the little finger of a hand that is spread apart, because at that stage the leaves are very toxic; **however, if it has grown** to the size of **a span, we have no** problem **with it.**[H]

אָמַר רַב פָּפָּא: לָא אֲמַרַן אֶלָּא דְּלָא אִישְׁתִּי שִׁיכְרָא, אֲבָל אִישְׁתִּי שִׁיכְרָא – לֵית לָן בַּהּ.

Rav Pappa said: We only stated this concern about eating onion leaves in a case where **one did not drink beer** afterward; **however, if he drank beer** afterward, **we have no** problem **with it.**

HALAKHA

Vinegar for an *eiruv* – חוֹמֶץ לְעֵירוּב: The minimum measure of vinegar needed to establish an *eiruv* is enough to use for dipping the food of two meals consisting of vegetables, although some authorities rule in accordance with the second version cited in the Gemara (Riaz; *Shiltei HaGibborim*; *Shulḥan Arukh, Oraḥ Ḥayyim* 386:6).

BACKGROUND

Ardiska – עַרְדִּיסְקָא: Ardiska, or Ardascus, refers to a settlement that was located not far from the town of Tiv'in, known as Tiv'on.

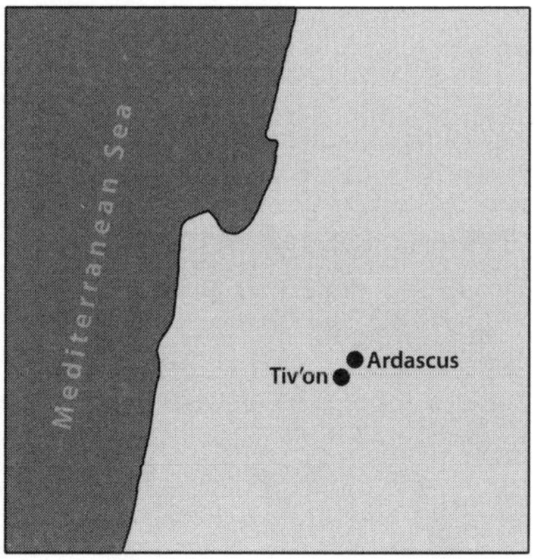

Northern Israel

HALAKHA

An *eiruv* of onions – עֵירוּב בִּבְצָלִים: One may not establish an *eiruv* with onion leaves that have not grown to the size of approximately 21 cm, the distance between the thumb and the end of the little finger (*Shulḥan Arukh, Oraḥ Ḥayyim* 386:5).

BACKGROUND

The toxins [*naḥash*] of an onion – נָחָשׁ שֶׁבְּבָצָל: The commentaries dispute the meaning of the word *naḥash* in this context. Most traditions identify it with the inflorescence of an onion stalk, which is somewhat similar to a snake [*naḥash*] with its long head and body. There is no definitive data concerning the measure of danger posed by eating onions in general or their undeveloped green leaves in particular. Although many people eat onion without any ill effects, onions do contain an oil called allyl propyl disulfide, $C_6H_{12}S_2$, which gives them their flavor and which can be toxic in large concentrations. Rashi defines this as the onion's *naḥash*. It has been proven that a relatively small portion of onions can lead to severe poisoning. Since the Gemara is discussing two meals consisting entirely of onions, it certainly poses a danger to all people. For particularly sensitive people, the danger might even be life-threatening.

Onion stalk with inflorescence

HALAKHA

The disqualification of a ritual bath through beer – פִּיסוּל מִקְוֶה בְּשֵׁיכָר: Three *log* of beer invalidate a ritual bath, in accordance with the opinion of Shmuel (Rambam *Sefer Tahara, Hilkhot Mikvaot* 7:4).

Dye-water in a ritual bath – מֵי צֶבַע: Three *log* of dye-water invalidate a ritual bath because of their volume, not because they change of appearance of the water in the ritual bath (Rambam *Sefer Tahara, Hilkhot Mikvaot* 7:8).

The measure of wine with regard to carrying out – שִׁיעוּר יַיִן לְהוֹצָאָה: The minimal measure of wine that determines liability when carried from one domain to another on Shabbat is a quarter of a quarter-*log* (Rambam *Sefer Zemanim, Hilkhot Shabbat* 18:2).

The amount of beer necessary for an *eiruv* – שִׁיעוּר שֵׁיכָר לְעֵירוּב: One may establish an *eiruv* with two-quarters of a *log* of beer, in accordance with the opinion of Rav Aḥa (Rambam *Sefer Zemanim, Hilkhot Eiruvin* 1:11).

תָּנוּ רַבָּנַן: לֹא יֹאכַל אָדָם בָּצָל מִפְּנֵי נָחָשׁ שֶׁבּוֹ. וּמַעֲשֶׂה בְּרַבִּי חֲנִינָא שֶׁאָכַל חֲצִי בָּצָל וַחֲצִי נָחָשׁ שֶׁבּוֹ, וְחָלָה וְנָטָה לָמוּת, וּבִקְּשׁוּ חֲבֵירָיו רַחֲמִים עָלָיו וְחָיָה, מִפְּנֵי שֶׁהַשָּׁעָה צְרִיכָה לוֹ.

The Sages taught in a *baraita*: **A person should not eat onion because of the toxins in it.**[BN] **There was an incident with Rabbi Ḥanina, who ate half an onion and half of its toxins, and he fell deathly ill, and his colleagues prayed for mercy for him,**[N] **and he survived.** He was rescued only **because the time needed him,** as his generation was in need of his teaching, but otherwise he would not have recovered.

אָמַר רַבִּי זֵירָא, אָמַר שְׁמוּאֵל: שֵׁכָר מְעָרְבִין בּוֹ, וּפוֹסֵל אֶת הַמִּקְוֶה בִּשְׁלֹשֶׁת לוּגִּין. מַתְקִיף לָהּ רַב כָּהֲנָא: פְּשִׁיטָא, וְכִי מַה בֵּין זֶה לְמֵי צֶבַע? דִּתְנַן, רַבִּי יוֹסֵי אוֹמֵר: מֵי צֶבַע פּוֹסְלִין אֶת הַמִּקְוֶה בִּשְׁלֹשֶׁת לוּגִּין! אָמְרִי: הָתָם – מַיָּא דִּצְבְעָא מִיקְּרִי, הָכָא – שִׁיכְרָא אִיקְּרִי.

Rabbi Zeira said that Shmuel said: One may establish an *eiruv* with beer, and it invalidates a ritual bath with a measure of **three *log*,** similar to drawn water.[HN] **Rav Kahana strongly objects to this:** This is **obvious, for what is the difference between this and dye-water? As we learned** in a mishna that **Rabbi Yosei says: Dye-water invalidates a ritual bath with** a measure of **three *log*,** like regular drawn water.[H] **They said:** There is a difference between the two cases, as **there,** the liquid **is called dye-water; here, it is called beer.**[N] Therefore, it might have been possible to argue that beer is not considered like water at all, in which case it would only invalidate a ritual bath if it changed the color of the water, and so Shmuel's novel teaching was necessary.

וּבְכַמָּה מְעָרְבִין? סָבַר רַב אַחָא בְּרֵיהּ דְּרַב יוֹסֵף קַמֵּיהּ דְּרַב יוֹסֵף לְמֵימַר: בִּתְרֵין רִבְעֵי שִׁכְרָא. כְּדִתְנַן: הַמּוֹצִיא יַיִן כְּדֵי מְזִיגַת הַכּוֹס, וְתָנֵי עֲלָהּ: כְּדֵי מְזִיגַת כּוֹס יָפֶה. מַאי כּוֹס יָפֶה? כּוֹס שֶׁל בְּרָכָה! וְאָמַר רַב נַחְמָן, אָמַר רַבָּה בַּר אֲבוּהּ: כּוֹס שֶׁל בְּרָכָה צָרִיךְ שֶׁיְּהֵא בּוֹ רוֹבַע רְבִיעִית, כְּדֵי שֶׁיִּמְזְגֶנּוּ וְיַעֲמוֹד עַל רְבִיעִית. וְכִדְרָבָא, דְּאָמַר רָבָא: כָּל חַמְרָא דְּלָא דָּרֵי עַל חַד תְּלָת מַיָּא – לָאו חַמְרָא הוּא.

The Gemara asks: And how much beer is needed to **establish an *eiruv*? Rav Aḥa, son of Rav Yosef, thought to say before Rav Yosef** as follows: **Two-quarters** of a *log* **of beer.** Rav Aḥa's reasoning is now spelled out in detail. **As we learned** in a mishna: If **one carries out wine** on Shabbat from a private domain to a public domain, he is liable if he carries out **enough** wine **for diluting a cup,** i.e., enough undiluted wine to fill a cup after it has been diluted with water.[H] **And a *baraita* was taught about** this mishna: **Enough** wine **for diluting a fine cup.** They inquired: **What** is meant by **a fine cup?** They answered: **A cup of blessing. And Rav Naḥman said that Rabba bar Avuh said: A cup of blessing must contain a quarter of a quarter-*log*** of wine, **so that** after one **dilutes** the wine with water, **it amounts to a** full **quarter-*log*. And** this measure is **in accordance with** the statement of **Rava** with regard to the strength of wine, **as Rava said: Any wine that is not** strong enough to require that it be **diluted** with **three** parts **water to one** part wine **is not** proper **wine.**

וְקָתָנֵי סֵיפָא: וּשְׁאָר כָּל הַמַּשְׁקִין בִּרְבִיעִית, וְכָל הַשּׁוֹפָכִין בִּרְבִיעִית. מִדְּהָתָם עַל חַד אַרְבַּע – הָכָא נַמִי עַל חַד אַרְבַּע.

And we learned in the latter clause of the aforementioned mishna: **And** one is liable for carrying out **all other liquids, and** similarly **all waste water,** in the measure of **a quarter-*log*.** Now, Rav Aḥa argues as follows: **Since there,** with respect to liability for carrying on Shabbat, the ratio is **one to four,** as one is liable for carrying out a quarter of a quarter-*log* of wine, and one is only liable for carrying out other liquids if one carries out a quarter-*log*; **here, too,** with respect to making an *eiruv*, the ratio of **one to four** should be maintained. Therefore, since Rav said that two-quarters of a *log* of wine are required for an *eiruv*, the minimum amount of beer one may use should be two full *log*.

וְלָא הִיא, הָתָם הוּא דְּבָצִיר מֵהָכִי לָא חֲשִׁיב, אֲבָל הָכָא – לָא, דַּעֲבִידִי אִינָשֵׁי דְּשָׁתוּ כָּסָא בְּצַפְרָא וְכָסָא בְּפַנְיָא, וְסָמְכִי עִילָּוַיְהוּ.

The Gemara rejects this argument: **And this is not so. There,** with regard to carrying on Shabbat, we require four times as much beer as wine because **less than that** amount, i.e., less than a quarter-*log* of beer, **is insignificant. However, here,** with regard to establishing an *eiruv*, this is **not** relevant, **as it is common for people to drink a cup** of beer **in the morning and a cup** of beer **in the evening, and they rely on them** as their meals, as beer is satisfying even in such quantities. Therefore, we should require only two-quarters of a *log* of beer for an *eiruv*.[H]

NOTES

Because of the toxins [*naḥash*] in it – מִפְּנֵי נָחָשׁ שֶׁבּוֹ: The word *naḥash* literally means snake. Some commentaries explain that the *naḥash* is referring here to a type of harmful worm found in onion leaves (Ritva).

And his colleagues prayed for mercy for him – וּבִקְּשׁוּ רַחֲמִים עָלָיו: Why is it necessary to specifically mention that Rabbi Ḥanina's generation needed him? Apparently, he acted improperly by eating something dangerous to his health, which the Sages warned against eating. It was therefore necessary to state that because of his importance they prayed for mercy for him nonetheless (Ritva).

The disqualification of a ritual bath – פְּסוּל מִקְוֶה: If a ritual bath lacks the requisite minimal measure of water, forty *se'a*, and three *log* of drawn water fall into it and complete the measure of forty *se'a*, the *mikva* is invalidated. However, if liquids fall into a ritual bath which already has the necessary amount of water, as long as they do not change its color, the ritual bath remains valid.

Beer – שֵׁיכָר: Beer is generally prepared by pouring water over a fermenting agent such as dates, grapes and their sediment, or fermented barley. The question raised in this context is whether or not beer ceases to be regarded as water when it becomes an alcoholic beverage, even though it is primarily water. See the Rashba and the Ritva for a discussion of some of the finer details of this *halakha*.

תְּמָרִים בְּכַמָּה? אָמַר רַב יוֹסֵף: תְּמָרִים בְּקַב. אָמַר רַב יוֹסֵף: מְנָא אָמִינָא לַהּ – דְּתַנְיָא: אָכַל גְּרוֹגָרוֹת וְשִׁילֵּם תְּמָרִים – תָּבוֹא עָלָיו בְּרָכָה.

The Gemara asks: **How many dates** are needed to establish an *eruv*?[H] **Rav Yosef said:** The minimal amount of **dates** one may use is **a *kav*. Rav Yosef said: From where do I say this *halakha*? As it was taught** in a *baraita*: If one inadvertently **ate dried figs** of *teruma*, **and paid dates** in compensation, **may a blessing come upon him.**

הֵיכִי דָּמֵי? אִילֵימָא לְפִי דָּמִים, דַּאֲכַל מִינֵּיהּ בְּזוּזָא וְקָא מְשַׁלֵּם לֵיהּ בְּזוּזָא – מַאי "תָּבֹא עָלָיו בְּרָכָה"? בְּזוּזָא אֲכַל, בְּזוּזָא קָא מְשַׁלֵּם! אֶלָּא לָאו לְפִי מִדָּה, דַּאֲכַל מִינֵּיהּ גְּרִיוָא דִּגְרוֹגָרוֹת דְּשָׁוְיָא זוּזָא, וְקָא מְשַׁלֵּם לֵיהּ גְּרִיוָא דִּתְמָרִים דְּשָׁוֵי אַרְבְּעָה. וְקָתָנֵי: "תָּבֹא עָלָיו בְּרָכָה", אַלְמָא: תְּמָרִים עֲדִיפִי.

The Gemara proceeds to clarify this ruling: **What are the circumstances** of this case? **If you say** that one paid **according to the value** of the figs he ate, e.g., **he ate a *zuz*** worth of figs **and he paid a *zuz*** worth of dates, **what is** the reason it says: **May a blessing come upon him? He ate a *zuz* and paid a *zuz*. Rather, is it not** that he paid **in accordance with the measure** of the figs eaten, e.g., that **he ate a *se'a* of dried figs worth one *zuz*, and he paid a *se'a* of dates worth four *zuz*. And it says: May a blessing come upon him. Apparently, dates are superior** to dried figs. Accordingly, since we learned above that one may establish an *eruv* with a *kav* of dried figs, a *kav* of dates should certainly suffice for the purpose of an *eruv*.

אֲמַר לֵיהּ אַבַּיֵּי: לְעוֹלָם דַּאֲכַל מִינֵּיהּ בְּזוּזָא, וְקָא מְשַׁלֵּם בְּזוּזָא. וּמַאי "תָּבֹא עָלָיו בְּרָכָה" – דַּאֲכַל מִינֵּיהּ מִידֵּי דְּלָא קָפֵיץ עֲלֵיהּ זְבִינָא, וְקָא מְשַׁלֵּם לֵיהּ מִידֵּי דְּקָפֵיץ עֲלֵיהּ זְבִינָא.

Abaye said to Rav Yosef: No proof can be brought from here. It can be argued that **he actually ate a *zuz*** worth of figs **and he paid a *zuz*** worth of dates. **And what** is the reason it says: **May a blessing come upon him? For he ate something that buyers are not eager** to buy, **and he paid him something that buyers are eager** to buy. Even though they are equal in value, the priest benefits, for it is easier for him to sell dates than to sell dried figs.

שְׁתִיתָא, אָמַר רַב אַחָא בַּר פִּנְחָס: תְּרֵי שַׁרְגּוּשֵׁי. כִּיסָּנֵי, אָמַר אַבַּיֵּי: תְּרֵי בּוּנֵי דְּפוּמְבְּדִיתָא.

With regard to ***shetita***, a dish made of roasted flour and honey, **Rav Aḥa bar Pineḥas said: Two large spoonfuls**[N] are needed for an *eruv*. With regard to **kisanei**, a type of roasted grain, **Abaye said: Two Pumbeditan *bunei*,** the name of a particular of measurement.

אָמַר אַבַּיֵּי, אָמְרָה לִי אֵם: הָנֵי כִּסָּאנֵי מַעֲלוּ לְלִיבָּא, וּמְבַטְּלֵי מַחְשַׁבְתָּא.

Having mentioned roasted grain, the Gemara tangentially relates that **Abaye said: Mother,** actually his foster mother, **told me: These roasted grains are good for the heart and drive away** worrisome **thoughts.**

וְאָמַר אַבַּיֵּי, אָמְרָה לִי אֵם: הַאי מַאן דְּאִית לֵיהּ חוּלְשָׁא דְּלִיבָּא לַיְיתֵי בִּישְׂרָא דְּאַטְמָא יְמִינָא דְּדִיכְרָא, וְלַיְיתֵי כַּבּוּיֵי דְּרָעִיתָא דְּנִיסָן. וְאִי לֵיכָּא כַּבּוּיֵי דְּרָעִיתָא – לַיְיתֵי סוּגְיָינֵי דְּעַרְבְתָא, וְנִיכַבְּבֵיהּ וְנֵיכוֹל, וְנִשְׁתֵּי בָּתְרֵיהּ חַמְרָא מַרְקָא.

And Abaye said: Mother told me about another remedy. **One who suffers from weakness of the heart should** go and **bring the meat of the right thigh of a ram, and** also **bring the dung of grazing cattle from** the month of **Nisan, and if there is no cattle dung he should bring willow twigs, and** then **roast** the meat on a fire made with the dung or twigs, **and eat it, and drink afterward** some **diluted wine.**[N] This will improve his condition.

אָמַר רַב יְהוּדָה, אָמַר שְׁמוּאֵל: כֹּל שֶׁהוּא לִיפְתָּן – כְּדֵי לֶאֱכוֹל בּוֹ. כֹּל שֶׁאֵינוֹ לִיפְתָּן – כְּדֵי לֶאֱכוֹל הֵימֶנּוּ. בָּשָׂר חַי – כְּדֵי לֶאֱכוֹל הֵימֶנּוּ. בָּשָׂר צָלִי, רַבָּה אָמַר: כְּדֵי לֶאֱכוֹל בּוֹ, וְרַב יוֹסֵף אָמַר: כְּדֵי לֶאֱכוֹל הֵימֶנּוּ.

Returning to the matter of quantities of food required for an *eruv*, **Rav Yehuda said** that **Shmuel said:** The minimum quantity for **anything that serves as a relish**[N] is **enough to eat** two meals **with it**, i.e., enough to serve as a relish for the bread eaten in two meals. **And** with regard to **anything that is not a relish,** but rather is a food in its own right, one must use **enough to eat** two meals **of it.**[H] The minimum quantity of **raw meat**[N] is **enough to eat** two meals **of it. Roasted meat** is the subject of a dispute: **Rabba said: Enough to eat** the bread of two meals **with it.** That is to say, roasted meat is not a food in itself, but rather it serves as relish for other foods. **And Rav Yosef said: Enough to eat** two meals **of it,**[H] as it is a food in its own right.

אָמַר רַב יוֹסֵף: מְנָא אָמִינָא לַהּ – דְּהָנֵי פָּרְסָאֵי אָכְלִי טַבָּהָקֵי בְּלָא נַהֲמָא. אֲמַר לֵיהּ אַבַּיֵּי: וּפָרְסָאֵי הֲווּ רוּבָּא דְּעָלְמָא?! וְהָתְנַן: בִּגְדֵי עֲנִיִּים לַעֲנִיִּים, בִּגְדֵי עֲשִׁירִים לַעֲשִׁירִים.

Rav Yosef said: From where do I say this *halakha*? For these Persians eat pieces of roasted **meat** [*tabahakki*][L] **without bread,** which shows that meat itself is a food. **Abaye said to him: But are the Persians a majority of the world?** The *halakha* follows the customary practice of most of the world and not that of particular locales. **Didn't we learn** the following in a *baraita*? **Clothing of the poor,**[H] i.e., pieces of cloth measuring three by three fingerbreadths, contracts impurity when in the possession of any **poor people** because poor people attach importance even to scraps of cloth of such small size. **Clothing of the wealthy** measuring at least three by three handbreadths contracts impurity in all cases, whether or not it is owned by **the wealthy.**[H]

HALAKHA

The amount of dates necessary for an *eruv* – שִׁיעוּר תְּמָרִים לְעֵירוּב: One may establish an *eruv* with a *kav* of dates, in accordance with the opinion of Rav Yosef, as Abaye only refuted Rav Yosef's proof, but not the position itself (Rambam *Sefer Zemanim, Hilkhot Eiruvin* 1:11).

The measure of two meals – שִׁיעוּר שְׁתֵּי סְעוּדוֹת: When relish is used for an *eruv*, the quantity required is enough for use as a condiment at two meals. The requisite quantity for any other food is enough to eat as two full meals by itself (*Shulḥan Arukh, Oraḥ Ḥayyim* 386:6).

The amount of meat necessary for an *eruv* – שִׁיעוּר בָּשָׂר לְעֵירוּב: The amount of raw meat required for an *eruv* is enough for two full meals comprised solely of meat, while the required measure of roasted meat is enough to accompany the bread eaten at two meals. This *halakha* is in accordance with the opinion of Rabba (*Shulḥan Arukh, Oraḥ Ḥayyim* 386:6).

Clothing of the poor – בִּגְדֵי עֲנִיִּים: In the house of a pauper, a piece of cloth measuring three by three fingerbreadths is susceptible to the ritual impurity imparted by the treading of a *zav* (Rambam *Sefer Tahara, Hilkhot Kelim* 22:20).

Clothing of the wealthy – בִּגְדֵי עֲשִׁירִים: A piece of cloth measuring three by three handbreadths is always susceptible to ritual impurity (Rambam *Sefer Tahara, Hilkhot Kelim* 22:23).

NOTES

Large spoonfuls [*shargushei*] – שַׁרְגּוּשֵׁי: Some commentaries explain this term as meaning handfuls.

Diluted wine – חַמְרָא מַרְקָא: Rabbeinu Ḥananel explains that this is wine that has not been transferred from one container to another but has remained in its original barrel.

Anything that serves as a relish – כֹּל שֶׁהוּא לִיפְתָּן: The principle is that all foodstuffs may be used for an *eruv* in the form and quantity in which they are generally consumed. If the food is eaten as the main portion of a meal, there must be enough for two meals. If it is a relish or seasoning, then there must be enough to season two meals. If it is eaten for dessert, there must be enough to eat it for dessert at two meals (Rabbeinu Yehonatan).

Raw meat – בָּשָׂר חַי: The Rashba and other commentaries explain that raw meat in this context is meat that has not been cooked but has been heavily salted and dried. The Ritva states that it does not refer to raw meat but to meat that has not been fully cooked. Still other commentaries maintain that the term is to be understood literally, since the mishna states that Babylonians were not particular and would eat raw meat. This is also implied by the Jerusalem Talmud (Rav Ya'akov Emden).

LANGUAGE

Pieces of meat [*tabahakki*] – טַבָּהָקֵי: Probably from the Middle Iranian word tabāhak, meaning stewed meat. The ancient Persians ate large quantities of meat, to the extent that bread was subordinate to the meat and was used as a mere side dish to accompany the meat.

NOTES

Openings for ritual impurity – פִּתְחֵי טוּמְאָה: If a person dies inside a house, the entire house becomes ritually impure. If the house does not have doorways, it is impure on all sides. If it does have doorways, the doorways become ritually impure, since it is possible that they will be used to remove the corpse from the house. However, if the intention is to carry the corpse out through a particular doorway, or if only one of the entrances is suitable for the task, only that opening becomes ritually impure. The others remain ritually pure.

HALAKHA

An opening of four handbreadths – פִּיתְחוֹ בְּאַרְבָּעָה: If there is a corpse in a house, even if the corpse is very large, an opening four handbreadths wide is considered the opening through which the corpse will be carried out (Rambam *Sefer Tahara*, *Hilkhot Tumat Met* 7:1).

אֲבָל בִּגְדֵי עֲשִׁירִים לַעֲנִיִּים – לָא!

But the clothing of the wealthy does **not** need to be three by three handbreadths in order to become ritually impure **for the poor** because even smaller pieces of cloth are significant for the poor. Therefore, the law with regard to the poor is not determined by the customary practice of the rich. So too, the law of *eiruv* pertaining to the rest of the world should not be determined by the customary practice of the Persians to eat roasted meat as a food in itself.

וְכִי תֵּימָא: הָכָא לְחוּמְרָא וְהָכָא לְחוּמְרָא, וְהָתַנְיָא: רַבִּי שִׁמְעוֹן בֶּן אֶלְעָזָר אוֹמֵר: מְעָרְבִין לְחוֹלֶה וְלְזָקֵן כְּדֵי מְזוֹנוֹ, וְלְרַעַבְתָּן בִּסְעוּדָה בֵּינוֹנִית שֶׁל כָּל אָדָם?! קַשְׁיָא.

And if you say: Both **here** the ruling is **stringent,** and **there** the ruling is **stringent,** i.e., with regard to ritual impurity the *halakha* is stringent with respect to the poor and declares scraps of cloth that are only three by three fingerbreadths impure, but with regard to *eiruv* the *halakha* requires enough roasted meat to suffice for two meals as a food in its own right, in accordance with the practice of the Persians, then there is a difficulty: **Wasn't it taught** in a *baraita* that **Rabbi Shimon ben Elazar says: One may establish an** ***eiruv*** **for an ill or elderly** person **with** an amount of **food that is enough for him** for two meals, and if he eats less than the average person due to his sickness or age, a smaller amount of food is required in order to establish an *eiruv* on his behalf; **however, for a glutton,** we do not require food in an amount that would satisfy him but merely enough food for two meals measured according to **an average meal for the typical person?** This indicates that the *halakha* with respect to an *eiruv* is lenient and not stringent. The Gemara concludes: Indeed, this is **difficult.**

וּמִי אָמַר רַבִּי שִׁמְעוֹן בֶּן אֶלְעָזָר הָכִי? וְהָתַנְיָא, רַבִּי שִׁמְעוֹן בֶּן אֶלְעָזָר אוֹמֵר: עוֹג מֶלֶךְ הַבָּשָׁן פִּיתְחוֹ כִּמְלוֹאוֹ!

The Gemara raises a difficulty with the aforementioned *baraita*: **Did Rabbi Shimon ben Elazar** really **say this? Wasn't it taught** in another *baraita* pertaining to the laws of ritual impurity that **Rabbi Shimon ben Elazar says: Og, king of the Bashan,** or any similar giant, requires an **opening as** big as **his full size?** If a person dies in a house and it is not clear how his corpse will be removed, all of the openings in the house are considered ritually impure,[N] as the corpse might be carried out through any one of them. If the corpse can fit through some of the openings but not through others, only the larger openings are ritually impure. Rabbi Shimon ben Elazar says that in the case of a giant the size of Og, king of the Bashan, one opening can only prevent the others from contracting impurity the others if it is large enough for Og's corpse to fit through. This indicates that the law is determined by the measure of each particular person and not by some general measure.

וְאַבַּיֵי: הָתָם הֵיכִי לִיעֲבִיד – הַדּוֹמֵי נְהַדְּמֵיהּ, [וְנַפְּקֵיהּ?!]

The Gemara asks: **And** what does **Abaye** say? How does he reconcile his position with regard to an *eiruv*, which maintains that we follow the customary practice of most of the world and not that of particular locales, with Rabbi Shimon ben Elazar's ruling with regard to the corpse of a giant? The Gemara answers: **There,** in the case of a giant, **what should we do? Should we cut** the corpse **into pieces and carry it out?** We have no choice but to carry it out through an opening large enough for the corpse to pass through. However, in the case of the food for the two meals of an *eiruv*, there is no such logistical constraint, and the law should be determined in accordance with the usual practice.

אִיבַּעְיָא לְהוּ: פְּלִיגִי רַבָּנַן עֲלֵיהּ דְּרַבִּי שִׁמְעוֹן בֶּן אֶלְעָזָר, אוֹ לָא? תָּא שְׁמַע, דְּאָמַר רַבָּה בַּר בַּר חָנָה, אָמַר רַבִּי יוֹחָנָן: עוֹג מֶלֶךְ הַבָּשָׁן פִּיתְחוֹ בְּאַרְבָּעָה.

A dilemma was raised before the Sages: **Do the Rabbis disagree with Rabbi Shimon ben Elazar, or not? Come** and **hear** a proof from that which **Rabba bar bar Ḥana said** that **Rabbi Yoḥanan said: Og, king of the Bashan,** requires **an opening of four** handbreadths[H] in order to save the other openings in the house from becoming ritually impure. This indicates that the Rabbis disagree with Rabbi Shimon ben Elazar.

הָתָם דְּאִיכָּא פְּתָחִים קְטַנִּים טוּבָא, וְאִיכָּא חַד דְּהָוֵי אַרְבָּעָה. דְּוַדַּאי כִּי קָא מְרַוַּח – בְּהַהוּא קָא מְרַוַּח.

The Gemara rejects this proof: **There,** we are dealing with a case **where there are many small openings, and there is** only **one that is four** handbreadths wide. Therefore, it may be assumed **with certainty that when one widens** one of the openings in order to remove the corpse from the house, **he will widen that** opening. Consequently, that opening is ritually impure while the others are not. However, if all the openings in the house are equal in size, they are all ritually impure, as we cannot know through which opening the corpse will be carried out.

אָמַר רַב חִיָּיא בַּר רַב אַשִׁי, אָמַר רַב: מְעָרְבִין בְּבָשָׂר חַי. אָמַר רַב שִׁימִי בַּר חִיָּיא: מְעָרְבִין בְּבֵיצִים חַיּוֹת. וְכַמָּה? אָמַר רַב נַחְמָן בַּר יִצְחָק: אַחַת. סִינַי אָמַר: שְׁתַּיִם.

Returning to the laws of *eiruv*, **Rav Ḥiyya bar Rav Ashi said that Rav said: One may establish an *eiruv* with raw meat** because it can be eaten when necessary, even though it is not ordinarily regarded as food. **Rav Shimi bar Ḥiyya said: One may** also **establish an *eiruv* with raw eggs.** The Gemara asks: **How many** eggs are required for an *eiruv*? **Rav Naḥman bar Yitzḥak said: One. Sinai,**[P] a nickname of Rav Yosef, **said: Two.**[H]

״הַנּוֹדֵר מִן הַמָּזוֹן – מוּתָּר בַּמַּיִם כו׳״. מֶלַח וּמַיִם הוּא דְּלָא אִיקְּרִי מָזוֹן, הָא כָּל מִילֵּי אִיקְּרִי מָזוֹן. לֵימָא תֶּיהֱוֵי תְּיוּבְתָּא דְּרַב וּשְׁמוּאֵל, דְּרַב וּשְׁמוּאֵל דְּאָמְרִי תַּרְוַיְיהוּ: אֵין מְבָרְכִין ״בּוֹרֵא מִינֵי מְזוֹנוֹת״ אֶלָּא עַל חֲמֵשֶׁת הַמִּינִין בִּלְבַד.

We learned in the mishna: **One who vows that nourishment** is prohibited to him **is permitted** to eat **water** and salt. The Gemara infers from this: **It is** only **salt and water** that **are not considered nourishment, but all** other food **items are considered nourishment. Let us say** that **this is a refutation of** the position of **Rav and Shmuel. As it was Rav and Shmuel who both said: One only recites the blessing: Who creates** the various **kinds of nourishment, over the five species** of grain **alone,** but not over other types of food.

וְלָא אוֹתְבִינֵיהּ חֲדָא זִימְנָא?! לֵימָא תֶּיהֱוֵי תְּיוּבְתַּיְיהוּ נַמִי מֵהָא!

The Gemara asks a question: **Did we not** already **refute** their position **on one occasion** from a different source? The Gemara answers: Indeed, we already refuted their view, but **let us say** that **there is a refutation of their** position **from here as well.**

אָמַר רַב הוּנָא: בְּאוֹמֵר: ״כָּל הַזָּן עָלַי״, מַיִם וּמֶלַח הוּא דְּלָא זָיְינִי, הָא כָּל מִילֵּי – זָיְינִי.

Rav Huna said: We can resolve the difficulty from the mishna by saying that it is referring to someone who vows and **says: Anything that nourishes** is prohibited **to me.** In that case, **it is water and salt** that are permitted to him, **as they do not nourish, but all** other food **items** are prohibited, as they **do nourish.** This inclusive formulation includes anything that provides even a small degree of nourishment; but the particular term *mazon*, nourishment or sustenance, used in the blessing over food, is reserved only for the five species of grain.[H]

וְהָאָמַר רַבָּה בַּר בַּר חָנָה: כִּי הֲוָה אָזֵילְנָא בָּתְרֵיהּ דְּרַבִּי יוֹחָנָן לְמֵיכַל פֵּירֵי דְּגִינּוֹסַר, כִּי הָוֵינַן בֵּי מְאָה – הֲוָה מְנַקְטִינַן לְכָל חַד וְחַד עֲשָׂרָה עֲשָׂרָה, כִּי הָוֵינַן בֵּי עֲשָׂרָה – הֲוָה מְנַקְטִינַן לְכָל חַד וְחַד מְאָה מְאָה, וְכָל מְאָה מִינַּיְיהוּ (לָא) הָוֵי מַחֲזִיק לְהוּ צַנָּא בַּת תְּלָתָא סָאוֵי. וַהֲוָה אָכֵיל לְהוּ לְכוּלְּהוֹן, וַאֲמַר: שְׁבוּעֲתָא דְּלָא טָעֵים לִי זִיוּנָא! אֵימָא מְזוֹנָא.

The Gemara asks: **Didn't Rabba bar bar Ḥana say: When we were following Rabbi Yoḥanan to eat of the fruits of Genosar,** very sweet fruits that grow in the region of the Sea of Galilee, **when we were** a group **of a hundred** people, **each and every** person **would take ten** fruits; and **when we were** a group **of ten, each and every** person **would take a hundred** fruits for him. **And each hundred of these** fruits **could not fit into a three-*se'a* basket. And** Rabbi Yoḥanan **would eat them all and** then **say: I swear that I have not** yet **tasted something that nourishes.** Didn't we say that only water and salt are excluded from the category of things that nourish? The Gemara corrects the rendition of the story: **Say** that he said as follows: I have not tasted **sustaining food,** but fruit is certainly considered something that nourishes.

אָמַר רַב הוּנָא, אָמַר רַב: ״שְׁבוּעָה שֶׁלֹּא אוֹכַל כִּכָּר זוֹ״ – מְעָרְבִין לוֹ בָּהּ. ״כִּכָּר זוֹ עָלַי״ – אֵין מְעָרְבִין לוֹ בָּהּ.

Rav Huna said that **Rav said:** If one said: **I swear that I shall not eat this loaf, one may** nonetheless **establish an *eiruv* for him with it** because the food used for an *eiruv* does not have to be edible for the particular individual the *eiruv* services. However, if one said: **This loaf** shall be forbidden **to me, one may not establish an *eiruv* for him with it,** as this formulation indicates that he is prohibiting himself to use or benefit from the loaf in any manner.[HN]

מֵיתִיבִי: הַנּוֹדֵר מִן הַכִּכָּר – מְעָרְבִין לוֹ בָּהּ. מַאי לָאו דְּאָמַר ״עָלַי״? לָא, דְּאָמַר ״זוֹ״.

The Gemara **raises an objection** based upon the following *baraita*: With regard to **one who vows** not to benefit **from a loaf, one may** nonetheless **establish an *eiruv* for him with it. What, is it not** referring to one **who said:** This loaf shall be forbidden **to me?** The Gemara answers: **No,** the *baraita* is only is referring to a case **where he said:** I swear that I shall not eat **this** loaf.

הָכִי נַמִי מִסְתַּבְּרָא, דְּקָתָנֵי סֵיפָא: אֵימָתַי – בִּזְמַן שֶׁאָמַר ״שְׁבוּעָה שֶׁלֹּא אֶטְעֲמֶנָּה״.

The Gemara comments: **So too, it is reasonable** to understand the *baraita* in this fashion, **as it was taught in the latter clause: When** do we apply this *halakha*? Only **when one said: I swear that I shall not taste it.**

PERSONALITIES

Sinai – סִינַי: Rav Yosef was given the nickname Sinai in contrast to his colleague, Rabba, who was called: The one who uproots mountains. Sinai denotes one who received the Torah itself, i.e., one who is exceedingly knowledgeable with regard to the *halakha* and whose positions are based on the most authoritative sources. The one who uproots mountains refers to one who employs sharp logical reasoning in deriving halakhic conclusions.

HALAKHA

An *eiruv* of raw eggs – עֵירוּב בְּבֵיצִים חַיּוֹת: One may establish an *eiruv* with raw eggs. Two eggs are required, in accordance with the opinion of Rav Yosef (*Shulḥan Arukh*, *Oraḥ Ḥayyim* 386:7).

What is permitted to one who vows that nourishment is prohibited to him – בַּמֶּה מוּתָּר הַנּוֹדֵר מִן הַמָּזוֹן: One who takes an oath and says: Anything that nourishes should be prohibited to me, is prohibited to eat anything other than water and salt (*Shulḥan Arukh*, *Yoreh De'a* 217:19).

A vow and *eiruv* – נֶדֶר וְעֵירוּב: If one vows that he is prohibited to eat or if he swears not to eat, he may still participate in an *eiruv ḥatzeirot*, a joining of courtyards (Rambam; Rashba). This ruling is not in accordance with the opinion of Rav Huna, since his is a minority opinion (Vilna Gaon). Some authorities rule that if an item is prohibited to a person, he may not use it for the *eiruv ḥatzeirot*. However, he may use it for the *eiruv teḥumin*, the joining of boundaries, which is established in order to enable him to travel for the performance of a mitzva (*Magen Avraham*). If one made the food prohibited by making a vow called a *konam*, in which one gives an item the prohibited status of a sacrificial offering, an *eiruv* may not be established with it because the food now resembles consecrated objects (Rema based on *Tosafot*; *Shulḥan Arukh*, *Oraḥ Ḥayyim* 386:8).

NOTES

A vow and an oath – נֶדֶר וּשְׁבוּעָה: The commentaries disagree whether the accepted distinction between a vow and an oath applies in this context or whether this is a special issue connected to two other disputes: Whether or not *mitzvot* were given for man's benefit, and whether or not an *eiruv* may be established exclusively in order to permit traveling for a purpose that does not constitute a mitzva (see Rashba and Ritva).

The basic difference between an oath [*shevua*] and a vow [*neder*] is as follows: In the case of an oath, one prohibits himself from performing a certain action, but the object itself does not become prohibited, even from his perspective. In the case of a vow, the situation is usually the opposite: One imposes a prohibited status on an object without restricting himself. This difference is particularly significant in cases where an object is utilized for the sake of a mitzva, but one took a vow or an oath not to benefit from it.

NOTES

A vow and consecration – נֶדֶר וְהֶקְדֵּשׁ: The main difference between a vow and consecration is the range of their application. A vow is a type of consecration for the one who took the vow, meaning that for him the prohibition is like that of consecrated objects. However, actual consecrated objects are prohibited to all people and not only to the one who consecrated them.

אֲבָל אָמַר ״עָלַי״ מַאי? הָכִי נַמִי דְּאֵין מְעָרְבִין לוֹ בָּהּ – אִי הָכִי, אַדְּתָנֵי ״כִּכָּר זוֹ הֶקְדֵּשׁ״ – אֵין מְעָרְבִין לוֹ בָּהּ לְפִי שֶׁאֵין מְעָרְבִין בְּהֶקְדֵּשׁוֹת, לִיפְלוֹג וְלִיתְנֵי בְּדִידָהּ: בַּמֶּה דְּבָרִים אֲמוּרִים – דְּאָמַר ״זוֹ״, אֲבָל אָמַר ״עָלַי״ – אֵין מְעָרְבִין לוֹ בָּהּ!

The Gemara asks: **But** if **he said:** This loaf shall be forbidden **to me, what** is the *halakha*? **So too, one may not establish an *eiruv* for him with it.** But **if so,** there is a difficulty. **Instead of teaching** in the continuation of the *baraita* that if one said: **This loaf is consecrated** property, **one may not establish an *eiruv* for him with it, as one may not establish an *eiruv* with consecrated** objects,[N] **let him make** an internal **distinction in the case** of a non-sacred loaf **itself** and state: **In what case is this statement said?** Only where **one said:** I swear that I shall not eat **this** loaf. **But if one said:** This loaf shall be forbidden **to me, one may not establish an *eiruv* for him with it.** This indicates that Rav Huna's understanding of the *baraita* is incorrect.

אָמַר לָךְ רַב הוּנָא: אֶלָּא מַאי, כָּל הֵיכָא דְּאָמַר ״עָלַי״ מְעָרְבִין? קַשְׁיָא רֵישָׁא!

Rav Huna could have **said to you: Rather, what** would you say, that **wherever** one **said:** This loaf shall be forbidden **to me, one may establish an *eiruv*** for him with it? If so, there is **a difficulty** from the **first clause** of the *baraita*, which states: When do we say this? Only when one said: I swear that I shall not taste it. That indicates that if one said: This loaf shall be forbidden to me, one may not establish an *eiruv* for him with it.

חַסּוּרֵי מִיחַסְּרָא וְהָכִי קָתָנֵי: הַנּוֹדֵר מִן הַכִּכָּר – מְעָרְבִין לוֹ בָּהּ, וַאֲפִילּוּ אָמַר ״עָלַי״ נַעֲשֶׂה כְּאוֹמֵר שְׁבוּעָה שֶׁלֹּא אֶטְעָמֶנָּה.

The Gemara answers that the *baraita* **is incomplete, and it teaches the following:** With regard to **one who vows** not to benefit **from a loaf, one may** nonetheless **establish an *eiruv* for him with it. And even if one said:** This loaf shall be forbidden **to me, it is as though he said: I swear that I shall not taste it.** Therefore, the loaf itself is only forbidden to him as food, but he can use it for the purpose of an *eiruv*.

מִכָּל מָקוֹם קַשְׁיָא לְרַב הוּנָא! הוּא דְּאָמַר כְּרַבִּי אֱלִיעֶזֶר. דְּתַנְיָא, רַבִּי אֱלִיעֶזֶר אוֹמֵר: ״שְׁבוּעָה שֶׁלֹּא אוֹכַל כִּכָּר זוֹ״ – מְעָרְבִין לוֹ בָּהּ, ״כִּכָּר זוֹ עָלַי״ – אֵין מְעָרְבִין לוֹ בָּהּ.

The Gemara comments: **Nevertheless,** the **difficulty** remains **according** to the opinion of **Rav Huna.** The Gemara answers: **He stated** his view **in accordance with** the opinion of **Rabbi Eliezer; as it was taught** in a *baraita* that **Rabbi Eliezer says:** If one said: **I swear that I shall not eat this loaf, one may establish an *eiruv* for him with it;** but if he said: **This loaf** shall be forbidden **to me, one may not establish an *eiruv* for him with it.**

וּמִי אָמַר רַבִּי אֱלִיעֶזֶר הָכִי? וְהָתַנְיָא, זֶה הַכְּלָל: אָדָם אוֹסֵר עַצְמוֹ בְּאוֹכֶל – מְעָרְבִין לוֹ בָּהּ, אוֹכֶל הַנֶּאֱסָר לוֹ לָאָדָם – אֵין מְעָרְבִין לוֹ בָּהּ. רַבִּי אֱלִיעֶזֶר אוֹמֵר: ״כִּכָּר זוֹ עָלַי״ – מְעָרְבִין לוֹ בָּהּ, ״כִּכָּר זוֹ הֶקְדֵּשׁ״ – אֵין מְעָרְבִין לוֹ בָּהּ, לְפִי שֶׁאֵין מְעָרְבִין לוֹ בְּהֶקְדֵּשׁוֹת!

The Gemara asks: **Did Rabbi Eliezer** really **say this? Wasn't it taught** in a *baraita*: **This is the principle:** With regard to **a person** who **prohibits himself from** eating a particular **food,** e.g., if one said: I swear that I shall not eat this loaf, **one may establish an *eiruv* for him with** that loaf. However, if the **food was prohibited to a person,** e.g., if he said: This loaf shall be forbidden to me, **one may not establish an *eiruv* for him with it. Rabbi Eliezer says:** If he said: **This loaf** shall be forbidden **to me, one may establish an *eiruv* for him with it.** However, if he said: **This loaf is consecrated** property, **one may not establish an *eiruv* for him with it, as one may not establish an *eiruv* for him with consecrated** objects. Therefore, Rabbi Eliezer does not distinguish between the two differently worded types of vows, but between a vow and consecration.

תְּרֵי תַּנָּאֵי, וְאַלִּיבָּא דְּרַבִּי אֱלִיעֶזֶר.

The Gemara answers: It must be explained that these are **two *tanna'im*** who both held **according to Rabbi Eliezer.** Two later *tanna'im* disagreed with each other in reporting Rabbi Eliezer's opinion.

״מְעָרְבִין לַנָּזִיר בְּיַיִן כו׳״. מַתְנִיתִין דְּלָא כְּבֵית שַׁמַּאי. דְּתַנְיָא, בֵּית שַׁמַּאי אוֹמְרִים: אֵין מְעָרְבִין לַנָּזִיר בְּיַיִן וּלְיִשְׂרָאֵל בִּתְרוּמָה. בֵּית הִלֵּל אוֹמְרִים: מְעָרְבִין לַנָּזִיר בְּיַיִן וּלְיִשְׂרָאֵל בִּתְרוּמָה. אָמְרוּ לָהֶן בֵּית הִלֵּל לְבֵית שַׁמַּאי: אִי אַתֶּם מוֹדִים

We learned in the mishna: **One may establish an *eiruv* for a nazirite with wine**[H] and for an Israelite with *teruma*, even though they themselves may not partake of these foods. The Gemara comments: **The mishna** was **not** taught **in accordance with** the opinion of **Beit Shammai, as it was taught** in a *baraita* that **Beit Shammai say: One may not establish an *eiruv* for a nazirite with wine and for an Israelite with *teruma*. Beit Hillel** disagree and **say: One may establish an *eiruv* for a nazirite with wine and for an Israelite with *teruma*. Beit Hillel said to Beit Shammai: Do you not concede**

HALAKHA

One may establish an *eiruv* for a nazirite with wine, etc. – מְעָרְבִין לַנָּזִיר בְּיַיִן וכו׳: One may establish an *eiruv* for a nazirite with wine and for an Israelite with ritually pure *teruma*. This ruling is as stated in the mishna, in accordance with the opinion of Beit Hillel (*Shulḥan Arukh, Oraḥ Ḥayyim* 386:8).

שֶׁמְּעָרְבִין לַגָּדוֹל בְּיוֹם הַכִּפּוּרִים?

that one may establish an *eiruv* for an adult even **on Yom Kippur,**[N] despite the fact that he may not eat on Yom Kippur? It must be because eating is permitted to a minor.

אָמְרוּ לָהֶן: אֲבָל. אָמְרוּ לָהֶן: כְּשֵׁם שֶׁמְּעָרְבִין לַגָּדוֹל בְּיוֹם הַכִּפּוּרִים, כֵּן מְעָרְבִין לַנָּזִיר בַּיַּיִן וּלְיִשְׂרָאֵל בִּתְרוּמָה.

Beit Shammai **said to them: Indeed** [*aval*],[L] it is so. Beit Hillel **said to them: Just as one may establish an *eiruv* for an adult on Yom Kippur, so too, one may establish an *eiruv* for a nazirite with wine and for an Israelite with *teruma*.**

וּבֵית שַׁמַּאי: הָתָם – אִיכָּא סְעוּדָה הָרְאוּיָה מִבְּעוֹד יוֹם, הָכָא – לֵיכָּא סְעוּדָה הָרְאוּיָה מִבְּעוֹד יוֹם.

And how do **Beit Shammai** explain the difference between these cases? The Gemara explains: **There,** with regard to Yom Kippur, **there is** at least **a meal that was fit** to be eaten by that person **while it was still day,** on the eve of Yom Kippur. **Here,** in the cases of wine for a nazirite and *teruma* for an Israelite, **there is no meal that was fit** to be eaten by them **while it was still day,** on Friday.

כְּמַאן – דְּלָא כַּחֲנַנְיָה. דְּתַנְיָא, חֲנַנְיָה אוֹמֵר: כׇּל עַצְמָן שֶׁל בֵּית שַׁמַּאי לֹא הָיוּ מוֹדִים בָּעֵירוּב, עַד שֶׁיּוֹצִיא מִטָּתוֹ וְכׇל כְּלֵי תַשְׁמִישָׁיו לְשָׁם.

The Gemara asks: **In accordance with whose** opinion was that entire *baraita* stated? It was **not** taught **in accordance with** the opinion of **Ḥananya, as it was taught** in another *baraita* that **Ḥananya says: The whole** view **of Beit Shammai,** i.e., their fundamental position, was that **they did not concede to** the very possibility of **joining** Shabbat borders [*eiruv teḥumin*] by simply placing food in a particular location. Rather, they hold that one's Shabbat residence remains the same **until** he literally moves his residence, such as if **he carries out his bed and his utensils to there,** to a new location.

כְּמַאן אָזְלָא הָא דְּתַנְיָא: עֵירֵב בִּשְׁחוֹרִים – לֹא יֵצֵא בִּלְבָנִים, בִּלְבָנִים – לֹא יֵצֵא בִּשְׁחוֹרִים. כְּמַאן? אָמַר רַב נַחְמָן בַּר יִצְחָק: חֲנַנְיָה הִיא, וְאַלִּיבָּא דְּבֵית שַׁמַּאי.

The Gemara asks: **In accordance with whose** opinion **is** the ruling **that was taught** in the following *baraita*: If **one established an *eiruv* in black** clothing, and Shabbat commenced while he was still dressed those clothes, **he may not go out in white** clothing. If one established the *eiruv* while dressed **in white, he may not go out in black. According to whose** opinion is this *halakha*? **Rav Naḥman bar Yitzḥak said: It is** the opinion of **Ḥananya, and** it is **in accordance with** the opinion of **Beit Shammai.**

וְלַחֲנַנְיָה, בִּשְׁחוֹרִים הוּא דְּלֹא יֵצֵא – הָא בִּלְבָנִים יֵצֵא? הָאָמַר: עַד שֶׁיּוֹצִיא מִטָּתוֹ וּכְלֵי תַשְׁמִישָׁיו לְשָׁם! הָכִי קָאָמַר: עֵירֵב בִּלְבָנִים וְהוּצְרַךְ לִשְׁחוֹרִים – אַף בִּלְבָנִים לֹא יֵצֵא. כְּמַאן? אָמַר רַב נַחְמָן בַּר יִצְחָק: חֲנַנְיָה הִיא, וְאַלִּיבָּא דְּבֵית שַׁמַּאי.

The Gemara asks: **And according to** the opinion of **Ḥananya,** is it **with black** clothing that **he may not go out, but in white** clothing **he may go out? Didn't** Ḥananya **say** that according to Beit Shammai an *eiruv* is not effective at all **until one carries out his bed and his utensils** to the place he wishes to establish as his residence? The Gemara answers: The wording of the *baraita* must be emended and **this is what it said:** If **one established an *eiruv*** while dressed **in white** clothing, **and he needed black** clothing but did not have it with him, **he may not go out even in white** clothing. **In accordance with whose** opinion was this *baraita* taught? **Rav Naḥman bar Yitzḥak said: It is** the opinion of **Ḥananya, and** it is **in accordance with** the opinion of **Beit Shammai.**

״סוּמָכוֹס אוֹמֵר בְּחוּלִּין״. וְאִילּוּ לַנָּזִיר בַּיַּיִן לָא פָּלֵיג, מַאי טַעְמָא – אֶפְשָׁר דְּמִתְשִׁיל אַנְּזִירוּתֵיהּ.

We learned in the mishna: **Summakhos** disagrees and **says:** One may not establish an *eiruv* for an Israelite with *teruma*, but only **with** regular, **non-sacred** food items. The Gemara notes: **But** with regard to the mishna's ruling that an *eiruv* may be established for **a nazirite with wine,** Summakhos **does not** appear to **disagree. What is the reason** for the distinction? The Gemara explains: A nazirite **can ask** a Sage to annul his vow and release him from **his nazirite status,**[N] and then he himself will be able to drink the wine.

אִי הָכִי תְּרוּמָה נַמִי אֶפְשָׁר דְּמִיתְשִׁיל עִילָּוֵיהּ! אִי מִתְשִׁיל עֲלָהּ – הָדְרָא לְטִיבְלָא.

The Gemara asks: **If so,** in the case of ***teruma* as well, one can ask** a Sage to annul **its** status. *Teruma* is consecrated through a verbal declaration by the one separating it, and that declaration, like other consecrations and vows, can be nullified by a Sage. The Gemara answers: Such a course of action would not help. **If one asks** a Sage to annul his declaration that turned the produce into *teruma*, the produce **will return to** its status as ***tevel***, produce from which the requisite dues and tithes were not separated, and he will still be prohibited to consume it.

NOTES

That one may establish an *eiruv* for an adult on Yom Kippur – שֶׁמְּעָרְבִין לַגָּדוֹל בְּיוֹם הַכִּפּוּרִים: It is unclear why Beit Hillel originally thought that Beit Shammai would agree in this case. Some commentaries explain that the question is actually referring to the laws of the joining of courtyards [*eiruv ḥatzeirot*], as certainly Beit Hillel and Beit Shammai agree that it is permissible to join courtyards for Yom Kippur, even though eating is prohibited (*Shem MiShimon*). Beit Shammai's answer, that the food is fit to be eaten before Yom Kippur, indicates that they do not accept the view that the laws of affliction that apply to Yom Kippur, including the prohibition of eating, begin before nightfall according to Torah law. If it were prohibited to eat before nightfall, the *eiruv* would not be valid according to Beit Shammai, even according to the opinion that an *eiruv* takes effect at the end of the day (see Rashba; Ritva).

Can ask to be released from his nazirite status – מִתְשִׁיל אַנְּזִירוּתֵיהּ: One may ask a Sage to annul a vow, oath, or consecration. One expresses regret at having made the vow or oath or at having consecrated certain items and asks the Sage to annul his statements. A vow that has been annulled is regarded as though it had never existed.

LANGUAGE

Indeed [*aval*] – אֲבָל: Generally used by the Sages to mean but or although. However, its biblical meaning is not entirely clear. In the language of the Sages, there are instances in which the word has a different connotation, e.g., indeed, or in truth. The same is true in the Aramaic translation of the Bible, in the few cases where this word appears in the Bible. According to its use in this context, the word is closely related to the Arabic بلى, *balā*, which also means indeed or in truth.

NOTES

Ḥaverim are not suspected of separating *teruma* from produce not situated near the produce – לֹא נֶחְשְׁדוּ חֲבֵירִים לִתְרוֹם שֶׁלֹּא מִן הַמּוּקָף: This statement should have been formulated as follows: It is prohibited to separate produce as *teruma* if it is not adjacent to the produce it comes to exempt. However, the phrase that is used in this context is different because it was the common rabbinic expression (Ritva). Separating *teruma* in this manner is prohibited because the produce it comes to exempt might have been lost, in which case the separation of the *teruma* does not take effect (Rashi).

What makes it necessary – וּמַאי פָּסְקָא: This expression is used where it is necessary to explain that a statement is referring to a unique and rare set of circumstances, even though there is no support whatsoever for this explanation in the formulation of the statement. In this case, the Gemara has explained that there is exactly the necessary amount of food that can be used for an *eiruv*. There is not even a single extra kernel of grain, which is the absolute minimum that one must separate as *teruma*. Since such a circumstance is clearly rare and surprising, the Gemara asks: Why it is necessary to claim that this is the case under discussion?

All in accordance with the particular person involved – הַכֹּל לְפִי מַה שֶּׁהוּא אָדָם: The required measure is reduced according to the size or eating habits of a person who is smaller or eats less than the average. However, a person who is bigger or eats more than average does not need to increase the measure in accordance with his size (*Ḥatam Sofer*).

HALAKHA

The amount required for an *eiruv* for different people – שִׁיעוּר עֵירוּב לַאֲנָשִׁים שׁוֹנִים: One may establish an *eiruv* for an invalid or for an elderly person with an amount of food that is enough for him. However, a glutton does not require more than two average meals for the typical person. This law is accepted by the *Shulḥan Arukh* and by all of the commentaries and halakhic authorities, in accordance with the opinion of Rabbi Shimon ben Elazar and the unattributed mishna in tractate *Kelim* (*Shulḥan Arukh, Oraḥ Ḥayyim* 409:7).

A priest in a *beit haperas* – כֹּהֵן בְּבֵית הַפְּרָס: One may establish an *eiruv* for a priest in a *beit haperas*. Although he is prohibited to enter such a field *ab initio*, since he may go there in times of need, the Sages allowed it (*Shulḥan Arukh, Oraḥ Ḥayyim* 409:7).

A person may blow on the dust in a *beit haperas* – מְנַפֵּחַ אָדָם בֵּית הַפְּרָס: One who has to pass through a *beit haperas* may blow upon the ground before each step. If he does not find a bone the size of a grain of barley, he retains his ritual purity and may offer the Paschal lamb. In addition, if the ground in a *beit haperas* is well-trodden, those who pass through it are permitted to offer the Paschal lamb. In the case of an obligation involving *karet*, like the offering of the Paschal lamb, the Sages were not strict with regard to the ritually impure status of a *beit haperas* (Rambam *Sefer Korbanot, Hilkhot Korban Pesaḥ* 6:8).

וְלִיפְרוֹשׁ עֲלָהּ מִמָּקוֹם אַחֵר! לֹא נֶחְשְׁדוּ חֲבֵירִים לִתְרוֹם שֶׁלֹּא מִן הַמּוּקָף.

The Gemara asks: **Let him separate *teruma* for** that produce **from** produce located **somewhere else** and thus permit it to be eaten. The Gemara answers: ***Ḥaverim*,** members of a group dedicated to the precise observance of mitzvot, **are not suspected of separating *teruma*** from produce that is **not** situated **near** the produce[N] it comes to exempt, as this is prohibited *ab initio*.

וְלִפְרוֹשׁ עֲלָהּ מִינֵּיהּ וּבֵיהּ! דְּלֵית בָּהּ שִׁיעוּרָא.

The Gemara asks: **Let him separate *teruma* from** the produce used for the *eiruv* **itself** and consequently permit the rest of the produce to be eaten. The Gemara answers: We are dealing with a case **where,** after removing *teruma*, **it would not contain the amount** required for an *eiruv*, i.e., one would be left with less than the quantity of food sufficient for two meals.

וּמַאי פָּסְקָא? אֶלָּא סוּמְכוֹס סָבַר לַהּ כְּרַבָּנַן, דְּאָמְרִי: כָּל דָּבָר שֶׁהוּא מִשּׁוּם שְׁבוּת – גָּזְרוּ עָלָיו בֵּין הַשְּׁמָשׁוֹת.

The Gemara asks: **What** makes it **necessary**[N] to say that the mishna is referring to this very unique case? **Rather,** we must retract all that was stated above and say as follows: **Summakhos agrees with** the opinion of **the Rabbis, who say: Anything that is** prohibited on Shabbat **due to a rabbinic decree** [***shevut***], the Sages **issued the decree** to apply even **during twilight.** Even though this period is of questionable status with regard to whether it is day or night, the Shabbat restrictions instituted by the Sages apply then as they do on Shabbat itself. Consequently, since it is prohibited to separate *teruma* on Shabbat, it is prohibited during the twilight period as well. Therefore, during twilight, when the *eiruv* would go into effect, it is impossible to cause it to become permitted to an Israelite.

כְּמַאן אָזְלָא הָא דִּתְנַן: יֵשׁ שֶׁאָמְרוּ הַכֹּל לְפִי מַה שֶּׁהוּא אָדָם: מְלֹא קוּמְצוֹ מִנְחָה, וּמְלֹא חׇפְנָיו קְטֹרֶת, וְהַשּׁוֹתֶה מְלֹא לוּגְמָיו בְּיוֹם הַכִּפּוּרִים, וּבִמְזוֹן שְׁתֵּי סְעוּדּוֹת לְעֵירוּב. כְּמַאן? אָמַר רַבִּי זֵירָא: סוּמְכוֹס הִיא, דְּאָמַר: מַאי דַּחֲזֵי לֵיהּ בָּעֵינַן.

The Gemara now asks: **In accordance with whose** opinion **is** the ruling **that we learned** in the following mishna: **There are** *halakhot* with regard to which **they stated** that measures **are all in accordance with the** particular **person** involved,[N] e.g, **the handful of** flour that a priest scoops out from **a meal-offering, and the handfuls of incense** the High Priest would offer on Yom Kippur, **and one who drinks a cheekful on Yom Kippur, and with regard to the** measure of **two meals'** worth of **nourishment for an *eiruv*.** All these measures are determined by the particular individual involved. **In accordance with whose** opinion is this *halakha*? **Rabbi Zeira said: It is** in accordance with the opinion of **Summakhos, who said: We require that which is fit for him,** the particular individual, and we do not follow a standard measure.

לֵימָא פְּלִיגָא אַדְּרַבִּי שִׁמְעוֹן בֶּן אֶלְעָזָר; דְּתַנְיָא, רַבִּי שִׁמְעוֹן בֶּן אֶלְעָזָר אוֹמֵר: מְעָרְבִין לְחוֹלֶה וְלַזָּקֵן כְּדֵי מְזוֹנוֹ, וְלָרַעַבְתָּן בִּסְעוּדָּה בֵּינוֹנִית שֶׁל כׇּל אָדָם!

The Gemara suggests: **Let us say** that the aforementioned mishna **disagrees with** the opinion of **Rabbi Shimon ben Elazar. As it was taught** in a *baraita*: **Rabbi Shimon ben Elazar says: One may establish an *eiruv* for an ill or elderly** person **with** an amount of **food that is enough for him** for two meals; and if he eats less than the average amount due to his sickness or age, a smaller amount of food is sufficient. **But for a glutton** we do not require food in an amount that would satisfy him; we measure on the basis of **an average meal for the typical person.**[H]

תַּרְגּוּמָא אַחוֹלֶה וְזָקֵן, אֲבָל רַעַבְתָּן – בָּטְלָה דַּעְתּוֹ אֵצֶל כׇּל אָדָם.

The Gemara answers: When the mishna says that the measure of food for two meals is determined by the particular person involved, **interpret** that as referring to **an ill or elderly** person. **But** with regard to **a glutton,** we do not determine the measure of food by his standard for a different reason, namely because **his opinion is rendered irrelevant by the opinions of all other people.** Therefore, there is no reason to be stringent with him and determine the measure according to his particular needs.

״וּלְכֹהֵן בְּבֵית הַפְּרָס״. דְּאָמַר רַב יְהוּדָה, אָמַר שְׁמוּאֵל: מְנַפֵּחַ אָדָם בֵּית הַפְּרָס וְהוֹלֵךְ. רַבִּי יְהוּדָה בַּר אַמֵּי מִשְּׁמֵיהּ דְּרַב יְהוּדָה אָמַר: בֵּית הַפְּרָס שֶׁנִּידַּשׁ טָהוֹר.

We learned in the mishna: One may establish an *eiruv* **for a priest in a *beit haperas*,**[H] an area in which there is doubt concerning the location of a grave or a corpse. The Gemara explains that the reason for this is as **Rav Yehuda said** that **Shmuel said:** In a time of need **a person may blow** on the dust in a ***beit haperas***[H] before taking each step, so that if there is a bone beneath the dust he will expose it and avoid it, **and** he may thus **walk** across the area. Similarly, **Rabbi Yehuda bar Ami said in the name of Rav Yehuda: A *beit haperas* that has been trodden** underfoot, creating a path, **is pure,** as we assume that it no longer contains any bones as large as a kernel of barley. Both of these statements indicate that the ritual impurity of a *beit haperas* is a stringency decreed by the Sages. Therefore, since there is a way to avoid becoming ritually impure there, even a priest may place his *eiruv* in a *beit haperas*.

״רַבִּי יְהוּדָה אוֹמֵר אַף בֵּית הַקְּבָרוֹת״. תָּנָא: מִפְּנֵי שֶׁיָּכוֹל לָחוֹץ, וְלֵילֵךְ בְּשִׁידָּה תֵּיבָה וּמִגְדָּל. קָא סָבַר: אֹהֶל זָרוּק שְׁמֵיהּ אֹהֶל.

We learned in the mishna that **Rabbi Yehuda says:** An *eiruv* may be established for a priest **even** in **a cemetery,** an area which the priest may not enter by Torah law. **It was taught:** This is permitted **because** the priest **can interpose and walk** between the graves inside **a carriage, a crate, or a cupboard.** These containers do not contract impurity because of their large size, and anything found inside of them remains pure. From here we see that **he holds** the following: **A moving tent[N] is called a tent,** and therefore the carriage, box, or cupboard are also considered tents. They shield a person carried in them from the impurity imparted by the graves in a cemetery.

וּבִפְלוּגְתָּא דְּהָנֵי תַּנָּאֵי; דְּתַנְיָא: הַנִּכְנָס לְאֶרֶץ הָעַמִּים בְּשִׁידָּה תֵּיבָה וּמִגְדָּל, רַבִּי מְטַמֵּא, רַבִּי יוֹסֵי בְּרַבִּי יְהוּדָה מְטַהֵר.

The Gemara notes that this matter is the subject of **a dispute between the following *tanna'im*, as it was taught** in a *baraita*: With regard to **one who enters the land of the nations,** i.e., any territory outside Eretz Yisrael, not on foot, but **in a carriage, a crate, or a cupboard,[H] Rabbi** Yehuda HaNasi **renders** him ritually **impure. Rabbi Yosei, son of Rabbi Yehuda, renders** him **pure.**

בְּמַאי קָמִיפַּלְגִי? מָר סָבַר: אֹהֶל זָרוּק – לָאו שְׁמֵיהּ אֹהֶל, וּמָר סָבַר: אֹהֶל זָרוּק – שְׁמֵיהּ אֹהֶל.

The Gemara explains: **With regard to what do they disagree? One Sage,** Rabbi Yehuda HaNasi, **holds** that **a moving tent is not called a tent.** The principle is that only something fixed can shield against ritual impurity, but if one is situated inside a portable vessel, the vessel contracts impurity and he becomes impure along with it. **And the other Sage,** Rabbi Yosei, son of Rabbi Yehuda, **holds** that **a moving tent is called a tent,** and it shields the person inside from contracting ritual impurity.

וְהָא דְּתַנְיָא, רַבִּי יְהוּדָה אוֹמֵר:

And with regard to **that which was taught** in a *baraita*: **Rabbi Yehuda says:**

NOTES

Moving tent – אֹהֶל זָרוּק: Any wooden vessel with a volume larger than forty *se'a* does not contract ritual impurity. Instead, it acts as a barrier against impurity and has the status of a tent. Therefore, if a corpse is located within it, anything situated underneath it contracts ritual impurity. In this context, the dispute is whether or not a portable item can be considered a tent (*Tosafot*).

HALAKHA

One who enters the land of the nations in a carriage, a crate, or a cupboard – הַנִּכְנָס לְאֶרֶץ הָעַמִּים בְּשִׁידָּה תֵּיבָה וּמִגְדָּל: One who enters a country outside of Eretz Yisrael in a carriage, crate, or cupboard is ritually impure. A moving tent is not called a tent, since the *halakha* is ruled in accordance with the opinion of Rabbi Yehuda HaNasi when he disagrees with his colleagues (Rambam *Sefer Tahara*, *Hilkhot Tumat Met* 11:5).

Perek **III**
Daf **31** Amud **a**

מְעָרְבִין לְכֹהֵן טָהוֹר בִּתְרוּמָה טְהוֹרָה בַּקֶּבֶר. הֵיכִי אָזֵיל – בְּשִׁידָּה תֵּיבָה וּמִגְדָּל.

One may establish an *eiruv* for a priest who is ritually **pure with *teruma* that is** ritually **pure** and resting **on a grave,** even though the location is impure and he cannot reach it. **How does he go** there? **In a carriage, crate, or cupboard,** which shield him from the ritual impurity.

וְהָא כֵּיוָן דְּאַחְתָּא אִיטַּמְיָא לָהּ! בְּשֶׁלֹּא הוּכְשְׁרָה, אוֹ שֶׁנִּילוֹשָׁה בְּמֵי פֵּירוֹת.

The Gemara asks: **Isn't** it true that **once** the *eiruv* **was placed** directly on the grave, the *teruma* **became defiled,** and ritually impure *teruma* is not fit to be eaten by anyone? The Gemara answers: We are dealing here with a case **where** the *teruma* **had not yet been rendered susceptible** to ritual impurity,[N] as it had not yet come into contact with a liquid. Produce that has yet to come into contact with a liquid does not contract impurity. **Or** we are dealing with bread **that was kneaded with fruit juice,** which is not one of the seven liquids that render a food susceptible to ritual impurity.

וְהֵיכִי מַיְיתֵי לָהּ? בִּפְשׁוּטֵי כְּלֵי עֵץ דְּלָא מְקַבְּלֵי טוּמְאָה.

The Gemara now asks: **How can he bring it** from where it is resting on the grave in order to eat it? The Gemara answers: **With flat wooden utensils** that are not shaped as receptacles and therefore **do not contract** ritual **impurity.**

וְהָא קָא מַאֲהִיל! דְּמַיְיתֵי לָהּ אַחוֹרֵיהּ.

The Gemara asks: **Doesn't** the utensil **cover** the grave? The Sages decreed that anyone who holds a utensil that is a handbreadth wide over a corpse or grave is ritually impure. The Gemara answers: **He may bring it on the edge[N]** of the utensil while holding the utensil sideways so that it does not form a cover that is a handbreadth wide over the grave.

אִי הָכִי מַאי טַעְמָא דְּרַבָּנַן? קָסָבְרִי: אָסוּר לִקְנוֹת בַּיִת בְּאִיסּוּרֵי הֲנָאָה.

The Gemara asks: **If** that is **so,** and there is a way for the *teruma* to remain ritually pure and for the priest to access it, **what is the reason** the Sages disagreed with Rabbi Yehuda and did not allow an *eiruv* to be established for a priest on a grave? The Gemara answers: **They hold** that **it is prohibited to acquire a home with items from which benefit is prohibited.** It is prohibited to derive benefit from a grave. Since one acquires a place of residence for Shabbat by means of the *eiruv*, it would be as if the priest acquired a home for himself with something from which he may not derive benefit.

NOTES

Had not yet been rendered susceptible to ritual impurity – בְּשֶׁלֹּא הוּכְשְׁרָה: The Torah states: "Of all food that may be eaten, that upon which water comes, shall be unclean" (Leviticus 11:34). Food that has not yet come into contact with water is not susceptible to ritual impurity. Therefore, even if it comes into contact with something that is ritually impure at any level of ritual impurity, the food itself does not become impure. The Sages had a tradition that the word water stated in the Torah in this context includes other liquids as well: Dew, wine, oil, blood, honey, and milk. Contact with any one of these liquids causes food to become susceptible to ritual impurity. However, dough kneaded with the juice of fruits other than olives or grapes does not become susceptible to ritual impurity.

He may bring it on the edge – דְּמַיְיתֵי לָהּ אַחוֹרֵיהּ: The Jerusalem Talmud explains that in this case one creates a hole in a carriage, crate, or cupboard and brings the *teruma* inside by means of thin wooden chips or poles. A wooden utensil that is less than a handbreadth wide does not contract impurity inside a tent. In addition, a wooden utensil that cannot serve as a receptacle does not contract impurity, even through contact with a ritually impure object.

מִכְּלָל דְּרַבִּי יְהוּדָה סָבַר: מוּתָּר?! קָסָבַר: מִצְוֹת לָאו לֵיהָנוֹת נִיתְּנוּ.

The Gemara asks: If so, does this prove **by inference that Rabbi Yehuda holds** that **it is permitted** to acquire a home with items from which benefit is prohibited? The Gemara answers: Rabbi Yehuda **holds** that **mitzvot were not given for benefit.**[N] The fulfillment of a mitzva is not in itself considered a benefit. Since the acquisition of a place of residence by means of an *eiruv* is a mitzva, as one may establish an *eiruv teḥumin* only for the sake of a mitzva, it is even permitted to establish one's *eiruv* in a place from which it is prohibited to benefit.

אֶלָּא הָא דַּאֲמַר רָבָא: מִצְוֹת לָאו לֵיהָנוֹת נִיתְּנוּ, לֵימָא כְּתַנָּאֵי אֲמָרָהּ לִשְׁמַעְתֵּיהּ? אָמַר לָךְ רָבָא: אִי סְבִירָא לְהוּ דְּאֵין מְעָרְבִין אֶלָּא לִדְבַר מִצְוָה – דְּכוּלֵּי עָלְמָא מִצְוֹת לָאו לֵיהָנוֹת נִיתְּנוּ. וְהָכָא בְּהָא קָמִיפַּלְגִי; מָר סָבַר: אֵין מְעָרְבִין אֶלָּא לִדְבַר מִצְוָה, וּמָר סָבַר: מְעָרְבִין אֲפִילּוּ לִדְבַר הָרְשׁוּת.

The Gemara suggests: **But** if so, with regard to **that which Rava said: Mitzvot were not given for benefit, let us say** that **he stated his** ***halakha*** only **in accordance with** the opinion of one side in a dispute between ***tanna'im***. The Gemara answers that **Rava** could have **said to you: If they hold that one may establish an** ***eiruv*** **only for the sake of a mitzva, all would agree** that the *eiruv* may be placed on a grave because **mitzvot were not given for benefit.** However, the dispute between Rabbi Yehuda and the Sages centers on a different aspect of the issue. **Here, they disagree with regard to this: One Sage**, Rabbi Yehuda, **holds: One may establish an** ***eiruv*** **only for the sake of a mitzva.**[N] Since mitzvot do not constitute forbidden benefit, it is therefore permitted to make use of the grave. **And one Sage**, i.e., the Rabbis, **holds: One may establish an** ***eiruv*** **even for a voluntary matter.** Establishing a Shabbat residence on the site of a grave by means of an *eiruv* made for a voluntary matter is regarded as forbidden benefit, and therefore it is prohibited.

אֶלָּא הָא דְּאָמַר רַב יוֹסֵף: אֵין מְעָרְבִין אֶלָּא לִדְבַר מִצְוָה – לֵימָא כְּתַנָּאֵי אֲמָרָהּ לִשְׁמַעְתֵּיהּ?

The Gemara suggests: **But** if so, with regard to **that which Rav Yosef said** as a general principle: **One may establish an** ***eiruv*** **only for the sake of a mitzva, let us say** that **he stated his** ***halakha*** **in accordance with** one side in a dispute between the ***tanna'im***.

אָמַר לָךְ רַב יוֹסֵף: דְּכוּלֵּי עָלְמָא אֵין מְעָרְבִין אֶלָּא לִדְבַר מִצְוָה, וּדְכוּלֵּי עָלְמָא מִצְוֹת לָאו לֵיהָנוֹת נִיתְּנוּ, וּבְהָא קָמִיפַּלְגִי; מָר סָבַר: כֵּיוָן דִּקְנָה לֵיהּ עֵירוּב – לָא נִיחָא לֵיהּ דְּמִינְטְרָא, וּמָר סָבַר: נִיחָא לֵיהּ דְּמִינְטְרָא, דְּאִי אִיצְטְרִיךְ אָכֵיל לֵיהּ.

The Gemara answers: **Rav Yosef** could have **said to you:** In fact, **all agree** that **one may establish an** ***eiruv*** **only for the sake of a mitzva, and all agree** that **mitzvot were not given for benefit, and they disagree with regard to this: One Sage**, Rabbi Yehuda, **holds: Once** he **acquired his** Shabbat residence at twilight by means of the ***eiruv***, **he is indifferent to its safeguarding**, as his main goal has already been achieved. He has no further need for the food used for the *eiruv*, and therefore, he receives no benefit from its placement on the grave. **And one Sage**, i.e., the Rabbis, **holds: It is pleasing to him that** the *eiruv* **is safeguarded, for if he needs** it the next day, **he can eat it.** According to this opinion, he would be making prohibited use of the grave to preserve his meal for the following day, and therefore the Sages prohibited placing an *eiruv* on a grave.[H]

מתני׳ מְעָרְבִין בִּדְמַאי, וּבְמַעֲשֵׂר רִאשׁוֹן שֶׁנִּטְּלָה תְּרוּמָתוֹ, וּבְמַעֲשֵׂר שֵׁנִי וְהֶקְדֵּשׁ שֶׁנִּפְדּוּ, וְהַכֹּהֲנִים בְּחַלָּה.

MISHNA **One may establish an** ***eiruv*** **with** ***demai***,[H] produce purchased from one who may not have separated the required tithes, **and** similarly, one may establish an *eiruv* **with** the **first tithe whose** ***teruma*** **has been taken** in order to be given to a priest, **and with** the **second tithe and consecrated articles that have been redeemed; and priests** may establish an *eiruv* **with** ***ḥalla***, the portion of dough that must be given to a priest.

אֲבָל לֹא בְּטֶבֶל, וְלֹא בְּמַעֲשֵׂר רִאשׁוֹן שֶׁלֹּא נִטְּלָה תְּרוּמָתוֹ, וְלֹא בְּמַעֲשֵׂר שֵׁנִי וְהֶקְדֵּשׁ שֶׁלֹּא נִפְדּוּ.

However, one may **not** establish an *eiruv* **with** ***tevel***, produce from which the priestly dues [*teruma*] and other tithes have not been separated, **nor with first tithe whose** ***teruma***, which must be given to a priest, **has not been taken, nor with** the **second tithe or consecrated articles that have not been redeemed.**

גמ׳ ״דְּמַאי״, הָא לָא חֲזֵי לֵיהּ! מִיגּוֹ דְּאִי בָּעֵי מַפְקַר לְהוּ לְנִכְסֵיהּ וְהָוֵי עָנִי, וַחֲזוּ לֵיהּ – הָשְׁתָּא נַמִי חֲזֵי לֵיהּ. דִּתְנַן: מַאֲכִילִין אֶת הָעֲנִיִּים דְּמַאי

GEMARA The Gemara asks: How can one establish an *eiruv* with ***demai***? **Isn't it unfit for him?**[N] Since it is prohibited to eat *demai*, how can it be used as an *eiruv*? The Gemara answers: **Since if he wants, he could declare his property ownerless, and he would be a poor** person, and the *demai* would then **be fit for him**, as a poor person is permitted to eat *demai*, **now too**, even though he has not renounced ownership of his property, **it is** considered **fit for him** to use as an *eiruv*. **As we learned** in a mishna: **One may feed the poor** ***demai***,

NOTES

Mitzvot were not given for benefit – מִצְוֹת לָאו לֵיהָנוֹת נִיתְּנוּ: The accepted ruling is that the fulfillment of mitzvot cannot be seen as a source of benefit, as Rashi says: They were not given to the Jewish people for benefit; rather, they were given as a yoke on their necks. Consequently, the prohibition against benefiting from a particular object does not prevent it from being used in the fulfillment of a mitzva. It is in cases such as the one described here that there is cause for concern, because a separate benefit exists, namely the establishment of an *eiruv teḥumin*, that is separate from the fulfillment of the mitzva which motivated him to establish the *eiruv*.

One may establish an ***eiruv*** **for the sake of a mitzva** – מְעָרְבִין לִדְבַר מִצְוָה: The term mitzva here is not limited to mitzvot mentioned explicitly in the Torah. It includes any activity related to a mitzva, the public good, or saving a life or property.

Demai**, isn't it unfit for him** – דְּמַאי הָא לָא חֲזֵי לֵיהּ: The commentaries explain (see *Tosafot*) that the Gemara is interpreting the mishna in accordance with all views, including that of Summakhos, since he does not disagree here. According to the opinion that one may establish an *eiruv* with something that is fit to be eaten by another person, it is acceptable to establish and eiruv with *demai*. Even though *demai* is unfit for the one establishing the *eiruv*, it is fit for someone else.

HALAKHA

An ***eiruv*** **in a cemetery** – עֵירוּב בְּבֵית הַקְּבָרוֹת: An *eiruv* may not be placed in a cemetery, as it is prohibited to derive benefit from graves. Even though mitzvot were not given for benefit, the person making the *eiruv* intends for the food to remain at this location should he need it the next day; therefore, it is prohibited to leave it there. The *halakha* is in accordance with the opinion of the Rabbis as clarified by the Gemara (*Shulḥan Arukh, Oraḥ Ḥayyim* 409:1).

One may establish an ***eiruv*** **with** ***demai*** – מְעָרְבִין בִּדְמַאי: One is permitted to establish an *eiruv* with *demai*, since it is fit to be eaten by a poor person (Rambam *Sefer Zemanim, Hilkhot Eiruvin* 1:15).

וְאֶת אַכְסַנְיָא דְּמַאי.

and one may also feed **soldiers** ***demai*****.**

אָמַר רַב הוּנָא: תָּנָא, בֵּית שַׁמַּאי אוֹמְרִים: אֵין מַאֲכִילִין אֶת הָעֲנִיִּים דְּמַאי, וּבֵית הִלֵּל אוֹמְרִים: מַאֲכִילִין אֶת הָעֲנִיִּים דְּמַאי.

Rav Huna said: It was taught that **Beit Shammai say: One may not feed the impoverished** ***demai*****. And Beit Hillel say: One may feed the impoverished** ***demai*****.** The *halakha* is in accordance with the opinion of Beit Hillel.

״וּבְמַעֲשֵׂר רִאשׁוֹן שֶׁנִּטְּלָה כו׳״. פְּשִׁיטָא! לָא צְרִיכָא שֶׁהִקְדִּימוֹ בְּשִׁבֳּלִין, וְנִטְּלָה מִמֶּנּוּ תְּרוּמַת מַעֲשֵׂר וְלֹא נִטְּלָה מִמֶּנּוּ תְּרוּמָה גְּדוֹלָה.

We learned in the mishna: One may establish an *eiruv* **with first tithe** whose *teruma* **has been taken.** The Gemara expresses surprise: **It is obvious** that if the *teruma* was already taken there is no problem. Why is it necessary to state it may be used for an *eiruv*? The Gemara answers: **It is only necessary** to teach this *halakha* in a case where the Levite **preceded** the priest while the grain was still **on the stalks,** i.e., the Levite took his tithe before the grain was threshed and before the priest took the *teruma*; **and the** ***teruma*** **of the tithes was taken from it** but ***teruma gedola*** **was not taken from it.** Therefore, since the *teruma* is generally separated first, a portion of the first tithe that the Levite took should have been separated as *teruma*.

וְכִדְרַבִּי אַבָּהוּ אָמַר רֵישׁ לָקִישׁ, דְּאָמַר רַבִּי אַבָּהוּ אָמַר רֵישׁ לָקִישׁ: מַעֲשֵׂר רִאשׁוֹן שֶׁהִקְדִּימוֹ בְּשִׁבֳּלִין – פָּטוּר מִתְּרוּמָה גְּדוֹלָה. שֶׁנֶּאֱמַר: ״וַהֲרֵמוֹתֶם מִמֶּנּוּ תְּרוּמַת ה׳ מַעֲשֵׂר מִן הַמַּעֲשֵׂר״, מַעֲשֵׂר מִן הַמַּעֲשֵׂר אָמַרְתִּי לָךְ, וְלֹא תְּרוּמָה גְּדוֹלָה וּתְרוּמַת מַעֲשֵׂר מִן הַמַּעֲשֵׂר!

And this is **in accordance with** the opinion that **Rabbi Abbahu** said that **Reish Lakish said, as Rabbi Abbahu said** that **Reish Lakish said: First tithe,** in a case **where** the Levite **preceded** the priest while the grain was still **on the stalks,**[H] **is exempt from** ***teruma gedola*****, as it is stated: "And you shall set apart from it a gift for the Lord, even a tenth part of the tithe"** (Numbers 18:26), from which the following inference is made: **A tenth part of the tithe,** i.e., the *teruma* of the tithe, **I told you,** the Levite, to separate. **And** I did **not** tell you to separate ***teruma gedola*** **and the** ***teruma*** **of the tithe.**

אָמַר לֵיהּ רַב פָּפָּא לְאַבָּיֵי: אִי הָכִי אֲפִילּוּ הִקְדִּימוֹ בִּכְרִי נָמֵי! אָמַר לֵיהּ: עָלֶיךָ אָמַר קְרָא: ״מִכֹּל מַעְשְׂרוֹתֵיכֶם תָּרִימוּ אֵת כָּל תְּרוּמַת ה׳״.

With regard to this matter, **Rav Pappa said to Abaye: If so, even** if the Levite **preceded** the priest after the kernels of grain were removed from the stalks and placed **in a pile,** the Levite should still not have to separate *teruma gedola*. Abaye **said to him: With regard to your** claim, **the verse states: "From all that is given to you, you shall set apart that which is the Lord's** ***teruma*****"** (Numbers 18:29). The inclusive phrase "from all" indicates that *teruma gedola* must be separated even from the first tithe in the case where the Levite precedes the priest after the grain has been collected in a pile.

וּמָה רָאִיתָ? הַאי אִידְגַן, וְהַאי – לָא אִידְגַן.

Rav Pappa asks: **And what did you see** that led you to expound one verse as exempting the Levite from separating *teruma gedola* from first tithe that has been separated while the grain was on the stalks, and to expound another verse as requiring *teruma gedola* to be separated when the Levite took his first tithe after the grain was collected in a pile? Abaye answers: **This** produce, which has been threshed and placed into piles, is completely processed and **has become grain,**[N] **and that** produce, which remained on the stalks, **did not** yet **become grain.** The wording of the biblical verses indicates that the requirement to separate *teruma* applies only to grain, whereas the produce is not considered grain until it has been threshed.

״וּבְמַעֲשֵׂר שֵׁנִי וְהֶקְדֵּשׁ שֶׁנִּפְדּוּ״. פְּשִׁיטָא! לָא צְרִיכָא, שֶׁנָּתַן אֶת הַקֶּרֶן וְלֹא נָתַן אֶת הַחוֹמֶשׁ. וְקָא מַשְׁמַע לַן: דְּאֵין הַחוֹמֶשׁ מְעַכֵּב.

The mishna also stated that one may establish an *eiruv* **with** the **second tithe and consecrated** food **that have been redeemed.** The Gemara asks: **It is obvious** that these foods may be used to establish an *eiruv*. The Gemara answers: This ruling **was only needed** for a case **where one** redeemed the second tithe or consecrated food and **paid the principle but did not pay the** additional **fifth** of their value, which must be paid when they are redeemed. **And** the mishna **teaches us** that the failure to pay **the** additional **fifth does not invalidate** the redemption. Once the principle is paid, even if payment of the additional fifth is still outstanding, the article is regarded as redeemed and may be used for mundane purposes.

HALAKHA

The Levite preceded the priest while the grain was still on the stalks, etc. – הִקְדִּימוֹ בְּשִׁבֳּלִין וכו׳: If a Levite came and took the first tithe before a priest received the *teruma*, while the produce was still on the stalks, the produce the Levite receives is exempt from *teruma*. However, if the produce was already threshed and in a pile, the Levite is obligated to separate *teruma* as well (*Tur, Yoreh De'a* 331).

NOTES

This has become grain – הַאי אִידְגַן: The Torah states, "And this shall be the priest's due…the first of your grain, of your wine and of your oil, and the first of the fleece of your sheep, shall you give to him" (Deuteronomy 18:3–4). These verses indicate that the priest's due, *teruma*, is only given from the produce once it reaches the stage at which it is called grain.

״אֲבָל לֹא בַּטֶּבֶל״. פְּשִׁיטָא! לָא צְרִיכָא, בְּטֶבֶל טָבוּל מִדְּרַבָּנַן, וּכְגוֹן שֶׁזְּרָעוֹ בְּעָצִיץ שֶׁאֵינוֹ נָקוּב.

The mishna further states: **But** one may not establish an *eiruv* **with** ***tevel***, produce from which the priestly dues and other tithes have not been separated. The Gemara asks: This too is **obvious,** as it is prohibited to eat or derive any benefit from *tevel.* The Gemara answers: This ruling **is only needed with regard to** ***tevel*** **that is considered** ***tevel*** **by rabbinic decree.** What is included in this category? **For example, if one planted** seeds **in an imperforated container,** one is exempt by Torah law from separting *teruma* and tithes from the resulting produce because Torah law does not consider produce grown in such a container to have grown from the ground.

״וְלֹא בְּמַעֲשֵׂר רִאשׁוֹן שֶׁלֹּא נִטְּלָה תְּרוּמָתוֹ״. פְּשִׁיטָא! לָא צְרִיכָא, שֶׁהִקְדִּימוֹ בַּכְּרִי וְנִטְּלָה מִמֶּנּוּ תְּרוּמַת מַעֲשֵׂר וְלֹא נִטְּלָה מִמֶּנּוּ תְּרוּמָה גְּדוֹלָה.

The mishna stated that one may **not** establish an *eiruv* **with first tithe whose** ***teruma*** **has not been taken.** The Gemara asks: **It is obvious,** as such produce is *tevel.* The Gemara answers: This ruling **is only needed** for a case where the Levite **preceded** the priest and took first tithe from **the pile, and** only ***teruma*** **of the tithe was taken from it,** but ***teruma gedola*** **was not taken from it,** and the produce is therefore still *tevel.*

מַהוּ דְּתֵימָא כְּדַאֲמַר לֵיהּ רַב פַּפָּא לְאַבַּיֵי, קָא מַשְׁמַע לָן כִּדְשַׁנֵּי לֵיהּ.

Lest you say the *halakha* in that case is **as Rav Pappa said to Abaye,** and the Levite is exempt from separating *teruma gedola,* and therefore the food may be used for an *eiruv,* the mishna **teaches us as** Abaye **responded to** Rav Pappa: If the Levite takes grain after it had been gathered in a pile, he must separate *teruma gedola.* Until he does so the produce may not be eaten.

״וְלֹא בְּמַעֲשֵׂר שֵׁנִי וְהֶקְדֵּשׁ שֶׁלֹּא נִפְדּוּ״. פְּשִׁיטָא!

We also learned in the mishna that one may **not** establish an *eiruv* **with** the **second tithe or consecrated** food **that have not been redeemed.** The Gemara asks: **It is obvious** that these items may not be used.

לֹא צְרִיכָא, שֶׁפְּדָאָן וְלֹא פְּדָאָן כְּהִלְכָתָן: מַעֲשֵׂר שֶׁפְּדָאוֹ עַל גַּב אֲסִימוֹן, וְרַחֲמָנָא אָמַר ״וְצַרְתָּ הַכֶּסֶף״ – כֶּסֶף שֶׁיֵּשׁ עָלָיו צוּרָה.

The Gemara answers: This ruling **is only needed** for a case **where he redeemed them,** but **did not redeem them properly,** e.g., in the case of **second tithe that was redeemed with an unminted coin** [*asimon*].[L] **And the Torah says** with regard to the redemption of the second tithe: **And bind up** [*vetzarta*] **the money** in your hand" (Deuteronomy 14:25). This is expounded to mean that the second tithe may only be redeemed with **money that has a form** [*tzura*] engraved **upon it;** however, unminted coins are not considered money for the purpose of redeeming the second tithe.

הֶקְדֵּשׁ – שֶׁחִילְּלוֹ עַל גַּב קַרְקַע, דְּרַחֲמָנָא אָמַר: ״וְנָתַן הַכֶּסֶף וְקָם לוֹ״.

With regard to **consecrated property,** the reference is to a case **where one redeemed it** by exchanging it **for land** instead of money, **as the Torah states: "He will give the money and it shall become his."**[N] Since the verse speaks of giving money, it may be inferred that consecrated property cannot be redeemed by giving the Temple treasury land of equivalent value.

מתני׳ הַשּׁוֹלֵחַ עֵירוּבוֹ בְּיַד חֵרֵשׁ שׁוֹטֶה וְקָטָן, אוֹ בְּיַד מִי שֶׁאֵינוֹ מוֹדֶה בָּעֵירוּב – אֵינוֹ עֵירוּב. וְאִם אָמַר לְאַחֵר לְקַבְּלוֹ מִמֶּנּוּ – הֲרֵי זֶה עֵירוּב.

MISHNA **If one sends his** ***eiruv*** **in the hands of a deaf-mute, an imbecile, or a minor,** all of whom are regarded as legally incompetent, **or in the hands of one who does not accept** the principle of ***eiruv,*** **it is not** a valid ***eiruv.***[H] But **if one told another** person **to receive it from him** at a specific location and set it down in that spot, **it is** a valid ***eiruv.*** The critical point in the establishment of an *eiruv* is that it must be deposited in the proper location by a competent person; but it is immaterial how the *eiruv* arrives there.

גמ׳ וְקָטָן לֹא?! וְהָאָמַר רַב הוּנָא: קָטָן גּוֹבֶה אֶת הָעֵירוּב! לָא קַשְׁיָא; כָּאן – בְּעֵירוּבֵי תְחוּמִין, כָּאן – בְּעֵירוּבֵי חֲצֵירוֹת.

GEMARA The Gemara asks: **Is a minor not** fit to set down an *eiruv*? **Didn't Rav Huna say: A minor may collect the** food for an ***eiruv*** from the residents of a courtyard and establish an *eiruv* on their behalf even *ab initio*?[H] The Gemara answers: This is **not difficult,** as **here,** where the mishna invalidates an *eiruv* placed by a minor, it is referring **to an** ***eiruv*** **of** Shabbat **borders.** These laws are relatively stringent, as they require that one establish a new place of residence, which a minor cannot do. **There,** where Rav Huna said that a minor may collect the food for an *eiruv,* he was referring **to an** ***eiruv*** **of courtyards.**[N] This type of *eiruv* is more lenient and may be established even by a minor, as all that is necessary is to join together domains that already exist.

LANGUAGE

Unminted coin [*asimon*] **– אֲסִימוֹן:** From the Greek word ἄσημον, *asimon*, meaning a coin-like piece of metal that does not have an impression on it.

NOTES

He will give the money and it shall become his – וְנָתַן הַכֶּסֶף וְקָם לוֹ: There is no such verse in the Bible. Apparently, the reference is to the following verse: "And if he that sanctified the field shall redeem it, then he shall add the fifth part of your valuation to it, and it shall become his" (Leviticus 27:19). In their citation, the Sages shortened the verse and slightly adjusted its wording in order to emphasize its relevance to the current discussion.

Eiruv **of Shabbat borders and** ***eiruv*** **of courtyards – עֵירוּבֵי תְחוּמִין וְעֵירוּבֵי חֲצֵירוֹת:** See Rashi and *Tosafot*, who explain the reason for the difference between the joining of Shabbat borders [*eiruv teḥumin*] and the joining of courtyards [*eiruv ḥatzeirot*]. It is indicated in the Jerusalem Talmud that nowadays, when most homes in a city are already joined together through the merging of alleyways, the joining of courtyards serves merely as a way to increase brotherly affection among Jews. Consequently, we are not particular about the agent who collects the food for the *eiruv.*

Rabbeinu Yehonatan explains that, in establishing an *eiruv ḥatzeirot*, the minor need not say anything. However, when one establishes an *eiruv teḥumin*, he must declare that a particular person designates this spot as his Shabbat residence; it is for this declaration, which is similar to an acquisition, that a minor is unfit. Some commentaries explain that with regard to *eiruv hatzeirot*, the intention of the person who sends the agent can transfer ownership of the food and thereby establish the *eiruv*. Therefore, there is no cause for concern if the agent is a minor. However, with regard to *eiruv teḥumin*, where the intention of the person who sends the agent is ineffective, a minor may not serve as a messenger (Rashba).

HALAKHA

Agents who are not qualified to establish an ***eiruv*** **– שָׁלִיחַ שֶׁאֵינוֹ רָאוּי לְעֵירוּב:** If one sends his *eiruv* with a deaf-mute, an imbecile, a minor, anyone who denies the principle of *eiruv*, or a gentile (Rabbeinu Yeruḥam), the *eiruv* is invalid (*Shulḥan Arukh, Oraḥ Ḥayyim* 409:8).

A minor with regard to ***eiruv ḥatzeirot*** **– קָטָן בְּעֵירוּבֵי חֲצֵירוֹת:** Minors, slaves, and individuals who are not legally competent may collect food for an *eiruv ḥatzeirot* and establish the *eiruv*, thereby allowing people to carry in the courtyard (*Tur, Oraḥ Ḥayyim* 366:10).

״אוֹ בְּיַד מִי שֶׁאֵינוֹ מוֹדֶה בָּעֵירוּב״. מַאן? אָמַר רַב חִסְדָּא: כּוּתַאי.

We learned in the mishna: **Or** if one sends his *eiruv* **in the hands of one who does not accept** the principle of ***eiruv***.[N] The Gemara asks: **Who is this? Rav Ḥisda said: A Samaritan [*Kuti*],** who does not accept the laws of the Sages with regard to *eiruv*.

״וְאִם אָמַר לְאַחֵר לְקַבְּלוֹ הֵימֶנּוּ – הֲרֵי זֶה עֵירוּב״. וְלֵיחוּשׁ דִּילְמָא לָא מַמְטֵי לֵיהּ? כִּדְאָמַר רַב חִסְדָּא: בְּעוֹמֵד וְרוֹאֵהוּ, הָכָא נַמִּי: בְּעוֹמֵד וְרוֹאֵהוּ.

The mishna also states: **And if he told another** person **to receive** the *eiruv* **from him, it is a** valid ***eiruv***. The Gemara challenges this statement: **Let us be concerned that perhaps** the minor or other incompetent person will **not bring** the *eiruv* to the other person. The Gemara responds: This may be answered **as Rav Ḥisda said** with regard to a different statement, that it was referring to a case **where he stands and watches him.**[H] **Here, too,** the mishna is referring to a case **where** the person sending the *eiruv* **stands and watches him** from afar until the *eiruv* reaches the person designated to receive it.

וְלֵיחוּשׁ דִּילְמָא לָא שָׁקִיל מִינֵּיהּ! כִּדְאָמַר רַב יְחִיאֵל: חֲזָקָה שָׁלִיחַ עוֹשֶׂה שְׁלִיחוּתוֹ, הָכָא נַמִּי: חֲזָקָה שָׁלִיחַ עוֹשֶׂה שְׁלִיחוּתוֹ.

The Gemara asks: But nonetheless, **let us be concerned that perhaps** the other person will **not take** the *eiruv* **from** the deaf-mute, imbecile, or minor and deposit it in the designated place. From a distance, one cannot see exactly what is happening. He only saw that the messenger arrived at his destination. The Gemara answers this question **as** follows: **Rav Yeḥiel said** in a different context that there is a legal **presumption** that **an agent fulfills his agency. Here, too,** there is a legal **presumption** that the **agent** appointed to accept the *eiruv* **fulfills his agency.**

וְהֵיכָא אִיתְּמַר דְּרַב חִסְדָּא וְרַב יְחִיאֵל? אַהָא אִתְּמַר; דְּתַנְיָא: נְתָנוֹ לַפִּיל וְהוֹלִיכוֹ, לַקּוֹף וְהוֹלִיכוֹ – אֵין זֶה עֵירוּב. וְאִם אָמַר לְאַחֵר לְקַבְּלוֹ הֵימֶנּוּ – הֲרֵי זֶה עֵירוּב. וְדִילְמָא לָא מַמְטֵי לֵיהּ? אָמַר רַב חִסְדָּא: בְּעוֹמֵד וְרוֹאֵהוּ. וְדִילְמָא לֹא מְקַבֵּל לֵיהּ מִינֵּיהּ? אָמַר רַב יְחִיאֵל: חֲזָקָה, שָׁלִיחַ עוֹשֶׂה שְׁלִיחוּתוֹ.

The Gemara asks: **Where were** these principles of **Rav Ḥisda and Rav Yeḥiel stated?** The Gemara answers: **They were stated with regard to** the following, **as it was taught** in a *baraita*: If **one gave** the *eiruv* **to** a trained **elephant, and it brought it** to the place where he wanted the *eiruv* deposited, or if he gave it **to a monkey,**[N] **and it brought it** to the proper location, **it is not** a valid ***eiruv***. **But if he told another** person **to receive it from** the animal, **it is** a valid ***eiruv***. The Gemara asks: **But perhaps** the animal **will not bring** the *eiruv* **to** the person appointed to receive it? **Rav Ḥisda said:** The *baraita* is referring **to** a case **where** the person sending the *eiruv* **stands and watches it** from afar until it reaches the person designated to receive the *eiruv*. The Gemara asks further: But **perhaps** the person appointed to receive the *eiruv* **will not accept it from** the elephant or monkey. **Rav Yeḥiel said:** There is a legal **presumption** that **an agent fulfills his agency.**

אָמַר רַב נַחְמָן: בְּשֶׁל תּוֹרָה – אֵין חֲזָקָה שָׁלִיחַ עוֹשֶׂה שְׁלִיחוּתוֹ,

Rav Naḥman said: With regard to Torah laws, we do **not** rely on the **presumption that an agent fulfills his agency;** rather, one must actually see the agent performing his mission.

NOTES

One who does not accept the principle of *eiruv* – מִי שֶׁאֵינוֹ מוֹדֶה בָּעֵירוּב: The reference is clearly not to a gentile, since a gentile is not fit to be an agent because of his dissimilarity to the one sending him. For this reason, the Gemara inquires as to the identity of the one who does not accept the principle of an *eiruv*. The example given is the Samaritan [*Kuti*]. Even though he accepts the Torah, since he does not agree with the concept of an *eiruv*. For this reason, he is unfit for this mission (Rav Ya'akov Emden). This rule was applicable even when *Kutim* were not regarded as gentiles for all purposes. The law of a *Kuti* applies equally to a Sadducee, who also does not accept the concept of *eiruv* (Ritva). With regard to the students of Beit Shammai, however, even though Ḥananya claims that they do not accept most of the laws of *eiruv*, if they accept upon themselves a mission of this kind, they will certainly fulfill it properly (*Beit Ya'akov*).

Gave it to a monkey – נְתָנוֹ לַקּוֹף: Some commentaries differentiate between two sets of circumstances: If one gave the *eiruv* to a trained monkey or elephant, there is certainly no agency, as they are not fit for such a role. However, if he placed it on their backs and observed that they placed the *eiruv* in a certain spot, and he said that he wishes to establish that location as his Shabbat residence, the *eiruv* is valid (Rashba).

HALAKHA

He told another…stands and watches him – אָמַר לְאַחֵר... עוֹמֵד וְרוֹאֵהוּ: If one sends his *eiruv* with a person unfit for the task or even places it on an elephant or monkey, and he sees the *eiruv* arrive at its destination, and he had told another person to accept the food and to place it down as an *eiruv*, the *eiruv* is valid. There is a presumption that an agent fulfills his mission (*Shulḥan Arukh*, *Oraḥ Ḥayyim* 409:8).

Perek **III**
Daf **32** Amud **a**

בְּשֶׁל סוֹפְרִים – חֲזָקָה, שָׁלִיחַ עוֹשֶׂה שְׁלִיחוּתוֹ. וְרַב שֵׁשֶׁת אָמַר: אֶחָד זֶה וְאֶחָד זֶה – חֲזָקָה, שָׁלִיחַ עוֹשֶׂה שְׁלִיחוּתוֹ.

However, **with regard to rabbinic** laws, we do rely on the **presumption** that **an agent fulfills his agency.**[H] **And Rav Sheshet** disagreed and **said:** With regard to **both this,** Torah law, **and that,** rabbinic law, we rely on the **presumption** that **an agent fulfills his agency.**

אָמַר רַב שֵׁשֶׁת: מְנָא אָמִינָא לָהּ – דִּתְנַן: מִשֶּׁקָּרַב הָעוֹמֶר הוּתַּר הֶחָדָשׁ מִיָּד.

Rav Sheshet said: From where do I say this? As we learned in a mishna: **Once the *omer* has been offered,** the grain from **the new crop is immediately permitted.**[N] The Torah prohibits eating from the new crop of grain until the *omer* sacrifice is offered on the second day of Passover (Leviticus 23:14); once the *omer* is offered, it is immediately permitted to partake of the new grain.

HALAKHA

The presumption with regard to an agent – חֲזָקַת שָׁלִיחַ: Although some authorities relied on the rule of the *ge'onim* that in matters of ritual law the *halakha* is in accordance with the opinions of Rav Sheshet rather than those of Rav Naḥman, it appears that in this instance most authorities rules in in accordance with the opinion of Rav Naḥman. They maintain that in cases of Torah law we are not lenient; we do not rely on the basis of a presumption that an agent fulfills his mission (Rambam *Sefer Zera'im*, *Hilkhot Terumot* 4:6).

NOTES

The prohibition to eat from the new crop of grain – אִיסּוּר חָדָשׁ: The year's newly harvested grain may not be eaten until the *omer* offering is brought, as stated in the Torah: "And you shall eat neither bread, nor parched corn, nor green ears, until that very day, until you have brought an offering to your God; it shall be a statute forever throughout your generations in all your dwellings" (Leviticus 23:14). During the Temple period, eating the new grain was dependent upon the offering alone, which typically took place early in the morning, on the first intermediate day of the festival of Passover. Outside of Jerusalem, everyone would rely on the presumption that by midday the *omer* sacrifice must have been offered.

HALAKHA

The time when the new crop is permitted – זְמַן הֶיתֵּר חָדָשׁ: Once the *omer* sacrifice has been offered, the new crop of grain may be eaten. People who live far from Jerusalem may partake of the new grain from midday onwards. Following the destruction of the Temple, the new crop of grain is forbidden until after the sixteenth of Nisan (Rambam *Sefer Kedusha, Hilkhot Ma'akhalot Assurot* 10:2).

The purification of a woman after childbirth or *ziva* – טַהֲרַת יוֹלֶדֶת וְזָבָה: A woman following childbirth and a *zava* would bring money to the Temple and place it in the designated box. After immersing, they are permitted to eat sacred foods at nightfall, since their purification sacrifices were certainly offered by then (Rambam *Sefer Korbanot, Hilkhot Meḥusrei Kappara* 1:12).

One who says to another: Go and gather for yourself figs from my fig tree – הָאוֹמֵר לַחֲבֵירוֹ צֵא וְלַקֵּט לְךָ תְּאֵנִים מִתְּאֵנָתִי: If one person said to another: Take figs for yourself from my fig tree, and he specified a particular amount, the presumption is that the owner must certainly have tithed the fruit. However, if he did not specify, then the recipient must separate the tithes. This applies when an *am ha'aretz* makes the offer to a *ḥaver*. However, if a *ḥaver* offers the figs to an *am ha'aretz*, and a different *ḥaver*, who heard this statement, wants to eat from the figs, he need not tithe the fruit as *demai* (see the language of the Rambam and the *Kesef Mishne*; Rambam *Sefer Zera'im, Hilkhot Ma'aserot* 10:10).

NOTES

A woman who is responsible to offer sacrifices following childbirth or after experiencing *ziva* – שֶׁיֵּשׁ עָלֶיהָ לֵידָה אוֹ זִיבָה: A woman after childbirth and a *zava* are both ritually impure and only achieve full purification after they have brought a special offering. A *zava* is a woman who experiences a flow of blood similar to her menstrual cycle on three consecutive days during a time when she is not due to experience menstrual bleeding. As long as these women have not brought their offerings, they are included in the category of one who lacks atonement, and they are prohibited to eat sacred foods. While there were several levels of sacrifices, the most common was a pair of turtledoves or pigeons, one for a burnt-offering and the other for a sin-offering.

BACKGROUND

The money in the collection box [*shofar*] – מָעוֹת בְּשׁוֹפָר: There were a large number of people who offered sacrifices in the Temple. In order to prevent mistakes, those arriving at the Temple would generally not bring the sacrificial animals with them. Rather, they would deposit their money in the Temple treasury and receive a receipt, for which they would receive, in a different chamber of the Temple, the appropriate sacrifice. Alternatively, they would place the money in one of the thirteen collection boxes in the Temple used for this and similar circumstances, as in the case of a woman after childbirth. Each box was called a *shofar* because it resembled a ram's horn in shape, with narrow openings that flared wider toward the bottom, to prevent theft from the boxes.

וְהָרְחוֹקִים מוּתָּרִים מֵחֲצוֹת הַיּוֹם וְאֵילָךְ. וְהָא חָדָשׁ דְּאוֹרָיְיתָא הוּא, וְקָתָנֵי: הָרְחוֹקִים מוּתָּרִין מֵחֲצוֹת הַיּוֹם וְאֵילָךְ. לָאו מִשּׁוּם חֲזָקָה שָׁלִיחַ עוֹשֶׂה שְׁלִיחוּתוֹ?

And those far from Jerusalem, who do not know whether or not the *omer* has already been offered, **are permitted** to eat from the new crop **from midday and on,** as the *omer* must surely have been offered by this time.[H] **Isn't** the prohibition to eat from **the new** crop **a Torah law? And** nevertheless, **it was taught: And those far** from Jerusalem **are permitted** to eat from the new crop **from midday and on. Is this not because** we may rely on the **presumption** that **an agent fulfills his agency?** The priests in the Temple serve as the agents of the entire Jewish people, and it may be assumed that they have performed the mission entrusted to them.

וְרַב נַחְמָן: הָתָם כִּדְקָתָנֵי טַעְמָא, לְפִי שֶׁיּוֹדְעִין שֶׁאֵין בֵּית דִּין מִתְעַצְּלִין בּוֹ.

The Gemara asks: **And** how does **Rav Naḥman,** who holds that with respect to Torah laws we may not rely on the presumption that an agent fulfills his agency, refute this proof? He can respond as follows: **There,** the agents may be trusted for **the reason that was** explicitly **taught: Because we know that the court will not be indolent** in offering the *omer* sacrifice; however, the same cannot be said of ordinary agents.

וְאִיכָּא דְּאָמְרִי, אָמַר רַב נַחְמָן מְנָא אָמֵינָא לַהּ – דְּקָתָנֵי טַעְמָא: לְפִי שֶׁיּוֹדְעִין שֶׁאֵין בֵּית דִּין מִתְעַצְּלִין בּוֹ. בֵּית דִּין הוּא דְּלָא מִתְעַצְּלִין בּוֹ, הָא שָׁלִיחַ מִתְעַצֵּל בּוֹ.

And some say a different version of this response: **Rav Naḥman said: From where do I say this** principle? **As it was taught** that **the reason** is **because we know that the court will not be indolent** in offering the *omer* past midday. From this we may infer: **It is the court** that **will not be indolent** with regard to missions entrusted to it, **but** an ordinary **agent may** indeed **be indolent** with regard to his mission. Therefore, we cannot rely upon an ordinary agent.

וְרַב שֵׁשֶׁת אָמַר לָךְ: בֵּית דִּין – עַד פַּלְגֵיהּ דְּיוֹמָא, שָׁלִיחַ – כּוּלֵּי יוֹמָא.

And Rav Sheshet could have **said to you** that this is not the correct inference; rather, we should infer as follows: It is only **the court** that is presumed to have executed its mission **by midday,** even though the mitzva to bring the *omer* offering lasts all day. However, an ordinary **agent,** who is not as diligent, is only presumed to have completed his mission by the end of **the entire day.**

אָמַר רַב שֵׁשֶׁת: מְנָא אָמֵינָא לַהּ – דְּתַנְיָא: הָאִשָּׁה שֶׁיֵּשׁ עָלֶיהָ לֵידָה אוֹ זִיבָה מְבִיאָה מָעוֹת וְנוֹתֶנֶת בַּשּׁוֹפָר, וְטוֹבֶלֶת וְאוֹכֶלֶת בְּקָדָשִׁים לָעֶרֶב. מַאי טַעְמָא – לָאו מִשּׁוּם דְּאָמְרִינַן חֲזָקָה שָׁלִיחַ עוֹשֶׂה שְׁלִיחוּתוֹ?

Rav Sheshet said: From where do I say my opinion? **As it was taught** in a *baraita*: **A woman who is responsible** to offer sacrifices following **childbirth or** after experiencing ***ziva***[N] (Leviticus 12, 15) **brings money and puts it in** the appropriate collection **box**[B] in the Temple, **immerses** in a ritual bath, **and** she may then **eat sacrificial food at nightfall.**[H] **What is the reason** that she is permitted to eat immediately at nightfall? **Is it not because we say** that there is a **presumption** that **an agent fulfills his agency,** and the priests certainly purchased the appropriate sacrifices with her money and offered them during the day?

וְרַב נַחְמָן – הָתָם כִּדְרַב שְׁמַעְיָה, דְּאָמַר רַב שְׁמַעְיָה: חֲזָקָה אֵין בֵּית דִּין שֶׁל כֹּהֲנִים עוֹמְדִים מִשָּׁם עַד שֶׁיִּכְלוּ כׇּל מָעוֹת שֶׁבַּשּׁוֹפָר.

The Gemara asks: **And** how does **Rav Naḥman** counter this proof? **There,** in the case of a woman who put money in the box, the reason she may rely on agency is **in accordance with** the statement of **Rav Shemaya, as Rav Shemaya said:** There is a legal **presumption** that **the court of priests would not leave** the Temple **until all the money in the** collection **box has been spent** on the purchase of sacrifices. We may rely only on the special court appointed to carry out this task, as it can be trusted. However, no proof may be brought from here with regard to an ordinary agent.

אָמַר רַב שֵׁשֶׁת: מְנָא אָמֵינָא לַהּ – דְּתַנְיָא: הָאוֹמֵר לַחֲבֵירוֹ "צֵא וְלַקֵּט לְךָ תְּאֵנִים מִתְּאֵנָתִי" – אוֹכֵל מֵהֶן עֲרַאי, וּמְעַשְּׂרָן וַדַּאי. "מַלֵּא לְךָ כַּלְכָּלָה זֶה תְּאֵנִים מִתְּאֵנָתִי" – אוֹכֵל מֵהֶן עֲרַאי, וּמְעַשְּׂרָן דְּמַאי.

Rav Sheshet said another proof: **From where do I say this? As it was taught** in a *baraita*: **One who says to another** person: **Go and gather for yourself figs from my fig tree,**[H] if he does not specify the amount that he should take, the gatherer **may eat casually from them** even without separating tithes. However, if one wishes to eat the figs as a regular, set meal, **he must** first **tithe them** as fruit that is known **with certainty** not to previously be tithed. In this case, it may be assumed that the owner of the fig tree did not separate tithes to exempt these figs, as he did not know how many the gatherer would take. However, if the owner of the fig tree said to him: **Fill this basket for yourself with figs from my fig tree, he may eat from them casually** without tithing, **and** before eating them as a regular meal, **he must tithe them** as ***demai,*** produce with regard to which we are unsure if the appropriate tithes have been separated. Since the owner of the tree knows how many figs the gatherer will take, it is possible that he has already separated tithes for these figs.

בְּמָה דְּבָרִים אֲמוּרִים – בְּעַם הָאָרֶץ, אֲבָל בְּחָבֵר – אוֹכֵל וְאֵינוֹ צָרִיךְ לְעַשֵּׂר, דִּבְרֵי רַבִּי. רַבָּן שִׁמְעוֹן בֶּן גַּמְלִיאֵל אוֹמֵר: בַּמֶּה דְּבָרִים אֲמוּרִים – בְּעַם הָאָרֶץ, אֲבָל בְּחָבֵר – אֵינוֹ אוֹכֵל עַד שֶׁיְּעַשֵּׂר, לְפִי שֶׁלֹּא נֶחְשְׁדוּ חֲבֵרִים לִתְרוֹם שֶׁלֹּא מִן הַמּוּקָף.

In what case **is this statement said?** Where the owner of the fig tree is **an *am ha'aretz*. But** if he is **a *ḥaver*,**[N] the gatherer **may eat** the figs, **and he need not tithe** them even as *demai*, as the owner certainly separated tithes for them from other produce; this is **the statement of Rabbi** Yehuda HaNasi. His father, **Rabban Shimon ben Gamliel, says** the opposite: **In what** case **is this statement said?** Where the owner of the fig tree is an ***am ha'aretz*. But** if he is **a *ḥaver*,** the gatherer **may not eat** the fruit **until he tithes** them **because *ḥaverim*,** who are meticulous in their observance of *halakha*, **are not suspected of separating *teruma*** and tithes **from** produce that is **not adjacent** to the produce they seek to exempt. Since the figs that have been picked are not adjacent to the owner's other figs, he has certainly not separated *teruma* and tithes on their account.

אָמַר רַבִּי: נִרְאִין דְּבָרַי מִדִּבְרֵי אַבָּא, מוּטָב שֶׁיֵּחָשְׁדוּ חֲבֵרִים לִתְרוֹם שֶׁלֹּא מִן הַמּוּקָף, וְלֹא יַאֲכִילוּ לְעַמֵּי הָאָרֶץ טְבָלִים.

Rabbi Yehuda HaNasi **said: My statement appears** to be more correct **than Father's statement: It is better that *ḥaverim* should be suspected of separating** *teruma* and tithes **from** produce that is **not adjacent** to the produce they seek to exempt, **and they should not feed *amei ha'aretz*** produce that is ***tevel*.**

עַד כָּאן לָא פְּלִיגִי אֶלָּא דְּמָר סָבַר נֶחְשְׁדוּ, וּמָר סָבַר לֹא נֶחְשְׁדוּ. אֲבָל כּוּלֵּי עָלְמָא – חֲזָקָה, שָׁלִיחַ עוֹשֶׂה שְׁלִיחוּתוֹ.

The Gemara infers: The *tanna'im* **disagreed only** with regard to the following point: **That one Sage,** Rabbi Yehuda HaNasi, **holds** that *ḥaverim* **are suspected** of tithing with produce that is not adjacent to the produce it comes to exempt, **and one Sage,** Rabban Shimon ben Gamliel, **holds** that **they are not suspected** of that. **But all** agree that we may rely on the **presumption** that **an agent fulfills his agency,** i.e., that the owner, who is regarded as an agent to tithe his produce so that no one will eat *tevel* on his account, can be relied upon to separate the tithes.

וְרַב נַחְמָן: הָתָם כִּדְרַב חֲנִינָא חוֹזָאָה, דְּאָמַר רַב חֲנִינָא חוֹזָאָה: חֲזָקָה הוּא עַל חָבֵר שֶׁאֵינוֹ מוֹצִיא דָּבָר שֶׁאֵינוֹ מְתוּקָּן מִתַּחַת יָדוֹ.

And Rav Naḥman can respond as follows: **There,** the owner can be trusted, **in accordance with** the statement of **Rav Ḥanina Ḥoza'a, as Rav Ḥanina Ḥoza'a said: There is** a legal **presumption with regard to a *ḥaver* that he does not release anything that is not tithed from his possession.** Therefore, we are not relying on a general presumption with regard to agents but on a presumption with regard to *ḥaverim*.

אָמַר מָר: בַּמֶּה דְּבָרִים אֲמוּרִים – בְּעַם הָאָרֶץ, אֲבָל בְּחָבֵר – אוֹכֵל וְאֵינוֹ צָרִיךְ לְעַשֵּׂר, דִּבְרֵי רַבִּי.

The previous *baraita* contained several puzzling elements. Now that the Gemara has completed its primary discussion, namely the presumption that an agent carries out his mission, it turns to a discussion of the *baraita* itself. **The Master said:** If one said to his fellow: Go and gather for yourself figs, **in what** case **is this statement said?** It is in a case where the owner of the fig tree is **an *am ha'aretz*. However,** if he is **a *ḥaver*,** the gatherer **may eat** the figs, **and he need not tithe** them; this is **the statement of Rabbi** Yehuda HaNasi.

הַאי עַם הָאָרֶץ דְּקָאָמַר לֵיהּ לְמַאן? אִילֵּימָא דְּקָאָמַר לְעַם הָאָרֶץ חַבְרֵיהּ – מְעַשְּׂרָן דְּמַאי? מִי צַיֵּית?! אֶלָּא בְּעַם הָאָרֶץ דְּקָאָמַר לֵיהּ לְחָבֵר. אֵימָא סֵיפָא: נִרְאִין דְּבָרַי מִדִּבְרֵי אַבָּא, מוּטָב שֶׁיֵּחָשְׁדוּ חֲבֵרִים לִתְרוֹם שֶׁלֹּא מִן הַמּוּקָף וְאַל יַאֲכִילוּ לְעַמֵּי הָאָרֶץ טְבָלִין. עַמֵּי הָאָרֶץ מַאי בָּעֵי הָתָם?

The Gemara asks: **This *am ha'aretz*,** who addressed his fellow man, **to whom did he speak? If you say that he spoke to his fellow *am ha'aretz*,** if so how are we to understand the statement that follows: **He must tithe them as *demai*? Would** an *am ha'aretz* **comply** with the admonition of the Sages[N] to suspect that the produce of his fellow *am ha'aretz* may not have been tithed? **Rather,** this must be referring **to an *am ha'aretz* who told a *ḥaver*** to gather figs from his fig tree, and the *ḥaver* will certainly tithe them. However, **say** that **the latter clause** of this *baraita*: **My statement appears** to be more correct **than Father's statement,** means the following: **It is better that *ḥaverim* should be suspected of separating** *teruma* and tithes **from** produce that is **not adjacent** to the produce they seek to exempt, **and they should not feed *amei ha'aretz*** produce that is ***tevel*. What is the relevance of *amei ha'aretz* there?** According to that explanation, the situation is the opposite. The person eating the figs is a *ḥaver*, and the owner of the fig tree is an *am ha'aretz*.

אָמַר רָבִינָא: רֵישָׁא בְּעַם הָאָרֶץ שֶׁאָמַר לְחָבֵר, סֵיפָא בְּחָבֵר שֶׁאָמַר לְעַם הָאָרֶץ וְחָבֵר אַחֵר שׁוֹמְעוֹ. רַבִּי

Ravina said: The first clause is referring **to an *am ha'aretz* who spoke to a *ḥaver*,** while **the latter clause** is referring **to a *ḥaver* who spoke to an *am ha'aretz*, and a different *ḥaver* heard him** speak, and the discussion relates not to the one gathering the figs but to whether the second *ḥaver* may partake of the figs if they are offered to him. The Gemara explains the disagreement according to this understanding: **Rabbi** Yehuda HaNasi

NOTES

Ḥaver – חָבֵר: A *ḥaver* was a member of a group or class of people that was very meticulous in its observance of several mitzvot that most commoners [*amei ha'aretz*] were not meticulous in observing. The difference was most pronounced in the practice of *ḥaverim* to eat even non-sacred food in a state of ritual purity and in practices concerning the separation of tithes. Torah scholars were typically *ḥaverim*, but not all *ḥaverim* were necessarily Torah scholars. There was a special ceremony for acceptance into this group, which was performed in the presence of *ḥaverim* who served as a kind of court for this purpose. The especially scrupulous practices of this group, all of whose members joined it out of their own free will in a desire to be more exacting in the performance of mitzvot, were not characteristic of all Jews. All agree that one may rely upon presumptions when dealing with *ḥaverim*.

Would an *am ha'aretz* comply with the admonition of the Sages – מִי צַיֵּית: Tithes would be separated from *demai* in order to eliminate any doubt as to whether the produce had been tithed. This represented a very meticulous level of observance, as most *amei ha'aretz* did in fact tithe their produce. Therefore, tithing *demai* was something of an affront to the seller or the provider of the produce, as it showed that the buyer did consider him reliable. Consequently, it can be assumed that an *am ha'aretz* would not agree to tithe the *demai*.

HALAKHA

If one placed his *eiruv* in a tree – נָתַן עֵירוּבוֹ בְּאִילָן: If one placed his *eiruv* in a tree or in a pit such that the *eiruv* is in a different domain than the one in which he establishes his Shabbat residence, and he is prohibited to carry the *eiruv* to his Shabbat residence, the *eiruv* is not valid. However, if one placed the *eiruv* in a location from which it is prohibited to carry only by rabbinic decree, the *eiruv* is valid, as stated in the mishna and in accordance with the statement of Rabbi Yehuda HaNasi in the Gemara (*Shulḥan Arukh, Oraḥ Ḥayyim* 409:2).

סָבַר: אוֹתוֹ חָבֵר אוֹכֵל וְאֵינוֹ צָרִיךְ לְעַשֵּׂר, דְּוַדַּאי עִישּׂוּרֵי מְעַשֵּׂר הַהוּא חָבֵר קַמָּא עִילָּוֵיהּ. וְרַבָּן שִׁמְעוֹן בֶּן גַּמְלִיאֵל אוֹמֵר: לֹא יֹאכַל עַד שֶׁיְּעַשֵּׂר, לְפִי שֶׁלֹּא נֶחְשְׁדוּ חֲבֵרִים לִתְרוֹם שֶׁלֹּא מִן הַמּוּקָף. וְאָמַר לֵיהּ רַבִּי: מוּטָב שֶׁיֵּחָשְׁדוּ חֲבֵרִים לִתְרוֹם שֶׁלֹּא מִן הַמּוּקָף, וְאַל יַאֲכִילוּ עַמֵּי הָאָרֶץ טְבָלִים.

holds: That *ḥaver*, who heard the first *ḥaver* speaking to the *am ha'aretz*, **may** immediately **eat** from the basket, **and he is not required to tithe** the produce, **as the first *ḥaver* certainly separated tithes for** the person who picked the figs, as he would not have caused an *am ha'aretz* to eat *tevel*. **And Rabban Shimon ben Gamliel** disagrees and **says:** That *ḥaver* **may not eat** of the fruit **until he has tithed** them, **for *ḥaverim* are not suspected of separating** *teruma* and tithes **from** produce that is **not adjacent** to the produce they seek to exempt. **And Rabbi** Yehuda HaNasi **said to him: It is better that *ḥaverim* should be suspected of separating** *teruma* and tithes **from** produce that is **not adjacent** to the produce they seek to exempt, **and they should not feed *amei ha'aretz*** produce that is ***tevel*.**

בְּמַאי קָמִיפַּלְגִי? רַבִּי סָבַר: נִיחָא לֵיהּ לְחָבֵר דְּלַעֲבֵיד הוּא אִיסּוּרָא קְלִילָא, וְלָא לִיעֲבַד עַם הָאָרֶץ אִיסּוּרָא רַבָּה. וְרַבָּן שִׁמְעוֹן בֶּן גַּמְלִיאֵל סָבַר: נִיחָא לֵיהּ לְחָבֵר דְּלֶיעֱבַד עַם הָאָרֶץ אִיסּוּרָא רַבָּה, וְאִיהוּ אֲפִילּוּ אִיסּוּרָא קְלִילָא לָא לִיעֲבַד.

The Gemara asks: **With regard to what** principle **do they disagree?** The Gemara answers: **Rabbi** Yehuda HaNasi **holds: It is preferable to a *ḥaver* that he commit a minor transgression,**[N] namely separating tithes from produce that is not adjacent to the produce they seek to exempt, so that **an *am ha'aretz* will not commit** the **major transgression** of eating *tevel* on his account. **And Rabban Shimon ben Gamliel holds: It is preferable to a *ḥaver* that an *am ha'aretz* commit a major transgression, and that he** himself **not commit even a minor transgression.**

מתני׳ נְתָנוֹ בְּאִילָן, לְמַעְלָה מֵעֲשָׂרָה טְפָחִים – אֵין עֵירוּבוֹ עֵירוּב, לְמַטָּה מֵעֲשָׂרָה טְפָחִים – עֵירוּבוֹ עֵירוּב. נְתָנוֹ בַּבּוֹר, אֲפִילּוּ עָמוֹק מֵאָה אַמָּה – עֵירוּבוֹ עֵירוּב.

MISHNA If **one placed** his *eiruv* **in a tree**[H] **above ten handbreadths** from the ground, **his *eiruv* is not** a valid ***eiruv***; if it is **below ten handbreadths, his *eiruv*** is a valid ***eiruv***. If **he placed** the *eiruv* **in a pit, even if it was a hundred cubits deep, his *eiruv*** is a valid ***eiruv*.**

גמ׳ יְתֵיב רַבִּי חִיָּיא בַּר אַבָּא וְרַבִּי אַסִּי וְרָבָא בַּר נָתָן, וִיתֵיב רַב נַחְמָן גַּבַּיְיהוּ, וְיָתְבֵי וְקָאָמְרִי: הַאי אִילָן דְּקָאֵי הֵיכָא? אִילֵימָא דְּקָאֵי בִּרְשׁוּת הַיָּחִיד – מַה לִּי לְמַעְלָה מַה לִּי לְמַטָּה? רְשׁוּת הַיָּחִיד עוֹלָה עַד לָרָקִיעַ!

GEMARA **Rabbi Ḥiyya bar Abba sat, and** with him sat **Rabbi Asi and Rava bar Natan, and Rav Naḥman sat beside them, and they sat and said: This tree** mentioned in the mishna, **where does it stand? If you say it stands in the private domain,**[N] **what** is the difference **to me** whether the *eiruv* is placed **above** ten handbreadths or **below** ten handbreadths? **The private domain ascends to the sky,** and there is no difference whether an object is above or below ten handbreadths.

וְאֶלָּא דְּקָאֵי בִּרְשׁוּת הָרַבִּים; דְּמִתְכַּוֵּין לִשְׁבּוֹת הֵיכָא? אִילֵימָא דְּנִתְכַּוֵּין לִשְׁבּוֹת לְמַעְלָה – הוּא וְעֵירוּבוֹ בְּמָקוֹם אֶחָד הוּא. אֶלָּא נִתְכַּוֵּין לִשְׁבּוֹת לְמַטָּה – וְהָא קָא מִשְׁתַּמֵּשׁ בְּאִילָן!

Rather, say **that** the tree **stands in the public domain;** but in that case the question arises: **Where** did the person **intend to establish his Shabbat residence? If you say that** he **intended to** establish his **Shabbat residence** in the tree **above, he and his *eiruv* are in one place.** Consequently, the *eiruv* should be valid, even if is at a height of more than ten handbreadths. **Rather,** say that he **intended to establish his Shabbat residence** on the ground **below;** but **isn't he making use of the tree**[N] if he accesses his *eiruv*? It is prohibited to make use of a tree on Shabbat, and therefore his *eiruv* should invalid even if it is less than ten handbreadths above the ground because it is inaccessible to him.

NOTES

It is preferable to a *ḥaver* that he commit a minor transgression – נִיחָא לֵיהּ לְחָבֵר דְּלַעֲבֵיד הוּא אִיסּוּרָא קְלִילָא: *Tosafot* and most of the commentaries discuss this issue and distinguish between various circumstances. Some commentaries state that where the other person is violating a prohibition anyway, there is no need to be concerned about him. However, if the other person would be acting unwittingly or because of circumstances beyond his control, one is permitted to transgress a minor prohibition in order to prevent him from violating a major prohibition. In addition, if the minor prohibition that one violates will lead to the fulfillment of a mitzva as well, there is additional room for leniency.

If you say it stands in a private domain – אִילֵימָא דְּקָאֵי בִּרְשׁוּת הַיָּחִיד: The question with regard to the fact that he is making use of the tree, which is prohibited in a private domain just as in a public domain, is relevant here as well (see Ritva). However, since this question is eventually raised and answered, the Gemara does not address it repeatedly.

Isn't he making use of the tree – וְהָא קָא מִשְׁתַּמֵּשׁ בְּאִילָן: The Rashba asks: What is prohibited about utilizing the tree in this circumstance? The *eiruv* is placed on the tree, and there is no need to move the tree at all to take the *eiruv* out of the tree, so why is this prohibited? Some commentaries answer that the very establishment of a Shabbat residence through an *eiruv* in a tree is considered utilizing the tree. However, this does not appear to be a convincing argument. Other authorities explain that while it is true that this case might not involve use of the tree, it is conceivable that there may be circumstances in which one places the *eiruv* in a spot where it cannot be reached without moving the entire tree or bending its branches (Ritva). However, other commentaries rule that even taking something that is located in a tree or putting something on a tree is considered utilizing the tree, and it is prohibited (see *Shulḥan Arukh, Oraḥ Ḥayyim* 336:1,13 and commentaries).

לְעוֹלָם דְּקָאֵי בִּרְשׁוּת הָרַבִּים, וְנִתְכַּוֵּין לִשְׁבּוֹת לְמַטָּה, וְרַבִּי הִיא, דְּאָמַר: כָּל דָּבָר שֶׁהוּא מִשּׁוּם שְׁבוּת לֹא גָּזְרוּ עָלָיו בֵּין הַשְּׁמָשׁוֹת.

The Gemara answers: **Actually,** we can accept the latter assumption **that** the tree **stands in the public domain, and that he intended to establish his Shabbat residence** on the ground **below,** in the public domain. **And** with regard to the prohibition against making use of a tree, this mishna **is** in accordance with the opinion of **Rabbi** Yehuda HaNasi, **who said: Anything that is** prohibited on Shabbat not by Torah law, but rather **due to a rabbinic decree** [*shevut*],[N] the Sages **did not issue the decree** to apply **during twilight,**[H] which is neither definitively day nor definitively night. Since using a tree is only prohibited due to a *shevut,* it is permitted to make use of the tree and remove one's *eiruv* from it during the twilight period, which is when the *eiruv* establishes the person's Shabbat residence. Therefore, the *eiruv* is valid, provided that it is below ten handbreadths. If, however, the *eiruv* is above ten handbreadths, it is invalid. At that height, removing the *eiruv* from the tree entails violation of the Torah prohibition of carrying from a private domain to a public domain, which is prohibited even during twilight.

אָמַר לְהוּ רַב נַחְמָן: יִשַּׁר, וְכֵן אָמַר שְׁמוּאֵל: אֲמַרוּ לֵיהּ: פָּתְרִיתוּ בָּהּ כּוּלֵּי הַאי?! אִינְהוּ נַמִי הָכִי קָא פָּתְרִי בָּהּ! [אֶלָּא הָכִי] אֲמַרוּ לֵיהּ: קָבְעִיתוּ לֵיהּ בִּגְמָרָא? אֲמַר לְהוּ: אִין. אִתְּמַר נַמִי, אָמַר רַב נַחְמָן, אָמַר שְׁמוּאֵל: הָכָא בְּאִילָן הָעוֹמֵד בִּרְשׁוּת הָרַבִּים עָסְקִינַן, גָּבוֹהַּ עֲשָׂרָה וְרָחָב אַרְבָּעָה, וְנִתְכַּוֵּין לִשְׁבּוֹת לְמַטָּה. וְרַבִּי הִיא, דְּאָמַר: כָּל דָּבָר שֶׁהוּא מִשּׁוּם שְׁבוּת לֹא גָּזְרוּ עָלָיו בֵּין הַשְּׁמָשׁוֹת.

Rav Naḥman said to them: Well said, and Shmuel said similarly with regard to this issue. **They said to him: Have you,** the Sages of Babylonia, **gone so far in your explanation** of the mishna? The Gemara asks: Why were the Sages of Eretz Yisrael so surprised? **They, too, explained** the mishna **in this** manner. **Rather, this is what they said to** Rav Naḥman: **Have you established this** explanation **as part of your** regular **study**[N] of the mishna? **He said to them: Yes.** Indeed, **it was also** explicitly **stated** that **Rav Naḥman said** that **Shmuel said: Here, we are dealing with a tree standing in the public domain,** and the tree is **ten** handbreadths **high and four** handbreadths **wide.** It thereby constitutes a private domain, **and** one **intended to establish his Shabbat residence below** in the public domain. **And** the mishna **is** in accordance with the opinion of **Rabbi** Yehuda HaNasi, **who said: Anything that is** prohibited on Shabbat not by Torah law, but rather **due to a rabbinic decree,** the Sages **did not issue the decree** to apply **during twilight.**

אָמַר רָבָא: לֹא שָׁנוּ אֶלָּא בְּאִילָן הָעוֹמֵד חוּץ לְעִיבּוּרָהּ שֶׁל עִיר, אֲבָל אִילָן הָעוֹמֵד בְּתוֹךְ עִיבּוּרָהּ שֶׁל עִיר – אֲפִילּוּ לְמַעְלָה מֵעֲשָׂרָה הֲרֵי זֶה עֵירוּב, דְּמָתָא כְּמַאן דִּמַלְיָא דָּמְיָא.

Rava said in continuation of this discussion: **They only taught** this law **with regard to a tree that stands beyond the outskirts of the city,** i.e., outside a radius of seventy and two-thirds cubits around the city. **However,** with regard to a **tree that stands within the outskirts of the city,**[H] **even** if the *eiruv* was placed **above ten** handbreadths, **it is a** valid *eiruv,* **as the city is considered as though it were filled in**[N] with earth, so that anything located at any height within the town itself or its outskirts is regarded as being in the same domain. Even though the person intended to establish his Shabbat residence below the tree in the public domain, we view the ground as raised to the height of the *eiruv,* and his *eiruv* is therefore valid even though he cannot actually remove it from the tree during the twilight period.

אִי הָכִי חוּץ לְעִיבּוּרָהּ שֶׁל עִיר נַמִי, כֵּיוָן דְּאָמַר רָבָא: הַנּוֹתֵן עֵירוּבוֹ – יֵשׁ לוֹ אַרְבַּע אַמּוֹת, הָוְיָא לָהּ רְשׁוּת הַיָּחִיד, וּרְשׁוּת הַיָּחִיד עוֹלָה עַד לָרָקִיעַ!

The Gemara asks: **If so,** if the tree stood **beyond the outskirts of the town,** there should **also** be no difference whether the *eiruv* is above or below the height of ten handbreadths. **Since Rava** himself **said: One who places his** *eiruv* in a particular location **has four cubits** surrounding him that are considered as a private domain, here too, the area should be considered **a private domain; and a private domain rises to the sky.** Since the tree stands within this area, all parts of the tree should be regarded as a private domain regardless of their height.

אָמַר רַב יִצְחָק בְּרֵיהּ דְּרַב מְשַׁרְשְׁיָא: הָכָא בְּאִילָן הַנּוֹטֶה חוּץ לְאַרְבַּע אַמּוֹת עָסְקִינַן,

Rav Yitzḥak, son of Rav Mesharshiya, said: Here, we are dealing with a tree that leans out[B] horizontally **beyond four cubits** from its trunk, and one placed the *eiruv* on a section that is beyond four cubits,

NOTES

Anything that is prohibited due to a *shevut* – כָּל שֶׁהוּא מִשּׁוּם שְׁבוּת: This rule is limited to cases involving a mitzva. However, if no mitzva is involved, the Sages did not permit violation of a *shevut* during the twilight period. This is true even when the act is prohibited only because two rabbinic prohibitions overlap.

Have you established this as part of your regular study – קָבְעִיתוּ לֵיהּ בִּגְמָרָא: In other words, is this resolution, which maintains that the mishna is referring to a tree four handbreadths wide standing in the public domain, regularly studied in the academies? Or was it stated only as an answer to the difficulty that was raised but was not widely known?

As the city is considered as though it were filled in – דְּמָתָא כְּמַאן דִּמַלְיָא דָּמְיָא: This principle is stated here only with regard to the laws of *eiruv teḥumin.* Since a town is generally filled with houses and people, it is all considered one solid unit up to a considerable height, and the person is considered to have established his Shabbat residence in the same area where he placed his *eiruv.* However, this rule is not applicable to the domains of Shabbat. Consequently, the person would not be able to remove his *eiruv* from the tree while standing on the ground, unless the entire area was a private domain.

HALAKHA

A *shevut* during twilight – שְׁבוּת בֵּין הַשְּׁמָשׁוֹת: An act prohibited by rabbinic decree [*shevut*] is not prohibited during the twilight period on Friday, provided that it is performed for the purpose of a mitzva (Rambam *Sefer Zemanim, Hilkhot Shabbat* 24:10; *Shulḥan Arukh, Oraḥ Ḥayyim* 307:22).

A tree that stands within the outskirts of the city – בְּאִילָן בְּתוֹךְ עִיבּוּרָהּ שֶׁל עִיר: The *halakha* does not accept Rava's distinction between a tree standing within the boundary of the town and one standing outside it (see Rabbeinu Ḥananel; *Shulḥan Arukh, Oraḥ Ḥayyim* 307:22).

BACKGROUND

A tree that leans out – אִילָן הַנּוֹטֶה:

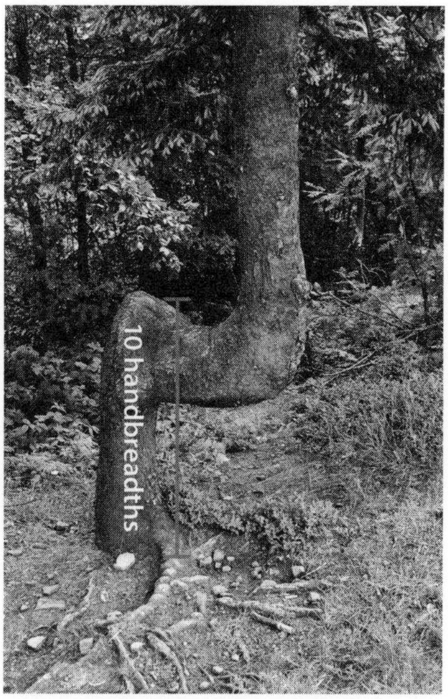

Tree leaning out horizontally before returning to an upright position

וְנִתְכַּוֵּין לִשְׁבּוֹת בְּעִיקָּרוֹ. וּמַאי לְמַעְלָה וּמַאי לְמַטָּה – דַּהֲדַר זָקֵיף.

and he intended to establish his Shabbat residence at its base. And what is the meaning of the terms **above and below,** as we said that this tree extends horizontally to the side, which indicates that it remains at a uniform height? After the tree leans horizontally beyond four cubits from the place of its roots, **it** rises once **again in an upright** position, and therefore the terms above and below are applicable.

וְהָא אִי בָּעֵי מַיְיתִי לַהּ דֶּרֶךְ עָלָיו!

The Gemara asks: **Isn't** it true that even if the *eiruv* is above ten handbreadths, **if one wants, he can** remove it from where it was deposited and **bring it by way of** the tree's **leaves,**[N] i.e., its branches that are above ten handbreadths, to within four cubits of the place where he intended to establish his Shabbat residence? Therefore, the *eiruv* should be valid even though it is above ten handbreadths.

כְּשֶׁרַבִּים מְכַתְּפִין עָלָיו, וְכִדְעוּלָּא, דְּאָמַר עוּלָּא: עַמּוּד תִּשְׁעָה בִּרְשׁוּת הָרַבִּים וְרַבִּים מְכַתְּפִין עָלָיו, וְזָרַק וְנָח עַל גַּבָּיו – חַיָּיב.

The Gemara answers: We are dealing with a unique situation **where** the horizontal section of the tree is used by **the masses** to **shoulder** their burdens **on it,** i.e., to temporarily rest their loads on it, so that they can adjust them and easily lift them up again; **and** the *halakha* in that case **is in accordance with** the opinion of **Ulla, as Ulla said:** With regard to **a pillar** that is **nine** handbreadths high and situated **in the public domain,**[H] **and the masses** use it to **shoulder** their loads **upon it,**[N] **and someone threw** an object from a private domain **and it came to rest upon it, he is liable,** as this pillar has the status of a public domain. Consequently, in the case of the tree, one may not bring the *eiruv* by way of the tree's branches, as the horizontal section of the tree has the status of a public domain, and one may not carry from one private domain to another via a public domain.

מַאי רַבִּי וּמַאי רַבָּנַן?

The Gemara previously cited the opinion of Rabbi Yehuda HaNasi that anything that is prohibited on Shabbat due to rabbinic decree is not prohibited during the twilight period. The Gemara now attempts to clarify the matter: **What is** the source that originally cites **Rabbi** Yehuda HaNasi's opinion, **and what is** the source which cites the opinion of **the Rabbis?**

דְּתַנְיָא: נְתָנוֹ בָּאִילָן, לְמַעְלָה מֵעֲשָׂרָה טְפָחִים – אֵין עֵירוּבוֹ עֵירוּב. לְמַטָּה מֵעֲשָׂרָה טְפָחִים – עֵירוּבוֹ עֵירוּב, וְאָסוּר לִיטְּלוֹ. בְּתוֹךְ שְׁלֹשָׁה – מוּתָּר לִיטְּלוֹ. נְתָנוֹ בְּכַלְכָּלָה וּתְלָאוֹ בָּאִילָן – אֲפִילּוּ לְמַעְלָה מֵעֲשָׂרָה טְפָחִים עֵירוּבוֹ עֵירוּב, דִּבְרֵי רַבִּי. וַחֲכָמִים אוֹמְרִים: כׇּל מָקוֹם שֶׁאָסוּר לִיטְּלוֹ – אֵין עֵירוּבוֹ עֵירוּב.

The Gemara cites the source of the disagreement: **As it was taught** in the *Tosefta*: **If one placed** his *eiruv* **in a tree above ten handbreadths** from the ground, **his** ***eiruv*** **is not** a valid ***eiruv***. If he placed it **below ten handbreadths, his** ***eiruv*** **is** a valid ***eiruv***, **but he is prohibited to take it** on Shabbat in order to eat it because it is prohibited to use the tree on Shabbat. However, if the *eiruv* is **within three** handbreadths[N] of the ground, **he is permitted to take it** because it is considered as though it were on the ground and not in a tree. If **one placed** the *eiruv* **in a basket and hung it on a tree, even above ten handbreadths, his** ***eiruv*** **is** a valid ***eiruv***; this is **the statement of Rabbi** Yehuda HaNasi. **And the Rabbis** disagree and **say:** In **any** situation in which the *eiruv* was placed in **a location where it is prohibited to take** it, **his** ***eiruv*** **is not** a valid ***eiruv***.

HALAKHA

A pillar nine handbreadths high in the public domain – עַמּוּד תִּשְׁעָה בִּרְשׁוּת הָרַבִּים: A pillar that is exactly nine handbreadths high (*Maggid Mishne*, citing the Ra'avad) and that many people use to shoulder their loads has the status of a public domain, even if it is not four handbreadths wide. According to the Rambam and Rashi, even a pillar that is between nine and ten handbreadths in height and that many people utilize to shoulder their loads has the status of a public domain (*Shulḥan Arukh, Oraḥ Ḥayyim* 345:10).

NOTES

Bring it by way of its leaves – מַיְיתִי לַהּ דֶּרֶךְ עָלָיו: All the commentaries struggle with this passage: What is the meaning of the phrase: By way of its leaves? Why is it impossible to remove the eiruv by way of the leaves when the masses shoulder their burdens on the tree? Some commentaries answer that the above phrase means by way of the tree itself, i.e., by rolling the object along the tree. One cannot roll it in this case because many people shoulder their burdens on it (*Me'iri*). Other commentaries offer a different approach: As long as one carries the object himself, he is prohibited to carry it even in the airspace of the public domain, even though it is not considered carrying in the public domain (Rashi).

A pillar nine handbreadths high, and the masses use it to shoulder their loads upon it – עַמּוּד תִּשְׁעָה וְרַבִּים מְכַתְּפִין: Generally, an object taller than three handbreadths is no longer considered like the ground itself. Therefore, a pillar that is nine handbreadths tall should be an exempt domain. Nevertheless, since the masses use it to adjust their loads, it attains the status of a public thoroughfare that is traversed by many people.

Within three handbreadths – בְּתוֹךְ שְׁלֹשָׁה: According to the principle of *lavud*, two solid surfaces are considered connected if the gap between them is less than three handbreadths. Therefore, the lowest three handbreadths of a tree are considered like the ground, and one is permitted to make use of them not only during the twilight period but even on Shabbat itself.

וַחֲכָמִים אוֹמְרִים אַהַיָּיא? אִילֵימָא אַסֵּיפָא – לֵימָא קָסָבְרִי רַבָּנַן צְדָדִין אֲסוּרִין? אֶלָּא אַרֵישָׁא.

The Gemara clarifies: With regard **to which** statement did **the Rabbis state** their opinion? **If you say** they were referring **to the latter clause** with respect to the basket hanging from the tree, **let us say that the Rabbis hold** that using even **the sides** of a tree **is prohibited,**[N] as making use of the basket is considered using the sides of a tree. **Rather,** the Rabbis' statement must refer **to the first clause,** in which Rabbi Yehuda HaNasi says that if one put the *eiruv* below ten handbreadths, his *eiruv* is valid, but he is prohibited to move it.

הַאי אִילָן הֵיכִי דָמֵי? אִי דְּלֵית בֵּיהּ אַרְבָּעָה – מְקוֹם פְּטוּר הוּא, וְאִי דְאִית בֵּיהּ אַרְבָּעָה כִּי נְתָנוֹ בְּכַלְכָּלָה מַאי הָוֵי?

The Gemara clarifies further: **This tree, what are its circumstances? If it is not four** by four handbreadths wide, **it is an exempt domain,** i.e., a neutral place with respect to the laws of carrying on Shabbat, from which an object may be carried into any other Shabbat domain. In that case, the *eiruv* should be valid even if it was placed higher than ten handbreadths in the tree. **And if it is four** by four handbreadths wide, **when one places it in a basket, what of it?** What difference does it make? In any event it is in a private domain.

אָמַר רָבִינָא: רֵישָׁא דְאִית בֵּיהּ אַרְבָּעָה, סֵיפָא דְּלֵית בֵּיהּ אַרְבָּעָה, וְכַלְכָּלָה מַשְׁלִימָתוֹ לְאַרְבָּעָה.

Ravina said: The first clause is referring to a case **where** the tree **is four** by four handbreadths wide. The *eiruv* is not valid if it was placed above ten handbreadths because the tree at that height constitutes a private domain, and the *eiruv* cannot be brought to the public domain below, where one wishes to establish his Shabbat residence. **The latter clause,** however, is referring to a case **where** the tree **is not four** by four handbreadths wide, **and the basket completes** the width of the tree at that spot **to four.**

NOTES

Let us say that the Rabbis hold that using the sides of a tree is prohibited – לֵימָא קָסָבְרִי רַבָּנַן צְדָדִין אֲסוּרִין: This question itself is puzzling. The rule that utilizing the sides of a tree is prohibited on Shabbat is accepted as *halakha*, and at the very least it should not be considered astonishing. Rabbeinu Ḥananel explains that the question relates to the suggestion that utilizing the sides of the tree should be prohibited during the twilight period, as it is only prohibited to use the sides of a tree on Shabbat itself, but not during twilight.

Perek **III**
Daf **33** Amud **b**

וְרַבִּי סָבַר לַהּ כְּרַבִּי מֵאִיר, וְסָבַר לַהּ כְּרַבִּי יְהוּדָה.

And Rabbi Yehuda HaNasi **holds in accordance with** the opinion of **Rabbi Meir, and he** also **holds in accordance with** the opinion of **Rabbi Yehuda.**

סָבַר לַהּ כְּרַבִּי מֵאִיר – דְּאָמַר: חוֹקְקִין לְהַשְׁלִים.

The Gemara clarifies: **He holds in accordance with** the opinion of **Rabbi Meir, who said** the following in the case of an arched gateway in which the lower, straight-walled section is three handbreadths high, and the entire arch is ten handbreadths high: Even if, at the height of ten handbreadths, the arch is less than four handbreadths wide, one considers it as if he **carves out** the space **to complete it,**[B] i.e., the arch has the legal status as though it were actually enlarged to a width of four handbreadths. Similarly, in our case the basket is taken into account and enlarges the tree to a width of four handbreadths.

וְסָבַר לַהּ כְּרַבִּי יְהוּדָה – דְּאָמַר: בְּעֵינַן עֵירוּב עַל גַּבֵּי מְקוֹם אַרְבָּעָה, וְלֵיכָּא.

And he also **holds in accordance with** the opinion of **Rabbi Yehuda, who said: We require** that the *eiruv* rest **on a place** that is **four** by four handbreadths wide, **and** here **there is not** a width of four handbreadths without taking the basket into account.

מַאי רַבִּי יְהוּדָה? דְּתַנְיָא, רַבִּי יְהוּדָה אוֹמֵר: נָעַץ קוֹרָה בִּרְשׁוּת הָרַבִּים וְהִנִּיחַ עֵירוּבוֹ עָלֶיהָ, גְּבוֹהַּ עֲשָׂרָה וּרְחָבָה אַרְבָּעָה – עֵירוּבוֹ עֵירוּב, וְאִם לָאו – אֵין עֵירוּבוֹ עֵירוּב.

The Gemara now asks: **What is** the source of the ruling of **Rabbi Yehuda? As it was taught** in a *baraita* that **Rabbi Yehuda says: If one stuck** a cross **beam** into the ground **in the public domain and placed his *eiruv* upon it,** if the cross beam is **ten** handbreadths **high and four** handbreadths **wide,** so that it has the status of a private domain, **his *eiruv* is a valid *eiruv*; but if not, his *eiruv* is not** a valid ***eiruv*.**

אַדְּרַבָּה, הוּא וְעֵירוּבוֹ בְּמָקוֹם אֶחָד! אֶלָּא הָכִי קָאָמַר: גָּבוֹהַּ עֲשָׂרָה – צָרִיךְ שֶׁיְּהֵא בְּרֹאשָׁהּ אַרְבָּעָה, אֵין גְּבוֹהָה עֲשָׂרָה – אֵין צָרִיךְ שֶׁיְּהֵא בְּרֹאשָׁהּ אַרְבָּעָה.

The Gemara expresses surprise: **On the contrary,** if the cross beam is not ten handbreadths high, why shouldn't his *eiruv* be valid? **He and his *eiruv* are in the same place,**[N] i.e., in the public domain. **Rather, this is what he said:** If the cross beam is **ten** handbreadths **high, it is necessary that its top be four** handbreadths wide, so that it can be considered its own domain; but if it is **not ten** handbreadths **high, it is not necessary that its top be four** handbreadths wide because it is considered part of the public domain.

BACKGROUND

He carves out the space to complete it – חוֹקְקִין לְהַשְׁלִים: See Background note on *Eiruvin* 11b, p. 56.

NOTES

He and his eiruv are in the same place – הוּא וְעֵירוּבוֹ בְּמָקוֹם אֶחָד: The early commentaries had a variant reading: Is his *eiruv* an *eiruv*? Isn't he in one place while his *eiruv* is in another place? Furthermore, with regard to the ruling that: If not, his *eiruv* is not an *eiruv*; on the contrary, he and his *eiruv* are in the same place.

According to this reading, the Gemara's question is: If a person wishes to establish his Shabbat residence in the public domain and his *eiruv* is placed in a private domain, why should his *eiruv* effectively establish his Shabbat residence? It is possible to explain, as Rashi does, in accordance with the opinion of Rava, which maintains that one who establishes an *eiruv teḥumin* creates a private domain for himself at the location of his *eiruv*. Therefore, he and his *eiruv* are in fact in the same place (see the Ritva).

כְּמַאן? דְּלָא כְּרַבִּי יוֹסֵי בְּרַבִּי יְהוּדָה; דְּתַנְיָא, רַבִּי יוֹסֵי בְּרַבִּי יְהוּדָה אוֹמֵר: נָעַץ קָנֶה בִּרְשׁוּת הָרַבִּים וְהִנִּיחַ בְּרֹאשׁוֹ טְרַסְקָל, וְזָרַק וְנָח עַל גַּבָּיו – חַיָּיב.

The Gemara poses a question: **In accordance with whose** opinion did Ravina offer his explanation, which maintains that we are dealing with a basket that completes the dimension of the tree to four handbreadths and yet it is not treated as a private domain? **It is not in accordance with** the opinion of **Rabbi Yosei, son of Rabbi Yehuda,**[N] **as it was taught** in a *baraita* that **Rabbi Yosei, son of Rabbi Yehuda, says:** If **one stuck a reed** into the ground **in the public domain, and placed a basket** [*teraskal*][LB] four by four handbreadths wide **on top of it,**[N] **and threw** an object from the public domain, **and it landed upon it, he is liable** for carrying from a public domain to a private domain. According to Rabbi Yosei, son of Rabbi Yehuda, if a surface of four by four handbreadths rests at a height of ten handbreadths from the ground, this is sufficient for it to be considered a private domain. Ravina's explanation of Rabbi Yehuda HaNasi's position, however, does not appear to accept this assumption.

אֲפִילּוּ תֵּימָא רַבִּי יוֹסֵי בְּרַבִּי יְהוּדָה, הָתָם – הָדְרָן מְחִיצָּתָא, הָכָא – לָא הָדְרָן מְחִיצָּתָא.

The Gemara refutes this and claims that this proof is not conclusive: **Even if you say** that Ravina's explanation is in accordance with the opinion of **Rabbi Yosei, son of Rabbi Yehuda,** a distinction can be made: **There,** in the case of the basket resting on a reed, the sides of the basket constitute **partitions** that **surround** the reed on all sides, and we can invoke the principle of: Lower the partition, according to which the partitions are viewed as extending down to the ground. Consequently, a kind of private domain is created within the public domain. **Here,** in the case of the basket hanging from the tree, the **partitions** of the basket **do not surround** the tree, and so they do not suffice to create a private domain.

רַבִּי יִרְמְיָה אָמַר: שָׁאנֵי כַּלְכָּלָה הוֹאִיל וְיָכוֹל לְנוֹטְתָהּ וְלַהֲבִיאָהּ לְתוֹךְ עֲשָׂרָה.

Rabbi Yirmeya said that the opinion of Rabbi Yehuda HaNasi in the *Tosefta* can be explained in an entirely different manner: **A basket is different, since one can tilt it**[N] **and** in that way **bring it to within ten** handbreadths of the ground. Without moving the entire basket, one can tilt it and thereby remove the *eiruv* in order to eat it, without carrying it from one domain to another.

יְתֵיב רַב פַּפָּא וְקָא אָמַר לְהָא שְׁמַעְתָּא. אֵיתִיבֵיהּ רַב בַּר שַׁבָּא לְרַב פַּפָּא: כֵּיצַד הוּא עוֹשֶׂה? מוֹלִיכוֹ בָּרִאשׁוֹן וּמַחְשִׁיךְ עָלָיו, וְנוֹטְלוֹ וּבָא לוֹ. בַּשֵּׁנִי מַחְשִׁיךְ עָלָיו וְאוֹכְלוֹ וּבָא לוֹ.

Rav Pappa sat and recited this ***halakha.*** **Rav bar Shabba raised an objection to Rav Pappa** from the following mishna: **What does one do** if a Festival occurs on Friday, and he wishes to establish an *eiruv* that will be valid for both the Festival and Shabbat? **He brings** the *eiruv* to the location that he wishes to establish as his residence **on** the eve of the **first** day, i.e., the eve of the Festival, **and stays** there **with it until nightfall,** the time when the *eiruv* establishes that location as his residence, **and** then **he takes it** with him **and goes away,**[N] so that it does not become lost before Shabbat begins, in which case he would not have an *eiruv* for Shabbat. **On** the eve of the **second** day, i.e., on Friday afternoon, he takes it back to the same place as the day before, and **stays** there **with it until nightfall,** thereby establishing his Shabbat residence; and then he may then **eat** the *eiruv* **and go away,** if he so desires.

LANGUAGE

Basket [*teraskal*] – טְרַסְקָל: Probably from the Greek word κάρταλλος, *kartallos,* with the consonants transposed. It means a basket with a pointed base.

BACKGROUND

A reed and a basket – קָנֶה וּטְרַסְקָל: According to the opinion of Rabbi Yosei, son of Rabbi Yehuda, the sides of the basket that have been placed on the reed are considered as though they extend down to the ground.

Basket placed on a reed

NOTES

It is not in accordance with Rabbi Yosei, son of Rabbi Yehuda – דְּלָא כְּרַבִּי יוֹסֵי בְּרַבִּי יְהוּדָה: Rabbeinu Ḥananel explains that this comment does not refer to the opinion of Rabbi Yehuda HaNasi. Rather, the reference is to a statement by Rabbi Yehuda, whose opinion with regard to an *eiruv* resting on a place four handbreadths wide at a height of ten handbreadths is contrary to the approach of his son, who holds that anything that is four handbreadths wide at a height of ten handbreadths constitutes a private domain (Rashba).

If one stuck a reed…and placed a basket on top of it – נָעַץ קָנֶה...וְהִנִּיחַ בְּרֹאשׁוֹ טְרַסְקָל: The dispute between Rabbi Yosei, son of Rabbi Yehuda, and the Rabbis is whether or not to evaluate partitions for a private domain in an entirely formalistic manner. Rabbi Yosei holds that since the basket has partitions at a height of ten handbreadths, they should be considered as partitions that descend all the way down to the ground. In this manner, they create a pillar four handbreadths wide and ten handbreadths high. The Rabbis claim that since these partitions do not form an actual physical barrier, they are insufficient to create a private domain.

Since one can tilt it – הוֹאִיל וְיָכוֹל לְנוֹטְתָהּ: In the Jerusalem Talmud it is explained that it is possible to turn the basket upside down. Once it has been turned upside down, all agree that its sides cannot be considered valid partitions and it cannot create a private domain, even according to Rabbi Yosei, son of Rabbi Yehuda.

He brings it on the first day…and takes it – מוֹלִיכוֹ בָּרִאשׁוֹן...וְנוֹטְלוֹ: The Gemara's implication is that if one wants to be sure that his *eiruv* will not be eaten or lost before Shabbat, he may remove it from its spot after it has established his place of residence for the first day and return it on the following day. However, in the Jerusalem Talmud it is stated that the *eiruv* must be removed, since one cannot establish an *eiruv* on Thursday for Shabbat if the sanctity of a Festival intervenes.

אַמַּאי? נֵימָא: כֵּיוָן דְּאִי בָּעֵי אַמְטוּיֵי מָצֵי מַמְטֵי לֵיהּ, אַף עַל גַּב דְּלָא אַמְטְיֵיהּ – כְּמַאן דְּאַמְטְיֵיהּ דָּמֵי!

Why must one actually bring the *eiruv* to the place where he wishes to establish his residence? **Let us say: Since if he wished to bring** the *eiruv* there **he could bring it, even though he did not bring it, it is considered as though he did bring it** there.[N] This follows the same reasoning proposed by Rav Yirmeya in the case of the basket: Since one can tilt it. The fact that this reasoning is not employed here indicates that the potential to do something is insufficient; rather, the deed must actually be done.

אָמַר רַבִּי זֵירָא: גְּזֵירָה מִשּׁוּם יוֹם טוֹב שֶׁחָל לִהְיוֹת אַחַר שַׁבָּת.

Rabbi Zeira said: The fact that one must bring his *eiruv* the day before to the spot that he wishes to establish as his place of residence, and the potential to bring it there does not suffice, is **a decree due to a Festival that occurs after Shabbat.** In that case, the *eiruv* is valid for the Festival only if it was brought there before Shabbat, for it cannot be carried there on Shabbat. Since one cannot actually bring the *eiruv* there, it cannot be said: It is considered as though he did bring it there because had he wished to bring the *eiruv* he could have. Consequently, the Sages decreed that in all cases, the *eiruv* is only valid if it was actually brought to the designated spot, lest one come to think that even on a Festival that occurs after Shabbat it need not be brought there.

אֵיתִיבֵיהּ: נִתְכַּוֵּין לִשְׁבּוֹת בִּרְשׁוּת הָרַבִּים, וְהִנִּיחַ עֵירוּבוֹ בְּכוֹתֶל, לְמַטָּה מֵעֲשָׂרָה טְפָחִים – עֵירוּבוֹ עֵירוּב, לְמַעְלָה מֵעֲשָׂרָה טְפָחִים – אֵין עֵירוּבוֹ עֵירוּב. נִתְכַּוֵּין לִשְׁבּוֹת בְּרֹאשׁ הַשּׁוֹבָךְ אוֹ בְּרֹאשׁ הַמִּגְדָּל, לְמַעְלָה מֵעֲשָׂרָה טְפָחִים – עֵירוּבוֹ עֵירוּב, לְמַטָּה מֵעֲשָׂרָה טְפָחִים – אֵין עֵירוּבוֹ עֵירוּב.

Rav bar Shabba **raised** another **objection** from a different *baraita*: With regard to one who **intended to establish his Shabbat residence in the public domain and placed his *eiruv* in a wall** that is more than four cubits away from that location; if he placed the *eiruv* **below** a height of **ten handbreadths** above the ground, **his *eiruv* is a valid *eiruv*;** but if he placed it **above ten handbreadths, his *eiruv* is not a** valid ***eiruv*** because he is in a public domain while his *eiruv* is in a private domain. If **one intended to establish his Shabbat residence on top of a dovecote or on top of** a large **cupboard,** if he placed the *eiruv* in the dovecote or cupboard **above ten handbreadths** from the ground, **his *eiruv* is** a valid ***eiruv*** because both he and his *eiruv* are in a private domain; but if he placed it **below ten handbreadths,** the area in which he placed his *eiruv* is considered a *karmelit*, and **his *eiruv* is not** a valid ***eiruv*** because he cannot transport his *eiruv* from there to his own domain on Shabbat.

וְאַמַּאי? הָכִי נַמִּי נֵימָא: הוֹאִיל וְיָכוֹל לְנוֹטְתוֹ וְלַהֲבִיאוֹ לְתוֹךְ עֲשָׂרָה! אָמַר רַבִּי יִרְמְיָה: הָכָא בְּמִגְדָּל מְסוּמָּר עָסְקִינַן.

Why should this be so? **Here too, let us say** that his *eiruv* should be valid even if it was placed below ten handbreadths, **since one can tilt** the cupboard **and bring it to within ten** handbreadths from the ground, in which case he and his *eiruv* would be in the same domain. **Rabbi Yirmeya said: Here, we are dealing with a cupboard that is nailed** to the wall so that it cannot be tilted.

רָבָא אָמַר: אֲפִילּוּ תֵּימָא בְּמִגְדָּל שֶׁאֵינוֹ מְסוּמָּר, וְהָכָא בְּמִגְדָּל אָרוֹךְ עָסְקִינַן, דְּאִי מַמְטֵי לֵיהּ פּוּרְתָּא אָזֵיל חוּץ לְאַרְבַּע אַמּוֹת.

Rava said: Even if you say that it is referring to **a cupboard that is not nailed** to the wall, **here, we are dealing with** a very **tall cupboard,** such **that were one to tilt it a little** in order to bring the top of the cupboard within ten handbreadths from the ground, the top of the cupboard **would project beyond** the **four cubits**[N] that constitute one's Shabbat residence.

הֵיכִי דָּמֵי? אִי דְּאִיכָּא כַּוְּותָא וּמִתְנָא – לַיְיתֵיהּ בְּכַוְּותָא וּמִתְנָא! דְּלֵית לֵיהּ כַּוְּותָא וּמִתְנָא.

The Gemara asks: **What,** exactly, **are the circumstances? If** it is referring to a case **where** the cupboard **has a window, and** one has **a rope** at hand,[N] **let him bring it by means of the window and rope.** In other words, let him lower the rope through the cupboard's window and bring the *eiruv* with it, and he will not have to move the entire cupboard. The Gemara answers: Here we are dealing with a case **where it does not have a window, and** he does not have **a rope** at hand.

"נְתָנוֹ בְּבוֹר – אֲפִילּוּ עָמוֹק מֵאָה אַמָּה וכו׳". הַאי בּוֹר דְּקָאֵי הֵיכָא? אִילֵימָא דְּקָאֵי בִּרְשׁוּת הַיָּחִיד –

We learned in the mishna: **If one placed** the *eiruv* **in a pit, even** if **it is a hundred cubits deep,** his *eiruv* is a valid *eiruv*. The Gemara asks: **This pit, where is it situated? If you say that it is situated in the private domain,**

NOTES

It is considered as though he did bring it there – כְּמַאן דְּאַמְטְיֵיהּ דָּמֵי: This question and those in the ensuing discussion are based on the assumption that something that has the potential to be done is considered as though it has already been done. As an aside, it should be noted that a similar assumption is mentioned in several talmudic sources and is termed: Anything suitable for mixing, mixing does not impede it.

The Gemara raises difficulties from a number of sources that indicate that the mere possibility that something can be done is not sufficient with regard to an *eiruv*. Rather, the action must actually be performed. With regard to the proof from the law of an *eiruv* on Shabbat and a Festival, some commentaries, such as Rashi, maintain that the proof is from the laws of *eiruvin* in general and not just from that unique case. However, the Ra'avad explains that the decisive proof comes from this particular case, since the *eiruv* is already found in that place, and one had already established that location as his Shabbat residence and intends to acquire his place of rest for the following day as well. Nevertheless, the possibility alone is insufficient.

Beyond four cubits – חוּץ מֵאַרְבַּע אַמּוֹת: It would seem that even if it is beyond four cubits, one can bring in the *eiruv*: Although it is prohibited to carry four cubits in the public domain, it is still possible to transfer it in increments of less than four cubits. Apparently, even Rabbi Yehuda HaNasi did not permit violating a rabbinic prohibition [*shevut*] of this kind (Ritva).

A window [*kavta*] and a rope [*mitna*] – כַּוְּותָא וּמִתְנָא: Some commentaries read these terms *lakhta* and *mitna*, according to a variant reading that appears elsewhere in the Talmud. A number of commentaries explain that *lakhta* refers to a type of handle at the end of a rope, while others state that it is a type of wheel like that at the top of a crane. The assumption is that beforehand one prepared a method of raising food to the top of the cupboard, and therefore he must have a *lakhta* and a *mitna* at hand to assist him in maneuvering objects within the cupboard. This is the reason why the Sages did not refer to a *lakhta* and *mitna* in the case of a tree. They are not typically used in such circumstances (Ra'avad).

HALAKHA

If one placed his *eiruv* on top of a reed – נְתָנוֹ בְּרֹאשׁ הַקָּנֶה: If one placed his *eiruv* on top of a reed or a growing plant, it is not a valid *eiruv* because he might come to break off part of the plant. However, if the reed had been detached and later reinserted into the ground, an *eiruv* placed on it is valid (*Shulḥan Arukh*, *Oraḥ Ḥayyim* 409:3).

NOTES

On top of a reed or on top of a pole – בְּרֹאשׁ הַקָּנֶה אוֹ הַקּוּנְדָּס: In the Jerusalem Talmud it is emphasized that according to Rabbi Yehuda HaNasi's opinion it is necessary to assume that a board four handbreadths wide rests on top of the reed. Therefore, the *eiruv* rests on a place four handbreadths wide (see Rashi).

Lest he break it off – שֶׁמָּא יִקְטוֹם: The Rambam explains that since reeds are thin and positioned closely together, one might pluck attached ones while pulling the detached ones, failing to differentiate between the two. Consequently, it is necessary for the reed to be reinserted into the ground in a different location.

פְּשִׁיטָא, רְשׁוּת הַיָּחִיד עוֹלָה עַד לָרָקִיעַ. וְכִי הֵיכִי דְּסָלְקָא לְעֵיל – הָכִי נָמֵי דְּנָחְתָּא לְתַחַת. וְאֶלָּא דְּקָאֵי בִּרְשׁוּת הָרַבִּים.

it is obvious, for **the private domain ascends to the sky, and just as it ascends upward, so too, it descends downward** to the bottom of the pit, even if it is more than ten handbreadths deep. **Rather,** we must say **that** the pit **is situated in the public domain.**

דְּנִתְכַּוֵּון לִשְׁבּוֹת הֵיכָא? אִי לְמַעְלָה – הוּא בְּמָקוֹם אֶחָד וְעֵירוּבוֹ בְּמָקוֹם אַחֵר הוּא, אִי לְמַטָּה – פְּשִׁיטָא, הוּא וְעֵירוּבוֹ בְּמָקוֹם אֶחָד!

The Gemara now clarifies: **Where** did one **intend to establish his Shabbat residence? If** he intended to establish his residence **above** the pit in the public domain, this is a case where **he is in one place and his *eiruv* is in another place,** i.e., in a private domain, and therefore his *eiruv* is not valid. Alternatively, **if** one intended to establish his Shabbat residence **below,** in the pit, **it is** also **obvious,** as **he and his *eiruv* are in one place.**

לָא צְרִיכָא, דְּקָאֵי בְּכַרְמְלִית, וְנִתְכַּוֵּון לִשְׁבּוֹת לְמַעְלָה, וְרַבִּי הִיא, דְּאָמַר: כָּל דָּבָר שֶׁהוּא מִשּׁוּם שְׁבוּת לֹא גָּזְרוּ עָלָיו בֵּין הַשְּׁמָשׁוֹת.

The Gemara answers: This ruling **is necessary only** in a case **where** the pit **is situated in a *karmelit*, and he intended to establish his Shabbat residence above** the pit in the *karmelit*. **And** with regard to the question of how this *eiruv* can be valid, as one cannot bring the *eiruv* from the pit to the *karmelit*, the answer is that the mishna was taught in accordance with the opinion of **Rabbi** Yehuda HaNasi, **who said:** With regard to **anything that is** prohibited on Shabbat **due to rabbinic decree** [***shevut***], **they did not issue the decree** to apply **during twilight.** Since carrying from the pit to the *karmelit* is only prohibited as a *shevut*, a person may carry from the pit to the *karmelit* during twilight, the time when the *eiruv* establishes one's Shabbat residence.

מתני׳ נְתָנוֹ בְּרֹאשׁ הַקָּנֶה אוֹ בְּרֹאשׁ הַקּוּנְדָּס, בִּזְמַן שֶׁהוּא תָּלוּשׁ וְנָעוּץ – אֲפִילּוּ גָּבוֹהַּ מֵאָה אַמָּה הֲרֵי זֶה עֵירוּב.

MISHNA If **one placed** his ***eiruv* on top of a reed**[H] **or on top of a pole** [***kundas***],[N] **when** the reed or pole **is detached** from its original place **and stuck** into the ground, **even** if it is **a hundred cubits high, it is** a valid ***eiruv***, as one can remove the reed or pole from the ground and take his *eiruv*.

גמ׳ רָמֵי לֵיהּ רַב אַדָּא בַּר מַתְנָא לְרָבָא: תָּלוּשׁ וְנָעוּץ – אִין, לֹא תָּלוּשׁ וְנָעוּץ – לֹא. מַנִּי – רַבָּנַן הִיא, דְּאָמְרִי: כָּל דָּבָר שֶׁהוּא מִשּׁוּם שְׁבוּת – גָּזְרוּ עָלָיו בֵּין הַשְּׁמָשׁוֹת, וְהָא אָמְרַתְּ רֵישָׁא רַבִּי, רֵישָׁא רַבִּי וְסֵיפָא רַבָּנַן?!

GEMARA Rav Adda bar Mattana raised a contradiction before Rava concerning two tannaitic rulings: The mishna states that if the reed **was detached** from its place of growth **and** then **stuck** into the ground, **yes,** the *eiruv* is valid. That indicates that if it **was not detached and** then **stuck** back into the ground, **no,** the *eiruv* is not valid. In accordance with **whose** opinion is this mishna? **It is** in accordance with the opinion of **the Rabbis, who say: Anything that is** prohibited on Shabbat **due to rabbinic decree** [***shevut***], such as using a tree on Shabbat, **they issued the decree** to apply even **during twilight.** Therefore, if the *eiruv* was on top of a reed that was still attached to the ground in its original place of growth, since it is prohibited by rabbinic decree to make use of trees on Shabbat, one cannot remove the *eiruv* from its place at the time that he must establish his Shabbat residence, and therefore his *eiruv* is invalid. But **didn't you say** that **the first clause,** i.e., the previous mishna, is in accordance with the opinion of **Rabbi** Yehuda HaNasi? How can you say that **the first clause** is in accordance with the opinion of **Rabbi** Yehuda HaNasi **and the latter clause** is in accordance with the opinion of **the Rabbis?**

אֲמַר לֵיהּ: כְּבָר רָמֵי לֵיהּ רָמִי בַּר חָמָא לְרַב חִסְדָּא, וְשַׁנִּי לֵיהּ: רֵישָׁא רַבִּי וְסֵיפָא רַבָּנַן.

Rava **said to** Rav Adda: **Rami bar Ḥama already raised this contradiction before Rav Ḥisda, and** Rav Ḥisda **answered him:** Indeed, **the first clause** is in accordance with the opinion of **Rabbi** Yehuda HaNasi, **and the latter clause** is in accordance with the opinion of the Rabbis.

רָבִינָא אָמַר: כּוּלָּהּ רַבִּי הִיא, וְסֵיפָא – גְּזֵירָה שֶׁמָּא יִקְטוֹם.

Ravina said: You can, in fact, say that **it is all Rabbi** Yehuda HaNasi, **and the latter clause,** i.e., the mishna that insists that the reed be detached and inserted, is not based upon the prohibition of utilizing trees on Shabbat. Rather, in that case there is a unique **decree lest he break it off**[N] from the ground if the reed is relatively soft. Therefore, the mishna requires one to use something that has already been detached from the ground and reinserted. However, the previous mishna is referring to someone who placed his *eiruv* in a tree, where this concern is not relevant.

הַהוּא פּוּלְמוֹסָא דַּאֲתָא לִנְהַרְדְּעָא, אֲמַר לְהוּ רַב נַחְמָן: פּוּקוּ עֲבִידוּ כְּבוּשֵׁי כְּבָשֵׁי בְּאַגְמָא, וּלְמָחָר נֵיזִיל וְנֵיתִיב עֲלַוַיְיהוּ.

The Gemara relates **that** a certain **army** [***pulmosa***][L] once **came to Neharde'a** and took quarters in the study hall, so that there was not enough room for the students. **Rav Naḥman said to** the students: **Go out and create** seats by **compressing** reeds **in the marshes,**[N] **and tomorrow,** on Shabbat, **we will go and sit on them** and study there.

אֵיתִיבֵיהּ רָמִי בַּר חָמָא לְרַב נַחְמָן, וְאָמְרִי לַהּ רַב עוּקְבָא בַּר אַבָּא לְרַב נַחְמָן: תָּלוּשׁ וְנָעוּץ – אִין, לֹא תָּלוּשׁ וְלֹא נָעוּץ – לָא.

Rami bar Ḥama raised an objection to Rav Naḥman, and some say that it was **Rav Ukva bar Abba** who raised the objection **to Rav Naḥman,** from the mishna that states that if the reed **was detached and** then **stuck** into the ground, **yes;** but if it **was not detached and not stuck** into the ground, **no.** This shows that it is not enough to compress the reeds, and they must actually be detached from the ground before they may be used on Shabbat.

אֲמַר לֵיהּ: הָתָם בְּעוּזְרָדִין. וּמְנָא תֵּימְרָא דְּשָׁנֵי לַן בֵּין עוּזְרָדִין לְשֶׁאֵין עוּזְרָדִין – דְּתַנְיָא: הַקָּנִין וְהָאֲטָדִין וְהָהִגִּין – מִין אִילָן הֵן, וְאֵינָן כִּלְאַיִם בַּכֶּרֶם. וְתַנְיָא אִידַּךְ: הַקָּנִים וְהַקִּידָּן וְהָאוּרְבָּנִין – מִין יָרָק הֵן, וְהֵן כִּלְאַיִם בַּכֶּרֶם. קַשְׁיָא אַהֲדָדֵי!

Rav Naḥman **said to him: There,** in the mishna, we are dealing with **hard** reeds, which may not be bent and used on Shabbat, unlike soft reeds. He adds: **And from where do you say that we distinguish between hard reeds and reeds that are not hard?**[N] **As it was taught** in a *baraita*: **Reeds, boxthorn,**[B] **and thistles**[H] **are species of trees, and** therefore they **are not** included in the prohibition of **food crops in a vineyard,** which applies only to herbs planted among vines. **And it was taught in another** *baraita*: **Reeds, cassia, and bulrushes are species of herbs, and** therefore **they are** included in the prohibition of **food crops in a vineyard.** These two *baraitot* **contradict one another,** as one states that reeds are trees, while the other says that they are considered herbs.

אֶלָּא שְׁמַע מִינַּהּ: כָּאן – בְּעוּזְרָדִין, כָּאן – בְּשֶׁאֵין עוּזְרָדִין, שְׁמַע מִינַּהּ.

Rather, conclude from this that we must distinguish between them as follows: **Here,** in the first *baraita*, it is referring **to hard** reeds, which are like trees; whereas **there,** in the second *baraita*, it is referring **to** reeds **that are not hard.** The Gemara concludes: Indeed, **conclude from this** that our resolution of the contradiction is correct.

וְקִידָּה מִין יָרָק הוּא? וְהָתְנַן: אֵין מַרְכִּיבִין פֵּיגָם עַל גַּבֵּי קִידָּה לְבָנָה, מִפְּנֵי שֶׁהוּא יָרָק בְּאִילָן! אָמַר רַב פַּפָּא: קִידָּה לְחוּד, וְקִידָּה לְבָנָה לְחוּד.

The Gemara raises a question with regard to the previously cited *baraita*: **Is cassia a type of herb? Didn't we learn** in a mishna: **One may not graft rue**[B] **to white cassia, as this** involves the grafting of **herbs to a tree?** This proves that white cassia is a tree. **Rav Pappa said:** There is no difficulty, as **cassia is distinct** and is considered a type of herb, **and white cassia is distinct** and is considered a type of tree.

מתני׳ נְתָנוֹ בְּמִגְדָּל וְאָבַד הַמַּפְתֵּחַ – הֲרֵי זֶה עֵירוּב. רַבִּי אֱלִיעֶזֶר אוֹמֵר: אִם אֵינוֹ יוֹדֵעַ שֶׁהַמַּפְתֵּחַ בִּמְקוֹמוֹ – אֵינוֹ עֵירוּב.

MISHNA **If one put** the *eiruv* **in a cupboard** and locked it, **and the key was lost,** so that he is now unable to open the cupboard and access the *eiruv*, **it is** nonetheless **a valid** *eiruv*. **Rabbi Eliezer says: If he does not know that the key is in its place, it is not** a valid *eiruv*.

גמ׳ וְאַמַּאי? הוּא בְּמָקוֹם אֶחָד וְעֵירוּבוֹ בְּמָקוֹם אַחֵר הוּא!

GEMARA The Gemara asks: **And why** should the *eiruv* be valid if the key was lost? **He is in one place and his** *eiruv* **is in a different place,** since he cannot access the *eiruv*.

LANGUAGE

Army [*pulmosa*] – פּוּלְמוֹסָא: From the Greek πόλεμος, *polemos*, meaning war or army.

BACKGROUND

Boxthorn [*atad*] – אָטָד: The *atad* is a species of *Lycium*, from the Solanaceae family. It is a prickly, tangled bush that grows up to a height of about 3 m. Boxthorn grows wild in the desert.

Boxthorn

Rue – פֵּיגָם: The common fringed rue, *Ruta chalepensis*, from the Rutaceae family, is a sharp-smelling bush, 50–70 cm tall. Its leaves divide into feathery lobes, about 10 cm in length. The plant has yellow flowers. Fringed rue is widely cultivated for its fragrance. Several potions that serve as folk medicines are extracted from it. However, the plant also grows wild in all parts of Eretz Yisrael, except the Negev, as well as in other Mediterranean countries.

Ruta chalepensis

HALAKHA

Reeds, boxthorns, and thistles – הַקָּנִין וְהָאֲטָדִין וְהָהִגִּין: Reeds, thornbushes, and thistles are types of trees. Therefore, their presence in a vineyard does not constitute a violation of the prohibition against food crops in a vineyard. There is no difference between hard and soft plants with regard to this prohibition. Rather, the primary factor is the species, as opposed to the softness or hardness of the plant. This ruling is in accordance with the principles established in the *Tosefta* (Radbaz; Rambam *Sefer Zera'im*, *Hilkhot Kilayim* 5:19).

NOTES

Compressing reeds in the marshes – כְּבוּשֵׁי כְּבָשֵׁי בְּאַגְמָא: The Ra'avad explains that Rav Naḥman told them to tread firmly over the reeds in the marsh so that the breakable reeds would be broken before Shabbat.

Hard reeds and reeds that are not hard – עוּזְרָדִין וְשֶׁאֵין עוּזְרָדִין: The straightforward meaning of Rav Naḥman's statement is that he classifies reeds according to their elasticity and softness: When the reed is soft, it is considered an herb, both to permit treading on it on Shabbat, as there is no prohibition against stepping on herbs, and with regard to the prohibition to plant it in a vineyard. With regard to the prohibition against diverse kinds, it is surprising that the same species can at times be considered an herb and at other times a tree. The Rashba explains that Rav Naḥman's intention was to differentiate between species of reeds: There are types of reeds that are hard and are defined as trees, and there are reeds that are soft and are considered herbs. It is possible that the Rambam understood this discussion in a similar manner.

NOTES

Cupboard of bricks – מִגְדָּל שֶׁל לְבֵנִים: The Gemara is trying to find a case that does not involve dismantling, as building and dismantling are primary categories of labor that are prohibited on Shabbat by Torah law. The consensus appears to be that a temporary construction made of layers of bricks is not subject to the prohibition of dismantling. Nevertheless, the Sages prohibited the dismantling of such a structure on Shabbat. They permitted dismantling it only on a Festival because on a Festival the prohibition is less severe than on Shabbat, and they also wanted to promote rejoicing on the Festival (see Ritva).

HALAKHA

A house filled with produce…was then breached – בַּיִת שֶׁמִּילְאָהוּ פֵּירוֹת...וְנִפְחַת: If a house filled with produce was breached, one is permitted to remove the produce via the opening. Apparently, this also applies to a bona fide house (*Magen Avraham*), as the produce itself was never set-aside [*muktze*] (*Shulḥan Arukh, Oraḥ Ḥayyim* 518:9).

רַב וּשְׁמוּאֵל דְּאָמְרִי תַּרְוַיְיהוּ: הָכָא בְּמִגְדָּל שֶׁל לְבֵנִים עָסְקִינַן; וְרַבִּי מֵאִיר הִיא, דְּאָמַר: פּוֹחֵת לְכַתְּחִילָּה וְנוֹטֵל. דִּתְנַן: בַּיִת שֶׁמִּילְאָהוּ פֵּירוֹת, סָתוּם וְנִפְחַת – נוֹטֵל מִמְּקוֹם הַפְּחָת. רַבִּי מֵאִיר אוֹמֵר: פּוֹחֵת וְנוֹטֵל לְכַתְּחִילָּה.

It was Rav and Shmuel who both said: Here, we are dealing with a cupboard made of bricks,[N] and the mishna is in accordance with the opinion of Rabbi Meir, who said: One may create a breach in a brick wall on Shabbat *ab initio*, and take produce from the other side. As we learned in a mishna: If a house filled with produce had been sealed and was then breached,[H] one may take out produce from the place of the breach. Rabbi Meir disagrees and says: One may even create a breach in the wall of the house and take produce *ab initio*. Consequently, according to Rabbi Meir it is permissible to make a hole in the cupboard in order to remove the produce found inside.

וְהָאָמַר רַב נַחְמָן בַּר אַדָּא, אָמַר שְׁמוּאֵל: בַּאֲוִירָא דְּלִיבְנֵי, הָכָא נַמִי – בַּאֲוִירָא דְּלִיבְנֵי.

The Gemara asks: Didn't Rav Naḥman bar Adda say that Shmuel said that that very mishna cited as a proof is referring to a structure built from layers of bricks piled one atop the other without cement or mortar between them, in which case making a hole cannot be considered dismantling a bona fide structure? The Gemara answers: Here too, we are dealing with a cupboard made from layers of bricks.

וְהָא אָמַר רַבִּי זֵירָא: בְּיוֹם טוֹב אָמְרוּ אֲבָל לֹא בְּשַׁבָּת! הָכָא נַמִי, בְּיוֹם טוֹב.

The Gemara raises another difficulty: Didn't Rabbi Zeira say: The Sages in the aforementioned mishna, who discussed the breaching of a wall, spoke only with regard to a Festival, but not with regard to Shabbat? Therefore, it cannot be derived from that mishna that it is permitted to breach the cupboard on Shabbat in order to access the food inside. The Gemara answers: Here too, the mishna is referring to a case where the person needed an *eiruv* for a Festival but not for Shabbat.

אִי הָכִי, הַיְינוּ דְּקָתָנֵי עֲלַהּ, רַבִּי אֱלִיעֶזֶר אוֹמֵר: אִם בָּעִיר אָבַד – עֵירוּבוֹ עֵירוּב, וְאִם בַּשָּׂדֶה אָבַד – אֵין עֵירוּבוֹ עֵירוּב. וְאִי בְּיוֹם טוֹב – מָה לִי עִיר מָה לִי שָׂדֶה?!

The Gemara asks: If it is so that the mishna is referring only to a Festival, there is a difficulty with that which was taught about it in the following *Tosefta*: Rabbi Eliezer says: If the key was lost in a city, his *eiruv* is a valid *eiruv*; and if it was lost in a field, his *eiruv* is not a valid *eiruv*, for within a city it is possible to carry the key by way of courtyards that have joined together in an *eiruv* or the like, but in a field it is impossible to carry it, as the field has the status of a *karmelit*. And if the mishna is referring to a Festival, what is the difference to me whether the key was lost in a city or a field? On a Festival there is no prohibition against carrying from a private to a public domain, and therefore if the key was lost even in a field, the *eiruv* should still be valid.

Perek **III**
Daf **35** Amud **a**

חִסּוּרֵי מִיחַסְּרָא וְהָכִי קָתָנֵי: נְתָנוֹ בְּמִגְדָּל, וְנָעַל בְּפָנָיו וְאָבַד הַמַּפְתֵּחַ – הֲרֵי זֶה עֵירוּב. בַּמֶּה דְּבָרִים אֲמוּרִים – בְּיוֹם טוֹב, אֲבָל בְּשַׁבָּת – אֵין עֵירוּבוֹ עֵירוּב. נִמְצָא הַמַּפְתֵּחַ, בֵּין בָּעִיר בֵּין בַּשָּׂדֶה – אֵין עֵירוּבוֹ עֵירוּב. רַבִּי אֱלִיעֶזֶר אוֹמֵר: בָּעִיר – עֵירוּבוֹ עֵירוּב, בַּשָּׂדֶה – אֵין עֵירוּבוֹ עֵירוּב.

The Gemara answers: The mishna is incomplete and it teaches the following: If one placed the *eiruv* in a cupboard and locked it, and the key is lost,[H] it is nonetheless a valid *eiruv*. In what case is this statement said? On a Festival; however, on Shabbat, his *eiruv* is not a valid *eiruv*. If the key is found,[H] whether in a city or in a field, his *eiruv* is not a valid *eiruv*. Rabbi Eliezer disagrees and says: If it is found in a city, his *eiruv* is a valid *eiruv*; but if it is found in a field, his *eiruv* is not a valid *eiruv*.

HALAKHA

If one placed the *eiruv* in a cupboard…and the key is lost – נְתָנוֹ בְּמִגְדָּל...וְאָבַד הַמַּפְתֵּחַ: If one placed his *eiruv* in a cupboard or in a house and locked it and then lost the key before Shabbat began, and if it is impossible to remove the *eiruv* without performing a labor prohibited by Torah law, the *eiruv* is not a valid *eiruv*. Some authorities rule that if one needs to perform only a labor prohibited by rabbinic decree to remove the *eiruv*, his *eiruv* is a valid *eiruv* (*Magen Avraham*; *Taz*). Other authorities dispute this ruling (*Tur*; *Shulḥan Arukh, Oraḥ Ḥayyim* 394:3).

If the key is found – נִמְצָא הַמַּפְתֵּחַ: If the key to the cupboard where the *eiruv* is located was misplaced, and it was then found in a place where one can carry it without transgressing a Torah prohibition, the *eiruv* is valid. This is the ruling even though one did not have the key during the twilight period (see *Shulḥan Arukh HaRav*; *Shulḥan Arukh, Oraḥ Ḥayyim* 394:3).

בָּעִיר עֵירוּבוֹ עֵירוּב – כְּרַבִּי שִׁמְעוֹן, דְּאָמַר: אֶחָד גַּגּוֹת וְאֶחָד חֲצֵירוֹת וְאֶחָד קַרְפֵּיפוֹת רְשׁוּת אַחַת הֵן לַכֵּלִים שֶׁשָּׁבְתוּ בְּתוֹכָן. בַּשָּׂדֶה אֵין עֵירוּבוֹ עֵירוּב – כְּרַבָּנַן.

The Gemara now explains the difference: If the key is found **in a city, his *eiruv*** is a valid ***eiruv* in accordance with** the opinion of **Rabbi Shimon, who said: Roofs, courtyards, and enclosed fields [*karpeifot*] are all one domain** with regard **to utensils that began Shabbat in them.** Accordingly, a utensil that was left on a roof at the beginning of Shabbat may be carried into a courtyard or a *karpef*. It is possible to transfer anything located in a city from one place to another in a similar manner. If, however, the key is found **in a field, his *eiruv* is not a** valid ***eiruv*, in accordance with** the opinion of **the Rabbis,**[N] due to the prohibition to carry in a *karmelit*. Although carrying there is merely a *shevut*, the *eiruv* is not valid.

רַבָּה וְרַב יוֹסֵף דְּאָמְרִי תַּרְוַיְיהוּ: הָכָא בְּמִגְדָּל שֶׁל עֵץ עָסְקִינַן; דְּמָר סָבַר: כְּלִי הוּא, וְאֵין בִּנְיָן בְּכֵלִים וְאֵין סְתִירָה בְּכֵלִים. וּמָר סָבַר: אֹהֶל הוּא.

The discussion above constitutes one understanding of the mishna. **Rabba and Rav Yosef,** however, **both said: Here, we are dealing with a wooden cupboard,** and the *tanna'im* disagree with regard to the following point: **The** first, anonymous **Sage,** who rules that the *eiruv* is valid, **holds** that the cupboard **is a utensil, and** that **there is no** prohibited labor of **building utensils, and** similarly, **there is no dismantling of utensils.** Since dismantling a utensil is not included in the prohibited labor of dismantling, one may make a hole in the cupboard in order to access the food used for the *eiruv*. **And** the other **Sage,** Rabbi Eliezer, who invalidates the *eiruv*, **holds** that the cupboard **is a tent.** A wooden implement of such a large size is no longer classified as a utensil; rather, it is considered a building, and therefore it is subject to the prohibitions against building and dismantling on Shabbat.

וּבִפְלוּגְתָּא דְּהָנֵי תַּנָּאֵי; דִּתְנַן: הִקִּישׁ עַל גַּבֵּי שִׁידָּה תֵּיבָה וּמִגְדָּל – טְמֵאִין. רַבִּי נְחֶמְיָה וְרַבִּי שִׁמְעוֹן מְטַהֲרִין.

And their dispute is parallel to **the dispute between these *tanna'im*, as we learned** in a mishna with regard to the ritual impurity of a *zav*: One of the unique laws of a *zav* is that he imparts impurity to an object simply by moving it, even if he does not touch it directly. If a *zav* **knocked on a carriage, crate, or cupboard,** even if he did not actually come into direct contact with them, **they are** nonetheless ritually **impure** because he caused them to move when he struck them. **Rabbi Neḥemya and Rabbi Shimon** disagree and **render** them **pure.**

מַאי לָאו בְּהָא קָמִיפַּלְגִי; מָר סָבַר כְּלִי הוּא, וּמָר סָבַר: אֹהֶל הוּא?

What, are they not disagreeing about this point: **The** first **Sage holds** that a carriage, crate, or cupboard **is** categorized as **a utensil,** and therefore it contracts ritual impurity when a *zav* causes it to move; **and the** other **Sage,** Rabbi Neḥemya and Rabbi Shimon, **holds** that **it is a tent,** and a building does not contract ritual impurity in any way from a *zav*?

אָמַר אַבַּיֵי: וְתִיסְבְּרָא?! וְהָתַנְיָא: אֹהֶל וְנִיסָּט – טָמֵא, כְּלִי וְאֵינוֹ נִיסָּט – טָהוֹר. וְקָתָנֵי סֵיפָא: וְאִם הָיוּ נִיסּוֹטִין – טְמֵאִים. זֶה הַכְּלָל: נִיסָּט מֵחֲמַת כֹּחוֹ – טָמֵא, מֵחֲמַת רְעָדָה – טָהוֹר!

Abaye said in refutation of this proof: **And** do **you think** that this is a reasonable explanation of the mishna? **Wasn't it taught** in a *baraita*: If a *zav* shook a real **tent, and it moved, it is** ritually **impure;** and if he shook **a utensil and it did not move, it is** ritually **pure?** This indicates that the critical factor is not whether the article is classified as a tent or as a utensil but whether or not it actually moves when shaken. Furthermore, **it was taught in the latter clause** of that *baraita*: **And if they moved, they are** ritually **impure,** and **this is the principle:** If a utensil or a tent **moved due to the** direct **force** of the *zav*, **it is** ritually **impure.** But if it moved **due to vibrations,**[NH] e.g., if the *zav* knocked on the floor or on the platform upon which the object is located, and the vibrations of the floor or the platform caused the object to move, **it is** ritually **pure,** as it was not moved by the direct force of the *zav*. Once again, the determining factor is not the object's classification as a tent or a utensil but whether it was actually moved by the *zav*.

אֶלָּא אָמַר אַבַּיֵי: דְּכוּלֵּי עָלְמָא: הֶיסֵּט מֵחֲמַת כֹּחוֹ – טָמֵא, מֵחֲמַת רְעָדָה – טָהוֹר. וְהָכָא בִּרְעָדָה מֵחֲמַת כֹּחוֹ עָסְקִינַן. וּבְהָא קָא מִיפַּלְגִי; דְּמָר סָבַר: הָוֵי הֶיסֵּט, וּמָר סָבַר: לָא הָוֵי הֶיסֵּט.

Rather, Abaye said that the dispute between the first *tanna* and Rabbi Neḥemya and Rabbi Shimon should be understood as follows: **All** agree that **movement due to** the direct **force** of the *zav* causes the object to become ritually **impure,** whether it is a tent or a utensil. Conversely, if the movement was **due to vibrations** of the floor or base, **it is** ritually **pure. And here, we are dealing with** a case where the object **vibrated because of** the direct **force** of the *zav*, i.e., where he banged upon the object itself, causing it to vibrate but not to move. **And** the *tanna'im* **disagree with regard to the following** point: **The** first **Sage holds** that this, too, **is** considered **movement; and the** other **Sage,** Rabbi Neḥemya and Rabbi Shimon, **holds** that vibration **is not** considered **movement.** Therefore, Abaye rejects Rabba and Rav Yosef's proof for their explanation of the mishna.

NOTES

His *eiruv* is not an *eiruv*, in accordance with the opinion of the Rabbis – אֵין עֵירוּבוֹ עֵירוּב כְּרַבָּנַן: Rabbi Zeraḥya HaLevi, Rabbeinu Yehonatan, and other commentaries explain that the Rabbis in this context are those who disagree with Rabbi Shimon with regard to carrying in a field. In pressing circumstances, Rabbi Shimon permits transporting an object by passing it from one person to another down a line of people. Therefore, the Gemara emphasizes that the *halakha* is not in accordance with Rabbi Shimon in this regard.

Movement and vibrations – הֶיסֵּט וּרְעָדָה: There are many details of these laws, and they are primarily addressed in tractate *Zavim*. The main point is the distinction between moving an object and merely causing it to vibrate. It would appear that when an object vibrates, its location does not noticeably change.

HALAKHA

Moved by his direct force and by vibrations – נִיסָּט מֵחֲמַת כֹּחוֹ וּמֵחֲמַת רְעָדָה: When a utensil is attached to the ground and other utensils are stacked on top of it, if the bottom utensil was moved by a *zav* and the stack of utensils fell off, they are ritually impure because they were moved by a *zav*. However, if the upper utensils only fell because the bottom utensil was caused to vibrate, but not actually move, they are not ritually impure (Rambam *Sefer Tahara, Hilkhot Metamei Mishkav UMoshav* 9:1).

וּמַתְנִיתִין בְּמַאי מוֹקְמִינַן לַהּ? אַבַּיֵי וְרָבָא דְּאָמְרִי תַּרְוַיְיהוּ: בִּמְנְעוּל וְקָטִיר בְּמִתְנָא עָסְקִינַן, וּבָעֵי סַכִּינָא לְמִיפְסְקֵיהּ.

The Gemara therefore proceeds to ask: If so, **how is the mishna** with regard to *eiruv* **to be interpreted?** The Gemara answers: **Abaye and Rava both said: We are dealing** here **with a lock** that is **tied with a leather strap,**[H] **and a knife is required to cut it**[N] if there is no key.

תַּנָּא קַמָּא סָבַר לָהּ כְּרַבִּי יוֹסֵי, דְּאָמַר: כָּל הַכֵּלִים נִיטָּלִין בַּשַּׁבָּת, חוּץ מִמַּסָּר הַגָּדוֹל וְיָתֵד שֶׁל מַחֲרֵישָׁה.

The anonymous **first *tanna* holds in accordance with** the opinion of **Rabbi Yosei, who said: All utensils may be moved on Shabbat, except for a large saw and the blade of a plow.**[H] Consequently, one may take a knife, cut the strap, and remove his *eiruv* from the cupboard.

וְרַבִּי אֱלִיעֶזֶר סָבַר לָהּ כְּרַבִּי נְחֶמְיָה, דְּאָמַר: אֲפִילּוּ טַלִּית, אֲפִילּוּ תַּרְוָוד – אֵין נִיטָּלִין אֶלָּא לְצוֹרֶךְ תַּשְׁמִישָׁן.

And Rabbi Eliezer holds in accordance with the opinion of **Rabbi Neḥemya, who said: Even a cloak,** and **even a spoon,** which are certainly used only for activities permitted on Shabbat, **may be moved** on Shabbat **only for the purpose of their** ordinary **use.** The same applies to a knife, which may be moved only in order to cut food, but not for any other purpose. Consequently, one cannot cut the strap around the lock of the cupboard, and therefore his *eiruv* is invalid unless the key is located in town and he can transport it via courtyards.

מתני׳ נִתְגַּלְגֵּל חוּץ לַתְּחוּם, נָפַל עָלָיו גַּל, אוֹ נִשְׂרַף, תְּרוּמָה וְנִטְמֵאת; מִבְּעוֹד יוֹם – אֵינוֹ עֵירוּב, מִשֶּׁחָשֵׁיכָה – הֲרֵי זֶה עֵירוּב.

MISHNA If one's *eiruv* **rolled beyond the** Shabbat **limit,**[H] and he no longer has access to his *eiruv* since he may not go beyond his limit, or **if a pile** of stones **fell on it, or if it was burnt,**[H] or if the *eiruv* was ***teruma* and it became** ritually **impure;** if any of these occurrences took place **while it was still day,** prior to the onset of Shabbat, **it is not** a valid ***eiruv,*** since one did not have an *eiruv* at twilight, which is the time one's Shabbat residence is established. However, if any of these occurred **after dark,** when it was already Shabbat, **it is** a valid ***eiruv,*** as it was intact and accessible at the time one's Shabbat residence is determined.

אִם סָפֵק, רַבִּי מֵאִיר וְרַבִּי יְהוּדָה אוֹמְרִים: הֲרֵי זֶה חַמָּר גַּמָּל.

If the matter is **in doubt,** i.e., if he does not know when one of the aforementioned incidents occurred, **Rabbi Meir and Rabbi Yehuda say: This** person **is** in the position of both **a donkey driver,** who must prod the animal from behind, **and a camel driver,**[N] who must lead the animal from the front, i.e., he is a person who is pulled in two opposite directions. Due to the uncertainty concerning his Shabbat border, he must act stringently, as though his resting place were both in his town and at the location where he placed the *eiruv*. He must restrict his Shabbat movement to those areas that are within two thousand cubits of both locations.

רַבִּי יוֹסֵי וְרַבִּי שִׁמְעוֹן אוֹמְרִים: סְפֵק עֵירוּב כָּשֵׁר. אָמַר רַבִּי יוֹסֵי: אַבְטוֹלְמוֹס הֵעִיד מִשּׁוּם חֲמִשָּׁה זְקֵנִים עַל סְפֵק עֵירוּב שֶׁכָּשֵׁר.

Rabbi Yosei and Rabbi Shimon disagree and **say: An *eiruv*** whose validity is **in doubt is** nevertheless **valid. Rav Yosei said:** The Sage **Avtolemos**[P] **testified in the name of five Elders that an *eiruv*** whose validity is **in doubt is valid.**

גמ׳ ״נִתְגַּלְגֵּל חוּץ לַתְּחוּם״. אָמַר רָבָא: לֹא שָׁנוּ אֶלָּא שֶׁנִּתְגַּלְגֵּל חוּץ לְאַרְבַּע אַמּוֹת, אֲבָל לְתוֹךְ אַרְבַּע אַמּוֹת – הַנּוֹתֵן עֵירוּבוֹ יֵשׁ לוֹ אַרְבַּע אַמּוֹת.

GEMARA We learned in the mishna: If one's *eiruv* **rolled beyond the** Shabbat **limit** prior to the onset of Shabbat, it is not a valid *eiruv*. **Rava said: They only taught** this in a case **where** one established his *eiruv* at the edge of his town's Shabbat limit and the *eiruv* **rolled more than four cubits** outside that limit; **however,** if it remained **within four cubits** of the Shabbat limit, it is a valid *eiruv*. The principle is that **one who places his *eiruv*** in a particular location **has four cubits** around it, since he has established his Shabbat residence there.

HALAKHA

A lock tied with a leather strap – מַנְעוּל וְקָטִיר בְּמִתְנָא: If one put his *eiruv* in a cupboard that was then locked with a knotted rope, since he can bring a knife and cut the rope, his *eiruv* is valid, in accordance with the opinions of Abaye and Rava (*Shulḥan Arukh, Oraḥ Ḥayyim* 409:4).

Utensils that may be moved on Shabbat – כֵּלִים הַנִּיטָּלִים בַּשַּׁבָּת: All utensils, even ones generally used for purposes prohibited on Shabbat, may be carried on Shabbat if one needs them in order to perform a permitted act or if one needs to use the place in which they are located. However, if one is generally careful not to handle the utensil for anything other than its primary purpose due to its importance and the concern for possible monetary loss, one may not move it on Shabbat, in accordance with the opinion of Rabbi Yosei (*Shulḥan Arukh, Oraḥ Ḥayyim* 308:1).

Rolled beyond the Shabbat limit – נִתְגַּלְגֵּל חוּץ לַתְּחוּם: If one's *eiruv* rolled beyond his Shabbat limit but remained within four cubits of the boundary, his *eiruv* is valid. If, however, it rolled more than four cubits past the limit, his *eiruv* is invalid, as stated in the mishna and in accordance with Rava's explanation (*Shulḥan Arukh, Oraḥ Ḥayyim* 409:5).

If the *eiruv* was lost or burnt – אָבַד הָעֵירוּב אוֹ נִשְׂרַף: If one's *eiruv* was lost or burnt prior to the onset of Shabbat, it is not a valid *eiruv*. However, if this happened after nightfall, it is a valid *eiruv*. In a case of doubt, it is an *eiruv*, in accordance with the opinions of Rabbi Yosei, Rabbi Shimon, and other Sages. A questionable *eiruv* is valid only if it is known with certainty that it was originally valid when it was placed in its spot. If a doubt arose at the outset, at the time of the placement of the *eiruv*, it is invalid (*Shulḥan Arukh, Oraḥ Ḥayyim* 409:6).

NOTES

A knife is required to cut it – בָּעֵי סַכִּינָא לְמִיפְסְקֵיהּ: The question is raised: If indeed the *halakha* is in accordance with Rabbi Yehuda HaNasi'a opinion that there is no concern with regard to rabbinic prohibitions during the twilight period before Shabbat, carrying the knife should be permitted, as even Rabbi Neḥemya agrees that it is merely a rabbinic prohibition. If Rabbi Yehuda HaNasi's opinion is not accepted, cutting the lock with a knife should be prohibited according to everyone, as that act itself constitutes a violation of a rabbinic decree. Rabbi Ovadya of Bartenura explains that Rabbi Yehuda HaNasi permits only an action that violates one rabbinic prohibition during twilight; if two rabbinic prohibitions are involved, he too prohibits the activity.

A donkey driver and a camel driver – חַמָּר גַּמָּל: The meaning of this expression, which appears several times in this tractate, derives from the differences in leading camels and donkeys. A donkey driver walks behind his donkey, every so often encouraging him from the rear, as a donkey is not generally accustomed to being pulled from the front. The opposite is true for a camel: One leads the camel by walking in front of it and pulling it. Consequently, the expression that a person must be both a donkey driver and a camel driver means that he must be in two places at once, both in front of and behind a particular object, and he is unable to move. A different interpretation of the expression is offered by the *Arukh*: One must pull a donkey and lead a camel when neither animal wants to move.

PERSONALITIES

Avtolemos – אַבְטוֹלְמוֹס: Almost nothing is known about Avtolemos. He was one of Rabbi Yosei's teachers, and Rabbi Yosei quotes his statements in the name of five Elders with regard to a variety of issues.

Some commentaries identify Avtolemos with Avtolemos ben Reuven, who was granted special permission by the Sages to dress and cut his hair in the gentile manner to facilitate his efforts on behalf of the Jewish people, as he had intimate ties with the Roman government. Avtolemos may be the son of Rabbi Reuven Ha'Itztrobuli, who also fulfilled a similar function in Rome.

”נָפַל עָלָיו גַּל וכו׳״. קָא סָלְקָא דַּעְתָּךְ דְּאִי בָּעֵי מָצֵי שָׁקֵיל לֵיהּ.

The mishna continues: If a **pile** of stones **fell on** the *eiruv*[H] prior to the onset of Shabbat, it is not a valid *eiruv*. **It** might **enter your mind** to say that the mishna is referring to a case **where if one wanted he could take** the *eiruv*, i.e., where it is physically possible to clear the stones and remove the *eiruv* from underneath them. The only reason he cannot do so is because of the rabbinic prohibition to handle items that are set-aside, such as stones, on Shabbat.

לֵימָא מַתְנִיתִין דְּלָא כְּרַבִּי, דְּאִי כְּרַבִּי – הָאָמַר: כָּל דָּבָר שֶׁהוּא מִשּׁוּם שְׁבוּת – לֹא גָּזְרוּ עָלָיו בֵּין הַשְּׁמָשׁוֹת!

If so, **let us say that the mishna is not in accordance with** the opinion of **Rabbi** Yehuda HaNasi. **As, if** you say that **it is in accordance with** the opinion of **Rabbi** Yehuda HaNasi, there is a difficulty: **Didn't he say** that with regard to **anything prohibited due to rabbinic decree, they did not issue the decree to apply during twilight?** The prohibition to handle items that are set-aside is also a rabbinic decree, and therefore, according to Rabbi Yehuda HaNasi, since the *eiruv* was accessible at twilight, it should be valid.

אֲפִילּוּ תֵּימָא כְּרַבִּי, לָא צְרִיכָא, דְּבָעֵי מָרָא וְחַצִּינָא.

The Gemara rejects this argument: **Even if you say** that the mishna **is in accordance with** the opinion of **Rabbi** Yehuda HaNasi, we can say that this ruling **was necessary only** in a case **where a hoe or a spade would be required** in order to remove the *eiruv* from under the stones, i.e., one would have to dig, which is a Shabbat labor prohibited by Torah law, not only by rabbinic decree.

וּצְרִיכִי, דְּאִי תָּנָא ״נִתְגַּלְגֵּל״ – מִשּׁוּם דְּלֵיתָא גַּבֵּיהּ. אֲבָל נָפַל עָלָיו גַּל, דְּאִיתֵיהּ גַּבֵּיהּ – אֵימָא לֶיהֱוֵי עֵירוּב.

The Gemara comments: **And** both rulings, the ruling concerning an *eiruv* that rolled beyond the Shabbat limit and the ruling concerning an *eiruv* that became buried under a pile of rocks, **are necessary. As, if** the mishna had only **taught** the case of the *eiruv* that **rolled** away, we might have said that the *eiruv* is invalid **because it is not near him, but** if **a pile** of rocks **fell on** the *eiruv*, since **it is near him,** you might **say that it should be** a valid ***eiruv*,** as one does not actually have to eat the *eiruv*.

וְאִי תָּנָא ״נָפַל עָלָיו גַּל״ – מִשּׁוּם דְּמִיכְסִי, אֲבָל נִתְגַּלְגֵּל, זִימְנִין דְּאָתֵי זִיקָא וּמַיְיתִי לֵיהּ, אֵימָא לֶיהֱוֵי עֵירוּב – צְרִיכָא.

And conversely, **if** the mishna had only **taught** the case where **a pile** of rocks **fell on** the *eiruv*, we might have said that the *eiruv* is invalid **because it is covered, but** in the case where it **rolled** away, since **sometimes a wind comes and brings it** back, **you might say that it should be a** valid *eiruv*. Therefore, it was necessary to teach both cases.

”אוֹ נִשְׂרַף, תְּרוּמָה וְנִטְמֵאת״. לָמָּה לִי? תָּנָא נִשְׂרַף –

The mishna further states: **Or** if the *eiruv* **was burnt,** or if the *eiruv* was ***teruma* that became** ritually **impure** before Shabbat, it is not a valid *eiruv*. The Gemara asks: **Why do I need** to teach these two cases? The essential point of both cases is the same: The *eiruv* is no longer fit to be eaten. The Gemara answers: The mishna **taught** the case where the *eiruv* **was burnt**

Perek **III**
Daf **35** Amud **b**

לְהוֹדִיעֲךָ כֹּחוֹ דְּרַבִּי יוֹסֵי. תָּנָא תְּרוּמָה וְנִטְמֵאת – לְהוֹדִיעֲךָ כֹּחוֹ דְּרַבִּי מֵאִיר.

to convey the far-reaching nature of Rabbi Yosei's statement, as he is lenient in a case of uncertainty whether the *eiruv* was burnt the previous day or only after nightfall, even though the *eiruv* is now entirely destroyed. Additionally, the mishna **taught** the case of ***teruma* that became** ritually **impure to convey the far-reaching nature of Rabbi Meir's** statement, as he is stringent even though the *teruma* itself is still present, and there is only an uncertainty about when it became impure.

HALAKHA

If a pile of stones fell on the *eiruv* – נָפַל עָלָיו גַּל: If a pile of stones fell on the *eiruv*, but one can still access it by moving the stones, it is a valid *eiruv*. However, if one must perform a labor prohibited by Torah law in order to access his *eiruv*, the *eiruv* is invalid (*Shulḥan Arukh*, *Oraḥ Ḥayyim* 394:2).

וְסָבַר רַבִּי מֵאִיר סְפֵיקָא לְחוּמְרָא?! וְהָתְנַן: טָמֵא שֶׁיָּרַד לִטְבּוֹל, סָפֵק טָבַל סָפֵק לֹא טָבַל, וַאֲפִילּוּ טָבַל, סָפֵק טָבַל בְּאַרְבָּעִים סְאָה סָפֵק לֹא טָבַל בְּאַרְבָּעִים סְאָה; וְכֵן שְׁנֵי מִקְוָואוֹת, בְּאַחַת יֵשׁ בָּהּ אַרְבָּעִים סְאָה וּבְאַחַת אֵין בָּהּ אַרְבָּעִים סְאָה, וְטָבַל בְּאַחַת מֵהֶן וְאֵינוֹ יוֹדֵעַ בְּאֵיזֶה מֵהֶן טָבַל – סְפֵיקוֹ טָמֵא.

The Gemara questions the mishna's ruling itself: **Does Rabbi Meir** really **hold** that in cases of **doubt** one must be **stringent? Didn't we learn** the following in a mishna: If a ritually **impure** person **descended to immerse** in a ritual bath,[H] and there is **doubt** whether he actually **immersed**[N] **or he did not immerse; and even if he** certainly **immersed,** there is **doubt** whether he **immersed in** a ritual bath containing **forty** ***se'a*** of water, the minimal amount of water necessary for the ritual bath to be valid, **or he did not immerse in forty** ***se'a*****; and similarly,** if there are **two** adjacent **ritual baths, one** of which **has forty** ***se'a*** of water **in it** and is therefore valid, **and one** of which **does not have forty** ***se'a*** of water **in it, and he immersed in one of them, but he does not know in which of them he immersed;** in each of these cases, owing to **one's doubt, he** remains ritually **impure?**

בַּמֶּה דְּבָרִים אֲמוּרִים – בְּטוּמְאָה חֲמוּרָה.

In what case is this statement, which maintains that in cases of doubt one is considered impure, **said?** It is said **with regard to severe** forms of ritual **impurity,** i.e., those imparted by a primary source of ritual impurity.

אֲבָל בְּטוּמְאָה קַלָּה, כְּגוֹן שֶׁאָכַל אוֹכָלִין טְמֵאִין וְשָׁתָה מַשְׁקִין טְמֵאִין, וְהַבָּא רֹאשׁוֹ וְרוּבּוֹ בְּמַיִם שְׁאוּבִין, אוֹ שֶׁנָּפְלוּ עַל רֹאשׁוֹ וְעַל רוּבּוֹ שְׁלֹשָׁה לוּגִּין מַיִם שְׁאוּבִין; וְיָרַד לִטְבּוֹל, סָפֵק טָבַל סָפֵק לֹא טָבַל, וַאֲפִילּוּ טָבַל – סָפֵק טָבַל בְּאַרְבָּעִים סְאָה סָפֵק לֹא טָבַל בְּאַרְבָּעִים סְאָה. וְכֵן שְׁנֵי מִקְוָואוֹת, בְּאַחַת יֵשׁ בָּהּ אַרְבָּעִים סְאָה וְאַחַת אֵין בָּהּ אַרְבָּעִים סְאָה, וְטָבַל בְּאַחַת מֵהֶן וְאֵינוֹ יוֹדֵעַ בְּאֵיזֶה מֵהֶן טָבַל – סְפֵיקוֹ טָהוֹר.

However, with regard to lenient forms of ritual **impurity** imposed only by rabbinic decree, **such as one who ate** half a half-loaf of **impure foods; and** similarly, **one who drank impure liquids; and one whose head and most of his body came under drawn water,** as opposed to spring water or rainwater, in which case the Sages decreed that person to be ritually impure; **or if three** ***log*** **of drawn water fell on one's head and most of his body,** in which case the Sages also decreed that person to be impure; **and** if in any of these cases **one descended to immerse** himself in a ritual bath to purify himself of the rabbinically decreed impurity, and there is **doubt** whether he actually **immersed or he did not immerse; and even if he** certainly **immersed,** there is **doubt** whether he **immersed in forty** ***se'a*** of water **or he did not immerse in forty** ***se'a*****; and similarly,** if there were **two ritual baths, one** of which **has forty** ***se'a*** of water **in it and one** of which **does not have forty** ***se'a*** of water **in it, and he immersed in one of them, but he does not know in which of them he immersed;** in all of these cases, owing to **his doubt, he is** ritually **pure.**

רַבִּי יוֹסֵי מְטַמֵּא.

Rabbi Yosei disagrees and **renders him** ritually **impure.** In any event, it is clear that, according to the unattributed mishna, which is generally presumed to reflect the opinion of Rabbi Meir, the *halakha* is lenient in cases of doubt relating to ritual impurity that is due to rabbinic decree. Why, then, doesn't Rabbi Meir agree that we should be lenient in cases of doubt relating to an *eiruv*, which is also of rabbinic origin?

קָסָבַר רַבִּי מֵאִיר: תְּחוּמִין דְּאוֹרַיְיתָא נִינְהוּ.

The Gemara answers: **Rabbi Meir holds** that the prohibitions relating to Shabbat **limits are** prohibited **by Torah law,** and therefore the uncertainties in the mishna involve a Torah prohibition, with regard to which one may not be lenient.

וְסָבַר רַבִּי מֵאִיר תְּחוּמִין דְּאוֹרַיְיתָא?! וְהָא תְּנַן: אִם אֵין יָכוֹל לְהַבְלִיעוֹ, בְּזוֹ אָמַר רַבִּי דּוֹסְתַּאי בַּר יַנַּאי מִשּׁוּם רַבִּי מֵאִיר: שָׁמַעְתִּי שֶׁמְּקַדְּרִין בֶּהָרִים.

The Gemara asks: **Does Rabbi Meir** really **hold** that the prohibitions of Shabbat **limits are** prohibited **by Torah law? Didn't we learn** in a mishna: When taking measurements related to Shabbat boundaries, if a fifty-cubit rope is held at either end by two people, the distance between them is deemed to be fifty cubits, even if the distance on the ground is greater, owing to inclines and depressions? If there is a hill or incline between them that **cannot be swallowed** by the fifty-cubit measuring rope, so that the usual mode of measurement cannot be used, **in this** situation, **Rabbi Dostai said in the name of Rabbi Meir: I heard that we pierce mountains,**[N] i.e., we measure the distance as if there were a hole from one side of the hill to the other, so that in effect we measure only the horizontal distance and ignore the differences in elevation.

וְאִי סָלְקָא דַּעְתָּךְ תְּחוּמִין דְּאוֹרַיְיתָא – מִי מְקַדְּרִין? וְהָא אָמַר רַב נַחְמָן, אָמַר רַבָּה בַּר אֲבוּהּ: אֵין מְקַדְּרִין לֹא בְּעָרֵי מִקְלָט וְלֹא בְּעֶגְלָה עֲרוּפָה – מִפְּנֵי שֶׁהֵן שֶׁל תּוֹרָה.

And if it should enter your mind to say that the prohibitions relating to Shabbat **limits are** prohibited **by Torah law, would** it be permitted to **pierce the mountains? Didn't Rav Naḥman say that Rabba bar Avuh said: We may not pierce** mountains **when** measuring the boundaries of **cities of refuge nor** when measuring which city is closest to a corpse and is therefore obligated to perform the rite of the **heifer whose neck is broken, because those** laws **are from the Torah;** therefore, a more stringent policy is used to measure the distances precisely?

HALAKHA

A ritually impure person descended to immerse in a ritual bath – טָמֵא שֶׁיָּרַד לִטְבּוֹל: If a ritually impure person descended to immerse himself, and a doubt arose with regard to his immersion, he is impure, since he retains his previous status of impurity until his status of purity has been clearly established. This ruling is in accordance with the opinion of Rabbi Yosei (*Be'er HaGola*). Some authorities maintain that this only applies to someone who was ritually impure by Torah law, but one who was ritually impure by rabbinic decree is presumed to have become pure, in accordance with the unattributed mishna and the Rambam's ruling (Vilna Gaon; *Shulḥan Arukh, Yoreh De'a* 201:71).

NOTES

There is doubt whether he immersed – סָפֵק טָבַל: As will be explained to a certain extent below (36a, p. 188), there are other aspects to this issue that merit clarification and elucidation beyond the discussion in the Gemara in this context. The primary issue is the strength of the legal presumption that everything retains its previous legal state until it is known with certainty that it is no longer in that state. In the case of an impure person who immersed himself, the presumption is one of ritual impurity. As long as he cannot prove that he immersed and purified himself, he retains his impure status. However, the application of these principles to the discussion with regard to *eiruv* is less clear, as there appear to be differing legal presumptions that would lead to different halakhic conclusions.

We pierce mountains – מְקַדְּרִין בֶּהָרִים: Thinking of mountains as if they were pierced allows measurements to be taken along a horizontal plane, ignoring the differences in elevation, and not along the ground. This method of measurement may not be used for measurements related to Torah law, e.g., measuring the area defined by the Torah as the outskirts of a city of refuge, which provides a safe haven for unwitting killers, and measuring to determine which town is closest to a corpse found in an open space and is therefore responsible to perform the rite of the heifer whose neck is broken [*egla arufa*]. In such cases, precise measurement along the ground is required.

People measuring the Shabbat limit while ignoring the difference in elevation

לָא קַשְׁיָא; הָא – דִּידֵיהּ, הָא – דְּרַבֵּיהּ. דַּיְקָא נַמִי, דְּקָתָנֵי: "בְּזוֹ אָמַר רַבִּי דּוֹסְתַּאי בַּר יַנַּאי מִשּׁוּם רַבִּי מֵאִיר שָׁמַעְתִּי שֶׁמְּקַדְּרִין בֶּהָרִים" – שְׁמַע מִינַּהּ.

The Gemara answers: This is **not difficult,** as there is no contradiction between the two statements. **This** statement, according to which Shabbat limits are by Torah law, **is his; that** statement, in which he is lenient, **is his teacher's.** The language of the mishna **is also precise** according to this explanation, **as we learned: In this** case, **Rabbi Dostai bar Yannai said in the name of Rabbi Meir: I have heard that we pierce mountains.** This formulation indicates that Rabbi Meir did not state his own opinion. Rather, he transmitted a ruling that he had heard from his teacher, even though he did not agree with it himself. The Gemara concludes: Indeed, **conclude from this** that this resolution is correct.

וְרָמֵי דְּאוֹרַיְיתָא אַדְּאוֹרַיְיתָא לְרַבִּי מֵאִיר;

The Gemara continues: There is still room **to raise a contradiction** between one ruling with regard to **Torah law and** another ruling with regard to **Torah law, according to** the opinion of **Rabbi Meir.**

דִּתְנַן: נָגַע בְּאֶחָד בַּלַּיְלָה, וְאֵינוֹ יוֹדֵעַ אִם חַי אִם מֵת, וּלְמָחָר הִשְׁכִּים וּמְצָאוֹ מֵת, רַבִּי מֵאִיר מְטַהֵר וַחֲכָמִים מְטַמְּאִין, שֶׁכׇּל הַטְּמָאוֹת כִּשְׁעַת מְצִיאָתָן!

As we learned in a mishna: If one **touched one** other person **at night, and he does not know whether** the person he touched was **alive or dead,**[H] **and the following day he arose and found him dead,** and he is in doubt as to whether or not he contracted ritual impurity as a result of having come into contact with a corpse, **Rabbi Meir renders him** ritually **pure.** It is assumed that the deceased was still alive until the point that it is known with certainty that he is dead. **And the Rabbis render him** ritually **impure because** it is assumed that **all** ritually **impure** items had already been in the same state as they were **at the time they were discovered.** Just as the deceased was found dead in the morning, so too, it may be presumed that he was dead when he was touched in the middle of the night. Therefore, Rabbi Meir is lenient even with respect to an uncertainty relating to a Torah law, and he holds that a person is presumed to be alive until it is known with certainty that he died. Why, then, is he stringent concerning doubt as to whether the *eiruv* had already become impure on the previous day or only after nightfall? Here too, one should assume that the *eiruv* is ritually pure until he knows with certainty that it became defiled, and so the *eiruv* should be valid, even if Shabbat limits are considered Torah law.

אָמַר רַבִּי יִרְמְיָה: מִשְׁנָתֵנוּ שֶׁהָיָה עָלֶיהָ שֶׁרֶץ כׇּל בֵּין הַשְּׁמָשׁוֹת. אִי הָכִי – בְּהָא לֵימָא רַבִּי יוֹסֵי סְפֵק עֵירוּב כָּשֵׁר?!

The Gemara answers: **Rabbi Yirmeya said: The mishna** is referring to a case **where a creeping animal** that imparts ritual impurity **was on the** *teruma*[N] that was used to establish the *eiruv* **for the entire twilight** period. The Gemara asks: **If so, in that case, would Rabbi Yosei say** that **an** ***eiruv*** whose validity is **in doubt is valid?** There is no uncertainty in this case.

רַבָּה וְרַב יוֹסֵף דְּאָמְרִי תַּרְוַיְיהוּ: הָכָא בִּשְׁתֵּי כִּיתֵּי עֵדִים עָסְקִינַן, אַחַת אוֹמֶרֶת: מִבְּעוֹד יוֹם נִטְמְאָה, וְאַחַת אוֹמֶרֶת: מִשֶּׁחֲשֵׁיכָה.

It was **Rabba and Rav Yosef who both said:** The doubt here does not result from the facts of the case themselves, but from conflicting testimonies and an inability to decide between them. **Here, we are dealing with two sets of witnesses,**[N] **one** of which **says:** The *teruma* **became impure while it was still day,** before the onset of Shabbat; **and one** of which **says:** The *teruma* became impure only **after nightfall.**

Perek **III**
Daf **36** Amud **a**

רָבָא אָמַר: הָתָם תְּרֵי חֲזָקֵי לְקוּלָּא, וְהָכָא חֲדָא חֲזָקָה לְקוּלָּא.

Rava said: That is not the way to resolve the apparent contradiction between the two rulings; rather, there is a difference between the cases with regard to the ritual impurity itself: **There,** with regard to touching a person who was later found dead, there are **two presumptions** supporting **leniency,** whereas **here,** with respect to the *teruma* being used for an *eiruv*, there is only **one presumption** supporting **leniency.** How so? With regard to one who touched another person who was later found to be dead, there are two presumptions of purity: Firstly, the person who was found dead was previously alive, and the presumption is that he remained in that state until we know with certainty that he was dead. Secondly, the one who touched that person was previously pure, and he remains in that presumptive state until we know with certainty that he became impure. Therefore, Rabbi Meir had adequate reason to be lenient. However, with regard to *teruma*, only one presumption exists, that the *teruma* was previously pure and presumably remained in that state until proven otherwise. Since there is no additional presumption, Rabbi Meir ruled stringently.

HALAKHA

If one touched a person who may be dead – נָגַע בִּסְפֵק מֵת: If one touched another person at night and does not know whether that person was alive or dead, and in the morning that person was found dead, the following distinction applies: If the doubt arose in a private domain, the person is ritually impure, in accordance with the opinion of the Rabbis. If the doubt arose in a public domain, he is ritually pure (Rambam *Sefer Tahara, Hilkhot She'ar Avot HaTumot* 18:14).

NOTES

A creeping animal was on the *teruma* – הָיָה עָלֶיהָ שֶׁרֶץ: The commentaries question Rashi's explanation that there was a dead creeping animal [*sheretz*] on the *teruma* throughout the twilight period. If so, what did Rabbi Yirmeya mean to say? The Rashba explains that there was a creeping animal, which was eventually discovered to be dead, on the *teruma*; however, it is not clear at what point it died.

Two sets of witnesses – שְׁתֵּי כִּיתֵּי עֵדִים: This issue is the topic of much discussion. The essential principle is that when two sets of witnesses give conflicting testimony, the matter is considered to be in doubt, and there is no room to take into consideration the preexisting circumstances or presumptions of legal status. This is unlike other circumstances of doubt, where in the absence of witnesses, the situation may be judged on the basis of the current state of affairs or on the basis of a preexisting legal status (see Rashba).

קַשְׁיָא דְּרַבִּי יוֹסֵי אַדְּרַבִּי יוֹסֵי!

All the difficulties raised above are based on the seemingly conflicting statements of Rabbi Meir. Yet it would appear that there is also **a contradiction between** one statement of **Rabbi Yosei and** another statement of **Rabbi Yosei,** for he was stringent with regard to the doubts involving ritual baths but lenient with regard to doubts involving *eiruv*.

אָמַר רַב הוּנָא בַּר חִינָּנָא: שָׁאנֵי טוּמְאָה, הוֹאִיל וְיֵשׁ לָהּ עִיקָּר מִן הַתּוֹרָה. שַׁבָּת נַמִי דְּאוֹרַיְיתָא הִיא! קָסָבַר רַבִּי יוֹסֵי: תְּחוּמִין דְּרַבָּנַן.

Rav Huna bar Ḥinnana said: The law with regard to ritual **impurity is different, since it has a basis in the Torah.** Therefore, Rabbi Yosei was stringent even with respect to immersion performed in order to remove impurity that is only of rabbinic origin. The Gemara asks: The prohibitions of **Shabbat** limits **are also** prohibited **by Torah law;** why isn't Rabbi Yosei stringent about them as well? The Gemara answers: **Rabbi Yosei holds:** The laws of Shabbat **limits** are by **rabbinic** law,[N] not by Torah law.

וְאִיבָּעֵית אֵימָא: הָא דִּידֵיהּ, הָא דְּרַבֵּיהּ. דַּיְקָא נַמִי, דְּקָתָנֵי: אָמַר רַבִּי יוֹסֵי ״אַבְטוֹלְמוֹס הֵעִיד מִשּׁוּם חֲמִשָּׁה זְקֵנִים שֶׁסְּפֵק עֵירוּב כָּשֵׁר״ – שְׁמַע מִינָּהּ.

And if you wish, say instead: **This** stringent ruling **is his; that** lenient ruling with regard to an *eiruv* **is his teacher's.** The Gemara comments: The language of the mishna **is also precise** according to this explanation, **as we learned** in the mishna that **Rabbi Yosei said:** The Sage **Avtolemos testified in the name of five Elders that an *eiruv*** whose validity is **in doubt is valid.**[N] This formulation indicates that Rabbi Yosei was merely reporting a ruling that he had heard from his teacher, although he may not have accepted it. The Gemara concludes: Indeed, **conclude from this** that this resolution of the contradiction is correct.

רָבָא אָמַר, הָתָם הַיְינוּ טַעְמָא דְּרַבִּי יוֹסֵי: הַעֲמֵד טָמֵא עַל חֶזְקָתוֹ, וְאֵימָא לֹא טָבַל.

Rava said that a different resolution of the contradiction may be suggested: **There,** with regard to ritual baths, **this is the reason** for **Rabbi Yosei's** opinion: **Keep the impure** person **in his presumptive state** of ritual impurity, **and say** that **he did not** properly **immerse** himself.

אַדְּרַבָּה, הַעֲמֵד מִקְוֶה עַל חֶזְקָתוֹ וְאֵימָא לֹא חָסַר! בְּמִקְוֶה שֶׁלֹּא נִמְדַּד.

The Gemara responds: **On the contrary, keep the ritual bath in its presumptive state** of validity **and say that** the ritual bath **was not lacking** the requisite measure of water. The Gemara answers: We are dealing here with **a ritual bath that had not been** previously **measured** to determine whether it contained forty *se'a*, and therefore it had no prior presumption of validity.

תַּנְיָא: כֵּיצַד אָמַר רַבִּי יוֹסֵי סְפֵק עֵירוּב כָּשֵׁר? עֵירֵב בִּתְרוּמָה, סָפֵק מִבְּעוֹד יוֹם נִטְמֵאת סָפֵק מִשֶּׁחֲשֵׁיכָה נִטְמֵאת, וְכֵן בְּפֵירוֹת – סָפֵק מִבְּעוֹד יוֹם נִתְקְנוּ, סָפֵק מִשֶּׁחֲשֵׁיכָה נִתְקְנוּ – זֶה הוּא סְפֵק עֵירוּב כָּשֵׁר.

It was taught in the *Tosefta*: **In what case did Rabbi Yosei say that an *eiruv*** whose validity is **in doubt is** nevertheless **valid?** For example, if **one established an *eiruv* with *teruma*** that had been ritually pure but later became impure, and there is **doubt whether it became impure while it was still day,** before the onset of Shabbat, or **whether it became impure** only **after nightfall, and similarly,** if one made an *eiruv* **with** untithed **produce** that was later tithed and thereby became permissible for eating, and there is **doubt whether it was rendered fit while it was still day,** before the onset of Shabbat, or **whether it was rendered fit** only **after nightfall, this is an *eiruv*** whose validity is **in doubt** which Rabbi Yosei said **is valid.**[H]

אֲבָל עֵירֵב בִּתְרוּמָה, סָפֵק טְהוֹרָה סָפֵק טְמֵאָה; וְכֵן בְּפֵירוֹת, סָפֵק נִתְקְנוּ סָפֵק לֹא נִתְקְנוּ – אֵין זֶה סְפֵק עֵירוּב כָּשֵׁר.

However, if one established an *eiruv* with *teruma* about which **there was doubt whether it was** ritually **pure or** ritually **impure** from the outset; **and similarly,** if one established an *eiruv* **with produce** about which **there was doubt** from the outset **whether it had been** tithed and thereby **rendered fit** or **whether it had not been** tithed and thereby **rendered fit, this is not** a case of **an *eiruv*** whose validity is **in doubt** that Rabbi Yosei said **is valid.**

מַאי שְׁנָא תְּרוּמָה – דְּאָמַר: הַעֲמֵד תְּרוּמָה עַל חֶזְקָתָהּ, וְאֵימָא טְהוֹרָה הִיא. פֵּירוֹת נַמִי, הַעֲמֵד טֶבֶל עַל חֶזְקָתוֹ, וְאֵימָא לֹא נִתְקְנוּ!

The Gemara raises a question in order to clarify the *Tosefta*: **What is different** about ***teruma***, with regard to which we say: **Keep the *teruma* in its presumptive state** of ritual purity, **and say** that **it was** still **pure** at the onset of Shabbat, since it had been previously pure and it is not known when it became impure? According to that reasoning, with regard to untithed **produce** [***tevel***] it should **also** be said: **Keep the untithed produce in its presumptive state,** as the produce had certainly been untithed originally, **and say that it was not** tithed and thereby **rendered fit** prior to the onset of Shabbat.

NOTES

The laws of Shabbat limits are by rabbinic law – תְּחוּמִין דְּרַבָּנַן: The halakhic authorities discussed at length whether it can be proven from here that the entire law of Shabbat limits is of rabbinic origin. Alternatively, it is possible that the two-thousand-cubit limit is of rabbinic origin, but the limit of twelve *mil* is a Torah law. This is the conclusion reached in the Jerusalem Talmud. Some commentaries state that the difference between two thousand cubits and twelve *mil* is so great that it is impossible to mistake the two, and therefore each has a separate set of laws (Ra'avad). Alternatively, since there is no way to adjust or circumvent the limit of twelve *mil* by means of an *eiruv*, it is impossible to mistake the two (Rashba).

An *eiruv* whose validity is in doubt is valid – סְפֵק עֵירוּב כָּשֵׁר: Some commentaries explain Rabbi Yosei's distinction as follows: In the first case, where the *teruma* was definitely impure, the doubt relates exclusively to the *eiruv* and its validity. The *halakha* is lenient in cases of doubt involving an *eiruv*. However, in the second case, the doubt relates to whether or not the *teruma* was impure, and not to the *eiruv*. The *halakha* is stringent in cases of doubt as to whether *teruma* is impure, even though in this instance the stringency will have implications with regard to the *eiruv* as well. Nevertheless, the relevant issue is not the status of the *eiruv* but that of the *teruma* (*Noda BeYehuda*). Other commentaries state that there is an additional presumption that invalidates the *eiruv*: It is presumed that a person stays in his house, and his presumptive Shabbat residence is there rather than at the location of his *eiruv* (Rashba).

HALAKHA

An *eiruv* whose validity is in doubt is valid – סְפֵק עֵירוּב כָּשֵׁר: An *eiruv* whose validity is in doubt can be considered valid only if it once had a presumption of validity, in accordance with the *Tosefta*'s explanation of Rabbi Yosei's opinion (*Shulḥan Arukh*, *Oraḥ Ḥayyim* 394:1, 409:6).

לָא תֵּימָא: "סָפֵק מִבְּעוֹד יוֹם נִתְקְנוּ", אֶלָּא אֵימָא: סָפֵק מִבְּעוֹד יוֹם נִדְמְעוּ, סָפֵק מִשֶּׁחֲשֵׁיכָה נִדְמְעוּ.

Rather, emend the wording of the *Tosefta*: **Do not say:** There is **doubt whether it was rendered fit while it was still day,** before the onset of Shabbat. **Rather, say:** There is **doubt whether** regular produce **became mixed** with untithed produce **while it was still day,** or **whether it became mixed** only **after nightfall.** In other words, one used regular food to establish his *eiruv*, but then *tevel* was mixed with that food, prohibiting the entire mixture from being consumed until tithes are separated for the *tevel*. However, there is doubt whether the produce became mixed with the *tevel* while it was still day, in which case the *eiruv* is invalid, or whether it became mixed only after nightfall, in which case the *eiruv* is valid. In that case, we say: Keep the produce in its presumptive state and say that it was not mixed with *tevel* during the day, and therefore the *eiruv* is valid.

בְּעָא רַב שְׁמוּאֵל בַּר רַב יִצְחָק מֵרַב הוּנָא: הָיוּ לְפָנָיו שְׁתֵּי כִכָּרוֹת, אַחַת טְמֵאָה וְאַחַת טְהוֹרָה, וְאָמַר: עֵירְבוּ לִי בַּטְּהוֹרָה בְּכׇל מָקוֹם שֶׁהִיא, מַהוּ?

Rav Shmuel bar Rav Yitzḥak raised a dilemma to Rav Huna: If **there were two loaves of** *teruma* **before** someone, **one** that was ritually **impure and one** that was ritually **pure,** and he did not know which one was pure; **and he said: Establish an** ***eiruv*** *teḥumin* **for me with the pure** loaf, **wherever it is,** i.e., even though I do not know which it is, I wish to establish my Shabbat residence at the location of the pure loaf, and those present placed both loaves in the same place, **what is** the *halakha*? Is this a valid *eiruv* or not?

תִּיבָּעֵי לְרַבִּי מֵאִיר, תִּיבָּעֵי לְרַבִּי יוֹסֵי; תִּיבָּעֵי לְרַבִּי מֵאִיר: עַד כָּאן לָא קָאָמַר רַבִּי מֵאִיר הָתָם – דְּלֵיכָּא טְהוֹרָה, הָכָא – הָא אִיכָּא טְהוֹרָה. אוֹ דִּילְמָא: אֲפִילּוּ לְרַבִּי יוֹסֵי לָא קָאָמַר אֶלָּא הָתָם, דְּאִם אִיתָא דְּהִיא טְהוֹרָה – יָדַע לַהּ, אֲבָל הָכָא – הָא לָא יָדַע לַהּ!

The Gemara clarifies: The question may **be asked according to** the stringent opinion of **Rabbi Meir,** and it may **be asked according to** the lenient opinion of **Rabbi Yosei.** The question may **be asked according to** the opinion of **Rabbi Meir** in the following manner: Perhaps **Rabbi Meir only stated** his stringent opinion with regard to a questionable *eiruv* **there, where there is no** *teruma* that is definitely **pure** present, but only *teruma* whose purity is in doubt. **Here,** however, **there** definitely **is a pure** loaf, and therefore even Rabbi Meir may agree to rule leniently. **Or perhaps** it may be argued that **even according to** the opinion of **Rabbi Yosei, he only said** that we are lenient with regard to an *eiruv* whose validity is in doubt in the case dealt with **there,** where, **if indeed** the *teruma* **is pure, he knows** where **it** is; **but here, he does not know** how to identify **it.**

אֲמַר לֵיהּ: בֵּין לְרַבִּי יוֹסֵי בֵּין לְרַבִּי מֵאִיר, בָּעֵינַן סְעוּדָה הָרְאוּיָה מִבְּעוֹד יוֹם – וְלֵיכָּא.

Rav Huna **said to** Rav Shmuel bar Rav Yitzḥak: **According to both** the opinion of **Rabbi Yosei and** the opinion of **Rabbi Meir, we require** that an *eiruv* consist of **a meal that is fit** to be eaten **while it is still day,** prior to the onset of Shabbat, **and** in this case **there is none.** Due to the uncertainty as to which loaf is pure and which is impure, neither of the two loaves may be eaten, and an *eiruv* made with food that may not be eaten while it is still day is not a valid *eiruv*.

בְּעָא מִינֵּיהּ רָבָא מֵרַב נַחְמָן: כִּכָּר זוֹ הַיּוֹם חוֹל וּלְמָחָר קֹדֶשׁ, וְאָמַר: עֵירְבוּ לִי בָּזֶה, מַהוּ? אֲמַר לֵיהּ: עֵירוּבוֹ עֵירוּב.

Rava raised another **dilemma to Rav Naḥman:** If one said: **This loaf** shall remain **unconsecrated today, and tomorrow** it shall be **consecrated,**[H] **and he** then **said: Establish an** ***eiruv*** **for me with this** loaf, **what is** the *halakha*? Do we say that since the twilight period's status as part of the previous day or part of the day that follows is questionable, the consecration of the loaf may take effect before the *eiruv* establishes one's Shabbat residence, and since an *eiruv* cannot be made with a consecrated object, the *eiruv* is not valid? Rav Naḥman **said to** Rava: In that case, **his** ***eiruv*** is a valid ***eiruv.***

הַיּוֹם קֹדֶשׁ וּלְמָחָר חוֹל, וְאָמַר: עֵירְבוּ לִי בָּזֶה, מַהוּ? אֲמַר לֵיהּ: אֵין עֵירוּבוֹ עֵירוּב. מַאי שְׁנָא?

Rava then asked about one who made the opposite statement: This loaf shall be **consecrated today, and tomorrow** it shall be **unconsecrated,** i.e., it shall be redeemed with money that I have in my house, **and he** then **said: Establish an** ***eiruv*** **for me with this** loaf, **what is** the *halakha*? Rav Naḥman **said to him: His** ***eiruv*** **is not** a valid ***eiruv.*** Rava asked him: **What is different** between the two cases? If we are lenient with regard to the twilight period, we should be lenient in both cases.

HALAKHA

Unconsecrated today and tomorrow consecrated – הַיּוֹם חוֹל וּלְמָחָר קֹדֶשׁ: If one said that a certain loaf should remain unconsecrated today but be consecrated tomorrow, and then he made an *eiruv* with it, the *eiruv* is valid, in accordance with the opinion of Rav Naḥman (*Shulḥan Arukh, Oraḥ Ḥayyim* 386:9).

BACKGROUND

Flask – לָגִין:

Flask from the talmudic period

NOTES

Teruma of the tithe when night falls – תְּרוּמַת מַעֲשֵׂר לִכְשֶׁתֶּחְשַׁךְ: The early commentaries ask, as Rav Naḥman said in response to Rava's question: Here, too, sanctification should not take effect because of the doubt involved. Several answers are offered. The Rashba explains that there is a difference between the expression tomorrow and the expression when night falls. When one says that the sanctification should take effect tomorrow, the implication is that it should take effect when the next day has clearly and definitely arrived. Therefore, the sanctification does not take effect when it is still unclear whether it is day or night. However, when one uses the expression when night falls, even Rav Naḥman agrees that it takes effect at the beginning of nightfall.

אָמַר לֵיהּ: לְכִי תֵּיכוֹל עֲלֵיהּ כּוֹרָא דְּמִלְחָא. הַיּוֹם חוֹל וּלְמָחָר קֹדֶשׁ – מִסְּפֵיקָא לָא נָחְתָא לֵיהּ קְדוּשָּׁה. הַיּוֹם קֹדֶשׁ וּלְמָחָר חוֹל – מִסְּפֵיקָא לָא פָּקְעָא לֵיהּ קְדוּשְּׁתֵיהּ מִינֵּיהּ.

Rav Naḥman **said to** Rava in jest: **After you eat a *kor* of salt over it,** and analyze the matter at length, you will be able to understand the difference. The difference is obvious: When one says that **today** the loaf shall remain **unconsecrated, and tomorrow** it shall be **consecrated,** we do **not** assume **out of doubt** that **sanctity has descended upon** the loaf. Therefore, the loaf remains in its presumptive state of being unconsecrated during the twilight period, and the *eiruv* is valid. With regard to the opposite case, however, when one says that **today** the loaf shall be **consecrated, and tomorrow** it shall be **unconsecrated,** we do **not** assume **out of doubt** that the loaf's **sanctity has departed from it.** The loaf remains in its presumptive state of consecration for the duration of the twilight period, and therefore the *eiruv* is invalid.

תְּנַן הָתָם: לָגִין טְבוּל יוֹם שֶׁמִּלְאוֹ מִן הֶחָבִית שֶׁל מַעֲשֵׂר טֶבֶל, וְאָמַר: הֲרֵי זֶה תְּרוּמַת מַעֲשֵׂר לִכְשֶׁתֶּחְשַׁךְ – דְּבָרָיו קַיָּימִין.

We learned in a mishna **there: If one filled a flask**[B] **that was immersed during the day** [***tevul yom***] but does not become fully ritually pure until night **from a barrel of tithe** that was still ***tevel,*** meaning that the produce inside was first tithe from which *teruma* of the tithe had not yet been separated, **and he said: Let** the contents of **this** flask **be *teruma* of the tithe** for the contents of the barrel **when night falls,**[N] **his statement takes effect.** If he were to say that the designated portion should immediately become *teruma* of the tithe, the *teruma* of the tithe would be defiled by the flask that is still a *tevul yom.* Once night falls, however, the flask is absolutely pure, and if the designation of the flask's contents as *teruma* of the tithe takes effect at that time, the produce remains pure. The mishna teaches that *teruma* of the tithe can be separated in this manner.

וְאִם אָמַר עֵירְבוּ לִי בָּזֶה – לֹא אָמַר כְּלוּם. אָמַר רָבָא, זֹאת אוֹמֶרֶת: סוֹף הַיּוֹם קוֹנֶה עֵירוּב.

The mishna continues: **And if he said: Establish an *eiruv* for me with** the contents of **this** flask, **he has not said anything,** as the contents of the flask are still *tevel.* **Rava said: That is to say** that **the end of the day** is when **the *eiruv* acquires** one's Shabbat residence. The critical time with respect to an *eiruv* is the last moment of Shabbat eve, rather than the first moment of Shabbat.

Perek **III**
Daf **36** Amud **b**

HALAKHA

A condition with regard to an *eiruv* – תְּנַאי בְּעֵירוּב: One may establish two *eiruvin* before the onset of Shabbat on two sides of a town and stipulate that if a certain event occurs on Shabbat, his *eiruv* will be on one side, as stated in the mishna. This ruling is in accordance with the opinion of the Rabbis, who accept the principle of retroactive designation (Vilna Gaon; *Shulḥan Arukh, Oraḥ Ḥayyim* 413:1).

דְּאִי סָלְקָא דַּעְתָּךְ תְּחִילַּת הַיּוֹם קוֹנֶה עֵירוּב – אִי אָמַר עֵירְבוּ לִי בָּזֶה, אַמַּאי לֹא אָמַר כְּלוּם?

As, **if it should enter your mind** that **an *eiruv* acquires** one's Shabbat residence at **the beginning of the day** of Shabbat, then **if he said: Establish an *eiruv* for me with** the produce in **this** flask, **why hasn't he said anything?** After nightfall, when Shabbat begins, the flask is already pure, and therefore the *teruma* of the tithe inside it is also pure and is suitable for an *eiruv*.

אָמַר רַב פָּפָּא: אֲפִילּוּ תֵּימָא תְּחִילַּת הַיּוֹם קוֹנֶה עֵירוּב – בָּעֵינַן סְעוּדָּה הָרְאוּיָה מִבְּעוֹד יוֹם, וְלֵיכָּא.

Rav Pappa said: This is no proof; **even if you say** that **an *eiruv* acquires** one's Shabbat residence at **the beginning of the day** of Shabbat, nonetheless, **we require a meal that is fit** to be eaten **while it is still day,** prior to the onset of Shabbat, in order for the *eiruv* to be valid, **and there is none** in this case. While it was still day, it was certainly prohibited to consume the contents of the flask, which were still *tevel*, and therefore it could not be used as an *eiruv*.

מתני׳ מַתְנֶה אָדָם עַל עֵירוּבוֹ, וְאוֹמֵר: אִם בָּאוּ גוֹיִם מִן הַמִּזְרָח – עֵירוּבִי לַמַּעֲרָב, מִן הַמַּעֲרָב – עֵירוּבִי לַמִּזְרָח, אִם בָּאוּ לְכָאן וּלְכָאן – לְמָקוֹם שֶׁאֶרְצֶה אֵלֵךְ, לֹא בָּאוּ לֹא לְכָאן וְלֹא לְכָאן – הֲרֵינִי כִּבְנֵי עִירִי.

MISHNA **A person may make a condition with regard to his *eiruv*** of Shabbat borders.[H] In other words, he need not decide in advance in which direction his *eiruv* should take effect. For example, he may deposit an *eiruv* on each of two opposite sides of his town, **and say: If gentiles come from the east, my *eiruv* is in the west,** so that I can escape in that direction; and if they come **from the west, my *eiruv* is in the east. If they come from here and from there,** i.e., from both directions, **I will go wherever I wish,** and my *eiruv* will retroactively take effect in that direction; and **if they do not come** at all, **neither from here nor from there, I will be like** the rest of **the inhabitants of my town** and give up both *eiruvin* that I deposited, leaving me with two thousand cubits in all directions from the town.

אִם בָּא חָכָם מִן הַמִּזְרָח – עֵירוּבִי לַמִּזְרָח, מִן הַמַּעֲרָב – עֵירוּבִי לַמַּעֲרָב, בָּא לְכָאן וּלְכָאן – לְמָקוֹם שֶׁאֶרְצֶה אֵלֵךְ, לֹא לְכָאן וְלֹא לְכָאן – הֲרֵינִי כִּבְנֵי עִירִי. רַבִּי יְהוּדָה אוֹמֵר: אִם הָיָה אֶחָד מֵהֶן רַבּוֹ – הוֹלֵךְ אֵצֶל רַבּוֹ, וְאִם הָיוּ שְׁנֵיהֶן רַבּוֹתָיו – לְמָקוֹם שֶׁיִּרְצֶה יֵלֵךְ.

Similarly, one may say: **If a Sage comes from the east**[N] and he is spending Shabbat beyond the boundaries of my town, **my *eiruv* is in the east,** so that I may go out to greet him there; and if he comes **from the west, my *eiruv* is in the west.** If one Sage **comes from here, and** another Sage comes **from there, I will go wherever I wish; and** if no Sage comes, **neither from here nor from there, I will be like** the rest of **the inhabitants of my town. Rabbi Yehuda says: If one of** the Sages coming from opposite directions **was his teacher, he may go** only **to his teacher,** as it is assumed that was his original intention. **And if they were both his teachers,** so that there is no reason to suppose that he preferred one over the other, **he may go wherever he wishes.**

גמ׳ כִּי אֲתָא רַבִּי יִצְחָק, תָּנֵי אִיפְּכָא כּוּלַּהּ מַתְנִיתִין. קַשְׁיָא גּוֹיִם אַגּוֹיִם, קַשְׁיָא חָכָם אַחָכָם.

GEMARA The Gemara relates that **when Rabbi Yitzḥak came** from Eretz Yisrael to Babylonia, **he taught all** of the laws in **the mishna in the opposite** manner. That is to say, according to him, if the gentiles came from the east, his *eiruv* would be to the east, and, conversely, if the Sage came from the east, his *eiruv* would be to the west. This is **difficult** because if this is correct, there is a contradiction **between** the ruling concerning **gentiles** in the mishna and the ruling concerning **gentiles** in the *baraita*, **and** similarly there is a contradiction **between** the ruling concerning **a Sage** in the mishna **and** the ruling concerning **a Sage** in the *baraita*.

גּוֹיִם אַגּוֹיִם לָא קַשְׁיָא; הָא – בְּפַרְהַגְבְּנָא, הָא – בְּמָרֵי דְמָתָא.

The Gemara answers: The apparent contradiction **between** the ruling concerning **gentiles** in the mishna **and** the ruling concerning **gentiles** in the *baraita* is **not difficult: This** case in the mishna is referring to **a tax collector [*parhagabena*],**[L] from whom one wishes to flee; whereas **that** case in the *baraita* is referring to **the lord of the town,**[N] with whom he wishes to speak. Therefore, there are times that one wants to go out toward the gentile, while at other times one wants to flee from him.

חָכָם אַחָכָם לָא קַשְׁיָא; הָא – בְּמוֹתִיב פִּירְקֵי, הָא – בְּמַקְרֵי שְׁמַע.

Similarly, the apparent contradiction **between** the ruling concerning **a Sage** in the mishna **and** the ruling concerning **a Sage** in the *baraita* is **not difficult: This** case in the mishna is referring to a scholar **who sits** and delivers public Torah **lectures,** and one wishes to come and learn Torah from him; whereas **that** case in the *baraita* is referring to one **who teaches** children how to **recite** the ***Shema*,**[N] i.e., one who teaches young children how to pray, of whom he has no need. The *baraita* teaches that if a scholar came from one direction to deliver a public lecture and the school teacher came from the opposite direction, his *eiruv* is in the direction of the scholar.

״רַבִּי יְהוּדָה אוֹמֵר: אִם הָיָה אֶחָד מֵהֶן וכו׳״. וְרַבָּנַן – זִימְנִין דְּנִיחָא לֵיהּ בְּחַבְרֵיהּ טְפֵי מֵרַבֵּיהּ.

We learned in the mishna that **Rabbi Yehuda says: If one of** the Sages **was** his teacher, he may go only to his teacher, as we can assume that this was his original intention. The Gemara asks: **And** what is the reason that **the Rabbis** do not accept this straightforward argument? The Gemara answers: The Rabbis maintain that **sometimes** one **prefers** to meet the Sage who is **his colleague rather than** the Sage who is **his teacher,** as sometimes one learns more from his peers than from his teachers.

אָמַר רַב: לֵיתָא לְמַתְנִיתִין מִדְּתָנֵי אַיּוֹ, דְּתָנֵי אַיּוֹ: רַבִּי יְהוּדָה אוֹמֵר: אֵין אָדָם מַתְנֶה עַל שְׁנֵי דְבָרִים כְּאֶחָד, אֶלָּא אִם (כֵּן) בָּא חָכָם לַמִּזְרָח – עֵירוּבוֹ לַמִּזְרָח, וְאִם בָּא חָכָם לַמַּעֲרָב – עֵירוּבוֹ לַמַּעֲרָב. אֲבָל לְכָאן וּלְכָאן – לֹא.

Rav said: This version of **the mishna** should **not** be accepted **because of what** the Sage **Ayo taught**[N] to the opposite effect, **as Ayo taught** the following *baraita*: **Rabbi Yehuda says: A person cannot make conditions about two things at once,** i.e., he cannot say that if one Sage comes from one direction and another Sage comes from the other direction, he will go wherever he wishes. **Rather,** he may say that **if a Sage came from the east, his *eiruv* is in the east, and if a Sage came from the west, his *eiruv* is in the west. But** he may **not** say that if one Sage came **from here, and** another Sage came **from there,** he will go wherever he wishes.

NOTES

If a Sage comes from the east – אִם בָּא חָכָם מִן הַמִּזְרָח: The early commentaries ask: How can the Sage come toward a town on Shabbat? Rashi answers that the Sage is spending Shabbat beyond the boundaries of the town, and the one placing the *eiruv* wishes to go out and greet him. However, before Shabbat he does not know from which direction the Sage will come, and he will only find out on Shabbat.

That case is referring to the lord of the town – הָא בְּמָרֵי דְּמָתָא: A number of commentaries state that this is a case where the one establishing the *eiruv* wishes to speak to the lord of the town with regard to the town's needs. This justifies establishing an *eiruv* because it is for the purpose of a mitzva. Rav Ya'akov Emden explains that the lord of the town is its ruler, and going out to greet him is part of the mitzva to greet a king.

That case is referring to one who teaches children how to recite the *Shema* – הָא בְּמַקְרֵי שְׁמַע: Why should one abandon the primary school teacher? Rashi explains that two Sages have arrived, one who will deliver a lecture and one who is a primary school teacher. Of the two, the individual naturally prefers the one who will deliver a lecture. One commentary explains simply that the one establishing the *eiruv* knows that the primary school teacher wishes to stay at his house. Since he does not have enough food for the guest, he leaves town in order to avoid the potentially embarrassing situation. As for the Sage who has come to deliver the lecture, his needs will be met by his fellow townsmen (Rav Ya'akov Emden).

The mishna should not be accepted because of what Ayo taught – לֵיתָא דְּמַתְנִיתִין מִדְּתָנֵי אַיּוֹ: The Gemara proceeds to explain that Ayo's statement is supported by a mishna and *Tosefta* in tractate *Demai*. If that is the source, why doesn't the Gemara point out the contradiction between the statements of Rabbi Yehuda in the mishna and in the *Tosefta* in *Demai*? It can be explained that there was room to distinguish between retroactive designation in cases involving Torah prohibitions, such as tithes, and retroactive designation with regard to rabbinic decrees, such as in the case of *eiruv*. However, according to Ayo's version, there is no need to make this distinction, and the potential contradiction is resolved (Rashba).

LANGUAGE

Guard [*parhagabena*] – פַּרְהַגְבְּנָא: From the Iranian pāhragbān, meaning guard.

HALAKHA

If one buys wine from among the *Kutim* – הַלּוֹקֵחַ יַיִן מִבֵּין הַכּוּתִים: If one buys wine from which *terumot* and tithes have not been separated, he must first separate *teruma* and tithes before he may drink the wine. If the wine is *tevel* only by rabbinic decree, he may drink first before physically separating the *teruma* and tithes, as the principle of retroactive clarification [*bereira*] may be applied with regard to rabbinic decrees (*Kesef Mishne*; Rambam *Sefer Zera'im*, *Hilkhot Ma'aserot* 7:1).

מַאי שְׁנָא לְכָאן וּלְכָאן דְּלָא – דְּאֵין בְּרֵירָה, לַמִּזְרָח לַמַּעֲרָב נָמֵי אֵין בְּרֵירָה!

The Gemara asks: **What is different** about a case in which one stipulated that if Sages came **from here and from there** he may go to whichever side he chooses, such **that** his *eiruv* **is not** effective? Apparently, this is due to the principle that **there is no retroactive designation,** meaning that a doubtful state of affairs cannot be clarified retroactively. However, according to this principle, when one established an *eiruv* **to the east** and **to the west** in order to be able to travel in the direction of one Sage who comes toward the town in a case where one does not know in advance from which direction he will come, we should **also** invoke the principle that **there is no retroactive designation.** Therefore, even if one deposited an *eiruv* at both ends of his town for the sake of one Sage who might come from either side, he should not be able to rely on what becomes clarified afterward and decide retroactively which *eiruv* he is interested in.

אָמַר רַבִּי יוֹחָנָן: וּכְבָר בָּא חָכָם.

Rabbi Yoḥanan said: This is not a true case of retroactive designation, as **the Sage had already come** by twilight but the person who established the *eiruv* did not yet know which side of the town the Sage had come toward. Therefore, at the time the *eiruv* establishes his Shabbat residence it is clear which *eiruv* the person wants, even though he himself will only become aware of that later.

אַדְּרַבָּה, לֵיתָא לְדְאַיּוֹ מִמַּתְנִיתִין!

The Gemara poses a question with regard to Rav's statement cited above: Why should we reject the mishna because of the *baraita*? **On the contrary,** let us say that the ruling of **Ayo** should **not** be accepted **because of the mishna.**

לָא סָלְקָא דַּעְתָּךְ, דְּהָא שָׁמְעִינַן לֵיהּ לְרַבִּי יְהוּדָה דְּלֵית לֵיהּ בְּרֵירָה. דִּתְנַן: הַלּוֹקֵחַ יַיִן מִבֵּין הַכּוּתִים,

The Gemara answers: **It should not enter your mind** to uphold the mishna's ruling because it contradicts other sources, **as we have** already **heard that Rabbi Yehuda does not** accept the principle of **retroactive designation. As it was taught** in the *Tosefta*: **One who buys wine from among the Samaritans** [***Kutim***],[H] who do not tithe their produce properly,

Perek **III**
Daf **37** Amud **a**

NOTES

He redeems [*meiḥel*] and he may immediately drink – מֵיחֵל וְשׁוֹתֶה: Two additional explanations have been put forward for the word *meiḥel* found in this context. The Rambam understands *meiḥel* in the sense of *mathil*, meaning begins, i.e., one is permitted to begin to drink. Rav Hai Gaon reads the word as *mohel*, which means dilutes. That is to say, one may dilute his wine with water and drink it (see also *Tosafot*).

אוֹמֵר: שְׁנֵי לוּגִּין שֶׁאֲנִי עָתִיד לְהַפְרִישׁ הֲרֵי הֵן תְּרוּמָה, עֲשָׂרָה מַעֲשֵׂר רִאשׁוֹן, תִּשְׁעָה מַעֲשֵׂר שֵׁנִי, וּמֵיחֵל וְשׁוֹתֶה מִיָּד, דִּבְרֵי רַבִּי מֵאִיר. רַבִּי יְהוּדָה וְרַבִּי יוֹסֵי וְרַבִּי שִׁמְעוֹן אוֹסְרִין.

may say: Two *log* of the hundred *log* present here, **which I will separate in the future,** when I have finished drinking, **shall be** the great ***teruma*** given to a priest; **ten** ***log*** shall be **first tithe;** and **nine** ***log***, which are a tenth of the remaining ninety *log*, shall be **second tithe. He** then **redeems** the second-tithe with money because in its sanctified state second tithe may only be consumed in Jerusalem, **and he may** then **immediately drink**[N] the wine, and the wine remaining at the end will be *teruma* and tithes. One may rely on the principle of retroactive designation and say that when he is finished drinking, the wine that is left becomes retroactively designated as *teruma* and tithes, such that the wine he drank was permitted for consumption. This is **the statement of Rabbi Meir.** However, **Rabbi Yehuda, Rabbi Yosei, and Rabbi Shimon prohibit** drinking the wine in this manner. Therefore, it would appear that Rabbi Yehuda rejects the principle of retroactive designation, contrary to the ruling of the mishna and in accordance with the opinion of Ayo.

עוּלָּא אָמַר: לֵיתָא לְאַיּוֹ מִמַּתְנִיתִין. וְאֶלָּא הָא דְּקָתָנֵי ״רַבִּי יְהוּדָה וְרַבִּי יוֹסֵי וְרַבִּי שִׁמְעוֹן אוֹסְרִין״?

Ulla also took note of this contradiction between the statements of Rabbi Yehuda, but he **said** the opposite: The statement of **Ayo** should **not** be accepted **because** it contradicts what is stated in **the mishna.** The Gemara raises a difficulty: **But that which was taught** in the *Tosefta*: **Rabbi Yehuda, Rabbi Yosei, and Rabbi Shimon prohibit** drinking the wine in this manner, indicates, as was demonstrated above, that Rabbi Yehuda rejects the principle of retroactive designation.

עוּלָּא זוּזֵי זוּזֵי קָתָנֵי: דִּבְרֵי רַבִּי מֵאִיר וְרַבִּי יְהוּדָה, רַבִּי יוֹסֵי וְרַבִּי שִׁמְעוֹן אוֹסְרִין.

Ulla taught the names of the authorities mentioned in the *Tosefta* dealing with wine **in pairs,** as follows: The allowance mentioned in the *Tosefta* is according to **the statement of Rabbi Meir and Rabbi Yehuda,** whereas **Rabbi Yosei and Rabbi Shimon prohibit** drinking the wine in this manner. Therefore, Rabbi Yehuda agrees with Rabbi Meir and accepts the principle of retroactive designation, in accordance with the mishna.

וְסָבַר רַבִּי יוֹסֵי אֵין בְּרֵירָה? וְהָתְנַן, רַבִּי יוֹסֵי אוֹמֵר: שְׁתֵּי נָשִׁים שֶׁלָּקְחוּ אֶת קִינֵּיהֶן בְּעֵירוּב, אוֹ שֶׁנָּתְנוּ קִינֵּיהֶן לַכֹּהֵן – אֵיזֶהוּ שֶׁיִּרְצֶה כֹּהֵן יַקְרִיב עוֹלָה, וּלְאֵיזֶה שֶׁיִּרְצֶה יַקְרִיב חַטָּאת!

To this point, it has been accepted that Rabbi Yosei clearly prohibits the procedure described in the *Tosefta*. Therefore, he apparently rejects the principle of retroactive designation. With regard to this point, the Gemara asks: **Does Rabbi Yosei** really **hold that there is no retroactive designation? Didn't we learn** in a mishna elsewhere that **Rabbi Yosei says:** If **two women took their birds' nests,**[N] pairs of turtledoves or pigeons as purification offerings following childbirth, **jointly** and without specifying which pair of birds was for which woman, **or if they gave their birds' nests to a priest** but did not inform him which birds were consecrated as sin-offerings and which as burnt-offerings, **whichever the priest wishes he may offer as a burnt-offering, and whichever he wishes he may offer as a sin-offering.**[H] Therefore, Rabbi Yosei must accept the principle of retroactive designation, such that when the priest offers any of the birds as a sacrifice, it is retroactively clarified that the bird had been selected for that woman and as that sacrifice.

אָמַר רַבָּה: הָתָם כְּשֶׁהִתְנוּ.

Rabba said: There is no proof from there, with regard to retroactive designation, as the mishna **there** deals with a special case, **where** the women **stipulated**[N] from the outset that the priest would decide which bird would be offered for which woman and as what sacrifice.

אִי הָכִי מַאי לְמֵימְרָא? קָא מַשְׁמַע לַן כִּדְרַב חִסְדָּא, דְּאָמַר רַב חִסְדָּא: אֵין הַקִּינִּין מִתְפָּרְשׁוֹת

The Gemara asks: **If so, what** need was there for the mishna **to say** anything? If they made an explicit stipulation to that effect, then the priest certainly has the power to fulfill their condition. The Gemara answers: The mishna nonetheless **teaches us** that the law is in accordance with the opinion of **Rav Ḥisda, as Rav Ḥisda said: Birds' nests become designated** as burnt-offerings or sin-offerings **only**

NOTES

Birds' nests [*kinnim*] – קִינִּים: The Torah states that after a certain period of time has passed, a woman who gave birth must offer a purification sacrifice in the Temple. This sacrifice consists of a lamb as a burnt-offering and a young pigeon or turtledove as a sin-offering. If she cannot afford the cost of the lamb, she may bring a nest [*ken*], which is a pair of turtledoves or young pigeons, one for a burnt-offering and the other for a sin-offering (see Leviticus 12:1–8). Similarly, a man suffering from an emission [*zav*] or a woman who experiences an irregular, unexpected flow of uterine blood for three days [*zava*] must bring a sacrifice as part of their purification process, which consists of two turtledoves or two young pigeons, one for a burnt-offering and the other for a sin-offering (Leviticus 15:14, 29). The laws relating to the offering of these sacrifices and the resolution of complications that might result from a mix-up of the birds are elucidated in the tractate *Kinnim*.

The mishna there is about a case where the women stipulated – הָתָם כְּשֶׁהִתְנוּ: Some commentaries explain that sacrifices of this kind include an automatic stipulation that the designation of one bird as a burnt-offering and the other as a sin-offering will be determined by the priest, and those who bring bird sacrifices rely on his decision (*Me'iri*).

HALAKHA

Designated birds' nests – הַפְרָשַׁת קִינִּים: If two women bought bird sacrifices in partnership, or if they jointly gave a priest money for such sacrifices, the priest offers whichever bird he selects as a sin-offering and whichever bird he selects as a burnt-offering, as the determination of which is the sin-offering and which is the burnt-offering is determined either by the owner at the time of purchase or by the priest at the time of the sacrifice. This ruling is in accordance with the opinion of Rav Ḥisda (Rambam *Sefer Avoda, Hilkhot Pesulei HaMukdashin* 8:8).

אֶלָּא אִי בִּלְקִיחַת בְּעָלִים אִי בַּעֲשִׂיַּית כֹּהֵן.

when they are purchased by their owner, if the owner explicitly consecrated it as a burnt-offering or sin-offering when he purchased it, **or through the actions of the priest** when he offers the birds as sacrifices. Therefore, even if the women did not verbalize their intentions, it is considered as if they had made a stipulation from the outset. Therefore, this case is not an instance of retroactive designation.

וְאַכַּתִּי, סָבַר רַבִּי יוֹסֵי אֵין בְּרֵירָה? וְהָתַנְיָא: עַם הָאָרֶץ שֶׁאָמַר לְחָבֵר "קַח לִי אֲגוּדָּה אַחַת שֶׁל יָרָק אוֹ גְּלוּסְקָא אַחַת" – אֵינוֹ צָרִיךְ לְעַשֵּׂר, דִּבְרֵי רַבִּי יוֹסֵי.

And still the question may be raised: Does **Rabbi Yosei** really **hold** that **there is no retroactive designation? Wasn't it taught** in a *baraita*: If **an *am ha'aretz*,** who is not known to be scrupulous in separating tithes, **said to a *ḥaver*,** one known to be meticulous in his observance of *halakha* and especially the laws of *teruma* and tithes, before the *ḥaver* went to the market to buy himself vegetables from another *am ha'aretz*: **Buy for me** as well **a bundle of vegetables or a cake [*geluska*],**[L] the *ḥaver* **does not need to tithe**[N] the food that he gives to the *am ha'aretz*.[H] The only reason the food needs to be tithed is because it is *demai*, and an *am ha'aretz* is not particular about that issue. This is **the statement of Rabbi Yosei.** It can be deduced from this ruling that Rabbi Yosei accepts the principle of retroactive designation, as the *ḥaver* purchased bundles of vegetables without specifying which was for himself and which was for the *am ha'aretz*, and when he gave one to the *am ha'aretz*, it became retroactively clear that he had purchased that bundle for the *am ha'aretz* from the start, and therefore he does not need to separate tithes from it as *demai*.

LANGUAGE

Cake [*geluska*] – גְּלוּסְקָא: From the Greek κόλλιξ, *kolix*, meaning cake or round bread.

NOTES

He does not need to tithe – אֵינוֹ צָרִיךְ לְעַשֵּׂר: Rabbeinu Ḥananel had a different reading: He eats and need not tithe. If the *ḥaver* tithed a portion of the produce and gave the rest to the *am ha'aretz* without precisely determining which portion he had tithed, it becomes retroactively determined that he tithed the portion he kept for himself and did not tithe the portion he gave to the *am ha'aretz*. In the Jerusalem Talmud it is indicated that the dispute does not concern retroactive designation because they disagree even in a case where one bought only a single vegetable bundle. Rather, the dispute is over whether the *ḥaver* is considered to be acting as the agent of the *am ha'aretz* or whether he is considered to have acquired the bundle, in which case he is obligated to tithe it due to the decree pertaining to *demai*.

HALAKHA

An *am ha'aretz* for whom a *ḥaver* bought produce – עַם הָאָרֶץ שֶׁקָּנָה חָבֵר עֲבוּרוֹ: If an *am ha'aretz* gave money to a *ḥaver* and asked him to buy a bundle of vegetables for him, the *ḥaver* may buy the produce and give it to him without tithing it. However, if the *ḥaver* bought the produce with different coins, he must tithe it before giving it to the *am ha'aretz* (Jerusalem Talmud; *Kesef Mishne*; Rambam *Sefer Zera'im, Hilkhot Ma'aserot* 10:8).

וַחֲכָמִים אוֹמְרִים: צָרִיךְ לְעַשֵּׂר! אֵיפוֹךְ.

And the Rabbis say: He must tithe it. Since we do not accept the principle of retroactive designation, everything that the *ḥaver* bought was bought for himself, and the fact that he later gave part of it to the *am ha'aretz* does not exempt him from his original obligation to separate tithes from the *demai*. In any case, it seems that Rabbi Yosei's opinion in this *baraita* contradicts his opinion in the *Tosefta* cited above with regard to wine. The Gemara answers: **Reverse** the opinons in the *baraita* and say that according to Rabbi Yosei he must tithe the produce he gives to the *am ha'aretz*, while the Rabbis permit him to proceed without tithing.

תָּא שְׁמַע: הָאוֹמֵר "מַעֲשֵׂר שֶׁיֵּשׁ לִי בְּבֵיתִי מְחוּלָּל עַל סֶלַע שֶׁתַּעֲלֶה בְּיָדִי מִן הַכִּיס", רַבִּי יוֹסֵי אוֹמֵר: מְחוּלָּל!

The Gemara attempts to bring another proof. **Come** and **hear** a proof from a different *Tosefta*: In the case of **one who says:** The second **tithe that I have in my house shall be redeemed upon the *sela*** coin **that will** happen to **come up in my hand** when I remove it **from the pouch,**[H] i.e., he did not have a particular coin in mind, **Rabbi Yosei says:** The second tithe **is redeemed.** When the coin is removed from the pouch, it is retroactively clarified that this is the coin that he had in his mind from the outset. This indicates that Rabbi Yosei accepts the principle of retroactive designation.

אֵיפוֹךְ, אֵימָא: רַבִּי יוֹסֵי אוֹמֵר: לֹא חִילֵּל. וּמַאי חָזֵית דְּאַפְּכַתְּ תַּרְתֵּי מִקַּמֵּי חֲדָא?! אֵיפוֹךְ חֲדָא מִקַּמֵּי תַּרְתֵּי!

The Gemara answers again: **Reverse** the attributions, and **say** that **Rabbi Yosei says: He has not redeemed** the second tithe. The Gemara raises a difficulty: **What did you see that you reversed two** sources **because of one,** and made the two *baraitot* conform to the mishna, which indicates that Rabbi Yosei holds that there is no retroactive designation? Perhaps **I should reverse one** source, i.e., the mishna, **because of** the **two** *baraitot* and say that in fact Rabbi Yosei accepts the principle of retroactive designation, and it is the lone source that indicates otherwise that must be revised.

הָא וַדַּאי אִיפְּכָא תַּנְיָא, דְּקָתָנֵי סֵיפָא: וּמוֹדֶה רַבִּי יוֹסֵי בְּאוֹמֵר "מַעֲשֵׂר שֶׁיֵּשׁ לִי בְּתוֹךְ בֵּיתִי יְהֵא מְחוּלָּל עַל סֶלַע חֲדָשָׁה שֶׁתַּעֲלֶה בְּיָדִי מִן הַכִּיס" – שֶׁחִילֵּל. מִדְּקָאָמַר הָכָא שֶׁחִילֵּל – מִכְּלָל דְּהָתָם לֹא חִילֵּל.

The Gemara answers: **This** *Tosefta* was **certainly taught in reverse,** as **the latter clause states: And Rabbi Yosei concedes with regard to one who says: The** second **tithe that I have in my house shall be redeemed with the new *sela*** coin **that will** happen to **come up in my hand** when I remove it **from the pouch, that he has redeemed** the second tithe. The Gemara makes the following inference: **From** the fact **that it said here that he has redeemed** the second tithe, it can be proven **by inference that there,** in the first clause of the *Tosefta*, **he did not redeem** the second tithe. Therefore, the wording found in the earlier part of the *baraita* is clearly incorrect and must be reversed.

הַאי סֶלַע חֲדָשָׁה הֵיכִי דָּמֵי? אִי דְּאִיכָּא תַּרְתֵּי תְּלָת, דְּיֵשׁ בְּרֵירָה – הַיְינוּ קַמַּיְיתָא! אֶלָּא דְּלֵיכָּא אֶלָּא חֲדָא – מַאי תַּעֲלֶה?

The Gemara raises a question with regard to the *halakha* cited in the *Tosefta*: **This new *sela*, what are its circumstances? If** it is referring to a situation **where there are two** or **three** coins in his pouch, so that it is not clear which coin he is referring to, **and there is** the possibility of **retroactive designation, this is** exactly the same as **the first** case. Why does he rule here, as opposed to the earlier case, that there is retroactive designation? **Rather,** it must refer to a situation **where he has only one** coin in his pouch. But if so, **what** is the meaning of the expression: **Will** happen to **come up?**

אַיְּידֵי דְּתָנֵי רֵישָׁא "תַּעֲלֶה" תְּנָא סֵיפָא נַמִי "תַּעֲלֶה".

The Gemara answers: In fact, it is referring to a case where one has only one coin in his pouch, and the wording of the latter clause is imprecise. **Since the first clause taught** the *halakha* using this expression: **Will** happen to **come up, the latter clause also taught** the *halakha* using this same expression: **Will** happen to **come up,** even though he was referring to the only new coin that he has in his pouch.

HALAKHA

One who redeems second tithe on the first coin – הַמְחַלֵּל עַל מַטְבֵּעַ רִאשׁוֹנָה: If one redeems the second tithe on the first coin that he will later remove from his pouch, the second tithe is redeemed. Apparently, this ruling only applies nowadays, when the obligation to separate tithes is a rabbinic enactment (*Kesef Mishne*; Rambam *Hilkhot Ma'aser Sheni* 4:15).

אָמַר לֵיהּ רָבָא לְרַב נַחְמָן: מַאן הַאי תַּנָּא דַּאֲפִילּוּ בִּדְרַבָּנַן לֵית לֵיהּ בְּרֵירָה? דְּתַנְיָא, אָמַר לַחֲמִשָּׁה: הֲרֵינִי מְעָרֵב עַל אֵיזֶה מִכֶּם שֶׁאֶרְצֶה, רָצִיתִי – יֵלֵךְ, לֹא רָצִיתִי – לֹא יֵלֵךְ, רָצָה מִבְּעוֹד יוֹם – עֵירוּבוֹ עֵירוּב, מִשֶּׁחֲשֵׁיכָה – אֵין עֵירוּבוֹ עֵירוּב.

Rava said to Rav Naḥman: Who is this ***tanna*** **who does not accept** the principle of **retroactive designation even concerning rabbinic decrees? As it was taught** in a *baraita*: If one person **said to five** people: **I am hereby establishing an** ***eiruv*** **for whichever one of you I will choose,** so that the person **I have chosen will** be able to **walk** two thousand cubits from the spot of the *eiruv*, whereas whomever **I have not chosen will not** be able to **walk** two thousand cubits from the location of the *eiruv*, the following distinction applies: If **he chose** the person for whom he was making the *eiruv* before Shabbat, **while it was still day, his** ***eiruv*** **is** a valid ***eiruv***; but if he only chose him **after nightfall, his** ***eiruv*** **is not** a valid ***eiruv***. The *tanna* of this *baraita* apparently rejects the principle of retroactive designation, even with regard to rabbinic enactments, as if that were not the case, the *eiruv* should be valid even if he only chose the person for whom he was making the *eiruv* after nightfall.

אִישְׁתִּיק וְלָא אָמַר לֵיהּ וְלָא מִידֵּי. וְלֵימָא לֵיהּ: תַּנָּא דְּבֵי אַיּוֹ הוּא! לָא שְׁמִיעַ לֵיהּ.

Rav Naḥman **was silent and did not say anything to** Rava. The Gemara asks: **And let** Rav Naḥman **say to him** that the *baraita* is the opinion of a Sage **of the school of Ayo,** in accordance with the opinion of Rabbi Yehuda, which maintains that even with regard to an *eiruv* there is no retroactive designation. The Gemara answers: **He did not accept** Ayo's version of Rabbi Yehuda's opinion and considered it incorrect.

רַב יוֹסֵף אֲמַר: תַּנָּאֵי שַׁקְלַתְּ מֵעָלְמָא?! תַּנָּאֵי הִיא. דְּתַנְיָא: הֲרֵינִי מְעָרֵב לְשַׁבָּתוֹת שֶׁל כָּל הַשָּׁנָה, רָצִיתִי – אֵלֵךְ, לֹא רָצִיתִי – לֹא אֵלֵךְ. רָצָה מִבְּעוֹד יוֹם – עֵירוּבוֹ עֵירוּב, מִשֶּׁחֲשֵׁיכָה; רַבִּי שִׁמְעוֹן אוֹמֵר: עֵירוּבוֹ עֵירוּב, וַחֲכָמִים אוֹמְרִים אֵין עֵירוּבוֹ עֵירוּב.

Rav Yosef said, in his unique style: Have **you removed the** ***tanna'im*** **from the world?** Is there no *tanna* who holds this position? The possibility of retroactive designation with regard to rabbinic enactments **is** a dispute among ***tanna'im***,[N] **as it was taught** in a *baraita*: One said: **I am hereby establishing an** ***eiruv*** **for the** ***Shabbatot*** **of the entire year,**[H] so that **if I want** to make use of it, **I will** be able to **walk** two thousand cubits from the *eiruv*, and **if I do not want** to do so, **I will not walk. If he wanted** to make use of the *eiruv* for a particular Shabbat **while it was still day, his** ***eiruv*** **is** a valid ***eiruv*** for that Shabbat. However, if he only decided **after nightfall** that he wanted the *eiruv* to be in effect, the *tanna'im* disagree: **Rabbi Shimon says: His** ***eiruv*** **is** a valid ***eiruv***; **and the Rabbis say: His** ***eiruv*** **is not** a valid ***eiruv***. This indicates that according to the Rabbis there is no retroactive designation, even with regard to *eiruvin*, while Rabbi Shimon holds that his *eiruv* is in effect because of the principle of retroactive designation.

וְהָא שָׁמְעִינַן לְרַבִּי שִׁמְעוֹן דְּלֵית לֵיהּ בְּרֵירָה, קַשְׁיָא דְּרַבִּי שִׁמְעוֹן אַדְּרַבִּי שִׁמְעוֹן! אֶלָּא אֵיפוֹךְ.

The Gemara asks: **Didn't we hear that Rabbi Shimon does not accept** the principle of **retroactive designation** in the case of wine from *Kutim*? The contradiction between one ruling of **Rabbi Shimon and** another ruling of **Rabbi Shimon** himself **is difficult.** The Gemara answers: **Rather, reverse** the opinions and say that it is Rabbi Shimon who holds that his *eiruv* is not valid, and therefore he can be identified as the *tanna* who holds that there is no retroactive designation at all, even with regard to rabbinic decrees.

מַאי קַשְׁיָא? דִּילְמָא, כִּי לֵית לֵיהּ לְרַבִּי שִׁמְעוֹן בְּרֵירָה – בִּדְאוֹרַיְיתָא, אֲבָל בִּדְרַבָּנַן – אִית לֵיהּ!

The Gemara asks: **What is the difficulty** here? **Perhaps it is with regard to Torah law that Rabbi Shimon does not accept** the principle of **retroactive designation, but with regard to rabbinic** decrees, **he does accept** the principle of retroactive designation. Therefore, it is not necessary to reverse the opinions.

קָסָבַר רַב יוֹסֵף: מַאן דְּאִית לֵיהּ בְּרֵירָה – לָא שְׁנָא בִּדְאוֹרַיְיתָא, לָא שְׁנָא בִּדְרַבָּנַן – אִית לֵיהּ. וּמַאן דְּלֵית לֵיהּ בְּרֵירָה – לָא שְׁנָא בִּדְאוֹרַיְיתָא, וְלָא שְׁנָא בִּדְרַבָּנַן – לֵית לֵיהּ.

The Gemara answers: **Rav Yosef holds** that **one who accepts** the principle of **retroactive designation accepts it** in all cases; **there is no difference** between **Torah law and rabbinic** decrees. **And one who does not accept** the principle of **retroactive designation does not accept it** at all; **there is no difference** between **Torah law and rabbinic** decrees.

רָבָא אֲמַר: שָׁאנֵי הָתָם, דְּבָעֵינַן רֵאשִׁית שֶׁשְּׁיָרֶיהָ נִיכָּרִין.

Rava said: The distinction between the case of the wine and the other cases is not related to the principle of retroactive designation. Rather, **there,** the case of the wine of a *Kuti*, **is different, as we require** that the *teruma* be **the first** of your produce, **whose remnants are recognizable.** Since *teruma* is called the first, if it is not clear which portion was separated and which portion is left over, the designation of part of the wine as *teruma* is not effective, despite the fact that Rabbi Shimon accepts the principle of retroactive designation.

NOTES

It is a dispute among the *tanna'im* – תַּנָּאֵי הִיא: Rav Yosef proves that there is a *tanna* who holds that there is no retroactive designation with regard to the laws of *eiruv*, even though they are rabbinic in origin. However, the following question has been asked: Why did Rav Yosef find it necessary afterward to reverse the opinions in the *baraita* to prove that Rabbi Shimon had that opinion, thereby entering himself into difficulties? Some commentaries explain that the discussion reversing the opinions is not part of Rav Yosef's statement (Maharshal). *Tosafot* explain that Rav Yosef wanted to identify the *tanna* by name and therefore proved that it was Rabbi Shimon's opinion. He had to prove it from this *baraita* rather than from any other source because not everyone accepts the principle that there is no difference between Torah law and rabbinic decrees with regard to retroactive designation. Consequently, at least the basis of his proof remains intact, even if the reversal of opinions is not accepted (Rashba).

HALAKHA

An *eiruv* for the entire year – עֵירוּב לְכָל הַשָּׁנָה: One may establish an *eiruv teḥumin* for the entire year, which will permit him to make use of it even if he decides to validate it only on Shabbat. The *halakha* is in accordance with the lenient opinion with regard to *eiruvin*, and there is retroactive designation with regard to rabbinic decrees (*Shulḥan Arukh*, *Oraḥ Ḥayyim* 413:1).

אמר ליה אביי: אלא מעתה, היו לפניו שני רמונים של טבל, ואמר: אם ירדו גשמים היום – יהא זה תרומה על זה, ואם לא ירדו גשמים היום – יהא זה תרומה על זה. הכי נמי, בין ירדו בין לא ירדו דאין בדבריו כלום?

Abaye said to him: Do you really think that this ruling is correct? **But if that is so, if there were two pomegranates** that were ***tevel* before him,**[N] **and he said: If rain falls today, this** pomegranate **shall be *teruma* for that** other pomegranate, **and if rain does not fall today, that** second pomegranate **shall be *teruma* for this** first one, **so too, whether** rain **fell or did not fall, there is no** significance to **his statement** because the remnants that are not *teruma* are not immediately recognizable.

וכי תימא הכי נמי – והתנן: תרומת הכרי הזה ומעשרותיו בתוכו, ותרומת מעשר זה בתוכו, רבי שמעון אומר: קרא השם!

And if you say that indeed, it **is so,** there is a difficulty. **Didn't we learn** in a mishna that if one says: **The *teruma* of this pile** of produce **and its tithes shall be inside it,** without specifying the location of the produce that he is designating for these purposes, **and** similarly, if one says about a pile of first-tithe produce: **The *teruma* of this tithe shall be inside it,** without specifying the location, **Rabbi Shimon says: He has given it a name,** i.e., the designation of the *teruma* and tithes take effect, even though it is impossible to distinguish between them and the permitted portion of the produce? Therefore, it is not necessary for the remnants of the act of separation to be recognizable.

שאני התם דאיכא סביביו.

Rava refutes this argument: **There,** with regard to a pile of produce, **it is different because there are** recognizable remnants **around it.** He specified that the *teruma* should be inside the heap, which indicates that it is in the middle of the pile, and therefore the produce on the perimeter of the pile is certainly not *teruma,* and some of the remnants of the act of separation are recognizable.

ואי בעית אימא כדקתני טעמא: אמרו לו לרבי מאיר: אי אתה מודה שמא יבקע הנוד ונמצא זה שותה טבלים למפרע? אמר להן: לכשיבקע.

And if you wish, you can reconcile the difference between the case of separating *teruma* from wine and the other cases and **say in accordance with the reason that was taught** in the case of the wine: The Rabbis **said to Rabbi Meir: Don't you concede** that **perhaps the** leather **flask will burst**[N] before he manages to separate the *teruma,* **and retroactively this** person would have been **drinking *tevel*?** Since he never ended up separating *teruma,* the wine remained *tevel* all along. Rabbi Meir **said to them: When it bursts,** I will consider the matter, but presently I am not concerned that the bottle might burst. Therefore, we see that these *tanna'im* do not disagree about the principle of retroactive designation but over the likelihood that the flask will burst.

ולמאי דסליק אדעתין מעיקרא דבעינן ראשית ששיריה ניכרין, מאי קאמרי ליה?

The Gemara now asks: **And according to what initially entered our minds,** which is **that we require** *teruma* that is **the first, whose remnants are recognizable what did** the Rabbis **say to** Rabbi Meir about that? That is the objection they should have raised against him.

הכי קאמרי ליה: לדידן – בעינן ראשית ששיריה ניכרין, לדידך –

The Gemara answers: **This is what they said to him: According to our** own opinion, **we require** *teruma* that is **the first, whose remnants are recognizable; according to your** opinion,

NOTES

If there were two pomegranates before him – היו לפניו שני רמונים: Some commentaries explain that the question of retroactive designation is based on the general principle that one cannot acquire or transfer ownership of something that has not yet come into the world. In other words, one cannot perform a legally valid act that relates to an object or state of affairs not currently in existence. Consequently, there is a distinction between the case of pomegranates and the separation of *terumot* and tithes from the leather flask. With regard to pomegranates, one can tithe them whenever one wishes. Their case does not constitute bona fide retroactive designation at all, as everything is already in existence. In the latter case, however, one is either not currently able to separate the *teruma* and tithes, e.g., if he is not in the same vicinity as the produce, or he is not permitted to do so, e.g., if it is Shabbat, and therefore it is considered something that has yet to come into the world (*Ketzot HaḤoshen*).

Perhaps the leather flask will burst – שמא יבקע הנוד: Some commentaries explain that this detail is not mentioned earlier in the discussion, even though it is written explicitly, because the Sages thought at first that if it is not a Torah prohibition, then there is no reason to be worried about the leather flask bursting, which is a far-fetched concern. Consequently, they considered it reasonable to suggest that the basic concern is the prohibition of *tevel* (*Yad Shlomo*).

אי אתה מודה שמא יבקע הנוד, ונמצא שותה טבלים למפרע? אמר להן: לכשיבקע.

don't you at least **concede** that we must be concerned that **perhaps the** leather **flask will burst, and retroactively this** person would have been **drinking *tevel*?** Rabbi Meir **said to them: When it bursts,**[N] I will consider the matter, but now I am not concerned about this possibility.

NOTES

When it bursts – לכשיבקע: This is not a Torah prohibition because the obligation to separate *teruma* from this barrel is only by rabbinic decree. Therefore, this doubt resembles all other doubts relating to rabbinic decrees, and one may be lenient (*Yad Shlomo*).

מתני׳ רַבִּי אֱלִיעֶזֶר אוֹמֵר: יוֹם טוֹב הַסָּמוּךְ לַשַּׁבָּת, בֵּין מִלְּפָנֶיהָ וּבֵין מִלְּאַחֲרֶיהָ – מְעָרֵב אָדָם שְׁנֵי עֵירוּבִין, וְאוֹמֵר: עֵירוּבִי בָּרִאשׁוֹן לַמִּזְרָח, וּבַשֵּׁנִי לַמַּעֲרָב. בָּרִאשׁוֹן לַמַּעֲרָב וּבַשֵּׁנִי לַמִּזְרָח, עֵירוּבִי בָּרִאשׁוֹן, וּבַשֵּׁנִי כִּבְנֵי עִירִי, עֵירוּבִי בַּשֵּׁנִי, וּבָרִאשׁוֹן כִּבְנֵי עִירִי.

MISHNA **Rabbi Eliezer says:** With regard to **a Festival adjacent to Shabbat,**[H] **whether before it,** on a Friday, **or after it,** on a Sunday, **a person** may **establish two** ***eiruvin*** of Shabbat borders [*teḥumin*] **and say** as follows: **My** ***eiruv*** **on the first** day shall be **to the east, and on the second** day **to the west.** Alternatively, one may say: **On the first** day it shall be **to the west and on the second** day **to the east.** Similarly, one may say: **My** ***eiruv*** shall apply **on the first** day, **but on the second** day I shall be **like** the rest of **the inhabitants of my town,** or: **My** ***eiruv*** shall apply **on the second** day, **but on the first** day I shall be **like** the rest of **the inhabitants of my town.**

וַחֲכָמִים אוֹמְרִים: אוֹ מְעָרֵב לְרוּחַ אַחַת, אוֹ אֵינוֹ מְעָרֵב כָּל עִיקָּר. אוֹ מְעָרֵב לִשְׁנֵי יָמִים, אוֹ אֵינוֹ מְעָרֵב כָּל עִיקָּר.

And the Rabbis disagree and **say** that such a split is impossible. Rather, **he either establishes an** ***eiruv*** **in one direction** for both days, **or he establishes no** ***eiruv*** **at all; either he establishes an** ***eiruv*** for the **two days, or he establishes no** ***eiruv*** **at all.**

כֵּיצַד יַעֲשֶׂה? מוֹלִיכוֹ בָּרִאשׁוֹן וּמַחְשִׁיךְ עָלָיו, וְנוֹטְלוֹ וּבָא לוֹ. בַּשֵּׁנִי מַחְשִׁיךְ עָלָיו וְאוֹכְלוֹ וּבָא לוֹ, וְנִמְצָא מִשְׂתַּכֵּר בַּהֲלִיכָתוֹ וּמִשְׂתַּכֵּר בְּעֵירוּבוֹ.

What does one do to establish an *eiruv* that will be valid for both the Festival and Shabbat? **He** or his agent **brings** the *eiruv* to the location that he wishes to establish as his residence **on** the eve of **the first** day, **and he stays** there **with it until nightfall,** the time when the *eiruv* establishes that location as his residence for the Festival, **and** then **he takes it** with him[N] **and goes away,** so that it will not become lost before the following evening, in which case he would not have an *eiruv* for the second day. **On** the eve of the **second** day, he takes it back to the same place as the day before, and **he stays** there **with it until nightfall,** thereby establishing his residence for Shabbat, and then he may **eat** the *eiruv* **and go away,** if he so desires. **Consequently, he benefits** in that he is permitted to **walk** in the direction that he desires, **and he benefits** in that he is permitted to eat **his** ***eiruv*****.**

נֶאֱכַל בָּרִאשׁוֹן – עֵירוּבוֹ לָרִאשׁוֹן וְאֵין עֵירוּבוֹ לַשֵּׁנִי.

However, if the *eiruv* **was eaten on the first** day, **his** ***eiruv*** is effective **for the first** day, **and his** ***eiruv*** **is not** effective **for the second** day.

אָמַר (לָהֶן) רַבִּי אֱלִיעֶזֶר: מוֹדִים אַתֶּם לִי שֶׁהֵן שְׁתֵּי קְדוּשּׁוֹת.

Rabbi Eliezer said to them: If so, **you agree with me that** Shabbat and a Festival **constitute two** distinct **sanctities,** as if not, the *eiruv* that went into effect during the twilight period on the eve of the first day should have remained in effect for both days, even if it was eaten during the first day. This being the case, you should also agree with me that one can make two separate *eiruvin* for the two days in two different directions.

גמ׳ לְרוּחַ אַחַת מַאי נִיהוּ – לִשְׁנֵי יָמִים, לִשְׁנֵי יָמִים מַאי נִיהוּ – לְרוּחַ אַחַת, הַיְינוּ קַמַּיְיתָא!

GEMARA The Gemara raises a difficulty with regard to the wording employed by the Rabbis: First, the Rabbis state that one may establish an *eiruv* **in one direction. What does this** mean? He must establish an *eiruv* in that direction **for two days.** Then they state that he may establish an *eiruv* **for two days. What does this** mean? He must establish an *eiruv* for the two days **in one direction.** If so, **this is** exactly the same as **the first** clause.

הָכִי קָאָמְרִי לֵיהּ רַבָּנַן לְרַבִּי אֱלִיעֶזֶר: אִי אַתָּה מוֹדֶה שֶׁאֵין מְעָרְבִין לְיוֹם אֶחָד חֶצְיוֹ לַצָּפוֹן וְחֶצְיוֹ לַדָּרוֹם? אָמַר לָהֶן: אֲבָל. כְּשֵׁם שֶׁאֵין מְעָרְבִין לְיוֹם אֶחָד חֶצְיוֹ לַדָּרוֹם וְחֶצְיוֹ לַצָּפוֹן – כָּךְ אֵין מְעָרְבִין לִשְׁנֵי יָמִים, יוֹם אֶחָד לַמִּזְרָח וְיוֹם אֶחָד לַמַּעֲרָב.

The Gemara explains: **This is what the Rabbis said to Rabbi Eliezer: Don't you concede that** in the case of **one day, one may not establish an** ***eiruv*** **for half** the day **to the north and** for **half of it to the south?**[N] Rabbi Eliezer **said to them: Indeed,** I agree. They then said to him: **Just as one may not establish an** ***eiruv*** **for one day, half** the day **to the north and half** the day **to the south, so too, one may not establish an** ***eiruv*** **for two** consecutive **days** of sanctity, **one day to the east and one day to the west.**

וְרַבִּי אֱלִיעֶזֶר: הָתָם – קְדוּשָּׁה אַחַת, הָכָא שְׁתֵּי קְדוּשּׁוֹת.

And how does **Rabbi Eliezer** respond? He holds as follows: **There,** one day constitutes **one sanctity,** and it is impossible to impossible to divide the day such that the *eiruv* applies to one direction for one half of the day and to another direction for the other half of the day. **Here,** where Shabbat and a Festival fall out on consecutive days, they are **two** separate **sanctities,** and therefore one can establish separate *eiruvin* for the two days.

HALAKHA

An ***eiruv*** **on a Festival that is adjacent to Shabbat – עֵירוּב בְּיוֹם טוֹב הַסָּמוּךְ לַשַּׁבָּת:** One may establish two *eiruvin* on the eve of a Festival adjacent to Shabbat and stipulate that his *eiruv* should apply to one day or both, to one direction or two. The *halakha* is in accordance with the opinion of Rabbi Eliezer (*Shulḥan Arukh, Oraḥ Ḥayyim* 416:1).

NOTES

He brings it…and he takes it with him – מוֹלִיכוֹ...וְנוֹטְלוֹ: Most commentaries agree that one is under no obligation to take the *eiruv* with him; this is merely good advice. If one is worried that his *eiruv* will be eaten over the course of the day, he should take it with him and bring it back the following day. However, in the Jerusalem Talmud it is indicated that one is obligated to take the *eiruv* and return it the next day because the *eiruv* cannot be established for both days at once (see Rashba).

Half the day to the north and half of it to the south – חֶצְיוֹ לַצָּפוֹן וְחֶצְיוֹ לַדָּרוֹם: Rabbeinu Yehonatan holds that the half to the north alludes to the night, according to the Gemara, because the sun is in the north during that time period. The half to the south is referring to the daylight hours. Therefore, the intention is that just as one cannot distinguish between the sanctities of the night and the day of a particular day, it is impossible to distinguish between the sanctities of two adjacent days.

HALAKHA

If one established an *eiruv* with his feet on the first day – עֵירֵב בְּרַגְלָיו בְּרִאשׁוֹן: If one established an *eiruv* by foot on a Festival adjacent to Shabbat, he may establish an *eiruv* by foot on the second day as well. However, if he made an *eiruv* with food and the food was eaten, he may not establish an *eiruv* the following day with different food, since it is prohibited to prepare from a Festival for Shabbat or vice versa. The *halakha* is in accordance with the opinion of Rabbi Yehuda HaNasi. However, if one established an *eiruv* for the first day with food, he may establish an *eiruv* for the second day on foot (*Shulḥan Arukh, Oraḥ Ḥayyim* 416:2).

NOTES

Due to preparation – מִשּׁוּם הֲכָנָה: Why doesn't Rabbi Eliezer base his ruling on the prohibition to purchase a house on Shabbat, since one acquires a new domain through establishing an *eiruv*? The commentaries answer that it is possible to refute this claim by differentiating between various types of acquisitions. Establishing an *eiruv teḥumin* is not considered to be a form of literal acquisition (Rashba).

אָמַר לָהֶן רַבִּי אֱלִיעֶזֶר: אִי אַתֶּם מוֹדִים שֶׁאִם עֵירֵב בְּרַגְלָיו בְּיוֹם רִאשׁוֹן – מְעָרֵב בְּרַגְלָיו בְּיוֹם שֵׁנִי, נֶאֱכַל עֵירוּבוֹ בְּיוֹם רִאשׁוֹן – אֵין יוֹצֵא עָלָיו בְּיוֹם שֵׁנִי.

Rabbi Eliezer said to the Rabbis: **Don't you concede that if one established an *eiruv* with his feet** by actually going to the place where he desires to establish an *eiruv* **on** the eve of **the first day**[H] and remaining there during the twilight period, as opposed to depositing food there beforehand, he nonetheless must **establish** another ***eiruv* with his feet on** the eve of **the second day,** and one *eiruv* does not suffice; similarly, if **his *eiruv* was eaten on the first day, he may not** rely **on it** and **go out** beyond the limit permitted to the rest of the inhabitants of his town **on the second day?**

אָמְרוּ לוֹ: אֲבָל. הָא לָאו שְׁתֵּי קְדוּשּׁוֹת הֵן. וְרַבָּנַן: סְפוּקֵי מְסַפְּקָא לְהוּ, וְהָכָא לְחוּמְרָא וְהָכָא לְחוּמְרָא.

The Rabbis **said to him: Indeed,** that is correct. Rabbi Eliezer then **said to them:** Then **isn't it** correct that **they are two** distinct **sanctities,** and therefore one should be permitted to establish two separate *eiruvin* for the two days? **And** how do **the Rabbis** respond? **They are in doubt** about this issue, **and** therefore their ruling **here is stringent** and prohibits establishing separate *eiruvin* for the two days in different directions, in case the two days are considered a single sanctity; **and** their ruling **here is stringent** and they require a separate *eiruv* for each day, in case the two days are considered distinct sanctities.

אָמְרוּ לוֹ לְרַבִּי אֱלִיעֶזֶר: אִי אַתָּה מוֹדֶה שֶׁאֵין מְעָרְבִין בַּתְּחִילָּה מִיּוֹם טוֹב לְשַׁבָּת? אָמַר לָהֶן: אֲבָל. הָא לָאו קְדוּשָּׁה אַחַת הִיא.

The Rabbis **said to Rabbi Eliezer: Don't you concede that one may not establish an *eiruv* initially on a Festival for Shabbat,** i.e., if a Festival occurs on a Friday and one forgot to establish an *eiruv* on the eve of the Festival, he may not establish an *eiruv* for Shabbat on the Festival itself? Rabbi Eliezer **said to them: Indeed,** that is correct. They said to him: Then **isn't it** correct that the two days constitute **one sanctity?**

וְרַבִּי אֱלִיעֶזֶר: הָתָם מִשּׁוּם הֲכָנָה.

The Gemara responds that **Rabbi Eliezer** holds that **there,** the *halakha* is so not because the two days constitute a single sanctity, but **due to** the prohibition of **preparation**[N] on a Festival for Shabbat, which includes establishing an *eiruv*.

תָּנוּ רַבָּנַן: עֵירֵב בְּרַגְלָיו בְּיוֹם רִאשׁוֹן – מְעָרֵב בְּרַגְלָיו בְּיוֹם שֵׁנִי. נֶאֱכַל עֵירוּבוֹ בְּיוֹם רִאשׁוֹן – אֵין יוֹצֵא עָלָיו בְּיוֹם שֵׁנִי, דִּבְרֵי רַבִּי.

The Sages taught in a *baraita*: **If one established an *eiruv* with his feet** by going to the place he wished to establish as his residence **on** the eve of **the first day** and remaining there during the twilight period, **he must** nevertheless **establish** another ***eiruv* with his feet on** the eve of **the second day.** Similarly, if he had established an *eiruv* by depositing food in the place he wished to establish as his residence, and **his *eiruv* was eaten on the first day, he may not** rely **on it** and **go out** beyond the limit permitted to the rest of the inhabitants of the town **on the second day.** This is **the statement of Rabbi** Yehuda HaNasi.

רַבִּי יְהוּדָה אוֹמֵר:

Rabbi Yehuda says:

Perek **III**
Daf **38** Amud **b**

הֲרֵי זֶה חַמָּר גַּמָּל.

This person **is** in the position of both **a donkey driver,** who must prod the animal from behind, **and a camel driver,** who must lead the animal from the front, i.e., he is pulled in two opposing directions. Since we are unsure whether the two days constitute one sanctity or two, he must act stringently as though the *eiruv* established for the first day is both effective and not effective for the second day, i.e., he must restrict his Shabbat movement to those areas where he would be permitted to go in both cases.

רַבָּן שִׁמְעוֹן בֶּן גַּמְלִיאֵל וְרַבִּי יִשְׁמָעֵאל בְּנוֹ שֶׁל רַבִּי יוֹחָנָן בֶּן בְּרוֹקָה אוֹמְרִים: עֵירֵב בְּרַגְלָיו בָּרִאשׁוֹן – אֵין מְעָרֵב בְּרַגְלָיו בַּשֵּׁנִי, נֶאֱכַל עֵירוּבוֹ בְּיוֹם רִאשׁוֹן – יוֹצֵא עָלָיו בַּשֵּׁנִי.

Rabban Shimon ben Gamliel and Rabbi Yishmael, son of Rabbi Yoḥanan ben Beroka, say: If **he established an *eiruv* with his feet on** the eve of **the first** day, **he** need **not establish an *eiruv* with his feet on** the eve of **the second** day, as his *eiruv* remains effective for the second day as well. Similarly, if he had made an *eiruv* by depositing food in the place where he wished to establish his residence, and **his *eiruv* was eaten on the first day, he may** still rely **on it** and **go out** beyond the limit permitted to the rest of the inhabitants of the town **on the second** day, as the two days constitute one sanctity; from the outset, the *eiruv* acquired his place of rest for both days.

אָמַר רַב: הֲלָכָה כְּאַרְבָּעָה זְקֵנִים הַלָּלוּ, וְאַלִּיבָּא דְּרַבִּי אֱלִיעֶזֶר דְּאָמַר: שְׁתֵּי קְדוּשּׁוֹת הֵן. וְאֵלּוּ הֵן אַרְבָּעָה זְקֵנִים: רַבָּן שִׁמְעוֹן בֶּן גַּמְלִיאֵל, וְרַבִּי יִשְׁמָעֵאל בְּרַבִּי יוֹחָנָן בֶּן בְּרוֹקָה, וְרַבִּי אֱלִיעֶזֶר בְּרַבִּי שִׁמְעוֹן, וְרַבִּי יוֹסֵי בַּר יְהוּדָה סְתִימְתָּאָה. וְאִיכָּא דְּאָמְרִי: חַד מִינַּיְיהוּ רַבִּי אֶלְעָזָר, וּמַפֵּיק רַבִּי יוֹסֵי בַּר יְהוּדָה סְתִימְתָּאָה.

Rav said: The *halakha* **is in accordance with** the opinion of **these four Elders**[N] **and in accordance with** the opinion of **Rabbi Eliezer, who said:** When Shabbat and a Festival occur on consecutive days, **they** constitute **two** distinct **sanctities.**[H] **And these are the four Elders: Rabban Shimon ben Gamliel; Rabbi Yishmael, son of Rabbi Yoḥanan ben Beroka; Rabbi Eliezer, son of Rabbi Shimon;** and **Rabbi Yosei bar Yehuda, the** one whose opinions were often recorded as **unattributed** *mishnayot.* **And there are** those **who say: One of them is Rabbi Elazar, and remove** from the list **Rabbi Yosei bar Yehuda, the** one whose statements were often recorded as **unattributed** *mishnayot.*

וְהָא רַבָּן שִׁמְעוֹן בֶּן גַּמְלִיאֵל וְרַבִּי יִשְׁמָעֵאל בַּר רַבִּי יוֹחָנָן בֶּן בְּרוֹקָה אִיפְּכָא שָׁמְעִינַן לְהוּ! אֵיפּוֹךְ.

The Gemara raises a difficulty: **Didn't we hear that Rabban Shimon ben Gamliel and Rabbi Yishmael, son of Rabbi Yoḥanan ben Beroka,** maintain **the opposite** opinion in the *baraita* cited above, namely that the two days constitute a single sanctity? The Gemara answers: **Reverse** the attributions in the *baraita.*

אִי הָכִי הַיְינוּ רַבִּי! אֵימָא: וְכֵן אָמַר רַבָּן שִׁמְעוֹן בֶּן גַּמְלִיאֵל וכו׳.

The Gemara asks: **If so, this is** exactly what **Rabbi** Yehuda HaNasi said. What is their dispute? The Gemara answers: **Say** that there is no disagreement between them, and the *baraita* should read as follows: **And so too, Rabban Shimon ben Gamliel said** that he agrees with what was stated above.

וְלִיחֲשׁוֹב נַמִי רַבִּי! רַבִּי תָּנֵי לָהּ וְלָא סָבַר לָהּ.

The Gemara now asks: **Let us also count Rabbi** Yehuda HaNasi among these Elders, as he too holds that the two days are distinct sanctities. The Gemara answers: **Rabbi** Yehuda HaNasi **taught this** opinion, **and** he himself **did not hold it** to be correct. He transmitted a ruling that he received from his teachers, but his own opinion was otherwise.

רַבָּנַן נַמִי תָּנוּ לָהּ וְלָא סָבְרִי לָהּ! רַב גְּמָרָא גְּמִיר לָהּ.

The Gemara raises a difficulty: If so, let us also say that **the Rabbis,** Rabban Shimon ben Gamliel, and Rabbi Yishmael **also taught** this law, **and** they themselves **did not hold it** to be correct. What proof is there that this represents their own opinions? The Gemara answers: **Rav** did not rely on the wording of these sources; rather, he **learned by** way of a definite **tradition** that these four Elders maintained this position.

כִּי נָח נַפְשֵׁיהּ דְּרַב הוּנָא, עַיֵּיל רַב חִסְדָּא לְמִירְמָא דְּרַב אַדְּרַב; מִי אָמַר רַב: הֲלָכָה כְּאַרְבָּעָה זְקֵנִים, וְאַלִּיבָּא דְּרַבִּי אֱלִיעֶזֶר דְּאָמַר שְׁתֵּי קְדוּשּׁוֹת הֵן?

The Gemara relates that **when Rav Huna,** Rav's preeminent student, **passed away,**[N] **Rav Ḥisda entered** the study hall **to raise a contradiction between** one statement of **Rav and** another statement of **Rav: Did Rav** actually **say:** The *halakha* **is in accordance with** the opinion of **the four Elders and in accordance with** the opinion of **Rabbi Eliezer, who said** that when Shabbat and a Festival fall out on consecutive days, **they** constitute **two** distinct **sanctities?**

וְהָא אִיתְּמַר: שַׁבָּת וְיוֹם טוֹב, רַב אָמַר: נוֹלְדָה בָּזֶה – אֲסוּרָה בָּזֶה!

Wasn't it stated that with regard to a case where **Shabbat and a Festival** occur on consecutive days, **Rav said:** An egg that **was laid on one is prohibited on the other,**[H] just as an egg that was laid on a Festival day is prohibited on that same day? This statement indicates that the two days constitute a single sanctity. How, then, can he say here that the *halakha* is in accordance with the opinion that they are two distinct sanctities?

אָמַר רַבָּה: הָתָם – מִשּׁוּם הֲכָנָה.

Rabba said that a distinction may be drawn between the cases: **There,** the egg is prohibited on the second day not because the two days constitute a single sanctity but **because of** the prohibition against **preparation,** i.e., because it is prohibited to prepare things on a Festival for Shabbat or on Shabbat for a Festival.

דְּתַנְיָא: ״וְהָיָה בַּיּוֹם הַשִּׁשִּׁי וְהֵכִינוּ״ – חוֹל מֵכִין לַשַּׁבָּת, וְחוֹל מֵכִין לְיוֹם טוֹב, וְאֵין יוֹם טוֹב מֵכִין לַשַּׁבָּת, וְאֵין שַׁבָּת מְכִינָה לְיוֹם טוֹב.

As it was taught in a *baraita*: The verse that states: **"And it shall come to pass, on the sixth day, when they shall prepare** that which they bring in" (Exodus 16:5), indicates as follows: On an ordinary **weekday one may prepare** what is needed **for Shabbat, and** similarly, on an ordinary **weekday one may prepare** what is needed **for a Festival.** However, on a **Festival one may not prepare for Shabbat, and** on **Shabbat one may not prepare for a Festival.** Therefore, an egg that was laid on a Festival is prohibited on Shabbat not because they constitute a single sanctity, but because it is prohibited to prepare on one sanctified day for another.

NOTES

Four Elders – אַרְבָּעָה זְקֵנִים: The source in which these four Elders expressed their opinion is not provided in the Babylonian Talmud. However, in the Jerusalem Talmud it is stated that the four Elders said that someone whose *eiruv* was eaten on the first day may not rely on it on the second day. Rav is referring to this ruling.

When Rav Huna passed away – כִּי נָח נַפְשֵׁיהּ דְּרַב הוּנָא: Due to a misunderstanding, relations between Rav Huna and Rav Ḥisda were strained, and they did not see each other for many years. Therefore, it was only after Rav Huna passed away that Rav Ḥisda came to the study hall to raise objections against Rav's statements (Rabbi Zvi Hirsch Chajes; Rabbi Elazar Landau).

HALAKHA

Two sanctities – שְׁתֵּי קְדוּשּׁוֹת: A Festival and Shabbat are considered two distinct sanctities with regard to *eiruvin* and other matters (*Shulḥan Arukh, Oraḥ Ḥayyim* 416:2).

An egg laid on a Festival – בֵּיצָה שֶׁנּוֹלְדָה בְּיוֹם טוֹב: If a Festival and Shabbat occur on consecutive days, an egg laid on one is prohibited on the other, due to the rabbinic prohibition against preparation (*Shulḥan Arukh, Oraḥ Ḥayyim* 503:1, 513:5).

אֲמַר לֵיהּ אַבַּיֵי: אֶלָּא הָא דִּתְנַן: כֵּיצַד הוּא עוֹשֶׂה – מוֹלִיכוֹ בָּרִאשׁוֹן, וּמַחְשִׁיךְ עָלָיו, וְנוֹטְלוֹ וּבָא לוֹ. בַּשֵּׁנִי מַחְשִׁיךְ עָלָיו, וְאוֹכְלוֹ וּבָא לוֹ. הָא קָא מֵכִין מִיּוֹם טוֹב לְשַׁבָּת!

Abaye said to him: But what about **that which we learned** in the mishna: **What does he do** if a Festival occurs on Friday, and he wishes to establish an *eiruv* that will be valid for the Festival and Shabbat? **He** or his agent **takes** the *eiruv* to the spot that he wishes to establish as his residence **on the** eve of **the first** day, **and he stays** there **with it until nightfall,** and then **he takes it** with him **and goes away. On the** eve of the **second** day, i.e., on Friday afternoon, he or his agent takes the *eiruv* back to the same place **and stays** there **with it until nightfall, and** then he may **eat** the *eiruv* **and go away,** if he so desires. **Isn't he preparing on a Festival for Shabbat?** According to Rabba, this should be considered a prohibited act of preparation.

אֲמַר לֵיהּ רַבָּה: מִי סָבְרַתְּ סוֹף הַיּוֹם קוֹנֶה עֵירוּב? תְּחִלַּת הַיּוֹם קוֹנֶה עֵירוּב, וְשַׁבָּת מְכִינָה לְעַצְמָהּ.

Rabba said to him: Do you think that the *eiruv* acquires one's residence **at the end of the day,** i.e., at the last moment of Shabbat eve, which in this case is a Festival, so that this would involve prohibited preparation? **The *eiruv* acquires** his residence **at the beginning of the day,** i.e., at the first moment of Shabbat, which means that no preparations were made for Shabbat on the Festival, **and** on **Shabbat** one may **prepare for** Shabbat **itself.**

אֶלָּא מֵעַתָּה יְעָרְבוּ בְּלָגִין!

Abaye asked: **But if that is so, one should** be able to **establish an *eiruv* with flasks** of wine that were filled from a barrel of first-tithe that was still *tevel* with respect to *teruma* of the tithe, and with regard to which one said: Let this wine in the flask be *teruma* of the tithe for the wine in the barrel only after nightfall. If you say that an *eiruv* acquires one's residence at the beginning of the day, why was it determined that one may not establish an *eiruv* with such wine?

בָּעֵינַן סְעוּדָה הָרְאוּיָה מִבְּעוֹד יוֹם, וְלֵיכָּא.

The Gemara answers: In that case the *eiruv* is not valid for a different reason: **We require a meal that is fit** to be eaten **while it is still day, and there is none,** as the wine in the flask remains *tevel* and therefore unfit for drinking until nightfall.

אֶלָּא הָא דִּתְנַן, רַבִּי אֱלִיעֶזֶר אוֹמֵר: יוֹם טוֹב הַסָּמוּךְ לַשַּׁבָּת, בֵּין מִלְּפָנֶיהָ וּבֵין מִלְּאַחֲרֶיהָ – מְעָרֵב אָדָם שְׁנֵי עֵירוּבִין. הָא בָּעֵינַן סְעוּדָה הָרְאוּיָה מִבְּעוֹד יוֹם, וְלֵיכָּא!

Abaye asked further: **But** what about **that which we learned** in a mishna: **Rabbi Eliezer says:** If **a Festival is adjacent to Shabbat, whether before it or after it, a person may establish two *eiruvin*.** Why are these *eiruvin* valid? **Don't we require a meal that is fit** to be eaten **while it is still day,**[N] **and there is none?** Since one established his *eiruv* in one direction for the first day, he can only travel within a two-thousand-cubit radius of that location. Therefore, if he established his *eiruv* for the second day in the opposite direction, he cannot access that *eiruv* during the first day.

מִי סָבְרַתְּ דְּמַנַּח לֵיהּ בְּסוֹף אַלְפַּיִם אַמָּה לְכָאן, וּבְסוֹף אַלְפַּיִם אַמָּה לְכָאן? לֹא, דְּמַנַּח לֵיהּ בְּסוֹף אֶלֶף אַמָּה לְכָאן, וּבְסוֹף אֶלֶף אַמָּה לְכָאן.

The Gemara responds: **Do you think that** we are dealing with a case where **he placed** one *eiruv* in the furthest possible spot **at the end of two thousand cubits in this** direction, **and** he placed the other *eiruv* in the furthest possible spot **at the end of two thousand cubits in that** direction, and he is therefore unable to go from one to the other on one day? **No,** the case is **that he placed** one *eiruv* **at the end of one thousand cubits in the this direction, and** he placed the other *eiruv* **at the end of one thousand cubits in that** direction,[HB] so that even after acquiring his residence on one side of the town by means of the first *eiruv*, he can still go to the spot where he left the other *eiruv* for the second day.

אֶלָּא הָא דְּאָמַר רַב יְהוּדָה: עֵירֵב בְּרַגְלָיו יוֹם רִאשׁוֹן – מְעָרֵב בְּרַגְלָיו יוֹם שֵׁנִי, עֵירֵב בַּפַּת בְּיוֹם רִאשׁוֹן – מְעָרֵב בַּפַּת בְּיוֹם שֵׁנִי, הָא קָא מֵכִין מִיּוֹם טוֹב לְשַׁבָּת!

Abaye raised yet another difficulty: **But** what about **that** which **Rav Yehuda said:** If **one established an *eiruv* with his feet** for the **first day, he may establish an *eiruv* with his feet** for the **second day;** and if **he established an *eiruv* with bread** on the **first day, he may establish an *eiruv* with bread** on the **second day?**[N] **Isn't he preparing from a Festival to Shabbat?**

אֲמַר לֵיהּ: מִי סָבְרַתְּ דְּאָזֵיל וְאָמַר מִידֵּי? דְּאָזֵיל וְשָׁתֵיק וְיָתֵיב.

Rabba **said to him: Do you think that one must go and say something** at the site of the *eiruv*, therefore performing an act of preparation? **He goes, and is silent, and sits** there,[NH] and he automatically acquires his residence without having to say or do anything. This does not fall into the category of prohibited preparation.

NOTES

A meal that is fit to be eaten while it is still day – סְעוּדָה הָרְאוּיָה מִבְּעוֹד יוֹם: *Tosafot* ask: The *halakha* is that food that may be eaten by some people, such as *teruma*, which may be eaten only by a priest, may be used by anyone to establish an *eiruv*. In this case as well, the *eiruv* is fit to be eaten by people on the other side of the town, so why shouldn't it be considered fit to be eaten?

The Rashba answers that the fact that other people may eat the food is only taken into account when the reason the person establishing the *eiruv* cannot eat it is due to a limitation that stems from the food itself. However, if the person is unable to eat the food for a reason that pertains to himself, the fact that it can be eaten by other people is irrelevant.

Nonetheless, according to Rabbeinu Yehonatan and Rabbi Zeraḥya HaLevi's versions of the text, this phrase does not appear. Instead, Abaye asks: Isn't he preparing while it is still day?

An *eiruv* on the first and the second – עֵירוּב בָּרִאשׁוֹן וּבַשֵּׁנִי: According to most commentaries, the question does not concern an *eiruv* established with bread but relates to an *eiruv* arranged by foot. According to this explanation, one who makes an *eiruv* with bread has no need to say anything more, for it was all said the day before, and the function of the bread is self-evident. Therefore, the question is only asked with regard to one who establishes an *eiruv* by foot. The *Me'iri* explains that, according to the Gemara's conclusion, one who makes an *eiruv* with bread must say so explicitly, and if he fails to do so, his *eiruv* is invalid. However, one may establish an *eiruv* by foot without saying anything.

Speech and silence – דִּיבּוּר וּשְׁתִיקָה: Since speech itself is not considered an action, even if one were to say that he is establishing an *eiruv*, why should this be considered a prohibited form of preparation? The explanation given is that in this case, since the act is only completed by means of speech, greater importance is attached to his statement. Consequently, the speaker is regarded as someone who actually prepares on a Festival for Shabbat.

HALAKHA

At the end of one thousand – בְּסוֹף אֶלֶף: If one wishes to establish two *eiruvin* for two days in different directions, he may not separate them by more than the distance which would allow him to reach on the first day the *eiruv* he prepared for the second day (*Shulḥan Arukh, Oraḥ Ḥayyim* 416:3).

He goes, and is silent, and sits there – דְּאָזֵיל וְשָׁתֵיק וְיָתֵיב: One who deposits an *eiruv* on a Festival for Shabbat should not go to the spot and declare that he is going to acquire a place of rest. Rather, he should sit there and remain silent. If he did speak, the *eiruv* is still valid (*Magen Avraham*; *Shulḥan Arukh, Oraḥ Ḥayyim* 416:2).

BACKGROUND

Two thousand and one thousand – אַלְפַּיִם וְאֶלֶף: If one lives at point A and established an *eiruv* at point B, he cannot walk to point C, where he had placed his second *eiruv*. However, if he placed one *eiruv* at point D, since the distance from there to point E totals two thousand cubits, he can reach that spot even if he established his residence at the site of his *eiruv*.

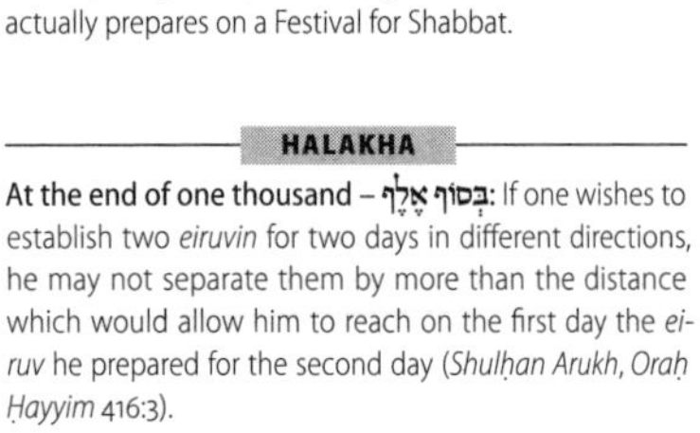

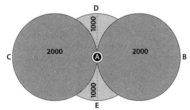

Diagram of different possibilities pertaining to establishment of a residence

כְּמַאן – כְּרַבִּי יוֹחָנָן בֶּן נוּרִי, דְּאָמַר: חֶפְצֵי הֶפְקֵר קוֹנִין שְׁבִיתָה?

Abaye asked: **In accordance with whose** opinion do you say that nothing must be said when establishing an *eiruv teḥumin*? It is **in accordance with** the opinion of **Rabbi Yoḥanan ben Nuri, who said:** A sleeping person acquires a Shabbat residence in the spot where he is sleeping. Even though he is comparable to ownerless property, **ownerless property** itself **acquires a Shabbat residence** and has its own Shabbat boundary, and there is no need for a person to establish a residence for it in a particular spot.

אֲפִילּוּ תֵּימָא רַבָּנַן. עַד כָּאן לָא פְּלִיגִי רַבָּנַן עֲלֵיהּ דְּרַבִּי יוֹחָנָן בֶּן נוּרִי – אֶלָּא בְּיָשֵׁן, דְּלָא מָצֵי אָמַר. אֲבָל בְּנֵיעוֹר, דְּאִי בָּעֵי לְמֵימַר מָצֵי אָמַר, אַף עַל גַּב דְּלָא אָמַר – כְּמַאן דַּאֲמַר דָּמֵי.

Rabba replied: **Even if you say** that my statement is in accordance with the opinion of **the Rabbis, the Rabbis disagree with Rabbi Yoḥanan ben Nuri only with regard to a sleeping person, who cannot say** anything, as he is asleep. Consequently, he cannot acquire a Shabbat residence. **However, with regard to** one who is **awake,** since **if he wanted to speak he could speak, even though he did not say** that he is acquiring his Shabbat residence, **he is considered as one who did say** that statement.

אֲמַר לֵיהּ רַבָּה בַּר רַב חָנִין לְאַבַּיֵי: אִי הֲוָה שְׁמִיעַ לֵיהּ לְמָר הָא דְּתַנְיָא: לֹא יְהַלֵּךְ אָדָם לְסוֹף שָׂדֵהוּ לֵידַע מַה הִיא צְרִיכָה, כַּיּוֹצֵא בּוֹ

Rabba bar Rav Ḥanin said to Abaye: If the Master, Rabba, **had heard that which was taught** in the following *baraita*: **A person may not walk to the end of his field**[H] on Shabbat **to determine what** work and repair **it requires,** which will be done after Shabbat. **Similarly,**

HALAKHA

A person may not walk to the end of his field – לֹא יְהַלֵּךְ אָדָם לְסוֹף שָׂדֵהוּ: It is prohibited to walk in one's fields on Shabbat for the purpose of determining what they will require after Shabbat. This rule only applies when it is evident that this is one's intention (*Magen Avraham*; *Shulḥan Arukh, Oraḥ Ḥayyim* 306:1).

Perek **III**
Daf **39** Amud **a**

לֹא יְטַיֵּיל אָדָם עַל פֶּתַח מְדִינָה כְּדֵי שֶׁיִּכָּנֵס לַמֶּרְחָץ מִיָּד – הֲדַר בֵּיהּ.

a person may not stroll at the entrance to the city toward the end of Shabbat or a Festival **in order to enter a bathhouse**[N] **immediately** upon the conclusion of Shabbat, then Rabba would have **retracted his** statement with regard to an *eiruv*. This *baraita* indicates that even walking on Shabbat for something one needs after Shabbat falls into the category of prohibited preparation.

וְלָא הִיא, שְׁמַע לֵיהּ וְלָא הֲדַר בֵּיהּ. הָתָם – מוֹכְחָא מִילְּתָא, הָכָא – לָאו מוֹכְחָא מִילְּתָא הִיא.

The Gemara rejects this argument: **And this is not** correct. Rabba **heard this** *baraita* **but did not retract** his ruling, as a distinction can be drawn between the cases. **There,** in the *baraita* pertaining to one who walks to the end of his field, or one who strolls at the entrance to the city, **it is clear** to all observers that he is doing so in order to determine what work the field needs after Shabbat, or to enter the bathhouse immediately after Shabbat, respectively. Whereas **here,** with regard to an *eiruv*, **it is not clear** to others that one's actions are for the purpose of establishing an *eiruv*.

אִי צוּרְבָא מֵרַבָּנַן הוּא – אָמְרִינַן: שְׁמַעְתָּא מְשַׁכְתֵּיהּ. וְאִי עַם הָאָרֶץ הוּא – אָמְרִינַן: חֲמָרָא אִירְכַס לֵיהּ.

The Gemara explains: **If he is a Torah scholar** [*tzurva merabbanan*],[L] **we,** the observers, would **say:** Perhaps **his study pulled him,** i.e., he was engrossed in his study and was not paying attention to where he was going. **And if he is an ignoramus, we** would **say:** Perhaps **he lost** his **donkey** and went to look for it. His actions give no indication that he is going to establish an *eiruv* for the following day, as establishing an *eiruv* does not require any recognizable action.

גּוּפָא, אָמַר רַב יְהוּדָה: עֵירֵב בְּרַגְלָיו בְּיוֹם רִאשׁוֹן – מְעָרֵב בְּרַגְלָיו בַּשֵּׁנִי. עֵירֵב בְּפַת בְּיוֹם רִאשׁוֹן – מְעָרֵב בְּפַת בְּיוֹם שֵׁנִי.

The Gemara now examines Rav Yehuda's statement **itself,** which was cited in the course of the previous discussion. **Rav Yehuda said:** If **one established an** *eiruv* **with his feet on** the eve of the **first day, he may establish an** *eiruv* **with his feet on** the eve of **the second** day as well. If **he established an** *eiruv* **with bread** that he deposited in the place where he wishes to acquire his place of rest **on** the eve of the **first day, he may establish an** *eiruv* **with bread on** the eve of the **second day** as well.

עֵירֵב בְּפַת בָּרִאשׁוֹן – מְעָרֵב בְּרַגְלָיו בַּשֵּׁנִי. עֵירֵב בְּרַגְלָיו בָּרִאשׁוֹן – אֵין מְעָרֵב בְּפַת בַּשֵּׁנִי, שֶׁאֵין מְעָרְבִין בַּתְּחִלָּה בְּפַת.

If **he established an** *eiruv* **with bread on** the eve of **the first** day, and his *eiruv* was eaten, he may change and **establish an** *eiruv* **with his feet on** the eve of **the second** day. However, if **he established an** *eiruv* **with his feet on** the eve of **the first** day, **he may not establish an** *eiruv* **with bread on** the eve of **the second** day, as **one may not initially establish an** *eiruv* **with bread** on a Festival for the sake of Shabbat because it is prohibited to prepare on a Festival for Shabbat.

NOTES

The entrance to the city and a bathhouse – פֶּתַח מְדִינָה וּמֶרְחָץ: The question may be asked: In these circumstances, why can't the same argument, that onlookers might conclude that one went to look for his donkey or was engrossed in his studies, be made? The difference in the case of a bathhouse is that one will not simply walk toward it; he will wait at the entrance to the bathhouse. However, this is not the case with regard to one who is establishing his *eiruv*, since he does not stay there but returns immediately (Maharam of Lublin).

LANGUAGE

Torah scholar [*tzurva meirabbanan*] – צוּרְבָא מֵרַבָּנַן: This refers to a Torah scholar, particularly a young scholar. Since ancient times, authorities have disagreed as to the linguistic source of this expression. Some relate the word *tzurva* to *tzarevet*, which connotes something hot and scorching like fire. This describes a young scholar's manner in his Torah studies (Rav Hai Gaon). Other commentaries explain that it means vigor and strength, and they find support for this interpretation from other talmudic expressions. The word would therefore be similar to the Arabic root ضرب, *d'rb*, which also denotes vigor and strength (Ran; *Arukh*).

HALAKHA

One who establishes an *eiruv* for two days – עירוב לְיוֹמַיִם: One who establishes an *eiruv* with bread for two days must use that same bread for both days, in accordance with the opinion of Shmuel (*Shulḥan Arukh, Oraḥ Ḥayyim* 416:2).

An *eiruv* for the days of Rosh HaShana – עירוב בִּימֵי רֹאשׁ הַשָּׁנָה: The two days of Rosh HaShana are considered as one day. Consequently, one may not establish separate *eiruvin* in two different directions for the two days, in accordance with the view of the Rabbis (*Shulḥan Arukh, Oraḥ Ḥayyim* 416:1–2).

NOTES

And the Rabbis…good advice – וְרַבָּנַן...עֵצָה טוֹבָה: The Ra'avad explains that the Gemara is saying as follows: What did Rav Yehuda and Shmuel add that was not already explained in the mishna? The Rabbis answer that from the mishna alone one may have assumed that this was merely good advice; therefore, Rav Yehuda and Shmuel taught that there is no other way to do it (see Rashba).

Strengthen us – הַחֲלִיצֵנוּ: In this context, the term *haḥalitzeinu* means grant us enthusiasm and strength. The root of the Hebrew word is used in this sense in several places in the Bible, such as "*ḥalutzim*" (Deuteronomy 3:18), meaning armed, and "*heiḥaltzu*" (Numbers 31:3), meaning arm yourselves. Both of these usages imply zeal and strengthening (Rabbeinu Yehonatan).

Whether today or tomorrow – אִם הַיּוֹם אִם לְמָחָר: If one would not employ this formulation, he would be lying in his prayer, since it is impossible for both today and tomorrow to occur on the first of the month (Rabbeinu Yehonatan).

And the Rabbis did not agree with him – וְלֹא הוֹדוּ לוֹ חֲכָמִים: The rationale is that if this conditional phrase appears in the prayer, the common people would make light of the sanctity of the two days, saying that they contain only questionable sanctity (Rabbeinu Yehonatan).

עֵירַב בַּפַּת בְּיוֹם רִאשׁוֹן – מְעָרֵב בַּפַּת בְּיוֹם שֵׁנִי. אָמַר שְׁמוּאֵל: וּבְאוֹתָהּ הַפַּת. אָמַר רַב אַשִׁי: דַּיְקָא נַמִי מַתְנִיתִין, דְּקָתָנֵי: כֵּיצַד הוּא עוֹשֶׂה? מוֹלִיכוֹ בָּרִאשׁוֹן, וּמַחְשִׁיךְ עָלָיו וְנוֹטְלוֹ – וּבָא לוֹ. בַּשֵּׁנִי מַחְשִׁיךְ עָלָיו וְאוֹכְלוֹ, וּבָא לוֹ.

With regard to the statement: If **he established an *eiruv* with bread on** the eve of the **first day, he may establish an *eiruv* with bread on** the eve of the **second day, Shmuel said:** Only **with the same bread. Rav Ashi said:** The wording of **the mishna is also precise** according to this understanding, **as we learned: What does he do** if a Festival occurs on Friday, and he wishes to establish an *eiruv* that will be valid for both the Festival and Shabbat? **He brings** the *eiruv* to the spot that he wishes to establish as his residence **on** the eve of **the first** day, **and he stays** there **with it until nightfall, and** then **he takes it** with him **and goes away. On** the eve of **the second** day, he takes the *eiruv* back to the same place as the day before, and **stays** there **with it until nightfall, and** then **he** may **eat** the *eiruv* **and go away.** The wording of the mishna indicates that he must establish his *eiruv* for the second day with the same bread that he used for the first day, as argued by Shmuel.[H]

וְרַבָּנַן – דִּילְמָא הָתָם עֵצָה טוֹבָה קָא מַשְׁמַע לַן.

The Gemara adds: **And the Rabbis,** who do not accept the opinion of Shmuel, argue that this is no proof, as **perhaps there,** the mishna is merely **teaching us good advice**[N] as to how one can rely on a single *eiruv* and avoid having to prepare an additional *eiruv* for the second day.

מתני׳ רַבִּי יְהוּדָה אוֹמֵר: רֹאשׁ הַשָּׁנָה, שֶׁהָיָה יָרֵא שֶׁמָּא תִּתְעַבֵּר – מְעָרֵב אָדָם שְׁנֵי עֵירוּבִין, וְאוֹמֵר: עֵירוּבִי בָּרִאשׁוֹן לַמִּזְרָח, וּבַשֵּׁנִי לַמַּעֲרָב. בָּרִאשׁוֹן לַמַּעֲרָב וּבַשֵּׁנִי לַמִּזְרָח. עֵירוּבִי בָּרִאשׁוֹן, וּבַשֵּׁנִי כִּבְנֵי עִירִי. עֵירוּבִי בַּשֵּׁנִי, וּבָרִאשׁוֹן כִּבְנֵי עִירִי, וְלֹא הוֹדוּ לוֹ חֲכָמִים.

MISHNA During the time period when the Jewish calendar was established by the court according to the testimony of witnesses who had seen the new moon, Rosh HaShana would be observed for only one day if witnesses arrived on that day, and for two days if witnesses failed to arrive and the month of Elul was declared to be an extended, thirty-day month. **Rabbi Yehuda says:** With regard to **Rosh HaShana, if one feared that** the month of Elul **might be extended,** and he wanted to travel in two different directions on the two days that could be Rosh HaShana, this **person may establish two *eiruvin* and say: My *eiruv* on the first** day shall be **to the east and on the second** day **to the west,** or alternatively: **On the first** day it shall be **to the west, and on the second** day **to the east.** Similarly, he may say: **My *eiruv*** shall apply **on the first** day, **but on the second** day I shall be **like** the rest of **the inhabitants of my town,** or alternatively: **My *eiruv*** shall apply **on the second** day, **but on the first** day I shall be **like** the rest of **the inhabitants of my town. And the Rabbis did not agree with him** that the two days of Rosh HaShana can be divided in such a manner.[H]

וְעוֹד אָמַר רַבִּי יְהוּדָה: מַתְנֶה אָדָם עַל הַכַּלְכָּלָה בְּיוֹם טוֹב רִאשׁוֹן, וְאוֹכְלָהּ בַּשֵּׁנִי.

And Rabbi Yehuda said further, with regard to the two days of Rosh HaShana that one observes because he does not know which is the real day of the Festival: **A person may make a condition** with regard to **a basket** of *tevel* produce **on the first day of the Festival** and say as follows: If today is the Festival and tomorrow is an ordinary weekday I will separate the *teruma* and tithes tomorrow, and I have performed nothing today; if today is an ordinary weekday, I hereby separate the appropriate *teruma* and tithes now. **He may** then **eat** the produce **on the second** day of the Festival, since one of his two acts of tithing was certainly performed on an ordinary weekday.

וְכֵן בֵּיצָה שֶׁנּוֹלְדָה בָּרִאשׁוֹן תֵּאָכֵל בַּשֵּׁנִי, וְלֹא הוֹדוּ לוֹ חֲכָמִים.

And similarly, an egg that was laid on the first day of the Festival **may be eaten on the second** day, since one of the days is certainly an ordinary weekday. **And the Rabbis did not agree with him** even with regard to these two days.

רַבִּי דּוֹסָא בֶּן הַרְכִּינָס אוֹמֵר: הָעוֹבֵר לִפְנֵי הַתֵּיבָה בְּיוֹם טוֹב שֶׁל רֹאשׁ הַשָּׁנָה, אוֹמֵר: "הַחֲלִיצֵנוּ ה׳ אֱלֹהֵינוּ אֶת יוֹם רֹאשׁ הַחֹדֶשׁ הַזֶּה אִם הַיּוֹם, אִם לְמָחָר". וּלְמָחָר הוּא אוֹמֵר: "אִם הַיּוֹם, אִם אֶמֶשׁ", וְלֹא הוֹדוּ לוֹ חֲכָמִים.

Rabbi Dosa ben Harekinas says: One who passes before the ark in the synagogue and leads the congregation in prayer **on** the first day of **the festival of Rosh HaShana says: Strengthen us,**[N] **O Lord our God, on this day of the New Moon, whether** it is **today or tomorrow.**[N] And similarly, **on the following day he says: Whether** Rosh HaShana is **today or yesterday. And the Rabbis did not agree with him**[N] that one should formulate his prayer in this conditional manner.

גמ׳ מַאן ״לֹא הוֹדוּ לוֹ״? אָמַר רַב: רַבִּי יוֹסֵי הִיא, דְּתַנְיָא: מוֹדִים חֲכָמִים לְרַבִּי אֱלִיעֶזֶר בְּרֹאשׁ הַשָּׁנָה שֶׁהָיָה יָרֵא שֶׁמָּא תִּתְעַבֵּר, מְעָרֵב אָדָם שְׁנֵי עֵירוּבִין, וְאוֹמֵר: עֵירוּבִי בָּרִאשׁוֹן לַמִּזְרָח וּבַשֵּׁנִי לַמַּעֲרָב. בָּרִאשׁוֹן לַמַּעֲרָב וּבַשֵּׁנִי לַמִּזְרָח. עֵירוּבִי בָּרִאשׁוֹן, וּבַשֵּׁנִי כִּבְנֵי עִירִי. עֵירוּבִי בַּשֵּׁנִי, וּבָרִאשׁוֹן כִּבְנֵי עִירִי. רַבִּי יוֹסֵי אוֹסֵר.

GEMARA **Who are** the Sages who **did not agree with** Rabbi Yehuda? **Rav said: It is** those who follow the opinion of **Rabbi Yosei, as it was taught** in the *Tosefta*: Even though **the Rabbis** disagree with him about a Festival and Shabbat that occur on consecutive days and say that one cannot make two separate *eiruvin* for the two days, they **concede to Rabbi Eliezer** with regard to **Rosh HaShana that if a person feared that** the month of Elul **might be extended, he may establish two** ***eiruvin*** **and say: My** ***eiruv*** **on the first** day shall be **to the east, and on the second** day **to the west,** or: **On the first** day it shall be **to the west, and on the second** day **to the east,** or: **My** ***eiruv*** shall apply **on the first** day, **but on the second** day I shall be **like** the rest of **the inhabitants of my town,** or: **My** ***eiruv*** shall apply **on the second** day, **but on the first** day I shall be **like** the rest of **the inhabitants of my town.** But **Rabbi Yosei prohibits** it.

אָמַר לָהֶן רַבִּי יוֹסֵי: אִי אַתֶּם מוֹדִים שֶׁאִם בָּאוּ עֵדִים מִן הַמִּנְחָה וּלְמַעְלָה, שֶׁנּוֹהֲגִין אוֹתוֹ הַיּוֹם קֹדֶשׁ וּלְמָחָר קֹדֶשׁ?

Rabbi Yosei said to the Rabbis: **Don't you concede that if witnesses came from the** time of ***minḥa*** **and on**[N] on the first day of Rosh HaShana and testified that they had seen the new moon, we do not rely on their testimony to sanctify that day as Rosh HaShana; rather, since their testimony was not given on time, **we observe that day as sanctified and** also **the following day as sanctified?** This indicates that the two days of Rosh HaShana are not observed out of doubt as to which is the proper day; rather, it is as though the two days are one long day that are imbued with one unified sanctity. Therefore, it should not be possible to divide them.

NOTES

If witnesses came from the time of *minḥa* and on – בָּאוּ עֵדִים מִן הַמִּנְחָה וּלְמַעְלָה: If witnesses came after the offering of the afternoon sacrifice, claiming they saw the new moon on the first day, their testimony is not examined, and the month and the Festival are not sanctified on that day. Rather, both that day and the following day are observed as Festival days. Therefore, the sanctity of the two days of Rosh HaShana is not based on doubt, but upon an independent rabbinic decree that both days are considered sanctified. In the Jerusalem Talmud this is phrased differently, in far stronger terms, stating that the sanctity of the two days of Rosh HaShana is a custom of the prophets and Rosh HaShana is different than the other Festivals, which are kept in the Diaspora for two days based on a doubt as to which day is the real day of the Festival.

וְרַבָּנַן – הָתָם כִּי הֵיכִי דְּלָא לְזַלְזוּלֵי בֵּיהּ.

And the Rabbis hold that **there,** the first day is not observed as a Festival by Torah law but due to rabbinic decree, **so that** people **will not demean** the day[N] in future years and end up desecrating the Festival should the witnesses come on time. However, by Torah law it is an ordinary weekday, and therefore one can establish two separate *eiruvin* for the two days.

״וְעוֹד אָמַר רַבִּי יְהוּדָה וכו׳״.

We learned in the mishna that in addition to his ruling with regard to *eiruvin* for the two days of Rosh HaShana, **Rabbi Yehuda said further** that the two days can be split with regard to a basket of *tevel* produce and an egg laid on the first day of the Festival.

וּצְרִיכָא, דְּאִי אַשְׁמְעִינַן רֹאשׁ הַשָּׁנָה – בְּהָא קָאָמַר רַבִּי יְהוּדָה מִשּׁוּם דְּלָא קָעָבֵיד מִידֵּי. אֲבָל כַּלְכָּלָה, דְּמֶיחֱזֵי כִּמְתַקֵּן טִיבְלָא – אֵימָא מוֹדֶה לְהוּ לְרַבָּנַן.

The Gemara comments: **And it** was **necessary** to teach us all three laws, as they could not have been derived from one another. **As, if he had** only **taught us** the *halakha* with regard to establishing an *eiruv* for the two days of **Rosh HaShana,** one might have said that only **in this** case does **Rabbi Yehuda say** his ruling **because** in this case **one does not** actually **do anything** on the Festival itself. **But** in the case of **a basket, where it appears as though one is rendering** ***tevel*** **fit** on a Festival, **say** that Rabbi Yehuda **concedes to the Rabbis** that it is decreed prohibited.

וְאִי אַשְׁמְעִינַן הָנֵי תַּרְתֵּי – מִשּׁוּם דְּלֵיכָּא לְמִיגְזַר עֲלַיְיהוּ, אֲבָל בֵּיצָה דְּאִיכָּא לְמִיגְזַר בָּהּ מִשּׁוּם פֵּירוֹת הַנּוֹשְׁרִין וּמִשּׁוּם מַשְׁקִין שֶׁזָּבוּ – אֵימָא מוֹדֶה לְהוּ לְרַבָּנַן, צְרִיכָא.

And had he taught us only **these two** *halakhot,* we might have said that Rabbi Yehuda is lenient **because there is no** reason **to issue a decree** prohibiting **them,** as the potential prohibitions involved are not so severe. **But** in the case of **an egg** that was laid on the first day of a Festival, **where there is** reason **to issue a decree** prohibiting **it,** as explained in tractate *Beitza,* **because of fruit that fall** from a tree or **due to liquids that oozed** from fruit on a Festival, both of which the Sages prohibited as a safeguard against violating Torah prohibitions, **say** that Rabbi Yehuda **concedes to** the opinion of **the Rabbis,** which maintains that this egg may not be eaten even on the second day of the Festival. It was therefore **necessary** to teach us all three cases.

NOTES

So that people will not demean the day – כִּי הֵיכִי דְּלָא לְזַלְזוּלֵי בֵּיהּ: Since the witnesses are not examined on that day, their testimony is technically disregarded, and the first day is actually an ordinary weekday. However, the Sages decreed that the remainder of the day should be observed as a Festival, so that people would not treat the day lightly in future years. This is the interpretation of the passage accepted by most of the commentaries.

Nevertheless, some commentaries explained the Gemara in the opposite manner: The first day is in fact the day sanctified as a Festival, since witnesses did come to testify about the new moon on that day, and the decree not to accept their testimony immediately does not cancel the sanctity of the day. The Sages, however, decreed that the following day should also be sanctified, so that people would not treat the Festival lightly when they saw that the Levites did not sing the Festival song at the offering of the afternoon sacrifice, when the witnesses had not yet arrived (Ra'avad).

תַּנְיָא, כֵּיצַד אָמַר רַבִּי יְהוּדָה מַתְנֶה אָדָם עַל הַכַּלְכָּלָה בְּיוֹם טוֹב רִאשׁוֹן וְאוֹכְלָהּ בַּשֵּׁנִי: הָיוּ לְפָנָיו שְׁתֵּי כַּלְכָּלוֹת שֶׁל טֶבֶל, אוֹמֵר: אִם הַיּוֹם חוֹל וּלְמָחָר קֹדֶשׁ – תְּהֵא זוֹ תְּרוּמָה עַל זוֹ, וְאִם הַיּוֹם קֹדֶשׁ וּלְמָחָר חוֹל – אֵין בִּדְבָרַי כְּלוּם, וְקוֹרֵא עָלֶיהָ שֵׁם וּמַנִּיחָהּ.

It was taught in a *baraita*: **How** is one to carry out what **Rabbi Yehuda said,** that **a person** may **make a condition** with regard to **a basket** of *tevel* produce **on the first day of the Festival and** then **eat** the produce **on the second** day? **If there were two baskets of *tevel*** produce **before him, he says** as follows: **If today is** an ordinary **weekday and tomorrow is sanctified, let this** basket **be *teruma* for that** basket; **and if today is sanctified and tomorrow** is an ordinary **weekday, my statement has no** significance. **And he bestows upon** the basket **the name of** *teruma,* **and sets it aside.**

וּלְמָחָר הוּא אוֹמֵר: אִם הַיּוֹם חוֹל – תְּהֵא זוֹ תְּרוּמָה עַל זוֹ, וְאִם הַיּוֹם קֹדֶשׁ – אֵין בִּדְבָרַי כְּלוּם, וְקוֹרֵא עָלֶיהָ שֵׁם וְאוֹכְלָהּ. רַבִּי יוֹסֵי אוֹסֵר. וְכֵן הָיָה רַבִּי יוֹסֵי אוֹסֵר בִּשְׁנֵי יָמִים טוֹבִים שֶׁל גָּלֻיּוֹת.

And on the next day he says as follows: **If today is** an ordinary **weekday, let this** basket **be *teruma* for that** basket; **and if today is sanctified, my statement has no** significance. **And He bestows upon** the basket **the name of** *teruma,* **and** he may then **eat** the produce in the other basket, as *teruma* has definitely been separated on a weekday.[H] **Rabbi Yosei prohibits** this. **And, so too, Rabbi Yosei would prohibit** this procedure even **on the two Festival days of the Diaspora,** even though the second day is only observed because of a doubt as to the proper day on which to observe the Festival.

הַהוּא בַּר טַבְיָא דַּאֲתָא לְבֵי רֵישׁ גָּלוּתָא, דְּאִתְּצִיד בְּיוֹם טוֹב רִאשׁוֹן שֶׁל גָּלֻיּוֹת, וְאִשְׁתַּחִיט בְּיוֹם טוֹב שֵׁנִי.

The Gemara relates that **a particular young deer was brought to the house of the Exilarch.** The deer **was trapped** by a gentile **on the first day of a Festival** observed **in the Diaspora and slaughtered on the second day of the Festival.**[H] The question arose whether it was permitted to eat it, based on the fact that one of these two days was certainly an ordinary weekday.

רַב נַחְמָן וְרַב חִסְדָּא אָכְלוּ, רַב שֵׁשֶׁת לֹא אָכַל. אָמַר רַב נַחְמָן: מַאי אַעֲבֵיד לֵיהּ לְרַב שֵׁשֶׁת דְּלָא אָכֵיל בִּישְׂרָא דְטַבְיָא? אֲמַר לֵיהּ רַב שֵׁשֶׁת: וְהֵיכִי אֵיכוֹל? דְּתָנֵי אִיסִי, וְאָמְרִי לָהּ אִיסִי תָּנֵי: וְכֵן הָיָה רַבִּי יוֹסֵי אוֹסֵר שְׁנֵי יָמִים טוֹבִים שֶׁל גָּלֻיּוֹת!

Rav Naḥman and Rav Ḥisda ate from it, but **Rav Sheshet did not eat** from it. **Rav Naḥman said** in a jesting manner: **What can I do for Rav Sheshet, who does not eat deer meat? Rav Sheshet said to him: How can I eat** it, **as Isi taught, and some say** that this should be read as a question: **Didn't Isi teach: And, so too, Rabbi Yosei would prohibit** this procedure even **on the two Festival days of the Diaspora?**

אֲמַר רָבָא: וּמַאי קוּשְׁיָא? דִּילְמָא הָכִי קָאָמַר: וְכֵן הָיָה רַבִּי יוֹסֵי אוֹסֵר בִּשְׁנֵי יָמִים טוֹבִים שֶׁל רֹאשׁ הַשָּׁנָה בַּגּוֹלָה. אִי הָכִי ״שֶׁל גָּלֻיּוֹת״?! ״בַּגּוֹלָה״ מִיבָּעֵי לֵיהּ!

Rava said: What is the difficulty? Perhaps this is what he said:[N] **And, so too, Rabbi Yosei would prohibit** this procedure even **on the two Festival days of Rosh HaShana in the Diaspora,**[N] but with regard to the two days of other Festivals observed in the Diaspora, he too would agree with Rabbi Yehuda and permit it. They said to him: **If so,** the phrase **of the Diaspora** is inappropriate. **It should have said in the Diaspora.**

אֲמַר רַב אַסִי: וּמַאי קוּשְׁיָא? דִּילְמָא הָכִי קָאָמַר: וְכֵן הָיָה רַבִּי יוֹסֵי עוֹשֶׂה אִיסּוּר שְׁנֵי יָמִים טוֹבִים שֶׁל גָּלֻיּוֹת, כִּשְׁנֵי יָמִים טוֹבִים שֶׁל רֹאשׁ הַשָּׁנָה לְרַבָּנַן דְּשָׁרוּ.

Rav Asi said: What is the difficulty? Perhaps this is what he said: And so too, Rabbi Yosei would treat the prohibition of such a procedure **on the two Festival days of the Diaspora as on the two Festival days of Rosh HaShana, according to** the opinion of **the Rabbis, who permit** it. In any case, the proof from this *baraita* is inconclusive.

אַשְׁכְּחֵיהּ רַב שֵׁשֶׁת לְרַבָּה בַּר שְׁמוּאֵל, אֲמַר לֵיהּ: תָּנֵי מָר מִידֵּי בִּקְדוּשּׁוֹת? אֲמַר לֵיהּ, תָּנֵינָא: מוֹדֶה רַבִּי יוֹסֵי בִּשְׁנֵי יָמִים טוֹבִים שֶׁל גָּלֻיּוֹת. אֲמַר לֵיהּ: אִי מַשְׁכַּחַתְּ לְהוּ – לָא תֵּימָא לְהוּ וְלָא מִידֵּי.

The Gemara further relates that afterward **Rav Sheshet met Rabba bar Shmuel** and **said to him: Has the Master learned anything with regard to** the two **sanctities** of a Festival and the like? Rabba bar Shmuel **said to him: We have learned** that **Rabbi Yosei concedes with regard to the two Festival days of the Diaspora.** Rav Sheshet **said to him: If you** happen to **meet** Rav Naḥman and Rav Ḥisda, who disagreed with me and ate the deer in the Exilarch's house, **do not tell them anything** of what you just told me, lest they use this *tannaitic* source to embarrass me about my refusal to eat.

אֲמַר רַב אַשִׁי, לְדִידִי אֲמַר לִי אַמֵימָר: הַהוּא בַּר טַבְיָא לָאו אִיתְצוּדֵי אִיתְּצִיד,

Rav Ashi said: Ameimar told me that the deer was not trapped on the Festival;

NOTES

Perhaps this is what he said – דִּילְמָא הָכִי קָאָמַר: Rashi points out that this is a difficult interpretation of Rabbi Yosei's statement, as it alters its straightforward meaning. However, it was difficult for the Sages to accept that Rabbi Yosei, whose halakhic opinion is generally accepted, would be stringent in this regard. Consequently, they preferred a far-fetched interpretation of his statement instead of a dubious halakhic ruling (see Rashba).

Days of Rosh HaShana in the Diaspora – יְמֵי רֹאשׁ הַשָּׁנָה בְּגוֹלָה: There is a good reason to emphasize that when the New Moon was announced based on the testimony of witnesses who appeared before the court, there was indeed a difference between the two days of Rosh HaShana in Jerusalem and Rosh HaShana in other parts of Eretz Yisrael and the Diaspora. In Jerusalem, Rosh HaShana was not always observed for two days. Often, witnesses would arrive in the early part of the first day, which was declared to be Rosh HaShana, and only that day would be observed. However, if witnesses did not arrive early in the day, the Festival would be observed for two days even in Jerusalem. Therefore, although all Festivals are observed for two days in the Diaspora due to the doubt as to which day had been declared as the New Moon, there is an additional reason to observe Rosh HaShana for a second day: It was possible that even in Jerusalem Rosh HaShana was being observed for a second day (Rashba).

HALAKHA

A condition with regard to a basket – תְּנַאי בְּכַלְכָּלָה: One may stipulate a condition and separate *teruma* from a basket of *tevel* produce on the first day of a Festival and then eat the produce on the second day. However, this rule only applies to the two Festival days observed outside of Eretz Yisrael but not to Rosh HaShana (Rambam *Sefer Zemanim, Hilkhot Yom Tov* 6:12).

Trapped on the first day and slaughtered on the second – שֶׁנִּיצּוֹד בְּרִאשׁוֹן וְנִשְׁחַט בַּשֵּׁנִי: An animal that was trapped by a gentile on the first day of a Festival may be eaten on the second Festival day observed outside of Eretz Yisrael, once the time necessary for trapping it has elapsed (see Rashi). The *Tur*, citing the Rosh, is stringent and prohibits eating the deer until the second Festival day has ended and the time necessary for trapping it has elapsed so that a Jew does not come to ask a gentile to trap it on a Festival. The custom is to be stringent in this matter but to practice leniency for the sake of guests (*Shulḥan Arukh, Oraḥ Ḥayyim* 515:1).

אֶלָּא מִחוּץ לַתְּחוּם אֲתָא. מַאן דַּאֲכַל סָבַר: הַבָּא בִּשְׁבִיל יִשְׂרָאֵל זֶה – מוּתָּר לְיִשְׂרָאֵל אַחֵר.

rather, it had already been caught beforehand, but it **came** to the Exilarch's house on the Festival **from outside the** Shabbat **limit**[H] and was slaughtered on that day. **The one** who **ate** from it, namely, Rav Naḥman and Rav Ḥisda, **holds:** Something **that comes** from outside the Shabbat limit **for one Jew**[HN] **is permitted to another Jew.** Since the deer was brought for the Exilarch, the Sages at his table were permitted to eat from it, and we do not prohibit them to derive benefit from something that a gentile did for another Jew.

וּמַאן דְּלָא אֲכַל סָבַר – כֹּל דְּאָתֵי לְבֵי רֵישׁ גָּלוּתָא – אַדַּעְתָּא דְכוּלְּהוּ רַבָּנַן אָתֵי.

And the one who **did not eat** from it, Rav Sheshet, **holds: Anything that comes to the house of the Exilarch comes with all the Sages in mind,** as it is known that the Exilarch invites them to dine with him on Festivals. Therefore, just as it was prohibited to the Exilarch himself, as it was brought from outside the Shabbat limit, so too, it was prohibited to all his guests.

וְהָא אַשְׁכְּחֵיהּ רַב שֵׁשֶׁת לְרַבָּה בַּר שְׁמוּאֵל וַאֲמַר לֵיהּ! לֹא הָיוּ דְּבָרִים מֵעוֹלָם.

The Gemara asks: **Didn't Rav Sheshet meet Rabba bar Shmuel and say to him** what he said, indicating that the issue is related to the question of whether the two days are considered distinct sanctities? The Gemara answers: According to Ameimar's version of the story, **that** encounter **never happened.**

הַהוּא לִיפְתָּא דְּאָתֵי לְמָחוֹזָא, נְפַק רָבָא חַזְיָא דִּכְמִישָׁא, שְׁרָא רָבָא לְמִיזְבַּן מִינֵּיהּ. אֲמַר: הָא וַדַּאי מֵאִיתְּמוֹל נֶעֶקְרָה.

The Gemara relates that a delivery of **turnip** was once **brought to** the town of **Meḥoza** by gentile merchants from outside the Shabbat limit on a Festival in the Diaspora. **Rava went out** to the market and **saw** that the turnips **were withered, and** therefore **he permitted** people **to buy them** immediately without having to wait the amount of time needed to bring similar items from outside the limit after the Festival. **He said: These** turnips **were** certainly **uprooted** from the ground **yesterday,** and no prohibited labor was performed with them today.

מַאי אָמְרַתְּ מִחוּץ לַתְּחוּם אַתְיָא – הַבָּא בִּשְׁבִיל יִשְׂרָאֵל זֶה מוּתָּר לֶאֱכוֹל לְיִשְׂרָאֵל אַחֵר, וְכׇל שֶׁכֵּן הַאי דְּאַדַּעְתָּא דְגוֹיִם אֲתָא.

What might **you say;** that **they came from outside the** Shabbat **limit** and should therefore be prohibited? The accepted principle is: Something **that comes for one Jew is permitted to be eaten by another Jew, and all the more so** with regard to **this** delivery of turnip, **which came with gentiles in mind,** i.e., for their sake rather than for the sake of Jews. Therefore, if they are purchased by Jews, no prohibition is violated.

כֵּיוָן דַּחֲזָא דְּקָא מַפְשׁוּ וּמַיְיתִי לְהוּ – אֲסַר לְהוּ.

The Gemara adds: **Once** Rava **saw that** the gentile merchants started to **bring increased** quantities of turnips on Festival days for the sake of their Jewish customers, **he prohibited** the inhabitants of Meḥoza to buy them, for it was evident that they were now being brought for Jews.

הָנְהוּ בְּנֵי גַנָּנָא דְּגָזוּ לְהוּ אַסָּא בְּיוֹם טוֹב שֵׁנִי, לְאוּרְתָּא שְׁרָא לְהוּ רָבִינָא לְאוֹרוֹחֵי בֵּיהּ לְאַלְתַּר. אֲמַר לֵיהּ רָבָא בַּר תַּחֲלִיפָא לְרָבִינָא: לֵיסַר לְהוּ מָר, מִפְּנֵי שֶׁאֵינָן בְּנֵי תוֹרָה!

The Gemara relates that **certain canopy makers,** who would braid myrtle branches into their canopies, once **cut myrtles on the second day of a Festival,** and **in the evening Ravina permitted** people **to smell them**[N] **immediately** at the conclusion of the Festival. **Rava bar Taḥalifa said to Ravina: The Master should prohibit them** to do this, **as they are not knowledgeable in Torah,**[N] and therefore we should be stringent with them lest they come to treat the sanctity of the second Festival day lightly.

מַתְקִיף לַהּ רַב שְׁמַעְיָה: טַעְמָא – דְּאֵינָן בְּנֵי תוֹרָה, הָא בְּנֵי תוֹרָה שָׁרֵי?! וְהָא בָּעֵינַן בִּכְדֵי שֶׁיֵּעָשׂוּ! אֲזַלוּ שַׁיְּילוּהּ לְרָבָא, אֲמַר לְהוּ: בָּעֵינַן בִּכְדֵי שֶׁיֵּעָשׂוּ.

Rav Shemaya strongly objects to this: The reason given here is **that they are not knowledgeable in Torah;** but if **they were knowledgeable in Torah, would it be permitted? Don't we require** them to wait **the time needed for** the myrtle's **preparation,** i.e., the time it takes to cut them? **They went and asked Rava. He said to them: We require** them to wait **the time needed for** the myrtle's **preparation.**

״רַבִּי דּוֹסָא אוֹמֵר הָעוֹבֵר לִפְנֵי הַתֵּיבָה כו׳״.

The mishna cited Rabbi Dosa's version of the Rosh HaShana prayer: **Rabbi Dosa says: He who passes before the ark** and leads the congregation in prayer on the first day of the festival of Rosh HaShana says: Strengthen us, O Lord our God, on this day of the New Moon, whether it is today or tomorrow.

HALAKHA

Objects that arrived from outside the Shabbat limit – חֲפָצִים מִחוּץ לַתְּחוּם: The person for whom a gentile brought an object from outside the Shabbat limit is prohibited to utilize the object until the first Festival day has concluded and the time required to bring a similar object from outside the limit has elapsed (*Shulḥan Arukh, Oraḥ Ḥayyim* 515:5).

That comes for one Jew – הַבָּא לְיִשְׂרָאֵל זֶה: An object brought in by a gentile from outside the limit for a specific Jew is permitted to be utilized by other Jews (*Shulḥan Arukh, Oraḥ Ḥayyim* 515:5).

NOTES

That comes for one Jew – הַבָּא בִּשְׁבִיל יִשְׂרָאֵל זֶה: The rationale for differentiating between the Jew for whom the service was provided and any other Jew is unclear because when a prohibited labor is performed, the benefit derived from it is equally prohibited to all people. Some commentaries explain that the reason is that the entire prohibition of boundaries is only rabbinic. Consequently, the Sages were not stringent and prohibited the item brought in from outside the limit only to the person for whom it was brought. An alternative explanation is that the whole prohibition is a decree lest the gentile bring something especially for the Jew. Since it is prohibited for this person, there is no concern that the gentile might act on behalf of another Jew whom he doesn't know (Rashi).

Permitted people to smell them – שְׁרָא לְאוֹרוֹחֵי בֵּיהּ: Why did Ravina allow them to smell the myrtle immediately, without waiting at all? One explanation is that the myrtle was not initially brought for its fragrance but to be used in the making of a wedding crown. Smelling it was merely a secondary usage, against which the Sages did not issue a decree (Rashba).

As they are not knowledgeable in Torah – מִפְּנֵי שֶׁאֵינָן בְּנֵי תוֹרָה: This was the rationale for various stringencies imposed in places where people had little knowledge of Torah. In their ignorance, they might come to treat certain laws lightly, unless extra restrictions were instituted in addition to those stringencies observed in communities that include many scholars.

NOTES

One remembrance counts for both this and that – זִכָּרוֹן אֶחָד עוֹלֶה לְכָאן וּלְכָאן: Since the Torah uses the term remembrance in relation to the New Moon, it seems that the New Moon, like Rosh HaShana, has both a general name, Day of Remembrance, and a particular name, New Moon. Therefore, it is better to mention that it is a Day of Remembrance without specifying, as this term includes both Rosh HaShana and the New Moon (*Ge'on Ya'akov*).

HALAKHA

The prayer of Rosh HaShana – תְּפִלַּת רֹאשׁ הַשָּׁנָה: The additional prayer of Rosh HaShana consists of nine blessings (*Tur, Oraḥ Ḥayyim* 582).

אֲמַר רַבָּה: כִּי הֲוֵינַן בֵּי רַב הוּנָא, אִיבַּעְיָא לָן: מַהוּ לְהַזְכִּיר שֶׁל רֹאשׁ חֹדֶשׁ בְּרֹאשׁ הַשָּׁנָה? כֵּיוָן דַּחֲלוּקִין בְּמוּסָפִין אָמְרִינַן, אוֹ דִילְמָא: זִכָּרוֹן אֶחָד עוֹלֶה לְכָאן וּלְכָאן?

Rabba said: When we were in the house of study **of Rav Huna, we raised the** following **dilemma: What is** the *halakha* with regard to whether it is proper **to mention the New Moon** during prayer **on Rosh HaShana?** The Gemara explains the two sides of the dilemma: Do we say that **since they have separate additional offerings,** as one additional offering is brought for the New Moon and another for Rosh HaShana, **we mention** them separately in prayer as well? **Or perhaps one remembrance counts for** both **this and that?**[N] The Torah is referring to both Rosh HaShana and the New Moon as times of remembrance, and therefore perhaps simply mentioning that it is a Day of Remembrance should suffice.

אֲמַר לָן; תְּנֵיתוּהָ, רַבִּי דּוֹסָא אוֹמֵר: הָעוֹבֵר לִפְנֵי הַתֵּיבָה כו׳. מַאי לָאו לְהַזְכִּיר?

Rav Huna **said to us: You have** already **learned** the answer to this question in the mishna, which states that **Rabbi Dosa says: He who passes before the ark** and leads the congregation in prayer on the first day and on the second day of Rosh HaShana mentions the New Moon in a conditional manner: On this day of the New Moon, whether it is today or tomorrow. But the Rabbis did not agree with him. **What, is it not** that the Rabbis disagree with Rabbi Dosa about the need **to mention** the New Moon during prayer on Rosh HaShana?

לֹא, לְהַתְנוֹת.

The Gemara refutes this proof: **No,** they disagree about whether **to make a condition.** The novelty in Rabbi Dosa's teaching was not that mention must be made of the New Moon, but that a condition must be made due to the day's uncertain status. The Rabbis disagree about that.

הָכִי נַמִי מִסְתַּבְּרָא, מִדְּקָתָנֵי בְּבָרַיְיתָא: וְכֵן הָיָה רַבִּי דּוֹסָא עוֹשֶׂה בְּרָאשֵׁי חֳדָשִׁים שֶׁל כָּל הַשָּׁנָה כּוּלָּהּ, וְלֹא הוֹדוּ לוֹ.

The Gemara comments: **So too, it is reasonable** to say that the dispute between Rabbi Dosa and the Rabbis relates to the condition and not to the very mention of the New Moon. This can be ascertained **from** the fact **that it was taught in a *baraita*: And so too, Rabbi Dosa would do** this **on** all **the New Moons** for which two days are kept out of doubt **the entire year; and** the Rabbis **did not agree with him.**

אִי אָמְרַתְּ בִּשְׁלָמָא לְהַתְנוֹת – מִשּׁוּם הָכִי לֹא הוֹדוּ לוֹ. אֶלָּא אִי אָמְרַתְּ לְהַזְכִּיר – אַמַּאי לֹא הוֹדוּ לוֹ?

Granted, if you say that the disagreement was about whether **to make a condition, that is why they did not agree with him** with regard to the New Moon throughout the year, as they did not accept the whole idea of a conditional prayer. **But if you say** the main point of contention was whether **to mention** the New Moon at all, **why didn't they agree with him** that the New Moon should be mentioned during prayer the rest of the year?

וְאֶלָּא מַאי – לְהַתְנוֹת? לָמָּה לִי לְאִיפְלוּגֵי בְּתַרְתֵּי?! צְרִיכָא, דְּאִי אַשְׁמְעִינַן רֹאשׁ הַשָּׁנָה, הֲוָה אָמִינָא: בְּהָא קָאָמְרִי רַבָּנַן דְּלָא – מִשּׁוּם דְּאָתֵי לְזַלְזוּלֵי בֵּיהּ, אֲבָל בְּרָאשֵׁי חֳדָשִׁים שֶׁל כָּל הַשָּׁנָה כּוּלָּהּ – אֵימָא מוֹדוּ לֵיהּ לְרַבִּי דּוֹסָא.

The Gemara asks: **Rather, what** is the disagreement about, whether or not **to make a condition? Why do I** need them **to disagree in two** cases? The issue is the same on Rosh HaShana as on any other New Moon. The Gemara answers: **It was necessary** to teach both cases, **as, if he had** only **taught us** the *halakha* with regard to **Rosh HaShana, I might have said** that only **in this** case **did the Rabbis say that one should not** mention the New Moon in a conditional manner **because people might come to demean** the day and perform prohibited labor. **But in** the case of an ordinary **New Moon throughout the year,** I might **say** that perhaps **they agree with Rabbi Dosa,** since labor is not prohibited on the New Moon, and therefore there is no reason for concern lest people come to treat it lightly.

וְאִי אִתְּמַר בְּהָא – בְּהָא קָאָמַר רַבִּי דּוֹסָא, אֲבָל בְּהַךְ – אֵימָא מוֹדֶה לְהוּ לְרַבָּנַן, צְרִיכָא.

And if the disagreement **had** only **been stated in this** case, in the case of an ordinary New Moon, one might say that only **in this** case **did Rabbi Dosa say** that a condition may be made. **But in that** other case of Rosh HaShana, I might **say** that **he agrees with the Rabbis,** due to concern lest people will come to treat the Festival lightly. It was therefore **necessary** to state the disagreement in both cases.

מֵיתִיבִי: רֹאשׁ הַשָּׁנָה שֶׁחָל לִהְיוֹת בְּשַׁבָּת, בֵּית שַׁמַּאי אוֹמְרִים: מִתְפַּלֵּל עֶשֶׂר, וּבֵית הִלֵּל אוֹמְרִים: מִתְפַּלֵּל תֵּשַׁע. וְאִם אִיתָא, בֵּית שַׁמַּאי אַחַת עֶשְׂרֵה מִבָּעֵי לֵיהּ!

The Gemara **raises an objection** based on the *Tosefta* that states that in the case of **Rosh HaShana that occurs on Shabbat, Beit Shammai say: One prays** an *Amida* that contains **ten** blessings, including the nine blessings ordinarily recited on Rosh HaShana and an additional blessing in which Shabbat is mentioned. **And Beit Hillel say: One prays** an *Amida* that contains **nine** blessings,[H] as Shabbat and the Festival are mentioned in the same blessing. **And if there were** an opinion that held that the New Moon must be separately mentioned in the Rosh HaShana prayer, then **it should** say that according to **Beit Shammai,** one must recite **eleven** blessings, i.e., nine for Rosh HaShana, one for Shabbat, and one for the New Moon.

אָמַר רַבִּי זֵירָא: שָׁאנֵי רֹאשׁ חֹדֶשׁ, מִתּוֹךְ שֶׁכּוֹלֵל לְשַׁחֲרִית וְעַרְבִית כּוֹלֵל נַמִי בְּמוּסָפִין.

Rabbi Zeira said: The New Moon is different, for while it must indeed be mentioned according to Beit Shammai, it does not require a separate blessing. **Since** the New Moon **is included** in the regular **morning and evening** prayers without a separate blessing, **it is included in the additional** prayer **as well** without a separate blessing.

וּמִי אִית לְהוּ לְבֵית שַׁמַּאי כּוֹלֵל, וְהָתַנְיָא: רֹאשׁ חֹדֶשׁ שֶׁחָל לִהְיוֹת בְּשַׁבָּת, בֵּית שַׁמַּאי אוֹמְרִים: מִתְפַּלֵּל שְׁמֹנֶה, וּבֵית הִלֵּל אוֹמְרִים: מִתְפַּלֵּל שֶׁבַע! קַשְׁיָא.

The Gemara asks: **And do Beit Shammai** accept the view that one should **include** the New Moon in the regular prayer? **Wasn't it taught** in a *baraita* that with regard to **a New Moon that occurs on Shabbat, Beit Shammai say: One** must **pray** an *Amida* that includes **eight** blessings in the additional prayer, including a separate blessing for the New Moon; **and Beit Hillel say: One must pray** an *Amida* that includes **seven** blessings, as Shabbat and the New Moon are mentioned in the same blessing? Therefore, according to Beit Shammai, we do not include the New Moon and other days in the same blessing, and the fact that the New Moon does not have its own blessing on Rosh HaShana is because one mention of remembrance counts for both Rosh HaShana and New Moon. The Gemara comments: Indeed, this is **difficult.**

וְכוֹלֵל עַצְמוֹ תַּנָּאֵי הִיא, דְּתַנְיָא: שַׁבָּת שֶׁחָל לִהְיוֹת בְּרֹאשׁ חֹדֶשׁ אוֹ בְּחוּלּוֹ שֶׁל מוֹעֵד, עַרְבִית שַׁחֲרִית וּמִנְחָה מִתְפַּלֵּל כְּדַרְכּוֹ שֶׁבַע, וְאוֹמֵר מֵעֵין הַמְּאוֹרָע בָּעֲבוֹדָה. רַבִּי אֱלִיעֶזֶר אוֹמֵר: בְּהוֹדָאָה. וְאִם לֹא אָמַר – מַחֲזִירִין אוֹתוֹ.

The Gemara comments: The issue of whether or not one should **include** the mention of the New Moon in the blessing pertaining to the sanctity of the day of Shabbat is **itself** the subject of a dispute between the ***tanna'im*, as it was taught** in a *baraita* with regard to a **Shabbat that occurs on a New Moon or on** one of **the intermediate days of a Festival:** For **the evening, morning, and afternoon prayers, one prays in his** usual **manner** and recites **seven** blessings, **and says** a passage pertaining to the **event** of the day, i.e. May there rise and come [*ya'aleh veyavo*], **during** the blessing of **Temple service. Rabbi Eliezer** disagrees and **says** that this passage is said **during** the blessing of **thanksgiving. And if he did not recite** it, **we require him to return** to the beginning of the prayer and repeat it.

וּבְמוּסָפִין מַתְחִיל בְּשֶׁל שַׁבָּת, וּמְסַיֵּים בְּשֶׁל שַׁבָּת, וְאוֹמֵר קְדוּשַּׁת הַיּוֹם בָּאֶמְצַע.

And in the additional prayer, one begins the fourth blessing, the special blessing for the additional service, **with Shabbat, and concludes** it **with Shabbat, and says** a passage referring to **the sanctity of the day** of the New Moon or the Festival **in the middle.** Therefore, only in the additional prayer is the New Moon included in the blessing for the sanctity of the day.

רַבָּן שִׁמְעוֹן בֶּן גַּמְלִיאֵל וְרַבִּי יִשְׁמָעֵאל בְּנוֹ שֶׁל רַבִּי יוֹחָנָן בֶּן בְּרוֹקָה אוֹמְרִים: כָּל מָקוֹם שֶׁזָּקוּק לְשֶׁבַע – מַתְחִיל בְּשֶׁל שַׁבָּת, וּמְסַיֵּים בְּשֶׁל שַׁבָּת, וְאוֹמֵר קְדוּשַּׁת הַיּוֹם בָּאֶמְצַע.

On the other hand, **Rabban Shimon ben Gamliel and Rabbi Yishmael, son of Rabbi Yoḥanan ben Beroka, say: Wherever** one is **obligated** to recite **seven** blessings, including the evening, morning, and afternoon prayers, **he begins** the fourth blessing **with Shabbat and concludes** it **with Shabbat, and he says** a passage referring to **the sanctity of the day** of the New Moon or the Festival **in the middle.** In their opinion, the New Moon is included in the blessing of the sanctity of the day in all the prayers of the day.

מַאי הֲוָה עֲלַהּ? אָמַר רַב חִסְדָּא: זִכָּרוֹן אֶחָד עוֹלֶה לוֹ לְכָאן וּלְכָאן. וְכֵן אָמַר רַבָּה: זִכָּרוֹן אֶחָד עוֹלֶה לוֹ לְכָאן וּלְכָאן.

Returning to the fundamental question of whether the New Moon must be mentioned separately on Rosh HaShana, the Gemara asks: **What** conclusion **was** reached **about this** issue? **Rav Ḥisda said: One** mention of **remembrance counts for** both **this and that. And so too, Rabba said: One** mention of **remembrance counts for** both **this and that.**

וְאָמַר רַבָּה: כִּי הֲוֵינָא בֵּי רַב הוּנָא, אִיבַּעְיָא לַן: מַהוּ לוֹמַר זְמַן בְּרֹאשׁ הַשָּׁנָה וּבְיוֹם הַכִּפּוּרִים? כֵּיוָן דְּמִזְּמַן לִזְמַן אָתֵי – אָמְרִינַן, אוֹ דִּילְמָא: כֵּיוָן דְּלָא אִיקְּרוּ רְגָלִים – לָא אָמְרִינַן? לָא הֲוָה בִּידֵיהּ.

Having discussed the Rosh HaShana prayers, the Gemara addresses related issues. **Rabba said: When I was in the house** of study **of Rav Huna, we raised the** following **dilemma: What is** the *halakha* with regard **to saying** the blessing for **time,** i.e., Who has given us life [*sheheḥeyanu*], **on Rosh HaShana and Yom Kippur?** The two sides of the dilemma are as follows: Do we say that **since** these Festivals **come at fixed times** of the year, **we recite** the blessing: Who has given us life, just as we would for any other joyous event that occurs at fixed intervals? **Or** do we say, **perhaps,** that **since** these Festivals **are not called pilgrim Festivals** [***regalim***], **we do not recite:** Who has given us life, as the joy that they bring is insufficient? Rav Huna **did not have** an answer **at hand.**

NOTES

Perhaps the child will come to be drawn after it – דִּילְמָא אָתֵי לְמִסְרַךְ: The early commentaries prove that if one were to give the wine to a small child, who does not understand, it would certainly not help. Since the child is not obligated to recite a blessing, there is no obligation to recite a blessing for him. Rather, the Gemara is referring to a child who has already reached the age of education with regard to blessings but has yet to reach the age of education for fasting (Rashba and others). Some ask: If we are so concerned that the child might become used to drinking wine on Yom Kippur that we do not give it to him, why doesn't that same concern apply to anything the child eats or drinks? The answer is that when the child grows up he will understand that he must refrain from eating for his own sake. However, he might come to see eating for the sake of the adults as part of the custom of the day (Rashba; *Me'iri*).

כִּי אֲתָאִי בֵּי רַב יְהוּדָה, אֲמַר: אֲנָא אַקְּרָא חַדְתָּא נַמִי אָמֵינָא זְמַן. אָמְרִי לֵיהּ: רְשׁוּת לָא קָא מִיבָּעֲיָא לִי, כִּי קָא מִיבָּעֲיָא לִי – חוֹבָה מַאי? אֲמַר לִי: רַב וּשְׁמוּאֵל דְּאָמְרִי תַּרְוַויְיהוּ אֵין אוֹמֵר זְמַן אֶלָּא בְּשָׁלֹשׁ רְגָלִים.

When I came to the house of study **of Rav Yehuda, he said: I recite** the blessing for **time** even **on a new gourd,** and I certainly recite the blessing on Rosh HaShana and Yom Kippur. **I said to him: I have no dilemma** about the fact that one has the **option** of reciting the blessing for time; **the dilemma I have is** about whether there is an **obligation** to recite the blessing. **What** is the *halakha* in this regard? Rav Yehuda **said to me** that **it was Rav and Shmuel who both said: One recites** the blessing for **time only on the three pilgrim Festivals.**

מֵיתִיבִי: ״תֶּן חֵלֶק לְשִׁבְעָה וְגַם לִשְׁמוֹנָה״, רַבִּי אֱלִיעֶזֶר אוֹמֵר: שִׁבְעָה – אֵלּוּ שִׁבְעָה יְמֵי בְרֵאשִׁית, שְׁמוֹנָה – אֵלּוּ שְׁמוֹנָה יְמֵי מִילָה. רַבִּי יְהוֹשֻׁעַ אוֹמֵר: שִׁבְעָה – אֵלּוּ שִׁבְעָה יְמֵי פֶסַח, שְׁמוֹנָה – אֵלּוּ שְׁמוֹנָה יְמֵי הֶחָג. וּכְשֶׁהוּא אוֹמֵר וְגַם – לְרַבּוֹת עֲצֶרֶת וְרֹאשׁ הַשָּׁנָה וְיוֹם הַכִּפּוּרִים.

The Gemara **raises an objection** based upon the following *baraita*: The verse states: **"Give a portion to seven, and also to eight"** (Ecclesiastes 11:2). **Rabbi Eliezer says: "Seven," these are the seven days of Creation; "eight," these are the eight days** until **circumcision. Rabbi Yehoshua says: "Seven," these are the seven days of Passover; "eight," these are the eight days of the festival** of *Sukkot*. **And when it says: "And also,"** like every other instance of the word "also" in the Torah, this comes **to include;** what it includes is ***Shavuot*, and Rosh HaShana, and Yom Kippur.**

מַאי לָאו לִזְמַן? לֹא, לִבְרָכָה.

What, is this exposition **not** coming **to** teach us that on these days one is obligated to recite the blessing for **time?** The Gemara responds: **No,** it is referring **to the blessing** recited over the special sanctity of the day.

הָכִי נַמִי מִסְתַּבְּרָא, דְּאִי סָלְקָא דַּעְתָּךְ לִזְמַן – זְמַן כָּל שִׁבְעָה מִי אִיכָּא? הָא לָא קַשְׁיָא, דְּאִי לָא מְבָרֵךְ הָאִידָּנָא – מְבָרֵךְ לְמָחָר וּלְיוֹם אוֹחֲרָא.

The Gemara comments: **So too, it is reasonable** to explain, **as if it would enter your mind** to say that it is referring **to** the blessing for **time, is there** a blessing for **time** that is recited **all seven** days of the Festival? It is recited only on the first day. The Gemara refutes this argument: **This is not difficult,** as it means **that if he does not recite the blessing** for time **now, he recites** the blessing **tomorrow or the following day,** as all seven days are part of the pilgrim Festival.

מִכָּל מָקוֹם בָּעֵינַן כּוֹס? לֵימָא מְסַיַּיע לֵיהּ לְרַב נַחְמָן, דְּאָמַר רַב נַחְמָן: זְמַן אוֹמְרוֹ אֲפִילּוּ בַּשּׁוּק. הָא לָא קַשְׁיָא – דְּאִיקְּלַע לֵיהּ כּוֹס.

The Gemara asks: **In any case, we require** that this blessing be recited over **a cup** of wine, and most people do not have cups of wine for the intermediate days of a Festival. **Let us say** that this **supports Rav Naḥman, as Rav Naḥman said:** The blessing for **time may be recited even in the market,** without a cup of wine. The Gemara responds: **This is not difficult,** as the case is that **he happened to have a cup;** but without a cup of wine, the blessing may not be recited.

הָתֵינַח עֲצֶרֶת וְרֹאשׁ הַשָּׁנָה, יוֹם הַכִּפּוּרִים הֵיכִי עָבֵיד? אִי מְבָרֵךְ עֲלֵיהּ וְשָׁתֵי לֵיהּ – כֵּיוָן דַּאֲמַר זְמַן קַבְּלֵיהּ עֲלֵיהּ, וְאָסַר לֵיהּ.

The Gemara asks: **Granted,** one can recite the blessing over a cup of wine on ***Shavuot*** **and Rosh HaShana;** but **what does one do on Yom Kippur? If** you say that **he should recite the blessing** over a cup of wine before the actual commencement of Yom Kippur **and drink it,** there is a difficulty: **Since he recited** the blessing for **time, he accepted** the sanctity of the day **upon himself, and** therefore **caused** the wine **to be prohibited to himself** by the laws of Yom Kippur.

דְּהָאֲמַר לֵיהּ רַב יִרְמְיָה בַּר אַבָּא לְרַב: מִי בָּדְלַתְּ? וַאֲמַר לֵיהּ: אִין, בָּדֵילְנָא.

As didn't Rav Yirmeya bar Abba say the following **to Rav,** upon observing him recite *kiddush* before the actual commencement of Shabbat: **Have you** therefore accepted the obligation to **abstain** from labor from this point on? **And he said to him: Yes, I have** accepted the obligation to **abstain** from labor. This indicates that once one recites *kiddush* and accepts upon himself the sanctity of the day, all the laws of the day apply to him. Accordingly, if one recited the blessing for time for Yom Kippur, he may no longer eat or drink.

לִבְרוֹךְ עֲלֵיהּ וְלַנְחֵיהּ – הַמְבָרֵךְ צָרִיךְ שֶׁיִּטְעוֹם! לֵיתְבֵיהּ לְיָנוֹקָא – לֵית הִלְכְתָא כְּרַב אַחָא, דִּילְמָא אָתֵי לְמִסְרַךְ.

And if you say that **he should recite the blessing over** a cup of wine **and leave it** and drink it only after the conclusion of Yom Kippur, this too is difficult, as the principle is that **one who recites a blessing** over a cup of wine **must taste** from it. If you say **that he should give it to a child,** who is not obligated to fast, this too is not feasible because **the *halakha* is not in accordance with** the opinion of **Rav Aḥa,** who made a similar suggestion with regard to a different matter, due to a concern that **perhaps** the child **will come to be drawn after** it.[N] The child might come to drink wine on Yom Kippur even in future years after he comes of age, and we do not institute a practice that might turn into a stumbling block.

מַאי הֲוֵי עֲלַהּ? שַׁדְּרוּהָ רַבָּנַן לְרַב יֵימַר סָבָא קַמֵּיהּ דְּרַב חִסְדָּא בְּמַעֲלֵי יוֹמָא דְּרֵישׁ שַׁתָּא, אֲמַרוּ לֵיהּ: זִיל חֲזֵי הֵיכִי עָבֵיד עוֹבָדָא, תָּא אֵימָא לָן. כִּי חַזְיֵיהּ אֲמַר לֵיהּ: דָּלוּיָה לְרְטִיבָה, רַפְסָא לֵיהּ בְּדוּכְתֵּיהּ. אַיְיתוּ לֵיהּ כָּסָא דְּחַמְרָא, קַדֵּישׁ וַאֲמַר זְמַן.

The Gemara asks: **What** conclusion **was** reached **about this** matter? Must one recite the blessing: Who has given us life, on Rosh HaShana and Yom Kippur? **The Sages sent Rav Yeimar the Elder before Rav Ḥisda on the eve of Rosh HaShana. They said to him: Go, see how he acts** in this regard and then **come and tell us. When** Rav Ḥisda **saw** Rav Yeimar, **he said to him** in the words of a folk saying: **One who picks up a moist log,** which is not fit for firewood, must want to do **something on the spot.**[N] In other words, you certainly have come to me with some purpose in mind, and not just for a visit. **They brought him a cup of wine, and he recited *kiddush* and** the blessing for **time.**[N]

וְהִלְכְתָא: אוֹמֵר זְמַן בְּרֹאשׁ הַשָּׁנָה וְיוֹם הַכִּפּוּרִים. וְהִלְכְתָא: זְמַן אוֹמְרוֹ אֲפִילּוּ בַּשּׁוּק.

The Gemara concludes: **The *halakha*** is that **one recites** the blessing for **time on Rosh HaShana and on Yom Kippur,**[H] and **the *halakha*** is that **one may recite** the blessing for **time even in the market,** as it does not require a cup of wine.

וְאָמַר רַבָּה, כִּי הֲוֵינַן בֵּי רַב הוּנָא אִיבַּעְיָא לַן: בַּר בֵּי רַב דְּיָתֵיב בְּתַעֲנִיתָא בְּמַעֲלֵי שַׁבְּתָא, מַהוּ לְאַשְׁלוֹמֵי? לָא הֲוָה בִּידֵיהּ. אֲתַאי לְקַמֵּיהּ דְּרַב יְהוּדָה וְלָא הֲוָה בִּידֵיהּ.

Having discussed a question that was raised during Rabba's student years, the Gemara now records another such question. **And Rabba** also **said: When we were in the house** of study **of Rav Huna, we raised the** following **dilemma: A student in his master's house who is fasting on Shabbat eve, what is** the *halakha* with regard to whether he has **to complete** the fast until the end of the day? Do we perhaps say that he must stop fasting before Shabbat, so as not to enter Shabbat weary from his fast?[H] Rav Huna **did not have** an answer **at hand. I** subsequently **came before Rav Yehuda, and he** too **did not have** an answer **at hand.**

אָמַר רָבָא: נַחְזֵיהּ אֲנַן, דְּתַנְיָא: תִּשְׁעָה בְּאָב שֶׁחָל לִהְיוֹת בְּשַׁבָּת,

Rava said: Let us look ourselves for an answer from the sources. **As it was taught** in a *baraita* in the case of **the Ninth of Av that occurs on Shabbat,**[H]

NOTES

He who picks up a moist log – דָּלוּיָה לִרְטִיבָה: Based on a variant reading of the Gemara, the *Arukh* explains as follows: When one sees another person picking up a moist log, which is unusable for firewood, it is a good idea to ask him what he is doing, in case he intends to strike him with it.

He recited *kiddush* and the blessing for time – קַדֵּישׁ וַאֲמַר זְמַן: How did the Sages understand from Rav Ḥisda's actions that one is obligated to recite the blessing over time on Rosh HaShana? Perhaps Rav Ḥisda holds that it is only optional to do so? One answer is that Rav Ḥisda recited the blessing after *kiddush* but before drinking the wine. If the blessing were not obligatory, he would not have recited it at that point and thereby caused an interruption between the blessing over the wine and the drinking of the wine. Therefore, the recitation of the blessing must be obligatory (*She'erit Berakha*).

HALAKHA

The blessing: Who has given us life, on Rosh HaShana and on Yom Kippur – שֶׁהֶחֱיָנוּ בְּרֹאשׁ הַשָּׁנָה וְיוֹם הַכִּפּוּרִים: One must recite the blessing for time, Who has given us life, on Rosh HaShana and Yom Kippur. On Yom Kippur one does not recite it over a cup of wine because of the concerns raised by the Gemara (*Shulḥan Arukh, Oraḥ Ḥayyim* 619:1).

Completing a fast on Shabbat eve – הַשְׁלָמַת תַּעֲנִית בְּעֶרֶב שַׁבָּת: One who accepted upon himself to fast on Shabbat eve must fast until the end of the day when the stars come out, unless he explicitly stipulated when accepting the fast that he would fast only until the completion of the communal prayers on Friday night. The Rema rules that in the case of a private fast, one need not fast until the stars appear. However, it is preferable that one state his intention explicitly when he accepts the fast. Nevertheless, a public fast must be completed, and this is the custom. When the Gemara states that he completes it, this means that he may complete it if he so desires; he may stop beforehand, if he so stipulated (*Mordekhai*; *Shulḥan Arukh, Oraḥ Ḥayyim* 249:4).

The Ninth of Av on Shabbat – תִּשְׁעָה בְּאָב בְּשַׁבָּת: If the Ninth of Av occurs on Shabbat or on Sunday, one eats the third Shabbat meal in the usual manner, which may include meat and wine. However, one must stop eating before sunset (Rema; *Shulḥan Arukh, Oraḥ Ḥayyim* 552:10).

Perek **III**
Daf **41** Amud **a**

וְכֵן עֶרֶב תִּשְׁעָה בְּאָב שֶׁחָל לִהְיוֹת בְּשַׁבָּת – אוֹכֵל וְשׁוֹתֶה כׇּל צׇרְכּוֹ, וּמַעֲלֶה עַל שׁוּלְחָנוֹ אֲפִילּוּ כִּסְעוּדַת שְׁלֹמֹה בִּשְׁעָתוֹ. חָל לִהְיוֹת תִּשְׁעָה בְּאָב בְּעֶרֶב שַׁבָּת – מְבִיאִין לוֹ כְּבֵיצָה וְאוֹכֵל, כְּדֵי שֶׁלֹּא יִכָּנֵס לַשַּׁבָּת כְּשֶׁהוּא מְעוּנֶּה.

and so too, on **the eve of the Ninth of Av that occurs on Shabbat,** one need not reduce the amount of food he eats; rather, **he may eat and drink as much as he requires and bring to his table a meal even like that of** King **Solomon in his time.**[N] **If the Ninth of Av occurs on Shabbat eve, we bring him an egg-bulk** of food toward end of the day, **and he eats** it, **so that he not enter Shabbat in a state of affliction.**

תַּנְיָא, אָמַר רַבִּי יְהוּדָה: פַּעַם אַחַת הָיִינוּ יוֹשְׁבִין לִפְנֵי רַבִּי עֲקִיבָא, וְתִשְׁעָה בְּאָב שֶׁחָל לִהְיוֹת בְּעֶרֶב שַׁבָּת הָיָה, וְהֵבִיאוּ לוֹ בֵּיצָה מְגוּלְגֶּלֶת וּגְמָעָהּ בְּלֹא מֶלַח. וְלֹא שֶׁהָיָה תָּאֵב לָהּ, אֶלָּא לְהַרְאוֹת לְתַלְמִידִים הֲלָכָה.

It was taught in a *baraita* that **Rabbi Yehuda said: We were once sitting before Rabbi Akiva, and it was the Ninth of Av that occurs on Shabbat eve, and they brought him a slightly cooked egg,**[N] **and he swallowed it without salt. And it was not that he desired it** so much that he ate it; **rather,** he did so **to show the students** the ***halakha*** that one need not complete the fast when the Ninth of Av occurs on Shabbat eve, so as not enter Shabbat in a state of affliction.

וְרַבִּי יוֹסֵי אוֹמֵר: מִתְעַנֶּה וּמַשְׁלִים. אָמַר לָהֶן רַבִּי יוֹסֵי: אִי אַתֶּם מוֹדִים לִי בְּתִשְׁעָה בְּאָב שֶׁחָל לִהְיוֹת בְּאֶחָד בְּשַׁבָּת, שֶׁמַּפְסִיק מִבְּעוֹד יוֹם? אָמְרוּ לוֹ: אֲבָל. אָמַר לָהֶם: מַה לִּי לִיכָּנֵס בָּהּ כְּשֶׁהוּא מְעוּנֶּה, מַה לִּי לָצֵאת מִמֶּנָּה כְּשֶׁהוּא מְעוּנֶּה?

And Rabbi Yosei says: He must fast and complete the fast. Rabbi Yosei **said to** the other Sages: **Don't you agree with me with regard to the Ninth of Av that occurs on Sunday, that one must stop** eating on Shabbat **while it is still day? They said to him: Indeed,** we agree. Rabbi Yosei **said to them: What** is the difference **to me between entering** Shabbat **in a state of affliction and leaving it in a state of affliction?** If one stops eating before Shabbat is over, he is spending part of Shabbat fasting, and yet even the Sages concede that one must do so.

NOTES

A meal like that of King Solomon in his time – כִּסְעוּדַת שְׁלֹמֹה בִּשְׁעָתוֹ: Rashi explains this expression in tractate *Ta'anit* (29b) in light of the story that Solomon was removed from his throne for a period of time and became a destitute, wandering pauper. Therefore, the Gemara states: Like that of King Solomon in his time, meaning at the time when he was a king.

And they brought him a slightly cooked egg – וְהֵבִיאוּ לוֹ בֵּיצָה מְגוּלְגֶּלֶת: Some commentaries explain that since Rabbi Akiva lived in the generation of Rabban Gamliel, he followed his opinion, as explained below. However, in the subsequent generation, Rabbi Akiva's students accepted Rabbi Yosei's opinion with the certainty that Rabbi Akiva would also have returned to the approach of his teacher, Rabbi Yehoshua (*Ge'on Ya'akov*). See *Tosafot* for an alternate tradition with regard to Rabbi Akiva's behavior.

אָמְרוּ לוֹ: אִם אָמַרְתָּ לָצֵאת מִמֶּנָּה – שֶׁהֲרֵי אָכַל וְשָׁתָה כׇּל הַיּוֹם כּוּלּוֹ, תֹּאמַר לִיכָּנֵס בָּהּ כְּשֶׁהוּא מְעוּנֶּה – שֶׁלֹּא אָכַל וְשָׁתָה כׇּל הַיּוֹם כּוּלּוֹ.

They said to him: There is a difference. **If you said** that one may **leave** Shabbat in a state of affliction, that is **because he ate and drank the entire day** and will not suffer if he fasts a few minutes at the end of the day. Can **you say** that it is the same **to enter** Shabbat **in a state of affliction,** when **he has not eaten or drunk** anything **the entire day?**

וְאָמַר עוּלָּא: הֲלָכָה כְּרַבִּי יוֹסֵי. וּמִי עָבְדִינַן כְּרַבִּי יוֹסֵי? וּרְמִינְהִי: אֵין גּוֹזְרִין תַּעֲנִית עַל הַצִּיבּוּר בְּרָאשֵׁי חֳדָשִׁים בַּחֲנוּכָּה וּבְפוּרִים, וְאִם הִתְחִילוּ – אֵין מַפְסִיקִין, דִּבְרֵי רַבָּן גַּמְלִיאֵל. אָמַר רַבִּי מֵאִיר: אַף עַל פִּי שֶׁאָמַר רַבָּן גַּמְלִיאֵל "אֵין מַפְסִיקִין", מוֹדֶה הָיָה שֶׁאֵין מַשְׁלִימִין, וְכֵן בְּתִשְׁעָה בְּאָב שֶׁחָל לִהְיוֹת בְּעֶרֶב שַׁבָּת.

And Ulla said: The ***halakha* is in accordance with** the opinion of **Rabbi Yosei,** and on the Ninth of Av that occurs on Shabbat eve one must complete the fast. The Gemara poses a question: **Do we** really **act in accordance with** the opinion of **Rabbi Yosei? And** the Gemara **raises a contradiction** based upon the following mishna: **We do not** initially **decree a fast upon the public on the New Moon, Hanukkah, or Purim,**[H] **and if** the community **had** already **begun** a cycle of fasts and one of them fell out on one of these days, **they do not interrupt** the series;[N] this is **the statement of Rabban Gamliel. Rabbi Meir said: Even though Rabban Gamliel said** that **they do not interrupt** the series, **he conceded that they do not complete** the fast on one of these days, **and so too,** the fast **on the Ninth of Av that occurs on Shabbat eve** is not completed.

וְתַנְיָא: לְאַחַר פְּטִירָתוֹ שֶׁל רַבָּן גַּמְלִיאֵל נִכְנַס רַבִּי יְהוֹשֻׁעַ לְהָפֵר אֶת דְּבָרָיו. עָמַד רַבִּי יוֹחָנָן בֶּן נוּרִי עַל רַגְלָיו וְאָמַר: חָזֵי אֲנָא דְּבָתַר רֵישָׁא גּוּפָא אָזֵיל, כׇּל יָמָיו שֶׁל רַבָּן גַּמְלִיאֵל קָבַעְנוּ הֲלָכָה כְּמוֹתוֹ, עַכְשָׁיו אַתָּה מְבַקֵּשׁ לְבַטֵּל דְּבָרָיו?! יְהוֹשֻׁעַ, אֵין שׁוֹמְעִין לְךָ, שֶׁכְּבָר נִקְבְּעָה הֲלָכָה כְּרַבָּן גַּמְלִיאֵל. וְלֹא הָיָה אָדָם שֶׁעִרְעֵר בַּדָּבָר כְּלוּם.

And it was taught in a related *baraita*: **Following the death of Rabban Gamliel, Rabbi Yehoshua entered** the study hall **to annul** Rabban Gamliel's **statement** with regard to fasts. **Rabbi Yoḥanan ben Nuri stood on his feet and said: I see that** the appropriate policy is that **the body must follow the head,** i.e., we must follow the statements of the earlier authorities and not deviate from established *halakha*. **All of Rabban Gamliel's life we established the *halakha* in accordance with his** opinion, and **now you seek to annul his statement? Yehoshua, we do not listen to you, as the *halakha* has already been established in accordance with** the opinion of **Rabban Gamliel. And there was no one who disputed**[N] **this statement in any way.** Therefore, this *baraita* demonstrates that when the Ninth of Av occurs on Shabbat eve, one must observe the fast but not complete it, and this was the accepted practice.

בְּדוֹרוֹ שֶׁל רַבָּן גַּמְלִיאֵל – עֲבוּד כְּרַבָּן גַּמְלִיאֵל, בְּדוֹרוֹ שֶׁל רַבִּי יוֹסֵי – עֲבוּד כְּרַבִּי יוֹסֵי.

The Gemara resolves the difficulty, arguing that this proof is not conclusive: Indeed, **in the generation of Rabban Gamliel they acted in accordance with** the opinion of **Rabban Gamliel,** but **in the generation of Rabbi Yosei they acted in accordance with** the opinion of **Rabbi Yosei,** and from then on, the *halakha* follows his view.

וּבְדוֹרוֹ שֶׁל רַבָּן גַּמְלִיאֵל עֲבוּד כְּרַבָּן גַּמְלִיאֵל? וְהָתַנְיָא, אָמַר רַבִּי אֶלְעָזָר (בֶּן) צָדוֹק: אֲנִי (הָיִיתִי) מִבְּנֵי סְנָאָב בֶּן בִּנְיָמִין, פַּעַם אַחַת חָל תִּשְׁעָה בְּאָב לִהְיוֹת בַּשַּׁבָּת, וּדְחִינוּהוּ לְאַחַר הַשַּׁבָּת וְהִתְעַנֵּינוּ בּוֹ וְלֹא הִשְׁלַמְנוּהוּ, מִפְּנֵי שֶׁיּוֹם טוֹב שֶׁלָּנוּ הָיָה. טַעְמָא דְּיוֹם טוֹב, הָא עֶרֶב יוֹם טוֹב מַשְׁלִימִין!

The Gemara asks: **And** is it correct that **in the generation of Rabban Gamliel they acted in accordance with** the opinion of **Rabban Gamliel? Wasn't it taught** in a *baraita* that **Rabbi Elazar ben Tzadok,** a contemporary of Rabban Gamliel, **said: I am a descendant of Sena'av ben Binyamin,** who observed a family festival on the tenth of Av. **One time, the Ninth of Av occurred on Shabbat, and we postponed it until after Shabbat,** as we do not observe the fast on Shabbat, **and we fasted on** Sunday **but did not complete** the fast **because** that day **was our Festival.**[N] This indicates that **the reason** they did not complete the fast is that the day itself was **a Festival** for them, **but** on **the eve of a Festival, they** would indeed **complete it.** This proves that even in the generation of Rabban Gamliel, they did complete fasts on the eve of Shabbat and Festivals.

אָמַר רָבִינָא: שָׁאנֵי יוֹם טוֹב שֶׁל דִּבְרֵיהֶם, מִתּוֹךְ שֶׁמִּתְעַנִּין בּוֹ שָׁעוֹת – מַשְׁלִימִין בּוֹ עַרְבִיּוֹת. שַׁבָּת, הוֹאִיל וְאֵין מִתְעַנִּין בָּהּ שָׁעוֹת – אֵין מַשְׁלִימִין בָּהּ עַרְבִיּוֹת.

Ravina said that this story poses no difficulty: **A rabbinic Festival is different,** as they are not as stringent as Shabbat or Festivals stated in the Torah, and the festival of the family of Sena'av was not a Festival from the Torah, but one established by the Sages. **Since one may fast on** such a Festival for a number of **hours,** i.e., one may fast on it for part of the day, **one** also **completes** a fast observed on the eve of such a Festival until the **evening.** With regard to **Shabbat,** however, **since one may not fast on it** even for several **hours, one does not complete** a fast observed on Shabbat eve.

HALAKHA

A fast on Hanukkah or Purim – תַּעֲנִית בַּחֲנוּכָּה וּבְפוּרִים: A public fast is never decreed for Hanukkah or Purim. Nevertheless, if the community already began to observe a cycle of fasts for some misfortune, and a fast day in the cycle of Monday, Thursday, and Monday occurs on Hanukkah or Purim, the fast is observed. This ruling is in accordance with the opinion of Rabban Gamliel, as the later Sages did not dispute this point (*Shulḥan Arukh, Oraḥ Ḥayyim* 572:2).

NOTES

And if they had begun they do not interrupt – וְאִם הִתְחִילוּ אֵין מַפְסִיקִין: The order of the public fasts decreed in times of drought is explained in tractate *Ta'anit*. It is with regard to this that they said that a cycle of fasts on Monday, Thursday, and Monday may not begin on the New Moon or on Hanukkah. However, if a cycle of fast days was already established, and one of the fast days occurred on the New Moon, the series is not interrupted.

And there was no one who disputed – לֹא הָיָה אָדָם שֶׁעִרְעֵר: We generally do not accept the argument that we have not seen a tradition being observed or did not hear someone argue about an existing tradition, as the rule is: The fact that we have not seen is not proof. However, this restriction applies only when there is someone who claims to have seen or heard something with regard to the tradition. If several people say that they have never seen something before and no one denies this, it is considered to be proof (*Maharik*).

It was our Festival – יוֹם טוֹב שֶׁלָּנוּ: This is explained at great length in tractate *Ta'anit*. The basic idea is as follows: In a particular time, when public funds were very scarce, several large families volunteered to sponsor the wood offering in the Temple. Over the course of time, even though the need for this donation passed, the custom remained. Each of these families observed the day on which it brought the wood to the Temple as a Festival on which fasting and eulogizing were prohibited.

אֲמַר רַב יוֹסֵף: לָא שְׁמִיעַ לִי הָא שְׁמַעְתָּא. אֲמַר לֵיהּ אַבַּיֵי: אַתְּ אָמְרַתְּ נִיהֲלַן, וְאַהָא אָמְרַתְּ נִיהֲלַן: אֵין גּוֹזְרִין תַּעֲנִית עַל הַצִּבּוּר בְּרָאשֵׁי חֳדָשִׁים וכו׳. וְאָמְרִינַן עֲלָהּ, אָמַר רַב יְהוּדָה, אָמַר רַב: זוֹ דִּבְרֵי רַבִּי מֵאִיר שֶׁאָמַר מִשּׁוּם רַבָּן גַּמְלִיאֵל, אֲבָל חֲכָמִים אוֹמְרִים: מִתְעַנֶּה וּמַשְׁלִים.

Rav Yosef said: I did not hear this ruling that the *halakha* is in accordance with the opinion of Rabbi Yosei. Rav Yosef had fallen ill and forgotten his learning and so was unable to remember that such a ruling had been issued. His student, **Abaye, said to him: You** yourself **told us** this *halakha*, **and** it was **with regard to this** point that **you told** it **to us,** as we learned in a mishna: **We do not** initially **decree a fast upon the public on the New Moon,** on Hanukkah, or on Purim. Rabbi Meir said: Even though Rabban Gamliel said that if the community had already begun a cycle of fasts, they do not interrupt the series, he conceded that they do not complete the fast on one of these days, and similarly, the fast of the Ninth of Av that occurs on Shabbat eve is not completed. **And we said with regard to** this mishna that **Rav Yehuda said** that **Rav said: This is the statement that Rabbi Meir said in the name of Rabban Gamliel. But the Rabbis say: One must fast and complete** the fast.

מַאי לָאו אַכּוּלְּהוּ? לָא, אַחֲנוּכָּה וּפוּרִים.

What? Does the Rabbis' ruling that one must complete the fast **not** refer **to all** the cases mentioned in the mishna, including that of the Ninth of Av that occurs on Shabbat eve? **No,** it was stated only with regard **to Hanukkah and Purim,** but one would not complete a fast on Shabbat eve.

הָכִי נָמֵי מִסְתַּבְּרָא,

The Gemara comments: **So too, it is reasonable** to explain that this ruling does not apply to Shabbat eve,

Perek **III**
Daf **41** Amud **b**

דְּאִי סָלְקָא דַּעְתָּךְ אַכּוּלְּהוּ – הָא בָּעֵי מִינֵּיהּ רַבָּה מֵרַב יְהוּדָה וְלָא פְּשַׁט לֵיהּ!

as, if it should enter your mind to say that Rav Yehuda said that the *halakha* is in accordance with the opinion of the Rabbis with regard **to all** the cases in the mishna, including that of the Ninth of Av that occurs on Shabbat eve, there is a difficulty: **Didn't Rabba raise a dilemma before Rav Yehuda** with regard to this issue, **and he did not answer him?** This demonstrates that he did not have a decisive ruling on this subject.

וּלְטַעְמִיךְ, הָא דְּדָרַשׁ מָר זוּטְרָא מִשְּׁמֵיהּ דְּרַב הוּנָא: הֲלָכָה, מִתְעַנֶּה וּמַשְׁלִים. הָא בְּעָא מִינֵּיהּ רַבָּה מֵרַב הוּנָא וְלָא פְּשַׁט לֵיהּ!

The Gemara responds: **And according to your opinion,** that the issue had not been resolved, there is a difficulty with **that** which **Mar Zutra expounded in the name of Rav Huna:** The ***halakha*** is that **one fasts and completes** the fast on Shabbat eve. **Didn't Rabba** also **raise** this **dilemma before Rav Huna, and he** too **did not answer him?** How could Mar Zutra have reported this halakhic ruling in the name of Rav Huna?

אֶלָּא: הָא – מִקַּמֵּי דִּשְׁמַעָהּ, וְהָא – לְבָתַר דִּשְׁמַעָהּ. הָכָא נַמִי, הָא – מִקַּמֵּי דִּשְׁמַעָהּ, הָא – לְבָתַר דִּשְׁמַעָהּ.

Rather, you must say that **this** dilemma that Rabba raised to Rav Huna was **before** Rav Huna **heard** Rav's ruling on the subject; whereas **this,** i.e., Rav Huna's statement as cited by Mar Zutra, was made **after he heard** Rav's ruling on the matter, and the problem was resolved for him. **Here, too,** with regard to Rav Yehuda, we can say that **this** dilemma that Rabba raised before Rav Yehuda was **before** Rav Yehuda **heard** Rav's ruling on the topic, and therefore he did not know how to answer Rabba; whereas **this,** i.e., Rav Yehuda's statement in the name of Rav, was made **after he heard it.**

דָּרַשׁ מָר זוּטְרָא מִשְּׁמֵיהּ דְּרַב הוּנָא: הֲלָכָה, מִתְעַנִּין וּמַשְׁלִימִין.

The Gemara repeats the statement cited above in passing: **Mar Zutra expounded in the name of Rav Huna:** The ***halakha*** is that **one fasts and completes** the fast on the eves of Shabbat and Festivals.

הדרן עלך בכל מערבין

Summary of **Perek III**

In this chapter, several of the *halakhot* of *eiruv* were discussed, primarily the *halakhot* of the joining of Shabbat boundaries. The issues raised were divided into distinct units that are related as far as preparation of the *eiruv* is concerned, not necessarily in terms of their intrinsic principles. With regard to the question of what may be used to establish an *eiruv*, the conclusion was that any item considered food in an amount sufficient for two meals, or alternatively any ingredient used in the consumption of two meals, e.g., spices, is suitable. This food must be suitable for human consumption, but there is no stipulation demanding that the one who placed the *eiruv* must actually be able to eat it. Even if for some reason he cannot, the *eiruv* is valid. However, neither water nor salt may be used for the *eiruv* since these are not considered food.

A second problem discussed with regard to the joining of Shabbat boundaries was: Who may establish the *eiruv*? The conclusion was that the one placing the *eiruv* must be of sound mind and acknowledge the *halakhot* of *eiruv*in. If he is not of sound mind, then he can only serve as an instrument for transferring the *eiruv*; however, he cannot serve as an emissary in placing the *eiruv*.

With regard to the joining of boundaries, it was stated that the person placing the *eiruv* must do so in a location where he has access to it, enabling him to take the food the moment the *eiruv* takes effect, during twilight on Shabbat eve. Therefore, one may not place the *eiruv* in a place from where it would be prohibited to take it on Shabbat. For example, if one places the food outside the domain where he establishes residence on Shabbat, or if he were to place it in a location that it is prohibited for him to enter, the *eiruv* would be invalidated.

Uncertainties arose due to the various restrictions that apply to the placement of the *eiruv*. Is the *eiruv* valid in a case where it is unclear whether the *eiruv* remained in place or was moved? Is it valid if it is not known whether the *eiruv* was eaten, destroyed, or became ritually impure, rendering it no longer fit for human consumption prior to the time when the *eiruv* took effect? In general, the resolution of those dilemmas was based on the ruling by the Sages: An *eiruv* whose validity is uncertain is nevertheless valid, since in principle the *halakhot* of *eiruv* are by rabbinic law.

The principle that one rules leniently in cases of *eiruv* since the *halakhot* are by rabbinic law resolved a different problem, which is the question of a conditional *eiruv*. An example is the case of an individual who seeks to establish residence not in one specific location, but rather places an *eiruv* in each of two different locations, stipulating that only later, on Shabbat, will he decide on which of the two he will rely. The dilemma that arises is whether or not one can rely on an indefinite *eiruv*. The halakhic conclusion was that even according to those who hold that there is no retroactive designation, i.e., the direction that one ultimately chooses was retroactively the direction that he originally intended, the *eiruv* is nevertheless valid. Since the *halakha* is by rabbinic law, the ruling is lenient and it is permitted to place a conditional *eiruv*.

Introduction to **Perek IV**

This chapter, too, deals with the *halakhot* of the joining of Shabbat boundaries; however, here the discussion focuses on different aspects of this topic.

The halakhic rulings in the previous chapter dealt primarily with cases of an individual who, although he already has a place of residence on Shabbat, seeks to establish residence elsewhere by means of an *eiruv*. This chapter discusses the case of an individual who does not have a bona fide place of residence, e.g., one traveling to another city, or one who establishes residence along the way. Similarly, this chapter deals with the legal status of one who intends to establish residence in a place other than the place where he is located at present, and also considers the *halakha* with regard to one who went outside his Shabbat limit and thereby forfeited his rights within that limit.

Addressing these questions necessitates an analysis of the fundamental problems with regard to the manner in which one acquires his Shabbat limit and the manner in which he loses it. One of the questions requiring consideration is the legal status of one who ventures beyond his Shabbat limit, whether unwittingly, intentionally, or for the purpose of performing a mitzva. Does he then acquire certain rights of residence in this other place? If so, what are they?

One of the essential questions discussed is: Does one's right to walk within the Shabbat limit stem from his decision and assertion: My residence is at such and such location, and in that way he acquires the right to walk two thousand cubits from that location? Or, is the Shabbat limit determined by the individual's very presence at a specific location?

A similar issue is the Shabbat limit as it applies to vessels and other objects. Is their Shabbat limit determined by their presence at a specific location? An example of this is the statement in the Gemara: Ownerless objects acquire residence. Or, perhaps, if they belong to a specific individual, the limit for these objects is determined by the limit of their owner.

An additional fundamental problem is with regard to the manner in which one acquires the *eiruv*. The joining of Shabbat boundaries is based upon one's decision to acquire residence at a given distance from his present location. The *eiruv* is generally established through the placement of food sufficient for two meals at the location where one seeks to acquire residence. However, the question arises: Are there other methods in which this may be accomplished? For example, does one's decision that he intends to establish residence at a specific location suffice even without placing the food there? Alternatively, is it sufficient for one merely to visit that location during the day, even if he neither stays there nor places an *eiruv*?

These problems require examination of the essence of the Shabbat limit, which will lead to a detailed understanding of how it takes effect, how it is acquired, and how it is lost. These are the topics discussed in this chapter.

מתני׳ מִי שֶׁהוֹצִיאוּהוּ נׇכְרִים אוֹ רוּחַ רָעָה – אֵין לוֹ אֶלָּא אַרְבַּע אַמּוֹת.

MISHNA With regard to **one whom gentiles** forcibly **took him out**[H] beyond the Shabbat limit, **or** if **an evil spirit**[N] took him out, i.e., he was temporarily insane, and found himself outside the Shabbat limit, he **has only four cubits** that he may walk from where he is standing.

הֶחֱזִירוּהוּ – כְּאִילּוּ לֹא יָצָא.

If the gentiles **returned him,** or if he came back while still under the influence of the evil spirit, **it is as though he had never left** his Shabbat limit, and he may move about within his original limit as before.

הוֹלִיכוּהוּ לְעִיר אַחֶרֶת, נְתָנוּהוּ בַּדִּיר אוֹ בַּסַּהַר, רַבָּן גַּמְלִיאֵל וְרַבִּי אֶלְעָזָר בֶּן עֲזַרְיָה אוֹמְרִים: מְהַלֵּךְ אֶת כּוּלָּהּ. רַבִּי יְהוֹשֻׁעַ וְרַבִּי עֲקִיבָא אוֹמְרִים: אֵין לוֹ אֶלָּא אַרְבַּע אַמּוֹת.

If the gentiles **brought him to a different city**[H] that was surrounded by walls, or if they **put him into a pen or a stable,** i.e., animal enclosures, the Sages disagree. **Rabban Gamliel and Rabbi Elazar ben Azarya say: He may walk** about **the entire** city, as the whole city is considered like four cubits. **Rabbi Yehoshua and Rabbi Akiva say: He has only four cubits** from where he was placed.

מַעֲשֶׂה שֶׁבָּאוּ מִפְּלַנְדַּרְסִין וְהִפְלִיגָה סְפִינָתָם בַּיָּם, רַבָּן גַּמְלִיאֵל וְרַבִּי אֶלְעָזָר בֶּן עֲזַרְיָה הִלְּכוּ אֶת כּוּלָּהּ, רַבִּי יְהוֹשֻׁעַ וְרַבִּי עֲקִיבָא לֹא זָזוּ מֵאַרְבַּע אַמּוֹת, שֶׁרָצוּ לְהַחְמִיר עַל עַצְמָן.

The mishna relates: There was **an incident where** all of these Sages **were coming from Pelandarsin,**[B] an overseas location, **and their boat set sail on the sea**[H] on Shabbat, taking them beyond their Shabbat limit. **Rabban Gamliel and Rabbi Elazar ben Azarya walked** about **the entire** boat, as they hold that the entire boat is considered like four cubits, while **Rabbi Yehoshua and Rabbi Akiva did not move beyond four cubits, as they sought to be stringent with themselves.**

פַּעַם אַחַת לֹא נִכְנְסוּ לַנָּמֵל עַד שֶׁחֲשֵׁיכָה, אָמְרוּ לוֹ לְרַבָּן גַּמְלִיאֵל: מָה אָנוּ לֵירֵד?

The mishna further relates that on **one occasion, they did not enter the port** [*namel*][L] **until after nightfall** on Shabbat eve. The others **said to Rabban Gamliel: What** is the *halakha* with regard to **alighting** from the boat at this time? In other words, were we already within the city's limit before Shabbat commenced?

אָמַר לָהֶם: מוּתָּרִים אַתֶּם, שֶׁכְּבָר הָיִיתִי מִסְתַּכֵּל וְהָיִינוּ בְּתוֹךְ הַתְּחוּם עַד שֶׁלֹּא חֲשֵׁיכָה.

He said to them: You are permitted to alight, **as I was watching,** and I observed that **we were** already **within the** city's **limit before nightfall.** We acquired our resting place in the city during the twilight period. Therefore, it is permitted to walk throughout the city even after nightfall.

גמ׳ תָּנוּ רַבָּנַן: שְׁלֹשָׁה דְּבָרִים מַעֲבִירִין אֶת הָאָדָם עַל דַּעְתּוֹ וְעַל דַּעַת קוֹנוֹ, אֵלּוּ הֵן: נׇכְרִים וְרוּחַ רָעָה, וְדִקְדּוּקֵי עֲנִיּוּת.

GEMARA Since the Gemara discussed one who stepped beyond the Shabbat limit due to an evil spirit, the Gemara cites a related *baraita,* in which **the Sages taught: Three matters cause a person to act against his** own **will and the will of his Maker, and they are: Gentiles, and an evil spirit, and the depths of** extreme **poverty.**

לְמַאי נָפְקָא מִינַּהּ? לְמִיבְעֵי רַחֲמֵי עֲלַיְיהוּ.

The Gemara asks: **What is the** practical halakhic **difference** that emerges from this statement? The Gemara answers: It is significant as it teaches one **to request mercy for** people[N] who suffer from those problems.

שְׁלֹשָׁה אֵין רוֹאִין פְּנֵי גֵיהִנָּם, אֵלּוּ הֵן: דִּקְדּוּקֵי עֲנִיּוּת וְחוֹלֵי מְעַיִין וְהָרָשׁוּת. וְיֵשׁ אוֹמְרִים: אַף מִי שֶׁיֵּשׁ לוֹ אִשָּׁה רָעָה.

The Gemara cites a related teaching: **Three** classes of people **do not see the face of Gehenna,** because the suffering that they bear in this world atones for their sins, and **they are:** Those suffering **the depths of** extreme **poverty,** those afflicted **with intestinal disease, and** those oppressed by **creditors. And some say: Even one who has an evil wife** who constantly harasses him.

וְאִידָּךְ – אִשָּׁה רָעָה מִצְוָה לְגָרְשָׁהּ.

The Gemara asks: **And** why don't **the other** Sages include one with an evil wife among those who will not be punished in Gehenna? The Gemara answers: They maintain that **it is a mitzva to divorce an evil wife.** Therefore, that source of distress can be remedied.

וְאִידָּךְ – זִימְנִין דִּכְתוּבָּתָהּ מְרוּבָּה. אִי נָמֵי: אִית לֵיהּ בָּנִים מִינַּהּ, וְלָא מָצֵי מְגָרֵשׁ לַהּ.

And why do **the other** Sages include an evil wife? The Gemara answers: **Sometimes** payment of **her marriage contract is** very **large,** and consequently he cannot divorce her since he cannot afford to pay it. **Alternatively, he has children from her,** and he cannot raise them himself, **and** therefore he **cannot divorce her.**

HALAKHA

One whom gentiles took him out – מִי שֶׁהוֹצִיאוּהוּ נׇכְרִים: If a person was taken out beyond his Shabbat limit by gentiles or by any other coercive force, he may walk only a distance of four cubits. However, if one was also forcibly returned to within the limit, it is as though he never left (*Shulḥan Arukh, Oraḥ Ḥayyim* 405:5).

If the gentiles brought him to a different city – הוֹלִיכוּהוּ לְעִיר אַחֶרֶת: If gentiles took a person beyond the Shabbat limit to a different city surrounded by a wall, he may walk throughout the entire city, since it is all considered like four cubits. According to some authorities, this also applies if the person was taken beyond the Shabbat limit to any city or enclosed area. The *halakha* is in accordance with the view of Rabban Gamliel, because Rav adopted his opinion. However, if the person went out to a different city knowingly, he is only permitted to walk a distance of four cubits in that place (Rambam; Ramban; Ran). Some commentaries dispute this and permit him to walk any distance in the entire city (*Tosafot*; Rashba; *Shulḥan Arukh, Oraḥ Ḥayyim* 405:6).

A boat in the sea – סְפִינָה בַּיָּם: One is permitted to walk about an entire boat, even if it sailed beyond the Shabbat limit. All of the Sages of the Talmud agreed that, in this regard, the *halakha* accords with Rabban Gamliel's opinion (*Shulḥan Arukh, Oraḥ Ḥayyim* 405:7).

NOTES

An evil spirit [*ruaḥ ra'a*] – רוּחַ רָעָה: Some commentaries explain the Hebrew phrase *ruaḥ ra'a* literally as an evil wind, meaning that the person was forced out of his Shabbat limit by tempestuous storm winds (Rav Natan Av HaYeshiva). The Rambam, in his Commentary on the Mishna, explains that any coercive force is called an evil spirit.

To request mercy for people – לְמִיבְעֵי רַחֲמֵי עֲלַיְיהוּ: Some commentaries explain that this statement has two ramifications: The first is for other people to pray on their behalf. The second is for the public to realize that even if these people acted improperly, they did not do so entirely out of their own free will. Therefore, they deserve pity rather than condemnation (*Ein Ya'akov*).

BACKGROUND

Pelandarsin – פְּלַנְדַּרְסִין: Variant readings indicate that the reference is to the Italian city of Brudisium, which is modern-day city of Brindisi in Calabria, Italy.

LANGUAGE

Port [*namel*] – נָמֵל: In some variant readings, this common word appears as *lamen*, which is similar to the Greek λιμήν, *limen*, meaning a port or a place on the shore for boats to anchor, as well as a beach and a border.

לְמַאי נָפְקָא מִינָּהּ? לְקַבּוֹלֵי מֵאַהֲבָה.

The Gemara asks: **What is the** practical halakhic **difference** that emerges from this statement? The Gemara answers: It is significant as it teaches one **to accept** those afflictions **with love,** knowing that they will exempt him from the punishment of Gehenna.

שְׁלֹשָׁה מֵתִין כְּשֶׁהֵן מְסַפְּרִין, וְאֵלּוּ הֵן: חוֹלֵי מֵעַיִין, וְחַיָּה, וְהַדְּרוֹקָן.

It was similarly taught: **Three** classes of people are liable to **die while conversing** with others, i.e., to die suddenly, although they appear to be in good health and are capable of engaging in conversation, **and they are: Those** afflicted **with intestinal sickness, and a woman in childbirth, and** one who is sick with **edema** [***hidrokan***].[L]

לְמַאי נָפְקָא מִינָּהּ? לְמַשְׁמוֹשֵׁי בְּהוּ זְוָודְתָא.

Once again the Gemara asks: **What is the** practical halakhic **difference** that emerges from this statement? The Gemara answers: It is significant as it teaches one **to prepare shrouds for them,** in case they need them suddenly.

אָמַר רַב נַחְמָן, אָמַר שְׁמוּאֵל: יָצָא לָדַעַת – אֵין לוֹ אֶלָּא אַרְבַּע אַמּוֹת. פְּשִׁיטָא! הַשְׁתָּא מִי שֶׁהוֹצִיאוּהוּ נׇכְרִים אֵין לוֹ אֶלָּא אַרְבַּע אַמּוֹת, יָצָא לָדַעַת מִיבַּעְיָא?!

The Gemara proceeds to analyze the mishna: **Rav Naḥman said** that **Shmuel said: If one knowingly went out** beyond the Shabbat limit, **he has only four cubits** that he may walk. The Gemara asks: This is **obvious. Now,** if with regard to **one whom gentiles** forcibly **took out** beyond the Shabbat limit, **he has only four cubits,** with regard to **one who knowingly went out, is it necessary** to teach that he has no more than four cubits within which he may walk?

אֶלָּא אֵימָא: חָזַר לָדַעַת – אֵין לוֹ אֶלָּא אַרְבַּע אַמּוֹת.

Rather, say that Rav Naḥman's statement means: If **he returned knowingly**[H] to within the Shabbat limit after having been taken out by gentiles, **he has only four cubits** within which he may walk, but no more.

הָא נַמִי תָּנֵינָא: הֶחֱזִירוּהוּ נׇכְרִים – כְּאִילּוּ לֹא יָצָא. הֶחֱזִירוּהוּ הוּא דִּכְאִילּוּ לֹא יָצָא, אֲבָל הוֹצִיאוּהוּ נׇכְרִים וְחָזַר לָדַעַת – אֵין לוֹ אֶלָּא אַרְבַּע אַמּוֹת!

The Gemara asks: **This, too, we learned** from a precise reading of the mishna: If the gentiles **returned him** to within the Shabbat limit **it is as though he had never left** the Shabbat limit, and he may move about as before. By inference, **it is** specifically when the gentiles themselves **returned him that it is as though he never left** his Shabbat limit. **However, if gentiles took him out, and** then he **returned knowingly** to his Shabbat limit, it is as though he left knowingly, and he **has only four cubits** within which he may walk.

אֶלָּא אֵימָא: יָצָא לָדַעַת וְהֶחֱזִירוּהוּ נׇכְרִים – אֵין לוֹ אֶלָּא אַרְבַּע אַמּוֹת.

Rather, say Rav Naḥman's statement as follows: If **he knowingly went out** beyond the Shabbat limit, **and was** later forcibly **returned**[H] **by gentiles** to within his limit, **he has only four cubits** that he may walk, although he was restored to within his limit against his will.

הָא נַמִי תָּנֵינָא: הוֹצִיאוּהוּ וְהֶחֱזִירוּהוּ – כְּאִילּוּ לֹא יָצָא. הוֹצִיאוּהוּ וְהֶחֱזִירוּהוּ הוּא דִּכְאִילּוּ לֹא יָצָא, אֲבָל יָצָא לָדַעַת – לֹא.

The Gemara raises a difficulty: **This, too, we learned from** a precise reading of the mishna: If gentiles forcibly **took him out and** later **returned him, it is as though he never left.** By inference, **it is** specifically when the gentiles themselves forcibly **took him out and** then themselves **returned him** that **it is as though he never left** the Shabbat limit. **However, if he knowingly went out, no,** that is not the *halakha*, even if he was later forcibly returned by gentiles.

מַהוּ דְּתֵימָא: לְצַדָדִין קָתָנֵי: מִי שֶׁהוֹצִיאוּהוּ נׇכְרִים וְחָזַר לָדַעַת – אֵין לוֹ אֶלָּא אַרְבַּע אַמּוֹת, אֲבָל יָצָא לָדַעַת וְהֶחֱזִירוּהוּ נׇכְרִים – כְּאִילּוּ לֹא יָצָא, קָא מַשְׁמַע לַן.

The Gemara answers: Rav Naḥman's statement is necessary **lest you say** that perhaps the mishna is not referring to one specific case, but rather **it is teaching disjunctively,**[N] i.e., referring to two separate cases, as follows: **One who was** forcibly **taken out** beyond the Shabbat limit **by gentiles and** later **returned knowingly has only four cubits** within which to walk. **But if he knowingly went out** beyond the Shabbat limit **and was** later forcibly **returned by gentiles, it is as though he had never left,** and he may move within his original limit as before. Therefore, Rav Naḥman **teaches us** that if he willingly went out beyond the Shabbat limit and was later forcibly returned by gentiles, it is considered as though he had returned knowingly, so that he has only four cubits within which to walk.

בָּעוּ מִינֵּיהּ מֵרַבָּה: הוּצְרַךְ לִנְקָבָיו מַהוּ? אָמַר לָהֶם: גָּדוֹל כְּבוֹד הַבְּרִיּוֹת שֶׁדּוֹחֶה אֶת לֹא תַעֲשֶׂה שֶׁבַּתּוֹרָה.

They raised a dilemma before Rabba: If a person who is restricted to an area of four cubits **needed to relieve himself** and no secluded spot is available, **what is** the *halakha*? **He said to them:** The Sages established a principle that **great** is **human dignity,**[N] **which** even **supersedes a negative precept of the Torah,** and therefore a person is permitted to overstep the Shabbat limit fixed by the Sages in order to relieve himself modestly.[HN]

LANGUAGE

Edema [*hidrokan*] – הַדְּרוֹקָן: From the Greek ὑδερικός, *hyderikos*, or ὑδρωπικός, *hydropikos*, which describes a condition where one's limbs become swollen and filled with water.

HALAKHA

If he returned knowingly – חָזַר לָדַעַת: If a person went out beyond the Shabbat limit and then returned, he may walk only a distance of four cubits, in accordance with the opinion of Rav Naḥman and the inference from the mishna (*Shulḥan Arukh*, *Oraḥ Ḥayyim* 405:5).

If he knowingly went out and was forcibly returned – יָצָא לָדַעַת וְחָזַר בְּאוֹנֶס: If a person knowingly went out beyond the Shabbat limit, but was forcibly returned to within the limit while outside the city, he can only walk a distance of four cubits. However, if he was brought back into the city itself, he may walk any distance in the entire city, since the entire city is considered to be like four cubits (*Shulḥan Arukh*, *Oraḥ Ḥayyim* 405:8).

If he went out of the Shabbat limit and needed to relieve himself – יָצָא מֵהַתְּחוּם וְנִצְרַךְ לִצְרָכָיו: If a person knowingly went out beyond the Shabbat limit, he is prohibited from leaving his four cubits. However, if he then needs to relieve himself, he may walk until he finds a private spot. It is advisable for the person to walk in the direction of his limit, for if he returns, it is as though he never left. Nevertheless, if he found a private spot before reaching his Shabbat limit, he may go no further (Rosh). Some authorities state that the permission only applies to defecation (*Tur*, citing the Rosh), while other authorities are also lenient if he needs to urinate (Rabbeinu Tam; *Shulḥan Arukh*, *Oraḥ Ḥayyim* 406:1).

NOTES

It is teaching disjunctively – לְצַדָדִין קָתָנֵי: This common expression means that, occasionally, two tannaitic statements are to be understood as disjunctive such that one cannot draw inferences from one to the other. Rather, each stands on its own and must be understood separately.

Great is human dignity – גָּדוֹל כְּבוֹד הַבְּרִיּוֹת: This principle is derived from the permission granted by the Torah to ignore the obligation to return lost property, if handling the lost article can be accomplished only in an undignified manner. The Gemara's conclusion is that, in most cases, human dignity overrides a rabbinic prohibition. In this context, the prohibition related to the Shabbat limit is only of rabbinic origin.

Human dignity – כְּבוֹד הַבְּרִיּוֹת: The authorities disagree whether or not the consideration of human dignity includes the person's own dignity as well. For example, since it would be an insult to his dignity to remain within four cubits of the spot where he relieved himself, he may move away for this reason (Rabbeinu Ḥananel; Rabbeinu Yehonatan; and others). An alternative approach is that perhaps human dignity only applies to the shame of having to relieve himself in front of others, or to the embarrassment and humiliation caused to others if he relieves himself in their presence (Rosh, based on Rav Hai Gaon).

אָמְרִי נְהַרְדְּעֵי: אִי פִּיקֵחַ הוּא – עָיֵיל לִתְחוּמָא, וְכֵיוָן דְּעָל – עָל.

The Sages of Neharde'a[P] **said: If** this person **is clever, he will enter** into his original Shabbat limit, **and since he** was permitted to **enter** it, **he entered,** and may remain there.

אָמַר רַב פַּפָּא: פֵּירוֹת שֶׁיָּצְאוּ חוּץ לַתְּחוּם וְחָזְרוּ, אֲפִילּוּ בְּמֵזִיד – לֹא הִפְסִידוּ אֶת מְקוֹמָן. מַאי טַעְמָא – אֲנוּסִין נִינְהוּ.

Rav Pappa said: With regard to **produce that was taken out**[N] **beyond the** Shabbat **limit and was** later **returned, even if** this was done **intentionally,** the produce **has not lost its place;** rather, it may still be carried within the entire limit. **What is the reason** for this *halakha*? It is that the produce did not go out willingly, but was taken **due to circumstances beyond its control.**

אֵיתִיבֵיהּ רַב יוֹסֵף בַּר שְׁמַעְיָה לְרַב פַּפָּא: רַבִּי נְחֶמְיָה וְרַבִּי אֱלִיעֶזֶר בֶּן יַעֲקֹב אוֹמְרִים: לְעוֹלָם אֲסוּרִין, עַד שֶׁיַּחְזְרוּ לִמְקוֹמָן שׁוֹגְגִין. בְּשׁוֹגֵג – אִין, בְּמֵזִיד – לָא!

Rav Yosef bar Shemaya raised an objection to the opinion of **Rav Pappa** from a *baraita*: **Rabbi Neḥemya and Rabbi Eliezer ben Ya'akov say:** It **is actually prohibited** to carry the produce beyond four cubits, **unless it was returned to its place unwittingly.** By inference, If it was returned **unwittingly, yes,** it is permitted, but if it was returned **intentionally,** it is **not.**

תַּנָּאֵי הִיא, דְּתַנְיָא: פֵּירוֹת שֶׁיָּצְאוּ חוּץ לַתְּחוּם, בְּשׁוֹגֵג – יֵאָכְלוּ, בְּמֵזִיד – לֹא יֵאָכְלוּ.

The Gemara answers: This **is** subject to a dispute between **the** *tanna'im*, **as it was taught** in a *baraita*: With regard to **produce that was taken out beyond the** Shabbat **limit,**[H] if it was taken out **unwittingly, it may be eaten;** but if it was taken out **intentionally, it may not be eaten.**

PERSONALITIES

The Sages of Neharde'a – נְהַרְדְּעֵי: The Gemara states elsewhere that anonymous statements attributed to the Sages of Neharde'a refer to Rav Ḥama from Neharde'a, who served as the head of the yeshiva of Neharde'a for several years following the passing of Rav Naḥman bar Yitzḥak. Apparently, Rav Ḥama was related to the house of the Exilarch, and for a time was his official scholar. It is also possible that he was the same Rav Ḥama who met with the king of Persia and discussed Torah matters with him.

NOTES

Produce that was taken out – פֵּירוֹת שֶׁיָּצְאוּ: Rashi and many other commentaries explain that this law only applies on a Festival, because then there is no prohibition against carrying from one domain to another, although the prohibition of limits applies. Therefore, it is permitted to carry the produce two thousand cubits, as long as it remains within the limit. On Shabbat, however, if the produce is not situated in a private domain, it may not be carried more than four cubits. In contrast, the Ramban suggests possible cases where this law could apply on Shabbat as well.

HALAKHA

Produce that was taken out beyond the Shabbat limit – פֵּירוֹת שֶׁיָּצְאוּ חוּץ לַתְּחוּם: If produce was unwittingly taken out beyond the Shabbat limit, one is permitted to eat it, but he may not carry it more than four cubits. If it was taken out intentionally, it is prohibited. However, the authorities disagree about this prohibition: Some authorities state that the rule applies to all people (Rosh; *Tosafot*), while other commentaries teach that it applies only to the one who took the produce beyond the limit (*Mordekhai*, citing Rabbi Meir of Rothenberg). If the produce was returned to its place, even intentionally, it may be eaten by anyone, even by the one who took it out. The *halakha* follows the anonymous first *tanna* since Rabbi Pappa decided in favor of his opinion (see *Tosafot*; *Shulḥan Arukh*, *Oraḥ Ḥayyim* 405:9).

Perek **IV**
Daf **42** Amud **a**

רַבִּי נְחֶמְיָה אוֹמֵר: בִּמְקוֹמָן – יֵאָכְלוּ, שֶׁלֹּא בִּמְקוֹמָן – לֹא יֵאָכְלוּ.

Rabbi Neḥemya says: If the produce was returned and is now **in its** original **place, it may be eaten;** but if it is **not in its** original **place,** i.e., if it is still beyond the Shabbat limit, **it may not be eaten.**

מַאי בִּמְקוֹמָן? אִילֵימָא בִּמְקוֹמָן בְּמֵזִיד, וְהָא קָתָנֵי בְּהֶדְיָא: רַבִּי נְחֶמְיָה וְרַבִּי אֱלִיעֶזֶר בֶּן יַעֲקֹב אוֹמְרִים: לְעוֹלָם אֲסוּרִין עַד שֶׁיַּחְזְרוּ לִמְקוֹמָן שׁוֹגְגִין. בְּשׁוֹגֵג – אִין, בְּמֵזִיד – לָא!

The Gemara clarifies: **What is** meant by: **In its place? If you say** that the produce was returned to **its place intentionally,** there is a difficulty, **as it was explicitly taught** in a *baraita*: **Rabbi Neḥemya and Rabbi Eliezer ben Ya'akov say:** It **is actually prohibited** to carry the produce beyond four cubits, **unless it was returned to its place unwittingly.** By inference, only if it was returned **unwittingly** is it **indeed** permitted, but if it was returned **intentionally,** it is **not** permitted.

אֶלָּא לָאו בִּמְקוֹמָן בְּשׁוֹגֵג, וְחַסּוּרֵי מִחַסְּרָא וְהָכִי קָתָנֵי: פֵּירוֹת שֶׁיָּצְאוּ חוּץ לַתְּחוּם, בְּשׁוֹגֵג – יֵאָכְלוּ, בְּמֵזִיד – לֹא יֵאָכְלוּ.

Rather, does it **not** mean that the produce was returned **to its place unwittingly, and** the *baraita* **is incomplete and it teaches the following:** With regard to **produce that was taken out beyond the** Shabbat **limit,** if it was taken out **unwittingly, it may be eaten;** but if it was taken out **intentionally, it may not be eaten.**

בַּמֶּה דְּבָרִים אֲמוּרִים – שֶׁלֹּא בִּמְקוֹמָן, אֲבָל בִּמְקוֹמָן – אֲפִילּוּ בְּמֵזִיד יֵאָכְלוּ. וַאֲתָא רַבִּי נְחֶמְיָה לְמֵימַר: אֲפִילּוּ בִּמְקוֹמָן נַמִי, בְּשׁוֹגֵג – אִין, בְּמֵזִיד – לָא!

In what case **is this statement said?** In a case where the produce is **not in its** original **place,** i.e., it is still beyond the Shabbat limit. **But** if it was returned and is now **in its** original **place, even** if it was returned **intentionally, it may be eaten. And Rabbi Neḥemya came to say: Even** if the produce was returned and is now **in its** original **place,** a distinction applies. If it was returned **unwittingly, yes,** it is permitted; but if it was returned **intentionally,** it is **not.**

לָא, בְּמֵזִיד בִּמְקוֹמָן – דְּכוּלֵּי עָלְמָא לָא פְּלִיגִי דְּאָסוּר. וְהָכָא – בְּשׁוֹגֵג שֶׁלֹּא בִּמְקוֹמָן פְּלִיגִי. תַּנָּא קַמָּא סָבַר: בְּשׁוֹגֵג שָׁרֵי שֶׁלֹּא בִּמְקוֹמָן, וְרַבִּי נְחֶמְיָה סָבַר: אֲפִילּוּ שׁוֹגֵג, בִּמְקוֹמָן – אִין, שֶׁלֹּא בִּמְקוֹמָן – לָא.

The Gemara rejects this explanation: **No,** this is not necessarily the case, as the *baraita* can also be explained as follows: If the produce was returned **intentionally to its place, everyone agrees,** i.e., both the first *tanna* and Rabbi Neḥemya, that **it is forbidden. However, here they disagree with regard to** produce that was **unwittingly** taken out beyond the Shabbat limit and was not returned, so that it is **not in its** original **place. The first *tanna* holds** that if the produce was taken out **unwittingly, it is permitted** to be eaten, even if it is **not in its** original **place.** However, **Rabbi Neḥemya holds** that **even** if the produce was taken out **unwittingly,** if it was returned **to its** original **place, it is** permitted; but if it was not returned **to its** original **place,** it is **not** permitted.

וְהָא מִדְּקָתָנֵי סֵיפָא: רַבִּי נְחֶמְיָה וְרַבִּי אֱלִיעֶזֶר בֶּן יַעֲקֹב אוֹמְרִים: לְעוֹלָם אֲסוּרִין עַד שֶׁיַּחְזְרוּ לִמְקוֹמָן שׁוֹגְגִין. שׁוֹגֵג – אִין, בְּמֵזִיד – לָא. מִכְּלָל דְּתַנָּא קַמָּא סָבַר: בְּמֵזִיד נַמִי שָׁרֵי, שְׁמַע מִינָּהּ.

The Gemara objects to this reading: **However, since the latter clause** of this *baraita* **teaches** that **Rabbi Neḥemya and Rabbi Eliezer ben Ya'akov say: Actually,** carrying the produce beyond four cubits **is prohibited, unless it was returned to its place unwittingly,** and by inference, only if it was **unwittingly** returned is it **indeed** permitted; however, if it was returned **intentionally,** it is **not** permitted. And since Rabbi Neḥemya maintains that produce that was intentionally returned to its place is forbidden, **by inference, the first *tanna* holds** that even if it was returned **intentionally, it is also permitted.** If so, the preceding explanation cannot be accepted, and the Gemara concludes: Indeed, **learn from here** that Rav Pappa's opinion is supported by the opinion of the first *tanna*.[N]

אָמַר רַב נַחְמָן, אָמַר שְׁמוּאֵל: הָיָה מְהַלֵּךְ וְאֵינוֹ יוֹדֵעַ תְּחוּם שַׁבָּת – מְהַלֵּךְ אַלְפַּיִם פְּסִיעוֹת בֵּינוֹנִיּוֹת, וְזוֹ הִיא תְּחוּם שַׁבָּת.

Rav Naḥman said that **Shmuel said:** If **one was walking** in a certain place **and does not know** where **the Shabbat limit** lies, **he may take two thousand medium strides**[N] in each direction from the spot he acquired as his place of residence, **and this is the Shabbat limit,** for a medium stride is approximately a cubit.[H]

וְאָמַר רַב נַחְמָן, אָמַר שְׁמוּאֵל: שָׁבַת בְּבִקְעָה, וְהִקִּיפוּהָ נָכְרִים מְחִיצָה בַּשַּׁבָּת – מְהַלֵּךְ אַלְפַּיִם אַמָּה, וּמְטַלְטֵל בְּכוּלָּהּ עַל יְדֵי זְרִיקָה.

And Rav Naḥman also **said** that **Shmuel said:** If **one established residence in a valley,**[B] **and gentiles surrounded** the entire area **with a partition**[H] for the purpose of residence **on Shabbat, he may walk** only **two thousand cubits**[N] in each direction, as he cannot rely on partitions that were not present when he acquired his place of residence. However, **he may carry in the entire** partitioned area,[N] as in any other private domain, even in the part that is beyond his two thousand cubits, but only **by means of throwing,** as he himself cannot accompany the object past two thousand cubits.

וְרַב הוּנָא אָמַר: מְהַלֵּךְ אַלְפַּיִם אַמָּה וּמְטַלְטֵל אַרְבַּע אַמּוֹת. וְנִיטַלְטֵל בְּכוּלָּהּ עַל יְדֵי זְרִיקָה!

Rav Huna said: He may walk two thousand cubits; however, even within this area **he may carry** objects only a distance of **four cubits,** as in a *karmelit*. The Gemara asks: **And let him** be permitted **to carry in the entire** partitioned area **by means of throwing.** Although he himself is limited in where he may walk, the partitions render it a private domain, and he should be permitted to carry in the entire area.

שֶׁמָּא יִמָּשֵׁךְ אַחַר חֶפְצוֹ.

The Gemara answers: The Sages prohibited this as a preventive measure, **lest he be drawn after his object.** It is prohibited for him to leave the two thousand cubit limit, but were he permitted to carry by means of throwing, he might follow his object and go out beyond his permitted limit.

בְּאַלְפַּיִם מִיהַת לִיטַלְטֵל כִּי אוֹרְחֵיהּ!

The Gemara asks: **Within two thousand** cubits, **at any rate, let him carry** the object **in his usual manner.** Since he may traverse this area, there should be no concern that he might come to be drawn after the object.

NOTES

The proof for Rav Pappa's opinion – הוֹכָחָה לְשִׁיטַת רַב פַּפָּא: The Gemara establishes that there is a tannaitic precedent for Rav Pappa's opinion based on an unstated opinion of the first *tanna*, inferred from the statement cited from Rabbi Neḥemya and Rabbi Eliezer ben Ya'akov. The latter *tanna'im* stipulate that only produce returned to its place unwittingly is permitted, while the first *tanna* does not address this case explicitly. However, once the latter *tanna'im* address this issue, the Gemara understands that they must be responding to the opinion of the first *tanna*. It then analyzes his opinion and infers that he disputes the claim cited from Rabbi Neḥemya and Rabbi Eliezer ben Ya'akov, and rules that even if the produce was returned intentionally, it is permitted. This inferred opinion of the first *tanna* of the *baraita* corresponds with Rav Pappa's statement, validating his opinion (see Rashba).

He may take two thousand medium strides – מְהַלֵּךְ אַלְפַּיִם פְּסִיעוֹת בֵּינוֹנִיּוֹת: This statement teaches, among other things, that one is permitted to count these two thousand strides on Shabbat. Although one is not permitted to count or measure on Shabbat, measuring the two thousand paces for the sake of a mitzva is permitted (Ritva). Incidentally, this statement also teaches that a stride of one cubit is an appropriate step for Shabbat. A longer stride is regarded as a large step, which the Sages said should not be taken on Shabbat (*Hagahot HaRosh*).

He may walk two thousand cubits – מְהַלֵּךְ אַלְפַּיִם אַמָּה: By Torah law, the entire area is regarded as a private domain and it is legally considered like four cubits, just like any other courtyard. Nevertheless, the Sages decreed that this is prohibited as a preventive measure (see *Tosafot*).

He may carry in the entire partitioned area – מְטַלְטֵל בְּכוּלָּהּ: This ruling refers to ownerless objects that are not limited by the place of residence of their owner. This is because an owner's Shabbat limit applies to his possessions as well.

BACKGROUND

If one established residence in a valley – שָׁבַת בְּבִקְעָה: The image depicts a valley surrounded by a partition, including the area within which the person is permitted to walk, as he established his place of residence there.

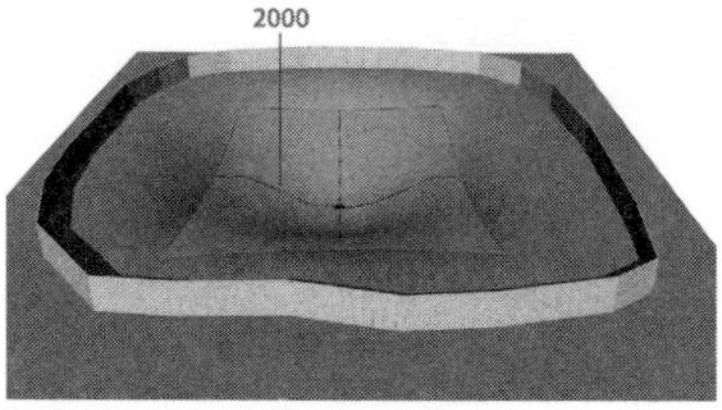

Shabbat limit for a valley surrounded by a partition

HALAKHA

Measuring the Shabbat limit – מְדִידַת תְּחוּם שַׁבָּת: If one is walking and does not know where the Shabbat limit is, he may walk two thousand medium strides, each of which is approximately two shoe lengths (*Magen Avraham*), as stated by Shmuel (*Shulḥan Arukh, Oraḥ Ḥayyim* 397:2).

If one established residence in a valley and gentiles surrounded it with a partition – שָׁבַת בְּבִקְעָה, וְהִקִּיפוּהָ נָכְרִים מְחִיצָה: If one established his Shabbat residence in a field and then gentiles surrounded it with a partition on Shabbat for the purpose of residence (Rashi), he may only walk two thousand cubits from his place of residence within the enclosure. However, he may carry in the entire area by means of throwing.

Some authorities rule stringently with regard to carrying within a Shabbat limit established in the valley. They hold that even in that area, he may throw but not carry (Rema, based on *Tosafot*; and others), since the concern of a partition that was breached in its entirety applies to Shmuel's opinion as well (Vilna Gaon). However, other authorities permit him to carry within this limit in the usual manner (Rashi; Rabbeinu Yehonatan; Rosh; *Tur*). Most later commentaries were lenient in this regard, based on the principle that the *halakha* follows the lenient opinion with regard to *eiruvin* (*Shulḥan Arukh HaRav*; *Shulḥan Arukh, Oraḥ Ḥayyim* 403:1).

מִשּׁוּם דְּהָוֵי כִּמְחִיצָה שֶׁנִּפְרְצָה בִּמְלוֹאָהּ לְמָקוֹם הָאָסוּר לָהּ.

The Gemara answers that this is prohibited due to another aspect of the laws of *eiruvin*, namely **because this is similar** to the case of **a partition that is breached in its entirety,** leaving the space open **to a place into which it is prohibited** to carry. Since he may not carry more than two thousand cubits, and the enclosed area is larger than two thousand cubits, the area that is permitted to him is breached in its entirety, left open to an area that is prohibited to him. Consequently, carrying is prohibited in the entire area, even by means of throwing.

חִיָּיא בַּר רַב אָמַר: מְהַלֵּךְ אַלְפַּיִם אַמָּה, וּמְטַלְטֵל בְּאַלְפַּיִם אַמָּה. כְּמַאן? דְּלָא כְּרַב נַחְמָן וְלָא כְּרַב הוּנָא!

However, **Ḥiyya bar Rav said:** In that case, **he may walk two thousand cubits, and he may** also **carry** objects **within** these **two thousand cubits.** The Gemara poses a question: **In accordance with whose** opinion did Ḥiyya bar Rav issue his ruling? It is **neither in accordance with** the opinion of **Rav Naḥman, nor in accordance with** the opinion of **Rav Huna,**[N] while this dispute would appear to leave no place for a third opinion.

אֵימָא: מְטַלְטֵל בְּאַרְבַּע. אִי הָכִי הַיְינוּ דְּרַב הוּנָא! אֵימָא: וְכֵן אָמַר רַבִּי חִיָּיא בַּר רַב.

The Gemara answers: **Read** Ḥiyya bar Rav's ruling as follows: **He may carry** objects only a distance of **four** cubits. The Gemara asks: **If so, this is** the same as the opinion **of Rav Huna.** The Gemara answers: **Read** it then as follows: **And similarly, Rabbi Ḥiyya bar Rav said.**

אֲמַר לֵיהּ רַב נַחְמָן לְרַב הוּנָא: לָא תִּיפְלוֹג עֲלֵיהּ דִּשְׁמוּאֵל, דְּתַנְיָא כְּוָותֵיהּ. דְּתַנְיָא:

Rav Naḥman said to Rav Huna: Do not argue with the opinion **of Shmuel** as cited by Rav Naḥman with regard to a field surrounded by a partition on Shabbat, **as it was taught** in a *baraita* **in accordance with his** opinion. **As it was taught** in a *baraita*:

NOTES

Neither in accordance with Rav Naḥman nor in accordance with Rav Huna – דְּלָא כְּרַב נַחְמָן וְלָא כְּרַב הוּנָא: If there is no decree against throwing due to a concern that one might carry, then throwing should be permitted in the entire field, in accordance with the opinion of Shmuel. On the other hand, if there is a decree against throwing, then it should apply even within the area of two thousand cubits, in accordance with the opinion of Rav Huna (Ritva). In the Jerusalem Talmud, the opinion of Rabbi Ḥiyya bar Rav remains an independent view, and is not aligned with the opinion of Rav Huna.

הָיָה מוֹדֵד וּבָא, וְכָלְתָה מִדָּתוֹ בַּחֲצִי הָעִיר – מוּתָּר לְטַלְטֵל בְּכָל הָעִיר כּוּלָּהּ, וּבִלְבַד שֶׁלֹּא יַעֲבוֹר אֶת הַתְּחוּם בְּרַגְלָיו. מַאי מְטַלְטֵל – לָאו עַל יְדֵי זְרִיקָה?

If a person **was measuring**[N] the two thousand cubits of his Shabbat limit from the spot where he deposited his *eiruv*, **and his measuring ended in the middle of the city,**[H] **he is permitted to carry throughout the city, provided that he does not overstep the limit by foot,** i.e., that he does not walk beyond his permitted limit in the middle of the city. If he cannot walk about on foot, **how can he carry** throughout the city? Is it **not by means of throwing?** This presents a difficulty for Rav Huna, who prohibits carrying by means of throwing in a place where it is prohibited to walk.

אָמַר רַב הוּנָא: לָא, עַל יְדֵי מְשִׁיכָה.

Rav Huna said: No, it means that he may carry in the city **by means of pulling,** i.e., he is permitted to pull objects from the other side of the city to the side where he is permitted to walk, for in this manner there is no concern that he might be drawn after the object, since he is bringing the object to him.

אָמַר רַב הוּנָא: הָיָה מוֹדֵד וּבָא, וְכָלְתָה מִדָּתוֹ בַּחֲצִי חָצֵר – אֵין לוֹ אֶלָּא חֲצִי חָצֵר.

Similarly, **Rav Huna said:** If a person **was measuring** the two thousand cubits of his Shabbat limit from the spot where he deposited his *eiruv*, **and his measuring ended in the middle of a courtyard, he has only half the courtyard** in which to walk.

פְּשִׁיטָא! אֵימָא: יֵשׁ לוֹ חֲצִי חָצֵר.

The Gemara raises a difficulty: It is **obvious** that he is not permitted to walk beyond his Shabbat limit. The Gemara answers: **Read** Rav Huna's statement as follows: **He has half a courtyard,** i.e., Rav Huna addresses a different aspect of the issue; namely, he permits carrying in half the courtyard.

הַאי נָמֵי פְּשִׁיטָא! מַהוּ דְּתֵימָא: לֵיחוּשׁ דִּלְמָא אָתֵי לְטַלְטוֹלֵי בְּכוּלָּהּ, קָא מַשְׁמַע לַן.

The Gemara asks: However, **this too is obvious,** for why should it be prohibited for him to carry in a private domain where he is permitted to walk? The Gemara answers: **Lest you say that we should be concerned that** if he is permitted to carry in half the courtyard, **he might come to carry in the entire** courtyard. **Consequently,** Rav Huna **teaches us** that this concern is not taken into account.

NOTES

If a person was measuring – מוֹדֵד וּבָא: There are three possible scenarios that can result from this measurement: If a person spent Shabbat within a partitioned enclosure, the entire area enclosed by the partitions is considered, for him, like four cubits. Consequently, after one exits the enclosure, even if it is a large city, he may still walk another two thousand cubits. The second possibility is that the area enclosed by partitions is fully within a person's Shabbat limit. The third option is a situation where the enclosure lay partially beyond his Shabbat limit. In that circumstance, he may not venture beyond his limit, even if it is located in the middle of a city or courtyard.

HALAKHA

His measuring ended in the middle of the city – כָּלְתָה מִדָּתוֹ בַּחֲצִי הָעִיר: If one's Shabbat limit ends in the middle of a city, a courtyard, or a house, he may throw items throughout that space. This principle is in accordance with the opinion of Shmuel because he is considered a greater authority than Rav Huna, and because Rav Naḥman also accepted Shmuel's opinion (Rambam *Sefer Zemanim*, *Hilkhot Shabbat* 27:8).

אָמַר רַב נַחְמָן, מוֹדֶה לִי הוּנָא: הָיָה מוֹדֵד וּבָא, וְכָלְתָה מִדָּתוֹ עַל שְׂפַת תִּקְרָה – מוּתָּר לְטַלְטֵל בְּכָל הַבַּיִת.

Rav Naḥman said: Rav **Huna agrees with me** that carrying is not prohibited in a comparable case, out of concern that the person be drawn after the object he is carrying: If a person **was measuring** the two thousand cubits of his Shabbat limit from the spot where he deposited his *eiruv*, **and his measuring ended at the edge of the roof**[N] of a house, most of which stood outside his Shabbat limit, **he is permitted to carry throughout the house** by means of throwing.

מַאי טַעְמָא – הוֹאִיל וְתִקְרַת הַבַּיִת חוֹבֶטֶת.

What is the reason that Rav Huna agrees in this case? **Because** the edge of **the roof of the house** is regarded as if it **presses** down vertically at the end of his Shabbat limit, thus creating a partition, and so there is no concern that he might pass beyond this partition and be drawn after his object.

אָמַר רַב הוּנָא בְּרֵיהּ דְּרַב נָתָן: כְּתַנָּאֵי; הוֹלִיכוּהוּ לְעִיר אַחֶרֶת וּנְתָנוּהוּ בְּדִיר אוֹ בְּסַהַר, רַבָּן גַּמְלִיאֵל וְרַבִּי אֶלְעָזָר בֶּן עֲזַרְיָה אוֹמְרִים: מְהַלֵּךְ אֶת כּוּלָּהּ. וְרַבִּי יְהוֹשֻׁעַ וְרַבִּי עֲקִיבָא אוֹמְרִים: אֵין לוֹ אֶלָּא אַרְבַּע אַמּוֹת.

Rav Huna, son of Rav Natan, said: The dispute between Shmuel and Rav Huna is **parallel to** a dispute between *tanna'im* recorded in the mishna: If the gentiles **brought him to a different city** beyond his Shabbat limit, **or if they put him in a pen or a stable,** the Sages disagree. **Rabban Gamliel and Rabbi Elazar ben Azarya say: He may walk about the entire** stable or pen. Since they are enclosed by a partition, their entire area is considered like only four cubits. **Rabbi Yehoshua and Rabbi Akiva say: He has only four cubits** from where he was deposited.

מַאי לָאו: רַבָּן גַּמְלִיאֵל וְרַבִּי אֶלְעָזָר בֶּן עֲזַרְיָה דְּאָמְרוּ מְהַלֵּךְ אֶת כּוּלָּהּ – דְּלָא גָּזְרִי הִילּוּךְ דִּיר וְסַהַר אַטּוּ הִילּוּךְ בַּבִּקְעָה,

Is it not the case that **Rabban Gamliel and Rabbi Elazar ben Azarya, who said: He may walk about the entire** area, **do not prohibit walking in a pen or a stable due to walking in a field** where one is limited to four cubits? Rather, they say that since the stable is surrounded by partitions, it is not similar to a field, in which a person may not leave his four cubits.

וּמִדְּהִילּוּךְ אַטּוּ הִילּוּךְ לָא גָּזְרִי – טִלְטוּל אַטּוּ הִילּוּךְ לָא גָּזְרִי.

And since they did not prohibit walking in a pen or a stable **due to** the limits imposed on **walking** in a field, **they would** certainly **not prohibit carrying** in a pen **due to** the limits imposed on **walking** in a field. Rather, they would permit a person to carry in a field that had been enclosed on Shabbat by gentiles, and even to throw into the part lying beyond his two thousand cubits, parallel to the opinion of Shmuel who did not decree against this.

וְרַבִּי יְהוֹשֻׁעַ וְרַבִּי עֲקִיבָא דְּאוֹמְרִים: "אֵין לוֹ אֶלָּא אַרְבַּע אַמּוֹת", דְּגָזְרִי הִילּוּךְ דִּיר וְסַהַר אַטּוּ הִילּוּךְ דְּבִקְעָה, וּמִדְּהִילּוּךְ אַטּוּ הִילּוּךְ גָּזְרִי – טִלְטוּל אַטּוּ הִילּוּךְ נַמִּי גָּזְרִי.

And is it not the case that **Rabbi Yehoshua and Rabbi Akiva, who say** that **he has only four cubits, prohibit walking in a pen or a stable due to** the limits imposed on **walking in a field? And since they prohibit walking** in a pen or a stable **due to** the limits imposed on **walking** in a field, **they would also prohibit carrying** past the two thousand cubit limit by means of throwing **due to** the limits imposed on **walking** past there, in accordance with Rav Huna's opinion.

מִמַּאי? דִּילְמָא, כִּי לָא גָּזְרִי רַבָּן גַּמְלִיאֵל וְרַבִּי אֶלְעָזָר בֶּן עֲזַרְיָה הִילּוּךְ סַהַר וְדִיר אַטּוּ הִילּוּךְ בִּקְעָה – הָנֵי מִילֵּי הָתָם דִּשְׁנֵי מְקוֹמוֹת הֵן,

The Gemara rejects this comparison: **From what** do you infer that this is the case? **Perhaps Rabban Gamliel and Rabbi Elazar ben Azarya did not prohibit walking in a pen or a stable due to** the limits imposed on **walking in a field,** but **this applies** only **there, because they are two** distinct **places.** In other words, the pen and stable are enclosed by partitions, while the field is not, and there is no reason to prohibit walking in one place out of concern that one might come to act improperly in a different place.

אֲבָל טִלְטוּל אַטּוּ הִילּוּךְ דְּמָקוֹם אֶחָד הוּא – הָכִי נַמִּי דְּגָזְרִי, גְּזֵירָה שֶׁמָּא יִמָּשֵׁךְ אַחַר חֶפְצוֹ.

However, as for the prohibition of **carrying due to** the limits imposed on **walking,** where **it is** all **one place,** might we **also** say **that** even Rabban Gamliel and Rabbi Elazar ben Azarya **would decree** against carrying **as a preventive measure, lest the person be drawn after his object** and come to walk in a place prohibited to him.

וְרַבִּי יְהוֹשֻׁעַ וְרַבִּי עֲקִיבָא נַמִּי מִמַּאי דְּמִשּׁוּם דְּגָזְרִי הוּא – דִּילְמָא מִשּׁוּם דְּקָא סָבְרִי: כִּי אָמְרִינַן "כָּל הַבַּיִת כּוּלּוֹ כְּאַרְבַּע אַמּוֹת דָּמֵי" – הָנֵי מִילֵּי הֵיכָא דְּשָׁבַת בַּאֲוִיר מְחִיצוֹת מִבְּעוֹד יוֹם,

The comparison can also be rejected from another angle: **And** with regard to **Rabbi Yehoshua and Rabbi Akiva too, from what** can it be inferred **that** they prohibit walking beyond four cubits **due to a decree? Perhaps** it is **because they hold** that **when we say that the entire house is considered like four cubits,** this **applies** only **where one acquired his place of residence within the airspace of** the **partitions** of the house **while it was still day,** i.e., prior to the onset of Shabbat.

NOTES

His measuring ended at the edge of the roof – כָּלְתָה מִדָּתוֹ עַל שְׂפַת תִּקְרָה: Some commentaries explain this case differently, namely, that it refers to a situation where his measuring ended inside the house. In that case, one may carry throughout the entire house by means of throwing. Since the house is closed off on all sides by partitions, it is considered halakhically like four cubits (Rabbeinu Ḥananel).

אֲבָל הֵיכָא דְּלָא שָׁבַת בַּאֲוִיר מְחִיצּוֹת מִבְּעוֹד יוֹם – לָא.

However, where he did not acquire his place of residence within the airspace of the **partitions** of the house **while it was still day,** the house, and all the more so the stable or pen, is **not** considered as four cubits; rather, it is measured based on the actual number of cubits it contains. Based on this explanation, this ruling indicates nothing with regard to the issue of throwing beyond the two-thousand cubit limit. Consequently, the Gemara rejects the link between the dispute of the *tanna'im* in the mishna and that of Rav Naḥman and Rav Huna.

אָמַר רַב: הִלְכְתָא כְּרַבָּן גַּמְלִיאֵל בְּדִיר וְסַהַר וּסְפִינָה. וּשְׁמוּאֵל אָמַר: הִלְכְתָא כְּרַבָּן גַּמְלִיאֵל בִּסְפִינָה, אֲבָל בְּדִיר וְסַהַר – לָא.

Rav said: The *halakha* is in accordance with the opinion of **Rabban Gamliel with regard to a pen, a stable, and a boat.**[H] **And Shmuel said: The *halakha* is in accordance with** the opinion of **Rabban Gamliel with regard to a boat,**[N] **but not with regard to a stable or a pen.**

דְּכוּלֵּי עָלְמָא מִיהַת הֲלָכָה כְּרַבָּן גַּמְלִיאֵל בִּסְפִינָה, מַאי טַעְמָא?

The Gemara poses a question: **At any rate, all agree,** i.e., both Rav and Shmuel, **that the *halakha* is in accordance with** the opinion of **Rabban Gamliel with regard to a boat. What is the reason** that the *halakha* is different in this case than in the other cases?

אָמַר רַבָּה: הוֹאִיל וְשָׁבַת בַּאֲוִיר מְחִיצּוֹת מִבְּעוֹד יוֹם.

Rabba said: This is **since he acquired his place of residence within the partitions** of the boat **while it was still day,** in which case it is reasonable to say that the entire boat is considered as if it is only four cubits.

רַבִּי זֵירָא אָמַר: הוֹאִיל וּסְפִינָה נוֹטַלְתּוֹ מִתְּחִילַּת אַרְבַּע וּמַנַּחְתּוֹ בְּסוֹף אַרְבַּע.

Rabbi Zeira said: This is **since the boat** constantly moves the person out of his four cubits, **lifting him**[N] **from the beginning of four** cubits **and placing him at the end of four** cubits. Since in any case he cannot restrict himself to any particular four cubits, even if he wished to do so, it is reasonable to say that he is permitted to walk about the entire boat.

מַאי בֵּינַיְיהוּ? אִיכָּא בֵּינַיְיהוּ שֶׁנִּפְחֲתוּ דּוֹפְנֵי סְפִינָה. אִי נַמִי, בְּקוֹפֵץ מִסְּפִינָה לִסְפִינָה.

The Gemara asks: **What is** the practical difference **between** these two explanations? The Gemara answers: **There is** a practical difference **between them** with regard to a case where **the walls of the boat were breached,** so that the person is no longer located between its partitions. **Alternatively,** there is a difference **with regard to** a case **where** the person **jumped from one boat to another,** so that he is no longer on the boat where he had acquired his place of residence. In both of these cases, Rabba's reason no longer applies, but Rabbi Zeira's reason does.

וְרַבִּי זֵירָא, מַאי טַעְמָא לָא אָמַר כְּרַבָּה? אָמַר לָךְ: מְחִיצּוֹת –

The Gemara asks: As for **Rabbi Zeira, what is the reason** that he **did not state** his opinion **in accordance with** the opinion of **Rabba,** whose explanation is more straightforward? The Gemara answers: He could have **said to you: The sides** of a boat are not regarded as proper partitions,

HALAKHA

He established residence on a boat – **שָׁבַת בִּסְפִינָה**: One who establishes residence on a boat may walk throughout the entire boat. If the walls of the boat are breached while it is at sea, he may still walk throughout the entire boat. However, if it has come to a stop, he may only walk four cubits (*Hagahot HaRosh*), in accordance with the opinion of Rabba, since the *halakha* accords with his opinion in disputes with Rabbi Zeira (*Shulḥan Arukh, Oraḥ Ḥayyim* 405:7).

NOTES

The *halakha* is in accordance with Rabban Gamliel with regard to a boat – **הִלְכְתָא כְּרַבָּן גַּמְלִיאֵל בִּסְפִינָה**: Proof for this opinion is offered in the Jerusalem Talmud from the statement with regard to Rabbi Yehoshua and Rabbi Akiva that they wished to be stringent upon themselves. This indicates that even they agree that the *halakha* is in accordance with the opinion of Rabban Gamliel, but they maintain that it is best to be stringent.

Since the boat lifts him – **הוֹאִיל וּסְפִינָה נוֹטַלְתּוֹ**: Rabbi Yehoshua and Rabbi Akiva do not accept Rabban Gamliel's reasoning in this context because, although the boat moves from one set of four cubits to another, the passengers themselves do not move on the boat. Therefore, the passengers do have a fixed, particular location that can be considered their four cubits (Ritva).

Perek **IV**
Daf **43** Amud **a**

לְהַבְרִיחַ מַיִם עֲשׂוּיוֹת.

for **they are** only **made to keep the water out;** that is to say, a boat's walls are not designed to turn it into a place of residence, but to protect it from the water. Therefore, they do not have the status of partitions made for the purpose of residence.

וְרַבָּה, מַאי טַעְמָא לָא אָמַר כְּרַבִּי זֵירָא? בִּמְהַלֶּכֶת – כּוּלֵּי עָלְמָא לָא פְּלִיגִי, כִּי פְּלִיגִי – בְּשֶׁעָמְדָה.

The Gemara asks: As for **Rabba, what is the reason he did not state** his opinion **in accordance with** the opinion of **Rabbi Zeira?** The Gemara answers: **With regard to** a boat **that is moving, all agree,** i.e., even Rabbi Yehoshua and Rabbi Akiva, that one is permitted to walk about the entire boat. **They disagree** only with regard to a boat **that is stationary.**[H] Rabban Gamliel holds that the boat's walls constitute effective partitions, whereas Rabbi Yehoshua disagrees.

HALAKHA

A boat that is moving and that is stationary – **סְפִינָה מְהַלֶּכֶת וְעוֹמֶדֶת**: One may walk throughout a moving boat even if its gunwales have been breached. However, if the boat stopped moving after its gunwales were breached, one may only walk a distance of four cubits on it, as the *halakha* is in accordance with the opinion of Rabba. If there is an area in the middle of the boat that is ten handbreadths deep, or a place that could be hollowed out to be ten handbreadths deep, that entire area is considered to be like four cubits (Rema; *Shulḥan Arukh, Oraḥ Ḥayyim* 405:7).

NOTES

Halakha…by inference that they disagreed – הִלְכְתָא מִכְּלָל דִּפְלִיגִי: Although the straightforward understanding of the mishna indicates that the *tanna'im* disputed the matter, a closer reading reveals that this is not stated explicitly. Therefore, the dispute is limited to the case of a pen and a stable. However, Rabbi Yehoshua and Rabbi Akiva may have agreed with Rabban Gamliel with regard to a boat, but they wished to be stringent with themselves in order to emphasize the severity of the prohibition involved, because it is fitting for a distinguished person to be stringent (Maharsha).

My father's brother determined – הִכְרִיעַ אֲחִי אַבָּא: The Rif maintains that this halakhic determination is not to be accepted for two main reasons. First, a halakhic ruling stated in a *baraita* or mishna is not automatically accepted. Consequently, any such statement is not binding. Second, Rabbi Yehoshua himself was a party to the dispute. Therefore, his determination of the dispute is not accepted, even if it differs from his own opinion. A compromise determination is only accepted as *halakha* if it was offered by a third party who had not been previously involved in the dispute.

Where he advances by way of a leap – דְּקָאָזֵיל בִּקְפִיצָה: The commentaries offer a variety of explanations for the case described here. One explanation is that the person leapt more than ten handbreadths beyond the Shabbat limit, and since he left the limit in a permitted manner, he may continue as far as he wants (see *Me'iri*). Several variant readings offer support for this explanation, as well as for the explanation that leaping refers to traveling by boat (see Ritva).

אָמַר רַב נַחְמָן בַּר יִצְחָק: מַתְנִיתִין נַמִי דַּיְקָא דְּבִמְהַלֶּכֶת לָא פְּלִיגִי, מִמַּאי? מִדְּקָתָנֵי: ״מַעֲשֶׂה שֶׁבָּאוּ מִפְּלַנְדַּרְסִין וְהִפְלִיגָה סְפִינָתָם בַּיָּם; רַבָּן גַּמְלִיאֵל וְרַבִּי אֶלְעָזָר בֶּן עֲזַרְיָה הִלְּכוּ אֶת כּוּלָּהּ, וְרַבִּי יְהוֹשֻׁעַ וְרַבִּי עֲקִיבָא לֹא זָזוּ מֵאַרְבַּע אַמּוֹת, שֶׁרָצוּ לְהַחְמִיר עַל עַצְמָן״.

Rav Naḥman bar Yitzḥak said: The mishna is also precise in its implication **that** the *tanna'im* **do not disagree with regard to a moving** boat. The Gemara asks: **From where** is this implied? **From that which is taught:** There was **an incident where** all of these Sages **were coming from Pelandarsin, and their boat set sail on the sea** on Shabbat, taking them out beyond their Shabbat limit. **Rabban Gamliel and Rabbi Elazar ben Azarya walked** about **the entire** boat, while **Rabbi Yehoshua and Rabbi Akiva did not move beyond four cubits, as they sought to be stringent with themselves.**

אִי אָמְרַתְּ בִּשְׁלָמָא בִּמְהַלֶּכֶת לָא פְּלִיגִי – הַיְינוּ דְּקָתָנֵי ״רָצוּ״ – דִּילְמָא עָמְדָה.

Rav Naḥman bar Yitzḥak explains: **Granted, if you say** that **they do not disagree with regard to a moving** boat, **that is why it is taught** that they **sought** to be stringent with themselves, i.e., they wished to practice stringency although they were under no obligation to do so, as they were concerned that **perhaps** the boat **will stand**, i.e., come to a stop.

אֶלָּא אִי אָמְרַתְּ פְּלִיגִי – הַאי ״רָצוּ לְהַחְמִיר״?! אִיסּוּרָא הוּא!

But if you say that **they disagree** even in the case of a boat that is moving, **this** phrase: **Sought to be stringent,** is problematic, for the mishna should not refer to a desire to be stringent, as according to their opinion **it is an** outright **prohibition.**

אָמַר רַב אַשִׁי: מַתְנִיתִין נַמִי דַּיְקָא, דְּקָתָנֵי סְפִינָה, דּוּמְיָא דְּדִיר וָסַהַר, מַה דִּיר וָסַהַר – דִּקְבִיעִי, אַף סְפִינָה נַמִי – דִּקְבִיעָא.

With regard to the previous issue, **Rav Ashi said: The mishna is also precise,** implying this point in another manner as well, **for it teaches** the law governing a boat **parallel to** the law governing **a pen and a stable. Just as a pen and a stable are fixed** in their place, **so too,** the mishna discusses **a boat that is fixed** in its place.

אֲמַר לֵיהּ רַב אַחָא בְּרֵיהּ דְּרָבָא לְרַב אַשִׁי: ״הִלְכְתָא כְּרַבָּן גַּמְלִיאֵל בִּסְפִינָה״, הִלְכְתָא – מִכְּלָל דִּפְלִיגִי?

Rav Aḥa, son of Rava, said to Rav Ashi: Rav and Shmuel both said that **the *halakha* is in accordance with Rabban Gamliel with regard to a boat,** and if they had to decide **the *halakha*,** then this proves **by inference that** the *tanna'im* **disagreed**[N] about the issue. This is difficult, as the words: They wished to be stringent upon themselves, imply that there was no fundamental dispute at all.

אִין, וְהָתַנְיָא: חֲנַנְיָא (בֶּן אֲחִי רַבִּי יְהוֹשֻׁעַ) אוֹמֵר: כׇּל אוֹתוֹ הַיּוֹם יָשְׁבוּ וְדָנוּ בִּדְבַר הֲלָכָה, אֶמֶשׁ הִכְרִיעַ אֲחִי אַבָּא: הֲלָכָה כְּרַבָּן גַּמְלִיאֵל בִּסְפִינָה, וַהֲלָכָה כְּרַבִּי עֲקִיבָא בְּדִיר וָסַהַר.

Rav Ashi replied: **Yes,** the *tanna'im* do in fact disagree about a boat that is standing. When the mishna says that Rabbi Yehoshua and Rabbi Akiva wished to be stringent upon themselves, implying that there is no real dispute, it is referring to a boat that is stationary. **And it was taught** in a *baraita*: **Ḥananya, son of Rabbi Yehoshua's brother, says: All that day** they spent on the boat, **they sat and discussed the matter of *halakha*;** and come **evening my father's brother,** i.e., Rabbi Yehoshua, **determined:**[N] The ***halakha* is in accordance with** the opinion of **Rabban Gamliel with regard to a** moving **boat,** i.e., one is permitted to walk about all of it. **And** the ***halakha* is in accordance with** the opinion of **Rabbi Akiva with regard to a pen and a stable,** i.e., one may only walk four cubits in them, and the same applies to a stationary boat.

בָּעֵי רַב חֲנַנְיָא: יֵשׁ תְּחוּמִין לְמַעְלָה מֵעֲשָׂרָה, אוֹ אֵין תְּחוּמִין לְמַעְלָה מֵעֲשָׂרָה?

Rav Ḥananya raised a dilemma: Does the prohibition of Shabbat **limits** apply **above ten** handbreadths from the ground, **or** perhaps does the prohibition of Shabbat **limits not** apply **above ten** handbreadths? In other words, does the Shabbat limit apply only close to the ground, in which case walking more than ten handbreadths above the ground, would be permitted?

עַמּוּד גָּבוֹהַּ עֲשָׂרָה וְרָחָב אַרְבָּעָה לָא תִּיבָּעֵי לָךְ – דְּאַרְעָא סְמִיכְתָּא הִיא.

The Gemara clarifies the case in which this dilemma arises: With regard to **a post ten** handbreadths **high and four** handbreadths **wide,** partly within the limit and partly outside of it, this case **should not be a dilemma for you.** Such a stable post **is** like **solid ground,** although it differs from the surrounding area in height; therefore, it is prohibited to walk from the part within the limit to the part outside of it.

כִּי תִּיבָּעֵי לָךְ – בְּעַמּוּד גָּבוֹהַּ עֲשָׂרָה וְאֵינוֹ רָחָב אַרְבָּעָה. אִי נַמִי, דְּקָאָזֵיל בִּקְפִיצָה.

The case **where** there **should be a dilemma for you** is that of **a post ten** handbreadths **high but not four** handbreadths **wide,** or the like. **Alternatively,** the case is one **where he advances by way of a leap**[N] in the air above ten handbreadths from the ground.

לִישָּׁנָא אַחֲרִינָא: בִּסְפִינָה מַאי?

The Gemara presents **another version** of the previous dilemma: **What is the** *halakha* **with regard to a boat** sailing on the surface of the water more than ten handbreadths from the sea or river bed? Does the prohibition of Shabbat limits apply or not?

אָמַר רַב הוֹשַׁעְיָא: תָּא שְׁמַע, מַעֲשֶׂה שֶׁבָּאוּ מִפְּלַנְדַּרְסִין וְהִפְלִיגָה סְפִינָתָם בַּיָּם וְכוּ׳. אִי אָמְרַתְּ בִּשְׁלָמָא יֵשׁ תְּחוּמִין – מִשּׁוּם הָכִי רָצוּ. אֶלָּא אִי אָמְרַתְּ אֵין תְּחוּמִין – אַמַּאי רָצוּ?

Rav Hoshaya said: Come and **hear** a resolution to this dilemma from what was taught in the mishna: **It once happened that** all of these Sages **were coming from Pelandarsin, and their boat set sail on the sea, etc. Granted, if you say** that the prohibition of Shabbat **limits applies** above ten handbreadths, **this is why** Rabbi Yehoshua and Rabbi Akiva **sought** to be stringent. **However, if you say** that the prohibition of Shabbat **limits** does not apply above ten handbreadths, **why did they seek** to be stringent?

כִּדְאָמַר רָבָא: בִּמְהַלֶּכֶת בִּרְקָק, הָכָא נַמִי – בִּמְהַלֶּכֶת בִּרְקָק.

The Gemara answers: It may be suggested **as Rava said** with regard to a parallel case, establishing that case as one where the boat was **moving through** shallow, **swampy water;**[H] **here, too,** we are dealing with a case **where** the boat **was moving through** shallow, **swampy water,** within ten handbreadths of the sea's bed, so that the prohibition of Shabbat limits certainly applies.

תָּא שְׁמַע: פַּעַם אַחַת לֹא נִכְנְסוּ לַנָּמֵל עַד שֶׁחֲשֵׁיכָה וְכוּ׳, אִי אָמְרַתְּ בִּשְׁלָמָא יֵשׁ תְּחוּמִין – שַׁפִּיר, אֶלָּא אִי אָמְרַתְּ אֵין תְּחוּמִין – כִּי לֹא הָיִינוּ בְּתוֹךְ הַתְּחוּם מַאי הָוֵי?

The Gemara cites another proof. **Come** and **hear** a resolution from the mishna: On **one occasion** on a Shabbat eve, **they did not enter the port until after nightfall, etc. Granted, if you say** that the prohibition of Shabbat **limits** applies above ten handbreadths, it was **well** that they asked whether or not they may disembark. **However, if you say** that the prohibition of Shabbat **limits does not apply** above ten handbreadths, even if Rabban Gamliel had told them: **We were not within the** city's **limit** before nightfall, **what** difference **would it** have made? They could have alighted from the boat, for the boat was above ten handbreadths, where the prohibition of Shabbat limits does not apply.

אָמַר רָבָא: בִּמְהַלֶּכֶת בִּרְקָק.

The Gemara answers that **Rava said:** The mishna refers to a case where the boat was **moving through** shallow, **swampy water** within ten handbreadths of the sea's bed.

תָּא שְׁמַע: הָנֵי שַׁב שְׁמַעְתָּא דְּאִיתְּאַמְרָן בְּצַפְרָא בְּשַׁבְּתָא קַמֵּיהּ דְּרַב חִסְדָּא בְּסוּרָא, בַּהֲדֵי פַּנְיָא בְּשַׁבְּתָא קַמֵּיהּ דְּרָבָא בְּפוּמְבְּדִיתָא.

The Gemara cites another proof: **Come** and **hear** a resolution from the incident involving **the seven teachings**[N] **that were** first **said on Shabbat morning before Rav Ḥisda in Sura** and then repeated **toward the conclusion of** that **Shabbat before Rava in Pumbedita,**[B] despite the fact that the distance between them is too great for someone to have traversed it on Shabbat.

מַאן אָמְרִינְהוּ? לָאו אֵלִיָּהוּ אָמְרִינְהוּ? אַלְמָא: אֵין תְּחוּמִין לְמַעְלָה מֵעֲשָׂרָה! לָא, דִּלְמָא יוֹסֵף שֵׁידָא אָמְרִינְהוּ.

Who said those teachings, and delivered them from one place to the other? Was it **not Elijah** the Prophet, who traveled from Sura to Pumbedita by way of a miraculous leap through the air above ten handbreadths from the ground, **who said them?**[N] **Apparently,** the prohibition of Shabbat **limits does not apply above ten** handbreadths, for Elijah would not have transgressed this prohibition. The Gemara rejects this argument: This is **no** proof; **perhaps Yosef the demon,**[N] who does not observe Shabbat, **reported these** teachings and brought them from Sura to Pumbedita.

תָּא שְׁמַע: הֲרֵינִי נָזִיר בַּיּוֹם שֶׁבֶּן דָּוִד בָּא – מוּתָּר לִשְׁתּוֹת יַיִן בְּשַׁבָּתוֹת וּבְיָמִים טוֹבִים,

The Gemara attempts to bring a different proof: **Come** and **hear** that which was taught in a *baraita*: With regard to one who said: **I will be a nazirite on the day that the son of David comes,** i.e., upon the arrival of the Messiah, **he is permitted to drink wine on Shabbat and Festivals,** for the Messiah will not arrive on one of those days.

HALAKHA

A boat in swampy water – **סְפִינָה בִּרְקָק**: A boat that is ten handbreadths above the bed of a river or the sea is not subject to the restrictions of Shabbat limits. One who is on such a boat on Shabbat may walk about the entire boat, even if it sails beyond the Shabbat limit (*Shulḥan Arukh*, *Oraḥ Ḥayyim* 404:1).

BACKGROUND

Sura and Pumbedita – **סוּרָא וּפוּמְבְּדִיתָא**: This map depicts the great distance between Sura and Pumbedita. Even via a direct aerial route, they are more than one hundred kilometers apart, a distance that a person cannot possibly walk in a single day.

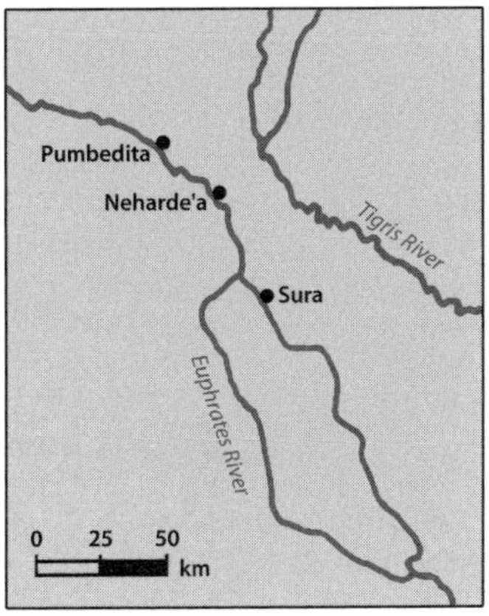

Map of Sura and Pumbedita region

NOTES

Seven teachings – **שַׁב שְׁמַעְתָּא**: The author of the *Me'iri* claims that these seven teachings are identical to the seven teachings mentioned in tractate *Ḥullin* (42b), all of which refer to the *halakhot* of animals with conditions that will cause them to die within twelve months [*tereifot*].

Was it not Elijah who said them – **לָאו אֵלִיָּהוּ אָמְרִינְהוּ**: The author of the *Me'iri* suggests that the Gemara is not referring here to Elijah the Prophet. Rather, it means that the person who taught these statements traveled quickly. He is referred to as Elijah due to the alacrity with which he performed his mission. The difficulty is that he traveled more than the length of two Shabbat limits, which could only take place above ten handbreadths. However, since the distance between Sura and Pumbedita is roughly one hundred kilometers by direct flight, it appears that the Gemara is indeed referring here to the Elijah the Prophet, who must have traveled by miraculous means.

Yosef the demon – **יוֹסֵף שֵׁידָא**: Yosef the demon and Yonatan the demon feature in another talmudic source as well. It is unclear in that context whether the reference is to the name of a demon or to a person who dealt with demons. Some commentaries explain that Yosef the demon did not transfer the teachings by actually traveling from one place to another. Rather, he possessed an apparatus that enabled him to transfer the information. Consequently, no proof can be brought from this case with regard to Shabbat limits (*Or Zarua*).

וְאָסוּר לִשְׁתּוֹת יַיִן כָּל יְמוֹת הַחוֹל.

However, he is prohibited to drink wine on all weekdays, in case the Messiah has come and he has not yet been informed.

אִי אָמְרַתְּ בִּשְׁלָמָא יֵשׁ תְּחוּמִין – הַיְינוּ דְּבְשַׁבָּתוֹת וּבְיָמִים טוֹבִים מוּתָּר. אֶלָּא אִי אָמְרַתְּ אֵין תְּחוּמִין, בְּשַׁבָּתוֹת וּבְיָמִים טוֹבִים אַמַּאי מוּתָּר?

The Gemara clarifies: **Granted, if you say that** the prohibition of Shabbat **limits applies** above ten handbreadths, **that is** why **on Shabbat and Festivals he is permitted** to drink wine, for the Messiah will certainly not arrive from outside the Shabbat limit on those days. **But if you say that** the prohibition of Shabbat **limits does not apply** above ten handbreadths, **why is he permitted** to drink wine **on Shabbat and Festivals?**

שָׁאנֵי הָתָם, דְּאָמַר קְרָא: ״הִנֵּה אָנֹכִי שֹׁלֵחַ לָכֶם אֵת אֵלִיָּה הַנָּבִיא וגו׳״ וְהָא לָא אֲתָא אֵלִיָּהוּ מֵאֶתְמוֹל.

The Gemara answers: **It is different there, as the verse stated: "Behold I will send you Elijah the prophet,** before the coming of the great and dreadful day of the Lord; and he shall turn the heart of the fathers to the children, and the heart of the children to their fathers" (Malachi 3:23–24). This verse teaches that Elijah will arrive the day before the coming of the Messiah. **Since Elijah did not come the previous day,** the Messiah will not come today, and therefore he may drink.

אִי הָכִי, בְּחוֹל כָּל יוֹמָא וְיוֹמָא נָמֵי לִישְׁתְּרֵי, דְּהָא לָא אֲתָא אֵלִיָּהוּ מֵאֶתְמוֹל! אֶלָּא אָמְרִינַן: לְבֵית דִּין הַגָּדוֹל אֲתָא. הָכָא נָמֵי – לֵימָא: לְבֵית דִּין הַגָּדוֹל אֲתָא!

The Gemara rejects this argument: **If so, on weekdays, too, he should be permitted** to drink wine **each and every day, as Elijah did not arrive the previous day. Rather,** the reason for the prohibition on weekdays must be that **we say** that Elijah may already have **arrived at the Great Court,** but it has not yet become a matter of public knowledge. Likewise, **here too we should say** that Elijah already **arrived** the previous day **at the Great Court,** on the eve of Shabbat or a Festival.

כְּבָר מוּבְטָח לָהֶן לְיִשְׂרָאֵל שֶׁאֵין אֵלִיָּהוּ בָּא לֹא בְּעַרְבֵי שַׁבָּתוֹת וְלֹא בְּעַרְבֵי יָמִים טוֹבִים מִפְּנֵי הַטּוֹרַח.

The Gemara answers: **It has already been promised to the Jewish people that Elijah will not come either on the eve of Shabbat or on the eve of a Festival, due to the trouble,** lest people go out to greet him and not have time to complete all their preparations for the sacred day.

קָא סָלְקָא דַּעְתָּךְ: מִדְּאֵלִיָּהוּ לָא אֲתָא – מָשִׁיחַ נָמֵי לָא אָתֵי, בְּמַעֲלֵי שַׁבְּתָא לִישְׁתְּרֵי! אֵלִיָּהוּ – לָא אָתֵי, מָשִׁיחַ אָתֵי. דְּכֵיוָן דְּאָתֵי מְשִׁיחָא – הַכֹּל עֲבָדִים הֵן לְיִשְׂרָאֵל.

The Gemara comments: **It might enter your mind** to say that **since Elijah will not come** on Shabbat eve due to the trouble involved, the **Messiah will also not come** then, and if so, **on Shabbat eve he should** also **be permitted** to drink wine. However, this reasoning is rejected: It is only **Elijah** who **will not arrive** on Shabbat eve, but the **Messiah** himself **may arrive,** for **once the Messiah comes, all** the nations **will be subservient to the Jewish people,** and they will help them prepare whatever is needed for Shabbat.

בְּחַד בְּשַׁבָּא לִישְׁתְּרֵי! לִפְשׁוֹט מִינַּהּ דְּאֵין תְּחוּמִין, דְּאִי יֵשׁ תְּחוּמִין – בְּחַד בְּשַׁבָּא לִישְׁתְּרֵי, דְּלָא אֲתָא אֵלִיָּהוּ בְּשַׁבָּת!

The Gemara raises a difficulty: **He should be permitted** to drink wine **on a Sunday,** for if Elijah cannot come on Shabbat, the Messiah will not come on a Sunday. **Let us resolve from here** that the prohibition of Shabbat **limits does not apply** above ten handbreadths, **as if** the prohibition of Shabbat **limits applies** above ten handbreadths, **on Sunday he should be permitted** to drink wine, **as Elijah cannot come on Shabbat.**

הַאי תַּנָּא סְפוֹקֵי מְסַפְּקָא לֵיהּ אִי יֵשׁ תְּחוּמִין אוֹ אֵין תְּחוּמִין, וּלְחוּמְרָא.

The Gemara answers: **This *tanna* was uncertain whether there is** a prohibition of Shabbat **limits** above ten handbreadths[H] **or** there is **no** prohibition of Shabbat **limits.** Therefore, he ruled **stringently** in this regard concerning Sunday.

דְּקָאֵי אֵימַת דְּקָא נָדַר? אִילֵימָא דְּקָאֵי בְּחוֹל – כֵּיוָן דְּחָל עֲלֵיהּ נְזִירוּת, הֵיכִי אָתְיָא שַׁבְּתָא וּמַפְקָעָא לֵיהּ?

The Gemara poses a question: **When did** the person who took the vow of naziriteship **arise** and **take** his **vow? If you say he arose** and took his vow **on a weekday, since** the vow of **naziriteship** already **took effect, how can Shabbat come and annul it?**[N] Naziriteship cannot take effect one day and be annulled on the next; rather, once it applies, it remains in effect for the entire period of his vow.

אֶלָּא דְּקָאֵי בְּשַׁבְּתָא, וְקָא נָדַר, וּבְיוֹם טוֹב וְקָא נָדַר, וְהַהוּא יוֹמָא דְּשָׁרֵי לֵיהּ, מִיכָּן וְאֵילָךְ – אָסִיר לֵיהּ.

Rather, it must be that **he arose on Shabbat and took** his **vow, or** else he arose **on a Festival and took** his **vow,** and it is only on **that day that he is permitted** to drink wine, as the Messiah will not come; but **from that day on he is prohibited** to drink wine, for once the naziriteship takes effect on a weekday, it remains in effect from that point onwards, even on Shabbat and Festivals.[H]

״פַּעַם אַחַת לֹא נִכְנְסוּ לַנָּמֵל וכו׳״.

It was taught in the mishna: On **one occasion, they did not enter the port**[N] until after nightfall on Shabbat eve, and they asked Rabban Gamliel whether they were permitted to alight from the boat. He told them that they were permitted to alight, for he had been watching, and he knew that they had entered within the city's limit before nightfall, and therefore they may walk throughout the city.

HALAKHA

Shabbat limits above ten handbreadths – **תְּחוּמִין לְמַעְלָה מֵעֲשָׂרָה**: The question of whether or not the prohibition of Shabbat limits applies above ten handbreadths is left unresolved by the Gemara. Consequently, anywhere that the prohibition is at most rabbinic, i.e., on the sea, on a river, or less than twelve *mil* from the location where one established Shabbat residence, the prohibition of Shabbat limits does not apply above ten handbreadths. Anywhere that the prohibition might be a Torah law, i.e., more than twelve *mil* from the location where one established Shabbat residence, one should be stringent (*Shulḥan Arukh, Oraḥ Ḥayyim* 404).

A nazirite at the time of the coming of the Messiah – **נְזִיר בְּעֵת בִּיאַת הַמָּשִׁיחַ**: If one took a vow to be a nazirite at the time of the coming of the Messiah on a weekday, the vow of naziriteship takes effect immediately and applies to him forever. If he took the vow on a Shabbat or a Festival, he only becomes a nazirite from the following day (Rambam *Sefer Hafla'a, Hilkhot Nezirut* 4:11).

NOTES

Can Shabbat come and annul it – **אָתְיָא שַׁבְּתָא וּמַפְקָעָא לֵיהּ**: Although Rashi explains this discussion differently, most early commentaries agree that the passage should be understood in accordance with the regular *halakhot* of naziriteship. Since naziriteship cannot take effect for just one day, and one who vows to be a nazirite without specifying the duration assumes nazirite obligations for a minimum of thirty days, it is impossible for Shabbat to release a person from a vow of being a nazirite. *Tosafot* offer a different reason: The person vowed on a day when the Messiah could possibly arrive, in which case his naziriteship would take effect on that day. Consequently, when Shabbat arrives, even though it is a day on which the Messiah cannot arrive, it cannot retroactively nullify the effect of his possibly becoming a nazirite.

On one occasion, they did not enter the port – **פַּעַם אַחַת לֹא נִכְנְסוּ לַנָּמֵל**: In the Jerusalem Talmud the following question is raised: According to Rabban Gamliel, why was it critical that they arrived before nightfall? Even if they entered the port after nightfall, they should still be permitted to walk two thousand cubits from it, like one who entered a pen or a stable. The answer is that the port in question was not surrounded by walls. In the Babylonian Talmud this issue is not discussed, apparently because the Gemara maintains that Rabban Gamliel measured the distance not for his own sake, but to assist his colleagues, Rabbi Yehoshua and Rabbi Akiva, who would disembark only if they had arrived within the city limits before Shabbat (Rashba; Ritva).

תָּנָא: שְׁפוֹפֶרֶת הָיְתָה לוֹ לְרַבָּן גַּמְלִיאֵל שֶׁהָיָה מַבִּיט וְצוֹפֶה בָּהּ אַלְפַּיִם אַמָּה בַּיַּבָּשָׁה, וּכְנֶגְדָּהּ אַלְפַּיִם בַּיָּם.

In order to clarify this issue, the Gemara cites that which was **taught** in a *baraita*: **Rabban Gamliel had a** special **tube**[B] **through which he would look and see** a distance of **two thousand cubits on land, and** also determine **a corresponding** distance of **two thousand cubits at sea.**

הָרוֹצֶה לֵידַע כַּמָּה עוּמְקוֹ שֶׁל גַּיְא מֵבִיא שְׁפוֹפֶרֶת וּמַבִּיט בָּהּ, וְיֵדַע כַּמָּה עוּמְקוֹ שֶׁל גַּיְא.

In general, **one who wishes to know the depth of a valley**[N] **can bring** such **a tube and look through it, and he will know the depth of the valley.**

וְהָרוֹצֶה לֵידַע כַּמָּה גּוֹבְהוֹ שֶׁל דֶּקֶל? מוֹדֵד קוֹמָתוֹ וְצִלּוֹ, וְצֵל קוֹמָתוֹ, וְיֵדַע כַּמָּה גּוֹבַהּ שֶׁל דֶּקֶל.

The Gemara cites another statement with regard to measurements: **One who wishes to know the height of a palm tree,** but does not want to actually climb the tree to measure it, **can measure his** own **height, and** the length of **his** own **shadow, and** the length of **the shadow of the height** of the palm tree, and calculate the proportions, **and he will know the height of the palm tree.**[B]

הָרוֹצֶה שֶׁלֹּא תִּשְׁרֶה חַיָּה רָעָה בְּצֵל קֶבֶר – נוֹעֵץ קָנֶה בְּאַרְבַּע שָׁעוֹת בַּיּוֹם, וְיִרְאֶה לְהֵיכָן צִלּוֹ נוֹטֶה, מְשַׁפֵּיעַ וְעוֹלֶה מְשַׁפֵּיעַ וְיוֹרֵד.

The Gemara cites related advice: If, out of honor for the dead, **one wishes that a wild beast should not rest in the shade of a grave, he should insert a reed** into the ground **at** the end of **the fourth hour of the day,** roughly ten o'clock in the morning, when it is hot in the sun and cooler in the shade, and beasts begin to seek shelter in the shade. **And** he should **observe in which direction the shadow** of the reed **inclines,** and then **slant** the gravestone **upwards and downwards** until he finds an angle at which it casts no shadow at that hour, and the beasts will not come to rest at the grave during the heat of the day.

נְחֶמְיָה בְּרֵיהּ דְּרַב חֲנִילַאי מְשַׁכְתֵּיהּ שְׁמַעְתָּא וּנְפַק חוּץ לַתְּחוּם. אֲמַר לֵיהּ רַב חִסְדָּא לְרַב נַחְמָן: נְחֶמְיָה תַּלְמִידָךְ שָׁרוּי בְּצַעַר.

The Gemara relates that **Neḥemya, son of Rav Ḥanilai, was** once so **engrossed in** his **learning** that he did not notice that **he was going out beyond** his Shabbat limit. **Rav Ḥisda said to Rav Naḥman: Your student Neḥemya is in distress,** as he is outside the Shabbat limit and cannot enter. What can we do for him?

אֲמַר לוֹ: עֲשֵׂה לוֹ מְחִיצָה שֶׁל בְּנֵי אָדָם וְיִכָּנֵס.

Rav Naḥman **said to him: Establish a human partition for him,**[NH] i.e., people who are permitted to go out there should line up and form human walls, through which he is permitted to walk and thereby **reenter** the Shabbat limit.

יָתֵיב רַב נַחְמָן בַּר יִצְחָק אֲחוֹרֵיהּ דְּרָבָא, וְיָתֵיב רָבָא קַמֵּיהּ דְּרַב נַחְמָן. אֲמַר לֵיהּ רַב נַחְמָן בַּר יִצְחָק לְרָבָא: מַאי קָא מִבַּעְיָא לֵיהּ לְרַב חִסְדָּא?

Rav Naḥman bar Yitzḥak sat behind Rava, and Rava sat in the first row **before Rav Naḥman. Rav Naḥman bar Yitzḥak said to Rava: What** precisely **was Rav Ḥisda's dilemma** that he addressed to Rav Naḥman with regard to Neḥemya's distress?

אִילֵימָא בְּדִמְלוֹ גַּבְרֵי עִסְקִינַן? וְקָא מִבַּעְיָא לֵיהּ: הִלְכְתָא כְּרַבָּן גַּמְלִיאֵל,

The Gemara explains: **If you say** that **we are dealing with** a case where the space between Neḥemya and the Shabbat limit could be **filled with people** who had established an *eiruv* and were permitted to go out beyond the Shabbat limit and establish a human partition for Neḥemya, **and** then it can be argued that **the dilemma** that **he raised** was: Is **the *halakha* in accordance with** the opinion of **Rabban Gamliel** that a person may walk throughout an enclosed area, although he had not established residence there before Shabbat while it was still day, and the same applies to a human partition of this kind;

BACKGROUND

Rabban Gamliel's tube – שְׁפוֹפֶרֶת שֶׁל רַבָּן גַּמְלִיאֵל: According to the *ge'onim* and the Rambam, Rabban Gamliel's tube refers to a geometrical measuring implement. It was a kind of precise protractor, similar to those used for astronomical measurements, i.e., a type of sextant, the early form of which was known as an astrolabe. By using it to find the angle between two surfaces, one can calculate angles with great precision, as well as perform reliable approximations of distances. In fact, a similar surveying implement is used even nowadays for most measurements required for mapping.

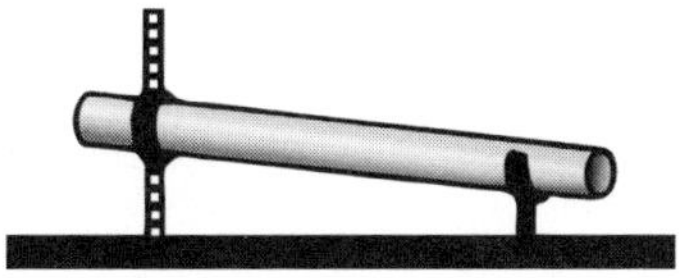

Sketch of a tube similar to the one used by Rabban Gamliel

A palm tree and its shadow – דֶּקֶל וְצִלּוֹ: The height of a palm tree can easily be measured by first determining the ratio between the height of a reed to the length of its shadow. Then, the shadow of the palm is measured, and its height can be calculated proportionally.

Reed, palm tree, and their respective shadows

HALAKHA

A human partition – מְחִיצָה שֶׁל בְּנֵי אָדָם: If someone unknowingly overstepped his Shabbat limit, it is permitted to line up a row of people who are allowed to walk there to serve as a partition, thereby allowing him to reenter his limit, as stated by Rav Naḥman (*Shulḥan Arukh, Oraḥ Ḥayyim* 405:4).

NOTES

One who wishes to know the depth of a valley – הָרוֹצֶה לֵידַע כַּמָּה עוּמְקוֹ שֶׁל גַּיְא: This statement is cited only incidentally. Since reference was made to Rabban Gamliel's special tube and its capabilities, the Gemara also mentions other ways that such a tube can be used for measurement, as well as other simple methods for calculating indirectly, i.e., without actually measuring the distances (*Me'iri*).

A human partition – מְחִיצָה שֶׁל בְּנֵי אָדָם: Rashi teaches that this partition was formed by people who had established a joining of boundaries [*eiruv*], allowing them to go out beyond the Shabbat limit. However, it is possible to explain that the partition was made by gentiles, who are not bound by the restrictions of Shabbat limits, and who can also form a partition in this manner (Rabbeinu Yehonatan).

אוֹ אֵין הֲלָכָה כְּרַבָּן גַּמְלִיאֵל? אוֹ דִּילְמָא: בִּדְלָא מְלוֹ גַּבְרֵי עָסְקִינַן, וְקָא מִבַּעְיָא לֵיהּ: הֲלָכָה כְּרַבִּי אֱלִיעֶזֶר אוֹ אֵין הֲלָכָה כְּרַבִּי אֱלִיעֶזֶר?

or is the ***halakha*** **not in accordance with** the opinion of **Rabban Gamliel? Or perhaps we are dealing with** a case where the space between Neḥemya and the Shabbat limit could **not be filled with people** who had established an *eiruv* and were permitted to establish a human partition for Neḥemya. In that case, there were enough people to establish partitions from where Neḥemya was standing to within two cubits from the limit, **and** the dilemma that Rav Ḥisda **raised** was: **Is the** ***halakha*** **in accordance with** the opinion of **Rabbi Eliezer,** who says that someone who went two cubits outside of his Shabbat limit may reenter it, **or is** the ***halakha*** **not in accordance with** the opinion of **Rabbi Eliezer?**[N]

פְּשִׁיטָא, בִּדְלָא מְלוֹ גַּבְרֵי עָסְקִינַן. דְּאִי סָלְקָא דַּעְתָּךְ בִּדְמְלוֹ גַּבְרֵי עָסְקִינַן – מַאי תִּיבְּעֵי לֵיהּ? הָאָמַר רַב: הֲלָכָה כְּרַבָּן גַּמְלִיאֵל בְּדִיר וְסַהַר וּסְפִינָה! אֶלָּא וַדַּאי: בִּדְלָא מְלוֹ גַּבְרֵי עָסְקִינַן, וּדְרַבִּי אֱלִיעֶזֶר קָמִיבַּעְיָא לֵיהּ.

The Gemara answers: This is **obvious that we are dealing with** a case where the space between Neḥemya and the Shabbat limit could **not be filled with people, as if it should enter your mind that we are dealing with** a case where the space between Neḥemya and the Shabbat limit could be fully **filled with people, what is** Rav Ḥisda's **dilemma? Didn't Rav say:** The ***halakha*** **is in accordance with** the opinion of **Rabban Gamliel with regard to a pen, a stable, and a boat? Rather,** we must be **dealing with** a case where the space between Neḥemya and the Shabbat limit could **not be filled with people, and** the dilemma that **he raised was** about the ruling **of Rabbi Eliezer.**

דַּיְקָא נַמִי, דְּקָאָמַר לֵיהּ "יִכָּנֵס". מַאי "יִכָּנֵס", לָאו בְּלֹא מְחִיצָה?

The Gemara comments: **This** interpretation is **also precise** and implicit in Rav Naḥman's answer, **for** Rav Naḥman **said to** Rav Ḥisda: Establish a human partition for him, and **let him reenter** his Shabbat limit. **Doesn't** the statement: **Let him reenter,** mean that he may reenter even **without a partition** along those two additional two cubits, i.e., that after he passes through the human partitions, he would still need to cross the remaining two cubits on his own without the benefit of a partition?

אֵיתִיבֵיהּ רַב נַחְמָן בַּר יִצְחָק לְרָבָא: נָפַל דּוֹפְנָהּ – לֹא יַעֲמִיד בָּהּ אָדָם בְּהֵמָה וְכֵלִים, וְלֹא יִזְקוֹף אֶת הַמִּטָּה לִפְרוֹס עָלֶיהָ סָדִין – לְפִי שֶׁאֵין עוֹשִׂין אֹהֶל עֲרַאי בַּתְּחִילָּה בְּיוֹם טוֹב, וְאֵין צָרִיךְ לוֹמַר בְּשַׁבָּת.

Rav Naḥman bar Yitzḥak raised an objection to the opinion of **Rava** with regard to the principle of making a human partition on Shabbat, from a *baraita*: **If the wall** of a *sukka* **fell** on a Festival or on Shabbat, thus rendering the *sukka* unfit for the mitzva, **one may not position people, animals or utensils there** in its place in order to form a wall, **nor may one turn a bed upright in order to spread a sheet over it,** which will thereby serve as a partition, **because one may not make a temporary tent for the first** time **on a Festival, and, needless to say,** this is prohibited **on Shabbat.** This indicates that a human partition may not be erected on Shabbat.

אֲמַר לֵיהּ: אַתְּ אָמְרַתְּ לִי מֵהָא, וַאֲנָא אָמִינָא לָךְ מֵהָא: עוֹשֶׂה אָדָם אֶת חֲבֵירוֹ דּוֹפֶן כְּדֵי שֶׁיֹּאכַל וְיִשְׁתֶּה וְיִשַׁן, וְיִזְקוֹף אֶת הַמִּטָּה, וְיִפְרוֹס עָלֶיהָ סָדִין כְּדֵי שֶׁלֹּא תִּפּוֹל חַמָּה עַל הַמֵּת וְעַל הָאוֹכָלִין.

Rava **said to him: You state to me** that this is prohibited **from this** *baraita*, **but I** can **state to you** that it is permitted **from this** other *baraita*: **A person may position his fellow as a wall,**[H] **so that he may eat, drink, and sleep** in a *sukka*, **and** he is likewise permitted to **turn a bed upright** in order to **spread a sheet over it, so that the sun should not beat down on a corpse, or on food.**

קַשְׁיָין אַהֲדָדֵי! לָא קַשְׁיָא; הָא – רַבִּי אֱלִיעֶזֶר, הָא – רַבָּנַן. דִּתְנַן: פְּקָק הַחַלּוֹן, רַבִּי אֱלִיעֶזֶר אוֹמֵר: בִּזְמַן שֶׁקָּשׁוּר וְתָלוּי – פּוֹקְקִין בּוֹ, וְאִם לָאו – אֵין פּוֹקְקִין בּוֹ. וַחֲכָמִים אוֹמְרִים: בֵּין כָּךְ וּבֵין כָּךְ פּוֹקְקִין בּוֹ.

The Gemara comments: If so, these two *baraitot* **contradict one another.**[N] The Gemara answers: This is **not difficult; this** *baraita* that teaches that it is prohibited reflects the opinion of **Rabbi Eliezer,** whereas **this** other *baraita* that teaches that it is permitted reflects the opinion of **the Rabbis. As we learned** in a mishna: With regard to **a window shutter**[N] that is not fixed to the wall with hinges, **Rabbi Eliezer says: If it is tied** to the wall **and hangs** from the window, **one may shut** the window **with it; but if not, one may not shut** the window **with it,** since one may not erect a tent, even a temporary one, on Shabbat. **But the Rabbis say: In either case, one may shut** the window **with it.** This indicates that the Rabbis permit constructing a temporary wall of this sort on Shabbat, and they also permit the construction of a temporary wall in the case of a *sukka*.

NOTES

Is the *halakha* not in accordance with the opinion of Rabbi Eliezer – הֲלָכָה כְּרַבִּי אֱלִיעֶזֶר אוֹ אֵין: The early commentaries note that the ruling that one can establish a human partition is justified only if one accepts the opinion of Rabban Gamliel on one issue as well as the opinion of Rabbi Eliezer on another. Namely, one must accept Rabban Gamliel's opinion with regard to one who spent Shabbat in a stable or a pen as well as Rabbi Eliezer's opinion with regard to incorporated boundaries (see *Tosafot* and Rashba).

Contradict one another – קַשְׁיָין אַהֲדָדֵי: Some commentaries explain this as a continuation of Rava's own words, i.e., he adds: Since these two *baraitot* appear to contradict each other, it is evident that this matter is subject to a dispute between the *tanna'im* (Ritva).

A window shutter – פְּקַק הַחַלּוֹן: According to Rava's first explanation, the mishna about a window shutter proves that, according to the opinion of the Rabbis, it is permitted to construct a temporary tent for the first time on Shabbat. Since an unattached shutter is comparable to a wall and the Rabbis permitted the shutter's use on Shabbat, this teaches that they permitted the construction of a similar wall on Shabbat.

HALAKHA

A person as the wall of a *sukka* – אָדָם כְּדוֹפֶן לַסּוּכָּה: A human being can serve as the wall of a *sukka*. If it is a Festival day, the person in question must not know that he is serving as a wall, since that would constitute a kind of permanent construction, which is prohibited on a Festival (*Taz*; *Shulḥan Arukh*, *Oraḥ Ḥayyim* 630:12).

וְהָא אִיתְּמַר עֲלָהּ, אָמַר רַבָּה בַּר בַּר חָנָה, אָמַר רַבִּי יוֹחָנָן: הַכֹּל מוֹדִים שֶׁאֵין עוֹשִׂין אֹהֶל עֲרַאי בַּתְּחִילָּה בְּיוֹם טוֹב, וְאֵין צָרִיךְ לוֹמַר בַּשַּׁבָּת. לֹא נֶחְלְקוּ אֶלָּא לְהוֹסִיף, שֶׁרַבִּי אֱלִיעֶזֶר אוֹמֵר: אֵין מוֹסִיפִין בְּיוֹם טוֹב, וְאֵין צָרִיךְ לוֹמַר בַּשַּׁבָּת. וַחֲכָמִים אוֹמְרִים: מוֹסִיפִין בַּשַּׁבָּת, וְאֵין צָרִיךְ לוֹמַר בְּיוֹם טוֹב!

The Gemara raises a difficulty: **But wasn't it stated with regard to this** dispute: **Rabba bar bar Ḥana said** that **Rabbi Yoḥanan said: All agree that one may not make a temporary tent**[H] **for the first** time **on a Festival, and, needless to say,** this is prohibited **on Shabbat.** The Rabbis and Rabbi Eliezer **disagree only with regard to adding** a temporary tent to a permanent structure, as in the case of a window shutter. **As Rabbi Eliezer says: One may not add** a temporary tent to a permanent structure even **on a Festival; and, needless to say,** this is prohibited **on Shabbat. And the Rabbis say: One may add** a temporary tent to a permanent structure **on Shabbat, and needless to say,** this is permitted **on a Festival.** This indicates that there is no opinion that grants license to construct a temporary wall for the first time.

אֶלָּא, לָא קַשְׁיָא; הָא – כְּרַבִּי מֵאִיר, הָא – כְּרַבִּי יְהוּדָה. דְּתַנְיָא: עֲשָׂאָהּ לַבְּהֵמָה דּוֹפֶן לַסּוּכָּה – רַבִּי מֵאִיר פּוֹסֵל, וְרַבִּי יְהוּדָה מַכְשִׁיר.

Rather, the Gemara resolves the contradiction differently: This is **not difficult,** as **this** *baraita* that permits the positioning of an animal or a person as a wall was taught **in accordance with** the opinion of **Rabbi Meir,** and **this** *baraita* that prohibits it was taught **in accordance with** the opinion of **Rabbi Yehuda. As it was taught** in a *baraita*: With regard to **one who positions an animal** to serve **as the wall of a** ***sukka,***[H] **Rabbi Meir deems it unfit,** out of concern that the animal might leave, whereas **Rabbi Yehuda deems it fit.**

רַבִּי מֵאִיר דְּקָא פָּסֵיל הָתָם – אַלְמָא: לֹא מְחִיצָה הִיא, הָכָא שָׁרֵי – דְּלָאו מִידֵּי קָא עָבֵיד.

Rabbi Meir, who deems the wall **unfit there,** with regard to a *sukka,* **apparently** holds that a partition established from a living creature **is not a partition** and he would **here,** in the case of Shabbat, rule that it is **permitted** to construct such a wall, as **he is not doing anything,** since it is not considered actual construction.

וְרַבִּי יְהוּדָה דְּקָא מַכְשִׁיר הָתָם – אַלְמָא: מְחִיצָה הִיא, הָכָא אָסַר.

However, **Rabbi Yehuda, who deems** the wall **to be fit there,** with regard to a *sukka,* **apparently** holds that it **is a proper partition;** and he would **here,** in the case of Shabbat, **prohibit** the construction of such a partition.

וְתִיסְבְּרָא?! אֵימַר דְּשָׁמְעַתְּ לֵיהּ לְרַבִּי מֵאִיר בְּהֵמָה, אָדָם וְכֵלִים מִי שָׁמְעַתְּ לֵיהּ?!

The Gemara raises a difficulty: **And** how can **you understand** it in that manner? **Say that you heard that Rabbi Meir** deemed the *sukka* to be unfit in the case where **an animal** was used to serve as a partition, but **did you hear** that he deemed the *sukka* to be similarly unfit if **a person or utensils** were used as walls? The reason that an animal may not be used as a partition, according to his opinion, is because it might leave. This concern does not apply to people or utensils, since a person is under his own control and can remain standing, and utensils do not move themselves. Since the *baraita* validates partitions established with people and utensils as well as animals, it cannot be based on the opinion of Rabbi Meir.

וְתוּ, רַבִּי מֵאִיר אַלִּיבָּא דְּמַאן? אִי אַלִּיבָּא דְּרַבִּי אֱלִיעֶזֶר – לְהוֹסִיף נַמִי אָסַר!

And furthermore, even if you do not differentiate as above, and instead assume that the consideration that the animal might leave is pertinent, **according to whose** opinion does **Rabbi Meir** state his opinion[N] with regard to constructing a temporary tent on Shabbat? **If** it is **according to** the opinion of his teacher **Rabbi Eliezer,** this is difficult, as **he even prohibited adding** a window shutter, i.e., a temporary tent, to a permanent structure.

אֶלָּא אַלִּיבָּא דְּרַבָּנַן – אֵימַר דְּאָמְרִי רַבָּנַן לְהוֹסִיף, לְכַתְּחִילָּה מִי אֲמוּר?!

Rather, you must say that he stated his opinion **in accordance with** the opinion of **the Rabbis.** However, even according to their opinion, **say that the Rabbis** only **said** that one is permitted **to add** a temporary tent to a permanent structure; but **did they say that** it is permitted to construct a partition or a tent **for the first time?**

אֶלָּא: הָא וְהָא רַבָּנַן, וְכֵלִים אַכֵּלִים לָא קַשְׁיָא; הָא – בְּדוֹפֶן שְׁלִישִׁית, הָא – בְּדוֹפֶן רְבִיעִית.

Rather, say that both **this** *baraita* **and that** *baraita* follow the opinion of **the Rabbis,** and this is the resolution of the various contradictions: With regard to the contradiction between the one ruling concerning **utensils** and the other ruling concerning **utensils,** this is **not difficult,** as **this** ruling that prohibits the construction of an additional wall refers **to the third wall** of a *sukka,* which renders it fit for the mitzva; whereas **this** other ruling that permits the construction of an additional wall refers **to the fourth wall** of a ***sukka,***[H] which is insignificant, as a *sukka* need not have four walls.

HALAKHA

A temporary tent – אֹהֶל עֲרַאי: One may not erect a temporary tent on Shabbat or a Festival, in accordance with the opinion of Rabbi Yoḥanan. However, one is permitted to add to a temporary tent and expand it, if it was already partly constructed and was at least a handbreadth wide the day before, in accordance with the opinion of the Rabbis (*Shulḥan Arukh, Oraḥ Ḥayyim* 315:1).

An animal as the wall of a ***sukka*** **– בְּהֵמָה דּוֹפֶן לַסּוּכָּה:** One is permitted to utilize an animal as the wall of a *sukka*, but only if it is tied so that it will not leave, and provided it will not shrink if it dies, in accordance with the opinion of Rabbi Yehuda (*Shulḥan Arukh, Oraḥ Ḥayyim* 630:11).

The fourth wall of a ***sukka*** **– דוֹפֶן רְבִיעִית בְּסוּכָּה:** A fourth wall of a *sukka*, or other walls that are not fixed permanently in place or do not serve to deem a *sukka* fit, may be erected in a temporary manner on a Shabbat or a Festival. In addition, it is permitted to instruct a person to stand in a position where he will serve as a wall that does not make the structure fit for a *sukka* or some other purpose, even if he knows that he is serving as a wall (*Shulḥan Arukh, Oraḥ Ḥayyim* 315:1 and 630:12, in the comment of the Rema).

NOTES

According to whose opinion does Rabbi Meir state his opinion – רַבִּי מֵאִיר אַלִּיבָּא דְּמַאן: This question is not generally asked with regard to the opinion of a *tanna*, as later *tanna'im* have the authority to dispute earlier *tanna'im*. Indeed, the question in this context does not concern his position vis-à-vis the opinion of a particular Sage. Rather, the question relates to his opinion on the issue of constructing a temporary wall on Shabbat. Since this question is a matter of dispute among *tanna'im*, the Gemara formulates the question so as to clarify which of these opinions Rabbi Meir accepts.

דִּיקָא נַמִי, דְּקָתָנֵי ״נָפַל דּוֹפְנָהּ״, שְׁמַע מִינָּהּ.

This interpretation **is also precise** in the wording of the *baraita*, **as the** *baraita* that prohibits the construction of an additional wall uses the following phrase: **If its wall fell.** This indicates a wall that is significant, i.e., a wall that renders it fit for use, rather than any wall, as stated in the *baraita* that permits it. The Gemara concludes: **Learn from this** that the correct resolution is to differentiate between the third and fourth wall of a *sukka*.

אֶלָּא אָדָם אַאָדָם קַשְׁיָא!

However, with regard to the contradiction between the one ruling concerning **a person** and the other ruling concerning **a person,** it is **difficult,** for one *baraita* states that one may not use a person as the wall of a *sukka*, while the other says that one may use a person as a wall and even states explicitly that he may do this: So that he may eat, drink and sleep in the *sukka*. That implies that this is permitted even if it is the third wall that is missing.

אָדָם אַאָדָם נַמִי לָא קַשְׁיָא; כָּאן – לָדַעַת, כָּאן – שֶׁלֹּא מִדַּעַת.

The Gemara answers: With regard to the contradiction between the one ruling concerning **a person** and the other ruling concerning **a person,** it is **also not difficult. Here,** where it is prohibited, the *baraita* refers to a case where that person **knowingly** served as a partition; whereas **here,** where it is permitted, it refers to a case where that person **unknowingly**[N] served as a partition, which is not the usual manner of building. This is not the case with regard to utilizing a utensil as a partition. Since the utensil lacks knowledge, it is considered a partition regardless of how it is placed, and it is prohibited in all cases.

וְהָא דְּרַבִּי נְחֶמְיָה בְּרֵיהּ דְּרַבִּי חֲנִילַאי לָדַעַת הֲוָה! שֶׁלֹּא מִדַּעַת הֲוָה.

The Gemara raises a difficulty: **However,** the case involving **Rabbi Neḥemya, son of Rabbi Ḥanilai, was** a case where people **knowingly** served as a partition, as the people were instructed to go out and serve as a human partition. The Gemara answers: In fact, that **was** a case where people **unknowingly** served as a partition, i.e., they were unaware why they were called, and were made into a partition without their knowledge.

רַב חִסְדָּא מִיהָא לָדַעַת הֲוָה! רַב חִסְדָּא שֶׁלֹּא מִן הַמִּנְיָן הֲוָה.

The Gemara asks: However, **Rav Ḥisda,** who gathered the people to that spot, **was in any case** present **knowingly.** The Gemara answers: While **Rav Ḥisda** was there knowingly, he **was not among the designated** people who served as a partition.

הָנְהוּ בְּנֵי גְנָנָא דְּאַעִילוּ מַיָּא בִּמְחִיצָה שֶׁל בְּנֵי אָדָם, נַגְדִּינְהוּ שְׁמוּאֵל. אָמַר: אִם אָמְרוּ שֶׁלֹּא מִדַּעַת יֹאמְרוּ לָדַעַת?!

The Gemara relates that there were **these members of a wedding** party who engaged the many people present **to bring water in** on Shabbat from a public domain to a private domain **through walls comprised of people** who knew that they were being used as partitions for that purpose. **Shmuel** instructed that **they** should **be flogged. He said** with regard to this matter: **If** the Sages **said** that a partition is effective when the people act **unknowingly,** does this mean that **they would** also **say** that this is permitted *ab initio* when they **knowingly** serve as a partition?

הָנְהוּ זִיקֵי דַּהֲוָה שָׁדְיָין בְּרִיסְתָּקָא דִּמְחוֹזָא, בַּהֲדֵי דְּאָתָא רָבָא מִפִּירְקֵיהּ אַעֲלִינְהוּ נִיהֲלֵיהּ. לְשַׁבְּתָא אַחֲרִיתִי בָּעֵי עַיְּילִינְהוּ. וַאֲסַר לְהוּ, דַּהֲוָה לֵיהּ כְּלָדַעַת, וְאָסוּר.

The Gemara relates that there **were** once **these flasks lying in the market** [*ristaka*][L] **of Meḥoza** on Shabbat and could not be moved. **When Rava was coming from his discourse** accompanied by a throng of people, his attendants **brought** the flasks **into his** house, as the crowd of people created human partitions, upon which the attendants capitalized for this purpose. **On another Shabbat they wanted to bring them in** again, **but** Rava **prohibited them** from doing so, reasoning: **This is like** the case where the people **knowingly** served as partitions, for presumably the people now knew that they were being used for this purpose, **and it is** therefore **prohibited.**[N]

לֵוִי אַעִילוּ לֵיהּ תִּיבְנָא, זְעֵירִי אַסְפַּסְתָּא, רַב שִׁימִי בַּר חִיָּיא מַיָּא.

The Gemara further relates that **Levi was brought straw** through human partitions comprised of people who were unknowingly used for this purpose, and in the same manner **Ze'eiri** was brought **fodder** [*aspasta*],[L] and **Rav Shimi bar Ḥiyya** was brought **water.**[H]

NOTES

Knowingly and unknowingly – לָדַעַת וְשֶׁלֹּא מִדַּעַת: There are different explanations as to why a human partition cannot be established on Shabbat with the knowledge of the participants. Some commentaries explain that a person who knows that he is being used as a partition attains the status of a permanent partition. Only a person who becomes a partition without intending to do so is considered to be a temporary structure (see Rashi and Rashba). Other authorities explain that the prohibition does not stem from the construction of a partition; rather, it is a desecration of the honor of Shabbat. If a person knowingly becomes a partition, then the public interprets this as a desecration of Shabbat. Consequently, it is prohibited (*Me'iri*).

The flasks of Meḥoza – זִיקֵי דִּמְחוֹזָא: The commentaries discuss the question of whether the flasks belonged to Rava, linking this question to a dispute with regard to the requirement that people establishing a partition do so unknowingly. Some authorities rule that the requirement that people who establish a partition be involved unknowingly only applies to the people who establish the partition, while others rule that the person who would derive benefit from the partition also needs to be unaware of its establishment. According to the latter approach, it is necessary to explain that Rav Neḥemya, the son of Rav Ḥanilai, was also unaware that the human partition was established for his sake (*Maggid Mishne*).

LANGUAGE

Market [*ristaka*] – רִיסְתָּקָא: This word is derived from Iranian and is related to the Middle Persian rastag, meaning a row of shops, and the New Persian rustāq, meaning market.

Fodder [*aspasta*] – אַסְפַּסְתָּא: From the Middle Persian aspast, which is derived from the Old Persian words asp, meaning horse, and asti, meaning fodder.

HALAKHA

A human partition – מְחִיצָה שֶׁל בְּנֵי אָדָם: It is only permitted to establish a human partition if the people involved are unknowingly used as a partition. If they know, or are likely to know, it is prohibited. This principle applies to Shabbat. On weekdays, with regard to other *halakhot* that require a partition, it is permitted to establish a human partition with the knowledge of the participants. Some authorities rule that not only must the people who form the partition be involved unknowingly, but the one who benefits from it must also be involved unknowingly (Rambam). Furthermore, one may not make use of the same people to create a human partition a second time, as by the second time they presumably know that they are involved. In addition, they may not be lined up in a row, for then they would certainly understand what is happening (*Shulḥan Arukh HaRav*; *Shulḥan Arukh*, *Oraḥ Ḥayyim* 362:5, 7 and 630:12).

מתני׳ מִי שֶׁיָּצָא בִּרְשׁוּת וְאָמְרוּ לוֹ ״כְּבָר נַעֲשָׂה מַעֲשֶׂה״ – יֵשׁ לוֹ אַלְפַּיִם אַמָּה לְכָל רוּחַ.

MISHNA With regard to **one who was permitted to leave** his Shabbat limit,[H] i.e., he went out to testify that he had seen the new moon or for some life-saving purpose, **and they said to him** along the way: **The action has already been performed,** and there is no need for you to travel for that purpose, **he has two thousand cubits in each direction** from the location where he was standing when this was told to him.

אִם הָיָה בְּתוֹךְ הַתְּחוּם – כְּאִילּוּ לֹא יָצָא. כָּל הַיּוֹצְאִים לְהַצִּיל חוֹזְרִין לִמְקוֹמָן.

If he was within his original **limit,** it is considered **as if he had not left** his limit, and he may return to his original location. The Sages formulated a principle: **All who go out to** battle and **save** lives **may return to their** original **locations** on Shabbat.

גמ׳ מַאי ״אִם הָיָה בְּתוֹךְ הַתְּחוּם כְּאִילּוּ לֹא יָצָא״? אָמַר רַבָּה, הָכִי קָאָמַר: אִם הָיָה בְּתוֹךְ תְּחוּם שֶׁלּוֹ – כְּאִילּוּ לֹא יָצָא מִתּוֹךְ בֵּיתוֹ דָּמֵי.

GEMARA The Gemara asks: **What is** the meaning of the statement: **If he was within** his original **limit, it is** considered **as if he had never left?** Given that he has not left his original boundary, it is clear that he remains within his original limit. **Rabba said:** The mishna **is saying as follows: If he was within his** original **limit, it is** considered **as if he had never left his house.** He is allowed to walk two thousand cubits in each direction from his house.

פְּשִׁיטָא! מַהוּ דְּתֵימָא: הוֹאִיל וְעָקַר עָקַר, קָא מַשְׁמַע לָן.

The Gemara asks: It is **obvious** that if he remained within his limit, he is considered as if he were in his house. Why is this statement necessary? The Gemara answers: **Lest you say** that, **since he moved** from his place with intention to leave his limit and go elsewhere, **he moved** and nullified his original place of residence. If so, his original place of residence would no longer determine his Shabbat limit, and instead he would have two thousand cubits in each direction from the location where he was standing when he was told that he need not travel. Therefore, the mishna **teaches us** that it is nonetheless considered as if he had never left his house.

רַב שִׁימִי בַּר חִיָּיא אָמַר, הָכִי קָאָמַר: אִם הָיוּ תְּחוּמִין שֶׁנָּתְנוּ לוֹ חֲכָמִים מוּבְלָעִין בְּתוֹךְ הַתְּחוּם שֶׁלּוֹ – כְּאִילּוּ לֹא יָצָא מִתְּחוּמוֹ.

Rav Shimi bar Ḥiyya said that the mishna is **saying as follows: If** he left his original Shabbat limit, but **the** new **limit** of two thousand cubits in each direction **that the Sages granted him is subsumed within his** original **limit,** so that if he walks those two thousand cubits, he can return to within his original limit, then **it is as if he had never left his** original **limit,** and he may return to his house.

בְּמַאי קָמִיפַּלְגִי? מָר סָבַר: הַבְלָעַת תְּחוּמִין מִילְּתָא הִיא, וּמָר סָבַר: לָאו מִילְּתָא הִיא.

The Gemara comments: **With regard to what** principle **do** Rabba and Rav Shimi bar Ḥiyya **disagree?** One **Sage,** Rav Shimi, **holds** that **the subsuming of** Shabbat **limits,** i.e., if one's original limit is subsumed within the new limit, one may pass from one to the other, **is something** significant and may be relied upon, whereas this **Sage,** Rabba, **holds** that **it is nothing** significant and cannot be relied upon.

אָמַר לֵיהּ אַבָּיֵי לְרַבָּה: וְאַתְּ לָא תִּסְבְּרָא דְּהַבְלָעַת תְּחוּמִין מִילְּתָא הִיא? וּמָה אִילּוּ שָׁבַת בִּמְעָרָה, שֶׁבְּתוֹכָהּ אַרְבַּעַת אֲלָפִים וְעַל גַּגָּהּ פָּחוֹת מֵאַרְבַּעַת אֲלָפִים אַמָּה, לֹא נִמְצָא מְהַלֵּךְ אֶת כּוּלָּהּ וְחוּצָה לָהּ אַלְפַּיִם אַמָּה?

Abaye said to Rabba: Do you not hold that **the subsuming of** Shabbat **limits is something** significant? **And what if he established residence in a cave**[N] that has entrances at its two ends, which **on the inside** of the cave **is four thousand** cubits across, **but atop its roof** it **is less than four thousand cubits** across?[B] Is it **not the case that he may walk the entire** length of the roof **and two thousand cubits outside it** in either direction? The entire interior of the cave is considered as if it were four cubits, and he is permitted to walk another two thousand cubits in each direction from each of its entrances. Consequently, he is permitted to walk along the roof, two thousand cubits from the eastern entrance in the direction of the western entrance and vice versa. However, since the distance across the roof is less than four thousand cubits, these two limits are subsumed within one another, and he is permitted to walk the entire length of the roof, given that when two limits are subsumed within one another, one may pass from one to the other.

HALAKHA

One who was permitted to leave his Shabbat limit – מִי שֶׁיָּצָא מִתְּחוּמוֹ בִּרְשׁוּת: If a person is permitted to leave his Shabbat limit, for example, to rescue or to heal someone, and is informed while en route that his assistance is not needed, he is permitted to walk two thousand cubits in any direction from the location where he stood when he was informed. If these two thousand cubits overlap with the two thousand cubits of his original limit, he may enter and proceed as though he had not left. The *halakha* is in accordance with the opinion of Rabbi Shimi bar Ḥiyya, since with regard to Rava's opinion there is an unresolved difficulty (Rif; Rosh; *Shulḥan Arukh, Oraḥ Ḥayyim* 407:2).

NOTES

Established residence in a cave – שָׁבַת בִּמְעָרָה: Apparently, all the Sages agreed with this ruling since it constitutes the foundation of Abaye's query, and Rabba's response does not indicate that he rejects it (*Ge'on Ya'akov*).

Several explanations have been offered for this *halakha*. Some commentaries explain that even if the roof of the cave is less than two thousand cubits long, when he walks beyond the roof, he can still walk a little more than two thousand cubits, in accordance with the discrepancy between the roof and the floor of the cave. This is because the roof is also considered part of the cave (*Me'iri*). The Ra'avad maintains that the roof of the cave is considered as if it was within the cave for the purpose of all Shabbat measurements, and as though the inner partitions of the cave rose up to the sky. The other early commentaries, however, did not agree with him, and it appears that this claim is also rejected in the Jerusalem Talmud (Rashba; Ritva).

BACKGROUND

A cave and its roof – מְעָרָה וְגַגָּהּ: This diagram depicts a cave underneath a relatively flat hill, with entrances on both sides. Since the Shabbat limit is determined from each entrance to the cave, one is permitted to walk on the hill from a distance of two thousand cubits from each entrance, and across the entire roof of the cave. This is due to the fact that before one leaves the limit delineated by one entrance, one enters the limit delineated by the other entrance.

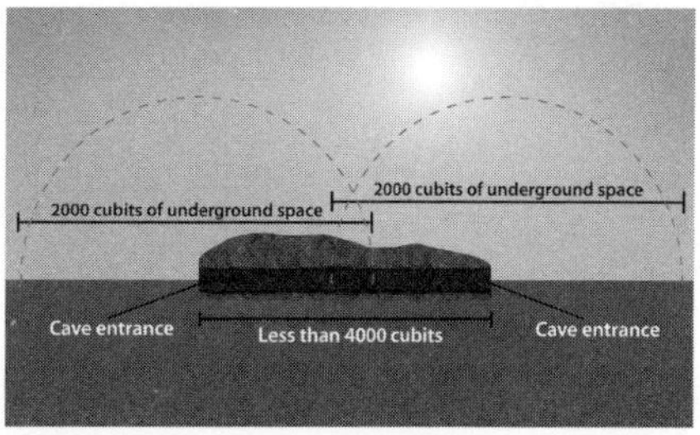

Cave with two entrances that are less than 4000 cubits apart

אֲמַר לֵיהּ: וְלָא שָׁנֵי לָךְ בֵּין הֵיכָא דִּשְׁבַת בַּאֲוִיר מְחִיצּוֹת מִבְּעוֹד יוֹם, לְהֵיכָא דְּלָא שָׁבַת בַּאֲוִיר מְחִיצּוֹת מִבְּעוֹד יוֹם?

Rabba **said to** Abaye: **Do you not distinguish between** a case **where** the person **established residence within the airspace of partitions** before Shabbat **while it was still day,** as in the case of the cave, **and** a case **where he did not establish residence within the airspace of partitions** before Shabbat **while it was still day,** as in the case of the mishna? The principle governing the Shabbat limits being subsumed in one another only applies in the former case, where both of the Shabbat limits were established before Shabbat, but not in the latter case, where the two limits were established at different times, one before Shabbat and one on Shabbat.

וְהֵיכָא דְּלָא שָׁבַת לָא?

Abaye raised a difficulty: **And** in a case **where he did not acquire** his place of residence within those partitions before Shabbat, does the principle governing the subsuming of limits **not** apply?

Perek **IV**
Daf **45** Amud **a**

HALAKHA

Those who are permitted to leave the limit – הַיּוֹצְאִים מִן הַתְּחוּם בִּרְשׁוּת: One who is permitted to travel beyond his Shabbat limit may travel two thousand cubits from his destination. If he reaches a town, he is considered an inhabitant of the town for the purpose of walking on Shabbat (*Shulḥan Arukh, Oraḥ Ḥayyim* 407:1).

NOTES

To save lives is different – לְהַצִּיל שָׁאנֵי: The Ritva explains that the Sages were certainly more lenient with one who went beyond the Shabbat limit for a lifesaving mission. However, the phrase: A person who was permitted to travel beyond his Shabbat limit, refers also to a midwife's attendance at a birth or to testimony with regard to the new month, where the same level of danger is not manifest.

וְהָתְנַן, רַבִּי אֱלִיעֶזֶר אוֹמֵר: שְׁתַּיִם יִכָּנֵס, שָׁלֹשׁ לֹא יִכָּנֵס. מַאי לָאו, רַבִּי אֱלִיעֶזֶר לְטַעְמֵיהּ, דְּאָמַר: וְהוּא בְּאֶמְצָעָן,

Didn't we learn in a mishna that **Rabbi Eliezer says:** If a person left his Shabbat limit by walking **two** cubits beyond it, **he may reenter** his original limit; but if he left his Shabbat limit by walking **three** cubits beyond it, **he may not reenter. What, is it not that Rabbi Eliezer follows his** standard line of **reasoning, in** that he **said** with regard to the four cubits a person is allotted wherever he is, he is set **in the middle of them,** i.e., he may walk two cubits in each direction?

וְאַרְבַּע אַמּוֹת דִּיהָבוּ לֵיהּ רַבָּנַן כְּמַאן דְּמִיבַלְעָן דָּמוּ, וְקָאָמַר ״יִכָּנֵס״, אַלְמָא: הַבְלָעַת תְּחוּמִין מִילְּתָא הִיא!

The Gemara explains that **the four cubits that the Sages gave** a person **are regarded** here **as being subsumed** within his original limit, **and** it is for this reason that **he said: He may reenter** his original limit. **Apparently** he is of the opinion that **the subsuming of** one Shabbat limit within another **is something** significant.

אֲמַר לֵיהּ רַבָּה בַּר בַּר חָנָה לְאַבָּיֵי: וּמִדְּרַבִּי אֱלִיעֶזֶר קָמוֹתְבַתְּ לֵיהּ לְמָר?! אֲמַר לֵיהּ: אִין, דִּשְׁמִיעַ לִי מִינֵּיהּ דְּמָר: עַד כָּאן לָא פְּלִיגִי רַבָּנַן עֲלֵיהּ דְּרַבִּי אֱלִיעֶזֶר – אֶלָּא לִדְבַר הָרְשׁוּת, אֲבָל לִדְבַר מִצְוָה – מוֹדוּ לֵיהּ.

Rabba bar bar Ḥana said to Abaye: Do you raise an objection against our Master, Rabba, **from** the statement of **Rabbi Eliezer?** But isn't the *halakha* in accordance with the opinion of Rabbi Eliezer? Abaye **said to him: Yes, as I heard from our Master** himself that **the Rabbis disagree with Rabbi Eliezer only** with regard to one who went beyond his limit **for a voluntary matter, but** with regard to one who went out **for a mitzva matter, they agree with him** about the subsuming of limits, i.e., that if one limit is subsumed in another, it is permitted to pass between them. This demonstrates that the *halakha* recognizes the principle of the subsuming of limits.

״וְכׇל הַיּוֹצְאִין לְהַצִּיל חוֹזְרִין לִמְקוֹמָן״. וַאֲפִילּוּ טוּבָא? וְהָא אָמְרַתְּ רֵישָׁא ״אַלְפַּיִם אַמָּה״ וְתוּ לָא!

The mishna teaches: **All who go out to save** lives **may return to their** original **locations** on Shabbat.[H] The Gemara asks: Does this mean that he may return to his original place **even** if he went out **more** than two thousand cubits beyond his limit? **Didn't the first clause say** that a person who was permitted to travel beyond his Shabbat limit is allotted **two thousand cubits, and no more?**

אָמַר רַב יְהוּדָה, אָמַר רַב: שֶׁחוֹזְרִין בִּכְלֵי זַיִין לִמְקוֹמָן. וּמַאי קוּשְׁיָא? דִּילְמָא לְהַצִּיל שָׁאנֵי?!

Rav Yehuda said that **Rav said:** What this means is **that they may return with** their **weapons to their** original **locations,** provided they are within two thousand cubits. The Gemara asks: **What is the difficulty** with returning home in this situation? **Perhaps** in the case where people went out **to** fight and **save** lives the law **is different,**[N] and they are allowed to go home even if they went more than two thousand cubits beyond the limit.

אֶלָּא אִי קַשְׁיָא הָא קַשְׁיָא: דִּתְנַן, בָּרִאשׁוֹנָה לֹא הָיוּ זָזִין מִשָּׁם כׇּל הַיּוֹם כּוּלּוֹ,

Rather, if there is a difficulty, this is the difficulty: As we learned in a mishna in tractate *Rosh HaShana,* **at first** they would take the witnesses who had come to Jerusalem from a distant place on Shabbat to testify that they had seen the new moon, and bring them into a special courtyard, **and they would not move from there the entire day.** This was in accordance with the law governing one who was permitted to go out beyond his limit, as once he fulfilled his mission, he was no longer permitted to move beyond four cubits.

הִתְקִין רַבָּן גַּמְלִיאֵל הַזָּקֵן שֶׁיְּהוּ לָהֶן אַלְפַּיִם אַמָּה לְכָל רוּחַ. וְלֹא אֵלּוּ בִּלְבַד אָמְרוּ, אֶלָּא אֲפִילּוּ חֲכָמָה הַבָּאָה לְיַלֵּד, וְהַבָּא לְהַצִּיל מִן הַגַּיִיס וּמִן הַנָּהָר וּמִן הַמַּפּוֹלֶת וּמִן הַדְּלֵיקָה – הֲרֵי הֵן כְּאַנְשֵׁי הָעִיר, וְיֵשׁ לָהֶן אַלְפַּיִם אַמָּה לְכָל רוּחַ.

However, **Rabban Gamliel the Elder instituted that they** should **have two thousand cubits in each direction,** so that witnesses not refrain from coming to testify. **And** it is **not only these** whom the Sages **said** are given two thousand cubits in the place that they have reached, **but even a midwife who comes to deliver** a child, **and one who comes to rescue** Jews **from** an invasion of gentile **troops or from a river or a collapsed building or a fire; they are like the inhabitants of the town** at which they arrive, **and they have two thousand cubits in each direction.**

וְתוּ לָא? וְהָא אָמְרַתְּ: כָּל הַיּוֹצְאִין לְהַצִּיל חוֹזְרִין לִמְקוֹמָן, אֲפִילּוּ טוּבָא!

The question may be raised: Are they given **no more** than two thousand cubits? **Didn't it say** in the mishna: **All who go out to save** lives **may return to their** original **locations** on Shabbat, which indicates that they may walk **even more** than two thousand cubits?

אָמַר רַב [יְהוּדָה, אָמַר רַב]: שֶׁחוֹזְרִין בִּכְלֵי זֵיינָן לִמְקוֹמָן. כִּדְתַנְיָא: בָּרִאשׁוֹנָה הָיוּ מַנִּיחִין כְּלֵי זֵיינָן בַּבַּיִת הַסָּמוּךְ לַחוֹמָה,

In response, **Rav Yehuda said** that **Rav said:** We must not infer from the mishna that they may go home even if they went out more than two thousand cubits from their limit, but rather **that they may return with** their **weapons**[H] **to their** original **locations,** provided that they are within two thousand cubits. **As it was taught** in the *Tosefta*: **At first** those returning from a rescue mission **would place their weapons in** the first house that they encountered upon their return, i.e., **the house nearest the wall,** to avoid carrying on Shabbat any more than necessary.

פַּעַם אַחַת הִכִּירוּ בָּהֶן אוֹיְבִים וְרָדְפוּ אַחֲרֵיהֶם, וְנִכְנְסוּ לִיטּוֹל כְּלֵי זֵיינָן, וְנִכְנְסוּ אוֹיְבִים אַחֲרֵיהֶן. דָּחֲקוּ זֶה אֶת זֶה, וְהָרְגוּ זֶה אֶת זֶה יוֹתֵר מִמַּה שֶּׁהָרְגוּ אוֹיְבִים. בְּאוֹתָהּ שָׁעָה הִתְקִינוּ שֶׁיְּהוּ חוֹזְרִין לִמְקוֹמָן בִּכְלֵי זֵיינָן.

Once, their **enemies noticed that they** were no longer carrying their weapons, **and** they **chased after them; and** the defenders **entered** the house **to take up their weapons** and fight, **and** their **enemies entered after them,** causing great confusion. In the chaos, the defenders began to **push one another, and** they **killed more of each other than** their **enemies killed** of them. **At that time** the Sages **instituted that they should return to their locations,** i.e., their destinations, **with their weapons.**

רַב נַחְמָן בַּר יִצְחָק אָמַר: לָא קַשְׁיָא; כָּאן – שֶׁנִּצְּחוּ יִשְׂרָאֵל אֶת אוּמּוֹת הָעוֹלָם, כָּאן – שֶׁנִּצְּחוּ אוּמּוֹת הָעוֹלָם אֶת עַצְמָן.

The Gemara cites an alternate resolution that **Rav Naḥman bar Yitzḥak said:** This is **not difficult. Here,** in the mishna in *Rosh HaShana* where they only permitted two thousand cubits, it is referring to a situation **where the Jews defeated the nations of the world,** i.e., the gentiles, in battle; in such a case there is no concern and they need not return to their original locations. Whereas **here,** in the mishna which indicates that the Sages permitted even more than two thousand cubits, it is referring to a situation **where the nations of the world defeated themselves,** i.e., the Jews, whom the Gemara refers to euphemistically as themselves; in such a case the Sages allowed the defeated soldiers to return to their original locations.

אָמַר רַב יְהוּדָה, אָמַר רַב: נָכְרִים שֶׁצָּרוּ עַל עֲיָירוֹת יִשְׂרָאֵל – אֵין יוֹצְאִין עֲלֵיהֶם בִּכְלֵי זֵיינָן, וְאֵין מְחַלְּלִין עֲלֵיהֶן אֶת הַשַּׁבָּת.

Since the Gemara discussed war on Shabbat, the Gemara cites **Rav Yehuda,** who **said** that **Rav said:** With regard to **gentiles who besieged Jewish towns, they may not go out** to fight **against them with their weapons, nor may they desecrate Shabbat** in any other way **due to them,** but rather they must wait until after Shabbat.

תַּנְיָא נַמִי הָכִי: נָכְרִים שֶׁצָּרוּ וכו׳. בַּמֶּה דְּבָרִים אֲמוּרִים – כְּשֶׁבָּאוּ עַל עִסְקֵי מָמוֹן. אֲבָל בָּאוּ עַל עִסְקֵי נְפָשׁוֹת – יוֹצְאִין עֲלֵיהֶן בִּכְלֵי זֵיינָן, וּמְחַלְּלִין עֲלֵיהֶן אֶת הַשַּׁבָּת.

That was also taught in a *baraita*, with a caveat: With regard to **gentiles who besieged, etc. In what** case **is this said?** It is said in a case **where** the gentiles **came** and besieged the town **with regard to monetary matters,** i.e., banditry. **However, if they came with regard to lives,** i.e., there is concern that the gentiles will attack, **they may go out against them with their weapons, and they may desecrate Shabbat due to them.**

וּבְעִיר הַסְּמוּכָה לַסְּפָר, אֲפִילּוּ לֹא בָּאוּ עַל עִסְקֵי נְפָשׁוֹת אֶלָּא עַל עִסְקֵי תֶּבֶן וָקַשׁ – יוֹצְאִין עֲלֵיהֶן בִּכְלֵי זֵיינָן, וּמְחַלְּלִין עֲלֵיהֶן אֶת הַשַּׁבָּת.

And with regard to a town that is located **near the border, even if** the gentiles **did not come with regard to lives, but** rather **with regard to matters of hay and straw,** i.e., to raid and spoil the town, **they may go out against them with their weapons, and they may desecrate Shabbat due to them,** as the border must be carefully guarded, in order to prevent enemies from gaining a foothold there.[H]

אָמַר רַב יוֹסֵף בַּר מַנְיוּמִי, אָמַר רַב נַחְמָן: וּבָבֶל כְּעִיר הַסְּמוּכָה לַסְּפָר דָּמְיָא. וְתַרְגּוּמָא – נְהַרְדְּעָא.

Rav Yosef bar Manyumi said that **Rav Naḥman said: And Babylonia is considered like a town** located **near the border,** and war may be waged there on Shabbat even if the gentiles came for financial gain. **And this means** the city of **Neharde'a,**[B] which was located near the border.

HALAKHA

Return with their weapons – חוֹזְרִים בִּכְלֵי זַיִין: Those who go beyond the Shabbat limit to rescue others are granted two thousand cubits from the place where they arrive. In a situation where there is fear of enemy reprisal, they may return to their original locations with their weapons (*Shulḥan Arukh, Oraḥ Ḥayyim* 407:3, 329:9).

War against gentiles on Shabbat – מִלְחָמָה בְּנׇכְרִים בְּשַׁבָּת: If foreign armies invade Jewish cities and lay siege to a town with intent to kill, or if their intention is uncertain (Rambam), the Jews may go to war against them, even if this entails the desecration of Shabbat. However, if the enemy's goal is strictly monetary gain, the defending Jews may not desecrate Shabbat. If the town is near the border, the Jews may go out and fight, even if the foreign army comes with the stated intention of plundering hay and straw, i.e., monetary gain. It is likewise permitted to wage a preemptive war on Shabbat, if there is reasonable intelligence that the gentiles are about to invade (Rema; *Shulḥan Arukh, Oraḥ Ḥayyim* 329:6).

BACKGROUND

Neharde'a – נְהַרְדְּעָא: The town of Neharde'a, located near the Euphrates River, was on the border of the Persian Empire for many years. It was conquered on several occasions by the Romans and by other bordering kingdoms.

דָּרַשׁ רַבִּי דּוֹסְתַּאי דְּמִן בִּירִי: מַאי דִּכְתִיב: ״וַיַּגִּידוּ לְדָוִד לֵאמֹר הִנֵּה פְלִשְׁתִּים נִלְחָמִים בִּקְעִילָה וְהֵמָּה שֹׁסִים אֶת הַגֳּרָנוֹת״.

Rabbi Dostai of the town **of Biri expounded: What is** the meaning **of that which is written: "And they told David, saying: Behold, the Philistines are fighting against Ke'ila,**[N] **and they rob the threshing floors"** (I Samuel 23:1), after which David asked God how he should respond.

תָּנָא: קְעִילָה עִיר הַסְּמוּכָה לַסְּפָר הָיְתָה, וְהֵם לֹא בָּאוּ אֶלָּא עַל עִסְקֵי תֶּבֶן וָקַשׁ. דִּכְתִיב: ״וְהֵמָּה שֹׁסִים אֶת הַגֳּרָנוֹת״, וּכְתִיב: ״וַיִּשְׁאַל דָּוִד בַּה׳ לֵאמֹר הַאֵלֵךְ וְהִכֵּיתִי בַּפְּלִשְׁתִּים הָאֵלֶּה וַיֹּאמֶר ה׳ אֶל דָּוִד לֵךְ וְהִכִּיתָ בַפְּלִשְׁתִּים וְהוֹשַׁעְתָּ אֶת קְעִילָה״.

It was taught in a *baraita*: **Ke'ila was a town** located **near the border,** and the Philistines **came only with regard to matters of hay and straw, as it is written: "And they rob the threshing floors." And** in the next verse **it is written: "Therefore David inquired of the Lord, saying: Shall I go and smite these Philistines? And the Lord said to David: Go and smite the Philistines, and save Ke'ila"** (I Samuel 23:2), which indicates that war may be waged in a border town on Shabbat, even with regard to monetary matters.

מַאי קָמִבַּעְיָא לֵיהּ? אִילֵּימָא אִי שָׁרֵי אִי אָסוּר – הֲרֵי בֵּית דִּינוֹ שֶׁל שְׁמוּאֵל הָרָמָתִי קַיָּים.

The Gemara refutes this proof by asking: **What is** David's **dilemma? If you say** that he had a halakhic question and was in doubt **whether it was permitted or prohibited** to fight the Philistines on Shabbat, it is possible to respond: **But the court of Samuel from Rama was** then **in existence,** and rather than inquire by way of the *Urim VeTummim* he should have inquired of the Great Sanhedrin.

אֶלָּא: אִי מַצְלַח אִי לָא מַצְלַח. דַּיְקָא נַמִי, דִּכְתִיב: ״לֵךְ וְהִכִּיתָ בַפְּלִשְׁתִּים וְהוֹשַׁעְתָּ אֶת קְעִילָה״, שְׁמַע מִינַּהּ.

Rather, he asked: **Will he succeed or will he not succeed** in his war? The Gemara comments: **This is also precise** in the language of the verse, **as it is written** in the response to David's query: **"Go and smite the Philistines, and save Ke'ila." Learn from this,** from the assurance that God gave David of his victory, that this was the subject of his inquiry.

מתני׳ מִי שֶׁיָּשַׁב בַּדֶּרֶךְ וְעָמַד וְרָאָה הֲרֵי (זֶה) הוּא סָמוּךְ לָעִיר – [הוֹאִיל] וְלֹא הָיְתָה כַּוָּונָתוֹ לְכָךְ – לֹא יִכָּנֵס, דִּבְרֵי רַבִּי מֵאִיר.

MISHNA With regard to **a person who was sitting along the road** on Shabbat eve toward nightfall, unaware that he was within the city's Shabbat limit, **and** when **he stood up** after Shabbat had already commenced, **he saw that he was near the town,** i.e., within its limit, **since he had not intended** to acquire his place of residence in the town, **he may not enter** it, but rather he measures two thousand cubits from his place; this is **the statement of Rabbi Meir.**

רַבִּי יְהוּדָה אוֹמֵר: יִכָּנֵס. אָמַר רַבִּי יְהוּדָה: מַעֲשֶׂה הָיָה וְנִכְנַס רַבִּי טַרְפוֹן בְּלֹא מִתְכַּוֵּין.

Rabbi Yehuda says: He may enter the town.[N] **Rabbi Yehuda said: It once happened that Rabbi Tarfon entered** a town on Shabbat **without intention** from the beginning of Shabbat to establish residence in the city.[H]

גמ׳ תַּנְיָא, אָמַר רַבִּי יְהוּדָה: מַעֲשֶׂה בְּרַבִּי טַרְפוֹן שֶׁהָיָה מְהַלֵּךְ בַּדֶּרֶךְ וְחָשְׁכָה לוֹ, וְלָן חוּץ לָעִיר. לְשַׁחֲרִית מְצָאוּהוּ רוֹעֵי בָקָר, אָמְרוּ לוֹ: רַבִּי, הֲרֵי הָעִיר לְפָנֶיךָ, הִכָּנֵס! נִכְנַס וְיָשַׁב בְּבֵית הַמִּדְרָשׁ, וְדָרַשׁ כׇּל הַיּוֹם כּוּלּוֹ.

GEMARA It was taught in a *baraita* that **Rabbi Yehuda said: It once happened that Rabbi Tarfon was walking along the way** on Shabbat eve, **and night fell upon him, and he spent the night outside the town. In the morning, cowherds** who came to graze their cattle outside the town **found him** and **said to him: Master, the town is before you; enter. He entered and sat in the study hall and taught the entire day.** This indicates that one is permitted to enter.

(אָמְרוּ לוֹ:) מִשָּׁם רְאָיָיה?! שֶׁמָּא בְּלִבּוֹ הָיְתָה, אוֹ בֵּית הַמִּדְרָשׁ מוּבְלָע בְּתוֹךְ תְּחוּמוֹ הָיָה.

The other Rabbis **said to** Rabbi Yehuda: Do you bring **proof from there? Perhaps he had it in mind** the day before to acquire residence in the city, **or** perhaps **the study hall was subsumed within his** Shabbat **limit.**[N] If the study hall was within two thousand cubits of the spot where he established residence, all agree that he may enter there.

מתני׳ מִי שֶׁיָּשַׁן בַּדֶּרֶךְ וְלֹא יָדַע שֶׁחֲשֵׁיכָה – יֵשׁ לוֹ אַלְפַּיִם אַמָּה לְכׇל רוּחַ, דִּבְרֵי רַבִּי יוֹחָנָן בֶּן נוּרִי.

MISHNA With regard to **one who was sleeping along the road** on Shabbat eve **and did not know that night had fallen,**[H] **he has two thousand cubits in each direction;** this is the statement of **Rabbi Yoḥanan ben Nuri,** who maintains that knowledge and awareness are not necessary for one to acquire residence, but rather, a person's presence in a given location establishes residence there.

וַחֲכָמִים אוֹמְרִים: אֵין לוֹ אֶלָּא אַרְבַּע אַמּוֹת. רַבִּי אֱלִיעֶזֶר אוֹמֵר: וְהוּא בְּאֶמְצָעָן.

But the Rabbis say: He has only four cubits, as since he did not knowingly acquire residence, he did not establish a Shabbat limit. **Rabbi Eliezer says:** He has only four cubits total **and he is in the middle of them,** i.e., he has two cubits in each direction.

NOTES

Ke'ila – קְעִילָה: *Tosafot* ask: What proof is there that this incident occurred on Shabbat? Ritva explains that the extra phrase "and they rob the threshing floors" adds a detail that is of no great significance for a weekday but is significant with regard to Shabbat.

He may enter the town – יִכָּנֵס: Some commentaries explain that one may walk a distance of four thousand cubits, because it is as though he had established an *eiruv* by walking two thousand cubits from where he was, and was then permitted to continue walking another two thousand cubits from there (Rabbeinu Ḥananel, and others). Most commentaries, however, reject this explanation. If one explicitly states that he will establish residence where he is, some authorities state that he thereby disables himself from acquiring residence in the city, and his current location remains his Shabbat residence (Ra'avad). Other authorities permit the person to walk four thousand cubits in this case as well, because the effectiveness of the *eiruv* does not derive from the act of acquisition; rather, it is derived from the assumption that he wishes to reach an inhabited place. This is his presumed intention, and the fact that he did not state it outright, and even that he said that he would establish residence in his place, was the result of being unaware that he was within the city's Shabbat limit (Rabbeinu Yehonatan).

The study hall was subsumed within his limit – בֵּית הַמִּדְרָשׁ מוּבְלָע בְּתוֹךְ תְּחוּמוֹ: Some commentaries refer to the Jerusalem Talmud, where Rabbi Yehuda answers that the fact that the *baraita* uses the phrase: In the morning, indicates that he really did not know where he was, and only when the sun rose did he discover his location.

HALAKHA

Established residence near a city – שָׁבַת סָמוּךְ לָעִיר: One who is located near a city when Shabbat begins is considered like the inhabitants of the town in terms of Shabbat limits, even if he is unaware that he is near the town. This is in accordance with the opinion of Rabbi Yehuda, whose opinion is accepted in the dispute with Rabbi Meir (*Shulḥan Arukh, Oraḥ Ḥayyim* 400:1).

One who was sleeping along the road and did not know that night had fallen – יָשַׁן בַּדֶּרֶךְ וְלֹא יָדַע שֶׁחֲשֵׁיכָה: If one is sleeping outside the city as Shabbat begins, he may travel two thousand cubits in each direction, in accordance with the opinion of Rabbi Yoḥanan ben Nuri, as this is the ruling stated in the Gemara (*Shulḥan Arukh, Oraḥ Ḥayyim* 401:1).

רַבִּי יְהוּדָה אוֹמֵר: לְאֵיזֶה רוּחַ שֶׁיִּרְצֶה יֵלֵךְ. וּמוֹדֶה רַבִּי יְהוּדָה, שֶׁאִם בֵּירֵר לוֹ – שֶׁאֵינוֹ יָכוֹל לַחֲזוֹר בּוֹ.

Rabbi Yehuda says: He may walk four cubits **in any direction he wishes. But Rabbi Yehuda agrees that if he selected for himself** the direction in which he wants to walk those four cubits, **he cannot retract** and walk four cubits in a different direction.

הָיוּ שְׁנַיִם, מִקְצָת אַמּוֹתָיו שֶׁל זֶה בְּתוֹךְ אַמּוֹתָיו שֶׁל זֶה – מְבִיאִין וְאוֹכְלִין בָּאֶמְצַע,

With regard to a case where **there were two** people in this situation, positioned in such a way that **part of the** four **cubits of one**[H] **were subsumed within the** four **cubits of the other, they may** each **bring** food **and eat** together in the shared area **in the middle,**

HALAKHA

Part of the cubits of one – מִקְצָת אַמּוֹתָיו שֶׁל זֶה: If two people are each restricted to a radius of four cubits, and the areas in which they are permitted to walk overlap, they may bring food and eat together in the middle (*Shulḥan Arukh*, *Oraḥ Ḥayyim* 349:4).

Perek **IV**
Daf **45** Amud **b**

וּבִלְבַד שֶׁלֹּא יוֹצִיא זֶה מִתּוֹךְ שֶׁלּוֹ לְתוֹךְ שֶׁל חֲבֵרוֹ.

provided that the one does not carry anything **from his** four-cubit limit **into that of his fellow.**

הָיוּ שְׁלֹשָׁה, וְהָאֶמְצָעִי מוּבְלָע בֵּינֵיהֶן – הוּא מוּתָּר עִמָּהֶן, וְהֵן מוּתָּרִין עִמּוֹ, וּשְׁנַיִם הַחִיצוֹנִים אֲסוּרִין זֶה עִם זֶה.

With regard to a case where there **were three** people in this situation, **and** certain parts of the four cubits of **the middle one were subsumed within** the respective limits of each of **the others,** so that he shared a certain area with each of them, **he is permitted** to eat **with** either of **them, and they are** both **permitted** to eat **with him; but the two outer ones are forbidden** to eat **with each other,** since they share no common area.

אָמַר רַבִּי שִׁמְעוֹן: לְמָה הַדָּבָר דּוֹמֶה – לְשָׁלֹשׁ חֲצֵירוֹת הַפְּתוּחוֹת זוֹ לָזוֹ, וּפְתוּחוֹת לִרְשׁוּת הָרַבִּים. עֵירְבוּ שְׁתַּיִם עִם הָאֶמְצָעִית – הִיא מוּתֶּרֶת עִמָּהֶן וְהֵם מוּתָּרוֹת עִמָּהּ, וּשְׁתַּיִם הַחִיצוֹנוֹת אֲסוּרוֹת זוֹ עִם זוֹ.

Rabbi Shimon said: To what is this comparable? It is like **three courtyards that open into one another, and** also **open into a public domain.** If **the two outer** courtyards **established an** ***eiruv*** **with the middle one,** the middle one **is permitted to** carry to the two outer ones, **and they are permitted to** carry to **it, but the two outer** courtyards **are prohibited** to carry from **one to** the **other,** as they did not establish an *eiruv* with one another.

גמ׳ בָּעֵי רָבָא: מַאי קָסָבַר רַבִּי יוֹחָנָן בֶּן נוּרִי? מִסְבַּר קָא סָבַר: חֶפְצֵי הֶפְקֵר קוֹנִין שְׁבִיתָה,

GEMARA **Rava raised a dilemma: What does Rabbi Yoḥanan ben Nuri hold?** Does **he hold** that **ownerless objects acquire residence** for Shabbat, i.e., even an article that does not belong to anyone acquires residence at the onset of Shabbat and can therefore be carried two thousand cubits in each direction?

וּבְדִין הוּא דְּלִיפְלוֹג בְּכֵלִים. וְהָא דְּקָמִיפַּלְגִי בְּאָדָם – לְהוֹדִיעֲךָ כּוֹחָן דְּרַבָּנַן, דְּאַף עַל גַּב דְּאִיכָּא לְמֵימַר: הוֹאִיל וְנֵיעוֹר קָנָה – יָשֵׁן נַמִי קָנָה, קָא מַשְׁמַע לָן דְּלָא.

And according to this understanding, Rabbi Yoḥanan ben Nuri **should by right have disagreed** with the Rabbis even **about utensils** that were left in the field, i.e., that according to the opinion of Rabbi Yoḥanan ben Nuri, ownerless utensils can be moved two thousand cubits in each direction. **And the reason that they disagreed about a person is to convey the far-reaching** nature of the stringent ruling **of the Rabbis, that although there is** room **to say: Since** a person who is **awake acquires** for himself two thousand cubits, **he also acquires** them if he is **sleeping,** the mishna nonetheless **teaches us that** the Rabbis did **not** accept this argument, and this is why the dispute is taught specifically with respect to a person.

אוֹ דִּילְמָא, קָסָבַר רַבִּי יוֹחָנָן בֶּן נוּרִי בְּעָלְמָא: חֶפְצֵי הֶפְקֵר אֵין קוֹנִין שְׁבִיתָה. וְהָכָא הַיְינוּ טַעְמָא: הוֹאִיל וְנֵיעוֹר קָנָה – יָשֵׁן נַמִי קָנָה?

Or perhaps we should understand his position differently, that **in general Rabbi Yoḥanan ben Nuri holds** that **ownerless objects do not acquire residence** of their own. **But here,** with regard to a person, **the reason is as follows: Since** a person who is **awake acquires** for himself two thousand cubits, **he also acquires** them if he is **sleeping.**

אָמַר רַב יוֹסֵף, תָּא שְׁמַע: גְּשָׁמִים שֶׁיָּרְדוּ מֵעֶרֶב יוֹם טוֹב, יֵשׁ לָהֶן אַלְפַּיִם אַמָּה לְכָל רוּחַ. בְּיוֹם טוֹב – הֲרֵי הֵן כְּרַגְלֵי כׇּל אָדָם.

Rav Yosef said: Come and **hear** a solution to this dilemma from the following *baraita*: **Rain that fell on the eve of a Festival has two thousand cubits in each direction,** meaning that one is permitted to carry the rainwater within a radius of two thousand cubits. But if the rain fell **on the Festival** itself, **it is like the feet of all people,** as it did not acquire residence, and consequently one is permitted to carry this water wherever he is permitted to walk.

NOTES

Rain near a city – בִּגְשָׁמִים הַסְּמוּכִין לָעִיר: Apparently, in this context the word near means just outside the city, such that the inhabitants of the city would have in mind to use the water. However, if the rain fell further from the city, even if it is within the Shabbat limit, it does not acquire two thousand cubits in each direction like the city's residents (*Me'iri*).

Like the feet of the one who draws the water – כְּרַגְלֵי הַמְמַלֵּא: According to some commentaries, there is no essential difference between the feet of all people and the feet of the one who drew the water. The practical implication is that the water enters the domain of the one who draws it, and its limit corresponds to his. According to this approach, even if the one drawing the water were to give it to another, its limit would remain that of the one who drew the water (Rashi and others). Some authorities maintain that the phrase: Like the feet of the one who draws, is referring to the feet of only the one who draws it; that is, as long as the water is in his possession it is prohibited to take it out of his limit unless he gives it to someone else. However, the phrase: Like the feet of all people, means that they may pass the water from one person to another without any limitation at all (Ra'avad).

אִי אָמְרַתְּ בִּשְׁלָמָא קָסָבַר רַבִּי יוֹחָנָן בֶּן נוּרִי חֶפְצֵי הֶפְקֵר קוֹנִין שְׁבִיתָה, הָא מַנִּי – רַבִּי יוֹחָנָן הִיא.

Granted, it is understandable **if you say that Rabbi Yoḥanan ben Nuri holds** that **ownerless objects acquire residence;** in accordance with **whose** opinion is **this** *baraita*? **It is** that of **Rabbi Yoḥanan** ben Nuri, and consequently the rain that fell on the eve of the Festival acquired residence in the spot where it fell.

אֶלָּא אִי אָמְרַתְּ חֶפְצֵי הֶפְקֵר אֵין קוֹנִין שְׁבִיתָה, הָא מַנִּי? לֹא רַבִּי יוֹחָנָן וְלֹא רַבָּנַן!

However, if you say that he maintains that **ownerless objects do not acquire residence,** in accordance with **whose** opinion is **this** *baraita*? **Neither** that of **Rabbi Yoḥanan** ben Nuri, **nor** that of **the Rabbis,** as it clearly indicates that rain acquires a place of residence even though it has no owner. Rather, we must say that Rabbi Yoḥanan ben Nuri is of the opinion that ownerless objects acquire residence, and this *baraita* is in accordance with his opinion.

יְתֵיב אַבַּיֵי וְקָאָמַר לָהּ לְהָא שְׁמַעְתָּא. אֲמַר לֵיהּ רַב סָפְרָא לְאַבַּיֵי: וְדִילְמָא בִּגְשָׁמִים הַסְּמוּכִין לָעִיר עָסְקִינַן, וְאַנְשֵׁי אוֹתָהּ הָעִיר דַּעְתָּם עִילָּוַיְיהוּ?

Abaye sat and recited this tradition. Rav Safra said to Abaye: Perhaps we are dealing with rain that fell **near a city,**[N] **and the inhabitants of that city had it in mind,** and that is why it acquires two thousand cubits in each direction.

אֲמַר לֵיהּ: לָא סָלְקָא דַּעְתָּךְ, דִּתְנַן: בּוֹר שֶׁל יָחִיד – כְּרַגְלֵי יָחִיד, וְשֶׁל אוֹתָהּ הָעִיר – כְּרַגְלֵי אוֹתָהּ הָעִיר, וְשֶׁל עוֹלֵי בָבֶל – כְּרַגְלֵי הַמְמַלֵּא.

Abaye **said to him: It should not enter your mind** that such an understanding is correct, **as we learned** in a mishna: **A cistern that belongs to an individual,** its water is **like the feet of that individual,** the owner of the cistern, in that it may be carried wherever he is permitted to walk. **And** a cistern **that belongs to a particular city,**[H] its water is **like the feet of** the people of **that city,** in that it may be carried wherever the inhabitants of that city may walk, i.e., two thousand cubits in each direction from the city. **And** a cistern **that belongs to pilgrims from Babylonia**[H] on the way to Eretz Yisrael, meaning that it belongs to all Jews and has no particular owner, its water is **like the feet of the one who draws** the water,[N] in that it may be carried wherever he is permitted to walk.

וְתַנְיָא: בּוֹר שֶׁל שְׁבָטִים יֵשׁ לָהֶן אַלְפַּיִם אַמָּה לְכָל רוּחַ. קַשְׁיָין אַהֲדָדֵי!

And it was taught in a *baraita*: **A cistern that belongs to** one of **the tribes** and has no particular owner, its water **has two thousand cubits in each direction.** If so, these two sources **contradict each other,** as the mishna teaches that water that belongs to the entire community does not establish residence, whereas the *tanna* of the *baraita* holds that it may be carried two thousand cubits from its place.

אֶלָּא לָאו שְׁמַע מִינַּהּ: הָא – רַבִּי יוֹחָנָן בֶּן נוּרִי, הָא – רַבָּנַן.

Rather, in order to resolve the contradiction, **learn from here: This** source, which states that the water may be carried two thousand cubits, was taught in accordance with the opinion of **Rabbi Yoḥanan ben Nuri,** who says that even ownerless objects acquire residence; **that** source, which states that water that does not belong to any particular person is like the feet of the one who draws it, was taught in accordance with the opinion of **the Rabbis,** who say that ownerless objects do not acquire residence.

כִּי אֲתָא לְקַמֵּיהּ דְּרַב יוֹסֵף, אֲמַר לֵיהּ: הָכִי קָאָמַר רַב סָפְרָא, וְהָכִי אַהֲדָרֵי לֵיהּ. אֲמַר לֵיהּ: וְאַמַּאי לָא תֵּימָא לֵיהּ מִגּוּפַהּ: אִי סָלְקָא דַּעְתָּךְ גְּשָׁמִים הַסְּמוּכִין לָעִיר עָסְקִינַן – הַאי יֵשׁ לָהֶן אַלְפַּיִם אַמָּה לְכָל רוּחַ?!

The Gemara relates that **when** Abaye **came before Rav Yosef, he said to him: This is what Rav Safra said, and this is what I answered him.** Rav Yosef **said to him: And why did you not answer him from the** *baraita* **itself? If it should enter your mind that we are dealing with rain** that fell **near a city,** how can you understand the statement **that** the rainwater **has two thousand cubits in each direction?**

HALAKHA

A cistern that belongs to an individual or a city – בּוֹר שֶׁל יָחִיד וְשֶׁל עִיר: Water collected in a private cistern may be carried only to a place where the owner of the cistern is permitted to walk. On the other hand, water collected in a public cistern, which belongs to all the inhabitants of a city, may be carried to wherever the inhabitants may walk. If one of the city's inhabitants establishes a joining of Shabbat limits [*eiruv*], one who lives outside the town may carry the water outside the limit with him (*Magen Avraham*, based on the Ran). Some authorities rule that if the inhabitants of the city establish *eiruvin* in several directions, those who live outside the city are prohibited to carry out of the city (*Shulḥan Arukh HaRav*; *Shulḥan Arukh, Oraḥ Ḥayyim* 397:14).

A cistern that belongs to pilgrims from Babylonia – בּוֹר...שֶׁל עוֹלֵי בָבֶל: There is no limitation on carrying water from a cistern that belongs to all Jews or from an ownerless cistern. The water has the status of the one who fills the cistern (*Shulḥan Arukh, Oraḥ Ḥayyim* 397:14).

הָא ״כְּרַגְלֵי אַנְשֵׁי אוֹתָהּ הָעִיר״ מִיבָּעֲיָא לֵיהּ!

According to your understanding, that the rainwater may be carried two thousand cubits because the inhabitants of the town had it in mind, the *baraita* **should have** said: The rainwater is **like the feet of the inhabitants of that city.** Rather, you must say that the inhabitants of the city did not acquire the water and that it may be carried within a radius of two thousand cubits, because the *baraita* was taught in accordance with the opinion of Rabbi Yoḥanan ben Nuri, that ownerless objects acquire residence.

אָמַר מָר: בְּיוֹם טוֹב – הֲרֵי הֵן כְּרַגְלֵי כָּל אָדָם. וְאַמַּאי? לִיקְנִי שְׁבִיתָה בְּאוֹקְיָינוֹס!

The Gemara further examines the *baraita* cited earlier. **The Master said:** If rain fell **on the Festival**[N] itself, **it is like the feet of all people.** The Gemara raises a difficulty: **And why** should this be? The water **should have acquired residence in the ocean [*okeyanos*]**,[L] where it was when the Festival began. And since the water went out on the Festival beyond its limit after it evaporated and formed into clouds, moving the water more than four cubits should be prohibited.

לֵימָא דְּלָא כְּרַבִּי אֱלִיעֶזֶר, דְּאִי כְּרַבִּי אֱלִיעֶזֶר – הָא אָמַר: כָּל הָעוֹלָם כּוּלּוֹ מִמֵּי אוֹקְיָינוֹס הוּא שׁוֹתֶה!

Let us say that this *baraita* was taught **not in accordance with** the opinion of **Rabbi Eliezer. Because if** it is **in accordance with** the opinion of **Rabbi Eliezer, he said: The entire world drinks from the waters of the ocean;** that is to say, evaporated ocean water is the source of rain.

אָמַר רַבִּי יִצְחָק: הָכָא בְּעָבִים שֶׁנִּתְקַשְּׁרוּ מֵעֶרֶב יוֹם טוֹב עָסְקִינַן.

Rabbi Yitzḥak said: Here we are dealing with clouds that were already **formed on the eve of the Festival.** Since these clouds were already formed before the Festival, the water did not acquire residence in the ocean or travel beyond its limit on the Festival.

וְדִילְמָא הָנָךְ אָזְלִי וְהָנָךְ אַחֲרִינֵי נִינְהוּ? דְּאִית לְהוּ סִימָנָא בְּגַוַּיְיהוּ.

The Gemara asks: **But perhaps those** clouds that had already been formed on the eve of the Festival **went** away, **and these** clouds, from which the rain fell, **are others** that did acquire residence in the ocean? The Gemara answers: We are dealing here with a case **where there is** an identifying **sign** that these are the same clouds and not others.[B]

וְאִיבָּעֵית אֵימָא: הָוֵי סְפֵק דִּבְרֵיהֶם, וּסְפֵק דִּבְרֵיהֶם לְהָקֵל.

And if you wish, say that there is another reason we are not concerned that these might be other clouds: **This** matter of whether or not they are the same clouds pertains to **an uncertainty** with respect to **a rabbinic law,** and the principle is that with regard to **an uncertainty** concerning **a rabbinic law,** one may follow the **lenient** understanding.

וְלִיקְנִי שְׁבִיתָה בְּעָבִים! תִּיפְשׁוֹט מִינָּהּ דְּאֵין תְּחוּמִין לְמַעְלָה מֵעֲשָׂרָה, דְּאִי יֵשׁ תְּחוּמִין – לִיקְנִי שְׁבִיתָה בְּעָבִים!

The Gemara asks: **Let** the water **acquire residence in the clouds,** where it was when the Festival began, and its limit should be measured from there. Since the *baraita* taught that the water is like the feet of all people, if so, **resolve from here** another dilemma, and say that **there is no** prohibition of Shabbat **limits above ten** handbreadths, and one is permitted to travel more than two thousand cubits above this height. **For if there is** a prohibition of Shabbat **limits** above ten handbreadths, **let** the water **acquire residence in the clouds.**

לְעוֹלָם אֵימָא לָךְ: יֵשׁ תְּחוּמִין, וּמַיָּא בְּעִיבָא מִיבְלַע בְּלִיעִי.

The Gemara rejects this argument: **Actually,** I can **say to you: There is** a prohibition of Shabbat **limits** even above ten handbreadths, **and the water** does not acquire residence in the clouds because it **is absorbed in the clouds.** Since water does not exist in its usual state within the clouds, but rather takes on a different form, it does not acquire residence there.

NOTES

Rain that fell on a Festival – גְּשָׁמִים שֶׁיָּרְדוּ בְּיוֹם טוֹב: The early commentaries ask: Why does rain that fell on a Festival have the status of the people? It can be argued that since the water came from a different place and did not acquire residence in its new place, it did not acquire residence at all. Therefore, it should be prohibited to carry it beyond four cubits. Some commentaries explain that reasoning of this kind applies only to one who has awareness and who is capable of acquiring residence for himself; if he fails to do so, he acquires no Shabbat residence. However, water, which has no awareness, can be limited only by the person who finds it and makes use of it. Other authorities state that since the water was previously moving continuously, it does not establish a place of residence, and it falls to the ground without having established a Shabbat residence (Rashba; see Maharshal).

LANGUAGE

Ocean [*okeyanos*] – אוֹקְיָינוֹס: From the Greek ὠκεανός, *okeanos*, meaning the Great Sea, or the ocean that surrounds the continents.

BACKGROUND

Identifying signs of clouds – סִימָנֵי הֶעָנָנִים: Although clouds change their shape constantly, which would seem to preclude associating any kind of marker with them, they do possess other markers apart from their shape. Clouds differ from one another by formation, color, and depth. These cloud markers are helpful in identifying different clusters of clouds, even though they do not distinguish any one particular cloud from the others.

כָּל שֶׁכֵּן דְּהָווּ לְהוּ נוֹלָד דַּאֲסִירִי!

The Gemara raises a difficulty: If the water was previously not in its current state, **all the more so should it be** considered as something that **came into being** [*nolad*] on the Festival, and consequently it is **prohibited** to carry it. Something that came into being or assumed its present form on Shabbat or Festivals is considered set-aside [*muktze*] and may not be handled on Shabbat or Festivals.

אֶלָּא מַיָּא בְּעָבִים מֵינָד נָיְידִי. הָשְׁתָּא דְּאָתֵית לְהָכִי – אוֹקְיָינוֹס נַמִי לָא לִיקְשׁוּ לָךְ, מַיָּא בְּאוֹקְיָינוֹס נַמִי מֵינַד נָיְידִי. וְתַנְיָא: נְהָרוֹת הַמּוֹשְׁכִין וּמַעְיָינוֹת הַנּוֹבְעִין – הֲרֵי הֵן כְּרַגְלֵי כׇּל אָדָם.

Rather, we should say: **The water in clouds** is **in** constant **motion** and therefore does not acquire residence there. The Gemara comments: **Now that you have arrived at this** answer, **the ocean should also not be difficult for you,** as the **water in the ocean is also in** constant **motion. And it was taught** in a *baraita*: **Flowing rivers and streaming springs are like the feet of all people,** as their waters do not acquire residence in any particular place.[H] The same law also applies to clouds and seas.

אָמַר רַבִּי יַעֲקֹב בַּר אִידִי, אָמַר רַבִּי יְהוֹשֻׁעַ בֶּן לֵוִי: הֲלָכָה כְּרַבִּי יוֹחָנָן בֶּן נוּרִי. אֲמַר לֵיהּ רַבִּי זֵירָא לְרַבִּי יַעֲקֹב בַּר אִידִי: בְּפֵירוּשׁ שְׁמִיעַ לָךְ, אוֹ מִכְּלָלָא שְׁמִיעַ לָךְ? אֲמַר לֵיהּ: בְּפֵירוּשׁ שְׁמִיעַ לִי.

Rabbi Ya'akov bar Idi said that **Rabbi Yehoshua ben Levi said: The *halakha* is in accordance with** the opinion of **Rabbi Yoḥanan ben Nuri,**[N] that one who was asleep at the beginning of Shabbat may travel two thousand cubits in every direction. **Rabbi Zeira said to Rabbi Ya'akov bar Idi:** Did **you hear** this *halakha* **explicitly** from Rabbi Yehoshua ben Levi, **or did you understand it by inference** from some other ruling that he issued? Rabbi Ya'akov bar Idi **said to him: I heard** it **explicitly** from him.

מַאי כְּלָלָא? דְּאָמַר רַבִּי יְהוֹשֻׁעַ בֶּן לֵוִי: הֲלָכָה כְּדִבְרֵי הַמֵּיקֵל בְּעֵירוּב.

The Gemara asks: From **what** other teaching could this ruling **be inferred?** The Gemara explains: From that **which Rabbi Yehoshua ben Levi said: The *halakha* is in accordance with the lenient** opinion **with regard to an *eiruv*.**[HN]

וְתַרְתֵּי לָמָּה לִי?

The Gemara asks: **Why do I need both?** Why was it necessary for Rabbi Yehoshua ben Levi to state both the general ruling that the *halakha* is in accordance with the lenient opinion with regard to an *eiruv*, and also the specific ruling that the *halakha* is in accordance with the opinion of Rabbi Yoḥanan ben Nuri on this issue?

אָמַר רַבִּי זֵירָא: צְרִיכִי, דְּאִי אַשְׁמְעִינַן הֲלָכָה כְּרַבִּי יוֹחָנָן בֶּן נוּרִי – הֲוָה אָמִינָא בֵּין לְקוּלָּא וּבֵין לְחוּמְרָא, קָא מַשְׁמַע לָן: הֲלָכָה כְּדִבְרֵי הַמֵּיקֵל בְּעֵירוּב.

Rabbi Zeira said: Both rulings **were necessary, as had he informed us** only that **the *halakha* is in accordance with** the opinion of **Rabbi Yoḥanan ben Nuri, I would have said** that the *halakha* is in accordance with him **whether this is a leniency,** i.e., that a sleeping person acquires residence and may walk two thousand cubits in every direction, **or** whether **it is a stringency,** i.e., that ownerless utensils acquire residence and can be carried only two thousand cubits from that place. **Consequently, he teaches us** that **the *halakha* is in accordance with the lenient** opinion **with regard to an *eiruv*,** so that we rule in accordance with Rabbi Yoḥanan ben Nuri only when it entails a leniency.

וְלֵימָא: ״הֲלָכָה כְּדִבְרֵי הַמֵּיקֵל בְּעֵירוּב״, ״הֲלָכָה כְּרַבִּי יוֹחָנָן בֶּן נוּרִי״ לָמָּה לִי?

The Gemara asks: **Let him state** only that **the *halakha* is in accordance with the lenient** opinion **with regard to an *eiruv*. Why do I need** the statement that **the *halakha* is in accordance with** the opinion of **Rabbi Yoḥanan ben Nuri?**

אִיצְטְרִיךְ, סָלְקָא דַּעְתָּךְ אָמִינָא: הָנֵי מִילֵּי – יָחִיד בִּמְקוֹם יָחִיד, וְרַבִּים בִּמְקוֹם רַבִּים. אֲבָל יָחִיד בִּמְקוֹם רַבִּים – אֵימָא לָא.

The Gemara answers: This ruling **was necessary** as well, for had he informed us only that the *halakha* is in accordance with the lenient opinion with regard to an *eiruv*, **it might have entered your mind to say** that **this statement applies only** to disputes in which **a single** authority disagrees **with** another **single** authority, **or several** authorities disagree with **several** other authorities. **But** when **a single** authority maintains a lenient opinion against **several** authorities who maintain a more stringent position, you might have **said** that we do **not** rule in his favor. Hence, it was necessary to state that the *halakha* is in accordance with the opinion of Rabbi Yoḥanan ben Nuri although he disputes the Rabbis.

אֲמַר לֵיהּ רָבָא לְאַבָּיֵי: מִכְּדִי, עֵירוּבִין דְּרַבָּנַן, מַה לִּי יָחִיד בִּמְקוֹם יָחִיד וּמַה לִּי יָחִיד בִּמְקוֹם רַבִּים?

Rava said to Abaye: Now, since the laws of *eiruvin* **are rabbinic** in origin, **what** reason is there for **me** to differentiate between a disagreement of **a single** authority **with a single** authority and a disagreement of **a single** authority **with several** authorities?

HALAKHA

Flowing water – **מַיִם זוֹרְמִים**: Flowing water, even if it is privately owned, has the legal status of the person who draws it. The wording of the Gemara indicates that if the water is moving, as in the case of flowing spring water, it has the legal status of the person who draws it even if it does not leave its place (*Shulḥan Arukh*, *Oraḥ Ḥayyim* 397:15).

The *halakha* is in accordance with the lenient opinion with regard to an *eiruv* – **הֲלָכָה כְּדִבְרֵי הַמֵּיקֵל בְּעֵירוּב**: Even a sleeping person establishes residence for the purpose of walking two thousand cubits in each direction, since the *halakha* is in accordance with the opinion of Rabbi Yoḥanan ben Nuri. However, ownerless objects have the halakhic status of the person who finds them and do not establish residence on their own, because the *halakha* is in accordance with the leniency of both opinions (*Shulḥan Arukh*, *Oraḥ Ḥayyim* 401:1).

NOTES

The *halakha* is in accordance with the opinion of Rabbi Yoḥanan ben Nuri – **הֲלָכָה כְּרַבִּי יוֹחָנָן בֶּן נוּרִי**: If the *halakha* is in accordance with Rabbi Yoḥanan ben Nuri only when he is lenient, and the *halakha* is in accordance with the Rabbis only where a leniency is involved, such as with regard to ownerless utensils, the result is two contradictory leniencies. Some commentaries answer that perhaps we rule in accordance with the opinion of Rabbi Yoḥanan ben Nuri, but not for his reason. Rather, since a sleeping person can establish residence when awake, he can also do so when asleep; a sleeping person establishes residence where he is. Ownerless objects, however, never establish residence (Rashba; Ritva).

The *halakha* is in accordance with the lenient opinion with regard to an *eiruv* – **הֲלָכָה כְּדִבְרֵי הַמֵּיקֵל בְּעֵירוּב**: The earlier and later commentaries discuss this principle, limiting it in several ways: They maintain that it applies only to an *eiruv*, but not to partitions, because the laws of partitions have a source in the Torah (Rivash). They further state that this principle does not apply to cases of unresolved dilemmas. Since the Sages did not resolve these dilemmas by applying this principle, leniency cannot be presumed (*Baḥ*, based on the Rif). The principle also cannot be applied if the doubt arises from two different explanations of the same statement (*Baḥ*). Some early commentaries claim that this principle refers only to disputes among the *tanna'im*, since their statements were known to Rabbi Yehoshua ben Levi and he could decide among them, but not to the words of *amora'im* (Ra'avad; see *Hagahot HaRosh*; *Me'iri*).

אֲמַר לֵיהּ רַב פַּפָּא לְרָבָא: וּבִדְרַבָּנַן לָא שָׁנֵי לָן בֵּין יָחִיד בִּמְקוֹם יָחִיד לְיָחִיד בִּמְקוֹם רַבִּים?

Rav Pappa said to Rava: Is there no difference with regard to rabbinic laws **between** a disagreement of **a single** authority **with a single** authority, **and** a disagreement of **a single** authority with **several** authorities?

וְהָתְנַן, רַבִּי אֱלִיעֶזֶר אוֹמֵר: כׇּל אִשָּׁה שֶׁעָבְרוּ עָלֶיהָ שָׁלֹשׁ עוֹנוֹת – דַּיָּיהּ שְׁעָתָהּ.

Didn't we learn in a mishna that **Rabbi Elazar says: Any woman who passed three** expected menstrual **cycles** without experiencing bleeding is presumed not to be menstruating. If afterward she sees blood, **it is enough** that she be regarded as ritually impure due to menstruation **from the time** that she examined herself[H] and saw that she had a discharge, rather than retroactively for up to twenty-four hours. The Rabbis, however, maintain that this *halakha* applies only to an older woman or to a woman after childbirth, for whom it is natural to stop menstruating, but not to a normal young woman for whom three periods have passed without bleeding.

וְתַנְיָא: מַעֲשֶׂה וְעָשָׂה רַבִּי כְּרַבִּי אֱלִיעֶזֶר. לְאַחַר שֶׁנִּזְכַּר אָמַר: כְּדַי הוּא רַבִּי אֱלִיעֶזֶר לִסְמוֹךְ עָלָיו בִּשְׁעַת הַדְּחָק.

And it was taught in a *baraita*: **It once happened that Rabbi** Yehuda HaNasi **ruled** that the *halakha* **is in accordance with** the opinion of **Rabbi Elazar. After he remembered** that Rabbi Elazar's colleagues disagree with him on this matter and that he had apparently ruled incorrectly, **he** nonetheless **said: Rabbi Elazar is worthy to rely upon in exigent circumstances.**[N]

מַאי "לְאַחַר שֶׁנִּזְכַּר"? אִילֵימָא לְאַחַר שֶׁנִּזְכַּר דְּאֵין הֲלָכָה כְּרַבִּי אֱלִיעֶזֶר, אֶלָּא כְּרַבָּנַן – בִּשְׁעַת הַדְּחָק הֵיכִי עָבֵיד כְּוָותֵיהּ?

The Gemara comments: **What is** the meaning of: **After he remembered? If you say** that it means **after he remembered** that **the *halakha* is not in accordance with** the opinion of **Rabbi Elazar but** rather **in accordance with** the opinion of **the Rabbis,** then **how could he rule in accordance with him** even **in exigent circumstances,** given that the *halakha* had been decided against him?

אֶלָּא: דְּלָא אִיתְּמַר הִלְכְתָא לֹא כְּרַבִּי אֱלִיעֶזֶר וְלֹא כְּרַבָּנַן, לְאַחַר שֶׁנִּזְכַּר דְּלָאו יָחִיד פְּלִיג עֲלֵיהּ אֶלָּא רַבִּים פְּלִיגִי עֲלֵיהּ, אָמַר: כְּדַי הוּא רַבִּי אֱלִיעֶזֶר לִסְמוֹךְ עָלָיו בִּשְׁעַת הַדְּחָק.

Rather, it must be that the ***halakha*** had **not been stated** on this matter, **neither in accordance with** the opinion of **Rabbi Elazar, nor in accordance with** the opinion of **the Rabbis. And after he remembered that it was not a single** authority who **disagreed with** Rabbi Elazar, **but** rather **several** authorities who **disagreed with him, he** nonetheless **said: Rabbi Elazar is worthy to rely upon in exigent circumstances.** This demonstrates that even with a dispute that involves a rabbinic decree, such as whether a woman is declared ritually impure retroactively, there is room to distinguish between a disagreement of a single authority and a single authority, and a disagreement of a single authority and several authorities.

אֲמַר רַב מְשַׁרְשִׁיָּא לְרָבָא, וְאָמְרִי לַהּ רַב נַחְמָן בַּר יִצְחָק לְרָבָא: וּבִדְרַבָּנַן לָא שָׁנֵי בֵּין יָחִיד בִּמְקוֹם יָחִיד, בֵּין יָחִיד בִּמְקוֹם רַבִּים?

Rav Mesharshiya said to Rava, and some say it was **Rav Naḥman bar Yitzḥak** who said **to Rava: Is there no difference with regard to rabbinic** laws **between** a disagreement of **a single** authority **with a single** authority, **and** a disagreement of **a single** authority **with several** authorities?

וְהָתַנְיָא: שְׁמוּעָה קְרוֹבָה נוֹהֶגֶת שִׁבְעָה וּשְׁלֹשִׁים, רְחוֹקָה – אֵינָהּ נוֹהֶגֶת אֶלָּא יוֹם אֶחָד.

Wasn't it was taught in a *baraita*: If a person receives **a proximate report** that one of his close relatives has died, **he practices** all the customs of the intense **seven** day mourning period as well as the customs of the **thirty** day mourning period. But if he receives **a distant** report, **he practices** only **one day** of mourning.

וְאֵי זוֹ הִיא קְרוֹבָה וְאֵיזוֹ הִיא רְחוֹקָה? בְּתוֹךְ שְׁלֹשִׁים – קְרוֹבָה, לְאַחַר שְׁלֹשִׁים – רְחוֹקָה, דִּבְרֵי רַבִּי עֲקִיבָא. וַחֲכָמִים אוֹמְרִים: אַחַת שְׁמוּעָה קְרוֹבָה וְאַחַת שְׁמוּעָה רְחוֹקָה נוֹהֶגֶת שִׁבְעָה וּשְׁלֹשִׁים.

What is considered a **proximate** report, **and what is** considered a **distant** report? If the report arrives **within thirty** days of the close relative's passing, it is regarded as **proximate,** and if it arrives **after thirty** days it is considered **distant;** this is **the statement of Rabbi Akiva. But the Rabbis say: Both** in the case of **a proximate report and** in the case of **a distant report,**[H] the grieving relative **practices** the **seven**-day mourning period **and** the **thirty**-day mourning period.

וְאָמַר רַבָּה בַּר בַּר חָנָה, אָמַר רַבִּי יוֹחָנָן: כׇּל מָקוֹם שֶׁאַתָּה מוֹצֵא יָחִיד מֵיקֵל וְרַבִּים מַחְמִירִין – הֲלָכָה כְּדִבְרֵי הַמַּחְמִירִין, הַמְרוּבִּים. חוּץ מִזּוֹ, שֶׁאַף עַל פִּי שֶׁרַבִּי עֲקִיבָא מֵיקֵל וַחֲכָמִים מַחְמִירִין – הֲלָכָה כְּדִבְרֵי רַבִּי עֲקִיבָא.

And Rabba bar bar Ḥana said that **Rabbi Yoḥanan said: Wherever you find** that **a single** authority **is lenient** with regard to a certain *halakha* **and several** other authorities **are stringent, the *halakha* is in accordance with the words of the stringent** authorities, who constitute **the majority, except for here, where despite** the fact that the opinion of **Rabbi Akiva is lenient and the** opinion of the **Rabbis** is more **stringent, the *halakha* is in accordance with** the opinion of **Rabbi Akiva.**

HALAKHA

A woman for whom it is enough that she be impure from the time she saw – אִשָּׁה שֶׁדַּיָּיהּ שְׁעָתָהּ: A woman approaching menopause who passes three expected menstrual cycles without experiencing bleeding and then sees blood is regarded as ritually impure only from the time that she examines herself and experiences menstrual flow. However, the law concerning a young woman is different. She is retroactively ritually impure for up to twenty-four hours, in accordance with the opinion of the Rabbis (Rambam *Sefer Tahara, Hilkhot Metamei Mishkav UMoshav* 4:1).

A proximate and a distant report – שְׁמוּעָה קְרוֹבָה וּרְחוֹקָה: One who receives a proximate report of the death of a close relative practices both the mourning customs observed for seven days and those observed for thirty days. One who receives a distant report practices mourning customs for only one day, with part of a day considered to be an entire day. Some authorities rule that although the laws governing the seven-day mourning period are not practiced in the case of a distant report concerning a father or mother, the other laws of mourning are observed (Ramban; *Shulḥan Arukh, Yoreh De'a* 402:1).

NOTES

In exigent circumstances – בִּשְׁעַת הַדְּחָק: The nature of the exigent circumstance referred to here is discussed by the commentaries (see Rashi and *Tosafot*). *Tosafot* explain that it refers to a case where the questioner departed, and it would be nearly impossible to find him and inform him that there had been a mistaken ruling.

NOTES

The *halakha* is in accordance with the lenient opinion with regard to mourning – הֲלָכָה כְּדִבְרֵי הַמֵּיקֵל בְּאֵבֶל: The rationale for this principle is that according to most commentaries and halakhic authorities, the mandate for mourning practices is not from Torah law. In addition, all the particulars of the laws of mourning are certainly instituted by rabbinic law, and consequently, the *halakha* is lenient about them. Nevertheless, certain limitations apply. For example, the principle applies to the laws of mourning but not to the laws of rending one's garments over the death of a relative (Ramban; *Baḥ*). In addition, this principle applies to only certain laws of mourning (Ramban; Rashba), and it is not operative with respect to an opinion that has been rejected by all authorities (*Baḥ*).

וְסָבַר לַהּ כִּשְׁמוּאֵל, דְּאָמַר שְׁמוּאֵל: הֲלָכָה כְּדִבְרֵי הַמֵּיקֵל בְּאֵבֶל.

And Rabbi Yoḥanan **holds like Shmuel, as Shmuel said: The *halakha* is in accordance with the lenient** opinion **with** regard to **mourning** practices,[N] i.e., wherever there is a dispute with regard to mourning customs, the *halakha* is in accordance with the lenient opinion.

בְּאֲבֵילוּת הוּא דְּאַקִּילוּ בָּהּ רַבָּנַן, אֲבָל בְּעָלְמָא – אֲפִילּוּ בִּדְרַבָּנַן שָׁנֵי בֵּין יָחִיד בִּמְקוֹם יָחִיד, בֵּין יָחִיד בִּמְקוֹם רַבִּים.

From here the Gemara infers: **It is** only **with regard to mourning** practices **that the Sages were lenient, but in general,** with regard to other areas of *halakha*, **even in the case of rabbinic** laws **there is a difference** between a disagreement of **a single** authority **with a single** authority and a disagreement of **a single** authority **with several** authorities. This being the case, Rabbi Yehoshua ben Levi did well to rule explicitly that the *halakha* is in accordance with the opinion of Rabbi Yoḥanan ben Nuri, even though he is a single authority who ruled leniently in dispute with the Rabbis.

Perek **IV**
Daf **46** Amud **b**

וְרַב פָּפָּא אָמַר: אִיצְטְרִיךְ, סָלְקָא דַּעְתָּךְ אָמִינָא: הָנֵי מִילֵּי – בְּעֵירוּבֵי חֲצֵירוֹת, אֲבָל בְּעֵירוּבֵי תְחוּמִין – אֵימָא לָא, צְרִיכָא.

Rav Pappa said a different explanation for the fact that Rabbi Yehoshua ben Levi made both statements: **It was necessary** for Rabbi Yehoshua ben Levi to inform us that the *halakha* is in accordance with the opinion of Rabbi Yoḥanan ben Nuri, because had he said only that the *halakha* follows the lenient opinion with regard to an *eiruv*, **it could have entered your mind to say** that **this statement applies only with regard to** the laws governing the ***eiruv* of courtyards,** which are entirely rabbinic in origin. **But with regard to** the more stringent laws governing the ***eiruv*** of Shabbat **limits,** you would have **said** that we should **not** rule leniently, and therefore **it was necessary** to make both statements.

וּמְנָא תֵּימְרָא דְּשָׁנֵי לַן בֵּין עֵירוּבֵי חֲצֵירוֹת לְעֵירוּבֵי תְחוּמִין – דִּתְנַן, אָמַר רַבִּי יְהוּדָה: בַּמֶּה דְּבָרִים אֲמוּרִים – בְּעֵירוּבֵי תְחוּמִין, אֲבָל בְּעֵירוּבֵי חֲצֵירוֹת – מְעָרְבִין בֵּין לָדַעַת וּבֵין שֶׁלֹּא לָדַעַת, שֶׁזָּכִין לָאָדָם שֶׁלֹּא בְּפָנָיו, וְאֵין חָבִין לָאָדָם אֶלָּא בְּפָנָיו.

The Gemara asks: **And from where do you say that we distinguish between an *eiruv* of courtyards and an *eiruv* of** Shabbat **limits? As we learned** in a mishna that **Rabbi Yehuda said: In what** case **is this statement said,** that an *eiruv* may be established for another person only with his knowledge? It was said **with regard to an *eiruv*** of Shabbat **limits, but with regard to an *eiruv* of courtyards, an *eiruv* may be established** for another person whether **with his knowledge or without his knowledge, as one may act in a person's interest in his absence; however, one may not act to a person's disadvantage in his absence.** One may act unilaterally on someone else's behalf when the action is to that other person's benefit; however, when it is to the other person's detriment, or when there are both advantages and disadvantages to him, one may act on the other person's behalf only if one has been explicitly appointed as an agent. Since an *eiruv* of courtyards is always to a person's benefit, it can be established even without his knowledge. However, with regard to an *eiruv* of Shabbat limits, while it enables one to walk in one direction, it disallows him from walking in the opposite direction. Therefore, it can be established only with his knowledge.

רַב אַשִׁי אָמַר: אִיצְטְרִיךְ, סָלְקָא דַּעְתָּךְ אָמִינָא: הָנֵי מִילֵּי – בְּשִׁיּוּרֵי עֵירוּב, אֲבָל בִּתְחִילַּת עֵירוּב – אֵימָא לָא.

Rav Ashi said that Rabbi Yehoshua ben Levi's need to issue two rulings can be explained in another manner: **It is necessary** for Rabbi Yehoshua ben Levi to inform us that the *halakha* is in accordance with the opinion of Rabbi Yoḥanan ben Nuri, as if he had said only that the *halakha* is in accordance with the lenient opinion with regard to an *eiruv*, **it could have entered your mind to say** that **this statement applies only with regard to the remnants of an *eiruv*,** i.e., an *eiruv* that had been properly established, where the concern is that it might subsequently have become invalid. **But with regard to an initial *eiruv*,** i.e., an *eiruv* that is just being established and has not yet taken effect, you might have **said** that we should **not** rule leniently, and therefore it was necessary to issue both rulings.

וּמְנָא תֵּימְרָא דְּשָׁנֵי לָן בֵּין שִׁיּוּרֵי עֵירוּב לִתְחִילַּת עֵירוּב – דִּתְנַן: אָמַר רַבִּי יוֹסֵי: בַּמֶּה דְּבָרִים אֲמוּרִים – בִּתְחִילַּת עֵירוּב, אֲבָל בְּשִׁיּוּרֵי עֵירוּב – אֲפִילּוּ כׇּל שֶׁהוּא.

The Gemara asks: **And from where do you say that we distinguish between the remnants of an *eiruv* and an initial *eiruv*? As we learned** in a mishna: **Rabbi Yosei said: In what** case **is this statement said,** that the Sages stipulated that a fixed quantity of food is necessary for establishing an *eiruv*? It is said **with regard to an initial *eiruv*,** i.e., when setting up an *eiruv* for the first time; **however, with regard to the remnants of an *eiruv*,** i.e., on a subsequent Shabbat when the measure may have become diminished, **even a minimal amount** suffices.[N]

וְלֹא אָמְרוּ לְעָרֵב חֲצֵירוֹת אֶלָּא כְּדֵי שֶׁלֹּא לְשַׁכֵּחַ תּוֹרַת עֵירוּב מִן הַתִּינוֹקוֹת.

And they said to establish an *eiruv* for courtyards only after all the inhabitants of the city merge their alleyways and become like the inhabitants of a single courtyard, **so that the law of *eiruv* should not be forgotten by the children,** who may not be aware of the arrangement that has been made with regard to the alleyways.

רַבִּי יַעֲקֹב וְרַבִּי זְרִיקָא אָמְרוּ: הֲלָכָה כְּרַבִּי עֲקִיבָא מֵחֲבֵירוֹ, וּכְרַבִּי יוֹסֵי מֵחֲבֵירָיו, וּכְרַבִּי מֵחֲבֵירוֹ.

Since the Gemara discussed the principles cited with regard to halakhic decision-making, it cites additional principles. **Rabbi Ya'akov and Rabbi Zerika said:** The ***halakha* is in accordance with** the opinion of **Rabbi Akiva** in disputes **with** any individual **Sage, and the *halakha* is in accordance with** the opinion of **Rabbi Yosei** even in disputes **with** other **Sages,**[N] **and the *halakha* is in accordance with** the opinion of **Rabbi** Yehuda HaNasi in disputes **with** any individual **Sage.**

לְמַאי הִלְכְתָא? רַבִּי אַסִּי אָמַר: הֲלָכָה, וְרַבִּי חִיָּיא בַּר אַבָּא אָמַר: מַטִּין, וְרַבִּי יוֹסֵי בְּרַבִּי חֲנִינָא אָמַר: נִרְאִין.

The Gemara asks: With regard **to what *halakha*** do these principles apply, meaning, to what degree are they binding? **Rabbi Asi said:** This is considered binding ***halakha*. And Rabbi Ḥiyya bar Abba said: One is inclined** toward such a ruling in cases where an individual asks, but does not issue it as a public ruling in all cases. **And Rabbi Yosei, son of Rabbi Ḥanina, said: It appears** that one should rule this way, but it is not an established *halakha* that is considered binding with regard to issuing rulings.[N]

כַּלָּשׁוֹן הַזֶּה אָמַר רַבִּי יַעֲקֹב בַּר אִידִי, אָמַר רַבִּי יוֹחָנָן: רַבִּי מֵאִיר וְרַבִּי יְהוּדָה – הֲלָכָה כְּרַבִּי יְהוּדָה, רַבִּי יְהוּדָה וְרַבִּי יוֹסֵי – הֲלָכָה כְּרַבִּי יוֹסֵי, וְאֵין צָרִיךְ לוֹמַר רַבִּי מֵאִיר וְרַבִּי יוֹסֵי – הֲלָכָה כְּרַבִּי יוֹסֵי. הָשְׁתָּא בִּמְקוֹם רַבִּי יְהוּדָה – לֵיתָא, בִּמְקוֹם רַבִּי יוֹסֵי מִיבַּעְיָא?!

Rabbi Ya'akov bar Idi said that **Rabbi Yoḥanan said:** In the case of a dispute between **Rabbi Meir and Rabbi Yehuda,** the ***halakha* is in accordance with** the opinion of **Rabbi Yehuda;** in the case of a dispute between **Rabbi Yehuda and Rabbi Yosei,** the ***halakha* is in accordance with** the opinion of **Rabbi Yosei; and, needless to say,** in the case of a dispute between **Rabbi Meir and Rabbi Yosei,** the ***halakha* is in accordance with** the opinion of **Rabbi Yosei.** As now, if **in disputes with Rabbi Yehuda,** the opinion of Rabbi Meir **is not** accepted as law, **need it** be stated that **in disputes with Rabbi Yosei,** Rabbi Meir's opinion is rejected? Rabbi Yehuda's opinion is not accepted in disputes with Rabbi Yosei.[N]

אָמַר רַב אַסִּי: אַף אֲנִי לוֹמֵד רַבִּי יוֹסֵי וְרַבִּי שִׁמְעוֹן – הֲלָכָה כְּרַבִּי יוֹסֵי. דְּאָמַר רַבִּי אַבָּא, אָמַר רַבִּי יוֹחָנָן: רַבִּי יְהוּדָה וְרַבִּי שִׁמְעוֹן – הֲלָכָה כְּרַבִּי יְהוּדָה. הָשְׁתָּא בִּמְקוֹם רַבִּי יְהוּדָה לֵיתָא, בִּמְקוֹם רַבִּי יוֹסֵי מִיבַּעְיָא?!

Rav Asi said: I also learn based on the same principle that in a dispute between **Rabbi Yosei and Rabbi Shimon,** the ***halakha* is in accordance with** the opinion of **Rabbi Yosei. As Rabbi Abba said** that **Rabbi Yoḥanan said:** In cases of dispute between **Rabbi Yehuda and Rabbi Shimon,** the ***halakha* is in accordance with** the opinion of **Rabbi Yehuda. Now,** if **where** it is opposed by **Rabbi Yehuda** the opinion of Rabbi Shimon **is not** accepted as law, **where** it is opposed by the opinion of **Rabbi Yosei,** with whom the *halakha* is in accordance against Rabbi Yehuda, **is it necessary** to say that the *halakha* is in accordance with the opinion of Rabbi Yosei?

אִיבַּעְיָא לְהוּ: רַבִּי מֵאִיר וְרַבִּי שִׁמְעוֹן מַאי? תֵּיקוּ.

The Gemara **raises a dilemma:** In a dispute between **Rabbi Meir and Rabbi Shimon,**[N] **what** is the *halakha*? No sources were found to resolve this dilemma, and it **stands** unresolved.

אָמַר רַב מְשַׁרְשִׁיָּא: לֵיתְנְהוּ לְהָנֵי כְּלָלֵי. מְנָא לֵיהּ לְרַב מְשַׁרְשִׁיָּא הָא?

Rav Mesharshiya said: These principles of halakhic decision-making **are not** to be relied upon. The Gemara asks: **From where does Rav Mesharshiya** derive **this** statement?

אִילֵימָא מֵהָא דִּתְנַן, רַבִּי שִׁמְעוֹן אוֹמֵר: לְמָה הַדָּבָר דּוֹמֶה – לְשָׁלֹשׁ חֲצֵירוֹת הַפְּתוּחוֹת זוֹ לָזוֹ וּפְתוּחוֹת לִרְשׁוּת הָרַבִּים, עֵירְבוּ שְׁתַּיִם הַחִיצוֹנוֹת עִם הָאֶמְצָעִית – הִיא מוּתֶּרֶת עִמָּהֶן, וְהֵן מוּתָּרוֹת עִמָּהּ, וּשְׁתַּיִם הַחִיצוֹנוֹת אֲסוּרוֹת זוֹ עִם זוֹ.

If you say that he derived it **from that which we learned** in the mishna that **Rabbi Shimon said: To what is this comparable?** It is like **three courtyards that open into one another, and** also **open into a public domain. If the two outer** courtyards **established an *eiruv* with the middle one,** the residents of the middle one **are permitted to** carry to the two outer ones, **and they are permitted to** carry to **it, but the** residents of the **two outer** courtyards **are prohibited to** carry from **one** to **the other,** as they did not establish an *eiruv* with one another.

NOTES

The remnants of an *eiruv* and an initial *eiruv* – שִׁיּוּרֵי עֵירוּב וּתְחִילַּת עֵירוּב: The distinction between an initial *eiruv* and the remnants of an *eiruv* refers to two clearly distinct stages. Namely, that there are different standards for the initial phase of acquiring residence in a given location, or establishing an *eiruv* in a given alleyway, than for the remainder of an *eiruv*, where the question is whether an *eiruv* that has been established remains valid. As stated here, it is more reasonable to be lenient with regard to the remainder of an *eiruv*.

The *halakha* is in accordance with the opinion of Rabbi Yosei even in disputes with other Sages – הֲלָכָה...כְּרַבִּי יוֹסֵי מֵחֲבֵירָיו: The different versions of this statement raise the question of whether the *halakha* accords with the opinion of Rabbi Yosei only in disputes with an individual Sage, or even in a dispute with two or more Sages. Many authorities (*Halakhot Gedolot*, Rav Sherira Gaon, Rif, Ri Migash, Rabbeinu Manoaḥ, and apparently the Rambam and Rabbi Yosef Karo as well) maintain that the *halakha* is in accordance with his opinion only in disputes with an individual Sage, but not in disputes with other Sages (see *Yad Malakhi*).

***Halakha*…one is inclined…it appears – הֲלָכָה...מַטִּין...נִרְאִין:** These expressions have been explained in several ways (see Rashi and *Tosafot*). The *ge'onim* explain that the word *halakha* means that this matter has been established as law and must be accepted. The phrase it appears indicates that the Sages discussed this issue and the words of one Sage appear more acceptable than the statements of his colleague. The phrase one is inclined means that without examining in detail all sides of the argument, the judgment tends towards a particular opinion.

Halakhic decision-making – קְבִיעַת הֲלָכוֹת: These rules of halakhic decision-making, namely, that the *halakha* is in accordance with the opinion of a particular Sage in disputes with a given colleague, whether with regard to one issue or all issues, were established by the Sages, who examined these disputes and usually found a principle in the statements of each Sage that led them to accept or reject his approach. Nevertheless, these fixed rules are limited in several ways. The Gemara itself explicitly states that where a contradictory *halakha* is stated by *amora'im* the principle does not apply, and it was only stated with regard to cases where no explicit ruling exists. Most authorities agree that even when there is no halakhic ruling in accordance with one opinion, but the Gemara's discussion favors a particular approach and accepts it as the basis of its discussion, the *halakha* follows suit. Some commentaries state that these principles do not apply to any issue that is not practical *halakha* nowadays, such as the laws related to the Temple. In addition, other principles occasionally override these fixed rules of halakhic decision-making. Examples include the principle of accepting the lenient opinion with regard to an *eiruv*, the rules listed in tractate *Eduyot*, and the acceptance of Rabbi Meir's decrees.

Rabbi Meir and Rabbi Shimon – רַבִּי מֵאִיר וְרַבִּי שִׁמְעוֹן: This dilemma is left unresolved in the Babylonian Talmud. Several authorities write that in these disputes, the stringent opinion is accepted with regard to Torah law, and the lenient opinion is accepted with regard to rabbinic law. However, in the Jerusalem Talmud it is stated that the *halakha* is in accordance with the opinion of Rabbi Shimon in disputes with Rabbi Meir. Apparently, Rav Sherira Gaon and the Ra'avad rule in accordance with the Jerusalem Talmud, as does Rambam, according to the *Leḥem Mishne* (see *Yad Malakhi*).

ואמר רב חמא בר גוריא, אמר רב: הלכה כרבי שמעון. ומאן פליג עליה – רבי יהודה. והא אמרת: רבי יהודה ורבי שמעון הלכה כרבי יהודה, אלא לאו שמע מינה: ליתנהו.

And Rav Ḥama bar Gurya said that **Rav said:** The ***halakha* is in accordance with** the opinion of **Rabbi Shimon; and who disagrees with** Rabbi Shimon on this matter? It is **Rabbi Yehuda. Didn't you say:** In disputes between **Rabbi Yehuda and Rabbi Shimon,** the ***halakha* is in accordance with** the opinion of **Rabbi Yehuda? Rather, can we not conclude from** this mishna that these principles should **not** be relied upon?

ומאי קושיא? דילמא: היכא דאיתמר – איתמר, היכא דלא איתמר – לא איתמר.

The Gemara rejects this argument: **What is the difficulty** posed by this ruling? **Perhaps where it is stated** explicitly to the contrary, **it is stated,** but **where it is not stated** explicitly to the contrary, **it is not stated,** and these principles apply.

אלא מהא, דתנן: עיר של יחיד ונעשית של רבים – מערבין את כולה. של רבים ונעשית של יחיד – אין מערבין את כולה, אלא אם כן עושה חוצה לה כעיר חדשה שביהודה, שיש בה חמשים דיורין, דברי רבי יהודה.

Rather, the proof is **from that which we learned** elsewhere in a mishna: **If a city that belongs to a** single **individual** subsequently **becomes** one that **belongs to many** people, **one may establish an** ***eiruv*** of courtyards **for all of it.** But if the city **belongs to many** people, **and it** falls into the possession **of a** single **individual, one may not establish an** ***eiruv*** **for all of it, unless he excludes** from the *eiruv* an area the size **of the town of Ḥadasha in Judea, which contains fifty residents;** this is **the statement of Rabbi Yehuda.**

רבי שמעון אומר:

Rabbi Shimon says:

Perek **IV**
Daf **47** Amud **a**

שלש חצירות של שני בתים. ואמר רב חמא בר גוריא, אמר רב: הלכה כרבי שמעון. ומאן פליג עליה – רבי יהודה. והא אמרת: רבי יהודה ורבי שמעון הלכה כרבי יהודה!

The excluded area need not be so large; rather, **three courtyards** each **containing two houses** are sufficient for this purpose. **And Rav Ḥama bar Gurya said** that **Rav said:** The ***halakha* is in accordance with** the opinion of **Rabbi Shimon; and who disagrees with** Rabbi Shimon on this matter? It is **Rabbi Yehuda. Didn't you say:** In a case where **Rabbi Yehuda and Rabbi Shimon** disagree, the ***halakha* is in accordance with** the opinion of **Rabbi Yehuda?** This teaches that one should not rely on these principles.

ומאי קושיא? דילמא הכא נמי, היכא דאיתמר – איתמר, היכא דלא איתמר – לא איתמר.

The Gemara rejects this argument as well: **What is the difficulty** here? **Perhaps here, too, where it is stated** explicitly that the *halakha* is in accordance with Rabbi Shimon, **it is stated,** but **where it is not stated** explicitly, **it is not stated,** and the principle that the *halakha* is in accordance with the opinion of Rabbi Yehuda applies.

אלא מהא, דתנן: המניח את ביתו והלך לשבות בעיר אחרת, אחד נכרי ואחד ישראל – אוסר לבני חצירות, דברי רבי מאיר.

Rather, the proof is **from that which we learned** elsewhere in a mishna: With regard to **one who left his house** without making an *eiruv* of courtyards, **and established residence** for Shabbat **in a different town, whether** he was **a gentile or a Jew,** his lack of participation **prohibits the** other **residents of the courtyards** in which he has a share to carry objects from their houses to the courtyard, because he did not establish an *eiruv* with them, and failure to include a house in the *eiruv* imposes restrictions upon all the residents of the courtyard. This is **the statement of Rabbi Meir.**

רבי יהודה אומר: אינו אוסר. רבי יוסי אומר: נכרי – אוסר, ישראל – אינו אוסר, מפני שאין דרך ישראל לבא בשבת. רבי שמעון אומר: אפילו הניח את ביתו והלך לשבות אצל בתו באותה העיר – אינו אוסר, שכבר הסיח דעתו.

Rabbi Yehuda says: His lack of participation **does not prohibit** the others to carry, since he is not present there. **Rabbi Yosei says:** Lack of participation in an *eiruv* by **a gentile** who is away **prohibits** the others to carry, because he might return on Shabbat; but lack of participation by **a Jew** who is not present **does not prohibit** the others to carry, **as it is not the way of a Jew to return on Shabbat** once he has already established his residence elsewhere. **Rabbi Shimon says: Even if he left his house and established residence** for Shabbat **with his daughter in the same town, his** lack of participation **does not prohibit** the residents of his courtyard to carry, even though he is permitted to return home, **because he has already removed it,** i.e., returning, **from his mind.**

וְאָמַר רַב חָמָא בַּר גּוּרְיָא, אָמַר רַב: הֲלָכָה כְּרַבִּי שִׁמְעוֹן. וּמַאן פָּלֵיג עֲלֵיהּ – רַבִּי יְהוּדָה. וְהָא אָמְרַתְּ רַבִּי יְהוּדָה וְרַבִּי שִׁמְעוֹן הֲלָכָה כְּרַבִּי יְהוּדָה!

And Rav Ḥama bar Gurya said that Rav said: The *halakha* is in accordance with the opinion of Rabbi Shimon. And who disagrees with him? It is Rabbi Yehuda. Didn't you say: When there is a dispute between Rabbi Yehuda and Rabbi Shimon, the *halakha* is in accordance with the opinion of Rabbi Yehuda? This teaches that one cannot rely upon these principles.

וּמַאי קוּשְׁיָא? דִּלְמָא הָכָא נַמִּי, הֵיכָא דְּאִיתְּמַר – אִיתְּמַר, הֵיכָא דְּלָא אִיתְּמַר – לָא אִיתְּמַר.

The Gemara rejects this argument again: **What is the difficulty** here? **Perhaps here, too, where it is** explicitly **stated** that the *halakha* is in accordance with the opinion of Rabbi Shimon, **it is stated;** but **where** such a ruling **is not stated, it is not stated,** and the principle that the *halakha* is in accordance with the opinion of Rabbi Yehuda is relied upon.

אֶלָּא מֵהָא, דִּתְנַן: וְזֶהוּ שֶׁאָמְרוּ הֶעָנִי מְעָרֵב בְּרַגְלָיו. רַבִּי מֵאִיר אוֹמֵר: אָנוּ אֵין לָנוּ אֶלָּא עָנִי.

Rather, the proof is **from that which we learned** in the mishna. **And that is what** the Sages meant when **they said: A pauper can establish an *eiruv* with his feet;** that is to say, he may walk to a place within his Shabbat limit and declare: Here shall be my place of residence, and then his Shabbat limit is measured from that spot. **Rabbi Meir says: We** apply this law **only to a pauper,** who does not have food for two meals; only such a person is permitted to establish his *eiruv* by walking to the spot that he wishes to acquire as his place of residence.

רַבִּי יְהוּדָה אוֹמֵר: אֶחָד עָנִי וְאֶחָד עָשִׁיר, לֹא אָמְרוּ מְעָרְבִין בְּפַת אֶלָּא לְהָקֵל עַל הֶעָשִׁיר, שֶׁלֹּא יֵצֵא וִיעָרֵב בְּרַגְלָיו.

Rabbi Yehuda says: This allowance applies **both to a pauper and to a wealthy person.** Indeed, **they said** that **one can establish an *eiruv* with bread only in order to** make placing an *eiruv* **easier for a wealthy person, so that he** need **not** trouble himself and **go out and establish an *eiruv* with his feet,** but the basic *eiruv* is established by walking to the spot one will acquire as his place of residence.

וּמַתְנֵי לֵיהּ רַב חִיָּיא בַּר אָשֵׁי לְחִיָּיא בַּר רַב קַמֵּיהּ דְּרַב: אֶחָד עָנִי וְאֶחָד עָשִׁיר. וְאָמַר לֵיהּ רַב: סַיֵּים בָּהּ נַמִּי: הֲלָכָה כְּרַבִּי יְהוּדָה.

And Rav Ḥiyya bar Ashi once **taught** this law **to Ḥiyya bar Rav in the presence of Rav,** saying: This allowance applies **both to a pauper and to a wealthy person, and Rav said to him:** When you teach this law, **conclude also with** this ruling: The ***halakha* is in accordance with** the opinion **of Rabbi Yehuda.**

תַּרְתֵּי לָמָּה לִי? וְהָא אָמְרַתְּ: רַבִּי מֵאִיר וְרַבִּי יְהוּדָה הֲלָכָה כְּרַבִּי יְהוּדָה!

The Gemara asks: **Why do I need a second** ruling? **Didn't you** already **say:** When there is a dispute between **Rabbi Meir and Rabbi Yehuda,** the ***halakha* is in accordance with** the opinion of **Rabbi Yehuda?** The fact that Rav needed to specify that the *halakha* is in accordance with the opinion of Rabbi Yehuda on this matter indicates that he does not accept the general principle that when there is a dispute between Rabbi Meir and Rabbi Yehuda, the *halakha* is in accordance with the opinion of Rabbi Yehuda.

וּמַאי קוּשְׁיָא? דִּילְמָא רַב לֵית לֵיהּ לְהָנֵי כְּלָלֵי?!

The Gemara rejects this reasoning: **What is the difficulty** here? **Perhaps Rav does not accept**[N] **these principles,** but the other Sages accept them.

אֶלָּא מֵהָא, דִּתְנַן: הַיְּבָמָה לֹא תַּחֲלוֹץ וְלֹא תִּתְיַיבֵּם עַד שֶׁיְּהוּ לָהּ שְׁלֹשָׁה חֳדָשִׁים.

Rather, the Gemara brings a proof **from that which we learned** in another mishna with regard to a woman waiting for her brother-in-law, i.e., a woman whose husband died without children but who is survived a by a brother. The brother-in-law is obligated by Torah law either to perform levirate marriage with his deceased brother's widow, or to free her to marry others by participating in *ḥalitza*. **The woman waiting for her brother-in-law may neither participate in *ḥalitza***[H] **nor undergo levirate marriage until three months have passed** following her husband's death, due to concern that she may be pregnant from him, in which case she is exempt from levirate marriage and *ḥalitza*. After the three-month waiting period it will become clear whether she is pregnant from her husband.

וְכֵן שְׁאָר כׇּל הַנָּשִׁים לֹא יִנָּשְׂאוּ וְלֹא יִתְאָרְסוּ עַד שֶׁיְּהוּ לָהֶן שְׁלֹשָׁה חֳדָשִׁים. אֶחָד בְּתוּלוֹת וְאֶחָד בְּעוּלוֹת, אֶחָד אַלְמָנוֹת וְאֶחָד גְּרוּשׁוֹת, אֶחָד אֲרוּסוֹת וְאֶחָד נְשׂוּאוֹת.

And similarly, all other women may not be married or even **betrothed until three months have passed**[N] following their divorce or the death of their husbands, **whether** they are **virgins or non-virgins, whether** they are **widows or divorcees,** and **whether** they became widowed or divorced when they were **betrothed or married.** In all cases, the woman may not marry for three months. Otherwise, if she is within the first three months of her pregnancy from her first husband, and she gives birth six months later, a doubt would arise as to the identity of the father. The Sages did not differentiate between cases where this concern is applicable and where it is not; rather, they fixed a principle that applies universally.

NOTES

Perhaps Rav does not accept – דִּילְמָא רַב לֵית לֵיהּ: Although the Gemara will ultimately accept this explanation, it rejects it at this stage, preferring to suggest that there is no dispute between Rav and Rabbi Yoḥanan rather than say that Rav does not accept these principles (Ritva).

The three months of differentiation – שְׁלֹשָׁה חוֹדְשֵׁי הַבְחָנָה: The purpose of the three-month waiting period between the first marriage and the second is to determine, in case she gives birth six months into her second marriage, whether the child she bears is the son of the first husband or the second. Two considerations determine the waiting period: The first is derived from the verse (Genesis 37:24) that indicates that a woman's pregnancy is noticeable after approximately three months. The second is based on the ambiguity that arises if she marries before three months have elapsed and a child is born seven months later. Such a child might have been born after seven months to the second husband, or possibly born after nine months to the first husband.

HALAKHA

The woman waiting for her brother-in-law may neither participate in *ḥalitza* – יְבָמָה לֹא תַּחֲלוֹץ: A widow must wait three months following the death of her husband before participating in the ceremony that frees her from the levirate bond [*ḥalitza*]. However, if she participates in the *ḥalitza* ceremony within this time period and is subsequently found not to be pregnant, her *ḥalitza* is valid. Some authorities maintain that the Sages invalidated such a *ḥalitza* (Rema; *Shulḥan Arukh, Even HaEzer* 164:1).

רַבִּי יְהוּדָה אוֹמֵר: נְשׂוּאוֹת – יִתְאָרְסוּ,

Rabbi Yehuda says: A woman who had been **married** when she became widowed or divorced **may be betrothed** immediately, as couples do not have relations during the period of their betrothal. However, she may not marry until three months have passed, in order to differentiate between any possible offspring from the first and second husband.

וַאֲרוּסוֹת – יִנָּשְׂאוּ, חוּץ מֵאֲרוּסָה שֶׁבִּיהוּדָה, מִפְּנֵי שֶׁלִּבּוֹ גַּס בָּהּ.

A woman who had only been **betrothed** when she became widowed or divorced **may be married** immediately, as it may be assumed that the couple did not have relations during the period of their betrothal. This is **except for a betrothed woman in Judea, because** there the bridegroom's **heart is bold,** as it was customary for couples to be alone together during the period of betrothal, and consequently there is a suspicion that they might have had relations, in which case she might be carrying his child. However, no similar concern applies in other places.

רַבִּי יוֹסֵי אוֹמֵר: כׇּל הַנָּשִׁים יִתְאָרְסוּ, חוּץ מִן הָאַלְמָנָה, מִפְּנֵי הָאִיבּוּל.

Rabbi Yosei says: All the women listed above **may be betrothed** immediately, because the decree applies only with regard to marriage; this is **except for a widow,** who must wait for a different reason, **because** of the **mourning** for her deceased husband.

וְאָמְרִינַן: רַבִּי אֱלִיעֶזֶר לָא עָל לְבֵי מִדְרָשָׁא, אַשְׁכְּחֵיהּ לְרַבִּי אַסִּי דַּהֲוָה קָאֵים. אֲמַר לֵיהּ: מַאי אַמוּר בְּבֵי מִדְרָשָׁא? אֲמַר לֵיהּ, הָכִי אֲמַר לֵיהּ יוֹחָנָן: הֲלָכָה כְּרַבִּי יוֹסֵי. מִכְּלָל דִּיחִידָאָה פָּלֵיג עֲלֵיהּ?

And we said with regard to this: It once happened that **Rabbi Eliezer did not come to the study hall. He met Rabbi Asi, who was standing,** and **said to him: What did they say** today **in the study hall? He said to him** that **Rabbi Yoḥanan said as follows:** The ***halakha*** **is in accordance with** the opinion of **Rabbi Yosei.** Rabbi Eliezer asked: **By inference,** can it be inferred from the fact that the *halakha* is in accordance with his opinion that only **a single** authority **disagrees with him?**

אִין, וְהָתַנְיָא: הֲרֵי שֶׁהָיְתָה רְדוּפָה לֵילֵךְ לְבֵית אָבִיהָ, אוֹ שֶׁהָיְתָה לָהּ כַּעַס עִם בַּעְלָהּ, אוֹ שֶׁהָיָה בַּעְלָהּ זָקֵן אוֹ חוֹלֶה, אוֹ שֶׁהָיְתָה הִיא חוֹלָה עֲקָרָה זְקֵנָה קְטַנָּה וְאַיְילוֹנִית וְשֶׁאֵינָהּ רְאוּיָה לֵילֵד, אוֹ שֶׁהָיָה בַּעְלָהּ חָבוּשׁ בְּבֵית הָאֲסוּרִין, הַמַּפֶּלֶת לְאַחַר מִיתַת בַּעְלָהּ – כּוּלָּן צְרִיכִין לְהַמְתִּין שְׁלֹשָׁה חֳדָשִׁים, דִּבְרֵי רַבִּי מֵאִיר. רַבִּי יוֹסֵי מַתִּיר לֵיאָרֵס וְלִינָּשֵׂא מִיָּד.

Rabbi Asi answered: **Yes, and** so **it was taught** in the following *baraita*: **If** a woman **was eager to go to her father's house** and did not remain with her husband during his final days, **or** if she **was angry with her husband** and they separated, **or** if **her husband was elderly or sick** and could not father children, **or** if **she was sick,** or **barren,** or **an elderly woman,** or **a minor, or a sexually underdeveloped woman** who is incapable of bearing children,[B] **or a woman who was unfit to give birth** for any other reason, **or** if **her husband was imprisoned in jail,** or if **she had miscarried after the death of her husband,** so that there is no longer any concern that she might be pregnant from him, **all** these women **must wait three months**[H] before remarrying or even becoming betrothed; this is **the statement of Rabbi Meir,** who maintains that this decree applies to all women, even when the particular situation renders it unnecessary. In all these cases **Rabbi Yosei permits** the woman **to be betrothed and to marry immediately.**

לָמָּה לִי? וְהָא אָמְרַתְּ רַבִּי מֵאִיר וְרַבִּי יוֹסֵי הֲלָכָה כְּרַבִּי יוֹסֵי!

The Gemara resumes its question: **Why do I need** Rabbi Yoḥanan to state that the *halakha* is in accordance with Rabbi Yosei? **Didn't you say:** In a dispute between **Rabbi Meir and Rabbi Yosei,** the ***halakha*** **is in accordance with** the opinion of **Rabbi Yosei,** and therefore the *halakha* should be in accordance with him here as well? This implies that the principle is not to be relied upon.

וּמַאי קוּשְׁיָא? דִּלְמָא לְאַפּוֹקֵי מִדְּרַב נַחְמָן אָמַר שְׁמוּאֵל, דְּאָמַר: הֲלָכָה כְּרַבִּי מֵאִיר בִּגְזֵירוֹתָיו.

The Gemara rejects this argument: **What is the difficulty** here? **Perhaps** this ruling **comes to exclude** what **Rav Naḥman said** that **Shmuel said:** Although there are many cases in which the *halakha* is not in accordance with the opinion of Rabbi Meir, nonetheless, the ***halakha*** **is in accordance with Rabbi Meir with respect to his decrees,**[N] i.e., in those cases where he imposed a restriction in a particular case due to its similarity to another case. For this reason Rabbi Yoḥanan had to say that the *halakha* here is in accordance with the opinion of Rabbi Yosei, notwithstanding its opposition to Rabbi Meir's decree.

BACKGROUND

A sexually underdeveloped woman – אַיְילוֹנִית: A sexually underdeveloped woman is incapable of giving birth, because she lacks certain secondary female sexual characteristics, probably as a result of a congenital defect of the hormonal system. In various places the Talmud discusses the definition of a sexually underdeveloped woman [*ailonit*] and the implications in Jewish law.

HALAKHA

Waiting before marriage – הַמְתָּנָה לִפְנֵי נִישּׂוּאִין: Any woman who was married or betrothed must wait three months to remarry after her husband's death or after her bill of divorce was written, or as some authorities rule, after she receives the bill of divorce (Rema, based on *Tur* and Rosh). This applies even if there is no reason to suspect that the woman is pregnant, such as if she lived apart from her husband or was incapable of conceiving. This is in accordance with the opinion of Rabbi Yoḥanan, who ruled in accordance with the opinion of Rabbi Meir. It is also in accordance with the principle stated by Shmuel that the *halakha* is in accordance with Rabbi Meir's decrees (see *Migdal Oz* and *Hagahot Maimoniyot*; *Shulḥan Arukh, Even HaEzer* 3:1).

NOTES

The *halakha* is in accordance with Rabbi Meir with respect to his decrees – הֲלָכָה כְּרַבִּי מֵאִיר בִּגְזֵירוֹתָיו: The early commentaries distinguish between Rabbi Meir's decrees and his monetary penalties. With regard to Rabbi Meir's decrees, the *halakha* is in accordance with his opinion; with regard to his monetary penalties, his rulings are not accepted. The rationale for this difference is that decrees involve specific cases which are prohibited due to their similarity to another case, but not prohibited in and of themselves. The concern is that leniency in one case would lead people to treat the prohibited case lightly and act leniently in that case as well. Fines, however, are punishments that go beyond the letter of the law. In this way, Rabbi Meir treats the offender in a stringent manner, to prevent him from sinning again (see *Tosefot HaRosh* and *Yad Malakhi*).

אֶלָּא מֵהָא, דְּתַנְיָא: הוֹלְכִין לְיָרִיד שֶׁל נׇכְרִים וְלוֹקְחִים מֵהֶן בְּהֵמָה וַעֲבָדִים וּשְׁפָחוֹת בָּתִּים שָׂדוֹת וּכְרָמִים, וְכוֹתֵב וּמַעֲלֶה בְּעַרְכָּאוֹת שֶׁלָּהֶן, מִפְּנֵי שֶׁהוּא כְּמַצִּיל מִיָּדָן.

Rather, the proof that these principles do not apply is **from that which was taught** in the following *baraita*: **One may go to a fair of** idolatrous **gentiles**[H] **and buy animals, slaves, and maidservants from them,**[N] as the purchase raises them to a more sanctified state; and he may buy **houses, fields, and vineyards** from them, due to the mitzva to settle Eretz Yisrael; **and he may write** the necessary deeds **and confirm** them **in their** gentile **courts**[N] with an official seal, even though this involves an acknowledgement of their authority, **because it is as though he were rescuing** his property **from their hands,** as the court's confirmation and stamp of approval prevents the sellers from appealing the sale and retracting it.

וְאִם הָיָה כֹּהֵן – מִטַּמֵּא בְּחוּצָה לָאָרֶץ לָדוּן וּלְעַרְעֵר עִמָּהֶן. וּכְשֵׁם שֶׁמִּטַּמֵּא בְּחוּצָה לָאָרֶץ, כָּךְ מִטַּמֵּא בְּבֵית הַקְּבָרוֹת.

And if he is a priest, he may become ritually impure by going **outside Eretz** Yisrael, where the earth and air are impure, in order **to litigate** with them **and to contest** their claims. **And just as** a priest **may become ritually impure** by going **outside Eretz** Yisrael, **so may he become ritually impure** for this purpose by entering **into a cemetery.**

בֵּית הַקְּבָרוֹת סָלְקָא דַּעְתָּךְ?! טוּמְאָה דְּאוֹרַיְיתָא הִיא!

The Gemara interrupts its presentation of the *baraita* to express surprise at this last ruling: **Can it enter your mind** to say that a priest may enter **a cemetery?** This would make him **ritually impure by Torah law.** How could the Sages permit a priest to become ritually impure by Torah law?

אֶלָּא בְּבֵית הַפְּרָס, דְּרַבָּנַן.

Rather, the *baraita* is referring to **an area where there is uncertainty with regard to the location of a grave or a corpse** [***beit haperas***], owing to the fact that a grave had been unwittingly plowed over, and the bones may have become scattered throughout the field. Such a field imparts ritual impurity only **by rabbinic law.**

וּמִטַּמֵּא לִישָּׂא אִשָּׁה וְלִלְמוֹד תּוֹרָה. אָמַר רַבִּי יְהוּדָה: אֵימָתַי – בִּזְמַן שֶׁאֵין מוֹצֵא לִלְמוֹד, אֲבָל מוֹצֵא לִלְמוֹד – לֹא יִטַּמֵּא.

The *baraita* continues: **And** a priest **may** likewise **become ritually impure** and leave Eretz Yisrael in order **to marry a woman or to study Torah** there. **Rabbi Yehuda said: When** does this allowance apply? When **he cannot find** a place **to study** in Eretz Yisrael. **But** if the priest can find a place **to study** in Eretz Yisrael, **he may not become ritually impure** by leaving the country.[H]

רַבִּי יוֹסֵי אוֹמֵר: אַף בִּזְמַן שֶׁמּוֹצֵא לִלְמוֹד נַמִי יִטַּמֵּא, לְפִי

Rabbi Yosei says: Even when he can find a place **to study** Torah in Eretz Yisrael, **he may also** leave the country and **become ritually impure, because**

HALAKHA

Going to a fair of gentiles – הֲלִיכָה לְיָרִיד: One is permitted to go to a market fair held in honor of idolatry in order to purchase things from the local farmers, especially if refraining from doing so would cause him significant financial loss. However, he may not buy from a merchant at such a fair, since part of his profits go to idolatry (*Shulḥan Arukh, Yoreh De'a* 149:3).

When may a priest become ritually impure – מָתַי מוּתָּר לְכֹהֵן לְהִיטַּמֵּא: A priest is permitted to become ritually impure with rabbinic impurity if he walks in an area where there is uncertainty with regard to the location of a grave or a corpse [*beit haperas*], or if he leaves Eretz Yisrael in order to marry a woman, learn Torah, or fulfill other mitzvot that he cannot perform in Eretz Yisrael (*Shulḥan Arukh, Yoreh De'a* 372:1).

NOTES

Buy animals…from them – לוֹקְחִים מֵהֶן בְּהֵמָה: An alternate rationale for this leniency is that animals and slaves and the other items listed here are not always readily available. The Sages waived their decrees in such cases of loss or irretrievable opportunity (Ritva).

Confirm in their courts – מַעֲלֶה בְּעַרְכָּאוֹת שֶׁלָּהֶן: The Sages prohibited litigation in gentile courts, even where they judge according to Jewish law, because this belittles the Jewish court and honors the gentile one. However, it is permitted in a case where the issue is of special importance.

Perek **IV**
Daf **47** Amud **b**

שֶׁאֵין מִן הַכֹּל זוֹכֶה אָדָם לִלְמוֹד. וְאָמַר רַבִּי יוֹסֵי: מַעֲשֶׂה בְּיוֹסֵף הַכֹּהֵן שֶׁהָלַךְ אֵצֶל רַבּוֹ לְצַיְדָּן לִלְמוֹד תּוֹרָה.

a person does not merit to learn from everyone, and it is possible that the only suitable teacher for him lives outside of Eretz Yisrael. **And Rabbi Yosei reported** in support of his position: **It once happened that Yosef the priest went to his teacher in Tzeidan,** outside Eretz Yisrael, **to learn Torah,** although the preeminent Sage of his generation, Rabban Yoḥanan ben Zakkai, lived in Eretz Yisrael.

וְאָמַר רַבִּי יוֹחָנָן: הֲלָכָה כְּרַבִּי יוֹסֵי. וְלָמָּה לִי? וְהָא אָמְרַתְּ: רַבִּי יְהוּדָה וְרַבִּי יוֹסֵי הֲלָכָה כְּרַבִּי יוֹסֵי!

And Rabbi Yoḥanan said about this: **The *halakha* is in accordance with** the opinion of **Rabbi Yosei.** The Gemara asks: **Why** was it necessary for Rabbi Yoḥanan to issue this ruling? **Didn't you say:** In disputes between **Rabbi Yehuda and Rabbi Yosei, the *halakha* is in accordance with** the opinion of **Rabbi Yosei,** and so it should be obvious that this *halakha* is in accordance with his opinion? Apparently, this principle is not accepted.

אָמַר אַבַּיֵי: אִיצְטְרִיךְ, סָלְקָא דַּעְתָּךְ אָמִינָא: הָנֵי מִילֵּי – בְּמַתְנִיתִין, אֲבָל בְּבָרַיְיתָא – אֵימָא לָא, קָא מַשְׁמַע לַן.

Abaye said: It **was** nonetheless **necessary** to issue this ruling, , it could have **entered your mind to say** that **this** principle **applies** only with regard to disputes **in the Mishna. But** with regard to disputes **in a *baraita*, say no,** the principle does not apply. Therefore, Rabbi Yoḥanan **is teaching us** that the *halakha* is in accordance with the opinion of Rabbi Yosei in this case as well.[N]

NOTES

In the Mishna but not in a *baraita* – בְּמִשְׁנָה, אֲבָל לֹא בִּבְרַיְיתָא: Rashi explains that it is possible that the opinions were reversed in a *baraita*, since *baraitot* were not always transmitted precisely. Elsewhere, the Sages express the concern not only about a reversal of the teachings, but also about a general lack of accuracy and inexact citation of the words of *tanna'im*. Consequently, the principles with regard to the Mishna do not always apply to the *baraitot*, even when the identity of the author is established. It is also possible that a principle was stated that takes into account everything stated in the *mishnayot*, whereas there is no way of knowing everything stated in all of the *baraitot*.

HALAKHA

Objects that belong to a gentile – חֶפְצֵי נָכְרִי: Objects that belong to a gentile establish residence in the spot where they are located, and it is permitted for a Jew to move them only two thousand cubits in each direction, in accordance with the opinion of Rabbi Yoḥanan and the conclusion of the Gemara (*Shulḥan Arukh, Oraḥ Ḥayyim* 401).

אֶלָּא הָכִי קָאָמַר: הָנֵי כְּלָלֵי לָאו דִּבְרֵי הַכֹּל נִינְהוּ, דְּהָא רַב לֵית לֵיהּ הָנֵי כְּלָלֵי.

Since no proof has been found to support Rav Mesharshiya's statement that there are no principles for issuing halakhic rulings, the Gemara emends his statement. **Rather, this** is what Rav Mesharshiya **is saying: These principles were not accepted by all** authorities, as in fact **Rav did not accept these principles,** as demonstrated above.

אָמַר רַב יְהוּדָה, אָמַר שְׁמוּאֵל: חֶפְצֵי נָכְרִי אֵין קוֹנִין שְׁבִיתָה.

The Gemara returns to addressing acquisition of residence. **Rav Yehuda said** that **Shmuel said: Objects belonging to a gentile do not acquire residence** and do not have a Shabbat limit, either on their own account or due to the ownership of the gentile. Accordingly, if they were brought into a town from outside its limits, a Jew may carry them two thousand cubits in each direction.

לְמַאן? אִילֵימָא לְרַבָּנַן – פְּשִׁיטָא! הָשְׁתָּא חֶפְצֵי הֶפְקֵר, דְּלֵית לְהוּ בְּעָלִים, אֵין קוֹנִין שְׁבִיתָה – חֶפְצֵי הַנָּכְרִי, דְּאִית לְהוּ בְּעָלִים מִיבַּעְיָא?!

The Gemara asks: **In accordance with whose** opinion was this statement made? **If you say** that it was made **in accordance with** the opinion of **the Rabbis,** it is **obvious. Now, if unclaimed objects, which do not have owners, do not acquire residence, is it necessary** to say that **a gentile's objects, which have an owner,** do not acquire residence?

אֶלָּא אַלִּיבָּא דְּרַבִּי יוֹחָנָן בֶּן נוּרִי. וְקָא מַשְׁמַע לָן: אֵימַר דְּאָמַר רַבִּי יוֹחָנָן בֶּן נוּרִי קוֹנִין שְׁבִיתָה – הָנֵי מִילֵּי חֶפְצֵי הֶפְקֵר, דְּלֵית לְהוּ בְּעָלִים. אֲבָל חֶפְצֵי הַנָּכְרִי, דְּאִית לְהוּ בְּעָלִים – לֹא.

Rather, this statement must have been made **in accordance with** the opinion of **Rabbi Yoḥanan ben Nuri, and** Shmuel **is teaching us** that when we **say** that **Rabbi Yoḥanan ben Nuri said** that objects **acquire residence, this applies only** to **unclaimed objects, which have no owners; but** it does **not** apply to **objects** belonging **to a gentile, which have owners.**

מֵיתִיבִי, רַבִּי שִׁמְעוֹן בֶּן אֶלְעָזָר אוֹמֵר: הַשּׁוֹאֵל כְּלִי מִן הַנָּכְרִי בְּיוֹם טוֹב, וְכֵן הַמַּשְׁאִיל לוֹ לַנָּכְרִי כְּלִי מֵעֶרֶב יוֹם טוֹב וְהֶחְזִירוֹ לוֹ בְּיוֹם טוֹב, וְהַכֵּלִים וְהָאוֹצָרוֹת שֶׁשָּׁבְתוּ בְּתוֹךְ הַתְּחוּם – יֵשׁ לָהֶן אַלְפַּיִם אַמָּה לְכָל רוּחַ. וְנָכְרִי שֶׁהֵבִיא לוֹ פֵּירוֹת מִחוּץ לַתְּחוּם – הֲרֵי זֶה לֹא יְזִיזֵם מִמְּקוֹמָן.

The Gemara raises an objection from a *baraita*. **Rabbi Shimon ben Elazar says:** With regard to a Jew **who borrowed a utensil from a gentile on a Festival, and similarly** with regard to a Jew **who lent a utensil to a gentile on the eve of a Festival and** the gentile **returned it to him on the Festival, and** likewise **utensils or bins that acquired residence within the** city's Shabbat **limit,** in all these cases the utensils **have,** i.e., can be moved, **two thousand cubits in each direction. But if a gentile brought** the Jew **produce from outside** the Shabbat **limit,** the Jew **may not move it from its place.**

אִי אָמְרַתְּ בִּשְׁלָמָא קָסָבַר רַבִּי יוֹחָנָן בֶּן נוּרִי חֶפְצֵי נָכְרִי קוֹנִין שְׁבִיתָה, הָא מַנִּי – רַבִּי יוֹחָנָן בֶּן נוּרִי הִיא.

Granted if you say that Rabbi Yoḥanan ben Nuri holds that **objects that belong to a gentile acquire residence,** one can say that **this** *baraita* is in accordance with **whose** opinion? **It is** in accordance with the opinion of **Rabbi Yoḥanan ben Nuri,** that even a gentile's objects acquire residence.

אֶלָּא אִי אָמְרַתְּ קָסָבַר רַבִּי יוֹחָנָן בֶּן נוּרִי חֶפְצֵי הַנָּכְרִי אֵין קוֹנִין שְׁבִיתָה, הָא מַנִּי? לֹא רַבִּי יוֹחָנָן בֶּן נוּרִי וְלֹא רַבָּנַן!

However, if you say that Rabbi Yoḥanan ben Nuri holds that **objects belonging to a gentile do not acquire residence,** in accordance with **whose** opinion is **this** *baraita*? It is **neither** in accordance with that of **Rabbi Yoḥanan ben Nuri nor** that of **the Rabbis.**

לְעוֹלָם קָסָבַר רַבִּי יוֹחָנָן בֶּן נוּרִי ״חֶפְצֵי הַנָּכְרִי קוֹנִין שְׁבִיתָה״, וּשְׁמוּאֵל דְּאָמַר כְּרַבָּנַן. וּדְקָאָמְרַתְּ לְרַבָּנַן פְּשִׁיטָא – מַהוּ דְּתֵימָא: גְּזֵירָה בְּעָלִים דְּנָכְרִי אַטּוּ בְּעָלִים דְּיִשְׂרָאֵל, קָא מַשְׁמַע לָן.

The Gemara answers: **Actually,** say that **Rabbi Yoḥanan ben Nuri holds** that **a gentile's objects acquire residence,** and that **Shmuel,** who said that they do not acquire residence, **spoke in accordance with** the opinion of **the Rabbis. And** with regard to **that which you said,** that **according to** the opinion of **the Rabbis,** it **is obvious** that a gentile's objects do not acquire residence, so this ruling need not have been stated at all. The Gemara answers: That is incorrect, as **you might have said** that the Sages should issue a **decree** in the case of **gentile owners** that his objects acquire residence in his location and that they may not be carried beyond two thousand cubits from that spot, lest people carry objects belonging to **a Jewish owners** beyond their two-thousand-cubit limit. Therefore, it **is teaching us** that no decree was issued.

וְרַב חִיָּיא בַּר אָבִין אָמַר רַבִּי יוֹחָנָן: חֶפְצֵי נָכְרִי קוֹנִין שְׁבִיתָה, גְּזֵירָה בְּעָלִים דְּנָכְרִי אַטּוּ בְּעָלִים דְּיִשְׂרָאֵל.

Rav Ḥiyya bar Avin, however, **said** that **Rabbi Yoḥanan said: Objects that belong to a gentile**[H] indeed **acquire residence,** due to the aforementioned **decree** issued in the case of **gentile owners due to** the case of **Jewish owners.**

הָנְהוּ דִּכְרֵי דְּאָתוּ לְמַבְרַכְתָּא, שְׁרָא לְהוּ רָבָא לִבְנֵי מְחוֹזָא לְמִיזְבַּן מִינַּיְיהוּ.

The Gemara relates that **certain rams were brought to** the town of **Mavrakhta** on Shabbat. **Rava permitted the residents of Meḥoza to purchase them**[N] and take them home, although Mavrakhta was outside the Shabbat limit of Meḥoza and could be reached by the residents of Meḥoza only by way of an *eiruv* of Shabbat limits.

אֲמַר לֵיהּ רָבִינָא לְרָבָא: מַאי דַּעְתִּיךְ – דְּאָמַר רַב יְהוּדָה, אָמַר שְׁמוּאֵל: חֶפְצֵי נׇכְרִי אֵין קוֹנִין שְׁבִיתָה,

Ravina said to Rava: What is your reasoning in permitting these rams? You must rely upon that which **Rav Yehuda said** that **Shmuel said: Objects belonging to a gentile do not acquire residence,** and so they are permitted even if they were brought to Meḥoza from outside the Shabbat limit.

וְהָא שְׁמוּאֵל וְרַבִּי יוֹחָנָן הֲלָכָה כְּרַבִּי יוֹחָנָן, וְאָמַר רַב חִיָּיא בַּר אָבִין אָמַר רַבִּי יוֹחָנָן: חֶפְצֵי נׇכְרִי קוֹנִין שְׁבִיתָה, גְּזֵירָה בְּעָלִים דְּנׇכְרִי אַטּוּ בְּעָלִים דְּיִשְׂרָאֵל!

Isn't the principle, in disputes between **Shmuel and Rabbi Yoḥanan,** that **the *halakha* is in accordance with** the opinion of **Rabbi Yoḥanan? And Rav Ḥiyya bar Avin** already **said** that **Rabbi Yoḥanan said: Objects that belong to a gentile acquire residence,** based on **a decree** in the case of **a gentile owner, due to** the case of **a Jewish owner.** The *halakha* is in accordance with his opinion.

הֲדַר אָמַר רָבָא: לִיזְדַּבְּנוּ לִבְנֵי מַבְרַכְתָּא. דְּכוּלַּהּ מַבְרַכְתָּא לְדִידְהוּ כְּאַרְבַּע אַמּוֹת דָּמְיָא.

Rava reconsidered and said: Let the rams **be sold** only **to the residents of Mavrakhta.**[N] Although the rams acquired residence, and may be moved only four cubits as they were taken beyond their Shabbat limit, the legal status of **all Mavrakhta is like four cubits for them.** However, they may not be sold to the residents of Meḥoza, as the *halakha* is in accordance with the opinion of Rabbi Yoḥanan.[H]

תָּנֵי רַבִּי חִיָּיא: חֵרֶם שֶׁבֵּין תְּחוּמֵי שַׁבָּת – צָרִיךְ

Rabbi Ḥiyya taught a *baraita*: **A water-filled ditch** [***ḥerem***][N] **that** lies **between** two **Shabbat limits requires**

NOTES

Acquisition on Shabbat – קִנְיָן בְּשַׁבָּת: The commentaries discuss the problematic aspect of the story itself: How could Rava have permitted buying and selling on Shabbat? Some commentaries answer that this case is not a standard purchase. Rather, shepherds who were well known to the locals entered the town and left various items in the possession of their Jewish acquaintances, without settling accounts on that day. The assumption is that the decree that prohibits buying and selling does not apply in that case (*Me'iri*; Rav Ya'akov Emden).

To the residents of Mavrakhta – לִבְנֵי מַבְרַכְתָּא: The assumption must be that these gentiles intended to bring the rams to the residents of Meḥoza, rather than Mavrakhta. This is because most authorities rule that a Jew may not utilize an object that was brought for him from outside the city, even if the whole city is considered like four cubits (Rashba).

Water-filled ditch [*ḥerem*] – חֵרֶם: Several explanations have been offered for this word (see *Tosafot*). One possibility is that the correct word is *ḥeres*, meaning a trench [*ḥaritz*], with the letter *tzaddi* interchanged with the letter *samekh*. However, most commentaries maintain that the word *ḥerem* is the correct version. According to some, the word *ḥerem* refers to a fishing net; a water trench is called a *ḥerem* because they would catch fish in it (Rabbeinu Yehonatan). According to others, it is derived from the verse: "One who is *ḥarum* or long-limbed" (Leviticus 21:18), in which the word *ḥarum* means sunken; and a sunken portion of the ground is also referred to as *ḥerem* (*Ge'on Ya'akov*).

HALAKHA

The objects of a gentile in a city – חֶפְצֵי נׇכְרִי בָּעִיר: If a gentile brings objects from outside the Shabbat limit to a city that is enclosed for the purpose of residence, it is permitted for a Jew to carry these objects within the city, in accordance with Rava's opinion (*Shulḥan Arukh, Oraḥ Ḥayyim* 401).

מְחִיצָה שֶׁל בַּרְזֶל לְהַפְסִיקוֹ. מְחַיֵּיךְ עֲלַיהּ רַבִּי יוֹסֵי בְּרַבִּי חֲנִינָא,

an iron partition to divide it into two separate areas, so that the residents of both places may draw water from it.[N] **Rabbi Yosei, son of Rabbi Ḥanina,** would **laugh at this** teaching,[N] as he deemed it unnecessary.

מַאי טַעְמָא קָא מְחַיֵּיךְ? אִילֵימָא מִשּׁוּם דְּתָנֵי לַהּ כְּרַבִּי יוֹחָנָן בֶּן נוּרִי לְחוּמְרָא, וְאִיהוּ סְבִירָא לֵיהּ כְּרַבָּנַן לְקוּלָּא? וּמִשּׁוּם דְּסָבַר לְקוּלָּא, מַאן דְּתָנֵי לְחוּמְרָא מְחַיֵּיךְ עֲלַהּ?

The Gemara asks: **Why did** Rabbi Yosei, son of Rabbi Ḥanina, **laugh? If you say** that it is **because** Rabbi Ḥiyya **taught** the *baraita* **stringently, in accordance with** the opinion of **Rabbi Yoḥanan ben Nuri,** saying that ownerless objects acquire a place of residence, **and** Rabbi Yosei, son of Rabbi Ḥanina **holds leniently, in accordance with** the opinion of **the Rabbis** and says that those objects do not acquire residence, this is difficult. Just **because he holds leniently, does he laugh at one who teaches stringently?**

אֶלָּא מִשּׁוּם דְּתַנְיָא: נְהָרוֹת הַמּוֹשְׁכִין וּמַעְיָינוֹת הַנּוֹבְעִין – הֲרֵי הֵן כְּרַגְלֵי כׇּל אָדָם.

Rather, he must have laughed for a different reason, **as it was taught** in a *baraita*: **Flowing rivers and streaming springs are like the feet of all people,** as the water did not acquire residence in any particular spot. Consequently, one who draws water from rivers and springs may carry it wherever he is permitted to walk, even if it had previously been located outside his Shabbat limit. According to Rabbi Yosei, son of Rabbi Ḥanina, the same *halakha* should apply to the water in the ditch.

וְדִילְמָא בִּמְכוּנָּסִין?

The Gemara rejects this argument: No proof can be brought from this ruling concerning rivers and springs, as **perhaps** we are dealing here with a ditch of still, **collected** water that belongs exclusively to the residents of that particular place.

NOTES

A water-filled ditch between Shabbat limits – חֵרֶם שֶׁבֵּין תְּחוּמֵי שַׁבָּת: According to some commentaries, Rabbi Ḥiyya maintains that going beyond the Shabbat limits is prohibited by Torah law. Consequently, a suspended partition is insufficient in that case, unlike the case of other water, where the carrying is prohibited by rabbinic law. Rabbi Yosei bar Ḥanina, however, maintains that going beyond the Shabbat limits is prohibited by rabbinic law. Therefore, a suspended partition suffices (*Kehillot Ya'akov*).

Laugh at this – מְחַיֵּיךְ עֲלֵיהּ: This expression, as an expression of objection to a particular opinion, is characteristic of Rabbi Yosei bar Ḥanina. It is stated in tractate *Sanhedrin* (17b): They laughed about this in the West, i.e., in Eretz Yisrael. Presumably, the reference there is to Rabbi Yosei bar Ḥanina.

אֶלָּא מִשּׁוּם דְּקָתָנֵי צָרִיךְ מְחִיצָה שֶׁל בַּרְזֶל לְהַפְסִיקוֹ. וּמַאי שְׁנָא קָנִים דְּלָא – דְּעָיְילִי בְּהוּ מַיָּא, שֶׁל בַּרְזֶל נַמִי – עָיְילִי בְּהוּ מַיָּא.

Rather, Rabbi Yosei, son of Rabbi Ḥanina, must have laughed for a different reason, **because** Rabbi Ḥiyya **taught** in his *baraita* that the ditch **requires an iron partition to divide it** into two separate sections. Rabbi Yosei, son of Rabbi Ḥanina, argued: **Why is** a partition of **reeds different, that** we should say it is **not** effective in that case? Apparently, it is **because water enters it** and passes from one limit to the other. But this is difficult, as **even** in the case of a partition **of iron, water enters it** and passes from one limit to another, as it cannot be hermetically sealed. If so, what does the iron accomplish that the reeds do not accomplish?

וְדִילְמָא צָרִיךְ וְאֵין לוֹ תַּקָּנָה קָאָמַר?

The Gemara raises a difficulty: **Perhaps** the *baraita* **is saying** as follows: A water-filled ditch that lies between two Shabbat limits **requires** an iron partition to divide it into two separate sections. **But there is no remedy,**[N] because it is impossible to hermetically seal a partition of that kind, and therefore its water may not be used.

מִשּׁוּם דְּקַל הוּא שֶׁהֵקִילוּ חֲכָמִים בַּמַּיִם.

Rather, you must say that Rabbi Yosei, son of Rabbi Ḥanina, laughed at Rabbi Ḥiyya's teaching for a different reason, **because the Sages were lenient with regard to water.** The Rabbis said that a minimal partition suffices in the case of water. Consequently, there should be no need for an iron partition.

כִּדְרַבִּי טַבְלָא, דִּבְעָא מִינֵּיהּ רַבִּי טַבְלָא מֵרַב: מְחִיצָה תְּלוּיָה, מַהוּ שֶׁתַּתִּיר בַּחוּרְבָּה?

This is **similar to** the case involving **Rabbi Tavla, as Rabbi Tavla asked of Rav: Does a suspended partition,** i.e., a partition that is suspended and does not reach the ground, **permit** carrying **in a ruin?** Do we say that the remnants of the walls that are suspended in the air are considered as though they descend to the ground and close off the area, so that it is regarded as a private domain?

אֲמַר לֵיהּ: אֵין מְחִיצָה תְּלוּיָה מַתֶּרֶת אֶלָּא בַּמַּיִם, קַל הוּא שֶׁהֵקִילוּ חֲכָמִים בַּמַּיִם.

Rav **said to him: A suspended partition** of this kind **permits** carrying **only** in the case of **water,** as **the Sages were lenient with regard to water.** Just as the Sages were lenient about water with respect to a suspended partition, so too they should be lenient here and not require an iron partition; rather, a minimal partition should suffice, even one made of reeds.

"וַחֲכָמִים אוֹמְרִים: אֵין לוֹ אֶלָּא אַרְבַּע וכו'". רַבִּי יְהוּדָה הַיְינוּ תַּנָּא קַמָּא!

The mishna taught: **And the Rabbis say** that if a person is sleeping at the onset of Shabbat and has no intention of acquiring residence in his location, **he has only four cubits,** whereas Rabbi Yehuda says he can walk four cubits in any direction he chooses. The Gemara asks: What is the dispute? The opinion of **Rabbi Yehuda is** the same as that of **the first *tanna*,** i.e., the Rabbis.

אָמַר רָבָא: שְׁמוֹנֶה עַל שְׁמוֹנֶה אִיכָּא בֵּינַיְיהוּ. תַּנְיָא נַמִי הָכִי: יֵשׁ לוֹ שְׁמוֹנֶה עַל שְׁמוֹנֶה, דִּבְרֵי רַבִּי מֵאִיר.

Rava said: There is a practical difference **between them,** as the Rabbis permit him to carry in an area of **eight by eight** cubits. Rabbi Yehuda maintains that he has only four cubits, in the direction of his choosing, whereas according to the Rabbis he has four cubits in every direction, which totals an area of eight by eight cubits. **That was also taught** explicitly in a *baraita*: **He has eight by eight** cubits; this is **the statement of Rabbi Meir,** which is the opinion of the Rabbis of the mishna.

וְאָמַר רָבָא: מַחֲלוֹקֶת לְהַלֵּךְ, אֲבָל לְטַלְטֵל – דִּבְרֵי הַכֹּל: אַרְבַּע אַמּוֹת – אִין, טְפֵי – לָא.

And Rava further **stated:** This **dispute** between Rabbi Meir and Rabbi Yehuda relates only **to walking, but as for carrying**[H] objects, **all agree** that to carry them **four cubits is indeed** permitted; but to carry them **more** than that is **not.**

וְהָנֵי אַרְבַּע אַמּוֹת הֵיכָא כְּתִיבָא?

The Gemara inquires about the basis of this law: **These four cubits** within which a person is always permitted to walk on Shabbat, **where are they written** in the Torah?

כִּדְתַנְיָא: "שְׁבוּ אִישׁ תַּחְתָּיו" – כְּתַחְתָּיו. [וְכַמָּה תַּחְתָּיו –] גּוּפוֹ שָׁלֹשׁ אַמּוֹת, וְאַמָּה כְּדֵי לִפְשׁוֹט יָדָיו וְרַגְלָיו, דִּבְרֵי רַבִּי מֵאִיר. רַבִּי יְהוּדָה אוֹמֵר: גּוּפוֹ שָׁלֹשׁ אַמּוֹת, וְאַמָּה כְּדֵי שֶׁיִּטּוֹל חֵפֶץ מִתַּחַת מַרְגְּלוֹתָיו, וּמַנִּיחַ תַּחַת מְרַאֲשׁוֹתָיו.

The Gemara answers: **As it was taught** in a *baraita*: The verse **"Remain every man in his place;** let no man go out of his place on the seventh day" (Exodus 16:29), means one must restrict his movement to an area **equal to his place. And how much is** the area of **his place?** A person's **body** typically measures **three cubits, and an** additional **cubit** is needed **in order** to allow him **to spread out his hands and feet,** this is **the statement of Rabbi Meir. Rabbi Yehuda says:** A person's **body** measures **three cubits, and an** additional **cubit** is needed **in order** to allow him **to pick up an object from under his feet and place it under his head,** meaning, to give him room to maneuver.

NOTES

A ditch requires it, but there is no remedy – צָרִיךְ וְאֵין לוֹ תַּקָּנָה: This expression appears in several places. The point is that when the Gemara uses the word requires it does not always mean that doing so is necessarily feasible in practice. Rather, it occasionally means that in principle a certain action is necessary. However, since it is impossible to perform that action, the matter in question remains prohibited.

HALAKHA

To walk and to carry – לְהַלֵּךְ וּלְטַלְטֵל: All people are permitted to walk and to carry objects within four cubits in the public domain, under all circumstances. However, the early and later commentaries dispute the exact measurement of these four cubits. With regard to walking, some authorities teach that the four cubits are measured with the person located at their center (Rema, citing the *Tur*). This ruling is in accordance with the statement of Rabbi Eliezer in the beginning of this mishna, which is the statement by the unattributed *tanna* cited before Rabbi Yehuda. Rabbi Eliezer states that since a total of four cubits are permitted, only two cubits are permitted in each direction (*Magen Avraham*; see the Vilna Gaon). The Rema, citing Rabbi Zeraḥya HaLevi and the Rashba, rules that he may walk four cubits in each direction, meaning that his limit is eight by eight cubits. This is in accordance with the opinion of the first *tanna* who disagrees with Rabbi Yehuda, who is lenient. With regard to carrying, four cubits and their diagonal are permitted (*Shulḥan Arukh, Oraḥ Ḥayyim* 397:1).

מַאי בֵּינַיְיהוּ? אִיכָּא בֵּינַיְיהוּ אַרְבַּע אַמּוֹת מְצוּמְצָמוֹת.

The Gemara asks: **What is** the practical difference **between them?** The Gemara answers: **There is** a practical difference **between them** in that Rabbi Yehuda provides him with **exactly four cubits**[N] but no more; whereas Rabbi Meir maintains that we do not restrict him in this manner, but rather he is provided with expansive cubits,[H] i.e., enough room to spread out his hands and feet, which measures slightly more than four cubits.

אֲמַר לֵיהּ רַב מְשַׁרְשְׁיָא לִבְרֵיהּ: כִּי עָיְילַתְּ לְקַמֵּיהּ דְּרַב פָּפָּא בְּעִי מִינֵּיהּ: אַרְבַּע אַמּוֹת שֶׁאָמְרוּ, בְּאַמָּה דִּידֵיהּ יָהֲבִינַן לֵיהּ, אוֹ בְּאַמָּה שֶׁל קֹדֶשׁ יָהֲבִינַן לֵיהּ?

Rav Mesharshiya said to his son: When you come before Rav Pappa, inquire of him as follows: The **four cubits** [*ammot*] mentioned here, **do we grant** them to each person measured **according to his own forearm** [*amma*], i.e., the distance from his elbow to the tip of his index finger, **or do we grant** them measured **according to the cubit** [*amma*] **used for consecrated** property, i.e., a standard cubit of six medium handbreadths for everyone?

אִם אָמַר לָךְ אַמּוֹת שֶׁל קֹדֶשׁ יָהֲבִינַן לֵיהּ – עוֹג מֶלֶךְ הַבָּשָׁן מַה תְּהֵא עָלָיו? וְאִם אָמַר לָךְ בְּאַמָּה דִּידֵיהּ יָהֲבִינַן לֵיהּ – אֵימָא לֵיהּ: מַאי טַעְמָא לָא קָתָנֵי לַהּ גַּבֵּי "יֵשׁ שֶׁאָמְרוּ הַכֹּל לְפִי מַה שֶּׁהוּא אָדָם"?

If he said to you that **we provide him** four cubits measured **according to the** standard **cubit used for consecrated** property, **what will be with regard to Og, king of the Bashan,** who is much larger than this? **And if he said to you** that **we provide him** four cubits measured **according to his own forearm, say to him: Why was** this *halakha* **not taught together with** the other matters whose measures are determined by the specific measure of the person involved, in the mishna that teaches: **These are** matters **with regard to which they stated** measures **all in accordance with the** specific measure of the **person** involved. This means that the measures are not fixed, but rather change in accordance with the person in question. If the four cubits are measured according to each person's forearm, this law should have been included in the mishna.

כִּי אֲתָא לְקַמֵּיהּ דְּרַב פָּפָּא, אֲמַר לֵיהּ: אִי דָּיְיקִינַן כּוּלֵּי הַאי, לָא הָוֵי תָּנֵינַן.

When Rav Mesharshiya's son **came before Rav Pappa,** the latter **said to him: Were we to be so precise,**[N] **we would not** be able to **learn** anything **at all,** as we would be too busy answering such questions.

לְעוֹלָם בְּאַמָּה דִּידֵיהּ יָהֲבִינַן לֵיהּ, וּדְקָא קַשְׁיָא לָךְ מַאי טַעְמָא לָא קָתָנֵי גַּבֵּי "יֵשׁ שֶׁאָמְרוּ" – דְּלָא פְּסִיקָא לֵיהּ, מִשּׁוּם דְּאִיכָּא נַנָּס בְּאֵבָרָיו.

In fact, we grant him four cubits measured **according to his own forearm. And as for that which was difficult for you, why was** this law **not taught** in the mishna that teaches: **These are** matters **with regard to which they stated** measures all in accordance with the specific measure of the person involved? It is because this law **is not** absolutely **clear-cut.** It occasionally must be adjusted, **since there may be** a person **whose limbs are small** in relation to his body. With regard to such a person, we do not measure four cubits according to the size of his own forearm, but rather by the standard cubits used for consecrated property.[H]

"הָיוּ שְׁנַיִם מִקְצָת אַמּוֹתָיו שֶׁל זֶה וכו'". לָמָּה לֵיהּ לְמֵימַר "לְמָה הַדָּבָר דּוֹמֶה"?

The mishna taught: **If there were two** people positioned in a way that **part of the** four **cubits of the one** were subsumed within the four cubits of the other, they each may bring food and eat together in the shared area in the middle. Rabbi Shimon likened this case to that of three courtyards that open one into another, where the two outer courtyards established an *eiruv* with the middle one. The Gemara asks: **Why does** Rabbi Shimon **need to** offer an analogy and **say: To what may this be likened,** and thus connect our case to a different issue?

הָכִי קָאָמַר לְהוּ רַבִּי שִׁמְעוֹן לְרַבָּנַן: מִכְּדִי, לְמָה הַדָּבָר דּוֹמֶה – לְשָׁלֹשׁ חֲצֵירוֹת הַפְּתוּחוֹת זוֹ לָזוֹ וּפְתוּחוֹת לִרְשׁוּת הָרַבִּים. מַאי שְׁנָא הָתָם דִּפְלִיגִיתוּ, וּמַאי שְׁנָא הָכָא דְּלָא פְּלִיגִיתוּ?

The Gemara explains: **This is what Rabbi Shimon said to the Rabbis: After all, to what is this similar? To three courtyards**[B] **that open into one another, and that** also **open into a public domain. What is different there that you disagree** with me and say that it is prohibited to carry from any one courtyard to any other, **and what is different here that you do not disagree** with me?

וְרַבָּנַן: הָתָם אָוּשֵׁי דִּיּוּרִין, הָכָא לָא אָוּשֵׁי דִּיּוּרִין.

And how do **the Rabbis** reply? **There** the **residents** of the courtyards **are numerous,**[N] and some might come to carry objects in a place where it is prohibited to do so; whereas **here** the **residents are not numerous,** and a mere three people can warn each other against Shabbat desecration.

NOTES

Exact cubits – אַמּוֹת מְצוּמְצָמוֹת: According to Rashi, Rabbi Meir's opinion is the more expansive, whereas Rabbi Yehuda's is more limiting. Other commentaries state the opposite: According to Rabbi Meir, an individual is given exactly four cubits, whereas Rabbi Yehuda provides him a certain extra space beyond the narrow confines of his body. Therefore, presumably, a little more is added to the four cubits (Rabbeinu Ḥananel; Rif; Rosh).

Were we to be so precise – אִי דָּיְיקִינַן כּוּלֵּי הַאי: Rav Mesharshiya did not draw an inference from the wording of the mishna itself, but rather from something not stated explicitly in the mishna. Consequently, Rav Pappa says that this method of inference should not be followed to its conclusion, as there are sometimes stylistic or other reasons for something to be omitted from a list. Omission from a list does not constitute absolute proof that the item is in a different category than the list items, and an inference of this kind sometimes leads to internal contradictions.

The residents are numerous [*avshi*] – אָוּשֵׁי דִּיּוּרִין: Rabbeinu Ḥananel has a version to the opposite effect, based on an alternate meaning of the word *avshi* as noisy, rather than numerous. As such, he explains that the residents are not noisy in the middle courtyard, because the courtyard is so big that its residents rarely hear one another. Therefore, if one of them is carrying in a place prohibited to him, the others might not know about it. However, with regard to the four cubits, the residents are noisy. Three people who are crowded within four cubits are aware of each other and can hear all of their movements (see Ritva).

HALAKHA

Expansive cubits – אַמּוֹת מְרוּוָחוֹת: The four cubits that the Sages permit one to walk are spacious ones (Rema). This is because, in disputes between Rabbi Yehuda and Rabbi Meir, the *halakha* is in accordance with the opinion of Rabbi Yehuda (Rif; Rosh); and because the *halakha* follows the lenient opinion with regard to *eiruv* (*Shulḥan Arukh*, *Oraḥ Ḥayyim* 397:1).

The measurement of cubits – מִידַּת הָאַמּוֹת: The four cubits are measured in accordance with one's size. However, one whose arms are small relative to the other limbs of his body is judged according to regular cubits, in accordance with the opinion of Rava (*Shulḥan Arukh*, *Oraḥ Ḥayyim* 397:1).

BACKGROUND

Three courtyards – שָׁלֹשׁ חֲצֵירוֹת:

Three courtyards that open into one another and into the public domain

"וּשְׁתַּיִם הַחִיצוֹנוֹת כו'". וְאַמַּאי? כֵּיוָן דְּעָרְבִי לְהוּ חִיצוֹנוֹת בַּהֲדֵי אֶמְצָעִית, הָוְיָא לְהוּ חֲדָא!

The mishna taught: If the residents of the two outer courtyards established an *eiruv* with the middle one, it is permitted to carry from the middle one to the two outer ones, and it is permitted to carry from the middle one to the two outer ones. **And** it is prohibited to carry from one of **the two outer** courtyards to the other, as they did not establish a joint *eiruv*. The Gemara asks: **Why** is it prohibited? **Since** the residents of the **outer** courtyards **established an *eiruv* with the middle one, they are** as **one,** and consequently, they should all be permitted with one another.

אָמַר רַב יְהוּדָה: כְּגוֹן שֶׁנָּתְנָה אֶמְצָעִית עֵירוּבָהּ בָּזוֹ וְעֵירוּבָהּ בָּזוֹ.

Rav Yehuda said: The mishna is referring to a case where the two outer courtyards did not place their *eiruv* in the middle courtyard; rather, to a case **where the** residents of the **middle** courtyard **placed** its first *eiruv* **in this** courtyard **and its** second *eiruv* **in that** courtyard, so that the *eiruv* of each of the other courtyards is not in the middle courtyard.

וְרַב שֵׁשֶׁת אָמַר: אֲפִילּוּ תֵּימָא שֶׁנָּתְנוּ עֵירוּבָן בָּאֶמְצָעִית, כְּגוֹן שֶׁנְּתָנוּהוּ

And Rav Sheshet said: Even if you say that the residents of each of the outer courtyards **placed their *eiruv* in the middle** courtyard, they are still not considered a single courtyard, as we are dealing **with a case where they placed** each *eiruv*

בִּשְׁנֵי בָתִּים.

in two separate **houses,** and consequently the two outer courtyards do not join together and become as one.[N]

כְּמַאן – כְּבֵית שַׁמַּאי, דְּתַנְיָא: חֲמִשָּׁה שֶׁגָּבוּ אֶת עֵירוּבָן וּנְתָנוּהוּ בִּשְׁנֵי כֵלִים, בֵּית שַׁמַּאי אוֹמְרִים: אֵין עֵירוּבָן עֵירוּב, וּבֵית הִלֵּל אוֹמְרִים: עֵירוּבָן עֵירוּב.

The Gemara asks: **In accordance with whose** opinion did Rav Sheshet state that an *eiruv* placed in two houses, even within the same courtyard, does not join the houses together? He must have said this in accordance **with** the opinion of **Beit Shammai, as it was taught** in a *baraita*: With regard to **five** people who **collected their *eiruv* and placed it in two** separate **utensils,** even in a single house, **Beit Shammai say: Their *eiruv* is not a** valid ***eiruv,*** as the two parts of the *eiruv* have not been deposited in the same place, **and Beit Hillel say: Their *eiruv* is a** valid ***eiruv*** as long as the entire *eiruv* was deposited in a single domain.

אֲפִילּוּ תֵּימָא בֵּית הִלֵּל; עַד כָּאן לָא קָאָמְרִי בֵּית הִלֵּל הָתָם – אֶלָּא בִּשְׁנֵי כֵלִים בְּבַיִת אֶחָד, אֲבָל בִּשְׁנֵי בָתִּים – לֹא.

The Gemara rejects this argument: **Even if you say** that this is in accordance with the opinion **of Beit Hillel, Beit Hillel** may have **stated** their opinion **only there, with regard to two utensils** that are located **in one house** and consequently, they join together. **However,** if the two utensils are located **in two** separate **houses,** even Beit Hillel agree that the *eiruv* is **not** valid.

אָמַר לֵיהּ רַב אַחָא בְּרֵיהּ דְּרַב אָוְיָא לְרַב אָשֵׁי: לְרַב יְהוּדָה קַשְׁיָא, וּלְרַב שֵׁשֶׁת קַשְׁיָא. לְרַב יְהוּדָה קַשְׁיָא, דְּאָמַר: כְּגוֹן שֶׁנָּתְנָה אֶמְצָעִית עֵירוּבָהּ בָּזוֹ וְעֵירוּבָהּ בָּזוֹ, וְכֵיוָן דְּעֵירְבָה אֶמְצָעִית בַּהֲדֵי חִיצוֹנָה – הָוְיָא לֵיהּ חֲדָא, וְכִי הָדְרָה וְעָרְבָה בַּהֲדֵי אִידָּךְ – שְׁלִיחוּתָהּ עָבְדָה!

Rav Aḥa, son of Rav Avya, said to Rav Ashi: The explanation **of Rav Yehuda is difficult**[N] and the explanation **of Rav Sheshet is difficult.** The explanation of **Rav Yehuda is difficult, as he said** that it is speaking **about a case where the middle** courtyard[H] **put its** first ***eiruv* in the one** courtyard **and its** second ***eiruv* in the other** courtyard. **However, once the middle** courtyard **establishes an *eiruv*** with one of the **outer ones, they are** regarded **as one,** so that **when it later establishes an *eiruv* with the other** outer courtyard, **it acts** also **on behalf** of the first outer courtyard, as both of them are treated like a single courtyard.

וּלְרַב שֵׁשֶׁת קַשְׁיָא: תֶּיהֱוֵי כַּחֲמִשָּׁה שֶׁשְּׁרוּיִין בְּחָצֵר אַחַת, וְשָׁכַח אֶחָד מֵהֶן וְלֹא עֵירֵב – דְּאָסְרִי אַהֲדָדֵי!

And the explanation **of Rav Sheshet is difficult.** Since the two outer courtyards placed their respective *eiruvin* in the middle courtyard, all are regarded as residents of the middle courtyard. And since each of the outer courtyards placed its *eiruv* in a different house, the case **should be** treated **like** that of **five** people **who lived in the same courtyard, one of whom forgot and did not join the *eiruv,* where they** all **prohibit one another** to carry in the courtyard. Similarly in this case, all should be prohibited to carry in the middle courtyard, the residents of the middle courtyard as well as the residents of the outer courtyards.

NOTES

The opinions of Rav Yehuda and Rav Sheshet – שִׁיטַת רַב יְהוּדָה וְרַב שֵׁשֶׁת: Most commentaries explain that Rav Sheshet accepts the statement of Rav Yehuda, while Rav Yehuda adds an additional point contested by Rav Sheshet (see Rashba; Rabbi Zeraḥya HaLevi). Some commentaries, however, state that these two opinions are not in conflict with one another. Rather, each Sage addresses a particular case, and they agree with one another (*Me'iri*).

The explanation of Rav Yehuda is difficult – לְרַב יְהוּדָה קַשְׁיָא: It is important to note that each of these questions applies exclusively to the Sage to whom it was addressed. Nevertheless, it can be asked why one difficulty is raised against Rav Yehuda while the other is directed at Rav Sheshet, since they both accept the same principle, and presumably the same question can be asked of them both. However, the difficulty that they all become like the inhabitants of a single courtyard poses no problem to Rav Sheshet's approach. By putting the *eiruv* in separate places, the residents of the outer courtyards demonstrated that they do not want all the courtyards to be considered one courtyard. The same is true of the opposite case. The difficulty with regard to residents situated in a courtyard is inapplicable to Rabbi Yehuda's approach, since he is of the opinion that it is the members of the middle courtyard who are considered as residents of the outer ones, rather than the other way around (Ritva).

HALAKHA

Three courtyards – שָׁלֹשׁ חֲצֵירוֹת: If there are three courtyards that open one into another and also into the public domain, and the outer courtyards each establish an *eiruv* with the inner one but not with each other, all of the residents are permitted to carry in each courtyard. However, this is not the case if the inhabitants of the middle courtyard place one *eiruv* in one outer courtyard and another *eiruv* in the other outer courtyard, or if both *eiruvin* are placed in the middle courtyard but in two different locations. The *halakha* is in accordance with the opinion of Rabbi Shimon, as well as with the opinion of Rav Sheshet. Furthermore, since Rav accepts the statement of Rav Yehuda while adding to it, the *halakha* is also according to Rav Yehuda (*Shulḥan Arukh*, *Oraḥ Ḥayyim* 378:1).

אָמַר לֵיהּ רַב אַשִׁי: לָא לְרַב יְהוּדָה קַשְׁיָא, וְלָא לְרַב שֵׁשֶׁת קַשְׁיָא; לְרַב יְהוּדָה לָא קַשְׁיָא: כֵּיוָן דְּעֵירְבָה לָהּ אֶמְצָעִית בַּהֲדֵי חִיצוֹנָה, וּשְׁתַּיִם חִיצוֹנוֹת בַּהֲדֵי הֲדָדֵי לֹא עֵירְבוּ – גַּלְיָא דַּעְתֵּיהּ דִּבְהָא נִיחָא לֵיהּ, וּבְהָא לָא נִיחָא לֵיהּ.

Rav Ashi said to him: It is not difficult according to the explanation **of Rav Yehuda and it is not difficult** according to the explanation of **Rav Sheshet. It is not difficult** according to the explanation of **Rav Yehuda, since the** residents of the **middle** courtyard **established an** ***eiruv*** **with** each of **the two outer** courtyards, **and the** residents of the **two outer** courtyards **did not establish an** ***eiruv*** **with one another.** The residents of each of the outer courtyards **indicated that it desired** to join **with** the middle courtyard, **but did not desire** to join **with** the other outer courtyard. Since the residents of the outer courtyards demonstrated that that they did not want to join together and form a common *eiruv*, they cannot be forced to do so.

וּלְרַב שֵׁשֶׁת לָא קַשְׁיָא: אִם אָמְרוּ דִּיּוֹרִין לְהָקֵל, יֹאמְרוּ דִּיּוֹרִין לְהַחְמִיר?!

And it is not difficult according to the explanation **of Rav Sheshet. If they said** that the people living in the outer courtyards are considered as **residents** of the middle courtyard **as a leniency,** so that they should be permitted to carry in the middle courtyard, does this mean that **they will say** that they are considered **residents** of the middle courtyard also **as a stringency,**[N] so that they should be prohibited from carrying in the middle courtyard as if they live there?

אָמַר רַב יְהוּדָה, אָמַר רַב: זוֹ דִּבְרֵי רַבִּי שִׁמְעוֹן. אֲבָל חֲכָמִים אוֹמְרִים: רְשׁוּת אַחַת מְשַׁמֶּשֶׁת לִשְׁתֵּי רְשׁוּיוֹת, אֲבָל לֹא שְׁתֵּי רְשׁוּיוֹת מְשַׁמְּשׁוֹת לִרְשׁוּת אַחַת.

Rav Yehuda said that **Rav said: This** statement in the mishna, that objects may be carried from either of the outer courtyards into the middle courtyard and also from the middle courtyard into either of the outer courtyards, **is the statement of,** i.e., in accordance with the opinion of, **Rabbi Shimon. But the Rabbis say: One domain serves two domains.**[N] That is to say, it is permitted to carry objects from either of the outer courtyards into the inner one, as no prohibition is imposed upon the outer courtyards, given that both established an *eiruv* with the middle courtyard. **But two domains do not serve one domain,** meaning that it is prohibited to carry objects from the middle courtyard into either of the two outer courtyards. The utensils of the middle courtyard are drawn after the other two, meaning that were he to bring them into one of the outer courtyards, he would be regarded as having removed them from the other.

כִּי אָמְרִיתָהּ קַמֵּיהּ דִּשְׁמוּאֵל, אֲמַר לִי:

Rav Yehuda relates: **When I recited** this teaching **before Shmuel, he said to me:**

NOTES

They will say they are residents as a stringency – יֹאמְרוּ דִּיּוֹרִין לְהַחְמִיר: *Tosafot* point out that there are occasions where the residents of the outer courtyard are considered residents of the middle courtyard as a stringency. In light of this, the statement should be understood as follows: The possibility of prohibiting the members of the outer courtyards from carrying in this case results from the *eiruv* that they placed, which apparently is not a proper *eiruv*. If it was a valid *eiruv*, it should serve as an *eiruv* for all of the residents. If it was an invalid *eiruv*, it should not render the inhabitants of the outer courtyard residents of the inner courtyard. As for the example of five residents of one courtyard, the *eiruv* serves as a leniency to unite them into one group. However, without an *eiruv*, their very presence there would render it prohibited for each of them to carry.

One domain serves two domains – רְשׁוּת אַחַת מְשַׁמֶּשֶׁת לִשְׁתֵּי רְשׁוּיוֹת: Most of the commentaries accept an alternate reading: One domain serves in two domains. This is the version of the *ge'onim*, which indicates that residents of the middle courtyard are permitted to utilize the outer courtyards, whereas the residents of the outer courtyards are prohibited to utilize the inner courtyard (Rabbeinu Tam in *Tosafot*; Rif; Rashba; Rosh). Other commentaries adopt Rashi's explanation with a slight variation. They prohibit the residents of the middle courtyard from utilizing the outer ones. Otherwise, there would be utensils in the outer courtyards that would be prohibited to the residents of those courtyards, and they would not be careful enough about them. Consequently, the Sages issued a decree (Ritva).

Perek **IV**
Daf **49** Amud **a**

אַף זוֹ דִּבְרֵי רַבִּי שִׁמְעוֹן, אֲבָל חֲכָמִים אוֹמְרִים: שְׁלָשְׁתָּן אֲסוּרוֹת.

This teaching, that carrying objects from either of the outer courtyards into the middle courtyard is permitted, is **also the statement of,** i.e., in accordance with, the opinion of **Rabbi Shimon. But the Rabbis say: All three** courtyards **are prohibited,** that is to say, carrying is prohibited from any of the courtyards to any of the others.

תַּנְיָא כְּוָותֵיהּ דְּרַב יְהוּדָה אַלִּיבָּא דִּשְׁמוּאֵל, אָמַר רַבִּי שִׁמְעוֹן: לְמָה הַדָּבָר דּוֹמֶה – לְשָׁלֹשׁ חֲצֵירוֹת הַפְּתוּחוֹת זוֹ לָזוֹ וּפְתוּחוֹת לִרְשׁוּת הָרַבִּים, עֵירְבוּ שְׁתַּיִם עִם הָאֶמְצָעִית – זוֹ מְבִיאָה מִתּוֹךְ בֵּיתָהּ וְאוֹכֶלֶת, וְזוֹ מְבִיאָה מִתּוֹךְ בֵּיתָהּ וְאוֹכֶלֶת, זוֹ מַחֲזֶרֶת מוֹתָרָהּ לְתוֹךְ בֵּיתָהּ, וְזוֹ מַחֲזֶרֶת מוֹתָרָהּ לְתוֹךְ בֵּיתָהּ.

It was taught in a *baraita* **in accordance with** the opinion of **Rav Yehuda, in accordance with** the opinion of **Shmuel. Rabbi Shimon said: To what is this comparable?** It is comparable **to three courtyards that open into one another, and that** also **open into a public domain. If the two** outer courtyards **established an** ***eiruv*** **with the middle** one, a resident of one of the outer courtyards **may bring** food **from a house** in that courtyard **and eat** it in the middle courtyard, **and** likewise a resident of the other courtyard **may bring** food **from a house** in that courtyard **and eat** it in the middle courtyard. And similarly, **this** resident **may bring leftovers** from the house where he ate **back into** the **house** in that courtyard, **and that resident may bring leftovers** from the house where he ate **back into** the **house** in this courtyard.

אֲבָל חֲכָמִים אוֹמְרִים: שְׁלָשְׁתָּן אֲסוּרוֹת.

However, the Rabbis say: All three courtyards **are prohibited.** Since the residents of the outer courtyards are prohibited to carry from one outer courtyard to the other, this results in a place where carrying is prohibited, and such a place prohibits carrying in all three courtyards.

BACKGROUND

Courtyard that is between two alleyways – חָצֵר שֶׁבֵּין שְׁנֵי מְבוֹאוֹת:

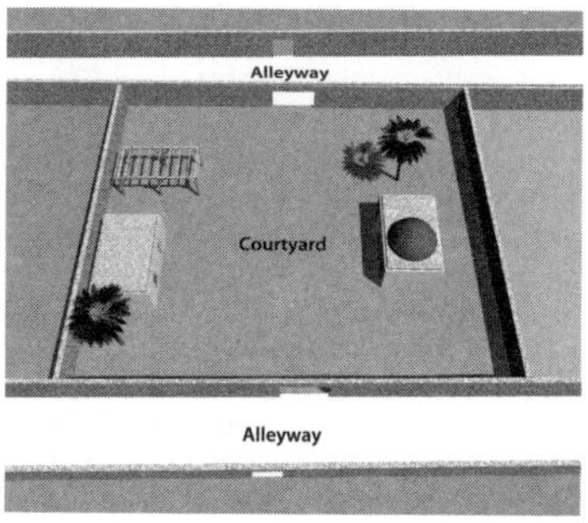

Courtyard that opens into two alleyways

NOTES

Established an *eiruv* with the alleyway which they were not accustomed to utilizing – עֵירְבָה עִם שֶׁאֵינָהּ רְגִילָה בּוֹ: When the residents of the courtyard established a joining of courtyards with the alleyway, which they were not accustomed to utilizing, they negated their utilization of the other alleyway. That would be the case all the more so if the residents established an *eiruv* with the alleyway they were accustomed to utilizing (Maharshal).

וְאָזְדָא שְׁמוּאֵל לְטַעְמֵיהּ, דְּאָמַר שְׁמוּאֵל: חָצֵר שֶׁבֵּין שְׁנֵי מְבוֹאוֹת, עֵירְבָה עִם שְׁנֵיהֶם – אֲסוּרָה עִם שְׁנֵיהֶם,

The Gemara notes that **Shmuel follows his** line of **reasoning** that he used elsewhere, as **Shmuel said:** With regard to **a courtyard that is between two alleyways,**[BH] if that courtyard **established an *eiruv* with both** alleyways, **it is prohibited with both of them.** Since the residents of the two alleyways are prohibited to carry from one to the other and the *eiruv* enables the residents of the two alleyways to carry in the courtyard, it is prohibited to carry from the courtyard into the alleyways, so that the residents of the alleyways do not transfer objects from one alleyway to the other via the courtyard.

לֹא עֵירְבָה עִם שְׁנֵיהֶם – אוֹסֶרֶת עַל שְׁנֵיהֶן.

If the courtyard **did not establish an *eiruv* with either** alleyway, **it prohibits** one to carry in **both of them.** Since the residents of the courtyard were accustomed to utilizing both alleyways and did not establish an *eiruv* with either alleyway, the result is that each alleyway has a courtyard that did not establish an *eiruv*, which prohibits carrying from the courtyard into either alleyway.

הָיְתָה בְּאֶחָד רְגִילָה וּבְאֶחָד אֵינָהּ רְגִילָה, זֶה שֶׁרְגִילָה בּוֹ – אָסוּר, וְזֶה שֶׁאֵינָהּ רְגִילָה בּוֹ – מוּתָּר.

If, however, the residents of the courtyard were **accustomed to utilizing** only **one** alleyway, while **they** are **not accustomed to utilizing**[H] **one** alleyway, then with regard to the alleyway **which** they are **accustomed to utilizing, it is prohibited** to carry there, as the residents of the courtyard did not establish an *eiruv* with it. **But** with regard to the alleyway, **which** they are **not accustomed to utilizing,** it **is permitted** to carry there, as the residents of the courtyard are not considered residents of that alleyway.

אָמַר רַבָּה בַּר רַב הוּנָא: עֵירְבָה עִם שֶׁאֵינָהּ רְגִילָה בּוֹ – הוּתַּר רְגִילָה לְעַצְמוֹ.

Rabba bar Rav Huna said: With regard to residents of a courtyard who **established an *eiruv* with** the alleyway, **which** they **were not accustomed to utilizing,**[N] the alleyway **which** they **were accustomed to utilizing is permitted** to establish an *eiruv* **on its own** without the courtyard. The residents of the courtyard have demonstrated their intention to use the other alleyway, despite their not being accustomed to doing so.

וְאָמַר רַבָּה בַּר רַב הוּנָא, אָמַר שְׁמוּאֵל: אִם עֵירְבָה רְגִילָה לְעַצְמוֹ, וְזֶה שֶׁאֵינָהּ רְגִילָה בּוֹ לֹא עֵירֵב, וְהִיא עַצְמָהּ לֹא עֵירְבָה – דּוֹחִין אוֹתָהּ אֵצֶל שֶׁאֵינָהּ רְגִילָה בּוֹ,

And Rabba bar Rav Huna said that **Shmuel said: If** the alleyway **which** the residents of the courtyard **were accustomed to utilizing established an *eiruv* on its own** without the courtyard, **while** the alleyway **which** they **were not accustomed to utilizing did not establish an *eiruv*, and** also the courtyard **itself did not establish an *eiruv*** with either alleyway, **we divert** the residents of the courtyard to use the alleyway, **which** they are **not accustomed to utilizing.** This is because there is one alleyway in which it is prohibited to carry due to the lack of an *eiruv*, and a second alleyway in which it is permitted to carry; while it is prohibited for the residents of the courtyard to carry. As explained above, were they to utilize the alleyway which they are accustomed to utilizing, the other residents of the alleyway would also be prohibited to carry from their courtyards into the alleyway, despite having established an *eiruv* for their own alleyway. However, if they use the other alleyway, the residents of that alleyway will not lose anything; since they did not establish an *eiruv*, it is prohibited for them to carry in that alleyway regardless.

HALAKHA

Courtyard that is between two alleyways – חָצֵר שֶׁבֵּין שְׁנֵי מְבוֹאוֹת: If the residents of a courtyard between two alleyways establish an *eiruv* with both alleyways, the residents are permitted to carry into each of the alleyways; and it is permitted to carry from each alleyway into the courtyard. However, it is prohibited to carry from one alleyway to the other via the courtyard, unless the residents of the two alleyways establish an *eiruv* in the same house in that courtyard. That is the ruling because the *halakha* is not in accordance with the opinion of Shmuel. Rather, it is in accordance with the opinion of Rabbi Shimon, with regard to courtyards. Therefore, in the case of alleyways as well, if the inhabitants of the courtyard did not establish an *eiruv* with each alleyway, it is prohibited to carry into either of them (*Shulḥan Arukh, Oraḥ Ḥayyim* 386:9).

Accustomed to utilizing and not accustomed to utilizing – רְגִילָה וְאֵין רְגִילָה: If the residents of a courtyard situated between two alleyways do not establish an *eiruv* with one of the alleyways, which they are accustomed to utilize, it is prohibited to carry into that alleyway. If they establish an *eiruv* with one alleyway, it is permitted to carry within the other alleyway. If the inhabitants of the alleyway that the residents of the courtyard are accustomed to utilizing establish a joining of courtyards for themselves, and the inhabitants of neither the courtyard nor the other alleyway establish an *eiruv*, the inhabitants of the courtyard are compelled to use the alleyway that does not have an *eiruv*. If they would utilize the other alleyway, and thereby prohibit its use, this would be behavior characteristic of Sodom, as stated by Shmuel and Rabba bar Rav Huna (*Shulḥan Arukh, Oraḥ Ḥayyim* 386:9).

וּכְגוֹן זֶה כּוֹפִין עַל מִדַּת סְדוֹם.

In a case such as this, one compels another to refrain from behavior **characteristic of Sodom.**[N] We force a person to waive his legal rights in order to prevent him from acting in a manner characteristic of the wicked city of Sodom. If one denies another use of his possessions, even though he would incur no loss or damage by granting use of his property, his conduct is considered to be characteristic of Sodom. The courts may sometimes compel such a person to waive his legal rights.

אָמַר רַב יְהוּדָה, אָמַר שְׁמוּאֵל: הַמַּקְפִּיד עַל עֵירוּבוֹ – אֵין עֵירוּבוֹ עֵירוּב. מַה שְּׁמוֹ – עֵירוּב שְׁמוֹ.

Rav Yehuda said that **Shmuel said:** With regard to **one who is particular about his *eiruv*,**[NH] i.e., that the other people should not eat of the food he contributed, **his *eiruv* is not a** valid ***eiruv*.** After all, **what is its name? Joining [*eiruv*] is its name,** indicating that it must be jointly owned [*me'urav*] by all the participants in the *eiruv*. If one person does not allow the other participants to eat of it, it does not belong to all of them and cannot be called an *eiruv*.

רַבִּי חֲנִינָא אָמַר: עֵירוּבוֹ עֵירוּב, אֶלָּא שֶׁנִּקְרָא מֵאַנְשֵׁי וַרְדִּינָא.

Rabbi Ḥanina said: Even in that case, **his *eiruv* is a** valid ***eiruv*, however,** that person **is called** one **of the men of Vardina.**[N] The men of Vardina were renowned misers, meaning that he is considered to be like them.

אָמַר רַב יְהוּדָה, אָמַר שְׁמוּאֵל: הַחוֹלֵק אֶת עֵירוּבוֹ – אֵינוֹ עֵירוּב.

Rav Yehuda also **said** that **Shmuel said:** With regard to **one who divides his *eiruv***[H] into two parts, his ***eiruv* is not a** valid ***eiruv*.** This is for the aforementioned reason that, by definition, an *eiruv* needs to be indicative of joining, and this *eiruv* is separated into different parts.

כְּמַאן – כְּבֵית שַׁמַּאי. דְּתַנְיָא: חֲמִשָּׁה שֶׁגָּבוּ אֶת עֵירוּבָן וּנְתָנוּהוּ בִּשְׁנֵי כֵלִים, בֵּית שַׁמַּאי אוֹמְרִים: אֵין זֶה עֵירוּב, וּבֵית הִלֵּל אוֹמְרִים: הֲרֵי זֶה עֵירוּב!

The Gemara asks: **In accordance with whose** opinion did Shmuel state this teaching? Could it be **in accordance with** the opinion of **Beit Shammai, as it was taught** in a *baraita*: With regard to **five** people who **collected their *eiruv* and placed it in two** separate **utensils, Beit Shammai say: This is not** a valid ***eiruv*, whereas Beit Hillel say: This is an *eiruv*.** It does not stand to reason that Shmuel would follow Beit Shammai, whose opinion is not accepted as normative law.

אֲפִילּוּ תֵּימָא בֵּית הִלֵּל: עַד כָּאן לָא קָאָמְרִי בֵּית הִלֵּל הָתָם אֶלָּא דִּמְלֵיין לְמָנָא וְאַיְיתַר, אֲבָל הֵיכָא דִּפְלַגֵּיהּ מִיפְלַג – לָא.

The Gemara answers: **Even if you say** that Shmuel stated his opinion in accordance with the opinion of **Beit Hillel, Beit Hillel stated** their opinion **only there, where the** first **utensil was filled and there was** still some food **left over,** and therefore, some of the leftover food had to be placed in a second utensil. **But where they divided it** from the outset, even Beit Hillel agree that the *eiruv* is **not** valid.

וְתַרְתֵּי לָמָּה לִי?! צְרִיכִי, דְּאִי אַשְׁמְעִינַן הָתָם – מִשּׁוּם דְּקָפֵיד, אֲבָל הָכָא – אֵימָא לָא.

The Gemara asks: **Why do I need two** rulings that are based on the same principle, i.e., that an *eiruv* must demonstrate joining? The Gemara answers: Both rulings were **necessary. As,** had the Gemara **taught us** the ruling only **there,** with regard to one who is particular about his *eiruv*, one might have said that the *eiruv* is not valid **because** the person **is particular** and expressly does not desire that his *eiruv* be eaten by others. **However here,** with regard to one who divides the *eiruv* into different parts, one might **say** that his portion should **not** be considered as separated from the rest.

וְאִי אַשְׁמְעִינַן הָכָא – מִשּׁוּם דִּפְלַגֵּיהּ מִיפְלַג, אֲבָל הָתָם – אֵימָא לָא, צְרִיכָא.

And had the Gemara **taught us** the ruling only **here,** with regard to one who divides his *eiruv*, one might have said that the *eiruv* is not valid **because he divided it up,** thereby physically separating himself from the others. **However there,** with regard to one who is particular about his *eiruv*, one might **say** that his portion should **not** be considered as separated from the rest, since no act of separation was performed. Consequently, both rulings were **necessary.**

אֲמַר לֵיהּ רַבִּי אַבָּא לְרַב יְהוּדָה בְּבֵי מַעְצַרְתָּא דְּבֵי רַב זַכַּאי: מִי אָמַר שְׁמוּאֵל ״הַחוֹלֵק אֶת עֵירוּבוֹ אֵינוֹ עֵירוּב״, וְהָאָמַר שְׁמוּאֵל: בַּיִת שֶׁמַּנִּיחִין בּוֹ עֵירוּב – אֵינוֹ צָרִיךְ לִיתֵּן אֶת הַפַּת. מַאי טַעְמָא – לָאו מִשּׁוּם דְּאָמַר: דְּכֵיוָן דְּמַנַּח בְּסַלָּא – כְּמַאן דְּמַנַּח הָכָא דָּמֵי, הָכִי נַמִי: כֵּיוָן דְּמַנַּח בְּסַלָּא כְּמַאן דְּמַנַּח הָכָא דָּמֵי!

Rabbi Abba said to Rav Yehuda in the olive press in Rav Zakkai's house: Did Shmuel actually **say** that in the case of **one who divides his *eiruv*, it is not** a valid ***eiruv*? Didn't Shmuel say** elsewhere: **The house in which the *eiruv* is placed**[H] **need not contribute bread** for the *eiruv*. The Gemara asks: **What is the reason** for this ruling? **Is it not because** Shmuel **maintains** that **since** there is bread **lying in a basket** somewhere in the house, **it is** regarded **as if it were placed here** with the rest of the *eiruv*? **Here too,** one should say that **since** the bread **is placed in a basket,** i.e., in one of the two utensils containing the *eiruv*, **it is** regarded **as if it were placed here** with the rest of the *eiruv*.

NOTES

One compels another to refrain from behavior characteristic of Sodom – כּוֹפִין עַל מִדַּת סְדוֹם: This coercion does not apply only in cases where the person does not lose anything. The Sages sometimes insisted that, for the public good, a person not establish an *eiruv*. This was true even if, according to the letter of the law, he could do so (*Tosafot*).

One who is particular about his *eiruv* – הַמַּקְפִּיד עַל עֵירוּבוֹ: Some commentaries explain that this refers to one who contributed his portion of the *eiruv* unwillingly, rather than freely. Since he is not pleased about the existence of the *eiruv*, there is a concern that he did not participate properly in establishing it, as is required (*Me'iri*).

The men of Vardina – אַנְשֵׁי וַרְדִּינָא: The *Arukh* explains that the residents of Vardina were known for being miserly. They would be particular with one another, even with regard to the difference between a large loaf of bread and a small one.

HALAKHA

One who is particular about his *eiruv* – הַמַּקְפִּיד עַל עֵירוּבוֹ: If one is particular that others not eat of his *eiruv*, he invalidates the *eiruv*. This is in accordance with the opinion of Shmuel, which is supported by the *baraita* (*Shulḥan Arukh*, *Oraḥ Ḥayyim* 366:5).

One who divides his *eiruv* – הַחוֹלֵק אֶת עֵירוּבוֹ: If one separates his *eiruv* from the other *eiruvin*, he invalidates the *eiruv*, unless one utensil is filled and part of the *eiruv* is placed in a different utensil, as stated by Shmuel (*Shulḥan Arukh*, *Oraḥ Ḥayyim* 366:4).

The house in which the *eiruv* is placed – בַּיִת שֶׁמַּנִּיחִים בּוֹ עֵירוּב: The residents of the house in which the *eiruv* is placed are not required to contribute bread, as stated by Shmuel (*Shulḥan Arukh*, *Oraḥ Ḥayyim* 366:3).

אָמַר לֵיהּ: הָתָם – אַף עַל פִּי שֶׁאֵין פַּת, מַאי טַעְמָא – דְּכוּלְּהוּ הָכָא דָּיְירִי.

Rav Yehuda **said to him: There** Shmuel validates the *eiruv* **although there is no bread** in the house in which the *eiruv* is deposited. And **what is the reason** for his ruling? It is **because** by placing food in a particular house, **all** the residents of the courtyard **are** regarded **as living here.** Therefore, those living in that house need not contribute bread for the *eiruv*, as they are certainly residents of the house.

אָמַר שְׁמוּאֵל: עֵירוּב מִשּׁוּם קִנְיָן.

Shmuel said: An *eiruv* that is deposited in a house is effective **due to** the principle of **acquisition,** as each person who contributes a portion of food acquires the right to a certain use of the residence and is considered one of its residents.

וְאִם תֹּאמַר: מִפְּנֵי מָה אֵין קוֹנִין בְּמָעָה – מִפְּנֵי שֶׁאֵינָהּ מְצוּיָה בְּעַרְבֵי שַׁבָּתוֹת.

And if you say: Why then **can one not acquire** this right **through** payment of a coin such as **a *ma'a***, but rather only through bread?[N] It is **because** a ***ma'a* is not** always **available on Shabbat eve,** as many people spend all of their available money for the necessities of Shabbat, and it is difficult to find money available at that hour.

הֵיכָא דְּעֵירַב מִיהוּ לִקְנֵי!

The Gemara asks: If so, according to Shmuel's opinion, in a case **where he established an *eiruv*** with money, **it should nonetheless acquire,** i.e., be valid. According to his opinion, there is no fundamental reason to invalidate the acquisition of rights in the residence through the payment of money, yet there is no indication that this position is valid.

גְּזֵירָה שֶׁמָּא יֹאמְרוּ מָעָה עִיקָּר, וּזְמַנִּין דְּלָא שְׁכִיחַ מָעָה, וְלָא אָתֵי לְאִיעֲרוּבֵי בְּפַת, דְּאָתֵי עֵירוּב לְאִיקַּלְקוֹלֵי.

The Gemara answers: Even Shmuel did not permit one to establish an *eiruv* with money, due to **a decree lest** people **say that a *ma'a* is essential, and sometimes a *ma'a* will not be available, and they will not come** to prepare **an *eiruv* with bread, and** the halakhic category of ***eiruv* will be forgotten.**

רַבָּה אָמַר: עֵירוּב מִשּׁוּם דִּירָה.

Rabba disagreed with Shmuel and **said: An *eiruv*** is effective **due to** the principle of **residence.** Each person who contributes a portion of food is considered as if he resides, for that Shabbat, in the residence in which the food is deposited.[H]

מַאי בֵּינַיְיהוּ? אִיכָּא בֵּינַיְיהוּ כְּלִי,

The Gemara asks: **What is** the practical, halakhic difference **between these** two understandings? The Gemara answers: **There is** a practical difference **between them** with regard to the question of whether an *eiruv* may be established with **a utensil.** If an *eiruv* is effective based on the principle of acquisition, in accordance with the opinion of Shmuel, then one should be able to establish an *eiruv* with a utensil; whereas, this would not constitute a valid *eiruv*, according to the opinion of Rabba.

וּפָחוֹת מִשָּׁוֶה פְּרוּטָה,

And another practical difference between them is with regard to whether an *eiruv* may be established with food that is **less than the value of a *peruta*.**[N] According to Shmuel's opinion, this would not be a valid *eiruv*, as there is no acquisition with something less than the value of a *peruta*; whereas according to Rabba's opinion, since an *eiruv* is effective by establishing a person's residence, this can be done even with an amount of food worth less than a *peruta*.

Perek **IV**
Daf **49** Amud **b**

וְקָטָן.

And there is another practical difference between them with regard to the question whether **a minor** may collect the *eiruv* from the residents of the courtyard and deposit it in one of the houses. According to Shmuel's opinion, this would not be a valid *eiruv*, for a minor cannot serve as an agent to effect acquisition, whereas according to Rabba's opinion, the *eiruv* is valid, as the food itself establishes the common residence for all the residents.

NOTES

Establishment of an *eiruv* with a *ma'a* – אֵין מְעָרְבִין בְּמָעָה: The early commentaries point out that, even if an *eiruv* works on the principle of acquisition, it is not clear that one can establish an *eiruv* with a *ma'a*, since courtyards and houses cannot be acquired in this manner. However, it can be argued that if bread can be utilized for an *eiruv*, it should also be possible to establish an *eiruv* with a *ma'a*, which can certainly be used for making purchases (*Me'iri*).

A utensil and less than the value of a *peruta* – כְּלִי וּפָחוֹת מִשָּׁוֶה פְּרוּטָה: Some early commentaries read these two details as a single case, i.e., a utensil worth less than a *peruta* (Rabbeinu Ḥananel and others). Most commentaries maintain that there is no difference between a utensil worth a *peruta* and one worth less, since it can be used as long as it has any value at all (see Rashba; *Me'iri*).

HALAKHA

Joining of courtyards – עֵירוּב חֲצֵרוֹת: An *eiruv* functions to establish residence and, therefore, it need not be worth a *peruta*. Nevertheless, it cannot be established with a utensil. In addition, a minor can collect the *eiruv* (Rashi),and it is even possible to establish an *eiruv* in a minor's house (*Tosafot*). Because the *halakha* is in accordance with Rabbi Yoḥanan's opinion in disputes with Shmuel, and since Rabba's opinion is in accordance with the opinion of Rabbi Yoḥanan, the *halakha* is in accordance with the opinion of Rabba. In addition, the Gemara's discussion seems to be in accordance with Rabba's opinion (*Shulḥan Arukh, Oraḥ Hayyim* 366:3).

אָמַר לֵיהּ אַבָּיֵי לְרַבָּה: לְדִידָךְ קַשְׁיָא, וְלִשְׁמוּאֵל קַשְׁיָא. הָא תַּנְיָא: חֲמִשָּׁה שֶׁגָּבוּ אֶת עֵירוּבָן, כְּשֶׁהֵם מוֹלִיכִין אֶת עֵירוּבָן לְמָקוֹם אַחֵר – אֶחָד מוֹלִיךְ לְכוּלָּן. הוּא נִיהוּ דְּקָא קָנֵי, וְתוּ לָא. הוּא נִיהוּ דְּקָא דָּיֵיר, וְתוּ לָא!

Abaye said to Rabba: It is difficult according to your opinion that an *eiruv* is effective based on the principle of residence, **and it is difficult according to** the opinion **of Shmuel** that it is effective based on the principle of acquisition. **As it was taught** in a *baraita*: With regard to **five** people **who collected their *eiruv*, when they take their *eiruv* elsewhere,** in order to establish an *eiruv* together with another courtyard, **one** person may **take it** there **for all of them.**[N] This indicates that **it is** only **that person who acquires** rights, **and nobody else,** and **it is** only **that person who gains residence, and nobody else.** In that case, how can the others rely on this *eiruv*?

אָמַר לֵיהּ: לָא לְדִידִי קַשְׁיָא, וְלָא לִשְׁמוּאֵל קַשְׁיָא: שְׁלִיחוּת דְּכוּלְּהוּ קָא עָבֵיד.

Rabba said **to him:** It is **neither difficult according to my** opinion, **nor** is it **difficult according to** the opinion of **Shmuel,** as, the person who takes the *eiruv* **acts as an agent,** effecting acquisition or determining residence **on behalf of all of them.**

אָמַר רַבָּה, אָמַר רַב חָמָא בַּר גּוּרְיָא, אָמַר רַב: הֲלָכָה כְּרַבִּי שִׁמְעוֹן.

With regard to the case of the three courtyards addressed above, **Rabba said** that **Rav Ḥama bar Gurya said** that **Rav said:** The ***halakha* is in accordance with** the opinion of **Rabbi Shimon** that it is permitted to carry from the middle courtyard into either of the two outer ones; and vice versa, however, it is prohibited to carry from one outer courtyard to the other.

מתני׳ מִי שֶׁבָּא בַּדֶּרֶךְ וְחָשְׁכָה לוֹ, וְהָיָה מַכִּיר אִילָן אוֹ גָּדֵר, וְאָמַר ״שְׁבִיתָתִי תַּחְתָּיו״ – לֹא אָמַר כְּלוּם.

MISHNA With regard to **one who was coming along the way** on Shabbat eve, **and it grew dark** while **he** was traveling,[N] **and he was familiar** with **a tree**[N] **or a fence** located two thousand cubits from his current location, and two thousand cubits from his house, **and he said: My residence is beneath** that tree, rather than in his present location, **he has not said anything,** as he did not establish a fixed location as his residence.

״שְׁבִיתָתִי בְּעִיקָּרוֹ״ – מְהַלֵּךְ מִמְּקוֹם רַגְלָיו וְעַד עִיקָּרוֹ אַלְפַּיִם אַמָּה, וּמֵעִיקָּרוֹ וְעַד בֵּיתוֹ אַלְפַּיִם אַמָּה. נִמְצָא מְהַלֵּךְ מִשֶּׁחֲשֵׁיכָה אַרְבַּעַת אֲלָפִים אַמָּה.

If, however, he said: **My residence is at** the tree's **trunk,** he acquired residence there, and he **may** therefore **walk from the place he is standing to the trunk** of the tree **two thousand cubits** away, **and from the trunk** of the tree **to his house,** an additional **two thousand cubits. Consequently, he walks after nightfall** a total of **four thousand cubits.**[H]

אִם אֵינוֹ מַכִּיר, אוֹ שֶׁאֵינוֹ בָּקִי בַּהֲלָכָה, וְאָמַר ״שְׁבִיתָתִי בִּמְקוֹמִי״ – זָכָה לוֹ מְקוֹמוֹ אַלְפַּיִם אַמָּה לְכָל רוּחַ.

If one is not familiar with a tree or any other noticeable landmark, **or if he is not an expert in the *halakha*,**[N] unaware that residence can be established from a distance, **and he said: My residence is at my** current **location,**[H] then his presence at **his** current **location acquires for him** the right to walk **two thousand cubits in each direction.**

עֲגוּלוֹת, דִּבְרֵי רַבִּי חֲנִינָא בֶּן אַנְטִיגְנוֹס. וַחֲכָמִים אוֹמְרִים: מְרוּבָּעוֹת, כְּטַבְלָא מְרוּבַּעַת, כְּדֵי שֶׁיְּהֵא נִשְׂכָּר לַזָּוִיּוֹת.

The manner in which the two thousand cubits are measured is the subject of a tannaitic dispute. These cubits are measured **circularly,** i.e., as a circle with a radius of two thousand cubits; this is **the statement of Rabbi Ḥanina ben Antigenos. And the Rabbis say:** These are measured **squarely,** i.e., **as a square tablet,**[N] with each side measuring four thousand cubits, **so that he gains the corners.** He is permitted to walk from the middle to the corners of the square as well, a distance of approximately 2,800 cubits.[H]

וְזוֹ הִיא שֶׁאָמְרוּ הֶעָנִי מְעָרֵב בְּרַגְלָיו. אָמַר רַבִּי מֵאִיר: אָנוּ אֵין לָנוּ אֶלָּא עָנִי. רַבִּי יְהוּדָה אוֹמֵר: אֶחָד עָנִי וְאֶחָד עָשִׁיר, לֹא אָמְרוּ מְעָרְבִין בְּפַת אֶלָּא לְהָקֵל עַל הֶעָשִׁיר, שֶׁלֹּא יֵצֵא וִיעָרֵב בְּרַגְלָיו.

And this is the meaning of that **which** the Sages **said: The pauper establishes an *eiruv* with his feet,** i.e., one who does not have the bread required to establish an *eiruv* may walk anywhere within his Shabbat limit and declare: This is my residence, and his Shabbat limit is measured from that location. **Rabbi Meir said: We have** this leniency in effect **only** for **a pauper,** who does not have food for two meals. However, one who has bread may only establish residence with bread. **Rabbi Yehuda says:** This leniency is in effect for **both a pauper and a wealthy person.** The Sages **said** that **one establishes an *eiruv* with bread only** in order **to be lenient with the wealthy** person, **so that he** need **not** exert himself and **go out and establish an *eiruv* with his feet.** Instead, he can appoint an agent to place bread for him in that location. This, however, does not negate the option of personally going to that location in order to establish residence without bread.

NOTES

One person may take it there for all of them – אֶחָד מוֹלִיךְ לְכוּלָּן: This means that the one taking the *eiruv* need not consult with the other parties to the *eiruv* to tell them where he will be placing their shared *eiruv*. Although it is reasonable to say that if one acts on his own accord, the place of residence should be established only for him, Rabba responds that he is acting as an agent for all parties to the *eiruv*. Even if the others are unaware of what he is doing, he is their agent (*Me'iri*).

And it grew dark while he was traveling – וְחָשְׁכָה לוֹ: Rabbeinu Yehonatan fills in the details of this case: As night approached, this tired traveler was reluctant to exert himself and continue walking. Instead, he decided to sleep or rest in that location until after nightfall.

And he was familiar with a tree – הָיָה מַכִּיר אִילָן: In this context, the Hebrew term does not mean that he recognizes the tree and can identify it. Rather, this person is aware of the existence of a particular tree, even if he cannot see it (*Ge'on Ya'akov*).

Or if he is not expert in the *halakha* – אוֹ שֶׁאֵינוֹ בָּקִי בַּהֲלָכָה: In this case, he did not establish his residence in error. Rather, there is no doubt that he established his residence in his present location. It is only if he was proximate to an inhabited area that one could claim that he erroneously acquired residence outside the town (Rabbeinu Yehonatan).

As a square tablet – כְּטַבְלָא מְרוּבַּעַת: These extra words indicate that there is no need for absolute precision in this regard. Rather, it suffices if it is almost squared, like the a tablet that one squares to the extent that he can although the result is not a perfect square (Rambam's Commentary on the Mishna).

HALAKHA

Rest in a particular location – שְׁבִיתָה בְּמָקוֹם מְסוּיָּים: One who was walking along the road before nightfall on Friday and said: Let my residence be alongside that tree trunk, or if he mentioned any other specific location within two thousand cubits of his current location, establishes residence in that place and may walk an additional two thousand cubits from there (*Shulḥan Arukh, Oraḥ Ḥayyim* 409:11).

My residence is at my current location – שְׁבִיתָתִי בִּמְקוֹמִי: If one says, let my residence be in my current location, he establishes residence there, and he may walk two thousand cubits in all directions (*Shulḥan Arukh, Oraḥ Ḥayyim* 397:1).

The measure of two thousand cubits – שִׁיעוּר אַלְפַּיִם אַמָּה: When the Sages spoke of two thousand cubits, they did not refer to a circle with a radius of two thousand cubits. Rather, they ruled that one is permitted to walk within a square-shaped area, which is four thousand cubits on each side. In that way, he gains the right to walk in the area in the corners (*Shulḥan Arukh, Oraḥ Ḥayyim* 399:10).

HALAKHA

My residence is beneath the tree – שְׁבִיתָתִי תַּחַת הָאִילָן: If one establishes residence in a location lacking clearly demarcated boundaries and which is more than four cubits wide, e.g., beneath a tree, if part of the tree is more than two thousand cubits away from his current location, he did not establish residence there. If the entire tree is within two thousand cubits, he acquired residence beneath the tree. However, the two thousand cubits from the tree are measured from the far side of the tree. The *halakha*, therefore, is stringent in both regards, as stated by Shmuel, because the *baraita* supports Rashi's understanding of Shmuel's opinion. The Rambam and the Rif have a different understanding of Shmuel's opinion. They rule that if he did not establish his place of residence in a particular location beneath the tree, he establishes residence in his present location and is prohibited to proceed any farther (*Shulḥan Arukh, Oraḥ Ḥayyim* 409:11).

NOTES

Shmuel's opinion – שִׁיטַת שְׁמוּאֵל: Rashi cites two explanations of Shmuel's opinion. The Rambam interprets this differently, and explains Shmuel opinion in the following manner. The person said nothing with regard to going to his house, and therefore did not establish residence beneath the tree at all. Instead, he established his residence in his present location. By failing to specify a particular location, it is as though he said nothing, and his residence is where he is standing (*Maggid Mishne*; see *Me'iri*).

גמ׳ מַאי "לֹא אָמַר כְּלוּם"?

GEMARA We learned in the mishna that one who declares his intention to establish residence beneath a tree, without specifying the precise location, has not said anything. The Gemara asks: **What is** the precise meaning of **he has not said anything?**

אָמַר רַב: לֹא אָמַר כְּלוּם כָּל עִיקָּר, דַּאֲפִילּוּ לְתַחְתָּיו שֶׁל אִילָן לָא מָצֵי אָזֵיל.

Rav said: He has not said anything at all, and has failed to establish residence anywhere, and **he may not even go to** the place **beneath** that **tree.** His failure to specify a particular location prevents him from establishing residence beneath the tree. The fact that he sought to establish residence someplace other than his present location prevents him from establishing residence at his present location. Accordingly, he may walk no more than four cubits from the place that he is standing.

וּשְׁמוּאֵל אָמַר: לֹא אָמַר כְּלוּם לְבֵיתוֹ, אֲבָל לְתַחְתָּיו שֶׁל אִילָן – מָצֵי אָזֵיל.

And Shmuel said: He has not said anything with regard to going **to his home,** if it is two thousand cubits past the tree; **however,** with regard to the area **beneath the tree,**[H] if its bough is entirely within two thousand cubits of his present location **he may** indeed **go** there.[N]

וְנַעֲשָׂה תַּחְתָּיו שֶׁל אִילָן חַמָּר גַּמָּל.

And when we learned in the mishna that he did not establish residence, it means that the legal status of the area **beneath the tree becomes** comparable to both **a donkey driver,** who walks behind the animal and prods it, **and a camel driver,** who walks before the animal and leads it in the sense that the tree is pulling him in both directions. Since he did not specify a particular location as his residence, any part of the area beneath the tree could be the place where he established residence.

בָּא לִמְדּוֹד מִן הַצָּפוֹן – מוֹדְדִין לוֹ מִן הַדָּרוֹם, בָּא לִמְדּוֹד מִן הַדָּרוֹם – מוֹדְדִין לוֹ מִן הַצָּפוֹן.

Therefore, if **he comes to measure** two thousand cubits **from the north** of the tree in order to ascertain whether or not he may go to his home, because of the uncertainty with regard to the precise location where he established residence, **one measures** the distance **for him** stringently **from the south.** And likewise if **he comes to measure** the distance to his home **from the south, one measures** the distance **for him from the north.**

Perek **IV**
Daf **50** Amud **a**

NOTES

Not precisely defined – דְּלָא מְסַיֵּים: This principle is significant primarily with regard to the *halakhot* of Shabbat boundaries. However, even though the *tanna'im* disagreed with regard to consecrations and vows, the *halakha* is that an object that is not defined can be consecrated. Therefore, Abaye did not raise an objection to the first version of Rabba's opinion (*Ge'on Ya'akov*).

Simultaneously – בְּבַת אַחַת: Rabba's opinion with regard to two matters taking effect simultaneously appears to be that this concept is moot, as no two phenomena can occur at precisely the same time. Therefore, simultaneity is merely uncertainty which of two events that occurred consecutively was first, as it is impossible to determine the actual order of events.

אָמַר רַבָּה: מַאי טַעְמָא דְּרַב – מִשּׁוּם דְּלָא מְסַיֵּים אַתְרֵיהּ.

Rabba said: What is the reason for Rav's statement that one who declares his intention to establish residence beneath a tree has said nothing at all? It is **because the place** he designated **is not** precisely **defined.**[N] Since he did not establish his residence in one particular location, he did not establish it at all.

וְאִיכָּא דְּאָמְרִי, אָמַר רַבָּה: מַאי טַעְמָא דְּרַב – מִשּׁוּם דְּקָסָבַר: כֹּל שֶׁאֵינוֹ בְּזֶה אַחַר זֶה – אֲפִילּוּ בְּבַת אַחַת אֵינוֹ.

And some say an alternative version of Rabba's statement. **Rabba said: What is the reason** for the statement of **Rav?** It is **Because he maintains: Anything that cannot** be accomplished **sequentially,** due to halakhic or practical considerations, **even simultaneously,**[N] **cannot** be accomplished, as one negates the other. In this case, since one cannot establish residence in an area of four cubits on one side of a tree and proceed to establish residence in an area of four cubits on the other side of the tree, neither can he simultaneously establish residence beneath a tree greater than four cubits.

מַאי בֵּינַיְיהוּ? אִיכָּא בֵּינַיְיהוּ: דְּאָמַר "לִיקְנוּ לִי בְּאַרְבַּע אַמּוֹת מִגּוֹ שְׁמוֹנֶה".

The Gemara asks: **What is** the practical difference **between these** two versions of Rabba's statement? The Gemara answers: **There is** a practical difference **between them** with regard to a case **where he said: Let** residence be **acquired for me** in **four cubits of the eight** or more cubits beneath that tree.

מַאן דְּאָמַר מִשּׁוּם דְּלָא מְסַיֵּים אַתְרֵיהּ – הָא לָא מְסַיֵּים אַתְרֵיהּ,

According to **the one who said** that it is **because the place** he designated **is not** precisely **defined,** here too, **the place** he designated **is not** precisely **defined,** as he failed to specify the precise location of the four cubits in which to establish his residence.

וּמַאן דְּאָמַר מִשּׁוּם כֹּל שֶׁאֵינוֹ בְּזֶה אַחַר זֶה אֲפִילּוּ בְּבַת אַחַת אֵינוֹ – הַאי כְּאַרְבַּע אַמּוֹת דָּמֵי, דְּהָכָא אַרְבַּע אַמּוֹת קָאָמַר.

And according to **the one who said** it is **because anything that cannot** be accomplished **sequentially even simultaneously** it **cannot** be accomplished, **this is** considered **as** if he established his residence in **four cubits, as here he stated** that he is designated only **four cubits** as his place of residence.

גּוּפָא, אָמַר רַבָּה: כָּל דָּבָר שֶׁאֵינוֹ בְּזֶה אַחַר זֶה – אֲפִילּוּ בְּבַת אַחַת אֵינוֹ. אֵיתִיבֵיהּ אַבָּיֵי לְרַבָּה: הַמַּרְבֶּה בְּמַעַשְׂרוֹת – פֵּירוֹתָיו מְתוּקָּנִין וּמַעַשְׂרוֹתָיו מְקוּלְקָלִין.

The Gemara proceeds to analyze **the matter** of Rabba's statement **itself. Rabba said: Anything that cannot** be accomplished **sequentially even simultaneously** it **cannot** be accomplished. **Abaye raised an objection to** the opinion of **Rabba** based on the *Tosefta*: **One who increases tithes,**[N] i.e., he tithes two-tenths instead of one-tenth, the remainder of **his produce is rendered** fit for consumption, as he properly tithed it; **however, his tithes are ruined,** as the additional tenth is neither a tithe nor is it tithed produce. It is not a tithe because tithe status applies only to one tenth, and neither is it tithed produce as it was not tithed. Since it is unclear which of the two-tenths is the actual tithe and which is not, this produce may neither be treated as a tithe nor as tithed produce.[H]

אַמַּאי? לֵימָא: כֹּל שֶׁאֵינוֹ בְּזֶה אַחַר זֶה – אֲפִילּוּ בְּבַת אַחַת אֵינוֹ!

According to Rabba's opinion, the question arises: **Why** should the produce be rendered fit for consumption? **Let us say** and apply his principle: **Anything that cannot** be accomplished **sequentially; even simultaneously** it **cannot** be accomplished. Since one may not designate two tenths sequentially, one tenth followed by a second tenth, likewise, he should be precluded from simultaneously designating two tenths of his produce as a tithe. Accordingly, it should be considered as though he had not designated any tithe at all, and therefore his produce should not be regarded as tithed.

שָׁאנֵי מַעֲשֵׂר דְּאִיתֵיהּ לַחֲצָאִין, דְּאִי אָמַר ״תִּקְדּוֹשׁ פַּלְגָא פַּלְגָא דְּחִיטְּתָא״ – קָדְשָׁה.

Gemara answers: The case of **a tithe is different, as** tithe status **takes effect partially,** i.e., on less than a unit of produce. **As if one said: Let half of each** grain of **wheat be designated** as tithed, **it is designated.** Just as one can designate an entire grain of wheat as a tithe, he can likewise designate half a grain. In this case too, when one tithes two tenths of the produce, the ruling is not that one tenth is actual tithe and the other tenth is untithed produce mixed with the tithe. Instead, half of each grain of the set-aside portion is designated as a tithe, while the other half of each grain is not. Accordingly, the remainder of the produce is tithed, as one tenth of the total has been designated as first tithe. However, the portion designated as the tithe is ruined, because it is impossible to identify which part of each grain is designated.

מַעְשַׂר בְּהֵמָה דְּלֵיתֵיהּ לַחֲצָאִין,

Another objection was raised against Rabba's opinion: Yet there is the case of the **animal tithe, which does take effect partially,** as one cannot consecrate half an animal for his tithe. Three times a year, the owner of a herd of kosher animals would gather all the animals born during the preceding period into an enclosure and let them out one by one. Every tenth animal would be marked with red paint to indicate that it was sacred. Only an entire animal could be consecrated as animal tithe, not a part of an animal.

וְאָמַר (רַבָּה): יָצְאוּ שְׁנַיִם בַּעֲשִׂירִי, וּקְרָאָן עֲשִׂירִי – עֲשִׂירִי וְאַחַד עָשָׂר מְעוֹרָבִין זֶה בָּזֶה!

And Rabba said: If **two** animals **emerged** from the enclosure together **as the tenth,**[H] **and he designated them** both as the **tenth, the tenth and eleventh** animals **are intermingled with each other.** One is sacred with the sanctity of the animal tithe, while the other remains a peace-offering, but there is no way to determine which is which. The question arises: If the principle that anything which cannot be accomplished sequentially; even simultaneously it cannot be accomplished applies, neither animal is consecrated, as one cannot designate both the tenth and the eleventh animals as the animal tithe, one after the other.

שָׁאנֵי מַעְשַׂר בְּהֵמָה דְּאִיתֵיהּ בְּזֶה אַחַר זֶה בְּטָעוּת.

The Gemara answers: The **animal tithe is different, as** two animals can indeed be designated as animal tithe **one after the other in** the case of **an error.** Although one cannot designate the tenth and eleventh animals as the animal tithe *ab initio*, if he did so in error they are both consecrated.

NOTES

One who increases tithes – הַמַּרְבֶּה בְּמַעַשְׂרוֹת: The *halakha* governing tithes differs from that of *teruma*. The Torah does not specify a particular amount that must be separated as *teruma*, or for several other priestly gifts. Consequently, any amount that the owner designates as *teruma* is consecrated with the sanctity of *teruma*. However, since tithes have a fixed measure, the sanctity of tithes does not apply to any amount beyond one-tenth.

HALAKHA

One who increases tithes – הַמַּרְבֶּה בְּמַעַשְׂרוֹת: If a person tithes too much, the remainder of his produce is regarded as tithed; however, the tithed portion is ruined. Therefore, one should tithe by measure and weight, rather than by estimate (*Shulḥan Arukh*, *Yoreh De'a* 331:76).

If two emerged as the tenth – יָצְאוּ שְׁנַיִם בַּעֲשִׂירִי: If two animals emerged together as the tenth, and he designated them both as the tenth, the tenth and the eleventh animals are intermingled. Therefore, the owner must wait until they develop a blemish, at which point they may be slaughtered and eaten as non-sacred meat (Rambam, *Sefer Korbanot*, *Hilkhot Bekhorot* 8:4).

דִּתְנַן: קָרָא לַתְּשִׁיעִי עֲשִׂירִי, וְלָעֲשִׂירִי תְּשִׁיעִי, וּלְאַחַד עָשָׂר עֲשִׂירִי – שְׁלָשְׁתָּן מְקוּדָּשִׁין.

As we learned in a mishna: If **one** erred and **designated the ninth** animal **as the tenth,**[N] and erred again and designated **the tenth as the ninth and the eleventh as the tenth,** all **three** animals **are consecrated.** The first is consecrated because it was designated as the tenth, the second because it actually is the tenth, while the third is also consecrated because it was designated as the tenth. Apparently, more than one animal can be consecrated as the animal tithe, if designated in error. Here too, a modicum of sanctity applies to the two animals that emerged together and were together designated as the tenth.[H]

וַהֲרֵי תּוֹדָה, דְּלֵיתָהּ בְּטָעוּת וְלֵיתָהּ בְּזֶה אַחַר זֶה; וְאִיתְּמַר: תּוֹדָה שֶׁנִּשְׁחֲטָה עַל שְׁמוֹנִים חַלּוֹת, חִזְקִיָּה אָמַר: קָדְשׁוּ עֲלֶיהָ אַרְבָּעִים מִתּוֹךְ שְׁמוֹנִים, רַבִּי יוֹחָנָן אָמַר: לֹא קָדְשׁוּ עֲלֶיהָ אַרְבָּעִים מִתּוֹךְ שְׁמוֹנִים.

The Gemara raises another objection to Rabba's principle. **But there is** the case of the forty loaves that accompany a **thanks-offering,**[N] **which are not** consecrated if they were designated **in error,**[N] **and** likewise **are not** consecrated if two sets of loaves were designated for the same offering **one after the other. And** yet **it is stated** that *amora'im* disagreed with regard to **a thanks-offering that was slaughtered** accompanied **by eighty loaves,** twice the required amount. **Ḥizkiya said: Forty of the eighty** loaves **are consecrated,** even though their identity cannot be determined; **Rabbi Yoḥanan said: Not** even **forty of** the **eighty** loaves **are consecrated.** It would appear that these *amora'im* disagree whether or not sanctity that cannot take effect in sequence can take effect simultaneously.

הָא אִיתְּמַר עֲלָהּ, אָמַר רַבִּי (זֵירָא): הַכֹּל מוֹדִים הֵיכָא דְּאָמַר ״לִיקַדְּשׁוּ אַרְבָּעִים מִתּוֹךְ שְׁמוֹנִים״ – דְּקָדְשִׁי, ״לֹא יִקָּדְשׁוּ אַרְבָּעִים אֶלָּא אִם כֵּן קָדְשׁוּ שְׁמוֹנִים״ – כּוּלֵּי עָלְמָא לָא פְּלִיגִי דְּלָא קָדְשׁוּ.

The Gemara rejects this contention. **Wasn't it stated with regard to** this dispute that **Rabbi Zeira said: Everyone,** both Ḥizkiya and Rabbi Yoḥanan, **concedes** that in a case **where** the donor **said: Let forty of the eighty** loaves **be consecrated, that** the forty **are consecrated;** and in a case where he said: **Let forty** loaves **only be consecrated if** all **eighty are consecrated, everyone agrees that they are not consecrated.** This is in accordance with Rabba's opinion.

כִּי פְּלִיגִי – בִּסְתָמָא. מָר סָבַר: לְאַחֲרָיוּת קָא מְכַוֵּין, וְעַל תְּנַאי אַיְיתִינְהוּ.

When Ḥizkiya and Rabbi Yoḥanan **disagree** is with regard a case where the donor designated eighty loaves **without stipulation** how many he wants consecrated. **One Sage,** Ḥizkiya, **maintains:** Although he designated eighty loaves, he seeks to consecrate only forty, and when he sets aside eighty loaves, **he** merely **intends to ensure** that he will have forty, **and he** therefore **brought** the extra loaves **on condition** that if the first forty loaves are lost or become ritually impure, the second forty will be consecrated in their place. Consequently, the first forty loaves are consecrated.[H]

NOTES

If he designated the ninth as the tenth – קָרָא לַתְּשִׁיעִי עֲשִׂירִי: Every tenth animal of those born that year is consecrated as the animal tithe. Special *halakhot* apply to this animal, which must be brought to Jerusalem, sacrificed, and eaten there. The Sages, however, derived from the verses that when the sanctity of the tithe is not properly declared, additional animals are occasionally consecrated as a result of his error. Therefore, if one designated the tenth animal as the tenth, sanctity cannot take effect on the eleventh. However, if one designated the tenth animal as the ninth, its sanctity did not fully take effect, and as a result the eleventh can also be consecrated as the animal tithe.

Thanks-offering – קָרְבַּן תּוֹדָה: The thanks-offering is specified in the Torah as a unique type of peace-offering. The Sages received a tradition, based on Psalms 107, with regard to the circumstances that obligate a person to bring a thanksgiving sacrifice. Along with the sacrifice, typically a sheep, one also brings a meal-offering in the form of forty loaves of four varieties, ten of each.

Thanks-offering, which are not consecrated in error – תּוֹדָה דְּלֵיתָהּ בְּטָעוּת: An error in the case of a thanks-offering would be, for example, if he consecrated forty black loaves of bread in his house, and he discovered they were actually white (Rashi; *Me'iri*), or if he used the thanksgiving loaves of another person for his own thanks-offering, as the loaves of one person cannot be consecrated through the offering of the thanks-offering of another (Ra'avad).

HALAKHA

If he designated the ninth as the tenth – קָרָא לַתְּשִׁיעִי עֲשִׂירִי: The *halakha* is that an error in counting can cause both the ninth and the eleventh animals, but no others, to be consecrated as the animal tithe. In that case, with regard to the ninth animal, one waits until it develops a blemish, at which point they may be slaughtered and eaten as non-sacred meat, and the eleventh animal is sacrificed as a peace-offering (Rambam, *Sefer Korbanot, Hilkhot Bekhorot* 8:1–2).

A thanks-offering with eighty loaves – תּוֹדָה עַל שְׁמוֹנִים חַלּוֹת: If one brought eighty loaves to accompany his thanks-offering, saying: Let forty of the eighty loaves be consecrated, he takes forty loaves for his thanks-offering, while the rest are redeemed and eaten as non-sacred bread. If one slaughtered the thanks-offering accompanied by eighty loaves without specifying, they are not consecrated. This is the Rambam's ruling, in accordance with the opinion of Rabbi Yoḥanan. The Ra'avad, however, rules that in the latter case only forty loaves are consecrated, in accordance with the opinion of Ḥizkiya, who was Rabbi Yoḥanan's teacher (See Rashba and *Kesef Mishne*; Rambam, *Sefer Avoda, Hilkhot Pesulei HaMukdashin* 12:15).

וּמָר סָבַר: לְקָרְבַּן גָּדוֹל קָא מְכַוֵּין.

And the other Sage, Rabbi Yoḥanan, **maintains:** He **intends** to bring **a large offering** of eighty loaves, and therefore none of the loaves are consecrated.

אָמַר אַבַּיֵי: לֹא שָׁנוּ אֶלָּא בְּאִילָן שֶׁתַּחְתָּיו שְׁתֵּים עֶשְׂרֵה אַמָּה, אֲבָל בְּאִילָן שֶׁאֵין שְׁתֵּים עֶשְׂרֵה אַמָּה – הֲרֵי מִקְצָת בֵּיתוֹ נִיכָּר.

Abaye said: They only taught Rav's ruling that one cannot establish residence beneath a tree without precisely defining a particular location, **with regard to a tree beneath which there are** at least **twelve cubits. However, with regard to a tree** beneath **which there are not twelve cubits,**[N] he can establish residence there, **as** at least **part of his residence is conspicuous.**[N] In that case, there is a partial overlap between the middle four cubits beneath the tree and the four cubits nearest him and the four cubits farthest from him, and consequently each necessarily contains at least part of his residence.

מַתְקִיף לַהּ רַב הוּנָא בְּרֵיהּ דְּרַב יְהוֹשֻׁעַ: מִמַּאי דְּבְאַרְבְּעֵי מְצִיעָתָא קָא מְסַיֵּים? דִּלְמָא בְּאַרְבְּעֵי דְּהַאי גִּיסָא וּבְאַרְבְּעֵי דְּהַאי גִּיסָא קָמְסַיֵּים!

Rav Huna, son of Rav Yehoshua, strongly objects to this: From where is it ascertained **that he designates** his residence **in the four middle** cubits, so that there is a partial overlap with both the nearest and the farthest cubits; **perhaps he designates** it in **the four** cubits **on this side or** in **the four** cubits **on the other side?** Since he does not know which location he designated as his residence, he did not establish residence anywhere beneath the tree.

אֶלָּא אָמַר רַב הוּנָא בְּרֵיהּ דְּרַב יְהוֹשֻׁעַ: לֹא שָׁנוּ אֶלָּא בְּאִילָן שֶׁתַּחְתָּיו שְׁמוֹנֶה אַמּוֹת, אֲבָל בְּאִילָן שֶׁתַּחְתָּיו שֶׁבַע אַמּוֹת – הֲרֵי מִקְצָת בֵּיתוֹ נִיכָּר.

Rather, Rav Huna, son of Rav Yehoshua, said: Abaye's statement must be emended. **They taught** this **only with regard to a tree that** has at least **eight cubits beneath it. However, with regard to a tree that** has only **seven cubits beneath it,**[H] even if one did not establish a particular location, he acquires residence, **as** at least **part of his residence is conspicuous,** as any four cubits must include at least one cubit of his residence.

תַּנְיָא כְּוָותֵיהּ דְּרַב, תַּנְיָא כְּוָותֵיהּ דִּשְׁמוּאֵל.

With regard to the dispute between Rav and Shmuel, the Gemara notes that one *baraita* **was taught in accordance with** the opinion of **Rav** and another *baraita* **was taught in accordance with** the opinion of **Shmuel.**

תַּנְיָא כְּוָותֵיהּ דְּרַב: מִי שֶׁבָּא בַּדֶּרֶךְ וְחָשְׁכָה לוֹ, וְהָיָה מַכִּיר אִילָן אוֹ גָּדֵר, וְאָמַר ״שְׁבִיתָתִי תַּחְתָּיו״ – לֹא אָמַר כְּלוּם. אֲבָל אִם אָמַר ״שְׁבִיתָתִי בְּמָקוֹם פְּלוֹנִי״ – מְהַלֵּךְ עַד שֶׁמַּגִּיעַ לְאוֹתוֹ מָקוֹם. הִגִּיעַ לְאוֹתוֹ מָקוֹם – מְהַלֵּךְ אֶת כּוּלּוֹ וְחוּצָה לוֹ אַלְפַּיִם אַמָּה.

The Gemara elaborates. A *baraita* **was taught in accordance with** the opinion of **Rav:** With regard to **one who was coming along the way** on Shabbat eve, **and it grew dark** while **he** was traveling, **and he was familiar** with **a tree or a fence** within two thousand cubits of his current location, **and he said: My residence is beneath** that tree, **he has not said anything** of legal consequence. **However, if he said: My residence is in such-and-such place, he walks until he reaches that place.** Once **he reached that place** that he established as his residence, **he walks** through **all of it and** another **two thousand cubits beyond it.**

בַּמֶּה דְּבָרִים אֲמוּרִים – בְּמָקוֹם הַמְסוּיָּים, כְּגוֹן שֶׁשָּׁבַת בְּתֵל שֶׁהוּא גָּבוֹהַּ עֲשָׂרָה טְפָחִים וְהוּא מֵאַרְבַּע אַמּוֹת וְעַד בֵּית סָאתַיִם.

In what case **are these matters,** that he establishes four cubits as his residence, and another two thousand cubits in each direction, **stated?** In a case where he selected **a well-defined,** clearly demarcated **place,**[H] i.e., a case **where he established** residence **on a mound ten handbreadths high, and its** area ranges **from** a minimum of **four cubits to** a maximum of **two** ***beit se'a.***

וְכֵן בִּקְעָה שֶׁהִיא עֲמוּקָּה עֲשָׂרָה וְהִיא מֵאַרְבַּע אַמּוֹת וְעַד בֵּית סָאתַיִם. אֲבָל בְּמָקוֹם שֶׁאֵין מְסוּיָּים – אֵין לוֹ אֶלָּא אַרְבַּע אַמּוֹת.

And, likewise, that is the *halakha* when he establishes residence on **a plain ten** handbreadths **deeper** than the surrounding area, **and its** area ranges **from** a minimum of **four cubits to** a maximum of **two** ***beit se'a.*** **However,** if he selected **a place that is not defined,** e.g., in the middle of a plain, he does not establish residence, and accordingly **he has only four cubits** in which to move.

הָיוּ שְׁנַיִם, אֶחָד מַכִּיר וְאֶחָד שֶׁאֵינוֹ מַכִּיר – זֶה שֶׁאֵינוֹ מַכִּיר מוֹסֵר שְׁבִיתָתוֹ לַמַּכִּיר, וְהַמַּכִּיר אוֹמֵר ״שְׁבִיתָתִי בְּמָקוֹם פְּלוֹנִי״.

If two people **were** walking together, **one** of whom is **familiar** with a particular location in the distance, **and one** of whom is **not familiar** with it, **the one who** is **not familiar** with it[H] **entrusts** his right to designate **his residence to the one** is **not familiar** with it, **and the one who** is **familiar** with it **says: My residence is in such-and-such place.**

NOTES

A tree beneath which there are not twelve cubits – בְּאִילָן שֶׁאֵין תַּחְתָּיו שְׁתֵּים עֶשְׂרֵה אַמָּה: According to Abaye, whenever it is possible to assume that one designated a particular location beneath a tree, that location becomes his established residence. Consequently, if there are less than twelve cubits beneath the tree, the assumption is that he is referring to the middle four cubits and he therefore acquires residence there. However, Rav Huna, son of Rabbi Yehoshua, maintains that the possibility of establishing residence at a specific location is insufficient to establish residence. Rather, it is only if his intention is clearly stated that his residence is established.

Part of his residence is conspicuous – הֲרֵי מִקְצָת בֵּיתוֹ נִיכָּר: The fact that part of his place of residence is conspicuous is relevant only with regard to acquiring residence beneath the tree. However, with regard to the measure of one's Shabbat limit from the tree, the *halakha* is applied stringently in either direction, comparable to that of both a donkey driver and a camel driver (Ra'avad).

HALAKHA

A tree that has only seven cubits beneath it – אִילָן שֶׁתַּחְתָּיו שֶׁבַע אַמּוֹת: If there are fewer than eight cubits beneath the tree it is considered a defined area, because part of his place of residence is recognizable. This is in accordance with the Rambam's opinion. The *Magen Avraham* writes that this ruling is even accepted by the *Shulḥan Arukh*, who rules in accordance with Shmuel's opinion as it was explained by Rashi, since all opinions, including that of Rav, accept it (*Shulḥan Arukh, Oraḥ Ḥayyim* 409:11).

A well-defined place – בְּמָקוֹם מְסוּיָּים: If a person established his residence in a place defined by its partitions, it is considered the equivalent of four cubits, and he may walk throughout the entire area and two thousand cubits beyond on one of two conditions: If it was enclosed for residence regardless of area or if it was less than two *beit se'a* (*Shulḥan Arukh, Oraḥ Ḥayyim* 396:3).

One of whom is familiar and one of whom is not familiar – מַכִּיר וְאֵינוֹ מַכִּיר: With regard to two people who were traveling together, one of whom is aware of a place where residence can be established, no farther than two thousand cubits from his present location, the one who is not aware of that place may entrust his right to select his residence to the one who is aware, and the latter says: My residence is in such-and-such place (*Shulḥan Arukh, Oraḥ Ḥayyim* 409:12).

בַּמֶּה דְּבָרִים אֲמוּרִים – כְּשֶׁסִּיֵּים אַרְבַּע אַמּוֹת שֶׁקָּבַע, אֲבָל לֹא סִיֵּים אַרְבַּע אַמּוֹת שֶׁקָּבַע – לֹא יָזוּז מִמְּקוֹמוֹ.

In what case **are these matters,** that he acquires four cubits as his residence and another two thousand cubits in each direction, **stated?** In a case **where he defined** the **four cubits that he** seeks to **establish** as his residence. **However,** if **he did not define** the **four cubits that he** seeks to **establish** as his residence, **he may not move from his** current **place,** as neither did he seek to establish residence there, nor did he acquire it in the location he sought to establish residence. This *baraita* is in accordance with the opinion of Rav opinion that one who fails to designate the four cubits he seeks to establish as residence has no residence at all.

לֵימָא תֶּיהֱוֵי תְּיוּבְתֵּיהּ דִּשְׁמוּאֵל! אָמַר לָךְ שְׁמוּאֵל: הָכָא בְּמַאי עָסְקִינַן – כְּגוֹן דְּאִיכָּא מִמְּקוֹם רַגְלָיו וְעַד עִיקָּרוֹ תְּרֵי אַלְפֵי וְאַרְבַּע גַּרְמִידֵי, דְּאִי מוֹקְמִית לֵיהּ בְּאִידָךְ גִּיסָּא דְּאִילָן – קָם לֵיהּ לְבַר מִתְּחוּמָא,

Gemara poses a question: **Let us say** that this *baraita* is a **conclusive refutation of** the opinion of **Shmuel?** The Gemara answers: There is no difficulty, as **Shmuel** could have **said to you: With what are we dealing here?** We are dealing **with a** special **case, where from the place he is standing to the trunk** of the tree **there is** a distance of **two thousand and four cubits,**[N] so that **if you were to establish** residence **on the other side of the tree, it would be situated outside** his Shabbat limit.[H]

אִי סִיֵּים אַרְבַּע אַמּוֹת – מָצֵי אָזֵיל, וְאִי לָא – לָא מָצֵי אָזֵיל.

Consequently, **if he designated** his **four cubits** on the near side of the tree **he may go** there; **and if not, he may not go** from the place he is standing. In other words, since he did not establish residence in a particular location, the concern is that he sought to establish it beyond his two thousand cubit limit.

תַּנְיָא כְּווֹתֵיהּ דִּשְׁמוּאֵל: טָעָה וְעֵירֵב לִשְׁתֵּי רוּחוֹת, כִּמְדוּמֶּה הוּא שֶׁמְּעָרְבִין לוֹ לִשְׁתֵּי רוּחוֹת, אוֹ שֶׁאָמַר לַעֲבָדָיו "צְאוּ וְעָרְבוּ לִי", אֶחָד עֵירֵב עָלָיו לַצָּפוֹן וְאֶחָד עֵירֵב עָלָיו לַדָּרוֹם – מְהַלֵּךְ לַצָּפוֹן כְּעֵירוּבוֹ לַדָּרוֹם, וְלַדָּרוֹם כְּעֵירוּבוֹ לַצָּפוֹן.

A *baraita* **was taught in accordance with** the opinion of **Shmuel. If one erred and established an** ***eiruv*** **in two directions**[N] at once, for example, if in his ignorance **he imagined that** it is permitted to **establish an** ***eiruv*** **in two directions,** that he may extend the distance that he may walk on Shabbat in two opposite directions, **or if he said to his servants: Go out and establish an** ***eiruv*** **for me,** without specifying the direction, and **one established an** ***eiruv*** **for him to the north, and one established an** ***eiruv*** **for him to the south, he may walk to the north as** far as he is permitted go based on **his** ***eiruv*** **to the south,** and he may walk **to the south as** far as he is permitted go based on **his** ***eiruv*** **to the north.** In other words, the assumption is that he established residence in both directions based on the *eiruv* in each direction, and he must therefore take both into consideration before moving.[H]

וְאִם מִיצְעוּ עָלָיו אֶת הַתְּחוּם – לֹא יָזוּז מִמְּקוֹמוֹ.

And consequently, **if** each *eiruv* was placed two thousand cubits in opposite directions **placing him in the middle of the limit,**[N] **he may not move from his** current **location,** as it is prohibited to venture beyond either limit. Apparently, even if one did not establish residence in a particular location, as in this case he has acquired residence in both places, nonetheless, the *halakha* is that residence has been established in his current location, in accordance with the opinion of Shmuel.

לֵימָא תֶּיהֱוֵי תְּיוּבְתֵּיהּ דְּרַב! רַב תַּנָּא הוּא וּפָלֵיג.

The Gemara poses a question: **Let us say** that this *baraita* is a **conclusive refutation of** the opinion of **Rav?** The Gemara answers: This *baraita* indeed differs with Rav's ruling. Nevertheless his opinion is not disqualified, as **Rav himself** had ***tanna*** status and therefore, unlike later *amora'im*, could **disagree** with opinions of *tanna'im*.[N]

"אָמַר שְׁבִיתָתִי בְּעִיקָּרוֹ – מְהַלֵּךְ מִמְּקוֹם רַגְלָיו וְעַד עִיקָּרוֹ אַלְפַּיִם אַמָּה, וּמֵעִיקָּרוֹ לְבֵיתוֹ אַלְפַּיִם אַמָּה. נִמְצָא מְהַלֵּךְ מִשֶּׁחֲשֵׁיכָה אַרְבַּעַת אֲלָפִים אַמָּה".

We learned in the mishna that if, however, **he said: My residence is at** the **trunk** of the tree, he established residence there, and he **may walk from the place that he is standing to the trunk** of the tree, up to **two thousand cubits, and from the trunk** of the tree **to his house** another **two thousand cubits. Ultimately, he may walk after nightfall** a total distance of **four thousand cubits.**

NOTES

Two thousand and four cubits – תְּרֵי אַלְפֵי וְאַרְבַּע גַּרְמִידֵי: According to Rashi's explanation, even Shmuel agrees that this person establishes his residence in the place he specified. However, since he is located outside the Shabbat limit in which he seeks to acquire residence at nightfall, he has only four cubits in which he may walk. Conversely, according to Rabbeinu Ḥananel, he does not establish residence if it is more than two thousand cubits away. Rather, he merely prevents himself from establishing residence in his current location, in accordance with the opinion of Rav.

If he established an ***eiruv*** **in two directions** – עֵירֵב לִשְׁתֵּי רוּחוֹת: Some commentaries question Rabba's opinion in light of this discussion. As Rabba maintains that anything that cannot be accomplished consecutively cannot be accomplished simultaneously either, how does this person establish an *eiruv* at all? The *halakha* should be that his limit is like that of the other the inhabitants of the town. The commentaries answer that there the issue of simultaneity is not relevant in this context. Even if he does not seek to establish his residence in two places simultaneously but acquired them one after the other, the *halakha* is stringent and he is subject to the restrictions of each *eiruv*, due to the uncertainty which came first (*Tosafot*, as cited by the Ritva).

If each ***eiruv*** **was placed two thousand cubits in opposite directions placing him in the middle of the limit** – אִם מִיצְעוּ עָלָיו אֶת הַתְּחוּם: Rashi states that the *baraita* supports Shmuel's opinion, because this person is permitted to walk to the north only as far as the *eiruv* in the south allows, and vice versa. The Ritva maintains that the primary proof for Shmuel's opinion from the *baraita* comes from the statement that if his two *eiruvin* placed him in the middle of his limit he no longer has permission to walk at all. This proves that he has fully acquired an *eiruv* and has been moved from his current location.

Rav himself had ***tanna*** **status and therefore could disagree with opinions of** ***tanna'im*** – רַב תַּנָּא הוּא וּפָלֵיג: Some commentaries explain that Rav is as important as one of the *tanna'im*. Consequently, he can even dispute the words of a *baraita*. However, it is more likely that the statement means that Rav actually was a *tanna*, since he is mentioned in several *baraitot*. In addition, there is a tradition in the name of Rav Hai Gaon that three *baraitot* cited in the Gemara include statements of Rav referring to him as Rabbi Abba. In any case, Rav remains an *amora*, because Shmuel and Rabbi Yoḥanan, who are not *tanna'im*, also disagree with him in various cases, and the *halakha* is occasionally in accordance with their opinion. In practical terms, this statement indicates that one cannot raise an objection to Rav's opinion from any *baraita*, as he is cited as a *tanna* in several *baraitot*. It is well-known that the Sages only used this answer as a last resort (see *Yad Malakhi*).

HALAKHA

Two thousand and four cubits – תְּרֵי אַלְפֵי וְאַרְבַּע גַּרְמִידֵי: If the entire tree beneath which a person established his residence was not within two thousand cubits of his present location, and he did not designate a defined location beneath it, he did not establish residence, even according to Shmuel (*Shulḥan Arukh, Oraḥ Ḥayyim* 409:11).

Two ***eiruvin*** – שְׁנֵי עֵירוּבִין: If one established two *eiruvin* in two different directions, whether due to ignorance or due to an error on the part of his messengers, it is as though he established his residence in two places, and he may only walk within the limits permitted to him by each (*Shulḥan Arukh, Oraḥ Ḥayyim* 412:1).

אָמַר רָבָא: וְהוּא דְּכִי רָהֵיט לְעִיקָּרוֹ מָטֵי. אָמַר לֵיהּ אַבַּיֵי: וְהָא חָשְׁכָה לוֹ קָתָנֵי!

Rava said: This *halakha* applies **only** in a case **where, were he to run to the trunk**[N] of the tree **he could reach it** before the onset of Shabbat. **Abaye said to him: But doesn't** the mishna **state: And it grew dark** while **he** was traveling, indicating that he is farther away than that?

חָשְׁכָה לְבֵיתוֹ, אֲבָל לְעִיקָּרוֹ שֶׁל אִילָן מָצֵי אָזֵיל. אִיכָּא דְּאָמְרִי, אָמַר רָבָא: חָשְׁכָה לוֹ – כִּי מַסְגֵּי קַלֵּי קַלֵּי, אֲבָל רָהֵיט – מָטֵי.

The Gemara answers: The mishna means that **it grew dark** while he was traveling so that he can no longer return **to his house** before nightfall; **however, he is able** to **go to the trunk** of the tree before Shabbat. **Some state** a different version of the previous statement. **Rava said:** The mishna means that **it grew dark** while **he** was traveling, so that **were he to walk very slowly** he could not reach his house; **however, if he runs, he can** still **arrive**[H] before Shabbat.

רַבָּה וְרַב יוֹסֵף הֲווּ קָא אָזְלִי בְּאוֹרְחָא. אֲמַר לֵיהּ רַבָּה לְרַב יוֹסֵף: תְּהֵא שְׁבִיתָתֵנוּ תּוּתֵי דִּיקְלָא דְּסָבֵיל אֲחוּהּ, וְאָמְרִי לַהּ: תּוּתֵי דִּיקְלָא דְּפָרֵיק מָרֵיהּ מִכַּרְגָּא.

Rabba and Rav Yosef were going together **along the way. Rabba said to Rav Yosef: Our residence will be beneath the palm that carries its brother,** the one with another palm tree leaning on it. **And some say** he said to him: Our residence will be **beneath the palm that spared its owner from the land tax [*karga*],**[L] the palm which yielded enough dates for its owner to pay his entire land tax.

יָדַע לֵיהּ מָר? אֲמַר לֵיהּ: לָא יָדַעְנָא לֵיהּ. אֲמַר לֵיהּ: סְמוֹךְ עָלַי. דְּתַנְיָא, רַבִּי יוֹסֵי אוֹמֵר: אִם הָיוּ שְׁנַיִם, אֶחָד מַכִּיר וְאֶחָד שֶׁאֵינוֹ מַכִּיר – זֶה שֶׁאֵינוֹ מַכִּיר מוֹסֵר שְׁבִיתָתוֹ לַמַּכִּיר, זֶה שֶׁמַּכִּיר אוֹמֵר ״תְּהֵא שְׁבִיתָתֵנוּ בְּמָקוֹם פְּלוֹנִי״.

Rabba asked: **Does the Master know** of that tree? Rav Yosef **said to him:** No, **I do not know** of it. **He said to him:** Then **rely on me, as it was taught** in a *baraita* that **Rabbi Yosei says: If two** people **were** walking together, **one** of whom is **familiar** with a particular location in the distance, **and one** is **not familiar** with it, **the one who** is **not familiar** with it **entrusts** his right to designate **his** residence **to the one who** is **familiar** with it, **and the one who** is **familiar** with it **says: My residence is in such-and-such place.**

וְלָא הִיא, לָא תְּנָא לֵיהּ כְּרַבִּי יוֹסֵי אֶלָּא כִּי הֵיכִי דְּלִיקַּבֵּל לַהּ מִינֵּיהּ, מִשּׁוּם דְּרַבִּי יוֹסֵי נִימּוּקוֹ עִמּוֹ.

The Gemara comments: **But it is not** so; that is not the opinion of Rabbi Yosei. Rabba **only taught it** as if it is **in accordance with** the opinion of **Rabbi Yosei so that** Rav Yosef **would accept it from him, due to** the fact that **Rabbi Yosei's reasoning** accompanies **his** rulings,[N] Since the *halakha* is usually in accordance with Rav Yosei's opinion, Rav Yosef would be less likely to raise doubts with regard to the ruling.

״אִם אֵינוֹ מַכִּיר אוֹ שֶׁאֵינוֹ בָּקִי וְכוּ׳״.

We learned in the mishna: **If one is not familiar** with a tree or any other noticeable landmark, **or if he is not an expert** in the *halakha*, unaware that residence can be established from a distance, and he said: My residence is at my current location, his presence at his current location acquires for him the right to walk two thousand cubits in each direction.

הָנֵי אַלְפַּיִם אַמָּה הֵיכָן כְּתִיבָן? דְּתַנְיָא: ״שְׁבוּ אִישׁ תַּחְתָּיו״ – אֵלּוּ אַרְבַּע אַמּוֹת, ״אַל יֵצֵא אִישׁ מִמְּקוֹמוֹ״ – אֵלּוּ אַלְפַּיִם אַמָּה.

The Gemara raises a fundamental question: **These two thousand cubits, where are** they **written** in the Torah?[N] The Gemara answers that it is **as it was taught** in a *baraita*: **"Remain every man in his place"** (Exodus 16:29); **these are** the **four cubits,** which constitute the minimum Shabbat limit, e.g., for one who ventured beyond his prescribed limit. **"Let no man go out of his place"** (Exodus 16:29); **these are** the **two thousand cubits** of the Shabbat limit for one who remains in his place. Unless otherwise specified, the measure of one's place is two thousand cubits.

HALAKHA

However, if he runs, he can still arrive – כִּי רָהֵיט מָטֵי: One can only establish residence in a distant location if he is capable of reaching it by nightfall, even if he can only do so by running. If he can reach the location by running, he need not actually run, but may proceed slowly. However, if one cannot reach it even by running, he does not establish it as his residence. This is in accordance with the second version of Rava's statement (*Shulḥan Arukh, Oraḥ Ḥayyim* 409:11).

LANGUAGE

Land tax [*karga*] – כַּרְגָּא: From the ancient Persian χαρακ, *xaray*, meaning land tax.

NOTES

Where, were he to run to the trunk of the tree – דְּכִי רָהֵיט לְעִיקָּרוֹ: One who establishes his *eiruv* with his feet only acquires his residence when he actually arrives in that place. Consequently, although the Sages were lenient with him and did not require his presence in the location when he establishes the *eiruv*, he must nevertheless arrive there by nightfall, or at least be in a position to do so.

Rabbi Yosei's reasoning accompanies his rulings – רַבִּי יוֹסֵי נִימּוּקוֹ עִמּוֹ: It is reasonable to rule in accordance with the opinion of Rabbi Yosei despite the fact that several Sages disagree with him, as several authorities accept Rabbi Yosei's opinion as the *halakha*, even when he is opposed by more than one of his colleagues. Since Rabba knew that this was clearly the *halakha*, he cited it in the name of the well-known Sage, so that his statement would be accepted. In our versions of the *Tosefta*, however, the opinion is explicitly ascribed to Rabbi Yosei.

These two thousand cubits, where are they written – אַלְפַּיִם הֵיכָן כְּתִיבָן: Even according to the majority of commentaries, who maintain that the two thousand cubit limit is rabbinic in origin, it still may be asked: On what did the Sages base their determination of this measurement? (Ritva).

מְנָא לָן? אָמַר רַב חִסְדָּא: לָמַדְנוּ מָקוֹם מִמָּקוֹם, וּמָקוֹם מִנִּיסָה, וְנִיסָה מִנִּיסָה, וְנִיסָה מִגְּבוּל, וּגְבוּל מִגְּבוּל, וּגְבוּל מִחוּץ, וְחוּץ מִחוּץ. דִּכְתִיב: ״וּמַדּוֹתֶם מִחוּץ לָעִיר אֶת פְּאַת קֵדְמָה אַלְפַּיִם בָּאַמָּה וגו׳״.

The Gemara asks: **From where do we** derive that this is the measure of one's place? **Rav Ḥisda said: We derive** this by means of a verbal analogy between the term **place** written here: "Let no man go out of his place," and **from** the term **place**[N] written with regard to an unwitting murderer: "Then I will appoint you a place to where he shall flee" (Exodus 21:13). This last verse mentions both place and fleeing, **and** the term **place** is derived **from** the term **fleeing. And** the term **fleeing** is derived **from** the term **fleeing,** written in a different verse with regard to the unwitting murderer: "But if the slayer shall at any time come outside the border of the city of his refuge, whither he has fled" (Numbers 35:26). **And** the term **fleeing** is derived **from** the term **border,** which appears in the same verse. **And** the term **border** is derived **from** the term **border,** as it states there: "And the avenger of blood find him outside [*miḥutz*] the borders of the city of his refuge" (Numbers 35:27). Since this verse mentions both the term border and the term outside, the term **border** is derived **from** the term **outside. And** the term **outside** is derived **from** the term **outside, as it is written** with regard to the Levite cities, which also served as cities of refuge: **"And you shall measure from outside [*miḥutz*] the city on the east side two thousand cubits,** and on the south side two thousand cubits, and on the west side two thousand cubits, and on the north side two thousand cubits" (Numbers 35:5). From this chain of identical terms, the meaning of the term place stated in connection with Shabbat is derived from the two thousand cubits mentioned with regard to the Levite cities.

וְנֵילַף ״מִקִּיר הָעִיר וָחוּצָה אֶלֶף אַמָּה״! דָּנִין ״חוּץ״ מִ״חוּץ״ וְאֵין דָּנִין ״חוּץ״ מִ״חוּצָה״.

The Gemara asks: **But let us derive** instead by means of a verbal analogy between the term outside in the verse: "Outside the borders of the city of refuge," and the term outside in the verse: **"From the wall of the city outward [*vaḥutza*] a thousand cubits"** (Numbers 35:4), that the Shabbat limit measures only a thousand cubits. The Gemara answers: **One derives** the meaning of the term **outside [*ḥutz*]** by means of a verbal analogy **from** another instance of the term **outside [*ḥutz*], but one does not derive** the meaning of the term **outside from** the term **outward [*ḥutza*].**

וּמַאי נָפְקָא מִינָּהּ? הָא תָּנָא דְּבֵי רַבִּי יִשְׁמָעֵאל: ״וְשָׁב הַכֹּהֵן״ ״וּבָא הַכֹּהֵן״ – זוֹ הִיא שִׁיבָה זוֹ הִיא בִּיאָה!

The Gemara raises a difficulty: **What is** significant about **the difference** between the two terms? **Didn't the school of Rabbi Yishmael teach** a verbal analogy with regard to leprosy of houses between the verse: **"And the priest shall return [*veshav*]"** (Leviticus 14:39) and the verse: **"And the priest shall come [*uva*]"** (Leviticus 14:44), from which it is derived that **this is** the *halakha* with regard to **returning,** i.e., it is after seven days; **this is** the same *halakha* with regard to **coming;** it is after seven days. Obviously, the less pronounced difference of one letter between *ḥutz* and *ḥutza*, should not prevent the teaching of a verbal analogy.

הָנֵי מִילֵּי – הֵיכָא דְּלֵיכָּא מִידֵּי דְּדָמֵי לֵיהּ, אֲבָל הֵיכָא דְּאִיכָּא מִידֵּי דְּדָמֵי לֵיהּ – מִדָּמֵי לֵיהּ יָלְפִינַן.

Gemara rejects this argument: **This applies** only **when there are no terms** that are **identical to it however, where there are terms** that are **identical to it, we derive** the verbal analogy **from** terms **identical to it,** rather than from the terms that are not precisely identical.

״אַלְפַּיִם אַמָּה עֲגוּלּוֹת״. וְרַבִּי חֲנִינָא בֶּן אַנְטִיגְנוֹס מַה נַּפְשָׁךְ, אִי אִית לֵיהּ גְּזֵירָה שָׁוָה – פֵּיאוֹת כְּתִיבָן, אִי לֵית לֵיהּ גְּזֵירָה שָׁוָה – אַלְפַּיִם אַמָּה מְנָא לֵיהּ?

The *tanna'im* of the mishna disagree whether the **two-thousand-cubit** limit granted to a person in every direction is measured as a **circle** or as a square tablet.[B] The Gemara poses a question: With regard to the opinion of **Rabbi Ḥanina ben Antigenos** that the limit is measured as a circle, **no matter what** you say, it is difficult. **If he is of the** opinion that there is a **verbal analogy** from the verse written with regard to the Levite cities it is difficult, because **sides** is the term **written,** indicating squared boundaries. And **if he is not of the** opinion that there is a **verbal analogy, from where does he** derive that the Shabbat limit is **two thousand cubits?**

לְעוֹלָם אִית לֵיהּ גְּזֵירָה שָׁוָה, וְשָׁאנֵי הָכָא דְּאָמַר קְרָא: ״זֶה יִהְיֶה לָהֶם מִגְרְשֵׁי הֶעָרִים״ – לָזֶה אַתָּה נוֹתֵן פֵּיאוֹת, וְאִי אַתָּה נוֹתֵן פֵּיאוֹת לְשׁוֹבְתֵי שַׁבָּת.

The Gemara answers: **Actually, he is of** the opinion that there is **a verbal analogy, but here,** with regard to the Levite cities, it **is different, as the verse says: "This shall be to them the open space of the cities"** (Numbers 35:5), from which it is inferred: **To this,** the open space of the city, **you** should **provide sides** and square it, **but you do not provide sides to those resting on Shabbat.** Instead, those who establish Shabbat residence are provided with a circular, two-thousand-cubit limit.[N]

NOTES

Place from place – מָקוֹם מִמָּקוֹם: The essence of the derivation is a verbal analogy between the term place in the verse: "Remain every man in his place," (Exodus 16:29) and the term place is the passage about the city of refuge (Exodus 21:13). The final proof is cited from the parallel between the cities of refuge and the Levite cities, whose limit of two thousand cubits is explicitly stated in the Torah. This is indeed how this *halakha* is derived in the Jerusalem Talmud.

The opinion of Rabbi Ḥanina ben Antigenos – שִׁיטַת רַבִּי חֲנִינָא בֶּן אַנְטִיגְנוֹס: In the Jerusalem Talmud it states that Rabbi Ḥanina ben Antigenos disagrees only with regard to the Shabbat limit of an individual. However, with regard to the Shabbat limit of cities, he agrees that they gain the corners, as was the case with the boundaries of the Levite cities.

BACKGROUND

Two thousand cubits – אַלְפַּיִם אַמָּה: There are different opinions with regard to the measurement of the two thousand cubit limit. According to the Rabbis, the two thousand cubits form a square, while Rabbi Ḥanina ben Antigenos maintains that they are circular. Some say that the two thousand cubits form a square, but since there is no indication of how to place the square, the authorities permitted to proceed to the edge of a circle whose diameter is the diagonal of a square whose sides are each two thousand cubits.

The diagonal shown in the diagram can be calculated by using the Pythagorean theorem. According to the theorem, the sum of the areas of the two squares on the legs (the right sides of the triangle) equals the area of the square on the hypotenuse (the longest side of a right triangle). Therefore, in our case the calculation is as follows: $2000^2 + 2000^2 = 8{,}000{,}000$, $\sqrt{8{,}000{,}000} = \sim 2828.427$.

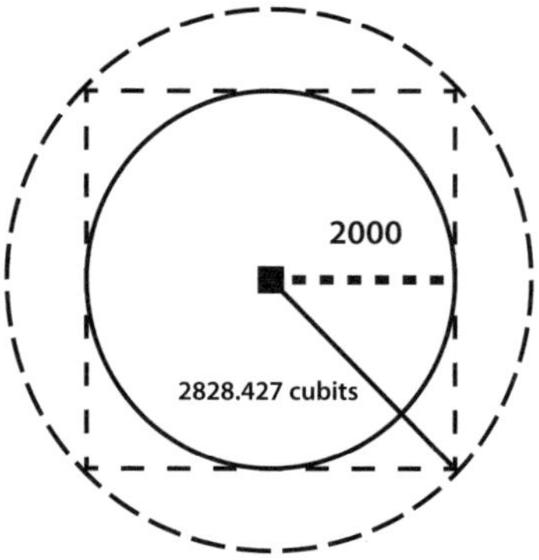

Different ways to measure the two-thousand-cubit limit

וְרַבָּנַן? תָּנֵי, רַב חֲנַנְיָה אוֹמֵר: כָּזֶה יְהוּ כׇּל שׁוֹבְתֵי שַׁבָּת.

The Gemara asks: **And** how do **the Rabbis** understand the emphasis placed on the word this in the verse? The Gemara answers: As **it was taught** in a *baraita* that **Rav Ḥananya says: Like this** measure **shall be** the calculations of measures for **all those who rest on Shabbat,** i.e., square.

אָמַר רַבִּי אַחָא בַּר יַעֲקֹב: הַמַּעֲבִיר אַרְבַּע אַמּוֹת בִּרְשׁוּת הָרַבִּים – אֵינוֹ חַיָּיב עַד שֶׁמַּעֲבִיר הֵן וַאֲלַכְסוֹנָן.

Rav Aḥa bar Ya'akov said: One who carries an object **four cubits in the public domain is only liable if he carries** it **four** cubits **with their diagonal.**[N] The four cubits mentioned in many places is only the basic measure by which the distance beyond which it is prohibited to carry is calculated. However, in practice, a person is liable only if he carries the object the length of the diagonal of a square with four-cubit sides.

אָמַר רַב פָּפָּא, בְּדַק לָן רָבָא: עַמּוּד בִּרְשׁוּת הָרַבִּים גָּבוֹהַּ עֲשָׂרָה וְרוֹחַב אַרְבָּעָה, צָרִיךְ הֵן וַאֲלַכְסוֹנָן, אוֹ לָא? וְאָמְרִינַן לֵיהּ: לָאו הַיְינוּ דְּרַב חֲנַנְיָה? דְּתַנְיָא, רַב חֲנַנְיָה אוֹמֵר: כָּזֶה יְהוּ כׇּל שׁוֹבְתֵי שַׁבָּת.

Rav Pappa said that **Rava** once **tested us** by asking:[N] With regard to **a pillar in the public domain, ten** handbreadths **high and four** handbreadths **wide, must** the width **be** four handbreadths **with their diagonal** in order to be regarded a private domain, **or not?**[H] **And we said to him: Is this not** that which was taught by **Rav Ḥananya? As it was taught** in a *baraita*: **Rav Ḥananya says: Like this** measure **shall be** that of **all those who rest on Shabbat,** indicating that the diagonal is the determining measure for the *halakhot* of rest on Shabbat.

״וְזֶה הוּא שֶׁאָמְרוּ הֶעָנִי מְעָרֵב בְּרַגְלָיו. אָמַר רַבִּי מֵאִיר: אָנוּ אֵין לָנוּ אֶלָּא עָנִי וכו׳״.

We learned in the mishna: **And this is** the meaning of that **which** the Sages **said: A pauper can establish an *eiruv* with his feet,** i.e., one who does not have the bread required to establish an *eiruv* may walk anywhere within his Shabbat limit and acquire residence. **We have** this leniency in effect **only** for **a pauper,** who does not have food for two meals. However, one who has bread may only establish residence with bread. Rabbi Yehuda says: This leniency is in effect for both a pauper and a wealthy person.

אָמַר רַב נַחְמָן: מַחְלוֹקֶת בִּ״מְקוֹמִי״, דְּרַבִּי מֵאִיר סָבַר: עִיקַּר עֵירוּב בְּפַת,

Rav Naḥman said: This **dispute** between Rabbi Meir and Rabbi Yehuda is **with regard to** a case where the person said: My residence is in **my** current **location. As Rabbi Meir maintains: The primary** ordinance and establishment **of *eiruv*** is **with bread.**

NOTES

They with their diagonal – הֵן וַאֲלַכְסוֹנָן: There are three opinions among the commentaries with regard to this basic issue. Rashi, *Tosafot*, and the Rashba explain that this additional diagonal depends on the direction in which one wishes to proceed. In other words, one may only walk two thousand cubits to the east or west, but to the northeast he may advance up to a little over two thousand eight hundred cubits. He adds that the same principle applies to all measures. Rabbeinu Tam and other commentaries contend that the calculation is based on the measurement with its diagonal in every direction, and that all the established measurements refer to the basic length, without the diagonal. Yet other commentaries maintain that one is only liable by Torah law for the measurement with its diagonal, but proceeding beyond the basic measure is prohibited by rabbinic law. Alternatively, they distinguished between the cases mentioned in this context, e.g., four cubits, and the other *halakhot* of Shabbat.

Rava tested us – בְּדַק לָן רָבָא: In other words, Rava tested us with regard to the ostensibly fixed measures of the Torah, e.g., four cubits, whether or not the diagonal should be added to them as well (Ritva).

HALAKHA

They with their diagonal – הֵן וַאֲלַכְסוֹנָן: One who carried an object four cubits in the public domain is only liable if he transfers it the length of the diagonal of a four cubit square, which is 5.6 cubits. It is permitted to carry it less than that distance (Rav Shimshon of Saens; *Tosafot*; Rosh; Rashba; Ra'avad). Some authorities state that it is only permitted to carry within a circle of a four-cubit radius. If one walked any further, he is exempt from punishment or from bringing a sin-offering, but it is prohibited to do so (Rambam, according to the *Maggid Mishne*; *Shulḥan Arukh, Oraḥ Ḥayyim* 349:2).

Perek **IV**
Daf **51** Amud **b**

עָנִי הוּא דְּאַקִילוּ רַבָּנַן עִילָוֵיהּ, אֲבָל עָשִׁיר – לָא.

Therefore, **it is** only **with regard to a pauper,** who does not have food for two meals, **that the Sages were lenient** and permitted him to establish residence merely by saying: My residence is in my current location. **However,** with regard to **a wealthy person** in his own house who has bread, **no,** they did not permit him to do so.

וְרַבִּי יְהוּדָה סָבַר: עִיקַּר עֵירוּב בְּרֶגֶל, אֶחָד עָנִי וְאֶחָד עָשִׁיר. אֲבָל ״בְּמָקוֹם פְּלוֹנִי״ – דִּבְרֵי הַכֹּל: עָנִי – אִין, עָשִׁיר – לָא.

And Rabbi Yehuda maintains: The primary ordinance **of *eiruv* is by foot,** i.e., by going and stating that he is establishing his residence in that location, and therefore it applies to **both a pauper and a wealthy person. However,** with regard a case when the person said: My residence is **in such-and-such place,** and he is not there, **everyone,** both Rabbi Meir and Rabbi Yehuda, **agrees** that for **a pauper** on the road on a Shabbat eve, **yes,** an *eiruv* may be established in that manner; however, for **a wealthy person, no,** an eiruv may not be established in that manner.[NH]

NOTES

A pauper and a wealthy person – עָנִי וְעָשִׁיר: The pauper mentioned in this context is not necessarily a person in dire financial straits. Rather, anyone traveling who intends to establish his residence in a location he has determined for himself is considered a pauper in terms of this *halakha*, as it can be assumed that he does not have with him all that he requires for a meal. The reverse is also true. One who is at home on Shabbat evening but establishes an *eiruv* in order to go the next day is considered a wealthy person. The proof is from the inhabitants of Siḥin mentioned in the *baraita*. Although they were going to receive charity, they were still considered wealthy with regard to the *eiruv* (Rashba).

HALAKHA

My residence in such-and-such place – שְׁבִיתָתִי בְּמָקוֹם פְּלוֹנִי: If one says, my residence is in such-and-such place, without going there or placing an *eiruv* there, it is only valid if he was on the road on Shabbat eve. It is not effective for one who remains at home, as per the opinion of Rabbi Naḥman, in accordance with the opinion of Rabbi Yehuda, and the explanation of the Rashba (Vilna Gaon; *Shulḥan Arukh, Oraḥ Ḥayyim* 409:13).

וזו היא שאמרו: מאן קתני לה – רבי מאיר, ואהייא קאי – א״אינו מכיר או שאינו בקי בהלכה״. ו״לא אמרו מערבין בפת אלא להקל״ מאן קתני לה – רבי יהודה.

And as for the mishna's statement: **And this is what** the Sages meant when **they said**[N] that a pauper can establish an *eiruv* with his feet, **who,** which Sage, **is teaching it?** It is **Rabbi Meir. And to which** clause of the mishna **is it referring?** It refers to the previous statement: If he is **not familiar** with a tree or any other noticeable landmark, **or if he is not an expert in the** ***halakha,*** and therefore is unaware that a residence can be established from a distance, and said: My residence is in my current location, he acquires two thousand cubits in each direction. **And** as for the statement in the continuation of the mishna: The Sages **said** that **one establishes an** ***eiruv*** **with bread only to be lenient**[N] **with the wealthy** person, **who,** which Sage, **is teaching it?** It is **Rabbi Yehuda,** who maintains that the option of establishing an *eiruv* by foot is available to the wealthy as well.

ורב חסדא אמר: מחלוקת ״במקום פלוני״, דרבי מאיר סבר: עני – אין, עשיר – לא. ורבי יהודה סבר: אחד עני ואחד עשיר. אבל ״במקומי״ – דברי הכל: אחד עני ואחד עשיר, דעיקר עירוב ברגל.

Rav Ḥisda, however, disagreed with Rav Naḥman and **said:** The **dispute** between Rabbi Meir and Rabbi Yehuda in the mishna is with regard to a person who said: My residence is **in such-and-such place,** in which case the his residence is neither acquired by foot nor with bread. **As Rabbi Meir maintains: A pauper, yes,** he establishes residence with an *eiruv* in that manner; however, **a wealthy person, no,** he does not. **And Rabbi Yehuda maintains: Both a pauper and a wealthy person** may establish an *eiruv* in that manner. **However,** in a case where one said: My residence is **in my** present **location, everyone,** both Rabbi Meir and Rabbi Yehuda, **agrees** that an *eiruv* of this kind is effective **both** for **a pauper and** for **a wealthy person,** as everyone agrees agree that **the primary** ordinance **of** ***eiruv*** **is by foot.**

״וזו היא שאמרו״, מאן קתני לה – רבי מאיר, ואהייא קאי – אהא: ״מי שבא בדרך וחשכה״. ״ולא אמרו מערבין בפת אלא להקל״ – מאן קתני לה – דברי הכל.

And as for the mishna's statement: **And this is what** the Sages meant when **they said** that **a pauper** can establish an *eiruv* by foot, **who is teaching it?** It is **Rabbi Meir. And to which** clause of the mishna **is it referring?** It is referring **to this** clause: **One who was coming along the way** on Shabbat eve, **and it grew dark** while **he** was traveling. According to Rabbi Yehuda, he could have established an *eiruv* even if he was in his house. And as for the statement in the continuation of the mishna: The Sages **said** that **one establishes an** ***eiruv*** **with bread only** in order **to be lenient with the wealthy** person, **who is teaching it? Everyone agrees** with this *halakha,* and it is taught according to both opinions.

תניא כוותיה דרב נחמן: אחד עני ואחד עשיר מערבין בפת. ולא יצא עשיר חוץ לתחום ויאמר ״שביתתי במקומי״ – לפי שלא אמרו מערבין ברגל אלא למי שבא בדרך וחשכה, דברי רבי מאיר.

The Gemara comments: A *baraita* **was taught in accordance with** the opinion of **Rav Naḥman,** who said that the dispute between Rabbi Meir and Rabbi Yehuda is with regard to one who said: My residence is in my present location. It was stated in the *baraita*: **Both a pauper and a wealthy person establish an** ***eiruv*** **with bread; however a wealthy person may not go out beyond the** Shabbat **limit and say: My residence is in my** present **location, because** the Sages **said** that **one can establish an** ***eiruv*** **by foot only** in the case of **a person who was coming along the way and it grew dark** while **he** was traveling. This is **the statement of Rabbi Meir.**

רבי יהודה אומר: אחד עני ואחד עשיר מערבין ברגל, ויצא עשיר חוץ לתחום ויאמר ״תהא שביתתי במקומי״, וזה הוא עיקרו של עירוב. והתירו חכמים לבעל הבית לשלח עירובו ביד עבדו, ביד בנו, ביד שלוחו בשביל להקל עליו.

Rabbi Yehuda says: Both a pauper and a wealthy person establish an ***eiruv*** **by foot. And a wealthy person will go out beyond the** Shabbat **limit and say: My residence is in my** present **location. And this is the primary** ordinance **of** ***eiruv.***[H] **However, the Sages permitted a homeowner to send his** ***eiruv*** **in the hand of his servant,** or **in the hand of his son,** or **in the hand of his agent,** in order **to be lenient with him,** so that he need not exert himself and go out and establish an *eiruv* by foot.[H] This *baraita* presents the dispute between Rabbi Meir and Rabbi Yehuda as it was delineated by Rav Naḥman.

אמר רבי יהודה: מעשה באנשי בית ממל ובאנשי בית גוריון בארומא, שהיו מחלקין גרוגרות וצימוקין לעניים בשני בצורת, ובאין עניי כפר שיחין ועניי כפר חנניה ומחשיכין על התחום, למחרת משכימין ובאין.

The *baraita* continues. **Rabbi Yehuda said:** There was **an incident involving the members of the household of** the **Memel** family **and members of the household of Guryon** family **in** the village of **Aroma,**[B] **who were distributing dried figs and raisins to the paupers in years of famine, and the paupers of the village of Siḥin and the paupers of the village of Ḥananya would come** to the edge of the Shabbat **limit at nightfall,** which was also within the Shabbat limit of Aroma, and then go home. **The following day they would rise early and go** to receive their figs and raisins. Apparently, one can establish an *eiruv* by foot, if he says: My residence is in my present location.

NOTES

This is what they said – וזו היא שאמרו: In addition to the words of the disputants, the mishna in this context includes two teachings apparently transmitted by the *tanna'im* but not part of their own statements: And this is what they said, a pauper can establish an *eiruv* by foot, and: They only said that one can establish an *eiruv* with bread in order to be lenient with a wealthy person. These two clauses do not appear to reflect the same opinion, but are traditions or parts of traditions cited by each of the disputants. Indeed, the two opposing explanations of the dispute explain these clauses differently.

They said that one establishes an *eiruv* with bread only to be lenient – לא אמרו מערבין בפת אלא להקל: The early commentaries ask: According to the opinion of Rabbi Ḥisda, that a person may sit in his house and say: My *eiruv* is in such-and-such place, what is the leniency of establishing an *eiruv* with bread? They answer that it remains a leniency for one who is not familiar with the place and therefore cannot establish his residence there. However, sending a messenger to place his meal there is also effective (See *Tosafot*; Rashba).

HALAKHA

An *eiruv* by foot – עירוב ברגל: If one arrived in a certain place, whether he was on the road or returning to his house in the evening, he may establish residence in that location. It is effective even if he did not explicitly state his intention, but merely had it in mind, in accordance with the opinion of Rabbi Yehuda, as explained by Rav Naḥman (*Shulḥan Arukh, Oraḥ Ḥayyim* 409:7).

Sending an *eiruv* – שליחת עירוב: A person may establish an *eiruv* for himself by means of a messenger, provided that the messenger is not a deaf-mute, an imbecile, a minor, or one who rejects the concept of an *eiruv* (*Shulḥan Arukh, Oraḥ Ḥayyim* 409:8).

BACKGROUND

The village of Aroma – כפר ארומה: Aroma, or Roma as it is called in other sources, was a small village in the vicinity of Tzippori, probably on the site of the modern town of Rameh.

אמר רב אשי: מתניתין נמי דיקא, דקתני: מי שיצא לילך לעיר שמערבין לה, והחזירו חברו – הוא מותר לילך, וכל בני העיר אסורין, דברי רבי יהודה.

Rav Ashi said: The formulation of the **mishna is also precise,**[N] in accordance with Rav Naḥman's explanation, **as it teaches: If** on a Shabbat eve **one set out to go to a city for which an** ***eiruv*** **is established** enabling him to go there on Shabbat, **and another** person **caused him to return** home, **he** himself **is permitted to go** to that city on Shabbat, **and** for **all the** other **residents of the town it is prohibited** to go there. This is **the statement of Rabbi Yehuda.**

והוינן בה: מאי שנא איהו ומאי שנא אינהו? ואמר רב הונא: הכא במאי עסקינן – כגון שיש לו שני בתים, ושני תחומי שבת ביניהן.

And we discussed this mishna and raised a difficulty: **What is different** about **him and what is different** about **them?** Why is he permitted to proceed to the other town while it is prohibited for the other residents to do so? **And Rav Huna said: We are dealing here with** a case **where he has** two **houses,** one in each city, **and** there is the distance of **two Shabbat limits,** four thousand cubits, **between them.**

איהו כיון דנפקא ליה לאורחא – הוה ליה עני,

With regard to **him, since he set out on his way, his** legal status **is** that of **a pauper,** as he did not intended to return to his first house, but to continue to his other house. Therefore, he can establish residence at the end of his Shabbat limit by verbal means alone.

והנך עשירים נינהו. אלמא: כל "במקום פלוני" עני – אין, עשיר – לא. שמע מינה.

And the legal status of **these** other inhabitants of his city, **is** that of **wealthy people,** as they are in their houses and have food. Consequently they can only establish residence at the end of their Shabbat limit by depositing food there prior the onset of Shabbat. **Apparently, everything** stated with regard to one who says: My residence is **in such-and-such place;** to **a pauper, yes,** it applies to **a wealthy person, no,** it does not apply. The Gemara concludes: Indeed, **learn from this** that this is the case.

מתני ליה רב חייא בר אשי לחייא בר רב קמיה דרב: אחד עני ואחד עשיר. אמר ליה רב: סיים בה נמי: הלכה כרבי יהודה.

Rav Ḥiyya bar Ashi was teaching the mishna to **Ḥiyya bar Rav before Rav.** He stated that this leniency applies **both to a pauper and to a wealthy person. Rav said to him: Conclude** your statement **also: The** ***halakha*** **is in accordance with** the opinion of **Rabbi Yehuda.**

רבה בר רב חנן הוה רגיל דאתי מארטיבנא לפומבדיתא,

The Gemara relates: **Rabba bar Rav Ḥanan was in the habit** of **coming from** his home in **Artibbena**[N] **to Pumbedita** on Shabbat.

Perek **IV**
Daf **52** Amud **a**

אמר: "תהא שביתתי בצינתא". אמר ליה אביי: מאי דעתיך – רבי מאיר ורבי יהודה – הלכה כרבי יהודה, ואמר רב חסדא: מחלוקת "במקום פלוני",

He **would declare** on Shabbat eve: **My residence is in Tzinta,** a settlement located between the Shabbat limits of the two places. **Abaye said to him: What is your opinion** that led you to act in that manner? Is it because in a dispute between **Rabbi Meir and Rabbi Yehuda, the** ***halakha*** **is in accordance with** the opinion of **Rabbi Yehuda, and Rav Ḥisda said:** The **dispute** between these two Sages is in a case where the person said: My residence is **in such-and-such place,** and you rely on Rabbi Yehuda and establish residence at a place between the two cities even though you are still at home?

והא רב נחמן ותניא כוותיה! אמר ליה: הדרי בי.

But didn't Rav Naḥman explain the dispute between Rabbi Meir and Rabbi Yehuda differently, **and** furthermore, a *baraita* **was taught in accordance with his** opinion. Rabba bar Rav Ḥanan **said to him: I retract** my opinion and will no longer do so.

אמר רמי בר חמא: הרי אמרו שבת יש לו ארבע אמות, הנותן את עירובו יש לו ארבע אמות או לא?

Rami bar Ḥama said: The Sages **have said** that one who **establishes** residence by foot **has four cubits** at that location, and another two thousand cubits beyond. However, with regard to **one who deposits his** ***eiruv*** in a certain place, there is a dilemma whether he **has four cubits** from the site of his *eiruv*, **or not.**

NOTES

The formulation of the mishna is also precise – מתניתין נמי דיקא: If the mishna can be explained only according to Rabbi Naḥman's opinion, how can Rabbi Ḥisda rule against an explicit mishna? The answer is that Rabbi Ḥisda maintains that the other inhabitants of the town cannot be included in an *eiruv* unless they declare their intentions. Consequently, for one who declares that he is establishing a residence for himself it is a valid *eiruv*, but not for the others (Ritva).

Was in the habit of coming from his home in Artibbena – דאתי מארטיבנא: Rabbeinu Ḥananel explains that he would go to Pumbedita to hear Rabbi Yosef's homily every Shabbat. Therefore, it is clear that he did not walk the day before. Rather, he spent Friday night in his own home, and walked to Artibbena the following day.

אָמַר רָבָא, תָּא שְׁמַע: לֹא אָמְרוּ מְעָרְבִין בְּפַת אֶלָּא לְהָקֵל עַל הֶעָשִׁיר, שֶׁלֹּא יֵצֵא וִיעָרֵב בְּרַגְלָיו, וְאִי אָמְרַתְּ אֵין לוֹ – הַאי לְהָקֵל?! לְהַחְמִיר הוּא!

Rava said: Come and **hear** a resolution from the mishna: The Sages **said** that **one establishes an *eiruv* with bread only to be lenient with the wealthy** person, **so that he** need **not** exert himself and **go out and establish an *eiruv* with his feet. And if you say** that one who establishes an *eiruv* with bread **does not have** four cubits, is **this** really **a leniency? It is a stringency.** Based on the mishna, apparently, all leniencies that apply to one who establishes an *eiruv* by foot must also apply to one who establishes an *eiruv* with bread.

אֲפִילּוּ הָכִי נִיחָא לֵיהּ, כִּי הֵיכִי דְּלָא נִטְרַח וְנֵיפּוֹק.

The Gemara rejects this argument: No proof can be cited from there, as **even** if he without the four cubits, **this is preferable to him, so that he** need **not exert himself and go out** and establish an *eiruv* by foot. Therefore, it can be said that establishing an *eiruv* with bread constitutes a leniency even if it entails the loss of four cubits.

מתני׳ מִי שֶׁיָּצָא לֵילֵךְ בְּעִיר שֶׁמְּעָרְבִין בָּהּ, וְהֶחֱזִירוֹ חֲבֵירוֹ – הוּא מוּתָּר לֵילֵךְ, וְכָל בְּנֵי הָעִיר אֲסוּרִין, דִּבְרֵי רַבִּי יְהוּדָה.

MISHNA If **a person set out to go**[NH] on a Shabbat eve **to a town for which an *eiruv* is established** in order to go there on Shabbat, **and another** person **caused him to return** home, **he** himself **is permitted to go** to that city on Shabbat, **and** for **all the** other **residents of the town it is prohibited** to go there. This is **the statement of Rabbi Yehuda.**

רַבִּי מֵאִיר אוֹמֵר: כֹּל שֶׁהוּא יָכוֹל לְעָרֵב וְלֹא עֵירֵב – הֲרֵי זֶה חַמָּר גַּמָּל.

Rabbi Meir says: Anyone who can establish an *eiruv*, and negated his residence in his original place, **and did not establish an *eiruv***, i.e., he did not at least state that he seeks to establish residence somewhere else, **is** likened to both **a donkey driver,** who walks behind the animal and prods it, **and a camel driver,** who walks before the animal and leads it, in the sense that he is pulled in two opposite directions. Due to the uncertainty with regard to the location of his Shabbat limit, his movement is restricted as though his residence was established in both his city and at a location along the way to the other city. He may not venture beyond two thousand cubits from either location.

גמ׳ מַאי שְׁנָא אִיהוּ וּמַאי שְׁנָא אִינְהוּ? אָמַר רַב הוּנָא: הָכָא בְּמַאי עָסְקִינַן – כְּגוֹן שֶׁיֵּשׁ לוֹ שְׁנֵי בָתִּים, וּבֵינֵיהֶן שְׁנֵי תְחוּמֵי שַׁבָּת.

GEMARA With regard to the mishna's statement that according to Rabbi Yehuda, he himself is permitted to go to the other city, while for all the rest of the residents of his city it is prohibited to do so, the Gemara asks: **What is different** about **him and what is different** about **them?** Why is he permitted to proceed to the other city, while they are not? **Rav Huna said: We are dealing here with** a case **where** that person **has two houses,** one in each town, **with** the distance of **two Shabbat limits,** four thousand cubits, **between them.**

אִיהוּ, כֵּיוָן דִּנְפַק לֵיהּ לְאוֹרְחָא – הֲוָה לֵיהּ עָנִי, וְהָנֵי עֲשִׁירֵי נִינְהוּ.

With regard to **him, since he set out on his way,**[H] **his** legal status **is** that of **a pauper,** as he did not intended to return to his first house but to continue to his other house, and he can therefore establish residence at the end of his Shabbat limit simply by declaring that he wishes to acquire residence in such-and-such place. **And** the legal status of **these** other inhabitants of his city, **is** that of **wealthy people,** as they are in their houses and have food. Consequently they can only establish residence at the end of their Shabbat limit by depositing food there prior the onset of Shabbat.

תַּנְיָא נַמִי הָכִי: מִי שֶׁיֵּשׁ לוֹ שְׁנֵי בָתִּים וּבֵינֵיהֶן שְׁנֵי תְחוּמֵי שַׁבָּת, כֵּיוָן שֶׁהֶחֱזִיק בַּדֶּרֶךְ – קָנָה עֵירוּב, דִּבְרֵי רַבִּי יְהוּדָה.

That was also taught in a *baraita*: With regard to **one who has two houses, with** the distance of **two Shabbat limits between them, once he set out on the way,** clearly demonstrating his intention to leave, although he did not explicitly say: My residence is at the end of my Shabbat limit, **he acquired an *eiruv*** there. This is **the statement of Rabbi Yehuda.**

יָתֵר עַל כֵּן אָמַר רַבִּי יוֹסֵי בְּרַבִּי יְהוּדָה: אֲפִילּוּ מְצָאוֹ חֲבֵירוֹ וְאָמַר לוֹ ״לִין פֹּה, עֵת חַמָּה הוּא, עֵת צִינָּה הוּא״ – לְמָחָר מַשְׁכִּים וְהוֹלֵךְ.

Furthermore, Rabbi Yosei, son of Rabbi Yehuda said: Even if another found him before he left, **and said to him: Spend the night here, it is a hot period,** or it **is a cold period** and inadvisable to set out now, **on the following day he may rise early and go** to the other town, as his intention to walk is sufficient.

NOTES

If a person set out to go – מִי שֶׁיָּצָא לֵילֵךְ: In the Jerusalem Talmud there are two explanations of this mishna, both of which involve a messenger sent to establish an *eiruv* for the community. According to the first explanation, the messenger established the *eiruv* for all of the town's residents except for the one who was persuaded to return. Therefore, the other residents are only permitted to go in the direction of their *eiruv*, while the one for whom the *eiruv* was not established is permitted to go in all directions. According to the second explanation, the messenger did not establish the *eiruv* for any of the town's residents. Rather, the one who left and returned established his *eiruv* by foot, while the other residents, who remained at home, did not establish an *eiruv* at all. This is in accordance with Rabbi Huna's opinion.

The Rambam, in his Commentary on the Mishna, states that this person was sent by the inhabitants of the town to establish an *eiruv* for them with food, but he established the *eiruv* by foot instead. He is permitted to use the *eiruv*, as he walked and stayed in that place, thereby establishing his residence there. However, the residents of the town, who did not place an *eiruv*, did not establish their residence through his agency. Only one who is familiar with that place can establish his residence there. The Bartenura understands the mishna in a similar fashion.

HALAKHA

If a person set out to go – מִי שֶׁיָּצָא לֵילֵךְ: If a messenger was sent before the onset of Shabbat by the residents of a town to establish an *eiruv* for them with food, and he returned without having established the *eiruv*, since he set out on the way, he established his residence in the location he intended and may walk there on Shabbat. It is prohibited for the other residents of the town to do so (Rambam and others; *Shulḥan Arukh*, *Oraḥ Ḥayyim* 410:3).

Since he set out on his way – כֵּיוָן דִּנְפַק לֵיהּ לְאוֹרְחָא: Only a pauper or one who was walking along the road may establish his residence in a particular location; however, the residents of a city who spend Shabbat evening in their homes may not do so (*Shulḥan Arukh*, *Oraḥ Ḥayyim* 410:1).

אָמַר רַבָּה: לוֹמַר – כּוּלֵּי עָלְמָא לָא פְּלִיגִי דְּצָרִיךְ, כִּי פְּלִיגִי – לְהַחֲזִיק.

Rabba said: With regard **to saying** that he is establishing residence at the end of his Shabbat limit, **everyone agrees** that this **is necessary,** as otherwise it could be understood that he is returning to his house because he changed his mind about establishing residence elsewhere. **When they disagree** is with regard to whether or not it is necessary for him actually to **set out** on his way. Rabbi Yehuda maintains that he must have set out on his way, whereas Rabbi Yosei, son of Rabbi Yehuda, maintains that he need not even set out on his way, as his intention to leave is sufficient.

וְרַב יוֹסֵף אָמַר: לְהַחֲזִיק – דְּכוּלֵּי עָלְמָא לָא פְּלִיגִי דְּצָרִיךְ, כִּי פְּלִיגִי – לוֹמַר.

And Rav Yosef said: With regard **to** actually **setting out** on his way, **everyone agrees** that this **is necessary. Where they disagree** is with regard to whether or not it is necessary for him **to say** that he is establishing his residence at the end of his Shabbat limit.

כְּמַאן אָזְלָא הָא דְּאָמַר עוּלָּא: מִי שֶׁהֶחֱזִיק בַּדֶּרֶךְ וְהֶחֱזִירוֹ חֲבֵירוֹ – הֲרֵי הוּא מוּחְזָר וּמוּחְזָק.

The Gemara asks: **In accordance with whose** opinion **is this** *halakha* that **Ulla stated? If a person set out on his way, and another persuaded him to return** home, **he is** considered **returned and** as considered **set out** on his way.

אִי מוּחְזָר – לָמָּה מוּחְזָק? וְאִי מוּחְזָק – לָמָּה מוּחְזָר?

The Gemara analyzes Ulla's statement itself: **If he is** considered **returned,** with the same legal status as the rest of the residents of his city and has not established residence elsewhere, **why** is he described as **set out** on his way? **And if** he is considered **set out** on his way, indicating that he established residence at the end of his Shabbat limit, **why is** he described as **returned?**

הָכִי קָאָמַר: אַף עַל פִּי שֶׁמּוּחְזָר – מוּחְזָק. כְּמַאן – כְּרַב יוֹסֵף, וְאַלִּיבָּא דְּרַבִּי יוֹסֵי בְּרַבִּי יְהוּדָה.

The Gemara answers: Emend Ulla's statement and explain that **this is** what **he is saying: Although he was returned** to his original place, he is nonetheless regarded as having **set out** on his way. **In accordance with whose** opinion did he state this ruling? **According to** the opinion of **Rav Yosef,** that everyone agrees he must set out on his way, **and in accordance with** the opinion of **Rabbi Yosei, son of Rabbi Yehuda,**[NH] that he need not declare he is establishing his residence at the end of his Shabbat limit.

רַב יְהוּדָה בַּר אִשְׁתְּתָא אַיְיתִי לֵיהּ כַּלְכַּלָּה דְּפֵירֵי לְרַב נָתָן בַּר אוֹשַׁעְיָא. כִּי הֲוָה אָזֵיל שַׁבְקֵיהּ עַד דְּנָחֵית דַּרְגָּא, אֲמַר לֵיהּ: בִּית הָכָא. לְמָחָר קְדֵים וְאָזֵיל.

The Gemara relates that **Rav Yehuda bar Ishtata** once **brought a basket of fruit to Rav Natan bar Oshaya** in a nearby town, four thousand cubits away, on Shabbat eve. **When he was going,** Rav Natan **left him until he descended one step, and** then **said to him: Lodge here** tonight. He allowed him start his journey so that he would be considered as having set out on his way. **On the following day** Rav Yehuda bar Ishtata **rose early and went** home.

NOTES

According to Rav Yosef, and in accordance with Rabbi Yosei – **כְּרַב יוֹסֵף, וְאַלִּיבָּא דְּרַבִּי יוֹסֵי בְּרַבִּי יְהוּדָה:** How can we be certain this is not according to Rabba in accordance with Rabbi Yehuda, as is stated on the following *amud* in a different context (see Rashi here)? One answer is that *amora'im* do not speak in vague formulations. If Ulla agreed with Rabba and Rabbi Yehuda, he would have said that someone persuaded him to return while he is establishing residence at the end of his Shabbat limit. Since Ulla did not explain it in this manner, he clearly maintains that there is no need to say anything at all (Rashba).

HALAKHA

To return and to set out – **לְהַחֲזִיר וּלְהַחֲזִיק:** If a person sets out on his way and then returns, he does not have to say that he seeks to establish his residence in a particular place. He need only intend to do so. Nevertheless, he must set out on his way, in accordance with the opinion of Rabbi Yosei, son of Rabbi Yehuda, as explained by Rabbi Yosef (*Shulḥan Arukh, Oraḥ Ḥayyim* 410:2).

Perek **IV**
Daf **52** Amud **b**

כְּמַאן – כְּרַב יוֹסֵף, וְאַלִּיבָּא דְּרַבִּי יוֹסֵי בַּר יְהוּדָה.

The Gemara comments: **In accordance with whose** opinion did Rav Natan bar Oshaya act? Apparently, it was **in accordance with** the opinion of **Rav Yosef** that everyone agrees that he must set out on his way, **and in accordance with** the opinion of **Rabbi Yosei bar Yehuda** that he need not declare that he is establishing his residence at the end of his Shabbat limit.

לָא, כְּרַבָּה וְאַלִּיבָּא דְּרַבִּי יְהוּדָה.

The Gemara rejects this suggestion: **No,** that is not necessarily so, as it is possible to say that he acted **according to** the opinion of **Rabba, and in accordance with** the opinion of **Rabbi Yehuda,** and Rav Yehuda bar Ishtata declared that he establishes his residence at the end of his Shabbat limit.

"רַבִּי מֵאִיר אוֹמֵר: כֹּל שֶׁיָּכוֹל לְעָרֵב כו'". הָא תְּנֵינָא חֲדָא זִימְנָא: סָפֵק, רַבִּי מֵאִיר וְרַבִּי יְהוּדָה אוֹמְרִים: הֲרֵי זֶה חַמָּר גַּמָּל!

We learned in the mishna that **Rabbi Meir says: Anyone who can establish an** ***eiruv,*** and negated his residence in his original place, and did not establish an *eiruv,* is likened to both a donkey driver and a camel driver. The Gemara asks: **Didn't we have** already **learned** it **once** before in another mishna: In a case of **uncertainty, Rabbi Meir and Rabbi Yehuda say: This** person **is** likened to both **a donkey driver** and **a camel driver.**[N] Here too, it is obvious that the same applies, as that is Rabbi Meir's opinion with regard to all uncertain cases.

NOTES

A donkey driver and a camel driver – **חַמָּר גַּמָּל:** Rabbi Sheshet explains that there is a difference between the two types of uncertainty; between an uncertainty whether or not he established an *eiruv,* and an uncertainty whether he established a place of residence in a different place or in his own location. Since likening one's status to that of a camel driver and a donkey driver is a great stringency, perhaps, when the uncertainty is whether or not he established an *eiruv* at all he should be considered like the rest of the inhabitants of his city (see the Ritva).

אמר רב ששת: לא תימא טעמא דרבי מאיר ספק עירב ספק לא עירב, הוא דהוי חמר גמל; אבל ודאי לא עירב – לא הוי חמר גמל,

Rav Sheshet said: It is necessary to state this ruling here as well, so that **you will not say the reason** for **Rabbi Meir's** statement only applies in a case where there is **uncertainty whether** one **established an *eiruv*** or **did not establish an *eiruv*,** and in **that** case **he is** in likened to both **a donkey driver** and **a camel driver. However,** in a case where there is **certainty** that he **did not establish an *eiruv* he is not** likened to both **a donkey driver** and **a camel driver,** but his Shabbat limit is the same as the rest of the residents of his city.

אלא: אפילו ודאי לא עירב – הוי חמר גמל. דהא הכא ודאי לא עירב, וקא הוי חמר גמל.

Rather, say that **even** in a case where there is **certainty** that he **did not establish an *eiruv*** he is sometimes likened to both **a donkey driver** and **a camel driver, as here he certainly did not establish an *eiruv*, and** yet **he is** likened to both **a donkey driver** and **a camel driver.** It was therefore necessary to state that even in that case, where there is no uncertainty whether or not he established the *eiruv*, but only with regard to the location of his residence, he nonetheless has the status of both a donkey driver and a camel driver.

מתני׳ מי שיצא חוץ לתחום – אפילו אמה אחת לא יכנס. רבי אליעזר אומר: שתים – יכנס, שלש – לא יכנס.

MISHNA **One who** intentionally, not for the purpose of performing a mitzva, **went out beyond** his Shabbat **limit,**[H] **even** if only **one** cubit, **may not reenter. Rabbi Eliezer says:** If he went out **two** cubits **he may reenter;** however, if he went out **three** cubits **he may not reenter.**

גמ׳ אמר רבי חנינא: רגלו אחת בתוך התחום ורגלו אחת חוץ לתחום – לא יכנס, דכתיב: ״אם תשיב משבת רגלך״, ״רגלך״ כתיב.

GEMARA **Rabbi Ḥanina said: If one of his feet was within the** Shabbat **limit, and his other foot was beyond the** Shabbat **limit, he may not reenter, as it is written: "If you turn away your feet [*raglekha*] due to Shabbat"**[N] (Isaiah 58:13). The word *raglekha* **is written** in defective form without the letter *yod*, and can therefore be read as **your foot** in the singular, indicating that Shabbat can be desecrated by the reentry of even a single foot.[H]

והתניא: רגלו אחת בתוך התחום ורגלו אחת חוץ לתחום – יכנס! הא מני – אחרים היא. דתניא, אחרים אומרים: למקום שרובו הוא נזקר.

The Gemara raises a difficulty: **But wasn't** the opposite **taught** in a *baraita*? If **one of his feet was within the** Shabbat **limit, and his other foot was beyond the** Shabbat **limit, he may reenter.** The Gemara answers: In accordance with **whose** opinion **is this** taught? **It is** in accordance with the opinion **of *Aḥerim*, as it was taught** in a *baraita*: ***Aḥerim* say: He is attributed to the place where the majority of his body** lies, and therefore, it is permitted for him to enter, as he stepped out with only one foot.

איכא דאמרי, אמר רבי חנינא: רגלו אחת בתוך התחום ורגלו אחת חוץ לתחום – יכנס, דכתיב: ״אם תשיב משבת רגלך״, ״רגליך״ קרינן.

The Gemara cites a different version of the previous discussion. **Some say** that **Rabbi Ḥanina said: If one of his feet was within the** Shabbat **limit, and his other foot was beyond the** Shabbat **limit, he may reenter, as it is written: "If you turn away your feet due to Shabbat"** (Isaiah 58:13). **We read** the word *raglekha* as **your feet,** in the plural, indicating that the entry of a single foot is permitted.

והתניא: לא יכנס! הוא דאמר כאחרים, דתניא: למקום שרובו הוא נזקר.

The Gemara raises a difficulty. **But wasn't** the opposite **taught** in a *baraita*: **He may not reenter?** The Gemara answers: Rabbi Ḥanina **stated** his opinion **in accordance with** the opinion of ***Aḥerim*, as it was taught** in a *baraita*: **He is attributed to the place where the majority of his body** is located, and it is therefore permitted to enter, as most of his body remains within the Shabbat limit.

״רבי אליעזר אומר: שתים – יכנס, שלש – לא יכנס״. והתניא, רבי אליעזר אומר: אחת – יכנס, שתים – לא יכנס! לא קשיא; הא – דעקר חדא וקם אתרתי, הא – דעקר תרתי וקם אתלת.

We learned in the mishna that **Rabbi Eliezer says:** If he went out **two** cubits **he may reenter;** however, if he went out **three** cubits **he may not reenter.**[N] The Gemara asks: **But wasn't it taught** otherwise in a *baraita*? **Rabbi Eliezer says:** If he went out **one** cubits **he may reenter;** however, if he went out **two** cubits **he may not reenter.** The Gemara answers: That is **not a difficulty. This,** the mishna, is referring to a case where **he moved** from **the first** cubit **and is** now **standing two** cubits out, and therefore it is permitted for him to reenter; **however that,** the *baraita*, is referring to a case where **he moved** from **the second** cubit **and is** now **standing three** cubits out. Consequently, it is prohibited for him to reenter.

HALAKHA

One who went out beyond his limit – **מי שיצא חוץ לתחום:** If a person intentionally went even one cubit beyond his Shabbat limit, he may not reenter, in accordance with the unattributed opinion of the first *tanna* in the mishna. According to the *Magen Avraham*, if he was forced out or if he did so to perform a mitzva, the ruling is lenient and his limit is incorporated within that of the town. This is in accordance with the explanation of Rashi and other commentaries (*Shulḥan Arukh*, *Oraḥ Ḥayyim* 405:1).

One foot beyond the Shabbat limit – **רגל אחת חוץ לתחום:** If a person had one foot beyond his Shabbat limit, he may reenter, in accordance with the second version of Rabbi Ḥanina's statement, because the *halakha* is in accordance with the second version, as it is supported by other sources. In addition, the *halakha* is in accordance with the lenient opinion in the *halakhot* of *eiruv* (*Shulḥan Arukh*, *Oraḥ Ḥayyim* 405:2).

NOTES

If you turn away your feet due to Shabbat – **אם תשיב משבת רגלך:** Rabbi Ḥanina interprets the verse as though it should be read literally, i.e., sometimes Shabbat is observed by turning away a foot that ventured beyond the Shabbat limit.

Two and three – **שתים ושלש:** The Gemara concludes that Rabbi Eliezer's ruling is based on the incorporation of Shabbat boundaries, i.e., each person has a limit of four cubits, two on each side. Consequently, if he is within two cubits, his own narrow limit is incorporated within the town limit, and it is as though he never left. If, however, he has ventured slightly further, his limit is merely contiguous with the town limit but not incorporated within it. As a result, he is not permitted to reenter (Ritva).

וְהָתַנְיָא, רַבִּי אֱלִיעֶזֶר אוֹמֵר: אֲפִילּוּ אַמָּה אַחַת לֹא יִכָּנֵס! כִּי תַּנְיָא הַהִיא – לְמוֹדֵד. דִּתְנַן: וּלְמוֹדֵד שֶׁאָמְרוּ נוֹתְנִין לוֹ אַלְפַּיִם אַמָּה – אֲפִילּוּ סוֹף מִדָּתוֹ כָּלָה בִּמְעָרָה.

The Gemara raises another difficulty. **But wasn't it taught** in a different *baraita* that **Rabbi Eliezer says: Even** if he went **one cubit** out, **he may not enter.** The Gemara answers: **When that** *baraita* **was taught** it was with regard to **one measuring** his limit by counting two thousand steps. **As we learned** in a mishna: **And for one** established residence in a particular place, and **is** now **measuring** his limit by counting out steps, **with regard to whom** the Sages **said one provides him** with **two thousand cubits, even if his measurement ended in a cave** he may not walk even one cubit beyond his measurement.

מתני׳ מִי שֶׁהֶחְשִׁיךְ חוּץ לַתְּחוּם – אֲפִילּוּ אַמָּה אַחַת לֹא יִכָּנֵס. רַבִּי שִׁמְעוֹן אוֹמֵר: אֲפִילּוּ חָמֵשׁ עֶשְׂרֵה אַמּוֹת יִכָּנֵס, שֶׁאֵין הַמְּשׁוֹחוֹת מְמַצִּין אֶת הַמִּדּוֹת מִפְּנֵי הַטּוֹעִין.

MISHNA With regard to **one** for **whom it grew dark**[N] while he was traveling **outside the** Shabbat **limit**[N] of the town where he was heading, **even** if he was only **one cubit** outside the limit **he may not enter** the town.[H] **Rabbi Shimon says: Even** if he was **fifteen cubits** beyond the limit **he may enter** the town, **because the surveyors do not precisely demarcate the measures;** rather, they mark the Shabbat limit within the two thousand cubits, **due to those who err.**[N]

גמ׳ תָּנָא: מִפְּנֵי טוֹעֵי הַמִּדָּה.

GEMARA With regard to the mishna's statement: Due to those who err, it is **taught** in a *baraita*: **Due to those who err in their measurement.** In other words, because the surveyors are concerned that they might have erred in their measurements, they are stringent and do not position the mark at the edge of the limit, but move it several cubits within the limit.

הדרן עלך מי שהוציאוהו

NOTES

One who went out and one for whom it grew dark – מִי שֶׁיָּצָא וּמִי שֶׁהֶחְשִׁיךְ: In the Jerusalem Talmud it is explicitly stated that there is no difference between someone who went out and one for whom it grew dark; the *tanna'im* disagree in both cases. Consequently, there are three opinions regarding this issue: The opinion of the first *tanna*, that of Rabbi Eliezer, and that of Rabbi Shimon. Some early commentaries explain differently (Rabbeinu Yehonatan and others).

If it grew dark for a person while beyond the limit – הֶחְשִׁיךְ חוּץ לַתְּחוּם: Apparently, he is permitted to walk another two thousand cubits from his location at nightfall. However, he may not enter the town itself, because he was not located within its limit when nighttime arrived. See the *Me'iri* and the opinions he cites.

Due to those who err – מִפְּנֵי הַטּוֹעִין: The Rambam, in his Commentary on the Mishna, indicates that this refers to the errors of the surveyors in their measurement, and that the fifteen cubits is not a fixed distance. Rather, if the topography is flat, the assumption is that they erred by less; if the terrain is shaped by hills and ravines, their error will be greater (Bartenura).

HALAKHA

One for whom it grew dark while outside the Shabbat limit – מִי שֶׁהֶחְשִׁיךְ חוּץ לַתְּחוּם: If night fell when a person was beyond a town's Shabbat limit, even if he was only one cubit beyond that limit, he may not enter the town. However, he has a full Shabbat limit from the residence that he established, in accordance with the unattributed opinion of the first *tanna* (*Shulḥan Arukh, Oraḥ Ḥayyim* 405:3).

Summary of
Perek IV

The focus in this chapter was primarily on the question of how an individual who does not have a specific permanent residence acquires his Shabbat limit. The Sages established that one who forfeited his Shabbat limit by venturing beyond that limit may proceed only four cubits, as that is the basic area at the disposal of every person at any time, even if he no longer has the right to the greater Shabbat limit of two thousand cubits. However, this holds true only for one who ventured beyond his Shabbat limit without justification. If there was a justified reason for leaving, e.g., to rescue someone, give testimony, or go to war, one establishes residence and acquires the Shabbat limit at his destination.

It was also concluded in this chapter that one acquires his Shabbat limit consciously or unconsciously. Indeed, even an individual who was sleeping in a specific location as Shabbat arrives acquires his Shabbat limit at that location, and he may walk two thousand cubits in any direction from there. Similarly, one who was adjacent to a city or some other place in which he desired to acquire residence, even if he did not know precisely where that residence would be, acquires that residence as long as he is near enough to that place that it is permitted to reach it.

There are two methods in which one may establish a joining of Shabbat boundaries without placing food at the new residence. The first method, which is effective regardless of the circumstances, is establishing an *eiruv* with one's feet. One who seeks to establish an *eiruv* can, during the day, go to the place that he seeks to acquire as his residence, and declare: I acquire residence at this location. This is effective even if he then returns home and sleeps there. At times, he acquires residence even without a declaration. This is effective because the *halakha* requiring placement of food in establishing residence was instituted as a leniency enabling one to establish an *eiruv* by means of an agent.

An alternative method of joining the boundaries is by declaring that one seeks to establish residence in a specific location, even without being present at that location. However, the Sages allowed the acquisition of residence in this manner, without placing food, only in cases where there is no other alternative. Therefore, this method may be employed by people traveling who must establish Shabbat residence en route. One sitting at home who is able to establish an *eiruv* employing one of the other methods may not acquire residence utilizing this method.

Index of **Background**

Index of **Background**

Index of **Language**

Index of **Personalities**

Image **Credits**

תלמוד בבלי
עירובין א

Shefa
ירושלים
KOREN

תלמוד בבלי

הוצאת קורן ירושלים

— מהדורת הדף היומי —

מסכת עירובין א

COMMENTARY BY

Rabbi Adin Even-Israel (Steinsaltz)

EDITOR-IN-CHIEF

Rabbi Dr Tzvi Hersh Weinreb

EXECUTIVE EDITOR

Rabbi Joshua Schreier

•

SHEFA FOUNDATION

KOREN PUBLISHERS JERUSALEM

מָבוֹי

מתני' *שֶׁהוּא א גָּבוֹהַּ(א) לְמַעְלָה מֵעֶשְׂרִים אַמָּה — יְמַעֵט, ר' יְהוּדָה אוֹמֵר: אֵינוֹ צָרִיךְ. וְהָרָחָב מֵעֶשֶׂר אַמּוֹת — יְמַעֵט. וְאִם יֵשׁ לוֹ צוּרַת הַפֶּתַח, אע"פ שֶׁהוּא רָחָב מֵעֶשֶׂר אַמּוֹת — אֵין צָרִיךְ לְמַעֵט.§

גמ' תְּנַן *הָתָם: בסוּכָּה שֶׁהִיא גְּבוֹהָה לְמַעְלָה מֵעֶשְׂרִים אַמָּה — פְּסוּלָה, וְרַבִּי יְהוּדָה מַכְשִׁיר. מַאי שְׁנָא גַּבֵּי סוּכָּה דְּתָנֵי "פְּסוּלָה" וְגַבֵּי מָבוֹי תָּנֵי תַּקַּנְתָּא? סוּכָּה דְּאוֹרַיְיתָא — תָּנֵי פְּסוּלָה, מָבוֹי דְּרַבָּנַן — תָּנֵי תַּקַּנְתָּא. וְאִיבָּעֵית אֵימָא: דְּאוֹרַיְיתָא נַמִי תָּנֵי תַּקַּנְתָּא, אֶלָּא: סוּכָּה דִּנְפִישִׁין מִילֵּיהּ — פָּסֵיק וְתָנֵי "פְּסוּלָה", מָבוֹי דְּלָא נְפִישִׁי מִילֵּיהּ — תָּנֵי תַּקַּנְתָּא. אָמַר רַב יְהוּדָה אָמַר רַב: חֲכָמִים לֹא לְמָדוּהָ אֶלָּא מִפִּתְחוֹ שֶׁל הֵיכָל, וְרַבִּי יְהוּדָה לֹא לְמָדָהּ אֶלָּא מִפִּתְחוֹ שֶׁל אוּלָם. דִּתְנַן: *גפִּתְחוֹ שֶׁל הֵיכָל גׇּבְהוֹ עֶשְׂרִים אַמָּה וְרׇחְבּוֹ עֶשֶׂר אַמּוֹת, *דוְשֶׁל אוּלָם גׇּבְהוֹ אַרְבָּעִים אַמָּה וְרׇחְבּוֹ עֶשְׂרִים אַמּוֹת. וּשְׁנֵיהֶן מִקְרָא אֶחָד דָּרְשׁוּ: °"וּשְׁחָטוֹ פֶּתַח אֹהֶל מוֹעֵד" (ויקרא ג). דְּרַבָּנַן סָבְרִי: קְדוּשַּׁת הֵיכָל לְחוּד, וּקְדוּשַּׁת אוּלָם לְחוּד. וְכִי כְּתִיב: "פֶּתַח אֹהֶל מוֹעֵד" — אַהֵיכָל כְּתִיב. וְרַבִּי יְהוּדָה סָבַר: *הֵיכָל וְאוּלָם קְדוּשָּׁה אַחַת הִיא, וְכִי כְּתִיב: "פֶּתַח אֹהֶל מוֹעֵד" — אַתַּרְוַיְיהוּ הוּא דִּכְתִיב. וְאִיבָּעֵית אֵימָא: לְר' יְהוּדָה נַמִי קְדוּשַּׁת אוּלָם לְחוּד, וּקְדוּשַּׁת הֵיכָל לְחוּד. וְהָכָא הַיְינוּ טַעְמָא דְּרַבִּי יְהוּדָה — דִּכְתִיב: "אֶל פֶּתַח אוּלָם הַבַּיִת". וְרַבָּנַן אִי הֲוָה כָּתַב: "אֶל פֶּתַח אוּלָם" — כִּדְקָאָמְרַתְּ, הַשְׁתָּא דִּכְתִיב: "אֶל פֶּתַח אוּלָם הַבַּיִת" — הַבַּיִת הַפָּתוּחַ לָאוּלָם. וְהָא כִּי כְּתִיב הַאי בַּמִּשְׁכָּן כְּתִיב! אַשְׁכַּחַן *מִשְׁכָּן דְּאִיקְּרִי מִקְדָּשׁ, וּמִקְדָּשׁ דְּאִיקְּרִי מִשְׁכָּן. דְּאִי לָא תֵּימָא הָכִי — הָא *דְּאָמַר רַב יְהוּדָה אָמַר שְׁמוּאֵל: השְׁלָמִים שֶׁשְּׁחָטָן קוֹדֶם פְּתִיחַת דַּלְתוֹת הַהֵיכָל — פְּסוּלִין, שֶׁנֶּאֱמַר: °"וּשְׁחָטוֹ פֶּתַח אֹהֶל מוֹעֵד" (שם) בִּזְמַן שֶׁפְּתוּחִין, וְלֹא בִּזְמַן שֶׁהֵן נְעוּלִים. וְהָא כִּי כְּתִיב הַהִיא בַּמִּשְׁכָּן כְּתִיב! אֶלָּא: אַשְׁכַּחַן מִקְדָּשׁ דְּאִיקְּרִי מִשְׁכָּן, וּמִשְׁכָּן דְּאִיקְּרִי מִקְדָּשׁ. בִּשְׁלָמָא מִקְדָּשׁ דְּאִיקְּרִי מִשְׁכָּן — דִּכְתִיב: °"וְנָתַתִּי (אֶת) מִשְׁכָּנִי בְּתוֹכְכֶם" (שם כו). אֶלָּא מִשְׁכָּן דְּאִיקְּרִי מִקְדָּשׁ מְנָלַן? אִילֵימָא מִדִּכְתִיב: °"וְנָסְעוּ הַקְּהָתִים נוֹשְׂאֵי הַמִּקְדָּשׁ וְהֵקִימוּ אֶת הַמִּשְׁכָּן עַד בּוֹאָם" (במדבר י) הַהוּא

רש"י

מָבוֹי שֶׁהוּא גָּבוֹהַּ. שֶׁהִנִּיחוּ אֶת הַקּוֹרָה לְמַעְלָה מֵעֶשְׂרִים אַמָּה. וְקוֹרָה זוֹ לְהַתִּיר לְטַלְטֵל לְתוֹכָהּ בָּאָה, דְּמִדְּאוֹרַיְיתָא אִיתְּסַר הוֹצָאַת רה"ר בַּשַּׁבָּת. וּמַה הִיא רה"ר – סְרַטְיָא וּפְלַטְיָא גְּדוֹלָה, כִּדְאָמְרִינַן בְּפֶרֶק "יְצִיאוֹת הַשַּׁבָּת" (שבת ד' ו:), שֶׁדּוֹמִין לְדִגְלֵי מִדְבָּר. דְּכָל מִילֵּי דְּשַׁבָּת מִמִּשְׁכָּן גָּמְרִינַן, וַעֲגָלוֹת שֶׁל לְוִיִּם בְּרוֹחַב י"ו אַמָּה אָזְלִי, כִּדְאָמְרִינַן בְּ"הַזּוֹרֵק" (שם ד' צט.), הִלְכָּךְ לָא הָוֵי רה"ר בְּלִיר מִי"ו אַמָּה רוֹחַב, וּמְפוּלָּשׁ מִב' רָאשִׁין. אֲבָל מָבוֹי קָצָר הוּא, וְאֵינוֹ רָחָב י"ו אַמָּה. וְאִי נַמִי רָחָב הוּא – אֵינוֹ מְפוּלָּשׁ, אֶלָּא רֹאשׁוֹ אֶחָד פָּתוּחַ לרה"ר וְרֹאשׁוֹ אֶחָד סָתוּם. דְּאִי הֲוָה מְפוּלָּשׁ – לָא הָוֵי מִשְׁתַּרֵי בְּקוֹרָה, כִּדְאָמְרִינַן בַּגְּמָ' *וְכֵיוָן דְּלָאו רה"ר הוּא – שָׁרֵי לְטַלְטוֹלֵי בֵּיהּ מִן הַתּוֹרָה בְּלִי שׁוּם תִּיקּוּן, וְרַבָּנַן גְּזוּר עֲלֵיהּ מִשּׁוּם דְּאָתֵי לְאִיחַלּוּפֵי בִּרה"ר, וְשַׁרְיוּהּ בְּתַקַּנְתָּא דְּלֶחִי אוֹ קוֹרָה, דְּלֶיהֱוֵי הֶיכֵּירָא, דְּלָא לֵיתֵי לְמִישְׁרֵי רה"ר גְּמוּרָה: יְמַעֵט. יַשְׁפִּיל, וְטַעְמָא מְפָרֵשׁ בַּגְּמָ': וְהָרָחָב מֵעֶשֶׂר אַמּוֹת יְמַעֵט. דְּזֶהוּ שִׁיעוּר רוֹחַב סְתָם פְּתָחִים, וְטְפֵי מֵהָכִי לָא מִיקְּרוּ פֶּתַח אֶלָּא פִּרְצָה, וַאֲנַן בָּעֵינַן פֶּתַח. וְצָרִיךְ לִנְעוֹץ קָנִים לְמַעֵט רוֹחַב כְּנִיסָתָהּ, וּלְהַעֲמִידָהּ עַל עֶשֶׂר אוֹ עַל פָּחוֹת: צוּרַת הַפֶּתַח. לֶחִי מִיכָּן וְלֶחִי מִיכָּן וְקוֹרָה (ס"א: וְקָנֶה) עַל גַּבֵּיהֶן:

[צורת הפתח]

גמ' דְּתָנֵי תַּקַּנְתָּא. דְּתָנֵי "יְמַעֵט" וְלָא תָּנָא "פָּסוּל": סוּכָּה. דְּטַעְמָא דִּידָהּ דְּאוֹרַיְיתָא, כִּדְאָמְרִי' הָתָם מִ"לְמַעַן יֵדְעוּ דוֹרוֹתֵיכֶם": תָּנֵי פְּסוּלָה. הוֹאִיל וּכְבָר מִימוֹת מֹשֶׁה נִיתְּנָה מִדָּה זוֹ, וּבָאוּ חֲכָמִים לְפָרֵשׁ לְךָ שֶׁאִם לֹא עָשָׂה כֵּן פְּסוּלָה שַׁיָּיךְ לְמִיתְנֵי בָּהּ לְשׁוֹן פַּסְלוּת. וְאַף עַל גַּב דְּמַהֲנְיָא בָּהּ תַּקַּנְתָּא, כׇּל כַּמָּה דְּלָא מְתַקַּן לָהּ – אִיקְרְיָא פְּסוּלָה: מָבוֹי. דְּכָל עִיקָּרֵיהּ דְּרַבָּנַן הוּא – לֹא שַׁיָּיךְ לְמֵימַר בֵּיהּ לְשׁוֹן פַּסְלוּת, שֶׁהֲרֵי כָּאן הִתְחִילוּ לְהַרְאוֹתְךָ עִסְקֵי מָבוֹי וְתוֹרוֹתָיו, וּמַאי "פָּסוּל" שַׁיָּיךְ לְמֵימַר? אַכַּתִּי לֹא הוֹדִיעוּךָ רַבָּנַן שִׁיעוּרֵיהּ בְּהָכִי, דְּלִיתְנֵי: אִם לֹא עָשָׂה כֵּן – פָּסוּל: דְּאוֹרַיְיתָא נַמִי תָּנֵי תַּקַּנְתָּא. בְּעָלְמָא, בְּמִילֵּי אַחֲרִינֵי: דִּנְפִישִׁי מִילֵּיהּ. דְּקָתָנֵי הָתָם: וְשֶׁאֵין לָהּ שָׁלֹשׁ דְּפָנוֹת, וְשֶׁאֵינָהּ גְּבוֹהָה עֲשָׂרָה, וְשֶׁחַמָּתָהּ מְרוּבָּה מִצִּלָּתָהּ: פָּסֵיק וְתָנֵי פְּסוּלָה. דְּהַשְׁתָּא מָצֵי כָּיֵיל וְתָנֵי לְהוּ כּוּלְּהוּ כַּחֲדָא. דְּאִי הֲוָה תָּנֵי תַּקַּנְתָּא לָא הֲוָה מָצֵי לְעָרוּבִינְהוּ וּלְמִתְנִינְהוּ. דִּבְשֶׁאֵין לָהּ שָׁלֹשׁ דְּפָנוֹת – בָּעֵי לְמִיתְנֵי יַעֲשֶׂה לָהּ דּוֹפֶן, וּבְשֶׁאֵינָהּ גְּבוֹהָה – בָּעֵי לְמִיתְנֵי יַגְבִּיהַּ, וּבְשֶׁחַמָּתָהּ מְרוּבָּה מִצִּלָּתָהּ – יוֹסִיף עַל סְכָכָהּ. וְאָמַר מָר: לְעוֹלָם יִשְׁנֶה אָדָם לְתַלְמִידוֹ דֶּרֶךְ קְצָרָה (פסחים ד' ג:): אֹהֶל מוֹעֵד. הוּא הַהֵיכָל, שֶׁשָּׁם הָיָה נָתוּן מִזְבַּח הַזָּהָב וְהַשֻּׁלְחָן וְהַמְּנוֹרָה, וּבְכוּלְּהוּ כְּתִיב "אֹהֶל מוֹעֵד": רַבָּנַן סָבְרִי. קְדוּשַּׁת אוּלָם לָאו כִּקְדוּשַּׁת הֵיכָל, וְכׇל עֲבוֹדוֹת הָאֲמוּרוֹת בַּהֵיכָל אִי הֲוָה עָבֵיד לְהוּ בָּאוּלָם שֶׁלְּפָנָיו, לָא מִיתַּכַּשְׁרִי. הִלְכָּךְ: לָא מִיקְּרִי "אֹהֶל מוֹעֵד", וְלָא אַשְׁכַּחַן קְרָא דְּלִיקְרִי לַפֶּתַח דִּילֵיהּ "פֶּתַח": אֶל פֶּתַח אוּלָם. אַלְמָא פִּיתְחָא אִקְרִי: הַבַּיִת הַפָּתוּחַ לָאוּלָם. וְהוּא הֵיכָל: וְהָא כִּי כְּתִיב. פֶּתַח אֹהֶל מוֹעֵד בַּמִּשְׁכָּן שֶׁהָיָה בַּמִּדְבָּר כְּתִיב, וְשָׁם לֹא הָיָה אוּלָם. וּפֶתַח הֵיכָל י' אַמּוֹת הוּא דְּגׇבְהוֹ, שֶׁהַקְּרָשִׁים לֹא הָיוּ אֶלָּא עֲשָׂרָה אַמּוֹת גׇּבְהָן: שְׁלָמִים שֶׁשְּׁחָטָן. שַׁחֲרִית, קוֹדֶם פְּתִיחַת דַּלְתוֹת הַהֵיכָל – פְּסוּלִין: הָא בַּמִּשְׁכָּן כְּתִיב. וּבְבֵית עוֹלָמִים מְנָא לָן: וְנָתַתִּי מִשְׁכָּנִי בְּתוֹכְכֶם. *וּכְשֶׁנֶּאֱמַר מִקְרָא זֶה כְּבָר הוּקַם הַמִּשְׁכָּן, שֶׁהֲרֵי בְּתוֹרַת כֹּהֲנִים נִכְתָּב, וְכׇל אוֹתוֹ הַסֵּפֶר בְּאֹהֶל מוֹעֵד נֶאֱמַר, כְּדִכְתִיב (ויקרא א): "וַיְדַבֵּר ה' אֵלָיו מֵאֹהֶל מוֹעֵד". וְעַל אֵיזֶה מִשְׁכָּן הָיָה מַבְטִיחָן עוֹד, אִם לֹא עַל הַמִּקְדָּשׁ: הַהוּא

תוספות

מבוי שהוא גבוה מעשרים אמה ימעט. הקשה מהר"י מאורליינ"ש: דהוה ליה לאשמועינן הכשר מבוי ברישא, שהוא בלחי וקורה, ואם הניח למעלה מעשרים – ימעט. ותירץ: דתנא ניחא ליה להתחיל בהאי לישנא, כמו שמתחלת מתניתין דסוכה. ולהכי פריך שפיר טפי בגמרא: מאי שנא גבי סוכה דתני פסולה:

סוכה דאורייתא תני פסולה. פרש"י: דשייך למיתני בה לשון פסול, הואיל ומימות משה ניתנה מדה זו. [אף על גב דבדאורייתא (ת"י) שייך נמי תקנתא]. ולישנא דאיבעית אימא בדאורייתא נמי תני תקנתא – לא אתי שפיר לפירושו. כי גם ללשון ראשון תני בדאורייתא תקנתא, ולא קאמר אלא דשייך למתני בה לשון פסולה. לכך נראה לפרש: סוכה דאורייתא תני פסולה, דלשון "ימעט" משמע חומרא בעלמא, ואתי למיטעי ולומר דדווקא לכתחלה, אבל בדיעבד שפיר דמי. אבל במבוי דרבנן אין לחוש. והא דאמרינן בפ' "במה מדליקין" (שבת ד' כב.): נר חנוכה שהניחה למעלה מעשרים אמה – פסולה, כסוכה וכמבוי, ואע"ג דנר חנוכה הוי דרבנן! נקט פסולה אגב סוכה דבתריה. א"נ: התם לא מצי למיתני ימעט – דהוה משמע כמו שהיא דולקת ימעט. וזה אינו, דאפילו למ"ד "הנחה עושה מצוה" צריך לכבותה ולהדליקה, שלא יאמר הרואה לצרכו הוא דאדלקה, כדאמרינן התם גבי הדליקה מבפנים והניחה מבחוץ:

דכתיב אל פתח אולם הבית. זה הפסוק אינו בשום מקום. ואור"י: דמלינו דכתיב (יחזקאל מ): "אולם הבית" ובקרא אחרינא (שם מז) כתיב: "פתח הבית", והוי כאלו נכתב בהדיא בחד קרא: "פתח אולם הבית", וקאמרי רבנן: אי כתב "פתח אולם" – כדקאמרת, פי': שלא היה כתוב בשום מקום "אולם הבית":

אשכחן משכן דאיקרי מקדש. ונפקא מינה שאינו דוחה את השבת, ושלא יכנס אדם שם באבק שעל רגליו. משמע דמשכן ומקדש גמרינן מהדדי. וכן בפ"ק דחולין (ד' כד.) גבי מומין שפסולין בכהנים ולוים בשנים דקאמר: יכול אף בשילה ובית עולמים כן. וקשה: דבפ"ב דשבועות (ד' טז:) מצריך תרי קראי, דקאמר: דלכתוב אידי ואידי מקדש וכו'. וכן בסוטה (ד' טז.) וביומא (ד' מד.) ובכמה דוכתי! ותירץ הר"ר נתנאל: דהכא לא צריך קרא, דעיקר דרשה אינה אלא על המקדש, דבמשכן לא היו דלתות. והיא דחולין סברא הוא – אם לא היה הפסוק שיפסלו אף בשילה, הואיל ואינו תלוי בקדושת המשכן:

שלמים ששחטן קודם פתיחת דלתות ההיכל פסולין. ואם תאמר: תיפוק ליה דנשחטו קודם תמיד של שחר, ואמרינן *"העולה" – עולה ראשונה, דתמיד של שחר נמי בעי פתיחת דלתות ההיכל, כדתנן *ב"תמיד נשחט" (פסחים ד' נח:): לא היה תמיד נשחט עד שהיה שומע קול שער שנפתח! וי"ל: דקרא ד"העולה" דווקא בהקטרה איירי, ולא בשחיטה, אי נמי: למצוה ולא לעכב, כדאמר בהדיא ב"התכלת" (מנחות ד' מט.). והא דתניא בתוספתא: *כל הזבחים שהקדימן לתמיד של שחר או עיכבן אחר תמיד של בין הערבים פסולין – היינו מדרבנן. אי נמי: הכא איצטריך כשנפתחו וחזרו וננעלו*):

*) [ועי' תוס' יומא כט: ד"ה אלא אפי' וכו' שכתבו דלשון התוספתא מוכח דפסולין מדאורייתא וע"ע תוספות פסחים נח: ד"ה העולה]

עין משפט נר מצוה

א א מיי' פי"ז מהלכות שבת הלכה יד סמג עשין דרבנן א טוש"ע א"ח סי' שסג סעיף כו:

ב ב מיי' פ"ד מהלכות סוכה הלכה א סמג עשין מג טוש"ע א"ח סי' תרלג סעיף א:

ג ג מיי' פ"ד מהלכות בית הבחירה הלכה ז סמג עשין קסג:

ד ד שם הלכה ח:

ה ה מיי' פ"ה מהל' מעשה הקרבנות הל' ה סמג עשין קפג:

רבינו חננאל

מבוי שהוא גבוה מעשרים אמה ימעט. תנא כיצד ממעטו נותן עליו קורה מכ' אמה ולמטה. תנן התם סוכה שהיא גבוהה מכ' אמה פסולה. מ"ש גבי סוכה תני פסולה ומ"ש גבי מבוי תני תקנתא וכו' ופשוטה היא. אמר רב יהודה אמר רב חכמים לא למדוה שעד כ' אמה כפתח הוא חשיב אלא מפתחו של היכל שהיה גובהו כ' אמה כדתנן במסכת מדות פתחו של היכל גובהו כ' ורחבו י' אמות ור' יהודה למד מן האולם דתנן ושל אולם גובהו מ' אמה ורוחבו כ' אמה ושניהם מהדרין אחד דרשו ושחטו פתח אהל מועד. רבנן סברי פתח אהל מועד ההיכל הוא דאקרי אהל מועד וההיא פתח פתח ההיכל הוא. ור' יהודה סבר קדושת אולם והיכל חדא מלתא הוא. וכולהו אהל מועד אקרי ואע"ג דההיא קרא ושחטו פתח אהל מועד במשכן כתיב וליכא התם אולם אשכחן דמשכן אקרו מקדש שנאמר ועשו לי מקדש ושכנתי בתוכם ככל אשר אני מראה אותך את תבנית המשכן ומקדש נמי אקרי משכן דכתיב ונתתי משכני בתוככם ותרווייהו חדא מילתא היא ארון נמי אקרי מקדש שנאמר ונסעו הקהתים נושאי המקדש אמרינן (מדילפי) [אדילפי] מפתח אהל

רב נסים גאון

מבוי דרבנן תאני תקנתא. בפרק עושין פסין (דף כא) אמר רב יהודה אמר שמואל בשעה שתיקן שלמה עירובין וידים יצתה בת קול ואמרה לו בני אם חכם לבך ודע כי כל דבר שאינו כתוב בקראי ואע"פ שהוא מתקנת נביאים דרבנן מיתקרי כי מפי השמועה שלהן קיבלנוהו ועירובין דרבנן לפי שאינם כתובים:

מסורת הש"ס

[דף ו:] | סוכה ב. | שם | מדות פ"ד מ"א | [שם פ"ג מ"ז] | [יומא מב: זבחים יד. נח: נט.] | שבועות טז: | זבחים נה: יומא כט. סב: | [ועי' ברש"י שבועות טז: שפירש באופן אחר] | [בפסחים נח:] | [נ"ל במסכת תמיד פ"ג משנה ז'] | [דפסחים פ"ד]

הגהות הב"ח

(א) במשנה מבוי שהוא גבוה מעשרים כו' ותיבת למעלה נמחק:

גליון הש"ס

רש"י ד"ה מבוי שהניחו את הקורה למעלה מכ'. וכ"כ הרע"ב ובחידושי למשניות כתבתי לתמוה הא מסקינן לקמן דחלל מבוי תנן וא"כ אפשר לקורה להיות מונח למעלה מכ' אלא דהחלל צריך שלא יהי' למעלה מכ' עוד כתבתי לתמוה במה דכתב רש"י בזה הדבור וכן הרע"ב ושריוה בתקנתא דלחי או קורה דליהוו היכר. הא קיי"ל דלחי העומד מאליו הוי לחי דקיי"ל לחי משום מחיצה: תום' ד"ה שלמים וכו' דתמיד של שחר נמי וכו'. עי' זבחים דף סא ע"א תוס' ד"ה קודם שיעמדו. בא"ד פסולין היינו מדרבנן. עי' הוריות דף ד ע"א ברש"י ד"ה ספק משתקיכה ובתו' שם:

— הַהוּא בָּאָרוֹן כְּתִיב. אֶלָּא מֵהָכָא: "וְעָשׂוּ לִי מִקְדָּשׁ וְשָׁכַנְתִּי בְּתוֹכָם". *בֵּין לְרַבָּנַן וּבֵין לְרַבִּי יְהוּדָה לֵילְפוּ מִפֶּתַח שַׁעַר הֶחָצֵר, דִּכְתִיב: "אוֹרֶךְ הֶחָצֵר מֵאָה בָאַמָּה וְרֹחַב חֲמִשִּׁים בַּחֲמִשִּׁים וְקוֹמָה חָמֵשׁ אַמּוֹת" וּכְתִיב: "וַחֲמֵשׁ עֶשְׂרֵה אַמָּה קְלָעִים לַכָּתֵף" וּכְתִיב: "וְלַכָּתֵף הַשֵּׁנִית מִזֶּה וּמִזֶּה לְשַׁעַר הֶחָצֵר קְלָעִים חֲמֵשׁ עֶשְׂרֵה אַמָּה", מַה לְּהַלָּן — חָמֵשׁ בְּרוֹחַב עֶשְׂרִים, אַף כָּאן חָמֵשׁ בְּרוֹחַב עֶשְׂרִים! "פֶּתַח שַׁעַר הֶחָצֵר" — אִיקְרִי, פֶּתַח סְתָמָא — לָא אִיקְרִי. וְאִיבָּעֵית אֵימָא: כִּי כְּתִיב: "קְלָעִים חֲמֵשׁ עֶשְׂרֵה אַמָּה *לַכָּתֵף" — בְּגוֹבְהָהּ הוּא דִּכְתִיב. גּוֹבְהָהּ?! וְהָא כְּתִיב: "וְקוֹמָה חָמֵשׁ אַמּוֹת"![(א)] הַהוּא מִשְּׂפַת מִזְבֵּחַ וּלְמַעְלָה. וְרַבִּי יְהוּדָה מִפִּתְחוֹ שֶׁל אוּלָם גָּמַר? וְהָא תְּנַן "וְהָרָחָב מֵעֶשֶׂר אַמּוֹת יְמַעֵט" וְלָא פָּלֵיג ר' יְהוּדָה! אָמַר *אַבַּיֵּי: פָּלֵיג בְּבָרַיְיתָא, דְּתַנְיָא: *וְהָרָחָב מִי' אַמּוֹת יְמַעֵט, ר' יְהוּדָה אוֹמֵר: אֵינוֹ צָרִיךְ לְמַעֵט. וְלִיפְלוֹג בְּמַתְנִי'! פָּלֵיג בְּגוֹבְהָהּ, וְה"ה לְרָחְבָּהּ. וְאַכַּתִּי, ר' יְהוּדָה מִפִּתְחוֹ שֶׁל אוּלָם גָּמַר? וְהָתַנְיָא: מָבוֹי שֶׁהוּא גָּבוֹהַּ מִכ' אַמָּה — יְמַעֵט, וְרַבִּי יְהוּדָה מַכְשִׁיר עַד מ' וְנ' אַמָּה. וְתָנֵי בַּר קַפָּרָא: עַד מֵאָה. בִּשְׁלָמָא לְבַר קַפָּרָא — גּוּזְמָא, אֶלָּא לְרַב יְהוּדָה מַאי גּוּזְמָא? בִּשְׁלָמָא[(ג)] לְרַבִּי יְהוּדָה, אַרְבָּעִים — גָּמַר מִפִּתְחוֹ שֶׁל אוּלָם, אֶלָּא נ' מְנָא לֵיהּ? א"ר חִסְדָּא: הָא מַתְנִיתָא אַטְעְיֵיהּ לְרַב, דְּתַנְיָא: *מָבוֹי שֶׁהוּא גָּבוֹהַּ מִכ' אַמָּה, יוֹתֵר מִפִּתְחוֹ שֶׁל הֵיכָל יְמַעֵט. הוּא סָבַר: מִדְּרַבָּנַן מִפִּתְחוֹ שֶׁל הֵיכָל גָּמְרִי, רַבִּי יְהוּדָה — מִפִּתְחוֹ שֶׁל אוּלָם גָּמַר. וְלָאו הִיא, ר' יְהוּדָה מִפִּתְחָא דְּמַלְכִּין גָּמַר. וְרַבָּנַן, אִי מִפִּתְחוֹ שֶׁל הֵיכָל גָּמְרִי — לִיבָּעוּ דְּלָתוֹת כַּהֵיכָל, אַלְמָה *תְּנַן: הֶכְשֵׁר מָבוֹי, ב"ש אוֹמְרִים: לֶחִי וְקוֹרָה, וּב"ה אוֹמְרִים: לֶחִי אוֹ קוֹרָה! דַּלְתוֹת הֵיכָל לִצְנִיעוּת בְּעָלְמָא הוּא דַּעֲבִידָן. אֶלָּא מֵעַתָּה, לָא תֵּיהַנֵּי לֵיהּ צוּרַת הַפֶּתַח, דְּהָא הֵיכָל צוּרַת הַפֶּתַח הֲוְיָא לוֹ, אֲפִילּוּ הָכִי עֶשֶׂר אַמּוֹת הוּא דְּרָוֵיחַ. אַלְמָה תְּנַן: אִם יֵשׁ לוֹ צוּרַת הַפֶּתַח, אע"פ שֶׁרָחָב מֵעֶשֶׂר אַמּוֹת — אֵינוֹ צָרִיךְ לְמַעֵט! מִידֵּי הוּא טַעְמָא אֶלָּא לְרַב — הָא *מַתְנֵי לֵיהּ רַב יְהוּדָה לְחִיָּיא בַּר רַב קַמֵּיהּ דְּרַב: אֵינוֹ צָרִיךְ לְמַעֵט. וְא"ל: אַתְנְיֵיהּ "צָרִיךְ לְמַעֵט". אֶלָּא מֵעַתָּה

לָא

רש"י

הַהוּא בָּאָרוֹן כְּתִיב. שֶׁהוּא מַשָּׂא בְּנֵי קְהָת. וְעַל שֵׁם שֶׁהוּא מְקוּדָּשׁ מִשְּׁאָר הַמַּשָּׂאוֹת קָרוּי "מִקְדָּשׁ": לֵילְפוּ מִפֶּתַח שַׁעַר הֶחָצֵר. אָרוֹחַב פָּרֵיךְ, דִּתְנַן בְּמַתְנִי': וְהָרָחָב מֵעֶשֶׂר אַמּוֹת יְמַעֵט. הָא אַשְׁכַּחַן פֶּתַח חָצֵר דַּהֲוֵי עֶשְׂרִים רוֹחַב, וְאִיקְרִי "פֶּתַח", דִּכְתִיב: "וְאֵת קַלְעֵי הֶחָצֵר וְאֶת מָסַךְ פֶּתַח שַׁעַר הֶחָצֵר" בְּפָרָשַׁת נָשֹׂא כְּתִיב. אֲבָל אַגּוֹבַהּ וּלְמִיפְסַל בְּגוֹבַהּ יוֹתֵר מֵה' אַמּוֹת — לָא מָצֵי פָּרֵיךְ, דְּהָא אַשְׁכַּחַן פֶּתַח הַהֵיכָל דְּגָבוֹהַּ כ' וְקָא קָרֵי לֵיהּ "פֶּתַח": רוֹחַב חֲצַר הַמִּשְׁכָּן נ' אַמָּה. וְהָא דִּכְתִיב "חֲמִשִּׁים בַּחֲמִשִּׁים" בְּפֶרֶק ב' (ד' כג:) מְפָרֵשׁ לָהּ, וּפִתְחָהּ בְּאֶמְצַע רָחְבָּהּ וּסְתָמוֹ בִּקְלָעִים ט"ו אַמָּה מִצַּד זֶה שֶׁל פֶּתַח וְט"ו אַמָּה מִצַּד זֶה שֶׁל פֶּתַח, נִשְׁאֲרוּ כ' אַמָּה רוֹחַב בָּאֶמְצַע, כִּדְכְתִיב: "חֲמֵשׁ עֶשְׂרֵה אַמָּה קְלָעִים לַכָּתֵף", וְכָתֵף הוּא צִידּוֹ שֶׁל פֶּתַח: מַה לְּהַלָּן. גּוֹבַהּ חָמֵשׁ, שֶׁהֲרֵי כָּל קַלְעֵי הֶחָצֵר סָבִיב לֹא הָיָה גּוֹבְהָן אֶלָּא חָמֵשׁ, כִּדִכְתִיב (שמות כז): "וְקוֹמָה חָמֵשׁ אַמּוֹת": בְּגוֹבְהָהּ הוּא דִּכְתִיב. שֶׁגָּבְהוּ הַקְּלָעִים הַמִּזְרָחִיּוֹת מִזֶּה וּמִזֶּה לַפֶּתַח ט"ו אַמָּה יוֹתֵר מִשְּׁאָר קַלְעֵי הֶחָצֵר, דַּהֲווּ לְהוּ גּוֹבַהּ כ' וְלָרוֹחַב לֹא נִיתְּנָה מִדָּה: הַהוּא. חָמֵשׁ אַמּוֹת: מִשְּׂפַת קְלָעִים וּלְמַטָּה. לְמַטָּה מֵאוֹתָן ט"ו שֶׁנֶּעֶדְפוּ מִזֶּה וּמִזֶּה לַפֶּתַח, הָיוּ עוֹד ה' גּוֹבַהּ שָׁוֶה לִשְׁאָר הַקְּלָעִים, וַעֲלֵיהֶן נִיתּוֹסְפוּ ט"ו בְּגוֹבַהּ מִב' עֶבְרֵי הַפֶּתַח דַּהֲווּ לְהוּ כ'. לִישָּׁנָא אַחֲרִינָא: בְּגוֹבְהָהּ הוּא דִּכְתִיב — דְּגוֹבַהּ כָּל קַלְעֵי הֶחָצֵר סָבִיב ט"ו אַמָּה, אֲבָל לְרוֹחַב הַפֶּתַח לֹא לָמַדְנוּ שִׁיעוּר. וּלְהַךְ לִישָּׁנָא גָּרְסִינַן בְּמַסְקָנָא: הַהוּא מִשְּׂפַת מִזְבֵּחַ וּלְמַעְלָה. שֶׁהַמִּזְבֵּחַ גּוֹבְהוֹ עֶשֶׂר וְהַקְּלָעִים גְּבוֹהוֹת מִמֶּנּוּ חָמֵשׁ, דַּהֲווּ לְהוּ ט"ו, כְּדֵי שֶׁלֹּא יְהֵא כֹּהֵן עוֹמֵד עָלָיו וַעֲבוֹדָה בְּיָדוֹ וְכָל הָעָם רוֹאִין אוֹתוֹ מִבַּחוּץ. וּשְׁתֵּיהֶן שָׁמַעְתִּי, וְזֶה עִיקָּר. וְכֵן מְפוֹרָשׁ בִּזְבָחִים בְּפ' "קָדְשֵׁי קָדָשִׁים" (ד' נט:). וְהַמְפָרֵשׁ לָשׁוֹן רִאשׁוֹן טוֹעֶה הוּא, שֶׁהָיָה סָבוּר דְּמַאן דְּפָרֵיךְ לֵילְפוּ מִפֶּתַח שַׁעַר הֶחָצֵר — אַגּוֹבְהָהּ פָּרֵיךְ, לְמִיפְסַל גּוֹבַהּ יוֹתֵר מֵחָמֵשׁ אַמּוֹת, וּמִשּׁוּם הָכִי אַהְדַּר לְאוֹקוֹמֵי פֶּתַח הֶחָצֵר בְּגוֹבַהּ כ': וְלָא פָּלֵיג ר' יְהוּדָה. וְאִי מֵאוּלָם גָּמַר לִיכַשַּׁר בְּרוֹחַב כ': וְתָנֵי בַּר קַפָּרָא. בְּמִילְּתֵיהּ דְּר' יְהוּדָה, עַד מֵאָה אַמָּה: בִּשְׁלָמָא לְבַר קַפָּרָא. אִיכָּא לְמֵימַר דְּר' יְהוּדָה מֵאוּלָם גָּמַר, וְלָא מַכְשַׁר בְּגוֹבַהּ מֵאַרְבָּעִים. וְהָא דְּתָנֵי בַּר קַפָּרָא ק' — גּוּזְמָא נָקַט, מִשּׁוּם דְּאַכְשַׁר ר' יְהוּדָה בְּיוֹתֵר מִכ' וּמִשְּׁלֹשִׁים נִרְאִים לְבַר קַפָּרָא גּוּזְמָא, וְנָקֵיט בְּמִילְּתֵיהּ טְפֵי: אַטְעְיֵיהּ לְרַב. דְּאָמַר לְעֵיל ר' יְהוּדָה לֹא לְמָדָהּ אֶלָּא מִפֶּתַח אוּלָם, הָא מַתְנִיתָא דִּלְקַמֵּיהּ אַטְעְיֵיהּ: פִּיתְחָא דְּמַלְכִּים. שָׁם פִּתְחֵי מְלָכִים גְּבוֹהִין הַרְבֵּה: לֶחִי. קָנֶה אוֹ לוּחַ נָעוּץ אֵצֶל כּוֹתֶל הָאֶחָד בְּרֹאשׁוֹ: לָא תֵּיהַנֵּי לֵיהּ צוּרַת הַפֶּתַח. לְהַכְשִׁיר רָחְבּוֹ בְּיוֹתֵר מֵעֲשָׂרָה:

לָא

תוספות

בין לרבנן ובין לרבי יהודה לילפו מפתח שער החצר. ארוחבה פריך, כדפי' בקונט'. דאגובהה לא מצי פריך, כיון דאשכחן דאיקרי פתח היכל ועזרה דהוו גביהי עשרים.(ג) ועוד: אי אגובהה פריך לא הוה משני מידי פתח שער החצר איקרי – דכל שכן לא איקרי "פתח" יותר מחמש, דשער גדול מפתח. אלא ארוחבה פריך, דלילפו משער החצר דהוה רוחב כ', כדמייתי מקרא. אע"ג דג' עמודים היו עומדים ברוחב הפתח, כדמוכחי קראי – מ"מ אתי אויר' דהאי גיסא ודהאי גיסא ומבטל ליה, כדאמר לקמן (ד' י:). ומשני: ד"פתח שער" – איקרי, "פתח" סתמא – לא איקרי. ואע"ג דבפרשת במדבר סיני מלינו דאיקרי נמי "פתח" סתמא – אין לחוש, הואיל ובשאר מקומות איקרי "פתח שער" וכענין זה מלינו ב"הקומץ רבה" (מנחות ד' לז.) דקאמר: מלינו ימין שנקראת "יד", דכתיב "כי ישית אביו יד ימינו". ואידך: "יד ימין" – איקרי, "יד" סתמא – לא איקרי. ואע"ג דבתר הכי כתיב "ויתמוך יד אביו":

ואיבעית[(א)] אימא כי כתיב. ט"ו אמות בגובה הוא דכתיב, אבל ברוחב אין שיעור מפורש, ואפשר שהיה הפתח רחב עשר או פחות. וגרסי' בתר הכי: משפת מזבח ולמעלה. והיינו כר' יוסי דבפ' "קדשי קדשים" (זבחים ד' נט:), דאמר: מזבח גובהו י' אמות, פי' שנים כאורכו, והקלעים סביב ט"ו, שלא יהא כהן עומד ועבודה בידו וכל העם רואין אותו. והא דכתיב בקלעים וקומה ה' אמות, היינו משפת מזבח ולמעלה. והא דכתיב במזבח (שמות כז) "ושלש אמות קומתו" – היינו משפת סובב ולמעלה. ור' יהודה פליג התם, ד"המזבח ג' אמות" – דברים ככתבן, והקלעים גובהן ה'. והאי שינויא בתרא דהכא לא משני לר' יהודה אלא לרבנן. דלר' יהודה קלעים ט"ו אמות לאו בגובהן כתיב. וא"ת: מאי פריך? שאני פתח החצר דהוה ליה צורת הפתח, שהכלונסות היו על גבי ווי עמודים שהקלעים תלויים בהן! וי"ל: דאמר לקמן (ד' יא.) דצורת הפתח שעשאה מן הצד לא עשה ולא כלום. ועוד: דלא קשה מידי, דאליבא דרב קיימינן ורב תני צריך למעט, אע"ג דאית ליה צורת הפתח. ולהכי נמי, כי פריך בסמוך: ור' יהודה מפתחו של אולם גמר והא תנן כו' ולא פליג ר' יהודה, ולא משני שאני אולם דה"ל צורת הפתח – משום דאליבא דרב קיימינן. אך קשה, דקראי מוכחי דברוחב כתיב! ונראה לריצב"א דמשמע ליה והרחב מי' אמות ימעט – אפילו אינו גבוה אלא חמש. ולהכי פריך היכא דאינו גבוה אלא ה' לילפו מפתח החצר, דאפילו רוחב כ' הוי פתח. ואין נראה למקשה ד"פתח שער" איקרי – כיון דנמוך כ"כ. ועוד: דבפ' מדבר סיני איקרי "פתח" סתמא, ואתי שפיר דגרס בכל הספרים מה להלן גבוה ה' ברוחב כ'. ומשני: דאפ"ה "פתח שער" איקרי הואיל ורחב כ"כ. והא דאיקרי בפרשת "במדבר סיני" "פתח" סתמא – אין לחוש, כדפי' לעיל. ואיבעית אימא: קלעים ט"ו אמה בגובה הוא דכתיב, כלומר: קרא ד"ויקהל" דההוא ודאי ע"כ בגובה נמי כתיב, דהא כתיב: "קלעים חמש עשרה אמה אל הכתף וגו'" וכתיב: "ולכתף השנית מזה ומזה לשער החצר". והשתא, אי לאו דקרא דלפניו בגובהה כתיב – לא הוצרך לכתוב מזה ומזה לשער החצר, כיון דככר פי' לד אחד. אלא וודאי קרא קמא איירי בגובה. והא דכתיב בקרא קמא: "עמודיהם שלשה" דמשמע דארוחבן קאי – י"ל דאדלבתריה קאי. ותדע, דהמקשה הביא קרא ד"תרומה" "חמש עשרה אמה קלעים", והמתרץ הביא קרא ד"ויקהל" "קלעים חמש עשרה אמה אל הכתף". וגם רב אשי שסידר התלמוד הביא למעלה "ולכתף השנית מזה ומזה" ד"ויקהל", ולא הביא קרא ד"תרומה" שהוא אלא הפסוק שהביא תחלה, דהיינו "ולכתף השנית חמש עשרה קלעים". והביאו בשביל שתירץ בזה הפסוק. והשתא ודאי הואיל וגובה היה כ"כ, פשיטא דנקרא "שער". ומתחלה לא הקשה אלא דלא משמע ליה דאיקרי "שער" בעבור גובהו חמש[ב]:

אמר אביי פליג בברייתא. משמע ולעולם מפתח אולם גמר, ומכשיר עד רוחב כ'. וקשה: דלקמן (ד' י.) אמר דלא מכשיר ר' יהודה אלא עד י"ג אמה ושליש[ג]: **עד** ארבעים וחמשים אמה. אין להקשות השתא נ' שרי, מ' מיבעיא? דאיכא למימר: מ' ונ' כדאמרי אינשי, כדמשמע בפרק "מפנין" (שבת ד' קכו:)*: **ליבעו** דלתות כהיכל. ואע"ג דאהל מועד שהיה נמי הפתח רחב י' לא היו דלתות, ואפי' הכי קרי ליה "פתח", היינו משום שלא היה גבוה אלא י'. א"נ: ע"כ אהל מועד שלא כדין נקרא "פתח", שהרי היה פרוץ במלואו דלא הוה ליה גיפופי: **אלא** מעתה לא תיהני ליה צורת הפתח. אבל לא תיהני ליה דלתות לא פריך. דפשיטא, הואיל ואית ליה דלתות והן ננעלות דהויא כמחילה מעלייתא. ולא שייך נמי למיפרך דליבעי צורת הפתח, דצורת הפתח לא הוי אלא משום נוי בעלמא. אבל האי פריך שפיר, דלא תהני ליה צורת הפתח; דאי הוה קרוי "פתח" אף כשגדול ביותר – ע"י צורת הפתח היה לו לעשותו שוה לאולם: **מידי** הוא טעמא אלא לרב. ואע"ג דברייתא נמי גמרה מהיכל, איכא למימר דפליגא אמתני'. א"נ: לא נקט היכל אלא לסימנא בעלמא, כדאמרינן בסמוך:

ורב

א) רש"ל כ' דהך ואיבע"א הוא דיבור אחד עם הך לעיל ב) [ועי' תוס' זבחים ס. ד"ה ואומר שהאריך בזה] ג) וי"ל דהתם תומרא בעלמא דיליף מפתחי בירתא (ת"י מהר"מ)

רבינו חננאל

מועד לילפי מפתח שער החצר שהיה גובהו ה' אמות ורוחבו כ' אמה שנאמר אורך החצר מאה באמה וגו' טול כ' אמה אחורי המשכן ול' אמה המשכן הרי נ' נשארו מן האורך של חצר המשכן ורוחב כולן רוחבן נ' פרנסתו החצר לאורכה וזו עוד מדת רחבת המשכן. רחבו עשר באמה ויש לו אחריו ריוח בצפון כ' אמה ובדרום י' אמה הרי נשאר במזרחו של משכן נ' אמה אורך בנ' רוחב שנאמר ורוחב החצר לפאת קדמה מזרחה חמשים אמה. עשו בקלעים ט"ו אמה מכן וט"ו אמה מכן הרי ל' אמה נשארו כ' אמה באמצע. (מהו) [וזהו] פתח המשכן ודחינן פתח שער אקרי פתח סתמא לא אקרי. איבעית אימא כי כתיב קלעים חמש עשרה אמה בגובה הוא דכתיב ואקשינן איני והכתיב בגובה של קלעים וקומה חמש אמות ופרכינן ההוא משפת המזבח ולמעלה ה' אמות. זו השמועה מפורשת בשחיטת קדשים ששחטן בראשו של מזבח בתחלתו. דתניא א"ל ר' יוסי ואתה אי אתה אומר כן והלא נאמר ואת מסך שער החצר אשר על המשכן ועל המזבח מקיש מזבח למשכן מה משכן י' אמות אף מזבח י' אמות ואומר חמש עשרה אמה קלעים וגו' הא מה אני מקיים וקומה ברוחב חמש אמות משפת מזבח ולמעלה שלא יהא כהן עומד במזבח ועבודה בידו והכל רואין אותו הכא נמי במזבח שכתוב בו רבוע יהיה המזבח ושלש אמות קומתו משפת סובב ולמעלה. ותנן עלה אמה וכנס אמה זהו יסוד. עלה חמשה וכנס אמה זהו סובב ומן הסובב ולמעלה ג' ואמה של קרנות הרי י' וקשיא לן מכ"מ ט"ו אמה הן אע"פ שתעשה קלעים בגובה בגובה כ' מנא ליה [ראקרי פתח] ופרקינן לעולם עד כ' אמה פתח אתקרי והאי דלא עבדו הכא משום דלא אצטריך דהא עלו בגובה מן המשכן חמש אמות מפני המזבח יתר מיכן לא איצטריכו: ואקשינן ור' יהודה מפתחו של אולם גמר והתניא מבוי שהוא גבוה מכ' אמה ימעט ר' יהודה מכשיר עד מ' ונ' אמה. אמר רב חסדא הא דתניא מבוי שהוא גבוה מכ' אמה יתר מפתחו של היכל אטעיתיה לרב הוא סבר מדרבנן מפתחו של היכל גמרי. ר' יהודה נמי מפתחו של אולם גמר ולא היא ר' יהודה [מפתחא] דמלכי גמר. ורבנן דגמרי מפתח ההיכל ליבעי דלתות כהיכל ודחינן לא דלתות לצניעותא עבידי דלא יהון חזיין מה דבגוא. אלא מעתה ליבעו תיקרה מעליא כי היכל

[וע"ע תוס' שבת ס: ד"ה השתא]

רב נסים גאון

והכתיב וקומה חמש אמות ההוא משפת מזבח ולמעלה. וזה גם הוא מן העיקר שאמרוהו בפרק המצניע (שבת קף לב:) דכתיב אשר על המשכן ועל המזבח מקיש מזבח למשכן מה משכן עשר אמות אף מזבח עשר אמות וכבר הזכרנו בפרק המצניע הדברים שנאמרו במסכת זבחים ואין אנו טורחין לחזור בהן: דתנן

מסורת הש"ס

שמות כה

שם כז

שם

שם לח

[נ"ל וכתיב ככל אשר אני מראה אותך את תבנית המשכן בין לרבנן כו' כ"א בשבועות טז:]

כ"א אל הכתף

[מנחות יז:]

[לקמן יז.]

[תוספ' פ"א]

לקמן יא.

[לקמן יא.]

הגהות הב"ח

(א) גמ' והכתיב וקומה חמש אמות (ההוא משפת מזבח ולמעלה) תא"מ ונ"ב ס"א ההוא משפת קלעים ולמטה: (ב) שם לר' יהודה מאי גוזמא בשלמא ארבעים כצ"ל ותיבות לרבי יהודה נמחק: (ג) תוס' ד"ה בין לרבנן וכו' כיון דאשכחן פתח היכל ועזרה דהוו גביהי עשרים דאיקרי פתח ועוד אי:

גליון הש"ס **גמ'** ובין לר"י לילפו מפתח שער החצר. לא ידעתי לפרש דמה קושיא על ר"י מה נוכל ללמוד מפתח החצר יותר מהלימוד מהאולם הא גם האולם היה רוחב יותר מי' ומזה פרכי' באמת א"כ ומוכחי מזה דר"י פליג על הרוחב עכ"פ איך שייך למינקט הקושיא לר"י לילף מפתח החצר מה עדיפות בזה מהילפותא מהאולם והלימוד מאולם הא צריך לענין גבוה יותר מכ' וצ"ע: **תום'** ד"ה אמר וכו' לקמן. לא ידעתי שעמו מזה קושיא והניחו בקושיא הא זהו אינו שם משנה או ברייתא רק לרב אחי סבר לומר כן ור"י לחי לה והיא הנותנת וא"כ י"ל מהילפותא דאביי סבר כר"י וגם הא ר"א לא אמר כן בהחלטו אלא לסבר לומר כן ואפשר דקיבל מר"י דוסיא הנותנת:

לָא תֵיהַנֵי לֵיהּ אֲמַלְתְּרָא, דְּהָא הֵיכָל אֲמַלְתְּרָא הָוְיָא לֵיהּ, וַאֲפִי' הָכִי עֶשְׂרִים אַמָּה הוּא דְּגָבוֹהַּ. דִּתְנַן: *אחָמֵשׁ אֲמַלְתְּרָאוֹת *שֶׁל מֵילָה הָיוּ עַל גַּבָּיו, זוֹ לְמַעְלָה מִזּוֹ, וְזוֹ לְמַעְלָה מִזּוֹ. וְהַאי מַאי תְּיוּבְתָּא, דִּילְמָא כִּי תַּנְיָא הַהִיא דַּאֲמַלְתְּרָאוֹת — בְּאוּלָם תַּנְיָא? וְהַאי מַאי קוּשְׁיָא?! דִּילְמָא תַּבְנִית הֵיכָל כְּתַבְנִית אוּלָם? אַלְמָה אָמַר רַבִּי אִילְעָא אָמַר רַב: רָחְבָּהּ ד' אע"פ שֶׁאֵינָהּ בְּרִיאָה, וְאִם יֵשׁ לָהּ אֲמַלְתְּרָא — אֲפִי' גְּבוֹהָה יוֹתֵר מֵעֶשְׂרִים אַמָּה אֵינוֹ צָרִיךְ לְמַעֵט. אָמַר רַב יוֹסֵף: אֲמַלְתְּרָא מַתְנִיתָא הִיא, מַאן קָתָנֵי לָהּ? אָמַר אַבַּיֵי: וְהָא *חָמָא בְּרֵיהּ דְּרַבָּה בַּר אֲבוּהּ קָתָנֵי לָהּ. וְתֶיהֱוֵי אֲמַלְתְּרָא מַתְנִיתָא, וְתִיקְשֵׁי לְרַב! אָמַר לָךְ רַב: דַּל אֲנָא מֵהָכָא, מַתְנְיָיתָא מִי לָא קַשְׁיָין אַהֲדָדֵי? אֶלָּא מַאי אִית לָךְ לְמֵימַר — תַּנָּאֵי הִיא, לְדִידִי נַמִי — תַּנָּאֵי הִיא. רַב נַחְמָן בַּר יִצְחָק אָמַר: בְּלָא רַב מַתְנְיָיתָא אַהֲדָדֵי לָא קַשְׁיָין; לְרַבָּנַן, קוֹרָה *טַעְמָא(א) מַאי — מִשּׁוּם הֶיכֵּרָא. וְהַאי דְּקָתָנֵי "יָתֵר מִפִּתְחוֹ שֶׁל הֵיכָל" — סִימָנָא בְּעָלְמָא. וְרַב נַחְמָן בַּר יִצְחָק, הָנִיחָא אִי לָא סְבִירָא לֵיהּ הָא דְּרַבָּה, אֶלָּא אִי סְבִירָא לֵיהּ הָא דְּרַבָּה, *דְּאָמַר רַבָּה: כְּתִיב: ◦"לְמַעַן יֵדְעוּ דוֹרוֹתֵיכֶם כִּי בַסֻּכּוֹת הוֹשַׁבְתִּי" עַד עֶשְׂרִים אַמָּה אָדָם יוֹדֵעַ שֶׁדָּר בַּסּוּכָּה, לְמַעְלָה מֵעֶשְׂרִים אַמָּה — אֵין אָדָם יוֹדֵעַ, מִשּׁוּם דְּלָא שָׁלְטָא בֵּיהּ עֵינָא. אַלְמָא: גַּבֵּי סוּכָּה נַמִי בְּהֶיכֵּרָא פְּלִיגִי, אִיפְלוּגֵי בְּתַרְתֵּי לָמָּה(ב) לִי? צְרִיכָא, דְּאִי אַשְׁמְעִינַן גַּבֵּי סוּכָּה — בְּהָא קָאָמַר ר' יְהוּדָה, כֵּיוָן דְּלִישִׁיבָה עֲבִידָא — שָׁלְטָא בֵּיהּ עֵינָא. אֲבָל מָבוֹי, דִּלְהִילּוּךְ עָבִיד — אֵימָא מוֹדֶה לְהוּ לְרַבָּנַן. וְאִי אַשְׁמְעִינַן בְּהָא — בְּהָא קָאָמְרִי רַבָּנַן, אֲבָל בְּהַךְ — אֵימָא מוֹדוּ לֵיהּ לְר' יְהוּדָה, צְרִיכָא. במַאי אֲמַלְתְּרָא? רַב חָמָא בְּרֵיהּ דְּרַבָּה בַּר אֲבוּהּ אָמַר: קִינֵּי. כִּי אֲתָא רַב דִּימִי אֲמַר, אָמְרִי בְּמַעַרְבָא: פִּסְקֵי דְּאַרְזָא. מַאן דְּאָמַר פִּסְקֵי דְּאַרְזָא — כ"ש קִינֵּי, מ"ד קִינֵּי אֲבָל פִּסְקֵי דְּאַרְזָא לָא. ומ"ד פִּסְקֵי דְּאַרְזָא(ג) מ"ט — מִשּׁוּם דְּנָפֵישׁ מָשְׁכֵיהּ, וְהָא סוּכָּה דְּנָפֵישׁ מָשְׁכֵיהּ, וְקָאָמְרִי רַבָּנַן דְּלָא! אֶלָּא: כֵּיוָן דְּקָא חֲשִׁיב — אִית לֵיהּ קָלָא.§ גמִקְצָת קוֹרָה בְּתוֹךְ עֶשְׂרִים וּמִקְצָת קוֹרָה לְמַעְלָה מֵעֶשְׂרִים, מִקְצָת סְכָךְ בְּתוֹךְ עֶשְׂרִים וּמִקְצָת סְכָךְ לְמַעְלָה מֵעֶשְׂרִים, אָמַר רַבָּה: בְּמָבוֹי — כָּשֵׁר, בַּסּוּכָּה — פָּסוּל. מַאי שְׁנָא בְּמָבוֹי דְּכָשֵׁר — דְּאָמְרִי' קְלוּשׁ, סוּכָּה נַמִי לֵימָא קְלוּשׁ! אִי קָלְשַׁתְּ הָוְיָא לָהּ חַמָּתָהּ מְרוּבָּה מִצִּילָּתָהּ. הָכָא נַמִי, אִי קָלְשַׁתְּ — הָוְיָא לָהּ קוֹרָה הַנִּיטֶּלֶת בָּרוּחַ. אֶלָּא: עַל כָּרְחָךְ נַעֲשׂוּ כִּשְׁפוּדִין שֶׁל מַתֶּכֶת, הָכָא נַמִי: עַל כָּרְחָךְ נַעֲשֵׂית צִילָּתָהּ מְרוּבָּה מֵחַמָּתָהּ! אָמַר רָבָא מִפַּרְזְקִי': סוּכָּה דְּלְיָחִיד הִיא — לָא מִדְּכַר, מָבוֹי דְּלְרַבִּים — מִדְּכְרִי אַהֲדָדֵי. רָבִינָא אָמַר: סוּכָּה דְּאוֹרַיְיתָא — אַחְמִירוּ בָּהּ רַבָּנַן, מָבוֹי דְּרַבָּנַן — לָא אַחְמִירוּ בֵּיהּ רַבָּנַן. רַב אַדָּא בַּר מַתָּנָה מַתְנֵי לְהָא שְׁמַעְתָּא דְּרַבָּה אִיפְּכָא; אָמַר רַבָּה: בְּמָבוֹי — פָּסוּל, בַּסּוּכָּה — כְּשֵׁירָה. מַאי שְׁנָא סוּכָּה דִּכְשֵׁירָה — דְּאָמְרִינַן קְלוּשׁ, בְּמָבוֹי נַמִי — לֵימָא קְלוּשׁ! אִי קָלְשַׁתְּ הָוֵי לָהּ קוֹרָה הַנִּיטֶּלֶת בָּרוּחַ. הָכָא נַמִי אִי קָלְשַׁתְּ — הָוְיָא לָהּ חַמָּתָהּ מְרוּבָּה מִצִּילָּתָהּ! אֶלָּא עַל כָּרְחָךְ נַעֲשֵׂית צִילָּתָהּ מְרוּבָּה מֵחַמָּתָהּ, הָכָא נַמִי: ע"כ נַעֲשׂוּ כִּשְׁפוּדִין שֶׁל מַתֶּכֶת! אָמַר רָבָא מִפַּרְזְקִיָא: ◦סוּכָּה דְּלְיָחִיד הִיא — רָמֵי אַנַּפְשֵׁיהּ וּמִדְּכַר, מָבוֹי דְּלְרַבִּי' הִיא — סָמְכִי אַהֲדָדֵי, וְלָא מִדְּכְרִי. *דְּאָמְרִי אֱינָשֵׁי: קִדְרָא דְּבֵי שׁוּתָּפֵי לָא חֲמִימָא וְלָא קְרִירָא. רָבִינָא אָמַר: סוּכָּה דְּאוֹרַיְיתָא — לָא בָּעֵי חִיזּוּק, מָבוֹי דְּרַבָּנַן — בָּעֵי חִיזּוּק. מַאי הָוֵי עֲלַהּ? רַבָּה בַּר רַב עוּלָּא אָמַר: זֶה וָזֶה פָּסוּל. רָבָא אָמַר: דזֶה וָזֶה כָּשֵׁר.

חָלַל

רש"י

לָא תֵיהַנֵי לֵיהּ אֲמַלְתְּרָא. לְאַכְשׁוּרֵי גּוֹבְהוֹ יוֹתֵר מִכ' לְקַמָּן מְפָרֵשׁ מַאי אֲמַלְתְּרָא, וְהֵיכָא תָּנֵי דִּמְהַנְיָא: שֶׁל מֵילָה. עֵץ שֶׁגְּדֵילִין בּוֹ מִילִין, וְהֵם עֲפָלִים, וּבלע"ז גלא"ם: אַלְמָה אָמַר ר' אִילְעָא כו'. הַשְׁתָּא קָא מַסֵּיק לְפִירְכֵיהּ, דְּאַשְׁכְּחַן דִּמְהַנְיָא אֲמַלְתְּרָא אַלִּיבָּא דְרַב, וּמֵעִיקָּרָא לָא שְׁבַקֵיהּ לְאַסּוּקֵי לְמִלְּתֵיהּ עַד דְּסָתַר לֵיהּ לִתְיוּבְתָּא: רְחָבָה ד'. אִם הָיְתָה קוֹרָה רְחָבָה ד' טְפָחִים, אע"פ שֶׁהִיא דַּקָּה וְאֵינָהּ חֲזָקָה לְקַבֵּל אָרִיחַ — כְּשֵׁירָה. וְהָא דִּתְנַן בְּמַתְנִי' (לקמן ד' יג:) בְּרִיאָה כְּדֵי לְקַבֵּל אָרִיחַ — כְּשֶׁאֵינָהּ רְחָבָה ד' טְפָחִים קָאָמַר: וְאִם יֵשׁ לָהּ אֲמַלְתְּרָא כו'. תַּרְתֵּי מִילֵּי קָאָמַר רַב, וּלְקוּלָּא: אָמַר רַב יוֹסֵף. הָא אֲמַלְתְּר' דְּאַיְיתוּהָ מִשְּׁמֵיהּ דְּרַב — לָאו רַב אֲמָרָהּ, דְּתִיקְשֵׁי דְּרַב אַדְּרַב, אֶלָּא מַתְנִיתָ' הִיא: וְתִיקְשֵׁי לְרַב. דְּהָא חָזֵינַן הָכָא דְּלָא גָּמְרִי רַבָּנַן מֵהֵיכָל, מִדְּקָתָנֵי דַּאֲמַלְתְּרָא מְהַנְיָא: דַּל אֲנָא מֵהָכָא. הַרִימֵנִי מִיכָּן כְּאִילּוּ שָׁתַקְתִּי וְלֹא אָמַרְתִּי דָּבָר זֶה: מַתְנְיָית' מִי לָא קַשְׁיָין אַהֲדָדֵי. דְּהָא תַּנְיָא לְעֵיל בְּהֶדְיָא מָבוֹי שֶׁהוּא גָּבוֹהַּ מִכ' יוֹתֵר מִפִּתְחוֹ שֶׁל הֵיכָל. אַלְמָא: רַבָּנַן מֵהָתָם גָּמְרִי: תַּנָּאֵי הִיא. תַּנָּא דִּלְעֵיל דִּסְבִירָא לֵיהּ דְּרַבָּנַן מֵהֵיכָל גָּמְרִי, וַאֲמַלְתְּרָא לָא מְהַנְיָא. וְהַאי תַּנָּא דַּאֲמַלְתְּרָא סָבַר: לָאו מֵהֵיכָל גָּמְרִי: לְדִידִי נַמִי תַּנָּאֵי הִיא. וְתַנָּא כְּתַנָּא דִּלְעֵיל אֲמַרִי: בְּלָא רַב. אִי לָא הֲוָה מְפָרֵשׁ רַב לְמַתְנִיתָא קַמַּיְיתָא, וְיָלֵיף מִינָּהּ דְּרַבָּנַן מֵהֵיכָל גָּמְרִי: מַתְנְיָיתָא אַהֲדָדֵי לָא קַשְׁיָין. דְּבֵין לְהַהִיא מַתְנִי' וּבֵין לְהָא מַתְנִיתִין דַּאֲמַלְתְּרָא: קוֹרָה לְרַבָּנַן טַעְמָא מַאי. בָּעוּ תּוֹךְ כ' אַמָּה: מִשּׁוּם הֶיכֵּר. דְּלֶיחֱזוּ אֱינָשֵׁי, וְלֵידְעוּ דְּתַקַּנְתָּא עֲבוּד, וְלָא לֵיתֵי לְאִיחְלוּפֵי בִּרה"ר: וּמִשּׁוּם הָכִי מְהַנְיָא אֲמַלְתְּרָא. דְּכֵיוָן דְּמִיסְתַּכְּלֵי בָּהּ אֱינָשֵׁי אֲפִי' לְמַעְלָה מִכ' אַמָּה — אִיכָּא הֶיכֵּרָא: וְהָא דְּקָתָנֵי. בְּמַתְנִיתָ' קַמַּיְיתָא יוֹתֵר מִפִּתְחוֹ שֶׁל הֵיכָל לָאו דְּגָמְרִי מֵהָתָם, אֶלָּא סִימָנָא בְּעָלְמָא נְקַט, שֶׁלֹּא תַּחֲלִיף גִּירְסָא דְּעֶשְׂרִים וְתֹאמַר לְמַעְלָה מִל' אוֹ מֵאַרְבָּעִים, יְהֵא פֶּתַח הֵיכָל סִימָן בְּיָדְךָ: אִי סְבִירָא לֵיהּ הָא דְּרַבָּה. דְּטַעְמַיְיהוּ דְּרַבָּנַן בְּסוּכָּה נַמִי מִשּׁוּם הֶיכֵּר: לָמָּה לְהוּ. לְרַבָּנַן וְלְר' יְהוּדָה לְפְלוּגֵי בְּתַרְתֵּי: מָבוֹי דִּלְהִילּוּךְ עָבִיד. כְּלוֹמַר: הַמְהַלֵּךְ אֵינוֹ מַבִּיט לְמַעְלָה: קִינֵּי.(ד) כְּגוֹן קִינֵּי עוֹפוֹת, הָיוּ בּוֹלְטִין מִתַּחַת הָאוּלָם לְמַעְלָה (מִל') מִן הַפֶּתַח: פִּסְקֵי דְּאַרְזָא. כְּלוּנְסוֹת שֶׁל אֶרֶז אֲרוּכִּין תְּחוּבִין בַּכּוֹתֶל, וְאַיְּידֵי דְּנָפֵישׁ מָשְׁכֵיהּ אוֹרֶךְ דִּידְהוּ חָזוּ לְהוּ אֱינָשֵׁי, וְאִיכָּא הֶיכֵּרָא: מַאן דְּאָמַר פִּסְקֵי. אִיכָּא הֶיכֵּרָא לְמָבוֹי: כָּל שֶׁכֵּן קִינֵּי. דְּאַיְּידֵי דַּחֲשִׁיבֵי, וּמִילְּתָא דִּתְמִיהָא הִיא מִסְתַּכְּלֵי בְּהוּ אֱינָשֵׁי, וְחָזוּ לַקּוֹרָה: מִקְצָת. עוֹבִי הַקּוֹרָה בְּתוֹךְ כ' וּמִקְצָתָהּ לְמַעְלָה, וְכֵן עוֹבִי סְכָכָהּ שֶׁל סוּכָּה: קְלוּשׁ. רוֹאִין כְּאִילּוּ נִיטַּל אוֹתוֹ הָעוֹבִי הַיּוֹצֵא לְמַעְלָה, וּתְהֵא קוֹרָה דַּקָּה: הַנִּיטֶּלֶת בָּרוּחַ. שֶׁהֲרֵי שִׁיעוּרָהּ חֲכָמִים בְּרִיאָה כְּדֵי לְקַבֵּל אָרִיחַ, וְאִי לָאו הָכִי — שָׁדֵי לֵיהּ זִיקָא, הִלְכָּךְ לָא חָשִׁיב: לָא מִידְּכַר. וְזִמְנִין דְּמִשְׁתַּקֵּיל מִקְצָת עוֹבִי הַסְּכָךְ הַנִּכְנָס לְתוֹךְ כ' וְקַיְימָא כּוּלָּהּ לְמַעְלָה מִכ': מִדְּכְרִי אַהֲדָדֵי. שֶׁאִם תִּרְקַב תַּחְתּוֹנָהּ שֶׁל קוֹרָה וְתַעֲמוֹד כּוּלָּהּ לְמַעְלָה מֵעֶשְׂרִים אַמָּה, מְתַקְּנֵי לָהּ: אֶלָּא. אַמַּאי מַכְשַׁרְתְּ בַּסּוּכָּה, מִשּׁוּם דְּע"כ הַשְׁתָּא צִילָּתָהּ מְרוּבָּה מֵחַמָּתָהּ דְּהָא רוֹאִין הוּא דְּקָאָמְרִי' וְלָא שְׁקִילְנָא מִינָּהּ מִידֵי: הָכָא נַמִי. חֲשׁוֹב אוֹתָהּ כִּשְׁפוּדִין כְּבֵידִין, דְּאִי נַמִי קְלִישִׁי — לָא שָׁדֵי לְהוּ זִיקָא, דְּהָא לָא מִידֵי שַׁקְלַתְּ מִינַּהּ, אֶלָּא רוֹאִין הוּא דְּקָאָמַר:

חָלַל

תוספות

ורב נחמן בר יצחק אי סבירא ליה הא דרבה כו'. לרבה גופיה הוה מצי למיפרך, דאית ליה בפרקין (ד' יג:) דקורה משום היכרא. אלא משום דרב נחמן מפרש בהדיא דפליגי בהיכר, פריך למה להו לאיפלוגי בתרתי: **אי** קלשת הוי לה חמתה מרובה מצילתה. מפר' ר"י: חמתה מרובה מצילתה ע"י שיבא הרוח ויפזר, עד שתהא חמתה מרובה מצילתה. דאי ע"י קלישה לחודה תהא חמתה מרובה — היכי מכשר' לה בלישנא בתרא? הא אין סכך פסול מצטרף בהדי סכך כשר. כדאמרי' בסוכה (ד' ט:) גבי העושה סוכתו תחת האילן. וקשיא: דאמר בפרק קמא דסוכה (ד' ד.): היתה גבוהה מכ' אמה, והוצין יורדין בתוך כ', אם צילתה מרובה מחמתה — כשירה, אם לאו — פסולה. ואמאי כשירה? והלא אי קלשת ליה, יפלו ההוצין למטה! וללישנא בתרא דהכא — אתי שפיר, ולרבא מפרזקיא נמי, דמפרש משום דסוכה דיחיד היא ולא מידכר — אתי שפיר, דגבי הוצין איכא למימר דיורדין הרבה למטה, דליכא למיגזר מידי. אבל לרבינא קשה, דמשמע דמשום סוכה דאורייתא פסולה משום אי קלשת כו'. וי"ל: דהתם איירי שיש הרבה הוצין, שיכולין להתקיים בקל על ידי סמיכה. ועוד נוכל לומר: הכא דאי קלשת ליה הוי חמתה מרובה ע"י קלישה לחוד, ומצטרף לסכך דלמעלה מכ', וללישנא בתרא דלא חשיב כל כך סכך פסול, הואיל והוי סכך כשר — אם היה למטה מכ'. אבל קשה: דגבי הוצין אמרי' ואם לאו פסול, וללישנא בתרא דהכא מכשרינן אפילו חמתה מרובה מצילתה! מיהו ללישנא קמא ניחא. אי נמי: גבי הוצין יש לפסול יותר, הואיל ואגודים עליונים והתחתונים זה בזה, דאי קלשת — יפול הכל: **אמר** רבה במבוי פסול. ל"ג "רב", דרב יליף מפתחו של היכל דהוי אללו כ':

חלל

ולא תיהני צורת הפתח (דאי) [דהיינו] קנה מיכן וקנה מיכן על גביהן ופרקינן שמועה זו דרבנן ילפי לה מפתחו של היכל *) מדקתני לה רבנן דבהא ליה רב לרב יהודה אתנייה לחייא ברי ואע"פ שיש שם צורת הפתח צריך למעט דצורת פתח לא מהני. תוב אקשינן ליבעו אמלתרא כי היכל כדתנן במס' מדות (פ"ג מ"ז) חמש אלמתראות (הן) של מילה היו על גבן כו'. פי' אמלתרא קורות לאחיזת הקיר. כגון וטור כרותות ארזים ובלישנא דרבנן למיסד בניינא. מילה שם האילן. ופירותיו נקראין מילין. כדגרסינן [בגיטין י"ט ע"ב] אין מי מילין ע"ג מילין. והשונה של מילת טועה הוא ודחינן [הא] דתני (המליא) [חמשה] מלתראות של מילה היו על גבן באולם היו וכל אחת אנירה על חברתה ואמרינן (ור"ל) [ודילמא] תבנית היכל כתבנית אולם הוא אלמה אמר רב הקורה אם רחבה ד' אע"פ שאינה בריאה ואם יש שם לו אמלתרא אין צריך למעט. לא תהני אמלתרא דהא גובה היכל לא היה יותר מכ' ואע"ג דהוה ליה אמלתרא ואמרינן ופריק רב יוסף אמלתרא לא רב אמרה מתניתא היא (ומאה) [וחמא] בריה דרבה בר אבוה קתני לה. ואי אמרת בין כך ובין כך קשיא לרב אמר לך רב והא תניא כוותיה דתניא מבוי שגבוה מכ' אמה יותר מפתחו של היכל ימעט אלא מאי אית לך למימר תנאי היא ופליגי אהדדי לדידי נמי תנאי היא ופליגי אהדדי ואנא דתני כי האי תנא. ודחינן ואמרינן בלא רב מתניתא לא פליגי אהדדי. קורה לרבנן משום היכר היא ואי איכא אמלתרא אין לך היכר גדול מזה והאי דתני פתחו של (אולם) [היכל] סימנא בעלמא הוא עד כ' כי היכי דלא ליחלוף לך ואמרינן ורב נחמן בר יצחק אי סביר לה להא דרבה דאמר למען ידעו דורותיכם כי בסוכות הושבתי וגו' עד כ' אמה אדם יודע שדר בצל סוכה וכו' באנו לפרש טעמא דהא מתניתא דתני אם יש אמלתרא אפילו למעלה מכ' אמה אין צריך למעט. ומאי אמלתרא חמא בריה בר אבוה א' קיני. פי' קורה ועליה כמין קיני העופות עליהם כעין הא דכתיב קנים תעשה את התבה במערבא אמרי פיסקא דארזא. פי' לוח ארז רחבה ד' טפחים (הגרסינן) [וגרסינן] בירושלמי. בענין אסקופה אבל אם יש שם רחב ד' אסורה. א"ל והדא אמלתרא אילו מלתרא שמא אינה מתרת כלל ואמלתרא זו שמתרת לא מפני רחבה אלא מפני חשיבותא וכל העובר נותן עיניו עליה מפני חשיבותא וכ"ש קנים שפוטרין לדברי הכל כי פליגי בפסקי דארזא. כך סוגיא דשמועה זו. מקצת קורה בתוך כ' ומקצת למעלה מכ' סכך מקצתה בתוך כ' ומקצתה למעלה מכ'. אמר רבה בסוכה פסולה ואמרינן אמאי [אמרינן] במבוי כשר דחזינן לה לקורה כמאן דקלישא וההוא דשריא למעלה מכ' כמאן דליתיה דמי. אי קלשת לה נמצאת קורה זו נטלת ברוח אלא רואין אותה כאילו היא שפוד של מתכת שהיא חזקה וכבדה וראויה לקבל אריח עליה. בסוכה נמי נימא דחזינן להאי סכך כמאן דקלישא ואעפ"כ בחזקתה קיימי וצילתה מרובה מחמתה היא ותהיה כשרה ופריק רבה מפרזקיא סוכה דיחיד כו'. ופריק רבינא סוכה דהיא מדאורייתא אחמרו בה רבנן מבוי דהוא מדרבנן לא אחמרו בה. רב אדא בר מתנה מתני איפכא אמר רבה בסוכה כשרה במבוי פסולה וכו' עד רבינא אמר סוכה דאורייתא לא בעי חיזוק מבוי דרבנן בעיא חיזוק. מאי הוי

*) [נ"ל רב הוא דאמר לה וכבר אמר רב לרבי יהודה וכו']

רב נסים גאון

דתנן חמש מלטריות היו על גביו. עיקר זו המשנה במסכת מדות בפרק ג' (משנה ז) פתחו של אולם גובהו ארבעים אמה ורחבו כ' אמה וחמש מלטריות של מילת היו על גביו התחתונה עודפת על הפתח אמה: אמת

עין משפט נר מצוה

ו א מיי' פ"ג מהלכות בית הבחירה הל' ח סמג עשין קסג:
ז ב מיי' פי"ז מהלכות שבת הלכה טו טוש"ע א"ח סי' שסג סעיף כו:
[גירסא משנה מילת וכן בערוך ערך מל י"ג]
ח ג ד מיי' שם הל' כז ופ"ד מהלכות סוכה הלכה יג סמג עשין מג טוש"ע א"ח שם וסימן תרלג ס"א:

מסורת הש"ס

מדות פ"ג מ"ז
גי' יעב"ץ רב חמא
[לקמן ה. ח: יב:]
סוכה ב.
[ב"ב כב:]
תורה אור: ויקרא כג

הגהות הב"ח

(א) גמ' מאי לאו משום היכרא: (ב) שם בתרתי למה להו צריכא: (ג) שם לארזא מ"ט אי משום: (ד) רש"י ד"ה קיני כמין קיני עופות:

גליון הש"ס

גמ' סוכה דליחיד רמי אנפשיה. עיין לקמן יח ע"א וברש"י ד"ה בור הרבים:

חלל סוכה תנן, חלל מבוי תנן. א"ל רב פפא לרבא: תניא דמסייע לך, מבוי שהוא גבוה מעשרים אמה יותר מפתחו של היכל — ימעט. והיכל גופו — חללו עשרים. איתיביה רב שימי בר רב אשי לרב פפא: *כיצד *היה עושה — מניח קורה משפת עשרים ולמטה. אימא "ולמעלה". והא "למטה" קתני! הא קמ"ל: דלמטה כלמעלה, מה למעלה — חללה עשרים, אף למטה — חללה עשרה.§ אמר אביי משמיה דרב נחמן: אמת סוכה ואמת מבוי — באמה בת חמשה. אמת כלאים — באמה בת ששה. "אמת מבוי — באמה בת חמשה". למאי הלכתא — לגובהו ולפירצת מבוי, והא איכא משך מבוי בארבע אמות דלקולא! כמאן דאמר *בארבעה טפחים. ואיבעית אימא: *בארבע אמות, ורוב אמות קאמר. "אמת סוכה באמה בת חמשה" למאי הלכתא — לגובהה ולדופן עקומה. והא איכא משך סוכה בארבע אמות, דלקולא. דתניא, *רבי אומר: אומר אני, כל סוכה שאין בה ד' אמות על ד' אמות — פסולה! כרבנן, דאמרי: "אפי' אינה מחזקת אלא ראשו ורובו ושולחנו". ואיבעית אימא: לעולם רבי היא, ורוב אמות קאמר. "אמת כלאים באמה בת ששה". למאי הילכתא — לקרחת הכרם ולמחול הכרם. דתנן: *קרחת הכרם, ב"ש אומרים: עשרים וארבע אמות, וב"ה אומרים: שש עשרה אמות. ומחול הכרם, בית שמאי אומרים: שש עשרה אמות, ובית הלל אומרים: שתים עשרה אמות. איזו היא קרחת הכרם — [א]כרם שחרב אמצעיתו, אין שם שש עשרה אמות — לא יביא זרע לשם, היו שם שש עשרה אמה — נותן לו כדי עבודתו וזורע את המותר. ואיזהו מחול הכרם — [ב]בין כרם לגדר; אין שם שתים עשרה אמה — לא יביא זרע לשם, היו שם שתים עשרה אמה — נותן לו כדי עבודתו וזורע את השאר. והא איכא רצופים בארבע אמות דלקולא, דתנן: *כרם הנטוע על פחות מארבע אמות, רבי שמעון אומר: אינו כרם, וחכמים אומרים: כרם, [ג]ורואין את האמצעיים כאילו אינם! כרבנן, דאמרי הוי כרם. ואיבעי' אימא: לעולם ר' שמעון, ורוב אמות קאמר. ורבא משמיה דר"נ אמר: [ד]כל אמות באמה בת ששה, אלא הללו שוחקות והללו עצבות. מיתיבי: כל אמות שאמרו חכמים באמה בת ששה, ובלבד שלא

רש"י

חלל סוכה תנן. עשרים אמות שהוזכרו בין במבוי בין בסוכה — אחללה קיימי: משפת כ' ולמטה. משמע שיהא עובי הקורה בתוך כ': הא קמ"ל. דשיעור שנתנו חכמים למטה מי' טפחים אחלל קאי, כשיעור שאמרו בכ' למעלה. והכי קאמר מתני' מניח את הקורה משפת כ' ולמעלה, וכן למטה אם בא לעשותו נמוך — מניחה משפת עשרה טפחים ולמעלה, דבפחות מעשרה לא הוי מבוי: אמת מבוי ואמת סוכה. אמות שהוזכרו במבוי ובסוכה — באמות קטנות שיערו. ואמות שהוזכרו בכלאים — באמות גדולות שיערו. ולקמן מפרש הי נינהו. ור"נ, מדקאמר הכא קטנות והכא גדולות — ש"מ: הכא חומרא והכא חומרא, דאי לא לחומרא — היכי מצי אמר הני גדולות והני קטנות? הא לא תנן בהו שיעורא: למאי הלכתא. משערים אלו שבמבוי בקטנות, דתיהוי חומרא: לגובהו. הנך עשרים שהוזכרו ליפסל בגובהו — מכי איכא כ' אמות קטנות פסלי אי מגבה לה טפי: ולפירצת מבוי. דקיימא לן בהאי פירקא פרצת מבוי ביו"ד אמות פסיל ליה, וקאמר רב נחמן דבעשר אמות קטנות מיפסיל: והא איכא. אמות שהוזכרו, במשך מבוי ד' אמות ואם ארכו פחות מד' אמות — פסיל ליה אביי לקמן בפירקין (ד' ה.), דאמר לקמן: היה פחות מיו"ד טפחים ובא להשלימו, עד כמה חוקק בו במשכו? רב יוסף אמר: ד' טפחים, אביי אמר: ד' אמות, דמשך מבוי בעינן ד' אמות. ובהני אמות אתיא מילתיה דרב נחמן לקולא, דמכשר ליה בד' אמות קטנות: כמ"ד. משך מבוי בארבעה טפחים סבירא ליה לרב נחמן, ולא הוזכרו אמות בשיעור משכו, ופלוגתא דאביי ורב יוסף היא: רוב אמות. הנזכרות במבוי קאמר רב נחמן דליהוי קטנות, ולא אכל אמות מבוי קאמר: לגובהה. שהוזכרו כ' אמות לפוסלה: ולדופן עקומה. דתנן (סוכה ד' יז.): בית שנפחת וסיכך ע"ג הפחת בסכך כשר, ותקרת העלייה נותרת סביב ומפסקת בין סכך כשר לדפנות, אם יש בין סכך כשר לדופן ד' אמות — פסולה, ולא אמרינן דופן עקומה פחות מד' אמות — כשירה, דאמרינן: חזינן ליה להאי סכך פסול כאילו הוא מן הדפנות שנעקמו למעלן ובאו עד סכך כשר, והרי אין כאן הפסק. וקא אתא רב נחמן למימר דבאמות קטנות משערינן ליה, ומיפסלא בעשרים טפחים — והיינו חומרא: והאיכא ארבע אמות. הנזכרות במשך סוכה, דאי מכשרת ליה בקטנות — איכא קולא. ורב נחמן כייל ואמר: כל אמות סוכה בקטנות, ואי אמר רב נחמן כרבי — הוי קולא: ואיבעית אימא. רב נחמן לעולם כרבי, והאי דאמר רב נחמן אמות סוכה בקטנות — לאו באמות דמשך סוכה, אלא בשאר אמות קאמר: לקרחת הכרם ולמחול הכרם. דכי משערת ליה בגדולות — חומרא היא: קרחת הכרם בית שמאי אומרים עשרים וארבע אמות. אם קרחתו עשרים וארבע אמות מותר לזרוע שם ואם פחות מכ"ד אמות אסור לזרוע שם, ולקמן מפרש מאי קרחת ומאי מחול: שחרב באמצעיתו. שהרי יש שם גפנים סביב הקרחה י"ו אמה על י"ו אמה, וכן, אם הלכה הקרחה על פני כל רוחב הכרם שאין שם גפנים אלא מב' לידי הקרחה בעינן י"ו — רוחב הקרחה: ואם לאו לא יביא זרע לשם. אפי' באמה האמצעית, דד' אמות שבצד הכרם מזה, וד' אמות שבצד זה אצל הכרם הוו עבודת הכרם. דתנן (כלאים פ"ו מ"א): כמה עבודת הכרם — (מלא) ד' אמות כמלא בקר וכלים. שהיו בוצרים אותה בשוורים ובעגלות, ובעת החרישה חורשים אותה בשוורים, הלכך כרם דמו. ואם נשארו ח' אמות בינתים, לבד אותן ד' לכל צד, דכי שדית פלגא להכא ופלגא להכא איכא ד' אמות מקום חשוב לכל חד — לא בטלי לגבי כרם, ומותר לזורען. ובציר מח' אמות שדי פלגא להכא ופלגא להכא — ליכא ד' אמות מקום חשוב, ובטיל לגבי כרם ולבית שמאי לא חשיב שדה פחות מח' אמות, הלכך כ"ד אמות בעינן: ד' לעבודת הכרם מכאן, וכנגדן מכאן, פשו י"ו, שדי ח' להכא וח' להכא — איכא שדה, ולא בטלי. אי נמי סבירא להו לבית שמאי עבודת הכרם ח' אמות: מחול הכרם בין כרם לגדר. דהיינו סביב כמו מחולות: יש שם י"ב אמות. לבית הלל נותן ד' אמות לעבודת הכרם, וזורע השאר: אין שם י"ב אמה לא יביא זרע לשם. דד' אמות דלהדי כרם — עבודת הכרם, וד' אמות דלהדי כותל, כיון דלא מיזדרעי משום דוושא דכותל — אפקורי מפקר להו. אמצעיות, אי איכא ד' אמות — חשיב, ואי לא — בטיל לגבי כרם[א]. והכא לא בעינן י"ו אמה, שאין האיסור אלא מצד אחד. והכי מפרש לה בפרק "כל גגות" (לקמן ד' צג.), וקא אמר רב נחמן דבאמות גדולות משערינן ולחומרא, ולא משתריא בקטנות: והא איכא רצופין. גפנים רצופין שסמוכה שורה לשורה יותר ממה שנתנו חכמים שיעור, שאם אין בין שורה לשורה ד' אמות אינו כרם. הואיל ואין לו כל צרכו להילוך עגלה, ומותר לזרוע בכולן לר' שמעון. ובהנך אמות אתיא מילתיה דרב נחמן לקולא, דאי איכא ד' אמות קטנות — אמרינן אינו כרם עד דאיכא גדולות: על פחות מד' אמות. שאין בין שורה לשורה ד' אמות — אינו כרם, ומותר לזרוע שם: ורואין את האמצעיים. הנטועין בתוך ריוח הראוי להיות בין שורה לשורה: כרבנן. סבירא ליה לרב נחמן: דאמרי כרם. הלכך לא הוזכרו אמות בכלאים לענין רצופים: הללו שוחקות. אמות כלאים מודדין בטפחים גדולים, ושל סוכה ומבוי עצבות מצומצמות לחומרא:
שלא

תוספות

חלל סוכה תנן. והא דאמר בסוכה (ד' ד.): והולין יורדין לתוך כ' — לאו דווקא, ואגב דנקט למעלה מכ' — נקט נמי בתוך כ', כלומר: בתוך הכשר כ': תניא דמסייע לך. אע"ג דהיכל באמת בת ששה, הכא ארבא קאי, דאית ליה לקמן דשל מבוי נמי באמת בת ששה. ואע"ג דהן עצבות — שמא של היכל נמי עצבות היו. א"נ: אפילו לאביי — לסימנא בעלמא נקט לענין אמות. אבל מ"מ מייתי, כמו שהיכל חללו עשרים באמות דידיה — הכי נמי מבוי באמות דידיה: כמאן דאמר בארבעה. פי': ומשהו יותר, דאין פתח פחות מד', ואי לא הוי משהו יותר — א"כ לא הוי ארכו יותר על רחבו, ואינו ניתר בלחי וקורה, כדאמרינן לקמן (ד' ה.). ואע"ג דאביי גופיה אית ליה לקמן (שם) דמשך מבוי בד' אמות — הכא אליבא דרב נחמן קאמר, וליה לא סבירא ליה: והא איכא רצופין דלקולא כו' כרבנן דאמרי כרם הוי. וא"ת: הא איכא הא דתנן במסכת כלאים (פ"ד מ"ד): גדר שנפרצה, עד י' אמות הרי הוא כפתח, יותר מכאן, כנגד הפרצה אסור! וי"ל: דרוב אמות קאמר: כרבנן דאמרי כרם הוי. אף על גב דרבנן מודים דלא הוי כרם היכא דכי נאמר רואין את האמצעים כאילו אינם — לא ישארו שתים כנגד שתים ואחת יוצאה זנב, אבל לא איירי אלא באמות שהוזכרו בפירוש, ולא באמות דמשתמע מכלל דבריהן: כל אמות שאמרו חכמים באמת בת ששה. לא איירי בהנך דכתיבי, כגון אמה יסוד ואמה סובב: ואלה

עין משפט נר מצוה

ט א מיי' פ"ז מהלכות כלאים הל' יא סמג לאוין רפ טוש"ע י"ד סי' רצו סעיף מב:

י ב מיי' שם הלכה יב וטוש"ע שם סעיף מג:

יא ג מיי' שם הלכה ג וטוש"ע שם סעיף לג:

יב ד מיי' פ"ז שם הל' יב ופי"ז מהל' שבת הל' לו סמג שם ועשין א טוש"ע א"ח סי' שמג סעיף א וטוש"ע י"ד סי' רצו סעיף סח:

רבינו חננאל

עלה רבה בר עולא אמר זה וזה פסול. רבא אמר זה וזה כשר. חלל סוכה וחלל מבוי תנן. תניא כרבא מבוי שהוא גבוהה מכ' אמה יותר מפתחו של היכל ימעט והא היכל חלליה עשרין הוא. ומותבינן עליה מהא דתניא כיצד ממעטו מניח קורה משפת כ' ולמטה ודחינן אימא מניח הקורה למעלה מכ' ואקשינן והא למטה קתני בהדיא ומשני קמ"ל דלמטה כלמעלה ומה למעלה למעלה מכ' אמות דנשאר חלל יתר מכ' אמה כך למטה למטה מעשרה טפחים שלא נשאר חלל שם י' טפחים פסולה. אמר אביי משמיה דרב נחמן אמת סוכה ואמת מבוי בת ה' טפחים. אמת כלאים בת ו' אמת מבוי למאי הלכתא לגובהה כ' אמה ולפירצת המבוי שהיא עד עשר אמות דגבהה דמבוי באמה בת ה' טפחים כ' אמה. הן ק' טפחים ואם הן ק' [טפחים] פסולה. ואילו היתה אמה בת ו' אינה פסולה עד ק"כ טפחים הנה לחומרא. וכן בפירצה כדבעינן למימר לקמן אם נשתייר בו פס ארבעה מתיר פרצה עד עשר. פי' אם הפירצה עד נ' טפחים שהן י' אמות (פסולה) מתירה ואם היא יתר מזה אפילו טפח (אמר) [אחד] פסלה (מתירה) [מחתירה] הנה גם זה לחומרא. ואקשינן והא [איכא] משכא פי' משכא רוחב כדבעינן למימר לקמן. משך החקיקה במבוי שהוא פחות מי' טפחים גובהו וחקק בו והשלימו לי' טפחים רוחב זה שחקק בכמה. אביי אמר בד' אמות הוה הכשר כל המבוי בחקיקת כ' טפחים ואילו היה באמה בת ו' טפחים אינו כשר עד שיהיו בחקיקתו כ"ד טפחים שהן ד' אמות בת ו' טפחים וכיון שהכשרת במבוי בכ' טפחים נמצא זה קולא ופרכינן רב נחמן דאמר כרב יוסף דסבר משך חקיקתו בד' טפחים ואין שם מדת אמה איבעית אימא לעולם כאביי ומאי אמות רוב אמות של מבוי באמה בת ו' טפחים אמה כלאים למאי הלכתא לקרחת הכרם ולמחול הכרם דתנן בכלאים בתחלת פרק רביעי בכרם שחרב באמצעיתו צריך להיות המקום החרב שאין בו גפנים י"ו אמה באמה בת ו' טפחים שהן צ"ו טפחים אם הוא פחות מזה השיעור אסור לזרוע באותו המקום שחרב. שאע"ג שאין בו גפנים מכלל הכרם הוא חשוב ולא תזרע כרמך כלאים

מסורת הש"ס

[נ"ל הוא] [לקמן ה.] [שם] סוכה ג. לקמן נג. כלאים פ"ד מ"א כלאים פ"ה מ"ב ב"ב לז: פג. קב: [פי' האלכסונות סמוכות מרווחות כדרך השוחק שפוסק שפתיו והעוצב מדביקן ערוך ערך סחק]

הגהות הב"ח

(א) רש"י ד"ה אין שם כו' אמה וכו' בטיל לגבי כרם (והכא לא). תא"מ ונ"ב ס"א והא דלא:

גליון הש"ס

גמ' לקרחת הכרם. ק"ל אמאי לא לקרחת ולעבודת הכרם שהוא נ"ל: רש"י ד"ה ולפירצת מבוי כו' בי' אמות פסל וכו' דבי' אמות קטנות. ליכנה קלילה הוא לה בי' אמות לא הוי פרצה רק ביותר מעשר: תום' ד"ה כמאן וכו'. דאין פתח פחות מד'. לקמן י"ב ע"א:

רב נסים גאון

אמת המבוי ואמת סוכה בת חמשה. בסדר טהרות במסכת כלים שנינו [בפ'] כל כלי בעלי בתים ב' אמות היו בשושן הבירה אחת על קרן מזרחית צפונית ואחת על קרן מזרחית דרומית שעל קרן מזרחית צפונית היתה יתירה על של משה חצי אצבע ושל קרן דרומית מזרחית היתה יתירה עליה חצי אצבע נמצאת יתירה על של משה אצבע ולמה אמרו אחת גדולה ואחת קטנה אלא שהאומנין נוטלין בקטנה וחוזרין בגדולה כדי שלא יבואו לידי מעילה ר"מ אומר כל האמות היו בבינוניות חוץ ממזבח הזהב והקרן והסובב והיסוד ר' יהודה אומר אמת הבנין ו' טפחים ושל כלים ה' ובתוספתא גרסי בפ' כלי עור [בכ"מ פ"ט דכלים] אצבע מארבע אצבעות בטפח טפח מו' טפחים באמה זרת האמורה בתורה חצי אמה של ו' טפחים ואי זו היא אמה בינונית זו אמה של ו' טפחים *) רבי מאיר אומר כל מדות שאמרו חכמים בכרם כגון חרבן הכרם ומחול הכרם ופיסקי ערים ומותר אפיפירות כולן באמה בת ו' טפחים חוץ ממזבח הזהב והקרן והסובב והיסוד שהן באמה בת ה' טפחים שנאמר (יחזקאל מג) אלה מדות המזבח שהיו למזבח ב' מדות יכול יהו כולן באמה של ה' טפחים תלמוד לומר (שם) באמות אמה אמה וטופח באמה שהיא יתירה על של חברתה טפח ובמס' מנחות בפ' שתי הלחם (דף צח) אמרו וכמה אמה בינונית אמר ר' יוחנן ו' טפחים ובפרק התכלת (שם דף מא) אמר רב פפא טפח דאורייתא ו' בקטנה ה' ותילתא בגדולה ד' בגודל ובמס' בכורות בפ' כל אלו מומין (דף לט) גרסי תאנא אצבע שאמרו אחת מארבע בטפח שלכל אדם ושאמרו [במס' כלים פי"ז] ב' אמות היו בשושן [הבירה] לזה נתכוונו לצורת שושן הבירה שהיתה במקדש על שער מזרחית כדתנן במדות בפרק א' שער המזרחי ועליה שושן הבירה צורה ובפ' שתי הלחם (דף צח) פירשו טעמא דמילתא דאמר מאי [טעמא] רב חסדא ורב יצחק בן אבדימי חד אמר כדי שידעו מהיכן באו וחד אמר כדי שתהא אימת מלכות עליהם ומכל הראיות שהזכרנו תבין שיעור הטפח ושיעור האמה הגדולה והבינונית

*) [שם בתוספתא הגי' אמה של ה' טפחים אבל פשוט דצ"ל שם של ו' כמו שגרס רבינו וכ"ה במנחות ד' צ"ח].

תורה אור

שלא יהו מכוונות. בשלמא לרבא – כי היכי דליהויין הללו שוחקות והללו עצבות. אלא לאביי קשיא! אמר לך אביי: אימא: "אמת כלאים באמה בת ששה". והא מדקתני סיפא "רשב"ג אומר: כל אמות שאמרו חכמים בכלאים באמה בת ששה, ובלבד שלא יהו מצומצמות" מכלל דתנא קמא כל אמות קאמר! אמר לך אביי: ולאו מי איכא רשב"ג דקאי כוותי? אנא דאמרי כרשב"ג. לאביי ודאי תנאי היא. לרבא מי לימא תנאי היא? אמר לך רבא: רשב"ג הא אתא לאשמועינן: אמת כלאים לא יצמצם. ולימא "אמת כלאים לא יצמצם", באמה בת ששה למעוטי מאי? לאו למעוטי אמת סוכה ואמת מבוי?! לא, למעוטי [א]אמה יסוד ואמה סובב. דכתיב: (יחזקאל מג) °"ואלה מדות המזבח באמות אמה אמה וטפח וחיק האמה ואמה רחב וגבולה אל שפתה סביב זרת האחד וזה גב המזבח". *"חיק האמה" – זה יסוד, "ואמה רחב" – זה סובב, "וגבולה אל שפתה סביב" – אלו הקרנות, "וזה גב המזבח" – זה מזבח הזהב. § *אמר ר' חייא בר אשי אמר רב: [ב]שיעורין חציצין ומחיצין הלכה למשה מסיני. שיעורין? דאורייתא הוא! דכתיב: (דברים ח) °"ארץ חטה ושעורה וגו'" *ואמר רב חנן: כל הפסוק הזה לשיעורין נאמר. חטה – לכדתנן: *[ג]הנכנס לבית המנוגע, וכליו על כתיפיו, *וסנדליו וטבעותיו בידיו – הוא והם טמאין מיד. [ד]היה לבוש כליו, וסנדליו ברגליו, וטבעותיו באצבעותיו – הוא טמא מיד, והן טהורין עד שישהא בכדי אכילת פרס, פת חיטין ולא פת שעורין, מיסב ואוכל בליפתן. שעורה – *דתנן: [ה]עצם כשעורה מטמא במגע ובמשא, ואינו מטמא באהל. גפן – כדי [ו]רביעית יין לנזיר. תאנה

רש"י

שלא יהו מכוונות. כדמפרש ואזיל: שיהו אמות כלאים שוחקות, ושל מבוי וסוכה עצבות: אלא לאביי קשיא. הא דקתני כל אמות באמה בת ששה: אימא אמת כלאים באמה בת ששה. והכי קאמר: כל אמות שאמרו בכלאים – באמה בת ששה, ובלבד שלא יהו מכוונות – מצומצמות אלא גדולות, בטפחים שוחקות: לאביי ודאי תנאי היא. דלא מצי לאוקמי לרבנן כוותיה דהא כל אמות קאמרי: לרבא מי לימא תנאי היא. מי אמרינן רבן שמעון בן גמליאל פליג עליה, למימר אמת כלאים באמה בת ששה. אבל שאר אמות, כגון סוכה ומבוי – באמה בת חמשה. או דילמא: פרושי קא מפרש רבן שמעון בן גמליאל למילתייהו דרבנן, דאמרי: ובלבד שלא יהו מכוונות, דיש מהן שוחקות ויש מהן עצבות, ולא פירשו איזה מהן שוחקות ואיזה מהן עצבות. ואתא איהו לפרושי: דהנך דכלאים ליהוו שוחקות, כדקתני: ובלבד שלא יהו מצומצמות. ולהכי אדכר כלאים, ולא למעוטי שאר אמות להיות בנות חמשה, אלא למעוטינהו דלא ליהוו שוחקות: הא אתא לאשמועינן אמת כלאים לא יצמצם. ולפרושי מילתיה דתנא קמא הוא דאתא ולא למעוטי שאר אמות מבת ששה: לא למעוטי אמה יסוד ואמה סובב. דלאו בנות ששה הן: באמות אמה אמה וטופח. באמות קטנות בת חמשה שיש באמה בת ו' בינונית אמה וטפח מאלו: חיק האמה. נמדד באמות קטנות, וכן אמה רוחב, וכן גבולו על שפתו זרת האחד, וזה גב המזבח – כולן באמות קטנות הללו: חיק האמה זה יסוד. "חיק" – על שם שהוא חיקויו ותיקונו של מזבח מלמטה: אלו הקרנות. שהן אמה על אמה. והאי דכתיב זרת האחד – מאמצעית רחבו של קרן מודד זרת, שהוא חצי אמה לכל רוח, דהוי אמה על אמה: וזה גב המזבח. כלומר: באמה קטנה זו נמדד האמה של מזבח הזהב, דכתיב ביה "אמה ארכו ואמה רחבו" (שמות ל) ובמסכת מנחות בפרק "שתי הלחם" (ד' נז:) מפרש ליה להאי קרא דאמה יסוד דקאמרי בקטנה – לאו ברוחב כניסת היסוד, אלא בגובה עלייתו. דאמר מר: עלה אמה וכנס אמה – זהו יסוד. אבל רוחב הכניסה באמה בת ששה. ואמה סובב – כניסה דילה באמה קטנה, ולא ה' אמות של עליית גובהה באמה קטנה. כדתנן: עלה חמש וכנס אמה – זה הסובב. וקרנות לא שנא גובהן ולא שנא רוחבן – באמה קטנה: הג"ה. כאשר מפורש בקונט' שמע רבינו מר' יעקב בר יקר, ועתה חזר בו, דקשיא ליה: מה שתרגם יונתן "אמה אמה וטפח" – אמתא דהיא אמתא ופשך, ונמלא דבאמה גדולה מיירי. ועוד: אם כדברי הזקן – לא היה לו לכתוב "וחיק" כי אם "חיק האמה". ופירש[א] לנו רבינו הכי: למעלה הזכיר מדות המזבח "והאריאל שתים עשרה אמה" ושאר מדותיו, ועתה כך אמר הכתוב: אלה מדות המזבח שאמרתי לך – הכל נמדדו באמה שהיא אמה וטפח. וחיק, שהיא יסוד – אינו נמדד אלא באמה שהיא אמה קטנה, ולא באמה שהיא אמה וטפח. ועתה דברי יונתן בן עוזיאל קיימין. כך שמעתי, ועיקר. ע"כ הג"ה: שיעורין. ששנו חכמים לכל דבר, כגון: כזית דם חלב פיגול ונותר, וכזית מן המת שמטמא באהל, ושאר שיעורין דמפרש לקמן: חציצין. חציצה הפוסלת בטבילה: ומחיצין. הלכות מחיצה שתהא גבוהה עשרה, וכן שאר הילכותיה – הלכה למשה מסיני: לשיעורין נאמר. וכל אלו משערין בהן דברים אחרים: כליו על כתיפיו וסנדליו וטבעותיו בידיו. שאינן מלובשין בו דרך מלבוש, דומיא דכליו על כתפיו: הוא והן טמאין מיד. שאף הן באין אל הבית, וכתיב "והבא אל הבית" (ויקרא יד): היה לבוש כליו. וכן כולם דרך לבישתן קרויין בגדיו וטפלין אליו. וכתיב (שם) "והאוכל בבית יכבס את בגדיו" ודרשינן בתורת כהנים מקרא, דהאי אוכל – לאו אכילה ממש הוא, אלא שישהא כדי שיעור אכילה. ובביאה בלא שהייה – אינו מטמא בגדים: פרס. ד' ביצים הן מזון סעודה בינונית, "פרס" – לשון פרוסה, ששיערוהו בחצי ככר האמור בעירוב, דבעינן מזון ב' סעודות. ותנן התם: חלייה לבית המנוגע, בפרק "כיצד" (לקמן ד' פב:): פת חיטין. אין שוהה בה כפת שעורין: מיסב. שהייה זו בהסיבה שיערוהו ולא בנאכלת בעמידה והולך ובא, שהוא שוהה באכילתו יותר: ואוכלה בליפתן. שנאכלת מהר: ואינו מטמא באהל. שום עצם בלא בשר, עד שיהא שם שדרה שלימה, או גולגולת, או רוב בנינו – ב' שוקיים וירך אחת, או רוב מניינו – קכ"ה אברים: רביעית יין לנזיר. לחייבו מלקות: גרוגרת

תוספות

ואלה מדות המזבח באמות אמה אמה וטופח. פי' בקונט': באמות קטנות, שיש באמה בינונית אמה וטפח מאלו. וקשה: דלא הוה ליה למיכתב "וחיק" בוי"ו, כיון דקאי(א) אאמות! ונראה כמו שפירש"י בפירוש יחזקאל, דפירש "באמות אמה" אמות גדולות, שיהא אמה וטופח בשל אמה בת ה'. וכן תרגם יונתן: באמתא דהיא אמתא ופשך. וקאי אשאר אמות המזבח, וחיק(ב) האמות הוו קטנות: גפן כדי רביעית יין לנזיר. פרש"י: לחייבו מלקות. וקשה דלא הוה דומיא דאחריני, דמשערינן בהו מילי אחריני! ונראה כפרש"י דסוכה (ד' ו. *), דפירש שאם אכל ענבים וחרצנים ולולבים מגפן – איכא למ"ד ברביעית. וזה ביין משערינן, שיקח כוס מלא יין ויטיל בו עלין ולולבין כשיעור מה שאכל, ואם יצא רביעית – חייב. ואם היה בא לשער במים היה יוצא רביעית בפחות, שאין נגדשין על שפת הכלי כמו יין. וכה"ג תניא בתוספתא: *כיצד יעשה? מביא כוס מלא יין, ומביא זית אגורי, ונותן לתוכו ושופע, אם שתה כיוצא בו – חייב, ואם לאו – פטור, דברי ר' עקיבא. רבי אלעזר בן עזריה אומר: אינו חייב עד שישתה רביעית יין. ואתיא לשמעתין כרבי אלעזר בן עזריה. ובפ' "ג' מינין" (נזיר ד' לד.) תנן: אינו חייב עד שיאכל ענבים כזית. משנה ראשונה אמרו: עד שישתה רביעית יין. רבי עקיבא אומר: אפי' נזיר ששרה פתו ביין, ויש בו כדי לצרף כזית – חייב. וקאמר בגמ': ת"ק מדמי להו אסורי נזיר אכילה לשתיה. פירוש: ת"ק, היינו משנה ראשונה – מדמה אכילה לשתיה, ובעי באכילת עלין ולולבין נמי רביעית. ונקט במתניתין שתייה – משום דאכילה מינה ילפינן. וטעמא משום דכתיב "לא ישתה" תרי זימני. ולא חש לפרש *)שם טעמא(ג) דר' עקיבא, כיון דאמר קרא "וענבים לחים ויבשים לא יאכל", מה אכילה בכזית – אף כל בכזית. והא דנקט אכילה במשנה אחרונה – משום דשתיה ילפינן מינה, וכל חד נקט מידי דיליף מיניה. וא"ת: ומ"מ, מאי נפקא מינה לשער ביין, והלא כלי המחזיק רביעית הוא בילה ומחלה, ומה שמפיל בילה ומחלה בין יין ובין מים, אם שיעור עלין ולולבין שאכל יפילו כל כך – חייב! וי"ל: דנפקא מינה אם יש כלי שמחזיק מה שמפיל בילה ומחלה מן היין, שלא ישער עלין ולולבין בכוס מלא מים עד שיתמלא הכלי – שזה הכלי אינו מחזיק בילה ומחלה מן המים, שאינן עבין כמו יין, ונמלא שאין הכלי זה רביעית. ודוחק. הגה"ה. וקשה: דשמעתין אתיא דלא כמשנה אחרונה. ועוד: דבספרים ישנים מלא ר"ת דגרסינן בנזיר (ד' לח:): תנא קמא לא מדמי להו לכל איסורי נזיר לאכילה. משמע להך גירסא דבאכילה לא פליגי, אלא הוי לכולי עלמא בכזית. וכן משמע בירושלמי דלא פליגי באכילה. דקאמר: משנה ראשונה

*) ולא חש לפרש אלא טעמא דר"ע. כצ"ל מהרש"א

מסורת הש"ס

מנחות נז:

סוכה ה: יומא פ.

ברכות מח: סוכה ה:

נגעים פי"ג מ"ט חולין עא: ת"כ פ' מצורע

אהלות פ"ב מ"ג

עין משפט נר מצוה

יג א מיי' פ"ב מהלכות בית הבחירה הל' ו:

יד ב מיי' פי"ד מהלכות מאכלות אסורות הלכה ב:

טו ג מיי' פט"ז מהל' טומאת צרעת הל' ז סמג עשין רלט:

טז ד שם הלכה ו:

יז ה מיי' פ"ג מהלכות טומאת מת הלכה ב סמג עשין רלח:

יח ו מיי' פ"ה מהלכות נזירות הלכה ב סמג לאוין רנ:

[וכפירש"י דברכות מח.]

[דנזירות פ"ז]

וסנדליו בידיו וטבעותיו בקומצו כ"ה בס"א

הגהות הב"ח

(א) תוס' ד"ה ואלה וכו' כיון דקאי אבאמות ונראה: (ב) בא"ד וחיק האמה הוו קטנות: (ג) ד"ה גפן וכו' ולא חש לפרש שם טעמא ורבי עקיבא. נ"ב ע"ש בדף ל"ח ע"ב:

הגהות הגר"א

[א] רש"י ד"ה הג"ה כאשר מפורש בקונט' וכו' כי אם חיק האמה ופי' כו'. נ"ב וג"ז ק' להו לאינו נזכר וחיק האמה באמה נמדד. אבל בתוספתא מפרש ר"מ בהדיא דכתיב אמה אמה כו' ב' מיני אמות א' אמה וא' באמה וטפח ומפר' והולך כו' והראל כו':

גליון הש"ס

רש"י ד"ה אלו הקרנות וכו' זרת שהוא חצי אמה. עי' לקמן דף כא ע"א ובתוס' שם ד"ה א' מג:

רבינו חננאל

קרינא ביה. וכן במחול הכרם [אם] אין בין גדר לכרם מקום מופנה מן הגפנים י"ב אמה באמה בת ו' טפחים אסור לזרוע באותו מקום הנה זה כולו לחומרא. הא איכא רצופין. פי' עקרי גפנים קרובין זה לזה דהוא לקולא דתנן בכלאים פ"א כרם הנטוע על פחות מד' אמות. פי' אם אין בין גפן לגפן ד' אמות שהן כ"ד טפחים אלא פחות מזה השיעור [אינו] כרם והזורע בו אינו עובר משום לא תזרע כרמך כלאים דברי ר"ש והנה כיון שיש בו כ' טפחים נמצאו בו ד' אמות באמה בת ה' טפחים ואתה מתירו לזרוע בו הנה לקולא. ופריק רב נחמן אלו דברי ר' שמעון הן ואנא דאמרי כרבנן דפליגי עליה ואמרי (הנה) [דהוי] זה כרם איבעית אימא אפי' כר' שמעון מאי אמות כלאים דקאמר אביי רוב אמות של כלאים באמה בת ו' טפחים היכא דאיכא לחומרא. אבל הני דרצופין באמה בת ה' טפחים. רבא אמר רב נחמן אמת סוכה ואמת מבוי נמי בת ו' הן. ומיהו טפחים עציבות. פי' האצבעות דחוקות זו עם זו. ושל כלאים. האצבעות שוחקות פי' מרווחות כדרך השוחק שפוסק שפתיו והעצב (וספיקם) [מדביקן]. ומותבינן (במבוי) *) כל אמות שאמרו באמה בת ו' טפחים ובלבד שלא יהו מכוונות. כלומר לא יהיו עציבות שוחקות ולא השוחקות עציבות כרבא אלא לאביי קשיא. ופריק אביי אנא דאמרי כרשב"ג ועמדה לאביי בתנאי. ורבא אמר לך כולי עלמא באמה בת ו' טפחים אית להו ולא פליגי אלא בצמצום. ת"ק סבר יצמצם **) אלא [הא] דקתני אמת כלאים בת ו' טפחים למעטי אמת יסוד ואמת סובב דכתיב ואלה מדות המזבח באמות אמה אמה וטופח וחיק האמה ואמה רוחב וגו' חיק האמה זה יסוד אמה [רוחב] זה סובב וזה מפורש במנחות באר היטב פרק שתי הלחם גלושות: אמר (רבה אמר) [ר' חייא] בר אשי אמר רב שיעורין חציצין ומחיצות הל"מ. שיעורין דאורייתא נינהו ארץ חטה ושעורה וגו' ואמר רבי יוחנן פסוק זה כולו לשיעורין נאמר חטה דתנן הנכנס לבית המנוגע וכליו על כו' פירשנוהו במסכת סוכה:

*) נראה דל"ל דמותבינן לאביי. **) נראה דחסר כאן וצ"ל ורשב"ג סבר דאמת כלאים לא יצמצם.

רב נסים גאון

והבינונית והקטנה ותבין מה שפירשו בפסוק שהביאו ראיה ממנו ואלה מדות המזבח וכי אמה וטפח פירוש שתהא יתירה על חברתה טפח: **עד** שישהה בכדי אכילת פרס. תמצא עיקר דיליה בתורת כהנים (ויקרא יד) והאוכל בבית אין לי אלא אוכל אם *) סופנו לרבות את האוכל אע"פ שאינו שוכב מה תלמוד לומר האוכל והשוכב אלא ליתן שיעור לאוכל כדי שיאכל שוכב וכמה הוא שיעור אכילת פרס פת חטים ולא

*) בתו"כ לפנינו הגי' אלא ליתן שיעור לשוכב כדי שיאכל וע"ש מה שדחקו הרא"ש והק"א בזה אבל גי' רבינו נכונה יותר ומזה למדו חז"ל דמשערין האכילה כאוכל בהסיבה.

תְּאֵנָה – [א]כִּגְרוֹגֶרֶת לְהוֹצָאַת שַׁבָּת, רִמּוֹן – כִּדְתְנַן: *[ב]כָּל כְּלֵי בַעֲלֵי בָתִּים שִׁיעוּרָן כְּרִימּוֹנִים. °"אֶרֶץ זֵית שֶׁמֶן (*וּדְבָשׁ)" אֶרֶץ שֶׁכָּל שִׁיעוּרֶיהָ כַּזֵּיתִים. "כָּל שִׁיעוּרֶיהָ" ס"ד?! וְהָאִיכָּא הָנֵי דַּאֲמָרַן! אֶלָּא אֵימָא: אֶרֶץ שֶׁרוֹב שִׁיעוּרֶיהָ כַּזֵּיתִים. דְּבָשׁ – [ג]כְּכוֹתֶבֶת הַגַּסָּה לְיוֹם הַכִּיפּוּרִים. וְתִיסְבְּרָא, שִׁיעוּרִין מִיכְתַּב כְּתִיבִי?! אֶלָּא: *הִלְכְתָא נִינְהוּ, וְאַסְמְכִינְהוּ רַבָּנַן אַקְּרָאֵי. חֲצִיצִין – דְּאוֹרָיְיתָא נִינְהוּ! דִּכְתִיב: *°"וְרָחַץ אֶת כָּל בְּשָׂרוֹ (בַּמַּיִם)" *[ד]– שֶׁלֹּא יְהֵא דָּבָר חוֹצֵץ בֵּין בְּשָׂרוֹ לַמַּיִם. 'בַּמַּיִם' – בְּמֵי מִקְוֶה, 'כָּל בְּשָׂרוֹ' – מַיִם [ה]שֶׁכָּל גּוּפוֹ עוֹלֶה בָּהֶן. וְכַמָּה הֵן – אַמָּה עַל אַמָּה בְּרוּם ג' אַמּוֹת. וְשִׁיעֲרוּ חֲכָמִים מֵי מִקְוֶה מ' סְאָה. כִּי אִיצְטְרִיךְ הִילְכְתָא – לִשְׂעָרוֹ, *וְכִדְרַבָּה בַּר רַב הוּנָא. דְּאָמַר רַבָּה בַּר רַב הוּנָא: [ו]נִימָא אַחַת קְשׁוּרָה – חוֹצֶצֶת, שָׁלֹשׁ – אֵינָן חוֹצְצוֹת, שְׁתַּיִם – אֵינִי יוֹדֵעַ. שְׂעָרוֹ נַמִי דְּאוֹרָיְיתָא הוּא, *דְּתַנְיָא: "וְרָחַץ אֶת כָּל בְּשָׂרוֹ" – אֶת הַטָּפֵל לִבְשָׂרוֹ, *וְזֶהוּ שֵׂעָר! כִּי אֲתַאי הִילְכְתָא – לְרוּבּוֹ וּלְמִיעוּטוֹ, וּלְמַקְפִּיד וּלְשֶׁאֵין מַקְפִּיד, וּכְדְר' יִצְחָק. *דְּאָמַר ר' יִצְחָק: [ז]דְּבַר תּוֹרָה, רוּבּוֹ וּמַקְפִּיד עָלָיו – חוֹצֵץ, וְשֶׁאֵינוֹ מַקְפִּיד עָלָיו – אֵינוֹ חוֹצֵץ. וְגָזְרוּ עַל רוּבּוֹ שֶׁאֵינוֹ מַקְפִּיד מִשּׁוּם רוּבּוֹ הַמַּקְפִּיד, וְעַל מִיעוּטוֹ הַמַּקְפִּיד מִשּׁוּם רוּבּוֹ הַמַּקְפִּיד. וְלִיגְזוֹר נַמִי עַל מִיעוּטוֹ שֶׁאֵינוֹ מַקְפִּיד מִשּׁוּם מִיעוּטוֹ הַמַּקְפִּיד, אִי נַמִי מִשּׁוּם רוּבּוֹ שֶׁאֵינוֹ מַקְפִּיד! *הִיא גּוּפָהּ גְּזֵירָה, וַאֲנַן נֵיקוּם וְנִיגְזוֹר גְּזֵירָה לִגְזֵירָה?! 'מְחִיצוֹת' – דְּאוֹרָיְיתָא נִינְהוּ, דְּאָמַר מָר: *אָרוֹן תִּשְׁעָה, וְכַפּוֹרֶת טֶפַח – הֲרֵי כָּאן עֲשָׂרָה! לָא צְרִיכָא,(א) *לְר' יְהוּדָה, דְּאָמַר: אַמַּת בִּנְיָן בְּאַמָּה בַּת שִׁשָּׁה, אַמַּת כֵּלִים בְּאַמָּה בַּת חֲמִשָּׁה. וּלְר"מ, דְּאָמַר: כָּל הָאַמּוֹת הָיוּ בְּבֵינוֹנִית, מַאי אִיכָּא לְמֵימַר? לְר' מֵאִיר, כִּי אֲתַאי הִילְכְתָא – לְגוֹד וּלְלָבוּד וּלְדוֹפֶן עֲקוּמָּה.§ הָיָה גָּבוֹהַּ מֵעֶשְׂרִים אַמָּה וּבָא לְמַעֲטוֹ כַּמָּה מְמַעֵט. "כַּמָּה מְמַעֵט"?! כַּמָּה דִּצְרִיךְ לֵיהּ! אֶלָּא: רָחְבּוֹ בְּכַמָּה? [ח]רַב יוֹסֵף אָמַר: טֶפַח. אַבַּיֵי אָמַר: אַרְבָּעָה. לֵימָא בְּהָא קָא מִיפַּלְגִי, דְּמַאן דְּאָמַר: טֶפַח, קָסָבַר: מוּתָּר לְהִשְׁתַּמֵּשׁ תַּחַת הַקּוֹרָה. וּמ"ד

[דברים ח] [ויקרא טו]

תורה אור

גְּרוֹגֶרֶת. הִיא תְּאֵנָה יְבֵשָׁה, וּבָהּ שִׁיעֲרוּ כָּל אוֹכֶל אָדָם לְעִנְיַן הוֹצָאַת שַׁבָּת, דִּתְנַן (שבת ד' עו:): הַמּוֹצִיא אוֹכָלִין כִּגְרוֹגֶרֶת: בַּעַל הַבַּיִת חָס עַל כֵּלָיו, וְאִם נִיקַּב כְּמוֹצִיא זַיִת – מַצְנִיעוֹ לָאֱגוֹזִים, כֶּאֱגוֹז – מַצְנִיעוֹ לְרִמּוֹנִים. לְפִיכָךְ, אִם נִיטְמָא וְנִיקַּב – עֲדַיִין טָמֵא עַד שֶׁיִּנָּקֵב כְּמוֹצִיא רִמּוֹן. וְהַיְינוּ שִׁיעוּרָן כְּרִמּוֹנִים. אֲבָל כְּלִי אוּמָּן הָעוֹמֵד לִימָּכֵר – טָהוֹר בְּנֶקֶב קָטָן: רוֹב שִׁיעוּרֶיהָ כַּזֵּיתִים. אֲכִילַת חֵלֶב וְדָם וְנוֹתָר וּפִיגּוּל וְטָמֵא וּנְבֵילָה וּבְהֵמָה טְמֵאָה וּבְשַׂר הַמֵּת לְהַאֲהִיל, וּמַגַּע נְבֵילוֹת: כָּל דְּבַשׁ הָאָמוּר בַּתּוֹרָה דְּבַשׁ תְּמָרִים וּכְדַאֲמַר הָתָם (בכורים פ"א מ"ג): אֵין מְבִיאִין בִּכּוּרִים כִּי אִם מִז' הַמִּינִין, וְלֹא מִתְּמָרִים שֶׁבֶּהָרִים וְלֹא מִפֵּירוֹת שֶׁבָּעֲמָקִים. אַלְמָא: פְּשִׁיטָא לֵיהּ לְתַנָּא דִּתְמָרִים מִז' הַמִּינִין, דְּהַיְינוּ דְּבַשׁ: בְּמַיִם בְּמֵי מִקְוֶה. הַמְכוּנָּסִין מַשְׁמַע. וְאַע"ג דְּלָאו חַיִּים, מִדְּלָא כְּתִיב חַיִּים: כָּל בְּשָׂרוֹ. מַשְׁמַע כָּל בְּשָׂרוֹ כְּאֶחָד: לִשְׂעָרוֹ. שֶׁתִּפְסוֹל בּוֹ חֲצִיצָה: וּכְדְרַבָּה. דְּאָמַר רַבָּה: חֲצִיצָה פּוֹסֶלֶת בְּשֵׂיעָר: נִימָא אַחַת קְשׁוּרָה חוֹצֶצֶת. דְּמָצֵי לְהַדּוּקָהּ שַׁפִּיר וְאֵין הַמַּיִם נִכְנָסִין בַּקֶּשֶׁר: שָׁלֹשׁ אֵינָן חוֹצְצוֹת. דְּלָא מִיהַדְקִי שַׁפִּיר וְעָיְילִי בְּהוּ מַיִם: דְּבַר תּוֹרָה. הֲלָכָה לְמֹשֶׁה מִסִּינַי בַּתּוֹרָה שֶׁבְּעַל פֶּה: רוּבּוֹ. רוֹב שְׂעָרוֹ. שֶׁאִם יֵשׁ בּוֹ דָּבָר הַחוֹצֵץ, כְּגוֹן דָּם יָבֵשׁ וּדְיוֹ וְטִיט יָבֵשׁ וְזֶפֶת יָבֵשׁ, אוֹ שֶׁקָּשׁוּר רוּבּוֹ אַחַת אַחַת: וּמַקְפִּיד עָלָיו. שֶׁמִּצְטַעֵר עַל לִיכְלוּךְ זֶה שֶׁבְּרֹאשׁוֹ: וְשֶׁאֵינוֹ מַקְפִּיד עָלָיו. הָוֵי כְּגוּפוֹ, וְאַע"ג דְּהָוֵי בְּרוּבּוֹ – לָא חָיֵיץ: וְגָזְרוּ עַל רוּבּוֹ שֶׁאֵינוֹ מַקְפִּיד. הוֹאִיל וְהָוֵי רוֹב, וְדָמֵי בְּמִקְצָת לַחֲצִיצָה דְּאוֹרַיְיתָא: וְעַל מִיעוּטוֹ הַמַּקְפִּיד. הוֹאִיל וְדָמֵי לֵיהּ בְּהַקְפָּדָה. וְגָזְרוּ – לָאו הֲלָכָה לְמֹשֶׁה מִסִּינַי הוּא, אֶלָּא גְּזֵירָה מִדְּרַבָּנַן. וְרוּבּוֹ הַמַּקְפִּיד לְחוּדֵיהּ הוּא דַּהֲוָה הֲלָכָה לְמֹשֶׁה מִסִּינַי: וְלִיגְזוֹר נַמִי עַל מִיעוּטוֹ שֶׁאֵינוֹ מַקְפִּיד עָלָיו מִשּׁוּם מִיעוּטוֹ הַמַּקְפִּיד. דְּדָמוּ לַהֲדָדֵי, דְּהַאי מִיעוּט וְהַאי מִיעוּט: אִי נַמִי. נִיגְזוֹר בּוֹ מִשּׁוּם רוּבּוֹ שֶׁאֵינוֹ מַקְפִּיד, דְּדָמֵי לַהֲדָדֵי – דְּהַאי אֵינוֹ מַקְפִּיד וְהַאי אֵינוֹ מַקְפִּיד: הִיא גּוּפָהּ גְּזֵירָה. מִשּׁוּם רוּבּוֹ הַמַּקְפִּיד כְּדַאֲמַר: אָרוֹן תִּשְׁעָה וְכַפּוֹרֶת טֶפַח. אָרוֹן גׇּבְהוֹ תִּשְׁעָה טְפָחִים, דִּכְתִיב (שמות כה) "וְאַמָּה וָחֵצִי קוֹמָתוֹ", וְכַפּוֹרֶת טֶפַח – הֲרֵי עֲשָׂרָה. וּכְתִיב "וְדִבַּרְתִּי אִתְּךָ מֵעַל הַכַּפּוֹרֶת", וְתַנְיָא בְּפ"ק דְּסוּכָּה (ד' ה.), ר' יוֹסֵי אוֹמֵר: לְעוֹלָם לֹא יָרְדָה שְׁכִינָה לְמַטָּה מֵעֲשָׂרָה, דִּכְתִיב "הַשָּׁמַיִם שָׁמַיִם לַה' וְהָאָרֶץ נָתַן לִבְנֵי אָדָם". וּלְמַטָּה מֵעֲשָׂרָה טְפָחִים חָשֵׁיב אֶרֶץ, דִּכְתִיב: "וְדִבַּרְתִּי אִתְּךָ מֵעַל הַכַּפּוֹרֶת", אַלְמָא: עֲשָׂרָה הָוֵי מְחִיצָּה, דִּלְמַעְלָה מֵעֲשָׂרָה לָא חָשֵׁיב לֵיהּ רְשׁוּת תַּחְתִּית, אֶלָּא רְשׁוּתָא אַחֲרִיתִי: אַמַּת בִּנְיָן. כְּגוֹן אַמּוֹת הַקְּרָשִׁים וְהַיְרִיעוֹת: אַמַּת כֵּלִים. כְּגוֹן אַמּוֹת הָאָרוֹן וְהַמִּזְבְּחוֹת וְהַשֻּׁלְחָן: בְּאַמָּה בַּת חֲמִשָּׁה. דְּהַשְׁתָּא לָא נָפְקָא לֵיהּ מֵאָרוֹן מִידֵי, דִּלְר' יְהוּדָה לֹא הָוֵי לָאָרוֹן בַּהֲדֵי כַּפּוֹרֶת אֶלָּא שְׁמֹנָה טְפָחִים וּמֶחֱצָה: בְּבֵינוֹנִית. בְּאַמָּה בַּת ו' בֵּינוֹנִית לְכָל אָדָם, וְיֵשׁ גְּדוֹלָה מִמֶּנָּה כְּדַאֲמַר בְּ"כֵּיצַד צוֹלִין" (פסחים פו.): שְׁתֵּי אַמּוֹת הָיוּ בְּשׁוּשַׁן הַבִּירָה, אַחַת יְתֵירָה עַל שֶׁל מֹשֶׁה חֲצִי אֶצְבַּע, וְאַחַת יְתֵירָה עָלֶיהָ חֲצִי אֶצְבַּע. נִמְצֵאת יְתֵירָה עַל שֶׁל מֹשֶׁה אֶצְבַּע: לְגוֹד. דְּאָמְרִי' בְּכַמָּה דּוּכְתֵּי גּוֹד אַחֵית גּוֹד אַסֵּיק וּפָחוֹת מִג' כְּלָבוּד. וּלְשׁוֹן "לָבוּד" כְּמוֹ סְנִיף – דָּבָר קָצָר שֶׁהוֹסִיפוּ עָלָיו וְהֶאֱרִיכוּהוּ: וּבָא לְמַעֲטוֹ. לַעֲשׂוֹת בִּנְיָן אִיצְטַבָּא אוֹ עָפָר תַּחַת הַקּוֹרָה בָּאָרֶץ לְמַעֵט גּוֹבַהּ הֶחָלָל: כַּמָּה מְמַעֵט. מַשְׁמַע: כַּמָּה יַגְבִּיהַּ הַקַּרְקַע: כַּמָּה דִּצְרִיךְ לֵיהּ. עַד שֶׁלֹּא יְהֵא הֶחָלָל יוֹתֵר עַל עֶשְׂרִים: רָחְבּוֹ. שֶׁל מִיעוּט לְהַרְחִיבוֹ לְתוֹךְ אוֹרֶךְ הַמָּבוֹי כַּמָּה: טֶפַח. כְּנֶגֶד רׇחְבָּהּ שֶׁל קוֹרָה וְתַחְתֶּיהָ: מַאן דְּאָמַר טֶפַח קָסָבַר מוּתָּר לְהִשְׁתַּמֵּשׁ תַּחַת הַקּוֹרָה. דְּאָמַר: חוּדוֹ הַחִיצוֹן יוֹרֵד וְסוֹתֵם, כִּדְמַשְׁמַע לְקַמָּן (ד' ח:). וְהִלְכָּךְ: כֵּיוָן דְּשִׁיעוּר עֶשְׂרִים אַמָּה מִשּׁוּם הֶיכֵּר הוּא – הֲרֵי יֵשׁ הֶיכֵּר לָעוֹמֵד עַל אוֹתוֹ טֶפַח שֶׁנִּגְבַּהּ תַּחַת הַקּוֹרָה: וּמַאן

ראשונה עד שישתה רביעית, *)דהא דרשינן "שכר" "שכר", דכתיב גבי שכר רביעית ההין, מה להלן רביעית – אף כאן רביעית. חזרו לומר: לא יאכל ולא ישתה, מה אכילה בכזית – אף שתיה בכזית, משמע דאכילה לכולי עלמא בכזית! ונראה לרבינו תם: דגרסינן בשמעתין גפן כדי כזית יין לנזיר. וקשה לפירוש רבינו תם: כך יכול לשער במים כמו ביין, במקום שיש זית אגורי ישים עלין ולולבין, אם יפילו שיעור עלין ולולבין שאכל כשיעור שיפיל הזית הן מים הן יין – חייב. ואי בשתיה איירי לחייבו אם שתה כשיעור מה שמפיל זית אגורי מן היין, דמשערין ביין שהוא דבר מועט, ולא במים – פשיטא, כיון דשתה יין שלא ישער אלא ביין, ומה צריך קרא? וגם לפ"ה, קשה: מאי נפקא מינה? ולי נראה: דלפ"ה לא קשה כלל, דרביעית של תורה הוא אצבעיים על אצבעיים כו', כדאמרינן ב"ערבי פסחים" (ד' קט.), וזהו מה שמפיל בילה ומחצה מן המים, לפי חשבון דמ' סאה דמקוה. והשתא משערינן עלין ולולבין שאכל כשיעור שיפילו מן היין כלי מלא אצבעיים על אצבעיים, שהוא שיעור גדול, ולא משערינן כשיעור שיפילו מן המים – שהוא דבר מועט. ע"כ הגה"ה: **כל** כלי בעלי בתים שיעורן ברמונים. גבי כלי עץ מתנייא במסכת כלים פרק י"ז (מ"א). אבל גבי כלי חרס תנן בפ"ג (מ"א) דכלים העשויים לאוכלים – שיעורן כזית. והא דאמר בסוף "המצניע" (שבת ד' צה.) חמש מדות בכלי חרס – ניקב כמוציא זית וכו' ועדיין כלי הוא לקבל בו רמונים – היינו היכא דייחדו לרמונים, אבל סתמא הוי כמוציא זית:

שיעורן ברמונים. בפרק י"ז, במסכת כלים (מ"ד) תנן: הרמונים שאמרו ג' אחוזים זה בזה. משמע דשיעורן בג' רמונים. וקשה: דבפרק "המצניע" (שבת ד' צה.) אמר: ניקב כמוציא רמון – טהור. משמע רמון אחד, ולקמן פ"ב (ד' כד.) בעי חזקיה: ניקב כמוציא זית וסתמו וחזר וניקב(ב) עד שהשלימו למוציא רמון, מהו? ולא קאמר ניקב כמוציא רמון וסתמו וחזר וניקב כמוציא רמון עד שהשלימו לג' רמונים מהו. וי"ל: דג' אחוזים – לא שיצאו ביחד, אלא זה אחר זה, וצריך נקב רחב להוציא ג' בזה אחר זה יותר ממה שהיה האחד לבד. אי נמי: ג' אחוזים – פירוש שגדילים ג' ביחד, והם רמונים בינונים, ולא מאותן שגדילין אחד או ב' יחד שהם גדולים, ולא מאותן שגדילין ד' או ה' ביחד שהם קטנים. ולעולם רמון אחד לבד קאמר:

הילכתא נינהו ואסמכינהו רבנן אקראי. בפרק בתרא דיומא (ד' פ.) א"ר יוחנן: שיעורין ועונשין הלכה למשה מסיני. והיה כתוב בספרים: שיעורין מכתב כתיבי, אימא שיעורין של עונשין. ולא גרסי' הכי, דהא מסקינן הכא דאסמכתא נינהו. ועוד: דלא הוה משני מידי, אלא גרסינן עונשין מכתב כתיבי אימא וכו': **דבר** תורה רובו ומקפיד עליו חוצץ. פי' בקונטרס: בשערו משמע, אבל בשרו – אפילו מיעוטו שאינו מקפיד חוצץ. וקשה לר"ת, דבפרק "הערל" (יבמות ד' עח. ושם) אמרינן: גויה מעוברת שנתגיירה, אין בנה צריך טבילה. וקאמר: אילימא משום דר' יצחק – הא אמר רב כהנא לא שנו אלא רובו, אבל כולו חוצץ. והשתא אדרבה, הוה ליה למימר כי אמר ר' יצחק – בשערו, בשרו מי אמר? ועוד: דפ' "דם חטאת" (זבחים ד' צח.) מייתי דם שעל בגדו חוצץ. ואם טבח הוא – אינו חוצץ. ועוד: אי בשערו דווקא – אם כן כשנאמר הלכה למשה מסיני הוצרך לומר שערו, רובו ומקפיד עליו חוצץ. אם כן שערו הוי הלכה למשה מסיני, ואמאי צריך קרא לשערו?* וכי האי גוונא פריך בכמה דוכתי:

מותר להשתמש תחת הקורה. פירש בקונטרס: דקסבר חודו החיצון יורד וסותם. ומאן דאסר, סבר חודו הפנימי יורד וסותם. ולא רצה לפרש(ג) דמר סבר היכירא לבני רשות הרבים, ומר סבר היכירא לבני מבוי. משום דקאמר בתר הכי, ואיבעית אימא: דכולי עלמא קורה משום היכירא, משמע דעד השתא לא הוי לכולי

יט א מיי' פי"ח מהל' שבת הלכה א:
כ ב מיי' פ"ו מהלכות כלים הלכה ב:
כא ג מיי' פ"ב מהל' שביתת עשור הל' א סמג לאוין סט טוש"ע א"ח סי' תריב סעיף א:
[בברכות מא: ליתא גם בילקוט ליתא]
כב ד מיי' פ"א מהל' מקוואות הלכה יב סמג עשין רמח טוש"ע י"ד סי' קנא סעיף א:
[נ"ל ורחץ במים את כו']
כג ה מיי' פ"ב שם הל' א סמג שם טוש"ע שם סי' רא סעיף א:
כד ו מיי' פ"ב שם הלכה טו סמג שם טוש"ע י"ד סי' קנא סעיף ה:
כה ז מיי' פ"א שם הלכה יב סמג שם טוש"ע שם סעיף א:
בס"י איתא לרבות את שערו אלא כי איצטריך הלכתא
כו ח מיי' פי"ז מהל' שבת הל' טז טוש"ע א"ח סי' שסג סעיף כו:

רבינו חננאל

היה גבוה מכ' אמה ובא למעטו ממעטו בגבהו עד שיעמידנו בכ'. ברחבו בכמה ממעטו רב יוסף אמר טפח כלומר שיעור רוחב הקורה. לימא בהא פליגי אביי ורב יוסף. רב יוסף אמר טפח [קסבר] מותר לו להשתמש תחת הקורה שנמצא משתמש במקום שהוא עשרים אביי אמר ד' טפחים [קסבר] שאסור לו להשתמש מן המבוי תחת הקורה שתחת הקורה כלחוץ דמי ומן הקורה ולפנים המבוי [מותר] לפיכך צריך מקום אחר זולתי תחת הקורה להיות בתוך עשרים שיהא מותר לו להשתמש בו מן המבוי ודחינן לא כולי עלמא מותר להשתמש תחת

רב נסים גאון

ולא פת שעורים וכו': **כי** אתאי הלכתא לגוד וללבוד ולדופן עקומה (אבל) לגוד זה כמו שאמרו בזו המסכתא ובמסכת סוכה גוד אסיק מחיצתא גוד אחית מחיצתא ולבוד זהו שאמרו כל פחות מג' כלבוד דמי ודופן עקומה מפורשת בפרק א' מסוכה (קף יז) בית שנפחת וסיכך על גביו אם יש בין הכותל ולסיכוך ד' אמות פסולה שאם יהיה הריחוק שביניהן פחות מד' אמות כשרה כי נידון זה הכותל של בית כאילו הוא סמוך לסיכוך ורואין כאילו הוא דופן עקומה

אלא וודאי הלכתא נאמרה סתמא והוי מוקמי' ליה לבשר להכי איצטריך קרא לשערו ואי לאו הלכתא ה"א כולו קמ"ל הלכתא לרובו בין לשערו בין לבשרו [ת"י]

שבת קב. קיב: סוכה ו. ברכות מא. לקמן כ"ד. כלים פי"ז מ"א
[בסוכה ו. ובברכות מא: איתא מדרבנן וקרא אסמכתא בעלמא]
[לקמן יד:] יומא לא. חגיגה יא. פסחים קט. [סוכה ו. ב"ק פב. ע"ש]
[סוכה ו. ע"ש נדה סז.]
סוכה ו. ע"ש
סוכה ו: נדה סז: יבמות עח.
[שבת יא: בילה ג. וש"נ]
[שבת נב. סוכה ד.]
[סוכה ה. ו. כלים פי"ז מ"ז מנחות לז]

הגהות הב"ח

(א) גמ' לא צריכא אלא לרבי יהודה: (ב) תוס' ד"ה שיעורן וכו' ניקב כמוציא זית וסתמו וחזר וניקב כמוציא זית וסתמו עד שהשלימו: (ג) ד"ה מותר וכו' ולא רצה לפרש. נ"ב ע"ל בסוף דף י"ב.

*) [בירושלמי לנזיר פ"ו איתא בזה"ל דהוין דרשין שכר מה שכר שנאמר להלן רביעית אף כאן רביעית ופי' בעל קרבן העדה להלן רביעית בביאת המקדש רביעית דבעי' שיהא מידי דמישתכר ובכן מלת ההין נדפס כאן הוא בטעות. וכן בתוס' סוכה ו. סד"ה גפן וכו' איתא על נכון]

וּמ"ד אַרְבָּעָה קָסָבַר: אָסוּר לְהִשְׁתַּמֵּשׁ תַּחַת הַקּוֹרָה. לֹא, דְּכוּלֵּי עָלְמָא קָסָבְרִי: מוּתָּר לְהִשְׁתַּמֵּשׁ תַּחַת הַקּוֹרָה, וּבְהָא קָא מִיפַּלְגִי: מָר סָבַר: *קוֹרָה מִשּׁוּם הֶיכֵּר, וּמָר סָבַר: קוֹרָה מִשּׁוּם מְחִיצָה. וְאִיבָּעֵית אֵימָא: דְּכוּלֵּי עָלְמָא קוֹרָה — מִשּׁוּם הֶיכֵּר, וְהָכָא בְּהֶיכֵּר שֶׁל מַטָּה וּבְהֶיכֵּר שֶׁל מַעְלָה קָא מִיפַּלְגִי; דְּמָר סָבַר: אָמְרִינַן "הֶיכֵּר שֶׁל מַטָּה כְּהֶיכֵּר שֶׁל מַעְלָה", וּמָר סָבַר: לָא אָמְרִינַן "הֶיכֵּר שֶׁל מַטָּה כְּהֶיכֵּר שֶׁל מַעְלָה". וְאִיבָּעֵית אֵימָא: דְּכוּלֵּי עָלְמָא אָמְרִינַן "הֶיכֵּר שֶׁל מַטָּה כְּהֶיכֵּר שֶׁל מַעְלָה" וְהָכָא בִּגְזֵירָה שֶׁמָּא יִפְחוֹת קָמִיפַּלְגִי.§ "הָיָה פָּחוֹת מֵעֲשָׂרָה טְפָחִים וְחָקַק בּוֹ לְהַשְׁלִימוֹ לַעֲשָׂרָה". כַּמָּה חוֹקֵק? כַּמָּה חוֹקֵק?! כַּמָּה דִּצְרִיךְ לֵיהּ! אֶלָּא: מִשְׁכּוֹ בְּכַמָּה? *רַב יוֹסֵף אָמַר: בְּד', *אַבַּיֵי אָמַר: בְּאַרְבַּע אַמּוֹת. לֵימָא בִּדְרַבִּי אַמִּי וְרַבִּי אַסִּי קָמִיפַּלְגִי; דְּאִיתְּמַר: מָבוֹי שֶׁנִּפְרַץ מִצִּידּוֹ כְּלַפֵּי רֹאשׁוֹ, אִיתְּמַר מִשְּׁמֵיהּ דְּר' אַמִּי וְר' אַסִּי: אִם יֵשׁ שָׁם פַּס ד' — מַתִּיר בְּפִירְצָה עַד עֶשֶׂר. וְאִם לָאו, פָּחוֹת מִשְּׁלֹשָׁה — מַתִּיר, שְׁלֹשָׁה — אֵינוֹ מַתִּיר. לְרַב יוֹסֵף — אִית לֵיהּ דְּרַבִּי אַמִּי, לְאַבַּיֵי — לֵית לֵיהּ דְּר' אַמִּי. אָמַר לָךְ אַבַּיֵי: הָתָם — סוֹף מָבוֹי, הָכָא — תְּחִלַּת מָבוֹי, אִי אִיכָּא אַרְבַּע אַמּוֹת — אִין, אִי לָא — לָא. אָמַר אַבַּיֵי: מְנָא אָמֵינָא לָהּ — דְּתַנְיָא: *אֵין מָבוֹי נִיתָּר בְּלֶחִי וְקוֹרָה עַד שֶׁיְּהוּ בָּתִּים וַחֲצֵרוֹת פְּתוּחִין לְתוֹכוֹ. וְאִי בְּד', הֵיכִי מַשְׁכַּחַתְּ לֵיהּ? וְכִי תֵּימָא: דְּפָתַח לָהּ בַּדּוֹפֶן הָאֶמְצָעִי — *וְהָאָמַר רַב נַחְמָן נְקִיטִינַן, אֵיזֶהוּ מָבוֹי שֶׁנִּיתָּר בְּלֶחִי וְקוֹרָה — כֹּל שֶׁאָרְכּוֹ יָתֵר עַל רָחְבּוֹ, *וּבָתִּים וַחֲצֵרוֹת פְּתוּחִין לְתוֹכוֹ. וְרַב יוֹסֵף? *דְּפָתַח לֵיהּ בְּקֶרֶן זָוִית. אָמַר אַבַּיֵי: מְנָא אָמֵינָא לָהּ — דְּאָמַר רָמִי בַּר *חָמָא אָמַר רַב הוּנָא: לֶחִי הַבּוֹלֵט מִדּוֹפְנוֹ שֶׁל מָבוֹי, פָּחוֹת מֵאַרְבַּע אַמּוֹת — נִידּוֹן מִשּׁוּם לֶחִי, וְאֵינוֹ צָרִיךְ לֶחִי אַחֵר לְהַתִּירוֹ. ד' אַמּוֹת — נִידּוֹן מִשּׁוּם מָבוֹי, וְצָרִיךְ לֶחִי אַחֵר לְהַתִּירוֹ. וְרַב יוֹסֵף: לְאַפּוֹקֵי מִתּוֹרַת לֶחִי — עַד דְּאִיכָּא אַרְבַּע אַמּוֹת, לְמֶיהֱוֵי מָבוֹי — אֲפִי' בְּאַרְבָּעָה טְפָחִים נַמִי הָוֵי מָבוֹי.§ גּוּפָא, אָמַר רָמִי בַּר חָמָא, אָמַר רַב הוּנָא: לֶחִי הַבּוֹלֵט מִדָּפְנוֹ שֶׁל מָבוֹי, פָּחוֹת

רש"י

וּמַאן דְּאָמַר אַרְבָּעָה קָסָבַר אָסוּר לְהִשְׁתַּמֵּשׁ תַּחַת הַקּוֹרָה. דְּחוּדָּהּ הַפְּנִימִי יוֹרֵד וְסוֹתֵם, וְרוֹחַב הַקּוֹרָה הָוֵי חוּץ לַסְּתִימָה. וְלַמִּשְׁתַּמְּשִׁים בַּמָּבוֹי אֵין לָהֶם הֶיכֵּר בַּקּוֹרָה, שֶׁהֲרֵי בַּגָּמוּךְ הֵן. הִלְכָּךְ, צָרִיךְ שֶׁיִּמָּשֵׁךְ לְתוֹךְ הַמָּבוֹי שֶׁתְּהֵא הַקּוֹרָה נִיכֶּרֶת לָהֶם כְּשֶׁיִּשְׁתַּמְּשׁוּ בְּאוֹתוֹ גּוֹבַהּ. וְכֵיוָן דְּאַפֵּיקְתֵּיהּ מִתַּחַת הַקּוֹרָה, צָרִיךְ שֶׁיְּהֵא מָקוֹם הַנִּיכָּר וְחָשׁוּב: לֹא דְּכוּלֵּי עָלְמָא מוּתָּר וּבְהָא פְּלִיגִי מָר סָבַר קוֹרָה. שֶׁתִּיקְּנוּ חֲכָמִים לַמָּבוֹי — מִשּׁוּם הֶיכֵּר בְּעָלְמָא הוּא, דְּלָא לֵיתֵי לְמִישְׁרֵי רְשׁוּת הָרַבִּים. וַהֲרֵי יֵשׁ כָּאן הֶיכֵּר בִּכְנִיסָתָן כְּשֶׁמִּשְׁתַּמְּשִׁין תַּחַת הַקּוֹרָה: וּמַאן דְּאָמַר אַרְבָּעָה קָסָבַר קוֹרָה. הַמַּתֶּרֶת בַּמָּבוֹי טַעְמָא מִשּׁוּם מְחִיצָּה, דְּאָמְרִי' חוּדָּהּ הַחִיצוֹן יוֹרֵד וְסוֹתֵם. וְאָמְרוּ רַבָּנַן דִּבְטְפֵי מֵעֶשְׂרִים לֹא אָמְרִי' יוֹרֵד וְסוֹתֵם. וְכֵיוָן דְּלָא הָוֵי מִיעוּט ד' — הָוֵי מְחִיצָּה הָעֲשׂוּיָה לְפָחוֹת מִד' וְקַיְימָא לָן בְּכָל דּוּכְתָּא דִּמְחִיצָּה שֶׁאֵינָהּ רְאוּיָה לְד' — לָאו מְחִיצָּה הִיא, דְּאֵין רְשׁוּת הַיָּחִיד לְפָחוֹת מִד' טְפָחִים וְאַע"פ שֶׁמּוּקָּף מְחִיצָּה שֶׁל עֲשָׂרָה טְפָחִים. וּבַגְּזוּזְטְרָאוֹת דַּחֲנַנְיָה בֶּן עֲקַבְיָא נַמִי הָכִי אָמְרִינַן, דְּאֵין מְחִיצּוֹת אֶלָּא אִם כֵּן יֵשׁ תּוֹךְ הֶחָלָל אַרְבָּעָה, בְּפֶרֶק "כֵּיצַד מִשְׁתַּתְּפִין" (ד' פו:): גְּזֵירָה שֶׁמָּא יִפְחַת. עַל יְדֵי דְּרִיסַת רַגְלַיִם יִפְחַת הַמִּיעוּט וְיַעֲמוֹד עַל פָּחוֹת מִטֶּפַח. הִלְכָּךְ בָּעֵינַן טְפֵי. וְכֵיוָן דְּאַפֵּיקְתֵּיהּ מֵהֶיכֵּר שֶׁל מַעְלָה — אוֹקְמֵיהּ אַאַרְבָּעָה, דַּחֲשִׁיבֵי בְּכָל דּוּכְתָּא: מִשְׁכּוֹ. שֶׁל חָקַק לְתוֹךְ אוֹרֶךְ הַמָּבוֹי בַּדָּבָר הַבּוֹלֵט כְּגוֹן מִיעוּט שַׁיָּיךְ לְמֵימַר רוֹחַב, וּבַדָּבָר הַשּׁוֹקֵעַ וּמַקִּיפוֹת אוֹתוֹ מְחִיצּוֹת כְּגוֹן חָקַק שַׁיָּיךְ לוֹמַר לְשׁוֹן מֶשֶׁךְ: רַב יוֹסֵף. דְּבָעֵי לְעֵיל טֶפַח, הָכָא בָּעֵי אַרְבָּעָה. דְּהָתָם דְּאַיְיתֵיהּ לַדּוֹפֶן, וּלְמַעוּטֵי קָאָתֵי, בְּהֶיכֵּר בְּעָלְמָא סַגֵּי. הָכָא דְּהַשְׁתָּא הוּא דְּמַשְׁוֵי לֵיהּ דּוֹפֶן, בֵּין לְרַב יוֹסֵף וּבֵין לְאַבַּיֵי בָּעֵינַן דְּלִיתְחֲזֵי הַאי דּוֹפֶן לְשִׁיעוּר הֶכְשֵׁר אוֹרֶךְ מָבוֹי שָׁלֵם. הִלְכָּךְ, לְרַב יוֹסֵף שִׁיעוּר מֶשֶׁךְ מָבוֹי בְּד' טְפָחִים, וְאַבַּיֵי סְבִירָא לֵיהּ: שִׁיעוּר מֶשֶׁךְ מָבוֹי בְּד' אַמּוֹת: שֶׁנִּפְרַץ מִצִּידּוֹ אֶחָד. מִן הַכְּתָלִים שֶׁבְּצַד אָרְכּוֹ: כְּלַפֵּי רֹאשׁוֹ. סָמוּךְ לַקּוֹרָה הַיְמָנָה וְלִפְנִים: אִם יֵשׁ שָׁם פַּס ד'. אִם נִשְׁתַּיֵּיר מִן הַכּוֹתֶל, אוֹ עָשָׂה פַּס ד' בִּמְקוֹם הַפִּרְצָה סָמוּךְ לַקּוֹרָה:

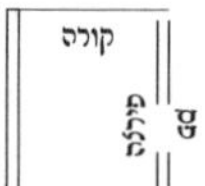

מַתִּיר פִּירְצָה. אַף עַל גַּב שֶׁנִּשְׁתַּיֵּיר שָׁם — עֲדַיִין פִּירְצָה עַד עֶשֶׂר, דְּכֵיוָן דְּיֵשׁ הֶכְשֵׁר אוֹרֶךְ מָבוֹי מִן הַקּוֹרָה עַד הַפִּירְצָה — לֹא בָּטֵל לֵיהּ תּוֹרַת פֶּתַח מִקַּמָּאֵי, וּבְמִלְּתֵיהּ קָאֵי, וְקוֹרָתוֹ מַתִּירָתוֹ. וּפִירְצָתָהּ מַתֶּרֶת, כֵּיוָן דְּלָאו יוֹתֵר מֵעֶשֶׂר תּוֹרַת פֶּתַח עָלֶיהָ. וּמָבוֹי אֵינוֹ נִפְסָל בִּפְתָחִים הַרְבֵּה. אִי נַמִי, שָׁבְקִי בְּנֵי מָבוֹי פִּתְחָא קַמָּא, וְנַפְקוּ וְעָיְילִי בְּהַהִיא פִּירְצָה, מִשּׁוּם דְּדֶרֶךְ קְצָרָה הִיא לָהֶם — אַפְּ"ה לֹא בָּטְלָה תּוֹרַת פֶּתַח וְקוֹרָה מִן הָרִאשׁוֹן, מִשּׁוּם דְּהָוֵי פֶּתַח לְד' הַסְּמוּכִין לוֹ. הוֹאִיל וְד' אוֹרֶךְ רְאוּיִין לְקוֹרָה, דְּיֵשׁ בָּהֶן הֶכְשֵׁר מָבוֹי: וְאִם לָאו. דְּאֵין שָׁם פַּס ד': פָּחוֹת מִג'. אִם הַפִּירְצָה פְּחוּתָה מִג': מַתִּיר. תִּיקּוּן הַמָּבוֹי אֶת הַמָּבוֹי. שֶׁהֲרֵי כְּלָבוּד דָּמֵי, וְאֵין כָּאן פִּירְצָה. וְאִם הַפִּירְצָה ג' — אֵינוֹ מַתִּיר דְּכֵיוָן דִּמְמַעֲטִין בְּנֵי מָבוֹי בְּהִילּוּכָן וּמְקַצְּרִין אֶת דַּרְכָּן דֶּרֶךְ אוֹתָהּ פִּירְצָה — חָיְישִׁינַן דִּילְמָא שָׁבְקִי פִּתְחָא רַבָּה וְעָיְילִי וְנָפְקִי בְּהַהִיא פִּירְצָה, וּבָטֵיל לֵיהּ פִּתְחָא קַמָּא, וּבָטְלָה קוֹרָה דִּידֵיהּ, וְאֵין קוֹרָה לְמָבוֹי זֶה. וְהַאי טַעְמָא מְפָרֵשׁ לְקַמָּן בְּפִירְקִין: וְאַבַּיֵי לֵית לֵיהּ דְּר' אַמִּי וּדְר' אַסִּי. דְּהָא הֶכְשֵׁר מָבוֹי בְּד' קָאָמַר. וְהָכָא נַמִי, אִי לֵיכָּא פַּס ד' אַמּוֹת — אֵין קוֹרָה זוֹ רְאוּיָה לְאוֹתוֹ הַפַּס, וְאֵין כָּאן קוֹרָה: סוֹף מָבוֹי. כְּגוֹן הָא דְּר' אַמִּי וְר' אַסִּי שֶׁכְּבָר הָיָה מָבוֹי וְאֵירַע בּוֹ פְּסוּל. ה"נ, דִּלְמֶיהְדַּר לְשַׁוְּיֵיהּ מָבוֹי סַגֵּי בְּד' טְפָחִים: תְּחִילַּת מָבוֹי. כְּגוֹן גַּבֵּי חָקַק, דְּהַשְׁתָּא קָמְתַקֵּן מָבוֹי: בָּתִּים וַחֲצֵרוֹת. בָּתִּים פְּתוּחִין לַחֲצֵירוֹת, וַחֲצֵירוֹת לַמָּבוֹי. שֶׁכֵּן הָיָה דַּרְכָּן שֶׁאֵין בָּתִּים פְּתוּחִין אֶלָּא לְחַצְרֵיהֶן. וְכָל חָצֵר הָאָמוּר בַּמִּשְׁנָה אֵינוֹ אֶלָּא לִפְנֵי הַבַּיִת, אֲבָל שֶׁאֲחוֹרֵי הַבַּיִת — מוּקְצֶה אוֹ רְחָבָה קָרֵי לֵיהּ: וְאִי אָמְרַתְּ בְּד' הָוֵי מָבוֹי הֵיאַךְ נִיתָּר. מִכְּדִי מִיעוּט חֲצֵירוֹת שְׁתַּיִם, וְאֵין פֶּתַח פָּחוֹת מִד' — וְאֵיךְ יִפְתַּח פֶּתַח רוֹחְבּוֹ אַרְבָּעָה, בְּמֶשֶׁךְ הַמָּבוֹי שֶׁאֵין בּוֹ אֶלָּא ד' הֵיכָא מְקוֹם הַפְּצִימִין? וְעוֹד: כּוּלּוֹ פָּרוּץ הוּא: וְכִי תֵּימָא דְּפָתַח לֵיהּ בַּדּוֹפֶן אֶמְצָעִית. וְכִי קָאָמַר רַב יוֹסֵף הֶכְשֵׁר בְּאוֹרֶךְ ד' — בְּמָבוֹי רָחָב מְאֹד קָאָמַר, וְיָכוֹל לִפְתּוֹחַ פֶּתַח הַחֲצֵירוֹת בַּדּוֹפֶן שֶׁמֵּאַחֲרָיו: וְהָאָמַר רַב נַחְמָן נְקִיטִינַן. מֵאֲבוֹתֵינוּ, מִנְהָג מֵרַבּוֹתֵינוּ: אָרְכּוֹ יָתֵר עַל רָחְבּוֹ. הָוֵי מָבוֹי, וְנִיתָּר בְּלֶחִי וְקוֹרָה. אֲבָל מְרוּבָּע — דִּין חָצֵר עָלָיו. וּלְקַמָּן: חָצֵר צְרִיכָה פַּס ד' אוֹ פַּס מַשֶּׁהוּ מִכָּאן וּפַס מַשֶּׁהוּ מִכָּאן, הֵיכָא דְּפְרִיצָה בִּמְלוֹאָהּ לִרְה"ר. וְכֵיוָן דְּאָמְרַתְּ ד' כָּשֵׁר — הֲרֵי רָחְבּוֹ ד' חָסֵר מַשֶּׁהוּ, וְאֵין שָׁם שִׁיעוּר פֶּתַח. דִּבְכוּלֵּי הַךְ מַסֶּכְתָּא אָמְרִי' דְּאֵין פֶּתַח פָּחוֹת מִד': דְּפָתַח לֵיהּ בְּקֶרֶן זָוִית. טֶפַח מִן הַפֶּתַח בַּדּוֹפֶן הָאֶמְצָעִי, וְג' טְפָחִים בַּדּוֹפֶן הַמֶּשֶׁךְ. וְכֵן בְּצִידּוֹ הַשֵּׁנִי, כָּזֶה*: לֶחִי הַבּוֹלֵט מִדּוֹפְנוֹ שֶׁל מָבוֹי. לְתוֹךְ רוֹחַב הַמָּבוֹי, וְלֹא נַעֲשָׂה שָׁם לְשֵׁם לֶחִי, אֶלָּא הוֹצִיא בִּנְיָינוֹ בְּפֶתַח בֵּיתוֹ כְּדֶרֶךְ שֶׁעוֹשִׂין מִשּׁוּם חִיזּוּק:

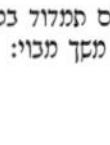

תוספות

לכולי עלמא משום היכרא. ואין להקשות לפירושו, הואיל וסברי קורה משום מחילה – א"כ מאי טעמא דמאן דאמר טפח? והא לא הוי מחילה לפחות מד' אין לחוש הואיל והוי דופן, אלא שבא למעטו, כדפי' בקונטר' בענין זה בסמוך*: **סוף** מבוי הכי נמי. פירוש: כיון שלא נפסלה שנשתייר שם פס ד', דמבוי כשר אינו יולא מתורת הכשר עד שיפחות, שלא ישאר שם ד'. אבל תחלת מבוי, דהיינו שלא נשתייר שם פס ד', שלריך לעשות לו הכשר – לריך ד' אמות. וכן משמע לישנא דקאמר אם יש שם פס ד' – מכלל דנשתייר שם פס ד' מיירי. ופרש"י אין נראה: **ואי** בארבעה היכי משכחת לה. אע"ג דד' דקאמר רב יוסף היינו דאיכא משהו טפי, דהמבוי אם אינו רוחב ד' אינו לריך לחי, כדרב אהילאי לקמן. ואי לא הוי טפי משהו – הוי ארכו כרחבו, מ"מ באותו משהו אין מקום לפלימין לעמוד: **דפתח** לי' בקרן זוית. פירש בקונט': טפח מן הפתח בדופן האמלעי, ושלשה טפחים בדופן המשך, וכן בלידו השני. ולא דק, דא"כ אין הפתח רחב אלא אלכסון של ג' טפחים על טפח, והנה עינינו רואות שאין (א) האלכסון של שלשה על אחד מגיע לאלכסון של טפח על טפח.

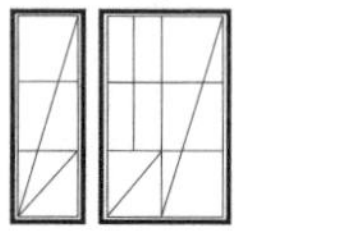

אמר אביי מנא אמינא לה. הא דלא מייתי ראייה מלקמן (ד' י.) דאמר שמואל משמיה דלוי: מבוי שרחבו כ' אמה עושה פס גבוה עשרה במשך ארבע אמות, ומעמידו לארכו של מבוי – שמא לחלק מבוי לב' מבואות מודה רב יוסף דלריך ד' אמות: **ורב** יוסף לאפוקי מתורת לחי עד דאיכא ד' אמות. קשה: דרב יוסף גופיה קאמר לקמן (ד' י.) על דברי רב הונא(ב) משך מבוי ארבע אמות, ודוחק לומר דהיינו לאפוקי מתורת לחי: **לחי** הבולט מדופנו של מבוי. אין פירושו כההיא דלקמן (ד' י.) לחי המושך מדופנו של מבוי, דהתם מושך חוץ למבוי לארכו של מבוי – דהא חשיב ליה שוה מבפנים. והכא בולט לרחבו של מבוי וסותמו דאמר לקמן דמבוי ז' ניתר בעומד מרובה על הפרוץ, ואביי הוה מצי לאתויי נמי מהתם:

פחות

עין משפט נר מצוה

כז א מיי' פי"ז מהל' שבת הלכה יא טוש"ע א"ח סי' שסה סעיף ד:
כח ב מיי' שם הלכה ט [וסג טו]:
כט ג טוש"ע א"ח סי' שסג סעיף כו:
ל ד מיי' שם הלכה טז טוש"ע שם:
לא ה מיי' שם הלכה יז טוש"ע א"ח סי' שסה סעיף א:
לב ו ז מיי' שם הל' ז סמג עשין דרבנן א טוש"ע א"ח סי' שסג סעיף כו:

רבינו חננאל

הקורה מיהו רב יוסף סבר היכר למטה כהיכר למעלה ובטפח נמי סגי ליה. אביי סבר לא [אמרינן היכר של מטה כהיכר של מעלה] איבעית אימא בגזירה שמא יפחת פליגי רב יוסף לא גזר. ואביי אמר פעמים שיפחת הלכך מצרכינן ליה ד' טפחים שאם יפחת יעמוד על טפח. היה פחות מי' טפחים ובא להשלימו לי' חוקקו כלומר מעמיק וחופר בקרקע עד שהשלימו לי'. משך כלומר רחב אותה החקיקה בכמה רב יוסף אמר בד' טפחים אביי אמר בד' אמות. לימא בהא פליגי דאתמר מבוי שנפרץ מצדו כלפי ראשו אתמר משמיה דר' אמי ור' אסי אם נשתייר בו פסל עומד שיש בו ד' טפחים מתיר פרצה עד עשר כלומר אפילו אם הוא רוחב הפרצה י' אמות כיון שהפסל זה עומד (ונמצא כפסל) והפרצה כפתח ומותר. רב יוסף אית ליה כר' אמי ור' אסי ואביי לית ליה ואמרינן בסוף מבוי כ"ע אית להו הא דר' אמי ור' אסי כי פליגי בתחלת מבוי רב יוסף סבר תחלת מבוי נמי בד' ואביי סבר בד' אמות. ובא אביי לברר דבריו מדבריו של רב דאמר אין מבוי ניתר בלחי וקורה עד שיהו בתים וחצרות פתוחים *) בו בקרן זוית. ואביי אמר לך פתחים בקרן זוית לא עבדי אינשי וכן עוד בא אביי לדקדק מהא דאמר לחי הבולט מדופנו של מבוי פי' בולט יוצא ועודף מבנין הכותל כגון כתיבת דינרין שהן בולטות האותיות ולא שוקעות אם זה הבולט

*) נראה דחסר כאן וצ"ל פתוחין לתוכו ואי בד' היכי משכחת לה ורב יוסף אמר לך דמשכחת לה שהיו פתוחין בו בקרן זוית.

רב נסים גאון

ונבשיר בו הסוכה: **אם** יש פס ד' מתיר פרצה עד עשרה עיקר דילה במשנה (דף טו) כל פרצה שהיא כי' אמות מותרות מפני שהיא כפתח יותר מיכן אסור:

ג"ל לחי ע"פ מהרש"ל ישן

הגהות הב"ח

(א) תום' ד"ה דפתח וכו' שאין האלכסון. נ"ב כלומר היתרון המרובע מהאלכסון למאי דאמרינן כל אמתא בריבוע אמתא ותרי חומשי באלכסונא הנה עינינו רואות דיתרון טפח ע"ט הוא יותר מהיתרון של ג' טפחים ע"ט והוא אם תמדוד בטפח ע"ט באלכסון ולא תמלא היתרון כ"א ב' חומשי טפח וכשתמדוד אלכסון של ג"ט על אחד לא יהיה היתרון כל כך וזה דבר ברור ונראה לעינים: (ב) ד"ה ורב יוסף וכו' על דברי רב הונא שמע מינה משך מבוי:

מסורת הש"ס

[לעיל ג. לקמן ח: יב:]
[לעיל ג:]
[שם]
שבת קל: ע"ש לקמן עג: ע"ש וש"נ
לקמן יב:
[שבת קלא. וש"נ]
[עי' תוס' לקמן ו. ד"ה דפתחא]
[גירס' הרא"ש אבא]

גליון הש"ס

גמ' ומ"ד קורה משום מחילה. עיין לקמן דף טו ע"א תוס' ד"ה אביי לטעמיה: **שם** מתיר בפרלה עד עשר. עיין לקמן דף י ע"ב תוס' ד"ה ואלכסונים: **רש"י** ד"ה ואי אמרת. מכדי מיעוט חלירות שתים. ק"ל בלאו הקדמה זו הא אף אי הוה סגי בחלר א' הוי הראיה נכונה והא באמת אף דבעי' ב' חלרות מ"מ אפשר בחלר א' מלד דופן זה וחלר א' בדופן כנגדו אלא דבאמת גם פתח אחד א"א באורך ד' וא"כ גם אם סגי בחלר א' ישנה לראיה זו: **תום'** ד"ה דפתח לי'. ולא דק. עיין ת' מהלכר"ח סי' יג:

לג א ב ג ד מיי' פי"ז מהלכות שבת הלכה כב טוש"ע א"ח סי' שסג סעיף יב:

רבינו חננאל

פחות מד' אמות נידון משום (לחי) [מבוי] ואין צריך לחי אחר להתירו ש"מ דשיעור מבוי ד' אמו' בעינן ורב יוסף אמר לך לא אתא לאשמעינן אלא כל דהוא מד' אמות ולמעלה נפיק ליה מתורת לחי והרי הוא כמבוי וצריך הוא לחי להתירו ולעולם אפילו ד' טפחים הוי מבוי. ומיבעיא לן הא דתני בבולט וצריך לחי להתירו אותו לחי היכן מעמיד. אם מעמידו בראשו של בולט נמצא מוסיף עליו. ופריק רב פפא דמוקים ליה כנגדו בכותל אחר שכנגדו. רב הונא א' לעולם אינו מעמידו אלא בראשו של בולט וכגון שבולטו יתר או פחות שיהא נראה או בולט או שוקע אבל משוה עם אותו לחי הבולט לו. אמר רב הונא בריה דרב יהושע לא אמרן אלא במבוי ח' אמות שנמצא הבולט ד' אמות ונמצאו עוד ד' אמות מבוי והכל צריכין דבר להתירו אבל מבוי ז' אמות וד' מהן לחי הבולט אין צריך לחי אחר להתירו אלא נידון בעומד מרובה על הפרוץ מק"ו וכו' ופרקינן מה לחצר שכן פרצתה בעשר דתנן חצר שנפרצה מב' רוחותיה כו' ואוקמה רב בעשר וכגון שנפרצה בקרן זוית דפתחא בקרן זוית לא עבדי אינשי. תאמר במבוי שפרצתו

רב נסים גאון

חצר שאינה ניתרת בלחי וקורה ניתרת במרובה עומד על הפרוץ. לפנינו בזה הפרק פרשו כי החצר צריכה פסין ואין מועיל לה לחי וקורה כלום וזהו שאמרו (דף יב) חצר ניתרת בפס אחד ר' אומר בב' פסין אמר ר' אסי אמר ר' יוחנן חצר צריכה ב' פסין וטעמו של דבר שהיא ניתרת בעומד מרובה על הפרוץ כי כל מחיצות של שבת צריכות עומד מרובה על הפרוץ חוץ מפסי ביראות כמו שאנו עומדין לפרשו וכל שכן המבוי שמועיל בו לחי וקורה שיועיל בו עומד מרובה על הפרוץ: מה לחצר שכן פרצתה בי' כבר הזכרנו מה שאמרה המשנה בזה הפרק כל פרצה שהיא כי' אמות כו' וגם בפרק חלון (דף עו) כותל שבין ב' חצרות גבוה י' טפחים נפרץ הכותל עד י' אמות מערבין שנים ואם רצו מערבין אחד מפני שהיא כפתח כבר נתברר לך כי פרצת חצר בי' ומה שאמרו פרצת מבוי בד' כבר מפורש אחר כן רב הונא אמר אחד זה ואחד זה בד':

גמרא

[א]פָּחוֹת מֵאַרְבַּע אַמּוֹת — נִידּוֹן מִשּׁוּם לֶחִי, וְאֵין צָרִיךְ לֶחִי אַחֵר לְהַתִּירוֹ. ד' אַמּוֹת — נִידּוֹן מִשּׁוּם מָבוֹי, וְצָרִיךְ לֶחִי אַחֵר לְהַתִּירוֹ. אוֹתוֹ לֶחִי הֵיכָן מַעֲמִידוֹ? אִי דְּמוֹקֵי לֵיהּ בַּהֲדֵי' — אוֹסְפֵי הוּא דְּקָא מוֹסִיף עֲלֵיהּ! אָמַר רַב פַּפָּא: [ב]דְּמוֹקֵי לֵיהּ לְאִידָךְ גִּיסָא. רַב הוּנָא בְּרֵיהּ דְּרַב יְהוֹשֻׁעַ אָמַר: אֲפִילּוּ תֵּימָא דְּמוֹקֵי לָהּ בַּהֲדֵי'. [ג]דְּמִטַּפֵּי בֵּיהּ, אוֹ דְּמִבַּצַּר בֵּיהּ. אָמַר רַב הוּנָא בְּרֵיהּ דְּרַב יְהוֹשֻׁעַ: לָא אֲמַרַן אֶלָּא בְּמָבוֹי שְׁמוֹנָה, אֲבָל בְּמָבוֹי שִׁבְעָה — נִיתָּר בְּעוֹמֵד מְרוּבֶּה עַל הַפָּרוּץ. וְקַל וָחוֹמֶר מֵחָצֵר. וּמָה חָצֵר שֶׁאֵינָהּ נִיתֶּרֶת בְּלֶחִי וְקוֹרָה — נִיתֶּרֶת בְּעוֹמֵד מְרוּבֶּה עַל הַפָּרוּץ, מָבוֹי שֶׁנִּיתָּר בְּלֶחִי וְקוֹרָה — אֵינוֹ דִּין שֶׁנִּיתָּר בְּעוֹמֵד מְרוּבֶּה עַל הַפָּרוּץ? מָה לְחָצֵר שֶׁכֵּן פִּרְצָתָהּ בְּעֶשֶׂר, תֹּאמַר בְּמָבוֹי שֶׁפִּרְצָתוֹ בְּאַרְבַּע! קָסָבַר רַב הוּנָא בְּרֵיהּ דְּרַב יְהוֹשֻׁעַ: מָבוֹי נַמִי, פִּרְצָתוֹ בְּעֶשֶׂר. לְמַאן קָאָמְרִינַן — לְרַב הוּנָא, וְהָא רַב הוּנָא פִּרְצָתוֹ בְּד' סְבִירָא לֵיהּ! רַב הוּנָא בְּרֵיהּ דְּרַב יְהוֹשֻׁעַ טַעְמָא דְּנַפְשֵׁיהּ קָאָמַר. רַב אַשִׁי אָמַר: אֲפִילּוּ תֵּימָא [ד]בְּמָבוֹי שְׁמוֹנָה נַמִי לָא צָרִיךְ לֶחִי. מַה נַּפְשָׁךְ, אִי עוֹמֵד נָפֵישׁ — נִיתָּר בְּעוֹמֵד מְרוּבֶּה עַל הַפָּרוּץ, וְאִי פָּרוּץ נָפֵישׁ — נִידּוֹן מִשּׁוּם לֶחִי מַאי אָמְרַתְּ — דְּשָׁווּ תַּרְוַיְיהוּ כִּי הֲדָדֵי, הֲוָה לֵיהּ סְפֵק דִּבְרֵיהֶן, *וּסְפֵק דִּבְרֵיהֶן לְהָקֵל. § אָמַר רַב חָנִין בַּר רָבָא, אָמַר רַב: מָבוֹי שֶׁנִּפְרַץ מִצִּידּוֹ

רש"י

פָּחוֹת מד' אַמּוֹת. בְּרוֹחַב הַמָּבוֹי נִידּוֹן מִשּׁוּם לֶחִי, וְסָמְכִינַן עֲלֵיהּ, וְאע"ג דְּלָאו לְשֵׁם לֶחִי אִיקְּבַע. דְּקַיְימָא לַן הִלְכְתָא כְּאַבַּיֵּי בְּלֶחִי הָעוֹמֵד מֵאֵלָיו, דְּכָשֵׁר: ד' אַמּוֹת. אִם הָיָה בּוֹלֵט לְתוֹךְ רוֹחַב הַמָּבוֹי ד' אַמּוֹת – נִידּוֹן מִשּׁוּם מָבוֹי. כְּלוֹמַר: כֵּיוָן דְּאוֹרֶךְ הֶכְשֵׁר מָבוֹי נִיתָּר בְּכָךְ בְּעָלְמָא, וּמִיקְּרֵי מָבוֹי – הָכָא נַמִי נָפֵיק מִתּוֹרַת לֶחִי, דְּלָא סָמְכִינַן עֲלֵיהּ, אע"ג דְּאִי עַבְדֵיהּ מִשּׁוּם לֶחִי הָוֵי כָּשֵׁר. דְּמִשּׁוּם דְּרִיבָּה בִּסְתִימָתוֹ לָא גָּרַע מִלֶּחִי מַשֶּׁהוּ, הָכָא כֵּיוָן דְּלָאו לְהָכִי אִיקְּבַע – אֲנַן בְּמַחֲשָׁבָה לָא מָצִינַן לְאַפּוּקֵיהּ מִתּוֹרַת כּוֹתֶל וּלְשַׁוּוֹיֵיהּ לֶחִי, דְּכֵיוָן דִּנְפַק לֵיהּ מִתּוֹרַת לֶחִי, וְנִמְצָא שֶׁאֵין תִּיקּוּן לְמָבוֹי זֶה, וְצָרִיךְ לֶחִי אַחֵר לְהַתִּיר הַמָּבוֹי. אַלְמָא: מִדְּקָתָנֵי דִּבְצִיר מִד' אַמּוֹת לָא הָוֵי מָבוֹי לְאַפּוּקֵי מִתּוֹרַת לֶחִי – שְׁמַע מִינָּהּ הֶכְשֵׁר מָבוֹי בְּד' אַמּוֹת: בַּהֲדֵיהּ. אֶצְלוֹ בְּרוֹחַב הַמָּבוֹי: בְּאִידָךְ גִּיסָא. אֵצֶל כּוֹתֶל הָאַחֵר, כְּנֶגְדּוֹ: דְּמִטַּפֵּי בֵּיהּ אוֹ דְּמִבַּצַּר בֵּיהּ. גָּבוֹהַּ מִמֶּנּוּ אוֹ נָמוּךְ מִמֶּנּוּ. א"נ: אוֹ עָב מִמֶּנּוּ אוֹ דַּק מִמֶּנּוּ, כְּדֵי שֶׁיִּמָּשֵׁךְ מִמֶּנּוּ וְלַחוּץ אוֹ הֵימֶנּוּ וְלִפְנִים: בְּמָבוֹי שְׁמוֹנֶה. שֶׁרָחָב שְׁמוֹנֶה אַמּוֹת, וְכָל שֶׁכֵּן אִם יוֹתֵר: אֲבָל בְּמָבוֹי שִׁבְעָה נִיתָּר. הַמָּבוֹי. וְאע"פ שֶׁאֵין זֶה לֶחִי – הוֹאִיל וּסְתִימַת הַפֶּתַח מְרוּבָּה עַל הַפָּרוּץ: וּמָה חָצֵר. מְרוּבַּעַת אוֹ רְחָבָּהּ יוֹתֵר עַל אוֹרְכָּהּ, שֶׁאֵינָהּ נִיתֶּרֶת בְּלֶחִי וְקוֹרָה, אִם נִפְרַץ כּוֹתֶל שֶׁעַל פְּנֵי רְשׁוּת הָרַבִּים עַל פְּנֵי כּוּלּוֹ, וְהֶעֱמִיד בּוֹ לֶחִי מַשֶּׁהוּ – אֵינוֹ מַתִּיר, אא"כ יֵשׁ בּוֹ פַּס ד' כִּדְאָמְרִינַן לְקַמָּן בְּפִרְקִין (ד' יב.): פַּסֵּי חָצֵר צְרִיכִין שֶׁיְּהֵא בָּהֶן אַרְבָּעָה: נִיתֶּרֶת בְּעוֹמֵד מְרוּבֶּה עַל הַפָּרוּץ. אֲפִילּוּ נִפְרְצוּ בָּהּ פְּרָצוֹת הַרְבֵּה בְּד' מְחִיצוֹתֶיהָ סָבִיב, וְנִשְׁתַּיֵּיר שָׁם מִן הָעוֹמֵד עַד שֶׁרַבּוּ עוֹמְדִים עַל הַפְּרוּצוֹת מוּתֶּרֶת בְּלֹא שׁוּם תִּיקּוּן: מָבוֹי שֶׁנִּיתָּר. פְּתִיחַת כּוֹתְלוֹ הַסָּמוּךְ לִרְשׁוּת הָרַבִּים בְּלֶחִי מַשֶּׁהוּ: אֵינוֹ דִּין שֶׁיְּהֵא נִיתָּר בְּעוֹמֵד מְרוּבֶּה עַל הַפָּרוּץ. בְּלֹא שׁוּם סִימָן אַחֵר. וּמִיהוּ, מָבוֹי שְׁמוֹנָה אע"ג דִּבְהַאי קַל וָחוֹמֶר נַמִי מָצֵי לְמִישְׁרְיֵיהּ, דְּהָא יוֹתֵר מֵאַרְבָּעָה טְפָחִים הָוֵי הַאי פַּס וְחָצֵר מִשְׁתַּרְיָיא בְּפַס ד' כֵּיוָן דְּלָאו לְשֵׁם לֶחִי הוּקְבַּע שָׁם וְלֹא לְשֵׁם תִּיקּוּן פַּס הוּקְבַּע שָׁם, כִּי הֵיכִי דְּיָצָא מִתּוֹרַת לֶחִי – יָצָא מִתּוֹרַת פַּס, וְלָא מִנְכְּרָא מִילְּתָא. וְאָמְרִינַן זֶהוּ פִּתְחוֹ, וְלֹא נַעֲשָׂה בּוֹ תִּיקּוּן לְהַתִּירוֹ: חָצֵר אֵין פִּירְצָתָהּ עֶשֶׂר אוֹסֶרֶת בָּהּ אא"כ הָוֵי מִלּוֹאוֹ בַּכּוֹתֶל אוֹ יוֹתֵר מֵעֶשֶׂר. וְהָכִי קַיְימָא לַן בְּמַתְנִיתִין (לקמן ד' טו:): כָּל פִּירְצָה שֶׁהִיא בְּעֶשֶׂר אַמּוֹת – מוּתֶּרֶת: תֹּאמַר בְּמָבוֹי. דְּאָמַר רַב הוּנָא בְּאַרְבַּע לְקַמָּן (ד' ו.): לְמַאן קָאָמְרִינַן לְרַב הוּנָא. הַאי ק"ו אַלִּיבָּא דְּמַאן קָאָמַר לֵיהּ רַב הוּנָא בְּרֵיהּ דְּרַב יְהוֹשֻׁעַ – אַלִּיבָּא דְּרַב הוּנָא רַבֵּיהּ תַּלְמִידֵיהּ דְּרַב. דְּהָא הַךְ שְׁמַעְתִּין דְּלֶחִי הַבּוֹלֵט רַב הוּנָא אֲמָרָהּ, וּמִילְּתֵיהּ דְּרַב הוּנָא קָא מְפָרֵשׁ רַב הוּנָא בְּרֵיהּ דְּרַב יְהוֹשֻׁעַ: פִּירְצָתוֹ בְּד' סְבִירָא לֵיהּ. לְקַמָּן בִּשְׁמַעְתִּין: טַעְמָא דְּנַפְשֵׁיהּ קָאָמַר. וְהָכִי קָאָמַר: בְּמָבוֹי שְׁמוֹנָה קָא מִסְתַּבְּרָא מִילְּתֵיהּ דְּרַב הוּנָא, אֲבָל בְּמָבוֹי שִׁבְעָה – לָא מִסְתַּבְּרָא כְּוָותֵיהּ, דְּאִיכָּא לְמִישְׁרְיֵיהּ בְּקַל וָחוֹמֶר: אִי עוֹמֵד מְרוּבֶּה עַל הַפָּרוּץ. שֶׁהָיוּ אַרְבַּע אַמּוֹתָיו שֶׁל לֶחִי שׁוֹחֲקוֹת, וְנִמְצָא פָּרוּץ חָסֵר מֵאַרְבַּע – הֲרֵי נִיתָּר בְּכָךְ: וְאִי פָּרוּץ מְרוּבֶּה. נִמְצָא שֶׁאֵין ד' שְׁלֵימוֹת בַּלֶּחִי, וְנִידּוֹן מִשּׁוּם לֶחִי, דְּהָא רוֹב בְּנֵי אָדָם אֵין יְכוֹלִין לְצַמְצֵם: מַאי אָמְרַתְּ. לְאוֹסְרוֹ דִּילְמָא נִמְצָא, וְכִי הֲדָדֵי נִינְהוּ, וְאֵין כָּאן לֶחִי – שֶׁהֲרֵי יֵשׁ בּוֹ אַרְבַּע אַמּוֹת, וְלֹא עוֹמֵד מְרוּבֶּה: הָוֵי סְפֵק דִּבְרֵיהֶם. שֶׁמָּא נִמְצָא וְאָסוּר, וְשֶׁמָּא לֹא נִמְצָא וּמוּתָּר. דְּטִלְטוּל מָבוֹי מִדְּרַבָּנַן הוּא, וּסְפֵק דִּבְרֵיהֶם לְהָקֵל: מִצִּידּוֹ

תוספות

פחות מארבע אמות נידון משום לחי. וסמכינן עליה. ואע"ג דלאו לשם לחי הוקבע, משום דקיימא לן כאביי בלחי העומד מאליו. ואפילו לר"ת דפסק כרבא – מ"מ הכא איירי אליבא דרב הונא, ואביי מרב הונא דייק לה לקמן בפירקין (ד' טו.). ונראה דרש"י מדקדק דמיירי הכא בלא הוקבע לשם לחי – מדמפליג בין ד' לפחות מד'. דאילו עבדיה לשם לחי – הוי כשר בכל ענין, דמשום דריבה בסתימתו לא גרע מלחי משהו, כדפי' רש"י בסמוך. אבל ההיא דלקמן (דף י.) דלחי המושך, הואיל והוי לאורך המבוי ואינו סותמו, דנידון משום מבוי – אפילו הוקבע לשם לחי. ולהכי כי דייק מיניה לקמן (ד' י.) שמע מיניה תלת – לא קאמר שמע מינה ד' דלחי העומד מאליו הוי לחי. ולקמן (דף ט.) פרש"י: ולרשב"ג ליהוי כנראה מבחוץ ושוה מבפנים, שכן דרך מעמידי לחי שמושכין קימע' כלפי חוץ – א"כ משמע דר"ל אע"ג דהוקבע לשם לחי – נידון משום מבוי:

ארבע אמות נידון משום מבוי. [א]אפילו למ"ד(א) (לקמן ד' טו.) לחי משום מחיצה – דהיה לו להועיל יותר אם סותמו, מ"מ היכר קצת בעינן. ואע"ג דהיכא דהעמידהו לשם לחי לפי' הקונטרס מועיל, אע"ג דאין היכירא – מ"מ י"ל כשהועמד לשם לחי יש קול, ואיכא היכירא:

אותו לחי היכן מעמידו. במבוי רחב יותר משמונה קא בעי, דברוחב ח' – היכן שיעמידנו הוי עומד מרובה: **קל** וחומר מחצר. אע"ג דחצר ומבוי שוין, דכשהן מרובעין צריכין פס ד', ואם ארכן יותר על רחבן – ניתרין בלחי וקורה. מכל מקום עביד קל וחומר שפיר, דבמקום דלא מהני לחי וקורה, דהיינו במרובעים, מהני עומד מרובה. ואמחיצה רביעית הוא דעביד קל וחומר, דליהני עומד מרובה. אבל שיועיל עומד מרובה בכל ד' מחיצות – ליכא למילף, דדיו לבא מן הדין להיות כנדון כמו לחי: **אינו** דין שיהא ניתר בעומד מרובה. פירש בקונט': ומיהו, במבוי ח' אע"ג דבהאי ק"ו נמי מצי למשרייה, דהא יותר מד' הוי האי פס וחצר משתריא בפס ד' – כיון דלאו לשם לחי הוקבע, ולא לשם תיקון פס הוקבע – כי היכי דאפקינן מתורת לחי, אפקינן נמי מתורת פס. ור"י פי': דאין סברא ללמוד לענין תורת פס מחצר. [ב]דבחצר הפס מהני משום מחיצה, משום הכי כל שכן דמהני היכא דסותמו טפי. אבל במבוי, שהקילו חכמים בלחי, אפי' למ"ד משום מחיצה – צריך שיהא שם לחי עליו. אבל לענין עומד מרובה – הוי ק"ו טוב, משום דהוי מחיצה גמורה, שמועיל בכל ד' דפנות. אבל לחי ופס לא מהני אלא במחיצה רביעית. וליכא למימר: פס ד' אמות יוכיח, דמהני בחצר ולא מהני במבוי, אף אני אביא עומד מרובה! דכיון שאין יכול ללומדו מק"ו – הכא נמי ליכא למימר תוכיח. ועוד: מה לפס ד' אמות שכן לא מהני אלא במחיצה רביעית, תאמר בעומד מרובה דמהני בכל ד': **תאמר** במבוי שפירצתו בארבע. וא"ת: והיא גופיה נילף מק"ו מחצר, שיהא פרצתו בעשר. ומאי טעמא דרב הונא דאמר בארבע? וי"ל: דלא שייך ק"ו אפרצת עשר, משום דהיא הנותנת, דבשביל שמבוי ניתר אפי' בלחי משהו – הוי פרצתו בד'. ואפילו לאידך לישנא, דאמר לקמן (ד' י.) גבי פסי בירא – כיון דאקילו בהו חד קולא אקילו בהו קולא אחריתי – התם משום עולי רגלים הקילו קולא יתירא מפני דוחקן. וא"ת: א"כ מאי פריך מה לחצר שכן פרצתו בי', מה פירכא היא זו? נימא: היא הנותנת, משום דלא התרתיו אלא בעומד מרובה – שרי עד עשר! וי"ל: דהיא הנותנת לא אמרי' אלא לסתור הק"ו, אבל לסתור הפירכא כדי לקיים הק"ו – לא אמר: **שפרצתו** בד'. וא"ת: ונעשה ק"ו מלחי וקורה שאין מועיל בחצר מהני במבוי, עומד מרובה כו'! וי"ל: דאיכא למימר פירכ' עשר תוכית. וליכא למימר דנילף שלא יועיל לחי וקורה למבוי, ועומד מרובה לחצר דגמירי לה מסיני דמהני, וכן שיועיל לחי וקורה לחצר ליכא למילף דגמירי דבעי פס ארבעה, ועוד, דמעומד מרובה ליכא למילף דמה לעומד מרובה דמהני בכל ד' דפנות, וממבוי נמי ליכא למילף, דמה למבוי שכן פרצתו בארבעה לרב הונא: **וספק** דבריהם להקל. וא"ת: תיפוק ליה דקיימא לן בפירקין (ד' טז:) דפרוץ כעומד מותר! וי"ל: דהכא(ב) קיימא לן אליבא דרב הונא בריה דרב יהושע, דאית ליה לקמן (ד' טו:) פרוץ כעומד אסור. וא"ת: ואמאי הוי ספק דבריהם, הא קיימא לן דבידי אדם אפשר לצמצם, דקיימא לן כרב פפא דאמר: פרוץ כעומד מותר. ואי לא אפשר לצמצם – ליחוש דילמא פרוץ מרובה. וכן בפרק ב' דחולין (ד' כח:) דפליגי במחצה על מחצה אי הוה כרוב, משמע דאפשר לצמצם. והא דאמרינן בפרק ג' דיבמות (ד' כח.): לא סתם לן תנא כר"י הגלילי, דאמר אפשר לצמצם – היינו בידי שמים. וב"הזורק" (גיטין ד' עח.) גבי ספק קרוב לו ספק קרוב לה, דאמר: וניחזי הי מינייהו קדים. וכ"ת: כשבאו שניהן בבת אחת

[שבת לד. לקמן מה: ביצה ג:]

הגהות הב"ח

(א) תוס' ד"ה ארבע וכו' למאן דאמר. נ"ב לקמן בדף יב ע"ב: (ב) ד"ה וספק וכו' דהכא קאי אליבא דרב הונא:

גליון הש"ס

תוס' ד"ה ארבע. אפילו למ"ד. נ"ל דמוכח כן דהא מרא דשמעתין הוא ר"ה ואיהו ס"ל לקמן דף טו דלחי העומד מאליו הוי לחי וחזו למ"ד לחי משום מחיצה עיי"ש: **ד"ה** אינו דין דבחצר הפס מהני משום מחיצה. עיין לקמן דף ט ע"ב תוס' ד"ה כותל:

אמִצִידוֹ – בְּעֶשֶׂר, מֵרֹאשׁוֹ – בְּד'. מַאי שְׁנָא מִצִּידּוֹ בְּעֶשֶׂר – דְּאָמַר פִּתְחָא הוּא, מֵרֹאשׁוֹ נַמִי – נֵימָא פִּתְחָא הוּא! א"ר הוּנָא בְּרֵיהּ דְּרַב יְהוֹשֻׁעַ: כְּגוֹן שֶׁנִּפְרַץ בְּקֶרֶן זָוִית, *דְּפִתְחָא בְּקֶרֶן זָוִית לָא עָבְדִי אֱינָשֵׁי. וְרַב הוּנָא אָמַר: אֶחָד זֶה וְאֶחָד זֶה בְּאַרְבָּעָה. וְכֵן א"ל רַב הוּנָא לְרַב חָנָן בַּר רָבָא: לָא תִּפְלוֹג עֲלַאי, דְּרַב אִיקְלַע לְדַמְחַרְיָא וַעֲבַד עוֹבְדָא כְּוָותִי. א"ל: רַב *בִּקְעָה מָצָא, וְגָדַר בָּהּ גָּדֵר. אָמַר רַב נַחְמָן בַּר יִצְחָק: כְּוָותֵיהּ דְּרַב הוּנָא מִסְתַּבְּרָא. דְּאִיתְּמַר: מָבוֹי עָקוּם, רַב אָמַר: בתּוֹרָתוֹ כִּמְפוּלָּשׁ, וּשְׁמוּאֵל אָמַר: תּוֹרָתוֹ כְּסָתוּם. בְּמַאי עָסְקִינַן? אִילֵימָא בְּיוֹתֵר מֵעֶשֶׂר – בְּהָא לֵימָא שְׁמוּאֵל תּוֹרָתוֹ כְּסָתוּם?! אֶלָּא לָאו – בְּעֶשֶׂר, וְקָאָמַר רַב: תּוֹרָתוֹ כִּמְפוּלָּשׁ. אַלְמָא: פִּירְצַת מָבוֹי מִצִּידּוֹ בְּד'. וְרַב חָנָן בַּר *רָבָא – שָׁאנֵי הָתָם, גדְּקָא בָּקְעִי בָּהּ רַבִּים. מִכְּלָל דְּרַב הוּנָא סָבַר אע"ג דְּלָא בָּקְעִי בָּהּ רַבִּים? מ"ש *מִדְּר' אַמִי וְרַב אַסִי? הָתָם – דְּאִיכָּא גִידוּדֵי, הָכָא – דְּלֵיכָּא גִידוּדֵי.§ ת"ר: כֵּיצַד מְעָרְבִין דֶּרֶךְ רה"ר – עוֹשֶׂה צוּרַת הַפֶּתַח מִכָּאן, וְלֶחִי *וְקוֹרָה מִכָּאן. *חֲנַנְיָה אוֹמֵר; ב"ש אוֹמְרִים: עוֹשֶׂה דֶּלֶת מִכָּאן וְדֶלֶת מִכָּאן, וּכְשֶׁהוּא יוֹצֵא וְנִכְנָס – נוֹעֵל. ב"ה אוֹמְרִים: עוֹשֶׂה דֶּלֶת מִכָּאן, וְלֶחִי וְקוֹרָה מִכָּאן. ורה"ר מִי מִיעַרְבָא? וְהָתַנְיָא: *יָתֵר עַל כֵּן א"ר יְהוּדָה: מִי

מִצִּידוֹ. בְּכוֹתֶל אָרְכּוֹ, וְלֹא אֵצֶל רֹאשׁוֹ, אֶלָּא שֶׁיֵּשׁ אַרְבָּעָה עוֹמֵד מִן הַפֶּתַח עַד הַפִּרְצָה: מֵרֹאשׁוֹ. שֶׁהָיָה מָבוֹי רָחָב כ' אַמָּה, וּסְתָמוֹ עֶשֶׂר אַמּוֹת, כִּדְתְנַן: וְהָרָחָב מֵעֶשֶׂר – יְמַעֵט, וְנִפְרְצָה פִּירְצָה בְּאוֹתָהּ סְתִימָה: לָא תִיפְלוֹג עֲלַאי. לוֹמַר דְּרַב מַכְשִׁר פִּירְצַת עֶשֶׂר בְּצִידוֹ, דְּהָא רַב אִיקְלַע לְדַמְחַרְיָא כו': בִּקְעָה מָצָא. עַמֵּי הָאֲרָצִים הָיוּ, וּמְזַלְזְלִין בְּמִצְוֹת, וְהֶחְמִיר עֲלֵיהֶן לַעֲשׂוֹת סְיָיג לְהַרְחִיקָן מִן הָעֲבֵירָה. כְּאָדָם הַגּוֹדֵר בִּקְעָה פְּרוּצָה לְשׁוֹמְרָהּ: מָבוֹי עָקוּם. וּשְׁנֵי פְּתָחָיו לִרְשׁוּת הָרַבִּים: כזה

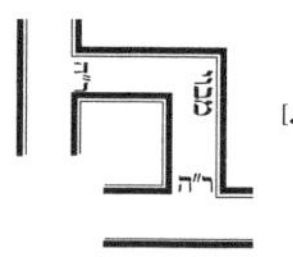

תּוֹרָתוֹ כִּמְפוּלָּשׁ. וּמָבוֹי הַמְפוּלָּשׁ לִרה"ר צָרִיךְ צוּרַת פֶּתַח מִכָּאן, וְלֶחִי אוֹ קוֹרָה מִכָּאן, כִּדְלְקַמָּן. אַף זֶה צָרִיךְ לִשְׁנֵי פְּתָחָיו לְצַד רְשׁוּת הָרַבִּים, לֶחִי לְכָל רוּחַ, וּבְעַקְמוּמִיתוֹ צָרִיךְ צוּרַת פֶּתַח, דְּפִילּוּשׁ שֶׁהוּא מְפוּלָּשׁ לַחֲבֵירוֹ, הָוֵי כִּמְפוּלָּשׁ לִרה"ר: תּוֹרָתוֹ כְּסָתוּם. וְאֵין צָרִיךְ בְּעַקְמוּמִיתוֹ כְּלוּם, אֶלָּא אֵלּוּ עוֹשִׂין לֶחִי לְפִתְחָן וְאֵלּוּ עוֹשִׂין לֶחִי לְפִתְחָן, דְּלָא מַצְרְכִינַן צוּרַת הַפֶּתַח אֶלָּא לִפְתָחִים הַמְפוּלָּשִׁין זֶה כְּנֶגֶד זֶה לִרְשׁוּת הָרַבִּים. ל"א: תּוֹרָתוֹ כְּסָתוּם – תּוֹרַת מָבוֹי סָתוּם, וְצָרִיךְ לַעֲשׂוֹת לֶחִי לְעַקְמוּמִיתוֹ, וְהַיְינוּ לֶחִי שֶׁעוֹשִׂים בְּמָבוֹי סָתוּם. וְזֶה קִבַּלְתִּי מִמּוֹרִי הַזָּקֵן ז"ל: אִילֵימָא בְּיוֹתֵר מֵעֶשֶׂר. שֶׁרוֹחַב פְּתִיחַת עַקְמוּמִיתוֹ יוֹתֵר מֵעֶשֶׂר: בְּהָא לֵימָא שְׁמוּאֵל כְּסָתוּם. וְנִיסַגֵּי בְּלֶחִי. הַאי לֶחִי בְּיוֹתֵר מֵעֶשֶׂר בְּמָבוֹי סָתוּם מִי מְהַנֵּי? וְלִלִישָּׁנָא קַמָּא, כֵּיוָן דְּיוֹתֵר מֵעֶשֶׂר הָוֵי כְּחַד מָבוֹי, וְכִי הַאי גַּוְונָא לָא לֵימָא שְׁמוּאֵל דְּלָאו מְפוּלָּשׁ הוּא: אֶלָּא לָאו בְּעֶשֶׂר. אַלְמָא: פִּירְצַת לְדִידֵן לְרַב בְּאַרְבָּעָה: מִכְּלָל דְּרַב הוּנָא. אֲפִי' בְּפִירְצָה דְּלָא בָּקְעִי רַבִּים, כְּגוֹן שֶׁפְּרוּצָה לְמָקוֹם מְטוּנָּף אוֹ לְמָקוֹם מְקוּלְקָל בִּפְחָתִים וְטִיט, וְאֵין דֶּרֶךְ רַבִּים מְצוּיִים לַעֲבוֹר בְּאוֹתָהּ פִּירְצָה – אֲסַר נַמִי בְּאַרְבָּעָה: מ"ש מִדְּר' אַמִי וּמִדְּרַב אַסִי. דְּאָמְרִינַן לְעֵיל: אִם יֵשׁ שָׁם פַּס אַרְבָּעָה מַתִּיר פִּירְצָה עַד עֶשֶׂר. אַלְמָא: פִּירְצַת מָבוֹי מִצִּידוֹ בְּעֶשֶׂר: הָתָם דְּאִיכָּא גִּידוּדֵי. שֶׁנִּשְׁתַּיֵּיר מִן הַכּוֹתֶל בַּיְּסוֹד ג' אוֹ ד' טְפָחִים גּוֹבַהּ עַל כָּל פְּנֵי הַפִּירְצָה, שֶׁאֵינָהּ נוֹחָה לַעֲבוֹר בָּהּ: הָכָא. דְּאָסְרִנָא אֲנָא בִּדְלֵיכָּא גִידוּדֵי. "גִּידוּד" – לְשׁוֹן שָׂפָה: ר"ה. מַשְׁמַע רָחָב שֵׁשׁ עֶשְׂרֵה אַמָּה, וְעִיר שֶׁמְּצוּיִין בָּהּ שִׁשִּׁים רִיבּוֹא וְאֵין בָּהּ חוֹמָה, (אוֹ) שֶׁהָיָה ר"ה שֶׁלָּהּ מְכוּוָן מִשַּׁעַר לְשַׁעַר שֶׁיְּהֵא מְפוּלָּשׁ, דּוֹמֶה לְדִגְלֵי מִדְבָּר: צוּרַת הַפֶּתַח מִכָּאן. בְּרֹאשׁוֹ אֶחָד: וְלֶחִי וְקוֹרָה. בְּסוֹף הָעִיר: יָתֵר עַל כֵּן. לְעֵיל מִינֵּיהּ אַיְירֵי, בְּבוֹנֶה עֲלִיָּיה מִבַּיִת לְבַיִת שֶׁבִּשְׁנֵי צִידֵּי רה"ר, וְכֵן גְּשָׁרִים הַמְפוּלָּשִׁין לִרה"ר דְּשָׁרֵי ר' יְהוּדָה לְטַלְטוּלֵי תּוּתֵיהּ מִשּׁוּם פִּי תִקְרָה יוֹרֵד וְסוֹתֵם, בְּפ' "כָּל גַּגּוֹת הָעִיר". וְקָאָמַר בְּבָרַיְיתָא: יָתֵר עַל כֵּן, אֲפִילּוּ הֵיכָא דְּלֵיכָּא פִּי תִקְרָה, הוֹאִיל

אחת, והא אי אפשר לנכנס התם נמי הואיל ולאו אדעתייהו לבא בבת אחת, הוי כבידי שמים! וי"ל: הואיל ואי אפשר לנכנס אלא ע"י טורח גדול – לא הטריחו לנכנס ולמדוד בספק דבריהם. וכן משמע מלשון הקונטרס, דפי': דרוב בני אדם אין יכולים לנכנס, והוי ספק נכנס ואסור, או לא נכנס ומותר. וה"ר שמעיה פי': דמצי למימר דבידי אדם נמי אי אפשר לנכנס, והא דפרוץ כעומד מותר – משום דהוי כעין ספק ספיקא, שמא עומד מרובה, ואפי' כי לא נפיש ושוו כי הדדי – מותר, והשתא שפיר קרי ליה ספק דבריהם. אך קשה: מאי איריא ספק דבריהם? אפי' בדאורייתא נמי שרי, כיון דההיתר קרוב מן האיסור. דמטעם זה בעי למישרי בשחיטה במחלה על מחלה! וי"ל: דהא דשרי הכא אי פרוץ נפיש – היינו בח' אמות מצומצמות, אבל שמא יש מעט יותר, ואפי' אי פרוץ נפיש איכא ד' אמות, ולכך לא שרי אלא בספק דבריהם. ואם תאמר: דבפרק ב' דבכורות (ד' יז:) אמר: נמצא מכוון בין שתי עיירות, לרבנן יביאו עגלה אחת ויתנו. והשתא כל אחת תביא עגלה לעצמה, דשמא קרובה היא ואפי' מצומצמות – הא אמר הקרובה אפילו קרובות! וי"ל: דממה נפשך סגי באחת, אם רחוקה היא – פטורה, ואי קרובה היא – יוצאה בשל תנאי. מאי אמרת דילמא מצומצמות היא – זה אינו מצוי: **מצידו** בעשר מראשו בארבעה. עשר אין פירושו כארבע'. דעשר כשל מטה, וארבעה כשל מעלה: **דפתחא** בקרן זוית לא עבדי אינשי. מיהו, אם עשא' כעין פתח במזוזות ומשקוף – הוי שפיר פתח, כדאמר לעיל (ד' ה.) דפתח ליה בקרן זוית: **אחד** זה ואחד זה בד'. אם נפרץ בקרן זוית. אבל אם נפרץ מראשו בלא קרן זוית, לא הוי בד', דלא פליג אדרב יהודה דאמר לקמן (ד' י:): מבוי שהוא רחב ט"ו אמות, מרחיק ב' אמות ועושה פס ג' אמות. והשתא הוי פירצה ב' אמות, ומצידו דהוי בד' – היינו משום דקא ממעט בהילוכא. אבל כשהפירצה בראשו – לא ממעט בהילוכא, דלא שבקי פתחא רבה ועיילי בפתחא זוטא: **רב** אמר תורתו כמפולש. פי' בקונטרס: דצריך לעשות צורת הפתח בעקמומיתו, דפילוש מה שמפולש לחבירו הוי כמפולש לרה"ר. ולשני פתחים לצד רה"ר יעשו לחי או קורה לכל אחד. ובמילתא דשמואל נמי דאמר תורתו כסתום פי' בשם רבו הזקן: תורת מבוי סתום, צריך לעשות בעקמומיתו, דהיינו לחי. מיהו, שם פי' פירוש אחר: תורתו כסתום – ואין צריך בעקמומיתו כלום. והלשון דחוק, דכיון דתורתו כסתום מה צריך לעשות בעקמומיתו? וכפירושו משמע, מדקאמר בסמוך: אי ביתר מעשר, בהא לימא שמואל תורתו כסתום? משמע דלרב אתי שפיר. ואי תורתו כמפולש קאי אפתחים, דהיינו שצריך לעשות צורת הפתח באחד הפתחים ובשני לחי, ולא בעקמומיתו – א"כ לרב נמי קשה, דאיך יועיל לחי מצד אחד או אפי' צורת הפתח ביותר מעשר? הא אית ליה לרב אע"פ שיש לו צורת הפתח צריך למעט! אבל אי אעקמומיתו קאי, כדפירש רש"י – אתי שפיר לרב, דסגי בצורת הפתח אפי' ביותר מי' הואיל ופתחי מבוי הפתוחים לרה"ר לא הוו יותר מעשר, דהא צ"ה מהני מן התורה אפילו לרב ביותר מי', כדאמרינן לקמן (ד' יא.) גבי כלאים. [ומיהו, יש לדחות: דהוי נמי מצי פריך לרב, אלא דמקשה אליבא דשמואל טפי בפשיטות]. ועוד יש ראיה *מההוא מבוי עקום דהוה בנהרדעא כו' ואצרכוה דלתות. ופירש"י: עקום כמין ח', וצריך ב' דלתות לשני עקמומית, דאי לאו הכי – די בדלת אחת. ומיהו ר"ח גרים: ואצרכוה דלת. וכן כתוב ברוב ספרים, ואפילו גרסינן דלתות איכא למימר דמפולש גמור הוה, ועקום באמצע, כזה

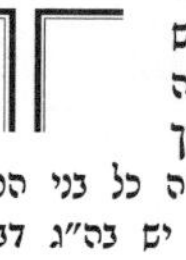

ופתוח בשלשה פתחים לרה"ר. דממה נפשך צריך לעשות דלתות. וגבי מבוי העשוי כנדל (לקמן ד' ח:) משמע נמי כפירוש הקונטרס, דקאמר: אלא עושה צ"ה לכולהו, פי': לצד מבוי הגדול, ואידך גיסא משתרי בלחי וקורה, היינו לצד רה"ר. וזה כפי' הקונט'. אבל אי קאי הא דקאמר עושה צ"ה לכולהו, היינו לצד רה"ר ואידך גיסא קאי אפתח מבוי גדול – אז לשון אידך גיסא לא אתי שפיר. ואין לתמוה למה יהיה מבוי עקום חמור ממפולש גמור, דסגי בצ"ה ולחי אחד – דבעינן שיראה צ"ה כל בני המבוי: **כיצד** מערבין דרך רה"ר. פ"ה: רה"ר רחב י"ו אמות, ומפולש משני צדדים משער לשער, ומצויין בה ששים רבוא. וכן יש בה"ג דבעינן דריסת ס' רבוא. וקשה לר"ת: דבשבת בפ' "הזורק" (ד' צח.) אמר דעגלות הוו תחתיהן וביניהן רה"ר, ותחתיהן לא היו ס' רבוא! ואומר ר"י: דמ"מ דרכן היה לצאת ולבא באותו דרך. ועוד הקשה: דבדגלי מדבר הוו טף ונשים לאין מספר, וכן קשה מערב רב! ויש לומר: דלא גמרי' ממשכן אלא מילתא דכתיבא במספרם: **ולחי** וקורה מכאן. אף על גב דלחי לא מהני ביותר מעשרה – יעשה לחי רחב עד שיתמעט האויר מעשרה: **יתר** על כן אמר ר' יהודה. פירש הקונטרס לעיל מיניה איירי בבונה עלייה כו', דשרי ר' יהודה לטלטל תחתיה משום פי תקרה יורד וסותם. וקאמר בברייתא יתר על כן אמר ר' יהודה, אע"ג דליכא פי תקרה – שרי ר' יהודה, הואיל ואיכא ב' מחיצות מעלייתא. והכי משמע בהדיא בתוספתא [במכילתין פ"ו], דאהא קאי יתר על כן:

מי

[לקמן לד:]
[לקמן ק: חולין קי.]
[גיר' הרא"ש אבא]
[לעיל ה.]
[לקמן יח:]
שבת ו. וקיז. לקמן יב. כב. נט: לה.

לד א מיי' פי"ז מהל' שבת הלי"ז וטוש"ע א"ח סי' שס"ה ס"ב:
לה ב מיי' פי"ז מהל' שבת הל' ג יט סמג עשין דרבנן א טוש"ע א"ח סי' שס"ד ס"ג:
לו ג טוש"ע א"ח סי' שסה סעיף ב:

רבינו חננאל

בד' ופרקינן סבר רב הונא בריה דרב יהושע פרצת מבוי נמי בעשר. רב אשי אמר אפילו תימא במבוי ח' לא צריך לחי מה נפשך אי עומד נפיש הרי הותר בעומד מרובה על הפרוץ אי פרוץ נפיש נידון משום לחי מאי אמרת כי הדדי נינהו הוי ספק דדבריהן וספק דדבריהן להקל. אמר רב נתן בר' אבא אמר רב פירצת מבוי מצדדין בעשר מאמצעיתו בקרן זוית בד' ורב הונא אמר בין מן הצדדין בין מן האמצע בד'. דרב איקלע לדמהדיא ועבד עובדא כוותיה א"ל גדר גדר כלומר לא שהלכה כך אלא ראה אותן שמקילין והחמיר עליהן. אמר רב נחמן בר יצחק כרב הונא מסתברא דהא אמר רב במבוי עקום כמין גומא ונפרץ בסופו שהוא כמו מצידו. ואמר תורתו כמו מפולש ואי אפשר לומר כשפרצתו יתר מעשר דהאמר שמואל תורתו כסתום. וביתר מעשר ליכא מאן דמכשר אלא ודאי בפחות מעשר ואמר רב כמפולש. אלמא פירצת מבוי מצדו בד' סבירא ליה לרב וכל שהוא יתר מארבעה הרי הוא כמפולש. ודחי רב חנן שאני מבוי עקום דקא בקעי ביה רבים. מכלל דרב הונא אע"ג דלא בקעי רבים אסור. מ"ש מדר' אמי ורבי אסי דאמר אם נשתייר בו פסל מתיר פירצה עד עשר. ופרקינן הא דר' אמי ור' אסי בדאית תמן גידורי: ת"ר כיצד מערבין רה"ר עושה צורת הפתח מיכן כו' עד בה"א עושה דלת מיכן ולחי או קורה מיכן. ואקשינן וכי מערבין רה"ר והתניא יתר על כן א"ר יהודה

גליון הש"ם

תום' ד"ה רב אמר וכו' דהא לה"פ מהני מן התורה עיין לקמן דף כב ע"א תוס' ד"ה והאר"י: **בא"ד** איכא למימר דמפולש גמור הוי. עיין לקמן דף י ע"ב תוס' ד"ה עושה פס:

ומהא [לקמן דף ח.] דבריך בודיא ואותיבו בעקמומיתו אין ראיה לפי' רי"ל דבי ראשו האחד לא לנו לעשות להם תיקון [רש"י]

מִי שֶׁהָיוּ לוֹ שְׁנֵי בָתִּים מִשְּׁנֵי צִידֵּי רה"ר — עוֹשֶׂה לֶחִי מִכָּאן וְלֶחִי מִכָּאן, אוֹ קוֹרָה מִכָּאן וְקוֹרָה מִכָּאן — וְנוֹשֵׂא וְנוֹתֵן בָּאֶמְצַע. אָמְרוּ לוֹ: אֵין מְעָרְבִין רְשׁוּת הָרַבִּים בְּכָךְ. וְכִי תֵּימָא: בְּכָךְ הוּא דְּלָא מִיעַרְבָא, הָא בִּדְלָתוֹת מִיעַרְבָא. *וְהָאָמַר רַבָּה בַּר *בַּר חָנָה, אָמַר רַבִּי יוֹחָנָן: [א]יְרוּשָׁלַיִם, אִילְמָלֵא דַּלְתוֹתֶיהָ נִנְעָלוֹת בַּלַּיְלָה חַיָּיבִין עָלֶיהָ מִשּׁוּם רְשׁוּת הָרַבִּים! וְאָמַר עוּלָּא: הָנֵי אַבּוּלֵי דִּמְחוֹזָא, אִילְמָלֵא דַּלְתוֹתֵיהֶן נִנְעָלוֹת — חַיָּיבִין עֲלֵיהֶן מִשּׁוּם רה"ר! אָמַר רַב יְהוּדָה, הָכִי קָאָמַר: [ב]כֵּיצַד מְעָרְבִין מְבוֹאוֹת הַמְפוּלָּשִׁין לִרְשׁוּת הָרַבִּים — עוֹשֶׂה צוּרַת הַפֶּתַח מִכָּאן, וְלֶחִי *וְקוֹרָה מִכָּאן. אִיתְּמַר, רַב אָמַר: [ג]הִילְכְתָא כְּתַנָּא קַמָּא, וּשְׁמוּאֵל אָמַר: *הֲלָכָה כַּחֲנַנְיָה. אִיבַּעְיָא לְהוּ: לַחֲנַנְיָה אַלִּיבָּא דְּבֵית הִלֵּל, צָרִיךְ לִנְעוֹל אוֹ אֵין צָרִיךְ לִנְעוֹל? ת"ש, דְּאָמַר רַב יְהוּדָה, אָמַר שְׁמוּאֵל: אֵינוֹ צָרִיךְ לִנְעוֹל. וְכֵן א"ר מַתָּנָה, אָמַר שְׁמוּאֵל: אֵינוֹ צָרִיךְ לִנְעוֹל. אִיכָּא דְּאָמְרִי, אָמַר רַב מַתָּנָה: בְּדִידִי הֲוָה עוּבְדָא, וְאָמַר לִי שְׁמוּאֵל: אֵין צָרִיךְ לִנְעוֹל. בָּעוּ מִינֵּיהּ מֵרַב עָנָן: צָרִיךְ לִנְעוֹל, אוֹ אֵין צָרִיךְ לִנְעוֹל? אָמַר לְהוּ: תָּא חֲזִי הָנֵי אַבּוּלֵי דִנְהַרְדְּעָא, דְּטִימָּן עַד פַּלְגַּיְיהוּ בְּעַפְרָא, וְעָיֵיל וְנָפֵיק מָר שְׁמוּאֵל, וְלָא אֲמַר לְהוּ וְלָא מִידֵּי. אֲמַר רַב כָּהֲנָא: הָנָךְ מְגוּפוֹת הֲוַאי. כִּי אֲתָא רַב נַחְמָן, אֲמַר: [ד]פַּנְיוּהּ לְעַפְרַיְיהוּ. לֵימָא קָסָבַר רַב נַחְמָן "צָרִיךְ לִנְעוֹל"? לָא, [ה]כֵּיוָן דִּרְאוּיוֹת לִנְעוֹל, אע"פ שֶׁאֵין נִנְעָלוֹת. *הַהוּא מָבוֹי עָקוּם דַּהֲוָה בִּנְהַרְדְּעָא, רְמִי עֲלֵיהּ חוּמְרֵיהּ דְּרַב וְחוּמְרֵיהּ דִּשְׁמוּאֵל, וְאַצְרְכוּהוּ דְּלָתוֹת. חוּמְרֵיהּ דְּרַב — דְּאָמַר "תּוֹרָתוֹ כִּמְפוּלָּשׁ". וְהָאָמַר רַב הֲלָכָה כְּת"ק! כִּשְׁמוּאֵל, דְּאָמַר: הֲלָכָה כַּחֲנַנְיָה. וְהָאָמַר שְׁמוּאֵל: תּוֹרָתוֹ כִּסְתוּם! כְּרַב, דְּאָמַר: תּוֹרָתוֹ כִּמְפוּלָּשׁ. וּמִי עָבְדִינַן כְּתְרֵי חוּמְרֵי? וְהָא תַּנְיָא: *לְעוֹלָם הֲלָכָה כְּבֵית הִלֵּל, וְהָרוֹצֶה לַעֲשׂוֹת כְּדִבְרֵי בֵית שַׁמַּאי — עוֹשֶׂה, כְּדִבְרֵי בֵית הִלֵּל — עוֹשֶׂה, מִקּוּלֵּי ב"ש וּמִקּוּלֵּי ב"ה — רָשָׁע, מֵחוּמְרֵי ב"ש וּמֵחוּמְרֵי ב"ה — עָלָיו הַכָּתוּב אוֹמֵר: °"הַכְּסִיל בַּחֹשֶׁךְ הוֹלֵךְ", אֶלָּא, אִי כְּב"ש — כְּקוּלֵּיהוֹן וּכְחוּמְרֵיהוֹן, אִי כְּב"ה — כְּקוּלֵּיהוֹן וּכְחוּמְרֵיהוֹן. הָא גּוּפָא קַשְׁיָא: אָמְרַתְּ "לְעוֹלָם הֲלָכָה כְּב"ה", וַהֲדַר אָמְרַתְּ: הָרוֹצֶה לַעֲשׂוֹת כְּדִבְרֵי ב"ש עוֹשֶׂה"! ל"ק; כָּאן — *קוֹדֶם בַּת קוֹל, כָּאן — לְאַחַר ב"ק. וְאִיבָּעֵית אֵימָא: הָא וְהָא לְאַחַר בַּת קוֹל, וְרַבִּי

הוֹאִיל וְאִיכָּא שְׁתֵּי מְחִיצּוֹת מַעַלְיָיתָא, מְחִיצַּת הַבַּיִת מִכָּאן וּמְחִיצַּת בַּיִת הַשֵּׁנִי מִכָּאן — סַגִּי בְּתַקַּנְתָּא פּוּרְתָּא: לֶחִי מִכָּאן. אֵצֶל פֶּתַח הַבַּיִת הָאֶחָד: וְלֶחִי מִכָּאן. אֵצֶל פֶּתַח הַשֵּׁנִי לְאוֹתוֹ בַּיִת עַצְמוֹ וְהָוְיָא סְתִימָה לִשְׁנֵי רָאשֵׁי רְשׁוּת הָרַבִּים, וּמוּתָּר לְטַלְטֵל מִבַּיִת לְבַיִת: יְרוּשָׁלַיִם. רְשׁוּת הָרַבִּים שֶׁלָּהּ מְכוּוָּן מִשַּׁעַר לְשַׁעַר, וּמְפוּלָּשׁ, וְיֵשׁ בָּהּ דְּרִיסַת שִׁשִּׁים רִיבּוֹא, וְרָחָב שֵׁשׁ עֶשְׂרֵה אַמָּה. וְאִילְמָלֵא שֶׁנּוֹעֲלִין דַּלְתוֹתֶיהָ בְּכָל לַיְלָה — חַיָּיבִין עָלֶיהָ בְּשַׁבָּת מִשּׁוּם רְשׁוּת הָרַבִּים. אֲבָל נְעִילַת דְּלָתוֹת מְשַׁוְיָא לָהּ כְּחָצֵר שֶׁל רַבִּים, וּמְעָרְבִין אֶת כּוּלָּהּ. וְכָל זְמַן שֶׁלֹּא עֵירְבוּ — הָוְיָא כַּרְמְלִית, וְלָא מִיחַיְּיבֵי עֲלַהּ. וְהָכִי נַמִי אָמְרִינַן בְּפֶרֶק בַּתְרָא (ד' קא.), דִּירוּשָׁלַיִם כַּרְמְלִית הִיא: אַבּוּלֵי דִּמְחוֹזָא. שַׁעֲרֵי הָעִיר מְכוּוָּנִים זֶה כְּנֶגֶד זֶה, וְהָיוּ בָּהּ שִׁשִּׁים רִיבּוֹא: חַיָּיבִין עָלֶיהָ כו'. אַלְמָא: נְעִילַת דְּלָתוֹת בָּעֵינַן בְּכָל לַיְלָה. וְהָכָא קָתָנֵי עוֹשֶׂה דֶּלֶת מִכָּאן וְלֶחִי וְקוֹרָה מִכָּאן לְבֵית הִלֵּל: צָרִיךְ לִנְעוֹל. אוֹתוֹ דֶּלֶת יָחִיד: אַבּוּלֵי דִנְהַרְדְּעָא. רָאשֵׁי מְבוֹאוֹת מְפוּלָּשִׁין לִרְשׁוּת הָרַבִּים הָווּ: דְּטִימָּן עַד פַּלְגַּיְיהוּ בְּעַפְרָא. = סְתוּמוֹת עַד חֶצְיָין בֶּעָפָר, וְאֵין אָדָם יָכוֹל לְנוֹעֲלָן מִפְּנֵי הֶעָפָר. "טַיְימָן" — כְּמוֹ "טְמוּנִין פְּלִשְׁתֵּי" (בראשית כו): מְגוּפוֹת הָיוּ. לֹא הָיוּ כּוּלָּן פְּתוּחוֹת, אֶלָּא סְגוּרוֹת וּפְתוּחוֹת בְּמִקְצָת. מְגוּפוֹת כְּמוֹ הֲגָפַת דְּלָתוֹת (ערכין ד' יא:): מָבוֹי עָקוּם. שְׁנֵי פְתָחָיו מְפוּלָּשִׁין לִרְשׁוּת הָרַבִּים אַחַת כְּגוֹן זֶה: אורך רשות הרבים

וְאַצְרְכוּהוּ דְּלָתוֹת. בִּשְׁנֵי עַקְמוּמִיתוֹ: תּוֹרָתוֹ כִּמְפוּלָּשׁ. וְכָאן שְׁנֵי פִּילוּשִׁין דרה"ר יֵשׁ: הֲלָכָה כְּת"ק. דְּלָא בָּעֵי דֶּלֶת אֶלָּא ל"ה: בַּת קוֹל. לְקַמָּן בְּפִירְקִין (ד' יג:) שֶׁיָּצְאָה בַּת קוֹל וְאָמְרָה הֲלָכָה כְּבֵית הִלֵּל:

מי שיש לו שני בתים כו'. פי': שתי חצירות, דאין מבוי ניתר בלחי עד שיהו חצירות פתוחות לתוכו. ובתוספתא גרסי' בהדיא: ב' חצירות: **וכי** תימא בבך הוא דלא מיערבא כו'. משמע דמסיק דאפי' בדלתות לא מיערבא. ואם כן איירי ברה"ר גמורה רוחב ט"ז אמות. וקשה: דלקמן בפירקין (ד' י.) אמרינן דלכל היותר לא התיר ר' יהודה אלא עד י"ג אמה ושליש! וי"ל: דמעיקרא ס"ד ודאי דמיירי ר' יהודה ברוחב ט"ז אמה, אבל לפי המסקנא דמשני כיצד מערבין מבואות המפולשות, הכי נמי ההיא דיתר על כן איירי במבוי המפולש, ואין רוחב ט"ז, ובכך הוא דלא מיערבא – הא בדלתות מיערבא. ולא קשה מירושלים – דהוי רוחב ט"ז אמה. ועי"ל: דמעיקרא נמי ידע שפיר דלא התיר ר' יהודה אלא עד י"ג אמה ושליש, ומ"מ הוי רה"ר גמורה – כגון שרשות הרבים אחת משני לידי המבוי רוחב ט"ז אמות, ואורך

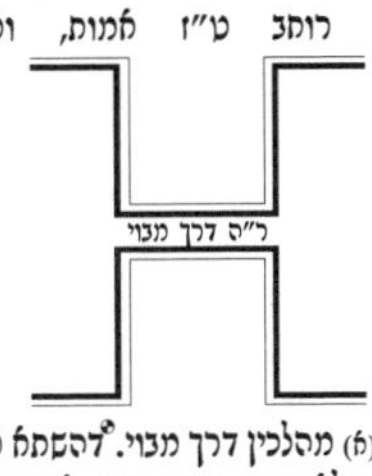

רה"ר (א) מהלכין דרך מבוי. °דהשתא אפי' במבוי דלא הוי רוחב ט"ז אמות הוי רה"ר גמורה, כיון דבשני לידי המבוי הוי רוחב ט"ז אמה. כמו בין העמודים, דאמר פ"ק דשבת (ד' ו.) דהוי רה"ר, אע"ג דלא הוי ט"ז אמה. אפי' למ"ד התם בין העמודים נידון ככרמלית – היינו משום דעמודים הן זה שלא כנגד זה, ולא ניחא תשמישתיה. ולא דמי למבואות המפולשות, דהתם רה"ר אינה עוברת במבוי, אלא ששני רה"ר

עוברות אצל הפתחים. ונ"ל לפי זה אע"ג דלר' יהודה לחי וקורה מהני מדרבנן לי"ג, ולרוחב י"ו לא מהני – מודה הוא דמדאורייתא אין חילוק בין י"ג לי"ו, וקסבר ב' מחיצות דאורייתא, ולכך פריך מירושלים, אע"ג דרחבה י"ו אמה; כיון דחייבין עליה משום רשות הרבים מדאורייתא – הוא הדין ברחבה י"ג, דמדאורייתא אין חילוק. ואם תאמר: כיון דאית ליה לרבי יהודה שתי מחיצות דאורייתא, אמאי איצטריך למיתני בברייתא פרק קמא דשבת (ד' ו.): זו היא רשות היחיד גמורה אחריך עמוק עשרה טפחים ורוחב ד' כו' למעוטי דרבי יהודה דיתר על כן – הא מדקתני ברישא "איזהו רשות הרבים סרטיא ופלטיא ומבואות המפולשות" שמעינן שפיר למעוטי דרבי יהודה. דלדידיה מבואות המפולשות לא הוו רה"ר הואיל ואיכא ב' מחיצות: ויש לומר דאי מרישא ה"א דטעמא דר' יהודה לאו משום שתי מחיצות, אלא משום דקסבר: לחי וקורה משום מחיצה, דאיכא מאן דסבר הכי בפירקין, להכי איצטריך זו היא רשות היחיד גמורה למעוטי דרבי יהודה, דלא הוי רשות היחיד דלחי וקורה לא חשיבי מחיצה:

והאמר רבה כו'. פ"ה: דפריך אמאי דשרינן לחי וקורה מצד אחד, ומדמצריך לנעילת דלת אינו נראה לו שהיה מקשה לו דאיכא לאוקומא נמי בננעלת. ואם תאמר: כיון דיש לו ב' מחיצות ושלישית בננעלת הוי ג' מחיצות ולקמן אמר דלכל היותר לב"ה שלש מחיצות דאורייתא! ויש לומר לפירושו: דהיינו דווקא היכא דאיכא ג' מחיצות גמורות הוו דאורייתא, אבל הכא דשלישית ע"י דלת – רביעית נמי צריך דלת. ולר"י נראה: דפריך משום דמשמע ליה דב"ה לא בעי נעילה, וכן אמר בסמוך דבברייתא לא מפרש בדברי ב"ה נעילה כמו בדברי ב"ש. וא"ת: והיכי פריך מר' יוחנן דאמר בפרק ב' דהוי אליבא דרבי יהודה, דאמר: אתו רבים ומבטלי מחיצתא, ופליגי עליה התם רבנן! ויש לומר: דפריך כי היכי דלר' יהודה בשם ד' מחיצות דלא חשיבי ליה מצריך נעילה, הכי נמי ב' מחיצות דלא חשיבי לרבנן יהיה צריך נעילה. וכן משמע בפרק שני (ד' כב.), דשתי מחיצות לרבנן כשם ד' מחיצות לרבי יהודה: **ומי** עבדינן כתרי חומרי. ואם תאמר: ומאי סלקא דעתך השתא כיון דלא סתרו אהדדי, וכי משום דהלכתא כוותיה בחד דוכתא יהא הלכה כמותו בכל מקום? ובכמה מקומות קיימא לן כמר בהא וכמר בהא! ויש לומר: דלא דמי, דהאי מבוי שרי בל"ה לכולי עלמא, וליכא מאן דמצריך דלתות: **כאן** לאחר בת קול. ואם תאמר: מאי שנא דלא קיימא לן כבת קול דרבי אליעזר ד"הזהב" (ב"מ ד' נט:)? ויש לומר: דהתם לא יצאה אלא לכבודו, כדמוכח התם. ועוד: דהתם היתה כנגד רבים, והתורה אמרה "אחרי רבים להטות". אבל הכא – אדרבה, בית הלל הוו רובא, ולא הוצרכו בת קול אלא משום דבית שמאי *הוו חריפי טפי. ואם תאמר: אם כן מאי קאמר ר' יהושע היא, דאמר אין משגיחין בבת קול, הלא לא אמר רבי יהושע אלא אבת קול דר"א! וי"ל: ד"לא בשמים היא" משמע דאין להשגיח כלל בשום בת קול:

כגון

רבינו חננאל

מי שיש לו ב' בתים מב' צדי רה"ר עושה לחי מיכן ולחי מיכן וכו' עד אמרו לו אין מערבין רה"ר בכך וכי תימא בכך הוא דלא מיערבא כלומר בלחי או קורה הא בדלתות מיערב אע"ג דאינן נגעלות. והאמר ר' יוחנן ירושלים אלמלא דלתותיה ננעלות בלילה חייבין עליה משום רה"ר פי' אע"פ שיש לה דלתות אילו [לא] היו דלתות ננעלות המטלטל בתוכה חייב משום מטלטל ברשות הרבים. (וכל אבולי) [וכן באבולי] דמחוזא ופריק רב יהודה הא דתנו רבנן לאו מערבין רשות הרבים עצמה קתני הכי קתני כיצד מערבין מבואות המפולשין לרה"ר עושה צורת הפתח מיכן ולחי או קורה מיכן. חנניה אומר (בית שמאי אומר) [ב"ה אומרים] עושה דלת מיכן ולחי או קורה מיכן. וכיון דאוקימנא במבואות המפולשין לרה"ר אמר רב הלכה כת"ק ושמואל אמר הלכה כחנניה איבעיא לחנניה ואליבא דב"ה צריך לנעול. ופשטנא אינו צריך מיהו צריך להיות דלתות ראויות לנעול ואם אינו נועל לא חיישינן. פי' מוגפות סגורות כגון (יגופו) [הגפת] הדלתות. טיימי סתומות טמונות. אבולי בלשון יון מבואות פי' עקום. להריפיה עטפה ההוא מבוי עקום דהוה בנהרדעא דרמי עליה חומריה דרב דאמר תורתו כמפולש וחומרי דשמואל דאמר הלכה כחנני' ואצרכוה דלתות. ומדשקיל וטרו כשמואל דאמר הלכה כחנניה ש"מ הלכה כשמואל בהא ואקשינן ומי עבדינן כתרין חומרי. והתניא לעולם הלכה כבית הלל והרוצה לעשות כב"ש עושה.

רב נסים גאון

כאן קודם בת קול כאן לאחר בת קול. בפירקין לקמן (דף יג) אמרו יצתה בת קול ואמרה הלכה כבית הלל ובגמ' דבני מערבא (ברכות פרק א [הלכה ד'] קידושין פ"א הלכה א יבמות סוף פ"א) היכן יצתה בת קול ר' ביבי בשם ר' יוחנן ביבנה יצאתה בת קול. ורבי יהושע היא דאמר אין משגיחין בבת קול בבבא מציעא בפרק הזהב (דף נט) אמרו עמד ר' יהושע על רגליו ואמר לא בשמים היא לאמר וכבר פירשנוהו בברכות: ובגולגלת

עין משפט נר מצוה

לז א מיי' פי"ד מהל' שבת הלכה א סמג עשין דרבנן א טוש"ע א"ח סי' שמה סעיף ז בהג"ה וסי' שסד סעיף ב:

לח ב ג מיי' פי"ז מהל' שבת הלכה ג סמג שם טוש"ע א"ח סי' שסד סעיף א:

לט ד ה מיי' פי"ד שם הלכה י וסמג שם טוש"ע שם ס"ב:

מסורת הש"ס

לקמן כב. קא.
[גיר' הרא"ש רב הונא]
[גיר' רי"ף ורא"ש או קורה]
[גיר' הרא"ש ואליבא דב"ה]
לקמן ח.
ר"ה יז: חולין מג. [תוס' סוכה פ"ב תוספ' עדיות פ"ב]
[עיין תוס' ערכין ב: ד"ה מי שתניה]
[יבמות יד.]

הגהות הב"ח

(א) תוס' ד"ה וכי תימא וכו' ואורך רה"ר מהלכת דרך מבוי:

גליון הש"ס

תום' ד"ה וכ"ת וכו' דהשתא אפילו במבוי דלא הוי רוחב י"ו אמה. עיין לקמן דף נט ע"א תוס' ד"ה עיר של יחיד:

*וְרַבִּי יְהוֹשֻׁעַ הִיא, *דְּלָא מַשְׁגַּח בְּבַת קוֹל. וְאִיבָּעֵית אֵימָא, הָכִי קָאָמַר: כָּל הֵיכָא דְּמַשְׁכַּחַתְּ תְּרֵי תַנָּאֵי וּתְרֵי אֲמוֹרָאֵי דִּפְלִיגִי אַהֲדָדֵי כְּעֵין מַחֲלוֹקֶת ב"ש וב"ה — לָא לֶיעֱבַד כִּי קוּלֵּיהּ דְּמָר וְכִי קוּלֵּיהּ דְּמָר, וְלָא כְּחוּמְרֵיהּ דְּמָר וְכִי חוּמְרֵיהּ דְּמָר. אֶלָּא: אוֹ כִּי קוּלֵּיהּ דְּמָר וּכְחוּמְרֵיהּ עָבֵיד, אוֹ כְּקוּלֵּיהּ דְּמָר וּכְחוּמְרֵיהּ עָבֵיד. מ"מ קַשְׁיָא! אָמַר ר"נ בַּר יִצְחָק: כּוּלֵּיהּ כְּרַב עֲבַדוּהּ, דְּאָמַר רַב הוּנָא, אָמַר רַב: "הֲלָכָה וְאֵין מוֹרִין כֵּן". וּלְרַב אַדָּא בַּר אַהֲבָה אָמַר רַב, דְּאָמַר: "הֲלָכָה וּמוֹרִין כֵּן", מַאי אִיכָּא לְמֵימַר? אָמַר רַב שֵׁיזְבִי: כִּי לָא עָבְדִינַן כְּחוּמְרֵי דְּבֵי תְרֵי — הֵיכָא דְּסָתְרִי אַהֲדָדֵי, כְּגוֹן שִׁדְרָה וְגוּלְגּוֹלֶת. דִּתְנַן: *הַשִּׁדְרָה וְהַגּוּלְגּוֹלֶת שֶׁחָסְרוּ, וְכַמָּה חֶסְרוֹן בַּשִּׁדְרָה? בש"א שְׁתֵּי חוּלְיוֹת, וב"ה אוֹמְרִים: [א]חוּלְיָא אַחַת, וּבַגּוּלְגּוֹלֶת, בש"א: כִּמְלֹא מַקְדֵּחַ, וב"ה אוֹמְרִים: [ב]כְּדֵי שֶׁיִּנָּטֵל מִן הַחַי וְיָמוּת. וְאָמַר רַב יְהוּדָה, אָמַר שְׁמוּאֵל: [ג]וְכֵן לְעִנְיַן טְרֵיפָה. אֲבָל הֵיכָא דְּלָא סָתְרִי אַהֲדָדֵי — עָבְדִינַן. וְהֵיכָא דְּסָתְרִי אַהֲדָדֵי לָא עָבְדִינַן?! מְתִיב רַב מְשַׁרְשְׁיָא: *מַעֲשֶׂה בְּרַבִּי עֲקִיבָא שֶׁלִּיקֵּט אֶתְרוֹג בְּאֶחָד בִּשְׁבָט, וְנָהַג בּוֹ ב' עִישּׂוּרִין, אֶחָד כְּדִבְרֵי ב"ש וְאֶחָד כְּדִבְרֵי ב"ה! *ר' עֲקִיבָא גְּמָרֵיהּ אִיסְתַּפֵּיק לֵיהּ, וְלָא יָדַע אִי בֵּית הִלֵּל בְּחַד בִּשְׁבָט אָמוּר, אִי בַּחֲמִיסַר בִּשְׁבָט אָמוּר, וַעֲבַד הָכָא לְחוּמְרָא וְהָכָא לְחוּמְרָא.§ יְתֵיב רַב יוֹסֵף קַמֵּיהּ דְּרַב הוּנָא, וְיָתֵיב וְקָאָמַר: אָמַר רַב יְהוּדָה, אָמַר רַב: [ד]מַחֲלוֹקֶת בִּסְרַטְיָא מִכָּאן וּסְרַטְיָא מִכָּאן וּפְלַטְיָא מִכָּאן וּפְלַטְיָא מִכָּאן. אֲבָל סְרַטְיָא מִכָּאן וּבִקְעָה מִכָּאן, אוֹ בִּקְעָה מִכָּאן וּבִקְעָה מִכָּאן — עוֹשֶׂה צוּרַת הַפֶּתַח מִכָּאן, וְלֶחִי וְקוֹרָה מִכָּאן. הַשְׁתָּא סְרַטְיָא מִכָּאן וּבִקְעָה מִכָּאן עוֹשֶׂה לוֹ צוּרַת הַפֶּתַח מִכָּאן, וְלֶחִי וְקוֹרָה מִכָּאן, בִּקְעָה מִכָּאן וּבִקְעָה מִכָּאן מִיבַּעְיָא?! הָכִי קָאָמַר: [ה]סְרַטְיָא מִכָּאן וּבִקְעָה מִכָּאן — נַעֲשָׂה כְּבִקְעָה מִכָּאן וּבִקְעָה מִכָּאן. וּמְסַיֵּים בָּהּ מִשְּׁמֵיהּ דְּרַב יְהוּדָה: אִם הָיָה מָבוֹי כָּלֶה לִרְחָבָה — א"צ כְּלוּם. אֲמַר לֵיהּ אַבַּיֵי לְרַב יוֹסֵף: הָא דְּרַב יְהוּדָה — דִּשְׁמוּאֵל הִיא.

דְּאִי

רש"י

ורבי יהושע. בפרק "הזהב" דבבא מציעא (ד' נט:): ואיבעית אימא. הרוצה לעשות דקתני – לאו בית שמאי ובית הלל דווקא נקט, על כרחיך כב"ה בעי למיעבד. אלא אפלוגתא דשאר תנאי בעלמא קאי, דפליגי בעלמא בשאר מילי, כגון אלו מחלוקת דבית שמאי ובית הלל. כלומר: כי היכי דפליגי בית שמאי ובית הלל בדברי מחלוקתן: מכל מקום. ברייתא (לא) מתרצה, וקשיא לנהרדעי דעבוד כתרי חומרי: הלכה. כתנא קמא: ואין מורין כן. אלא כחנניה, דבעי דלתות: דסתרן אהדדי. תרי תנאי דפליגי, מר מחמיר ומר מיקל, וטעמא דחומריה דמר בהאי הוי קולא בדוכתא אחריתי, וטעמא דקוליה דמר בהאי הוי חומרא בדוכתא אחריתי – מאן דעביד בהנך תרי דוכתי לחומרא מיקרי כסיל, דהא חד טעמא הוא דהכא הוי חומרא והכא הוי קולא. ואי ההוא טעמא סבירא ליה – ליעביד כקוליה וכחומריה: כגון שדרה וגולגולת. של מת, דאיפליגו בה. דלבית שמאי לא הוי חסרון אלא בב' חוליות, ואם חסרה חוליא אחת – עדיין מטמא באהל, וגבי טריפה נמי לא הוי חסרון, וכשירה. והוי טעמא דבית שמאי חומרא לגבי מת. ולבית הלל דאמרי חסרון הוא – הוי חומרא לגבי טריפה ומאן דעביד בטריפה כבית הלל וכבית שמאי במת הוי כסיל, דהא סתרין עובדי אהדדי. דהכא הוי חסרון, והכא לא הוי חסרון: השדרה והגולגולת. גבי טומאת אהל במת תנן: כמה חסרון בשדרה, ותלא מתורת שדרה ותידון כשאר עצם כשעורה שאינו מטמא באהל: כמלא מקדח. וכדי שינטל מן החי וימות, מפרש להו בבכורות בפ' שלישי: אבל היכא דלא סתרן חומרי אהדדי. כגון הכא, דפליגי בתרי מילי דתליין בתרי טעמא, מר מחמיר בהא עקום ומר מחמיר בהא מפולש, ולא סתרן חומרי אהדדי – עבדינן: שליקט אתרוג. כל האילן קרוי אתרוג: שני עישורין. שניה יוצאה ושלישית נכנסת, הואי שנה שניה לשמיטה מעשר ראשון ושני, והשלישית מעשר ראשון ומעשר עני: אחד כדברי בית שמאי. דאמרי באחד בשבט ראש השנה לאילן, וכבר נכנסת שלישית: ואחד כדברי בית הלל. דאמרי עד חמשה עשר בו לא הוי ראש השנה, ועדיין שניה היא: גמריה איסתפיק ליה. וכוליה כב"ה עבד: מחלוקת. דמבואות המפולשין דת"ק וחנניה: סרטיא ופלטיא. שתיהן רה"ר, כדאמרינן ב"יציאות השבת" (שבת ד' ו.): איזהו רה"ר – סרטיא ופלטיא. סרטיא – דרך הילוך בני אדם. פלטיא – רחוב לשווקים. והיכא דשני ראשין מפולשין ברשות הרבים הוא דפליג חנניה, ואמר בעי דלת: בקעה. כרמלית היא, ואיסורא דרבנן הוא:(א) ומסיים בה. רב יוסף משמיה דרב יהודה סתמא, ולא פירש לו רב יהודה לרב יוסף ממי קבל האי סיום, דאם היה סוף המבוי הזה המפולש לרה"ר כלה לרחבה, ודרך הרחבה היה המבוי מפולש שנפרץ כותל הרחבה שכנגדו לרה"ר*. רחבה – היקף חצר שאחורי בתים קרי רחבה, מוקפת ארבע מחיצות: אין צריך כלום. לתקן אותה פתיחה של צד הרחבה, אלא ראש המפולש לרה"ר צריך לחי או קורה כתורת מבוי סתום. ועל כרחיך בדנפרצה נמי רחבה כנגד פרצת המבוי בכותל שכנגדו לרה"ר קאמר לאשמועינן, ואמפולשין דלעיל קאי. דאי ברחבה סתומה לגמרי – פשיטא, דהא סתימה מעלייתא היא. והא ליכא למימר דמשום בני רחבה איצטריך לאשמועינן דלא אסרי אבני מבוי, ואפילו לא עירבו עמהן – דהא נמי פשיטא דרחבה לא בעיא לערובי, דסתם רחבה אין בה דיורין לצאת ולבא, ואין תשמישה תדיר(ב), כדאמרינן בפרק שני (ד' כה.): מאן דשרי לטלטולי מן המבוי לתוכה – משום דלית בה דיורין. והלכתא כוותיה, דקיימא לן*) בכל התורה רב אחא לחומרא ורבינא לקולא, והלכתא כרבינא לקולא בר מאומצא, ביעי, ומזריקי. ורחבה לאו דוקא נקט, והוא הדין לחצר שיש בה דיורין ועירבו, אלא עובדא ברחבה היתה, כדאמרינן לקמן: עובדא הוה בדורא דרעוותא כו' כל כניסה ויליאה דבתים שבהש"ס דרך החצר הוא, וחצר לפני הבתים: הא דר"י. הא דסיימת משמיה דרב יהודה ולא פירש לך ממאן גמריה, כדמפרש ברישא דמילתיה משמיה דרב – האי סיומא ע"כ משמואל רביה גמריה:

במלואו

*) [פסחים עב:]

תוספות

כגון שדרה וגולגולת. משמע דוכן לטרפה אתרוייהו קאי. ואם תאמר: מאי קאמרי ב"ה כדי שינטל מן החי וימות, לב"ש נמי מיית בשיעורא דידהו! ועוד: מאי קמ"ל רב יהודה דאמר וכן לטרפה לענין גולגולת, כיון דמיית בה! וי"ל: דרגילות הוא למות על ידי נטילה בחסרון מועט מעל ידי רקיבה וחולי. וא"ת: וב"אלו טרפות" (חולין ד' מב:) דפריך: והאיכא בסג"ר ושב שמעתתא, והסמ"ך הוי חסרון בשדרה. ואמאי לא פריך נמי מגולגולת? וי"ל: דחסרון גולגולת דטריפה – היינו משום דסוף הקרום של מוח ליפסק, והוי בכלל י"ח טריפות. אבל שדרה לא הוי משום דסוף החוט ליפסק, דאפילו למטה מפרסות דליכא טרפות בפסיקת החוט, איירי:

(ומיהו כמה בני אדם שניטל הרבה מעלם גולגלתם ולא ניקב הקרום וחיו. ול"ל: דחסרון הגולגולת הוי עם קרום העליון. ואע"ג דאיכא למ"ד דבבהמה בכה"ג בנקיבת קרום העליון טריפה – היינו משום דסוף התחתון ליפסק. אבל באדם אין סופו ליפסק, לפי שהוא קשה וחזק באדם יותר מבהמה, ולכך לריך חסרון העלם. אבל למ"ד עד דאינקיב תתאה – אדם ובהמה שוים, דבין באדם בין בבהמה כי נפסק העלם עם הקרום – סוף התחתון ליפסק):

ונהג בו ב' עישורים. מפרש בירושלמי שעישר על תנאי, וחללו, ונתנו לענייס: בקעה מכאן ובקעה מכאן מיבעיא. ולא משמע ליה דאתא לאשמועינן דאפ"ה בעי לורת הפתח, אלא אתי לאשמועינן דסגי בלורת הפתח: אם היה מבוי כלה לרחבה אינו צריך כו'. פירש רש"י: דנפרלה רחבה כנגדו איירי, דאל"כ – מאי אשמועינן? דלאשמועינן דאין רחבה אוסרת על המבוי – לא אילטריך, דרחבה לית בה דיורין, כדאמרינן בפ' ב' (ד' כד:) גבי רחבה דהוה בפוס נהרא, מאן דשרי – משום דלית בה דיורין. והלכתא כרבינא לקולא *. ועוד: דאין לריך כלום – משמע דקאי אאיסור פילוש דאיירי ביה. לכך נראה דנפרלה כנגדו איירי. והא דנקט רחבה ולא נקט חלר – משום דבעי למימר אין לריך כלום, אפילו לא עירבו. אבל חלר דאית ביה דיורין – אסור עד שיערבו, דסבר נראה מבחוץ ושוה מבפנים אינו נידון משום לחי ופתח, ובכלה לאמלע רחבה איירי.

הגה"ה: אפילו מאן דאסר איכא למימר דאיירי ברחבה שכל אחד היה חלקו מבורר בה ברחבה ואיכא למיחש שמא כל אחד יכנס בחלקו כדאמר בסמוך(ג). ע"כ:

ולא חשיב ליה כמפולש – משום דיליאתו מן המבוי יש מקום לנטות לכאן ולכאן, ולא אתי למישרי מפולש:

דאי

עין משפט נר מצוה

מ א ב מיי' פ"ב מהל' טומאת מת הלכה ח סמג עשין רלג:

מא ג מיי' פ"י מהלכות שחיטה הלכה ב ה סמג עשין סג טוש"ע י"ד סי' ל' סעיף ב וכסי' נד סעיף ד:

מב ד ה מיי' פי"ז מהל' שבת הלכה ג י סמג עשין א טוש"ע א"ח סי' שס"ד סעיף א [ע"ש בכ"מ וכמ"מ]:

[ועי' תוס' גיטין נו: ד"ה וניקר ותוס' חולין מב: ד"ה ואמר ותוס' ב"ק נח. ד"ה נעביד ותוס' בכורות לז. ד"ה כדי]

מסורת הש"ס

[ברכות נב. פסחים קיד. יבמות יד. ב"מ נט: חולין מד.]

חולין מב: אהלות פ"ב מ"ג בכורות לז:

ר"ה יד. יבמות טו. [תוספתא שביעית סוף פ"ג]

[ר"ה יד:]

הגהות הב"ח

(א) רש"י ד"ה ומסיים וכו' הל"א עם ד"ה אין לריך וכו': (ב) כדאמרינן בפרק שני. נ"ב ריש דף כה וע"ש בפרש"י דף כד ע"ב: (ג) תוס' ד"ה אם היה וכו' בהג"ה שמא כל אחד יכנה בחלקו כדאמר בסמוך. נ"ב פירוש דקאמר ברחבה ליחיד זימנין דמימלך ובני לה בתי כו' כלומר דחיישי' דילמא עבדי בה דיורין ואסרי אהדדי היינו דקאמר לקמן ומאן דאסר זמנין דהוו בה דיורין ואתי לטלטולי:

גליון הש"ס

גמ' אמר לי' אביי לר"י הא דר"י דשמואל היא. לקמן דף פה ע"א יבמות יח ע"א כתובו' דף יב ע"ב:

רבינו חננאל

כב"ה עושה ובלבד שלא יעשה כקולי זה וכקולי זה או כחומרי זה וכחומרי זה. ופרקינן הא דעבוד דלת בהאי מבוי עקום כוליה כרב עבוד דאע"ג דאמר רב הלכה כת"ק (א') [הא אמר] אין מורין כן אלא כב"ה ואליבא דחנניה דאמר עושה דלת ולרב אדא בר אהבה דאמר הלכה ומורין כן פריק רב שיזבי כי לא עבדינן כתרי חומרי כגון שדרה שנעקרה צלע מעיקרא טריפה. דסתרי אהדדי דחיסרון בשדרה *) חוליא וצלע בהדא ונעקרה צלע בלא חוליא אבל תרי חומרי דלא סתרי אהדדי עבדינן. וכבר פירשנו שמועה זו בפרק אלו טרפות [באהלות תנן] כמה חסרון בשדרה כדי שינטל מן החי וימות. ולענין טרפה תנן זה הכלל כל שאין כמוה חיה טרפה וכיון שאתה עושה חוליא אחת טריפה ולענין טומאה [אם חסר] חוליא אחת [אתה] מטמא באהל דהן סותרין זה את זה. **) פי' תרי חומרי דסתרי אהדדי כגון שדרה וגולגולת דתנן בתרוייהו כדי שינטל מן החי וימות. גבי טומאה תנן כמה חסרון בשדרה ולא יהא מטמא באהל בש"א ב' חוליות ובה"א אחת. וחלוקתם דב"ש סברי לא מיית עד דאשתלפי מיניה תרי חוליות. וב"ה סברי כשתנטל חוליא אחת מיית וכאלו הותזה ראשו ואם נחמיר כב"ה לחשבו מת ולטמא במגע מת ולכשימות לגמרי [אינו] מטמא באהל שכבר חסר כדי שינטל מן החי וימות. ואם כשניטלה ממנו חוליא אחת אינו מת אלא חי הוא [כב"ש] אינו מטמא במגע. אבל לטמויי במגע כב"ה ובאהל כב"ש לא אפשר דהא העיקר דסמכא דתרוייהו עליה כדי שיטול מן החי וימות ואי אפשר ***) לחלל בשעה אחת לב"ש חי ולב"ה מת. וכיון ששנינו בטריפה נמי זה הכלל כל שאין כמוה חיה טרפה שמפרכסין טמאין [אף] כזנב הלטאה שמפרכסת. ומי שנטלה ממנו חוליא אחת לב"ה כאילו הותזו ראשיהן: יתיב רב יוסף וקאמר הא דת"ר כיצד מערבין ואוקימנא במבואות המפולשות לרה"ר מחלוקת ת"ק וחנניה בסרטיא או פלטיא מיכן. אבל סרטיא מיכן ובקעה מיכן עושה צורת הפתח מיכן ולחי או קורה מיכן ומסיים בה משמיה דרב יהודה אם היה מבוי

*) דברי רבינו כמסורסין ונראה דל"ל כגון שדרה שניטל ממנה חוליא בלא צלע או שנעקר צלע ממנה ותלי חוליא בהדה טרפה (עי' חולין נ"ב) דסתרי אהדדי אבל תרי חומרי כו': **) אולי צריך להגי' פי' אחר תרי חומרי דסתרי כו'. ***) נראה דל"ל ולא אפשר כלל לומר בשעה אחת הוא כחי כב"ש וגם הוא כמת כב"ה.

רב נסים גאון

ובגולגולת בית שמי אומרים כמלא מקדח. במשנה שנו באיזה מקדח אמרו בקטן של רופאים דברי ר' מאיר וחכמים אומרים בגדול של לשכה בפרק ב' דאהלות ובית הלל אומרים כדי שינטל מן החי וימות תמצא פירוש שלו במסכת בכורות בפרק על אלו מומין שוחטין את הבכור (קף לז) יתיב רב חסדא ומיבעיא ליה כדי שינטל מן החי כמה אמר רב תחליפא בר אבדימי הכי אמר שמואל כסלע: מעשה בר' עקיבא שליקט אתרוג באחד בשבט ונהג בו ב' עישורין כו' ובגמ' דבני מערבא (ר"ה פרק א הלכה ב) גרסי מה עשה קרא שם למעשר שני ופדאו ונתנו לעני ועל זו הדרך ישיג בקשתו לרווחא דמילתא שרצה לעשות לפנים משורת הדין כדי להנצל מן הספק ממה נפשך לפי שקרא עליו שם מעשר שני ואחר כך פדאו ונתנו לעניים והניח הכסף שמור אצלו עד שיאכלנו בירושלים לפנים מן החומה לפי מה שפרט בו הכתוב (דברים יד) ונתתה הכסף בכל אשר תאוה נפשך שאם יהיו בית הלל הם שאמרו באחד בשבט ראש השנה לאילן זה המעשר שהפריש מעשר עני הוא וכבר נטלו מי שהוא ראוי לו ואם בט"ו בשבט אמרו הרי שנה שניה עדיין לא יצאת וזה המעשר שהפריש מעשר שני הוא וחייב לאכלו הוא או כספו בירושלים ולפיכך פדאהו בכסף ואכל כספו לפנים מן החומה כראוי לו כדי להנצל מן הספק:

אי

מג א ב מיי' פי"ז מהל' שבת הלכה יח סמג עשין דרבנן א טוש"ע א"ח סי' שסה סעיף ג:

דְּאִי דְּרַב — קַשְׁיָא דְּרַב אַדְּרַב בְּתַרְתֵּי. דְּאָמַר רַב יִרְמְיָה בַּר אַבָּא, אָמַר רַב: [א]מָבוֹי שֶׁנִּפְרַץ בִּמְלוֹאוֹ לֶחָצֵר, וְנִפְרְצָה חָצֵר כְּנֶגְדּוֹ — חָצֵר מוּתֶּרֶת וּמָבוֹי אָסוּר. וְאַמַּאי? לֶיהֱוֵי כְּמָבוֹי שֶׁכָּלֶה לָרְחָבָה! אֲמַר לֵיהּ: אֲנָא לָא יָדַעְנָא; עוּבְדָּא הֲוָה בְּדוּרָא דְּרַעֲוָתָא מָבוֹי שֶׁכָּלֶה לִרְחָבָה הֲוָה, וַאֲתָא לְקַמֵּיהּ דְּרַב יְהוּדָה וְלָא אַצְרְכֵיהּ וְלָא מִידֵּי. וְאִי קַשְׁיָא מִשְּׁמֵיהּ דְּרַב — תֶּיהֱוֵי מִשְּׁמֵיהּ דִּשְׁמוּאֵל, וְלָא קַשְׁיָא מִידֵּי. הָשְׁתָּא דַּאֲמַר לֵיהּ רַב שֵׁשֶׁת לְרַב שְׁמוּאֵל בַּר אַבָּא, וְאָמְרִי לֵיהּ לְרַב יוֹסֵף בַּר אַבָּא: אַסְבְּרָא לָךְ, כָּאן — שֶׁעֵירְבוּ, כָּאן — שֶׁלֹּא עֵירְבוּ. דְּרַב אַדְּרַב נַמִי לָא קַשְׁיָא, כָּאן — [ב]שֶׁעֵירְבוּ בְּנֵי חָצֵר עִם בְּנֵי מָבוֹי, כָּאן — שֶׁלֹּא עֵירְבוּ.

וּלְמַאי

רש"י

בִּמְלוֹאוֹ. כּוֹתֶל אֶמְצָעִי עַל פְּנֵי כּוּלּוֹ: וְנִפְרְצָה חָצֵר כְּנֶגְדּוֹ. בְּפָחוֹת מֵעֶשֶׂר: חָצֵר מוּתֶּרֶת. דִּלְדִידָהּ לָא הָוֵי בִּמְלוֹאָהּ, וְנִשְׁתַּיְּירוּ בָּהּ גִּיפּוּפִין מִכָּאן וּמִכָּאן. לְפִיכָךְ לְגַבֵּי דִידָהּ פְּתָחִים נִינְהוּ, וְלָא אָסְרִי עֲלָהּ בְּנֵי מָבוֹי – שֶׁאֵין מָבוֹי אוֹסֵר עַל חֲצֵירוֹת הַפְּתוּחִין לוֹ. אֲבָל חֲצֵירוֹת אוֹסְרִין בְּמָבוֹי, שֶׁהֲרֵי דְּרִיסַת רַגְלֵיהֶם עָלָיו. וּרְשׁוּת הָרַבִּים נַמִי לָא אָסַר עֲלָהּ, דְּחָצֵר הַפָּתוּחַ לוֹ כְּפֶתַח הוּא: וּמָבוֹי אָסוּר. קס"ד מִדְּנָקַט וְנִפְרְצָה חָצֵר כְּנֶגְדּוֹ מִשּׁוּם דְּמִיחֲזֵי כְּמָבוֹי מְפוּלָּשׁ קָא אָסַר לֵיהּ, וְלָאו מִשּׁוּם דְּנִפְרַץ לֶחָצֵר. וְרַב יְהוּדָה, מִדְּנָקַט רְחָבָה אַשְׁמְעִינַן דְּמִשּׁוּם מְפוּלָּשׁ לָא מִיתְּסַר, וּבִרְחָבָה לֵיכָּא דִּיּוּרִין דְּלִיתַּסְרוּ עֲלֵיהּ. אֲבָל אִי הֲוָה כָּלֶה לֶחָצֵר – אָסְרִי עֲלֵיהּ. וּלְקַמָּן מְפָרֵשׁ טַעֲמַיְיהוּ. וְהַיְינוּ דְּקַשְׁיָא דְּרַב אַדְּרַב בְּתַרְתֵּי, אִי מִשּׁוּם מְפוּלָּשׁ אִי מִשּׁוּם הַנִּפְרָץ לֶחָצֵר וְאָסְרִי עֲלֵיהּ בְּנֵי חָצֵר, דְּנִפְרַץ הַמָּבוֹי בִּמְלוֹאוֹ לִרְשׁוּת הָאֲסוּרָה לוֹ: לָא יָדַעְנָא. מִמַּאן גְּמָרָהּ: בְּדוּרָא דְּרַעֲוָתָא. כְּפַר רוֹעִים: שֶׁכָּלֶה לִרְחָבָה. וּרְחָבָה נִפְרְצָה בַּכּוֹתֶל שֶׁכְּנֶגְדָּהּ: אַסְבְּרָא לָךְ. מִילְּתֵיהּ דְּרַב, דִּגְמִירְנָא לָהּ מִינֵּיהּ: כָּאן שֶׁעֵירְבוּ כָּאן שֶׁלֹּא עֵירְבוּ. כְּלוֹמַר: הַאי מָבוֹי אָסוּר דְּקָאָמַר רַב יֵשׁ חִילּוּק בַּדָּבָר, שֶׁפְּעָמִים אָסוּר וּפְעָמִים מוּתָּר. עֵירְבוּ בְּנֵי הֶחָצֵר עִם בְּנֵי מָבוֹי – בְּנֵי מָבוֹי מוּתָּרִין, דְּהָא דְּאָסַר לֵיהּ רַב – לָאו מִשּׁוּם מְפוּלָּשׁ קָאָסַר לֵיהּ, כִּדְמוֹקְמִינַן לְקַמָּן בְּזֶה שֶׁלֹּא כְּנֶגֶד זֶה. וְהַאי נִפְרְצָה חָצֵר כְּנֶגְדּוֹ – מִשּׁוּם רְבוּתָא דְּחָצֵר נָקַט, דְּאַף עַל גַּב דְּרַבִּים נִכְנָסִין לָהּ בְּזוֹ וְיוֹצְאִין לָהּ בְּזוֹ – אֲפִילּוּ הָכִי שַׁרְיָא, הוֹאִיל וְנִפְרְצָה בְּפָחוֹת מֵעֶשֶׂר, דַּחֲשִׁיב כְּפֶתַח חָצֵר. אֲבָל אִיסּוּר מָבוֹי לָאו מִשּׁוּם [פִּירְצָה] דְּכוֹתֶל שֶׁכְּנֶגְדּוֹ הוּא, אֶלָּא מִשּׁוּם דִּבְנֵי חָצֵר אָסְרִי עֲלֵיהּ כִּי לָא עֵירְבוּ. דְּכֵיוָן דִּלְדִידֵיהּ הָוֵי מְלוֹאוֹ – פִּירְצָה הוּא, וְדִיּוּרֵי חָצֵר אוֹסְרִין עָלָיו, וְהוּא אֵינוֹ אוֹסֵר עֲלֵיהֶן. כִּדְאָמְרִינַן בְּפֶרֶק "כָּל גַּגּוֹת הָעִיר" (לקמן ד' צב.) גַּבֵּי חָצֵר גְּדוֹלָה שֶׁנִּפְרְצָה לִקְטַנָּה: דִּיּוּרֵי גְּדוֹלָה בִּקְטַנָּה, כְּלוֹמַר: אוֹסְרִים בִּקְטַנָּה, דְּדִידְהוּ הוּא, דִּבְטֵלָה לְגַבָּהּ. וְאֵין דִּיּוּרֵי קְטַנָּה בִּגְדוֹלָה – דִּלְגַבֵּי גְּדוֹלָה פֶּתַח הוּא, וּשְׁתֵּי חֲצֵירוֹת שֶׁיֵּשׁ בֵּינֵיהֶן פֶּתַח לָא אָסְרָן אַהֲדָדֵי, כִּדְאָמְרִינַן בְּפֶרֶק "חַלּוֹן" (לקמן ד' עו:): נִפְרַץ הַכּוֹתֶל עַד עֶשֶׂר אַמּוֹת, אִם רָצוּ – מְעָרְבִין שְׁנַיִם, וְאִם רָצוּ – מְעָרְבִין אֶחָד, מִפְּנֵי שֶׁהוּא כְּפֶתַח, וּשְׁנֵיהֶם מוּתָּרִין זֶה בָּזֶה: דְּרַב אַדְּרַב נַמִי לָא תִּיקְשֵׁי. כְּלוֹמַר: מֵהָשְׁתָּא מָצֵינַן לְמֵימַר דְּרַב יְהוּדָה בְּדוּרָא דְּרַעֲוָתָא כְּרַב עֲבַדוּהּ, כִּדְאָמְרִינַן כָּאן שֶׁעֵירְבוּ וְכָאן שֶׁלֹּא עֵירְבוּ, וּבִרְחָבָה לֵיכָּא דִּיּוּרִין לְמֵיסְרֵי אַמָּבוֹי:

וּלְמַאי

תוספות

דאי דרב קשיא אדרב בתרתי דאמר רב מבוי שנפרץ במלואו לחצר ונפרצה חצר כנגדו חצר מותרת. דבני מבוי לא אסרי – עלה דאין דריסתם עלה, ורשות הרבים נמי לא אסרה – דלא הוי פרצה יותר מעשר, והוי פתח. ומבוי אסור משום פילוש, דהעומד במבוי רואה רשות הרבים כנגדו, ואינו רואה שיכול לנטות לכאן ולכאן. ומדנקט נפרצה חצר כנגדו – משמע דוקא שנפרצה חצר כנגדו אסור, משום דהוי כמפולש. אבל אם לא נפרצה, אפילו אם לא עירבו – מותר, אע"ג דנפרץ המבוי במלואו לחצר, משום דקסבר: נראה מבחוץ ושוה מבפנים – נידון משום לחי ופתח, ומתני' דגדולה מותרת וקטנה אסורה – מוקי לה בנכנסין כותלי קטנה לגדולה. וליכא למימר דאסור משום מפולש ומשום שנפרץ במלואו ולא עירבו קאמר – דא"כ הוה ליה למינקט רחבה, דהוה משמע דאסור משום מפולש וגם הוה משמע מדנקט רחבה ולא נקט חצר מכלל דבחצר יש עוד איסור אחר, דהיינו משום שלא עירבו. אבל השתא דנקט חצר – משמע אפילו איסור דלא עירבו דשייך בחצר ליכא, אלא משום שנפרצה חצר כנגדו. והיינו דקשיא דרב אדרב בתרתי, דרב סבר נידון משום לחי ופתח ואסור משום מפולש, ורב יהודה סבר דאין אסור משום מפולש, ונראה מבחוץ ושוה מבפנים – אינו נידון משום לחי ופתח. אסברא לך כאן שעירבו. כלומר: רב לא אסר מטעם מפולש, ולא נקט נפרצה חצר כנגדו – אלא משום שריותא דחצר, אע"ג דרבים נכנסין לה בזו ויוצאין לה בזו – שריא. אבל מבוי – אסור, אפילו לא נפרצה חצר כנגדו, משום דנפרץ במלואו לחצר ולא עירבו. וסבר: נראה מבחוץ – אינו נידון משום לחי ופתח. ודווקא נפרץ במלואו, אבל אי לא הוה נפרץ במלואו – שרי, אע"ג דלא עירבו, כיון דאינה רגילה בו. כדאמר ונפרץ – משמע דאינה רגילה בו. והוא הדין *דהוה מצי למינקט במבוי פתוח לחצר דאסור, כיון דרגילה בו, אע"ג דלא הוי במלואו. אלא אי נקט הכי לא הוה קמ"ל רב מידי, דכיון דפתח גמור הוא – פשיטא דלא אתו רבים ומבטלי מחיצתא. אי נמי: לא הוה מצי למינקט בפתוח לחצר, דאע"ג דרגילה בו הוה שרי, הואיל ולבני חצר יש להם דרך לרה"ר בלא מבוי – דכגון זו כופין אותו על מדת סדום, כדאמרינן ב"מי שהוציאוהו" (לקמן ד' מט.) גבי חצר שבין שני מבואות.

*__בעירבו__ קמיפלגי בדרב יוסף. דהיינו כלה לאמצע רחבה. ורב יוסף מפרש מילתיה דרב יהודה הא דאמר אין צריך כלום. ותירוץ דכאן בעירבו – לא תירצו בימי רב יוסף. וסבר רב יוסף דנראה מבחוץ לרב נידון משום לחי, כדס"ד מעיקרא אליבא דרב. והכי נמי דייק רב יוסף ממלתיה דרב הונא, דהוא תלמידיה דרב דנדון משום לחי. אך קשה: דלא שייך למימר קמיפלגי בדרב יוסף, הואיל ולא איירו במה שבא רב יוסף לחדש והיינו דאסור בצידי רחבה! וי"ל: דאי לאו מילתיה דרב יוסף ה"א דפליגי נמי בצידי רחבה, והוה קשה היכי שרי שמואל בצידי רחבה היכא דאיכא תרתי לריעותא, שצידו אחד מפולש עד רה"ר וצידו השני נמי, אע"ג דנראה מבחוץ – האמר שמואל דאין נידון משום לחי! לכך הוצרך להביא דרב יוסף דבכלה לאמצע רחבה פליגי, דלא הוי תרתי לריעותא. וגם לרב נמי הוה קשה, הואיל וסבר דנידון משום לחי – אמאי אסר משום מפולש? דהוה סברא לומר דהא בהא תליא. ולכך מייתי דרב יוסף, דלאו הא בהא תליא, דבכלה לצידי רחבה – אסור לכולי עלמא, אפילו למאן דאמר נידון משום לחי. וטעמא, משום דלמפולש לא מהני לחי(א) אלא לר' יהודה. והא דלא משני לעיל דרב יהודה בכלה לאמצע, ודרב בכלה מן הצד, או כאן בזה כנגד זה וכאן בזה שלא כנגד זה – משום דהאמת תירץ לו, דהא רב ששת לא מחמת קושיא תירץ, אלא קבלה היתה בידו. כך יש לפרש לפי שיטת רש"י. ור"י מפרש: דרחבה דהכא לא הויא כרחבה דפ' שני (ד' כד:), דהתם מיירי ביתירה מבית סאתים ולא הוקף לדירה והויא כרמלית, ואין מטלטלין בה אלא בד'. אבל רחבה דהכא אינו כן – דא"כ הוה כלה לבקעה, אלא מיירי בדאית בה דיורין, מדמפליג בין עירבו ובין לא עירבו דלא גרע מחורבה, דאמר בפרק "הדר" (לקמן ד' עד.) דאסור, כ"ש רחבה דאית ביה דיורין טפי מחורבה. והיתה אסורה אי לאו דס"ד השתא דסבר רב יהודה נראה מבחוץ נידון משום לחי. וקס"ד השתא מדלא מפליג רב יהודה בשריותא – משמע דשרי בכל ענין, אפילו כלה לצידי רחבה ונפרצה(ב) חצר כנגדו ואפילו לא עירבו. ועוד: מדאיירי רב יהודה בנפרצה כנגדו ואיצטריך לאשמועינן דלא הוי מפולש – א"כ על כרחך ס"ל נראה מבחוץ ושוה מבפנים נדון משום לחי, דאי לא חשיב לחי – אמאי שרי בכלה לצידי רחבה? דלאמצע רחבה פשיטא דלא הוי מפולש, וא"כ איכא תרתי לריעותא: שצידו אחד מפולש עד רשות הרבים, וצידו השני נמי נהי דנראה מבחוץ – הא לא חשיב לחי. אלא וודאי חשיב לחי, והשתא לא הוי תרתי לריעותא [דחשיב] לחי מצד אחד, כדאמר לקמן (ד' ט.): ולימא לבוד מרוח אחת ותשתרי. ונקט רחבה משום דעובדא הכי הוה, והוא הדין חצר. אע"ג דרב יוסף קאמר משמיה דרב יהודה והוא מוקי לה לקמן בכלה לאמצע רחבה, אבל בצידי רחבה אסור – ההוא לא שנו הוי לפי המסקנא. השתא ס"ד אסור משום מפולש בכלה לצידי חצר, ונפרצה כנגדו אפילו עירבו. דבכלה לאמצע אין סברא לאסור משום פילוש, מדקאמר ונפרץ חצר כנגדו ואסור בשלא עירבו, אפילו בכלה לאמצע ולא נפרצה חצר כנגדו. מדנקט "במלואו" משמע דאסור משום דנפרץ במלואו, דהיינו בלא עירבו, ובדלא נפרצה כנגדו. דאי בנפרצה ובעירבו – מאי אריא ונפרץ במלואו, דאפילו לא נפרץ במלואו הוי כמפולש, ולא מהני לחי עד דאיכא צורת הפתח. ועוד: מדנקט חצר ולא נקט קרפף דלית בה דיורין – משמע משום דיורין שבחצר בא נמי לאסור. ועוד: דאי לא אסור אלא משום פילוש, הוה ליה למימר: מבוי שנפרץ במלואו לצידי חצר. מדלא נקט הכי – משמע דבכלה לאמצע נמי מיירי, ואסור משום דלא עירבו, וסבר: נראה מבחוץ ושוה מבפנים – אינו נידון משום לחי. ומיהו, מדאסר בצידי חצר משום פילוש – אין להוכיח דסבר דאינו נידון משום לחי, דאפילו נידון משום לחי הוי מפולש, דהא רב יוסף אסר בצידי רחבה לכ"ע, אפילו למ"ד נידון משום לחי. דרב אדרב נמי ל"ק כאן בעירבו. פי': הא דרב יהודה בכלה לאמצע, כדמפרש רב יוסף אע"ג דלא מפליג בשריותא – אין לחוש, דכיון דתרווייהו מילתיה דרב מה שסתם כאן פירש כאן. ועוד: כיון דסבר רב נראה מבחוץ לא הוי לחי, לא חש לפרש דאיירי בכלה לאמצע רחבה. דבכלה מן הצד הוי תרתי לריעותא. אע"ג דרב יוסף אית ליה נראה מבחוץ נידון משום לחי, כדדייק לקמן ממלתיה דרב הונא – מ"מ אוקי מילתיה דרב יהודה בעירבו, משום דרב יהודה תחלת דבריו אמר משמיה דרב, ונראה לרב יוסף דהסיום נמי הוי משמיה דרב אע"פ שסתם א"ר יהודה כו' ולא פירש משם מי אמר. וכן רב יוסף אמר בסתם משמיה דרב יהודה, מ"מ היה נראה לו שגם זה מדברי רב, ורב סבר אינו נידון משום לחי. והשתא אתי שפיר דקמפלגי במה שבא רב יוסף לחדש. ומיהו, רבינו חננאל מיישב דאתי שפיר דקא מיפלגי בדרב יוסף, דרב יהודה שרי אפילו זה כנגד זה כרב יוסף, ורב כרבה דבעי זה שלא כנגד זה. ולקמן נמי משמע דרבה פליג אדרב יוסף, דפריך: ולרבה דאמר זה כנגד זה אסור. מיהו, ה"ל למימר דרבה ודרב יוסף איכא בינייהו:

זורקין

ולימא למימר דנקט הכי לאשמועי' דאם אינה רגילה בו מותר דא"כ מאי פריך לקמן מאי קמ"ל רב

שייך לדף ח ומהר"מ כתב דקך ד"ה בעירבו עם ד"ה דאי וד"ה אם כולם ליבור אחד

הגהות הב"ח

(א) תוס' ד"ה בעירבו וכו' דלמפולש לא מהני לחי אלא. נמחק תיבת אלא ובעו"ה נמחק ג"כ מה שנ"ב: (ב) בא"ד כלה לצידי רחבה ונפרצה רחבה כנגדו:

גליון הש"ס

גמ' אנא לא ידענא עובדא הוי. לקמן דף יב ע"א ב"ב דף נד ע"ב ושם דף פב ע"ב: **תוס'** ד"ה בעירבו ור"י מפרש. בחידושי כתבתי דלא זכיתי להבין הא באמת דהסיא עובדא היה בכלה לאמצע רחבה דהא למסקנא בכלה לצידי לכ"ע אסור ואיך לא אצרכה ר"י ולא מידי וכיון שכן למה דהיה סבר ר"י תחלה דפלוגתייהו רק בצידי דבאמצע ליכא חידוש ושריא לכ"ע איך הביא ראי' מההוא עובדא הא שם היה בכלה באמצע וה' יאיר עיני: **בא"ד** אפי' לא נפרץ במלואו נמי הוי כמפולש. וק"ל הא כמו דהרחבה וחצר לא הוי כמפולש מכח הגיפופין שלהן ה"נ המבוי בלא נפרץ במלואו:

רבינו חננאל

כלה לרחבה אינו צריך כלום. פי' רחבה זו יש בה בתים ודיורין והיא מפולשת לרה"ר א"ל אביי לרב יוסף הא דרב יהודה אינה כרב דכיון דאמר רב מבוי שנפרץ במילואו לחצר ונפרצה כנגדו חצר לרה"ר החצר מותרת ומבוי אסור. אמאי אסור וליהוי כמבוי שכלה לרחבה אלא אינה כרב אלא כשמואל וא"ל אנא עובדא חזיתי לרב יהודה דלא אצטריך למבוי שכלה לרחבה ולא כלום ואי קשיא משמיה דרב ליהוי כשמואל ולא היא לרב נמי לא קשיא כיון דפרשה רב ששת הא דאמר רב חצר מותרת ומבוי אסור בשלא עירבו בני חצר עם בני מבוי. אבל אם עירבו מבוי נמי מותר. הכא נמי בשעירבו בני מבוי

וּלְמַאי דְּסָלֵיק אַדַּעְתִּין מֵעִיקָּרָא דְּבֵין עֵירְבוּ וּבֵין שֶׁלֹּא עֵירְבוּ פְּלִיגֵי. דַּאֲפִילּוּ בְּעֵירְבוּ אָסַר רַב. וְטַעֲמָא מִשּׁוּם מְפוּלָּשׁ, וְדַוְקָא נִפְרְצָה [חָצֵר] כְּנֶגְדּוֹ קָאָמַר, – הָא לָאו הָכִי לָא מִיתְּסַר מָבוֹי מִשּׁוּם בְּנֵי חָצֵר. וְהָא דְּרַב יְהוּדָה – דִּשְׁמוּאֵל הִיא, וְשָׁרֵי בְּעֵירְבוּ כְּגוֹן רְחָבָה דְּלָא בָּעֲיָא עֵירוּב. וְאַע"ג דְּנִפְרְצָה רְחָבָה כְּנֶגְדּוֹ, וְאָסַר בְּלֹא עֵירְבוּ גַּבֵּי חָצֵר אֲפִילּוּ לֹא נִפְרְצָה, מִדְּנָקַט רְחָבָה וְלָא נָקַט חָצֵר: בְּעֵירְבוּ. דְּאִיסּוּרָא מִשּׁוּם פִּירְצָה שֶׁכְּנֶגְדּוֹ הִיא: בְּמַאי פְּלִיגֵי. מַאי טַעְמָא דְּרַב דְּחָשֵׁיב לֵיהּ מְפוּלָּשׁ, וּמַאי טַעְמָא דִּשְׁמוּאֵל דְּלָא קָרֵי לֵיהּ מְפוּלָּשׁ? בְּשֶׁלֹּא עֵירְבוּ. כִּי לֹא נִפְרְצָה מַאי טַעְמָא דִּשְׁמוּאֵל, דְּאָמַר בְּנֵי חָצֵר אָסְרִי? וּמַאי טַעְמָא דְּרַב, דְּאָמַר לָא אָסְרִי? בְּנִרְאֶה מִבַּחוּץ וְשָׁוֶה מִבִּפְנִים. דִּפְלִיגִי בֵּיהּ אֲמוֹרָאֵי לְקַמָּן בְּפִירְקִין (ד' ט:), אִיכָּא לְמַאן דְּאָמַר נִדּוֹן כְּנִרְאֶה מִשְּׁנֵי לְצָדָדִין, וְאִיכָּא לְמַאן דְּאָמַר אֵינוֹ נִידּוֹן, וְהָכָא נַמִי, הָנָךְ גִּיפּוּפֵי דְּאִית לְחָצֵר הָעוֹדְפִים עַל רוֹחַב פִּירְצַת הַמָּבוֹי נִרְאִין מִבַּחוּץ לְאוֹתָן הָעוֹמְדִים בֶּחָצֵר, וְלָא מֶיחֱזֵי כּוֹתֶל פָּרוּץ בִּמְלוֹאוֹ. וְיוֹתֵר מֵעֶשֶׂר נַמִי לָא הָוֵי. הִלְכָּךְ, אַע"ג דְּשָׁוֶה מִבִּפְנִים, שֶׁהָעוֹמְדִין בַּמָּבוֹי אֵין רוֹאִין אוֹתוֹ וְנִרְאֶה לָהֶם כּוֹתֶל פָּרוּץ בִּמְלוֹאוֹ – אֲפִילּוּ הָכִי, לְרַב מְהַנֵּי הָנֵי גִּיפּוּפֵי לְשַׁוּוֹיֵיהּ פִּתְחָא לְגַבֵּי מָבוֹי, כִּי הֵיכִי דְּמְשַׁוּוּ לֵיהּ פִּתְחָא לְגַבֵּי חָצֵר. וְהָא דִּתְנַן קְטַנָּה אֲסוּרָה – מוֹקִים לֵיהּ רַב בְּנִכְנָסִין כּוֹתְלֵי קְטַנָּה לִגְדוֹלָה, דְּלֵיכָּא נִרְאֶה מִבַּחוּץ וְהָוְיָא פְּרוּצָה בִּמְלוֹאָהּ. אֲבָל הָכָא – פִּיתְחָא הוּא אַף לַמָּבוֹי, וְלָא אָסְרֵי בְּנֵי חָצֵר לַמָּבוֹי. וְאַע"ג דִּשְׁאָר חֲצֵירוֹת הַפְּתוּחוֹת לְמָבוֹי בְּפֶתַח הָגוּן וַדַּאי אוֹסְרוֹת עָלָיו, זוֹ הוֹאִיל וְאֵינָהּ רְגִילָה בּוֹ שֶׁהֲרֵי סָתוּם הָיָה מִתְּחִלָּה – אֵינָהּ אוֹסֶרֶת עָלָיו, כִּדְאָמַר בְּפ' "מִי שֶׁהוֹצִיאוּהוּ" (לקמן ד' מט.): שֶׁאֵינָהּ רְגִילָה בּוֹ – מוּתָּר, וּשְׁמוּאֵל סָבַר: אֵין נִידּוֹן מִשּׁוּם שִׁיּוּר לְמָבוֹי, וּפִירְצָה הִיא, וְדִיוּרֵי חָצֵר אוֹסְרִין עָלָיו אִם לֹא עֵירְבוּ: וּבְשֶׁעֵירְבוּ. דְּאִיסּוּרָא מִשּׁוּם פִּירְצָה שֶׁכְּנֶגְדּוֹ הוּא, פְּלִיגֵי בִּדְרַב יוֹסֵף דְּאָמַר לֹא שָׁנוּ דְּאֵין צָרִיךְ כְּלוּם אֶלָּא שֶׁכָּלֶה מָבוֹי לְאֶמְצַע רְחָבָה, דְּכֵיוָן דְּרוֹחְבָּהּ שֶׁל רְחָבָה עוֹדֵף עַל הַמָּבוֹי לְכָל צַד – נִרְאֶה שֶׁהַמָּבוֹי לָרְחָבָה כָּלֶה, וְאֵינוֹ מוֹשֵׁךְ עַד רְשׁוּת הָרַבִּים שֶׁכְּנֶגְדּוֹ, וְלָא אָתֵי לְמִיסְרֵי מְפוּלָּשׁ. וְרַב סָבַר: אֲפִילּוּ הָכִי, כֵּיוָן דְּהָעוֹמֵד בַּמָּבוֹי רוֹאֶה לְב' רָאשֵׁי רְשׁוּת הָרַבִּים, וּבָקְעֵי רַבִּים מֵרְשׁוּת הָרַבִּים זוֹ לִרְשׁוּת הָרַבִּים זוֹ דֶּרֶךְ מָבוֹי וּרְחָבָה – אָסוּר: אֲבָל כָּלֶה לְצִידֵּי רְחָבָה. שֶׁכּוֹתֶל אוֹרֶךְ הַמָּבוֹי שָׁוֶה לְאֶחָד מִכּוֹתְלֵי

וּלְמַאי דְּסָלֵיק אַדַּעְתִּין מֵעִיקָּרָא, בֵּין שֶׁעֵירְבוּ וּבֵין שֶׁלֹּא עֵירְבוּ פְּלִיגִי; בְּעֵירְבוּ בְּמַאי פְּלִיגִי, בְּשֶׁלֹּא עֵירְבוּ בְּמַאי פְּלִיגִי? בְּשֶׁלֹּא עֵירְבוּ פְּלִיגִי בְּ"נִרְאֶה מִבַּחוּץ וְשָׁוֶה מִבִּפְנִים". בְּעֵירְבוּ – קָמִיפַּלְגִי בִּדְרַב יוֹסֵף, דְּאָמַר רַב יוֹסֵף: לֹא שָׁנוּ [א]אֶלָּא שֶׁכָּלָה לְאֶמְצַע רְחָבָה. אֲבָל כָּלָה לְצִידֵּי רְחָבָה – אָסוּר. אָמַר רַבָּה: הָא דְּאָמְרַתְּ "לְאֶמְצַע רְחָבָה מוּתָּר", לָא אֲמַרַן אֶלָּא [ב]זֶה שֶׁלֹּא כְּנֶגֶד זֶה, אֲבָל זֶה כְּנֶגֶד זֶה – אָסוּר. אָמַר רַב מְשַׁרְשְׁיָא: הָא דְּאָמְרַתְּ "זֶה שֶׁלֹּא כְּנֶגֶד זֶה מוּתָּר", לָא אֲמַרַן אֶלָּא [ג]רְחָבָה דְּרַבִּים, אֲבָל רְחָבָה דְּיָחִיד – זִימְנִין דְּמִימְלַךְ עֲלָהּ וּבָנֵי לָהּ בָּתִּים, וְה"ל כְּמָבוֹי שֶׁכָּלָה לָהּ לְצִידֵּי רְחָבָה – וְאָסוּר. וּמְנָא תֵּימְרָא דְּשָׁנֵי לָן בֵּין רְחָבָה דְּרַבִּים לִרְחָבָה דְּיָחִיד – *דְּאָמַר רָבִין בַּר רַב אַדָּא, אָמַר רַבִּי יִצְחָק: מַעֲשֶׂה בְּמָבוֹי אֶחָד שֶׁצִּידּוֹ אֶחָד כָּלֶה לַיָּם וְצִידּוֹ אֶחָד כָּלֶה לָאַשְׁפָּה, וּבָא מַעֲשֶׂה לִפְנֵי רַבִּי וְלֹא אָמַר בָּהּ לֹא הֶיתֵּר וְלֹא אִיסּוּר. אִיסּוּר לֹא אָמַר בָּהּ – דְּהָא קָיְימִי מְחִיצוֹת, הֶיתֵּר לֹא אָמַר בָּהּ – חָיְישִׁינַן: שֶׁמָּא תִּינָּטֵל אַשְׁפָּה, וְיַעֲלֶה הַיָּם שִׂרְטוֹן. וּמִי חָיְישִׁינַן שֶׁמָּא תִּינָּטֵל אַשְׁפָּה? *וְהָתְנַן: אַשְׁפָּה בִּרְשׁוּת הָרַבִּים גְּבוֹהָהּ י' טְפָחִים, חַלּוֹן שֶׁעַל גַּבָּהּ זוֹרְקִין לָהּ בְּשַׁבָּת, אַלְמָא: שָׁנֵי [ד]בֵּין אַשְׁפָּה דְּרַבִּים לְאַשְׁפָּה דְּיָחִיד. הָכָא נַמִי, שָׁנֵי בֵּין רְחָבָה דְּרַבִּים לִרְחָבָה דְּיָחִיד. וְרַבָּנַן מַאי? אָמַר רַב יוֹסֵף בַּר אַבְדִּימִי, תָּנָא: וַחֲכָמִים אוֹסְרִין. אָמַר רַב נַחְמָן: הֲלָכָה כְּדִבְרֵי חֲכָמִים. אִיכָּא דְּאָמְרִי, אָמַר רַב יוֹסֵף בַּר אַבְדִּימִי, תָּנָא: [ה]וַחֲכָמִים מַתִּירִין. אָמַר רַב נַחְמָן: אֵין הֲלָכָה כְּדִבְרֵי חֲכָמִים. מָרֵימָר פָּסֵיק לָהּ לְסוּרָא בְּאוּזְלֵי, *אָמַר: חָיְישִׁינַן שֶׁמָּא יַעֲלֶה הַיָּם שִׂרְטוֹן. הַהוּא מָבוֹי עָקוֹם דַּהֲוָה בְּסוּרָא, כָּרוּךְ בּוּדְיָא, אוֹתִיבוּ בֵּיהּ בְּעַקְמוּמִיתֵיהּ. אָמַר רַב חִסְדָּא: הָא לָא כְּרַב וְלָא כִּשְׁמוּאֵל. לְרַב דְּאָמַר "תּוֹרָתוֹ כִּמְפוּלָּשׁ" – צוּרַת הַפֶּתַח בָּעֵי, לִשְׁמוּאֵל דְּאָמַר "תּוֹרָתוֹ כְּסָתוּם" – הָנֵי מִילֵּי לֶחִי מְעַלְּיָא, אֲבָל הַאי כֵּיוָן דְּנָשֵׁיב בֵּיהּ זִיקָא וְשָׁדֵי לֵיהּ – לָא כְּלוּם הוּא. וְאִי נָעֵיץ בֵּיהּ סִיכְתָא וְחַבְרֵיהּ – חַבְרֵיהּ.§ גּוּפָא, אָמַר רַב יִרְמְיָה בַּר אַבָּא, אָמַר רַב: מָבוֹי שֶׁנִּפְרַץ בִּמְלוֹאוֹ לְחָצֵר, וְנִפְרְצָה חָצֵר כְּנֶגְדּוֹ – חָצֵר מוּתֶּרֶת, וּמָבוֹי אָסוּר. אֲמַר לֵיהּ רַבָּה בַּר עוּלָּא לְרַב בֵּיבָי בַּר אַבַּיֵי: רַבִּי, לָא מִשְׁנָתֵנוּ הִיא זוֹ? *"חָצֵר קְטַנָּה שֶׁנִּפְרְצָה לִגְדוֹלָה – גְּדוֹלָה מוּתֶּרֶת וּקְטַנָּה אֲסוּרָה, מִפְּנֵי שֶׁהִיא כְּפִתְחָהּ שֶׁל גְּדוֹלָה". אֲמַר לֵיהּ: אִי מֵהָתָם הֲוָה אָמִינָא: *הָנֵי מִילֵּי – הֵיכָא דְּלָא קָא דָּרְסִי בָּהּ רַבִּים, אֲבָל הֵיכָא דְּקָא דָּרְסִי בָּהּ רַבִּים – אֵימָא אֲפִילּוּ חָצֵר נַמִי. וְהָא נַמִי תְּנֵינָא: *[ו]חָצֵר שֶׁהָרַבִּים נִכְנָסִין לָהּ בָּזוֹ וְיוֹצְאִין לָהּ בָּזוֹ – רה"ר לְטוּמְאָה, [ז]ורה"י לְשַׁבָּת. אִי מֵהָתָם הֲוָה אָמִינָא: הָנֵי מִילֵּי – זֶה שֶׁלֹּא כְּנֶגֶד זֶה, אֲבָל

אוֹרֶךְ הָרְחָבָה וְנִרְאֶה כְּמָבוֹי אָרוֹךְ, וּמוֹשֵׁךְ עַד רה"ר שֶׁכְּנֶגְדּוֹ – מֵיחֱזֵי כִּמְפוּלָּשׁ, וְאָסוּר: אֲבָל זֶה כְּנֶגֶד זֶה. פִּרְצַת חָצֵר כְּנֶגֶד הַמָּבוֹי אָסוּר. וְהַאי "כְּנֶגְדּוֹ" דְּקָאָמַר רַב, וְאוֹקִימְנָא טַעְמָא דְּאִיסּוּר מָבוֹי בְּשֶׁלֹּא עֵירְבוּ הָא עֵירְבוּ מוּתָּר, הַאי "כְּנֶגְדּוֹ" לָאו דַּוְקָא, אֶלָּא כָּל כּוֹתֶל שֶׁכְּנֶגְדּוֹ קָרֵי הָכִי. וּבְלִידֵּי רְחָבָה, אֲפִילּוּ זֶה שֶׁלֹּא כְּנֶגֶד זֶה – אָסוּר, מִשּׁוּם דְּכוֹתֶל רְחָבָה מַאֲרִיךְ הַמָּבוֹי, וַהֲוֵי כְּמָבוֹי אָרוֹךְ עַד כּוֹתֶל(א) רְחָבָה שֶׁכְּנֶגְדּוֹ, וְאָסוּר, מִידֵּי דַּהֲוָה אַמָּבוֹי עָקוֹם שֶׁיֵּשׁ יוֹתֵר מֵעֶשֶׂר בְּעַקְמוּמִיתוֹ, דִּלְכוּלֵּי עָלְמָא אָסוּר, וְאַע"פ שֶׁאֵין פְּתָחָיו מְכוּוָּנִין. הָכָא נַמִי, מִשֶּׁנִּכְנָס לָרְחָבָה הֲרֵי כָּל רוֹחַב הָרְחָבָה הָוֵי עַקְמוּמִית גְּדוֹלָה וּרְחָבָה הַרְבֵּה, וְדָמֵי כְּמָבוֹי הַמְפוּלָּשׁ דֶּרֶךְ עַקְמוּמִית: וּבָנֵי לָהּ בָּתִּים. בָּרְחָבָה, בָּרוֹחַב הָעוֹדֵף עַל הַמָּבוֹי, וּמַשְׁוֵי כּוֹתְלֵי אוֹרְכָּהּ לְכוֹתֶל אוֹרֶךְ הַמָּבוֹי: צִידּוֹ אֶחָד יָם וְצִידּוֹ אֶחָד אַשְׁפָּה. וְרֹאשׁוֹ אֶחָד סָתוּם כִּשְׁאָר מָבוֹי, וְרֹאשׁוֹ אַחֵר לִרְשׁוּת הָרַבִּים מְתוּקָּן בְּלֶחִי וְקוֹרָה: אַשְׁפָּה. גְּבוֹהָה עֲשָׂרָה (*וְיֵשׁ) שְׂפָתוֹ גָּבוֹהַּ עֲשָׂרָה: וְיַעֲלֶה הַיָּם שִׂרְטוֹן. שֶׁל חוֹל וַאֲבָנִים אֵצֶל שְׂפָתוֹ, כִּי כֵּן דַּרְכּוֹ, וּמִתְקַצֵּר רוֹחַב הַיָּם וְנַעֲשָׂה קַרְקַע כְּרוֹחַב פַּרְסָה אוֹ יוֹתֵר: וּמִי חָיְישִׁינַן כו'. הַתַּלְמוּד הוּא דִּמְפָרֵשׁ מִלְּתֵיהּ דְּ"מְנָא תֵּימְרָא" וְאָזֵיל: זוֹרְקִין לָהּ בְּשַׁבָּת. וְלָא חָיְישִׁינַן שֶׁמָּא תִּתְמַעֵט אַשְׁפָּה מֵעֲשָׂרָה, וְנִמְצָא זוֹרְקִין לִרְשׁוּת הָרַבִּים: לְאַשְׁפָּה דְּיָחִיד. וְהַהִיא אַשְׁפָּה דְּרַבֵּי – אַשְׁפָּה דְּיָחִיד הֲוַאי: וְרַבָּנַן. שֶׁהָיוּ בְּדוֹרוֹ שֶׁל רַבִּי, מַאי הֲווּ אָמְרִי בֵּיהּ בְּהַהוּא מָבוֹי: פָּסֵיק לֵיהּ לְסוּרָא בְּאוּזְלֵי. הַיָּם הָיָה סָמוּךְ לְסוּרָא מֵאַחֲרֶיהָ, וְרָאשֵׁי הַמְּבוֹאוֹת מְפוּלָּשִׁין לַיָּם, וְהָיָה מָרֵימָר עוֹשֶׂה רְשָׁתוֹת וּמִכְמוֹרוֹת לְכָל הַמְּבוֹאוֹת, וְלֹא רָצָה לִסְמוֹךְ עַל מְחִיצַּת הַיָּם: אָמַר שֶׁמָּא יַעֲלֶה הַיָּם שִׂרְטוֹן. וּמִטַּלְטְלֵי נַמִי בַּמְּבוֹאוֹת כִּדְמֵעִיקָּרָא: פָּסֵיק. מַפְסִיק בֵּינָהּ לְבֵין הַיָּם בִּמְחִיצּוֹת אוּזְלֵי: בּוּדְיָא. = מַחֲצֶלֶת: וְאוֹתִיבוּ בֵּיהּ בְּעַקְמוּמִיתֵיהּ. בְּנֵי רֹאשׁוֹ אַחֵר עָשׂוּ לֶחִי לְפִתְחָן וְהַמַּחֲצֶלֶת לְעַקְמוּמִיתוֹ, וּבְנֵי רֹאשׁוֹ אַחֵר לֹא עָשׂוּ לְפִתְחָן לֶחִי: הנ"מ לֶחִי מְעַלְּיָא. כְּשֶׁיֵּשׁ לְחַיִּים מִשְּׁנֵי רָאשִׁין. וְלִלְשׁוֹן מוֹרִי צָרִיךְ עַקְמִימוּתוֹ לֶחִי, לְבַד מֵאוֹתָן שֶׁבִּשְׁנֵי רָאשָׁיו: סִיכְתָא. = קבילי"א בְּלַעַ"ז: גּוּפָא אָמַר ר' יִרְמְיָה כו'. וְאוֹקְמַהּ כְּשֶׁלֹּא עֵירְבוּ. וְאִיסּוּרָא דְּמָבוֹי – מִשּׁוּם דְּאָסְרִי עֲלֵיהּ בְּנֵי הֶחָצֵר הוּא: לָאו מִשְׁנָתֵנוּ הִיא. הֶיתֵּר חָצֵר תְּנֵינָא, וְאִיסּוּר מָבוֹי תְּנֵינָא: חָצֵר קְטַנָּה שֶׁנִּפְרְצָה. בִּמְלוֹאָהּ לִגְדוֹלָה – גְּדוֹלָה מוּתֶּרֶת, וְלָא אָסְרֵי בְּנֵי קְטַנָּה עִילָּוֵיהּ, דִּלְגַבֵּי גְּדוֹלָה פֶּתַח הוּא דְּיֵשׁ לָהּ שִׁיּוּר מִכָּאן וּמִכָּאן. וַהֲווּ כִּשְׁתֵּי חֲצֵירוֹת וּפֶתַח אֶחָד בֵּינֵיהֶן, דְּלָא אָסְרָן אַהֲדָדֵי. וּלְקַמָּן מוֹקֵי לָהּ בְּשֶׁאֵין קְטַנָּה רְחָבָה יוֹתֵר מֵעֶשֶׂר, דְּאִי יוֹתֵר מֵעֶשֶׂר לָא הָוֵי פֶּתַח גַּבֵּי גְּדוֹלָה: וּקְטַנָּה אֲסוּרָה. דִּלְדִידָהּ לָאו פֶּתַח הוּא אֶלָּא פִּירְצָה, וְנַעֲשֵׂית רְשׁוּתָן שֶׁל בְּנֵי גְּדוֹלָה, שֶׁהֲרֵי נִתְעָרְבָה עִמָּהֶן: א"ל. רַב(ב) הֶיתֵּר חָצֵר אַשְׁמְעִינַן, וְאַע"ג דְּנִפְרְצָה בַּכּוֹתֶל הַשֵּׁנִי, דְּדָרְסִי רַבִּים מֵרְשׁוּת הָרַבִּים זוֹ לרה"ר זוֹ דֶּרֶךְ חָצֵר וּמָבוֹי. דְּאִי מֵהָתָם, הֲוָה אָמֵינָא: מִשּׁוּם דְּלָא דָּרְסִי רַבִּים דְּהָא גְּדוֹלָה לֹא נִפְרְצָה בַּכּוֹתֶל הַשֵּׁנִי: רה"ר לְטוּמְאָה. וּסְפֵיקָא טָהוֹר, דְּהָא סְפֵק טוּמְאָה מִסּוּטָה גָּמְרִינַן. וּבְסוֹטָה בְּכִי הַאי חָצֵר – לָאו מְקוֹם יִיחוּד וּסְתִירָה הוּא:

אֲבָל

זורקין לה בשבת. משמע שהאשפה רחוקה מן הכותל ודרך למעלה מעשרה זורקין לה, דהוו מקום פטור, ואית דגרס שופכין:

לאו משנתנו היא זו חצר קטנה וכו'. וא"ל דקמ"ל דנראה מבחוץ ושוה מבפנים אינו נידון משום לחי, דמתני' איכא לאוקמה בנכנסין כותלי קטנה לגדולה, דאם כן – הוי ליה לרב לפרושי מתני' דלא איירי בנכנסין. או הוי ליה למימר בהדיא: נראה מבחוץ אינו נידון משום לחי:

מבוי

וא"ת מ"מ אמאי אצטריך למימר למבוי אסור וי"ל דקמ"ל דנראה מבחוץ אינו נידון משום לחי:

רבינו חננאל

עם בני רחבה ולמאי דסליק ארעתין מעיקרא דרב בין עירבו ובין לא עירבו אוסר במאי פליגי ואמרינן בשלמא עירבו בנראה מבחוץ ושוה מבפנים. שמואל סבר הרי הוא לחי ומותר ורב סבר לא הוי לחי בשעירבו פליגי במבוי שכלה לאמצע לרחבה שמואל סבר לה כרב יוסף דאמר אפילו פלוש מבוי כנגד פילושיה של רוחבה כיון שהוא באמצע רוחבה שרי. ורב יוסף כרבה דאמר אפילו באמצע רחבה זו כנגד זו אסור. אמר רב משרשיא זה שלא כנגד זה באמצע רחבה לא אמרן שמותר אלא ברחבה דרבים אבל רחבה דיחיד אסור מ"ט זימנין דמימליך ומלי ליה האי אמצע רחבה בתי והוה ליה פילושא בצידי הרחבה ורחבה זו היא כמו שאמרנו שיש בה דיורין ואינה מוקפת כולה אלא יש לה פתח פתוח לרה"ר. ומנא תימרא דשני בין רחבה דרבים לרחבה דיחיד. דאמר [רבין בר רב אדא אמר ר"י] מעשה במבוי דצדו אחד כלה לים וצדו אחד לאשפה ולא אמר בו ר' איסור דהא קיימא מחיצות. היתר נמי לא אמר בו שמא תנטל אשפה מזה הצד ויעלה הים שרטון מן הצד האחר ונמצא מבוי מפולש לרה"ר משני צדדין. פי' שרטון כדכתיב ויגרשו מימיו רפש וטיט. פעמים שמגרש הים בזעפו על שפתו רפש וטיט ומתקבץ על שפתו ועולה כמין גבשושית וכשנם הים ישאר זה הטיט ומתייבש ונעשה קרקע מהלך לבני אדם לרה"ר ואקשינן ומי חיישינן שמא תינטל אשפה והתנן בסוף מסכת זו [דף לט ע"ב] אשפה ברה"ר גבוה י' טפחים חלון שע"ג וכו' הנה ר' לא אמר בו לא איסור ולא היתר רבנן מאי (ואמר ת"ק) [ואמרינן תנא] וחכמים אוסרין. ואמר רב נחמן הלכה כחכמים. מרימר פסיק לסורא באוזלי ולא חייש שמא יעלה הים שרטון. ההוא מבוי עקום דהוה בסורא כרכו בודיא. פי' מחצלת אותיבו בשפתיה דמבוי. אמר רב חסדא הא דלא כרב דאמר תורתו כמפולש דאי כרב צורת הפתח בעי. ואי כשמואל דאמר בסתום לחי מעליא או קורה בעיא. ואי נקש ביה סיכא וחבריה בטינא לשמואל מיהא שפיר דמי משום דאינה מחיצה הניטלת ברוח. פי' ואם תקע בבודיא זו יתד וחיברו בטיט שפיר דמי. אמרו משמיה דרב מבוי שנפרץ במלואו. פי' נפרץ הכותל האמצעי כולו לחצר ונפרצה חצר כנגדו ברה"ר חצר מותרת ומבוי אסור. מבוי אסור משום דהוא מפולש לרה"ר אבל חצר מותרת אפילו לטלטל בה

מד א ב ג מיי' וסמג שם טוש"ע א"ח שם:
מה ד ה מיי' שם הלכה ה וסמג שם טוש"ע א"ח סי' שסג סעיף כט:
מו ו מיי' פ"כ מהלכות שאר אבות הטומאות הלכה ג:
מז ז מיי' פי"ז מהלכות שבת הלכה יח וסמג שם טוש"ע א"ח סי' שסד סעיף ד:

לקמן לט:

שם ע"ש

גי' ר"ח אמר לא חיישינן [וכ"ה גיר' הערוך בערך אזל] ועי' במ"מ פי"ז מהלכות שבת

לקמן ט: לב. לג: ע"ש

לקמן כב: תוספתא פ"ז דטהרות

[נ"ל ויש]

הגהות הב"ח

(א) רש"י ד"ה אבל זה וכו' כמבוי ארוך עד כותל (רחבה) תז"מ ונ"ב ס"א אין זה: (ב) שם ד"ה אמר ליה רב ביבי היתר:

מח א מיי' פי"ז מהל' שבת הלכה יט סמג עשין דרבנן א טוש"ע א"ח סי' שסד ס"ה:
מט ב מיי' שם הלכה כ טוש"ע א"ח סי' שסג סעיף ל:
נ ג מיי' שם הלכה יא סמג עשין דרבנן א טוש"ע א"ח סי' שסה סעיף ד:
נא ד מיי' שם הלכה כג טוש"ע א"ח סי' שסג סעיף יד:

אֲבָל זֶה כְּנֶגֶד זֶה — אֵימָא לָא. וּלְרַבָּה דְּאָמַר "זֶה כְּנֶגֶד זֶה אָסוּר" הָא דְּרַב בְּמַאי מוֹקֵי לָהּ? בְּזֶה שֶׁלֹּא כְּנֶגֶד זֶה. תַּרְתֵּי לָמָּה לִי? אִי מֵהָתָם הֲוָה אָמִינָא: הָנֵי מִילֵּי — לִזְרוֹק, אֲבָל לְטַלְטֵל — אֵימָא לָא, קמ"ל. אִיתְּמַר, מָבוֹי הֶעָשׂוּי כַּנָּדָל, אָמַר אַבַּיֵי: עוֹשֶׂה צוּרַת הַפֶּתַח לְגָדוֹל, וְהָנָךְ כּוּלְּהוּ מִישְׁתָּרוּ בְּלֶחִי וְקוֹרָה. א"ל רָבָא: כְּמַאן — כִּשְׁמוּאֵל, דְּאָמַר: "תּוֹרָתוֹ כְּסָתוּם" לָמָּה לֵיהּ צוּרַת הַפֶּתַח? וְעוֹד; הָא *הַהוּא מָבוֹי עָקוּם דַּהֲוָה בִּנְהַרְדְּעָא, וְחָשׁוּ לָהּ לְדְרַב! אֶלָּא אָמַר רָבָא: [א]עוֹשֶׂה צוּרַת הַפֶּתַח לְכוּלְּהוּ לְהַאי גִּיסָא, וְאִידָּךְ גִּיסָא מִישְׁתָּרוּ בְּלֶחִי וְקוֹרָה. אָמַר רַב כָּהֲנָא בַּר תַּחְלִיפָא מִשְּׁמֵיהּ דְּרַב כָּהֲנָא בַּר מְנְיוּמִי מִשְּׁמֵיהּ דְּרַב כָּהֲנָא בַּר מַלְכִּיו(א) מִשְּׁמֵיהּ דְּרַב כָּהֲנָא רַבֵּיהּ דְּרַב, וְאָמְרִי לָהּ רַב כָּהֲנָא בַּר מַלְכִּיו הַיְינוּ רַב כָּהֲנָא רַבֵּיהּ דְּרַב: מָבוֹי שֶׁצִּידּוֹ אֶחָד אָרוֹךְ וְצִידּוֹ אֶחָד קָצָר, פָּחוֹת מֵאַרְבַּע אַמּוֹת — מַנִּיחַ אֶת הַקּוֹרָה בַּאֲלַכְסוֹן, אַרְבַּע אַמּוֹת — אֵינוֹ מַנִּיחַ אֶת הַקּוֹרָה אֶלָּא כְּנֶגֶד הַקָּצָר. רָבָא אָמַר: [ב]אֶחָד זֶה וְאֶחָד זֶה — אֵינוֹ מַנִּיחַ אֶת הַקּוֹרָה אֶלָּא כְּנֶגֶד הַקָּצָר. וְאֵימָא טַעֲמָא דִּידִי, וְאֵימָא טַעֲמָא דִּידְהוּ. אֵימָא טַעֲמָא דִּידִי: *קוֹרָה טַעֲמָא מַאי — מִשּׁוּם הֶיכֵּר, וּבַאֲלַכְסוֹן לָא הָוֵי הֶיכֵּר; וְאֵימָא טַעֲמָא דִּידְהוּ: *קוֹרָה מִשּׁוּם מַאי — מִשּׁוּם מְחִיצָּה, וּבַאֲלַכְסוֹן נַמִי הָוֵי מְחִיצָּה. אָמַר רַב כָּהֲנָא: הוֹאִיל וּשְׁמַעְתָּא דְּכָהֲנֵי הִיא — אֵימָא בָּהּ מִילְּתָא: הָא דְּאָמְרַתְּ מַנִּיחַ הַקּוֹרָה בַּאֲלַכְסוֹן — לָא אֲמַרַן אֶלָּא שֶׁאֵין בַּאֲלַכְסוֹנוֹ יוֹתֵר מֵעֶשֶׂר, אֲבָל יֵשׁ בַּאֲלַכְסוֹנוֹ יוֹתֵר מֵעֶשֶׂר — דִּבְרֵי הַכֹּל אֵינוֹ מַנִּיחַ אֶלָּא כְּנֶגֶד הַקָּצָר. אִיבַּעְיָא לְהוּ: מַהוּ לְהִשְׁתַּמֵּשׁ תַּחַת הַקּוֹרָה? רַב וְרַבִּי חִיָּיא וְר' יוֹחָנָן אָמְרוּ: [ג]מוּתָּר לְהִשְׁתַּמֵּשׁ תַּחַת הַקּוֹרָה. שְׁמוּאֵל וְרַבִּי שִׁמְעוֹן בַּר רַבִּי וְר"ש בֶּן לָקִישׁ אָמְרוּ: אָסוּר לְהִשְׁתַּמֵּשׁ תַּחַת הַקּוֹרָה. לֵימָא בְּהָא קָמִיפַּלְגִי, דְּמָר סָבַר: קוֹרָה מִשּׁוּם הֶיכֵּר, וּמָר סָבַר קוֹרָה מִשּׁוּם מְחִיצָּה. לָא, דְּכוּלֵּי עָלְמָא — קוֹרָה מִשּׁוּם הֶיכֵּר, וְהָכָא בְּהָא קָמִיפַּלְגִי; דְּמָר סָבַר: הֶיכֵּירָא מִלְּגָיו, וּמָר סָבַר: הֶיכֵּירָא מִלְּבַר. וְאִיבָּעֵית אֵימָא: דְּכוּלֵּי עָלְמָא "מִשּׁוּם מְחִיצָּה", וְהָכָא בְּהָא קָמִיפַּלְגִי: דְּמָר סָבַר: חוּדוֹ הַפְּנִימִי יוֹרֵד וְסוֹתֵם, וּמָר סָבַר: חוּדוֹ הַחִיצוֹן יוֹרֵד וְסוֹתֵם. אָמַר רַב חִסְדָּא: הַכֹּל מוֹדִים בְּבֵין לְחָיַיִם שֶׁאָסוּר. בְּעָא מִינֵּיהּ רָמִי בַּר חָמָא מֵרַב חִסְדָּא: [ד]נָעַץ שְׁתֵּי יְתֵידוֹת בִּשְׁנֵי כּוֹתְלֵי מָבוֹי מִבַּחוּץ, וְהִנִּיחַ קוֹרָה עַל גַּבֵּיהֶן מַהוּ? א"ל: לְדִבְרֵי הַמַּתִּיר — אָסוּר, לְדִבְרֵי הָאוֹסֵר — מוּתָּר. רָבָא אָמַר: לְדִבְרֵי הָאוֹסֵר, נַמִי אָסוּר. בְּעֵינַן קוֹרָה ע"ג מָבוֹי, וְלֵיכָּא. אֵיתִיבֵיהּ רַב אַדָּא בַּר מַתְּנָה *לְרָבָא: הָיְתָה קוֹרָתוֹ מְשׁוּכָה

רש"י

אֲבָל זֶה כְּנֶגֶד זֶה. לָא הָוְיָא לָהּ חָצֵר רְשׁוּת הַיָּחִיד לַשַּׁבָּת. הַשְׁתָּא אַשְׁמְעִינַן דִּכְנֶגְדּוֹ, וַאֲפִילּוּ הָכִי מוּתֶּרֶת: וּלְרַבָּה. דְּאָמַר לְעֵיל: אֲבָל זֶה כְּנֶגֶד זֶה – הָוֵי מָבוֹי מְפוּלָּשׁ וְאָסוּר (אֲפִילּוּ חָצֵר), הָא דְּרַב בְּמַאי מוֹקִים לָהּ בְּזֶה שֶׁלֹּא כְּנֶגֶד זֶה, וְעַל כָּרְחָךְ "כְּנֶגֶד" דְּקָאָמַר רַב לָאו דַּוְוקָא, דְּהָא אוֹקִימְנָא טַעְמֵיהּ דְּרַב בְּשֶׁלֹּא עֵירְבוּ, אֲבָל עֵירְבוּ – אֲפִילּוּ מָבוֹי מוּתָּר: תַּרְתֵּי לָמָּה לִי. הָא תְּנָא לָהּ: חָצֵר שֶׁהָרַבִּים נִכְנָסִין לָהּ בָּזוֹ כו' וּמִילְּתֵיהּ דְּרַב לְמִשְׁתַּרְיֵיהּ חָצֵר מִינָּהּ, מִשְׁתַּמְּעָא וַאֲפִילּוּ זֶה כְּנֶגֶד זֶה, וְכָל שֶׁכֵּן בְּזֶה שֶׁלֹּא כְּנֶגֶד זֶה. וְאִיסּוּר מָבוֹי – מֵאֵילָךְ מַתְנִיתִין דְּחָצֵר קְטַנָּה שָׁמְעִינַן: אִי מֵהָתָם. מֵחָצֵר שֶׁהָרַבִּים נִכְנָסִין לָהּ כו' דְּקָתָנֵי "רְשׁוּת הַיָּחִיד לַשַּׁבָּת": הֲוָה אָמִינָא. הַאי דְּקָרֵי לֵיהּ רה"י: לִזְרוֹק. כְּלוֹמַר: מִדְּאוֹרַיְיתָא רה"י הוּא, וְהַזּוֹרֵק מֵרה"ר לְתוֹכוֹ חַיָּיב: אֲבָל לְטַלְטֵל. בְּתוֹכוֹ: אֵימָא לָא. מִשְׁתַּרְיָא, וּמִדְּרַבָּנָן דְּלִיגְזוֹר רַבָּנַן עֲלֵיהּ: קמ"ל. רַב, מוּתֶּרֶת: נָדָל. שֶׁרֶץ שֶׁיֵּשׁ לוֹ רַגְלַיִם הַרְבֵּה. כִּדְתַנְיָא בְּתוֹרַת כֹּהֲנִים (פרשת שמיני): "מַרְבֵּה רַגְלַיִם" זֶה נָדָל. מָבוֹי הֶעָשׂוּי כַּנָּדָל – שֶׁפְּתוּחִין לוֹ מְבוֹאוֹת הַרְבֵּה, וְרָאשֵׁיהֶן פְּתוּחִין לִרְשׁוּת הָרַבִּים, וְרֹאשׁוֹ פָּתוּחַ לִרְשׁוּת הָרַבִּים אַחֵר: עוֹשֶׂה צוּרַת פֶּתַח לַגָּדוֹל. בְּאֶחָד מִשְּׁנֵי רָאשִׁין, וְהָאֲחֵרִים קְטַנִּים מִשְׁתְּרוּ בְּלֶחִי וְקוֹרָה בְּרָאשֵׁיהֶן עַל פְּנֵי רְשׁוּת הָרַבִּים: כְּמַאן כִּשְׁמוּאֵל. דְּאָמַר מָבוֹי עָקוּם תּוֹרָתוֹ כְּסָתוּם. דְּהָא כָּל מְבוֹאוֹת קְטַנִּים הַלָּלוּ מְבוֹאוֹת עֲקוּמּוֹת הֵן, נִכְנָס בְּדֶרֶךְ זֶה וְיוֹצֵא בְּדֶרֶךְ זֶה. וְקָאָמְרַתְּ: לָא בָּעֵי תִּיקּוּן לַעֲקְמוּמִיתוֹ, כִּשְׁמוּאֵל: ה"ג: לָמָּה לִי צוּרַת פֶּתַח. אַמַּאי אַצְרְכַת צוּרַת פֶּתַח לַגָּדוֹל? הָא אִיהוּ נַמִי אֵין פִּילּוּשָׁיו מְכוּוָּנִין: וְעוֹד הָא הַהוּא מָבוֹי(ב). דַּהֲוָה בְּאַתְרֵיהּ דִּשְׁמוּאֵל בִּנְהַרְדְּעָא וְחָשׁוּ לֵיהּ לְדְרַב; כִּדְאָמַר לְעֵיל רְמוּ עֲלֵיהּ חוּמְרֵיהּ דְּרַב וְחוּמְרֵיהּ דִּשְׁמוּאֵל: עוֹשֶׂה צוּרַת פֶּתַח לְכוּלְּהוּ. הַקְּטַנִּים: מֵהַךְ גִּיסָא. בַּעֲקְמוּמִיתָן לְצַד מָבוֹי גָּדוֹל: וְאִידָךְ גִּיסָא. *לִרְשׁוּת הָרַבִּים מִישְׁתְּרֵי בְּלֶחִי אוֹ קוֹרָה: צִידּוֹ אֶחָד אָרוֹךְ. וְנִמְשָׁךְ כּוֹתְלוֹ לִרְשׁוּת הָרַבִּים יוֹתֵר מִכּוֹתֶל הַשֵּׁנִי *כָּזֶה: אִם פָּחוֹת מֵאַרְבַּע אַמּוֹת.

עוֹדֵף זֶה עַל חֲבֵירוֹ מַנִּיחַ קוֹרָה בַּאֲלַכְסוֹן, וְיִשְׁתַּמֵּשׁ כָּאן בַּאֲרוּכָּה וְכָאן בַּקְּצָרָה: אַרְבַּע אַמּוֹת אֵינוֹ מַנִּיחַ קוֹרָה. עַל רֹאשׁ כּוֹתֶל הָאָרוֹךְ, אֶלָּא כּוֹנֵס לִפְנִים מֵרֹאשׁוֹ כְּנֶגֶד רֹאשׁ כּוֹתֶל הַקָּצָר וּמַנִּיחָהּ:

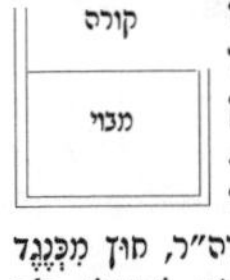

וּבַאֲלַכְסוֹן לָא הָוֵי הֶיכֵּירָא. שֶׁהָרוֹאֶה בְּנֵי מָבוֹי נִמְשָׁכִין וּמִשְׁתַּמְּשִׁין בִּרה"ר, חוּץ מִכְּנֶגֶד כּוֹתֶל הַקָּצָר אוֹמֵר מוּתָּר לְהִשְׁתַּמֵּשׁ בִּרְשׁוּת הָרַבִּים לְפִי שֶׁאֵין אוֹתוֹ הָעוֹדֵף דּוֹמֶה שֶׁיְּהֵא מִן הַמָּבוֹי: שֶׁאֵין בַּאֲלַכְסוֹנוֹ יוֹתֵר מֵעֶשֶׂר. שֶׁהַמָּבוֹי קָצָר לִרְחָבּוֹ הַרְבֵּה, וְאֵין בְּרוֹחְבּוֹ, וּבְאַרְבַּע אַמּוֹת הַנִּמְשָׁכִין לְהִצְטָרֵף, יוֹתֵר מֵעֶשֶׂר. נִמְצָא פִּתְחוֹ רָחָב מֵעֶשֶׂר, שֶׁהֲרֵי כָּל יוֹתֵר מֵעֶשֶׂר תַּחַת הַקּוֹרָה הָוֵי פֶּתַח: מַהוּ לְהִשְׁתַּמֵּשׁ תַּחַת הַקּוֹרָה. אֲבָל מְבוֹאוֹת קָאֵי: קוֹרָה מִשּׁוּם מְחִיצָּה. וְחוּדּוֹ הַפְּנִימִי יוֹרֵד וְסוֹתֵם. הִלְכָּךְ אָסוּר, דְּמִן הַמְּחִיצָּה וְלִפְנִים בָּעֵי אִשְׁתַּמּוּשֵׁי: מָר סָבַר הֶיכֵּירָא. לְהָנָךְ מִגַּוַּואי בָּעֵינַן, וְצַד הַפְּנִימִי הָוֵי לְהוּ הֶיכֵּר, וְאָסוּר לְהִשְׁתַּמֵּשׁ מִן הַהֶיכֵּר וְלַחוּץ: מִלְּבַר. לִבְנֵי רְשׁוּת הָרַבִּים, דְּהַיְינוּ לַד הַחִיצוֹן: מָר סָבַר חוּדּוֹ הַפְּנִימִי יוֹרֵד וְסוֹתֵם. נִמְצָא תַּחַת הַקּוֹרָה מִן הַמְּחִיצָּה וְלַחוּץ וְאָסוּר: הַכֹּל מוֹדִים. בְּמָבוֹי שֶׁאֵין בּוֹ קוֹרָה, וְהִכְשִׁירוּ בְּלֶחִי – שֶׁאָסוּר לְהִשְׁתַּמֵּשׁ בֵּין לְחָיַיִם, כְּלוֹמַר: כְּנֶגֶד הַלֶּחִי וְהַאי דְּנָקַט בֵּין לְחָיַיִם – אַמְּבוֹאוֹת טוּבָא קָאֵי: נָעַץ שְׁתֵּי יְתֵידוֹת. = קבילי"ש נְעוּצוֹת בַּכּוֹתֶל בְּעוֹדוֹ שֶׁלְּצַד רְשׁוּת הָרַבִּים, וְנִמְצֵאת קוֹרָה שֶׁעֲלֵיהֶן בּוֹלֶטֶת וְנִמְשֶׁכֶת לַחוּץ יוֹתֵר מִן הַכְּתָלִים, וְחוּדָּהּ הַפְּנִימִי דָּבוּק וְסָמוּךְ לַכּוֹתֶל כָּזֶה:

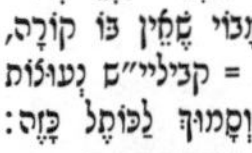

לְדִבְרֵי הָאוֹסֵר. לְהִשְׁתַּמֵּשׁ תַּחַת הַקּוֹרָה בְּכָל מְבוֹאוֹת, דְּטַעְמָא מִשּׁוּם חוּדּוֹ הַפְּנִימִי יוֹרֵד וְסוֹתֵם: מַתִּיר. כָּאן לְהִשְׁתַּמֵּשׁ בַּמָּבוֹי הָיָה מַגַּב הַךְ קוֹרָה שֶׁאֵינָהּ עַל גַּבֵּי מָבוֹי, דְּכֵיוָן דְּחוּדּוֹ הַפְּנִימִי סוֹתֵם – נִמְצֵאת סְתִימַת הַקּוֹרָה דְּבוּקָה לַכְּתָלִים, וּסְתִימָה מַעַלְיָיתָא הִיא: לְדִבְרֵי הַמַּתִּיר. לְהִשְׁתַּמֵּשׁ תַּחַת הַקּוֹרָה, אַלְמָא: חִיצוֹן יוֹרֵד וְסוֹתֵם, אוֹסֵר כָּל הַמָּבוֹי הַזֶּה עַד שֶׁיָּבִיאוּ קוֹרָה אַחֶרֶת. דְּאֵין הַסְּתִימָה מְחוּבֶּרֶת לַכְּתָלִים, וְיֵשׁ אֲוִיר בֵּינֵיהֶם. וְהָכָא לָאו מְחִיצָּה מַמָּשׁ הוּא לְהַכְשִׁיר הֶפְסֵק אֲוִיר שֶׁמִּכָּאן וּמִכָּאן ע"י לָבוּד:

תוספות

מבוי העשו כנדל. פי' רבינו חס: שמבואות קטנים פתוחים למבוי גדול משני לדדין. ואינן זה כנגד זה, דאם כן הוו מפולשין. וכענין זה הם כרגלי הנדל שיש לו ב' שורות של רגלים מימין ומשמאל, והם זה שלא כנגד זה:

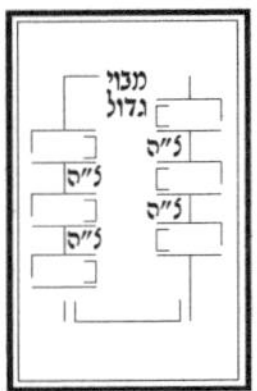

והא ההוא מבוי עקום דהוה בנהרדע' ורמו עליה חומריה דרב. ממאי(ג) דחשו נמי לדשמואל לא פריך ויצטרך דלתות – דהא דחשו משום דנהרדעא אתריה דשמואל הוה, אבל מדחשו לדרב באתריה דשמואל פריך שפיר: מניח את הקורה באלכסון. פ"ה: משתמש כאן בארוכה וכאן בקצרה. והדין עמו שפי' כן, דאי לא תימא הכי – אמאי מניח את הקורה באלכסון? הא בעינן קורה לכל הפחות דבוקה במבוי, כדאמר בסמוך גבי ב' יתידות בשני כותלים כו' לדברי המתיר אסור. ואף על פי שכאן מונח ראשו האחד על גבי המבוי – אין סברא לחלק. וא"ת: והיכי שרי להשתמש נגד הארוך? הא אין כאן אלא ג' מחילות! וי"ל: דאית ליה קורה משום מחילה, ומאן דאית ליה משום מחילה הוי אפילו דאורייתא, כדמוכח בפירקין. אי נמי: כיון דלידו האחד ארוך משתמש לא בקעי בה רבים, ולא גזרו ביה רבנן, הואיל ובטל לגבי מבוי אע"ג דאית ביה ד' על ד': הכל מודים בבין לחיים דאסור. טעמא משום דלחי הוי אפילו משהו, ואתי לאפוקי. אבל בקורה דרחבה טפח – ליכא למיחש. אבל אין לפרש דטעמא דרב חסדא משום דסבר קורה משום היכר, ולחי משום מחילה, ומשום היכר.(ד) ובין לחיים אסור ואינו יכול להשתמש אלא מן המחילה שלפנים – דהא אביי אית ליה לעיל (ד' ה.) גבי היה גבוה מכ' ובא למעטו לחד לישנא קורה משום מחילה, וכ"ש לחי. וקא אמר בסמוך: מסתברא מילתיה דר' יוחנן תחת הקורה, אבל בין לחיים – אסור. ורבא נמי אית ליה בפירקין דתרווייהו משום היכירא. ובסמוך מודה רבא דאסור להשתמש בין לחיים היכא דרחב ארבעה:

רבינו חננאל

בה. דקיי"ל בחצר אע"פ שרבים בוקעין בה מותר לטלטל. אתמר מבוי העשוי כנדל. פי' מבוי ארוך שמשני צדדין יש לו מבואות קטנים פתוחין מיכן ומיכן כגון רגלי השרץ הנקרא נדל. ויש לו רגלים הרבה משוכות מהנה ומהנה כדתניא עד כל מרבה רגלים זה נדל. אסקה רבא דהלכתא כוותיה. עושה צורת הפתח לכולהו אחד גיסא לכל חד וחד ואידך גיסא מישתרי בלחי וקורה. והא דרבא שייכא כרב דסבר מבוי עקום תורתו כמפולש וקאמר רב במבוי המפולש לרה"ר הלכה כת"ק דאמר עושה צורת הפתח מיכן ולחי או קורה מיכן. הא דאמר רב כהנא רביה דרב מבוי שצדו אחד ארוך וצדו אחד קצר. פחות מד' אמות מניח קורה באלכסון. פי' אם עודף צד הארוך על הצד הקצר ד' אמות כאילו מבוי בפני עצמו הוא וצריך מחיצות כנגדו. פחות מד' אמות חשוב כמו פירצת מבוי ומחיצות של מבוי פוטרות אותו. ואסיקנא בשיש באלכסונו יותר מעשר אמות דברי הכל אינו מניח את הקורה אלא כנגד הקצר. וכן אם בא לעשות לחי אינו עושה אותו אלא כנגד הקצר. הא דאיבעיא לן מהו להשתמש תחת הקורה רב ור' חייא ור' יוחנן אמרי מותר וקיימא כוותייהו. וסוגיא

מסורת הש"ס

רש"ל מ"ז ועי' במהרש"א
[לעיל ו:]
[לעיל ה. וש"נ]
[שם]
גס לרב חסדא פריך [ת"י]

הגהות הב"ח

(א) גמ' משמי' דרב כהנא בר מלכיו (משמיה דרב כהנא רביה דרב וכו' רביה דרב) תא"מ ונ"ב ס"א משמיה דרב כהנא רבה ואמרי לה רב כהנא בר מלכיו היינו רב כהנא רבה: (ב) רש"י ד"ה ועוד הא ההוא מבוי עקום דהוה: (ג) תום' ד"ה והא ההוא וכו' דהא דחשו לדשמואל משום: (ד) ד"ה הכל וכו' קורה משום היכר ולחי משום מחילה ומשום הכי בין לחיים אסור דאינו יכול:

אִיפכ' מסתבר' דטוב לעשות ל"ה בפילושו לרה"ר ובעקמימותו לחי וא"ש לשמואל לפירו' שני של רש"י א"נ יותר בקל הוא לעשות ל"ה בעקמימותו ולחי אחד מכל לד מלעשות פעמיי' ל"ה ולחי באמצע [הר"ח בן הרי"ק]

גליון הש"ס

ברש"י ד"ה נדל. כדתניא בתורת כהנים. והוא בחולין דף סז ע"ב: תוס' ד"ה מניח את הקורה. משום מחילה הוי אפי' לאורייתא. עי' לקמן דף פו ע"א תד"ה קורה: בא"ד לא בקעי. עי' בר"ן פ"ק דסוכה דף רלא ע"ב ד"ה גרסינן:

*) דקאמר סברי קורה משום היכר הני סבירא להו היא והיכרא מלבר. וא"ת משום מחיצה הני סברי חודה החיצון סותם ולפיכך מותר להשתמש תחת הקורה. וכן בין לחיים נמי מותר להשתמש כר' יוחנן דאמר לתנא דר' זכאי דהוה תני תחת הקורה ובין לחיים בכרמלית פוק תני לברא. כלומר זו אינה משנה. הכיר כלומר בין הקורה ובין הלחיים משום היכר הן ועג"ע דא"ל רב הונא בריה דרב יהושע לרבא ואת לא תסברא דכיון דלחיים אסור והאמר משמיה דר' יוחנן מבוי שרצפו בלחיים. ס"א נפרץ בלחיים פחות מד' טפחים אליבא דרשב"א אמרינן לבוד בר' מפחים אשתמש עם חודה הפנימי של פימי דאמר לא אמרינן לבוד בכי האי גוונא אשתמש עם חודה הפנימי של חוצן ודוכלי עלמא בין לחיים אסור. ופרקינן דפתוח לכרמלית ואקשינן אבל לרה"ר מאי שרי. יציבא בארעא וכו'. כלומר ברה"ר מותר בכרמלית אסור. ופרקינן (האיך) מצא מין את מינו ונעור. בעא מיניה רמי בר חמא מרב חסדא נעץ ב' יתדות בב' כותלי מבוי מבחוץ והביא קורה על גבן שנמצאת הקורה ע"ג היתדות מחוץ לכותלי המבוי מהו (זה) להשתמש במבוי וכו'. א"ל לדברי רב ור' חייא ור' יוחנן דשרו להשתמש תחת הקורה דסברי חודה של קורה החיצונה מתרת הכא אסור דהא היכירא החיצונה חוץ למבוי הוא ואין בו מחיצות מבוי לפיכך המבוי אסור. ולדברי הני דאסרי דסברי דהפנימית מתרת הכא שרי דהא (קורה) [חודה] הפנימית פותח' מתחלת המבוי הנה רב חסדא אוקמא

*) [נראה דל"ל וסוגיא דגמ' הכי דלאו קורה משום היכר לחוד הסוגיה להו לסכירא מלבר וא"ת משום מחילה סו'.]

משׁוּכָה או תְלוּיָה; *[א]פָּחוֹת מִג' — אֵין צָרִיךְ לְהָבִיא קוֹרָה אַחֶרֶת, ג' — צָרִיךְ לְהָבִיא קוֹרָה אַחֶרֶת. *רשב"ג אוֹמֵר: פָּחוֹת מִד' — אֵין צָרִיךְ לְהָבִיא קוֹרָה אַחֶרֶת, ד' — צָרִיךְ לְהָבִיא קוֹרָה אַחֶרֶת. מַאי לָאו — מְשׁוּכָה מִבַּחוּץ, וּתְלוּיָה מִבִּפְנִים! לֹא, אִידִי וְאִידִי מִבִּפְנִים; מְשׁוּכָה — מֵרוּחַ אַחַת, וּתְלוּיָה — מִשְּׁתֵּי רוּחוֹת. *מַהוּ דְּתֵימָא: מֵרוּחַ אַחַת אָמְרִינַן לָבוּד, מִשְּׁתֵּי רוּחוֹת לָא אָמְרִינַן לָבוּד, קמ"ל. רַב אַשִׁי אָמַר: מְשׁוּכָה וְהִיא תְּלוּיָה. וְהֵיכִי דָּמֵי — [ב]כְּגוֹן שֶׁנָּעַץ שְׁתֵּי יְתֵידוֹת עֲקוּמוֹת עַל שְׁנֵי כּוֹתְלֵי מָבוֹי, שֶׁאֵין בְּגוֹבְהָן ג', וְאֵין בְּעַקְמוּמִיתָן ג'. מַהוּ דְּתֵימָא: אוֹ *"לָבוּד" אָמְרִינַן אוֹ "חָבוּט" אָמְרִינַן, לָבוּד וְחָבוּט לָא אָמְרִינַן, קמ"ל. תָּנֵי ר' זַכַּאי קַמֵּיהּ דְּר' יוֹחָנָן: בֵּין לְחָיַיִם וְתַחַת הַקּוֹרָה — נִידּוֹן כְּכַרְמְלִית. אֲמַר לֵיהּ: פּוֹק תְּנִי לְבָרָא. אֲמַר אַבַּיֵי: מִסְתַּבְּרָא מִילְּתֵיהּ דְּר' יוֹחָנָן תַּחַת הַקּוֹרָה, אֲבָל בֵּין לְחָיַיִן — אָסוּר. וְרָבָא אֲמַר: [ג]בֵּין לְחָיַיִם נַמִי מוּתָּר. אֲמַר רָבָא: מְנָא אָמִינָא לָהּ — *דְּכִי אֲתָא רַב דִּימִי, א"ר יוֹחָנָן: מָקוֹם שֶׁאֵין בּוֹ ד' עַל ד' — מוּתָּר לִבְנֵי רה"ר וְלִבְנֵי רה"י לְכַתֵּף עָלָיו, וּבִלְבַד שֶׁלֹּא יַחֲלִיפוּ. וְאַבַּיֵי — הָתָם בְּגָבוֹהַּ ג'. אֲמַר אַבַּיֵי: מְנָא אָמִינָא לָהּ — *דְּאָמַר רַב חָמָא בַּר גּוּרְיָא, אָמַר רַב: תּוֹךְ הַפֶּתַח צָרִיךְ לֶחִי אַחֵר לְהַתִּירוֹ. וְכִי תֵּימָא דְּאִית בֵּיהּ ד' עַל ד'. וְהָאָמַר רַב חָנִין* בַּר רָבָא אָמַר רַב: תּוֹךְ הַפֶּתַח, אע"פ שֶׁאֵין בּוֹ ד' עַל ד' — צָרִיךְ לֶחִי אַחֵר לְהַתִּירוֹ. וְרָבָא — [ד]הָתָם דְּפָתוּחַ לְכַרְמְלִית, אֲבָל לרה"ר מַאי — שָׁרֵי? *יַצִּיבָא בְּאַרְעָא וְגִיּוֹרָא בִּשְׁמֵי שְׁמַיָּא! אִין, *מָצָא מִין אֶת מִינוֹ *וְנֵיעוֹר. א"ל רַב הוּנָא בְּרֵיהּ דְּרַב יְהוֹשֻׁעַ לְרָבָא: וְאַתְּ לָא תִסְבְּרָא דְּבֵין לְחָיַיִן אָסוּר? וְהָאָמַר רַבָּה בַּר בַּר חָנָה, אָמַר ר' יוֹחָנָן: מָבוֹי שֶׁרְצָפוֹ בִּלְחָיַיִן פָּחוֹת מִד' — בָּאנוּ לְמַחֲלוֹקֶת רשב"ג וְרַבָּנָן. לְרשב"ג דְּאָמַר אָמְרִינַן לָבוּד — מִשְׁתַּמֵּשׁ עַד חוּדּוֹ הַפְּנִימִי שֶׁל לֶחִי הַפְּנִימִי, לְרַבָּנַן דְּאָמְרִי לָא אָמְרִינַן לָבוּד — מִשְׁתַּמֵּשׁ עַד חוּדּוֹ הַפְּנִימִי שֶׁל חִיצוֹן. אֲבָל בֵּין לְחָיַיִן — דְּכוּלֵּי עָלְמָא אָסוּר! וְרָבָא — הָתָם נַמִי דְּפָתוּחַ לְכַרְמְלִית. אֲבָל לרה"ר מַאי — שָׁרֵי? יַצִּיבָא בְּאַרְעָא וְגִיּוֹרָא בִּשְׁמֵי שְׁמַיָּא! אִין, מָצָא מִין אֶת מִינוֹ וְנֵיעוֹר.

רַב

כזה

רש"י

מְשׁוּכָה. מַשְׁמַע: רְחוֹקָה הִיא מִן הַכְּתָלִים: אוֹ תְלוּיָה. שֶׁאֵין רָאשֶׁיהָ מוּנָּחִים עַל גַּבֵּי הַכְּתָלִים, אֶלָּא תְּלוּיָה בָּאֲוִיר – שֶׁקְּצָרָה מִשְּׁתֵּי רוּחוֹתֶיהָ. וּכְגוֹן שֶׁנָּעַץ קָנֶה כָּל שֶׁהוּא בְּאֶמְצַע פֶּתַח הַמָּבוֹי, וְנָתַן עַל גַּבּוֹ אֶת הַקּוֹרָה, *כָּזֶה: רַבָּן שִׁמְעוֹן סְבִירָא לֵיהּ בְּכָל דּוּכְתָּא פָּחוֹת מִד' כְּלָבוּד דָּמֵי: מְשׁוּכָה מִבַּחוּץ. שֶׁנִּמְשְׁכָה לְתוֹךְ רְשׁוּת הָרַבִּים, כְּגוֹן הַאי דְּבָעֵינַן דִּלְעֵיל דִּשְׁתֵּי יְתֵידוֹת: תְּלוּיָה מִבִּפְנִים. שֶׁקְּצָרָה מִשְּׁתֵּי רוּחוֹת, וְאֵינָהּ מַגַּעַת לַכְּתָלִים אֶלָּא נִתְלֵית בָּאֲוִיר, וְאָמְרִינַן לָבוּד לְהַאֲרִיךְ רָאשֶׁיהָ: אִידִי וְאִידִי מִבִּפְנִים. וְתַרְוַיְיהוּ בְּקוֹרָה קְצָרָה עָסְקִינַן: מְשׁוּכָה מֵרוּחַ אַחַת. רֹאשָׁהּ אֶחָד עַל הַכּוֹתֶל, וְרֹאשָׁהּ הַשֵּׁנִי אֵינוֹ מַגִּיעַ לַכּוֹתֶל שֶׁכְּנֶגְדּוֹ: רַב אַשִׁי אָמַר. מִשּׁוּם ב' רוּחוֹת לָא אִיצְטְרִיכָא לֵיהּ, דְּכֵיוָן דְּתָנָא מְשׁוּכָה מֵרוּחַ אַחַת – הוּא הַדִּין מִשְּׁתֵּי רוּחוֹת. אֶלָּא חֲדָא קָתָנֵי: מְשׁוּכָה וְהִיא תְּלוּיָה, שֶׁקְּצָרָה הִיא מֵהַגִּיעַ לַכְּתָלִים. וְעוֹד: שֶׁתְּלוּיָה הִיא לְמַעְלָה מִגּוֹבַהּ כּוֹתְלֵי הַמָּבוֹי: וְהֵיכִי דָּמֵי כְּגוֹן שֶׁנָּעַץ שְׁתֵּי יְתֵידוֹת עֲקוּמוֹת עַל גַּבֵּי ב' כּוֹתְלֵי מָבוֹי. וַעֲקַמִימוּתֵיהֶן נוֹטוֹת זוֹ כְּלַפֵּי זוֹ לִהְיוֹתָן סָנִיף לְהַאֲרִיךְ הַקּוֹרָה מִשְּׁנֵי צִדֶּיהָ כְּשֶׁתִּנָּתֵן עֲלֵיהֶם, וְהֵם עַצְמָם אֵינָם רְאוּיוֹת לְהֶכְשֵׁר קוֹרָה שֶׁאֵין בָּהֶן רוֹחַב טֶפַח כְּשִׁיעוּר הֶכְשֵׁר קוֹרָה דְּמַתְנִיתִין: וְאֵין בְּעַקְמוּמִיתָן שְׁלֹשָׁה. וְאִיכָּא לְמֵימַר לָבוּד מֵרָאשֵׁי הַקּוֹרָה וְלַכְּתָלִים, וְאֵין בְּגוֹבְהָן שֶׁל יְתֵידוֹת מִמַּעַל לַכְּתָלִים שְׁלֹשָׁה טְפָחִים. דְּאִי הֲוָה בְּגוֹבְהָן שְׁלֹשָׁה טְפָחִים – הֲוָה מִיפַּסְלָא, דְּקוֹרָה עַל גַּבֵּי כְתָלִים בָּעֵינַן. אֲבָל הַשְׁתָּא בְּפָחוֹת מִשְּׁלֹשָׁה אָמְרִינַן חָבוּט = הַשְׁפֵּל, כְּאִילּוּ מוּנַּחַת עַל הַכּוֹתֶל: לָבוּד. לְשׁוֹן סָנִיף לְהַאֲרִיךְ, וּבְלַע"ז אפש"ק: נִידּוֹן בְּכַרְמְלִית. וְאָסוּר לְטַלְטֵל שָׁם: מִסְתַּבְּרָא מִילְּתֵיהּ דְּר' יוֹחָנָן. דְּאָמַר: פּוֹק תְּנִי לְבָרָא. אֶלָּא מוּתָּר הוּא אַתַּחַת קוֹרָה קָאָמַר לֵיהּ, דְּקָסָבַר: חוּדּוֹ הַחִיצוֹן יוֹרֵד וְסוֹתֵם: אֲבָל בֵּין לְחָיַיִם. בְּמָבוֹי שֶׁאֵין שָׁם קוֹרָה – מוֹדֶה דְּאָסוּר: מָקוֹם שֶׁאֵין בּוֹ ד' עַל ד'. עוֹמֵד בֵּין רְשׁוּת הָרַבִּים לִרְשׁוּת הַיָּחִיד, הוֹאִיל וְלֵיכָּא מָקוֹם חָשׁוּב – לָאו רְשׁוּת בְּאַנְפֵּי נַפְשֵׁיהּ הוּא, וּבָטֵיל לְהָכָא וּלְהָכָא. וְהַיְינוּ מְקוֹם פְּטוּר: לְכַתֵּף עָלָיו. מַשָּׂאוֹת: וּבִלְבַד שֶׁלֹּא יַחֲלִיפוּ. דְּלָא לֵימְרוּ דְּקָא מְעַיֵּיל מֵרְשׁוּת הָרַבִּים לִרְשׁוּת הַיָּחִיד, וְאָתֵי לְמִישְׁרֵי הוֹצָאָה בְּשַׁבָּת. וּבֵין לְחָיַיִם נַמִי, אֲפִילּוּ חָשְׁבַהּ לֵיהּ מָקוֹם בִּפְנֵי עַצְמוֹ – בָּטֵל לְהָכָא וּלְהָכָא, וְשָׁרֵי: בְּגָבוֹהַּ שְׁלֹשָׁה. דְּמִינְכְּרָא אֲבָל בֵּין לְחָיַיִם דְּלָא מִינְכְּרָא דּוּכְתָּא, אִי שָׁרֵית לְטַלְטֵל הָתָם – אָתֵי לְהַחֲלִיף וּלְאַפּוּקֵי לִרְשׁוּת הָרַבִּים: תּוֹךְ הַפֶּתַח. כְּגוֹן מָבוֹי שֶׁיֵּשׁ פַּצִּימִין רְחָבִים לְפִתְחוֹ מִכָּאן וּמִכָּאן, וְהֵן הֵן לְחָיַיִם שֶׁלּוֹ – צָרִיךְ לְהַעֲמִיד לֶחִי אַחֵר מִבַּחוּץ, אִם יִרְצֶה לְהִשְׁתַּמֵּשׁ בֵּין הַפַּצִּימִין: דְּאִית בְּהוּ אַרְבַּע. בְּרוֹחַב הַפַּצִּימִין בְּמֶשֶׁךְ הַמָּבוֹי, דְּכָל ד' רְשׁוּת בְּאַנְפֵּי נַפְשֵׁיהּ הִיא, וְכַרְמְלִית הִיא וּמִדְּרַבָּנָן אֲסוּרָה: לְכַרְמְלִית. לְבִקְעָה, דְּשַׁיָּיךְ וּמִצְטָרֵף לְמִינוֹ שֶׁחוּלָּה לוֹ: יַצִּיבָא. אֶזְרָחִי: מָצָא. כַּרְמְלִית שֶׁבֵּין לְחָיַיִם, שֶׁלֹּא הָיָה בּוֹ שִׁיעוּר כַּרְמְלִית: אֶת מִינוֹ. שֶׁחוּלָּה לוֹ: וְנֵיעוֹר. נִתְחַזֵּק עַל יְדֵי מִינוֹ, וְנֵיעוֹר מִשְּׁנָתוֹ שֶׁהָיָה בַּתְּחִלָּה בָּטֵל אֵצֶל שֶׁאֵינוֹ מִינוֹ. וְדוּגְמָתוֹ בִּבְכוֹרוֹת (ד' כב.): טוּמְאָה שֶׁבָּטְלָה וְחָזְרָה וְנֵיעוֹרָה: אֲבָל פָּתוּחַ לִרְשׁוּת הָרַבִּים. שֶׁלֹּא זֶה מִינוֹ וְלֹא זֶה מִינוֹ, וּלְכָאן וְכָאן בְּטֵלָה: וְאַתְּ לָא תִסְבְּרָא דְּבֵין לְחָיַיִם. לְר' יוֹחָנָן אָסוּר: וְהָאָמַר ר' יוֹחָנָן מָבוֹי שֶׁרְצָפוֹ בִּלְחָיַיִם. בְּמֶשֶׁךְ הַמָּבוֹי מֵרֹאשׁוֹ לְצַד סוֹפוֹ בִּשְׁתַּיִם וְשָׁלֹשׁ אַמּוֹת: בִּפְחוֹת מֵאַרְבָּעָה. שֶׁאֵין בֵּין לֶחִי לְלֶחִי ד' אֲבָל יֵשׁ בֵּינֵיהֶן ג': בָּאנוּ לְמַחֲלוֹקֶת רַבָּן שִׁמְעוֹן וְרַבָּנַן. דְּאִיפְּלִגוּ לְעֵיל בְּמִשְּׁלֹשָׁה וְעַד ד' אִי אָמְרִינַן לָבוּד אוֹ לָא. מֵאוֹתוֹ מַחֲלוֹקֶת אָנוּ לְמֵידִין שֶׁאַף בְּהֶכְשֵׁר מָבוֹי זֶה יֵשׁ מַחֲלוֹקֶת בֵּינֵיהֶן. וְרַבִּי יוֹחָנָן לָא מְפָרֵשׁ מִילְּתֵיהּ. וְהַשְׁתָּא קָא מְפָרֵשׁ רַב הוּנָא בְּרֵיהּ דְּרַב יְהוֹשֻׁעַ דְּעַל כָּרְחֵיךְ הָא דְּקָאָמַר רַבִּי יוֹחָנָן דְּשַׁיְּיכָא פְּלוּגְתָּא דְּרַבָּן שִׁמְעוֹן וְרַבָּנַן הָכָא – לָא מַשְׁכַּחַתְּ לָהּ אֶלָּא בְּתַשְׁמִישׁ שֶׁכְּנֶגֶד הַלְּחָיַיִם, דִּלְרַבָּן שִׁמְעוֹן הָווּ כּוּלְּהוּ כְּחַד לֶחִי וְאֵין מִשְׁתַּמֵּשׁ בַּמָּבוֹי אֶלָּא עַד חוּדּוֹ הַפְּנִימִי שֶׁל לֶחִי הַפְּנִימִי, אֲבָל מִשָּׁם וְלַחוּץ – הָוֵי בֵּין לְחָיַיִם וְאָסוּר. וּלְרַבָּנַן לָא הָוֵי כְּחַד לֶחִי, וּבַלֶּחִי הַחִיצוֹן מִשְׁתְּרֵי מָבוֹי וּמוּתָּר לְהִשְׁתַּמֵּשׁ בְּכָל הַמָּבוֹי עַד חוּדּוֹ הַפְּנִימִי שֶׁל חִיצוֹן, דִּכְנֶגֶד חִיצוֹן לְחוּדֵיהּ הָוֵי בֵּין לְחָיַיִם. אַלְמָא: לְרַבִּי יוֹחָנָן בֵּין לְחָיַיִם אָסוּר. דְּאִי בֵּין לְחָיַיִם לְרַבִּי יוֹחָנָן מוּתָּר, מַאי שַׁיְּיכָא פְּלוּגְתַּיְיהוּ דְּרַבָּן שִׁמְעוֹן וְרַבָּנַן לְהָכָא? בֵּין הָווּ כּוּלְּהוּ כְּחַד, בֵּין לָא הָווּ כּוּלְּהוּ כְּחַד – כְּנֶגֶד כּוּלָּם הוּא מִשְׁתַּמֵּשׁ:

רַב

מבוי קורה

תוספות

שאין בגובהן שלשה. ואם תאמר: והא אמר בסוף פרק "הישן" (סוכה ד' כב.) דכי יש ברחבו טפח אמר חבוט ורמי אפילו ביתר מג'. וקורה דרחבה טפח נימא נמי חבוט ורמי אפילו גבוה מג'! ובלאו הכי קשה: אמאי לא שריא אפילו ביתר מג', כיון דקורה תוך עשרים? וי"ל: דהכא בעינן קורה על גבי מבוי, וביתר מג' לא הוי היכר. תדע, דהא משוכה מבחוץ, אפילו בפחות מג' לא אמרינן לבוד: **תוך** הפתח צריך לחי אחר להתירו. לאו משום דנחשב כמבוי בפני עצמו, דאין מבוי ניתר בלחי וקורה אלא אם כן ארכו יתר על רחבו ובתים וחצירות פתוחין לתוכו: **ורבא** התם הוא דפתוח לכרמלית. ואם תאמר: בפרק קמא דשבת (ד' ו.), גבי אחרים אומרים: אסקופה משמשת שתי רשויות, פתח פתוח כלפנים פתח נעול כלחוץ. ופריך מהא דאמר רב:* צריך לחי אחר להתירו. ומשני: הכא באסקופת מבוי עסקינן. ואמאי לא משני התם דפתוחה לכרמלית, וההוא דאחרים — בפתוח לרה"ר? וי"ל: דאי בפתוח לרה"ר, כיון דאין בו ארבע על ארבע – הוי מקום פטור, ואפילו פתח נעול נמי כלפנים. ותדע, דלאביי נמי לוקמא בגובה שלשה דהוי מקום פטור, כדאמרינן לעיל – אלא משום דאם כן אפילו נעול נמי. **לרשב"ג** דאמר לבוד משתמש עד חודו הפנימי. זו אינו מדברי רבי יוחנן, דהא רב אשי מפרשה בע"א. ואם תאמר: אם כן מאי פריך לרבא? הוא יפרש דפליגי שרצפו בלחיים רחבים ארבע, דרבא מודה לעיל ברחבים ארבע דאסור. ואפילו באין רחבים ד' פליגי, ומשכחת פלגותא דרשב"ג אומר לבוד, והרי בין כולם יש ד' ואסור להשתמש כנגדו. ולרבנן דאמרי לא אמרינן לבוד — משתמש עד חודו החיצון של לחי החיצון. וי"ל:* כיון דכשאין כ"א ב' לחיים, ובכל א' משהו, ושניהם רצופים בפחות מד' — לא משכחת פלוגתייהו דרשב"ג ורבנן. ולא משכחת פלוגתייהו אלא כשיש ד', הוה ליה לרבי יוחנן לפרושי במילתיה בהדיא: מבוי שרצפו בלחיים בפחות מד' *במשך ד'. אע"ג דרב אשי מוקי לה במשך ד' אמות, כיון שאמר ר' יוחנן מבוי שרצפו — הוי כאילו פירש בהדיא ד' אמות, דמשך מבוי ד' אמות: ולרשב"ג

רבינו חננאל

אוקמא בפלוגתא רבא אמר לדברי הכל מבוי אסור בעינא קורה ע"ג מבוי וליכא ומותיב עליה רב אדא מהא דתניא היתה קורתו משוכה או תלויה פחות מג' אין צריך קורה אחרת. ג' צריך קורה אחרת. רשב"ג אומר אם יש ביניהן ארבעה צריך קורה אחרת ואמרינן מאי משוכה לאו משוכה חוץ למבוי ונתונה ע"ג יתידות כי האי גוונא. וקתני דאם הקורה נתונה בפחות מג' אין צריך קורה אחרת. ומותר לטלטל במבוי. ומשני רבא לא אידי ואידי בין משוכה בין תלויה מבפנים של מבוי הוא מיהו משוכה מרוח אחת כגון שנתן קורה ע"ג המבוי ויוצאה מכותל זה ואינה נוגעת בכותל שכנגדה במבוי פחות מג' טפחים כלבוד דמי וכאילו ע"ג ב' כותלין היא נתונה ואין צריך קורה אחרת וכו'. תלויה כגון שזו הקורה תלויה באמצע מבוי ואינה נתונה לא בכותל זה ולא בכותל זה אם היא בפחות מג' טפחים מיכן ומיכן אין צריך קורה אחרת. דקיי"ל דאמרינן לבוד מב' רוחות. רב אשי אמר משוכה והיא תלויה היכי דמי כגון שנעץ ב' יתדות עקומות כגון עקמומית של אגמון שאין בגובהו ג' ולא בעקמימותו ג' ותלה הקורה בחבל ביניהן והיא תלויה ומשוכה כלומר רחוקה מב' כותלי המבוי וקיי"ל דאמרינן גוד אסיק מחיצה מן הקורה ולמעלה. ותוב אמרינן חבוט רמי ביתדות כדי להראות כאילו נתפשטה עקמומית להשוות לקורה כדי שתהיה הקורה על ב' הכתלים. וקיי"ל כרבא דהא רב אשי דהוא בתרא מתרץ למתניתא דא כוותיה. כיון דאמר רבא בין הקורה ובין הלחיים מותר להשתמש. א"ל רב אשי *) דהוא הונא בריה דרב יהושע אוג לא תסברין דבין לחיים אסור והא [אמר] רבה בר בר חנה א"ר יוחנן מבוי שרצפו בלחיים פחות פחות מד' פי' כותל של מבוי בכל [שיעור] פחות מד' טפחים מרחיב בעובי הכותל כשיעור טפח ונראה לחי. וכך מושך בענין הזה רוב אורכו של מבוי. וא"ר (יוסי) [יוחנן] בכה"ג באנו למחלוקת רשב"ג ורבנן שחולקין בהא דתניא היה קורה משוכה או תלויה פחות מג' א"צ קורה אחרת כו'. עד כ"ע בין לחיים אסור ושני (רבה) [רבא] במבוי שפתוח לכרמלית משום דמצא

*) ד' רכיט בכאן אם לא עגיה בדבריו כמ"ש בגמרא לאו מובן כלל ואולי דגי' אחרת הוה לו בכאן ול"ע:

עין משפט נר מצוה

נב א ב מיי' פי"ז מהל' שבת הלכה כד טוש"ע א"ח סי' שסו סעיף כה:

נג ג ד מיי' שם הלכה יא סמג עשין דרבנן א טוש"ע א"ח סי' שסה סעיף ז:

מסורת הש"ס

[לקמן יד.]

[לקמן יז. עז: עו. פז: סוכה כב.]

[סוכה טז:]

[בערוך ערך גד שני גריס גוד]

שבת ח: לקמן עז. פה: פז: קא:

שבת ט.

[בשבת איתא רב חמא בר גוריא]

[יומא מז. ב"ק מב.]

[ע"ז עג. בכורות כב. כג.]

[דף ט.]

[עי' רש"י בע"ז עג. בד"ה מנא האריך לפרש מלה זו]

וה"ה דה"מ לשנוי' דרבא סבר משך מבוי בד' וכן הוה מצי לאוקמא פלוגתא בשרצפ' עד סוף המבוי לרשב"ג דאמר לבוד לא הוי נראה מבפנים [ת"י]

גליון הש"ס

גמ' א"ל פוק תני לברא. שבת דף קו ע"א ברש"י ד"ה זיל קרי יב ע"ב יומא דף מג ע"ב:

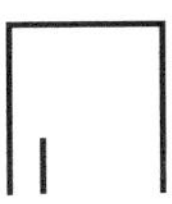

נד א מיי' פי"ז מהלכו' שבת הלכה כב טוש"ע א"ח סי' שסג סעיף ט:

רַב אַשִׁי אָמַר: כְּגוֹן שֶׁרְצָפוֹ בִּלְחָיַיִם פָּחוֹת מֵאַרְבָּעָה, בְּמֶשֶׁךְ אַרְבַּע אַמּוֹת. לְרַבָּן שִׁמְעוֹן בֶּן גַּמְלִיאֵל דְּאָמַר "אָמְרִינַן לָבוּד" — הָוֵה לֵיהּ מָבוֹי, וְצָרִיךְ לֶחִי אַחֵר לְהַתִּירוֹ. וּלְרַבָּנַן דְּאָמְרִי לָא אָמְרִינַן לָבוּד — לֹא צָרִיךְ לֶחִי אַחֵר לְהַתִּירוֹ. וּלְרַבָּן שִׁמְעוֹן בֶּן גַּמְלִיאֵל, לֶהֱוֵי כְּנִרְאֶה מִבַּחוּץ וְשָׁוֶה מִבִּפְנִים! מִידֵּי הוּא טַעְמָא אֶלָּא לְר' יוֹחָנָן, הָא כִּי אֲתָא רָבִין אֲמַר רַבִּי יוֹחָנָן: נִרְאֶה מִבַּחוּץ וְשָׁוֶה מִבִּפְנִים — אֵינוֹ נִידּוֹן מִשּׁוּם לֶחִי. *אִיתְּמַר; נִרְאֶה מִבִּפְנִים וְשָׁוֶה מִבַּחוּץ — נִידּוֹן מִשּׁוּם לֶחִי. נִרְאֶה מִבַּחוּץ וְשָׁוֶה מִבִּפְנִים, רַבִּי חִיָּיא וְרַבִּי שִׁמְעוֹן בְּ"ר. חַד אָמַר: [א]נִידּוֹן מִשּׁוּם לֶחִי, וְחַד אָמַר: אֵינוֹ נִידּוֹן מִשּׁוּם לֶחִי. תִּסְתַּיֵּים דְּר' חִיָּיא הוּא דְּאָמַר "נִידּוֹן מִשּׁוּם לֶחִי", דְּתָנֵי *רַבִּי חִיָּיא: כּוֹתֶל שֶׁצִּידּוֹ אֶחָד כָּנוּס מֵחֲבֵירוֹ, בֵּין שֶׁנִּרְאֶה מִבַּחוּץ וְשָׁוֶה מִבִּפְנִים, וּבֵין שֶׁנִּרְאֶה מִבִּפְנִים וְשָׁוֶה מִבַּחוּץ — נִידּוֹן מִשּׁוּם לֶחִי, תִּסְתַּיֵּים. וְרַבִּי יוֹחָנָן מִי לָא שְׁמִיעַ לֵיהּ הָא?! אֶלָּא: שְׁמִיעַ לֵיהּ, וְלָא סָבַר לַהּ, רַבִּי חִיָּיא נַמִּי, לֹא סָבַר לַהּ?! הַאי מַאי?! בִּשְׁלָמָא ר' יוֹחָנָן לֹא סָבַר לַהּ — מִשּׁוּם הָכִי לָא תָּנֵי לַהּ, אֶלָּא ר' חִיָּיא — אִי אִיתָא דְּלָא סָבַר לַהּ, לָמָּה לֵיהּ לְמִיתְנָא? אָמַר רַבָּה בַּר רַב הוּנָא: נִרְאֶה מִבַּחוּץ וְשָׁוֶה מִבִּפְנִים — נִידּוֹן מִשּׁוּם לֶחִי. אָמַר רַבָּה: *וּמוֹתְבִינַן אַשְׁמַעְתִּין *"חָצֵר קְטַנָּה שֶׁנִּפְרְצָה לִגְדוֹלָה — גְּדוֹלָה מוּתֶּרֶת וּקְטַנָּה אֲסוּרָה, מִפְּנֵי שֶׁהִיא כְּפִתְחָהּ שֶׁל גְּדוֹלָה". וְאִם אִיתָא, קְטַנָּה נַמִּי תִּשְׁתְּרֵי בְּנִרְאֶה מִבַּחוּץ וְשָׁוֶה מִבִּפְנִים! אָמַר ר' זֵירָא: בְּנִכְנָסִין כּוֹתְלֵי קְטַנָּה לִגְדוֹלָה. וְלֵימָא "לָבוּד" וְתִשְׁתְּרֵי! וְכִי תֵּימָא דְּמִפַּלְגֵי טוּבָא — וְהָא *תָּנֵי רַב אַדָּא בַּר אֲבִימִי *קַמֵּיהּ דְּר' חֲנִינָא:(א) קְטַנָּה בְּעֶשֶׂר, גְּדוֹלָה בְּאַחַת עֶשְׂרֵה! אָמַר רָבִינָא: בְּמוּפְלָגִין מִכּוֹתֶל זֶה בִּשְׁנַיִם, וּמִכּוֹתֶל זֶה בְּד'. וְלֵימָא לָבוּד מֵרוּחַ אַחַת, וְתִשְׁתְּרֵי!
רַבִּי

רב אשי אמר. לעולם בין לחיים לרבי יוחנן מותר. והאי דקאמר רבי יוחנן דשייכא פלוגתייהו דרבן שמעון ורבנן להכא — כגון דהוה משך רליפה זו ד' אמות באורך המבוי: לרבן שמעון. יש לבוד בפחות מד' והוה ליה חד לחי. ואמרינן לעיל (ד' ה.): ד' אמות נידון משום מבוי, ויצא מתורת לחי: וצריך לחי אחר להתירו. מבוי זה שבין לחיים. אבל מלחי הפנימי ואילך מיהו שרי לטלטולי במבוי, דלהנהו ודאי נראה לחי, ועודיו נידון להם בלחי, וניתר בו מבוי, כך שמעתי. ולי נראה: שאפילו מפנימי ולפנים אינו ניתר, דלחי הפנימי ולפנים לר' יוחנן אינו מתיר כלל. אבל לרבנן — כל חד וחד בתנפי נפשיה הוא, ומשתרי מבוי בלחי קמא: ולרבן שמעון. נהי נמי דכולי חד הוא, ונידון משום מבוי — אפילו הכי, היכי שמע רבי יוחנן מדרבן שמעון דבעי לחי אחר להתירו? לישתרי האי מבוי בנראה מבחוץ ושוה מבפנים. דהא מסתמא כי אוקמא ללחי קמא משכו קימעא כלפי חוץ. שכן דרך כל מעמידי לחיים כדי שיראה. *כזה

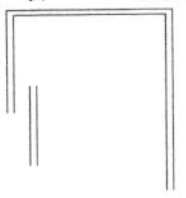

מבפנים ומבחוץ שהוקבע שם לשם לחי. דאם אינו מושך קצת רוחב הלחי להלאה מכותלי המבוי מעט, אלא בשוה להן,

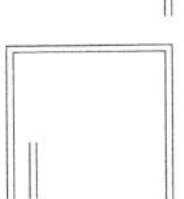

*כזה נראה כמוסיף על רוחב עובי כותל המבוי ואינו ניכר מבחוץ שהוא לחי, אלא בפנים ניכר שאינו מן הכתלים לפי שחודו נראה בפנים. וכיון דראשון קצתו נמשך לחוץ, כי הדר השוהו מבפנים ברליפת לחיים הללו ועשאו כותל — מיהא לישתרי מבוי בההיא בליטה קמייתא הנראית מבחוץ, דהא קאמרינן לקמן: נראה מבחוץ ושוה מבפנים נידון משום לחי: מידי הוא טעמא. כלומר: מי מותבינן האי תיובתא אלא לר' יוחנן, דיליף מלבוד דרבן שמעון פסולא להאי מבוי: אינו נידון. הלכך: אי אמרינן לבוד — בעי לחי אחרינא: "איתמר" גרסינן: נראה מבפנים ושוה מבחוץ. שהעמיד הלחי רחבו לצד אורכו של מבוי, ולא משך קצת רחבו קימעא כלפי חוץ אלא השוה חודו החיצון לעובי כותלי המבוי, ודומה כמי שמוסיף על רוחב הכתלים, ואינו נראה מבחוץ כלחי.

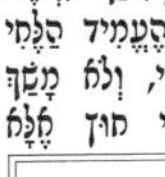

אבל חודו הפנימי נראה מבפנים שעביו בולט לתוך רוחב המבוי כזה: נראה מבחוץ ושוה מבפנים. שמשך כל הלחי לחוץ, וחודו הפנימי(ב) נכנס בכותלי המבוי ואינו נראה מבפנים, אלא דומה כמוסיף על אורך הכותל. אבל מבחוץ ניכר שאינו מכותל המבוי שהרי נמשך להלאה מרוחב הכותל כזה:

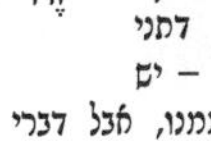

כותל שצידו אחד כנוס מחבירו. שנכנס הבנין ומיעטו מעביו, דהשתא בולט ויוצא ממנו כמין עמוד שקורין פליי"ר: בין. שכניסתו נראית בפנים א] ושוה מבחוץ, כזה:

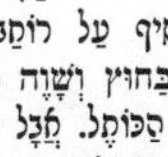

ששקוע הכותל מאחריו ונראית הפגימה בפנים: בין שנראה מבחוץ ושוה מבפנים. כגון ששקוע הכותל מלפניו, שאין הכניסה נראית לעומדים בפנים, אלא לבני רשות הרבים כזה:

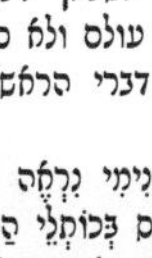

ורבי יוחנן. דקאמר לעיל בהדיא אינו נידון: מי לא שמיע ליה הא. מתני' דר' חייא, ואפ"ה לא סבר לה, הכא נמי היכי(ג) מסיימא מיניה דר' חייא הוא דקאמר נידון? דילמא איהו נמי שמיע ליה, ולא סבר לה: חצר קטנה שנפרצה לגדולה קטנה נמי תשתרי. דלא ליסרו בני גדולה עלייהו, אלא ליהוי נמי פתחה לגבה, להיות כשני חצירות ופתח ביניהם ואע"ג דשוה מבפנים, שהעומד בתוכה רואה כל כותלי אורכה שוין, שאין שם מכותל רחבה לפיאותיה כלום והוי מלואה — הרי מבחוץ בתוך הגדולה נראין לה שיורין(ד), וכותל זה מכאן ומכאן, אותו עודף שהגדולה עודפת על הקטנה, דהא גדולה בהו משתריא משום דלדידה נראית מבפנים: בנכנסין כותלי קטנה. ובולטין לתוך הגדולה בשפים וג' אמות, דהנך גיפופי דפשו להו מגדולה שעומדין מאחרי פירצת הקטנה נראין שלא מאותו כותל היה: ונימא לבוד ותשתרי. כזה:

כלומר: אי נראה מבחוץ מהני ליהוי כאלו ראשי כניסה של כותלי קטנה סנופי' לצד כותלי אורך, כזה:

הגדולה דהדר הוה להו הכניסה ליה גיפופי נראין מבחוץ. דקס"ד: אין הגדולה רחבה מן הקטנה אלא מעט פחות מג' לכאן, ופחות מג' לכאן, דהשתא אין ריוח שבין הכניסות לכותלי אורכה ג' טפחי' וכלבוד דמי: וכי תימא דמיפלגי. כניסות מחיצות הקטנה מכותל אורך של גדולה טובא. טפי משלשה, שהיתה גדולה רחבה מן הקטנה הרבה: קטנה בעשר וגדולה בי"א. שאין גדולה עודפת על הקטנה אלא אמה אחת, הרי שלשה טפחים לכאן ושלשה טפחים לכאן. ועובי כניסות הכתלים ממעטין את השלשה מכל צד, דאיכא לבוד: במופלגין מכותל זה בשנים ומזה בארבע. שלא היתה קטנה מכוונת כנגד אמצעיתה של גדולה, אלא משוכה שני טפחים לצד אחד ויש מהאמה עודפת שני טפחים לכאן, וארבעה לכאן. והכניסות דקות, ונשאר מצד אחד יותר משלשה ריוח: ונימא לבוד מרוח אחת. והרי כאן שיור אחד נראה מבחוץ, ותשתרי ביה קטנה, דנישוייה להאי פירצה פתח — דהא עשר הוא דהויא:
רבי

ולרשב"ג להוי כנראה מבחוץ ושוה מבפנים. פ"ה: דמסתמא דלחי קמא משכו קימעא כלפי חוץ, שכן דרך כל מעמידי לחי שמושכין קצת כלפי חוץ כדי שיראה מבחוץ ומבפנים שהוקבע לשם לחי. ויותר נראה לפרש: שמשכו קצת כלפי פנים, דהא משמע בכולי שמעתא דבעי למישרי נרבא עד חודו החיצון של לחי, והיכי הוה שרי אי מושכו כלפי חוץ דהיינו לרשות הרבים, דאיך יתיר את רה"ר? דסתם מבוי אורך כתליו שוין: **כותל** שצדו אחד כנום משל חבירו בין שנראה כו'. כאן פ"ה: שתקע הכותל מלפניו, ולעיל פירש: נראה מבחוץ — שמשך כל הלחי לחוץ, וחודו הפנימי נכנס בעובי הכותל ואינו נראה מבפנים אלא מבחוץ. ונראה דלכך שינה: דלעיל איירי בלחי שמעמידין אצל כותל, ודרך להעמידו לצד פנים, ומייתי לה נמי אמבוי שרצפו בלחיים דהיינו לצד פנים. אבל הכא מיירי בכותל שצידו אחד כנום משל חבירו, ודרך לעשות בנין כענין זה כשיש שני מבואות זה אצל זה או בית וחצר אצל המבוי, שפעמים מאריכין כותל שאצלו יותר מכותל המבוי. ומה שפירש כאן – ניחא טפי. דלפי' הקונטרס לעיל קשה: דאי חשיב נראה מבחוץ כשהלחי לצד הפנימי(ה) – היכי משני לקמן בנכנסין כותלי קטנה לגדולה? אכתי נראה מבחוץ הוא, דגיפופי גדולה נראין שהן עובי כותלי קטנה. ומה שנכנס לתוך הגדולה הוי כלחי, שפירש הקונטרס ואין לומר בנכנסין ארבע אמות שיוצאין מתורת לחי דאין זה שייך בחצר. ומיהו, אי הוי דווקא הא דאמר לקמן בעשר ושני טפחים סגי – אתי שפיר, דמיירי כשאין(ו) בעוביו טפח. וריצב"א מיישב: בנכנסין כותלי קטנה לגדולה מיירי שיש היכר איזו הם כותלי קטנה, כגון שכותלי קטנה הולכים בשיפוע ממזרח למערב כמו שעושין לכתלים בראשיהן, וכותלי גדולה שיפועם מצפון לדרום: **אי** לא סבר לה למה ליה למתנייה. אע"ג דבפ' "יוצא דופן" (נדה ד' מו:) אשכחן רבי יוסי דתני ברייתא דסדר עולם ולא סבר לה – יש לומר דהיינו דברי הראשונים ממנו, אבל דברי דבר פלוגתא לא תני:

[סוכה יט.]
לקמן טו. [תוספתא פ"א]
[קידושין ג: וש"נ]
[לעיל ח. וש"נ]
נ"א קמיה דר' חנינא ואמרי לה קמיה דר' חנינא בר פפא
לקמן יב. ע"ש

רבינו חננאל

דמצא מין את מינו וניעור. אבל אם היה פתוח לרה"ר מותר. רב אשי אמר כגון שרצפו פחות פחות מד' במשך ד' אמות לרשב"ג דאמר כל פחות מד' טפחים אמרינן לבוד הוא נידון אותן ד' אמות הרצופות בלחיים כאילו מבוי בפ"ע הוא. וצריך לחי אחר להתירו ור' יוחנן הוא דאמר מבוי שצרפו בלחיים באנו למחלוקת רשב"ג ורבנן: ולמה אומר לדברי רשב"ג צריך לחי אחר להתירו. *) נראה מבחוץ ושוה מבפנים הוא לית ליה לר' יוחנן דכי האי גוונא נידון משום לחי דכי אתא רבין אמר אפי' נראה מבחוץ ושוה מבפנים אינו נידון משום לחי. תני ר' חייא כותל שצידו אחד כנום מחבירו פי' כגון כותל רחב ועשה ראשו צר ונראה מבחוץ כמו לחי ושוה מבפנים או רחב מראשו והניח מעוביו כמו טפח כגון שהתחיל רחב הכותל ד' טפחים והניח טפח והיצר ובנה נידון משום לחי. ואע"ג דר' יוחנן שמיעא ליה הא מתניתא (ר') [דר'] חייא כיון דלא ס"ל כוותה משום הכי לא תני לה אבל ר' חייא אי לאו דסבר לה כוותיה למה לי למיתנייה. אקשי רבא למ"ד נידון משום לחי והתנן חצר גדולה שנפרצה לקטנה גדולה מותרת וקטנה אסורה ואמאי קטנה אסורה תשתרי בנראה מבחוץ ושוה מבפנים. ודחי ר' זירא בנכנסין כותלי קטנה בגדולה ג' טפחים שאינו נראה הנותר מן הכותל של גדולה כמו לחי שהרי יוצא ג' ואינו נראה מכללו. (ואמרינן ודלמא לבוד כאמ' כזה כותל קטנה היוצא ג' כאילו לבוד בכותל. בנכנסין כותלי קטנה בגדולה ג' טפחים שאינו נראה הנותר מן הכותל של גדולה כמו לחי שהרי יוצא ג' ואינו נראה אכלט). ואמרי' ולימא לבוד. כלומר ראה כותל קטנה היוצא ג' כאילו לבוד בכותל של גדולה ויהיה כותל של קטנה כלחי. וכי תימא כי אמרי' לבוד היכא דהוא פחות מג' טפחים והאי כותל של קטנה איפלג מכותל של גדולה טובא והא תני אדא קטנה בעשר גדולה בי"א הנה אין ביניהן אלא אמה אמה בלבד ודחי רבינא במופלגת

*) [נראה דל"ל והא נראה מחוץ ושוה מבפנים הוא משום דנראה מבחוץ ושוה מבפנים לית ליה לר"י]:

הגהות מהר"ב רנשבורג

א] רש"י ד"ה בין שכניסתו נראית בפנים וכו'. נ"ב עי' מהרש"ל והציורים נדפסו בטעות וכבר הארכתי בזה בחידושי. ושוב ראיתי בקרבן נתנאל בפרקין סי' יא תקנם על נכון. והנה הנם סוף מסכת עירובין מצוירים שם:

הגהות הב"ח

(א) גמ' קמיה דר' חנינא בר פפי קטנה בעשר: (ב) רש"י ד"ה נראה מבחוץ וכו' וחודו הפנימי נכנס בעובי כותל המבוי: (ג) ד"ה מי לא שמיע וכו' הכא נמי היכי מסתיימא מינה: (ד) ד"ה חצר קטנה וכו' לה שיורי מכותל זה: (ה) תום' ד"ה כותל וכו' דאי חשיב נראה מבחוץ כשהלחי לצד הפנימי ואין נראה לצד המבוי אלא לעומדי' אחורי המבוי היכי משני לקמן: (ו) בא"ד בעשר וב' טפחים סגי אתי שפיר דמיירי כשאין באורכן טפח. נ"ב פי' באורכן של כותלים הנכנסין לקטנה אין באורכן טפח ולא חשיב פס הכותל עצמו אם לא בדאיכא טפח:

רַבִּי הִיא, דְּאָמַר: בָּעֵינַן שְׁנֵי פַסִּין. דְּתַנְיָא: *חָצֵר נִיתֶּרֶת בְּפַס אֶחָד, רַבִּי אוֹמֵר: בִּשְׁנֵי פַסִּין. הַאי מַאי?! אִי אָמְרַתְּ בִּשְׁלָמָא "נִרְאֶה מִבַּחוּץ וְשָׁוֶה מִבִּפְנִים — אֵינוֹ נִידּוֹן מִשּׁוּם לֶחִי", וְרַבִּי סָבַר לָהּ כְּר' יוֹסֵי, וּדְרַבִּי זֵירָא וּדְרָבִינָא לֵיתָא — מִשּׁוּם הָכִי: קְטַנָּה בְּעֶשֶׂר, וּגְדוֹלָה בְּאַחַת עֶשְׂרֵה, מִשּׁוּם דְּר' סָבַר לָהּ כְּר' יוֹסֵי. אֶלָּא אִי אָמְרַתְּ "נִרְאֶה מִבַּחוּץ וְשָׁוֶה מִבִּפְנִים — נִידּוֹן מִשּׁוּם לֶחִי", וּדְרַבִּי זֵירָא וּדְרָבִינָא אִיתָא, וְר' לָא סָבַר לָהּ כְּר' יוֹסֵי — גְּדוֹלָה בְּאַחַת עֶשְׂרֵה לָמָּה לִי? מִמַּה נַּפְשָׁךְ: אִי לְמִשְׁרַיֵיהּ לִגְדוֹלָה קָאָתֵי — בְּעֶשֶׂר וּשְׁנֵי טְפָחִים סַגְיָא. וְאִי לְמֵיסְרָהּ לִקְטַנָּה קָאָתֵי — לְאַשְׁמוֹעִינַן דְּמַפְלְגֵי טוּבָא! אֶלָּא לָאו שְׁמַע מִינָּהּ: נִרְאֶה מִבַּחוּץ וְשָׁוֶה מִבִּפְנִים — אֵינוֹ נִידּוֹן מִשּׁוּם לֶחִי, שְׁמַע מִינָּהּ. *אָמַר רַב יוֹסֵף: לָא שְׁמִיעַ לִי הָא שְׁמַעְתָּא. אָמַר לֵיהּ אַבַּיֵי: אַתְּ אֲמַרְתְּ נִיהֲלַן, וְאַהָא אֲמַרְתְּ נִיהֲלַן; דְּאָמַר רָמִי בַּר אַבָּא, אָמַר רַב הוּנָא: לֶחִי הַמּוֹשֵׁךְ עִם דָּפְנוֹ שֶׁל מָבוֹי, פָּחוֹת מִד' אַמּוֹת — נִידּוֹן מִשּׁוּם לֶחִי וּמִשְׁתַּמֵּשׁ עִם חוּדוֹ הַפְּנִימִי, ד' אַמּוֹת — נִידּוֹן מִשּׁוּם מָבוֹי, וְאָסוּר לְהִשְׁתַּמֵּשׁ בְּכוּלּוֹ. וְאַתְּ אֲמַרְתְּ לַן עֲלַהּ: שְׁמַע מִינָּהּ תְּלָת; שְׁמַע מִינָּהּ: בֵּין לְחָיַיִן אָסוּר, וּשְׁמַע מִינָּהּ: מֶשֶׁךְ מָבוֹי בְּאַרְבַּע, וּשְׁמַע מִינָּהּ: נִרְאֶה מִבַּחוּץ וְשָׁוֶה מִבִּפְנִים — נִידּוֹן מִשּׁוּם לֶחִי. וְהִלְכְתָא: נִרְאֶה מִבַּחוּץ וְשָׁוֶה מִבִּפְנִים — נִידּוֹן מִשּׁוּם לֶחִי. *תְּיוּבְתָּא וְהִלְכְתָא?! אִין, מִשּׁוּם דְּתָנֵי רַבִּי חִיָּיא כְּוָותֵיהּ. § "וְהָרָחָב מֵעֶשֶׂר יְמַעֵט". § אָמַר אַבַּיֵי, *תָּנָא: [א]וְהָרָחָב מֵעֶשֶׂר יְמַעֵט, ר' יְהוּדָה אוֹמֵר: אֵינוֹ צָרִיךְ לְמַעֵט. וְעַד כַּמָּה? סָבַר רַב אַחִי קַמֵּיהּ דְּרַב יוֹסֵף לְמֵימַר: עַד שְׁלֹשׁ עֶשְׂרֵה אַמָּה וּשְׁלִישׁ. וְקַל וָחוֹמֶר מִפַּסֵּי בִירָאוֹת, *וּמַה פַּסֵּי בִירָאוֹת שֶׁהִתַּרְתָּה בָּהֶן פָּרוּץ מְרוּבֶּה עַל הָעוֹמֵד — לֹא הִתַּרְתָּה בָּהֶן יוֹתֵר מִשְּׁלֹשׁ עֶשְׂרֵה אַמָּה וּשְׁלִישׁ, מָבוֹי שֶׁלֹּא הִתַּרְתָּה בּוֹ פָּרוּץ מְרוּבֶּה עַל הָעוֹמֵד — אֵינוֹ דִּין שֶׁלֹּא תַּתִּיר בּוֹ יוֹתֵר מִשְּׁלֹשׁ עֶשְׂרֵה אַמָּה וּשְׁלִישׁ! וְהִיא הַנּוֹתֶנֶת, פַּסֵּי בִירָאוֹת שֶׁהִתַּרְתָּה בָּהֶן פָּרוּץ מְרוּבֶּה עַל הָעוֹמֵד — לֹא תַּתִּיר בָּהֶן יוֹתֵר מִשְּׁלֹשׁ עֶשְׂרֵה אַמָּה וּשְׁלִישׁ, מָבוֹי שֶׁלֹּא הִתַּרְתָּה בּוֹ פָּרוּץ מְרוּבֶּה עַל הָעוֹמֵד — תַּתִּיר בּוֹ יוֹתֵר מִי"ג אַמּוֹת וּשְׁלִישׁ! אִי נַמִי לְאִידָךְ גִּיסָא: פַּסֵּי בִירָאוֹת דְּאַקִילַתְּ בְּהוּ חַד קוּלָּא — אַקִּיל בְּהוּ קוּלָּא אַחֲרִינָא, מָבוֹי כְּלָל כְּלָל לֹא. תָּנֵי לֵוִי: מָבוֹי שֶׁהוּא רָחָב עֶשְׂרִים אַמָּה, נוֹעֵץ קָנֶה בְּאֶמְצָעִיתוֹ, וְדַיּוֹ. הוּא תָּנֵי לָהּ וְהוּא אָמַר לָהּ: דְּאֵין הֲלָכָה כְּאוֹתָהּ מִשְׁנָה. אִיכָּא דְּאָמְרִי, אָמַר שְׁמוּאֵל מִשְּׁמֵיהּ דְּלֵוִי: אֵין הֲלָכָה כְּאוֹתָהּ מִשְׁנָה. אֶלָּא הֵיכִי עָבֵיד? אָמַר שְׁמוּאֵל מִשְּׁמֵיהּ דְּלֵוִי: עוֹשֶׂה

רַבִּי הִיא דְּאָמַר בָּעֵינַן. ב' שִׁיּוּרִין לְחָצֵר שֶׁל עֶשֶׂר הַנִּפְרֶצֶת בִּמְלוֹאָהּ: חָצֵר נִיתֶּרֶת בְּפַס אֶחָד. אִם נִפְרְצָה לִרְשׁוּת הָרַבִּים, וְנִשְׁתַּיֵּיר בָּהּ מִצַּד א' – מוּתֶּרֶת. וּבְשֶׁאֵין הַפִּירְצָה יוֹתֵר מֵעֶשֶׂר עָסְקִינַן; דְּאִי יוֹתֵר מֵעֶשֶׂר, לָא מְהַנֵּי לֵיהּ מְחִיצָּה לְהַאי חָצֵר: הַאי מַאי אִי אָמְרַתְּ בִּשְׁלָמָא. מַתְנִי' כִּדַהֲוָה שָׁמְעִינַן לָהּ מֵעִיקָּרָא בִּמְכוּוֶּנֶת קְטַנָּה כְּנֶגֶד אֶמְצָעִיתָהּ שֶׁל גְּדוֹלָה, וּמֵהַטַּעַם הַיְּתֵירָה נִשְׁאֲרוּ שְׁלֹשָׁה לְכָאן וּשְׁלֹשָׁה לְכָאן, וְי"ל נִרְאֶה מִבַּחוּץ וְשָׁוֶה מִבִּפְנִים מִשְּׁנֵי רוּחוֹת – וַאֲפִילּוּ הָכִי קְטַנָּה אֲסוּרָה, דְּנִרְאֶה מִבַּחוּץ וְשָׁוֶה מִבִּפְנִים לָא מְהַנֵּי[א]. וְרַבִּי בִּשְׁנֵי פַסִּין דְּחָצֵר כְּרַבִּי יוֹסֵי סָבַר לָהּ, דְּאָמַר בְּמַתְנִי' *אֵין לֶחִי פָּחוֹת מֵרוֹחַב שְׁלֹשָׁה, וְכָל שֶׁכֵּן פַּסִּין דְּחָצֵר דְּבָעֵי רוֹחַב כִּדְבָעֵי רַבִּי יוֹסֵי בְּלֶחִי: וּדְרָבִינָא. דְּאוֹקְמָא בְּמוּפְלָגִין מִזֶּה בִּשְׁנַיִם וּמִזֶּה בְּאַרְבָּעָה – לֵיתָא, דְּא"כ לָא הֲוָה מִשְׁתַּרְיָא גְּדוֹלָה, דְּפַס ב' טְפָחִים לָא מְהַנֵּי. וְכֵיוָן דְּלֵיתָא לִדְרָבִינָא – לֵיתָא נַמִי לִדְר' זֵירָא, דְּאוֹקְמָא בְּנִכְנָסִין. דְּכֵיוָן דִּמְכוּוֶּנֶת שְׁלֹשָׁה מִכָּאן וּשְׁלֹשָׁה מִכָּאן – כְּנִיסָה מַאי מְהַנְּיָא? הָא כִּי נִכְנָסִין נַמִי אִיכָּא *לְמִשְׁרַיֵיהּ[ב] בְּנִרְאֶה מִבַּחוּץ וְשָׁוֶה מִבִּפְנִים מִבּ' רוּחוֹת, וְלָא שָׁרֵינַן לָהּ. דְּמוֹקְמִינַן לֵיהּ בְּנִרְאֶה מִבַּחוּץ וְשָׁוֶה מִבִּפְנִים אֵינוֹ נִידּוֹן מִשּׁוּם לֶחִי – מִשּׁוּם הָכִי יָהֵיב תַּנָּא שִׁיעוּר לְעוֹדְפָהּ שֶׁל גְּדוֹלָה שֶׁתְּהֵא יְתֵירָה עַל הַקְּטַנָּה אַמָּה, כִּי הֵיכִי דְּנֶיהֱווּ לָהּ לַגְּדוֹלָה שְׁלֹשָׁה מִכָּאן וּשְׁלֹשָׁה מִכָּאן – מִשּׁוּם דְּרַבִּי שְׁנֵי פַסִּין בָּעֵי וְרָחְבֵּי' שְׁלֹשָׁה כְּרַבִּי יוֹסֵי, וּמִשּׁוּם הֶיתֵּר גְּדוֹלָה נָקֵט לָהּ: אֶלָּא אִי אָמְרַתְּ נִרְאֶה מִבַּחוּץ. מְהַנֵּי וּקְטַנָּה דַּאֲסִירָא הַיְינוּ טַעְמָא מִשּׁוּם דְּאִיתָא לִדְרַבִּי זֵירָא בְּנִכְנָסִין, וְלִדְרָבִינָא בְּמוּפְלָגִין וְלֵיכָּא לְבוּד מִשְּׁנֵי רוּחוֹת, וַאֲפִילּוּ הָכִי גְּדוֹלָה מִשְׁתַּרְיָא בְּגִיפּוּפִין הַנִּשְׁאָרִין לָהּ מֵאֲחוֹרֵי הַכְּנִיסוֹת, וְאַף עַל פִּי שֶׁרוֹחַב הָאֶחָד אֵינוֹ אֶלָּא ב' טְפָחִים, דְּלָא סָבַר לָהּ כְּר' יוֹסֵי: גְּדוֹלָה בְּי"א. דְּיָהֵיב תַּנָּא שִׁיעוּרָא לְעוֹדְפָהּ אַמָּה לָמָּה לִי: אִי לְמִשְׁרַיֵיהּ לִגְדוֹלָה. דְּלֶיהֱוֵי לָהּ שִׁיּוּר מִשְּׁנֵי צְדָדִין קָאָתֵי: בְּעֶשֶׂר וּשְׁנֵי טְפָחִים סַגֵּי. דְּהָא רַבִּי לָא סָבַר לָהּ כְּר' יוֹסֵי: וְאִי לְמֵיסְרָהּ לִקְטַנָּה קָאָתֵי. כְּדֵי שֶׁיִּרְחֲקוּ כּוֹתְלֵי אוֹרֶךְ הַגְּדוֹלָה מִכְּנִיסָתָהּ שֶׁל קְטַנָּה ד' טְפָחִים מִצַּד הָאֶחָד, דְּלָא לֵימְלֵי לְמֵימַר לָבוּד לְמִשְׁרַיֵיהּ, וּלְאַגְמוּרֵיהּ דְּאִי לָאו הָכִי הֲוָה שָׁרֵינַן לָהּ בִּקְטַנָּה בְּנִרְאֶה מִבַּחוּץ ע"י לָבוּד: לִישְׁמְעִינַן. גְּדוֹלָה רְחָבָה הַרְבֵּה, וּמִיפְלְגֵי טוּבָא, דְּהָוֵי מִילְּתָא דִּפְסִיקָא. דְּהָא לָאו מִילְּתָא דִּפְסִיקָא הִיא, הוֹאִיל וּמוּפְלָג' מִכּוֹתֶל זֶה בִּשְׁלֹשָׁה וּמִכּוֹתֶל זֶה בִּשְׁלֹשָׁה. וְאִי הַגְּדוֹלָה רְחָבָה הַרְבֵּה הֲוָה תָּנֵי, הֲוָה גָּמְרִינַן מִינָּהּ טְפֵי דְּמִשּׁוּם הַפְלָגָה מִיתַּסְרָא. וְהָא לֵיכָּא לְמֵימַר דְּדָק תַּנָּא בְּשִׁיעוּרִין לְאַשְׁמוּעִינַן דִּבְהָכִי הוּא דְּמִיתַּסְרָא, וּבְצִיר מֵהָכִי לָא דְּהָא בִּ' וְד' טְפָחִים נַמִי מִיתַּסְרָא וּכְגוֹן דְּמוּפְלֶגֶת בַּחֲצִי טֶפַח מִכָּאן וּבִשְׁלֹשָׁה וַחֲצִי מִכָּאן, דְּמִשְׁתַּרְיָא גְּדוֹלָה בְּגִיפּוּף מַשֶּׁהוּ מִכָּאן וּשְׁלֹשָׁה וַחֲצִי מִכָּאן, וּקְטַנָּה מִיתַּסְרָא – דְּלֵיכָּא לָבוּד מִשְּׁנֵי רוּחוֹת: אֶלָּא לָאו שְׁמַע מִינָּהּ. עַל כָּרְחָךְ דַּוְקָא שְׁלֹשָׁה מִכָּאן וּשְׁלֹשָׁה מִכָּאן לְמִשְׁרַיֵיהּ לַגְּדוֹלָה נָקֵט לָהּ, וְאַפ"ה קְטַנָּה אֲסוּרָה, דְּנִרְאֶה מִבַּחוּץ לָא מְהַנֵּי שְׁמַע מִינָּהּ: לָא שְׁמִיעַ לִי הָא שְׁמַעְתָּא. דְּרַבָּה בַּר רַב הוּנָא מֵרַב הוּנָא אֲבוּהּ, דְּנִרְאֶה מִבַּחוּץ נִידּוֹן מִשּׁוּם לֶחִי: לֶחִי הַמּוֹשֵׁךְ עִם דּוֹפְנוֹ שֶׁל מָבוֹי. לַחוּץ, שֶׁנִּרְאֶה כְּמַאֲרִיךְ אֶת דּוֹפֶן הַמָּבוֹי שֶׁמַּעֲמִיד חוּדוֹ כְּנֶגֶד עוֹבִי הַדּוֹפֶן, דְּמִיכְסֵי חוּדוֹ בְּעוֹבְיוֹ שֶׁל דּוֹפֶן דְּשָׁוֶה מִבִּפְנִים וְנִרְאֶה מִבַּחוּץ שֶׁאֵין חוּדוֹ שֶׁל לֶחִי מְכַסֶּה כָּל עוֹבִי הַדּוֹפֶן שֶׁרָחָב מִמֶּנּוּ: בְּכוּלּוֹ. בְּכָל הַמָּבוֹי, שֶׁהֲרֵי אֵין כָּאן לֶחִי: שְׁמַע מִינָּהּ מֶשֶׁךְ מָבוֹי אַרְבַּע. מִדְּקָאָמַר נִידּוֹן מִשּׁוּם מָבוֹי: בֵּין לְחָיַיִם אָסוּר. מִדְּקָאָמַר עַד חוּדוֹ הַפְּנִימִי: וּשְׁמַע מִינָּהּ נִרְאֶה מִבַּחוּץ וְשָׁוֶה מִבִּפְנִים נִידּוֹן מִשּׁוּם לֶחִי. מִדְּקָאָמַר נִידּוֹן מִשּׁוּם לֶחִי: תְּיוּבְתָּא וְהִלְכְתָא. דְּהָא אוֹתְבִינֵיהּ מֵחָצֵר קְטַנָּה שֶׁנִּפְרְצָה לִגְדוֹלָה: דְּתָנֵי רַבִּי חִיָּיא כְּוָותֵיהּ. כּוֹתֶל שֶׁצִּידּוֹ אֶחָד כָּנוּס כו': עַד כַּמָּה. יְהֵא רָחָב וְלָא יְהֵא צָרִיךְ לְמַעֵט לְרַבִּי יְהוּדָה: פַּסֵּי בִירָאוֹת שֶׁהִתַּרְתָּה בָּהֶן. שְׁלֹשׁ עֶשְׂרֵה אַמָּה וּשְׁלִישׁ, דִּתְנַן בְּפֶרֶק שֵׁנִי (לקמן יז:): עוֹשִׂין פַּסִּין לַבִּירָאוֹת שֶׁבִּרְשׁוּת הָרַבִּים, וְהֵן עֲמוּקִין עֲשָׂרָה וְאָסוּר לְמַלְּאוֹת מֵהֶן וּלְהַנִּיחַ עַל שְׂפָתָן שֶׁמּוֹצִיא מֵרְשׁוּת הַיָּחִיד לִרְשׁוּת הָרַבִּים, וְהִתִּירוּ חֲכָמִים לַעֲשׂוֹת אַרְבָּעָה דְּיוֹמְדִין לְאַרְבַּע פֵּיאוֹת, וּלְשַׁוּוֹיֵהּ בֵּין הַפַּסִּין רְשׁוּת הַיָּחִיד וּמוּתָּר לְמַלְּאוֹת וְשָׁרֵי רַבִּי יְהוּדָה לְהַרְחִיק זֶה מִזֶּה מְלֹא שְׁנֵי רְבָקוֹת שֶׁל אַרְבָּעָה אַרְבָּעָה בָּקָר. וְעוֹבְיָהּ שֶׁל פָּרָה אַמָּה וּשְׁנֵי שְׁלִישֵׁי אַמָּה, דְּהָווּ לְהוּ שְׁלֹשׁ עֶשְׂרֵה אַמָּה וּשְׁלִישׁ לִשְׁמוֹנָה בָּקָר: וְהִיא הַנּוֹתֶנֶת. מִדָּה זוֹ שֶׁאַתָּה מֵבִיא בָּהּ אִיסּוּר לְיוֹתֵר מִשְּׁלֹשׁ עֶשְׂרֵה אַמָּה וּשְׁלִישׁ לְמָבוֹי, מִשּׁוּם טַעְמָא דְּלָא הִתַּרְתָּה בּוֹ פָּרוּץ מְרוּבֶּה עַל הָעוֹמֵד – הִיא הַנּוֹתֶנֶת טַעַם לְהֶיתֵּר, דְּהָתָם הוּא דְּאִיכָּא עוֹמֵד מוּעָט – מִשּׁוּם הָכִי לֹא הִתַּרְתָּה בּוֹ יוֹתֵר מִשְּׁלֹשׁ עֶשְׂרֵה אַמָּה וּשְׁלִישׁ, אֲבָל מָבוֹי דְּרוּבּוֹ סָתוּם שָׁרֵי בֵּיהּ טְפֵי: אִי נַמִי לְאִידָךְ גִּיסָא. דְּלָא תֵּיתֵי לֵיהּ מִפַּסֵּי בִירָאוֹת. דְּאִילּוּ הָתָם הוּא דְּהֵקַלְתָּ בָּהּ קוּלָּא, דְּמַכְשַׁרְתְּ לֵיהּ בְּפָרוּץ מְרוּבֶּה עַל הָעוֹמֵד – אַקִּיל נַמִי קוּלָּא אַחֲרִיתָא, דְּלֶהֱוֵי חָשׁוּב פֶּתַח עַד שְׁלֹשׁ עֶשְׂרֵה אַמָּה וּשְׁלִישׁ: כְּלָל כְּלָל לָא. טְפֵי מֵעֶשֶׂר לָא: אֵין הֲלָכָה כְּאוֹתָהּ מִשְׁנָה. דְּאָתֵי אֲוִירָא דְּהַאי גִּיסָא וּדְהַאי גִּיסָא וּמְבַטֵּל לֵיהּ לַקָּנֶה:

וּמַעֲמִידוֹ

רבי היא דאמר בעינן שני פסין דתניא וכו'. משמע לרבנן אפילו בחלר מרובעת סגי בפס משהו, דבמרובעת פליגי, כמו שאפרש לקמן(ג). ושני טפחים סגי. הלי ב' טפחים לאו דוקא, דהא אמרינן (לקמן ד' יב.) בשתי רוחות משהו לכאן ומשהו לכאן. ואין סברא לומר דמשהו לאו דוקא, כדאמרינן פרק "חלון" (לקמן ד' פ.) גבי שיתופי מבואות וצריך להגביה כל שהוא, וכמה כל שהוא – טפח, דאם כן הוה ליה לפרושי כי התם. אי נמי: בפס גמור סגי בשני משהויין, אבל כותל עלמו לא חשיב פס אם לא ברוחב טפח, דאין היכר כל כך בכותל כמו בפס גמור:

[לקמן דף יד:]

לקמן יב.

ס"א למשריי' בלבוד מב' רוחות דהא איכא פחות מג' מכאן ומכאן מיהו כי אמרי' לבוד ונראה מבחוץ משכחת להו לב' פסין של ג' בסדר עובי הכותל ואפ"ה לא שרינן לה דמוקמינן ליה בנראה מבחוץ ושוה מבפנים אינו וכו'. (ח"מ)

[לעיל ב:]

הגהות הב"ח

(א) רש"י ד"ה האי מאי וכו' ושוה מבפנים לא מהני לאינו נדון משום לחי ורבי בשני פסין דחלר: (ב) ד"ה ודרבינא וכו' הא כי נכנסין נמי איכא למשרייה בלבוד משתי רוחות כל"ל ותיבות בנראה מבחוץ ושוה מבפנים נמחק: (ג) תום' ד"ה רבי הוא וכו' שאפרש לקמן. נ"ב בדף י"ב ד"ה ורב נחמן:

נה א מיי' פי"ז מהל' שבת הלכה יד סמג עשין דרבנן א טוש"ע א"ח סי' שסג סעיף כו:

[לקמן מא. סו: עג. פט: נדרים מא. מכות ד. נדה לט. סג:]

[לקמן טז: כתובות מא: ב"ק טו:]

וא"ת ומה לפסי בירלות שכן לריך שם ד' מחילות ולכך לא התרת בהן יותר מי"ג אמות ושליש תאמר במבוי דסגי בג' וי"ל דאין חילוק בין ד' לג' אפילו ב' מחילות חשיבי לר' יהודה שפיר משם ד' מחילות כדאמר לקמן בפרק ב [דף כב.]

רבינו חננאל

במופלגת מכותל זה ד' טפחים ומכותל זה ב' טפחים ור' היא דצריך בחצר שני פסין דתניא חצר מתרת בפס אחד ר' אומר בב' פסין. עכשיו א"ת דר' זירא דאמר בנכנסין כותלי קטנה בגדולה ג' ליתא. ודרבינא נמי דאמר במופלגת [מכותל זה] ד' ומכותל זה ב' ליתא ולעולם אין נכנסין כותליה ולא אחד מהן רחוק ד' טפחין וכותליהן שוין וזו י"א אמה וזו י' אמה נמצאת הגדולה יתירה על הקטנה ג' טפחים מיכן וג' טפחים מיכן. ומתני' ר' היא ור' סבר לה כר' יוסי דאמר רוחבן של לחיים ג' טפחים לכל א' ולחיים מעליא הוו ואמאי קטנה אסורה דנראה מבחוץ ושוה מבפנים אינו נידון משום לחי. אלא אי אמרת נראה מבחוץ ושוה מבפנים נידון משום לחי ודר' זירא ודרבינא איתא ור' לא סבר לה כרבי יוסי אמאי תנא אדא גדולה בי"א קטנה בי' דאי לאסור קטנה קתני לאשמעינן אפילו מפלגא טובא אי למשרי גדולה לשמעינן דגדולה יתירה על הקטנה שני משהויין משהו מיכן ומשהו מיכן דהוויין לחיים של גדולה כדתנן רחבן ועוביין כל שהוא אלא לאו ש"מ נראה מבחוץ ושוה מבפנים אינו נידון משום לחי ש"מ. אמר רב יוסף לא שמיעא לי הא שמעתא כבר פירשנוהו. הא דאמר רב יוסף לא שמיעא לי הא שמעתא במקומות הרבה דבר זה מפורש בנדרים. כד חלש רב יוסף איעקר תלמודיה ואנשייה מצעריה ועד איתפח אהדרי ליה אביי. היינו דאמר את אמרת לן. ואהא אמרה לחי המושך עם דופנו של מבוי פחות מד' אמות נידון משום לחי ומשמש עם חודו הפנימי ד' אמות נידון משום מבוי וצריך לחי אחר להתירו כו' ואסיקנא והלכתא נידון משום לחי: **פיסקא** והרחב מ' אמות למעט. ואמרינן הא דאמר ר' יהודה [דא"צ] למעט אם הוא רחב כמה אליבא דר' יהודה אין צריך למעט. ובאנו לפרש טעמיה דר"י מפסי בירואות דמתיר התם רחב בין הדיומדין כמלא ב' רבקות של ד' ד' בקר. הנה ח' פרות וכל פרה מפורש כי עוביה אמה וב' שלישי אמה נמצא המקום שמכיל ח' פרות ח' אמה ונשאר עדיין מעובי הפרות ב' שלישי אמה לכל פרה והן ח' פרות הלא ט"ז שליש ה' אמה ושליש אמה וא' ק"ו מפסי בירואות ומה פסי בירואות שהתרתה בהן פרוץ י"ג אמה ושליש על העומד והוא הדיומד שהוא רחבו ג' טפחים ג' מיכן וג' מיכן וזהו הפרוץ מרובה על העומד. מבוי שלא התרתה בו פרוץ מרובה על העומד. ודחינן היא הנותנת כלומר זו היא הראייה שהבאת ללמד ממנה. מראה כי חילוף מה שאמרת: הא דתני לוי מבוי שרחב כ' אמות נועץ קנה באמצעיתו ודיו כו' לית הלכתא כוותיה

רב נסים גאון

אי אמרת בשלמא נראה מבחוץ ושוה מבפנים אין נידון משום לחי ור' סבר לה כר' יוסי זה הדבר חוזר על מה שאמר ר' יוסי במשנה בפירקין (דף יד) ברוחב הלחיים ר' יוסי אומר רחבן ג' טפחים: **אמר** רב יוסף לא שמיע לי הא שמעתתא אמר ליה אביי את אמרתה יהלן ואהא אמרת ניהלן. תמצא במס' נדרים בפרק אין בין מודר הנאה מחברו (דף מא) רב יוסף חלש אייקר ליה תלמודיה אהדריה אביי קמיה ובכל דוכתא היינו דאמר רב יוסף לא שמיעא לי הא שמעתא: **פסי** בירואות שהתרתה כאן פרוץ מרובה על העומד לא התרתה בהן יתר מי"ג אמה ושליש. עיקר שלו בפרק ב' (דף יז) דתנן עושין פסין לבירואות ד' דיומדין נראין כח' ולפי שרוחב הדיומד ו' טפחים שהן אמה נמצא לשני הדיומדין ב' אמות (וכהן) [וע"י כן] הותר לטלטל ביניהן בפרוץ מרובה על העומד ובתלמוד ארץ ישראל (פרק עושין פסין ה"א) גרסי' שבכ"מ עומד מרובה על הפרוץ וכאן הקלתה עליו שיהא הפרוץ רבה על העומד והחמרתה עליו בדבר זה שבכ"מ עושה פס של [ד"ט וכאן של ו"ט] (י"ט) ופירוש י"ג אמה ושליש שביניהם הוא ששנינו (בסוף המסכת) [במשנת עושין פסין] ר' יהודה אומר של ד' ד' קשורות ולא מותרות נמצא בין ב' הדיומדין רוחב שיעור ח' פרות כשתתן לכל אחת מהפרות ב' אמות פחות שליש וכשתצרפנו לח' ימצא י"ג אמה ושליש ומיכן אמרו לא התרתה בהן יותר מי"ג אמה ושליש ומה שאמרו מבוי שלא התרתה בו פרוץ מרובה על העומד כבר מפורש הוא בזה הפרק במשנה (דף טו) ובלבד שלא יהו פרצות יתירות על הבנין ובברייתא יש עוד ואם היה פרוץ מרובה על העומד אף כנגד העומד אסור וזה כלל לכל מחיצות שבת חוץ מפסי בירואות כמו שביארנו שהיא מיוחדת:

ומאי

נו א מיי' פי"ז מהלכות שבת הלכה לא סמג שם טוש"ע או"ח סי' שסג סעיף לג:
נז ב ג ד מיי' שם טוש"ע שם סעיף לד:
נח ה מיי' פט"ז שם הלכה טז ופי"ז הלכה יד סמג שם טוש"ע או"ח סי' שסב סעיף י וסי' שסג סעיף כו:

ר"מ גריס ומבוי עקום כמין ח דאצרכו לחות לא הוי

א עוֹשֶׂה פַּס גָּבוֹהַּ עֲשָׂרָה בְּמֶשֶׁךְ אַרְבַּע אַמּוֹת, וּמַעֲמִידוֹ לְאׇרְכּוֹ שֶׁל מָבוֹי. אִי נַמִּי כִּדְרַב יְהוּדָה, דְּאָמַר רַב יְהוּדָה: מָבוֹי שֶׁהוּא רָחָב חֲמֵשׁ עֶשְׂרֵה אַמָּה — ב מַרְחִיק שְׁתֵּי אַמּוֹת וְעוֹשֶׂה פַּס שָׁלֹשׁ אַמּוֹת. וְאַמַּאי? יַעֲשֶׂה פַּס אַמָּה וּמֶחֱצָה, וְיַרְחִיק שְׁתֵּי אַמּוֹת, וְיַעֲשֶׂה פַּס אַמָּה וּמֶחֱצָה. שְׁמַע מִינָּהּ: עוֹמֵד מְרוּבֶּה עַל הַפָּרוּץ מִשְּׁתֵּי רוּחוֹת — לָא הָוֵי עוֹמֵד! לְעוֹלָם אֵימָא לָךְ "הָוֵי עוֹמֵד", ג וְשָׁאנֵי הָכָא — דְּאָתֵי אֲוִירָא דְּהַאי גִּיסָּא וַאֲוִירָא דְּהַאי גִּיסָּא וּמְבַטֵּל לֵיהּ. וְיַעֲשֶׂה פַּס אַמָּה, וְיַרְחִיק אַמָּה, וְיַעֲשֶׂה פַּס אַמָּה וְיַרְחִיק אַמָּה וְיַעֲשֶׂה פַּס אַמָּה, ש"מ: *עוֹמֵד כְּפָרוּץ — אָסוּר! לְעוֹלָם אֵימָא לָךְ "מוּתָּר", וְשָׁאנֵי הָכָא — דַּאֲתָא אֲוִירָא דְּהַאי גִּיסָּא וּדְהַאי גִּיסָּא וּמְבַטֵּל לֵיהּ. וְיַרְחִיק אַמָּה, וְיַעֲשֶׂה פַּס אַמָּה וּמֶחֱצָה וְיַרְחִיק אַמָּה וְיַעֲשֶׂה פַּס אַמָּה וּמֶחֱצָה! ד אִין הָכִי נַמִּי, וְכוּלֵּי הַאי לָא אַטְרַחוּהּ רַבָּנַן. וְלִיחוּשׁ דִּלְמָא שָׁבֵיק פִּיתְחָא רַבָּה, וְעָיֵיל בְּפִיתְחָא זוּטָא! אָמַר *רַב אַדָּא בַּר מַתָּנָה: חֲזָקָה, אֵין אָדָם מַנִּיחַ פֶּתַח גָּדוֹל וְנִכְנָס בְּפֶתַח קָטָן. וּמַאי שְׁנָא מִדְּרַבִּי אַמִּי וּדְרַבִּי אַסִי? הָתָם קָא מְמַעֵט בְּהִילּוּכָא, הָכָא לָא קָא מְמַעֵט בְּהִילּוּכָא. *תְּנַן הָתָם: *עוֹר *הָעַסְלָא וְחָלָל שֶׁלּוֹ — מִצְטָרְפִין בְּטֶפַח. מַאי "עוֹר הָעַסְלָא"? אָמַר רַבָּה בַּר בַּר חָנָה, א"ר יוֹחָנָן: עוֹר כִּיסּוּי שֶׁל בֵּית הַכִּסֵּא. וְכַמָּה? כִּי אֲתָא רַב דִּימִי, אֲמַר: אֶצְבָּעַיִים מִכָּאן וְאֶצְבָּעַיִים מִכָּאן, וְאֶצְבָּעַיִים רֶיוַח בָּאֶמְצַע. כִּי אֲתָא רָבִין, אֲמַר: אֶצְבַּע וּמֶחֱצָה מִכָּאן, וְאֶצְבַּע וּמֶחֱצָה מִכָּאן, וְאֶצְבַּע רֶיוַח בָּאֶמְצַע. א"ל אַבַּיֵי לְרַב דִּימִי: מִי פְּלִיגִיתוּ? א"ל: לָא, הָא — בְּרַבְרְבָתָא, הָא — בְּזוּטְרָתָא, וְלָא פְּלִיגִי. א"ל: לָאֵי, פְּלִיגִיתוּ, וּבְעוֹמֵד מְרוּבֶּה עַל הַפָּרוּץ מִשְּׁתֵּי רוּחוֹת פְּלִיגִיתוּ; לְדִידָךְ — הָוֵי עוֹמֵד, מִשְּׁתֵּי רוּחוֹת, לְרָבִין, מֵרוּחַ אַחַת — הָוֵי עוֹמֵד, מִשְּׁתֵּי רוּחוֹת — לָא הָוֵי עוֹמֵד. דְּאִי סָלְקָא דַּעְתָּךְ לָא פְּלִיגִיתוּ — לְרָבִין הָכִי אִיבָּעֵי לֵיהּ לְמֵימַר: אֶצְבַּע וּשְׁלִישׁ מִכָּאן, וְאֶצְבַּע וּשְׁלִישׁ מִכָּאן, וְאֶצְבַּע וּשְׁלִישׁ רֶיוַח בָּאֶמְצַע. וְאֶלָּא מַאי — פְּלִיגִינַן, לְדִידִי הָכִי אִיבָּעֵי לִי לְמֵימַר: אֶצְבַּע וּשְׁנֵי שְׁלִישִׁים מִכָּאן, וְאֶצְבַּע וּשְׁנֵי שְׁלִישִׁים מִכָּאן, וְאֶצְבָּעַיִים וּשְׁנֵי שְׁלִישִׁים רֶיוַח בָּאֶמְצַע! אֶלָּא אִי אִיכָּא לְמֵימַר דִּפְלִיגִינַן — בְּפָרוּץ כְּעוֹמֵד פְּלִיגִינַן.§ ה "אִם יֵשׁ לוֹ צוּרַת הַפֶּתַח אַף עַל פִּי שֶׁרָחָב מֵעֶשֶׂר אֵינוֹ צָרִיךְ לְמַעֵט".§ אַשְׁכַּחַן צוּרַת הַפֶּתַח דִּמְהַנְיָא בְּרׇחְבּוֹ, וְאַמַּלְתְּרָא דִּמְהַנְיָא בְּגׇבְהוֹ. אִיפְּכָא

רש"י

וּמַעֲמִידוֹ לְאוֹרְכּוֹ שֶׁל מָבוֹי. בְּאֶמְצַע הַפֶּתַח דְּכֵיוָן דְּאִיכָּא הֶכְשֵׁר מָבוֹי בְּאוֹרְכּוֹ שֶׁל פַּס הָווּ לְהוּ כִּשְׁתֵּי מְבוֹאוֹת, וְנַעֲשָׂה הַפֶּתַח הָאֶחָד לְמָבוֹי זֶה וְהַפֶּתַח הַשֵּׁנִי לַמָּבוֹי הַשֵּׁנִי: מַרְחִיק שְׁתֵּי אַמּוֹת. מִן הַכּוֹתֶל, וּמַתְחִיל לַעֲשׂוֹת שָׁם פַּס, וְעוֹשֵׂהוּ מִשָּׁלֹשׁ אַמּוֹת לִסְתּוֹם הַפֶּתַח, וְנִמְצְאוּ חָמֵשׁ אַמּוֹת אֵלּוּ סְתוּמוֹת, שֶׁפִּרְצַת שְׁתֵּי הָאַמּוֹת נִיתֶּרֶת בְּעוֹמֵד מְרוּבֶּה עֲלֵיהֶן. וְהֵיכָא דְּהָוֵי רוֹחַב כ' יַעֲשֶׂה כֵּן אַף לַצַּד הַשֵּׁנִי, אוֹ יַעֲשֶׂה פַּס שֵׁשׁ אַמּוֹת וְיַרְחִיק ד' אַמּוֹת, וְנִיתָּר לִידוֹ אֶחָד בְּעוֹמֵד מְרוּבֶּה עַל הַפָּרוּץ: וְאַמַּאי. מַצְרְכַתְּ לֵיהּ לִסְתּוֹם ג' הָאַמּוֹת כְּאֶחָד: יַעֲשֶׂה פַּס אַמָּה וּמֶחֱצָה. לְפֵיאָה אֵצֶל הַכּוֹתֶל, וְיַרְחִיק ב' אַמּוֹת וְיַעֲשֶׂה פַּס אַמָּה וּמֶחֱצָה אֵצֶל פֶּתַח גָּדוֹל. וְכֵיוָן דְּלָא שָׁרֵית לֵיהּ בְּהָכִי, מִשּׁוּם דְּפָרוּץ מְרוּבֶּה עַל הָעוֹמֵד שֶׁמִּכָּאן וְעַל הָעוֹמֵד שֶׁמִּכָּאן אֶלָּא א"כ תִּצְטָרֵף יַחַד, לִהְיוֹת שְׁנֵיהֶן רָבִין עָלָיו — שָׁמְעִי' מִינָּהּ מִדְּלָא מִצְטָרֶפֶת לְהוּ עוֹמֵד מְרוּבֶּה עַל הַפָּרוּץ בֵּין ב' הָרוּחוֹת כְּשֶׁמִּצְטָרְפִים — לָא הָוֵי עוֹמֵד מְרוּבֶּה, אֶלָּא זִיל לְגַבֵּי כׇּל חַד וְחַד וְנִמְצָא פָּרוּץ רָבֶה עָלָיו וּמְבַטְּלוֹ, וְנִמְצָא פֶּתַח רָחָב מֵעֶשֶׂר: לְעוֹלָם אֵימָא לָךְ. בְּעָלְמָא, אִי לָא הֲוָה קָאֵי עוֹמֵד זֶה בֵּין שְׁנֵי פְּרָצִים — מִצְטָרְפִין הָעוֹמְדִין לְבַטֵּל פָּרוּץ הַיְחִידִי. אֲבָל הָכָא — אָתֵי אֲוִירָא דְּהַאי גִּיסָא דְּב' הָאַמּוֹת, וַאֲוִירָא דְּפֶתַח הַגָּדוֹל — וּמְבַטְּלֵי לֵיהּ לַפַּס אַמָּה וּמֶחֱצָה שֶׁבֵּינֵיהֶן: שְׁמַע מִינָּהּ פָּרוּץ כְּעוֹמֵד אָסוּר. וּפְלוּגְתָּא דְּרַב פַּפָּא וְרַב הוּנָא בְּרֵיהּ דְּרַב יְהוֹשֻׁעַ הִיא בְּשִׁילְהֵי פִּירְקִין, וְשָׁמַעְתְּ מֵהָכָא דְּרַב יְהוּדָה כְּרַב הוּנָא סְבִירָא לֵיהּ. וּלְפִיכָךְ, כׇּל אַמַּת פָּרוּץ אוֹסֶרֶת עוֹמֵד שֶׁאֶצְלָהּ, וְנִמְצָא שֶׁאֵין כָּאן סְתִימָה: דְּהַאי גִּיסָא. פֶּתַח גָּדוֹל: וּדְהַאי גִּיסָא. אַמָּה הַפָּרוּץ, וּמְבַטֵּל לֵיהּ לָאַמָּה הָעוֹמֵד שֶׁאֵצֶל הַפֶּתַח: וְיַרְחִיק אַמָּה מִן הַכּוֹתֶל וְיַעֲשֶׂה פַּס אַמָּה וּמֶחֱצָה כו'. דְּהַשְׁתָּא לָא מִצְטָרֵף אֲוִיר אַמָּה עִם אֲוִיר הַפֶּתַח לְבַטֵּל אַמָּה וּמֶחֱצָה, דְּהָא בָּטֵיל לֵיהּ אֲוִיר דְּזוּטָר מִינֵּיהּ. וְהָכִי הָוֵי שַׁפִּיר טְפֵי, שֶׁלֹּא תְּהֵא פִּירְצָה שְׁתֵּי אַמּוֹת כְּאַחַת: אִין הָכִי נַמִּי. דְּהָכִי שַׁפִּיר טְפֵי, וְכוּלֵּי הַאי לָא אַטְרְחוּהּ: דִּילְמָא שָׁבֵיק פִּתְחָא רַבָּה. וּבָטֵיל תּוֹרַת פֶּתַח מִינֵּיהּ, וּבָטֵיל לֶחִי הַמְתוּקָּן בּוֹ, וְנִמְצָא מָבוֹי זֶה בְּלֹא תִּיקּוּן: מַאי שְׁנָא מִדְּר' אַמִּי וְר' אַסִי. דְּאָמְרִי לְעֵיל (ד' ה.) בְּמָבוֹי שֶׁנִּפְרַץ מִצִּידּוֹ כְּלַפֵּי רֹאשׁוֹ ג' אֵינוֹ מַתִּיר, וְאַף עַל גַּב דְּאֵין פִּירְצָה פְּחוּתָה מֵעֶשֶׂר אַמּוֹת אוֹסֶרֶת בְּמָבוֹי — קָאָסְרִי לֵיהּ אִינְהוּ, מִשּׁוּם דִּלְמָא עָיְילֵי וְנָפְקִי בְּהַהִיא פִּירְצָה שְׁלֹשָׁה, וּבָטֵיל קָמָא מִפֶּתַח, וּבָטֵיל תִּיקּוּנוֹ: הָתָם. אִיכָּא לְמֵיחַשׁ לְהָכִי, מִשּׁוּם דְּהַהִיא פִּירְצָה קְטַנָּה מִצִּידּוֹ שֶׁל מָבוֹי הִיא, וּמְמַעֲטִי בְּהִילּוּכָא. אֲבָל הָכָא — בְּרֹאשׁ הַמָּבוֹי הוּא, וְלָא מְמַעֲטִי בְּהִילּוּכָא: עוֹר הָעַסְלָא. כִּדְמְפָרֵשׁ: עוֹר הֶעָשׂוּי לְבֵית הַכִּסֵּא שֶׁל שָׁרִים. חֲלַל הַנֶּקֶב שֶׁבּוֹ מִצְטָרֵף לִהְיוֹת עוֹמֵד טֶפַח שָׁלֵם, וְאִם יֵשׁ תַּחְתָּיו כַּזַּיִת מֵת. וְכֵלִים מְטַמְּאִים בְּאֹהֶל, וּבְפָחוֹת מִטֶּפַח אֵין אֹהֶל, דִּתְנַן (אהלות פ"ג משנה ז): טֶפַח עַל טֶפַח בְּרוּם טֶפַח מֵבִיא אֶת הַטּוּמְאָה: וְכַמָּה. יְהֵא בַּנֶּקֶב שֶׁיְּהֵא בָּטֵל אֵצֶל הָעוֹמֵד שֶׁסְּבִיבָיו, בִּמְנָחוֹת פֶּרֶק "הַתְּכֵלֶת" (ד' מא:) אָמְרִינַן: טֶפַח דְּאוֹרַיְיתָא ד' בְּגוּדָל, חָמֵשׁ בְּאֶצְבַּע, שֵׁית בְּזוּטַרְתִּי: בְּרַבְרְבָתָא. בְּגוּדָל: בְּזוּטַרְתִּי. בְּאֶצְבַּע קְטַנָּה: לְדִידָךְ הָוֵי עוֹמֵד. דְּהָא אֵין בְּאֶחָד מִן הָעוֹמְדִין לְבַטֵּל הֶחָלָל, עַד שֶׁיִּצְטָרְפוּ שְׁנֵיהֶן לְבַטְּלוֹ: לְרָבִין. דְּנָקַט הֶחָלָל פָּחוֹת מִן אֶחָד הָעוֹמְדִין: לָא הָוֵי עוֹמֵד. לְהִצְטָרֵף לְבַטֵּל הַפָּרוּץ: לְדִידִי הָכִי מִיבָּעֵי לִי לְמֵימַר כו'. וְלִמְינְקַט חָלָל יוֹתֵר עַל כׇּל אֶחָד מֵהָעוֹמְדִין, וְאַף עַל פִּי כֵן לִיצְטָרְפֵי לִרְבּוֹת עָלָיו וּלְבַטְּלוֹ. אֲבָל הַשְׁתָּא מִשּׁוּם דְּפָרוּץ כְּעוֹמֵד הוּא בְּכׇל חַד וְחַד: אֶלָּא אִי פְּלִיגִינַן בְּפָרוּץ כְּעוֹמֵד פְּלִיגִינַן. דִּלְרָבִין דְּנָקַט אֶצְבַּע וּמֶחֱצָה מִכָּאן, וְאֶצְבַּע רֶיוַח בָּאֶמְצַע, וּמְמַעֵט לֵיהּ לַפָּרוּץ מֵעוֹמֵד שֶׁבְּצַד אֶחָד לָא הָוֵי עוֹמֵד, אֶלָּא אִם כֵּן כׇּל אֶחָד וְאֶחָד מְרוּבֶּה עַל הַפָּרוּץ: רָחָב מֵעֶשֶׂר: וְאַמַּלְתְּרָא דִּמְהַנְיָא בְּגוֹבְהָהּ. לְהַכְשִׁיר גָּבוֹהַּ מֵעֶשְׂרִים: דִּמְהַנְיָא בְּרׇחְבָּהּ. לְהַכְשִׁיר רָחָב מֵעֶשֶׂר: הַפָּרוּץ: אַתְנְיֵיהּ

תוספות

עושה פס גבוה עשרה במשך ד' אמות. אי איכא מראש הפס של צד פנים עד הכותל אמצעי של מבוי יותר מעשר – צריך למבוי זה צורת הפתח, דהוי כמבוי עקום. ואע"ג דאליבא דשמואל קיימינן, כדפרישית לעיל(א) אי ביתר מעשר בהא לימא שמואל תורתו כסתום – דאפתיחה עקמומית קאי. וריצב"א פי': דהכא אפילו ביתר מעשר לא מיקרי מפולש, דכיון דשני הפתחים לרה"ר אחד, והעומד בפתח זה לא יסבב לבא סביב [הפס] לפתח אחר. אבל במבוי עקום יש בשני ראשי' בכל צד רה"ר, ורגילות לילך דרך מבוי מצד זה לצד אחר – משום הכי הוי מפולש. *ומבוי עקום דאצריכוה דלתות דהוי כמו לא הוי פתוח בשני פתחים לרה"ר אחד, או יפרש שהוא מפולש משלש רוחות, ובאמצע עקום, כפי' ר"י:

ועושה פס שלש אמות. וצריך לחי אחר, דהאי פס לא מהני הואיל ומופלג מן הכותל שלש, דאמר לקמן דלא הוי לחי. ומשום הכי פריך מדר' אמי ומדר' אסי, שהיה לו להתבטל לאותו התקון:

ואמאי יעשה פס אמה ומחצה. פי' רש"י: דאמאי אצרכיה פס ג' אמות יחד. משמע שהמקשה בא להקל עליו. ולא משמע הכי, מדמשני לקמן: כולי האי לא אטרחוה רבנן. משמע שהמקשה להחמיר עליו בא. וכענין זה משמע שהיו כל הקושיות. לכך נראה דפריך: ויעשה פס אמה ומחצה, דהכי עדיף טפי דכשיש גיפופי לצד זה ולצד זה, נראה יותר פתח:

עור העסלא וחלל שלו מצטרפין. היינו כשהטומאה והכלי תחת העור, כדאמרינן בפ"ק דסוכה (ד' יח.): ארובה בבית ובה פותח טפח, טומאה בבית – מה שכנגד ארובה טהור, טומאה נגד ארובה – כל הבית כולו טהור. ומ"מ, מצטרף האויר כמו אויר סוכה דמצטרפין, ואין ישנים תחתיו. ואין לחשוב האויר כסתום מטעם לבוד – דהלכתא גמירי לה גבי טומאה דלא אמרינן לבוד. ולהכי נמי קאמר בסמוך אצבעיים מכאן כו'. ואי אמרת לבוד סגי במשהו מכאן ומשהו מכאן:

ואצבעיים ושני שלישים ריוח באמצע. לא שייך בעור העסלא שהוא כלי אתי אוירא דהאי גיסא ואוירא דעלמא ומבטל ליה – אלא במחילות קבועות, כדלעיל, ולקמן בפירקין *גבי מקיפין בחבלים. וריצב"א מפרש: דאוירא דעלמא לא אמר דאתי ומבטל ליה, אלא באויר שאני חושבו כסתום, כההיא דלעיל דחשיב האויר של עשר כסתום. ובמקיפין בחבלים אוירא דלמעלה מעשר חשוב כסתום. אבל האויר שאינו מן המחילה – אינו מבטל. וכן משמע (לעיל ה.) דקאמרי רבי אמי ורבי אסי: יש שם פס ארבע – מתיר פירצה עד עשר, ולא אמרינן אתי אוירא דהאי גיסא ודעלמא ומבטלי ליה, אם לא שנחלק בין תחילת מבוי לסוף מבוי:

איפכא

[לקמן טו: סוכה טו.]

[ליתא בפוס משנה ולפיכך מלת תקן צריך תיקון]

[גיר' הרא"ש רב יהודה]

בתוספתא דכלים ב"ב פ"א *) [בערוך ליתא האסלא ע"ש פי' בא' ריכות]

[דף טז:]

הגהות הב"ח

(א) תוס' ד"ה עושה וכו' כדפרישית לעיל גבי אי ביתר:

רב נסים גאון

ומאי שנא מדר' אמי ור' אסי. חזור על הדבר שהקדימו בראש הפרק (דף ה) דאיתמר מבוי שנפרץ מצדו כלפי ראשו איתמר משמיה דר' אמי ומשמיה דר' אסי אם יש שם פס ד' מתיר פרצה עד י':

רבינו חננאל

והיכי עביד הא. אמר *) אביי עושה פס גבוה י' טפחים במשך ד' אמות כלומר ארוך ד' אמות ומעמידו באמצע מבוי לארכו של מבוי אי נמי כרב יהודה דאמר מבוי שרחב ט"ו אמות מרחיק אמתים ועושה פס ג' אמות ומקשינן ויעשה פס אמה ומחצה וירחיק ב' אמות ויעשה פס אמה ומחצה שמעינן מינה עומד מרובה על הפרוץ משתי רוחות לא הוי עומד. ודחינן שאני (התם) [הכא] דקא אתיא אוירא דהאי גיסא ודהאי גיסא ומבטל ליה. ויעשה פס אמה וירחיק אמה [וכו']: ומ"ש מדר' אמי ומדר' אסי דאמרי מבוי שנפרץ מצדו כלפי ראשו אם נשתייר פס ד' מתיר פירצה עד עשר. ודחינן התם ממעט בהלוכה: תנן בתוספתא בכלים פרק י"ט. עור אסלא וחלל שלו מצטרפין לטפח וכאילו סתום הוא כולו ומאהיל פי' עור אסלא כסא של ברזל ועושין בו בב' קצותיו רצועות מעור של בקר חזקות רחבות מאצבע ולמעלה וביניהן חלל. ויושב אדם עליו בשעה שצריך לנקביו והרעי נופל מן החלל על העביט של רעי וזהו עור אסלא. עור כסא של בית הכסא הוא עור שהוא מכסה לאסלא. וכך שמה בלשון יון אסלא. אמר רב דימי אצבעיים שיעור רוחב הרצועה מיכן ואצבעיים מיכן ואצבעיים שיעור רוחב הרצועה מיכן ואצבעיים חלל באמצע. ורבין אמר אצבע ומחצה מיכן ואצבע ומחצה מיכן ואצבע חלל באמצע. ואסיקנא דלא פליגי. רב דימי אמר באצבעות קטנות שהן ו' בטפח ורבין אמר באצבעות גדולות כגודל שהן ד' בטפח כי פליגי בעומד מרובה על הפרוץ משתי רוחות לרב דימי דאמר אצבעיים מיכן ואצבעיים מיכן ואצבעיים ריוח אי מצרפת אצבעיים ואצבעיים מב' רוחות נמצאו מרובות על החלל דהני ד' אצבעות והחלל בב' אבל אם לא תצטרף לא תמצא מרוח אחד עומד מרובה על הפרוץ דהני אצבעיים והני אצבעיים אינון. אבל (רבא) [רבין] דאמר אצבע ומחצה מיכן ואצבע ומחצה מיכן ואצבע ריוח באמצע אמר לך אי איכא עומד מרובה על הפרוץ מרוח אחת אין אבל מב' רוחות לא מצרפי דאי ס"ד לא פליגי (רמי) [רבין] ורב דימי הכי הוה להו למימר אצבע ושליש מיכן ואצבע ושליש מיכן ואצבע ושליש ריוח באמצע ודחינן אלא מאי אית לך דפליגי אי הכי איבעיא לי' למימר אצבע ושני שלישים מכאן ואצבע ושני שלישים מכאן ואצבעיים וב' שלישי' ריוח באמצע שהן ג' אצבעות ושליש שנמצא העומד מב' רוחותיה העומד מרובה על הפרוץ [ב'] שליש אצבע אלא כי פליגי בעומד כפרוץ רב דימי אמר עומד כפרוץ הוי עומד (רבא) [רבין] אמר לא הוי עומד ורחבה מי' אמות אם יש לו צורת הפתח אין צריך למעט. א"ל רב לרב יהודה תני צריך למעט.

*) [שמואל משמיה דלוי]

איפכא מאי? ת"ש, דתניא: מבוי שהוא גבוה מעשרים אמה — ימעט ואם יש לו צורת הפתח — אינו צריך למעט. אמלתרא ברחבו מאי? תא שמע, דתניא: מבוי שהוא גבוה מעשרים אמה — ימעט והרחב מעשר — ימעט, ואם יש לו צורת הפתח — אינו צריך למעט, ואם יש לו אמלתרא — אינו צריך למעט. מאי לאו אסיפא? לא, ארישא. *מתני ליה רב יהודה לחייא בר רב קמיה דרב: "אינו צריך למעט". א"ל: *אתנייה: "צריך למעט". אמר רב יוסף, מדברי רבינו נלמד: חצר שרובה פתחים וחלונות — אינה ניתרת בצורת הפתח. מ"ט — הואיל ויותר מעשר אוסר במבוי, ופרוץ מרובה על העומד אוסר בחצר, מה יותר מעשר האוסר במבוי — אינו ניתר בצורת הפתח, אף פרוץ מרובה על העומד, האוסר בחצר — אינו ניתר בצורת הפתח. מה ליותר מעשר האוסר במבוי — שכן לא התרת בו אצל פסי ביראות לר"מ, תאמר בפרוץ מרובה על העומד האוסר בחצר — שכן התרת אצל פסי ביראות לדברי הכל. לימא מסייע ליה: *דפנות הללו שרובן פתחים וחלונות — מותר, ובלבד שיהא עומד מרובה על הפרוץ. "שרובן" ס"ד?! אלא אימא: שריבה בהן פתחים וחלונות, ובלבד שיהא עומד מרובה על הפרוץ. אמר רב כהנא: כי תניא ההיא — בפיתחי שימאי. *מאי פיתחי שימאי? פליגי בה רב רחומי ורב יוסף; חד אמר: דלית להו שקפי, וחד אמר: דלית להו תיקרה. ואף ר' יוחנן סבר לה להא דרב. דאמר רבין בר רב אדא, א"ר יצחק: מעשה באדם אחד מבקעת בית חורתן שנעץ ד' קונדיסין בארבע *פינות השדה, ומתח זמורה עליהם, ובא מעשה לפני חכמים, והתירו לו לענין כלאים. ואמר ר"ל: כדרך שהתירו לו לענין כלאים — [ב]כך התירו לו לענין שבת. ר' יוחנן אמר: לכלאים — התירו לו, לענין שבת — לא התירו לו. במאי עסקינן? אילימא מן הצד — והאמר רב חסדא: [ג]צורת הפתח שעשאה מן הצד — לא עשה ולא כלום. אלא על גבן; ובמאי? אילימא בעשר — בהא לימא ר' יוחנן "בשבת לא"?! אלא לאו — ביתר מעשר! לא, לעולם בעשר ומן הצד, ובדרב חסדא קא מיפלגי. ורמי דר' יוחנן אדר' יוחנן, ורמי דריש לקיש אדריש לקיש. דאמר ריש לקיש משום ר' יהודה בר' חנינא:

פיאה

רש"י

אתנייה צריך למעט. אפילו יש לו צורת פתח: מדברי רבינו. רב, דאמר צורת פתח לא מהניא: שרובה פתחים. כארבע דפנותיה: אינה ניתרת בצורת פתח. ואפילו פתחים קטנים מעשר. כי היכי דלא מהניא צורת פתח לשוויה יותר מעשר פתחא — לא מהני נמי לפרוץ מרובה על העומד בפתחים קטנים: מה ליותר מעשר. דין הוא שלא יועיל צורת פתח בו — שכן חמור איסורו, שלא הותר בשום מקום בשבת, ואפילו בפסי ביראות. ואליבא דרבי מאיר, דאמר בפ' שני (לקמן יח:): ובינייהן כמלא שתי רבקות של ג' ג' בקר. דהיינו עשר אמות, דכל פרה אמה ושני שלישי אמה: תאמר בפרוץ מרובה על העומד. בפרצות של עשר או פחות, שהרי הותר בפסי ביראות. ואפילו לרבי מאיר דמחמיר בהו ואסר ביותר מעשר — מיהו פרוץ מרובה מודי דשרי. וכ"ש לר' יהודה דמכשיר בי"ג אמה ושליש: לימא מסייע ליה. למ"ד לא מהניא צורת הפתח בעומד פחות מן הפרוץ: שרובן ס"ד. כיון דרובן פתחים וחלונות, הוה ליה פרוץ מרובה, והיכי מצי תו למיתני "ובלבד שיהא עומד מרובה": אלא שריבה בהן. שעשה בהן הרבה פתחים, וחלונות סביב סביב — מותר, ובלבד שיהא בין פתח לפתח יותר מכדי פתח. אלמא: עומד מרובה על הפרוץ בעינן, ואע"ג דאיכא צורת פתח בכולהו: פיתחי שימאי. פתחין שוממין. ל"א: פתחים מקולקלין שמחוסרין תיקון, כמו זקן אשמאי* חסר מתורה: שיקפי. מזוזות שנחלנו אבניהם מכאן ומכאן, אבן יוצאת ואבן נכנסת, ואין זו צורת פתח: תיקרה. שאין כלום בנין למעלה מן הפתח, אלא כל הכותל חלוק כפתח עד ראשו. כזה

וצורת פתח שאמרו — קנה מכאן וקנה מכאן וקנה על גביהן: סבר לה להא דרב. דלא מהני צורת פתח ליותר מעשר במבוי: בית חורתן. שם מקום: ומתח זמורה על גביהן. מזה לזה, כעין צורת פתח: לענין כלאים. שאם יש גפנים בתוך הקונדסין — מותר לזרוע סמוך להן חוץ למחיצה. כדתנן: *היה גדר בינתיים — זה סומך לגדר מכאן, וזה סומך לגדר מכאן: לענין שבת. לטלטל בתוכו: מן הצד. שמתח הזמורה מזה לזה באמצעיתו. ולא על ראשיהן: לא עשה כלום. *ולענין שבת, אמאי התירו לו: בשבת לא. הא בעשר — לכולי עלמא פתחא הוא: ובדרב חסדא פליגי. ריש לקיש לית ליה דרב חסדא, ורבי יוחנן אית ליה דרב חסדא. וקסבר: כי אמר רב חסדא — לשבת, אבל לכלאים — אפילו מן הצד הוי צורת פתח, דשבת חמור מכלאים:

פיאה

תוספות

איפכא מאי. כלומר: מי מהניא צורת הפתח בגובהה. וקשיא לר"ת: דהא צורת הפתח הוי קנה מכאן וקנה מכאן וקנה על גביהן. דל קנה דעל גביהן, ליתכשר בקנה דמכאן ומכאן, דהוי כלחי משהו! וי"ל: דמיבעיא ליה היכא דלא מהני לחי, כמו במפולש או ביתר מעשר, דבעי צורת הפתח. או לר' יוסי, דבעי לחי רוחב ג'. ובהכי מיתוקמא נמי ברייתא דמייתי: **חצר** שרובה פתחים וחלונות. ובפחות מעשר. דאי ביתר מעשר — אפילו בעומד מרובה, הא אתנייה רב צריך למעט. ובד' דפנותיה איירי, דמשני לדדין מודה רב דמהני צורת הפתח,(א) דאמרינן לעיל*: הלכה כת"ק. וקשיא: דמהאי בנין אב, אפילו מחיצה רביעית יש ללמוד דלא מהני צורת הפתח, כי היכי דלא מהני ביתר מעשר אפילו במחיצה אחת! וי"ל: דאין ללמוד אלא על ד' מחיצות, דמחיצה אחת ביתר מעשר הוי כמו פרוץ מרובה בד' מחיצות, דמה שאוסר ביתר מעשר — משום דלא מיקרי פתח, ולא מהני ליה צורת הפתח — גם לפרוץ מרובה מד' רוחות לא יועיל צורת הפתח, דפתחא בד' רוחות לא עבדי אינשי. אבל אמחיצה אחת דעבדי פתח — פשיטא דמהני צורת הפתח, ועל זה אין שייך ללמוד: **מה** יתר מעשר האוסר במבוי. ואין להקשות: מה למבוי שכן פרצתו(ב) בד'! דיתר מעשר נמי אסר בחצר, ולא נקט מבוי אלא משום דרב איירי ביה: **פתחי** שימאי. *פר"ח: פתחי ארץ ישראל, שהוא ארץ בני שם: **אילימא** בעשר בהא לימא ר' יוחנן בשבת לא. אין להקשות דמאי פריך, דילמא סבר כנהרדעא(ג) דאצרכוהו ללחות אפילו בעשר! דביתר מעשר שמואל נמי מודה דהוי כמפולש. דכאן איירי בבקעה שהיא כרמלית, דליכא מאן דפליג שלא יועיל צורת הפתח, כדאמרינן לעיל (ד' ז.). אך קשה: דהא רב יוסף אסר לעיל אפילו בעשר, הואיל ופרוץ מרובה, ואפילו בכלה לבקעה איירי, דומיא דיתר מעשר דאסר ואפילו בכלה לבקעה. מדמייתי מרבי יוחנן דאיירי בבקעה. א"כ, מה פריך בהא: לימא ר' יוחנן, כיון דרב יוסף סבר הכי! וי"ל: דאין לחוש לדברי רב יוסף, הואיל ונדחו. וא"ת: הואיל ומהני צורת הפתח מכל ד' רוחות, א"כ גבי פסי ביראות למה הוצרכו לארבעה דיומדין, ולא הוי שרי אלא לבהמה, בין לר"מ ובין לר' יהודה היה להם לעשות ד' קונדסין וזמורה על גביהן — לרב בעשר, ולמתני' ביתר מעשר! וגבי שיירא נמי, אמאי צריך שלשה חבלים זה למעלה מזה או קנים פחות פחות מג'? יעשו צורת הפתח מד' רוחות! ואומר ר"י: לפי שלא היה מתקיים כל כך, משום דאתו גמלי ושדו ליה. וגם, בקל יכול ליפול ברוח שאינה מצויה, לפי שהיו צריכין להגביהו מן הגמלים הנכנסים שם לשתות, וכן בשיירא. ועוד: דבשיירא אין להתיר כמו בחצר שמוקף לדירה. וריצב"א מפרש: דהכא לא איירי בד' דפנות, וה"פ: כך התירו לענין שבת במפולש, דהיינו ב' מחיצות. דד' מחיצות לענין שבת הוי כד' מחיצות לענין כלאים. דבכלאים אין חילוק בין ב' לד'. והשתא פריך שפיר: בהא לימא רבי יוחנן בשבת לא? דבד' מחיצות אין לחוש אם פרוץ מרובה. והשר מקוצי מפרש, דהכי פירושא: בהא לימא רבי יוחנן בשבת לא — אי לית ליה דרב דאמר ביתר מעשר לא מהני צורת הפתח, דהא דאמר רב יוסף צורת הפתח לא מהניא בפרוץ מרובה — היינו מדברי רב דאסר ביתר מעשר, אלא לאו ביתר מעשר ס"ל לרבי יוחנן כרב דלא מהני צורת הפתח, ולכך אפילו בעשר קאמר רבי יוחנן בשבת דלא מהני צורת הפתח, משום דפרוץ מרובה לרב יוסף אסור אפילו ע"י צורת הפתח, דאית ליה בנין אב:

הכא

עין משפט נר מצוה

נט א טור א"ח סי' שסג:
ס ב מיי' פט"ז מהל' שבת הלכה טז סמג שם טוש"ע א"ח סי' שסב סעיף י וסי' שסג סעיף כו:
סא ג מיי' פט"ז הלכה כ ופי"ז הלכה לה מהל' שבת סמג שם טוש"ע א"ח סי' שסב סעיף יא:

מסורת הש"ס

[לעיל ב:]
[עי' תוס' לקמן יז. ד"ה אתנייה]
[קידושין לב:]
מנחות לג: ע"ש
[גירסת הערוך בערך פיאה א' פיאות]
[ב"ב כו.]
ס"א ולענין כלאים
[דף ו:]
לקמן טז:
[ועי' תוספות קידושין לב: ד"ה זקן וכו']

הגהות הב"ח

(א) תוס' ד"ה חצר וכו' דאמרינן לעיל. נ"ב דף ז ע"ב: (ב) ד"ה מה וכו' שכן פרצתו. נ"ב עי' לעיל דף ו: (ג) ד"ה אילימא וכו' כנהרדעי. נ"ב לעיל סוף דף ו:

גליון הש"ס

גמ' רי"ו לכלאים התירו. עיין לקמן דף לג ע"א תוד"ה תלוי.

רבינו חננאל

אמלתרא אסיקנא דלא מהניא ברחבה. אמר רב יוסף מדברי רבינו. רב דאמר צריך למעט נלמד חצר שרובה פתחים וחלונות אינה ניתרת בצורת הפתח הואיל ויותר מעשר אסור במבוי. ופרוץ מרובה על העומד אסור בחצר שיש לה צורת הפתח. מה יותר מעשר האוסר במבוי אינו [ניתר] לדברי רב בצורת הפתח אף פרוץ מרובה על העומד כו'. (פי') מה ליתר מעשר שכן לא התרת' בו אצל פסי ביראות לר' מאיר [פי'] דאמר ב' דביקות של בקר נמצאו רחב ו' פרות כשעומדות בשורה אחת זו אצל זו עובי כל פרה ופרה אמה וב' שלישי אמה. נמצא בשש פרות עשר אמות לר' מאיר אבל לר' יהודה דאמר ח' פרות הן י"ג אמות ושליש אבל פרוץ מרובה על העומד לדברי הכל מותר. פי' הדיומת רחבו ו' טפחים ובין דיומת לדיומת פרוץ לר' מאיר י' אמות ולר' יהודה י"ג אמות ושליש לימא מסייע ליה לרב דפנות הללו שרבה בהן פתחים וחלונות כשרות ובלבד שיהא עומד מרובה על הפרוץ. ודחה רב כהנא ואמר הא דתני בפתחים וחלונות הללו עד שיהא עומד מרובה על הפרוץ משום דפתחים הללו פיתחי שימאי נינהו דלית להו תקרה או משקוף. פי' שימאי של א"י שהיא ארץ בני שם. ואף ר' יוחנן סבר לה להא דרב דאמר הרחב מעשר אמות אע"פ שיש לו צורת הפתח צריך למעט דצורת הפתח ביותר מעשר אינה ניתרת. ואמרינן מעשה באחד מבקעת בית חוורתן שנעץ ד' קונדסין בד' פינות השדה כענין דאמרין ובין אלו קונדסין קנים זה אצל זה בפחות מג' טפחים כדי שתהיה כמו מחיצה ומתח זמורה עליהן בשביל שלא יושממו ויפלו זולתי מקום הפתח. ואמר ריש לקיש כשם שהיא מחיצה לכלאים כך היא מחיצה לשבת ור' יוחנן אמר לכלאים התירו ולא לשבת. במאי עסקינן אי נימא בעושה פתחו בלא תקרה אלא קנה מיכן וקנה מיכן והאמר רב חסדא צורת הפתח שעשאה מן הצד לא עשה כלום אלא לעולם שעשה קנה מיכן וקנה מיכן וקנה אחר עליהן. וכי האי גוונא צורת הפתח מעליא הוא. ואם רוחב זה הפתח עשר אמות אמאי א"ר יוחנן אבל לא לשבת אלא כגון שיש בפתחו יתר מעשר. וא"ר יוחנן אע"פ שיש שם צורת הפתח (עשר אמות) כיון דפתחו יתר מעשר לא עשה כלום ש"מ דר' יוחנן כרב סבירא ליה דאמר דהרחב מעשר אמות ימעט. ודחינן לא לעולם לא נתן קנה על גביהן ולא עשה הפתח אלא קנה מיכן וקנה מיכן וזהו צורת הפתח מן הצד. כלומר יש לו מזוזות מן הצדדין ואין תקרה על גביהן ובדרב חסדא פליגי דאמר העושה צורת הפתח מן הצד לא עשה כלום. ר' יוחנן אית ליה דרב חסדא. ר"ל לית ליה

וכיון

סב א ב מיי' פט"ז מהלכות שבת הלכה יט סמג עשין א טוש"ע א"ח סי' שסב סעיף יא:
סג ג מיי' פ"ו מהלכות מזוזה הלכה ד סמג עשין כג טוש"ע י"ד סי' רפו סעיף ב ובהגה אלפס בהלכות מזוזה דף טו:]
סד ד מיי' פי"ז מהל' שבת הלכה ב סמג עשין א טוש"ע א"ח סי' שסג סעיף ג וסעיף יד:

פֵּאָה מוּתֶּרֶת לְעִנְיַן כִּלְאַיִם, אֲבָל לֹא לַשַּׁבָּת. וְר' יוֹחָנָן אָמַר: כִּמְחִיצוֹת לַשַּׁבָּת — דְּלָא, כָּךְ מְחִיצוֹת לְכִלְאַיִם — דְּלָא. בִּשְׁלָמָא דְּרֵישׁ לָקִישׁ אדר"ל לָא קַשְׁיָא, הָא — דִּידֵיהּ, הָא — דְּרַבֵּיהּ. אֶלָּא דְּרַבִּי יוֹחָנָן אַדְּר' יוֹחָנָן קַשְׁיָא! אִי אָמְרַתְּ בִּשְׁלָמָא: הָתָם — עַל גַּבָּן, הָכָא — מִן הַצַּד, שַׁפִּיר. אֶלָּא אִי אָמְרַתְּ אִידִי וְאִידִי מִן הַצַּד, מַאי אִיכָּא לְמֵימַר? לְעוֹלָם אִידִי וְאִידִי מִן הַצַּד, הָתָם — בְּעֶשֶׂר, הָכָא — בְּיוֹתֵר מֵעֶשֶׂר. וּמְנָא תֵּימְרָא דְּשָׁנֵי לַן בֵּין עֶשֶׂר לְיוֹתֵר מֵעֶשֶׂר — דְּאָמַר לֵיהּ רַבִּי יוֹחָנָן לְרֵישׁ לָקִישׁ: לֹא כָּךְ הָיָה הַמַּעֲשֶׂה שֶׁהָלַךְ רַבִּי יְהוֹשֻׁעַ אֵצֶל ר' יוֹחָנָן בֶּן נוּרִי לִלְמוֹד תּוֹרָה, אַף עַל פִּי שֶׁבָּקִי בְּהִלְכוֹת כִּלְאַיִם, וּמְצָאוֹ שֶׁיּוֹשֵׁב בֵּין הָאִילָנוֹת וּמָתַח זְמוֹרָה מֵאִילָן לְאִילָן. וְאָמַר לוֹ: רַבִּי, אִי גְּפָנִים כָּאן מַהוּ לִזְרוֹעַ כָּאן? אָמַר לוֹ: בְּעֶשֶׂר — מוּתָּר, בְּיוֹתֵר מֵעֶשֶׂר — אָסוּר. בְּמַאי עָסְקִינַן? אִילֵימָא עַל גַּבָּן — יוֹתֵר מֵעֶשֶׂר אָסוּר — וְהָתַנְיָא: *הָיוּ שָׁם קָנִין הַדּוֹקְרָנִין, וְעָשָׂה לָהֶן פֵּאָה מִלְמַעְלָה, אֲפִי' בְּיוֹתֵר מֵעֶשֶׂר — מוּתָּר! אֶלָּא לָאו מִן הַצַּד, וְקָאָמַר לֵיהּ: בְּעֶשֶׂר — מוּתָּר, יוֹתֵר מֵעֶשֶׂר — אָסוּר. שְׁמַע מִינַּהּ.§ גּוּפָא, אָמַר רַב חִסְדָּא: צוּרַת הַפֶּתַח שֶׁעֲשָׂאָהּ מִן הַצַּד — לֹא עָשָׂה וְלֹא כְלוּם. וְאָמַר רַב חִסְדָּא: צוּרַת הַפֶּתַח שֶׁאָמְרוּ — [א]צְרִיכָה שֶׁתְּהֵא בְּרִיאָה כְּדֵי לְהַעֲמִיד בָּהּ דֶּלֶת, וַאֲפִילּוּ דֶּלֶת שֶׁל קַשִּׁין. אָמַר רֵישׁ לָקִישׁ מִשּׁוּם ר' יַנַּאי: צוּרַת הַפֶּתַח צְרִיכָה הֶיכֵּר צִיר. *מַאי "הֶיכֵּר צִיר"? אָמַר רַב אָוְיָא: אַבְקָתָא. אַשְׁכְּחִינְהוּ רַב אַחָא בְּרֵיהּ דְּרַב אָוְיָא לְתַלְמִידֵי דְּרַב אַשִׁי, אֲמַר לְהוּ: אָמַר מָר מִידֵּי בְּצוּרַת הַפֶּתַח? אָמְרוּ לֵיהּ: לֹא אָמַר וְלֹא כְלוּם. תָּנָא: צוּרַת הַפֶּתַח שֶׁאָמְרוּ — קָנֶה מִכָּאן וְקָנֶה מִכָּאן וְקָנֶה עַל גַּבֵּיהֶן. צְרִיכִין לִיגַּע אוֹ אֵין צְרִיכִין לִיגַּע? רַב נַחְמָן אָמַר: [ב]אֵין צְרִיכִין לִיגַּע. וְרַב שֵׁשֶׁת אָמַר: צְרִיכִין לִיגַּע. אֲזַל רַב נַחְמָן וַעֲבַד עוּבְדָּא בֵּי רֵישׁ גָּלוּתָא כִּשְׁמַעְתֵּיהּ, א"ל רַב שֵׁשֶׁת לְשַׁמָּעֵיהּ רַב גַּדָּא: זִיל, שְׁלוֹף שְׁדִינְהוּ. אֲזַל, שְׁלַף שַׁדִּינְהוּ. אַשְׁכַּחוּהוּ דְּבֵי רֵישׁ גָּלוּתָא, חַבְשׁוּהוּ. אֲזַל רַב שֵׁשֶׁת קָם אַבָּבָא, א"ל: גַּדָּא, פּוֹק תָּא! נְפַק וַאֲתָא. אַשְׁכְּחֵיהּ רַב שֵׁשֶׁת לְרַבָּה בַּר שְׁמוּאֵל, אֲמַר לֵיהּ: תָּנֵי מָר מִידֵּי בְּצוּרַת הַפֶּתַח? א"ל: אִין, *תָּנֵינָא; כִּיפָּה, ר"מ מְחַיֵּיב בִּמְזוּזָה וַחֲכָמִים פּוֹטְרִין. וְשָׁוִין [ג]שֶׁאִם יֵשׁ בְּרַגְלֶיהָ עֲשָׂרָה שֶׁהִיא חַיֶּיבֶת. אָמַר אַבָּיֵי: הַכֹּל מוֹדִים אִם גְּבוֹהָה עֲשָׂרָה וְאֵין בְּרַגְלֶיהָ שְׁלֹשָׁה, אִי נַמִּי: יֵשׁ בְּרַגְלֶיהָ שְׁלֹשָׁה וְאֵין גְּבוֹהָה עֲשָׂרָה — וְלֹא כְלוּם. כִּי פְּלִיגִי — בְּיֵשׁ בְּרַגְלֶיהָ ג' וּגְבוֹהָה עֲשָׂרָה וְאֵין רְחָבָה אַרְבָּעָה, וְיֵשׁ בָּהּ לָחוֹק לְהַשְׁלִימָהּ לְאַרְבָּעָה. *ר' מֵאִיר סָבַר: חוֹקְקִין לְהַשְׁלִים, וְרַבָּנַן סָבְרִי: אֵין חוֹקְקִין לְהַשְׁלִים. א"ל:(א) *אִי מַשְׁכְּחַתְּ לְהוּ — לָא תֵּימָא לְהוּ לְבֵי רֵישׁ גָּלוּתָא וְלָא מִידֵּי מֵהָא מַתְנִיתָא דְּכִיפָּה.§

מתני' *הֶכְשֵׁר מָבוֹי; ב"ש אוֹמְרִים: לֶחִי וְקוֹרָה, וּב"ה אוֹמְרִים: אוֹ לֶחִי אוֹ קוֹרָה. רַבִּי אֱלִיעֶזֶר אוֹמֵר: לְחָיַיִן. מִשּׁוּם ר' יִשְׁמָעֵאל אָמַר תַּלְמִיד אֶחָד לִפְנֵי ר"ע: לֹא נֶחְלְקוּ ב"ש וּב"ה עַל מָבוֹי שֶׁהוּא פָּחוֹת מֵאַרְבַּע אַמּוֹת שֶׁהוּא נִיתָּר אוֹ בְּלֶחִי אוֹ בְּקוֹרָה, עַל מַה נֶּחְלְקוּ — עַל רָחָב מֵאַרְבַּע אַמּוֹת וְעַד עֶשֶׂר, שֶׁב"ש אוֹמְרִים לֶחִי וְקוֹרָה, וּב"ה אוֹמְרִים: אוֹ לֶחִי אוֹ קוֹרָה. א"ר עֲקִיבָא: עַל זֶה וְעַל זֶה נֶחְלְקוּ.§ **גמ'** כְּמַאן? *דְּלָא כַּחֲנַנְיָה וְלָא כְּתַנָּא קַמָּא! אָמַר רַב יְהוּדָה, הָכִי קָאָמַר: "הֶכְשֵׁר מָבוֹי סָתוּם כֵּיצַד? ב"ש אוֹמְרִים: לֶחִי וְקוֹרָה, וּב"ה אוֹמְרִים: [ד]אוֹ לֶחִי אוֹ קוֹרָה". "ב"ש אוֹמְרִים: לֶחִי וְקוֹרָה", לְמֵימְרָא דְּקָא סָבְרִי ב"ש אַרְבַּע מְחִיצוֹת דְּאוֹרָיְיתָא? לֹא, לִזְרוֹק — מִשָּׁלֹשׁ הוּא דְּמִיחַיַּיב, לְטַלְטֵל — עַד דְּאִיכָּא אַרְבַּע. "ב"ה אוֹמְרִים אוֹ לֶחִי אוֹ קוֹרָה", לֵימָא קָא סָבְרִי ב"ה שָׁלֹשׁ מְחִיצוֹת דְּאוֹרָיְיתָא? לֹא, לִזְרוֹק — מִשְּׁתַּיִם הוּא דְּמִיחַיַּיב, לְטַלְטֵל — עַד דְּאִיכָּא שָׁלֹשׁ.§ "ר' אֱלִיעֶזֶר אוֹמֵר: לְחָיַיִן".§ אִיבַּעְיָא לְהוּ: ר' אֱלִיעֶזֶר לְחָיַיִן וְקוֹרָה קָאָמַר, אוֹ דִּילְמָא לְחָיַיִן בְּלֹא קוֹרָה קָאָמַר? ת"ש: [ה]*מַעֲשֶׂה בְּרַבִּי אֱלִיעֶזֶר שֶׁהָלַךְ אֵצֶל רַבִּי יוֹסֵי בֶּן פְּרִידָא תַּלְמִידוֹ לְאוֹבְלִין

רש"י

פִּיאָה. קְלִיעַת הַזְּמוֹרָה הַמְּתוּחָה מִקּוּנְדָּס לַחֲבֵירוֹ. וְדוּגְמָתוֹ פֵּיאָה נָכְרִית בְּמַסֶּכֶת שַׁבָּת (ד' סד:): הָא דְּרַבֵּיהּ. הָךְ בַּתְרַיְיתָא מִשּׁוּם ר' יְהוּדָה בְּר' חֲנִינָא אֲמָרָהּ, וְלֵיהּ לָא סְבִירָא לֵיהּ: אִי אָמְרַתְּ בִּשְׁלָמָא. קַמַּיְיתָא עַל גַּבָּן – מִשּׁוּם הָכִי שָׁרֵי לְעִנְיַן כִּלְאַיִם, וּבְיוֹתֵר מֵעֶשֶׂר. דְּאִי בְּעֶשֶׂר – לָא מָצֵי לְמֵימַר אֲבָל לֹא לְשַׁבָּת, וְעַל כָּרְחָךְ כְּרַב סְבִירָא לֵיהּ שַׁפִּיר: וּמְנָא תֵּימְרָא דְּשָׁנֵי לַן. בְּכִלְאַיִם, בֵּין עֶשֶׂר לְיוֹתֵר מֵעֶשֶׂר מִן הַצַּד: אע"פ שֶׁבָּקִי. רַבִּי יְהוֹשֻׁעַ בְּהִלְכוֹת כִּלְאַיִם, שָׁאַל מִמֶּנּוּ דָּבָר זֶה: קָנִים הַדּוֹקְרָנִין. מְסוּפִּין כְּדֶקֶר = יָתֵד הַנָּעוּץ בַּקַּרְקַע: כְּדֵי לְהַעֲמִיד בָּהּ דֶּלֶת. כָּל שֶׁהוּא, וַאֲפִילּוּ יָכוֹל לְהַעֲמִיד בָּהּ דֶּלֶת שֶׁל קַשִּׁין – דַּיָּהּ קַשִּׁין שֶׁל שִׁבֳּלִים: אַבְקָתָא. חוֹר שֶׁצִּיר הַדֶּלֶת סוֹבֵב בּוֹ. וְאַף עַל פִּי שֶׁאֵינָהּ צְרִיכָה דֶּלֶת, מִיהוּ חָזְיָא לְדֶלֶת בָּעֵינַן: צְרִיכִין לִיגַּע. קָנֶה שֶׁעַל גַּבָּן לַקָּנִים שֶׁבַּצְּדָדִין, אוֹ אֲפִילּוּ תְּלוּיָה לְמַעְלָה מֵהֶן בָּאֲוִיר: עוּבְדָּא בֵּי רֵישׁ גָּלוּתָא. שֶׁהִקִּיף לְהַתִּיר רְחָבָה לְטַלְטֵל בָּהּ, וְעָשָׂה בָּהֶן פְּתָחִים הַרְבֵּה יוֹתֵר מֵעֶשֶׂר, וְעָשָׂה לָהֶן פֵּיאָה, וְלֹא נָגְעוּ לַקָּנִים שֶׁל מַטָּה: כִּיפָּה. שַׁעַר הֶעָשׂוּי כְּכִיפָּה: וַחֲכָמִים פּוֹטְרִים. מִפְּנֵי שֶׁלְּמַעְלָה בָּעִיגּוּל הוּא מֵיצַר, וְאֵינוֹ רָחָב אַרְבָּעָה, וְאֵין פֶּתַח פְּחוּתָה מד' רוֹחַב: וְשָׁוִין שֶׁאִם יֵשׁ בְּרַגְלֶיהָ עֲשָׂרָה. גּוֹבַהּ, קוֹדֶם שֶׁיַּתְחִיל לְעַגֵּל: חַיֶּיבֶת. דְּהָא יֵשׁ בָּהּ עֲשָׂרָה גּוֹבַהּ בְּרוֹחַב אַרְבָּעָה. וַאֲפִילּוּ כָּל הָעִיגּוּל סָתוּם – נִשְׁאָר שָׁם שִׁיעוּר פֶּתַח כָּשֵׁר. אַלְמָא: אֵין צְרִיכִין לִיגַּע, דְּהָא הַכְשֵׁירָהּ דְּפֶתַח בְּרַגְלֶיהָ הִיא, וְהָעִיגּוּל מַפְסִיק בֵּין תִּקְרָה הָעֶלְיוֹנָה לַמְּזוּזוֹת, וְקָתָנֵי חַיֶּיבֶת: אַבַּיֵּי לְפָרוֹשֵׁי פְּלוּגְתַּיְיהוּ אֲתָא. לִישָּׁנָא אַחֲרִינָא: "וְאָמַר אַבַּיֵּי" גָּרְסִינַן וּמִפֵּירוּשׁ דְּאַבַּיֵּי יָלְפִינַן דְּאֵין צְרִיכִין לִיגַּע: הַכֹּל מוֹדִים גְּבוֹהָה עֲשָׂרָה וְאֵין בְּרַגְלֶיהָ שְׁלֹשָׁה דְּלָא כְלוּם. דְּכָל בְּצִיר מִשְּׁלֹשָׁה גּוֹבַהּ – אַרְעָא סְמִיכְתָּא הִיא, וְאֵין שָׁם מִפֶּתַח זֶה כְּלוּם שֶׁיְּהֵא רוֹחַב אַרְבָּעָה: אִי נַמִּי יֵשׁ בְּרַגְלֶיהָ גּוֹבַהּ שְׁלֹשָׁה. וּסְתָם רַגְלֶיהָ רוֹחַב ד' וְאֵין גּוֹבְהָהּ עֲשָׂרָה. וְלֹא כְלוּם, דְּכָל פָּחוֹת מֵעֲשָׂרָה לֹא כְלוּם, וְלָאו פֶּתַח הוּא: כִּי פְּלִיגִי דְּיֵשׁ בְּרַגְלֶיהָ שְׁלֹשָׁה. דְּנָפֵיק מִתּוֹרַת אַרְעָא סְמִיכְתָּא בְּהֶכְשֵׁר פֶּתַח אַרְבָּעָה רוֹחַב, וְגוֹבְהָהּ עֲשָׂרָה עִם הָעִיגּוּל, וְאֵינָהּ רְחָבָה אַרְבָּעָה מֵעוּגָּל וּלְמַעְלָה: וְיֵשׁ בָּהּ לָחוֹק. וְלִסְתּוֹר הָעִיגּוּל וּלְהַרְחִיבוֹ לְאַרְבָּעָה בְּלֹא נְפִילַת רֹאשׁ הָעִיגּוּל הָעֶלְיוֹן, שֶׁהַבִּנְיָן אָרוֹךְ לְכָאן וּלְכָאן, וְאֵין הַבִּנְיָן כָּלֶה מִכָּאן וּמִכָּאן לְמִדַּת הַשַּׁעַר: חוֹקְקִין לְהַשְׁלִים. הוֹאִיל וּגְובַהּ שְׁלֹשָׁה יֵשׁ הֶכְשֵׁר רוֹחַב פֶּתַח – רוֹאִין שִׁבְעָה הָעֶלְיוֹנִים כְּאִילּוּ הֵן חֲקוּקִין מִכִּפְנִים, וּרְחָבִים לְמִדַּת הָרַגְלַיִם: **מתני'** עַל מָבוֹי שֶׁהוּא פָּחוֹת מֵאַרְבַּע אַמּוֹת. רוֹחַב פִּתְחוֹ: **גמ'** כְּמַאן דְּלָא כַּחֲנַנְיָה כו'. דְּקָא סָלְקָא דַּעְתֵּיהּ דְּהָכִי קָאָמַר: הֶכְשֵׁר מָבוֹי מְפוּלָּשׁ, ב"ש אוֹמְרִים כו': ד' מְחִיצוֹת דְּאוֹרָיְיתָא. הֲלָכָה לְמֹשֶׁה מִסִּינַי הִיא בִּמְחִיצוֹת, דִּבְצִיר מד' מְחִיצוֹת לָא הָוֵי רְשׁוּת הַיָּחִיד. מִשּׁוּם הָכִי בָּעֵי לֶחִי וְקוֹרָה, דְּתֶיהֱוֵי מְחִיצָה מַעַלְיָיתָא: לִזְרוֹק. מֵרה"ר לְתוֹכוֹ, מִשָּׁלֹשׁ הוּא דְּמִיחַיַּיב. דְּשָׁלֹשׁ מְחִיצוֹת דְּאוֹרָיְיתָא לְשַׁוּוּיֵהּ רה"י, אֲבָל לְטַלְטֵל בְּתוֹכוֹ – גְּזוּר רַבָּנַן עַד דְּאִיכָּא אַרְבַּע: לְאוֹבְלִין

כיפה

יש לחוק רגלים

אין לחוק רגלים

תוספות

הכא ביתר מעשר. והשתא לא צריכי לשנויי לריש לקיש הא דידיה הא דרביה.

כי פליגי בשיש ברגליה שלשה וגבוהה עשרה. והא דאמרינן בפרק קמא דשבת (ד' ז:): זרק למעלה מי' והלכה ונחה בחור כל שהוא – באנו למחלוקת ר' מאיר ורבנן דפליגי בחוקקין להשלים. אומר ר"י: דמיירי בחורין שדרכן לעשות בשעת בנין, שמפולשין לרשות הרבים ולצד רשות היחיד רחבין ארבעה על ארבעה, דבענין אחר לא הוה אמרינן לרבי מאיר חוקקין כדמשמע הכא: בפסי

רבינו חננאל

וכיון דאסיקנא דבפתח מן הצד פליגי אמרי איני והאמר ר"ל משום ר' יהודה בן חנינא פיאה מותרת לענין כלאים אבל לא לשבת. ור' יוחנן אמר כשם שאינן מחיצות לשבת כך אינן מחיצות לכלאים. בשלמא ר"ל לא קשיא הא דידיה הא דרביה אלא ר' יוחנן קשיא. ופריק ר' יוחנן הכא אמר לכלאים והכא אמר אפילו לכלאים אינה מותרת בשלמא אי אמרת הכא דקאמר מותרת לכלאים בשעשה צורת הפתח על גבן והכא עשה מן הצד לפיכך זה שעל גבן מותרת וזה שמן הצד אינה מותרת. אלא אי אמרת אידי ואידי מן הצד קשיא. ושנינן לעולם תרוייהו מן הצד והא דאמר [המחרת לכלאים] בפתח שהוא בעשר. והא דאמר אינה מותרת ביותר מעשר. והיינו דא"ל ר' יוחנן לר"ל לא כך היה המעשה שהלך ר' יהושע בן קרחה אצל ר' יוחנן בן נורי ללמוד תורה אע"פ שהיה בקי בהלכות כלאים ומצאו יושב בין האילנות כו' ואסיקנא אלא לאו מן הצד וש"מ עשר מותר יותר מי' אסור. ירושלמי (בפירקין הל"ט) ר"ל בשם רבי יהודה בן חנינא פיאה נעץ ד' קנים בד' זויות הכרם וקשר גמי מלמעלה מציל משום פיאה. א"ר יוחנן כמחיצות שבת כך מחיצות כלאים. א"ר יוחנן מעשה שהלך ר' יהושע בן קרחה אצל ר' יוחנן בן נורי והראהו שדה אחת (תוותחה) [ובית הבירה] היתה נקראת והיו שם פרצות יותר מעשר והיה נוטל עצים וסותם בהן הדוקרין וסותם עד שמעמעט פחות מעשר. אמר כזו כך מחיצות שבת ואסיקנא א"ר אבהו כל אילין מיליא לענין מיסב ומיתן הא להורות אסירי. תניא היו שם קנין דוקרנין פי' נעוצין ועשה להן פיאה מלמעלה אפי' ביתר מעשר מותר: גופא אמר רב חסדא צורת הפתח שעשאה מן הצד פי' בלא תקרה ולא משקוף אלא מזוזות בלבד לא עשה כלום

ויש שמפרש פתחא מן הצד כגון קנה עומד כנגד הקונדס הנעוץ בזווית ונתן קנה על גביהן צדו אחד על הקנה וצדו אחד על הקונדס שנמצא כצורת פירצה ולא כצורת פתח שהרי לא עשה לה מזוזות אלא הקונדס נתן במקום מזוזות: תנא קנה מיכן וקנה מיכן וקנה על גביהן ואמר רב חסדא צריכה שתהא בריאה כדי לקבל דלת ואפי' של קשין. וא"ר ינאי צריכה היכר ציר והיא (אבקתין) [אבקתא] פי' ידות כדמתרגמינן שתי ידות תרתין צירין וכתיב הדלת תסוב על צירה והוא החלל החקוק על המשקוף להכניס בו ציר הדלת כדגרסינן (במכות כג) בענין הרצועה שמלקין בה. אלא אמר רבא אבקתא אית בה. פי' נקבין שמקויצין בהן הרצועה כי בעו מרפו בה מפקי לה. וכי בעו (מלקט) [מיקטר] בה לפום גבראי: איבעיא להו צריכין ליגע או לא. פי' הקנים העשויין במזוזות צריכין ליגע בקנה שעל גביהן הנתון במשקוף או כיון שהקנים הללו הוו י' טפחים ולמעלה והקנה שהוא במשקוף אינן נוגעין בו אלא הוא [מונח] על אחרים גבוהין מאלו והם מופרדין זה מזה יותר מד' אמות או קרובים פחות מד' טפחים מאי אמר רב נחמן אין צריכין ליגע. עבד רב נחמן עובדא שעשה צורת הפתח שלא היו מגיעין ב' הקנים העשויין כמזוזות על הקנה העליון העשוי במשקוף. ואמר רב ששת לגדא שמעי' (זו) [זיל] שדינהו ושדנהו חבשוה עבדי דרב נחמן לגדא. קם רב ששת אאבבא ואמר ליה גדא פוק ושבקוה ונפק. אשכח רב ששת לרבה בר שמואל א"ל תני מר משנה בצורת הפתח. אין תנינא כיפה ר"מ מחייב במזוזה וחכמים פוטרין ושוין שאם יש ברגליה עשרה טפחים שחייבת. הנה כיפה זו כגון שיש ברגליה י' טפחים ומשם ולמעלה עוקם הבנין כמו קשת ועולה והאבנים (שבשאי) [שבראשי] כיפה אע"פ כי אינן מגיעות לרגליה שהן המזוזות נקרא פתח ושער לדברי הכל חייבת במזוזה (וחכמים פוטרין ושוין שאם יש) שמעינן מינה שאע"פ שאינן מגיעות המזוזות למשקוף שער מעליא הוא כרב נחמן. א"ל רב ששת אי משכחת להו לאלו שחלקו עלי לא תימא להו הא מתניתא. כלומר אני אחזור בי מעצמי. אמר אביי הכל מודים אם כיפה זו רחבה ד' טפחים ואין ברגליה ג' ולא כלום היא דכל פחות מג' כלבוד דמי. (ואפילו סבר ליכא). וכן יש ברגליה ג' ואינה רחבה ד' ולא כלום היא דכל פחות מד' לא הוי מקום. כי פליגי דיש ברגליה ג' ורחבה ד' ואין גבוה עשרה ויש בה לחוק ולהשלימה לעשרה. ר' מאיר סבר הואיל ויש בה לחוק ולהשלימה לעשרה רואין אותו כאלו הוא חקוק ויש בה ברגליה עשרה וחייבת במזוזה כי פתח מעליא הוא. ורבנן סברי הואיל ואינו חקוק לא אמרינן רואין כאילו הוא חקוק השתא מיהא אין ברגליה עשרה: פיסקא הכשר מבוי ב"ש אומרים לחי וקורה כו'. ואמרינן מתניתין דקא תני לחי וקורה. ובה"א או לחי או קורה קס"ד דמתניתין במבוי מפולש לרה"ר לפיכך אמרינן כמאן כת"ק דברייתא דקתני עושה צורת פתח מיכן ולחי או קורה מיכן ולא כחנניה דתני לב"ש דתניא דלת מיכן ולב"ה דלת מיכן ולחי או קורה מיכן. ופרקינן א"ר יהודה הכי קאמר הכשר מבוי סתום בג' רוחותיה כיצד מערבין בו בש"א לחי וקורה ובה"א או לחי או קורה כו' דייקינן מדקתני במתני' הכשר מבוי דמשמע בו בש"א לחי וקורה הויא לה מחיצה רביעית כדתנן ועוד א"ר יהודה מערבין למבוי המפולש כו' ואמר רבה התם לא תימא טעמא משום דסבר ב' מחיצות דאורייתא אלא משום דסבר פי תקרה יורד וסותם ולחי משום היכר. הלכך לב"ש ליתא לרה"י שמותר לטלטל בה עד דאיכא ד' מחיצות אבל ג' מבוי הוא ואע"פ שאין מטלטלין בו שאינה רה"י גמורה כרה"י דמי ואסור לזרוק מתוכו לרה"ר או מרה"ר לתוכו: ולב"ה ג' מחיצות דאורייתא לטלטל וכשם שלחי משום היכר כך קורה משום היכר ובשתי מחיצות נמי מבוי הוא מיהו לזרוק בו מרה"ר אסור כדאמרינן דהוא כרה"י ולטלטל בו עד שיהו ג' ובדרבנן חצרות של רבים ומבואות שאינן מפולשין בין ערבו בין לא ערבו הזורק בתוכו חייב. ר' אליעזר אומר לחיין וקורה קאמר ולב"ש חולק או לב"ה חולק ולחיים בלא קורה קאמר ולא אפשטא בהדיא. א"ר

[לקמן עז. תוספ' כלאים פ"ד]
[מנחות לג.]
יומא יא:
[יומא שם שבת ז: ק. לקמן לג: קא.]
שבת קיז. לעיל ב:
[תוספתא פ"א]

הגהות הב"ח

(א) גמ' אי משכחת להו לבי ריש גלותא לא תימא להו ולא מידי:

גליון הש"ס

גמ' נפק ואתא. אשכחי' רב ששת כעין זה לקמן דף לט ע"ב וכב"ק דף לא ע"ב:

לאובלין ומצאו שיושב במבוי שאין לו אלא לחי אחד. אמר לו: בני, עשה לחי אחר. אמר לו: וכי לסותמו אני צריך?! א"ל: יסתם, ומה בכך. אמר רשב"ג: לא נחלקו ב"ש וב"ה על מבוי שהוא פחות מארבע אמות שאינו צריך כלום, על מה נחלקו – על רחב מארבע אמות ועד עשר; שב"ש אומרים: לחי וקורה, וב"ה אומרים: או לחי או קורה. קתני מיהת: "וכי לסותמו אני צריך", אי אמרת בשלמא לחיין וקורה – משום הכי אמר: "וכי לסותמו אני צריך", אלא אי אמרת לחיין בלא קורה – מאי "לסותמו"? הכי קאמר: וכי לסותמו בלחיין אני צריך. אמר מר, אמר רבן שמעון בן גמליאל: לא נחלקו ב"ש וב"ה על מבוי שפחות מארבע אמות שאינו צריך כלום. והא אנן תנן, משום רבי ישמעאל אמר תלמיד אחד לפני ר"ע: לא נחלקו ב"ש וב"ה על מבוי שהוא פחות מארבע אמות, שהוא ניתר או בלחי או בקורה! אמר רב אשי, הכי קאמר: אינו צריך לחי וקורה כב"ש, ולא לחיין כר' אליעזר, אלא או לחי או קורה כבית הלל. וכמה? אמר *רב אחלי, ואיתימא רב יחיאל: [א]עד ארבעה. אמר רב ששת, אמר רב ירמיה בר אבא, אמר רב: מודים חכמים לרבי אליעזר בפסי חצר. ורב נחמן אמר: הלכה כר' אליעזר בפסי חצר. [°]אמר רב נחמן בר יצחק: מאן מודים – ר'. *הלכה מכלל דפליגי, [מאן פליג עליה –] רבנן. דתניא: *חצר ניתרת בפס אחד. רבי אומר: בשני פסין. אמר רבי אסי, אמר רבי יוחנן: חצר צריכה שני פסין. אמר ליה רבי זירא לרבי אסי: מי אמר רבי יוחנן הכי? והא אתה הוא דאמרת משמיה דר' יוחנן: פסי חצר צריכין שיהא בהן ד'! וכי תימא ארבעה מכאן וארבעה מכאן – והתני *רב אדא בר אבימי קמיה דרבי חנינא, ואמרי לה קמיה דר' חנינא בר פפי: קטנה – בעשר, וגדולה – באחת עשרה! כי סליק רבי *זירא מימי, פרשה: [ב]ברוח אחת – בארבעה, משתי רוחות – משהו לכאן ומשהו לכאן. והדתני(א) אדא בר אבימי – רבי היא, וסבר לה כרבי יוסי. אמר רב יוסף, אמר רב יהודה, אמר שמואל: חצר ניתרת בפס אחד. אמר ליה אביי לרב יוסף: מי אמר שמואל הכי? והא אמר ליה שמואל לרב חנניה בר שילא: את לא תעביד עובדא אלא או ברוב דופן או בשני פסין! אמר ליה: ואנא לא ידענא, דעובדא הוה (ב)בדורה דרעותא, לשון ים הנכנס לחצר הוה, ואתא לקמיה דרב יהודה ולא אצרכיה אלא פס אחד. אמר ליה: לשון ים קאמרת – קל הוא שהקלו חכמים במים. *כדבעא מיניה רבי טבלא מרב: מחיצה תלויה, מהו שתתיר בחורבה? אמר ליה: [ג]אין מחיצה תלויה מתרת אלא במים, קל הוא שהקלו חכמים במים, מכל מקום קשיא! כי אתו רב פפא ורב הונא בריה דרב יהושע מבי רב, פירשוה: מרוח אחת – בארבעה, משתי רוחות – משהו לכאן ומשהו לכאן. אמר רב פפא: אי קשיא לי – הא קשיא לי; דאמר ליה שמואל לרב חנניה בר שילא: את לא תעביד עובדא אלא או ברוב דופן או בשני פסין. למה לי רוב דופן? בפס ארבעה סגי! וכי תימא מאי ברוב דופן – בדופן שבעה, דבארבעה הוה ליה רוב דופן. למה לי ארבעה? בשלשה ומשהו סגי! דהא אמר רב אחלי, ואיתימא רב יחיאל: עד ארבעה! איבעית אימא: כאן – בחצר, כאן במבוי. ואיבעית אימא: דרב אחלי גופיה תנאי היא. תנו רבנן: [ד]לשון ים הנכנס לחצר – אין ממלאין הימנו בשבת אלא אם כן יש לו מחיצה גבוה י' טפחים. בד"א – שפירצתו ביותר מעשרה, אבל עשרה – אין צריך כלום. ממלא הוא דלא ממלאינן, הא טלטולי – מטלטלינן. והא נפרצה חצר במלואה למקום האסור לה!

הכא

רש"י

לאובלין. מקום: הכי קאמר אינו צריך(ג) לא לחי ולא קורה כו'. והאי כלום דקאמר – אהנך תוספת דמוספי בית שמאי ורבי אליעזר אדבית הלל קאי: וכמה. יהא פחות רוחבו מארבע אמות, ויהא צריך תיקון: עד ארבעה. טפחים, אפילו אינו רחב אלא אמה או חמשה או ארבעה טפחים – צריך לחי, אבל בפחות מארבעה – אינו צריך כלום: בפסי חצר. אם נפרצה למקום האסור לה, צריכה שיור משני לידיה: מאן מודים. דקאמר ר' ירמיה – רבי. ומאי הלכתא דקאמר רב נחמן, דמשמע מכלל דפליגי אף בפסי חצר: מאן פליג עליה רבנן. בני מחלוקתו של רבי: וגדולה באחת עשרה. דליכא אלא שלשה מכאן ושלשה מכאן, וקתני "גדולה מותרת": מימי. עלה מן הים: רבי היא וסבר לה כר' יוסי. דאמר: *לחי רחב שלשה טפחים בעי. ורבי יוחנן אליבא דרבנן קאמר, דפס דקאמרי רבנן – ארבעה טפחים הוא, ובשני רוחות סגי בשני משהויין: לשון ים שנכנס לחצר הוה. ופרצו הדופן במלואו: ולא אצרכוה אלא פס אחד. בראש הכותל, ומותר למלאות מן המים לפנים ממקום המחיצה. ולא אמרינן: קא ממלא מכרמלית לרשות היחיד: שהקילו חכמים במים. למלאות מהן ע"י תיקון כל שהוא: כדבעא מיניה כו'. אלמא: יש להקל במים [מה] שאין [כן] במקום אחר. להכי נקט חורבה – דדרכה להיות שם מחיצות תלויות: אלא במים. כגון גזוזטרא שהיא למעלה מן הים, בפרק "כיצד משתתפין" (לקמן ד' פז:). מכל מקום. דשמואל אדשמואל קשיא: פירשוה. לדשמואל האי דקאמר בפס אחד – היינו ארבעה טפחים, והאי דקאמר שני פסים – בקטנים כל דהו: בשלשה ומשהו סגי. דאימעיט מארבעה, ותו לא בעי מידי: דהא אמר רב אחלאי. לעיל, דפחות מארבעה לא צריך כלום: כאן בחצר. חצר מרובע, או רחבו יותר מארכו. אע"ג דאימעיט מארבעה – לא סגי בהכי: מבוי. ארכו יותר על רחבו: דרב אחלאי תנאי היא. לקמן(ז) מפרש להו. וליכא למיקם עלה דמילתא, הילכך בעינן רוב הדופן עומד: שנכנס לחצר. דרך פירצת הכותל. וכשלא נפרץ במלואו עסקינן, מדמפליג בעשרה ליותר מעשרה: אלא אם כן. עשו מחיצה לגדור פירצת כותל החצר עד עשרה: אבל עשרה אין צריך כלום. שהרי יש שיור מכאן ומכאן: מימלא הוא דלא ממלאינן. משום דמטלטל מכרמלית לרשות היחיד: הא טלטולי מטלטלינן. בהאי חצר: במלואה. לאו דווקא, אלא כל יותר מעשרה קרי ליה "מלואה":

דאית

תוספות

בפסי חצר. וקשה: דגבי מבוי נקט לשון לחי, וגבי חצר נקט לשון פס בכולה שמעתא, אף על גב דשניהם משהו.

ורב נחמן אמר הלכה כר' אליעזר בפסי חצר. והא דלא קאמר הלכה כרבי בפסי חצר דהא סבר כרבי אליעזר, כדקאמרינן: ומודים חכמים, היינו רבי, לר' אליעזר, והוה ניחא טפי דאיהו איירי בחצר – אלא*: דניחא ליה למנקט ר' אליעזר, שנזכר במשנתנו. וצריך לומר דרבי ורבנן בחצר מרובעת פליגי, דלרבנן סגי להו בפס משהו ולרבי צריך שני פסין של שני משהויין. דאי בארוכה יתר על רחבה פליגי – קשיא דרב נחמן אדרב נחמן – דהכא פסיק כרבי, ובסוף שמעתא קאמר רב נחמן: נקיטינן דחצר שארוכה יתר על רחבה – ניתרת בלחי משהו. אלא ודאי במרובע פליגי, וצריך שני פסין של שני משהויין, או בפס אחד של ארבעה. כדאמר רב נחמן בסוף שמעתא, דחצר מרובעת ניתרת בפס ארבעה. ודלא כפירוש הקונטרס, שפירש בסמוך: מרוח אחת – בד', משתי רוחות – משהו לכאן ומשהו לכאן. דהוי כרבנן, דלרבנן סגי בפס אחד ומשהו, כדפירשנו. אלא כרבי אתי, דהכי הילכתא:

וכי תימא בדופן שבעה דבארבעה הוי רוב דופן. והשתא, אי נקט ארבעה – לא הוי משמיענו חדוש יותר מברוב דופן. דאדרבה, השתא דנקט ברוב דופן – הוי רבותא טפי, דאע"ג דלא הוי ארבעה – סגי. הואיל ואיכא רוב דופן למה לי ארבעה. פירוש: למה אטעיה – להצריך ארבעה, בשלשה ומשהו סגי! דהשתא לא הוי צריך אפילו רוב דופן, כיון שנתמעט האויר מארבעה. ויש ספרים דגרסי: למה לי רוב דופן? ולפי זה אתי שפיר בפשיטות*. ואית ספרים דלא גרסי "רוב דופן" אלא "למה לי בתלתא ומשהו סגי" והיא היא:

הכא

עין משפט נר מצוה

סה א מיי' פי"ז מהלכות שבת הלכה ט סמג עשין דרבנן א טור ש"ע א"ח סי' שסג סעיף כח:

סו ב מיי' פט"ו מהלכות שבת הלכה יב סמג שם טוש"ע א"ח סי' שסג סעיף ב:

או שמא משום דאדא בר אבימי צריך לר' רחבים (ד') [ג'] ומודים חכמים דקאמר היינו שצריך ב' [ת"י]

סז ג מיי' שם הלכה יג וסמג שם טוש"ע א"ח סי' שנה סעיף ג:

סח ד מיי' שם הלכה יא וסמג שם טוש"ע א"ח סי' שנו סעיף ב:

[לקמן יג.]

ואם היינו גורסי' בצ"ר מארבעה סגי הוי א"ש טובא אך לא נמצא בשום ספר

[גירס' הערוך בערך ימי ר' אבא]

מסורת הש"ס

[לקמן יז:]

שבת קו: וש"נ]

לעיל י:

[ב"ב סו:]

שבת קא. לקמן טז: מח. פו:

הגהות הב"ח

(א) גמ' והא דתני רב אדא בר אבימי: (ב) שם לעובדא הוה בדורא דרעותא (ג) רש"י ד"ה הכי קאמר אינו צריך לחי וקורה כצ"ל ותיבת לא נמחק: (ד) ד"ה דרב אחלי וכו' לקמן. נ"ב ברים דף יג:

גליון הש"ס

גמ' א"ר נחמן בר יצחק מאן מודים. עי' גיטין דף לא ע"ב תד"ה אנא ל"ל. ולקמן דף מג ע"ב תד"ה יתיב ולקמן דף יח ע"ב תד"ה מתקיף:

רב נסים גאון

והאי דתני אדא בר אבימי רבי היא וסבר לה כר' יוסי הוא שאמר ר' יוסי במשנה (דף יז) בשביל הלחיים רחבן ג' שכבר פירשנוהו:

רבינו חננאל

א"ר שמעון בן גמליאל לא נחלקו ב"ש וב"ה על מבוי שהוא פחות מד' אמות שאין צריך כלום. איני והא תנן משום ר' ישמעאל אמר תלמיד אחד לא נחלקו ב"ש וב"ה על פחות מד' אמות שהוא (או) [ניתר] בלחי או בקורה. ופריק רב אשי דרשב"ג הכי קתני אינו צריך לחיים כר' אליעזר ולא לחי וקורה כב"ש אלא או לחי או קורה כב"ה. למטה עד כמה אהלי ואיתימא רב (יהואל) [אהלי] עד ארבעה. פי' מבוי שהוא רחב מארבע אמות ולמעלה צריך לחי וקורה עד עשר אמות אבל למטה מד' אמות עד ד' טפחים צריך לחי או קורה אבל אם פתחו של מבוי רחבו מארבעה טפחים ולמטה אין צריך לא לחי ולא קורה אלא מותר בולא כלום. סוגיין דכי היכי דמצריך ר' אליעזר במבוי לחיים הכי נמי מצריך לחצר שני פסין ואמר רב נחמן בר יצחק מאן מודים רבי ומאן חולקין עליו רבנן. דתניא חצר ניתרת בפס אחד. רבי אומר בב' פסין א"ר אסי א"ר יוחנן חצר צריכה ב' פסין ואסיקנא שני פסין בב' רוחות משהו לכאן ומשהו לכאן. מצד אחד צריך פס ארבעה. והא דתני איבומי חצר קטנה בעשר גדולה בי"א איקימנא לר' דמצריך ב' פסין וסבר לה כר' יוסי דאמר לחיים שאמרו רחבן ג' טפחים שצריך לחי ג' מיכן ולחי ג' מיכן הרי אמה שעודפת הגדולה על הקטנה. הא דאמר שמואל חצר מותרת בפס אחד. אסיקנא עובדא הוה בדורא דרעותא בלשון ים שנכנס לחצר ולא אצרכה רב יהודה אלא פס אחד משום קל הוא שהקילו חכמים במים. אמר רב פפא קשיא לי הא דא"ל שמואל לרב חנניה בר שילא את לא תעביד עובדא. אלא או ברוב דופן או בב' פסין. למה לן רוב דופן פס ארבעה סגיא. וכי תימא הכא בחצר שהיא שבעה עסקינן ועבד ארבעה ושבק תלתא הא עביד תלתא *) ושבק ד' לא. והאמר אהלי ואי תימא רב אהלי. במבוי אבל בחצר לא: ת"ר לשון ים שנכנס לחצר אין ממלאין הימנה בשבת אא"כ עשו לה מחיצה גבוהה עשרה טפחים. בד"א ביותר מעשר אבל בעשר אין צריך כלום. ומקשינן

*) [ומשהו ושבק פחות ד' לא. כ"ה לפי הנוסחא בגמ' שלפנינו]

הכא במאי עסקינן דאית ליה גידודי.§ אמר רב יהודה: מבוי שלא נשתתפו בו, הכשירו בלחי – הזורק לתוכו חייב, הכשירו בקורה – הזורק לתוכו פטור. מתקיף לה רב ששת: טעמא דלא נשתתפו בו, הא נשתתפו בו – אפילו הכשירו בקורה נמי חייב. וכי כבר זו עשה אותו רשות היחיד או רשות הרבים? והתניא: חצירות של רבים ומבואות שאינן מפולשין, בין עירבו ובין לא עירבו – הזורק לתוכן חייב! אלא אי איתמר – הכי איתמר, אמר רב יהודה: מבוי שאינו ראוי לשיתוף, [א]הכשירו בלחי – הזורק לתוכו חייב. הכשירו בקורה – הזורק לתוכו פטור. אלמא קסבר: *לחי משום מחיצה, וקורה משום היכר. וכן אמר רבה: לחי משום מחיצה *וקורה משום היכר. ורבא אמר: אחד זה ואחד זה משום היכר. איתיביה רבי יעקב בר אבא לרבא: הזורק למבוי, יש לו לחי – חייב, אין לו לחי – פטור! הכי קאמר: אינו צריך אלא לחי, הזורק לתוכו – חייב, לחי ודבר אחר – הזורק לתוכו פטור. איתיביה: *יתר על כן אמר רבי יהודה: מי שיש לו שני בתים בשני צידי רשות הרבים עושה לחי מכאן ולחי מכאן, או קורה מכאן וקורה מכאן, ונושא ונותן באמצע. אמרו לו: אין מערבין רשות הרבים בכך! התם קסבר רבי יהודה: שתי מחיצות דאורייתא. אמר רב יהודה, אמר רב: מבוי שארכו כרחבו אינו ניתר בלחי משהו. אמר רב חייא בר אשי, אמר רב: מבוי שארכו כרחבו אינו ניתר בקורה טפח. אמר רבי זירא: כמה מכוונן שמעתא דסבי; כיון דארכו כרחבו – הוה ליה חצר, וחצר אינה ניתרת בלחי וקורה אלא בפס ארבעה. אמר רבי זירא: אי קשיא לי – הא קשיא לי, ליהוי האי לחי כפס משהו ונשתרי! אישתמיטתיה הא דאמר ר' אסי אמר ר' יוחנן: פסי חצר צריכין שיהא בהן ארבעה. *אמר רב נחמן: [ב]נקטינן, איזהו מבוי שניתר בלחי וקורה – כל שארכו יתר על רחבו, *ובתים וחצרות פתוחים לתוכו. [ג]ואיזו היא חצר שאינה ניתרת בלחי וקורה אלא בפס ארבעה – כל שמרובעת. מרובעת – אין, עגולה – לא?! הכי קאמר: אי ארכה יתר על רחבה – הוה ליה מבוי, ומבוי בלחי וקורה סגיא, ואי לא – הוה לה חצר. וכמה? סבר שמואל למימר: עד דאיכא פי שנים ברחבה. אמר ליה רב, הכי אמר חביבי: אפילו משהו.§ "משום רבי ישמעאל אמר תלמיד אחד כו'".§

ר"ע

רש"י

דאית ליה גידודי. מה שנשאר מן הפרצה בגובה עשרה אבל הים כיסהו: הכשירו בלחי. תיקנו בלחי: הזורק לתוכו. מרשות הרבים: חייב. דקסבר: לחי משום מחיצה: הכשירו בקורה הזורק לתוכו פטור. דקורה משום היכר. וקסבר: ארבעה מחיצות דאורייתא, בין לקולא בין לחומרא: חצירות של רבים. שפתוחין בתים הרבה לחצר, ואוסרים בני הבתים זה על זה, שאין יכולין להוציא מן הבתים לחצר בלא עירוב – מפני שהבית רשות מיוחדת לו, וחצר רשות חבירו מושל בה. ונמצא מוציא מרשות לרשות. ורבנן גזור שלא להוציא מרשות היחיד לרשות היחיד – גזירה דילמא אתי לאפוקי מרשות היחיד לרשות הרבים. אבל בחצר – מותר לטלטל בה, כדאמרינן במסכת שבת בפ' "רבי אליעזר אומר אם לא הביא כלי כו'" (דף קל:): שאינו ראוי לשיתוף. מפולש: לחי משום מחיצה. וקסבר: שלש מחיצות דאורייתא: הזורק למבוי כו'. אלמא: לחי משום מחיצה: אינו צריך אלא לחי. שאינו מפולש: חייב. ואע"ג דלית ליה לחי, דשלש מחיצות דאורייתא: לחי ודבר אחר. נורת הפתח כתורת מפולש: הזורק לתוכו פטור. ואע"ג דעבד לחי: יתר על כן. לעיל מיניה איירי, בבונה עלייה על גבי שני בתים בפ' "כל גגות" (לקמן פה.): לחי מכאן כו'. אלמא: לחי משום מחיצה. ואפילו רבנן לא פליגי עליה אלא ברשות הרבים, אבל במבוי מפולש – לא: שתי מחיצות. של שני בתים, לבד הלחיים. והלחיים דקא מצריך ר' יהודה – משום היכר בעלמא: בלחי משהו. אלא בפס ארבעה, כחצר: בקורה טפח. כשאר מבוי. ומר אמר חדא, ומר אמר חדא, ולא פליגי: כמה מכוונין. לסייען הוא בא: ובתים וחצירות. שתי חצירות פתוחות לתוכו, ובית פתוח לכל חצר שכן היו דירותיהן: לפני כל בית היה חצר: עגולה לא. בתמיה: משום דעגולה היא משתריא בלחי משהו: ואי לא הויא לה חצר. ובעיא פס. והאי מרובעת – לאו למעוטי עגולה אתא, אלא למעוטי ארכה יתר על רחבה: וכמה. יהא אורכה יותר, דנפקא לה מדין חצר ומשתריא בלחי משהו: עד דאיכא פי שנים. הואיל וחצר היתה לא נפקא מדינא עד דאיכא פי שנים: חביבי. ר' חייא, שהוא אחי אביו ואמו של רב:

רבי

תוספות

הכא במאי עסקינן דאית ליה גידודי. פירש רש"י: אבל הים כיסהו. וקשיא: דמכל מקום מאי שנא דלענין טלטול חשיבי מחילות, ולענין מילוי לא חשיבי? וי"ל דהכי פירושו: מילוי הוא דלא ממלינן – פירוש דאסור לטלטל[א] מבית לחצר. ונקט מילוי – משום דעיקר תשמיש מחצר לבית הוא המילוי. אבל טלטולי הוא דמטלטלין בחצר. ואמאי – כו'. ומשני: דאית ליה גידודי, וניכרת מחילה לבני חצר, ולבני בית שהם רחוקים – אינה ניכרת, ועבידי מיא ומשום הכי אסור. וקשה: דבפרק "כילד משתתפין" (לקמן ד' פו.) משמע דאתי שפיר דלא בעינן שיראו ראשי קנים, אי לאו משום דרב יהודה קפיד אערובי מיא. והשתא, הך ברייתא נמי סברה הכי! ויש לומר: דהוה מצי למימר וליטעמיך. וריב"ן מפרש: דמיירי בחצר שנפרצה מערב שבת, והמים באו בשבת. וקאמר, הכא במאי עסקינן – דאית ליה גידודי, ולהכי מטלטלין: דשבת הואיל והותרה הותרה, אע"ג דהשתא אין המחילות ניכרות. אבל למלאות מן המים שבאו בשבת – לא שייך הואיל והותרה הותרה. ורשב"ס ור"ת פירשו: דאית ליה גידודי – [שיש גדודים] גבוהים עשרה ליס[ב] בתוך החצר, ולכך מטלטלין בחצר. אבל למלאות מן המים – אסור, דמקום המים נפרץ במלואו ליס, והים הוי כרמלית. [ג]ואין לחוש שמא יעלה הים שרטון – שגדודים גבוהים יותר, או שהם רחוקים משפת הים ביותר הרבה. והשר מקוצי מפרש, דהכי פירושו: מילוי הוא דלא ממלינן – הוא הדין טלטול, ונקט מילוי – משום דקתני בברייתא "אין ממלאים". אבל טלטולי מטלטלינן – אם הלכו להם המים, ואמאי וכו', דאית ליה גידודי ולהכי שרי בשאין המים, אבל כשיש המים ומחילה אינה ניכרת ועבידי מיא – אסור. וא"ת: ואמאי אסור הכא למלאות? והא קתני בתוספתא (פ"ו): גזוזטרא שהיא למעלה מן המים – אין ממלאים הימנה בשבת, אלא אם כן עשה מחילה גבוה עשרה למטה מן המים, ואע"פ שהמים לפין על גבה. אלמא: אף על גב דאין מחילה ניכרת ממלאין הימנה. ושמא יש לומר: דהתם שהמחילות עשויות לשם מים – עדיפי מגידודי דהכא. ורילב"א פירש כרש"י: דאית ליה גידודי, אבל הים כסהו, ולהכי לא ממלינן דילמא אזיל דלי לאידך גיסא חוץ לחצר. וטעמא דעבידי מיא – אין אסור אלא משום דילמא אזיל דלי לאידך גיסא, ולא משום דאין המחילות ניכרות. ובעשר דהוי כפתח – לא חיישינן, דאיכא היכרא. אבל טלטולי מטלטלינן אע"ג דאין מחילות ניכרות. והשתא אתי שפיר ההיא דתוספתא*:

איתיביה יתר על כן. [ד]ואפילו רבנן לא אסרי, אלא דמדרבנן בעו שלש מחילות גמורות: **כמה** מכוונים כו' אלא בפס ארבעה. אית דלא גריס "ארבעה", משום דהשתא סלקא דעתיה דרבי זירא דסגי בפס משהו. ואין לחוש, דמשום מסקנא נקט ארבעה. **להוי** כפס משהו ולישתרי. ואף על גב דרבי זירא גופיה קאמר לעיל: מרוח אחת בארבעה – לבתר הכי שמעה:

ובתים וחצירות פתוחים לתוכו. שתי חלירות למבוי, ושתי בתים לכל חצר וחצר. והכי איתא בפרק "רבי אליעזר דמילה" (שבת ד' קלא.). ואם תאמר: חצר שאינה מרובעת היכי משתרי בלחי וקורה? הא אין בתים וחלירות פתוחים לתוכה! ואין לומר לחצר דיש בה דיורין לא בעי בתים וחלירות, אבל מבוי דרחוק מדיורין, שחצר מפסיק בין הבתים למבוי – משום הכי בעינן דיורין מרובין שתי חלירות ושני בתים לכל חצר. דהא בפרק "הדר" (לקמן ד' עג:) אמר רב: אין מבוי ניתר בלחי וקורה כו', ושמואל אמר: אפילו בית אחד וחצר אחת. ופירש רש"י התם: בית אחד במבוי בלא חצר, וחצר אחת עם הבתים. וכיון דטעמיה דרב משום דיורין – רב נמי מודה, כיון דאיכא בית במבוי – אפילו ליכא שום חצר דשרי בלחי וקורה. וכפי' הקונטרס צריך לפרש, דאין לפרש בית אחד וחצר אחת – היינו בית אחד בחצר, דהא קאמר רבי יוחנן התם: אפילו חורבה. וקאמר בתר הכי: דלא חיישינן דלמא אתי לאפוקי מנא דבתים לחורבה. משמע: דלא בעי למימר חורבה שבחצר, דאם כן – ליכא בתים. אלא חורבה בלא חצר קאמר. והכי נמי לשמואל, דאמר אפילו בית אחד וחצר אחת. ונראה לפרש משום דמבוי קרוב לרה"ר יותר מחצר, בעי בתים וחלירות:

עין משפט נר מצוה

סט א מיי' פי"ז מהל' שבת הלכה ט:

ע ב מיי' שם הלכה ז וסמג שם טוש"ע א"ח סי' שסג סעיף כו:

עא ג מיי' שם הלכה ח וטוש"ע שם סעיף כז:

רבינו חננאל

ומקשינן בלשון ים דאסיר הא בחצר שרי לטלטולי והרי נפרצה החצר למקום האסור לה ושנינן בחצר דאית לה גידודי שהן כמו לחיים. אמר רב יהודה מבוי הראוי לשיתוף. פי' כגון מבוי מפולש ועשה בראשו האחת דלת ובראשו האחרת לחי או קורה לפיכך ראוי הוא עכשיו לשיתוף אם הכשירו בלחי הלחי במקום מחיצות חשוב. ונמצא בו ד' מחיצות לפיכך הזורק מרה"ר לתוכו חייב. אבל הכשירו בקורה שהיא משום היכר ואין בו אלא ב' מחיצות ודלת הזורק לתוכו פטור. וכן אמר רבה לחי משום מחיצה וקורה משום היכר. ורבא אמר אחד זה ואחד זה משום היכר ואקשינן לרבא מיהא הזורק למבוי יש לו לחי חייב. אין לו לחי פטור. מאי לאו יש לו הכשירו בלחי אין לו לחי אין הכשירו בלחי אלא בקורה. קשיא לרבא ומשני רבא הכי קתני מבוי שיש לו ג' מחיצות ואינו מחוסר אלא לחי והכשירו עכשיו בלחי חייב אבל מחוסר לחי ומחיצה פטור. (איני דמבוי) [ומבוי] שיש לו (ג) [ב] מחיצות בהכשירו בב' ראשין בלחיים או בקורות פטור והתניא יתר על כן א"ר יהודה מי שיש לו ב' בתים מב' צידי רה"ר עושה לחי מיכן ולחי מיכן כו' ומשני קסבר ר' יהודה ב' מחיצות דאורייתא. אמר רב יהודה אמר רב מבוי שארכו כרחבו אינו ניתר בלחי משהו וגם אינו ניתר בקורה מ"מ כיון שארכו כרחבו הוה ליה כחצר וחצר אינה ניתרת בלחי אלא בפס ארבעה. אמר רב נחמן נקטינן איזהו מבוי שניתר בלחי וקורה כל שארכו יתר על רחבו ובתים וחצירות פתוחין לתוכו. ואיזו היא חצר שאינה ניתרת בלחי וקורה כל שמרובעת ואפילו עגולה לאפוקי ארוכה וקטנה ואפילו ארכה יתירה על רחבה משהו: **פיסקא** משום ר' ישמעאל אומר תלמיד אחד בפני ר'

רב נסים גאון

אמר ליה רב הכי אמר חביבי. ותמצא בירורו בפרק אור לארבעה עשר בתחילת מסכת פסחים (דף ד) רב בר אחוה דר' חייא ובר אחתיה הוא ובבבא בתרא בפר' חזקת הבתים (דף מח) תמצא ג"כ ההוא גברא דהוה דר בקשתא בעליתא אתא לקמיה דר' חייא אמר ליה אי אית לך סהדי דדר בה איהו מיקמך אפי' חד יומא מוקימנא לה בידך ואי לא לא אנא רב הוה יתיבנא קמיה דחביבי: תלמיד

מסורת הש"ס

וא"ת והיכא ס"ד דלחי משום מחיצה הא אגמריה רחמנא למשה לא תפרוץ רובה ושמא במחיצה ג' או ד' לא אגמריה [תו"י]

שבת ו. קיז. לעיל ו. לקמן כב. נט: נה.

לעיל ה.

[שבת קלה. וש"נ]

הגהות הב"ח

(א) תוס' ד"ה הכא וכו' פירוש דאסור לטלטל מבית לחצר ונקט מילוי: (ב) בא"ד גבוהים עשרה ליס בתוך החצר וכו': (ג) בא"ד ואין לחוש. נ"ב עיין בדף ח ע"ב: (ד) ד"ה איתיביה וכו' רבנן לא אמרי' אלא:

*) ולפע"ג דהכא לאמר דביש אין צריך לנקט כלום והתם כענין אפילו בית שירלו ראשי קנים התם משום דנראה כממלאה מרשות חבירו ועוד דאיכא למיחש דילמא אזיל דלי לאידך גיסא וגם נפרץ במילואו והכוסי' דתוספ' מיירי בענין דליכא למיחש דילמא אזיל דלי לאידך גיסא [מ"י]

גליון הש"ס **גמ'** אלמא קסבר לחי משום מחיצה וקורה משום היכר. עי' לעיל ח ע"ב תוד"ה מניח ולקמן דף פו ע"א תד"ה קורה: **גמ'** ורבא אמר אחד זה ואחד זה. עיין בהרא"ש פ"ק דסוכה סי' ט: **רש"י** ד"ה לחי מכאן. אלמא לחי משום מחיצה. ק"ל הא הקושי' לכ"ע דמדברי ר"י מוכח דאפילו קורה משום מחילה. ויש לדחוק דלענין קורה ברייתא דלעיל דקתני זורק לתוך מבוי יש לו לחי חייב משמע דווקא לחי ולא קורה פליג בזה עלה ר"י אבל לענין לחי לא מלינו מאן דפליג: **תד"ה** הכ"ע. משום דר"י קפיד אערובי מיא. לא זכיתי להבין דעירובי מיא שייך בבור שבין ב' חלירות דמים שבלב השני בא לכאן דרך המחילה ואסור לשאוב דשבתו בחצר חבירו ואסור להביאם לביתו. אבל הכא מה בכך דשבתו בכרמלית הא עתה שבאו תוך החצר נעשה רה"י גמורה ואינו עוקר מכרמלית. אם נבא לדון כיון דבבית לא מנכרא מחיצות הוי כליתנהו למחילה א"כ גם בלא טעמא דעירובי מיא אסור דמים שבחצר נפרצו למקום האסור לה וא"כ ענין עירובי מיא לא שייך הכא כלל וה' יאיר עיני: **תד"ה** איתיביה. ואפי' רבנן כו'. תמוה לי הא מלינו מאן דפליג על ר"י בברייתא פ"ק דשבת דף ו' זהו רה"י גמורה וכו' ואמאי קרי לה גמורה ואמרי' עלה אבל לזרוק מודו וכו' אבל לזרוק מודו קמ"ל הרי מברייתא זו מוכח או דרבנן דר"י פליגי עלה אפי' לזרוק או דעכ"פ הך ברייתא פליג עלה וכפשטא דמלתא דמכח הברייתא שמעי' דרבנן פליגי עליה אפי' לזרוק וא"כ איך כתבו ואפילו רבנן וכו' ומאי פריך הש"ס וצ"ע:

תורה אור

"ר"ע אומר: עַל זֶה וְעַל זֶה נֶחְלְקוּ כו'". § ר"ע הַיְינוּ תַּנָּא קַמָּא! אִיכָּא בֵּינַיְיהוּ *דְּרַב אַחְלַי וְאִיתֵימָא רַב יְחִיאֵל, וְלָא מְסַיְּימִי. תַּנְיָא, אָמַר ר"ע: לֹא אָמַר ר' יִשְׁמָעֵאל דָּבָר זֶה, אֶלָּא אוֹתוֹ תַּלְמִיד אָמַר דָּבָר זֶה — וַהֲלָכָה כְּאוֹתוֹ תַּלְמִיד. הָא גּוּפָהּ קַשְׁיָא: אָמְרַתְּ "לֹא א"ר יִשְׁמָעֵאל דָּבָר זֶה" — אַלְמָא לֵית הִלְכְתָא כְּוָותֵיהּ, וַהֲדַר אָמְרַתְּ "הֲלָכָה כְּאוֹתוֹ תַּלְמִיד"! אָמַר רַב יְהוּדָה, אָמַר שְׁמוּאֵל: לֹא אֲמָרָהּ ר' עֲקִיבָא אֶלָּא *לְחַדֵּד בָּהּ הַתַּלְמִידִים. וְר"נ בַּר יִצְחָק אָמַר: נִרְאִין אִיתְּמַר. א"ר יְהוֹשֻׁעַ בֶּן לֵוִי: כָּל מָקוֹם שֶׁאַתָּה מוֹצֵא מִשּׁוּם רַבִּי יִשְׁמָעֵאל אָמַר תַּלְמִיד אֶחָד לִפְנֵי ר"ע — אֵינוֹ אֶלָּא ר"מ, שֶׁשִּׁימֵּשׁ אֶת ר' יִשְׁמָעֵאל וְאֶת ר"ע. *דְּתַנְיָא, אָמַר ר"מ: כְּשֶׁהָיִיתִי אֵצֶל ר' יִשְׁמָעֵאל הָיִיתִי מַטִּיל קַנְקַנְתּוֹם לְתוֹךְ הַדְּיוֹ וְלֹא אָמַר לִי דָּבָר. כְּשֶׁבָּאתִי אֵצֶל רַבִּי עֲקִיבָא, אֲסָרָהּ עָלַי. אִינִי?! וְהָאָמַר רַב יְהוּדָה, אָמַר שְׁמוּאֵל מִשּׁוּם ר' מֵאִיר: כְּשֶׁהָיִיתִי לוֹמֵד אֵצֶל ר' עֲקִיבָא הָיִיתִי מַטִּיל קַנְקַנְתּוֹם לְתוֹךְ הַדְּיוֹ וְלֹא אָמַר לִי דָּבָר. וּכְשֶׁבָּאתִי אֵצֶל ר' יִשְׁמָעֵאל, אָמַר לִי: בְּנִי, מַה מְּלַאכְתְּךָ? אָמַרְתִּי לוֹ: לַבְלָר אֲנִי. אָמַר לִי: בְּנִי, הֱוֵי זָהִיר בִּמְלַאכְתְּךָ, שֶׁמְּלַאכְתְּךָ מְלֶאכֶת שָׁמַיִם הִיא, שֶׁמָּא אַתָּה מְחַסֵּר אוֹת אַחַת אוֹ מְיַיתֵּר אוֹת אַחַת — נִמְצֵאתָ מַחֲרִיב אֶת כָּל הָעוֹלָם כּוּלּוֹ. אָמַרְתִּי לוֹ: דָּבָר אֶחָד יֵשׁ לִי וְ'קַנְקַנְתּוֹם' שְׁמוֹ, שֶׁאֲנִי מַטִּיל לְתוֹךְ הַדְּיוֹ. אָמַר לִי: וְכִי מַטִּילִין קַנְקַנְתּוֹם לְתוֹךְ הַדְּיוֹ? וַהֲלֹא אָמְרָה תּוֹרָה *°"וְכָתַב" °"וּמָחָה" — כְּתָב שֶׁיָּכוֹל לִמְחוֹת. מַאי קא"ל, וּמַאי קָא מְהַדַּר לֵיהּ? הָכִי קא"ל: לָא מִבַּעְיָא בַּחֲסֵירוֹת וּבִיתֵירוֹת [דְּלָא טָעֵינָא] דְּבָקִי אֲנָא, *אֶלָּא אֲפִילּוּ מֵיחַשׁ לִזְבוּב נַמִי, דִּילְמָא אָתֵי וְיָתֵיב אַתָּגֵיהּ דְּדל"ת וּמָחֵיק לֵיהּ וּמְשַׁוֵּי לֵיהּ רי"ש, דָּבָר אֶחָד יֵשׁ לִי וְקַנְקַנְתּוֹם שְׁמוֹ שֶׁאֲנִי מַטִּיל לְתוֹךְ הַדְּיוֹ. קַשְׁיָא שִׁימּוּשׁ אַשִּׁימּוּשׁ, קַשְׁיָא אֲסָרָהּ אַאֲסָרָהּ! בִּשְׁלָמָא שִׁימּוּשׁ אַשִּׁימּוּשׁ לָא קַשְׁיָא; מֵעִיקָּרָא אֲתָא לְקַמֵּיהּ דְּר"ע, וּמִדְּלָא מָצֵי לְמֵיקַם אַלִּיבֵּיהּ — אֲתָא לְקַמֵּיהּ דְּרַבִּי יִשְׁמָעֵאל וּגְמַר גְּמָרָא, וַהֲדַר אֲתָא לְקַמֵּיהּ דְּר"ע וּסְבַר סְבָרָא. אֶלָּא אֲסָרָהּ אַאֲסָרָהּ קַשְׁיָא! קַשְׁיָא. תַּנְיָא רַבִּי יְהוּדָה אוֹמֵר, ר"מ הָיָה אוֹמֵר: [א]לַכֹּל מַטִּילִין קַנְקַנְתּוֹם לְתוֹךְ הַדְּיוֹ, חוּץ מִפָּרָשַׁת סוֹטָה. וְרַבִּי יַעֲקֹב אוֹמֵר מִשְּׁמוֹ: [ב]חוּץ מִפָּרָשַׁת סוֹטָה שֶׁבַּמִּקְדָּשׁ. מַאי בֵּינַיְיהוּ? אָמַר רַב יִרְמְיָה: לִמְחוֹק לָהּ מִן הַתּוֹרָה אִיכָּא בֵּינַיְיהוּ. וְהָנֵי תַּנָּאֵי כִּי הָנֵי תַּנָּאֵי; דְּתַנְיָא: [ג]אֵין מְגִילָּתָהּ כְּשֵׁירָה לְהַשְׁקוֹת בָּהּ סוֹטָה אַחֶרֶת. ר' אַחַי בַּר יֹאשִׁיָּה אָמַר: מְגִילָּתָהּ כְּשֵׁירָה לְהַשְׁקוֹת בָּהּ סוֹטָה אַחֶרֶת. אָמַר רַב פַּפָּא: דִּילְמָא לֹא הִיא; עַד כָּאן לָא קָאָמַר ת"ק הָתָם — אֶלָּא כֵּיוָן דְּאִינְתִּיק לְשׁוּם רָחֵל, תּוּ לָא הָדְרָא מִינַּתְקָא לְשׁוּם לֵאָה. *אֲבָל גַּבֵּי תּוֹרָה דִּסְתָמָא מִיכְּתְבָא — הָכִי נַמִי דִּמְחַקִּינַן. אָמַר רַב נַחְמָן בַּר יִצְחָק: דִּילְמָא לֹא הִיא; עַד כָּאן לָא קָאָמַר רַבִּי אַחַי בַּר יֹאשִׁיָּה הָתָם — אֶלָּא דְּאִיכְּתִיב מִיהַת לְשׁוּם סוֹטָה בְּעוֹלָם, אֲבָל גַּבֵּי תּוֹרָה דִּלְהִתְלַמֵּד כְּתִיבָא — הָכִי נַמִי דְּלָא מְחַקִּינַן. וְלֵית לֵיהּ לְרַבִּי אַחַי בַּר יֹאשִׁיָּה הָא דִּתְנַן: *[ד]כָּתַב [גֵּט] לְגָרֵשׁ אֶת אִשְׁתּוֹ, וְנִמְלַךְ

רש"י

רַבִּי עֲקִיבָא הַיְינוּ ת"ק. *דְּקָתָנֵי: הֶכְשֵׁר מָבוֹי ב"ש אוֹמְרִים כו' וְלָא מַפְלִיג בֵּין קָצָר לְרָחָב: דְּרַב אַחְלַי. מָבוֹי פָּחוֹת מֵאַרְבָּעָה טְפָחִים. חַד מִינַּיְיהוּ אִית לֵיהּ דְּבְאַרְבָּעָה, וּמֵאַרְבָּעָה וּלְמַעְלָה פְּלִיגִי, אֲבָל פָּחוֹת מֵאַרְבָּעָה — אֵין צָרִיךְ כְּלוּם: וְלָא מְסַיְּימִי. הֵי מִינַּיְיהוּ אִית לֵיהּ דְּרַב אַחְלַי, וְהֵי מִינַּיְיהוּ לֵית לֵיהּ לִדְרַב אַחְלַי. וְהַיְינוּ דְּאָמַר לְעֵיל: דְּרַב אַחְלַי גּוּפֵיהּ תַּנָּאֵי הִיא: לֹא רַבִּי יִשְׁמָעֵאל אָמַר דָּבָר זֶה. מוּחְזָק אֲנִי בּוֹ שֶׁהוּא חָכָם, וּמֵעוֹלָם לֹא אָמַר דָּבָר זֶה: לֹא אֲמָרָהּ רַבִּי עֲקִיבָא. לְהָאי הֲלָכָה כְּאוֹתוֹ תַּלְמִיד, אֶלָּא לְחַדֵּד אֶת הַתַּלְמִידִים שֶׁיָּשִׂימוּ לִבָּם לַתּוֹרָה וְיֹאמְרוּ פִּלְפּוּל מִלִּבָּם, לְפִיכָךְ שִׁיבְּחוֹ בִּפְנֵיהֶם: נִרְאִין אִיתְּמַר. נִרְאִין דִּבְרֵי אוֹתוֹ תַּלְמִיד: קַנְקַנְתּוֹם. = אדרימנ"ט: אֲסָרָהּ עָלַי. וּלְקַמָּן מְפָרֵשׁ: מְחַסֵּר אוֹת אַחַת. "וַה' אֱלֹהִים אֱמֶת" אִם תְּחַסֵּר אל"ף — הֲרֵי אַתָּה מַחֲרִיב. "וַיְדַבֵּר ה'" אִם תּוֹסִיף אוֹת אַחַת וְתִכְתּוֹב "וַיְדַבְּרוּ" — נִמְצֵאתָ מַחֲרִיב: דָּבָר אֶחָד יֵשׁ לִי. לְקַמָּן מְפָרֵשׁ מַאי קָמְהַדַּר לֵיהּ: כְּתָב שֶׁיָּכוֹל לִמְחוֹק. וְקַנְקַנְתּוֹס רִישּׁוּמוֹ נִיכָּר מְאֹד: מַאי קָאָמַר לֵיהּ. רַבִּי יִשְׁמָעֵאל: וּמַאי קָא מְהַדַּר לֵיהּ. רַבִּי מֵאִיר אַזְהַר לֵיהּ עַל חָסֵר וְיָתֵר, וּמְהַדַּר לֵיהּ קַנְקַנְתּוֹס יֵשׁ לִי: קַשְׁיָא שִׁימּוּשׁ אַשִּׁימּוּשׁ. דְּקָאָמַר לְעֵיל: קַמֵּיהּ רַבִּי יִשְׁמָעֵאל שִׁימֵּשׁ תְּחִילָּה, וְהָכָא תָּנֵי אִיפְּכָא: רַבִּי עֲקִיבָא הָיָה חָרִיף טוּבָא, וְלָא מָצֵי ר' מֵאִיר לְמֵיקַם אַלִּיבֵּיהּ: וּגְמַר גְּמָרָא. מִשְׁנָיוֹת שֶׁקִּיבֵּל מֵרַבּוֹתָיו: וַהֲדַר אֲתָא לְקַמֵּיהּ דְּרַבִּי עֲקִיבָא. שֶׁהָיָה חָרִיף לְפַלְפֵּל וּלְדַקְדֵּק בַּמֶּה שֶׁלָּמַד, לְהָשִׁיב תְּשׁוּבוֹת וּמִשְׁנָיוֹת זוֹ עַל זוֹ וּלְתָרֵץ: חוּץ מִפָּרָשַׁת סוֹטָה. אֲפִילּוּ בְּסֵפֶר תּוֹרָה: דְּקָסָבַר: אִם בָּא לִמְחוֹק לָהּ מִן הַתּוֹרָה — מוֹחֵק: שֶׁבַּמִּקְדָּשׁ. מְגִילָּה שֶׁל כָּל סוֹטָה וְסוֹטָה: אֵין מְגִילָּתָהּ כְּשֵׁירָה כו'. סוֹטָה שֶׁנִּכְתְּבָה מְגִילָּתָהּ, וְאָמְרָה טְמֵאָה אֲנִי וּפְטוּרָה — אֵין מְגִילָּתָהּ כְּשֵׁירָה לְסוֹטָה אַחֶרֶת. אַלְמָא: כְּתִיבָה לִשְׁמָהּ בָּעֵינַן. וְה"ה נַמִי דְּאֵין מוֹחֲקִין לָהּ מִן הַתּוֹרָה: וְנִמְלַךְ

תוספות

על זה ועל זה נחלקו. לא שייך למימר הכא טעמיה דב"ש אתא לאשמעינן, דכיון דאמר ת"ק לא נחלקו — בדין הוא שיש לו להשיב, ולומר נחלקו: **ולא** מסיימי. לא שייך כאן *תנא בתרא לטפויי קאתי, כיון דאיכא תנא דאפסקיה. **לחדד** בו את התלמידים. אין לפרש כמו בשאר דוכתי: לידע אם ידעו להשיב על דבריו. דמאחר שאמר שלא אמר ר' ישמעאל דבר זה מעולם — היו יודעים שלא אמר *כי אם לשבחו:

קנקנתום. פירש הקונטרס אדרמינ"ט. ורשב"ס פירש דקנקנתוס היא קרקע ירוקה, שקורין אותה וידריו"ל. וכן בערוך. ור"ת נמי פוסק כן בתיקון ספר תורה, דמותר לתת אדרמינ"ט לתוך הדיו לספר תורה לכולי עלמא — דלאו היינו קנקנתוס. וא"ת: דבמסכת נדה (ד' יט.) תנן: שחור כחרת. ומפרש *התם: חרתא דאושכפי. ובפ"ב דגיטין (ד' יט.) קאמר דקנקנתוס הוא חרתא דאושכפי, אם כן משמע שהוא שחור, ואילו וידריו"ל ירוקה היא ודומה לזכוכית, ועל שם זכוכית נקראת וידריו"ל! ולפי' הקונטרס ניחא. ור"י מפרש: דאחר שטוחנים אותה יפה לתת לתוך הדיו — אז היא משחרת: **או** מייתר אות אחת. כמו "בראשית ברא" — בראו. ורבינו מאיר קבל מרבותיו: כמו "הוה על הוה" (יחזקאל ז) — שהטיל יו"ד על האחרון:

חוץ מפרשת סוטה. ור' ישמעאל שהיה אוסר בכל התורה כולה — שמא היה דורש גזירה שוה מסוטה, או כתיבה כתיבה, או ג"ש אחרת. אי נמי: מדרבנן: **אבל** תורה דסתמא כתיבא ה"נ דמחקינן. משמע: אע"ג דסוטה בעי כתיבה לשמה — מוחקין לה מן התורה. ותימה: דלענין גט פסלינן פרק שני דגיטין (שם:) גבי ההוא דשקל ספר תורה ויהביה לדביתהו, דאמר רב יוסף: למאי ניחוש להו? אי משום כריתות דאית בה — בעינן "וכתב לה" — לשמה, וליכא! וי"ל: דרב יוסף לית ליה סברא דרב פפא דהכא. אי נמי: סבר לה כמאן דאמר אין מוחקין לה מן התורה. וא"ת: והיכי מכשר הכא רב פפא בספר תורה, אפילו למאן דבעי לשמה, והא תנן בריש "כל הגט" (שם ד' כד.) שמע קול סופרים מקרין איש פלוני מגרש פלונית — פסול לגרש בו. ומוקי לה בגמ': בסופרים העשויין להתלמד. וספר תורה נמי חשיב לה הכא כעשויין להתלמד. ומשמע דלכולהו תנאי אית להו מתני' דהתם, מדפריך: ולית ליה לר' אחא בר יאשיה הא דתנן? וכו' — וי"ל: דלהתלמד דהתם — לא נכתב כלל להכשר הגט, אבל ספר תורה — כותב בסתמא, לדעת כן שאם יצטרכו — ימחקו ממנה פרשת סוטה. ומיהו, קשיא: דלגבי גט אפילו בענין זה פסול, ולא חשיב לשמה. דהא אפילו כתבו הסופר לשמה בלא צווי הבעל — פסול לגרש בו. דהא תניא ב"מי שאחזו" (שם ד' עב.): כתב סופר לשמה, וחתמו עדים לשמה ונתנו לה — הרי הוא פסול, עד שישמעו קולו שאמר לסופר כתוב, ולעדים חתמו. והתם פסול משום דלא חשיב לשמה, ולא משום דבעינן שליחות בכתיבה, דהא סוף פ"ב דגיטין (ד' כג:) מכשירים כתיבת חש"ו בגדול עומד על גביו, אע"ג דלאו בני שליחות נינהו! וי"ל: דלעולם חשיב לשמה, והתם פסול מדרבנן. וגבי סוטה לא שייך לפסול מדרבנן. א"נ: בסוטה אין הכהן שעליו לכתוב מקפיד אם יכתוב שום אדם לשמה שלא ברשותו, ומסתמא ניחא ליה. אבל גבי גט — מסתמא לא ניחא ליה לבעל:

עשייה

מסורת הש"ס

ל' דמתניתין דקתני הכשר כו'

[לעיל יב.]

[ברכות לג: וש"נ]

סוטה כ. ע"ש

במדבר ה

שם

[סוטה יז:]

ומהר"ם אומר שזכובי' בורחי' ממנו להכי קא"ל קנקנתום יש לי וליכא למיחש לזכובי' [ת"י]

וצריך לחלק בין נכתב לנותן דבכתיבה בעינן שליחות אבל בכתיבה לא בעינן שליחות משום דמסתמא איירי קרא שכל אדם יכול לגרש את אשתו ואפי' ידיו קטועות [ת"י]

עין משפט נר מצוה

[כלאי' ב"ב לג.]

עב א ב מיי' פ"א מהל' תפילין הלכה ד ופ"ג מהלכות סוטה הלכה ח ופ"ד שם הלכה ט סמג עשין כד נה טוש"ע י"ד סי' רעא סעיף ו:

אלא לשבחו אלא כמו שפירש הקונטרס כל"ל ס"א רש"ל ול"ע מה יש בין הלכה לנראין כיון דלשבחו אומר כן אם אמר הלכה מה נראה שבחו יותר [ת"י]:

עג ג מיי' פ"ג מהלכות סוטה הלכה ח ופ"ד הלכה ד והלכה יא סמג שם:

[וכן כתבו תוס' בגיטין יט. ואפשר דבגרסתם היה כתוב אבל לפנינו שם לא נמצא]

עד ד מיי' פ"ג מהלכות גירושין הלכה ב סמג שם ועשין כ טוש"ע אה"ע סי' קלא סעיף ב

רבינו חננאל

עקיבא וכו'. א"ר עקיבא על זה ועל זה נחלקו. פי' בין על המבוי שיש בארכו מד' אמות ולמעלה ובין על מבוי שהוא פחות מד' אמות נחלקו ב"ש וב"ה. ואמרינן ת"ק סתם קאמר על כל מבוי. ור' עקיבא סתם אמר על כל מבוי מה בינייהו ופרקינן דרב אהלי [איכא בינייהו] דאמר למטה עד ד' כלומר אם הוא מבוי שרוחב פתחו מד' טפחים ולמטה אינו צריך לא לחי ולא קורה. ולא מסיימי. אריב"ל כל מקום שאתה מוצא משום ר' ישמעאל אומר תלמיד אחד בפני ר' עקיבא אינו אלא ר' מאיר ששימש את ר' ישמעאל ואת ר' עקיבא דתניא א"ר מאיר כשהייתי למד תורה אצל ר' ישמעאל הייתי מטיל קנקנתום לתוך הדיו וכשבאתי אצל ר' עקיבא אסרו עלי. איני והא [אמר רב יהודה אמר שמואל] משמיה דר"מ כשהייתי למד תורה אצל ר' עקיבא וכו' ואסיקנא לא קשיא מעיקרא אתא קמיה דר' עקיבא כיון דלא מצי למיקם אליביה אתא לקמיה דר' ישמעאל גמר גמרא והדר אתא לקמיה דר' עקיבא וסבר סברא. תניא ר' יהודה אומר ר' מאיר היה אומר לכל מטילין קנקנתום חוץ מפרשת סוטה שבמקדש מפני שצריך

גיטין כ. סוטה כ:

וְנִמְלַךְ, וּמְצָאוֹ בֶּן עִירוֹ וְאָמַר: שִׁמְךָ כְּשְׁמִי וְשֵׁם אִשְׁתְּךָ כְּשֵׁם אִשְׁתִּי – פָּסוּל לְגָרֵשׁ בּוֹ! הָכִי הָשְׁתָּא?! הָתָם °"וְכָתַב לָהּ" כְּתִיב – בָּעֵינַן כְּתִיבָה לִשְׁמָהּ, הָכָא "וְעָשָׂה לָהּ" כְּתִיב – בָּעֵינַן עֲשִׂיָּה לִשְׁמָהּ, עֲשִׂיָּה דִּידָהּ מְחִיקָה הִיא. א"ר אַחָא בַּר חֲנִינָא: גָּלוּי וְיָדוּעַ לִפְנֵי מִי שֶׁאָמַר וְהָיָה הָעוֹלָם שֶׁאֵין בְּדוֹרוֹ שֶׁל רַבִּי מֵאִיר כְּמוֹתוֹ, וּמִפְּנֵי מָה לֹא קָבְעוּ הֲלָכָה כְּמוֹתוֹ – שֶׁלֹּא *יָכְלוּ חֲבֵירָיו לַעֲמוֹד עַל סוֹף דַּעְתּוֹ. שֶׁהוּא אוֹמֵר עַל טָמֵא טָהוֹר וּמַרְאֶה לוֹ פָּנִים, עַל טָהוֹר טָמֵא וּמַרְאֶה לוֹ פָּנִים. תָּנָא: לֹא ר"מ שְׁמוֹ, אֶלָּא *רַבִּי נְהוֹרַאי שְׁמוֹ. וְלָמָּה נִקְרָא שְׁמוֹ ר"מ – שֶׁהוּא מֵאִיר עֵינֵי חֲכָמִים בַּהֲלָכָה. *וְלֹא *נְהוֹרַאי שְׁמוֹ, אֶלָּא רַבִּי נְחֶמְיָה שְׁמוֹ, וְאָמְרִי לָהּ: רַבִּי אֶלְעָזָר בֶּן עֲרָךְ שְׁמוֹ. וְלָמָּה נִקְרָא שְׁמוֹ נְהוֹרַאי – שֶׁמַּנְהִיר עֵינֵי חֲכָמִים בַּהֲלָכָה. אָמַר *רַבִּי: הַאי דִּמְחַדַּדְנָא מֵחַבְרַאי – דַּחֲזִיתֵיהּ לְרַבִּי מֵאִיר מֵאֲחוֹרֵיהּ. [א]וְאִילּוּ חֲזִיתֵיהּ מִקַּמֵּיהּ – הֲוָה מְחַדַּדְנָא טְפֵי. דִּכְתִיב: °"וְהָיוּ עֵינֶיךָ רוֹאוֹת אֶת מוֹרֶיךָ". א"ר אַבָּהוּ, א"ר יוֹחָנָן: תַּלְמִיד הָיָה לוֹ לְר"מ וְסוּמְכוֹס שְׁמוֹ, שֶׁהָיָה אוֹמֵר עַל כָּל דָּבָר וְדָבָר שֶׁל טוּמְאָה אַרְבָּעִים וּשְׁמוֹנָה טַעֲמֵי טוּמְאָה, וְעַל כָּל דָּבָר וְדָבָר שֶׁל טָהֳרָה אַרְבָּעִים וּשְׁמוֹנָה טַעֲמֵי טָהֳרָה. תָּנָא: תַּלְמִיד וָתִיק הָיָה בְּיַבְנֶה שֶׁהָיָה מְטַהֵר אֶת הַשֶּׁרֶץ בְּמֵאָה וַחֲמִשִּׁים טְעָמִים. *אָמַר *רָבִינָא: אֲנִי אָדוּן וַאֲטַהֲרֶנּוּ; וּמַה נָּחָשׁ שֶׁמֵּמִית וּמַרְבֶּה טוּמְאָה – טָהוֹר, שֶׁרֶץ שֶׁאֵין מֵמִית וּמַרְבֶּה טוּמְאָה לֹא כ"ש? וְלֹא הִיא, מַעֲשֶׂה קוֹץ בְּעָלְמָא קָעָבֵיד. א"ר אַבָּא, אָמַר שְׁמוּאֵל: שָׁלֹשׁ שָׁנִים נֶחְלְקוּ ב"ש וּב"ה, הַלָּלוּ אוֹמְרִים הֲלָכָה כְּמוֹתֵנוּ וְהַלָּלוּ אוֹמְרִים הֲלָכָה כְּמוֹתֵנוּ.[א] *יָצְאָה בַּת קוֹל וְאָמְרָה: *אֵלּוּ וָאֵלּוּ דִּבְרֵי אֱלֹהִים חַיִּים הֵן, וַהֲלָכָה כְּב"ה. וְכִי מֵאַחַר שֶׁאֵלּוּ וָאֵלּוּ דִּבְרֵי אֱלֹהִים חַיִּים, מִפְּנֵי מָה זָכוּ ב"ה לִקְבּוֹעַ הֲלָכָה כְּמוֹתָן – מִפְּנֵי שֶׁנּוֹחִין וַעֲלוּבִין הָיוּ וְשׁוֹנִין דִּבְרֵיהֶן וְדִבְרֵי ב"ש. וְלֹא עוֹד אֶלָּא שֶׁמַּקְדִּימִין דִּבְרֵי ב"ש לְדִבְרֵיהֶן. כְּאוֹתָהּ שֶׁשָּׁנִינוּ: *"מִי שֶׁהָיָה רֹאשׁוֹ וְרוּבּוֹ בַּסּוּכָּה וְשֻׁלְחָנוֹ בְּתוֹךְ הַבַּיִת בֵּית שַׁמַּאי פּוֹסְלִין וּב"ה מַכְשִׁירִין. אָמְרוּ ב"ה לְב"ש: לֹא כָּךְ הָיָה מַעֲשֶׂה שֶׁהָלְכוּ זִקְנֵי ב"ש וְזִקְנֵי ב"ה לְבַקֵּר אֶת רַבִּי יוֹחָנָן בֶּן הַחוֹרָנִית, וּמְצָאוּהוּ יוֹשֵׁב רֹאשׁוֹ וְרוּבּוֹ בַּסּוּכָּה וְשֻׁלְחָנוֹ בְּתוֹךְ הַבַּיִת. אָמְרוּ לָהֶן בֵּית שַׁמַּאי: אִי *מִשָּׁם רְאָיָה?! אַף הֵן אָמְרוּ לוֹ: אִם כָּךְ הָיִיתָ נוֹהֵג לֹא קִיַּימְתָּ מִצְוַת סוּכָּה מִיָּמֶיךָ". לְלַמֶּדְךָ, שֶׁכָּל הַמַּשְׁפִּיל עַצְמוֹ – הקב"ה מַגְבִּיהוֹ, *וְכָל הַמַּגְבִּיהַּ עַצְמוֹ – הקב"ה מַשְׁפִּילוֹ. כָּל הַמְחַזֵּר עַל הַגְּדוּלָּה – גְּדוּלָּה בּוֹרַחַת מִמֶּנּוּ, וְכָל הַבּוֹרֵחַ מִן הַגְּדוּלָּה – גְּדוּלָּה מְחַזֶּרֶת אַחֲרָיו. *וְכָל הַדּוֹחֵק אֶת הַשָּׁעָה – שָׁעָה דּוֹחַקְתּוֹ, וְכָל הַנִּדְחֶה מִפְּנֵי שָׁעָה – שָׁעָה עוֹמֶדֶת לוֹ. ת"ר: שְׁתֵּי שָׁנִים וּמֶחֱצָה נֶחְלְקוּ ב"ש וּב"ה, הַלָּלוּ אוֹמְרִים: נוֹחַ לוֹ לָאָדָם שֶׁלֹּא נִבְרָא יוֹתֵר מִשֶּׁנִּבְרָא, וְהַלָּלוּ אוֹמְרִים: נוֹחַ לוֹ לָאָדָם שֶׁנִּבְרָא יוֹתֵר מִשֶּׁלֹּא נִבְרָא. נִמְנוּ וְגָמְרוּ: נוֹחַ לוֹ לָאָדָם שֶׁלֹּא נִבְרָא יוֹתֵר מִשֶּׁנִּבְרָא, עַכְשָׁיו שֶׁנִּבְרָא – יְפַשְׁפֵּשׁ בְּמַעֲשָׂיו. וְאָמְרִי לַהּ: *)יְמַשְׁמֵשׁ בְּמַעֲשָׂיו.§ **מתני'** *ג הַקּוֹרָה שֶׁאָמְרוּ – רְחָבָה כְּדֵי לְקַבֵּל אָרִיחַ. וְאָרִיחַ חֲצִי לְבֵנָה שֶׁל שְׁלֹשָׁה טְפָחִים. דַּיָּיהּ לַקּוֹרָה שֶׁתְּהֵא רְחָבָה טֶפַח כְּדֵי לְקַבֵּל אָרִיחַ *לְרׇחְבּוֹ. רְחָבָה כְּדֵי לְקַבֵּל אָרִיחַ, דוּבְרִיאָה כְּדֵי לְקַבֵּל אָרִיחַ. רַבִּי יְהוּדָה אוֹמֵר: רְחָבָה אַף עַל פִּי שֶׁאֵין בְּרִיאָה. הָיְתָה שֶׁל קַשׁ וְשֶׁל קָנִים – רוֹאִין אוֹתָהּ כְּאִילּוּ הִיא שֶׁל מַתֶּכֶת. עֲקוּמָּה – רוֹאִין אוֹתָהּ כְּאִילּוּ הִיא פְּשׁוּטָה, עֲגוּלָּה – רוֹאִין אוֹתָהּ כְּאִילּוּ הִיא מְרוּבַּעַת. *כָּל שֶׁיֵּשׁ בְּהֶיקֵּיפוֹ שְׁלֹשָׁה טְפָחִים – יֵשׁ בּוֹ רוֹחַב טֶפַח.§ **גמ'**

*) [פי' ימשמש מעיקרא שיהא זהיר מהחטא או אם חטא יפשפש מעשיו ויחזור בתשובה. ערוך ערך פשפש א']

רש"י

וְנִמְלַךְ. וְחָזַר בּוֹ מִלְּגָרֵשׁ אוֹתָהּ: פָּסוּל. אַלְמָא: "וְכָתַב לָהּ" מַשְׁמַע לִשְׁמָהּ. הָכִי נַמִּי: כְּתִיב "וְעָשָׂה לָהּ" – מַשְׁמַע לִשְׁמָהּ: הָתָם כְּתִיב לָהּ. לְגַבֵּי כְּתִיבָה: הָכָא. כְּתִיב "לָהּ" לְגַבֵּי עֲשִׂיָּה. עֲשִׂיָּה – הַיְינוּ מְחִיקָה: עַל סוֹף דַּעְתּוֹ. לֹא יָכְלוּ לְהָבִין בְּאֵיזֶה דְּבָרָיו נְכוֹנִים. וּבְאֵיזֶה אֵין דְּבָרָיו נְכוֹנִים שֶׁהָיָה נוֹתֵן דַּעַת מְיוּשָּׁב וְהָגוּן עַל אֵין הֲלָכָה כַּהֲלָכָה: דַּחֲזִיתֵיהּ לְרַבִּי מֵאִיר מֵאֲחוֹרֵיהּ. כְּשֶׁלָּמַדְתִּי לְפָנָיו יָשַׁבְתִּי בְּשׁוּרָה שֶׁל אַחֲרָיו: נָחָשׁ שֶׁמֵּמִית. אָדָם וּבְהֵמָה, וּמֵבִיא טוּמְאָה בָּעוֹלָם: טָהוֹר. כְּשֶׁמֵּת. דְּהָא שְׁמוֹנָה שְׁרָצִים כְּתִיבִי: הָכִי גָּרְסִינַן: מַעֲשֶׂה קוֹץ בְּעָלְמָא קָעָבֵיד: עֲלוּבִין. סַבְלָנִין: וְשׁוֹנִין דִּבְרֵיהֶן וְדִבְרֵי ב"ש. כְּשֶׁהָיוּ ב"ש מְבִיאִין רְאָיָה לְדִבְרֵיהֶם מִן הַתּוֹרָה, וּב"ה מְבִיאִין רְאָיָה מִמִּקְרָא אַחֵר, וְהָיוּ ב"ה דּוֹרְשִׁין אֶת הַמִּקְרָא שֶׁל ב"ש לָמָּה בָּא, וְלֹא הָיָה קַל בְּעֵינֵיהֶם. כְּאוֹתָהּ שֶׁשָּׁנִינוּ בְּמַסֶּכֶת בְּרָכוֹת (ד' י:), ב"ש אוֹמְרִים: בָּעֶרֶב כָּל אָדָם יַטּוּ וְיִקְרְאוּ וּבַבֹּקֶר יַעֲמוֹד, שֶׁנֶּאֱמַר "בְּשׇׁכְבְּךָ וּבְקוּמֶךָ". וּב"ה אוֹמְרִים: כָּל אָדָם קוֹרֵא כְּדַרְכּוֹ, שֶׁנֶּאֱמַר "וּבְלֶכְתְּךָ בַדֶּרֶךְ" אִם כֵּן לָמָּה נֶאֱמַר "בְּשׇׁכְבְּךָ וּבְקוּמֶךָ" – בְּשָׁעָה שֶׁדֶּרֶךְ בְּנֵי אָדָם שׁוֹכְבִין וּבְשָׁעָה שֶׁדֶּרֶךְ בְּנֵי אָדָם עוֹמְדִין: שֶׁמַּקְדִּימִין דִּבְרֵי ב"ש לְדִבְרֵיהֶן. דְּקָאָמְרִי לְהוּ: מַעֲשֶׂה שֶׁהָלְכוּ זִקְנֵי ב"ש וְהַדַר זִקְנֵי ב"ה: הַדּוֹחֵק אֶת הַשָּׁעָה. מִתְיַגֵּעַ לְהַעֲשִׁיר וּלְהִתְגַּדֵּל, וְרוֹאֶה שֶׁאֵינוֹ מַצְלִיחַ, וְאעפ"כ חוֹזֵר וְהוֹלֵךְ לְמֶרְחַקִּים, וּמַכְנִיס עַצְמוֹ לִגְבוֹהוֹת: שָׁעָה עוֹמֶדֶת לוֹ. לְאַחַר זְמַן עֲתִידָה לַעֲמוֹד לוֹ שָׁעָה מַצְלַחַת: יְפַשְׁפֵּשׁ מַעֲשָׂיו. שֶׁעָשָׂה כְּבָר, וְיִבְדּוֹק עֲבֵירוֹת שֶׁבְּיָדוֹ, וְיִתְוַדֶּה וְיָשׁוּב: יְמַשְׁמֵשׁ בְּמַעֲשָׂיו. כְּגוֹן: אִם בָּא מִצְוָה לְיָדוֹ יְחַשֵּׁב הֶפְסֵד מִצְוָה כְּנֶגֶד שְׂכָרָהּ, וְלֹא יַנִּיחַ(א) לַעֲשׂוֹתָהּ בִּשְׁבִיל הַהֶפְסֵד, שֶׁהֲרֵי שְׂכָרָהּ עָתִיד לָבוֹא. וְאִם בָּאת לְיָדוֹ עֲבֵירָה – יְחַשֵּׁב שְׂכָרוֹ שֶׁמִּשְׂתַּכֵּר בָּהּ עַכְשָׁיו כְּנֶגֶד הֶפְסֵדָהּ הֶעָתִיד לִיפָּרַע מִמֶּנּוּ: **מתני'** רְחָבָה כְּדֵי לְקַבֵּל אָרִיחַ. שֶׁתְּהֵא דּוֹמָה לִקְבִיעוּת לִבְנוֹת עָלֶיהָ בִּנְיָן: וְאָרִיחַ חֲצִי לְבֵנָה שֶׁל ג' טְפָחִים. נִמְצָא אָרִיחַ טֶפַח וּמֶחֱצָה רוֹחַב: דַּיָּיהּ לַקּוֹרָה בְּרוֹחַב טֶפַח כְּדֵי לְקַבֵּל אָרִיחַ זֶה בְּרׇחְבּוֹ. וּבַגְּמָרָא פָּרֵיךְ: טֶפַח וּמֶחֱצָה בָּעֵי: הָיְתָה שֶׁל קַשׁ כו'. ר' יְהוּדָה קָאָמַר לָהּ: עֲקוּמָּה. שֶׁאֵין אָרִיחַ יָכוֹל לַעֲמוֹד עָלֶיהָ: עֲגוּלָּה. וְאֵין אָרִיחַ יָכוֹל לַעֲמוֹד עָלֶיהָ. אֲבָל עָבָה הִיא, שֶׁאִם תְּחַלֵּק – יְהֵא רְחָבָהּ טֶפַח: רוֹאִין אוֹתָהּ כְּאִילּוּ הִיא(ב) מְרוּבַּעַת. נִפְסֶלֶת אוֹ חֲלוּקָה, וְאִי זוֹ הִיא מִדַּת עֲגוּלָּה לְהַכְשִׁיר: כָּל שֶׁיֵּשׁ בְּהֶיקֵּיפָהּ ג' טְפָחִים. שֶׁצְּרִיכָה חוּט אָרוֹךְ ג' טְפָחִים לְהַקִּיפָהּ סָבִיב – בְּיָדוּעַ שֶׁיֵּשׁ בָּהּ רוֹחַב טֶפַח אִם תְּחַלֵּק:

תוספות

עשייה דידה מחיקה היא. ואם תאמר: אם כן למה אין מוחקין לה מן התורה? ואומר ר"י: משום דכתיב "וכתב את האלות האלה" דבעינן שתהא כתיבה לשם אלה: **שיודע** לטהר את השרץ. תימה: מאי חריפות הוא לטהר את השרץ שהתורה טמאתו בהדיא?! ואומר רבינו תם: לענין טומאת נבילות איירי, שלא יטמא כזית ממנו במשא. דהא כתיב "או בנבלת חיה" ושרץ אע"פ שרוחש – הוי בכלל חיה, כמו נחש. דדרשינן בסנהדרין בפרק "ארבע מיתות" (ד' נט:) "ובכל חיה הרומשת" – זה נחש. ויליף רבינא ק"ו מנחש, דילא מכלל נבלת חיה, דממעט ליה בתורת כהנים מטומאת נבילות מ"וכל הולך על גחון". וכי מסיק ולא היא, וסותר הקל וחומר – מ"מ אתי במה מלינו שפיר מנחש דלא הוי בכלל חיה – ה"נ כל שרצים שרוחשין לא הוו בכלל חיה. ולא מצא ר"י בתורת כהנים שממעט בשום מקום נחש מטומאת נבילות. ועוד קשיא לר"י: דבהדיא ממעט בת"כ כל שרצים מטומאת נבילות, דקתני התם: היא מטמאה במשא ואין שרצים מטמאים במשא. שיכול, ומה בהמה שלא עשה הכתוב דמה כבשרה מטמאה במשא, שרץ שעשה דמו כבשרו – אינו דין שיטמא במשא, ת"ל: "היא" – ולא שרץ. ומיהו, י"ל: אע"ג דאיכא מיעוטא – עביד נמי ק"ו. אבל קשיא: היכי אתי רבינא לבטל הק"ו שבתורת כהנים ואי לאו דאיכא מיעוטא בהדיא. אדרבה, הוה עבדינן ק"ו דתורת כהנים! ועוד: דעל ק"ו דרבינא איכא למיפרך: מה לנחש – שכן טהור אפילו במגע בכעדשה*: **נוח** לו לאדם שלא נברא. והא דאמרינן בפ"ק דע"ז (ד' ה.): בואו ונחזיק טובה לאבותינו, *שאילמלי הן לא חטאו לא באנו לעולם. הא מפרש התם, אימא: כמי שלא באנו לעולם. א"נ: הכא איירי בסתם בני אדם, אבל צדיק – אשריו ואשרי דורו: ובלבד

רבינו חננאל

למוחקה. א"ר (חנינא) [חמא] בר חנינא גלוי וידוע מפני מי שאמר והיה העולם שאין בדורו של ר"מ כמותו. ומפני מה לא קבעו הלכה כמותו שלא עמדו חביריו על סוף דעתו שהיה מראה כאילו מטמא את הטהור ומראה לו פנים וכו' ור' מייאשא היה שמו ולמה נקרא שמו ר' מאיר שהיה מאיר פנים בהלכה. וכן ר' אלעזר בן ערך נקרא ר' נהוראי. אמר רב האי דעדיפנא מחבריי דחזיתיה לר' מאיר לאחוריה. פי' שהייתי קטן ולא הגעתי לישב בשורה שלפניו אלא הייתי יושב בשורה שלאחריו. ואילו הייתי זוכה לישב לפניו הוינא עדיף טפי. שנאמר והיו עיניך רואות את מוריך. ותלמיד היה לו לר' מאיר וסומכוס שמו שהיה ר"מ אומר על כל דבר טומאה מ"ח טעמי טומאה ועל כל טהרה מ"ח טעמי טהרה. תנא תלמיד וותיק היה ביבנה שהיה מטהר את השרץ מק"נ טעמים אמר רבינא אני אדון ואטהרנו מה נחש שממית וכו': **שלש** שנים חלקו ב"ש וב"ה הללו אומרים הלכה כמותנו והללו אומרים הלכה כמותנו יצתה בת קול ואמרה הללו והללו דברי אלהים חיים הן אלא שהלכה כב"ה ומפני מה זכו להיות הלכה כמותן מפני שנוחין בהלכה ועלובין הן ושונין דבריהם ודברי ב"ש ולא עוד אלא שמקדימין דברי ב"ש לדבריהן. דתנן מי שהיה ראשו ורובו בסוכה ושלחנו בתוך הבית כו'. ללמדך שכל המשפיל עצמו הקב"ה [מגביהו] וכל המגביה עצמו [הקב"ה] מנמיכו. וכל המחזר אחר השררה השררה בורחת ממנו. וכל הבורח ממנה היא מחזרת אחריו. וכל הדוחק את השעה שעה דוחקתו והנדחה מפני השעה שעה עומדת לו. ת"ר שנתים ומחצה נחלקו ב"ש וב"ה ובסוף נמנו וגמרו נוח לו למי שלא נברא. פי' מי שנכנס בצורך העולם יותר ממי

עין משפט נר מצוה

עה א מיי' פ"ד מהלכות ת"ת הלכה ב טוש"ע י"ד סי' רמו סעיף ט:

עו ב מיי' פ"ו מהלכות סוכה הלכה ח סמג עשין מג טוש"ע א"ח סי' תרלד סעיף ד:

עז ג ד מיי' פי"ז מהל' שבת הלכה יג סמג עשין א טוש"ע א"ח סי' שסג סעיף יז:

לא קאי על ר"מ אלא על רבי נהוראי המוזכר בתלמוד

הגהות מהר"ב רנשבורג

[א] גמ' יצאה בת קול ואמרה אלו ואלו דברי אלהים חיים הן. נ"ב עי' פירושו ביבין שמועה דף כט ע"ב ודף פה ע"ב ועי' גם בריטב"א כאן:

[ועי' תוס' סנהדרין יז. ד"ה שיודע]

[שאלמלא נ"ל עיין תוס' מגילה כא. ד"ה אלמלא]

מסורת הש"ס

[לקמן נג.]

שם העולם

שבת קמז: ע"ש

[בתוספות למנחות' קד. ד"ה מורייתא כתבו דאית לגרסי רב]

הגהות הב"ח

(א) רש"י ד"ה ימשמש וכו' ולא יניח מלעשותה: (ב) ד"ה רואין אותה כאילו היא חלוקה או נפסלת ומרובעת הס"ד:

גליון הש"ס

גמ' אמר רבינא אני אדון ואטהרנו. עי' תשובת רמ"א סי' קז: **שם** יצאה בת קול ואמרה אלו ואלו דברי אלהים חיים. עי' רש"י כתובות דף נז ע"א ד"ה הא קמ"ל:

[גיטין ו:]

ברכות יא. סוכה ג. ז: כח.

[שבת כט: וש"נ]

[עי' לקמן נד. ובנדרים נה.]

[ברכות סד.]

ב"ב ג:

ס"א לארכו

[לקמן עו. סוכה ז: ב"ב יד: אהלות פי"ב מ"ו]

דברים כד

ישעיהו ל

[בה אלף דבר ג' באלף פתח]

רב נסים גאון

תלמיד אחד היה לו לר' מאיר וסומכוס שמו שהיה אומר על כל דבר ודבר של טומאה מ"ח טעמי טומאה ועל כל דבר ודבר של טהרה מ"ח טעמי טהרה. ישנו בפרק ארבעה ראשי שנים הם (ר"ה כא) כשהזכיר ר' אבהו (תהלים יב) כסף צרוף בעליל לארץ מזוקק שבעתים אמרו פליגי בה רב ושמואל חד אמר נ' שערי בינה נבראו בעולם וכולם ניתנו לו למשה בסיני חסר א' שנאמר (שם ח) ותחסרהו מעט מאלהים לפי שפירש מזוקק שבעתים שבעה כפולים שבעה פעמים שיעלה חשבונם מ"ט ויהיה פירוש ותחסרהו מעט בשביל האחד שחסר מן הנ' ובתלמוד סנהדרין דבני מערבא (פרק ד הלכה ב) גרסי' כדי שתהא התורה נדרשת מ"ט פנים טמא ומ"ט פנים טהור רבא בר מריה בשם ר' יצחק נתן לו הקב"ה למשה את התורה מ"ט פנים טהור ומ"ט פנים טמא דכתיב (שיר השירים ב) ודגלו עלי אהבה שלמה אמרו ודגלו עלי אהבה פירו' ודגלו בגימטריא מ"ט וכן הוא אומר אמרות ה' אמרות טהורות כסף צרוף בעליל לארץ מזוקק שבעתים: **כל** הדוחק את השעה שעה דוחקתו וכל הנדחה מפני השעה שעה עומדת לו. מרבה ורב יוסף ותמצא פירושו בסוף מס' ברכות: דהויא

גמ' טפח?! טפח ומחצה בעי! כיון דרחב לקבל טפח, אידך חצי טפח מלבין ליה בטינא, משהו מהאי גיסא ומשהו מהאי גיסא, וקיימא. אמר רבה בר רב הונא: קורה שאמרו — צריכה שתהא בריאה כדי לקבל אריח, [א]ומעמידי קורה אינן צריכין שיהיו בריאין כדי לקבל קורה ואריח. [א] ורב חסדא אמר: אחד זה ואחד זה צריכין שיהיו בריאין כדי לקבל קורה ואריח. אמר רב ששת: [ב]הניח קורה על גבי מבוי, ופרס עליה מחצלת, והגביה מן הקרקע שלשה — קורה אין כאן, מחיצה אין כאן. קורה אין כאן — דהא מיכסיא, מחיצה אין כאן — דהויא לה מחיצה שהגדיים בוקעין בה. *ת"ר: [ג]קורה היוצאה מכותל זה ואינה נוגעת בכותל זה, [ד]וכן שתי קורות אחת יוצאה מכותל זה ואחת יוצאה מכותל זה ואינן נוגעות זו בזו. *פחות משלשה — אין צריך להביא קורה אחרת, שלשה — צריך להביא קורה אחרת. *רבן שמעון בן גמליאל אומר: פחות מד' — אין צריך להביא קורה אחרת, ארבע — צריך להביא קורה אחרת. [ה]וכן ב' קורות המתאימות, לא בזו כדי לקבל אריח ולא בזו כדי לקבל אריח, אם מקבלות אריח לרחבו טפח — אין צריך להביא קורה אחרת, ואם לאו — צריך להביא קורה אחרת. רשב"ג אומר: אם מקבלת אריח לארכו שלשה — אין צריך להביא קורה אחרת, ואם לאו — צריך להביא קורה אחרת. היו אחת למעלה ואחת למטה, ר' יוסי בר' יהודה אומר: [ו]רואין את העליונה כאילו היא למטה, ואת התחתונה כאילו היא למעלה, ובלבד שלא תהא עליונה למעלה מכ' אמה ותחתונה למטה מעשרה. אמר אביי: ר' יוסי בר' יהודה סבר לה כאבוה בחדא, ופליג עליה בחדא. סבר לה כאבוה בחדא — דאית ליה רואין, ופליג עליה בחדא — דאילו ר' יהודה סבר: למעלה מעשרים, ור' יוסי ברבי יהודה סבר: בתוך כ' — אין, למעלה מכ' — לא.§ "ר' יהודה אומר: רחבה אע"פ שאינה בריאה".§ מתני ליה רב יהודה לחייא בר רב קמיה דרב: רחבה אע"פ שאינה בריאה. א"ל: אתנייה רחבה ובריאה. והאמר ר' אילעאי, אמר רב: [ז]רחבה ארבעה אע"פ שאינה בריאה! רחבה ארבעה שאני.§ "היתה של קש כו'".§ מאי קמ"ל — דאמרינן רואין, היינו הך! מהו דתימא: במינה — אמרינן, שלא במינה — לא אמרינן, קמ"ל.§ "עקומה רואין אותה כאילו היא פשוטה".§ פשיטא! קמ"ל כדרבי זירא; דאמר ר' זירא: [ח]היא בתוך המבוי ועקמומיתה חוץ למבוי, היא בתוך עשרים ועקמומיתה למעלה מעשרים, היא למעלה מעשרה ועקמומיתה למטה מעשרה, רואין, כל שאילו ינטל עקמומיתה ואין בין זה לזה שלשה — אין צריך להביא קורה אחרת, ואם לאו — צריך להביא קורה אחרת. הא נמי פשיטא! היא בתוך מבוי ועקמומיתה חוץ למבוי איצטריכא ליה, מהו דתימא: ליחוש דילמא אתי לאמשוכי בתרה, קמ"ל.§ [ט]"עגולה רואין אותה כאילו היא מרובעת".§ הא תו למה לי? סיפא איצטריכא ליה: כל שיש בהיקפו ג' טפחים יש בו רחב טפח. מנא הני מילי? א"ר יוחנן, אמר קרא: °"ויעש את הים מוצק עשר באמה משפתו עד שפתו עגל סביב וחמש באמה קומתו וקו שלשים באמה יסוב אותו סביב". והא איכא שפתו! אמר רב פפא: שפתו שפת פרח שושן כתיב ביה, דכתיב: °"ועביו טפח ושפתו (א)כמעשה כוס פרח שושן אלפים בת יכיל". והאיכא משהו! כי קא חשיב — מגואי קא חשיב. *תניא *רבי חייא: ים שעשה שלמה היה מחזיק מאה וחמשים מקוה טהרה. מכדי, מקוה כמה הוי — ארבעים סאה, כדתניא: °"ורחץ את *בשרו במים

סוכה יח. כב. [תוספ' פ"א]
[לעיל ט.]
[שם וש"נ]
מלכים א ז
[שם]
*[נ"ל תני]
[פסחים קט:]
ויקרא טו
*[עי' פסחים קט.]

גמ' מלבין לה. לקורה בטינא, ממרח בטיט בשיפוע מלא אצבע מכאן וכנגדו מכאן, ומשוה אותה לקורה. מלבין לשון לבנים: ומעמידי הקורה. אם הניחה על גבי יתידות — אין צריכין שיהו בריאין לקבל קורה ואריח, אלא לקבל קורה לבד. דהא לא יהבי אריח עלה. ובקורה הוא דבעינן קביעות, כי היכי דתיהוי היכר מעליא. אבל מעמידיה — לא תלי היכירא בדידהו: אחד זה ואחד זה. קורה בעינן בריאות דאריח, ומעמידיה בעו בריאות דקורה ואריח: מחצלת. להיות מחיצה לייפות כח התירו: שהגדיים בוקעין בה. הואיל וגובהה שלשה הויא מחיצה תלויה ואינה מתרת: המתאימות. שהשכיבן זו אצל זו כמו תאומים: אחת למעלה ואחת למטה. ואין שתיהם כדי לקבל אריח זו אצל זו, אלא שאחת מעמידים [שלה] גבוהים משל חברתה, וגבוהים ממנה: רואין את העליונה כו'. עד שיהא זו אצל זו בשוה: למעלה מעשרים אמה. מן הקרקע דאין שם הכשר קורה: ולא תחתונה למטה מי'. סמוך לקרקע: דאית ליה רואין.(ב) נמי כאבוה, דאמר במתני' רואין אותה כאילו היא של מתכת: היינו הך. דתנא ברישא רחבה אע"פ שאינה בריאה, ולמה לי תו היתה של קש דאינה בריאה, רואין אותה כאילו היא של מתכת: בריאה במינה אמרינן. שרגיל להיות באותו המין בריאה, כגון קורה של עץ — כי אינה בריאה נמי אמרינן רואין, כאילו היא בריאה. אבל של קש ושל קנים דאינה בריאה במינה — אימא: לא אמרינן רואין: פשיטא. דהכא נמי אמרינן רואין, דמאי שנא הא מדרישא: משפתו עד שפתו. חללו שלו, לבד עובי דופנותיו, עשר אמות. וכתיב "וקו שלשים באמה יסוב אותו", אלמא: לכל אמה רוחב בעיגולא, איכא שלש אמות היקף: והאיכא עובי שפתו. דהוה עדיף על י' של חלל, ואפילו הכי "וקו שלשים" הוא דבעי, ותו לא: פרח שושן. דק מאד כפרח שושן זו: ועביו טפח. בשולי דפנותיו, אבל מלמעלה — דק מאד, כמעשה שפת כוס פרח שושן: מגוואי קא חשיב. קרא, להוא קו ל' להיקף דגוואי קא חשיב ליה, שאין עובי שפתו מוקף בו, אלא קו שלשים הוא מקיף חלל שלשים: מקוה טהרה. ארבעים סאה: במים

ובלבד שלא תהא עליונה למעלה מעשרים. בפ' "הישן" (סוכה כב.) פריך מהכא למאן דאמר כל היכא דלית ביה טפח לא אמרינן חבוט רמי. ומשני: תריץ הכי, ובלבד שלא תהא עליונה למעלה מכ', אלא בתוך כ' ותחתונה סמוכה לה בפחות משלשה. וקשה: דאדפריך מר' יוסי בר' יהודה, לסייעינן מרבנן דלית להו רואין: ואומר ר"י: דטעמי' דרבנן לאו משום דלית להו חבוט רמי בפחות מטפח, אלא משום דבעי קורה ראויה לקבל אריח, ופסלי קורה הנופלת ברוח. ושתי קורות המתאימות, אפילו בפחות משלשה — משום דבעי קורה ראויה לקבל אריח:

אתנייה רחבה ובריאה. פירש רשב"ס: ואין מחלוקת בדבר. וקשה: דאז יש למחוק כל בבא דרואין! אלא נראה שהיה *מהפך דברי רבי יהודה לרבנן. וא"ת: מאי פריך מרבי אילעאי? דילמא כרבנן ס"ל?! וי"ל: דלא מתוקם מילתיה כרבנן, דהא רחבה ארבעה קאמ', ולרבנן דיה שתהא רחבה טפח, ואפילו אינה בריאה. אלא על כרחך כדרבי יהודה. וס"ד דקים ליה לר' אילעאי דר' יהודה בעי רחבה ד', אבל אין צריך שתהא בריאה. ומשני: רחבה ארבעה שאני. אבל ברחבה טפח בעי ר' יהודה שתהא בריאה. *ומיהו, קשיא: כיון דגם דברי רבנן מהפך, הוה ליה(ג) למימר מילתיה ארבנן, ולמימר אתנייה: רחבה אע"פ שאינה בריאה, כמילתייהו דרבנן! ונראה לרבינו תם: דרב יהודה מתני ליה אמילתיה דרבנן, ואמר ליה רב: אתנייה רחבה ובריאה, כמו במתני'. אלא שהתלמוד המתין לסדר הגמרא זו עד שסיים פלוגתייהו. והשתא פריך מר' אלעאי, דמסתמא הוי כרבנן. ולפי זה יש להוכיח דאין הלכה כרב, דקאמר לעיל (ד' יא.) אתנייה: צריך למעט. דהמשנה לא נשנית כמו שהגיה, וכאן נשנית כמו שהגיה. וכן פסקו הגאונים, וה"ג:

והאיכא משהו. משמע שהחשבון מלומלם וכן בפ"ק דב"ב (ד' יד:) גבי שני טפחים שנשתיירו בארון ששם ספר תורה מונח — שהיא בהיקפה ששה טפחים. ופריך: כיון דלאמצעיתו נגלל, נפיש ליה משני טפחים! וכן בתר הכי, דמשני בספר דעזרה לתחלתו נגלל, ופריך: אכתי תרי בתרי היכי יתיב. משמע דמלומלם לגמרי, וקשיא: דאין החשבון מדוקדק לפי חכמי המדות: כמה

עח א טוש"ע א"ח שם סעיף יח: [א] [מיי' שם]
עט ב מיי' שם הלכה כג טוש"ע שם סעיף כד:
פ ג ד מיי' שם הלכה כד טוש"ע שם סעיף כא:
פא ה מיי' שם הלכה כה טוש"ע שם סעי' כב:
פב ו מיי' שם טוש"ע שם סעיף כג:
פג ז [עיין מ"מ בפי"ז הלכה יג] שם סעיף יז:

והר"ח בשם ה"ר אביגדור הגיה דלא קאי לא ארבנן ולא אר' יהודה אלא רב יהודה הוי מתני לחייא ברי' דרב דהכי הלכתא דלא בעי' בריאה כר' יהודה וא"ל אתניי' רחבה דהלכתא רחבה טו' ובריאה כרבנן ופריך והא"ר אילעי אמר רב דהלכתא רחבה ד' אע"פ כו' [ת"י]

ועי"ל דאדרב יהודה פריך מר' אילעאי אמר רב דמסתמא רב יהודה ידע כל דברי רב לפי שהיה תלמידו וא"כ ההיא מילתא דרב כמאן אתי' דלרבנן לא צריך ולרבי יהודה בעינן בריאה ומשני דרחבה שאני ומודה ר' יהודה דלא בעינן בריאה ואתי כר' יהודה [ת"י]

פד ח מיי' שם הלכה כו טוש"ע שם סעיף כ:
פה ט מיי' שם טוש"ע שם סעיף יט:

הגהות הב"ח
(א) גמ' כמעש' שפת כוס פרח: (ב) רש"י ד"ה דאית ליה רואין כאבוה דאמר כנ"ל ותיבת נמי נמחק: (ג) תום' ד"ה אתנייה וכו' מהפך הוה ליה לאסוקי ארבנן מילתייהו ולמימר אתנייה:

רבינו חננאל

שנברא ועכשיו שנברא ימשמש במעשיו ואמרי לה יפשפש במעשיו: מתני' הקורה שאמרו רחבה כו'. כיון שנתפרש במשנה כי שיעור קורה כדי לקבל אריח שהיא חצי לבנה של ג' טפחים נמצא האריח טפח ומחצה. למה שנינו דיה לקורה טפח. טפח ומחצה בעי כשיעור אריח. ומשנינן כי משוי האריח על הקורה מעדיף אצבע בגודל מיכן וכמותו מצד אחר ממלאהו בטיט ועומד. פי' בריאה חזקה. ואמר רב חסדא אחד הקורה ואחד מעמיד הקורה כנגד כותלי המבוי צריכין להיות בריאין כדי לקבל קורה ואריח שעליה. שמועה דרב ששת פשוטה היא. ת"ר קורה היוצאת מכותל צפוני ואינה נוגעת בכותל דרומי שיש כנגדו אלא יש ביניהן ריוח וכן ב' קורות אחת יוצאה מכותל צפוני ואחת יוצאה מכותל דרומי ואין מגיעות הקורות [וא"ז] אלא יש ריוח ביניהן. אם אותו הריוח פחות מג' טפחים כלבוד דמי וא"צ קורה אחרת (אלא) [אבל] אם אותו הריוח ג' טפחים צריך קורה אחרת למלאות הריוח ההוא. רשב"ג אומר ד' טפחים צריך להביא קורה אחרת פחות מד' אין צריך דסבר כל פחות מד' טפחים כלבוד דמי וכן ב' קורות דקות משוכות ע"ג המבוי שאין אחת מהן בריאה לקבל אריח לארכו ג' טפחים [פחות מג'] אין צריך להביא קורה אחרת כו'. היו ב' קורות אחת למעלה ואחת למטה ממנה ואין אחת מהן בריאה [כדי] לקבל אריח ר' יוסי אומר רואין את העליונה כאילו היא למטה. פי' חבוט רמי ורואין את התחתונה כאילו היא למעלה. פי' אמרינן גוד אסיק מחיצתא. ובלבד שלא תהא העליונה למעלה מכ' אמה שיצאה מתורת פתחו של היכל ולא תהיה עוד התחתונה למטה מעשרה טפחים שיצאת מתורת מחיצה. אמר אביי ר' יוסי סבר לה כר' יהודה אבוה בחדא דאית ליה רואין. פי' *) פצימין שרואין בהן. ופליג על אבוה בחדא. דאילו לר' יהודה אפילו הקורה אם היא נתונה למעלה מעשרים מכשיר. ר"י אמר רחבה אע"פ שאינה בריאה. אמר רבינא לא היא אלא [בעינן] בריאה. אלא אם רחבה הקורה ד' טפחים אינה צריכה בריאה. היתה של קש או של קנים מהו דתימא רואין אותה כאילו היא של קש אמיץ וחזק שהוא מינו אמרינן אבל בדבר שאינו מינו לא קמ"ל רואין אותה כאילו היא של מתכת עקומה כר' זירא דאמר הקורה במבוי ועקמומיתה חוץ למבוי היא בתוך עשרים ועקמומותה למעלה **) (מי' טפחים) ועקמומיתה למטה מי' טפחים רואין כל שאילו תינטל עקמומיתה ואין בין זה לזה ג' אמרינן כלבוד דמי ואין צריך קורה אחרת כו': פיסקא כל שיש בהיקפו שלשה טפחים יש בו רוחב טפח מנא לן א"ר יוחנן דאמר קרא ויעש את הים מוצק עשר באמה משפתו אל שפתו עגול סביב וחמש באמה קומתו וקו שלשים באמה (היינו עשר אמות ועוד. ופירק מגוואי חשיב). פי' רוחב חלל הים עשר באמה רחבו והיקפו שלשים באמה ואקשינן והא איכא עובי השפתים שנמצא הים עשר אמות ועוד. ופירק מגוואי חשיב. פי' רוחב חלל הים עשר באמה וכן מדת היקף סביבותיו מבפנים הוא מחשב שנמצא ברוחב עשרה להיקף. איבעית אימא שפתו דק היה

*) [אלו ג' תיבות פצימין שרואין בהן הם מסוללי הבנה וצ"ע]. **) [נ"ל למעלה מעשרים היא למעלה מעשרה ועקמומיתה למטה מעשרה וכו'].

רב נסים גאון

דהויא לה מחיצה שהגדיים בוקעין בה. עיקר בירור זה בתוספת כלאים (פ"ג) והיא הברייתא האמורה בזה הפרק הבא לפנינו (דף טז) כל שהוא פחות מג' צריך שלא יהא בין זה לזה ג' שלא יזדקר הגדי בבת ראש וכבר בירורנוהו בפרק הזורק במסכת שבת: אמר אביי ר' יוסי בר' יהודה סבר לה כאבוה בחדא היא שאמר במשנה היתה של קש או של קנים רואין אותה כאילו היא של מתכת ור' יוסי בנו השוה עמו בזה הדבר כמו שהזכיר בזו הברייתא בכאן ר' יוסי בר' יהודה אומר רואין את העליונה כאילו היא למטה ברואין השוו שניהן ובגובה המבוי יתר מכ' אמה היתה חלוקה ביניהן שר' יוסי היה סובר צריך למעט כי כן אמר ובלבד שלא תהא עליונה למעלה מכ' אמה ור' יהודה אביו היה מכשיר במבוי שגבוה למעלה מכ' אמה כדתנן (ריש מסכתא) מבוי שגבוה למעלה מכ' אמה ימעט ור' יהודה אומר אינו צריך

פו א מיי' פ"ג מהלכות כלים הלכה ב:
פז ב מיי' פי"ז מהלכות שבת הלכה יב טוש"ע א"ח סי' שסג סעיף ג:
פח ג מיי' שם הלכה כ טוש"ע שם סעיף לא:
פט ד מיי' שם הלכה כב טוש"ע שם סעיף י:
צ ה מיי' פ"ח מהל' ברכות הלכה א סמג עשין כז טוש"ע א"ח סי' רד סעיף ז:

כמה מרובע יתר על העגול רביע. מפורש ב"כילד מעברין" (לקמן ד' נו:): **ש"מ** גודשא תלתא. אומר ר"ת: דנפקא מינה לענין מקח וממכר, אם התנה לתת לו סאה גדושה, או לתקן לו כלי המדה. **פוק** חזי. פ"ה: וכבר נהגו בלחי משהו. וכיון דאין הלכה כרבי יוסי בלחי – כ"ש בהילמי. דאפילו רב הונא בר חיננא דפליג בלחיים מודה בהילמי, ושרי לעשות מי מלח בשבת בשביל ליתן על עופות ללוין. ואם נותן מלח על עופות ואח"כ נותן משקין עליהם – הוי שרי אפילו לרבי יוסי, שהשמנונית ממתיק את המלח, כדתנן בפ' "שמנה שרצים" (שבת ד' קח:) ואלו הן מי מלח המותרים – נותן שמן בתחילה לתוך המים או לתוך המלח:
תא

תורה אור

*בַּמַּיִם" — בְּמֵי מִקְוֶה. "כָּל בְּשָׂרוֹ" — מַיִם שֶׁכָּל גּוּפוֹ עוֹלֶה בָּהֶן. וְכַמָּה הֵן — אַמָּה עַל אַמָּה בְּרוּם שָׁלֹשׁ אַמּוֹת. וְשִׁיעֲרוּ חֲכָמִים מֵי מִקְוֶה אַרְבָּעִים סְאָה. כַּמָּה הָווּ לְהוּ חֲמֵשׁ מְאָה גַּרְמִידֵי, לִתְלָת מְאָה מְאָה, לִמְאָה וַחֲמִשִּׁין חַמְשִׁין, בְּאַרְבַּע מְאָה וְחַמְשִׁין סַגְיָא! הָנֵי מִילֵּי בְּרִיבּוּעָא, יָם שֶׁעָשָׂה שְׁלֹמֹה עָגוֹל הָיָה. *מִכְּדִי, כַּמָּה מְרוּבָּע יָתֵר עַל הָעִגּוּל — רְבִיעַ; לְאַרְבַּע מְאָה — מְאָה לִמְאָה — עֶשְׂרִים וַחֲמִשָּׁה, הָנֵי מֵאָה וְעֶשְׂרִים וַחֲמִשָּׁה הָווּ לְהוּ! תָּנֵי רָמִי בַּר יְחֶזְקֵאל: יָם שֶׁעָשָׂה שְׁלֹמֹה שָׁלֹשׁ אַמּוֹת תַּחְתּוֹנוֹת מְרוּבָּעוֹת וּשְׁתַּיִם עֶלְיוֹנוֹת עֲגוּלוֹת. נְהִי דְּאִיפְּכָא לָא מָצֵית אָמְרַתְּ, דִּ"שְׂפָתוֹ עָגֹל" כְּתִיב, אֶלָּא אֵימָא חֲדָא! לָא סָלְקָא דַּעְתָּךְ, דִּכְתִיב: °"אַלְפַּיִם בַּת יָכִיל", בַּת כַּמָּה הָוְיָא — שָׁלֹשׁ סְאִין, דִּכְתִיב: °"מַעְשַׂר הַבַּת מִן הַכֹּר". דַּהֲוָה לְהוּ שִׁיתָּא אַלְפֵי גַּרְוֵי. וְהָא כְּתִיב: °"מַחֲזִיק בַּתִּים שְׁלֹשֶׁת אֲלָפִים"! הַהוּא לְגוּדְשָׁא. *אָמַר אַבַּיֵי, שְׁמַע מִינַּהּ: הַאי גּוּדְשָׁה תִּלְתָּא הָוֵי. *וּתְנַן נַמִּי: אשִׁידָּה תֵּיבָה וּמִגְדָּל, כַּוֶּורֶת הַקַּשׁ, וְכַוֶּורֶת הַקָּנִים, וּבוֹר סְפִינָה אֲלֶכְּסַנְדְּרִית, אע"פ שֶׁיֵּשׁ לָהֶן שׁוּלַיִם וְהֵן מַחֲזִיקוֹת אַרְבָּעִים סְאָה בַּלַּח, שֶׁהֵן כּוֹרַיִים בְּיָבֵשׁ — טְהוֹרִין.§ **מתני'** בלְחָיַין שֶׁאָמְרוּ — גּוֹבְהָן עֲשָׂרָה טְפָחִים, וְרָחְבָּן וְעוֹבְיָין כָּל שֶׁהוּא. ר' יוֹסֵי אוֹמֵר: רָחְבָּן ג' טְפָחִים.§ **גמ'** "לְחָיַין שֶׁאָמְרוּ כו'". לֵימָא תְּנַן סְתָמָא כְּר"א, *דְּאָמַר לְחָיַין בָּעֵינַן! לָא, מַאי לְחָיַין — לְחָיַין דְּעָלְמָא. אִי הָכִי קוֹרָה נַמִּי נִיתְנֵי קוֹרוֹת, וּמַאי קוֹרוֹת — קוֹרוֹת דְּעָלְמָא! הָכִי קָאָמַר: אוֹתָן לְחָיַין שֶׁנֶּחְלְקוּ בָּהֶן ר' אֱלִיעֶזֶר וַחֲכָמִים — גּוֹבְהָן עֲשָׂרָה טְפָחִים, וְרוֹחְבָּן וְעוֹבְיָין כָּל שֶׁהוּא. *וְכַמָּה כָּל שֶׁהוּא? תָּנֵי רַבִּי חִיָּיא: אֲפִילּוּ כְּחוּט הַסַּרְבָּל. תָּנָא: *עָשָׂה לֶחִי לַחֲצִי מָבוֹי — אֵין לוֹ אֶלָּא חֲצִי מָבוֹי. פְּשִׁיטָא! אֶלָּא אֵימָא: גיֵשׁ לוֹ חֲצִי מָבוֹי. הָא נַמִּי פְּשִׁיטָא! מַהוּ דְּתֵימָא: לֵיחוּשׁ דִּילְמָא אָתֵי לְאִישְׁתַּמּוּשֵׁי בְּכוּלֵּיהּ, קמ"ל. אָמַר רָבָא: דעָשָׂה לֶחִי לַמָּבוֹי וְהִגְבִּיהוֹ מִן הַקַּרְקַע שְׁלֹשָׁה, אוֹ שֶׁהִפְלִיגוֹ מִן הַכּוֹתֶל שְׁלֹשָׁה — לֹא עָשָׂה וְלֹא כְלוּם. אֲפִילּוּ לרשב"ג דְּאָמַר *אָמְרִינַן לָבוּד — הָנֵי מִילֵּי לְמַעְלָה; אֲבָל לְמַטָּה, כֵּיוָן דַּהֲוְיָא מְחִיצָה שֶׁהַגְּדָיִין בּוֹקְעִין בָּהּ — לָא קָאָמַר.§ "ר' יוֹסֵי אוֹמֵר רָחְבָּן ג' טְפָחִים".§ אָמַר רַב יוֹסֵף, אָמַר רַב יְהוּדָה, אָמַר שְׁמוּאֵל: אֵין הֲלָכָה כְּר' יוֹסֵי לֹא *בְּהִילְמֵי וְלֹא בִּלְחָיַין. אֲמַר לֵיהּ רַב הוּנָא בַּר חִינָּנָא: בְּהִילְמֵי אָמְרַתְּ לָן, בִּלְחָיַין לָא אָמְרַתְּ לָן. מַאי שְׁנָא בְּהִילְמֵי — דִּפְלִיגִי רַבָּנַן עֲלֵיהּ, לְחָיַין נַמִּי פְּלִיגִי רַבָּנַן עֲלֵיהּ! א"ל: שָׁאנֵי לְחָיַין, מִשּׁוּם דְּקָאֵי רַבִּי כְּוָותֵיהּ. רַב רַחוּמֵי מַתְנֵי הָכִי, אָמַר רַב יְהוּדָה בְּרֵיהּ דְּרַב שְׁמוּאֵל [בַּר שִׁילַת] מִשְּׁמֵיהּ דְּרַב: אֵין הֲלָכָה כְּרַבִּי יוֹסֵי לֹא בְּהִילְמֵי וְלֹא בִּלְחָיַין. א"ל: אָמְרַתְּ? אָמַר לְהוּ: לָא. אָמַר רָבָא: הָאֱלֹהִים! אֲמָרָהּ, וּגְמִירְנָא לָהּ מִינֵּיהּ. וּמַאי טַעְמָא קָא הָדַר בֵּיהּ — מִשּׁוּם דְּר' יוֹסֵי *נִימוּקוֹ עִמּוֹ. אֲמַר לֵיהּ רָבָא בַּר רַב חָנָן לְאַבַּיֵי: הִילְכְתָא מַאי? א"ל: פּוּק חֲזֵי מַאי עַמָּא דְּבַר. אִיכָּא דְּמַתְנֵי לָהּ אַהָא; *הַשּׁוֹתֶה מַיִם לִצְמָאוֹ אוֹמֵר: ה"שֶׁהַכֹּל נִהְיֶה בִּדְבָרוֹ", ר' טַרְפוֹן אוֹמֵר: "בּוֹרֵא נְפָשׁוֹת רַבּוֹת וְחֶסְרוֹנָן" *עַל כָּל מַה שֶּׁבָּרָאתָ. א"ל רַב חָנָן לְאַבַּיֵי: הִלְכְתָא מַאי? א"ל: *פּוּק חֲזֵי מַאי עַמָּא דְּבַר.
אִיתְּמַר

מ"א ז | יחזקאל מה | ד"ה ב ד

בַּמַּיִם. מַשְׁמַע מַיִם מְחוּבָּרִין יַחְדָּיו: כַּמָּה הָווּ לְהוּ. לְהָנָךְ עֶשֶׂר עַל עֶשֶׂר בְּרוּם חָמֵשׁ אַמּוֹת, כַּמָּה גּוֹבַהּ יֵשׁ בָּהֶן בְּאַמָּה עַל אַמָּה בְּרִיבּוּעוֹ שֶׁל מִקְוֶה: ת"ק גַּרְמִידֵי. כֵּיצַד? חַלְּקֵהוּ לְעֶשֶׂר רְצוּעוֹת – הֲרֵי לְכָל רְצוּעָה עֶשֶׂר אַמּוֹת אוֹרֶךְ, בְּרוֹחַב אַמָּה, וְרוּם חָמֵשׁ. חָתְכֵם לַחֲתִיכוֹת שֶׁל אַמָּה אַמָּה – הֲרֵי מֵאָה חֲתִיכוֹת שֶׁל אַמָּה עַל אַמָּה בְּרוּם חָמֵשׁ אַמּוֹת. שִׂים זוֹ עַל זוֹ אַמָּה עַל אַמָּה בְּרוּם חָמֵשׁ – הֲוֵה ת"ק אַמּוֹת: לִתְלָת מְאָה. גּוֹבַהּ: מְאָה. מִקְוָאוֹת, שָׁלֹשׁ אַמּוֹת לְמִקְוֶה: הָנֵי מִילֵּי בְּרִיבּוּעַ. אִם הָיָה מְרוּבָּע, שֶׁיְּהֵא בּוֹ אוֹרֶךְ וְרוֹחַב לְצְדָדִין כְּבְאֶמְצָעִיתוֹ, וְיִהְיוּ רְצוּעוֹתָיו שָׁווֹת בְּי' י' אַמּוֹת לִרְצוּעָה, כִּדְפָרֵישִׁית: יָם שֶׁעָשָׂה שְׁלֹמֹה עָגוֹל הָיָה. כִּדְכְתִיב "עָגֹל סָבִיב" וְנִמְצָא שֶׁאֵין אוֹרֶךְ הָרְצוּעוֹת עֶשֶׂר אַמּוֹת, אֶלָּא רְצוּעָה הָאֶמְצָעִית לְבַדָּהּ. דְּכָל דָּבָר עָגוֹל רָחָב בְּאֶמְצָעִיתוֹ, וְקָצָר לְכָל צְדָדָיו: מִכְּדִי כַּמָּה מְרוּבָּע יָתֵר עַל הָעִגּוּל רְבִיעַ. דְּהָא כָּל עִיגּוּל שֶׁרָחְבּוֹ אַמָּה יֵשׁ בּוֹ הֶיקֵּף שָׁלֹשׁ אַמּוֹת, כִּדְתְנַן בְּמַתְנִי', וְאִם הָיָה מְרוּבָּע אַמָּה עַל אַמָּה – הָיָה לוֹ הֶיקֵּף ד' אַמּוֹת, אַמָּה לְכָל רוּחַ. נִמְצָא: מְרוּבָּע יָתֵר עַל הָעִגּוּל רְבִיעַ. הִלְכָּךְ: הַאי יָם עָגוֹל דְּשִׁעֲרִינוּהּ בְּחָמֵשׁ מֵאוֹת אַמִּין בִּמְרוּבָּע – בָּעֵינַן לְבַצּוֹרֵי רִבְעָא מִינַּיְיהוּ אִימְעִיט לְהוּ אַרְבַּע מְאָה לִתְלָת מְאָה דְּאִינּוּן מֵאָה מִקְוָאוֹת, וְלִמְאָה אַמִּין דְּאִישְׁתַּיֵּיר – הָווּ עֶשְׂרִים וְחָמֵשׁ מִקְוָאוֹת, אַרְבַּע אַמּוֹת לְמִקְוֶה – דְּהָנֵי אַרְבַּע תְּלָת הוּא דַּהֲווּ, שֶׁהֲרֵי אַמּוֹת קְצָרוֹת הֵן: שָׁלֹשׁ אַמּוֹת תַּחְתּוֹנוֹת מְרוּבָּעוֹת. וְיֵשׁ בָּהֶן י' רְצוּעוֹת שֶׁל י' עַל י' שֶׁהֵן מֵאָה אַמָּה בְּרוּם ג' בְּרוֹחַב אַמָּה, דְּהַיְינוּ תְּלָת מְאָה אַמִּין גּוֹבַהּ, בְּאַמָּה עַל אַמָּה – וְהֵן ק' מִקְוָאוֹת: וּב' עֶלְיוֹנוֹת עֲגוּלוֹת. וְאִי הָווּ מְרוּבָּעוֹת הָווּ לְהוּ מָאתָן גַּרְמִידֵי, הָשְׁתָּא דְּאִינּוּן עֲגוּלוֹת, כִּי בָּצְרַתְּ רִיבְעָא – פָּשׁוּ לָהֶן ק"נ, דְּאִינּוּן נ' מִקְוָאוֹת: נְהִי דְּאִיפְּכָא לָא מָצֵית אָמְרַתְּ. דְּלֶיהֱוֵי תַּחְתּוֹנוֹת עֲגוּלוֹת וְעֶלְיוֹנוֹת מְרוּבָּעוֹת – ד"שְׂפָתוֹ עָגֹל" כְּתִיב. אֶלָּא שְׁתַּיִם עֲגוּלוֹת מְנָא לָן? דִּילְמָא חֲדָא הוּא דַּהֲוְיָא עֲגוּלָּה, וְתוּ לָא, וְטָפֵי מִק"נ מִקְוָאוֹת הוּא מַחֲזִיק: לָא סָלְקָא דַּעְתָּךְ. שֶׁיְּהֵא מַחֲזִיק יוֹתֵר מִק"נ מִקְוָאוֹת: מַעְשַׂר הַבַּת מִן הַכּוֹר. כּוֹר שְׁלֹשִׁים סְאִין, וְכִי הָוֵי הַבַּת מַעֲשֵׂר דִּילֵיהּ – אִשְׁתַּכַּח דְּג' סְאִין הָוְיָא: דַּהֲווּ לְהוּ. הָנָךְ אַלְפַּיִם בַּת: ו' אֲלָפִים סְאִין. שֶׁהֵן ק"נ מִקְוָאוֹת. ד' אֲלָפִים הָוֵי מ' מֵאוֹת סְאִין, שֶׁהֵן ק' מִקְוָאוֹת שֶׁל מ' סְאִין, וְאַלְפַּיִם סְאִין נ' מִקְוָאוֹת: מַחֲזִיק בַּתִּים שְׁלֹשֶׁת אֲלָפִים. בַּיָּם שֶׁעָשָׂה שְׁלֹמֹה כְּתִיב, בְּדִבְרֵי הַיָּמִים: לְגוּדְשָׁא. כְּשֶׁמּוֹדְדִין בּוֹ יָבֵשׁ: שִׁידָּה. כְּמִין אַרְגָּז תָּלוּי בָּעֲגָלָה, לְמֶרְכַּב נָשִׁים חֲשׁוּבוֹת: מִגְדָּל. = מנשטי"ר: וּבוֹר סְפִינָה אֲלֶכְּסַנְדְּרִית. עוֹשֶׂה בָּהּ כְּעֵין בּוֹר, וְנוֹתֵן שָׁם מַיִם מְתוּקִים: טְהוֹרִין. לְפִי שֶׁגְּדוֹלִים יוֹתֵר מִדַּאי, וְאֵין תּוֹרַת כְּלִי עֲלֵיהֶן, שֶׁהֲרֵי אֵינָן מִטּוּלְטָלִין מָלֵא וְרֵיקָן: שֶׁהֵן כּוֹרַיִים בְּיָבֵשׁ. שֶׁאָדָם יָכוֹל לִגְדּוֹשׁ. אַלְמָא: גּוּדְשָׁא תִּילְתָּא. וּבִכְלִי שֶׁגּוֹבְהוֹ כַּחֲצִי אָרְכּוֹ וְרָחְבּוֹ קָאָמַר, כַּיָּם:

מתני' גמ' לְחָיַין דְּעָלְמָא. אַכָּל מְבוֹאוֹת קָאֵי: אִי הָכִי. רֵישָׁא דְּקָתָנֵי "הַקּוֹרָה שֶׁאָמְרוּ כו'" לִיתְנֵי נַמִּי "הַקּוֹרוֹת שֶׁאָמְרוּ", וְאֵימָא: מַאי קוֹרוֹת – קוֹרוֹת דְּעָלְמָא: לְחָיַין שֶׁנֶּחְלְקוּ בָּהֶן ר"א וַחֲכָמִים. דְּלר"א תַּרְתֵּי, וּלְרַבָּנַן חֲדָא – וְזֶהוּ שִׁיעוּרָן, כִּדְמְפָרֵשׁ. מִיהוּ סְתָמָא לָא כְּמַר דַּיְיקָא וְלָא כְּמַר דַּיְיקָא: הַסַּרְבָּל. = קו"ט: לַחֲצִי מָבוֹי. שֶׁהִכְנִיס הַלֶּחִי לִפְנִים הַרְבֵּה עַד חֲצִי אוֹרְכּוֹ שֶׁל מָבוֹי, כָּזֶה:

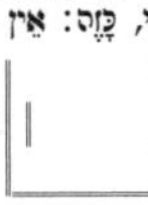

אֵין לוֹ אֶלָּא חֲצִי מָבוֹי. שֶׁאָסוּר לְהִשְׁתַּמֵּשׁ אֶלָּא מִן חֶלְיוֹ וְלִפְנִים: יֵשׁ לוֹ. דְּאֵין לוֹ לָא אִיצְטְרִיךְ לְאַשְׁמְעִינַן, אֶלָּא הָא אֲתָא לְאַשְׁמְעִינַן: דְּהֵימֶנּוּ וְלִפְנִים מִיהָא מוּתָּר לְהִשְׁתַּמֵּשׁ: לְמַעְלָה. כְּגוֹן קוֹרָה הַיּוֹצְאָה מִכּוֹתֶל זֶה וְאֵינָהּ נוֹגַעַת לְכוֹתֶל אַחֵר, דְּאִיפְּלִיגוּ בָּהּ רשב"ג וְרַבָּנַן (לעיל ע"א): הִילְמֵי. בְּמַסֶּכֶת שַׁבָּת, בְּפֶרֶק "שְׁמֹנָה שְׁרָצִים" [דף קח:]: הִילְמֵי שלמוייר"א בְּלַע"ז: מִשּׁוּם דְּקָאֵי רַבִּי כְּוָותֵיהּ. *לְעֵיל. וְהָא דְּתָנֵי חֲדָא בַּר מִנְיוֹמֵי – רַבִּי הִיא, וְסָבַר לָהּ כְּר' יוֹסֵי, כִּדְאוֹקִימְנָא בְּחָצֵר קְטַנָּה שֶׁנִּפְרְצָה לִגְדוֹלָה: נִימוּקוֹ עִמּוֹ. טַעֲמֵי רְאָיוֹתָיו מֵבִיא לוֹ בְּכָל מָקוֹם, בְּמַסֶּכֶת גִּיטִּין (ד' סז.) מָנֵי שִׁבְחָן שֶׁל חֲכָמִים, וְזֶהוּ שִׁבְחוֹ שֶׁל ר' יוֹסֵי: הִילְכְתָא מַאי. בִּלְחָיַין: עַמָּא דְּבַר. מַה נָּהֲגוּ הָעָם, וּכְבָר נָהֲגוּ בְּלֶחִי מַשֶּׁהוּ: לִצְמָאוֹ. לְאַפּוּקֵי מָאן דַּחֲנַקְתֵּיהּ אוּמְצָא: שֶׁהַכֹּל נִהְיֶה בִּדְבָרוֹ. לְפָנָיו וּלְאַחֲרָיו לֹא כְלוּם: ר"ט אוֹמֵר בּוֹרֵא נְפָשׁוֹת רַבּוֹת. וַאֲנִי שָׁמַעְתִּי דְּר"ט בָּא לְחַיֵּיב אַף בְּרָכָה אַחֲרָיו "בּוֹרֵא נְפָשׁוֹת רַבּוֹת", וְלָא נְהִירָא(א) דְּאָמְרִינַן בְּמַסֶּ' נִדָּה (ד' נא:): יֵשׁ טָעוּן בְּרָכָה לְפָנָיו וְאֵין טָעוּן בְּרָכָה לְאַחֲרָיו, וְאָמְרִינַן: לְאֵתוּיֵי *מַאי? וְהָוֵינַן בָּהּ: וּלְרַב פַּפָּא דִּמְבָרֵךְ אַמַּיָּא כו' וְלָא אָמְרִינַן וּלְרַבִּי טַרְפוֹן דִּמְחַיֵּיב אַמַּיָּא, מַאי אִיכָּא לְמֵימַר. אֶלָּא נִרְאֶה לִי: דְּרַבִּי טַרְפוֹן אַלְּפָנָיו קָאָמַר:
הָעוֹמֵד

[לעיל ד: וש"נ]
[ב"ב כז. קא: לקמן נו: עז: סוכה ח. אהלות פי"ב מ"ו]
שבת לה. וקנ"ע
שבת לה. כלים פט"ו מ"א אהלות פ"ח מ"ו ומ"ג
לעיל יא:
[ב"ב קו. חולין קכד. קלו: נדה סו:]
[תוספתא פ"א]
[לקמן עז:]
שבת קח:
ברכות מד:
[לקמן נח. וע"ש פרק י' גיטין מז. בכורות לז.]
[שם מה. וש"נ]
ד' תיבות אלו מיותרים גם במשנה דברכות מד. אינן ועיין בביאור לא"ח מהגאון מהרא"ו ז"ל סי' תנט ס"ק ה
דף י. ודף יב.
[נ"ל מה]

הגהות הב"ח

(א) רש"י ד"ה ר' טרפון וכו' ולא נהירא לומר דקאי ר' טרפון אלא אלפניו ולא אלאחריו ואמרינן במס' נדה:

גליון הש"ס

גמ' אפילו כחוט הסרבל. עי' לקמן דף פ ע"ב תד"ה אבל קורה. ובתוס' סוכה דף ... עד:

רבינו חננאל

כמין שפת כום פרח שושן. וכיון דהוא משהו לא חשיב ליה. תני ר' חייא ים שעשה שלמה מחזיק ק"נ מקוה טהרה. דתניא ורחץ את בשרו במים מי מקוה. כל בשרו. מים שכל גופו עולה בהן וכמה הן אמה על אמה ברום שלש. ושיערו חכמים מ' סאה. (מורט לחשוב) [ומוזה צא וחשוב] הים היאך עולין בו ק"נ מקוה ואמרינן מכדי הים כמה הוי רחבו עשר על עשר וקומתו (מ"ה) [ה'] אמה י' אמות על עשר אמות ברוחב בגובה אמה הרי הן ק' אמות בתברייתא ויש בים גובה ה' אמות. כשתוציא לכל אמה גובה בעשר על עשר רוחב ק' אמה נמצא בים כולו ת"ק אמה אורך בגובה אמה אחת ושיעור המקוה אמה על אמה רחב ברום ג' אמות. נמצאו בש' אמות ק' מקוה נשתיירו עדיין מחשבון הים ק"ק אמה ק"נ חמשים מקוה היה דיי לים ת"נ למה ג' אמות יתירות. ודחינן כי זה החשבון עשר אמה על עשר אמה אי האמה בתברייתא במרובע אבל בים שהוא עגול אין חשבון זה (כולו) [כלל] ואקשינן אי הכי דמרובע יתר על העגול רביע. ואנו חשבינן ת"ק אמה בים במרובע חסר רביע נמצאת מדת העיגול שע"ה אמה. ש' אמה ק' מקוה ועוד [ע"ה] אמה כ"ה מקוה בכל שלש אמות מקוה. הנה לא תמצא בים אלא קכ"ה מקוה. איך תני ר' חייא ק"נ מקוה ושנינן ג' מאות התחתונות מרובעות שהן ק' מקוה. וב' אמות העליונות עגולות והן במרובעים כשתוציא ג' אמה נשתיירו ק"נ אמה (הך) [היינו] נ' מקוה ג' אמות לכל מקוה ולא יתכן שתאמר העליונות מרובעות דכתיב משפתו אל שפתו עגול. וגם לא יתכן שתאמר דכי פחות מב' אמות הוא עגול שנא' אלפים בת יכיל והבת היא ג' סאין שנא' מעשר הבת מן הכור. והכור י' איפות. והאיפה ג' סאין וכתיב האיפה והבת תוכן אחד יהיה שנמצא (לאלפים) [ששת אלפים] סאין מכיל הים. והמקוה מ' סאה נמצא ששת אלפים סאה ק"נ מקוה בכל מקוה מ' סאה ואין חשבון זה עולה אלא כשיהיו ג' אמות התחתונות מרובעות ושתי אמות העליונות עגולות. כתוב אחד אומר אלפים בת יכיל וכתוב אחד אומר שלשת אלפים: ספינה אלכסנדרית אע"פ שיש להם שוליים ומחזיקים מ' סאה בלח שהן כוריים ביבש טהורין. פי' שאינן יכולין להטלטל מלאין ורקנין כוריים הן ס' סאין (כלבוד) [כי כור] ל' סאין נמצא היבש כשיגדש עודף על הלח שאינו יכול להגדש כ' סאה על ל' של לח והוא השליש: **פיסקא** לחיים שאמרו גובהו עשרה טפחים ורוחבן ועוביין כל שהוא וכמה כל שהוא תני ר' חייא אפילו כחוט הסרבל פי' חוט הסרבל חוט חזק כפול שתופרין בו הסרבל כדכתיב כפיתו בסרבליהון. תנא עשה לחי לחצי מבוי יש לו חצי מבוי פי' עשה לחי לחצי המבוי לארכו ונשתייר חצי המבוי החיצון בלא לחי יש לו להשתמש מן הלחי ולפנים במבוי ולא גזרינן דלמא אתי לאשתמושי אפילו בחיצון. אמר רבא עשה לחי והגביהו מן הקרקע ג' טפחים או הרחיקו מן הכותל ג"ט (סימן) [כיון] דהיא מחיצה שהגדיים בוקעין בה לא עשה כלום. אמרי משמיה דשמואל אין הלכה כר' יוסי בהילמי ולא בלחיים. אין הלכה כר' יוסי בלחיים דבעי רוחב כל לחי ג' טפחים וא"ל רב הונא בר חיננא אמרת לן בהילמי דאין הלכה כר' יוסי *) (ולא בלחיים). ואמרינן מ"ש והא בין בהילמי בין בלחיים פליגי עליה ואמרן משום דקאי ר' כוותיה בענין חצר גדולה שנפרצה לקטנה ואוקמה גדולה בי"א אמה וקטנה בעשר וכר' דאמר בענין ב' פסין וסבר לה כר' יוסי דאמר כל פס רחבו ג"ט ומדחזינן דר' קאי כוותיה ותוב [דרב רחומי דמתני'] דרב דאמר רב יהודא משמיה דרב אין הלכה כר' יוסי [לא] בהילמי ולא בלחיים הדר ביה משום דר' יוסי נימוקו עמו. ש"מ הלכתא כוותיה בלחיים. ואביי דאמר לרבא בר רב חנן כדבעא מיניה הלכתא מאי
*) נ"ל בלחיים לא אמרת לן.

רב נסים גאון

צריך ולפי דעתו אפי' עליונה למעלה מעשרים אמה רואין אותה כאילו היא למטה: **אין** הלכה כר' יוסי לא בהילמי ולא בלחיים ובלחיים הוא שאמר ר' יוסי בבאן רחבן ג' טפחים ובהילמי שנו במסכת שבת בפרק ח' שרצים (דף קח) אמר ר' יוסי והלא היא הילמי בין מרובה בין מעוטה:

איתמר: לחי העומד מאליו, אביי אמר: הוי לחי. רבא אמר: לא הוי לחי. היכא דלא סמכינן עליה מאתמול — כולי עלמא לא פליגי דלא הוי לחי. כי פליגי — היכא דסמכינן עליה מאתמול. אביי אמר: ^א^הוי לחי, דהא סמכינן עליה מאתמול. רבא אמר: לא הוי לחי, כיון דמעיקרא לאו אדעתיה דהכי עבידי — לא הוי לחי. קא סלקא דעתך כי היכי דפליגי בלחי פליגי נמי במחיצה. ת"ש: *^ב^העושה סוכתו בין האילנות, ואילנות דפנות לה — כשירה! הכא במאי עסקינן — שנטען מתחילה לכך. אי הכי, פשיטא! מהו דתימא: ליגזור דילמא אתי לאישתמושי באילן, קמ"ל. ת"ש: *היה שם אילן או גדר או חיצת הקנים — נידון משום דיומד. הכא נמי במאי עסקינן — שעשאן מתחילה לכך. אי הכי מאי קמ"ל? [קמ"ל: חיצת הקנים קנה קנה פחות משלשה טפחים, *כדבעא מיניה אביי מרבה. ת"ש: *אילן המסיך על הארץ, אם אין נופו גבוה מן הארץ ג' טפחים — מטלטלין תחתיו. הכא נמי במאי עסקינן — שנטעו מתחילה לכך. אי הכי ליטלטל בכולו, אלמה אמר רב הונא בריה דרב יהושע: אין מטלטלין בו אלא בית סאתים! משום דהוי דירה שתשמישה לאויר, וכל דירה שתשמישה לאויר אין מטלטלין בה אלא בית סאתים. ת"ש: *^ג^שבת בתל שהוא גבוה עשרה, והוא מארבע אמות ועד בית סאתים. וכן בנקע שהוא עמוק עשרה, והוא מארבע אמות ועד בית סאתים, וקמה קצורה ושיבולות מקיפות אותה — מהלך את כולה וחוצה לה אלפים אמה. וכי תימא, הכא נמי שעשה מתחילה לכך — בשלמא קמה, לחיי. אלא תל ונקע מאי איכא למימר? אלא: ^ד^במחיצות כולי עלמא לא פליגי דהויא מחיצה, כי פליגי בלחי. אביי לטעמיה, דאמר: לחי משום מחיצה, ומחיצה העשויה מאליה הויא מחיצה. ורבא לטעמיה, דאמר: *לחי משום היכר. אי עבידא בידים — הויא היכר, ואי לא — לא הוי היכר. ת"ש: אבני גדר היוצאות מן הגדר, מובדלות זו מזו פחות משלשה — אין צריך לחי אחר, שלשה — צריך לחי אחר. הכא נמי, שבנאן מתחילה לכך. אי הכי, פשיטא! מהו דתימא למיסר בניינא הוא דעבידא, קמ"ל. ת"ש, *דתני ר' חייא: כותל שצידו אחד כנוס מחבירו, בין שנראה מבחוץ ושוה מבפנים, ובין שנראה מבפנים ושוה מבחוץ — נדון משום לחי. הכא נמי שעשאו מתחילה לכך. אי הכי מאי קמ"ל? הא קמ"ל: נראה מבחוץ ושוה מבפנים — נדון משום לחי. ת"ש: דרב הוה יתיב בההוא מבואה, הוה יתיב רב הונא קמיה. אמר ליה לשמעיה: זיל אייתי לי כוזא דמיא. עד דאתא נפל לחייא. אחוי ליה בידיה, קם אדוכתיה. אמר ליה רב הונא: לא סבר לה מר לסמוך אדיקלא? אמר: *דמי האי מרבנן כמאן דלא פרשי אינשי שמעתא. מי סמכינן עליה מאתמול? טעמא — דלא סמכינן, הא סמכינן — הוי לחי! לימא אביי ורבא בדלא סמכינן עליה פליגי, הא סמכינן עליה — הוה לחי? לא ס"ד, דההוא ברקא דהוה בי בר חבו, דהוו פליגי בה אביי ורבא כולי שנייהו. § מתני' ^ה^בכל עושין לחיין, אפילו בדבר שיש בו רוח חיים, *ורבי מאיר אוסר. *^ו^ומטמא משום גולל, ורבי

רש"י

העומד מאליו. שלא הוקבע שם לשם תיקון מבוי, דלא הזמינוהו לכך: היכא דלא סמכינן עליה מאתמול. שהיה שם לחי אחר, ונפל בשבת: לאישתמושי באילן. ויעלה ויתלוש ביום טוב: היה שם. בפסי בירות, תניא בפרק שני: חיצת הקנים. קנים מחוברים. חיצת שהיו נטועים כסדר מחיצה: דיומד. מפרש בפ' שני: *דיו עמודין — עמוד אחד נראה כשנים, שעשאו כמרזב ונוטה אחד ממחיצותיו לדרום ואחד למערב. דכי עביד ד' דיומדין לד' הפיאות — יש לכל מחיצה ב' אמות עומד, אמה מכאן ואמה מכאן: כזה

כדבעא מיניה. בפרק שני[א]: המסיך. נופו נוטה סמוך לארץ. ראש הנוף בפחות מג' לקרקע, ועיקרו — במקום שמחובר לאילן, גבוה עשרה: אין מטלטלין בו. אם היה היקפו יותר מבית סאתים כחצר המשכן. ושיעור זה נתנו חכמים לכל היקף המתוקן ואינו מתוקן כל צרכו, כגון למחיצה שאין בה שתי וערב בהאי פירקא (ד' טז:), ולהיקף שלא הוקף לדירה בפ' שני (ד' כד.), והכא נמי, אי בעומד מאליו מוקמת לה שפיר כו' — הואיל ולאו להכי עבידא, יהבו ביה רבנן האי שיעורא: משום דהוי דירה שתשמישה לאויר. לעולם שנטעו מתחילה לכך, והיקף לדירה הוא, אבל דירה זו אינה עשויה לנורך תוכה אלא לנורך אויר שחוצה לה, לדור שם שומרי השדות, ועשויי' להציל מן החמה, ואין מטלטלין בדירה זו אלא בית סאתים, כדתניא בפ' שני (ד' כג.): כלל אמר ר"ש בן אלעזר: כל אויר שתשמישו לדירה, כגון דיר וסהר ומוקצה וחצר, ואפילו י' כורים — מותר. וכל דירה שתשמישה לאויר, כגון בורגנין שבשדות, בית סאתים — מותר, יותר מבית סאתים — אסור, דלאו דירה הוא, דעל כרחו הוא דר שם: שבת בתל. קדש עליו היום, וקנה שם שביתתו: גבוה עשרה. דאמרינן: גוד אסיק מחיצותיו כל סביבותיו, והרי הוא מוקף: וכן נקע. אחד מנקיקי הסלעים: והוא מד' אמות עד בית סאתים. הואיל ושבת באויר מחיצותיו נעשית ביתו, וכולו כארבע אמותיו הוא. הלכך: מהלך את כולו וחוצה לו אלפים אמה. אבל אי הוה טפי מבית סאתים — אין מחיצותיו מועילות לו, שהיקף שאינו עשוי לדירה אינו מועיל אלא לבית סאתים, להכי נקט מארבע אמות ואילך, דאם היה פחות מד' אמות — מאי מהלך את כולו איכא? ומחיצותיו מאי מהניי? דבלאו מחיצה נמי, מקום לכל אדם ד' אמות, בפרק "מי שהוציאוהו" (לקמן ד' מא:): ושיבולות מקיפות אותה. שהניח גבוליה סביב מלקצור, ושבלים גבוהין י' עסקינן: תל ונקע מאי איכא למימר. מימות עולם הן: היוצאות מן הגדר. זו למעלה מזו: למיסר בניינא. שאם ירצה לעשות מחיצה מכותל זה לכותל שכנגדו יתקשר באבנים הללו, שכן דרך הבנאין לעשות. ובענין אחר אינו יכול לדבק בנין חדש בבנין ישן: לסמוך אדיקלא. דקל היה עומד אצל פתח המבוי: הא סמכינן הוי לחי. אלמא: הלכה כאביי: לימא בדלא סמכינן עליה פליגי. ואביי דשרי קשיא ליה האי עובדא דרב לא סמך אדיקלא, ואנן קים לן הלכתא כאביי בלחי העומד מאליו: ומתרץ לא ס"ד. דוודאי בדסמכינן עליה פליגי, אבל לא סמכינן — דברי הכל אינו לחי, כההוא עובדא דדיקלא דרב: ברקא. יליע: דהוה בי בר חבו. והיה עמוד הסומך את הגליע עומד בראש מבוי אחר: ואפליגו בה כולי שנייהו. אביי שרי למיסמך עליה, ורבא אסר. אלמא: בדסמכינן עליה פליגי. והלכתא כאביי בהא, דזו היא אחת מיע"ל קג"ס שהלכה כאביי: מתני' ומטמא משום גולל. אם עשאו גולל לקבר מטמא לעולם באהל כמת עצמו, ואפי' ניטל משם. דתניא בפ' "בהמה המקשה" (חולין עב.): "וכל אשר יגע על פני השדה" לרבות גולל ודופק:

תוספות

תא שמע העושה סוכתו. בפ' "הישן" (סוכה ד' כד:) מוקי לה דעביד לה בהולא ודפנא, דלא תקשי לרב אחא בר יעקב, דאמר: כל מחילה שאינה יכולה לעמוד ברוח, פירוש: שהרוח מנענעת' לכאן ולכאן — אינה מחילה. ואמאי כשרה? והא קאזיל ואתי! ולפי זה לא פריך הכא מידי, והוה מצי למימר: ולטעמיך. אי נמי: משמע ליה דמיירי בכל ענין, בין הוי רוב דופן מעובי האילן שאינו הולך ברוח, בין דהוי רוב דופן מן הנוף: אי הכי מאי למימרא. ולא סגי בשינויא דלעיל, דלא הוה נקט תרתי אטו חדא: תל ונקע מאי איכא למימר. ולא תקשי מכאן למ"ד (ג): מחילה שאינה עשויה בידי אדם לא שמה מחילה — דלא אתיא למעוטי אלא דבר שאינו ראוי להעשות בידי אדם, כגון בעלי חיים: אביי לטעמיה. היינו לחד לישנא דלעיל גבי היה גבוה מכ' ובא למעטו (ד' ה.), דקסבר: דאפילו קורה משום מחילה, וכל שכן לחי, ואותו לשון תופס עיקר. ורבא לטעמיה, דאמר לעיל*: אחד זה ואחד זה משום היכר. ור"ח לא גרס "לטעמיה" אלא גרס בהדיא "אביי אמר: לחי משום מחילה ורבא אמר לחי משום היכר". לא סבר לה מר למסמך אדיקלא. אף על גב דרב הונא אית ליה בפירקין (ד' י.) שבת הואיל והותרה הותרה, ולא נריך למסמך אדיקלא — הא מסיק לקמן דמודה רב הונא היכא דליתנהו למחילות, דלא אמרינן הואיל והותרה הותרה. אי נמי: הכא לפי דברי רב היה מקשה:

רבינו חננאל

א"ל פוק חזי היאך עמא דבר איכא דמתני לה על השותה מים לצמאו אומר שהכל נהיה בדברו. אתמר לחי העומד מאליו כגון אילן וכיוצא בו. אביי אמר הוי לחי רבא אמר לא הוי לחי וסברוה כי היכי דפליגי בלחי הכי פליגי במחיצות. ת"ש העושה סוכתו (על) [בין] האילנות והאילנות דפנות [לה] כשרה ודחי רבא הכי הכא במאי עסקינן כשעשאו לאילן בתחלה לשום דופן והא אתא לאשמעינן דלא גזרינן דלמא אתי להשתמושי בי"ט באילן. וכן נמי דחי במחיצת הקנים דתנינן דנידון משום דיומד כשעשאו מתחלה לכך. אי הכי מאי למימרא כלומר אם מתחלת עשאו לכך הא פשיטא היא ודחי לכדבעא אביי מרבה אצטריכא ליה וכדבעינן למימר לקמן. תא שמע מהא דתנן בהמוצא תפילין. אילן המיסך על הארץ כו'. ודחי הכא נמי כשעשאו לכך. אי הכי האי מחיצה מעלייתא היא. אלמה אמר רב הונא בריה דרב יהושע אין מטלטלין בו אלא בבית סאתים ומשני משום דהויא דירה שתשמישה לאויר כו'. ת"ש שבת בתל גבוה י' והוא מד' אמות ועד בית סאתים מפני שהיא דירה שתשמישה לאויר ואין לה אלא בית סאתים. וכן בנקע עמוק י' כו' עד וקמה קצורה או שיבולות מקיפות אותה מהלך את כולה וחוצה לה אלפים אמה הנה התל והנקע אי אפשר לומר בהן שעשאן מתחלה לכך. ופרקינן במחיצות כ"ע לא פליגי דמחיצה העשויה מאליה היא מחיצה. כי פליגי בלחי אביי אמר לחי משום מחיצה ומחיצה העשויה מאליה הויא מחיצה ורבא אמר לחי משום היכר ואי עשאו לכך הוי היכר ואי לא לא הוי היכר. ת"ש אבנים היוצאות מן הגדר ונראות בולטות ומובדלות זו מזו פחות משלשה אין צריך לחי אחר וכו'. *) פי' לאיסר בניינא. ת"ש דרב ורב הונא הוו יתבי במבוי א"ל רב לשמעיה אייתי לי מיא עד דאתו שמעא נפל הלחי א"ל רב קום אדוכתיך א"ל רב הונא ולסמוך מר אדיקלא. א"ל וכי סמכינן עליה מאתמול מכלל דאילו סמכינן עליה הוו לחי. לימא אביי ורבא בדלא סמך עליה מאתמול פליגי. ודחינן לה דההוא ברקא חלילה. פירוש בנין כמותא ומפורש בהמוכר את הבית. דהוה בדבי רב הונא על פי המבוי וחלקו בו אביי ורבא כל שנותם: בכל עושין לחיים כו'.

*) [נראה דצ"ל כאן ודחי ה"נ שבנאן מתחילה לכך א"ה פשיטא מהו דתימא למיסר בניינא].

תניא

עין משפט נר מצוה

צא א מיי' פי"ז מהל' שבת הלכה כב סמג עשין א טוש"ע א"ח סי' שסג סעיף יא:
צב ב מיי' פ"ד מהל' סוכה הלכה ה סמג עשין מג טוש"ע א"ח סי' תרל סעיף י:
צג ג מיי' פט"ז מהל' שבת הלכה כב ופכ"ז הלכה ד' ופ"ז מהלכות עירובין הלכה ד' סמג לאוין סה ועשין דרבנן א טוש"ע א"ח סי' שנו סעיף ב:
צד ד מיי' פט"ז מהל' שבת הלכה כב טוש"ע א"ח סי' שסב סעיף ג:
צה ה מיי' פי"ז מהל' שבת הלכה יב סמג עשין דרבנן א טוש"ע א"ח סי' שסג סעיף ג:
צו ו מיי' פ"ו מהלכות טומאת מת הלכה ד:

מסורת הש"ס

(דף יח.) | סוכה כד: | לקמן יט: [סוכה כד:] | [לקמן יט:] | [דף יג:] | לקמן עט: סוכה כד: | [לעיל יב:] | לעיל ט: [תוספתא פ"א] | [גיטין לט. ב"מ יא: ב"ב פד: חולין ה:] | [במשנה שבמשניות איתא ר' יוסי אוסר] | [ב"ב כב.] | [מנחות כא.] | [חולין עב.]

הגהות הב"ח

(א) רש"י ד"ה כדבעא מיניה בפ' שני. נ"ב סוף דף יט: (ב) תוס' ד"ה תל וכו' למ"ד מחילה. נ"ב בפרק הישן:

רב נסים גאון

מחיצת קנים קנה קנה פחות משלשה איצטריכא ליה כדבעא מיניה אביי מרבה. עיקר זו הבעיא בפרק עושין פסין (דף יט):

גליון הש"ס

גמ' וכל דירה שתשמישה לאויר. לקמן דף כב ע"א:

צז א מיי' פ"ד מהלכות גירושין הלכה ג סמג עשין נ טור שו"ע אה"ע סי' קכד סעיף ב:
צח ב ג מיי' פ"א שם הלכה ו וג סמג שם:
צט ד ה מיי' שם פ"ח הלכה יא ויב סמג שם טוש"ע אה"ע סי' קמג סעיף כ וכו':
ק ו ז מיי' פט"ז מהל' שבת הלכה טז טוש"ע א"ח סי' שסב סעיף ט:
קא ח ט י מיי' פ"ה מהלכות סוכה הלכה יא סמג עשין מג טוש"ע א"ח סי' תרלא סעיף ח:

וְר' מֵאִיר מְטַהֵר. [א]וְכוֹתְבִין עָלָיו גִּיטֵּי נָשִׁים, וְר' יוֹסֵי הַגְּלִילִי פּוֹסֵל.§ **גמ'** *תַּנְיָא, ר' מֵאִיר אוֹמֵר: כָּל דָּבָר שֶׁיֵּשׁ בּוֹ רוּחַ חַיִּים אֵין עוֹשִׂין אוֹתוֹ לֹא דּוֹפֶן לַסּוּכָּה, וְלֹא לֶחִי לַמָּבוֹי, לֹא פַּסִּין לַבִּירָאוֹת, וְלֹא גּוֹלֵל לַקֶּבֶר. מִשּׁוּם רַבִּי יוֹסֵי הַגְּלִילִי אָמְרוּ: אַף אֵין כּוֹתְבִין עָלָיו גִּיטֵּי נָשִׁים. מַאי טַעְמָא דְּרַבִּי יוֹסֵי הַגְּלִילִי? *דְּתַנְיָא: °"סֵפֶר", (דברים כד) אֵין לִי אֶלָּא סֵפֶר, מִנַּיִין לְרַבּוֹת כָּל דָּבָר – ת"ל °"וְכָתַב לָהּ" (שם) מִכָּל מָקוֹם. אִם כֵּן מַה ת"ל "סֵפֶר" – לוֹמַר לָךְ: מַה סֵפֶר דָּבָר שֶׁאֵין בּוֹ רוּחַ חַיִּים וְאֵינוֹ אוֹכֶל, אַף כָּל דָּבָר שֶׁאֵין בּוֹ רוּחַ חַיִּים וְאֵינוֹ אוֹכֶל. וְרַבָּנַן: מִי כְּתִיב "בְּסֵפֶר"? "סֵפֶר" כְּתִיב – לְסִפִּירוּת דְּבָרִים בְּעָלְמָא הוּא דַּאֲתָא. וְרַבָּנַן, הַאי "וְכָתַב לָהּ" מַאי דָּרְשִׁי בֵּיהּ? הַהוּא מִבָּעֵי לֵיהּ: *[ב]בִּכְתִיבָה מִתְגָּרֶשֶׁת, וְאֵינָהּ מִתְגָּרֶשֶׁת בְּכֶסֶף. סָלְקָא דַּעְתָּךְ אָמִינָא: הוֹאִיל וְאִיתַּקַּשׁ יְצִיאָה לַהֲוָיָה, מַה הֲוָיָה בְּכֶסֶף אַף יְצִיאָה בְּכֶסֶף – קמ"ל. וְר' יוֹסֵי הַגְּלִילִי, הַאי סְבָרָא מְנָא לֵיהּ? נָפְקָא לֵיהּ מִ"סֵּפֶר כְּרִיתוּת" – סֵפֶר כּוֹרְתָהּ וְאֵין דָּבָר אַחֵר כּוֹרְתָהּ. וְרַבָּנַן, הַאי "סֵפֶר כְּרִיתוּת" מִיבָּעֵי לֵיהּ לְדָבָר [ג]הַכּוֹרֵת בֵּינוֹ לְבֵינָהּ. *לִכְדְתַנְיָא: [ד]הֲרֵי זֶה גִּיטֵּךְ עַל מְנָת שֶׁלֹּא תִּשְׁתִּי יַיִן, [ה]עַל מְנָת שֶׁלֹּא תֵּלְכִי לְבֵית אָבִיךְ לְעוֹלָם – אֵין זֶה כְּרִיתוּת. כָּל שְׁלֹשִׁים יוֹם – הֲרֵי זֶה כְּרִיתוּת. וְרַבִּי יוֹסֵי הַגְּלִילִי נָפְקָא לֵיהּ מִ"כָּרֵת" "כְּרִיתוּת". וְרַבָּנַן, "כָּרֵת" "כְּרִיתוּת" לָא דָּרְשִׁי.§

מתני' שַׁיָּירָא שֶׁחָנְתָה בַּבִּקְעָה וְהִקִּיפוּהָ כְּלֵי בְהֵמָה – מְטַלְטְלִין בְּתוֹכָהּ, וּבִלְבַד שֶׁיְּהֵא גָּדֵר גָּבוֹהַּ עֲשָׂרָה טְפָחִים, וְלֹא יְהוּ פִּירְצוֹת יְתֵרוֹת עַל הַבִּנְיָן. [ו]כָּל פִּירְצָה שֶׁהִיא כְּעֶשֶׂר אַמּוֹת – מוּתֶּרֶת, מִפְּנֵי שֶׁהִיא כְּפֶתַח, יָתֵר מִכָּאן – אָסוּר.§ **גמ'** אִיתְּמַר: *פָּרוּץ כְּעוֹמֵד, רַב פַּפָּא אָמַר: [ז]מוּתָּר. רַב הוּנָא בְּרֵיהּ דְּרַב יְהוֹשֻׁעַ אָמַר: אָסוּר. רַב פַּפָּא אָמַר: מוּתָּר, הָכִי אַגְמְרֵיהּ רַחֲמָנָא לְמֹשֶׁה: לֹא תִּפְרוֹץ רוּבָּהּ. רַב הוּנָא בְּרֵיהּ דְּרַב יְהוֹשֻׁעַ אָמַר: אָסוּר, הָכִי אַגְמְרֵיהּ רַחֲמָנָא לְמֹשֶׁה: גְּדוֹר רוּבָּהּ. תְּנַן: וְלֹא יְהוּ פִּירְצוֹת יְתֵרוֹת עַל הַבִּנְיָן, הָא כַּבִּנְיָן – מוּתָּר! לָא תֵּימָא הָא כַּבִּנְיָן מוּתָּר, אֶלָּא אֵימָא: אִם בִּנְיָן יָתֵר עַל הַפִּירְצָה – מוּתָּר. אֲבָל כַּבִּנְיָן מַאי? אָסוּר? אִי הָכִי, לִיתְנֵי: "לֹא יְהוּ פִּירְצוֹת כַּבִּנְיָן"! קַשְׁיָא. ת"ש: *[ח]הַמְקָרֶה סוּכָּתוֹ בַּשַּׁפּוּדִין אוֹ בַּאֲרוּכוֹת הַמִּטָּה, אִם יֵשׁ רֶיוַח בֵּינֵיהֶן כְּמוֹתָן – כְּשֵׁירָה! הָכָא בְּמַאי עָסְקִינַן – כְּשֶׁנִּכְנָס וְיוֹצֵא. וְהָא אֶפְשָׁר לְצַמְצֵם! אָמַר רַבִּי אַמִי: [ט]בְּמַעְדִּיף. רָבָא אָמַר: [י]אִם הָיוּ נְתוּנִין עֵרֶב – נוֹתְנוֹ שְׁתִי, שְׁתִי – נוֹתְנוֹ עֵרֶב. ת"ש: שַׁיָּירָא שֶׁחָנְתָה בַּבִּקְעָה וְהִקִּיפוּהָ בִּגְמַלִּין, בְּאוּכָּפוֹת, בַּעֲבִיטִין

וְרַבִּי מֵאִיר מְטַהֵר. וְטַעְמָא דְּרַבִּי מֵאִיר מְפָרֵשׁ בְּמַסֶּכֶת סוּכָּה בְּכוּלְּהוּ, מִשּׁוּם דְּקָסָבַר: כָּל מְחִיצָּה הָעוֹמֶדֶת בְּרוּחַ חַיִּים – אֵינָהּ מְחִיצָּה: **גמ'** וְלֹא גּוֹלֵל לַקֶּבֶר. כְּלוֹמַר: אִם עֲשָׂאוֹ גּוֹלֵל – אֵין שֵׁם גּוֹלֵל חָל עָלָיו לְטַמֵּא. גּוֹלֵל הוּא כִּיסּוּי שֶׁנּוֹתְנִין דַּף עַל הַמֵּת: סֵפֶר. "וְכָתַב לָהּ סֵפֶר כְּרִיתוּת", "סֵפֶר" מַשְׁמַע קְלָף, כִּדְכְתִיב "וַאֲנִי כּוֹתֵב עַל הַסֵּפֶר בַּדְּיוֹ". וַהֲדַר קָרֵי לֵיהּ מְגִילָּה כִּדְכְתִיב (ירמיה לו) "אַחֲרֵי שְׂרֹף [הַמֶּלֶךְ] אֶת הַמְּגִילָּה": מִנַּיִין לְרַבּוֹת כָּל דָּבָר. שֶׁיִּכְתּוֹב הַגֵּט עָלָיו: אִי הֲוָה כְּתִיב "וְכָתַב לָהּ כְּרִיתוּת בְּסֵפֶר" – הֲוָה מַשְׁמַע מְגִילָּה. אֲבָל הַשְׁתָּא דִּכְתִיב "סֵפֶר" הַאי "סֵפֶר" – סִפִּירוּת דְּבָרִים הוּא. וְהָכִי מַשְׁמַע, וְכָתַב לָהּ דִּבְרֵי כְּרִיתוּת. אֲבָל לֹא קָבַע לוֹ מָקוֹם לְכוֹתְבוֹ, וּמִמֵּילָא מַשְׁמַע בְּכָל מָקוֹם שֶׁיִּרְצֶה יִכְתְּבֶנּוּ: וְכָתַב לָהּ מַאי דָּרְשִׁי בֵּיהּ. כֵּיוָן דְּסֵפֶר לָאו קְלָף מַשְׁמַע, מִמֵּילָא הָא לָא קָבַע לֵיהּ קְלָף, וּבְכָל דָּבָר מַשְׁמַע. וְלָמָּה לֵיהּ לְמִיכְתַּב "וְכָתַב" לְרַבּוֹת כָּל דָּבָר, לִכְתּוֹב "וְנָתַן לָהּ סֵפֶר כְּרִיתוּת": וְאֵינָהּ מִתְגָּרֶשֶׁת בְּכֶסֶף. אִם נָתַן לָהּ כֶּסֶף וְאָמַר: הִתְגָּרְשִׁי בּוֹ: וְהָיְתָה לְאִישׁ אַחֵר. הַיְינוּ קִדּוּשִׁין: מַה הֲוָיָה בְּכֶסֶף. דְּגָמְרִינַן בְּמַסֶּכֶת קִידּוּשִׁין (דף ב.) 'קִיחָה' 'קִיחָה' מִשְּׂדֵה עֶפְרוֹן: מִסֵּפֶר כְּרִיתוּת. מִדִּכְתִיב כְּרִיתוּת סָמוּךְ לְסֵפֶר: לְדָבָר הַכּוֹרֵת בֵּינוֹ לְבֵינָהּ. שֶׁלֹּא יַטִּיל תְּנַאי בַּגֵּט שֶׁיִּקָּשְׁרוּ יַחַד, אֶלָּא דִּבְרֵי הַבְדָּלָה יְהוּ: לְעוֹלָם אֵין זֶה כְּרִיתוּת. דְּהָא כָּל יָמֶיהָ קְשׁוּרָה בּוֹ, שֶׁמֵּחֲמָתוֹ הִיא נִמְנַעַת מִלִּשְׁתּוֹת יַיִן. וּתְנַאי זֶה תָּלוּי וְהוֹלֵךְ לְעוֹלָם, וְאֵין זֶה הַבְדָּלָה. אֲבָל מִכָּאן וְעַד שְׁלֹשִׁים יוֹם – הֲרֵי זֶה כְּרִיתוּת מִיָּד, שֶׁהֲרֵי דִּבְרֵי הַבְדָּלָה הֵן לְסוֹף שְׁלֹשִׁים יוֹם וּמוּתֶּרֶת מִיָּד לְאִישׁ אַחֵר: **מתני'** וְלֹא יְהוּ פִּרְצוֹת יְתֵירוֹת עַל הַבִּנְיָן. וַאֲפִילּוּ הֵן פִּרְצוֹת קְטַנּוֹת פְּחוּתוֹת מֵעֶשֶׂר: כָּל פִּרְצָה שֶׁהִיא כְּעֶשֶׂר מוּתֶּרֶת מִפְּנֵי שֶׁהִיא כְּפֶתַח. וְשֶׁיְּהֵא בָּעוֹמֵד רַב עֲלֵיהֶן: יָתֵר מִכָּאן אֲסוּרָה. פִּרְצָה אַחַת אוֹסֶרֶת כָּל הַהֶיקֵּף, אֲפִילּוּ כּוּלּוֹ עוֹמֵד, כִּדְמְפָרֵשׁ בַּבָּרַיְיתָא לְקַמָּן: **גמ'** פָּרוּץ כְּעוֹמֵד. כָּל הַהֶיקֵּף כּוּלּוֹ עָשׂוּי כֵּן: אַגְמְרֵיהּ רַחֲמָנָא לְמֹשֶׁה. כִּדְאָמַר בְּרֵישׁ פִּירְקִין (דף ד.): מְחִיצּוֹת וְהִלְכוֹתֵיהֶן הֲלָכָה לְמֹשֶׁה מִסִּינַי: שַׁפּוּדִין וַאֲרוּכוֹת הַמִּטָּה פְּסוּלִין לְסַכֵּךְ בָּהֶן, לְפִי שֶׁכֵּלִים הֵן וּמְקַבְּלִין טוּמְאָה. וּתְנַן (סוכה דף יא.): כָּל דָּבָר הַמְקַבֵּל טוּמְאָה אֵין מְסַכְּכִין בּוֹ: אֲרוּכוֹת. = אשפונד"ש: אִם יֵשׁ רֶיוַח בֵּינֵיהֶן כְּמוֹתָן. לְסַכֵּךְ שָׁם בִּסְכָךְ כָּשֵׁר. אַלְמָא: פָּרוּץ כְּעוֹמֵד מוּתָּר. דְּהָא הָכָא פָּסוּל כְּכָשֵׁר הוּא, וְשָׁרֵי. וְקַשְׁיָא נַמִי הָא לְרַב הוּנָא: בְּנִכְנָס וְיוֹצֵא. שֶׁיְּהֵא שַׁפּוּד יָכוֹל לִיכָּנֵס וְלֵיצֵא בָּרֶיוַח שֶׁבֵּינְתַיִם, דְּהַשְׁתָּא הָוֵי רֶיוַח טְפֵי מִשִּׁיעוּר שַׁפּוּד, וְאֵינוֹ מְלוּמְצָם: וְהָא אֶפְשָׁר לְצַמְצֵם. דְּקס"ד דְּהַאי דְּקָא מְתָרֵץ בִּנְכְנָס וְיוֹצֵא הָכִי קָמְתָרֵץ: דְּכָל כְּמוֹתָן בִּנְכְנָס וְיוֹצֵא הוּא, דְּאֵין דֶּרֶךְ לְצַמְצֵם, לְכָךְ פָּרֵיךְ: וְהָא אֶפְשָׁר לְצַמְצֵם וּלְכַוֵּין שֶׁלֹּא יְהֵא לוֹ רֶיוַח יוֹתֵר וַאֲנַן כְּמוֹתָן תְּנַן: אָמַר ר' אַמִי. מַתְנִיתִין בְּלֹא צִמְצֵם אֶלָּא בְּמַעְדִּיף רֶיוַח יוֹתֵר מִשִּׁיעוּר שַׁפּוּדִין. וּ"כְמוֹתָן" דְּקָתָנֵי – כְּשִׁיעוּר שַׁפּוּדִין בִּנְכְנָס וְיוֹצֵא: אִם הָיוּ. שַׁפּוּדִין נְתוּנִין שְׁתִי – נוֹתֵן לְסַכֵּךְ כָּשֵׁר עֵרֶב, דַּאֲפִילּוּ לֹא הֶעֱדִיף הָרֶיוַח אִיכָּא סְכָךְ כָּשֵׁר טְפֵי, דְּכֵיוָן דְּנוֹתְנוֹ עֵרֶב אִי אֶפְשָׁר לַעֲמוֹד אֶלָּא אִם כֵּן רֹאשׁוֹ אֶחָד מוּנָּח עַל הַשַּׁפּוּד מִכָּאן, וְרֹאשׁוֹ אֶחָד מוּנָּח עַל הַשַּׁפּוּד מִכָּאן:
עֲבִיטִין

תלמוד לומר וכתב לה מכל מקום. וא"ת: ולימא, "וכתב לה" – כלל, "ספר" – פרט, אין בכלל אלא מה שבפרט: ספר – אין, מידי אחרינא – לא! וי"ל: "ונתן בידה" חזר וכלל. אף על גב דלא מייתי בברייתא אלא כללא קמא – אין לחוש, דכה"ג איכא בקדושין בפ"ק (ד' כא:), דקתני בברייתא: אין לי אלא מרצע, הסול והסירא מנין? ת"ל: "ולקחת" – כל דבר הנקח ביד, ומשמע בתר הכי דמכלל ופרט וכלל דריש, דקאמר "ונתת באזנו" – חזר וכלל: **מה** ספר דבר שאין בו רוח חיים. בפ' "בכל מערבין" (לקמן ד' כז:) גבי מעשר שני [בבקר ובצאן] נקט לד של פרי מפרי וגדולי קרקע. ובפרק קמא דסוכה (ד' יא:) גבי חגיגה נקט: מה חגיגה דבר שאינו מקבל טומאה וגדולו מן הארץ – הכל לפי מה שדומה לחכמים:

ורבנן האי וכתב לה מאי עבדי. אע"ג דאיצטריך למדרש: "וכתב לה" – לשמה, תרי "וכתב לה" כתיבי. והא דדרשינן ב"המגרש" (גיטין ד' פז.): "וכתב לה" ולא לה ולחברתה – התם דריש מ"לה" ד"וכתב" דהכא:

בכתיבה מתגרשת ולא בכסף. הך דרשה לא אתיא אלא לרבא, אבל לאביי נפקא ליה בפרק קמא דקדושין (ד' ה.) מסברא, דאין סניגור נעשה קטיגור. ומכל מקום, לאביי נמי איצטריך "וכתב" – בכתיבה מתגרשת ולא בחליצה. והא דדריש לה בריש קדושין (ד' ג:) דאינה יוצאה בחליצה מ"ספר כורתה" – ההיא דרשה כר' יוסי הגלילי, כדמשמע הכא. ונקט לה – משום דהויא דרשה פשוטה טפי, וכן דרך התלמוד. כדאשכחן ב"החובל" (ב"ק ד' פז.) דמייתי קרא ד"בנעוריה בית אביה" לגבי חבלה. וריש קדושין (ד' ג:) קאמר דבהפרת נדרים הוא דכתיב, ובריש פרק "אחד דיני ממונות" (סנהדרין ד' לד:) דריש דראיית נגעים ביום מ"וביום הראות בו", דהיינו כאביי דפ"ק דמועד קטן, (ד' ח.) ושביק דרשה דרבא דדריש התם מדכתיב "לי" ולא לאורי*:

על מנת שלא תלכי לבית אביך. תימה: דהא אם מת אביה *לא חשיב תו בית אביה, כדתניא בנדרים ב"השותפין" (ד' מו.): קונם לביתך שאני נכנס, שדך שאני לוקח. מת או מכרו לאחר – מיד מותר! וי"ל: דבית אביה קרויים כל יוצאי חלציו, כדכתיב בתמר (בראשית לח): "שבי אלמנה בית אביך" אע"ג דקרא מוכחי שכבר מת שם*:

ורבי יוסי הגלילי(א) מכרת כריתות. קשה לר"י: דבגיטין בריש "המגרש" (ד' פג:) קאמר על רבנן דרבי אלעזר בן עזריה דכרת כריתות לא דרשי, ורבי יוסי הגלילי הוא בכלל הנהו רבנן! וי"ל: דהתם קאמר דלא דרשי להאי דרשה, ולא בעי למימר דלא דרשי ליה כלל:

פרוץ כעומד. מכאן משמע דאפשר לצמצם, כדפירש' לעיל*, ומפרק שני דחולין (ד' לח:) דמוקי קרא ד"תחת אמו" פרט ליתום – זה פירש למיתה וזה פירש לחיים. ואם אי אפשר לצמצם – אמאי איצטריך למעוטי? מספיקא הייתי אוסר, דילמא מתה אמו והדר ילדתו והוה ליה יוצא דופן! אין לדקדק דשבקינן לקרא דדחיק. ואיצטריך, לשאם יבא אליהו ויאמר. ויש להביא ראיה מפרק "בהמה המקשה" (חולין דף ע.) גבי בעיא דהלכו באיברים אחר הרוב, דמוקי לה כגון שילא חציו ברוב אבר, ואם אי אפשר לצמצם – מאי קמיבעי ליה? ממה נפשך טעון קבורה, שמא יצא רובו: **רש"י** גרים והא אפשר לצמצם. פירוש: כיון דאפשר לצמצם – אית לן למימר כמותו דווקא קאמר. אמר רבי אמי: במעדיף, כלומר: מתניתין בלא צמצם, וכמותו דקתני – ביוצא ונכנס, ותימה:
דאין

סוכה כג:
שם כד: גיטין כא:
שם
קידושין ה.
סוכה כד: יומא יג. גיטין כא: פג:
לעיל י: סוכה טו
סוכה שם

[וע"ע תוספות שבת דף קכת. ד"ה ונתן וכו']
ושמא אפ"ה אין זה כריתות כיון דבשעת גירושין אינו יודע שימות אביה קודם [ת"י]
[עי' תוס' סוכה כב: בד"ה על מנת]

הגהות הב"ח
(א) תום' ד"ה ור' יוסי הגלילי נפקא ליה מכרת:

רבינו חננאל
תניא היה ר' מאיר אומר כל דבר שיש בו רוח חיים אין עושין אותו לא דופן לסוכה ולא לחי למבוי ולא פסין לביראות כו' משום ר' יוסי הגלילי אמרו אף אין כותבין עליו גיטי נשים דתניא ספר אין לי אלא ספר מנין לרבות כל דבר ת"ל וכתב לה כו': מתני' שיירא שחנתה בבקעה וכו'. אתמר פרוץ כעומד רב פפא אמר מותר הכי אגמריה רחמנא למשה לא תפרוץ רובה רב הונא בריה דרב יהושע אמר אסור הכי אגמריה רחמנא למשה גדור רובה ודייקינן מדקתני במתני' לא יהו פרוצות יתירות על הבנין ולא קתני לא יהו פרוצות כבנין ש"מ פרוץ כבנין שרי כרב פפא. ת"ש המקרה סוכתו בשפודין או בארוכות המטה אם יש ריוח ביניהן כמותן כשרה ש"מ פרוץ כעומד שרי. ודחינן מאי כמותן כמלא נכנס ויוצא שהוא יותר כמעט. ואקשינן *) והא אי אפשר לצמצם כלומר אם מרחיב בנכנס ויוצא כשאתה נותן הפסל ביניהן נמצאת אתה דוחק באחד. ושנינן במעדיף כדי שלא יבואו לידי דוחק. רבא אמר מניח כדי שיעור נכנס ויוצא וממלאהו מסכך כשר. אם היו השפודין נתונין לאורך בשתי נותן הסכך הכשר על גבן לרוחב הסוכה בערב. ת"ש שיירה שחנתה בבקעה והקיפוה גמלים

*) [דברי רבינו ז"ל וגירסתו יתפרשו ע"פ התוס' כאן בד"ה רש"י גרים ע"ש]

בַּעֲבִיטִין, בִּשְׁלִיפִין, בְּקָנִים, בְּקוֹלָחוֹת — מְטַלְטְלִין בְּתוֹכָהּ, וּבִלְבַד שֶׁלֹּא יְהֵא בֵּין גָּמָל לְגָמָל כִּמְלֹא גָּמָל, וּבֵין אוּכָּף לְאוּכָּף כִּמְלֹא אוּכָּף, וּבֵין עָבִיט לְעָבִיט כִּמְלֹא עָבִיט. הָכָא נַמִי, כְּשֶׁנִּכְנָס וְיוֹצֵא. תָּא שְׁמַע: *נִמְצֵאתָ אַתָּה אוֹמֵר שָׁלֹשׁ מִדּוֹת בַּמְּחִיצוֹת: [א]כֹּל שֶׁהוּא פָּחוֹת מִשְּׁלֹשָׁה — צָרִיךְ שֶׁלֹּא יְהֵא בֵּין זֶה לָזֶה שְׁלֹשָׁה, כְּדֵי שֶׁלֹּא יִזְדַּקֵּר הַגְּדִי בְּבַת רֹאשׁ. כֹּל שֶׁהוּא ג' [ב]וּמִג' עַד ד' — צָרִיךְ שֶׁלֹּא יְהֵא בֵּין זֶה לָזֶה כִּמְלוֹאוֹ, כְּדֵי שֶׁלֹּא יְהֵא פָּרוּץ כְּעוֹמֵד. וְאִם הָיָה פָּרוּץ מְרוּבֶּה עַל הָעוֹמֵד — אַף כְּנֶגֶד הָעוֹמֵד אָסוּר. כֹּל שֶׁהוּא ד' וּמֵאַרְבָּעָה עַד עֶשֶׂר אַמּוֹת — צָרִיךְ שֶׁלֹּא יְהֵא בֵּין זֶה לָזֶה כִּמְלוֹאוֹ, שֶׁלֹּא יְהֵא פָּרוּץ כְּעוֹמֵד. וְאִם הָיָה פָּרוּץ כְּעוֹמֵד — כְּנֶגֶד הָעוֹמֵד מוּתָּר, כְּנֶגֶד הַפָּרוּץ אָסוּר. וְאִם הָיָה עוֹמֵד מְרוּבֶּה עַל הַפָּרוּץ — אַף כְּנֶגֶד הַפָּרוּץ מוּתָּר. נִפְרְצָה בְּיוֹתֵר מֵעֶשֶׂר — אָסוּר. *הָיוּ שָׁם קָנִים הַדּוּקְרָנִים וְעוֹשֶׂה לָהֶן פֵּיאָה מִלְמַעְלָה — אֲפִילּוּ בְּיוֹתֵר מֵעֶשֶׂר מוּתָּר. קָתָנֵי מִיהַת רֵישָׁא מִג' וְעַד ד', וּבִלְבַד שֶׁלֹּא יְהֵא בֵּין זֶה לָזֶה כִּמְלוֹאוֹ, תְּיוּבְתָּא דְּרַב פַּפָּא! אָמַר לָךְ רַב פַּפָּא: מַאי מְלוֹאוֹ — נִכְנָס וְיוֹצֵא. הָכִי נַמִי מִסְתַּבְּרָא, מִדְּקָתָנֵי: אִם הָיָה פָּרוּץ מְרוּבֶּה עַל הָעוֹמֵד — אַף כְּנֶגֶד הָעוֹמֵד אָסוּר. הָא כְּעוֹמֵד — מוּתָּר. שְׁמַע מִינָּהּ. לֵימָא תֶּיהֱוֵי תְּיוּבְתֵּיהּ דְּר"ה בְּרֵיהּ דְּרַב יְהוֹשֻׁעַ! אָמַר לָךְ: וְלִיטַעְמִיךְ, אֵימָא סֵיפָא: אִם הָיָה עוֹמֵד מְרוּבֶּה עַל הַפָּרוּץ — אַף כְּנֶגֶד הַפָּרוּץ מוּתָּר. הָא כְּפָרוּץ — אָסוּר. סֵיפָא קַשְׁיָא לְרַב פַּפָּא, רֵישָׁא קַשְׁיָא לְר"ה בְּרֵיהּ דְּרַב יְהוֹשֻׁעַ. סֵיפָא לְרַב פַּפָּא לָא קַשְׁיָא — *אַיְּידֵי דִּתְנָא רֵישָׁא "פָּרוּץ מְרוּבֶּה עַל הָעוֹמֵד" תְּנָא סֵיפָא "עוֹמֵד מְרוּבֶּה עַל הַפָּרוּץ". רֵישָׁא לְרַב הוּנָא בְּרֵיהּ דְּרַב יְהוֹשֻׁעַ לָא קַשְׁיָא, אַיְּידֵי דְּבָעֵי לְמִיתְנֵי סֵיפָא "עוֹמֵד מְרוּבֶּה עַל הַפָּרוּץ" תְּנָא רֵישָׁא "פָּרוּץ מְרוּבֶּה עַל הָעוֹמֵד". בִּשְׁלָמָא לְרַב פַּפָּא — מִשּׁוּם הָכִי לָא עָרֵיב לְהוּ וְתָנֵי לְהוּ, אֶלָּא לְרַב הוּנָא בְּרֵיהּ דְּרַב יְהוֹשֻׁעַ לִיעָרְבִינְהוּ וְלִיתְנִינְהוּ: כֹּל שֶׁהוּא פָּחוֹת מִשְּׁלֹשָׁה וּשְׁלֹשָׁה — צָרִיךְ שֶׁלֹּא יְהֵא בֵּין זֶה לָזֶה שְׁלֹשָׁה! מִשּׁוּם דְּלָא דָּמֵי פְּסוּלָא דְּרֵישָׁא לִפְסוּלָא דְּסֵיפָא; פְּסוּלָא דְּרֵישָׁא — כְּדֵי שֶׁלֹּא יִזְדַּקֵּר הַגְּדִי בְּבַת אַחַת, פְּסוּלָא דְּסֵיפָא — שֶׁלֹּא יְהֵא פָּרוּץ כְּעוֹמֵד. פָּחוֹת מִשְּׁלֹשָׁה מַנִּי — רַבָּנַן הִיא, דְּאָמְרִי: *פָּחוֹת מִשְּׁלֹשָׁה אָמְרִינַן לָבוּד, שְׁלֹשָׁה — לָא אָמְרִינַן לָבוּד. אֵימָא סֵיפָא: כֹּל שֶׁהוּא שְׁלֹשָׁה וּמִשְּׁלֹשָׁה וְעַד אַרְבָּעָה — אֲתָאן

עֲבִיטִין. כַּר שֶׁתַּחַת אוּכַּף הַגָּמָל. כִּדְמְתַרְגְּמִינַן (בראשית לא) "בְּכַר הַגָּמָל" בַּעֲבִיטָא דְּגַמְלָא: שְׁלִיפִין. מַשׂוּאוֹת: קוֹלָחוֹת. קַלְחֵי יְרָקוֹת: נִמְצֵאתָ אַתָּה אוֹמֵר כו'. רֵישָׁא בְּמַסֶּכֶת כִּלְאַיִם (פ"ד משנה ד') תָּנֵינַן לָהּ: כָּל שֶׁהוּא פָּחוֹת מִג'. כָּל גָּדֵר הֶעָשׂוּי בְּקָנִים עוֹמְדִין פָּחוֹת מֵרוֹחַב ג': צָרִיךְ שֶׁלֹּא יְהֵא בֵּין זֶה לָזֶה ג' כְּדֵי שֶׁלֹּא יִזְדַּקֵּר הַגְּדִי בְּבַת רֹאשׁ. כְּלוֹמַר: לְהֶדְיָא, בְּלֹא עִכּוּב. דִּדְקִירַת גְּדִי מְבַטֵּל לָהּ מִתּוֹרַת לָבוּד. וְאִם אֵין בֵּין זֶה לָזֶה ג' — אֲפִי' פָּרוּץ מְרוּבֶּה עַל הָעוֹמֵד, כְּגוֹן קָנִים שֶׁל ג' אֶצְבָּעוֹת וְרֶיוַח ג' טְפָחִים בֵּין זֶה לָזֶה — כָּשֵׁר, דְּכָל רֶיוַח פָּחוֹת מִג' אָמְרִי' לָבוּד, וְכוּלּוֹ הָוֵי עוֹמֵד: וּמִג' וְעַד ד'. וְלֹא ד' בִּכְלָל: צָרִיךְ שֶׁלֹּא יְהֵא בֵּין זֶה לָזֶה כִּמְלוֹאוֹ. וְכָל כַּמָּה דְּלָא הָוֵי כִּמְלוֹאוֹ, אע"ג דְּהָוֵי רֶיוַח שְׁלֹשָׁה — כֵּיוָן דְּעוֹמֵד רָבֶה עָלָיו לֵיכָּא לְמֵימַר אָתֵי אֲוִירָא דְּהַאי גִּיסָא וּדְהַאי גִּיסָא וּמְבַטֵּל לֵיהּ, וְהָווּ לְהוּ פְּתָחִים: וְאִם הָיָה פָּרוּץ כו'. לְקַמָּן מְתָרֵץ לָהּ: אִם הָיָה פָּרוּץ כְּעוֹמֵד הֲוָה לֵיהּ לְמִיתְנֵי: אַף כְּנֶגֶד הָעוֹמֵד אָסוּר. לִזְרוֹעַ, דְּלָא חָלֵים עוֹמֵד בְּפָחוֹת מִד' לְמִישְׁרֵי כְּנֶגְדּוֹ הֵיכָא דְּפָרוּץ רָבֶה עָלָיו: וְעַד עֶשֶׂר. וְעֶשֶׂר בִּכְלָל. אֲבָל יוֹתֵר מִי' כְּגוֹן עוֹמֵד י"ב אוֹ ט"ו — לָא מָצֵי לְמִיתְנֵי שִׁיעוּר פִּירְצָתוֹ בִּמְלוֹאוֹ, דַּאֲפִי' בְּצִיר מִמְּלוֹאוֹ, דְּאִיכָּא פִּירְצָה יוֹתֵר מֵעֲשָׂרָה *מִיתְּסַר כּוּלּוֹ, כִּדְתָנֵי סֵיפָא: כְּנֶגֶד הָעוֹמֵד מוּתָּר. הוֹאִיל וְהֶיקֵּף חָשׁוּב הוּא וְה"ה אִם הָיָה פָּרוּץ מְרוּבֶּה. וּלְקַמָּן מְתָרֵץ לָהּ. הֲרֵי כָּאן שָׁלֹשׁ מִדּוֹת, בְּמִדָּה רִאשׁוֹנָה דְּקָנִים פְּחוּתִים מִג' — לָא קָפְדִינַן אַמְּלוֹאוֹ, כֵּיוָן דִּמְלוֹאוֹ לָא הָוֵי פִּירְצָה שְׁלֹשָׁה. וַאֲפִי' אַיּוֹתֵר מִמְּלוֹאוֹ לָא קָפְדִינַן, עַד דְּאִיכָּא פִּירְצָה שְׁלֹשָׁה. וּבְמִדָּה שְׁנִיָּה קָפְדִינַן אַמְּלוֹאוֹ, דְּהָא אִיכָּא שִׁיעוּר פִּירְצָה לְמֶיהֱוֵי קָרוּי אֲוִיר, וְאָתֵי אֲוִיר הַמְּרוּבֶּה וּמְבַטֵּל לָעוֹמֵד, דַּאֲפִי' כְּנֶגְדּוֹ אֵינוֹ מַתִּיר. וּבְמִדָּה שְׁלִישִׁית דְּאִיכָּא עוֹמֵד חָשׁוּב — אֲוִיר לָא מְבַטֵּל לָהּ לְגַמְרֵי, וּמַתִּיר מִיהָא כְּנֶגְדָּהּ: וְאִם הָיָה עוֹמֵד מְרוּבֶּה כו'. אַכּוּלָּהּ קָאֵי, וַאֲפִי' אַעוֹמֵד מִג' וְעַד ד' דְּהָא קָתָנֵי בָּהּ נַמִי צָרִיךְ שֶׁלֹּא יְהֵא בֵּין זֶה לָזֶה כִּמְלוֹאוֹ, הָא בְּצִיר מִמְּלוֹאוֹ — שָׁרֵי: נִפְרְצָה בְּיוֹתֵר מִי' אָסוּר. וַאֲפִי' כּוּלּוֹ עוֹמֵד: הָיוּ שָׁם קָנִים הַדּוּקְרָנִין. מְשׁוּפִּין כְּדֶקֶר, נְעוּצִין בָּאָרֶץ, וְעָשָׂה לָהֶן פֵּאָה קְלוּעָה מִלְמַעְלָה מִזֶּה לָזֶה: אֲפִי' בְּיוֹתֵר מֵעֶשֶׂר אַמּוֹת מוּתָּר. דְּלוּרַת הַפֶּתַח מְהַנְיָא בְּכִלְאַיִם אַף לְיוֹתֵר מֵעֶשֶׂר: מַאי מְלוֹאוֹ נִכְנָס וְיוֹצֵא. וְהָכִי מַשְׁמַע בָּרַיְיתָא: כָּל שֶׁהוּא ג' וּמִג' וְעַד ד' — צָרִיךְ שֶׁלֹּא יְהֵא בֵּין זֶה לָזֶה מִילּוּאוֹ נִכְנָס וְיוֹצֵא, שֶׁלֹּא יְהֵא פָּרוּץ כְּעוֹמֵד בְּנִכְנָס וְיוֹצֵא, דַּהֲוָה לֵיהּ פָּרוּץ מְרוּבֶּה. וְאִם הָיָה פָּרוּץ מְרוּבֶּה עַל הָעוֹמֵד — אַף כְּנֶגֶד הָעוֹמֵד אָסוּר, הוֹאִיל וְהוּקַּף בְּדָבָר שֶׁאֵינוֹ חָשׁוּב, שֶׁאֵין בּוֹ רוֹחַב ד': אַיְּידֵי דִּתְנָא רֵישָׁא פָּרוּץ מְרוּבֶּה עַל הָעוֹמֵד. אָסוּר. דְּלָא סַגְיָא דְּלָא קָתָנֵי לָהּ לְגַלּוּיֵי אַמְּלוֹאוֹ דְּלָאו מְצוּמְצָם קָאָמַר, דְּקמ"ל: הָא כְּעוֹמֵד — מוּתָּר אַף כְּנֶגֶד הַפָּרוּץ: תְּנָא סֵיפָא עוֹמֵד מְרוּבֶּה עַל הַפָּרוּץ. אע"ג דְּלָא אִיצְטְרִיךְ לֵיהּ, דְּהָא מִגּוּפָהּ שָׁמְעַתְּ מִינָּהּ דַּאֲפִי' יֵשׁ עוֹמֵד כְּפָרוּץ שָׁרֵי, מִדְּתָנָא לֵיהּ שֶׁלֹּא יְהֵא פָּרוּץ כְּעוֹמֵד. וְתָרְצִינַן לָהּ בְּנִכְנָס וְיוֹצֵא, הָא בִּמְצוּמְצָם — שָׁרֵי; וְכ"שׁ עוֹמֵד מְרוּבֶּה עַל הַפָּרוּץ. אֶלָּא מִשּׁוּם רֵישָׁא תְּנָא סֵיפָא, וְלָא מִשּׁוּם לְמֵידַק מִינָּהּ: הָא כְּפָרוּץ אָסוּר: רֵישָׁא לְרַב הוּנָא לָא קַשְׁיָא אַיְּידֵי דְּבָעֵי לְמִיתְנֵי סֵיפָא עוֹמֵד מְרוּבֶּה עַל הַפָּרוּץ. מוּתָּר, דְּלָא סַגֵּי דְּלָא קָתָנֵי לָהּ, דְּקמ"ל הָא כְּפָרוּץ אָסוּר: תָּנֵי נַמִי רֵישָׁא פָּרוּץ מְרוּבֶּה עַל הָעוֹמֵד. אע"ג דְּלָא אִיצְטְרִיךְ, דְּהָא אֲפִי' כְּעוֹמֵד נַמִי אָסוּר: בִּשְׁלָמָא לְרַב פַּפָּא. דְּאָמַר פָּרוּץ כְּעוֹמֵד מוּתָּר: מִשּׁוּם הָכִי לָא עָרֵיב. ג' בַּהֲדֵי פָּחוֹת מִג' וּלְמִיתְנֵי כָּל שֶׁהוּא פָּחוֹת מִג' וְג' — צָרִיךְ שֶׁלֹּא יְהֵא בֵּין זֶה לָזֶה ג'. דְּלָא מָצֵי לְמֵימַר צָרִיךְ שֶׁלֹּא יְהֵא בֵּין זֶה לָזֶה ג' דְּכֵיוָן דְּעוֹמֵד ג' — לָא אִיכְפַּת לָן אִי פָּרוּץ נַמִי ג' דְּהָא פָּרוּץ כְּעוֹמֵד מוּתָּר. וּמִשּׁוּם הָכִי אַפְסְקֵיהּ לְאַתְנְיֵיהּ גַּבֵּי פָּחוֹת מִד' לְמִיתְנָא בֵּיהּ כִּמְלוֹאוֹ, דְּלֶיהֱוֵי מַשְׁמַע בְּנִכְנָס וְיוֹצֵא: אֶלָּא לְרַב הוּנָא. דְּאָמַר פָּרוּץ כְּעוֹמֵד אָסוּר, אֲפִי' כְּנֶגֶד הָעוֹמֵד: לִיעָרֵב. ג' בַּהֲדֵי פָּחוֹת מִג' וְלִיתְנֵי: צָרִיךְ שֶׁלֹּא יְהֵא בֵּין זֶה לָזֶה ג' טְפָחִים: מִשּׁוּם דְּלָא דָּמֵי. פְּסוּלָא דְּפָחוֹת מִג' לִפְסוּלָא דְּג' דִּפְסוּלָה דְּפָחוֹת מִג' — לָא הָוֵי מָצֵי לְמִיתְלֵי בְּפָרוּץ מְרוּבֶּה עַל הָעוֹמֵד, דְּכָל כַּמָּה דְּלָא הָוֵי פָּרוּץ ג' אע"ג דְּעוֹמֵד טֶפַח וּפָרוּץ טְפָחַיִים — כָּשֵׁר. וּמִכִּי מְטָא פָּרוּץ לִשְׁלֹשָׁה אַשְׁמְעִי' דְּבְהָכִי מִקְרֵי פָּרוּץ, מִשּׁוּם יִזְדַּקֵּר גְּדִי: פְּסוּלָא דְּסֵיפָא. הֵיכָא דְּעוֹמֵד ג' — לָא מִיפְּסַל מִשּׁוּם דִּיקּוּר גְּדִי, דְּאִי הֲוָה עוֹמֵד מְרוּבֶּה לָא הֲוָה חָיְישִׁינַן לִגְדִי אֶלָּא מִשּׁוּם מַאי מִיפְּסִיל בְּפָרוּץ ג' — מִשּׁוּם דְּהָוֵי פָּרוּץ כְּעוֹמֵד וְתַנָּא לְאַגְמוּרֵי מִדּוֹת דִּמְחִיצָה קָאָתֵי, וּמִכִּי מָצֵי לְחַדּוּשֵׁי טַעְמֵיהּ וּלְמִתְלְיֵיהּ בִּפְסוּלָא אַחֲרִינָא — תַּנְיֵיהּ: פָּחוֹת מִג' מַנִּי רַבָּנַן הִיא. מִדְּקָא מַפְלִיג בֵּין פָּחוֹת מִג' לְג' — ש"מ רַבָּנַן הִיא, דְּמִפַּלְגֵי נַמִי בֵּין פָּחוֹת מִג' לְג': אֵימָא סֵיפָא כָּל שֶׁהוּא ג' וּמִג' וְעַד ד'. מִדְּקָא מַפְלִיג בֵּין פָּחוֹת מִד' לְד' דְּקָאָמַר: פָּחוֹת מִד' אִם פָּרוּץ יָתֵר עָלָיו — אַף כְּנֶגֶד הָעוֹמֵד אָסוּר, וְד' גּוּפֵיהּ קָתָנֵי סֵיפָא דְּמַתִּיר כְּנֶגְדּוֹ, וְאַף עַל גַּב דְּפָרוּץ יָתֵר עָלָיו. ש"מ: רַבָּן שִׁמְעוֹן בֶּן גַּמְלִיאֵל הִיא:
אֲתָאן

דאין זה סוגיית התלמוד, דמשני במעדיף ואינו חושש על קושייתו. ועוד קשה: דפי' בדרבא אם היו נתונין שתי נותנין ערב, ואיכא סכך כשר טפי. ובפ"ק דסוכה (ד' ט:) תנן גבי העושה סוכתו תחת האילן: אם היה הסיכוך הרבה מהן, או שקלגן – כשירה. ומוקי לה בגמרא כשחבטן. ופ"ה שם: כשעירבן ואין ניכר איזהו פסול ואיזהו כשר. ועוד: דדוחק הוא לאמוראי מסקי אליבא דמ"ד פרוץ כעומד אסור, דלא קי"ל הכי. ועוד: דלא פריך בסמוך כי מוקי נמי ביוצא ונכנס גבי שיירא, והא אפשר לנמלס – והתם ליכא לשנויי לרבא כי הכא, ונראה כגירסת ר"ת, דגרים: והא אי אפשר לנמלס, שיסתום כל האויר ונמלא שאין הכשר מרובה על האויר ועל הפסול, או אפי' כמוהו, ופריך לכולי עלמא. ומשני ר' אמי: במעדיף, שבודאי יסתום כל האויר. ורבא אמר: אפי' תימא שאינו מעדיף, אם היו נתונין שתי נותנו ערב – ואז נסתם כל האויר. אבל אין לפרש דדווקא כעניין זה אהני לרבא, ולא במעדיף, דגזר דילמא לא יעדיף. דבכל הספרים גרסי' בפ"ק דסוכה (ד' טו:), רבא אמר: אפי' תימא בשאינו מעדיף:

מארבעה עד עשר גרסי' ולא גרסינן עד ארבע אמות:

אימא סיפא כל שהוא שלשה ומג' ועד ד' כו'. סיפא גופה היה יכול להקשות דלא אתיא כרבנן, כדקאמר התלמוד מדלא מתיר עומד שלשה כנגדו. וכרשב"ג נמי לא אתיא, מדקאמר "וצריך שלא יהא בין זה לזה כמלואו" ולרשב"ג אפי' יותר ממלואו אין בכך כלום, כיון דליכא ד' – כלבוד דמי. אלא כך דרך התלמוד, שמתחיל קושיא מרישא כשיכול. וכה"ג איכא פ' "כירה" (ד' לט:) גבי חמין שהוחמו בשבת*:
והלכתא

[ועי' תוס' שבת לט: ד"ה אלא פניו]

רבינו חננאל

גמלים או באוכפין כו' עד ובלבד שלא יהא בין גמל לגמל כמלוא גמל כו' ודחינן הכא נמי כמלוא נכנס [ויוצא] ת"ש נמצאת אומר ג' מדות במחיצות כל שהוא פחות מג' צריך שלא יהא בין זה לזה שלשה שלא יזדקר הגדי בבת ראש [כל שהוא] שלשה ומשלשה ועד ארבעה צריך שלא יהא בין זה לזה כמלואו שלא יהא פרוץ כעומד. ואם היה פרוץ מרובה על העומד אף כנגד העומד אסור כל שהוא מארבעה ולמעלה עד עשרה צריך שלא יהא בין זה לזה במלואו שלא יהא פרוץ כעומד ואם היה פרוץ כעומד כנגד עומד מותר. כנגד פרוץ אסור. ואם היה עומד מרובה על הפרוץ אף כנגד (עומד אסור) הפרוץ נמי מותר. נפרצה יותר מעשר אסור. היה לו קנים מדקרין ועשה להן פאה מלמעלה אפילו ביתר מותר. קתני מיהא רישא כל שהוא שלשה ומג' ועד ארבעה צריך שלא יהא בין זה לזה כמילואו. פ' צריך שלא יהא (כמילואו) [פרוץ כעומד] קשיא לרב פפא. ודחי כמלוא [כמלואו] נכנס ויוצא שהוא יותר כמעט ואמרינן הכי נמי מסתברא דמלואו יתר הוא כמעט מדקתני ואם היה פרוץ מרובה על העומד. פרוץ מרובה על העומד הוא דאסור הא כעומד מותר ואמרינן רישא קשיא לרב הונא בריה דרב יהושע סיפא קשיא לרב פפא ושנינן להו ופשוטה היא. ואמרינן בשלמא לרב פפא מוקים לה לרישא כל שהוא פחות משלשה צריך שלא יהא בין זה לזה שלשה שאם היה העומד פחות משלשה והפרוץ שלשה אסור שנמצא הפרוץ מרובה על העומד לפיכך אסור הא זה כמו זה או אפי' הפרוץ מרובה על העומד כיון שהפרוץ אינו ג' טפחים אלא פחות מותר. ומציעתא דקתני צריך שלא יהא בין זה לזה כמלואו מוקים לה כמלוא נכנס ויוצא שהוא יותר כמעט הא זה כמו זה מותר משום הכי לא מערב. ותני להו ברישא אפילו פרוץ מרובה על העומד שרי ומציעתא אי הוי פרוץ מרובה אסור. אלא לרב הונא בריה דרב יהושע דלא שנא ג' ולא שנא פחות מג' פרוץ כעומד אסור ליערבינהו וליתנינהו כל שהן פחות משלשה ושלשה צריך שלא יהא

תוספתא דכלאים פ"ד
[לעיל יח: תוספתא דכלאים פ"ד]
ולי נראה דלא מיתסר אלא כנגד הפירל' כיון דהוי עומד חשוב כמו בפרוץ מרובה דלא מיתסר כנגד העומד ובהדיא תנן במסכת כלאים גדר שנפרץ עד י' אמה הרי הוא כפתח יתר מכאן כנגד הפרלה אסור [ת"י]
[שבת ל. וש"נ]
[לקמן עט:]

קב א מיי' פ"ז מהל' כלאים הלכה טו טוש"ע י"ד סי' רל"ו סעיף מ"ה:
קג ב מיי' שם וטוש"ע שם סעיף מ:

קד א ב ג מיי' פט"ז מהל' שבת הל' יח סמג עשין א טוש"ע או"ח סי' שסב ס"ה:
קה ד ה מיי' שם הל' יב וסמג שם טוש"ע או"ח סי' שם סעיף א:

[עי' לעיל ד' י' ע"ב תוס' ד"ה ואנבעיים]

[נ"ל עוביין וכן איתא במשנה שבמשניות ובירו' ובכרי"ף]

אַתָאן לְרַבָּן שִׁמְעוֹן בֶּן גַּמְלִיאֵל, דַּאֲמַר: *פָּחוֹת מֵאַרְבָּעָה לָבוּד! דְּאִי רַבָּנַן – מִשְּׁלֹשָׁה וְעַד אַרְבָּעָה?! שְׁלֹשָׁה וְאַרְבָּעָה חַד הוּא! אָמַר אַבַּיֵי: מִדְּרֵישָׁא רַבָּנַן סֵיפָא נַמִי רַבָּנַן, וּמוֹדוּ רַבָּנַן דְּכָל לְמִישְׁרָא כֶּנֶגְדּוֹ, אִי אִיכָּא מָקוֹם אַרְבָּעָה – חָשִׁיב, וְאִי לָא – לָא חָשִׁיב. רָבָא אָמַר: מִדְּסֵיפָא רַבָּן שִׁמְעוֹן בֶּן גַּמְלִיאֵל רֵישָׁא נַמִי רַבָּן שִׁמְעוֹן בֶּן גַּמְלִיאֵל,[א] וְכִי אָמַר רַבָּן שִׁמְעוֹן בֶּן גַּמְלִיאֵל אָמְרִי' לָבוּד – *הנ"מ לְמַעְלָה, אֲבָל לְמַטָּה הֲוָה לֵיהּ כִּמְחִיצָה שֶׁהַגְּדָיִים בּוֹקְעִין בָּהּ – לָא אָמְרִי' לָבוּד. תָּא שְׁמַע: *דְּפָנוֹת הַלָּלוּ שֶׁרוּבָּן פְּתָחִים וְחַלּוֹנוֹת – מוּתָּר, וּבִלְבַד שֶׁיְּהֵא עוֹמֵד מְרוּבֶּה עַל הַפָּרוּץ. שֶׁרוּבָּן סָלְקָא דַּעְתָּךְ?! אֶלָּא: שֶׁרִיבָּה בָּהֶן פְּתָחִים וְחַלּוֹנוֹת מוּתָּר, וּבִלְבַד שֶׁיְּהֵא עוֹמֵד מְרוּבֶּה עַל הַפָּרוּץ. הָא כְּפָרוּץ – אָסוּר! תְּיוּבְתָּא דְּרַב פָּפָּא – *תְּיוּבְתָּא. וְהִילְכְתָא כְּוָותֵיהּ דְּרַב פָּפָּא. תְּיוּבְתָּא וְהִילְכְתָא?! אִין, מִשּׁוּם דְּדַיְיקָא מַתְנִי' כְּוָותֵיהּ, דִּתְנַן: לֹא יִהְיוּ פְּרָצוֹת יְתֵירוֹת עַל הַבִּנְיָן. הָא כַּבִּנְיָן – מוּתָּר.§

מתני' אמַקִּיפִין שְׁלֹשָׁה חֲבָלִים זֶה לְמַעְלָה מִזֶּה וְזֶה לְמַעְלָה מִזֶּה, וּבִלְבַד שֶׁלֹּא יְהוּ בֵּין חֶבֶל לַחֲבֵירוֹ שְׁלֹשָׁה טְפָחִים. שִׁיעוּר חֲבָלִים *וְעוּבְיָין – יָתֵר עַל טֶפַח, כְּדֵי שֶׁיְּהֵא הַכֹּל עֲשָׂרָה טְפָחִים. מַקִּיפִין בְּקָנִים, וּבִלְבַד שֶׁלֹּא יְהֵא בֵּין קָנֶה לַחֲבֵירוֹ שְׁלֹשָׁה טְפָחִים. בַּשַּׁיָּירָא דִּבְּרוּ, דִּבְרֵי ר' יְהוּדָה. וַחֲכָמִים אוֹמְרִים: בלֹא דִּבְּרוּ בַּשַּׁיָּירָא, אֶלָּא בַּהוֹוֶה. כָּל מְחִיצָה שֶׁאֵינָהּ שֶׁל שְׁתִי וְשֶׁל עֵרֶב – אֵינָהּ מְחִיצָה, דִּבְרֵי רַבִּי יוֹסֵי בְּר' יְהוּדָה. גוַחֲכָמִים אוֹמְרִים: אֶחָד מִשְּׁנֵי דְּבָרִים.§

גמ' אָמַר רַב הַמְנוּנָא, אָמַר רַב: הֲרֵי אָמְרוּ עוֹמֵד מְרוּבֶּה עַל הַפָּרוּץ בִּשְׁתִי – הָוֵי עוֹמֵד. בָּעֵי רַב הַמְנוּנָא: בְּעֵרֶב מַאי? אָמַר אַבַּיֵי, תָּא שְׁמַע: שִׁיעוּר חֲבָלִים וְעוּבְיָין יָתֵר עַל טֶפַח, שֶׁיְּהוּ הַכֹּל עֲשָׂרָה טְפָחִים. וְאִי אִיתָא – לָמָּה לִי יָתֵר עַל טֶפַח? לִיעֲבִיד פָּחוֹת מִשְּׁלֹשָׁה וְחֶבֶל מַשֶּׁהוּ, פָּחוֹת מִשְּׁלֹשָׁה וְחֶבֶל מַשֶּׁהוּ, פָּחוֹת מֵאַרְבָּעָה וְחֶבֶל מַשֶּׁהוּ! וְתִיסְבְּרָא, הַאי פָּחוֹת מֵאַרְבָּעָה הֵיכָא מוֹקִים לֵיהּ? אִי מוֹקִים לֵיהּ תַּתַּאי – הֲוָה לֵיהּ כִּמְחִיצָה שֶׁהַגְּדָיִים בּוֹקְעִין בָּהּ, אִי מוֹקִים לֵיהּ עִילָּאֵי – אָתֵי אֲוִירָא דְּהַאי גִּיסָּא וּדְהַאי גִּיסָּא וּמְבַטֵּל לֵיהּ. אִי מוֹקִים לֵיהּ בְּמִיצְעֵי – הֲוָה לֵיהּ עוֹמֵד מְרוּבֶּה עַל הַפָּרוּץ מִשְּׁתֵּי רוּחוֹת. שָׁמְעַתְּ מִינַּהּ: עוֹמֵד מְרוּבֶּה עַל הַפָּרוּץ מִשְּׁתֵּי רוּחוֹת הָוֵי עוֹמֵד! אֶלָּא רַב הַמְנוּנָא הָכִי קָא מִיבַּעְיָא לֵיהּ: כְּגוֹן דְּאַיְיתִי מַחֲצֶלֶת דְּהָוְיָ ז' וּמַשֶּׁהוּ, וְחָקַק בָּהּ ג' וְשָׁבַק בָּהּ ד' וּמַשֶּׁהוּ, וְאוֹקְמֵיהּ בְּפָחוֹת מִג'. רַב אַשִׁי אָמַר: מְחִיצָה תְּלוּיָה אִיבַּעְיָא לֵיהּ, *כִּדְבָעָא מִינֵּיהּ רַבִּי טַבְלָא מֵרַב: מְחִיצָה תְּלוּיָה מַהוּ שֶׁתַּתִּיר בְּחוּרְבָּה? א"ל: אֵין מְחִיצָה תְּלוּיָה מַתֶּרֶת אֶלָּא בַּמַּיִם, קַל הוּא שֶׁהֵקֵלּוּ חֲכָמִים בַּמַּיִם.§ "מַקִּיפִין בַּקָּנִים וְכוּ'": בַּשַּׁיָּירָא – אִין, בְּיָחִיד – לָא. וְהָתַנְיָא, ר' יְהוּדָה אוֹמֵר: כָּל מְחִיצוֹת שַׁבָּת לֹא הִתִּירוּ לְיָחִיד יוֹתֵר מִבֵּית סָאתַיִם! כִּדְאָמַר רַב נַחְמָן, וְאִיתֵּימָא רַב בֵּיבָי בַּר אַבַּיֵי: לֹא נִצְרְכָא אֶלָּא לִיתֵּן לָהֶן כָּל צָרְכָּן, ה"נ: לִיתֵּן לָהֶן כָּל צָרְכָּן. הֵיכָא אִיתְּמַר דְּרַב נַחְמָן וְאִיתֵּימָא רַב בֵּיבָי בַּר אַבַּיֵי – אַהָא דִּתְנַן: כָּל מְחִיצָה שֶׁאֵינָהּ שֶׁל שְׁתִי וָעֵרֶב – אֵינָהּ מְחִיצָה, דִּבְרֵי ר' יוֹסֵי בְּר' יְהוּדָה. וּמִי א"ר יוֹסֵי בְּר' יְהוּדָה הָכִי? וְהָתַנְיָא: אֶחָד יָחִיד וְאֶחָד שַׁיָּירָא לַחֲבָלִים, וּמַה בֵּין יָחִיד לַשַּׁיָּירָא? יָחִיד – נוֹתְנִין לוֹ בֵּית סָאתַיִם, שְׁנַיִם – נוֹתְנִין לָהֶם בֵּית סָאתַיִם, ג' – נַעֲשׂוּ שַׁיָּירָא, וְנוֹתְנִין לָהֶן בֵּית שֵׁשׁ, דִּבְרֵי ר' יוֹסֵי בְּרַבִּי יְהוּדָה. וַחֲכָמִים אוֹמְרִים: אֶחָד יָחִיד וְאֶחָד שַׁיָּירָא נוֹתְנִין לָהֶן כָּל צָרְכָּן, דוּבִלְבַד שֶׁלֹּא יְהֵא בֵּית סָאתַיִם פָּנוּי. אָמַר רַב נַחְמָן, וְאִיתֵּימָא רַב בֵּיבָי בַּר אַבַּיֵי: לֹא נִצְרְכָא אֶלָּא לִיתֵּן לָהֶן כָּל צָרְכָּן.§ דָּרַשׁ רַב נַחְמָן מִשּׁוּם רַבֵּינוּ שְׁמוּאֵל: יָחִיד נוֹתְנִין לוֹ בֵּית סָאתַיִם, ב' נוֹתְנִין לְהוּ בֵּית סָאתַיִם, ג' – נַעֲשׂוּ שַׁיָּירָא, וְנוֹתְנִין לָהֶן בֵּית שֵׁשׁ. שָׁבְקַתְּ רַבָּנַן וַעֲבַדְתְּ כְּר' יוֹסֵי בְּרַבִּי יְהוּדָה?! הֲדַר אוֹקִים רַב נַחְמָן אָמוֹרָא עֲלֵיהּ וְדָרַשׁ: *דְּבָרִים שֶׁאָמַרְתִּי לִפְנֵיכֶם טָעוּת הֵן בְּיָדִי, בְּרַם כָּךְ אָמְרוּ: היָחִיד – נוֹתְנִין לוֹ בֵּית סָאתַיִם, שְׁנַיִם – נוֹתְנִין לָהֶן בֵּית סָאתַיִם, שְׁלֹשָׁה – נַעֲשׂוּ שַׁיָּירָא, וְנוֹתְנִין לָהֶן כָּל צָרְכָּן.
רֵישָׁא

והלכתא כרב פפא. אין לתמוה דהכא קי"ל פרוץ כעומד מותר, ובפ"ב דחולין (ד' כט.) מסיק לכ"ע מחלה על מחלה אינו כרוב ומייתי עלה ההיא דתנור, והכא לא מייתי לה. ושמא יש לחלק בין מחיצות לאיסור וטומאה:

אי מוקי לה בי מיצעי הוה ליה עומד מרובה על הפרוץ מב' רוחות. ולא הוה ליה עומד – משום דאתי אוירא דהאי גיסא ודהאי גיסא ומבטל ליה לעילאי. *וקשה להשר מקולי: דהכתי נעביד פחות מג' וחבל משהו, ופחות מג' וחצי וחבל משהו ופחות מג' וחבל חצי טפח ומשהו, ולמה לי עוביו יתר על טפח? ושמא בענין זה אתי למיטעי:
עירב

אַתָאן לְרשב"ג וְכוּ'. כְּלוֹמַר: עַד ד' וְלֹא ד' בִּכְלָל. דְּהָא תְּנָא בָּבָא אַחֲרִיתִי: כָּל שֶׁהוּא ד' וּמִד' עַד י' אַמּוֹת – אֲתָאן לְרשב"ג, דְּקָא מַפְלִיג נַמִי בֵּין פָּחוֹת מִד' לְד': ה"ג: דְּאִי רַבָּנַן מִג' וְעַד ד' ג' וְד' חַד הוּא. מִג' וְעַד ד' בִּתְמִיָּה: הֵיכִי מַפְלִיג ד' מִג' דְּקָתָנֵי עַד וְלֹא עַד בִּכְלָל, דְּתָנֵי סֵיפָא כָּל שֶׁהוּא ד' וְכוּ' – הָא לְרַבָּנָן ג' וְד' חַד הוּא: הָנֵי מִילֵּי לְמַעְלָה. כְּעֵין קוֹרָה: מתני' מַקִּיפִין ג' חֲבָלִים. הַשַּׁיָּירָא שֶׁחָנְתָה בְּבִקְעָה קָאֵי: זֶה לְמַעְלָה מִזֶּה. עַל גַּבֵּי יְתֵדוֹת סָבִיב. מִן הַתַּחְתּוֹן לַקַּרְקַע פָּחוֹת מִג' וְהָוֵי כּוּלּוֹ עוֹמֵד, דִּכְלָבוּד דָּמֵי. וּמִמֶּנּוּ לָאֶמְצָעִי פָּחוֹת מִג' – הֲרֵי שִׁשָּׁה עוֹמֵד פָּחוֹת ב' מַשֶּׁהוּיִין בִּשְׁנֵי הָאֲוִירִין. וּמֵאֶמְצָעִי לָעֶלְיוֹן פָּחוֹת מִשְּׁלֹשָׁה – הֲרֵי בִּשְׁלֹשָׁה אֲוִירִין תִּשְׁעָה עוֹמֵד, פָּחוֹת שְׁלֹשָׁה מַשֶּׁהוּיִין: שִׁיעוּר עוֹבִי הַחֲבָלִים יוֹתֵר עַל טֶפַח. שְׁלֹשָׁה מַשֶּׁהוּיִין כְּדֵי שֶׁיְּהוּ הַכֹּל עֲשָׂרָה טְפָחִים: וּמַקִּיפִין בְּקָנִים. נְעוּצִים וְעוֹמְדִים – זוֹ הִיא מְחִיצָה שֶׁל שְׁתִי. אֲבָל שֶׁל חֲבָלִים הָוְיָא מְחִיצָה שֶׁל עֵרֶב: בַּשַּׁיָּירָא דִּבְּרוּ. הֵקִילּוּ אֶצְלָן, שֶׁאֵינָן צְרִיכִין אֶלָּא אוֹ שְׁתִי אוֹ עֵרֶב, שְׁתִי – כְּגוֹן קָנִים, עֵרֶב – כְּגוֹן חֲבָלִים. אֲבָל לְיָחִיד לֹא הֵקִילּוּ עַד שֶׁיְּהֵא בָּהּ שְׁתִי וָעֵרֶב: כָּל מְחִיצָה שֶׁאֵינָהּ כו'. רַבִּי יוֹסֵי פָּלֵיג עֲלֵיהּ דַּאֲבוּהּ דְּמַתְנִי' וְקָאָמַר דַּאֲפִילּוּ לַשַּׁיָּירָא בָּעֵינַן שְׁתִי וָעֵרֶב: אֶחָד מִשְּׁנֵי דְּבָרִים. אוֹ שְׁתִי אוֹ עֵרֶב: גמ' הֲרֵי אָמְרוּ עוֹמֵד מְרוּבֶּה עַל הַפָּרוּץ בִּשְׁתִי הָוֵי עוֹמֵד. אע"ג דְּאִיכָּא פְּרָצוֹת, כִּדְתְנַן לְעֵיל: וְלֹא יְהוּ פְּרָצוֹת יְתֵירוֹת עַל הַבִּנְיָן, וּסְתָם כְּלֵי בְּהֵמָה שֶׁל שְׁתִי הוּא, שֶׁעוֹמֵד עַל גַּבֵּי קַרְקַע: בְּעֵרֶב מַאי. מֵחֲבָלִים דְּמַתְנִי' לֵיכָּא לְמֵילַף הֶכְשֵׁירָה, דְּהָתָם כּוּלּוֹ עוֹמֵד הוּא, דִּכְלָבוּד דָּמֵי: לִיעֲבִיד. אֲוִיר הָאֶחָד פָּחוֹת מִשְּׁלֹשָׁה, וְחֶבֶל מַשֶּׁהוּ. וְכֵן שֵׁנִי דְּהָוֵי לְהוּ שִׁשָּׁה עוֹמֵד, וְהָאֲוִיר הַשְּׁלִישִׁי פָּחוֹת מִשְּׁלֹשָׁה וְחֶבֶל מַשֶּׁהוּ, וְתִתְכַּשֵּׁר פִּירְצַת הַד' בְּעוֹמֵד שֶׁל שִׁשָּׁה: שֶׁהַגְּדָיִים בּוֹקְעִין בָּהּ. וַאֲפִילּוּ לְמַעְלָה מִמֶּנּוּ עוֹמֵד י' טְפָחִים שְׁלֵימִין, הָא קַיְימָא לָן מְחִיצָה תְּלוּיָה אֵינָהּ מַתֶּרֶת: עִילָּאֵי. בָּאֲוִיר הַשְּׁלִישִׁי שֶׁהוּא עֶלְיוֹן: אָתֵי אֲוִירָא. דְּמִן הַחֶבֶל וְלָרָקִיעַ: וּדְהַאי גִּיסָא. שֶׁמִּמֶּנּוּ וְלָאֶמְצָעִי דְּהָוֵי נַמִי אֲוִיר, כֵּיוָן דְּהָוֵי יוֹתֵר מִשְּׁלֹשָׁה – וּמְבַטֵּיל לֵיהּ לְחֶבֶל, וְאֵין כָּאן אֶלָּא ו' תַּחְתּוֹנִים: וְאִי מוֹקֵי לָהּ בְּאֶמְצָעִי. אֵין כָּאן עוֹמֵד מְרוּבֶּה עַל הַפָּרוּץ אֶלָּא אִם כֵּן תְּצָרֵף שְׁתֵּי רוּחוֹת לְבַטְּלוֹ: אֶלָּא. כֵּיוָן דְּלָא מַשְׁכַּחַתְּ לָהּ רַב הַמְנוּנָא הָכִי קָמִיבַּעְיָא לֵיהּ: וְשָׁבַק בָּהּ ד'. שְׁלֵימִין לְמַעְלָה, וּמַשֶּׁהוּ לְמַטָּה: וְאוֹקְמֵיהּ. לְהָךְ גִּיסָא דְּמַשֶּׁהוּ פָּחוֹת מִג' סָמוּךְ לַקַּרְקַע, דְּהָשְׁתָּא הֲוָה לֵיהּ עוֹמֵד מְרוּבֶּה עַל הַפָּרוּץ מֵרוּחַ אַחַת. וַאֲוִירָא דְּהַאי גִּיסָא וּדְהַאי גִּיסָא – נַמִי לֵיכָּא לְמֵימַר, הוֹאִיל וְעוֹמֵד מְרוּבֶּה עַל הָאֲוִיר דִּתוּתֵיהּ מִינֵּיהּ: מְחִיצָה תְּלוּיָה מִיבַּעְיָא לֵיהּ. מַחֲלֶלֶת עֲשָׂרָה שֶׁהִגְבִּיהָהּ מִן הַקַּרְקַע שְׁלֹשָׁה אוֹ יוֹתֵר, מִיבַּעְיָא לֵיהּ לְרַב הַמְנוּנָא אִי מְבַטֵּל לָעוֹמֵד לַפָּרוּץ שֶׁמִּתַּחְתָּיו הוֹאִיל וּפָחוֹת מִמֶּנּוּ, אוֹ לָא: אֶלָּא בַּמַּיִם. לְהַתִּיר לְמַלְּאוֹת, כְּגוֹן גְּזוּזְטְרָא שֶׁהִיא לְמַעְלָה מִן הַמַּיִם, בְּפֶרֶק "כֵּיצַד מִשְׁתַּתְּפִין" (לקמן ד' פז:): כָּל מְחִיצוֹת שַׁבָּת. בְּהָנָךְ מְחִיצוֹת רְעוּעוֹת שֶׁהֵן דִּשְׁתִי אוֹ דְּעֵרֶב קָאָמַר, שֶׁהִתִּירוּם לָרַבִּים ע"י הַדְּחָק: לֹא הִתִּירוּם לְיָחִיד. אִי הִקִּיף בָּהֶן יוֹתֵר מִבֵּית סָאתַיִם. וְאַף עַל גַּב שֶׁהוּקַּף לְדִירָה. שֶׁהֲרֵי לָדוּר בָּהֶן בְּלֵילֵי שַׁבָּת הִקִּיפוּם מֵעֶרֶב שַׁבָּת, הָא בֵּית סָאתַיִם מִיהָא שָׁרֵי: לִיתֵּן לָהֶן כָּל צָרְכָּן. דְּהָא דְּקָאָמַר רַבִּי יְהוּדָה בַּשַּׁיָּירָא דִּבְּרוּ וְלֹא לְיָחִיד לִיתֵּן לוֹ כָּל צָרְכּוֹ – בְּהָנָךְ מְחִיצוֹת קָאָמַר, אֲבָל בֵּית סָאתַיִם – וַדַּאי יָהֲבִינַן לֵיהּ, הוֹאִיל וּלְדִירָה הִקִּיפָהּ. וּבְהָא שַׁיָּירָא עֲדִיפָא – דְּיָהֲבִינַן לְהוּ כָּל צָרְכָּן: לַחֲבָלִים. מוּתָּר בְּהֶיקֵּף חֲבָלִים, אע"פ שֶׁאֵין כָּאן אֶלָּא עֵרֶב: נוֹתְנִים לוֹ בֵּית סָאתַיִם. בִּמְחִיצָה זוֹ, אֲבָל בִּמְחִיצָה מְעַלְּיָיתָא – כַּמָּה דְּבָעֵי: שֶׁלֹּא יְהֵא בֵּית סָאתַיִם פָּנוּי. שֶׁלֹּא יַקִּיפוּ יוֹתֵר מִכְּדֵי צָרְכָּן בֵּית סָאתַיִם: לִיתֵּן לָהֶם כָּל צָרְכָּן. הָא דְּקָאָמַר רַבִּי יוֹסֵי דְּמַתְנִי' דְּאֵינָהּ מְחִיצָה – אֵינָהּ מְחִיצָה לְכָל צָרְכָּן, אֲבָל מְחִיצָה הִיא לְבֵית סָאתַיִם לְאֶחָד, וּלְבֵית שֵׁשׁ לַשַּׁיָּירָא:
רֵישָׁא

רבינו חננאל

יהא בין זה לזה כמילואו. (ורמינן) [ושנינן] רישא קתני פחות מג' תורת לבודין סיפא דקתני כל שהוא ארבעה ומארבעה ועד ארבעה אמות ועד עשר תורת מחיצה משום הכי לא מתני ליה. ת"ש דפנות הללו שריבה בהן פתחין וחלונות כשרין ובלבד שיהא עומד מרובה על הפרוץ. תיובתא דרב פפא תיובתא והלכתא כרב פפא דפרוץ כעומד מותר משום דדייקא מתני' כוותיה דקתני לא יהא פרצות יתירות על הבנין. יתירות הוא דאסיר הא כבנין שרי ואף על גב דסלקא בתיובתא: **מתני'** מקיפין שלשה חבלים וכו'. ובעי רב המנונא עומד מרובה על הפרוץ בשתי ודאי הוה עומד בערב מאי כגון דאייתי מחצלת שבעה ומשהו וחקק בה שלשה ושבק בה ד' מלמעלה ומשהו מלמטה וג' באמצע ולא אפשיט. ואתינן למיפשטא מהא. ת"ש שעור חבלים עוביין יתר על טפח כדי שיהא הכל י' טפחים כו' רב אשי אמר מחיצה תלויה איבעיא ליה ופשטא אין מחיצה תלויה מתרת אלא במים קל הוא שהקילו חכמים במים. מקיפין בקנים ובלבד שלא יהא בין קנה לחבירו ג' טפחים בשיירא דברו דברי ר' יהודה. ואקשינן בשיירא אין ביחיד לא והתניא ר' יהודה אומר במחיצות לא התירו ליחיד אלא בית סאתים שהן ע' אמה ושיריים על ע' אמה ושיריים. הנה דין זה של מחיצות אפי' ליחיד. ופרקי' מתני' דקתני בשיירא ולא ליחיד ליתן להן כל צרכן. פי' קסבר ר' יהודה לשיירא נותנין לה כל צרכה אבל ליחיד אין נותנין לו אלא בית סאתים בלבד וכרב ביבי דאמר (בהא) [אהא] דתנן כל מחיצה שאינה של שתי ושל ערב אינה מחיצה דברי ר' יוסי בר"י איני והא תניא אחד יחיד ואחד שיירא בחבלים. ומה בין יחיד לשיירא יחיד נותנין לו בית סאתים שנים נותנין להם בית סאתים שלשה נעשו שיירא ונותנין להם בית שש דברי ר' יוסי בר' יהודה וחכ"א אחד יחיד ואחד שיירא נותנין להם כל צרכן ובלבד שלא יהא בית סאתים פנוי הנה ר' יוסי בר' יהודה מתיר במחיצה אע"פ שאינה של שתי ושל ערב. ופריק רב ביבי אין שתי בלא ערב או ערב בלא שתי הויא מחיצה מיהו אין נותנין לשיירא כל צרכה עד שתהא מחיצה עשויה שתי וערב. דרש רב נחמן [מחיצה] שתשמישה לאויר יחיד נותנין לו בית סאתים כחצר המשכן שהוא ק' אמה על נ' רוחב וזהו בית סאתים ונקראת חצר [והעמודים] ועליהם קלעים כדרך הולכי מדברות לפיכך למדו מן המשכן שנים נותנין להם בית סאתים כמאן כר' יוסי בר' יהודה הואיל ואבוה קאי כוותיה. דתניא ר' יהודה אומר במחיצות שבת לא התירו ליחיד אלא סאתים (ועוד) שלשה נעשו שיירא ונותנין להן

[לעיל ט. וש"נ]
[לעיל יד:]
לעיל יח.
[לעיל י. וש"נ]

גליון הש"ס

גמ' אמר אביי מדרישא. כעין זה בב"ק דף מ ע"ב:

שבת קא. לעיל יב. ולקמן מח. פו:

הגהות מהר"ב רנשבורג

[א] גמ' וכי אמר רשב"ג אמרי' לבוד הני מילי למעלה. עי' ריטב"א ליישב מאי דקשה מדלעיל דף ט. ודו"ק:

[שבת סג: וש"נ]

רישא רבי יוסי ברבי יהודה וסיפא רבנן! אין, משום דקאי אבוה בשיטתיה. אמר רב גידל, אמר רב: שלשה, בחמש – אסורין, בשבע – מותרין. אמרו ליה: אמר רב הכי? אמר להו: אורייתא נביאי וכתיבי, דאמר רב הכי. אמר רב אשי: מאי קשיא? דילמא הכי קאמר: הוצרכו לשש והקיפו בשבע – אפי' בשבע מותרין, לא הוצרכו אלא[א] לחמש והקיפו [ב]בשבע – אפי' בחמש אסורין. ואלא הא דקתני "ובלבד שלא יהא בית סאתים פנוי", מאי לאו פנוי מאדם? לא, פנוי מכלים. איתמר: שלשה ומת אחד מהן, שנים *ונתוספו עליהן. רב הונא ורבי יצחק, חד אמר: שבת גורמת, וחד אמר: דיורין גורמין. תסתיים דרב הונא הוא דאמר שבת גורמת. דאמר רבה: *בעאי מרב הונא, ובעאי מרב יהודה: עירב דרך הפתח ונסתם הפתח, דרך החלון ונסתם החלון, מהו? ואמר לי: שבת הואיל והותרה – הותרה. תסתיים. לימא רב הונא ורבי יצחק בפלוגתא דרבי יוסי ורבי יהודה קמיפלגי. *דתנן: חצר שנפרצה משתי רוחותיה, וכן בית שנפרץ משתי רוחותיו, וכן מבוי שניטלו קורותיו או לחייו – מותרין לאותה שבת ואסורין לעתיד לבא, דברי רבי יהודה. ר' יוסי אומר: אם מותרין לאותה שבת – מותרין לעתיד לבא, ואם אסורין לעתיד לבא – אסורין לאותה שבת. לימא רב הונא דאמר כר' יהודה, ורבי יצחק דאמר כר' יוסי? אמר לך רב הונא: אנא דאמרי אפי' לר' יוסי, עד כאן לא קאמר רבי יוסי התם – אלא דליתנהו למחיצות, הכא – איתנהו למחיצות. ור' יצחק אמר: אנא דאמרי אפי' לר' יהודה, עד כאן לא קאמר ר' יהודה התם אלא דאיתנהו לדיורין, הכא ליתנהו לדיורין. § "וחכמים אומרים אחד משני דברים". § היינו ת"ק! איכא בינייהו יחיד בישוב. §

מתני' ארבעה דברים פטרו במחנה: מביאין עצים מ"מ, ופטורין מרחיצת ידים, ומדמאי, ומלערב. §

גמ' ת"ר: *מחנה היוצאת למלחמת הרשות – מותרין בגזל עצים יבשים. ר' יהודה בן תימא אומר: אף חונין בכל מקום, ובמקום שנהרגו שם נקברין. § "מותרין בגזל עצים יבשים". § האי תקנתא דיהושע הוה, *דאמר מר: עשרה תנאים התנה יהושע: שיהו מרעין בחורשין ומלקטין עצים משדותיהן! התם בהיזמי והיגי, הכא בשאר עצים. אי נמי: התם במחוברין, הכא בתלושין. אי נמי: התם בלחין, הכא ביבשים. § "ר' יהודה בן תימא אומר: אף חונין בכל מקום ובמקום שנהרגים שם נקברים". § פשיטא, מת מצוה הוא, *ומת מצוה קונה מקומו! לא צריכא, אף על גב דאית
מיס

רש"י

רישא רבי יוסי ברבי יהודה. דקאמר יחיד בית סאתים, דאי רבנן – אפי' ליחיד כל צרכו יהבינן: אין משום דקאי אבוה בשיטתיה. גבי יחיד קאמר רבי יהודה נמי דאין נותנין לו אלא בית סאתים, במחיצת שתי או ערב: שלשה בחמש אסורין. כלומר: פעמים ג' אנשים אסורין אפילו בחמש סאין, ופעמים שמותרין אפילו בשבע: אורייתא נביאי וכתיבי. שבועה הוא: הוצרכו לשש והקיפו לשבע. שתי בלא ערב, מותרין דליכא בית סאתים פנוי: לא הוצרכו אלא לה' והקיפו לז' אפילו בה' נמי אסורין. דהשתא לא מהני מחיצות, הואיל והוקפו לבית סאתים יותר מכדי צרכן: מאי לאו פנוי מאדם. כגון שלשה שהקיפו ח' סאין, דכי יהבת לכל חד בית סאתים אכתי פשו להו בית סאתים פנוי בלא בעלים, אבל ז' – לא, דכי יהבת בית סאתים לכל חד לא פש ליה אלא חד בית סאה בלא בעלים: לא פנוי מכלים. כלומר: שיש בין המחיצות בית סאתים פנוי, שלא היו צריכין לו. ואע"ג דאינהו שלשה, אם אין צריכין אלא לבית סאתים והקיפו ד' סאין – נמי בטלי מחיצות: ומת אחד מהן. ביום השבת: וניתוספו עליהן. בשבת: שבת גורמת. שלשה ומת אחד מהן, הואיל וגורמת שבת להתיר – מותרין השנים אפי' לר' יהודה. שנים והקיפו יותר מבית סאתים אע"פ שניתוספו עליהן דיורין – אסורין לרבי יהודה, הואיל וכשנכנסה שבת גרמה לאיסור: דיורין גורמין. ג' ומת אחד מהן, דבתר דיורין – אסורין אם הקיפו יותר מבית סאתים. שנים ונתוספו עליהן – מותרין, דאיכא דיורין: עירב דרך הפתח ונסתם הפתח. אם היו ב' חצרות ופתח ביניהם ועירבו(א) דרך הפתח ונסתם הפתח, או אם היו ב' חנויות ופתח ביניהם דעירבו על דעת הפתח ועכשיו נסתם בשבת, שנפלה כנגדו מפולת: מהו. מי שרי לאשתמושי דרך שאר חלונות הפתוחות מד' שאין ראויות לעירוב, כדאמרי' בפ' "חלון" (לקמן דף עו.): חצר שנפרצה. בשבת: משתי רוחותיה. מפרש בפרק "כל גגות" (שם ד' לד:) מאי טעמא נקט מב' רוחותיה: שניטלה קורתו או לחיו. בשבת: מותרין לאותה שבת. דאמרי' הואיל והותרה – הותרה: רבי יוסי אומר אם מותרין כו'. ומפרשינן בפ' "כל גגות" (שם ד' לה.) דר' יוסי לאיסור, והכי קאמר: כשם שאסורים לעתיד לבא כך אסורין לאותה שבת, אלמא: לא אמרי' הואיל והותרה הותרה כדרבי יצחק: היינו תנא קמא. רבנן קמאי, דאמרי לא דברו בשיירא אלא בהווה, ולעולם יחיד נמי מותר: איכא בינייהו יחיד בישוב. דתנא קמא דקאמר לא דברו בשיירא אלא בהווה, ולעולם יחיד נמי מותר – יחיד דומיא דשיירא, דבדרך ולא בישוב. הואיל ויכול לעשות מחיצה הוגנת. ורבנן בתראי – אמילתיה דרבי יוסי ב"ר יהודה קא מהדרי, דקאמר איהו אינה מחיצה לא בדרך ולא בישוב, ואמרי ליה רבנן; אחד משני דברים, או שתי או ערב מחיצה היא, אחד יחיד ואחד רבים, בין בדרך בין בישוב: מתני' במחנה. היוצאת למלחמה: מביאין עצים. ואין חוששין לגזל: ומלערב. עירובי חצירות, אם הקיפו אלו ואלו ומחיצה מפסקת ביניהם, ויש שם פתח – אין צריכין לערב: גמ' למלחמת הרשות. סתם מלחמת רשות, ממלחמת יהושע ואילך שהיא היתה מלחמת מצוה: עצים יבשים. וכל שכן לחים: עשרה תנאים. בבא קמא בפ' "מרובה" (דף פ.): שיהו מרעין בחורשין. שיהא כל אדם מוליך בהמותיו לרעות ביער של חבירו, ולא יקפיד בעל היער, משום דלאו לקלירה קאי: הכא בתלושין. אע"פ שתלשום הבעלים לצרכן להיסק, ויש בהם משום גזל אצל אחרים – מותר לאנשי מחנה: מת מצוה קונה מקומו. אחד מי' תנאין שהתנה יהושע הוא:
דאית

תוספות

עירב דרך הפתח. נראה לר"י דהלכה כרב הונא, דשבת הואיל והותרה הותרה. דתניא כוותיה בפרק "הדר" (לקמן ד' ע:): כל שהותר למקצת שבת כו'. ואין לומר דרבי יצחק יעמיד הברייתא אליבא דרבי יהודה – דהא מוקי נפשיה אפילו כר' יהודה בשמעתין. ואביי נמי סבירא ליה הכי בפרק "כל גגות" (לקמן ד' לג:). ומיהו, היכא דליתנהו למחיצות – אסור, כדמסיק הכא: אנא דאמרי אפי' כר' יוסי, עד כאן לא קאמר רבי יוסי אלא משום דליתנהו למחיצות. ורב נמי פסיק כרבי יוסי בסוף פרק "כל גגות" (שם) וכן שמואל בנפרצה לרה"ר. ואע"ג דרב פסיק כר' יוסי אפי' באיתנהו למחיצות, כדמוכח גבי שתי חצירות ונפל כותל שביניהם, דהתם הוי שפיר איתנהו למחיצות, דהכתי איכא מחיצות חיצונות שעל ידיהן נעשה החצר רה"י, ומשום הכי מייתי מחצר [גדולה] שנפרצה על בעיא דרב הושעיא בפרק "כל גגות", (ד' לג:) מ"מ נראה דבהא הילכתא כרב הונא, כדפרישית. ונראה לר"י: שאם עירבו(ג) לצורך *שניהן מבית לבית, ונסתם הפתח בשבת – דשרי, כרב הונא. ואפילו נסתם באמצע השבוע ואח"כ נפתח בשבת – שרי, דחזר העירוב למקומו. וראיה מדאמר בפ' "הזורק" (שבת ד' קא:) ספינות קשורות זו בזו – מערבין ומטלטלין מזו לזו, נפסקו – נאסרו, חזרו ונתקשרו – חזרו להתירן הראשון. ועוד: דלמסקנא דשמעתין דמוקי ר' יצחק נפשיה כר' יהודה ושרי אפי' במבוי שניטלה קורתו – כ"ש דיתיר בעירבו דרך הפתח. דהא בפרק "הדר" (לקמן ד' ע:) קאמר: כל שהותר למקצת שבת כו', לאתויי עירב דרך הפתח. וזה הכלל לאתויי מבוי שנטלה קורתו. משמע דאי לא דתני זה הכלל – לא הוי שרינן מבוי שניטלה קורתו, אע"ג דהוי שרינן עירב דרך הפתח ונסתם. ורשב"א אומר: דמהתם נמי יש להוכיח דהלכה כרב הונא, דההיא סוגיא כרב הונא דקפיד אמחיצה טפי, כדאמר הכא: עד כאן לא קאמר רבי יוסי כו'. ולהכי, אי לאו זה הכלל – לא הוי שרינן מבוי שניטלה קורתו, אע"ג דשרינן עירב דרך הפתח ונסתם, דאילו רבי יצחק קפיד טפי אדיורין:

קורותיו או לחייו. בפירוש רש"י בכתיבת ידו נמצא כתוב: "קורתו או לחיו", והדין עמו. ואע"ג דאליבא דרבי יהודה קיימינן, ואשכחת לה לדידיה *מבוי ניתר בשתי קורות או שני לחיים כמו במפולש – מ"מ למה לי למינקט קורותיו, כיון דבקורה אחת או בלחי אחד נאסר המבוי:

התם במחוברים. להאי שינויא נמי איירי בהיזמי והיגי, דלא התקין יהושע אלא היזמי והיגי המחוברים ולחים, כדאמר בהדיא ב"מרובה" (ב"ק דף פא.):

עין משפט נר מצוה

קו א מיי' פט"ז מהל' שבת הל' יח סמג עשין א טוש"ע או"ח סי' שס"ב ס"ה:
קז ב מיי' שם הל' יג וטוש"ע שם ס"ב:
קח ג מיי' פ"ג מהל' עירובין הלכה כה טוש"ע א"ח סי' שעד סעיף א:
קט ד מיי' פ"ו מהל' מלכים הל' יג סמג עשין קיח:
קי ה מיי' פ"ה מהל' נזקי ממון הל' ג טוח"מ סי' רעד:
קיא ו ז מיי' פ"ו מהל' מלכים הל' יב:

רבינו חננאל

להן כל צרכן אמר רב גידל אמר רב שלשה מותרין בשבע ואסורין בחמש. פירשה רב אשי *) נותנין להן כל צורכן כגון שהוצרכו לשש מותרין אפילו בשבע אבל אם הקיפו שבע ולא הוצרכו אלא לחמש אפילו בחמש אסורין ואלא דקתני נותנין להן כל צורכן בין מעט בין הרבה ובלבד שלא יהא בית סאתים בלבד פנוי מאי לאו פנוי מאדם והנה זה אין פנוי מאדם דהא שלשה בני אדם הן וכל אחד יש לו בית סאתים לא נשאר פנוי אלא בית סאה ואסיקנא פנוי מכלים לפיכך כשהוקפו לחמש ונשארו סאתים פנוים מכלים נאסרו אפילו בחמש: אתמר שבתו שנים וניתוספו עליהן בשבת אחד כיון שעכשיו ג' הרי הן נעשו שיירה ונותנין להן כל צרכן או דלמא כיון שלא קנו שביתה שלשתן כאחד אינן אלא כיחידים ואין נותנין להן אלא סאתים וכן שלשה שקנו שביתה ומת א' מהן בשבת מאי כשיירה הן או כיחידים. רב הונא אמר שבת גורמת. פירוש הכל הולך בשעה שקנה שביתה אם יחידין מה שניתוספו עליהן אין חוששין להן ואם שיירה קנו שביתה ומת אחד מהן השנים הנשארים יש להן כל צרכן ולא חיישינן להאי דמית. ור' יצחק אמר דיורין גורמת. פי' הכל לפי הדיורין ואם יחידין יחידין אם שיירה שיירה. לימא רב הונא ור' יצחק בפלוגתא דר' יהודה ור' יוסי פליגי דתנן חצר שנפרצה משתי רוחותיה בית כו' ופשוטה היא. **פסקא** וחכמים אומרים אחד משני דברים. היינו ת"ק דקתני לא דברו אלא בהווה ופרקינן איכא בינייהו יחיד בישוב לת"ק בישוב לא דפליגי על ת"ק דהוא ר' יהודה דאמר (הוא ר' יהודה) בשיירה וחלקו עליו הם אפילו ביחיד מיהו במקום השיירות במדבר אבל בישוב לא ורבנן בתראי אמרי אפילו בישוב וקיי"ל כוותייהו: [מתני'] ד' דברים פטורין במחנה כו'. וכמה הן מחנה. ירושלמי ר' יוחנן אומר עשרה שנא' [ש"א כ"ה] ויבואו נערי דוד וידברו אל נבל וגו' מהו וינוחו נעשו מחנה ר"י בן פזי אומר עשרה עד למחנה גדול (במחנה) [כמחנה] אלהים [דה"א י"ב] וכמה מחנה אלהים עשרה תני בשם ר' יהודה י"ב אלף כמחנה ישראל. ת"ר מחנה היוצאת למלחמת הרשות מותרין בגזל עצים יבשים כו'. עשרה דברים שהתנה יהושע מפורשין בסוף פרק מרובה ואוקימנא מותרין בגזל עצים ואפילו בשאר עצים דלא היזמי והיגי נינהו ואפילו תלושין ואפילו יבשין. ר' יהודה

*) [אולי צ"ל פעמים שנותנין להן אפי' יותר מכדי צרכן כגון שהוצרכו וכו'].

הגהות הב"ח

(א) רש"י ד"ה עירב דרך הפתח וכו' ופתח ביניהם ועירבו על דעת הפתח ועכשיו כו"ל ותיבות דרך הפתח ונסתם הפתח או אם היו ב' חנויות ופתח ביניהם לעירבו נמחק: (ג) תוס' ד"ה עירב וכו' ונראה לר"י שאם עירבו. נ"ב עי' באשר"י:

הגהות הגר"א

[א] לחמש. נ"ב לשלש כ"א: [ב] (בשבע אפי') תא"מ. (לפי הגר"א):

גליון הש"ס

גמ' דר"ה הוא דאמר שבת גורמת. עיין לקמן דף מב. תד"ה וניטלטל:

מסורת הש"ס

[לקמן עט:] [לקמן לג.] [לקמן לד.] [תוס' פ"ב] [סוטה מה: ב"ק פא. סנהדרין מז:]

רב נסים גאון

משום דקאי אבוה בשיטתיה. חוזרין אלו הדברים על דברי ר' יהודה שאמרו כבר במחיצות שבת לא התירו ליחיד אלא בית סאתים פירוש שתי בלא ערב ולא היה מתיר ר' יהודה לתת ליחיד כל צרכו אלא אם תהיה שתי וערב יחדיו ובזה הוא שוה עם ר' יוסי בנו שאמר נותנין לו בית סאתים: י' דברים התנה יהושע תמצא פי' כולן בבבא קמא בפר' מרובה (פ:) ובגמרא דמגילה דבני מערבא:

תורה אור

דְּאִית לֵיהּ קוֹבְרִין, *דְּתַנְיָא: [א]אֵיזֶהוּ מֵת מִצְוָה — כֹּל שֶׁאֵין לוֹ קוֹבְרִין, קוֹרֵא וַאֲחֵרִים עוֹנִין אוֹתוֹ — אֵין זֶה מֵת מִצְוָה. *וּמֵת מִצְוָה קָנָה מְקוֹמוֹ? וְהָתַנְיָא: *[ב]הַמּוֹצֵא מֵת מוּטָּל בְּסַרְטְיָא — מְפַנֵּיהוּ לִימִין אִסְרַטְיָא אוֹ לִשְׂמֹאל אִסְרַטְיָא. שָׂדֶה בּוּר וּשְׂדֵה נִיר — מְפַנֵּיהוּ לִשְׂדֵה בּוּר, שְׂדֵה נִיר וּשְׂדֵה זֶרַע — מְפַנֵּיהוּ לִשְׂדֵה נִיר, הָיוּ שְׁתֵּיהֶן נִירוֹת, שְׁתֵּיהֶן זְרוּעוֹת, שְׁתֵּיהֶן בּוּרוֹת — מְפַנֵּהוּ לְכָל רוּחַ שֶׁיִּרְצֶה. אָמַר רַב בֵּיבָי: הָכָא [ג]בְּמֵת מוּטָּל עַל הַמֵּיצַר עָסְקִינַן, מִתּוֹךְ שֶׁנִּיתְּנָה רְשׁוּת לְפַנּוֹתוֹ מִן הַמֵּיצַר(א) — מְפַנֵּיהוּ לְכָל רוּחַ שֶׁיִּרְצֶה.§ [ד]"וּפְטוּרִין מֵרְחִיצַת יָדַיִם".§ אָמַר אַבַּיֵי: [ה]לֹא שָׁנוּ אֶלָּא מַיִם רִאשׁוֹנִים, אֲבָל מַיִם אַחֲרוֹנִים — חוֹבָה. *אָמַר רַב חִיָּיא בַּר אַשִׁי: מִפְּנֵי מָה אָמְרוּ מַיִם אַחֲרוֹנִים חוֹבָה — מִפְּנֵי שֶׁמֶּלַח סְדוֹמִית יֵשׁ, שֶׁמְּסַמֵּא אֶת הָעֵינַיִם. אָמַר אַבַּיֵי: וּמִשְׁתַּכְחָא כְּקוֹרְטָא בְּכוֹרָא. א"ל רַב אַחָא בְּרֵיהּ דְּרָבָא לְרַב אַשִׁי: כָּיֵיל מִילְחָא מַאי? א"ל: [הָא] לָא מִיבַּעְיָא.§ "וּמִדְּמַאי".§ *דִּתְנַן: [ו]מַאֲכִילִין אֶת הָעֲנִיִּים דְּמַאי וְאֶת אַכְסַנְיָא דְּמַאי. אָמַר רַב הוּנָא: תָּנָא, בֵּית שַׁמַּאי אוֹמְרִים: אֵין מַאֲכִילִין אֶת הָעֲנִיִּים דְּמַאי וְאֶת אַכְסַנְיָא דְּמַאי. וּבֵית הִלֵּל אוֹמְרִים: מַאֲכִילִין אֶת הָעֲנִיִּים דְּמַאי וְאֶת אַכְסַנְיָא דְּמַאי.§ "וּמִלְּעָרֵב".§ אָמְרִי דְּבֵי רַבִּי יַנַּאי: [ז]לֹא שָׁנוּ אֶלָּא עֵירוּבֵי חֲצֵירוֹת, אֲבָל עֵירוּבֵי תְחוּמִין — חַיָּיבִין. דְּתָנֵי רַבִּי חִיָּיא: [ח]לוֹקִין עַל עֵירוּבֵי תְחוּמִין דְּבַר תּוֹרָה. מַתְקִיף לָהּ רַבִּי יוֹנָתָן: וְכִי לוֹקִין עַל לָאו שֶׁבְּ"אַל"? מַתְקִיף רַב אַחָא בַּר יַעֲקֹב: אֶלָּא מֵעַתָּה דִּכְתִיב: °"אַל תִּפְנוּ אֶל הָאוֹבוֹת וְאֶל הַיִּדְּעוֹנִים" ה"נ דְּלָא לָקֵי? רַבִּי יוֹנָתָן הָכִי קַשְׁיָא לֵיהּ: *לָאו שֶׁנִּיתָּן לְאַזְהָרַת מִיתַת ב"ד, וְכָל *לָאו שֶׁנִּיתָּן לְאַזְהָרַת מִיתַת בֵּית דִּין אֵין לוֹקִין עָלָיו. אָמַר רַב אַשִׁי: מִי כְּתִיב "אַל יוֹצִיא"? °"אַל יֵצֵא" כְּתִיב.§ (ויקרא יט; שמות טז)

הֲדְרָן עֲלָךְ מָבוֹי

עוֹשִׂין [ט]פַּסִּין לַבֵּירָאוֹת, אַרְבָּעָה דְּיוּמָדִין נִרְאִין כִּשְׁמוֹנָה, דִּבְרֵי ר' יְהוּדָה. ר"מ אוֹמֵר: שְׁמוֹנָה נִרְאִין כִּשְׁנֵים עָשָׂר, אַרְבָּעָה דְּיוּמָדִים וְאַרְבָּעָה פְּשׁוּטִין. [י]גּוֹבְהָן עֲשָׂרָה טְפָחִים וְרוֹחְבָּן שִׁשָּׁה, וְעוֹבְיָים כָּל שֶׁהוּא. *וּבֵינֵיהֶן כִּמְלֹא שְׁתֵּי רְבָקוֹת שֶׁל שָׁלֹשׁ שָׁלֹשׁ בָּקָר, דִּבְרֵי ר"מ. ר' יְהוּדָה אוֹמֵר: [כ]שֶׁל *אַרְבַּע. קְשׁוּרוֹת וְלֹא מוּתָּרוֹת, אַחַת נִכְנֶסֶת וְאַחַת יוֹצֵאת. [ל]מוּתָּר לְהַקְרִיב לַבְּאֵר וּבִלְבַד שֶׁתְּהֵא פָּרָה רֹאשָׁהּ וְרוּבָּהּ בִּפְנִים וְשׁוֹתָה. [מ]מוּתָּר לְהַרְחִיק

[נ"ל ארבע ארבע קשורות] [לפנינו בגמ' אי' לא מוליא מכלל פי']

רש"י

דְּאִית לֵיהּ קוֹבְרִין. שֶׁיֵּשׁ לוֹ יוֹרְשִׁין: בְּאִיסְרַטְיָא. דֶּרֶךְ כְּבוּשָׁה: מְפַנֵּיהוּ. וְאִי סָלְקָא דַּעְתָּךְ קָנָה מְקוֹמוֹ, הֵיכִי מָצֵי לְמִשְׁקְלֵיהּ מֵהָתָם: בְּמֵת מוּטָּל עַל הַמֵּיצַר. שֶׁמּוּשְׁכָּב בְּרוֹחַב הַדֶּרֶךְ מִמֵּיצַר לְמֵיצַר. מִתּוֹךְ שֶׁנִּיתָּן רְשׁוּת לְפַנּוֹתוֹ מִפְּנֵי כֹּהֲנִים וְעוֹשֵׂי טְהָרוֹת שֶׁלֹּא יַאֲהִילוּ עָלָיו, מְפַנֵּיהוּ לְכָל רוּחַ שֶׁיִּרְצֶה: שֶׁמֶּלַח סְדוֹמִית יֵשׁ כו'. וְאָמוּר רַבָּנַן (ברכות דף מ.): אַחַר כָּל אֲכִילָתְךָ אֱכוֹל מֶלַח. וּמִשּׁוּם מֶלַח שֶׁטָּבַל בּוֹ אֶצְבָּעוֹ תִּיקְּנוּ מַיִם אַחֲרוֹנִים: כִּי קוֹרְטָא בְּכוֹרָא. בְּכוֹר מֶלַח יֵשׁ מְעַט מֵאוֹתוֹ מֶלַח סְדוֹמִית, כְּמִין קוֹרֶט קָטָן: כָּיֵיל מִלְחָא מַאי. מוֹדֵד מֶלַח לַחֲמָרִים, צָרִיךְ לִיטּוֹל יָדָיו אוֹ לֹא: כָּל שֶׁכֵּן. דְּצָרִיךְ: אַכְסַנְיָא. חַיִל הַבָּא לְמֶלֶךְ יִשְׂרָאֵל לְהִלָּחֵם עַל אוֹיְבֵיהֶם, וְיִשְׂרְאֵלִים הֵם: דְּמַאי. סָפֵק מְעוּשָּׂר סָפֵק אֵינוֹ מְעוּשָּׂר. דְּרוֹב עַמֵּי הָאָרֶץ מְעַשְּׂרִין הֵן, וְחוּמְרָא דְּרַבָּנַן הִיא, וְגַבֵּי הָנָךְ אַקִּילוּ רַבָּנַן: לוֹקִין עַל עֵירוּבֵי תְחוּמִין. דִּכְתִיב "אַל יֵצֵא אִישׁ מִמְּקוֹמוֹ", וּמֵהָכָא יָלְפִינַן תְּחוּמִין בְּפ' "מִי שֶׁהוֹצִיאוּהוּ" (לקמן דף נא.): (שֶׁבְּאַל). לָאו שֶׁנִּיתָּן לְאַזְהָרַת מִיתַת ב"ד הוּא, דְּס"ד אַל יוֹצִיא הוּא, וְנָפְקָא לָן הוֹצָאָה מֵרְשׁוּת לִרְשׁוּת מִינֵּיהּ, וְהַהִיא אַב מְלָאכָה הִיא, וּמְמִיתִין עָלֶיהָ: וְכָל לָאו שֶׁנִּיתָּן לְאַזְהָרַת. שֶׁלֹּא יַעֲשֶׂה כֵּן, שֶׁמִּתְחַיֵּיב עָלָיו מִיתַת ב"ד — אֵין לוֹקִין עָלָיו, אֲפִי' לֹא הִתְרוּ בּוֹ לְמִיתָה וְהִתְרוּ בּוֹ לְמַלְקוֹת, דְּהָשְׁתָּא לָא מִיקְטִיל — אֲפִי' הָכִי לָא לָקֵי, דִּלְאַזְהָרַת מִיתָה נִיתַּן וְלֹא לְמַלְקוֹת: אַל יֵצֵא כְּתִיב. וְאֵין כָּאן לְשׁוֹן הוֹצָאַת מַשּׂוֹי:

הֲדְרָן עֲלָךְ מָבוֹי שֶׁהוּא גָּבוֹהַּ

עוֹשִׂין פַּסִּין לַבֵּירָאוֹת. שֶׁבִּרְשׁוּת הָרַבִּים וּבֵירָאוֹת עַצְמָן רְשׁוּת הַיָּחִיד הֵן, שֶׁעֲמוּקִים עֲשָׂרָה. וְאֵין יָכוֹל לְמַלְאוֹת מֵהֶן, וְעוֹשִׂים פַּסִּין אֵלּוּ לְהָכִין לָהֶן הֶיקֵּף שֶׁיְּהוּ הַפַּסִּין הַלָּלוּ עוֹשִׂין אֶת סְבִיבוֹת הַבּוֹר רְשׁוּת הַיָּחִיד וִימַלֵּא וְיוֹלִיא וְיַנִּיחַ שָׁם וְתִיכָּנֵס בְּהֶמְתּוֹ וְיַשְׁקֶנָּה: דְּיוּמָדִין. עַמּוּדִין הַנִּרְאִין כִּשְׁנַיִם, שֶׁעָשׂוּי כְּמַרְזֵב שֶׁלָּנוּ. וּכְשֶׁנּוֹעֲצוֹ בַּקַּרְקַע לְפִאַת דְּרוֹמִית מַעֲרָבִית נוֹטֶה(ג) דּוֹפְנוֹ אֶחָד *לַמִּזְרָח וְלִידוֹ אֶחָד* לַצָּפוֹן. וְהַשֵּׁנִי לְפִאַת מַעֲרָבִית צְפוֹנִית נוֹטֶה לִידוֹ אֶחָד *לַמִּזְרָח וְלִידוֹ אֶחָד *לַדָּרוֹם. וּכְשֶׁנּוֹתֵן אַרְבַּעְתָּן לְד' הַפֵּיאוֹת, נִמְצָא לְכָל רוּחַ ב' אַמּוֹת דּוֹפֶן אַמָּה כְּנֶגֶד אַמָּה, וְהָרֶיוַח בֵּינְתַיִם: פְּשׁוּטִין. בָּאֶמְצַע נוֹתֵן לְכָל רוּחַ לוּחַ רְחָבָה אַמָּה. וּבַגְּמָרָא מְפָרֵשׁ בְּאֵיזֶה בּוֹר בָּעֵי ר' מֵאִיר פְּשׁוּטִין, דְּהָא מוֹדֶה ר' מֵאִיר שֶׁיָּכוֹל לְהַנִּיחַ י' אַמּוֹת רֶיוַח בֵּינְתַיִם, כִּדְמְפָרֵשׁ וְאָזֵיל: וּבֵינֵיהֶם שְׁתֵּי רְבָקוֹת וְכוּ'. דְּהַיְינוּ עֶשֶׂר אַמּוֹת, כִּדְמְפָרֵשׁ בַּגְּמָרָא. וְאִם פָּחוֹת — כ"ש שֶׁהוּא יָפֶה: קְשׁוּרוֹת. חוּמְרָא הוּא, לְמַעֵט מֵרֶיוַח שֶׁבֵּינְתַיִם: וְלֹא מוּתָּרוֹת. בַּגְּמָרָא פָּרֵיךְ: הַיְינוּ קְשׁוּרוֹת: אַחַת נִכְנֶסֶת וְאַחַת יוֹצֵאת. קוּלָּא הוּא, דְּלָא בָּעֵינַן עֶשֶׂר מְלוּמְלָמוֹת אֶלָּא שׁוֹחֲקוֹת: מוּתָּר לְהַקְרִיב. פַּסִּים לַבְּאֵר, וְלַעֲשׂוֹת הַהֶיקֵּף קָצָר: וּבִלְבַד שֶׁתְּהֵא. מִשְּׂפַת הַבְּאֵר עַד בֵּין הַפַּסִּין כְּדֵי רֹאשָׁהּ וְרוּבָּהּ שֶׁל פָּרָה. אֲבָל בְּצִיר מֵהָכִי — לָא, דִּילְמָא מַמְשִׁיךְ אַחַר פָּרָתוֹ וּמַפִּיק לַדְּוָולָא חוּץ לַמְּחִיצָּה, וְקָא מַפֵּיק מֵרְשׁוּת הַיָּחִיד לִרְשׁוּת הָרַבִּים:

לְהַרְחִיק

תוספות

מים אחרונים חובה. עכשיו לא נהגו במים אחרונים, דאין מלח סדומית מלוי בינינו. אי נמי: לפי שאין אנו רגילים לטבל אלבעותינו במלח אחר אכילה: **ואת** אכסניא דמאי. פ"ה: וישראלים הם. מיהו בירושלמי איכא פלוגתא, דאיכא דמוקי לה בנכרים, ואפ"ה איצטריך לאשמועינן דמאכילין אותם דמאי, דטבל אסור בהנאה, *ובדמאי הקילו:

אמר רב הונא תנא בית שמאי אומרים. לא שייך כאן להקשות וכי טעמא דב"ש אתא לאשמועינן, דקמ"ל: דאי משכחת תנא דאמר אין מאכילין — לא תיחוש לה, דב"ש הוא. וכה"ג אמרי' בפרק בתרא דיבמות (דף קכב.):

אל תפנו אל האובות הכי נמי דלא לקי. וא"ת: אין הכי נמי, דהא לאו שאין בו מעשה הוא! וי"ל: דפריך למ"ד לוקין עליו. אי נמי: עקימת שפתיו הוי מעשה. **לאו** שניתן לאזהרת מיתת ב"ד. פ"ה(ג): כמו אל יוליא הוא, ונפקא לן הוצאה מרשות לרשות מינה. ומשני: "אל יצא" כתיב, ואין כאן לשון הוצאת משוי. וקשה לפי': מה צריך כלל להזכיר דהוי לאו שניתן לאזהרת מיתת ב"ד? כיון דמקשה מכח דבעי למימר דאתי קרא להוצאה ולא לתחומין! ועוד: מה מקשה ר' יונתן, והא ר' עקיבא ס"ל *תחומין דאורייתא, ונפקא ליה ב"מי שהוציאוהו" (לקמן דף נא.) מ"אל יצא". ואם בא ר' יונתן לומר דמסתבר כמ"ד דרבנן — על זה לא היה חולק רב אשי, דהא בכל דוכתא פשיטא ליה להתלמוד דעירובי תחומין דרבנן, כדאמר בפרק "בכל מערבין" (שם דף לז:). דא"ל רבא לרב נחמן: מאן האי תנא דאפילו בדרבנן לית ליה ברירה. ובפרק "מי שהוציאוהו" (שם דף מו.) א"ל רבא לאביי: מכדי, עירובי תחומין דרבנן, מה לי יחיד במקום רבים כו'. ועוד: דמשמע בכל דוכתא דהוצאה כתיב ביה בשבת, דבפר' "כילד צולין" (פסחים דף פה:) אמרי' המוליא בשר פסח מחבורה לחבורה — אינו חייב עד שיניח, הוצאה כתיב ביה כשבת. ולא מצינו לשון הוצאה בשבת אלא מהאי קרא ד"אל יצא איש". ובפרק קמא דהוריות (דף ד.) יש ספרים דגרסי בהדיא: והא הוצאה כתיב *"אל יצא איש ממקומו". ונראה לפרש: דבין ר' יונתן ובין רב אשי נפקא להו הוצאה מ"אל יצא" כדמשמע בכל מקום. והכי משמע פשטי' דקרא: שאל יצא בשבת עם כליו ללקוט את המן כדרך שעושין בחול. וסבר ר' יונתן: אפי' למ"ד תחומין דאורייתא — לא לקי, דכיון דמהאי קרא נמי נפקא לן איסור הוצאה דהוי מיתת ב"ד. ורב אשי משני: מי כתיב "אל יוליא"? דהוי עיקר קרא בהוצאה, דאז ודאי לא היו לוקין עליו אע"ג דלתחומין נמי אתי. "אל יצא" כתיב, וכיון דעיקרו בלשון יליאה — לוקין עליו, אע"ג דאתי נמי לאיסור הוצאה. ואע"ג דהוצאה נפקא לן בריש "הזורק" (שבת דף צו:) מ"ויכלא העם מהביא" — איצטריך תרי קראי, חד — להוצאת עני, וחד — להוצאת בעל הבית. ומשום דהוצאה מלאכה גרועה היא איצטריך תרי קראי, כדפרישית בשבת (דף ב. ד"ה "פשט"). והא דמשמע הכא דאי הוה עיקר קרא בהוצאה כמו בתחומין לא הוה לקי לכולי עלמא, אע"ג דבתחומין ליכא מיתה וב"מרובה" (ב"ק דף עד:) גבי עדים שהוכחשו בנפש ולבסוף הוזמו, משמע דלוקין למאן דאמר אין נהרגים, משום דלא חשיב לאו שניתן לאזהרת מיתת בית דין, ושם מפורש.

הדרן עלך מבוי שהוא גבוה

עושין ארבעה דיומדין. והא דאמר לעיל (דף טו:) הכי אגמריה רחמנא למשה לא תפרוץ רובה — היינו היכא דליכא שם ד' מחילות כי הכא, דהואיל ואיכא בכל לד אמה מכאן ואמה מכאן — חשיב פתח.

וארבעה פשוטין. וליכא למימר הכא דאתי אוירא דהאי גיסא ודהאי גיסא ומבטלי ליה, דלגבי עולי רגלים הקילו(ד) ואוקמא אדאורייתא. [ואפשר דדוקא בפשוטין דרחבי' אמה לא אמרי' מדאוריי' דלא אתי אוירא ומבטל ליה, דהא גבי עמודי האלר פירש בריש מס' דאתי אוירא ומבטל להו מדאוריי'. ת"י] [**וביניהן** כמלא שתי רבקות. לא סגי בהך פלוגתא, ואצטריך דלעיל דמהני פשוטין לר"מ, ולא אמרי' אתי אוירא ומבטל ליה. ת"י]:

אפי'

עין משפט נר מצוה

קיב א מיי' פ"ג מהלכות אבל הלכה ח' סמ"ג לאוין רלה טוש"ע י"ד סי' שעד סעיף ג [וברב אלפס ריש הלכות טומאה' דף סג.]

[ועי' תוס' ברכות מז. ד"ה ומאכילין]:

קיג ב ג מיי' פ"ח מה' טומאת מת הלכה ז' ופ"ה מהל' נזקי ממון הלכה ג' טוש"ע י"ד סי' שסד סעי' ג' וטור חו"מ סי' רעד:

קיד ד ה מיי' פ"ו מהל' ברכות הל' ג ופ"ז מהל' מלכים הלכה יג טוש"ע או"ח סימן קנח סעיף ח:

קטו ו מיי' פ"י מהלכות מעשר הלכה יא ופ"ו מהל' מלכים שם:

קטז ז מיי' פ"ו מה' מלכי' שם ופ"א מהל' עירובין הל' ג טוש"ע או"ח סי' שסו סעי' ב:

קיז ח מיי' פכ"ז מהלכות שבת הלכ' א סמג לאוין סה:

א ט י כ מיי' פי"ז מהל' שבת הלכה כז:

ב ל מ מיי' שם הלכה כט:

[סוטה כז:]

רבינו חננאל

יהודה בן תימא אומר אף חונין בכל מקום ובמקום שנהרגין שם נקברין ואע"פ שאינן מת מצוה. ואיזו הוא מת מצוה כל שאין לו קוברין. אבל קורא ואחריו עונין אותו אין זה מת מצוה. ופטורין מרחיצת ידים. אמר אביי לא שנו אלא מים הראשוני' אבל מים אחרונים חובה. מפני שיש מלח סדומית ומסמא את העינים ומשתכחא קורטא בכורא ואפילו מדד מלחא צריך נ"י. ופטורין מדמאי שהם אכסניא ודומים כעניים. ותנן מאכילין את העניים דמאי ואת האכסניא דמאי וכן א' ב"ה. ופטורין מלערב. ואוקימנא בעירובי חצירות. ואקשינן ויש חצירות במחנה ופרקינן כדתניא מה בין שיירא למחנה אלא אהלים שבשיירא חייבין בעירוב אהלים שבמחנה פטורין מן העירוב ושאר (שאר) [שיירא] שאין להם אהלי' הרי הן כשרויין שבחצר. אבל בעירובי תחומין אפי' במחנה חייבין דתני ר' חייא לוקין על עירובי תחומין דבר תורה דכתיב אל יצא איש ממקומו ביום השביעי. ואקשינן וכי לוקין על לאו שבאל (ולאו) [ולא] אלא מעתה דכתיב אל תפנו אל האובות ואל הידעונים וגו' הכי נמי דלא לקי הכי קשיא לן לאו שניתן לאזהרת מיתת ב"ד [הוא] וכל לאו שניתן לאזהרת מיתת ב"ד אין לוקין עליו: מתקיף ליה רב אשי מי כתיב אל יוציא אל יצא כתיב ואל יצא קרינן. פי' בהוצאת חפץ אזהרת מיתת ב"ד ביציאת תחומין אין שם מיתה:

הדרן עלך מבוי.

עושין פסין לביראות ד' דיומדין הואין כח' דברי ר' יהודה כו':

מסורת הש"ס

יבמות פט: נזיר מג:

[ב"ק פ"א:]

שם

חולין קה: [ע"ש שמביא בשם רב יהודה בר' דרב חייא וע' תוס' חולין קה. ד"ה מים לאשונים גרסו הכא אבל מים אחרונים חובה דאמר וכו']

ברכות מז. שבת קכז: דמאי פ"ג מ"א לקמן לא. פסחים לה: סוכה לה:

ס"א וכי לוקין על לאו של שביתה [שבת קנד. ב"ק עד: סנהדרין פו: מכות יג: שבועות ז.]

נ"ל למערב

נ"ל לדרום

נ"ל למערב

נ"ל ללפון. כ"א בפי' ה"ר יהונתן

הגהות הב"ח

(א) גמ' מפניהו לכל רוח שירלה נ"ב וע"ע סנהדרין דף מ"ז ע"ב: (ב) רש"י ד"ה דיומדין וכו' נוטה לידו אחד למזרח: (ג) תוס' ד"ה לאו שניתן וכו' פ"ה דס"ד אל יוליא הוא: (ד) תוס' ד"ה וארבעה וכו' דלגבי עולי רגלים הקילו ואוקמוה אדאורייתא:

גליון הש"ס

גמ' אלא מעתה דכתי' אל תפנו אל האובות. בס' המצות להרמב"ם ל"ת י הגירס' כאן אל תפנו אל האלילים: **מתני'** ורוחבן ששה ועוביין כו'. עיין סוכה דף ד' ע"ב תוד"ה דיומד:

להרחיק כל שהוא, ובלבד שירבה בפסין. ר' יהודה אומר: עד בית סאתים. אמרו לו: לא אמרו בית סאתים אלא לגנה ולקרפף, אבל אם היה דיר או *סהר או מוקצה או חצר — אפילו בית חמשת כורין אפילו בית עשרה כורין — מותר. ומותר להרחיק כל שהוא, ובלבד שירבה בפסין:§ גמ' לימא מתני' דלא כחנניא, דתניא: עושין פסין לבור וחבלין לשיירא. וחנניא אומר: חבלין לבור, אבל לא פסין. אפי' תימא חנניא, בור לחוד באר לחוד. איכא דאמרי: מדלא קתני חנניא אומר עושין חבלין לבור ופסין לבאר — מכלל דלחנניא לא שנא בור ולא שנא באר, חבלין — אין, פסין — לא. לימא מתני' דלא כחנניא! אפילו תימא חנניא, למאי דקאמר ת"ק קא מהדר ליה. לימא מתני' דלא כר"ע, *דתנן: אחד באר הרבים ובור הרבים ובאר היחיד — עושין להן פסין, אבל בור היחיד עושין לו מחיצה גבוה עשרה טפחים, דברי ר"ע. ואילו הכא קתני לביראות, לביראות — אין, לבורות — לא. אפי' תימא ר"ע, באר מים חיים דפסיקא ליה — לא שנא דרבים ול"ש דיחיד, קתני, בור מכונסין, דלא פסיקא ליה — לא קתני. לימא מתני' דלא כר' יהודה בן בבא, *דתנן רבי יהודה בן בבא אומר: אין עושין פסין אלא לבאר הרבים בלבד. ואילו הכא קתני לביראות, ל"ש דרבים ול"ש דיחיד! אפי' תימא ר' יהודה בן בבא, מאי ביראות — ביראות דעלמא. מאי דיומדין? א"ר ירמיה בן אלעזר: דיו עמודין.§ [א]ד"יו למ"נודה שב"ח זונ"ית נתק"לקל במיד"ה שלש"ה סימן.§ *תנן התם, ר' יהודה אומר: כל השיתין פטורין חוץ מן הדיופרא. מאי דיופרא? אמר עולא: אילן העושה דיו פירות בשנה. *א"ר ירמיה בן אלעזר: דיו פרצוף פנים היה לו לאדם הראשון, שנאמר: °"אחור וקדם צרתני". תהלים קלט
בראשית ב כתיב: °"ויבן ה' אלהים את הצלע וגו'", רב ושמואל; חד אמר: *פרצוף, וחד אמר: זנב. בשלמא למ"ד פרצוף — היינו דכתיב: "אחור וקדם צרתני", אלא למ"ד זנב — מאי "אחור וקדם צרתני"? כדר' אמי, דא"ר אמי: אחור למעשה בראשית, וקדם לפורענות. בשלמא אחור למעשה בראשית — דלא איברי עד מעלי שבתא, אלא וקדם לפורענות מאי היא? אילימא משום קללה — הא בתחילה נתקלל נחש, ולבסוף
יד
שם ז נתקללה חוה, ולבסוף נתקלל אדם! אלא למבול, דכתיב: °"וימח את כל היקום אשר על פני האדמה מאדם ועד בהמה וגו'". בשלמא למ"ד פרצוף — היינו דכתיב:
שם ב °"וייצר" תרין יודי"ן. אלא למ"ד זנב — מאי "וייצר"? כדר"ש בן פזי, *דא"ר שמעון בן פזי:
שם ה אוי לי מיצרי אוי לי מיוצרי. בשלמא למאן דאמר פרצוף — היינו דכתיב: °"זכר ונקבה בראם", אלא למאן דאמר זנב — מאי "זכר ונקבה בראם"? לכדר' אבהו,
שם א *דר' אבהו רמי, כתיב: "זכר ונקבה בראם", וכתיב: °"(כי) בצלם אלהים ברא אותו" — °בתחילה עלתה במחשבה לבראות שנים, ולבסוף לא נברא אלא אחד. בשלמא למאן דאמר פרצוף — היינו דכתיב: °"ויסגור בשר תחתנה". אלא למאן דאמר זנב — מאי "ויסגור בשר תחתנה"? אמר רב זביד, ואיתימא ר' ירמיה, ואיתימא רב נחמן בר יצחק: °לא נצרכה אלא למקום חתך. בשלמא למ"ד זנב — היינו דכתיב: "ויבן", אלא למ"ד פרצוף — מאי "ויבן"? לכדר' שמעון בן מנסיא, *דדריש ר"ש בן מנסיא: "ויבן ה' אלהים את הצלע" — מלמד שקילעה הקב"ה לחוה והביאה לאדם הראשון, שכן בכרכי הים קורין לקלעיתא בנייתא. דבר אחר: "ויבן ה' אלהים", אמר רב חסדא, ואמרי לה במתניתא תנא: מלמד שבנאה הקב"ה לחוה כבנין
אוצר

רש"י

להרחיק כל שהוא. כל מה שקבלו לעשות היקף גדול: ובלבד שירבה בפסין. דכל כמה דמרחיק מבור — מגדיל ריוח שבין דיומד לדיומד, וצריך להרבות בפסין עד שלא יהא בין פשוט לפשוט, ובין פשוט לדיומד יותר מי' אמות לר' מאיר, או מי"ג אמה ושליש לרבי יהודה: לגינה ולקרפף. שאין הקיפן לדירה. תורה אור קרפף — היקף גדול חוץ לעיר להכניס שם עצים לאוצר: אבל אם היה דיר. של בהמות, שעושין בשדות, היום כאן והיום כאן כדי לזבל בגללי הבהמות: סהר. לבהמות של עיר: מוקצה. רחבה שאחורי הבתים: וחצר. שלפני הבתים. דכל הני הקיפן לדירה הוא. והני פסי ביראות נמי, הואיל ומימיהן ראויין לשתיית אדם — תשמיש דירה מעלייתא הוא: גמ' חבלים לשיירא. כדתנן בפ"ק (דף טז:): מקיפין שלשה חבלים, דכולה עומד הוא. אבל פסין לשיירא — לא, דהוי פרוץ מרובה (א), ולא הותר אלא לבור משום בהמת עולי רגלים, כדמפרש לקמן: בור. מים מכונסין, ועבידי דפסקי, ומשום הכי אסר חנניא, דזמנין דפסקי מיא ובטלי מחיצות, ולא הותרו פסי ביראות אלא מפני מימיהן של בהמת עולי רגלים: באר. מים חיים. וביראות דמתניתין, מדלא קתני בורות — במים חיים קאמר: בור הרבים. אי פסקי מיא °מדכרי אהדדי, ולא מטלטלי התם: באר היחיד. דלא פסקי מיא: לבורות לא. ואפילו דרבים: מכונסין דלא פסיקא ליה. דאיכא בור הרבים דמהני, ואיכא בור דיחיד דלא מהני — לא קתני: ואילו הכא ביראות קתני. דמשמע תרי, חד דרבים וחד דיחיד: ביראות דעלמא. אכל ביראות קאי, ולעולם דרבים: השיתין. מיני תאנים רעות, כדאמר במס' ברכות (דף מ:): פטורין. מן הדמאי, דכיון דרעות הן — לא חש עלייהו עם הארץ, ועישרן: חוץ מן הדיופרא. שהוא חשוב: דיו פירות. טוענין ב' פעמים בשנה: אחור וקדם צרתני. מלפנים ומאחור צרת לי צורת פנים: הצלע. בין לרב בין לשמואל לשון לדדין, כמו "ולצלע המשכן השנית" (שמות כו): פרצוף. חילקו לשנים, שהיה זכר מכאן ונקבה מכאן: זנב. היה לו לאדם הראשון, ונטלו ממנו, ובראה את חוה: מאי אחור וקדם צרתני. דמשמע ב' צורות: מאדם ועד בהמה. אדם הוזכר בפורענות תחילה: ה"ג: היינו דכתיב וייצר בתרין יודין. דמשמע ב' צורות: אוי לי מיצרי. שמצערני אם אעשה רצון יוצרי: אוי לי מיוצרי. אם אעשה רצון יצרי: זכר ונקבה בראם. משמע: מתחילת בריאתו היה זכר ונקבה זכר מצד זה ונקבה מצד זה: ברא אותו. משמע חד: ויבן. משמע שהיתה מחוסרת בנין: מאי ויבן. בנויה ועומדת היתה: שקילעה. קליעת שיער:
אוצר

תוספות

אפילו י' כורין מותר. פ"ה: והני פסי בירא‍ות נמי, הואיל ומימיהן ראויין לשתיית אדם — תשמיש דירה מעלייתא היא. ואין להקשות: א"כ, אמאי אמר בגמרא מתני' דלא כרבי עקיבא מדלא קתני בורות. דילמא נקט בירא‍ות — דאפי' י' כורין שרי(ב). וי"ל: דמתניתין ר' יהודה היא, דלא שרי אפי' בבאר אלא בית סאתים. וא"ת: ומאי שנא גבי שיירא דבעו רבנן שלא יהא בית סאתים פנוי, והכא גבי פסין דגריעי טפי מחבלים כדאמר בגמרא, לא אצרכיה שלא יהא בית סאתים פנוי? וי"ל: דגבי שיירא, הואיל ונעשה לצורך שעה — לא הוי חשיב מוקף לדירה כמו פסין. אי נמי: גבי עולי רגלים הקילו, והחשיבו פסין כמו מחיצה גמורה, כמו שהקילו לענין פרוץ מרובה על העומד. ומ"מ, צריך לפרש כפירוש הקונטרס דחשיבי פסין מוקפין לדירה אע"פ שאין אדם דר שם, דאל"ה — תקשה מתני' לרב הונא בר' *חיננא, דבעי למימר בפ' "הדר" (לקמן דף סז:) דמחילה שאינה מוקפת לדירה — לא שמה מחילה. דפריך לר' יוחנן, דאמר: מחילה היא, אלא שמחוסרת דיורין: בור לחוד ובאר לחוד. המקשה נמי היה יודע שיש חילוק בין בור לבאר, דמתני' היא. אלא שהיה מדקדק לפרש, מדלא פירש במילתיה ופסין לבאר — מכלל דלא מפליג, כמו שמדקדק בסמוך. וה"ה דהוה מצי למימר מתניתין דלא כתנא קמא, דבמתני' קתני דווקא באר ולא בור: בור לחוד. פירש רש"י: בור מים מכונסין, דעבידי דפסקי. ואע"ג דלקמן בפירקא קאמר טעמא דבעינן מים חיים, משום דבעינן מידי דחזי לאדם — האי טעמא לא שייך אלא לר' יהודה בן בבא, דאמר: אין עושין פסין אלא לבאר הרבים לבד. וטעמא משום דבעי מידי דחזי לאדם. דאי משום דלא פסקי — אפילו בור רבים נמי, דאין לחוש דילמא פסקי. אבל שאר תנאים טעמייהו משום דלא פסקי, דאי בעי מידי דחזי לאדם — אפילו בור הרבים נמי לא: בשלמא למ"ד פרצוף היינו כו'. מכאן היה מקשה ריב"ס על פ"ה דפירש בריש כתובות (דף ח.): ב' יצירות הוו, ולכך בריך שתים "יוצר האדם" ו"אשר יצר". דהוי כמ"ד זנב. ועוד, דבתר הכי קאמר התם: לכ"ע חדא יצירה הוי, מר סבר: בתר מחשבה אזלינן, ומר סבר בתר מעשה אזלינן והיינו כמ"ד זנב, דאליבא דידיה דרשינן הנהו קראי כרבי אבהו. לכן נראה דשתי יצירות הואי — היינו כמאן דאמר פרצוף:
*צ"ל חנינא

רבינו חננאל

ואמרינן לימא מתניתין דלא כחנניא דתניא חנניא אומר חבלין לבור ולא פסין. ואוקימנא אפי' תימא חנניא אימור דאמר חנניא חבלין ולא פסין לבור לבאר מי אמר כו' לימא מתניתין דלא כר"ע דתניא אחד באר הרבים ובור הרבים ובאר היחיד עושין להם פסים כו' אפי' תימא ר"ע באר דפסיקא ליה לא שנא דרבים ולא שנא דיחיד [קתני] מכונסין דלא פסיקא ליה כו' לימא מתניתין דלא כר' יהודה בן בבא דתנן ר' יהודה בן בבא אומר אין עושין פסין אלא לבאר הרבים בלבד כו'. ומתניתין קתני לביראות לא שנא דרבים ולא שנא דיחיד. אפי' תימא מתני' ר"י בן בבא מאי ביראות דתנן במשנתנו ביראות דרבים אין ביראות דיחיד לא. ומאי ביראות [ביראות] דעלמא. מאי דיומדין אמר ר' ירמיה דיו עמודין פי' ב' עמודין כלומר נראין כשנים. תנן ר' יהודה אומר כל השיתין פטורין חוץ מן הדיופרא אמר עולא אילן שעושה ב' פירות בשנה כו'. דיו פרצופין היו לו לאדם הראשון שנאמר אחור וקדם צרתני. ויבן ה' אלהים את הצלע רב ושמואל חד אמר פרצוף וחד אמר זנב. ר' אבהו רמי כתיב זכר ונקבה בראם וכתיב בצלם אלהים ברא אותו בתחלה עלה במחשבה ליבראות שניהם כאחד ולבסוף בראו יחידי. ויבן מלמד שקילעה לחוה שכן בכרכי הים היו קורין לקלעיתא

רב נסים גאון

פרק ב כל השיתין פטורין. תמצא פירושו בברכות בפרק כיצד מברכין על הפירו' (דף מ') שיתין אמר רבה בר בר חנה א"ר יוחנן תאיני ובגמרא דבני מערבא (שביעית פ"ה הל"א) מהוצאת העלין ועד הפגין ג' יום:

הגהות הב"ח

(א) רש"י ד"ה חבלים וכו' פרוץ מרובה לא דלא הותר: (ב) תום' ד"ה אפילו וכו' שרי די"ל דמתניתין:

הגהות הגר"א

[א] גמ' דיו מנודה שבח יונה בית שתי נתקלל במדה שלשה. סימן כצ"ל (והוא סימן לכל מימרות דר' ירמיה ב"א על הפיסקא):

גליון הש"ס

גמ' בתחלה עלתה במחשבה. עי' ר"ה דף כז ע"א תוס' ד"ה כמאן מצלי': שם לא נצרכה אלא למקום חתך. כעין זה חולין דף סח ע"ב: רש"י ד"ה בור הרבים וכו' מדכרי אהדדי. עי' לעיל דף ג ע"א:

מסורת הש"ס

משנה שבמשניות הגי' סחר]
לקמן כב:
שם
דמאי פ"א מ"א
ברכות סא. ע"ש
[פי' גוף. ערוך]
ברכות סא.
כתובות ח. ע"ש ברכות שם
שם ב
ברכות סא. נדה מה: ע"ש שבת לג.

תורה אור

אוֹצָר, מָה אוֹצָר זֶה רָחָב מִלְּמַטָּה וְקָצָר מִלְּמַעְלָה כְּדֵי לְקַבֵּל אֶת הַפֵּירוֹת — אַף הָאִשָּׁה רְחָבָה מִלְּמַטָּה וּקְצָרָה מִלְּמַעְלָה כְּדֵי לְקַבֵּל אֶת הַוָּלָד. "וַיְבִיאֶהָ אֶל הָאָדָם" — מְלַמֵּד שֶׁעָשָׂה הקב"ה שׁוֹשְׁבִינוּת לְאָדָם הָרִאשׁוֹן, מִכָּאן לַגָּדוֹל שֶׁיַּעֲשֶׂה שׁוֹשְׁבִינוּת לְקָטָן וְאַל יֵרַע לוֹ. וּלְמַאן דְּאָמַר פַּרְצוּף — הֵי מִינַּיְיהוּ סַגִּי בְּרֵישָׁא? אָמַר רַב נַחְמָן בַּר יִצְחָק: מִסְתַּבְּרָא דְּזָכָר סַגִּי בְּרֵישָׁא. דְּתַנְיָא: [א]לֹא יְהַלֵּךְ אָדָם אֲחוֹרֵי אִשָּׁה בַּדֶּרֶךְ, וַאֲפִי' הִיא אִשְׁתּוֹ. נִזְדַּמְּנָה עַל הַגֶּשֶׁר — יְסַלְּקֶנָּה לַצְּדָדִין. וְכָל הָעוֹבֵר אֲחוֹרֵי אִשָּׁה בְּנָהָר — אֵין לוֹ חֵלֶק לָעוֹלָם הַבָּא.§ תָּנוּ רַבָּנַן: *הַמַּרְצֶה מָעוֹת לְאִשָּׁה מִיָּדוֹ לְיָדָהּ אוֹ מִיָּדָהּ לְיָדוֹ בִּשְׁבִיל שֶׁיִּסְתַּכֵּל בָּהּ, אֲפִילּוּ דּוֹמֶה לְמֹשֶׁה רַבֵּינוּ שֶׁקִּיבֵּל תּוֹרָה מֵהַר סִינַי — לֹא יִנָּקֶה מִדִּינָהּ שֶׁל גֵּיהִנָּם. וְעָלָיו הַכָּתוּב אוֹמֵר: °"יָד לְיָד לֹא יִנָּקֶה רָע" (משלי יא) — לֹא יִנָּקֶה מִדִּינָהּ שֶׁל גֵּיהִנָּם. אָמַר רַב נַחְמָן: מָנוֹחַ עַם הָאָרֶץ הָיָה, שֶׁנֶּאֱמַר: °"וַיָּקָם וַיֵּלֶךְ מָנוֹחַ אַחֲרֵי אִשְׁתּוֹ" (שופטים יג). מַתְקִיף לָהּ רַב נַחְמָן בַּר יִצְחָק: אֶלָּא מֵעַתָּה, גַּבֵּי אֶלְקָנָה דִּכְתִיב: *"וַיֵּלֶךְ אֶלְקָנָה אַחֲרֵי אִשְׁתּוֹ" הָכִי נַמִי? וְגַבֵּי אֱלִישָׁע דִּכְתִיב: °"וַיָּקָם וַיֵּלֶךְ אַחֲרֶיהָ" (מלכים ב ד) הָכִי נַמִי? אֶלָּא: אַחֲרֵי דְּבָרֶיהָ וַעֲצָתָהּ, הָכָא נַמִי: אַחֲרֵי דְּבָרֶיהָ וַעֲצָתָהּ. אָמַר רַב אַשִׁי: וּלְמַאי דְּאָמַר רַב נַחְמָן, מָנוֹחַ עַם הָאָרֶץ הָיָה, אֲפִילּוּ בֵּי רַב נַמִי לֹא קָרָא. דִּכְתִיב: °"וַתָּקָם רִבְקָה וְנַעֲרוֹתֶיהָ וַתִּרְכַּבְנָה עַל הַגְּמַלִּים וַתֵּלַכְנָה אַחֲרֵי הָאִישׁ" (בראשית כד) — וְלֹא לִפְנֵי הָאִישׁ. אָמַר רַבִּי יוֹחָנָן: אַחֲרֵי אֲרִי וְלֹא אַחֲרֵי אִשָּׁה, אַחֲרֵי אִשָּׁה וְלֹא אַחֲרֵי עֲבוֹדָה זָרָה, אֲחוֹרֵי עֲבוֹדָה זָרָה [ב]וְלֹא אֲחוֹרֵי בֵּית הַכְּנֶסֶת בְּשָׁעָה(א) שֶׁמִּתְפַּלְּלִין. וְאָמַר ר' יִרְמְיָה בֶּן אֶלְעָזָר: כָּל אוֹתָן הַשָּׁנִים שֶׁהָיָה אָדָם הָרִאשׁוֹן בְּנִידּוּי הוֹלִיד רוּחִין וְשֵׁידִין וְלִילִין, שֶׁנֶּאֱמַר: °"וַיְחִי אָדָם שְׁלֹשִׁים וּמְאַת שָׁנָה וַיּוֹלֶד בִּדְמוּתוֹ כְּצַלְמוֹ" (שם ה), מִכְּלָל דְּעַד הָאִידָּנָא לָאו כְּצַלְמוֹ אוֹלִיד. מֵיתִיבִי, הָיָה ר' מֵאִיר אוֹמֵר: אָדָם הָרִאשׁוֹן חָסִיד גָּדוֹל הָיָה, כֵּיוָן שֶׁרָאָה שֶׁנִּקְנְסָה מִיתָה עַל יָדוֹ יָשַׁב בְּתַעֲנִית מֵאָה וּשְׁלֹשִׁים שָׁנָה, וּפֵירֵשׁ מִן הָאִשָּׁה מֵאָה וּשְׁלֹשִׁים שָׁנָה, וְהֶעֱלָה זַרְזֵי תְּאֵנִים עַל בְּשָׂרוֹ מֵאָה וּשְׁלֹשִׁים שָׁנָה?! כִּי קָאָמְרִינַן הַהוּא — בְּשִׁכְבַת זֶרַע דְּאִתְחֲזָא לְאוֹנְסֵיהּ. וְא"ר יִרְמְיָה בֶּן אֶלְעָזָר: מִקְצָת שִׁבְחוֹ שֶׁל אָדָם אוֹמְרִים בְּפָנָיו, וְכוּלּוֹ שֶׁלֹּא בְּפָנָיו. מִקְצָת שִׁבְחוֹ בְּפָנָיו — דִּכְתִיב: °"כִּי אוֹתְךָ רָאִיתִי צַדִּיק לְפָנַי בַּדּוֹר הַזֶּה" (שם ז), כּוּלּוֹ שֶׁלֹּא בְּפָנָיו — דִּכְתִיב: °"נֹחַ אִישׁ צַדִּיק תָּמִים הָיָה בְּדֹרֹתָיו" (שם ו). וְא"ר יִרְמְיָה בֶּן אֶלְעָזָר: מַאי דִּכְתִיב: °"וְהִנֵּה עֲלֵה זַיִת טָרָף בְּפִיהָ" (שם ח) — *אָמְרָה יוֹנָה לִפְנֵי הקב"ה: רבש"ע, יִהְיוּ מְזוֹנוֹתַי מְרוֹרִין כַּזַּיִת וּמְסוּרִין בְּיָדְךָ, וְאַל יִהְיוּ מְתוּקִין כִּדְבַשׁ וּתְלוּיִן בְּיַד בָּשָׂר וָדָם. כְּתִיב הָכָא "טָרָף" וּכְתִיב הָתָם °"הַטְרִיפֵנִי לֶחֶם חֻקִּי" (משלי ל). וְא"ר יִרְמְיָה בֶּן אֶלְעָזָר: [ג]כָּל בַּיִת שֶׁנִּשְׁמָעִין בּוֹ דִּבְרֵי תוֹרָה בַּלַּיְלָה — שׁוּב אֵינוֹ נֶחְרָב, שֶׁנֶּאֱמַר: °"וְלֹא אָמַר אַיֵּה אֱלוֹהַּ עֹשָׂי נֹתֵן זְמִרוֹת בַּלָּיְלָה" (איוב לה). וְאָמַר רַבִּי יִרְמְיָה בֶּן אֶלְעָזָר: מִיּוֹם שֶׁחָרַב בֵּית הַמִּקְדָּשׁ דַּיּוֹ לָעוֹלָם שֶׁיִּשְׁתַּמֵּשׁ בִּשְׁתֵּי אוֹתִיּוֹת, שֶׁנֶּאֱמַר: °"כֹּל הַנְּשָׁמָה תְּהַלֵּל יָהּ הַלְלוּיָהּ" (תהלים קנ). *וְאָמַר רַבִּי יִרְמְיָה בֶּן אֶלְעָזָר: נִתְקַלְּלָה בָּבֶל — נִתְקַלְּלוּ שְׁכֵנֶיהָ, נִתְקַלְּלָה שׁוֹמְרוֹן — נִתְבָּרְכוּ שְׁכֵנֶיהָ. נִתְקַלְּלָה בָּבֶל נִתְקַלְּלוּ שְׁכֵנֶיהָ — דִּכְתִיב: °"וְשַׂמְתִּיהָ לְמוֹרַשׁ קִפֹּד וְאַגְמֵי מָיִם" (ישעיהו יד). נִתְקַלְּלָה שׁוֹמְרוֹן נִתְבָּרְכוּ שְׁכֵנֶיהָ — דִּכְתִיב: °"וְשַׂמְתִּי שֹׁמְרוֹן לְעִי הַשָּׂדֶה לְמַטָּעֵי (מיכה א)

רש"י

אוֹצָר רָחָב מִלְּמַטָּה וְקָצָר מִלְּמַעְלָה. שֶׁאִם הָיָה רָחָב מִלְמַעְלָה, כְּשֶׁהוּא מְמַלְּאוֹ מַכְבִּיד מַשָּׂאוֹי הַפֵּירוֹת עַל הַכְּתָלִים, וּמַטֶּה אוֹתָם: רְחָבָה מִלְּמַטָּה. חֲלַל בֵּית הָרֶחֶם שֶׁלָּהּ: שׁוֹשְׁבִינוּת. שֶׁנִּשְׁתַּדֵּל בַּחִיתּוּנוֹ, לְשַׂמְּחוֹ וּלְהִתְעַסֵּק בְּצָרְכֵי סְעוּדַת חוּפָּה: סַגֵּי. מְהַלֵּךְ: וַאֲפִילּוּ הִיא אִשְׁתּוֹ. שֶׁהוּא גְּנַאי לוֹ: נִזְדַּמְּנָה לוֹ עַל הַגֶּשֶׁר. וְהִיא מְהַלֶּכֶת לְפָנָיו: יְסַלְּקֶנָּה לַצְּדָדִין. וְיַעֲבוֹר לְפָנֶיהָ: בְּנָהָר. דְּמַדְלְיָא לְמָנָא, וּמִסְתַּכֵּל בִּבְשָׂרָהּ, וּבְאֵשֶׁת אִישׁ קָאָמַר: הַמַּרְצֶה. מוֹנֶה: יָד לְיָד. הַמַּרְצֶה מִיָּד לְיָד, אֲפִי' הוּא כְּמוֹ מֹשֶׁה שֶׁקִּבֵּל תּוֹרָה מִיַּד הקב"ה לְיָדוֹ: עַם הָאָרֶץ הָיָה. דְּלֹא גָּמַר דֶּרֶךְ אֶרֶץ דְּמַתְנִי' דְּקָתָנֵי לְעֵיל: לֹא יְהַלֵּךְ אָדָם אֲפִילּוּ אַחֲרֵי אִשְׁתּוֹ: אֶלְקָנָה. נָבִיא הָיָה, כִּדְתַנְיָא בְּסֵדֶר עוֹלָם: "וַיָּבֹא אִישׁ הָאֱלֹהִים אֶל עֵלִי" — זֶה אֶלְקָנָה. י' נְבִיאִים נִקְרְאוּ "אִישׁ הָאֱלֹהִים" וְהוּא א' מֵהֶם. וְלֵיכָּא לְמֵימַר עַם הָאָרֶץ הָיָה: וּלְמַאי דְּקָאָמַר רַב נַחְמָן. דְּהַאי "אַחֲרֵי" אַחֲרֵי מַמָּשׁ קָאָמַר: בֵּי רַב. מִקְרָא [שֶׁקּוֹרִין] תִּינוֹקוֹת שֶׁל בֵּית רַבָּן: וְלֹא אַחֲרֵי אִשָּׁה. אֵשֶׁת אִישׁ: וְלֹא אַחֲרֵי עֲבוֹדָה זָרָה. שֶׁמָּא יִמָּשֵׁךְ אַחֲרֶיהָ, וּכְתִיב "הַרְחֵק מֵעָלֶיהָ דַרְכֶּךָ", וְאָמְרִי' (ע"ז דף יז.): זוֹ הָאַפִּיקוֹרְסוּת: וְלֹא אֲחוֹרֵי בֵּית הַכְּנֶסֶת בִּשְׁעָ' שֶׁהַצִּיבּוּר מִתְפַּלְּלִין. שֶׁנִּרְאֶה כְּכוֹפֵר, שֶׁעוֹמֵד מֵאַחֲרֶיהָ וְאֵינוֹ נִכְנָס: בְּנִדּוּי. שֶׁיָּשַׁב מֵאָה וּשְׁלֹשִׁים שָׁנָה נָזוּף, מִפְּנֵי שֶׁגָּעַר בּוֹ הקב"ה, דִּכְתִיב "הֲמִן הָעֵץ וגו'" וְקִלְּלוֹ: זַרְזֵי תְּאֵנָה. חֲגוֹרוֹת, וּמְתַרְגְּמִינַן זְרָזִין (בראשית ג): שִׁכְבַת זֶרַע דְּחַזָא לְאוֹנְסֵיהּ. נַעֲשָׂה שֵׁידִין וְרוּחִין וְלִילִין מִינֵי מַזִּיקִין: אוֹמְרִים מִקְצָת שִׁבְחוֹ כו'. כְּלוֹמַר: דֶּרֶךְ אֶרֶץ הוּא, שֶׁאַע"פ שֶׁאָדָם מְשַׁבֵּחַ אֶת חֲבֵרוֹ, שֶׁלֹּא בְּפָנָיו הַרְבֵּה, אֵין מַרְבֶּה בְּשִׁבְחוֹ לְפָנָיו, מִפְּנֵי שֶׁנִּרְאֶה כְּמַחֲנִיף(ב): בְּפָנָיו. כְּתִיב "צַדִּיק": שֶׁלֹּא בְּפָנָיו. כְּתִיב "צַדִּיק תָּמִים": טָרָף בְּפִיהָ. מַאֲמַר פִּיהָ, בִּיקְּשָׁה שֶׁיְּהֵא זַיִת טֶרֶף שֶׁלָּהּ — וְהַיְינוּ מָזוֹן: בָּשָׂר וָדָם. נֹחַ: וְלֹא אָמַר אַיֵּה אֱלוֹהַּ עוֹשָׂי. לֹא הוּצְרַךְ לְהִתְאוֹנֵן וְלוֹמַר אַיֵּה עוֹשַׂי וַהֲרֵינִי חָרֵב, מִי שֶׁנּוֹתֵן זְמִירוֹת שֶׁל תּוֹרָה בַּלַּיְלָה. וּלְהָכִי נָקַט לַיְלָה — שֶׁהַקּוֹל נִשְׁמָע מֵרָחוֹק: מִיּוֹם שֶׁחָרַב בֵּית הַמִּקְדָּשׁ. וּפָסְקוּ הַכֹּהֲנִים מִלְּבָרֵךְ בַּשֵּׁם הַמְּפוֹרָשׁ, כִּדְאָמַר בְּ"אֵין דּוֹרְשִׁין" *שֶׁהָיוּ מְבָרְכִין בַּשֵּׁם הַמְּפוֹרָשׁ: דַּיּוֹ לָעוֹלָם שֶׁיִּשְׁתַּמֵּשׁ בְּשֵׁם ב' אוֹתִיּוֹת. בֵּין לְשַׁבֵּחַ לְפָנָיו, בֵּין לְבָרֵךְ אִישׁ אֶת חֲבֵירוֹ, דִּכְתִיב "כֹּל הַנְּשָׁמָה תְּהַלֵּל יָהּ". כְּלוֹמַר: זֶה הַשֵּׁם שֶׁכָּל הַנְּשָׁמָה כּוּלָּהּ רָאוּי לְהִשְׁתַּמֵּשׁ בּוֹ. מִכְּלָל דְּשֵׁם בֶּן אַרְבַּע אוֹתִיּוֹת וְשֵׁם הַמְּפוֹרָשׁ — לֹא לְכָל הַנְּשָׁמָה נִיתַּן, אֶלָּא לַכֹּהֲנִים בִּלְבַד. דִּכְתִיב (דברים י) "וּלְבָרֵךְ בִּשְׁמוֹ", וּכְתִי' (במדבר ו) "וְשָׂמוּ אֶת שְׁמִי" — הַמְיוּחָד לִי: נִתְקַלְּלוּ שְׁכֵנֶיהָ. מִקְּלָלָתָהּ: נִתְבָּרְכוּ שְׁכֵנֶיהָ. מִקְּלָלָתָהּ: לְמוֹרַשׁ קִפּוֹד. וְשָׁם הוֹלְכוֹת הַחַיּוֹת רָעוֹת, וּמַזִּיקוֹת מְקוֹמוֹת הַסְּמוּכוֹת לָהּ, דְּאוֹי לָרָשָׁע וְאוֹי לִשְׁכֵנוֹ [סוכה נו:]: לְמַטָּעֵי

תוספות

יד לְיָד לֹא ינקה רע. לאו היינו קרא דדריש בסוטה (דף ד:) לענין גסות הרוח, דהתם דריש מקרא *ד"תועבת ה' כל גבה לב יד ליד וגו'", וקרא דהכא היינו "יד ליד לא ינקה רע וזרע צדיקים נמלט": מתקיף לה רב נחמן בר יצחק. מכאן משמע דרב נחמן בר יצחק לאו היינו רב נחמן סתמא*: ולא אחורי בית הכנסת בשעה שהצבור מתפללין. בתוספתא דמגילה [פרק ג] תניא: אין פותחין בתי כנסיות אלא למזרח, שכן מצינו במשכן שנא' [במדבר ג]: "והחונים לפני המשכן קדמה וגו' מזרחה וגו'". ונראה דקסבר האי תנא דשכינה במערב, והיו משתחוים למערב או היתה א"י ובהמ"ק במערבם, דכתיב [דה"ב ו]: "(ויתפללו) [והתפללו] דרך ארצם", וכתיב [דניאל ו]: "וכוין פתיחן ליה בעיליתיה נגד ירושלם". והשתא לכאורה נראה דאחורי בית הכנסת היינו לצד הארון. ומיהו, אין נראה, (*דבסוף פרק) קמא דברכות (דף ו:) אמרינן: ההוא גברא דהוה מצלי אחורי בי כנישתא, א"ל אליהו: כדו בר קיימת קמי מרך. פירוש: כשתי רשויות. וקאמר: לא שנו אלא דלא קא מהדר אפיה לבי כנישתא, אבל מהדר אפיה לבי כנישתא – לית לן בה. ואם היה עומד לצד הארון – כ"ש דאי מהדר אפי' לבי כנישתא *דמחזי כשני רשויו', שהצבור משתחוי' למזרח והוא משתחוה למערב. ועוד, דאמר התם בפר' "הרואה" (דף סא.): אסור לו לאדם לעבור אחורי בית הכנסת בשעה שהצבור מתפללין, ולא אמרן אלא דליכא פיתחא אחרינא, אבל איכא פיתחא אחרינא – לית לן בה. א"כ משמע, לפי שעובר לפני הפתח ואינו נכנס! ונראה דאחורי בית הכנסת היינו לצד פתח ביהכ"נ, וקורא "אחורי" – לפי שהוא אחורי העם: מרורין כזית. °היינו אילן של זית, והוא מר. ואילן נמי מקרי זית, דכתיב [שמות טו]: "ויורהו ה' עץ", °ודרשינן: זה זית, שאין לך מר באילנות כמו זית*: כל הנשמה. פר"ח: קרי ביה הַנְּשַׁמָּה בדגש: נתברכו שכיניה. והא דאמר [בת"כ פ' בחוקותי]: "ושממו עליה אויביכם" שזו היא מדה טובה שאינה טוענת פירות בשעה שאין שרויין בה – כאן היו בני יהודה שכיניה. אי נמי: שאינה מוציאה כל כך כמו כשהם עליה.

עין משפט נר מצוה

[משלי טז]

[עי' תוס' גיטין לא: ד"ה אלא ולקמן מג: ד"ה יתיב וב"ב מו: ד"ה שלח]

ג א מיי' פכ"א מהלכות אסורי ביאה הלכה כב סמג לאוין קכה טוש"ע אה"ע סימן כא סעיף א:

ד ב מיי' פ"ו מהלכות תפלה הל"א סמג עשין יט טוש"ע או"ח סימן צ סעיף ח:

ה ג מיי' פ"ג מהל' ת"ת הלי"ג טור או"ח סימן רלח טוש"ע יו"ד סימן רמו סעיף כב:

[צ"ל דבפרק]

[ואפשר כיון דהופך פניו כלפי ארון לא מיחזי כב' רשויות [תו"י בשם מורי הרב דודי ז"ל]

[כתבו תוספות בברכות סא. ד"ה אלא מעתה גבי אלקנה דכתיב וילך אלקנה אחרי אשתו וגו' שיבוש הוא שאין פסוק זה בכל המקרא ול"ג ליה ע"כ שוב מצאתי ברש"ל ישן דפוס קראקא שנת ושלו"ה בברכות סא. הארוך לקיים הגי' ע"פ פסוקים מלוקטים הרבה ונכנס בגדר דחוקה למאד ולבסוף הודה בעצמו דלפי פרש"י בשופטים דפלגש בגבעה היה בתחילת ימי השופטים א"א לקיים הגירסא בשום אופן ע"ש ומעתה פי' רש"י דהכא בסוגיין ד"ה אלקנה נביא היה כדתניא וכו' צריך לפני ולפנים]

[ופ"ע תוס' פסחים לו. ד"ה מה]

[יומא לב ובכמה]

מסורת הש"ס

ברכות סא מס' כלה פ"א

[סנהדרין קח: ע"ש]

[ברכות נח.]

הגהות הב"ח

(א) גמ' בשעה שהצבור מתפללין: (ב) רש"י ד"ה אומרים מקצת וכו' כמחניף בפניו בפניו כתיב כצ"ל והד"א:

גליון הש"ס

גמ' וא"ר בן אלעזר כל בית שנשמעין בו ד"ת בלילה. עי' סנהדרין דף צב ע"א וע"ש דף קח ע"ב ושם איתא א"ר אלעזר: תוס' ד"ה מרורין כזית היינו אילן. עי' פסחים דף לו ע"א תוס' ד"ה מה מרור: בא"ד ודרשי' זה זית. מכילתא פרשת בשלח:

רבינו חננאל

בנייתא. ויביאה מלמד שעשה הקדוש ברוך הוא שושבינות לאדה"ר מיכן לגדול שעושה שושבינות לקטן ואל ירע לו: תניא לא יהלך אדם אחורי אשה בשוק ואפי' היא אשתו ואפילו אחותו נזדמנה לו על הגשר יסלקנה לצדדין וכל העובר על הנהר אחורי אשה אין לו חלק לעולם הבא: ת"ר המרצה מעות ליד האשה בשביל להסתכל בה אפי' הוא כמשה רבינו לא ינקה מדינה של גיהנם ועליו הכתוב אומר יד ליד לא ינקה רע. פי' [אפי' הוא כמשה רבינו] שקיבל התורה מידו של הקדוש ב"ה לא ינקה מדין גיהנם: מנוח עם הארץ היה שנא' וילך מנוח אחרי אשתו. והלא באלקנה כתיב וילך אלקנה אחרי אשתו. ובאלישע כתיב ויקם וילך אחריה. אלא מאי אחריה אחרי דבריה ואחרי עצתה. אמר ר"י אחרי ארי ולא אחרי אשה אחרי אשה *) ולא אחורי בהכ"נ. אחורי בהכ"נ ולא אחורי בית ע"ז. בשעה שהצבור מתפללין. היה ר"מ אומר אדה"ר חסיד גדול היה כיון שראה שנקנסה עליו מיתה ישב בתענית ק"ל שנה ופירש מן חוה והעלה זרדי תאנים על בשרו. ופרקינן שכבת זרע דחזה לאנסו. פי' קרי נעשו שידין ולילין: אומר מקצת שבחו של אדם בפניו וכולו שלא בפניו כו'. אמר' יונה רבון העולמים יהיו מזונותי מרורין כזית ומסורין בידך ואל יהיו מתוקין כדבש ומסורין בידי בו"ד כו'. כל בית שנשמעין ממנו דברי תורה בלילה אינו חרב שנאמר ולא אמרו איה אלוה עושי נותן זמירות בלילה. א"ר ירמיה בן אלעזר מיום שחרב ביהמ"ק דיו לעולם שישתמש בב' אותיות שנא' כל הנשמה תהלל יה פי' הנשמה [בדגש] דכתיב (יחזקאל לו) הארץ הלזו הנשמה פי' משנעשית א"י נשמה הילולו של הקב"ה בחצי השם והוא ככל השם ומפורש במנחות בגמ' דהקומץ. וי"א כיון שאין אומרים שם ככתבו אלא במקדש ובמדינה בכינויו וחציו ככלו. כיון שנחרב ביהמ"ק מהללין שבח הק' בחו"ל בחצי השם שהוא חשוב ככלו: נתקללה בבל נתקללה שכניה שנאמר ושמתיה למורש קיפוד ואגמי מים וטאטאתיה במטאטא השמד. נתקללה שומרון נתברכו

*) נ"ל ולא אחורי בית ע"ז אחרי ע"ז ולא אחורי בהכנ"ס בשעה שהצבור מתפללין.

למטעי כרם". וא"ר ירמיה בן אלעזר: בא וראה שלא כמדת הקב"ה מדת בשר ודם; מדת בשר ודם, מתחייב אדם הריגה למלכות — מטילין לו חכה לתוך פיו כדי שלא יקלל את המלך, מדת הקב"ה אדם מתחייב הריגה למקום — שותק, שנאמר: °"לך דומיה תהלה". ולא עוד אלא שמשבח, שנאמר "תהלה". ולא עוד אלא שדומה לו כאילו מקריב קרבן, שנאמר: °"ולך ישולם נדר". היינו דא"ר יהושע בן לוי: מאי דכתיב: °"עוברי בעמק הבכא מעין ישיתוהו גם ברכות יעטה מורה"; "עוברי" — אלו בני אדם שעוברין על רצונו של הקב"ה, "עמק" — שמעמיקין להם גיהנם, "הבכא" — שבוכין ומורידין דמעות כמעיין של שיתין, "גם ברכות יעטה מורה" — שמצדיקין עליהם את הדין, ואומרים לפניו: רבונו של עולם, יפה דנת, יפה זכית, יפה חייבת, ויפה תקנת גיהנם לרשעים, גן עדן לצדיקים. איני?! והאמר רבי שמעון בן לקיש: רשעים אפילו על פתחו של גיהנם אינם חוזרין בתשובה, שנאמר: °"ויצאו וראו בפגרי האנשים הפושעים בי וגו'", "שפשעו" לא נאמר, אלא "הפושעים" — שפושעים והולכין לעולם! ל"ק; הא — בפושעי ישראל, הא — בפושעי גוים. הכי נמי מסתברא, דא"כ קשיא דר"ל אדריש לקיש. *דאמר ריש לקיש: פושעי ישראל אין אור גיהנם שולטת בהן, ק"ו ממזבח הזהב: מה מזבח הזהב שאין עליו אלא כעובי דינר זהב עמד כמה שנים ולא שלטה בו האור, פושעי ישראל שמליאין מצות כרמון, שנאמר: °"כפלח הרמון רקתך", ואמר ר"ש בן לקיש" אל תיקרי "רקתך" אלא "ריקתיך", שאפי' ריקנין שבך מליאין מצות *כרמון — עאכ"ו. אלא הא דכתיב: "עוברי בעמק הבכא" — ההוא דמחייבי ההיא שעתא בגיהנם, ואתי אברהם אבינו ומסיק להו ומקבל להו, בר מישראל שבא על הגויה דמשכה ערלתו ולא *מבשקר ליה. מתקיף לה רב כהנא: השתא דאמרת "הפושעים" דפשעי ואזלי, אלא מעתה דכתיב: "המוציא והמעלה" דמסיק ודמפיק הוא?! אלא דאסיק ואפיק, הכי נמי דפשעי הוא. ואמר רבי ירמיה (*בר) אלעזר: שלשה פתחים יש לגיהנם, אחד במדבר, ואחד בים, ואחד בירושלים. במדבר, דכתיב: °"וירדו הם וכל אשר להם חיים שאולה". בים, דכתיב: °"מבטן שאול שועתי שמעת קולי". בירושלים, דכתיב: °"נאם ה' אשר אור לו בציון ותנור לו בירושלים". ותנא דבי רבי ישמעאל: "אשר אור לו בציון" — זו גיהנם, "ותנור לו בירושלים" — זו פתחה של גיהנם. ותו ליכא? והאמר *ר' מריון, אמר ר' יהושע בן לוי, ואמרי לה תנא רבה בר מריון בדבי רבי יוחנן בן זכאי: שתי תמרות יש בגי בן הנום ועולה עשן מביניהן, וזו היא ששנינו ציני הר הברזל כשירות, וזו היא פתחה של גיהנם! דילמא היינו דירושלים. א"ר יהושע בן לוי: ז' שמות יש לגיהנם, ואלו הן: שאול ואבדון, ובאר שחת, ובור שאון, וטיט היון, וצלמות, וארץ התחתית. שאול — דכתיב: °"מבטן שאול שועתי שמעת קולי". אבדון — דכתיב: °"היסופר בקבר חסדך אמונתך באבדון". באר שחת — דכתיב: °"כי לא תעזוב נפשי לשאול לא תתן חסידך לראות שחת". ובור שאון וטיט היון — דכתיב: °"ויעלני מבור שאון מטיט היון". וצלמות — דכתיב: °"יושבי חושך וצלמות". וארץ התחתית — גמרא הוא. ותו ליכא? והאיכא גיהנם! גיא שעמוקה (*כגיהנם) שהכל יורד לה על עסקי(א) הנם.*) והאיכא "תפתה", דכתיב: °"כי ערוך מאתמול תפתה"! ההוא — שכל המתפתה ביצרו יפול שם. גן עדן, אמר ריש לקיש: אם בארץ ישראל הוא — בית שאן פתחו, ואם בערביא — בית גרם פתחו, ואם בין הנהרות הוא — דומסקנין פתחו. בבבל, אביי משתבח בפירי דמעבר ימינא, רבא משתבח בפירי דהרפניא.§ "וביניהן כמלוא שתי וכו'". פשיטא, כיון דתנא ליה דקשורות הוו אנן ידעינן דלא הוו מותרות! מהו דתימא: קשורות כעין קשורות, אבל ממש לא, קמ"ל "ולא מותרות".§ "אחת נכנסת ואחת יוצאת". תנא: רבקה נכנסת ורבקה יוצאת.§ ת"ר: כמה ראשה ורובה של פרה — שתי אמות. וכמה עוביה של פרה — אמה ושני שלישי אמה, שהן

*) [בעי"י הגי' חנם עי' במהרש"א בח"א]

רש"י

למטעי כרם. ויהנו שכיניה, ושבח הוא לה שנזכרת לטובה: חכה. עץ, שפותח פיו שלא יכול לדבר: לך דומיה. הכל שותקין כנגדך: שדומה עליו כו'. נותנין לו יסורין שמקבלן מאהבה: ולך ישולם נדר. אותה דומיה שהוא דומה ביסורין, דומה לו כשילום נדר: מעין ישיתוהו. כמעין של שיתין נקב שבבנין המזבח שניסוך היין של ספלים יורד לתוכו כל השנה, כדאמרי' ב"לולב וערבה" (סוכה מט.): הפושעי' בי. עדיין, ואפי' בשעת פורענותם ואשם: דא"כ. דהא דר"ל בפושעי ישראל מוקי לה להאי קרא, דכתיב "ואשם לא תכבה", קשיא דידיה אדידיה: ולא מבשקר. אינו מכירו שהוא יהודי, דמשכה ערלתו ודומה לו כמי שאינו נימול: המוציא והמעלה. "המוציא אתכם מארץ מצרים" (ויקרא כב), וכן "המעלה אתכם מארץ מצרים" (שם יא): דפשעי. בחייהם: מבטן שאול. יונה בן אמתי קאמר ליה: בדבי רבן יוחנן בן זכאי. ברייתא שנסדרה בבית מדרשו כעין תוספתא שסידר ר' חייא ור' אושעיא: ציני. דקלים: כשרין. ללולב: טיט היון. הוא רפש לטבוע בו, ובלע"ז פנ"ק. וסתם טיט היינו שראוי לבנין: שחת ובאר שחת. חדא מילתא היא: על עסקי הנם. ערוות: תפתה. גיהנם, דכתיב בההוא קרא "מדורתה אש ועצים הרבה": בית שאן פיתחו. שפירותיו מתוקין מכל ארץ ישראל: משתבח בפירות דעבר ימינא. משתבח בפירות של עבר הנהר פרת בדרומו: רבקה נכנסת ורבקה יוצאת. ולא פרה נכנסת ופרה יוצאת, דא"כ לא הוו להו קשורות: כמה ראשה ורובה של פרה. שנתנו חכמים שיעור להרחקת פסין מן הבור שיהו רחוקין כדי ראשה ורובה, כדתנן במתני':

תוספות

[פושעי ישראל אין אור שולטת בהן ק"ו ממזבח הזהב. תימה: דבמס' חגיגה (דף כז.) עביד ק"ו מסלמנדרא, דתלמידי חכמים אין אור שולטת בהן מק"ו! וי"ל: דפושעי ישראל פניהם משחירי', ואלו תלמידי חכמי' כלל וכלל לא.] בר מבא וכו'. לא שייך למחשביה ב"הזהב" (ב"מ דף נח:) גבי שלשה יורדין לגיהנם ואין עולין, דזה עולה כשקיבל דינו. והא דלא חשיב התם פושעי ישראל בגופן והצדוקין כו' דאין עולין — לפי שעשויים בברייתא. *ואע"ג דמלבין פני חבירו חשיב ליה ותני ליה במס' אבות — מ"מ אשמעינן דמכנה שם הוי מלבין, אע"ג דדש ביה בשמיה:

דילמא היינו דירושלים. כדכתיב: (יהושע טו): "גיא בן הנם וגו' ירושלים". ולא גרסינן היינו דמדבר: באר שחת כדכתיב: "כי לא תעזוב נפשי לשאול לא תתן חסידך לראות שחת". [והיינו באר שחת, ומהאי קרא הוה מצי לאתויי דשמו שאול, והא דלא מייתי קרא: *"ואתה אלהים תורידם לבאר שחת" — דהאי קרא בקבר כתיב, כדמוכח סיפא דקרא: "אנשי דמים ומרמה לא יחצו ימיהם":

וצלמות דכתיב יושבי חשך וצלמות. האי קרא בתהלים כתיב, גבי *ארבעה צריכין להודות. ונראה כספרים דגרסי "בטרם אלך ולא אשוב אל ארץ חשך וצלמות" (איוב י). ["תחתית" גרס, ד"תחתית" כתיב ביחזקאל (ל"א), כשהראה הקב"ה שכל הגוים יורדים לגיהנם כתיב שם "אל ארץ תחתית"]:

והאיכא תפתה. תימה דלא חשב עלוקה! ור"ת מפרש: דעלוקה שם הכס, כמו לאיתיאל. והא דמוקי ליה במסכת עבודה זרה (דף יז.) בגיהנם — היינו משום דכתיב בתריה: "שאול ועוצר רחם". ומיהו, קשה: דבפסיקתא לא חשיב להם בשמות שלמה, וגם בג' דברי'(ב) וד' דברים(ג) הכתובים באותו ספר לא חשיב עלוקה. ואע"ג דלא חשיב נמי יקא — היינו משום דשמא הוי בכלל אגור. והפייט *נמי יסדו בשם גיהנם בזולת "אין צור חלף יקדו בההבי עלק": אם בין הנהרות הוא. משמע דבין הנהרו' לאו היינו בבל. ודלא כפ"ה שפי' ב"י' יוחסין" (קדושין דף עב.) גבי בין הנהרות הרי הוא כגולה ליוחסין. ובפירקין (דף כג:) נמי אמרי': בבל נמי מקיף לה פרת מחד גיסא ודגלת מחד גיסא:

רבינו חננאל

נתברכו שכניה שנאמר ושמתיה לעי השדה למטעי כרם לשכניה: עוברי בעומק הבכא וגו' עוברי אלו בני אדם שעוברין על רצונו של מקום. בעמק שמעמיקין להם גיהנם שעה אחת. ואתי אברהם ומציל להו לבר מהבא על הגוי' דמשכ' ערלתיה כר"ל דאמר אין אור שולטת בפושעי ישראל ק"ו ממזבח הזהב. ורשעים אפילו על פתח גיהנם אין חוזרין בתשובה ברשעי או"ה הוא. ג' פתחים יש לגיהנם וכו': מתני' וביניהן כמלא ב' רבקות. פי' מלשון עגלי מרבק (מלאכי ג) של ג' בקר דברי ר"מ.

הגהות הב"ח

(א) גמ' על עסקי חנם: (ב) תום' ד"ה והא איכא וכו' וגם בג' דברי'. נ"ב כלומר במדרש של ג' דברים: (ג) בא"ד וארבע דברים בשמות שלמה הכתובין באותו ספר:

גליון הש"ס

רש"י ולא מבשקר אינו מכירו. וכן לא בשקרוה יבמות דף קכ ע"א: שם על עסקי חנם עריות כצ"ל. וכדאיתא ביומא פרק יוה"כ נאכל במצרים חנם זה עריות מהרש"א:

מסורת הש"ס

תהלים סה | שם | שם פד | [ר"ה יז.] | ישעיהו סו | חגיגה כז. ע"ש | שיר ו | [סנהדרין לז. וש"נ] | [פי' ולא ניכר הבריות ולבקר בהיכלו תרגום ולבקר בהיכלי' (תהלי' כז) ערוך ערך בקר] | במדבר טז | יונה ב | ישעיהו לא | [סוכה לב: ע"ש] | יונה ב | תהלים פח | שם מ | שם קז | [צ"ל כגיהנם] | ישעיהו ל | [תהלים נה.] | [ברכות נד:] | [לשבת חנוכה]

ו א מיי' פי"ז מהלכות שבת הלכ"ז:
ז ב שם הלכה כט:
ח ג ד ה שם הלכה כח:

שהן כעשר אמות. לא שייך למיפרך מניינא אתא לאשמעינן, כדפריך בפ"ק דקדושין (דף יז.) – כיון דלא השמיענו מנין פרות: **בבור** שתים עשרה כ"ע לא פליגי. הוה מצי למנקט בבור אחת עשרה ושליש ומשהו, ולא דק: **רב** פפא ברייתא לא שמיע ליה. והא דמשני לעיל אברייתא יתירות על שלש עשרה – היינו בתר דשמעה: **ואם** איתא זו היא מחיצה וזו היא מחיצה מיבעי ליה. קשה: דהכא פשיטא ליה דהארכת דיומדין עדיפי מפשוטין, ולעיל איבעיא דר"מ משמע ליה איפכא! וי"ל: דלעיל בעי היכי, דכי נמי נאריך בדיומדין – יהיה פרוץ מרובה. דאז פשוטין עדיפי דאיכא היכר טפי. אבל הכא איירי ברחב הרבה, שאם נאריך הדיומדין יהיה עומד מרובה, כדקתני: אי אתה מודה בדיר וסהר ומוקצה, שאפילו בית י' כורין או יותר מותר. לכך פריך שפיר: זו מחיצה וזו מחיצה מבעי ליה:

ההדרן

שֶׁהֵן כְּעֶשֶׂר, דִּבְרֵי ר"מ. ר' יְהוּדָה אוֹמֵר: כִּשְׁלֹשׁ עֶשְׂרֵה אַמָּה וּכְאַרְבַּע עֶשְׂרֵה אַמָּה. "כְּעֶשֶׂר"? הָא עֶשֶׂר הָוְיָין! מִשּׁוּם דְּבָעֵי לְמִיתְנָא סֵיפָא "כִּשְׁלֹשׁ עֶשְׂרֵה"(א) כִּשְׁלֹשׁ עֶשְׂרֵה טְפֵי הָוְיָין, מִשּׁוּם דְּבָעֵי לְמִתְנֵי "כְּאַרְבַּע עֶשְׂרֵה" — וּכְאַרְבַּע עֶשְׂרֵה הָא לָא הָוְיָא! אָמַר רַב פַּפָּא: [א]יְתֵירוֹת עַל שְׁלֹשׁ עֶשְׂרֵה, וְאֵינָן מַגִּיעוֹת לְאַרְבַּע עֶשְׂרֵה. א"ר פַּפָּא: בְּבוֹר שְׁמוֹנֶה דְּכ"ע לָא פְּלִיגִי דְּלָא בָּעֵינַן פְּשׁוּטִין, בְּבוֹר שְׁתֵּים עֶשְׂרֵה, דְּכ"ע לָא פְּלִיגִי דְּבָעֵינַן פְּשׁוּטִין. כִּי פְּלִיגִי — מִשְּׁמוֹנֶה עַד שְׁתֵּים עֶשְׂרֵה. לְר' מֵאִיר בָּעֵינַן פְּשׁוּטִין, לְר' יְהוּדָה לָא בָּעֵינַן פְּשׁוּטִין. וְרַב פַּפָּא מַאי קמ"ל? תָּנֵינָא! רַב פַּפָּא *בָּרַיְיתָא לָא שְׁמִיעַ לֵיהּ, וְקמ"ל כְּבָרַיְיתָא.§ ארי"ך יות"ר בת"ל חיצ"ת חצ"ר שיבש"ה סִימָן.§ בְּעָא מִינֵּיהּ אַבַּיֵי מֵרַבָּה: הֶאֱרִיךְ בְּדְיוֹמָדִין כְּשִׁיעוּר פְּשׁוּטִין, לְר"מ מַהוּ? א"ל: תְּנֵיתוּהָ, וּבִלְבַד שֶׁיַּרְבֶּה בְּפַסִּין. מַאי לָאו דְּמַאֲרִיךְ בְּדְיוֹמָדִין? לָא, [ב]דְּמַפֵּישׁ וְעָבֵיד פְּשׁוּטִין. א"ה, הַאי "וּבִלְבַד שֶׁיַּרְבֶּה בְּפַסִּין", "עַד שֶׁיַּרְבֶּה פַּסִּין" מִיבָּעֵי לֵיהּ! תְּנֵי: *עַד שֶׁיַּרְבֶּה פַּסִּין. א"ד, א"ל: תְּנֵיתוּהָ, וּבִלְבַד שֶׁיַּרְבֶּה בְּפַסִּין, מַאי לָאו דְּמַפֵּישׁ וְעָבֵיד פְּשׁוּטִין? לָא, דְּמַאֲרִיךְ בְּדְיוֹמָדִין. הָכִי נַמִי מִסְתַּבְּרָא, מִדְּקָתָנֵי "וּבִלְבַד שֶׁיַּרְבֶּה בְּפַסִּין" — ש"מ. בְּעָא מִינֵּיהּ אַבַּיֵי מֵרַבָּה: יוֹתֵר מִשְּׁלֹשׁ עֶשְׂרֵה אַמָּה וּשְׁלִישׁ לְר' יְהוּדָה מַהוּ? פְּשׁוּטִין עָבֵיד אוֹ בְּדְיוֹמָדִין מַאֲרִיךְ? א"ל: תְּנֵיתוּהָ, *כַּמָּה הֵן מְקוּרָבִין — כְּדֵי רֹאשָׁהּ וְרוּבָּהּ שֶׁל פָּרָה, וְכַמָּה מְרוּחָקִין — אֲפִי' כּוֹר וַאֲפִי' כּוֹרַיִים, ר' יְהוּדָה אוֹמֵר: בֵּית סָאתַיִם — מוּתָּר, יוֹתֵר מִבֵּית סָאתַיִם — אָסוּר. אָמְרוּ לוֹ לְר' יְהוּדָה: אִי אַתָּה מוֹדֶה בְּדִיר וְסַהַר וּמוּקְצֶה וְחָצֵר אֲפִילוּ בַּת חֲמֵשֶׁת כּוֹרִים וַאֲפִי' בַּת עֲשָׂרָה כּוֹרִים שֶׁמּוּתָּר? אָמַר לָהֶן: זוֹ מְחִיצָה, וְאֵלּוּ פַּסִּין. וְאִם אִיתָא — זוֹ מְחִיצָה וְזוֹ הִיא מְחִיצָה מִיבָּעֵי לֵיהּ! הָכִי קָאָמַר: זוֹ תּוֹרַת מְחִיצָה עָלֶיהָ, וּפִרְצוֹתֶיהָ בְּעֶשֶׂר, וְאֵלּוּ תּוֹרַת פַּסִּין עֲלֵיהֶן, וּפִרְצוֹתֵיהֶן בִּשְׁלֹשׁ עֶשְׂרֵה אַמָּה וּשְׁלִישׁ. בְּעָא מִינֵּיהּ אַבַּיֵי מֵרַבָּה: תֵּל הַמִּתְלַקֵּט עֲשָׂרָה מִתּוֹךְ אַרְבַּע נִידּוֹן מִשּׁוּם דְּיוֹמָד, אוֹ אֵינוֹ נִידּוֹן מִשּׁוּם דְּיוֹמָד? א"ל: תְּנֵיתוּהָ, ר' שִׁמְעוֹן בֶּן אֶלְעָזָר אוֹמֵר: *[ג]הָיְתָה שָׁם אֶבֶן מְרוּבַּעַת, רוֹאִין, כֹּל שֶׁאִילּוּ תֵּחָלֵק וְיֵשׁ בָּהּ אַמָּה לְכָאן וְאַמָּה לְכָאן — נִידּוֹן מִשּׁוּם דְּיוֹמָד, וְאִם לָאו — אֵינוֹ נִידּוֹן מִשּׁוּם דְּיוֹמָד. רַבִּי יִשְׁמָעֵאל בְּנוֹ שֶׁל רַבִּי יוֹחָנָן בֶּן בְּרוֹקָה אוֹמֵר: הָיְתָה שָׁם אֶבֶן עֲגוּלָּה, רוֹאִין, כֹּל שֶׁאִילּוּ תֵּחָקֵק וְתֵחָלֵק וְיֵשׁ בָּהּ אַמָּה לְכָאן וְאַמָּה לְכָאן — נִידּוֹן מִשּׁוּם דְּיוֹמָד, וְאִם לָאו — אֵינוֹ נִידּוֹן מִשּׁוּם דְּיוֹמָד. בְּמַאי קָא מִיפַּלְגִי? מָר סָבַר: חַד רוֹאִין אָמְרִינַן, תְּרֵי רוֹאִין — לָא אָמְרִינַן. וּמָר סָבַר: אֲפִי' תְּרֵי רוֹאִין נַמִי אָמְרִינַן. *בְּעָא מִינֵּיהּ אַבַּיֵי מֵרַבָּה: חִיצַּת הַקָּנִים, קָנֶה קָנֶה פָּחוֹת מִשְּׁלֹשָׁה נִידּוֹן מִשּׁוּם דְּיוֹמָד אוֹ לָאו? אֲמַר לֵיהּ: *תְּנֵיתוּהָ, [ד]הָיָה שָׁם אִילָן אוֹ גָּדֵר אוֹ חִיצַּת הַקָּנִים — נִידּוֹן מִשּׁוּם דְּיוֹמָד. מַאי לָאו [ה]קָנֶה קָנֶה פָּחוֹת מִשְּׁלֹשָׁה! לָא, גּוּדְרִיתָא דְּקָנֵי. אִי הָכִי הַיְינוּ אִילָן! וְאֶלָּא מַאי — קָנֶה קָנֶה פָּחוֹת מִשְּׁלֹשָׁה, הַיְינוּ גָּדֵר! אֶלָּא מַאי אִית לָךְ לְמֵימַר — תְּרֵי גַּוְונֵי גָּדֵר, הָכָא נַמִי: תְּרֵי גַּוְונֵי אִילָן. אִיכָּא דְּאָמְרִי: גּוּדְרִיתָא דְּקָנֵי קָא מִיבַּעְיָא לֵיהּ, גּוּדְרִיתָא דְּקָנֵי מַאי? א"ל: תְּנֵיתוּהָ, הָיָה שָׁם גָּדֵר אוֹ אִילָן אוֹ חִיצַּת הַקָּנִים — נִידּוֹן מִשּׁוּם דְּיוֹמָד, מַאי לָאו גּוּדְרִיתָא דְּקָנֵי? לָא, קָנֶה קָנֶה פָּחוֹת מִשְּׁלֹשָׁה. אִי הָכִי, הַיְינוּ גָּדֵר! וְאֶלָּא מַאי — גּוּדְרִיתָא דְּקָנֵי, הַיְינוּ אִילָן! אֶלָּא מַאי אִית לָךְ לְמֵימַר — תְּרֵי

שֶׁהֵן כְּעֶשֶׂר. אַמּוֹת, שִׁשָּׁה בָּקָר. וּלְקַמָּן פָּרֵיךְ: מַאי כְּעֶשֶׂר? הָא עֶשֶׂר מְכוּוָּנוֹת הֵן: כִּי"ג וְי"ד. שְׁמוֹנָה בָּקָר יָצְאוּ מִכְּלַל שְׁלֹשׁ עֶשְׂרֵה, וְלִכְלַל י"ד לֹא בָּאוּ. דְּי"ג אַמָּה וּשְׁלִישׁ הֵן: בְּבוֹר רָחָב שְׁמוֹנֶה. אֲפִי' לְר"מ לָא בָּעֵינַן פְּשׁוּטִין, דְּכִי מַרְחִיק כְּדֵי רֹאשָׁהּ וְרוּבָּהּ, דְּהַיְינוּ שְׁתֵּי אַמּוֹת לְכָל רוּחַ — נִמְצָא הֶחָלָל שֶׁבֵּין ב' הַמְּחִיצוֹת שְׁתֵּים עֶשְׂרֵה אַמָּה, וְהַפַּסִּין רָחְבָּן אַמָּה לְכָל רוּחַ זֶה כְּנֶגֶד זֶה — נִמְצָא בֵּין פַּס לְפַס שִׁיעוּר פֶּתַח עֶשֶׂר אַמּוֹת, וְר' מֵאִיר בְּהָכִי שָׁרֵי: בְּבוֹר שְׁתֵּים עֶשְׂרֵה. דְּכִי מַרְחִיק שְׁתֵּי אַמּוֹת מִכָּאן וּכְנֶגְדָּם מִכָּאן יֵשׁ חֲלַל הַמְּחִיצָה י"ו אַמָּה, וּמֵהֶן שְׁתֵּי אַמּוֹת עוֹמֵד, הֲרֵי בֵּין זֶה לָזֶה י"ד פָּרוּץ — וְכוּלֵּי הַאי לָא שָׁרֵי רַבִּי יְהוּדָה, וּבָעֵינַן פְּשׁוּטִין לְכָל צַד, דְּמִכָּל צַד וָצַד אִיכָּא י"ד אַמּוֹת. וּלְקַמָּן מְפָרֵשׁ הֵיכָא מַשְׁוֵי לְהוּ: תָּנֵינָא. לְדְרַב פַּפָּא בְּמַתְנִי' דְּקָתָנֵי לְר' מֵאִיר שִׁשָּׁה בָּקָר. וּלְר' יְהוּדָה שְׁמוֹנָה בָּקָר וּמִמֵּילָא שָׁמְעִינַן דְּר"מ שָׁרֵי בְּהַבְדָּלַת עֶשֶׂר, וְר' יְהוּדָה שָׁרֵי בְּהַבְדָּלַת שְׁלֹשׁ עֶשְׂרֵה אַמָּה וּשְׁלִישׁ, וְכִי קָבָעֵי ר' מֵאִיר פְּשׁוּטִין — בְּיוֹתֵר מֵעֶשֶׂר קָאָמַר: רַב פַּפָּא הָךְ בָּרַיְיתָא. דִּתְנָא שִׁיעוּרָא דְּעוֹבִי הַפָּרוֹת לָא שְׁמִיעַ לֵיהּ, וּבְמַתְנִי' לָא פָּרֵישׁ לְהוּ, וַאֲתָא רַב פַּפָּא לְפָרוּשֵׁי לָךְ מַתְנִיתִין דְּשִׁיעוּרָא דְּר' מֵאִיר עֶשֶׂר אַמּוֹת, וּדְר' יְהוּדָה שְׁלֹשׁ עֶשְׂרֵה אַמָּה וּשְׁלִישׁ, וְהִסְכִּים רַב פַּפָּא מִדַּעְתּוֹ לְמַה שֶּׁשָּׁנִינוּ בְּבָרַיְיתָא דְּרֹאשָׁהּ וְרוּבָּהּ שְׁתֵּי אַמּוֹ' וְעוֹבְיָהּ אַמָּה וּשְׁנֵי שְׁלִישֵׁי אַמָּה: הֶאֱרִיךְ בְּדְיוֹמָדִין. יוֹתֵר מֵאַמָּה לְכָל צַד, עַד שֶׁהֶעֱמִיד רֶיוַח שֶׁבֵּינְתַיִם עַל עֶשֶׂר אַמּוֹת: מַהוּ. דַּוְוקָא פְּשׁוּטִין קָאָמַר, דְּכֵיוָן דְּהִרְחִיקָן יוֹתֵר מִשִּׁיעוּר חֲכָמִים בָּעֵינַן הֶיכֵּר בֵּינֵי בֵּינֵי, וְלָא סַגִּי בְּהַאֲרָכַת דְּיוֹמָדִין. אֶלָּא מַרְחִיק פּוּרְתָּא מִן הַפַּס וְנוֹתֵן שָׁם פָּשׁוּט, וְכֵן לְאִידָךְ גִּיסָא, מִשּׁוּם דְּלֶיהֱוֵי הֶיכֵּירָא. אוֹ דִילְמָא: כֵּיוָן דְּסוֹף סוֹף עֶשֶׂר רֶיוַח הוּא דְּאִיכָּא — לָא מִיתְּסַר: לְר' יְהוּדָה. דְּלָא אַדְכַּר פְּשׁוּטִין, הֵי עֲדִיפָא לֵיהּ: פְּשׁוּטִין עֲדִיפֵי לֵיהּ וּמְרוּחָקִין מִן הַדְּיוֹמָדִין י"ג אַמָּה לְמֶיהֱוֵי הֶיכֵּירָא בֵּינֵי בֵּינֵי, וְלָא סַגִּי בְּהַאֲרָכַת דְּיוֹמָדִין, אוֹ הַאֲרָכַת דְּיוֹמָדִין עֲדִיפָא דְּלָא לֵיתֵי אֲוֵירָא דְּהַאי גִּיסָא וּדְהַאי גִּיסָא וּלְבַטְּלָהּ: כַּמָּה הֵן מְקוֹרָבִין. לַבּוֹר: אֲפִילוּ כּוֹר. וּבִלְבַד שֶׁיַּרְבֶּה בְּפַסִּין: יוֹתֵר מִבֵּית סָאתַיִם אָסוּר. שֶׁזֶּה שִׁיעוּר הֶיקֵּף שֶׁלֹּא כְּתִיקְנוֹ: דִּיר. מוּקָּף לְדִירָה, שֶׁהָרוֹעֶה דָּר שָׁם בַּלַּיְלָה: זוֹ מְחִיצָה. שְׁלֵימָה הִיא: וְאֵלּוּ פַּסִּין הֵן. וּבֵין כָּל אֶחָד וְאֶחָד שְׁלֹשׁ עֶשְׂרֵה אַמּוֹת, וְאֵין עוֹמֵד אֶלָּא פַּס אַמָּה בֵּין כָּל שְׁלֹשׁ עֶשְׂרֵה וּשְׁלֹשׁ עֶשְׂרֵה. אַלְמָא: לְרַבִּי יְהוּדָה פְּשׁוּטִין עָבֵיד, דְּאִי בְּדְיוֹמָדִין מַאֲרִיךְ – הָא מְחִיצָה הִיא: וּפִירְצָתָהּ. אוֹסֶרֶת בְּיוֹתֵר מֵעֶשֶׂר: וְאֵלּוּ תּוֹרַת פַּסִּין עֲלֵיהֶן. וְיֵשׁ י"ג אַמָּה בֵּין הַאֲרָכָה לְהַאֲרָכָה. הִלְכָּךְ, בְּיוֹתֵר מִבֵּית סָאתַיִם – לָא מִיתַּכְשַׁר: תֵּל הַמִּתְלַקֵּט י'. טְפָחִים: מִתּוֹךְ ד'. אַמּוֹת תֵּל מְשׁוּפָּע אֲבָל מִדְרוֹנוֹ זָקוּף, קוֹדֶם שֶׁיִּמָּשֵׁךְ ד' אַמּוֹת עָלָה וְנִתְלַקֵּט גּוֹבְהוֹ לִי' טְפָחִים וְקַיְ"ל בְּ"הַזּוֹרֵק" בְּמַסֶּ' שַׁבָּת (דף ק.) דִּלְעִנְיַן שַׁבָּת הָוֵי רְשׁוּת הַיָּחִיד, הָכָא מַאי? אִי קָאֵי בִּמְקוֹם א' מִן הַדְּיוֹמָדִין מִי הָוֵי כִּדְיוֹמָד אוֹ לָא? וּלְהָכִי נָקֵט מִתּוֹךְ ד' – שֶׁאִם הָיָה מִדְרוֹנוֹ מְשׁוּפָּע יָפֶה וְאֵינוֹ מִתְלַקֵּט לְגוֹבַהּ עֲשָׂרָה עַד שֶׁיִּמָּשֵׁךְ יוֹתֵר מִד' אַמּוֹת, וַאֲפִי' עָלָה גּוֹבְהוֹ לְשִׁפּוּעַ לְעֶשֶׂר אַמּוֹת – אַרְעָא סְמִיכְתָּא הִיא: מְרוּבַּעַת. אַמָּה עַל אַמָּה, וְאֵינָהּ מְחוּסֶּרֶת אֶלָּא חֲלִיקָה שֶׁיִּבָּטֵל עוֹבִי שֶׁבֵּינְתַיִם וְתֵיעָשֶׂה כְּמַרְזֵב, דּוֹפֶן לְכָאן וְדוֹפֶן לְכָאן: עֲגוּלָּה. מְחוּסֶּרֶת חֲקִיקָה לַחְקוֹק וְלִיטּוֹל בְּלִיטַת עִיגּוּל וּלְהַשְׁווֹת אֶמְצָעָהּ לְפֵיאוֹתֶיהָ וּתְהֵא מְרוּבַּעַת, וַעֲדַיִין הִיא מְחוּסֶּרֶת חֲלִיקָה: אָמְרִי' נַמִי תְּרֵי רוֹאִין. לְר' יִשְׁמָעֵאל. וְתֵל נַמִי כְּאֶבֶן עֲגוּלָּה דָּמֵי, לְתַנָּא קַמָּא לָא אָמְרִינַן תְּרֵי רוֹאִין: חִיצַּת קָנִים. שֶׁעֲשָׂאָהּ לְכָאן וּלְכָאן כְּעֵין דְּיוֹמָד: גּוּדְרִיתָא דְּקָנֵי. קָנִים מְחוּבָּרִין הַרְבֵּה בְּעֵץ א' סָמוּךְ לָאָרֶץ, וּלְמַעְלָה הֵן מִתְפָּרְשִׁין: תְּרֵי גַּוְונֵי אִילָן. אַשְׁמְעִי' אִילָן שָׁלֵם דְּאִיכָּא לְמֵימַר יֵחָלֵק וְיֵחָקֵק, וְאַשְׁמְעִי' הַאי אַע"ג דְּלֵיכָּא לְמֵימַר הָכִי שָׁרֵי, הוֹאִיל וְתַחְתָּיו אֶחָד* הוּא כִּדְיוֹמָד, אֲבָל קָנֶה(ב) פָּחוֹת מִג' – לָא: מַאי לָאו גּוּדְרִיתָא דְּקָנֵי. וּש"מ, דְּאַע"ג דְּאֵין עוֹבְיוֹ(ג) ד' בְּגוֹבַהּ עֲשָׂרָה – אָמְרִינַן רוֹאִין: לָא קָנֶה קָנֶה פָּחוֹת מִג'. דַּעֲשׂוּי כִּדְיוֹמָד מַמָּשׁ, וּבְלָא רוֹאִין אִיכָּא תִּיקּוּן מְעַלְיָא:

אָמַר

[שבת יט: וש"נ]
ס"א ובלבד שירבה
[תוספ' פ"א]
[תוספ' פ"א]
[לעיל טו.]
שם [סוכה כד:]
[גי' מהרש"ל וכוה]

רבינו חננאל

ר' יהודה אומר של ד' ד' בקר. תנא רבקה נכנסת רבקה יוצא'. ת"ר כמה ראשה ורובה של פרה אמתים. וכמה עוביה של פרה אמה וב' שלישי אמה שהן כעשר אמות. ר' יהודה אומר כי"ג וכי"ד נמצא לר"מ עובי שש פרות כל פרה אמה וב' שלישי אמה עשר אמות. ולר' יהודה דתני ח' פרות י"ג אמה ושליש. אמר רב פפא בבור שמונה דברי הכל [דלא בעינן] פשוטין דהא אפילו לרבי מאיר דאית ליה עשר אמות בין הדיומד פש ליה תרתי אמתי ריוח לכל רוח דמעייל ליה לפרה ראשה ורובה התם ומשקה לה. דדיומדין הללו יש להם ו' טפחים אילך וו' טפחים אילך נמצא לר' מאיר שיעור הדיומדין ב' אמות ובין הדיומדין כעשר אמות הרי י"ב אמות על י"ב אמות. וכ"ש לר' יהודה דפש ליה ה' אמות ושליש. בבור י"ב אמות דברי הכל בעינן פשוטי' דאפילו לר' יהודה [לא] פש ליה אלא אמתא ושליש כי פליגי בבור דאית ביה יתר מח' אמות עד י"ב אמה. ולא כל י"ב אמה בכלל אלא י"א אמה ושליש לר"מ בעי פשוטין לר' יהודה לא בעי פשוטין. פשיטא ופריק רב פפא לא שמיעא ליה הא ברייתא דיהיב שיעור דפרה בארכיה ועביה וקא מפרש כי הא ברייתא. בעא מניה אביי מרבה האריך בדיומדין הקבועין בזוית כשיעור פשוטין. פי' הפסין העומדין בזוית נקראין דיומדין מפני שהן מרובעים ונראין ששה טפחים לזה הצד וששה טפחים לצד האחר. והפס העומד באמצע נקרא פשוט עתה אם האריך בפס שבזוית כשיעור י"ב טפחים מהו ואסיקנא ללישנא קמא דלא כדיומדין דמו. ועוד בעא מיניה יתר מג' אמה ושליש אמה לר' יהודה במה ממעט פשוטין עביד או מאריך בדיומדין ואתא למיפשטה מהא דתניא וכמה הן הפסים מקורבין לבאר כדי ראשה ורובה של פרה. וכמה הן מרוחקין מן הבאר אפי' כור ואפילו כורים. ר' יהודה אומר בית סאתי' מותר. יתר מבית סאתים אסור. אמרו לו אי אתה מודה בדיר או בסהר מוקצה וחצר אפי' בית י' כורין שמותר. אמר להן אלו כולן יש בהן מחיצה לפיכך מטלטלין בכולן אבל בביראות פסין מלא מחיצות וא"ת בדיומדין מאריך להו גם אלו מחיצות הן. ושנינן הכי קאמר הללו דיר מוקצה חצר סהר תורת מחיצה עליהן ופרצתן בעשר. אבל ביראות תורת פסין עליהם ופרצתן בי"ג אמה ושליש. בעא מיניה אביי מרבה תל המתלקט עשרה מתוך ד' נידון משום דיומד אי לא. א"ל תניתוה. היתה אבן מרובעת בראש הזוית רואין כל שאילו תחלק ויש בה אמה לכאן ואמה לכאן נידון משום דיומד. ואי לאו אינו נידון משום דיומד ר' ישמעאל ב"ר יוחנן בן ברוקא אומר אפילו היא אבן עגולה רואין כל שאילו תחלק ותחקק וישבה אמה לכאן ואמה לכאן נידון משום דיומד [שמעינן] (מי') דתל המתלקט י"ט גובה מתוך ד' אמות אורך נידון משום דיומד. ותוב בעא מיניה חיצת הקני' קנה קנה פחות מג' טפחי' נידון משום דיומד אי לא ופשט ליה מהא דתניא היה שם אילן או גדר או חיצת הקנים נידון משום דיומד והא חיצת הקנים דקתני לאו חיצת קנים (פחות) קנה קנה פחות משלשה הן. ודחי לא. האי חיצת קנים גודרייתא דקני הן. פי' עיקרי הקנים שהן מחוברין כולן כאילו קנה א' אי הכי היינו אילן כלומר גודרייתא (דקני) דומין לאילן שעיקרו א' ואמרי' מפורין כו' עד תרי גווני

הגהות הב"ח

(א) גמ' משום דבעי למיתני סיפא כשלש עשרה תנא רישא כעשר כשלש עשרה הא טפי הויין: (ב) רש"י ד"ה תרי גווני וכו' אבל קנה קנה פחות: (ג) ד"ה מאי לאו וכו' דאין עוביו שלשה בגובה עשרה:

תְּרֵי גַּוְונֵי אִילָן, הָכָא נַמִי — תְּרֵי גַּוְונֵי גָּדֵר. בְּעָא מִינֵּיהּ אַבַּיֵי מֵרַבָּה: חָצֵר שֶׁרֹאשָׁהּ נִכְנָס לְבֵין הַפַּסִּין, מַהוּ לְטַלְטֵל מִתּוֹכָהּ לְבֵין הַפַּסִּין, וּמִבֵּין הַפַּסִּין לְתוֹכָהּ? א"ל: מוּתָּר. שְׁתַּיִם מַאי? אֲמַר לֵיהּ: אָסוּר. אָמַר רַב הוּנָא: שְׁתַּיִם אֲסוּרִין, וַאֲפִילּוּ עֵירְבוּ, גְּזֵירָה שֶׁמָּא יֹאמְרוּ "עֵירוּב מוֹעִיל לְבֵין הַפַּסִּין". רָבָא אָמַר: עֵירְבוּ מוּתָּר. א"ל אַבַּיֵי לְרָבָא, תַּנְיָא דִּמְסַיַּיע לָךְ: [א]חָצֵר שֶׁרֹאשָׁהּ אֶחָד נִכְנָס לְבֵין הַפַּסִּין — מוּתָּר לְטַלְטֵל מִתּוֹכָהּ לְבֵין הַפַּסִּין, וּמִבֵּין הַפַּסִּין לְתוֹכָהּ, אֲבָל שְׁתַּיִם — אָסוּר. בד"א — שֶׁלֹּא עֵירְבוּ, אֲבָל עֵירְבוּ — מוּתָּרִין. לֵימָא תֶּיהֱוֵי תְּיוּבְתָּא דְּרַב הוּנָא! אָמַר לָךְ רַב הוּנָא: הָתָם דְּהַדְרָן וְעָרְבָן. בְּעָא מִינֵּיהּ אַבַּיֵי מֵרַבָּה: יָבְשׁוּ מַיִם בַּשַּׁבָּת מַהוּ? א"ל: [ב]כְּלוּם נַעֲשֵׂית מְחִיצָּה אֶלָּא בִּשְׁבִיל מַיִם, מַיִם אֵין כָּאן — מְחִיצָּה אֵין כָּאן. בָּעֵי רָבִין: יָבְשׁוּ מַיִם בַּשַּׁבָּת וּבָאוּ בַּשַּׁבָּת מַהוּ? א"ל אַבַּיֵי: יָבְשׁוּ בַּשַּׁבָּת לָא תִּיבָּעֵי לָךְ. דְּבָעֵי מִינֵּיהּ דְּמָר וּפְשַׁט לִי דַּאֲסִיר. [ג]בָּאוּ נַמִי לָא תִּיבָּעֵי לָךְ דַּהֲוָה לֵיהּ מְחִיצָּה הָעֲשׂוּיָה בַּשַּׁבָּת, *וְתַנְיָא: [ד]כָּל מְחִיצָּה הָעֲשׂוּיָה בַּשַּׁבָּת, בֵּין בְּשׁוֹגֵג בֵּין בְּמֵזִיד, בֵּין בְּאוֹנֶס בֵּין בְּרָצוֹן — שְׁמָהּ מְחִיצָּה. וְלָאו אִיתְּמַר עֲלָהּ, אָמַר ר"נ: לֹא שָׁנוּ אֶלָּא לִזְרוֹק, אֲבָל לְטַלְטֵל — לֹא! [ה]כִּי אִיתְּמַר דְּר"נ — אַמֵּזִיד אִיתְּמַר. אָמַר ר"א: [ו]הַזּוֹרֵק לְבֵין פַּסֵּי הַבֵּירָאוֹת — חַיָּיב. א"ל: פְּשִׁיטָא! אִי לָאו מְחִיצָּה הִיא הֵיכִי מִשְׁתְּרֵי לֵיהּ לְמַלְּאוֹת?! לָא צְרִיכָא, [ז]דַּעֲבַד כְּעֵין פַּסֵּי בֵירָאוֹת בִּרה"ר, וְזָרַק לְתוֹכָהּ — חַיָּיב. הָא נַמִי פְּשִׁיטָא! אִי לָאו דִּבְעָלְמָא מְחִיצָּה הִיא — גַּבֵּי בּוֹר הֵיכִי מִשְׁתְּרֵי לֵיהּ לְטַלְטְלֵי? [ח]לָא צְרִיכָא, אע"ג דְּקָא בָּקְעִי בָּהּ רַבִּים. וּמַאי קמ"ל — דְּלָא אָתוּ רַבִּים וּמְבַטְּלִי מְחִיצָּתָא, הָא א"ר אֶלְעָזָר חֲדָא זִימְנָא! *דִּתְנַן, רַבִּי יְהוּדָה אוֹמֵר: אִם הָיְתָה דֶּרֶךְ רה"ר מַפְסַקְתָּן, יְסַלְּקֶנָּה לִצְדָדִין, וַחכ"א: אֵינוֹ צָרִיךְ. *רַבִּי יוֹחָנָן וְר"א דְּאָמְרִי תַּרְוַיְיהוּ: כָּאן הוֹדִיעֲךָ כֹּחָן שֶׁל מְחִיצוֹת. אִי מֵהָתָם — הֲוָה אָמִינָא: כָּאן — וְלָא סְבִירָא לֵיהּ, קָא מַשְׁמַע לָן: כָּאן — וּסְבִירָא *לֵיהּ. וְלֵימָא הָא וְלָא בָּעֵי הַךְ! *חֲדָא מִכְּלָל חֲבֶירְתָּהּ אִיתְּמַר.§ "מוּתָּר לְהַקְרִיב לַבְּאֵר וְכוּ'".§ *תְּנַן הָתָם: לֹא יַעֲמוֹד אָדָם בִּרְשׁוּת הָרַבִּים וְיִשְׁתֶּה בִּרְשׁוּת הַיָּחִיד, בִּרְשׁוּת הַיָּחִיד וְיִשְׁתֶּה בִּרְשׁוּת הָרַבִּים, אֶלָּא אִם כֵּן מַכְנִיס רֹאשׁוֹ וְרוּבּוֹ לַמָּקוֹם שֶׁהוּא שׁוֹתֶה. וְכֵן

רש"י

אָמַר לֵיהּ מוּתָּר. דְּהָא לֵיכָּא דִּיּוּרִין בֵּין הַפַּסִּין דְּלִיסְרוּ עֲלַיְיהוּ, דְּלֶיהֱוֵי מוֹצִיא מֵרְשׁוּתוֹ לִרְשׁוּת חֲבֵירוֹ: שְׁתַּיִם מַאי. שְׁתַּיִם זוֹ אֵצֶל זוֹ, וּמְחִיצָּה בֵּינֵיהֶן, וּשְׁתֵּיהֶן רֹאשָׁן בֵּין הַפַּסִּין: אָסוּר. לְטַלְטֵל מִתּוֹכָן לְבֵין הַפַּסִּין, כִּדְמְפָרֵשׁ(א) טַעְמָא רַב הוּנָא: וַאֲפִילּוּ עֵירְבוּ. דֶּרֶךְ הַפֶּתַח שֶׁבַּמְּחִיצָּה שֶׁבֵּינֵיהֶן, דְּהַשְׁתָּא חֲדָא נִינְהוּ וְלָא אָסְרָן אַהֲדָדֵי – אֲסוּרוֹת לְטַלְטֵל מִתּוֹכָן לְבֵין הַפַּסִּין, גְּזֵירָה שֶׁמָּא יֹאמְרוּ עֵירוּב מוֹעִיל בֵּין הַפַּסִּין לְשַׁתֵּף חֲצֵירוֹת יַחַד. שֶׁהָרוֹאֶה אוֹתָן מְטַלְטְלִין מִתּוֹכָן לְבֵין הַפַּסִּין לֹא יָדַע דְּיֵשׁ פֶּתַח בֵּינֵיהֶן, וְסָבַר: הַאי דְּלָא אָסְרָן אַהֲדָדֵי בְּתוֹךְ בֵּין הַפַּסִּין, כִּשְׁאָר שְׁתֵּי חֲצֵירוֹת הַפְּתוּחוֹת לְמָבוֹי אֶחָד שֶׁאָסוּר לְהוֹצִיא לַמָּבוֹי אֶלָּא א"כ נִשְׁתַּתְּפוּ – ה"נ מִשּׁוּם דְּנָתְנוּ עֵירוּבָן בֵּין הַפַּסִּין, לְשַׁתֵּף כְּשִׁיתּוּף שְׁאָר מָבוֹי. וְאָתוּ לְמִשְׁרֵי נַמִי לְהַכְנִיס וּלְהוֹצִיא מִבֵּין הַפַּסִּין לַחֲצֵירוֹת כִּי לֵיכָּא פֶּתַח בֵּינֵיהֶן, וְיָהֲבֵי עֵירוּב בְּחַצֵּרוֹת דֶּרֶךְ בֵּין הַפַּסִּין. וְהוּא וַדַּאי לָא מְהַנֵּי, דְּכִי תַּקִּינוּ רַבָּנַן שִׁיתּוּפֵי מְבוֹאוֹת – בְּמָבוֹי סָתוּם תַּקּוּן, וְאָרְכּוֹ יָתֵר עַל רָחְבּוֹ, וְזֶה מְפוּלָּשׁ לְאַרְבָּעָה צְדָדִין: עֵירְבוּ מוּתָּרִין. דְּכֵיוָן דְּעֵירְבוּ דֶּרֶךְ פֶּתַח שֶׁבֵּינֵיהֶן, וְחַד רְשׁוּתָא הוּא – דְּלָא אָסְרָן אַהֲדָדֵי, לְהָךְ גְּזֵירָה לָא חָיְישִׁינַן: דְּהַדְרָן וְעָרְבָן.

פירלה

שֶׁמַּפְרְלָה בֵּינֵיהֶן פִּירְלָה גְּדוֹלָה בְּסוֹפָהּ, שֶׁגָּלוּי לַכֹּל שֶׁרְשׁוּת אַחַת הִיא: יָבְשׁוּ מַיִם בַּשַּׁבָּת מַהוּ. לְטַלְטֵל בֵּין הַפַּסִּין. מִי אָמְרִינַן שַׁבָּת הוֹאִיל וְהוּתְּרָה הוּתְּרָה, אוֹ דִּילְמָא כֵּיוָן דְּהֶיתֵּר פַּסִּין אֵינוֹ אֶלָּא מִשּׁוּם מַיִם, וַהֲרֵי יָבְשׁוּ – וְאָסוּר. וְאַכָּל פַּסֵּי בֵירָאוֹת קָאֵי: כְּלוּם נַעֲשֵׂית מְחִיצָּה. כְּלוֹמַר: כְּלוּם הוּתְּרָה מְחִיצָּה כָּזוֹ אֶלָּא מִשּׁוּם מַיִם: יָבְשׁוּ מַיִם בַּשַּׁבָּת. וְחָזְרוּ וּבָאוּ גְּשָׁמִים בּוֹ בַּיּוֹם, מַאי? מִי אָמְרִינַן: חָזְרוּ פַּסִּין לְהֶיתֵּרָן הָרִאשׁוֹן לְטַלְטֵל מִתּוֹכָן: מִינֵּיהּ דְּמָר. רַבָּה, שֶׁהָיָה רַבּוֹ: וּבָאוּ מַיִם בַּשַּׁבָּת לָא קָמִבָּעֲיָא לִי. דְּמוּתָּר, דְּהָא קַיְימָא לָן כָּל מְחִיצָּה הַנַּעֲשֵׂית בַּשַּׁבָּת שְׁמָהּ מְחִיצָּה: לֹא שָׁנוּ. דִּשְׁמָהּ מְחִיצָּה: אֶלָּא לִזְרוֹק. שֶׁהַזּוֹרֵק מֵרְשׁוּת הָרַבִּים לְתוֹכָהּ חַיָּיב, דְּמִדְּאוֹרַיְיתָא וַדַּאי מְחִיצָּה הִיא: אֲבָל לְטַלְטֵל אָסוּר. דְּרַבָּנַן גְּזוּר עֲלֵיהּ: אַמֵּזִיד אִיתְּמַר. וּקְנָסָא קְנָסוּהָ. אֲבָל שׁוֹגֵג – מוּתָּר. וְהָא דְּנַעֲשֵׂית מֵאֵלֶיהָ – כָּל שֶׁכֵּן דְּמוּתָּר: הַזּוֹרֵק. מֵרְשׁוּת הָרַבִּים לְבֵין הַפַּסִּין שֶׁל בֵּירָאוֹת: חַיָּיב. חַטָּאת, דִּרְשׁוּת הַיָּחִיד מְעַלְיָיתָא הוּא: אִי לָאו מְחִיצָּה. מִדְּאוֹרַיְיתָא הִיא, לְשַׁוְּיֵהּ מִיהָא רְשׁוּת הַיָּחִיד לִזְרִיקָה: הֵיכִי שָׁרוּ רַבָּנַן לְמַלְּאוֹת. וּלְהוֹצִיא מֵרה"י לִרה"ר מִשּׁוּם דּוֹחַק: כְּעֵין פַּסֵּי בֵירָאוֹת. וְאֵין שָׁם בּוֹר: מַפְסַקְתָּן. שֶׁאֵין שָׁם דֶּרֶךְ אֶלָּא בֵּין הַפַּסִּין – יְסַלְּקֶנָּה לִצְדָדִין, דְּאָתֵי דְּרִיסַת רַבִּים וּמְבַטְּלֵי מְחִיצּוֹת. חֲכָמִים כַּמָּה גָּדוֹל כֹּחָן שֶׁל מְחִיצּוֹת, דְּלָא מִיבַּטְלֵי מִשּׁוּם בְּקִיעַת רַבִּים: מוּתָּר לְהַקְרִיב כו'. פָּרֵישְׁנָא לָהּ לְכוּלָּהּ מַתְנִי' בְּרֵישׁ פִּירְקִין: אֶלָּא א"כ הִכְנִיס רֹאשׁוֹ וְרוּבּוֹ. דְּחָיְישִׁי' שֶׁמָּא יִמָּשֵׁךְ גּוּפוֹ לִמְקוֹם רַגְלָיו, וְיוֹצִיא הַכְּלִי עִמּוֹ: וְכֵן

תוספות

דהדרן וערבן. והכי פירושו: שתים אסורות אפי' עירבו, ואם עירבו כו', דהיינו: כלומר, דהדרן וערבן, מותרות כשעירבו:

מחיצה אין כאן. אע"ג דאביי אית ליה: *שבת הואיל והותרה הותרה – מודה הכא, משום דליכא מחילות:

כי איתמר דרב נחמן אמזיד איתמר. והא דאמרינן בשבת בפרק "הזורק" (ד' קא:): ספינות שנתקשרו מערב שבת והותרו, וחזרו ונתקשרו, בין שוגגין ובין מזידין ובין מוטעין ובין אנוסין – חזרו להיתרן הראשון(ב). במזיד לא חזרו לגמרי להיתרן הראשון לטלטל, אלא דהוו רשות היחיד דאורייתא. אי נמי – לא קאי אמזיד:

קמ"ל כאן וסבירא ליה. ומיהו, לר' יוחנן ודאי כאן ולא ס"ל, כדאמרי' לקמן.

לא יעמוד אדם. בפרק בתרא (ד' צט.) מוקי לה בחפצים הצריכין לו, וגזרי' דלמא יכניס אצלו. וקשיא: דתיפוק ליה דקא מעייל מרשות הרבים לרשות היחיד, כמו משתין ורק מרשות הרבים לרה"י דאסרינן לקמן! ורש"י תירץ לקמן: דלא דמי למשתין ורק, דשותה עביד עקירה והנחה בחד רשותא, דמשקין נחין בתוך פיו שהוא מקום פטור. ואע"ג דחוזרין ונבלעין – אין לחוש, הואיל ונחו במקום פטור. ואע"ג דבמקום שאין בו ד' על ד'(ג) (אמות) אמרינן ובלבד שלא יחליפו – התם גזרינן דילמא אתי לאפוקי בהדיא, אבל הכא – אי אפשר כלל שלא ינוחו מעט בפיו קודם שיבלעם. אבל במשתין ורק – לא חשיב פיו מקום פטור, כיון דפיו וגופו הן במקום א'. ולפי זה היה מותר להוציא ראשו מרה"ר ולרוק, כיון דפיו במקום אחר הוי מקום פטור. והא דמבעיא לן בפרק בתרא (ד' צט.) הוא ברה"י ופי האמה ברה"ר מהו? היינו משום דמי רגלים מיד כשנעקרו מגופו שוב אין נחים בפי האמה. אבל מפ"ק דשבת (ד' ג:) קשיא; דקאמרינן התם: אדרבה, משתשיכה דאי שדי(ד) ליה אתי לידי חיוב חטאת – לא קנסינן. והשתא, היכי אתי לידי חיוב חטאת? הואיל ונחו בידו שהוא מקום פטור! וי"ל: דלא חשיב הנחה במקום פטור אלא בדבר שהוא נוטל ממקומו, אבל התם שהכלי נח מאליו – לא חשיב הנחה במקום פטור. ולפי זה אסור להוציא ראשו ברה"ר ולרוק. וא"ת: אכתי אפשר דלא אתי לידי חיוב חטאת כגון שיתן מידו זאת לידו אחרת! וי"ל: דאיירי כשהנקב קטן, שלא יוכל להכניס בו שתי ידיו. ועוד נראה לפרש: דלא דמי למשתין ורק, דהכא כשבולעם מיד חשיבי כנחין, אע"ג דאינם נחים עד שיגיעו למעיו – משום דמבטלי אגב גופו, והוי עקירה והנחה בחד רשותא. והכי נמי אמר רבא בפ' "המוציא" (שבת ד' פ.): הוציא שתי אותיות וכתבן כשהוא מהלך – חייב, דכתיבתן זו היא הנחתן. ואתי נמי שפיר מתניתין דאמרו לו *גבי יש אוכל אכילה אחת כו', ר' מאיר אומר: אם היה שבת והוציא בפיו – חייב. והשתא היכי חשיב הוצאה בהדי הנך? הא בעידנא דמיחייב עלייהו דהיינו בשעת הנחת גרון אכתי לא מיחייב אהוצאה עד שינוחו במעיו! אלא, אהוצאה נמי מחייב משעת בליעה, דחשיב כמונח: וכי

רבינו חננאל

גווני אילן איכא דאמרי (הכל) [בכה"ג] (פשט) [פשוט] ליה גודדייתא דקני בעא מיניה. ותוב בעא מיניה חצר שראשה אחד נכנס לבין הפסין מותר לטלטל מתוכה לבין הפסין ומבין הפסין לתוכה אבל ב' חצירות נכנסות לבין הפסין אסור. אמר רב הונא ואפי' עירבו חצרות זו עם זו גזירה שמא יאמרו עירוב מועיל לבין הפסין כו' (ורבה) [ורבא] אמר עירבו מותר ותניא כוותיה חצר שראשה אחד נכנס לבין הפסין מותר לטלטל בתוכה לבין הפסין וכו' ושתים אסור בד"א בשלא עירבו [אבל עירבו] מותר ורב הונא משני בהדרן ועירבן כלומר אלו ב' חצרות הנכנסות לבין הפסין הדרן מתערבן או כגון שביטל אחד מהן רשותו לחבירו והויין כחדא. אבל אי לא הדרן ומתערבו אסור וזו שנויה היא. והלכתא כרבא: בעא מיניה אביי מרבה יבשו מים בשבת מותר לטלטל בין הפסין או לא. ופשיט ליה לא נעשו פסין מחיצות אלא בשביל המים יבשו המים בטלו המחיצות ואמר אביי באו מים בשבת לא קא מיבעיא לי דהא כל מחיצה שנעשית בשבת בין במזיד בין בשוגג שמה מחיצה הלכך כיון שבאו מים מותר. והא דאמר רב נחמן לא שנו אלא לזרוק אבל לטלטל אסור במזיד אתמר. והני מיא לא במזיד הביאום. אלא מימי המטר וכיוצא בהן באו מעצמן: א"ר אלעזר הזורק מבין רה"ר לבין פסי בירות חייב וכן העושה כמין פסי בירות ברה"ר וזרק לתוכו חייב דכרה"ר דמי ואע"ג דבקעי ביה [רבים דתנן] ואם היתה דרך הרבים מפסיקתה יסלקנה לצדדין וחכמים אומרים אין צריך ר' יוחנן ור' אלעזר דאמרי תרוויהו כאן הודיעוך כוחן של מחיצות דאע"ג דבקעי ביה [רבים] כיון דקיימי מחיצתא כרה"י דמי: **פיסקא** מותר להקריב לבאר כו'. תנן התם בסוף המסכתא לא יעמוד ברה"ר וישתה ברה"י אלא אם כן הכניס ראשו ורובו למקום שהוא שותה כו'

עין משפט נר מצוה

ט א ב ג שם הלכה לד:

[לקמן לג:]

י ד ה מיי' שם הל' לד ופט"ז שם הל' כב טוש"ע א"ח סי' שסב סעיף ג:

יא ו ז ח מיי' פי"ז שם הלכה לג:

מסורת הש"ס

שבת קא: לקמן כב.

שבת ו: לקמן כב.

[לקמן שם]

[מגילה כט: וש"נ]

[שם]

שבת יא. ע"ש לקמן לג.

הגהות הב"ח

(א) רש"י ד"ה אסור לטלטל וכו' כדמפרש רב הונא טעמא הס"ד: (ב) תום' ד"ה כי איתמר כו' להיתרן הראשון וכן מתחלות כו'. במזיד לא חזרו: (ג) ד"ה לא יעמוד וכו' ואע"ג דבמקום שאין בו ד' על ד' אמרינן כצ"ל ותיבת אמות נמחק: (ד) בא"ד אדרבה משתשיכה דאי שדי להו אתי לידי חיוב חטאת:

יב א מיי' פי"ג מהל' שבת הלכה יב:
יג ב מיי' פי"ז מהל' שבת הלכה כט:
יד ג שם הלכה ל:

וכן בגת. גבי אדם הא אמר דבעי ראשו ורובו; גבי פרה, מי בעינן לה ראשה ורובה או לא? כל היכא דקא נקיט מנא ולא נקיט לה – לא תיבעי לך דבעי ראשה ורובה מלגיו. כי תבעי לך – היכא דנקיט מנא ונקיט לה, מאי? א"ל: תניתוה, ובלבד שתהא הפרה ראשה ורובה מבפנים ושותה. מאי לאו דנקיט לה ונקיט מנא! לא, דנקיט מנא ולא נקיט לה. וכי נקיט מנא ולא נקיט לה מי שרי? והתניא: *לא ימלא אדם מים ויתן בשבת לפני בהמתו, אבל ממלא הוא ושופך, והיא שותה מאיליה! הא איתמר עלה, *אמר אביי: הכא באבוס העומד ברשות הרבים, גבוה י' טפחים ורוחב ד' וראשו אחד נכנס לבין הפסין, גזרה דילמא חזי ליה לאבוס דמקלקל ואתי לתקוניה ודרא ליה לדוולא בהדיה, וקא מפיק מרשות היחיד לרשות הרבים. וכי האי גוונא מי מיחייב? *והאמר רב ספרא, אמר ר' אמי, אמר ר' יוחנן: [א]המפנה חפציו מזוית לזוית ונמלך עליהן והוציאן – פטור, שלא היתה עקירה משעה ראשונה לכך! אלא זמנין דמתקן ליה והדר מעייל ליה, וקא מעייל מרשות הרבים לרשות היחיד. איכא דאמרי: גבי אדם – הא קאמרינן דסגי ליה בראשו ורובו. גבי פרה מי סגי לה בראשה ורובה, או לא? היכא דנקיט מנא ונקיט לה – לא תיבעי לך דסגי לה בראשה ורובה, אלא כי תיבעי לך דנקיט מנא ולא נקיט לה, מאי? אמר ליה: תניתוה, ובלבד שתהא פרה ראשה ורובה מבפנים ושותה. מאי לאו [ב]דנקיט מנא ולא נקיט לה! לא, דנקיט מנא ונקיט לה. והכי נמי מסתברא, דאי נקיט מנא ולא נקיט לה מי שרי?! והתניא: לא ימלא אדם מים ויתן לפני בהמתו, אבל ממלא ושופך והיא שותה מאיליה! הא איתמר עלה, אמר אביי: הכא באבוס העומד ברשות הרבים גבוה עשרה טפחים ורוחב ארבעה, וראשו נכנס לבין הפסין, דזמנין דחזי ליה לאבוס דמקלקל ואתי לתקוניה, ודרי ליה לדוולא בהדיה וקא מפיק מרשות היחיד לרשות הרבים. וכי האי גוונא מי מיחייב? והאמר רב ספרא, אמר ר' אמי, אמר ר' יוחנן: המפנה חפציו מזוית לזוית ונמלך עליהן והוציאן – פטור, שלא היתה עקירה משעה ראשונה לכך! אלא, זמנין דמתקן ליה והדר מעייל ליה, וקא מעייל ליה מרה"ר לרשות היחיד. תא שמע: גמל שראשו ורובו מבפנים – אובסין אותו מבפנים. והא איבוס כמאן דנקיט מנא ונקיט לה דמיא, וקא בעינן ראשה ורובה! אמר רב אחא בר רב הונא, אמר רב ששת: שאני גמל הואיל וצוארו ארוך. ת"ש: בהמה שראשה ורובה בפנים – אובסין אותה מבפנים. והא אבוס כמאן דנקיט מנא ונקיט לה(א) וקא בעינן ראשו ורובו! מאי בהמה נמי דקתני – גמל. והתניא בהמה והתניא גמל! *מידי גבי הדדי תניא?! תנ"ה: ר"א אוסר בגמל, הואיל וצוארו ארוך. [ג]א"ר יצחק בר *אדא: לא הותרו פסי ביראות אלא לעולי רגלים בלבד. והתניא: לא הותרו פסי ביראות אלא לגבי בהמה בלבד! מאי בהמה – בהמת עולי רגלים, אבל אדם
מטפם

וכי (ג)לא נקיט לה מי שרי. קשה: דאין זה סוגיית התלמוד; דלעיל קאמר היכא דנקיט מנא ולא נקיט לה – לא תבעי לך דבעינן ראשה ורובה. והשתא פריך מי שרי? וי"ל: לא משום דפשיטא ליה קאמר הכי, אלא אפי' אם תימצי לומר דשרי – לא שרי אלא בראשה ורובה.

והתניא לא ימלא. גבי פסי בירות מיתניא, ומשמע דקאי אמתני', ואע"ג דאיכא ראשה ורובה. ועל כרחך בדלא נקיט לה איירי, דאי בדנקיט לה איירי – אם כן מה הועילו ראשה ורובה של פרה?

אמר אביי הכא באיבוס העומד ברה"ר. פירוש: שהבהמה אוכלת מן האיבוס ברה"ר אצל הפסין. וקא משמע לן דלא ימלא דלי ויתננו על ראש האיבוס ויאחזנו בידו, דילמא חזי לראש האיבוס שברה"ר נתקלקל, וילך שם עם הדלי ומפיק מרשות היחיד לרשות הרבים. אלא שופך לפניה, דכי נמי חזי לראש האיבוס שנתקלקל ואזיל להתם – הא לית ליה מידי בידיה. דהא כששפך הניח הדלי בין הפסין. ובחנם דחק רש"י לפרש שהבהמה עומדת בבית. ויש ספרים שכתוב בהן, וכן גירסת רבינו חננאל: דלמא חזי לאיבוס דמקלקל, ומפיק ליה לדווליה בהדיה. פירוש: שלא יכול להניח הדלי בראש האיבוס שבין הפסין, ומפיק לה לדווליה דרך האיבוס, דעומד אדם ברה"ר ומטלטל ברה"י, וחזי ליה לאידך גיסא דמקלקל ומנח ליה, וקא מפיק ליה מרה"י לרה"ר. ומנח ליה – פי': על ארעא ברה"ר, עד דמתקן ליה לאיבוס:

אובסין האי אובסין לאו דוקא, אלא כלומר: מלעיטין. דתנן בפ' בתרא דשבת (ד' קנה:): אין אובסין את הגמל אלא מלעיטין:
מידי

וכן בגת. מפרש בפ' בתרא (דף לט:) לענין מעשר, דכל כמה שהוא בגת – שותין בלא מעשר על הגת, אבל להוציא מן הגת – שתיית קבע הוא. ועל הגת, אפי' מוזגו בחמין דהויא לה קבע – לא חשיב ליה קבע התם: גבי בהמה. המשקה בהמתו ברה"י, והיא עומדת ברה"ר, מהו: היכא דנקיט מנא. שהיא שותה בו: ולא נקיט. לאוחרה באפסר, שלא תוכל לעקם ראשה בחוץ: לא תיבעי לך. דודאי חיישינן שמא תעקם את ראשה, ותוליך את הכלי אחריה: וכי לא נקיט לה מי שרי. לאחוז הכלי בפסי בירות, ואע"ג דעשויין כתיקנן שהפרה ראשה ורובה בפנים: לא ימלא אדם מים ויתן לפני בהמתו. ויאחוז הכלי בידו בעוד שהיא שותה. ולקמן בברייתא במשמעתין היא גבי פסי בירות. ועל כרחך בדלא נקיט לה הוא, דאי נקיט לה הוא ואפ"ה אסור – למה הוצרכו ראשה ורובה בפנים? אלא פשיטא בדלא נקיט לה, ומתני' דשרי – בדנקיט לה, וקתני: ראשה ורובה מבפנים: הא איתמר עלה כו'. כלומר: כי בעינן ראשה ורובה – בדלא נקיט לה, וכי הוי ראשה ורובה – שרי. וברייתא דקתני לא ימלא ויתן הוא עצמו לבהמתו – הא תרלה אביי לקמן דלאו בבהמה העומדת ברה"ר וראשה ורובה בין הפסין עסקינן, אלא בבהמה העומדת בבית וחלונות פתוחות לה לרה"ר, ואיבוס מתוקן לה(ב) לפניה ברה"ר גבוה עשרה ורחב ד' דהוי רה"י. ונותן לה שם תבן ומספוא מרה"י. וראש האיבוס נכנס לבין הפסין. ואשמעינן דלא ימלא מן הבור ויגביה הדלי על ראש האיבוס וילך דרך רה"ר, ויטלטל הדלי על האיבוס לפני בהמה. ואע"ג דקיי"ל: עומד אדם ברה"ר ומטלטל ברה"י ב"המוצא תפילין" (לקמן ד' צח:) – הכא אסור: דילמא. כי בעי לאנוחי דלי על ראש האיבוס, חזי ליה לאיבוס דמקלקל בראשו שברה"ר, ומינשי ודרי ליה לדווליה בהדיה, ואזיל לתקוניה וקא מפיק מבין הפסין לרה"ר. הלכך לא יניחנו ויטלטלנו, אלא שופך על האיבוס והמים הולכין עד הבהמה מאליהן: וכי האי גוונא מי מיחייב. כי עקר מרה"י אדעתא לאנוחיה ברה"י, ואינשי ואפקיה לרה"ר, מי מיחייב מדאורייתא, דליגזור רבנן בדלא אפקיה, משום דלא ליתי להכי: שלא היתה עקירה כו'. ובשבת מלאכת מחשבת אסרה תורה, שנתכוין לכך אלא ששגג בשבת, כסבור שהיום חול או מלאכה זו מותרת. אבל כי לא נתכוין – פטור מחטאת. וכיון דאי נמי אתי לידי כך ליכא חיובא דאורייתא – לא איבעי לן למיגזר היתירא משום הא: והדר מעייל ליה. לדוולא לאיבוס לבתר דתקניה, וקא עקר ליה מרה"ר אדעתא לאנוחי ברה"י: לא תיבעי לך דסגי בראשה ורובה. דהא מתני' היא בדנקיט מנא. דאי לאו דנקיט מנא קמיה – למה הצריכו ראשה ורובה בפנים? אבל הא מספקא לן: דדילמא מתני' בדנקיט לה הוא: אובסין אותה מבפנים. מפרש בפרק "מי שהחשיך" (שבת ד' קנה:) שאוחז לה מספוא הרבה על כרחה בבית הבליעה, יותר מכדי אכילתה, עד שנעשה כאיבוס במעיה כשיוליכה למדבר, ומתיירא שלא תמצא מאכל: והא איבוס כמאן דנקיט מנא ונקיט לה הוא. שאם אינו אוחז בצוארו אינו יכול לתחוב, וקא בעי ראשו ורובו. ותיפשוט בעיא קמייתא דלישנא קמא: מידי גבי הדדי תני להו. דתנא בהמה לא תנא גמל, ומאי בהמה – גמל: איתמר נמי לא גרסי': צוארו ארוך. *ואע"ג דרוב גופו מבפנים, אם יתקפנו *ויעקר צוארו יגיע *עד רשות הרבים: בהמת עולי רגלים. אבל אדם, אפי' עולי רגלים – לא הותר לדלות ולשתות, שיכול ליכנס לפנים ולשתות:
מטפם

[לקמן כח.]
[שם]
שבת ה: כתובות לא. ע"ש
[שבת יח. גיטין סז. ב"מ לד. לב.]
[גי' הרא"ש אמי
[נ"ל ויעקס]

רבינו חננאל

[גבי] אדם הא תנן דבעי להכנים ראשו ורובו למקום שהוא שותה. פרה מאי מי בעינן להכנים ראשה ורובה למקום ששותה [ואי לא והיכא דנקיט לה למנא ולא נקיט לה לבהמה. לא תיבעי לן דודאי בעינן להכנים ראשה ורובה למקום ששותה] כי תיבעי לן היכא דנקיט לה למנא ונקיט לה לבהמה מאי. ת"ש ובלבד שתהא פרה ראשה ורובה בפנים ושותה מאי לאו דנקיט מנא ונקיט לה כו'. [איכא דאמרי גבי] אדם הא קאמרינן דסגי ליה בראשו ורובו בהמה מאי היכא דנקיט לה למנא ונקיט לה לבהמה דברי הכל סגי ליה בראשה ורובה כי תיבעי לן היכא דנקיט מנא ולא נקיט לה מאי. ת"ש ובלבד שתהא פרה ראשה ורובה לפנים ושותה מאי לאו דנקיט מנא ולא נקיט לה ודחינן לא דנקיט מנא ונקיט לה הכי נמי מסתברא דאי לא נקיט לה מי שרי לה לאשקויה. והתניא לא ימלא אדם מים ויתן לפני בהמתו אבל ממלא הוא ושופך והיא שותה מאיליה ודחינן הא אתמר עלה דהא ברייתא אמר אביי הכא באיבום העומד ברה"ר גבוה עשרה ורחב ד' שהוא רה"י וראשו אחד נכנס לבין הפסין עסקינן חיישינן דלמא נפיק ומסגי עילולא ומפיק ליה [לדוולא] בהדיה ומנח ליה כ"א בארעא וקא מפיק מרה"י לרה"ר ואקשינן ומאן דמפיק כי האי גוונא מי מיחייב והא אמר ר' יוחנן המפנה חפצים מזוית לזוית ונמלך עליהן

הגהות הב"ח

(א) גמ' ונקט לה דמיא וקא בעינן לאשו: (ב) רש"י ד"ה הא איתמר וכו' ואבוס מתוקן לה לפניה ברשות הרבים כזה:

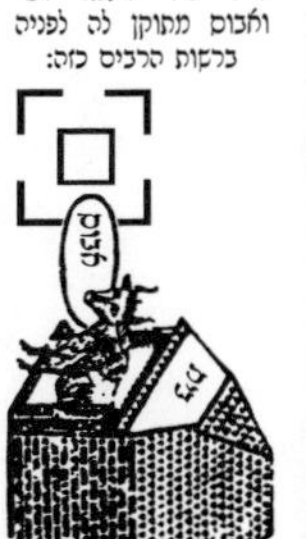

(ג) תום' ד"ה וכי נקיט מנא ולא נקיט לה מי שרי:

ואי לאו דרוב כצ"ל [ח"מ]

עד רה"ר ואהכי בעי ראשו ורובו אע"ג דנקיט לה כצ"ל [רש"ל]

מטפס ועולה מטפס ויורד. איני?! והאמר רב(א) יצחק, אמר רב יהודה, אמר שמואל: לא הותרו פסי ביראות אלא לבאר מים חיים בלבד. ואי לבהמה — מה לי חיים מה לי מכונסין? בעינן מידי דחזי לאדם. גופא: לא הותרו פסי ביראות אלא לבהמה בלבד, אבל אדם מטפס ועולה מטפס ויורד, ואם היו רחבין — אפילו לאדם נמי. *ולא ימלא אדם מים ויתן לפני בהמתו, אבל ממלא הוא ושופך לפני בהמה ושותה מאיליה. מתקיף לה רב ענן: אם כן מה הועילו פסי ביראות? מה הועילו?! למלאות מהן! אלא: מה הועיל ראשה ורובה של פרה? *אמר אביי: הכא במאי עסקינן — באיבוס העומד ברה"ר, גבוה עשרה ורוחב ארבעה וראשו נכנס לבין הפסין וכו'. אמר רב ירמיה בר אבא, אמר רב: אין בורגנין בבבל ולא פסי ביראות בחו"ל. בורגנין בבבל לא — דשכיחי בידקי, פסי ביראות בחו"ל לא — דלא שכיחי מתיבתא. אבל איפכא עבדינן. א"ד, אמר רב ירמיה בר אבא, אמר רב: אין בורגנין ופסי ביראות, לא בבבל ולא בחו"ל, בורגנין בבבל לא — דשכיחי בידקי, בחו"ל נמי לא — דשכיחי גנבי. פסי ביראות בבבל לא — דשכיחי מיא, בחוץ לארץ נמי לא — דלא שכיחי מתיבתא. א"ל רב חסדא למרי בריה דרב הונא בריה דרב ירמיה בר אבא: אמרי אתיתו מברנש לבי כנישתא דדניאל דהוה תלתא פרסי בשבתא, אמאי סמכיתו — אבורגנין, הא אמר אבוה דאבוה משמיה דרב אין בורגנין בבבל! נפק ואחוי ליה הנהו מתוותא, דמבלען בשבעים אמה ושיריים.§ אמר רב חסדא, דריש מרי בר מר: מאי דכתיב:

תהלים קיט "לכל תכלה ראיתי קץ רחבה מצותך מאד", דבר זה אמרו דוד ולא פירשו, אמרו איוב ולא פירשו, אמרו יחזקאל ולא פירשו, עד שבא זכריה בן עדו ופירשו. אמרו דוד ולא פירשו, דכתיב: "לכל תכלה ראיתי קץ רחבה מצותך מאד", אמרו איוב

איוב יא ולא פירשו — דכתיב: "ארוכה מארץ מדה ורחבה מני ים", אמרו יחזקאל ולא פירשו —

יחזקאל ב *דכתיב: "ויפרש אותה לפני והיא כתובה פנים ואחור וכתוב אליה קנים והגה והי". "קינים" — זו פורענותן של צדיקים בעולם הזה,

שם לב וכן הוא אומר: "קינה היא וקוננוה". "והגה" — זו מתן שכרן של צדיקים לעתיד לבא, וכה"א:

תהלים צב "עלי הגיון בכנור". "והי" — זו היא פורענותן של

יחזקאל ז רשעים לעתיד לבא, וכן הוא אומר: "הוה על הוה תבא". עד שבא זכריה בן עדו

זכריה ה ופירשו, דכתיב: "ויאמר אלי מה אתה רואה ואומר אני רואה מגילה עפה ארכה עשרים באמה ורחבה עשר באמה". וכי פשטת לה הויא לה עשרין בעשרין, וכתיב: "היא כתובה פנים ואחור". וכי קלפת לה כמה הויא לה —

ישעיהו מ ארבעין בעשרין, וכתיב: "מי מדד בשעלו מים ושמים בזרת תכן וגו'". נמצא כל העולם כולו אחד משלשת אלפים ומאתים בתורה. ואמר רב חסדא, דריש

ירמיהו כד מרי בר מר: מאי דכתיב: "והנה שני דודאי תאנים מועדים לפני היכל ה' הדוד האחד תאנים טובות מאד כתאני הבכורות

רש"י

מטפס. אוחז בידיו וברגליו בכתלים ונכנס ויוצא. מטפס = קרפי"ר בלע"ז: מידי דחזי לאדם. כיון דמים משוי להו מחיצה – בעינן מים חשובין: אם היו רחבין. ואינו יכול לטפס – מותר לו למלאות ולשתות: ויתן לפני בהמתו. הוא עצמו אינו מותר לאחוז הכלי לפניה: מה הועילו. בתמיה: הרי הועילו למלאות מן הבור, שהוא רשות היחיד: אין בורגנין בבבל. דאמר ב"כיצד מעברין" (לקמן ד' נה:): אם היו בורגנין חוץ לעיר בתוך ע' אמה ושירים – מתעברין עמה, ומודדין תחום העיר משם ולהלן. ומה הן בורגנין – סוכות שעושין שומרי העיר, ואינו דבר קבוע. וקאמר ר' ירמיה: הנך בורגנין אין בבבל. כלומר: ואין מתעברין עם העיר, דבבבל איכא בדקי דמיא ושטפי להו, הלכך לא חשיבי מידי: בחוצה לארץ. בשאר ארצות לבד מבבל: דלא שכיחי מתיבתא. להיות תלמידים הולכים מעיר לעיר ללמוד תורה, ופסי ביראות לא הותרו אלא לעולי רגלים ולכיוצא בהן, שהולכין לדבר מצוה: דשכיחי גנבי. דגנבי להו, הלכך לא חשיבי להיות בתים: דשכיחי מיא. ולא הותרו פסי ביראות אלא למקום שצריכין מי גשמים לכנסן ולשתות מהן, דאיכא דוחק: אמרי דקאתיתו מברנש לבי כנישתא דדניאל. שמעתי שאומרי' עליכם שאתם באין מברניש לבי כנישתא דדניאל בשבת. מקום היה בבבל ששם היה מתפלל דניאל דכתיב "וכוין פתיחן ליה בעיליתיה": אמאי קא סמכיתו אבורגנין. שיש בורגנין משבעים אמה לשבעים אמה: מתוותא. עיירות חריבות, ונשארו שם מחיצות מן הבתים. ואמרי' התם בפ' "כיצד מעברין" (שם נה:): נפש שאין נפרצה, דהיינו מצבת קבר – מתעברת עם העיר, ואע"פ שאינה בית ממש: בשבעים אמה ושירים. שני שלישי אמה, דהוא שיעור בית סאתים כחצר המשכן. כדאמרי' לקמן (ד' נז.): נותנין קרפף לעיר, דכל שבעים אמה ושירים סמוך לעיר הוי עיר: לכל תכלה ראיתי קץ. דסוף כל דבר יש קץ, למצוא סופו. אבל מצותך רחבה מאד, ואין קץ לתכלה שלה: לא פירשו. איזהו קץ שיעורה: ויפרוש אותה לפני. מגילת תורה שבעל פה הראהו: וכן הוא אומר. דקינים לשון פורענות הוא: והגה. לשון שמחה: עשרים באמה. אמה של הקדוש ברוך הוא: ורחבה עשר. כשהיא עפה, היינו כפולה: כי פשטת. לכפילתה, הויא עשרים בעשרים: כי קלפת לה. דתשים קליפה זו בראש חבירתה, שיהא כל כתיבה מצד אחד: חויא לה ארבעי'. אורך, ברוחב כ': ושמים בזרת תכן. מדת עולם חצי אמה על חצי אמה. צא וחשוב כמה חצי אמה על חצי אמה יש במגילה, ותמצא שלשת אלפים ומאתים. כיצד? עשה מעשרים אמה רוחב רצועות של רוחב חצי אמה – הרי כאן ארבעים רצועות, וכל אחת ארבעים אמה לאורכה של מגילה – הרי אלף ושש מאות אמה אורך שהן שלשת אלפים ומאתים זרתות: דודאי תאנים. סירות נחושת מלאות תאנים: מועדים. = מוכנים:

תוספות

מידי דחזי לאדם בעינן. ואובסין את הגמל דלעיל – היינו נמי במידי דחזי לאדם. אי נמי איירי ברה"י, ולא בין הפסין. אי נמי הואיל ותחילת התיקון הוי במידי דחזי לאדם – שרי בכל ענין לצורך בהמה. וא"ת: אמאי בעינן מידי דחזי לאדם כיון דלא שרי אלא לצורך בהמה! וי"ל: שאם דלה לצורך בהמה, ונשתיירו שם – שרי לאדם. והא דאמרינן בסמוך: ואם היו רחבים – לאדם נמי שרי היינו, לדלות לכתחילה לצורך אדם. אי נמי: הא דאמרינן לא הותרו אלא לצורך בהמה – היינו תחילת התיקון. אבל בשכבר נתקן לצורך בהמה – שרי אף לצורך אדם לכתחילה לדלות. ואם היו רחבים – שרי לתקן אפי' לצורך אדם. ואתי שפיר הא דאמר לעיל: אגר שראשה נכנס לבין הפסין מותר לטלטל מתוכה לבין הפסין, ומבין הפסין לתוכה – היינו השתא אפי' לצורך אדם:

מה הועילו ראשה ורובה של פרה. וא"ת: הועילו בדנקיט מנא ונקיט לה, דאמר לעיל דשרי. וברייתא איירי בדלא נקיט לה, כדמוכח לעיל! וי"ל: דרב ענן משמע ליה לא ימלא – אפילו בדנקיט מנא ונקיט לה. אי נמי: סבירא ליה דבנקיט מנא ונקיט לה – לא בעינן ראשה ורובה:

אחוי ליה הנך מתוותא. משמע דכפרים קטנים מקרו מתוותא. דהואיל ולא היו ידועים מכלל דקטנים היו. ובפרק קמא דגטין (ד' ז.) קרי לעיירות גדולות מתוותא. דקא אמרי': מתוותא דארעא דישראל קא חשיב, גבי קינה ודימונה ועדעדה. ומתוך כך נראה דאין להקפיד מה שכותבין בגט "מתא פלוני", בין עיר גדולה בין עיר קטנה. ומיהו, בקונטרס פי' כאן: מתוותא – עיירות חריבות. ולפי זה אין ראיה, דשמא גדולות היו, ולפי שנחרבו לא היו ידועות:

אחד משלשת אלפים ומאתים בתורה. בסלוק *"אז ראית וספרת" יסד רבי אליעזר הקליר: אלפים וארבע מאות בעולם מאריכה. וזהו לפי שעושה זרת שליש אמה, כמו שיסד: "והזרת מותחת עד שנים בסיט וארבעה אצבעות הוא הטפח והסיט". ולפי חשבון דשמעתא הוי זרת חצי אמה, וכל אמה כשתחלקנה לשתי וערב יש בה ארבע זרתות. אך תימה: כי לפי חשבונו היה לו לחלק אמה לתשעה חלקים, ואז יהיה בכל חלק זרת על זרת כי העולם זרת על זרת, ואז יעלה לשבעת אלפים ומאתים והוא עושה העולם זרת על אמה, וזה מנין לו(ב)? וגם סובר ד"וכל בשליש עפר הארץ" – היינו שליש אמה, והוא עצמו יסד: "גיא וכל עפרה בגרדה הכילו", משמע דאצבע שלישי, היינו אצבע הקרוי אמה, קרי ליה "גרדה", ורצה לפרש "וכל בשליש" באצבע שלישי. ובמסכת יומא (ד' יט:) קרי "גרדה" אצבע שאצל הגודל, ו"גרדה" היינו גרה דדא, של אגודל*):

מפני

*) [וע"ע תוס' מנחות לה: ד"ה וכמה]

עין משפט נר מצוה

טו א מיי' פי"ז מהל' שבת הל' ל:

טז ב ג ד מיי' שם הל' ל והלכה לב:

יז ה מיי' פ"ה מהל' שבת הלכה ג סמג לאוין סה טוש"ע א"ח סי' שמה סעיף ו:

מסורת הש"ס

[עי' תוס' פסחים כ. ד"ה יכנס ותוס' כ"ק ס: ד"ה לשעלם]

[לעיל כ:]

[שם]

הגהות הב"ח

(א) גמ' מטפס ויורד איני והא אמר רב יוסף אמר ר' יהודה אמר שמואל כו' נ"ב ע"ל ראש דף כ"ג: (ב) תוס' ד"ה אחד וכו' וזה מניין לו ואם סובר דוכל שליש היינו שליש אמה הוא עצמו וכו' משמע דאצבע שליש דהיינו:

גליון הש"ס

גמ' א"ר יהודה אמר שמואל לא הותרו פסי ביראות. עיין שבת דף כ' ע"ב תוס' ד"ה א"ה: רש"י ד"ה ושמים. חצי אמה על חצי אמה. עיין לעיל דף ד ע"א ברש"י ד"ה אלו הקרטות:

רבינו חננאל

והוציאו פטור שלא היתה עקירה משעה ראשונה לכך ואמרינן חיישינן דלמא בתר דמנח ליה הדר מעייל ליה וקא מעייל מרה"ר לרה"י. ת"ש גמל שראשו ורובו לפנים אובסין אותו בפנים והא איבוס כמאן דנקיט למנא [ונקיט לה] דמי. וקא בעי ראשו ורובו של גמל. ודחי ר' אלעזר שאני גמל הואיל וצוארו ארוך: תניא לא התירו פסי ביראות אלא לעולין לרגל ואוקימנא לבהמת עולי רגלים בלבד אבל אדם מטפס ויורד ושותה מטפס ועולה. פי' מטפס מסתרך מלשון שממית בידים תתפש והיא בהיכלי מלך ואם הבורות רחבין שאין יכולין לטפס ולירד אפילו לאדם נמי. פי' אם היו הבורות רחבות שאין אדם יכול לטפס ולירד מותר למלאות גם לאדם ולא ימלא אדם ויתן לפני בהמתו אבל ממלא הוא ושופך והיא שותה מאיליה ואקשינן א"כ מה הועיל ראשה ורובה של פרה ואוקמה אביי (באותו) [באיבום] העומד ברה"ר. איני והא אמרי משמיה דשמואל לא הותרו פסי ביראות אלא לבאר מים חיים בלבד. ואי לבהמה מים חיים למה לי ושנינן דלמא בעינן מידי דחזי לאדם. איכא דאמרי אמר רב יהודה בר אבא אמר רב אין בורגנין ולא פסי ביראות לא בבבל ולא בחוצה לארץ. פי' בורגנין כמין סוכות עשוין בשדות לאצור בהן תבואה ובמקום שמצוים בדיקי דמיא דמזמנין דסלקי ושטפי להו לא עבדי וכן אין חיישי משום גנבי לא שבקי פירי הלכך בורגנין בבבל דשכיחי בדיקי דמיא ובחוצה לארץ שכיחי גנבי לא עבדי בורגנין. פסי ביראות נמי בבבל שכיחי מיא בכל מקום ולא צריכי להשקות ממי הבארות ובחוצה לארץ נמי לא שכיחי מתיבתא ולא צריכי לפרקא במקום עולי רגלים. א"ל רב חסדא למרי בריה דרב הונא אמרי דקא אתיתו בשבת מברנש לבי כנישתא דדניאל ג' פרסי אמאי סמכיתו אבורגנין והאמר אבוה דאימך אין בורגנין בבבל כלומר אין תורת בורגנין בבבל. נפק אחוי ליה הנהו מתוותא. פי' כגון כפרים שסמוכין זה לזה בתוך ע' אמות ושירים וכאלו הללו תלתא פרסי חדא מדינה היא כיון דלית בינייהו יתר רחב משבעים אמה ושירים כדתנן וכן ג' כפרים המשולשים אם יש בין ב' החיצונים קמ"א אמה ושליש אמה עשה האמצעי את שלשתן להיות אחד: כתוב לכל תכלה ראיתי קץ רחבה מצותך מאד אמר דוד ולא פירשו וכן איוב וכן יחזקאל עד שבא זכריה בן עדו ופירשו ויאמר אלי מה אתה רואה ואומר אני רואה מגלה עפה ארכה עשרים באמה ורחבה עשרה באמה. פי' עפה כפולה כדמתרגמינן רבוע יהיה כפול ארבעה יהא עיף כי פשטת לה כמה הויא עשרים בעשרים והיא כתובה פנים ואחור כי קלפת להו משוית ליה לאחור בהדי פנים כמה הויא ארבעין בעשרין וכתיב שמים בזרת תכן נמצא העולם כולו זרת על זרת [שהן] ארבעין אמה בעשרין משתכח (בברייתא) [באורייתא] ת"ת אמה וכל אמתא אית בה ד' זרתות ב' זרתות אורך וב' זרתות רוחב. נמצא אורך המגילה שלשת אלפים ומאתים זרת ברוחב זרת וזו היא שיעור התורה נמצא שיעור העולם זרת והוא הג' אלפים ומאתים חלקים בתורה: הדוד האחד תאנים טובים מאד אלו צדיקים גמורים והתאנים הרעות רשעים גמורים כו':

הַבַּכּוּרוֹת וְהַדּוּד הָאֶחָד תְּאֵנִים רָעוֹת מְאֹד אֲשֶׁר לֹא תֵאָכַלְנָה מֵרוֹעַ". תְּאֵנִים הַטּוֹבוֹת — אֵלּוּ צַדִּיקִים גְּמוּרִים, תְּאֵנִים הָרָעוֹת — אֵלּוּ רְשָׁעִים גְּמוּרִים. וְשֶׁמָּא תֹּאמַר אָבַד סִבְרָם וּבָטַל סִיכּוּיָם — ת"ל: "הַדּוּדָאִים נָתְנוּ רֵיחַ", אֵלּוּ וָאֵלּוּ עֲתִידִין שֶׁיִּתְּנוּ רֵיחַ. דָּרַשׁ רָבָא: מַאי דִּכְתִיב: °"הַדּוּדָאִים נָתְנוּ רֵיחַ" — אֵלּוּ בַּחוּרֵי יִשְׂרָאֵל שֶׁלֹּא טָעֲמוּ טַעַם חֵטְא. "וְעַל פְּתָחֵינוּ כָּל מְגָדִים" — אֵלּוּ בְּנוֹת יִשְׂרָאֵל שֶׁמַּגִּידוֹת פִּתְחֵיהֶן לְבַעֲלֵיהֶן. ל"א: שֶׁאוֹגְדוֹת פִּתְחֵיהֶן לְבַעֲלֵיהֶן. "חֲדָשִׁים גַּם יְשָׁנִים דּוֹדִי צָפַנְתִּי לָךְ", אָמְרָה כְּנֶסֶת יִשְׂרָאֵל לִפְנֵי הקב"ה: רִבּוֹנוֹ שֶׁל עוֹלָם, הַרְבֵּה גְּזֵירוֹת גָּזַרְתִּי עַל עַצְמִי יוֹתֵר מִמַּה שֶּׁגָּזַרְתָּ עָלַי — וְקִיַּימְתִּים. א"ל רַב חִסְדָּא לְהַהוּא מִדְּרַבָּנַן דַּהֲוָה קָא מְסַדֵּר אַגָּדְתָא קַמֵּיהּ: מִי שְׁמִיעַ לָךְ "חֲדָשִׁים גַּם יְשָׁנִים" מַהוּ? אֲמַר לֵיהּ: אֵלּוּ מִצְוֹת קַלּוֹת וְאֵלּוּ מִצְוֹת חֲמוּרוֹת. א"ל: *וְכִי תּוֹרָה פְּעָמִים פְּעָמִים נִיתְּנָה? אֶלָּא הַלָּלוּ מִדִּבְרֵי תּוֹרָה, וְהַלָּלוּ מִדִּבְרֵי סוֹפְרִים. דָּרַשׁ רָבָא: מַאי דִּכְתִיב: °"וְיוֹתֵר מֵהֵמָּה בְּנִי הִזָּהֵר עֲשׂוֹת סְפָרִים הַרְבֵּה וגו'" — בְּנִי! הִזָּהֵר בְּדִבְרֵי סוֹפְרִים יוֹתֵר מִדִּבְרֵי תוֹרָה. שֶׁדִּבְרֵי תוֹרָה יֵשׁ בָּהֶן עֲשֵׂה וְלֹא תַעֲשֶׂה, וְדִבְרֵי סוֹפְרִים — *כָּל הָעוֹבֵר עַל דִּבְרֵי סוֹפְרִים חַיָּיב מִיתָה. שֶׁמָּא תֹּאמַר אִם יֵשׁ בָּהֶן מַמָּשׁ מִפְּנֵי מָה לֹא נִכְתְּבוּ — אָמַר קְרָא "עֲשׂוֹת סְפָרִים הַרְבֵּה אֵין קֵץ". °"וְלַהַג הַרְבֵּה יְגִיעַת בָּשָׂר". א"ר פָּפָּא בְּרֵיהּ דְּרַב אַחָא בַּר אַדָּא מִשְּׁמֵיהּ דְּרַב אַחָא בַּר עוּלָּא: מְלַמֵּד שֶׁכָּל הַמַּלְעִיג עַל דִּבְרֵי חֲכָמִים נִידּוֹן בְּצוֹאָה רוֹתַחַת. מַתְקִיף לָהּ רָבָא: מִי כְּתִיב "לַעַג"? "לַהַג" כְּתִיב! אֶלָּא: כָּל הַהוֹגֶה בָּהֶן טוֹעֵם טַעַם בָּשָׂר. תָּנוּ רַבָּנַן: מַעֲשֶׂה בְּר"ע שֶׁהָיָה חָבוּשׁ בְּבֵית הָאֲסוּרִין וְהָיָה ר' יְהוֹשֻׁעַ הַגַּרְסִי מְשָׁרְתוֹ. בְּכָל יוֹם וָיוֹם הָיוּ מַכְנִיסִין לוֹ מַיִם בְּמִדָּה. יוֹם אֶחָד מְצָאוֹ שׁוֹמֵר בֵּית הָאֲסוּרִין, אָמַר לוֹ: הַיּוֹם מֵימֶיךָ מְרוּבִּין, שֶׁמָּא לַחְתּוֹר בֵּית הָאֲסוּרִין אַתָּה צָרִיךְ! שָׁפַךְ חֶצְיָין, וְנָתַן לוֹ חֶצְיָין. כְּשֶׁבָּא אֵצֶל ר"ע, אָמַר לוֹ: יְהוֹשֻׁעַ, אֵין אַתָּה יוֹדֵעַ שֶׁזָּקֵן אֲנִי וְחַיַּי תְּלוּיִין בְּחַיֶּיךָ? סָח לוֹ כָּל אוֹתוֹ הַמְּאוֹרָע. אָמַר לוֹ: תֵּן לִי מַיִם שֶׁאֶטּוֹל יָדַי. אָמַר לוֹ: לִשְׁתּוֹת אֵין מַגִּיעִין, לִיטּוֹל יָדֶיךָ מַגִּיעִין?! אָמַר לוֹ: מָה אֶעֱשֶׂה שֶׁחַיָּיבִים עֲלֵיהֶן מִיתָה, מוּטָב אָמוּת מִיתַת עַצְמִי וְלֹא אֶעֱבוֹר עַל דַּעַת חֲבֵירַי. אָמְרוּ: לֹא טָעַם כְּלוּם עַד שֶׁהֵבִיא לוֹ מַיִם וְנָטַל יָדָיו. כְּשֶׁשָּׁמְעוּ חֲכָמִים בַּדָּבָר, אָמְרוּ: מָה בְּזִקְנוּתוֹ כָּךְ — בְּיַלְדוּתוֹ עַל אַחַת כַּמָּה וְכַמָּה. וּמָה בְּבֵית הָאֲסוּרִין כָּךְ — שֶׁלֹּא בְּבֵית הָאֲסוּרִין עַל אַחַת כַּמָּה וְכַמָּה. *אָמַר רַב יְהוּדָה, אָמַר שְׁמוּאֵל: בְּשָׁעָה שֶׁתִּיקֵּן שְׁלֹמֹה [א]עֵירוּבִין וּנְטִילַת יָדַיִם, יָצְתָה בַּת קוֹל וְאָמְרָה: °"בְּנִי אִם חָכַם לִבֶּךָ יִשְׂמַח לִבִּי גַם אָנִי", וְאוֹמֵר: °"חֲכַם בְּנִי וְשַׂמַּח לִבִּי וְאָשִׁיבָה חֹרְפִי דָבָר". דָּרַשׁ רָבָא: מַאי דִּכְתִיב: °"לְכָה דוֹדִי נֵצֵא הַשָּׂדֶה נָלִינָה בַּכְּפָרִים נַשְׁכִּימָה לַכְּרָמִים נִרְאֶה אִם פָּרְחָה הַגֶּפֶן פִּתַּח הַסְּמָדַר הֵנֵצוּ הָרִמּוֹנִים שָׁם אֶתֵּן אֶת דֹּדַי לָךְ". "לְכָה דוֹדִי נֵצֵא הַשָּׂדֶה" — אָמְרָה כְּנֶסֶת יִשְׂרָאֵל לִפְנֵי הקב"ה: רבש"ע, אַל תְּדִינֵנִי כְּיוֹשְׁבֵי כְרַכִּים שֶׁיֵּשׁ בָּהֶן גָּזֵל וַעֲרָיוֹת וּשְׁבוּעַת שָׁוְא וּשְׁבוּעַת שֶׁקֶר. "נֵצֵא הַשָּׂדֶה" — בֹּא וְאַרְאֲךָ תַּלְמִידֵי חֲכָמִים שֶׁעוֹסְקִין בַּתּוֹרָה מִתּוֹךְ הַדְּחָק. "נָלִינָה בַּכְּפָרִים" אַל תִּקְרִי "בַּכְּפָרִים" אֶלָּא "בַּכּוֹפְרִים" — בֹּא וְאַרְאֲךָ אוֹתָם שֶׁהִשְׁפַּעְתָּ לָהֶן טוֹבָה וְהֵן כָּפְרוּ בָּךְ. "נַשְׁכִּימָה לַכְּרָמִים" — אֵלּוּ בָּתֵּי כְנֵסִיּוֹת וּבָתֵּי מִדְרָשׁוֹת. "נִרְאֶה אִם פָּרְחָה הַגֶּפֶן" — אֵלּוּ בַּעֲלֵי מִקְרָא. "פִּתַּח הַסְּמָדַר" — אֵלּוּ בַּעֲלֵי מִשְׁנָה. "הֵנֵצוּ הָרִמּוֹנִים" — אֵלּוּ בַּעֲלֵי גְמָרָא. "שָׁם אֶתֵּן אֶת דֹּדַי לָךְ" — אַרְאֲךָ כְּבוֹדִי וְגוֹדְלִי, שֶׁבַח בָּנַי וּבְנוֹתַי. אָמַר רַב הַמְנוּנָא: מַאי דִּכְתִיב: °"וַיְדַבֵּר שְׁלֹשֶׁת אֲלָפִים מָשָׁל וַיְהִי שִׁירוֹ חֲמִשָּׁה וָאָלֶף" — מְלַמֵּד שֶׁאָמַר שְׁלֹמֹה עַל כָּל דָּבָר וְדָבָר שֶׁל תּוֹרָה שְׁלֹשֶׁת אֲלָפִים מָשָׁל, עַל כָּל דָּבָר וְדָבָר שֶׁל סוֹפְרִים חֲמִשָּׁה וָאֶלֶף טְעָמִים. דָּרַשׁ רָבָא: מַאי דִּכְתִיב: °"וְיוֹתֵר שֶׁהָיָה קֹהֶלֶת חָכָם עוֹד לִימַּד דַּעַת אֶת הָעָם [וְ]אִיזֵּן וְחִקֵּר תִּיקֵּן מְשָׁלִים הַרְבֵּה". "לִימַּד דַּעַת אֶת הָעָם" — דְּאַגְמְרֵיהּ בְּסִימָנֵי טְעָמִים, וְאַסְבְּרֵהּ בְּמַאי דְּדָמֵי לֵיהּ. "[וְ]אִיזֵּן וְחִקֵּר תִּיקֵּן מְשָׁלִים הַרְבֵּה" — *אָמַר עוּלָּא, אָמַר רַבִּי *אֱלִיעֶזֶר: בַּתְּחִילָּה הָיְתָה תוֹרָה דּוֹמָה *לִכְפִיפָה שֶׁאֵין לָהּ אָזְנַיִם, עַד שֶׁבָּא שְׁלֹמֹה וְעָשָׂה לָהּ אָזְנַיִם. "קְוֻצּוֹתָיו תַּלְתַּלִּים". אָמַר רַב חִסְדָּא, אָמַר מָר עוּקְבָא: מְלַמֵּד שֶׁיֵּשׁ לִדְרוֹשׁ עַל כָּל קוֹץ וָקוֹץ תִּילֵּי תִילִּים שֶׁל הֲלָכוֹת. "שְׁחוֹרוֹת כָּעוֹרֵב" — [ב]בְּמִי אַתָּה מוֹצְאָן — בְּמִי שֶׁמַּשְׁכִּים

רש"י

הַבַּכּוּרוֹת. תְּאֵנִים חֲשׁוּבוֹת הַמְמַהֲרוֹת לְהִתְבַּשֵּׁל: שֶׁאוֹגְדוֹת. קוֹשְׁרוֹת פִּתְחָן לְצוֹרֶךְ בַּעֲלֵיהֶן, שֶׁאֵין נִבְעָלוֹת לַאֲחֵרִים אוֹגְדוֹת לְשׁוֹן אֲגוּדָּה ל"א: שֶׁמַּגִּידוֹת פִּתְחֵיהֶן. כְּשֶׁרוֹאָה דָּם אוֹמֶרֶת לְבַעְלָהּ, וּפוֹרֵשׁ הֵימֶנָּה: חֲדָשִׁים. דִּבְרֵי סוֹפְרִים: גַּם יְשָׁנִים. דִּבְרֵי תוֹרָה: דּוֹדִי צָפַנְתִּי. וְשָׁמַרְתִּי כָּל אֵלֶּה לָךְ לִשְׁמָךְ: פְּעָמִים פְּעָמִים נִיתְּנָה. שֶׁתְּהֵא זוֹ חֲדָשָׁה וְזוֹ יְשָׁנָה: דִּבְרֵי סוֹפְרִים. חֲדָשִׁים, שֶׁנִּתְחַדְּשׁוּ בְּכָל דּוֹר וָדוֹר לִגְדּוֹר גָּדֵר וּסְיָיג: וְיוֹתֵר מֵהֵמָּה. לְעֵיל מִינֵּיהּ כְּתִיב "דִּבְרֵי חֲכָמִים כַּדָּרְבֹנוֹת" — אֵלּוּ דִּבְרֵי תוֹרָה שֶׁנִּמְסְרוּ לְמֹשֶׁה עַל פֶּה, שֶׁנֶּחְלְקוּ בָהֶן חַכְמֵי יִשְׂרָאֵל לְאַחַר שֶׁנִּתְמַעֵט הַלֵּב וְשָׁכְחוּ. כִּדְכְתִיב בְּסֵיפֵיהּ דִּקְרָא "נִתְּנוּ מֵרוֹעֶה אֶחָד" זֶה מֹשֶׁה. וּכְתִיב בַּתְרֵיהּ "וְיוֹתֵר מֵהֵמָּה בְּנִי הִזָּהֵר" מִמַּה שֶּׁנִּיתָּן בְּסִינַי בִּכְתָב, שֶׁהוּא עִיקָּר — בְּנִי הִזָּהֵר בְּאֵלּוּ שֶׁבְּעַל פֶּה, שֶׁגַּם הֵם עִיקָּר. אֶלָּא לְכָךְ לֹא נִכְתְּבוּ — שֶׁאֵין קֵץ לַעֲשׂוֹת סְפָרִים הַרְבֵּה בְּכָל אֵלֶּה: עֲשֵׂה וְלֹא תַעֲשֶׂה. יֵשׁ בָּהֶן שֶׁאֵין בָּהֶן חִיּוּב מִיתָה. אֲבָל דִּבְרֵי סוֹפְרִים — חַיָּיבִין מִיתָה עַל כּוּלָּן, כִּדְכְתִיב (קהלת י) "וּפוֹרֵץ גָּדֵר יִשְּׁכֶנּוּ נָחָשׁ": וְלַהַג הַרְבֵּה. הַמַּלְעִיג עֲלֵיהֶן — בִּיגִיעוֹת בָּשָׂר נִידּוֹן: כָּל הַהוֹגֶה בָּהֶן. בְּכָל שָׁעָה שֶׁאָדָם מְחַזֵּר בְּדִבְרֵי תוֹרָה מוֹצֵא בָּהֶן טַעַם: הַגַּרְסִי. שֵׁם מָקוֹם. ל"א: שֶׁהָיָה טוֹחֵן גְּרִיסִים: וְחַיַּי תְּלוּיִין בְּחַיֶּיךָ. שֶׁאֵין לִי אֶלָּא מַה שֶּׁאַתָּה נוֹתֵן וּמְזַמֵּן לִי: בְּיַלְדוּתוֹ. שֶׁהָיָה יָכוֹל לְקַבֵּל טוֹרַח וְעִינּוּי: שְׁלֹמֹה תִּיקֵּן עֵירוּבֵי חֲצֵירוֹת. וְגָזַר שֶׁלֹּא לְהוֹצִיא מֵרְשׁוּת הַיָּחִיד לִרְשׁוּת הַיָּחִיד חֲבֵירוֹ, לַעֲשׂוֹת סְיָיג וְהַרְחָקָה לְאִיסּוּר תּוֹרָה, שֶׁלֹּא יָבוֹא לְהַתִּיר מֵרְשׁוּת הָרַבִּים לִרְשׁוּת הַיָּחִיד. וְהַיְינוּ דִּכְתִיב "וְאִיזֵּן וְחִקֵּר תִּיקֵּן מְשָׁלִים" — שֶׁעָשָׂה אָזְנַיִם לַתּוֹרָה, כְּאָזְנֵי כְלִי שֶׁאוֹחֲזִין אוֹתוֹ בָּם: וְיָדַיִם. נְטִילַת יָדַיִם, לַעֲשׂוֹת סְיָיג לִטְהָרוֹת: כְּרַכִּים. מְקוֹם שְׁוָוקִים הֵן, וְיִשּׁוּב גָּדוֹל, וְרֶגֶל רוֹכְלִין וְסוֹחֲרִין מְצוּיָה שָׁם — לְפִיכָךְ גָּזֵל וַעֲרָיוֹת נוֹהֵג בָּהֶן: הַשָּׂדֶה. בְּנֵי (א)בָגָא וְעוֹבֵד אֲדָמָה, וְעוֹסְקִין בַּתּוֹרָה מִתּוֹךְ דּוֹחַק: סְמָדַר. גָּדוֹל מִפֶּרַח, כָּךְ מִשְׁנָה מְפוֹרֶשֶׁת יוֹתֵר מִן הַמִּקְרָא: הֵנֵצוּ הָרִמּוֹנִים. גָּדְלוּ כָּל צָרְכָּן, וּכְבָר הַנֵּץ גָּדַל סְבִיבוֹתָיו, כְּעֵין שׁוֹמֵר שֶׁיֵּשׁ לֶאֱגוֹזִים קְטַנִּים: מָשָׁל. טַעַם: אַגְמְרֵיהּ בְּסִימָנֵי טְעָמִים. קָבַע לָהּ מָסוֹרֶת וְסִימָנִין, בֵּין בִּתֵיבוֹת הַמִּקְרָא בֵּין בְּגִירְסָא שֶׁל מִשְׁנָה: וְעָשָׂה לָהּ אָזְנַיִם. שֶׁתִּיקֵּן עֵירוּבִין וְיָדַיִם, וְגָזַר עַל הַשְּׁנִיּוֹת לַעֲרָיוֹת כִּדְמְפָרֵשׁ בִּיבָמוֹת (כא.). וְע"י כָּךְ אוֹחֲזִין יִשְׂרָאֵל בַּמִּצְוֹת, שֶׁנִּתְרַחֲקוּ מִן הָעֲבֵירָה כְּדֶרֶךְ שֶׁנּוֹחַ לֶאֱחוֹז בִּכְלִי שֶׁיֵּשׁ לוֹ בֵּית יָד מִשֶּׁאֵין לוֹ: שֶׁמַּשְׁכִּים

תוספות

מפני מה לא נכתבו.[א] * וגם בהלכה למשה מסיני לא נתנו, כדי שלא ישתכחו.

מוטב אמות מיתת עצמי. אף על גב דבפ' קמא (ד' יז.) אמר: ארבעה דברים פטורין במחנה, רחילת ידים. וכל שכן במקום סכנה — מחמיר על עצמו היה:

בשעה שתיקן שלמה עירובין ונטילת ידים. אף על גב דתיקן נמי שניות, כדאמר בפרק שני דיבמות (ד' כא.), הא דלא חשיב הכא — משום דלאו בבת אחת תיקן, ואחר בת קול תיקן. ומדכתיב: "איזן וחקר תיקן משלים הרבה" — משמע נמי שהרבה תקנות עשה: אלך

עין משפט נר מצוה

יח א מיי' פ"א מהל' עירובין הל' ב סמג עשין א:

יט ב מיי' פ"ג מהלכות ת"ת הל' יב טוש"ע י"ד סי' רמו סעיף כא:

[עי' שו"ת חות יאיר סי' קלב כוונת תוס' בזה]

רבינו חננאל

חדשים גם ישנים דודי צפנתי לך הן דברי תורה ודברי סופרים. בני הזהר עשות ספרים. פי' הזהר בדברי סופרים [יותר] מד"ת. שדברי תורה עשה ולא תעשה ודברי סופרים העובר על דברי חכמי' חייב מיתה. כדתנן [ברכות י"א] אמרו לו לר' טרפון כדיי היית לחוב בעצמך שעברת על דברי בית הלל וכל המלעיג על דברי חכמים נידון בצואה רותחת: ת"ר מעשה בר' עקיבא שהיה חבוש בבית האסורים ולא מצא מים ליטול ידיו ואמר מה אעשה העובר על דברי חכמים חייב מיתה אמר מוטב לי שאמות מיתת עצמי ואל אעבור על דעת חבירי כו'. בשעה שתיקן שלמה עירובין וגזר טומאה על הידים כדמפרש בתחלת שבת. יצתה בת קול ואמרה לו בני אם חכם לבך ישמח לבי גם אני [ואומר] חכם בני שמח לבי ואשיבה חורפי דבר. נשכימה לכרמים אלו [בתי] כנסיות ומקדש. נראה אם פרחה הגפן אלו בעלי מקרא. פתח הסמדר אלו בעלי משנה הנצו הרמונים אלו בעלי התלמוד. על כל דבר ודבר של תורה אמר ג' אלפים משל ועל כל דבר ודבר של סופרים אמר ג' אלפים *) טעמים שנאמר ויהי שירו חמשה ואלף. קווצותיו תלתלים שחורות כעורב במי אתה מוצא תלי תלים של הלכות במי

*) [אולי ט"ס הוא וצ"ל חמשה ואלף כמו דאיתא לפנינו בגמ']

גליון הש"ס

תום' ד"ה מפני. לא נתנו כדי שלא ישתכחו. עיין תשובת חו"י סי' לב:

הגהות מהר"ב רנשבורג

[א] תום' ד"ה מפני וכו' וגם בהל"מ לא נתנו כדי שלא ישתכחו. עי' יבמות דף עז ע"ב תום' ד"ה הלכה ובשו"ת חו"י סימן קל"ב ובשו"ת חוט השני סי' נג:

הגהות הב"ח

(א) רש"י ד"ה השדה בני בגא ועובדי:

מסורת הש"ס: [חולין קא:] · ברכות ז: · יבמות כא. · ס"א לקופה · [נ"ל אלעזר]

שיר ז · קהלת יב · שם · משלי כג · שם כז · שיר ז · מלכים א ד · קהלת יב

שֶׁמַּשְׁכִּים וּמַעֲרִיב עֲלֵיהֶן לְבֵית הַמִּדְרָשׁ. רַבָּה אָמַר: בְּמִי שֶׁמַּשְׁחִיר פָּנָיו עֲלֵיהֶן כְּעוֹרֵב. רָבָא אָמַר: בְּמִי שֶׁמֵּשִׂים עַצְמוֹ אַכְזָרִי עַל בָּנָיו וְעַל בְּנֵי בֵיתוֹ כָּעוֹרֵב. כִּי הָא דְּרַב אַדָּא בַּר מַתְנָא הֲוָה קָאָזֵיל לְבֵי רַב, אֲמַרָה לֵיהּ דְּבֵיתְהוּ: יְנוּקֵי דִידָךְ מַאי אַעֲבֵיד לְהוּ? אָמַר לָהּ: מִי שְׁלִימוּ קוּרְמֵי בְּאַגְמָא? °"וּמְשַׁלֵּם לְשׂוֹנְאָיו אֶל פָּנָיו לְהַאֲבִידוֹ", א"ר יְהוֹשֻׁעַ בֶּן לֵוִי: אִילְמָלֵא מִקְרָא כָּתוּב אִי אֶפְשָׁר לְאוֹמְרוֹ, *כִּבְיָכוֹל כְּאָדָם שֶׁנּוֹשֵׂא מַשּׂוֹי עַל פָּנָיו וּמְבַקֵּשׁ לְהַשְׁלִיכוֹ מִמֶּנּוּ. "לֹא יְאַחֵר לְשׂוֹנְאוֹ", א"ר אִילָא: לְשׂוֹנְאָיו הוּא דְּלֹא יְאַחֵר, אֲבָל יְאַחֵר לְצַדִּיקִים גְּמוּרִים. וְהַיְינוּ *דְּא"ר יְהוֹשֻׁעַ בֶּן לֵוִי: מַאי דִּכְתִיב: °"אֲשֶׁר אָנֹכִי מְצַוְּךָ הַיּוֹם לַעֲשׂוֹתָם", הַיּוֹם לַעֲשׂוֹתָם — וְלֹא לְמָחָר לַעֲשׂוֹתָם, הַיּוֹם לַעֲשׂוֹתָם — לְמָחָר לְקַבֵּל שְׂכָרָם. *א"ר חַגַּי, וְאִיתֵימָא ר' שְׁמוּאֵל בַּר נַחְמָנִי: מַאי דִּכְתִיב: °"אֶרֶךְ אַפַּיִם" אֶרֶךְ אַף מִבָּעֵי לֵיהּ! אֶלָּא: אֶרֶךְ אַפַּיִם לַצַּדִּיקִים, אֶרֶךְ אַפַּיִם לָרְשָׁעִים.§ "רַבִּי יְהוּדָה אוֹמֵר: עַד בֵּית סָאתַיִם וכו'".§ אִיבַּעְיָא לְהוּ: בּוֹר וּפַסִּין קָאָמַר אוֹ דִילְמָא בּוֹר וְלֹא פַּסִּין קָאָמַר? אָדָם נוֹתֵן עֵינָיו בְּבוֹרוֹ, וְלָא גָּזְרִינַן דִּילְמָא אָתֵי לְטַלְטוֹלֵי יוֹתֵר מִבֵּית סָאתַיִם בְּקַרְפֵּף. אוֹ דִילְמָא: אָדָם נוֹתֵן עֵינָיו בִּמְחִיצָּתוֹ, וְגָזְרִינַן דִּילְמָא אָתֵי לְאִיחַלּוּפֵי יוֹתֵר מִבֵּית סָאתַיִם בְּקַרְפֵּף! ת"ש: כַּמָּה הֵן מְקוֹרָבִין — כְּדֵי רֹאשָׁהּ וְרוּבָּהּ שֶׁל פָּרָה. וְכַמָּה הֵן מְרוּחָקִין — אֲפִי' כּוֹר, אֲפִי' כּוֹרַיִים. ר' יְהוּדָה אוֹמֵר: בֵּית סָאתַיִם — מוּתָּר, יָתֵר מִבֵּית סָאתַיִם — אָסוּר. אָמְרוּ לְרַבִּי יְהוּדָה: אִי אַתָּה מוֹדֶה בְּדִיר וְסַהַר מוּקְצֶה וְחָצֵר אֲפִילּוּ בֵּית חֲמֵשֶׁת כּוֹרִים וּבֵית עֲשֶׂרֶת כּוֹרִים שֶׁמּוּתָּר? אָמַר לָהֶם: זוֹ מְחִיצָּה, וְאֵלּוּ פַּסִּין. ר"ש בֶּן אֶלְעָזָר אוֹמֵר: בּוֹר בֵּית סָאתַיִם אַבֵּית סָאתַיִם — מוּתָּר, וְלֹא אָמְרוּ לְהַרְחִיק אֶלָּא כְּדֵי רֹאשָׁהּ וְרוּבָּהּ שֶׁל פָּרָה. הָא מִדְּקָאָמַר ר"ש בֶּן אֶלְעָזָר בּוֹר וְלֹא פַּסִּין — מִכְּלָל דְּרַבִּי יְהוּדָה בּוֹר וּפַסִּין קָאָמַר! וְלֹא הִיא, ר' יְהוּדָה בּוֹר בְּלֹא פַּסִּין קָאָמַר. אִי הָכִי, הַיְינוּ דְּר' שִׁמְעוֹן בֶּן אֶלְעָזָר! אִיכָּא בֵּינַיְיהוּ אָרִיךְ וְקַטִּין. כְּלָל אָמַר רַבִּי שִׁמְעוֹן בֶּן אֶלְעָזָר: [א]כָּל אֲוִיר שֶׁתַּשְׁמִישׁוֹ לְדִירָה, כְּגוֹן דִּיר וְסַהַר מוּקְצֶה וְחָצֵר, אֲפִילּוּ בֵּית חֲמֵשֶׁת כּוֹרִים וּבֵית עֲשֶׂרֶת כּוֹרִים — מוּתָּר. °וְכָל דִּירָה שֶׁתַּשְׁמִישָׁהּ לָאֲוִיר, כְּגוֹן בּוּרְגָּנִין שֶׁבַּשָּׂדוֹת, בֵּית סָאתַיִם — מוּתָּר, יָתֵר מִבֵּית סָאתַיִם — אָסוּר.§ מתני' *ר' יְהוּדָה אוֹמֵר: אִם הָיָה דֶּרֶךְ רְשׁוּת הָרַבִּים מַפְסַקְתָּן — יְסַלְּקֶנָּה לַצְּדָדִין. וַחֲכָמִים אוֹמְרִים: [ב]אֵינוֹ צָרִיךְ.§ גמ' רַבִּי יוֹחָנָן וְר' אֶלְעָזָר דְּאָמְרִי תַּרְוַיְיהוּ: כָּאן הוֹדִיעֲךָ כּוֹחָן שֶׁל מְחִיצוֹת. כָּאן וּסְבִירָא לֵיהּ! *וְהָאָמַר רַבָּה בַּר בַּר חָנָה, א"ר יוֹחָנָן: יְרוּשָׁלַיִם אִילְמָלֵא דַּלְתוֹתֶיהָ נִנְעָלוֹת בַּלַּיְלָה חַיָּיבִין עָלֶיהָ מִשּׁוּם רְשׁוּת הָרַבִּים! אֶלָּא: כָּאן וְלָא ס"ל. וְרָמֵי דְּר' יְהוּדָה אַדְּר' יְהוּדָה, וְרָמֵי דְּרַבָּנַן אַדְּרַבָּנַן. *דְּתַנְיָא: יָתֵר עַל כֵּן א"ר יְהוּדָה: מִי שֶׁהָיוּ לוֹ שְׁנֵי בָתִּים מִשְּׁנֵי צִידֵּי רְשׁוּת הָרַבִּים — עוֹשֶׂה לוֹ לֶחִי מִכָּאן וְלֶחִי מִכָּאן, אוֹ קוֹרָה מִכָּאן וְקוֹרָה מִכָּאן, וְנוֹשֵׂא וְנוֹתֵן בָּאֶמְצַע. אָמְרוּ לוֹ: אֵין מְעָרְבִין רְשׁוּת הָרַבִּים בְּכָךְ. קַשְׁיָא דְּר' יְהוּדָה אַדְּרַבִּי יְהוּדָה, קַשְׁיָא דְּרַבָּנַן אַדְּרַבָּנַן! דְּר' יְהוּדָה אַדְּרַבִּי יְהוּדָה לָא קַשְׁיָא, הָתָם: דְּאִיכָּא שְׁתֵּי מְחִיצוֹת מַעַלְיָיתָא, הָכָא — לֵיכָּא שְׁתֵּי מְחִיצוֹת מַעַלְיָיתָא. דְּרַבָּנַן אַדְּרַבָּנַן [נַמִי] לָא קַשְׁיָא: הָכָא — אִיכָּא שֵׁם אַרְבַּע מְחִיצוֹת, הָתָם — לֵיכָּא שֵׁם ד' מְחִיצוֹת. א"ר יִצְחָק בַּר יוֹסֵף א"ר יוֹחָנָן: אֶרֶץ יִשְׂרָאֵל אֵין חַיָּיבִין עָלֶיהָ מִשּׁוּם רה"ר. יְתֵיב רַב דִּימִי וְקָאָמַר לֵיהּ לְהָא שְׁמַעְתָּא. א"ל אַבַּיֵי לְרַב דִּימִי: מ"ט? אִילֵימָא

שֶׁמַּשְׁכִּים וּמַעֲרִיב. "שְׁחוֹרוֹת" – לְשׁוֹן שַׁחֲרִית, "כָּעוֹרֵב" – לְשׁוֹן עַרְבִית: עוֹרֵב אַכְזָרִי עַל בָּנָיו כִּדְכְתִיב (תהלים קמז) "לִבְנֵי עוֹרֵב אֲשֶׁר יִקְרָאוּ", וְהקב"ה מְזַמֵּן לָהֶן יַתּוּשִׁים וְנִכְנָסִין לְתוֹךְ פִּיהֶן: קוּרְמֵי. יְרָקוֹת, לִישָּׁנָא אַחֲרִינָא: (א) גַּמֵּי לַח. כִּי עָקְרַתְּ לְהַהוּא רַכִּיכָא דְּאִית בֵּיהּ וְטַחֲנֵי לֵיהּ וְעָבְדֵי רִיפְתָּא, בְּחָלָ"ף בֵּי"ת דְּר' מָכִיר מְלָאכְתִּיו: אֶל פָּנָיו. שֶׁל הקב"ה, וְדוֹמֶה לוֹ כְּמַשּׂאוֹי לְפָנָיו: וְלֹא לְמָחָר לַעֲשׂוֹתָם. שֶׁלְּאַחַר מִיתָה לֶעָתִיד לָבוֹא, אִם בָּא לְקַיֵּים מִצְוֹת – אֵינוֹ מוֹעִיל. דְּמִי שֶׁטָּרַח בְּעֶרֶב שַׁבָּת – יֹאכַל בְּשַׁבָּת, כִּדְאָמַר בְּמַסֶּ' ע"ז*: אַפַּיִם. מַשְׁמַע: פָּנִים, בֵּין שׂוֹחֲקוֹת בֵּין זְעוּמוֹת, אַפַּיִם שׂוֹחֲקוֹת מַאֲרִיךְ וּמְאַחֵר לַצַּדִּיקִים לֶעָתִיד לָבֹא, וְאַפַּיִם זְעוּמוֹת מַאֲרִיךְ לָרְשָׁעִים, וּמְאַחֵר פּוּרְעָנוּתָם לָעוֹה"ב: בּוֹר וּפַסִּין. רוֹחַב הַבּוֹר עִם חֲלַל הֶיקֵּף הַפַּסִּין הַרְחוֹקִין שְׁתֵּי אַמּוֹת: אוֹ דִילְמָא בּוֹר. לְחוֹדֵיהּ שָׁרֵי בְּבֵית סָאתַיִם, לְבַד הַרְחָקַת ב' אַמּוֹת: אָדָם נוֹתֵן עֵינָיו בְּבוֹרוֹ. וְאִם בָּא לִלְמוֹד מִכָּאן הֶיתֵּר לְמָקוֹם אַחֵר – מִן הַבּוֹר הוּא לָמֵד, וַהֲרֵי אֵינוֹ אֶלָּא בֵּית סָאתַיִם, הִלְכָּךְ, אע"פ שֶׁהוּקַּף יוֹתֵר עַל כֵּן – לָא אָתוּ לְמִישְׁרֵי קַרְפֵּף יוֹתֵר מִבֵּית סָאתַיִם דְּעָלְמָא, שֶׁלֹּא הוּקַּף לְדִירָה: אוֹ דִילְמָא בִּמְחִיצָּתוֹ אָדָם נוֹתֵן עֵינָיו. וְאִם בָּא לִלְמוֹד מִכָּאן הֶיתֵּר לְמָקוֹם אַחֵר – מִן הַמְּחִיצָּה יִלְמוֹד, הִלְכָּךְ, אָתֵי לְמִישְׁרֵי בְּעָלְמָא יוֹתֵר מִבֵּית סָאתַיִם, אִי שָׁרֵית הָכָא: לֹא אָמְרוּ לְהַרְחִיק. הַהֶיקֵּף לְבַד בֵּית סָאתַיִם שֶׁל רוֹחַב הַבּוֹר, אֶלָּא שְׁתֵּי אַמּוֹת: אָרִיךְ וְקַטִּין. ק' עַל נ' דְּהָווּ סָאתַיִם כַּחֲצַר הַמִּשְׁכָּן לְר' יְהוּדָה, אע"פ שֶׁאֵינוֹ מְרוּבָּע – מוּתָּר, וּבִלְבַד שֶׁלֹּא יְהֵא בֵּין אָרְכּוֹ וְרָחְבּוֹ יוֹתֵר מִבֵּית סָאתַיִם. וּלְר"ש בָּעֵינַן מְרוּבָּע, כִּדְאָמַר בְּהֶדְיָא: בֵּית סָאתַיִם עַל בֵּית סָאתַיִם, דְּהָוֵי שִׁבְעִים אַמָּה וְשִׁירַיִים עַל שִׁבְעִים אַמָּה וְשִׁירַיִים, כִּדְאָמַר בְּהַאי פִּירְקִין (ד' כג.) קָטִין = קָצָר בְּרָחְבּוֹ: כָּל אֲוִיר. אַף עַל פִּי שֶׁאֵינוֹ מְקוֹרֶה, אִם תַּשְׁמִישׁוֹ לְדִירַת אָדָם לִכְנִיסָה וִיצִיאָה תָּמִיד: וְכָל דִּירָה. שֶׁהִיא מְכוּסָּה בְּגַג, וְהִיא עֲשׂוּיָה לִשְׁמִירַת אֲוִיר שֶׁחוּצָה לָהּ: מתני': גמ' חַיָּיבִין עָלֶיהָ. אַלְמָא: אָתוּ רַבִּים וּמְבַטְּלֵי מְחִיצָּה: הָכָא אִיכָּא שֵׁם ד' מְחִיצוֹת. שֶׁיֵּשׁ שְׁתֵּי אַמּוֹת (ב) הֶיכֵר הֶיקֵּף דּוֹפֶן לְכָל רוּחַ: *סוּלָּמָא דְּצוֹר. סֶלַע הַר גָּבוֹהַּ סָבִיב לַעֲלוֹת

אֶרֶךְ אפים לצדיקים ולרשעים. אפים שוחקות מאריך לצדיקים עד לעתיד, וזעומות לרשעים. ומאחר פורענותם עד לעולם הבא, וגם זה לטובה – שיש להם שהות לחזור בתשובה כדמשמע ב"חלק" (סנהדרין ד' קיא.) דהוי נמי לטובה [ע' תוס' ב"ק נ. ד"ה ארך].

אוֹ דלמא בור בלא פסין קאמר. פירוש ופסין לא יהו מרוחקין מן הבור אלא כדי ראשה ורובה של פרה. אבל אין לפרש דפסין נמי, אי בעי מרחיק עד בית סאתים, מדקאמרי' בסמוך: אי הכי – מאי בינייהו? בין לר"ש בין לר' יהודה. ולפי זה טובא איכא בינייהו, דר' שמעון לא שרי(ג) אלא להרחיק כדי ראשה ורובה של פרה, ור' יהודה מתיר עד בית סאתים! אלא ודאי גם ר' יהודה לא שרי להרחיק אלא כדי ראשה ורובה של פרה, אע"ג דאדם נותן עיניו בבורו ולא במחיצה – אין להתיר יותר:

בּוֹר ופסין קאמר. והא דאמר בפרקין (ד' כה.) קרפף יותר מבית סאתים ובנה(ד) עמוד גבוה י' ורחב ד' מיעטו, ה"נ האי בור למה לא הוי מיעוט? וי"ל: דהתם במחילות טובות, אבל בפסין – לא התירו בין הכל אלא בית סאתים:

וְהָא א"ר יוחנן ירושלים אלמלא דלתותיה. ואם תאמר: שאני ירושלים דהוה רחבה שש עשרה אמות, ופסין ליכא אלא י"ג ושליש! וי"ל: הואיל והיה לירושלים צורת הפתח, דחשיב כמחילה, כדאמר בפ"ק (ד' יא.): ואם יש לו צורת הפתח – א"צ למעט, לא היה לרבים דבקעי לבטל המחילה. ואפילו לרב דאתנייה "צריך למעט", מודה הוא דמן התורה מהני. תדע, דהא פיאה מתרת בכלאים אפילו יותר מעשר. ולפי פירוש אחר דפירשתי (ד' ו.) גבי יתר(ה) על כן – ניחא:

חַיָּיבִין עליה משום רשות הרבים. וא"ת: כיון דמסקינן דרבי יוחנן סבר ליה כרבי יהודה, אמאי חייבין עליה משום רשות הרבים? הא אית ליה שתי מחילות דאורייתא! וי"ל: דירושלים היתה מפולשת מארבע לצדדין, וחייבין עליה משום רה"ר לעומד באמצע הפילוש דליכא מחילה:

קַשְׁיָא דרבי יהודה אדר' יהודה. קא סלקא דעתיה דמקשה דלרבי יהודה שלש מחילות דאורייתא, ולחי וקורה משום מחילה, אלמא לא אתו רבים ומבטלו מחילה! דאי שתי מחילות דאורייתא – לא הוה פריך מידי. ומשני: קסבר שתי מחילות דאורייתא. אי נמי: אפילו קסבר שלש מחילות דאורייתא – לא אתו רבים ומבטלי מחילה שלישית, כיון דאיכא שתי מחילות שלימות:

דְּרַבָּנַן אדרבנן נמי לא קשיא. הוה מצי לשנויי דרבנן לא פליגי אדרבי יהודה אלא מדרבנן, אבל מדאורייתא – מודו ליה:

אילימא

עין משפט נר מצוה

כ א מיי' פט"ז מהל' שבת הל' ד' וה' סמג לאוין סה טור ש"ע א"ח סי' שנח סעיף א:

כא ב מיי' פי"ז מהל' שבת הלכה לג:

רבינו חננאל

שמשכימין ומעריבין עליהן בבהמ"ד רבה אמר במי שמשחירין פניהם כעורב. רבא אמר במי שמתאכזר על בניו כעורב. כדרב אדא בר אהבה דכד הוה אזיל בי רב הוה אמרה ליה דביתהו ינוקי מאי אעביד להו הוה אמר לה איכא קראי באגמא. פי' ירקות שדה באגם יאכלו מהם. אשר אנכי מצוך [היום היום לעשותם] ולא היום לקבל שכרם כו'. ארך אפים לצדיקים ולרשעים כו': **מתני'** ר' יהודה אומר עד בית סאתים כו' איבעיא להו ר' יהודה בור ופסין קאמר או דלמא בור בית סאתים זולתי פסין קאמר אדם עיניו בבורו ולא גזר דלמא אתי לטלטולי בקרפף דעלמא יתר מבית סאתים או דלמא עיניו במחיצתו שהן הפסין וכיון שהן יתר מבית סאתים גזר פסין אטו קרפף מאי. ת"ש כמה הן מקורבין כדי ראשה ורובה של פרה. וכמה יהא רחוקין מן הבאר אפי' כוריים מותר כו'. ר' יהודה אומר בית סאתים מותר כו' ר' שמעון בן אלעזר אומר באר שהוא בית סאתים אינו מותר להרחיק מן באר אלא כדי ראשה ורובה של פרה מדתני ר' שמעון בן אלעזר אומר בור בית סאתים על בית סאתים מכלל דר' יהודה באר ופסין בית סאתים קאמר. ודחינן לא ר' יהודה נמי בור בלא פסין קאמר ובבור ארוך וצר פליגי ר' שמעון בן אלעזר בעי ארכו כרחבו ור' יהודה לא חייש כלל אמר ר' שמעון בן אלעזר כל אויר שתשמישה לבית דירה כגון דיר וסהר ומוקצה וחצר אפילו עשרת כורים מותר. פי' דיר כדתנן הכונס צאן לדיר ותנן בענין מעשר בהמה כונסן לדיר סהר כגון רחבה שעושין אחורי העיירות ומקיפין אותה להכנים פירות וכיוצא בהן עראי. מוקצה מקום גבוה הוא שנעשה מוקצה מן רה"ר ומן הכרמלית והללו יש בהן ריוח כמו הבקעה כדתנן הוליכוהו לעיר אחרת ונתנוהו בדיר או בסהר ואמרינן גזירה הילוך דדיר וסהר אטו הילוך דבקעה. קרפף הוא כעין כתלים בלא קירוי והיא נקראת אילוסא של חצר *) וכל שתשמישה לאויר כגון בורגנין [בית סאתים מותר] יתר מבית סאתים אסור זו פשוטה היא: **מתני'** ר' יהודה אומר אם היה דרך הרבים מפסקתה יסלקנה לצדדין. וחכמים אומרים אינו צריך. ר' יוחנן ור' אלעזר דאמרי תרווייהו כאן הודיע כחן של מחיצות שאע"פ שמפסיקין אותן העוברים והשבים כמו רה"ר שיש שם מחיצות נעשה כרה"י ומקשינן ר' יוחנן אמר כאן וסבירא ליה והאמר רבה בר בר חנה אמר ר' יוחנן ירושלים אלמלי דלתותיה ננעלות בלילה חייבין עליה משום רה"ר והנה ירושלים הרי היא מוקפת חומה שהיא חומה מעליא. וא"ר יוחנן אילולי שדלתותיה ננעלות בלילה ואין מפסיקין בה משום כך היא כרשות היחיד אבל אילו לא היו דלתותיה ננעלות כיון שמפסיקין אותה דרך הרבים כרשות הרבים היא ותורת רשות הרבים בה ומחיצותיה אינן מועילות בה אלא כאן ולא סבירא ליה. בכאן הנוסחאות מתחלפות. אמר ר' יוחנן ארץ ישראל אין חייבין עליה משום רשות הרבים אמר ליה רב דימי מאי טעמא אי

*) אולי כוונתו לל' הש"ס דב"ב דף ס"ז המוכר את החצר לא מכר אלא מילוסא של חצר ואפשר דרבינו גרס שם אילוסא באל"ף:

מסורת הש"ס

[דף ג.]

[עי' פי' רש"י חגיגה יג: וביומא ג: ובמגילה כח.]

ע"א ג. ד:

ב"ק נ. ע"ש

דברים ז

שם

שמות לד

שבת ו: [לעיל כ.]

לעיל ו. ולקמן קא.

שבת ו. קיז. לעיל ו. יב: לקמן נט: ודף לה.

לע"ב

הגהות הב"ח

(א) רש"י ד"ה קורמי ירקות לישנא אחרינא קורמא גמי לח: (ב) ד"ה הכא איכא וכו' שתי אמות היקף כצ"ל ותיבת היכר נמחק: (ג) תום' ד"ה או דילמא וכו' לא שרי להרחיק אלא כדי ראשה: (ד) ד"ה בור וכו' ובנה בו עמוד גבוה י' ורחב ד' ומיעטו הוי מיעוט והכא נמי האי: (ה) ד"ה והא אמר וכו' גבי יותר. נ"ב דף ו ע"ב בד"ה וכי תימא:

גליון הש"ס

גמ' וכל דירה שתשמישה לאויר. לעיל דף טו ע"א ועי' ברכות דף כה ע"ב וברבינו יונה: **תום'** ד"ה והא"ר כו'. דאתנייה צריך למעט מודה הוא דמן התורה מהני. ע"ל דף ו ע"א תד"ה רב אמר:

רב נסים גאון

רבא אמר במי שמתאכזר על בניו כעורב. עיקר דיליה מהא דכתיב (תהלים קמז) ולבני עורב אשר יקראו וזה הדבר ידוע הוא כי העורב יטוש את אפרוחיו כל זמן שעדיין לא העלו אברה ולאחר שתעלה עליהן אברה והן משחירין הוא חוזר אליהן וכתיב נמי (איוב לח) מי יכין לעורב צידו ובכתובות בפרק נערה שנתפתתה הקשו (דף מט) ועורבא בעי בניה והכתיב לבני עורב אשר יקראו לא קשיא הא בחוורי והא באוכמי:

והא

כב א מיי' פי"ד מהל' שבת הלכה ד סמג לאוין סה טוש"ע א"ח סי' שמה סעיף יד:
כג ב מיי' פי"ב מהל' שאר אבות הטומאות הלכה ג:
כד ג מיי' פי"ז מהל' שבת הלכה לג:
כה ד מיי' שם הל' לח:

אילימא משום דמקיף לה סולמא דצור מהך גיסא ומחתנא דגדר מהך גיסא – בבל נמי מקיף לה פרת מהך גיסא ודיגלת מהאי גיסא. דכולא עלמא נמי מקיף אוקיינוס! דילמא מעלות ומורדות קאמרת?! א"ל: *קרקפנא חזיתיה לרישך בי עמודי כי א"ר יוחנן להא שמעתא. איתמר נמי, כי אתא רבין א"ר יוחנן, ואמרי לה א"ר אבהו, א"ר יוחנן: [א]מעלות ומורדות שבארץ ישראל אין חייבין עליהן משום רה"ר, לפי שאינן כדגלי מדבר. בעא מיניה רחבה מרבא: תל המתלקט עשרה מתוך ארבע, ורבים בוקעין בו, חייבין עליו משום רה"ר או אין חייבין עליו? אליבא דרבנן לא תיבעי לך, השתא ומה התם דניחא תשמישתיה, אמרי רבנן לא אתו רבים ומבטלי לה מחיצתא, הכא דלא ניחא תשמישתיה – לא כל שכן. כי תיבעי לך אליבא דר' יהודה, מאי? התם הוא דניחא תשמישתיה, הכא הוא דלא ניחא תשמישתיה – לא אתו רבים ומבטלי מחיצתא, או דילמא לא שנא? א"ל: חייבין. ואפי' עולין לו בחבל? א"ל: אין. ואפילו במעלות בית מרון? א"ל: אין. איתיביה: *חצר שהרבים נכנסין לה בזו ויוצאין(א) בזו – רה"ר לטומאה ורשות היחיד לשבת. מני? אילימא רבנן – השתא ומה התם דניחא תשמישתיה אמרי רבנן לא אתו רבים ומבטלי מחיצתא, הכא דלא ניחא תשמישתיה – לא כ"ש! אלא לאו – ר' יהודה היא! לא, לעולם רבנן, ורה"ר לטומאה איצטריכא ליה. ת"ש: *מבואות המפולשות בבורות בשיחין ובמערות רשות היחיד לשבת, [ב]ורשות הרבים לטומאה. בבורות סלקא דעתך?! אלא: לבורות. רשות היחיד לשבת ורשות הרבים לטומאה. מני? אילימא רבנן – השתא ומה התם דניחא תשמישתיה – אמרי לא אתו רבים ומבטלי לה, הכא דלא ניחא תשמישתיה לא כ"ש? אלא לאו ר' יהודה היא! לא, לעולם רבנן, ורה"ר לטומאה איצטריכא ליה. ת"ש: *שבילי בית גילגול וכיוצא בהן רשות היחיד לשבת, ורה"ר לטומאה. ואיזהו שבילי בית גילגול? אמרי דבי ר' ינאי: כל שאין העבד יכול ליטול סאה של חיטין וירוץ לפני סרדיוט. מני? אילימא רבנן – השתא ומה התם דניחא תשמישתא אמרי רבנן לא אתו רבים ומבטלי לה מחיצתא, הכא דלא ניחא תשמישתא לא כל שכן? אלא לאו רבי יהודה היא! א"ל: שבילי בית גילגול קאמרת – יהושע *אוהב ישראל היה, עמד ותיקן להם דרכים וסרטיא, כל היכא דניחא תשמישתא – מסרה לרבים, כל היכא דלא ניחא תשמישתא – מסרה ליחיד: §

מתני' *אחד בור הרבים ובאר הרבים ובאר היחיד עושין להן פסין, אבל לבור היחיד עושין לו מחיצה גבוה י' טפחים, דברי ר' עקיבא. ר' יהודה בן בבא אומר: [ג]אין עושין פסין אלא לבאר הרבים בלבד, [ד]ולשאר עושין חגורה גבוה עשרה טפחים. §

גמ'

רש"י

*[לעלות בו לא"י והוא גבוה י' טפחים: ומחתנא. מורד חריץ עמוק י' טפחים ורחב ד' סביב א"י מאידך גיסא] והוי לה מחיצה. ונהי דאסור לטלטולי מדרבנן – מיהו לאו רה"ר דאורייתא היא לאחיובי עליה: מעלות ומורדות שבה קאמרת. שאין חייבין עליהם משום רה"ר, דלא ניחא דריסה דידהו, ולא הוי רה"ר: קרקפנא. בעל הגולגולת, כלומר: אדם חשוב: עמודי. של בית מדרש של ר' יוחנן: שאינן כדגלי מדבר. דארץ חלקה היתה, שהענן משוה אותה: ואפי' עולין לו בחבל. בעיא היא, ורחבה קאמר לה: מעלות בית מרון. זקופין מאד, ומעלה קצרה, ומהלכין בה בזה אחר זה ולא שנים יחד, כדאמרי' בר"ה (ד' יח.): "כבני מרון", כמעלות בית מרון: חצר שהרבים נכנסין לה. דרך פתחים או פרצות של עשר: דלא ניחא תשמישתי'. לרבים לדריסה. שהפתחין קצרין, וגידודין יש באסקופה. ופשיטא דלא מבטלה בקיעת רבים למחיצות: אלא לאו ר' יהודה. ואשמעי' דהיכא דלא ניחא תשמישתיה – מודי: בבורות סלקא דעתך. היכי הוי מבוי בתוך הבור: לבורות. שיש בור בראשו אחד, ובשפה (ב)אחת קצרה מהלכין שם עד שעוברין: שבילי בית גילגול. מעלה גבוהה וזקופה היא בארץ ישראל: יהושע אוהב ישראל היה. ובמעלות ומורדות דארץ ישראל מודינא לך דאין חייבין עליהן, וכי אמינא לך דחייבין – בשאר ארצות קאמינא: מתני' בור הרבים. אי פסקי מיא מדכרי אהדדי: באר היחיד. נמי שרי דהא לא פסקי מיא: לבאר הרבים. דאיכא תרתי למעליותא: חגורה. היקף של חבלים:

תוספות

אילימא משום דמקיף סולמא דצור. הוה מצי לאקשויי מר' יוחנן גופיה, דאמר לעיל: ירושלים, אלמלא דלתותיה נעולות בלילה – חייבין עליה משום רה"ר. ושמא: התם הוי אליבא דר' יהודה, דאית ליה דאתו רבים ומבטלי מחיצה, והכא אליבא דרבנן.

דילמא מעלות ומורדות קאמרת. ודווקא בארץ ישראל, כדמפרש טעמא בסמוך: יהושע אוהב ישראל היה. אבל בחוצה לארץ – חייב ואליבא דר' יהודה, אבל לרבנן – אפי' בחוצה לארץ פטור, דלא אתו רבים ומבטלי מחיצה. ותימה: דלרבנן כל ארץ ישראל תעשה רה"י ע"י סולמא דצור ומחתנא דגדר. ובבל נמי, דמקיף לה דיגלת, ולא אתו רבים ומבטלי מחיצתן! ולר' יוחנן, דאמר בפרק "הדר" (לקמן ד' סז:): קרפף יותר מבית סאתים שלא הוקף לדירה, אפי' כור ואפי' כוריים – הזורק לתוכו חייב. והוא הדין אפי' לאלף כורים, דמה שיעור יהיה? וי"ל: דמחיצה שאינה עשויה בידי אדם לא חשיבא מחיצה כולי האי, ואפי' רבנן מודו דאתו רבים ומבטלי מחיצה:

קרקפנא חזיתיה לרישך. רישך – היינו רבה, שהיה רבו של אביי. והוי כמו "רישך בקרירי ורישא דרישך בחמימי" (שבת ד' נה.). ומצינו שהלך רבה לארץ ישראל ללמוד תורה לפני ר' יוחנן בסוף פרק "שני דייני גזירות" (כתובות ד' קיא.). אבל אביי עצמו לא מצינו שהלך ללמוד תורה שם. *[ועוד: שלא ראה אביי את ר' יוחנן, אבל רבה תלמידו של רבי יוחנן הוה.]*

תל המתלקט כו'. לא הוה שמיע ליה הא דא"ר יוחנן: מעלות ומורדות שבארץ ישראל כו', אבל בחוצה לארץ – חייבין:

מני אילימא רבנן. וא"ת: לימא לעולם רבנן, וקמשמע לן דאפילו לטלטל שרי. דמפסי בירחות לא שמעינן, דבעולי רגלים הקילו! וי"ל: דעדיפא קא משני*:

אלא לאו ר' יהודה. וא"ת: ולוקמא כגון שיש שתי מחיצות גמורות, דבההיא ודאי מודה ר' יהודה! וי"ל: דע"כ בנפרצה מד' רוחות. דאי בנפרצה מב' רוחות – מאי איריא דלא ניחא תשמישתיה, אפי' ניחא תשמישתיה נמי, כדפריך לרבנן:

תא שמע מבואות המפולשות. במסכת טהרות (פ"ו מ"ו) גרסי': בגיתות, והיינו בורות שתחת הגיתות. פי' רבינו חננאל: וכגון שהבור רחוק מן הכותל ג' טפחים מכל צד, והולכין דרך כאן וכאן. וקא משמע לן דאפי' הכי לא בטלי מחיצה, דאי בור הולך מכותל לכותל – פשיטא דהוי רה"י. והא דנקט בור ולא נקט מחיצה מופלגת ג' מן הכותל – משום דבבור הוי חדוש טפי, דאע"ג שרשות הרבים נמי מהלכת בתוכו – אפי' הכי הוי רשות היחיד לשבת:

ואיזהו שבילי בית גלגול כו'. ואם תאמר: והא ע"כ שבילי בית גלגול היו מתלקטים עשרה מתוך ארבע, הואיל והוי רשות היחיד לשבת, וא"כ מה צריך הכא לאתויי דר' ינאי? ועוד קשיא: דאמאי לא משני רשות הרבים לטומאה איצטריכא ליה, כדמשני לעיל?! ויש לומר: דמשום הכי מייתי מדר' ינאי, דמשמע דעיקר חידושא הוי שהוא רשות היחיד לשבת, מדלא אמרינן: אפילו אין העבד יכול לרוץ כו'. אפ"ה – הוי רשות הרבים. ואם תאמר: ולמה לי אין העבד יכול לרוץ? אפי' יכול נמי הוי רשות היחיד, כיון שמתלקט עשרה מתוך ארבע! ויש לומר: דבעינן שלא יהא ניחא תשמישתיה, שלא יהא עשוי כעין מדרגה, דלא תהוי מחיצתא נדרסת, דאמר בפרק "כל גגות" (לקמן ד' פט:) *דלא הויא מחיצתא*):

יהושע אוהב ישראל היה. דוקא שבילי בית גלגול דלא ניחא תשמישתיה כלל, כדמפרש ר' ינאי שאין העבד יכול לרוץ. אבל מבוי מפולש לבורות, וחצר שרבים נכנסים לה בזו ויוצאין בזו – הוי רה"ר לר"י, אע"ג דהוו של יחיד. הואיל וניחא תשמישתיה וראוי למוסרו לרבים – הוו רה"ר לר' יהודה ע"י בקיעת רבים, ולהכי לא קאמר אלא דמשמע דצריך עדיין לשנויא דלעיל: **חגורה** פירוש: מחיצה:

והא

*) א"נ אי עבד יכול לרוץ הוה ניחא תשמישתיה ואתו רבים ומבטלי מחיצתא לרבי יהודה ולא מסרה ליחיד [תוספות ישנים]:

א"נ כיון דלא נפרצה אלא מב' רוחות ולא ניחא תשמישתיה פשיטא דלרבנן דאמרו לא אתו רבים ומבטלי מחיצה דשריא אפי' לטלטל. א"נ מלישנא דברייתא לא משמע היתר טלטול כדאמר עלה לעיל אי מהתם ה"א ה"מ לזרוק וכו' [תוספות ישנים כ"י]:

רבינו חננאל

נימא (דא"י כגון מוקצה שאמרנו) [משום] דחד גיסא דסולמא דצור גבוה וחד גיסא מחתנא דגדר בבל נמי חד גיסא מקף לה פרת וחד גיסא מקף לה דיגלת כל העולם כולו מקף ליה אוקייאנוס. פי' בחר אלמוחים. דלמא מעלות ומורדות דא"י שהן מוקצין [אין חייבין] עליהן משום רשות הרבים א"ל קרקפנא כלומר גולגולת גדולה מבין העמודין של בית המדרש ראיתי ראשך כשאמר ר' יוחנן זו השמועה וכן א"ר אבהו אמר רבי יוחנן מעלות שבארץ ישראל כמו תל שהוא מוקצה וכיוצא בו ומורדות כגון חריצין מרווחין וכיוצא בהן אין חייבין עליהן משום רה"ר לפי שאינן כדגלי מדבר שהיו העגלות מהלכין בהן והיו הדרכים משוין בלא רצפין ובלא נקבין ובלא פתחים. בעא מיניה רחבה מרבה תל המתלקט י' טפחים גובה מתוך ד' אמות ורבים בוקעין בו כלומר עוברין ושבין ע"ג התל ההוא מהו. אליבא דרבנן דפטרי בפסין אע"ג דפסקי להו רבים לא תיבעי לך דהא לא חיישינן להפסק' ורה"י היא כי תיבעי לך אליבא דר' יהודה אמר יסלקנה לצדדין דהפסקה מבטלת למחיצות מאי התם בפסין דניחא תשמישתיה אמרינן דהפסקה מבטלת דהא דשו בה רבים לפיכך היא כרה"ר. אבל הכא דלא ניחא תשמישתיה אפי' (היא) [דמפסק] אפסקתא אמרינן בטלה דעתיה ואסיקנא *) אפסקת דר' יהודה מבטלת למחיצות ואפי' לא ניחא תשמישתיה אלא עולין לאותו התל ולכל (מוציא) [כיוצא] בו בחבל וכן אפי' מעלות של בית חורון ומותבינן עליה מהא חצר שהרבים נכנסין בו בצד זה ויוצאין בצד אחר כנגדו רה"י לשבת ורה"ר לטומאה שספק נגע בה ספק לא נגע בה טהור דקיי"ל ספק טומאה ברה"י טמא ברה"ר טהור. מאי לאו ר"י היא וקתני רה"י לשבת ודחינן לא רבנן היא ורה"ר לטומאה אצטריכא ליה: ת"ש מבואות המפולשין לבורות שיחין ומערות כו' כגון שיש חוץ למבוי בור או שיח כו' שנכנסין למבוי מצד זה ויוצאין מצד האחר למלאות מים מן הבור או מן השיח או מן המעבר שחוץ למבוי על פני המבוי רה"י לשבת ורה"ר לטומאה. פי' שביל מקום מעבר צר כדמתרגמי' במשעול הכרמים בשביל כרמיא (משעול משעול) כלומר אין זה יכול ליכנס עד שיצא חבירו כלומר אין מכיל המעבר שני בני אדם. בית גדגד**). מלשון גידוד חמשה ומחיצה חמשה. ואמרינן דבי ר' ינאי כל שאין העבד יכול ליטול סאה של חיטין וירוץ לפני סרדיוט זהו שביל בית דגדגד כל מקום צר. ופרקינן יהושע אוהב היה לישראל ותיקן להם דרכים וסרטאות כל היכא דניחא תשמישתיה מסרה לרבים. וכל היכא דלא ניחא תשמישתיה לא מסרה לרבים: [מתני'] ר' יהודה בן בבא אומר אין עושין פסין אלא לבור ברה"ר בלבד

אמר

*) נראה דצ"ל דלר' יהודה הפסקת רבים מבטלת למחיצות. **) עי' בערוך ערך גלגל ג'.

גירסת רש"ל
[יבמות עח.]

הגהות הב"ח

(א) גמ' ויוצאין בזו ורשות היחיד לשבת ורשות הרבים לטומאה מני: (ב) רש"י ד"ה לבורות וכו' ובשפה קצרה כצ"ל ותיבת אחת נמחק:

לעיל ח. תוספ' דטהרות פ"ו
רש"ל
[עיין תוס' יבמות עח. ד"ה חזיתיה]
טהרות פ"ו [מ"ו וסם אי' השבילין]
שם
[מנחות סט.]
[לעיל יח.]
[עיין לג: תוס' ד"ה חייב]

גמ' אָמַר רַב יוֹסֵף, אָמַר רַב יְהוּדָה, אָמַר שְׁמוּאֵל: הֲלָכָה כְּר' יְהוּדָה בֶּן בָּבָא. וְאָמַר רַב יוֹסֵף, אָמַר רַב יְהוּדָה, אָמַר שְׁמוּאֵל: לֹא הוּתְּרוּ פַּסֵּי בִירָאוֹת אֶלָּא לִבְאֵר מַיִם חַיִּים בִּלְבַד. וּצְרִיכָא, דְּאִי אַשְׁמְעִינַן הֲלָכָה כְּר' יְהוּדָה בֶּן בָּבָא – הֲוָה אָמִינָא דְּרַבִּים, וַאֲפִילּוּ מְכוּנָּסִין. וְהַאי דְּקָתָנֵי בְּאֵר הָרַבִּים – לְאַפּוּקֵי מִדְּר' עֲקִיבָא. קָא מַשְׁמַע לָן דְּלֹא הוּתְּרוּ פַּסֵּי בִירָאוֹת אֶלָּא לִבְאֵר מַיִם חַיִּים. וְאִי אַשְׁמְעִינַן בְּאֵר מַיִם חַיִּים – הֲוָה אָמִינָא: לָא שְׁנָא דְּרַבִּים וְלָא שְׁנָא דְּיָחִיד, קָא מַשְׁמַע לָן: הֲלָכָה כְּרַבִּי יְהוּדָה בֶּן בָּבָא.§

מתני' וְעוֹד אָמַר ר' יְהוּדָה בֶּן בָּבָא: הַגִּינָּה וְהַקַּרְפֵּף שֶׁהֵן שִׁבְעִים אַמָּה וְשִׁירַיִים עַל ע' אַמָּה וְשִׁירַיִים, הַמּוּקָּפוֹת גָּדֵר גָּבוֹהַּ עֲשָׂרָה טְפָחִים – מְטַלְטְלִין בְּתוֹכָהּ, וּבִלְבַד שֶׁיְּהֵא בָּהּ שׁוֹמֵירָה אוֹ בֵּית דִּירָה, אוֹ שֶׁתְּהֵא סְמוּכָה לָעִיר. ר' יְהוּדָה אוֹמֵר: אֲפִילּוּ אֵין בָּהּ אֶלָּא בּוֹר וְשִׁיחַ וּמְעָרָה מְטַלְטְלִין בְּתוֹכָהּ. [א] רַבִּי עֲקִיבָא אוֹמֵר: אֲפִילּוּ אֵין בָּהּ אַחַת מִכָּל אֵלּוּ מְטַלְטְלִין בְּתוֹכָהּ, וּבִלְבַד שֶׁיְּהֵא בָּהּ שִׁבְעִים אַמָּה וְשִׁירַיִים עַל שִׁבְעִים אַמָּה וְשִׁירַיִים. רַבִּי אֱלִיעֶזֶר אוֹמֵר: אִם הָיְתָה אָרְכָּהּ יָתֵר עַל רָחְבָּהּ אֲפִי' אַמָּה אַחַת – אֵין מְטַלְטְלִין בְּתוֹכָהּ. [ב] רַבִּי יוֹסֵי אוֹמֵר: אֲפִילּוּ אָרְכָּהּ פִּי שְׁנַיִם בְּרָחְבָּהּ מְטַלְטְלִין בְּתוֹכָהּ. א"ר אֶלְעַאי, שָׁמַעְתִּי מֵרַבִּי *אֱלִיעֶזֶר: וַאֲפִילּוּ הִיא כְּבֵית כּוֹר. וְכֵן שָׁמַעְתִּי מִמֶּנּוּ: אַנְשֵׁי חָצֵר שֶׁשָּׁכַח אֶחָד מֵהֶן וְלֹא עֵירֵב – בֵּיתוֹ אָסוּר מִלְּהַכְנִיס וּלְהוֹצִיא לוֹ, אֲבָל לָהֶם מוּתָּר. *וְכֵן שָׁמַעְתִּי מִמֶּנּוּ שֶׁיּוֹצְאִין *בְּעַרְקַבְלִין בַּפֶּסַח, וְחָזַרְתִּי עַל כָּל תַּלְמִידָיו *וּבִקַּשְׁתִּי לִי חָבֵר וְלֹא מָצָאתִי.§

גמ' מַאי תַּנָּא דְּקָתָנֵי "וְעוֹד"? אִילֵימָא מִשּׁוּם דְּתָנָא לֵיהּ חֲדָא לְחוּמְרָא וְקָתָנֵי אַחֲרִיתִי מִשּׁוּם הָכִי קָתָנֵי "וְעוֹד" – וְהָא רַבִּי יְהוּדָה דְּתָנָא לֵיהּ חֲדָא לְחוּמְרָא וְקָתָנֵי אַחֲרִיתִי, וְלָא קָתָנֵי "וְעוֹד"! הָתָם אַפְסְקוּהּ רַבָּנַן, הָכָא לָא אַפְסְקוּהּ רַבָּנַן. וְכָל הֵיכָא דְּאַפְסְקוּהּ רַבָּנַן לָא קָתָנֵי "וְעוֹד"? וְהָא רַבִּי אֱלִיעֶזֶר דְּסוּכָּה, דְּאַפְסְקוּהּ רַבָּנַן וְקָתָנֵי *"וְעוֹד"! הָתָם בְּמִילְּתֵיהּ הוּא דְּאַפְסְקוּהּ, הָכָא בְּמִילְּתָא אַחֲרִיתִי אַפְסְקוּהּ.§ "רַבִּי עֲקִיבָא אוֹמֵר: אֲפִילּוּ אֵין בָּהּ אֶחָד מִכָּל אֵלּוּ מְטַלְטְלִין בְּתוֹכָהּ".§

רַבִּי

רש"י

גמ' הֲוָה אָמִינָא דְּרַבִּים אֲפִי' מְכוּנָּסִין. שָׁרֵי ר"י בֶּן בָּבָא, וְהַאי דְּקָאָמַר בְּאֵר הָרַבִּים – מִשּׁוּם ר' עֲקִיבָא דְּאָמַר: בְּאֵר הַיָּחִיד שָׁרֵי, וְאָתָא אִיהוּ לְמֵימַר: אע"ג דְּמַיִם חַיִּים נִינְהוּ, דְּרַבִּים – אִין, דְּיָחִיד – לָא. וְהָכִי קָאָמַר: אֵין עוֹשִׂין פַּסִּין אֲפִילּוּ לִבְאֵר, אֶלָּא שֶׁל רַבִּים: מתני' שׁוֹמֵירָה. סוּכַּת שׁוֹמְרִין. וְאע"ג דְּהוּקַּף לְדִירָה – בֵּית סָאתַיִם הוּא דְּשָׁרֵי, טְפֵי לָא: סְמוּכָה לָעִיר. דְּהוֹאִיל וּקְרוֹבָה לְבֵיתוֹ, דַּעְתּוֹ לְהִשְׁתַּמֵּשׁ בָּהּ תָּמִיד, וּכְהוּקַּף לְדִירָה דָּמֵי: וּבִלְבַד שֶׁתְּהֵא שִׁבְעִים אַמָּה וְשִׁירַיִים עַל ע' אַמָּה וְשִׁירַיִים. וְלֹא יוֹתֵר. וּבַגְּמָרָא פָּרֵיךְ: תַּנָּא קַמָּא נַמִי הָכִי קָאָמַר: אִם הָיָה אָרְכָּהּ יוֹתֵר עַל רָחְבָּהּ אֲפִילּוּ אַמָּה אַחַת. אע"ג דְּמִיעֵט רָחְבָּהּ וְהוֹסִיף בְּאָרְכָּהּ, וְאֵין בְּכוּלָּהּ אֶלָּא בֵּית סָאתַיִם – אֵין מְטַלְטְלִין. דִּמְרוּבַּע הוּא דְּשָׁרוּ רַבָּנַן הֵיכָא דְּלֹא הוּקַּף לְדִירָה: אַנְשֵׁי חָצֵר שֶׁשָּׁכַח כו'. וּלְמָחָר בִּיטֵּל רְשׁוּתוֹ לַחֲבֵרוֹ (א), שֶׁהִיא אוֹסֶרֶת עֲלֵיהֶן מִלְּהוֹצִיא מִבָּתֵּיהֶן לֶחָצֵר: בֵּיתוֹ אָסוּר לְהַכְנִיס וּלְהוֹצִיא. לֶחָצֵר, לְצָרְכּוֹ: אֲבָל לָהֶן מוּתָּר. לְהָבִיא כְּלֵי בָּתֵּיהֶן לְבֵיתוֹ דֶּרֶךְ חָצֵר: בְּעַרְקַבְלִין. שֵׁם מָרוֹר: וּבִקַּשְׁתִּי לִי חָבֵר. לִשְׁלֹשָׁה דְּבָרִים הַלָּלוּ, אִם שְׁמָעָן מִפִּיו, וְלֹא מָצָאתִי. וּבַגְּמָרָא מְפָרֵשׁ דְּגַבֵּי גִּינָּה וְקַרְפֵּף לָא שָׁרוּ יוֹתֵר מִבֵּית סָאתַיִם, וְגַבֵּי אַנְשֵׁי חָצֵר סָבְרֵי דְּאַף לָהֶם אָסוּר בֵּיתוֹ, אֲבָל מִבָּתֵּיהֶן לֶחָצֵר – מוּתָּר. וּבַגְּמָ' מְפָרֵשׁ פְּלוּגְתַּיְיהוּ. וּבְעַרְקַבְלִין סָבְרֵי דְּלָאו מָרוֹר הוּא: גמ' מַאי תַּנָּא. רַבִּי יְהוּדָה בֶּן בָּבָא, בְּגִינָּה וְקַרְפֵּף דִּלְעֵיל: דְּקָאָמַר וְעוֹד. דְּמַשְׁמַע דְּאָמַר לְעֵיל בָּהּ חוּמְרָא אַחֲרִיתִי: אִילֵימָא מִשּׁוּם דְּאָמַר חֲדָא לְחוּמְרָא. גַּבֵּי פַּסִּין, דְּאָמַר דְּאֵין עוֹשִׂין אוֹתָן אֶלָּא לִבְאֵר הָרַבִּים. וְהַשְׁתָּא קָאָמַר חוּמְרָא אַחֲרִיתִי, דְּאע"ג דְּהוּקַּף לְדִירָה לָא שָׁרֵי טְפֵי מִבֵּית סָאתַיִם: וְהָא רַבִּי יְהוּדָה בַּר אֶלְעַאי דִּתְנָא לְעֵיל* חֲדָא לְחוּמְרָא. דְּאָמַר עַד בֵּית סָאתַיִם – אִין, טְפֵי – לָא. וַהֲדַר תָּנָא אַחֲרִיתִי: *יַסְלְקֶנָּה לִצְדָדִין. וְלָא תָּנָא "וְעוֹד" – מִשּׁוּם דְּלָאו בַּחֲדָא מִלְּתָא הִיא, דְּרֵישָׁא אַיְירֵי בְּמִדַּת הֶיקֵּף, וְסֵיפָא אַיְירֵי בְּבִיטּוּל מְחִיצּוֹת: אַפְסְקוּהּ רַבָּנַן. דְּקָא תָּנֵי אָמְרוּ לוֹ: לֹא אָמְרוּ בֵּית סָאתַיִם אֶלָּא לְגִינָּה כו': וְכָל הֵיכָא דְּאַפְסְקוּהּ רַבָּנַן לָא הֲוָה תָּנֵי בָּהּ וְעוֹד. אִי שַׁיָּיךְ לְמֵימַר בָּהּ, כְּגוֹן הֵיכָא דְּרֵישָׁא וְסֵיפָא בַּחֲדָא מִילְּתָא: וְהָא ר' אֱלִיעֶזֶר דְּסוּכָּה. דִּתְנַן בְּמַסֶּכֶת סוּכָּה (ד' כז.), ר' אֱלִיעֶזֶר אוֹמֵר: י"ד סְעוּדוֹת חַיָּיב אָדָם לֶאֱכוֹל בַּסּוּכָּה. וַחֲכָמִים אוֹמְרִים: אֵין לַדָּבָר קִצְבָּה. וְעוֹד אָמַר ר' אֱלִיעֶזֶר: מִי שֶׁלֹּא אָכַל לֵילֵי יו"ט הָרִאשׁוֹן יַשְׁלִים לֵילֵי יוֹם טוֹב הָאַחֲרוֹן. אַלְמָא: מִשּׁוּם דְּרֵישָׁא וְסֵיפָא בִּסְעוּדָה דְּסוּכָּה, וּבְחֶשְׁבּוֹנָן אַיְירֵי – תָּנָא: "וְעוֹד" אע"ג דְּאַפְסְקוּהּ. וּשְׁמַע מִינָּהּ: הַאי דְּלָא תָּנָא בִּדְרַבִּי יְהוּדָה "וְעוֹד" – מִשּׁוּם דְּלָא דָּמֵי הוּא, וּבִדְרַבִּי יְהוּדָה בֶּן בָּבָא לָמָּה לִי דְּתָנֵי לֵיהּ: הָתָם. גַּבֵּי סוּכָּה בְּמִלְּתֵיהּ אַפְסְקוּהּ, לָא אַהַדְרוּ לֵיהּ רַבָּנַן אֶלָּא בִּסְעוּדוֹת. אֲבָל רַבִּי יְהוּדָה דְּמַתְנִי' – לָא אַיְירֵי אֶלָּא בְּפַסֵּי בִירָאוֹת בֵּית סָאתַיִם, וְאַהֲדַרוּ רַבָּנַן בְּגִינָּה וְקַרְפֵּף וְדִיר וָסַהַר. וּלְעוֹלָם טַעְמֵיהּ מִשּׁוּם הַפְסָקָה. וּלְר' יְהוּדָה בֶּן בָּבָא דְּלָא אַפְסְקֵיהּ – תָּנָא "וְעוֹד":

רַבִּי

תוספות

והא דנקט באר הרבים לאפוקי מר' עקיבא. וא"ת: א"כ הוה ליה למימר בור הרבים. וע"כ באר היחיד לא – דא"כ היינו רבי עקיבא. וי"ל: דאורחא דמלתא למיתני מענין שממעט דהיינו באר היחיד. אי נמי: הא דקאמר דרבים אפילו מכונסין, לאו אר"י בן בבא קאי, אלא אשמואל:

לא שנא דרבים ולא שנא כו'. יכול להיות דהוי כר' יהודה בן בבא. והא דנקט ר' יהודה בן בבא באר הרבים, היינו לאפוקי בור הרבים: **שהוא** ע' אמה ושיריים. וא"ת: ולילף מהר הבית ועזרת נשים, שהיה קל"ה אמה ועזרת ישראל היה קפ"ז! וי"ל: דכל מילי דשבת ממשכן גמרינן להו. אי נמי: העזרות חשיבי מוקפין לדירה, שהיו שומרים בה כל הלילה:

ובלבד שיהא בה שומירה. נראה לפרש דפחות מע' אמה נמי צריך שומירה או בית דירה. וביתר מבית סאתים – לא סגי בשומירה ובית דירה, אלא פתח ולבסוף הוקף הקרפף לצורך הבית. אבל אין לומר דבשבעים אמה דוקא צריך שומירה, אבל בפחות א"צ כלום, וביתר אין סגי בשומירה, דאין סברא שיהא ג' חלוקים בג' משהויין. והא נמי אין לומר דביתר מע' נמי סגי בשומירה, ולא אתא למימר אלא דבציר משבעים אמה ושיריים לא צריך כלל – דאם כן במאי פליג ר' עקיבא, לפירוש ר"ת דפירש דר' יהודה בן בבא איירי בדבר מועט, ור' עקיבא לא איירי. דלתרוייהו בע' אמה ושיריים, ודבר מועט – צריך שומירה, ובפחות מכאן לא צריך. ואפי' לפי' רש"י, דפי': היינו תנא קמא, דאמרו לו לר' יהודה – מ"מ גם לפי' נראה דרבי יהודה בן בבא נמי אית ליה דבר מועט כמו תנא קמא, דמשום הכי איצטריך לרבי עקיבא לחזור ולשנות: ובלבד שיהא בה ע' אמה כו'. ועוד: אי ביתר מבית סאתים נמי איירי ר"י בן בבא – א"כ היכי קאמר ר"י אפילו אין בה אלא בור ושיח ומערה משמע דלר"י נמי אין חילוק בין סאתים ליתר. ורבי יהודה גופיה קאמר לעיל, גבי פסין: עד בית סאתים. ועוד, לר"ת דפי' היינו תנא קמא – היינו ר"י בן בבא. כלומר: ואמאי הוצרך לשנות ובלבד כו'. כיון דקאי ארבי יהודה בן בבא, והא אצטריך דלא נימא דשרי אפילו ביתר מבית סאתים, כיון דר' יהודה בן בבא איירי ביתר מבית סאתים! לכך נראה כדפרישית. ומה שפירש רש"י: אפילו בהוקף לדירה לא שרי רבי יהודה בן בבא ביתר מבית סאתים – אין נראה, אלא בפתח ולבסוף הוקף – מהני אפי' ביתר מבית סאתים, דהא שרו רבנן לעיל בדיר וסהר ומוקצה אפי' בי' כורים. וכמה אלירות ומבואות שהיו בירושלים יתרות על בית סאתים, וכי יאסור ר' יהודה בן בבא בכולם לטלטל? ודווקא א) בשומירה הוא דקאמר דלא מהני ביתר מבית סאתים, אבל פתח ולבסוף הוקף – מהני אפי' יותר. ולרש"י, שמא יש לחלק: דבדיר וסהר ומוקצה וחצר, לפי שתשמישתן רב(ב) יותר – אפי' י' כורין, אבל קרפף – אפי' פתח ולבסוף הוקף לא מהני ביתר מבית סאתים:

אילימא משום(ג) דתני חדא לחומרא. פירוש: דשייך(ב) למיתני ועוד, אע"ג דלא הוו תרוייהו מענין א'. וכ"ש היכא דהוו תרוייהו מענין א', אף על גב דלא הוו תרוייהו לחומרא. כמו בסוכה (דף כז.) ובפרק רביעי דמגילה (דף כח.)ג) כדפ"ה: **הכא** במלתא אחריתי אפסקוה. תימה: דבפרק "המביא כדי יין" (ביצה דף לג. ושם) קתני ועוד, ואע"ג דאפסיק במילתא אחריתי. דקתני, ר' אליעזר אומר: נוטל אדם קיסם מלפניו [לחצוץ בו שיניו] ומגבב מן החצר ומדליק, וחכ"א: מגבב מלפניו ומדליק. וקתני בתר הכי: אין מוציאין את האור לא מן העצים כו'. ומפסיק בבא שלימה. וקתני בתר הכי: ועוד א"ר אליעזר, עומד אדם על המוקצה כו'. ומיהו, רש"י מהפך שם המשנה והגמ'. אך לר"ת, שאומר שאין צריך להפך, דמילתא דאור קא מסיים ואזיל, קשה! וי"ל: דהתם הוו תרי קולי, ושייך למיתני "ועוד" אע"ג דאפסיק במילתא אחריתי, דכה דהיתירא עדיף:

רבי

א) [בשומירה ובית דירה דהוי גרועה הוא דקאמר כצ"ל רש"ל מתוס' שנ"ז] ב) למיתני ועוד אע"ג דלא הוי מענין אחד אבל הא פשיטא לי דשייך למיתני ועוד היכא דהוי תרוייהו כו' [רש"ל] ג) [וע"ש תוס' ד"ה ועוד]

עין משפט נר מצוה

כו [א טוש"ע א"ח סי' שנח סעיף א]:
כז [ב טוש"ע שם]:

מסורת הש"ס

[נ"ל אליעזר וכ"ה בגמ' לקמן ובכל הספרים]

[במשנה שבמשניות א' עקרבנין ופי' הרמב"ם וכן הרב מברטנורה שהוא ירק שעלין שלו דומות לעקרב וגירסת הערוך עקרבלין ובפסחים איתא עקרבלין]

פסחים לט. ע"ש

[עי' תוס' לקמן כו: ד"ה ולא מצאתי כו']

[לעיל כב.]

[סוכה כז.]

רבינו חננאל

אמר רב יוסף אמר רב יהודה אמר שמואל הלכה כרבי יהודה בן בבא. ועוד אמר לא הותרו פסי ביראות אלא לבאר הרבים בלבד. וצריכא דאי אשמעינן הלכה כרבי יהודה בן בבא הוה אמינא דרב אפילו במכונסין ואפילו מלוחין ולאפוקי מדרבי עקיבא דאמר אחד בור הרבים ואחד בור היחיד עושין להן פסין קמ"ל לא הותרו פסי ביראות אלא לבאר מים חיים בלבד. ואי אשמעינן שמואל באר מים חיים הוה אמינא לא שנא דרבים ולא שנא דיחיד וכר"ע קמ"ל הלכה כר' יהודה בן בבא: **מתני'** ועוד א"ר יהודה בן בבא הגינה והקרפף כו' מאי תנא דקתני ועוד וכי תימא איידי דתנא רבי יהודה בן בבא אומר אין עושין פסין אלא לבאר הרבים דהוא לחומרא משום הכי קתני ועוד דהיא לחומרא. והא רבי יהודה דתנא אין עושין פסין אלא עד בית סאתים דהיא לחומרא

הגהות הב"ח

(א) רש"י ד"ה אנשי חצר וכו' רשותו לחבירו שהיתה אוסרת: (ב) תוס' ד"ה ובלבד כו' מותר אפי' י' כורין כו': (ג) תוס' ד"ה אילימא משום וכו' אלא דיבור זה נדפס בזה הלשון גליון ולרש"י שמא יש לחלק דבדיר וסהר ומוקצה וחצר לפי שתשמישתה מותר אפי' עשר כורים אבל קרפף אפי' פתח ולבסוף הוקף לא מהני ביתר מבית סאתים:

והדר קתני אם היתה דרך הרבים מפסקתה יסלקנה לצדדין דהיא נמי לחומרא ולא קתני ועוד ופרקינן התם גבי ר"י אפסקוה רבנן דקתני אמרו לו לא אם אמרו בית סאתים [וכו'] אבל גבי ר' יהודה בן בבא לא אפסקוה לפיכך קתני ועוד. ואקשינן וכל היכא דאפסקוה לא קתני ועוד והא ר' אליעזר דסוכה בפרק הישן בסוכה תחת המטה דקאמר ר' אליעזר אומר י"ד סעודות חייב אדם לוכל בסוכה ואפסקוה רבנן דקתני וחכמים אומרים אין לדבר קצבה וקתני ועוד אמר ר' אליעזר מי שלא אכל לילי יו"ט הראשון ישלים ופרקינן התם במלתיה אפסקוה דקתני וחכ"א אין לדבר קצבה חוץ מלילי יו"ט הראשון כלומר כאלו לא אפסקוה אבל הכא הוא קאמר לענין פסין והן אמרו לו גינה וקרפף וכיון דאפסקוה במלתא אחריתי לפיכך לא קתני ועוד. אקשינן ר' יהודה בן בבא קתני ע' אמה ושיריים ור"ע קתני ע' אמה ושיריים

רב נסים גאון

והא גבי ר' אליעזר דסוכה דאפסקוה רבנן וקאמר ועוד זהו שאמר ר' אליעזר במסכת סוכה בפרק הישן תחת המטה (דף כז) ר' אליעזר אומר ארבע עשרה סעודות חייב אדם לוכל בסוכה אחת ביום ואחת בלילה וחכמים אומרים אין לדבר קצבה חוץ מלילי יום טוב הראשון בלבד ועוד אמר רבי אליעזר מי שלא אכל כו':

איכא

כח א ב מיי' פ"ו מהל' שבת הלכה ד סמג עשין א טוש"ע א"ח סי' שנח סעיף א:

רבי עקיבא היינו תנא קמא! איכא בינייהו דבר מועט. דתניא, ר' יהודה אומר: דבר מועט יש על שבעים אמה ושירים, ולא נתנו חכמים בו שיעור. [א]וכמה שיעור סאתים – כחצר המשכן. מנא הני מילי? אמר רב יהודה: דאמר קרא: °"ארך החצר מאה באמה ורחב חמשים בחמשים", אמרה תורה: *טול חמשים וסבב חמשים. *פשטיה דקרא במאי כתיב? אמר אביי: העמד משכן על שפת חמשים, כדי שיהא חמשים אמה לפניו, ועשרים אמה לכל רוח ורוח. § "ר"א אומר: אם היתה ארוכה כו'". § והתניא, ר"א אומר: אם היתה ארוכה יתר על פי שנים ברחבה אפי' אמה אחת אין מטלטלין בתוכה! אמר רב ביבי בר אביי: כי תנן נמי מתני', °[יתר על] פי שנים ברחבה תנן. אי הכי היינו ר' יוסי! איכא בינייהו ריבועא דריבעוה רבנן. § "ר' יוסי אומר כו'". איתמר, אמר רב יוסף, אמר רב יהודה, אמר שמואל: הלכה כר' יוסי. ורב ביבי אמר רב יהודה,* אמר שמואל: הלכה כר' עקיבא. [ב]ותרווייהו לקולא. וצריכא, דאי אשמעינן הלכה כרבי יוסי – הוה אמינא עד דאיכא שומירה או בית דירה, קמ"ל הלכה כר' עקיבא. ואי אשמעינן הלכה כר"ע – הוה אמינא דאריך וקטין לא, קמ"ל הלכה כר' יוסי. *קרפף שהוא יותר מבית סאתים שהוקף לדירה, נזרע רובו – הרי הוא כגינה, ואסור. נטע רובו – הרי הוא כחצר, ומותר. "נזרע רובו", אמר רב הונא בריה דרב יהושע: לא אמרן אלא יותר מבית סאתים, אבל בית סאתים – מותר. כמאן – כרבי שמעון; דתנן, *ר' שמעון אומר: אחד גגות ואחד חצירות ואחד קרפיפות רשות אחת הן לכלים ששבתו בתוכן, ולא לכלים ששבתו בתוך הבית. לר"ש נמי, כיון דנזרע רובו – הוי ההוא מיעוטא בטיל

תורה אור

רבי עקיבא היינו ת"ק. דאמרו לו: לא אמרו בית סאתים אלא לגינה ולקרפף, אבל אם היה כו' אלמא: היכא דאיכא בית דירה – אפי' טובא, ובשלא הוקף לדירה – בית סאתים, כר"ע: איכא בינייהו דבר מועט. שבית סאתים יתר על שבעים אמה ושיריים רבועים, כדתני לקמן. לתנא קמא – שרי בבית סאתים שלימים, ולר' עקיבא – שבעים ושיריים על שבעים ושיריים, ותו לא, כדקא אמרי' בהדיא: וכמה הן סאתים – כחצר המשכן: דבר מועט. לקמן מפרש לה: מנא הני מילי. דמרבעינן ליה לחצר המשכן לשער בו איסור שבת: מאי בחמשים. הא רוחב חמשים וארכו מאה, דהכי כתיבי במדות הקלעים: "ולפאת צפון באורך קלעים מאה אורך ורוחב החצר לפאת קדמה מזרחה חמשים אמה": אלא אמרה תורה טול חמשים. שארכו יתר על רחבו, וסבב חמשים הנותרים – דהוו להו שבעים אמות וד' טפחים מרובעין. כיצד: עשה מהן חמש רצועות של עשר אמה רוחב, וארכן חמשים. הסבב האחת למזרח והאחת למערב – הרי רחבה שבעים וארכה חמשים. עוד יש אחת לצפון ואחת לדרום – הרי שבעים על שבעים. אלא שהקרנות פגומין לכל קרן וקרן עשר על עשר מפני התוספת שהוספת, טול מן החמשים ד' חתיכות של י' על י' ויש בד' קרנות – ונתמלאו. נשארה רצועה אחת של עשר על עשר אמות שהיא ששים טפחים על ששים טפחים, ועשה אותן ל' רצועות של שני טפחים – (הרי ל'[א] רצועות, אורך כל אחת ואחת עשר אמה), שכולן הן ג' מאות אמות, תן ע' לכל רוח – *הרי שבעים וד' טפחים על שבעים וד' טפחים, אלא שהקרנות פגומין טפחיים על טפחיים. נשארו בידך עשרים אמה, טול מהן שמונה טפחים ויש לקרנות ונתמלאו, ונשארו בידך י"ח אמה וד' טפחים ברוחב טפחיים – והיינו דבר מועט. שאם באת לחלקו ולהקיף בהן[א], אין מגיע התוספת לרוחב ב' שלישי אצבע. דהא בעית למעבד מיניה רצועה של רפ"ג *אמות *וד' טפחים אורך, להקיף ארבע הרוחות: פשטיה דקרא. לענין משכן: במאי כתיב. בחמשים דקרא, מאי היא: העמד משכן על שפת. שכלין שם החמשים של חצר, משנכנסים לה בפתחה של מזרח: כדי שיהו חמשים אמה. של חצר לפני המשכן: ועשרים לכל רוח. שהמשכן ארכו ל' כדכתיב (שמות כו) "עשרים קרשים". ורוחב הקרש אמה וחצי. ורחבו של משכן תופש עשר אמות, כדכתיב: "ששה קרשים" שהן תשע אמות, "ושני קרשים למקוצעות" שהן ג' אמות רוחב, והאמה מכאן והאמה מכאן לכסות עוביין של קרשים של צלע(ג) ארכו אמה וחצי אמה מכאן וחצי אמה מכאן להשלים ולמלא החלל לעשר. וכשאתה מעמידו לסוף חמשים ובאמצע רחבה של חצר, נשארו מהחמשים על חמשים של חצר עשרים אמות לשלש הרוחות. אלא שעובי הקרשים ממעט מהן אמה(ג) לכל צד. והכא חללה חשיב, ועובי הכתלים בכלל העשרים של כל רוח. ולפניו למזרחו לא היו קרשים, אלא מסך והיינו וילון: ארכה יתר משנים ברחבה. כחצר המשכן הוא דשרי, ואע"ג דלא מרבעה – והיינו אורך כשנים ברוחב. אבל טפי משנים ברוחב – לא מישתרי: היינו רבי יוסי. דאמר: ארכה אפילו פי שנים ברחבה: איכא בינייהו ריבועא דריבעוה רבנן. ר"א סבר: ארכה יותר משנים ברחבה אין מטלטלין. ומיהו, עיקרה ארכה פי שנים ברחבה, כדכתיב, ולית ליה ריבועא ומיהו אי מרבעא לא מיתסרא בהכי, כדקתני: אם היה ארכה יותר משנים ברחבה – אין מטלטלין. הא בציר מפי שנים – מטלטלין. ורבי יוסי סבר, מרובעת עיקר, ולכתחילה אורויי מורינן הכי. ומיהו, אפילו ארכה פי שנים ברחבה – שריא. ומדקאמר "אפי'" – מכלל דמעיקרא לאו הכי הוא: הלכה כרבי יוסי. דלא בעי מרובעת: והלכה כר' עקיבא. דלא בעי מוקפת לדירה: ותרווייהו. הנך שמעתתא דשמואל, לקולא: הוה אמינא. דשמואל דירה בעי כר"י בן בבא, ובארכה יותר על רחבה כרבי יוסי סבר לה: אריך וקטין לא. דהא ר"ע מרובע בעי: נזרע רובו. בזרעונים – ביטל דירתו. דזרעונים לא דיירי אינשי, והוה ליה גינה – ואסור לטלטל אף בשאינו נזרע, דבטיל ליה לגבי רובא. אבל בנוטע אילנות – לא ביטל דירתו, דאורחא להתעופף בצל אילנות תמיד: אלא. שיש באותו מקום זריעה יותר מבית סאתים, דנעשה כרמלית. דקרפף יותר מבית סאתים שלא הוקף לדירה כרמלית היא, ושאינו נזרע – הוי חצר פרוצה במלואה לכרמלית, לפיכך כולו אסור: אבל בית סאתים. דבלאו דירה שרי באנפי נפשיה – הכא נמי שרי. ואף על גב דמקום זריעה הוי קרוי קרפף, ושאינו נזרע הוי חצר ופרוצין זה לזה, שאין מחיצה ביניהן – אפילו הכי לא אסרי אהדדי, הואיל ודחד גברא הוא. ורבי שמעון היא, דאמר רשות קרפף וחצר לא אסרי אהדדי, אפילו היא של ב' בעלי בתים: כדתנן רבי שמעון אומר אחד חצרות ואחד קרפיפות ואחד גגות רשות אחד הן. לטלטל מזה לזה לכלים ששבתו בתוכן, ואפילו הן של בעלים הרבה. אבל לא לכלים ששבתו בתוך הבית והוציאן לחצר – אסור להוציאן מחצר לקרפף או לגג, דבית וקרפף שתי רשויות הן, ואפילו דחד גברא: בטיל

ס"א הרי ר"פ אמות

רבי עקיבא היינו ת"ק. פ"ה: היינו ת"ק דאמרו לו לר"י. וקשיא: דהוה מצי למימר אריך וקטין איכא בינייהו, דרבי עקיבא קאמר בהדיא ע' אמה על ע' אמה, ובאמרו לו לא קא אמר ומסתמא לא פליגי אר' יהודה בהא דאית ליה לעיל אפילו אריך וקטין. ועוד: דילמא בעו בור שיח ומערה! ומיהו, י"ל: דמשני שפיר. ומ"מ נראה כפר"ח: דהיינו ת"ק – היינו רבי יהודה בן בבא. פי', כיון דרבי יהודה בן בבא איירי בשבעים אמה ושיריים על שבעים אמה וכו' – מה הוצרך ר"ע תו לשנות ובלבד שיהא בה כו'? ומשני: איכא בינייהו דבר מועט. דלר' עקיבא לית ליה, לר' יהודה אית ליה. והא דקתני בסמוך ר"י אומר דבר מועט יש, ולא נתנו בו חכמים שיעור, היינו שלא חשו לגמרם, ולעולם אית ליה. דכולהו תנאי שהוזכרו לפני ר"ע נראה דאית להו דבר מועט: **דבר** מועט יש. והא דלא חשיב ליה ב"כילד מעברין" (לקמן ד' נז.) דקתני גבי ג' כפרים: אם יש בין החיצונות מאה וארבעים אמה ואמה אחת ושליש – לא חש לגמרם. אי נמי: אתיא כר"ע, דלית ליה דבר מועט: **פשטיה** דקרא במאי כתיב. משמע דטול חמשים וסבב חמשים הוי אסמכתא בעלמא. ומיהו, ב"כילד מעברין" (לקמן דף נח.) פריך: והא מבעי ליה דיטול חמשים כו'(א)! **והתניא** רבי אליעזר אומר. והוא הדין דהוה מצי למיפרך דאם כן היינו רבי עקיבא, אלא דניחא ליה למיפרך דרבי אליעזר אדרבי אליעזר: **אי** הכי היינו ר' יוסי. אף על גב דמעיקרא איכא למיפרך נמי היינו ר"ע – מ"מ היינו רבי יוסי ליכא למיפרך(ב): **איכא** בינייהו רבועא דרבעוא רבנן. פ"ה: דרבי אליעזר בעי לכתחילה אורכה פי שנים ברחבה, ורבי יוסי בעי לכתחילה מרובעת. וקשיא: דאין שייך כאן לכתחילה ודיעבד. דאי כבר הוקף לכתחילה – לכ"ע שרי, ואם בא להקיף – ג) וכי נאמר לו שלא יקיף? אלא: למר כדאית ליה, ולמר כדאית ליה. ונראה כפירוש רבינו חננאל, דפירש: דרבעוה רבנן – היינו פלוגתא ד"מי שהוציאוהו" (לקמן ד' מט:) דר' חנינא בן אנטיגנוס ורבנן, גבי האומר: שביתתי במקומי יש לו אלפים אמה לכל רוח, עגולות – דברי ר' חנינא בן אנטיגנוס, וחכ"א: מרובעות כטבלא מרובעת, כדי שיהא נשכר לזויות. והשתא, לר"א אי ארכה יתר ע"פ שנים ברחבה אפילו באלכסון – אין מטלטלין כרבי חנינא. ורבי יוסי לטפויי קאתי, וקאמר דמטלטלין(ד): [נזרע רובו. ונראה לר"ת דדוקא קרקע יותר מבית סאתים, אבל בבית סאתים – אפילו נזרע כולו לא בטלי דירתו, דהא לר' יהודה בן בבא דמחמיר בנזרע כולו מודה דמהני לגינה שומירה, אע"ג דסתם גינה היא כולה זרועה. ומיהא מיבעיא ליה ביתר מבית סאתים אם ביטל דירתו אף בדיר וסהר ומוקצה, דשמא לפי שתשמישו רב אינו מתבטל משום זריעה. כי גם לרש"י צריך לחלק בין דיר וסהר ומוקצה וחצר לקרפף]: **לרבי** שמעון כיון דנזרע רובו ה"ל מיעוט בטל. נראה(ד) דמכ"ש פריך, לגבי רוב, דמדקאמר נזרע רובו והיינו ביתר מבית סאתים, משמע: הא מיעוטו – שרי אפילו ביתר מבית סאתים, היינו משום דבטל לגבי רובו אפילו לקולא, כל שכן היכא דרובא נזרע אפילו בית סאתים, דנימא דבטל לגבי רובא לחומרא: לא

רבינו חננאל

מאי בינייהו ופרקינן דבר מועט איכא בינייהו דתניא ר' יהודה אומר דבר מועט יש מן חוץ לע' אמה ושיריים ולא נתנו בו חכמים שיעור: כמה הוא בית סאתים. ק' אמה ברוחב נ' בחצר המשכן מנ"ל דאמר רב יהודה אמר קרא אורך החצר מאה באמה ורוחב חמשים בחמשים אמרה תורה טול חמשים מן המאה וסבב אותן על חמשים הנשארות מן המאה ולכשתסבבם נמצאות שבעים אמה ושיריים על שבעים אמה ושיריים: **ירושלמי** ר' שמואל בר נחמן בשם ר' נתן. מחצר המשכן למדו דהויא לה ארך ק' אמה ורחב ג' אמה ג' זמנין מאה אמין הוויין בתרייתא ה' אלפין אמין. ע' אמין על ע' אמין בתרייתא חמשה אלפין (פרוו) [פרא] מאה. ותנינן ע' אמה ושיריים ותני שמואל שיריים הללו הן שני שלישי אמה וכך הצעה של משנה ע' אמה וב' שלישי אמה על ע' אמה וב' שלישי אמה דאינון ע' (תלתולין) [תלתותין] באורכה וע' (תלתולין) [תלתותין] בפותיא הא מאה וארבעין (תלתולין) [תלתותין] דאינון צ' אמתא ותלת אמין ותילתא דאמתא אפיק מינייהו ארבעה תשעין לארבע רוחתא אישתיירו תשסרי [תלתותין] חסיר תשעה הדא הוא דתני יש בו דבר קל ולא יכלו חכמים לעמוד עליו והוא חלק מי"ב חלקים לאמה. וחצי אצבע מחמש אצבעות לטפח. נמצא ע' אמה וב' שלישי אמה וחלק מי"ב חלקים באמה וחצי אצבע מה' אצבעות לטפח על ע' אמה וב' שלישי אמה וחלק מי"ב חלקים באמה. [וחצי אצבע מ"ה אצבעות לטפח] כיון דאמרינן שיטול ג' וסבב ג' אמרי' פשטיה דקרא היכי הוא ופשיט אביי אמרה תורה העמד משכן על שפת נ' נמצא אורך המשכן ל' אמות שהן כ' קרשים כל קרש אמה וחצי הרי ל' אמה ואחורי המשכן במערב כ' אמה ריוח הרי נ' אמה ורוחב המשכן י' אמות וריוח כ' אמות בצפון וכ' אמה בדרום הרי נ' אמה נמצא המשכן עם הריוח שלו נ' אמה לכל רוח בג' רוחותיו צפון ומערב ודרום חמשים בחמשים וחמשים בחמשים לפני המשכן חצר הרי מאה אורך בחמשים: **מתני'** ר' אליעזר אומר אם אורכה יתירה על רוחבה אפי' אמה אחת. אוקימנא אם היה אמה יתירה על פי שנים כרחבה אפי' אמה אחת אין מטלטלין בתוכה. ר' יוסי אומר אם היה אורכה אפילו כשנים כרוחבה מטלטלין בתוכה. ואקשינן ר' יוסי היינו ר' אליעזר ופרקינן איכא בינייהו ריבועא [דריבעוה] רבנן דתנן עגולות דברי ר' חנניה בן אנטיגנוס וחכמים אומרים מרובעות כטבלא

רב נסים גאון

איכא בינייהו ריבועא דרבנן. עיקר דיליה בפרק מי שהוציאוהו גוים (דף מט) אם אינו מכיר או אינו בקי בהלכה ואמר שביתתי במקומי זכה לו מקומו אלפים אמה לכל רוח עגולות דברי רבי חנניה בן אנטיגנוס וחכמים אומרים מרובעות כטבלה מרובעת אמר

לקמן נח.

[כתובות קיא: קידושין פ: חולין ו. קנב. ערכין לח:]

לקמן לה. עד. פט. ולח. שבת קל:

[עי' תוס' ד"ה וכלבד] [ערבוב גירסאות יש כאן לאי גרסינן וד' טפחים ע"ב לא גרסי' רפ"ב ע"ב לא גרסי' רפ"ב ועיין במהרש"א]

הגהות הב"ח

(א) רש"י ד"ה אלא אמרה תורה טול וכו' הרי ל' רצועות של ב' טפחים רוחב לאורך כל אחת וכו' למעבד מינייהו רצועה של רפ"ב אמות וד' טפחים אורך להקיף: (ב) ד"ה ועשרים לכל רוח וכו' של צלע לארכו ולאמה וכו' (ג) בא"ד לכל צד והכלה כללה קחשיב ועובי הכתלים: (ד) תוס' ד"ה לר' שמעון וכו' נראה דמכת כ"ש פריך וכו' והיינו משום דבטל:

הגהות הגר"א

[א] רש"י ד"ה אלא אמרה תורה טול וכו' אין מגיע התוספת לרוחב וכו'. נ"ב והוא לאצבע בקירוב ול' מ"ח באצבע ע"ז והרבעה טפחי' ולאצבע משתייר שלש אמה:

גליון הש"ס

גמ' יתר ע"פ שנים ברחבה תנן. עיין לקמן דף כה ע"ב תוס' ד"ה לקרפף:

א) [ועיין תוס' ב"ב קמז. ד"ה מנין ותוס' סוטה לב: סד"ה ורבי] ב) [ועיין תוס' שבת קכ:] ג) [וכי מאות הן שילטרך לכתחלה לעשות כך והא לא איירי אלא בהכשר קרפף שהוא בנוי כבר רש"ל מתוס' שנז] ד) [ועיין ברב אלפס דף נה.]

בָּטֵיל לֵיהּ לְגַבֵּי רוּבָּהּ, וַהֲוָה לֵיהּ קַרְפֵּף יוֹתֵר מִבֵּית סָאתַיִם — וְאָסוּר. אֶלָּא, אִי אִיתְּמַר הָכִי אִיתְּמַר: הָא מִיעוּטָא שָׁרֵי. אָמַר רַב הוּנָא בְּרֵיהּ דְּרַב יְהוֹשֻׁעַ: לָא אֲמַרַן אֶלָּא דְּלָא הָוֵי בֵּית סָאתַיִם, אֲבָל בֵּית סָאתַיִם — אָסוּר. כְּמַאן — כְּרַבָּנַן. וְרַב יִרְמְיָה מִדִּיפְתִּי מַתְנֵי לְקוּלָּא: [א]הָא מִיעוּטָא — שָׁרֵי. אָמַר רַב הוּנָא בְּרֵיהּ דְּרַב יְהוֹשֻׁעַ: לָא אֲמַרַן אֶלָּא בֵּית סָאתַיִם, אֲבָל יוֹתֵר מִבֵּית סָאתַיִם — אָסוּר, כְּמַאן — כְּר"ש. § "נָטַע רוּבּוֹ — הֲרֵי הוּא כֶּחָצֵר, וּמוּתָּר". § אָמַר רַב יְהוּדָה, אָמַר אֲבִימִי: וְהוּא שֶׁעֲשׂוּיִין אִיצְטַבְלָאוֹת. וְרַב נַחְמָן אָמַר: [ב]אע"פ שֶׁאֵין עֲשׂוּיִין אִיצְטַבְלָאוֹת. מָר יְהוּדָה אִיקְלַע לְבֵי רַב הוּנָא בַּר יְהוּדָה; חַזְנְהוּ לְהָנְהוּ דְּלָא עֲבִידִי אִיצְטַבְלָאוֹת, וְקָא מְטַלְטְלֵי בְּגַוַּיְיהוּ. אֲמַר לֵיהּ: לָא סָבַר לַהּ מָר לְהָא דַּאֲבִימִי? אֲמַר לֵיהּ: אֲנָא כְּרַב נַחְמָן סְבִירָא לִי. אָמַר רַב נַחְמָן, אָמַר שְׁמוּאֵל: קַרְפֵּף יוֹתֵר מִבֵּית סָאתַיִם שֶׁלֹּא הוּקַּף לְדִירָה, כֵּיצַד הוּא עוֹשֶׂה? [ג]פּוֹרֵץ בּוֹ פִּירְצָה יוֹתֵר מֵעֶשֶׂר, וְגוֹדְרוֹ וּמַעֲמִידוֹ עַל עֶשֶׂר, וּמוּתָּר. אִיבַּעְיָא לְהוּ: פָּרַץ אַמָּה וְגָדַר אַמָּה [וּפָרַץ אַמָּה וְגָדְרָהּ] עַד שֶׁהִשְׁלִימוֹ לְיוֹתֵר מֵעֶשֶׂר, מַהוּ? א"ל: [ד]לָאו הַיְינוּ דִּתְנַן: *[ה]כָּל כְּלֵי בַּעֲלֵי בָתִּים שִׁיעוּרָן כְּרִמּוֹנִים. וּבָעֵי חִזְקִיָּה: נִיקַּב כְּמוֹצִיא זַיִת וּסְתָמוֹ, וְחָזַר וְנִיקַּב כְּמוֹצִיא זַיִת וּסְתָמוֹ עַד שֶׁהִשְׁלִימוֹ לְמוֹצִיא רִמּוֹן, מַהוּ? וְא"ל רַבִּי יוֹחָנָן: רַבִּי, שָׁנִיתָ לָנוּ: [ו]*סַנְדָּל(א) שֶׁנִּפְסְקָה אַחַת מֵאׇזְנָיו וְתִיקְּנָהּ — טָמֵא מִדְרָס, נִפְסְקָה שְׁנִיָּה וְתִיקְּנָהּ — טָהוֹר בָּהּ מִן הַמִּדְרָס, אֲבָל טָמֵא מַגַּע מִדְרָס. וְאָמַרְתְּ עֲלָהּ מַאי שְׁנָא רִאשׁוֹנָה — דְּהָא קָיְימָא שְׁנִיָּה, שְׁנִיָּה נָמֵי הָא *קָיְימָא רִאשׁוֹנָה! וְאָמַרְתְּ לַן עֲלָהּ: פָּנִים חֲדָשׁוֹת בָּאוּ לְכָאן. הָכָא נָמֵי פָּנִים חֲדָשׁוֹת בָּאוּ לְכָאן. *קָרֵי עֲלֵיהּ: לֵית דֵּין בַּר אֱנָשׁ! אִיכָּא דְּאָמְרִי: כְּגוֹן דֵּין בַּר נַשׁ! אָמַר רַב כָּהֲנָא: [ז]רְחָבָה שֶׁאֲחוֹרֵי הַבָּתִּים, אֵין מְטַלְטְלִין בּוֹ אֶלָּא בְּד' אַמּוֹת. וְאָמַר רַב נַחְמָן: [ח]אִם פָּתַח לוֹ פֶּתַח — מוּתָּר לְטַלְטֵל בְּכוּלּוֹ, פֶּתַח מַתִּירוֹ. וְלָא אֲמַרַן אֶלָּא שֶׁפָּתַח וּלְבַסּוֹף הוּקַּף, אֲבָל הוּקַּף וּלְבַסּוֹף פָּתַח — לֹא. פָּתַח וּלְבַסּוֹף הוּקַּף, פְּשִׁיטָא! לָא צְרִיכָא, דְּאִית בֵּיהּ בֵּי דָרֵי. מַהוּ דְּתֵימָא: אַדַּעְתָּא דְּבֵי דָרֵי *עֲבַדֵיהּ, קמ"ל. קַרְפֵּף יוֹתֵר מִבֵּית סָאתַיִם שֶׁהוּקַּף לְדִירָה וְנִתְמַלֵּא מַיִם, סְבוּר רַבָּנַן לְמֵימַר כִּזְרָעִים דָּמוּ — וַאֲסִיר. אֲמַר לְהוּ רַב אַבָּא *אֲבוּהּ *דְּרַב בְּרֵיהּ דְּרַב מְשַׁרְשִׁיָּא: הָכִי אָמְרִינַן מִשְּׁמֵיהּ דְּרָבָא: [ט]מַיִם כִּנְטָעִים דָּמוּ — וְשָׁרֵי.

אָמַר

רש"י

בָּטֵיל לְגַבֵּי רוּבָּהּ. וְהָוֵי כְּאִילּוּ נִזְרַע כּוּלּוֹ: וַהֲוָה לֵיהּ קַרְפֵּף יוֹתֵר מִבֵּית סָאתַיִם. וְאַע"ג דְּהוּקַּף לְדִירָה — חָשׁוּב כְּלֹא הוּקַּף לְדִירָה. דְּהָא הָוֵי כּוּלּוֹ גִּינָּה, וּבְגִינָּה לָא מְהַנֵּי הוּקַּף לְדִירָה: דְּלָא הָוֵי. הַהוּא מִיעוּט דְּנִזְרַע בֵּית סָאתַיִם, דְּלָא חֲשִׁיב לְהִבָּדֵל מִן הֶחָצֵר וּלְהִקָּרוֹת לוֹ שֵׁם לְבַדּוֹ: אֲבָל בֵּית סָאתַיִם. נִקְרָא קַרְפֵּף שֶׁלֹּא הוּקַּף לְדִירָה. וְאַע"ג דְּאִילּוּ הֲוָה בְּאַנְפֵּי נַפְשֵׁיהּ כְּבֵית סָאתַיִם לָא מִיתְּסַר, הָכָא דְּנִפְרַץ לְחָצֵר וְחָצֵר נִפְרְצָה לוֹ — קַיְימָא לָן דְּאָסוּר לְטַלְטֵל מִקַּרְפֵּף לְחָצֵר, דְּהָוֵי רְשׁוּת הַנִּפְרְצָה לְמָקוֹם הָאָסוּר לָהּ וְאוֹסְרִין הָרְשׁוּיוֹת זוֹ לָזוֹ וְאֵין מְטַלְטְלִין לֹא בָּזֶה וְלֹא בָּזֶה: כְּמַאן. אָמְרִי' דִּשְׁתֵּי רְשׁוּיוֹת נִינְהוּ: כְּרַבָּנַן. דִּפְלִיגִי עֲלֵיהּ דְּר"ש בְּפ' "כָּל גַּגּוֹת" (דף פט.), וְאָמְרִי: כָּל חַד וְחַד רְשׁוּת לְעַצְמוֹ. וְאַע"ג דְּלֵיכָּא דִּיּוּרִין בְּהוּ דְּלִיסְרוּ אַהֲדָדֵי — אֵין מְטַלְטְלִין מִזֶּה לָזֶה: לְקוּלָּא. דַּאֲפִילּוּ הַמִּיעוּט בֵּית סָאתַיִם דְּמִיקְרֵי קַרְפֵּף, כֵּיוָן דְּבְאַנְפֵּי נַפְשֵׁיהּ שָׁרֵי, הַשְׁתָּא נָמֵי שָׁרֵי, — וְלָא אָסְרֵי אַהֲדָדֵי. דְּאִילּוּ הָיְתָה מְחִיצָּה בֵּינֵיהֶן — הֲוָה שָׁרֵי לְטַלְטוּלֵי מִזֶּה לָזֶה כְּר"ש, וְהַשְׁתָּא דְּנִפְרְצוּ זֶה לָזֶה — לֹא נִפְרְצוּ לִרְשׁוּת הָאָסוּר לָהּ. אֲבָל יוֹתֵר מִבֵּית סָאתַיִם — נַעֲשָׂה כַּרְמְלִית, וּבְהָא אֲפִילּוּ ר"ש מוֹדֶה דְּאֵין מְטַלְטְלִין מֵחָצֵר לְקַרְפֵּף יוֹתֵר מִבֵּית סָאתַיִם שֶׁלֹּא הוּקַּף לְדִירָה. וְהָכָא דְּנִפְרְצוּ זֶה לָזֶה — הֲרֵי כָּל אֶחָד נִפְרַץ לְמָקוֹם הָאָסוּר לוֹ: אִיצְטַבְלָאוֹת. נְטוּעִין שׁוּרוֹת שׁוּרוֹת, וְנָאֶה לָשֶׁבֶת שָׁם: לְבֵי רַב הוּנָא. יוֹתֵר מִבֵּית סָאתַיִם הֲוָה, וְהוּקַּף לְדִירָה, וְנִיטַּע אַחֲרֵי כֵן: קַרְפֵּף יוֹתֵר מִבֵּית סָאתַיִם שֶׁלֹּא הוּקַּף לְדִירָה. וְאַחֲרֵי כֵן בָּנָה אֶצְלוֹ דִּירָה, וְאָמְרִי' לְקַמָּן: הוּקַּף שֶׁלֹּא לְדִירָה וּלְבַסּוֹף פָּתַח לוֹ פֶּתַח לְדִירַת בֵּיתוֹ — לָא מְהַנֵּי: כֵּיצַד הוּא עוֹשֶׂה פּוֹרֵץ לוֹ פִּרְצָה יוֹתֵר מֵעֶשֶׂר. דְּהָוֵי כְּמִי שֶׁאֵין בּוֹ מְחִיצּוֹת, וְגוֹדֵר וְסוֹתֵם אוֹתָהּ פִּירְצָה וּמַעֲמִידָהּ עַל עֶשֶׂר, וְהָוֵי כְּפָתַח וּלְבַסּוֹף הוּקַּף לְדִירָה שֶׁנִּפְתְּחָה לוֹ. דִּלְעוֹלָם בָּעֵינַן שֶׁיִּגְדּוֹר יוֹתֵר מֵעֶשֶׂר אַמּוֹת. דְּאִי פָּרֵיץ עֶשֶׂר לְבַד וּגְדָרָהּ — לָא חֲשִׁיב הַהוּא הֶיקֵּף לְשֵׁם דִּירָה, אֶלָּא כְּמִי שֶׁעָשָׂה פֶּתַח. דְּעַד עֶשֶׂר לְעוֹלָם הָוֵי פֶּתַח: פָּרַץ אַמָּה. אֵצֶל סְתִימָה, וּגְדָרָהּ. וְעוֹד פָּרַץ אַמָּה אֵצֶל סְתִימַת אַמָּה הַחֲדָשָׁה וּגְדָרָהּ, דְּלֹא פָּרַץ י' אַמּוֹת כְּאֶחָד וְלֹא גָּדַר עֶשֶׂר אַמּוֹת בְּבַת אַחַת אֶלָּא מְעַט הָיָה פּוֹרֵץ וְגוֹדֵר מִיָּד: עַד שֶׁהִשְׁלִימוֹ לְיוֹתֵר מֵעֶשֶׂר. מִי אָמְרִינַן: כֵּיוָן דְּלֹא פָּרַץ י' בְּבַת אַחַת וְלֹא גָּדַר בְּבַת אַחַת — לָא הָוְיָא הֶיקֵּף בָּזוֹ לְשֵׁם דִּירָה. אוֹ דִּילְמָא: כֵּיוָן דְּהַשְׁתָּא מִיהָא הָוֵי הַחִידּוּשׁ שֶׁל הֶיקֵּף יוֹתֵר מֵעֶשֶׂר — חֲשִׁיב הֶיקֵּף לְשֵׁם דִּירָה: כָּל כְּלֵי בַּעֲלֵי בָתִּים. לְגַבֵּי כְּלֵי עֵץ תְּנֵינַן לָהּ בְּמַסֶּכֶת כֵּלִים (פי"ז מ"א): שִׁיעוּרָן בְּרִמּוֹנִים. לִיטָּהֵר מִטּוּמְאָתָן, אֲבָל פָּחוֹת מִכָּאן — חָיֵיס עֲלֵיהּ וְלָא מְבַטֵּיל לֵיהּ. שִׁיעוּרָן כְּרִמּוֹנִים — נִיקַּב כְּמוֹצִיא רִמּוֹן טָהוֹר: וְחָזַר וְנִיקַּב. אֵצֶל הַסְּתִימָה: וְתִיקְּנָהּ. הוּא הַדִּין כִּי לֹא תִּיקְּנָהּ נָמֵי עֲדַיִין טְמֵא מִדְרָס הוּא. וְהָא דְּנָקַט תִּיקְּנָהּ — לְרַבּוּתָא, דְּאִי לָאו הָכִי — תּוּ לָא אִיצְטְרִיךְ לְמֵימַר נִפְסְקָה הַשְּׁנִיָּה וְכוּ': (ב) טָהוֹר מִן הַמִּדְרָס. דְּתוּ לָא הָוֵה כְּלִי, וְלָא חֲזֵי לְמִדְרָס מִלְּטַמֵּא תּוּ אָדָם וְכֵלִים: אֲבָל. כְּלִי הוּא דַּחֲזֵי לְתַשְׁמִישׁ אַחֲרִינָא, וַעֲדַיִין טוּמְאַת מַגַּע מִדְרָס עָלָיו, שֶׁהֲרֵי בִּשְׁעַת פְּרִישָׁתוֹ (ג) מִן הָאוֹזֶן שֶׁעֲדַיִין הוּא מִדְרָס לְקַבֵּל טוּמְאָה לְטַמֵּא כֵּלִים קִיבֵּל טוּמְאָה מֵאָבִיו. וְהָוֵי רִאשׁוֹן לְטוּמְאָה, וּמְטַמֵּא אוֹכָלִין וּמַשְׁקִין: פָּנִים חֲדָשׁוֹת. אֵין אָזְנַיִם הַלָּלוּ מִמֶּנּוּ, וּמִשֶּׁנִּיתַּקְּנוּ — לֹא דְּרָסָן הַזָּב. וּמִטּוּמְאָה הָרִאשׁוֹנָה טִיהֲרוֹ — שֶׁהֲרֵי אֵין זֶה סַנְדָּל רִאשׁוֹן: לֵית דֵּין בַּר נַשׁ. אֶלָּא מַלְאָךְ: כְּגוֹן דֵּין בַּר נַשׁ. אָדָם גָּדוֹל: רְחָבָה שֶׁאֲחוֹרֵי הַבָּתִּים. וְאֵין פֶּתַח הַבַּיִת פָּתוּחַ לָהּ — הָוְיָא מוּקֶּפֶת שֶׁלֹּא לְדִירָה, וְאִי יוֹתֵר מִבֵּית סָאתַיִם הָיָה — אֵין מְטַלְטֵל בָּהּ אֶלָּא בְּאַרְבַּע אַמּוֹת: וְאִם פָּתַח לוֹ פֶּתַח. מִן הַבַּיִת: פְּשִׁיטָא. דִּכְפָתַח וּלְבַסּוֹף הוּקַּף שָׁרֵי, שֶׁהֲרֵי הוּקַּף לְשֵׁם פֶּתַח: לָא צְרִיכָא דְּאִית בֵּיהּ בֵּי דָרֵי. גּוֹרֶן אַחַר הַבַּיִת קוֹדֶם הֶיקֵּף הָרְחָבָה: מַהוּ דְּתֵימָא אַדַּעְתָּא דְּבֵי דָרֵי פְּתָחֵיהּ. וְלָאו אַדַּעְתָּא לְהַקִּיף שָׁם רְחָבָה:

דחזו

תוספות

לא אמרן אלא דלא הוי בית סאתים. אע"ג דלרבנן קרפף פחות מבית סאתים דינו כקרפף בית סאתים(ד) לטלטל ממנו לחצר, משום דאין סברא שיהו שלשה חילוקים בשלשה משהויין – הכא לא אסר מיעוט הנזרע לרוב שאינו נזרע במה שפרוץ לו במלואו. דכיון שהוא פחות מבית סאתים – לא חשיב, ובטל לגבי רוב שאינו נזרע, אבל בית סאתים – חשיב טפי, ולא בטיל. ובנזרע רובו, אפי' לא הוי בית סאתים – אסור, דבטיל(ה) לגבי רובו, והוה כנזרע כולו: **סנדל** שנפסקה וכו'. הוא הדין בלא תקנה נמי דטמא מדרס. דאי כשנפסקה פרחה לה טומאה – תו לא הדרה לה, דלא מצינו טומאה ישנה חוזרת אלא בכלי מתכות, כדמפרש בסוף פ"ק דשבת (ד' טז.). והא דנקט ותקנה – פ"ה: לאשמועינן, אע"ג דתקנה, כי נפסקה שניה – טהורה מן המדרס, דפנים חדשות באו לכאן: **אבל** טמא מגע מדרס. פירש הקונטרס: משום דעדיין כלי הוא לאשתמושי ביה תשמישתא אחרינא. ולפירושו, אפילו נפסקה שניה טמא מגע מדרס. וקשה, דתנן בהדיא, בסיפא דהך משנה במסכת כלים בפרק כ"ו (מ"ד): לא הספיק לתקן ראשונה עד שנפסקה שניה – טהורה. ור"י חזר בו, והגיה: אבל טמא מגע מדרס – דעדיין כלי הוא, וחזי למילתא קמייתא, דהא איתקנה ראשונה. ולפירושו איצטריך למיתני ברישא ותיקנה, דאי לא נתקנה – כי נפסקה שניה אינה טמאה אפילו מגע מדרס. ואגב דתני ברישא – תני נמי בסיפא. ומיהו, תימה: מתי בא לו מגע מדרס? דאם בא לו מגע מדרס ומדרס יחד, כגון שדרס עליו הזב ברגלו יחף, או אפי' במנעל ולא הפסיק בפשוטי כלי עץ – א"כ איכא פנים חדשות למגע מדרס כמו למדרס! ולפי' ר"י קמא ניחא, דאפילו נפסקו ב' אזנים – טמא מגע מדרס, הואיל וחזי לתשמיש אחרינא. ובפרק "אלו קשרים" (שבת דף קיב:) פ"ה: דטמא מגע מדרס – לפי שנגע בעצמו כשהיה אב הטומאה. ולא נהירא, דטומאת בית הסתרים היא. דלא קיימא לן כרבי מאיר דאמר מטמא, מדפריש בפשיטות בפרק "בהמה המקשה" (חולין דף עג:) וב"העור והרוטב" (שם דף קכט:): טומאת בית הסתרים היא! ומה שפירש כאן נמי, דבשעת פרישתו מאוזן קיבל טומאה מאביו – אינו נראה. דבפרק "בהמה המקשה": (שם דף עג:) אמרינן: דבעינן באות מבגד גדול. ואין לומר דכשתיקן אוזן ראשון, לאחר שתפר אליה נעשית מחוברת, ובא לה טומאת מדרס שבטלה לסנדל. וכשחזר ותפר אליה השניה – בא לסנדל מגע מדרס מן האוזן, ותו ליכא פנים חדשות. דא"כ תפשוט בעיין ד"הקומץ רבה" (מנחות דף כד.) דלא אמרינן שבע לה טומאה. ולהר"ר שמעון מיינבי"א, דמפרש: דלא אמרינן שבע לה טומאה היכא דטומאה בא לו מגופו – אתי שפיר. ועוד יש לומר: דלאוזן בא מגע מדרס ומדרס יחד כשתפרה לסנדל, והסנדל בטל לאוזן, דאי אפשר להיות טומאה לזה בלא זה. וכיון שבאו לה כאחד – אין שייך לומר גביה שבע לה טומאה. וריצב"א אומר: דלא שייך גבי מגע פנים חדשות, דאפילו נפסקו שתי אזניו – ראוי לקבל טומאת מגע אם מיחדו לתשמיש אחר, ולא נתבטל תורת יחוד מכאן, דכל שעה ושעה מתקנו ודעתו להשתמש בו. אבל לנועלו, אם נפסקו שתי אזניו, אפילו מיחדו – בטלה דעתו אצל כל אדם:

פשיטא לא צריכא דאית ביה בי דרי. אדרב נחמן, דאמר: אם פתח בו פתח מותר לטלטל פריך, דמפרש הש"ס בפתח ולבסוף הוקף, ואהא פריך פשיטא. אבל אתלמוד דמפרש לא אמרן לא פריך, דקמ"ל הוקף ולבסוף פתח לא מהני, לאפוקי מהני אמוראי דלקמן (ד' כה:) גבי אבורנקי: לא

עין משפט נר מצוה

כט א ב מיי' פט"ז שם הלכה ו טוש"ע שם סעיף ט:
ל ג ד מיי' שם הל' ה וטוש"ע שם ס"ב:
לא ה מיי' פ"ז מהל' כלים הלכה ב:
לב ו מיי' פ"ז שם הלכה יב:
לג ז ח מיי' פט"ז מהל' שבת הלכה י טור ש"ע א"ח סי' שנט:
לד ט מיי' שם הלכה ו טוש"ע א"ח סי' שנח סעיף יא:

רבינו חננאל

מרובעות כדי שיהא נשכר הזויות לר' אליעזר דאמר אם היה אורכה יתר על שנים ברחבה אפילו אמה אם היא מרובעת לא שרי לטלטולי בה דכי (אשכחת) [משחת] לה באלכסונא מזוית לזוית (אשתכרו) [אשתכחו] טפי מן שנים ברחבה כר' חנינא בן אנטיגנוס. [דכתיב] זה יהיה לכם גבול לזה אתה (אומר) נותן פיאות ואי אתה נותן פיאות לשובתי שבת. ואילו ר' יוסי דאמר אפילו אורכה כשנים ברחבה [אפי'] מרובע [שרי] דיליף ממשכן דהוא ארכו ק' אמה ורחבו נ' אמה שנמצא ארכו מרובע כשנים ברחבו אע"ג דאלכסונו טפי מן שנים ברחבה שרי כרב אחא דאמר המעביר ד' אמות ברה"ר אינו חייב עד שיעביר הן ואלכסונן ואמר רב פפא בדיק לן רבא עמוד ברשות הרבים גבוה י' ורחב ד' מי בעינן הן ואלכסונן אי לא ופשטנא מיהא דתני רב חנינא כזה יהיו כל שובתי שבת ובהא אסיקנא הלכתא כרבי עקיבא והלכתא כר' יוסי ותרוויהו לקולא דאפי' אריך וקטין ואפילו לא יש בה שומירה ולא בית דירה שרי. קרפף יותר מבית סאתים שהוקף לדירה אם ניטע רובו הרי הוא כחצר פי' לא אפקיה מתורת חצר דעבידי אינשי דנטעי אילנות בחצר. ועדיין תורת חצר עליו. אבל אם נזרע רובו בא זריעתו ודחה את ההקפה שהקיפו לשם דירה לפיכך אמרו הרי הוא כגינה ותנן לא אמרו בית סאתים אלא בגינה ובקרפף אבל יתר מיכן אסור. וזה כיון שהוא יתר מבית סאתים אסור דהא זריעתו אפקיה מתורת דירה. אמר רב הונא בריה דר' יהושע לא אמרו שבאה זריעתה ובטלה תורת הקפתו לדירה אלא בזמן שהוא יתר מבית סאתים אבל בית סאתים מותר. דתנן אחד גגות אחד חצרות ואחד קרפיפות [רשות אחת הן] לכלים ששבתו בתוכן ולא לכלים ששבתו בתוך הבית ואקשינן לר' שמעון נמי אפילו בית סאתים כיון שנזרע רובו בטיל ליה מיעוטו לגבי רובו וחשיב כמי שלא הוקף לדירה כיון שזרעו ליהוי כי קרפף יתר מבית סאתים שלא הוקף לדירה כשם שזריעתו עשאתו כשדה כך תעשהו ביתר מבית סאתים אלא אי אתמר הכי אתמר הא נזרע מיעוטו שרי: אמר רב הונא כו' רב ירמיה מדפתי מתני לה לקולא נזרע רובו הרי הוא כגינה ואסור. הא

מסורת הש"ס

לעיל ד: ברכות מח. סוכה ו. שבת קיב: כלים פי"ז מ"א

שם פכ"ו מ"ד שבת קיב:

ס"א קמתקנא

[שבת קיב: ע"ז ע:]

ס"א פתח

(נ"ל אחוה)

גי' יעב"ץ דרבא

הגהות הב"ח

(א) גמרא סנדל שנפסקה וכו': (ב) רש"י ד"ה טהור מן המדרס וכו': (ג) שם ד"ה אבל וכו' מן האוזן: (ד) תוס' ד"ה לא אמרן וכו' כקרפף בית סאתים: (ה) בא"ד דבטיל לגבי רובו:

מיעוטו שרי. אמר רב הונא בריה דר' יהושע לא אמרו אלא בית סאתים הא יתר מבית סאתים אפילו שלא נזרע אלא מיעוטו אסור *) כמאן כרבנן: **איצטבלאות.** עיקר המלה ארוות סוסים הוא בלשון יווני ופירושו כי נוטעין אילנות זה בצד זה כגון העמדת סוסים בתוך אורותיהם זה בצד זה ואסיקנא דאע"ג דאינה עשויה איצטבלאות מותר כרב נחמן: אמר רב נחמן אמר שמואל קרפף יתר מבית סאתים שלא הוקף לדירה פורץ בו פרצה יתר מעשר אמות וחוזר וגודרו לשם דירה ודיו וחשוב כאילו הקיפו כולו לשם דירה וכן אם פרץ אמה וגדרה לשם דירה ועוד פרץ אמה וגדרה לשם דירה עד שהשלים יתר מי' אמות גדר לשם דירה נעשה כאילו

*) [לפי הגהתו מן הסוגיא לרבנן אפילו בית סאתים אסור ואולי טס"ה וצ"ל כמאן כר"ש וכמו שהגיה בגמ'].

אמר אמימר: [א]והוא דחזיין לתשמישתא, אבל לא חזיין לתשמישתא – לא. אמר רב אשי: ודחזיין לתשמישתא נמי לא אמרן אלא שאין בעומקו יותר מבית סאתים, אבל אם יש בעומקו יותר מבית סאתים – אסור. [ב]ולאו מילתא היא, מידי דהוה אכריא דפירי. ההיא רחבה דהואי בפום נהרא דחד גיפא הוה פתיח למתא, וחד גיפא הוה פתיח לשביל של כרמים, ושביל של כרמים הוה סליק לגודא דנהרא. אמר אביי: היכי נעביד? לעביד ליה מחיצה אגודא דנהרא – אין עושין מחיצה על גבי מחיצה. ולעביד ליה צורת הפתח אפומא דשביל של כרמים – אתו גמלי שדיין ליה. אלא אמר אביי: ליעביד לחי אפיתחא דשביל של כרמים, דמגו דמהניא לשביל של כרמים – מהני נמי לרחבה. אמר ליה רבא: יאמרו לחי מועיל לשביל של כרמים דעלמא! אלא אמר רבא: [ג]עבדינן ליה לחי לפיתחא דמתא, דמגו דמהני לחי למתא – מהני נמי לרחבה. הלכך, טלטולי במתא גופה – שרי, טלטולי ברחבה גופה – שרי, ממתא לרחבה ומרחבה למתא – פליגי בה רב אחא ורבינא, חד אסר וחד שרי. מאן

רש"י

דחזו לתשמישתא. לשתיה, דאין לך דירה מעולה מזו: שאין בעומקו יותר על בית סאתים. כלומר: שאין עומקו של מים נפשט ברוחב יותר על בית סאתים. ועומקו של סתם מים לבטל מקומו מדין קרקע – י' טפחים, כדאמרינן במסכת שבת (דף ק:): ואם היה רקק מים וכו' כמה רקק מים, פחות מי' טפחים: כריא דפירי. כרי של פירות, גבוה עשרה ורוחב כרוחב בית כור – לא בטלה תורת דירה משם. ומים הראוין לשתיה – כפירות דמי. ל"א: מידי דהוה אכריא דפירי – שוחה עמוקה שמצניעין שם פירות, שאע"פ שעמוקין שם הרבה – נוטלים מהן בשבת: ההיא רחבה. יותר מבית סאתים הוה ולא הוקפה לדירה: פום נהרא. שם מקום: חד גיפא פתוח למתא. למבוי שבעיר שכלה לרחבה זו: שביל של כרמים. דיורין היו בו: היכי ניעביד. למשרינהו לכולהו. שהרי רחבה זו כרמלית היא, ואוסרת כל המבוי, ואת השביל שיש לו שלש מחיצות. דהא גודא דנהרא מחיצה מעלייתא היא, שגובהה עשרה, אבל הרחבה אוסרתן – לפי שפרוצין הן במילואן לכרמלית. והא דאמרינן בפ"ק (ד' ז.): אם היה מבוי כלה לרחבה אין צריך כלום – במוקפת לדירה והיו בה דיורין קאמר, כדמפליג התם בין עירבו ללא עירבו. אבל רחבה כרמלית – אסור, כדאמרינן בההיא שמעתא: בקעה מכאן ובקעה מכאן כו': היכי ניעביד. להתיר את כולם, שהיו רוצין מעכשיו להשתמש בהם בני העיר ולהיותה מוקפת לדירה, ושוב לא תיהוי כרמלית, ותהא היא בכולן מותרת. ואמרינן לעיל: הוקף ולבסוף פתח – לא מהני. וגדר של אבנים היתה רחבה זו מוקפת, וקשה להם לפרוץ פירצה יותר מעשר ולגדרה לדירה אדעתא דלישתמשו בה בני מבוי ושביל מהשתא, וליהוי כפתח ולבסוף הוקף כדשמואל: ניעביד ליה מחיצה. של קנים: אגודא דנהרא. כלומר: להוי שביל כמוסף על הרחבה, דניהוי רחבה ושביל חד, וניהוי הך מחיצה דעבדינן בשביל אדעתא דדירה דלישתמשו מהשתא בני שביל ברחבה כאילו עבדינן לה ברחבה גופה לדירה, דהוי פתח ולבסוף הוקף: אין עושין מחיצה על גבי מחיצה. כיון דגודא גבוה עשרה, כל מה שמוסיפין עליה – הגבהת אותה מחיצה עצמה הויא. שהרי אם היה מגביה כל מחיצת הרחבה לדירה – לא מהני עד שיפרוץ בה פירצה האוסרתה, ויחזור ויגדור לדירה: ליעביד ליה צורת הפתח אפומא דשביל של כרמים. דפתוח לרחבה. דמגו דמהני לשביל, שלא יהא פרוץ לרחבה, שאפילו היה פתוח לרה"ר מועיל לו – ליהני נמי לרחבה, להיות לה תוספת זה היקף לדירה: אתו גמלי. הבאין לשתות מן העיר דרך מבוי לרחבה ומשם לשביל ולנהר: שדיין ליה. שהיה פתח השביל צר להן, ועכשיו הוא דוחקן: לחי. הנעוץ בארץ, ועביו משהו ואין גמלין נוגעין בו: דמיגו דמהני לשביל. לטלטל בו, דלא הוי השתא פרוץ לכרמלית: מהני נמי לרחבה. להיות לה היקף לדירה, ויתירנה לטלטל בה. ובלאו מיגו לא מישתריא, דהא פתח שבין רחבה לשביל לא היה יותר מעשר, וכל כמה דסתים ליה לדירה – לאו כלום היא, דהא כל פתח סתימה מעלייתא היא, וסתום ועומד הוא: לשביל של כרמים דעלמא. דלא סליק לגודא דנהרא, והוי ליה כמבוי מפולש, ויאמרו שאין צריך תיקון אלא בראשו אחד, כי האי: דמיגו דמהני למתא. לטלטל במבוי, כדאמרינן בפרק קמא (דף ז.): סרטיא מכאן ובקעה מכאן – עושה צורת הפתח מכאן ולחי או קורה מכאן. והכא נמי: ליעבדו בראש המבוי הפתוח לרשות הרבים צורת פתח, והאי לחי דלצד הרחבה שרי ליה: טלטולי במתא גופה שרי. דהא שרינן לה בהאי לחי, ואפילו היא והרחבה אסורים זה עם זה – שניהן משתמשין לעצמן כשתי חצירות ופתח ביניהן, וכן ברחבה גופה: דלית

תוספות

לא אמרן אלא שאין בעומקו יותר מבית סאתים. פי': שאין בעומקו עשרה ביותר מבית סאתים ברוחב, דהנך דעמוקין עשרה הוו כזרעים, ואתיא כרבי שמעון דקיימא לן כוותיה. דלרבנן, אפילו בית סאתים אסור, כדאמרינן לעיל. ומיירי כגון דהוי מיעוט מים העמוקים י'. דאי הוו רובא – הנך שאין עמוקין עשרה – הוי מיעוט, ובטלים לגבי רוב ואסור, כדאמרינן לעיל. ור"י מפרש: דאפילו רוב מים עמוקין נמי שרו. כיון דליכא אלא בית סאתים, בין עמוקים ובין שאינם עמוקים – לא חשיבי כזרעים, אלא דמו לנטעים, דדמו לבור. ומיהו, ביותר מבית סאתים – אסור, שאין דרך שוחה מליאה מים לעשות יותר מבית סאתים, וחשיבי כזרעים. אע"ג דגבי בור, אפי' רבי יהודה לא אסר ביותר מבית סאתים במחילות גמורות, אלא דווקא בפסין כדקאמר לעיל (דף יט:) זו מחילה ואלו פסין – היינו דווקא בבור המתוקן כהלכתו, אבל שוחה – לא:

(א) ההיא רחבה דהוה בפום נהרא דחד גיפא פתוח למתא וחד גיפא פתוח לשביל. פירש הקונטרס: דרחבה זו כרמלית. והיתה אוסרת המבוי. ואע"פ שבראשו האחד היה לו צורת הפתח או היה סתום, וגם את השביל שהיו לו שלש מחילות, דגודא דנהרא מחילה מעליא היא. ואף ע"ג דלרחבה היו גפופין, כדמוכח הסוגיא – לא מהניא למבוי ולשביל – משום דנראה מבחוץ ושוה מבפנים נידון משום לחי, דכיון דלא מהני לרחבה גופה – כל שכן דלא מהני למבוי ולשביל. ושביל, פירש הקונטרס דאית ביה דיורין. ואתי שפיר הא דקאמרינן בסמוך דמהני לחי לשביל. ואי אין בתים וחצירות פתוחים לתוכו – לא הוה משתרי בלחי. וכאן חזר בו רש"י ממה שפירש בפ"ק (דף ז:) דרחבה דהתם לית בה דיורין:

ליעביד מחיצה אגודא דנהרא. וניהוי שביל כמוסיף על הרחבה, ותיהוי שביל ורחבה חד, ותיהוי הך מחילה כאילו עבדינן לה ברחבה! ונראה דהיה שם רוחב יותר מעשר, ולכך על ידי המחילה נחשב מוקף לדירה. דאי בעשר – בלאו הכי הוי סתום ועומד, אפילו אם היה פרוץ במלואו לנהרא – היה די בלחי משהו. אלא היה יותר מעשר, ולכך לא היה מהני אפי' צורת הפתח לרב:

אין עושין מחיצה על גבי מחיצה. וא"ת: הא אמרי' לקמן (דף כה.) שאם עשה מחילה ע"ג התל – הועיל, שבאויר מחילות העליונות הוא דר! וי"ל: שהיה שם תל גבוה עשר מן השביל. ולפי זה אתי שפיר הא דלא חיישינן שמא יעלה הנהר שרטון, אפילו אם לא נחלק בין ים לשאר נהרות. וא"ת: ויעשו מחילות ברחוק ד' טפחים דאמר לקמן דמועיל. וי"ל: דלא רצו לקצר השביל:

לעביד צורת הפתח אפומא דשביל. פירש רש"י: דפתוח לרחבה. מיגו דמהני לשביל – מהני נמי לרחבה. וקשה: דמשמע דלא צריך למיגו עד לקמן. ועוד: דמה לו להזכיר צורת הפתח כלל, כיון דסגי בלחי כדקאמר אביי גופיה! ועוד: למה שינה הלשון, דמעיקרא קאמר אפומא דשביל, וגבי לחי קאמר אפיתחא. ועוד: דפריך "יאמרו לחי מהני לשביל של כרמים היכא דהוי מפולש", ואיך יטעו בין שביל זה, דאית ליה גדודי, לשביל דעלמא! ועוד: שצריך לפרש שיש שם תל גבוה עשרה – כל שכן שלא יטעו. לכך נראה לפרש: דשביל של כרמים אין בו דיורין, כדמוכח ב"הדר" (לקמן דף עד.), דקאמר: א"ר יוחנן אפילו בשביל של כרמים? א"ל: לא אמר ר' יוחנן אלא בחורבה, דחזיא לדירה. אבל בשביל של כרמים – לא אמר. ואפי' הכי מהניא ליה לחי, דבני מבוי היו משתמשין שם. ובמבוי הרבה בתים וחצירות היו. וליעבד מחילה אגודא דנהרא – היינו מעבר הנהר. וה"ה צורת הפתח, דהוי כמחילה. והנהר לא היה רחב יותר מעשר, ומעבר הנהר היו גידודין גבוהים עשרה, [ומצד השביל היה נמוך.] והשתא אתי שפיר הא דקאמר אין עושין מחילה על גבי מחילה כו' – כי מצד השביל היה נמוך. והשתא נמי לא חיישינן לשרטון – דלעולם יהיה מתלקט י' מתוך ד': ולעביד צורת הפתח אפומא דשביל. פירוש: אגודא דנהרא בנמוך. ושם לא רצו לעשות מחילה ולסתום השביל, שדרך שם משקין הגמלים: ולעביד לחי אפיתחא דשביל לצד הרחבה כו'(ג) מיגו דמהני. פירוש: השתא ודאי בלא מיגו לא מהני: יאמרו לחי מהני בשביל של כרמים דעלמא. שאין בני מבוי משתמשין שם, שלא יעלו על דעתם דהכא מהני משום מבוי. אי נמי, י"ל: יאמרו דלחי מהני בשביל של כרמים דעלמא, שהוא מפולש. דלא יסיקו אדעתייהו דגדודין שמעבר הנהר מהני: טלטולי ברחבה גופיה שרי. פירוש: הכלים ששבתו בתוכה, וכן בשביל: מאן

עין משפט נר מצוה

לה א ב מיי' שם וטוש"ע שם:

לו ג ד מיי' פט"ז מהל' שבת הלכה יח:

רבינו חננאל

כאילו הוקף כולו לשם דירה ומותר לטלטל בכולו ואפילו הוא בית י' כורין. כי הא דתנן כל כלי בעלי בתים שיעורן כרמונים כלומר אם נקבו כמוציא רימון טהרו. ובעי חזקיה ניקב במוציא זית וסתמו וחזר וניקב במוציא זית וסתמו עד שהשלימו למוציא רמון וא"ל ר' יוחנן רבי לא משנתנו היא זו סנדל שנפסקה אחת מאוני' ותקנה טמאה מדרס נפסקה שניה ותקנה טהור מלטמא מדרס כו'. ואמרת לן פנים חדשות באו לכאן. הכא נמי פנים חדשות באו לכאן כלומר אינם הן הן אינם אלא כאילו אחרות חדשות באו עכשיו קרי חזקיה על ר' יוחנן לית דין בר נש כמלאך הוא חשוב שמבין ומוציא אלו החכמות. אמר רב כהנא רחבה שאחורי בתים אין מטלטלין בה אלא בד' אמות. אמר ר"נ אם פתח מן הבתים לתוכו פתח מותר לטלטל בכולו. ודווקא פתח ולבסוף הקיף דהויא לה הקפה לדירה אבל הקיף שלא לשם דירה ולבסוף פתח לא ואמרינן פתח מן הבתים פתח ואח"כ הקיפה צריכה למימר דהא ודאי לדירה היא ופרקינן כגון דאית ליה בההוא רחבה בי דרי. פי' גורן לדוש עליו תבואה מהו דתימא האי פתח לגורן הוא דעבדיה קמ"ל דכיון דאית ליה פתח האי דאקיף לדירה הוא דאקיף קרפף יתר מבית סאתים שהוקף לדירה ונתמלא מים כנטיעים דמי ומותר לטלטל בכולו. דכולו כחצר דמי דאיכא מאן דעביד בחצירו בריכה של מים ואפי' יש בעומקו של מים יותר מבית סאתים מותר מידי דהוה אכריא דפירי. פי' יתכן שיעשה אדם בחצרו כרי של פירות עודף ועולה גבוה מן הקרקע של חצר יתר מבית סאתים: ההיא רחבה דהוה בפום נהרא. פי' על שפת הנהר מסתברא דרחבה דרבים הואי. חד גיפא פתוח למתא וחד גיפא פתוח לשביל של כרמים ושביל פתוח לגודא דנהרא. אמר אביי היכי נעביד ניעביד ליה מחיצה אגודא דנהרא גודא היא כמו מחיצה ואין עושין מחיצה על גבי מחיצה נעביד צורת הפתח אפומא דשביל של כרמים אתו גמלי שדיין ליה אלא נעביד לחי אפומא דשביל של כרמים וכו' ודחאה רבא ואסקא רבא דעביד לחי בהך גיפא דלהדי מתא מיגו דמהני האי לחי למתא. פליגי בה רב אחא ורבינא חד אסר וחד שרי.

הגהות הב"ח

(א) תוס' ד"ה ההיא רחבה וכו' וגם אוסרת את השביל כצ"ל והד"א עם ד"ה ליעבד וד"ה אין עושין וד"ה לעביד וד"ה ולעבד וד"ה ולעבד וד"ה יאמרו: (ב) ד"ה ולעביד לחי וכו' לצד הרחבה למיגו דמהני כו' השתא ודאי בלא מיגו לא מהני אבל יאמרו לחי מהני:

*שני דבורים המתחילים לעביד צ"ה והדיבור ג' ולעביד לחי הד"א [ר"מ]

כיון דלרחבה דסמיכא טפי לא מהני אי לאו מיגו בשביל אלא אמר רבא לתו לא אסרה רחבה על השביל ודירת בני מתא היתה בכולן ותו ליכא למימר לחי מהני כו' דילפי שפיר דדיורי מתא מהני גם לשביל כיון דגם הרחבה מותרה בדיורי מתא והוה ליה השתא רחבה ושביל כחדא והאי לחי מהני לתרווייהו: [ת"י כ"ז]:

מַאן דְּשָׁרֵי – דְּהָא לֵיכָּא דִּיוּרִין, וּמַאן דְּאָסַר – זִימְנִין דְּהָוֵי בָּהּ דִּיוּרִין, וְאָתֵי לְטַלְטוּלֵי. [א]קַרְפֵּף יוֹתֵר מִבֵּית סָאתַיִם שֶׁלֹּא הוּקַּף לַדִּירָה וּבָא לְמַעֲטוֹ, מִיעֲטוֹ בָּאִילָנוֹת – לָא הָוֵי מִיעוּט, בָּנָה בּוֹ עַמּוּד גָּבוֹהַּ עֲשָׂרָה וְרָחָב ד' – הָוֵי מִיעוּט. פָּחוֹת מִג' – לָא הָוֵי מִיעוּט. מִג' וְעַד ד', רַבָּה אָמַר: [ב]הָוֵי מִיעוּט, וְרָבָא אָמַר: לָא הָוֵי מִיעוּט. רַבָּה אָמַר: הָוֵי מִיעוּט – דְּהָא נָפֵיק לֵיהּ מִתּוֹרַת לָבוּד. רָבָא אָמַר: לָא הָוֵי מִיעוּט – כֵּיוָן דְּלָא הָוֵי מָקוֹם ד' – לָא חֲשִׁיב. הִרְחִיק מִן הַכּוֹתֶל ד' וְעָשָׂה מְחִיצָה – הוֹעִיל, פָּחוֹת מִג' – לֹא הוֹעִיל. מִג' וְעַד ד', רַבָּה אָמַר: [ג]הוֹעִיל, רָבָא אָמַר: אֵינוֹ מוֹעִיל. רַבָּה אָמַר: הוֹעִיל – דְּהָא נָפֵיק לֵיהּ מִתּוֹרַת לָבוּד. רָבָא אָמַר: אֵינוֹ מוֹעִיל – כֵּיוָן דְּלָא הָוֵי מָקוֹם ד' – לָא חֲשִׁיב. רַב שִׁימִי מַתְנֵי לְקוּלָּא: טָח בּוֹ טִיט וְיָכוֹל לַעֲמוֹד בִּפְנֵי עַצְמוֹ – הָוֵי מִיעוּט. אֵינוֹ יָכוֹל לַעֲמוֹד בִּפְנֵי עַצְמוֹ, רַבָּה אָמַר:[ד] הָוֵי מִיעוּט, רָבָא אָמַר: [ד]לָא הָוֵי מִיעוּט. רַבָּה אָמַר: הָוֵי מִיעוּט – הַשְׁתָּא מִיהָא קָאֵי. רָבָא אָמַר: לָא הָוֵי מִיעוּט – כֵּיוָן דְּלָא יָכוֹל לְמֵיקַם בִּפְנֵי עַצְמוֹ – לָאו כְּלוּם הוּא. הִרְחִיק מִן הַתֵּל ד' וְעָשָׂה מְחִיצָה – הוֹעִיל. פָּחוֹת מִג' אוֹ עַל שְׂפַת הַתֵּל, רַב חִסְדָּא וְרַב הַמְנוּנָא; חַד אָמַר: הוֹעִיל, וְחַד אָמַר: לֹא הוֹעִיל. תִּסְתַּיֵּים דְּרַב חִסְדָּא אָמַר הוֹעִיל. דְּאִתְּמַר: הָעוֹשֶׂה מְחִיצָה עַל גַּבֵּי מְחִיצָה, אָמַר רַב חִסְדָּא: בְּשַׁבָּת – הוֹעִיל, [ה]בְּנִכְסֵי הַגֵּר – לֹא קָנָה. וְרַב שֵׁשֶׁת אָמַר: [ו]אַף בְּשַׁבָּת נַמִי לֹא הוֹעִיל, תִּסְתַּיֵּים. אָמַר רַב חִסְדָּא: וּמוֹדֶה לִי רַב שֵׁשֶׁת [ז]שֶׁאִם עָשָׂה מְחִיצָה עַל הַתֵּל שֶׁהוֹעִיל. מַאי טַעְמָא – הוֹאִיל וּבַאֲוִיר מְחִיצוֹת הָעֶלְיוֹנוֹת הוּא דָּר. בָּעֵי רַבָּה בַּר בַּר חָנָה: נִבְלְעוּ מְחִיצוֹת הַתַּחְתּוֹנוֹת וְהָעֶלְיוֹנוֹת קַיָּימוֹת, מַהוּ? לְמַאי? אִי לְנִכְסֵי הַגֵּר – הַיְינוּ דְּיִרְמְיָה בִּירָאָה, *דְּאָמַר יִרְמְיָה בִּירָאָה, אָמַר רַב יְהוּדָה: [ח]הַאי מַאן דִּשְׁדָא לִיפְתָּא *אַפִּילָא(פי' בקעי') דְּאַרְעָא דְּגֵר, וַאֲתָא יִשְׂרָאֵל אַחֲרִינָא רְפַק בָּהּ פּוּרְתָּא – בַּתְרָא קָנֵי, קַמָּא לָא קָנֵי. מ"ט? בְּעִידָּנָא דִּשְׁדָא – לָא קָא שְׁבַח, כִּי קָא שְׁבָחָא מִמֵּילָא קָא מַשְׁבְּחָא. [ט]וְאֶלָּא לְעִנְיַן שַׁבָּת – הָוֵי מְחִיצָה הַנַּעֲשָׂה בְּשַׁבָּת, *וְתַנְיָא: כָּל מְחִיצָה הַנַּעֲשָׂה בְּשַׁבָּת, בֵּין בְּשׁוֹגֵג בֵּין בְּמֵזִיד – שְׁמָהּ מְחִיצָה. לָאו אִיתְּמַר עֲלָהּ, אָמַר רַב נַחְמָן: לֹא שָׁנוּ אֶלָּא לִזְרוֹק, אֲבָל לְטַלְטֵל – אָסוּר. כִּי אִיתְּמַר דְּרַב נַחְמָן – אַמֵּזִיד אִיתְּמַר. הַהִיא אִיתְּתָא דַּעֲבָדָה מְחִיצָה עַל גַּבֵּי מְחִיצָה בְּנִכְסֵי הַגֵּר, אֲתָא הַהוּא גַּבְרָא רְפַק בָּהּ פּוּרְתָּא. אֲתָא לְקַמֵּיהּ דְּרַב נַחְמָן, אוֹקְמָהּ בִּידֵיהּ. אֲתַת אִיהִי וְקָא צָוְוחָא קַמֵּיהּ. אֲמַר לָהּ: מַאי אִיעֲבִיד לִךְ דְּלָא מַחְזְקַתְּ כִּדְמַחְזְקִי אֱינָשֵׁי? [י]קַרְפֵּף בֵּית שָׁלֹשׁ, וְקֵירָה בּוֹ בֵּית סְאָה; *רָבָא אָמַר: אֲוִיר קֵירוּיוֹ מְיַיתְּרוֹ, וְרַבִּי זֵירָא אָמַר: [כ]אֵין אֲוִיר קֵירוּיוֹ מְיַיתְּרוֹ. לֵימָא *רָבָא וְרַבִּי זֵירָא בִּפְלוּגְתָּא דְּרַב וּשְׁמוּאֵל קָא מִיפַּלְגִי? *דְּאִיתְּמַר, אַכְסַדְרָה בְּבִקְעָה, רַב אָמַר: [ל]מוּתָּר לְטַלְטֵל בְּכוּלָּהּ, וּשְׁמוּאֵל אָמַר: אֵין מְטַלְטְלִין אֶלָּא בְּד' אַמּוֹת. רַב אָמַר: מוּתָּר לְטַלְטֵל בְּכוּלָּהּ – אָמְרִינַן: פִּי תִקְרָה יוֹרֵד וְסוֹתֵם. וּשְׁמוּאֵל אָמַר: אֵין מְטַלְטְלִין אֶלָּא בְּאַרְבַּע אַמּוֹת – לָא אָמְרִי' פִּי תִקְרָה יוֹרֵד וְסוֹתֵם.

אִי

רש"י

דְּלֵית בָּהּ דִּיוּרִין. שֶׁיֶּאֶסְרוּ עַל בְּנֵי מָבוֹי. הִלְכָּךְ רְשׁוּת בְּנֵי מָבוֹי הוּא, וּבְנֵי שְׁבִיל לָא אָסְרֵי עֲלָהּ – דְּהָוֵי כְּחָצֵר קְטַנָּה שֶׁנִּפְרְצָה לִגְדוֹלָה דִּגְדוֹלָה מוּתֶּרֶת וּקְטַנָּה אֲסוּרָה. וּשְׁבִיל לָא מְתַקְּנִינַן לֵיהּ – גְּזֵרָה שֶׁמָּא יֹאמְרוּ לֶחִי מוֹעִיל לִשְׁבִיל דְּעָלְמָא: בְּאִילָנוֹת לֹא הָוֵי מִיעוּט. דְּדֶרֶךְ קַרְפֵּף לִהְיוֹת בּוֹ אִילָנוֹת, וְלָא בָּטֵיל לֵיהּ(א) הֶיקֵּף קַמָּא: בָּנָה בּוֹ עַמּוּד. וַאֲפִילּוּ בָּאֶמְצַע, וּבְכָךְ נִתְמַעֵט מִבֵּית סָאתַיִם: פָּחוֹת מִג' טְפָחִים. אֲפִי' נִתְמַעֵט מִבֵּית סָאתַיִם, כְּמַאן דְּלֵיתֵיהּ דָּמֵי: דְּהָא נָפְקָא לֵיהּ מִתּוֹרַת לָבוּד. כְּלוֹמַר: דְּהָא חָשֵׁיב לֵיהּ ג' בְּעָלְמָא לְמֵיפַק מִתּוֹרַת לָבוּד, הִלְכָּךְ ה"נ חֲשִׁיבֵי וְלָא בָּטֵיל: הִרְחִיק מִן הַכּוֹתֶל. שֶׁל קַרְפֵּף ד' טְפָחִים, וְעָשָׂה מְחִיצָּה (ב) לְדִירָה: הוֹעִיל. מְחִיצָּה זוֹ לִהְיוֹת הֶיקֵּף חָדָשׁ, וְהָוֵי פֶּתַח וּלְבַסּוֹף הוּקַּף: פָּחוֹת מִג' לֹא הוֹעִיל. דְּהָוֵי כִּמְחִיצָּה עַל גַּבֵּי מְחִיצָּה. וְלֹא בְּנִתְמַעֵט מִבֵּית סָאתַיִם מַיְירֵי, מִדְּלָא נָקַט מִיעוּט. וְאֵינוֹ מִיעוּט, דְּאִי נִתְמַעֵט – וַדַּאי הָוֵי מִיעוּט, שֶׁאֲפִילּוּ הוֹסִיף עַל עוֹבִי הַכְּתָלִים עַד שֶׁנִּתְמַעֵט – שַׁפִּיר דָּמֵי, כִּדְלְקַמָּן, אֶלָּא לְמֵיהֱוֵי פֶּתַח וּלְבַסּוֹף הוּקַּף מַיְירֵי: מַתְנֵי לְקוּלָּא. לְהָךְ פְּלוּגְתָּא דִּלְעֵיל. וְאָמַר: דְּבִשְׁלֹשָׁה דְּנָפֵק לֵיהּ מִתּוֹרַת לָבוּד – כּוּלְּהוּ מוֹדוּ דְּעַמּוּד הָוֵי מִיעוּט, וּמְחִיצָּה הָוְיָא מְחִיצָּה לְדִירָה, וְלֹא כְּמוֹסִיף, וּבְפָחוֹת מִשְּׁלֹשָׁה פְּלִיגֵי: טָח בְּטִיט. וְהוֹסִיף עַל עוֹבִי הַכְּתָלִים עַד שֶׁנִּתְמַעֵט. וְהַאי לָאו רַבָּה בַּר שִׁימִי קָאָמַר לָהּ, אֶלָּא מִילְּתָא בְּאַנְפֵּי נַפְשֵׁיהּ הִיא: וְיָכוֹל לַעֲמוֹד. הַטִּיט בִּפְנֵי עַצְמוֹ, שֶׁעָשׂוּי בְּעוֹבִי, שֶׁאֲפִילּוּ יִנָּטֵל כּוֹתֶל הָרִאשׁוֹן יָכוֹל זֶה לַעֲמוֹד: הָוֵי מִיעוּט וְלֹא הָוֵי מִיעוּט גְּרַס הָכָא: הִרְחִיק מִן הַתֵּל. שֶׁבַּקַּרְפֵּף, וְיֵשׁ מִן הַתֵּל עַד הַמְּחִיצָּה יוֹתֵר מִבֵּית סָאתַיִם הַרְבֵּה, וְעָשָׂה מְחִיצָּה לְדִירָה אֵצֶל הַתֵּל בְּרִחוּק ד' טְפָחִים, וַעֲדַיִין יֵשׁ יוֹתֵר מִבֵּית סָאתַיִם בֵּין יְשָׁנָה לַחֲדָשָׁה. אֲבָל זוֹ – לְדִירָה עֲשָׂאָהּ: הוֹעִיל. וְהַכֹּל מוּתָּר: לֹא הוֹעִיל. דְּהָוְיָא מְחִיצָּה עַל גַּבֵּי מְחִיצָּה: וְחַד אָמַר הוֹעִיל. דְּקָסָבַר: מְחִיצָּה ע"ג מְחִיצָּה מְהַנְּיָא לִהְיוֹת הֶיקֵּף לְדִירָה: בְּנִכְסֵי הַגֵּר. שֶׁמֵּת וְאֵין לוֹ יוֹרְשִׁין, אֵין זוֹ חֲזָקָה לִקְנוֹת. וְאִם בָּא אַחֵר וְהֶחֱזִיק בָּהֶן – קָנָה הָאַחֲרוֹן: בְּשַׁבָּת. כְּגוֹן לְעִנְיַן הֶיקֵּף לְדִירָה, שֶׁבַּתְּחִילָּה הָיְתָה מְחִיצָּה הוֹגֶנֶת אֶלָּא שֶׁלֹּא הוּקְּפָה לְדִירָה: הָכִי גָּרְסִינַן: מוֹדֶה לִי רַב שֵׁשֶׁת שֶׁאִם עָשָׂה מְחִיצָּה עַל הַתֵּל. וְלָא גָּרְסִי': עַל שְׂפַת. וְהָכִי פֵּי' אַף עַל גַּב דִּפְלִיג, וְאָמַר דְּלָא מִישְׁתְּרֵי קַרְפֵּף בְּהָכִי – הַיְינוּ טַעְמָא: שֶׁהַדָּר בַּקַּרְפֵּף, בַּאֲוִיר מְחִיצוֹת הַתַּחְתּוֹנוֹת דָּר, אֲבָל אִם הָיָה תֵּל יוֹתֵר מִבֵּית סָאתַיִם וְעָשָׂה מְחִיצוֹת סָבִיב עָלָיו לְהִשְׁתַּמֵּשׁ(ג) עַל גּוֹבַהּ הַתֵּל: הוֹאִיל. וְהַדָּר עַל הַתֵּל דָּר בַּאֲוִיר מְחִיצוֹת הָעֶלְיוֹנוֹת, וְלָא מְהַנֵּי לֵיהּ תַּחְתּוֹנוֹת מִידֵּי – הִלְכָּךְ לָאו מְחִיצָּה עַל גַּבֵּי מְחִיצָּה הִיא: בָּעֵי רַבָּה. לְמ"ד: אֵין מְחִיצָּה עַל גַּבֵּי מְחִיצָּה, נִבְלְעוּ הַתַּחְתּוֹנוֹת בַּקַּרְקַע, שֶׁהָיָה הֶעָפָר רַךְ וְתִיחוּחַ וְנִתְבַּע הַכּוֹתֶל כְּבַת אַחַת בְּשַׁבָּת וְלֹא נָפַל, אֶלָּא נִבְלַע, וְהָעֶלְיוֹנוֹת קַיָּימוֹת, מַהוּ: אִי לְנִכְסֵי הַגֵּר. קָא מִיבַּעְיָא לֵיהּ, אִי לֹא קָדַם אַחֵר וְהֶחֱזִיק בָּהֶן עַד שֶׁנִּבְלְעוּ הַתַּחְתּוֹנוֹת, וְנִמְצָא שֶׁאֵין בּוֹ אֶלָּא מְחִיצוֹת שֶׁעָשָׂה לוֹ זֶה, וּמַעַכְשָׁיו קָנוּי לוֹ: דִּשְׁדָא לִיפְתָּא אַפִּילָא. נָטַע לֶפֶת בְּגוּמָא שֶׁמָּצָא בְּקַרְקַע הַגֵּר. וְלֹא חֲפָרָהּ הוּא, דְּאִי חֲפָרָהּ – בְּמַכּוֹשׁ רִאשׁוֹן קָנָה: לָא קָא שְׁבַח. וְלָאו חֲזָקָה הִיא. וְאַף, נָעַל גָּדַר וּפָרַץ כָּל שֶׁהוּא, תְּנַן (ב"ב דף מב.), מִידֵּי דִּמְהַנֵּי הָוֵי חֲזָקָה: מִמֵּילָא שְׁבַח. וְהַהִיא שַׁעְתָּא לָאו אִיהוּ מַחֲזִיק בָּהּ אֶלָּא לֶפֶת הוּא דִּשְׁבַח וְאָזֵיל, וְהָכָא נַמִי, כֵּיוָן דִּבְשַׁעְתָּא דְּהֶחֱזִיק לָאו חֲזָקָה הִיא, כִּי הַדּוּר הָווּ מְחִיצוֹת מִמֵּילָא הוּא דְּהָווּ, וְלָאו אִיהוּ דְּעָבֵיד: אֶלָּא לְעִנְיַן שַׁבָּת. אִי מִשְׁתְּרֵי בָּעֶלְיוֹנוֹת, שֶׁהָיוּ בְּטֵילוֹת עַד עַכְשָׁיו: לִזְרוֹק. לְחוּמְרָא: וְקֵירָה בּוֹ בֵּית סְאָה. קֵירוּי גַּג: אֲוִיר קֵירוּיוֹ מְיַיתְּרוֹ. סָפֵק הַמְּקוֹרָה מִיחַשְּׁבָה בַּהֲדֵי אִידָךְ כְּאִילּוּ לֹא קֵירוּהוּ, וְאַכַּתִּי הָוֵי יוֹתֵר מִבֵּית סָאתַיִם: אֵין אֲוִיר קֵירוּיוֹ מְיַיתְּרוֹ. דְּאָמְרִינַן: פִּי תִקְרָה יוֹרֵד וְסוֹתֵם: אַכְסַדְרָה. מְקוֹרָה בְּגַג חָלָק כַּעֲלִיּוֹת שֶׁלָּנוּ, וְאֵינוֹ מְשׁוּפָּע, וְהִיא קֵירוּי שֶׁבְּכָל הַתַּלְמוּד:

ה"ג

תוספות

מאן דשרי דהא לית ביה דיורין. ובשביל(ד) – לית ביה דיורין דליתסרו עליה. ולפירוש הקונטרס דאית ביה דיורין – לא אסרו עלה משום גיפופי: **ומאן** דאסר זימנין דאית ביה דיורין. שהבתים שאצל הרחבה יפתחו מבתיהן לרחבה, ויאסרו הרחבה על בני מתא להוציא בה כלים ששבתו בתוכה, ומשום הכי אסור לטלטל ממתא לרחבה, דשמא יטלטלו גם לאחר פתיחת הדיורין בלא עירוב כמו עתה. אבל רחבה גופיה – שרי, שהרי אף לאחר שיפתחו מותר לטלטל כלים ששבתו בתוכה:

שאם עשה מחיצה על שפת התל שהועיל. רש"י לא גריס "על שפת התל", דהוה משמע לאותן הדריס למטה. אלא גריס "על התל", והועיל לאותן הדריס על התל. ומיהו, צריך לפרש דמיירי על שפת התל שאם הרחיקו ד' מן השפה – אין שם חידוש, דהכי נמי למטה אם הרחיק הועיל:

אכסדרה בבקעה. רש"י פירש לקמן: דאכסדרה פרולה מארבעה רוחותיה. והשתא אתי שפיר הא דנקט בבקעה – שאין שם מחיצות, ולא נקט בחצר. וגרס לקמן בפרק "כל גגות" (דף לד.) דמשני שמואל אדשמואל כי לית ליה בד', אבל בג' – אית ליה. וקשיא לפירושו, דבסוכה אמרינן: דאפילו בשתי רוחות זה כנגד זה לא אמרינן פי תקרה יורד וסותם, משום דהוי כמבוי מפולש. ומפרש ר"ת: דאכסדרה אית לה שלשה מחיצות, כדאמרינן בפרק "לא יחפור" (ב"ב דף כה:): עולם דומה לאכסדרה, ורוח צפונית אינה מסובבת. וגרס בפרק "כל גגות" (לקמן דף לד:): כי לית ליה – בשלש, אבל בד' אית ליה. פירוש: שיש ג' מחיצות ומעט מן הרביעית. ורב אית ליה פי תקרה יורד וסותם אפי' בשתי מחיצות, ובזה שלא כנגד זה. והא דלא נקט אכסדרה בחצר – משום דסתם אכסדרה בחצר יש לה ג' מחיצות, להכי נקט בקעה, דאפי' כי ליכא אלא שתי מחיצות אמר רב: פי תקרה יורד וסותם:

אי

רבינו חננאל

מאן דשרי דהא לית בה דיורין וכחצר דמיא ומאן דאסר גזר דלמא מיתבי בה דיורין וקי"ל הלכתא כמאן דמיקל ושרי ולא חיישינן לדיורין וכבר פירשנוה למעלה *) (ורחבה) [דברחבה] דרבים הוא (ולא) [דלא] חיישינן אבל ברחבה דיחיד זמנין דמימליך ובני בתי ודייר בה דיורין. קרפף יתר מבית סאתים שלא הוקף לדירה ובא למעטו באילנות לא הוי [מיעוט] דהא נטיעת אילנו' בחצר כחצר דמו כדאמרן. עמוד גבוה י' טפחים ורחב ד' טפחים הוי מיעוט פחות מג' לא הוי מיעוט וכן סלקא סוגיא דשמעתא ד' הוי מיעוט פחות לא. הרחיק מן התל ד' ועשה בו מחיצה הועיל בו. פי' התל הוא מקום שלא הוקף לדירה ואם הרחיק משפת התל ד' טפחים ועשה בו מחיצה לדירה הותר לו לטלטל בכולו. אבל בפחות מג' וכן העושה מחיצה על שפת התל לא דאין מחיצה שעשה עכשיו מבטלת גידור התל שהוא מחיצתו המוקף שלא לדירה אלו דברי רב ששת ורב חסדא אמר העושה מחיצה ע"ג מחיצה בשבת הועיל בנכסי הגר לא קנה ורב ששת אמר אפילו בשבת לא הועיל. ואמר רב חסדא מודה לי רב ששת בעושה מחיצה על שפת התל ודר בתל שהועיל הואיל ובמחיצות העליונות הוא דר ומותר לטלטל בכולו. והלכתא כרב חסדא בין בשבת דהוא לקולא בין בנכסי הגר דהא רב נחמן קאי כוותיה. בעי רבה בר חנן אליבא דרב ששת נבלעו מחיצות התחתונות והעליונות קיימות מהו כמחיצה ע"ג מחיצה הוי אי לא ופשיט אביי לענין שבת הא קי"ל כל מחיצה שנעשית בשבת בין בשוגג בין במזיד שמה מחיצה ואפילו רב נחמן דאמר לא שנו אלא לזרוק אבל לטלטל אסור. לא אמר אלא במתכוין לעשות מחיצה כדי לטלטל הוא דאסר אבל כי האי גוונא אפילו רב נחמן שרי. אי בנכסי הגר הא אמרינן האי מאן דשדא ליפתא בי (פילחי) [פילי] בארעא דגר לא עבד ולא מידי. מ"ט בעידנא דשדא האי ליפתא לא משבחא ולא מידי בתר הכי כי קא משבחא ממילא שבחא. האי נמי בעידנא דעבד מחיצה ע"ג מחיצה לא הועיל בתר דנבלעו התחתונות בעליונות לא עשה הוא כלום הלכך לא קנה בנכסי הגר כלום כי האי גוונא. האי אתתא דעבדא מחיצה ע"ג מחיצה בנכסי הגר אתא ההוא גברא רפק ביה פורתא. אוקמה רב נחמן בידיה לההוא דרפק בנכסי הגר אתא היא צווחא קמיה ולא אשגח בה אמר לה לא מחזקת כדמחזקי אינשי. קרפף בית ג' סאין וקירה בו בית סאה. רבה אמר וכאילו יתר מבית סאתים הוא ואסור. ור' זירא אמר אין קירויו מייתרו אלא הקרוי מפסיק בינתים וזה אין בו יותר מבית סאתים ומותר. לימא בפלוגתא דרב ושמואל פליגי דאתמר אכסדרה בבקעה רב אמר מותר לטלטל בכולה אמרינן פי תקרה יורד וסותם והויא לה רשות היחיד ושמואל אמר אין מטלטלין בה אלא בארבע אמות כרשות הרבים לא אמרינן פי תקרה יורד וסותם

ר'

*) [אולי צ"ל לעיל דף ח' בהא דאמרינן שם דברחבה דיחיד חיישינן דלמא מימליך ע"ש].

עין משפט נר מצוה

לז א מיי' פט"ז מהל' שבת הלכה ח טוש"ע א"ח סי' שנח סעיף ד:
לח ב מיי' שם טוש"ע שם סעיף ה:
לט ג מיי' שם טוש"ע שם סעיף ו:
[לט] [ד מיי' שם הלכה ט]:
מ ד טוש"ע שם ס"ז:
מא ה מיי' פ"ב מהלכות זכייה ומתנה הלכה יא סמג עשין פג טוש"ע ח"מ סי' רעה סעיף כג:
מב ו ז מיי' פי"ז מהל' שבת הל' ט טוש"ע א"ח סי' שנח סעיף ח:
מג ח מיי' פ"ב מהל' זכייה הל' י טוש"ע ח"מ סי' רעה סעיף כב:
מד ט מיי' פט"ז מהל' שבת הל' כב טוש"ע א"ח סי' שנח סעיף ח:
מה י מיי' פט"ז מהל' שבת הלכה ז סמג עשין א טוש"ע א"ח סי' שנח סעיף יב:
מו כ מיי' פי"ז מהל' שבת הלכה לה סמג עשין א:

הגהות הב"ח

(א) רש"י ד"ה באילנות וכו' ולא בטיל ליה היקף קמא תא"מ ונ"ב ס"א משום קמא: (ב) ד"ה הרחיק וד"ה הועילה מחילה הס"א: (ג) ד"ה הכי גרסינן וכו' על גובה התל הועיל הואיל והדר כנ"ל והס"א: (ד) תוס' ד"ה מאן דשרי וכו' ובשביל נמי לית ביה. [ובכת"י הגי' וכ"ש שביל דלית כו']:

גליון הש"ס

גמ' קרפף בית שלש וקירה בו בית סאה. עי' לקמן דף ל ע"א תוס' ד"ה אלא שתי:

ב"ב נג: ושם איתא רבי ירמיה וכ"ה בגיטין לז.

שבת קא: לעיל כ.

[נ"ל רבה]

[לקמן ל. לד: סוכה יח:]

אִי דַּעֲבִידָא כִּי אַכְסַדְרָה – הָכִי נַמִי. הב"ע – דַּעֲבָדָה כִּי *אוּרְזִילָא. אָמַר רַבִּי זֵירָא: [א]וּמוֹדִינָא בְּקַרְפֵּף שֶׁנִּפְרַץ בִּמְלוֹאוֹ לֶחָצֵר, שֶׁאָסוּר. מ"ט – הוֹאִיל וַאֲוִיר חָצֵר מְיַיתְּרוֹ. מַתְקִיף לָהּ רַב יוֹסֵף: וְכִי אֲוִיר הַמּוּתָּר לוֹ אוֹסְרוֹ?! א"ל אַבַּיֵי: כְּמַאן – *כְּרַבִּי שִׁמְעוֹן, לְרַבִּי שִׁמְעוֹן נַמִי, הָא אִיכָּא אֲוִיר מְקוֹם מְחִיצוֹת! דְּאָמַר רַב חִסְדָּא: קַרְפֵּף שֶׁנִּפְרַץ בִּמְלוֹאוֹ לֶחָצֵר – חָצֵר מוּתֶּרֶת וְקַרְפֵּף אָסוּר. חָצֵר מַאי טַעְמָא – דְּאִית לֵיהּ גִּיפּוּפֵי, וְהָא זִמְנִין דְּמַשְׁכַּחַתְּ לָהּ אִיפְּכָא! אֶלָּא: מִשּׁוּם דְּאָמְרִינַן זֶה – אֲוִיר מְחִיצוֹת מְיַיתְּרוֹ, וְזֶה – אֵין אֲוִיר מְחִיצוֹת מְיַיתְּרוֹ. הַהוּא בּוּסְתָּנָא דַּהֲוָה סְמִיךְ לְגוּדָא דְּאַפַּדְנָא, נְפַל אֲשִׁיתָא בָּרַיְיתָא דְּאַפַּדְנָא. סָבַר רַב בֵּיבָי לְמֵימַר: לִיסְמוֹךְ אַגּוּדָא גַּוָּויָאתָא. אֲמַר לֵיהּ רַב פַּפִּי: *מִשּׁוּם דַּאֲתוּ *מִמּוּלָאֵי אָמְרִיתוּ מִילֵּי מוּלַיְיאתָא?! [ב]הָנָךְ מְחִיצוֹת, לְגַוַּאי – עֲבִידָן, לְבַרַּאי – לָא עֲבִידָן. הַהִיא *אַבְוַורְנְקָא דַּהֲוָה לֵיהּ לְרֵישׁ גָּלוּתָא בְּבוּסְתָּנֵיהּ, א"ל לְרַב הוּנָא בַּר חִינָּנָא: לִיעֲבִיד מָר תַּקַּנְתָּא, דִּלְמָחָר נֵיכוּל נַהֲמָא הָתָם. אֲזַל עֲבַד קָנֶה קָנֶה פָּחוֹת מִשְּׁלֹשָׁה. אֲזַל רָבָא שַׁלְפִינְהוּ

רש"י

ה"נ. אַפִּי' רַבָּה מוֹדֶה כְּרַב, דְּפִי תִקְרָה יוֹרֵד וְסוֹתֵם: וְהָכָא. דְּפָלֵיג רַבָּה – דַּעֲבִיד קִירוּי כִּי אוּרְזִילָא, יָלִיעַ גַּג מְשׁוּפָּע דְּלֵיכָּא פֶּה: וּמוֹדִינָא בְּקַרְפֵּף. בֵּית סָאתַיִם: שֶׁנִּפְרַץ בִּמְלוֹאוֹ לֶחָצֵר. שֶׁאֲוִיר חָצֵר מְיַיתְּרוֹ, וְעוֹשֵׂהוּ יוֹתֵר מִבֵּית סָאתַיִם, וְאָסוּר. וְגַבֵּי קִירוּי דְּשָׁרֵינָא – מִשּׁוּם פִּי תִקְרָה יוֹרֵד וְסוֹתֵם: וְכִי אֲוִיר הַמּוּתָּר לוֹ אוֹסְרוֹ. וַהֲרֵי חָצֵר זוֹ מִתְּחִילָּה הָיְתָה מוּתֶּרֶת לְטַלְטֵל הֵימֶנָּה לַקַּרְפֵּף, כְּר' שִׁמְעוֹן. וְעַכְשָׁיו שֶׁנִּפְרַץ לְמָקוֹם הַמּוּתָּר לוֹ, נֶאֱסַר לוֹ. וּמִשּׁוּם יִיתּוּר לֵיכָּא לְמֵימַר, דְּהָא כָּל חָצֵר מוּקֶּפֶת לְדִירָה הָוֵי: כְּמַאן. הָוֵי אֲוִיר הַמּוּתָּר לוֹ – כְּר"ש: לְר"ש נַמִי. מִיתְּסַר קַרְפֵּף מִשּׁוּם מְקוֹם מְחִיצּוֹת שֶׁנִּיטְּלוּ, וְנִיתּוֹסַף עַל הָאֲוִיר וְעוֹשֵׂהוּ יוֹתֵר מִבֵּית סָאתַיִם, שֶׁבַּתְּחִילָּה הָיְתָה בֵּית סָאתַיִם מְצוּמְצָם: וְנִפְרְצָה חָצֵר כְּנֶגְדּוֹ. לֹא גָּרַס דְּכוּלָּהּ שְׁמַעְתְּתָא: דְּאִיכָּא גִּיפּוּפֵי. וְאִי לָאו הָכִי אָסְרִי אַהֲדָדֵי. וּכְרַבָּנַן דִּפְלִיגִי אַדְּר' שִׁמְעוֹן נָקַט לָהּ. וּבְשֶׁאֵין הַפִּרְצָה יְתֵירָה עַל עֶשֶׂר, אַמַּאי נָקַט הֶיתֵּר בְּחָצֵר וְאִיסּוּר בְּקַרְפֵּף? וְהָא מָצֵי לְמֵימַר נַמִי אִיפְּכָא, כְּגוֹן שֶׁקַּרְפֵּף גָּדוֹל מִן הֶחָצֵר – דְּהָוֵי לֶחָצֵר מִילּוּאָהּ, וּבַקַּרְפֵּף אִיכָּא גִּיפּוּפֵי: אֶלָּא. מִדְּנָקַט אִיסּוּר בְּקַרְפֵּף – ש"מ כְּר"ש ס"ל, דְּמִשּׁוּם שְׁתֵּי רְשׁוּיוֹת לָא מִיתְּסַר. וְטַעְמָא מִשּׁוּם יִיתּוּר בֵּית סָאתַיִם הוּא, דִּמְקוֹם מְחִיצּוֹת מְיַיתְּרָן. דְּבְחָצֵר לָא אָסַר וּבְקַרְפֵּף אָסַר. וְלָא מָצֵי לְמִינְקַט אִיפְּכָא – דְּכִי הָוֵי חָצֵר מְלוֹאוֹ וּבְקַרְפֵּף גִּיפּוּפֵי תַּרְוַיְיהוּ מִשְׁתְּרוּ, דְּכְר"ש ס"ל דְּכוּלְּהוּ רְשׁוּת אַחַת הֵן וְיִיתּוּר בְּקַרְפֵּף נַמִי לֵיכָּא, הוֹאִיל וְאִיכָּא גִּיפּוּפֵי: זֶה אֲוִיר מְחִיצוֹת מְיַיתְּרוֹ. וְקַרְפֵּף יִיתּוּר קָאָסַר בֵּיהּ, יִיתּוּר דִּמְקוֹם מְחִיצָּה. וְאִילּוּ יִיתּוּר דַּאֲוִיר חָצֵר לָא אָסַר לֵיהּ – דְּחָצֵר מוּקֶּפֶת לְדִירָה הָוֵי, וְלָא הָוֵי יִיתּוּר: וְזֶה. חָצֵר: אֵין אֲוִיר מְחִיצוֹת מְיַיתְּרוֹ. כְּלוֹמַר: אֵין יִיתּוּר אוֹסֵר בּוֹ, דְּחָצֵר אִית בֵּיהּ *דִּיוּרָא, הִלְכָּךְ, אִי נָקֵיט אִיפְּכָא לָא מִיתְּסַר חָצֵר כְּר"ש: בּוּסְתָּנָא. פַּרְדֵּס, דְּהָוֵי נָטוּעַ אִילָנוֹת: דַּהֲוֵי סָמוּךְ לְגוּדָא דְּאַפַּדְנָא. *וְהִיא הָיְתָה לוֹ [(א)] הֶיקֵּף לְדִירָה הַהוּא גּוּדָא, שֶׁהָיָה בּוֹ פֶּתַח פָּתוּחַ לְצַד פַּרְדֵּס סָמְכוּ הֶיקֵּף הַפַּרְדֵּס דְּהָוֵי מוּקָּף לְדִירָה. וְיוֹתֵר מִבֵּית סָאתַיִם הֲוָה: אַגּוּדָא גַּוָּואֵי. הֲרֵי יֵשׁ עוֹד מְחִיצּוֹת פְּנִימוֹת לַבַּיִת, וְהֵן יְהוּ מְחִיצּוֹת לַפַּרְדֵּס: מִמּוּלָאֵי. מְקוּטָּעִים. מִבֵּית עֵלִי, דְּאַבַּיֵי אֲבוּהּ דְּרַב בֵּיבָי, מִבֵּית עֵלִי אֲתָא, כִּדְאָמְרִינַן בְּמַסֶּכֶת ר"ה (דף יח.). מוּלַיְיתָא – קְטוּעוֹת בְּלֹא רַגְלַיִם: לְבָרַאי לָא עֲבִידָן. וְנִהְי דְּפִירְצָה לֵיכָּא, הֶיקֵּף דִּירָה מִיהָא לֵיתָא בַּפַּרְדֵּס, דְּהָוֵי יוֹתֵר מִבֵּית סָאתַיִם: אַבְוַורְנְקֵי. אִילָן שֶׁנּוֹפוֹ מְרוּבֶּה, וְנוֹטְעִין אוֹתוֹ הַשָּׂרִים וְעוֹשִׂין אִיצְטַבָּאוֹת תַּחְתָּיו סְבִיבוֹתָיו, לְהִתְלוֹנֵן תַּחְתָּיו בִּימוֹת הַחַמָּה, וְלִשְׂמוֹחַ שָׁם: בְּבוּסְתָּנָא. וְיוֹתֵר מִבֵּית סָאתַיִם שֶׁלֹּא הוּקַּף לְדִירָה הָיָה הַפַּרְדֵּס: נֵיכוּל נַהֲמָא הָתָם. תַּחַת הָאִילָן: עֲבַד קָנֶה קָנֶה פָּחוֹת מִשְּׁלֹשָׁה טְפָחִים. הֶיקֵּף, כְּגוֹן מְחִיצּוֹת קָנִים ד' מְחִיצּוֹת כְּחֶדֶר לְהָנִיחַ שָׁם בַּלַּיְלָה הַמַּאֲכָל וְלָדוּר שָׁם הַשּׁוֹמֵר, וּלְמָחָר יְטַלְטְלוּהוּ בְּכָל הַפַּרְדֵּס, דְּהָא אִית בֵּיהּ שׁוֹמִירָה וּבֵית דִּירָה: שַׁלְפִינְהוּ

תוספות

(ג) **אי** דעבידא כי אכסדרה הכי נמי. פירוש: שהיתה מוקפת משלש או משתי רוחותיה*: **הכא** במאי עסקינן דעביד כי ערסלא. שהיתה פרוצה מד' רוחות. וערסלא – מטה. דתרגום "כמלונה במקשה" – כערסלא (ישעיה א). והם חבלין המתוחין מאילן לאילן כסדר המטה, והשומר שוכב עליה בלילה ויושב בצלו ביום. ורש"י גרס: כי ארזילא – משופע, דלית לה פה. ולא אמרי' פי תקרה יורד וסותם: **וכי** אויר המותר לו אוסרו. הרי נפרץ במלואו למקום המותר לו. ויתור נמי ליכא – דהא כל חצירות מוקפות לדירה הם. א"ל אביי: כמאן – כר' שמעון, דלרבנן דאמרי שתי רשויות הן – נפרץ במלואו למקום האסור לו. ולדידהו נמי אויר החצר האסור לו מייתרו, אע"ג דחצר מוקף לדירה – דהיינו למה שבתוכו, אבל לקרפף שהוא רשות אחרת – לא חשיב מוקף לדירה, ומייתרו. אבל לר"ש שפיר דמי, דחדא רשותא היא, והוי אויר מותר. וא"ת: מדקאמר כמאן – כר"ש, לר"ש נמי כו'. משמע דמילתיה דר' זירא אתי בפשיטות כרבנן. ואי אתי כרבנן, אמאי נקט הואיל ואויר חצרו מייתרו? תיפוק ליה משום דנפרץ במלואו למקום האסור לו! וי"ל: דאשמעינן דאסור נמי משום דאויר חצר מייתרו. ונפקא מינה, שאם נפרץ מצד אחד לרה"ר – צריך צורת הפתח מכאן ולחי מכאן. אבל מטעמא דנפרץ במלואו למקום האסור לו – לא הוה צריך אלא לחי לצד רה"ר, כדמשמע בפ"ק (דף ז:) דמבוי שנפרץ במלואו לחצר – אין צריך כלום, אפי' לא עירבו. אי נמי: אשמעינן דמייתרו והוי כרמלית, ואם נפרץ לכרמלית אחר – מותר לטלטל ב' אמות מזה וב' אמות מזה. אבל אם לא היה מייתרו, אע"ג דנפרץ למקום האסור לו – לא חשיב כרמלית, ואסור לטלטל הימנו לכרמלית אחר כו'. וכן פי' רש"י פרק "כל גגות" (לקמן דף צ:), גבי הא דפריך לשמואל אליבא דרבנן לטלטל מגג לקרפף:

קרפף שנפרץ במלואו לחצר חצר מותרת וקרפף אסור. ושלא נפרץ – ביתר מעשר, דביתר מעשר חצר נמי אסורה. וקשה למהר"י: דעל כרחך בקרפף בית סאתים איירי, מדקאמרי': הואיל ואויר מחילה מייתרו – א"כ הוה ליה ארכה יותר הרבה על פי שנים ברחבה, וזה לא מצינו שום תנא דמתיר! וי"ל: דמקום שנפרצה לא הוי יותר מעשר, אבל מכאן ואילך מתרחבת והולכת. א"נ: בית סאתים לא שרינא ארכה יותר על פי שנים ברחבה, אבל במשהו פחות מבית סאתים – שרי טפי: **זימנין** דמשכחת לה איפכא. אי אתי כרבנן. וכגון שהקרפף גדול מן החצר. ומדנקט איסור בקרפף – ש"מ דכר"ש אתיא. דמשום שתי רשויות לא מיתסר, אלא משום ייתור אויר. דבמקום מחילות דבחצר לא אסר, ובקרפף אסר. ולא מצי למנקט איפכא, דאי הוה בחצר מלואו ובקרפף גיפופי – תרוייהו משתרו, דר"ש סבר דכולהו רשות אחד הן. ויתור בקרפף נמי ליכא, הואיל ואיכא גיפופי, כך פי' רש"י. וא"ת: ולוקמה לעולם כרבנן, והא דלא אמרי' איפכא – משום דבחצר ליכא איסור משום ייתור אלא פירצת מלואו. וי"ל: דא"כ היה לו לפרש דקרפף אסור משום דאויר חצר מייתרו, אי כרבנן אתי, ולא מצי למימר איפכא. ולכך הוצרך לאתויי דרב חסדא, דהוי כר"ש. דממילתיה דר' זירא אין להוכיח דהוי כר"ש, מדלא אמרינן איפכא – משום דבעי למימר אע"ג דבקירה בה בית סאה לא הוי ייתור, מודינא הכא דהוי ייתור – משום הכי לא *מצי למימר איפכא: **ההוא** בוסתנא דהוה סמוך לאגודא דאפדנא. והוקף ולבסוף פתח, והרחיקו ד' ועשו אשיתא, והיה בה נמי פתח לבוסתנא. נפל אשיתא, וסבר רב ביבי: דכיון דפעם אחת היתה מוקפת לדירה, אע"פ שנפלה – שרי, הואיל ופתוחה נמי לאפדנא. ואע"ג דפתח דאפדנא הוי לאחר שהוקף, דלא יצא מהיתרו. ומסיק דגודא דאפדנא אינו מועיל. ורש"י לא פירש כן: **ההוא** אבוורנקא.

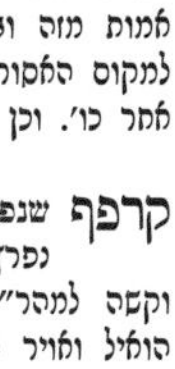

פירש רש"י* לשון שני שמצא בהלכות גדולות ונראה לו עיקר: דאבוורנקא כמין אכסדרה או קובה שעושין למלכים בתוך הפרדס. אזל רב הונא עבד קנה קנה פחות משלשה, ולא רצה לסמוך אאבוורנקא משום דהוקף ולבסוף ישב, ומשום דהויא מחילה העשויה לנחת ולצניעות, כדמסיק. ועביד שביל דקנה קנה פחות מג' מפתח הבוסתנא עד אבוורנקי, אם האבוורנקא היתה עומדת בתוך הפרדס. אבל אם היתה עומדת מצד הפרדס – לא היה צריך לעשות שביל, אלא לחלק הבוסתנא ולמעטה מסאתים, אע"ג דהיקף האבוורנקי היה עשוי לנחת ולצניעות – היה מותר לטלטל כלים ששבתו בו. והנהו פירי *דבי תורי היו יותר מבית סאתים, משום הכי הוצרכו לערב ערסייתא. או לא יכלו לערב יחד לכלים ששבתו בבית. ורבא שלפינהו, והיה סבור שהיקף האבוורנקי חשוב כמוקף לדירה, אף על גב דהוקף ולבסוף ישב. וצריך לומר שידעו שרבא היה מתיר מחמת האבוורנקי, ולא מחמת שהוקף ולבסוף פתח מהני. כיון דהקשו לו מאדרכלין, והמחילות העשויות לנחת – דהא לא שייך למיפרך אהוקף ולבסוף פתח. או שמא לא היה פתוח שם שום בית. א"נ: נוכל לומר אבוורנקא ישב ולבסוף הוקף היה, והם לא ידעו אם רבא סמך על הוקף ולבסוף פתח, ובית היה פתוח לו, או על האבוורנקא. והקשה לו מעיר חדשה, דהוקף ולבסוף ישב לא מהני – כל שכן הוקף ולבסוף פתח. ואחרי כן הקשה לו (דאם כן) דאבוורנקא לא חשיב מחילה משום דעשוי לנחת ולצניעות. ורבינו נתנאל מפרש: דעביד קנה קנה פחות משלשה – היינו שהרחיק מן הכותל ארבע, להתיר כל הבוסתנא, והיה הבית פתוח לו. דהשתא הוי כפתח ולבסוף הוקף. ורבא סבר דלא צריך כלום משום אבוורנקא, אע"ג דהוקף ולבסוף פתח לא מהני – הוקף ולבסוף ישב מהני:

מערב

רבינו חננאל

ר' זירא כרב דאמר פי תקרה יורד וסותם וזה המקורה נמי אמרי' פי תקרה יורד וסותם ואין בזה שאינו מקורה אלא בית סאתים ורבה כשמואל דאמר אכסדרה ורה"ר רשות אחת הן ואין מטלטלין בהן אלא בד' אמות ואין ביניהן מחיצה מפסקת ודחינן דכי איעביד האי קירוי כי אכסדרה בג' מחיצות הכי נמי דחלוקתן כחלוקת רב ושמואל וקיי"ל הלכתא כוותיה דרב הכא במאי עסקינן דעביד כי ארזלא. פי' ערסלא כדמתרגם כמלונה במקשה כערסלא מבתותא והוא חבלים מתוחים מאילנות לאילנות כמין מטה לשכב עליהן (היושב) בלילה ויושב תחת צילה ביום ותחתיהן פתוח כולו ובהכי אמר רבה קירויו מייתרו שביניהם פתוח לגמרי ור' זירא אמר אין קירוי מייתרו אלא המקום הקירוי חלוק הוא זה מזה. וקיי"ל כר' זירא דמיקיל בעירובין ולפיכך אמר ר' זירא אע"ג דפליגנא בהא קירוי דעביד (כימדולא) [כארזלא] שהוא פרוץ מתחתיו מכל צד ומותר מודינא בקרפיף שנפרץ במילואו לחצר שאין מטלטלין בו באותו קרפיף אלא בד' אמות הואיל ואויר מחיצות החצר מייתרו. ומתקיף לה רב יוסף וכי אויר של חצר שמותר לטלטל בכל החצר אוסר. א"ל אביי [כמאן] כר"ש דאמר אחד גגות ואחד חצרות ואחד קרפיפות לכלים ששבתו בתוכן. הנה לר' שמעון הקרפיף והחצר רשות אחת הן לר' שמעון נמי איכא אויר מחיצות והוא מקום הכותל שנפרץ שאינו בכלל החצר ונצטרף עתה עם הקרפף ונעשה יתר מבית סאתים. ומנא תימרא דאמר רב חסדא קרפף שנפרץ במילואו לחצר ונפרצה חצר כנגדו חצר מותרת וקרפף אסור חצר מ"ט מותרת משום דאיכא גיפופי. פי' גיפופי דחשיבי כפסין זמנין דמשכחת לה איפכא כלומר זימנין דמשכחת גיפופי בקרפף ולא בחצר אלא משום דאמר זה הקרפף אויר מחיצות מייתרו דאע"ג דאיכא מחיצות כיון דהוא יתר מבית (סאה) [סאתים] אסור ובחצר מחיצותיה מתירין אותה אפי' בבית י' כורין וקיי"ל דהלכתא כוותיה דרב באכסדרן וכר' זירא בקרפף: **ההוא** בוסתנא דהוה סמיך גודא לאשיתא דאפדנא נפל גודא דבוסתנא סבר רב ביבי למיסמך אאישיתא דאפדנא. ודחה רב ואמר אשיתא לאפדנא עביד לבוסתנא לא עביד ופשוטה היא: **ריש** גלותא נטע (טורנקיא) [בורנקיא] נטיעה. כדגרסינן איזהי נטיעה של שמחה זה הנוטע (אטורנקי) [אבורנקי] של מלכים. והיתה זאת הגינה יתר מבית סאתים מוקפת גדר גבוה י' טפחים סביבותיה ולא היתה בה שומירה ולא בית דירה. וא"ל ריש גלותא לרב הונא בר חננא זיל תקון דוכתא דניכרוך ביה ריפתא בשבת התם ביקש להתיר לו לטלטל בכל הגן אפילו במקום האילנות דהוה חד גיסא נטיעות וחד גיסא זרעים. אזל רב הונא עבד קנה קנה פחות מג' בחדא גיסא מן הנטיעות ועד הבנין שבנה (כגון) [בגן] אחרי נטיעתו וסמך בהאי גיסא אחריתי בנגדר של גן שהוא

עין משפט נר מצוה

[מב' רוותיה הכ"ע כו' הל"ה רש"ל]

מז א מיי' פט"ו מהל' שבת הלכה ז סמג עשין א טור וש"ע א"ח סי' שנח סעיף יג:

מח ב שם סעיף יד:

[יבמות עו. וש"נ]

[גירסת הערוך אבורנקי וכן גירסת תוס' לעיל דף כב. ד"ה פשיטא]

מסורת הש"ס

[ארזילא פירש ערסלא. ערוך פי' ככל פירוש שכתבו התוס' דהכא]

[לעיל כג:]

[פי' גאון זה נאמר על אדם גדול מפני שהוא גדול מדבר גדולות. ערוך ערך מל ז']

(והיא היתה לו אחת ממחיצותיו וע"ש ההוא גודא כו' פרדס הוקף הספרדס כו' כל"ל רש"ל)

הגהות הב"ח

(א) רש"י ד"ה דהוה סמוך לגודא דאפדנא היא היתה לו אחת ממחיצותיו ועל שם ההוא גודא שהיה בו פתח פתוח לצד פרדס הוקף כל"ל ותיבת סמכו נמחק: (ב) תוס' ד"ה אי וכו' הכא הס"ד:

רב נסים גאון

אמר ליה אביי כמאן כר' שמעון וזהו שאמר ר' שמעון בפרק כל גגות העיר (דף פט.) אחד גגות ואחד חצרות ואחד קרפיפות:

בס"ד בעי

[לקמן כו. ד"ה להרע]

א"ג האבורנקי היה ע"י קנים ומגו דמהני קנה להיות מחילה לעלמו מהני נמי לאשוויה אבורנקי מוקף לדירה [תו' ומי רש"ל]

מט א מיי' פכ"ח מהל' שבת הל' ה טוש"ע א"ח סי' שנח סעיף יא:
נ ב ג מיי' פט"ו מהל' שבת הלכה טו סמג עשין א טוש"ע א"ח סי' שסב סעיף ח:

שַׁלְפִינְהוּ. אֲזַל רַב פַּפָּא וְרַב הוּנָא בְּרֵיהּ דְּרַב יְהוֹשֻׁעַ נָקְטִינְהוּ מִבַּתְרֵיהּ. לְמָחָר אֵיתִיבֵיהּ רָבִינָא לְרָבָא: אעִיר חֲדָשָׁה מוֹדְדִין לָהּ מִישִׁיבָתָהּ, וִישָׁנָה מֵחוֹמָתָהּ. אֵיזוֹ הִיא חֲדָשָׁה וְאֵיזוֹ הִיא יְשָׁנָה? חֲדָשָׁה – שֶׁהוּקְּפָה וּלְבַסּוֹף יָשְׁבָה, יְשָׁנָה – יָשְׁבָה וּלְבַסּוֹף הוּקְּפָה. וְהַאי נַמִי, כְּהוּקְּפָה וּלְבַסּוֹף יָשְׁבָה דָּמֵי. א"ל רַב פַּפָּא לְרָבָא; וְהָאָמַר רַב אַסִּי: במְחִיצּוֹת אַדְרְכָלִין לֹא שְׁמָהּ מְחִיצָּה. אַלְמָא: כֵּיוָן דְּלִצְנִיעוּתָא עֲבִידָא לָהּ – לָא הָוְיָא מְחִיצָּה. ה"נ, כֵּיוָן דְּלִצְנִיעוּתָא עֲבִידָא – לָא הָוְיָא מְחִיצָּה(א). וְאָמַר רַב הוּנָא בְּרֵיהּ דְּרַב יְהוֹשֻׁעַ לְרָבָא, וְהָאָמַר רַב הוּנָא: גמְחִיצָּה *הָעֲשׂוּיָה לְנַחַת – לֹא שְׁמָהּ מְחִיצָּה, דְּהָא *רַבָּה בַּר אֲבוּהּ מְעָרֵב לָהּ לְכוּלָּהּ מְחוֹזָא עַרְסָיָיתָא עַרְסָיָיתָא מִשּׁוּם *פִּירָא דְּבֵי תוֹרֵי; וְהָא פִּירָא דְּבֵי תוֹרֵי כִּמְחִיצָּה הָעֲשׂוּיָה לְנַחַת דָּמְיָא! קָרֵי עֲלַיְיהוּ רֵישׁ גָּלוּתָא: °"חֲכָמִים הֵמָּה לְהָרַע וּלְהֵיטִיב לֹא יָדָעוּ". § "א"ר אֶלְעַאי: שָׁמַעְתִּי מֵר"א וַאֲפִי' בֵּית כּוֹר". § מַתְנִיתִין דְּלָא כַּחֲנַנְיָה. דְּתַנְיָא, חֲנַנְיָה אוֹמֵר: וַאֲפִילּוּ הִיא אַרְבָּעִים סְאָה כְּאִסְטְרַטְיָא שֶׁל מֶלֶךְ. א"ר יוֹחָנָן: וּשְׁנֵיהֶם מִקְרָא אֶחָד דָּרְשׁוּ, שֶׁנֶּאֱמַר: °"וַיְהִי יְשַׁעְיָהוּ לֹא יָצָא אֶל חָצֵר הַתִּיכוֹנָה", כְּתִיב "הָעִיר" וְקָרֵינַן "חָצֵר" מִכָּאן לְאִסְטְרַטְיָא שֶׁל מֶלֶךְ, שֶׁהָיוּ כַּעֲיָירוֹת בֵּינוֹנִיּוֹת. בְּמַאי קָמִיפַּלְגִי? מָר סָבַר: עֲיָירוֹת בֵּינוֹנִיּוֹת הָוְיָין בֵּית כּוֹר, וּמ"ס מ' סְאָה הָוְיָין. וִישַׁעְיָהוּ מַאי בָּעֵי הָתָם? אָמַר רַבָּה בַּר בַּר חָנָה, אָמַר ר' יוֹחָנָן: מְלַמֵּד שֶׁחָלָה חִזְקִיָּה, וְהָלַךְ יְשַׁעְיָהוּ וְהוֹשִׁיב יְשִׁיבָה עַל פִּתְחוֹ. מִכָּאן לְת"ח שֶׁחָלָה שֶׁמּוֹשִׁיבִין יְשִׁיבָה עַל פִּתְחוֹ. וְלָאו מִילְּתָא הִיא, דִּילְמָא אָתֵי לְאִיגְרוּיֵי בֵּיהּ שָׂטָן. § "וְכֵן שָׁמַעְתִּי הֵימֶנּוּ: אַנְשֵׁי חָצֵר שֶׁשָּׁכַח אֶחָד וְלֹא עֵירֵב – בֵּיתוֹ אָסוּר". § *וְהָתְנַן: בֵּיתוֹ אָסוּר לְהוֹצִיא וּלְהַכְנִיס לוֹ וְלָהֶן! אָמַר רַב הוּנָא בְּרֵיהּ דְּרַב יְהוֹשֻׁעַ, אָמַר רַב שֵׁשֶׁת: לָא קַשְׁיָא; הָא

תורה אור: ירמיהו ד; מ"ב כ

לקמן ס.

רש"י

שלפינהו. דלא ס"ל הא תקנתא: נקטינהו מבתריה. שלא יחזור רב הונא ויתקנם: איתיביה. לסיועיה דשפיר עבד: עיר חדשה מודדין לה מישיבתה. אם מוקפת חומה ואינה מיושבת כולה, כשבא למדוד תחומיה – לא ימדוד לה מן החומה אלא מן הבתים, דחומתה לאו חומה היא לשוויה כולה כד' אמות, הואיל וישיבתה חדשה שקדמה חומתה לישיבתה. אבל ישנה, שישובה ישנה וקדם לחומתה – מודדין לה מחומתה: והאי נמי. האי פרדס הרי הוקף ימים רבים, וכך השומירה נעשה עכשיו, והיקף הפרדס לאו אדעתא דהך דירה הוה ודמי כי הוקף ולבסוף ישב: א"ל רב פפא לרבא. לסיועיה: אדרכלין. בנאים, שעושים מחיצה לגל סדינותיהם כשבונים בחמה: כיון דלצניעותא היא. ולמחר סתרי לה – לאו כלום היא. והא נמי לצניעותא – דיום ולילה בעלמא היא דעבידא, ולאו דירה היא: לנחת. שלא לדור שם, אלא להשתמר מה שמניחו שם: ערסייתא. שכונות שכונות לבד, ובכל שכונה היו מבואות הרבה ולא התיר את העיר כולה ביחד, ואע"פ שהיתה עיר קטנה שאין נכנסין בה ששים ריבוא. ותנן לקמן (דף נט.): עיר של יחיד מערבין את כולה, והיינו של יחיד – שאינה דומה לדגלי מדבר של ששים ריבוא: משום פירא דבי תורי. שוחה עמוקה היתה בין שכונה לשכונה, ושם היו מניחין גרעיני תמרים לאכול השוורים. והעיר אין לה חומה ומבואות של (בין) [בתי] השכונות מפולשים,

ועשו מחיצות לראשי המבואות לכל צד שחוץ לעיר להשתמר הגרעינין, ולא חשיב ליה מחיצה לצרף את המבואות ולעשות העיר אחת, ואע"פ שמחיצה של קיימא היתה: פירא. שוחה. כמו פירא דכוורי במס' תענית (דף כד.). והך מחיצה דרב הונא כעשויה לנחת דמיא, שאינה נעשית לדירה תמיד לצאת ולבא בה: להרע. לאסור. ובתשובת הגאונים מצאתיה בלשון אחר, וישר בעיני מאד. ההוא בוסתנא קרפף יותר מבית סאתים שלא הוקף לדירה הוה, ואבוורנקא כמין אכסדרה או קובה שבונין המלכים בתוך פרדס שלהן, ועומד באמצע פרדס. ולא הוליך ריש גלותא אלא לטלטל מפתח בוסתנא שהיה אצל הבית עד האבוורנקא. ועבד רב הונא בר חיננא כמין שביל מן הפתח עד האבוורנקא גדר מכאן וגדר מכאן בקנה קנה פחות מג' להפסיק בין הדרך לבוסתנא, ויטלטל באותו שביל. ורבא כי שלפינהו – לא לאסור אלא להקל עליו, דס"ל דשרי לטלטולי בכולה בוסתנא, דכיון דבנה ליה אבוורנקא בבוסתנא שוייה לכולה בוסתנא חצר לאבוורנקא, והוי מוקף לדירה. ואתו תלמידי דרבא רב פפא ורב הונא בריה דרב יהושע נקטינהו, דלא ליהדר רב הונא בר חיננא וליתקנינהו. והיא שעתא לא אדכור להו דלאו שפיר עביד דשלפינהו, ולמחר אדכור ואותבוה. כדאמר: למחר איתיביה רבינא לרבא עיר חדשה כו' והאי בוסתנא נמי כהוקף ולבסוף ישב דמי, שקודם נטיעתו מקיפין אותו ולאחר שגדל האילן עשו האבוורנקא סביב – הלכך, שפיר עבד רב הונא בר חיננא. ורב פפא אותביה ממחיצת אדרכלין, דהא מחיצה דאבוורנקא נמי לצניעות עבידא וכן לנחת, להשתמש להניח בה טליתותיהן ולבושיהן שפושטים שם ושאר כלי תשמישם. קרי עלייהו על רב פפא ורב הונא בריה דרב יהושע שלא נזכרו אתמול, וסתרו תיקונו של רב הונא בר חיננא, ועכשיו נעשו חכמים לאסור עליו. "ולהיטיב לא ידעו" אתמול, וכן עיקר: כאיסטרטיא של מלכים. רחבה שאחורי פלטין, ושם היו מטיילים תמיד. אלמא: איכא דירה בהכי: ושניהן. ר' אלעאי וחנניה: התיכונה. אחרי פלטין של חזקיה. דאי חצר שלפני בתים הואי – "התיכונה" הוה קרי לה, ואע"ג דגדולה היא כעיר, קרי לה חצר, ולא הוקפה לדירה: מאי בעי התם. ברחבה שאחורי פלטין, שאינה לדרך יציאה: להושיב ישיבה. של תלמידים, לעסוק בתורה על פתחו, שלא יהא רשות למלאך המות ליכנס שם: שטן. מלאך המות: דכי חזי (דמיגלו) בהדי הדדי מיגרי בהו): אנשי חצר ששבח אחד מהן כו'. ודאי מתני' כשביטל להן רשות שהיה לו בחצר מיירי. דאי לא בטיל – אף בחצר אסורים לטלטל מבתיהן, שהבתים לכל אחד ואחד הן, והחצר רשות כולן וחלקו אוסר עליהן. ואשמעינן ר' אלעאי דהמבטל רשות חצירו רשות ביתו נמי ביטל, ונעשה אורח אצלן. לפיכך אף ביתו מותר להן. אבל הוא אסור להכניס ולהוציא מביתו לחצר. ואף על פי שהוא מותר להכניס ולהוציא מפתח בתיהן לחצר כדתנן בפרק "הדר" (דף סט:): ושלהן מותר לו ולהן, כשאר כל אדם הנכנס לחצר חבירו ומותר לו להוציא מפתח חבירו לחצר – דהא רשותא דחד הוא. והכא נמי, כיון (*דבטל הוא דירתו) מביתו (*מיהא) אסור הוא להוציא, ולא אמרינן כיון דביטל להו רשות ביתו הוי ביתו כבתיהן. דבשלמא מבתיהן, אם הוא מכניס ומוציא – איכא למימר כאינש בעלמא הוא. אבל מביתו – חוזר ומחזיק ברשותו הוא – ואוסר עליהם והן עליו. כדתנן בפרק "הדר": מי שנתן רשותו והוציא, בין בשוגג בין במזיד – הרי זה אוסר: והא תנן. לקמן בפרק "הדר": ביתו אסור להכניס ולהוציא לו ולהן. ואמרינן התם: ביתו הוא דאסור להם, הא חצירו – שריא להוציא מבתיהן לחצר שרשותו שולט בה. ה"ד? אי דלא ביטל – חצירו אמאי שריא? ואוקימנא כשביטל רשות חצירו, ולא ביטל רשות ביתו. וקסבר: המבטל רשות חצירו – רשות ביתו לא ביטל. לפיכך, חצר כולה שלהן היא, וביתו מיוחדת לאסור להן להוציא מרשותו לרשותן: מתני'

נ"א שאינה עשויה

[פי' תריץ קרובלין בו הבהמות ערוך ערך פרא]

לקמן סט:

[ברש"י שבע"י איתא דמיגרו בהדיה מגרי בהו]

[נ"ל דבטל להו דירתם הוי] [נ"ל מיהו]

תוספות

מערב לכולה מחוזא ערסייתא. פי' רש"י: לא התיר לערב כולה יחד, אע"ג שהיתה עיר קטנה. ותנן לקמן(ג): עיר של יחיד – מערבין את כולה. וקשיא: דבפ' "כילד מעברין" (לקמן דף ס.) אמרינן דשל רבים הוא דקאמר רבה בר אבוה מערב לכולה מחוזא ערסייתא, דכל חד וחד הוי שיור לחבריה. ועיר של יחיד לא בעי שיור, אם לא שהיתה של רבים קודם. אלא ודאי של רבים היתה(ג). ולעיל (ו:) נמי משמע שהיתה של רבים גבי אבולי דמחוזא, דאמר: אילמלא דלתותי' נעולות בלילה – הוי חייב עליה משום רה"ר. משמע דהיו שם ס' רבוא. מ"מ, אי לאו משום פירי דבי תורי – היו יכולין לערב כל העיר יחד, והוו משיירי נ' דיורין לר' יהודה, או שלש חצירות לר' שמעון: דבי תורי. פירש הקונטרס: דמחוזא עיר שאין לה חומה, ועשו מחיצה בראשי מבואות לכל צד לשמור גרעינין, ולא חשיב מחיצה להצטרף המבואות ולעשות כל העיר כאחת, לפי שההיקף לא נעשה בעבור העיר אלא לשמור פירא דבי תורי. ומשמע שר"ל שהוקף קודם ישוב העיר, דאם הוקף אחרי כן – אז נעשה גם בעבור העיר, והוו מחיצה מעלייתא. וקשיא: דלישנא משמע שאם נסתלקה משם הפירא – דהוי מחיצה מעלייתא, ולפי' הקונט', אף אם לא היה הפירא – לא היה ניתר, כיון דהוקף ולבסוף ישב. ועוד: מה שפי' בקונטרס דמחוזא לית לה חומה – לא נהירא, דאמר לעיל: אבולא דמחוזא, אילמלא דלתותיה נעולות בלילה. ונראה דמוקפת חומה היתה אחר שנתיישבה, והיו יכולין לערב יחד אי לאו פירא דבי תורי שהיתה בין ערסא לערסא לאורך המבוי והיתה יתירה מבית סאתים ועמוקה י', ולא היו יכולים לערב מערסא לערסא לפי שלא היו יכולין לטלטל מזה לזה, דהפירא הוי קרפף יותר מבית סאתים. ולא דמי לכריא דפירי דלעיל – דראוין למאכל אדם ואע"ג דיש להו מחיצות – אינם מועילים כלום, דמחיצות העשויות לנחת הם. ורש"י פי' ב"כילד מעברין" (לקמן דף ס.) משום פירא שמפסיק, ואין יכולין להלך משכונה לשכונה, והוי כחריץ שבין ב' חצירות. דאמרינן לקמן (דף עח:) שמערבין שתים ואין מערבין אחת, והכא [לא משמע בפירא אלא] משום דהויא מחיצה עשויה לנחת: והתנן ביתו אסור לו ולהם. וליכא למימר דמתניתין דמבטל בהדיא רשות ביתו – דאם כן, מאי לא מצאתי לי חבר? אי נמי: משמע ליה דמתניתין איירי אפילו בסתם: ולא

רבינו חננאל

גבוה י' טפחים דלהוי כאלו הוקף לדירה. אזל רבא שלפינהו להנהו קני סבר צריך להקיף גדר בהאי גיסא (לדירה אחריתי) [אחריתי לדירה] למחר בשבת אותיביה רבינא לרבא עיר חדשה *) מונין לה מישיבתה ואיזו עיר חדשה שישבה ולבסוף הוקפה ואיזו היא ישנה [שמודדין לה מחומתה]. שהוקפה ולבסוף נתיישבה דכיון דחומה נעשית תחלה כל בנין שבונים בפנים סמוכין על החומה שהיא מחיצה החיצונה והאי [נמי] כהוקף ולבסוף ישב דמי דהא בניינא דאיתבני בהדין בוסתנא בתרא הכי סמיכי להו אגדר דבוסתנא וכי עבד רב הונא קנה קנה פחות מג' בהאי גיסא דהוו בה זרעים שפיר עבד דגיסא אחריתי לא בעיא מחיצה דהא קיימי מחיצתה דבוסתנא דאינון חומה לכל בניינא דמתבי לגואי כגון חומת העיר. ואישתיק רבא וסייעיה רב פפא וא"ל אמאי שתקת הא אמר רב אסי האי מחיצת אדרכלין לאו שמיה מחיצה. פי' כי אינה עשויה מחיצה לשדה אלא **) למסע החיות מקנה קנה פחות מג' כמו מחיצת אדרכלין היא דעבידא לצניעותא בעלמא ואינה מחיצה שמתרת לטלטל בתוכה בשבת כמו מחיצה של שיירות להולכי דרכים ובא רב הונא בריה דר' יהושע נמי וסייעיה לרבא ואמר מחיצה זו אינה עשוי' (לעות) [לנחת] פי' להיות קבועה לעולם כבנין אלא ארעי הוא. ואמר רב הונא כל מחיצה שמתרת לטלטל בשבת ***) כמו מחיצה שאינה עשויה (לעות) [לנחת] אינה מחיצה. ועוד הא רבא בר אבוה מערב למחוזא ערסתא. ערסתא מחיצה שהיו עושין דקבעין וקיימין ועשויות לנחת. פי' ערסתא שכונו' שכונות. וכיון שהסכימו כלן כרבא. וכי מה שעשה רב הונא [היה] שלא כהוגן הוה קרי עליהו חכמים המה להרע וגו'. פי' פירא תורי באר דמחמא ואו' כי היא רסן העיר הגדולה וכבר ראינו פי' לרבותינו הגאונים זולתי זה אבל אנו כתבנו הפי' שהוא קבלה בידינו: מתני' א"ר אלעאי שמעתי מר"א אליעזר שאפילו בית כור. מתניתא דלא כחנניה דתניא חנניה אומר ארבעים סאה כאסטרטיא של מלך. ותנן בית כור שהוא ל' סאה א"ר חנן ושניהם מקרא אחד דרשו ויהי ישעיהו לא יצא חצר התיכונה. כתיב עיר וקרי' חצר מיכן לחצר של מלכים שהיא בעיירות בינוניות ובהא פליגי תנא דידן סבר עיירות בינוניות שלשים סאה וחנניה סבר מ' סאה. אמר רבה בר בר חנה א"ר יוחנן שחלה חזקיהו ובא ישעיה והושיב ישיבה על פתחו מיכן לת"ח שחלה שמושיבין ישיבה על פתחו ולאו מלתא היא דלמא מגרי שטן: פיסקא וכן שמעתי ממנו אנשי חצר ששכח אחד מהן ולא עירב ביתו אסור להכניס ולהוציא. לו אבל להם מותר והתנן ביתו אסור לו ולהן. ופרקינן

הגהות הב"ח

(א) גמ' לא הוי מחיצה אמר ליה רב הונא: (ב) תוס' ד"ה מערב וכו' ותנא לקמן נ"ב דף נט: (ג) בא"ד ודאי של רבים היתה ומכל מקום אי לאו כ"ל ומן תיכת ולעיל נמי משמע וכו' עד ס' רבוא הוא גליון:

*) גי' רבינו הוא להיפך גמ' דילן דחדשה הוא שישבה ולבסוף הוקפה וישנה שהוקפה ולבסוף ישבה וצ"ע: **) [נראה דכאן נ"ל אלא לצניעותא ושני תיבות אלו למחק] ולמסע החיות נ"ל לקמן גבי פירא דבי תורי ועי' בערוך ערך פרא. ***) נראה דנ"ל שאינה כמו מחיצה שעשויה לנחת.

הָא — ר"א, וְהָא — רַבָּנַן. כְּשֶׁתִּימְצֵי לוֹמַר, לְדִבְרֵי ר' אֱלִיעֶזֶר הַמְבַטֵּל רְשׁוּת חֲצֵירוֹ — רְשׁוּת בֵּיתוֹ בִּיטֵּל. *לְרַבָּנַן, [א]הַמְבַטֵּל רְשׁוּת חֲצֵירוֹ — רְשׁוּת בֵּיתוֹ לֹא בִּיטֵּל. פְּשִׁיטָא! אָמַר *רַחֲבָה: אֲנָא וְרַב הוּנָא בַּר חִינָּנָא תַּרְגִּימְנָא: לֹא נִצְרְכָא אֶלָּא לַחֲמִשָּׁה שֶׁשְּׁרוּיִן בְּחָצֵר אֶחָד, וְשָׁכַח אֶחָד מֵהֶן וְלֹא עֵירֵב. לְדִבְרֵי ר"א, כְּשֶׁהוּא מְבַטֵּל רְשׁוּתוֹ — אֵין צָרִיךְ לְבַטֵּל לְכָל אֶחָד וְא'. לְרַבָּנַן, *[ב]כְּשֶׁהוּא מְבַטֵּל רְשׁוּתוֹ — צָרִיךְ לְבַטֵּל לְכָל אֶחָד וְאֶחָד. *כְּמַאן אָזְלָא הָא דְּתַנְיָא: חֲמִשָּׁה שֶׁשְּׁרוּיִן בְּחָצֵר אֶחָד וְשָׁכַח אֶחָד מֵהֶן וְלֹא עֵירֵב, כְּשֶׁהוּא מְבַטֵּל רְשׁוּתוֹ — אֵין צָרִיךְ לְבַטֵּל רְשׁוּת לְכָל אֶחָד וְאֶחָד. כְּמַאן — כְּר"א. רַב כָּהֲנָא מַתְנֵי הָכִי. רַב טַבְיוֹמֵי מַתְנֵי הָכִי: כְּמַאן אָזְלָא הָא דְּתַנְיָא ה' שֶׁשְּׁרוּיִם בְּחָצֵר אֶחָד וְשָׁכַח אֶחָד מֵהֶן וְלֹא עֵירֵב, כְּשֶׁהוּא מְבַטֵּל רְשׁוּתוֹ — אֵינוֹ צָרִיךְ לְבַטֵּל רְשׁוּת לְכָל אֶחָד וְאֶחָד. כְּמַאן? אָמַר רַב הוּנָא בַּר יְהוּדָה, אָמַר רַב שֵׁשֶׁת: כְּמַאן — כְּר"א. א"ל רַב פַּפָּא לְאַבַּיֵי: לְר"א, אִי אָמַר "לָא מְבַטֵּילְנָא", וּלְרַבָּנַן אִי אָמַר "מְבַטֵּילְנָא", מַאי? טַעְמָא דְּר"א — מִשּׁוּם דְּקָסָבַר: הַמְבַטֵּל רְשׁוּת חֲצֵירוֹ — רְשׁוּת בֵּיתוֹ בִּיטֵּל, וְהַאי אָמַר "אֲנָא לָא מְבַטֵּילְנָא". אוֹ דִּילְמָא: טַעְמָא דְּר"א מִשּׁוּם *דְּבַיִת בְּלָא חָצֵר לָא עָבְדִי אֱינָשֵׁי דְּדָיְירֵי וְכִי קָאָמַר לָא מְבַטֵּילְנָא — לָאו כָּל כְּמִינֵיהּ, אע"ג דְּאָמַר דָּיְירְנָא, לָאו כְּלוּם קָאָמַר. וּלְרַבָּנַן, אִי אָמַר "מְבַטֵּילְנָא" מַאי טַעְמָא דְּרַבָּנַן? מִשּׁוּם דְּקָסָבְרִי הַמְבַטֵּל רְשׁוּת חֲצֵירוֹ רְשׁוּת בֵּיתוֹ לֹא בִּיטֵּל — וְהַאי אָמַר "מְבַטֵּילְנָא". אוֹ דִּילְמָא: טַעְמָא דְּרַבָּנַן מִשּׁוּם דְּלָא עָבֵיד אִינִישׁ דִּמְסַלֵּק נַפְשֵׁיהּ לְגַמְרֵי מִבַּיִת וְחָצֵר, וְהָוֵי כִּי אוֹרֵחַ לְגַבַּיְיהוּ. וְהַאי כִּי אָמַר מְבַטֵּילְנָא — לָאו כָּל כְּמִינֵיהּ קָאָמַר. א"ל: בֵּין לְרַבָּנַן בֵּין לְר"א, [ג]כֵּיוָן דְּגַלֵּי דַּעְתֵּיהּ — גַּלֵּי.§ "וְכֵן שָׁמַעְתִּי מִמֶּנּוּ שֶׁיּוֹצְאִים בְּעַרְקַבְלִין בַּפֶּסַח".§ מַאי עַרְקַבְלִין? *אָמַר רֵישׁ לָקִישׁ: אַצְוָותָא חֲרוּזְיָאתָא.§

הֲדְרָן עֲלָךְ עוֹשִׂין פַּסִּין

בַּכֹּל *[ד]מְעָרְבִין וּמִשְׁתַּתְּפִין — חוּץ מִן הַמַּיִם וּמִן הַמֶּלַח. וְהַכֹּל נִיקָּח בְּכֶסֶף מַעֲשֵׂר — חוּץ מִן הַמַּיִם וּמִן הַמֶּלַח. *הַנּוֹדֵר מִן הַמָּזוֹן — מוּתָּר *בַּמֶּלַח וּבַמַּיִם. *מְעָרְבִין לַנָּזִיר בַּיַּיִן, וּלְיִשְׂרָאֵל בִּתְרוּמָה. סוּמְכוֹס אוֹמֵר: בְּחוּלִּין. וּלְכֹהֵן בְּבֵית הַפְּרָס, ר' יְהוּדָה אוֹמֵר: אֲפִי' *בֵּין הַקְּבָרוֹת, מִפְּנֵי

מַתְנִי' ר"א. כִּדְאָמַר ר' אֱלְעַאי: שָׁמַעְתִּי מֵר"א: רְשׁוּת בֵּיתוֹ בִּיטֵּל. וְאע"ג דְּלָא פָּרֵישׁ בְּהֶדְיָא רְשׁוּת בֵּיתוֹ, דְּהָא וַדַּאי מַתְנִי' בִּדְלָא פֵּירֵשׁ, דְּאִי פֵּירֵשׁ — לָא מָצֵי לְמֵימַר ר' אֱלְעַאי בִּקַּשְׁתִּי לִי חָבֵר וְלֹא מְצָאתִי, דְּהָא כ"ע מוֹדוּ דְּשָׁרֵי: פְּשִׁיטָא. דִּבְהָכִי פְּלִיגִי, וְלָמָּה לֵיהּ לְרַב שֵׁשֶׁת לוֹמַר "כְּשֶׁתִּימְצֵי לוֹמַר": אָמַר רַחֲבָה אֲנָא וְרַב הוּנָא בַּר חִינָּנָא תַּרְגִּימְנָא. לְהַאי "כְּשֶׁתִּימְצֵי לוֹמַר" דְּרַב שֵׁשֶׁת לְמַאי אִיצְטְרִיךְ: ה"ג: לֹא נִצְרְכָה אֶלָּא לַחֲמִשָּׁה שֶׁשְּׁרוּיִן בְּחָצֵר כו'. דְּאַשְׁמְעִינַן רַב שֵׁשֶׁת לָשׁוּם לֵב לְהָבִין טַעַם מַחֲלוֹקְתָּן וְלִלְמוֹד הֵימֶנּוּ דָּבָר אַחֵר, דְּלְר' אֱלִיעֶזֶר מְבַטֵּל, בְּעַיִן יָפָה מְבַטֵּל. וְלָא אָמְרִינַן חָצֵר דְּגַלֵּי — גַּלֵּי, בַּיִת דְּלָא גַּלֵּי — לָא גַּלֵּי, וְנֵילַף מִינָּהּ דְּהֵיכָא דְּבַטֵּיל לְחַד מִינַּיְיהוּ — בַּטֵּיל לְכוּלְּהוּ, וְלָא אָמְרִינַן לְמַאן דְּגַלֵּי — גַּלֵּי, לְמַאן דְּלָא גַּלֵּי — לָא גַּלֵּי. וּלְרַבָּנַן צָרִיךְ לְבַטֵּל לְכָל אֶחָד וְאֶחָד. כִּי הֵיכִי דִּלְגַבֵּי בַּיִת סְבִירָא לְהוּ דְּמַאי דְּלָא פָּרֵישׁ — לָא בַּטֵּיל, הָכָא נַמִי: לְמַאן דְּלָא פָּרֵישׁ — לָא בַּטֵּיל, וְכוּלָּן אֲסוּרִין. דְּאע"ג דְּהַאי דְּבַטֵּיל לֵיהּ עֵירֵב עִם חֲבֵירוֹ — כִּי עֵירֵב מֵאֶתְמוֹל אַדַּעְתָּא דְּהַהִיא חוּלְקָא לָא עֵירֵב, דְּהַהִיא שַׁעְתָּא לָאו דִּידֵיהּ הוּא. וְדִכְוָותֵיהּ תַּנְיָא בְּ"הַדָּר" (לקמן דף ע:): אֶחָד מִן הַשּׁוּק שֶׁמֵּת וְהָיָה לוֹ בַּיִת בֶּחָצֵר, וְהִנִּיחַ רְשׁוּתוֹ לְאֶחָד מִבְּנֵי הֶחָצֵר מִבְּעוֹד יוֹם, דְּהַיְינוּ קוֹדֶם שֶׁעֵירְבוּ, דְּכִי עֵירֵב אַדַּעְתָּא דְּהַהִיא חוּלְקָא נַמִי עֵירֵב — אֵינוֹ אוֹסֵר, מִשֶּׁחֲשֵׁיכָה — הֲרֵי זֶה אוֹסֵר: רַב כָּהֲנָא מַתְנֵי הָכִי. לְהַאי "כְּשֶׁתִּימְצֵי לוֹמַר" דְּרַב שֵׁשֶׁת אַמַּתְנִיתִין. וְרַחֲבָה וְרַב הוּנָא הוּא דְּתַרְגְּמוּהּ לְאַגְמוֹרֵינַן מִינָּהּ אַחֲמִשָּׁה שֶׁעֵירְבוּ בֶּחָצֵר כו' הוּא דְּאָתָא: וְרַב טַבְיוֹמֵי מַתְנֵי. דְּרַב שֵׁשֶׁת בְּהֶדְיָא אֲמָרָהּ עֲלָהּ: כְּר' אֱלִיעֶזֶר. דְּאָמַר: מְבַטֵּל, בְּעַיִן יָפֶה מְבַטֵּל: לְרַבִּי אֱלִיעֶזֶר. דְּאָמַר: מִסְּתָמָא בִּיטֵּל רְשׁוּת בֵּיתוֹ: אִם אָמַר. בְּהֶדְיָא לָא בַּטֵּילְנָא רְשׁוּת בֵּיתוֹ, מִי הָוֵי בֵּיתוֹ מוּתָּר לָהֶן, אוֹ לָא: וּלְרַבָּנַן. דְּאָמְרִי: מִסְּתָמָא לָא בִּיטֵּל רְשׁוּת בֵּיתוֹ, אָמַר בְּהֶדְיָא מְבַטֵּילְנָא לְכוּ אַף רְשׁוּת בֵּיתוֹ, מְבַטֵּיל אִי לָא: בֵּיתָא בְּלָא חָצֵר. כֵּיוָן דְּאָסַר עַצְמוֹ בַּחֲצֵרוֹ שֶׁבִּיטֵּל לָהֶם: לָאו כָּל כְּמִינֵיהּ. דְּכֵיוָן דְּלֵית לֵיהּ חָצֵר — דִּירַת בַּיִת לָא כְּלוּם הִיא לְדִידֵיהּ: וְהַאי כִּי אָמַר מְבַטֵּילְנָא. בָּטְלָה דַּעְתּוֹ אֵצֶל כָּל אָדָם, וְלֹא בִּיטֵּל אֶלָּא חָצֵר: אַצְוָותָא חַרְזְיָיתָא. סִיב עָבֶה הַגָּדֵל סָבִיב הַדֶּקֶל, וְנִכְרָךְ וְעוֹלֶה בּוֹ כְּלוּלְבֵי גְּפָנִים. חַרְזְיָיתָא. תְּכוּפוֹת הַרְבֵּה יַחַד כְּמַחֲרוֹזוֹת, וְטַעַם מָרוֹר בּוֹ:

הֲדְרָן עֲלָךְ עוֹשִׂין פַּסִּין

בַּכֹּל מְעָרְבִין. עֵירוּבֵי חֲצֵירוֹת[א] וּתְחוּמִין: וּמִשְׁתַּתְּפִין. בְּמָבוֹי: חוּץ מִן הַמַּיִם וּמִן הַמֶּלַח. דְּלָאו מִידֵּי דְּמָזוֹן הֵן. וְטַעְמָא דְּעֵירוּב — מִשּׁוּם דְּדַעְתּוֹ וְדִירָתוֹ בִּמְקוֹם מְזוֹנוֹתָיו הוּא, וְכֵיוָן שֶׁנָּתְנוּ כָּל בְּנֵי הֶחָצֵר כְּדֵי מָזוֹן בְּבַיִת אֶחָד — נַעֲשָׂה כְּאִילּוּ כּוּלָּן דָּרִים בְּתוֹכוֹ, וְנִמְצְאוּ כּוּלָּן רְשׁוּת אַחַת וכו' וְכֵן בְּעֵירוּבֵי תְחוּמִין — נַעֲשָׂה כְּמִי[ב] שֶׁשָּׁבַת שָׁם, וּמִשָּׁם יֵשׁ לוֹ אַלְפַּיִם אַמָּה לְכָל רוּחַ, הִלְכָּךְ, דְּבַר מָזוֹן בָּעֵינַן: בְּכֶסֶף מַעֲשֵׂר. בְּתוֹךְ יְרוּשָׁלַיִם, כְּשֶׁהוּא מוֹצִיאוֹ [לְצוֹרֶךְ מַאֲכָלוֹ] כִּדְכְתִיב (דברים יד): "וְנָתַתָּה הַכֶּסֶף בְּכֹל אֲשֶׁר תְּאַוֶּה נַפְשְׁךָ": חוּץ מִן הַמַּיִם וּמֶלַח. בַּגְּמָרָא מְפָרֵשׁ טַעְמָא, דְּלָאו פְּרִי מִפְּרִי הוּא: מְעָרְבִין לַנָּזִיר. עֵירוּבֵי תְחוּמִין: בַּיַּיִן. וְאַף עַל גַּב דְּלָא חֲזֵי לְדִידֵיהּ חֲזֵי לְאַחֲרִינֵי, וְכֵיוָן דִּמְזוֹנָא הוּא גַּבֵּי אַחֲרִינֵי — שָׁרוּ לֵיהּ רַבָּנַן: וּלְיִשְׂרָאֵל בִּתְרוּמָה. דְּהָא חַזְיָא לְכֹהֵן: סוּמְכוֹס אוֹמֵר בְּחוּלִּין. אֲבָל לֹא בִּתְרוּמָה, דְּמִידֵּי דַּחֲזִי לֵיהּ בָּעֵינַן. וּבַגְּמָרָא מְפָרֵשׁ מַאי טַעְמָא לָא פָּלֵיג סוּמָכוֹס אַיַּיִן לַנָּזִיר: וּלְכֹהֵן בְּבֵית הַפְּרָס. סְתָמָא הִיא, וְלָאו סוּמָכוֹס קָאָמַר לָהּ: מַנִּיחִין עֵירוּב לַכֹּהֵן בְּבֵית הַפְּרָס, אע"ג דְּבָעֵינַן דְּמָצֵי לְמֵיזַל וּלְמִשְׁקְלֵיהּ וּמֵיכְלֵיהּ הָתָם, דְּאִי לָא מָצֵי אָזֵיל הָתָם — הֵיכִי קָנֵי שְׁבִיתָה בְּהַהוּא דּוּכְתָּא לְמֶהֱוֵי כְּאִילּוּ שָׁבַת שָׁם[ג]? בְּבֵית הַפְּרָס שַׁפִּיר דָּמֵי, דִּסְפֵיקָא דְּרַבָּנַן הוּא, וּמוּתָּר לִיכָּנֵס ע"י נִפּוּחַ: לָחוּץ

---

*ולא מצאתי לי חבר. היינו דוקא בתלמידיו. דתניא ב"כל שעה" (פסחים דף לט.): עד שבאתי אצל ר"א בן יעקב והודה לדברי. אי נמי: לא מצא חבר ששמע מר"א קאמר.

אצוותא חרוזייתא. פירש בקונטרס: סיב עבה הגדל סביב הדקל ונכרך ועולה כלולבי גפנים. ואין נראה לר"י, דבפ' "כל שעה" (פסחים דף לט.) אמרי': מה מצה מין זרעים — אף מרור מין זרעים. והתם אמרינן דחרחבינא אצוותא דדיקלא. ואפשר דהן ב' מינין, ושניהן נכרכין סביב הדקל*:

הדרן עלך עושין פסין

בבל מערבין. פי' בקונט': עירובי חצירות ותחומין. ואין נראה, דבעירובי חצירות בעינן פת לכולי עלמא בפרק "הדר" (לקמן דף עא:), וכל האי פירקא מוכח דאיירי בתחומין:

ולכהן בבית הפרס. וא"ת: בפסחים (דף צב.) אמר: אונן ומצורע ובית הפרס בעושי פסח לא העמידו דבריהם במקום כרת. פירוש: לא העמידו דבריהם לטמאותו, משום דאיכא כרת אם לא יעשה פסח. והכא משמע דאפי' בשביל עירוב לא העמידו דבריהם. והתם נמי, ע"י בדיקה דרב יהודה איירי, דקאמר אבית הפרס. כדתנן: ושוין ב"ש וב"ה שבודקין לאוכלי פסחים ואין בודקין לאוכלי תרומה. וקאמר: מאי בודקין? א"ר יהודה, אמר שמואל: מנפח אדם בבית הפרס והולך לו. ואף ע"ג דמפרש התם בפרק בתרא דאהלות (משנה ד) אהך משנה: כיצד הוא בודק — מביא עפר שהוא יכול להסיטו, ונותן לתוך כברה שנקביה דקין וממחה. אם יש עלם כשעורה — טמא. ההיא בדיקה מיירי אם כבר עבר, ובדיקת דרב יהודה איירי אם רוצה לעבור. וה"פ: מאי בודקין אם רוצה לעבור. וי"ל: דהא דקאמרינן התם דלא העמידו דבריהם במקום כרת — היינו משום דאיכא נמי כרת לעושי פסח בטומאה, ולכך דוקא לעושי פסח לא העמידו דבריהם, אע"ג דאיכא כרת כיון דאי לא עביד(ד) נמי פסח איכא כרת. אבל אין בודקין לאוכלי תרומה, אף על גב דליכא כרת לאוכלי תרומה בטומאה — כיון דאיכא מיתה העמידו דבריהם. והכי אמרינן ב"חומר בקדש" (חגיגה דף כה:): לעושי פסח לא העמידו דבריהם במקום כרת, פי': אפי' במקום כרת. לאוכלי תרומה — העמידו דבריהם במקום מיתה, פי': אף על גב דליכא כרת אלא מיתה, כדפרישית. אבל הכא, דטומאת כהן ליכא כרת אלא לאו — לא העמידו דבריהם במקום מצוה. דאפי' אם מערבין לדבר הרשות — אורחא דמלתא הוא לערב לדבר מצוה, כדאמר בפ' "כיצד משתתפין" (לקמן דף פב.) ובמצוה רבה, אפי' בלא ניפוח התירו כגון ללמוד תורה ולישא אשה ולדון ולערער עמהם כדי להציל מידם. כדאמר במס' ע"ג (דף יג.) ובפרק "מי שהוציאוהו" (לקמן דף מז.) דמדלא מייתי התם הא דרב יהודה — משמע דבלא ניפוח איירי. ולכך נקט נמי הנך מלות, ולא נקט אחריני. וכן מצינו דמשום כבוד הבריות התירו לטמא בטומאה דרבנן ב"מי שמתו" (ברכות דף יט:) גבי מדלגין היינו ע"ג ארונות:

מפני

[שייך לעיל במשנה]

נא א ב מיי' פ"ב מהל' עירובין הלכה א סמג עשין א טוש"ע א"ח סי' שפ סעיף א:
נב ג מיי' שם הל' ב טוש"ע שם ס"ב:
א ד מיי' פ"א מהלכות עירובין הל' ח סמג עשין א טוש"ע א"ח סי' שפו סעיף ה:

עיין תוס' סוכה לו: ד"ה בסיב

רבינו חננאל

ופרקינן מתני' ר' אליעזר אידך רבנן ואסיקנא בה' השרויין בחצר אחת ושכח אחד ולא עירב לדברי ר' אליעזר אין צריך לבטל רשות לכל אחד ואחד לדברי חכמים צריך לבטל רשות לכל אחד ואחד. א"ל רב פפא לאביי לר' אליעזר אי פריש ואמר רשות חצרי בטלתי רשות ביתי לא בטלתי ולרבנן אי פריש ואמר רשות חצרי ורשות ביתי מאי. ופשטנא בין לרבנן ובין לר' אליעזר כיון דגלי גלי: ערקבלין פי' ירקות שמם אצותא חרזיתא. ירקות שיוצאין בהן בפסח:

הדרן עלך עושין פסין

פ"ג בבל מערבין ומשתתפין חוץ מן המים ומן המלח כו'.

הגהות הב"ח

(א) רש"י ד"ה בכל מערבין עירובי חלירות. נ"ב כן מוקי לה בדף פ"א ע"ש: (ב) ד"ה חוץ וכו' רשות אחת וכן בעירובי תחומין נעשה כמי שבת שם ומשם: (ג) ד"ה ולכהן וכו' כאלו שבת שם דהא ביתו הוא ולא מלי למידר שם בבית הפרס שפיר דמי: (ד) תוס' ד"ה ולכהן וכו' אע"ג דאיכא כרת כיון דאי לא עביד פסח נמי איכא כרת:

[נ"ל במים ובמלח וכ"א בברכות לט:]

גליון הש"ס

גמ' כשהוא מבטל רשות צריך לבטל לכל אחד ואחד. עיין לקמן דף סג ע"ב תוס' ד"ה בטילו רשותייכו:

לקמן סט:
ס"א רבא
לקמן ע.
כל זה עד כמאן כר"א בס"א אינו רש"ל
[לקמן סח:]
[פסחים לט. ע"ש]
לקמן פח. קידושין לד.
[ברכות לט:]
פסחים כג. [לקמן כח.]
ס"א בבית

לָחוּץ. לַעֲשׂוֹת מְחִיצָּה בֵּינוֹ וּבֵין הַקֶּבֶר שֶׁלֹּא יַאֲהִיל עָלָיו. וּכְגוֹן בְּשִׁידָּה תֵּיבָה וּמִגְדָּל, יִכָּנֵס שָׁם מִבְּעוֹד יוֹם בַּעֲגָלוֹת אִם יִרְצֶה, אַלְמָא: חֲזֵי לֵיהּ: גמ' אֵין לְמֵידִין מִן הַכְּלָלוֹת. כָּל הֵיכָא דִּתְנַן כְּלָל לָא אָמְרִי' דַּוְקָא הוּא, דְּאִיכָּא כְּלָל. דְּלָא דָּק בְּמִילְּתֵיהּ, וְאִיכָּא מִילֵּי דְּלֵיתַנְהוּ בְּהַהוּא כְּלָל, כִּי הָנָךְ דְּאָמְרִינַן לְקַמָּן: וַאֲפִילּוּ בְּמָקוֹם שֶׁנֶּאֱמַר בּוֹ חוּץ. מִדָּבָר פְּלוֹנִי, דְּאִיכָּא לְמֵימַר מִדְּאַפְּקֵיהּ לְהַאי – וַדַּאי דָּק בִּכְלָלֵיהּ – אֲפִילּוּ הָכִי לָא יָלְפִינַן מִינֵּיהּ, דִּדְלְמָא שַׁיֵּיר וְלָא אַפֵּיק כָּל מַאי דְּבָעֵי: מִדְּקָאָמַר. רַבִּי יוֹחָנָן "אֲפִי'", מִכְּלָל דְּכִי אָמַר' לְמִילְּתֵיהּ – לָאו הָכָא אֲמָרָהּ. דְּהָכָא נֶאֱמַר בּוֹ חוּץ, וּמִמִּילְּתֵיהּ מַשְׁמַע דְּאַכְּלָל שֶׁלֹּא נֶאֱמַר בּוֹ חוּץ אֲמָרָהּ וּמש"ה אָמַר "אֲפִי'". כְּלוֹמַר: לָא מִיבַּעְיָא הֵיכָא דְּלֹא נֶאֱמַר בּוֹ חוּץ, אֶלָּא אֲפִי' בְּמָקוֹם שֶׁנֶּאֱמַר בּוֹ חוּץ: וְנָשִׁים פְּטוּרוֹת. בְּפֶרֶק קַמָּא דְּקִידּוּשִׁין (דף לד.) יָלֵיף טַעְמָא: מַצָּה. לַיְלָה הָרִאשׁוֹנָה חוֹבַת עֲשֵׂה הִיא: "בָּעֶרֶב תֹּאכְלוּ מַצּוֹת" (שמות יב), וּשְׁאָר כָּל הַיָּמִים, אִם רָצָה לְהִסְתַּפֵּק בְּבָשָׂר בְּלֹא לֶחֶם – אֵין חוֹבָה עָלָיו לֶאֱכוֹל: שִׂמְחָה. "וְשָׂמַחְתָּ אַתָּה וּבֵיתֶךָ" (דברים יד), הֲרֵי נָשִׁים בְּמַשְׁמַע. וּמַצָּה נַמִי חוֹבָה לְנָשִׁים, בְּמַס' פְּסָחִים (דף מג.) מֵהֶיקֵּישָׁא דְּ"לֹא תֹאכַל עָלָיו חָמֵץ, שִׁבְעַת יָמִים תֹּאכַל עָלָיו מַצּוֹת", כֹּל שֶׁיֶּשְׁנוֹ בְּבַל תֹּאכַל חָמֵץ – יֶשְׁנוֹ בְּקוּם אֱכוֹל מַצָּה. וְנָשִׁים יֶשְׁנָן בְּבַל תֹּאכַל חָמֵץ, דְּכָל מִצְוֹת לֹא תַעֲשֶׂה נָשִׁים מוּזְהָרוֹת כַּאֲנָשִׁים, (א) בְּפ"ק דְּקִידּוּשִׁין (דף כט.): הַקְהֵל. בְּמוֹעֵד שְׁנַת הַשְּׁמִטָּה בְּחַג הַסּוּכּוֹת הַמֶּלֶךְ עוֹמֵד עַל בִּימָה וְקוֹרֵא לִפְנֵיהֶן מִצְוַת מִשְׁנֵה תּוֹרָה, כִּדְאִיתָא בְּסוֹטָה (דף מא.). וּכְתִיב: "הָאֲנָשִׁים וְהַנָּשִׁים וְהַטַּף": תַּלְמוּד תּוֹרָה. נָשִׁים פְּטוּרוֹת, דִּכְתִיב: "וְלִמַּדְתֶּם אוֹתָם אֶת בְּנֵיכֶם" – וְלֹא בְּנוֹתֵיכֶם: פְּרִיָּה וּרְבִיָּה. דִּכְתִיב: "פְּרוּ וּרְבוּ וּמִלְאוּ (ב) וְכִבְשׁוּהָ" – אִישׁ דַּרְכּוֹ לִכְבּוֹשׁ, וְאֵין אִשָּׁה דַּרְכָּהּ לִכְבּוֹשׁ (יבמות דף סה:): פִּדְיוֹן. בְּנוֹ הַבְּכוֹר, חוֹבָה עַל הָאָב וְלֹא עַל הָאֵם (ג), בְּקִידּוּשִׁין (דף כט.) שָׁמְעִינַן לָהּ, מִדִּכְתִיב "תִּפְדֶּה" קָרֵי בֵּיהּ "תִּפָּדֶה", כֹּל שֶׁחַיָּיב לִיפָּדוֹת – חַיָּיב לִפְדּוֹת אֶת בְּנוֹ, וְאִשָּׁה אֵינָהּ בִּכְלָל פִּדְיוֹן עַצְמָהּ, דִּכְתִיב (שמות יג): "בְּכוֹר בָּנֶיךָ תִּפְדֶּה" – וְלֹא בְּנוֹתֶיךָ – אֵינָהּ נַמִי בְּמִצְוַת פִּדְיוֹן בְּנָהּ הַבְּכוֹר: כֹּל שֶׁנִּישָּׂא עַל גַּבֵּי הַזָּב. עֶלְיוֹנוֹ שֶׁל זָב, דִּכְתִיב (ויקרא טו): "בְּכֹל אֲשֶׁר יִהְיֶה תַחְתָּיו". וְאָמַר בְּפֶרֶק "בְּנוֹת כּוּתִים" (נדה דף לג.) מַאי "תַּחְתָּיו"? אִי נֵימָא תַּחְתָּיו דְּזָב – הַיְינוּ מִשְׁכָּב, אֶלָּא בְּכֹל אֲשֶׁר יִהְיֶה הַזָּב תַּחְתָּיו דְּזָב – וְהַיְינוּ עֶלְיוֹנוֹ שֶׁל זָב: חוּץ מִן הָרָאוּי לְמִשְׁכָּב וּמוֹשָׁב. אֲבָל שֶׁאֵינוֹ רָאוּי – טָהוֹר, כִּדְאָמַר בְּ"אוֹמֶר בַּקּוֹדֶשׁ" (חגיגה דף כג:): יָכוֹל כָּפָה סְאָה וְיָשַׁב עָלֶיהָ יְהֵא טָמֵא – תַּלְמוּד לוֹמַר: "וְהַיּוֹשֵׁב עַל הַכְּלִי אֲשֶׁר יֵשֵׁב עָלָיו" – מִי שֶׁמְּיוּחָד לִישִׁיבָה, יָצָא זֶה שֶׁאֵינוֹ מְיוּחָד לִישִׁיבָה, שֶׁאוֹמְרִים: עֲמוֹד וְנַעֲשֶׂה מְלַאכְתֵּנוּ: וְהָאָדָם. דִּכְתִיב: "וְהַנּוֹשֵׂא אוֹתָם" – אַף הַזָּב בְּמַשְׁמַע "אוֹתָם": תַּפּוּס. דְּאוּכָּף אַרְצוֹ"ן בְּלַע"ז: שֶׁכְּשֶׁרוֹכֵב תּוֹפֵס בְּאוֹתוֹ עֵץ שֶׁנִּקְרָא אַרְצוֹ"ן, וּלְהָכִי מְטַמֵּא מִשּׁוּם מֶרְכָּב: חַד מַתְנֵי אַעֵירוּב וְחַד מַתְנֵי אַמַּעֲשֵׂר. הַאי "לֹא שָׁנוּ" דְּקָאָמְרִינַן לְקַמָּן: מַיִם וּמֶלַח. הַמְעוֹרָבִין, מָזוֹן הֵן לְטַבֵּל בָּהֶן פִּתּוֹ: פֵּירָא בָּעֵינַן. כִּדְלְקַמָּן (עמוד ב'), מִכְּלָל וּפְרָט: כִּי אֲתָא רַבִּי יִצְחָק מַתְנֵי. לְהַאי "לֹא שָׁנוּ" אַמַּעֲשֵׂר: דְּשׁוּמְנָא דְּפֵירָא. אֲפִילּוּ כְּשֶׁאֵין קִרְבֵי דָגִים מְעוֹרָבִים בּוֹ – יֵשׁ שָׁם קְצָת מִשַּׁמְנָן עִם הַמַּיִם וּמֶלַח: אֲבָל מַיִם וּמֶלַח. דְּעָלְמָא, דְּלָאו צִיר הוּא – לֹא אָמַר: לֹא

מִפְּנֵי שֶׁיָּכוֹל *לָחוּץ וְלֵילֵךְ וְלֶאֱכוֹל.§ **גמ'** *א"ר יוֹחָנָן: אֵין לְמֵידִין מִן הַכְּלָלוֹת וַאֲפִילּוּ בְּמָקוֹם שֶׁנֶּאֱמַר בּוֹ חוּץ. מִדְּקָאָמַר: "אֲפִי' בְּמָקוֹם שֶׁנֶּאֱמַר בּוֹ חוּץ", מִכְּלָל דְּלָאו הָכָא קָאֵי, הֵיכָא קָאֵי? הָתָם קָאֵי: *כָּל מִצְוַת עֲשֵׂה שֶׁהַזְּמַן גְּרָמָא אֲנָשִׁים חַיָּיבִין וְנָשִׁים פְּטוּרוֹת, וְשֶׁלֹּא הַזְּמַן גְּרָמָא – אֶחָד נָשִׁים וְאֶחָד אֲנָשִׁים חַיָּיבִין. וּכְלָלָא הוּא דְּכָל מִצְוַת עֲשֵׂה שֶׁהַזְּמַן גְּרָמָא נָשִׁים פְּטוּרוֹת?! הֲרֵי מַצָּה שִׂמְחָה וְהַקְהֵל, דְּמִצְוַת עֲשֵׂה שֶׁהַזְּמַן גְּרָמָא הוּא – וְנָשִׁים חַיָּיבוֹת. וְכָל מִצְוַת עֲשֵׂה שֶׁלֹּא הַזְּמַן גְּרָמָא נָשִׁים חַיָּיבוֹת? הֲרֵי תַּלְמוּד תּוֹרָה, פְּרִיָּה וּרְבִיָּה, וּפִדְיוֹן הַבֵּן, דְּמִצְוַת עֲשֵׂה שֶׁלֹּא הַזְּמַן גְּרָמָא – וְנָשִׁים פְּטוּרוֹת! אֶלָּא אָמַר רַבִּי יוֹחָנָן: אֵין לְמֵידִין מִן הַכְּלָלוֹת, וַאֲפִילּוּ בְּמָקוֹם שֶׁנֶּאֱמַר בּוֹ חוּץ. אָמַר אַבַּיֵי, וְאִיתֵּימָא רַבִּי יִרְמְיָה: אַף אֲנַן נַמִי תְּנֵינָא; *עוֹד כְּלָל אַחֵר אָמְרוּ: אכֹּל שֶׁנִּישָּׂא עַל גַּבֵּי הַזָּב – טָמֵא, בוְכֹל שֶׁהַזָּב נִישָּׂא עָלָיו – טָהוֹר, חוּץ מִן הָרָאוּי לְמִשְׁכָּב וּמוֹשָׁב גוְהָאָדָם. וְתוּ לֵיכָּא?! וְהָא אִיכָּא מֶרְכָּב! הַאי מֶרְכָּב הֵיכִי דָּמֵי? אִי דְּיָתֵיב עֲלֵיהּ – הַיְינוּ מוֹשָׁב! אֲנַן הָכִי קָאָמְרִינַן: הָא אִיכָּא גַּבָּא דְּאוּכְפָּא, *דְּתַנְיָא: דהָאוּכָּף טָמֵא מוֹשָׁב, וְהַתָּפוּס טָמֵא מֶרְכָּב. אֶלָּא שְׁמַע מִינָּהּ: אֵין לְמֵידִין מִן הַכְּלָלוֹת, וַאֲפִילּוּ בְּמָקוֹם שֶׁנֶּאֱמַר בּוֹ חוּץ. אָמַר רָבִינָא, וְאִיתֵּימָא רַב נַחְמָן: אַף אֲנַן נַמִי תְּנֵינָא: בַּכֹּל מְעָרְבִין וּמִשְׁתַּתְּפִין, חוּץ מִן הַמַּיִם וְהַמֶּלַח.[א] וְתוּ לֵיכָּא?![ב] [א] וְהָא אִיכָּא הכְּמֵיהִין וּפִטְרִיּוֹת! אֶלָּא שְׁמַע מִינָּהּ: אֵין לְמֵידִין מִן הַכְּלָלוֹת, וַאֲפִי' בְּמָקוֹם שֶׁנֶּאֱמַר בּוֹ חוּץ.§ "הַכֹּל נִיקָּח בְּכֶסֶף מַעֲשֵׂר כו'".§ ר' *אֱלִיעֶזֶר [נ"א אלעזר] וְר' יוֹסֵי בַּר חֲנִינָא, חַד מַתְנֵי אַעֵירוּב וְחַד מַתְנֵי אַמַּעֲשֵׂר. חַד מַתְנֵי אַעֵירוּב: ול"ש אֶלָּא מַיִם בִּפְנֵי עַצְמוֹ וּמֶלַח בִּפְנֵי עַצְמוֹ, דְּאֵין מְעָרְבִין – אֲבָל בְּמַיִם וּמֶלַח מְעָרְבִין. וְחַד מַתְנֵי אַמַּעֲשֵׂר: לֹא שָׁנוּ אֶלָּא מַיִם בִּפְנֵי עַצְמוֹ וּמֶלַח בִּפְנֵי עַצְמוֹ דְּאֵין נִיקָּחִין, אֲבָל מַיִם וּמֶלַח – נִיקָּחִין בְּכֶסֶף מַעֲשֵׂר. מַאן דְּמַתְנֵי אַמַּעֲשֵׂר – כ"ש אַעֵירוּב, וּמַאן דְּמַתְנֵי אַעֵירוּב – אֲבָל זאַמַּעֲשֵׂר לֹא. מ"ט – פֵּירָא בָּעֵינַן. כִּי אֲתָא רַבִּי יִצְחָק, מַתְנֵי אַמַּעֲשֵׂר. מֵיתִיבִי, הֵעִיד ר' יְהוּדָה בֶּן גָּדִישׁ לִפְנֵי ר"א: שֶׁל בֵּית אַבָּא הָיוּ לוֹקְחִין צִיר בְּכֶסֶף מַעֲשֵׂר. אָמַר לוֹ: שֶׁמָּא לֹא שָׁמַעְתָּ אֶלָּא כְּשֶׁקִּרְבֵי דָגִים מְעוֹרָבִין בָּהֶן. וַאֲפִילּוּ רַבִּי יְהוּדָה בֶּן גָּדִישׁ לֹא קָאָמַר אֶלָּא בְּצִיר, דְּשׁוּמְנָא דְּפֵירָא הִיא, אֲבָל מַיִם וּמֶלַח – לֹא! אָמַר רַב יוֹסֵף: לֹא

מפני שיכול לחוץ ולילך ולאכול. אבל אי לאו הכי – לא הוי עירוב, אע"ג דחזי לישראל – משום דהוי הוא במקום אחד ועירובו במקום אחר. והיינו טעמא דת"ק דלא הוי עירוב, ולא משום דס"ל כסומכוס. ומיהו, ר' יהודה משמע דסבר כסומכוס, מדקאמר "ולאכול". וכן קאמר בברייתא לקמן (דף לא.): מערבין לכהן טהור בתרומה טהורה – משמע דבעי מידי דחזי ליה: **כל** שנישא על גבי הזב. אם נפרש דבהיסט איירי, שמסיט כולו – הוי "כל" דוקא. ובכמה דוכתי קרי להיסט משא. אבל אי מיירי בעליונו של זב, שאינו מסיט כולו (ד) ושמקצתו נגרר בארץ, דלאו היסט הוא כדאמר (ת"כ פ' מצורע): איזהו מגע שהוא ככולו – הוי אומר זה היסטו. מספקא לר"י אי שייך בכל דבר, או לא. דעליונו של זב נפקא לן מ"בכל אשר יהיה תחתיו הזב" (ה) אי הוי דומיא דמשכב ומושב, שאינו נוהג אלא בדבר הראוי לכך, או לא: **כל** שהזב נישא עליו טהור. אומר רבינו תם דטהור מטומאה חמורה – דאינו מטמא אדם וכלים, אבל טמא טומאה קלה – כגון לטמא אוכלין ומשקין. אף על גב דאינו ראוי למשכב ומושב. ומייתי ראיה מפרק "דם הנדה" (דף נד:), דקאמרינן: אי מה היא עושה משכב ומושב כו' (ו). אף (*מדוה) [נ"א דמה] נמי עושה משכב ומושב לטמא אדם לטמא בגדים. ומשני: אמר קרא היא ולא דמה. אי מה היא מטמאה באבן מסמא, אף מדוה נמי. והשתא, כיון שמיעט דמה מדין משכב ומושב מאי קאמרינן תו דליטמא באבן מסמא? והא אבן מסמא היינו משכב ומושב, דמטעם משכב ומושב הוא דמיטמא. כדקתני בתורת כהנים: אפילו עשרה כלים זה על זה, ואפילו על גבי אבן מסמא מניין? תלמוד לומר: כל המשכב. ואבן מסמא מפרש רבינו תם: דהיינו אבן גדולה שיש כלים תחתיה, ואין מרגישין הכלים בכובד הזב היושב על האבן, שבלא הזב האבן כבידה ביותר. ומפרש התם רבינו תם דהכי פירושו: אי מה היא כו'. כלומר: דנהי שמיעטת דמה מטומאה חמורה, אכתי מניין שלא יטמא טומאה קלה? אף על גב דממעט ממשכב ומושב, צריך למעט מטומאה קלה. והיינו, משום דאפילו דבר שאינו ראוי למשכב ומושב מטמא טומאה קלה. ואין נראה, דבהדיא כתיב בתורת כהנים, תניא: "כל אשר ישכב עליו הזב יטמא" יכול יטמא דבר שאינו ראוי לשכיבה – לא, מה היא אינה מטמאה כו'. יכול הוא והיא לא יטמאו טומאה חמורה, אבל יטמאו טומאה קלה – תלמוד לומר "משכב". אלמא: מידי דלא חזי למשכב ומושב – טהור לגמרי. ונראה לפרש דמה שמרבה בתורת כהנים אבן מסמא מ"וכל המשכב" – היינו דוקא לטומאה קלה. ושמא בשום מקום ממעט לה מטומאה חמורה. אבל מידי דלא חזי למשכב ומושב – אפי' טומאה קלה ליכא. ולכן, אע"ג דמיעט דמה מדין משכב ומושב – לענין טומאה חמורה, עדיין צריך למעט מדין אבן מסמא, שהוא לענין טומאה קלה: **אי** דיתיב עלה היינו מושב. תימה: דבקרא כתיב מרכב ומושב, ודינן חלוק זה מזה! *)וי"ל: דנהי דקרא מחלק בין ישיבה דרכיבה לישיבה דעלמא, מ"מ התנא דקאמר חוץ מן הראוי למשכב ומושב – כל עניני ישיבות קאמר, ולא נימא דלא דק בכללי', משום הכי קאמר היינו מושב: **אבל** במים ומלח מערבין. בסמוך מוקי בשנותן לתוכן שמן. וקשה: דתיפוק לי משום שמן, כדפריך לקמן (עמוד ב') אמעשר. והכא לא שייך סיועה דסתם! ויש לומר: דהכא איצטריך, דאף על גב דלא הוי מן השמן מזון שתי סעודות: **מאן** דמתני אמעשר כ"ש אעירוב. וקשה: הא איכא כמיהין ופטריות וכפניות ופולין יבישין, דאמרינן לקמן דאין מערבין

*) [דסגוג במרכב אין טעון לרבוב בגדים כלמותה בתורת כהנים עי' תוס' פסחים ג. ד"ה שהרי]

רבינו חננאל

א"ר יוחנן אין למדין מן הכללות ואפילו במקום שנאמר בהן חוץ פי' כל מקום שיאמר כל אינו ממש. ואפילו אם יפרש ויאמר חוץ מכך וכך לא תאמר כיון שאמר חוץ אין לך דבר היוצא מן הכלל הזה אלא המפורשין אלא יש הרבה זולתן יוצאין מזה הכלל. ואסיקנא בקדושין תנן כל מצות עשה שהזמן גרמא נשים פטורות ואנשים חייבין כו' והתם א"ר יוחנן אין למדין מן הכללות ואפי' במקום שנאמר בהן חוץ. אמר אביי אף אנן נמי תנינא במסכת זבים פ"ה עוד כלל אמרו כל הנישא ע"ג הזב טמא. וכל שהזב נישא עליו טהור חוץ מן הראוי למשכב ולמושב והאדם ואקשינן כללא הוא ותו ליכא. והא איכא מרכב ואמרינן מרכב מאי ניהו איכוף אדייתיב עליה היינו מושב. ולטעמיך מי לא כתיב מושב וכתיב מרכב אלא מרכב (גברא) [גבא] דאוכפא דבהדי דרכיב מחית ידיה עליה ותנן בתוספתא בכלים [בב"ב] פרק ב' האיכוף מטמא מושב והתופס שלו מטמא מרכב ושאר כל החופיות שבצדדין אם היו רחבות טפח טמאין יש מי שמפרש התפויות הזונות והן העצים הנתונים בטיפשא שבאחור ושלפנים. כדכתיב (מלכים א' כב) והזונות רחצו והן פיני המרכב שניטנפו מן הדם. פי' האיכוף העץ שאחורי הסרג והתפוס העץ שלפניו שאוחז בידו בעת שהוא עולה לרכוב והנה אלו לא מושב ולא מרכב וטמאין ש"מ אין למדין מן הכללות. וכן שנינו בכל מערבין חוץ מן המים ומן המלח והא איכא כמיהין ופטריות נמי כמו (המים ומן המלח) [מים ומלח] ואמרינן לא שנו אלא מים בפ"ע ומלח בפ"ע אבל שניהן יחד ניקחין. מאן דמתני אמעשר שניקחין כ"ש אעירוב שמערבין בו'. כי אתא ר' יצחק מתני אמעשר ואותבינן עליה מהא דתניא העיד ר' יהודה בן גדיש לפני ר' אליעזר של בית אבא היו לוקחין ציר בכסף מעשר. אמרו לו שמא לא שמעתה [אלא] בציר שקרבי דגים מעורבין בהן. ואפי' ר' יהודה בן גדיש לא אמר [אלא] בציר דשומנא דפירא הוא אבל מים ומלח דברי הכל

עין משפט נר מצוה:
ב א מיי' פ"א מהלכות משכב ומושב הל' א' ופ"ו הלכה ג והלכה ו:
ג ב מיי' פ"ו שם הל' ו' ופ"ו הלכה ח:
ד ג מיי' פ"א שם הל' א' ופ"ו הל' ו ופ"ח הלכה ב:
ה ד מיי' פכ"ה מהל' כלים הלכה כ:
ו ה ו מיי' פ"א מהל' עירובין הלכה ח סמג עשין א טוש"ע א"ח סי' שפו סעיף ה:
ז ז מיי' פ"ז מהלכות מעשר שני הלכה ד סמג עשין קלו:

לקמן כט. קידושין לד.

מסורת הש"ס:
גירסת ירושלמי ובמשנה שבמשניות ליליך לחוץ וגירסת רי"ף ללאת לחוץ וגירסת הרא"ש לחוץ ולאכול
[קידושין שם כט. וש"נ]
זבים פ"ה מ"ב
תוספתא דכלים ב"ב פ"ב

הגהות הב"ח
(א) רש"י ד"ה שמחה וכו' מוזהרות כאנשים דהוקשו נשים לאנשים לכל עונשים שבתורה בפרק קמא דקידושין: (ב) ד"ה פריה ורביה וכו' ומלאו את הארץ וכבשוה: (ג) ד"ה פדיון וכו' ולא על האם דמכתיב תפדה וקרי ביה תפדה כל שחייב לפדות את עצמו חייב וכו': (ד) תוס' ד"ה כל שנושא וכו' שאינו מסיט כו' כגון שמקצתו: (ה) בא"ד תחתיו הזב אי הוי דומית: (ו) ד"ה כל שהזב וכו' מה הוא עושה משכב ומושב לטמא אדם לטמא בגדים כו' ומשני וכו' אף מדוה נמי וכו' לטמא באבן מסמא והשתא כיון וכו' תלמוד לומר כל המשכב:

הגהות הגר"א
[א] גמ' חוץ מן המים והמלח. נ"ב וכו': [ב] והאיכא כמיהין ופטריות. נ"ב תו"כ פ"א פסקא ח:

הגהות מהר"ב רנשבורג [א] גמ' הא איכא כמיהין ופטריות. נ"ב וכו' כל"ל כמו שכתב הגאון מהר"א ווילנא. וביאור לדבריו בביאורו לש"ע א"ח סי' שפ"ו ס"ק ט' יעו"ש באורך דקושית הש"ס קאי על ניקח בכסף מעשר. וכמיהין ופטריות אינן נקחין כדאיתא בתורת כהנים פ"א פסקא ח' אבל לענין עירוב לא שייך כלל דמה"ט אם מבושלין הוו מאכל ומערבין בהם כמבואר ואם הם חיין לא ... ודפח"ח אף שהוא דלא כרי"ף והרמב"ם. וע"ע גם בתוספתא ד"ה מאן דמתני וכו' לסברי דניקחין בכסף מעשר נגד מה שכתב הגאון ז"ל. וי"ל:

ח א ב שם הלכה י:
ט ג מיי' פ"ח שם הלכה א:
י ד מיי' שם הלכה ב:
יא ה מיי' פ"ו שם הלכה ו:
יב ו מיי' שם הל' ג:

לֹא נִצְרְכָה *אֶלָּא שֶׁנָּתַן לְתוֹכָן שֶׁמֶן. אֲמַר לֵיהּ אַבַּיֵי: וְתִיפּוֹק לֵיהּ מִשּׁוּם שֶׁמֶן! לָא צְרִיכָא [ב] שֶׁנָּתַן דְּמֵי מַיִם וּמֶלַח בְּהַבְלָעָה. וּבְהַבְלָעָה מִי שָׁרֵי? אִין, וְהָתַנְיָא, בֶּן בַּג בַּג אוֹמֵר: "בַּבָּקָר" – [ג] מְלַמֵּד שֶׁלּוֹקְחִין בָּקָר עַל גַּב עוֹרוֹ, (דברים יד) "וּבַצֹּאן" – מְלַמֵּד שֶׁלּוֹקְחִין צֹאן עַל גַּב גִּיזָּתָהּ, "וּבַיַּיִן" – מְלַמֵּד [ד] שֶׁלּוֹקְחִין יַיִן עַל גַּב קַנְקַנּוֹ, "וּבַשֵּׁכָר" – מְלַמֵּד [ה] שֶׁלּוֹקְחִין תֶּמֶד מִשֶּׁהֶחְמִיץ. א"ר יוֹחָנָן: מַאן דִּמְתַרְגֵּם לִי "בַּבָּקָר" אַלִּיבָּא דְּבֶן בַּג בַּג – *מוֹבִילְנָא מָאנֵיהּ אַבַּתְרֵיהּ לְבֵי מַסּוּתָא. מַאי טַעְמָא? כּוּלְּהוּ צְרִיכִי, לְבַר מִ"בַּבָּקָר" דְּלָא צָרִיךְ. מַאי צְרִיכִי? דְּאִי כָּתַב רַחֲמָנָא "בַּבָּקָר", הֲוָה אָמִינָא: בָּקָר הוּא דְּמִזְדַּבַּן עַל גַּב עוֹרוֹ, מִשּׁוּם דְּגוּפֵיהּ הוּא, אֲבָל צֹאן עַל גַּב גִּיזָּתָהּ דְּלָאו גּוּפֵיהּ הוּא – אֵימָא לָא. וְאִי כָּתַב רַחֲמָנָא "בַּצֹּאן" עַל גַּב גִּיזָּתָהּ – הֲוָה אָמִינָא: מִשּׁוּם דִּמְחוּבָּר בָּהּ, אֲבָל יַיִן ע"ג קַנְקַנּוֹ – אֵימָא לָא. וְאִי כָּתַב רַחֲמָנָא "בַּיַּיִן" הֲוָה אָמִינָא: מִשּׁוּם דְּהַיְינוּ נְטִירוּתֵיהּ, אֲבָל תֶּמֶד מִשֶּׁהֶחְמִיץ דְּקִיוְהָא בְּעָלְמָא הוּא – אֵימָא לָא, כָּתַב רַחֲמָנָא "שֵׁכָר". וְאִי כָּתַב רַחֲמָנָא "בַּשֵּׁכָר" – הֲוָה אָמִינָא: מַאי שֵׁכָר – דְּבֵילָה קְעִילִית, דְּפֵירָא הוּא, אֲבָל יַיִן עַל גַּב קַנְקַנּוֹ – אֵימָא לָא. וְאִי כָּתַב רַחֲמָנָא יַיִן עַל גַּב קַנְקַנּוֹ – דְּהַיְינוּ נְטִירוּתֵיהּ, אֲבָל צֹאן עַל גַּב גִּיזָּתָהּ – אֵימָא לָא, כָּתַב רַחֲמָנָא "צֹאן" דַּאֲפִילּוּ עַל גַּב גִּיזָּתָהּ. "בַּבָּקָר" לָמָּה לִי? וְכ"ת: אִי לֹא כָּתַב רַחֲמָנָא "בַּבָּקָר" הֲוָה אָמִינָא: צֹאן עַל גַּב עוֹרָהּ – אִין, עַל גַּב גִּיזָּתָהּ – לָא, כָּתַב רַחֲמָנָא "בַּבָּקָר" לְאַתּוּיֵי עוֹרוֹ. אִיַּיתַר לֵיהּ "צֹאן" לְאַתּוּיֵי גִּיזָּתָהּ. אִי לֹא כָּתַב רַחֲמָנָא "בָּקָר" – לָא הֲוָה אָמִינָא צֹאן עַל גַּב עוֹרָהּ אִין עַל גַּב גִּיזָּתָהּ לָא. דְּאִם כֵּן – לִכְתּוֹב רַחֲמָנָא "בָּקָר" דְּמִמֵּילָא אִיַּיתַר לֵיהּ צֹאן! וְכֵיוָן דִּכְתַב רַחֲמָנָא "צֹאן", דַּאֲפִילּוּ עַל גַּב גִּיזָּתָהּ – "בַּבָּקָר" לָמָּה לִי? הַשְׁתָּא צֹאן עַל גַּב גִּיזָּתָהּ מִיזְדַּבְּנָא, בָּקָר עַל גַּב עוֹרוֹ מִיבַּעְיָא?! [א] הַיְינוּ דְּקָאָמַר רַבִּי יוֹחָנָן: מַאן דִּמְתַרְגֵּם לִי בַּבָּקָר אַלִּיבָּא דְּבֶן בַּג בַּג, מוֹבִילְנָא מָאנֵיהּ לְבֵי מַסּוּתָא. בְּמַאי קָא מִיפַּלְגִי רַבִּי יְהוּדָה בֶּן גָּדִישׁ וְר"א וְהָנֵי תַּנָּאֵי דִּלְקַמָּן? ר' יְהוּדָה בֶּן גָּדִישׁ וְר"א דָּרְשִׁי רִבּוּיֵי וּמִיעוּטֵי, וְהָנֵי תַּנָּאֵי דָּרְשִׁי כְּלָלֵי וּפְרָטֵי. ר' יְהוּדָה בֶּן גָּדִישׁ וְר"א דָּרְשִׁי רִיבּוּיֵי וּמִיעוּטֵי: (שם) "וְנָתַתָּה הַכֶּסֶף בְּכֹל אֲשֶׁר תְּאַוֶּה נַפְשְׁךָ" – רִיבָּה, "בַּבָּקָר וּבַצֹּאן וּבַיַּיִן וּבַשֵּׁכָר" – מִיעֵט, "וּבְכֹל אֲשֶׁר תִּשְׁאָלְךָ נַפְשֶׁךָ" – חָזַר וְרִיבָּה. רִיבָּה וּמִיעֵט וְרִיבָּה – רִיבָּה הַכֹּל. מַאי רַבֵּי – רַבֵּי כָּל מִילֵּי, וּמַאי מִיעֵט – לר"א מִיעֵט צִיר, לר' יְהוּדָה בֶּן גָּדִישׁ מִיעֵט מַיִם וּמֶלַח. וְהָנֵי תַּנָּאֵי דָּרְשִׁי כְּלָלֵי וּפְרָטֵי, *דְּתַנְיָא: "וְנָתַתָּה הַכֶּסֶף בְּכֹל אֲשֶׁר תְּאַוֶּה נַפְשְׁךָ" – כְּלָל, "בַּבָּקָר וּבַצֹּאן וּבַיַּיִן וּבַשֵּׁכָר" – פְּרָט, "וּבְכֹל אֲשֶׁר תִּשְׁאָלְךָ נַפְשֶׁךָ" – חָזַר וְכָלַל. כְּלָל וּפְרָט וּכְלָל – אִי אַתָּה דָּן אֶלָּא כְּעֵין הַפְּרָט; [ו] מָה הַפְּרָט מְפוֹרָשׁ – פְּרִי מִפְּרִי וְגִידּוּלֵי קַרְקַע, אַף כֹּל – פְּרִי מִפְּרִי וְגִידּוּלֵי קַרְקַע. וְתַנְיָא אִידָךְ: מָה הַפְּרָט מְפוֹרָשׁ – וְלַד וְלָדוֹת הָאָרֶץ, אַף כֹּל – וְלַד וְלָדוֹת הָאָרֶץ. מַאי בֵּינַיְיהוּ? אָמַר אַבַּיֵי: דָּגִים אִיכָּא בֵּינַיְיהוּ, לְמַאן דְּאָמַר: פְּרִי מִפְּרִי וְגִידּוּלֵי קַרְקַע – הָנֵי דָּגִים גִּידּוּלֵי קַרְקַע נִינְהוּ. לְמַאן דְּאָמַר וְלַד וְלָדוֹת הָאָרֶץ – דָּגִים מִמַּיָּא אִיבְרוּ. וּמִי אָמַר אַבַּיֵי דָּגִים גִּידּוּלֵי קַרְקַע נִינְהוּ? וְהָאָמַר אַבַּיֵי:

אָכַל

דברים יד · שם · ב"ק נד: סג. נזיר לה:

רש"י

לֹא נִצְרְכָה. הָא דְּמַתְנֵי ר' יִצְחָק מַיִם וּמֶלַח הַמְעוֹרָבִין נִיקָּחִין אֶלָּא כְּשֶׁנָּתַן לְתוֹכָן שֶׁמֶן: בְּהַבְלָעָה. בִּשְׁבִיל הַמַּיִם וְהַמֶּלַח קָנָה הַשֶּׁמֶן בְּיוֹקֶר, וְהִבְלִיעַ בּוֹ דְּמֵיהֶן. וְכִי הַאי גַּוְונָא שָׁרֵי רַבִּי יִצְחָק: וְהָתַנְיָא. בִּנְיחוּתָא: הוֹאִיל וּכְתִיב: "בְּכֹל אֲשֶׁר תְּאַוֶּה נַפְשְׁךָ" לָמָּה לִי לְמִיכְתַּב "בַּבָּקָר בַּצֹּאן וּבַיַּיִן וּבַשֵּׁכָר"? אֶלָּא לִדְרָשׁוֹת: "בַּבָּקָר" – לְלַמֶּדְךָ שֶׁלּוֹקְחִים בָּקָר אַגַּב עוֹרוֹ, וְיֵצֵא הָעוֹר לְחוּלִּין, וְאֵין צָרִיךְ לְמוֹכְרוֹ וְלַחֲזוֹר וּלְאָכְלוֹ בִּירוּשָׁלַיִם: אַגַּב גִּיזּוֹתֶיהָ. אע"ג דְּאִיכָּא תַּרְתֵּי, עוֹר וְגִיזָּה דְּנָפְקִי לְחוּלִּין: אַגַּב קַנְקַן. חָבִית שֶׁל חֶרֶס שֶׁהַיַּיִן שָׁמוּר בְּתוֹכוֹ, וְיֵצֵא הַקַּנְקַן לְחוּלִּין: תֶּמֶד. שֶׁנּוֹתְנִים מַיִם בְּחַרְצַנִּים, וּלְכְשֶׁהֶחְמִיץ, שֶׁנִּגְמְרָה תְּסִיסָתוֹ – הָוֵי כְּיַיִן. אַלְמָא: מִדְּקָתָנֵי "בַּבָּקָר" אַגַּב עוֹרוֹ – אַלְמָא: בְּהַבְלָעָה שָׁרֵי, וְאע"ג דְּעוֹר בְּאַנְפֵּי נַפְשֵׁיהּ לָא חֲזֵי. דְּמִידֵּי דְּמַאֲכָל בָּעֵינַן, כְּדִכְתִיב "וְאָכַלְתָּ": מַאן דִּמְתַרְגֵּם בָּקָר. דְּלִיצְטְרִיךְ לְמִיכְתְּבֵיהּ, אַלִּיבָּא דְּבֶן בַּג בַּג כו': עוֹרוֹ. הַמְחוּבָּר לַבָּשָׂר, וְאֵינוֹ יָכוֹל לְהַפְשִׁיטוֹ מֵחַיִּים: אֲבָל גִּיזָּה. יָכוֹל לְגוֹזְזָהּ מֵחַיִּים, וַהֲוָה אָמִינָא דְּלִיתְּסַר, דְּלָא גּוּפָא דְּפֵירָא הוּא: קִיוְהָא. כְּמוֹ: "תִּקְהֶינָה שִׁנָּיו" (ירמיהו לא), כְּלוֹמַר: לָאו פֵּירָא מַמָּשׁ הוּא, אֶלָּא מַיִם בְּעָלְמָא שֶׁנִּכְנָס בָּהֶן קִיוְהָא שֶׁל חַרְצַנִּים, אֵיגְרו"ם בלע"ז: וְאִי כָּתַב שֵׁכָר הֲוָה אָמִינָא. הַבְלָעָה לְעוֹלָם אֲסִירָא, וְהַאי שֵׁכָר – לָאו תֶּמֶד הוּא דְּנֵילַף מִינֵּיהּ דְּיָהֵיב דָּמִים שֶׁל מַיִם בְּהַבְלָעָה. אֶלָּא, הַאי שֵׁכָר – דְּבֵילָה קְעִילִית הִיא, מֵאוֹתוֹ מָקוֹם, דִּמְשַׁכְּרָא. כִּדְאָמְרִינַן בִּכְרֵיתוֹת (דף יג:): אָכַל דְּבֵילָה קְעִילִית וְנִכְנַס לַמִּקְדָּשׁ – חַיָּיב: דְּאִם כֵּן. דְּ"צֹאן" לָאו לְמִישְׁרֵי גִּיזּוֹת הוּא דַּאֲתָא, אֶלָּא עוֹר, לָא הֲוָה כָּתֵיב קְרָא "צֹאן" אֶלָּא "בָּקָר" – דְּלֵית לֵיהּ גִּיזּוֹת: בְּמַאי קָא מִיפַּלְגִי רַבִּי יְהוּדָה וְרַבִּי אֱלִיעֶזֶר. דְּאָמְרִי תַּרְוַיְיהוּ: דָּגִים נִיקָּחִין, וּבְצִיר הוּא דִּפְלִיגִי: וְהָנֵי תַּנָּאֵי דִּלְקַמָּן. דְּדָרְשִׁי פְּרִי מִפְּרִי וְגִידּוּלֵי קַרְקַע וּוְלַד וְלָדוֹת הָאָרֶץ, וְתַרְוַיְיהוּ מְמַעֲטִי דָּגִים וְכ"ש צִיר: ה"ג: לר"א מִיעֵט צִיר וּלְרַבִּי יְהוּדָה מִיעֵט מַיִם וּמֶלַח. דְּלָאו צִיר: ה"ג. דְּתַנְיָא וְנָתַתָּה הַכֶּסֶף וגו': פְּרִי מִפְּרִי. עֵגֶל נוֹלָד מֵאִמּוֹ, וְכֵן שֶׂה, וַעֲנָבִים מֵחַרְצַנִּים, שֶׁזּוֹרְעִין הַחַרְצַנִּים: וְגִידּוּלֵי קַרְקַע. שֶׁכּוּלָּן נִיזּוֹנִין וּגְדֵילִין מִן הַקַּרְקַע: וְלַד וְלָדוֹת הָאָרֶץ. שֶׁנִּבְרְאוּ מִן הָאָרֶץ בְּמַעֲשֵׂה בְרֵאשִׁית: דָּגִים. גִּידּוּלֵי קַרְקַע נִינְהוּ, קָסָבַר שֶׁהַדָּגִים נִיזּוֹנִין מִן הַקַּרְקַע:

[ב"מ מח. סנהדרין סב:]

תוספות

מערבין בהן אף על גב דמסתמא נקנין בכסף מעשר. דפרי מפרי הן וגידולי קרקע! ויש לומר: הא דאין מערבין בהן – היינו משום דלא חזו אלא ע"י תיקון, וגבי עירוב צריך שיהו ראויין לאכילה בשעה שהעירוב חל. אבל לטמא טומאת אוכל, או ליקח בכסף מעשר – שפיר דמי, כיון דחזו על ידי תיקון. אבל דבר שאין צריך תיקון, אם ניקח בכסף מעשר – כל שכן דמערבין בו, וכן משני לקמן *אכפניות, דלענין טומאת אוכל – שאני, דראוי למתקן על ידי האור, ומתני' דמעילה דקתני ובמזון שתי סעודות לעירוב, וכבילה לטמא טומאת אוכלין דמשמע דהא בהא תליא, כדאמר לקמן – *היינו בדבר שאין צריך תיקון. ורבא, דאמר וכי מערבין בתפוחים – לאחודי הסוא מדרבנן עבד, דהא אטו מי לא הוה ידע דניקח בכסף מעשר, דהוי פירי מפירי וגדולי קרקע דאין לומר דמיירי בתפוחים של יער דצריך למתקן – דאם כן לא מייתי שפיר ממתני' דמעילה:

[דף כח:] · [דף כט.]

הוה אמינא מאי שכר דבילה קעילית. כל הני דרשות מיתורא דביתי"ן דריש, דפרטי צריכי לפרט וכלל, דממה נפשך צריכי תרי מינייהו, כדאמר בפרק קמא דקדושין (דף יז.) גבי הענקה. דאי כתיב צאן – הוה אמינא גידולי קרקע לא, ואי כתיב גורן – הוה אמינא בעלי חיים לא. ושאר פרטי נמי, שמא צריכי לשום דרשה. ועוד, דבשבועות פ"ג (דף כג.) ובפרק בתרא דיומא (דף עו.) פריך: ואימא דבילה קעילית! ומשני: גמר שכר שכר מנזיר. והכא נפקא לן מדמרבינן יין אגב קנקן. אלא התם אצטריך שכר שכר – דלא נימא שכר גופיה דבילה קעילית היא. והכא – אבי"ת דבשכר קאי. וקשה: דהיכי קאמר הכא דה"א דבי"ת דבשכר לדבילה קעילית אתא – הא מכלל ופרט נפקא, דהוו פירי מפירי! ועוד הקשה מה"ר שמואל: דהיכי בעי למימר התם דשכר גופיה לדבילה קעילית, והאמר הכא דאי לאו יתור דיין אגב קנקן, ה"א דבי"ת דבשכר לדבילה קעילית! ויש לומר: דשכר גופיה בעי למימר לדבילה קעילית בעינן, והכא בדבילה מעורבת עם המים, שכך רגילים לתקנם וחשיב טפי מתמד. ואם תאמר: אמאי לא מוכח התם דשתיה בכלל אכילה, מדמרבינן תמד, ואמר רחמנא "ואכלת"! וליכא למימר ע"י אניגרון – כדאמרינן התם דמידי דמשכר בעינן, הואיל ואתי מריבויא דבשכר! וי"ל: ד"ואכלת" לא קאי אביתי"ן, אלא אגופיה דקרא. דהא עור וגיזה וקנקן לאו בני אכילה נינהו:

הוה אמינא צאן על גב עורו אין. ואם תאמר: והא נפקא לן מיין אגב קנקן, דעור נמי חשיב שומר, כדאמרי' ב"העור והרוטב" (חולין דף קיח.)! וי"ל: דעור לא הוי כל כך שומר לבשר, דמשהופשט – לא הוי שומר, אבל יין – אי אפשר בלא קנקן:

נירעה

רבינו חננאל

הכל לא ופריק רב יוסף הא דתני ר' יצחק כגון שנתן שמן על גבי המליח והבליע לו דמי מים ומלח בשמן. פי' ששוה השמן לבדו חצי איסר. וא"ל הריני קונה מאצלך השמן לבדו באיסר והמים והמלח בחנם. ומנ"ל דכי האי גוונא שרי דתניא בן בג בג אומר ונתתה הכסף בכל אשר תאוה נפשך בבקר ובצאן וגו' לא הי' לו לומר בבקר ללמד שלוקחין בקר על גבי עורו. פי' מבליע דמי עור בבשר: בצאן כו'. א"ר יוחנן מאן דמתרגם לי בבקר אליבא דבן בג בג מובילנא מאניה בתריה לבי מסותא. פי' אני משמשו כתלמיד לרב מ"ט הני כלהו בצאן וביין ובשכר צריכ' [לבד] מבבקר דלא הוה צריך דאתי מהני אמאי כתביה רחמנא ולא אשתכח ליה תרגומא ובמאי פליגי יהודה בן גדיש דמרבה ליקח ציר במעות מעשר שני ור' אליעזר דאוסר והני תנאי דבעינא למימר לקמן ואמרי' (נמי) יהודה בן גדיש ור' אליעזר דרשי התורה ברבויי ומיעוטי כתיב ונתתה הכסף בכל אשר תאוה נפשך ריבה כל דבר שתתאוה וחזר וכתב בבקר ובצאן ביין ובשכ' מיעט כל דבר ולא התיר אלא [אלו] בלבד. עוד חזר וכללו בכל אשר תשאלך נפשך חזר וריבה לן כל דבר שתשאלך נפשך ריבה ומיעט וריבה למדנו כל שהוא בתורה כעניין הזה דרשינן לא חזר ריבוי באחרונה אלא שריבה הכל. מאי רבי רבי הכל אי הכי מיעוט למאי אתא ואמרינן אתא לר' אליעזר למעט [ציר] קסבר בעינן עיקר פירי והאי שומנא דפירי הוא ליהודה בן גדיש למעוטי מים ומלח. הני תנאי דרשי כללי ופרטי דתניא ונתתה הכסף בכל אשר תאוה נפשך כלל בבקר ובצאן וביין ובשכר ופרט ובכל אשר תשאלך נפשך חזר וכלל כלל ופרט וכלל אי אתה דן אלא כעין הפרט מה הפרט מפורש פרי מפרי וגדולי קרקע אף כל פרי מפרי וגדולי קרקע האי תנא דספרי דבי רב ודבי ר' ישמעאל תנא מה הפרט מפורש וולד וולדות הארץ אף כל וולד וולדות האר[ץ] מאי בינייהו אמר אביי דגים איכא בינייהו. האי תנא דמרבי כל דהוא פרי מפרי וגדולי קרקע מרבי אפי' דגים דהני נמי גדולי קרקע נינהו. ואקשינן דאביי אדאביי אי דגים גדולי קרקע נינהו אמ[ר] אכל

הגהות מהר"ב רנשבורג

[א] גמ' היינו דקאמר ר' יוחנן מאן דמתרגם בבקר אליבא דבן בג בג עי' ב"ק דף נד ע"א תוס' ד"ה חמור דבור וכו' וכו' ד"ה חמור וכו' ד' נה ע"א תוס' ד"ה חמור וכו' ונ"ע שלא הקשו מן בבלי דהכא ולא שייך תירוצם:

*א אבל פוטיתא — לוקה ארבע, נמלה — לוקה חמש, ב צירעה — לוקה שש. ואם איתא, פוטיתא נמי לילקי משום: "השרץ השורץ על הארץ"! אלא אמר רבינא: עופות איכא בינייהו. למאן דאמר פרי מפרי וגידולי קרקע — ג הני נמי גידולי קרקע נינהו. למאן דאמר ולד ולדות הארץ — הני עופות *מן הרקק נבראו. מאן דמרבי עופות מאי טעמיה, ומאן דממעיט עופות מאי טעמיה? מאן דמרבי עופות קסבר: כללא בתרא דווקא, פרט וכלל נעשה כלל מוסף על הפרט. ואיתרבו להו כל מילי, ואהני כללא קמא למעוטי כל דלא דמי ליה משני צדדין. ומאן דממעט עופות קסבר: כללא קמא דווקא, כלל ופרט — ואין בכלל אלא מה שבפרט, הני — אין, מידי אחרינא — לא. ואהני כללא בתרא לרבויי כל דדמי ליה משלשה צדדין.§ א"ר יהודה משמיה דרב שמואל בר שילת משמיה דרב: מערבין בפעפועין ובחלגלוגות ובגודגדניות, אבל לא בחזיז, ולא ד בכפניות. ובגודגדניות מי מערבין? והתניא: גודגדניות, מרובי בנים — יאכלו, חשוכי בנים — לא יאכלו, ה ואם הוקשו לזרע — אף מרובי בנים לא יאכלו! תרגמא אשלא הוקשו לזרע, ומרובי בנים. ואיבעית אימא: לעולם לחשוכי בנים — דהא חזו למרובי בנים. מי לא תנן: *מערבין לנזיר ביין ולישראל בתרומה. אלמא: אע"ג דלא חזי להאי — חזי להאי. הכא נמי: אע"ג דלא חזי להאי — חזי להאי. ואיבעית אימא: כי קאמר רב — בהנדקוקי מדאי. ובחזיז לא?! והאמר רב יהודה, א"ר: כשות וחזיז מערבין בהן, ומברכין עליהן "בורא פרי האדמה"! לא קשיא; הא — מקמי *דאתא רב לבבל, הא — לבתר דאתא רב לבבל. ובבבל הויא *רובא דעלמא?! *והתניא: ו הפול והשעורה ז והתילתן שזרען לירק — בטלה דעתו אצל כל אדם, לפיכך: זרען חייב וירקן פטור. ח השחליים והגרגיר שזרען לירק — מתעשרין ירק וזרע, זרען לזרע — מתעשרין זרע וירק. כי קאמר רב — בדגנונייתא

[תוספתא פ"ב דמעשרות]

רש"י

פוטיתא. שרץ המים קטן שאין בו כזית. ואפ"ה, כיון דבריה היא — אכילה היא ולוקה ד' מלקיות. בשרץ המים כתיב(א) בתורת כהנים: "אל תשקצו את נפשותיכם בכל השרץ השורץ ולא תטמאו בהם" — הרי כאן שנים, וכלל בהן בין שרץ הארץ בין שרץ המים, ומשום "מבשרם לא תאכלו" ומשום "וכל אשר אין לו סנפיר וקשקשת לא תאכלו": נמלה. שהוא שרץ הארץ — לוקה ה': תרתי — הא דאמרן: ו"כל הולך על גחון לכל השרץ השורץ על הארץ לא תאכלום" — הרי ג', "וכל השרץ השורץ על הארץ שקץ הוא לא יאכל" — הרי ד', "ולא תטמאו את נפשותיכם בכל השרץ הרומש על הארץ" — הרי ה'. כולן בפרשת "ויהי ביום השמיני": צרעה לוקה שש. שהיא שרץ העוף. ולקי בכל הני חמשה, מוסף עליו "וכל שרץ העוף *שקץ הוא לא יאכל", במשנה תורה. *והאי דכתיב ב"קדושים תהיו": "ולא תשקצו את נפשותיכ' בבהמה ובעוף ובכל אשר תרמוש" — לא חשיב ליה, דבבהמה וחיה ועוף גדולים משתעי, ולא בשרצים דלא כתיב בהו. שרץ, לשון 'שרץ', דבר שהוא נד בארץ ואינו נראה אלא ע"י שירוצו וריחושו מפני קוטנו: ואם איתא. דדגים גידולי קרקע נינהו, פוטיתא נמי לילקי משום שרץ הארץ גרס. ולא גרס, לילקי ה' דשבע בעי למילקי, חמש דשרץ הארץ ושתים דשרץ המים: מאי טעמא דמאן דמרבי עופות קסבר. כל היכא דאיכא כלל ופרט וכלל — כללא בתרא עיקר, ובתריה אזלינן: והוה ליה פרט וכלל ונעשה כלל מוסיף על הפרט ומרבי כל מילי. וכללא קמא דאתי למעוטי, ולמימר דנדרשי' בכלל ופרט ואין בכלל אלא מה שבפרט, ולא נרבי מידי — לא אזלינן בתריה. ומיהו, אהני פורתא למימר: דכי מרבי כללא בתרא — לא כל מילי מרבי, אלא כעין הפרט מאי דדמי ליה מב' לצדדין, דהוי פרי מפרי וגידולי קרקע. ומיתרבי נמי עופות בהאי דינא, ולמעוטי דגים דלא דמו ליה אלא בחד צד, בפרי מפרי: ומאן דממעט עופות קסבר. כל היכא דאיכא כלל ופרט כללא קמא דווקא, ואין בכלל אלא מה שבפרט, וממעטי כל מילי ואפי' מאי דדמי ליה בפרטא. והדר כתב כללא בתרא — לאפוקי ממיעוטא דכללא קמא במקצת, ולאתויי מיהא מידי דדמי לפרטא בכל ג' צדדין. דהוי פרי מפרי, וגידולי קרקע, וולד ולדות הארץ: פעפועין. = ירקות שקורין קקול"י בל' ארמי, יוטלי"ש בלע"ז: חלגלוגות. = פולפי"ר בלע"ז: גודגדניות. = אליינדר"א בלע"ז: חזיז. = שחת של תבואה כשהוא ירק, וגוזזין ואוכלין אותו: כפניות. = תמרים רעות שלא בישלו כל צרכן: גודגדניות. ממעיטין את הזרע: ואם הוקשו. הקלחין כעץ, שכבר נמח בהן זרעו — קשין הקלחין לכל אדם: תרגמא. להא דאמר רב מערבין — אשלא הוקשו, וזה המערב בהן יש לו בנים, דהשתא חזו ליה: הנדקוקי מדאי. גודגדניות שבמדי יפות הן: כשות. = הומלי"ן: בבבל אוכלין חזיז, וכי אתא רב לבבל וחזא דאכלי להו, אמר: מערבין, ומעיקרא אמר דאין מערבין: לירק. לאכול בירקן: זרען חייב. במעשר, ואע"פ שלא זרען מתחילה לכך: וירקן פטור. דלאו מידי הוא: שחליים. קרישו"ן: הגרגיר. אורוג"א נאכל בין זרע ובין ירק: כי קאמר רב. דמערבין בהן: בדגנונייתא

תוספות

צירעה לוקה שש. פי' בקונט' דהא דכתיב בקדושים: "לא תשקצו וגו' ובכל אשר תרמש האדמה" — בגדולים משתעי, דלא כתיב שרץ. וקשה, דבפרק ד' מיתות (סנהדרין דף נט:) דרשינן: "ובכל חיה הרומשת" — זה נחש. משמע דרמישה נמי הוי דבר הרוחש כמו נחש ההולך על גחונו. ומפרש ה"ר יעקב דאורלינ"ש: דבמעילה פרק "קדשי מזבח" (דף טז:) מוקי האי קרא דוקא בשמונה שרצים, כדכתיב "אשר הבדלתי לכם לטמא" — במובדלין דבר הכתוב: אהני כללא קמא למעוטי כל דלא דמי ליה משני צדדים. וא"ת: דבנזיר, בפ' "ג' מינין" (דף לה:) אמר: מאי איכא בין תרי פרטי וכללא לתרי כללי ופרטא? תרי כללי ופרטא, אי איכא דדמי ליה אפי' בחד צד — מרבינן, תרי פרטי וכללא עד דדמי ליה משני צדדין. משמע, דבחד צד סגי! וי"ל: דשני צדדין דהכא הוי כחד צד דהתם. דשני צדדין, פרי מפרי וגידולי קרקע — שוין הן. ובפ"ק דקדושין (דף כד:) גבי שן ועין דריש; מה הפרט מפורש מומין שבגלוי ואינו חוזר — הא נמי צדדין שוין. והא דפריך התם למימר מה הפרט מפורש — מומין שבגלוי ובטל ממלאכה, ואינו חוזר — היינו למאן דאמר כללא קמא דווקא — דע"כ צד דבטל ממלאכתו גרוע מהנך. מדקמשני "לחפשי ישלחנו" ריבויא הוא. ואם שוה הוא — אמאי מרבינן ליה טפי משאר צדדין? וכי האי סוגיא איתא בחולין (דף סו.) בסוף "אלו טריפות" גבי ארבה, וכריש "אלו מומין" (בכורות דף לז.) גבי פסח או עור. ואתו כולהו כמאן דאמר כללא קמא דווקא, כדפירש'. ועוד אומר ר"י: דאתא שפיר אפי' למ"ד כללא בתרא דווקא, ולדידיה נמי צריך שידמה בכל צדדין החשובין, אע"פ שהא' חשוב מחבירו — רק שלא יהיה צד גרוע יותר מדאי. אבל למאן דאמר כללא קמא דוקא — מצריך שיהא דומה אף בצד גרוע הרבה. והדבר מסור לחכמים להכיר איזהו צד גרוע שחולקין בו:

ובבבל הויא רובא דעלמא והתניא כו'. תימה: אמאי לא משני כדמשני בפ' "חבית" (שבת ד' קמד:) מי דמי: ערביא אתרא, הכא — בטלה דעתו אצל כל אדם! וי"ל: דהתם ודאי שייך לחלק, דכולי עלמא נמי, אם היו להם גמלים הרבה כמו בערביא — היו מקיימין קוצים בשדותיהן, ולכך יש חשיבות באתרא. אבל בית מנשיא, אע"פ שכל העולם נמי, אם היו להם רמונים היו סוחטין — כיון דלא הוי אלא חד גברא בטלה דעתו. אבל הכא שבכל העולם יש חזיז ולא אכלי — אין לחלק בין אתרא לגברא. ולהכי נמי לקמן (דף כט:) דפריך: ופרסאי הוו רובא דעלמא, ולא מייתי מהך ברייתא דליבטלו פרסאי לגבי רובא דעלמא — דאין לי לבטלם, כיון דרוב בשר יש להם. ושאר העולם נמי אם הוי להם רוב בשר — היו אוכלים בלא לחם דומיא דערביא. ומייתי שפיר מבגדי עניים דלא בעי שיעור עשירים, כיון שפחות חשוב בעיניהן. ועוד, דמדמי השיעורים להדדי. ולא שייך נמי לאתויי לקמן ההיא דחבית. [וע"ע תוס' שבת נב: ד"ה ואת"ל]

לפיכך זרען חייב וירקן פטור. אין להקשות: מאי "לפיכך" — הא קתני דבטלה דעתו! דאיכא למימר: בטלה דעתו לענין דמתעשר אחר הבאת שליש, כדין זרע, או לענין תורם מן הרעה על היפה: לזרע מתעשרין זרע וירק. תימה: אמאי לא עירב ותני להו: זרען לזרע או לירק — מתעשרין זרע וירק! ואומר ר"י: דהיכא דזרען לירק — הוי ירק עיקר, ומתעשר הכל אחר לקיטה כירק, בין ירק בין זרע. ואם זרע לזרע — מתעשר הכל לשעבר, אחר זמן הראוי למעשר זרע, ולא בתר לקיטה. ולהכי תנא ברישא ירק וזרע, ובסיפא זרע וירק. דברישא ירק עיקר, ובסיפא זרע עיקר. ונפקא מינה נמי לענין מן הרעה על היפה, דכשירק עיקר — הוי ירק יפה, וכשזרע עיקר — הוי זרע יפה. והוי מן הזורע על הירק מן היפה על הרעה, וכן משמע בירושלמי בפרק [רביעי] דמעשרות: ראשונים

רבינו חננאל

אבל פוטיתא דהוא דג טמא לוקה משום אאל"ס *) [ארבעה לאוין] נילקו נמי משום שרץ השורץ על הארץ ומשני רבינא לא תימא דגים איכא בינייהו דדגים ודאי אליבא דאביי לאו גידולי קרקע נינהו אלא אימא עופות איכא בינייהו. האי תנא מרבי להו דגידולי קרקע נינהו ואידך תנא ממעט להו דלא וולד וולדות נינהו (רבא) [אלא] מרקק מים איברו ואמרינן מכדי הני תרי תנאי כללי ופרטי דרשי מ"ט האי ממעט לעוף והאי מרבה ליה ואמרינן האי תנא דמרבי ליה לעוף קסבר כללא בתרא דווקא דהדר וכתב ובכל אשר תשאלך נפשך דהוה פרט וכלל דנעשה כלל מוסיף על הפרט ואיתרבי להו כל מילי **) אהני כללא קמא למעוטי כל דדמי ליה מב' צדדין והן פרי מפרי וגדולי קרקע ולא דמי להו מב' צדדין כגון מים ומלח כמיהין ופטריות שאינן פרי מפרי וכגון דגים שהן פרי מפרי אינן גידולי קרקע ומרבי אפילו עופות שהן פרי מפרי וגדולי קרקע. ואידך תנא סבר כללא קמא דווקא דהוה ליה כלל ופרט ותורת כל כלל ופרט אין בכלל אלא מה שפרט הני דפריש קרא אין מידי אחרינא לא אהני כללא בתרא לרבויי כל דדמי ליה בג' צדדין והן פרי מפרי וגדולי קרקע ותולדת ברייתו מן הארץ למעוטי מים ומלח וכמיהין ופטריות כדאמרן ולעופות נמי אע"ג דאינן פרי מפרי וגדולי קרקע מרקק מים נבראו ואינן דומין לבקר וצאן שהן פרי מפרי וגדולי קרקע ותולדת ברייתו מן הארץ וכענין שמועה זו היא במס' נזיר (דף לה ע"ב) וסוגיא חדא היא לתרווייהו כאשר פירשנו. וכן בענין מבית המקדש (בסוכה נ ע"ב) ר' דריש לה בכללי ופרטי ומרבי כל מיני מתכות וממעט של עץ. ור' יוסי בר' יהודה דריש ליה ברבויי ומיעוטי ואינו ממעט אלא של חרס בלבד. וכל אחד דורש הלשון שקבל מרבותיו: ירושלמי בכאן בעירובין [ובמע"ש] בפ' מעשר שני ניתן לאכילה

עין משפט נר מצוה

יג א מיי' פ"ב מהלכות מאכלות אסורות הל' כג [וברב אלפס סוף פרק ג דחולין ד' רפב. ובר"ח שם סימן סט]:
יד ב מיי' שם הל' כד:
טו ג מיי' פ"ז מהל' מעשר שני הל' יב:
טז ד ה טוש"ע או"ח סי' שפו סעיף ט:
יז ו מיי' פ"ב מהלכות תרומות הלכה ז:
יח ז שם הלכה ח:
יט ח שם הלכה ה:

מסורת הש"ס

מכות טז: פסחים כד.
[חולין כז: ע"ש]
[צ"ל טמא]
הרי שם רש"ל
[לעיל כו:]
[עי' תוס' גיטין ו. ותוס' ב"ק פ. ד"ה מכי אתא]
[שבת נב. וש"נ]

הגהות הב"ח

(א) רש"י ד"ה פוטיתא וכו' ד' מלקיות בשרץ המים כתיב מבשרם לא תאכלו כו"כ בויהי ביום השמיני ולאו שני במשנה תורה וכל אשר אין לו סנפיר וקשקשת לא תאכלו וכתיב בת"כ אל תשקצו את נפשותיכם וכו' בין שרץ המים הס"ד:

רב נסים גאון

פ"ג בכל מערבין אמר רב יהודה בריה דרב שמואל בר שילת משמיה דרב מערבין בפעפועין ובחלגלוגות ובגודגדניות פירשו בגמ' דבני מערבא והכי גרסי בעון קומוי אילין אינון אמר לון קקולי והנדקוקי ופרפחיני:

בסופו. מתני' ר' עקיבא ולא ר' ישמעאל דר' ישמעאל דרש ונתתה הכסף בכל אשר תאוה נפשך כלל בבקר ובצאן וביין ובשכר פרט ובכל אשר תשאלך נפשך חזר וכלל. כלל ופרט וכלל אי אתה דן אלא כעין הפרט מה הפרט מפורש וולד וולדות הארץ אף כל וולד וולדות הארץ. ר' עקיבא דריש מה הפרט מפורש פרי וולד פרי ומכשר פרי אף כל פרי ולד פרי ומכשר פרי מה נפק מבינייהו עופות דגים וחגבים וכמיהין ופטריות לר' ישמעאל אין נקחין בכסף מעשר לר' עקיבא נקחין ... *) כלל ופרט וכלל ... ***) ...

*) אולי הוא ר"ת וכל אשר אין לו סנפיר וגו'. **) נראה דצ"ל כל מילי דדמי ליה מב' צדדין והן פרי מפרי וגדולי קרקע ואהני כללא קמא למעוטי מאי דלא דמי להו וכו'. ***) נראה שחסר כאן ...

בְּדַרְגְּנוּנָיְיתָא. זֶרַע גַּרְגִּיר לְמַאי חֲזִי? א"ר יוֹחָנָן: שֶׁכֵּן רִאשׁוֹנִים שֶׁלֹּא הָיָה לָהֶן פִּלְפְּלִין, שׁוֹחֲקִין אוֹתוֹ וּמַטְבִּילִין בּוֹ אֶת הַצָּלִי. *ר' זֵירָא כִּי הֲוָה חָלִישׁ מִגִּרְסֵיהּ הֲוָה אָזֵיל וְיָתֵיב אַפִּיתְחָא דְּרַב יְהוּדָה בַּר אַמִי, אֲמַר: כִּי נָפְקִי וְעָיְילִי רַבָּנַן — אֵיקוּם מִקַּמַּיְיהוּ וַאֲקַבֵּל בְּהוּ אַגְרָא. נְפַק אֲתָא יָנוּקָא דְּבֵי רַב, א"ל: מַאי אַגְמְרָךְ רַבָּךְ? א"ל: כְּשׁוּת — "בּוֹרֵא פְּרִי הָאֲדָמָה", חָזִיז — "שֶׁהַכֹּל נִהְיָה בִּדְבָרוֹ". אֲמַר לֵיהּ: אַדְּרַבָּה, אִיפְּכָא מִסְתַּבְּרָא: הַאי — מֵאַרְעָא קָא מִרְבֵּי, וְהַאי — מֵאַוִּירָא קָא מִרְבֵּי. [א]וְהִלְכְתָא כְּיָנוּקָא דְּבֵי רַב. מ"ט? הַאי — גְּמַר פֵּירֵי, וְהַאי — לָאו גְּמַר פֵּירֵי. וּמַאי דְּקָאָמְרַתְּ הַאי מֵאַרְעָא קָא רָבֵי וְהַאי מֵאַוִּירָא קָא רָבֵי — לֹא הִיא. כְּשׁוּת נַמִי מֵאַרְעָא קָא רָבֵי, דְּהָא קָא חָזֵינַן דְּקָטְלִינַן לָהּ לְהִיזְמָתָא וּמַיְיתָא(א) כְּשׁוּתָא. וּבְכַפְנִיּוֹת אֵין מְעָרְבִין? וְהָתַנְיָא: *[ב]קוֹר נִיקָּח בְּכֶסֶף מַעֲשֵׂר, [ג]וְאֵין מְטַמֵּא טוּמְאַת אוֹכָלִין. וְכַפְנִיּוֹת נִקָּחוֹת בְּכֶסֶף מַעֲשֵׂר, [ד]וּמְטַמְּאוֹת טוּמְאַת אוֹכָלִים. רַבִּי יְהוּדָה אוֹמֵר: *קוֹר הֲרֵי הוּא כָּעֵץ לְכָל דְּבָרָיו, אֶלָּא [ה]שֶׁנִּיקָּח בְּכֶסֶף מַעֲשֵׂר. וְכַפְנִיּוֹת — הֲרֵי הֵן כַּפֵּרִי לְכָל דִּבְרֵיהֶם, אֶלָּא [ה]שֶׁפְּטוּרוֹת מִן הַמַּעֲשֵׂר. הָתָם בִּדְנִיסְחָנֵי. אִי הָכִי, בְּהָא לֵימָא רַבִּי יְהוּדָה פְּטוּרוֹת מִן הַמַּעֲשֵׂר? *וְהָתַנְיָא: אָמַר רַבִּי יְהוּדָה: לֹא הוּזְכְּרוּ פַּגֵּי בֵיתְיוֹנִי אֶלָּא לְעִנְיַן מַעֲשֵׂר בִּלְבַד; פַּגֵּי בֵיתְיוֹנִי וְאָהִינֵי דְּטוֹבִינָא חַיָּיבִין בְּמַעֲשֵׂר. אֶלָּא לְעוֹלָם לָאו בְּנִיסְחָנֵי, וּלְעִנְיַן טוּמְאַת אוֹכָלִין שָׁאנֵי. כְּדְאָמַר רַבִּי יוֹחָנָן: הוֹאִיל וְרָאוּי לְמַתְּקָן ע"י הָאוּר. הָכָא נַמִי: הוֹאִיל וְיָכוֹל לְמַתְּקָן ע"י הָאוּר. וְהֵיכָא אִתְּמַר דְּרַבִּי יוֹחָנָן — אַהָא: *דְּתַנְיָא, שְׁקֵדִים הַמָּרִים, קְטַנִּים — חַיָּיבִין, גְּדוֹלִים — פְּטוּרִין. מְתוּקִים, גְּדוֹלִים — חַיָּיבִין, קְטַנִּים — פְּטוּרִין. רַבִּי *שִׁמְעוֹן בְּרַבִּי יוֹסֵי אוֹמֵר מִשּׁוּם אָבִיו: זֶה וָזֶה לִפְטוֹר, וְאָמְרִי לָהּ: זֶה וָזֶה לְחִיּוּב. א"ר אִילְעָא:(ב) הוֹרָה רַבִּי חֲנִינָא בְּצִיפּוֹרִי כְּדִבְרֵי הָאוֹמֵר זֶה וָזֶה לִפְטוֹר. וּלְמַאן דְּאָמַר זֶה וָזֶה לְחִיּוּב, לְמַאי חֲזֵי? א"ר יוֹחָנָן: הוֹאִיל וְרָאוּי לְמַתְּקָן ע"י הָאוּר. אָמַר מָר, רַבִּי יְהוּדָה אוֹמֵר: קוֹר הֲרֵי הוּא כָּעֵץ לְכָל דְּבָרָיו, אֶלָּא שֶׁנִּיקָּח בְּכֶסֶף מַעֲשֵׂר. הַיְינוּ תַּנָּא קַמָּא! אָמַר אַבַּיֵי: שְׁלָקוֹ וְטִגְּנוֹ אִיכָּא בֵּינַיְיהוּ. מַתְקִיף לָהּ רָבָא: מִי אִיכָּא לְמַאן דְּאָמַר שְׁלָקוֹ וְטִגְּנוֹ לֹא? וְהָתַנְיָא: *הָעוֹר וְהַשִּׁילְיָא אֵין מְטַמְּאִין טוּמְאַת אוֹכָלִין, [ו]עוֹר שֶׁשְּׁלָקוֹ, וְשִׁילְיָא שֶׁחִישֵּׁב עָלֶיהָ מְטַמְּאִין טוּמְאַת אוֹכָלִין! אֶלָּא אָמַר רָבָא: אִיכָּא בֵּינַיְיהוּ בְּרָכָה. דְּאִתְּמַר: *קוֹר, רַב יְהוּדָה אָמַר: "בּוֹרֵא פְּרִי הָאֲדָמָה", וּשְׁמוּאֵל אָמַר: "שֶׁהַכֹּל נִהְיָה בִּדְבָרוֹ". רַב יְהוּדָה אָמַר "בּוֹרֵא פְּרִי הָאֲדָמָה" — אוּכְלָא הוּא. וּשְׁמוּאֵל אָמַר "שֶׁהַכֹּל נִהְיָה בִּדְבָרוֹ" — כֵּיוָן שֶׁסּוֹפוֹ לְהַקְשׁוֹת לָא מְבָרְכִינַן עִילָּוֵיהּ "בּוֹרֵא פְּרִי הָאֲדָמָה". א"ל שְׁמוּאֵל לְרַב יְהוּדָה: שִׁינָּנָא, כְּוָותִיךְ מִסְתַּבְּרָא, דְּהָא [ח]צְנוֹן שֶׁסּוֹפוֹ לְהַקְשׁוֹת וּמְבָרְכִינַן עֲלֵיהּ "בּוֹרֵא פְּרִי הָאֲדָמָה". וְלֹא הִיא, צְנוֹן — נָטְעִי אֱינָשֵׁי אַדַּעְתָּא דְּפוּגְלָא, דִּיקְלָא — לָא נָטְעִי אֱינָשֵׁי אַדַּעְתָּא דְּקוּרָא. וְאע"ג דְּקַלְּסֵיהּ שְׁמוּאֵל לְרַב יְהוּדָה, [ט]הִלְכְתָא כְּוָותֵיהּ דִּשְׁמוּאֵל.§ גּוּפָא, אָמַר רַב יְהוּדָה, אָמַר רַב: כְּשׁוּת וְחָזִיז מְעָרְבִין בָּהֶן, וּמְבָרְכִין עֲלֵיהֶם "בּוֹרֵא פְּרִי הָאֲדָמָה". כְּשׁוּת בְּכַמָּה? כִּדְאָמַר רַב יְחִיאֵל: כִּמְלֹא הַיָּד, [י]הָכָא נַמִי — כִּמְלֹא הַיָּד. חָזִיז בְּכַמָּה? אָמַר רַבָּה בַּר טוֹבִיָּה בַּר יִצְחָק, אָמַר רַב: כִּמְלֹא אוּזִילְתָּא דְּאִיכָּרֵי. אָמַר רַב חִלְקִיָּה בַּר טוֹבִיָּה: מְעָרְבִין *בְּקַלְיָא. בְּקַלְיָא ס"ד?! אֶלָּא: בְּיַרְקָא דְּקַלְיָא. וְכַמָּה? אָמַר רַב יְחִיאֵל: כִּמְלֹא הַיָּד. רַבִּי יִרְמְיָה נְפַק לְקִירְיָיתָא, בָּעוּ מִינֵּיהּ: מַהוּ לְעָרֵב בְּפוֹלִין לַחִין. לָא הֲוָה בִּידֵיהּ. כִּי אֲתָא לְבֵי מִדְרְשָׁא אֲמַרוּ לֵיהּ, הָכִי אָמַר רַבִּי יַנַּאי: [כ]מְעָרְבִין בְּפוֹלִין לַחִין. וְכַמָּה? אָמַר רַב יְחִיאֵל: כִּמְלֹא הַיָּד. אָמַר רַב הַמְנוּנָא: [ל]מְעָרְבִין בִּתְרָדִין חַיִּין. אִינִי?! וְהָאָמַר רַב חִסְדָּא: סִילְקָא חַיָּא קָטִיל גַּבְרָא חַיָּא!
ההוא

רש"י

בדרגנונייתא. כְּחָזִיז שֶׁגָּדֵל בְּגִינָּה, דְּכוּלֵּי עָלְמָא אָכְלֵי לְהוּ: כְּשׁוּת. גָּדֵל בְּהִיזְמֵי, וְאֵין לוֹ שׁוֹרֶשׁ בַּקַּרְקַע, אֶלָּא מֵהִיזְמֵי נָמַח: כְּשׁוּת גְּמַר פְּרִי. וְנִקְרָא פְּרִי: דְּקָטְלֵי לְהִיזְמָתָא. שֶׁקּוֹצְצִין הַהִיזְמֵי וּמַיְיתֵי כְּשׁוּתָא. אַלְמָא: אִי לָא יָנְקָא מֵאַרְעָא — לָא רָבְיָא: קוֹר. דָּבָר רַךְ הַנּוֹסָף עַל הַדֶּקֶל בְּכָל שָׁנָה, וְקוֹדֶם שֶׁיַּגִּיעוּ יְמוֹת הַגְּשָׁמִים וְיִתְקַשֶּׁה וְיֵעָשֶׂה עֵץ — קָרֵי לֵיהּ "קוֹר", וְטוֹב לְמַאֲכָל הוּא: נִיקָּח בְּכֶסֶף מַעֲשֵׂר. דִּפְרִי מִפְּרִי, וְגִדּוּלֵי קַרְקַע הוּא: וְאֵינוֹ מְטַמֵּא טוּמְאַת אוֹכָלִין. וַאֲפִילּוּ חִישֵּׁב עָלָיו לַאֲכִילוֹ, דְּלָאו אוֹכֶל הוּא: קוֹר הֲרֵי הוּא כָּעֵץ כו'. לְקַמָּן פָּרֵיךְ: הַיְינוּ ת"ק: אֶלָּא שֶׁפְּטוּרוֹת מִן הַמַּעֲשֵׂר. דְּלָא נִגְמְרָה מְלַאכְתָּן. וּלְתַנָּא קַמָּא חַיָּיבוֹת, דִּלְכָל מִילֵּי פֵּירוֹת נִינְהוּ. וּמִדְּקָתָנֵי מְטַמְּאוֹת טוּמְאַת אוֹכָלִים — אַלְמָא אוֹכֶל נִינְהוּ: הָתָם. דְּקָתָנֵי מְטַמְּאוֹת: בִּדְנִיסְחָנֵי. דְּקָלִים זְכָרִים שֶׁעוֹשִׂין כַּפְנִיּוֹת, וְאֵינָם נַעֲשִׂים תְּמָרִים לְעוֹלָם. וְכַפְנִיּוֹת הוּא גְּמַר פֵּירָן, וְלוֹקְטִים אוֹתָן בְּנִיסָן, וְהָנְהוּ אוֹכְלָא נִינְהוּ, וְכִי קָאָמַר רַב — בִּדְקָלִים נְקֵיבוֹת, שֶׁכַּפְנִיּוֹת שֶׁלָּהֶן נַעֲשִׂים תְּמָרִים, הִלְכָּךְ הַשְׁתָּא לָא גְּמַר פְּרִי הוּא: לֹא הוּזְכְּרוּ וכו'. בְּתוֹסֶפְתָּא דִּשְׁבִיעִית (פ"ז) הִיא, וּמַיְיתֵי בִּגְמָרָא דִּפְסָחִים בְּפֶרֶק "מָקוֹם שֶׁנָּהֲגוּ"(ג): אוֹכְלִים בִּתְאֵנִים עַד שֶׁיִּכְלוּ פַּגֵּי בֵיתוֹנִי, רַבִּי יְהוּדָה אוֹמֵר כו': בֵּיתוֹנִי. מָקוֹם: פַּגֵּי. תְּאֵנִים הֵן שֶׁלֹּא נִתְבַּשְּׁלוּ: אָהִינֵי. הֵן כַּפְנִיּוֹת. וְהָנָךְ דְּטוֹבִינָא כּוּלָּם זְכָרִים הֵן, וּמִשּׁוּם הָכִי חַיָּיבִין בְּמַעֲשֵׂר דִּגְמַר פֵּירָא הוּא, וְכָל שֶׁכֵּן דִּגְמַר פֵּירָא הוּא לְשְׁאָר מִילֵּי: וְיָכוֹל לְמַתְּקָן. אַף עַל פִּי שֶׁעַכְשָׁיו בְּקַטְנוּתָן מָרִין הֵן, אֲבָל לְעִנְיַן עֵירוּב בָּעֵינַן מִידֵּי דַּחֲזֵי בְּהַהִיא שַׁעְתָּא, וְהָנֵי הָא לָא מַתְקִינְהוּ. וּלְעִנְיַן מַעֲשֵׂר — מִשּׁוּם דְּלָא גְּמַר פֵּירָא הוּא: קְטַנִּים חַיָּיבִין. מִשּׁוּם שֶׁהוּא גְּמַר פְּרִי שֶׁלָּהֶן, שֶׁכְּשֶׁגְּדֵלִין נַעֲשִׂין מָרִים: וּגְדוֹלִים פְּטוּרִין. מִמַּעֲשֵׂר, דְּלָאו אוֹכֶל נִינְהוּ: מְתוּקִין קְטַנִּים פְּטוּרִין. דְּלָא נִגְמְרוּ: זֶה וָזֶה לִפְטוֹר. מָרִים בֵּין גְּדוֹלִים וּבֵין קְטַנִּים, גְּדוֹלִים — דְּלָא אוֹכְלָא, קְטַנִּים — דְּלָא פֵּירָא: שְׁלָקוֹ. מְבוּשָּׁל הַרְבֵּה: וְטִיגְּנוֹ. בְּשֶׁמֶן, פריי"ט בְּלַעַ"ז. לְרַבִּי יְהוּדָה אֲפִי' שְׁלָקוֹ וְטִיגְּנוֹ אֵינוֹ טָמֵא, וְתַנָּא קַמָּא אִם שְׁלָקוֹ וְטִיגְּנוֹ מְטַמֵּא דְּלָא(ד) קָאָמְרֵי הֲרֵי הוּא כָּעֵץ: עוֹר שֶׁשְּׁלָקוֹ מְטַמֵּא. אֲבָל בְּמַחֲשָׁבָה גְּרֵידָתָא — לֹא: וְשִׁילְיָא. אֲפִי' בְּמַחֲשָׁבָה גְּרֵידָתָא. וְכֵיוָן דִּמְהַנְּיָא שְׁלִיקָה לְעוֹר — כ"ש לְקוֹר דַּחֲזֵי לַאֲכִילָה מֵעִיקָּרָא: בְּרָכָה אִיכָּא בֵּינַיְיהוּ. לְתַנָּא קַמָּא "בּוֹרֵא פְּרִי הָאֲדָמָה", לְרַבִּי יְהוּדָה "שֶׁהַכֹּל", דְּסוֹפוֹ לְהַקְשׁוֹת: אַדַּעְתָּא דְּפוּגְלָא. לְאוֹכְלוֹ כְּשֶׁהוּא רַךְ: כְּשׁוּת בְּכַמָּה. הָוְיָא לָהּ מְזוֹן ב' סְעוּדוֹת, דְּאָמְרִינַן לְקַמָּן (דף פ:): מְזוֹן שְׁתֵּי סְעוּדוֹת לְעֵירוּב: אוּזִילְתָּא. = ווי"ל בְּלַעַ"ז — אֲגוּדוֹת יָרָק שֶׁכּוֹרְכִין הָאִיכָּרִים: קַלְיָא. = קֶלַח שֶׁל עֵשֶׂב, וְקָשֶׁה כָּעֵץ: לְקִירְיָיתָא. כְּפָרִים, לִרְאוֹת בִּתְבוּאָתוֹ*:
בשיל

תוספות

ראשונים שלא היה להן פלפלין. הקשה ה"ר שמעון: א"כ, מהאי טעמא נמי פלפלין חייבין במעשר, ואם כן מטמאין טומאת אוכלין. דהא בהא תליא, כדאמר בפ' "בא סימן" (נדה דף נ:), והתם בגמרא* מייתי: נמנו וגמרו שאין פלפלין מטמאין טומאת אוכלין! וי"ל: דהא דגרגיר חייב במעשר – לאו משום דמטבילין בו, אלא משום כששוחקין אותו חזי למיכל בעיניה, אבל אין רגילות לשוחקו כדי לאוכלו בעיניה אלא כדי לטבל בו, אבל פלפלין, גם כי נשחקו לא חזו בעינייהו, ופטורין מן המעשר*:

והאי לאו גמר פירא הוא. והא דאמר רב יהודה אמר רב: כשות וחזיז מברכין עליהן "בפה"א" – הא אוקימנא בדגנונייתא:

קור ניקח בכסף מעשר ואין מטמא טומאת אוכלים. תימה: דבפ' "בא סימן" (נדה דף נא:) פריך גבי קושט וחימוס וראשי בשמים, אי נקחין בכסף מעשר ליטמאו טומאת אוכלין. ומסיק: דנמנו וגמרו שאין נקחין בכסף מעשר ואין מטמאין טומאת אוכלין. והכא קתני דקור ניקח בכסף מעשר ואין מטמא טומאת אוכלין! וי"ל: ודאי, התם אי חזי לאכילה – הוי אוכל, ושפיר קרינן ביה "מכל האוכל אשר יאכל". אבל הכא קור לא מיקרי אוכל – כיון דסופו להקשות, ולא נטעי דיקלא אדעתא דקורא. ומכל מקום, ניקח בכסף מעשר – דהשתא הוא רך, והוי פרי מפרי אע"ג דלא הוי אוכל:

הואיל וראוי למתקן ע"י האור. וקור, אף על גב דחזי ע"י שליקה וטיגון לא מטמא טומאת אוכלין, משום דהוי כעץ בעלמא, אלא דחזי ע"י שליקה כמו עור דבסמוך. אבל הכא, דבקל יכול למתקן – חשיב אוכל, ואף קודם מיתוק מטמא טומאת אוכלין: זה וזה לפטור ואמרי לה זה וזה לחיוב. אמרים גדולים וקטנים קאי. אבל אין לפרש דקאי אקטנים מרים ומתוקים – דבסוף פ"ק דחולין (דף כה:) גרסינן ברוב ספרים: ולמ"ד זה וזה לחיוב – גדולים למאי חזו?

איכא ביניהו ברכה. דלתנא קמא מברך "בפה"א". ואע"ג דלענין ברכה מיקרי פרי, מכל מקום לא חשיב לטמא טומאת אוכלין:
מאי

עין משפט נר מצוה

כ א טוש"ע א"ח סי' רד סעיף א:
[דף נא:]
כא ב מיי' פ"ז מהל' מעשר שני הל' ח:
כב ג מיי' פ"א מהל' טומאת אוכלין הלכה י:
כג ד שם הלכה יג:
[וע"ע תוס' יומא פא: ד"ה שהפלפלין ותוס' נדה נ. ד"ה כל שחייב]
כד ה מיי' פ"ב מהלכות מעשר הלכה ה:
כה ו מיי' פ"א מהל' מעשר הלכה ט ופ"ב הלכה ה סמג עשין קלה:
כו ז מיי' פ"ב מהלכות טומאת אוכלין הל' טו סמג עשין קלו:
כז ח טוש"ע א"ח סי' רג סעיף ח:
[תוספתא מ"ש פ"א ותוספתא טבול יום פ"ה ע"ש]
כח ט מיי' פ"ח מהל' ברכות הלכה ו סמג עשין כז טוש"ע א"ח סי' רד סעיף א:
כט י מיי' פ"א מהל' עירובין הלכה יא סמג עשין א:
ל כ ל מיי' וסמג שם טוש"ע א"ח סי' שפו סעיף ז:

מסורת הש"ס

[ברכות כח. ע"ש]
עוקצין פ"ג מ"ז ע"ש
פסחים נג. ע"ש תוספתא פ"ז דשביעית
חולין כה:
[נ"ל ישמעאל]
[חולין עז:]
ברכות לו. [וגם אי' קורא]
בב"מ פה. רש"י ד"ה לקרייתי פי' לעירי
[קליא הוא עשב ששורפין וטוחנין אותו בבורית ורוחצין ידיהן כמו קלם מלך בבל ואלו הירקות ירקות שדה הנאכלים הם ערוך ערך קליא א']

הגהות הב"ח

(א) גמ' ומייתא כשותא נ"ב ומייתא לשון מיתה כלומר יבש הכשות. ערוך ערך כשות: (ב) שם אמר ר' אילעא אמר ר' יהודה הורה ר' חנינא: (ג) רש"י ד"ה לא הוזכרו וכו' בפ' מקום נ"ב דף נג ע"א: (ד) ד"ה וטיגנם וכו' דלא אמרי הרי:

רבינו חננאל

זרע גרגיל למאי חזי א"ר יוחנן ראשונים שלא היה להן פלפלין שוחקין זרע גרגיל ומטבילין בו בשר צלי. ואסיקנא כישות מברכין עליה בורא פרי האדמה דמארעא קא רבי דהא חזינן דקטלי הזמתא ומייתא כשותא והיא גמר פירא אבל חוץ שהכל נהיה בדברו דהא לא גמר פירא לפיכך אמר רב אין מערבין בחזיז דדברא כדאוקימנא וגם לא בכפניות ואקשינן בכפניות לא [מערבין] והתניא קור אלגומר ניקח בכסף מעשר ואינו מטמא טומאת אוכלין כפניות נלקחות בכסף מעשר ומטמאין טומאת אוכלין כו' ופרקינן כי תניא זו הברייתא כפניות הרי הן כפרי לכל דבריהן אלא שפטורין מן המעשר בדניסחני. פי' הן הכפניות הללו שיוצאין בניסן העשויות להיאכל כפניות כי הן דקלין ידועין שפירותיהן נאכלין כפניות (נאכלין) ואינן מתקיימין להיגמר תמרים אבל שאר דקלים כפניות היוצאות אחר ניסן שראויות להיות תמרים. עכשיו כפגין חשובין ולא נגמרו. ואקשינן אי הכי בהא נימא ר' יהודה פטורה מן המעשר. והתניא א"ר יהודה לא הוזכרו פגי ביתיוני אלא לענין מעשר. ביתוני פי' מקום ואהיני דבוובניא. פי' בוסר חייבין במעשר. פי' כיון שכן דרכם להיאכל חייבין במעשר שכבר נגמרה מלאכתן הכא נמי בכפניות דניסחני הרי נגמרה מלאכתן אמאי פטורין מן המעשר לר' יהודה ומפרקינן לעולם דלאו דניסחני אלא כפניות שהן פגין קתני וכי קתני כפניות הרי הן כפרי לענין טומאת אוכלין קתני מ"ט הואיל ויכול לתקן ע"י האור ולעשותן אוכל וכו' יוחנן דאמר בשחיטת חולין פרק ראשון בשקדים המרים הואיל ויכול לתקן ע"י האור והא דאמר ר' (יוחנן) יהודה קור דהוא אמגומר הרי הוא כעץ לכל דבריו היינו ת"ק דאמר [אין מטמא טומאת אוכלין] ואתא אביי לפרק שלקו וטיגנו איכא בינייהו דר' יהודה סבר אפילו שלקו וטיגנו אינו מטמא טומאת אוכלין שאע"פ שהעור אינו אוכל כיון דהא עץ הוא ות"ק סבר כיון דטיגנו מטמא ודחה רבא האי פריקא מדתניא עור ששלקו ושיליא שחשב עליה מטמא טומאת אוכלין אע"פ שהעור אינו אוכל כיון ששלקו נעשה אוכל אמר רבה ברכה איכא בינייהו (ר' יהודה סבר) [ת"ק] כיון דאכיל שויא אוכלא ובריך עליה בפה"א. ושמואל אמר כיון שסופו להקשות לאו אוכלא. והלכתא כשמואל דדיקלא אדעתא דקורא לא נטעי אינשי אבל צלף דאיכא אינשי דנטעי לשיתאי תנן על מיני נצפה על העלין ועל התמרות אומר בורא פרי האדמה ועל האביונות ועל הקפריסין אומר בורא פרי העץ. אמר רב ששת כישות וחזין מערבין בהן ומברכין עליהן בורא פרי האדמה ואוקימנא בדגנוניתא ואמרי כישות בכמה. פי' כמה שיעור הוא בעירוב ופשטנא כדאמר רב יחיאל בפולין לחין מלא היד וכן נמי מלא יד כישות בכמה ופשיטנא כמו איזולתא דאכירי. פי' איסורייתא והן חבילות של חמן שקושרין אותו האיכרים הם עובדי האדמה: מערבין בירקא דקיליא כי יש ירקות ששורפין אותן ומערבין אפרן בבורית שמעבירין הכתם ונקרא ירקא דקיליא כדכתיב אשר קלם מלך בבל באש. ואלו הירקות ירקות שדה הנאכלין הן ולפיכך אמר מערבין בהן בכמה מלא היד וכן פולין לחין. אמר רב יחיאל מלא היד אמר רב המנונא מערבין בתרדין חיין איני והא אמרינן סילקא חייא קטיל גברי חייא ופרקינן
ההוא

[א]ההוא בבשיל ולא בשיל, איכא דאמרי, אמר רב המנונא: אין מערבין בתרדין חיין, דאמר רב חסדא: סילקא חייא קטיל גברא חייא. והא קא חזינן דקא אכלי ולא מייתי! התם בבשיל ולא בשיל. אמר רב חסדא: *תבשיל של תרדין יפה ללב וטוב לעינים, וכל שכן לבני מעיים. אמר אביי: והוא דיתיב אבי תפי ועביד *תוך תוך. אמר רבא: *הריני כבן עזאי בשוקי טבריא. אמר ליה ההוא מרבנן לרבא: תפוחים בכמה? אמר ליה: וכי מערבין בתפוחים? ולא?! *והתנן: [ב]כל האוכלין מצטרפין לפסול את הגויה בחצי פרס, [ג]ובמזון שתי סעודות לעירוב, [ד]וכביצה לטמא טומאת אוכלים! והאי מאי תיובתא? אילימא משום דקתני "כל האוכלין" והני בני אכילה נינהו – *והאמר רבי יוחנן: אין למדין מן הכללות ואפילו במקום שנאמר בו חוץ! אלא משום דקתני: "ובמזון שתי סעודות לעירוב וכביצה לטמא טומאת אוכלין", והני נמי בני טמויי טומאת אוכלין נינהו. וכמה? אמר ר"נ: [ה]תפוחים בקב. מיתיבי, ר"ש בן אלעזר אומר: [ו]עוכלא תבלין, וליטרא ירק, ועשרה אגוזין, וחמשה אפרסקין, ושני רמונים, ואתרוג אחד. ואמר גורסק בר דרי משמיה דרב מנשיא בר שגובלי משמיה דרב: [ז]וכן לעירוב. והני נמי ליהוו כי אפרסקין? הני חשיבי והני לא חשיבי. אמר רב יוסף: שרא ליה מריה לרב מנשיא בר שגובלי, אנא אמריתא ניהליה אמתני' והוא אמרה אברייתא. *דתנן: [ח]אין פוחתין לעני בגורן מחצי קב חטין וקב שעורין. רבי מאיר אומר: חצי קב שעורין, וקב וחצי כוסמין, וקב גרוגרות, [ט]או מנה דבילה. רבי עקיבא אומר: פרס. [י]וחצי לוג יין, ר"ע אומר: רביעית. [כ]ורביעית שמן, ר"ע אומר: שמינית. ושאר כל הפירות, אמר אבא שאול: [ל]כדי שימכרם ויקח בהן מזון שתי סעודות. ואמר רב: וכן לעירוב. ומאי אולמיה דהאי מהך? אילימא משום דקא תני בהך תבלין, ותבלין לאו בני אכילה נינהו – אטו הכא מי לא קתני חטין ושעורין, ולאו בני אכילה נינהו. אלא משום דקתני חצי לוג יין. ואמר רב: [מ]מערבין(א) בשתי רביעיות של יין. מדבעינן כולי האי – ש"מ כי אמר רב וכן לעירוב – אהא מתני' קאמר, ש"מ. אמר מר: ובמזון שתי סעודות לעירוב. סבר רב יוסף למימר: עד דאיכא סעודה מהאי וסעודה מהאי. אמר ליה רבה: אפילו למחצה לשליש ולרביע. גופא, אמר רב: מערבין בשתי רביעיות של יין. ומי בעינן כולי האי? והתניא, רבי שמעון בן אלעזר אומר: יין – כדי לאכול בו, [נ]חומץ – כדי לטבל בו, זיתים ובצלים – כדי לאכול בהן שתי סעודות. התם [ס]בחמרא מבשלא. אמר מר: חומץ כדי לטבל בו. אמר רב גידל, אמר רב: כדי לטבל בו מזון שתי סעודות של ירק. איכא דאמרי, אמר רב גידל אמר רב: ירק הנאכל בשתי סעודות. אמר מר: זיתים ובצלים, כדי לאכול בהן מזון שתי סעודות. ובבצלים מי מערבין? והתניא, *אמר ר' שמעון בן אלעזר: פעם אחת *שבת רבי מאיר בערדיסקא, ובא אדם אחד לפניו. אמר לו: ר', עירבתי בבצלים לטיבעין. והושיבו ר' מאיר בארבע אמות שלו. לא קשיא; הא – בעלים, הא – באימהות. דתניא: אכל בצל והשכים ומת – אין אומרין ממה מת. ואמר שמואל: לא שנו אלא בעלים, אבל באימהות – לית לן בה, ובעלין נמי לא אמרן, אלא דלא

רש"י

בשיל ולא בשיל. קטיל גברא: איכא דאמרי אמר רב המנונא וכו' והא חזינן אינשי דאכלי ולא מייתי התם בבשיל ולא בשיל. כי קאמר רב המנונא אין מערבין – בבשיל ולא בשיל: אבי תפי. בכירה, מקום שפיתת הקדירה: ועביד תוך תוך. שמבושל יפה ונצטמק כולו עד שנימוח, וכשהוא רותח דומה כמשמיע קול זה, תוך תוך*: הריני כבן עזאי בשוקי טבריא. יומא דבדיחא הוה ליה לרבא, ואמר להו לתלמידיו: השתא לילי דעתאי, והריני מזומן להשיב בחריפות לכל מי שישאלני, כבן עזאי, שהיה דורש בשוקי טבריא, ולא היה בימיו עוקר הרים כמותו [*והיה אומר: כל חכמי ישראל לפני כקליפת השום, חוץ מן הקרח הזה]: לפסול את הגויה. אם אכל אוכלין טמאין, אע"ג שאין אוכל מטמא אדם במגע אי אכיל מינייהו חצי פרס דהיינו שני ביצים – נפסל מלאכול בתרומה, כדתנן בפירקין דלקמן (דף פב:): ואוכלי חצייה – לפסול את הגויה. חצייה – היינו פרס, ל' פרוסה, וחצי חצייה – היינו חצי פרס: אלא משום דתני. עירוב דומיא דטומאת אוכלין, דמשמע: כל שהוא מטמא טומאת אוכלין – יש לו מזון שתי סעודות חזי לעירוב, ותפוחין בני טמויי נינהו: ר' שמעון בן אלעזר. במעשר עני שמחלקו לעניים הרבה על הגורן קאי, וקאמר: אין פוחתין לעני בגורן מהאי שיעור, דכתיב: "ונתת ללוי לגר ליתום ולאלמנה", ובציר מהכי לא הוי נתינה: עוכלא. שמינית שבליטרא, וליטרא הוא לוג: וכן לעירוב. דחלק עני בגורן נמי מזון שתי סעודות היא, כדאמר לקמן: ה"ג: והני נמי ליהוי כאפרסקין. ותיסגי בחמשה: חשיבי. ואמרינן לקמן: כל שהוא ליפתן – כדי לאכול בו. אלמא: לאו ממש סעודות, דליהוי כולה סעודתא מההוא מינא בעינן, אלא כל מידי לפום חשיבותיה. אם ליפתן שאדם רגיל ללפת בו את הפת – [שיעורו כדי ללפת בו את הפת] לשתי סעודות, ואם דבר הרגיל לבא בקינוח סעודה הוא – שיעורו בכדי שאדם רגיל להביא קינוח לב' סעודות: שרי ליה מריה. ימחול לו אדונו, על דבר זה, לרבי מנשיא: דאנא אמריתא ניהליה. להא דאמר רב "וכן לעירוב" אמתני' כדמפרש ואזיל, והוא אגמריה לגורסק בר דרי אברייתא: אין פוחתין לעני בגורן. ממעשר עני, אם יש לו הרבה לחלק, ובאו עניים הרבה והוא מחלק לכל אחד – אל יפחות לו משיעור זה, דנתינה בעינן. והתם קתני: היה לו דבר מועט – נותן לפניהם והן מחלקין ביניהן: מחצי קב חיטין. ואם שעורין – קב, ואם כוסמין – קב ומחצה: דבילה. לאחר שנדרסין בעיגול קרי להו דבילה, ושוב אינו מוכר במדה אלא במשקל: פרס. חצי מנה: ומאי אולמיה דהאי מהך. דאיקפד רב יוסף אדרב מנשיא, דקאמר אברייתא במאי דאיירי מתניתין לא איירי ברייתא, ולא סתרן אהדדי; הני שיעורייהו בהכי והני שיעורייהו בהכי: לאו בני אכילה נינהו. וסבירא ליה לרב יוסף דאין מערבין בהן, הלכך, "וכן לעירוב" לאו עלה אתמר: אלא משום דקתני חצי לוג יין. דהיינו שתי רביעיות, ושמעינן ליה לרב גבי עירוב נמי דקאמר הכי: וסעודה מהאי. ב' אוכלין מצטרפין לעירוב אבל ג' וד' דליכא סעודה מכל חד – לא: יין כדי לאכול בו. לשרות בו פת מזון ב' סעודות: חומץ כדי לטבל בו. בשר, מזון ב' סעודות: כדי לאכול בהן. ללפת בהן את הפת דב' סעודות: התם. דקתני יין כדי לאכול בו: בחמרא מבושל. קאמר, דחשוב ללפת בו אבל חמרא בעלמא – בעינן להיות בו שתיית ב' סעודות, והיינו ב' רביעיות: מזון ב' סעודות ירק. שכל הסעודה מן הירק: ירק הנאכל לב' סעודות. בפת: בערדיסקא ובא אדם אחד לפניו. בשבת מחוץ לתחום, על ידי עירוב שעירב ממקומו לטיבעין, והיה ערדיסקא באלפים אמה שבין עירובו לטיבעין: והושיבו ר' מאיר בד' אמות. ואסר לו לצאת ולזוז ממקומו מד' אמותיו שהיה עומד בהן בשעת שאלה, דקסבר: לאו עירוב הוא, ונמצא יוצא חוץ לתחום בלא עירוב, ותנן לקמן בפ' "מי שהוציאוהו" (דף מא:): אין לו אלא ד' אמות: עלין. לא חשיבי, ורעים לאכול: דלא

תוספות

מאי אולמיה דהאי מהאי. נראה לפרש דקים ליה להתלמוד דרב יוסף לא שמעיה דרב אמתני' בפירוש, אלא משום טעם דקדק רב יוסף דאמר רב אמתני'. ולהכי קאמר: מאי אולמיה דהאי מהאי, מאיזה כח בא לדקדק? ומשני: משום דקתני מתני' חצי לוג יין, ואמר רב מערבין בשתי רביעיות יין. והך מילתא לא אמר רב בפירוש, אלא מכללא דההיא דוכן לעירוב איתמר. א"כ שמע מינה דוכן לעירוב אמתני' איתמר, דאי אברייתא – מנא ליה דסבר רב מערבין בשתי רביעיות יין, דהא פשיטא דאין ללמוד זה מזה מדלא אמר כל שיעורי עירוב כשיעורי מתנות עניים: **חומץ** כדי לטבל בו. היינו רביעית כדאמרינן בפרק "הדר" (דף סח.) וליקנו להו רביעתא דחלא בחביתא: **והושיבו** ר' מאיר בד' אמותיו. חוץ לעיר היה. דבעיר היה מהלך את כולה, כדאמר ב"מי שהוציאוהו" (דף מא:). אי נמי: סבר לה כרבי יהושע דאמר: אין לו אלא ארבע אמות. ואין לומר משום דרבי מאיר קניס שוגג אטו מזיד, דהא בדאורייתא לא קניס. ואית ליה בפירקין [דף לה:] דתחומין דאורייתא. ועוד: כיון דחשבינן כל העיר כארבע אמות – אפילו במזיד נמי מהלך את (את) כולה, דמזיד נמי אית ליה ארבע אמות. בתוספות רבינו יהודה:

עין משפט נר מצוה

לא א שם סעיף ה:
לב ב מיי' פ"ד מהל' טומאת אוכלין הלכה ג:
לג ג מיי' פ"א מהלכות עירובין הל' ט סמג עשין א טוש"ע א"ח סי' שפו סעיף ד:
לד ד מיי' פ"ד מהלכות טומאת אוכלין הל' ג:
לה ה ו ז מיי' פ"א מהל' עירובין הלכה יא ופ"ו מהל' מתנות עניים הל' ח סמג עשין א טוש"ע א"ח סי' שפו סעיף ז:
לו ח ט י כ ל מיי' פ"ו מהלכות מתנות עניים שם:
לז מ נ ס מיי' פ"א מהל' עירובין הלכה יא סמג עשין א טוש"ע א"ח סי' שפו סעיף ו:

רבינו חננאל

ההוא בבשיל ולא בשיל: אמר רבא הריני כבן עזאי בשוקי טבריא. פי' רבא משתבח ואמר הריני [ידוע] בחכמה (ידוע) בעירובין כמו שהיה בן עזאי ידוע בחכמתו בשוקי טבריא. שאלו ההוא מרבנן שיעור תפוחים בעירוב כמה א"ל רבא וכי מערבין בתפוחין א"ל ההוא מרבנן ולא והתנן במס' מעילה פרק ד' כל האוכלין מצטרפין לפסול את הגויה כבחצי פרס. וכמזון ב' סעודות לעירוב קתני מיהת כל האוכלין ואפי' התפוחין נמי בכללן שגם הם אוכלין הן. ודחאו רבא הא"ר יוחנן אין למדין מן הכללות כלומר האי דקתני כל לאו דווקא הוא. ואמרינן לאו (מכלל) [מכל] אלא מדקתני ובמזון ב' סעודות לעירוב וכביצה לטמא טומאת אוכלין. והני נמי בני טמויי נינהו ללמד דווקא קתני ולא מצא רבא תשובה. ופי' רב נחמן תפוחין (בעירובין) [בקב]. וכן הלכה ומותיב עלה מיהא דתני בפאה בפרק האחרון. בירושלמי וקרוב לענין הזה בספרי דבי רב. ר"ש בן אלעזר אומר עוכלא תבלין וליטרא ירק עשרה אגוזין וה' אפרסקין ב' רמונים ואתרוג אחד ואמר גורסק בר דרי משום (דרבנן) [דרב] וכן לעירוב ואם איתא ניהוי ה' תפוחים כשיעור אפרסקין ה'. ושנינן תפוחין דשכיחי קב אפרסקין דלא שכיחי ה' אמר רב יוסף שארי לי' מריה לרב מנשיא בר שגובלי דאנא אמריתא ניהלי' האי דאמר רב וכן לענין [עירוב] אמתניתין דתנן בסוף פאה אין פוחתין לעניים בגורן מחצי קב חטין וקב שעורין ר' מאיר אמר חצי קב וקב וחצי כוסמין וקב גרוגרת או מנה דבילה [ר"ע אומר] פרס חצי לוג יין. ר' עקיבא אומר רביעית. רביעית שמן ר' עקיבא אומר שמינית ושאר כל הפירות אמר אבא שאול כדי שימכרם ויקח בהן מזון ב' סעודות והוא אמר הא דרב וכן לעירוב (בזו) [על זו] הברייתא ומאי אולמיה דמתני' מברייתא משום דתני בברייתא תבלין ותבלין לאו בני אכילה ולאו בני עירוב נינהו אטו מתני' [מי לא] תני חיטין ושעורין דלאו בני אכילה נינהו אלא משום דתני במתני' חצי לוגין ואמר רב מערבין בב' רביעיות של יין ש"מ כי אמר רב וכן לעירוב אמתני' קאמר ש"מ ואם הוא יין מבושל אמר רב כדי לאכול בו חומץ כדי לטבול בו. זיתים ובצלים כדי לאכול בהן ב' סעודות וכמזון ב' סעודות לעירוב סבר רב יוסף עד דאיכא סעודה מהאי וסעודה מהאי מצטרפין ואסיקנא [דאפילו למחצה ולשליש ולרביע] (חומץ כדי לטבול בו) [בצלים כדי לאכול מהן] מזון ב' סעודות הני מילי באימהות אבל בעלין לא ועלין

מסורת הש"ס

[ועי' רש"י פסחים עד. ד"ה רבי ישמעאל]
ברכות לט. [בכורות נח.]
ס"א
[פסחים עד:]
[קידושין כ. סוטה מה. ערכין ל:]
מעילה יז: כריתות יג. [מקוואות פ"י מ"ז]
לעיל כז. קידושין לד.
פאה פ"ח מ"ה
[תוספתא פ"ז]
[לפנינו איתא היינו יושבין לפני ר"מ]

הגהות הב"ח

(א) גמ' בשתי רביעיות של יין (מדבעינן כולי האי) תא"מ ונ"ב ס"א איתו:

גליון הש"ס

רש"י ד"ה הריני כבן עזאי וכו' והיה אומר כל חכמי ישראל וכו' בכורות נח ע"א: **תום'** ד"ה מאי אולמי' וכו' דקים ליה להש"ס. כעין זה בתוס' בשבת דף ט ע"ב ד"ה הא לן וש"נ:

עין משפט נר מצוה

לח א שם סעיף ה:
לט ב מיי' פ"ז מהל' מקוואות הלכה ד: [דף ג:]
מ ג שם הלכה ה:
מא ד מיי' פי"ו מהל' שבת הלכה ב:
מב ה ו מיי' פ"א מהל' עירובין הלכה יא:
מג ז ח מיי' שם הל' י ופ"ז שם הלכה ז טוש"ע א"ח סי' שפו סעיף ו:
מד ט מיי' פכ"ב מהל' כלים הלכה ו:
מה י שם הלכה כג:

גמרא

א° דלא *אבציל זירתא, אבל °אבציל זירתא — לית לן בה. אמר רב פפא: לא אמרן אלא דלא אישתי שיכרא, אבל אישתי שיכרא — לית לן בה. תנו רבנן: לא יאכל אדם בצל מפני *נחש שבו. ומעשה ברבי חנינא שאכל חצי בצל וחצי נחש שבו, וחלה ונטה למות, ובקשו חביריו רחמים עליו וחיה, מפני שהשעה צריכה לו.§ א"ר זירא, אמר שמואל: שכר מערבין בו, ב ופוסל את המקוה בשלשת לוגין.(א) מתקיף לה רב כהנא: פשיטא, וכי מה בין זה למי צבע? *דתנן, רבי יוסי אומר: ג מי צבע פוסלין את המקוה בשלשת לוגין! אמרי: התם — מיא דצבעא מיקרי, הכא — שיכרא איקרי. ובכמה מערבין? סבר רב אחא בריה דרב יוסף קמיה דרב יוסף למימר: בתרין רבעי שכרא. *כדתנן: ד המוציא יין כדי מזיגת הכוס, ותני עלה: כדי מזיגת כוס יפה. מאי כוס יפה? כוס של ברכה! ואמר ר"נ, אמר רבה בר אבוה: כוס של ברכה צריך שיהא בו רובע רביעית, כדי שימזגנו ויעמוד על רביעית. וכדרבא, *דאמר רבא: כל חמרא דלא דרי על חד תלת מיא — לאו חמרא הוא. וקתני סיפא: ושאר כל המשקין ברביעית, וכל השופכין ברביעית. מדהתם על חד ארבע — הכא נמי על חד ארבע. ולא היא, התם הוא דבציר מהכי לא חשיב, *אבל הכא — ה לא, דעבידי אינשי דשתו כסא בצפרא וכסא בפניא, וסמכי עילוייהו. תמרים בכמה? אמר רב יוסף: ו תמרים בקב. אמר רב יוסף: מנא אמינא לה — *דתניא: אכל גרוגרות ושילם תמרים — תבוא עליו ברכה. היכי דמי? אילימא לפי דמים, דאכל מיניה בזוזא וקא משלם ליה בזוזא — מאי "תבא עליו ברכה"? בזוזא אכל, בזוזא קא משלם! אלא לאו לפי מדה, דאכל מיניה גריוא דגרוגרות דשויא זוזא, וקא משלם ליה גריוא דתמרים דשוי ארבעה. וקתני: "תבא עליו ברכה", אלמא: תמרים עדיפי. אמר ליה אביי: לעולם דאכל מיניה בזוזא, וקא משלם בזוזא. ומאי "תבא עליו ברכה" — דאכל מיניה מידי דלא קפיץ עליה זבינא, וקא משלם ליה מידי דקפיץ עליה זבינא. *שתיתא, אמר רב אחא בר פנחס: תרי שרגושי. כיסאני, אמר אביי: תרי בוני דפומבדיתא. *אמר אביי, אמרה לי אם: הני כסאני מעלו לליבא, ומבטלי מחשבתא. ואמר אביי, אמרה לי אם: האי מאן דאית ליה חולשא דליבא לייתי בישרא דאטמא ימינא דדיכרא, ולייתי כבויי דרעיתא דניסן. ואי ליכא כבויי דרעיתא — לייתי סוגייני דערבתא, וניכבביה וניכול, ונשתי בתריה חמרא מרקא.§ אמר רב יהודה, אמר שמואל: ז כל שהוא ליפתן — כדי לאכול בו. כל שאינו ליפתן — כדי לאכול הימנו. בשר חי — כדי לאכול הימנו. בשר צלי, רבה אמר: ח כדי לאכול בו, ורב יוסף אמר: כדי לאכול הימנו. אמר רב יוסף: מנא אמינא לה — דהני פרסאי אכלי *טבהקי בלא נהמא. אמר ליה אביי: *ופרסאי הוו *רובא דעלמא?! *והתנן: ט בגדי עניים לעניים, י בגדי עשירים לעשירים, אבל

רש"י

(ב) דלא אבציל זירתא. שלא גדלו זרת [יש להן אֹרס] בבצל: נחש שבו. אֹרס שרף הבצל: ופוסל את המקוה. כשאר מים שאובין: מתקיף לה רב כהנא מה בין זה למי צבע. ופשיטא דפוסל: שיכרא מיקרי. וסד"א אין עליו שם מים: תרין ריבעי שיכרא. תרי לוגין, דלוג רובע קב: המוציא יין. בשבת: כדי מזיגת כוס. כמו שנותנין יין חי בכוס כדי למוזגו במים: רובע רביעית. רובע לוג יין חי: וקתני סיפא. דהמוציא יין, ושאר כל המשקין הוצאתן ברביעית, דהיינו לוג: ומדהתם. בהוצאת שבת בעינן על חד דיין ארבע דשיכרא, דביין תני רובע רביעית ובשאר כל המשקין תני רביעית: הכא נמי. גבי עירוב בעינן ארבע, ואמר רב לעיל: מערבין בשני רביעית יין. אלמא: בשיכרא תרי לוגי בעינן: דשתי כסא. של רביעית לוג שכר בצפרא, וכסא בפניא, וסמיך עלייהו: אכל גרוגרות. של תרומה בשוגג: בזוזא. בשוה זוז: וקא משלם ליה. תמרים היקרים מגרוגרת, ולא שילם לו לפי מדה אלא לפי דמים: אלמא תמרים עדיפי. ותנן לעיל גבי עני בגורן: קב גרוגרות, ואמר רב: וכן לעירוב. וכ"ש תמרים, דודאי סגי להו בהכי: א"ל אביי. מהא לא תשמע דתמרים עדיפי. לעולם גרוגרות עדיפי, ולפי דמים משלם. ומאי ברכה — דקפיץ עליה זבינא — לוקחים. ולענין עירוב בעינן טפי מקב: שתיתא. מאכל שעושין מקמח קלי שנתייבש בתנור, ונותנין דבש לתוך התבשיל: שרגושי. = תרוודין: כיסני. = קליות: בוני. = מדות: מחשבתא. = דאגה: כבויי דרעייתא דניסן. = לפיתי בקר: סוגייני דערבתא. = קיסמין של ערבה: וניכבביה. יעשה מהן גחלת, ויצלה בהן אותו בשר וניכול: חמרא מרקא. יין מזוג: כדי לאכול בו. כל שהוא לפתן שיעורו כדי לאכול בו ללפת בו את הפת מזון ב' סעודות: כדי לאכול הימנו. שיהו כל שתי הסעודות ממנו: בשר חי. אינו לפתן, ובעינן כדי לאכול ממנו: בשר צלי. פליגי ביה אי הוי ליפתן אי לא: טבהקי. = חתיכות: בגדי עניים. שלש על שלש, מקבלין טומאה לעניים: בגדי עשירים. שלשה על שלשה מקבלין טומאה אף לעשירים:

ה"ג

תוספות

מפני נחש שבו. פ"ה: אֹרס של שרף בצל. ור"ת פי': העמוד שבתוכו, שמתעגל בתוכו כמין גבעול, ומתקבלין בו זרע הבצל – אותו העמוד נקרא נחש של בצל: **הכא** שכר איקרי. ואפ"ה פוסל המקוה. והא דאמר בפ"ק דמכות [דף ג:] *דיין מזוג אינו פוסל את המקוה אפילו כשיש בו ג' לוגין מים שאובין – משום דחמרא מזיגא מיקרי, שאני שכר דכל עיקרו אינו אלא מים. ועוד דהתם מיקרי חמרא מזיגא ושם חמרא עילוי', ופירי לא פסיל המקוה: **כדי** שימזגנו ויעמוד על רביעית. משמע דכוס של ברכה טעון מזיגה. וכן בפרק "ג' שאכלו" (ברכות נ:) וב"המוכר פירות" (ב"ב דף צז.) אמר: ואין מברכין עליו עד שיתן לתוכו מים. ותימה: דבפרק "שלשה שאכלו" (ברכות נא.) אמרינן: עשרה דברים נאמרו בכוס של ברכה ותשיב חי! ותירץ רש"י: ד"חי" דקאמר – היינו שיתננו חי בכוס, ואחר כך ימזוג, לאפוקי שלא ימזגנו בכוס זה ויתננו בכוס אחר שמברך עליו. ור"ת מפרש: ד"חי" היינו מזוג ולא מזוג, דאמר בפרק "בן סורר ומורה" (סנהדרין דף ע.) אינו חייב עד שישתה יין חי, ומוקי לה במזוג ולא מזוג. ונותן בו קצת מים בתחילת הברכה, ובברכת הארץ מוסיף עליו מים עד שיהא מזוג כראוי, כדאמר בפ' "ג' שאכלו" (ברכות נא.) שמוסיף בברכת הארץ, והיינו מים, ולא כמו שפירש שם בקונט' שמוסיף יין. ובני נרבונה מפרשים ד"חי" קאי אכוס, ולאפוקי כוס שבור. דכולהו עשרה דברים קאי אכוס. ושייך חי בכוס, כדאמר (ב"ק נד.): שבירתן זו היא מיתתן. ובפרק בתרא דמכות (דף טז:) אמר: ריסק ט' נמלין ואחד חי, ר"ל: אותו חי שלם*: **ויעמוד** על רביעית. נראה כמו שפי' רש"י ב"המוציא" (שבת דף עו:) דכוס של ברכה צריך שיהא בה רובע רביעית הלוג, כדי שימזגנו ויעמוד על רביעית הלוג. ולא כטועים שמפרשים רובע רביעית הקב, דהיינו רביעית הלוג כדי שימזגנו ויעמוד על רביעית הקב – דהיינו לוג. דהא בנזיר בפרק "שלשה מינים" (דף לח.) חשיב הך דשאר משקין ברביעית דמייתי הכא, ומשמע הכא וב"המוציא" (שבת דף עו.) דהיינו שיעור כוס יפה אחר מזיגתו. והנהו דחשיב בנזיר – הוי רביעית הלוג, מדחשיב רביעית שמן לנזיר, דיליף מקרא בהתודה דהוי חצי שיעור של תודה. ותנן בפ' "שתי מדות" (מנחות דף פח:): חצי לוג שמן לתודה. ועוד, תני התם: ז' מדות של לח היו במקדש, רביעית הלוג מה היא משמשת – רביעית מים למצורע, רביעית שמן לנזיר. וחשיב נמי רביעית דם מטמא באהל – דהיינו רביעית הלוג, כדמשמע בפרק "כ"ג" בנזיר (דף נג.), דאמר: חצי קב עצמות, וחצי לוג דם – לכל, רובע קב עצמות ורביעית דם – לא לכל. ופריך נמי התם: ותו ליכא? והאיכא מי רביעית נוטלין מהן לידים, והיינו מי רביעית הלוג, כדמוכח במס' ידים (פ"א מ"א): **כל** חמרא דלא דרי על חד תלת. והא דאמר ב"דיני ממונות" (סנהדרין דף לז.): אל יחסר המזג, שאם נצרך אחד מהם לצאת רואין אם יש שם כ"ג – דמשמע דמזוג הוי שני חלקים מים! אומר ר"י: דקרא איירי ביין השרוני, דהוי ב' חלקים מים. דליכא לאוקמא קרא בסתם מזוג, רביעית דסנהדרין למאי חזי? אבל שליש חזי לדיני נפשות, ליהוי סנהדרי קטנה*: **אלמא** תמרים עדיפי. ואם תאמר: כיון דעדיפן, דילמא לא בעינן קב? ויש לומר: דמייתי ראיה דיותר מקב לא בעי: **בגדי** עניים. דווקא בטומאת מדרס יש חילוק בין עניים לעשירים, דביחוד תליא מילתא, ואין דרך עשיר לייחד פחות משלשה על שלשה טפחים. ואם ייחד – בטלה דעתו. אבל בטומאת מת אין חילוק, ואף לעשירים הוי בשלש על שלש. דבפרק "במה מדליקין" (שבת דף כו:) תניא: שלש על שלש מניין? תלמוד לומר: "והבגד" ולא מפליג בין עניים לעשירים. ועוד, דבמסכת כלים פרק כ"ז (משנה ב) תנן: דבגד מטמא שלשה על שלשה למדרס, ושלש על שלש למת. ועל כרחך בעשירים מיירי, דבעניים תנן בפכ"ח (משנה ח): בגדי עניים, אף על פי שאין בהם שלשה על שלשה – טמאין מדרס. כך פר"ת, ודלא כפ"ה דסוף "כירה" (שבת דף מז.): שלש על שלש לא מטמא ביד עשיר כלל. לימא

הגהות הב"ח

(א) גמ' מתקיף לה רב כהנא וכי מה כנ"ל ותיבת פשיטא נמחק: (ב) רש"י ד"ה דלא אבציל זירתא שלא גדל זרת בבצל ועוד יש להן ארס הס"ד:

גליון הש"ס

גמ' דלא אבציל זירתא. עין תי"ט פ"ז מ"ד דשבת: שם אבציל. בתוס' חולין נט ע"ב ד"ה והרי היה להם הגירסא כאן אפציל וכתבו דהוי כמו אבציל:

מסורת הש"ס

[עי' תוס' חולין נט: ד"ה והרי לבן]
[עמ"ש הערוך בערך נתן]
מכות ג: מקוואות פ"ז מ"ג
שבת עו.
שם עו: כ"ב צ:
אבל הכא עבידי אינשי כנ"ל
פסחים לב.
[ברכות לח.]
[קידושין לא: וש"נ]
[ע' תוס' לעיל כח. ד"ה ובכל]
[לעיל כח. שבת לב. קמד:]
[נ"ל והתניא]
[וע' תוס' ברכות נ: ד"ה מודים]
[ועי' עוד תוס' שבת עז. ד"ה לאמר]

רבינו חננאל

ועלין נמי לא אמרן אלא דלא אפציל זיתא (זירתא) אבל אפציל לית לן בה *) פי' נחש שבבצל העמוד שבתוכו שמתעגל בראשו כמין גבעול ומתקבץ בו זרע הבצל אותו העמוד נקרא נחש של בצל: א"ר זירא אמר שמואל שכר מערבין בו ופוסל את המקוה בג' לוגין. ואתקיף רב כהנא עליה הא פשיטא מ"ש ממי צבע דתנן ר' יוסי אומר מי צבע פוסלין את המקוה בג' לוגין ומשני איצטריך משום דהני מיא דצבעא מיקרו והמים פוסלין שהן שאובין אבל [הכא] שיכרא מיקרי. שיעור שיכרא לעירוב בכמה ואתינן למימר תרי רבעא שיכרא שאם תמזגם יעמוד בב' לוגין על חד תמניא. בהוצאת שבת פי' בהוצאת שבת המוציא רובע רביעית [חייב] נמצא ב' רביעיות של עירוב ח' חלקים כהוצאת שבת דתנן המוציא יין כדי מזיג' כוס ואוקימנ' בכוס של ברכ' (אומרים כוס של ברכה) ואמרינן כוס של ברכה צריך שיהא בו רובע רביעית כדי שימזגנו ויעמוד על רביעית כדרבא דאמר כל חמרא דלא דרי מקבל על חד תלת מיא לאו חמרא הוא וקתני סיפא ושאר המשקין ברביעית ומדהתם על חד ארבעה הכא נמי על חד ארבעה דאינון תמניא רביעיות (בב') [דאינון ב'] לוגין ולא היא התם בציר מהכא מרובע רביעית לא חשיב אבל הכא גבי עירוב עבידי אינשי דשתו כסא דשכרא בצפרא דהוא רביעית מזוג וכסא דשכרא בפנייא וסמכי עלוייהו. תמרים בכמה אמר רב יוסף קב דייק רב חסדא מהא דתניא אין פותחין לעני בגורן מקב גרוגרות ואמר רב וכן לעירוב וסבר תמרי דעדיפי הן לא כל שכן ומנא אמינא לה דתניא אכל גרוגרות ושלם תמרין תבא עליו ברכה ונדחת זו הראייה שלו: פי' שתיתא אסוויק/תרין שרגושי הן מדות קטנות אינן ידועות עכשיו כיסאני תרי כוני כוני נמי מדות הן כדגרסינן בכתובות פרק **) כונא בפרוטה ואינון מיני תרגימא כדתניא בתוספתא בברכות הביאו לפניו מיני תרגימא מברך עליהן בורא מיני. כסנין פ' (עובדא) [בשרא] דאטמא אבר הירך חמרא מרקא השוקט על שמריו כדכתיב ושוקט הוא על שמריו ולא הורק מכלי אל כלי אמר רב יהודה אמר שמואל כל דבר שהוא לפתן לאחר כדי לאכול בו ב' סעודות וכל הנאכל כמות שהוא כדי לאכול הימנו ב' סעודות בשר חי כדי לאכול הימנו ב' סעודות בשר צלי רבה אמר כדי לאכול בו רב יוסף אמר כדי לאכול הימנו דהא פרסאי [אכלי] טבהקי פי' בשר צלי בלא נהמא ואקשיה עליה אביי ופרסאי הוו רובא דעלמא כלומר מפני שהפרסיים אוכלין בשר צלי בלא פת נעשה כל העולם כולו כמותם ועלתה לרב יוסף בקשיא

*) [נראה שחסר בדברי רבינו וצ"ל ת"ר לא יאכל אדם בצל מפני נחש שבו פי' נחש וכו']. **) [אלמנה ניזונת דף נט ע"ב כונא בונא].

רב נסים גאון

שכר מערבין בו ופוסל את המקוה בג' לוגין עיקר דיליה במסכת מקוואות (פרק ב משנה ז) ר' אליעזר העידו מפי שמעיה ואבטליון ששלשת לוגים מים שאובין פוסלין המקוה ואיתה בגמ' דריצאות השבת אומר רביעית מים שאובין בין בתחילה בין בסוף שיעורן בג' לוגין ובמסכת עדיות בפרק א' (מ"ג) (דף טו.): תרין כוני היא שמה של מידה ואיתה בכתובות בפרק אלמנה ניזונת (דף נט) באתרא דכיילי בכנא

אבל בגדי עשירים לעניים — לא! וכי תימא: הכא לחומרא והכא לחומרא, והתניא: *רבי שמעון בן אלעזר אומר: מערבין לחולה *ולזקן כדי מזונו, ולרעבתן בסעודה בינונית של כל אדם?! קשיא. ומי אמר ר"ש בן אלעזר הכי? והתניא, רבי שמעון בן אלעזר אומר: עוג מלך הבשן פיתחו כמלואו![א] ואביי: התם היכי ליעביד — הדומי נהדמיה, [ונפקיה?!] איבעיא להו: פליגי רבנן עליה דרבי שמעון בן אלעזר, או לא? ת"ש, דאמר רבה בר בר חנה, אמר רבי יוחנן: עוג מלך הבשן [א]פיתחו בארבעה. התם דאיכא פתחים קטנים טובא, ואיכא חד דהוי ארבעה. דודאי כי קא מרוח — בההוא קא מרוח. אמר רב חייא בר רב אשי, אמר רב: מערבין בבשר חי. אמר רב שימי בר חייא: מערבין בביצים חיות. וכמה? אמר רב נחמן בר יצחק: אחת. סיני אמר: [ב]שתים.§ [ג]"הנודר מן המזון — מותר במים כו'".§ *מלח ומים הוא דלא איקרי מזון, הא כל מילי איקרי מזון. לימא תיהוי תיובתא דרב ושמואל, דרב ושמואל דאמרי תרוייהו: אין מברכין "בורא מיני מזונות" אלא על חמשת המינין בלבד. *ולא אותביניה חדא זימנא?! לימא תיהוי תיובתייהו נמי מהא! אמר רב הונא: [ד]באומר: "כל הזן עלי", מים ומלח הוא דלא זייני, הא כל מילי — זייני. *והאמר רבה בר בר חנה: כי הוה אזילנא בתריה דרבי יוחנן למיכל פירי דגינוסר, כי הוינן בי מאה — הוה מנקטינן לכל חד וחד עשרה עשרה, כי הוינן בי עשרה — הוה מנקטינן לכל חד וחד מאה מאה, וכל מאה מינייהו (לא) הוי מחזיק להו צנא בת תלתא סאוי. והוה אכיל להו לכולהון, ואמר: שבועתא דלא טעים לי זיונא! אימא מזונא. אמר רב הונא, אמר רב: "שבועה שלא אוכל ככר זו" — מערבין לו בה. "ככר זו עלי" — אין מערבין לו בה. מיתיבי: הנודר מן הככר — מערבין לו בה. מאי לאו דאמר "עלי"? לא, דאמר "זו". הכי נמי מסתברא, דקתני סיפא: אימתי — בזמן שאמר "שבועה שלא אטעמנה". אבל אמר "עלי" מאי? הכי נמי דאין מערבין לו בה — א"ה, אדתני "ככר זו הקדש" — אין מערבין לו בה [ו]לפי שאין מערבין בהקדשות, ליפלוג וליתני בדידה: במה דברים אמורים — דאמר "זו", אבל אמר "עלי" — אין מערבין לו בה! אמר לך רב הונא: אלא מאי, כל היכא דאמר "עלי" מערבין? קשיא רישא! חסורי מיחסרא והכי קתני: הנודר מן הככר — מערבין לו בה, ואפילו אמר "עלי" נעשה כאומר שבועה שלא אטעמנה. מכל מקום קשיא לרב הונא! הוא דאמר כרבי אליעזר. דתניא, רבי אליעזר אומר: "שבועה שלא אוכל ככר זו" — מערבין לו בה, "ככר זו עלי" — אין מערבין לו בה. ומי א"ר אליעזר הכי? והתניא, זה הכלל: אדם אוסר עצמו באוכל — מערבין לו בה, אוכל הנאסר לו לאדם — אין מערבין לו בה. רבי אליעזר אומר: [ה]"ככר זו עלי" — מערבין לו בה, "ככר זו הקדש" — אין מערבין לו בה, לפי שאין מערבין לו בהקדשות! תרי תנאי, ואליבא דרבי אליעזר.§ "מערבין לנזיר ביין כו'".§ מתני' דלא כב"ש. דתניא, ב"ש אומרים: אין מערבין לנזיר ביין ולישראל בתרומה. ב"ה אומרים: [ו]מערבין לנזיר ביין ולישראל בתרומה. אמרו להן ב"ה לב"ש: אי אתם מודים שמערבין

רש"י

ה"ג: אבל בגדי עשירים לעניים לא. כלומר: לעניים לא בעינן בגדי עשירים, אלא כיון דלדידהו חזו — אזלי בתרייהו, הכא נמי, אע"ג דלפרסאי לאו ליפתן הוא, כיון דלדידן הוי ליפתן — ניסגי בשיעור זוטא: הכא לחומרא. דכיון דחזו להו, מקבלי טומאה: והכא לחומרא. דעד דהוי ליפתן לכ"ע, ליבעי שיעורא רבה: והתניא. גבי עירוב, דכיון דחזו לזקן ולחולה, אף על גב דלכל אדם לא הוי מזון שתי סעודות — מערבין מיהא למאן דחזי. וגבי רעבתן דאכיל טפי — סגי בבינונית, אלמא: לקולא אזלינן: פתחו במלואו. להציל על שאר פתחים, ואי ליכא פתח דחזי ליה — כל חור מלא אגרוף שבכתלים טמאין: הדומי ניהדמיה. ינתחוהו לאיברין: פליגי רבנן. במת בבית: פתחים קטנים. פחותין מד': בההוא מרווח. הלכך מציל על כולן אבל כולן שוין, בד' או בי' אמות — כולן טמאין, דלא ידעי בהי מרווח ומפיק. ואפילו נפתח אחד מהן והאחרים סגורין, או חישב עליו להוציאו באחד מהן. דתנן בגמרא במסכת ביצה (דף לח:): הוא טמא[א] וכולן טהורים — ה"מ היכי דהאי חזי ליה, ואפילו כולהו חזי ליה אבל היכא דליכא חד חזי ליה, ובעי מרווח וכולן שוין — לא ידעינן בהי מרווח: סיני. קרי רב *יוסף, לפי שהיה בקי במשניות וברייתות: ולאו אותביניה חדא זימנא. ב"כילד מברכין" (דף לה:): באומר כל הזן עלי. מתני' דאסר ליה בכל מילי לאו דאמר יאסר עלי מזון — דודאי לא מיקרי מזון אלא ה' מינין, דהוו מין דגן, דזייני וסעדי ליבא. אלא כגון דאמר "יאסר עלי כל הזן", דמשמע כל דבר המשביע דכל מילי זייני חוץ ממים ומלח, אבל מיסעד לא סעדי ולא מיקרו מזון: גינוסר. ארץ ים כינרת, ופירותיה מתוקין: דלא טעים לי זיונא. לא אכלתי לשובע, ועדיין אני רעב: זיונא ס"ד. לא גרסינן הכא, אלא במס' ברכות, והכא גרסינן: אימא מזונא: מערבין לו בה. דלא נדר אלא מאכילה. ואי משום דלא חזיא ליה — הא חזיא לאחריני, מידי דהוה אנזיר ביין: ככר זו עלי. משמע: כל דבר הנאתה קאסר עליה: מאי לאו דאמר עלי. ושמע מינה דלא אסר איניש אדעתיה אלא דרך עיקר הנאתה, וכי נדר — אדעתא דאכילה נדר: לא דאמר הרי זו. "שבועה שלא אוכל ככר זו": הקדש. ודאי אסר בכל הנאות, ואינו ראוי לשום אדם: בדידיה. בככר של חולין: אלא מאי כל היכא דאמר עלי מערבין. דלא משמע אלא אכילה: קשיא רישא. דקתני: אימתי — בזמן שאמר "שבועה שלא אטעמנה", דמשמע: הא אמר "עלי" — לא. ומשני: הא לא קשיא, דחסורי מיחסרא כו' עד נעשה כאומר כו' דלא מסיק אדעתיה לאסור עליו אלא דרך הנאתה, דהיינו אכילה: אדם אוסר עצמו באוכל. שתלה הנדר במעשה שהוא עושה בעצמו, דהיינו שלא אוכל: מערבין לו בה. דהא הנאה דממילא היא, ולאו איהו עביד: אוכל הנאסר על האדם. כגון "ככר זו תיאסר עלי", או "שבועה שלא אהנה מככר זו", דהשתא לא תלה האיסור במעשה שבגופו, אלא אפילו הנאה דממילא — אין מערבין לו בה. ל"א: "ככר זו עלי" מערבין לו בה — דאמר לקמן (דף לא.): אין מערבין אלא לדבר מצוה, ומצות לאו ליהנות ניתנו. הלכך, משום הנאה לא איכפת לן. ואי משום דלא חזיא ליה — הא חזיא לאחרים, דומיא דנזיר ביין. ככר זו הקדש — לא חזיא לא לדידיה ולא לאחריני, ואנן סעודה הראויה בעינן, כדלקמן. זה עיקר:

שמערבין

תוספות

לימא תהוי תיובתא. ואם תאמר: והא מאן דפליג ארב ושמואל לא פליג אלא באורז ודוחן, וא"כ תקשה לכולהו! ועוד: תיקשי ליה מתניתין ד"כילד מברכין" (ברכות דף מ:) דיש כמה דברים דמברכין עליו "שהכל" או "בפ"ה"! וי"ל: דדווקא לרב ושמואל פריך דלא חשיבי אורז ודוחן, אף על גב דקבעי נמי סעודתא עלייהו, א"כ סבירא להו דכל מילי לא מיקרו מזון אלא ה' מינין בלבד. אבל מאן דפליג עלייהו, סבר שפיר דכל מילי איקרו מזון, אך דלא תקנו "בורא מיני מזונות" אלא הך דקבעי סעודתא עלייהו ואאורז ודוחן קבעי נמי: ככר זו עלי אין מערבין לו בה. תימה לר"י: אמאי נקט בהאי שבועה ובהאי נדר? בשבועה גופה או בנדר גופיה הוה מצי לפלוגי דהיכא דאסר עליה באכילה – מערבין לו בה, בהנאה – אין מערבין לו בה. ועוד: דאמר לקמן (דף לא.): לכ"ע אין מערבין אלא לדבר מצוה, ומצות לאו ליהנות ניתנו, משמע דליכא תנא דפליג – והא רבי אליעזר דבסמוך, דאמר: ככר זו עלי, דאין מערבין לו בה משום דאסור בהנאה. אם כן סבר דמערבין לו לדבר הרשות, או מצות ליהנות ניתנו! ונראה כרשב"ם, דמפרש: דאין מערבין לו בה – אפי' אמר קונם אכילת ככר זו עלי. משום דקונם הוי כעין הקדש ואתי לאחלופי בהקדש אבל אמר שבועה, אפילו אמר שבועה שלא אהנה מככר זו, כיון דלא מיחלף בהקדש – מערבין לו בה. דאין מערבין אלא לדבר מצוה, ומצות לאו ליהנות ניתנו. ונקט שבועה שלא אוכל – דאפי' הכי בקונם אין מערבין לו בה. וקשה לפירושו: דכי פריך בסמוך לרב הונא ליפלוג וליתני בדידיה – לישני דהכי קאמר: אבל אמר עלי – נעשה כאומר ככר זו הקדש, ואין מערבין לו בה. ולפי' הקונטרס ניחא, דאין לו לתלות בהקדשות דאסירי לדידיה ולאחריני. ויש לומר: דלא מצי לשנויי הכי משום דמסיים בה לפי שאין מערבין בהקדשות, משמע דווקא בהקדשות – אבל בקונמות מערבין:

תרומה

רבינו חננאל

מהא דתניא ר' שמעון בן אלעזר אומר מערבין לחולה ולזקן כדי מזונו ולרעבתן כדי סעודה בינונית של כל אדם. ומי א"ר שמעון בן אלעזר הכי שאם הוא משונה מרוב בני אדם מעמידין אותו במדה של בינונים והתניא רבי שמעון בן אלעזר אומר עוג מלך הבשן פתחו כמלואו. כלומר אם יש כמלואו וחישב להוציאו ממנו מטהר שאר פתחי הבית ואם לאו כל הפתחים טמאין. ודחינן התם גבי עוג משום דלא אפשר היכי נעביד ננתחי אברים אברים וניפקיה [איבעיא להו] מי פליגי עליה אי לא. ת"ש דאמר רבה בר בר חנה א"ר יוחנן עוג מלך הבשן פתחו בד' ש"מ פליגי עליה ודחי אביי התם כגון דאיכא פתחים קטנים טובא ואיכא חד דרויח ד' טפחים ודאי כי מרוח ופתח פתחא לאפוקיה מיניה בהאיך רבה מוסיף קמרוות. משום דרב אמרו מערבין בבשר חי ובביצים חיים וכמה אמר רב נחמן סיני [אמר] שתים. ומפורש בסוף הוריות רב יוסף סיני רבה עוקר הרים: ירושלמי בכל מערבין ומשתתפין חוץ מן המים ומן המלח. א"ר יסא מפני שאין הגוף ניזון מהן ר' לוי אמר שהן מין קללה. פי' מים מי המבול מלח מכת סדום. משנה בכלים פרק כ"ז. בגדי עניים אע"פ שאין להם ג' על ג' הרי אלו טמאין מדרס: מתני' הנודר מן המזון מותר במים ומלח. ואקשינן וכי כל מילי איקרו מזון (כדאהני) [כדאתני] דהא רב ושמואל דאמרי תרווייהו אין מברכין בורא מיני מזונות אלא על ה' מינין הללו חיטין ושעורין וכוסמין ושבולת שועל ושיפון ולא אתותבו חדא זימנא נימא מיהא נמי תהוי עלייהו תיובתא ופריק ר' יוחנן מתני' בנודר ואמר כל דבר הזן אסור עליו ואקשינן תוב וכי כל מילי זייני חוץ ממים ומלח והא ר' יוחנן הוה אכיל מפירות גינוסר טובא והוה משתבע דלא טעים לי זיונא ופרקינן לא תימא זיונא אלא תימא מזונא. אמר רב הונא שבועה שלא אוכל ככר זו מערבין עליו בה (ככר זו מערבין עליו בה) וככר זו עלי אין מערבין לו בה. ומקשינן עליה ומוקמינן ליה רב הונא דאמר כר' אליעזר דתניא ר' אליעזר אומר שבועה שלא אוכל זו מערבין לו בה ככר זו עלי אין מערבין לו בה ומי א"ר אליעזר הכי והתניא זה הכלל כל שהאוכל נאסר על האדם אין מערבין לו בה אוסר עצמו באוכל מערבין לו בה ר' אליעזר אומר ככר זו עלי אסורה מערבין לו בה. ככר זו הקדש אין מערבין לו בה לפי שאין מערבין בהקדשות ופריק תרי תנאי אליבא דר' אליעזר: **פיסקא** מערבין לנזיר ביין ולישראל בתרומה. תניא בית שמאי אומר אין מערבין לנזיר ביין ולא לישראל בתרומה ובית הלל אומרים מערבין. אמרו בית הל% לבית שמאי אי אתם מודים

עין משפט נר מצוה

מו א מיי' פ"ז מהל' טומאת מת הל' ח:

מז ב מיי' פ"א מהל' עירובין הל' ... סמג עשין א טוש"ע א"ח סי' שפו סעיף ז:

מח ג ד טוש"ע י"ד סי' רז סעיף יט:

מט ה ו מיי' פ"א מהל' עירובין הל' יד טוש"ע א"ח סי' שפו סעיף ח:

מסורת הש"ס

[תוספתא פ"ו]

[לפנינו איתא אסטנים וקטן]

רש"ל מ"ז

ברכות לה:

[סוף מסכת ברכות וסוף מסכת הוריות]

[פסחים קכ.]

ברכות מד.

הגהות הב"ח

(א) רש"י ד"ה בההוא מרווח וכו' הוא טמא. נ"ב ע"ל פרק הדר דף סח ע"א:

גליון הש"ס

גמ' לפי שאין מערבין בהקדשות. כעין זה שבת ד' לא ע"א וש"נ:

הגהות מהר"ב רנשבורג

[א] גמ' ואביי התם היכי ליעבד הדומי נהדמיה. נ"ב פי' בתמיה וכי נגוליה כולי האי לאתחב לחתיכות ועי' ריטב"א:

רב נסים גאון

בכבנא כנא כנא בפרותה: עוג מלך הבשן פתחו בד'. עיקרו באהלות בפ"ג (משנה ו) כזית מן המת פתחו [בטפח] והמת בית פתחיו בד' טפחים: אמר רב נחמן בר יצחק סיני אמר ב'. היינו רב יוסף וביורוא דמילתא בסוף מסכת

נ א טוש"ע א"ח סי' תטו סעיף ז:
נא ב מיי' פ"ו מהל' עירובין הלכה יז טור ש"ע א"ח סי' תטו סעיף ח:
נב ג ד מיי' פ"ו מהל' קרבן פסח הל' ח:
נג ה ו מיי' פ"א מהל' טומאת מת הל' ה:

שֶׁמְּעָרְבִין לַגָּדוֹל בְּיוֹם הַכִּפּוּרִים? אָמְרוּ לָהֶן: אֲבָל. אָמְרוּ לָהֶן: כְּשֵׁם שֶׁמְּעָרְבִין לַגָּדוֹל בְּיוֹם הַכִּפּוּרִים, כֵּן מְעָרְבִין לַנָּזִיר בְּיַיִן וּלְיִשְׂרָאֵל בִּתְרוּמָה. וּבֵית שַׁמַּאי: הָתָם – אִיכָּא סְעוּדָה הָרְאוּיָה מִבְּעוֹד יוֹם, הָכָא – לֵיכָּא סְעוּדָה הָרְאוּיָה מִבְּעוֹד יוֹם. כְּמַאן – דְּלָא כַּחֲנַנְיָה. דְּתַנְיָא, חֲנַנְיָה אוֹמֵר: כָּל עַצְמָן שֶׁל בֵּית שַׁמַּאי לֹא הָיוּ מוֹדִים בָּעֵירוּב, עַד שֶׁיּוֹצִיא מִטָּתוֹ וְכָל כְּלֵי תַּשְׁמִישָׁיו לְשָׁם. כְּמַאן אָזְלָא הָא דְּתַנְיָא: עֵירֵב בִּשְׁחוֹרִים – לֹא יֵצֵא בִּלְבָנִים, בִּלְבָנִים – לֹא יֵצֵא בִּשְׁחוֹרִים. כְּמַאן? אָמַר רַב נַחְמָן בַּר יִצְחָק: חֲנַנְיָה הִיא, וְאַלִּיבָּא דְּב"ש. וְלַחֲנַנְיָה, בִּשְׁחוֹרִים הוּא דְּלָא יֵצֵא – הָא בִּלְבָנִים יֵצֵא? הָאָמַר: עַד שֶׁיּוֹצִיא מִטָּתוֹ וּכְלֵי תַשְׁמִישָׁיו לְשָׁם! הָכִי קָאָמַר: עֵירֵב בִּלְבָנִים וְהוּצְרַךְ לִשְׁחוֹרִים – אַף בִּלְבָנִים לֹא יֵצֵא. כְּמַאן? אָמַר רַב נַחְמָן בַּר יִצְחָק: חֲנַנְיָה הִיא, וְאַלִּיבָּא דְּבֵית שַׁמַּאי. § "סוּמְכוֹס אוֹמֵר בְּחוּלִּין". § וְאִילּוּ לַנָּזִיר בְּיַיִן לָא פָּלֵיג, מַאי טַעְמָא – אֶפְשָׁר דְּמִתְשִׁיל אַנְּזִירוּתֵיהּ. אִי הָכִי תְּרוּמָה נַמִי אֶפְשָׁר דְּמִיתְשִׁיל עִילָּוֵיהּ! אִי מִתְשִׁיל עֲלָהּ – הָדְרָא לְטִיבְלָא. וְלִיפְרוֹשׁ עֲלָהּ מִמָּקוֹם אַחֵר! *לֹא נֶחְשְׁדוּ חֲבֵירִים לִתְרוֹם שֶׁלֹּא מִן הַמּוּקָּף. וְלִפְרוֹשׁ עֲלָהּ מִינַּהּ וּבַהּ! דְּלֵית בַּהּ שִׁיעוּרָא. וּמַאי פַּסְקָא? אֶלָּא סוּמְכוֹס סָבַר לַהּ כְּרַבָּנַן, *דְּאָמְרִי: כָּל דָּבָר שֶׁהוּא מִשּׁוּם שְׁבוּת – גָּזְרוּ עָלָיו בֵּין הַשְּׁמָשׁוֹת. כְּמַאן אָזְלָא הָא *דִּתְנַן: יֵשׁ שֶׁאָמְרוּ הַכֹּל לְפִי מַה שֶּׁהוּא אָדָם: מְלֹא קוּמְצוֹ מִנְחָה, וּמְלֹא חׇפְנָיו קְטֹרֶת, וְהַשּׁוֹתֶה מְלֹא לוּגְמָיו בְּיוֹם הַכִּפּוּרִים, וּבִמְזוֹן שְׁתֵּי סְעוּדוֹת לָעֵירוּב. כְּמַאן? א"ר זֵירָא: סוּמְכוֹס הִיא, דְּאָמַר: מַאי דַּחֲזֵי לֵיהּ בָּעֵינַן.[א] לֵימָא פְּלִיגָא אַדְּרַבִּי שִׁמְעוֹן בֶּן אֶלְעָזָר; דְּתַנְיָא, *ר"ש בֶּן אֶלְעָזָר אוֹמֵר: אמְעָרְבִין לַחוֹלֶה *וְלַזָּקֵן כְּדֵי מְזוֹנוֹ, וְלָרַעַבְתָּן בִּסְעוּדָה בֵּינוֹנִית שֶׁל כׇּל אָדָם! תַּרְגּוּמָא אַחוֹלֶה וְזָקֵן, אֲבָל רַעַבְתָּן – בָּטְלָה דַּעְתּוֹ אֵצֶל כׇּל אָדָם. § ב"וּלְכֹהֵן בְּבֵית הַפְּרָס". § *דְּאָמַר רַב יְהוּדָה, אָמַר שְׁמוּאֵל: גמְנַפֵּחַ אָדָם בֵּית הַפְּרָס וְהוֹלֵךְ. *רַבִּי יְהוּדָה בַּר אַמֵּי מִשְּׁמֵיהּ דְּרַב יְהוּדָה אָמַר: דבֵּית הַפְּרָס שֶׁנִּידַּשׁ טָהוֹר. § "רַבִּי יְהוּדָה אוֹמֵר אַף בֵּית הַקְּבָרוֹת". § תָּנָא: מִפְּנֵי שֶׁיָּכוֹל לָחוֹץ, וְלֵילֵךְ בְּשִׁידָּה תֵּיבָה וּמִגְדָּל. קָא סָבַר: אֹהֶל זָרוּק שְׁמֵיהּ אֹהֶל. וּבִפְלוּגְתָּא דְּהָנֵי תַּנָּאֵי; *דְּתַנְיָא: הַנִּכְנָס לְאֶרֶץ הָעַמִּים בְּשִׁידָּה תֵּיבָה וּמִגְדָּל, רַבִּי המְטַמֵּא, רַבִּי יוֹסֵי בְּרַבִּי יְהוּדָה מְטַהֵר. בְּמַאי קָמִיפַּלְגִי? מ"ס: ואֹהֶל זָרוּק – לָאו שְׁמֵיהּ אֹהֶל, וּמ"ס: אֹהֶל זָרוּק שְׁמֵיהּ אֹהֶל. *וְהָא דְּתַנְיָא, רַבִּי יְהוּדָה אוֹמֵר: מְעָרְבִין

[פ"י מ"ב פסחים צב: ברכות יט:]

רש"י

שֶׁמְּעָרְבִין לַגָּדוֹל. לְמִי שֶׁהוּא גָּדוֹל שֶׁהֵבִיא שְׁתֵּי שְׂעָרוֹת שֶׁחַיָּיב בְּעִנּוּי. וְאַע"ג דִּלְדִידֵיהּ לָא חֲזֵי לֵיהּ – הוֹאִיל וַחֲזֵי לְקָטָן שֶׁאֵינוֹ בַּר עוֹנְשִׁין: אֲבָל. אֱמֶת: מִבְּעוֹד יוֹם. שֶׁל עֶרֶב יוֹם הַכִּפּוּרִים: כְּמַאן דְּלָא כַּחֲנַנְיָה. הָא מַתְנִי' דְּמַשְׁמַע שֶׁהָיוּ בֵּית שַׁמַּאי מוֹדִין בְּעֵירוּב, דְּלָא כַּחֲנַנְיָה: עֵירֵב בִּשְׁחוֹרִים. הָיָה לָבוּשׁ שְׁחוֹרִים וְהָלַךְ וְיָשַׁב בְּסוֹף אַלְפַּיִם אַמָּה עַד שֶׁקָּנָה שָׁם שְׁבִיתָה שֶׁקִּידֵּשׁ עָלָיו הַיּוֹם, וְחָזַר לְבֵיתוֹ: כׇּל כְּלֵי תַּשְׁמִישׁוֹ. מַשְׁמַע דְּאִי לָא אַפֵּיק כׇּל צׇרְכֵי תַּשְׁמִישׁ, לָא הָוֵי עֵירוּב לְדִידֵיהּ: דְּמִיתְשִׁיל אַנְּזִירוּתֵיהּ. יִשְׁאַל לְחָכָם וְיַתִּיר לוֹ נִדְרוֹ, וִיהֵא יַיִן רָאוּי לוֹ: מִיתְשִׁיל עֲלֵיהּ. וְיִפְתַּח בַּחֲרָטָה: לֹא נִתְכַּוַּונְתִּי לְכָךְ. וּתְנַן (נזיר דף לא.): הֶקְדֵּשׁ טָעוּת אֵינוֹ הֶקְדֵּשׁ: הָדְרָא לְטִבְלָא. וְטֶבֶל לָא חֲזֵי: וְלִיפְרוֹשׁ עָלֶיהָ מִמָּקוֹם אַחֵר. לְבָתַר דְּמִתְשִׁיל עֲלַהּ וְהָדְרָא לְטִבְלָא, בֵּין הַשְּׁמָשׁוֹת בִּשְׁעַת קְנִיַּית עֵירוּב מָצֵי לְמֵימַר: פֵּירוֹת שֶׁיֵּשׁ לִי בְּבֵיתִי יְהוּ תְּרוּמָה עַל זוֹ, וְאִשְׁתַּכַּח דְּאִית לֵיהּ תַּקַּנְתָּא דְּתִתְחֲזֵי לֵיהּ: מוּקָּף. סָמוּךְ כְּמוֹ: "מַקִּיפִין בְּבוּעֵי" (חולין מו:) – שֶׁסּוֹמְכִים זוֹ לָזוֹ, וְרוֹאִין אִם דּוֹמוֹת זוֹ לָזוֹ. וּכְמוֹ: "מַקֶּפֶת וְקוֹרֵא לָהּ שֵׁם" דְּמַסֶּכֶת נִדָּה בְּפֶרֶק בַּתְרָא (דף עא:): שֶׁלֹּא מִן הַמּוּקָּף. מִדָּבָר שֶׁאֵינוֹ סָמוּךְ לוֹ בְּאוֹתוֹ כְּלִי, דְּלֶיהֱוֵי מִינֵּיהּ וּבֵיהּ: דְּלֵית לֵיהּ שִׁיעוּרָא. שֶׁמְּזוֹן ב' סְעוּדוֹת מְלוּמְצָמוֹת הָיָה, וְאִי מַפְרִישׁ תְּרוּמָה מִינֵּיהּ כׇּל דְּהוּ – בָּצַר לֵיהּ שִׁיעוּר עֵירוּב: וּמַאי פַּסְקָא. בִּתְמִיָּה, כְּלוֹמַר: מַאי הַאי תֵּירוּצָא? וְכִי פַּסְקָא תַּנָּא לְמִילְּתֵיהּ דְּאֵין אָדָם נוֹתֵן עֵירוּבוֹ אֶלָּא בִּמְצוּמְצָם, דְּנָקֵט סְתָם בְּמִילְּתֵיהּ הָכִי: סָבַר לַהּ כְּרַבָּנַן. דִּפְלִיגִי עֲלֵיהּ דְּרַבִּי, לְקַמָּן בְּפִירְקִין (דף לד:): גָּזְרוּ עָלָיו בֵּין הַשְּׁמָשׁוֹת. כִּשְׁבַּת עַצְמָהּ, וְהַגְבָּהַת תְּרוּמָה שְׁבוּת הִיא, וְכֵיוָן דְּמֵעִיקָּרָא לֹא תַּקְנָהּ, וּבָעֵית לְמֵימַר אִי בָּעֵי הָוֵי חֲזֵי לְהַהוּא שַׁעְתָּא דְּמִתְשִׁיל עֲלַהּ כׇּל מָקוֹם שֶׁהִיא וְהָדְרָה לְטִבְלָא. וַהֲדַר אָמַר: תְּרוּמָתָהּ בִּצְפוֹן שֶׁבָּהּ, וּמַעֲשֵׂר רִאשׁוֹן בִּדְרוֹמָהּ. וְכֵן כּוּלָּם. אִם כֵּן מְתַקֵּן לֵיהּ בֵּין הַשְּׁמָשׁוֹת וְקָעָבַר אַשְּׁבוּת, וּקְנִיַּית עֵירוּב כְּשֶׁזֶּה נִכְנָס וְזֶה יוֹצֵא: יֵשׁ שֶׁאָמְרוּ. יֵשׁ דְּבָרִים שֶׁאָמְרוּ שִׁיעוּרָן לְפִי מַה שֶּׁהוּא אָדָם. וְאֵין שִׁיעוּרָן שָׁוֶה בַּכֹּל: מְלֹא חׇפְנָיו קְטֹרֶת. בְּיוֹם הַכִּפּוּרִים: תַּרְגּוּמָא. לְהָא דְּתָלֵי שִׁיעוּרָא בָּאָדָם עַצְמוֹ – אַחוֹלֶה וְזָקֵן וּלְקוּלָּא, וְלֹא אַרַעַבְתָּן וּלְחוּמְרָא דִּבְטֵלָה דַּעְתּוֹ: מְנַפֵּחַ אָדָם בֵּית הַפְּרָס. שָׂדֶה שֶׁנֶּחְרַשׁ בָּהּ קֶבֶר, דְּכוּלָּהּ סְפֵיקָא מִשּׁוּם עֲצָמוֹת הִיא, וַעֲצָמוֹת בְּלֹא בָּשָׂר אֵינוֹ מְטַמֵּא בְּאֹהֶל, וּכְשֶׁמְּנַפֵּחַ לִפְנֵי רַגְלָיו, אִם יֵשׁ שָׁם עֶצֶם גָּדוֹל – נִרְאֶה מֵאֵלָיו, וְעֶצֶם קָטָן – נִרְאֶה בִּנְפִיחָה, וְאֵינוֹ מַסִּיטוֹ בְּרַגְלָיו: שֶׁנִּידַּשׁ. בִּדְרִיסַת רַגְלֵי בְּנֵי אָדָם: טָהוֹר. שֶׁכְּבָר נִידַּשׁוּ עֲצָמוֹת שֶׁבּוֹ וְנִפְחֲתוּ מִכַּשְּׂעוֹרָה: אֹהֶל זָרוּק. אֹהֶל הַמִּיטַּלְטֵל: שְׁמֵיהּ אֹהֶל. וְחוֹצֵץ בֵּינוֹ לְבֵין הַטּוּמְאָה: אֶרֶץ הָעַמִּים. מְטַמְּאָה בְּאֹהֶל: שִׁידָּה. מֶרְכֶּבֶת נָשִׁים, עֲגָלָה עֲשׂוּיָה כְּקוּפְסָא: מִגְדָּל. מִשְׁטי"ר: אֹהֶל זָרוּק לָאו שְׁמֵיהּ אֹהֶל. וְכׇל שֶׁאֵינוֹ אֹהֶל אֵינוֹ חוֹצֵץ: שְׁמֵיהּ אֹהֶל. וְחוֹצֵץ. וּבִגְדוֹלָה עָסְקִינַן, שֶׁמַּחְזֶקֶת מ' סְאָה בְּלַח שֶׁהֵם כּוֹרַיִים בְּיָבֵשׁ. דְּאִי קְטַנָּה – כְּלִי הִיא וּמְקַבֶּלֶת טוּמְאָה וְלָא חָיְילָא. וְרַבָּנַן דְּמַתְנִי' כְּרַבִּי סְבִירָא לְהוּ, וּבֵין לְרַבִּי יְהוּדָה וּבֵין לְרַבָּנַן כְּסוּמָכוֹס סְבִירָה לְהוּ, דְּאָמַר: מִידֵּי דַּחֲזֵי לֵיהּ לְמֵיכְלֵיהּ בְּהַהִיא שַׁעְתָּא בָּעֵינַן: מְעָרְבִין

תוספות

תרומה נמי אפשר דמתשיל[ב] ולא מצי לאוקמה בתרומה ביד כהן דתו לא מצי לאתשולי עליה, כדאמר בפרק "הנודר מן הירק" (נדרים דף נט.) – מדקתני בחולין, משמע דווקא בחולין. אבל בתרומה, אפי' ביד ישראל לא: ולפרוש עליה ממקום אחר. השתא ס"ד דכל דבר שהוא משום שבות לא גזרו עליו בין השמשות. ואף על גב דרבה דאית ליה הכנה אמרינן בפירקא (דף לח:) דתחילת היום קונה עירוב, וכוותיה קיימא לן – מ"מ מותר לתקן הטבל, דלא גזרו עליו בין השמשות עד שתהא לילה ניכרת וידוע. והא דתנן ב"במה מדליקין" (שבת דף לד.) דספק חשיכה אי מעשרין את הודאי – והיינו כרבנן דר' אפ"ה קס"ד דהך מתני' דהכא – אתיא כרבי, משום דאיכא משניות טובא דמוקי להו התלמוד לקמן כרבי. וא"ת: אם כן, אמאי קתני מתני' אבל לא בטבל, הא חזי לתקוני בין השמשות! ואין לומר דההיא אתיא דלא כרבי, מדפריך לקמן (דף לד:) רישא רבי וסיפא רבנן, ולא פריך רישא וסיפא רבנן ומציעתא רבי! ועוד: דפריך לקמן אבל לא בטבל פשיטא! משמע דליכא מאן דפליג, ומיהו, °איכא למימר: הא דפריך פשיטא – היינו משום דמרישא שמעינן לה, דקתני: מערבין בדמאי דמשמע אבל לא בטבל. וי"ל: דאינו מועיל מה שראוי לתקנו אלא במידי דחזי השתא לשום אדם, כגון תרומה דחזיא לכהנים. ותדע, דאמר לעיל דאין מערבין בהקדשות – אף על גב דאפשר לאיתשולי עלייהו: לא נחשדו חברים. אע"ג דמשום כבוד שבת שרי, כדאמר ב"האשה רבה" (יבמות דף לג.) – היינו שצריך לאכול אותן פירות בשבת, אבל הכא מיירי דאין צריך לאוכלן בשבת. ואע"ג *דאין מערבין אלא לדבר מצוה – לא התירו לתרום שלא מן המוקף אלא לכבוד שבת, ולא לצורך מצוה אחרת: אלא סומכוס סבר לה כרבנן. ואם תאמר: מהאי טעמא נמי נזיר לא יערב ביין, כיון דשבות הוא לשאול על הנדרים בשבת, כדאמרינן פרק "מי שהחשיך" (שבת דף קמ.)! וי"ל: דלצורך שבת נשאלין, כדאמרינן התם והאי הוי צורך שבת – שיהיה מותר לשתות יין בשבת: תרגומא אחולה ואזקן. וא"ת: ולוקמא נמי כרבנן דסומכוס. "והכל לפי מה שהוא אדם" – אחולה ואזקן. דלרבנן מערבין חולה וזקן כדי מזונן, דמקילי טפי מסומכוס דאמרי: אפילו במידי דלא חזי ליה מערבין משום דחזי לאחריני, כל שכן דמערבין במידי דחזי ליה אע"ג דלא חזי לאחריני. וי"ל: דלרבנן אין מערבין לחולה ולזקן כדי מזונן, אלא בסעודה בינונית. דהא כיון דלא בעו מידי דחזי ליה – אם כן לחולה וזקן מערבין נמי אפי' במאכל דלא חזי להו, אלא לבריא – ובמידי דלא חזי לדידהו ע"כ שיעורו בסעודה בינונית, וא"כ גם במידי דחזי להו בעינן שיעור סעודה בינונית. דאין סברא שיהא לרבנן ב' שיעורין לחולה ולזקן. א"נ הכל לפי מה שהוא אדם – משמע נמי לאפוקי ישראל בתרומה. והא דנקט תרגומא אחולה ואזקן – הוא הדין דהוה מצי למינקט אישראל בתרומה, אלא נקט חולה וזקן משום דרשב"א איירי ביה: ומר סבר אהל זרוק שמיה אהל. דוקא כשמונח הוי אהל, אבל בשעת זריקה, אפילו רבי יוסי ברבי יהודה מטמא. דבאותה שעה לא חשיב אהל כלל, מידי דהוה אעוף פורח ואטלית המנפנפת, דתנן באהלות (פ"ח מ"ה) דאין מביאין ואין חוצצין. והכי נמי קתני

[לקמן לא. פי"ח]

רבינו חננאל

שמערבין לאדם גדול. פי' כיון שהוא אדם גדול בשנים חייב במצות. ביוה"כ מערבין לו ערובי תחומין ועירובי חצרות אע"פ שאסורה לו אכילה ביוה"כ וכשם שמערבין לגדול ביוה"כ ואין בו ביום אכילה כך מערבין לנזיר ביין ולישראל בתרומה ואע"פ שהן אסורין בהן וב"ש התם בענין גדול ביוה"כ בשעה שמערבין לו בה איכא סעודה הראויה לו הני נזיר ביין וישראל בתרומה ליכא בשעת עירוב סעודה ראויה להם. הא דמערבין לגדול דלא כחנניא (ותניא) [דתניא] חנניא אומר כל עצמן של ב"ש לא היו מודים בעירוב עד שיוציא מטתו וכל כלי תשמישו לשם. מאן תנא דהא דתניא עירב בלבנים והוצרך בשחורים אף בלבנים לא יצא חנינא היא ואליבא דב"ש: סומכוס אומר בחולין ואילו לנזיר ביין לא פליגי למאי משום דיין חזי לשאר בנ"א שאינן נזירים תרומה נמי חזיא לכהנים אלא נזיר משום דאפשר דמיתשיל על נזירותו ושרו ליה. תרומה נמי אפשר דמיתשיל עלה ונפקא לחולין ואמרינן תרומה אי מיתשיל עלה הדרא לטבלא ועדיין היא אסורה לישראל ואמרינן אפשר (עליו) [לאפרושי עלה] דהא תרומה ממקום אחר נשארה זו כולה חולין ודחינן לא יתכן להוציא עליה תרומה ממקום אחר דלא נחשדו חברים לתרום שלא מן המוקף. פי' אין תורמין על פירות שהן בכאן מפירות שהן מונחין במקום אחר ואינן מוקפין. כלומר ההיקף שמקיפין על כולן נמצא כאילו נוגעין אלו באלו ונמצא תורם מצד זו לצד זו ואמרינן אפשר דמיתשיל עלה ומפריש ממנה והנשארת ראויה היא לאכילתו כמו היין לנזיר לאחר שישאל על נזירותו ודחינן לא פליג סומכוס אלא בתרומה שהיא מעוטה שאם ישאל עליה ותחזור לטבלא ויפריש ממנה תרומה לא תשאר בה מזון ב' סעודות. ואקשינן אמאי פסקה כלומר דחאה לתרומה (או) [מן] העירוב לגמרי ושנה בחולין בלבד היה לו לומר בר"א בתרומה מועטת אבל בתרומה מרובה שאם יוציא תרומתה ממנה ותשאר ממנה מזון ב' סעודות מערבין לו בה. אלא סומכוס סבר לה כרבנן דפליגי על ר' בשמועה שאחרי שמועה (ניתנו) [דנתנו] באילן כו' דאכל דבר שהוא משום שבות גזרו עליו בין השמשות ותקנת הטבל (משום) [שבות] הוא כמאן אולא [הא] דתנן יש שאמרו הכל לפי מה שהוא אדם. קומץ מנחה ומלא חפניו קטורת והשותה מלא לוגמיו ביוה"כ ובמזון ב' סעודות לעירוב סומכוס (אי) [היא] דאמר מאי דחזי ליה בעינן דאי רבנן כיון דחזי ליה לאחריני אע"ג דלא חזי ליה שפיר דמי: לימא דלא כר"ש בן אלעזר דאמר מערבין לחולה ולזקן כדי מזונו. ולרעבתן בבינוני של כל אדם. ואמרינן אפילו תימא מתני' דקתני במסכת כלים פרק ט"ז יש שאמרו הכל לפי מה שהוא אדם וקתני בה במזון ב' סעודות לעירוב אחולה ואזקן קתני כר' אלעזר בר' שמעון ותני ר' אלעזר בר' שמעון בהני כדי מזונו אבל רעבתן אפי' האי תנא מודה [משערינן] בבינוני משום דבטלה דעתו אצל כל אדם. לכהן בבית [הפרם] ואמרינן בית הפרם מנפח אדם מנפח ומפריח עפר תיחות. וכיון שנגלה עפר ולא ראה עצם תחתיו טהור וכן אם נידש אותו בית הפרם כיון שנדרם ברגלי העוברין והשבין אלו היה שם עצם ודאי נדרם ונתמעט [ונטהר] המקום: **מתני'** רבי יהודה אומר אפי' בבית הקברות כו'.

מסורת הש"ס

[לקמן לב. גיטין ל: חולין ז: נדה עא:]
לקמן לד:
כלים פי"ז מי"א ע"ש [לקמן מח.]
[תוספ' פ"ו]
[לפנינו איתא אסטנים וקטן]
כתובות כח: פסחים צב: ברכות יט: נדה נז: מו"ק ה: בכורות כט. חגיגה כה:
גיטין ח: חגיגה כה. נזיר נה.
רש"ל גורס תנא ר"י אומר

גליון הש"ס

תוס' ד"ה ולפרוש וכו' איכא למימר הא דפריך פשיטא היינו משום דמרישא שמעינן. עי' תוס' פסחים כ' ע"ב ד"ה עבר זמנו:

רב נסים גאון

מסכת ברכות ובסוף מסכת הוריות רב יוסף סיני ורבה עוקר הרים: **לא** נחשדו חברים לתרום שלא מן המוקף עיקר דילה במשנה במסכת חלה בפרק א' (משנה ט) החלה והתרומה חייבין עליה מיתה וחומש ואין ניטלין מן הטהור על הטמא אלא מן המוקף וזה הדבר בתרומה גדולה אבל בתרומת מעשר לא כמא דמפרש במשנת ביכורים בפרק ב' (מ"ה) תרומת מעשר לביכורים בשתי דרכים ולתרומה בב' דרכים ניטלת מן הטהור על הטמא ושלא מן המוקף כביכורים ובגמ' דבני מערבא בפרק (א') [ב'] דתרומות גרסי' כל הדברים למדין ומלמדין תרומת מעשר מלמדת ואינה למידה תרומת מעשר לימדה על תרומה גדולה

הגהות מהר"ב רנשבורג [א] לימא פליגי אדרבי שמעון בן אלעזר. נ"ב מתני' דאמרה הכל לפי מה שהוא אדם אדרשב"א דלא משער לרעבתן בדידיה ומשני תרגמא אחולה וזקן אמרה המשנה לפי מה שהוא ולא ארעבתן דבטלה דעתו וכו' וכ"כ ריטב"א: [ב] תוס' ד"ה תרומה וכו' ולא מצי לאוקמי בתרומה ביד כהן וכו'. נ"ב לפמ"ש בנדרים שם בפי' הרא"ש בשם הר"א מיץ לק"מ ישוב"ה ודו"ק:

מְעָרְבִין לְכֹהֵן טָהוֹר בִּתְרוּמָה טְהוֹרָה בַּקֶּבֶר. הֵיכִי אָזֵיל — בְּשִׁידָּה תֵּיבָה וּמִגְדָּל. וְהָא כֵּיוָן דְּאַחְתָּא אִיטַּמְיָא לָהּ! בְּשֶׁלֹּא הוּכְשְׁרָה, אוֹ שֶׁנִּילוֹשָׁה בְּמֵי פֵּירוֹת. וְהֵיכִי מַיְיתִי לָהּ? בִּפְשׁוּטֵי כְּלֵי עֵץ דְּלָא מְקַבְּלֵי טוּמְאָה. וְהָא קָא מַאֲהִיל! דְּמַיְיתֵי לָהּ אֲחוֹרֵיהּ. אִי הָכִי מ"ט דְּרַבָּנַן? קָסָבְרִי: אָסוּר לִקְנוֹת בַּיִת בְּאִיסּוּרֵי הֲנָאָה. *מִכְּלָל דְּר' יְהוּדָה סָבַר: מוּתָּר?! קָסָבַר: מִצְוֹת לָאו לֵיהָנוֹת נִיתְּנוּ, אֶלָּא *הָא דְּאָמַר רָבָא: מִצְוֹת לָאו לֵיהָנוֹת נִיתְּנוּ, לֵימָא כְּתַנָּאֵי אֲמָרָהּ לִשְׁמַעְתֵּיהּ? אָמַר לָךְ רָבָא: אִי סְבִירָא לְהוּ דְּאֵין מְעָרְבִין אֶלָּא לִדְבַר מִצְוָה — דְּכוּלֵּי עָלְמָא מִצְוֹת לָאו לֵיהָנוֹת נִיתְּנוּ. וְהָכָא בְּהָא קָמִיפַּלְגִי; מ"ס: אֵין מְעָרְבִין אֶלָּא לִדְבַר מִצְוָה, וּמ"ס: מְעָרְבִין אֲפִילּוּ לִדְבַר הָרְשׁוּת. אֶלָּא הָא *דְּאָמַר רַב יוֹסֵף: אֵין מְעָרְבִין אֶלָּא לִדְבַר מִצְוָה — לֵימָא כְּתַנָּאֵי אֲמָרָהּ לִשְׁמַעְתֵּיהּ? אָמַר לָךְ רַב יוֹסֵף: דְּכוּלֵּי עָלְמָא אֵין מְעָרְבִין אֶלָּא לִדְבַר מִצְוָה, וּדְכוּלֵּי עָלְמָא מִצְוֹת לָאו לֵיהָנוֹת נִיתְּנוּ, וּבְהָא קָמִיפַּלְגִי; מ"ס: *כֵּיוָן דְּקָנָה לֵיהּ עֵירוּב — לָא נִיחָא לֵיהּ דְּמִינְטְרָא, וּמ"ס: [א]נִיחָא לֵיהּ דְּמִינְטְרָא, דְּאִי אִיצְטְרִיךְ אָכֵיל לֵיהּ.§

מתני' [ב]מְעָרְבִין בִּדְמַאי, וּבְמַעֲשֵׂר רִאשׁוֹן שֶׁנִּטְּלָה תְּרוּמָתוֹ, וּבְמַעֲשֵׂר שֵׁנִי וְהֶקְדֵּשׁ שֶׁנִּפְדּוּ, וְהַכֹּהֲנִים *בְּחַלָּה. אֲבָל לֹא בְּטֶבֶל, וְלֹא בְּמַעֲשֵׂר רִאשׁוֹן שֶׁלֹּא נִטְּלָה תְּרוּמָתוֹ, וְלֹא בְּמַעֲשֵׂר שֵׁנִי וְהֶקְדֵּשׁ שֶׁלֹּא נִפְדּוּ.§ **גמ'** *"דְּמַאי", הָא לָא חֲזִי לֵיהּ! מִיגּוֹ דְּאִי בָּעֵי מַפְקַר לְהוּ לְנִכְסֵיהּ וְהָוֵי עָנִי, וַחֲזוּ לֵיהּ — הַשְׁתָּא נַמִי חֲזִי לֵיהּ. *דִּתְנַן: מַאֲכִילִין אֶת הָעֲנִיִּים דְּמַאי וְאֶת

[רש"י]

מְעָרְבִין לְכֹהֵן טָהוֹר בִּתְרוּמָה טְהוֹרָה בַּקֶּבֶר. וְכ"שׁ בְּחוּלִּין, דְּאִי נַמִי מִיטַּמּוּ — חֲזוּ לֵיהּ, אֶלָּא אֲפִי' בִּתְרוּמָה, דְּאִי מִטַּמְּאָה לָא חַזְיָא לֵיהּ — אֶפְשָׁר לְמֶיעֱבַד תַּקַּנְתָּא, כִּדְמְפָרֵשׁ וְאָזֵיל. וְדַוְקָא נָקַט טָהוֹר בִּטְהוֹרָה, אֲבָל בִּטְמֵאָה — לָא, דְּלָא חַזְיָא לֵיהּ לָא לְכֹהֵן טָמֵא וְלָא לְכֹהֵן טָהוֹר, וְכֹהֵן טָמֵא בִּטְהוֹרָה נַמִי לָא, דְּלָא חַזְיָא לֵיהּ: הֵיכִי אָזֵיל בְּשִׁידָּה תֵּיבָה וּמִגְדָּל וְהָא כֵּיוָן דְּאַחְתָּא מִיטַּמְיָא לֵיהּ. כְּלוֹמַר: נְהִי דְּלְר' יְהוּדָה אֲפִילּוּ בְּבֵית הַקְּבָרוֹת אִיכָּא תַּקַּנְתָּא לְמֵיזַל בְּשִׁידָּה תֵּיבָה וּמִגְדָּל, וְכ"שׁ קֶבֶר יְחִידִי שֶׁיָּכוֹל לַעֲמוֹד אֶצְלוֹ. אֶלָּא מִיהָא, תְּרוּמָה מִכִּי מַנְחָהּ הָתָם מִטַּמְּאָה בְּאָהֳלוֹ שֶׁל קֶבֶר: בְּמֵי פֵּירוֹת. שֶׁאֵין מַכְשִׁירִין: וְהֵיכִי מַיְיתִי לָהּ. לְאוֹכְלָהּ, דְּהָא רַבִּי יְהוּדָה רָאוּי לְאוֹכְלוֹ בָּעֵי מִדְּנָקַט טָהוֹר בִּטְהוֹרָה — וְלָא אַכְשַׁר טָמֵא בִּטְהוֹרָה מִשּׁוּם דְּחַזְיָא לְאַחֲרִינֵי. וְעוֹד: מִדְּתָנֵי בְּמַתְנִיתִין "לָחוּץ וְלֶאֱכוֹל": בִּפְשׁוּטֵי כְּלֵי עֵץ דְּלָא מְקַבְּלֵי טוּמְאָה. אֲבָל בְּמִידֵּי דִּמְקַבֵּל טוּמְאָה — לָא, דְּה"ל כְּלֵי טְמֵא מֵת, שֶׁהוּא אַב הַטּוּמְאָה, דְּמִיטַּמֵּא מֵחֲמַת אֹהֶל וּמְטַמֵּא לֵיהּ לָאָדָם, וְטָמֵא אָסוּר בִּתְרוּמָה טְהוֹרָה, וְקָאֵי עֲלֵיהּ בְּמִיתָה. וְאַע"ג דְּלֵית בֵּיהּ פּוֹתֵחַ טֶפַח, דְּמַיְיתֵי לֵיהּ אֲחוֹרֵיהּ כִּדְמְפָרֵשׁ לְקַמָּן, קי"ל (שבת דף יז.) בִּי"ח דָּבָר, שֶׁכָּל הַמִּטַּלְטְלִין מְבִיאִין אֶת הַטּוּמְאָה עַל עַצְמָן, כְּשֶׁהֶאֱהִילוּ עַל מֵת בְּכָל שֶׁהֵן, וּמְטַמֵּא לֵיהּ אָדָם הָאוֹחֲזוֹ, וְתוּ לָא חַזְיָא לֵיהּ תְּרוּמָה: וְהָא קָא מַאֲהִיל. קס"ד כְּשֶׁיֵּשׁ בַּכְּלִי פּוֹתֵחַ טֶפַח, אוֹ בְּהֶקֵּיפוֹ טֶפַח, וְגָזְרוּ עַל הָאָדָם הַנּוֹשְׂאוֹ בְּעוֹבֵי הַמַּרְדֵּעַ בְּ"אֵילּוּ הַשַּׁבָּת" (שם): דְּמַיְיתֵי לֵיהּ *אֲחוֹרֵיהּ. דִּכְלִי שֶׁאֵין בְּחוּדּוֹ טֶפַח לָאו אֹהֶל הוּא: אִי הָכִי מ"ט דְּרַבָּנַן. בְּקֶבֶר יְחִידִי. נְהִי דְּאִיפְּלְגוּ בְּמַתְנִיתִין בְּבֵית הַקְּבָרוֹת, וְלָא סְבִירָא לְהוּ דְּתֶיהֱוֵי חֲצִיצָה בְּאוֹהֶל זָרוּק — אֲבָל הָכָא יָכוֹל לַעֲמוֹד עַל שְׂפָתוֹ, וִידִיחֶנּוּ אֶצְלוֹ: אָסוּר לִקְנוֹת בַּיִת בְּאִיסּוּרֵי הֲנָאָה. בְּקֶבֶר. וְהָא הֲנָאָה הִיא, דְּמִשְׁתַּמְּרֵי בֵּיהּ לְמֵיפַק חוּץ לַתְּחוּם, וְכָל תַּשְׁמִישֵׁי הַמֵּת אֲסוּרִין בַּהֲנָאָה. דְּנָפְקָא לָן בְּסַנְהֶדְרִין (דף מז:) מִ"וַתָּמָת שָׁם מִרְיָם", וְגָמַר "שָׁם" "שָׁם" מֵעֶגְלָה עֲרוּפָה. וַאֲפִילּוּ בְּיִשְׂרָאֵל נַמִי אָסְרֵי רַבָּנַן, וְהָא דְּתָנֵי כֹּהֵן — לְהוֹדִיעֲךָ כֹּחוֹ דְּרַבִּי יְהוּדָה: מִצְוֹת לָאו לֵיהָנוֹת נִתְּנוּ. וְאֵין מְעָרְבִין אֶלָּא לִדְבַר מִצְוָה, לָלֶכֶת לְבֵית הָאֵבֶל אוֹ לְבֵית הַמִּשְׁתֶּה כִּדְלְקַמָּן: הָא דְּרָבָא. בְּמַסֶּכֶת רֹאשׁ הַשָּׁנָה (דף כח.): תּוֹקְעִין בְּשׁוֹפָר שֶׁל עוֹלָה: רַבָּנַן סָבְרִי מְעָרְבִין אֲפִילּוּ לִדְבַר הָרְשׁוּת. וְהִלְכָּךְ הֲנָאָה הִיא: הָא דְּרַב יוֹסֵף. בְּ"כֵּיצַד מִשְׁתַּתְּפִין" (דף פב.): כֵּיוָן דְּקָנָה לֵיהּ עֵירוּב. בֵּין הַשְּׁמָשׁוֹת, תּוּ לָא אִיכְפַּת לֵיהּ בִּנְטִירוּתָא. וְעַד קְנִיַּית עֵירוּב, אִי נַמִי נִיחָא לֵיהּ — לָאו הֲנָאָה הִיא, דְּמִשּׁוּם מִצְוָה הוּא: **מתני'** בִּדְמַאי. כְּכָּר שֶׁלְּקָחוֹ מֵעַם הָאָרֶץ וְלֹא הִפְרִישׁ מִמֶּנּוּ דְּמַאי: וְלֹא בְּמַעֲשֵׂר שֵׁנִי וְהֶקְדֵּשׁ שֶׁלֹּא נִפְדּוּ. וְאַע"ג דְּמָצֵי פָּרֵיק לְהוּ, הַשְׁתָּא מִיהָא לָא מְפָרֵק: **גמ'** אַכְסַנְיָא

[תוספות]

קתני בברייתא דמייתי בנזיר בפרק "כהן גדול" (דף נה.), ר' יוסי ברבי יהודה אומר: תיבה שהיתה מלאה כלים. זרקה באהל המת – טמאה, ואם היתה מונחת – טהורה. וא"ת: למ"ד אהל זרוק לא שמיה אהל, מה היו מועילים דלתות שתחת התינוקות מפני קבר התהום, כדאמר בפרק "הישן" (סוכה ד' כא.), הא אהל זרוק הוא! ואומר ר"ת: שיסבור שלא היו מביאין דלתות, אלא שוורים שכריסם רחבה, כדא"ר יהודה התם. והשוורים רחמנא קרינהו אהל, דכתיב: "ובעצמות וגידים תסוככני" (איוב י), ורשב"א מפרש: דלתות על גב שוורים לכ"ע הוי אהל, דתנן באהלות (פ"ו מ"א): אדם וכלים נעשים אהל לטמא אבל לא לטהר. פירוש: מביאין טומאה, ואין מפסיקין בין טומאה שתחתיהם לכלים שעליהם. ולא איירי באדם וכלים שעושים עצמן אהלים, אלא כדמפרש התם: כגון נדבך של אבנים או דלתות על האדם או על הכלים, אפילו כלי גללים וכלי אבנים וכלי אדמה. ומשמע דסבר דאהל זרוק לא שמיה אהל, דאי שמיה אהל – כשנתן הנדבך על גבי הכלים אמאי לא יהיה חשוב אהל להפסיק? והא כלי עצמו נעשה אהל להפסיק כשאינו מקבל טומאה, כגון שידה תיבה ומגדל למ"ד שמיה אהל. וקתני סיפא: נתון על גבי אבנים שאינם כלים, או על דבר שיש בו רוח חיים, דומיא דשוורים בפרק "הישן" (סוכה ד' כא.): טומאה תחתיו – כלים שעליו טהורין כו'. משמע דבענין זה הוי אהל לכ"ע: **היכי אזיל** בשידה תיבה ומגדל. פירש: נהי דלר' יהודה איכא תקנה אפילו בבית הקברות, על ידי שידה תיבה ומגדל, ובקבר יחידי נמי שגזרו *שתופס ד' אמות סביביו – משום הרחקה, כ"ש דמלי אזיל בשידה תיבה ומגדל. ולקמן פריך: מאי טעמייהו דרבנן בקבר יחידי? נהי דבבית הקברות גדול לא הוי חצילה, הכא דלא הויא אלא הרחקה – אמאי פליגי? הא מלי אזיל בשידה תיבה ומגדל, דאין לך הרחקה גדולה מזו: **בשלא** הוכשרה. ולספרים דגרסי או שנילושה במי פירות – ה"פ: בשלא הוכשרה – כגון שעירב בפירות, או בפת שנילושה במי פירות: **בפשוטי** כלי עץ. משמע דלא מקבלי טומאה אפילו מדרבנן, וכן תנן במס' כלים (פ"ב מ"א), ומייתי לה בפ"ק דשבת (ד' טז.): כלי עץ וכלי זכוכית – פשוטיהם טהורים ומקבליהם טמאין. וע"כ פשוטין טהורים אפי' מדרבנן, דכלי זכוכית אפילו יש להן בית קבול – אין להן טומאה אלא מדרבנן, כדאמר בשבת. וכן משמע בכמה דוכתי, דטהורין פשוטי כלי עץ אפי' מדרבנן. וקשה: דב"המוכר בית" (ב"ב דף סו.) אומר: שאני פשוטי כלי עץ למדרבנן, גבי דף של נחתומין. והתם לא איירי בהנך דחזו למדרסות – דהנהו מקבלי טומאה דאורייתא, דכל המטמא מדרס מטמא טומאת מת, כדילפינן בב"ק פ"ב (דף כה.) ק"ו מפכים קטנים.

(*)ורשב"א פירש התם: דאין לחוש, כיון דמסקנא לא קיימא הכי, דמוקי לה בדף של מתכת. ור"י מפרש: דכלי עץ שהם רחבים כעין דף, ורגילין להניח עליהם ספלים – גזרו רבנן עלייהו טומאה, משום דדמו למקבלי כלי עץ. אבל פשוטי כלי עץ שאינם רחבים – טהורין אפילו מדרבנן. וי"מ: דדף של נחתומים וכיוצא בזה שהם שימושי אדם, ומשמשין שימושי אדם – גזרו רבנן בהן טומאה, כדמוכח בתורת כהנים בפרשת "ביום השמיני", דממעט סולם וקולב מ"כלי עץ" ולא כל כלי עץ, ומרבה שולחן וטבלא ודולבקי מ"כל". וקאמר: ומה ראית? ת"ל: "שק". מה שק מיוחד, שהם תשמישי אדם ומשמשי תשמישי כו'. וע"כ כשאין ראויין למדרס איירי, מדלא נקט כסא ומטה. ועוד: דמ"וכל המשכב" ה"ל לרבויינהו. וכשאין להן בית קבול נמי איירי, מדלא קאמר מה שק מיטלטל מלא וריקן. אלמא: מקבלי טומאה מדרבנן. ואף על גב דדריש מקרא – אסמכתא בעלמא הוא, ועיקר דרשה דרשינן ל"מה שק מטלטלין מלא וריקן". וכמה מדרשות יש בת"כ דהוי רק אסמכתא. ותדע, דבפרק "שתי הלחם" (מנחות דף צו:) אמר רבי יוחנן: לדברי האומר מסגרת למטה היתה, פי' ברגלים ולא בשולחן – טבלא המתהפכת טמאה, כדדרשינן מ"על השולחן הטהור" – מכלל דאיכא שהוא טמא. ולדברי האומר למעלה היתה – טבלא המתהפכת תיבעי לך. דשל מקדש מקבל טומאה – לפי שיש לו בית קיבול, וצריך קרא דהטהור מכלל שהוא טמא שהיו מגביהין אותו לעולי רגלים, שלא תאמר עשוי לנחת הוא. והשתא אמאי תיבעי, תיפשוט מדרשה דת"כ! אלא ש"מ: אסמכתא בעלמא היא, כדפרישית. והא דמשמע התם דטבלא המתהפכת עדיפא לקבל טומאה דאורייתא משאר פשוטי כלי עץ – היינו כדפ"ה, משום דראוי להשתמש מב' לדדין:

דמאי הא לא חזי ליה. נראה דלסומכוס דווקא פריך. דלרבנן, אף על גב דלא חזי ליה – הא חזי לעניים. ואם תאמר: ולסומכוס, הא חזי ליה, דמלי לאפרושי מיניה וביה אפילו לרבנן דרבי, דספק חשיכה מעשרין הדמאי! ויש לומר: דמשמע ליה מתניתין אפילו ליכא אלא שתי סעודות מצומצמות, דמסתמא מתניתין איירי בכל ענין, ולעיל (דף ל:) נמי דפריך מאי פסקא – משום דמשמע ליה דמתניתין איירי אפילו ביתר משתי סעודות. ומיהו בפרק "מפנין" (שבת דף קכז:) פריך נמי הכי גבי טלטול, ומשני כי הכא: מיגו דמפקר כו'. והתם הוה מלי למימר דחזי לעניים, אלא משום דהתם מיבעי ליה לשנויי כי הכא, ובפרק "כל שעה" (פסחים דף לה:) ובפרק "שלשה שאכלו" (ברכות דף מז.):

(*) [נ"ל ורשב"ם]

רשב"א

[עין משפט נר מצוה]

נד א מיי' פ"ו מהל' עירובין הלכה יז טוש"ע א"ח סימן תט סעיף א:

נה ב מיי' פ"א מהלכות עירובין הלכה טז:

רבינו חננאל

תנא מפני שיכול לחוץ בשידה תיבה ומגדל. פי' אלו עשויות לנחת היושב בתוכן והמת תחתיהן. ואילו מאהיל עליו היושב בתוכן טהור. שאלו חוצצין בפני הטומאה ואמרינן קסבר האי תנא אהל זרוק שמיה אהל כדתניא הנכנס לארץ העמים בשידה תיבה ומגדל ר' מטמא קסבר אהל זרוק [לאו] שמיה אהל ואינו חוצץ בפני הטומאה וכאלו הוא מאהיל עליהן לפיכך היושב בתוכן טמא ר' יוסי ב"ר יהודה (מטמא) [מטהר] קסבר אהל זרוק שמיה אהל לפיכך היושב בתוכם טהור ואע"פ שאפשר לאלו שידה תיבה ומגדל להיזרק ממקום למקום א"ר יוסי ב"ר יהוד' אהל הן וחוצצין ואין הטומאה בוקעת ועולה בהן: **תניא** ר' יהודה אומר מערבין לכהן טהור ותרומה טהורה בקבר. אמרינן כהן טהור היכי עייל בקבר והא קא מטמא. ופרקינן עייל בשידה תיבה ומגדל כר' יוסי בריה. ואקשינן תרומה זו כיון שנתנה על הקבר נטמאת ופרקינן ככר זו של תרומה במי פירות נילושה ומי פירות אין מכשירין וכיון שלא הוכשרה (להו) [לאו] בת אטמויי היא. תוב אמרינן היכי מעייל לה בשידה תיבה ומגדל אי דמפיק ידיה ושקיל לה מן הקבר הא איטמא. ושנינן דמייתי לה בפשוטי כלי עץ דלא מקבלי טומאה והא מאהיל זה כלי עץ הפשוט (יניח אחר) [אם יניח צדו אחד] עליו וצדו אחר על הקבר ותנן כל המטלטלין המאהילין על הקבר מביאין טומאה על האדם הנושאין בעובי המרדע והוא טפח ושנינן דמייתי לה להאי ככר אחודיה דהאי כלי עץ הפשוט

רב נסים גאון

שניטלת מן המוקף והיא ניטלת שלא מן המוקף ומניין שתרומת מעשר ניטלת שלא מן המוקף מכל מעשרותיכם אפילו אחד ביהודה ואחד בגליל: **אלא** סומכוס סבר לה כרבנן דאמר דבר שהוא משום שבות גזרו עליו בין השמשות. עיקר דיליה בהא ברייתא דבהדין פירקא (דף לג) פליגו בה רבי ורבנן דאמרינן עלה מאי רבי ומאי רבנן דתניא נתנו באילן למעלה מי' טפחים כו' וחכמים אומרים בכל מקום שאסור ליטלו אין עירובו עירוב: **בית** הפרס. כבר פירשנוהו קודם לכן וה"נ עצם כשעורה שמטמא כבר פירשנוה קודם לכן במסכת שבת: **שנילושה** במי פירות. עיקרו הוא שאמר הכתוב (ויקרא יא) מכל האוכל אשר יאכל אשר יבא עליו מים יטמא (תורת כהנים) אין לי אלא מים הטל והיין והשמן והדם והדבש והחלב מניין ת"ל וכל משקה יכול מי תותים ומי רמונים ושאר כל מיני פירות שיש להם שם לווי ועוד ממה שאמר הכתוב אחר כן וכי יותן מים על זרע ואמרו בפירושו הרי זה בא ללמד על השרץ שלא יטמא את הזרעים אלא לאחר הכשר מים מניין לעשות שאר משקין כמים ת"ל מים מים אמורין למעלה ומים אמורין למטה מה מים אמורין למעלה עשה בהן שאר משקין כמים אף מים האמורין למטה נעשה בהן שאר משקין כמים וזו ראיה על כל המשקין שנידונין בהכשר מים ומאי היא ז' המשקין כמו שפירשום בכאן כך פירשום עוד במשנת מכשירין בפ' (מכשירין פ"ו) ז' משקין הן הטל והיין והשמן והדם וחלב ודבש דבורים ואמרו תולדות למים היוצא מן העין ומן האוזן ובתוספתא שבת (פרק ט) גרסי מניין לדם שהוא משקה שנא' (במדבר כג) ודם חללים ישתה ומניין ליין שהוא משקה שנאמר (דברים לב) ודם ענב תשתה חמר מניין לדבש שהוא משקה שנאמר (שם) ויניקהו דבש מסלע מניין לשמן שהוא משקה שנאמר (ישעיה כה) משתה שמנים משתה שמרים מניין לחלב שהוא משקה שנאמר (שופטים ד) ותפתח את נאד החלב ותשקהו מניין לטל שהוא משקה שנאמר (שם ו) וימץ טל מן הגזה מלא הספל מים מניין לדם נדה שהוא משקה שנאמר (ויקרא כ) מקור דמיה ואומר (זכריה יג) ביום ההוא יהיה מקור נפתח מנין לדמעת עין שהוא משקה שנאמר (תהלים פ) ותשקמו בדמעות שליש ואומר (ירמיה ט) ועפעפינו יזלו מים כל אלו שהכתובין הם שקרויים משקה אבל מי פירות יצאו מכלל אלו המשקין ואינם מכשירין את הזרעים לטומאה ואיתא נמי בתוספ' מכשירין (פרק ג) מי פירות מטמאין ולא מכשירין ובתו' עוקצים עיסה שנילושה במי פירות טהורה שאין לך שמחובר לאוכלין אלא משקין ובמס' דחלה (פ"ב משנה ב) עיסה שנילושה במי פירות חייבת בחלה ונאכלת בידים מסואבות ובמס' תרומות (פ"ה מ"ב) נמי שנינו וחכ"א תעלה ותאכל ניקודים או קליות או תלוש במי פירות ואיתא נמי בתלמוד בבורות בפרק (דף כב) ובב"ב בפ' לא יחפור (יט) איתא מדאקשינן ותיפוק ליה דהוה ליה דבר שהוא מקבל טומאה ואינו חוצץ ופרקינן בשנילושה במי פירות: **היכי** מייתי לה בפשוטי כלי עץ דלא מקבלי טומאה. עיקר דילה במשנה במס' כלים בפ"ב כלי עץ כלי עור כלי עצם כלי זכוכית פשוטיהם טהורין ומקבליהן טמאים ובתוס' שחיטת חולין (פ"א) גולמי כלי עץ טמאים ופשוטיהן (טמאין) [טהורין] ואיתא בסוף גמ' דהכל שוחטין (דף כה): **עיקר** דברי רבא לאו ליהנות ניתנו במס' ר"ה בפ' ראוהו ב"ד (דף כח) ובמס' חולין בפ' כיסוי הדם (דף פט) בסופו ועיקר דברי רב יוסף אין מערבין אלא לדבר מצוה בתחילת פ' כיצד משתתפין (פב) האשה

[מסורת הש"ס]

ר"ה כח. | לקמן פב. | [לקמן עח:] | ס"א ובתרומה | נ"ל אחוריה | ברכות מז. שבת קכז: פסחים לה: סוכה לה: | דמאי פ"ג מ"א לעיל יז: | [נזיר נה.]

גליון הש"ס

גמ' מכלל דר"י סבר מותר. מצות לאו ליהנות. עי' לקמן דף עח ע"ב תוס' ד"ה אשירה: תו' ד"ה ומ"ס אהל זרוק וכו' עודי אבן חגיגה דף כה ע"ב ד"ה היכי אזיל וכו' דלא הוי אלא הרחקה. עי' ב"ב דף קח ע"א תוס' ד"ה ותנו:

וְאֶת אַכְסַנְיָא(א) דְּמַאי. אָמַר רַב הוּנָא: תָּנָא, בֵּית שַׁמַּאי אוֹמְרִים: אֵין מַאֲכִילִין אֶת הָעֲנִיִּים דְּמַאי, וּבֵית הִלֵּל אוֹמְרִים: מַאֲכִילִין אֶת הָעֲנִיִּים דְּמַאי.§ "וּבְמַעֲשֵׂר רִאשׁוֹן שֶׁנִּטְּלָה כו'".§ פְּשִׁיטָא! לָא צְרִיכָא שֶׁהִקְדִּימוֹ בַּשִּׁבֳּלִין, וְנִטְּלָה מִמֶּנּוּ תְּרוּמַת מַעֲשֵׂר וְלֹא נִטְּלָה מִמֶּנּוּ תְּרוּמָה גְּדוֹלָה. וּכְדְר' אַבָּהוּ אָמַר רֵישׁ לָקִישׁ, דְּאָמַר ר' אַבָּהוּ אָמַר רֵישׁ לָקִישׁ: *מַעֲשֵׂר רִאשׁוֹן שֶׁהִקְדִּימוֹ בַּשִּׁבֳּלִין — פָּטוּר מִתְּרוּמָה גְּדוֹלָה. שֶׁנֶּאֱמַר: °"וַהֲרֵמוֹתֶם מִמֶּנּוּ תְּרוּמַת ה' מַעֲשֵׂר מִן הַמַּעֲשֵׂר", מַעֲשֵׂר מִן הַמַּעֲשֵׂר אָמַרְתִּי לְךָ, וְלֹא תְּרוּמָה גְּדוֹלָה וּתְרוּמַת מַעֲשֵׂר מִן הַמַּעֲשֵׂר! א"ל רַב פַּפָּא לְאַבַּיֵי: *אִי הָכִי אֲפִילּוּ הִקְדִּימוֹ בַּכְּרִי נַמִּי! א"ל: עָלֶיךָ אָמַר קְרָא:(ג) °"מִכֹּל מַעְשְׂרוֹתֵיכֶם תָּרִימוּ אֵת כָּל תְּרוּמַת ה'". וּמָה רָאִיתָ? הַאי אִידְגַּן, וְהַאי — לָא אִידְגַּן.§ "וּבְמַעֲשֵׂר שֵׁנִי וְהֶקְדֵּשׁ שֶׁנִּפְדּוּ".§ פְּשִׁיטָא! לָא צְרִיכָא, שֶׁנָּתַן אֶת הַקֶּרֶן וְלֹא נָתַן אֶת הַחוֹמֶשׁ. וְקמ"ל: דְּאֵין הַחוֹמֶשׁ מְעַכֵּב.§ "אֲבָל לֹא בְּטֶבֶל".§ פְּשִׁיטָא! לָא צְרִיכָא, בְּטֶבֶל טָבוּל מִדְּרַבָּנַן, וּכְגוֹן שֶׁזְּרָעוֹ בְּעָצִיץ שֶׁאֵינוֹ נָקוּב.§ "וְלֹא בְּמַעֲשֵׂר רִאשׁוֹן שֶׁלֹּא נִטְּלָה תְּרוּמָתוֹ".§ פְּשִׁיטָא! לָא צְרִיכָא, שֶׁהִקְדִּימוֹ בַּכְּרִי וְנִטְּלָה מִמֶּנּוּ תְּרוּמַת מַעֲשֵׂר וְלֹא נִטְּלָה מִמֶּנּוּ תְּרוּמָה גְּדוֹלָה. מַהוּ דְּתֵימָא כִּדְאָמַר לֵיהּ רַב פַּפָּא לְאַבַּיֵי, קמ"ל כִּדְשַׁנֵּי לֵיהּ.§ "וְלֹא בְּמַעֲשֵׂר שֵׁנִי וְהֶקְדֵּשׁ שֶׁלֹּא נִפְדּוּ".§ פְּשִׁיטָא! לָא צְרִיכָא, שֶׁפְּדָאָן וְלֹא פְּדָאָן כְּהִלְכָתָן: מַעֲשֵׂר שֶׁפְּדָאוֹ עַל גַּב *) אֲסִימוֹן, וְרַחֲמָנָא אָמַר °"וְצַרְתָּ הַכֶּסֶף" — *כֶּסֶף שֶׁיֵּשׁ עָלָיו צוּרָה. הֶקְדֵּשׁ — שֶׁחִילְּלוֹ עַל גַּב קַרְקַע, דְּרַחֲמָנָא אָמַר: *"וְנָתַן הַכֶּסֶף וְקָם לוֹ".§

מתני' [ב]הַשּׁוֹלֵחַ עֵירוּבוֹ בְּיַד חֵרֵשׁ שׁוֹטֶה וְקָטָן, אוֹ בְּיַד *מִי שֶׁאֵינוֹ מוֹדֶה בָּעֵירוּב — אֵינוֹ עֵירוּב. וְאִם אָמַר לְאַחֵר לְקַבְּלוֹ מִמֶּנּוּ — הֲרֵי זֶה עֵירוּב.§ **גמ'** וְקָטָן לֹא?! וְהָאָמַר רַב הוּנָא: קָטָן גּוֹבֶה אֶת הָעֵירוּב! לָא קַשְׁיָא; כָּאן — [ג]בְּעֵירוּבֵי תְחוּמִין, כָּאן — [ד]בְּעֵירוּבֵי חֲצֵירוֹת.§ "אוֹ בְּיַד מִי שֶׁאֵינוֹ מוֹדֶה בָּעֵירוּב".§ מַאן? אָמַר רַב חִסְדָּא: כּוּתַאי.§ "וְאִם אָמַר לְאַחֵר לְקַבְּלוֹ הֵימֶנּוּ — הֲרֵי זֶה עֵירוּב".§ וְלֵיחוּשׁ דִּילְמָא לָא מַמְטֵי לֵיהּ? כִּדְאָמַר רַב חִסְדָּא: בְּעוֹמֵד וְרוֹאֵהוּ, [ה]ה"נ: בְּעוֹמֵד וְרוֹאֵהוּ. וְלֵיחוּשׁ דִּילְמָא לָא שָׁקֵיל מִינֵּיהּ! כִּדְאָמַר רַב יְחִיאֵל: חֲזָקָה *שָׁלִיחַ עוֹשֶׂה שְׁלִיחוּתוֹ, הָכָא נַמִּי: חֲזָקָה שָׁלִיחַ עוֹשֶׂה שְׁלִיחוּתוֹ. וְהֵיכָא אִיתְּמַר דְּרַב חִסְדָּא וְרַב יְחִיאֵל? אַהָא אִתְּמַר; דְּתַנְיָא: [ו]*נְתָנוֹ לַפִּיל וְהוֹלִיכוֹ, לַקּוֹף וְהוֹלִיכוֹ — אֵין זֶה עֵירוּב. וְאִם אָמַר לְאַחֵר לְקַבְּלוֹ הֵימֶנּוּ — הֲרֵי זֶה עֵירוּב. וְדִילְמָא לָא מַמְטֵי לֵיהּ? אָמַר רַב חִסְדָּא: בְּעוֹמֵד וְרוֹאֵהוּ. וְדִילְמָא לֹא מְקַבֵּל לֵיהּ מִינֵּיהּ? אָמַר רַב יְחִיאֵל: חֲזָקָה, שָׁלִיחַ עוֹשֶׂה שְׁלִיחוּתוֹ. אָמַר רַב נַחְמָן: [ז]בְּשֶׁל תּוֹרָה — אֵין חֲזָקָה שָׁלִיחַ עוֹשֶׂה שְׁלִיחוּתוֹ, בְּשֶׁל

*) [כסף שאין עליו צורה מלשון סומא שאין לו עינים. ערוך]

אַכְסַנְיָא. חַיָּילוֹת מַלְכֵי יִשְׂרָאֵל שֶׁמַּטִּילִין אוֹתָן עַל בְּנֵי הָעִיר לְזוּנָן, וְהָווּ לְהוּ כַּעֲנִיִּים, שֶׁהֲרֵי אֵינָן בְּבָתֵּיהֶן: שֶׁהִקְדִּימוֹ בַּשִּׁבֳּלִין. לִתְרוּמָה גְּדוֹלָה. דְּמִן הַתּוֹרָה הַתְּרוּמָה קוֹדֶמֶת לַמַּעֲשֵׂר, דְּ"רֵאשִׁית" קְרָאָהּ רַחֲמָנָא, וּמִן הַמּוּתָר הוּא נוֹתֵן מַעֲשֵׂר רִאשׁוֹן לַלֵּוִי, וְעַכְשָׁיו הֶעֱרִים הַלֵּוִי וְקִדְּמוֹ כְּדֵי שֶׁלֹּא יְחַסְּרֶנּוּ כֹּהֵן אֶחָד מִנ' בַּמַּעֲשֵׂר: מִכֹּל מַעְשְׂרוֹתֵיכֶם. בַּלְוִיִּם כְּתִיב: תָּרִימוּ אֶת(ג) כָּל תְּרוּמַת ה'. אֲפִילּוּ תְּרוּמָה גְּדוֹלָה: וּמָה רָאִיתָ. דְּמוֹקְמַתְ קְרָא דְּחִיּוּב בְּהִקְדִּימוֹ בַּכְּרִי, וּקְרָא דִּפְטוּר בְּהִקְדִּימוֹ בַּשִּׁבֳּלִים: הַאי. הִקְדִּימוֹ בַּכְּרִי אִידְגַּן, וְכֵיוָן דְּנִקְרָא "דָּגָן" נַעֲשָׂה טֶבֶל לִתְרוּמָה, כִּדְכְתִיב (דברים יח): "רֵאשִׁית דְּגָנְךָ": וְהַאי לָא אִידְגַּן. וְכִי שַׁקְלֵיהּ לֵוִי — עֲדַיִין לֹא הָיָה טָבוּל לִתְרוּמָה: וְלֹא בְּמַעֲשֵׂר רִאשׁוֹן שֶׁלֹּא נִטְּלָה תְּרוּמָתוֹ. קס"ד בִּתְרוּמַת מַעֲשֵׂר קָאָמַר, וְקָא פָּרֵיךְ: פְּשִׁיטָא: לֹא נִצְרְכָה שֶׁהִקְדִּימוֹ בַּכְּרִי. וְהָא תְּרוּמָה דְּקָאָמַר — הַיְינוּ תְּרוּמָה גְּדוֹלָה, דַּחֲזֵי לְאַפְרוֹשֵׁי מִינֵּיהּ מִקַּמֵּי דְּלִיפְרְשֵׁי מַעֲשֵׂר מִינֵּיהּ, קָאָמַר: כִּדְאָמַר לֵיהּ רַב פַּפָּא לְאַבַּיֵי. לְעֵיל בִּשְׁמַעְתִּין: אֲסִימוֹן. = מָעָה בְּלֹא צוּרָה, פנטו"ן בְּלַעַ"ז: וְנָתַן הַכֶּסֶף. בְּמַקְדִּישׁ שָׂדֵהוּ כְּתִיב: "וְיָסַף חֲמִישִׁית כֶּסֶף עֶרְכְּךָ" (ויקרא כז): **מתני'** שֶׁאֵינוֹ מוֹדֶה בָּעֵירוּב. כּוּתִי: **גמ'** גּוֹבֶה אֶת הָעֵירוּב. מִבְּנֵי חָצֵר, וּמְעָרֵב עֲלֵיהֶם: עֵירוּבֵי חֲצֵירוֹת. דְּעָרוּבֵי רְשׁוּתַיְיהוּ בְּעָלְמָא הוּא, הִלְכָּךְ מִמֵּילָא מִיעֲרַב וְאע"ג דְּאֵין מַעֲשֵׂה הַקָּטָן כְּלוּם — לֹא אִיכְפַּת לָן. כִּדְתְנַן לְקַמָּן (דף עא.): בַּעַל הַבַּיִת שֶׁהָיָה שׁוּתָּף עִם שְׁכֵנָיו — א"צ לְעָרֵב. אֲבָל עֵירוּבֵי תְחוּמִין — אַקְנוּיֵי שְׁבִיתָה הוּא, וְקָטָן לָא אַלִּים לְמִיקְנֵי: *לְקַבֵּל הֵימֶנּוּ. קוֹדֶם שֶׁיַּגִּיעַ שָׁם, וְהַמְקַבְּלוֹ עֵירֵב עָלָיו: דִּילְמָא לָא מַמְטֵי לֵיהּ. קָטָן עַד לְיָדוֹ שֶׁל מְקַבֵּל: בְּעוֹמֵד וְרוֹאֵהוּ. עַד שֶׁמּוֹלִיכוֹ: וְדִלְמָא הַהוּא לָא שָׁקֵיל מִינֵּיהּ. וְלֹא מְעָרֵב לֵיהּ, אַף עַל פִּי שֶׁהִבְטִיחוֹ: קוֹף וּפִיל. פְּעָמִים שֶׁהֵן מְלוּמָּדִים: בְּשֶׁל תּוֹרָה אֵין חֲזָקָה כו'. כְּלוֹמַר: לֹא סָמְכִינַן אַחֲזָקָה, עַד דְּחָזֵינַן דַּעֲבַד: בְּשֶׁל

(ד) **רשב"א** גרים "מכל מתנותיכם תרימו" דאיירי בתרומה גדולה. אבל "מכל מעשרותיכם *תרימו" בתרומת מעשר קמיירי:

ומה ראית. מפרש ריב"א: מה ראית לחלק בין הקדימו בכרי להקדימו בשבלין, אימא בהקדימו בכרי נמי פטור מתרומה גדולה הואיל ולא הוקבע עדיין למעשר. וקרא ד"מכל מתנותיכם" — אתי לחיובי בראה פני הבית, אבל לא יתכן לפרש האי ומה ראית, נימא איפכא לחייב הקדימו בשבלין ולפטור הקדימו בכרי — דאין זו סברא:

וקא משמע לן דאין חומש מעכב. וא"ת: אמאי לא פשיט מהכא בפרק "הזהב" (ב"מ דף נד.) דאין החומש מעכב? וי"ל: משום דאיכא למידחי, ולאוקומי כשנתן החומש. ואף על גב דמילתא דפשיטא היא — אגב מעשר ראשון נקט מעשר שני:

שפדאו על גב אסימון. פ"ה: מעה בלא צורה, והא דמחללין מעשר שני על אסימון, לר' דוסא טפי ממעות הניתנין לסימן לבית המרחץ בפרק "הזהב" (ב"מ דף מז:) — היינו משום דאסימון עשוי במשקל ורוחב כראוי, ואינו מחוסר אלא צורה, ובדבר קל יטביעו כמה מהם. וקשה לר"ת, דבפרק "במה אשה" (שבת דף סה.) אמר: אי משום צורתא — ליעבד לה פולסא. משמע דיש עליו צורה. וב"הזהב" אמר: מאי אסימון — פולסא! וי"ל לפ"ה דקרי אסימון לכל דבר שאינו עשוי כהלכתו, או של כסף ואין עליו צורה, או של עץ ויש עליו צורה:

ונתן הכסף וקם לו. ואף על גב דבעלמא שוה כסף ככסף — הכא איכא מיעוטא, דדרשינן האי קרא בכלל ופרט וכלל, וכן משמע בבכורות, דתנן בפרק "יש בכור" (דף נא.): אין פודין לא בעבדים כו' ולא בהקדשות. ומפרש בגמרא: ולא הקדש בכל אלו. וגבי בכור דריש בכלל ופרט. וא"ת, דאמרינן במעילה (דף יד.): בונין בחול ואח"כ מקדישין, אלמא מחללין מעות הקדש על הבנין! וי"ל: דלענין זה חשיב תלוש ולבסוף חברו תלוש. אי נמי: התם חשיב תלוש טפי, כיון דאי לא קדיש עומד לתלישה:

כאן בעירובי תחומין. פ"ה: עירובי תחומין — אקנויי שביתה הוא, וקטן לא אליס למיקני. וקשה: דבפרק בתרא דמעילה (דף כא.) אמר, גבי שלא ביד חרש שוטה וקטן: עשה שליחותו — בעל הבית מעל. ופריך: והא לאו בני שליחות נינהו! ומשני: עשאוהו כההיא דנתנו על הפיל והוליכו, על הקוף והוליכו, הרי זה עירוב. אלמא: איתעביד שליחותייהו, הכא נמי איתעביד שליחותיהו. אלמא: אפילו על הקוף ופיל הרי זה עירוב! ועוד, לפירושו, משמע דאי הוה אליס למיקני — הוה מהימני ליה, והוי עירוב. וא"כ, היכי פריך בסמוך ודילמא לא ממטי, ודלמא לא שקיל מיניה? דכיון דמהימני ליה — ממטי ליה, ואי לא שקלי מיניה יחזור! לכן נראה לפרש: דעירובי תחומין הואיל ואסמכוה אקרא — חמירי, ולא הימנוהו רבנן, ולא הוי עירוב אם לא בעומד ורואהו. וההיא דמעילה דנתנו על הקוף דהוי עירוב — מיירי נמי בעומד ורואהו. דכשאינו עומד ורואהו — לא הוי עירוב, כדתניא בשמעתין: נתנו לקוף והוליכו — אין זה עירוב. ולכך קתני במעילה על הקוף — משמע דאינו סומך על חכמתו. והכא בשמעתין קתני לקוף — משמע דסומך עליהם. °ואף על גב דבפ"ק דפסחים (דף ד:) אמר גבי בדיקת חמץ המניהו רבנן בדרבנן — היינו בבית שלהם, דרמי עלייהו, אבל שליחות — איכא למימר דמייאשי. וכעין זה פ"ה לקמן גבי חזקה על חבר, ובירושלמי נמי מחלק בין אמר לא וערב, בין אמר לא ואערב לך:

וליחוש דילמא לא שקיל מיניה כדאמר רב יחיאל. וא"ת: מאי קא פריך ומאי קא משני? הא מדיוקא דמתני' שמעינן דחזקה שליח עושה שליחותו, דקתני: ביד חרש שוטה וקטן — אין זה עירוב, הא ביד פיקח — הרי זה עירוב! וי"ל: דהתם סומך עליו לגמרי. אבל הכא, שאמר להם לקבל מהם, דלא סמיך עליו בכל השליחות — ממנע ולא עביד. משום הכי פריך, ומשני: דאפילו הכי חזקה שליח עושה שליחותו: **והיכא** איתמר דרב חסדא וכו'. וא"ת: אמאי לא איתמר מילתייהו אמתניתין דהכי נמי צריך לשנויי אמתניתין! י"ל: דס"ל דטעם דמתניתין דאין זה עירוב — לאו משום דלא מהימני, אלא משום דלא אלימי למיקני(ה) תחומין. והשתא לא קשה מידי אמתניתין, דמהימני להו, °ובריית' דמעילה*) דקתני אפי' לפיל הוי עירוב — לא שמיע להו. ומתניתין דמעילה איכא לשנויי שינויא אחרינא דמשני התם — דעשאוהו כמעטן של זיתים, דהא דניחא ליה חשיב כמעשה:

[ע"ש כא. בתוס' ד"ה נתנו וכו'].

רג

*) דברי ירושלמי אלו שייך למעלה קודם ד"ה מערבין. **) אולי צ"ל כר"א אמר ר"ל שהקדימו בשיבולין וכבר פירשנוה כנ"ל ואולי פירש כן בפ"ו על ברכות דף מ"ז ע"ב:

עין משפט נר מצוה

נו א מיי' פ"ג מהל' תרומות הל' יג טור י"ד סימן שלא:

נז ב ג מיי' פ"ו מהל' עירובין הלכה כב סמג עשין א טוש"ע א"ח סימן תט סעיף ח:

נח ד מיי' פ"א מהל' עירובין הלכה טז סמג שם טוש"ע א"ח סי' שסו סעיף י:

נט ה ו מיי' פ"ו שם הלכה כב סמג שם טוש"ע א"ח סימן תט סעיף ח:

ס ז מיי' פ"ד מהלכות תרומות הלכה ו:

רבינו חננאל

דלית ביה עובי המרדע אי הכי לית ליה אורחא לטמאה אמאי אסרי רבנן ואמרינן רבנן סברי אסור בית שביתה באיסורי הנאה שנמצא נהנה מהן ואקשינן וכי ר"י שרי ליהנות מאיסורי הנאה ופרקינן דכ"ע אסרי ליה (פת) [בית] באיסורי הנאה והכא בדרבא מצות לא ליהנות ניתנו פליגי. דברי רבא מפורשין בשחיטת חולין פרק כסוי הדם בסופו וכ"ע כרב יוסף סבירא להו דאמר אין מערבין אלא לדבר מצוה דדייקינן ממתני' כל איש ילך לבית האבל ולבית המשתה. רבי יהודה סבר הקונה שביתה בעירוב במקום איסורי הנאה שרי דלא נמצא נהנה מן האיסור דעירוב זה מצוה היא. ואית ליה הא דרבא דאמר מצות לא ליהנות ניתנו. גרסי' בר"ה פרק ראוהו ב"ד וכל ישראל בענין התוקע בשופר של עולה ובשופר של שלמים ואסיק' הדר אמר רבא אחד זה ואחד זה מצות לאו ליהנות ניתנו. רבנן לית להו דרבא. ואקשינן נימא דרבא תנאי היא. ושנינן לא כ"ע אית להו לרבא ובדרב יוסף פליגי דאמר בתחלת פרק כיצד משתתפין בתחומין אין מערבין אלא לדבר מצוה ואקשינן תוב נימא הא דרב יוסף תנאי היא ושנינן לא כ"ע אית להו דרב יוסף הכא בהא פליגי ר' יהודה סבר כיון דקנה ליה עירוב אסוחי מסחא דעתא מההוא ככר. ואי אבד ליה לא אכפת ליה הלכך לאו הנאה אית ליה כד מנטרא בקבר ולפיכך שרי ולא מתהני מאיסורי הנאה ולא מידי. ורבנן סברי אפ"ה בתר דקנה עירוב ואיתעבידנא לה מצוה ניחא ליה דמינטר האי ככר בקבר ואי אצטריך לה אכיל לה דאשתכח דקא מתהני מן הקבר בתר דאתעביד לה מצות עירוב הלכך אסרי: מערבין בדמאי דהא חזי ליה כב"ה דאמרו מאכילין את העניים דמאי ואי בעי מפקר לכולהו נכסי וחזו ליה. *) ירושלמי לכהן בבית הפרס ועתה אפי' בבית הקברות ראוי לעבור על השבות. וכ"ש ראוי הוא ליכנס בשידה תיבה ומגדל ולעשות לו חור פחות מטפח (ולחטוב ובקיסם) [ולתחוב בקיסם] ולאכול. ובמעשר ראשון כר' **) וכבר פירשנוה השולח עירובו ביד חש"ו אינו עירוב אוקימנא בעירובי תחומין אבל בעירובי חצרות קי"ל כרב הונא דאמר קטן גובה את העירוב מאי אינון

[ברכות מז. שבת קכז: פסחים לה: ביצה יג:]

תמורה ה:

[ר"ן שייך לעיל במשנה]

[ב"מ מז:]

[עי' בתוספות שבת קכז:]

[לקמן סח:]

[נזיר יב. גיטין סד. חולין יב.]

[מעילה כא. ע"ש]

תורה אור: במדבר יח | שם יח | דברים יד

הגהות הב"ח

(א) גמ' ואת האכסניא דמאי ולמאי רב הונא: (ב) שם אמר קרא תרימו את תרומת ה' מכל מעשרותיכם ומה ראית: (ג) רש"י ד"ה מכל וכו' בלוים כתיב תרימו תרומת ה' מכל מעשרותיכם אפילו תרומה גדולה: (ד) תוס' ד"ה רשב"א גרים וכו' דלא צריך להתחיל תרימו את תרומת ה' מכל מעשרותיכם בתרומה גדולה כצ"ל ותיבת תרימו נמחק: (ה) ד"ה והיכא וכו' דלא אלימי למיקני שביתה והשתא:

גליון הש"ס תום' ד"ה כאן. ואע"ג דבפ"ק דפסחים. בתו' כתבתי לתמוה דהתם מעידים שבדקו ומאמינים להם בדרבנן וה"נ י"ל דאם באו ואמרו הנחנו העירוב נאמנים אבל הכא הא לא מיירי מזו אלא שלחם לערב דבזה אפשי' בשולח לגדול צריכים לבא עליו מדין חזקה שליח עושה שליחותו וזה חזקה לא מהמנינן בקטן וכו'. **תום'** ד"ה והיכא ובריית' דמעילה וכו'. לא הוו צריכי לזה כיון דעל מתניתין לחוד הא צריך לשנויי דהא מכח צריך לבריית' דמעילה מש"ה דייקו יותר על דך בריית' לחודיה. מ"ש במהרש"א לא ידענא וכו'. בעניי לא ידענא מאי קושיא הא י"ל דזהו מפשט פשיטא הא השי"ס דקוף ופיל לא מהימני:

בשל סופרים — חזקה, שליח עושה שליחותו. ורב ששת אמר: אחד זה ואחד זה — חזקה, שליח עושה שליחותו. א"ר ששת: מנא אמינא לה — דתנן: *[א]משקרב העומר הותר החדש מיד. *והרחוקים מותרים מחצות היום ואילך. והא חדש דאורייתא הוא, וקתני: הרחוקים מותרין מחצות היום ואילך. לאו משום חזקה שליח עושה שליחותו? ורב נחמן: התם כדקתני טעמא, לפי שיודעין שאין בית דין מתעצלין בו. ואיכא דאמרי, אמר רב נחמן מנא אמינא לה — דקתני טעמא: לפי שיודעין שאין ב"ד מתעצלין בו. ב"ד הוא דלא מתעצלין בו, הא שליח מתעצל בו. ורב ששת אמר לך: ב"ד — עד פלגיה דיומא, שליח — כולי יומא. אמר רב ששת: מנא אמינא לה — [ב]דתניא: האשה שיש עליה לידה או זיבה מביאה מעות ונותנת בשופר, וטובלת ואוכלת בקדשים *לערב. מאי טעמא — לאו משום דאמרינן חזקה שליח עושה שליחותו? ורב נחמן — התם כדרב שמעיה, *דאמר רב שמעיה: חזקה אין ב"ד של כהנים עומדים משם עד שיכלו כל מעות שבשופר. אמר רב ששת: מנא אמינא לה — דתניא: האומר לחבירו "צא ולקט לך תאנים מתאנתי" — אוכל מהן עראי, ומעשרן ודאי. "מלא לך כלכלה זה תאנים מתאנתי" — אוכל מהן עראי, ומעשרן דמאי. [ג]במה דברים אמורים — בעם הארץ, אבל בחבר — אוכל ואינו צריך לעשר, דברי רבי. רבן שמעון בן גמליאל אומר: במה דברים אמורים — בעם הארץ, אבל בחבר — אינו אוכל עד שיעשר, לפי *שלא נחשדו חברים לתרום שלא מן המוקף. אמר רבי: נראין דברי מדברי אבא, מוטב שיחשדו חברים לתרום שלא מן המוקף, ולא יאכילו לעמי הארץ טבלים. עד כאן לא פליגי אלא דמר סבר נחשדו, ומר סבר לא נחשדו. אבל כולי עלמא — חזקה, שליח עושה שליחותו. ורב נחמן: התם כדרב חנינא חוזאה, *דאמר רב חנינא חוזאה: חזקה הוא על חבר שאינו מוציא דבר שאינו מתוקן מתחת ידו. [[ג"ז, ט. סוטה מח.]] אמר מר: במה דברים אמורים — בעם הארץ, אבל בחבר — אוכל ואינו צריך לעשר, דברי רבי. האי עם הארץ דקאמר ליה למאן? אילימא דקאמר לעם הארץ חבריה — מעשרן דמאי? מי ציית?! אלא בעם הארץ דקאמר ליה לחבר. אימא סיפא: נראין דברי מדברי אבא, מוטב שיחשדו חברים לתרום שלא מן המוקף ואל יאכילו לעמי הארץ טבלין. עמי הארץ מאי בעי התם? אמר רבינא: [ד]רישא בעם הארץ שאמר לחבר, סיפא בחבר שאמר לעם הארץ וחבר אחר שומעו. רבי סבר [[נ"ל לא ימתור]]

רש"י

בשל סופרים. סמכינן אחזקת שליח, דאי נמי לא עביד — לא חמיר איסורא, כגון עירובי תחומין: הרחוקין. מירושלים, שאינן יודעין אם עדיין קרב העומר — מותרין מחצות היום. אלמא: סמכינן אכהנים שהן שלוחינו, ועבדי שליחותייהו ומקרבי ליה: התם כדתני טעמא כו'. ואפי' דינא סמכינן, אבל אשליח בעלמא — לא: שליח כולי יומא. נטריה, ומכי מטא לאורתא סמכינן עליה דודאי לא עבר היום עד שעשה הבטחתו: מעות. דמי שתי תורים: ונותנת בשופר. שכתוב עליו קינין, ששם נותנין מעות קיני חובה. כדתנן בשקלים (פ"ו משנה ה): י"ג שופרות כו': וטובלת. דתנן (חגיגה כא.): האונן והמחוסר כפורים צריכין טבילה לקודש: ואוכלת בקדשים לערב. אלמא: חזקה כהנים עושין שליחותן, הואיל והדבר תלוי בהן שהנשים סומכות עליהן שלא יעבור היום עד שיקנו קינין בכל מעות שבאותו שופר, ויקריבו, כדי שלא יאכלו הנשים קדשים בטומאת הגוף, *שהוא בכרת: ורב נחמן. אמר לך: הא נמי חזקה דבי דינא הוא: צא ולקט לך תאנים מתאנתי. ולא נתן מדה ללקיטתו: אוכל. המלקט מן הנלקטות: עראי. בלא מעשר, וכשבא לאכלן קבע — מעשרן ודאי מעשרות ודאין תרומה גדולה, וכל דיני הפרשה. שאין ספק לומר שמא בעל הבית עישר עליהן ממקום אחר, דהא לא ידע כמה ליקט: אבל אמר לו מלא לך כלכלה זו. הואיל ונותן זה יודע כמה לוקט, יש לומר שמא זה הנותן חושש שמא יסמוך עליו שיתן לו דבר היתר, ומעשר עליהן ממקום אחר. הילכך, מלקט זה אוכל מהן עראי בלא מעשר, וכשבא לאוכלן קבע — אין צריך לעשרן ודאי, אלא דמאי[(א)] יפריש, ויאכל הוא בעצמו המעשרות של לוי ושל עני, כשאר לוקח פירות מעם הארץ שמחזיקן בספק מעושרין. אף אלו ספק מעושרין הן, ותורת דמאי עליהן: בד"א. דספק הן, ודמאי מיהא בעי לאפרושי: בעם הארץ. שהנותן עם הארץ הוא, ואינו חושש ב"לפני עור": אבל בחבר. ודאי מעושרין הן ואין צריך לעשרן אפילו דמאי: רשב"ג אומר בד"א. דסגי בדמאי — בזמן שהנותן עם הארץ, וחשוד לתרום שלא מן המוקף: אבל. היה הנותן חבר לא יאכל קבע הלוקט, עד שיעשרם מעשרות ודאי. רבי בנו של רשב"ג הוה: ואל יאכילו לעמי הארץ טבלים. לקמן מפרש הי ניהו עם הארץ: לא נחשדו. לתרום שלא מן המוקף. הא לאו הכי — ודאי הוה סמכינן על בעל הבית זה, שהוא שליח על כך שמוטל עליו לעשר מה שהוא נותן, ואל יאכיל איסור לעם הארץ: מתחת ידו. דהואיל ופירי דידיה הוא, עליה דידיה רמי, וחייש ל"לפני עור". אבל שליח דקביל עליה מחבירו — איכא למימר דמייאש. ולא עביד, דסבר: ההוא לא סמיך עלי: מי ציית לך. לעשורי ספק, הא עם הארץ חבריה מהימן ליה טפי מינך: רישא דקתני מעשרן דמאי בעם הארץ דקאמר ליה לחבר סיפא כו'. והכי קאמר: במה דברים אמורים דלוקט צריך לעשרן דמאי — בעם הארץ שאמר לו לחבר לקט, דאיכא לספוקי אי עישר עלייהו האי בעל הבית אי לא. אבל בחבר שאמר לעם הארץ לקט בכלכלה זו, וחבר אחר שמע ממנו — אוכל, ואינו צריך לעשר דמאי. דודאי כיון דנותן חבר ולוקט עם הארץ — חייש הנותן דלא ליכלינהו בטבלייהו, ותורם אף שלא מן המוקף, דמוטב יחשדו חברים וכו': איסורא

מנחות סח. | [ר"ה ל. מנחות סח. סוכה מא.] | [מנחות כז. ע"ש] | פסחים ל: | [לעיל ל: וש"נ]

תוספות

רב ששת אמר חזקה שליח עושה שליחותו. הרב רבינו שמשון מפולירר"א פוסק כרב ששת. דבה"ג פוסק דהלכה כרב נחמן בדיני, וכרב ששת באיסורי. ולר"ת נראה דהלכה כרב נחמן, דבפ' "התקבל" (גיטין דף סד.) אמר: בעל אמר לגירושין, ושליש אמר לגירושין, והיא אומרת נתן לי ואבד — אין דבר שבערוה פחות משנים. ופריך מהא דאמר האומר לחבירו צא וקדש לי אשה סתם(ב) — אסור בכל הנשים שבעולם, אלמא: חזקה שליח עושה שליחותו! ומשני: ה"מ — לחומרא, אבל לקולא — לא. ובפ"ק דחולין (דף יב.) נמי מסיק: לעולם אין חזקה שליח עושה שליחותו, והאומר לשלוחו צא ותרום לי והלך ומצא תרום — אין חזקתו תרום, דילמא אינים אחרינא שמע ותרם. ואע"ג דהתם רב נחמן קאמר לה, מ"מ סליק התלמוד התם הכי, וההוא דבעא מיניה קיבלה. ועוד דרב שמעיה דבסמוך סבר נמי כרב נחמן, דלרב ששת לא היה צריך לחזקת(ג) כהנים. ואומר ר"י: דמכל זה אין ראיה, דרב ששת נמי לית ליה חזקה שליח עושה שליחותו אלא במקום שאם לא יעשה שליחותו יבא המשלח לידי עבירה אם יסמוך עליו. ולכך, בגט אין השליח חושש ליתן גט. והיא דחולין נמי, אינו חושש לשחוט ולתרום — שאם לא יתרום יראה המשלח שאינו תרום, ולא אסיק אדעתיה שמא אחר ישמע ויתרום. ודרב שמעיה נמי, איכא למימר דלא אמר כדי ליתן טעם למה סומכין על הכהנים, אלא ליישב דברי רב, דאמר בפ' "האשה" (יבמות דף ס:): אין שוחטין וזורקין על טמא שרץ, אף על גב דמקוה לפנינו, דילמא פשע ולא טביל. אבל שוחטין וזורקין על מחוסר כפורים, ואע"ג דהוי נמי מחוסר מעשה — דליכא למיחש דילמא פשע, כדרב שמעיה, והתם נמי מייתי לה:

הרחוקים מותרין. אף על גב דע"כ צריכין להקריב משום מצות העומר — מ"מ מייתי ראיה מהא דשרו רחוקין מחצות ואילך, אף על גב דיש שהות כל היום אלא שממהרין, לפי שיודעין שהרחוקין סומכין עליהן. וכן גבי קיני זבה ויולדת, אף על גב דמצווין להקריב באותו יום — מיהא לא מיחייבי אי לאו משום שסומכות עליהן, וחזקה שליח עושה שליחותו:

האומר לחברו צא ולקוט לך. בפרק "לולב" (סוכה דף לט.) גבי הלוקח לולב מחבירו בשביעית, מגיה שם רש"י: מעם הארץ, משום דלא הוה קרי ליה חבירו. ואין צריך להגיה, דהכא מוקי לה בעם הארץ שאמר לחבר, אע"ג דקתני "לחברו" ובשבת פרק "השואל" (דף קנ.) [[נ"ל לא ימתור]] אמר: *אומר אדם לחברו לא ושכור לי פועלים, ומוקי לה בחברו נכרי:

תאנים מתאנתי. אף על גב דמעשר פירות מדרבנן, ורב נחמן מודה דבשל סופרים חזקה שליח עושה שליחותו, כיון דעיקר שם מעשר מן התורה — חשיב לה [ב]כשל תורה: ולא

עין משפט נר מצוה

סא א מיי' פ"י מהל' מאכלות אסורות הלכה ב:

סב ב מיי' פ"א מהל' מחוסרי כפרה הלכה יב:

סג ג ד מיי' פ"י מהל' מעשר הלכה י:

[הא דהכא דוקא לערב ולעיל גבי עומר שרי מחצות עי' תוס' חגיגה כא. ד"ה האונן וכו' ותוס' זבחים נח: ד"ה טבול]

רבינו חננאל

שאינן מודים בעירוב אמר רב חסדא כותאי אם אמר לאחד לקבלו ממנו ועומד ורואהו כדרב חסדא עד שמגיע אצלו הרי זה עירוב. ואקשי' ודלמא האי לא קביל מיניה. ושנינן חזקה שליח עושה שליחותו. וזה כיון שא"ל לקבלו ממנו ונתרצה לקבלו חזקה שקבל כדרב יחיאל האי דרב חסדא ורב יחיאל אהא אתמר דתניא נתנו לפיל או לקוף והוליכו אינו עירוב ואם אמר לאחר לקבלו ממנו [הרי זה עירוב] *) ודלמא לא מקביל ליה. אמר רב יחיאל חזקה שליח עושה שליחותו ומקבלו. אמר רב נחמן בשל סופרים אמרינן חזקה שליח עושה שליחותו אבל בשל תורה עד שיתברר שעשה שליחותו ורב ששת אמר אחד זה ואחד זה חזקה שליח עושה שליחותו. אמר רב ששת מנא אמינא לה דתנן במנחות משקרב העומר מותר בחדש מיד. והרחוקין מחצות היום כו' ופשוטה היא [וכו']. ורב ששת ב"ד אין מתעצלין ושרי מחצות היום אבל גבי שליח כל היום. יתר מזה אמרינן חזקה שליח עושה שליחותו. אמר רב ששת מנא אמינא לה דתניא באשה שיש עליה לידה או זיבה מביאה מעות לקינה ונותנת בשופר וטובלת ואוכלת [בקדשים] לערב מאי טעמא לאו משום דאמרינן חזקה שליח עושה שליחותו ודחי רב נחמן ואמר התם כדרב שמעיה דאמר חזקה אין ב"ד עומדין משם עד שיכלו כל המעות שבשופר. אמר רב ששת מנא אמינא לה דתניא האומר לחבירו צא ולקט לך תאנים [מתאנתי] אוכל מהן עראי ומעשרן ודאי. בד"א בעם הארץ אבל חבר אוכל ואין צריך לעשר דברי רבי רשבג"א לא יאכל עד שיעשר לפי שלא נחשדו חברים לתרום [שלא] מן המוקף. א"ר נוחין דברי מדברי אבא מוטב שיחשדו חברים לתרום שלא מן המוקף ואל יאכילו לעמי הארץ טבלא. ודייק רב ששת מנה ואו' עד כאן לא פליגי ר' ואבא אלא בנחשדו. אבל כ"ע חזקה שליח עושה שליחותו. (וכמו) [וכיון] דאמר ליה לקט לי ודאי ליקט ודחי רב נחמן הכי לאו משום דחזקה שליח עושה שליחותו אלא כדרב [חנינא חוזאה] חזקה היא הדבר שאין מוציא דבר שאינו מתוקן מתחת ידו לפי' א"ר אם החבר אמר לע"ה ודאי עשר עליהן מביתו לפי' אוכל עם הארץ וא"צ לעשר. ואבוה א' [לא] נחשדו חברים לתרום מביתיה (בעלמא) [על מה] שהוא בשדה. אמר מר בד"א שמעשרין דמאי בעם הארץ האי עה"א [דקאמר ליה למאן] אי לע"ה כמותו לקוט לי [לא] לעשר כלל לא וודאי ולא דמאי אלא ע"ה דא' לחבר אותו חבר

*) [נ"ל ודלמא לא ממטי ליה אמר רב חסדא בעומד ורואהו].

הגהות הב"ח

(א) רש"י ד"ה אבל אמר וכו' לעשרן ודאי אלא דמאי דהא אמרינן שמא הנותן עישר אלא יפריש ויאכל הוא: (ב) תוס' ד"ה רב ששת וכו' אשה סתם ומת שלוחו אסור בכל הנשים: (ג) בא"ד לא היה צריך לחזקת ב"ד כהנים:

גליון הש"ס

תוס' ד"ה תאנים מתאנתי וכו' כשל תורה. עי' לקמן דף לז ע"ב תוס' ד"ה מאן האי תנא:

רב נסים גאון

האשה שיש עליה לידה או זיבה מביאה מעות ונותנת בשופר. פי' שופר האמור כאן היא תיבה שמקבצין לתוכה מעות של קינין כמפורש במס' שקלים (פ"ו מ"ה) י"ג שופרות היו במקדש וכתוב עליהן תקלין חדתין תקלין עתיקין ולזה נתכוונו במס' גיטין בפרק הניזקין (דף ס) והא שיפורא דמעיקרא בי רב יהודה ולבסוף בי רבה ולבסוף בי רב יוסף ולבסוף בי אביי ולבסוף בי רבא:

סָבַר: אוֹתוֹ חָבֵר אוֹכֵל וְאֵינוֹ צָרִיךְ לְעַשֵּׂר, דְּוַדַּאי עִישּׂוּרֵי מְעַשֵּׂר הַהוּא חָבֵר קַמָּא עִילָּוֵיהּ. וְרַבָּן שִׁמְעוֹן בֶּן גַּמְלִיאֵל אוֹמֵר: לֹא יֹאכַל עַד שֶׁיְּעַשֵּׂר, לְפִי *שֶׁלֹּא נֶחְשְׁדוּ חֲבֵרִים לִתְרוֹם שֶׁלֹּא מִן הַמּוּקָּף. וְאָמַר לֵיהּ רַבִּי: מוּטָב שֶׁיֵּחָשְׁדוּ חֲבֵרִים לִתְרוֹם שֶׁלֹּא מִן הַמּוּקָּף, וְאַל יַאֲכִילוּ עַמֵּי הָאָרֶץ טְבָלִים. בְּמַאי קָמִיפַּלְגִי? רַבִּי סָבַר: נִיחָא לֵיהּ לְחָבֵר דְּלַעֲבֵיד הוּא אִיסּוּרָא *קְלִילָא, וְלָא לִיעֲבַד עַם הָאָרֶץ אִיסּוּרָא רַבָּה. וְרַבָּן שִׁמְעוֹן בֶּן גַּמְלִיאֵל סָבַר: נִיחָא לֵיהּ לְחָבֵר דְּלֶיעֱבַד עַם הָאָרֶץ אִיסּוּרָא רַבָּה, וְאִיהוּ אֲפִי' אִיסּוּרָא קְלִילָא לָא לִיעֲבַד.§

מתני' [א]נְתָנוֹ בָּאִילָן, לְמַעְלָה מֵעֲשָׂרָה טְפָחִים — אֵין עֵירוּבוֹ עֵירוּב, לְמַטָּה מֵעֲשָׂרָה טְפָחִים — עֵירוּבוֹ עֵירוּב. נְתָנוֹ בַּבּוֹר, אֲפִילּוּ עָמוֹק מֵאָה אַמָּה — עֵירוּבוֹ עֵירוּב.§

גמ' יְתֵיב רַבִּי חִיָּיא בַּר אַבָּא וְרַבִּי אַסִּי וְרָבָא בַּר נָתָן, וִיתֵיב רַב נַחְמָן גַּבַּיְיהוּ, וְיָתְבֵי וְקָאָמְרִי: הַאי אִילָן דְּקָאֵי הֵיכָא? אִילֵימָא דְּקָאֵי בִּרְשׁוּת הַיָּחִיד — מָה לִי לְמַעְלָה מָה לִי לְמַטָּה? *רְשׁוּת הַיָּחִיד עוֹלָה עַד לָרָקִיעַ! וְאֶלָּא דְּקָאֵי בִּרְשׁוּת הָרַבִּים; דְּמִתְכַּוֵּין לִשְׁבּוֹת הֵיכָא? אִילֵימָא דְּנִתְכַּוֵּין לִשְׁבּוֹת לְמַעְלָה — הוּא וְעֵירוּבוֹ בְּמָקוֹם אֶחָד הוּא. אֶלָּא(א) נִתְכַּוֵּין לִשְׁבּוֹת לְמַטָּה — וְהָא קָא מִשְׁתַּמֵּשׁ בָּאִילָן! לְעוֹלָם דְּקָאֵי בִּרה"ר, וְנִתְכַּוֵּין לִשְׁבּוֹת לְמַטָּה, וְרַבִּי הִיא, *דְּאָמַר: [ב]כָּל דָּבָר שֶׁהוּא מִשּׁוּם שְׁבוּת לֹא גָּזְרוּ עָלָיו בֵּין הַשְּׁמָשׁוֹת. אָמַר לְהוּ רַב נַחְמָן: *יִשַּׁר, *וְכֵן אָמַר שְׁמוּאֵל.(ב) אֲמַרוּ לֵיהּ: פַּתְרִיתוּ בָּהּ כּוּלֵּי הַאי?! אִינְהוּ נַמִי הָכִי קָא פָּתְרִי בָּהּ! [אֶלָּא הָכִי] אֲמַרוּ לֵיהּ: קָבְעִיתוּ לֵיהּ בִּגְמָרָא? אֲמַר לְהוּ: אִין. אִתְּמַר נַמִי, אָמַר רַב נַחְמָן, אָמַר שְׁמוּאֵל: הָכָא בְּאִילָן הָעוֹמֵד בִּרְשׁוּת הָרַבִּים עָסְקִינַן, גָּבוֹהַּ עֲשָׂרָה וְרָחָב אַרְבָּעָה, וְנִתְכַּוֵּין לִשְׁבּוֹת לְמַטָּה. וְרַבִּי הִיא, דְּאָמַר: כָּל דָּבָר שֶׁהוּא מִשּׁוּם שְׁבוּת לֹא גָּזְרוּ עָלָיו בֵּין הַשְּׁמָשׁוֹת. אָמַר רָבָא: [ג]ל"ש אֶלָּא בְּאִילָן הָעוֹמֵד חוּץ לְעִיבּוּרָהּ שֶׁל עִיר, אֲבָל אִילָן הָעוֹמֵד בְּתוֹךְ עִיבּוּרָהּ שֶׁל עִיר — אֲפִילּוּ לְמַעְלָה מֵעֲשָׂרָה הֲרֵי זֶה עֵירוּב, דְּמָתָא כְּמַאן דִּמְלְיָא דָּמְיָא. אִי הָכִי חוּץ לְעִיבּוּרָהּ שֶׁל עִיר נַמִי, כֵּיוָן דְּאָמַר רָבָא: *הַנּוֹתֵן עֵירוּבוֹ — יֵשׁ לוֹ אַרְבַּע אַמּוֹת, הָוְיָא לָהּ רְשׁוּת הַיָּחִיד, וּרְשׁוּת הַיָּחִיד עוֹלָה עַד לָרָקִיעַ! אָמַר רַב יִצְחָק בְּרֵיהּ דְּרַב מְשַׁרְשְׁיָא: הָכָא בְּאִילָן הַנּוֹטֶה חוּץ לְאַרְבַּע אַמּוֹת עָסְקִינַן, וְנִתְכַּוֵּין

[שבת מג: וש"נ] [ועי' תוס' פסחים פח: ד"ה כופין] [לקמן לה. וש"נ]

איסורא קלילא. שלא מן המוקף: איסורא רבה. לאכול טבלים: מתני' למעלה מעשרה טפחים כו'. מפרש בגמרא: נתנו בבור כו'. מפרש בגמרא: גמ' אי דנתכוין. לקנות שביתתו על אילן: הוא ועירובו במקום אחד. ואפילו למעלה מי' עירובו עירוב: אלא דנתכוין לשבות למטה. תירוצא הוא. הילכך, למעלה מעשרה – אין עירובו עירוב, דבמקום שנתכוין לשבות, שם היא שביתתו, וכיון דאי הוה בעי למישקל עירוביה ומיכליה בשעה שהעירוב זוכה לו, דהיינו בין השמשות – לא מצי שקיל, דמייתי מרשות היחיד לרשות הרבים – לא הוה עירובו עירוב. וכגון דאילן רחב ד' והוי למעלה מי' דידיה רשות היחיד. למטה מי' – עירובו עירוב. ואע"ג דלמטה מי' כרמלית הוא, דכל ג' עד ט' ברוחב ד' כרמלית היא, כדאמרן ב"יציאות השבת" (שבת דף ח.), וקא מייתי ליה מכרמלית לרה"ר – הא מוקמי לה כרבי, דאמר: כל דבר שהוא משום שבות לא גזרו עליו בין השמשות: והא משתמש באילן. כי שקיל ליה, ואמאי עירובו עירוב אפילו למטה מעשרה? והא לא מצי שקיל ליה, דשימוש אילן שבות הוא, כדתנן (ביצה דף לו:), אלו הן משום שבות: לא עולין באילן. והוא הדין דמצי למיפרך: והא קא מייתי מכרמלית לרשות הרבים. אלא כיון דהא שבות והא שבות, חדא מינייהו נקט: בין השמשות. שהיא שעת קניית עירוב. וכיון דההיא שעתא מצי שקיל ליה – נמצאת סעודה הראויה לו באותה שעה(ג), ותו לא איכפת לן. לא גזרו עליו בין השמשות, דכיון דבין השמשות ספיקא הוא, ושבות דרבנן הוא – לא גזור. ולקמן (לג.) מפרש מאי רבי ומאי רבנן: עיבורה של עיר. כל בית שישנו בתוך שבעים אמה ושיריים לעיר קרי עיבורה של עיר בפרק "כיצד מעברין" (לקמן דף נז.): אבל באילן העומד בתוך עיבורה של עיר. כגון שהיה עיר בתוך אלפים אמה של עירו, והיה רוצה לילך עוד אלפים, והניח עירובו באותה העיר באילן העומד בתוך עיבורה של עיר: אפי' למעלה מעשרה. והוא נתכוין לשבות למטה – עירובו עירוב: דמתא. מתוך שהיא מוקפת יישוב מחיצות ואינה מגולה – חזינא לה כמאן דמליא עפרא, והוי כמאן דנתכוין לשבות למעלה מעשרה. ואע"ג דאי בעי למשקליה לא מצי שקיל, דהא אילן רשות היחיד ותחתיו רשות הרבים – חזינן למקום שביתתו כאילו הוא גבוה, למיהוי כאילו נתכוין לשבות למעלה, ויקנה לו העירוב: כיון דאמר רבא הנותן את עירובו כו'. לקמן בהאי פירקא (דף לה.) גבי נתגלגל חוץ לתחום דקתני מתניתין: אינו עירוב, ואמר רבא: לא שנו אלא שנתגלגל חוץ לתחום ארבע אמות, אבל תוך ארבע אמות – הנותן את עירובו יש לו ארבע אמות. כלומר: ארבע אמות שסביביו הוו ליה כמוקפות מחיצות, וכי היכי דהנותן את עירובו בבית שמקבלתו בתחום ומקבלתו חוץ לתחום מהלך את כולו וחוצה לו אלפים אמה, דהוי כל הבית כאילו הוא בתוך תחומו, כדאמרינן לקמן ב"כיצד מעברין" (דף סא.): אנשי עיר גדולה מהלכין את כל עיר קטנה כו', הא נמי: כל ארבע אמות הוו להו כבית ומצי לאיתויי מחוץ לתחום. בתוך התחום. אלמא: לרבא כרשות היחיד הן לו: ורשות היחיד עולה עד לרקיע. ואפילו נתנו למעלה מעשרה – הוא ועירובו ברשות היחיד הן. ונהי דלאו רשות היחיד ממש נינהו, לגבי איסורא דאורייתא למשקליה מאילן להתם דהא ליכא מחיצה – מיהו לענין מיהוי הוא ועירובו במקום אחד – הוי חד רשותא, דומיא דנותן בעיבורה של עיר, דחזי ליה רבא כמאן דמליא: באילן. שנופו נוטה חוץ לארבע אמות(ז), שהוא סוף התחום, והניח עירובו בנופו חוץ לד' אמות: והוא

ולא ליעבד עם הארץ איסורא רבה. והא דמסיק פ"ק דשבת (דף ד.) גבי הדביק פת בתנור, דאין אומרים לאדם חטא בשביל שיזכה חברך – הכא שאני, שהוא גורם לו לעבור, שהוא אומר לו לקוט וסבור שעשרן. ומיהו קשה: דבפרק "תמיד נשחט" (פסחים דף נט.) אמר: אין לך דבר שמתעכב אחר תמיד של בין הערבים אלא קטרת ונרות בכל השנה. ופסח ומחוסר כפורים בערבי פסחים בלבד, שטובל ואוכל פסחו לערב. וקעברי כהני אעשה דהשלמה שאין בו כרת כדי שיקיים זה מצות עשה שיש בו כרת! וכן אמר הכא בפרק בתרא (דף קג:) דכהן דעלתה לו יבלת – חברו חותכו לו בשיניו כדי שיעשה עבודתו, ואף ע"ג דאי לאו עבודתו היה אסור. והתם לא שרינן רדיית הפת שהיא מדרבנן! ואומר ר"י: יש לחלק בההיא דהדביק, לפי שפשע שהדביק סמוך לחשיכה. ואע"ג דהוי שוגג איבעי ליה לאסוקי אדעתיה. אבל בהנך דלא פשע מידי – שרי. והא דשרי (גיטין דף לח:) בחציה שפחה וחציה בת חורין לשחררה כשנהגו בה מנהג הפקר, אע"ג שעובר בעשה – לא דמי פריצות דידהו למדביק פת בתנור. שאותו לא היה אנוס כלל, אבל שפחה האסורה לעבדים ולבני חורין והיא להוטה אחר זנות – אי אפשר שלא תכשיל בני אדם, ודמו לאונסין. ועוד: דהוה ליה כמצוה דרבים, כדמשני (שם:) גבי ר' אליעזר ששיחרר עבדו להשלימו לעשרה מצוה דרבים שאני*: **מה** לי למעלה מה לי למטה. השתא דאכתי לא אסיק אדעתיה דאתי כרבי, הוי מצי לאקשויי דבין למעלה ובין למטה לא יהיה עירוב, משום דמשתמש באילן. אלא דפריך: כיון דלמטה הוי עירוב, ולא איכפת לן במה שמשתמש באילן – למעלה נמי ליהוי עירוב, דהוא ועירובו במקום אחד הוא: **דרה"י** עולה עד לרקיע. לא הוי צריך להאי טעמא דרשות היחיד עולה עד לרקיע, דאי נמי הוי מקום פטור – הוא ועירובו במקום אחד, אלא האמת אומר: **הא** קמשתמש באילן. פירש רש"י: דהוא הדין דהוה מצי למיפרך והא קמייתי מכרמלית לרשות הרבים. אלא חדא מב' פירכי נקט. ומהר"י מפרש: דהוי מצי לשנויי דקאי בכרמלית. **והא** אמר רבא הנותן עירובו יש לו ד' אמות. לכל רוח כאילו מוקפת מחיצה. וכיון דחשבינן עיבורה של עיר כמאן דמליא, אע"פ שהוא רשות הרבים לפי שהוא כמוקף לבני העיר, שהוא חשוב בכלל העיר כד' אמות לענין תחום שבת, וכן לנותן שם עירובו (לקמן דף ס:) – גם חוץ לעיבורו של עיר יש לו ארבע אמות במקום שביתתו, בלא חשבון אלפים אמה יחשב נמי כמאן דמליא*): **הכא** באילן שנוטה חוץ לד' אמות. פירש רש"י: הלכך למטה מעשרה – עירובו עירוב, דמצי לאתויי פחות מארבע אמות עד תוך ארבע אמותיו. ולא הוצרך לפרש כן אלא משום שרוצה להכשיר אפילו הניחו ברחוק הרבה מארבע אמותיו, דאם לא היה נוטה אלא שלש אמות או שתי אמות חוץ לארבע אמותיו יכול להביאו בבת אחת. ומהר"י מפרש: דאפילו במופלג טובא יכול להוליכו בבת אחת עד מקום שביתתו, דכיון דעוקרו מכרמלית – שוב אינו מתחייב בהנחתו אלא משום שבות: דהדר

*) [ועי' תוס' לקמן מז: ד"ה דכולא]

עין משפט נר מצוה

סד א ב מיי' פכ"ד מהל' שבת הלכה י ופ"ו מהל' עירובין הלכה ט י סמג עשין א טוש"ע א"ח סי' שז סעיף כב וסימן שמב ס"א וסימן תט ס"ב:
סה ג מיי' שם הלכה ח טור ש"ע שם:

רבינו חננאל

חבר מעשר דמאי חייש שמא ע"ה שא' לו לקט לי עשר עליהן מביתו הוה ליה ספק לפי' [מעשר] דמאי אי הכי [הא] דתני רבי מוטב שיחשדו חברים לתרום שלא מן המוקף ואל יאכילו לעם הארץ טבלין. בעל התאנה שהוא התורם ע"ה הוא והמלקט ואוכל הוא חבר ואוקמוה רבינא רישא בע"ה דאמר לחבר לפיכך מעשרין דמאי וסיפא בחבר שאמר לע"ה וחבר אחר שומע וסבר [רבי] החבר ששומע לחבר שאמר לע"ה מלא לך כלכלה זו [אוכל]. (אבל) [אותו] החבר ששמע וא"צ לעשר דבודאי ההוא חבר קמא דא"ל מלא לך כלכלה זו עישורי מעשר עילויה מביתיה ואע"ג שאינו מן המוקף. סבר ניחא ליה למיעבד איסורא קלילא לתרום שלא מן המוקף. ולא ליעבדיה לע"ה איסורא רבה אכילת טבלים ואבוה סבר לא נחשדו חברים לתרום שלא מן המוקף ולא חייש החבר (כע"ה) [לע"ה] אע"פ דעביד איסורא רבה ולא ליעבד הוא איסורא קלילא: **מתני'** נתנו באילן למעלה מי"ט אינו עירוב וכו' אוקימנא באילן העומד ברה"ר ואם נתן עירובו למטה מעשרה טפחים כיון שנתכוון לשבות למטה הוא ועירובו במקום אחד הן. ואקשינן והא המשתמש באילן. ושנינן מתני' רבי היא ותשמיש באילן משום שבות הוא דתנן אלו הן (מב') [משום] שבות לא עולין באילן כו' ורבי סבר כל דבר שהוא משום שבות לא גזרו עליו בין השמשות וקניית העירוב בין השמשות הוא והנה בין השמשות לא היה אסור להשתמש באילן שנמצא אותה העת שקנה עירוב הוא ועירובו במקום אחד. אמר להו רב נחמן לר' (אחא) חייא בר אבא ולר' (יוסי) [אסי] ולרבא בר נתן ישר וכן אמר שמואל וכי כולי האי אתון קבעי פותרא בגמ'. אמר רבא לא שנו אלא באילן העומד חוץ לעיבורה של עיר. אבל בתוך עיבורה של עיר אפילו למעלה מי' עירובו עירוב דעיר כמאן (דמידליא מיא) [דמליא דמיא] אי הכי חוץ לעיבורה של עיר נמי (דקא') [דהא] אמר רבא המניח עירובו יש לו ד' אמות הויא רה"י ורה"י עולה עד לרקיע ושנינן הכא באילן הנוטה חוץ לד' אמות עסקינן ונתכוון לשבות בעיקרו.

רב נסים גאון

אלא דנתכוון לשבות למטה הא קא משתמש באילן. במסכת יום טוב בפרק משילין (דף לו) אמרו אלו הן משום שבות [לא עולין באילן] לא גזרו עליו רבנן בין השמשות (רבנן) כלומר שימוש אילן:

מסורת הש"ס

[לעיל ל: וש"נ]

[פי' מעטו. יוקח לא מעט מים תרגום יונתן קליל מיא. ערוך ערך קל ב']

[לקמן לד: שבת ז.]

שבת ח: [לקמן לד: לה: עח:]

[נ"ל יישר וכ"א ברכות מב: שבת נג. סג: פסחים נג: ב"מ נא. סנהדרין ק. שבועות מ. מה: חולין יז: עה: עו:]

הגהות הב"ח

(א) גמ' אלא דנתכוון לשבות: (ב) שם וכן אמר שמואל ייסר אמרו ליה: (ג) רש"י ד"ה בין השמשות וכו' באותה שעה היא ותו לא: (ד) ד"ה באילן שנופו נוטה חוץ לד' אמות (שהוא סוף התחום) תא"מ ונ"ב ס"א אין זה:

גליון הש"ס

תוס' ד"ה הכא באילן שנוטה וכו' דכיון דעוקרו מכרמלית. עי' סוכה דף מג. תוספות ד"ה ועבירנו:

וְנִתְכַּוֵּין לִשְׁבּוֹת בְּעִיקָּרוֹ. וּמַאי לְמַעְלָה וּמַאי לְמַטָּה — דַּהֲדַר זָקֵיף. וְהָא אִי בָּעֵי מַיְיתִי לָהּ דֶּרֶךְ עָלָיו! כְּשֶׁרַבִּים מְכַתְּפִין עָלָיו, וְכִדְעוּלָּא, *דְּאָמַר עוּלָּא: אעַמּוּד תִּשְׁעָה בִּרְשׁוּת הָרַבִּים וְרַבִּים מְכַתְּפִין עָלָיו, וְזָרַק וְנָח עַל גַּבָּיו — חַיָּיב.§ מַאי רַבִּי וּמַאי רַבָּנַן? דְּתַנְיָא: נְתָנוֹ בָּאִילָן, לְמַעְלָה מֵעֲשָׂרָה טְפָחִים — אֵין עֵירוּבוֹ עֵירוּב. לְמַטָּה מֵעֲשָׂרָה טְפָחִים — עֵירוּבוֹ עֵירוּב, וְאָסוּר לִיטְּלוֹ. בְּתוֹךְ שְׁלֹשָׁה — מוּתָּר לִיטְּלוֹ. נְתָנוֹ בְּכַלְכָּלָה וּתְלָאוֹ בָּאִילָן — אֲפִילּוּ לְמַעְלָה מֵעֲשָׂרָה טְפָחִים עֵירוּבוֹ עֵירוּב, דִּבְרֵי רַבִּי. וַחֲכָמִים אוֹמְרִים: כָּל מָקוֹם שֶׁאָסוּר לִיטְּלוֹ — אֵין עֵירוּבוֹ עֵירוּב. וַחכ"א אַהַיָּיא? אִילֵימָא אַסֵּיפָא — לֵימָא קָסָבְרִי רַבָּנַן צְדָדִין אֲסוּרִין? אֶלָּא אַרֵישָׁא. הַאי אִילָן הֵיכִי דָּמֵי? אִי דְּלֵית בֵּיהּ אַרְבָּעָה — מְקוֹם פְּטוּר הוּא, וְאִי דְּאִית בֵּיהּ אַרְבָּעָה כִּי נְתָנוֹ בְּכַלְכָּלָה מַאי הָוֵי? אָמַר רָבִינָא: רֵישָׁא דְּאִית בֵּיהּ אַרְבָּעָה, סֵיפָא דְּלֵית בֵּיהּ אַרְבָּעָה, וְכַלְכָּלָה מַשְׁלִימָתוֹ לְאַרְבָּעָה. וְרַבִּי

רש"י

והוא נתכוין לשבות בעיקרו. הלכך, למטה מי' עירובו עירוב, דמצי נפיק ליה חוץ לד' אמותיו כמה דבעי, ולמשקליה ואייתוייה(א) פחות מד' אמות עד לתוך ד' אמותיו. ואע"ג דמשוינן להו ניהליה רשות היחיד לגבי קניית עירוב להקל — לאו רה"י גמורה היא, שלא יוכל להביא מחוצה להן לתוכן. דהא לאו מחיצה איכא, ולא חילוק רשות איכא. ומאן קא משוי להו בית — עירוב הוא דמשוי ליה. וכי איכוון — לבית דהיתרא איכוון, ולא לשוויה בית דאיסורא. למעלה מי' אין עירובו עירוב, דהא כי נפיק ושקליה מייתי מרה"י לרה"ר. ולקמן פריך: הא אי בעי מייתי ליה דרך עליו: ומאי למעלה ומאי למטה. בדבר הנוטה שוה הוא, ואי למעלה אית ביה — למטה לית ביה, ולא שייך ביה לשון מעלה ומטה, אלא לשון גבוה ונמוך, והכי איבעיא ליה למיתני: נתנו באילן גבוה י' — אין עירובו עירוב, אין גבוה עשרה — עירובו עירוב. ומדתני מעלה ומטה — משמע דזקוף, ויכול להניח למעלה בגובהו, או למטה בשיפולו: דהדר זקיף. בסוף נטייתו, ומשכחת ביה מעלה ומטה בזקיפתו. כגון דנטייתו כולה למטה מי' דאי למעלה מי' — לא משכחת בזקיפתו מעלה ומטה: והא אי בעי מייתי ליה דרך עליו. כי הוי חוץ לד' אמות נמי, ולמעלה מי' כיון דד' אמותיו עולות עד לרקיע רה"י(ב) — הרי יכול לעלות לאילן עד למעלה מעשרה וליטלו, דהא כל האילן מעשרה ולמעלה רה"י, ומביאנו למקום שביתתו: כשרבים מכתפין. על נטיית הנוף שחוץ לד' אמותיו הנמוכה מי' דהויא רה"ר כדעולא. וכי מייתי ליה למעלה מעשרה דרך אוירה של נטייה — עובר באויר רה"ר, וקיימא לן במושיט מרשות היחיד לרה"י דרך אויר רה"ר — אפילו למעלה מי' חייב, דתנן בפרק "הזורק" (שבת צו.): היו שתיהן בדיוטא אחת — הזורק פטור, המושיט חייב, שכך היתה עבודת הלוים: עמוד ט'. דוקא נקט ט' כדאמר ב"יציאות השבת" (דף ח.) דפחות מג' ארעא סמיכתא היא, דדרסי לה רבים. מג' עד ט' — לא מדרס דרסי לה מפני גובהה, ולא כתופי מכתפי עלה מפני שנמוכה לכתף. הלכך, לאו רה"ר היא אלא כרמלית, ט' — חזיא לכתופי, והוי רה"ר. עשרה — רה"י: וזרק. מתחילת ארבע לסוף ד': ונח על גביו חייב. דהויא לה עקירה והנחה מתחילת ד' לסוף ד' ברה"ר. אבל אין רבים מכתפין עליו, אע"ג דזרק ד' אמות ברשות הרבים, כיון דלא הויא הנחה ברה"ר — פטור: למעלה מעשרה אין עירובו עירוב. וכדאוקימנא מתניתין בנתכוין לשבות בעיקרו, ונופו נוטה חוץ לארבע אמות, והדר זקיף: ואסור ליטלו. אפילו האי דלמטה מעשרה אסור ליטלו למחר בשבת אם רצה לאוכלו, משום דמשתמש באילן — ואפילו הכי קני ליה עירוב בין השמשות. דכיון דשמוש אילן שבות דרבנן הוא, לא גזרו עליו בין השמשות. ואי הוה בעי למשקליה, ההיא שעתא מצי שקיל. כל איסור שבת ויו"ט דהוי מדרבנן קרי שבות: בתוך ג'. הניח עירובו באילן למטה משלשה סמוך לקרקע: מותר ליטלו. בשבת, דכל למטה משלשה אפילו באילן לא גזרו עליו, דהוי כארעא סמיכתא. והכי נמי תנן בפרק בתרא (דף צט:): היו שרשיו גבוהין מן הארץ ג' — לא ישב עליהן: נתנו בכלכלה כו' **אפילו** למעלה מעשרה עירובו עירוב. לקמן מפרש בשאין האילן רחב ד'. ו"אסור ליטלו" לא גרסינן. דאי גרסינן — אמאי מתמה לקמן אדרבנן, ואמר: לימא קא סברי רבנן צדדין אסורין, ואדרבי לא מתמה? ומשום דקיימי רבנן עליה, ואמרין כל מקום שאסור ליטלו כו' — לפיכך נכתב בספרים(ג). ואי גרסינן ליה — טעמא משום דקסבר צדדין אסורין: **אילימא אסיפא.** דקאמר רבי: נתנו בכלכלה עירובו עירוב. ואמרי ליה רבנן: הואיל וסוף אסור ליטלו בשבת משום שימוש אילן — אין עירובו עירוב, דגזרו על השבות בין השמשות: **נימא** קסברי רבנן **צדדין** דאילן **אסורין.** כגון הכא, דאינו משתמש באילן עצמו אי הוה שקיל לעירובו אפילו בשבת — בכלכלה הוא דמשתמש, שהוא לידי אילן. ופלוגתא היא בפ' "מי שהחשיך" (שבת דף קנד:), איכא למ"ד אסור ואיכא למ"ד מותר. והשתא נימא מהכא לדדין אסורין, וניהוי ההוא דשרי כיחיד במקום רבים, ותיהוי הך מתניתא סייעתא למאי דפסקינן התם הלכתא לדדין אסורים: **אלא ארישא.** קיימי רבנן, דקאמר רבי: נתנו באילן למטה מעשרה — עירובו עירוב, ואסור ליטלו. ואמרי ליה רבנן: אע"ג דהוא ועירובו ברה"ר, כיון דאסור ליטלו בשבת משום אילן — אסור ליטלו בין השמשות שהוא ספק ואין עירובו עירוב: **אי דלית ביה ארבעה.** רוחב: מקום **פטור הוא.** דכל פחות מרוחב ד' קי"ל ביציאות השבת דלא הוי רשות בפני עצמו, ובטל אגל רה"ר ואגל רה"י אם עומד ביניהן. כדאמרינן (שם דף ו.): עומד אדם על האסקופה, נוטל מן העני ונותן לו, מבעל הבית ונותן לו. ואפילו איסורא דרבנן ליכא. והכא, כי נתנו למעלה מעשרה — לאו ברה"י הוא, ואמאי אין עירובו עירוב? הרי יכול ליטלו לרשות הרבים: **ואי דאית ביה ד'.** ומשום הכי קאסר ליה רישא, סיפא אמאי מהני ליה כלכלה? הא רשות היחיד הוא, ואסור: **רישא דאית ביה ד'.** ומשום הכי: למעלה מי' — אין עירובו עירוב, דהוא ברה"ר ועירובו ברה"י: **סיפא דלית** ביה ד'. ומשום הכי לאו רה"י היא, וכלכלה דנקט — משום דרבי סבר לה כר' יהודה, דאמר: עירוב המונח למעלה מי' לא הוי עירוב, ואפילו נתכוין לשבות למעלה, אלא א"כ מונח על גבי מקום ארבעה. הלכך, אי לאו כלכלה — ליכא עירוב על גבי מקום ארבעה, אלא כלכלה משלימתו לארבעה: וסבר

תוספות

דהדר זקיף. וא"ת: והיכי חשיב למעלה מעשרה רה"י? הא גדיים בוקעין בו תחתיו! ואפילו ר' יוסי בר' יהודה לא שרי אלא בהדרן מחילות. וי"ל: דמיירי כגון שסתום תחת הזקיפה, דלא מלי בקעי. אי נמי: כגון שיש גובה י' באותו זקיפה, דחשיב רה"י אע"ג דגדיים בוקעין, כמו עגלות. כדאמר ב"הזורק" (שבת צט.) דהוי רה"י, אע"ג דתחתיהן הוי רה"ר: **והא** אי בעי מייתי לה דרך עליו. פ"ה: דיכול לעלות באילן עד למעלה מעשרה וליטלו, דהא כל האילן מעשרה ולמעלה רה"י, ויביאנו אללו למקום שביתתו. יש סבורים שר"ל שגם האויר שהוא למעלה מי', אפילו כנגד הנטייה שהיתה פחותה מי' — הוי רה"י. ולא עלה זה על דעת רש"י, דלא הוי רה"י אלא כרמלית, ומה שפירש: ויביאנו למקום שביתתו — אין לומר דהיינו לעיקרו של אילן, דהא רה"ר גמורה. ואע"ג דד' אמותיו חשבינן כרה"י — היינו דוקא למהוי הוא ועירובו במקום אחד, אבל להתיר להביא שם מרה"י או לאסור מרה"ר שם — לא חשיב רה"י, דהא לית ליה מחילות ולא חלק רשות. ומשני: כשרבים מכתפים עליו — על נטיית הנוף הנמוכה מי', דהוי רה"ר כדעולא. וקיימא לן במושיט מרה"י לרה"י דרך אויר רה"ר — אפילו למעלה מעשרה חייב, דתנן ב"הזורק" (שם דף צו.): היו שתיהן בדיוטא אחת — הזורק פטור והמושיט חייב, שכך היתה עבודת הלוים. ונראה דלאו מושיט הוא, אלא מעביר את העירוב רחוק חוץ לד' אמות, וחייב אפילו זה כנגד זה. כדאי' ב"הזורק" (שם דף צז.), א"ר אלעזר: המוליא משוי למעלה מעשרה — חייב, שכן משא בני קהת, ומקום עקירתו והנחתו הוי רה"י. וקשה: אכתי, אי בעי זריק ליה עד נגד מקום השביתה, דזורק פטור! ור"י מפרש: והא אי בעי מייתי ליה דרך עליו — היינו שיניחנו על הנטייה שהיא כרמלית, ויחזור ויביאנו לעיקרו של אילן שהוא מקום שביתתו ממש! ומשני: כשרבים מכתפין עליו, דהשתא לא מלי מנח ליה על נטייה, דהוי מוליא מרה"י לרה"ר. והואיל ואי בעי זריק ליה עד נגד מקום השביתה — ליכא למימר, דכי זריק ליה נמי אכתי לא הוי עירוב אלא משום דד' אמות חשידי רה"י, ועולה עד לרקיע — וכולי האי וודאי לא אמרינן "הואיל". אך קשה: דאכתי משכחת לה דאינו חייב — כגון בזה עוקר וזה מניח*. אי נמי: דכי מטי ליה עד מקום הנטייה יניח על ידו או על כתיפו למעלה מי'. דהא דמחייב ב"הזורק" מעביר למעלה מעשרה — היינו דוקא בדלא נח למעלה מעשרה. דהכי מוקי לה ההיא דפ"ק דשבת (דף ח:) גבי אסקופה, דאם נטל ונתן — שלשתן פטורין. ופריך: נימא תהוי תיובתא דרבא, דאמר: המעביר חפץ כו'. ומשני: התם לא נח, הכא נח. ונראה לי דבכל הנהו, כיון דבקל יבא לידי איסור דאורייתא — אפילו רבי מודה דגזרו עליו בין השמשות, כדאמרינן לקמן (דף לד:) גבי קנה דרכיך, דגזר שמא יקטום: **אי** דאית ביה ארבעה כי נתנו בבלבלה מאי הוי. דכיון דהאילן רשות היחיד — הויא ליה כלכלה חורי רה"י — ובחורי רשות היחיד אין לחוש אם גדיים בוקעים בו: **וכלכלה** משלימתו לד'. פירש"י: אף על גב דבראשו הוי ד' — לא הוי רה"י, הואיל ואין בתחתיו רוחב ד'. ולא הוי רה"י אלא אם כן מתחיל להיות רחב ארבעה בתוך ג' הסמוכין לארץ. ולא נראה, דבשלהי פ' "הזורק" (שבת דף קא.) אמר: עמוד גבוה י' ובראשו רחב ארבע, אם למטה(ד) רוחב כותל שלשה, זרק ונח על גביו — חייב. כיון דרוחב שלשה לא בקעי גדיים, וצריך לומר: באין בתחתיתו ג': ורבי

*א"נ בלאחר יד [ח"מ]

רבינו חננאל

ומאי למעלה ומאי למטה דהדר זקיף אי הוי למטה מעשרה טפחים עירובו עירוב למעלה מעשרה טפחי' אין עירובו עירוב. דהוא במקום (אחד) [אחר]. ועירובו במקום אחד. ואמרינן והא אי בעי מייתי ליה דרך עליו. פי' עליו על גופו של אדם. ובן עזאי דאמר מהלך כעומד דמי וי"א הא לא אפשר דגרסינן בהמוצא תפילין לימא הוי תיובתא דרבא דאמר המעביר חפץ מתחלת ד' לסוף ד' והעבירו דרך עליו וכו' ופי' עליו על כפיפתו של אילן. כשרבים מכתפין עליו. וכדעולא דאמר עמוד ט' ברה"ר ורבים מכתפין עליו וזרק ונח ע"ג חייב. מאי רבי ומאי רבנן דתניא נתנו באילן (אפילו) למעלה מעשרה טפחים [אין] עירובו עירוב למטה מעשרה טפחים עירובו עירוב ואסור לטלטלו. נתנו בכלכלה ותלאו באילן אפי' למעל' מעשרה טפחים עירובו עירוב ואסור לטלטלו דברי רבי וחכ"א כל מקום שאסור לטלטלו אין עירובו עירוב. רבנן אהייא אי נימא אסיפא אנתנו בכלכלה נימא רבנן סברי צדדין אסורין להשתמש בהן שהכלכלה התלויה באילן בצידי האילן היא ואע"ג דגרסינן בסוף שבת והלכתא צדדין אסורין ה"מ בשבת עצמה אבל בין השמשות לא גזרו בהו רבנן בצדדין איסורא אלא ארישא נתנו על האילן עצמו היכי דמי אי דלית ביה רוחב ד' טפחים פחות מד' אמות כו' ופירשה רבינא [רישא] דאית ביה ד"ט סיפא דלית ביה ד' טפחים מקום פטור הוא ואי דאית ביה ד'

עין משפט נר מצוה

סו א מיי' פ"ד מהלכות שבת הלכה ח סמג לאוין סה טוש"ע א"ח סי' שמה סעיף י:

מסורת הש"ס

שבת ח.

הגהות הב"ח

(א) רש"י ד"ה והוא נתכוון וכו' ואייתוה פתו' פחות מד' אמות כנ"ל והד"א עם דיבור הקודם: (ב) ד"ה והא אי בעי וכו' לרקיע רה"י הוא והרי יכול: (ג) ד"ה נתנו בכלכלה וכו' לפיכך נכתב בספרים (ואי גרסי' וכו' אסורים) תא"מ ונ"ב ס"א אין זה: (ד) תוס' ד"ה וכלכלה וכו' אם למטה הוי רוחב שלשה כנ"ל תיבת כותל נמחק: [והגריעב"ץ גרס קלר שלשה]:

רב נסים גאון

לימא קסברי רבנן צדדין אסורין. איתא במס' שבת בפרק מי שהחשיך לו בדרך (דף קנד) דהוינן בה בצדדי בהמה וצדדי אילן אי כאילן עצמו וכבהמה עצמה דאמו ואסור להשתמש בהן בשבת אי לא ובסיפה פסקו ההלכה ואמרו הלכתא צדדין אסורין צידי צדדין מותרין ואית דמקשי עלה ואמר וכי מאחר שנפסקה הלכה כי הצדדין אסורין למה מתמיהין בכאן בעירובין לימא קא סברי רבנן צדדין אסורין וחוזרין ודוחין אותה לפי הפירוק שפירקו בסוף ויש לי לפרק על זו הקושיא ולומר כי זה שאמרו בעירובין לימא קסברי רבנן צדדין אסורין אלו הדברים חוזרין לעיקר דברי רבנן כל שהוא משום שבות לא גזרו *) עליו בין השמשות וכשהגיעו הדברים לצדדים התמיהו ואמרו לימא קא סברי רבנן צדדין אסורין בין השמשות וחזרו ודחו כי בין השמשות לא גזרו רבנן אלא על אילן גופו אבל על צדדים [לא גזרו] אלא

*) [נראה דל"ל גזרו עליו בהסמ"ש].

וְרַבִּי סָבַר לָהּ כְּר' מֵאִיר, וְסָבַר לָהּ כְּר' יְהוּדָה. סָבַר לָהּ כְּרַבִּי מֵאִיר – דְּאָמַר: *חוֹקְקִין לְהַשְׁלִים. וְסָבַר לָהּ כְּר' יְהוּדָה – דְּאָמַר: בָּעֵינַן עֵירוּב עַל גַּבֵּי מְקוֹם אַרְבָּעָה, וְלֵיכָּא. מַאי רַבִּי יְהוּדָה? דְּתַנְיָא, רַבִּי יְהוּדָה אוֹמֵר: נָעַץ קוֹרָה בִּרְשׁוּת הָרַבִּים וְהִנִּיחַ עֵירוּבוֹ עָלֶיהָ, גָּבוֹהַּ י' וּרְחָבָה ד' – עֵירוּבוֹ עֵירוּב, וְאִם לָאו – אֵין עֵירוּבוֹ עֵירוּב. אַדְּרַבָּה, הוּא וְעֵירוּבוֹ בְּמָקוֹם אֶחָד!(א) אֶלָּא הָכִי קָאָמַר: גָּבוֹהַּ עֲשָׂרָה – צָרִיךְ שֶׁיְּהֵא בְּרֹאשָׁהּ אַרְבָּעָה, אֵין גְּבוֹהָה עֲשָׂרָה – אֵין צָרִיךְ שֶׁיְּהֵא בְּרֹאשָׁהּ אַרְבָּעָה. כְּמַאן? דְּלָא כְּרַבִּי יוֹסֵי בְּרַבִּי יְהוּדָה; *דְּתַנְיָא, רַבִּי יוֹסֵי בְּרַבִּי יְהוּדָה אוֹמֵר: נָעַץ קָנֶה בִּרה"ר וְהִנִּיחַ בְּרֹאשׁוֹ טְרַסְקָל, וְזָרַק וְנָח עַל גַּבָּיו – חַיָּיב. אֲפִילּוּ תֵּימָא רַבִּי יוֹסֵי בְּרַבִּי יְהוּדָה, הָתָם – הָדְרָן מְחִיצָּתָא, הָכָא – לָא הָדְרָן מְחִיצָּתָא. רַבִּי יִרְמְיָה אָמַר: שָׁאנֵי כַּלְכָּלָה הוֹאִיל וְיָכוֹל לְנַטּוֹתָהּ וְלַהֲבִיאָהּ לְתוֹךְ עֲשָׂרָה. יָתֵיב רַב פָּפָּא וְקָא אָמַר לְהָא שְׁמַעְתָּא. אֵיתִיבֵיהּ רַב בַּר שַׁבָּא לְרַב פָּפָּא: *כֵּיצַד הוּא עוֹשֶׂה? מוֹלִיכוֹ בָּרִאשׁוֹן וּמַחְשִׁיךְ עָלָיו, וְנוֹטְלוֹ וּבָא לוֹ. בַּשֵּׁנִי מַחְשִׁיךְ עָלָיו וְאוֹכְלוֹ וּבָא לוֹ. אַמַּאי

רש"י

וְסָבַר לָהּ כְּר' מֵאִיר. דְּאָמַר גַּבֵּי כִּיפָּה בְּפֶרֶק קַמָּא (דף יא:): חוֹקְקִין לְהַשְׁלִים. וּמִיהוּ רְשׁוּת הַיָּחִיד גְּמוּרָה לָא הָוֵי – כֵּיוָן דְּאֵין בְּתַחְתִּיתוֹ שֶׁל אִילָן רֹחַב ד' אע"ג דִּבְרֹאשׁוֹ רֹחַב אַרְבָּעָה דְּכַלְכָּלָה מַשְׁלִימָה לַעֲשָׂרָה לָא הָוֵי רְשׁוּת הַיָּחִיד, אא"כ מַתְחִיל לִהְיוֹת רָחְבּוֹ אַרְבָּעָה מִתּוֹךְ ג' הַסְּמוּכִים לַקַּרְקַע. דְּהָכִי אָמְרִינַן בְּ"הַזּוֹרֵק" (שבת דף קא.) גַּבֵּי בּוֹלִיַיְתָא דְּמֵישָׁן, וְהֵן סְפִינוֹת שֶׁשּׁוּלֵיהֶן חַדִּים וְאֵין בְּשׁוּלֵיהֶן רוֹחַב ד' וּלְמַעְלָה הֵן הוֹלְכוֹת וּמַרְחִיבוֹת הַרְבֵּה וּמְחִיצּוֹתָן גְּבוֹהוֹת י' – אֵין מְטַלְטְלִין בָּהֶן אֶלָּא בְּאַרְבַּע אַמּוֹת, דְּלָאו רה"י נִינְהוּ. וְאע"ג דִּגְבוֹהִים עֲשָׂרָה וּרְחָבִין אַרְבָּעָה מִלְמַעְלָה, הוֹאִיל וּבְשׁוּלֵיהֶן לָא הָוֵי אַרְבָּעָה. וְהָכָא גַּבֵּי אִילָן נָמֵי טַעְמָא מִשּׁוּם הָכִי הוּא. וְתֵדַע שֶׁזֶּהוּ הַטַּעַם, מִדְּקָאָמַר לְקַמָּן: כְּמַאן – דְּלָא כְּר' יוֹסֵי בַּר ר' יְהוּדָה וכו' וּבְ"הַזּוֹרֵק" נָמֵי מוֹתְבִינַן עֲלָהּ דְּהַהִיא מֵהָא דְּר' יוֹסֵי: בָּעֵינַן עֵירוּב עַל גַּבֵּי מְקוֹם ד' וְלֵיכָּא. בְּלָא כַּלְכָּלָה: ה"ג: גְּבוֹהָה עֲשָׂרָה וּרְחָבָה ד' עֵירוּבוֹ עֵירוּב וְאִם לָאו אֵין עֵירוּבוֹ עֵירוּב. גְּבוֹהָה י' וּרְחָבָה אַרְבָּעָה – עֵירוּבוֹ עֵירוּב, אע"ג דִּרה"י הִיא הַךְ קוֹרָה, וְהוּא נִתְכַּוֵּון לִשְׁבּוֹת בִּרְשׁוּת הָרַבִּים – הָא אֲמַרַן: הַנּוֹתֵן אֶת עֵירוּבוֹ יֵשׁ לוֹ אַרְבַּע אַמּוֹת, וּרְשׁוּת הַיָּחִיד עוֹלָה עַד לָרָקִיעַ. וְגַבֵּי אִילָן הוּא דְּלָא הָוֵי עֵירוּב, כִּדְאוֹקִימְנָא בְּנוֹפוֹ נוֹטֶה חוּץ לְד"א, אֲבָל הָכָא דְּלֵיכָּא נוֹף – שַׁפִּיר דָּמֵי: וְאִם לָאו אֵין עֵירוּבוֹ עֵירוּב. קס"ד דְּהָכִי קָאָמַר: וְאִם לָאו, דְּאֵינָהּ גְּבוֹהָה עֲשָׂרָה אוֹ שֶׁאֵינָהּ רְחָבָה אַרְבָּעָה, אֵין עֵירוּבוֹ עֵירוּב וּלְהָכִי מַתְמְהִינַן, אֵינָהּ גְּבוֹהָה עֲשָׂרָה? אַדְּרַבָּה, כ"ש דְּעֵירוּבוֹ עֵירוּב, דִּכְשֶׁאֵינָהּ גְּבוֹהָה י' הָוְיָא כְּמַאן דְּמַנְּחָא בִּרְשׁוּת הָרַבִּים: אֶלָּא. הַאי "וְאִם לָאו" דְּקָתָנֵי לָאו אַגְּבוֹהָהּ קָאֵי, אֶלָּא אַרוֹחַב קָאֵי. וְהָכִי קָאָמַר גְּבוֹהָה י' וְהִנִּיחָהּ בְּרֹאשָׁהּ, אִם יֵשׁ בְּרָחְבָּהּ ד' הָוֵי מָקוֹם חָשׁוּב לְהַנָּחַת עֵירוּב – עֵירוּבוֹ עֵירוּב. וּמִשּׁוּם דְּהוּא בִּרה"ר וְעֵירוּבוֹ בִּרה"י לָא מִיתְסַר, כִּדְאָמַר דְּהַנּוֹתֵן אֶת עֵירוּבוֹ יֵשׁ לוֹ ד' אַמּוֹת. וְאִם לָאו, דִּגְבוֹהָה י' וְאֵינָהּ רְחָבָה ד' – אֵין עֵירוּבוֹ עֵירוּב, דְּכֵיוָן דִּגְבוֹהָה עֲשָׂרָה וְאֵין הָעֵירוּב מוּנָּח עַל גַּבֵּי מְקוֹם ד' – הֲוָה לֵיהּ כְּמוּנָּח בָּאֲוִיר. וּמִדּוּקְיָא שָׁמְעִינַן הָא אֵינָהּ גְּבוֹהָה עֲשָׂרָה, אֲפִילּוּ אֵינָהּ רְחָבָה ד' – עֵירוּבוֹ עֵירוּב, דְּכֵיוָן דִּלְמַטָּה מֵעֲשָׂרָה – הָוְיָא לָהּ כְּמַאן דְּמַנְּחָה אַאַרְעָא דָּמְיָא, דְּכָל לְמַטָּה מִי' קְלוּטָה כְּמָה שֶׁהוּנְּחָה דָּמְיָא: גְּבוֹהָה עֲשָׂרָה. דְּמִידַּלְיָא מֵרה"ר, צָרִיךְ שֶׁיְּהֵא בְּרוֹחְבָּהּ אַרְבָּעָה, שֶׁיְּהֵא שָׁם מָקוֹם חָשׁוּב: אֵינָהּ גְּבוֹהָה עֲשָׂרָה אֵין צָרִיךְ שֶׁיְּהֵא רוֹחְבָּהּ ד'. דַּאֲפִילּוּ פָּחוֹת מִד' עֵירוּבוֹ עֵירוּב, דְּכָל לְמַטָּה מֵעֲשָׂרָה כְּמַאן דְּמַנְּחָא אַאַרְעָא הִיא: כְּמַאן. מַתְרֵץ רַבִּינָא לְעֵיל, אע"ג דְּחוֹקְקִין לְהַשְׁלִים וְאִיכָּא רוֹחַב ד' – לָא הָוֵי רה"י, מִשּׁוּם דְּאֵין בְּעִיקָּרוֹ ד' – דְּלָא כְּר' יוֹסֵי בַּר' יְהוּדָה: טְרַסְקָל. סַל רָחָב ד' וְזָרַק מֵרְשׁוּת הָרַבִּים וְנָח עַל גַּבָּיו – חַיָּיב, שֶׁהֲרֵי זָרַק מֵרְשׁוּת הָרַבִּים לרה"י. אַלְמָא: אע"ג דְּקָנֶה אֵינוֹ רָחָב ד' – הָוֵי רה"י, הוֹאִיל וְעֶלְיוֹנוֹ ד' דְּאָמְרִינַן: גּוֹד אַחֵית. וְהָכִי מְפָרֵשׁ בְּ"הַזּוֹרֵק": הָתָם הָדְרָן מְחִיצּוֹת. הַטְּרַסְקָל סוֹבֶבֶת אֶת הַקָּנֶה, שֶׁהֲרֵי תָּחוּב בְּאֶמְצָעִיתוֹ. וְכִי אָמְרִינַן גּוֹד אַחֵית מְחִיצּוֹת הַטְּרַסְקָל עַד הַקַּרְקַע – נִמְצָא קָנֶה מוּקָּף מְחִיצּוֹת שֶׁחָלָלוֹ אַרְבָּעָה, וְתוּ לֵיכָּא לְמֵימַר מִידֵי: הָכָא לָא הָדְרָן מְחִיצּוֹת. דְּכַלְכָּלָה אֵינָהּ מַקֶּפֶת אֶת עָבְיוֹ שֶׁל אִילָן, וְכִי אָמְרִינַן גּוֹד אַחֵית – אַכַּתִּי אִית לָן לְמֵימַר חוֹקְקִין לְהַשְׁלִים לְאִיצְטְרוּפֵי כַּלְכָּלָה בַּהֲדֵי אִילָן, וְתַרְתֵּי לָא אָמְרִינַן. וְאִית דִּמְפָרְשִׁי: כְּמַאן דְּלָא כְּר' יוֹסֵי – אַנָּעַץ קוֹרָה קָאֵי. דְּקא"ר יְהוּדָה: קוֹרָה שֶׁאֵין בְּרָחְבָּהּ ד' מִלְמַעְלָה – לָא הָוֵי רה"י, וְאָמְרִינַן: הָא דְּלָא כְּר' יוֹסֵי, דְּאָמַר טְרַסְקָל הָוֵי רְשׁוּת הַיָּחִיד. וּמוֹקְמִית לָהּ בְּשֶׁאֵין רָחָב אַרְבָּעָה. וְלָאו מִילְּתָא הִיא; חֲדָא: דְּבַהֲדְיָא מְפוֹרָשׁ בְּ"הַזּוֹרֵק" וּמוֹתְבִינַן מִינָּהּ אַדְּרַב הוּנָא, דְּאַיְירֵי בְּבוֹלִיַיְתָא דְּמֵישָׁן שֶׁרְחָבוֹת לְמַעְלָה וּקְצָרוֹת לְמַטָּה. וְאוֹתְבִינַן: וְנֵימָא גּוֹד אַחֵית מְחִיצָּתָא, מִי לָא תַּנְיָא ר' יוֹסֵי בַּר ר' יְהוּדָה כו' אַלְמָא: טַעְמָא מִשּׁוּם גּוֹד אַחֵית הוּא, וְנִמְצָא תַּחְתּוֹנוֹ שֶׁל קָנֶה מוּקָּף מְחִיצּוֹת בַּחֲלַל אַרְבָּעָה. וְאִי כְּשֶׁאֵין טְרַסְקָל רָחָב ד' כִּי אָמְרִינַן גּוֹד אַחֵית – מַאי הָוֵי? וְעוֹד: בְּכָל דּוּכְתָּא דְּקָאָמַר פָּחוֹת מִד' לָאו רְשׁוּת הוּא – אַמַּאי לָא אָמְרִינַן: כְּמַאן – דְּלָא כְּרַבִּי יוֹסֵי בַּר' יְהוּדָה, כִּדְקָאָמַר הָכָא: רַבִּי יִרְמְיָה אָמַר. לְעוֹלָם מַתְנִיתִין דִּלְעֵיל רֵישָׁא וְסֵיפָא בְּרוֹחַב ד' וּדְקָא קַשְׁיָא לָךְ כִּי נָתְנוֹ בְּכַלְכָּלָה מַאי הָוֵי: שָׁאנֵי בְּכַלְכָּלָה. הוֹאִיל וַעֲרוּכָה הִיא, יָכוֹל לְנַטּוֹתָהּ וְלָא יַעַקְרֶנָּה מִתְּלִיָּיתָהּ, וְיַטֶּה רֹאשָׁהּ אֶחָד עַד שֶׁיְּהֵא לְתוֹךְ י' וְיִטּוֹל אֶת עֵירוּבוֹ: מְתִיב רַב בַּר שַׁבָּא כֵּיצַד הוּא עוֹשֶׂה. מַתְנִיתִין(ב) הִיא בְּיו"ט שֶׁלִּפְנֵי הַשַּׁבָּת וְרָצָה לְעָרֵב לִשְׁנֵי הַיָּמִים, כֵּיצַד הוּא עוֹשֶׂה? מוֹלִיכוֹ בָּרִאשׁוֹן בְּעֶרֶב יו"ט לְסוֹף אַלְפַּיִם, וְעַל יְדֵי שְׁלוּחוֹ קָאָמַר. דְּאִי אִיהוּ גּוּפֵיהּ – בְּלָא פַּת נָמֵי קָנֵי לֵיהּ שְׁבִיתָה, כֵּיוָן דְּהָתָם יָתֵיב וְקָדֵישׁ עֲלֵיהּ יוֹמָא: וּמַחְשִׁיךְ עָלָיו. עַד שֶׁיִּקְנֶה לוֹ הָעֵירוּב: וְנוֹטְלוֹ וּבָא לוֹ. שֶׁאִם יַנִּיחֶנּוּ שָׁם שֶׁמָּא יֹאבַד, וְשׁוּב אֵין לוֹ עֵירוּב לְיוֹם הַמָּחֳרָת. כִּדְקָתָנֵי מַתְנִיתִין: נֶאֱכַל עֵירוּבוֹ בָּרִאשׁוֹן – עֵירוּבוֹ לָרִאשׁוֹן וְאֵין עֵירוּבוֹ לַשֵּׁנִי. וְחוֹזֵר וּמוֹלִיכוֹ בַּשֵּׁנִי שֶׁהוּא עֶרֶב שַׁבָּת, וּמַחְשִׁיךְ עָלָיו וְאוֹכְלוֹ שָׁם אִם יִרְצֶה, דְּלַהֲבִיאוֹ אִי אֶפְשָׁר, דְּשַׁבָּת הוּא. וְאִם יו"ט אַחַר הַשַּׁבָּת הוּא – עַל כָּרְחוֹ יַנִּיחֶנּוּ שָׁם ע"ש, וּלְמָחָר יֵלֵךְ וְיִרְאֶה אִם עֲדַיִין יֶשְׁנוֹ שָׁם, וְיַחְשִׁיךְ עָלָיו יְהֵא לוֹ עֵירוּב לַשֵּׁנִי, וְאִם אָבַד – יֵשֵׁב בְּבֵיתוֹ. קָתָנֵי מִיהַת: הַמְעָרֵב צָרִיךְ לְהוֹלִיךְ עֵירוּבוֹ לְסוֹף אַלְפַּיִם, וְאַמַּאי צָרִיךְ לְהוֹלִיכוֹ מִשֶּׁעֲשָׂאוֹ לְשֵׁם עֵירוּב? נֵימָא: אַף עַל גַּב דְּלָא אַמְטְיֵיהּ – כְּמַאן דְּאַמְטְיֵיהּ דָּמֵי. דְּהָא אָמְרַתְּ: הוֹאִיל וְיָכוֹל לְנַטּוֹתָהּ. וְהָא הָכָא כְּמַאן דְּלָא אַמְטְיֵיהּ הִיא, דְּהָא הוּא בִּרה"ר וְעֵירוּבוֹ בִּרְשׁוּת הַיָּחִיד, וְקָאָמְרַתְּ: הוֹאִיל וְיָכוֹל לְנַטּוֹתָהּ, וּמַה לִּי הוֹאִיל וְיָכוֹל לְנַטּוֹתָהּ, וּמַה לִּי יָכוֹל לַהֲבִיאָהּ. וְהַאי דִּנְקַט לְאוֹתוּבֵי מַתְנִיתִין דְּיוֹם טוֹב וְשַׁבָּת – מִשּׁוּם דְּלָא תְּנַן בְּמִשְׁנָה אַחֲרִיתִי הוֹלָכַת עֵירוּב בְּהֶדְיָא כִּי הָכָא: א"ר

תוספות

ורבי סבר כר' מאיר דאמר חוקקין להשלים וכרבי יהודה דבעי עירוב על מקום ד'. וא"ת: והך כלכלה היכי דמי? אם היא שוה לגבי האילן או תלויה למטה בפחות מג' לגבי האילן: אם היא שוה לגבי האילן – א"כ אמאי צריך חקיקה? ואם היא תלויה למטה מג' לגבי האילן – א"כ היכי פריך לעיל ואי אית ביה ד' כי נתנו על הכלכלה מאי הוי? הא לא חשיב רשות היחיד אפילו יש באילן ד', אם לא מטעם חקיקה דרחוקה מגב האילן! וי"ל: כגון שפי הכלכלה שוה לגבי האילן, ומ"ה הוי חורי רה"י, והעירוב מונח בשולי הכלכלה שהיא רחוקה ג', ולהכי צריך חקיקה. והא דלא מוקי שהעירוב בפי הכלכלה, או שהכלכלה רחבה ד' ומכל מקום לא הוי רה"י, הואיל והגדיים בוקעין בו! וי"ל: דא"כ במאי דנקט כלכלה לא השמיענו מידי, דלינקוט עמוד שיש בראשו ד' ואין בתחתיתו ג'. ואף על גב דאשמעינן דלדדין אסורין – לא הוי ליה למתנייה הכא, כיון שבעירוב לא השמיענו כלום. אלא ודאי נקט כלכלה לאשמעינן דחוקקין להשלים, ובעינן עירוב על מקום ד', וא"ת: אכתי למה ליה למימר כלל, סבר לה כרבי מאיר וסבר לה כר' יהודה? לימא, לעולם אימא לך דלא בעינן עירוב על גבי מקום ד', והכא כשהכלכלה שוה לראשו של אילן, וקמ"ל דלא חשיב רשות היחיד אפילו לרבי יוסי ברבי יהודה דחשיב טרסקל רשות היחיד – משום דהתם הדרן מחיצתא! ונראה לפרש דמשמע ליה דווקא נתנו על כלכלה הוי עירוב, הא נתנו על גבי אילן – לא הוי עירוב, מדקתני נתנו בכלכלה, ולא קתני תלאו לכלכלה באילן ונתן שם עירובו. הלכך: ע"כ איירי דשולי הכלכלה רחוק שלשה מגב האילן:

כמאן דלא כר' יוסי בר' יהודה. לספרים דגרסי בסמוך התם (כי) הדרן מחיצתא, אבל בקורה לא הדרן מחיצתא, דמשמע דקאי אברייתא דנעץ קורה, ומשמע ליה דאיירי אפילו חוץ לארבע אמותיו דומיא דמתניתין, אפילו הכי הוי עירוב. דכיון דאין בתחתיתו ג' אע"ג דראשו ד' – לא הוי רשות היחיד, דגדיים בוקעים בו. ולהכי קאמר דלא כרבי יוסי ברבי יהודה: **הואיל** ויכול לנטותו ולהביאו תוך עשרה. פירש רבינו שמואל: דהאי אמורא סבר לה כרבנן, דאמרי ב"המצניע" (שבת דף צב.) אגד כלי שמיה אגד. וכיון דאגד כלי למעלה מיו"ד כשנח העירוב למטה(ג) – אין בהנחה זו איסור הוצאה, הואיל ואחר שנח ברה"ר יכול ליטלו ולאוכלו. ומיהו, אפילו לא שמיה אגד אין כאן איסור הוצאה, הואיל ונח בכלכלה למטה מעשרה דהוי כרמלית אם רוחב ד', ואין בהטייה זו איסור דאורייתא: **איתיביה** רב בר שבא כו'. לפ"ה דפי' לעיל גבי אילן הנוטה חוץ לד"א דלמטה מיו"ד הוי עירוב הואיל ומצי לאתויי פחות מארבע – צריך לחלק בין הואיל דהכא להואל: **מוליכו**: פ"ה ועל ידי שלוחו קאמר. דאיהו אפילו בלא פת קני ליה שביתה. ופי' כן משום דבסוף "מי שהוציאוהו" (לקמן נא:)(ד) פסקינן כרב נחמן, ואליבא דרבי יהודה דאחד עני ועשיר מערב ברגליו: ואמאי

רבינו חננאל

וכלכלה משלימתו לד' טפחים ור' סבר לה כר' יהוד' דאמר בעינן עירוב ע"ג מקום (פטור) ד' וליכ' ד' טפחים (לא). מאי ר' יהודה דתניא נעץ קורה ברה"ר להניח עירובו עליה גבוהה י' טפחים ורחבה ד' עירובו עירוב אין גבוה י' טפחים אין צריך בראשו ד' ואפי' אין בראשו ד' הוא ועירובו במקום אחד הן [כמאן דלא] כר' יוסי בר' יהודה דתניא רבי יוסי ב"ר יהודה אומר נעץ קנה ברה"ר והניח בראשו טרסקל ורק ונח ע"ג חייב כלומר דרה"י היא. ור' יהודה סבר גבוה י' ואינו רחב *) ד' רה"ר היא דתני עירובו עירוב. ודחינן אפילו תימא ר' יוסי כאבוה סבירא ליה ושני טרסקל הואיל והדרן מחיצתא אבל (לא) עמוד או קורה דלא הדרן מחיצתא לאו כרה"י היא ר' ירמיה אמר שאני כלכלה הואיל ויכול לנטותה ולהביאה בתוך עשרה טפחים אע"ג שלא הביאה כמי שהביאה נחשבת. אי הכי הא דתנן כיצד היה עושה מוליכו בראשון מחשיך עליו נוטלו ובא לו

*) [נראה דל"ל גבוה י' ואינו רחב ד' למטה רה"ר היא כל"ל ולגי' רבינו פירושו הוא כמו שכתב התוס' בד"ה כמאן וכו"ק]:

רב נסים גאון

אלא בשבת עצמה אבל בבין השמשות לא גזרו: **סבר** לה כר' מאיר דאמר חוקקין להשלים כבר פירשנוהו לשעבר:

(שבת ז: ק. לעיל יא: לקמן קא: יומא יא.)

שבת ה. קא.

לקמן לח.

הגהות הב"ח

(א) גמ' ועירובו במקום אחד הוא אלא: (ב) רש"י ד"ה מתיב רב וכו' מתני' היא. נ"ב לקמן לח: (ג) תום' ד"ה הואיל וכו' כשנח העירוב למטה מעשרה אין בהנחה: (ד) ד"ה מוליכו וכו' דבסוף מי שהוציאוהו. נ"ב דף נא ע"ב ועי' שם דאחד עני ואחד עשיר אפי' לא תשכה לו בדרך:

אַמַּאי? נֵימָא: כֵּיוָן דְּאִי בָּעֵי אַמְטוּיֵי מָצֵי מַמְטֵי לֵיהּ, אע"ג דְּלָא אַמְטְיֵיהּ – כְּמַאן דְּאַמְטְיֵיהּ דָּמֵי! א"ר זֵירָא: גְּזֵירָה מִשּׁוּם י"ט שֶׁחָל לִהְיוֹת אַחַר שַׁבָּת. אֵיתִיבֵיהּ: נִתְכַּוֵּון לִשְׁבּוֹת בִּרה"ר, וְהִנִּיחַ עֵירוּבוֹ בַּכּוֹתֶל, לְמַטָּה מֵעֲשָׂרָה טְפָחִים – עֵירוּבוֹ עֵירוּב, לְמַעְלָה מִי' טְפָחִים – אֵין עֵירוּבוֹ עֵירוּב. נִתְכַּוֵּון לִשְׁבּוֹת בְּרֹאשׁ הַשּׁוֹבָךְ אוֹ בְּרֹאשׁ הַמִּגְדָּל, לְמַעְלָה מִי' טְפָחִים – עֵירוּבוֹ עֵירוּב, לְמַטָּה מִי' טְפָחִים – אֵין עֵירוּבוֹ עֵירוּב. וְאַמַּאי? הָכִי נַמִי נֵימָא: הוֹאִיל וְיָכוֹל לִנְטוֹתוֹ וְלַהֲבִיאוֹ לְתוֹךְ עֲשָׂרָה! א"ר יִרְמְיָה: הָכָא בְּמִגְדָּל מְסוּמָּר עָסְקִינַן. רָבָא אָמַר: אֲפִילּוּ תֵּימָא בְּמִגְדָּל שֶׁאֵינוֹ מְסוּמָּר, וְהָכָא בְּמִגְדָּל אָרוֹךְ עָסְקִינַן, דְּאִי מַמְטֵי לֵיהּ פּוּרְתָּא (א) אָזֵיל חוּץ לְאַרְבַּע אַמּוֹת. הֵיכִי דָּמֵי? אִי דְּאִיכָּא כַּוְּותָא וּמִתְנָא – לַיְיתֵיהּ בְּכַוְּותָא וּמִתְנָא! דְּלֵית לֵיהּ כַּוְּותָא וּמִתְנָא. § "נְתָנוֹ בַּבּוֹר – אֲפִילּוּ עָמוֹק מֵאָה אַמָּה וכו'". § הַאי בּוֹר דְּקָאֵי הֵיכָא? אִילֵימָא דְּקָאֵי בִּרְשׁוּת הַיָּחִיד – פְּשִׁיטָא

א"ר זֵירָא. הָא דְּאַצְרְכוּ רַבָּנַן לְכָל הַמְעָרְבִין לְהוֹלִיךְ עֵירוּבָן לִמְקוֹם שְׁבִיתָתָן – גְּזֵירָה מִשּׁוּם יו"ט אַחַר הַשַּׁבָּת דְּאִי בָּעֵי לְאַמְטוּיֵיהּ בְּשַׁבָּת לְעֶרֶב לְיוֹם הַמָּחֳרָת – לָא מָצֵי מַמְטֵי לֵיהּ, וְצָרִיךְ לְהוֹלִיכוֹ מֵעֶרֶב שַׁבָּת. וְאִי אָמְרַתְּ בְּעָלְמָא נִשְׁבְּקֵיהּ בְּבֵיתֵיהּ מִשּׁוּם הוֹאִיל – הָכִי נַמִי אָתֵי לְמִיסְמַךְ עֲלֵיהּ, וְנָפֵיק עַל עֵירוּב שְׁבִיתָתוֹ בְּיו"ט אַחַר הַשַּׁבָּת, וְהָתָם אֲפִילּוּ הוֹאִיל לֵיכָּא: וְהִנִּיחַ עֵירוּבוֹ בַּכּוֹתֶל. סָמוּךְ לִמְקוֹם שְׁבִיתָתוֹ חוּץ לְאַרְבַּע אַמּוֹת קָאָמַר, וּכְדְאוֹקִימְנָא בְּאִילָן. דְּאִי תּוֹךְ אַרְבַּע אַמּוֹת – אֲפִילּוּ לְמַעְלָה מִי' נַמִי עֵירוּבוֹ עֵירוּב. דְּהַנּוֹתֵן אֶת עֵירוּבוֹ יֵשׁ לוֹ אַרְבַּע אַמּוֹת: לְמַטָּה מֵעֲשָׂרָה עֵירוּבוֹ עֵירוּב. וְאַע"ג דְּעֵירוּבוֹ חוּץ לְאַרְבַּע אַמּוֹתָיו מָצֵי שָׁקֵיל לֵיהּ וְאַיְתוּיֵי פָּחוֹת פָּחוֹת מֵאַרְבַּע אַמּוֹת, דְּהָא אֲפִילּוּ בְּשַׁבָּת לָא אָסִיר כִּי הַאי גַּוְונָא אֶלָּא מִשּׁוּם שְׁבוּת דְּרַבָּנַן וְהָכָא דְּבֵין הַשְּׁמָשׁוֹת הוּא – לָא גְּזוּר: לְמַעְלָה מֵעֲשָׂרָה אֵינוֹ עֵירוּב. דְּאִי נָפֵיק חוּץ לְאַרְבַּע אַמּוֹתָיו קָאֵי בִּרה"ר, וְלָא מָצֵי לְמִשְׁקְלֵיהּ מֵרה"י, דְּהוּא בִּרה"ר וְעֵירוּבוֹ בִּרה"י. וְהָכָא לֵיכָּא לְמֵימַר כְּמַאן דְּמָלֵי – דְּהָא חוּץ לְאַרְבַּע אַמּוֹתָיו הוּא: נִתְכַּוֵּון לִשְׁבּוֹת שְׁבִיתָתוֹ בְּרֹאשׁ הַמִּגְדָּל. וְהוּא גָּבוֹהַּ הַרְבֵּה וְהִנִּיחַ עֵירוּבוֹ לְתוֹכוֹ: אִם לְמַעְלָה מֵעֲשָׂרָה הִנִּיחוֹ עֵירוּבוֹ עֵירוּב. וְאַע"פ שֶׁאֵינוֹ יָכוֹל לִיטְּלוֹ מִשָּׁם וְלַהֲבִיאוֹ לִמְקוֹם שְׁבִיתָתוֹ, דְּהָא מַמְטֵי לֵיהּ מֵרה"י לִרה"י דֶּרֶךְ אֲוִיר רה"ר, וְקַיְימָא לָן [שבת צו.] *בְּמוֹשִׁיט דַּאֲפִילּוּ לְמַעְלָה מִי' חַיָּיב – הֲרֵי יָכוֹל לֵירֵד וּלְאוֹכְלוֹ בַּמָּקוֹם שֶׁהוּא מוּנָּח שָׁם, דְּכֵיוָן דִּלְמַעְלָה מֵעֲשָׂרָה הוּא הָוֵי כְּבִמְקוֹם שְׁבִיתָתוֹ מַמָּשׁ, דְּכָל לְמַעְלָה מֵעֲשָׂרָה עַד לָרָקִיעַ חֲדָא רְשׁוּתָא הִיא: לְמַטָּה מִי'. כְּגוֹן שֶׁיֵּשׁ עֲלִיּוֹת לַמִּגְדָּל זוֹ לְמַעְלָה מִזּוֹ, וְהִנִּיחוֹ בָּעֲלִיָּיה שֶׁלְּמַטָּה מִי' דְּהָוְיָא כַּרְמְלִית: אֵין עֵירוּבוֹ עֵירוּב. דְּהָא לָא מָצֵי לְמִישְׁקְלֵי מֵהַהוּא כַּרְמְלִית וְאַיְתוּיֵי לְרֹאשׁ הַמִּגְדָּל שֶׁשּׁוֹבֵת שָׁם, מִשּׁוּם אֲוִיר רה"ר דְּמַמְטֵי לֵיהּ דֶּרֶךְ אֲוִיר רה"ר לִרְשׁוּת הַיָּחִיד. וְאִי נָחֵית וְאָכַל לֵיהּ הָתָם – נָפֵיק לֵיהּ מִמְּקוֹם שְׁבִיתָתוֹ, וַאֲנַן סְעוּדָה הָרְאוּיָה מִבְּעוֹד יוֹם בִּמְקוֹמוֹ בָּעֵינַן: וְאַמַּאי. לְמַטָּה מִי' אֵינוֹ עֵירוּב? נֵימָא: הוֹאִיל וְיָכוֹל לִנְטוֹת הַמִּגְדָּל וּלְהוֹלִיכוֹ לְמַטָּה, וְנִמְצָא מְקוֹם שְׁבִיתָתוֹ מוּטָּל לָאָרֶץ בִּרְשׁוּת הָרַבִּים וְשָׁקֵיל לֵיהּ מִכַּרְמְלִית, וְאָכֵיל לֵיהּ בִּמְקוֹם שְׁבִיתָתוֹ. דְּהָא לָא גָּזְרוּ עַל הַשְּׁבוּת, דְּהָא עַל כָּרְחָךְ רַבִּי הִיא, מִדְּקָתָנֵי רֵישָׁא: הִנִּיחַ עֵירוּבוֹ בַּכּוֹתֶל לְמַטָּה מֵעֲשָׂרָה – עֵירוּבוֹ עֵירוּב, וְאַף עַל גַּב דְּהוּא בִּרה"ר וְעֵירוּבוֹ בְּכַרְמְלִית: בְּמִגְדָּל הַמְסוּמָּר. תָּקוּעַ בְּמַסְמְרוֹת בַּכּוֹתֶל וְאֵינוֹ יָכוֹל לִנְטוֹת: בְּמִגְדָּל אָרוֹךְ. הַרְבֵּה, יוֹתֵר מִד' אַמּוֹת: דְּכִי מַמְטֵי לֵיהּ. לַמִּגְדָּל עַד דְּהָוֵי רֹאשׁוֹ לְמַטָּה מִי' – נָפֵיק לֵיהּ רֹאשׁוֹ חוּץ לְד' אַמּוֹת מִמָּקוֹם שֶׁהָיָה הַמִּגְדָּל יוֹשֵׁב בַּתְּחִילָּה, וְכִי שָׁקֵיל לֵיהּ וְאַמְטֵי לֵיהּ עַד רֹאשׁ הַמִּגְדָּל וְאָכֵיל לֵיהּ – אִישְׁתַּכַּח דְּלָא קָאֵי בְּד' אַמּוֹת שֶׁנִּתְכַּוֵּון לִשְׁבּוֹת בָּהֶן: וְאִי אִיכָּא כַּוְּותָא וּמִיתְנָא כו'. כַּוְּותָא חַלּוֹן, מִיתְנָא = חֶבֶל. אִם אֲרוּבָּה בְּרֹאשׁ הַמִּגְדָּל וְיֵשׁ חֶבֶל בְּיָדוֹ וְקָשׁוּר בָּעֵירוּב, וַאֲפִילּוּ כְּשֶׁהוּא בְּכַרְמְלִית לְמַטָּה מִי' יְבִיאֶנּוּ אֶצְלוֹ דֶּרֶךְ תּוֹכוֹ שֶׁל מִגְדָּל, דְּהָא מִכַּרְמְלִית לִרְשׁוּת הַיָּחִיד הוּא:(ב) ל"א שָׁמַעְתִּי, וְעִיקָּר: נִתְכַּוֵּון לִשְׁבּוֹת בְּרֹאשׁ הַמִּגְדָּל אוֹ בְּרֹאשׁ הַשּׁוֹבָךְ – אַהִנִּיחַ עֵירוּבוֹ בַּכּוֹתֶל קָאֵי. וְקָתָנֵי דְּהַשְׁתָּא הָוֵי אִיפְּכָא, דְּאִי לְמַעְלָה מִי' הִנִּיחוֹ בַּכּוֹתֶל – עֵירוּבוֹ עֵירוּב, שֶׁהַמִּגְדָּל אֵצֶל הַכּוֹתֶל וְיָכוֹל לַהֲבִיאוֹ אֶצְלוֹ, וְאֵין הֶפְסֵק בֵּינֵיהֶן. לְמַטָּה מִי' כְּגוֹן בְּטֶפַח תְּשִׁיעִי וְרַבִּים מְכַתְּפִין עָלָיו וְהָוֵי רה"ר – אֵין עֵירוּבוֹ עֵירוּב, דְּלָא מָצֵי מַיְיתֵי לֵיהּ מֵרה"ר לִרה"י. וְאַמַּאי? לֵימָא: הוֹאִיל וְיָכוֹל לִנְטוֹת הַמִּגְדָּל שֶׁל מְקוֹם שְׁבִיתָה וּלְהָבִיאוֹ לְתוֹךְ רה"ר, דְּנֶיהֱוֵי רֹאשׁ הַמִּגְדָּל כַּרְמְלִית דְּרָחָב ד' וְאֵינוֹ גָּבוֹהַּ י' נָפֵק לֵיהּ מִחוּץ לְד' אַמּוֹת – מַרְחִיק רֹאשׁ הַמִּגְדָּל מִן הָעֵירוּב אַרְבַּע אַמּוֹת וְלָא מָצֵי לְמִשְׁקְלֵיהּ וּלְאַיְתוּיֵי לְרֹאשׁ הַמִּגְדָּל, וְנִמְצָא מַעֲבִירוֹ ד' אַמּוֹת בִּרה"ר. אִי נַמִי: נִמְצֵאת שְׁבִיתָתוֹ מִתְרַחֶקֶת(ג) אַרְבַּע אַמּוֹתָיו הָרִאשׁוֹנוֹת וְאֵין זֶה מְקוֹמוֹ. מִתְנָא = חֶבֶל, כַּוְּותָא = חַלּוֹן. אִם יֵשׁ חַלּוֹן בַּמִּגְדָּל כְּנֶגֶד מָקוֹם שֶׁהָעֵירוּב שָׁם, וְיֵשׁ חֶבֶל קָטָן בְּיָדוֹ וְקָשׁוּר חֶבֶל בָּעֵירוּב מִבְּעוֹד יוֹם, אֲפִילּוּ כְּשֶׁהוּא בִּרה"ר לְמַטָּה מִי' וְרֹאשׁ הַשֵּׁנִי יְהֵא בַּמִּגְדָּל – יְבִיאֶנּוּ אֶצְלוֹ, דְּכֵיוָן דְּאִיגּוּדוֹ בְּיָדוֹ אֵינוֹ אֶלָּא מִשּׁוּם שְׁבוּת כִּי מַיְיתֵי לֵיהּ מֵרה"ר לִרה"י, כִּדְתְנַן בְּרֵישׁ "הַמּוֹצֵא תְּפִילִּין"* [דף צז:]: הָיָה קוֹרֵא בְּרֹאשׁ הַגַּג וְנִתְגַּלְגֵּל הַסֵּפֶר מִיָּדוֹ, אֲפִילּוּ בָּאָרֶץ עַצְמוֹ – גּוֹלְלוֹ אֶצְלוֹ, שֶׁאֵין לְךָ דָּבָר שֶׁהוּא מִשּׁוּם שְׁבוּת עוֹמֵד בִּפְנֵי כִּתְבֵי הַקּוֹדֶשׁ. אַלְמָא: הֵיכָא דְּאִיגּוּדוֹ בְּיָדוֹ – שְׁבוּת בְּעָלְמָא הוּא. וְאָתְיָא כְּרַבִּי, דְּאָמַר: לֹא גָּזְרוּ עַל הַשְּׁבוּת בֵּין הַשְּׁמָשׁוֹת:

ה"ג

ואמאי נימא כיון דאי בעי לאמטויי מצי ממטי ליה כו'. פ"ה: הא דנקט לאוקמיה ממתניתין דיו"ט ושבת משום דלא תנא במשנה אחריתי הולכת עירוב בהדיא כדהכא. ולר"י נראה: דדוקא מי"ט פריך, אבל מהא דבעיר הולכת עירוב להכא לערב בערב שבת – לא מצי למיפרך, דהא בין השמשות שהוא שעת קניית עירוב לא מצי לאמטויי התם משום איסור הוצאה. ואין ליישב דברי רש"י דודאי מהולכת עירוב של כל השנה [לא] היה יכול להקשות למה היה צריך להוליכו עד מקום השביתה – לא היה צריך רק להוציאו מביתו ולהניחו ברשות הרבים במקום קרוב, כשיעור שני תילתי מיל או שלשה רביעי מיל או חצי מיל שהם שיעורי בין השמשות, למר כדאית ליה ולמר כדאית ליה, דאי בעי ממטי ליה פחות פחות מד' עד מקום השביתה. דהא לרבנן דר' לא מצי לאמטויי פחות פחות מד' אמות הלכך צריך להוליכו עד מקום השביתה. ולרבי נמי איכא למימר דהא דצריך להוליכו עד מקום השביתה – היינו כששביתתו ברה"י הוא, ויש רה"ר בין ביתו למקום שביתתו. ועוד נראה לר"י: דאף כששביתתו ברה"ר צריך להוליכו גם לרבי עד מקום שביתתו, דמודה רבי שיש להחמיר בשבות בפחות מארבע אמותיו, כמו שמודה בקנה דגוזר שמא יקטום משום דבקל יבא לידי איסור שבת דאורייתא. וה"ה דבהאי שבות נמי יש להחמיר וכי משני גזירה משום יו"ט אחר שבת כו' – הוה מצי לשנויי גזרינן אטו כל שבת דעלמא. דבכמה דוכתין [ביצה יח.] *אמר גזירה יו"ט אטו שבת, אלא דעדיפא למגזר יו"ט אטו יו"ט. א"נ: אע"ג דבעלמא גזרינן, בעירוב דמקילינן טפי לא הוה גזרינן יו"ט אטו שבת: **גזירה** אטו יו"ט שחל להיות אחר השבת. והא דאמר לעיל* [דף לב:] גבי אילן: כל דבר שהוא משום שבות לא גזרו עליו בין השמשות, ולא גזרינן משום יו"ט שחל להיות אחר השבת או לפני השבת, דאז ממה נפשך אסור להשתמש באילן. היינו משום דהתם היא גופא לא הויא אלא משום שבות, ואינו אסור ליטלו אלא מדרבנן. אבל הכא, דביו"ט שחל להיות אחר השבת אי אפשר להוליכו משום איסור הוצאה דאורייתא – גזרי' שאר יו"ט אטו הא.

הגה"ה

אבל כששביתתו ברה"ר לא יצטרך להוליכו עד מקום השביתה וע"כ כן צ"ל האמת לפירוש הקונ' דאי לעולם צריך להוליכו עד מקום השביתה א"כ תיקשי ליה מרבי ולא יכול לתרץ מה שמתרץ גזירה אטו י"ט שלאחר שבת. ע"כ:

או בראש המגדל למטה מעשרה אין עירובו עירוב. פי' בקונט' בלשון ראשון: דלא מצי למשקלי' מכרמלית ולאיתויי לראש המגדל שובת שם, דממטי ליה דרך אויר רה"ר לרה"י. וקשה: דאמאי אינו עירוב? הא ליכא איסורא דאורייתא וכרבי אתיא. מדפריך בתר הכי: אי איכא כוותא ומתנא – ה"נ. ואע"ג דאגודו בידו איכא נמי איסורא דרבנן! לכך נראה דלא הוי כרמלית אלא רה"ר, כגון שהוא בטפח תשיעי ורבים מכתפין עליו, או בחורי (ד) רה"ר דהוי כרה"ר. וצ"ע: דכי נמי הוי רה"ר, אם בכה"ג הוי מושיט, הואיל ואינו מושיט דרך קרקע רה"ר. ואי לא הוי מושיט – צ"ל דמיירי שאי אפשר להושיט מראש המגדל וליטול אלא דרך כוותא שכנגד העירוב צריך להביאו לתוך המגדל ומשם יביאנו למקום שביתתו: **הכי** נמי נימא הואיל ויכול לנטותו. נראה לר"י דקסבר התלמוד דכי נמי יטה ראש המגדל – הוי שביתתו בראש המגדל, כ"ז שאין ראש התחתון זז ממקומו. דאם בשמטה ראש המגדל שביתתו לעולם במקום שהיה ראשו בתחילה כשהיה זקוף, דהיינו כנגד הראש התחתון – א"כ מאי משני הכא במגדל ארוך עסקינן, דאי ממטי ליה קא נפיק חוץ לד' אמות, מה לנו במה שיצא ראש העליון חוץ לד' אמות, כיון שאין שביתתו שם! אלא ודאי שביתתו לעולם *בראש המגדל, ולהכי במגדל ארוך אי אפשר לנטותו, דאי ממטי ליה נפיק ליה חוץ לד' אמות, ונמצא מרוחק מעירובו ארבע אמות ולא יוכל להביא עירובו לראש המגדל אפילו לרבי, כדפי' לעיל דמודה בשבות בפחות מד' אמות דאסור. אי נמי: אינו עירוב, כדפ"ה משום שנמצא שביתתו מתרחקת מד' אמות הראשונות, ואין זה מקומו והוי כאלו מסיר כל המגדל ממקומו הראשון ומעמידו חוץ לד' אמות, דהשתא שביתתו בקרקעית המגדל שהיה בתחילה, והואיל (ה) ושקיל ליה כוליה האי ודאי לא אמרו: **אי איכא כוותא ומתנא.** הא דלא פריך לעיל נמי הכי גבי אילן – משום דאין דרך מתנא להיות גבי אילן. ואין לומר דנייתי, דכולי האי ודאי לא אמרינן "הואיל". אי נמי יש לומר: דהשתא דוקא פריך, מכיון דאמר הואיל ויכול לנטותו:

אי

בראש המגדל ארוך ולהכי בראש המגדל א"א לנטותו כצ"ל [מהר"ס]

רבינו חננאל

אמאי נימא כיון דיכול למיזל ולאמטויי לעירובו אע"ג דלא אזל ואמטייה כמאן דאזיל ואמטייה דמי. ופריק ר' זירא גזירה משום יו"ט אחר השבת שאינו יכול לילך בעירובו בשבת לפיכך הצריכוהו דלא תהוי עירוב עד דממטייה ליה. איתיביה נתכוון לשבות ברה"ר ונתן עירובו בכותל למעלה מעשרה טפחים אין עירובו עירוב שהוא ברה"ר ועירובו ברה"י נתכוון לשבות בראש השובך או בראש המגדל אם עירובו בכותל למעלה מעשרה הוא עירובו עירוב למטה מי' אין עירובו עירוב שהרי הוא ברה"י ועירובו ברה"ר ואמאי נימא כיון דיכול לנטות את המגדל ולהביאו בתוך עשרה כמאן דאמטיי חזי והרי הוא נמי ברה"ר הוא שובת ואמאי קתני אין עירובו עירוב ופריק ר' ירמיה הכא במגדל מסומר עסקינן דלא יכול למינטיה. רב פפא אמר אפילו תימא במגדל [שאינו] מסומר והכא במגדל ארוך עסקינן דאי מנטליה נפיק חוץ לד' אמות והרי אמרו המניח עירובו יש לו ד' אמות וכו' ואסיקנא דלית ליה כוותא ומתנא לאיתויי עירוב גביה: **נתנו** בבור אפילו עמוק ק' אמה הרי

הגהות הב"ח

(א) גמ' דאי ממטי ליה פורתא נפיק ליה חוץ: (ב) רש"י ד"ה ל"א שמעתי נ"ל לא שמעתי וכו': (ג) מתרחקת מד' אמותיו: (ד) תום' ד"ה או בראש וכו' או בחורי רה"י דהוי כרה"י ול"ע: (ה) ד"ה הכי נמי וכו' והואיל ואי שקיל ליה:

סז א ב מיי' פ"ו מהל' עירובין הלכה י טור שו"ע א"ח סי' תט סעיף ג:
סח ג מיי' פ"ב מהלכות כלאים הלכה יט:
סט ד מיי' פ"ב מהל' י"ט הלכה ט טור שו"ע א"ח סי' תקיח סעיף ט:

פְּשִׁיטָא, *רה"י עוֹלָה עַד לָרָקִיעַ. וְכִי הֵיכִי דְּסָלְקָא לְעֵיל — ה"נ דְּנָחְתָא לְתַחַת. וְאֶלָּא דְּקָאֵי בִּרְשׁוּת הָרַבִּים. דְּנִתְכַּוֵּין לִשְׁבּוֹת הֵיכָא? אִי לְמַעְלָה(א) — הוּא בְּמָקוֹם אֶחָד וְעֵירוּבוֹ בְּמָקוֹם אַחֵר הוּא, אִי לְמַטָּה — פְּשִׁיטָא, הוּא וְעֵירוּבוֹ בְּמָקוֹם אֶחָד! לָא צְרִיכָא, דְּקָאֵי בְּכַרְמְלִית, וְנִתְכַּוֵּין לִשְׁבּוֹת לְמַעְלָה, וְרַבִּי הִיא, דְּאָמַר: *כׇּל דָּבָר שֶׁהוּא מִשּׁוּם שְׁבוּת לֹא גָּזְרוּ עָלָיו בֵּין הַשְּׁמָשׁוֹת.§ **מתני'** אנָתְנוֹ בְּרֹאשׁ הַקָּנֶה אוֹ בְּרֹאשׁ הַקּוּנְדָּס, בִּזְמַן שֶׁהוּא תָּלוּשׁ וְנָעוּץ — אֲפִילּוּ גָּבוֹהַּ ק' אַמָּה הֲרֵי זֶה עֵירוּב.§ **גמ'** רָמֵי לֵיהּ רַב אַדָּא בַּר מַתְנָא לְרָבָא: תָּלוּשׁ וְנָעוּץ — אִין, לֹא תָּלוּשׁ וְנָעוּץ — לָא. מַנִּי — רַבָּנַן הִיא, *דְּאָמְרִי: כׇּל דָּבָר שֶׁהוּא מִשּׁוּם שְׁבוּת — גָּזְרוּ עָלָיו בֵּין הַשְּׁמָשׁוֹת, וְהָא אָמְרַתְּ רֵישָׁא רַבִּי, רֵישָׁא רַבִּי וְסֵיפָא רַבָּנַן?! א"ל: כְּבָר רָמֵי לֵיהּ רָמִי בַּר חָמָא לְרַב חִסְדָּא, וְשַׁנֵּי לֵיהּ: רֵישָׁא רַבִּי וְסֵיפָא רַבָּנַן. רָבִינָא אָמַר: כּוּלָּהּ רַבִּי הִיא, וְסֵיפָא — בגְּזֵירָה שֶׁמָּא יִקְטוֹם.§ הַהוּא פּוּלְמוּסָא דַּאֲתָא לִנְהַרְדְּעָא, אֲמַר לְהוּ רַב נַחְמָן: פּוּקוּ עֲבִידוּ כְּבוּשֵׁי כַּבְשֵׁי בְּאַגְמָא, וּלְמָחָר נֵיזִיל וְנֵיתִיב עֲלָוַיְהוּ. אֵיתִיבֵיהּ רָמִי בַּר חָמָא לְרַב נַחְמָן, וְאָמְרִי לָהּ רַב עוּקְבָא בַּר אַבָּא לְרַב נַחְמָן: תָּלוּשׁ וְנָעוּץ — אִין, לֹא תָּלוּשׁ וְלֹא נָעוּץ — לָא. א"ל: הָתָם בְּעוּזְרְדִין. וּמְנָא תֵּימְרָא דְּשָׁנֵי לָן בֵּין עוּזְרְדִין לְשֶׁאֵין עוּזְרְדִין — *דְּתַנְיָא: גהַקָּנִין וְהָאֲטָדִין וְהָהִגִּין — מִין אִילָן הֵן, וְאֵינָן כִּלְאַיִם בַּכֶּרֶם. וְתַנְיָא אִידָךְ: ‏הַקָּנִים וְהַקִּידָן וְהָאוּרְבָּנִין — מִין יָרָק הֵן, וְהֵן כִּלְאַיִם בַּכֶּרֶם. קַשְׁיָא אַהֲדָדֵי! אֶלָּא ש"מ: כָּאן — בְּעוּזְרְדִין, כָּאן — בְּשֶׁאֵין עוּזְרְדִין, ש"מ. וְקִידָה מִין יָרָק הוּא?! *וְהָתְנַן: אֵין מַרְכִּיבִין פֵּגָם ע"ג קִידָה לְבָנָה, מִפְּנֵי שֶׁהוּא יָרָק בְּאִילָן! אָמַר רַב פָּפָּא: קִידָה לְחוּד, וְקִידָה לְבָנָה לְחוּד.§ **מתני'** נְתָנוֹ בְּמִגְדָּל *וְאָבַד הַמַּפְתֵּחַ — הֲרֵי זֶה עֵירוּב. ר"א אוֹמֵר: אִם אֵינוֹ יוֹדֵעַ שֶׁהַמַּפְתֵּחַ בִּמְקוֹמוֹ — אֵינוֹ עֵירוּב.§ **גמ'** וְאַמַּאי? הוּא בְּמָקוֹם אֶחָד וְעֵירוּבוֹ בְּמָקוֹם אַחֵר הוּא! רַב וּשְׁמוּאֵל דְּאָמְרִי תַּרְוַיְיהוּ: הָכָא בְּמִגְדָּל שֶׁל לְבֵנִים עָסְקִינַן; וְר"מ הִיא, דְּאָמַר: פּוֹתֵחַ לְכַתְּחִילָּה וְנוֹטֵל. *דִּתְנַן: דבַּיִת שֶׁמִּילְּאָהוּ פֵּירוֹת, סָתוּם וְנִפְחַת — נוֹטֵל מִמְּקוֹם הַפְּחָת. ר' מֵאִיר אוֹמֵר: פּוֹחֵת וְנוֹטֵל לְכַתְּחִילָּה. וְהָאָמַר *רַב נַחְמָן בַּר אַדָּא, אָמַר שְׁמוּאֵל: *בַּאֲוִירָא דְּלִיבְנֵי, הָכָא נַמִי — בַּאֲוִירָא דְּלִיבְנֵי. וְהָא אָמַר רַבִּי זֵירָא: *בְּיוֹ"ט אָמְרוּ אֲבָל לֹא בְּשַׁבָּת! ה"נ, בְּיו"ט. אִי הָכִי, הַיְינוּ דְּקָתָנֵי עֲלָהּ, *ר"א אוֹמֵר: אִם בָּעִיר אָבַד — עֵירוּבוֹ עֵירוּב, וְאִם בַּשָּׂדֶה אָבַד — אֵין עֵירוּבוֹ עֵירוּב. וְאִי בְּיוֹם טוֹב — מַה לִּי עִיר מַה לִּי שָׂדֶה?!
חַסּוּרֵי

הכי גרסינן: **פשיטא** רשות היחיד עולה עד לרקיע וכי היכי דסלקא לעיל ה"נ **נחתא** לתחת. ומאי אפילו בור עמוק עשרה – רה"י היא: בבור דקאי בכרמלית. כגון בקעה, דהיינו שדות, דהוי בור רה"י ושפתו כרמלית: **מתני'** קונדס. = פל"ו בלע"ז, ואינם מחוברים.

ובגמ' פריך: והאמרת רישא רבי היא, דאמר: לא גזרו במחובר בין השמשות: **אפילו** גבוה מאה אמה. הואיל ואינו רחב ד' למטה – לאו רשות היחיד הוה. ואע"ג דלמעלה ד' דהא עירוב על גבי מקום ד' בעינן: **גמ'** תלוש ונעוץ. הוא דהוי עירוב, אבל מחובר – לא הוה עירוב, משום דכי(ב) בעי לאשקליה משתמש באילן: גזירה **שמא** יקטום. לפי שהקנה רך הוא איכא למיגזר שמא יקטום כי שקיל ליה. אבל אילן קשה הוא. ובין השמשות לשמא יעלה ויתלוש לא חיישינן, אבל לקטימת קנה ודאי היא, איידי דרכיכא מיקטמא. ולאו שבות הוא אלא מלאכה, דמיחייב משום קוצר: **פולמוסא**. חיל המלך, היה מקום דחוק לתלמידים מפני אנשי החיל: כבושי כבשי **באגמא**. לאו וכפו הקנים זה על זה הרבה כמין כסאות לישב עליהן: **לא** תלוש ונעוץ **לא**. אלמא: קנים כאילן הן, ואסור להשתמש עליהן: (ג)**עוזרדין**. שהוקשה כבר – הרי הן כאילן. וכי שרינן בשאינן עוזרדין – בעוד הקנים רכין, דהוו כירק, ובירק לא הזכירו חכמים שבות: **עוזרדין** אטדין והיגין מיני קוצים הן: **קידן**. = בושם ששמו קידה: **אורבנין**. = אורשרי"ש: קשיא. קנים אקנים: **פגם**. = רוד"א:
מתני' ואבד המפתח עירובו עירוב. ובגמרא מפרש לה. וכגון שהמגדל ברה"י. דאי הוה ביה מפתח – לא הוה ביה שום איסור, דהוא ועירובו ברה"י: **גמ'** ואמאי. נהי דתרווייהו ברה"י נינהו, כיון דלא מצי שקיל ליה – הוה ליה כשני מקומות: **של** לבנים. שנוח לסותרו. וכדבעי לאוקומי באוירא דליבני, סדורות זו ע"ג זו בלא טיט ביניהן, דלאו סתירה היא: **דר"מ**. במס' ביצה (לג:): **ונפחת**. מאליו, אפילו ביו"ט עצמו: **נוטל** ממקום הפחת. ולא מיתסר משום מוקצה, וסתמא כר"ש: **אף** פוחת לכתחילה. כדמוקי לה באוירא דליבני, דלאו סתירת אהל היא: **אם** בעיר **אבד**. המפתח: **עירובו** עירוב. דאי משכח ליה מצי מייתי ליה דרך חצירות וגגות וקרפיפות, שכולן רשות אחת הן כר"ש: **ואם** בשדה אין עירובו עירוב. דאי נמי משכח ליה – לא מצי לאיתויי ליה וג' מחלוקות בדבר: לת"ק בין בעיר בין בשדה – עירובו עירוב, דמצי סבר ליה. ולר' אליעזר דמתני' בין בעיר בין בשדה – אין עירובו עירוב, דמיספר לא מצי סבר, ולית ליה דר"מ. ולאיתויי נמי לא מצי אי הוה משכח ליה, דלית ליה דר"ש *דגגות וקרפיפות רשות אחת הן. ור' אליעזר דברייתא סבר לה כרבי שמעון. אי נמי: ר' אליעזר דמתניתין לא איירי אלא בשדה, והוא ניהו רבי אליעזר דברייתא: אבל

אי למעלה אמאי וכו'. הוה מצי למימר משום דהנותן עירובו יש לו ד' אמות, אלא דבעי לשנויי אפילו נתכוון לשבות חוץ לד' אמות מן הבור, דומיא דרישא. ולעיל גבי אילן לא רצה לתרץ דנתכוון לשבות חוץ לארבע אמות, דרגילות הוא לשבות בעיקרו של אילן:

והאורבנין. פ"ה: אורשרי"ש. ואינו נראה, דאותו כשהוקשה נעשה עץ גמור, והוה ליה למחשב בברייתא דלעיל ולחלק בין עוזרדין לשאינן עוזרדין כדמפליג גבי קנים. ונראה לי שהוא שם מין ירק:

ואמאי הוא במקום אחד ועירובו במקום אחר. וא"ת: והא השתא ס"ד דבמגדל עץ איירי דהוי כלי. מדקא משני הכא במגדל של לבנים עסקינן. ועוד: דסתם מגדל שבהתלמוד של עץ, וא"כ מאי פריך? הרי מותר לשבר את הכלי וליטול מה שבתוכו, כדתנן בפ' "חבית" (שבת דף קמו.): שובר אדם את החבית ליטול ממנה גרוגרות. וטעמא, כדאמר בסמוך* – משום דאין בנין וסתירה בכלים! וי"ל: דמשמע ליה במגדל גדול, דשייך ביה בנין וסתירה. דאי בקטן דהוי כלי – מ"ט דר"א דפליג? ועוד: דבכלי נמי שייך בנין וסתירה, כדאמר ב"הבונה" (שם דף קב.) האי מאן דעייל שופתא בקופינא דמרא – חייב משום בונה. והא דקאמר בסמוך דמר סבר כלי הוא ואין בנין בכלים כו' – היינו בהנהו דאמר נוטלין אבל לא מחזירין, דלא הוי בנין וסתירה גמורה, או כדמוקי במסקנא במנעול קטיר במיתנא ומדמוקי לה בקטיר במיתנא – משמע דווקא בהכי שרי, אבל לשבר הכלי ולקלקלו – אסור, דשפיר שייך בנין וסתירה בכלים. והא דשרי לשבר החבית – הא מוקי לה בביצה פרק "המביא" (דף לג:) במוסתקי. פירוש: חתיכות המדובקות יחד. ואף על גב דאליבא דרבי אליעזר דאמר קטמו להריח בו פטור אבל אסור מוקי לה במוסתקי. דפריך: ולית ליה לר"א שובר אדם את החבית וכו'. לרבנן נמי צריך לאוקמא הכי, דמודים אי הוה חייב חטאת לאלות בו שיניו דהוי אסור בקטמו להריח. והא דבעי לרב ששת בפרק "חבית" (שבת דף קמו.): מהו למברז חביתא בבורטיא – במוסתקי איירי. ומיהו, בירושלמי קאמר אמתני' דהכא, הדא דתימא במגדל של אבן, אבל במגדל של עץ נעשה כשובר את החבית ליטול ממנה גרוגרות. משמע דבלא מוסתקי נמי שרי בכלי של עץ:

נוטל ממקום הפחת. פירש"י: ולא מיתסר משום מוקצה, דסתמא כר"ש. וקשה למהר"י, דאמר בריש ביצה (דף ב:): דביו"ט סתם לן תנא כרבי יהודה, הא סתם לן תנא כר"ש נמי והך סתמא עדיפא, דהויא בתראה? ומיהו, רש"י תירץ בביצה דהא דנוטל ממקום הפחת לא חשיב מוקצה – הואיל ולא הוי מוקצה אלא משום פסיתא, דהוי דרבנן דמוקי באוירא דליבני. וכן נמי אמרינן ב"המביא" (שם דף לד:) טבל מוכן הוא אצל שבת, שאם עבר ותקנו – מתוקן. משמע דלא חשיב מוקצה כיון דלא רכיב עליה איסורא דאורייתא. ולמהר"י נראה לתרץ: דהך לא חשיב סתמא דלא מצי למיתני דברי ר"ש – דאפשר דר"ש סובר דפותח לכתחילה כר"מ, אבל ההיא דשבת (ד' קנו:) דמסתכין את הדלועין דמצי למיתני בה דברי ר"ש ולא קתני, חשיב ודאי סתמא: **והאמר** ר' זירא ביו"ט אמרו וכו'. והוה מצי לאוקמ' כרבי, דבהכי אוירא דליבני לית(ד) ליה איסורא אלא מדרבנן, כדאמר ב"המביא" (ביצה לה:) כיון דטרגינהו אקלינהו. אלא דניחא ליה לאוקומה כרבנן, כרבא דאוקי לעיל סיפא כרבנן. ועי"ל: דאם כן טעמא דר"א דאסר משום דסבר כרבנן, ולא ניחא ליה לאוקמא פלוגתייהו בפלוגתא דרבי ורבנן:
חסורי

(דף לה.)
תוספתא פ"ג דכלאים
[גירסת ירושלמי ורי"ף ורא"ש ונעל בפניו]
[גירסת הערוך אארא ופירוש לבינים סדורים זה אצל זה או זה ע"ג זה קורין לו כך בלשון פרסי]

[לעיל לב: וש"נ]
[שם וש"נ]
[לעיל לג:]
כלאים פ"א מ"ח ע"ש
ביצה לג:
[שם ע"ש]
[ביצה שם]
[תוספתא פ"ב ושם איתא רבי אלעזר]
[לקמן פט.]

הגהות הב"ח

(א) גמ' אי למעלה אמאי הוא במקום אחד: (ב) רש"י ד"ה תלוש וכו' משום דכי שקיל ליה משתמש: (ג) ד"ה עוזרדין שהוקשה וכו' שבות הס"ד ואח"כ מ"ה אטדין והיגין עוזרדין נינהו: (ד) תוס' ד"ה והאמר וכו' דליבני לית ביה איסורא:

גליון הש"ס

גמ' ותניא אידך הקנים והקידן. עי' בר"ש פ"א מ"ח דכלאים:

רבינו חננאל

זה עירוב כו'. אוקימנא בבור העומד בכרמלית ונתכוון לשבות למעלה ורבי היא דקאמר כל משום שבות לא גזרו רבנן עליו בין השמשות: **נתנו** בראש הקנה כו' עד בתלוש ונעוץ ש"מ דלא התירו בעירוב אלא בתלוש ונעוץ מכלל דבמחובר לקרקע אסור כמאן כרבנן דפליגי על ר' ואמרי כל משום שבות גזרו עליו בין השמשות ואקשינן רישא דתני נתנו באילן אוקימנא לר' סיפא דתני נתנו בראש הקנה שהוא תלוש ונעוץ לרבנן רישא רבי וסיפא רבנן. אמר רב חסדא אין רישא רבי וסיפא רבנן רבינא אמר כולה רבי היא. ובקנה מחובר אמאי לא גזרו גזרה כיון דהוא אינו יכול לנטותו שמא יקטמנו. ההוא פולמוסא דאתי לנהרדעא אמר רב נחמן לתלמידיו פוקו כבשו כבשוה באגמא. פי' כבשו כופו הקנים שבאגם ותנו עליהן עפר כדי שיהו נוחים לישב עליהן בשבת. והקשו עליו איך אתה מורה לעשות כן וכי מותר להשתמש בקנים המחוברים לקרקע והא אנן תנן תלוש ונעוץ אין מחובר לא. ופריק מתני' בקנים עוזרדין חזקים שהן כמין אילן. ואם יבא להשוות בהן. כיון שהן חזקים ואינו יכול לנטותן וליטול העירוב שעל ראשו. גזרה שמא יקטום. כי קאמינא בקנים דקים שהן עוזרדין שהן כמין ירק ונוחים להרכיבם ולנטותם ולא אתי לקוטמתן דהני לאו מין אילן נינהו ולא גזרו בהו רבנן. ובירק נמי דמפריך ליתנהו דהא קשין הן לאו מיפרכו לפיכך לא גזרו בהו והביא ראיה לדבריו ממשנתנו דתנן הקנים מין אילן הן ותנן הקנים מין ירק הן. קשיין אהדדי ופריק הא דתני מין אילן בעוזרדין והא דתניא מין ירק בשאינן עוזרדין. ואסיקנא קידה מין ירק הוא. אבל קידה לבנה מין (ירק) [אילן] הוא. ויש מי שאמר אלקסט: **מתני'** נתנו במגדל ונעל בפניו ואבד המפתח כו'. ואקשינן כיון שאין יכול ליטלו הוא במקום אחד ועירוב במקום אחר הוא. אמאי תנן (אין) עירובו עירוב. ופרקינן רב ושמואל דאמר מתני' של בנין ור' מאיר היא דאמר במס' יו"ט בבית שמלא פירות סתום [ונפחת] פותח לכתחלה ונוטל הכא נמי פותח לכתחלה ונוטל העירוב. ודחינן להא בבית שהוא מלא פירות וסתום וא"ר מאיר פותח לכתחלה ונוטל. תנא ביו"ט אמרו
ולא

חַסּוּרֵי מִיחַסְּרָא וְהָכִי קָתָנֵי: נָתְנוּ בְּמִגְדָּל, וְנָעַל בְּפָנָיו וְאָבַד הַמַּפְתֵּחַ — הֲרֵי זֶה עֵירוּב. בַּמֶּה דְּבָרִים אֲמוּרִים — בְּיוֹם טוֹב, אֲבָל בְּשַׁבָּת — אֵין עֵירוּבוֹ עֵירוּב. נִמְצָא הַמַּפְתֵּחַ, בֵּין בָּעִיר בֵּין בַּשָּׂדֶה — אֵין עֵירוּבוֹ עֵירוּב. רַבִּי אֱלִיעֶזֶר אוֹמֵר: בָּעִיר — עֵירוּבוֹ עֵירוּב, בַּשָּׂדֶה — אֵין עֵירוּבוֹ עֵירוּב. בָּעִיר עֵירוּבוֹ עֵירוּב — כְּר' שִׁמְעוֹן, *דְּאָמַר: אֶחָד גַּגּוֹת וְאֶחָד חֲצֵירוֹת וְאֶחָד קַרְפֵּיפוֹת רְשׁוּת אַחַת הֵן לַכֵּלִים שֶׁשָּׁבְתוּ בְּתוֹכָן. (א) בַּשָּׂדֶה אֵין עֵירוּבוֹ עֵירוּב — כְּרַבָּנַן. רַבָּה וְרַב יוֹסֵף דְּאָמְרִי תַּרְוַיְיהוּ: *הָכָא בְּמִגְדָּל שֶׁל עֵץ עָסְקִינַן; דְּמָר סָבַר: כְּלִי הוּא, *וְאֵין בִּנְיָן בְּכֵלִים וְאֵין סְתִירָה בְּכֵלִים. וּמָר סָבַר: אֹהֶל הוּא. וּבִפְלוּגְתָּא דְּהָנֵי תַּנָּאֵי; *דִּתְנַן: הִקִּישׁ עַל גַּבֵּי שִׁידָּה תֵּיבָה וּמִגְדָּל — טְמֵאִין. רַבִּי נְחֶמְיָה וְרַבִּי שִׁמְעוֹן מְטַהֲרִין. מַאי לָאו בְּהָא קָמִפַּלְגִי; מָר סָבַר כְּלִי הוּא, וּמָר סָבַר: אֹהֶל הוּא? אָמַר אַבַּיֵי: וְתִיסְבְּרָא?! וְהָתַנְיָא: אֹהֶל וְנִיסָּט — טָמֵא, כְּלִי וְאֵינוֹ נִיסָּט — טָהוֹר. וְקָתָנֵי סֵיפָא: *וְאִם הָיוּ נִיסּוֹטִין — טְמֵאִים. זֶה הַכְּלָל: נִיסָּט מֵחֲמַת כֹּחוֹ — טָמֵא, מֵחֲמַת רְעָדָה — טָהוֹר! אֶלָּא אָמַר אַבַּיֵי: דְּכ"ע: הֶיסֵּט מֵחֲמַת כֹּחוֹ — טָמֵא, מֵחֲמַת רְעָדָה — טָהוֹר. וְהָכָא בִּרְעָדָה מֵחֲמַת כֹּחוֹ עָסְקִינַן. וּבְהָא קָא מִיפַּלְגִי; דְּמָר סָבַר: הָוֵי הֶיסֵּט, וּמָר סָבַר: לָא הָוֵי הֶיסֵּט. וּמַתְנִיתִין בְּמַאי מוֹקְמִינַן לָהּ? אַבַּיֵי וְרָבָא דְּאָמְרִי תַּרְוַיְיהוּ: בְּמַנְעוּל וְקָטִיר בְּמִתְנָא עָסְקִינַן, וּבָעֵי סַכִּינָא לְמִיפְסְקֵיהּ. תַּנָּא קַמָּא סָבַר לָהּ כְּרַבִּי יוֹסֵי, דְּאָמַר: *כָּל הַכֵּלִים נִיטָּלִין בְּשַׁבָּת, חוּץ מִמַּסָּר הַגָּדוֹל וְיָתֵד שֶׁל מַחֲרֵישָׁה. וְרַבִּי אֱלִיעֶזֶר סָבַר לָהּ כְּרַבִּי נְחֶמְיָה, *דְּאָמַר: אֲפִי' טַלִּית, אֲפִי' תַּרְוָוד — אֵין נִיטָּלִין אֶלָּא לְצוֹרֶךְ תַּשְׁמִישָׁן.§

מתני' נִתְגַּלְגֵּל חוּץ לַתְּחוּם, נָפַל עָלָיו גַּל, אוֹ נִשְׂרַף, תְּרוּמָה וְנִטְמֵאת; מִבְּעוֹד יוֹם — אֵינוֹ עֵירוּב, מִשֶּׁחֲשֵׁיכָה — הֲרֵי זֶה עֵירוּב. אִם *סָפֵק, ר"מ וְר' יְהוּדָה אוֹמְרִים: הֲרֵי זֶה חַמָּר גַּמָּל. ר' יוֹסֵי וְר"ש אוֹמְרִים: סְפֵק עֵירוּב כָּשֵׁר. אָמַר ר' יוֹסֵי: אַבְטוֹלְמוֹס הֵעִיד מִשּׁוּם חֲמִשָּׁה זְקֵנִים עַל סְפֵק עֵירוּב שֶׁכָּשֵׁר.§

גמ' "נִתְגַּלְגֵּל חוּץ לַתְּחוּם". אָמַר רָבָא: לֹא שָׁנוּ אֶלָּא שֶׁנִּתְגַּלְגֵּל חוּץ לְאַרְבַּע אַמּוֹת, אֲבָל לְתוֹךְ ד' אַמּוֹת — *הַנּוֹתֵן עֵירוּבוֹ יֵשׁ לוֹ ד' אַמּוֹת.§ "נָפַל עָלָיו גַּל וכו'".§ קָא ס"ד דְּאִי בָּעֵי מָצֵי שָׁקֵיל לֵיהּ, לֵימָא מַתְנִיתִין דְּלָא כְּרַבִּי, דְּאִי כְּרַבִּי — הָאָמַר: *כָּל דָּבָר שֶׁהוּא מִשּׁוּם שְׁבוּת — לֹא גָּזְרוּ עָלָיו בֵּין הַשְּׁמָשׁוֹת! אֲפִילּוּ תֵּימָא כְּרַבִּי, לָא צְרִיכָא, דְּבָעֵי מָרָא וַחֲצִינָא. וּצְרִיכִי, דְּאִי תָּנָא "נִתְגַּלְגֵּל" — מִשּׁוּם דְּלֵיתָא גַּבֵּיהּ. אֲבָל נָפַל עָלָיו גַּל, דְּאִיתֵיהּ גַּבֵּיהּ — אֵימָא לֶיהֱוֵי עֵירוּב. וְאִי תָּנָא "נָפַל עָלָיו גַּל" — מִשּׁוּם דְּמִיכְּסֵי, אֲבָל נִתְגַּלְגֵּל, זִימְנִין דְּאָתֵי זִיקָא וּמַיְיתֵי לֵיהּ, אֵימָא לֶיהֱוֵי עֵירוּב — צְרִיכָא.§ "אוֹ נִשְׂרַף, תְּרוּמָה וְנִטְמֵאת".§ לָמָּה לִי? תָּנָא נִשְׂרַף — לְהוֹדִיעֲךָ

רש"י

אֲבָל בַּשַּׁבָּת אֵין עֵירוּבוֹ עֵירוּב. דְּלָא שָׁרוּ לֵיהּ רַבָּנַן לְמִיסְתַּר: נִמְצָא הַמַּפְתֵּחַ. בְּשַׁבָּת: אֵין עֵירוּבוֹ עֵירוּב. דְּלֵית לֵיהּ דְּר"ש. וְהָא דְּר"ש בְּפ' "כָּל גַּגּוֹת"*: וְאֵין סְתִירָה בְּכֵלִים. וְאִי בָּעֵי סָתַר לֵיהּ: הִקִּישׁ. זָב בְּאֶגְרוֹפוֹ עַל גַּבֵּי שִׁידָּה כו': טְמֵאִים. מִפְּנֵי שֶׁהֱסִּיטָן. וּכְגוֹן שֶׁהָיָה לָבוּשׁ בֵּית יָד דְּלָא מְטַמֵּא בִּנְגִיעָה. אִי נַמִי: שֶׁהִקִּישׁוֹ בַּחֲתִיכַת עֵץ שֶׁבְּיָדוֹ: אֹהֶל הוּא. וְלָא מְקַבֵּל טוּמְאָה: וְתִסְבְּרָא. דְּטַעְמָא מִשּׁוּם אֹהֶל וְלָאו אֹהֶל הוּא: וְנִיסָּט. שֶׁאֵינוֹ תָּקוּעַ יָפֶה, וּכְשֶׁמַּקִּישׁ בּוֹ נִיסָּט — טָמֵא. וְאִם כְּלִי הוּא, שֶׁמְּחוּבָּר וְתָקוּעַ אוֹ כָּבֵד הַרְבֵּה שֶׁאֵינוֹ נִיסָּט מֵחֲמָתוֹ — טָהוֹר: וְקָתָנֵי נַמִי סֵיפָא. דְּקַמַּיְיתָא דְּהִקִּישׁ ע"ג שִׁידָּה, אִם הָיוּ נִיסָּטִין — טְמֵאִין אֲפִילּוּ לְר' נְחֶמְיָה וְר"ש, אַלְמָא: טַעֲמַיְיהוּ לָאו מִשּׁוּם אֹהֶל הוּא: זֶה הַכְּלָל נִיסָּט מֵחֲמַת כֹּחוֹ. שֶׁהֱסִּיט אֶת הַכְּלִי אוֹ אֶת הָאֹהֶל מַמָּשׁ, שֶׁנִּיתְּקוּ מִמּוֹשָׁבוֹ מַשֶּׁהוּ: מֵחֲמַת רְעָדָה. שֶׁטָּפַח בְּרַגְלָיו בַּקַּרְקַע, וּמֵחֲמַת נִיעֲנוּעַ הַקַּרְקַע נִיסָּט הַכְּלִי, אַף עַל פִּי שֶׁנִּיתַּק מִן הָאָרֶץ — טָהוֹר, דְּלָאו כּוֹחוֹ הוּא: דְּכוּלֵּי עָלְמָא. אֲפִילּוּ לְר' נְחֶמְיָה, הֶסִּיט מַמָּשׁ מֵחֲמַת כֹּחוֹ — טָמֵא, וַאֲפִילּוּ אֹהֶל: מֵחֲמַת רְעָדָה טָהוֹר. וַאֲפִילּוּ הוּא כְּלִי: וְהָכָא בִּרְעָדָה מֵחֲמַת כֹּחוֹ. שֶׁהִקִּישׁ עֲלֵיהֶן מַמָּשׁ, וְלֹא נִתְּקָן וְלֹא הוּסְטוּ, אֶלָּא רָעֲדוּ: וּמַתְנִי'. דְּעֵירוּב בְּמַאי מוֹקְמִינַן לָהּ, דְּהָא לְכ"ע אִי גָּדוֹל הוּא — אֹהֶל הוּא, וְאַמַּאי עֵירוּבוֹ עֵירוּב? אִי קָטָן שֶׁאֵינוֹ מַחֲזִיק מ' סְאָה בְּלַח — כְּלִי הוּא, וּמַאי טַעְמָא דְּר' אֱלִיעֶזֶר: קְטִיר בְּמִתְנָא. קָשׁוּר הַמַּנְעוּל בְּחֶבֶל: וּבָעֵי סַכִּינָא לְמִיפְסְקֵיהּ. דְּאִי הֲוָה מָצֵי לְמִיפְסְקֵיהּ בִּידֵיהּ — שַׁפִּיר דָּמֵי אֲפִי' לְר' אֱלִיעֶזֶר, דְּאֵין חֲתִיכָ' אֲסוּרָה אֶלָּא בִּמְחוּבָּר, אֲבָל הָכָא מְקַלְקֵל הוּא, וְשָׁרֵי. כִּדְתַנְיָא בְּמַסֶּכֶת בֵּיצָה (דף לג:): חוֹתָמוֹת שֶׁבַּכֵּלִים מַתִּיר וּמַפְקִיעַ וְחוֹתֵךְ. וְאע"ג דְּהָכָא אֹהֶל הוּא, וְאָמְרִינַן הָתָם שֶׁבַּקַּרְקַע אָסוּר לַחְתּוֹךְ — גְּזֵירָה דְּרַבָּנַן הִיא, דְּמֶיחֱזֵי כְּסוֹתֵר וְלֹא סוֹתֵר בִּנְיָן מַמָּשׁ הוּא. דְּהָא פְּתִיחַת דֶּלֶת בְּעָלְמָא הוּא, כֵּיוָן דִּשְׁבוּת הוּא — לֹא גָּזְרוּ עָלָיו בֵּין הַשְּׁמָשׁוֹת: אֶלָּא לְצוֹרֶךְ תַּשְׁמִישָׁן. וְעִיקַּר תַּשְׁמִישׁוֹ שֶׁל סַכִּין לֹא לַחְתּוֹךְ חֲבָלִים הוּא, אֶלָּא לֶחֶם וּבָשָׂר וְאוֹכְלִין. וְהָכִי פְּלִיגִי: תַּנָּא קַמָּא לֵית לֵיהּ דְּרַבִּי נְחֶמְיָה, הִלְכָּךְ, עֵירוּבוֹ עֵירוּב — דְּפָסֵיק לֵיהּ לְמִיתְנָא. רַבִּי אֱלִיעֶזֶר אוֹמֵר: אִם בָּעִיר אָבַד — הֲרֵי זֶה עֵירוּב, דְּכִי מִדְּכַר לֵיהּ מַיְיתֵי לֵיהּ דֶּרֶךְ קַרְפֵּיפוֹת. וְאִם בַּשָּׂדֶה — אֵינוֹ עֵירוּב, דְּמִיפְסִיק מַנְעוּל לָא מָצֵי, כְּדְרַבִּי נְחֶמְיָה:

מתני' נִתְגַּלְגֵּל חוּץ לַתְּחוּם אֵינוֹ עֵירוּב. הוֹאִיל וְיֵשׁ מִבֵּיתוֹ שֶׁהוּא לָן שָׁם עַד עֵירוּבוֹ יוֹתֵר מֵאַלְפַּיִם אַמָּה. דְּמִמָּה נַפְשָׁךְ כָּל הֵיכָא דְּקָנֶה שְׁבִיתָה אִי בְּבֵיתוֹ אִי בְּעֵירוּבוֹ — לָא מָצֵי לְמֵיזַל וּלְמִשְׁקְלֵיהּ: נָפַל עָלָיו גַּל. מְפָרֵשׁ בַּגְּמָ' דְּבָעֵי מָרָא וַחֲצִינָא לְפַנּוֹיֵי, דְּהָוְיָא מְלָאכָה וְלָא שְׁבוּת: תְּרוּמָה וְנִטְמֵאת. דְּלָא חַזְיָא לָא לְדִידֵיהּ וְלָא לְאַחֲרִינֵי: מִשֶּׁחֲשֵׁיכָה. כְּבָר קָנָה עֵירוּב בֵּין הַשְּׁמָשׁוֹת, וְשַׁבָּת הוֹאִיל וְהוּתְּרָה הוּתְּרָה: סָפֵק. אִם מִבְּעוֹד יוֹם אִם מִשֶּׁחֲשֵׁיכָה: הֲרֵי זֶה חַמָּר גַּמָּל. דְּמִסְּפְקָא לָן אִי קָנֵי לֵיהּ זֶה עֵירוּב וְהָכָא הָוֵי בֵּיתוֹ, וּמֵהָכָא יֵשׁ לוֹ אַלְפַּיִם אַמָּה לְכָל רוּחַ וְהִפְסִיד אַלְפַּיִם שֶׁמֵּעֵבֶר בֵּיתוֹ וָהָלְאָה אוֹ שֶׁמָּא לֹא קָנָה עֵירוּב, וּמִבֵּיתוֹ יֵשׁ לוֹ אַלְפַּיִם לְכָל רוּחַ וְלֹא קָנָה לְעֵבֶר עֵירוּבוֹ כְּלוּם. וּמֵחֲמַת סָפֵק זֶה נֶאֱסַר לֵילֵךְ אֶלָּא אַלְפַּיִם אַמָּה שֶׁבֵּין בֵּיתוֹ לְעֵירוּבוֹ, דְּמִמָּה נַפְשָׁךְ בְּהָנָךְ מִשְׁתְּרֵי. אֲבָל אַלְפַּיִם שֶׁמֵּעֵירוּבוֹ וְאֵילָךְ — לָא, דִּילְמָא לֹא קָנָה עֵירוּב. וּמִבֵּיתוֹ וְאֵילָךְ נַמִי לָא — דִּלְמָא קָנָה עֵירוּב. נִמְצָא זֶה מוֹשְׁכוֹ כָּאן לֵילֵךְ, וְזֶה מוֹשְׁכוֹ לְכָאן. כְּאָדָם הַמַּנְהִיג חֲמוֹר וְגָמָל, שֶׁהַחֲמוֹר הוֹלֵךְ לְפָנָיו וְזֶה מַנְהִיגוֹ, וְהַגָּמָל הוּא מוֹשֵׁךְ — וְצָרִיךְ לִפְנוֹת לְפָנָיו וּלְאַחֲרָיו:

גמ' הַנּוֹתֵן אֶת עֵירוּבוֹ. הוֹאִיל וְנִתְכַּוֵּין לִקְנוֹת שָׁם שְׁבִיתָה יֵשׁ לוֹ אַרְבַּע אַמּוֹת, דְּהוֹאִיל וְהָנְהוּ אַרְבַּע אַמּוֹת מִיבַּלְעָן בִּתְחוּמָא — הָווּ לְהוּ כִּתְחוּמָא, וַהֲוֵי כְּנוֹתֵן אֶת עֵירוּבוֹ בְּבֵית שֶׁבְּסוֹף הַתְּחוּם שֶׁאֲפִילּוּ הוּא אֶלֶף אַמָּה מְהַלֵּךְ אֶת כּוּלָּהּ וְחוּצָה לָהּ אַלְפַּיִם אַמָּה: דְּאִי בָּעֵי שָׁקֵיל לֵיהּ. וְקָתָנֵי מַתְנִיתִין אֵינוֹ עֵירוּב מִשּׁוּם טִלְטוּל אֲבָנִים, דִּשְׁבוּת דְּרַבָּנַן הוּא:

תוספות

חסורי מיחסרא והכי קתני. פ"ה: וג' מחלוקות בדבר. ולא דק, דמתניתין איירי ביום טוב, ופליגי אי מצי סתר ליה אי לאו. ובריי' כשנמצא בשבת, ופליגי בדר"ש. והא דתניא בתוספתא (פרק שני) דעירובין: ומודים חכמים לרבי אליעזר בבני אלר ובני מרפסת שנגבו עירובן ונתנוהו בבית, אע"פ שיודעין שאין המפתח במקומו שעירובו עירוב. היינו טעמא — דבעירובי חצירות הקילו. ומיהו, נראה דאנמצא מפתח בשבת, קאי מדקאמר ומודים חכמים לרבי אליעזר וביו"ט, כי לא נמצא מפתח — אדרבה חכמים הקילו טפי, והוה ליה למימר איפכא, ומודה רבי אליעזר לחכמים: **בעיר** עירובו עירוב. בנמצא בשבת, אף על פי שהיה אבוד בין השמשות. וקתני סיפא **אם** היו ניסטין טמאין. מהך סיפא לחוד לא מצי למידק, דמצי למימר דמחמת רעדה הוא דפליגי. דיש חלוק בין אהל לכלי, אבל בהיסט — אהל נמי טמא. לכך מייתי ברייתא דמחמת רעדה נמי אין חילוק בין אהל לכלי. וברייתא לחוד נמי לא סגיא, דהוה אמינא דאתיא לא (ב) כרבי נחמיה ולא כרבי שמעון, להכי אייתי סיפא דמילתייהו:

ומתני' במאי מוקי ליה. ולא בעי לאוקומ' בפלוגתא דאין בנין בכלים, משום דפלוגתא דב"ש וב"ה היא בפרק(ג) ב' דביצה (ד' כב.):

בעי סכינא למיפסקיה. פ"ה: דאי ביד — הוה שרי אפילו(ד) רבי אליעזר, דמקלקל הוא. דתניא במסכת ביצה (דף לג:): חותמות שבכלים — מתיר ומפקיע וחותך. ואף על גב דהכא אהל הוא, ואמר שבקרקע אסור — גזירה דרבנן הוא, דמיחזי כסותר ולא סותר בנין ממש הוא, דהא פתיחת דלת בעלמא הוא. וכיון דשבות הוא — לא גזרו עליו בה"ש. ואינו נראה, דכי נמי סבר רבי אליעזר כרבי נחמיה — שרי דטלטול סכין לא אסור אלא מדרבנן. לכך י"ל דהכא כלי הוא ואי הוה מצי למפסקיה ביד — הוה שרי, אבל בסכינא אסור, כרבי נחמיה, ולית ליה דרבי. ומכאן מדקדק ר"י: דחותמות שבכלים מתיר ומפקיע וחותך, היינו דוקא כעין קשר של מיתנא, אבל פותח של עץ או של מתכת — אסור לשבר, דבכלי נמי יש בנין וסתירה כדפ"ל*:

נתגלגל חוץ לתחום. אפילו תחומין דרבנן. ואפילו לרבי, דאמר: כל דבר שהוא משום שבות לא גזרו עליו בין השמשות — מכל מקום לא הוי עירוב. אף על גב דבין השמשות מצי למישקליה ולאיתויי, כיון דאם קנה שביתה במקום שנתגלגל העירוב היה עומד עתה חוץ לתחום, ואין לו אלא ארבע אמות — הילכך תקנו רבנן שלא יהיה עירוב אלא כשהוא בתוך התחום: ספק

עין משפט נר מצוה

ע א ב מיי' פ"ו מהל' עירובין הלכה א טור א"ח סי' שצו:

עא ג מיי' פ"ט מהל' משכב ומושב הלכה א:

עב ד מיי' פ"א מהל' עירובין הלכה כב ופ"ו הלכה י סמג לאוין סה טוש"ע א"ח סי' שלד סעיף ג וסי' תט סעיף ד וסימן שיד סעיף ז וטור סי' תקיט:

עג ה מיי' פכ"ה מהל' שבת הלכה ט סמג שם טוש"ע א"ח סי' שח סעיף א:

עד ו ז מיי' פ"א מהל' עירובין הלכה כא ופ"ו הלכה יב סמג עשין א טוש"ע א"ח סי' שלד סעיף א ב וסי' תט סעיף ו:

[שבת קכב: ביצה יא: כב:]

עה ח מיי' פ"ו מהל' עירובין הלכה יא טוש"ע שם סי' תט סעיף ה:

עו ט מיי' פ"ו שם הלכה יד טוש"ע א"ח סי' שלד סעיף ב:

רבינו חננאל

ולא בשבת. ופרקינן מתני' נמי ביו"ט קתני ואקשינן אי הכי הא דתני עלה ר' אליעזר אמר אי בעיר אבד עירובו עירוב כו' ואי ביו"ט שרי ליה לאתויי מה לי בעיר ומה לי בשדה. ותרוץ הכי חסורי מחסרא והכי קתני נתנו במגדל ונעל בפניו ואבד המפתח הרי זה עירוב בד"א ביו"ט אבל בשבת אין עירובו עירוב נמצא המפתח בין בעיר בין בשדה עירובו עירוב. ר' אליעזר אומר בעיר עירובו עירוב דיכול לאתויי דרך גגות כר"ש דתנן ר"ש אומר אחד גגות ואחד חצרות ואחד קרפיפות (וכלים) [רשות אחת הן לכלים] ששבתו בתוכן. נמצא המפתח בשדה אין עירובו עירוב [דלא] כר"ש דתני (לקמן צ"ה) בהמוציא תפילין בשדה נותנן לחבירו וחבירו לחבירו עד שמגיע לחצר החיצונה אלא כרבנן דאסרי ורבה ורב יוסף אוקמוה למתני' במגדל עץ. ואמאי עירובו עירוב [דאין בנין] ואין סתירה בכלים וכיון שיש לו לסתור ולהוציא העירוב נמצא הוא ועירובו במקום אחד ובהא פליגי ר' אלעזר ורבנן רב ושמואל סברי מן מגדל של עץ אהל הוא ואסור לסותרו ורבה ורב יוסף [סברי] כלי הוא. ובפלוגתא דהני תנאי דתנן במס' זבין פ' ד' הקיש הזב על הדלת של שידה של תיבה ושל מגדל טמאין ר' נחמיה ור' שמעון מטהרין מאי לאו בהא קמיפלגי דת"ק סבר כלי הוא ונטמא. ור' נחמיה ור' שמעון סברי אהל הוא. ודחי אביי כללא הוא דבכלי טמא ובאהל טהור. והתניא אהל הניסט טמא. כלי ואינו ניסט טהור. וקתני סיפא אם היו הניסטין דלת ומגדל טמאין. זה הכלל ניסט מחמת כחו טמא מחמת רעדה טהור אלא אמר אביי כ"ע היסט מחמת כחו טמא והכא ברעדה מחמת כחו פליגי כגון שהכה הזב במקום ונתרעד כלי מחמת ההכאה ההיא ת"ק סבר הוי היסט ור' נחמיה ור' שמעון סברי לא הוי היסט ואסיקנא למתניתין דקתני אבד המפתח במנעל דקטיר במתנא ובעי סכינא למפסקיה. (אבד הסכין) ובהא פליגי ר' אלעזר סבר לה כר' נחמיה דאמר אפי' טלית ואפי' תרווד אין ניטלין אלא לצורך תשמישן ולפיכך אסור ורבנן סברי כל הכלים ניטלין לצורך ושלא לצורך: **מתני'** נתגלגל חוץ לתחום כו' אמר רבא לא שנו אלא שנתגלגל חוץ מד' אמות אבל נתגלגל לתוך ד' אמות אפי' מבעוד יום עירובו עירוב דהוא ועירובו במקום אחד הן שכל המניח עירובו יש לו ד' אמות. נפל עליו גל ובעי מרא וחצינא לפקחו ספק. ר' מאיר אומר הרי זה חמר גמל. פירוש דרך חמור בהנהגה ודרך גמל במשיכה ומי שיש לו חמור וגמל ונתן חמור מאחוריו למושכו והגמל

הגהות הב"ח

(א) גמ' לכלים ששבתו בתוכן (בשדה וכו' כרבנן) תא"מ ונ"ב ס"א אין זה: (ב) תוס' ד"ה וקתני וכו' דהוה אמינא דאתיא לא כר' נחמיה ור"ש ומתניתין וכו': (ג) ד"ה ומתניתין וכו' היא בפרק קמא דביצה: (ד) ד"ה בעי וכו' שרי אפי' לרבי אליעזר:

[דף פט.] [לעיל כג: וש"נ] [עי' תוס' שבת קכב: ד"ה הא ותוס' לעיל לד: ד"ה ואמאי] [זבים פ"ד מ"ג [תוס' שם פ"ד]] [שם כתוספתא אבל במשנה ליתא] [שבת קכב: וע' שבת קנז.] [שבת לו. קכב: קמו. ביצה לב. תוספתא שבת פט"ו] [לקמן נב:] [לעיל לב: ועי' לקמן נב.] [לעיל לב: וש"נ]

רב נסים גאון ר' אליעזר אומר בעיר עירובו עירוב כר' שמעון בשדה אין עירובו עירוב כרבנן. עיקר דילה בפרק כל גגות העיר כו' (דף פט) וחכמים אומרים כל אחד ואחד רשות בפני עצמו ר' שמעון אומר אחד גגות ואחד חצרות ואחד

גליון הש"ס **גמ'** בשדה אין עירובו עירוב כרבנן. רש"ל מוחק זה והרז"ה כתב כרבנן היינו רבנן דלקמן דף לה ע"ב דלא ס"ל הירא דנותנו לחבירו וחבירו לחבירו: **מתני'** הרי זה חמר גמל. עי' לקמן דף מט ע"ב תד"ה ואפילו וכו' ולקמן דף נב ע"ב ברש"י ד"ה אלא אפילו:

להודיעך כחו דרבי יוסי. תנא תרומה ונטמאת – להודיעך כחו דרבי מאיר. וסבר ר"מ ספיקא לחומרא?! *והתנן: [א]טמא שירד לטבול, ספק טבל ספק לא טבל, ואפילו טבל, ספק טבל בארבעים סאה ספק לא טבל בארבעים סאה; וכן שני מקוואות, באחת יש בה ארבעים סאה ובאחת אין בה ארבעים סאה, וטבל באחת מהן ואינו יודע באיזה מהן טבל – ספיקו טמא. *במה דברים אמורים – בטומאה חמורה. אבל בטומאה קלה, כגון שאכל אוכלין טמאין ושתה משקין טמאין, והבא ראשו ורובו במים שאובין, או שנפלו על ראשו ועל רובו שלשה לוגין מים שאובין, וירד לטבול; ספק טבל ספק לא טבל, ואפילו טבל – ספק טבל בארבעים סאה ספק לא טבל בארבעים סאה. וכן שני מקוואות, באחת יש בה ארבעים סאה ואחת אין בה ארבעים סאה, וטבל באחת מהן ואינו יודע באיזה מהן טבל – ספיקו טהור. רבי יוסי מטמא. קסבר ר"מ: תחומין דאורייתא נינהו. וסבר ר"מ תחומין דאורייתא?! והא *תנן: אם אין יכול להבליעו, בזו אמר רבי דוסתאי בר ינאי משום ר"מ: שמעתי שמקדרין בהרים. ואי ס"ד תחומין *דאורייתא – מי מקדרין? והא *אמר רב נחמן, אמר רבה בר אבוה: אין מקדרין לא בערי מקלט ולא בעגלה ערופה – מפני שהן של תורה. לא קשיא; הא – דידיה, הא – דרביה. דיקא נמי, דקתני: "בזו אמר רבי דוסתאי בר ינאי משום רבי מאיר שמעתי שמקדרין בהרים" – ש"מ. ורמי דאורייתא אדאורייתא לרבי מאיר; דתנן: *נגע באחד בלילה, ואינו יודע אם חי אם מת, ולמחר השכים ומצאו מת, ר"מ מטהר וחכמים [ב]מטמאין, שכל הטמאות כשעת מציאתן! אמר רבי ירמיה: משנתנו (א)*שהיה עליה שרץ כל בין השמשות. אי הכי – בהא לימא רבי יוסי ספק עירוב כשר?! רבה ורב יוסף דאמרי תרוייהו: הכא בשתי כיתי עדים עסקינן, אחת אומרת: מבעוד יום נטמאה, ואחת אומרת: משחשיכה. רבא

רש"י

להודיעך כחו דר' יוסי. דאע"ג דאינו בעולם – לא מיתסר: להודיעך כחו דר"מ. דאע"ג דישנה בעולם, וי"ל העמידנה בבין השמשות על חזקתה, וקודם לכן טהורה היתה – אפ"ה לא אמרינן חזקה לקולא: בטומאה חמורה. שניטמא בטומאה המטמאתו מן התורה, כגון באב הטומאה: אבל טומאה קלה. דרבנן היא, ואיזו טומאת דברי סופרים לטמאות אדם – כגון אכל חצי פרס אוכלין טמאין, והבא ראשו ורובו כו' מי"ח דבר הן בגזירות השבת: ואפילו טבל. י"ל בו ספק, כגון ספק טבל בארבעים סאה, שהיה מקוה לפניו ונמצא חסר, ואין אנו יודעים אם בשעת טבילה היה שלם ואח"כ חיסר, או לא: וכן ב' מקוואות. שאנו בקיאים בא' מהן שלא היו בו מ' סאה מעולם: ספיקו טהור. וסתם משנה ר"מ: ור' יוסי מטמא. ולקמן מקשינן דר' יוסי אדר' יוסי: תחומין דאורייתא. וספיקא דאורייתא לחומרא: אם אינו יכול להבליעו. בפרק "כיצד מעברין" (נז:) היא: היה מודד ורוצה לסיים תחומי העיר ולעשות שם סימן, ותנן: אין מודדין אלא בחבל של נ' אמה, והגיע לגיא או לגדר משופע ויכול להבליעו, בחבל של נ' אמה – מבליעו, ואף על פי ששיפועו מרבה את הדרך. ואם היה מודד שיפועו מכאן ועלייתו לעבר השני – יש בו ק' או ר' אמות – לא איכפת לן, הואיל ומשפתו אל שפתו אין יותר מנ' אמה. ואם אינו יכול להבליעו בחבל של חמשים אמה: בזו אמר ר' דוסתאי בר רבי ינאי משום ר"מ שמעתי שמקדרין בהרים. לא מבליעו בחבל ארוך יותר מנ', דהתנן: אין מודדין אלא בחבל של נ' אמה, ולא מודד כל מדרונו כמות שהוא בחבל של חמשים בקרקע חלקה – דאיכא חומרא טפי, אלא מודדו בחבלים קטנים של ארבע אמות, ואוחזין בו ב' בני אדם בב' ראשי החבל. התחתון נותן ראש החבל כנגד לבו, והעליון כנגד מרגלותיו, ומשתכרין בכל ארבע אמות כשיעור חצי קומת אדם. ולשון 'מקדרין' – כמו 'נוקבין', דמשוה מדת הסדר כאילו הוא נקוב במקום מעמד רגלי העליון, ונמצא לבו במקום שרגליו עומדות עכשיו, וכשנותן החבל עכשיו כנגד מרגלותיו – ה"ל כאילו נותן אותו כנגד לבו בקרקע חלקה, כדרך כל המודדין: אין מקדרין בעגלה ערופה. כשבא למדוד הערים שסביבות החלל לידע איזו היא קרובה מכוון – מודד את ההרים ואת הגאיות כמות שהן, ואף על פי שהמדרון מרבה את המדה ומרחיק את העיר: וכן בתחום ערי מקלט. דקי"ל: *כשם שהעיר קולטת כך תחומה קולט: שמעתי. ר' מאיר קאמר ליה. ו"שמעתי" איכא למימר: שמעתי מרבותי, ולדידיה לא ס"ל: נגע באחד. באדם אחד: ר"מ מטהר. דאמר: אוקמיה אחזקי' ואתמול חי היה. אלמא: בספיקא דאורייתא ואיכא חזקה לקולא – אזיל ר"מ בתר חזקה. ומתני' נמי, ניזיל בתר חזקה, ומעיקרא כי הנח התם – טהור הואי: כל בין השמשות. מתחילתו ועד סופו, דודאי איטמי מבעוד יום, דתחילת בין השמשות מערב שבת הוא: בהא לימא כו'. הא ודאי מבעוד יום איטמי. ומתני' קתני: מבעוד יום אין עירובו עירוב דברי הכל: אחת אומרת מבעוד יום כו'. ובהא פליגי; ר' יוסי סבר: אוקי תרי לבהדי תרי, ואוקי תרומה אחזקה קמייתא. וכי הנחה – טהורה הואי. רבי מאיר סבר: כיון דאיכא כת דמפקא ליה מחזקיה, בספיקא דאורייתא לא אזלינן בתר חזקה. אבל בנוגע באחד בלילה, דאין כת מוציאתו מחזקתו – מוקמינן ליה כל הלילה בחזקתו, ובתר שעת מציאתו לא אזלינן, דאיכא למימר השתא הוא דמיית: רבא

תוספות

ספק לא טבל ואפילו טבל כו'. הך ספק ספיקא נקט משום רבותא דסיפא, דאפ"ה בטומאה קלה טהור. וריב"א מפרש: דאו או קתני, ואפילו טבל – היינו או שטבל. מדפריך בתר הכי: אדרבה, ואימא העמד מקוה על חזקתו ואימא לא חסר. והא לא שייך למיפרך אספק טבל או לא טבל? אלא: או או קתני, ופריך אספק טבל בארבעים סאה ספק לא טבל:

(*ספיקו טהור). ר"מ ברה"ר איירי, כדתני' בתוספתא [טהרות פ"ו]: ר"מ מטהר שספק טומאה ברה"ר טהור: כל הטמאות כשעת מציאתן. תימה: דבריש נדה (ב.) תנן, ב"ש אומר: כל הנשים דיין שעתן. ואפילו הלל וחכמים דמטמאין מעת לעת או מפקידה לפקידה – היינו דווקא לתרומה וקדשים, או לקדש דווקא לחד לישנא – אבל לחולין טהור לכ"ע. ואמאי לא אמרינן דכל הטמאות כשעת מציאתן כי הכא, ולא הוה לן לאוקמה אשה על חזקתה! ועוד: דהתם מטהרינן לה אפילו ברשות היחיד, כדמוכח התם בשמעתא קמייתא, והכא מטמאין אפילו ברה"ר, כדמוכח בתוספתא שהבאתי! וכ"ת: דהכא לא מוקמינן אחזקיה משום דלא נבדק מבעוד יום אם היה חי, כדקתני סיפא *ומודים חכמים לר"מ ברואהו חי מבערב וכו' – דאשה נמי כיון דשכיחי בה דמים כאינה בדוקה דמיא, כדאמרינן בנדה (דף ד.). ואור"י: דכל הטמאות כשעת מציאתן לא הוי אלא לתרומה וקדשים, כמו מעת לעת שבנדה. ולפי זה צריך ליישב סוגיא דנדה, ושם פי' שמאי נמי אית ליה דכל הטמאות כשעת מציאתן, והא דמטהר מעת לעת אפילו לקדשים – היינו משום דחשיב אשה כבדוקה. אי נמי, משום בטול פריה ורביה, כדאמר התם (דף ג:). וא"ת: ולר"מ דמטהר ברה"ר, מאי שנא דבמעת לעת דמטמא אפילו ברה"ר, כדאמר בירושלמי? וי"ל: באשה דאיכא ריעותא מגופה – החמירו טפי: אמר ר' ירמיה משנתנו כשהיה עליה כו'. וא"ת: ומאי קושיא דר"מ אדר' מאיר, דבמתני' הא דלא אוקמיה תרומה אחזקה – לאו משום דהשתא היא טמאה, אלא משום דאיכא חזקה אחרת כנגדה, דמוקמינן לגברא בחזקת שלא עירב, ולקמן נמי, דקאמר היינו טעמא דרבי יוסי העמד טמא על חזקתו ואימא לא טבל. במתני' נמי, נימא: העמד אדם על חזקת תחום ביתו, ואימא לא עירב. ואי הוה אמרינן דחזקה שלא עירב לא חשיב ליה התלמוד חזקה – אתי שפיר. ומיהו רש"י פי' לקמן: העמד טמא על חזקתו – חזקה לחומרא איכא, ולקולא ליכא אבל במתני' איכא חזקה לקולא, דהעמד תרומה על חזקתה, ואיכא נמי חזקה לחומרא דהעמד אדם על חזקת תחום ביתו, ואימא לא עירב. ובדרבנן אזלינן לקולא. והכי נמי י"ל דניחא ליה לשנויי אפי' סבר ר"מ עירובי תחומין דרבנן, דהשתא לא מצי לשנויי הכי משום דמתני' איכא חזקה לחומרא, דכיון דאיכא נמי חזקה לקולא הוי מצי למימר דהוי עירוב דספיקא דרבנן לקולא, משום הכי מוקי מתני' בשני כיתי עדים דלא שייך למימר הכי כיון דאיכא כת דמפקי ליה מחזקתה, ורבה ורב יוסף אתו לפרושי דברי רבי ירמיה: בהא לימא רבי יוסי ספק עירוב כשר. הוה מצי למיפרך: בהא לימא רבי מאיר ורבי יהודה הרי זה חמר גמל? אלא דעדיפא טפי פריך:

עז א מיי' פ"י מהל' מקואות הלכה ו סמג עשין רמח טוש"ע י"ד סי' רא סעיף עא:
עח ב מיי' פי"ח מהל' אבות הטומאות הלכה יד:

[נ"ל ר' מאיר מטהר וכ"כ בספר נודע ביהודה ח"א סוף סי' סה דף סט ע"ד ע"ש] וכ"ה בס"י

[בתוספתא שם]

מקוואות פ"ב מ"א
[שם מ"ב]
לקמן נח.
[ביצה לו: סוטה לג:]
לקמן נח:
טהרות פ"ה מ"ז נדה ד.
[מכות יא:]

הגהות הב"ח

(א) גמ' משנתנו כשהיה:

גליון הש"ס

גמ' שהיה עליה שרץ כל ביהש"מ אי הכי בהא לימא ר"י. תמוה לי דלמאי מוקי שהיה השרץ עליה כל ביהש"מ לוקי בפשיטות דנפל עליה בתוך ביה"ש ואנן ידעינן הזמן שנפל עליה דל"ש לומר אוקמי אחזקה אלא דלא ידעינן אם עתה לילה או יום. ובהא שפיר אמר ר' יוסי דספק עירוב כשר וצ"ל וה' יאיר עיני:

רבינו חננאל

לפניו להנהיגו לא זה מהלך במשיכה ולא הגמל בהנהגה נמצא אדם שבניהם יושב בלא הליכה לפיכך עשו כמו משל זה שאין לו רשות להלוך כמו חמר גמל ואקשינן וכי ר' מאיר בדבר שהוא ספק מחמיר והתניא טמא שירד לטבול ספק טבל ספק לא טבל כו' עד ספיקו טהור דברי ר' מאיר ור' יוסי מטמא. ופרקינן קסבר ר' מאיר תחומין דאורייתא שהן כגון טומאה חמורה שספיקה טמא. ור' יוסי אמר העיד אבטילם משום ה' זקנים על ספק העירוב שהוא כשר בזה הספק בלבד מיקל אבל בשאר ספיקות אפילו בטומאה קלה. כגון שאכל אוכלין טמאין ושתה משקין טמאין כו' ספיקו טמא. ואקשינן תוב וסבר ר' מאיר תחומין דאורייתא והתנן אם אינו יכול להבליעו בזו א"ר דוסתאי ב"ר ינאי משום ר' מאיר שמעתי שמקדרין בהרים פי' מקדרין חותכין כדתנן בפסחי' ובמוקדשין קודר בקופיץ. וגרסינן נמי בשבת קודר את כל האזכרות ולא קדירה ממש היא אלא אומרים בדעת כאלו קודרין את ההרים ואי ס"ד דסבר ר' מאיר תחומין דאוריי' היכי מקדרינן והא' רב נחמן אמר רבה בר אבוה אין מקדרין לא בערי מקלט לתת להם מדת מגרשיהם ולא בעגלה ערופה לראות איזו עיר הקרובה אל החלל מפני שהן של תורה ופרקינן לא קשיא הא מתני' דאוקימנא בתחומין דאורייתא דידיה. והא דקתני מקדרין דמשמע תחומין לאו דאורייתא דרבה. ודייקינן מדקתני משום ר' מאיר שמעינן מינה ר' מאיר הוא דשמע מרבותיו שמקדרין ורמינן תוב ור' מאיר ספיקא דאורייתא לחומרא סבירא ליה דקתני תרומה ונטמאת ספק מבעוד יום או משחשיכה אינו עירוב והתנן נגע באחד בלילה ואינו יודע אם חי אם מת לשחר השכים ומצאו מת. ר' מאיר מטהר וחכמים מטמאין שכל הטומאות כשעת מציאתן ופריק ר' ירמיה משנתנו כשהיה השרץ על התרומה כל בין השמשות ודחינן להאי פירוקא אי כשהיה השרץ על התרומה בין השמשות בהא לימא ר' יוסי ספק עירוב כשר.

רב נסים גאון

ואחר קרפיפות לכלים ששבתו בתוכן: אין מקדרין לא בעגלה ערופה ולא בערי מקלט. עגלה ערופה הוא שכתוב (דברים כא) ומדדו אל הערים אשר סביבות החלל וערי מקלט הוא ששנינו בפרק אלו הן הגולין (מכות דף יא) כשם שהעיר קולטת כך תחומה קולט והיו מדקדקין במדידת העיר הקרובה אל החלל ובתחום ערי מקלט ולא היו מקדרין מפני שהן מן התורה ושמא יוסיפו על השיעור הקצוב להם:
אלא

רַבָא אָמַר: הָתָם תְּרֵי חֲזָקֵי לְקוּלָּא, וְהָכָא חֲדָא חֲזָקָה *לְקוּלָּא. קַשְׁיָא דְּר' יוֹסֵי אַדְּר' יוֹסֵי! אָמַר רַב הוּנָא בַּר חִינָּנָא: שָׁאנֵי טוּמְאָה, הוֹאִיל וְיֵשׁ לָהּ עִיקָּר מִן הַתּוֹרָה. שַׁבָּת נַמִי דְּאוֹרַיְיתָא הִיא! קָסָבַר ר' יוֹסֵי: *תְּחוּמִין דְּרַבָּנַן. וְאִיבָּעֵית אֵימָא: (א)הָא דִּידֵיהּ, הָא דְּרַבֵּיהּ. דַּיְקָא נַמִי, דְּקָתָנֵי: א"ר יוֹסֵי "אַבְטוּלְמוֹס הֵעִיד מִשּׁוּם חֲמִשָּׁה זְקֵנִים שֶׁסְּפֵק עֵירוּב כָּשֵׁר" — ש"מ. רָבָא אָמַר, הָתָם הַיְינוּ טַעְמָא דְּרַבִּי יוֹסֵי: הַעֲמֵד טָמֵא עַל חֶזְקָתוֹ, וְאֵימָא לֹא טָבַל. אַדְּרַבָּה, הַעֲמֵד מִקְוֶה עַל חֶזְקָתוֹ וְאֵימָא לֹא חָסַר! בְּמִקְוֶה שֶׁלֹּא נִמְדַּד. תַּנְיָא: *אכֵּיצַד אָמַר ר' יוֹסֵי סְפֵק עֵירוּב כָּשֵׁר? עֵירֵב בִּתְרוּמָה, סָפֵק מִבְּעוֹד יוֹם נִטְמֵאת סָפֵק מִשֶּׁחֲשֵׁיכָה נִטְמֵאת, וְכֵן בְּפֵירוֹת — סָפֵק מִבְּעוֹד יוֹם נִתְקְנוּ, סָפֵק מִשֶּׁחֲשֵׁיכָה נִתְקְנוּ — זֶה הוּא סְפֵק עֵירוּב כָּשֵׁר. אֲבָל עֵירֵב בִּתְרוּמָה, סָפֵק טְהוֹרָה סָפֵק טְמֵאָה; וְכֵן בְּפֵירוֹת, סָפֵק נִתְקְנוּ סָפֵק לֹא נִתְקְנוּ — אֵין זֶה סְפֵק עֵירוּב כָּשֵׁר. מַאי שְׁנָא תְּרוּמָה — דְּאָמַר: הַעֲמֵד תְּרוּמָה עַל חֶזְקָתָהּ, וְאֵימָא טְהוֹרָה הִיא. פֵּירוֹת נַמִי, הַעֲמֵד טֶבֶל עַל חֶזְקָתוֹ, וְאֵימָא לֹא נִתְקְנוּ! לָא תֵּימָא: "סָפֵק מִבְּעוֹד יוֹם נִתְקְנוּ", אֶלָּא אֵימָא: סָפֵק מִבְּעוֹד יוֹם נִדְמְעוּ, סָפֵק מִשֶּׁחֲשֵׁיכָה נִדְמְעוּ. בְּעָא רַב שְׁמוּאֵל בַּר רַב יִצְחָק מֵרַב הוּנָא: הָיוּ לְפָנָיו שְׁתֵּי כִּכָּרוֹת, אַחַת טְמֵאָה וְאַחַת טְהוֹרָה, וְאָמַר: עֵירְבוּ לִי בַּטְּהוֹרָה בְּכָל מָקוֹם שֶׁהִיא, מַהוּ? תִּיבָּעֵי לְרַבִּי מֵאִיר, תִּיבָּעֵי לְר' יוֹסֵי; תִּיבָּעֵי לְר"מ: עַד כָּאן לָא קָאָמַר ר"מ הָתָם — דְּלֵיכָּא טְהוֹרָה, הָכָא — הָא אִיכָּא טְהוֹרָה. אוֹ דִּילְמָא: אֲפִילּוּ לְרַבִּי יוֹסֵי לָא קָאָמַר אֶלָּא הָתָם, דְּאִם אִיתָא דְּהִיא טְהוֹרָה — יָדַע לָהּ, אֲבָל הָכָא — הָא לֹא יָדַע לָהּ! אָמַר לֵיהּ: בֵּין לְר' יוֹסֵי בֵּין לְרַבִּי מֵאִיר, *בבָּעֵינַן סְעוּדָה הָרְאוּיָה מִבְּעוֹד יוֹם — וְלֵיכָּא. בְּעָא מִינֵּיהּ רָבָא מֵרַב נַחְמָן: כִּכָּר זוֹ הַיּוֹם חוֹל וּלְמָחָר קֹדֶשׁ, וְאָמַר: עֵירְבוּ לִי בָּזֶה, מַהוּ? א"ל: געֵירוּבוֹ עֵירוּב. הַיּוֹם קֹדֶשׁ וּלְמָחָר חוֹל, וְאָמַר: עֵירְבוּ לִי בָּזֶה, מַהוּ? א"ל: דאֵין עֵירוּבוֹ עֵירוּב. מַאי שְׁנָא? א"ל: *לְכִי תֵּיכוֹל עֲלֵיהּ כּוֹרָא דְּמִלְחָ'. הַיּוֹם חוֹל וּלְמָחָר קֹדֶשׁ — מִסְּפֵיקָא לָא נָחְתָא לֵיהּ קְדוּשָּׁה. הַיּוֹם קֹדֶשׁ וּלְמָחָר חוֹל — מִסְּפֵיקָא לָא פָּקְעָא לֵיהּ קְדוּשָּׁתֵיהּ מִינֵּיהּ. *תְּנַן הָתָם: *)לָגִין טְבוּל יוֹם שֶׁמִּלְאוֹ מִן הֶחָבִית שֶׁל מַעֲשֵׂר טֶבֶל, וְאָמַר: הֲרֵי זֶה תְּרוּמַת מַעֲשֵׂר לִכְשֶׁתֶּחְשַׁךְ — דְּבָרָיו קַיָּימִין, וְאִם אָמַר עֵירְבוּ לִי בָּזֶה — הלֹא אָמַר כְּלוּם. אָמַר רָבָא, זֹאת אוֹמֶרֶת: סוֹף הַיּוֹם קוֹנֶה עֵירוּב.

דְּאִי

*) פי' כדיס

רש"י

רָבָא אָמַר. גַּבֵּי נֶגַע בְּאֶחָד נַמִי, אֲפִילּוּ יֵשׁ שְׁנֵי כִּיתֵּי עֵדִים חֲלוּקוֹת אַחַת אוֹמֶרֶת קוֹדֶם שֶׁנָּגַע בּוֹ מֵת, וְאַחַת אוֹמֶרֶת עַכְשָׁיו מֵת — הָוֵי נַמִי ר"מ מְטַהֵר, וַאֲפִילּוּ הָכִי לָא תִּיקְשֵׁי: הָתָם תְּרֵי חֲזָקֵי נִינְהוּ. לְטַהֵר. וּמִשּׁוּם הָכִי אָזְלִינַן לְקוּלָּא, דְּאוֹקֵי תְּרֵי לְגַבֵּי תְּרֵי, וְהַעֲמֵד מֵת עַל חֶזְקָתוֹ רִאשׁוֹנָה כָּל הַלַּיְלָה, וְחַי הֲוָה. וְעוֹד: הַעֲמֵד נוֹגֵעַ עַל חֶזְקָתוֹ רִאשׁוֹנָה, וְטָהוֹר הָיָה: הָכָא. בְּמַתְנִיתִין, חֲדָא חֲזָקָה הוּא. דְּאִיכָּא לְמֵימַר: הַעֲמֵד תְּרוּמָה עַל חֶזְקָתָהּ. וּמִשּׁוּם חֲדָא חֲזָקָה לָא מָרְעִינַן סַהֲדֵי, הִלְכָּךְ, אָזְלִינַן לְחוּמְרָא: קַשְׁיָא דְּר' יוֹסֵי. דְּבָרַיְיתָא דְּקָתָנֵי בִּסְפֵק טָבַל וּבִסְפֵק לֹא טָבַל וּבְטוּמְאָה דְּרַבָּנַן אֲבָל אוֹכְלִין כו' וְרַבִּי יוֹסֵי מְטַמֵּא, וּמַתְנִי' קָתָנֵי סְפֵק עֵירוּב כָּשֵׁר, וַאֲפִילּוּ תְּחוּמִין דְּרַבָּנַן תִּיקְשֵׁי: הוֹאִיל וְיֵשׁ לָהּ עִיקָּר מִן הַתּוֹרָה. דְּיֵשׁ טוּמְאָה מִן הַתּוֹרָה, וְיֵשׁ לְהַחְמִיר בִּסְפֵק טְבִילָתָהּ, לְהָכִי אַחְמוּר רַבָּנַן אַף בִּסְפֵק טְבִילַת טוּמְאָה דְּרַבָּנַן, דְּלָא לֵיתֵי לְזַלְזוּלֵי בִּסְפֵק טְבִילַת טוּמְאָה דְּאוֹרַיְיתָא: שַׁבָּת נַמִי דְּאוֹרַיְיתָא הִיא. אַתְּחוּמִין פָּרֵיךְ, לְמֵימַר דִּתְחוּמִין דְּאוֹרַיְיתָא, וּכְר' עֲקִיבָא בְּמַסֶּ' סוֹטָה(ב) (דף ל:): וּמְשַׁנֵּי קָסָבַר ר' יוֹסֵי תְּחוּמִין דְּרַבָּנַן. וּמִשּׁוּם דְּלָא לֵיתוּ לְזַלְזוּלֵי בִּשְׁאָר סְפֵיקוֹת דִּמְלֶאכֶת שַׁבָּת לֵיכָּא לְמִיגְזַר, דְּלָא דָּמוּ מְלָאכוֹת לִתְחוּמִין. אֲבָל טוּמְאוֹת דָּמוּ לַהֲדָדֵי: דִּידֵיהּ. מַחְמִיר אֲפִילּוּ בִּסְפֵק דְּרַבָּנַן, וּמַתְנִיתִין דְּרַבֵּיהּ אַבְטוּלְמוֹס הִיא: הַעֲמֵד טָמֵא עַל חֶזְקָתוֹ. כּוּלֵּיהּ חֲזָקָה, לְחוּמְרָא — אִיכָּא, לְקוּלָּא — לֵיכָּא. אֲבָל מַתְנִי' אִיכָּא חֲזָקָה לְקוּלָּא וּלְחוּמְרָא; הַעֲמֵד אָדָם עַל חֶזְקַת תְּחוּם בֵּיתוֹ (ג)וְאָמַר לֹא עֵירֵב, הַעֲמֵד תְּרוּמָה עַל חֶזְקָתָהּ וְעֵירֵב, וּבִדְרַבָּנַן לְקוּלָּא אָזְלִינַן: שֶׁלֹּא נִמְדְּדָה. מִתְּחִילָּתָהּ וְלֹא עָמְדָה בְּחֶזְקַת כַּשְׁרוּת: עֵירֵב בִּתְרוּמָה. טְהוֹרָה וְנִטְמֵאת מִשֶּׁהִנִּיחָהּ שָׁם: סָפֵק מִבְּעוֹד יוֹם נִטְמֵאת סָפֵק מִשֶּׁחֲשֵׁיכָה נִטְמֵאת. אָמְרִינַן: אוֹקְמֵהּ בֵּין הַשְּׁמָשׁוֹת אַחֶזְקַתְ' קַמַּיְיתָא וּטְהוֹרָה הֲוַאי, וְהַשְׁתָּא מִשֶּׁחֲשֵׁיכָה הוּא דְּאִיטַּמֵּי: וְכֵן בְּפֵירוֹת. שֶׁל טֶבֶל: סָפֵק מִבְּעוֹד יוֹם נִתְקְנוּ. לְאַחַר שֶׁהִנִּיחָן שָׁם: סָפֵק מִשֶּׁחֲשֵׁיכָה נִתְקְנוּ. וְלֹא קָנָה עֵירוּב, כִּדְתְנַן בְּמַתְנִי': אֲבָל לֹא בַּטֶּבֶל, וּלְקַמָּן פָּרֵיךְ בְּהַאי: מַה חֶזְקַת כַּשְׁרוּת אִיכָּא דְּמַכְשַׁר רַבִּי יוֹסֵי, דְּהָא אִיכָּא לְמֵימַר הַעֲמֵד טֶבֶל עַל חֶזְקָתוֹ: סָפֵק טְמֵאָה סָפֵק טְהוֹרָה. דְּקוֹדֶם שֶׁהִנִּיחָהּ שָׁם נוֹלַד לָהּ סָפֵק וְלֹא הָיָה שָׁם חֶזְקַת הֶכְשֵׁר עֵירוּב מֵעוֹלָם: מַאי שְׁנָא תְּרוּמָה. דְּרֵישָׁא סָפֵק מִבְּעוֹד יוֹם נִיטְמָא סָפֵק מִשֶּׁחֲשֵׁיכָה דְּמַכְשַׁר ר' יוֹסֵי מִשּׁוּם חֲזָקָה קַמַּיְיתָא: פֵּירוֹת. סָפֵק מִבְּעוֹד יוֹם נִתְקְנוּ סָפֵק מִשֶּׁחֲשֵׁיכָה, נוֹקְמִינְהוּ נַמִי אַחֲזָקָה קַמַּיְיתָא דְּטֶבֶל הָווּ, וְלִיפְסוֹל: נִדְמְעוּ. חוּלִּין הָווּ מֵעִיקָּרָא מְתוּקָּנִין וְנָפְלָה בָּהֶן תְּרוּמָה וְנִדְמְעוּ וְהַאי תַּנָּא סָבַר לָהּ כְּסוּמָכוֹס דְּאָמַר (לעיל כו:): אֵין מְעָרְבִין לְיִשְׂרָאֵל בִּתְרוּמָה, הִלְכָּךְ, אִם מִבְּעוֹד יוֹם נִדְמְעוּ אַף עַל גַּב דַּחֲזֵי לְכֹהֲנִים אֵין עֵירוּבוֹ עֵירוּב. ל"א: נִדְמְעוּ — שֶׁנָּפַל לְתוֹכָן טֶבֶל, דְּלָא חֲזֵי אֲפִילּוּ לְכֹהֵן: עֵירְבוּ לִי בַּטְּהוֹרָה בְּכָל מָקוֹם שֶׁהִיא. וְהַנִּיחוּם שְׁתֵּיהֶן יַחַד בְּסוֹף הַתְּחוּם. וּבְכִכָּרוֹת שֶׁל תְּרוּמָה עָסְקִינַן, דְּאִי בְּחוּלִּין — חוּלִּין טְמֵאִין מוּתָּרִין הֵן, דְּלָאו כָּל אָדָם אוֹכֵל חוּלָּיו בְּטָהֳרָה: דְּלֵיכָּא טְהוֹרָה. וְדָאִית, דְּשֶׁמָּא מִבְּעוֹ"י נִטְמֵאת: אוֹ דִּילְמָא אֲפִילּוּ ר' יוֹסֵי. לָא מַכְשַׁר בְּמַתְנִי' אֶלָּא מִשּׁוּם דְּאִי טְהוֹרָה הִיא הָא יָדַע לָהּ הֵיכָא הִיא, וְאֵיזוֹ הִיא סְעוּדָּתוֹ. וּמִשּׁוּם סְפֵק טוּמְאָה לָא מִיפַּסְלָא, דְּאָמַר אוֹקְמָא אַחֲזָקָה: אֲבָל הָכָא לֹא יָדַע. הֵי נִיהוּ סְעוּדָּתוֹ: בָּעֵינַן סְעוּדָּה הָרְאוּיָה מִבְּעוֹ"י וְלֵיכָּא. וְאֵין עֵירוּבוֹ כְּלוּם, דַּאֲפִילּוּ חֲמָר גַּמָּל לָא הָוֵי. דְּבִשְׁלָמָא מַתְנִי' — סְעוּדָּה הָרְאוּיָה הֲוַאי, וְהַשְׁתָּא הוּא דְּאִיתְיְלִיד בָּהּ סָפֵק: כִּכָּר זוֹ כו'. אָמַר עַל כִּכָּר אַחַת בְּע"שׁ: הַיּוֹם יְהֵא חוֹל וּלְמָחָר יְהֵא קֹדֶשׁ, וְעֵירֵב שְׁלוּחוֹ בָּהּ: מַהוּ. הוֹאִיל וּבֵין הַשְּׁמָשׁוֹת סָפֵק הוּא, חָיְישִׁינַן דִּילְמָא קוֹדֶם קְנִיַּית עֵירוּב חָל עָלֶיהָ הֶקְדֵּשׁ, וְאֵין מְעָרְבִין בְּהֶקְדֵּשׁ, אוֹ לָא אָמְרִינַן הָכִי: הַיּוֹם תְּהֵא קוֹדֶשׁ וּלְמָחָר תְּהֵא חוֹל. עַל מָעוֹת שֶׁיֵּשׁ לִי בַּבַּיִת, מַהוּ? מִי אָמְרִינַן כִּי מְטָא בֵּין הַשְּׁמָשׁוֹת — נָפַק לֵיהּ מִקְּדוּשָּׁתֵיהּ וְקָנָה עֵירוּב, אוֹ לָא: וּמַאי שְׁנָא. הָא בֵּין הַשְּׁמָשׁוֹת סְפֵיקָא הוּא, מַאי שְׁנָא הָכָא לְקוּלָּא וְהָכָא לְחוּמְרָא: לְכִי תֵּיכוּל עֲלָהּ כּוֹרָא דְּמִילְחָא. לִכְשֶׁתִּמְדּוֹד כּוֹר שֶׁל מֶלַח עַל דָּבָר זֶה וְתִתְּנֵהוּ לִי, אוֹמַר לְךָ טַעֲמוֹ: הַיּוֹם חוֹל וּלְמָחָר קֹדֶשׁ. וּבֵין הַשְּׁמָשׁוֹת דִּקְנִיַּית עֵירוּב סְפֵיקָא הוּא, וּמִסְּפֵיקָא לָא תַּפְקִיעַ מִמִּילְּתֵיהּ קַמַּיְיתָא, וְכֵן סֵיפָא: שֶׁל מַעֲשֵׂר. רִאשׁוֹן, שֶׁהָיָה עֲדַיִין טֶבֶל שֶׁלֹּא הִפְרִישׁ הַלֵּוִי מִמֶּנּוּ תְּרוּמַת מַעֲשֵׂר, וַהֲרֵי הוּא בְּמִיתָה בְּעוֹדוֹ טֶבֶל, וַאֲפִילּוּ לְכֹהֲנִים, וְלָא חֲזֵי לְעֵירוּב. וּלְגַבֵּי לָגִין טְבוּל יוֹם בְּעוֹדוֹ טֶבֶל לָא פָּסֵיל, דִּטְבוּל יוֹם מוּתָּר בִּנְגִיעָה לְחוּלִּין וּלְמַעֲשֵׂר. וְאַף עַל גַּב דִּפְתִיכָא בֵּיהּ תְּרוּמָה שֶׁלֹּא הוּרְמָה, וְאָמַר הֲרֵי זוֹ שֶׁבַּלָּגִין תְּרוּמַת מַעֲשֵׂר עַל הֶחָבִית לִכְשֶׁתֶּחְשַׁךְ, וְעֵירֵב שְׁמָשׁוֹ שֶׁהִיא כְּשֵׁרָה לִתְרוּמָה: דְּבָרָיו קַיָּימִין. וְהַתְּרוּמָה טְהוֹרָה: וְאִם אָמַר עֵירְבוּ לִי בַּלָּגִין זֶה לֹא אָמַר כְּלוּם.: הוֹאִיל וְכִי מְטָא בֵּין הַשְּׁמָשׁוֹת אֲלַפְנֵי טֶבֶל הָוֵה: תְּחִלַּת בֵּין הַשְּׁמָשׁוֹת, שֶׁהוּא סוֹף הַיּוֹם: קוֹנֶה עֵירוּב: וְסוֹף הַיּוֹם שֶׁל ע"שׁ טֶבֶל הוּא:

דְּאִי

תוספות

*הכא בשתי כיתי עדים. דר' מאיר לית ליה אוקי תרי בהדי תרי כו'. אע"ג דבפרק שני דכתובות (דף כ.) אמרינן אוקי תרי בהדי תרי °אפילו בדאורייתא — הכא שאני, דהשתא ודאי טמאה היא:

אדרבה העמד מקוה על חזקתו. הוה מצי לשנויי: הרי חסר לפניך, כדאמר פר' קמא דנדה (דף ג:), אלא דלא איירי הכא במקוה שנמדד ונמצא חסר:

במקוה שלא נמדד. וא"ת: והא רבי יוסי מטמא אפילו טהרות אם נגע בהן. דלענין דאמרינן ליה זיל טבול — אפילו ר"מ מודה, °כדאמרינן גבי ספק טומאה ברשות הרבים. וא"כ אדרבה נימא אוקי טהרות על חזקתן! וי"ל: דבספיקא דרבנן כי הכא לא אמרינן זיל טבול לרבי מאיר, ופליגי אגברא אי בעי טבילה, אבל טהרות מודה רבי יוסי דלא מטמאינן. וכן איתא במסכת מקואות (פ"ב משנה ב), °דקתני: ורבי יוסי מטמא *שספק ליטמא טמא לטמא אחרים טהור:

אבל עירב בתרומה ספק טמאה ספק טהורה. כגון שהיו ב' ליטורין לפניו, אחד היה תרומה טמאה ואחד היה תרומה טהורה, ועירב באחד מהן — דליכא חזקה כלל:

ספק נדמעו. נראה כפ"ה בלשון שני נדמעו טבל בחולין, ולא כסתם דימוע שבהתלמוד. אבל לשון ראשון שפירש נדמעו תרומה בחולין, ואתיא כסומכוס — אין נראה, דהא קתני בברייתא דמערבין בתרומה. ודוחק לומר דמיירי בתרומה לכהן:

מאי שנא. ואם תאמר: והא רבא גופיה קאמר בסמוך: זאת אומרת סוף היום קונה עירוב. ואם סוף היום קונה עירוב — אתיא דרב נחמן שפיר, ואמאי קמיבעיא ליה מאי שנא? ויש לומר: דע"כ דרבא אית ליה דתחלת היום קונה עירוב, דהא פסיק בריש ביצה (דף ד:) כרב, דאמר: נולדה בזה, אסורה בזה. וטעמא דרב משום הכנה, ומאן דאית ליה הכנה סבר תחילת היום קונה עירוב, כדמוכח בפירקין (דף לח:). ורבא דאמר זאת אומרת סוף היום קונה עירוב — אליבא דברייתא קאמר, וליה לא ס"ל:

דאי

[נ"ל אבל ספק ליטמא ולטמא אחרים טהור]

רבינו חננאל

ופריק רבה ורב יוסף משנתינו בב' כתי עדים אחת אומרת מבעוד יום נטמאת התרומה ואחת אומרת משחשכה. ופריק רבא פירוק אחר. התם תרי חזקה לקולא חדא העמד חי על חזקתו ואימור לא היה מת באותה שעה שנגע בו. שניה העמד טהור על חזקתו ואימור לא נטמא *) [והכא] אמרינן ספיקו טמא דאדרבה העמד גברא על חזקתו ואימור לא עירב בסעודה הראויה. קשיא דר' יוסי אדר' יוסי הכא במתני' קתני ספק עירוב [כשר] והתם בברייתא קתני ספק טומאה (כשר) [טמא] ופרקינן שאני טומאה דאפילו טומאה קלה יש לה עיקר מן התורה. לפיכך א"ר יוסי אפילו ספיקו טמא. אבל בעירוב תחומין דרבנן נינהו. אי [בעית] תימא הא דידיה ומתני' דרביה ופשוטה היא. רבא א' בשלמא התם העמד טמא על חזקתו ואימור לא טבל שלא נתברה טבילתו כהוגן. אבל הכא מאי איכא לך למימר העמד גברא על חזקתו ואימור לא עירב הרי עירב. מאי איכא **) שמא משחשכה לא אתי שמא ודאי. מקוה נמי א"ת העמד מקוה על חזקתו ואימור לא חסר. איכא למימר הכי במקוה (שלא נמדדה) [שנמדדה] אבל במקוה (שלא נמדדה) [שלא נמדדה] ונמצאת חסרה היכי יכלת למימר הכי לפיכך קתני טמא: ת"ר כיצד א"ר יוסי ספק עירוב כשר. עירב בתרומה ספק מבעוד יום נטמאת ספק לא נטמאת וכן בפירות ספק נדמעו וספק לא נדמעו אבל עירב בתרומה ספק נטמאת מבעוד יום ספק משחשכה נטמאת. וכן בפירות ספק מבע"י ספק משחשכה אין זה ספק עירוב כשר: היו לפניו ב' ככרות אחת טמאה ואחת טהורה ואמ' עירובו בטהורה כ"מ שהיא אסיקנא בין לר"מ בין לר"י אינו עירוב בעינן סעודה הראויה מבעוד יום וליכא. בעא מיניה [רבא] מר"נ ככר זה היום חול ולמחר קודש וא' עירובו בזה מהו. ופשט ליה הוי עירוב כו' מ"ש בתר יומא

עין משפט נר מצוה

שייך לדף הקודם
עט א ב מיי' פ"ו מהל' עירובין הלכה טו טוש"ע א"ח סי' שצד סעיף ז וסי' תנו סעיף א:
פ ג ד ה מיי' שם הלכה טז טוש"ע א"ח סי' שצד סעיף ז:

מסורת הש"ס

ס"א לחומרא
[לקמן נט. סוטה ל:]
[תוספתא פ"ב]
[לקמן ע"ב ודף לח.]
שבת ד. חולין יב. קיב.
[טבול יום פ"ד מ"ד]

הגהות הב"ח

(א) גמ' ואיבעית אימא לא קשיא הא דידיה: (ב) רש"י ד"ה שבת נמי וכו' במס' סוטה. נ"ב דף כז: ובגמ' שם דף ל ע"ב: (ג) ד"ה העמד טמא וכו' תחום ביתו ואומר לא:

גליון הש"ס

גמ' קסבר ר"י תחומין דרבנן. עיין הגהת אשר"י ספ"ק דעירובין. תוס' ד"ה הכא. ק"ל התם אמרינן כן לענין ממון [illegible] בדאורייתא. [illegible]

*) [נראה דחסר כאן ונ"ל והכא חדא חזקה לקולא דהעמד תרומה על חזקתה ואימור לא נטמאת ולכן אמרינן כו'] **) [נראה דל"ל מאי איכא למימר שמא משחשכה לא אתי שמא ומוציא מידי ודאי.] [illegible]

דאי סלקא דעתך תחילת היום קונה עירוב — אי אמר עירבו לי בזה, אמאי לא אמר כלום? אמר רב פפא: אפילו תימא תחילת היום קונה עירוב — *בעינן סעודה הראויה מבעוד יום, וליכא.§ **מתני'** [א]מתנה אדם על עירובו, ואומר: אם באו גוים מן המזרח — עירובי למערב, מן המערב — עירובי למזרח, אם באו *לכאן ולכאן — למקום שארצה אלך, לא באו לא לכאן ולא לכאן — הריני כבני עירי. [ב]אם בא חכם מן המזרח — עירובי למזרח, מן המערב — עירובי למערב, בא לכאן ולכאן — למקום שארצה אלך, לא לכאן ולא לכאן — הריני כבני עירי. רבי יהודה אומר: אם היה אחד מהן רבו — הולך אצל רבו, ואם היו שניהן רבותיו — למקום שירצה ילך.§ **גמ'** כי אתא רבי יצחק, תני איפכא כולה מתניתין. קשיא גוים אגוים, קשיא חכם אחכם. גוים אגוים לא קשיא; הא — בפרהגבנא, הא — *במרי דמתא. חכם אחכם לא קשיא; הא — במותיב פירקי, הא — במקרי שמע.§ "ר' יהודה אומר: אם היה אחד מהן וכו'".§ ורבנן — זימנין דניחא ליה בחבריה טפי מרביה. אמר רב: ליתא למתניתין מדתני איו, *דתני איו: ר' יהודה אומר: אין אדם מתנה על שני דברים כאחד, אלא אם (כן) בא חכם למזרח — עירובו למזרח, ואם בא חכם למערב — עירובו למערב. אבל לכאן ולכאן — לא. מאי שנא לכאן ולכאן דלא — *דאין ברירה, למזרח למערב נמי אין ברירה! אמר רבי יוחנן: וכבר בא חכם. אדרבה, ליתא לדאיו ממתניתין! לא סלקא דעתך, דהא שמעינן ליה לרבי יהודה דלית ליה ברירה. *דתנן: *הלוקח יין מבין הכותים, אומר

רש"י

דאי אמרת תחילת היום. של שבת קונה עירוב, דהיינו סוף בין השמשות קונה עירוב, אמאי לא אמר כלום: **מתני'** מתנה אדם על שני עירובין, אחד לסוף אלפים למזרח ביתו ואחד לסוף אלפים אמה למערב ביתו: ואומר אם באו גוים מן המזרח. וצריך אני לברוח מפניהם — יקנה לי עירובי שבמערב, ויהיו לי במערב ביתי ד' אלפים אמה, אע"ג דלא אתו עד למחר — אמרינן: יש ברירה, דבין השמשות קנה לו עירובו דאידך גיסא: הריני כבני עירי. אלפים מעירי לכל רוח, ואין צריך להשתכר כאן ולהפסיד כאן: בא חכם למזרח. חוץ לתחום עירי, ורוצה אני ללמוד תורה מפיו ועכשיו איני יודע לאיזה צד יבא, ולמחר אשמע מבני אדם הבאים משם לכאן על ידי עירוב: רבי יהודה אומר. אם באו לכאן ולכאן, ואחד מהן רבו — ילך אצל רבו ולא אצל חכם, דקים לן בגוויה דבשעת קניית עירוב דעתיה למקני ליה ההוא עירוב דלצד רבו. ומיהו, איהו הוא דלא ידע לאיזה מן הצדדין יבא, והשתא דידע להתם ליזיל: **גמ'** תני איפכא. איתי מתניתא בידיה דתני איפכא: בורח מן החכם, ומתנה: אם בא חכם למזרח — עירובו למערב כו' ולגבי נכרים תני דלהוא צד דליתו נכרים לקני עירוביה: פרהגבני. גבאי המס ובורח מפניהם: מרי דמתא. צריך הוא לפייס או לצעוק: מותיב פירקי. לדרוש ברבים, דעת האדם לילך ולשמוע: מקרי שמע. כלומר: מלמדי תינוקות להתפלל. ומתניתין דר' יצחק בדאתו בי תרי, חד להאי גיסא וחד להאי גיסא. ומתני' אדמותיב פירקי קאי. והכי קאמר: בא מותיב פירקי למזרח, או בא לכאן ולכאן דתרווייהו מותיבי פירקי — למקום שארצה אלך. ולכשיתברור לו למחר, אמרינן: הוברר הדבר דבשעת קניית עירוב דעתיה אההוא חכם הוה. ודר' יצחק קאי אמקרי שמע, והכי קאמר: בא מקרי שמע למזרח — עירובי אדמותיב פירקי למערב, בא מקרי שמע למערב — עירובי אדמותיב פירקי למזרח, בא לכאן ולכאן, תרווייהו מותיבי פירקי או שניהן שוין — למקום שארצה אלך. כך שמעתי: ורבנן. דפליגי אדר' יהודה, דאפילו אחד מהן רבו ילך לאיזה שירצה: דזמנין דניחא ליה לאיניש בחבריה טפי מרביה. וי"ל ברירה אף כאן: ליתא למתני'. דקתני לר' יהודה. היו שניהן רבותיו — למקום שירצה ילך. אלמא: אית ליה לר' יהודה ברירה. דהא עירוב מאתמול קנה, ואיהו השתא הוא דקא בריר ליה, ואמרינן: הוברר הדבר דמאתמול נמי דעתיה להאי הוה: ליתא למתניתין. אינה עיקר, מדתני איו. הואיל ואשכחן מתני' דתני איו דלאו הכי הוא: איו. שם חכם: על שני דברים. לומר בא לכאן ולכאן למקום שארצה אלך, דאין ברירה אלא על אחד ואינו יודע להיכן יבא, יכול להתנות ולומר בא חכם למזרח כו': מאי שנא לכאן ולכאן. דתלה עצמו לומר באיזה שארצה אלך, דלא שרי רבי יהודה: דאין ברירה. דכי בריר למחר, אמרינן: שמא אתמול כי קנה עירוב לאו דעתיה אהך הוה, אלא אאידך: מזרח ומערב נמי. בשלא בא אלא אחד. וקא סלקא דעתך השתא דבין השמשות עדיין לא בא חכם למזרח, שעדיין היה רחוק מן העירוב ששה אלפים פחות שתי אמות, ומשחשיכה הלך אלפים ונכנס לתוך ארבעה אלפים של עיר. וזה שהניח עירובו ותלה בדעת החכם, ואמר אם יבוא למזרח עירובי למזרח ואם לא יבא לא לכאן ולא לכאן הריני כבני עירי ולא יהא עירוב, ולמחר שמע שבא למזרח מי יאמר דבשעת קניית עירוב היה דעת החכם ליכנס לתוך ד' אלפים של עיר? דילמא לא היה בדעתו לזוז, ולא קנה עירובו של זה. ור' יהודה קאמר דקני, דאמרינן: הוברר הדבר דסופו הוכיח שבין השמשות היה דעתו לכאן: א"ר יוחנן וכבר בא חכם. מתניתין בהכי עסקינן שבא חכם כבר קודם בין השמשות, אבל זה לא היה יודע להיכן בא, או אם בא או לא. ולמחר כשנשמע לו גלויי מילתא בעלמא הוא, ואיגלאי מילתא דההוא עירוב קנה. ואין זו סמך על ברירת ספק, אלא קנייה ודאית — שהרי אמר לצד החכם יקנה לי העירוב, והחכם כבר בא קודם קניית העירוב, וקנה: אדרבה ליתא לדאיו. דמתניתין עיקר, והיא ברייתא היא: לא סלקא דעתך. לאפוקי להאי דאיו: הלוקח יין מבין הכותים. קודם שגזרו על יינם כדמפרש ב"שחיטת חולין". וסתם כותים לא מפרשי תרומה, ואין לזה כלים להפריש לתוכן תרומה ומעשר: אומר

תוספות

דאי סלקא דעתך תחילת היום קונה עירוב. ואם תאמר: נימא משום דמספיקא לא פקע טבל, ומספיקא לא נחתא תרומה כדאמר לעיל! ואור"י: דלא דמי, דודאי כי אמר היום חול ולמחר קדש — מקפיד שלא תחול על העירוב *קדושת היום, אבל הכא — רוצה הוא שתחול עליו שם תרומה מיד אם היה יכול, ואינו אומר לכשתחשך — אלא שתלא לגין מתורת טבול יום: **ואם** היו שניהן רבותיו. אצטריך לאשמועינן אפילו אחד רבו מובהק:

לא ס"ד דשמעינן ליה לר' יהודה דלית ליה ברירה דתנן כו'. ואם תאמר: אכתי ליתא לדאיו, ולההיא דהלוקח מקמי מתניתין דהכא, ומתני' ד"מי שאחזו" (גיטין דף עג.) דמה היא באותן הימים, דדייקינן מינה בריש "כל הגט" (שם דף כה:) דאית ליה לרבי יהודה ברירה, ומקמי ברייתא ד"מרובה" (ב"ק דף סט.) דקאמר רבי יהודה: שחרית אומר בעל הבית כל מה שילקטו כו' — דבכל הני אית ליה לרבי יהודה ברירה! ויש לומר: דרב מחלק בין תולה בדעת אחרים בין תולה בדעת עצמו, כמו שמחלק אביי בריש "כל הגט" וההיא דגיטין וד"מרובה" — הוי תולה בדעת אחרים, והתם אית ליה ברירה. אבל תולה בדעת עצמו — לית ליה ברירה. ולהכי קאמר דליתא למתניתין דקתני דאית לרבי יהודה ברירה, אפילו בתולה בדעת עצמו מקמי דאיו, ומקמי ההיא ד"הלוקח". והאי דפריך אההיא דאיו מאי שנא דלכאן ולכאן דאין ברירה — לא לרב פריך, דלדידיה דמחלק בין תולה בדעת עצמו בין תולה בדעת אחרים אתי שפיר, אלא למי שאינו מחלק פריך. ור' יוחנן דמשני: וכבר בא חכם — נמי אין מחלק, ולדידיה ודאי ליתא לדאיו(א) מקמי כל הנהו. ומיהו, קשה: דבסוף ביצה (דף לז:) גבי ב' שלקחו בהמה וחבית בשותפות מדקדק דרבי יוחנן לית ליה ברירה מדמפרש מלתיה דאיו. והא ע"כ לרבי יוחנן ליתא לדאיו, כדפי'! וי"ל: דודאי הוה מצי לשנויי הכי, אלא ניחא ליה לשנויי לעולם לא תיפוך. אי נמי: נהי דלר' יוחנן ליתא לדאיו, דאמר דלר' יהודה אין ברירה — מכל מקום מוכח שפיר דר' יוחנן לית ליה ברירה, מדמשני ליה. אבל קשה, דאפילו בתולה בדעת אחרים נמי שמעינן לרבי יהודה דלית ליה ברירה. דתנן בשקלים, ומייתי לה ב"הוציאו לו" (יומא דף נה.), דקאמר ר' יהודה: לא היו שופרות לקיני חובה מפני התערובות, ומפרש התם טעמא משום חטאת שמתו בעליה, ומשום דלית ליה ברירה כדמוכח בההיא דאיו. והשתא הא לר' יוחנן ליתא לדאיו, ולרב אית ליה ברירה לרבי יהודה בתולה בדעת אחרים! וי"ל: דהא דאית ליה ברירה לרבי יהודה בתולה בדעת אחרים — ה"מ כשמתנה, אבל בלא תנאי — אינו מועיל: **דתנן** הלוקח יין מבין הכותים. "דתניא" גרסינן. דבמשנה בדמאי פ"ז (משנה ד) ליכא אלא מלתיה דר"מ לחוד. ואע"ג דר' מאיר גזר על יינן, כדאמר פ"ק דחולין (דף ו.) — זאת נשנית קודם גזירה. ואף על גב דרבי יוסי ור"ש סבירא להו כותים גירי אריות הם, כדאמר במנחות פרק "ר' ישמעאל" (דף סו.): תורמין משל נכרים על של כותים, מ"מ, כיון דפרשי מע"ז — הם טפי משאר אומות, ומחזיקים בתורה שבכתב ולא היו עובדין אלהיהם כמו שעשו בבית ראשון — לא גזרו על יינן. ואע"ג דגזרו על פתן כמו לרבי מאיר קודם גזירה — שהיה פתן אסור ויינן מותר. אי נמי: הכא איירי כשטיהר ישראל יינו של כותי: שני

רבינו חננאל

טבל טבול לתרומת מעשר היה ואין מערבין בטבל לפיכך לא אמר כלום. דאי ס"ד תחלת היום והוא תחלת לילי שבת הוא דקונה עירוב כיון שהעריב שמש נתקן הטבל אמאי אין עירובו עירוב. רב פפא אמר אפי' תימא תחלת היום קונה עירוב בעינן סעודה הראויה לו מבעוד יום וליכא דכל היום טבל היה: **מתני'** מתנה אדם על עירובו ואומר אם באו גוים למזרח עירובי (למזרח) [למערב] למערב וכו' כי אתא רב יצחק מתני איפכא אם באו גוים מן המזרח עירובי למזרח למערב עירובי למערב ואמרינן קשיא גוים אגוים כלומר מתני' [תנן] באו מן המזרח ובורח מהן למערב (ורישא) [ובריתא] באו מן המזרח והולך עליהם ופרקינן לא קשיא מתני' *) בפרהגבנאי פי' אנשים הטורדין כגון דגרסי' (בב"ק קי"ז) בהאי שותה קם חד מסרה לפרהגבאנא דמלכא ובורח מהן מן המזרח למערב. והא דקתני ר' יצחק למרי מתא והולך אליו להקביל פניו ולהתקרב לו. וכן בא חכם למזרח במותיב פירקיה. פי' דרשן הוא בא לשמוע דברי תורה והא דקתני ר' יצחק בא חכם למזרח עירובי (למזרח) למערב במקרי שמע. חזן שמתרחק ממנו מפני שאינו צריך לו ומפורש כך בתלמוד א"י באו גוים מן המזרח עירובי למערב אית תנאי תנן במזרח מאן דמר במזרח באילן טקסיווט מאן דמר במערב באילן רומאי. בא חכם מן המזרח עירובי במזרח אית תנאי תנן במערב. מאן דמר במזרח באילן חכימיא. מ"ד במערב ברגיל: פיסקא ר' יהודה אומר אם היה אחד (מעין) [מהן] רבו ילך אצל רבו ואם הוו שניהם רבותיו ילך למקום שירצה כיון שילך לאחד מהן נתברר כי על זה היה עירובו מאתמול אלמא אית ליה ברירה אמר רב ליתא למתני' מדתני איו דברי ר' יהודה לכאן ולכאן דלא דאין ברירה. אלא אם בא חכם במזרח עירובי במזרח עירובי למערב (או) כר' יוחנן דאמר וכבר בא חכם ונתברר כי על דבר ברור עירב. ואמרינן ואמאי לא דחינן דברי איו דאמר לית ליה ברירה לר' יהודה (ומוקמינן) [מקמיה] מתניתין דפריש אית ליה לר' יהודה בריה ודחינן הכי לא ס"ד דהא איכא מתניתא אחריתי

*) עיין ערוך ערך פרהגבן.

עין משפט נר מצוה

פא א מיי' פ"ח מהל' עירובין הלכה ג סמג עשין א:

נ"ל קדושה

פב ב מיי' שם טוש"ע א"ח סי' תיג:

[נ"ל דתניא עי' תוס']

מסורת הש"ס

[לקמן לח:]

[גי' ירושלמי ומשנה שבמשניות מכאן ומכאן]

[עי' תוס' לקמן פב. ד"ה אין]

ביצה לז: חולין יד: [יומא נו:]

[לקמן עח: חולין קלה: כ"ב כז:]

ב"ק סט: תוספתא דמאי פ"ז סוכה כג: יומא נה: מגילה כב. חולין יד. גיטין כה.

הגהות הב"ח

(א) תוס' ד"ה לא ס"ד וכו' ולדידיה ודאי ליתא לדאיו והההיא דהלוקח מקמי כל:

גליון הש"ס

גמ' הא במרי דמתא. עי' לקמן דף פ ע"א תוד"ה אין מערבין:

אומר: שני לוגין שאני עתיד להפריש הרי הן תרומה, עשרה מעשר ראשון, תשעה מעשר שני, ומיחל ושותה מיד, דברי ר"מ. ר' יהודה ור' יוסי ור' שמעון [א]אוסרין. עולא אמר: ליתא לאיו ממתני'. ואלא הא דקתני "ר' יהודה ורבי יוסי ורבי שמעון אוסרין"? עולא *זוזי זוזי קתני: דברי רבי מאיר ור' יהודה, ר' יוסי ור' שמעון אוסרין. וסבר ר' יוסי אין ברירה? *והתנן, רבי יוסי אומר: [ב]שתי נשים שלקחו את קיניהן בעירוב, או שנתנו *קיניהן לכהן – איזהו שירצה כהן יקריב עולה, ולאיזה שירצה יקריב חטאת! אמר רבה: התם כשהתנו. אי הכי מאי למימרא? קמ"ל כדרב חסדא, *דאמר רב חסדא: [ג]אין הקינין מתפרשות אלא

רש"י

אומר שני לוגין שאני עתיד להפריש תרומה. מן המשנה: הרי הן. בתוכו: ומיחל. מעשר שני שהוא יכול לתקן מיד בלא הפרשה לאחר שקרא עליו שם יחללנו בכל מקום שהוא על המעות, ושותה מיד. ולאחר זמן יפריש התרומה והמעשר. ואמרינן: הוברר הדבר שזהו תרומה: אוסרין. קס"ד השתא דטעמייהו משום דקסברי אין ברירה: [זוזי. זוגי]: בעירוב. בשותפות: לאיזה. מן הקינין שירצה, ב' הפרידות יקריב עולות לשתי הנשים, ואת קן הא' יקריב שתיהן חטאות לשתי הנשים. וכ"ש אם בא לחלק כל קן וקן פרידה לעולה ופרידה לחטאת דשפיר דמי. אלמא: מדקא אמר שמותר ליקח קיניהן בעירוב – מכלל דיש ברירה, דאמרינן: הוברר הדבר שזו הפרידה שהקריב לשמה של זו שלה היא, דשם בעלים בעינן. דאי אין ברירה – איכא למימר חטאת ועולה שהקריב לה לא שלה היו אלא של חברתה, וקרבן הקרב בשנוי בעלים קי"ל בפסחים (דף ס:) ובזבחים (דף ב.) דאינו עולה לבעלים וכ"ש בחטאת שלא לשמה או שלא לשם בעליה – לגמרי מיפסלא, וקביעות שם בעלים אינו תלוי בכהן: כשהתנו. הנשים ביניהן, שכל מי שיקריב הכהן לשמה יהא שלה: אי הכי מאי למימרא. כיון דמדעת כהן תלוי: קמ"ל כדרב חסדא. שאע"פ שהיה כל קן וקן בפני עצמו, אלא שלקחום ביחד, וסד"א על כרחו מכל קן צריך לעשות חטאת ועולה, ולא יוכל לעשות מן הקן הא' שתי עולות לשתי הנשים, ומקן השני ב' חטאות, דלאו אדעתא דהכי יהבינהו, קא משמע לן: כיון דלא אקבעינהו בהדיא בשעת לקיחה, לאמר "פרידה זו חטאת ופרידה זו עולה" – אפילו קבעום לאחר לקיחה, יכול הכהן לעשות כמה שירצה: אין הקינין. של כל מחוסרי כפרה, מתפרשות איזו עולה ואיזו חטאת: אלא

תוספות

שני לוגין שאני עתיד להפריש. ואע"ג דע"ה לא נחשדו על תרומה גדולה. כדאמרינן בסוטה (דף מח.): כותים אפילו תרומה גדולה אין מפרישין. ואע"ג דבפרק "שלשה שאכלו" (ברכות דף מז:) אמרינן דכותאי עשורי מעשרי כראוי, דבמאי דכתיב מזהר זהירי – ה"מ לאכול לעצמן, אבל למכור לאחרים – לא מעשרי, דלא דרשי "לפני עור לא תתן מכשול" אלא כפשטיה. ואע"ג דאינן חשודין על הגזל – הכא לא חשיב ליה גזל, דהוי ממון שאין לו תובעין. ועוד: דכל זמן שלא הופרש אינו דומה שיהא גזל, שעדיין לא נתחייב ליתן לכהן או ללוי. ותדע, דע"ה לא נחשדו על הגזל וחשידי על המעשרות. ועוד, דסמכי אהא דדרשינן בבבא מציעא (דף פח:): "עשר תעשר ואכלת" – ולא מוכר:

עשרה מעשר ראשון ותשעה מעשר שני. לאו דוקא עשרה ותשעה, דאחר שהסיר שני לוגין לתרומה גדולה פשו להו מאה נכי ב':

מיחל. פ"ה: מחלל על מעות ושותה מיד בלא הפרשה. ואינו נראה, דאינו יכול לחלל. דדוקא בסיפא דהך מתני' גבי דמאי קתני: ומחלל על מעות, משום דקבע לו מקום – דהוי כמו הפרשה. דקתני התם: מעשר שני בצפונו או בדרומו. ובע"ש בין השמשות איירי, כדקתני *בתוספתא וקדש עליו היום. ולכך, בדמאי יכול לקבוע עליו מקום – דספק חשיכה מעשרין את הדמאי. אבל בכותים, דודאי לא מעשרי – הוי ודאי. ולהכי לא קתני גבי כותים מעשר שני בצפונו או בדרומו כדקתני על דמאי, ולא קתני נמי הכא ומחלל על מעות כדקתני גבי דמאי. אלא "ומיחל", פירוש: *מתחיל. או כמו שפי' רבינו תם ד"מיחל" כמו מיהל בה"א, פירוש: מזוג, כמו "סבאך מהול במים" (ישעיה א), ואחר השבת מפריש מעשר ראשון ושני. כדקתני בתוספתא: עשרה הבאין אחריהן, תשעה הבאין אחריהן, דכיון שאין יכול לקבוע לו מקום, אם היה שותה בלא הפרשה – היה שותה טבלים למפרע:

דברי ר"מ. משמע דאית ליה לר"מ ברירה. ולר' יהודה נמי קאמר רבה במסקנא דאית ליה ברירה. והכא אסר משום דחייש לבקיעת נוד, ואילו בפ' "יש בכור" (בכורות דף מח.) גבי נתנו עד שלא חלקו מוקי רבא ר"מ ור' יהודה כרב אסי, דאמר האחין מחצה יורשין ומחצה לקוחות. אלמא: מספקא להו! ויש לחלק בין הכא, שמברר דבריו ומתנה בפירוש, ואומר "שאני עתיד להפריש" להיא דאחין שחלקו, דאינו מברר דבריו כלום. וב"מרובה" (ב"ק דף סט:), דפריך דר' יוחנן אדר' יוחנן, דבההיא דכל המתלקט אית ליה ברירה ובההיא דאחין שחלקו שמעינן דלית ליה ברירה. וחוזר בו התלמוד מדבריו מתוך קושיא זו – הוה מצי לחלק כדפרי'. אלא דניחא ליה למימר לעולם כל הנלקט כדקתני במתניתין, וניחא ליה למימר לעולם לא תיפוך, כדפי' לעיל. ועוד: דלא מצי לחלק הכי, דהא ר' יוחנן לית ליה ברירה אפילו היכא דמברר בריש "כל הגט"*:

רבי יוסי ור"ש אוסרין. משמע דר' יוסי לית ליה ברירה. וכן בסמוך, גבי מעשר שני שיש לי בביתי מחולל על סלע שתעלה בידי מן הכיס. וקשה: דשמעינן לר' יוסי דאית ליה ברירה ב"מי שאחזו" (גיטין דף עג:). דתנן, ר' יוסי אומר: מגורשת ואינה מגורשת. ולכי מיית הוי גיטא. אלמא: יש ברירה. דהכי דייקינן בריש "כל הגט" (שם דף כה:) לר"י, ופ"ה התם: אע"ג דתנאי הוא לריך ברירה, כיון דאין בידו ובשעת התנאי ספק הוא, והתנאי מתקיים מאליו, ואי לאו משום ברירה – לא הוי גט. והכי נמי בשמעתא חשיב ברירה אם בא חכם למזרח כו', ואע"ג דמתנה. וכן בריש "כל הגט"*: הריני בועליך ע"מ שירצה אבא כו'. והא דאמרי בשמעתין הרי זה תרומה על זה אם ירדו גשמים כו' – ה"נ לא הוי תרומה, דפשיטא ליה דהויא תרומה – היינו למאן דאית ליה ברירה קאמר. ולמאן דמחלק בין תולה בדעת עצמו לדעת אחרים – ניחא, אבל למאן דלא מחלק – קשה! וי"ל: דהתם בגיטין עומד הדבר להתברר בודאי, שהרי יחיה או ימות. אבל הכא – יכול להיות שלא יבא לידי הפרשה, או לא יעלה סלע מן הכיס. תימה: למאי דסלקא דעתך דלר' יהודה לית ליה ברירה, א"כ סבר האחין שחלקו לקוחות הן ומחזירין זה לזה ביובל כר' יוחנן, וא"כ לא משכחת דמייתי בכורים אלא חד בר חד עד יהושע בן נון, דאין להן אלא קנין פירות. ור' יהודה אית ליה ב"החובל" (ב"ק דף פ.) דלאו כקנין הגוף דמי גבי דין יום או יומים. ולר' יוסי נמי לא משכחת לה, דס"ל דאין ברירה וגבי דין יום או יומים מספקא ליה אם קנין פירות כקנין הגוף דמי אם לאו. וכה"ג דייק התלמוד בסוף "השולח" (גיטין דף מח.)! ותירץ ר"י: דמדין יום או יומים אין ללמוד בעלמא, דהתם כתב קרא "כספו" ו"תחתיו", ולהכי לא מייתי ב"השולח" כי מייתי ההיא דשדה אחוזה:

אוסרין. הקשה השר מקוצי: דהכא משמע אי טעמא דר"י משום בקיעת הנוד ליתא לדאיו מקמי מתני'. ואילו בפ"ק דחולין (דף יד:) בשמעתין דנסבין חברייא למימר דר"י היא, מייתי דאיו בתר דמוקי טעמא דר"י משום בקיעת הנוד. ושם פירשתי* מה שנ"ל. *והתניא ר' יוסי אומר. הוה מצי לשנויי דהתם בתולה בדעת אחרים:

לאיזו שירצה כהן. פי' בקונטרס: אלמא אית ליה ברירה, דאי לית ליה ברירה – איכא למימר חטאת שהקריב לא שלה היה אלא לחבירתה וקרבן הקרב בשנוי בעלים פסול. ואין נראה להסר, דהא מוכח בריש זבחים (דף ג:) דסתמא לשמה קאי א"כ בלא ברירה אפשר להקריב לו בסתם. ונראה דמוכח דאי אין ברירה איכא למימר כל קן רחל הקריב למעלה וכל קן לאה הקריב למטה והקריב עולה למטה וחטאת למעלה:

כשהתנו. פי' הקונטרס: שהתנו הנשים שכל שיקריב לשמה יהא שלה. וקשה לפירושו: דהיינו ברירה גמורה שתולה בדעת הכהן, שאותו שיעשה יתברר שהוא שלה. דכיון שנתערבו הקינין, אי אפשר כלל בלא ברירה. ונראה לר"י לפרש: כשהתנו הנשים בשעת לקיחה זה יהיה שלי וזה יהיה שלך, וכן בנתנו דמי קיניהן לכהן בעירוב, ונתנם למוכר ופירש בשעת לקיחה קן זה לזו, וקן זה לזו. ונמצא שלא נתערבו הקינין אלא המעות. ופריך: אי הכי, מאי למימרא? דכיון שלא נתערבו הקינין פשיטא דשריא. ומשני: מהו דתימא דנגזור התנו אטו לא התנו, דכיון שנותנין הדמים בעירוב יקחו גם כן הקינין בעירוב – ואז אי אפשר בלא ברירה, קמשמע לן דלא גזרינן. וכדרב חסדא גרסינן, פירוש: וקמ"ל נמי כדרב חסדא. ותרתי קמ"ל, מדנקט שתי נשים ולא נקט באשה אחת – משמע דאתא לאשמעינן דלא גזרינן התנו אטו לא התנו. ואי לא אתא לאשמעינן נמי כדרב חסדא לא הוה ליה למתני לאיזה שירצה יקריב עולה ולאיזה שירצה יקריב חטאת, דלא הוה צריך להזכיר עולה וחטאת אלא יקריב של לאה ללאה, ושל רחל לרחל:
אלא

מסורת הש"ס

קינין פ"א מ"ד

גירסת המשנ' שם דמי קיניהן

ריתות כח. יומא מה. [נזיר כו:]

[גיטין ד' כה.]

[שם]

[בד"ה התם]

[נ"ל והתנן]

עין משפט נר מצוה

פג א מיי' פ"ז מהל' מעשר הלכה א סמג עשין קלה:

פד ב ג מיי' פ"ח מהל' פסולי המוקדשין הלכה ח:

[במגילה טז. איתא אייתא זוזא מביתיה פירש"י זוזא זוג ובכתובות עא. איתא זוגי זוגי קתני גם בערוך לא נמצא מלת זוזא]

בתוספתא [דמאי פ"ז] ועדיין לא קדש עליו כנ"ל

[וז"ל הערוך ערך חל ומיחל ושותה פ"א מתחיל ושותה פי' אומר שני לוגין שאני עתיד להפריש הרי הן בתחתית הנוד וכן המעשר אחריהן כו' ורב האי פירש מוהל ושותה כמו סבאך מהול במים ודע עוד דביומא נו. כתבו תוס' בשם הרב משולם מה שכתבו כאן ובגיטין כה: בשם רבינו תם]

רבינו חננאל

אחריתי דלית ליה לר' יהודה ברירה (הא) [מהא דתנן] הלוקח יין מבין הכותים אומר ב' לוגין שאני עתיד להפריש הרי הן תרומה עשרה מעשר ראשון תשעה מעשר שני. ומיחל ושותה דברי ר' מאיר. ור' יהודה ור' יוסי ור' שמעון אוסרין ואקשינן וסבר ר' יוסי אין ברירה והא תנן ר' יוסי אומר ב' נשים [שלקחו את קיניהן] בעירוב או שנתנו דמי קיניהן בעירוב איזה מהן שירצה מקריב עולה. פי' כיון שהקריבה לחטאת נתברר כי זו שלקחה מתחלה לחטאת וכן העולה אלמא אית ליה לר' יוסי ברירה. ופריק רבה (כשהיתה) [כשהתנו] ביניהן בכך. ועל כן א"ר יוסי איזה שירצה מקריב חטאת. ומאי אתא לאשמעינן כדרב חסדא דאמר אין

פה א מיי' פ"ו מהלכות מעשר הלכה ח:
פו ב מיי' פ"ד מהלכות מ"ש הלכה טו:
פז ג ד מיי' פ"ו מהל' עירובין הלכה כ סמג עשין א' טוש"ע א"ח סימן תיג:

אלא אי בלקיחת בעלים אי בעשיית כהן. ואכתי, סבר ר' יוסי אין ברירה? (א) והתניא: *עם הארץ שאמר לחבר "קח לי אגודה אחת של ירק או גלוסקא אחת" — [א]אינו צריך לעשר, דברי רבי יוסי. וחכ"א: צריך לעשר! איפוך. תא שמע: *האומר "מעשר שיש לי בביתי מחולל על סלע שתעלה בידי מן הכים", רבי יוסי אומר: [ב]מחולל! איפוך, אימא: רבי יוסי אומר: לא חילל. ומאי חזית דאפכת תרתי מקמי חדא?! איפוך חדא מקמי תרתי! הא ודאי איפכא תניא, דקתני סיפא: ומודה רבי יוסי באומר "מעשר שיש לי בתוך ביתי יהא מחולל על סלע חדשה שתעלה בידי מן הכים" — שחילל. מדקאמר הכא שחילל — מכלל דהתם לא חילל. האי סלע חדשה ה"ד? אי דאיכא תרתי תלת, דיש ברירה — היינו קמייתא! אלא דליכא אלא חדא — מאי תעלה? איידי דתני רישא "תעלה" תנא סיפא נמי "תעלה". א"ל רבא לרב נחמן: מאן האי תנא דאפילו בדרבנן לית ליה ברירה? דתניא, אמר לחמשה: הריני מערב על איזה מכם שארצה, רציתי — ילך, לא רציתי — לא ילך, רצה מבעו"י — עירובו עירוב, משחשיכה — אין עירובו עירוב. אישתיק ולא א"ל ולא מידי. ולימא ליה: תנא דבי איו הוא! לא שמיע ליה. *רב יוסף אמר: תנאי שקלת מעלמא?! תנאי היא. דתניא: הריני מערב לשבתות של כל השנה, רציתי — אלך, לא רציתי — לא אלך. רצה מבעוד יום — עירובו עירוב, משחשיכה; רבי שמעון אומר: [ג]עירובו עירוב, וחכמים אומרים אין עירובו עירוב. והא שמעינן לרבי שמעון דלית ליה ברירה, קשיא דרבי שמעון אדר"ש! אלא איפוך. מאי קשיא? דילמא, [ד]כי לית ליה לר' שמעון ברירה — בדאורייתא, אבל בדרבנן — אית ליה! (ב) קסבר רב יוסף: מאן דאית ליה ברירה — ל"ש בדאורייתא, ל"ש בדרבנן — אית ליה. ומאן דלית ליה ברירה — ל"ש בדאורייתא, ול"ש בדרבנן — לית ליה. *רבא אמר: שאני התם, דבעינן ראשית *ששיריה ניכרין. א"ל אביי: אלא מעתה, היו לפניו שני רמונים של טבל, ואמר: אם ירדו גשמים היום — יהא זה תרומה על זה, ואם לא ירדו גשמים היום — יהא זה תרומה על זה. ה"נ, בין ירדו בין לא ירדו דאין בדבריו כלום? וכ"ת הכי נמי — *והתנן: תרומת הכרי הזה ומעשרותיו בתוכו, ותרומת מעשר זה בתוכו, ר"ש אומר: קרא השם! שאני התם דאיכא סביביו. ואב"א כדקתני טעמא: *אמרו לו לר"מ: אי אתה מודה שמא יבקע הנוד ונמצא זה שותה טבלים למפרע? אמר להן: לכשיבקע. ולמאי דסליק אדעתין מעיקרא דבעינן ראשית ששיריה ניכרין, מאי קאמרי ליה? הכי קאמרי ליה: לדידן — בעינן ראשית ששיריה ניכרין, לדידך —
אי

אלא דליכא אלא חדא. וקמ"ל דלא גזרינן אטו היכא דאיכא תרתי או תלת: **מאן** האי תנא דאפילו בדרבנן לית ליה ברירה. הוי מצי למימר רבי יוסי דאגודה של ירק היא, דהוי מדרבנן, ושמא: כיון דעיקר מעשר מן התורה חשיב ליה כדאורייתא כדפ"ל (דף לב: בד"ה תאנים) גבי לקט תאנים מתאנתי:
אלא איפוך. בלא איפוך הוה אשכחן תנא דבדרבנן לית ליה ברירה – רבנן דר"ש. אלא דבעי לאוכוחי בהדיא שם התנא, ולהכי מוכח דמבעיא לן למימר איפוך ולכך קאמר אלא. ומיהו, לפי זה לא אתי שפיר הא דקאמר בסמוך: קסבר מאן דלית ליה ברירה לא שנא בדרבנן לא שנא בדאורייתא. ***קסבר**(ד) רב יוסף. וא"ת: דהכא מסיק רב יוסף דלרבי שמעון אין ברירה, ובריש "כל הגט" (גיטין דף כה:) אית ליה ברירה, גבי הריני בועליך על מנת שירצה אבא! וי"ל: דרב יוסף מחלק בין תולה בדעת עצמו לתולה בדעת אחרים, כרב משרשיא דהתם. ורבא דלא מחלק התם – מסיק הכא דלרבי שמעון יש ברירה. וטעמא דאסר – משום דבעינן ראשית ששיריה ניכרין:
אלא מעתה היו לפניו שני רמונים. וא"ת: וליפרוך ה"נ אי הוי טעמא משום דאין ברירה! וי"ל: דאי טעמא משום דאין ברירה הוא – אין תימ', דודאי כיון דאין ברירה הכי נמי דלא הויא תרומה. אבל אי מטעמא דבעינן ראשית ששיריה ניכרין – ה"נ דבשני רמונין לא הויא תרומה. והא בשני רמונים לא מסתברא שפיר האי טעמא. ומיהו, אי אמר התם האי טעמא דראשית – ה"נ אית לן למימר גבי רמונים. דלא מסתבר לפלוגי בהו. והא דמייתי מתרומת הכרי בתוכו, ר' שמעון אומר קרא שם. למאי דלא ידע דאיכא סביביו, הוי מצי לאקשויי נמי לטעמא דאין ברירה. ומהר"י מפרש: דאי טעמא דרבי שמעון משום דאין ברירה – אתי שפיר, דודאי היתה אחת מהן תרומה ומותר הכהן לאכלן ואע"ג דאין ברירה, דחד מינייהו ודאי תרומה. אבל אטעמא דראשית – פריך שפיר. הכי נמי דלא הוי כלל תרומה, ויהיה כהן אסור לאכלן. וכן בההיא דתרומת הכרי בתוכו קרא שם, וכהן מצי אכיל לכל מה שבתוך הכרי אע"ג דאין ברירה: **ולמאי** דסליק אדעתין מעיקרא דבעיא ראשית ששיריה ניכרין. הכי נמי הוה מצי למימרא (*לטעמא דברירה:
*) לטעמא דאין ברירה כצ"ל. ח"מ:
אי

אלא אי בלקיחת בעלים. שאמרו בשעת לקיחה: זו אני לוקח לעולה וזו לחטאת: **או בעשיית כהן.** אבל אם לקחום סתם, ואחר כך קרא עליהן שם – אין השם חל עליהן, ויכול הכהן לשנותן. וקרא דריש רב חסדא בסדר יומא*: "ולקחה שתי תורים או שני בני יונה אחד לעולה ואחד לחטאת", וכתיב גבי כהן: "ועשה הכהן את האחד חטאת והאחד עולה", אלמא: אין שם עולה וחטאת חל עליהן אלא בלקיחה או בעשייה: **עם הארץ שאמר לחבר.** שהיה חבר הולך לשוק ליקח לו ירק לעצמו, ואמר לו עם הארץ: (ג)קח גם לי אגודת ירק. אין צריך חבר לעשר דמאי מאותה שנתן לעם הארץ. אע"פ שלקח שלו ושל עם הארץ סתם, ולא פירש כשקנאן: זה לי וזה לעם הארץ, והוא מעם הארץ לקחן – יש ברירה, כשנותנו לעם הארץ שזו לצורכו לוקחה, ואין חבר זה מוכרה לו: **וחכמים אומרים צריך לעשר.** דאין ברירה. וי"ל: זו לצורך חבר לוקחה, והוא חוזר ומחליפה לעם הארץ, וחבר אינו רשאי למכור לעם הארץ דבר שאינו מתוקן: **רבי יוסי אומר חילל.** וכי סליק סלע בידיה אמרינן: יש ברירה, שזה שחילל מעשר שני עליה דאי אין ברירה, לא אמר מידי, אלא אמרינן: דהא סלע דסלקא בידיה השתא לא הוה דעתיה להחליף ואישתכח דקא אכיל מעשר שני בלא פדייה: **דאפכת תרתי.** אגודה וחילול: **מקמי חדא.** יין מבין הכותים: **דקתני סיפא.** דהך דחילול: **סלע חדשה.** ואין שם אלא היא. ולקמן פריך: מאי תעלה: **שחילל.** דכיון דאין שם חדשה אלא היא, מוכרא מלתא: **אי דאיכא תרתי תלת.** חדשות, היינו קמייתא, ואמאי חילל: **מאן האי תנא.** דבעי למימר דלית ליה ברירה אפילו בעירוב דמדרבנן הוא: ה"ג: **על איזה מהן שארצה רציתי ילך לא רציתי לא ילך רצה מבעוד יום כו' משחשיכה אינו עירוב.** דילמא בין השמשות לא הוה דעתיה להאי: **תנא דבי איו.** אליבא דר' יהודה, דבעירוב נמי קאמר אין ברירה: **לא שמיע ליה.** ומהנך תנאי דלעיל לא מצי אמר, דכולהו מילי דאורייתא נינהו: **רציתי אלך לא רציתי לא אלך.** היה מוצא עירובו בסוף אלפים למזרח במקום המשתמר, והרי הוא מניחו שם עכשיו לכל השנה כולה, שכשבת שירצה יקנה לו עירובו ובשבת שלא ירצה יהיה כבני עירו ולא יקנה לו העירוב להפסידו אלפים אמה שבמערב: **עירובו עירוב.** ויש ברירה, דבין השמשות דעתיה הכי הוה: **והא שמעינן לר"ש.** גבי יין הבא מבין הכותים: **רבא אמר.** טעמא דרבי שמעון ביין לאו משום דאין ברירה הוא, דאית ליה ברירה. אלא משום דקרייה רחמנא לתרומה: "ראשית דגנך ותירושך" – מכלל שתהא מובדלת תרומה משיריה בשעה שקורא עליה שם שתהא היא נראית ראשית ואלו שיריה: **היו לפניו שני רמונים כו'.** בהדיא הוי ליה למיפרך מהא דלקמן, דתנן: תרומת הכרי כו' אלא הלכתא דעלמא נקט, כלומר: אם באתה לדרוש בדבים אליבא דר"ש – אתה דורש על אחד שהיו לפניו שני רמונים כו': **אין בדבריו כלום.** הואיל ובשעת קריאת השם אינו ניכר איזו תרומה ואיזו שיריה. דהא הכא גבי יין ניכרין שיריה לאחר זמן כי הכא, וקאסר ר' שמעון: **בתוכו.** באמצעיתו תהא תרומתו כדי שיעור תרומה ומעשריו תהא להקיף סביביו: **ותרומת מעשר בתוכו.** מילתא אחריתי היא. כלומר: או אם היה כרי של מעשר, ואמר תהא תרומת מעשר שלו בתוכו – קרא שם. ועד עכשיו, אם אכל ממנו לא היה בו אלא איסור של טבל, ומעתה אם אכלו – לוקה עליו משום תרומה ומשום מעשר שני חוץ לירושלים, ואם נטמא ואכלו – חייב משום אוכל תרומה בטומאה: **דאיכא סביביו.** שיריה ניכרים דאיהו "בתוכו" קאמר: **ואיבעית אימא.** ר' שמעון אית ליה ברירה. וגבי יין דקאסר – לאו משום דקסבר אין ברירה, אלא כדקתני טעמא: **שמא יבקע הנוד** קודם שיפריש הימנו, ונמצא ששתה טבלין למפרע. דבשלמא כי מפריש לה לאחר זמן – איכא למימר: הך דמטא השתא לחלק (*בהן) יש ברירה, דמעיקרא בתוך הנוד נמי דידיה הואי משעת קריאת שם, וחולין שתה. אבל כי בקע הנוד ולא איברר לה תרומה מיניה – מאי יש ברירה איכא למימר? הא אפילו לבסוף לאו לכלל תרומה אתאי: **לכשיבקע.** נעיין בדבר לאוסרו, כלומר: דלא חיישינן להכי, דלא שכיח, דאי בעי מסר ליה לשומר:
מתני'

רבינו חננאל

הקינין מתפרשות אלא או בלקיחת בעלים או בעשיית כהן קמ"ל ר' יוסי כרב חסדא דמעשיית כהן הקינין מתפרשות ולעולם בשהתנו כי עשיית כהן תזכה כל אחת בשלה אבל ברירה לית ליה. ת"ש עם הארץ שאמר לחבר קח לי אגודת ירק אחת אוכל ואינו צריך לעשר. דברי ר' יוסי כו' פי' ע"ה שאמ' לחבר קנה לי כמו שתקנה לעצמך והלך וקנה ב' ועישר על אחת מהן ואחרי כן נתן לע"ה אחת הנשארת לו א"ר יוסי אוכל ואינו צריך לעשר עליה נתברר כיון שלקחה כי המעשר שהוציא מקודם על זו הוציאו והנה אית ליה ברירה ופרקינן איפוך [ותריץ] הכי אינו אוכל עד שיעשר וחכמים פוטרין. ת"ש האומר מעשר שני שיש לי יהא מחולל על המעות כו' ואמר' אפך ואימא לא חלל דברי ר' יוסי ממאי מדקתני סיפא מודה ר' יוסי דאומר מעשר שני שיש לי יהא מחולל על סלע חדשה שתעלה בידי מן הכים שחילל מדקתני סיפא חילל מכלל דרישא לא חילל קאמר ואיך קאתיא סיפא בדלית ליה בכים אלא אותה סלע חדשה בלבד ואיידי דתני רישא תעלה תנא סיפא נמי תעלה [ואף] דלא הוה צריך. א"ל רבא לרב נחמן מאן האי תנא דאפילו דעירוב דהוא מדרבנן לית ליה ברירה דתניא האומר הריני מערב לחמשה על איזה מהן שארצה רצה מבעו"י עירובו עירוב רצה משחשכה אין עירובו עירוב. ואין ברירא. אישתיק. ולימא ליה איו הוא לא שמיעא ליה הא מתניתא דהוא תני לה איו. רב יוסף אמר תנאי (דרישא) *)הריני מערב לרוח אחת לכל שבתות השנה רציתי אלך [לא] רציתי לא אלך אלא הריני כבני עירי רצה מבעו"י עירובו עירוב משחשכה ר' שמעון אומר עירובו עירוב וחכ"א אין עירובו עירוב והא שמעינן ליה לר' שמעון דאמר בהלוקח יין מבין הכותים שני לוגין שאני עתיד להפריש הרי הן תרומה ר' שמעון אסר דלית ליה ברירא. ופרקינן אפך ואימא ר' שמעון אומר אין עירובו עירוב וחכ"א אומרים עירובו עירוב ואמרינן אמאי אפכת דלמא כי לית ליה לר' שמעון ברירה בתרומה דהיא דאורייתא אבל בעירוב דהוא מדרבנן אית ליה ברירה ודחינן לא מאן דלית ליה ברירה לא שנא בין דרבנן לית ליה ברירה ומאן דתני דאית ליה בין בדאורייתא בין בדרבנן אית ליה. רבא אמר היינו טעמא דר' שמעון דהלוקח יין מבין הכותים וקסבר תרומה אקרי ראשית וכל ראשית יש לו אחרית ידוע הלכך בעינן תרומה ששיריה נכרין וכיון שהנוד היין שיש בתוכו כולו מעורב ואינו ניכר בין ראשית לשיריה אע"פ **) שא' תרומה ולאו משום דלית ליה ברירה. אלא מעתה היה לפניו ב' רמונים ואמר אם ירדו גשמים היום זה תרומה על זה ואם לא ירדו היום יהא זה תרומה על זה הכי נמי כיון דבעת אמירתו אינה נבררת התרומה ולא שיריה הכי נמי דלא הוי תרומה. וכי תימא הכי נמי והתנן האומר תרומת הכרי הזה בתוכו ומעשרותיו בתוכו ותרומת מעשר בתוכו ר"ש [אומר] קרא השם והנה הכרי מעורב כולו כמו היין בנוד ואמר ר"ש (אמרו) קרא השם פי' תרומתו תרומה. ופרקינן כיון שהזכיר בתוכו נעשו סביבותיו שירים ניכרים. [ואיבעית] אימא טעמא דר"ש לאו משום דלית ליה ברירה אלא כדקתני סיפא אמרו לו לר"מ אי אתה מודה שמא יבקע הנוד ונשפכה אותה שקרא תרומה ונמצאת כי מה ששתה טבלים היה שותה למפרע. ואמר להן ר' מאיר לכשיבקע הנוד וישפוך היין אחרי כן אם ישתה הם טבלים. אבל כ"ז שהנוד קיים אינם טבלים. כי התרומה בקרקעית הנוד היא שומרה. ולמאי דסליק אדעתין מעיקרא דבברירה פליגי מאי קאמרי ליה. הכי קאמרי ליה לדידן אין ברירא לדידך אינך מודה כו' ופשוטה היא:
מתני'

*) נראה דצ"ל דתניא הריני מערב וכו'. **) נראה דצ"ל אעפ"י שאמר דהכרי הן תרומה אינו כלום.

תוספתא פ"ד דמעשר שני

רש"י כתב דקה קסבר ר' יוסף שייך לעיל והוא דבור אחד עם הך דלעיל וכצ"ל ל"ש בדרבנן ול"ש בדאורייתא והכ"ל קסבר ר' יוסף וא"ת וכו'

[דף מח.]
[ספ"ו דדמאי ע"ש]
[שבת נג: וש"נ]
[עתוס' גיטין כו. ד"ה התם]
[פסחים לג:]
תרומות פ"ג מ"ה
יומא נו: גיטין כו. סוכה כג. חולין יד: [תוספתא דמאי פ"ז]
[נ"ל כהן]

הגהות הב"ח

(א) גמ' והתניא עם הארץ. נ"ב דומה לזה כתב הרי"ף פ"ו דמס' דמאי וע"ש: (ב) שם קסבר מאן דאית ליה כל"ל ותיבת רב יוסף נמחק: (ג) רש"י ד"ה עם הארץ וכו' שאמר להארץ (קח גם לי אגודת ירק) תא"מ ונ"ב ס"א קח לי אגודת ירק ועשר: (ד) תוס' ד"ה קסבר. מאן כו' וא"ת דהכא מסיק ר' יוסף דלר' שמעון לית ליה לר' ברירה:

גליון הש"ס

גמ' שאני התם דבעינן ראשית ששיריה ניכרין. עי' מכות דף יט ע"ב ברש"י ד"ה תרומה בטבליה.

אִי אַתָּה מוֹדֶה שֶׁמָּא יִבָּקַע הַנּוֹד, וְנִמְצָא שׁוֹתֶה טְבָלִים לְמַפְרֵעַ? אָמַר לָהֶן: לִכְשֶׁיִּבָּקַע.§ **מתני'** [א]רַבִּי אֱלִיעֶזֶר אוֹמֵר: יו"ט הַסָּמוּךְ לַשַּׁבָּת, בֵּין מִלְּפָנֶיהָ וּבֵין מִלְּאַחֲרֶיהָ – מְעָרֵב אָדָם שְׁנֵי עֵירוּבִין, וְאוֹמֵר: עֵירוּבִי* בָּרִאשׁוֹן לַמִּזְרָח, וּבַשֵּׁנִי לַמַּעֲרָב. בָּרִאשׁוֹן לַמַּעֲרָב וּבַשֵּׁנִי לַמִּזְרָח, עֵירוּבִי בָּרִאשׁוֹן, וּבַשֵּׁנִי כִּבְנֵי עִירִי, עֵירוּבִי בַּשֵּׁנִי, וּבָרִאשׁוֹן כִּבְנֵי עִירִי. וַחכ"א: אוֹ מְעָרֵב לְרוּחַ אַחַת, אוֹ אֵינוֹ מְעָרֵב כָּל עִיקָּר. אוֹ מְעָרֵב לִשְׁנֵי יָמִים, אוֹ אֵינוֹ מְעָרֵב כָּל עִיקָּר. *[ב]כֵּיצַד יַעֲשֶׂה? מוֹלִיכוֹ בָּרִאשׁוֹן וּמַחְשִׁיךְ עָלָיו, וְנוֹטְלוֹ וּבָא לוֹ. בַּשֵּׁנִי מַחְשִׁיךְ עָלָיו וְאוֹכְלוֹ וּבָא לוֹ, וְנִמְצָא מִשְׂתַּכֵּר בַּהֲלִיכָתוֹ וּמִשְׂתַּכֵּר בְּעֵירוּבוֹ. נֶאֱכַל בָּרִאשׁוֹן – עֵירוּבוֹ לָרִאשׁוֹן וְאֵין עֵירוּבוֹ לַשֵּׁנִי. אָמַר (*לָהֶן) ר' אֱלִיעֶזֶר: מוֹדִים אַתֶּם לִי שֶׁהֵן שְׁתֵּי קְדוּשׁוֹת.§ **גמ'** לְרוּחַ אַחַת מַאי נִיהוּ – לִשְׁנֵי יָמִים, לִשְׁנֵי יָמִים מַאי נִיהוּ – לְרוּחַ אַחַת, הַיְינוּ קַמַּיְיתָא! הָכִי קָאָמְרִי לֵיהּ רַבָּנַן לְר' אֱלִיעֶזֶר: אִי אַתָּה מוֹדֶה שֶׁאֵין מְעָרְבִין לְיוֹם אֶחָד חֶצְיוֹ לַצָּפוֹן וְחֶצְיוֹ לַדָּרוֹם? אָמַר לָהֶן: אֲבָל. כְּשֵׁם שֶׁאֵין מְעָרְבִין לְיוֹם אֶחָד חֶצְיוֹ לַדָּרוֹם וְחֶצְיוֹ לַצָּפוֹן – כָּךְ אֵין מְעָרְבִין לִשְׁנֵי יָמִים, יוֹם אֶחָד לַמִּזְרָח וְיוֹם אֶחָד לַמַּעֲרָב. וְר"א: הָתָם – קְדוּשָּׁה אַחַת, הָכָא ב' קְדוּשׁוֹת. אָמַר לָהֶן ר"א: אִי אַתֶּם מוֹדִים שֶׁאִם עֵירֵב בְּרַגְלָיו בְּיוֹם רִאשׁוֹן – מְעָרֵב בְּרַגְלָיו בְּיוֹם שֵׁנִי, נֶאֱכַל עֵירוּבוֹ בְּיוֹם רִאשׁוֹן – אֵין יוֹצֵא עָלָיו בְּיוֹם שֵׁנִי. אָמְרוּ לוֹ: אֲבָל. הָא לָאֵיי ב' קְדוּשׁוֹת הֵן. וְרַבָּנַן: סְפוּקֵי מְסַפְּקָא לְהוּ, וְהָכָא לְחוּמְרָא וְהָכָא לְחוּמְרָא. אָמְרוּ לוֹ לְרַבִּי אֱלִיעֶזֶר: אִי אַתָּה מוֹדֶה שֶׁאֵין מְעָרְבִין בַּתְּחִילָּה מִיו"ט לַשַּׁבָּת? אָמַר לָהֶן: אֲבָל. הָא לָאֵיי קְדוּשָּׁה אַחַת הִיא. וְרַבִּי אֱלִיעֶזֶר: הָתָם מִשּׁוּם הֲכָנָה. ת"ר: *[ג]עֵירֵב בְּרַגְלָיו בְּיוֹם רִאשׁוֹן – מְעָרֵב בְּרַגְלָיו בְּיוֹם שֵׁנִי. נֶאֱכַל עֵירוּבוֹ בְּיוֹם רִאשׁוֹן – אֵין יוֹצֵא עָלָיו בְּיוֹם שֵׁנִי, דִּבְרֵי רַבִּי. ר' יְהוּדָה אוֹמֵר:

הֲרֵי

רש"י

מתני' מְעָרֵב אָדָם שְׁנֵי עֵירוּבִין. אִם הָיָה צָרִיךְ יוֹם רִאשׁוֹן לֵילֵךְ לְכָאן, וְיוֹם שֵׁנִי לֵילֵךְ לְכָאן, יָכוֹל לְעָרֵב לַמִּזְרָח וְלַמַּעֲרָב עֶרֶב יו"ט הָרִאשׁוֹן: וְאוֹמֵר עֵירוּבִי. שֶׁל מִזְרָח יִקְנֶה לִי הַיּוֹם לְצוֹרֶךְ מָחָר, וְעֵירוּבִי שֶׁל מַעֲרָב יִקְנֶה לִי בְּבֵין הַשְּׁמָשׁוֹת דִּלְמָחָר לְצוֹרֶךְ יוֹם שֵׁנִי. דְּקָסָבַר רַבִּי אֱלִיעֶזֶר: שַׁבָּת וְיו"ט לָאו כְּחַד יוֹמָא אֲרִיכָא נִינְהוּ, אֶלָּא שְׁתֵּי קְדוּשׁוֹת, וּלְכָל חַד יוֹמָא אִית לֵיהּ חֲדָא שְׁבִיתָה, וּבְכָל חֲדָא מִיקַּנְיָא לֵיהּ שְׁבִיתָה לְאֵיזֶה צַד שֶׁיִּרְצֶה. וּבִיה"ש דְּקַמָּא לְדִידֵיהּ הוּא דְּקָנֵי, וְלֹא לְיוֹם ב': עֵירוּבִי בָּרִאשׁוֹן וּבַשֵּׁנִי כִּבְנֵי עִירִי כו'. כְּלוֹמַר: וְאִם לֹא הָיָה רוֹצֶה לֵילֵךְ אֶלָּא בְּאֶחָד מִן הַצְּדָדִין בְּיוֹם רִאשׁוֹן, וּבַשֵּׁנִי אֵין צָרִיךְ לָזוּז מִתְּחוּמוֹ לֹא לְכָאן וְלֹא לְכָאן, וְאֵינוֹ רוֹצֶה לְהַפְסִיד *לֹא אַלְפַּיִם שֶׁל תְּחוּמוֹ מִכָּאן וְלֹא אַלְפַּיִם שֶׁל תְּחוּמוֹ מִכָּאן – יְעָרֵב עֵירוּב אֶחָד לְצַד שֶׁהוּא רוֹצֶה לֵילֵךְ בּוֹ בְּיוֹם רִאשׁוֹן, וְיֹאמַר: עֵירוּבִי זֶה יִקְנֶה לִי לְצוֹרֶךְ מָחָר, וּבַשֵּׁנִי הֲרֵינִי כִּבְנֵי עִירִי שֶׁלֹּא עֵירְבוּ. אוֹ אִם הָיָה צָרִיךְ לֵילֵךְ בַּשֵּׁנִי וְלֹא בָּרִאשׁוֹן, יֹאמַר: עֵירוּבִי זֶה יִקְנֶה לִי בִּיה"ש שֶׁל מָחָר, וּבָרִאשׁוֹן אֶהְיֶה כִּבְנֵי עִירִי: אוֹ מְעָרֵב לְרוּחַ אַחַת. לְצוֹרֶךְ שְׁנֵי יָמִים: אוֹ אֵינוֹ מְעָרֵב כָּל עִיקָּר. אֲפִילּוּ לְצַד אֶחָד, לִהְיוֹת בְּאֶחָד מִן הַיָּמִים כִּבְנֵי עִירוֹ: אוֹ מְעָרֵב לְב' יָמִים. וּבַגְּמָרָא פָּרִיךְ: הַיְינוּ לְרוּחַ אַחַת: מוֹלִיכוֹ. הַשָּׁלִיחַ: בָּרִאשׁוֹן. עֶרֶב יו"ט שֶׁלִּפְנֵי הַשַּׁבָּת: וּמַחְשִׁיךְ עָלָיו. עַד שֶׁיִּקְנֶה הָעֵירוּב: וְנוֹטְלוֹ וּבָא לוֹ. שֶׁמָּא יֹאבַד, וְשׁוּב אֵין לוֹ עֵירוּב בַּשֵּׁנִי. כִּדְקָתָנֵי נֶאֱכַל עֵירוּבוֹ בָּרִאשׁוֹן וכו' וְחוֹזֵר וּמוֹלִיכוֹ בַּשֵּׁנִי כו': מִשְׂתַּכֵּר בַּהֲלִיכָתוֹ. כְּלוֹמַר: קָנָה לוֹ הֲלִיכָה לְיוֹם מָחָר: וּמִשְׂתַּכֵּר בְּעֵירוּבוֹ. שֶׁאוֹכְלוֹ וּבְיו"ט אַחַר שַׁבָּת דְּלֹא אֶפְשָׁר בְּהָכִי – מוֹלִיכוֹ בָּרִאשׁוֹן, וְחוֹזֵר וְהוֹלֵךְ שָׁם בַּשֵּׁנִי לִרְאוֹת אִם קַיָּים עֵירוּבוֹ, וּמַחְשִׁיךְ עָלָיו, וְאִם רָצָה – יֹאכְלֶנּוּ אַחֲרֵי כֵן: מוֹדִים אַתֶּם לִי שֶׁהֵן ב' קְדוּשׁוֹת. דְּקָאָמְרִיתוּ אֵין עֵירוּב לַשֵּׁנִי. דְּאִי קְדוּשָּׁה אַחַת – ה"ל כְּחַד יוֹמָא אֲרִיכָא וְיִקְנֶה בֵּין הַשְּׁמָשׁוֹת שֶׁל רִאשׁוֹן לִשְׁנֵיהֶן, וְכֵיוָן דִּשְׁתֵּי קְדוּשׁוֹת הֵן – יָכוֹל לְעָרֵב נַמִּי לְב' רוּחוֹת: **גמ'** לְרוּחַ אַחַת. דְּקָתָנֵי מַתְנִי': מַאי נִיהוּ. פְּשִׁיטָא דְּלִשְׁנֵי יָמִים קָאָמַר. כִּנְיוּתָא: וְלִשְׁנֵי הַיָּמִים. דְּקָתָנֵי: מַאי נִיהוּ. פְּשִׁיטָא לִי דִּלְרוּחַ אַחַת קָאָמַר. וְא"כ תַּרְתֵּי לָמָּה לִי? הַיְינוּ קַמַּיְיתָא: אִי אַתָּה מוֹדֶה בְּיוֹם אֶחָד. דִּמְעָרֵב לְרוּחַ אַחַת, אוֹ אֵינוֹ מְעָרֵב כָּל עִיקָּר. לְב' יָמִים נַמִּי, אוֹ מְעָרֵב כְּמוֹ לְיוֹם אֶחָד אוֹ אֵינוֹ מְעָרֵב כָּל עִיקָּר: אֲבָל. אֱמֶת. כְּמוֹ "אֲבָל שָׂרָה", וּמְתַרְגֵּם: "קוּשְׁטָא" (בראשית יז): שֶׁאִם עֵירֵב בְּרַגְלָיו. שֶׁלֹּא הָיָה לוֹ פַּת לְשַׁגֵּר ע"י שָׁלִיחַ וּלְעָרֵב וְהָלַךְ הוּא בְּעַצְמוֹ וְיָשַׁב לְסוֹף אַלְפַּיִם אַמָּה עַד שֶׁקָּדַשׁ עָלָיו הַיּוֹם, וְקָנָה שְׁבִיתָה וְחָזַר וְלָן בְּבֵיתוֹ: מְעָרֵב בְּרַגְלָיו בַּשֵּׁנִי. צָרִיךְ לְעָרֵב בְּרַגְלָיו אַף בַּשֵּׁנִי, וְאֵינוֹ יָכוֹל לָצֵאת בַּשֵּׁנִי חוּץ לַתְּחוּם ע"י קִנְיָיה הָרִאשׁוֹנָה. אוֹ אִם נֶאֱכַל עֵירוּבוֹ הַמְעָרֵב בְּפַת וְנֶאֱכַל עֵירוּבוֹ בְּיוֹם רִאשׁוֹן לְאַחַר שֶׁקָּנָה הָעֵירוּב, אִי אַתֶּם מוֹדִים לִי שֶׁאֵינוֹ יוֹצֵא עָלָיו בַּשֵּׁנִי ע"י אוֹתָהּ קִנְיָיה: הָא לָאֵיי. ר' אֱלִיעֶזֶר קָמְהַדַּר לָהּ, וְקָאָמַר: וַדַּאי אַף לְדִבְרֵיכֶם ב' קְדוּשׁוֹת הֵן. וְלָא גָּרְסִינַן "לָאֵיי אַפְנוּיֵי מוּפְנֵי", דְּאֵינוֹ דּוֹרֵשׁ לֹא פָּסוּק וְלֹא ג"ש, דִּבְכוּלֵּי הַתַּלְמוּד "הֵן" תַּרְגּוּם שֶׁל "לָאֵיי": וְרַבָּנַן מְסַפְּקָא לְהוּ. בְּשַׁבָּת וְיו"ט, אִי קְדוּשָּׁה אַחַת נִינְהוּ אִי שְׁתֵּי קְדוּשׁוֹת: וְעָבְדֵי הָכָא לְחוּמְרָא. דְּאֵין יָכוֹל לְעָרֵב לִשְׁנֵי רוּחוֹת, דִּלְמָא חֲדָא קְדוּשָּׁה הִיא: וְהָכָא לְחוּמְרָא. דְּאִי נֶאֱכַל בָּרִאשׁוֹן דְּאֵין עֵירוּב לַשֵּׁנִי, דִּלְמָא ב' קְדוּשׁוֹת הֵן: אִי אַתָּה מוֹדֶה שֶׁאֵין מְעָרְבִין בַּתְּחִילָּה מִיו"ט לַשַּׁבָּת. אִם לֹא עֵירֵב בֵּין הַשְּׁמָשׁוֹת שֶׁל עֶרֶב יו"ט, וְהוֹלֵךְ לָצֵאת בַּשַּׁבָּת, אִי אַתָּה מוֹדֶה שֶׁאֵינוֹ יָכוֹל לְעָרֵב מִיו"ט לַשַּׁבָּת? אַלְמָא: קְדוּשָּׁה אַחַת הִיא, וַהֲרֵי הוּא כְּיוֹם אֶחָד שֶׁאֵינוֹ יָכוֹל לְעָרֵב בַּחֲצִי הַיּוֹם, אִם לֹא עֵירֵב בֵּין הַשְּׁמָשׁוֹת: מִשּׁוּם הֲכָנָה. שֶׁמְּכִין מִיו"ט לַשַּׁבָּת, וְלֹא מִשּׁוּם טַעְמָא דְּחַד יוֹמָא הוּא: אֵין יוֹצֵא עָלָיו בַּשֵּׁנִי. וַהֲרֵי הוּא כִּבְנֵי עִירוֹ. דְּוַדַּאי שְׁתֵּי קְדוּשׁוֹת הֵן, וְאֵין עָלָיו חֲשַׁשׁ סָפֵק:

הֲרֵי

תוספות

אי אתה מודה שמא יבקע הנוד. תימה: להנהו דמפרשי טעמייהו משום דאין ברירה, או משום ראשית כו' – כיון דקתני סיפא אי אתה מודה שמא יבקע הנוד, מנא להו דלא הוה טעמא מש"ה? וי"ל: דידע התלמוד שאין זה עיקר טעם. ואע"פ שהן עצמן לא היו חושבים זה הטעם עיקר, מ"מ היו שואלין אותו לדעת מה ישיב. וכענין זה יש בזבחים (דף עז:) גבי איברים תמימים שנתערבו באיברים בעלי מומין, דרבי אליעזר אומר יקרב ורואה אני את בשר של בעל מום כאילו הן עצים. ואין זה עיקר טעמו, דבנרבע ורובע מודה רבי אליעזר, וטעם בעל מום – משום דכתיב: "מום בם לא ירצו", הא על ידי תערובות – ירצו. ור' אליעזר דקאמר: רואה אני כאילו הן עצים היה שואל לחכמים למה לא יכשירו מאותו טעם. אע"פ שהוא בעצמו לא היה חושש לאותו טעם. וכהנה רבות בתלמוד*:

אמרו לו אבל. לא לגמרי מודו לו לר' אליעזר, דלר' אליעזר הוי כבני עירו, ולרבנן כיון דמספקא להו הוי כחמר גמל:

ורבי אליעזר התם משום הכנה. וא"ת: ולמה לי טעמא משום הכנה, תיפוק לי' דאסור למיקני שביתה בשבת. פי': ביו"ט, כיון דביו"ט אסור לצאת חוץ לתחום, כדאמר פרק ב' דביצה (דף יז.) דאין מניחין עירובי תחומין מיו"ט לחבירו. ואע"ג דהתם לא שייך ביה הכנה, דהא נולדה בזה מותרת בזה! ואור"י: דאצטריך לטעמא דהכנה, משום דמאן דשרי התם למיקני שביתה בשבתא. א"נ: משום דרבנן הקשו לר' אליעזר גם מעירובי חצירות, ולכן צריך לתרץ משום הכנה. תדע, דהכנה נמי שייך בעירובי חצירות, דהא רב פוסק בשמעתין כר' אליעזר דשתי קדושות הן, ורב גופיה פסיק בריש פרק ב' דביצה (דף טז:) דהלכה כת"ק, דאמר: יו"ט שחל להיות בע"ש אין מערבין לא עירובי תחומין ולא עירובי חצירות. וכיון דשתי קדושות הן – אמאי אין מערבין? ע"כ משום הכנה. ומיהו התם דקאמר רבי מערבין עירובי חצירות אבל לא עירובי תחומין – מ"ט? דמהדרי עירובי חצירות – משמע דלית ליה הכנה, וא"כ למה אין מערבין עירובי תחומין? ולמאן דאסר למקני שביתה בשבתא – ניחא. אבל למאן דשרי, קשה! ושמא י"ל: דבהכי פליגי רבי ורבנן, דרבי סבר: לא שייך איסור הכנה בעירובי חצירות, כיון דביום טוב שרי להוציא מחצר לחצר: **משום** הכנה. איסור הכנה דאורייתא היא, כדילפינן לקמן בשמעתין. ומה שאופין מיו"ט לשבת משום עירובי תבשילין – מפרש רבה בפרק "אלו עוברין" (פסחים דף מו:): משום הואיל ומקלעי ליה אורחין. וא"ת: והיכי בעי ב"אלו עוברין" (שם) למימר דר' אליעזר לית ליה "הואיל" – א"כ לדידיה איך אופין מיו"ט לשבת? הא אית ליה איסור הכנה הכא בשמעתין! וי"ל: דההיא ד"אלו עוברין" דאסר למיקני שביתה בשבתא, ואז לא צריכין לטעמא דהכנה כדפי'. ועירובי חצירות נמי סבר ההיא ד"אלו עוברין" דמערבין לר' אליעזר מיו"ט לשבת, כיון דלית ליה הכנה. וא"ת: הא אכתי מוכח בפ"ק דביצה (דף ד.) דאית ליה לר' אליעזר הכנה, גבי ביצה שנולדה בשבת דקאמר רבי אליעזר: עדיין היא מחלוקת, ב"ש אומרים תיאכל ביו"ט וב"ה אומרים לא תיאכל! וי"ל: דרבי אליעזר סבר כב"ש, *דשמותי הוא. ועוד דתניא בפ"ק דביצה (שם) דר' אליעזר אומר תיאכל היא ואמה. וריצב"א אומר: דלא שייך הכנה באפיה ובישול, דאין זה אלא תיקון בעלמא שמתקן המאכל, ולא שייך הכנה אלא לענין ביצה ועירוב, שהוא דבר חדש:

אמר

עין משפט נר מצוה

פח א מיי' פ"ח מהל' עירובין הלכה ה סמג עשין א טוש"ע א"ח סי' תיו סעיף א:

פט ב ג מיי' שם הלכה ח ט טוש"ע שם סעיף ב:

מסורת הש"ס

[ר' ירושלמי ורי"ף בה: בראשון והשני וכן כלס]

[עי' תוי"ט ד"ה ובשני]

צ"ל לג. [ע"ש לקמן לט. ע"ש]

[צ"ל להם]

[תוספתא פ"ד]

[ועי' תוס' סוכה כד. ד"ה רבי יהודה]

[פי' מתלמידי ב"ש עי' תוס' שבת קל: ד"ה דר"א שמותי הוא]

רבינו חננאל

מתני' ר' אליעזר אומר יו"ט הסמוך לשבת בין מלפניה בין מלאחריה מערב שני עירובין ואומר כו'. תניא אמרו לו לר' אליעזר אין אתה מודה שאין מערבין ליום אחד חציו לצפון וחציו לדרום אמר להם אבל אמרו כשם שאין מערבין ליום אחד חציו לצפון וחציו לדרום כך אין מערבין לב' ימים (אם) [יום] אחד לצפון (ואם) [ויום] אחד לדרום. אמר להם (אם) [יום] אחד חדא קדושה היא (ואפשר) [ואי אפשר] לחלקו הכא בב' ימים ב' קדושות הן אמרו לו אי אתה מודה שאין מערבין לכתחלה מיו"ט לשבת אמר להן אבל. והא לאיי קדושה אחת הן א"ל התם משום הכנה שאין יו"ט מכין לשבת. אמר להם ר' אליעזר אי אתם מודים שאם עירב ברגליו בראשון מערב ברגליו בשני נאכל כו' ומפורש בפ' מי שהוציאוהו גוים דתנן מי שבא בדרך והיה מכיר אילן או גדר כו' ואמרינן בגמרא זהו שאמרו העני מערב ברגליו ולא יצא העשיר חוץ לעיר ויאמר שביתתי במקומי לפי שלא התירו לערב ברגליו [אלא] למי שבא בדרך וחשכה לו לדברי ר"מ ר' יהוד' אומר אחד עני ואחד עשיר כו': ת"ר עירב ברגליו בראשון מערב ברגליו בשני נאכל עירובו בראשון [אין] יוצא עליו בשני דברי רבי ר'

צ א מיי' פ"ח מהל' עירובין הל' ח ט סמג עשין א טוש"ע א"ח סי' תי"ז סעיף ב:
צא ב ג מיי' פ"ח מהל' יו"ט הלכה יט סמג לאוין עה טוש"ע א"ח סי' תקיג סעיף א וסי' תקכז סעיף ה:
צב ד מיי' פ"ח מהל' עירובין הלכה יא יב יג טוש"ע א"ח סי' תטז סעיף ג:
צג ה מיי' שם הלכה ט טוש"ע שם סעיף ב:
צד ו מיי' פכ"ד מהל' שבת הלכה ב סמג לאוין סה טוש"ע א"ח סי' שו סעיף א:

הֲרֵי זֶה חַמָּר גַּמָּל. רשב"ג וְר' יִשְׁמָעֵאל בְּנוֹ שֶׁל ר' יוֹחָנָן בֶּן בְּרוֹקָה אוֹמְרִים: עֵירֵב בְּרַגְלָיו בָּרִאשׁוֹן — אֵין מְעָרֵב בְּרַגְלָיו בַּשֵּׁנִי, נֶאֱכַל עֵירוּבוֹ בְּיוֹם רִאשׁוֹן — יוֹצֵא עָלָיו בַּשֵּׁנִי. *אָמַר רַב: הֲלָכָה כְּד' זְקֵנִים הַלָּלוּ, וְאַלִּיבָּא דר"א דְּאָמַר: אב' קְדוּשׁוֹת הֵן. וְאֵלּוּ הֵן ד' זְקֵנִים: רשב"ג, וְר' יִשְׁמָעֵאל *בְּר' יוֹחָנָן בֶּן בְּרוֹקָה, וְר"א בְּר"ש, וְר' יוֹסֵי בַּר יְהוּדָה סְתִימְתָּאָה. וְאִיכָּא דְּאָמְרִי: חַד מִינַּיְיהוּ רַבִּי אֶלְעָזָר, וּמַפֵּיק ר' יוֹסֵי בַּר יְהוּדָה סְתִימְתָּאָה. וְהָא רשב"ג וְרַבִּי יִשְׁמָעֵאל *בַּר רַבִּי יוֹחָנָן בֶּן בְּרוֹקָה אִיפְּכָא שָׁמְעִינַן לְהוּ! אֵיפוֹךְ. אִי הָכִי הַיְינוּ רַבִּי! אֵימָא: וְכֵן אָמַר רשב"ג וכו'. וְלִיחֲשׁוֹב נַמִי רַבִּי! רַבִּי *תָּנֵי לָהּ וְלָא סָבַר לָהּ. רַבָּנַן נַמִי תָּנוּ לָהּ וְלָא סָבְרִי לָהּ! רַב גְּמָרָא גְּמִיר לָהּ. כִּי נָח נַפְשֵׁיהּ דְּרַב הוּנָא, עָיֵיל רַב חִסְדָּא לְמִירְמָא דְּרַב אַדְּרַב; מִי אָמַר רַב: הֲלָכָה כְּד' זְקֵנִים, וְאַלִּיבָּא דר"א דְּאָמַר שְׁתֵּי קְדוּשּׁוֹת הֵן? וְהָא *אִיתְּמַר: שַׁבָּת וְיו"ט, רַב אָמַר: בנוֹלְדָה בָּזֶה — אֲסוּרָה בָּזֶה! אָמַר רַבָּה: הָתָם — מִשּׁוּם הֲכָנָה. *דְּתַנְיָא: °"וְהָיָה בַּיּוֹם הַשִּׁשִּׁי וְהֵכִינוּ" — גחוֹל מֵכִין לַשַּׁבָּת, וְחוֹל מֵכִין לְיו"ט, וְאֵין יו"ט מֵכִין לַשַּׁבָּת, וְאֵין שַׁבָּת מְכִינָה לְיוֹם טוֹב. א"ל אַבָּיֵי: אֶלָּא הָא דִּתְנַן: כֵּיצַד הוּא עוֹשֶׂה — מוֹלִיכוֹ בָּרִאשׁוֹן, וּמַחְשִׁיךְ עָלָיו, וְנוֹטְלוֹ וּבָא לוֹ. בַּשֵּׁנִי מַחְשִׁיךְ עָלָיו, וְאוֹכְלוֹ וּבָא לוֹ. הָא קָא מֵכִין מִיו"ט לַשַּׁבָּת! א"ל רַבָּה: מִי סָבְרַתְּ סוֹף הַיּוֹם קוֹנֶה עֵירוּב? תְּחִלַּת הַיּוֹם קוֹנֶה עֵירוּב, וְשַׁבָּת מְכִינָה לְעַצְמָהּ. אֶלָּא מֵעַתָּה יְעָרְבוּ בְּלָגִין! בָּעֵינַן סְעוּדָה הָרְאוּיָה מִבְּעוֹד יוֹם, וְלֵיכָּא. אֶלָּא הָא דִּתְנַן, ר"א אוֹמֵר: יו"ט הַסָּמוּךְ לַשַּׁבָּת, בֵּין מִלְּפָנֶיהָ וּבֵין מִלְּאַחֲרֶיהָ — מְעָרֵב אָדָם שְׁנֵי עֵירוּבִין. הָא *בָּעֵינַן סְעוּדָה הָרְאוּיָה מִבְּעוֹד יוֹם, וְלֵיכָּא! מִי סָבְרַתְּ דְּמַנַּח לֵיהּ בְּסוֹף אַלְפַּיִם אַמָּה לְכָאן, וּבְסוֹף אַלְפַּיִם אַמָּה לְכָאן? לֹא, דדְּמַנַּח לֵיהּ בְּסוֹף אֶלֶף אַמָּה לְכָאן, וּבְסוֹף אֶלֶף אַמָּה לְכָאן. אֶלָּא הָא דְּאָמַר רַב יְהוּדָה: עֵירֵב בְּרַגְלָיו יוֹם רִאשׁוֹן — מְעָרֵב בְּרַגְלָיו יוֹם שֵׁנִי, עֵירֵב בַּפַּת בְּיוֹם רִאשׁוֹן — מְעָרֵב בַּפַּת בְּיוֹם שֵׁנִי, הָא קָא מֵכִין מִיו"ט לַשַּׁבָּת! א"ל: מִי סָבְרַתְּ דְּאָזֵיל וְאָמַר מִידֵּי? הדְּאָזֵיל וְשָׁתֵיק וְיָתֵיב. כְּמַאן — כְּרַבִּי יוֹחָנָן בֶּן נוּרִי, *דְּאָמַר: חֶפְצֵי הֶפְקֵר קוֹנִין שְׁבִיתָה? *אֲפִילּוּ תֵּימָא רַבָּנַן. עַד כָּאן לָא פְּלִיגִי רַבָּנַן עֲלֵיהּ דְּרַבִּי יוֹחָנָן בֶּן נוּרִי — אֶלָּא בְּיָשֵׁן, דְּלָא מָצֵי אָמַר. אֲבָל בְּנֵיעוֹר, דְּאִי בָּעֵי לְמֵימַר מָצֵי אָמַר, אע"ג דְּלָא אֲמַר — כְּמַאן דַּאֲמַר דָּמֵי. א"ל רַבָּה בַּר רַב חָנִין לְאַבָּיֵי: אִי הֲוָה שְׁמִיעַ לֵיהּ לְמָר הָא דְּתַנְיָא: ולֹא יְהַלֵּךְ אָדָם לְסוֹף שָׂדֵהוּ לֵידַע מַה הִיא צְרִיכָה, כַּיּוֹצֵא בּוֹ לֹא

תורה אור

הֲרֵי זֶה חַמָּר גַּמָּל. דִּלְמָא חֲדָא קְדוּשָּׁה הִיא וְקָנָה עֵירוּב לִשְׁנֵי יָמִים, וְהִפְסִיד אַלְפַּיִם שֶׁכְּנֶגֶד עֵירוּבוֹ וְכָאן לֹא קָנָה כְּלוּם אֶלָּא אַלְפַּיִם שֶׁהָיוּ לוֹ בְּלֹא עֵירוּב. *וְדִלְמָא ב' קְדוּשּׁוֹת הֵן, וְלֹא קָנָה עֵירוּבוֹ אֶלָּא לְיוֹם אֶחָד, וְדִינוֹ לִהְיוֹת בַּשֵּׁנִי כִּבְנֵי עִירוֹ וְאֵין לוֹ כָּאן אֶלָּא אַלְפַּיִם. וּמִמָּה נַפְשָׁךְ בְּהָנָךְ אַלְפַּיִם אַמָּה מִשְׁתְּרֵי: אֵין מְעָרֵב בְּרַגְלָיו בַּשֵּׁנִי. א"ל לְעָרֵב, דְּוַדַּאי קְדוּשָּׁה אַחַת נִינְהוּ וּכְחַדָא יוֹמָא אֲרִיכָא הָוֵי: חַד מִינַּיְיהוּ ר' אֶלְעָזָר. כָּל ר' אֶלְעָזָר סְתָם בַּתַּלְמוּד שֶׁהוּא תַּנָּא, ר' אֶלְעָזָר בֶּן שַׁמּוּעַ הוּא: סְתִימְתָּאָה. קָרֵי כָּל מִי שֶׁרָאָה רַבִּי דְּבָרָיו בִּמְקוֹמוֹת הַרְבֵּה וּשְׁנָאָן בַּמִּשְׁנָה סְתָם: אִיפְּכָא שָׁמְעִינַן לְהוּ. לְעֵיל: וְכֵן א"ר שִׁמְעוֹן. נֶאֱכַל עֵירוּבוֹ בָּרִאשׁוֹן – אֵין יוֹצֵא עָלָיו בַּשֵּׁנִי: וְלִיחְשׁוֹב נַמִי רַבִּי. דְּשָׁמְעִינַן לֵיהּ לְעֵיל בְּהֶדְיָא: תָּנֵי לָהּ וְלָא סָבַר לָהּ. וּלְדִבְרֵי ר' אֱלִיעֶזֶר קָאָמַר: רַבָּנַן נַמִי. הָנָךְ רַבָּן שִׁמְעוֹן וְר' יִשְׁמָעֵאל נְהִי דְּקָתָנֵי "וְכֵן" דִּלְמָא תָּנוּ וְלָא סָבְרִי לָהּ: רַב גְּמָרָא גְּמִיר לָהּ. מֵרַבֵּיהּ, דְּהָנָךְ אַרְבָּעָה זְקֵנִים סְבִירָא לְהוּ כְּר"א. אֲבָל רַבִּי תָּנֵי וְלָא סָבַר לָהּ: מִי סָבְרַתְּ סוֹף הַיּוֹם. שֶׁל ע"ש קוֹנֶה עֵירוּב. דְּהָוֵי יו"ט מֵכִין לַשַּׁבָּת: יְעָרְבוּ בְּלָגִין. לָגִין טְבוּל יוֹם, דִּתְנַן לְעֵיל בְּפִירְקִין (דף לו.) שֶׁמִּילְּאָהוּ מִן הֶחָבִית שֶׁל טֶבֶל, וְאָמַר "הֲרֵי זֶה תְּרוּמַת מַעֲשֵׂר" – לִכְשֶׁתֶּחְשַׁךְ דְּבָרָיו קַיָּימִין וְאִם אָמַר עֵירְבוּ לִי בָּהּ – לֹא אָמַר כְּלוּם. אַלְמָא: סוֹף הַיּוֹם קוֹנֶה עֵירוּב, וְאַכַּתִּי טֶבֶל הוּא: ה"ג: אֶלָּא הָא דִּתְנַן ר' אֱלִיעֶזֶר כו'. הָא בָּעֵינַן סְעוּדָה הָרְאוּיָה מִבְּעוֹד יוֹם, וְלֵיכָּא: מְעָרֵב אָדָם שְׁנֵי עֵירוּבִין. וְקס"ד: זֶה לְסוֹף אַלְפַּיִם לַמִּזְרָח וְזֶה לְסוֹף אַלְפַּיִם לַמַּעֲרָב. וְכִי קָנָה לוֹ יוֹם רִאשׁוֹן לַמִּזְרָח, אִי הֲוָה בָּעֵי לְמֵיזַל לְמַעֲרַב הָעִיר פְּסִיעָה אַחַת – לָא מָצֵי אָזֵיל, דִּמִּמְּקוֹם עֵירוּבוֹ יֵשׁ לוֹ אַלְפַּיִם אַמָּה לְכָל רוּחַ וַהֲרֵי מֵעֵירוּבוֹ וְעַד עִירוֹ הָוֵי אַלְפַּיִם. וְכָל עִירוֹ מִיהָא מָצֵי אָזֵיל דְּכוּלָּהּ לְדִידֵיהּ, °כֵּיוָן דְּלָן בָּהּ כְּד' אַמּוֹת דָּמְיָא לֵיהּ. אֲבָל טְפֵי – לָא מָצֵי אָזֵיל לֵיהּ. וְהֵיכִי קָנֵי לֵיהּ עֵירוּב דְּמַעֲרָב בְּבֵין הַשְּׁמָשׁוֹת? הָא בָּעֵינַן סְעוּדָה הָרְאוּיָה מִבְּעוֹד יוֹם, וְהָא אִי הֲוָה בָּעֵי לְמֵיזַל וּמֵיכְלֵיהּ מִבְּעוֹד יוֹם – לָא מָצֵי אָזֵיל: בְּסוֹף אַלְפַּיִם. דְּתוּ לֵית לֵיהּ לַצַּד שֶׁכְּנֶגְדּוֹ בְּיוֹם רִאשׁוֹן כְּלוּם: לֹא דְּמַנַּח לֵיהּ בְּסוֹף אֶלֶף כו'. דְּלָא הֲוָה צָרִיךְ לְמֵיזַל לֹא בָּרִאשׁוֹן וְלֹא בַּשֵּׁנִי אֶלָּא שְׁלֹשָׁה אֲלָפִים, וְנָתַן עֵירוּבוֹ בְּסוֹף אֶלֶף לְכָל צַד. הִילְכָּךְ, בְּיוֹם רִאשׁוֹן אע"פ שֶׁקָּנָה עֵירוּבוֹ לַמִּזְרָח – יָכוֹל לֵילֵךְ אֵצֶל עֵירוּבוֹ בַּמַּעֲרָב, דְּהָא מִמְּקוֹם עֵירוּבוֹ שֶׁבַּמִּזְרָח עַד עֵירוּב שֶׁבַּמַּעֲרָב אַלְפַּיִם הוּא דְּהָווּ: עֵירֵב בַּפַּת בָּרִאשׁוֹן מְעָרֵב בַּפַּת בַּשֵּׁנִי. לְקַמָּן מְפָרֵשׁ: בְּאוֹתוֹ פַּת: וְהָא קָא מֵכִין. כְּשֶׁמְּעָרֵב בְּרַגְלָיו בַּשֵּׁנִי מִיו"ט לַשַּׁבָּת. בִּשְׁלָמָא מְעָרֵב בַּשֵּׁנִי בַּפַּת נִיחָא דִּתְחִילַּת הַיּוֹם קוֹנֶה עֵירוּב, וְעֵירוּב דְּפַת שְׁתִיקָה מֵאֵילָא קָנֵי. אֶלָּא עֵירֵב בְּרַגְלָיו, ס"ד דְּבָעֵי לְמֵימַר שְׁבִיתָתִי בִּמְקוֹמִי, וְלָא מָצֵי לְכַוֵּין תְּחִילַּת הַיּוֹם וּבָעֵי לְמֵימַר מִבְּעוֹד יוֹם, וְאִישְׁתַּכַּח דְּמֵכִין בַּאֲמִירָתוֹ מִיו"ט לַשַּׁבָּת: רַבִּי יוֹחָנָן בֶּן נוּרִי. לְקַמָּן בְּ"מִי שֶׁהוֹצִיאוּהוּ"* קָאָמַר דְּיָשֵׁן קוֹנֶה שְׁבִיתָתוֹ, וְאַף עַל גַּב דְּהָוֵי כְּחֶפְצֵי הֶפְקֵר בְּעָלְמָא, שֶׁאֵין אָדָם מַקְנֶה לָהֶם שְׁבִיתָה: בְּנֵיעוֹר גָּרְסִינַן: אִי הֲוָה שְׁמִיעַ לֵיהּ לְמָר. לְרַבָּה, דִּמְתָרֵץ וְאָזֵיל כָּל הָנָךְ תֵּירוּצֵי, וְקָאָמַר דְּמִשּׁוּם דְּלָא אָמַר מִידֵּי שָׁרֵי, וְאַף עַל גַּב דְּאָזַל הָתָם מִבְּעוֹד יוֹם: לֹא יְהַלֵּךְ. בְּשַׁבָּת: לֵידַע מַה הִיא צְרִיכָה. אַחַר הַשַּׁבָּת: לֹא

אמר רבה משום הכנה דתניא. ר"ת מחק מספרו "דתניא", משום דאמר בריש ביצה (דף ב:): רבה לטעמיה, דאמר רבה: "והיה ביום הששי והכינו", ואי ברייתא היא – מאי קאמר לטעמיה? ואין זו קושיא, דנקט לטעמיה – משום דרבה הביא הברייתא תחילה לבית המדרש. ואין להקשות מן הברייתא לרבי יוחנן דלית ליה הכנה בפ"ק דביצה (דף ד.) דילמא לא מיתני בי רבי חייא ורבי אושעיא. ועוד: דאיכא פלוגתא דתנאי בפ"ק דביצה (דף ג.). ורש"י פירש בביצה דרבה לטעמיה, דאמר אליביה ב"אלו עוברין" (פסחים מז:) דמוקצה דאורייתא מהאי קרא. ולא נהירא, ועוד: דמשמע התם דהדר ביה:

ואין יו"ט מכין לשבת. דקרא משמע: ביום הששי שהיה יורד המן. ואמר במדרש (מכילתא פרשת בשלח) דדרשינן שלא ירד מן לישראל בשבתות וימים טובים. ויש מדרשים חלוקים דדרשי' "ויברך" "ויקדש", ברכו במן וקדשו במן. וב"אתה קדשת וברכתו מכל הימים וקדשתו מכל הזמנים" – משמע דירד מן ביו"ט*, ולפי זה צ"ל ד"הששי" משמע המבורר, דהיינו חול. כמו "הירך" – המיומנת שבירך (חולין דף צא.):

והא בעינן סעודה. וא"ת: והא ראויה היא לאותן שבתחומו, כמו שמערבין לישראל בתרומה כיון שראויה לכהנים! וי"ל: דכמו שצריך בלילה, דהיינו שעת קניית העירוב שיהא הוא ועירובו תוך התחום, דאם נתגלגל העירוב חוץ לתחום לא הוי עירוב – ה"נ צריך שתהא תוך תחומו מבעוד יום. והא דקאמר: והא בעינן סעודה הראויה מבעוד יום וליכא – תימה, דמשמע דניחא ליה אי לא בעינן סעודה הראויה מבעוד יום, ואע"ג דסבר סוף היום קונה עירוב, ואמאי? כיון דס"ד דמנח אלפים לכאן ואלפים לכאן, היכי קנייה ליה סוף היום עירוב ושביתתו, הא עדיין בסוף היום ד' אלפים רחוק מעירובו!

הא קא מכין מיו"ט לשבת. וא"ת: אמאי לא פריך לרב יהודה גופיה ממלתיה דנפשיה, דע"כ אית ליה הכנה, מדקאמר: אין מערבין תחילה בפת. והא קאמר עירב ברגליו ביום ראשון – מערב ברגליו ביום שני! וי"ל: דהא דקאמר מערב ברגליו ביום שני – ברייתא דלעיל קתני לה, דפליגי בה רבי יהודה ורשב"ג. והא דקא מייתי מלתיה דרב יהודה – לפי שלא היתה ידוע להם. תדע, דלקמן קאמר אמלתא דרב יהודה אמר שמואל: ובאותו הפת. והיכי מפרש שמואל מלתיה דרב יהודה שהיה תלמידו? אלא ודאי רב יהודה ברייתא קתני:

כמאן כרבי יוחנן בן נורי. וא"ת: והא ר' יוחנן בן נורי לא אמר אלא בישן חוץ לתחום, אבל תוך התחום – הרי הוא כרגלי אנשי אותה העיר! וי"ל: דהתם משום דסתמא דעתו להיות כאנשי אותה העיר: וכן

[ביצה ד.] בנו של כצ"ל בנו של כצ"ל [נדה מו:] [ביצה ד.] ביצה כ: ע"ש [לעיל לו.] לקמן מה: וש"נ ס"א ויש לו אלפים

[וע"ע תוס' פסחים קטז. ד"ה מה ותוס' ביצה ב: ד"ה והיה]

רבינו חננאל

יהודה אומר הרי זה חמר גמל. רשב"ג ור' ישמעאל בנו של ר' יוחנן בן ברוקה אומרים עירב ברגליו בראשון [אין] מערב ברגליו בשני נאכל עירובו בראשון (אינו) יוצא עליו בשני אמר רב הלכה כד' זקנים: רשב"ג ור' ישמעאל בנו של ר' יוחנן בן ברוקה ור' אלעזר בר' שמעון סתימתאה ור' יוסי ב"ר יהודה סתימתאה וכולהו אליבא דר' אליעזר דאמר ב' קדושות הן ואקשינן והא רשב"ג ור' ישמעאל בנו של ר' יוחנן בן ברוקה איפכא שמענא להו כלומר דלא כר' אליעזר דאמר ב' קדושו' הן דהא קאמרי עירב ברגליו בראשון אין מערב ברגליו בשני נאכל עירובו בראשון יוצא עליו בשני. (אמר רב הלכה כד' זקנים. רשב"ג ור' ישמעאל בנו של ר' יוחנן בן ברוקה ור' אלעזר בר' שמעון סתימתאה ור' יוסי ב"ר יהודה סתימתאה) שמעי' מינה דקדושה אחת סבירא להו ופרקינן רב איפכא הוה תני לה להא מתניתא וכן היה רשב"ג אומר וכו' (לר' יוחנן בן ברוקה אחד) עירב ברגליו בראשון מערב ברגליו בשני כו'. אי הכי היינו ר' ליחשוב נמי בהדי הני זקנים רב גמרי גמיר דר' מיתנא הוה תני להא מתניתא דב' קדושות הן ולא סבר לה הכי ומקשי רב חסדא מי אמר רב הלכתא ב' קדושות הן והא אמר רב שבת ויו"ט ביצה שנולדה בזה אסורה בזה. ופריק רבא לעולם ב' קדושות הן והתם לא קאסר רב אלא משום הכנה דאין יו"ט מכין לשבת כ"ש שבת ליו"ט. ואלא הא דתנן כיצד עושה מוליכו בראשון וכו' מחשיך עליו ואוכלו ובא לו הא מכין. שקונה עירוב מיום [טוב] לשבת. ודחינן מי סברת סוף ע"ש קונה עירוב ושבת היא שמכינה לעצמה. (היכי) [אי הכי] אמאי בלגין טבול יום שמילאוהו מחבית של מעשר טבל כו' אם תחלת היום קונה עירוב אמאי לא עירב ומשנינן התם דבעינן סעודה הראויה מבעו"י וליכא דהא מבעו"י טבל הוה ואין מערבין בטבל. אלא הא דתנן ר' אליעזר אומר יו"ט הסמוך לשבת בין מלפניו בין מלאחריו מערב ב' עירובין וא' עירובו הראשון למזרח והשני למערב הנה נמצא מניח עירוב מיו"ט לשבת שביו"ט היה במזרח וחזר בשבת במערב. ומשני מי סברת דמנח ליה בסוף אלפים אמה במזרח ולבסוף אלפים אמה במערב שנמצא כאילו מעתיק העירוב מיו"ט לשבת דמנח ליה מערב יו"ט בסוף אלף אמה לכאן ובסוף אלף אמה לכאן. ואלא הא דאמר רב יהודה עירב ברגליו בראשון מערב ברגליו בשני עירב בפת בראשון מערב בפת בשני. הא (מאי) [מכין] מיו"ט לשבת מי סברת דאזיל ברגליו ואמר מידי לא אלא אזיל ויתיב ושתיק וכן בפת וכיון דקדיש יומא קנה עירוב דכיון דאיבעי למימר שביתתי במקומי מצי אמר אע"ג דלא אמר כמאן דאמר דמי. וא' (מי) [אי] הוה שמיעא ליה לרבא דאמר מי סברת דאזיל ואמר מידי (דלא) [אלא] אזיל ושתיק. משמע דאית ליה למיזל ואע"ג דמכוון למיקנא

גליון הש"ס

רש"י ד"ה מערב אדם שני עירובין כו' כיון דלן בה כד' אמות. עי' לקמן דף ס ע"ב תד"ה אין אלו:

רב נסים גאון

אלא מעתה יערבו בלגין היינו מתני' שהזכירוה לשעבר (דף לו) לגין טבול יום שמלאהו מן החבית של מעשר טבל כו': כמאן כר' יוחנן בן נורי. בפרק מי שהוציאוהו גוים (דף מה) דתנן מי שישן בדרך ולא ידע עד שחשכה יש לו אלפים אמה לכל רוח דברי ר' יוחנן בן נורי ופירושו בתלמוד כי מדבריו אלו נתברר שהיה סובר דחפצי הפקר קונין שביתה. אמר ליה רבא בר רב חנה לאביי אי הוה שמיעא ליה למר כלפי רבא הוא אומר דאמר דאזיל ושתיק יתיב והוא רבה בר נחמני רבו דאביי: ביצה

לא יטייל אדם. בשבת או ביו"ט סמוך לחשיכה עד פתח מדינה, כדי להתקרב למרחץ להיות מזומן ליכנס כשתחשך מיד. אלמא: אף על גב דהילוך גרידא עביד ולא אמר מידי – אסור. וגבי עירוב אי בדיבורא הוה אסור משום הכנה – בשתיקותא נמי הוה אסור: מוכחא מילתא. מאי בעי בשדהו, אם לא לידע מה היא צריכה. ורחמנא אמר: "ממצוא חפצך וגו'" (ישעיה נח). וכן בפתח המדינה. אבל חוץ לעיר עד התחום – לא מוכחא מילתא דלערוביה לצורך מחר קאזיל. ולא מסקי אינשי אדעתייהו. אלא, אי צורבא מרבנן הוא – אמרינן שמעתא משכחיה, שממהר בה ואין דעתו עליו: חמרא אירכס ליה. ואזיל לעיוני. דאפילו בשבת מותר להשיבו מתוך התחום לביתו. אבל מידי דאסיר ליה למיעבד בשבת – אסיר ליה לזמוני נפשיה להאוה מידי: עירב בפת בראשון. ונאכל עירובו מערב ברגליו בשני: שאין מערבין בתחילה בפת. מי"ט לשבת משום הכנה, דקרי ליה השתא שם עירוב: דיקא נמי. באותה פת דקרא עליה שם מאתמול והשתא קא שתיק. אבל לא בפת אחרת, דבעי למיקרי שם עירוב השתא: ורבנן. אביי ורבה בר חנן, דקא מתמהי לעיל אהכנה דרבה, ולא ילפי מהא מתני' דדיקא כוותיה. דמשמע בפת אחרת לא – אלמא: הכנה היא: אמרי לך. דילמא מתני' עצה טובה קמ"ל, הא דקתני נוטלו ובא לו – שלא יאבד ויפסיד פתו ויטרח באחרת. ולעולם, אי בעי – מערב באחרת. ודקתני אין עירוב לשני – בקנייה קמייתא קאמר, אי לא הדר מערב: מתני' שמא תתעבר. בגולה קיימי, שמא יעשו ב"ד הגדול אלול מעובר ויהיו שני ימים טובים, והוא צריך לילך בראשון לצד אחד ובשני לצד אחר: מערב שני עירובין. ומניחן בעי"ט, זה לכאן וזה לכאן, ואומר כו' כדלעיל: ולא הודו לו חכמים. דקסברי: קדושה אחת הן: מתנה אדם על הכלכלה. של טבל ביו"ט ראשון של ר"ה, ואומר: אם היום חול – תהא זו תרומה על אלו, ואם היום קדש – אין בדברי כלום. דאין מגביהין תרומה בי"ט, דשבות דרבנן היא, במסכת ביצה.* ולמחר אומר: אם אתמול קדש והיום חול – תהא זו שאמרתי אתמול תרומה על אלו, ואם היום קדש ואתמול חול – כבר היא תרומה מאתמול. ואוכל הכלכלה המתוקנת, ומשייר התרומה: ולא הודו לו חכמים. דסברי דתרווייהו קדושה אחת היא, ואין מגביהין בהן תרומה: החליצנו. זרזנו. ו"החליצנו" – כמו "נחלץ חושים" (במדבר לב): אם היום אם מחר. אם היום הוא – החליצנו היום, ואם מחר – מחר: ולא הודו לו חכמים. בגמ' מפרש: אי אתנאה קאי, וקא סברי לאו ספק הוא אלא יום ראשון הוא ראש חדש, או אזכרון קאי, וקסברי דאין מזכירין של ר"ח בראש השנה: גמ' מודים חכמים. אע"ג דפליגי עליה דר"א בשבת ויו"ט הכא מודו דב' ימים טובים של ר"ה ב' קדושות הן, דחד מינייהו חול, ומשום ספיקא דלא ידעינן אי עברוהו ב"ד וקדשו ירחא ביום ל"א והוה ליה ראשון חול, או ביום ל' נקבע, והוי שני חול הוא דעבדי להו: ור' יוסי אוסר. דקסבר: לאו משום ספיקא דשמא באו עדים ביום ל' ספק ביום ל"א לחודיה איתקון, אלא אף משום שמא באו עדים מן המנחה ולמעלה איתקון, דתרווייהו קדישי. דאמור רבנן שהיו מצפין ביום ל' של אלול שמא יבאו עדים שנראית הלבנה בו, ויקדשו ב"ד את החדש היום, ונוהגין אותו היום קדש שמא י"ט הוא. ותניא: תמיד של ר"ה, שחרית קרב כהלכתו תמיד של חול ושיר של חול המתוקן ליום ב' בשבת שהיו הלוים אומרים במקדש ביום הראשון" כו' [תמיד פ"ז מ"ד]. בתמיד של בין הערבים אומר שיר אחר: הסירותי מסבל שכמו כדאמרינן בפרק בתרא של ר"ה (ד' ל:) ואם באו עדים אחר תמיד של בין הערבים, שכבר קרב בשיר של חול – תיקנו שיהיו מקדשין החדש מחר, ומיום המחרת מונין קביעתו, כדי לומר שיר הראוי לי"ט. ומ"מ, גמר יום שלשים נוהגין קדש כתחלתו, שכך תקנו שיהו נוהגין אותו היום קדש ואפילו גמרו של יום, ואע"פ שיודעין שידחה ליום המחרת, ולמחר קדש. והרחוקים מב"ד נוהגין שני ימים טובים – לאו משום ספק נראית לבנה ביום ל' והוי שני חול ספק ביום ל"א והוי ראשון חול קא עבדי, אלא משום שמא באו עדים אחר תמיד של בין הערבים ונהגו ב"ד שניהן קדש קא עבדי. אלמא: שניהן קדש: אי אתם מודים כו'. כדפרישית. אלמא: אנן דתקינן מב"ד מספקא לן דילמא הכי הוה, ותרווייהו קדש:
ורבנן

וכן ביצה שנולדה ביום ראשון. פי': לא הודו לו שתאכל אפילו בשני. דקדושה אחת היא. ובריש ביצה (דף ג.) דפריך למאן דגזר ביצה משום משקין שזבו, קשה דר' יהודה דהכא אדרבי יהודה דפ' "חבית" (שבת קמג.). דתנן, ר' יהודה אומר: אם לאוכלין – היוצא מהן מותר. ומשני, אמר ר' יוחנן: מוחלפת השיטה. צריך לומר: ההיא ד"חבית" מחליף, דהך דהכא אם היה מחליף – לא היה מרויח כלום, דרבנן מחמירי טפי. והא דאמר רבי יוחנן בפ' "חבית" (דף קמג:): הלכה כר' יהודה – היינו לפי מה שהיתה המשנה שנויה, כדאמר ב"הגוזל עצים" (ב"ק ד' צו:) ולמאי דאפכיתו ותניתו – הלכה כר"מ. ובלאו הכי אין סברא להפוך כאן כל השבות. ואין להאריך*: מודים חכמים לר' אליעזר. תימה: דסברת חכמים הפוכה ממה דקי"ל כרב, דפסיק לעיל כד' זקנים דשבת וי"ט ב' קדושות הן. ובב' ימים טובים של ר"ה קי"ל נמי כוותיה, דנולדה בזה אסורה בזה – והיינו אפכא מסברת חכמים: אי אתם מודים לי שאם באו עדים כו'. תימה לרבה, דאמר בפ"ק דביצה (דף ה.): מתקנת רבי יוחנן בן זכאי שהתקין שיהו מקבלין עדות החדש כל היום כולו, ביצה שרי. וכי לא נחלקו ר' יוסי ור' יהודה אלא בזמן שבהמ"ק קיים ולא לדורות? וי"ל: דנפקא מינה אף על גב דפליגי בא"י בזמן שבהמ"ק קיים, כדמשמע לישנא דקתני: שהיה ירא שמא תתעבר, מ"מ, נפקא מינה פלוגתייהו גבי לאחר חורבן לבני בבל. דהא דקאמר רבה מתקנת ריב"ז ביצה שריא – היינו דוקא לבני א"י, כדקתני התם בהדיא: הא לן והא להו, לפי שיש להם היכירא שנשתנה להן המנהג אחר חורבן, שהיו מקבלים עדות כל היום. אבל לבני בבל שלא נשתנה להם המנהג, דלעולם עושין ב' ימים – ביצה אסורה. דכמו שבזמן שבהמ"ק קיים היה נחשב להם ב' ימים קדושה אחת – הוא הדין לאחר חורבן, דאין ניכר להם שום שינוי בין קודם חורבן בין לאחר חורבן. והא דקאמר לקמן: וכן היה רבי יוסי אוסר בשני ימים טובים של גליות, ומפרש רבא דה"ק: וכן היה רבי יוסי אוסר בשני ימים טובים של ר"ה בגולה – לאו היינו אליבא דרבה. דלדידיה עיקר פלוגתייהו בהכי. אלא רבא לטעמיה, דאמר פ"ק דביצה (דף ה:): אף מתקנת ריב"ז ואילך ביצה אסורה. דמי לא מודה ריב"ז שאם באו עדים מן המנחה ולמעלה, פירוש: סמוך לחשיכה כל כך שאין שהות ביום כדי לקבל עדות, שנוהגין היום קדש ולמחר קדש. שאע"פ שיודעין שלא יקדשוהו היום. אלמא: קדושה אחת היא, שאע"פ שבטלה תקנתא ראשונה אחר חורבן, שהיו מקבלין עדות החדש כל היום – מסתמא לא בטלה לגמרי, דבסמוך לחשיכה אין פנאי לקבל עדות, ונוהגין אותו היום קדש כו'. ורש"י ורבינו חננאל פירשו שם כל אחד ואחד לפי שיטת גירסתו, ול"נ

לא יטייל אדם על פתח מדינה כדי שיכנס למרחץ מיד – הדר ביה. ולא היא, שמע ליה ולא הדר ביה. התם – מוכחא מילתא, הכא – לאו מוכחא מילתא היא. אי צורבא מרבנן הוא – אמרי': שמעתא משכתיה. ואי עם הארץ הוא – אמרי': חמרא אירכס ליה. גופא, אמר רב יהודה: [א]עירב ברגליו ביום ראשון – מערב ברגליו בשני. עירב בפת ביום ראשון – מערב בפת ביום שני. עירב בפת בראשון – מערב ברגליו בשני. עירב ברגליו בראשון – אין מערב בפת בשני, שאין מערבין בתחלה בפת. עירב בפת ביום ראשון – מערב בפת ביום שני. אמר שמואל: [ב]ובאותה הפת. אמר רב אשי: דיקא נמי מתני', דקתני: *כיצד הוא עושה? מוליכו בראשון, ומחשיך עליו ונוטלו – ובא לו. בשני מחשיך עליו ואוכלו, ובא לו. ורבנן – דילמא התם *עצה טובה קמ"ל. § **מתני'** ר' יהודה אומר: ראש השנה, שהיה ירא שמא תתעבר – מערב אדם שני עירובין, ואומר: (א)עירובי *בראשון למזרח, ובשני למערב. בראשון למערב ובשני למזרח. עירובי בראשון, ובשני כבני עירי. עירובי בשני, ובראשון כבני עירי, [ג]ולא הודו לו חכמים. *ועוד אמר ר' יהודה: מתנה אדם על הכלכלה ביו"ט ראשון, ואוכלה בשני. וכן ביצה שנולדה בראשון תאכל בשני, ולא הודו לו חכמים. ר' דוסא בן הרכינס אומר: העובר לפני התיבה ביו"ט של ר"ה, אומר: "החליצנו ה' אלהינו את יום ראש החדש הזה אם היום, אם למחר". ולמחר הוא אומר: "אם היום, אם אמש", ולא הודו לו חכמים. § **גמ'** מאן "לא הודו לו"? אמר רב: ר' יוסי היא, דתניא: *מודים חכמים לר"א בר"ה שהיה ירא שמא תתעבר, מערב אדם שני עירובין, ואומר: עירובי בראשון למזרח ובשני למערב. בראשון למערב ובשני למזרח. עירובי בראשון, ובשני כבני עירי. עירובי בשני, ובראשון כבני עירי. ר' יוסי אוסר. אמר להן ר' יוסי: אי אתם מודים *שאם באו עדים מן המנחה ולמעלה, שנוהגין אותו היום קדש ולמחר קדש?
ורבנן

צה א ב מיי' פ"ח מהל' עירובין הלכה ט טוש"ע א"ח סי' תטז סעיף ב:
צו ג מיי' שם הלכה ה וטוש"ע א"ח שם ס"א:

[וע"ע תוס' ביצה ג. ד"ה ר' יוחנן]

רבינו חננאל

למיקנא מקום הא דתניא לא יטייל אדם בתוך שדהו לידע מה היא צריכה וכיוצא בו לא יטייל אדם על פתח מדינה כדי שתחשך ויכנס למרחץ מיד הוה הדר ביה. ודחינן לא לעולם הוה שמיעא ליה הא מתניתא (הוה) [ולא] הדר ביה דאמר התם מוכחא מלתא דאדעתא דהכי מטייל ולפיכך אסור. אבל הכא לא מוכחא מלתא (דצורבא) [דאי צורבא] מרבנן הוא האי דאזיל ויתיב התם מאן דחזי ליה א' שמעתא משכחיה ואתא הכא לעיוניה בה. אי עם הארץ [הוא] א' חמרא אירכס ליה ואתא הכא לאהדוריה: גופא אמר רב יהודה עירב ברגליו בראשון מערב ברגליו בשני. עירב בפת בראשון מערב בפת בשני. עירב (ברגליו) [בפת] בראשון מערב (בפת) [ברגליו] שני. עירב (בפת) [ברגליו] בראשון אינו מערב בפת בשני לפי שאין מערבין בתחלה בפת ביום השני. עירב בפת בראשון מערב בפת בשני. אמר שמואל ובאותו הפת. אמר רב אשי מתני נמי דייקא שאין מערבין בשני אלא בפת שעירב בו בראשון דתנן [כיצד] הוא עושה מוליכו בראשון כו': מתני' ר' יהודה אומר ר"ה שהיה ירא שמא תתעבר מערב ב' עירובין ואומר עירובי הראשון למזרח כו' ולא הודו לו חכמים ואוקימנא מאן לא הודו לו חכמים ר' יוסי דאמרינן ר' יהודה אומר לא נחלקו ר' אליעזר וחכמים בהא דתניא מודים חכמים לר' אליעזר בר"ה שהיה מתיירא שמא תתעבר שמערב ב' עירובין ואומר עירובי הראשון למזרח ושני למערב כו' ור' יוסי אוסר אמר להם ר' יוסי אי אתם מודים שאם באו עדים מן המנחה ולמעלה שנוהגים אותו יום קודש ולמחר קודש

[לעיל לח. ע"ש]
[כתובות פא: נז. גיטין כב: ב"ב כח: כט. קית. קס: חולין קלו:]
[גי' ירושלמי ורי"ף בה"א הראשון והשני]
ביצה ג.
תוספתא פ"ד
דף לו:
ביצה ה:

הגהות הב"ח

(א) במשנה ואומר אם עירובי כצ"ל וכן בגמ':

ורבנן – התם כי היכי דלא לזלזולי ביה.§ "ועוד א"ר יהודה וכו'".§ וצריכא, דאי אשמעינן(א) ר"ה – בהא קאמר ר' יהודה משום דלא קעביד מידי. אבל כלכלה, דמיחזי כמתקן טיבלא – אימא מודה להו לרבנן. ואי אשמעינן הני תרתי – משום דליכא למיגזר עלייהו, אבל ביצה דאיכא למיגזר בה *משום פירות הנושרין *ומשום משקין שזבו – אימא מודה להו לרבנן, צריכא.§ תניא, כיצד א"ר יהודה מתנה אדם על הכלכלה ביו"ט ראשון ואוכלה בשני: אהיו לפניו שתי כלכלות של טבל, אומר: אם היום חול ולמחר קדש – תהא זו תרומה על זו, ואם היום קדש ולמחר חול – אין בדברי כלום, וקורא עליה שם ומניחה. ולמחר הוא אומר: אם היום חול – תהא זו תרומה על זו, ואם היום קדש – אין בדברי כלום, וקורא עליה שם ואוכלה. ר' יוסי אוסר. וכן היה ר' יוסי אוסר בשני ימים טובים של גליות. ההוא בר טביא דאתא לבי ריש גלותא, דאתציד ביו"ט ראשון של גליות, ואשתחיט ביו"ט שני. בר"נ ורב חסדא אכלו, רב ששת לא אכל. אמר ר"נ: מאי אעביד ליה לרב ששת דלא אכיל בישרא דטביא? א"ל רב ששת: והיכי איכול? דתני איסי, ואמרי לה איסי תני: וכן היה ר' יוסי אוסר שני ימים טובים של גליות! אמר רבא: ומאי קושיא? דילמא ה"ק: וכן היה ר' יוסי אוסר בשני יו"ט של ר"ה בגולה. א"ה "של גליות"?! "בגולה" מיבעי ליה!(ג) א"ר אסי: ומאי קושיא? דילמא הכי קאמר: וכן היה ר' יוסי עושה איסור שני ימים טובים של גליות, כשני ימים טובים של ראש השנה לרבנן דשרו. *אשכחיה רב ששת לרבה בר שמואל, אמר ליה: תני מר מידי בקדושות? אמר ליה, תנינא: מודה רבי יוסי בשני ימים טובים של גליות. אמר ליה: *אי משכחת להו – לא תימא להו ולא מידי. אמר רב אשי, לדידי אמר לי אמימר: ההוא בר טביא לאו איתצודי איתציד, אלא

רש"י

ורבנן. אמרי לך: התם נמי כיון דנדחה ליום המחרת, הוי ראשון חול ולא הוי קודש אלא חד. והאי דתקון לגמור היום בקדושה – כי היכי דלא לזלזולי ביום ל' של שנה האחרת דאי שרייא להו לעשות בו מלאכה מן המנחה ולמעלה, כשיודעין שידחה – אתו למיעבד ביה נמי קודם המנחה, ושמא יבואו עדים קודם המנחה, ויהא היום קדש, ונמצא שעשו מלאכה בי"ט: וצריכי. לר' יהודה לאורויי דב' קדושות הן בהנך תלת מילי, לענין עירוב וכלכלה וביצה: הכי גרסינן: אבל כלכלה דמיחזי כמתקן טיבלא אימא לא: ביצה. שנולדה בי"ט איתסר בכלל גזירת פירות הנושרין, שגזרו עליהן שמא יעלה ויתלוש. ויש שאוסרי' בכלל משקין שזבו מן הענבים שגזרו עליהן משום שמא יסחוט, והך פלוגתא בשמעתא קמייתא דביצה: וקורא עליה שם. בתנאי כמו שאמרנו: ולמחר הוא אומר. על אותה עצמה שתהא תרומה על חברתה: וקורא עליה שם. על אותה של תרומה: ואוכלה. לחברתה: וכן היה ר' יוסי אוסר בשני ימים טובים של גליות. כגון ב' ימים של פסח ועצרת וסוכות. שהתורה אמרה יום אחד שבתון, ובגולה עושין שני ימים. מפני שרחוקין מב"ד, ואין יודעין אם הוקבעו תשרי וניסן ביום שלשים או ביום ל"א. ואף על גב דמשום ספק, וחד מינייהו חול – אפ"ה מחמיר בהו ר' יוסי. והנך דר"ה לא קרי להו של גליות – מפני שאף בירושלים פעמים היו נעשין ב' ימים, וכגון שבאו עדים מן המנחה ולמעלה: בר טביא. לבי: דאיתציד בי"ט ראשון של גליות. ועל ידי נכרים: רב נחמן ורב חסדא אכלו. ממה נפשך: אי אתמול חול – הרי מותר, ואי אתמול קודש – הרי היום חול, והרי המתינו בכדי שיעשה: לא אכל. משום דקא סבר קדושה אחת היא: דתני איסי. בניחותא: ואמרי לה איסי תני. ובלשון תימה, כלומר: איסי תני וכו' והיכא איכול: ומאי קושיא. דילמא הך סיפא נמי אראש השנה קאי. והכי קאמר: וכן היה רבי יוסי אוסר בר"ה בגולה כל ראשי שנים, כאותו שהיו עושים בירושלים כשבאים העדים מן המנחה ולמעלה: של גליות. משמע בהני שאין נעשים שנים אלא בגולה: אמר רב אסי ומאי קושיא דילמא. האי אוסר ה"ק וכן היה ר' יוסי עושה איסור שני ימים טובים של גליות קל, כאיסור שני ימים של ר"ה לרבנן דפליגי עליו, ואמרי מותר. כדתניא לעיל: מודים חכמים לר' אליעזר. ומוטב לתרוצי הכי מילתיה, ולא נוקי שבשתא בר' יוסי. דקי"ל ר' יוסי נימוקו עמו, והאי חומרא בלא טעמא הוא: תנינא מודה ר"י בשני ימים טובים של גליות. דב' קדושות הן: אי משכחת להו. לרב נחמן ורב חסדא: לא תימא להו. להאי מילתא, דמיכספי לי על דלא אכלית מיניה: פסק. ושמעינן מדרב נחמן ורב חסדא ומדרבה בר שמואל ומדרב ששת דהדר ביה, ומדרבא *דקאמר במסכת ביצה (ד' יז.): מניח אדם עירובי תבשילין ועירובי תחומין מי"ט לחבירו ומתנה, ומדרב דקאמר במסכת ביצה (ד' ד:): בב' ימים טובים של גליות ביצה שנולדה בזה – מותרת בזה. וקבעי הלכתא כוותיה, דדבר הניצוד או הנלקט מן המחובר ביום טוב הראשון של גליות – ממתין לערב בכדי שיעשו, ומותר. דמכולהו שמעינן דאחד מהן חול. דאי מספקא לן בקדושה אחת – מאי מיפתרי בהו ביצה? ואי משום דביצה איסורא דרבנן היא – הא לא אישתרי בשני ימים טובים של ר"ה. ועוד: קי"ל במסכת ביצה (ד' ד.) דספיקא דרבנן בדבר שיש לו מתירין אסור. ועוד: לידת גדי מלאכה דאורייתא היא, ושרייא. ובהלכות גדולות אסר. ויליף טעמא מדקבע רב פפא הילכתא: נכרי שהביא דורון לישראל כו' ומוקי דהאי לערב אסורין בכדי שיעשו – לערב של מוצאי יום טוב שני קאמר, דליהוי ראוי לעשות קאמר. ובעיני נראה שאינו כן, אלא כדקתם ואמר לערב סתם – אי ביום טוב ראשון הביאו – ימתין לערב בכדי שיעשו, ואוכלו. ולפיכך צריך להמתין, דשמא היה היום קדש ולמחר חול, ובעי המתנה בכדי שיעשו. ואי הוה איפכא – כל שכן דאף בלא המתנה היו מותרין. ואי ביום שני הביאום – ימתין לערב בכדי שיעשו, דשמא היום קדש הוא. ותדע דעיקר מילתיה דרב פפא לערב יום טוב ראשון איתמר, דאמר לקמן (דף מ.): הנהו בני גננא דגזו להו נכרים אסא ביום טוב שני, לאורתא שרא להו *רבינא לאורותי לאלתר. אלמא קסבר: כי בעינן בכדי שיעשו – ביום טוב ראשון, דהא קים לן בקביעא דירחא דראשון עיקר. והא דעבדינן תרי יומי – משום דשלחו מתם הזהרו כו'. אבל יום טוב שני דקיל – לא בעינן בכדי שיעשו. ומסקנא קבעינן הילכתא אף בי"ט שני בכדי שיעשו, דלא ליתו לזלזולי ביה. ותשובת הגאון יש בידי כן. עד כאן פסק: לאו איתצודי איתציד. דודאי פשיטא ליה לרב ששת דשרי בשני:
אלא

תוספות

ול"נ. וא"ת: נהרדעי דאמרי התם* ביצה מותרת, דלא חיישינן דילמא עברוה לאלול, כמאן סברוה? דלר' יהודה, אפילו אי עברוה לא הוי קדושה אחת. ואי כרבי יוסי – הא קאסר הכא! וי"ל: דנהרדעי סברי דלעולם בבבל ביצה שריא, אפילו בתקנה ראשונה. דדוקא במקום ב"ד, אי עברוה לאלול חשיב קדושה אחת. אבל שלא במקום ב"ד, דעבדי לעולם שני ימים הוו שתי קדושות, דאזלינן בתר רוב שנים שאין מעוברות, כדאמרינן במס' ר"ה (דף כא.) לענין יום הכפורים שאין עושין אלא יום אחד. ואף על גב דרבי יוסי סבר אפילו בבבל קדושה אחת הוו, כדאמר: ומודה רבי יוסי בשני ימים טובים של גליות. משמע דבשני ימים טובים של ר"ה הוו קדושה אחת – נהרדעי לא סבירא להו בהא כרבי יוסי: אי משכחת להו לא תימא להו. רש"י פסק דדבר הנילוד או הנלקט ביו"ט ראשון של גליות, דממתין בי"ט שני בכדי שיעשו, ושרי. דודאי קי"ל בשני י"ט של גליות דשתי קדושות הן, כדמוכח הכא. ובפרק קמא דביצה (ד' ד:) נמי פסקינן: נולדה בזה מותרת בזה, אלמא: דשתי קדושות הן. והא דפסיק רב פפא הלכתא בריש "אין לדין" (שם ד' כד:) דנכרי שהביא דורון לישראל כו' ולערב בכדי שיעשו – פי' בקונטרס דהיינו לערב די"ט ראשון. ומותר ממה נפשך, דאי יום ראשון קדש – יום שני חול, דהא שרינן ביצה ולבי הנילוד בי"ט ראשון לאוכלו בי"ט שני. ולקמן* נמי, גבי הנהו גננא דשרי להו רבינא לאורתא לאורוחי ביה לאלתר – אלמא קסבר דכי בעינן בכדי שיעשו – היינו מי"ט ראשון. דטעם בכדי שיעשו מפרש הקונטרס ב"אין לדין" (שם ד' כד:) כדי שלא יהנה ממלאכת י"ט. ולפי טעם זה ודאי יש להתיר לעי"ט ראשון בכדי שיעשו. דמה נפשך לא יהנה ממלאכת יו"ט, כדפי'. ולפי זה נמי אין צריך להמתין כשיעור שילך וילוד ויביא ויתלוש ויביא, אלא שיעור תלישה לבד, שהוא ברגע אחד קטן – דאז לא יהנה ממלאכת י"ט. ודוקא בדבר הנעשה בשביל ישראל צריך להמתין בכדי שיעשו. אבל בפירות הנושרין, או שעשה הנכרי בשביל עצמו – אין צריך בכדי שיעשו, כדאמר בשבת בפ' "שואל" (ד' קנא.): אם רוב נכרים בעיר – במוצאי שבת רוחץ בה מיד. ומבשל בשבת דאמר בשוגג יאכל (שבת ד' לח.), אע"ג דנהנה ממלאכת שבת, כיון דמילתא דלא שכיחא – לא גזרו ביה רבנן. ובה"ג מפרש: דצריך להמתין עד מוצאי יו"ט(ג) בכדי שיעשו. וטעם כדי שיעשו יש לפרש: משום שמא יאמר ישראל לנכרי לעשות ביום טוב, כדי שיאכל לאלתר במוצאי יום טוב. וזה אין שייך אלא בדבר הנעשה בשביל ישראל, כדמשמע נמי בפרק "שואל" (שם ד' קנא.). והשיא בר טוביא – מיירי באיתציד מאליו, על ידי שהיו מצודות פרוסות מערב יום טוב. ולא נכרי שהביא דורון לישראל הוה. ורבינא דשרי לאורותי ביה לאלתר – שמא
לית

רבינו חננאל

הנה אע"ג דנתעבר החדש תרווייהו קדושה אחת היא ורבנן התם לא נהגו קדושה בו ביום אלא כי היכי דלא ליזלזלו ביה (וליכא) [אי ליכא] סהדי אמרי' אי אתון סהדי מן המנחה ולמעלה הלא חול הוא. *) השתא בחזקת חול לפיכך התקינו שיהיו לעולם אותו היום נוהגין (אותו היום) קודש: ת"ר כיצד אר"י מתנה אדם על הכלכלה של פירות ביו"ט הראשון ואוכלה בשני. היו לפניו ב' כלכלות של טבל אומר אם היום קדש אין בדברי כלום. אם חול הוא תהא זו תרומה על זו וקורא עליה שם. ואומר ור' יוסי אוסר וכן היה ר' יוסי אוסר להתנות מיו"ט לחבירו בשני ימים טובים של גליות: ההוא טביא (דאתבציר) [דאיתציד] ביום טוב הראשון של גליות ואתאי לריש גלותא ואישתחיט ביו"ט שני. רב נחמן ורב חסדא אכלו ורב ששת לא אכל אמר היכי איכול (ומתני) [דתני] וכן היה ר' יוסי אוסר בשני יו"ט של גליות מאן פליג עליה ר' יהודה [ור"י] ור' יוסי הלכה כר' יוסי ואתא [רבה] לפרושי דברי איסי ואמר ודלמא הכי קתני איסי וכן היה ר' יוסי אוסר להתנות מיו"ט לחבירו בב' יו"ט של ר"ה [בגולה]. אבל בב' יו"ט של גליות מודה ליה לר' יהודה ונדחו דברי רבה. ואתא רב אשי לפרושי ואמר ודלמא לא קאי ר' יוסי (בהא) [אהא] מתני' דתני ר' יהודה אלא (לרבנן פליג) [האי ארבנן דפליגי] והכי קתני וכן היה ר' יוסי עושה איסור שני י"ט של גליות כאיסור ב' יו"ט של ר"ה. **) ולרבנן היא דפליג דשרו בכלי ולא אתבררא שפיר אשכחיה רב ששת לרב שמואל א"ל תני מר מידי בקדושות. א"ל תנינא מודה ר' יוסי לחכמים בב' ימים של

*) נראה דל"ל ולכן גם השתא בחזקת חול הוא לפיכך תקנו שיהיו נוהגין לעולם אותו היום קודש: **) נראה דל"ל לרבנן דפליגי ושרו בכלכלה:

עין משפט נר מצוה

(דף ו.)

צז א מיי' פ"ו מהלכות יום טוב הלכה יב:

צח ב מיי' פ"א מהלכות יו"ט הלכה כד סמג לאוין סה ועה טור ש"ע א"ח סי' תקטו סעיף א:

רב נסים גאון

ביצה דאיכא למיגזר בה משום פירות הנושרין ומשום משקים שזבו איתא בתחלת מסכת יום טוב:

הגהות הב"ח

(א) גמ' דאי אשמעינן רישא בהא קאמר ר' יהודה: (ב) שם בגולה מיבעי ליה (אמר רב אסי) תא"מ ונ"ב ס"א רב אשי: (ג) תום' ד"ה אי משכחת וכו' עד מוצאי יו"ט שני בכדי שיעשו וכו' לאלתר במוצאי יו"ט שני וזה אין שייך:

גליון הש"ס

גמ' אשכחיה רב ששת לרבה בר שמואל. כעין זה לעיל יח ע"ב ובב"ק לח ע"ב:

מסורת הש"ס

[ביצה כ:] שם ג.

[לעיל יח: ב"ק לח.]

נ"ל ומרב וכ"ה ברש"י שבר"ן:

כד"י רבא וכן שם בגמ'

אֶלָּא מִחוּץ לַתְּחוּם אֲתָא. מַאן דַּאֲכַל *סָבַר: *הַבָּא בִּשְׁבִיל יִשְׂרָאֵל זֶה — מוּתָּר לְיִשְׂרָאֵל אַחֵר. וּמַאן דְּלָא אֲכַל סָבַר — אכֹּל דְּאָתֵי לְבֵי רֵישׁ גָּלוּתָא — אַדַּעְתָּא דְּכוּלְּהוּ רַבָּנַן אָתֵי. וְהָא אַשְׁכַּחֵיהּ רַב שֵׁשֶׁת לְרַבָּה בַּר שְׁמוּאֵל וַא"ל:(ב) *לֹא הָיוּ דְּבָרִים מֵעוֹלָם. הַהוּא לִיפְתָּא דְּאָתֵי לְמְחוֹזָא, נְפַק רָבָא חַזְיָא דִּכְמִישָׁא, שְׁרָא רָבָא לְמִיזְבַּן מִינֵּיהּ. אֲמַר: הָא וַדַּאי מֵאִיתְמוֹל נֶעֶקְרָה. מַאי אָמְרַתְּ מִחוּץ לַתְּחוּם אֲתְיָא — בהַבָּא בִּשְׁבִיל יִשְׂרָאֵל זֶה מוּתָּר לֶאֱכוֹל לְיִשְׂרָאֵל אַחֵר, וְכָל שֶׁכֵּן הַאי דְּאַדַּעְתָּא דְּגוֹיִם אֲתָא. כֵּיוָן דַּחֲזָא דְּקָא מַפְּשִׁי וּמַיְיתִי לְהוּ — אֲסַר לְהוּ. § הָנְהוּ בְּנֵי גְּנָנָא דְּגָזוּ לְהוּ אָסָא בְּי"ט שֵׁנִי, לְאוֹרְתָּא שְׁרָא לְהוּ רָבִינָא לְאוֹרוֹחֵי בֵּיהּ לְאַלְתַּר. א"ל רָבָא בַּר תַּחְלִיפָא לְרָבִינָא: לֵיסַר לְהוּ מָר, מִפְּנֵי שֶׁאֵינָן בְּנֵי תוֹרָה! מַתְקִיף לָהּ רַב שְׁמַעְיָה: טַעְמָא — דְּאֵינָן בְּנֵי תוֹרָה, הָא בְּנֵי תוֹרָה שָׁרֵי?! וְהָא בָּעֵינַן בִּכְדֵי שֶׁיֵּעָשׂוּ! אֲזַלוּ שַׁיְילוּהּ לְרָבָא, אֲמַר לְהוּ: גבָּעֵינַן בִּכְדֵי שֶׁיֵּעָשׂוּ. § "ר' דּוֹסָא אוֹמֵר הָעוֹבֵר לִפְנֵי הַתֵּיבָה כו'". § אֲמַר רַבָּה: כִּי הֲוֵינַן בֵּי רַב הוּנָא, אִיבַּעְיָא לַן: מַהוּ לְהַזְכִּיר שֶׁל רֹאשׁ חֹדֶשׁ בְּרֹאשׁ הַשָּׁנָה? כֵּיוָן דַּחֲלוּקִין בְּמוּסָפִין אָמְרִינַן, אוֹ דִּילְמָא: זִכָּרוֹן אֶחָד עוֹלֶה לְכָאן וּלְכָאן? אֲמַר לַן; תְּנֵיתוּהָ, רַבִּי דּוֹסָא אוֹמֵר: הָעוֹבֵר לִפְנֵי הַתֵּיבָה כו'. מַאי לָאו לְהַזְכִּיר? לֹא, לְהַתְנוֹת. הָכִי נַמִּי מִסְתַּבְּרָא, מִדְּקָתָנֵי בִּבְרַיְיתָא: וְכֵן הָיָה ר' דּוֹסָא עוֹשֶׂה בְּרָאשֵׁי חֳדָשִׁים שֶׁל כָּל הַשָּׁנָה כּוּלָּהּ, וְלֹא הוֹדוּ לוֹ. אִי אָמְרַתְּ בִּשְׁלָמָא לְהַתְנוֹת — מִשּׁוּם הָכִי לֹא הוֹדוּ לוֹ. אֶלָּא אִי אָמְרַתְּ לְהַזְכִּיר — אַמַּאי לֹא הוֹדוּ לוֹ? וְאֶלָּא מַאי — לְהַתְנוֹת? לָמָּה לִי לְאִיפְלוּגֵי בְּתַרְתֵּי?! צְרִיכָא, דְּאִי אַשְׁמְעִינַן ר"ה, הֲוָה אָמִינָא: בְּהָא קָאָמְרִי רַבָּנַן דְּלָא — מִשּׁוּם דְּאָתֵי לְזִלְזוּלֵי בֵּיהּ, אֲבָל בְּרָאשֵׁי חֳדָשִׁים שֶׁל כָּל הַשָּׁנָה כּוּלָּהּ — אֵימָא מוֹדוּ לֵיהּ לְר' דּוֹסָא. וְאִי אִתְּמַר בְּהָא — בְּהָא קָאָמַר ר' דּוֹסָא, אֲבָל בְּהָךְ — אֵימָא מוֹדֶה לְהוּ לְרַבָּנַן, צְרִיכָא. מֵיתִיבִי: *רֹאשׁ הַשָּׁנָה שֶׁחָל לִהְיוֹת בְּשַׁבָּת, בֵּית שַׁמַּאי אוֹמְרִים: מִתְפַּלֵּל עֶשֶׂר, וּבֵית הִלֵּל אוֹמְרִים: גמִתְפַּלֵּל תֵּשַׁע. וְאִם אִיתָא, בֵּית שַׁמַּאי אַחַת עֶשְׂרֵה מִבָּעֵי לֵיהּ! אָמַר

אֶלָּא מִחוּץ לַתְּחוּם קָאָתָא. וּבוֹ בַּיּוֹם: וְהָא אַשְׁכַּחֵיהּ רַב שֵׁשֶׁת כו'. וְאִי בּוֹ בַּיּוֹם, אַמַּאי מְשַׁיֵּיל לֵיהּ אִי קְדוּשָּׁה אַחַת אוֹ ב' קְדוּשּׁוֹת: דְּקָא מַפְּשִׁי. נָכְרִים וּמַיְיתִי. אָמַר: הָנֵי וַדַּאי אַדַּעְתָּא דְּיִשְׂרָאֵל מַפְּשִׁי וּמַיְיתוּ, וְאָסַר לְהוּ: בְּנֵי גְנָנָא. קוֹשְׁרֵי כִּילוֹת לַחֲתָנִים, וְנוֹתְנִים שָׁם הֲדַס: לְפִי שֶׁאֵינָן בְּנֵי תוֹרָה. וְאָתוּ לְזַלְזוּלֵי בְּיוֹם טוֹב שֵׁנִי: כֵּיוָן דַּחֲלוּקִין בְּמוּסָפִין. שֶׁמַּקְרִיבִין מוּסְפֵי רֹאשׁ חֹדֶשׁ וּמוּסְפֵי רֹאשׁ הַשָּׁנָה, כִּדְכְתִיב (במדבר כט): "מִלְּבַד עוֹלַת הַחֹדֶשׁ": אָמְרִינַן. בַּתְּפִלָּה נַמִּי: "אֶת יוֹם רֹאשׁ הַחֹדֶשׁ הַזֶּה וְאֶת יוֹם הַזִּכָּרוֹן הַזֶּה": זִכָּרוֹן אֶחָד. "אֶת יוֹם הַזִּכָּרוֹן הַזֶּה" דְּרַחֲמָנָא קַרְיֵיהּ "זִכָּרוֹן", דִּכְתִיב: "זִכְרוֹן תְּרוּעָה" [וּבְר"ח נַמִּי כְּתִיב: "וְהָיוּ לָכֶם לְזִכָּרוֹן"]: מַאי לָאו. "לֹא הוֹדוּ" אַלְּהַזְכִּיר קָאֵי, דְּלֹא הוֹדוּ לוֹ לְהַזְכִּיר שֶׁל ר"ח בְּרֹאשׁ הַשָּׁנָה: לְהַתְנוֹת. אִם הַיּוֹם אִם לְמָחָר, אֶלָּא סְתָמָא לֵימָא, וְכֵן יוֹם הַמָּחֳרָת: בְּרָאשֵׁי חֳדָשִׁים שֶׁל כָּל הַשָּׁנָה. שֶׁהוּא סָפֵק אִם עִיבְּרוּהָ בֵּית דִּין: לְזַלְזוּלֵי. אִי מַחְזְקִינַן לֵיהּ סָפֵק אָתוּ לְזַלְזוּלֵי *בַּשְּׁנִי אֲבָל כִּי אָמְרִינַן סְתָמָא — מַחְזְקִינַן לְהוּ בִּקְדוּשָּׁה אַחַת: אֲבָל בִּשְׁאָר חֳדָשִׁים. דְּשָׁרוּ בִּמְלָאכָה, וְלֵיכָּא לְמֵיחַשׁ לְזִלְזוּלֵי — אֵימָא מוֹדוּ לֵיהּ: מִתְפַּלֵּל עֶשֶׂר. שָׁלֹשׁ רִאשׁוֹנוֹת וְג' אַחֲרוֹנוֹת, וְשֶׁל שַׁבָּת בִּפְנֵי עַצְמָהּ — הֲרֵי שֶׁבַע. וּקְדוּשַּׁת הַיּוֹם וְכוֹלֵל עִמָּהּ מַלְכֻיּוֹת — הֲרֵי שְׁמוֹנָה, וְזִכְרוֹנוֹת וְשׁוֹפָרוֹת: וּבֵית הִלֵּל אוֹמְרִים מִתְפַּלֵּל תֵּשַׁע. דְּכוֹלֵל שַׁבָּת וְיוֹם טוֹב בִּבְרָכָה אַחַת, וְחוֹתֵם: "מְקַדֵּשׁ הַשַּׁבָּת וְיִשְׂרָאֵל וְיוֹם הַזִּכָּרוֹן": וְאִם אִיתָא. דְּמַזְכִּיר שֶׁל רֹאשׁ חֹדֶשׁ לְבֵית שַׁמַּאי, דְּבָעֵי לְכָל חַד בְּרָכָה בִּפְנֵי עַצְמָהּ — י"א מִבָּעֵי לֵיהּ: אָמַר

לית ליה בכדי שיעשו כלל, אפילו בי"ט ראשון. או שמא אית ליה בי"ט ראשון שהוא מדאורייתא בכדי שיעשו במוצאי י"ט שני. ומבשל בשבת אתי שפיר דיאכל — דליכא למיגזר אטו שמא יבשל בשבת. ולפי טעם זה היה צריך להמתין במוצאי י"ט שני כשיעור [שילך] ויתלוש ויביא. דאי כדי שיתלוש לבד — איכא למיחש שמא יאמר לנכרי בי"ט לתלוש, כדי שיאכל במוצאי י"ט אחר שעה מועטת. ושמא יש לומר דכולי האי לא החמירו חכמים. וריב"א אומר: דבירושלמי (א) דנדה משמע דטעם כדי שיעשו כדפרש"י. דתניא התם: לא תמלא אשה קדירה עססיות ותורמוסין ותתנם לתוך התנור עם חשיכה, ואם עשתה כן — למוצאי שבת אסורין בכדי שיעשו. ומפרש התם בתר הכי: מפני שהניית שבת עליו. וכיון דממתין בכדי שיעשו — אינו נהנה ממלאכת שבת כלום. ובשבת וי"ט אף לפרש"י אסור מזה לזה אף בדבר הבא מחוץ לתחום בשביל ישראל. ובדבר הנילוד והנלקט — אפילו שלא בא בשביל ישראל יש לאסור בשבת וי"ט משום הכנה, מידי דהוה אביצה שנולדה בזה אסורה בזה. וכן משמע בריש ביצה (ד' ד.), דמשמע התם דרב דאסר ביצה אסר נמי עלים שנשרו מן הדקל ושירי מדורה ושירי פתילה ושמן שכבה בשבת. ומפרש בירושלמי דרב אוסר להדליק בי"ט. ובהלכות גדולות בהלכות י"ט כתב: דאע"ג דדבר הנילוד והנלקט בי"ט בשביל ישראל — אסור עד מוצאי י"ט שני, בדבר הבא מחוץ לתחום בשביל ישראל — שרי בי"ט שני מידי דהוה אביצה שנולדה בזה מותרת בזה. ונראה שדקדקו מדקאמר ב"אין לדין" (שם ד' כד:) ולערב אסורים בכדי שיעשו — אאם יש [במינו] במחובר, ולא קאמר נמי על הבא מחוץ לתחום. משמע דאין צריך בו בכדי שיעשו. וטעמא משום דבתחום הקילו כעין שהקילו לענין הבא בשביל ישראל זה מותר לישראל אחר. ומיהו, לביצה ודאי לא מדמינן — דבביצה לא שייך שמא יאמר לנכרי, כמו בדבר הבא מחוץ לתחום: **אדעתא** דכולהו רבנן קאתו. נראה לריב"א דהכי הלכתא, דקיימא לן כרב ששת כלפי רב נחמן באיסורי. וכלפי רב חסדא נמי הלכתא כוותיה, שהיה גדול ממנו. כדאשכחן בכמה דוכתי: בעי רב חסדא מרב ששת. ובפ' "הדר" (לקמן ד' סז.) נמי אמר: רב חסדא ורב ששת כי הוו פגעו אהדדי רב חסדא מירתע ספוותיה ממתני' דרב ששת, ורב ששת מירתע כוליה גופיה מפלפוליה דרב חסדא. ואמר בסוף הוריות (ד' יד.): סיני ועוקר הרים — סיני עדיף. דהכל צריכין למרי חיטיא. הלכך: דבר הבא מחוץ לתחום בשביל ישראל — אסור לכל בני ביתו לאכול, דאדעתא דכולהו קאתי: **הא** ודאי מאתמול נעקרה. אבל אי היום נעקרה — אסור, אע"ג דאדעתא דנכרים אתו. וטעמא משום מוקצה. ואפילו לר"ש דלית ליה מוקצה — הכא מודה, כיון דלא לקטן מאתמול — אקצינהו. ודמי לגרוגרות וצמוקין. וכן משמע בריש "המביא" בביצה (ד' ל:) דכל היכא דאין יושב ומצפה — אית ליה לר"ש מוקצה. וכן פירש הקונטרס בריש "אין לדין" (שם ד' כד:) גבי נכרי שהביא דורון לישראל. וא"ת: דבפ"ק דחולין (ד' יד.) גבי השוחט בשבת משמע דלא הוי מוקצה לר"ש, ואפילו לר' יהודה בעי למימר מעיקרא דלא הוי מוקצה! וי"ל דמיירי ביושב ומצפה שמא ישחטנו חרש שוטה וקטן ואחרים רואין אותו. וא"ת: למה ליה טעמא בריש ביצה (ד' ג.) גבי פירות הנושרין שמא יעלה ויתלוש? תיפוק ליה משום מוקצה! וי"ל: כגון דאית ליה עורבים, דהוי מוכן לעורבים. והא דאמרינן בפ' "כל כתבי" (שבת ד' קכב.) דאין מעמידין בהמה על גבי מוקצה בשבת, פירוש: עשבים שנתלשו בשבת — הא פרשינן התם כגון שהיו עומדין בשעת חיבורן במקום שהבהמה לא היתה יכולה לבא שם. אי נמי: דצריך טעמא שמא יעלה ויתלוש, לר"ש ביושב ומצפה. וא"ת: טעמא דמוקצה למה ליה? תיפוק ליה משום שמא יעלה ויתלוש! וי"ל: דשמא יעלה ויתלוש לא הוי אלא בפירות האילן, שקלים ליתלוש. אבל לפחות, דבעי מרא וחצינא — לא. וכן במשקין, דגזרינן שמא יסחוט, לפי שקלים ליסחוט. ודגים שנצודו בי"ט — אסורין משום מוקצה כגרוגרות וצמוקין, ולא משום דגזרינן שמא יצוד. ותדע, דבסוף "כל כתבי" (שם ד' קכב.) גבי מילא מים לבהמתו, ונכרי שהדליק הנר ועשה כבש — לא אסרינן לישראל לירד אחריו גזירה שמא יעשנו. והא דמדמי בפ"ק דחולין (ד' יד:) שמא ישחוט לשמא יסחוט — הוה מצי למידחי דלא דמו כדפי', אלא דבלאו הכי דחי ליה שפיר: **זכרון** אחד עולה. דבראש השנה כתיב "זכרון תרועה" ובראש חדש כתיב בפרשת "בהעלותך" גבי חצוצרות "והיו לכם לזכרון". פי' רשב"ם: *דאין צריך להזכיר מקראות של מוסף, לא די"ט ולא דר"ח. כדאמר *)רב חיננא א"ר בשילהי ר"ה (ד' לה.): כיון שאמר "ובתורתך כתוב לאמר" — שוב אינו צריך, גבי מלכיות זכרונות ושופרות. ואם התחיל — צריך לסיים. והא דתנן: הפוחת לא יפחות משלש — היינו בהתחיל. והוא הדין נמי במקראות דקרבנות, ואם בא להזכיר — מזכיר אף של ר"ח. ור"ת מפרש: דההיא דרב חיננא — דווקא במלכיות זכרונות ושופרות, אבל דמוסף צריך להזכיר לעולם. אבל דר"ח אין צריך כלל להזכיר, דנפטר במה שאמר "מלבד עולת החדש ומנחתה". והגיה במחזורו "ושני שעירים לכפר ושני תמידים כהלכתם". ולר' יצחק אין נראה לחלק בין מלכיות זכרונות ושופרות למקראות דמוסף, ויש גאונים קדמונים שאין מניחין לומר "ובראשי חדשיכם" דלא ליתי לזלזולי במועדות וי"ט ראשון של ר"ה, דיאמרו יום שני עיקר כמו בראשי חדשים של כל השנה, ואתי לממני מועדות מיום שני. ואין נראה לר"י, דבכולהו שמעתא ליכא דחש להאי זלזולא. ובערוך בערך "חדש": איזה הוא חג שהחדש מתכסה בו — הוי אומר זה ר"ה. פי': שאין אומר "ובראשי חדשיכם" לא בתפלה ולא(ג) בזולתה. [וע"ע תוס' ביצה טז. ד"ה איזהו ותוס' ר"ה. ח. ד"ה "שהחדש", ועוד שם בתו' לה.]:

*) [לפנינו איתא שם חננאל]

לית

צט א ב מיי' פ"ב מהל' יו"ט הלכה י וטור ש"ע א"ח סי' תקטו ס"ה:
ק ג מיי' שם הלכה י:
קא ד מיי' פ"ב מהל' תפלה הלכה ה ו סמג עשין יט טור א"ח סי' תקפב:

רבינו חננאל

גליות וכן הלכה: ההוא לפתא דאתיוה גוים למחוזא ביו"ט שני של גליות חזייה רבא דאכמשא אמר הא ודאי מאיתמול (מעיקרא) [נעקרה] הויא לה כההוא טביא דאיתציד ביום טוב ראשון ואשתחיט ביו"ט שני. מאי חיישת דלמא מחוץ לתחום אתאי היום הא קי"ל בהא כל דבר הבא מחוץ לתחום בשביל ישראל זה מותר לישראל אחר לאכול אותו וכ"ש הדא לפתא דאדעתא דגוים אתאי דידעי דהאידנא יומא טבא הוא לאזבוני ושרא לישראל למזבן מיניה כיון (דחזא ביו"ט אחרי') [דחזו גוים אחרים] הוו אמרי ישראל נמי האידנא ביום [טוב] שני זבני והוו מפשי ואייתו. אמר הא ודאי מדעתא דישראל מפשי ואייתי הדר אסר להו למזבן כלל. והא אסא דגזו לה גוים ביו"ט אסיקנא אפילו הן בני תורה דאסיר לאורתא לישראל לאורוחיה ביה לאלתר [אלא] משהי ביה בכדי שיעשו פי' כשיעור שילך ישראל משחשכה בגן ויגזז ויביא ואחר שהיית שיעור זה שרי: **מתני'** ר' דוסא אומר העובר לפני התיבה ביו"ט של ר"ה אומר החליצנו את יום רה"ח הזה כו' איבעיא להו מהו להזכיר מוסף של ר"ח עם מוסף של ר"ה כיון דחלוקין במוספין מדכרינן או דלמא זכרון אחד לכאן ולכאן ואתינן למיפשטא ממתניתין מדקתני ר' דוסא החליצנו את יום ראש החדש הזה ש"מ ודחינן לא ר' דוסא להתנות איירי לומר אם היום אם למחר *) אבל להזכיר אינו מזכיר אלא זכרון אחד. ואמרינן הכי נמי מסתברא דלא איירי ר' דוסא אלא להתנות מדקתני ר' דוסא (עוסק) [עושה] בראשי חדשים של כל השנה כולהו כו'. ואסיקנא זכרון אחד עולה לכאן ולכאן: **ירושלמי** ר' יעקב בר אחא בשם ר' יוסי העובר לפני התיבה ביו"ט של ר"ה אינו צריך להזכיר של ר"ח פי' אינו צריך להזכיר מוסף של ר"ח. וקי"ל כי הא מתני' שבת שחלה להיות בר"ח או בחולו של מועד ערבית שחרית ומנחה מתפלל כבכל שבת. ובמוספין מתחיל בשל שבת ומסיים בשל שבת ואמרינן קדושת היום באמצע

*) לכאורה הדבר פשוט דמאי דדחינן לא להתנות אר"בנן קאי דר' דוסא הא בהדיא אמר דצריך להזכיר של ר"ח ואולי למש"כ רבינו דהאיבעיא אינו אלא אם צריך להזכיר מוסף של ר"ח עם מוסף ר"ה אפשר דגם ר' דוסא יש למבעיא ועדיין צ"ע:

[ביצה כה.]

[עי' תוס' שבת קכב. ד"ה ואם ותוס' ביצה כה. ד"ה הבא]

[ב"מ מ"ט: ע"ז כב.]

[נ"ל בשניהם ולפי זה לא צריכין לדוחק שכתב הרש"א]

הגהות הב"ח

(א) בתד"ה אי משכחת וכו' דבירושלמי דנדה משמע: (ב) גמ' לרבה בר שמואל וא"ל וכו' לא היו: (ג) תום' סוף ד"ה זכרון וכו' ולא זולתה. נ"ב פי' בכל מקומות זולת התפלה דהיינו בבקר בענין הקרבנות וכן בהפטרה:

[תוספ' ברכות פ"ג ותוספתא ר"ה סוף פ"ב]

גליון הש"ם

גמ' לא היו דברים מעולם. ע"ג כב ע"א ב"מ מט ע"ב יבמות לה ע"ב תד"ה כ"ע ל"פ ב"ב קנד ע"ב תד"ה ברם נראין בכורות ד ע"ב תד"ה אלא אי אתמר נדה כל ע"א תד"ה אמר ר"פ:

ורש"י פי' נמי התם כיון שאמר נעשה ונקריב לפניך כמו שכתבת בתורתך שוב א"צ לומר מקראות מוספין אלא שבשם רבותיו פירש דקאי אמלכיות זכרונות ושופרות [רש"ל בשם גליון]

אָמַר רַבִּי זֵירָא: שָׁאנֵי ר"ח, מִתּוֹךְ שֶׁכּוֹלֵל לְשַׁחֲרִית וְעַרְבִית כּוֹלֵל נַמִי בְּמוּסָפִין. וּמִי אִית לְהוּ לְב"ש כּוֹלֵל, וְהָתַנְיָא: ר"ח שֶׁחָל לִהְיוֹת בְּשַׁבָּת, ב"ש אוֹמְרִים: מִתְפַּלֵּל שְׁמוֹנֶה, וּב"ה אוֹמְרִים: [א]מִתְפַּלֵּל שֶׁבַע! קַשְׁיָא.§ וְכוֹלֵל עַצְמוֹ תַּנָּאֵי הִיא, *דְּתַנְיָא: שַׁבָּת שֶׁחָל לִהְיוֹת בְּר"ח אוֹ בְּחוּלּוֹ שֶׁל מוֹעֵד, [ב]עַרְבִית שַׁחֲרִית וּמִנְחָה מִתְפַּלֵּל כְּדַרְכּוֹ שֶׁבַע, וְאוֹמֵר מֵעֵין הַמְּאוֹרָע בָּעֲבוֹדָה. ר' אֱלִיעֶזֶר אוֹמֵר: בַּהוֹדָאָה. וְאִם לֹא אָמַר – מַחֲזִירִין אוֹתוֹ. וּבְמוּסָפִין [ג]מַתְחִיל בְּשֶׁל שַׁבָּת, וּמְסַיֵּים בְּשֶׁל שַׁבָּת, וְאוֹמֵר קְדוּשַּׁת הַיּוֹם בָּאֶמְצַע. רשב"ג וְר' יִשְׁמָעֵאל בְּנוֹ שֶׁל ר' יוֹחָנָן בֶּן בְּרוֹקָה אוֹמְרִים: כָּל מָקוֹם שֶׁזָּקוּק לְשֶׁבַע – מַתְחִיל בְּשֶׁל שַׁבָּת, וּמְסַיֵּים בְּשֶׁל שַׁבָּת, וְאוֹמֵר קְדוּשַּׁת הַיּוֹם בָּאֶמְצַע. מַאי הֲוָה עֲלָהּ? א"ר חִסְדָּא: [ד]זִכָּרוֹן אֶחָד עוֹלֶה לוֹ לְכָאן וּלְכָאן. וְכֵן אָמַר רַבָּה: זִכָּרוֹן אֶחָד עוֹלֶה לוֹ לְכָאן וּלְכָאן.§ וְאָמַר רַבָּה: כִּי הֲוֵינָא בֵּי רַב הוּנָא, אִיבַּעְיָא לָן: מַהוּ לוֹמַר זְמַן בְּרֹאשׁ הַשָּׁנָה וּבְיוֹם הַכִּפּוּרִים? כֵּיוָן דְּמִזְּמַן לִזְמַן אָתֵי – אָמְרִינַן, אוֹ דִּילְמָא: כֵּיוָן דְּלָא אִיקְּרוּ רְגָלִים – לָא אָמְרִינַן? לָא הֲוָה בִּידֵיהּ. כִּי אֲתַאי בֵּי רַב יְהוּדָה, אֲמַר: אֲנָא [ה]אַקָּרָא חַדְתָּא נַמִי אָמֵינָא זְמַן. א"ל: רְשׁוּת לָא קָא מִיבַּעְיָא לִי, כִּי קָא מִיבַּעְיָא לִי – חוֹבָה מַאי? א"ל: רַב וּשְׁמוּאֵל דְּאָמְרִי תַּרְוַויְיהוּ אֵין אוֹמֵר זְמַן אֶלָּא בְּשָׁלֹשׁ רְגָלִים. מֵיתִיבִי: °"תֶּן חֵלֶק לְשִׁבְעָה וְגַם לִשְׁמוֹנָה", ר' אֱלִיעֶזֶר אוֹמֵר: שִׁבְעָה – אֵלּוּ ז' יְמֵי בְרֵאשִׁית, שְׁמוֹנָה – אֵלּוּ ח' יְמֵי מִילָה. ר' יְהוֹשֻׁעַ אוֹמֵר: שִׁבְעָה – אֵלּוּ שִׁבְעָה יְמֵי פֶּסַח, שְׁמוֹנָה – אֵלּוּ שְׁמוֹנָה יְמֵי הֶחָג. וּכְשֶׁהוּא אוֹמֵר וְגַם – לְרַבּוֹת עֲצֶרֶת וְר"ה וְיוה"כ. מַאי לָאו לִזְמַן? לָא, לִבְרָכָה. הָכִי נַמִי מִסְתַּבְּרָא, דְּאִי ס"ד לִזְמַן – זְמַן כָּל שִׁבְעָה מִי אִיכָּא? הָא לָא קַשְׁיָא, דְּאִי לָא מְבָרֵךְ הָאִידָּנָא – מְבָרֵךְ לְמָחָר וּלְיוֹם אוּחְרָא. מ"מ בָּעֵינַן כּוֹס? לֵימָא מְסַיֵּיעַ לֵיהּ לְר"נ, דְּאָמַר *ר"נ: זְמַן אוֹמְרוֹ אֲפִילּוּ בַּשּׁוּק. הָא לָא קַשְׁיָא – דְּאִיקְּלַע לֵיהּ כּוֹס. הָתֵינַח עֲצֶרֶת וְר"ה, יוֹם הַכִּפּוּרִים הֵיכִי עָבֵיד? אִי מְבָרֵךְ עֲלֵיהּ וְשָׁתֵי לֵיהּ – כֵּיוָן דַּאֲמַר זְמַן קַבְּלֵיהּ עֲלֵיהּ, וְאָסַר לֵיהּ. *דְּהָאֲמַר לֵיהּ רַב יִרְמְיָה בַּר אַבָּא לְרַב: מִי בָּדְלַתְּ? וְא"ל: אִין, בְּדֵילְנָא. לִבְרוֹךְ עֲלֵיהּ וְלַנְחֵיהּ – *הַמְבָרֵךְ צָרִיךְ שֶׁיִּטְעוֹם! לֵיתְבֵיהּ לְיָנוֹקָא – לֵית הִלְכְתָא כְּרַב אַחָא,(א) דִּילְמָא אָתֵי לְמִסְרַךְ. מַאי הָוֵי עֲלָהּ? שַׁדְרוּהָ רַבָּנַן לְרַב *יֵימַר סָבָא קַמֵּיהּ דְּרַב חִסְדָּא בְּמַעֲלֵי יוֹמָא דְּרֵישׁ שַׁתָּא, אֲמַרוּ לֵיהּ: זִיל חֲזִי הֵיכִי עָבֵיד עוּבְדָא, תָּא אֵימָא לָן. כִּי חַזְיֵיהּ א"ל: דָּלוּיֵהּ לִרְטִיבָה, רַפְסָא לֵיהּ בִּדוּכְתֵּיהּ. אַיְיתוּ לֵיהּ כָּסָא דְּחַמְרָא, קַדֵּישׁ וַאֲמַר זְמַן. [ו]וְהִלְכְתָא: אוֹמֵר זְמַן בְּר"ה וּבְיוה"כ. וְהִלְכְתָא: זְמַן אוֹמְרוֹ אֲפִילּוּ בַּשּׁוּק.§ וַאֲמַר רַבָּה, כִּי הֲוֵינַן בֵּי רַב הוּנָא אִיבַּעְיָא לָן: [ז]בַּר בֵּי רַב דְּיָתֵיב בְּתַעֲנִיתָא בְּמַעֲלֵי שַׁבְּתָא, מַהוּ לְאַשְׁלוֹמֵי? לָא הֲוָה בִּידֵיהּ. אֲתָאִי לְקַמֵּיהּ דְּרַב יְהוּדָה וְלָא הֲוָה בִּידֵיהּ. אֲמַר רָבָא: נַחֲזֵייהּ אֲנַן, דְּתַנְיָא: *[ח]ט' בְּאָב שֶׁחָל לִהְיוֹת בַּשַּׁבָּת, וְכֵן

תורה אור: קהלת יא

רש"י

אמר ר' זירא. לעולם צריך להזכיר. ומיהו, לבית שמאי ברכה באנפי נפשה לראש חדש לא בעי. ולאו משום דזכרון דראש השנה עולה לו, דמשמע דכיון דראש השנה הוא היינו ראש חדש. דאי הוה נמי שבת וראש חדש ולאו ראש השנה – לא בעי ליה ברכה בפני עצמה, אלא חותם: "מקדש השבת וישראל וראשי חדשים". והלכך, בראש השנה נמי חותם: "מקדש ישראל ויום הזכרון וראשי חדשים". ואע"ג דבשבת וראש השנה בעי לכל חד ברכה בפני עצמה – בראש חדש מודו, דמתוך שכולל ברכתו בתוך ברכת היום שחרית וערבית, ואפילו בשאר שבתות. דהכא ודאי אפילו לבית שמאי פשיטא לן דלא בעי לכל חד ברכה לעצמו. דהא אי הוה מיקלע בחול אין לו ברכה שחרית וערבית, אלא אומר "יעלה ויבא" בעבודה. והלכך, כי מיקלע בשבת, אפילו למאן דאמר לקמן דבשבת לא מדכרינן דראש חדש בעבודה אלא בברכת היום – מיכלל הוא דכיילינן, ולאו בפני עצמה: כולל נמי במוספין. לבית שמאי. ואע"ג דבחול אית ליה ברכה במוספין לעצמו – הכא מיכלל הוא דכיילינן הואיל וכולל שחרית וערבית. אבל שאר ימים טובים, דאית להו ברכה ערבית ושחרית כי מיקלעי בחול – בהני פליגי בית שמאי כי מיקלעי בשבת מצרכי להו ברכה בעצמן, לכל תפלותיהם: ומי אית להו לבית שמאי כולל. בברכת המוספין של ראש חודש דאיקלע בשבת: מתפלל שמנה. של ראש חדש ושל שבת ובמוספין קאמר: קשיא. וש"מ: כיון דבשאר שבתות קא בעו ב"ש ברכה לראש חדש, ובר"ה לא בעו – דטעמא משום דזכרון דראש השנה עולה לו. וש"מ אפילו מכלליה ואדכורי נמי לא בעינן: וכולל עצמו. דשחרית וערבית בראש חדש שחל להיות בשבת: תנאי היא. דאיכא תנא דאפילו כולל לית ליה, אלא אומר "יעלה ויבא" בעבודה כבחול. אבל בברכת היום אינו נזכר כלל, אפילו לכוללו: ומתחיל בשל שבת. "ותתן לנו את יום המנוח הזה", ומסיים בשל שבת "מקדש השבת" ותו לא. ומיהו, במוספים באמצע ברכה הוא נכלל. אבל שחרית וערבית – אינו נכלל אפילו באמצע, והאי תנא לית ליה כולל שחרית וערבית:

כל מקום שזקוק לשבע. ואפילו שחרית וערבית: קדושת היום. של ראש חדש עם של שבת. כגון: "את יום המנוח הזה ואת יום ראש חדש הזה", ואם מועד הוא: "את יום השבת הזה ואת יום חג פלוני הזה". (פסק: ובמסכת ביצה קבעינן הלכתא דלא כי הני תנאי דמסיימי בשל שבת לחודיה במוספין, אלא אף קדושת היום בעי לאדכורי בחתימה: "מקדש השבת וישראל והזמנים", ובראש חדש: "מקדש השבת וישראל וראשי חדשים". אבל במאי דקאמר שחרית וערבית מתפלל כדרכו, ואומר מעין המאורע בעבודה – הלכתא כוותיה. וגבי כולל דשחרית וערבית קבעינן אין הלכה כאותו הזוג, דאמרי: כל מקום שזקוק לשבע כולל. בפרק שני דביצה)*: מאי הוי עלה. מהו להזכיר של ראש חדש בראש השנה: אקרא חדתא. כשאני רואה דלעת חדשה משנה לשנה אמינא זמן: אלו שבעת ימי בראשית. השבת נבחר מתוכה: שמונה ימי מילה. השמיני נבחר מתוכה: אלו ז' ימי הפסח. שאתה צריך לתת חלק לכולם, ולקמן מפרש מאי חלק: לברכה. דמברכים כל יומא "מקדש ישראל והזמנים": מכל מקום כוס בעינן. לעיל מהדר לאוקומי הכי נמי מסתברא, דאי ס"ד זמן זמן – כל ז' מי איכא, ודקאמר דאי לא אמר האידנא, אומר למחר וליומא אחרינא – האי נמי ליתא, דהא כוס יין בעי לומר הברכה עליו. וסתמא דאינשי, יומא קמא אית להו כוס – אבל בשאר יומא לכולי עלמא לית להו: הא לא קשיא דמיקלע ליה כוס. ולעולם אזמן קאי, ולרב נחמן לא תסייעיה: תינח עצרת וראש השנה. איכא למימר דזמן אכוס קאמר ליה. אלא יום הכפורים, אי בזמן מוקמת ליה – על כרחיך סייעתא לרב נחמן היא, דעל הכוס היכי ליעביד? אי מברך עליה ושתי ליה וכו': מי בדלת. פעם אחת נתקשרו שמים בעבים, והתפלל רב של שבת מבעוד יום, ואמר ליה רב ירמיה לרב: מי בדלת מן המלאכה משקבלת עליך שבת? ואמר ליה: אין, בדילנא: ליתביה לינוקא. לשתותו, לאחר שיברך עליו. דהאי שיטעום דקאמר – לאו דווקא קאמר אמברך, דהוא הדין כי שתי אחרינא. דטעמא משום דגנאי הוא לכוס של ברכה שלא יהנה אדם ממנו לאלתר, שתהא ברכת היין ד"בורא פרי הגפן" שלא לצורך. ומכי טעם ליה אחרינא – שפיר דמי. וכדתניא נמי בגמרא דפרק "ראוהו בית דין" (ר"ה כט:): לא יפרוס אדם פרוסה לאורחין אלא אם כן אוכל עמהם, שהרי הן יכולין לעשות, אבל פורס הוא לבניו ולבני ביתו כדי לחנכן במצות. ואף על פי שהוא לא טעם אלא בניו – שפיר דמי, ואף על פי שבירך עליה ברכת "המוציא": *דרב אחא בר יעקב. לא איתפרש: דאתי למסרך. התינוק לאחר המנהג זה, ולשתות ביום הכפורים אחר שיגדיל: מאי הוי עלה. צריך לומר זמן בראש השנה וביום הכפורים, או לא: בר חוייה. רב חסדא לרב ייבא: אמר ליה דלויה לרטיבא רפסא ליה בדוכתיה. המגביה עץ לח שאינו ראוי להיסק בידוע שצריך למקומו, הואיל ואליו אינו צריך, שעל חנם לא הגביהו. כלומר: על חנם לא באת לכאן:

תוספות

לית הלכתא כרב אחא בר יעקב. פירש רש"י ולא איתפרש. ור"ח פי': דבפרק "תולין" (שבת ד' קלט.) גבי כשות' פריך: וליתיב לינוקא דישראל, ומשני: דילמא אתי למיסרך, וקים לן דרב אחא בר יעקב הקשה אותה קושיא*: **דלמא** אתי למיסרך. אומר רבינו שמואל: דוקא גבי זמן שהוא קבוע חיישינן דלמא אתי למיסרך. אבל אם אירע ברית מילה בט' באב או ביו"כ, דלא הוי אלא אקראי בעלמא – לא חיישינן דלמא אתי למיסרך. ומעשה היה בתופה בעשרה בטבת נתנו הכוס לתינוק לשתות. [ומעשה היה בברית מילה ברבינו יעקב בר יקר שחל עשרה באב בא' בשבת, והוא היה אב"ד, ולוה להתפלל מנחה גדולה, ורחצו ואכלו מפני שי"ט שלהן היה, כדכתיב: "שש אנכי כו'". והאי דלא מברכינן "שהחיינו" – משום לערא דינוקא. תוס' שאנ"ץ]:

עין משפט נר מצוה

קב א מיי' פ"ב מהל' תפלה הלכה יא סמג עשין יט טוש"ע א"ח סי' תכה סעיף ג:

[ועי' תוס' שבת קלט. ד"ה וליתן]

קג ב מיי' שם טוש"ע שם סעיף א:

קד ג מיי' שם טור ש"ע שם סעיף ג:

קה ד מיי' פ"ב מהלכות תפלה הלכה ה סמג עשין כט טוש"ע א"ח סי' תקפב סעיף ו [וברב אלפס שבועות סוף פ"א דף רפז]:

קו ה מיי' פ"י מהלכות ברכות הלכה ב סמג עשין כז טוש"ע א"ח סי' רכה סעיף ג:

קז ו מיי' פכ"ט מהל' שבת הלכה כג סמג עשין יט טוש"ע א"ח סי' תריט סעיף א:

קח ז (מיי' פ"א מהל' תענית הל"ו) טוש"ע א"ח סי' רמט סעיף ג ד:

קט ח מיי' פ"ה מהל' תענית הלכה ח סמג עשין ג טוש"ע א"ח סי' תקנב סעיף י:

רבינו חננאל

*) וכן הלכתא כהני תנאי כ"מ שזקוק לשבע (כגון שבת) ואפילו בערבית שחרית ומנחה מתחיל בשל שבת ואומר קדושת היום באמצע [ומסיים] בשל שבת והני מילי בר"ח וחוה"מ אבל ביום טוב אפילו בערבית ובשחרית ובמנחה מתחיל בשל שבת ומסיים בשל **) שבת ואומר קדושת היום באמצע: ירושלמי ר' יסא משלח כתוב לון אע"פ ששלחנו לכם סידרי מועדות אל תשנו מנהג אבותיכם נוחי נפש רב חסדא ורבה דאמרי תרווייהו זכרון אחד עולה לכאן ולכאן: **אמר** רבה איבעיא להו מהו להזכיר זמן בר"ה וביום הכפורים ואמר [ליה] רב ושמואל דאמרי תרווייהו אין אומרים זמן אלא בשלש רגלים בלבד. ומותבינן מהא תן חלק לשבעה גם לשמונה ר' אליעזר אומר שבעה אלו ז' ימי בראשית שמונה אלו ח' ימי מילה ר' יהושע אומר שבעה אלו ז' ימי הפסח שמנה אלו ח' ימי החג כשהוא אומר וגם לרבות גם עצרת ור"ה ויוה"כ מאי לאו הני כולהו עיקר לקדש אותן בזמן. (אתה) [ואתי] וגם לרבות גם עצרת מפני שהוא יום אחד ור"ה ויוה"כ שאין בהן לא ז' ולא ח' שתתן להן חלק בזמן הנה יש בהן זמן. ודחי רב ושמואל לא לעולם זמן אין בהן אלא מהו החלק שתתן להן הזכרה בברכת המזון כמו פסח וסוכות. הכי נמי מסתברא דר"ה ויוה"כ אין בהן זמן משום דליכא זמן אלא בכוס. אי אמרת דאיקלע ליה כוס. תינח ר"ה אלא יוה"כ היכי ליעביד [אי] מייתי כוס ומברך עליה ומדכר זמן ושתי ליה מכי אמר זמן קבליה ליוה"כ עליה ואתסר בשתיה. דא"ל רב ירמיה לרב כיון דאת מצלי של שבת מבעו"י (אבדלת) [אי בדלת] וקבלת לשבת עלך וא"ל בדילנא. ליבריך אכסא ולישבקיה המברך צריך שיטעום ליתביה לינוקא ולישתיה דלאו בר חייובא הוא לית הלכתא כרב אחא בר יעקב דשרי בכי האי גוונא. דחיישינן דלמא אתי ינוקא למיסרך וישתה כוס ברכה כי האי גוונא ביוה"כ והוא גדול. כיוצא בו גרסינן בשבת פ' ר"א אומר תולין כו' (דף קלט.) ליתן לינוקא דישראל אתי למיסרך כו' ואסיקנא הלכתא אומר זמן בר"ה וביוה"כ וזמן אומר אפי' בשוק ולא צריך כוס. אמר רבא איבעיא לן בני בי רב דיתבי בתעניתא במעלי שבתא ובמעלי יומא טבא מהו למיתב כולי יומא בתעניתא ושקלי בה טובא

*) נראה דל"ל ולית הילכתא כהני תנאי דהא בהדיא אמר רב הונא בביצה דף י"ז ע"א דאין הלכה כאותו הזוג וכן מסיק רבינו בעצמו בהדיא לקמן דדוקא ביו"ט מתחיל בשל שבת ומסיים בשל שבת:

**) עיין בפ"ב דיו"ט שם דפסק הש"ס דהילכתא כרבי דאף חותם בה מקדש השבת וישראל והזמנים ודברי רבינו צ"ע:

מסורת הש"ס

ביצה יז. [תוספתא ברכות פ"ג] ע"ש תוספתא איירי בר"ח וחוה"מ בחול

[סוכה מז:]

ברכות כז:

[שם נב. פסחים קה:]

[בשאלתות סוף וזאת הברכה איתא רב ייבא סבא וכן גירסת רש"י לפנינו]

תענית כט:

[דף יז.]

עי' בנדה מז:

הגהות הב"ח

(א) גמ' לית הלכתא כרב אחא בר יעקב דילמא אתי למסרך. נ"ב עיין בפרק תולין דף קלט ע"ב תוס' ד"ה וליתן ליה.

גליון הש"ס

רש"י ד"ה דרב אחא ב"י לא איתפרש. ועי' ברכות נה ע"ב תוס' ד"ה מתן שמעת ליה וש"נ.

קי א ב מיי' פ"א מהל' תעניות הלכה ו סמג עשין ג טוש"ע א"ח סי' תקעב סעיף ב:

וְכֵן עֶרֶב תִּשְׁעָה בְּאָב שֶׁחָל לִהְיוֹת בְּשַׁבָּת — אוֹכֵל וְשׁוֹתֶה כָּל צָרְכּוֹ, וּמַעֲלֶה עַל שׁוּלְחָנוֹ אֲפִילּוּ כִּסְעוּדַּת שְׁלֹמֹה בִּשְׁעָתוֹ. חָל לִהְיוֹת תִּשְׁעָה בְּאָב בְּעֶרֶב שַׁבָּת — מְבִיאִין לוֹ כַּבֵּיצָה וְאוֹכֵל, כְּדֵי שֶׁלֹּא יִכָּנֵס לַשַּׁבָּת כְּשֶׁהוּא מְעוּנֶּה. (א)תַּנְיָא, אָמַר רַבִּי יְהוּדָה: פַּעַם אַחַת הָיִינוּ יוֹשְׁבִין לִפְנֵי ר"ע, וְתִשְׁעָה בְּאָב שֶׁחָל לִהְיוֹת בְּע"ש הָיָה, וְהֵבִיאוּ לוֹ בֵּיצָה מְגוּלְגֶּלֶת וּגְמָעָהּ בְּלֹא מֶלַח. וְלֹא שֶׁהָיָה תָּאֵב לָהּ, אֶלָּא לְהַרְאוֹת לַתַּלְמִידִים הֲלָכָה. וְרַבִּי יוֹסֵי אוֹמֵר: מִתְעַנֶּה וּמַשְׁלִים. אָמַר לָהֶן ר' יוֹסֵי: אִי אַתֶּם מוֹדִים לִי בְּט' בְּאָב שֶׁחָל לִהְיוֹת בְּאֶחָד בַּשַּׁבָּת, שֶׁמַּפְסִיק מִבְּעוֹד יוֹם? אָמְרוּ לוֹ: *אֲבָל. אָמַר לָהֶם: מַה לִּי לִיכָּנֵס בָּהּ כְּשֶׁהוּא מְעוּנֶּה, מַה לִּי לָצֵאת מִמֶּנָּה כְּשֶׁהוּא מְעוּנֶּה? אָמְרוּ לוֹ: אִם אָמַרְתָּ לָצֵאת מִמֶּנָּה — שֶׁהֲרֵי אָכַל וְשָׁתָה כָּל הַיּוֹם כּוּלּוֹ, תֹּאמַר לִיכָּנֵס בָּהּ כְּשֶׁהוּא מְעוּנֶּה — שֶׁלֹּא אָכַל וְשָׁתָה כָּל הַיּוֹם כּוּלּוֹ. וְאָמַר עוּלָּא: הֲלָכָה כְּרַבִּי יוֹסֵי. וּמִי עָבְדִינַן כְּרַבִּי יוֹסֵי? וּרְמִינְהִי: *אֵין אגּוֹזְרִין תַּעֲנִית עַל הַצִּיבּוּר בְּרָאשֵׁי חֳדָשִׁים בַּחֲנוּכָּה וּבְפוּרִים, וְאִם הִתְחִילוּ — אֵין מַפְסִיקִין, דִּבְרֵי ר"ג. אָמַר ר"מ: אַף עַל פִּי שֶׁאָמַר רַבָּן גַּמְלִיאֵל "אֵין מַפְסִיקִין", מוֹדֶה הָיָה שֶׁאֵין מַשְׁלִימִין, וְכֵן בְּט' בְּאָב שֶׁחָל לִהְיוֹת בְּע"ש. וְתַנְיָא: לְאַחַר פְּטִירָתוֹ שֶׁל (*רשב"ג) נִכְנַס ר' יְהוֹשֻׁעַ לְהָפֵר אֶת דְּבָרָיו. עָמַד רַבִּי יוֹחָנָן בֶּן נוּרִי עַל רַגְלָיו וְאָמַר: חָזֵי אֲנָא דְּבָתַר רֵישָׁא גּוּפָא אָזֵיל, כָּל יָמָיו שֶׁל רַבָּן גַּמְלִיאֵל קָבַעְנוּ הֲלָכָה כְּמוֹתוֹ, עַכְשָׁיו אַתָּה מְבַקֵּשׁ לְבַטֵּל דְּבָרָיו?! יְהוֹשֻׁעַ, אֵין שׁוֹמְעִין לְךָ, שֶׁכְּבָר נִקְבְּעָה הֲלָכָה כְּר"ג. וְלֹא הָיָה אָדָם שֶׁעִרְעֵר בַּדָּבָר כְּלוּם. בְּדוֹרוֹ שֶׁל רַבָּן גַּמְלִיאֵל — עֲבוּד כְּר"ג, בבְּדוֹרוֹ שֶׁל רַבִּי יוֹסֵי — עֲבוּד כְּרַבִּי יוֹסֵי. וּבְדוֹרוֹ שֶׁל ר"ג עֲבוּד כְּר"ג? *וְהָתַנְיָא, א"ר אֶלְעָזָר *(בֶּן) צָדוֹק: אֲנִי (הָיִיתִי) מִבְּנֵי סְנָאָב בֶּן בִּנְיָמִין, פַּעַם אַחַת חָל תִּשְׁעָה בְּאָב לִהְיוֹת בַּשַּׁבָּת, וּדְחִינוּהוּ לְאַחַר הַשַּׁבָּת וְהִתְעַנִּינוּ בּוֹ וְלֹא הִשְׁלַמְנוּהוּ, מִפְּנֵי שֶׁיּוֹ"ט שֶׁלָּנוּ הָיָה. טַעְמָא דְּיוֹ"ט, הָא עֶרֶב יוֹ"ט מַשְׁלִימִין! אָמַר רָבִינָא: שָׁאנֵי יוֹ"ט שֶׁל דִּבְרֵיהֶם, מִתּוֹךְ שֶׁמִּתְעַנִּין בּוֹ שָׁעוֹת — מַשְׁלִימִין בּוֹ עַרְבִיּוֹת. שַׁבָּת, הוֹאִיל וְאֵין מִתְעַנִּין בָּהּ שָׁעוֹת — אֵין מַשְׁלִימִין בָּהּ עַרְבִיּוֹת. *אָמַר רַב יוֹסֵף: לָא שְׁמִיעַ לִי הָא שְׁמַעְתָּא. אָמַר לֵיהּ אַבַּיֵי: אַתְּ אָמַרְתְּ נִיהֲלַן, וְאַהָא אָמְרַתְּ נִיהֲלַן: אֵין גּוֹזְרִין תַּעֲנִית עַל הַצִּבּוּר בְּרָאשֵׁי חֳדָשִׁים וכו'. וְאָמְרִינַן עֲלָהּ, *אָמַר רַב יְהוּדָה, אָמַר רַב: זוֹ דִּבְרֵי רַבִּי מֵאִיר שֶׁאָמַר מִשּׁוּם רַבָּן גַּמְלִיאֵל, אֲבָל חֲכָמִים אוֹמְרִים: מִתְעַנֶּה וּמַשְׁלִים. מַאי לָאו אַכּוּלְּהוּ? לָא, אַחֲנוּכָּה וּפוּרִים. הָכִי נַמִי מִסְתַּבְּרָא, דְּאִי

[נ"ל בן ברבי]

רש"י

וְכֵן עֶרֶב תִּשְׁעָה בְּאָב שֶׁחָל לִהְיוֹת בַּשַּׁבָּת. אע"פ שֶׁאָז חָל לִהְיוֹת בְּחוֹל לֹא יֹאכַל שְׁנֵי תַבְשִׁילִין וְלֹא יֹאכַל בָּשָׂר וְלֹא יִשְׁתֶּה יַיִן — עַכְשָׁיו שֶׁהוּא שַׁבָּת אוֹכֵל כָּל צָרְכּוֹ: בִּשְׁעָתוֹ. שֶׁהָיְתָה שְׁעָתוֹ עוֹמֶדֶת לוֹ בְּמַלְכוּתוֹ, דְּמֶלֶךְ וְהֶדְיוֹט הֲוָה: מְגוּלְגֶּלֶת. צְלוּיָה רַכָּה: לְהַרְאוֹת הֲלָכָה. שֶׁאֵין מַשְׁלִימִין תַּעֲנִית עֶרֶב שַׁבָּת: שֶׁהוּא מַפְסִיק. סְעוּדָּה: מִבְּעוֹד יוֹם. שֶׁצָּרִיךְ לֶאֱכוֹל מִבְּעוֹד יוֹם, וּמְקַבֵּל תַּעֲנִית עָלָיו מִשֶּׁגָּמַר לֶאֱכוֹל, וְאע"פ שֶׁהוּא שַׁבָּת: אֲבָל. בֶּאֱמֶת: וּמַה לִּי לִיכָּנֵס כְּשֶׁהוּא מְעוּנֶּה. כְּגוֹן שֶׁהִשְׁלִים בְּעֶרֶב שַׁבָּת תַּעֲנִיתוֹ: וּמַה לִּי לָצֵאת מִמֶּנָּה כְּשֶׁהוּא מִתְעַנֶּה. שֶׁמַּתְחִיל תַּעֲנִיתוֹ מִבְּעוֹד יוֹם: וְאִם הִתְחִילוּ. שֶׁהִתְחִילוּ לְהִתְעַנּוֹת כ' אוֹ ל' יוֹם, וְנִכְנְסוּ בָּהֶן יְמֵי חֲנוּכָּה אוֹ רֹאשׁ חֹדֶשׁ: שֶׁאֵין מַשְׁלִימִין. תַּעֲנִית בַּחֲנוּכָּה וְרֹאשׁ חֹדֶשׁ, לְהִתְעַנּוֹת כָּל הַיּוֹם: וְכֵן בְּתִשְׁעָה בְּאָב שֶׁחָל בְּע"ש. נַמִי אֵין מַשְׁלִימִין: לְבַטֵּל אֶת דְּבָרָיו. וְלוֹמַר מַשְׁלִימִין: חָזֵי אֲנָא דְּבָתַר רֵישָׁא גּוּפָא אָזֵיל. רוֹאֶה אֲנִי בְּדִין וּבְדָת שֶׁצְּרִיכִין אָנוּ לְהַלֵּךְ אַחַר דִּבְרֵי הָרִאשׁוֹנִים: וְלֹא הָיָה אָדָם כו'. אַלְמָא: אֵין מַשְׁלִימִין: בְּדוֹרוֹ שֶׁל ר' יוֹסֵי. דַּהֲוָה בָּתַר הָכִי שֶׁבַּקוּהוּ לְדר"ג וְקָבְעוּ הֲלָכָה כְּרַבִּי יוֹסֵי דְּמוּתָּר: מִבְּנֵי סְנָאָב בֶּן בִּנְיָמִין. מִשְׁפָּחָה הִיא מִשֵּׁבֶט בִּנְיָמִין, שֶׁנָּפַל לָהֶן גּוֹרָל לְקָרְבַּן עֵצִים בִּי' בְּאָב בִּימֵי עֶזְרָא, וְיוֹ"ט הָיָה לָהֶם לְעוֹלָם, כִּדְתְנַן בְּפֶרֶק בַּתְרָא דְּתַעֲנִית: לְאַחַר הַשַּׁבָּת. שֶׁהוּא עֲשָׂרָה בְּאָב וַהֲוֵי יוֹ"ט שֶׁלָּנוּ: טַעְמָא דְּיוֹ"ט. הָא בְּשָׁאָר ט' בְּאָב הָיוּ מַשְׁלִימִין, אע"פ שֶׁכָּל ט' בְּאָב הֲוֵי עֶרֶב יוֹ"ט שֶׁלָּהֶם. וְרַבִּי אֶלְעָזָר בַּר צָדוֹק בְּדוֹרוֹ שֶׁל רַבָּן גַּמְלִיאֵל הֲוָה, כִּדְתַנְיָא בְּבֵיצָה (דף כב:): א"ר אֶלְעָזָר בְּר' צָדוֹק: פְּעָמִים הַרְבֵּה נִכְנַסְתִּי אַחַר אַבָּא לְבֵית ר"ג: שָׁאנֵי יוֹם טוֹב (ב)דְּרַבָּנַן. כְּגוֹן הַאי קָרְבַּן עֵצִים, הוֹאִיל וְקַל הוּא — שֶׁמִּתְעַנִּין בּוֹ לְשָׁעוֹת. כִּדְקָתָנֵי: וְהִתְעַנִּינוּ בּוֹ. לְפִיכָךְ מַשְׁלִימִין בּוֹ עַרְבִיּוֹת, כְּלוֹמַר: מוּתָּר לְהַשְׁלִים עֶרֶב אוֹתוֹ יוֹם טוֹב, וְלִיכָּנֵס לְתוֹכוֹ כְּשֶׁהוּא מְעוּנֶּה. דְּהָא אֲפִילּוּ בְּעִיקָּרוֹ מוּתָּר לְהִתְעַנּוֹת בּוֹ קְצָת הַיּוֹם. אֲבָל שַׁבָּת שֶׁאָסוּר לְהִתְעַנּוֹת בּוֹ קְצָת לְשׁוּם תַּעֲנִית — אָסוּר נַמִי לְהַשְׁלִים בּוֹ עַרְבִיּוֹת, שֶׁהַמַּשְׁלִים ע"ש מִתְעַנֶּה בְּמִקְצָת שַׁבָּת: לָא שְׁמִיעַ לִי הָא שְׁמַעְתָּא. דְּקָבַע עוּלָּא לְעֵיל הֲלָכָה כְּר' יוֹסֵי: אַתְּ אָמַרְתְּ נִיהֲלַן. ר' יוֹסֵף חָלָה וְשָׁכַח תַּלְמוּדוֹ, וְהָיָה אַבַּיֵי תַּלְמִידוֹ מַזְכִּירוֹ: זוֹ דִּבְרֵי ר' מֵאִיר. דְּאָמַר לְעֵיל מִשּׁוּם ר"ג מוֹדֶה הָיָה שֶׁאֵין מַשְׁלִימִין. וְכֵן ט' בְּאָב שֶׁחָל לִהְיוֹת עֶרֶב שַׁבָּת אֲבָל חֲכָמִים אוֹמְרִים מִתְעַנֶּה וּמַשְׁלִים: מַאי לָאו. חֲכָמִים אַכּוּלְּהוּ קָיְימִי, בֵּין אַחֲנוּכָּה וּפוּרִים בֵּין אַעֶרֶב שַׁבָּת. וּמִדְּאַגְמָרֵיהּ רַב לְר' יוֹסֵי בִּלְשׁוֹן חֲכָמִים — ש"מ הֲלָכָה כְּרַבִּי יוֹסֵי:

[עי' פירש"י לעיל לח. ד"ה אבל]
[תענית טו:]
[נ"ל ר' גמליאל]
תענית יב.
[לעיל י. וש"נ]
תענית יח.

תוספות

[ביצה מגולגלת. כפי' ר"ח, קבלה בידינו כי ר' עקיבא אותה שנה מסוכן היה, והביאו לר"ע הרופאים לגמע ביצה מגולגלת באחרית היום, ור' יהודה לא דקדק, לפיכך סמך על מה שראה ולא ידע העיקר על מה עשה כך. ותמוז דהאי שתא מלייה מליוה, לפיכך חל תשעה באב בערב שבת, וחסרו אב ובא ר"ה בשבת. תוס' שאנ"ץ]:

אי אתם מודים בתשעה באב. וא"ת: והא אמר שמואל בפרק "מקום שנהגו" (פסחים דף נד:): תשעה באב — בין השמשות שלו מותר! וי"ל: דמ"מ מתחיל מבעוד יום, לפי שאי אפשר לכוין תחילת הלילה. ועוד: דר' יוסי סבירא ליה *בין השמשות כהרף עין ואין אדם יכול לעמוד עליו. ואין לפרש דהכי קאמר: דהיכא דהפסיק סעודתו דהוי כמו קבלת תענית בשבת — דהא לא מצי קביל תענית בשבת עליה. ועוד: דאמרינן דאפילו יוה"כ דתוספת שלו דאורייתא שרי לאכול, אע"פ שכבר הפסיק. כדאמרינן *באיכה רבתי: ר' יהודה בן בתירא אזל לנציבין בערבא צומא, רבא אזל ריש כנישתא לזמוני ליה. א"ל: כבר אכלי ופסקי. א"ל: אשגחאי עלי, דלא לימא גברא רבא הוא דלא אשגח עילויה. אזיל עמיה. ומסיק התם: דאכל מכל עיגול חד פתיתא ומכל *מאכל פת אחד ומכל חבית חד כוס:

מודה היה שאין משלימין. משמע דרבנן דפליגי עליה סברי דאפילו מפסיקין. ולקמן אמרינן: זו דברי ר' מאיר שאמר משום ר"ג, אבל חכמים אומרים: מתענה ומשלים. אלמא אדרבה דלרבנן — משלימין. ושמא הנהו חכמים דפליגי אדרבי מאיר סברי דמשלימין. והכא קאמר מודה לרבנן — דפליגי ארבן גמליאל, והנהו סבירא להו דמפסיקין:

מבני סנאב בן בנימין. "סנאה" גרסינן, ולא גרסינן "סנאב", דהכי כתיב בעזרא(ב), ועל שם שבטו נקרא "בן בנימין". דגבי עלי מערכה חשיב ליה בפרק ד' דתענית (דף כו.), וכל הנהו דחשיב התם בני ארח בן יהודה בני דוד בן יהודה — כולם על שם שבטן. ואע"ג דר' אלעזר בן צדוק כהן היה, כדמוכח בפרק "כל פסולי המוקדשין" (בכורות דף לו.) גבי רבי אלעזר *בר צדוק הוה ליה בוכרא וכו' — שמא אמו היתה מבנימין, או חתנם היה והיה עמהם בסייעתם:

שאני ימים טובים מדבריהם מתוך שמתענין בו שעות משלימין בו ערביות. והא דאמרינן בסוף פ"ק דר"ה (דף יט.): דימים הכתובים במגילת תענית אסורין בין לפניהם בין לאחריהם, ותנן נמי במסכת תענית בפרק שני (דף טז:): כל הכתובים במגילת תענית דלא למספד בהון — לפניו אסור, ולאחריו מותר. ועשרה באב כתיב בהנהו דלא למספד בהון — משמע דיו"ט דדבריהם נמי אסור להתענות בו ערביות! הני מילי תענית דרשות, אבל תענית חובה, כגון תשעה באב — מתענין. וא"ת: והיכי פשיט לעיל מרבי יוסי דאיירי בתענית חובה, על בני בי רב דיתבי בתענית, דמשמע דאיירי בתענית הרשות? וכן משמע בשאלתות *דמיירי בכל תעניות. ומנהג נמי דאפילו בתענית הרשות משלימין. ובירושלמי נמי אמרינן במסכת תענית בשם רב הונא: אפילו יחיד הגוזר על עצמו בע"ש תענית — מתענה ומשלים! וי"ל: דשפיר מוכח לעיל, דכיון דאמר ר' יוסי מתענה ומשלים, אע"ג דתענית ט' באב לא דחי שבת — ש"מ דדמה שנכנס בשבת כשהוא מעונה לא חשיב כמתענה בשבת. וא"כ בתענית הרשות נמי שרי להשלים. אבל ערב יום טוב דדבריהם — שייך לפלוגי בין תשעה באב לתענית הרשות, דמה שאסור להתענות בערב יו"ט דדבריהם — לאו משום דחשוב כמתענה ביו"ט, דהא לאחריו נמי אסור אף על גב דאין מתענין ביו"ט, אלא משום דעשו חיזוק ביו"ט דדבריהם שלא יבא להתענות ביו"ט עצמו. וכי גזרו — בתענית רשות, אבל בתשעה באב — לא גזרו:

והלכתא

[ברכות כ:]
[תבשיל חד פת כנ"ל רש"ל]
[לפנינו בבכורות איתא רבי צדוק וכן איתא בברכות כז: ועי' תוס' יומא עט: ותוס' סוכה כו: ד"ה נטלו ותוס' חולין קז. ד"ה מאי]
[פרקת כרלאשי' ס"ס א']

הגהות הב"ח

(א) גמ' כשהוא מעונה תניא. תז"מ וג"כ ס"א ותניא: (ב) רש"י ד"ה שאני יום טוב דדבריהם כגון האי:

גליון הש"ס

תוס' ד"ה אי אתם מודים וכו' אע"פ שכבר הפסיק כדאמרינן. עי' תענית דף ל ע"ב תוס' ד"ה כל העושה: בא"ד באיכה רבתי. בפסוק ויגרס בחצץ שני:

רבינו חננאל

טובא והא דתניא ט' באב שחל להיות בערב שבת והביאו לפני ר' עקיבא ביצה מגולגלת בלא מלח וגמאה וכו' קבלה בידינו כי ר' עקיבא באותה שעה מסוכן היה והביאו לפני ר' עקיבא הרופאים לגמוע ביצה מגולגלת בלא מלח באחרית היום ור' יהודה לא דקדק לפי' סמך על מה שראה ולא ידע העיקר מפני מה עשה כך. ופסח דההיא שתא יום ה' היה. ותמוז דההיא שתא מילויי מליוה. לפיכך חל ט' באב להיות בע"ש וחיסרו אב. ובאותה השנה בא ר"ה להיות בשבת וכבר פירשנוהו ביאור זה יפה במס' תענית והא דאמרי' בדורו של ר"ג עבוד כר"ג ואקשינן והתנן א"ר אלעזר ב"ר צדוק אני הייתי מבני סנאב בן בנימין כו' ואסיק' טעמא דיו"ט שלנו ומפני כך לא השלמנו הא ערב יו"ט מתענה ומשלים בט' באב שחל להיות בע"ש: (ור"מ היא) [זו דברי ר"מ] דאמר הכי אבל חכ"א דר"ג אומר מתענה ומשלים וקיי"ל כר' יוסי וכדדרש מר זוטרא משמיה דרב הונא הלכה מתענה ומשלים. פי' דליוה לרטיבא (ופסא ליבחכתיה) [רפסא ליה בדוכתא]. כיון שראה שמרימין עץ לח שאינו ראוי לשרפה. אמר שמא יש לו תחתיו דבר טמון או שמא להכות בו אדם מתכוון לכך שואל מה עסקך וכן כיון שראה *) ומדקדק: ירושלמי מודים חכמים לר' יהודה בב' יו"ט של ר"ה שהן מתקנת נביאים הראשונים מי גרם לי להיות שומר ב' יו"ט בסוריא על שם שלא שמרתי יום אחד בא"י. סבורה אני שמקבלת שכר על השנים ואיני מקבלת שכר אלא על אחד. וה"ה לב' חלות בסוריא ר' יוחנן קרי עלייהו וגם אני נתתי להם חקים לא טובים: **הדרן עלך בכל מערבין**

*) [אינו מובן כוונת ד' רבינו בזה ואולי דחיסור לשון יש כאן וצ"ע].

רב נסים גאון

אמר ר' אלעזר בר' צדוק אני מבני סנאה בן בנימין פעם אחת חל ט' באב להיות בשבת ודחינוהו לאחר שבת והתענינו בו ולא השלמנוהו מפני שיום טוב שלנו היה. עיקרו במס' תעניות בפרק ב' פרקים (דף טו) זמן עצי כהנים והעם בתשעה כו' בה' באב בני פרעוש בן יהודה בשבעה בו בני רכב בן בנימין והיה יום י' של חודש אב יום טוב שלהן שמביאין בו קרבן עצים ולפיכך לא השלימו בו

דְּאִי סָלְקָא דַּעְתָּךְ אַכּוּלְּהוּ. אֲמָרָהּ רַב יְהוּדָה: הָא בָּעֵי מִינֵּיהּ רַבָּה מֵרַב יְהוּדָה. כִּדְאָמְרִינַן לְעֵיל: אֲתָא לְקַמֵּיהּ דְּרַב יְהוּדָה, וְלָא הֲוָה בִּידֵיהּ: מִתְעַנֶּה וּמַשְׁלִים. בְּעֶרֶב שַׁבָּת: הָא בָּעֵי רַבָּה מֵרַב הוּנָא. לְעֵיל, וְלָא פְּשַׁט לֵיהּ: לְבָתַר דִּשְׁמַעָהּ. רַב הוּנָא מֵרַב לְהַאי "אֲבָל חֲכָמִים אוֹמְרִים" הֲדַר אַגְמָרֵיהּ לְמָר זוּטְרָא(א) וּמִקַּמֵּיהּ דְּלִישְׁמְעֵיהּ בְּעָא רַבָּה מִינֵּיהּ וְלָא פְּשַׁט לֵיהּ: הָכָא נַמִי. דְּרַב יְהוּדָה לָא תִּיקְשֵׁי: הָא מִקַּמֵּי דִּשְׁמַעָהּ. מֵרַב: הָא לְבָתַר דִּשְׁמַעָהּ. רַב הוּנָא וְרַב יְהוּדָה תַּלְמִידֵי דְּרַב הָווּ: הָדְרָן עֲלָךְ בַּכֹּל מְעָרְבִין

דְּאִי סָלְקָא דַּעְתָּךְ אַכּוּלְּהוּ — הָא בָּעֵי מִינֵּיהּ רַבָּה מֵרַב יְהוּדָה וְלָא פְּשַׁט לֵיהּ! וּלְטַעְמִיךְ, הָא דְּדָרַשׁ מָר זוּטְרָא מִשְּׁמֵיהּ דְּרַב הוּנָא: הֲלָכָה, מִתְעַנֶּה וּמַשְׁלִים. הָא בְּעָא מִינֵּיהּ רַבָּה מֵרַב הוּנָא וְלָא פְּשַׁט לֵיהּ! אֶלָּא: הָא — מִקַּמֵּי דִּשְׁמַעָהּ, וְהָא — לְבָתַר דִּשְׁמַעָהּ. הָכָא נַמִי, הָא — מִקַּמֵּי דִּשְׁמַעָהּ, הָא — לְבָתַר דִּשְׁמַעָהּ. *דָּרַשׁ מָר זוּטְרָא מִשְּׁמֵיהּ דְּרַב הוּנָא: אהֲלָכָה, מִתְעַנִּין וּמַשְׁלִימִין.§

הָדְרָן עֲלָךְ בַּכֹּל מְעָרְבִין

מִי בשֶׁהוֹצִיאוּהוּ נָכְרִים אוֹ רוּחַ רָעָה — אֵין לוֹ אֶלָּא ד' אַמּוֹת. הֶחֱזִירוּהוּ — כְּאִילּוּ לֹא יָצָא. הוֹלִיכוּהוּ לְעִיר אַחֶרֶת, נְתָנוּהוּ בְּדִיר אוֹ בְּסַהַר, ר"ג וְר' אֶלְעָזָר בֶּן עֲזַרְיָה אוֹמְרִים: גמְהַלֵּךְ אֶת כּוּלָּהּ. רַבִּי יְהוֹשֻׁעַ וְר"ע אוֹמְרִים: אֵין לוֹ אֶלָּא ד' אַמּוֹת.§ מַעֲשֶׂה שֶׁבָּאוּ *מִפְּלַנְדְּרְסִין וְהִפְלִיגָה סְפִינָתָם בַּיָּם, דר"ג וְרַבִּי אֶלְעָזָר בֶּן עֲזַרְיָה הִלְּכוּ אֶת כּוּלָּהּ, ר' יְהוֹשֻׁעַ וְר"ע לֹא זָזוּ מִד"א, שֶׁרָצוּ לְהַחְמִיר עַל עַצְמָן. פַּעַם אַחַת לֹא נִכְנְסוּ לַנָּמֵל עַד שֶׁחֲשֵׁיכָה, אָמְרוּ לוֹ לְרַבָּן גַּמְלִיאֵל: מָה אָנוּ לֵירֵד? אָמַר לָהֶם: *מוּתָּרִים אַתֶּם, שֶׁכְּבָר הָיִיתִי מִסְתַּכֵּל וְהָיִינוּ בְּתוֹךְ הַתְּחוּם עַד שֶׁלֹּא חֲשֵׁיכָה.§ גמ' ת"ר: ג' דְּבָרִים מַעֲבִירִין אֶת הָאָדָם עַל דַּעְתּוֹ וְעַל דַּעַת קוֹנוֹ, אֵלּוּ הֵן: נָכְרִים וְרוּחַ רָעָה, וְדִקְדּוּקֵי עֲנִיּוּת. לְמַאי נָפְקָא מִינָּהּ? לְמִיבְעֵי רַחֲמֵי עֲלַיְיהוּ. ג' אֵין רוֹאִין פְּנֵי גֵיהִנָּם, אֵלּוּ הֵן: דִּקְדּוּקֵי עֲנִיּוּת וְחוֹלֵי מֵעַיִין וְהָרָשׁוּת. וְיֵשׁ אוֹמְרִים: אַף מִי שֶׁיֵּשׁ לוֹ אִשָּׁה רָעָה. וְאִידָךְ — אִשָּׁה רָעָה מִצְוָה לְגָרְשָׁהּ. וְאִידָךְ — *זִימְנִין דִּכְתוּבָּתָהּ מְרוּבָּה. אִי נַמִי: אִית לֵיהּ בָּנִים מִינָּהּ, וְלָא מָצֵי מְגָרֵשׁ לָהּ. לְמַאי נָפְקָא מִינָּהּ? לְקַבּוֹלֵי מֵאַהֲבָה. שְׁלֹשָׁה מֵתִין כְּשֶׁהֵן מְסַפְּרִין, וְאֵלּוּ הֵן: חוֹלֵי מֵעַיִין, וְחַיָּה, וְהִדְרוֹקָן. לְמַאי נָפְקָא מִינָּהּ? לְמַשְׁמוֹשֵׁי בְּהוּ *זַוְודְתָא.§ אָמַר רַב נַחְמָן, אָמַר שְׁמוּאֵל: יָצָא לָדַעַת — אֵין לוֹ אֶלָּא אַרְבַּע אַמּוֹת. פְּשִׁיטָא! הַשְׁתָּא מִי שֶׁהוֹצִיאוּהוּ נָכְרִים אֵין לוֹ אֶלָּא ד' אַמּוֹת, יָצָא לָדַעַת מִיבַּעְיָא?! אֶלָּא האֵימָא: חָזַר לָדַעַת — אֵין לוֹ אֶלָּא ד"א. הָא נַמִי תְּנֵינָא: הֶחֱזִירוּהוּ נָכְרִים — כְּאִילּוּ לֹא יָצָא. הֶחֱזִירוּהוּ הוּא דִּכְאִילּוּ לֹא יָצָא, אֲבָל הוֹצִיאוּהוּ נָכְרִים וְחָזַר לָדַעַת — אֵין לוֹ אֶלָּא ד"א! אֶלָּא אֵימָא: ויָצָא לָדַעַת וְהֶחֱזִירוּהוּ נָכְרִים — אֵין לוֹ אֶלָּא ד"א. הָא נַמִי תְּנֵינָא: הוֹצִיאוּהוּ וְהֶחֱזִירוּהוּ — כְּאִילּוּ לֹא יָצָא. הוֹצִיאוּהוּ וְהֶחֱזִירוּהוּ הוּא דִּכְאִילּוּ לֹא יָצָא, אֲבָל יָצָא לָדַעַת — לֹא. זמַהוּ דְּתֵימָא: לַצְּדָדִין קָתָנֵי: מִי שֶׁהוֹצִיאוּהוּ נָכְרִים וְחָזַר לָדַעַת — אֵין לוֹ אֶלָּא ד' אַמּוֹת, אֲבָל יָצָא לָדַעַת וְהֶחֱזִירוּהוּ נָכְרִים — כְּאִילּוּ לֹא יָצָא, קמ"ל. בָּעוּ מִינֵּיהּ מֵרַבָּה: הוּצְרַךְ לִנְקָבָיו מַהוּ? אָמַר לָהֶם: *חגָּדוֹל כְּבוֹד הַבְּרִיּוֹת שֶׁדּוֹחֶה אֶת לֹא תַעֲשֶׂה שֶׁבַּתּוֹרָה. אָמְרִי נְהַרְדְּעֵי: *טאִי פִּיקֵּחַ הוּא — עָיֵיל לִתְחוּמָא, וְכֵיוָן דְּעָל — עָל. א"ר פָּפָּא: פֵּירוֹת שֶׁיָּצְאוּ חוּץ לַתְּחוּם וְחָזְרוּ, יאֲפִילּוּ בְּמֵזִיד — לֹא הִפְסִידוּ אֶת מְקוֹמָן. מ"ט — אֲנוּסִין נִינְהוּ. אֵיתִיבֵיהּ רַב יוֹסֵף בַּר שְׁמַעְיָה לְרַב פָּפָּא: ר' נְחֶמְיָה וְר' אֱלִיעֶזֶר בֶּן יַעֲקֹב אוֹמְרִים: לְעוֹלָם אֲסוּרִין, עַד שֶׁיַּחְזְרוּ לִמְקוֹמָן שׁוֹגְגִין. בְּשׁוֹגֵג — אִין, בְּמֵזִיד — לָא! תַּנָּאֵי הִיא, דְּתַנְיָא: כפֵּירוֹת שֶׁיָּצְאוּ חוּץ לַתְּחוּם, בְּשׁוֹגֵג — יֵאָכְלוּ, בְּמֵזִיד — לֹא יֵאָכְלוּ.

רַבִּי

רש"י

מִי שֶׁהוֹצִיאוּהוּ נָכְרִים. חוּץ לַתְּחוּם: אוֹ רוּחַ רָעָה. שֶׁנִּכְנַס בּוֹ שֵׁד, וְנִטְרְפָה דַּעְתּוֹ, וְיָצָא חוּץ לַתְּחוּם. וְאַחַר כָּךְ נִשְׁתַּפָּה, וַהֲרֵי הוּא חוּץ לַתְּחוּם: הֶחֱזִירוּהוּ. לְתוֹךְ הַתְּחוּם: כְּאִילּוּ לֹא יָצָא. וַהֲרֵי כָּל הָעִיר לוֹ כְּד' אַמּוֹת כְּבַתְּחִילָּה, וְחוּצָה לָהּ אַלְפַּיִם אַמָּה לְכָל רוּחַ: הוֹלִיכוּהוּ לְעִיר אַחֶרֶת. וַהֲרֵי הִיא מוּקֶּפֶת מְחִיצּוֹת: אוֹ שֶׁנְּתָנוּהוּ בְּדִיר אוֹ בְּסַהַר. שֶׁהֵן מוּקָּפִין, וְהֶיקֵּיפָן גָּדוֹל: מְהַלֵּךְ אֶת כּוּלָּהּ. דְּהוֹאִיל וּמוּקֶּפֶת מְחִיצּוֹת, הֲרֵי הִיא כְּד' אַמּוֹת: מִפְּלַנְדְּרְסִין. שֵׁם מָקוֹם: וְהִפְלִיגָה. כְּשֶׁהִיא מִתְרַחֶקֶת מִשְּׂפַת הַיָּם וְנִכְנֶסֶת לָאֶמְצָעִי קָרֵי לֵיהּ הַפְלָגָה. וּלְשׁוֹן לע"ז הוּא, שֶׁקּוֹרִין לִשְׁלוּלִית הַיָּם פיל"ג: הִלְּכוּ אֶת כּוּלָּהּ. הָיוּ מְהַלְּכִין בְּכָל הַסְּפִינָה, דְּאַעַ"פ שֶׁהַסְּפִינָה הוֹלֶכֶת בַּשַּׁבָּת וְיָצְאוּ חוּץ לַתְּחוּם — הָווּ כְּמִי שֶׁיָּצָא חוּץ לַתְּחוּם וְנִיתַּן בְּדִיר אוֹ בְּסַהַר, שֶׁהַסְּפִינָה מְחִיצּוֹת לָהּ: שֶׁרָצוּ לְהַחְמִיר. בַּגְּמָרָא מְפָרֵשׁ: לַנָּמֵל. פורט"ו בלע"ז. שֶׁשָּׁם הַסְּפִינוֹת יוֹצְאוֹת מִן הַיָּם לִשְׂפָתוֹ: מַה אָנוּ לֵירֵד. מִן הַסְּפִינָה לְתוֹךְ הָעִיר, כְּלוֹמַר: בָּאנוּ מִחוּץ לַתְּחוּם מִשֶּׁחֲשֵׁיכָה: גמ' וְהָרָשׁוּת. מִי שֶׁיֵּשׁ לוֹ נוֹגְשִׂין: לְקַבְּלִינְהוּ מֵאַהֲבָה. דִּמְכַפְּרֵי עֲלֵיהּ: כְּשֶׁהֵן מְסַפְּרִים. אַף עַל פִּי שֶׁיֵּשׁ בָּהֶן חִיּוּת הַרְבֵּה, שֶׁמְּדַבְּרִים — אעפ"כ מֵתִין פִּתְאוֹם: הִדְרוֹקָן. חוֹלִי הַפֶּה(ב), מוּסג"א: זַוְודְתָא. לְזַמֵּן תַּכְרִיכִין: חָזַר לָדַעַת. מִי שֶׁהוֹלִיאוּהוּ נָכְרִים וְחָזַר לָדַעַת לְתוֹךְ הַתְּחוּם — לָא הָוֵי כְּהֶחֱזִירוּהוּ דִּתְנַן בְּמַתְנִיתִין כְּאִילּוּ לֹא יָצָא: מַהוּ דְּתֵימָא. מַתְנִי' לַצְּדָדִין קָתָנֵי, וְהֶחֱזִירוּהוּ דְּסֵיפָא — מִילְּתָא בְּאַפֵּי נַפְשֵׁיהּ הִיא, וְלָאו אַהוֹצִיאוּהוּ נָכְרִים קָאֵי. וְהָכִי קָאָמַר: מִי שֶׁהוֹצִיאוּהוּ נָכְרִים, בֵּין כְּשֶׁהוּא עוֹמֵד בַּחוּץ בֵּין שֶׁחָזַר לָדַעַת — אֵין לוֹ אֶלָּא ד' אַמּוֹת. וּמִי שֶׁהָיָה חוּץ לַתְּחוּם וְהֶחֱזִירוּהוּ נָכְרִים, בֵּין שֶׁהָיְתָה יְצִיאָתוֹ רִאשׁוֹנָה לָדַעַת בֵּין שֶׁלֹּא לָדַעַת אֶלָּא בְּאוֹנֶס — הָוֵי כְּאִילּוּ לֹא יָצָא: קמ"ל. ר"נ דְּסֵיפָא דְּמַתְנִיתִין אַרֵישָׁא מְהַדַּר: הוּצְרַךְ לִנְקָבָיו. זֶה שֶׁהוֹלִיאוּהוּ נָכְרִים, מַהוּ לָצֵאת מִד' אַמּוֹתָיו: אֶת לֹא תַעֲשֶׂה שֶׁבַּתּוֹרָה. לָאו דְּ"לֹא תָסוּר" (דברים יז), וּתְחוּמִין נַמִי דְּרַבָּנַן: אִי פִּיקֵּחַ הוּא. הַאי דְּנִצְרָךְ לִנְקָבָיו וְיָהֲבוּ לֵיהּ רַבָּנַן רְשׁוּת לְמֵיפַק חוּץ לְאַרְבַּע אַמּוֹתָיו: עָיֵיל לִתְחוּמָא וְכֵיוָן דְּעָל עָל. וּמוּתָּר כְּאִילּוּ לֹא יָצָא, דְּהָא בִּרְשׁוּת עָל, וְלָא גָּרַע מֵהֶחֱזִירוּהוּ: פֵּירוֹת שֶׁיָּצְאוּ חוּץ לַתְּחוּם וְחָזְרוּ. בְּיוֹם טוֹב, לֹא הִפְסִידוּ מְקוֹמָן, וְכָל הָעִיר לָהֶן כְּד' אַמּוֹת. וְיֵשׁ לָהֶן לְכָל רוּחַ אַלְפַּיִם אַמָּה אִם יו"ט הוּא, וְאִי שַׁבָּת — מוּתָּרִין לַאֲכִילָה בַּמָּקוֹם שֶׁחָזְרוּ: אֲנוּסִים הָיוּ. עַל יְדֵי הַמּוֹלִיכָן: אֲסוּרִין. לָזוּז אוֹתָן מֵאַרְבַּע אַמּוֹתֵיהֶן, וְלֹא לְאוֹכְלָן אֲפִילּוּ חָזְרוּ, אֶלָּא אִם כֵּן חָזְרוּ שׁוֹגְגִין, אֲבָל מֵזִיד — לֹא: הָכִי גָּרְסִינַן: תַּנָּאֵי הִיא, דְּתַנְיָא: פֵּירוֹת שֶׁיָּצְאוּ חוּץ לַתְּחוּם בְּשׁוֹגֵג — יֵאָכְלוּ. וְלָא גָּרְסִינַן הָכָא "וְחָזְרוּ": בְּשׁוֹגֵג יֵאָכְלוּ. בַּמָּקוֹם שֶׁהֵן שָׁם, אִם יֵשׁ אָדָם שֶׁעֵירֵב לְאוֹתוֹ צַד, אוֹ שֶׁהָיוּ בְּנֵי עִיר אַחֶרֶת סְמוּכִים:

רַבִּי

תוספות

והלכתא מתענה ומשלים. פירוש: אם ירלה להשלים, דשרי להשלים. דבעיא הוא אי שרי להשלים אי לא:

[ומורי אמר לי בשם ה"ר ידידיה: דאפילו ר' יוסי ל"פ אלא דיכול להשלים, מיהו, גם ר' יוסי מודה אי אינו רוצה להשלים — הרשות בידו. ור' יהודה אמר אסור להשלים. ואין נ"ל. מדקאמר ר' יוסי: אי אתה מודה לי בט' באב שחל להיות באחד בשבת שהוא מתחיל מבע"י. והתם ע"כ דחייב קאמר, דומיא דהכי ע"ש דחייב להשלים קאמר.] [רש"ל בשם תוס' שאנ"ץ]:

הדרן עלך בכל מערבין

מי שהוציאוהו. על דעתו ועל דעת קונו. ואע"ג דאיכא נמי כשפים, שמכחישין פמליא של מעלה — נראה דהוי בכלל רוח רעה. ויצר הרע אע"ג דמשמע בפ' "ואלו מגלחין" (מו"ק ד' ח.) דפעמים שילרו מתגבר עליו ואינו יכול לכופו — מ"מ אדם יכול ליזהר שלא יבא לידי כך: **הרשות.** פי' רבינו חננאל: עול מלכות גוים, כדאמר במסכת אבות (פ"ב מ"ג): הוו זהירין ברשות. ורש"י פירש: נושה. **לצדדין** קתני. אחזר לדעת לא רצה לתרץ כך לצדדין קתני — דסוף סוף אהחזירוהו צ"ל לעולם לצדדין קתני. (ועוד:) דניחא ליה לפרש שיתקיימו דברי רב נחמן הראשונים. **לא** הפסידו את מקומן. אע"ג דהכא מחוץ לתחום אסור למי שנשתלח לו — הני מילי התם דאיתיה חוץ לתחום, אבל הכא דהשתא הם במקומן — שרי אפילו להאי דאפקה. ולא דמי למבשל בשבת *במזיד לא יאכל — דהתם הוי איסור דאורייתא: **במזיד** לא יאכלו. משמע: לשום אדם לא יאכלו, ואף על גב דהכא בשביל ישראל זה מותר לישראל אחר, כיון שנעשה איסור על ידי ישראל — החמירו:

מכלל

עין משפט נר מצוה

קיא א מיי' פ"א מהל' תעניות הל"ו טוש"ע א"ח סי' רמט סעיף ד:

א ב מיי' פכ"ז מהלכות שבת הלכה יב סמג לאוין סו טור ש"ע א"ח סי' תה סעיף ה:

ב ג מיי' שם טוש"ע שם סעיף ו:

ג ד מיי' שם הלכה יג טוש"ע שם סעיף ז:

ד ה מיי' שם הלכה יב טוש"ע שם סעיף ה:

ה ו ז מיי' שם הלכה יג טוש"ע שם סעיף ח:

ו ח ט מיי' שם הלכה טו סמג שם טור ש"ע א"ח סי' תו:

ז י כ מיי' פ"ה מהלכות י"ט הלכה י טוש"ע א"ח סי' תה סעיף ט:

ר"מ מ"ז

שבת לח.

[וז"ל רש"י בע"ז יז. ד"ה כזוודתא תכריכין לידה לדרך (בראשית מב) מתרגמינן זוודין לאורחא ותכריכין הן לידה לדרך למתים עכ"ל]

רבינו חננאל

פ"ד מי שהוציאוהו גוים או רוח רעה אין לו אלא ד' אמות. החזירוהו כאלו לא יצא כו': גוים ורוח רעה ועניות מעבירין את האדם על דעתו ועל דעת המקום. פי' גוים ורוח רעה כופין אותו בעל כרחו. עניות נמי דכתיב פן אורש וגנבתי למאי נפקא מיניה לבקש רחמים ויצילהו הקב"ה מהן ועוד דקדוקי עניות וחולי מעים והרשות כיון שיש להן יסורין בעוה"ז אין רואין פני גיהנם. וי"א אף מי שיש לו אשה רעה למנ"מ לקבולי מאהבה. פי' הרשות עבודת השרים והשלטונים. זוותא תכריכין. אמר רב נחמן אמר שמואל יצא לדעת אין לו אלא ד' אמות אסיקנא היכא דיצא לדעת אע"פ שהחזירוהו גוים בע"כ כיון דיציאתו לדעת היתה אין לו אלא ד' אמות. בעו מיניה מרבא כיון דתנן מי שהוציאוהו גוים או רוח רעה אין לו אלא ד' אמות אם הוצרך לנקביו פי' השתנת מים והוצאת רעי מה יעשה ופשיט ליה יצא חוץ ויעשה צרכיו הגדול כבוד הבריות שדוחה את ל"ת שבתורה שנאמר באבדה (אחר) [במקום אחד] לא תוכל להתעלם וכת' והתעלמת מהם ואמרו חכמים פעמים שאתה מתעלם. כיצד זקן ואינו לפי כבודו. הנה התירה התורה לזקן להתעלם ואע"ג דכתיב בה לאו. אמרי נהרדעי ואם זה שהוצרך לנקביו הוא חכם ויודע שהנכנס בתחומו אפי' מזיד כיון שתחלתו אנוס הוא אם חזר בתחומו כאילו לא יצא ויש לו אלפים אמה לכל רוח וילך ויעשה צרכיו באותו מקום שיצא ממנו ואם יזדמן לו ליכנס בתחומו ונכנס בתחומו ישב שם ודומה כאילו הגוים החזירוהו ויש לו אלפים אמה לכל רוח וזהו פי' כיון דעל על ואמר רב פפא פירות שיצאו חוץ לתחום וחזרו אפילו במזיד לא הפסידו את מקומן. מ"ט אנוסים נינהו כלומר לאו בני דעה נינהו ומותבי על רב פפא מדברי ר' נחמיה ור' אליעזר בן יעקב ופריק תנאי היא דתניא פירות שיצאו חוץ לתחום וחזרו כו' ואסיקנא דכ"ע מזיד לא והכא בשוגג שלא במקומן פליגי ת"ק סבר דשוגג שלא במקומו שרי

מסורת הש"ס

תענית יח:

[גי' הערוך מפרנדסין וכן איתא במשנה שבמשניות]

[ועי' תוס' לקמן מג: ד"ה מותרין]

[עירובין קג:]

ברכות יט: שבת פא: לג: מנחות לז: [מגילה ג:]

הגהות הב"ח

(א) רש"י ד"ה לבתר וכו' למר זוטרא מקמי דשמעה ובעא רבה: (ב) רש"י ד"ה הדרוקן חולי הפה. נ"ב במס' שבת פרק במה מדליקין דף לג מבואר להדיא שהיא חולי הבטן וז"ל הגמ' שם שנדון בהדרוקן שנא' ומכות חדרי בטן ע"כ:

גליון הש"ס

גמ' אי פקח הוא. עי' לקמן דף מד ע"ב תוס' ד"ה ומר סבר: רש"י ד"ה הוליכוהו לעיר אחרת וכו' מוקפת מחיצות. עי' לקמן דף מז ע"ב בתוס' ד"ה לסולה:

רב נסים גאון

מי שהוציאוהו אמר להו גדול כבוד הבריות שדוחה את לא תעשה שבתורה. כבר פירשנוהו למעלה דהני מילי בלאו דלא תסור אבל לאו דאורייתא לא דחי ופירושו בברכות בפרק מי שמתו מוטל לפניו (דף יט) וקא פריש' טיבן של דברים לשעבר: סליק בכל מערבין ניהלן כבר אמרתה את אביי ליה אמר שמעתא הא לי שמיעא לא יוסף רב אמר התענית. בו

רַבִּי נְחֶמְיָה אוֹמֵר: בִּמְקוֹמָן — יֵאָכְלוּ, שֶׁלֹּא בִּמְקוֹמָן — לֹא יֵאָכְלוּ. מַאי בִּמְקוֹמָן? אִילֵימָא בִּמְקוֹמָן בְּמֵזִיד, וְהָא קָתָנֵי בְּהֶדְיָא: רַבִּי נְחֶמְיָה וְרַבִּי אֱלִיעֶזֶר בֶּן יַעֲקֹב אוֹמְרִים: לְעוֹלָם אֲסוּרִין עַד שֶׁיַּחְזְרוּ לִמְקוֹמָן שׁוֹגְגִין. בְּשׁוֹגֵג — אִין, בְּמֵזִיד — לָא! אֶלָּא לָאו בִּמְקוֹמָן בְּשׁוֹגֵג, וְחַסּוֹרֵי מִחַסְּרָא וְהָכִי קָתָנֵי: פֵּירוֹת שֶׁיָּצְאוּ חוּץ לַתְּחוּם, בְּשׁוֹגֵג — יֵאָכְלוּ, בְּמֵזִיד — לֹא יֵאָכְלוּ. בַּמֶּה דְּבָרִים אֲמוּרִים — שֶׁלֹּא בִּמְקוֹמָן, אֲבָל בִּמְקוֹמָן — אֲפִילּוּ בְּמֵזִיד יֵאָכְלוּ. וַאֲתָא ר' נְחֶמְיָה לְמֵימַר; אֲפִי' בִּמְקוֹמָן נַמִי, בְּשׁוֹגֵג — אִין, בְּמֵזִיד — לָא! לָא, בְּמֵזִיד בִּמְקוֹמָן — דְּכוּלֵּי עָלְמָא לָא פְּלִיגִי דְּאָסוּר. וְהָכָא — בְּשׁוֹגֵג שֶׁלֹּא בִּמְקוֹמָן פְּלִיגִי. תַּנָּא קַמָּא סָבַר: בְּשׁוֹגֵג שָׁרֵי שֶׁלֹּא בִּמְקוֹמָן, וְרַבִּי נְחֶמְיָה סָבַר: אֲפִילּוּ שׁוֹגֵג, בִּמְקוֹמָן — אִין, שֶׁלֹּא בִּמְקוֹמָן — לָא. וְהָא מִדְּקָתָנֵי סֵיפָא: רַבִּי נְחֶמְיָה וְרַבִּי אֱלִיעֶזֶר בֶּן יַעֲקֹב אוֹמְרִים: לְעוֹלָם אֲסוּרִין עַד שֶׁיַּחְזְרוּ לִמְקוֹמָן שׁוֹגְגִין. שׁוֹגֵג — אִין, בְּמֵזִיד — לָא. מִכְּלָל דְּת"ק סָבַר: בְּמֵזִיד נַמִי שָׁרֵי, שְׁמַע מִינַּהּ.§ אָמַר רַב נַחְמָן, אָמַר שְׁמוּאֵל: הָיָה מְהַלֵּךְ וְאֵינוֹ יוֹדֵעַ תְּחוּם שַׁבָּת — [א]מְהַלֵּךְ אַלְפַּיִם פְּסִיעוֹת בֵּינוֹנִיּוֹת, וְזוֹ הִיא תְּחוּם שַׁבָּת. וְאָמַר רַב נַחְמָן, אָמַר שְׁמוּאֵל: [ב]שָׁבַת בְּבִקְעָה, וְהִקִּיפוּהָ נָכְרִים מְחִיצָה בַּשַּׁבָּת — מְהַלֵּךְ אַלְפַּיִם אַמָּה, וּמְטַלְטֵל בְּכוּלָּהּ עַל יְדֵי זְרִיקָה. וְרַב הוּנָא אָמַר: מְהַלֵּךְ אַלְפַּיִם אַמָּה וּמְטַלְטֵל ד' אַמּוֹת. וְנִיטַּלְטֵל בְּכוּלָּהּ עַל יְדֵי זְרִיקָה! שֶׁמָּא יִמָּשֵׁךְ אַחַר חֶפְצוֹ. בְּאַלְפַּיִם מִיהַת לִיטַּלְטֵל כִּי אוֹרְחֵיהּ! מִשּׁוּם דְּהָוֵי כִּמְחִיצָה שֶׁנִּפְרְצָה בִּמְלוֹאָהּ לְמָקוֹם הָאָסוּר לָהּ. חִיָּיא בַּר רַב אָמַר: מְהַלֵּךְ אַלְפַּיִם אַמָּה, וּמְטַלְטֵל בְּאַלְפַּיִם אַמָּה. כְּמַאן? דְּלָא כְּרַב נַחְמָן וְלָא כְּרַב הוּנָא! אֵימָא: מְטַלְטֵל בְּאַרְבַּע. אִי הָכִי הַיְינוּ דְּרַב הוּנָא! אֵימָא: וְכֵן אָמַר רַבִּי חִיָּיא בַּר רַב. א"ל רַב נַחְמָן לְרַב הוּנָא: לָא תִּיפְלוֹג עֲלֵיהּ דִּשְׁמוּאֵל, דְּתַנְיָא כְּוָותֵיהּ. דְּתַנְיָא:
הָיָה

רַבִּי נְחֶמְיָה אוֹמֵר בִּמְקוֹמָן. אִם חָזְרוּ לִמְקוֹמָן — יֵאָכְלוּ. אֲבָל שֶׁלֹּא בִּמְקוֹמָן, כָּל זְמַן שֶׁהֵן חוּץ לַתְּחוּם — לֹא יֵאָכְלוּ: מַאי בִּמְקוֹמָן. דְּשָׁרֵי רַבִּי נְחֶמְיָה, הֵיכִי חָזְרוּ: אִי נֵימָא. אֲפִילּוּ בְּמֵזִיד, דְּחָשֵׁיב לְהוּ אֲנוּסִין וְהָוֵי כְּהוֹצִיאוּהוּ נָכְרִים וְהֶחֱזִירוּהוּ: וְהָתַנְיָא. אַחֲרִיתִי בְּהֶדְיָא: רַבִּי אֱלִיעֶזֶר וְרַבִּי נְחֶמְיָה אָמְרֵי לְעוֹלָם אֲסוּרִין כו': אֶלָּא לָאו. עַל כָּרְחָךְ הַאי בִּמְקוֹמָן — בְּשׁוֹגֵג קָאָמַר, מִכְּלָל דְּת"ק אַף בְּמֵזִיד שָׁרֵי הֵיכָא דְּחָזְרוּ, וְתַרְתֵּי קוּלָּא אִית לֵיהּ: וְחַסּוֹרֵי מִחַסְּרָא כו' שֶׁלֹּא בִּמְקוֹמָן. שֶׁלֹּא חָזְרוּ הוּא דִּבְמֵזִיד לֹא יֵאָכְלוּ, אִם יָצְאוּ בְּמֵזִיד, אֲבָל חָזְרוּ בִּמְקוֹמָן (וְהֵוּ) — בְּמֵזִיד נַמִי יֵאָכְלוּ: וַאֲתָא רַבִּי נְחֶמְיָה לְמֵימַר. הַאי "בְּשׁוֹגֵג — יֵאָכְלוּ, בְּמֵזִיד — לֹא יֵאָכְלוּ" דְּקָאָמַר, אַשֶּׁלֹּא בִּמְקוֹמָן — אֵינוֹ כֵּן, אֶלָּא אַמְּקוֹמָן אִיתְּמַר. דְּאִם חָזְרוּ לִמְקוֹמָן בְּשׁוֹגֵג — יֵאָכְלוּ, אִם בְּמֵזִיד — לֹא יֵאָכְלוּ. וְת"ק אִית לֵיהּ דְּרַב פַּפָּא: לֹא בְּמֵזִיד. אֲפִי' בִּמְקוֹמָן, לְת"ק אָסוּר. וּמַתְנִי' לָא תְּחַסַּר' אֶלָּא כִּדְקָתָנֵי. דְּלָא אַיְירֵי תַּנָּא קַמָּא בַּחֲזָרָה כְּלָל, וְרַבִּי נְחֶמְיָה אַשֶּׁלֹּא בִּמְקוֹמָן אֲתָא לְאִפְלוּגֵי. דְּקָאָמַר תַּנָּא קַמָּא שׁוֹגֵג יֵאָכְלוּ, וַאֲתָא רַבִּי נְחֶמְיָה לְמֵימַר הַאי חִילּוּק דְּיָהַבְתְּ בֵּין שׁוֹגֵג לְמֵזִיד — לָאו אַשֶּׁלֹּא בִּמְקוֹמָן אִיתְּמַר, אֶלָּא בִּמְקוֹמָן. וְהָכִי קָאָמַר ר' נְחֶמְיָה: חָזְרוּ בִּמְקוֹמָן יֵאָכְלוּ — בְּהַאי שׁוֹגֵג דְּקָאָמְרַתְּ, אֲבָל שֶׁלֹּא בִּמְקוֹמָן — אֲפִילּוּ בְּשׁוֹגֵג לֹא יֵאָכְלוּ: וְהָא מִדְּתָנֵי. בְּהַךְ אַחֲרִיתִי לְעוֹלָם אֲסוּרִין כו' — מִכְּלָל דִּבְתַרְתֵּי פְּלִיגִי. וְתַנָּא קַמָּא בְּמֵזִיד בִּמְקוֹמָן נַמִי שָׁרֵי, דְּאִי חֲדָא קוּלָּא הוּא דְּמֵיקֵל וְר' נְחֶמְיָה בְּהַהוּא הוּא דְּפָלֵיג — הָכִי אִיבָּעֵי לֵיהּ לְמִיתְנֵי, כִּדְתָנָ' בְּקַמַּיְיתָא: בִּמְקוֹמָן — יֵאָכְלוּ, שֶׁלֹּא בִּמְקוֹמָן — לֹא יֵאָכְלוּ, וַאֲנָא יָדַעְנָא דְּאַשּׁוֹגֵג דְּשָׁרֵי תַּנָּא קַמָּא שֶׁלֹּא בִּמְקוֹמָן, קָאָתָא רַבִּי נְחֶמְיָה לְמֵימַר, הָא דְּשׁוֹגֵג דְּשָׁרֵי בִּמְקוֹמָן הוּא דְּשָׁרֵי, שֶׁלֹּא בִּמְקוֹמָן לֹא. וּמִדִּתְנַן לְעוֹלָם אֲסוּרִין עַד שֶׁיַּחְזְרוּ שׁוֹגְגִין — שְׁמַע מִינָּהּ: [(א)]לְת"ק דְּשָׁרֵי הֵיכָא דְּאִיכָּא חֲדָא לְהֶתֵּירָא, כְּגוֹן שׁוֹגֵג שֶׁלֹּא בִּמְקוֹמָן אוֹ מֵזִיד בִּמְקוֹמָן, כֵּיוָן דְּאִיכָּא חֲדָא לְטִיבוּתָא. וְקָאָמַר רַבִּי נְחֶמְיָה: לְעוֹלָם אֲסוּרִים עַד דְּאִיכָּא תַּרְתֵּי לְהֶתֵּירָא — שׁוֹגֵג וּבִמְקוֹמָן, וּלְעוֹלָם תַּנָּאֵי הִיא: פְּסִיעָה בֵּינוֹנִית. דֶּרֶךְ הֲלִיכָתוֹ שֶׁל אָדָם אַמָּה: שָׁבַת בְּבִקְעָה. יֵשׁ לוֹ מִמְּקוֹמוֹ אַלְפַּיִם אַמָּה לְכָל רוּחַ: וְהִקִּיפוּהָ נָכְרִים מְחִיצוֹת בַּשַּׁבָּת. וּלְדִירָה כְּגוֹן שֶׁהִקִּיפוּהָ לָדוּר בְּתוֹכָהּ דְּאִי לָאו הָכִי, בְּיוֹתֵר מִבֵּית סָאתַיִם לָא מִשְׁתַּרְיָא לְטַלְטוּלֵי בָּהּ אֶלָּא ד' אַמּוֹת: מְהַלֵּךְ בָּהּ אַלְפַּיִם. דְּלָא מְהַנֵּי לֵיהּ הָנָךְ מְחִיצוֹת לִהְיוֹתָהּ לוֹ כְּד' אַמּוֹת. דְּכִי אָמְרִינַן כָּל הַבַּיִת כּוּלּוֹ כְּד' אַמּוֹת — הֵיכָא דְּשָׁבַת בָּאֲוִיר מְחִיצוֹת מִבְּעוֹד יוֹם, אֲבָל הָכָא דִּבְשָׁעַת שְׁבִיתָה לָא הָווּ מְחִיצוֹת — לָא. וַאֲפִי' לְרַבָּן גַּמְלִיאֵל, דְּאָמַר בְּהוֹצִיאוּהוּ נָכְרִים וּנְתָנוּהוּ בְּדִיר אוֹ בְּסַהַר, דְּאַע"ג דְּלָא שָׁבַת בַּאֲוִיר מְחִיצוֹת נַעֲשִׂית לוֹ כְּאַרְבַּע אַמּוֹת, וּמְהַלֵּךְ אֶת כּוּלָּהּ — הָתָם הוּא דְּמֵי שֶׁהוֹצִיאוּהוּ נָכְרִים אֵין לוֹ אֶלָּא אַרְבַּע אַמּוֹת — הֵקִילּוּ חֲכָמִים אֶצְלוֹ לִהְיוֹת לוֹ הֶיקֵּף מְחִיצוֹת כְּאַרְבַּע אַמּוֹת. אֲבָל הַקּוֹנֶה שְׁבִיתָה, שֶׁיֵּשׁ לוֹ אַלְפַּיִם אַמָּה — לֹא הֵקִילּוּ חֲכָמִים אֶצְלוֹ לִהְיוֹת לוֹ הֶיקֵּף מְחִיצוֹת כְּאַרְבַּע אַמּוֹת, אֶלָּא אִם כֵּן שָׁבַת בַּאֲוִירָן. וְתֵדַע, דְּהָא רַב הוּנָא וְחִיָּיא בַּר רַב תַּלְמִידֵי דְּרַב נִינְהוּ, וְאָמַר רַב: הֲלָכָה כְּרַבָּן גַּמְלִיאֵל בְּדִיר וְסַהַר, וְהָכָא אָסְרֵי כִּשְׁמוּאֵל. וּבְמַתְנִי' נַמִי הָכִי תְּנַן לְקַמָּן, בְּפֶרֶק "כֵּיצַד מְעַבְּרִין" (דף סא.): וּמוֹדֶה שֶׁאָמְרוּ נוֹתְנִין לוֹ אַלְפַּיִם אַמָּה — אֲפִילּוּ סוֹף מִדָּתוֹ כָּלָה בִּמְעָרָה, אֵינָהּ לוֹ כְּאַרְבַּע אַמּוֹת. וְאִילּוּ הוֹצִיאוּהוּ נָכְרִים וּנְתָנוּהוּ בָּהּ — מְהַלֵּךְ אֶת כּוּלָּהּ, וְהָא דִּבְרֵי הַכֹּל הִיא: וּמְטַלְטֵל בְּכוּלָּהּ. אֲפִי' חוּץ לְאַלְפַּיִם שֶׁאֵין לוֹ רְשׁוּת לְהַלֵּךְ — מוּתָּר לְטַלְטֵל ע"י זְרִיקָה. כְּלוֹמַר: מוּתָּר לִזְרוֹק שָׁם, דְּקַיְימָא לָן: מְחִיצָּה הָעֲשׂוּיָה בַּשַּׁבָּת שְׁמָהּ מְחִיצָּה, וּמִמֵּילָא שָׁמְעִינַן דְּבְתוֹךְ אַלְפַּיִים מְטַלְטֵל כְּדַרְכּוֹ, דְּהָא מְחִיצוֹת נִינְהוּ: וּמְטַלְטֵל בְּאַרְבַּע אַמּוֹת. כְּאִילּוּ לֹא הָיְתָה שָׁם מְחִיצָּה. וּטְפֵי מֵאַרְבַּע לָא, וַאֲפִילּוּ בִּזְרִיקָה. דְּלָא שָׁנֵי לָן בֵּין טַלְטוּל כִּי אוֹרְחֵיהּ, לְטַלְטוּל דִּזְרִיקָה אֶלָּא בְּמָקוֹם שֶׁמּוּתָּר לְטַלְטֵל וְאָסוּר לְהַלֵּךְ, כְּגוֹן מִתּוֹךְ הַתְּחוּם לְחוּץ הַתְּחוּם. אֲבָל בְּמָקוֹם שֶׁהוּא מוּתָּר לְהַלֵּךְ, אִי שָׁרֵי לְטַלְטֵל בִּזְרִיקָה — שָׁרֵי נַמִי לְטַלְטֵל כִּי אוֹרְחֵיהּ, וְאִי אֲסִיר — תַּרְוַיְיהוּ אֲסִירִי. וְכֵיוָן דְּאָסַר לֵיהּ רַב הוּנָא לְטַלְטֵל בְּאַלְפַּיִם שֶׁלּוֹ, אֲפִילּוּ זְרִיקָה נַמִי אָסוּר, וְטַעְמָא מְפָרֵשׁ וְאָזֵיל: וּמַקְשִׁינַן לְרַב הוּנָא: וְנִטַּלְטֵל בְּכוּלָּהּ. וַאֲפִילּוּ חוּץ לְאַלְפַּיִם, ע"י זְרִיקָה. דְּהָא קַיְימָא לָן מְחִיצָּה הַנַּעֲשֵׂית בַּשַּׁבָּת מְחִיצָּה הִיא, בְּפ"ב (דף כ.). וְנְהִי דְּאִיהוּ לָא מָצֵי אָזֵיל, כֵּיוָן דְּלֹא שָׁבַת בַּאֲוִירָהּ לָא הָוֵי לָהּ כְּאַרְבַּע אַמּוֹת, אֲבָל מִכָּל מָקוֹם מְחִיצוֹת נִינְהוּ: שֶׁמָּא יִמָּשֵׁךְ אַחַר חֶפְצוֹ. חוּץ לְאַלְפַּיִם. הִלְכָּךְ, גָּזְרִינַן טַלְטוּל בִּזְרִיקָה אַטּוּ הִילּוּךְ: בְּאַלְפַּיִם מִיהַת. שֶׁהוּא מוּתָּר לְהַלֵּךְ בָּהֶן, וְלֵיכָּא לְמִיגְזַר בְּהוּ מִשּׁוּם שֶׁמָּא יִמָּשֵׁךְ אַחַר חֶפְצוֹ נִיטַּלְטֵל כִּי אוֹרְחֵיהּ טִלְטוּל גָּמוּר. וְכָל שֶׁכֵּן זְרִיקָה, דְּהָא מְחִיצוֹת מַעַלְיָיתָא נִינְהוּ. וּמְשַׁנֵּי: כֵּיוָן דְּחוּץ לְאַלְפַּיִם אָסוּר לְטַלְטֵל אֲפִילּוּ בִּזְרִיקָה, מִשּׁוּם שֶׁמָּא יִמָּשֵׁךְ אַחַר חֶפְצוֹ, וְכָל שֶׁכֵּן כִּי אוֹרְחֵיהּ — דְּהָא אֵין יָכוֹל לְהַלֵּךְ שָׁם וּלְטַלְטֵל, מִיתְּסַר נַמִי בְּאַלְפַּיִם מִשּׁוּם דְּהָוֵי אַלְפַּיִם דִּילֵיהּ נִפְרָצִין לְחוּץ לְאַלְפַּיִם דַּאֲסִירֵי לֵיהּ, מִשּׁוּם גְּזֵרָה שֶׁמָּא יִמָּשֵׁךְ. דְּהָא אֵין הֶפְסֵק בֵּינֵיהֶן, וְהָוְיָא מְחִיצָּה הַנִּפְרֶצֶת בִּמְלוֹאָהּ לְמָקוֹם הָאָסוּר לָהּ: וּמְטַלְטֵל בְּאַלְפַּיִם. אֲפִילּוּ כִּי אוֹרְחֵיהּ, וְחוּץ לְאַלְפַּיִם לֹא, אֲפִילּוּ בִּזְרִיקָה: לֹא כְּרַב נַחְמָן וְלֹא כְּרַב הוּנָא. וּמַה נַּפְשָׁךְ; אִי גָּזַר שֶׁמָּא יִמָּשֵׁךְ — אֲפִילּוּ אַלְפַּיִם נִיתַּסְרוּ מִשּׁוּם מְחִיצָּה הַנִּפְרֶצֶת לְמָקוֹם הָאָסוּר לָהּ, וְאִי לֹא גָּזַר שֶׁמָּא יִמָּשֵׁךְ — לְטַלְטֵל חוּץ לְאַלְפַּיִם בִּזְרִיקָה: עֲלֵיהּ דִּשְׁמוּאֵל. דְּרַב נַחְמָן מִשְּׁמֵיהּ דִּשְׁמוּאֵל אֲמָרָהּ: דְּתַנְיָא כְּוָותֵיהּ. דְּלָא גָּזְרִינַן שֶׁמָּא יִמָּשֵׁךְ:
הָיָה

מכלל דתנא קמא במזיד נמי שרי. נראה דהלכתא כתנא קמא ואף על גב דקיימא לן: משנת רבי אליעזר קב ונקי — הכא לא קיימא לן כוותיה אלא כרבנן, כיון דסבר רב פפא כרבנן. ואף בשוגג שלא במקומן נראה דהלכתא כת"ק דשרי, מדקאמרינן: במזיד במקומן כולי עלמא לא פליגי דאסור, כי פליגי — בשוגג שלא במקומן. ואם כן, דרב פפא דשרי במזיד במקומן — כ"ש דשרי בשוגג שלא במקומן. ועוד: דקיימא לן דלא קנסינן שוגג אטו מזיד, לא בדאורייתא ולא בדרבנן. מיהו, על כרחך הא דאסר ראב"י שוגג שלא במקומן — לאו משום דקניס שוגג אטו מזיד, דהא במקומן לא קניס שוגג אטו מזיד. אלא משום כיון דאין להן אלא ארבע אמות, גזרינן דילמא אתי להוציאן חוץ לארבע אמותיהן. וכן איתא בירושלמי. דקאמר, ר' נחמיה דאמר: עד שיחזרו למקומן שוגגין — אתיא כר"מ, דאמר: המבשל בשבת בשוגג יאכל ואף ע"ג דהבא בשביל ישראל זה מותר לישראל אחר, ואמרינן לקמן (דף מז:) דחפצי גוים קונין שביתה, ולא גזרינן שמא יוציא חוץ לעיר — יש לחלק בין עיר לארבע אמות. ועוד: דכשנעשה ע"י נכרים לא החמירו. ועוד: הא דחפצי נכרי קונין שביתה היינו דגזרו בעלים דנכרים אטו בעלים דישראל, ומשום הכי לא גזרינן שמא יוציא, דלא גזרינן גזירה לגזירה: ונכרים שהקיפוה מחיצות. בירושלמי מוקי לה כרבי יהושע, ומיהו בקונט' פי' דאתיא נמי כר"ג, דאמר: נתנוהו בדיר או בסהר — מהלך את כולה. ואע"ג דלא שבת באויר מחיצות מבעוד יום. דלא הקילו חכמים אלא התם דאין לו אלא ארבע אמות, אבל הכא דיש לו אלפים — לא הקילו: ומטלטל בכולה ע"י זריקה. נראה לר"י דאף תוך אלפים מטלטל ע"י זריקה. אבל כי אורחיה אינו מטלטל אלא ארבע אמות. דלענין טלטול כי אורחיה נפרצה למקום האסור לה: וניטלטל בכולה ע"י זריקה. אע"ג דרב הונא אית ליה בסוף פ"ק (דף יז.) דשבת גורמת, והכא נאסר בתחילת שבת — לא דמי להכא, דרב הונא מודה במחילה גמורה העשויה בשבת דשמה מחילה:
לא

ח א מיי' פכ"ז מהל' שבת הלכה ד סמג לאוין סו טוש"ע א"ח סי' שצז סעיף א:
ט ב מיי' שם הל' ח סמג שם טוש"ע א"ח סי' תג:

רבינו חננאל

ור' נחמיה אמר אפילו בשוגג נמי במקומו אין שלא במקומו לא. איני והא מדקתני בהאי ר' נחמיה ור' אלעזר בן יעקב אומרים לעולם אסורין עד שיחזרו למקומן שוגגין. מכלל דת"ק סבר במזיד נמי שרי אלא לאו ש"מ תנאי היא ש"מ. אמר רב נחמן אמר שמואל מי שאינו יודע תחום שבת מהלך אלפים פסיעות בינוניות וזהו תחום שבת: ועוד אמר רב נחמן אמר שמואל שבת בבקעה והקיפוה גוים מחיצה בעביטין ואוכפות ומשואות וכיוצא בהן בשבת מהלך בה אלפים אמה ומטלטל בכולה ע"י זריקה. רב הונא אמר מהלך בה אלפים אמה דאינון תחומיה ומטלטל בה בד' אמות דאע"ג דניקפה מחיצה נעשית כאילו נפרצה המחיצה הרביעי' במלואה למקום האסור לה שהוא חוץ לתחומו ואילו היתה ההקפה באלפים אמה או פחות היה מותר לטלטל בכולה אבל כיון שהיא יתר נעשית כאלו נפרצה במקום האסור לו וע"י זריקה נמי אינו מטלטל גזרה שמא ימשוך אחר חפצו ויצא חוץ לתחומו ואסיקנא וכן א"ר חייא בר רב כרב הונא. א"ל רב נחמן לרב הונא לא תפלוג עליה דשמואל דאמר מהלך בה אלפים אמה ומטלטל בכולה ע"י זריקה דהא תניא כוותיה היה מודד ובא וכלתה מדתו בחצי העיר מותר לטלטל בכל

י א ב מיי' שם הל' ח:
יא ג שם הלכה ט:
יב ד ה טוש"ע א"ח סי' [illegible]

*היה מודד ובא, וכלתה מדתו בחצי העיר – מותר לטלטל בכל העיר כולה, ובלבד שלא יעבור את התחום ברגליו. במאי מטלטל – לאו על ידי זריקה?(א) אמר רב הונא: לא, על ידי משיכה. אמר רב הונא: היה מודד ובא, וכלתה מדתו בחצי חצר – אין לו אלא חצי חצר. פשיטא! אימא: יש לו חצי חצר. האי נמי פשיטא! מהו דתימא: *ליחוש דלמא אתי לטלטולי בכולה, קמ"ל. אמר רב נחמן, מודה לי הונא: היה מודד ובא, וכלתה מדתו על שפת תקרה – מותר לטלטל בכל הבית. מאי טעמא – הואיל ותקרת הבית חובטת. אמר רב הונא בריה דרב נתן: כתנאי; הוליכוהו לעיר אחרת ונתנוהו בדיר או בסהר, רבן גמליאל ורבי אלעזר בן עזריה אומרים: מהלך את כולה. ורבי יהושע ורבי עקיבא אומרים: אין לו אלא ארבע אמות. מאי לאו: רבן גמליאל ורבי אלעזר בן עזריה דאמרו מהלך את כולה – דלא גזרי הילוך דיר וסהר אטו הילוך בבקעה, ומדהילוך אטו הילוך לא גזרי – טלטול אטו הילוך לא גזרי. ור' יהושע ור' עקיבא דאומרים: "אין לו אלא ארבע אמות", דגזרי הילוך דיר וסהר אטו הילוך דבקעה, ומדהילוך אטו הילוך גזרי – טלטול אטו הילוך נמי גזרי. ממאי? דילמא, כי לא גזרי רבן גמליאל ורבי אלעזר בן עזריה הילוך סהר ודיר אטו הילוך בקעה – הני מילי התם דשני מקומות הן, אבל טלטול אטו הילוך דמקום אחד הוא – ה"נ דגזרי, גזירה שמא ימשך אחר חפצו. ורבי יהושע ור' עקיבא נמי ממאי דמשום דגזרי הוא – דילמא משום דקא סברי: כי אמרינן *"כל הבית כולו כארבע אמות דמי" – הני מילי היכא דשבת באויר מחיצות מבעוד יום, אבל היכא דלא שבת באויר מחיצות מבעו"י – לא. אמר רב: הלכתא כרבן גמליאל בדיר וסהר וספינה. ושמואל אמר: הלכתא כרבן גמליאל בספינה, אבל בדיר וסהר – לא. דכולי עלמא מיהת הלכה כרבן גמליאל בספינה, מאי טעמא? אמר רבה: הואיל ושבת באויר מחיצות מבעוד יום. ר' זירא אמר: הואיל וספינה נוטלתו מתחילת ארבע ומנחתו בסוף ארבע. מאי בינייהו? איכא בינייהו שנפחתו דופני ספינה. אי נמי, בקופץ מספינה לספינה. ורבי זירא, מאי טעמא לא אמר כרבה? אמר לך: מחיצות – להבריח

היה מודד ובא. הנותן עירובו, ובא לילך ממקום עירובו אלפים, וכלתה מדתו בחצי עיר אחרת שעירבו את כולה, אי נמי ביו"ט: שלא יעבור תחום. אלפים ממקום עירובו ברגליו, דכיון דלא שבת בתוכה – לא הויא ליה כד' אמות: במאי מטלטל. בכל העיר, הואיל ותני שלא יעבור את התחום ברגליו: לאו על ידי זריקה. אלמא: לא גזרינן שמא ימשך: לא במשיכה לא גרסי' ומאן דגריס לה, הכי קאמר: ורב הונא אמר לך האי דקתני מותר לטלטל בכל העיר כולה, במשיכה קאמר, שמושך מחוץ לאלפים לתוך אלפים, דהתם ליכא למיגזר שמא ימשך דלאו חפציו הוא, עד דמייתי ליה לגואי. וכי מייתי ליה – תו לא מפיק ליה: הכי גרסינן: אמר רב הונא היה מודד ובא וכלתה מדתו בחצי חצר אין לו אלא חצי חצר להלך: פשיטא. דהא כלו אלפים שלו: אימא יש לו חצי חצר. אותו חצי של חצר שבתוך תחומו מותר להלך כי(ב) אורחיה, והתירא איצטריכא לאשמועינן, ולאו איסורא דאידך פלגא: הא נמי פשיטא. דפלגא דבתוך מדתו אית ליה: (ה"ג: אמר רב הונא: היה מודד ובא וכלתה מדתו בחצי חצר – אין לו אלא חצי חצר: פשיטא. דהא שמעינן ליה לרב הונא דגזר שמא ימשך: אימא יש לו חצי חצר. אותו חצי חצר שבתוך תחומו מותר לטלטל כי אורחיה, והתירא איצטריך לאשמועי' ולאו איסורא דאידך פלגא: הא נמי פשיטא. דפלגא, דבתוך מדתו – שרי, דלא דמי לשבת בבקעה, דהתם – איכא למיסר לטלטולי אפי' בתוך אלפים משום טעמא דנפרצה, דההיא ודאי נפרצה למקום האסור לה שהרי מחיצות הללו לא היו כאן מבעוד יום והיתה אסורה לכל אדם. וכשהוקפה בשבת והועילו לזה שבתוכו לאלפים – הועילו לו ולא לחוץ אלפים שהן חוץ מתחומו. והאי חוץ לאלפים – לא היה לו שום היתר אלא שום אדם, הלכך, הוי מקום האסור, ואוסר! אבל חצר – אין לומר בה חילוק פירצה למקום האסור, דהא מבעוד יום חדא היא, וגבי דאסרי להאי לטלטולי חוץ לאלפים ע"י זריקה, משום שמא ימשך, אבל בתוך מדת תחומו – מותר לטלטולי כי אורחיה): מודה לי הונא. אע"ג דגזר שמא ימשך: היה מודד ובא וכלתה מדתו על שפת תקרה. כנגד שפת הקירוי, והבית חוץ למדתו הוא. וכגון שנפרץ כותל הבית שנשתייר מלמעלה קירוי, ונפרץ בית לחצר שבפניה, דלא הוי בית נפרץ למקום האסור: מותר לטלטל בכל הבית. ע"י זריקה. ואע"פ שאסור ליכנס לתוכה ברגליו, והכא לא גזרינן שמא ימשך, הואיל ותקרות הבית חובטות, כלומר: נראות כיורדות וסותמות ואיכא היכר ולא ממשיך, שהרי עיניו נותן בתקרה, וסימן הוא ששם כלתה מדתו: כתנאי. אי גזרינן שמא ימשך אי לא: דלא גזרינן הילוך דיר וסהר. היכא דנתנוהו נכרים בו: אטו הילוך דבקעה. דאין בה מחיצות, דהתם אין לו אלא ד' אמות. כדתנן בריש פירקין: ובדיר וסהר, אע"ג דלא שבת באויר מחיצותיהן מבעוד יום – כארבע אמות דמיין ליה, הואיל ובאונס יצא מתחומו: ומדהילוך. דיר וסהר אטו הילוך דבקעה לא גזרינן: טלטול אטו הילוך. כגון שבת בבקעה ביו"ט, שהילוך אסור לו חוץ לאלפים במקום שביתתו, וטלטול דזריקה מותר בלא מחיצות: לא גזרינן. שלא יטלטל בזריקה חוץ לאלפים אטו הילוך, שמא ימשך אחר חפצו כרב נחמן. ואף על גב דשבת בבקעה והקיפוה נכרים לא סבירא להו כוותיה, דהא לדידהו אע"ג דלא שבת באויר מחיצות שרי, בהא מיהא כרב נחמן קיימי, דלא גזרי' שמא ימשך, אי נמי: כששבת בבקעה נמי סבירא להו כוותיה, דהא דשרו ליה הכא – משום דנאנס הוא: שני מקומות הן. ולא דמי אהדדי. דיר וסהר יש להן מחיצות, בקעה אין לה מחיצה, הלכך, לא מיחלפי: אבל טלטול אטו הילוך. כגון ששבת בבקעה ביו"ט, אימא דגזרי שלא יטלטל בזריקה חוץ לאלפים שמא ימשך אחר חפצו. דהא חד מקום הוא, ולית להו דרב נחמן כלל: אבל היכא דלא שבת. לא הוי כארבע אמות, ולהכי לא מישתרי בהילוך. אבל טלטול דזריקה לעולם אימא לך דשרי ליה בכל הדיר וסהר בזריקה, ולא גזרינן שמא יזוז וימשך: הואיל ושבת. הויא לה ספינה כארבע אמות: נוטלתו מתחילת ארבע ומניחתו לסוף ארבע. כלומר: משיצא זה חוץ לתחום לא נקט ליה ארבע אמות, דספינה כל שעה היא מהלכת בכל קפילה וקפילה יותר מארבע אמות, נמצא שאין לה תורת ארבע אמות כלל, שלא עמד פסיעה אחת בתוך ארבע אמות, הלכך, לא קנו לו ארבע אמות. לישנא אחרינא: כגון שהספינה הולכת למזרח והוא מהלך בתוכה למערב, שהספינה מחזירתו כל שעה לתוך ארבע אמותיו. וקשיא לי: תינח הליכה, אבל אם חזר לראש האחר היכי מישתרי? ובמתני' לא חילק רבן גמליאל בין שהוא מהלך לצד זה בין שהוא מהלך לצד שהספינה מהלכת. וזהו לשון דודי ר' שמעון מפי הרב. ל"א: כלומר, כשעוקר את רגלו קודם שיניחנה, הספינה מוליכתו מד' אמות שלו ונכנס לתוך ארבע אמות אחרות על כרחו, והוה ליה כמי שהוליכוהו נכרי חוץ מארבע אמותיו ונתנוהו לתוך ארבע אמות אחרות, שנותנין לו ארבע אמות, וכן לעולם. וזה עיקר: מאי בינייהו. בין רבה לר' זירא: שנפחתו דופני הספינה. ובטלו המחיצות. דרבה – ליתא, דר' זירא – איתא: אי נמי בקופץ מספינה לספינה. [illegible] דרבה – אין יכול להלך(ג) בזו, ולר' זירא – שרי: להבריח

לא ע"י משיכה. כי שקיל מבראי לגואי ליכא למיחש שמא ימשך אחר חפצו, אלא כשזורק מגואי לבראי דמרחיק החפץ ממנו. והא דאמר רב הונא: אין מטלטלין אלא בארבע – היינו כלפי צד(ד) אבראי לטלטל כי אורחיה או לזרוק, דלענין זה נפרצה במלואה למקום האסור לה. אבל במשיכה – מטלטל בכל מקום, דלענין זה לא נפרצה במלואה למקום האסור לה. וכענין זה יש ב"כל גגות" (לקמן דף פט.) דאסר רב לטלטל טפי מארבע בכלים דבית לגג, אע"ג דכלים דגג שרי לטלטל בכל הגגין כרבי שמעון, והוי למקום המותר לו:

וכלתה מדתו בחצי חצר גרסינן. דאי העיר שמעינן ליה *ממתני' ד"כילד מעברין" (לקמן דף סא.), וא"ת: חצר נמי פשיטא, דמאי שנא ממערה? דתנן ב"כילד מעברין" (שם): ולמודד שאמרו נותנין לו אלפים אמה, שאפי' כלתה מדתו במערה. דמשמע דיש לו חצי מערה! ואין לומר דהתם איירי בכלתה מדתו בסוף המערה – מדקאמר בגמרא (שם): סוף העיר איצטריכא ליה, דלא תנן. וי"ל: דמערה לא שכיחא בה כלים, ושייך למיגזר טפי בחצר מבמערה:

[אמר רב הונא היה מודד ובא. ותימה לי: לרב הונא היכי מטלטל בחצי חצר? הא נפרץ למקום האסור לו ורש"י פי': להלך. וקשה: לי' לטלטולי לא משמע להלך. ועוד: הא אשמעינן לעיל בבקעה דמהלך אלפים, ולא גזרי' דילמא אתי להלוכי חוץ לאלפים! וי"ל: לענין טלטול יש לחלק בין בקעה לחצר, כיון דלגבי אחריני חשיב מחיצה – בחצר לא חשיב נפרץ למקום האסור לה, ואי להלך כפי' רש"י, איצטריך רב הונא לאשמעינן, אע"ג דשייך טפי למיגזר בחצר מבבקעה – אפ"ה לא גזרינן. תוספות שאנ"ץ]:

כתנאי (או) הוליכוהו לעיר אחרת. קצת קשה: דהשתא בעי לאוקומי שמואל כר"ג, ושמואל לא פסיק לקמן כר"ג אלא בספינה! וי"ל: דהוה מצי למימר וליטעמיך:

אבל היכא דלא שבת באויר מחיצות מבעוד יום. וא"ת: והרי ספינה, דשבת באויר מחיצות מבעוד יום ומוכיח לקמן דפליגי! וי"ל: דקסבר מחיצות להבריח מים עשויות:

ורבי זירא מ"ט לא אמר כרבה. פירוש: ויתיר אפי' בהעמדה. וא"ת: מאי קבעי? מההוא טעמא דלית להו לר' יהושע ור' עקיבא, מאותן סברות לית להו לדידהו דהדדי! וי"ל: דלר' יהושע ור' עקיבא ניחא, דאית להו בכל מקום שהוא חוץ לתחום דאין לו אלא ד' אמות, ולא מפלגי בין דיר וסהר וספינה. אבל רבה ורבי זירא דמפלגי בין דיר וסהר וספינה בעי שפיר, מר אמאי לא אמר כמר, שמטעם זה יש לחלק ביניהם: כי

ממתניתין דכילד מעברין ובדדייק שם בסוף פרקא אבל בחצר שייך למגזר בי' דילמא אתי לטלטולי בכולה ובעיר פשיטא וא"ת חצר כו' [כ"ה בס"א רש"ל]

רבינו חננאל

העיר כולה ובלבד שלא יעבור התחום ברגליו. ופי' ובלבד שלא יעבור חצי העיר [השניה] ממקום שכלתה מדתו שם ואקשינן וכי מאחר שאינו עובר חצי העיר היאך מטלטל בכל העיר כולה אלא לאו ע"י זריקה הוא דמטלטל בכל העיר ש"מ. ולענין הילוך ברגליו כ"ע לא פליגי שאין לו להלך ברגליו אלא כמה שקנה שביתה מבעוד יום ומחיצה שנעשית בשבת לא מהניא ליה להילוך כי לא שבת מעיקרא באויר מחיצות כי פליגי בטלטול שמואל סבר דינה כי השתא כיון דהשתא מוקפת מחיצות שרי לטלטולי בכל המחיצות כולן מיהו עד אלפים אמה במקום שיש לו רשות להלך מטלטל כדרכו. א) וחוץ לאלפים אמה עד סוף המחיצות מטלטל ע"י זריקה ורב הונא דאמר אין מטלטל אלא בד' אמות קסבר כל מחיצה שנעשית בשבת ב) לאו מחיצה היא דאע"ג דחייא בר רב קאי כרב הונא קיי"ל כשמואל דתניא כוותיה. אמר רב הונא היה מודד ממקום שקנה בו שביתה אלפים אמה ובא וכלתה מדתו בחצי חצר יש לו חצי חצר ולא גזרינן דלמא אתי לטלטולי בכולה חצר אמר רב נחמן מודה לי הונא היה מודד ובא וכלתה מדתו בשפת תקרה מותר לטלטל בכל הבית ג) הואיל ותקרת הבית חובטת. פי' כיון שנכנס מן הבית המקורה מקצתו בתוך מדתו הותר לו לטלטל בכל הבית ד) כשם שאם כלתה מדתו תחת חצי התקרה יש לו לטלטל לבעל התחום עד סופה כך אם כלתה מדתו בסוף העיר ונותר בקצה העיר כלום נשכר אותו בעל התחום וישנה לו עד סופה דתנן (לקמן סא) היה מודד ובא [נותנין לו אלפים אמה שאפילו סוף מדתו כלה במערה] אמר רב הונא בריה דרב נתן כתנאי דתנן הוליכוהו לעיר אחרת ונתנוהו לדיר או לסהר כו' מאי לאו רבן גמליאל ור' אלעזר בן עזריה דאמרי מהלך את כולה דלא גזרו הילוך דדיר וסהר דאינון מוקפין מחיצות אטו בקעה. ומדהילוך דבקעה אטו הילוך לא גזרו טלטול נמי אטו הילוך לא גזרי ושמואל דאמר כוותיהון ור' יהושע ור' עקיבא דאמרי אין לו אלא ד' אמות היינו טעמא משום דגזרי הילוך דדיר דהוא מוקף מחיצות אטו בקעה דאינה מוקפת מחיצות ומדהילוך אטו הילוך גזרי טלטול אטו הילוך נמי גזרי ורב הונא דאמר כוותיהו ודחינן ממאי דלמא כי לא גזר רבן גמליאל ור' אלעזר

לקמן ס: ע"ש

[illegible] רש"ל

כתב רש"ל מן ה"ג עד ד"ה מודה לי הונא מפני אחרים

[ברכות כה:]

הגהות הב"ח

(א) גמ' לאו על ידי זריקה ורב הונא אמר לך לא על ידי משיכה: (ב) רש"י ד"ה אימא יש וכו' מותר להלך ולטלטל (כי אורחיה) תא"מ ונ"ב ס"א אין זה: (ג) ד"ה אי נמי וכו' אין יכול להלך לזו: (ד) תוס' ד"ה לא וכו' כלפי צד דמבראי:

א) [illegible] ב) [illegible] ג) [illegible] ד) [illegible]

להבריח מים עשויות. ורבה, מאי טעמא לא אמר כרבי זירא? במהלכת – כולי עלמא לא פליגי, כי פליגי – בשעמדה. אמר רב נחמן בר יצחק: מתני' נמי דיקא דבמהלכת לא פליגי, ממאי? מדקתני: "מעשה שבאו מפלנדרסין והפליגה ספינתם בים; רבן גמליאל ורבי אלעזר בן עזריה הלכו את כולה, ורבי יהושע ורבי עקיבא לא זזו מארבע אמות, שרצו להחמיר על עצמן". אי אמרת בשלמא במהלכת לא פליגי – היינו דקתני "רצו" – דילמא עמדה. אלא אי אמרת פליגי – האי "רצו להחמיר"?! איסורא הוא! אמר רב אשי: מתניתין נמי דיקא, דקתני ספינה, דומיא דדיר וסהר, מה דיר וסהר – דקביעי, אף ספינה נמי – דקביעא. אמר ליה רב אחא בריה דרבא לרב אשי: "הלכתא כרבן גמליאל בספינה", *הלכתא – מכלל דפליגי? אין, והתניא: חנניא(א) (בן אחי רבי יהושע) אומר: כל אותו היום ישבו ודנו בדבר הלכה, אמש הכריע אחי אבא: הלכה כרבן גמליאל בספינה, והלכה כרבי עקיבא בדיר וסהר.§ בעי רב חנניא: *יש תחומין למעלה מעשרה, או אין תחומין למעלה מעשרה? עמוד גבוה עשרה ורחב ארבעה לא תיבעי לך – דארעא סמיכתא היא. כי תיבעי לך – בעמוד גבוה עשרה ואינו רחב ארבעה. אי נמי, דקאזיל בקפיצה. לישנא אחרינא: בספינה מאי? אמר רב הושעיא: ת"ש, מעשה שבאו מפלנדרסין והפליגה ספינתם בים וכו'. אי אמרת בשלמא יש תחומין – משום הכי רצו. אלא אי אמרת אין תחומין – אמאי רצו? כדאמר רבא: במהלכת ברקק, הכא נמי – במהלכת ברקק. תא שמע: [א]פעם אחת לא נכנסו לנמל עד שחשיכה וכו', אי אמרת בשלמא יש תחומין – שפיר, אלא אי אמרת אין תחומין – כי לא היינו בתוך התחום מאי הוי? אמר רבא: [ב]במהלכת ברקק. תא שמע: הני שב שמעתא דאיתאמרן בצפר' בשבתא קמיה דרב חסדא בסורא, בהדי פניא בשבתא קמיה *דרבא בפומבדיתא. מאן אמרינהו? לאו אליהו אמרינהו? אלמא: אין תחומין למעלה מעשרה! לא, דלמא יוסף שידא אמרינהו. תא שמע: הריני נזיר ביום שבן דוד בא – מותר לשתות יין בשבתות ובימים טובים, ואסור

רש"י

להבריח מים עשויות. ולא חשיבי מחיצות לעשות ספינה כולה כארבע אמות: אמר לך במהלכת. דאיכא למימר האי טעמא דספינה נוטלתו אפילו ר"ע מודי דשרי: כי פליגי בשעמדה. ובשעת עמידתה קנו להו ד' אמותיהן. (וללישני בתראי על שעת עמידה נחלקו,) ואפ"ה שרי ר"ג משום אויר מחיצות: היינו דקתני רצו להחמיר. דמשמע דשרי אפילו לרבי עקיבא. אלמא: כי אסרי – לאו במהלכת אסרי לר"ע, ואינהו הוא דאחמור אנפשייהו, דדלמא עמדה פתאום ולאו אדעתן: אלא אי אמרת. בשעמדה דברי הכל אסור, דמחיצות לא חשיבי. ובמהלכת הוא דפליגי – מאי רצו? הא לר' עקיבא ורבי יהושע בין מהלכת בין עמדה איסורא הוא: דיקא נמי. דבעמדה פליגי: מכלל דפליגי. בספינה, בתמיה. והא רצו קתני ומנא להו לרב ושמואל דפליגי בספינה: אין והתניא. בניחותא. ופליגי בשעמדה. והא דקתני רצו – אמהלכת: רבי חנניא בן אחי רבי יהושע(ב) (הלכה כר"ג בספינה. כעין ספינתו, שהיתה מהלכת, דלא חיישינן לשמא עמדה. ומיהו, אפילו בשעמדה פליג רבן גמליאל דומיא דדיר וסהר, ואין הלכה כמותו אלא במהלכת. אבל עמדה דהיינו דיר וסהר – הלכה כר' עקיבא): כל אותו היום. שהיו בספינה: אחי אבא. רבי יהושע: אמש. לערב: יש תחומין. איסור תחומין למעלה מעשרה, כדמפרש ואזיל: בעמוד גבוה עשרה ורחב ארבעה. ונכנס ראשו א' לתוך התחום לא תיבעי לך דאיסור תחומין נוהג בו, ולא יעלה על ראשו שבתוך התחום ויצא לראשו אחר – דהא חזי להילוך, והילוך מעליא הוא: ואין רחב ד'. דלא ניחא תשמישתיה: בקפיצה. בשם. מי הוי הילוך, אי לא: סתם ספינה למעלה מעשרה מהלכת ואינה נחה, ודמי לקפיצה באויר ואפ"ה אסור: אמאי רצו. הא אין בו שום איסור אפילו עמדה: ברקק. פחות מעשרה, רקק בלע"ז גרבל"א: יוסף שידא. דלא מינטר שבתא: בשבתות וי"ט. דודאי לא אתי משיח האידנא: ואסור

רש"ל מ"ז | רש"ל מ"ז | [שבת קו: ש"נ] | [לקמן מה:] | נ"ל דרבה

תוספות

כי פליגי בשעמדה. השתא הדר ביה ממאי דקאמרינן: איכא בינייהו שנפחתו דופני הספינה וקופץ. דהשתא לרבה נמי מהלך את כולה, דמודה רבה לרבי זירא במהלכת. וא"ת: דהכא לית ליה לרבה אליבא דשמואל דמחיצות להבריח מים עשויות, ובפרק "כל גגות" (לקמן דף צ.) קאמר שמואל בספינה: אין מטלטלין בה אלא בד' אמות, משום דמחיצות להבריח מים עשויות! וי"ל: דהתם ביתירות מבית סאתים, ומטעם להבריח מים עשויות לא חשיבא כמוקפת לדירה והכא בפחות מבית סאתים, דלא בעינן מוקפת לדירה, אי נמי: הדר ביה כדאמרינן התם: **האי** רצו איסורא הוא. ורבי זירא לא חש לאותה קושיא, ומפרש שרצו להחמיר על עצמן כשמעתייהו. אי נמי: היה סובר ר' זירא דאין תחומין למעלה מעשרה, ורצו משום שמא תהלך ברקק, כדאמרינן בסמוך: **הלכה** כרבנן גמליאל בספינה. פסק רשב"ם: דמותר ליכנס בספינה מבע"י בערב שבת, אפילו שהספינה הולכת חוץ לתחום בשבת, דספינה ממילא אזלא ואיהו לא מידי עביד, ובלבד שלא יצא חוץ לספינה, והספינה כולה ארבע אמות. והא דתניא סוף פ"ק דשבת (דף יט.): אין מפליגין בספינה פחות משלשה ימים – אתיא כב"ש, דלא שרו לעשות מלאכה בערב שבת אלא בכדי שיעשו מבעוד יום. אבל לב"ה דשרו עם השמש, אע"פ שהמלאכה נעשית בשבת – שרי ליכנס. ואע"ג דבההיא ברייתא פליגי רבי ורבן שמעון בן גמליאל – אליבא דב"ש פליגי. וכן משמע בירושלמי דהך ברייתא כב"ש, דקתני: אין מפליגין ליס הגדול לא בחמישי ולא בערב שבת, ב"ש אומרים: אפי' ברביעי, וב"ה מתירין. משמע דשרי אפי' בערב שבת. וקאי את"ק, דאי אבית שמאי – היינו ת"ק! ועוד פסק רשב"ם: שאפי' בשבת שרי ליכנס, כיון דלאו מידי קא עביד, אך אין לו אלא ארבע אמות כיון דלא שבת באויר מחיצות מבעוד יום. ואע"ג דב"ה לא שרו אלא עם השמש אבל בשבת לא – היינו משום דדמי לאמירה דנכרי שבות. ואין נראה, דבפרק "תולין" (שם דף קלט:) משמע דאסור, גבי ההוא צורבא מרבנן דאזיל ונייס במברא ועבר לאידך גיסא וסייר פירי, ואמר: למינס קא מיכוונא. ושרי משום דהערמה *דרבנן הוא, וצורבא מרבנן לא אתי למיעבד לכתחילה. משמע דאסור לכתחילה, ואפילו לתוך התחום, מדאין מזכיר שם יציאתו חוץ לתחום, ומשמע דסייר פירי לית בו איסורא, דאפי' בשכר שרי, כדאמרינן (שם ד' קנא.): שמור לי פירותי שבתחומך ואני אשמור פירותיך שבתחומי. וטעם שאסור ליכנס בספינה, אומר ריצב"א: משום דדמי לשט בנהר, ואסור גזירה שמא יעשה חבית של שייטין. אי נמי: שמא ינהיג הספינה, והוי כמוליכה ארבע אמות בכרמלית. וריצב"א מדקדק נמי מירושלמי שהבאתי שאסור ליכנס בספינה בשבת, מדלא קאמר ת"ק לא בשבת ולא בערב שבת, דהוה משמע דב"ה מתירין אפילו בשבת, כי היכי דנקט ולא בערב שבת משום ב"ה. ואור"י: דאותן בני אדם שמדליקין נרות בספינה בערב שבת ואוכלין שם וסומכין על כך להפליג בספינה בשבת – לא שפיר עבדי, דסוף סוף הם מפליגין בשבת. ומה שפירש רשב"ם שמי שנכנס בספינה בשבת אין לו אלא ארבע אמות – אין נראה, דקיימא לן כרב דאמר: אפילו דיר וסהר דלא שבת באויר מחיצות – הלכה כר"ג. מדפריך לקמן (ד' מד.) בפשיטות גבי נחמיה בן חנילאי: פשיטא דבלא מלו גברי עסקינן, דאי בדמלו מאי תיבעי? והאמר רב: הלכה כר"ג בדיר וסהר! ולקמן (ד' מז:) נמי, גבי הנהו דכרי דאתו למברכתא דחשבינן כל העיר כארבע אמות – היינו כרב. אע"ג דרב חננאל פסיק כשמואל, והביא ראיה מחנניה דאמר: אמש הכריע (בן) אחי אבא כו' – אין הלכה כן. דהא אמרינן בשבת פרק "כירה" (ד' מ.): הכרעה דברייתא לאו הכרעה היא. ועוד: דלאו אבא רבי יהושע, והחולק אינו יכול להכריע. וכן פסק רב אלפס דקיימא לן כרב באיסורי. ועוד רצה רשב"ם להתיר ליכנס בקרון בשבת וגוי מוליכו חוץ לתחום. וחזר בו, משום שמא יפגעו בו ליסטים או שמא ישכח וירד, ואין לו אלא ארבע אמות. ואומר ר"י: דאפילו ליכנס בו בערב שבת אסור, דדוקא בספינה שרי ליכנס בערב שבת, אבל הכא כיון דאפשר לו לירד – אסור. מיהו, בספינה אין לו להחמיר אפילו נזדמן לו יבשה שיכול לירד – לא פלוג רבנן בספינה. ועוד: אם בהמה מנהיג בקרון – פשיטא דאסור להשתמש בבעלי חיים, שמא יחתוך זמורה: ואסור

עין משפט נר מצוה

יג א ב מיי' פכ"ז מהל' שבת הלכה ג טור ש"ע א"ח סי' תד:

רבינו חננאל

אלעזר בן עזריה הילוך דדיר אטו הילוך דבקעה משום דדיר ובקעה ב' מקומות נינהו דיר לחוד ובקעה לחוד ולא גזרי מקום אטו מקום אבל טלטול אטו הילוך דחד מקום הוא אמרינן גזרה שמא ימשך אחר חפצו הכי נמי דגזרי. ור' יהושע ור' עקיבא נמי ממאי דמשום דגזרי הוא דלמא משום דסברי כי אמרינן כל העיר כד' אמות דמיא היכא דשבת באויר מחיצות מבע"י אבל היכא דלא שבת באויר מחיצות מבעוד יום כגון האי שנתנוהו בזה הדיר גוים בשבת אין לו אלא ד' אמות ולאו משום דגזרי הילוך דיר אטו הילוך דבקעה. וכן טלטול אטו הילוך נמי לא גזרי ולא קמה הא דרב הונא בר נתן: אמר רב הלכה כר"ג בדיר וסהר וספינה שמהלך את כולה. ושמואל אמר הלכה כמותו בספינה בלבד שמהלך את כולה מ"ט רבה אמר הואיל ושבת באויר מחיצות מבע"י שהרי הוא יושב מע"ש בזו הספינה ר' זירא אמר הואיל וספינה נוטלתו מתוך ד' ומנחתו לסוף ד' ולעולם לא עקר והניח חוץ לד' אמות ואמרינן מאי בינייהו איכא בינייהו שנפחתו דופני הספינה לרבה אסור לר' זירא מותר אי נמי בקופץ מספינה לספינה לרבה דאמר הואיל ולא שבת באויר מחיצות מבע"י אסור האי נמי דקפץ לאו באויר הני מחיצות שבת דהא מספינה אחרת קפץ ולר' זירא מותר. רבה אמר בספינה מהלכת כ"ע לא פליגי דשרי. כי פליגי בעומדת. ודייקא מתני' כוותיה דקתני והפליגה ספינתן בים אי אמרת בשלמא במהלכת לא פליגי היינו דקתני רצו להחמיר על עצמן מכלל דשרי אלא אי אמרת פליגי האי רצו איסורא הוא. ורב אשי נמי דייק מדקתני לספינה גבי דיר וסהר דומיא דידהו מה דיר וסהר דקביעי וקיימי אף ספינה נמי קביעה וקיימה ואע"ג דרב ושמואל הלכתא כרב באיסורי בהא קי"ל כשמואל דהא תניא כוותיה דתניא חנניא אומר כל אותו היום ישבו ודנו בהלכה לאמש הכריע אחי אבא בינייהו וא' נראין דברי ר"ג בספינה ודברי ר' עקיבא בדיר וסהר: בעי רב חנניא יש תחומין למעלה מי' טפחים אם לא בעמוד גבוה י' ורחב ד' לא תיבעי לך דכי ארעא סמיכתא דמי כי תיבעי לך עמוד גבוה י' ואין רחב ד' טפחים אי נמי דקא אזיל בקפיצה ואתנא ממתני' למיפשטא דקתני והפליגה ספינתם בים וקתני רצו להחמיר על עצמן בשלמא אי אמרת יש תחומין למעלה מי' היינו טעמא דרצו להחמיר חיישינן דלמא עמדה דבמהלכת כ"ע לא פליגי דשרי ומשום חשש שמא עמדה ויש תחומין למעלה רצו להחמיר אלא אי אמרת אין תחומין למעלה מי' ואפי' עמדה שרי אמאי קתני רצו. ואוקימנא מתני' בספינה המהלכת ברקק שפחות מי' טפחים מים. ת"ש פעם אחת לא נכנסו לנמל עד כו'. ואי אמרת אין תחומין למעלה מי' [כי לא היינו בתוך התחום מאי הוי] ואוקמה רבה בספינה שהיתה מהלכת ברקק מקום שאין שם מים י' טפחים וכאלו בקרקע הים נמשכת. ת"ש מהנך שמעתתא. דאיתאמרן בצפרא דשבתא בסורא בי רב חסדא ובהדי פניא איתאמרן בבי רבה בפומבדיתא לאו אליהו אמרן. ובקפיצה הלך. וש"מ אין תחומין למעלה מי' טפחים ודחינן לא יוסף שידה אמרן. ת"ש

הגהות הב"ח

(א) גמ' והתניא חנניא אומר כל אותו כצ"ל ותיבת בן אחי רבי יהושע נמחק: (ב) רש"י ד"ה רבי חנניא בן אחי רבי יהושע לישנא אחרינא הלכה כרבן גמליאל:

יד א מיי' פכ"ז מהל' שבת הלכה ג טוש"ע א"ח סי' תד:
טו ב מיי' פ"ד מהל' נזירות הלכה יא:
טז ג מיי' פט"ז מהל' שבת הלכה כג ופ"ז הלכה יד טוש"ע א"ח סי' תה סעיף ד:

תורה אור

ואסור לשתות יין כל ימות החול. אי אמרת בשלמא יש תחומין – היינו דבשבתות ובימים טובים מותר. אלא אי אמרת אין תחומין, בשבתות ובימים טובים אמאי מותר? שאני התם, דאמר קרא: °"הנה אנכי שלח לכם את אליה הנביא וגו'" (מלאכי ג) והא לא אתא אליהו מאתמול. אי הכי, בחול כל יומא ויומא נמי לישתרי, דהא לא אתא אליהו מאתמול! אלא אמרינן: לבית דין הגדול אתא. הכא נמי – לימא: לבית דין הגדול אתא! *כבר מובטח להן לישראל שאין אליהו בא לא בערבי שבתות ולא בערבי ימים טובים מפני הטורח. קא סלקא דעתך: מדאליהו לא אתא – משיח נמי לא אתי, במעלי שבתא לישתרי! אליהו – לא אתי, משיח אתי. דכיון דאתי משיחא – הכל עבדים הן לישראל. בחד בשבא לישתרי! לפשוט מינה דאין תחומין, דאי יש תחומין – בחד בשבא לישתרי, דלא אתא אליהו בשבת! האי תנא [א]ספוקי מספקא ליה אי יש תחומין או אין תחומין, ולחומרא. דקאי אימת דקא נדר? אילימא דקאי בחול – כיון דחל עליה נזירות, היכי אתיא שבתא ומפקעא ליה? אלא [ב]דקאי בשבתא, וקא נדר, וביום טוב וקא נדר, וההוא יומא דשרי ליה, מיכן ואילך – אסיר ליה.§ "פעם אחת לא נכנסו לנמל וכו'".§ תנא: שפופרת היתה לו לרבן גמליאל שהיה מביט וצופה בה אלפים אמה ביבשה, וכנגדה אלפים בים. הרוצה לידע כמה עומקו של גיא מביא שפופרת ומביט בה, וידע כמה עומקו של גיא. והרוצה לידע כמה גובהו של דקל? מודד קומתו וצלו, וצל קומתו, וידע כמה גובה של דקל. הרוצה שלא תשרה חיה רעה בצל קבר – נועץ קנה בד' שעות ביום, ויראה להיכן צלו נוטה, משפיע ועולה משפיע ויורד. נחמיה בריה דרב חנילאי משכתיה שמעתא ונפק חוץ לתחום. אמר ליה רב חסדא לרב נחמן: נחמיה תלמידך שרוי בצער. אמר לו: [ג]עשה לו מחיצה של בני אדם ויכנס. יתיב רב נחמן בר יצחק אחוריה דרבא, ויתיב רבא קמיה דרב נחמן. א"ל רב נחמן בר יצחק לרבא: מאי קא מבעיא ליה לרב חסדא? אילימא בדמלו גברי עסקינן? וקא מבעיא ליה: הלכתא כרבן גמליאל,

או

רש"י

ואסור כל ימות החול. דילמא אתי: לפני בא יום ה'. לפני ביאת בן דוד יבא אליהו לבשר: מפני הטורח. שמניחין צרכי שבת והולכין להקביל פניו: עבדים הן. ואין לישראל טורח, דאיכא דטרח להו: בחד בשבא לישתרי. דודאי לא אתי משיח היום, דהא אתמול בשבת לא אתא אליהו. ומדקאסר ליה – ליפשוט דחייש לדילמא אתא אליהו ואין תחומין למעלה מעשרה: ומשנינן: מהא לא תיפשוט דאין תחומין, דדילמא ספוקי מספקא ליה להאי תנא, דדילמא אין תחומין ומש"ה אסר בחד בשבא, ולחומרא, אבל מפשט לא פשיטא ליה, דאילף התירא מיניה: כיון דחל עליה נזירות. בע"ש, ומספקא דילמא אתי משיח היום לב"ד הגדול, היכי מישתרי לשתות למחר בשבת? ליחוש דילמא אתא לב"ד הגדול מאתמול: דקאי בשבת וקא נדר בי"ט וקא נדר. כלומר: כשקיבל נדר זה היה שבת או י"ט, והיינו דקתני מותר לשתות בשבתות וימים טובים – אותה שבת או אותו י"ט שנדר, אבל מכאן ואילך – אסור, ואפי' בשבת, דילמא אתא אתמול בן דוד וחל עליה נזירות: שפופרת. קנה חלול. וכשהוא ארוך אין צופין בו למרחוק, וכשהוא קצר צופין בו יותר. והיתה שפופרת של רבן גמליאל מתוקנת למדת לפיית אלפים או בים או ביבשה: כמה עומקו של גיא מביא שפופרת ומביט בה. ביבשה. וימדוד כמה אמות הוא יכול לצפות בה, ואח"כ ילך על שפת הגיא ויצפה בה לעומקו, ויתרחק לאחוריו עד שיבחין שבמקום שכלה עומקו של גיא שם כלה לפיית השפופרת, שאם יתרחק עוד מעט לא יראה את קרקעית הגיא, וידע שעומקו של גיא והרחקתו שנתרחק משפתו הוי כמדת לפיית השפופרת: גובהו של דקל. ומתיירא לעלות בו ולמודדו: ימדוד צלו. של דקל: וצל קומתו. של עצמו, ופעמים שהצל רבה על המילא, ופעמים שהמילא רבה על הצל, כשחמה עומדת בגובה הרקיע צל כל דבר הוי קטן, וכשחמה בשיפולו הוי צל ארוך. הלכך, מודד אף צל קומתו, ולפי מה שיראה שירבה צל קומתו על קומתו, ידע שריבוי צל הדקל על הדקל – או כפלים או שליש או רביע: הרוצה שלא תשרה חיה רעה בצל קבר. כעין מצבה היו מציבין על הקבר כעין שאנו מגביהין וצוברין בו עפר, ומשפע לכאן ולכאן. והיירא שלא תבא חיה רעה להסתופף בצל הקבר מפני חום השמש, ויריח את המת ויחטטנו: נועץ קנה בד' שעות. כשבא לעשות הבנין ינעוץ קנה בארבע שעות ביום, שאותה שעה מתחיל השמש להתחמם והצל נוטה ונוח, כדאמרינן בברכות (ד' כז.): "וחם השמש ונמס", איזו שעה שהשמש חם והצל נוטה – הוי אומר זה ארבע שעות. ולפיכך חיות מתאוות לצל באותה שעה, ולאותו צד שיראה זה שהצל הקנה נוטה – ישפע הבנין, ויעשה שיפוע ארוך שלא יהא נוטה לו צל. ואע"פ שכשתסוב החמה יהיה לו צל לצד אחר, כיון דבההיא שעתא ליכא צל – תו לא אתיא חיה להתלונן בצילו. דההיא שעתא אזלא עד דמשכחא. ועוד, דלאחר ארבע שעות – אף הצל חם, ולא איכפת לה לחיה בצל: בדמלו גברי. שהיו לו אנשים הרבה שיכולין לצאת חוץ לתחום, כגון שעירבו לעשות לו מחיצה מכאן ומחיצה מכאן, ממקום שהוא שם עד התחום: הלכה כרבן גמליאל. דליהנו ליה מחיצות שלא שבת בהן מבעוד יום, כדאמר לעיל גבי דיר וסהר. או דילמא פשיטא ליה דהלכה כרבן גמליאל, והכא הוא דלא מלו ליה גברי עד תוך התחום, אלא עד ד' אמות סמוך לתחום:

וקמיבעיא

תוספות

ואסור לשתות יין כל ימי החול. וא"ת: מאי שנא דלא אסרינן כהן לשתות לעולם יין, כדאמרינן בסנהדרין (ד' כב:): אבל מה אעשה שתקנתו קלקלתו, פי': שעברו כמה שנים שלא נבנה הבית. ואמאי לא חיישינן לבן דוד כי הכא? וי"ל: דהתם ליכא איסורא, דאפשר בכהן אחר או יישן מעט, אבל הכא, אי אתי – עובר על נזירותו. ובפ"ק דנדה (ד' ה:) נמי אמרינן: חיישינן לשמא יבנה. ור"ת מפרש: ביום שבן דוד בא – שראוי לבא. והשתא לא קשיא מידי. וניחא נמי מה שמקשינן: אמאי אסור, והלא משיח בן יוסף יש לו לבא תחילה ועדיין לא בא? אבל קשה: האי דפריך בסמוך, בחול נמי לשתרי דהא לא אתא אליהו מאתמול – מ"מ היה ראוי לבא! וי"ל: דלפי המסקנא פריך, דמוקמינן דקאי בשבת וקנדר, משום הכי פריך בחול לשתרי יום שנדר בו, שאינו ראוי לבא באותו יום, הואיל ולא אתא אליהו מאתמול:

דלא אתא אליהו בשבת. וא"ת: ודלמא אתי בערב שבת ויבשר בשבת? וי"ל: דקרא "הנני שולח לכם את אליה הנביא לפני בא יום ה'" משמע ביום שבא יבשר:

האי תנא ספוקי מספקא ליה. (א)והיא דתנן בפרק קמא דפסחים (ד' יג.), דקאמר: לדבריך אף תלויות לא ישרפו שמא יבא אליהו ויטהרם – איכא למימר נמי: מספקא ליה. והא שמשיב* כבר מובטח להם לישראל שאין אליהו בא בשבת ולא בערב שבת ולא בערב יו"ט, נראה לי דהכי פירושו: כי היכי דלא בא לא בערב שבת ולא בערב י"ט מפני הטורח של תקון סעודה, הכי נמי בשבת קודם אכילה, מפני טורח סעודת שבת:

*מותרין אתם שכבר הייתי מסתכל בשפופרת וכו'. אפילו לרבי מאיר, דאמר לקמן: מי שישב בדרך ועמד והרי הוא סמוך לעיר, אם לא היתה כוונתו לכך – לא יכנס, הכא מתכוונים היו לשבות בעיר, והיו סומכים על שפופרת של ר"ג:

יתיב רב נחמן בר יצחק אחוריה דרבא ויתיב רבא קמיה דרב נחמן. הכא °משמע דרב נחמן בר יצחק לאו היינו רב נחמן סתם, וכן בכמה מקומות. ודלא כפ"ה דסוף פרק "כל הגט" (גיטין ד' לא:), דקאמר רב נחמן בר יצחק: אנא לא צריכנא להו, פירוש: לבי ריש גלותא, ופ"ה התם: משום דהוי חתנו של ריש גלותא. דהא רב נחמן סתם הוי חתנו של ריש גלותא, כדמוכח ב"העור והרוטב" (חולין ד' קכד.). אלא הא דקאמר לא צריכנא – משום דעשיר היה. ורב נחמן סתם הוא רב נחמן בר יעקב, דהא רב נחמן סתם היה חבירו דרב ששת, ובירושלמי מוכח דרב נחמן בר יעקב היה חבירו דרב ששת. וגם בשום מקום בתלמוד אינו מזכיר בפירוש רב נחמן בר יעקב אלא אבל רב נחמן בר רב חסדא, או רב נחמן בר יצחק*:

ויתיב רבא וקמבעיא ליה גרסינן. ול"ג: אמר ליה רב נחמן בר יצחק. דהכא פשיטא ליה במחילה של בני אדם שמותר לעשות. ובתר הכי פריך רב נחמן בר יצחק לרב מנפל דופנה דאסור לעשות:

אילימא בדלא מלו גברי. ואם תאמר: כי לא מלו גברי נמי, ילך אל מקום שהמחילה מגעת ואחר כך יעשה היקף אחר, עד שיגיע לתחום! ויש לומר: כיון שכבר עשו פעם אחת ידעו שלדעת כן עשו, ואסור מכאן ואילך כדמסיק בסמוך בשמעתין:

או

[שם יג. וע"ש וברש"י דהתם ד"ה לא בערבי שבתות וכו']

[שייך במשנה לעיל מח.]

פסחים יג.

הגהות הב"ח

(א) תוס' ד"ה האי תנא וכו' והיינו דתנן בפ"ק דפסחים נ"ב דף יג ועיין מ"ש שם:

גליון הש"ס

תוס' ד"ה יתיב רב נחמן בר יצחק וכו' משמע דרב נחמן בר יצחק לאו היינו ר"נ עי' לעיל דף יח ע"ב תוס' ד"ה מתקיף ולקמן עב ע"ב:

[ועי' תוס' ב"ב מו: ד"ה שלח וכתוב: גיטין לח: ד"ה אנא ותוס' לעיל יח: ד"ה מתקיף]

רבינו חננאל

ת"ש הריני נזיר יום שבן דוד בא בו אסור לשתות יין כל ימות החול דכל יומא איכא למימר האידנא לייתי ומותר בשבתות וי"ט דליכא למיחש דלמא אתי ש"מ יש תחומין בקפיצה למעלה מעשרה ודחינן לא משום דבעי מיתא אליהו מאתמול כו' ופשוטה היא מינה דאין תחומין דאי יש תחומין כיון דאליהו לא אתא בשבת משיח נמי לא אתא [בחד] בשבת בחד בשבת מיהו נשתרי. ואמרינן תנא ספוקי מספקא ליה ומחמיר הכי והכי דקאי אימת ונדר אי נימא בחול כיון דחל נזירות עליה היכי אתיא שבת ומפקעה ליה דקתני ומותר בשבת אלא בשבת נדר או בי"ט וההוא יומא בלחוד הוא דשרי מיכן ואילך אסור ואפי' בשבתות וי"ט: מתני' פעם אחת לא נכנסו לנמל עד שחשכה כו'. מנא ידע תנא שפופרת היתה לו לר"ג שהיה צופה ומביט בה אלפים אמה ביבשה וכנגדן אלפים בים. פי' כעין שפופרת עשויה מנחושת היתה לו לר"ג ושיער בה אלפים אמה ביבשה והיתה אצלו לשער בה בים. ומפורש כך בירושלמי *) מצופית היתה לו לר"ג והיה משער בה עיניו למישור אלפים אמה והיה משער בה בים ולמה ליה למימר והיינו בתוך התחום עד שלא חשכה והא ר"ג שרי משחשיכה אם נכנסו לנמל כגון דיר וסהר תפתר כשהיה (בלמין) [בנמל] יתר מבית סאתים ולא יהיו מחיצות גבוהות עשרה ולא יהיו פרצות יותר מעשר ולא יהא עומד כנגד עומד ופרוץ כנגד פרוץ. הרוצה לידע כמה עומקו של גיא מביא שפופרת ומביט בה קרקעית הגיא וחוזר וצופה ומביט בה למעלה במישור. אם רואה במישור ק' אמה יודע שעומקו של גיא ק' אמה. וכן כשיעור הזה הרוצה לידע גובהו של דקל. תני ר' חייא הרוצה שלא תשרה חיה רעה בצל קברו נועץ קנה משעה רביעית ביום ורואה היכן נוטה צילו משפיע ועולה משפיע ויורד פי' משעה ד' כיום החמה נכנסת לישוב והבריות מבקשות הצל ומשפע ועולה כלומר מיצר מלמעלה ויורד כגון מדרון שלא יהא לו צל כל היום כולו. נחמיה בר רבא בר חנילאי משכתיה שמעתא בשבת ויצא חוץ לתחום. א"ל רב חסדא לרב נחמן נחמיה תלמידך שרוי בצער חוץ לתחום א"ל לך ועשה לו מחיצה של בני אדם ויכנס דקי"ל דמחיצה שנעשית

בשבת

*) וע"ש בק"ע ופ"מ פי' ד' הירושלמי הזה.

וקמיבעיא ליה הלכה כר"א. דקאמר במתניתין(א): מי שיצא חוץ לתחום שתי אמות – יכנס: דיקא נמי. דבדלא מלו גברי הוה: דאמר ליה. רב נחמן: עשה לו מחיצה של בני אדם ויכנס, למה ליה למימר יכנס – אלא הכי קאמר: יעשה המחיצה [עד] השפים, ואחר כך יכנס הוא מעצמו בלא מחיצה: נפל דופנה. של סוכה:

ולא יזקוף את המטה. שיש לו בסוכה כנגד הפרצה. ואע"ג דלא מיחזי כבנין, דדומה כמתכוין לפנות לו מקום הסוכה – אפי' הכי אסור. וקשה להנך דשרו לעשות מחיצה של בני אדם בשבת: כדי שיאכל וישתה ויישן. עיקר מלותה של סוכה בג' דברים הללו: ויזקוף את המטה כו'. אלמא: שרי. ופרכינן: קשיין אהדדי: ואם לא אין פוקקין בו. דדמי לבונה, שמוסיף על סתימת הבית. ואף על פי שעראי הוא, שהרי יחזור ויפתחנו: והא אתמר עלה. דאפי' רבנן לא שרו אלא להוסיף, כגון פקק חלון דתוספת בעלמא הוא. ובברייתא שרי למיעבד דופן לכתחילה: ר' מאיר פוסל. מפרש במסכת סוכה [דף כא.] שמא תברח: דלאו מידי קא עביד. דכיון דלא מתקן לסוכה, אע"ג דעביד אהל – שרי. דקסבר: עושין אהל עראי. והואיל דלא מתקן סוכה – אינו אלא אהל עראי, ושרי. ואכתי טובא איכא למיפרך עלה; דהא "כדי שיאכל וישתה ויישן" קתני, אלמא: לתקנה לסוכה קאתי! הא פרכינן עליה פירכי טובא, עד דמפקינן ליה מטעמא: אימור דשמעת ליה לרבי מאיר. דפסיל: בהמה. משום שמא תברח: אדם. שיש בו דעת לעמוד, או כלים שאין זזין ממקומן – מי שמעת ליה? והאי תנא אדם וכלים הוא דקתני, עושה את חבירו דופן ויזקוף את המטה: ותו. נהי דלא מתקן לה לסוכה: ר' מאיר. דמוקמת להא דשריא אליביה, ומשום דלא הוי תיקון מחיצה ואהל, דלאו הכשר מחיצה: אליבא דמאן. דשרי ר' מאיר, לא קאמר כר"א רביה ולא כרבנן. דהא פקק החלון אין בו מצות סוכה, ולא שרו רבנן אלא להוסיף: אלא הא והא רבנן. והא דקתני נפל דופנה לא יעמיד בה כו': בדופן שלישית. דבשתי דפנות אין קרוי אהל, וכי עביד בה דופן שלישית – משוי ליה אהל. ומודו רבנן דאין עושין אהל עראי בתחילה. והא דתני מותר – בדופן רביעית, דבלאו הכי הוי אהל, והאי תוספת בעלמא הוא, ורבנן לטעמייהו, דאמרי מוסיפין אהל בשבת: דיקא נמי. דהא דקתני אסור בדופן שלישית קאי: דקתני נפל דופנה. דמשמע דופן שהיא מותרת בה, ורביעית לא הויא תיקון סוכה, דתנן (סוכה ד' ב.): ושאין לה שלש דפנות – פסולה, הא בג' – כשירה: אלא

או אין הלכה כר"ג? או דילמא: בדלא מלו גברי עסקינן, וקא מבעיא ליה: הלכה כרבי אליעזר או אין הלכה כר"א? פשיטא, בדלא מלו גברי עסקינן. דאי סלקא דעתך בדמלו גברי עסקינן – מאי תיבעי ליה? האמר רב: הלכה כר"ג בדיר וסהר וספינה! אלא ודאי: בדלא מלו גברי עסקינן, ודר' אליעזר קמיבעיא ליה. דיקא נמי, דקאמר ליה "יכנס". מאי "יכנס", לאו בלא מחיצה? איתיביה ר"נ בר יצחק לרבא: נפל דופנה – לא יעמיד בה אדם בהמה וכלים, ולא יזקוף את המטה לפרוס עליה סדין – לפי שאין עושין אהל עראי בתחילה ביו"ט, ואין צריך לומר בשבת. א"ל: את אמרת לי מהא, ואנא אמינא לך מהא: [א]עושה אדם את חבירו דופן כדי שיאכל וישתה וישן, ויזקוף את המטה, ויפרוס עליה סדין כדי שלא תפול חמה על המת ועל האוכלין. קשיין אהדדי! ל"ק; הא – ר"א, הא – רבנן. דתנן: *פקק החלון, ר"א אומר: בזמן שקשור ותלוי – פוקקין בו, ואם לאו – אין פוקקין בו. וחכ"א: בין כך ובין כך פוקקין בו. והא איתמר עלה, *אמר רבה בר בר חנה, א"ר יוחנן: [ב]הכל מודים שאין עושין אהל עראי בתחילה ביום טוב, וא"צ לומר בשבת. לא נחלקו אלא להוסיף, שר' אליעזר אומר: אין מוסיפין ביום טוב, ואין צריך לומר בשבת. וחכמים אומרים: [ג]מוסיפין בשבת, ואין צריך לומר ביום טוב! אלא, ל"ק; הא – כרבי מאיר, הא – כרבי יהודה. דתניא: *עשאה לבהמה דופן לסוכה – רבי מאיר פוסל, ור' יהודה [ד]מכשיר. רבי מאיר דקא פסיל התם – אלמא: לא מחיצה היא, הכא שרי – דלאו מידי קא עביד. ורבי יהודה דקא מכשיר התם – אלמא: מחיצה היא, הכא אסר. ותיסברא?! אימר דשמעת ליה לרבי מאיר בהמה, אדם וכלים מי שמעת ליה?! ותו, רבי מאיר אליבא דמאן? אי אליבא דרבי אליעזר – להוסיף נמי אסר! אלא אליבא דרבנן – אימר דאמרי רבנן להוסיף, לכתחילה מי אמור?! אלא: הא והא רבנן, וכלים אכלים ל"ק; [ה]הא – בדופן שלישית, הא – בדופן רביעית. דיקא נמי, דקתני "נפל דופנה", שמע מינה.
אלא

או דילמא בדמלו גבי עסקינן. והשתא, אפי' אי אין הלכה כרבי אליעזר – יכנס. וא"ת: כיון דאמרי רבנן אפי' אמה אחת לא יכנס, אע"פ שד' אמות שלו מובלעות בתוך התחום ראשון – ה"נ כי מלו גברי מחילות, ומגיעות תוך התחום לא יכנס! ויש לומר: דלא דמי, דהכא כשתסלק מחילה דגברי וכבר יצא ע"י מחילה מארבע אמות שנתנו לו חכמים(ב), ומעתה היה ליתן לו ארבע אמות אחרות. וכיון שהוא בתחום ראשון – לא ניתן לו ד' אמות אחרות, אלא חוזר לתחומו הראשון. אבל בהבלעת ד' אמות, שלא הפסיד בכניסתו ד' אמות – לא יכנס:

דאי בדמלו מאי תבעי ליה. ואף על גב דרבי מאיר פוסל לקמן בהמה לדופן סוכה, פשיטא ליה דהלכה כרבי יהודה. אבל אין לפרש דבאדם אפי' רבי מאיר מודה, דלא שייך ביה שמא יברח – דלאו היינו טעמא דר' מאיר כדמסיק פרק "הישן" (סוכה ד' כג.). והא דפריך לקמן: אדם וכלים מי שמעינן ליה – היינו למאן דמפרש בסוכה דטעמא דרבי מאיר חיישינן שמא תברח: **כדי** שלא תפול חמה על המת. והא דאמרינן בפרק "כירה" (שבת ד' מג:): אין עושין מחילה למת בשביל מת, הא דשרי הכא היינו כדמפרש התם – באין בני אדם ויושבין בלדו וכו'. ור"י מפ': דהכא הוי שפיר בשביל חי, שאם יסריח המת יצטרכו לצאת מן הסוכה:

פקק החלון. בפ' "כל הכלים" (שבת דף קכה:) פ"ה: דהאי חלון הוי למעלה בגג, אבל מן הלד – לא שייך איסור אהל. והביא ראיה מפ' "כל גגות" (לקמן ד' צד.) גבי רב ושמואל דהוו יתבי בההוא חלר, נפל גודא(ג) ביני וביני. אמר שמואל: נגודו ליה גלימא. אהדריה רב לאפיה. ופריך: לשמואל, למה לי למעבד הכי? והאמר: זה מטלטל עד עיקר מחילה כו'. ומשני: דשמואל עביד לצניעות בעלמא. משמע, שאם היה שמואל אוסר לטלטל כרב – לא הוה קשה מידי. דהיכי שרי למיעבד הכי, אלמא: לא חשיב אהל בדפנות מן הלד. והא דקפיד רב – לא אעשיית מחילות, אלא משום דקסבר אסור לטלטל הסדין בתוכה. ובפ"ק דסוכה, (ד' טז:) גבי עובדא דשכחו ולא הביאו ס"ת מערב שבת, למחר פרסו סדינין על גבי עמודין והביאו ס"ת וקראו בו. ופריך: פרסו לכתחילה? ומי שרי? והאמר מר: הכל מודים שאין עושין אהל עראי בתחלה בשבת. רש"י ל"ג אלא פרסו סלקא דעתך. פירוש: איך הביאו דרך רשות הרבים. ומשני: אלא שמלאו סדינין פרוסין. ואין נראה למחוק הספרים. ועוד: מאי קשיא ליה איך הביאוס? דלמא הביאוס דרך מלבושים. ועוד: דבשמעתין מוכח דמן הלד שייך עשיית אהל, דאעשיית דופן מייתי ליה. ועוד דלשון חלון שייך בכותל ובגג קרי ליה ארובה כדתנן (בילה דף לה:): משילין פירות דרך הארובה. ונראה לר"ת דמן הלד שייך עשיית אהל, והיכא שהמחילה מועלת להתיר – חשוב עשיית אהל בתחלה, כההיא דפירסו סדינין ולרב דאסר לטלטל בכל גגות – שייך עשיית אהל לכתחילה. ואעשיית מחילות קפיד, והוי כדופן ג' של סוכה דחשבינן ליה הכא אהל, אבל לשמואל דשרי לטלטל – לא חשיב אלא תוספת אהל, כמו דופן רביעית של סוכה דחשיב ליה תוספת, משום דבלאו הכי מישתרי. ואי הוה אסיר שמואל, כל שכן דהוה פריך ליה היכי שרי למיעבד הכי. ומאן דשרי תוספת אהל – למעלה נמי שרי, כדמוכח ב"המוצא תפילין" (לקמן דף קב.) גבי הני דיכרי דיממא בעו טולא ובלילא בעו אוירא, ובפ' "הישן" (סוכה דף כז:) גבי ר"א ששבת בסוכתו של ר' יוחנן: **רבי** מאיר דקפסיל התם אלמא לאו מחיצה היא. השתא בעי למימר דאיירי בדופן שלישית, אפ"ה לא חשיב אלא תוספתא בעלמא לר"מ דקפסיל. וקשה, הא קתני בהדיא התם כדי שישתה ויאכל ויישן. ובקונטרס פי': דהוה מצי למפרך, אלא בלאו הכי פריך שפיר. אך מ"מ קשה, דמאי פריך בסמוך: אימר דאמור רבנן להוסיף, לכתחילה מי אמור. הא אמר דלר"מ דקפסיל לא חשיב אלא תוספת בעלמא! ע"כ יש לומר: דהיינו ודאי דפריך, מדקאמר כדי שיאכל וישתה ויישן – אלמא מיתכשר סוכה בהכי, דעיקר מלות סוכה בג' דברים הללו. ואם כן הרי עשיית אהל לכתחילה הוא. אך קשה להשר מקוצי: דהשתא כי משני הא ר"מ הא ר' יהודה – לא תירך כלום אמעשה דנחמיה! ונראה לפרש דה"פ: כיון דפוסל ר"מ לז' ימי סוכה שאינה יכולה לעמוד שם כל ז', גבי נחמיה שרי לכתחילה. אע"ג דמהני לא חשיב אלא תוספת בעלמא, כיון שאותה מחילה אינה ראויה לז'. וכן הא דקתני: כדי שיאכל וישתה ויישן – שרי, דליכא למיחש שמא תברח לפי שעה. ובתר הכי פריך: אימר דאמור רבנן להוסיף, לכתחילה מי אמור, דכיון דמהני אפי' לשעה – חשיב עשיית אהל לכתחלה, כמו פקק החלון:
כל

עין משפט נר מצוה

יז א מיי' פ"ד מהל' סוכה הלכה טז טוש"ע א"ח סי' תרל סעיף יב:
יח ב מיי' פכ"ב מהל' שבת הלכה כז סמג לאוין סה טוש"ע א"ח סי' שטו ס"א:
יט ג מיי' שם טוש"ע שם סעיף ב:
כ ד מיי' פ"ד מהלכות סוכה הל' טז טוש"ע א"ח סי' תרל סעיף יא:
כא ה מיי' שם טוש"ע שם סעיף יב בהג"ה וסימן שטו סעיף א:

רבינו חננאל

בשבת הויא מחיצה. רב נחמן כשמעתיה. ואסיקנא לעולם פשיטא ליה לרב חסדא דהלכתא כר"ג דשרי להלך בכולה ולא בעיא אלא הכא דלא מלי גברא עד התחום וא"ל רב נחמן זיל עביד ליה מחיצה של בני אדם ויהלך נחמיה עד שיגיע בב' אמות קרוב לתחומו ויכנס אלו ב' אמות בלא מחיצה כר' אליעזר דאמר מי שיצא חוץ לתחום ב' אמות יכנס. ג' לא יכנס. ומותבינן עליה מהא דתניא נפלה דפנה לא יעמיד בה לא אדם ולא בהמה ולא כלים כו' הנה אין עושין מחיצה מבני אדם בתחלה ביו"ט ק"ו בשבת א"ל איני והתניא עושה אדם את (חביתו) [חבירו] דופן כד שיאכל וישתה וישן (ואכוף) [ויזקוף] המטה ויפרוש עליה סדין כדי שלא תפול חמה על המת ועל האוכלין ואמרינן אי הכי קשיין אהדדי. ואתינן לפרוקי הא ר' אליעזר הא רבנן ונדחה הדין פירוקא. ואסיקנא הא דתניא עושה אדם את (חביתו) [חבירו] דופן ר' מאיר היא (דתנן) [דתניא] עשאה לבהמה דופן לסוכה ר' מאיר פוסל ור' יהודה מכשיר ר' מאיר דפסיל התם ואמר לאו מחיצה הוא קא שרי הכא דלא עביד ולא כלום. לר' יהודה דמכשיר התם אלמא מחיצה היא (הכא דקתני) [קתני הכא] לא יעמיד בה אדם דמחיצה היא דעביד ואסירי ואקשינן ותסברא דלר"מ ולר' יהודה נינהו אימור דשמעת להו דפליגי בבהמה אבל אדם וכלים מי שמעת להו *) דעבדי בהו מחיצה ונדחה גם זה. ואסיקנא אלא הני מתניתא תרווייהו לרבנן נינהו [דפליגי] על רבי אלעזר [וס"ל] דשרי להוסיף אאהלי עראי בשבת וכ"ש ביו"ט וכלין אכלין ל"ק הא דתניא אין עושין בדופן

*) [לכאורה צ"ל דלא עבדי בהו מחילה].

רב נסים גאון

וקא מיבעיא ליה הלכה כר' אלעזר או אין הלכה כר' אלעזר היינו דאמר ר' אלעזר בהדין פירקא (דף נב) במשנה מי שיצא חוץ לתחום אמה אחת לא יכנס ר' אלעזר אומר ב' יכנס ג' לא יכנס:

מסורת הש"ס:
שבת קכה: קלז: סוכה כז:
שבת שם [תוספ' סוכה פ"א לקמן פו:]
סוכה כג:

הגהות הב"ח

(א) רש"י ד"ה וקמבעיא ליה וכו' לאמר במתני'. נ"ב לקמן דף נב ע"ב: (ב) תוס' ד"ה או דילמא וכו' חכמים מעתה היה ראוי ליתן לו: (ג) ד"ה פקק וכו' דביני ביני אמר להו שמואל שקילו גלימא נגידו ביה אהדרי רב:

כב א מיי' פ"ד מהל' סוכה הל' ט"ו ופט"ז מהל' שבת הל' כב טוש"ע א"ח סי' שסב סעיף ה וסי' תה ס"ד וסי' תרל סעיף יב:
כג ב מיי' פט"ז שם טוש"ע א"ח סי' שסב סעיף ז:
כד ג מיי' שם טוש"ע שם סעיף ה:
כה ד ה מיי' פכ"ז מהל' שבת הל' יז סמג לאוין סו טוש"ע א"ח סי' תז סעיף ב:

אֶלָּא אָדָם אַאָדָם קַשְׁיָא! אָדָם אַאָדָם נַמִּי לָא קַשְׁיָא; אכָּאן – לָדַעַת, כָּאן – שֶׁלֹּא מִדַּעַת. וְהָא דְּרַבִּי נְחֶמְיָה בְּרֵיהּ דְּרַבִּי חֲנִילַאי לָדַעַת הֲוָה! שֶׁלֹּא מִדַּעַת הֲוָה. רַב חִסְדָּא מִיהָא לָדַעַת הֲוָה! רַב חִסְדָּא שֶׁלֹּא מִן הַמִּנְיָן הֲוָה.§ הָנְהוּ בְּנֵי גְּנָנָא בדְּאַעִילוּ מַיָּא בִּמְחִיצָה שֶׁל בְּנֵי אָדָם, נַגְדִּינְהוּ שְׁמוּאֵל. אָמַר: אִם אָמְרוּ שֶׁלֹּא מִדַּעַת יֹאמְרוּ לָדַעַת?! הָנְהוּ זִיקֵי דַּהֲוָה שַׁדְיָין בְּרִיסְתְּקָא דִּמְחוֹזָא, בַּהֲדֵי דַּאֲתָא רָבָא מִפִּירְקֵיהּ אַעֲלִינְהוּ נִיהֲלֵיהּ. לְשַׁבְּתָא אַחֲרִיתִי בָּעֵי עַיְּילִינְהוּ. וַאֲסַר לְהוּ, גדַּהֲוָה לֵיהּ כְּלָדַעַת, וְאָסוּר. לֵוִי אַעִילוּ לֵיהּ תִּיבְנָא, זְעֵירִי אַסְפַּסְתָּא, רַב שִׁימִי בַּר חִיָּיא מַיָּא.§ **מתני'** דמִי שֶׁיָּצָא בִּרְשׁוּת וְאָמְרוּ לוֹ "כְּבָר נַעֲשָׂה מַעֲשֶׂה" – יֵשׁ לוֹ אַלְפַּיִם אַמָּה לְכָל רוּחַ. אִם הָיָה בְּתוֹךְ הַתְּחוּם – כְּאִילּוּ לֹא יָצָא. *כָּל הַיּוֹצְאִים לְהַצִּיל חוֹזְרִין לִמְקוֹמָן.§ **גמ'** מַאי "אִם הָיָה בְּתוֹךְ הַתְּחוּם כְּאִילּוּ לֹא יָצָא"? אָמַר רַבָּה, הָכִי קָאָמַר: אִם הָיָה בְּתוֹךְ תְּחוּם שֶׁלּוֹ – כְּאִילּוּ לֹא יָצָא מִתּוֹךְ בֵּיתוֹ דָּמֵי. פְּשִׁיטָא! מַהוּ דְּתֵימָא: הוֹאִיל וְעָקַר עָקַר, קמ"ל.

רַב שִׁימִי בַּר חִיָּיא אָמַר, הָכִי קָאָמַר: האִם הָיוּ תְּחוּמִין שֶׁנָּתְנוּ לוֹ חֲכָמִים מוּבְלָעִין בְּתוֹךְ הַתְּחוּם שֶׁלּוֹ – כְּאִילּוּ לֹא יָצָא מִתְּחוּמוֹ. בְּמַאי קָמִיפַּלְגִי? מָר סָבַר: הַבְלָעַת תְּחוּמִין מִילְּתָא הִיא, וּמָר סָבַר: לָאו מִילְּתָא הִיא. א"ל אַבַּיֵי לְרַבָּה: וְאַתְּ לָא תִּסְבְּרָא דְּהַבְלָעַת תְּחוּמִין מִילְּתָא הִיא? וּמָה אִילּוּ שָׁבַת בִּמְעָרָה, שֶׁבְּתוֹכָהּ אַרְבַּעַת אֲלָפִים וְעַל גַּגָּהּ פָּחוֹת מֵאַרְבַּעַת אֲלָפִים אַמָּה, לֹא נִמְצָא מְהַלֵּךְ אֶת כּוּלָּהּ וְחוּצָה לָהּ אַלְפַּיִם אַמָּה? אֲמַר לֵיהּ: וְלָא שָׁנֵי לָךְ בֵּין הֵיכָא דְּשָׁבַת בַּאֲוִיר מְחִיצוֹת מִבְּעוֹד יוֹם, לְהֵיכָא דְּלֹא שָׁבַת בַּאֲוִיר מְחִיצוֹת מִבְּעוֹד יוֹם? וְהֵיכָא דְּלֹא שָׁבַת לֹא? וְהָתְנַן

אֶלָּא אָדָם אַאָדָם קַשְׁיָא. דְּבִשְׁלָמָא מִטָּה אַמִּטָּה אִיכָּא לְתָרוּצָא כִּדְקָאָמְרַתְּ, דְּהָא דְּתָנֵי וְיִזְקוֹף אֶת הַמִּטָּה – בְּדוֹפֶן רְבִיעִית קָאָמַר. דְּהָא קָתָנֵי שֶׁלֹּא תִּפּוֹל חַמָּה עַל הַמֵּת וְעַל הָאוֹכָלִין, אַלְמָא: לָאו לְאַכְשׁוּרֵי סוּכָּה אָתֵי, אֶלָּא אָדָם, הָא קָתָנֵי "כְּדֵי שֶׁיֹּאכַל וְיִשְׁתֶּה וְיִישַׁן", אַלְמָא: לְמֵיפַּק בֵּיהּ חוֹבַת סוּכָּה אוֹקְמֵיהּ הָתָם, דְּג' דְּבָרִים הַלָּלוּ הֵן מִצְוַת סוּכָּה. אַלְמָא: דּוֹפֶן שְׁלִישִׁי הָוְיָא חֲסֵירָה, דְּאִי דּוֹפֶן רְבִיעִית – לָא הֲוָה מִיפַּסְלָא בָּהּ כִּדְאָמְרִי'. וְאַע"ג דְּעָבֵיד אֹהֶל – שָׁרֵי: לָדַעַת. שֶׁהָעוֹמֵד שָׁם יוֹדֵעַ שֶׁלְּשֵׁם מְחִיצָּה הֶעֱמִידוּהוּ שָׁם אָסוּר: שֶׁלֹּא לָדַעַת. מוּתָּר. דְּמִשּׁוּם עֲשִׂיַּית אֹהֶל לֵיכָּא לְמֵימַר, דְּאֵין דֶּרֶךְ בִּנְיָן בְּכָךְ. אֲבָל כְּלִי – דֶּרֶךְ בִּנְיָן בְּכָךְ הוּא, הִלְכָּךְ, דּוֹפֶן שְׁלִישִׁית אָסוּר: שֶׁלֹּא לָדַעַת הֲוָה. לֹא יָדְעוּ הָאֲנָשִׁים עַל מַה קִבְּלוּם שָׁם: רַב חִסְדָּא מִיהָא. שֶׁעָשָׂה הַמְּחִיצָּה, וְנִקְבַּע שָׁם בְּא' מֵהֶן, הָא יָדַע: שֶׁלֹּא מִן הַמִּנְיָן הֲוָה. בְּעוֹשֵׂי הַמְּחִיצָּה: דְּאַעִילוּ מַיָּא. מֵרְשׁוּת הָרַבִּים לרה"י, וְהוּקְבְּעוּ לְשָׁם לָדַעַת, שֶׁהוֹדִיעוּם שֶׁלְּכָךְ הֵם נִקְבָּלִין: זִיקֵי. = נוֹדוֹת. וְשֶׁל רָבָא הָווּ: רִיסְתְּקָא. רְחוֹב הָעִיר, רה"ר: בַּהֲדֵי דְּאָתֵי רָבָא מִפִּירְקֵיהּ. וְהָיָה גְּדוּד דְּשׁוֹמְעֵי הַדְּרָשָׁה בָּאִין אַחֲרָיו, נְטָלָן שַׁמָּשׁ וֶהֱבִיאָן בְּתוֹךְ מְחִיצּוֹת הַבָּאִין: אַסְפַּסְתָּא. שַׁחַת שֶׁל תְּבוּאָה: **מתני'** מִי שֶׁיָּצָא בִּרְשׁוּת. כְּגוֹן לְעֵדוּת הַחֹדֶשׁ, אוֹ לְהַצִּיל מִן הַגַּיִּים וּמִן הַנָּהָר, אוֹ חֲכָמָה הַבָּאָה לְיַלֵּד: כְּבָר נַעֲשָׂה מַעֲשֶׂה. וְאֵינְךָ צָרִיךְ לֵילֵךְ: יֵשׁ לוֹ אַלְפַּיִם אַמָּה לְכָל רוּחַ. מִמָּקוֹם שֶׁנֶּאֱמַר לוֹ: כְּאִילּוּ לֹא יָצָא. מְפָרֵשׁ בַּגְּמָ': חוֹזְרִין לִמְקוֹמָן. מְפָרֵשׁ בַּגְּמָ': **גמ'** מַאי כְּאִילּוּ לֹא יָצָא. הָא וַדַּאי לֹא יָצָא, דְּהָא עֲדַיִין בְּתוֹךְ הַתְּחוּם הוּא: ה"ג: אָמַר רַבָּה הָכִי קָאָמַר וְאִם הָיָה בְּתוֹךְ הַתְּחוּם שֶׁלּוֹ כְּאִילּוּ לֹא יָצָא מִבֵּיתוֹ דָּמֵי. כְּלוֹמַר: הַאי "כְּאִילּוּ לֹא יָצָא" – אַבֵּיתוֹ קָאֵי, וְהָכִי קָאָמַר: אִם הָיָה עֲדַיִין בְּתוֹךְ תְּחוּם בֵּיתוֹ – חוֹזֵר לְבֵיתוֹ, וַהֲרֵי הוּא כְּאִילּוּ לֹא עָקַר רַגְלָיו, לְכָךְ יֵשׁ לוֹ מִבֵּיתוֹ אַלְפַּיִם אַמָּה לְכָל רוּחַ כְּבַתְּחִילָּה. וְלָא אָמְרִינַן מִמָּקוֹם שֶׁנֶּאֱמַר לוֹ יֵשׁ לוֹ אַלְפַּיִם אַמָּה לְכָל רוּחַ: פְּשִׁיטָא. דְּכֵיוָן דַּעֲדַיִין לֹא יָצָא מִן הַתְּחוּם, כְּאִילּוּ הוּא בְּבֵיתוֹ דָּמֵי: מַהוּ דְּתֵימָא כֵּיוָן דְּעָקַר. לָצֵאת בִּרְשׁוּת, וְרַבָּנַן תַּקּוּן לֵיהּ מִמָּקוֹם שֶׁנֶּאֱמַר לוֹ אַלְפַּיִם לְכָל רוּחַ – הָכָא נַמִּי, אַע"ג דְּקָאֵי בִּתְחוּמוֹ – לִימְדּוֹד לֵיהּ מֵהָתָם, וְאִי בָּעֵי לְמֵיפַּק – לֵיפּוֹק, קמ"ל: רַב שִׁימִי בַּר חִיָּיא אָמַר הָכִי קָאָמַר אִם הָיוּ תְּחוּמִין שֶׁנָּתְנוּ לוֹ חֲכָמִים מוּבְלָעִין בְּתוֹךְ הַתְּחוּם שֶׁלּוֹ כְּאִילּוּ לֹא יָצָא מִתְּחוּמוֹ דָּמֵי. כְּלוֹמַר: מַתְנִי' בְּשֶׁכְּבָר יָצָא מִתְּחוּמוֹ עָסְקִינַן, וּכְאִילּוּ לֹא יָצָא(א) – אַתְּחוּמִין קָאֵי, כִּדַהֲוָה ס"ד מֵעִיקָּרָא. וּמַאי אִם הָיָה בְּתוֹךְ הַתְּחוּם – ה"ק: אִם הָיוּ אוֹתָן אַלְפַּיִם הַנְּתוּנוֹת לוֹ לְכָל רוּחַ מָקוֹם שֶׁנֶּאֱמַר לוֹ נִכְנָסוֹת לְתוֹךְ אַלְפַּיִם שֶׁל תְּחוּם בֵּיתוֹ – כְּאִילּוּ לֹא יָצָא מִתְּחוּמוֹ דָּמֵי, וְהוֹלֵךְ עַד בֵּיתוֹ, וַהֲרֵי הוּא כְּבַתְּחִילָּה: רַב שִׁימִי סָבַר הַבְלָעָה מִילְּתָא הִיא. וְכֵיוָן דְּמִיבְלְעָן בִּתְחוּמֵיהּ, וּמַמְטוּ לֵיהּ לְגוֹ תְּחוּמֵיהּ – הָווּ לְהוּ כְּחַד תְּחוּמָא, וּכְמַאן דְּלָא נָפֵיק מִתְּחוּמָא הוּא, וְרַבָּה סָבַר לָאו מִילְּתָא הִיא, הִלְכָּךְ, לָא מָצֵי לְתָרוּצֵי כְּאִילּוּ לֹא יָצָא דְּמַתְנִי' בְּשֶׁכְּבָר יָצָא חוּץ לַתְּחוּם, דְּאִם יָצָא – הִפְסִיד שְׁבִיתַת בֵּיתוֹ, וְקָנָה לוֹ מִמָּקוֹם שֶׁנֶּאֱמַר לוֹ. וְרַבָּה לֵית לֵיהּ הָא דְּתָנוּ נְהַרְדָּעֵי לְעֵיל (דף מא:): וְאִי פִּיקֵּחַ הוּא – עָיֵיל לִתְחוּמוֹ, וְכֵיוָן דְּעָל עָל. וְאִית דְּגָרְסִי בְּלִישָּׁנָא אַחֲרִינָא דְּבֵין רַבָּה וּבֵין רַב שִׁימִי בְּשֶׁכְּבָר יָצָא מִתְּחוּמוֹ מוֹקֵי לֵיהּ, וּבְתַרְוַיְיהוּ גָּרְסִי': אִם הָיוּ תְּחוּמִין שֶׁנָּתְנוּ לוֹ חֲכָמִים מוּבְלָעִין בְּתוֹךְ הַתְּחוּם שֶׁלּוֹ. אֶלָּא, בְּדְרַבָּה גָּרְסִינַן: כְּאִילּוּ לֹא יָצָא מִבֵּיתוֹ, וּבִדְרַב שִׁימִי גָּרְסִינַן: כְּאִילּוּ לֹא יָצָא מִתְּחוּמוֹ. וּבְהָא פְּלִיגִי: דִּלְרַבָּה לָא מְשַׁוְּיָא לְהוּ הַבְלָעָה כְּחַד תְּחוּמָא, שֶׁיִּהְיוּ לוֹ כָּל הַיּוֹם כּוּלּוֹ ח' אֶלֶף אַמָּה. אֶלָּא: כִּי מַמְטוּ לֵיהּ תְּחוּמִין הַנִּיתָּנִין לוֹ עַד תּוֹךְ תְּחוּמוֹ – הָוֵי כְּאִילּוּ לֹא יָצָא מִבֵּיתוֹ כְּלָל, וְלֹא קָנָה שְׁבִיתָה בְּמָקוֹם אַחֵר, וְיֵשׁ לוֹ אַלְפַּיִם מִבֵּיתוֹ לְכָל רוּחַ כְּבַתְּחִילָּה. וְרַב שִׁימִי סָבַר: כְּאִילּוּ לֹא יָצָא מִבֵּיתוֹ לָא אָמְרִינַן אֶלָּא וַדַּאי קָנָה שְׁבִיתָה בַּמָּקוֹם שֶׁנֶּאֱמַר לוֹ, אֲבָל כְּאִילּוּ לֹא יָצָא מִתְּחוּמוֹ אָמְרִי' וְלֹא הִפְסִיד תְּחוּמוֹ הָרִאשׁוֹן, וְיֵשׁ לוֹ קָרוֹב לְח' אֶלֶף. כְּגוֹן, מִמָּקוֹם שֶׁנֶּאֱמַר לוֹ וְלַמִּזְרָח אַלְפַּיִם, וְלַמַּעֲרָב אַלְפַּיִם, וּמִשָּׁם וּלְבֵיתוֹ אַלְפַּיִם, וּמִבֵּיתוֹ וּלְהַלָּן אַלְפַּיִם. דְּהַבְלָעַת תְּחוּמִין מְשַׁוְּיָא לְהוּ לְכוּלְּהוּ תְּחוּמֵי כַּחֲדָא תְּחוּמָא. וְרַבָּה סָבַר לָאו מִילְּתָא הִיא לְשַׁוְּינְהוּ תְּחוּמָא חַד, הִלְכָּךְ, עַל כָּרְחָךְ לָא מִיתּוֹקַם כְּאִילּוּ לֹא יָצָא אַתְּחוּם גְּרֵידָא, וְלוֹמַר תְּחוּמוֹ לֹא הִפְסִיד, אֲבָל יוֹצֵא חָשְׁבִינַן לֵיהּ לְקוּלָּא דְּיֵשׁ לוֹ שְׁבִיתָה אַף בַּמָּקוֹם שֶׁנֶּאֱמַר לוֹ. אֶלָּא, כְּאִילּוּ לֹא יָצָא לְגַמְרֵי קָאָמַר, וַהֲרֵי הוּא כְּבַתְּחִילָּה: וּמַה אִילּוּ שָׁבַת בִּמְעָרָה שֶׁתּוֹכָהּ ד' אֲלָפִים וְעַל גַּגָּהּ פָּחוֹת מִד' אֲלָפִים לֹא נִמְצָא כו'. כְּלוֹמַר: אִי אַתָּה מוֹדֶה שֶׁמְּהַלֵּךְ אֶת גַּגָּהּ וְחוּצָה לָהּ אַלְפַּיִם לְכָל צַד. סְתָם מְעָרָה ב' פְּתָחִים יֵשׁ לָהּ בְּב' קְלוֹתֶיהָ, פֶּתַח לַמִּזְרָח וּפֶתַח לַמַּעֲרָב. מִפֶּתַח הַמִּזְרָח נוֹתֵן לוֹ חוּצָה לָהּ לְצַד מִזְרָח אַלְפַּיִם, וּלְצַד גַּגָּהּ אַלְפַּיִם. וְכֵן מִפֶּתַח הַמַּעֲרָב נוֹתֵן חוּצָה לָהּ לְצַד הַמַּעֲרָב אַלְפַּיִם, וּלְצַד גַּגָּהּ אַלְפַּיִם. וְכֵיוָן דְּגַגָּהּ פָּחוֹת מִד' אֲלָפִים, *כֵּיוָן שֶׁכּוֹתָלֶיהָ מְשׁוּפָּעִין לְצַד גַּגָּהּ וּמִתְרַחֲבוֹת מִלְּמַטָּה בְּקַרְקָעִיתָהּ, (כזה)

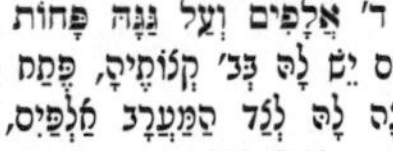

נִמְצָא אַלְפַּיִם שֶׁיֵּשׁ לוֹ עַל גַּגָּהּ כְּשֶׁיָּצָא מִפֶּתַח מִזְרָחִי נִבְלָעוֹת בְּתוֹךְ אַלְפַּיִם שֶׁיֵּשׁ לוֹ עַל גַּגָּהּ כְּשֶׁיּוֹצֵא מִפֶּתַח הַמַּעֲרָב, וְאִי אַתָּה מוֹדֶה שֶׁאִם בָּא לָצֵאת בְּאֵיזֶה מֵהֶן שֶׁיִּרְצֶה, שֶׁיָּכוֹל לְהַלֵּךְ כָּל גַּגָּהּ וְחוּצָה לָהּ אַלְפַּיִם אַמָּה לְכָל צַד, מִשּׁוּם דְּהַבְלָעַת תְּחוּמִין מְשַׁוֵּי לִתְחוּמֵי שְׁנֵי הַיְּצִיאוֹת כְּחַד. וְאִילּוּ הֲוָה גַּגָּהּ ד' אֲלָפִים שְׁלֵימוֹת, וְיָצָא בְּפֶתַח מִזְרָח – אֵינוֹ יָכוֹל לְהַלֵּךְ לְצַד גַּגָּהּ אֶלָּא אַלְפַּיִם, וְאִם הָיָה רוֹצֶה לְהַלֵּךְ בְּאַלְפַּיִם מַעֲרָבִיּוֹת – הָיָה צָרִיךְ לַחֲזוֹר עַל הָעָקֵב, וְלִיכָּנֵס בַּמְּעָרָה וְלַחֲזוֹר וְלָצֵאת דֶּרֶךְ פֶּתַח מַעֲרָבִי. אַלְמָא: מִילְּתָא הִיא, וְקַשְׁיָא לְתַרְוַיְיהוּ לִישָּׁנֵי: וְלָא שָׁנֵי לָךְ בּוֹ. הָכָא נַמִּי ב' תְּחוּמִין מֵחֲמַת שְׁבִיתָה חֲדָא קָמָתוּ לָהּ, וְכֵיוָן דְּמִיבְלְעֵי לְעֵיל הָווּ חַד תְּחוּמָא. אֲבָל בְּגֵי מַתְנִי' לֹא שָׁבַת בַּאֲוִיר מְחִיצוֹת שְׁבִיתָה הַשְּׁנִיָּה, הִלְכָּךְ, כֵּיוָן דְּקָנֵי לָהּ שְׁבִיתָה בַּתְרַיְיתָא – תּוּ לֵית לֵיהּ שְׁבִיתָה קַמַּיְיתָא. וְהֵיכָא דְּיָצָא חוּץ לַתְּחוּם אֵין לוֹ אֶלָּא מִמָּקוֹם שֶׁנֶּאֱמַר לוֹ אַלְפַּיִם, וַאֲפִי' נִכְנְסוּ לְתוֹךְ תְּחוּמוֹ אֵינוֹ הוֹלֵךְ מִמָּקוֹם שֶׁכָּלוּ שָׁם וָהָלְאָה כְּלוּם. וּלְלִישָּׁנָא אַחֲרִינָא הָכִי מְפָרֵשׁ: כֵּיוָן דְּלֹא שָׁבַת בַּאֲוִיר מְחִיצוֹת שְׁנִיָּה לָא יָהֲבִינַן לֵיהּ ב' שְׁבִיתוֹת, אֶלָּא אוֹ הַאי אִית לֵיהּ אוֹ הַאי אִית לֵיהּ. אִם מוּבְלָעוֹת – אִית לֵיהּ שְׁבִיתַת בֵּיתוֹ, וְאֵין לוֹ מִמָּקוֹם שֶׁנֶּאֱמַר לוֹ אֶלָּא כְּדֵי לָבֹא וְלִיכָּנֵס בִּתְחוּמוֹ. וְאִם אֵינָן מוּבְלָעוֹת – קָנָה מְקוֹמוֹ וְהִפְסִיד בֵּיתוֹ. וּלְשׁוֹן הָרִאשׁוֹן נִרְאֶה הָגוּן: וְהָא

כל היוצאין להציל חוזרין למקומן. הא דלא חשיב ליה בפ"ק דבילה (דף יא:) גבי הנך ג' דהתירו סופן משום תחילתן – דזה אינו חידוש, וכל הנהו צריכי, כדאמרינן התם:

ומר סבר הבלעת תחומין לאו מילתא היא. פ"ה: ולית ליה לרבה הא דנהרדעי דאמרי לעיל (דף מא:) אי פקח הוא עייל לתחומי' וכיון דעל על. ולר"י נראה דאית ליה הא דנהרדעי, כיון שנכנס בתחומו מפני כבוד הבריות, ויצא מד' אמותיו כיון שצריך ליתן לו ד' אמות חדשות – יכול לחזור ולקנות תחומו הראשון. אבל הכא, מכיון שיצא חוץ מתחומו וקנה לו תחום אחר – לא הותר ליעקר *מתחום שקבע, כדפי' לעיל. דאי לאו הכי, תיקשי לה מתני' לנהרדעי דאמרי *אפי' אמה אחת לא יכנס, ואף על גב דע"י ארבע אמותיו נכנס לתחומו הראשון, ולא אמר כיון דעל על: ומדרכי

רבינו חננאל

שלישית אדם אאדם נמי ל"ק הא דתניא עושין שלא לדעת כלומר שלא יתכוון בתחלה לעשות מחיצה והא דתניא לא יעשה לדעת. ואקשינן איני והא רב חסדא לדעת הוה. וא"ל רב נחמן זיל עביד ופרקינן רב חסדא שלא מן המנין הוה כלומר לא נמנה רב חסדא עם אותם דמלו להו למחיצה דהנהו כולם שלא לדעת הוו: הנהו בני גננא. פי' בני החופה דעייל אסא מחוץ לתחום נגדינהו מר שמואל אמר להו אי אמור דאמור רבנן שלא לדעת. לדעת מי אמור. הנהו (דייקינן) [זיקי] דחמרא דהוו (שדי) [שדיין] בדסקרתא דמחוזא [בהדי] דאתא רבא מפירקא עיילינהו בשבת אחריתי נמי הוו בעו לעיילי אמר להו. א"כ הוו להו לדעת ואסיר. לוי עיילו ליה תיבנא. זעירי אספסתא רב אשי מיא. והני כולהו שלא לדעת: מתני' מי שיצא ברשות כו'. ואם היה בתוך התחום כאילו לא יצא. מאי קאמר אמר רבה הכי קאמר אם היה בתוך התחום שלו כאילו לא יצא מביתו דמי פשיטא. מהו דתימא כיון דעקר רגליו לצאת חוץ לתחום אע"ג דלא יצא כמי דיצא דמי ונאסר בתחומו קמ"ל. רב שימי אמר הכי קתני אם אותו המקום שהלך בו תחומו מובלע בתוך התחום שלו כלומר הוא פחות מאלפים אמה. כיון שנתנו לו חכמים אלפים אמה לכל רוח מהלך באותן אלפים אמה שהן כנגד תחומו ועייל בתחומו וכיון שנכנס חזר ברשות שהיתה לו מקודם שיצא. קסבר רב שימי הבלעת תחומין מלתא היא. ורבה סבר הבלעת תחומין לאו מלתא היא. א"ל [אביי] לרבה ואת לא תסברא דהבלעת תחומין מלתא היא. ומה אילו שבת במערה שיש בה ד' אלפים אמה ועל גגה פחות מד' אלפים אמה לא נמצא מהלך את כולה וחוצה לה אלפים אמה. ודחי שאני הכא דהא מחיצות מבעוד יום ואקשינן והיכא דלא שבת באויר מבע"י לא והתנן

[במשנה שבמשניות איתא שכל וע"ש בפירוש הר' מברטנורה וכן בפירוש הרמב"ם וכ"ה ברב אלפס]

מתחום שקנה כדפי' כצ"ל

[לקמן נב:]

גי' רש"ל כגון

וְהָא תְּנַן רַבִּי אֱלִיעֶזֶר אוֹמֵר. מִי שֶׁיָּצָא חוּץ לַתְּחוּם שְׁתֵּי אַמּוֹת – יִכָּנֵס, אֲבָל ג' – לֹא יִכָּנֵס. מַאי הַאי שִׁיעוּרָא דְּנָקַט? לָאו ר' אֱלִיעֶזֶר לְטַעְמֵיהּ דְּאָמַר בְּמַתְנִיתִין גַּבֵּי ד' אַמּוֹת שֶׁנָּתְנוּ חֲכָמִים לַיּוֹצֵא חוּץ לַתְּחוּם דְּהוּא בְּאֶמְצָעָן, שֶׁיֵּשׁ לוֹ לְכָל צִדָּיו ב' אַמּוֹת. וּלְפִיכָךְ, זֶה שֶׁיָּצָא ב' אַמּוֹת חוּץ לַתְּחוּם, כֵּיוָן דְּב' אַמּוֹתָיו דְּבוּקוֹת לוֹ בִּתְחוּמוֹ – סְבִירָא לֵיהּ לְרַבִּי אֱלִיעֶזֶר דִּכְמַאן דְּמוּבְלָעַן בִּתְחוּמֵיהּ דָּמוּ, וּמוּתָּר לִיכָּנֵס. אַלְמָא: מִילְּתָא הִיא. לְלִישָּׁנָא קַמָּא הָוְיָא תְּיוּבְתֵּיהּ, אֲבָל לְלִישָּׁנָא בַּתְרָא לָא נְהִירָא לִי, דְּהָא לָא קָאָסְרִי לֵיהּ לְמֶהְדַּר. וּמַאן דְּגָרֵיס לָהּ מְפָרֵשׁ דְּכֵיוָן דְּהָא לָא הָווּ מוּבְלָעוֹת אֶלָּא דְּבוּקוֹת, וַאֲפִילּוּ הָכִי שָׁרֵי – שְׁמַע מִינָּהּ הַבְלָעָה דָּבָר גָּדוֹל הוּא, וְהֵיכָא דְּמִיבְלְעָן – חַד תְּחוּמָא הָוֵי: וּמִדְּרַבִּי אֱלִיעֶזֶר אוֹתַבְתְּ לֵיהּ לְמָר. הָא פְּלִיגִי רַבָּנַן עֲלֵיהּ בְּמַתְנִי': לִדְבַר מִצְוָה מוֹדוּ לֵיהּ. וּמַתְנִי' דְּמִי שֶׁיָּצָא בִּרְשׁוּת דְּבַר מִצְוָה הוּא, וְקָאָמַר רַבָּה לְעֵיל דְּהַבְלָעָה לָא מְהַנְיָא: וַאֲפִילּוּ טוּבָא. יוֹתֵר מֵאַרְבַּעַת אֲלָפִים?! בִּתְמִיָּה: וְהָאָמַרְתְּ רֵישָׁא: הֵיכָא דְּלָא מִיבַּלְעָן – אַלְפַּיִם אִית לֵיהּ, וְתוּ לָא: אָמַר רַב יְהוּדָה אָמַר רַב. לָא תֵּימָא אֲפִי' טוּבָא, דְּלָא שָׁרֵי אֶלָּא אַלְפַּיִם. וְהָא אֲתָא לְאַשְׁמְעִינַן דְּחוֹזְרִין בִּכְלֵי זַיְינָן, וְלָא אָמְרִינַן כֵּיוָן דְּנַעֲשָׂה מַעֲשֶׂה יַשְׁלִיכוּ כְּלֵי זַיְינָן מֵעֲלֵיהֶן, וְלֹא יְחַלְּלוּ שַׁבָּת בַּחֲזָרָתָן. וְטַעְמָא מְפָרֵשׁ לְקַמָּן: דִּילְמָא לְהַצִּיל שָׁאנֵי. וּמִי שֶׁיָּצָא בִּרְשׁוּת דְּמַתְנִיתִין – אִיכָּא לְאוֹקְמֵי בְּעֵדוּת הַחֹדֶשׁ, וּבַחֲכָמָה הַבָּאָה לְיַלֵּד. אֲבָל הַבָּא לְהַצִּיל מֵאוֹיְבִים – יֵשׁ לָחוּשׁ שֶׁמָּא אוֹיְבִים יִרְדְּפוּ אַחֲרָיו, הִלְכָּךְ, אֲפִי' טוּבָא נַמִי יִכָּנְסוּ לָעִיר: לֹא הָיוּ זָזִין מִשָּׁם. בַּיּוֹצְאִין חוּץ לַתְּחוּם לְהָעִיד עַל הַחֹדֶשׁ מַיְירֵי, בְּמַסֶּכֶת ר"ה (דף כג:). לֹא הָיוּ זָזִין, דְּמִי שֶׁיָּצָא חוּץ לַתְּחוּם אֵין לוֹ אֶלָּא ד' אַמּוֹת: וְהַבָּא לְהַצִּיל מִן הַגַּיִּים כו'. וְקָאָמַר: אַלְפַּיִם וְתוּ לָא. וּמַתְנִי' קָתָנֵי כָּל הַיּוֹצְאִין לְהַצִּיל חוֹזְרִין לִמְקוֹמָן, וַאֲפִי' טוּבָא: מַנִּיחִים כְּלֵי זַיְינָן. בַּחֲזִירָתָן, בַּבַּיִת הַחִיצוֹן שֶׁמּוּנָּחִין חוּץ לַחוֹמָה: הִכִּירוּ בָּהֶן אוֹיְבִים. שֶׁיָּצְאוּ חוּץ לָעִיר, וְרָדְפוּ אַחֲרֵיהֶן: נִכְנְסוּ. הַיּוֹצְאִין לִיטּוֹל כְּלֵי זַיְינָן וְהַבַּיִת צַר, וְדָחֲקוּ זֶה אֶת זֶה: נִצְּחוּ יִשְׂרָאֵל. אַלְפַּיִם וְתוּ לָא: נִצְּחוּ אוּמּוֹת הָעוֹלָם. חוֹזְרִין לִמְקוֹמָן אֲפִי' טוּבָא: אֵין יוֹצְאִין עֲלֵיהֶן. כִּדְמְפָרֵשׁ לְקַמָּן כְּשֶׁבָּאוּ נָכְרִים עַל עִסְקֵי מָמוֹן: לַסְּפָר. עִיר שֶׁמַּבְדֶּלֶת בֵּין גְּבוּל יִשְׂרָאֵל לִגְבוּל הָאוּמּוֹת, יוֹצְאִין עֲלֵיהֶם שֶׁמָּא יִלְכְּדוּהָ וּמִשָּׁם תְּהֵא נוֹחָה הָאָרֶץ לִיכָּבֵשׁ לִפְנֵיהֶם: תַּרְגּוּמָא. אֵי זוֹ הִיא עִיר בְּבָבֶל דַּהֲוְיָא סְמוּכָה לַסְּפָר: נְהַרְדְּעָא. שֶׁהָיְתָה סְמוּכָה לַנָּכְרִים מִצַּד אֶחָד, וְלַעֲיָירוֹת שֶׁיּוֹשְׁבִין בָּהֶן בְּנֵי גוֹלָה מִצַּד שֵׁנִי: וְהֵם לֹא בָּאוּ כו'. וְאַף עַל פִּי כֵן מָסַר דָּוִד עַצְמוֹ לְהַצִּיל: אִי שָׁרֵי אִי אָסוּר. וְשַׁבָּת הָיְתָה: הֲרֵי שְׁמוּאֵל וּבֵית דִּינוֹ קַיָּים. וּמִידֵּי דְּאִיסּוּר וְהֶיתֵּר לָא מְשַׁיְּילֵי בְּאוּרִים וְתוּמִּים: וְהוֹשַׁעְתָּ. אַלְמָא: מְבַשְּׂרֵי לֵיהּ דְּנָצַח: מתני' מִי שֶׁיָּשַׁב בַּדֶּרֶךְ. לָנוּחַ, שֶׁהָיָה עָיֵיף וְלֹא הָיָה יוֹדֵעַ שֶׁהוּא בִּתְחוּם הָעִיר, וְחָשְׁכָה לוֹ שָׁם וּכְשֶׁעָמַד רָאָה שֶׁהוּא סָמוּךְ לָעִיר וּבִתְחוּמָהּ: לֹא יִכָּנֵס לָעִיר. לִהְיוֹת כְּאַנְשֵׁי הָעִיר אֶלָּא מִמָּקוֹם שֶׁחָשְׁכָה לוֹ מוֹדֵד אַלְפַּיִם פְּסִיעוֹת בֵּינוֹנִיּוֹת, וְעַד מָקוֹם שֶׁכָּלוּ יִכָּנֵס: בְּלֹא מִתְכַּוֵּין. שֶׁלֹּא הָיָה יוֹדֵעַ כְּשֶׁחָשְׁכָה לוֹ שֶׁהוּא בִּתְחוּם הָעִיר, וְלֹא נִתְכַּוֵּין לִהְיוֹת שְׁבִיתָתוֹ בָּעִיר אֶלָּא בִּמְקוֹמוֹ: גמ' בְּלִבּוֹ הָיְתָה. כְּשֶׁיָּשַׁב שָׁם הָיָה יוֹדֵעַ שֶׁהוּא בְּתוֹךְ אַלְפַּיִם לִמְקוֹם שְׁבִיתָתוֹ: מתני' אֵין לוֹ אֶלָּא ד' אַמּוֹת. הוֹאִיל וְיָשֵׁן הָיָה לֹא נִתְכַּוֵּין לִקְנוֹת שְׁבִיתָה: וְהוּא בְּאֶמְצָעָן. שֶׁל ד' אַמּוֹת. כְּלוֹמַר: ב' אַמּוֹת יֵשׁ לוֹ לְכָל צִדָּיו: לְאֵיזֶה רוּחַ שֶׁיִּרְצֶה. יִטּוֹל ד' אַמּוֹת, וְאַחַר שֶׁבֵּירֵר לוֹ לְצַד זֶה – אֵין יָכוֹל לַחֲזוֹר וְלִבְרוֹר לְצַד אַחֵר: הָיוּ שְׁנַיִם. עוֹמְדִין זֶה רָחוֹק מִזֶּה ו' אַמּוֹת, דְּמִיבַּלְעָן ב' אַמּוֹת שֶׁל כָּל אֶחָד בְּתוֹךְ שֶׁל חֲבֵרוֹ: מְבִיאִין וְאוֹכְלִין. בְּתוֹךְ אוֹתָן ב' אַמּוֹת: וּבִלְבַד

תורה אור

*וְהָתְנַן, ר"א אוֹמֵר: שְׁתַּיִם יִכָּנֵס, שְׁלֹשָׁה לֹא יִכָּנֵס. מַאי לָאו, רַבִּי אֱלִיעֶזֶר לְטַעְמֵיהּ, דְּאָמַר: וְהוּא בְּאֶמְצָעָן, וְאַרְבַּע אַמּוֹת דִּיהָבוּ לֵיהּ רַבָּנַן כְּמַאן דְּמִיבְלָעַן דָּמוּ, וְקָאָמַר "יִכָּנֵס", אַלְמָא: הַבְלָעַת תְּחוּמִין מִילְּתָא הִיא! א"ל רַבָּה בַּר בַּר *חָנָה לְאַבַּיֵי: וּמִדְּר"א קָמוֹתַבְתְּ לֵיהּ לְמָר?! אֲמַר לֵיהּ: אִין, דְּשַׁמְעִי לִי מִינֵּיהּ דְּמָר: עַד כָּאן לָא פְּלִיגִי רַבָּנַן עֲלֵיהּ דְּר"א – אֶלָּא לִדְבַר הָרְשׁוּת, אֲבָל לִדְבַר מִצְוָה – מוֹדוּ לֵיהּ.§ "וְכָל הַיּוֹצְאִין לְהַצִּיל חוֹזְרִין לִמְקוֹמָן".§ וַאֲפִי' טוּבָא? וְהָא אָמַרְתְּ רֵישָׁא "אַלְפַּיִם אַמָּה" וְתוּ לֹא! אָמַר רַב יְהוּדָה, אָמַר רַב: שֶׁחוֹזְרִין בִּכְלֵי זַיְינָן לִמְקוֹמָן. וּמַאי קוּשְׁיָא? דִּילְמָא לְהַצִּיל שָׁאנֵי?! אֶלָּא אִי קַשְׁיָא הָא קַשְׁיָא: דִּתְנַן, *בָּרִאשׁוֹנָה לֹא הָיוּ זָזִין מִשָּׁם כָּל הַיּוֹם כּוּלּוֹ, הִתְקִין ר"ג הַזָּקֵן [א]שֶׁיֵּשׁ לָהֶן אַלְפַּיִם אַמָּה לְכָל רוּחַ. וְלֹא אֵלּוּ בִּלְבַד אָמְרוּ, אֶלָּא אֲפִי' חֲכָמָה הַבָּאָה לְיַלֵּד, [ב]וְהַבָּא לְהַצִּיל מִן הַגַּיִּים וּמִן הַנָּהָר וּמִן הַמַּפּוֹלֶת וּמִן הַדְּלֵיקָה – הֲרֵי הֵן כְּאַנְשֵׁי הָעִיר, וְיֵשׁ לָהֶן אַלְפַּיִם אַמָּה לְכָל רוּחַ. וְתוּ לֹא? וְהָא אָמַרְתְּ: כָּל הַיּוֹצְאִין לְהַצִּיל חוֹזְרִין לִמְקוֹמָן, אֲפִילּוּ טוּבָא! [ג]אָמַר רַב [יְהוּדָה, אָמַר רַב]: שֶׁחוֹזְרִין בִּכְלֵי זַיְינָן לִמְקוֹמָן. כִּדְתַנְיָא: *בָּרִאשׁוֹנָה הָיוּ מַנִּיחִין כְּלֵי זַיְינָן בַּבַּיִת הַסָּמוּךְ לַחוֹמָה, פַּעַם אַחַת הִכִּירוּ בָּהֶן אוֹיְבִים וְרָדְפוּ אַחֲרֵיהֶם, וְנִכְנְסוּ לִיטּוֹל כְּלֵי זַיְינָן, וְנִכְנְסוּ אוֹיְבִים אַחֲרֵיהֶן. דָּחֲקוּ זֶה אֶת זֶה, וְהָרְגוּ זֶה אֶת זֶה יוֹתֵר מִמַּה שֶּׁהָרְגוּ אוֹיְבִים. בְּאוֹתָהּ שָׁעָה הִתְקִינוּ שֶׁיְּהוּ חוֹזְרִין לִמְקוֹמָן בִּכְלֵי זַיְינָן. רַב נַחְמָן בַּר יִצְחָק אָמַר: ל"ק; כָּאן – שֶׁנִּצְּחוּ יִשְׂרָאֵל אֶת אוּמּוֹת הָעוֹלָם, כָּאן – [ד]שֶׁנִּצְּחוּ אוּמּוֹת הָעוֹלָם אֶת עַצְמָן. אָמַר רַב יְהוּדָה, אָמַר רַב: [ה]נָכְרִים שֶׁצָּרוּ עַל עֲיָירוֹת יִשְׂרָאֵל – אֵין יוֹצְאִין עֲלֵיהֶם בִּכְלֵי זַיְינָן, וְאֵין מְחַלְּלִין עֲלֵיהֶן אֶת הַשַּׁבָּת. תַּנְיָא נַמִי הָכִי: נָכְרִים שֶׁצָּרוּ וכו'. *[ו]בַּמֶּה דְּבָרִים אֲמוּרִים – כְּשֶׁבָּאוּ עַל עִסְקֵי מָמוֹן. אֲבָל בָּאוּ עַל עִסְקֵי נְפָשׁוֹת – יוֹצְאִין עֲלֵיהֶן בִּכְלֵי זַיְינָן, וּמְחַלְּלִין עֲלֵיהֶן אֶת הַשַּׁבָּת. וּבְעִיר הַסְּמוּכָה לַסְּפָר, אֲפִילּוּ לֹא בָּאוּ עַל עִסְקֵי נְפָשׁוֹת אֶלָּא עַל עִסְקֵי תֶּבֶן וָקַשׁ – יוֹצְאִין עֲלֵיהֶן בִּכְלֵי זַיְינָן, וּמְחַלְּלִין עֲלֵיהֶן אֶת הַשַּׁבָּת. *אָמַר רַב יוֹסֵף בַּר מַנְיוּמֵי, אָמַר רַב נַחְמָן: וּבָבֶל כְּעִיר הַסְּמוּכָה לַסְּפָר דָּמְיָא. וְתַרְגּוּמָא – נְהַרְדְּעָא. דָּרַשׁ רַבִּי דּוֹסְתַּאי דְּמִן בִּירִי: מַאי דִּכְתִיב: °"וַיַּגִּידוּ לְדָוִד לֵאמֹר הִנֵּה פְלִשְׁתִּים נִלְחָמִים בִּקְעִילָה וְהֵמָּה שֹׁסִים אֶת הַגְּרָנוֹת". תְּנָא: קְעִילָה עִיר הַסְּמוּכָה לַסְּפָר הָיְתָה, וְהֵם לֹא בָּאוּ אֶלָּא עַל עִסְקֵי תֶּבֶן וָקַשׁ. דִּכְתִיב: "וְהֵמָּה שֹׁסִים אֶת הַגְּרָנוֹת", וּכְתִיב: °"וַיִּשְׁאַל דָּוִד בַּה' לֵאמֹר הַאֵלֵךְ וְהִכֵּיתִי בַּפְּלִשְׁתִּים הָאֵלֶּה וַיֹּאמֶר ה' אֶל דָּוִד לֵךְ וְהִכִּיתָ *בַפְּלִשְׁתִּים וְהוֹשַׁעְתָּ אֶת קְעִילָה". מַאי קָמִבַּעְיָא לֵיהּ? אִילֵימָא אִי שָׁרֵי אִי אָסוּר – הֲרֵי בֵּית דִּינוֹ שֶׁל שְׁמוּאֵל הָרָמָתִי קַיָּים. אֶלָּא: אִי מַצְלַח אִי לָא מַצְלַח. דַּיְקָא נַמִי, דִּכְתִיב: "לֵךְ וְהִכִּיתָ בַפְּלִשְׁתִּים וְהוֹשַׁעְתָּ אֶת קְעִילָה", ש"מ.§ **מתני'** *מִי שֶׁיָּשַׁב בַּדֶּרֶךְ וְעָמַד וְרָאָה הֲרֵי (זֶה) הוּא סָמוּךְ לָעִיר – [הוֹאִיל] וְלֹא הָיְתָה כַּוָּונָתוֹ לְכָךְ – לֹא יִכָּנֵס, דִּבְרֵי רַבִּי מֵאִיר. ר' יְהוּדָה אוֹמֵר: [ז]יִכָּנֵס. א"ר יְהוּדָה: מַעֲשֶׂה הָיָה וְנִכְנַס רַבִּי טַרְפוֹן בְּלֹא מִתְכַּוֵּין.§ **גמ'** תַּנְיָא, א"ר יְהוּדָה: מַעֲשֶׂה בְּרַבִּי טַרְפוֹן שֶׁהָיָה מְהַלֵּךְ בַּדֶּרֶךְ וְחָשְׁכָה לוֹ, וְלָן חוּץ לָעִיר. לְשַׁחֲרִית מְצָאוּהוּ רוֹעֵי בָקָר, אָמְרוּ לוֹ: רַבִּי, הֲרֵי הָעִיר לְפָנֶיךָ, הִכָּנֵס! נִכְנַס וְיָשַׁב בְּבֵית הַמִּדְרָשׁ, וְדָרַשׁ כָּל הַיּוֹם כּוּלּוֹ. (אָמְרוּ *לוֹ:) *מִשָּׁם רְאָיָה?! שֶׁמָּא בְּלִבּוֹ הָיְתָה, אוֹ בֵּית הַמִּדְרָשׁ מוּבְלָע בְּתוֹךְ תְּחוּמוֹ הָיָה.§ **מתני'** [ח]מִי שֶׁיָּשַׁן בַּדֶּרֶךְ וְלֹא יָדַע *שֶׁחֲשֵׁיכָה – יֵשׁ לוֹ אַלְפַּיִם אַמָּה לְכָל רוּחַ, דִּבְרֵי ר' יוֹחָנָן בֶּן נוּרִי. וַחֲכָמִים אוֹמְרִים: אֵין לוֹ אֶלָּא אַרְבַּע אַמּוֹת. ר"א אוֹמֵר: וְהוּא בְּאֶמְצָעָן. ר' יְהוּדָה אוֹמֵר: לְאֵיזֶה רוּחַ שֶׁיִּרְצֶה יֵלֵךְ. וּמוֹדֶה ר' יְהוּדָה, שֶׁאִם בֵּירַר לוֹ – שֶׁאֵינוֹ יָכוֹל לַחֲזוֹר בּוֹ. [ט]הָיוּ שְׁנַיִם, מִקְצָת אַמּוֹתָיו שֶׁל זֶה בְּתוֹךְ אַמּוֹתָיו שֶׁל זֶה – מְבִיאִין וְאוֹכְלִין בָּאֶמְצַע, וּבִלְבַד

ומדרבי אליעזר קמותבת ליה למר. משמע דרבה אמר: אנא דאמר כרבנן. וזה קשה ללשון שני דרש"י, דרבה אית ליה הבלעת תחומין מילתא היא לענין ליכנס, ולרבנן לית להן הבלעה כלל:

אי מצלח אי לא מצלח. וא"ת: א"כ היכא דריש ר' דוסתאי דמחללין עליו השבת? דלמא חול היה. אי משום דמספקא ליה, דכתיב: "וישאל דוד" – הא מסקינן אי מצלח אי לא מצלח. ויש לומר: דמוכחא מילתא מדקאמר נלחמים בקעילה, דקרי ליה מלחמה ומסר דוד נפשיה עליה, אע"פ שלא באו אלא על עסקי תבן וקש – שמע מינה דמחללין עליה נמי את השבת:

כו א מיי' פכ"ז מהל' שבת הל' יז סמג לאוין סו טוש"ע א"ח סי' תז סעיף א:
כז ב ג ד מיי' שם וטוש"ע שם ס"ג וסי' שכט סעיף ט:
כח ה ו מיי' פ"ב מהל' שבת הלכה כג סמג לאוין סה סו טוש"ע א"ח סי' שכט סעיף ו[ז] [וברב אלפס שבת פ"א ח.]:
כט ז מיי' פכ"ז מהל' שבת הלכה ט סמג עשין א טוש"ע א"ח סי' ת:
ל ח מיי' שם הלכה ד טור ש"ע א"ח סי' תא:
לא ט מיי' פי"ב מהל' שבת הלכה טז סמג לאוין סה טוש"ע א"ח סי' שמט ס"ד:

לקמן נב: | ר"ה כג: | [תוספ' פ"ג] | [תוספתא שם] | [ב"ק פ"ג.] | שמואל א כג | שם | בכ"י את פלשתים וכן למטה | [גירסת השאלתות מי שישן בדרך ועמד והרי הוא סמוך וכו'] | [שבת כט: וש"נ] | [בירושלמי ובכי"ף עד שחשכה] | [גירסת השאלתות פרשת בשלח סי' מח אמר לי' ר' עקיבא משום ראיה וכו']

רבינו חננאל

והתנן ר' אלעזר אומר שתים יכנס והנה זה עכשיו יצא חוץ לתחום ולאו מבע"י שבת [באויר] במחיצות מאי לאו ר"א לטעמיה דאמר מי שישן ולא ידע עד שחשכה יש לו ד' אמות והוא באמצען והני ד' אמות [illegible] דיהבו ליה רבנן כמאן דמיבלען בתחומיה דמי לפיכך תני שתים יכנס א"ל ומדר' אלעזר מותבת ליה לרבה א"ל [אין] דשמיעא לי מיניה דמר דרבה דאמר עד כאן לא פליגי רבנן עליה דר' אלעזר דאמרי מי שיצא חוץ לתחום אפי' [אמה] אחת לא יכנס אלא לדבר הרשות אבל לדבר מצוה מודו ליה ומתני בדבר מצוה היא דקתני *) מי שיצא חוץ לתחום אפי' [אמה] אחת לא יכנס לא לדבר הרשות. פי' ברשות ב"ד: **מתני'** כל היוצאין להציל חוזרין למקומן אוקימנא חוזרין בכלי זיינם למקומן. רב נחמן בר יצחק אמר בזמן שיד ישראל תקיפה על אומות העולם אלפים אמה ותו לא. ובזמן שיד גוים תקיפה על ישראל אפילו טובא. אמר רב יהודה אמר רב גוים שצרו על עיירות של ישראל מחללין עליהן את השבת ויוצאין עליהן בכלי זיין תניא נמי הכי כו' בד"א שבאו על עסקי נפשות אבל באו על עסקי ממון אין יוצאין עליהן בכלי זיין ואין מחללין עליהן את השבת ובעיר הסמוכה לספר פי' על שפת הים. אפילו לא באו אלא על עסקי תבן מחללין עליהן השבת ויוצאין בכלי זיין. אמר רב נחמן בבל כעיר הסמוכה לספר דמיא תרגימא נהרדעא. קעילה עיר הסמוכה לספר היתה והן לא באו אלא על עסקי תבן וקש וישאל דוד בה' האלך כו' ויאמר ה' אל דוד לך והכית בפלשתים והושעת את קעילה מאי קמבעיא ליה כו': **מתני'** מי שישן בדרך ועמד והרי הוא קרוב לעיר כו' פי' כיון שהיה בדעתו מתחלה לילך בזו העיר אע"פ שעכשיו לא הזכיר כלום. אמר רבי יהודה דינו כדין שיצא לילך בעיר שמערבין בו שמותר לו לילך עד אותה העיר. אם היה בתוך ד' אלפים אמה שנמצא כאילו עירב ברגליו וכך נכנס רבי טרפון בלא מתכוין ב' תחומי שבת כאילו עירב ברגליו. תניא אמר ר' יהודה מעשה ברבי טרפון שחשכה לו לילי שבת ולן חוץ לעיר כו' א"ל ר' יעקב שמא ר' טרפון בלבו היה לכנס או שמא ההוא בהמ"ד מובלע בתחומו היה: **מתני'** מי שישן בדרך ולא ידע עד שחשכה וכו':

בעי'

*) דברי רבינו אלו כמו שהם לפנינו הם מקולקלי הכונה ונראה דצ"ל מי שיצא ברשות ואמרו לו כו' ופי' ברשות ב"ד כצ"ל.

עין משפט נר מצוה

לב א מיי' פ"ה מהל' י"ט הלכה יד סמג עשין א טוש"ע א"ח סי' תצז סעיף יד:

לג ב מיי' שם טוש"ע שם סעיף טז:

וּבִלְבַד שֶׁלֹּא יוֹצִיא זֶה מִתּוֹךְ שֶׁלּוֹ לְתוֹךְ שֶׁל חֲבֵרוֹ. הָיוּ שְׁלֹשָׁה, וְהָאֶמְצָעִי מוּבְלָע בֵּינֵיהֶן — הוּא מוּתָּר עִמָּהֶן, וְהֵן מוּתָּרִין עִמּוֹ, וּשְׁנַיִם הַחִיצוֹנִים אֲסוּרִין זֶה עִם זֶה. *אָמַר רַבִּי שִׁמְעוֹן: לְמָה הַדָּבָר דּוֹמֶה — לְשָׁלֹשׁ חֲצֵירוֹת הַפְּתוּחוֹת זוֹ לָזוֹ, *וּפְתוּחוֹת לרה"ר. עֵירְבוּ שְׁתַּיִם עִם הָאֶמְצָעִית — הִיא מוּתֶּרֶת עִמָּהֶן וְהֵם מוּתָּרוֹת עִמָּהּ, וּשְׁתַּיִם הַחִיצוֹנוֹת אֲסוּרוֹת זוֹ עִם זוֹ.§

גמ' בָּעֵי רָבָא: מַאי קָסָבַר ר' יוֹחָנָן בֶּן נוּרִי? מִסְבַּר קָא סָבַר: *חֶפְצֵי הֶפְקֵר קוֹנִין שְׁבִיתָה, וּבְדִין הוּא דְּלִיפְלוֹג בְּכֵלִים. וְהָא דְּקָמִיפַּלְגִי בְּאָדָם — לְהוֹדִיעֲךָ כּוֹחָן דְּרַבָּנַן, דְּאע"ג דְּאִיכָּא לְמֵימַר: הוֹאִיל וְנֵיעוֹר קָנָה — יָשֵׁן נַמִּי קָנָה, קמ"ל דְּלָא. אוֹ דִּילְמָא, קָסָבַר ר' יוֹחָנָן בֶּן נוּרִי בְּעָלְמָא: חֶפְצֵי הֶפְקֵר אֵין קוֹנִין שְׁבִיתָה. וְהָכָא הַיְינוּ טַעְמָא: הוֹאִיל וְנֵיעוֹר קָנָה — יָשֵׁן נַמִּי קָנָה? אָמַר רַב יוֹסֵף, ת"ש: גְּשָׁמִים שֶׁיָּרְדוּ מֵעי"ט, יֵשׁ לָהֶן אַלְפַּיִם אַמָּה לְכָל רוּחַ. בְּי"ט — הֲרֵי הֵן כְּרַגְלֵי כָּל אָדָם. אִי אָמְרַתְּ בִּשְׁלָמָא קָסָבַר רַבִּי יוֹחָנָן בֶּן נוּרִי חֶפְצֵי הֶפְקֵר קוֹנִין שְׁבִיתָה, הָא מַנִּי — ר' יוֹחָנָן הִיא. אֶלָּא אִי אָמְרַתְּ חֶפְצֵי הֶפְקֵר אֵין קוֹנִין שְׁבִיתָה, הָא מַנִּי? לָא רַבִּי יוֹחָנָן וְלָא רַבָּנַן! יָתֵיב אַבַּיֵי וְקָאָמַר לָהּ לְהָא שְׁמַעְתָּא. א"ל רַב סַפְרָא לְאַבַּיֵי: וְדִילְמָא °בִּגְשָׁמִים הַסְּמוּכִין לָעִיר עָסְקִינַן, וְאַנְשֵׁי אוֹתָהּ הָעִיר דַּעְתָּם עִילָּוַיְיהוּ? אֲמַר לֵיהּ: לָא ס"ד, אדִּתְנַן: *בּוֹר שֶׁל יָחִיד — כְּרַגְלֵי יָחִיד, וְשֶׁל אוֹתָהּ הָעִיר — כְּרַגְלֵי אוֹתָהּ הָעִיר, בוְשֶׁל עוֹלֵי בָבֶל — כְּרַגְלֵי הַמְמַלֵּא. וְתַנְיָא: בּוֹר שֶׁל שְׁבָטִים יֵשׁ לָהֶן אַלְפַּיִם אַמָּה לְכָל רוּחַ. קַשְׁיָין אַהֲדָדֵי! אֶלָּא לָאו ש"מ: הָא — רַבִּי יוֹחָנָן בֶּן נוּרִי, הָא — רַבָּנַן. כִּי אֲתָא לְקַמֵּיהּ דְּרַב יוֹסֵף, א"ל: הָכִי קָאָמַר רַב סַפְרָא, וְהָכִי אַהְדְּרֵי לֵיהּ. אֲמַר לֵיהּ: וְאַמַּאי לָא תֵּימָא לֵיהּ מִגּוּפַהּ: אִי סָלְקָא דַּעְתָּךְ גְּשָׁמִים הַסְּמוּכִין לָעִיר עָסְקִינַן — הַאי יֵשׁ לָהֶן אַלְפַּיִם אַמָּה לְכָל רוּחַ?! הָא "כְּרַגְלֵי אַנְשֵׁי אוֹתָהּ הָעִיר" מִיבָּעֵיא לֵיהּ!§ אָמַר מָר: בְּיוֹם טוֹב — הֲרֵי הֵן כְּרַגְלֵי כָל אָדָם. וְאַמַּאי? לִיקְנֵי שְׁבִיתָה בְּאוֹקְיָינוֹס! לֵימָא דְּלָא כְּרַבִּי אֱלִיעֶזֶר, דְּאִי כְּר' אֱלִיעֶזֶר — *הָא אָמַר: כָּל הָעוֹלָם כּוּלּוֹ מִמֵּי אוֹקְיָינוֹס הוּא שׁוֹתֶה! אָמַר ר' יִצְחָק: הָכָא בְּעָבִים שֶׁנִּתְקַשְּׁרוּ מֵעֶרֶב יוֹם טוֹב עָסְקִינַן. וְדִילְמָא הָנָךְ אָזְלִי וְהָנָךְ אַחֲרִינֵי נִינְהוּ? דְּאִית לְהוּ סִימָנָא בְּגַוַּיְיהוּ. וְאִיבָּעֵית אֵימָא: הָוֵי סְפֵק דְּדִבְרֵיהֶם, *וּסְפֵק דְּדִבְרֵיהֶם לְהָקֵל. וְלִיקְנֵי שְׁבִיתָה בְּעָבִים! תִּיפְשׁוֹט מִינָּהּ *דְּאֵין תְּחוּמִין לְמַעְלָה מִי', דְּאִי יֵשׁ תְּחוּמִין — לִיקְנֵי שְׁבִיתָה בְּעָבִים! לְעוֹלָם אֵימָא לָךְ: יֵשׁ תְּחוּמִין, וּמַיָּא בְּעִיבָא מִיבְלַע בְּלִיעֵי.

כָּל

רש"י

וּבִלְבַד. שֶׁלֹּא יִפְשׁוֹט זֶה יָדוֹ לְתוֹךְ שְׁתַּיִם הַחִיצוֹנוֹת, שֶׁאֵין לוֹ בָּהֶם כְּלוּם, וְיוֹצִיא לְשָׁם פִּתּוֹ אוֹ חֶפְצוֹ. דַּחֲפָצָיו כְּרַגְלָיו, דִּתְנַן (ביצה לז.): הַבְּהֵמָה וְהַכֵּלִים כְּרַגְלֵי הַבְּעָלִים. *דְּכָל ד' אַמּוֹת דְּכָל חַד שַׁוְּינְהוּ רַבָּנַן לְגַבֵּיהּ כִּרְשׁוּת הַיָּחִיד, וְאָסוּר לְהַכְנִיס וּלְהוֹצִיא מֵחוּצָה לָהֶן לְתוֹכָן. וְלָא דָּמֵי לְהָיָה מוֹדֵד וּבָא וְכָלְתָה מִדָּתוֹ בַּחֲצֵי הָעִיר, דְּתַנְיָא לְעֵיל (דף מב:) דְּמוּתָּר לְטַלְטֵל בְּכָל הָעִיר ע"י זְרִיקָה, וּבִלְבַד שֶׁלֹּא יַעֲבוֹר הַתְּחוּם בְּרַגְלָיו. דְּאַף ע"ג דְּאָסוּר לְהַלֵּךְ, מוּתָּר לְהוֹצִיא, דְּהָתָם כּוּלָּהּ חֲדָא רְשׁוּתָא הוּא, וְאִי נַמִּי כָּלְתָה מִדָּתוֹ חוּץ לָעִיר — מוּתָּר לְטַלְטֵל מִחוּץ לִתְחוּמוֹ לְתוֹךְ תְּחוּמוֹ שְׁתֵּי אַמּוֹת בָּזֶה וּשְׁתֵּי אַמּוֹת בָּזֶה, דְּכוּלָּהּ רְשׁוּת הָרַבִּים הוּא דְּאַלְפַּיִם דִּידֵיהּ לָא שַׁוְּינְהוּ רְשׁוּת הַיָּחִיד לְגַבֵּיהּ. דְּהָא אָסוּר לְטַלְטוּלֵי בְּהוּ אֲבָל ד' אַמּוֹת דְּיוֹצֵא חוּץ לַתְּחוּם וּדְנוֹתֵן אֶת עֵירוּבוֹ וּדְקוֹנֶה שְׁבִיתָה בְּרַגְלָיו — שַׁוְּינְהוּ רַבָּנַן לְגַבֵּיהּ כִּרְשׁוּת הַיָּחִיד, וְאָסוּר לְהוּ מִדְּרַבָּנַן לְטַלְטֵל מִתּוֹכָן לְחוּץ לָהֶן: וְהָאֶמְצָעִי מוּבְלָע בֵּינֵיהֶם. ג' אַמּוֹתָיו בְּתוֹךְ שֶׁל זֶה, וּב' אַמּוֹתָיו בְּתוֹךְ שֶׁל זֶה: מוּתָּר עִם כָּל אֶחָד. פּוֹנֶה לְכָאן וּמִשְׁתַּמֵּשׁ עִם זֶה, וּפוֹנֶה לְכָאן וּמִשְׁתַּמֵּשׁ עִם זֶה: לְשָׁלֹשׁ חֲצֵירוֹת. זוֹ אֵצֶל זוֹ: פְּתוּחוֹת לִרְשׁוּת הָרַבִּים. דְּכָל אַחַת רְשׁוּת לְעַצְמָהּ, וְאֵין לָהֶן דְּרִיסַת הָרֶגֶל זוֹ עַל זוֹ. דְּאִי הָווּ לְהוּ זוֹ לִפְנִים מִזּוֹ — אֲסָרָה פְּנִימִית אַחִיצוֹנָה, דַּאֲפִי' בִּפְנֵי עַצְמָהּ אֲסוּרָה כָּל אַחַת לְהִשְׁתַּמֵּשׁ: **גמ'** חֶפְצֵי הֶפְקֵר. כֵּלִים שֶׁאֵין לָהֶם בְּעָלִים, וַחֲשֵׁיכָה לָהֶן בְּמָקוֹם אֶחָד אע"ג שֶׁלֹּא נִתְכַּוֵּין לָהֶן אָדָם לְהַקְנוֹתָן שְׁבִיתָה: קוֹנִין שְׁבִיתָה. בִּמְקוֹמָן, וְאֵין אָדָם יָכוֹל לְטַלְטְלָן מִשָּׁם יוֹתֵר מֵאַלְפַּיִם לְכָל רוּחַ וַאֲפִילּוּ עֵירֵב לְצַד אַחֵר: דְּלִיפַּלְגוּ בְּכֵלִים. שֶׁל הֶפְקֵר וְהַאי אָדָם יָשֵׁן שֶׁלֹּא נִתְכַּוֵּין לִשְׁבִיתָה — כְּכֵלִים שֶׁל הֶפְקֵר דָּמֵי: בְּיוֹם טוֹב. אִם יָרְדוּ בְּי"ט: הֲרֵי הֵן כְּרַגְלֵי כָּל אָדָם. שֶׁלֹּא הָיְתָה לָהֶן שְׁבִיתָה בֵּין הַשְּׁמָשׁוֹת, וּלְכָל צַד שֶׁעֵירֵב הָאָדָם יָכוֹל לִיטְּלָן: הָא מַנִּי. דְּקָתָנֵי: מֵעֶרֶב י"ט יֵשׁ לָהֶן אַלְפַּיִם וְאֵינָן כְּרַגְלֵי כָּל אָדָם, אַלְמָא: חֶפְצֵי הֶפְקֵר קוֹנִין שְׁבִיתָה: לָא ס"ד. לְאוֹקְמֵי טַעְמָא מִשּׁוּם דַּעַת אַנְשֵׁי הָעִיר, אֶלָּא טַעְמָא מִשּׁוּם דְּחֶפְצֵי הֶפְקֵר קוֹנִין שְׁבִיתָה: דִּתְנַן. נַמִּי בְּדוּכְתָּא אַחֲרִיתִי. וּמַתְנִי' קַשְׁיָין אַהֲדָדֵי וְעַל כָּרְחָךְ חֲדָא מִינַּיְיהוּ תּוֹקְמָא כְּר' יוֹחָנָן בֶּן נוּרִי, וְתִיפְשׁוֹט דְּחֶפְצֵי הֶפְקֵר קוֹנִין שְׁבִיתָה: כְּרַגְלֵי אוֹתוֹ יָחִיד. בַּעַל הַבּוֹר. וְאִם לָקַח מֵהֶם אָדָם אַחֵר — אֵין יָכוֹל לְהוֹלִיכָן אֶלָּא לְמָקוֹם שֶׁזֶּה יָכוֹל לְהוֹלִיכָן. וְאִם עֵירֵב הוּא לַמִּזְרָח — אֵין יָכוֹל זֶה לְהוֹלִיכָן חוּץ לָעִיר בְּצַד מַעֲרָב אֲפִילּוּ פְּסִיעָה אַחַת: כְּרַגְלֵי אוֹתָהּ הָעִיר. אַלְפַּיִם לְכָל רוּחַ. וְאִם עֵירֵב זֶה לַמַּעֲרָב אוֹ לַמִּזְרָח — אֵין יָכוֹל זֶה לְהוֹלִיכָן חוּץ לְאַלְפַּיִם: וְשֶׁל עוֹלֵי בָבֶל. שֶׁבַּדֶּרֶךְ, שֶׁעוֹלִים מִבָּבֶל לא"י, וְהוּא שֶׁל הֶפְקֵר: כְּרַגְלֵי הַמְמַלֵּא. דְּכָל מִילֵּי דְּהֶפְקֵירָא מַאן דְּמַגְבַּהּ לֵיהּ קָנֵי, וַאֲפִילּוּ נָתַן לַאֲחֵרִים לְאַחַר שֶׁמִּילְּאָן לְצוֹרְכּוֹ — הֲרֵי הֵן כְּרַגְלָיו. אַלְמָא: מִידֵי דְּהֶפְקֵירָא אֵין קוֹנִין שְׁבִיתָה: וְתַנְיָא אִידָךְ בּוֹר שֶׁל שְׁבָטִים. דְּהַיְינוּ שֶׁל עוֹלֵי בָבֶל, יֵשׁ לָהֶם אַלְפַּיִם לְכָל רוּחַ. אַלְמָא: קָנוּ שְׁבִיתָה, דְּאֵינָן כְּרַגְלֵי כָּל אָדָם: כִּי אֲתָא. אַבַּיֵי לְקַמֵּיהּ דְּרַב יוֹסֵף: יֵשׁ לָהֶן. מַשְׁמַע דְּאִינְהוּ גּוּפַיְיהוּ קָנוּ לְהוּ שְׁבִיתָה. וְלָאו מִשּׁוּם דַּעַת אַנְשֵׁי הָעִיר, דְּאִי מִשּׁוּם דַּעַת אַנְשֵׁי הָעִיר — הָא לִישָּׁנָא בָּעֵי לְמֵימַר: הֲרֵי הֵן כְּרַגְלֵי אוֹתָהּ הָעִיר, דְּהַיְינוּ נַמִּי אַלְפַּיִם לְכָל רוּחַ: לִיקְנוּ שְׁבִיתָה בְּאוֹקְיָינוֹס. שֶׁשָּׁבְתוּ שָׁם אֶמֶשׁ, וְהַיּוֹם שֶׁאֲבוּ הֶעָבִים וַהֲרֵי יָצְאוּ חוּץ לַתְּחוּם וְאֵין לָהֶם אֶלָּא אַרְבַּע אַמּוֹת: דִּילְמָא הָנָךְ. שֶׁרָאָה אֶמֶשׁ קְשׁוּרוֹת אָזְדוּ לְעָלְמָא: וְהָנֵי אַחֲרִינֵי נִינְהוּ. וְנִתְקַשְּׁרוּ הַיּוֹם, וְקָנוּ אֶמֶשׁ שְׁבִיתָה בָּאוֹקְיָינוֹס, וְלִיתַּסְרוּ: וְלִיפְשׁוֹט. מִדְּקָתָנֵי בְּמַיִם שֶׁקָּנוּ שְׁבִיתָה אֶמֶשׁ בֶּעָבִים וְיָרְדוּ הַיּוֹם דְּמוּתָּר לְהוֹלִיכָן כְּרַגְלֵי כָּל אָדָם, אַלְמָא: אֵין אִיסּוּר תְּחוּמִין לְמַעְלָה מֵעֲשָׂרָה: מִיבְלַע בְּלִיעֵי. וּכְמַאן דְּלֵיתִנְהוּ דָּמוּ, וְלָא קָנוּ לְהוּ שְׁבִיתָה אֶמֶשׁ:

כ"ש

תוספות

להודיעך כחן דרבנן. ואם תאמר: וליפלגו בכלים להודיעך כחו דר' יוחנן בן נורי, אע"ג דליכא למימר בהן: הואיל וניעור קני שביתה, וכח דהתירא עדיף! וי"ל: הא דקנו להו שביתה – לאו קולא היא אלא חומרא היא, דאדרבה לרבנן דלא קנו הוי קולא – דהוי כרגלי המוצאן, ויכול להוליכן למקום עירובו, והכי מוכח בשמעתא דאין דין אדם וכלים שוין, למ"ד אין קונין שביתה. ולקמן נמי קרי ליה חומרא, דקאמר: צריכא, אי אשמעינן הלכה כרבי יוחנן בן נורי – ה"א בין לקולא בין לחומרא. פי': קולא גבי אדם, וחומרא גבי כלים:

ביום טוב הרי הן כרגלי כל אדם. פי': כאותו שיזכה בהן ראשון, ואם נתנן לאחר – הרי הן כרגלי הראשון. אבל אין לפרש דלעולם הרי הן כרגלי כל אדם שהן בידו – דהא בור עולי בבל אמרינן בסמוך דהוי כרגלי הממלא. אלמא: כל היכא דלא קנו שביתה הרי הן כרגלי הזוכה ראשון. ולקמן [דף מו.], דתניא גבי נהרות המושכין ומעיינות הנובעין הרי הן כרגלי כל אדם, ובתוספתא דמסכת ביצה [פ"ד] קתני בהדיא: הרי הן כרגלי הממלא*. משמע °דהכל אחד:

[לפנינו הגיר' כל אדם]

ליקנו שביתה באוקיינוס. ואפילו אם אין תחומין למעלה (א) והעבים שותין מאותו שלמעלה שגבוהין מי', כיון שכל המים מחוברין יחד – חשובין כאילו מונחין בארץ. ולא דמו לספינה ששטה על המים. וכיון דקנו שביתה באוקיינוס, אע"פ שבאו למעלה מי' – אין להם אלא ד' אמות, דהרי הן חוץ לתחום ובעובדא דר"ג דפריך [לעיל מג.] ואי אין תחומין למעלה מי' כי לא היו בתוך התחום מאי הוי? היינו משום שגם בין השמשות בשעת קניית שביתה היו למעלה מי', ולא קנו שביתה בשום מקום ולכך כשבאו בתוך י' – היה להם שביתה, והיה להם אלפים אמה לכל רוח:

לימא דלא כרבי אליעזר. וא"ת: ולרבי יהושע נמי, דאמר מן הכיפה הוא שותה – ליקנו שביתה התם אי יש תחומין למעלה מי'! ויש לומר: אפילו יש תחומין – לא שייך קנין שביתה ברקיע:

איבעית אימא הוי ספק דדבריהם. אף ע"ג דהוי דבר שיש לו מתירין, ואמר רב אשי בריש ביצה (דף ד.) דדבר שיש לו מתירין (ב) אפי' באלף לא בטיל אפילו בספק דבריהם – בעירוב הקילו:

כל

רבינו חננאל

בעי רבה טעמא דר' יוחנן בן נורי משום דקסבר חפצי הפקר קונין שביתה ובדין הוא דנפלגו בעלמא בחפצי הפקר והאי דמיפלגי הכא כו' או דלמא בעלמא סבר דחפצי הפקר אין קונין שביתה והכא היינו טעמא הואיל וניעור קנה שביתה ישן נמי קנה שביתה. ת"ש גשמים שירדו בעיו"ט יש להם אלפים אמה לכל רוח ביו"ט הרי הן כרגלי כל אדם אי אמרת דסבר ר' יוחנן בן נורי דחפצי הפקר קונין שביתה הנה גשמים שירדו (בערב שבת) [מערב יו"ט] שקנו שביתה כר' יוחנן בן נורי אלא אי אמרת ר' יוחנן בן נורי נמי סבר חפצי הפקר אין קונין שביתה הא מתניתין מאן קתני לה ודחי רב ספרא ואמר ודלמא בגשמים שירדו סמוך לעיר וקנו אותם אנשי העיר כו' ודחאה רב יוסף ואמר אי הכי כרגלי אנשי אותה העיר הוה ליה למימר. ואסיקנא מהא דתנן בור של עולי בבל כרגלי הממלא. ותניא אידך בור של שבטים אלפים אמה לכל רוח קשיא אהדדי ופריקנא ברייתא לר' יוחנן בן נורי דסבר חפצי הפקר קונין שביתה לפיכך יש להן אלפים אמה לכל רוח. מתניתין דקתני כרגלי הממלא לרבנן: ביו"ט כרגלי כל אדם אקשינן אמאי לריב"נ ליקנו שביתה באוקיאנוס דהא א"ר אלעזר כל העולם כולו ממי אוקייאנוס הוא שותה. ופריק רב יצחק בעבים שנתקשרו מעיו"ט. כלומר כבר נעקרו המים מאוקייאנוס ונבלעו בעבים וכו'. ואסיקנא כל מידי דנייד לא קני שביתה ומיא דאוקייאנוס מינד נייד. לפיכך לא קני להו שביתה דתניא נהרות המושכין ומעיינות הנובעין הרי הן כרגלי כל אדם

מסורת הש"ס

ע' רש"ל ורש"א

לקמן [מו:] עא. לח.

[עי' תוס' לקמן מח. ד"ה ופתוחות]

[לעיל לח: לקמן מז: לז: ביצה לח: ע"ש ברש"י]

ביצה לט.

תענית ט:

[שבת לד. וש"נ]

[לעיל מג.]

הגהות הב"ח

(א) תוס' ד"ה ליקנו וכו' והעבים שותין: (ב) ד"ה איבעית וכו' דאפי' באלף:

גליון הש"ס

גמ' בגשמים הסמוכים לעיר. עי' לקמן דף מז ע"ב תוס' ד"ה והכלים: **תוס'** ד"ה בי"ט וכו' דהכל אחד. עי' לקמן דף לז ע"ב תוס' ד"ה הכא בחבית:

רב נסים גאון

דאי ר' אלעזר האמר כל העולם כולו מאוקינוס הוא שותה איתא לדר' אלעזר בהדא ברייתא הכתובה בפ"א דמס' תענית (דף ט) תניא ר"א אומר כי העולם כולו מאוקינוס הוא שותה שנא' (בראשית ב) ואד יעלה מן הארץ

כל שכן דהוו להו נולד(א) דאסירי! אלא מיא בעבים מינד ניידי. השתא דאתית להכי – אוקיינוס נמי לא ליקשו לך, מיא באוקיינוס נמי מינד ניידי. *ותניא: א נהרות המושכין ומעיינות הנובעין – הרי הן כרגלי כל אדם. אמר רבי יעקב בר אידי, אמר רבי יהושע בן לוי: הלכה כרבי יוחנן בן נורי. אמר ליה רבי זירא לרבי יעקב בר אידי: *בפירוש שמיע לך, או מכללא שמיע לך? אמר ליה: בפירוש שמיע לי. מאי כללא? דאמר רבי יהושע בן לוי: הלכה כדברי המיקל בעירוב. ותרתי למה לי? אמר רבי זירא: צריכי, דאי אשמעינן הלכה כר' יוחנן בן נורי – הוה אמינא בין לקולא ובין לחומרא, ב קמ"ל: הלכה כדברי המיקל בעירוב. וליממא: "הלכה כדברי המיקל בעירוב", "הלכה כרבי יוחנן בן נורי" למה לי? איצטריך, ס"ד אמינא: הני מילי – יחיד במקום יחיד, ורבים במקום רבים. אבל יחיד במקום רבים – אימא לא. אמר ליה רבא לאביי: מכדי, עירובין דרבנן, מה לי יחיד במקום יחיד ומה לי יחיד במקום רבים? אמר ליה רב פפא לרבא: ובדרבנן לא שני לן בין יחיד במקום יחיד ליחיד במקום רבים? *והתנן, רבי (ג)אלעזר אומר: כל אשה שעברו עליה שלש עונות – דייה שעתה. *ותניא: מעשה ועשה רבי כר' אלעזר. לאחר שנזכר אמר: כדי הוא רבי אלעזר לסמוך עליו בשעת הדחק. מאי "לאחר שנזכר"? אילימא לאחר שנזכר דאין הלכה כרבי אלעזר, ג אלא כרבנן – בשעת הדחק היכי עביד כוותיה? אלא: דלא איתמר הלכתא לא כרבי אלעזר ולא כרבנן, לאחר שנזכר דלאו יחיד פליג עליה אלא רבים פליגי עליה, אמר: כדי הוא רבי אלעזר *לסמוך עליו בשעת הדחק. אמר רב משרשיא לרבא, ואמרי לה רב נחמן בר יצחק לרבא: ובדרבנן לא שני בין יחיד במקום יחיד, בין יחיד במקום רבים? *והתניא: שמועה קרובה נוהגת שבעה ושלשים, רחוקה – אינה נוהגת אלא יום אחד. ואי זו היא קרובה ואיזו היא רחוקה? בתוך שלשים – קרובה, לאחר שלשים – רחוקה, דברי רבי עקיבא. וחכמים אומרים: אחת שמועה קרובה ואחת שמועה רחוקה נוהגת שבעה ושלשים. ואמר רבה בר בר חנה, אמר רבי יוחנן: כל מקום שאתה מוצא יחיד מיקל ורבים מחמירין – הלכה כדברי המחמירין, חוץ מזו, שאע"פ שרבי עקיבא מיקל וחכמים מחמירין – ד הלכה כדברי רבי עקיבא. וסבר לה כשמואל, דאמר *שמואל: הלכה כדברי המיקל באבל. באבילות הוא דאקילו בה רבנן, אבל בעלמא – אפילו בדרבנן שני בין יחיד, בין יחיד במקום רבים.

ורב

רש"י

כל שכן דהוו להו נולד ואסירי. אפילו לטלטלן במקומן: הרי הן כרגלי כל אדם. כיון דניידי לא קנו שביתה, ואפילו הן של יחיד אינן כרגליו: בפירוש שמיע לך. מר' יהושע בן לוי: או מכללא. דשמיע לך מיניה מילתא אחריתי, ודייקת מינה דכר' יוחנן בן נורי סבירא ליה: ומאי כללא. מאיזה כלל הוה ס"ד מעיקרא דשמעת ליה לר' יהושע בן לוי, דנימא מילתא דנידוק לה מינה: בעירוב. בכל משפטיו, ותחומין מהלכות עירובין הן: בין לקולא. כגון אדם ישן, דאי לא קנה שביתה לא נפיק מד' אמות: לחומרא. כגון כלי הפקר. אי אמרת קונין שביתה – אסור להוליכן למקום שעירב זה המוליכן, אלא אלפים הוא דאית להו לכל רוח: קמ"ל כדברי המיקל. באדם הוא דהלכתא כוותיה, דכיון דניעור קנה – ישן נמי קנה. אבל בכלים לית הלכתא כוותיה: אבל יחיד במקום רבים. כגון ר' יוחנן בן נורי דפליגי רבנן עליה, אימא לית הלכתא כוותיה: ר' אליעזר. גרסינן: כל אשה שעברו עליה שלש עונות. דהיינו ל' יום, דעונה סתם לפריסת נדה משלשים יום לשלשים יום, וכל אשה שעברו עליה תשעים יום ולא ראתה – נסתלקו דמיה. ואם ראתה אחרי כן – אמרינן השתא הוא דראתה דם, ולא מטמינן טהרות שנתעסקה בהן למפרע, כשאר נשים שדמיהן מלויין שמטמאות טהרות למפרע מעת לעת. כדאמר במס' נדה (דף ג.) דחיישינן שמא כותלי בית הרחם העמידוהו, ותנן (שם ח.): כל הנשים מטמאות בבית החיצון. ופליגי רבנן עליה, ואמרי דאין הפסקת ג' עונות סילוק אלא לזקנה שעברו עליה ג' עונות סמוך לזקנתה, אבל בילדה – לא: כרבי אלעזר. וטיהר אף בילדה שעברו עליה ג' עונות: אחר שנזכר. משמע דנזכר דלאו שפיר עביד: שעת הדחק. שני בצורת הוו, ואיכא הפסד טהרות: מאי כשנזכר. אילימא נזכר דאיתמר בפלוגתייהו הלכה כרבנן, וכשנעשה המעשה לא היה זכור ועכשיו נזכר אמאי לא אהדר עובדא: אלא. האי דלא אהדר משום דלא איתמר הלכתא לא כמר ולא כמר, ומאי נזכר – לאחר שנזכר דרבים פליגי עליה, דהוה ליה למיעבד כרבים, אמר: כדי הוא רבי אליעזר לסמוך עליו בשעת הדחק, ולא אהדר עובדא. הא לאו בשעת הדחק – לא. אלמא: אע"ג דמעת לעת גזירה דרבנן היא, בעי למיעבד כרבים: נוהגת שבעה. לרחיצה ולתכבוסת, ושלשים לתספורת ולגיהוץ מיום שנשמע לו: וסבר לה. רבי יוחנן כשמואל: ה"ג:

תוספות

כל שכן דהוי ליה נולד ואסיר. ואע"ג דמשקין בפירי נמי אמרינן בפסחים (דף לג:) דמבלע בליעי, אפ"ה לא מתסרי משום נולד, אי לא גזרינן שמא יסחוט. דמים בעבים בליעי טפי, ואינה ניכרין כמו משקין בפירי. ואפילו לא היו ניכרין משקין בפירי כלל לא חשיבי נולד, כיון דמעיקרא נמי הוי אוכל – אוכלא דאיפרת הוא. וא"ת: ולימא הא רבי שמעון היא, דלית ליה מוקצה ולית ליה נולד, כדאיתא בריש ביצה (דף ב.)! וי"ל: דבנולד כה"ג, דדבר חדש שלא בא לעולם כל עיקר – מודה רבי שמעון, וכן באפר כירה שהוסק ביום טוב נראה דמודה ר"ש דאסור לכסות בו, אא"כ ראוי לצלות בו ביצה, כדאמר בפרק קמא דביצה (דף ח.):

נהרות המושכין. פ"ה: אפי' הן של יחיד. ונראה שדקדק דאי הוה של רבים דווקא – מאי איריא נהרות? אפי' מים מכונסים נמי אמרי' לעיל כרגלי הממלא, והיינו כרגלי כל אדם דהכא, כדפרישי' לעיל *דהכל אחד. וכן מוכח בפרק בתרא דביצה (דף לט.) דבשל יחיד מיירי, דפריך מהך דהכא אמתני' דהתם. דקתני: בור של יחיד כרגלי היחיד. ומיהו, שם לא פירש רש"י כרגלי הממלא וכרגלי כל אדם בענין אחד. ור"ת מפרש: אפילו מיירי בשל רבים מדקדק שפיר, דדווקא משום דניידי לא קנו שביתה – אבל מכונסים דקנו שביתה – יש להם אלפים אמה לכל רוח, כרבי יוחנן בן נורי:

הוה אמינא בין לקולא בין לחומרא. הוה ליה למימר דאיצטריך הלכה כדברי המיקל לפסוק הלכה בכל מקומות, אלא דניחא ליה למימר דאפילו להך מילתא גופה איצטריך:

קמ"ל הלכה כדברי המיקל בעירוב. דלענין אדם – הלכה כרבי יוחנן בן נורי דקני שביתה. ולענין כלים – הלכה כרבנן דלא קנו שביתה, והרי הן כרגלי כל אדם. ולא הוי תרי קולי דסתרי אהדדי, דקיימא לן כרבנן דאמרי אין חפצי הפקר קונין שביתה. וישן היינו טעמא – הואיל וניעור קני, ישן נמי קני, כדפ"ה. ואפילו אם לא היה משמעינן רבי יהושע בן לוי אלא הלכה כדברי המיקל בעירוב לחוד, הוה משמע מדבריו דהלכתא כדברי שניהם להקל:

לסמוך עליו בשעת הדחק. פי' הקונטרס: דשנת בצורת הוה, ואיכא הפסד טהרות. ואי אפשר לומר כן, דבדחק כה"ג אפי' רבנן מודים, כדאמר בפ"ק דנדה (ד' ט:): אין שעת הדחק ראיה. ומפרש התם: מאי שעת הדחק – שנת בצורת הוה. ואיכא דאמרי דטהרות אפיש ועבוד, וחשו רבנן להפסד טהרות*:

דאמר שמואל הלכה כדברי המיקל באבל. אפילו ביחיד במקום רבים נראה דלעולם הלכה כדברי המיקל באבל, וחוץ מזו לאו למעוטי שאר מקומות דאבל קאמר, כדקאמר אבילות הוא דאקילו ביה רבנן. וכן מוכיח בהדיא פרק בתרא דמו"ק (דף יט:) גבי אבא שאול ורבנן, גבי קובר את מתו ג' ימים לפני הרגל, וגבי בא ממקום קרוב פלוגתא *דרשב"ג ורבנן (דף כב.). וא"ת: כיון דאפי' יחיד במקום רבים אמר שמואל הלכה כדברי המיקל באבל, למה ליה לשמואל למיפסק בפרק בתרא דמו"ק (דף כד.) *כרשב"ג, דאמר: ר"ה ויום הכפורים כרגלים? ויש לומר: דקמ"ל אפי' ביחיד במקום רבים, כדאמר לעיל. ונראה, אפי' ביום ראשון של אבילות דהוי דאורייתא, כדאמר בה"ג – דהלכה כדברי המיקל באבל, מידי דהוי כהלכה כדברי המיקל בעירוב. דמשמע לעיל דאפילו הוי דאורייתא – הלכה כדברי המיקל. מדקאמר, מכדי עירובין דרבנן מה לי יחיד במקום וכו'. משמע דאי הוה דאורייתא – ניחא דלריכי. וכן מוכח בפ' "יש בכור" (בכורות דף מט.) גבי פלוגתא דר"ע ורבנן, דאמר רב אשי: הכל מודים לענין אבילות דיום ל' כשלפניו. דאמר שמואל: הלכה כדברי המיקל באבל, ואפילו ביום ראשון אינו נוהג אבילות. וזה לשון ה"ג: היכא דשכיב שכיבא ביום טוב ראשון, או ביום טוב שני, או בחולו של מועד, או בי"ט ראשון של יום טוב אחרון – אינו נוהג אבילות

עד

רבינו חננאל

א"ר יעקב בר אידי אריב"ל הלכה כריב"נ במי שישן ולא ידע עד שחשכה יש לו אלפים אמה לכל רוח ותוב אריב"ל הלכה כדברי המיקל בעירוב. ש"מ דלית הלכתא כר' יוחנן אלא לקולא אבל היכא דאיכא לחומרא כגון חפצי הפקר דקנו שביתה ולית ליה למוצאם להוציאם חוץ לאלפים אמה שלהן לא אלא כרגלי כל אדם. ולא פי' הלכתא כריב"נ אלא משום דפליג בהדי רבים. אמר רבה מכדי עירוב דרבנן הוא מה לי יחיד במקום יחיד ומה לי יחיד במקום רבים הכל אחד הוא. ואמרינן וכל מדרבנן לא שאני לן בין יחיד במקום יחיד ובין יחיד במקום רבים והתנן בתחלת נדה ר' אלעזר אומר כל אשה שעברו עליה ג' עונות פי' הווסת שלה שהיתה ווסתה לראות כל ט"ו יום הפסיקה ועכשיו עברו עליה ג' פעמים ט"ו יום ולא ראתה ואע"ג דאינה זקינה שיש לומר נסתלקו דמים חדל להיות לה אורח כנשים. ואח"כ ראתה דייה שעתה ואין מטמאין אותה מעת לעת ותניא מעשה ועשה רבי כר' אליעזר סבר יחיד פליג עליה לאחר שנזכר עליה ולא אתמר הלכתא לא כמר ולא כמר. אמר כדי ר' אליעזר לסמוך עליו בשעת הדחק. מאי שעת הדחק פירשוה רבנן אשה שהפסיקה ג' עונות ואמרינן עונה בינונית שלשים יום *) אפי' שהעבדה טהרות ואח"כ ראתה דם. איכא דאמרי שנת בצורת היתה ועשתה טהרות ונדחק הדבר לרבי להפסידם. ולהחזיקה בטומאה לאחר מעת לעת ופסק כר' אלעזר דייה שעתה. והנה זה מדרבנן הוא דאמר רבא מאי דרבנן כדרב יהודה אמר שמואל דאמר חכמים תקנו לבנות ישראל להיות בודקות עצמן שחרית וערבית בשחרית להכשיר טהרות שעשתה בלילה. בערבית להכשיר טהרות שעשתה ביום וזו הואיל ולא בדקה הפסידוה עונה יתירה וטומאות מעת לעת (הני) [הוא] מדרבנן ושני בין יחיד ליחיד ובין יחיד לרבים ותוב אתו רבנן אחריני למידק ולאחוויי דשני (כדתנן) [בדרבנן] בין יחיד ליחיד בין יחיד לרבים מהא דתניא שמועה קרובה שהיא בתוך שלשים יום נוהגת ז' ימי אבילות ולגיהוץ כיוצא בו ל' יום. ושמועה רחוקה שהיא לאחר ל' יום אינה נוהגת אלא יום אחד דברי ר"ע וחכ"א בין קרובה בין רחוקה נוהגת ז' ול'. ואמרינן כ"מ שאתה מוצא יחיד מיקל ורבים מחמירין הלכה כרבים חוץ מזו שאע"פ ר"ע יחיד הוא במקום רבים ומיקל הלכתא כוותיה. דאמר שמואל הלכה כדברי המיקל [באבל] באבילות הוא דאקילו רבנן (ואמרינן כיחיד) [אפי' ביחיד] במקום רבים אבל בעלמא לא. ואפי' בדרבנן הרי שני בין יחיד ליחיד ורבים ופריק רב פפא לכולהו

*) [נ"ל ואפילו למעבדה טהרות].

עין משפט נר מצוה

לד א מיי' שם וטוש"ע שם סעיף טו:
לה ב מיי' שם טוש"ע א"ח סי' תח:
לו ג מיי' פ"ד מהל' טומאת משכב ומושב הלכה ה סמג עשין רמג:
לז ד מיי' פ"ז מהל' אבל הלכה א סמג עשין ב טוש"ע י"ד סי' תב סעיף א:

מסורת הש"ס

[לקמן מח.] שבת קכח: ביצה לט.
[ברכות ט. וש"נ ע"ש]
נדה ז:
שם ו. ט:
[ברכות ט. וש"נ]
מ"ק כ.
[מו"ק יח. יט: כ. כב. כו: בכורות מט. חולין כ.]
[נ"ל דר"ש]
[נ"ל כר"ג]

הגהות הב"ח

(א) גמ' דהוו להו נולד דאסירי: (ב) שם והתנן רבי אליעזר כצ"ל וכן בכל העמוד:

עד דנפקי יומא טבא כולהו. אבל יומא בתרא דרבנן, מסלק סליק למנין ז' אבל אבילות לא נהיג ביה כלל. אבל שכיב שכיבא בי"ט שני של י"ט אחרון, כיון דעיקר אבילות יום ראשון – נהיג ביה אבילות, וסליק למנין ז', דהכי אסמכוה רבנן דעיקר אבילות יום ראשון הוא, דכתיב: "ואכלתי חטאת היום" – היום אסור ולמחר מותר. וכתיב: "ואחריתה כיום מר". וכיון דיום ראשון דאבילות דאורייתא, ויום טוב אחרון ספיקא דרבנן – אתי עשה ודאי דאורייתא דיחיד, וחייל על עשה ספק דרבים דרבנן. והא דאמרינן בכתובות (דף ד.): מכניסין את המת לחדר ונוהג ז' ימי המשתה, ואחר כך נוהג ז' ימי אבילות – אלמא דלא דחי יומא קמא דאבילות מועד דרבנן – שאני מועד דחתן עדיף טפי:

ואין חבין לאדם שלא בפניו. וא"ת: והיכי מוכח מהכא דעירובי תחומין חמירי? הלא אין הטעם תלוי בחומר, אלא משום דאין חבין לאדם שלא בפניו! ויש לומר: מ"מ מוכח שפיר דחמירי טפי, דאפילו ידעינן גבי עירובי תחומין דלמחר דעתו לילך באותו צד, אפי' הכי, כיון דאיכא קצת חוב שמפסיד במה שאינו יכול לילך לצד אחר אם ירצה – לא הוי עירוב. ובעירובי חצירות אע"ג דאיכא קצת נמי חובה, שמערבין בפת שלו שלא מדעתו, כדאמר בפ' "חלון" (לקמן דף פ.): אחד מבני מבוי שרגיל להשתתף באין בני אדם ונוטלין הימנו שיתופו בע"כ, וצריך שימחול להם פתן אם ירצו לנאת, כדאמר ב"הדר" (לקמן ד' סח.): כיון דאי בעי ליה מינאי ולא יהבינא בטל שיתוף, והיינו משום דחמירי טפי: **שלא** לשכח תורת עירוב מן התינוקות. פ"ה: אבל עיקר עירוב בתחומין הוא. ומשנה היא זו לקמן בפרק "חלון" (דף פ:), ושם פירש הקונט' בענין אחר: ולא אמרו לערב בחצירות לאחר שנשתתפו אלא שלא לשכח תורת עירובי חצירות מן התינוקות, מדורות הבאין. הלכך מקילין ביה בשיורי עירוב. והכי משמע, דתניא לקמן בפרק "הדר" (דף עא:): מערבין בחצירות ומשתתפין במבוי שלא לשכח תורת עירוב מן התינוקות. ולר"י נראה דפי' דהכא עיקר, דההיא דפרק "חלון" לא איירי כלל בעירובי חצירות, אלא אשיתופי מבואות קאי. דקתני רישא: כיצד משתתפין כו', ולמה אמרו לערב בחצירות. היינו פירוש אשיתופי מבואות, וקרי שיתוף מבוי עירובי חצירות בכמה דוכתי: **כרבי** יוסי מחבירו. והא דאמר לקמן (דף מז.): אמר ר' יוחנן הלכה כר' יוסי, מכלל דיחידאה פליג עליה – אתיא כר' יעקב בר אידי*: **רבי** אסי אמר הלכה. פ"ה: ודרשינן בפירקא. ומ"ד מטין – מורינן ולא דרשינן בפירקא. ונראין – היינו דאי עביד הכי לא מהדרינן עובדא, אבל לא מורינן. וקשה לפירושו: דאפי' לא איתמר נראין, לא מהדרינן עובדא, כיון דלא איתמר הלכתא לא כמר ולא כמר! לכן נראה לי: דהלכה – דאי עביד כאידך מהדרינן, ומטין – אורויי נמי אורינן, ואם בא למיעבד עובדא כאידך מחינן בידיה. ומיהו, אי עביד עובדא – לא מהדרינן. ונראין – מורין, ואי בעי למעבד כאידך – לא מחינן בידיה. וכן משמע בפרק "הכותב" (כתובות פד.) גבי דנו דייני כר' טרפון. וא"ת: אדרבה ב"יש נוחלין" (ב"ב דף קכד:) משמע דלמ"ד מטין היינו דיעבד מטין כהני תנאי, אבל לכתחלה עבדינן כאידך, גבי בכור נוטל פי שנים בשבח ששבחו נכסים לאחר מיתת אביו. דאמר רבא: הלכתא אסור לעשות כדברי רבי, ואם עשה – עשוי. קסבר מטין איתמר. וי"ל: דמטין דהתם היינו לענין חבריו, דפליגי התם רבנן עליה. ויש סובר הלכה כרבי מחברו ולא מחבריו, דאתמר "הלכה כחבריו" ורבא סבר "מטין כחבריו" אתמר ולא הלכה כחבריו:

ה"ג: רב פפא אמר איצטריך. ולעיל קאי, אדרבי יהושע בן לוי, איצטריך ליה למימר הלכה כרבי יוחנן(ג). ואע"ג דאמר הלכה כדברי המיקל בעירוב: אבל בעירובי תחומין לא כו'. והא דרבי יוחנן בן נורי, באיסור תחומין קאי: א"ר יהודה כו'. לקמן בפרק "חלון" (פא:): בד"א. דאין מערבין לו לאדם אלא לדעתו, שנתרצה: בעירובי תחומין. דשמא חוב לו להפסיד אלפים למזרח, על מנת להשתכר באלפים למערב: עירובי חצירות. אין שם הפסד אלא ריוח: הני מילי. דהלכה כמיקל בעירובי חצירות: בשיורי עירוב. שהניח עירוב במקום המשתמר לכמה שבתות, ונתמעט האוכל משיעור ב' סעודות, מקילין ביה לאכשורי: אבל. במחלוקת של תחילת עירוב לא ניזיל בתר מיקל. והא דרבי יוחנן בן נורי כתחילת עירוב דמי: בד"א. דצריך שיעור לעירובי חצירות, או מזון שתי סעודות בין כולן, או כגרוגרת לכל אחד בתחילת עירוב: כל שהוא. לכל אחד: ולא אמרו לערב בחצירות אלא שלא לשכח את התינוקות. שלא לשכח תורת עירוב מדורות הבאין. אבל עיקר עירוב בתחומין הוא: הלכה כרבי עקיבא מחברו. בכל דוכתא: למאי הלכתא. לענין מה נאמרה שמועה זו, שפסקו הלכה סתם. בכל מקומות יש לסמוך עליה להורות הלכה למעשה כן, או דלמא מסברא בעלמא קאמרי כן, אבל(ד) הלכתא מכללא לא סמכינן עליה למילף: רבי אסי אמר הלכה. ממש קאמרי רבי יעקב ורבי זריקא, למיגמר מעשה מיניה ומיעבד כר' עקיבא היכא דיחיד פליג עליה, וכר' יוסי אפילו במקום רבים: מטין. רבי יעקב ור' זריקא לאו הלכה ממש פסקי, אלא מטין ההוראה אחר רבי יוסי, ואפי' במקום רבים. דאורויי מורינן לאדם יחיד לעשות כר' יוסי, אבל מדרש בפירקי ברבים לא דרשינן: נראין. אורויי לא מורינן, ואם עשה כרבי יוסי – לא מהדרי' עובדא: כלשון הזה אמר ר' יעקב בר אידי. כי האי לישנא דאיתמר הך דרבי יעקב ורבי זריקא, איתמר נמי הך דרבי יעקב בר אידי, למר הלכה ולמר מטין ולמר נראין: להני כללי. דכללינן לעיל: פלוני ופלוני – הלכה כפלוני בכל מקום. אלא היכא דמסתבר כמר – הלכתא כוותיה, והיכא דמסתבר בדוכתא אחריתי כאידך – עבדינן כוותיה: למה הדבר דומה. מתניתין היא (לעיל דף מה:): היא מותרת עמהן. ופליגי רבנן עליה בברייתא, ואמרי: שלשתן אסורות: מאן פליג עליה רבי יהודה. דהוא הוי סתם בר פלוגתיה. ל"א: מאן פליג עליה – רבי יהודה, דהוא איירי לעיל מיניה. רבי יהודה אומר: לאיזה רוח שירצה. ועלה תני: היו שנים מקלת כו' אמר ר"ש: למה הדבר דומה. ואמרינן* דהכי קאמר להו רבי שמעון לרבנן: מכדי למה הדבר דומה כו' מאי שנא התם דפליגיתו עלי' אלמא: הנך רבנן דאיירי לעיל מיניה בד' אמות דשביתה, איפלוג נמי בחצירות: היכא דאיתמר. בהדיא הלכה כרבי שמעון – איתמר. וכי קיילינן רבי יהודה ור"ש הלכה כרבי יהודה – להיכא דלא איתמר הלכתא לא כמר ולא כמר: שלש

(א)ורב פפא אמר: איצטריך, ס"ד אמינא: הני מילי – בעירובי חצירות, אבל בעירובי תחומין – אימא לא, צריכא. ומנא תימרא דשני לן בין עירובי חצירות לעירובי תחומין – *דתנן, א"ר יהודה: במה דברים אמורים – בעירובי תחומין, אבל בעירובי חצירות – מערבין בין לדעת ובין שלא לדעת, שזכין לאדם שלא בפניו, ואין חבין לאדם אלא בפניו. רב אשי אמר: איצטריך, ס"ד אמינא: הני מילי – בשיורי עירוב, אבל בתחילת עירוב – אימא לא. ומנא תימרא דשני לן בין שיורי עירוב לתחילת עירוב – *דתנן: א"ר יוסי: במה דברים אמורים – בתחילת עירוב, אבל בשיורי עירוב – אפילו כל שהוא. ולא אמרו לערב חצירות אלא כדי שלא לשכח תורת עירוב מן התינוקות. רבי יעקב ורבי זריקא [א] אמרו: *הלכה כרבי עקיבא מחבירו, וכרבי יוסי מחבריו, *וכרבי מחבירו. למאי הלכתא? *רבי אסי אמר: הלכה, ורבי חייא בר אבא אמר: מטין, ור' יוסי בר' חנינא אמר: נראין. כלשון הזה א"ר יעקב בר אידי, אמר ר' יוחנן: *ר' מאיר ור' יהודה – הלכה כרבי יהודה, רבי יהודה ורבי יוסי – הלכה כרבי יוסי, ואצ"ל *ר"מ ור' יוסי – הלכה כרבי יוסי. השתא במקום רבי יהודה – ליתא, במקום רבי יוסי מיבעיא?! אמר רב אסי: אף אני לומד רבי יוסי ור' שמעון – הלכה כרבי יוסי. דאמר רבי אבא, אמר רבי יוחנן: *רבי יהודה ורבי שמעון – הלכה כר' יהודה. השתא במקום רבי יהודה ליתא, במקום רבי יוסי מיבעיא?! איבעיא להו: ר"מ ור"ש מאי? תיקו. אמר רב משרשיא: ליתנהו להני כללי. מנא ליה לרב משרשיא הא? אילימא מהא דתנן, *ר"ש אומר: למה הדבר דומה – לג' חצירות הפתוחות זו לזו ופתוחות לרשות הרבים, עירבו שתים החיצונות עם האמצעית – היא מותרת עמהן, והן מותרות עמה, ושתים החיצונות אסורות זו עם זו. *ואמר רב חמא בר גוריא, אמר רב: הלכה כרבי שמעון. ומאן פליג עליה – רבי יהודה. והא אמרת: רבי יהודה ורבי שמעון הלכה כרבי יהודה, אלא לאו ש"מ: ליתנהו. ומאי קושיא? דילמא: היכא דאיתמר – איתמר, היכא דלא איתמר – לא איתמר. אלא מהא, *דתנן: עיר של יחיד ונעשית של רבים – מערבין את כולה. של רבים ונעשית של יחיד – אין מערבין את כולה, אלא אם כן עושה חוצה לה(ב) כעיר חדשה שביהודה, שיש בה חמשים דיורין, דברי רבי יהודה. רבי שמעון אומר: שלש

[ברכות לג:]

רבינו חננאל: לכולהו ואפילו למאי דאקשינן איהו נמי וא' איצטריך ר' יהושע למימר הלכתא כריב"נ אפי' בעירובי תחומין דאי לא פריש הוה אמינא כי אריב"ל הלכתא כדברי המיקל בעירובי חצרות אבל בעירובי תחומין לא קמ"ל דהלכתא כריב"נ אפילו בעירובי חצרות ומנא תימרא דשני לן בין עירובי תחומין לעירובי חצרות דלא משמע בהאי וה"ה להאי דתנן א"ר יהודה בד"א בעירובי תחומין אבל בעירובי חצרות כו'. רב אשי בא לומר איצטריך לומר הלכה כריב"נ שלא תאמר בשירי העירוב אריב"ל הלכה כדברי המיקל בעירוב אבל בתחלה אימא לא קמ"ל הלכתא כריב"נ דהוא כמו תחלת העירוב: ר' יעקב ור' זריקא אמרי הלכתא כר"ע מחבירו. וכר' יוסי (מחבירו) [מחביריו]. וכרבי מחבירו ר' (יוסי) [אסי] אמר הלכת' אתמר ר' חייא בר אבא אמר מטין אתמר. ור' יוסי בר' חנינא אמר נראין אתמר. א"ר יעקב בר אידי משום ר' יוחנן ר"מ ור' יהודה הלכה כר' יהודה ר' יהודה ור' יוסי הלכתא כר' יוסי. וכ"ש ר"מ ור' יוסי הלכתא כר' יוסי. ור' אבא אמר רבי יוחנן ר' יהודה ור"ש הלכתא כר"י. אמר רב אשי ר' יוסי ור"ש הלכה כר"י אבעיא להו ר"מ ור"ש הלכתא כמאן תיקו. בא רב (אשי) משרשיא לדחות דברי ר' אבא שאמר משמיה דר' יוחנן ואמר ליתנהו להני כללי מדתנן אמר ר"ש למה הדבר דומה לג' חצרות הפתוחות זו לזו ופתוחות לרה"ר ועירבו שתיהן עם האמצעית כו' ואמר (רבא) [רב חמא בר גוריא אמר רב] הלכה כר"ש מאן פליג עליה ר' יהודה. והא"ר יוחנן ר"י ור"ש הלכה כר"י [ומאי קושיא] היכא דלא איתמר עלה בפירוש הלכה (כר"ש) [כר"י] אבל היכא דאתמר לא א"ר יוחנן. ואקשינן נמי מהא דתנן ר"ש אומר

הגהות הב"ח

(א) גמ' רב פפא כצ"ל ואות ו' נמחק: (ב) שם עיר חדשה כך שמה חדשה. ע"ל דף ס ע"א: (ג) רש"י ד"ה ה"ג רב פפא וכו' הלכה כרבי יוחנן בן נורי ואע"ג: (ד) ד"ה למאי הלכתא וכו' קאמרי כן אבל לא סמכינן עליה למילף הלכתא מכללא הס"ד:

[וע' תוס' לקמן פג: ד"ה שבעת]

הגהות מהר"י לנדא

א] גמ' אמרו הלכה כרבי עקיבא מחברו וכו'. עי' בתוי"ט בפ"ג דכלים משנה ב מ"ש בשם מהרי"ק:

[לקמן פ: פא: נה.]
לקמן פ:
[כתובות פד:]
[פסחים כז. כתובות כא. נא. ב"ב קכד:]
[לקמן נב. כתובות סו:]
[סנהדרין כז.]
[ביצה כז. בכורות יח.]
[לעיל מה:]
[לקמן מט: ס.]
לקמן נט:
[לקמן מח.]

גליון הש"ס

גמ' אר"י ר"מ ור"י הלכה כר"י. עי' זבחים דף ו ע"ב תוס' ד"ה אחד:

שָׁלֹשׁ חֲצֵירוֹת שֶׁל שְׁנֵי בָתִּים. *וְאָמַר רַב חָמָא בַּר גּוּרְיָא, אָמַר רַב: הֲלָכָה כְּרַבִּי שִׁמְעוֹן. וּמַאן פָּלֵיג עֲלֵיהּ – רַבִּי יְהוּדָה. וְהָא אָמְרַתְּ: רַבִּי יְהוּדָה וְר"ש הֲלָכָה כְּרַבִּי יְהוּדָה! וּמַאי קוּשְׁיָא? דִּילְמָא הָכָא נַמִי, הֵיכָא דְּאִיתְּמַר – אִיתְּמַר, הֵיכָא דְּלָא אִיתְּמַר – לָא אִיתְּמַר. אֶלָּא מֵהָא, דִּתְנַן: *הַמַּנִּיחַ אֶת בֵּיתוֹ וְהָלַךְ לִשְׁבּוֹת בְּעִיר אַחֶרֶת, אֶחָד נׇכְרִי וְאֶחָד יִשְׂרָאֵל – אוֹסֵר לִבְנֵי חֲצֵירוֹת, דִּבְרֵי רַבִּי מֵאִיר. רַבִּי יְהוּדָה אוֹמֵר: אֵינוֹ אוֹסֵר. רַבִּי יוֹסֵי אוֹמֵר: נׇכְרִי – אוֹסֵר, יִשְׂרָאֵל – אֵינוֹ אוֹסֵר, מִפְּנֵי שֶׁאֵין דֶּרֶךְ יִשְׂרָאֵל לָבֹא בְּשַׁבָּת. רַבִּי שִׁמְעוֹן אוֹמֵר: אֲפִילּוּ הִנִּיחַ אֶת בֵּיתוֹ וְהָלַךְ לִשְׁבּוֹת אֵצֶל בִּתּוֹ בְּאוֹתָהּ הָעִיר – אֵינוֹ אוֹסֵר, שֶׁכְּבָר הִסִּיחַ דַּעְתּוֹ. וְאָמַר רַב חָמָא בַּר גּוּרְיָא, אָמַר רַב: *הֲלָכָה כְּר"ש. וּמַאן פָּלֵיג עֲלֵיהּ – ר"י. וְהָא אָמְרַתְּ רַבִּי יְהוּדָה וְר"ש הֲלָכָה כְּרַבִּי יְהוּדָה! וּמַאי קוּשְׁיָא? דִּלְמָא הָכָא נַמִי, הֵיכָא דְּאִיתְּמַר – אִיתְּמַר, הֵיכָא דְּלָא אִיתְּמַר – לָא אִיתְּמַר. אֶלָּא מֵהָא, *דִּתְנַן: וְזֶהוּ שֶׁאָמְרוּ הֶעָנִי מְעָרֵב בְּרַגְלָיו. רַבִּי מֵאִיר אוֹמֵר: אָנוּ אֵין לָנוּ אֶלָּא עָנִי. רַבִּי יְהוּדָה אוֹמֵר: אֶחָד עָנִי וְאֶחָד עָשִׁיר, לֹא אָמְרוּ מְעָרְבִין בְּפַת אֶלָּא לְהָקֵל עַל הֶעָשִׁיר, שֶׁלֹּא יֵצֵא וִיעָרֵב בְּרַגְלָיו. *וּמַתְנֵי לֵיהּ רַב חִיָּיא בַּר אַשִׁי לְחִיָּיא בַּר רַב קַמֵּיהּ דְּרַב: אֶחָד עָנִי וְאֶחָד עָשִׁיר. וְאָמַר לֵיהּ רַב: סַיֵּים בָּהּ נַמִי: הֲלָכָה כְּרַבִּי יְהוּדָה. תַּרְתֵּי לָמָּה לִי? וְהָא אָמְרַתְּ: ר"מ וְרַבִּי יְהוּדָה הֲלָכָה כְּרַבִּי יְהוּדָה! וּמַאי קוּשְׁיָא? דִּילְמָא רַב לֵית לֵיהּ לְהָנֵי כְּלָלֵי? אֶלָּא מֵהָא, *דִּתְנַן: [א]הַיְבָמָה לֹא תַחֲלוֹץ וְלֹא תִתְיַיבֵּם עַד שֶׁיְּהוּ לָהּ שְׁלֹשָׁה חֳדָשִׁים. [ב]וְכֵן שְׁאָר כׇּל הַנָּשִׁים לֹא יִנָּשְׂאוּ וְלֹא יִתְאָרְסוּ עַד שֶׁיְּהוּ לָהֶן שְׁלֹשָׁה חֳדָשִׁים. אֶחָד בְּתוּלוֹת וְאֶחָד בְּעוּלוֹת, אֶחָד אַלְמָנוֹת וְאֶחָד גְּרוּשׁוֹת, אֶחָד אֲרוּסוֹת וְאֶחָד נְשׂוּאוֹת. ר' יְהוּדָה אוֹמֵר: נְשׂוּאוֹת – יִתְאָרְסוּ, וַאֲרוּסוֹת – יִנָּשְׂאוּ, חוּץ מֵאֲרוּסָה שֶׁבִּיהוּדָה, מִפְּנֵי שֶׁלִּבּוֹ גַּס בָּהּ. ר' יוֹסֵי אוֹמֵר: כׇּל הַנָּשִׁים יִתְאָרְסוּ, חוּץ מִן הָאַלְמָנָה, מִפְּנֵי הָאִיבּוּל. *וְאָמְרִינַן: רַבִּי *אֶלְעָזָר [נ"ל אלעזר] לָא עַל לְבֵי מִדְרְשָׁא, אַשְׁכְּחֵיהּ לְרַבִּי אַסִי דַּהֲוָה קָאֵים. אֲמַר לֵיהּ: מַאי אֲמוּר בְּבֵי מִדְרְשָׁא? אֲמַר לֵיהּ, הָכִי א"ר יוֹחָנָן: הֲלָכָה כְּרַבִּי יוֹסֵי. מִכְּלָל דִּיחִידָאָה פָּלֵיג עֲלֵיהּ? אִין, *וְהָתַנְיָא: [ג]הֲרֵי שֶׁהָיְתָה רְדוּפָה לֵילֵךְ לְבֵית אָבִיהָ, אוֹ שֶׁהָיְתָה לָהּ כַּעַס עִם בַּעְלָהּ, אוֹ שֶׁהָיָה בַּעְלָהּ זָקֵן אוֹ חוֹלֶה, אוֹ שֶׁהָיְתָה הִיא חוֹלָה עֲקָרָה זְקֵנָה קְטַנָּה וְאַיְילוֹנִית וְשֶׁאֵינָהּ רְאוּיָה לֵילֵד, אוֹ שֶׁהָיָה בַּעְלָהּ חָבוּשׁ בְּבֵית הָאֲסוּרִין, הַמַּפֶּלֶת לְאַחַר מִיתַת בַּעְלָהּ – כּוּלָּן צְרִיכִין לְהַמְתִּין ג' חֳדָשִׁים, דִּבְרֵי ר"מ. רַבִּי יוֹסֵי מַתִּיר לֵיאָרֵס וְלִינָּשֵׂא מִיָּד. לָמָּה לִי? וְהָא אָמְרַתְּ ר"מ וְרַבִּי יוֹסֵי הֲלָכָה כְּר' יוֹסֵי! וּמַאי קוּשְׁיָא? דִּלְמָא לְאַפּוֹקֵי מִדְּרַב נַחְמָן אָמַר שְׁמוּאֵל, דְּאָמַר: *הֲלָכָה כְּרַבִּי מֵאִיר *בִּגְזֵירוֹתָיו. אֶלָּא מֵהָא, *דְּתַנְיָא: [ד]הוֹלְכִין לַיָּרִיד שֶׁל נׇכְרִים וְלוֹקְחִים מֵהֶן בְּהֵמָה וַעֲבָדִים וּשְׁפָחוֹת בָּתִּים שָׂדוֹת וּכְרָמִים, וְכוֹתֵב וּמַעֲלֶה בְּעַרְכָּאוֹת שֶׁלָּהֶן, מִפְּנֵי שֶׁהוּא כְּמַצִּיל מִיָּדָן. [ה]וְאִם הָיָה כֹּהֵן – מִטַּמֵּא בְּחוּצָה לָאָרֶץ לָדוּן וּלְעַרְעֵר עִמָּהֶן. וּכְשֵׁם שֶׁמִּטַּמֵּא בְּחוּצָה לָאָרֶץ, כָּךְ מִטַּמֵּא בְּבֵית הַקְּבָרוֹת. בֵּית הַקְּבָרוֹת ס"ד?! טוּמְאָה דְּאוֹרָיְיתָא הִיא! אֶלָּא בְּבֵית הַפְּרָס, דְּרַבָּנַן. וּמִטַּמֵּא לִישָּׂא אִשָּׁה וְלִלְמוֹד תּוֹרָה. א"ר יְהוּדָה: אֵימָתַי – בִּזְמַן שֶׁאֵין מוֹצֵא לִלְמוֹד, אֲבָל מוֹצֵא לִלְמוֹד – לֹא יִטַּמֵּא. ר' יוֹסֵי אוֹמֵר: [ו]אַף בִּזְמַן שֶׁמּוֹצֵא לִלְמוֹד נַמִי יִטַּמֵּא, לְפִי שֶׁאֵין

הכי גרסינן: רבי יוסי מתיר ליארס ולינשא מיד. ואין להאריך כאן: והכלים

שלש חצירות. לקמן ב"כיצד מעברין" (דף נט.) וקאמר ר' יהודה: עיר של רבים ונעשית של יחיד שנתמעטו אוכלוסיה מעבור ברחובותיה ס' ריבוא ולא דמיא השתא לדגלי מדבר – אין מערבין את כולה יחד, אלא אם(א) שייר חוצה לה כ' דיורין שלא יערבו עמה, למיהוי היכר לעיר של רבים, דלא ליערבו כולה אלא מבואות מבואות. ר"ש אומר: דיו לשייר ג' חצירות של ב' ב' בעלי בתים: אוסר על בני חצירות. שלא יוציאו מבתיהן לחצר מפני שיש לו רשות בחצר, ואע"פ שאינו בעיר – אוסר עליהן אם לא עירב קודם שהלך: ר' יהודה אומר אינו אוסר. הואיל ואינו בעיר: נכרי אוסר. אף על פי שאינו בעיר, שהרי יכול לבא ואין זה(ב) היסח מן הלב. אבל ישראל – משהלך מכאן ולא בא מערב שבת – הסיח לביתו מלבו כל השבת, שהרי לא יבא. הלכך, כמאן דלית ליה להך דירה בעלים דמי: לשבות אצל בתו. מאמש אפילו באותה העיר: רבי יהודה פליג עליה. דקאמר: בעיר אחרת – אינו אוסר, הא באותה העיר – אוסר. ורבי יוסי נמי פליג עליה, אלא חד מינייהו נקט: וזהו שאמרו. בפירקין היא (דף מט:): אנו אין לנו. "שיכול לקנות שביתה ברגליו בלא עירוב פת" – אלא עני. כלומר: מי שהוא בדרך ואין עמו פת: אחד עשיר. היושב בביתו, אם רצה לילך בעצמו ולהחשיך שם על התחום – קונה לו שביתה: שלא יצא. מפני הטורח – ויערב ברגליו. אלא התירו לשלוח עירוב בפת ע"י שלוחו: ומתני ליה רב חייא בר אשי. למתני' לחייא בר רב קמיה דרב: אחד עני ואחד עשיר. מילתיה דרבי יהודה: למה ליה. למיפסק הלכה כרבי יהודה(ג) דרבי מאיר פליג עליה? הא כיילת לעיל – להיכא דלא איתמר הלכה לא כמר ולא כמר – עבדינן כרבי יהודה: רב לית ליה להני כללי. ומשום דרב לית ליה קאמרת ליתנהו?! והא ר' יוחנן קאמר להו, והלכה כר' יוחנן: היבמה לא תחלוץ. בתוך ג' חדשים למיתת בעלה. מפרש טעמא ביבמות: שמא מעוברת היא, וחליצת מעוברת אינה חליצה. וא"ת: תחלוץ בתוך ג' ותמתין עד לאחר ג' שאם תמצא מעוברת – אינה צריכה חליצה, אם תלד וולד של קיימא. ואם לא תמצא מעוברת – אינה צריכה חליצה אחרת. ואם תלד וולד שאינו של קיימא – תחלוץ פעם שניה שמא יהא וולד של קיימא, ואינה חליצה לאוסרה לכהונה. ונמצא מצריכה כרוז לכהונה. ולילכרזה! דלמא איכא דהוי בחליצה ולא הוי בהכרזה, וסבר: שרו חלוצה לכהן: ולא תתייבם. שמא מעוברת היא, ונמצא בא על אשת אחיו שיש לה בנים, והרי היא עליו בכרת. אבל לאחר שלשה – דניכר בה שאינה מעוברת, או תחלוץ או תתייבם: שאר כל הנשים כו'. שמא תלד בתוך תשעה למיתת בעלה, ספק בן תשעה לאחרון, ספק בן שבעה לראשון. ובעינן הבחנה, כדאמרינן ביבמות (דף מב.): שמא ייבם אשת אחיו מאמו. ועוד יש איסורין הרבה: ולא יתארסו. גזור רבנן אירוסין אטו נשואין: אחת בתולות כו'. מפרש התם (שם:): אחת שנישאו לזה כשהן בתולות, ואחת שנישאו לזה כשהן בעולות, שנתאלמנה או נתגרשה מבעלה זה, בין מן האירוסין בין מן הנשואין – צריכות להמתין אחר הגט או אחר המיתה ג' חדשים: אחת ארוסות. אף על גב דארוסה לא בת עיבורי היא, גזור רבנן ארוסה אטו נשואה: "דברי ר"מ" לא גרסי' אלא סתמא היא: יתארסו. מיד, דהא לא מיעברא מספי תוך ג' – ואם תלד בתוך ט' – ודאי דראשון הוא, דאי מאחרון – בן שבעה הוא ולא חיי: והארוסות. שנתאלמנו או שנתגרשו מן האירוסין – ינשאו מיד, דהא לא מיעברא מראשון: חוץ מן הארוסה שביהודה. שהיו רגילין ליחד חתן וכלה קודם כניסתן לחופה, כדאמרינן בכתובות (דף יב.): גם בה. רגיל בה ומכירה ומרוצה לו: כל הנשים יתארסו. אתנא קמא פליג דאסר אפי' ליארס. ואדרבי יהודה פליג, דשרי ארוסה לינשא: חוץ מן האלמנה מפני האיבול. שאסורה ליארס כל ימי אבלה, אבל גרושה – תיארס מיד: הלכה כר' יוסי. דמתיר ליארס מיד: ואמרינן. מכלל דהך סתמא דתנינא לעיל אחת ארוסות ואחת נשואות – יחידאה היא: והתניא. בניחותא: רדופה לילך לבית אביה. תדירה לדור בבית אביה בעיר אחרת, ואינה רגילה עם בעלה: חולה. ואינה מקבלת טורח תשמיש: עקרה. מחמת מזל, שכבר נישאת לג' בני אדם ולא ילדה להן, והוחזקה עקרה: איילונית. ממעי אמה, ויש לה סימנין שאין לה שערות ולא דדין. ולשון "איילונית" – דוכרניתא, כאיל זה שאינו יולד*: ושאינה ראויה לילד. מחמת משקה סם: דברי ר"מ. אלמא: ר"מ הוא דגזר בהאיך דפשיטא לן דאינה מעוברת, וה"ה לארוסה: ולמה ליה. לר' יוחנן למימר הלכה כר' יוסי, דהא איהו גופיה כייל לעיל ר"מ ורבי יוסי הלכה כר' יוסי. אלא ש"מ: לא אמר ר' יוחנן להני כללי, אלא הנך אמוראי אמרינהו מנפשייהו: ומאי קושיא דלמא. אע"ג דכיילינהו ר' יוחנן, איצטריך ליה למיפסק בהא משום דהוה רבי מאיר מחמיר, ואמר שמואל: הלכה כרבי מאיר בגזירותיו בכל מקום שהחמיר. ואתא רבי יוחנן לאפוקי לדשמואל מיהא, דבהא הלכה כרבי יוסי: ליריד. שוק הנקבע ליום חג של גוים ולוקחין מהן בתים ושדות מפני שממעיטן. אי נמי: משום ישוב א"י: בהמה ועבדים ושפחות. מפני שמכניסן לקדושה: ומעלה. השטר: בערכאות שלהן. לפני דייניהן לחתום. ואע"פ שהוא חשיבות להן, ואיכא למיחש דלמא אזלי ומודו – אפ"ה שרי: מפני שהוא כמציל מידם. שלא יחזור הנכרי ויערער על המכירה: בית הקברות ס"ד. הא עבר בלאו: שאינו מוצא ללמוד. באתרו: שלא

[לקמן מט: ס.] לקמן סב: פו. ע"ש [לקמן פו. ע"ש] לקמן מט: [לקמן נח:] יבמות מא. [שם מב:] [כתובו' ס: ע"ש יבמות מב: ע"ש תוספ' יבמות פ"ו] [ע"ש כמה שינויים] [כתובו' נז. ס:] מו"ק יא. ע"א יג. [כתובות יא.]

[עי' תוס' ביצה כז. ד"ה אלא ר"מ ותוס' יבמות לז. ד"ה מי עביד ותוס' ב"ק ל: ד"ה וחכמים ותוס' ב"מ עב. ד"ה קונסין ותוס' ב"ב לד: סד"ה וחכמים ותוס' זבחים קד. ד"ה אר"ע ותוס' בכורות כח. ד"ה ר"מ]

לח א מיי' פ"א מהל' יבום הלכה יט סמג עשין כב טוש"ע אה"ע סי' קסד ס"א וסי' יג ס"ב:
לט ב ג מיי' פי"א מהל' גירושין הל' יח סמג עשין נ טוש"ע אה"ע סי' יג סעיף א:
מ ד מיי' פ"ט מהל' ע"ז הלכה יד סמג לאוין מח טור ש"ע י"ד סי' קמט סעיף ג [וברב אלפס הלכות טומאה דף סה]:
מא ה ו מיי' פ"ג מהל' אבל הלכה יד סמג לאוין רלג טור ש"ע י"ד סי' שעב סעיף א [וברב אלפס שם]:

הגהות הב"ח
(א) רש"י ד"ה שלש וכו' אלא אם כן שייר: (ב) ד"ה גוי וכו' ואין זה שהסיח לביתו מן הלב: (ג) ד"ה למה ליה וכו' כרבי יהודה היכא דר"מ פליג:

גליון הש"ס
גמ' והא אמרת ר"י ור"ש הלכה כר"י. עי' תוס' לקמן דף סה ע"ב ד"ה איקלעו: גמ' בבית הפרס דרבנן ומטמא. עי' בכורות דף כט ע"א תוס' ד"ה היכי אזיל:

רבינו חננאל
ג' חצרות של ב' בתים כו' ופרקינן כדפרקינן לעילא. ואקשינן מהא דתנן ר"י אומר אחד עני ואחד עשיר לא אמרו מערבין [בפת] אלא להקל על העשיר שלא יהא צריך לצאת ולערב ברגליו ומתני ליה רב חייא בר אשי לחייא בר רב קמיה דרב אחד עני ואחד עשיר וא"ל רב אתניה הלכה כר' יהודה כלומר קבעה במשנתנו הלכתא כר' יהודה ואי איתא להא דר' יוחנן למה ליה למתנייה במתני' אע"ג דלא תנא הא ידוע דהלכתא כר' יהודה דהא ר' מאיר פליג עליה ודחינן דלמא רב פליג על ר' יוחנן ואמר ליתנהו להני כללי ורב ור' יוחנן הלכה כר' יוחנן אלא מהא דתנינן היבמה לא תחלוץ ולא תתייבם עד שיהו לה ג' חדשים וכן שאר כל הנשים לא יתארסו עד שיהו להן ג' חדשים אחד בתולות ואחד בעולות אחד אלמנות ואחד גרושות כו' ר' יוסי אומר כל הנשים יתארסו חוץ מאלמנה מפני האיבול. וא"ר (יוסי) [אסי] א"ר יוחנן הלכה כר' יוסי ואמר מכלל דיחיד פליג עליה אין והתניא הרי שהיתה רדופה לילך לבית אביה או שהיתה לה כעס מבעלה או שהיה בעלה זקן או חולה או שהיתה [היא] חולה או קטנה או איילונית או עקרה או זקנה שאינה ראויה לילד והמפלת לאחר מיתת בעלה צריכה להמתין ג' [חדשים] דברי ר"מ ר' יוסי מתיר ליארס ולהנשא מיד למה ליה לר' יוחנן למימר הלכה כר' יוסי והא ר' יוחנן הוא דאמר ר' יהודה ור' יוסי הלכה כר' יוסי וכ"ש ר"מ ור' יוסי שהלכה כר' יוסי אלא ש"מ ליתנהו להני כללי ודחינן (למאי) [ומאי] קשיא ודלמא לעולם איתנהו להני כללי ר' יוחנן לא אצטריך למימר הכא הלכה אלא כדי לאפוקי מרב נחמן אמר שמואל דאמר הלכה כר"מ בגזירותיו. והא גזרה היא דגזר עקרה ואיילונית ומי שאינה ראויה לילד ואפי' המפלת לאחר מיתת בעלה אטו ראויה לילד אתא לדחויי מהא דרב נחמן אמר שמואל ואמר הלכתא כר' יוסי (ופליג) [דפליג] על ר"מ אלא מהא דתניא הולכין ליריד של גוים ולוקחין מהן בהמה עד (דמטי) [ומטמא] ללמד תורה ולישא אשה. אר"י אימתי בזמן שאינו מוצא ללמד בטהרה יטמא [ר"י אומר אף בזמן שמוצא ללמוד נמי יטמא] לפי שאין

שֶׁאֵין מִן הַכֹּל זוֹכֶה אָדָם לִלְמוֹד. וְאָמַר ר' יוֹסֵי: מַעֲשֶׂה בְּיוֹסֵף הַכֹּהֵן שֶׁהָלַךְ אֵצֶל רַבּוֹ לְצַיְדָן לִלְמוֹד תּוֹרָה. וְאָמַר ר' יוֹחָנָן: הֲלָכָה כְּרַבִּי יוֹסֵי. וְלָמָּה לִי? וְהָא אָמַרְתְּ: רַבִּי יְהוּדָה וְר' יוֹסֵי הֲלָכָה כְּר' יוֹסֵי! אָמַר אַבָּיֵי: אִיצְטְרִיךְ, סד"א: *הָנֵי מִילֵּי — בְּמַתְנִי', אֲבָל בְּבָרַיְיתָא — אֵימָא לָא, קמ"ל. אֶלָּא הָכִי קָאָמַר: הָנֵי כְּלָלֵי לָאו ד"ה נִינְהוּ, דְּהָא רַב לֵית לֵיהּ הָנֵי כְּלָלֵי.§ אָמַר רַב יְהוּדָה, אָמַר שְׁמוּאֵל: חֶפְצֵי נָכְרִי אֵין קוֹנִין שְׁבִיתָה. לְמַאן? אִילֵימָא לְרַבָּנַן — פְּשִׁיטָא! הָשְׁתָּא חֶפְצֵי הֶפְקֵר, דְּלֵית לְהוּ בְּעָלִים, אֵין קוֹנִין שְׁבִיתָה — חֶפְצֵי הַנָּכְרִי, דְּאִית לְהוּ בְּעָלִים מִיבָּעֲיָא?! אֶלָּא אַלִּיבָּא דְּר' יוֹחָנָן בֶּן נוּרִי. וְקמ"ל: אֵימַר *דְּאָמַר ר' יוֹחָנָן בֶּן נוּרִי קוֹנִין שְׁבִיתָה — הָנֵי מִילֵּי חֶפְצֵי הֶפְקֵר, דְּלֵית לְהוּ בְּעָלִים. אֲבָל חֶפְצֵי הַנָּכְרִי, דְּאִית לְהוּ בְּעָלִים — לָא. מֵיתִיבִי, ר"ש בֶּן אֶלְעָזָר אוֹמֵר: הַשּׁוֹאֵל כְּלִי מִן הַנָּכְרִי בְּיוֹם טוֹב, וְכֵן הַמַּשְׁאִיל לוֹ לְנָכְרִי כְּלִי מֵעיו"ט וְהֶחֱזִירוֹ לוֹ בְּיוֹם טוֹב, וְהַכֵּלִים וְהָאוֹצָרוֹת שֶׁשָּׁבְתוּ בְּתוֹךְ הַתְּחוּם — יֵשׁ לָהֶן אַלְפַּיִם אַמָּה לְכָל רוּחַ. וְנָכְרִי שֶׁהֵבִיא לוֹ פֵּירוֹת מִחוּץ לַתְּחוּם — הֲרֵי זֶה לֹא יְזִיזֵם מִמְּקוֹמָן. אִי אָמְרַתְּ בִּשְׁלָמָא קָסָבַר רַבִּי יוֹחָנָן בֶּן נוּרִי חֶפְצֵי נָכְרִי קוֹנִין שְׁבִיתָה, הָא מַנִּי — ר' יוֹחָנָן בֶּן נוּרִי הִיא. אֶלָּא אִי אָמְרַתְּ קָסָבַר רַבִּי יוֹחָנָן בֶּן נוּרִי חֶפְצֵי הַנָּכְרִי אֵין קוֹנִין שְׁבִיתָה, הָא מַנִּי? לָא ר' יוֹחָנָן בֶּן נוּרִי וְלָא רַבָּנַן! לְעוֹלָם קָסָבַר רַבִּי יוֹחָנָן בֶּן נוּרִי "חֶפְצֵי הַנָּכְרִי קוֹנִין שְׁבִיתָה", וּשְׁמוּאֵל דְּאָמַר כְּרַבָּנַן. וּדְקָאָמְרַתְּ לְרַבָּנַן פְּשִׁיטָא — מַהוּ דְּתֵימָא: גְּזֵירָה בְּעָלִים דְּנָכְרִי אַטּוּ בְּעָלִים דְּיִשְׂרָאֵל, קמ"ל. וְרַב חִיָּיא בַּר אָבִין אָמַר רַבִּי יוֹחָנָן: [א]חֶפְצֵי נָכְרִי קוֹנִין שְׁבִיתָה, גְּזֵירָה בְּעָלִים דְּנָכְרִי אַטּוּ בְּעָלִים דְּיִשְׂרָאֵל. הָנְהוּ דִּכְרֵי דַּאֲתוּ לְמַבְרַכְתָּא, שְׁרָא לְהוּ רָבָא לִבְנֵי מְחוֹזָא לְמִיזְבַּן מִינַּיְיהוּ. א"ל רָבִינָא לְרָבָא: מַאי דַּעְתִּיךְ — דְּאָמַר רַב יְהוּדָה, אָמַר שְׁמוּאֵל: חֶפְצֵי נָכְרִי אֵין קוֹנִין שְׁבִיתָה, וְהָא שְׁמוּאֵל וְר' יוֹחָנָן הֲלָכָה כְּר' יוֹחָנָן, וְאָמַר רַב חִיָּיא בַּר אָבִין אָמַר ר' יוֹחָנָן: חֶפְצֵי נָכְרִי קוֹנִין שְׁבִיתָה, גְּזֵירָה בְּעָלִים דְּנָכְרִי אַטּוּ בְּעָלִים דְּיִשְׂרָאֵל! [ב]הֲדַר אֲמַר רָבָא: לִיזְדַּבְּנוּ לִבְנֵי מַבְרַכְתָּא. דְּכוּלָּהּ מַבְרַכְתָּא לְדִידְהוּ כְּד' אַמּוֹת דָּמְיָא. תָּנֵי רַבִּי חִיָּיא: [ג]חֵרֶם שֶׁבֵּין תְּחוּמֵי שַׁבָּת — צָרִיךְ מְחִיצָּה

רש"י

שֶׁלֹּא מִן הַכֹּל אָדָם זוֹכֶה לִלְמוֹד. אֵין אָדָם זוֹכֶה לִלְמוֹד מִכָּל מְלַמְּדָיו. יֵשׁ רַב שֶׁמִּשְׁנָתוֹ סְדוּרָה בְּפִיו, וְשׁוֹנֶה לְתַלְמִידָיו דֶּרֶךְ קְצָרָה: לְצַיְדָן. חוּצָה לָאָרֶץ: סד"א הָנֵי מִילֵּי. דְּקַיי"ל רַבִּי יוֹחָנָן הֲלָכָה כְּרַבִּי יוֹסֵי: בְּמַתְנִיתִין. דְּדַוְקָא הִיא: אֲבָל בְּבָרַיְיתָא. דִּילְמָא אִיחְלִיף דְּרַבִּי יְהוּדָה לְדְרַבִּי יוֹסֵי, וּדְרַבִּי יוֹסֵי לִדְרַבִּי יְהוּדָה: אֵימָא לָא. לִסְמוֹךְ עֲלָהּ. לְהָכִי צָרִיךְ לְמֵימַר הֲלָכָה, וּלְעוֹלָם אִיתְנְהוּ לְהָנֵי כְּלָלֵי: אֶלָּא הָכִי קָאָמַר. רַב מְשַׁרְשְׁיָא כו': דְּהָא רַב לֵית לֵיהּ לְהָנֵי כְּלָלֵי. כִּדְאָמַר לְעֵיל, מִדְּאִיצְטְרִיךְ לֵיהּ לְמֵימַר סַיְּיעָ בָּהּ נַמִי הֲלָכָה כְּר' יְהוּדָה: אֵין קוֹנִין שְׁבִיתָה. וַהֲרֵי הֵן כְּרַגְלֵי כָּל אָדָם. וְאִם בָּאוּ מִחוּץ לַתְּחוּם לְתוֹךְ הָעִיר — מוּתָּר לְהוֹלִיכָן לְכָל רוּחַ: חֶפְצֵי הֶפְקֵר. דְּאִיכָּא לְמֵימַר לִיקְנוּ מִנַּפְשַׁיְיהוּ, אָמְרִי רַבָּנַן דְּאֵין קוֹנִין: חֶפְצֵי הַנָּכְרִי דְּאִית לְהוּ בְּעָלִים. וַהֲרֵי הֵן כְּמוֹתָן, וּבַעֲלֵיהֶן לֵית לְהוּ שְׁבִיתָה, דְּלָאו בְּנֵי שְׁבִיתָה נִינְהוּ מִיבָּעֲיָא: [א]הַשּׁוֹאֵל כְּלִי מִן הַנָּכְרִי. וְגַן עִירוֹ הֲוָה: וְכֵן הַמַּשְׁאִיל לוֹ כְּלִי מֵעֶרֶב יוֹם טוֹב. וְקָנָה שְׁבִיתָה אֵצֶל הַנָּכְרִי בְּתוֹךְ תְּחוּם הָעִיר: וְהַכֵּלִים וְהָאוֹצָרוֹת. שֶׁעֲשָׂאוּם אוֹצָר: יֵשׁ לָהֶן אַלְפַּיִם לְכָל רוּחַ. וַאֲפִילּוּ הֵן שֶׁל הֶפְקֵר. וּכְלִי שֶׁקָּנָה שְׁבִיתָה אֵצֶל הַנָּכְרִי וְהֶחֱזִירוֹ לַבְּעָלִים וְעֵירְבוּ בְּעָלָיו לַמִּזְרָח אוֹ לַמַּעֲרָב אֵין יָכוֹל לְהוֹלִיכוֹ מֵאַלְפַּיִם: לֹא יְזִיזֵם מִמְּקוֹמָן. דְּקָנוּ שְׁבִיתָה בִּמְקוֹמָן, וַהֲרֵי יָצְאוּ חוּץ לַתְּחוּם וְאֵין לָהֶן אֶלָּא אַרְבַּע אַמּוֹת: הָא מַנִּי. דְּקָתָנֵי: חֶפְצֵי הַנָּכְרִי קוֹנִין שְׁבִיתָה, ר' יוֹחָנָן בֶּן נוּרִי. כְּלוֹמַר: ר' שִׁמְעוֹן בֶּן אֶלְעָזָר אַלִּיבָּא דְּר' יוֹחָנָן בֶּן נוּרִי אָמַר: לְעוֹלָם סָבַר רַבִּי יוֹחָנָן[ב] חֶפְצֵי נָכְרִי. כְּחֶפְצֵי הֶפְקֵר. וְהָא ר' יוֹחָנָן בֶּן נוּרִי: וּשְׁמוּאֵל דְּאָמַר. לְעֵיל, אֵין קוֹנִין — כְּרַבָּנַן, דְּאָמְרִי בְּחֶפְצֵי הֶפְקֵר דְּאֵין קוֹנִין: דִּיכְרֵי. אֵילִים: מַבְרַכְתָּא. שֵׁם מָקוֹם: מְחוֹזָא. עִיר הַסְּמוּכָה לְמַבְרַכְתָּא בְּתוֹךְ ד' אֲלָפִים, וּמְעָרְבִין מִזּוֹ לָזוֹ: לְמִיזְבַּן מִינַּיְיהוּ. וְלַאֲיְיתִינְהוּ לִמְחוֹזָא. וְאַף עַל פִּי שֶׁהֱבִיאוּם הַנָּכְרִים מִחוּץ לַתְּחוּם, דְּקָסָבַר חֶפְצֵי הַנָּכְרִי אֵין קוֹנִין שְׁבִיתָה: כְּאַרְבַּע אַמּוֹת דָּמֵי. כִּדְתְנַן *בְּמַתְנִיתִין: הוֹלִיכוּהוּ לְעִיר אַחֶרֶת אוֹ נְתָנוּהוּ בְּדִיר וְסַהַר כו' וּפָסְקִינַן לְעֵיל, *אָמַר רַב: הֲלָכָה כְּרַבָּן גַּמְלִיאֵל בְּדִיר וְסַהַר וּסְפִינָה, וְהוּא הַדִּין לְעִיר שֶׁיֵּשׁ לָהּ מְחִיצּוֹת: חֵרֶם. מְצוּדַת דָּגִים, וּמַפְסִיק בְּמַיִם בֵּין ב' תְּחוּמִין שֶׁל ב' עֲיָירוֹת. וַחֲבֵרוֹ "מְצוֹדִים וַחֲרָמִים" (קהלת ז), וּכְתִיב "עַל כֵּן יְזַבֵּחַ לְחֶרְמוֹ" (חבקוק א), וְגָדֵר שֶׁל קָנִים הוּא: צָרִיךְ לַעֲשׂוֹת מְחִיצָּה שֶׁל בַּרְזֶל. שֶׁלֹּא יַעַבְרוּ מַיִם שֶׁל תְּחוּם זֶה לְתוֹךְ תְּחוּם זֶה. דְּכָל מַה שֶּׁבְּתוֹךְ תְּחוּם הָעִיר אֵין קוֹנֶה שְׁבִיתָה בִּמְקוֹמוֹ לִהְיוֹת לוֹ מִמְּקוֹמוֹ אַלְפַּיִם אַמָּה לְכָל רוּחַ. אֶלָּא בָּתַר הָעִיר גָּרֵיר. וְאִם הוּא בְּסוֹף הַתְּחוּם — אֵין יָכוֹל לָזוּז מִשָּׁם וְלַחוּץ, וְאֵין בְּנֵי תְּחוּם זֶה יְכוֹלִין לְמַלְּאוֹת מִתּוֹךְ תְּחוּם עַצְמוֹ, מִפְּנֵי עֵירוּב מַיִם שֶׁל תְּחוּם הָאַחֵר: *ה"ג: אִי נֵימָא מִשּׁוּם דְּתָנֵי לָהּ כְּרַבִּי יוֹחָנָן בֶּן נוּרִי וּלְחוּמְרָא וְאִיהוּ לְקוּלָּא סָבַר וּמִשּׁוּם דִּסְבִירָא לֵיהּ לְקוּלָּא כָּל דְּתָנֵי לְחוּמְרָא מְחַיֵּיךְ עֲלֵיהּ. בִּתְמִיָּה: אִי נֵימָא מִשּׁוּם דְּרַבִּי חִיָּיא תָּנֵי לְמַתְנִיתִין כְּר' יוֹחָנָן בֶּן נוּרִי, דְּאָמַר: "חֶפְצֵי הֶפְקֵר קוֹנִין שְׁבִיתָה בְּתוֹךְ[ג] תְּחוּמִין", וְרַבִּי יוֹסֵי בַּר חֲנִינָא סְבִירָא לֵיהּ כְּרַבָּנַן — לְקוּלָּא, דְּאָמְרִי: "אֵין קוֹנִין שְׁבִיתָה וַהֲרֵי הֵן כְּרַגְלֵי כָּל אָדָם":

תוספות

והכלים והאוצרות ששבתו בתוך התחום יש להם אלפים אמה לכל רוח. פ"ה: ואפילו הן של הפקר. משמע דלא מיבעיא אם יש להם בעלים. וקשה: דאי יש להם בעלים — הרי הן כרגלי הבעלים. ואפי' אם נעמידם כגון שהבעלים בעיר אחרת, דהשתא לא הוי כרגלי הבעלים. ומ"מ, בני שביתה הם יותר מן ההפקר ויש להן אלפים אמה לכל רוח. מ"מ אין נראה להעמיד כלל דיש להם בעלים, דיש להם בעלים מה לי תוך התחום מה לי חוץ לתחום? ונראה דבשל הפקר איירי, והא דנקט תוך התחום — לאשמעינן דאפ"ה לא קני שביתת העיר. וא"ת: ומאי שנא דהכא יש להן אלפים אמה לכל רוח, דמשמע ממקומן, מדלא קתני כרגלי אנשי העיר. וגבי גשמים שסמוכים לעיר הוי כרגלי אנשי העיר, כדאמרינן לעיל (דף מה:)? וי"ל: דהתם אנשי העיר דעתם עליהם, דגשמים ידועים לכל בני העיר. אבל אוצרות דהפקר, אם היו ידועים — כבר היו זוכין בהן. ועוד: שמא יש לחלק, משום דהתם בסמוכין וקרובין — דעתן עליהן, והכא ברחוקים, אלא שהן בתוך התחום. ומיהו, נראה דאלפים אמה לאו ממקומן קאמר אלא מן העיר, כמו בגשמים דלעיל. דהא מוכח גבי חרם שבין שתי תחומי שבת דלרבי יוחנן (ד)חפצי הפקר שבתוך התחום קונין שביתת העיר, אפילו אין דעת אנשי העיר עליהם, כמו שאפרש בסמוך. וברייתא דהכא כר' יוחנן בן נורי. וליכא למיפרך: האי כרגלי אנשי העיר מבעי' ליה, כדפריך לעיל. כיון דהזכיר הכא תוך התחום, משמע שפיר דאלפים אמה לכל רוח מן העיר קאמר. ואף על גב דכייל להו בהדי שואל כלי מן הנכרי, ונכרי אם עומד חוץ לעיר מונין לו אלפים ממקומו — סתמא דמלתא נכרי בעיר עומד:

דכולה מברכתא כד' אמות דמיא. בריש פירקא פ"ה: והוליכו לעיר אחרת והרי מוקפת מחיצות — משמע דלא חשיב כד' אמות לענין להלך את כולה אלא במוקפת מחיצות, דומיא דדיר וסהר, והא מברכתא צריך לומר דמוקפת מחיצות הויא. ואע"ג דגבי נותן עירובו באילן (לעיל דף לג:) פריך: חוץ לעיבורה של עיר נמי, כיון דאמר רבא הנותן עירובו יש לו ד' אמות וכו', משמע דתוך עיבורה של עיר נמי הוי טעמא לפי שנעשית לו כל העיר ועיבורה כארבע אמות, אף על פי שאין שם מחילה — ה"מ לשובת שם או נותן שם עירובו, שיש לו אלפים אמה לכל רוח ונחשב הכל כד' אמות אפילו חוץ למחילות, כיון שהוא בעיבורה של עיר. אבל בבא מחוץ לתחום — אינו נחשב כד' אמות בלא היקף מחילות. ואומר ר"י: דבעי נמי דתהוי מוקפת לדירה, דלא עדיף משבת באויר מחילות שיש לו אלפים אמה לכל רוח — אפילו הכי לא חשיב לגביה כארבע אמות בהיקף יותר מבית סאתים שלא הוקף לדירה, כדאמר בשבת בתל ונקע. וצריך ליזהר בדבר הבא מחוץ לתחום בשביל ישראל זה, דשרי לישראל אחר, או שבא בשביל נכרי — שלא יטלטלנו חוץ לד"א בעיר שאין לה מחילות שמוקפת לדירה:

חרם. לשון מצודות וחרמים, שבין שני תחומי שבת צריך מחילה של ברזל שלא יעברו מים מתחום זה לתחום זה, דכל מה שבתוך תחום העיר אין לו שביתה במקומו להיות לו אלפים לכל רוח ממקומו, אלא בתר קרתא גרירא. כך פ' הקונט', וכן פר"ת. אלא דפי' "חרם" לשון "והחרים ה' לשון ים" (ישעיה יא) — כשמעלה הים שרטון ומתייבש נשארים נקעים מלאים מים, וחרם הוא נקע מלא מים. וכן פר"ח* חרם לשון חריץ. וא"ת: אמאי מוקי לה כרבי יוחנן בן נורי? הא לרבנן נמי אמר לעיל (מה:) גבי גשמים הסמוכים לעיר דהוו כרגלי אנשי העיר! וי"ל: דהכא דמימשכי מתחום זה לתחום זה — בטלה דעתם, והוי כחפצי הפקר דאין קונין שביתה לרבנן, והוו כרגלי הזוכה. אבל לר' יוחנן דקנו שביתה כשהן בתוך תחום העיר, קונין שביתת העיר אף ע"פ שאין דעת אדם עליהם קונה. אבל אין לפרש דלר' יוחנן(ה) קונין שביתה במקומן, ומה שצריך מחילה של ברזל — היינו כדי להכניסם לעיר, לפי שמקצת המים רחוקים מן העיר יותר מאלפים אמה, דאם כן — אמאי נקט בין שני תחומין? אפילו אי ליכא עיר שניה לא מצו להכניס מים לעיר שחוץ לתחום. ועוד: אפילו מחילה של ברזל לא תועיל להכניסם לעיר מסוף אלפים אמה, שהרי בתחלת העיר כלו האלפים של מים:

רבי

עין משפט נר מצוה

מב א ב מיי' פ"ה מהל' י"ט הלכה י סמג עשין א טור ש"ע א"ח סימן תא:

מג ג מיי' פט"ו מהל' שבת הל' יג טוש"ע א"ח סי' תב:

רבינו חננאל

שאין מכל אדם זוכה ללמוד וא"ר יוסי מעשה ביוסף הכהן שהלך אחר רבו לצידן ללמוד תורה וא"ר יוחנן הלכה כר' יוסי למה לי למימר הלכה כר"י והא רבי יהודה פליג עליה ואיהו הוא דאמר ר' יהודה ור' יוסי הלכה כר' יוסי ופרקינן *) אלא אמר רב משרשיא הכי קאמר הני כללי לאו דברי הכל הן דהא רב לית ליה הני כללי אבל רבי יוחנן אית ליה. ורב הוא דפליג עליה וקיי"ל כר' יוחנן: אמר רב יהודה אמר שמואל חפצי הגוי אין קונין שביתה. פי' אם תשאל מן הגוי ביו"ט הרי הוא כרגלי השואל ואין אומרים שקנה שביתה. ואמרינן אי לרבנן פשיטא אלא אפי' לריב"נ ומותבינן עליה ר' שמעון בן אלעזר אמר השואל כלי מן הגוי וכן גוי ששאל כלי מישראל בעיו"ט והחזירו ביו"ט וכלים ואוצרות ששבתו בתוך התחום יש להן אלפים אמה לכל רוח וכן הגוי שהביא פירות מחוץ לתחום הרי זה לא יזיזם ממקומם אי אמרת בשלמא ר' יוחנן בן נורי סבר חפצי הגוי קונין שביתה היינו דקתני יש להן אלפים אמה לכל רוח אלא אי אמרת אין קונין שביתה אמאי כו'. ואסיקנא דודאי ריב"נ סבר חפצי הגוי קונין שביתה ורשב"א דאמר כריב"נ ושמואל דאמר חפצי הגוי אין קונין שביתה כרבנן. (ואמרינן האי נמי) [ודקאמרת הא] פשיטא. ופרקינן אצטריך מהו דתימא גזרינן בעלים דגוי לקנות להן שביתה אטו בעלים דישראל שאם תאמר חפצי הגוי דאית להו בעלים לא קנו שביתה אתי למימר אפילו חפצי ישראל דאית להו בעלים לא קנו שביתה קמ"ל דלא גזרינן אלא חפצי הגוי אין להם שביתה. רב חייא בר אבין אמר ר"י חפצי הגוי קונין שביתה גזירה בעלים דגוי אטו בעלים של ישראל: הנהו דכרי דאתו למברכתא. פי' מברכתא שם הכפר. והביאו שם גוים אלים בשוק של בהמות למכור ביו"ט שרא להו רבא לבני מחוזא שבאו ע"י עירוב למברכתא למזבן מינייהו ולאייתינהו למחוזא כשמואל דאמר חפצי הגוי אין קונין שביתה אלא הרי הן כרגלי כל אדם א"ל רבינא והאמר ר' יוחנן חפצי הגוי קונין שביתה ושמואל ור"י הלכה כר' יוחנן והדר רבא ואסר להן לבני מחוזא דלא הוו אתו למברכתא אלא ע"י עירוב. [כי] בין מברכתא למחוזא יותר מאלפים אמה הוה. ואפילו אם היו בתוך התחום (א') [אחר] כי (אלו) הצאן קנו שביתה בחוץ קודם שיבואו למברכתא ושרא רבא לבני מברכתא למזבן מינייהו דאע"ג דאיכא למימר הני דיכרי קנו שביתה במקום רחוק מ"מ יש להן לטלטל אותן בד' אמות ומברכתא כולה כמו ד' אמות היא הלכך שרי להו למשקל מינייהו.

תני

*) הדבר פשוט דחסר בדברי רבינו וצ"ל אמר אביי איצטריך סד"א הנ"מ במתני' אבל בברייתא אימא לא קמ"ל אלא אמר וכו'.

מסורת הש"ס

[עי' תוס' מנחות לח: ד"ה מי קאמר]

ביצה לח: לעיל לח: מה: לקמן נז:

[לעיל מא:]

[דף מב:]

[שייך לדף מח.]

[וכ"כ הערוך ערך חרם]

הגהות הב"ח

(א) רש"י ד"ה השואל וד"ה וכן וד"ה והכלים וד"ה יש להן הכל דיבור אחד: (ב) ד"ה לעולם סבר ר' יוחנן ב"נ חפצי: (ג) ד"ה ה"ג וכו' בתוך תחומן ורבי יוסי: (ד) תד"ה והכלים וכו' דלר"י ב"נ חפצי הפקר: (ה) ד"ה חרם וכו' דלרבי יוחנן בן נורי קונין:

מְחִיצָה שֶׁל בַּרְזֶל לְהַפְסִיקוֹ. מְחַיֵּיךְ עֲלֵיהּ ר' יוֹסֵי בְּר' חֲנִינָא, מַאי טַעְמָא קָא מְחַיֵּיךְ? אִילֵימָא מִשּׁוּם דְּתָנֵי לָהּ כְּר' יוֹחָנָן בֶּן נוּרִי לְחוּמְרָא, וְאִיהוּ סְבִירָא לֵיהּ כְּרַבָּנַן לְקוּלָּא? וּמִשּׁוּם דְּסָבַר לְקוּלָּא, מַאן דְּתָנֵי לְחוּמְרָא מְחַיֵּיךְ עֲלָהּ? אֶלָּא מִשּׁוּם *דְּתַנְיָא: נְהָרוֹת הַמּוֹשְׁכִין וּמַעְיָינוֹת הַנּוֹבְעִין — הֲרֵי הֵן כְּרַגְלֵי כׇּל אָדָם. וְדִילְמָא בְּמִכּוֹנָּסִין? אֶלָּא מִשּׁוּם דְּקָתָנֵי צָרִיךְ מְחִיצָה שֶׁל בַּרְזֶל לְהַפְסִיקוֹ. וּמַאי שְׁנָא קָנִים דְּלָא — דְּעָיְילִי בְּהוּ מַיָּא, שֶׁל בַּרְזֶל נַמִי — עָיְילִי בְּהוּ מַיָּא. וְדִילְמָא *צָרִיךְ וְאֵין לוֹ תַּקָּנָה קָאָמַר? אֶלָּא מִשּׁוּם דְּקַל הוּא שֶׁהֵקִילוּ חֲכָמִים בְּמַיִם. כִּדְרַבִּי טַבְלָא, *דִּבְעָא מִינֵּיהּ רַבִּי טַבְלָא מֵרַב: מְחִיצָה תְּלוּיָה, מַהוּ שֶׁתַּתִּיר בַּחוּרְבָּה? א"ל: אֵין מְחִיצָה תְּלוּיָה מַתֶּרֶת אֶלָּא בַּמַּיִם, קַל הוּא שֶׁהֵקִילוּ חֲכָמִים בַּמַּיִם. § "וַח"א: אֵין לוֹ אֶלָּא אַרְבַּע וכו'". § רַבִּי יְהוּדָה הַיְינוּ ת"ק! אָמַר רָבָא: שְׁמוֹנֶה עַל שְׁמוֹנֶה אִיכָּא בֵּינַיְיהוּ. תנ"ה: יֵשׁ לוֹ שְׁמוֹנֶה עַל שְׁמוֹנֶה, דִּבְרֵי ר"מ. וְאָמַר רָבָא: [א]מַחֲלוֹקֶת לְהַלֵּךְ, אֲבָל לְטַלְטֵל — דִּבְרֵי הַכֹּל: אַרְבַּע אַמּוֹת — אִין, טְפֵי — לָא. וְהָנֵי ד' אַמּוֹת הֵיכָא כְּתִיבָא? כִּדְתַנְיָא: °"שְׁבוּ אִישׁ תַּחְתָּיו" — כְּתַחְתָּיו. [וְכַמָּה תַּחְתָּיו —] גּוּפוֹ שָׁלֹשׁ אַמּוֹת, וְאַמָּה כְּדֵי לִפְשׁוֹט יָדָיו וְרַגְלָיו, דִּבְרֵי ר' מֵאִיר. ר' יְהוּדָה אוֹמֵר: גּוּפוֹ שָׁלֹשׁ אַמּוֹת, וְאַמָּה כְּדֵי שֶׁיִּטּוֹל חֵפֶץ מִתַּחַת מַרְגְּלוֹתָיו, וּמַנִּיחַ תַּחַת מְרַאֲשׁוֹתָיו. מַאי בֵּינַיְיהוּ? אִיכָּא בֵּינַיְיהוּ אַרְבַּע אַמּוֹת מְצוּמְצָמוֹת. אֲמַר לֵיהּ רַב מְשַׁרְשְׁיָא לִבְרֵיהּ: כִּי עָיְילַתְּ לְקַמֵּיהּ דְּרַב פַּפָּא בְּעִי מִינֵּיהּ: אַרְבַּע אַמּוֹת שֶׁאָמְרוּ, בְּאַמָּה דִּידֵיהּ יָהֲבִינַן לֵיהּ, אוֹ בְּאַמָּה שֶׁל קֹדֶשׁ יָהֲבִינַן לֵיהּ? אִם אָמַר לָךְ אַמּוֹת שֶׁל קֹדֶשׁ יָהֲבִינַן לֵיהּ — עוֹג מֶלֶךְ הַבָּשָׁן מַה תְּהֵא עָלָיו? וְאִם אָמַר לָךְ בְּאַמָּה דִּידֵיהּ יָהֲבִינַן לֵיהּ — אֵימָא לֵיהּ: מַאי טַעְמָא לָא קָתָנֵי לָהּ גַּבֵּי *"יֵשׁ שֶׁאָמְרוּ הַכֹּל לְפִי מַה שֶּׁהוּא אָדָם"? כִּי אֲתָא לְקַמֵּיהּ דְּרַב פַּפָּא, א"ל: אִי דָּיְיקִינַן כּוּלָּא הַאי, לָא הָוֵי תָּנֵינַן. [ב]לְעוֹלָם בְּאַמָּה דִּידֵיהּ יָהֲבִינַן לֵיהּ, וּדְקָא קַשְׁיָא לָךְ מַאי טַעְמָא לָא קָתָנֵי גַּבֵּי "יֵשׁ שֶׁאָמְרוּ" — דְּלָא פְּסִיקָא לֵיהּ, מִשּׁוּם דְּאִיכָּא נַנָּס בְּאֵבָרָיו. § "הָיוּ שְׁנַיִם מִקְצָת אַמּוֹתָיו שֶׁל זֶה וכו'". § לָמָּה לֵיהּ לְמֵימַר "לָמָּה הַדָּבָר דּוֹמֶה"? הָכִי קָאָמַר לְהוּ רַבִּי שִׁמְעוֹן לְרַבָּנַן: מִכְּדֵי, לָמָּה הַדָּבָר דּוֹמֶה — לְשָׁלֹשׁ חֲצֵירוֹת הַפְּתוּחוֹת זוֹ לָזוֹ וּפְתוּחוֹת לִרְ"ה. מַאי שְׁנָא הָתָם דִּפְלִיגִיתוּ, וּמ"ש הָכָא דְּלָא פְּלִיגִיתוּ? וְרַבָּנַן: הָתָם אָווֹשִׁי דִּיּוּרִין, הָכָא לָא אָווֹשִׁי דִּיּוּרִין. § [ג]"וּשְׁתַּיִם הַחִיצוֹנוֹת כו'". § וְאַמַּאי? כֵּיוָן דְּעָרְבִי לְהוּ חִיצוֹנוֹת בַּהֲדֵי אֶמְצָעִית, הָוְיָא לְהוּ חֲדָא! אָמַר רַב יְהוּדָה: [ד]כְּגוֹן שֶׁנָּתְנָה אֶמְצָעִית עֵירוּבָהּ בָּזוֹ וְעֵירוּבָהּ בָּזוֹ. וְרַב שֵׁשֶׁת אָמַר: אֲפִילּוּ תֵּימָא שֶׁנָּתְנוּ עֵירוּבָן בָּאֶמְצָעִית, [ה]כְּגוֹן שֶׁנְּתָנוּהוּ בִּשְׁנֵי

רש"י

מְחִיצָה שֶׁל בַּרְזֶל נַמִי עָיְילִי בָּהּ מַיָּא. מִתַּתַּאי, דְּהָא סְתָם מְחִיצָה י' טְפָחִים הִיא, וְלָא מָטְיָא עַד קַרְקָעִית הַמַּיִם. וַאֲפִילּוּ מַגַּעַת לְקַרְקָעִית הַמַּיִם — אִי אֶפְשָׁר שֶׁלֹּא יִכָּנְסוּ הַמַּיִם מִתַּחְתֶּיהָ: אֶלָּא. מִשּׁוּם הָכִי מְחַיֵּיךְ עֲלֵיהּ: דְּקַל הוּא שֶׁהֵקִילוּ חֲכָמִים בְּמַיִם. בִּמְחִיצָה כׇּל דְּהוּ, וּבִלְבַד שֶׁיְּהֵא בָּהּ י' מְהַנְיָא בָּהּ, וְאַע"ג דְּעָיְילִי בָּהּ מַיָּא מֵעִילָּאֵי וּמִתַּתָּאֵי: כִּדְבְעָא מִינֵּיהּ ר' טַבְלָא כו'. וְכִי הֵיכִי דִּמְחִיצָּה תְּלוּיָה מְהַנְיָא — מְחִיצַּת הַקָּנִים נַמִי מְהַנְיָא, דְּמַה לִי מִיעָרְבִי מַיָּא מִתַּתַּאי, מַה לִי מִיעָרְבִי בֵּין קָנֶה לַחֲבֵרוֹ: הַיְינוּ תַּנָּא קַמָּא. ר' יְהוּדָה, דְּאָמַר לְאֵיזֶה רוּחַ שֶׁיִּרְצֶה יֵשׁ לוֹ ד' אַמּוֹת — הַיְינוּ תַּנָּא קַמָּא, רַבָּנַן דִּפְלִיגִי עֲלֵיהּ דְּר' יוֹחָנָן בֶּן נוּרִי: שְׁמוֹנֶה עַל שְׁמוֹנֶה אִיכָּא בֵּינַיְיהוּ. דְּרַבָּנַן סָבְרִי: ד' לְכׇל לְדָדִין, הַיְינוּ שְׁמוֹנֶה עַל שְׁמוֹנֶה. וְר' יְהוּדָה סָבַר: לְחַד רוּחַ וְתוּ לָא, כִּדְקָתָנֵי: וּמוֹדֶה ר' יְהוּדָה לְר' אֱלִיעֶזֶר, שֶׁאִם בֵּירֵר לוֹ שְׁתַּיִם לְכָאן וּשְׁתַּיִם לְכָאן — שֶׁאֵין יָכוֹל לַחֲזוֹר בּוֹ. וְכֵן אִם בֵּירֵר אַרְבַּעְתָּן לְרוּחַ אַחַת: מַחֲלוֹקֶת. דְּר' מֵאִיר, דְּשָׁרֵי שְׁמוֹנֶה עַל שְׁמוֹנֶה לְהִילּוּךְ: לְרַבִּי יְהוּדָה מְצוּמְצָמוֹת, וּלְרַבִּי מֵאִיר גְּדוֹלוֹת, דְּפִישּׁוּט יָדַיִם וְרַגְלַיִם יוֹתֵר מֵאַמָּה הוּא: בְּאַמָּה דִּידֵהּ. אִישׁ לְפִי מַה שֶּׁגּוּפוֹ אָרוֹךְ, יֵשׁ לוֹ ד' אַמּוֹת בְּאַמָּתוֹ הָאֲרוּכָּה: שֶׁל קֹדֶשׁ. לְכׇל אָדָם אַמּוֹת שָׁוֶה, שֶׁל ו' טְפָחִים בֵּינוֹנִים, לְמִדַּת שְׁתֵּי אַמּוֹת *שֶׁהָיוּ בְּשׁוּשַׁן הַבִּירָה שֶׁנַּעֲשׂוּ לְמִדַּת אַמָּתוֹ שֶׁל מֹשֶׁה: גַּבֵּי יֵשׁ שֶׁאָמְרוּ. מִשְׁנָה הִיא(א) בְּמַסֶּ' כֵּלִים (פ' י"ז משנה יא). יֵשׁ שֶׁאָמְרוּ הַכֹּל לְפִי מַה שֶּׁהוּא אָדָם: מְלֹא קוּמְצוֹ מִנְחָה, מְלֹא חׇפְנָיו קְטֹרֶת, מְלֹא לוּגְמָיו בְּיוֹם הַכִּפּוּרִים, וּבִמְזוֹן שְׁתֵּי סְעוּדוֹת לְעֵירוּב. וְלִיתְנֵי נַמִי: ד' אַמּוֹת לַיּוֹצֵא חוּץ לַתְּחוּם: אִי הֲוָה דָּיְיקִינַן כּוּלֵּי הַאי. בְּכוּלֵּי הַתַּלְמוּד, לָא הֲוֵי מָצִינוּ לְתָרוּצֵי כׇּל דִּיּוּקֵי, וְלָא הֲוָה תָּנֵינַן: מִשּׁוּם דְּאִיכָּא נַנָּס בְּאֵיבָרָיו. שֶׁגּוּפוֹ בֵּינוֹנִי וְאַמָּתוֹ קְצָרָה, וְלָא סַגִּי לֵיהּ בְּאַמָּה דִּידֵיהּ, וּבָעֵי לְמֵיהַב לֵיהּ בְּאַמָּה שֶׁל קֹדֶשׁ: הָיוּ שְׁנַיִם כו'. מַתְנִיתִין פָּרֵישְׁנָא לְעֵיל: מַאי שְׁנָא הָתָם דִּפְלִיגִיתוּ. דְּאָמְרוּ רַבָּנַן לְקַמָּן* בִּשְׁמַעְתִּין: שְׁלׇשְׁתָּן אֲסוּרִין לְטַלְטֵל זוֹ עִם זוֹ: אָווֹשִׁי דִּיּוּרִין. דִּיּוּרֵי הַחֲצֵרוֹת רַבִּים, וְלָא יָדְעִי כּוּלָּן לְהִזָּהֵר, וְאָתוּ לְטַלְטוּלֵי כֵּלִים שֶׁשָּׁבְתוּ בַּחִיצוֹנָה לְתוֹךְ חִיצוֹנָה אַחֶרֶת דֶּרֶךְ אֶמְצָעִית: הָכָא. גַּבֵּי ג' אֲנָשִׁים יְכוֹלִין הַחִיצוֹנִים לִיזָּהֵר, דְּהָא מוּעָטִין נִינְהוּ וְלָא אָוְושִׁי: שְׁתַּיִם הַחִיצוֹנוֹת אֲסוּרוֹת זוֹ עִם זוֹ. כֵּלִים שֶׁשָּׁבְתוּ בָּזוֹ אָסוּר לְהַכְנִיס לָזוֹ דֶּרֶךְ אֶמְצָעִית, שֶׁנִּמְצָא שֶׁיָּצְאוּ מֵרְשׁוּתָן לִרְשׁוּת הָאָסוּר לָהֶן: ה"ג: אַמַּאי כֵּיוָן דְּעָרְבִי חִיצוֹנוֹת בַּהֲדֵי אֶמְצָעִית הָווּ לְהוּ חֲדָא. *(וְלִישְׁתְּרוּ כּוּלָּם, דְּדָמֵי כְּמַאן דְּדָיְירֵי הָתָם. דּוּמְיָא דִּבְנֵי חָצֵר שֶׁעֵירְבוּ, וְיָהֲבֵי כּוּלְּהוּ עֵירוּבָן בְּבַיִת אֶחָד דְּדָמוּ כְּאִילּוּ דָּרוּ כּוּלְּהוּ בְּאוֹתוֹ בַּיִת. וְחָצֵר דְּהַהוּא בַּיִת הָוְיָא, וּמִשְׁתְּרֵי בָּהּ. הָכָא נַמִי, דָּמוּ כְּמַאן דְּדָיְירֵי כּוּלְּהוּ בֶּחָצֵר הָאֶמְצָעִית וכו') וְקס"ד: כְּגוֹן שֶׁנָּתְנוּ שְׁתֵּיהֶן עֵירוּבָן בָּאֶמְצָעִית, שֶׁזֶּהוּ מִשְׁפַּט עֵירוּבֵי חֲצֵירוֹת. סְתָם חָצֵר יֵשׁ בָּהּ בָּתִּים הַרְבֵּה, וּצְרִיכוֹת בְּנֵי הַבָּתִּים לְעָרֵב יַחַד, לְפִי שֶׁהַבַּיִת מְיוּחָד לְכׇל אֶחָד וְהֶחָצֵר רְשׁוּת כּוּלָּן, וְאָסוּר לְהוֹצִיא מֵרְשׁוּת לִרְשׁוּת דְּהַיְינוּ מִן הַבָּתִּים לֶחָצֵר, בְּלֹא עֵירוּב. וּכְשֶׁהֶחָצֵר פְּתוּחָה לְחָצֵר אַחֶרֶת, וְרוֹצִין לַעֲשׂוֹתָן רְשׁוּת אַחַת — נוֹטְלִין הָעֵירוּב שֶׁגָּבוּ מִן הַבָּתִּים, וְנוֹתְנִין אוֹתוֹ בְּאֶחָד מִבָּתֵּי חָצֵר אַחֶרֶת: וְכִי הֲדַרָה אֶמְצָעִית וְעֵירְבָה בַּהֲדֵי אִידָךְ שְׁלִיחוּתָהּ דְּחִיצוֹנָה עֲבָדָה. לָא גָּרְסִינַן הָכָא עַד לְקַמָּן: שֶׁנָּתְנָה אֶמְצָעִית עֵירוּבָהּ בָּזוֹ וּבְזוֹ. דְּדַמְיָא אֶמְצָעִית כְּאִילּוּ דָּרָה בָּהֶן, וְאֵין דִּיּוּרֵי חִיצוֹנוֹת בָּאֶמְצָעִית, לְמֵימְרָא דְּכִי הֲדָדֵי נִינְהוּ:

*) [וע"ע תוס' שבת נב. ד"ה אישתכח ותוס' פסחים קט: ד"ה ברוס]

תוספות

רבי יהודה היינו תנא קמא. וא"ת: דילמא ר' אליעזר ור' יהודה לא פליגי אתנא קמא, אלא לפרושי מלתיה קאתו? וכן מצינו פרק "כ"ג" (סנהדרין דף כא.)* גבי "לא ירבה לו נשים", ובריש מתני' בריש "חזקת הבתים" (ב"ב דף כח.). ואומר ר"י: דע"כ ר' אליעזר לא מפרש מילתיה דתנא קמא אלא פליג עליה, דהא ת"ק קאי אר' יוחנן בן נורי, דאמר: יש לו אלפים אמה לכל רוח, ולא הוי באמצעיתו. הכי נמי, ד' אמות לת"ק. וא"ת: א"כ, מאי פריך היינו ת"ק, כיון דתנא קמא ארבי יוחנן בן נורי קאי, ויש לו ד' אמות לכל רוח! וי"ל: דסבר המקשה אע"ג דאלפים דרבי יוחנן(ב) הוי לכל רוח, דהוו ד' אלפים על ד' אלפים – ד' אמות דת"ק הוו ד' אמות בין הכל, דומיא דטלטול ארבע אמות ברשות הרבים דהוי פי' ד' אמות לכל רוח שירצה, כמו שאמר ר' יהודה. לכך פריך היינו ת"ק. ור"ח גרים: חכמים היינו ת"ק. פי': ת"ק דריש פרקין, דמי שהוציאוהו נכרים אין לו אלא ד' אמות. ואע"ג דאינם מענין אחד – מ"מ פריך, דחכמים דפליגי ארבי יוחנן בן נורי לא היה להם להזכיר ד' אמות אלא אין לו אלפים, ומסתמא דיש(ג) לו ד' אמות לכל רוח:

גופו ג' אמות. וא"ת: אמאי בעינן גבי היזק ראייה מחיצה ד' אמות ב"השותפין" (ב"ב דף ב:)? וי"ל: דפעמים שיש גבשושית סמוך לכותל, ופעמים נמי שמגביה עקיבו ועומד על אצבעות רגליו. ועוד: הא דאמר הכא גופו ג' אמות – היינו בלא ראשו. וכן משמע ב"המצניע" (שבת דף צב.), דאמר: המוציא משוי למעלה מיו"ד – חייב, שכן משא בני קהת. דאמר מר: ארון תשעה וכפרת טפח, וגמירי: כל טונא דמידלי במוטה – תילתא מלעיל ותרתי תילתי מלתחת. אישתכח דלמעלה מי' הוה קאי(ד). ובכתף היו נושאים אותו ודל מי"ח טפחים ב' תילתי דארון וכפרת – היינו ששה וב' שלישי טפח, ונשתיירו עד הקרקע י"א טפחים ושליש. אבל אם אדם עם ראשו רק י"ח טפחים – יגיע הארון עד למטה מיו"ד, דראש וצואר מחזיק יותר מטפח ושליש וגבי כוכין בעינן נמי ד' אמות, בפרק "המוכר פירות" (ב"ב דף ק:) – היינו עם ראשו ועובי דפי הארון. ושיעור מקוה דהוי אמה על אמה ברום שלש אמות – לאו משום שלא יהא גובה האדם יותר מג' אמות, אלא משנכנס במים המים עולין, וגם קצת ירכין ראשו. והא דכתיב בתרגום מגילת אסתר: "פרשנדתא איטליב על תלת אמין", וכן כולם – התם קטועי ראש הוו*):

ופתוחות לרה"ר. דאי לאו הכי, אותם שיש להם דריסת הרגל על חבירתה אוסרת עליה: אבל

תורה אור
שמות טז

לעיל מו. שבת קלה: ביצה לט.
[ברכות טו: וש"נ]
שבת קא. לעיל יב. טז: לקמן פו:
[פסחים פו.]
לעיל ל: כלים פי"ז מי"א

עין משפט נר מצוה

[וע"ע תוס' פסחים פג. ד"ה ר"ש עוד שם קטז: ד"ה והתוס' ותוס' מו"ק כד. ד"ה וחכמים ותוס' זבחים פ"ג. ד"ה המזבח]

מד א ב מיי' פי"ב מהל' שבת הלכה טו סמג לאוין סה טוש"ע א"ח סי' שמט סעיף ו וסי' שנו סעיף א:

מה ג ד ה מיי' פ"ד מהלכות עירובין הלכה כג טור ש"ע א"ח סי' שעח סעיף א:

רבינו חננאל

תני ר' חייא. חרם פי' כמו חריץ שבין שני תחומי שבת מלא מים צריך מחיצה של ברזל להתיר המים חציין לתחום זה וחציין לתחום זה. מחיך עלה ר' יוסי בר' חנינא ואמרינן אמאי מחיך אי נימא משום דר' חייא סבר לה כריב"נ דאמר חפצי הפקר קונה שביתה. והני מיא קנו שביתה. ור' יוסי ס"ל לקולא. כל דמתנא להו לחומרא (מתיר) [מחייך] עליה. אלא אמאי מחיך משום הא דתניא בהדיא נהרות המושכין ומעינו' הנובעין הרי הן כרגלי כל אדם. ודלמא מיא דבחרם שבין ב' תחומי שבת מכונסין הוו ומשום הכי תני דקנו שביתה אלא למה הוה מחיך משום דא' צריך מחיצה של ברזל. ואנן קיי"ל שהקילו חכמים על המים דאפילו תלויה מחיצה מתרת: מתני' וחכ"א אין לו אלא ד' אמות ואקשינן היינו ת"ק דתנן מי שהוציאוהו גוים או רוח רעה אין לו אלא ד' אמות. ש"מ דכל השבת שלא לדעת אין לו אלא ד' אמות ופריק רבא ח' על ח' איכא בינייהו והכין הוא (בונבא) [כוונת] דמתני' וחכמים אומרים אין לו אלא ארבע אמות לכל רוח. שהן ח' על ח' ופריש בתלמוד א"י [מי] שבירר לו מבעו"י וקדיש עליו היום. ושמעיניה מן הדא דלא יכנס דברי ר"מ ר' יהודה אמר [יכנס] לא על הדא אתאמרת אלא ארישא דפירקא. מי שהוציאוהו גוים או רוח רעה איתאמרת עליה. א"ר בון מודה ר' יודה שאם בירר לו שאינו יכול לחזור בו תנ"ה יש לו ח' על ח' דברי ר' מאיר כלומר ד' אמות לכל רוח ישנן ח' על ח' אמות. אמר רבה מחלוקת להלך פי' אפילו רבי יוחנן בן נורי לא התיר לו (להלך אלא) [אלא להלך] אלפים אמה. אבל לטלטל דברי הכל ד' אמות אין טפי לא. והני ד' אמות היכא כתיבי כדתניא שבו איש תחתיו. כתחתיו. וכמה תחתיו. גופו ג' אמות ואמה כדי פישוט ידיו ורגליו והני ד' מצומצמו' דברי ר' מאיר ר' יהודה אומר אמה אחת כדי שיהא נוטל חפץ ממראשותיו ויניח מרגלותיו. והני ד' מרווחות ולא מצומצמות ובעו לה הני ד' אמות דיהבי ליה באמה דידיה או באמה של קודש. ואי אמרת באמה דידיה אמאי לא תני לה במס' כלים פרק ט"ז יש שאמרו הכל מה שהוא אדם קומץ מנחה וחופני הקטורת והשותה מלא לוגמיו ביוה"כ כו' ליתני בהדייהו ד' אמות באמה שלו ואי משום דאיכא ננס באבריו. פי' יש אדם ארוך ואמתו קצרה שאינו ד' אמות באמתו כתחתיו ניתני במשנה חוץ מן ננס באבריו שאין נותנין לו באמתו ואסיק' א"ל רב פפא לבריה דרב משרשיא אי אתינא לדקדק כולי האי לא תנינן: מתני' היו שנים מקצת אמותיו של זה בתוך אמותיו של זה מביאין באמצע שלא יוציא כו' עד ושתים החיצונות אסורות זו עם זו. פי' כגון שיש ביניהן ג' אמות וכל אחד מהן יושב בב' אמות שלו ונשאר לו ב' אמות בזה הצד שביניהם וכל אחד ואחד מותר לו לטלטל בב' אמות הקרובות לו נמצא באחת האמצעית שביניהן מותרין לטלטל. ה"ק להו ר' שמעון לרבנן מכדי למה"ד לשלש [חצירות כו'] מ"ש הכא דלא פלגיתו ומ"ש התם בעלמא פלגיתו עלי ורבנן התם בחצרות לא אושי דיורין כלומר יתכן שישכחו בעלי חצרות ויטלטלו החיצונות מזו לזו. הכא אושי דיורין כי אלו ג' האנשים הנה הם יושבים שלשתן ביחד ואם יבואו החיצונים לטלטל זה מזה לזה האמצעי מזכירן כי אסורין לו ונמנעים משום דאושי דיורין. אבל בחצרות חיישינן דלמא מטלטל ולאו אדעתייהו: ושתים החיצונות אסורות זו עם זו. אקשינן עלה אמאי כיון דערביה לה חדא מן החיצונות בהדי אמצעית הויא לה כאלו הכא דרא לשתריא בהדי אמצעית ופריק רב יהודה כגון שנתנה האמצעית עירוב בזו ובזו דלא מכרעא היכא היא דיירה. רב ששת אמר אפי' תימא שנתנו עירובן אחת מהן באמצעית וכגון

הגהות הב"ח

(א) רש"י ד"ה גבי יש שאמרו משנה היא. נ"ב לעיל דף ל ע"ב מייתי לה תלמודא: (ב) תוס' ד"ה רבי יהודה וכו' דאלפים דרבי יוחנן ב"נ הוו לכל רוח דהוו ד' אלפים: (ג) בא"ד ומסתמא דיש להם ד"א ומשני דהכא אמות לכל רוח: (ד) ד"ה גופו וכו' דבכתף היו נושאים:

בִּשְׁנֵי בָתִּים. כְּמַאן — כְּבֵית שַׁמַּאי, דְּתַנְיָא: *חֲמִשָּׁה שֶׁגָּבוּ אֶת עֵירוּבָן וּנְתָנוּהוּ בִּשְׁנֵי כֵלִים, בֵּית שַׁמַּאי אוֹמְרִים: אֵין עֵירוּבָן עֵירוּב, וּבֵית הִלֵּל אוֹמְרִים: עֵירוּבָן עֵירוּב. אֲפִילּוּ תֵּימָא בֵּית הִלֵּל; עַד כָּאן לָא קָאָמְרִי בֵּית הִלֵּל הָתָם — אֶלָּא בִּשְׁנֵי כֵלִים בְּבַיִת אֶחָד, אֲבָל בִּשְׁנֵי בָתִּים — לֹא. א"ל רַב אַחָא בְּרֵיהּ דְּרַב אַוְיָא לְרַב אַשִׁי: לְרַב יְהוּדָה קַשְׁיָא, וּלְרַב שֵׁשֶׁת קַשְׁיָא. לְרַב יְהוּדָה קַשְׁיָא, דְּאָמַר: כְּגוֹן שֶׁנָּתְנָה אֶמְצָעִית עֵירוּבָהּ בָּזוֹ וְעֵירוּבָהּ בָּזוֹ, וְכֵיוָן דְּעֵירְבָה אֶמְצָעִית בַּהֲדֵי חִיצוֹנָה — הָוְיָא לֵיהּ חֲדָא, וְכִי הָדְרָה וְעָרְבָה בַּהֲדֵי אִידָךְ — שְׁלִיחוּתָהּ עָבְדָה! וּלְרַב שֵׁשֶׁת קַשְׁיָא: תֶּיהֱוֵי כַּחֲמִשָּׁה שֶׁשְּׁרוּיִין בְּחָצֵר אַחַת, וְשָׁכַח אֶחָד מֵהֶן וְלֹא עֵירֵב — דְּאָסְרִי אַהֲדָדֵי! א"ל רַב אַשִׁי: לָא לְרַב יְהוּדָה קַשְׁיָא, וְלָא לְרַב שֵׁשֶׁת קַשְׁיָא; לְרַב יְהוּדָה ל"ק: כֵּיוָן דְּעֵירְבָה לָהּ אֶמְצָעִית בַּהֲדֵי חִיצוֹנָה, וּשְׁתַּיִם חִיצוֹנוֹת בַּהֲדֵי הֲדָדֵי לֹא עֵירְבוּ — גָּלְיָא דַּעְתֵּיהּ דִּבְהָא נִיחָא לֵיהּ, וּבְהָא לָא נִיחָא לֵיהּ. וּלְרַב שֵׁשֶׁת לָא קַשְׁיָא: אִם אָמְרוּ דִּיּוֹרִין לְהָקֵל, יֹאמְרוּ דִּיּוֹרִין לְהַחְמִיר?! אָמַר רַב יְהוּדָה, אָמַר רַב: זוֹ דִּבְרֵי ר' שִׁמְעוֹן. אֲבָל חֲכָמִים אוֹמְרִים: רְשׁוּת אַחַת(א) מְשַׁמֶּשֶׁת לִשְׁתֵּי רְשׁוּיוֹת, אֲבָל לֹא שְׁתֵּי רְשׁוּיוֹת מְשַׁמְּשׁוֹת לִרְשׁוּת אַחַת. כִּי אָמְרִיתָהּ קַמֵּיהּ דִּשְׁמוּאֵל, אֲמַר לִי:
אַף

רש"י

בִּשְׁנֵי בָתִּים. דְּהַשְׁתָּא לָא מִיחַבְּרָן חִיצוֹנוֹת בַּהֲדָדֵי: חֲמִשָּׁה שֶׁגָּבוּ עֵירוּבָן. שֶׁהָיוּ דָּרִין בְּחָצֵר אַחַת, וְגָבוּ מִכָּל אֶחָד אֶת עֵירוּבוֹ לְהַתִּיר אֶת חֲצֵירָן לְהוֹצִיא מִבָּתֵּיהֶן לֶחָצֵר: בִּשְׁנֵי כֵלִים. בְּבַיִת אֶחָד: הָכִי גָּרְסִינַן: כֵּיוָן דְּעֵירְבָה אֶמְצָעִית בַּהֲדֵי חִיצוֹנָה הָוְיָא לָהּ חֲדָא וְכִי הֲדַר' עֵירְבָה בַּהֲדֵי אִידָךְ שְׁלִיחוּתָהּ עֲבַדָה. שְׁלִיחוּתָהּ דְּחִיצוֹנָה עֲבַדָה, וְאִישְׁתַּכַּח דְּכוּלְּהוּ כִּי הֲדָדֵי עֵירְבוּ, וְכוּלְּהוּ לִישְׁתַּרְיָן. וְלָא גָּרְסִינַן: "וְאִידָךְ מִיהָא לִישְׁתְּרֵי". וְאִית דְּגָרְסִי לָהּ, וּמְפָרְשִׁי: חִיצוֹנָה שֶׁעֵירְבָה עִמָּהּ מִיהָא תִּישְׁתְּרֵי בַּחִיצוֹנָה הָאַחֶרֶת, וְזוֹ תֵּיאָסֵר בָּהּ. וְאִי אֶפְשָׁר לוֹמַר כֵּן, דְּכֵיוָן דִּשְׁלִיחוּתָהּ עֲבַדָה — הָווּ לְהוּ כּוּלְּהוּ חֲדָא רְשׁוּתָא, וְכוּלְּהוּ שַׁרְיָין: לְרַב שֵׁשֶׁת קַשְׁיָא. כֵּיוָן דְּנָתְנוּ שְׁתֵּיהֶן עֵירוּבָן בָּאֶמְצָעִית — הָעֵירוּב מֵבִיא דִּיּוּרֵיהֶן לְתוֹכָהּ, וְהָווּ לְהוּ כְּאִילּוּ דָּרִין כּוּלָּן בָּאֶמְצָעִית. וְכֵיוָן דְּעֵירוּבָן נָתוּן בִּשְׁנֵי בָתִּים — נִמְצָא שֶׁלֹּא עֵירְבוּ שְׁתַּיִם הַחִיצוֹנוֹת זוֹ עִם זוֹ, וַהֲוֵי כַּחֲמִשָּׁה שֶׁשְּׁרוּיִן בְּחָצֵר אַחַת וְשָׁכַח אֶחָד מֵהֶן וְלֹא עֵירֵב עִם כּוּלָּן יַחַד, דְּכָל הֶחָצֵר אֲסוּרָה. וַאֲפִילּוּ עֵירֵב עִם אֶחָד מֵהֶן, דְּהָא גַּבֵּי חֲמִשָּׁה(ב) דְּחָצֵר אַחַת תַּנְיָא לְעֵיל, לְבֵית הִלֵּל דְּבִשְׁנֵי כֵלִים הוּא דַּהֲוֵי עֵירוּב, אֲבָל בִּשְׁנֵי בָתִּים — לֹא. וְאע"פ שֶׁעֵירְבוּ הַשְּׁנַיִם יַחַד לְעַצְמָן וְהַשְּׁלֹשָׁה לְעַצְמָן. וְהָכָא נַמִי, כֵּיוָן דְּלָא מִצְטָרְפִי, דְּקָתָנֵי שְׁתַּיִם הַחִיצוֹנוֹת אֲסוּרוֹת זוֹ עִם זוֹ — אֶמְצָעִית גּוּפָהּ תִּיתְסַר בְּדִידָהּ, שֶׁכּוּלָּן אוֹסְרִין עָלֶיהָ: אִם אָמְרוּ דִּיּוּרִין. שֶׁל זוֹ בָּזוֹ ע"י הָעֵירוּב לְהָקֵל לְהַתִּירָן יַחַד, יֹאמְרוּ שֶׁהָעֵירוּב מֵבִיא הַדִּיּוּרִין לְתוֹכָהּ כְּדֵי לֶאֱסוֹר עָלֶיהָ? הָא לָא דָּיְירִי מַמָּשׁ בְּגַוָּהּ, דְּלִיבָּעֵי עֵירוּבָן בְּבַיִת אֶחָד. הִלְכָּךְ, אע"ג דְּחִיצוֹנִים לֹא עֵירְבוּ אַהֲדָדֵי — חִיצוֹן וְאֶמְצָעִי מִיהָא מִצְטָרְפִי וְלָא אָסְרִי אַהֲדָדֵי: זוֹ דִּבְרֵי רַבִּי שִׁמְעוֹן. דְּהִיא מוּתֶּרֶת עִמָּהֶן וְהֵן עִמָּהּ: אֲבָל חֲכָמִים אוֹמְרִים. דְּלָא שְׁנָא נָתְנוּ שְׁתֵּיהֶן עֵירוּבָן בָּאֶמְצָעִית, לָא שְׁנָא נָתְנָה אֶמְצָעִית עֵירוּבָן בָּזוֹ וּבָזוֹ — הִיא אֲסוּרָה עִמָּהֶן, וְהֵן מוּתָּרִין עִמָּהּ: רְשׁוּת אַחַת מְשַׁמֶּשֶׁת לִשְׁתֵּי רְשׁוּיוֹת. כֵּלִים שֶׁשָּׁבְתוּ בַּחִיצוֹנוֹת מוּתָּרוֹת בָּאֶמְצָעִית, דְּהָא הַחִיצוֹנוֹת לֹא עֵירְבוּ אֶלָּא עִם זוֹ, וְאֵין רְשׁוּת אַחֶרֶת מוֹשַׁכְתָּן לְצַד אַחֵר: וְאֵין ב' רְשׁוּיוֹת מְשַׁמְּשׁוֹת לִרְשׁוּת אַחַת. דְּכֵיוָן דִּשְׁתֵּי חִיצוֹנוֹת לֹא עֵירְבוּ יַחַד לַעֲשׂוֹת רְשׁוּת אַחַת, אֶלָּא רְשׁוּיוֹת חֲלוּקוֹת הֵן, וְאֵין כֹּחַ בָּאֶמְצָעִית לְהִשְׁתַּמֵּשׁ לֹא בָּזוֹ וְלֹא בָּזוֹ דְּזוֹ מוֹשַׁכְתָּהּ לְכָאן, וְזוֹ מוֹשַׁכְתָּהּ לְכָאן וּשְׁנֵי דִּיּוּרִין לָא יָהֲבִינַן לָהּ, וְדָמְיָא כְּאִילּוּ הִיא מֵהַךְ חָצֵר הַחִיצוֹנָה שֶׁלֹּא עֵירְבָה בַּהֲדֵי אִידָךְ חִיצוֹנָה, וְאוֹסַרְתָּהּ. וְכֵן נַמִי כִּי אָזְלָא לְאִידָךְ חָצֵר דְּעֵירְבָה נַמִי בַּהֲדָהּ — אוֹסַרְתָּהּ אִידָךְ חִיצוֹנָה. אֲבָל הֵיכָא דְּעֵירְבוּ שְׁלָשְׁתָּן — הָווּ כּוּלְּהוּ חֲדָא רְשׁוּתָא:
אַף

תוספות

אבל בשני בתים לא. והא דלא מוקי לה רב יהודה כרב ששת – לאו דקסבר דאפילו בשני בתים הוי עירוב לב"ה, דהא אפילו כלים קאמר רב יהודה לקמן* דחולק עירובו אינו עירוב. דעד כאן לא קאמרי ב"ה אלא דמלי' למנא ואייתר. והא דלא מוקי כרב ששת – משום דפריך בסמוך לרב ששת דניהוי כחמשה ששרויין בחצר אחת – וקסבר דאמר דיורין להחמיר:

לרב יהודה דאמר כגון שנתנה אמצעית עירובה בזו וכו'. לרב ששת לא שייך למיפרך הכי, דכיון שנתנו עירובן באמצעית ולא נתנו עירובן יחד אלא בשני בתים – גלי אדעתייהו דלא ניחא להו לחיצונות להשתתף ביחד. אבל כשנתנה אמצעית עירובה בזו ובזו – ליכא גלוי דעתייהו התם כולי האי. אי נמי: לרב יהודה, כיון שנתנה עירובה בזו ובזו – נעשה כאלו דרה בחיצונות בבתיהם, ונעשית לכל אחת ואחת להיות שלוחה. ולרב ששת – אין האמצעית נעשית שליח, דאדרבה כולן דיירין בה:

יאמרו דיורין להחמיר. והא דאמר בפרק "הדר" (לקמן דף סו:): נתנו עירובן בפנימית ושכח אחד מן הפנימית ולא עירב – שתיהן אסורות, משום דלא מצי מבטל לפנימית, דאיכא חיצונה דאסרי עלייהו – שאני התם דפשעה:

רשות אחת משתמשת לשתי רשויו' ואין שתי רשויות משתמשות לרשות אחת. כן גרס הקונטרס. ומפרש הקונט': שהחיצונות משתמשות באמצעית, ופי' "משתמשות" – כמו משמשת. אבל אמצעית אסורה בשתיהן, דזו מושכתה לכאן וזו מושכתה לכאן, וב' דירות לא יהבינן לה, כיון דחיצונות לא עירבו יחד – רשויות חלוקות הן. והא דקאמר שמואל אף זו דברי ר"ש – פי': דר"ש דווקא בענין זה התיר. והא דקאמר ואזדא שמואל לטעמיה – משום דסבירא ליה "הלכה כדברי המיקל בעירוב". ואי סבירא ליה כרב, דאמר אמצעית נמי שרי לר"ש בשתיהן – לא היה אומר עירבה עם שתיהן אסורה עם שתיהן. וקשה: דלפי' היה לו ליגרוס "משמשות", שב' רשויות משתמשות בה! ועוד קשה: דקאמרינן לעיל [ע"א] דה"ק להו ר"ש לרבנן מ"ש גבי חצירות דפליגיתו כו'. ולרב מה ענין זה לזה? והא רבנן לא גזרו כלל, דהא שרו חיצונות באמצעית. ומאי קמשני נמי התם אוושא דיורין. ועוד: דלא שמעינן ליה לשמואל בשום מקום דקאמר "הלכה כדברי המיקל בעירוב" אלא ריב"ל הוא דקאמר הכי לעיל. ואדרבה שמואל הוא דאית ליה בפרק "חלון" (לקמן דף פא:): כל מקום שאמר רבי יהודה בעירוב – הלכה כמותו. ובר פלוגתא דר"ש דהכא – היינו ר' יהודה כדאמר לעיל. ומיהו, בהא י"ל: כיון דלא נזכר כאן ר' יהודה בפי' – ליתא (ג)בההיא כללא דפסיק שמואל לקמן*. אלא היכא שנזכר בהדיא. ועוד: לשון "אף" לא אתי שפיר. כמו שהקשה בעצמו, דהוי עדיף טפי אי לא הוה תני "אף". דבהאי לישנא איכא למטעי, דמשמע דתרוייהו שרי. ועוד: לפי' נחלקו רב ושמואל בפירוש לשון המשנה "שהיא מותרת עמהן והן מותרות עמה". לכן נראה לר"ת: דרשות אחת משתמשת לב' רשויות, דאמצעית משתמשת בחיצונה – דליכא למיגזר (בחיצונה) כולי האי שתוציא האמצעית כלי החיצונה מזו לזו. אבל החיצונות אסורות עם האמצעית – דילמא אתי להחליף כלים ששבתו בחיצונה זו לחיצונה זו. אבל אין לפרש טעמא דרבנן דחיצונות אסורות באמצעית משום דחיצונות אוסרות זו על זו כיון דלא עירבו יחד, או משום הכי אסורות החיצונות באמצעית משום דאין דיורי חיצונות באמצעית, אבל אמצעית תשמש בחיצונות דעירובה מרגלתה בשתיהן. ורב יהודה לטעמיה, דמוקי לעיל כגון שנתנה אמצעית עירובה בזו ובזו. דא"כ לא הוי אתי שפיר הא דאמר ר"ש לרבנן: מ"ש התם דפליגתו. אלא ודאי טעמא משום דגזרינן. וקאמר שמואל: דאף זו דברי ר' שמעון, דשרי חיצונות ואמצעית זו בזו. אבל לרבנן שלשתן אסורות. והשתא הוי שמואל לטעמיה, דאמר: עירבה עם שתיהן – אסורה עם שתיהן כרבנן דאמרי שלשתן אסורות, דהיינו ר' יהודה. ושמואל פסיק כר' יהודה בעירוב. אבל לרב אינה אסורה עם שתיהן, דאפילו לרבנן שרי לאמצעית להשתמש עמהן. וקשה למהר"י: ד"אסורה עם שתיהן" משמע אבל הם מותרין עמה, מדלא קתני "אוסרת על שתיהן" כמו בסיפא, אע"ג דאיכא למימר דאשמעינן דאסורה עם שתיהן אע"ג דליכא למיגזר כולי האי, וכ"ש דהם אסורות עמה דאיכא למיגזר טפי. ומ"מ, כיון דלא מתסרי להשתמש יחד אלא משום גזירה – אינה אוסרת על שתיהן. מכל מקום כיון דלא קאמר "עירבה עם שתיהן אינה אוסרת על שתיהן" דהוה משמע וכולן אסורות זו עם זו, אלא נקט "אסורה עם שתיהן" משמע ודאי דאבל הם מותרין עמה. ועוד קשה: דבפרק "כל גגות" (לקמן דף צא.) אמר* שמואל, הלכה כר' שמעון דאמר: גגות חצירות וקרפיפות רשות אחד הן לכלים ששבתו בתוכן בין עירבו בין לא עירבו. משום דרבי שמעון לטעמיה דהכא לא גזר. ונראה לפרש: דהא דקאמר שמואל דלרבנן שלשתן אסורות – הוי מתרי טעמי. חיצונות באמצעית – משום גזירה שמא יוליכו כלי חיצונה זו לחיצונה אחרת, ואמצעית בחיצונות ליכא למיגזר שמא תוליך האמצעית כלי חיצונה זו לאחרת, דסתמא דמילתא כי משתמש איניש – במאי דידיה קמשתמש ולא במאי דחבריה, כדמפרש לקמן (דף עד.) גבי שתי חצירות וחורבה אחת ביניהן. ואי משום יוליכו [בני] החיצונות כליהן באמצעית – הא ליכא למגזר, דהוי גזירה לגזירה, אלא טעמא דאסורה האמצעית בחיצונות – שזו מושכתה לכאן וזו לכאן. ור"ש פליג אתרוייהו. והשתא הוי שמואל לטעמיה דפסיק לקמן כר' יהודה בעירוב, ולכך קאמר אסורה עם שתיהן – כרבנן, דהיינו ר' יהודה. וטעמא משום דזו מושכת' לכאן וזו לכאן. כדפרישית. אבל הם מותרות עמה – דבהא סבר כר"ש, דלא גזר. וכדפסק בפרק "כל גגות" דהלכה כר"ש, דבין עירבו ובין לא עירבו לא גזר:
זו

רבינו חננאל

וכגון שנתנו בו בב' בתים כדתניא ה' שגבו עירובן כו' עד כאן לא אמרי ב"ה דהוי עירוב אלא בב' כלים בבית אחת דבית אחת מצרפן אבל בב' בתים דברי הכל עירוב ואמרי' לר' יהודה קשיא דדחי שנתנה האמצעית בעירוב בזו ובזו. אמאי כיון שעירבה האמצעית בהדי חדא מן החיצונות הויא להו תרווייהו חדא רשותא כי הדרא מערבא בהדי אידך שליחותא קא עבדא. ולרב ששת נמי קשיא כיון שחלקה ונתנוהו בב' בתים מכל מקום הויין להו כב' בתים. ניהוי כה' ששרויין בחצר אחת ושכח אחת מהן ולא עירב דאסרי אהדדי ופרקינן לרב יהודה לא קשיא כגון במערבא (באמצעית) [אמצעית] בהדי חיצונה ולא אזלא הא חיצונה בהדיה גלאי דעתא בהדי אמצעית לחודא היא דניחא לה לעירובי אבל בהדי אידך חיצונה לא לפיכך לא אמרינן שליחותא קא עבדא. לרב ששת נמי לא קשיא אם באו הללו ג' אמות של זה בתוך ג' של זה מותרין החיצוני' והקילו עליהם משום דאוושא דיורין כמו שאמרנו נחמיר עליהן כמו ה' ששרויין בחצר אחת ושכח אחד מהן ולא עירב כולם אסורים שיהו גם אלו אסורין אם חשבנום כחצר אחת להקל נחשבת כחצר אחת להחמיר. אמר רב יהודה אמר רב דברי ר' שמעון כי שתים החיצונות אסורות אבל חכ"א רשות אחת משתמש עם ב' רשויות אין ב' רשויות משתמשות עם רשות אחת ושמואל אמר לדברי חכמים שלשתן

הגהות הב"ח

(א) גמ' רשות אחת משתמשת לשתי וכו' ב' רשויות משתמשות לרשות: (ב) רש"י ד"ה לרב ששת וכו' חמשה בחצר: (ג) תוס' ד"ה רשות וכו' בפי' ליתא להאי כללא:

[לקמן מט: ע"ש]
[מט. ע"ש]
נ"ל רב

אַף זוֹ דִּבְרֵי ר' שִׁמְעוֹן, אֲבָל חֲכָמִים אוֹמְרִים: שְׁלָשְׁתָּן אֲסוּרוֹת. תַּנְיָא כְּוָותֵיהּ דְּרַב יְהוּדָה אַלִּיבָּא דִּשְׁמוּאֵל, א"ר שִׁמְעוֹן: לְמָה הַדָּבָר דּוֹמֶה — לְשָׁלֹשׁ חֲצֵירוֹת הַפְּתוּחוֹת זוֹ לָזוֹ וּפְתוּחוֹת לרה"ר, עֵירְבוּ שְׁתַּיִם עִם הָאֶמְצָעִית — זוֹ מְבִיאָה מִתּוֹךְ בֵּיתָהּ וְאוֹכֶלֶת, וְזוֹ מְבִיאָה מִתּוֹךְ בֵּיתָהּ וְאוֹכֶלֶת, זוֹ מַחֲזֶרֶת מוּתֶּרֶת לְתוֹךְ בֵּיתָהּ, וְזוֹ מַחֲזֶרֶת מוּתֶּרֶת לְתוֹךְ בֵּיתָהּ. אֲבָל חֲכָמִים אוֹמְרִים: שְׁלָשְׁתָּן אֲסוּרוֹת. וְאָזְדָא שְׁמוּאֵל לְטַעְמֵיהּ, דְּאָמַר שְׁמוּאֵל: חָצֵר שֶׁבֵּין שְׁנֵי מְבוֹאוֹת, עֵירְבָה עִם שְׁנֵיהֶם — אֲסוּרָה עִם שְׁנֵיהֶם, [א]לֹא עֵירְבָה עִם שְׁנֵיהֶם — אוֹסֶרֶת עַל שְׁנֵיהֶן. הָיְתָה בְּאֶחָד רְגִילָה וּבְאֶחָד אֵינָהּ רְגִילָה, זֶה שֶׁרְגִילָה בּוֹ — אָסוּר, וְזֶה שֶׁאֵינָהּ רְגִילָה בּוֹ — מוּתָּר. אָמַר רַבָּה בַּר רַב הוּנָא: [ב]עֵירְבָה עִם שֶׁאֵינָהּ רְגִילָה בּוֹ — הוּתַּר רְגִילָה לְעַצְמוֹ. וְאָמַר רַבָּה בַּר רַב הוּנָא, אָמַר שְׁמוּאֵל: [ג]אִם עֵירְבָה רְגִילָה לְעַצְמוֹ, וְזֶה שֶׁאֵינָהּ רְגִילָה בּוֹ לֹא עֵירֵב, וְהִיא עַצְמָהּ לֹא עֵירְבָה — דּוֹחִין אוֹתָהּ אֵצֶל שֶׁאֵינָהּ רְגִילָה בּוֹ, וּכְגוֹן זֶה *כּוֹפִין עַל מִדַּת סְדוֹם. אָמַר רַב יְהוּדָה, אָמַר שְׁמוּאֵל: [ד]הַמַּקְפִּיד עַל עֵירוּבוֹ — *אֵין עֵירוּבוֹ עֵירוּב. מַה שְּׁמוֹ — עֵירוּב שְׁמוֹ. ר' חֲנִינָא אָמַר: עֵירוּבוֹ עֵירוּב, אֶלָּא שֶׁנִּקְרָא מֵאַנְשֵׁי וַרְדִּינָא. אָמַר רַב יְהוּדָה, אָמַר שְׁמוּאֵל: [ה]הַחוֹלֵק אֶת עֵירוּבוֹ — אֵינוֹ עֵירוּב. כְּמַאן — כְּבֵית שַׁמַּאי. דְּתַנְיָא: *חֲמִשָּׁה שֶׁגָּבוּ אֶת עֵירוּבָן וּנְתָנוּהוּ בִּשְׁנֵי כֵלִים, ב"ש אוֹמְרִים: אֵין זֶה עֵירוּב, וּב"ה אוֹמְרִים: הֲרֵי זֶה עֵירוּב! אֲפִילּוּ תֵּימָא ב"ה: [ו]עַד כָּאן לָא קָאָמְרִי ב"ה הָתָם אֶלָּא דְּמַלְיָין לְמָנָא וְאַיְיתַר, אֲבָל הֵיכָא דִּפְלַגֵיהּ מִיפְלַג — לָא. וְתַרְתֵּי לָמָּה לִי?! צְרִיכִי, דְּאִי אַשְׁמְעִינַן הָתָם — מִשּׁוּם דְּקָפֵיד, אֲבָל הָכָא — אֵימָא לָא. וְאִי אַשְׁמְעִינַן הָכָא — מִשּׁוּם דִּפְלַגֵיהּ מִיפְלַג, אֲבָל הָתָם — אֵימָא לָא, צְרִיכָא. אֲמַר לֵיהּ ר' אַבָּא לְרַב יְהוּדָה בְּבֵי מַעֲצַרְתָּא דְּבֵי רַב זַכַּאי: מִי אָמַר שְׁמוּאֵל "הַחוֹלֵק אֶת עֵירוּבוֹ אֵינוֹ עֵירוּב", וְהָאָמַר שְׁמוּאֵל: [ז]בַּיִת שֶׁמַּנִּיחִין בּוֹ עֵירוּב — אֵינוֹ צָרִיךְ לִיתֵּן אֶת הַפַּת. מ"ט — לָאו מִשּׁוּם דְּאָמַר: דְּכֵיוָן דְּמַנַּח בְּסַלָּא — כְּמַאן דְּמַנַּח הָכָא דָּמֵי, ה"נ: כֵּיוָן דְּמַנַּח בְּסַלָּא כְּמַאן דְּמַנַּח הָכָא דָּמֵי! א"ל: הָתָם — אע"פ שֶׁאֵין פַּת, מ"ט — דְּכוּלְּהוּ הָכָא דָּיְירִי. אָמַר שְׁמוּאֵל: עֵירוּב מִשּׁוּם קִנְיָן. וְא"ת: מִפְּנֵי מָה אֵין קוֹנִין בְּמָעָה — מִפְּנֵי שֶׁאֵינָהּ מְצוּיָה בְּעַרְבֵי שַׁבָּתוֹת. הֵיכָא דְּעֵירֵב מִיהוּ לִקְנֵי! גְּזֵירָה שֶׁמָּא יֹאמְרוּ מָעָה עִיקָּר, וְזִמְנִין דְּלָא שְׁכִיחַ מָעָה, וְלָא אָתֵי לְאִיעָרוֹבֵי בְּפַת, דְּאָתֵי עֵירוּב לְאִיקַּלְקוּלֵי. רַבָּה אָמַר: [ח]עֵירוּב מִשּׁוּם דִּירָה. מַאי בֵּינַיְיהוּ? אִיכָּא בֵּינַיְיהוּ כְּלִי, וּפָחוֹת מִשָּׁוֶה פְּרוּטָה, וְקָטָן

רש"י

אַף זוֹ דִּבְרֵי ר' שִׁמְעוֹן. אֲפִילּוּ לְהִשְׁתַּמֵּשׁ שְׁתֵּיהֶן עִמָּהּ, ר' שִׁמְעוֹן הוּא דְּשָׁרֵי, דְּהָא אֲפִילּוּ אֶמְצָעִית בִּשְׁתֵּיהֶן נַמִי שָׁרֵי, אֲבָל לְרַבָּנַן — פְּלִיגֵי בְּכוּלָּהּ, וְאָמְרוּ שְׁלָשְׁתָּן אֲסוּרִין זוֹ עִם זוֹ. ל"א: אַף זוֹ דִּבְרֵי ר"ש — ר' שִׁמְעוֹן גּוּפֵיהּ לָא שָׁרֵי אֶלָּא חִיצוֹנוֹת בָּאֶמְצָעִית. וְקַשְׁיָא לִי: הָא תְּנַן בְּמַתְנִיתִין "הִיא מוּתֶּרֶת עִמָּהֶן"! וְעוֹד: מַאי "אַף"? הָכִי אִיבָּעֵי לֵיהּ לְמֵימַר: "זוֹ דִּבְרֵי ר"ש", "אַף" מַשְׁמַע דְּבַתְרַוְייהוּ שָׁרֵי. וְלָשׁוֹן אַחֲרוֹן זֶה שָׁמַעְתִּי. וְכֵן עִיקָּר. וְהִיא מוּתֶּרֶת עִמָּהֶן — דְּמַתְנִיתִין מְתָרֵץ לָךְ שְׁמוּאֵל דְּבְהֶיתֵּר שִׁימּוּשׁ שֶׁבָּאֶמְצָעִית קָאָמַר, דּוּמְיָא דְּהוּא מוּתָּר עִמָּהֶן דְּרֵישָׁא. וְאַיְּידֵי דִּתְנָא רֵישָׁא הוּא מוּתָּר עִמָּהֶן — תָּנֵי נַמִי סֵיפָא. וְ"אַף זוֹ" הָכִי מַשְׁמַע: אַף ר' שִׁמְעוֹן הַמֵּיקֵל אוֹסֵר בָּזוֹ, דְּאֵין אֶמְצָעִית מוּתֶּרֶת בַּחִיצוֹנוֹת. אַף אִיסּוּר זֶה ר"ש נַמִי אֲמָרוֹ כְּרַבָּנַן. וְאַלִּישָּׁנָא קַמָּא קַשְׁיָא מַאי "וְאָזְדָא שְׁמוּאֵל לְטַעְמֵיהּ"? אִי נַמִי הֲוָה אָמַר כְּרַב הֲוָה מָצֵי נַמִי לְמֵימַר: לְרַבָּנַן, עֵירְבָה עִם שְׁתֵּיהֶן — אֲסוּרָה עִם שְׁתֵּיהֶן, דְּאֵין ב' רְשׁוּיוֹת מִשְׁתַּמְּשׁוֹת לִרְשׁוּת אַחַת: תַּנְיָא כְּוָותֵיהּ דִּשְׁמוּאֵל. דַּאֲפִילּוּ ר"ש לָא הִתִּיר אֶמְצָעִית בַּחִיצוֹנוֹת, כִּדְקָתָנֵי "זוֹ מְבִיאָה מִתּוֹךְ בֵּיתָהּ כו'", וְאִילּוּ אֶמְצָעִית בַּחִיצוֹנוֹת לָא קָאָמַר: וְאָזְדָא שְׁמוּאֵל לְטַעְמֵיהּ. דְּאָמַר: אַף לְר"ש אֵין שְׁתֵּי רְשׁוּיוֹת מִשְׁתַּמְּשׁוֹת לִרְשׁוּת אַחַת: לְמָה הַדָּבָר דּוֹמֶה. אַשְּׁלֹשָׁה שֶׁשָּׁבְתוּ בַּדֶּרֶךְ קָאֵי: זוֹ מְבִיאָה. בָּאֶמְצָעִית וְאוֹכֶלֶת וְזוֹ מְבִיאָה בָּאֶמְצָעִית וְאוֹכֶלֶת: חָצֵר שֶׁבֵּין שְׁנֵי מְבוֹאוֹת. פְּתוּחָה לִשְׁנֵיהֶן: ה"ג: עֵירְבָה עִם שְׁנֵיהֶן אֲסוּרָה עִם שְׁנֵיהֶן. אֲפִילּוּ לְרַבִּי שִׁמְעוֹן, וְהַיְינוּ שְׁמוּאֵל לְטַעְמֵיהּ, דְּאָמַר שְׁמוּאֵל: הֲלָכָה כְּדִבְרֵי הַמֵּיקֵל בְּעֵירוּב. וְאִי הֲוָה שָׁרֵי ר"ש בְּהָא — לָא הֲוָה אָמַר שְׁמוּאֵל אֲסוּרָה עִם שְׁנֵיהֶן: לֹא עֵירְבָה עִם שְׁנֵיהֶן. לֹא עֵירְבָה לֹא עִם זוֹ וְלֹא עִם זוֹ: אוֹסֶרֶת עַל שְׁנֵיהֶן. מִלְּהוֹצִיא מֵחַלְּרוֹתֵיהֶן לַמָּבוֹי. וּכְגוֹן שֶׁרְגִילָה כָּל יְמוֹת הַחוֹל לָצֵאת וְלָבֹא בִּשְׁנֵיהֶן דֶּרֶךְ פְּתָחִים, דְּרִיסַת הָרֶגֶל שֶׁיֵּשׁ לָהּ אוֹסַרְתָּן, כִּדְמְפָרֵשׁ. דְּאִי לָא הָוְיָא רְגִילָה אֶלָּא בְּחַד, לָא אָסְרָה אַחִידָךְ. וְאַע"ג דִּרְגִילָה עִם שְׁנֵיהֶן — זוֹ הִיא תַּקָּנָתָהּ, מְעָרֶבֶת עִם הָאֶחָד וְגַלְּיָא דַּעְתָּהּ שֶׁנִּסְתַּלְּקָה מִן הָאַחֵר, וּמוּתָּר הָאֶחָד לְעַצְמוֹ: הָיְתָה בְּאֶחָד רְגִילָה. לָצֵאת וְלָבֹא כָּל שָׁעָה, וּבְאֶחָד אֵינָהּ רְגִילָה וְלֹא עֵירְבָה לֹא עִם זוֹ וְלֹא עִם זוֹ, זֶה שֶׁרְגִילָה בּוֹ — אָסוּר שֶׁחָצֵר זוֹ אוֹסֶרֶת עָלָיו, דְּמֵינֵיהּ הוּא וַהֲרֵי לֹא עֵירְבָה. וְהָאַחֵר מוּתָּר — שֶׁאֵינָהּ הֵימֶנּוּ: הוּתַּר רְגִילָה לְעַצְמוֹ. דְּהָא סַלְּקָא נַפְשָׁהּ מִינֵּיהּ: וְזֶה שֶׁאֵינָהּ רְגִילָה בּוֹ לֹא עֵירֵב. אֲפִילּוּ בִּפְנֵי עַצְמוֹ: וְהִיא נַמִי לֹא עֵירְבָה. לֹא עִם זֶה וְלֹא עִם זֶה: דּוֹחִין אוֹתָהּ אֵצֶל שֶׁאֵינָהּ רְגִילָה. שֶׁלֹּא לֶאֱסוֹר עַל זֶה שֶׁעֵירֵב, הוֹאִיל וְהַאי לָא מַפְסְדָא מִידֵי דְּהָא לֹא עֵירֵב: מִדַּת סְדוֹם. דַּאֲפִילּוּ מִידֵי דְּלָא חָסֵר בֵּיהּ לָא מְהַנֵּי לַחֲבֵרֵיהּ וְהָכָא עַל כָּרְחֵיהּ דְּמַיְין לֵיהּ גַּבֵּיהּ: מִדַּת סְדוֹם. שֶׁלִּי שֶׁלִּי: הַמַּקְפִּיד עַל עֵירוּבוֹ. אִם יֹאכַל אֶחָד מִבְּנֵי חֲבוּרָה אֶת הַפַּת שֶׁנָּתַן הוּא: עֵירוּב שְׁמוֹ. שֶׁיְּהוּ כּוּלָּן מְעוֹרָבִין וּמְרוּצִּין בּוֹ, שֶׁלֹּא יִמְחֶה זֶה בַּחֲבֵירוֹ, אֶלָּא שׁוּתָּפוּת נוֹחָה וַעֲרֵיבָה: אַנְשֵׁי וַרְדִּינָא. צִיקָנִין הָיוּ: הַחוֹלֵק. בִּשְׁנֵי כֵּלִים, אֵינוֹ עֵירוּב מִשּׁוּם הַאי טַעְמָא גּוּפֵיהּ, דְּמָה שְּׁמוֹ — עֵירוּב שְׁמוֹ: דְּמַלְיָא לְמָנָא וְאַיְיתַר. שֶׁלֹּא יָכוֹל הַכְּלִי לְהַחֲזִיק כָּל הָעֵירוּב, וְלֹא חִילְּקוּ מִדַּעַת. וְכִי קָאָמַר שְׁמוּאֵל — כְּגוֹן שֶׁחִילְּקוּ מִדַּעַת: וְתַרְתֵּי לָמָּה לִי. לִשְׁמוּאֵל, הוֹאִיל וְתַרְוַיְיהוּ חַד טַעְמָא דְּקָפֵיד וְחוֹלֵק: דְּמִיפְלַג פַּלְגֵיהּ. וּבָטֵל שְׁמֵיהּ, דְּעֵירוּב מַשְׁמַע מְעוֹרָב: שֶׁמַּנִּיחִין בּוֹ עֵירוּב. אַרְבָּעָה שֶׁגָּבוּ עֵירוּבָן וּנְתָנוּהוּ בְּבַיִת חֲמִישִׁי, אֵין צָרִיךְ לְהַנִּיחַ שָׁם פִּיתּוֹ: לָאו מִשּׁוּם דְּכֵיוָן דְּמַנַּח לֵיהּ. לְבַעַל הַבַּיִת רִיפְתָּא בְּסַלָּא דִּידֵיהּ שֶׁהוּא אוֹכֵל מִמֶּנּוּ, כְּמַאן דְּמַנַּח בַּכְּלִי עִם הָעֵירוּב דָּמֵי: דְּכוּלְּהוּ הָכָא דָּיְירִי. מִשּׁוּם פִּיתָּן הָוְיָא לְהוּ דִּירָתָן, וכ"ש בַּעַל הַבַּיִת שֶׁהוּא דָּר שָׁם מַמָּשׁ בְּתוֹכוֹ. וַאֲפִילּוּ אֵין לוֹ פַּת בְּכָל הַבַּיִת — שַׁפִּיר דָּמֵי: עֵירוּב. שֶׁהוּא מְצָרְפָן טַעְמָא מִשּׁוּם קִנְיָן, שֶׁמַּקְנֶה לְהוּ בַּעַל הַבַּיִת רְשׁוּתוֹ, וְנִמְצְאוּ כּוּלָּם בְּעָלִים בְּבַיִת זֶה שֶׁהָעֵירוּב מוּנָּח בּוֹ, וְכָל חָצֵר מְשׁוּעְבֶּדֶת לִרְשׁוּתָם זוֹ, וְאַחַת הִיא: וּמִפְּנֵי מָה אֵין מְעָרְבִין בְּמָעָה. לִיתֵּן כָּל אֶחָד וְאֶחָד מָעָה וּמְעוֹתָיו יִקְנוּ לוֹ רְשׁוּת חֲבֵירוֹ: לְאִיקַּלְקוּלֵי. לְהִשְׁתַּכַּח תּוֹרַת עֵירוּב: מִשּׁוּם דִּירָה. שֶׁדַּעְתּוֹ שֶׁל אָדָם עַל פִּיתּוֹ, וְהָוּוּ לְהוּ כְּאִילּוּ דָּיְירֵי בְּהַהוּא בֵּיתָא. וְאֵין בֶּחָצֵר זוֹ אֶלָּא דִּירָה אַחַת, וַהֲרֵי כָּל רְשׁוּת הֶחָצֵר מְיוּחֶדֶת לְבַיִת זֶה: הָכִי גָּרְסִינַן: אִיכָּא בֵּינַיְיהוּ כְּלִי וְשֶׁאֵין בּוֹ שָׁוֶה פְּרוּטָה וְקָטָן. לְמַאן דְּאָמַר מִשּׁוּם קִנְיָן — יְכוֹלִין לִקְנוֹת בְּסוּדָר כְּדֶרֶךְ שְׁאָר קִנְיָן, וְאֵין יְכוֹלִין לִקְנוֹת בְּפַת שֶׁאֵין בּוֹ שָׁוֶה פְּרוּטָה, וַאֲפִילּוּ הָוְיָא מְזוֹן ב' סְעוּדוֹת. וְאֵין יָכוֹל לַעֲשׂוֹת הַקָּטָן שָׁלִיחַ לְעָרֵב עָלָיו עֵירוּבֵי חֲצֵירוֹת — דְּלָאו בַּר מַקְנֶה וְאַקְנוּיֵי הוּא. וּלְמ"ד מִשּׁוּם דִּירָה — לָא מְהַנֵּי קִנְיַן סוּדָר, וּמְעָרְבִין בְּאוֹכֶל שֶׁאֵין בּוֹ שָׁוֶה פְּרוּטָה, וְקָטָן גּוֹבֶה אֶת הָעֵירוּב — דְּפַת מְשַׁוְּיָא לְהוּ חֲדָא דִּירָה, וְקָטָן לָאו מִידֵי עָבֵיד: לְמָקוֹם

תוספות

זו מביאה מתוך ביתה ואוכלת. לפ"ה דווקא נקט, אבל אמצעית בחיצונות – לא. ולר"ת איכא למימר דלרבותא נקט, דכ"ש אמצעית בחיצונות דליכא למגזר כולי האי. ולפי' מהר"י נקט הא – משום דמהא פריך לרבנן מאי שנא התם דפליגיתו וגזריתו, והכא לא גזריתו. מכדי למה הדבר דומה כו':

עירוב משום קנין. פירוש: דבהאי פת מיקני רשות להדדי אע"ג דפירי לא עבדי חליפין, מ"מ קנו בתורת דמים. וא"ת: והתנן לקמן ב"הדר" (דף עא.) בעל הבית שהיה שותף לשכיניו, לזה ביין ולזה בשמן – אין צריך לערב. ואמר ב"הדר" (דף עג:) נמי: בני חבורה שהיו מסובין וקדש עליהם היום, סומכין על הפת שעל השולחן משום עירוב. ולמ"ד משום דירה – אתי שפיר! וי"ל: דכיון שיש קירוב דעת ביניהן – עשאוה חכמים כאילו הקנו זה לזה: **מפני** שאינה מצויה. ובשאר דברים נמי אין מערבין עירובי חצירות, אלא בפת דשכיח טפי. וגבי שיתוף הקילו שלא להצריך פת, ושרי בשאר דברים דשכיחי קצת. אבל במעה דלא שכיח כלל – לא: **איכא** בינייהו כלים ופחות משוה פרוטה. דלמ"ד משום קנין – אין מערבין בפחות משוה פרוטה אע"ג דאיכא מזון ב' סעודות. וא"ת: וכי איכא שוה פרוטה, להוי עירוב אע"ג דליכא מזון ב' סעודות. דהא אפילו בכלי הוי עירוב, למ"ד משום קנין. אם כן מה צריך ב' סעודות? וי"ל: כשמפרש ועושה דרך קנין – לא בעי חזי לאכילה, וקונה אפילו בכלי. אבל בסתם, כמו שרגילין לערב שאין מפרשין ומדקדקין לעשות דרך קנין – בעי נמי שיהא בו חשיבות אוכל: וקטן

עין משפט נר מצוה

מו א ב ג מיי' פ"ה מהל' עירובין הלכה ז ח ט טוש"ע א"ח סי' שפו סעיף ט:

מז ד מיי' שם הלכה ב' טוש"ע א"ח סי' שסו סעיף ה:

מח ה ו מיי' פ"א מהל' עירובין הלכה יח סמג עשין א טור ש"ע א"ח שם סעיף ד:

מט ז ח מיי' שם הלכה טז טור ש"ע שם סעיף ג:

רבינו חננאל

אסורות תניא כשמואל אמר רבי שמעון למה הדבר דומה לג' חצרות הפתוחות זו לזו כו' עד חכ"א שלשתן אסורות ואודא שמואל לטעמיה דאמר שמואל חצר שבין ב' מבואות עירבה עם שניהם אסורה עם שניהם כחכמים דאמרי שלשתן אסורות זו עם זו. לא עירבה עם שניהן אוסרת על שניהן. במבוי אחד רגילה לערב עמו ובא' אין רגילה. המבוי שהיא רגילה לערב עמו אסור והאחד שאינה רגילה עמו מותר ואם חזרה חצר זו וערבה עם מי שלא היתה רגילה לערב עמו הותר המבוי שהיתה רגילה בו שכבר סילקה עצמה מן המבוי הזה וחזרה על האחר. ואם עירבו בני המבוי שהיתה רגילה חצר זו לערב עמהן וזו החצר לא עירבה עמהן ולא עם בני מבוי האחר. וגם בני אותו מבוי אפי' לעצמם לא עירבו. דוחין זו החצר שלא עירבה עמהם אצל המבוי שלא עירב וא' מכלל אותו מבוי הוא שבני אותו מבוי אין מפסידין כלום [כי] בלא זו נמי אסורין הן דהא לא עירבו כי מצטרפא בהדייהו למשרא בני המבוי שהיתה רגילה בו שפיר דמי דכגון זה כופין על מדת סדום. אמר שמואל המקפיד על עירובו פי' המדקדק שלא יתערב לו עם אחרים כדי שלא יקח פחות משלו אינו עירוב לפי שלא נקרא עירוב אלא שמתערב ר' חנינא אמר עירובו עירוב אלא שנקרא מאנשי וורדינא פירוש אנשי וורדאן היו ידועין בציקנות ובצרות עין. אמר רב יהודה אמר שמואל החולק עירובו בב' כלים אפילו לב"ה אין עירובו עירוב ע"כ לא קאמר ב"ה דעירובו עירוב אלא היכא דמליא למנא ואותיר אבל (פלגיא הוא) [היכא דפלגיה] מיפלג אין עירובו עירוב. ומי אמר שמואל הכי שהחולק לעירוב אינו עירוב והא אמר שמואל בית שמניחין בו עירוב אין צריך ליתן פת עמהן מ"ט לאו משום דאמרינן פת דמנחא בסלא כמאן דמנחא בהדי עירוב דמי ושנינן לא הכי קאמר שמואל אין צריך להיות לו פת בבית מ"מ כולהו אחת דיירי כלומר (עירובין) [כל העירובין] קיבצם אצלו בזה הבית לפיכך הוא א"צ כלום. אמר שמואל עירוב משום קנין מקום. (וא"ת מה אמר) [מפני מה] אין קונין במעות לפי שאין מצויין בע"ש ואקשינן אי הכי אי עירב במעות ליהוי עירוב. אלמ' הנותן מעה לנחתום כדי שיזכה בעירוב *) כו' ודחינן דלמא אתי למימר מע' עיקר וזימנין דליכא מע' ולא מיערב בפת

*) [לא זכו לא מעותיו לקמן דף פא ע"א]

מסורת הש"ס

[ב"ב יב: נט. קסח.]

[לקמן סח.]

[לעיל מח:]

וקטן. פ"ה: דלמ"ד משום קנין, אין קטן יכול לעשות שליח לערב עליו עירובי חצירות, דלאו בר קנין הוא. וקשה לפי': דלהוי כנשתתפו, כמו בעל הבית שנעשה שותף לחבירו. ועוד: דבפרק "בכל מערבין" (לעיל דף לח:) אמר רב הונא: קטן גובה העירוב. ודוחק לומר דפליג. ועוד: דשמואל גופיה דאמר הכא משום קנין, קאמר בפ' "המקבל" (גיטין דף סד:) דקטן זוכה לאחרים בשיתופי מבואות דרבנן! ויש לדחות: דהכא בקטן לגמרי, והתם נמי מחלק בין קטן גמור ובין שאינו קטן גמור. ונראה לר"ת כמו שפר"ח: דבבית של קטן מיירי הכא. ונראה דהלכה כרבה דאמר עירוב משום דירה, דבפ' "הדר" (לקמן דף סו.) קאמר ר' יוחנן: שוכר כמערב דמי. ומפרש: מה מערב בפחות משוה פרוטה. וקיימא לן כרבי יוחנן לגבי דשמואל. ועוד: דהתם מפרש התלמוד הכי, ואם כן כך הלכה: **ואמר** שביתתי במקומי זכה. ואומר ר"י: דבלא אמירה נמי קני, כדאמרינן בפ' "בכל מערבין" (לעיל דף לח:). אבל ניעור דאי בעי מלי אמר, אע"ג דלא אמר – כמאן דאמר דמי. ויש לחלק: שאני התם שהולך לשם כך על התחום כדי לערב. אבל מדפליגי רבנן על רבי יוחנן(ה) בישן, משמע דבניעור מודו דקני אע"ג דלא אמר. ולעיל (דף מה.) דתנן: מי שישב בדרך ועמד, והרי הוא סמוך לעיר, הואיל ולא היתה כוונתו לכך – לא יכנס. ומוכח בגמרא דקני שביתה במקומו, כעובדא דר' טרפון דקאמר: בית המדרש מובלע בתוך תחומו היה. והא דנקט "ואמר" אטו כשאומר שביתתי במקום פלוני, או אגב דסיפא העני מערב ברגליו אבל עשיר לא, אפי' אמר. וכה"ג איכא ב"שנים אוחזין" (ב"מ דף יא.): ראה אותן רצין אחר צבי שבור אחר גוזלות שלא פרחו, ואמר: זכתה לי שדי – זכתה לו. והתם נמי, אפי' לא אמר קני. כדאמר התם בגמ' *גבי ד' אמות דתקינו ליה רבנן דליקנו. ואי תקינו ליה רבנן דליקנו – כי לא אמר מאי הוי? ונקט "ואמר" משום סיפא שהיה לבי רץ כדרכו, אפי' אמר – לא אמר כלום: **ואפילו** לתחתיו של אילן לא מצי אזיל. דממקום רגליו עקר דעתיה, ותחת האילן נמי לא קנה, לכך לא יזוז ממקומו. ואם תאמר: בפרק "בכל מערבין" (לעיל דף לה.) גבי נתגלגל חוץ לתחום קאמר: ספק – הרי זה חמר גמל, ויש לו מביתו עד עירובו אלפים. ולא אמר ולא יזוז ממקומו! ואומר ר"י: דהתם בעומד בעירו לא עקר דעתיה מעירו, ודעתו שאם לא יקנה שם שביתה – שיהיה לו תחום ביתו. ***מאי** טעמא דרב כל שאינו בזה אחר זה אפילו בבת אחת אינו. ושמואל וברייתא דלקמן* דתניא כוותיה – אית להו דרבה בעלמא, והכא בתחומין הקילו, דאין להחמיר בהן. דאין לומר דפליגי, דהא הכא משמע לכאורה דהילכתא כשמואל, מדדחיק לומר אליבא דרב תנא הוא ופליג. ומתניתין בפ"ב דקדושין (דף נ:) במקדש אשה ובתה לא מתוקמא אלא אליבא דרבה, למאי דפסיק התם דקדושין שאין מסורים לביאה הוו קדושין. ועוד י"ל: דהכא סבר כיון דאמר שביתתי תחת האילן, והשביתה הוי ד' אמות – הוי כאילו אמר ליקנו לי ד' מגו תמני, ומודה שמואל במפרש ואומר "שביתתי תהא בכל ח' אמות שתחת האילן" דלא קני. וברייתא נמי דלקמן דטעה ועירב בשתי רוחות, אע"ג דנתכוון לערב בשתי רוחות כאחת, י"ל: דכל המערב בשתי רוחות כאחת מסופק הוא בלבו, ודעתו שאם לא יקנו לו שביתת שתיהן – יקנה באחת מהן, להכי הוי עירוב באחת מהן:

וְקָטָן. אֲמַר לֵיהּ אַבַּיֵי לְרַבָּה: לְדִידָךְ קַשְׁיָא, וְלִשְׁמוּאֵל קַשְׁיָא. הָא תַּנְיָא: *חֲמִשָּׁה שֶׁגָּבוּ אֶת עֵירוּבָן, כְּשֶׁהֵם מוֹלִיכִין אֶת עֵירוּבָן לְמָקוֹם אַחֵר — אֶחָד מוֹלִיךְ *לְכוּלָּן. הוּא נִיהוּ דְּקָא קָנֵי, וְתוּ לָא. הוּא נִיהוּ דְּקָא דָּיֵיר, וְתוּ לָא! אֲמַר לֵיהּ: לָא לְדִידִי קַשְׁיָא, וְלָא לִשְׁמוּאֵל קַשְׁיָא: שְׁלִיחוּת דְּכוּלְּהוּ קָא עָבֵיד. אָמַר רַבָּה, *אָמַר רַב חָמָא בַּר גּוּרְיָא, אָמַר רַב: אהֲלָכָה כְּרַבִּי שִׁמְעוֹן.§

מתני' במִי שֶׁבָּא בַּדֶּרֶךְ *וְחָשְׁכָה לוֹ, וְהָיָה מַכִּיר אִילָן אוֹ גָּדֵר, וְאָמַר "שְׁבִיתָתִי תַּחְתָּיו" — לֹא אָמַר כְּלוּם. "שְׁבִיתָתִי בְּעִיקָּרוֹ" — מְהַלֵּךְ מִמְּקוֹם רַגְלָיו וְעַד עִיקָּרוֹ אַלְפַּיִם אַמָּה, וּמֵעִיקָּרוֹ וְעַד בֵּיתוֹ אַלְפַּיִם אַמָּה. נִמְצָא מְהַלֵּךְ מִשֶּׁחֲשֵׁיכָה אַרְבַּעַת אֲלָפִים אַמָּה. אִם אֵינוֹ מַכִּיר, אוֹ שֶׁאֵינוֹ בָּקִי בַּהֲלָכָה, וְאָמַר "שְׁבִיתָתִי בִּמְקוֹמִי" — גזָכָה לוֹ מְקוֹמוֹ אַלְפַּיִם אַמָּה לְכָל רוּחַ. עֲגוּלוֹת, דִּבְרֵי ר' חֲנִינָא בֶּן אַנְטִיגְנוֹס. וַחֲכָמִים אוֹמְרִים: דמְרוּבָּעוֹת, כְּטַבְלָא מְרוּבַּעַת, כְּדֵי שֶׁיְּהֵא נִשְׂכָּר לַזָּוִיוֹת. *וְזוֹ הִיא שֶׁאָמְרוּ הֶעָנִי מְעָרֵב בְּרַגְלָיו. *אָמַר ר"מ: אָנוּ אֵין לָנוּ אֶלָּא עָנִי. רַבִּי יְהוּדָה אוֹמֵר: אֶחָד עָנִי וְאֶחָד עָשִׁיר, לֹא אָמְרוּ מְעָרְבִין בַּפַּת אֶלָּא לְהָקֵל עַל הֶעָשִׁיר, שֶׁלֹּא יֵצֵא וִיעָרֵב בְּרַגְלָיו.§ **גמ'** מַאי "לֹא אָמַר כְּלוּם"? אָמַר רַב: לֹא אָמַר כְּלוּם כָּל עִיקָּר, דַּאֲפִילּוּ לְתַחְתָּיו שֶׁל אִילָן לָא מָצֵי אָזֵיל. וּשְׁמוּאֵל אָמַר: הלֹא אָמַר כְּלוּם לְבֵיתוֹ, אֲבָל לְתַחְתָּיו שֶׁל אִילָן — מָצֵי אָזֵיל. וְנַעֲשָׂה תַּחְתָּיו שֶׁל אִילָן חַמָּר גַּמָּל. בָּא לִמְדּוֹד מִן הַצָּפוֹן — מוֹדְדִין לוֹ מִן הַדָּרוֹם, בָּא לִמְדּוֹד מִן הַדָּרוֹם — מוֹדְדִין לוֹ מִן הַצָּפוֹן.

לְמָקוֹם אַחֵר. שֶׁרָצוּ לְעָרֵב עִם חָצֵר אַחֶרֶת, נוֹתְנִין בְּתוֹכָהּ עֵירוּבָן זֶה שֶׁגָּבוּ לְהַתִּיר חֲצֵירָן: אֶחָד מֵהֶן מוֹלִיךְ ע"י כּוּלָּן. בִּשְׁבִיל כּוּלָּן, וַאֲפִי' נָתַן הוּא לְבַדּוֹ פַּת אַחַת בִּשְׁבִילָן, הוֹאִיל וְהוּא כְּבָר עֵירֵב עִם חֲבֵירָיו – קוֹנֶה לְצוֹרֶךְ כּוּלָּן: כְּר"ש. דְּהִיא מוּתֶּרֶת עִמָּהֶן וְהֵן מוּתָּרִין עִמָּהּ: **מתני'** מִי שֶׁבָּא בַּדֶּרֶךְ וְחָשְׁכָה לוֹ. גָּרְסִינַן: וְהָיָה מַכִּיר אִילָן אוֹ גָּדֵר. וְהוּא בְּסוֹף אַלְפַּיִם מִמְּקוֹם רַגְלָיו, וּמֵהָאִילָן לְבֵיתוֹ אַלְפַּיִם: וְאָמַר שְׁבִיתָתִי תַּחְתָּיו. וּמִשָּׁם יִהְיוּ לִי אַלְפַּיִם. דְּאַע"ג דְּהַשְׁתָּא קָדֵישׁ יוֹמָא(א) – מָצֵי לְמֵיזַל אַלְפַּיִם עַד הָתָם דְּהוּא מְקוֹם שְׁבִיתָתוֹ, וּמִשּׁוּם הָכִי יֵשׁ לוֹ אַלְפַּיִם לְכָאן וְאַלְפַּיִם לְצַד בֵּיתוֹ(ב): לֹא אָמַר כְּלוּם. טַעְמָא מְפָרֵשׁ בַּגְּמָ': גָּדֵר. חוֹמַת אֲבָנִים: אָמַר שְׁבִיתָתִי בְּעִיקָּרוֹ. וְיוֹדֵעַ הוּא שֶׁמֵּעִיקָּרוֹ וְעַד בֵּיתוֹ אֵין יוֹתֵר מֵאַלְפַּיִם – קָנָה לוֹ שְׁבִיתָה בְּעִיקָּרוֹ, הוֹאִיל וְסִיֵּים אֶת מְקוֹמוֹ. וְאוֹתָהּ שְׁבִיתָה קוֹנָה לוֹ אַלְפַּיִם לְצַד רַגְלָיו, וְאַלְפַּיִם לְצַד בֵּיתוֹ: וְאִם אֵינוֹ מַכִּיר. אִילָן אוֹ גָּדֵר: אוֹ אֵינוֹ בָּקִי בַּהֲלָכָה. וְאֵינוֹ יוֹדֵעַ שֶׁיּוֹעִיל לוֹ, וְלֹא אָמַר כֵּן: פְּלוּגְתָּא דְּר' חֲנִינָא בֶּן אַנְטִיגְנוֹס וְרַבָּנַן – בַּגְּמָ' מְפָרֵשׁ: וְזֶהוּ שֶׁאָמְרוּ. כְּגוֹן זֶה שֶׁהוּא בָּא בַּדֶּרֶךְ וְאֵין עִמּוֹ פַּת, דְּהַשְׁתָּא עָנִי הוּא – לוֹ הִתִּירוּ חֲכָמִים לְעָרֵב בְּרַגְלָיו בְּלֹא פַּת: וְאֶחָד עָשִׁיר. הַיּוֹשֵׁב בְּבֵיתוֹ וְרוֹצֶה לֵילֵךְ וּלְהַחְשִׁיךְ עַל הַתְּחוּם וְלִקְנוֹת שְׁבִיתָה מוּתָּר: לְהָקֵל עַל הֶעָשִׁיר. שֶׁיּוּכַל לְשַׁגֵּר ע"י שָׁלִיחַ וְלֹא יִטְרַח הוּא עַצְמוֹ: **גמ'** לֹא אָמַר כְּלוּם כָּל עִיקָּר. וְלֹא יָזוּז מִמְּקוֹמוֹ, שֶׁהֲרֵי בִּמְקוֹם רַגְלָיו אֵין לוֹ שְׁבִיתָה, שֶׁהֲרֵי עָקַר דַּעְתּוֹ וְלִבּוֹ מִכָּאן. וְתַחַת הָאִילָן נַמִי לֹא קָנָה שְׁבִיתָה – דְּהָא לֹא סִיֵּים. וְאַע"פ שֶׁכָּל תַּחְתָּיו שֶׁל נוֹף הָאִילָן לְתוֹךְ אַלְפַּיִם אַמָּה לִמְקוֹם רַגְלָיו, מְפָרְשִׁי' טַעְמָא דְּרַב לְקַמָּן: הוֹאִיל וְלֹא פֵּירֵשׁ אֵיזוֹ ד' אַמּוֹת בָּחַר לוֹ בְּתַחְתָּיו שֶׁל אִילָן – לָאו שְׁבִיתָה הִיא: וּשְׁמוּאֵל אָמַר לֹא אָמַר כְּלוּם לְבֵיתוֹ אֲבָל לְתַחְתָּיו שֶׁל אִילָן מָצֵי אָזֵיל. לְקַמָּן מְפָרֵשׁ, דְּהָכִי אָמַר שְׁמוּאֵל לְמִילְּתֵיהּ – כְּגוֹן דְּקָאֵי כָּל נוֹפוֹ שֶׁל אִילָן בְּתוֹךְ אַלְפַּיִם(ג) לִמְקוֹם רַגְלָיו, דְּכָל ד' אַמּוֹת שֶׁאַתָּה נוֹתֵן לִשְׁבִיתָה [תַּחְתָּיו] כּוּלָּן רְאוּיוֹת לוֹ. הִלְכָּךְ, לְבֵיתוֹ לֹא אָמַר כְּלוּם – דְּהָא בֵּיתוֹ רָחוֹק מֵעִיקָּרוֹ אַלְפַּיִם, כִּדְתָנֵי בְּמַתְנִיתִין מֵעִיקָּרוֹ וְעַד בֵּיתוֹ אַלְפַּיִם, וְשֶׁמָּא הוּא בָּחַר לוֹ אַרְבַּע אַמּוֹת הָרִאשׁוֹנוֹת שֶׁתַּחַת הָאִילָן אוֹתָן שֶׁל לִידוֹ, וּמִשָּׁם עַד בֵּיתוֹ יֵשׁ יוֹתֵר מֵאַלְפַּיִם כָּל רוֹחַב נוֹף הָאִילָן. אֲבָל לְתַחְתָּיו שֶׁל אִילָן – מָצֵי אָזֵיל, דְּמִמָּה נַפְשָׁךְ כָּל ד' אַמּוֹת שֶׁאַתָּה נוֹתֵן לוֹ תַּחְתָּיו לִשְׁבִיתָה נוֹתְנוֹת עַד מְקוֹם רַגְלָיו אַלְפַּיִם אַמָּה: וְנַעֲשָׂה תַּחְתָּיו שֶׁל אִילָן. רוֹחַב נְטִיַּית נוֹפוֹ שֶׁל אִילָן, אִם הוּא רָחָב כ' אוֹ ל' אַמָּה – נַעֲשָׂה לוֹ חַמָּר גַּמָּל, כְּלוֹמַר: מוֹשְׁכוֹ לְכָאן וּלְכָאן: בָּא לִמְדּוֹד מִן הַצָּפוֹן. בְּסוֹף נְטִיַּית הַנּוֹף לְצַד בֵּיתוֹ אַלְפַּיִם, כְּדֵי שֶׁיַּגִּיעַ לְבֵיתוֹ: מוֹדְדִים לוֹ מִן הַדָּרוֹם. וְאוֹמֵר: שֶׁמָּא אַרְבַּע רִאשׁוֹנוֹת שֶׁל צַד רַגְלָיו בָּחַר לוֹ תַּחַת הָאִילָן, וּמִשָּׁם מוֹדְדִין לוֹ אַלְפַּיִם וּלְבֵיתוֹ, וְנִמְצָא רָחוֹק שְׁלֹשִׁים אַמָּה: בָּא לִמְדּוֹד מִן הַדָּרוֹם. מִד' אַמּוֹת רִאשׁוֹנוֹת אַלְפַּיִם לְצַד רַגְלָיו, כְּדֵי שֶׁיָּכוֹל לַחֲזוֹר לַאֲחָרָיו מִמְּקוֹם רַגְלָיו שְׁלוֹשִׁים אַמָּה: מוֹדְדִין לוֹ מִן הַצָּפוֹן. שֶׁמָּא ד' אַמּוֹת שֶׁל סוֹף הָאִילָן לְצַד בֵּיתוֹ בָּחַר לוֹ, וּמִשָּׁם עַד מְקוֹם רַגְלָיו יֵשׁ לוֹ אַלְפַּיִם, וְאֵין יָכוֹל לַחֲזוֹר לַאֲחָרָיו אֲפִילּוּ פְּסִיעָה. אֲבָל אַרְבַּע' אֲלָפִים יֵשׁ לוֹ מִמְּקוֹם רַגְלָיו לְצַד בֵּיתוֹ פָּחוֹת שְׁלֹשִׁים אַמָּה מִמַּה נַּפְשָׁךְ, וּמְקוֹם רוֹחַב הָאִילָן הוּא מַפְסִיד מִפְּנֵי שֶׁלֹּא פֵּירֵשׁ: ל"א: וּשְׁמוּאֵל אָמַר לֹא אָמַר כְּלוּם לְבֵיתוֹ, שֶׁאֵין לוֹ מִן הָאִילָן לְצַד בֵּיתוֹ כְּלוּם, אֲבָל לְתַחְתָּיו שֶׁל אִילָן מָצֵי אָזֵיל. דְּקָסָבַר שְׁמוּאֵל דְּקָנָה לוֹ שְׁבִיתָה בְּב' הַמְּקוֹמוֹת: הוֹאִיל וְלֹא סִיֵּים ד' אַמּוֹתָיו – אֵין לוֹ מָקוֹם הַמְיוּחָד לוֹ(ד) לֹא תַּחַת הָאִילָן וְלֹא בִּמְקוֹם רַגְלָיו, אֶלָּא אוֹ כָּאן אוֹ כָּאן וּמִמַּה נַּפְשָׁךְ, אַלְפַּיִם שֶׁמִּמְּקוֹם רַגְלָיו עַד הָאִילָן יֵשׁ לוֹ. וּכְשֶׁהִגִּיעַ לְתַחַת הָאִילָן – נַעֲשָׂה לוֹ חַמָּר גַּמָּל. בָּא לִמְדּוֹד לוֹ מִן הַצָּפוֹן מִן הָאִילָן לְבֵיתוֹ – מוֹדְדִין לוֹ מִן הַדָּרוֹם, מִמְּקוֹם רַגְלָיו. בָּא לִמְדּוֹד מִמְּקוֹם רַגְלָיו כְּדֵי לַחֲזוֹר לַאֲחָרָיו אַלְפַּיִם – מוֹדְדִין לוֹ מִן הָאִילָן. זֶה שָׁמַעְתִּי. וְיֵשׁ תְּשׁוּבוֹת וְגִימְגּוּמִין יוֹתֵר מִדַּאי לְפִי לְשׁוֹן הַתַּלְמוּד וְהִילּוּכוֹ. חֲדָא, דְּקָא מְשַׁיֵּיל מ"ט דְּרַב, הֲוָה לְשַׁיּוּלֵיהּ טְפֵי טַעְמָא דִּשְׁמוּאֵל דְּמִילְּתֵיהּ דְּרַב מִסְתַּבֵּר טְפֵי, דִּבִמְקוֹם רַגְלָיו לֹא רָצָה לִקְנוֹת וְתַחַת הָאִילָן לֹא קָנָה – דְּלָא יָדְעִי' מַאי סִיֵּים. אֲבָל שְׁמוּאֵל, מַאי סְבִירָא לֵיהּ? אִי קְנִיָּיה הִיא, בְּלֹא סִיּוּם לִקְנֵי הָתָם, וְאִי לָאו קְנִיָּיה הִיא, לָא לִיקְנֵי לָא הָכָא וְלָא הָתָם. דְּהָא כָּאן לֹא רָצָה לִקְנוֹת. וַאֲפִילּוּ ר' יוֹחָנָן בֶּן נוּרִי לָא קָאָמַר אֶלָּא חֶפְצֵי הֶפְקֵר, אוֹ יָשֵׁן. אֲבָל זֶה שֶׁאָמַר בְּפֵירוּשׁ אֵינִי רוֹצֶה לִקְנוֹת כָּאן – הֵיאַךְ יִקְנֶה? וְעוֹד: מַאי "נַעֲשָׂה תַּחְתָּיו שֶׁל אִילָן חַמָּר גַּמָּל"? הָכִי אִיבְּעֵי לֵיהּ לְמֵימַר: וּשְׁמוּאֵל אָמַר הֲרֵי זֶה חַמָּר גַּמָּל. וְעוֹד: מַאי מִן הַצָּפוֹן וּמִן הַדָּרוֹם? בְּמָקוֹם אֶחָד יֵשׁ לוֹמַר מִצְּפוֹנוֹ וּמִדְּרוֹמוֹ, אֲבָל בִּשְׁנֵי מְקוֹמוֹת לֹא שַׁיָּיךְ הַאי לִישָּׁנָא: מאי

עין משפט נר מצוה

נ א מיי' פ"ד מהלכות עירובין הלכה ד ופ"ה הלכה ז טוש"ע א"ח סי' שעח סעיף א' וסי' שפו סעיף ט:

נא ב מיי' פ"ז שם הלכה ה סמג עשין א טוש"ע א"ח סי' תט סעיף יא:

נב ג מיי' פכ"ז מהל' שבת הלכה ב סמג לאוין סה טוש"ע א"ח סי' שצז סעיף א:

נג ד מיי' וסמג שם טוש"ע א"ח סי' שלט סעיף י:

נד ה מיי' פ"ז מהלכות עירובין הלכה ה סמג עשין א טוש"ע א"ח סי' תט סעיף יא.

רבינו חננאל

בפת. רבה אמר עירוב משום דירה איכא בינייהו שנתן לשכנו כלי שאין בו שוה פרוטה לשמואל [הוי עירוב] דהא קנין איתיה בפחות משוה פרוטה לרבה לא הוי עירוב אי נמי *) קטן לשמואל לא הוי עירוב דאין קנין לקטן לרבה הוי עירוב דהא משום דירה הוא וקטן נמי אית ליה דירה ומקשה אביי על תרווייהו מהא דתניא ה' שגבו את עירובן כשמוליכין אותו למקום אחר אחד מוליך ע"י כולן למ"ד משום קניין האי דמוליך העירוב (לא) קא קני (ולא) וקא דייר [ותו לא]. ופריק רבה אליבא דידיה ואליבא דשמואל שליחותא דכולהו קא עביד. אמר רבה אמר רב חמא בר גוריא אמר רב הלכה כרבי [שמעון] דאמר הא למה זה דומה לג' חצרות וכו': **מתני'** מי שבא בדרך ומכיר אילן או גדר ואמר שביתתי תחתיו לא אמר כלום מאי לא אמר כלום רב אמר לא אמר כלום כל עיקר דאפילו לתחתיו של אילן לא מצי אזיל דהא (עיקר) [עקר] שביתתו ממקומו באומרו שביתתי תחת האילן פלוני ותחת אותו אילן לא קנה שביתה דהא לא סיים מקום שביתתו דמקום שביתתו הן הד' האמות המקום שמותר לו לטלטל ומשם מודד תחומו וכיון שאין לו מקום אין לו תחום ושמואל אמר לא אמר כלום שאינו יכול להלך מן האילן לביתו אם הוא בתוך אלפים אמה מן האילן אבל אל האילן יש לו להלך קסבר שמואל אם במקומו קנה שביתה יש לו להלך אלפים אמה עד תחתיו של אילן. ואם תחת האילן קנה יש לו להלך שם אבל כיון שיגיע אל תחת האילן אין לו לזוז ממקומו בא למדוד מן הצפון אומר לו מן הדרום תחומך. אמר

*) [עי' תוס' כאן ד"ה לקטן שכ' בשם רבינו ז"ל דבבית של קטן מיירי הכא ופי' דאם יש לקטן בית בחצר אינו יכול לערב עמהם משום דאין קנין לקטן].

מסורת הש"ס

לקמן עב: ע"ש

ס"א ע"י כולן

[לעיל מו: לקמן ס.]

[בירושלמי והיה ירא שמא תחשך]

[לעיל מז.]

[בירושלמי ר"מ אומר אין לנו]

[שייך לדף נ.]

[דף נ:]

גליון הש"ס

תום' ד"ה ואפי' לתחתיו וכו' ואר"י דהתם בעומד בעירו וכו' כה"ג ברש"י לקמן דף ס ע"א ד"ה ואסור:

הגהות הב"ח

(א) רש"י ד"ה ואמר שביתתי וכו' קדיש יומא מלינא למיזל וכו' מקום שביתתי ומשם יש לי אלפים כצ"ל ותיבת הכי נמחק: (ב) בא"ד לצד ביתי הס"ד: (ג) ד"ה ושמואל אמר וכו' כגון דקאי כל נופו של אילן בתוך אלפים: X כזה

(ד) ד"ה ל"א ושמואל וכו' מקום המיוחד לא תחת כצ"ל ותיבת לו נמחק:

(ה) תום' ד"ה ואמר וכו' על רבי יוחנן ב"נ בישן וכו' ולעיל נמי דתנן מי שישב:

אָמַר רַבָּה: מ"ט דְּרַב — מִשּׁוּם דְּלָא מְסַיֵּים אַתְרֵיהּ. וְאִיכָּא דְּאָמְרִי, אָמַר רַבָּה: מ"ט דְּרַב — מִשּׁוּם דְּקָסָבַר: *כֹּל שֶׁאֵינוֹ בְּזֶה אַחַר זֶה — אֲפִילּוּ בְּבַת אַחַת אֵינוֹ. מַאי בֵּינַיְיהוּ? אִיכָּא בֵּינַיְיהוּ: דְּאָמַר "לִיקְנוּ לִי בְּאַרְבַּע אַמּוֹת מִגּוֹ שְׁמוֹנֶה". מַאן דְּאָמַר מִשּׁוּם דְּלָא מְסַיֵּים אַתְרֵיהּ — הָא לָא מְסַיֵּים אַתְרֵיהּ, וּמַאן דְּאָמַר מִשּׁוּם כֹּל שֶׁאֵינוֹ בְּזֶה אַחַר זֶה אֲפִילּוּ בְּבַת אַחַת אֵינוֹ — הַאי כְּאַרְבַּע אַמּוֹת דָּמֵי, דְּהָכָא אַרְבַּע אַמּוֹת קָאָמַר. גּוּפָא, *אָמַר רַבָּה: כָּל דָּבָר שֶׁאֵינוֹ בְּזֶה אַחַר זֶה — אֲפִילּוּ בְּבַת אַחַת אֵינוֹ. אֵיתִיבֵיהּ אַבָּיֵי לְרַבָּה: **[א]הַמַּרְבֶּה בְּמַעַשְׂרוֹת — פֵּירוֹתָיו מְתוּקָּנִין וּמַעַשְׂרוֹתָיו מְקוּלְקָלִין. אַמַּאי? לֵימָא: כֹּל שֶׁאֵינוֹ בְּזֶה אַחַר זֶה — אֲפִילּוּ בְּבַת אַחַת אֵינוֹ! שָׁאנֵי מַעֲשֵׂר דְּאִיתֵיהּ לַחֲצָאִין, דְּאִי אָמַר "תִּקְדּוֹשׁ פַּלְגָּא פַּלְגָּא דְּחִיטְּתָא" — קָדְשָׁה. וַהֲרֵי מַעֲשַׂר בְּהֵמָה דְּלֵיתֵיהּ לַחֲצָאִין,(א) *וְאָמַר (*רַבָּה): [ב]יָצְאוּ שְׁנַיִם בָּעֲשִׂירִי, וּקְרָאָן עֲשִׂירִי — עֲשִׂירִי וְאַחַד עָשָׂר מְעוֹרָבִין זֶה בָּזֶה! שָׁאנֵי מַעֲשַׂר בְּהֵמָה דְּאִיתֵיהּ בְּזֶה אַחַר זֶה בְּטָעוּת. *דִּתְנַן: [ג]קָרָא לַתְּשִׁיעִי עֲשִׂירִי, וְלָעֲשִׂירִי תְּשִׁיעִי, וּלְאַחַד עָשָׂר עֲשִׂירִי — שְׁלָשְׁתָּן מְקוּדָּשִׁין. וַהֲרֵי תּוֹדָה, דְּלֵיתָהּ בְּטָעוּת וְלֵיתָהּ בְּזֶה אַחַר זֶה; *וְאִיתְּמַר: תּוֹדָה שֶׁנִּשְׁחֲטָה עַל שְׁמוֹנִים חַלּוֹת, חִזְקִיָּה אָמַר: קָדְשׁוּ עָלֶיהָ מ' מִתּוֹךְ שְׁמוֹנִים, ר' יוֹחָנָן אָמַר: [ד]לֹא קָדְשׁוּ עָלֶיהָ מ' מִתּוֹךְ שְׁמוֹנִים. הָא אִיתְּמַר עֲלַהּ, אָמַר ר' (*זֵירָא): [ה]הַכֹּל מוֹדִים הֵיכָא דְּאָמַר "לִיקַּדְשׁוּ אַרְבָּעִים מִתּוֹךְ שְׁמוֹנִים" — דְּקָדְשִׁי, "לֹא יִקָּדְשׁוּ אַרְבָּעִים אֶלָּא אִם כֵּן קָדְשׁוּ שְׁמוֹנִים" — כּוּלֵּי עָלְמָא לָא פְּלִיגִי דְּלָא קָדְשׁוּ. כִּי פְּלִיגִי — בִּסְתָמָא. מָר סָבַר: לַאֲחָרָיוּת קָא מְכַוֵּין, וְעַל תְּנַאי אַיְיתִינְהוּ.

ומ"ש

רש"י

מאי טעמא דרב. בשלמא לשמואל ללישנא קמא מיסתברא מילתיה, דמכל מקום קנה שביתה תחת האילן, אבל אין אנו יודעין איזו ד' אמות קנה – הלכך, ידו על התחתונה ומפסיד מארבע' אלפים כשיעור תחתיו של אילן, בא למדוד מכאן מודדין לו מכאן: משום דלא סיים אתריה. וכיון דלא סיים – לא קני ליה מידי: כל שאינו בזה אחר זה אפילו בבת אחת אינו. דכיון דאם סיים ד' לפוניות אינו יכול לחזור בו, לברור ד' דרומיות להיות לו שביתה כאן וכאן, כי אמר נמי כולהו כחדא, כגון הכא דאמר שביתתי תחתיו – לא אמרינן ליקנו: ארבע מינייהו מגו תמני. להכי נקט מגו תמני, דלקמן מוקמינן באילן שיש תחתיו ח' אמות: המרבה במעשרות. אחד מחמש או מח': פירותיו. שסילק לצד אחר – חולין מתוקנין הן, אבל המעשרות שנותן ללוי – מקולקלין הן, שהרי טבל מעורב בהן. כשנתן קב השמיני לא חל שם המעשר אלא על הראוי למעשר, והשאר טבל הוא. דמעשר בהדיא אמר רחמנא שיעור אחד מעשרה. ולא דמי לתרומה שניטלת בעין יפה ובעין רעה ובבינונית, דבתרומה לא כתיב בה שיעור: אמאי. פירותיו מתוקנין: נימא כל שאינו בזה אחר זה. דאילו הוה מפריש מעשר כהלכתו והדר שקל תו וקרייה עליה שם מעשר, על חולין שניתקנו כבר – לא חייל עליה שם מעשר והשתא נמי כי אפריש האי טופיינא עם מעשר – לא ליחול שם מעשר אפילו על הראוי למעשר כי היכי דאמר גבי שביתה דלא קני ארבע מינייהו מגו תמני כי לא אמר ארבע בהדיא: שאני מעשר. דלהכי פירותיו מתוקנין, דעל כל גרגר וגרגר שבו חל השם עליו לפי חשבון הראוי למעשר. כגון: הפריש אחד מחמשה – קדש כל גרגר חציו. אבל גבי שביתה ליכא למימר דשייכא בכל תחתיו של אילן, דארבע אמות כהדדי בעינן: דאי אמר תיקדוש פלגא פלגא דחיטתא קדשה. והאי כיון דאפריש כפלים וקרא עליה שם מעשר – כמאן דאמר: תיקדוש כל חיטתא לפלגא: והרי מעשר בהמה דליתי לחצאין. דאי אמר: חצי טלה זה חולין וחציו מעשר – לא אמר כלום ליקדש לחצאין. ד"כל אשר יעבור תחת השבט העשירי יהיה קודש" אמר רחמנא (יהיה כולו קדוש לשם מעשר). וליתיה נמי בזה אחר זה, שאם קרא לעשירי "עשירי" ולאחד עשר "עשירי" – אינו קדוש. וכי קרא לשנים "עשירי" בבת אחת – אמרינן דחד מינייהו מעשר גמור, דאמר רבה: עשירי ואחד עשר מעורבין זה בזה, דחד מינייהו מעשר, ואידך הוי אחד עשר שקראו עשירי ואילו הוה ידע ביה, כגון שטעה וקרא לעשירי "תשיעי" ולאחד עשר "עשירי" – קיימא לן דעשירי מעשר, ואחד עשר קרב שלמים. ומה בין שלמים למעשר? שהשלמים טעונין סמיכה ונסכים ותנופת חזה ושוק, ונפדין במומן, ותמורתן קריבה. מה שאין כן במעשר. והשתא דקראן בבת אחת ולא ידע הי עשירי גמור והי אחד עשר שנקרא עשירי – בעו תרוייהו תנופת חזה ושוק וסמיכה. ולבי אומר דאינו מברך על התנופה ועל הסמיכה, דלא ליהוי ברכה לבטלה. ונסכים בעי קרבן אחד על תנאי, ויאמר: אם זה שלמים – יהיו על זה, ואם לאו – יהיו על חברו. אלמא: מדחל שם מעשר אחד מינייהו – שמע מינה: אע"ג דלא קדיש אחד עשר, אם קרא לעשירי "עשירי" דהוי עשירי וקרא לאחד עשר "עשירי" – אפילו הכי, כי קראן בבת אחת – קדיש חד מינייהו בעשירי: שאני מעשר בהמה דאיתיה בזה אחר זה בטעות. כגון אם טעה בעשירי וקראו "תשיעי" ולאחד עשר "עשירי" – קדוש אחד עשר משום קריאת השם, וקרב שלמים. דתנן כו' ובפרק בתרא דבכורות ילפינן מקראי. הלכך, כי קראן כאחד – לא מעכב י"א על העשירי מלחול עליו שם גמור, דהא י"א גופיה זימנין דקדוש בקריאת שם מעשר, כגון היכא דקרייה לעשירי שלפניו "תשיעי". והא דרבה – בפרק בתרא דבכורות: והרי תודה. דלחמי תודה מ' חלות, כדאמר במנחות (דף עז.): דליתה בטעות. אם הפריש לחמי תודתו, וטעה, וסבור שלא הפריש, וחזר וקרא שם על מ' חלות אחרות – לא קדשי. דהא טעה, ותנן: הקדש טעות – אינו הקדש, במסכת נזיר (דף לא.). וליתה נמי בזה אחר זה, שאם הפריש מ' לתודתו ושחט הזבח עליהן, וחזר והפריש לה מ' אחרות – לא קדשי, וכי שחטה על שמונים בבת אחת – אמר חזקיה דקדשי מ' מתוך שמונים. שחיטת התודה מקדשת הלחם, כדתניא במנחות (דף עח:): קרבנו על זבח – מלמד שאין הלחם קדוש אלא על הזביחה: יקדשו ארבעים. הא מ' קאמר, וגבי שביתה נמי: הא אמרן דאי אמר לקנו לי ארבע מתוך תמני – קני: לאחריות קא מכוין. שאם יאבדו או יטמאו אלין יפטור באלין, והוה ליה כאומר יקדשו ארבעים מתוך שמונים:

ורבי

תוספות

כל שאינו בזה אחר זה אפילו בבת אחת אינו. ואומר ר"י: דלא דמי לתמורת עולה ושלמים אע"ג דליתא בזה אחר זה איתא בבת אחת, כדאיתא ב"כילד מעריכין" (תמורה כה:) ובפרק שני דזבחים (דף ל.) – דהתם אפשר להתקיים שניהן, כדאמר התם: דתרעה עד שתסתאב, ותמכר, ויביא בדמי חציה עולה ובדמי חציה שלמים. אבל הכא לא קנו כל ח' אמות, והי מינייהו מייתית? דאי קני הני ד' – לא קני הני ד'. ובמקדש אשה ובתה, אי תפסי קדושין בהא – לא תפסי בהא. וכן כל הני דמייתי בסמוך ובפרק ב' דקידושין (דף נא.), וכן "קיים ליכי ומופר ליכי" בנדרים (דף סט.). ועוד פי' ר"י טעם אחר, ולא נתיישב לפירושו ההיא דנדרים: **שאני** מעשר דאיתיה לחצאין דאי אמר תיקדוש פלגא פלגא דחיטתא קדשה. כדפירש בקונטרס, שהמעשר על כל גרגיר שבו חל השם לפי החשבון הראוי למעשר, כגון: הפריש אחד מחמשה – קדש כל גרגיר חציו. אבל גבי שביתה ליכא למימר הכי, דהא ארבע אמות כי הדדי בעינן, ומיהו קשה, הא דפריך: והא מעשר בהמה דליתיה לחצאין, כי איתיה נמי לחצאין תיקשי ליה אמאי עשירי ואחד עשר מעורבין זה בזה? כי מטעם חצאין לא היה ראוי להיות מעשר רק חצי של כל אחד ואחד, כמו במעשר דגן, כדפירש הקונטרס! וי"ל: נהי דאיתיה לחצאין, הוה קשיא ליה קושיא אחריתי, מכל מקום הך פירכא דפריך אמאי שניהן קדושין כל עיקר לא הוה מצי לאקשויי. ולר"י נראה לפרש הכי: שאני מעשר דאיתיה לחצאין, פירוש: בזה אחר זה שאם אמר "סאה אחת(ב) מהם מעשר" כל חצי חטה וחטה, ואחר כך אמר גם כן בסאה האחרת – חל מעשר בשתיהן במקצת. וכיון דאיתא לחצאין בזה אחר זה – גם בבת אחת ישנה, להיות חל מעשר על סאה אחת, והאחרת תהיה טבל: **ואמר** רבה יצאו שנים בעשירי כו'. וא"ת: דלמא התם היינו טעמא – משום דאי אפשר לצמצם, והאחד יצא תחילה ואפילו בלא קריאת שם הוא הקדוש, כדאמר בפרק בתרא דבכורות (דף ס:) עשירי מאליו הוא קדוש! וי"ל: דע"כ סבר רבה דאפשר לצמצם שיצאו שניהם בבת אחת, דאי אי אפשר לצמצם והאחד יצא תחילה – אם כן הוה ליה למימר עשירי וחולין מעורבין זה בזה, דאפילו יצא עשירי בשתיקה ואחר כך יצא אחד עשר וקרא לו עשירי – אין אחד עשר קדוש כלל, דהא לא נעקר שם עשירי ממנו. ועוד י"ל: דאפילו סבר אי אפשר לצמצם, כיון דאין יכול להכיר איזה יצא קודם לחברו, ונתכוון לקרות שניהם עשירי – קדשו תרוייהו. ולא דמי לקרא לעשירי עשירי ולאחד עשר עשירי. והכא מבתרא פריך דאינו קדוש אלא מחמת דבורו. והראשון נראה לי עיקר: **עשירי** ואחד עשר מעורבין זה בזה. הגיה רש"י בפירוש כתב ידו דשניהם ירעו, לפי שאין מתן דמיהם שוה, שהשלמים טעונין ד' מתנות ומעשר מתנה אחת, הלכך ירעו, ויחלל(ג) מעות בדמי היפה שבהן, ויאמר: כל מקום שהם שלמים – יהא מחולל על דמים האלו, ויאכל שניהם במומן בתורת מעשר:

ומר

עין משפט נר מצוה

נה א מיי' פ"א מהל' מעשר הלכה יד סמג עשין קלג טוש"ע י"ד סי' שלא סעיף טו:

נו ב מיי' פ"ו מהלכות בכורות הלכה ד:

נז ג מיי' שם הלכה ה:

נח ד ה מיי' פי"ב מהל' פסולי המוקדשין הלכה טו:

מסורת הש"ס

[קידושין נ: נדרים סט:]

[שם]

קידושין נא. מנחות נד: תוספתא דמאי פ"ח

קידושין שם. בכורות ס:

גם זה שם

קידושין נא. מנחות עח:

[בקידושין ובכורות איתא רבא]

[בקידושין איתא ר"י בן לוי]

רש"ל מוחק זה

הגהות הב"ח

(א) גמ' בהמה דליתיה לחצאין וליתיה בזה אחר זה ואמר רבה יצאו: (ב) תוס' ד"ה שאני וכו' שאם אמר סאה אחת זה כל חצי חטה וחטה יהא מעשר ואח"כ אמר: (ג) ד"ה עשירי וכו' ויחלל במעות:

גליון הש"ס

רש"י ד"ה והרי מעשר בהמה כו' חזה ושוק וסמיכה. עי' בשער המלך פ"ג הלכה יג מהל' מעשה הקרבנות:

רבינו חננאל

אמר רבה מ"ט דרב דאמר לא אמר כלום כל עיקר משום דלא מסיים אתריה קסבר כל מאן דלא מסיים אתריה לא קנה שביתה במקום. ומי שלא קנה שביתה במקום ידוע ומסויים דומה למי שיצא חוץ לתחום מאחר שקדש היום שאין לו אלא ד' אמות בלבד. איכא דאמרי טעמא דרב משום דכל דבר שאינו בזה אחר זה אפילו בבת אחת אינו. פי' כיון שאין לאדם לקנות ד' אמות מקום שביתה אחרי שקנה במקום אחר כך אין לו לקנות שיעור ב' מקומות בבת אחת והוא תחת האילן שיש תחתיו שיעור כמה מקומות כל ד' אמות מקום ולברור אחר כך איזה מקום שירצה. והוא כגון קידושי אשה ובתה כשם שאחר שיקדש אחת מהן אינו יכול לחזור ולקדש האחרת. כך אם יאמר בבת אחת *) (מכם). ואמרינן מאי איכא בין תרי לישני דרבה איכא בינייהו כגון דאיכא תחתיו דאילן ח' אמות ואמר שביתתי תחת ד' אמות מהני ח' למאן דאמר דהא לא מסיים אתריה האי נמי לא מסיים אתריה דלא אמר לא בצפון ולא בדרום. ולמאן דאמר כל שאינו בזה אחר זה כו' כיון דאמר ליקניין לי ד' אמות מהני ח' הרי כאילו בזה אחר זה קאמר דראשון מיהא קני ולא דמי לבת אחת. ומותיב אהא דרבה דאמר כל שאינו בזה אחר זה אפי' בבת אחת אינו [מהא דתניא] המרבה במעשרות פירותיו מתוקנין ומעשרותיו מקולקלין הנה אם הוציא מן הכור מעשר שלו איפה אחת וחזר אח"כ והפריש איפה אחרת השניה חולין הנה המעשר אינו בזה אחר זה ואם הפריש בבת אחת ב' איפות קנה מעשר וישנו בבת אחת מדקתני פירותיו מתוקנין קשיא לרבה. ופריק רבה שאני מעשר הואיל ואיתיה לחצאין דאי אמר תקדוש פלגא דחיטתא קדשה כאלו ישנו בזה אחר זה. פי' אילו אמר חצי כל חטה מאילו ב' איפות מעשר הן קדשו וכיון שאי אפשר לברר איזהו חציו הקדוש נתפס גם חצי האחר. ומשום דמשכחת לה דמקדש זה אחר זה. משום הכי מקדשו בבת אחת. ואקשינן והרי מעשר בהמה דליתא לחצאין דנוקמה בזה אחר זה ואיתנהו בבת אחת כדרבא דאמר עשירי ואחד עשר מעורבין זה בזה. ושנינן מעשר בהמה שאני דמשכחת לה בזה אחר זה בטעות דתנן קרא לתשיעי עשירי כו' ואקשינן תוב והרי תודה דליתה בטעות ולא בזה אחר זה ואתמר תודה ששחטה על פ' חלות חזקיה אמר קדשו מ' מתוך פ' ופירק רבא הא אתמר עלה א"ר זירא הכל מודים היכא דא' קדשו מ' מתוך פ' דקדשי כי היכי דאמינא אנא היכא דאמר ליקנו לי ד' אמות מהני ח' דקני ופריק רבא ואוקמה לטע' [דרבה] אמר

רב נסים גאון

תודה שנשחטה על שמונים חלות חזקיה אמר קדשו מ' מתוך שמונים כי לחם התודה ארבעים חלות ואיתא בתורת כהנים נמצא לחמה של תודה ארבעים חלות נוטל מהן ד' וניתן לכהן ובמס' מנחות בפרק התודה (דף עח) תמצא גם שם פירושו:

*) [עי' תוס' כאן ד"ה לקטן שכ' בשם רבינו ז"ל דבבית של קטן מיירי הכא ופי' דאם יש לקטן בית בחצר אינו יכול לערב עמהם משום דאין קנין לקטן]. *) [דשניהם מקודשות לי לא אמר כלום].

נט א מיי' פ"ז מהלכות עירובין הלכה ו טור ש"ע א"ח סי' תט סעיף יא:
ס ב מיי' פכ"ז מהלכו' שבת הלכה ט ופ"ז מהלכות עירובין הלכה ד' טוש"ע א"ח סי' שנו סעיף ב:
סא ג מיי' פ"ז מהלכות עירובין הלכה ז טוש"ע א"ח סי' תט סעיף יב:
סב ד מיי' שם הלכה ו טוש"ע שם סעיף יא:
סג ה מיי' פ"ח מהלכות עירובין הלכה א טור ש"ע א"ח סי' תיב:

וּמ"ס: לְקָרְבָּן גָּדוֹל קָא מְכַוֵּין. אָמַר אַבַּיֵי: לֹא שָׁנוּ אֶלָּא בְּאִילָן שֶׁתַּחְתָּיו י"ב אַמָּה, אֲבָל בְּאִילָן שֶׁאֵין תַּחְתָּיו י"ב אַמָּה — הֲרֵי מִקְצָת בֵּיתוֹ נִיכָּר. מַתְקִיף לָהּ רַב הוּנָא בְּרֵיהּ דְּרַב יְהוֹשֻׁעַ: מִמַּאי דִּבְאַרְבְּעֵי מְצִיעֲתָא קָא מְסַיֵּים? דִּלְמָא בְּאַרְבְּעֵי דְּהַאי גִּיסָּא וּבְאַרְבְּעֵי דְּהַאי גִּיסָּא קָמְסַיֵּים! אֶלָּא אָמַר רַב הוּנָא בְּרֵיהּ דְּרַב יְהוֹשֻׁעַ: אלֹא שָׁנוּ אֶלָּא בְּאִילָן שֶׁתַּחְתָּיו ח' אַמּוֹת, אֲבָל בְּאִילָן שֶׁתַּחְתָּיו ז' אַמּוֹת — הֲרֵי מִקְצָת בֵּיתוֹ נִיכָּר. תַּנְיָא כְּוָותֵיהּ דְּרַב, תַּנְיָא כְּוָותֵיהּ דִּשְׁמוּאֵל. תַּנְיָא כְּוָותֵיהּ דְּרַב: מִי שֶׁבָּא בַּדֶּרֶךְ וְחָשְׁכָה לוֹ, וְהָיָה מַכִּיר אִילָן אוֹ גָּדֵר, וְאָמַר "שְׁבִיתָתִי תַּחְתָּיו" — לֹא אָמַר כְּלוּם. אֲבָל אִם אָמַר "שְׁבִיתָתִי בְּמָקוֹם פְּלוֹנִי" — מְהַלֵּךְ עַד שֶׁמַּגִּיעַ לְאוֹתוֹ מָקוֹם. בהִגִּיעַ לְאוֹתוֹ מָקוֹם — מְהַלֵּךְ אֶת כּוּלּוֹ וְחוּצָה לוֹ אַלְפַּיִם אַמָּה. בד"א — בְּמָקוֹם הַמְסוּיָּים, כְּגוֹן שֶׁשָּׁבַת בְּתֵל שֶׁהוּא גָּבוֹהַּ י' טְפָחִים וְהוּא מֵד"א וְעַד בֵּית סָאתַיִם. וְכֵן בְּקָעָה שֶׁהִיא עֲמוּקָּה י' וְהִיא מֵד"א וְעַד בֵּית סָאתַיִם. אֲבָל בְּמָקוֹם שֶׁאֵין מְסוּיָּים — אֵין לוֹ* אֶלָּא ד"א. *גהָיוּ שְׁנַיִם, אֶחָד מַכִּיר וְאֶחָד שֶׁאֵינוֹ מַכִּיר — זֶה שֶׁאֵינוֹ מַכִּיר מוֹסֵר שְׁבִיתָתוֹ לַמַּכִּיר, וְהַמַּכִּיר אוֹמֵר "שְׁבִיתָתִי בְּמָקוֹם פְּלוֹנִי". בד"א — כְּשֶׁסִּיֵּים ד"א שֶׁקָּבַע, אֲבָל לֹא סִיֵּים ד"א שֶׁקָּבַע — לֹא יָזוּז מִמְּקוֹמוֹ. לֵימָא תֶּיהֱוֵי תְּיוּבְתֵּיהּ דִּשְׁמוּאֵל! אָמַר לָךְ שְׁמוּאֵל: הָכָא בְּמַאי עָסְקִינַן — דכְּגוֹן דְּאִיכָּא מִמְּקוֹם רַגְלָיו וְעַד עִיקָּרוֹ תְּרֵי אַלְפֵּי וְאַרְבַּע גַּרְמִידֵי, דְּאִי מוֹקְמִית לֵיהּ בְּאִידָךְ גִּיסָּא דְּאִילָן — קָם לֵיהּ לְבַר מִתְּחוּמָא, אִי סִיֵּים ד"א — מָצֵי אָזֵיל, וְאִי לָא — לָא מָצֵי אָזֵיל. תַּנְיָא כְּוָותֵיהּ דִּשְׁמוּאֵל: הטָעָה וְעֵירֵב לִשְׁתֵּי רוּחוֹת, כִּמְדוּמֶּה(א) הוּא שֶׁמְּעָרְבִין לוֹ לִשְׁתֵּי רוּחוֹת, אוֹ שֶׁאָמַר לַעֲבָדָיו "צְאוּ וְעָרְבוּ לִי", *אֶחָד עֵירֵב עָלָיו לַצָּפוֹן וְאֶחָד עֵירֵב עָלָיו לַדָּרוֹם — מְהַלֵּךְ לַצָּפוֹן כְּעֵירוּבוֹ לַדָּרוֹם, וְלַדָּרוֹם כְּעֵירוּבוֹ לַצָּפוֹן. וְאִם מִיצְּעוּ עָלָיו אֶת הַתְּחוּם — לֹא יָזוּז מִמְּקוֹמוֹ. לֵימָא תֶּיהֱוֵי תְּיוּבְתֵּיהּ דְּרַב! *רַב תַּנָּא הוּא וּפָלֵיג.§ "אָמַר שְׁבִיתָתִי בְּעִיקָּרוֹ — מְהַלֵּךְ מִמְּקוֹם רַגְלָיו וְעַד עִיקָּרוֹ אַלְפַּיִם אַמָּה, וּמֵעִיקָּרוֹ לְבֵיתוֹ אַלְפַּיִם אַמָּה. נִמְצָא מְהַלֵּךְ מִשֶּׁחֲשֵׁיכָה ד' אֲלָפִים אַמָּה".§
אָמַר

ומר סבר לקרבן גדול מכוין. הקשה הר"ר אפרים: ל"ל לפרושי טעמא דר' יוחנן משום דלקרבן גדול קמכוין? תיפוק ליה דר"י לית ליה ברירה, דקסבר האחין שחלקו לקוחות הן, בפרק "מרובה" (ב"ק סט:)! ואומר ר"י: דלא שייך כאן ברירה, דלא צריכי לבירורן [א] דקדשי כל היכא דאיתנהו בתערובתן. וא"ת: והא צריך ארבע מהן ליתן לכהן לתרומת לחמי תודה! ואומר ר"י: דאם הן לבדן — יכול להפריש ד' מכל מ' ומ'. אבל אם כולן יחד — אי אפשר לתקן אם לא יפריש י"א מכל מין ומין דהא כל מין ומין, יש לו עשרה חולין ועשרה קדושות, ואז א"א שלא תהא אחת תרומה מן הקדושות:
כזה

וְר' יוֹחָנָן סָבַר לְקָרְבָּן גָּדוֹל מְכַוֵּין. וְהָא לָא אֶפְשָׁר. וְאַדְּאַרְבְּעִין מִינַּיְיהוּ לָא אָמְרִינַן דְּלִקַּדְשׁוּ, אֲבָל גַּבֵּי שְׁבִיתָה, כִּי אָמַר תַּחְתָּיו — מַאי אַחֲרָיוּת אִיכָּא? הַהוּא וַדַּאי לְכוּלְּהוּ אִיכַּוֵּין, וְאֵין שְׁבִיתָה אֶלָּא בְּד' לָא אָמְרִינַן לִקְנוּ לֵיהּ בְּד' מִינַּיְיהוּ: ל"ש. (דְּלָא אָמַר כְּלוּם) אַדְּרַב קָאֵי: י"ב אַמָּה. אוֹ יוֹתֵר, דְּאִיכָּא לְמֵימַר ד' דְּהַאי גִּיסָא אוֹ דְּהַאי גִּיסָא אוֹ מִילְעֵי, הִלְכָּךְ, לָא מְסַיְּימִי: אֲבָל בְּי"א הֲרֵי מִקְצָת בֵּיתוֹ נִיכָּר. יֵשׁ לְךָ לִבְרוֹר שִׁיעוּר שְׁבִיתָה בְּתוֹךְ י"א הַלָּלוּ, שֶׁעַל כָּרְחֲךָ מִקְצָת בֵּיתוֹ בְּתוֹכָם הוּא. וּמַאי נִינְהוּ — אַרְבַּע מְלִיעָתָא, דְּאִי בְּדִידְהוּ אָמַר — שַׁפִּיר, וְאִי בִּדְהַאי גִּיסָא אוֹ בִּדְהַאי גִּיסָא — הֲרֵי חֲלִי אַמָּה מֵאֵלּוּ וּמֵאֵלּוּ בְּתוֹכָם שֶׁל אֶמְצָעִיּוֹת, הִלְכָּךְ, הָוֵי סִיּוּמָא לִקְנוֹת בַּיִת. וּמִיהוּ, בָּא לִמְדּוֹד מִן הַצָּפוֹן — מוֹדְדִין לוֹ מִן הַדָּרוֹם כו': וּמִמַּאי דִּבְאַרְבְּעֵי מְצִיעֲתָא כו'. כְּלוֹמַר: מִי הִבְדִּיל לְךָ אֶמְצָעִיּוֹת מִתּוֹךְ הַשְּׁאָר, וּמַה בְּכָךְ אִם מִקְצָת בַּיִת נִיכָּר בָּהֶן? הֲרֵי י"ל: דְּהַאי גִּיסָא בָּחַר לֵיהּ, אוֹ דְּהַאי גִּיסָא בָּחַר לֵיהּ, וְאֵינוֹ יוֹדֵעַ אֶת אֵלּוּ. וְכֵיוָן דְּאִיכָּא לְסַפּוּקֵי בְּהָנֵי וּבְהָנֵי, וְאֵין אֵלּוּ נִבְלָעוֹת בְּאֵלּוּ — אֵין כָּאן סִיּוּם: ח' אַמּוֹת. דְּאִיכָּא לְמֵימַר דְּהַאי גִּיסָא בָּחַר, אוֹ דְּהַאי גִּיסָא וְלָא הָוֵי סִיּוּם: אֲבָל ז' אַמּוֹת. עַל כָּרְחֲךָ מִקְצָת בֵּיתוֹ נִיכָּר בְּאוֹתָהּ אַמָּה אֶמְצָעִית, דְּא"א שֶׁלֹּא בֵּירְרָהּ לוֹ(ב). וְאִי בְּאֶמְצַע הָאִילָן בָּחַר לֵיהּ ד"א — הֲרֵי הִיא מֵהֶן וְאִי מֵהַאי גִּיסָא [אוֹ מֵהַאי גִּיסָא] — הֲרֵי הִיא מֵהֶן. הִלְכָּךְ, קָנָה שָׁם בַּיִת, וּמִיהוּ בָּא לִמְדּוֹד כו': שְׁבִיתָתִי בְּמָקוֹם פְּלוֹנִי. כִּדְמְפָרֵשׁ וְאָזֵיל שֶׁהָיָה אוֹתוֹ מָקוֹם מוּקָּף מְחִיצּוֹת, וְרָאוּי לִהְיוֹת כּוּלּוֹ כְּד' אַמּוֹת. הִלְכָּךְ, לָא צָרִיךְ לְסַיּוּמֵי בֵּיהּ ד"א, דְּכוּלֵּיהּ כְּד"א, וּמְהַלֵּךְ אֶת כּוּלּוֹ וְחוּצָה לוֹ אַלְפַּיִם אַמָּה: בד"א. דִּמְהַלֵּךְ אֶת כּוּלּוֹ לְבַד מֵאַלְפַּיִם שֶׁחוּצָה לוֹ: בְּמָקוֹם הַמְסוּיָּים. שֶׁמְּיוּחָד וְחָלוּק מִשְּׁאָר הַבִּקְעָה שֶׁיֵּשׁ לוֹ מְחִיצּוֹת, וְהוּא מד"א עַד בֵּית סָאתַיִם. דִּבְצִיר מֵהַאי מַאי מְהַלֵּךְ אֶת כּוּלּוֹ אִיכָּא? בְּלָאו מְחִיצּוֹת נַמִי ד' קָנֵי לֵיהּ לִשְׁבִיתָה. וְאִם יוֹתֵר מִבֵּית סָאתַיִם, הוֹאִיל וְלֹא הוּקַּף לְדִירָה — לָא מְהַנְיָין לֵיהּ מְחִיצּוֹת לְשַׁוְּייֵהּ כְּד"א: אֲבָל מָקוֹם שֶׁאֵינוֹ מְסוּיָּים. כְּלוֹמַר: שֶׁאֵינוֹ כּוּלּוֹ רְשׁוּת אַחַת שֶׁל ד"א, כְּגוֹן שֶׁאֵין לוֹ מְחִיצּוֹת, אוֹ שֶׁיֶּשְׁנוֹ יוֹתֵר מִב' סָאתַיִם: אֵין לוֹ. בְּתוֹכוֹ אֶלָּא ד"א לְבַד מֵאַלְפַּיִם מִשָּׁם וָהָלְאָה, וּבָעֵי לְסַיּוּמֵי בֵּיהּ הֵי מִינַּיְיהוּ, כִּדְמְפָרֵשׁ וְאָזֵיל לְקַמָּן. וְכִי מְסַיֵּים לְהוּ קָנֵי לְהוּ, וּמְהַלֵּךְ מִשָּׁם וָהָלְאָה אַלְפַּיִם אַמָּה. וְתוֹךְ מְחִיצּוֹת עוֹלֶה לוֹ מִן הַמִּנְיָן: בד"א. דִּבְמָקוֹם שֶׁאֵינוֹ מְסוּיָּים קָנֵי לֵיהּ מִיהָא ד"א לִשְׁבִיתָה, וְאַלְפַּיִם מֵהֶן לְכָל רוּחַ: בִּמְסַיֵּים ד"א. שֶׁקָּבַע(ג) בְּד' בָּהֶן, שֶׁהָיָה לוֹ בָּהֶן סִימָן אִילָן אוֹ אֶבֶן, וְאָמַר בְּאוֹתָן ד' תְּהֵא שְׁבִיתָתִי: לֹא יָזוּז מִמְּקוֹמוֹ. אֲפִילּוּ פְּסִיעָה אַחַת מד"א שֶׁל מְקוֹם רַגְלָיו, דְּאֵין לוֹ שְׁבִיתָה לֹא כָּאן וְלֹא כָּאן. דִּבִמְקוֹם רַגְלָיו לֹא רָצָה לִקְנוֹת, וְכָאן שֶׁרָצָה — לֹא סִיֵּים, וְהַיְינוּ כְּרַב: הָכָא בְּמַאי עָסְקִינַן. דְּקָתָנֵי "לֹא יָזוּז" כְּגוֹן דְּאִיכָּא מִמְּקוֹם רַגְלָיו עַד עִיקָּרוֹ תְּרֵי אַלְפֵי וְד' גַּרְמִידֵי, תְּרֵי אַלְפֵי לִתְחוּמָא וְד' לִשְׁבִיתָה כּוּלָּן כָּלִין מִמְּקוֹם רַגְלָיו וְעַד עִיקָּרוֹ, וַעֲדַיִין נוֹף דְּאִידָךְ גִּיסָא דְּאִילָן נוֹטֶה חוּץ לְכוּלָּן: דְּאִי מוֹקְמַתְּ לֵיהּ בְּאִידָךְ גִּיסָא דְּאִילָן קָם לֵיהּ לְבַר מִתְּחוּמָא. שֶׁאִם אַתָּה נוֹתֵן לוֹ שְׁבִיתָה תַּחַת הַנּוֹף שֶׁבָּעֵבֶר הַשֵּׁנִי — נִמְצָא מְקוֹם רַגְלָיו שֶׁהָיָה עוֹמֵד שָׁם בְּשָׁעָה שֶׁחָשְׁכָה לוֹ חוּץ לִתְחוּמוֹ, שֶׁהֲרֵי רָחוֹק מִמְּקוֹם שְׁבִיתָתוֹ יוֹתֵר מֵאַלְפַּיִם וְד"א. הִלְכָּךְ, סִיֵּים לוֹ ד"א בְּצַד זֶה שֶׁל אִילָן — מָצֵי אָזֵיל שַׁפִּיר, אֲבָל לֹא סִיֵּים לוֹ — י"ל בָּעֵבֶר הַשֵּׁנִי בָּחַר, וַהֲרֵי הוּא עַכְשָׁיו חוּץ לִתְחוּמוֹ, וְאֵין לוֹ אֶלָּא ד"א. וְכִי אָמַר שְׁמוּאֵל דְּלִיקְנֵי שְׁבִיתָה תַּחַת הָאִילָן אע"ג דְּלֹא סִיֵּים וּמָצֵי אָזֵיל — כְּגוֹן שֶׁכָּל תַּחְתָּיו שֶׁל אִילָן בְּתוֹךְ אַלְפַּיִם וְד"א, דְּכָל ד' דִּיהָבַתְּ לֵיהּ לִשְׁבִיתָה תַּחְתָּיו מָטֵי תְּחוּמַיְיהוּ עַד מְקוֹם רַגְלָיו, הִלְכָּךְ, שְׁבִיתָה קָנָה לוֹ שָׁם, אֲבָל אֵינוֹ יוֹדֵעַ אִם בִּצְפוֹנוֹ אוֹ בִּדְרוֹמוֹ, וּלְפִיכָךְ יָדוֹ עַל הַתַּחְתּוֹנָה, בָּא לִמְדּוֹד מִצְּפוֹנוֹ שֶׁל אִילָן לְצַד בֵּיתוֹ אַלְפַּיִם — מוֹדְדִין לוֹ מִדְּרוֹמוֹ, וּמְקַצְּרִין לוֹ(ד) כָּל תְּחוּמוֹ כָּל שִׁיעוּר תַּחְתָּיו שֶׁל אִילָן, וְלֹא יַגִּיעַ לְבֵיתוֹ. בָּא לִמְדּוֹד מִן הַדָּרוֹם שֶׁל אִילָן וְלַחֲזוֹר לַאֲחוֹרָיו מִמְּקוֹם רַגְלָיו כְּמִדַּת תַּחְתָּיו שֶׁל אִילָן — מוֹדְדִין לוֹ מִצְּפוֹנוֹ שֶׁל אִילָן, וְכָלָה הַתְּחוּם בִּמְקוֹם רַגְלָיו: טָעָה וְעֵירֵב לְב' רוּחוֹת. לַדָּרוֹם וְלַצָּפוֹן: כִּמְדוּמֶּה(ה) הוּא. שֶׁמּוּתָּר לַעֲשׂוֹת כֵּן, וְלֵילֵךְ שַׁחֲרִית כָּאן וְעַרְבִית כָּאן. וְכֵיוָן שֶׁנִּתְכַּוֵּין לִשְׁתֵּיהֶן, וְהָאַחַת הוּא דְּקָנְתָה לוֹ, וְאֵינוֹ יוֹדֵעַ אֵיזוֹ הִיא — נוֹתְנִין עָלָיו חוּמְרֵי זוֹ וְחוּמְרֵי זוֹ: מְהַלֵּךְ לַצָּפוֹן כְּעֵירוּבוֹ לַדָּרוֹם וְלַדָּרוֹם כְּעֵירוּבוֹ לַצָּפוֹן. מְהַלֵּךְ לְבֵיתוֹ לַצָּפוֹן כְּשִׁיעוּר תְּחוּם שֶׁמַּנִּיחַ לוֹ עֵירוּבוֹ שֶׁל דָּרוֹם לְצַד צָפוֹן, וּמְהַלֵּךְ לַדָּרוֹם מִבֵּיתוֹ כְּשִׁיעוּר תְּחוּם שֶׁמַּנִּיחַ לוֹ עֵירוּב שֶׁל צָפוֹן לְצַד דָּרוֹם. כְּגוֹן: אִם לֹא הוּצְרַךְ לָלֶכֶת אֶלָּא ג' אֲלָפִים לְכָאן וְג' אֲלָפִים לְכָאן, וְהִנִּיחַ עֵירוּב בְּסוֹף אֶלֶף אַמָּה לְכָאן וּבְסוֹף אֶלֶף אַמָּה לְכָאן, דְּלֶיהֱוֵי לֵיהּ מִמְּקוֹם עֵירוּבוֹ אַלְפַּיִם — מוּתָּר לֵילֵךְ אֶלֶף אַמָּה מִבֵּיתוֹ לְכָאן וּלְכָאן. דְּמֵעֵירוּבוֹ יֵשׁ לוֹ אַלְפַּיִם אַמָּה לְכָל רוּחַ, הִלְכָּךְ, אַלְפַּיִם שֶׁיֵּשׁ לוֹ לַצָּפוֹן מֵעֵירוּבוֹ שֶׁבַּדָּרוֹם כָּלוֹת לוֹ לְסוֹף אֶלֶף לִצְפוֹן בֵּיתוֹ, וְאַלְפַּיִם שֶׁיֵּשׁ לוֹ לַדָּרוֹם מֵעֵירוּבוֹ שֶׁבַּצָּפוֹן כָּלוֹת לוֹ לְסוֹף אֶלֶף אַמָּה לִדְרוֹם בֵּיתוֹ: וְאִם מִיצְּעוּ עָלָיו אֶת הַתְּחוּם. עָלָיו = בִּשְׁבִילוֹ, מִילְּאוּ הַתְּחוּם, שֶׁהִנִּיחַ כָּל אֶחָד עֵירוּב לְסוֹף אַלְפַּיִם, דְּהַשְׁתָּא הֲוָה לֵיהּ עֵירוּב [עִירוֹ] בְּאֶמְצַע ב' תְּחוּמִין, תְּחוּם שָׁלֵם מִן הַמַּעֲרָב לְבֵיתוֹ וּתְחוּם שָׁלֵם מִן הַמִּזְרָח, דְּנִתְכַּוְּונוּ לִקְנוֹת מִן הָעֵירוּב אַלְפַּיִם וָהָלְאָה: לֹא יָזוּז מִמְּקוֹמוֹ. מִבֵּיתוֹ, וַאֲפִילּוּ כִּבְנֵי עִירוֹ אֵינוֹ — דְּהָא לֹא נִתְכַּוֵּין לִקְנוֹת שְׁבִיתָה אֶלָּא בִּמְקוֹם הָעֵירוּבִין, וְאֵינוֹ יוֹדֵעַ אֵי זֶה מֵהֶן קָנָה. זֶה עֵירוּב הַדָּרוֹם מַפְסִידוֹ אַלְפַּיִם שֶׁל צָפוֹן, וְזֶה עֵירוּב הַצָּפוֹן מַפְסִידוֹ אַלְפַּיִם שֶׁל דָּרוֹם. קָתָנֵי מִיהַת: מְהַלֵּךְ לַצָּפוֹן כְּעֵירוּבוֹ לַדָּרוֹם, אַלְמָא: הֵיכָא דְּמִסְתַּפְּקָא לָן בְּהֵי נִיחָא לֵיהּ — תָּלִינַן בְּתַרְוַיְיהוּ לְחוּמְרָא. וּמִיהוּ, בְּמַאי דִּשְׁבָקוֹ שָׁרֵי לֵיהּ לְמֵיזַל. וְאע"ג דְּלֹא סִיֵּים בְּהֵי נִיחָא לֵיהּ. וְהַיְינוּ כִּשְׁמוּאֵל, דְּאָמַר: הֵיכָא דְּמִסְתַּפְּקָא לָן בְּהֵי ד"א דְּאִילָן קָנָה שְׁבִיתָה חוּמְרֵי דְּתַרְוַיְיהוּ יָהֲבִינַן לֵיהּ: לֵימָא תֶּיהֱוֵי תְּיוּבְתֵּיהּ דְּרַב. דְּאָמַר: הֵיכָא דְּלֹא סִיֵּים לֹא יָזוּז מִמְּקוֹמוֹ, דִּבִמְקוֹם רַגְלָיו לֹא רָצָה לִקְנוֹת, וְתַחַת הָאִילָן הוֹאִיל וְאִיכָּא לְמֵימַר הָכִי וְאִיכָּא לְמֵימַר הָכִי — לֹא קָנָה לָא הָנֵי וְלָא הָנֵי, דְּהָא הָכָא אָמְרִינַן אַף עַל גַּב דְּאִיכָּא לְמֵימַר הָכִי וְאִיכָּא לְמֵימַר הָכִי — קָנָה בְּאֶחָד מִן הָעֵירוּבִין, וּמוּתָּר לְהַלֵּךְ בְּמָקוֹם שֶׁבִּשְׁנֵיהֶם נוֹתְנִים לוֹ, דְּאִי לְרַב, אֲפִילּוּ לֹא מִילְּאוּ אֶת הַתְּחוּם — לֹא יָזוּז מִמְּקוֹמוֹ. דִּבְבֵיתוֹ לֹא רָצָה לִקְנוֹת, וּבִשְׁבִיתוֹת הָעֵירוּבִין לָא סִיֵּים בְּהֵי נִיחָא לֵיהּ. וְלָשׁוֹן שֶׁשָּׁמַעְתִּי קַשְׁיָא לִי: מַאי דּוֹחְקֵיהּ לְמֵימַר "רַב תַּנָּא הוּא וּפָלֵיג"? מִכְּדֵי פְּלוּגְתַּיְיהוּ דְּרַב וּשְׁמוּאֵל בְּמַאי דְּרַב סָבַר לֹא קָנָה לוֹ מְקוֹם רַגְלָיו וְלֹא תַּחַת הָאִילָן, וְלִשְׁמוּאֵל קָנָה אוֹ מְקוֹם רַגְלָיו אוֹ תַּחַת הָאִילָן, וּמוֹתְבִינַן לְרַב מֵהָא דְּקָתָנֵי דְּקָנָה אוֹ לַצָּפוֹן אוֹ לַדָּרוֹם, וּמְהַלֵּךְ כְּרַגְלֵי שְׁנֵיהֶן. מִי דָּמְיָא הָא לִדְרַב? הָכָא אִיכַּוֵּין לְתַרְוַיְיהוּ. וְגַבֵּי עֲבָדִים נַמִי — תַּרְוַיְיהוּ שְׁלִיחוּתַיְיהוּ עֲבוּד, וּבִשְׁתֵּי שְׁבִיתוֹת אִי אֶפְשָׁר. מִיהוּ, חֲדָא מִינַּיְיהוּ קָנְיָא, וּמִדְּלָא יָדִיעַ הֵי קָנְיָא — נוֹתְנִין חוּמְרֵי שְׁתֵּיהֶן עָלָיו, וְאִידָךְ שָׁרֵי מִמָּה נַפְשָׁךְ. אֲבָל הָתָם — בִּמְקוֹמוֹ לֹא רָצָה לִקְנוֹת, וְתַחַת הָאִילָן סָבַר רַב דְּכֵיוָן דְּלֹא סִיֵּים לָאו קְנִיָּיה הִיא, הִלְכָּךְ, אֵין לוֹ שְׁבִיתָה כְּלָל. וא"ת: הַיְינוּ תְּיוּבְתֵּיהּ, אַמַּאי לָא קָנֵי הָתָם תַּחַת הָאִילָן אוֹ אַרְבַּע צְפוֹנִיּוֹת אוֹ אַרְבַּע דְּרוֹמִיּוֹת, וְלֵיתִיב עֲלֵיהּ חוּמְרֵי תַּרְוַיְיהוּ וְאִידָךְ לִישְׁתְּרֵי מִמָּה נַפְשָׁךְ. אִם כֵּן — לִשְׁמוּאֵל נַמִי הָוְיָא תְּיוּבְתֵּיהּ, דְּהָא מְפָרֵשׁ בְּהַהוּא לִישָּׁנָא דְּלִשְׁמוּאֵל אֵין לוֹ מִן הָאִילָן וָהָלְאָה כְּלוּם, וְאַמַּאי? מִמָּה נַפְשָׁךְ, מִתְּחִילַּת אִילָן לְצַד רַגְלָיו לֵיתִיב לֵיהּ אַלְפַּיִם לְצַד בֵּיתוֹ:
וְהוּא

רבינו חננאל

אמר אביי לא שנו אלא באילן שיש תחתיו י"ב אמה שיש לומר כל ד' אמות מקום בפ"ע ואינו מסיים איזהו אבל באילן שתחתיו י"א אמה הרי מקצת ביתו ניכר כיון שאין תחת האילן שיעור ג' בתים ד' אמות לכל בית יש לומר ד' אמות שבאמצע הן מקום שביתתו ואם תתן לו מקום שביתה באמצע הרי כל ביתו ניכר אלא אם תנוח ד' אמות מצד אחד ותתן לו הז' אמות שנשארו (תתן לו) אם ד' אמצעיות תתן לו נשארו ג' החיצונות. ואם ד' החיצונות תתן לו נשארו באמצע ג' אמות מכל פנים נמצאת אמה אחת מכל בית. ודחינן ממאי דמד' מציעתא קא מסיים ולא אפשר דלא מינכר מקצת בייתיה דלמא מארבעי דבצפון או דארבעי דבדרום קא מסיים אבל במיצעי כלל לא דליכא מקצת ביתו ניכר. ואסיקנא לא שנו [אלא] באילן שתחתיו ח' אמות אבל באילן שתחתיו ז' אמות כיון דבית שביתתו לא פחות מד' אמות בין מצד אחד ובין מצד אחר אתה מודד לו ד' אמות אמה אחת מביתו ודאי ניכר תניא כוותיה דרב מי שהיה בדרך והיה מכיר אילן או גדר כו'. עד בד"א שסיים ד' אמות שקבע אבל לא סיים ד' אמות שקבע הרי זה לא יזוז ממקומו. לימא תהוי תיובתא דשמואל ומוקים שמואל להא ברייתא כגון דהוי ממקום רגליו ועד עיקר האילן תרי אלפי גרמידי וד' גרמידי וכיון דאמר שביתתי תחת האילן והוא ממקום רגליו ועד עיקר האילן אלפים וד' אמות נמצאו ד' אמות שתחת האילן חוץ לתחומו ואין אדם קונה שביתה חוץ לתחומו לפיכך אין לו אלא ד' אמות (דתניא) [והא דתניא] הגיע לאותו מקום מהלך את כולו וחוצה לו אלפים אמה אימתי בזמן שהוא בתוך אלפים אמות שלו אבל אם היה אותו מקום חוץ לאלפים אמה שלו אין לו אלא ד' אמות שהוא עומד בהן אבל (הן) [אם היו] ממקום רגליו ועד עיקרו של אילן אלפים מכוונות מהלך את כולן עד שמגיע תחת האילן ונעשה שם חמר גמל דהא לא סיים מקום שביתתו ויש לומר שבאותן ד' אמות שהיה עומד בהן מבעו"י שהן עכשיו לו לאלפים אמות בהו קנה שביתה ועכשיו יצא חוץ לתחום ואין לו אלא ד' אמות בלבד. תניא כוותיה דשמואל טעה ועירב לב' רוחות כמדומה שמערבין לב' רוחות או שאמר לעבדיו צאו ועירבו עלי אחד עירב לו לצפון ואחד עירב לו לדרום מהלך בצפון כרגלי מי שעירב עליו לדרום וכו'. הנה טעה ועירב לב' רוחות דומה לזה שטעה ועירב ברגליו לקנות שביתה תחת האילן ולא קתני לא יזוז ממקומו אלא אומר מהלך בצפון כרגלי מי שעירב עליו לדרום כשמואל דאמר מהלך אלפים אמה קשיא לרב. ופרקינן רב תנא הוא וחולק תנא על תנא. ונתברר לדברי רב כי אם יש תחת האילן מז' אמות ולמטה כיון שיש לו מכללם ד' אמות מכל פנים מקצת ביתו ניכר שקנה שביתה והוא כגון תל גבוה עשרה טפחים שהוא מד' אמות ועד בית סאתים או נקע עמוק י' טפחים וכל מי שאין שביתתו ידוע סבר שאין לו מד' אמות שלו [כלום]. פי' מיצעו עליו את התחום. כגון שערבו לו בתוך אלפים שבצפון והעתיקו ממנו האלפים אמה שהיה לו בדרום ונתנום לו האלפים שבצפון לילך בצפון ד' אלפים ולא נשאר לו בדרום כלום נמצא אסור בכל הדרום. וכן עוד עירב עליו כענין הזה שפירשנו בדרום ולא השאיר לו (בדרום) [בצפון] כלום נמצא עירובו ספק כאן וספק כאן ואסור בצפון ובדרום שכשיבא לילך בצפון אומר לו עירובו בדרום ואין לו בצפון כלום וכשיבא בדרום דוחין אותו ואומר עירובו בצפון לפיכך לא יזוז ממקומו אבל אם נתנו עירובו בתוך אלפים מהלך בצפון כשיעור המקום שנתנו

רש"ל מ"ז

הגהות הב"ח

(א) גמ' כמדומה היה שמערבין: (ב) רש"י ד"ה אבל ז' וכו' שלא בירירה לו לאי באמצע: (ג) ד"ה במסיים ד' אמות שקבע בהן כצ"ל ותיבת כד' נמחק: (ד) ד"ה דאי מוקמת וכו' ומקצרין כל תחומו כצ"ל ותיבת לו נמחק: (ה) ד"ה כמדומה היה שמותר:

[לקמן נא.]

ביצה לז: ע"ש

[כתובות ח. גיטין לח: ב"ב מב. סנהדרין פג: חולין קכב:]

הגהות מהר"ב רנשבורג

[א] תוס' ד"ה ומר סבר וכו' ואומר ר"י וכו' לבירורן. עי' מנחות עח ע"ב תוס' ד"ה ליקדשו וכו' ודו"ק:

אָמַר רָבָא: [א]וְהוּא דְּכִי רָהֵיט לְעִיקָּרוֹ מָטֵי. א"ל אַבַּיֵי: וְהָא חָשְׁכָה לוֹ קָתָנֵי! חָשְׁכָה לְבֵיתוֹ, אֲבָל לְעִיקָּרוֹ שֶׁל אִילָן מָצֵי אָזֵיל. אִיכָּא דְּאָמְרִי, אָמַר רָבָא: חָשְׁכָה לוֹ — כִּי מַסְגֵּי קַלֵּי קַלֵּי, אֲבָל רָהֵיט — מָטֵי. רַבָּה וְרַב יוֹסֵף הָווּ קָא אָזְלִי בְּאוֹרְחָא. א"ל רַבָּה לְרַב יוֹסֵף: תְּהֵא שְׁבִיתָתֵנוּ תּוּתֵי דִּיקְלָא דְּסָבֵיל אֲחוּהּ, וְאָמְרִי לָהּ: תּוּתֵי דִּיקְלָא דְּפָרֵיק מָרֵיהּ מִכַּרְגָּא. יָדַע לֵיהּ מָר? א"ל: לָא יָדַעְנָא לֵיהּ. אֲמַר לֵיהּ: סְמוֹךְ עָלַי. דְּתַנְיָא, רַבִּי יוֹסֵי אוֹמֵר: *אִם הָיוּ שְׁנַיִם, אֶחָד מַכִּיר וְאֶחָד שֶׁאֵינוֹ מַכִּיר — זֶה שֶׁאֵינוֹ מַכִּיר מוֹסֵר שְׁבִיתָתוֹ לַמַּכִּיר, זֶה שֶׁמַּכִּיר אוֹמֵר "תְּהֵא שְׁבִיתָתֵנוּ בְּמָקוֹם פְּלוֹנִי". וְלָא הִיא, לָא תְּנָא לֵיהּ *כְּר' יוֹסֵי אֶלָּא כִּי הֵיכִי *דְּלִיקַבֵּל לָהּ מִינֵּיהּ, מִשּׁוּם דְּר' יוֹסֵי נִימוּקוֹ עִמּוֹ.§ "אִם אֵינוֹ מַכִּיר אוֹ שֶׁאֵינוֹ בָּקִי וְכוּ'".§ הָנֵי אַלְפַּיִם אַמָּה הֵיכָן כְּתִיבָן? דְּתַנְיָא: (שמות טז) °"שְׁבוּ אִישׁ תַּחְתָּיו" — אֵלּוּ אַרְבַּע אַמּוֹת, "אַל יֵצֵא אִישׁ מִמְּקוֹמוֹ" — אֵלּוּ אַלְפַּיִם אַמָּה. מְנָא לָן? אָמַר רַב חִסְדָּא: לָמַדְנוּ מָקוֹם מִמָּקוֹם, וּמָקוֹם מִנִּיסָה, וְנִיסָה מִנִּיסָה, וְנִיסָה מִגְּבוּל, וּגְבוּל מִגְּבוּל, וּגְבוּל מִחוּץ, וְחוּץ מִחוּץ. דִּכְתִיב: (במדבר לה) °"וּמַדּוֹתֶם מִחוּץ לָעִיר אֶת פְּאַת קֵדְמָה אַלְפַּיִם בָּאַמָּה וגו'". (שם) וְנֵילַף °"מִקִּיר הָעִיר וָחוּצָה אֶלֶף אַמָּה"! דָּנִין "חוּץ" מֵ"חוּץ" וְאֵין דָּנִין "חוּץ" מֵ"חוּצָה". וּמַאי נָפְקָא מִינָּהּ? *הָא תָּנָא דְּבֵי רַבִּי יִשְׁמָעֵאל: (ויקרא יד) °"וְשָׁב הַכֹּהֵן" (שם) °"וּבָא הַכֹּהֵן" — זוֹ הִיא שִׁיבָה זוֹ הִיא בִּיאָה! הָנֵי מִילֵּי — הֵיכָא דְּלֵיכָּא מִידֵּי דְּדָמֵי לֵיהּ, אֲבָל הֵיכָא דְּאִיכָּא מִידֵּי דְּדָמֵי לֵיהּ — מִדְּדָמֵי לֵיהּ יָלְפִינַן.§ "אַלְפַּיִם אַמָּה עֲגוּלוֹת".§ וְרַבִּי חֲנִינָא בֶּן אַנְטִיגְנוֹס מַה נַּפְשָׁךְ, אִי אִית לֵיהּ ג"ש — פֵּיאוֹת כְּתִיבָן, אִי לֵית לֵיהּ גְּזֵירָה שָׁוָה — אַלְפַּיִם אַמָּה מְנָא לֵיהּ? (במדבר לה) לְעוֹלָם אִית לֵיהּ גְּזֵירָה שָׁוָה, וְשָׁאנֵי הָכָא דְּאָמַר קְרָא: °"זֶה יִהְיֶה לָהֶם מִגְרְשֵׁי הֶעָרִים" — לָזֶה אַתָּה נוֹתֵן פֵּיאוֹת, וְאִי אַתָּה נוֹתֵן פֵּיאוֹת לְשׁוֹבְתֵי שַׁבָּת. וְרַבָּנַן? תָּנֵי, רַב חֲנַנְיָה אוֹמֵר: כָּזֶה יְהוּ כָּל שׁוֹבְתֵי שַׁבָּת. א"ר אַחָא בַּר יַעֲקֹב: [ב]הַמַּעֲבִיר ד"א בִּרה"ר — אֵינוֹ חַיָּיב עַד שֶׁמַּעֲבִיר הֵן וַאֲלַכְסוֹנָן. א"ר פַּפָּא, *בָּדֵיק לָן רָבָא; עַמּוּד בִּרה"ר גָּבוֹהַּ י' וְרוֹחַב ד', צָרִיךְ הֵן וַאֲלַכְסוֹנָן, אוֹ לֹא? וְאָמְרִינַן לֵיהּ: לָאו הַיְינוּ דְּרַב חֲנַנְיָה? דְּתַנְיָא, רַב חֲנַנְיָה אוֹמֵר: כָּזֶה יְהוּ כָּל שׁוֹבְתֵי שַׁבָּת.§ "וְזֶה הוּא שֶׁאָמְרוּ הֶעָנִי מְעָרֵב בְּרַגְלָיו. אָמַר ר' מֵאִיר: אָנוּ אֵין לָנוּ אֶלָּא עָנִי וכו'".§ אָמַר רַב נַחְמָן: מַחֲלוֹקֶת בִּ"מְקוֹמִי", דְּר"מ סָבַר: עִיקַּר עֵירוּב בְּפַת, עָנִי

רש"י

וְהוּא דְּכִי רָהֵיט מָטֵי. הָא דְּקָתָנֵי מַתְנִי' דְּאִם סִיֵּים קָנָה שְׁבִיתָה בְּעִיקָּרוֹ הוּא דְּכִי הֲוָה רָהֵיט מָטֵי הָתָם קוֹדֶם שֶׁתֶּחְשַׁךְ – הָתָם מְהַנְּיָא אֲמִירָה. וְאִי קָנֵי הָתָם מָצֵי לְמֵיזַל לְבֵיתוֹ בְּנַחַת: חָשְׁכָה *לוֹ. [נ"ל לביתו] לֵילֵךְ עַד בֵּיתוֹ אֲפִילּוּ בִּמְרוּצָה אֲבָל לְעִיקָּרוֹ הֲוָה מָטֵי בִּמְרוּצָה אִי הֲוָה רָהֵיט: מַסְגֵּי קַלֵּי. הוֹלֵךְ מְעַט מְעַט: דְּסָבֵיל אֲחוּהּ. אִילָן אַחֵר הָיָה נִסְמָךְ עָלָיו: דְּפָרֵיק מָרֵיהּ מִכַּרְגָּא. טוֹעֵן פֵּירוֹת הַרְבֵּה וּמוֹכְרָן, וּפוֹרֵעַ מֵהֶן הַמַּס: לָא יָדַעְנָא לֵיהּ. אֵינִי מַכִּיר אוֹתוֹ אִילָן: מוֹסֵר שְׁבִיתָתוֹ לַמַּכִּיר. אוֹמֵר שְׁבִיתָתִי עִמְּךָ: וְלָא הִיא. הָא דְּאָמַר לֵיהּ מִשְּׁמֵיהּ דְּר' יוֹסֵי לֵיתָא, דְּלָא תַּנְיָא לֵיהּ בְּשֵׁם ר' יוֹסֵי אֶלָּא סְתָמָא תַּנְיָא לֵיהּ לְעֵיל, וּמִשּׁוּם הָכִי אֲמָרָהּ בְּשֵׁם ר' יוֹסֵי כִּי הֵיכִי דְּלִיקַבְּלָהּ מִינֵּיהּ: ה"ג: וְלָא הִיא לָא תַּנְיָא לֵיהּ כְּדְר' יוֹסֵי: נִימּוּקוֹ עִמּוֹ. טַעְמוֹ. בְּמַסֶּכֶת גִּיטִּין (דף סז.) מוֹנֶה שִׁבְחָן שֶׁל חֲכָמִים – וְאָמַר: ר"י נִימּוּקוֹ עִמּוֹ. נִים וְקוֹ – דָּבָר יָשָׁר כְּקַו הַמִּשְׁקוֹלֶת: אֵלּוּ ד' אַמּוֹת. לַיּוֹצֵא חוּץ לַתְּחוּם: מָקוֹם מִמָּקוֹם וּמָקוֹם מִנִּיסָה. פָּסוּק שֶׁנֶּאֱמַר בּוֹ מָקוֹם וְלֹא נֶאֱמַר בּוֹ נִיסָה, דָּנִין אוֹתוֹ מִפָּסוּק אַחֵר שֶׁנֶּאֱמַר בּוֹ מָקוֹם וְנִיסָה. כְּגוֹן "אַל יֵצֵא אִישׁ מִמְּקוֹמוֹ" דָּנִין מִ"וְשַׂמְתִּי לְךָ מָקוֹם אֲשֶׁר יָנוּס שָׁמָּה", מַה לְהַלָּן כְּתִיב נִיסָה "אֲשֶׁר יָנוּס", אַף מִקְרָא דְּ"אַל יֵצֵא אִישׁ מִמְּקוֹמוֹ" מְרַבֵּי בֵּיהּ נִיסָה, וַהֲוֵי כְּמַאן דִּכְתִיב בֵּיהּ נִיסָה. וַהֲדַר דָּנִין נִיסָה מִנִּיסָה, וְנִיסָה מִגְּבוּל. כְּלוֹמַר: דָּנִין נִיסָה זוֹ שֶׁלֹּא נֶאֱמַר בּוֹ גְּבוּל, מִנִּיסָה שֶׁנֶּאֱמַר בּוֹ גְּבוּל. דִּכְתִיב מִ"גְּבוּל עִיר מִקְלָטוֹ אֲשֶׁר יָנוּס" וּמְרַבִּינַן נַמִי בְּאִידָךְ נִיסָה דְּ"אַל יֵצֵא אִישׁ מִמְּקוֹמוֹ" כְּאִילּוּ כְּתִיב בֵּיהּ גְּבוּל. וַהֲדַר דָּנִין גְּבוּל מִגְּבוּל וּגְבוּל מִחוּץ, דָּנִין גְּבוּל זֶה שֶׁלֹּא נֶאֱמַר בּוֹ חוּץ, מִגְּבוּל שֶׁנֶּאֱמַר בּוֹ חוּץ, שֶׁנֶּאֱמַר: "וּמָצָא אוֹתוֹ גּוֹאֵל הַדָּם מִחוּץ לִגְבוּל". וּמְרַבִּינַן חוּץ מִג"ש לְהַאי גְּבוּל דְּ"אַל יֵצֵא אִישׁ מִמְּקוֹמוֹ", וַהֲדַר דָּנִין הַאי חוּץ מִחוּץ דְּ"וּמַדּוֹתֶם מִחוּץ לָעִיר" דִּכְתִיב בֵּיהּ: "אַלְפַּיִם בָּאַמָּה": וְשָׁב הַכֹּהֵן וּבָא הַכֹּהֵן. בְּתוֹרַת כֹּהֲנִים שְׁנוּיָה בְּנִגְעֵי בָּתִּים. בַּשָּׁבוּעַ שֶׁל הֶסְגֵּר רִאשׁוֹן כְּתִיב: "וְשָׁב הַכֹּהֵן בַּיּוֹם הַשְּׁבִיעִי וְרָאָה וְהִנֵּה פָּשָׂה הַנֶּגַע בְּקִירוֹת הַבָּיִת", וּכְתִיב בַּתְרֵיהּ: "וְחִלְּצוּ אֶת הָאֲבָנִים וְאֶת הַבַּיִת יַקְצִיעַ מִבַּיִת" "יִקְצוּ עֲפַר הַבַּיִת סָבִיב הַקִּיר" "וְעָפָר אַחֵר יִקַּח וְטָח אֶת הַבָּיִת". וּכְתִיב: "וְאִם יָשׁוּב הַנֶּגַע וּפָרַח בַּבַּיִת וגו' וְנָתַץ אֶת הַבַּיִת". וְתַנְיָא: "וּפָרַח", יָכוֹל לֹא יְהֵא טָמֵא עַד שֶׁיַּחֲזוֹר וְיִפְשֶׂה – ת"ל: "צָרַעַת מַמְאֶרֶת" "צָרַעַת מַמְאֶרֶת" לְג"ש, מַה צָּרַעַת מַמְאֶרֶת הָאֲמוּרָה בִּבְגָדִים – טִימֵּא אֶת הַחוֹזֵר אע"פ שֶׁאֵינוֹ פּוֹשֶׂה, אַף צָרַעַת מַמְאֶרֶת הָאֲמוּרָה בְּבָתִּים – טִימֵּא אֶת הַחוֹזֵר אע"פ שֶׁאֵינוֹ פּוֹשֶׂה. יָכוֹל חָזַר וּפָרַח בּוֹ בַּיּוֹם יְהֵא טָמֵא – נֶאֱמַר: "וְשָׁב הַכֹּהֵן" וְנֶאֱמַר: "וְאִם יָשׁוּב הַנֶּגַע", מַה שִּׁיבָה הָאֲמוּרָה לְהַלָּן – בְּסוֹף שָׁבוּעַ, אַף שִׁיבָה הָאֲמוּרָה כָּאן – בְּסוֹף שָׁבוּעַ. לָמַדְנוּ שֶׁנּוֹתֵן לוֹ שָׁבוּעַ אַחַר הַחֲלִיצָה וּקְצִיָּה וּטִיחָה, אִם חָזַר הַנֶּגַע – נוֹתְצוֹ, וְאִם לֹא חָזַר – מְטַהֲרוֹ. אֵין לִי אֶלָּא חוֹלֵץ וְקוֹצֶה וְטָח וְנוֹתֵן שָׁבוּעַ אֶלָּא בְּפוֹשֶׂה בַּשָּׁבוּעַ שֶׁל הֶסְגֵּר רִאשׁוֹן, מִנַּיִין לְנֶגַע שֶׁעָמַד בְּעֵינָיו בָּרִאשׁוֹן שֶׁלֹּא פָּשָׂה, וְהַכֹּהֵן לֹא חָלַץ, וְלֹא קָצָה וְלֹא טָח, וְהִמְתִּין שָׁבוּעַ שֵׁנִי וּפָשָׂה בַּשָּׁבוּעַ שֵׁנִי – מִנַּיִין שֶׁהוּא חוֹלֵץ וְקוֹצֶה וְטָח וְנוֹתֵן לוֹ שָׁבוּעַ וְאֵינוֹ נוֹתְצוֹ מִיָּד – ת"ל: "וּבָא הַכֹּהֵן(א) וְהִנֵּה פָּשָׂה וגו'". וְאע"ג דְּהַאי קְרָא בַּתְרֵיהּ דְּ"אִם יָשׁוּב הַנֶּגַע" כְּתִיב, דְּמַשְׁמַע דִּבְנֶגַע הַחוֹזֵר קָאֵי – מַפְּקִינַן לֵיהּ הָתָם מֵהַאי מַשְׁמָעוּת, וּמְרַבִּינַן נְתִיצָה לְנֶגַע הַחוֹזֵר וְאע"פ שֶׁלֹּא פָּשָׂה. וְהַאי "וּבָא הַכֹּהֵן וְרָאָה וְהִנֵּה פָּשָׂה" דְּמַשְׁמַע דְּבָעֵי פִּשְׂיוֹן – מוֹקְמִינַן לֵיהּ בְּנֶגַע שֶׁעָמַד בָּרִאשׁוֹן וּפָשָׂה בַּשֵּׁנִי. וְאע"ג דִּכְתִיב נְתִיצָה בַּתְרֵיהּ – יָלֵיף בִּג"ש, נֶאֱמַר כָּאן בְּפָשָׂה בַּשֵּׁנִי "וּבָא הַכֹּהֵן", וְנֶאֱמַר בְּפָשָׂה בָּרִאשׁוֹן "וְשָׁב הַכֹּהֵן"*) – הִיא שִׁיבָה הִיא בִּיאָה. כְּלוֹמַר: זוֹ כָּזוֹ, מַה לְהַלָּן חוֹלֵץ וְקוֹצֶה וְטָח וְנוֹתֵן לוֹ שָׁבוּעַ – אַף כָּאן חוֹלֵץ וְקוֹצֶה וְטָח וְנוֹתֵן לוֹ שָׁבוּעַ. וְאִם חָזַר שׁוּב – בָּעֵי נְתִיצָה, אַלְמָא: אע"ג דְּלָאו שִׁיבָה הִיא, כֵּיוָן דְּשִׁיבָה וּבִיאָה חֲדָא מִילְּתָא הִיא, דְּתַרְוַיְיהוּ מַשְׁמַע שֶׁבָּא מִבֵּיתוֹ לְבֵית הַמְנוּגָּע – דַּיְינִינַן גְּזֵירָה שָׁוָה מִינַּיְיהוּ: אִי אִית לֵיהּ ג"ש. דְּמָקוֹם מִנִּיסָה וְחוּץ מִחוּץ, כִּדְאָמַר לְעֵיל: פֵּיאוֹת כְּתִיב. דִּכְתִיב "פְּאַת"*) (נֶגֶב) וּפְאַת מַשְׁמַע מְרוּבָּע: הֵן וַאֲלַכְסוֹנָן. ד"א וח' חוּמְשֵׁי אַמָּה, דַּאֲמַרַן: כָּזֶה יִהְיוּ כָּל שׁוֹבְתֵי שַׁבָּת, פֵּיאוֹת תֵּן לָהֶן וְגַבֵּי הַעֲבָרָה לֵיכָּא לְמֵיתַב פֵּיאוֹת. אֶלָּא כִּי הַאי גַּוְונָא שֶׁנּוֹתְנִין לָהֶן שִׁיעוּר אֲלַכְסוֹנָן. דְּהָא לֵיכָּא לְמֵימַר בְּהוּ רִבּוּעַ וְעִיגּוּל: בָּדֵיק לָן. מְנַסֶּה אוֹתָנוּ: מִי בָּעֵינַן הֵן וַאֲלַכְסוֹנָן. שֶׁיְּהֵא רָחָב ד' בְּרִיבּוּעַ, שֶׁתּוּכַל לִמְצוֹא בּוֹ אֲלַכְסוֹן, דְּדָבָר עָגוֹל אֵין לוֹ אֲלַכְסוֹן: מַחֲלוֹקֶת בִּמְקוֹמִי. גָּרְסִינַן בְּיו"ד, מַחֲלוֹקֶת דְּר' מֵאִיר וְר' יְהוּדָה דְּקָא שָׁרֵי ר' יְהוּדָה אֲפִילּוּ לְעָשִׁיר לְעָרֵב בְּרַגְלָיו – בְּאוֹמֵר "שְׁבִיתָתִי בִּמְקוֹמִי" – וְזֶהוּ שֶׁאָמְרוּ דְּמַתְנִי' לְקַמָּן מְפָרֵשׁ אַהֵיכָא קָאֵי, אִי אַמַּכִּיר אִילָן דְּקָתָנֵי דְּאָמַר שְׁבִיתָתִי בְּמָקוֹם פְּלוֹנִי, אוֹ אַאֵינוֹ בָּקִי דְּקָתָנֵי דְּאָמַר שְׁבִיתָתִי בִּמְקוֹמִי: [נ"ל קדמה]

תוספות

כזה יהו כל שובתי שבת. פ"ה: דגבי העברה ליכא למיתב פיאות אלא כה"ג, שנותנין שיעור אלכסון, דהא ליכא למימר בהן ריבוע ועיגול. ור' שמואל מפרש: שמרביעין ד' אמות ברשות הרבים כריבוע עולם, ואם מעביר או זורק ממזרח למערב או מצפון לדרום – חייב בד"א לחודיה, ואם לאלכסונו של עולם – אינו חייב עד שיזרוק או יעביר ד"א ואלכסונן. ועמוד נמי ברה"ר גבוה י' (ב)ורחב ד' דבעינן נמי ד' על ד' מרובעים – היינו כשמעמיד אלכסון העמוד לאלכסון העולם, אבל העמיד האלכסון ממזרח למערב ומצפון לדרום – לא סגי בד' על ד' מרובעות. ועיר עגולה נמי אמרינן ב"כילד מעברין" (לקמן דף נו.) דמרבעה בריבוע עולם. ור"ת מפרש: דלכל צד נותנין האלכסון בזריקה ובהעברה ובתחום שבת, ועמוד נמי צריך שיהא בו שש פחות ב' חומשין. והא דמזכיר בכל דוכתא ד' אמות – היינו משום דנפיק מינייהו האלכסון. וכוורת דפ"ק דשבת (ד' ח.) שהיא עגולה ואין לה אלכסון – נקט רחבה ו', דאי הוה נקט ד' הוה משמע דלא בעי אלכסון. ול"נ, דפיאות דשבת ילפינן מערי הלוים, והתם אין נותנין פיאות אלא לפיאות העולם, כדמוכח ב"כילד מעברין" (לקמן דף נו:) דקאמר נמלא מגרש רביע*: ואהיכא

עין משפט נר מצוה

סד א מיי' פ"ז מהל' עירובין הלכה ג סמג עשין א טוש"ע א"ח סי' תט סעיף יא:

סה ב מיי' פ"ב מהל' שבת הלכה ט סמג לאוין סה טור ש"ע א"ח סי' שמט סעיף ב:

רש"ל מ"ז

עי' מג"א סי' קנו

[וע"ע תוס' יומא סז. ד"ה וכולן וכו']

מסורת הש"ס

[נ"ל לביתו]

[תוספתא פ"ג ע"ש לעיל נ:]

[בתוס' פ"ג איתא להדיא ר' יוסי אומר אם היו שנים וכו']

נדה כב: [יומא כ: יבמות יז: נזיר ה. מכות יג: הוריות ח. מנחות מה: בכורות לג. חולין פה.]

[פסחים נה: מ"ק יג. כתובות סא. נדרים נ: מנחות לה. חולין קלג.]

*) [לפי גירס' רש"ל ושב הכהן הס"ל ואח"כ מ"ה היא שיבה כו']

הגהות הב"ח

(א) רש"י ד"ה ושב הכהן וכו' ת"ל ובא הכהן ולראה והנה: (ב) תד"ה כזה כו' גבוה עשרה ורחב ארבעה דסגי נמי בארבעה על ארבעה וכו' אבל כשמעמיד האלכסון העמוד ממזרח למערב ומצפון:

כזה

רבינו חננאל

שנתנו עירובו בדרום. פי' אם נתן עירובו בצפון בסוף אלף אמה יש לו לילך בצפון ג' אלפים אמה אלפים תחומו שבצפון ואלף שהעתיק לו מן הדרום נשאר לו בדרום אלף אמה וכענין הזה בצפון: פיסקא מהלך ממקום רגליו ועד עיקרו אלפים אמה. אמר רבה והוא כי רהיט מטי תותי האילן קודם שקדש היום והאי דקתני והיה ירא שמא תחשך לביתו אבל לאילן מצי אזיל. אי נמי כי מסגי קליל קליל. אבל אם רהיט מטי. פי' דקלא דסבילא דקל נפל על דקל אחר והיה עמסו והיה נקרא דקלא דסביל אחוה. דקלא דפריק מריה ביה דקל גדול והיה עושה פירות הרבה והיה בעליו מוכרם ופורע המס שעליו. והיה נקרא דקלא דפריק מריה. כלומר פודה בעליו מן המס שעליו. הא דא"ל רבה לרב יוסף משום דר' יוסי תניא ר' יוסי אמר [אם היו] שנים אחד מכיר אילן או גדר או מקום ואחד אינו [מכיר] מוסר שביתתו למכיר. והמכיר אומר תהא שביתתנו במקום פלוני זו הברייתא לא שנאה ר' יוסי אלא אמר רבה משום דר' יוסי כדי שיקבלוהו ממנו רב יוסף משום דר' יוסי נימוקו עמו: מתני' אם אינו מכיר או אם אינו בקי בהלכות כו'. הני אלפים אמה היכא כתיבן דתניא שבו איש תחתיו אלו ד' אמות אל יצא איש ממקומו אלו אלפים אמה מנ"ל אמר רב חסדא למדנו מקום ממקום כתיב הכא אל יצא איש ממקומו ביום השביעי וכתיב התם ושמתי לך מקום אשר ינוס שמה מה זה מקום שיש בו ניסה אף זה מקום (אילן יש בו כתוב) [הוי כמו שכתוב בו] ניסה וילפינן ניסה מן ניסה כתיב הכא ניסה וכתיב התם ואם יצא יצא הרוצח אל גבול עיר מקלטו אשר ינוס שמה מה ניסה זו יש בה גבול אף ניסה זו יש בה גבול ויליף גבול מגבול כתיב הכא גבול וכתיב התם ומצא אותו גואל הדם מחוץ לגבול עיר מקלטו ויליף מחוץ ממחוץ ומדותם מחוץ לעיר את פאת קדמה אלפים באמה ואת פאת נגב אלפים באמה וגו' ואקשינן אדיליף מחוץ ממחוץ באלפים נילף מחוץ מחוצה אלף אמה סביב שנא' מקיר העיר וחוצה אלף אמה סביב ודחינן דנין מחוץ ממחוץ ואין דנין מחוץ ממחוצה. ואקשינן על ר' חנינא בן אנטיגנוס דתני במתני' אלפים אמה לכל רוח עגולות מה נפשך אי בג"ש גמר מהני אלפים אמה מרובעות הוה ליה למימר דהא בקרא פאת כתיבי. פי' פאת קדמה ופאת נגב ופאת ים ופאת צפון ולא אשכחת לה פיאות אלא (בקובע) [במרובע] ואי לא גמיר גזירה [שוה] אלפים תחום שבת מנא ליה ופרקינן לעולם גמיר ג"ש ושאני מגרשי ערי הלוים דכתיב בהו זה יהיה לכם מגרשי הערים כלומר לזה אתה נותן פיאות ועושה אותן מרובעות ואי אתה נותן פיאות לשובתי שבת דגמירי מיניה. ורבנן דבעי מרובעות סברי כדתני רב חנינא זה יהיה לכם כזה יהיו כל שובתי שבת. פי' רבנן סברי פיאות הן הזוית וקיי"ל כל אמתא בריבועא אמתא ותרי חומשי באלכסונא הלכך ד' אמות שאמרו חכמים הן ה' אמות וג' חומשי אמה וכן למדידת ד' אלפים אמה תחום שבת. אמר רב אחא בר יעקב המעביר ד' אמות ברה"ר אינו חייב עד שיעביר ד' אמות ואלכסונן שהן ו' אמות פחות ב' חומשין. אמר רב פפא בדיק לן רבא עמוד ברה"ר גבוה י' ורחב ד' אי בעינן הן ואלכסונן אי לא ואמר לן לאו היינו דתני רב חנינא כזה יהיו כל שובתי שבת: מתני' וזהו שאמרו העני מערב ברגליו ר"מ אומר אין לנו אלא העני ר' יהודה אומר אחד עני ואחד עשיר לא אמרו מערבין [בפת] אלא

עָנִי הוּא דַּאֲקִילוּ רַבָּנַן עִילָּוֵיהּ, אֲבָל עָשִׁיר — לָא. וְרַבִּי יְהוּדָה סָבַר: עִיקַּר עֵירוּב בָּרֶגֶל, אֶחָד עָנִי וְאֶחָד עָשִׁיר. [א]אֲבָל "בִּמְקוֹם פְּלוֹנִי" — דִּבְרֵי הַכֹּל: עָנִי — אִין, עָשִׁיר — לָא. וְזוֹ הִיא שֶׁאָמְרוּ: מַאן קָתָנֵי לָהּ — ר"מ,(א) וְאַהַיָּיא קָאֵי — אַ"אֵינוֹ מַכִּיר אוֹ שֶׁאֵינוֹ בָּקִי בַּהֲלָכָה". וְ"לֹא אָמְרוּ מְעָרְבִין בַּפַּת אֶלָּא לְהָקֵל" מַאן קָתָנֵי לָהּ — רַבִּי יְהוּדָה. וְרַב חִסְדָּא אָמַר: מַחֲלוֹקֶת "בִּמְקוֹם פְּלוֹנִי", דְּר' מֵאִיר סָבַר: עָנִי — אִין, עָשִׁיר — לָא. וְרַבִּי יְהוּדָה סָבַר: אֶחָד עָנִי וְאֶחָד עָשִׁיר. אֲבָל "בִּמְקוֹמִי" — דִּבְרֵי הַכֹּל: אֶחָד עָנִי וְאֶחָד עָשִׁיר, דְּעִיקַּר עֵירוּב בָּרֶגֶל. "וְזוֹ הִיא שֶׁאָמְרוּ", מַאן קָתָנֵי לָהּ — ר"מ, וְאַהַיָּיא קָאֵי — אַהָא: "מִי שֶׁבָּא בַּדֶּרֶךְ וְחָשְׁכָה". "וְלֹא אָמְרוּ מְעָרְבִין בַּפַּת אֶלָּא לְהָקֵל" — מַאן קָתָנֵי לָהּ — דִּבְרֵי הַכֹּל. תַּנְיָא כְּוָותֵיהּ דְּרַב נַחְמָן: אֶחָד עָנִי וְאֶחָד עָשִׁיר מְעָרְבִין בַּפַּת. וְלֹא יֵצֵא עָשִׁיר חוּץ לַתְּחוּם וְיֹאמַר "שְׁבִיתָתִי בִּמְקוֹמִי" — לְפִי שֶׁלֹּא אָמְרוּ מְעָרְבִין בָּרֶגֶל אֶלָּא לְמִי שֶׁבָּא בַּדֶּרֶךְ וְחָשְׁכָה, דִּבְרֵי רַבִּי מֵאִיר. רַבִּי יְהוּדָה אוֹמֵר: [ב]אֶחָד עָנִי וְאֶחָד עָשִׁיר מְעָרְבִין בָּרֶגֶל, וְיֵצֵא עָשִׁיר חוּץ לַתְּחוּם וְיֹאמַר "תְּהֵא שְׁבִיתָתִי בִּמְקוֹמִי", וְזֶה הוּא עִיקָּרוֹ שֶׁל עֵירוּב. [ג]וְהִתִּירוּ חֲכָמִים לְבַעַל הַבַּיִת לִשְׁלֹחַ עֵירוּבוֹ בְּיַד עַבְדּוֹ, בְּיַד בְּנוֹ, בְּיַד שְׁלוּחוֹ בִּשְׁבִיל לְהָקֵל עָלָיו. א"ר יְהוּדָה: מַעֲשֶׂה בְּאַנְשֵׁי בֵּית מָמָל וּבְאַנְשֵׁי בֵּית גּוּרְיוֹן בַּאֲרוֹמָא, שֶׁהָיוּ מְחַלְּקִין גְּרוֹגָרוֹת וְצִימּוּקִין לַעֲנִיִּים בִּשְׁנֵי בַּצּוֹרֶת, וּבָאִין עֲנִיֵּי כְּפַר שִׁיחִין וַעֲנִיֵּי כְּפַר חֲנַנְיָה וּמַחְשִׁיכִין עַל הַתְּחוּם, לְמָחֳרַת מַשְׁכִּימִין וּבָאִין. אָמַר רַב אַשִׁי: מַתְנִיתִין נַמִּי דַּיְקָא, דְּקָתָנֵי: *מִי שֶׁיָּצָא לֵילֵךְ לְעִיר שֶׁמְּעָרְבִין לָהּ, וְהֶחֱזִירוֹ חֲבֵרוֹ — הוּא מוּתָּר לֵילֵךְ, וְכָל בְּנֵי הָעִיר אֲסוּרִין, דִּבְרֵי רַבִּי יְהוּדָה. וְהָוֵינַן בָּהּ: *מַאי שְׁנָא אִיהוּ וּמַאי שְׁנָא אִינְהוּ? וְאָמַר רַב הוּנָא: הָכָא בְּמַאי עָסְקִינַן — כְּגוֹן שֶׁיֵּשׁ לוֹ שְׁנֵי בָּתִּים, וּשְׁנֵי תְּחוּמֵי שַׁבָּת בֵּינֵיהֶן. אִיהוּ כֵּיוָן דִּנְפַק לֵיהּ לְאוֹרְחָא — הָוֵה לֵיהּ עָנִי, וְהָנָךְ עֲשִׁירִים נִינְהוּ. אַלְמָא: כֹּל "בְּמָקוֹם פְּלוֹנִי" עָנִי — אִין, עָשִׁיר — לָא. ש"מ. *מַתְנֵי לֵיהּ *רַב חִיָּיא בַּר אַשִׁי לְחִיָּיא בַּר רַב קַמֵּיהּ דְּרַב: אֶחָד עָנִי וְאֶחָד עָשִׁיר. א"ל רַב: סַיֵּים בָּהּ נַמִּי: הֲלָכָה כְּר' יְהוּדָה. רַבָּה בַּר רַב חָנָן הֲוָה רָגִיל דְּאָתֵי מֵאַרְטִיבְנָא לְפוּמְבְּדִיתָא, אָמַר

עָנִי הוּא דְּאַקִילוּ רַבָּנַן גַּבֵּיהּ. הַבָּא בַּדֶּרֶךְ וְאֵין עִמּוֹ פַּת הוּא דְּאַקִילוּ רַבָּנַן גַּבֵּיהּ לוֹמַר "שְׁבִיתָתִי בִּמְקוֹמִי" כְּשֶׁאֵינוֹ מַכִּיר אִילָן אוֹ גָּדֵר, אוֹ לְמַכִּיר לוֹמַר "שְׁבִיתָתִי בְּמָקוֹם פְּלוֹנִי": אֲבָל עָשִׁיר. כְּגוֹן יוֹשֵׁב בְּבֵיתוֹ — לֹא זוֹ וְלֹא זוֹ: עִיקַּר עֵירוּב בָּרֶגֶל. שְׁבִיתָתִי תַּחְתַּי, אֲפִילּוּ לְעָשִׁיר אִם יָצָא וְהֶחְשִׁיךְ — זֶהוּ עִיקַּר מִצְוַת עֵירוּב, כִּדְתָנֵי לֹא אָמְרוּ לְעָרֵב בַּפַּת כו' אַלְמָא: עִיקַּר תַּקָּנַת עֵירוּב לְר' יְהוּדָה בָּרֶגֶל הִיא: זֶהוּ שֶׁאָמְרוּ חֲכָמִים. דְּמַשְׁמַע דְּעִיקַּר תַּקַּנְתָּא לָאו הָכִי הֲוַאי, אֶלָּא קוּלָּא בְּעָלְמָא הוּא שֶׁאָמְרוּ אֵצֶל הֶעָנִי לְעָרֵב בְּרַגְלָיו: מַאן קָאָמַר לֵיהּ ר"מ. דְּאָמַר: עִיקַּר עֵירוּב בַּפַּת: וְאַהֵיכָא קָאֵי אַאֵינוֹ מַכִּיר אוֹ שֶׁאֵינוֹ בָּקִי בַּהֲלָכָה. וְאָמַר שְׁבִיתָתִי תַּחְתַּי — עֲלָהּ קָאָמַר ר"מ: וְזֶהוּ שֶׁאָמְרוּ. כְּלוֹמַר: דַּאֲפִילּוּ לְהַאי דְּאָמַר בִּמְקוֹמִי — קוּלָּא הוּא דְּאַקִילוּ רַבָּנַן גַּבֵּיהּ, אֲבָל לֹא זֶהוּ עִיקַּר תַּקָּנַת עֵירוּב: וְלֹא אָמְרוּ לְעָרֵב בַּפַּת. דְּמַשְׁמַע דְּעִיקַּר עֵירוּב כִּי אִיתְּקַן בָּרֶגֶל אִיתְּקַן, וְלֹא אָמְרוּ בַּפַּת אֶלָּא לְהָקֵל עַל הֶעָשִׁיר: מַחֲלוֹקֶת בְּמָקוֹם פְּלוֹנִי. דְּאֵין כָּאן לֹא עֵירוּב בַּפַּת וְלֹא עֵירוּב בָּרֶגֶל, אֶלָּא אֲמִירָה בְּעָלְמָא, עֲלָהּ קָאָמַר ר"מ עָנִי אִין עָשִׁיר לָא: אֲבָל בִּמְקוֹמִי דִּבְרֵי הַכֹּל אֶחָד עָנִי וְאֶחָד עָשִׁיר. דְּעִיקַּר עֵירוּב בָּרֶגֶל: ה"ג: וְזֶהוּ שֶׁאָמְרוּ. דְּמַשְׁמַע דְּאֵין זֶה עִיקַּר עֵירוּב, אֶלָּא קוּלָּא הוּא דְּאָמַר לֶעָנִי. עַל כָּרְחֲךָ ר"מ קָאָמַר לָהּ וְאַע"ג דְּמוֹקְמִינַן לָהּ בְּמִי שֶׁבָּא בַּדֶּרֶךְ וְחָשְׁכָה לוֹ, וְהָיָה מַכִּיר אִילָן אוֹ גָּדֵר וְאָמַר שְׁבִיתָתִי בְּעִיקָּרוֹ, וְהַאי אֲפִילּוּ לְר' יְהוּדָה לֹא זֶהוּ עִיקַּר מִצְוָתוֹ — אפ"ה לָא מָצֵינַן לְאוֹקְמָא כְּר' יְהוּדָה, מִשּׁוּם דְּקָתָנֵי בָּהּ עָנִי. וְאִילּוּ ר' יְהוּדָה אֶחָד עָנִי וְאֶחָד עָשִׁיר קָאָמַר: אַמִּי שֶׁבָּא בַּדֶּרֶךְ וְחָשְׁכָה לוֹ. וְהָיָה מַכִּיר אִילָן, וְאָמַר "שְׁבִיתָתִי בְּעִיקָּרוֹ" דְּקָתָנֵי: קָנָה שָׁם שְׁבִיתָתוֹ. וַעֲלָהּ קָאָמַר: זֶה הוּא שֶׁאָמְרוּ הֶעָנִי מְעָרֵב בְּרַגְלָיו. דְּהָא קוּלָּא לֶעָנִי הוּא דְּאַקֵּיל, לֹא שֶׁיְּהֵא זֶה עִיקַּר עֵירוּב, אֶלָּא בְּאוֹמֵר "שְׁבִיתָתִי בִּמְקוֹמִי", וְר' יְהוּדָה אָמַר: אֲפִילּוּ לְעָשִׁיר שֶׁהָיָה יוֹשֵׁב בְּבֵיתוֹ וְאָמַר שְׁבִיתָתִי בְּסוֹף אַלְפַּיִם הֵקִילּוּ נַמִּי. וְאַף עַל גַּב דְּעִיקַּר עֵירוּב בִּמְקוֹמִי הוּא: וְלֹא אָמְרוּ. דְּמַשְׁמַע עִיקַּר עֵירוּב אֵינוֹ בַּפַּת, אֶלָּא לְהָקֵל עַל הֶעָשִׁיר הוּא דְּאִיתְּקוּן — סְתָמָא הִיא וְד"ה, וְלָאו מַסְקָנָא דְּמִילְּתֵיהּ דְּר"י הִיא. דְּהָא רַבִּי מֵאִיר נַמִּי מוֹדֶה בָּהּ דְּעִיקַּר עֵירוּב בָּרֶגֶל בִּמְקוֹמִי: תַּנְיָא כְּוָתֵיהּ דְּר"נ. דְּאָמַר מַחֲלוֹקֶת בִּמְקוֹמִי, דַּאֲפִילּוּ הֵיכָא דְּאָמַר בִּמְקוֹמִי — לְר"מ עָשִׁיר לֹא, וְר' יְהוּדָה נַמִּי לָא שָׁרֵי לְעָשִׁיר אֶלָּא "בִּמְקוֹמִי" אֲבָל בְּמָקוֹם פְּלוֹנִי — לֹא: ה"ג: וְלֹא יֵצֵא עָשִׁיר חוּץ לַתְּחוּם וְיֹאמַר תְּהֵא שְׁבִיתָתִי בִּמְקוֹמִי. וְהַאי חוּץ לַתְּחוּם — לָאו דַּוְקָא, אֶלָּא בְּסוֹף הַתְּחוּם. וְאִי דַּוְוקָא חוּץ לַתְּחוּם — בְּתוֹךְ ד' אַמּוֹת קָאָמַר, שֶׁבּוֹ שְׁבִיתָתוֹ: שֶׁלֹּא אָמַר לְעָרֵב בָּרֶגֶל. אֲפִילּוּ כִּי הַאי גַּוְונָא דְּאָמַר בִּמְקוֹמִי, אֶלָּא לְמִי שֶׁבָּא בַּדֶּרֶךְ כו' — אַלְמָא: לְר"מ אֲפִילּוּ "בִּמְקוֹמִי" עָנִי — אִין, עָשִׁיר — לָא: וְיֵצֵא עָשִׁיר חוּץ לַתְּחוּם. אִם יִרְצֶה: וְיֹאמַר שְׁבִיתָתִי בִּמְקוֹמִי. אַלְמָא: לְר' יְהוּדָה לָא שָׁרֵי לְעָשִׁיר אֶלָּא "בִּמְקוֹמִי", כְּרַב נַחְמָן: א"ר יְהוּדָה מַעֲשֶׂה בְּאַנְשֵׁי בֵּית מָמָל וּבְאַנְשֵׁי בֵּית גּוּרְיוֹן בַּאֲרוֹמָא. מָקוֹם: גְּרוֹגָרוֹת. תְּאֵנִים יְבֵשִׁים: צִימּוּקִין. עֲנָבִים יְבֵשִׁים שֶׁנִּתְיַיבְּשׁוּ וְנִצְטַמְּקוּ: עֲנִיֵּי כְּפַר שִׁיחִין. סְמוּכִין לָהֶן לַאֲרוֹמָא בְּתוֹךְ ד' אֲלָפִים: וּמַחְשִׁיכִין עַל הַתְּחוּם וכו'. אַלְמָא: עִיקַּר עֵירוּב בָּרֶגֶל, וּ"בִמְקוֹמִי". וְאַע"ג דַּעֲנִיִּים הָיוּ, הוֹאִיל וּבְבֵיתָם אִיתְנְהוּ — כַּעֲשִׁירִים דָּמוּ, דְּאָ"אְ לָהֶם בְּלֹא מָזוֹן ב' סְעוּדוֹת, וְאַעפ"כ הָיוּ מְעָרְבִין בְּרַגְלָן וּמַחְשִׁיכִין, דְּהַיְינוּ "בִּמְקוֹמִי" כְּרַב נַחְמָן(ג). אַלְמָא: עִיקַּר עֵירוּב בָּרֶגֶל, וּמַחְשִׁיכִין עַל הַתְּחוּם. וְאַע"ג דִּלְגַבֵּי עֵירוּב עֲשִׁירִים הֵן, דְּהָא מִבֵּיתָם יוֹצְאִין עַל כָּךְ, וְיֵשׁ לָהֶן פַּת — אפ"ה שָׁרֵי, כִּי לֵית לֵיהּ שָׁלִיחַ לְעָרֵב(ג) בְּרַגְלָיו: מַתְנִי' נַמִּי דַּיְקָא. כְּרַב נַחְמָן דִּלְר' יְהוּדָה בְּמָקוֹם פְּלוֹנִי עָשִׁיר — לֹא, וְכִי פָּלֵיג אַדְּר"מ "בִּמְקוֹמִי" הוּא דְּפָלֵיג: מִי שֶׁיָּצָא. כָּל דְּהוּ וְהֶחֱזִיק בַּדֶּרֶךְ לָעִיר, שֶׁמְּעָרְבִין שֶׁסְּמוּכָה לְעִירוֹ לְסוֹף ד' אֲלָפִים — וְיָכוֹל אָדָם לֵילֵךְ מִזּוֹ לָזוֹ ע"י עֵירוּב: וְהֶחֱזִירוֹ חֲבֵירוֹ. דְּא"ל: עֵת חַמָּה הוּא, עֵת לַיְּלָה הוּא, כִּדְלְקַמָּן (נב.): הוּא מוּתָּר לֵילֵךְ. לְמָחָר, לְאוֹתָהּ עִיר אַחֶרֶת, וְכָל בְּנֵי עִירוֹ אֲסוּרִין: שֶׁיֵּשׁ לוֹ ב' בָּתִּים. אֶחָד בָּזֶה וְאֶחָד בָּזֶה, וְהָיָה רוֹצֶה לֵילֵךְ לְבֵיתוֹ שֶׁבָּעִיר אַחֶרֶת מֵעֶ"שׁ, וְלִשְׁבּוֹת שָׁם בַּשַּׁבָּת. וְלֹא יָצָא מִבֵּיתוֹ אַדַּעְתָּא דִּקְנִיַּית שְׁבִיתָה בְּסוֹף הַתְּחוּם וְלַחֲזוֹר, אֶלָּא אַדַּעְתָּא לְמֵיזַל עַד הָתָם, וְהֶחֱזִירוֹ חֲבֵירוֹ: אִיהוּ כֵּיוָן דִּנְפַק לְאוֹרְחָא. מִשּׁוּם הֲלִיכָה מַמָּשׁ, וְלֹא מִשּׁוּם לְעָרֵב בְּרַגְלָיו — הָוֵי לֵיהּ עָנִי, וְיָכוֹל לוֹמַר שְׁבִיתָתִי בְּסוֹף הַתְּחוּם, וִיסַיֵּים מָקוֹם הַנִּיכָּר לוֹ שָׁם. וּפְלוּגְתָּא דְּאָמוֹרָאֵי הִיא לְקַמָּן (שם) אִיכָּא לְמ"ד דַּאֲפִילּוּ לֹא אָמַר נַמִּי(ד), כֵּיוָן דְּאָזֵן סָהֲדֵי דְּהָתָם בָּעֵי לְמֵיזַל — כְּמַאן דְּאָמַר דָּמֵי. וְע"כ בִּדְלָא אָמַר מִידֵי עָסְקִינַן. חֲדָא: דְּלָא קָתָנֵי "וְאָמַר שְׁבִיתָתִי בְּמָקוֹם פְּלוֹנִי", וְעוֹד: מִדְּפָלֵיג ר"מ עֲלַהּ, וְאָמַר הֲרֵי זֶה חַמָּר גַּמָּל — ש"מ בִּדְלָא אָמַר שְׁבִיתָתִי בְּמָקוֹם פְּלוֹנִי עָסְקִינַן. דְּהָא ר"מ מוֹדֶה בְּעָנִי. וְא"ת: ר"מ עָשִׁיר חָשֵׁיב לֵיהּ לְהַאי, דְּמִשּׁוּם דְּהֶחֱזִיק בַּדֶּרֶךְ פּוּרְתָּא לָא מְשַׁוֵּי לֵיהּ עָנִי, א"כ דְּעָשִׁיר חָשֵׁיב לֵיהּ ר"מ, חַמָּר גַּמָּל אַמַּאי? הָא בְּבֵיתוֹ לֹא רָצָה לִקְנוֹת, דְּהָא אָמַר שְׁבִיתָתִי בְּסוֹף הַתְּחוּם, וְשָׁם לֹא יָכוֹל — דְּהָא לָאו עָנִי הוּא, וְלֹא יָזוּז מִמְּקוֹמוֹ מִיבְּעֵי לֵיהּ! אֶלָּא בִּדְלָא אָמַר עָסְקִינַן, וְר"מ נַמִּי עָנִי מְשַׁוֵּי לֵיהּ וּמִשּׁוּם דְּלֹא אָמַר כְּלוּם מְסַפְּקָא לֵיהּ אִי דַּעְתּוֹ לִקְנוֹת שְׁבִיתָה בְּסוֹף הַתְּחוּם, אוֹ שֶׁמָּא חָזַר בּוֹ לְגַמְרֵי מִלֵּילֵךְ לְמָחָר לְאוֹתָהּ הָעִיר, וְדַעְתּוֹ לִקְנוֹת שְׁבִיתָה בְּבֵיתוֹ. הִלְכָּךְ, חַמָּר גַּמָּל הוּא: הָנָךְ עֲשִׁירִים נִינְהוּ. וַאֲפִילּוּ אָמְרוּ "שְׁבִיתָתֵנוּ בְּמָקוֹם פְּלוֹנִי" אָסוּר. דְּאִי לֹא אָמְרוּ — פְּשִׁיטָא. אַלְמָא: כָּל בְּמָקוֹם פְּלוֹנִי לְר' יְהוּדָה, עָנִי — אִין, עָשִׁיר — לָא, וּלְהָכִי נְקַט יֵשׁ לוֹ ב' בָּתִּים. דְּאִי לָא הֲוָה לֵיהּ בֵּיתָא הָתָם — לָא הֲוָה אָמְרִינַן כִּי לֹא אָמַר כְּמַאן דְּאָמַר דָּמֵי, דִּדְלְמָא קָא הָדַר בֵּיהּ: הֲלָכָה כְּרַבִּי יְהוּדָה. וּכְרַב נַחְמָן בִּמְקוֹמִי: הֲוָה אָתֵי מֵאַרְטִיבְנָא. רָגִיל דְּאָתֵי בְּכָל שַׁבָּת מֵאַרְטִיבְנָא לְפוּמְבְּדִיתָא וְהָיָה

ואהיכא קא אאינו מכיר. ולא בעי למימר דקאי אמי שבא בדרך וחשכה לו, ודברי הכל — דמוכחא מתני' דבמאי דפליגי ר"מ ורבי יהודה איירי: **ולא** אמרו לערב בפת אלא להקל מאן קתני לה דברי הכל. וא"ת: ולר' יהודה מאי להקל איכא? כיון שאפילו בבית יכול לומר שביתתי במקום פלוני! וי"ל: דהאי להקל — היכא דליכא אילן או גדר ומקום מסויים, במקום שרוצה לקנות שביתה:

ויצא עשיר חוץ לתחום. קשה לר"י דמדקרי ליה עשיר — דמשמע שרוצה לחזור וללון בביתו ואיך יכול לחזור? והלא אין לו אלא אלפים מעירובו לצד עירו, ואפילו אם ביתו הוא הראשון בכניסתו לצד עירו — לא יהיה לו בתוך ביתו אלא ד' אמות, ואטו בשופטני עסקינן שילון בביתו ולא יהיה לו אלא ד"א? ונראה לר"י: דהא "חוץ לתחום" — היינו חוץ לעיבורה של עיר. וכה"ג איכא ב"כילד מעברין" (לקמן דף ס.). ועוד אומר ר"י: דהאי דקאמר ויצא עשיר חוץ לתחום — לא שרוצה לקנות שביתה חוץ לתחום, אלא שרוצה לחזור ולקנות שביתה בתוך התחום. ונקט הכי משום רבי מאיר, דקתני "לא יצא עשיר חוץ לתחום", וקמ"ל: אע"פ דיצא חוץ לתחום, ודמי השתא לבא בדרך — ואפ"ה אין יכול לערב ברגליו, דכיון דכל עיקר יציאה זו לא היה אלא כדי לערב. ואגב דנקט רבי מאיר, נקט נמי רבי יהודה:

סו א מיי' פ"ז מהלכות עירובין הלכה ב ג סמג עשין א טור ש"ע א"ח סי' תט סעיף יג:
סז ב מיי' שם הלכה א טוש"ע שם סעיף ז:
סח ג מיי' שם טור ש"ע שם סעיף ח:

רבינו חננאל

אלא להקל על העשיר וכו' אמר רב נחמן מחלוקת (במקומו) [במקומי] דכיון דאמר שביתתי במקומי דין אין צריך עירוב אחר בפת דר' מאיר סבר עני אין עשיר לא ור' יהודה סבר אחד עני ואחד עשיר אבל במקום פלוני דברי הכל עני אין עשיר לא. אלמא קסבר ר' מאיר עיקר עירוב בפת וזהו שאמרו אאינו ניכר או אינו בקי בהל' קאי ולא אמרו מערבין בפת אלא להקל על העשיר ר' יהודה קתני לה והלכה כר' יהודה וקיי"ל כרב נחמן דתניא כוותיה דתניא זהו שאמרו (מפני) העני מערב ברגליו ולא יצא העשיר חוץ לתחום ויאמר שביתתי במקומי לפי שלא התירו לערב ברגליו אלא למי שבא בדרך וחשכה לו דברי ר"מ. ר' יהודה אומר אחד עני ואחד עשיר מערבין ברגל ויוצא העשיר חוץ לעיר לתחום (ואמר) [ויאמר] שביתתי תהא במקומי וזהו עיקרו של עירוב והתירו לבעל הבית לשלח עירובו ביד בנו ביד עבדו ביד שלוחו בשביל להקל עליו אמר רב אשי אף אנן נמי תנינן להא דרב נחמן דתנן מי שיצא לילך לעיר שמערבין בה פירוש שיש לו לילך בה ע"י עירוב והחזירו חבירו [הוא] מותר שעירב ברגליו וכל בני העיר אסורין. ופירשה רב הונא כגון שיש לו ב' בתים וביניהם ב' תחומי שבת שהן ד' אלפים אמה. איהו דעקר נפשיה הוה ליה כעני דכל הבא בדרך עני הוא חשוב שאין פת מצויה לרוב עוברי דרכים וכבר הותר לו לערב ברגליו. וכיון שאמר שביתתי במקום (ב') התחומין קנה לו התם שביתה ויש לילך מביתו זה (שלזבו) [שלן בו] לביתו האחר בסמוך אלפים אמה אבל בני העיר כיון שלא החזיקו בדרך הוו להו עשירים. ואף על גב (דאמרינן) [דאמרי] שביתתנו במקום פלוני לא קנו שביתה התם דלא התירו לערב במקום פלוני בדבור אלא עני אבל עשיר לא. תניא כפירושא דרב הונא: מתני לה רב חייא בר אשי לחייא בר רב אחד עני ואחד עשיר א"ל רבא תנייה הלכתא כרב יהודה. רבא בר חנן רגיל דאתא מאנטוכיא לפומבדיתא לפירקיה דרב יוסף ואמר שביתתי במתא

[לקמן נב.]
[שם]
[לעיל מז.]
[גירסת הרא"ש רב חמא

הגהות הב"ח

(א) גמ' ר' מאיר ואהייא ... תז"מ ונ"ב גירסת רש"... ואהיכא: (ב) רש"י ד"... ומחשיכין וכו' דהיי... במקומי כרב נח... ומחשיכין על התחום כל... ותיבת אלמא עיקר עירו... ברגל נמחק: (ג) בא"ד ... לית ליה שליח לערב ב... יערב ברגליו: (ד) ד"... איהו כיון וכו' איכא למ... דאמר דאפי' לא אמר נ... ועל כרחך בדלא אמר אי... מערב מידי עסקינן כי... דאזן סהדי דהתם ב... למיזל כמאן דאמר ד... חדא דלא קתני:

אמר: "תהא שביתתי בצינתא". א"ל אביי: מאי דעתיך – *ר"מ ורבי יהודה – הלכה כרבי יהודה, ואמר רב חסדא: מחלוקת "במקום פלוני", והא ר"נ ותניא כוותיה! א"ל: הדרי בי. אמר רמי בר חמא: הרי אמרו שבת יש לו ד"א, *הנותן את עירובו יש לו ד"א או לא? אמר רבא, ת"ש: לא אמרו מערבין בפת אלא להקל על העשיר, שלא יצא ויערב ברגליו, ואי אמרת אין לו – האי להקל?! להחמיר הוא! אפילו הכי ניחא ליה, כי היכי דלא נטרח וניפוק. § מתני' *א מי שיצא לילך בעיר שמערבין *בה, והחזירו חבירו – הוא מותר לילך, וכל בני העיר אסורין, דברי רבי יהודה. ר"מ אומר: כל שהוא יכול לערב ולא עירב – הרי זה חמר גמל. § גמ' *מאי שנא איהו ומאי שנא אינהו? אמר רב הונא: הכא במאי עסקינן – כגון שיש לו שני בתים, וביניהן שני תחומי שבת. איהו, ב כיון דנפק ליה לאורחא – הוה ליה עני, והני עשירי נינהו. תניא נמי הכי: מי שיש לו שני בתים וביניהן שני תחומי שבת, כיון שהחזיק בדרך – קנה עירוב, דברי ר' יהודה. יתר על כן אמר ר' יוסי בר' יהודה: ג אפילו מצאו חבירו ואמר לו "לין פה, עת חמה הוא, עת צינה הוא" – למחר משכים והולך. אמר רבה: לומר – כולי עלמא לא פליגי דצריך, כי פליגי – להחזיק. ורב יוסף אמר: להחזיק – דכ"ע לא פליגי דצריך, כי פליגי – לומר. כמאן אזלא הא דאמר עולא: מי שהחזיק בדרך והחזירו חבירו – הרי הוא מוחזר ומוחזק. אי מוחזר – למה מוחזק? ואי מוחזק – למה מוחזר? הכי קאמר: אע"פ שמוחזר – מוחזק. כמאן – כרב יוסף, ואליבא דרבי יוסי ברבי יהודה. רב יהודה בר אישתתא איתי ליה כלכלה דפירי לרב נתן בר אושעיא. כי הוה אזיל שבקיה עד דנחית דרגא, אמר ליה: בית הבא. למחר קדים ואזיל.

כמאן

והיה יושב ערב שבת בביתו, ואומר שביתתי בצינתא. מקום מסוים היה בין שני התחומין: מאי דעתיך. דעשיר את, ואמרת שביתתי במקום פלוני: והא אמר רב נחמן. דלא שרי ר' יהודה אלא במקומי. ותניא כוותיה דרב נחמן לעיל*: שבת. שקונה שביתה ברגליו, יש לו ד' אמות לקניית בית, לבד מאלפים לכל רוח: להחמיר הוא. דמפסיד ארבע אמות: **מתני'** מי שיצא. מעירו, לילך בעיר אחרת שמערבין בה שסמוכה לעירו בתוך ד' אלפים: הוא מותר לילך. ואע"פ שלא אמר כלום, כדפירשתי לעיל, דכיון שיש לו לשם בית – ודאי לא עקר דעתו מהליכתו, ונתכוון לקנות שביתה בסוף התחום, והוי כעני האומר שביתתי במקום פלוני, וקנה. דהא עני הוא, דהחזיק בדרך. ולרבי מאיר ודאי עני הוא. ואי אמר – הוי קני. אבל השתא דיכול היה לערב ולומר שביתתי במקום פלוני, ולא אמר – מספקא לן אי הוה דעתו לקנות שביתה בסוף התחום או בביתו, והרי זה חמר גמל שאין לו אלא אלפים שבין ביתו לסוף התחום. אבל אלפים שמעבר ביתו לצד השני – הפסיד, דשמא בסוף התחום קנה, ומסוף התחום נמי לא קנה אלפים לצד עיר האחרת – שמא לא קנה שביתה כאן כי אם בביתו: **גמ'** תניא נמי הכי. דכשיש לו ב' בתים וביניהן שני תחומי שבת עסקינן: כיון שהחזיק בדרך קנה עירוב. אף אם לא אמר "שביתתי בסוף התחום" וחזר: יתר על כן. אפילו לא החזיק בדרך, אלא אמר לצאת, והחזירו חברו ואמר "לין פה": לומר כ"ע לא פליגי דצריך. שיאמר לו חברו "לין פה" כדקתני מתניתין בדר' יהודה "והחזירו חברו" דהשתא ודאי משום לינה וחמה הוא דהדר ביה, ודעתיה למקני שביתה בסוף התחום, ואע"פ שלא אמר. אבל אם חזר מעצמו – איכא למימר נמלך, ולא קנה שביתה לשם. דאפילו גלוי דעתא ליכא, והרי הוא כבני עירו: כי פליגי להחזיק. והיינו יתר על כן אפילו לא החזיק בדרך, אלא שאמר לו חברו "לין פה" ששמע ממנו שהיה רוצה לצאת, ואמר לו לין פה בביתך הלילה משום לינה: ורב יוסף אמר להחזיק כ"ע לא פליגי דצריך כי פליגי לומר. "לין פה" דלר' יהודה, אם החזיק בדרך, אע"פ שלא אמר לו חברו "לין פה", אלא שחזר מעצמו – כמאן דאמר "שביתתי במקום פלוני" דמי. ו"החזירו חברו" דקתני מתני' לר"י – לאו דוקא, דה"ה לחזור מעצמו, אלא אורחא דמילתא נקט. אבל ר' יוסי בר' יהודה תרוייהו בעי, חזקה ואמירה. (והכי קאמר: מצאו חברו שהתחיל לצאת, ואמר לו חברו "לין פה עמדי הלילה", וקסבר רב יוסף: ר' יוסי בר' יהודה להחמיר, ולא תנן בברייתא "יתר על כן" ו"אפילו", אלא הכי תנן: "ר' יוסי אומר מצאו חברו כו'"). כך שמעתי. והרבה גמגומין יש, *דקשיא ליה לר' יוסי מאי "יתר על כן", ומאי "אפילו". ויש מתרצין: דרבי יוסי לא בעי חזקה כולי האי כדר' יהודה. אבל אמרי נואש הן, דפסיעה אחת חוץ לביתו הויא חזקה, ובציר מהכי ליכא חזקה. ועוד: רב יוסף אמר דבחזקה לא פליגי אלא בלומר, וא"כ אף בחזקה פליגי. ל"א, ולא שמעתיו: אמר רבה: לומר "שביתתי בתוך התחום" – כ"ע לא פליגי דצריך זה החוזר לומר כן, וכי פליג ר' יוסי ואתא לאקולי – אחזקה פליג. דשמעיה לר' יהודה דאמר החזיק, ואתא איהו למימר אפילו מצאו חברו שהיה רוצה להחזיק, ולא הניחו – קנה עירוב. ובלבד שיאמר שביתתי לשם, דהואיל והיה רוצה לצאת חשבינן ליה כיוצא, והוי עני. ורב יוסף אמר: להחזיק לא פליגי, דודאי חזקה בעינן, דאי לא החזיק – לא הוי עני. כי פליגי לומר דר' יהודה בעי שיאמר שביתתי לשם, וארישא דמתניתין קאי, דפריש בה ואמר שביתתי בעיקרו. ולא איצטריך למיהדר ומיתנייא בסיפא. ואתא ר' יוסי למימר: אפילו לא אמר מידי – קני, הואיל והחזיק, דגלוי דעתא קנייה היא. וא"ת: כיון דלרבי יהודה באומר "שביתתי במקום פלוני" קאמר, אמאי פליג ר"מ עליה ומשוי ליה חמר גמל? ר"מ לית ליה חזקה כי האי גוונא, אלא בא בדרך ממש. אבל האי – כעשיר משוי ליה. וקסבר ר"מ: כל שהוא עשיר, והיה לו לערב בפת ולא עירב בפת אלא באמירה – הפסיד באמירתו אלפים שהיה לו לעבר הלז מביתו, שסילק עצמו מרוח זו. ובמקום שביתתו לא נשתכר, דלאו עירוב הוא, ואין לו אלא אלפים הללו. ונראין הדברים דר' מאיר אכל מי שהוא עשיר פליג. ובאומר שביתתי במקום פלוני, מדקתני: כל שיש בידו לערב כו' דאי ס"ד ר"מ עני משוי ליה להאי, וטעמא משום דמספקא לן היכא ניחא ליה הואיל ולא אמר – אם כן מאי "כל"? הא לא משכחת לה הך ספיקא אלא בהך לחודיה שיצא וחזר, ו"הרי זה חמר גמל" מיבעי ליה: מוחזר. משמע שלא קנה שביתה כלל: מוחזק. משמע דקנה: כמאן. ללישנא קמא דפרשי דרב יוסף אליבא דר' יוסי, תרתי בעי: אמירה דלין פה, וחזקה. הכי בעי ליה כמאן אזלא הא דעולא, דבעי תרתי שהחזיק – היינו חזקה, והחזירו חברו – היינו "לין פה": כרב יוסף אליבא דר' יוסי בר' יהודה. דבעי תרתי. והוא הדין לרבה אליבא דר' יהודה, אלא חדא מינייהו נקט. וללישנא בתרא הכי פירושא: כמאן אזלא הא דעולא דלא בעי למימר שביתתי במקום פלוני, דקאמר: אע"פ שמוחזר דמשמע לגמרי – כרב יוסף, ואליבא דרבי יוסי ברבי יהודה, דאמר לא בעינן לומר. (הג"ה: ואהך לישנא ליכא למימר כרבה ואליבא דר' יהודה דבין רבה ובין רב יוסף תרוייהו סבירא להו דר' יהודה תרתי בעי. עד כאן): אישתתא. שם אדם: כי הוה אזיל. לביתיה ובתוך ד' אלפים הוה: נחת דרגא. מעלה מן הכבש שהיה יורד מן העלייה, דהוה ליה החזיק בדרך: בית הבא. "לין פה":

כמאן

האי להקל להחמיר הוא. ואם תאמר: תיקשי ליה לשמואל דסוף "כילד מעברין" (לקמן דף סא:) דאמר: שבת בעיר חריבה, לרבנן – מהלך את כולה וחוצה לה אלפים אמה. הניח עירובו בעיר חריבה – אין לו ממקומו אלא אלפים אמה! וי"ל: מכל מקום בסתמא כי אורחיה, כשאין נותן עירובו בעיר חריבה, הוי להקל.

לומר כ"ע לא פליגי דצריך. פי' ר"ת: לומר עת חמה הוא, ועת צינה הוא. דכיון שהחזירו מטעם זה, אם כן כיון דעתו לילך כשתעבור חמה וצינה, ולא יצא מתורת עני. אבל אם בלא טעם החזירו – אם כן לגמרי נתייאש מלילך, ויצא מתורת עני אע"פ שהחזיק בדרך. ורב יוסף אמר: להחזיק – כולי עלמא לא פליגי דצריך, כי פליגי – לומר. דסבר רב יוסף: כיון שמחמת חמה וצינה הוא חוזר – אם כן נתייאש לגמרי מלילך, ולא קנה העירוב לרבי יהודה אלא כחוזר בלא טעם. יתר על כן אמר ר' יוסי, דאפילו הכי קנה עירוב. והוה ליה לרב יוסף למנקט כי פליגי באומר, אלא נקט במילתיה דרב יוסף לומר אגב מילתיה דרבה. ודייק רב יוסף מדלא הזכיר ר' יהודה "עת צינה ועת חמה" ורבי יוסי הזכיר:

***כמאן** אזלא הא דאמר עולא. אף על פי שמוחזר מוחזק כמאן כרב יוסף, ואליבא דרבי יוסי. מלשון "אע"פ" דייק דחזר מחמת חמה וצינה, ולא קנה עירוב לרבי יהודה, וכרבה לא אתיא, דלכ"ע בעי רבה שיאמר עת צינה הוא. ואי דאמר עת צינה – לא שייך לשון "אע"פ". ופי' זה דחוק. ופי' אחרון דרש"י נראה לר"י עיקר:

כמאן

עין משפט נר מצוה

סט א מיי' פ"ז מהל' עירובין הלכה ח טור ש"ע א"ח סי' תי סעיף ג:

ע ב ג מיי' שם טור ש"ע שם סעיף א:

[לפי גירסת רש"ל שלשה דבורי תוס' ד"ה לומר וד"ה כמאן וד"ה כמאן בעמוד ב' הם ד"א]

מסורת הש"ס

[דף נח:]

[לעיל מז. כתובות ס:]

[עי' לעיל לב: לה. במימרא דרבא]

[לעיל נח:]

גי' רש"ל לה

[לעיל נח:]

רש"ל מ"ז

[נ"ל כי קשיא לר"י וכו']

גליון הש"ס

גמ' יש לו ד' אמות או לא. עיין לקמן דף ס ע"ב ד"ה כאן שכלתה וכו': גמ' אפי' הכי ניחא ליה. עיין לעיל דף לב ע"ב ודף לה ע"א:

רבינו חננאל

פלוני א"ל אביי כמאן כרב חסדא דאמר מחלוקת במקום פלוני ור' יהודה מתיר והא רב נחמן [פליג] עליה ותניא כוותיה. א"ל הדרי בי אמר רמי בר חמא הרי אמרו שבת יש לו ד' אמות. פי' *) המניח עירובו יש לו ד' אמות אי לא ופשיט רבא דיש לו מדתנן לא אמרו לערב בפת כלומר להניח עירובו בפת אלא להקל על העשיר מכלל שזה וזה שוין ואי אמרת המניח עירובו אין לו ד' אמות האי להקל להחמיר הוא שהרי הפסיד ד' אמות אלא ש"מ יש לו ורמי בר חמא (סברא) [סבר] הא ניחא ליה דלא נטרח: מתני' מי שיצא לילך לעיר שמערבין בה כו' כבר פירשנוה למעלה. תניא כוותיה דרב הונא מי שיש לו ב' בתים וביניהן ב' תחומי שבת כיון שהחזיק בדרך קנה עירוב במקום שסיים שביתתו דברי ר' יהודה יתר על כן (ור') [אמר ר'] יוסי ב"ר יהודה אפי' מצאו חבירו וא"ל לין פה עת חמה או עת צנה הוא. למחר משכים והולך. אמר רבה אם החזיק שצריך לומר שביתתי במקום פלוני כ"ע לא פליגי דצריך דכיון דהוא אזיל באורחא אע"פ שהחזיק צ"ל. כי פליגי במי שאמר שביתתי במקום פלוני אם צריך להחזיק ר' יהודה אמר צריך. ר' יוסי ב"ר יהודה אמר אינו צריך. ורב יוסף אמר האומר שביתתי במקום פלוני צריך נמי להחזיק כ"ע לא פליגי דודאי צריך כי פליגי במחזיק אם צריך לומר נמי שביתתי במקום פלוני אי לא ר' יהודה אמר צריך ר' יוסי ב"ר יהודה אמר (אינו צריך) כיון שהחזיק בדרך אע"פ שלא אמר שביתתי במקום פלוני קנה שביתה במקום. ואסיקנא כרב יוסף דרב יהודה בר אישתיתא איתי לרב נתן בר הושעיה כלכלה דפירי כי אזיל שבקיה עד דנחית לדרגא והחזיק להוליכה. א"ל בית הבא וקדים זיל כדרב יוסף

*) נראה דחסר כאן וצ"ל פי' שבת מי שקנה שביתה ברגליו יש לו ד"א לבד מאלפים לכל רוח.

[שייך לע"א]

[נ"ל למוחזר וכ"ה בדפוס ויניציא משנת רפ"ח]

עא א מיי' פ"ז מהלכ' עירובין הלכה ח' טוש"ע א"ח סימן ת"י סעיף ב:

עב ב מיי' פכ"ז מהל' שבת הלכה יא סמג לאוין סו טוש"ע א"ח סי' תה סעיף א:

עג ג מיי' שם טוש"ע שם סעיף ב:

עד ד מיי' שם טוש"ע שם סעיף ג:

א ה מיי' פכ"ח מהל' שבת הלכה ו סמג שם טור ש"ע א"ח סי' שלח סעיף ו:

רבינו חננאל

יוסף אליבא דר' יוסי ב"ר יהודה. ר' מאיר אומר כל מי שיש לערב ולא עירב הרי זה חמר גמל הא תו למה לי תנינא ספק ר' מאיר ור' יהודה אומרים הרי זה חמר גמל ופרקינן אצטריך סד"א התם דהוא ספק אמרי חמר גמל אבל הכא דודאי לא עירב לא אלא הרי הוא כבני העיר [קמ"ל] כיון שיצא לילך והחזיק בדרך עקר רשותיה מן העיר ובמקום שרצה לילך לא קנה שביתה דהא לא עירב בפת ולאו עני הוא דקתני (כמחזיק) [החזיק] הלכך לא יזוז ממקומו. מי שיצא חוץ לתחום אפי' אמה אחת כו' איכא דאמר א"ר חנינא רגלו אחת בתוך התחום והאחרת חוץ לתחום יכנס. שנאמר אם תשיב משבת רגלך רגליך קרינן. והתניא לא יכנס ההיא אחרים היא דא' למקום שכלו (מ"ז). פיסקא ר' אליעזר אומר ב' יכנס ג' לא יכנס והתניא ר' אליעזר אומר א' יכנס ב' לא יכנס. ופרקינן הא דקתני אחת יכנס ב' לא יכנס כגון שיצא אמה אחת ועומד בשניה יכנס אבל אם מצא שתים ועומד בשלישית לא יכנס ומשני הכי קתני ב' פי' אם עומד בשתים יכנס עומד בשלש לא יכנס והא דתניא אפילו אמה אחת לא יכנס במודד כלומר אין לו להוסיף על מדתו. כדתנן ולמודד שאמרו נותנין לו אלפים ומודד:

הדרן עלך מי שהוציאוהו

כיצד מעברין את הערים נכנס פגום יוצא כו'.

כמאן כרב יוסף ואליבא דרבי יוסי. פירש הקונטרס: דמאע"פ דייק, דמשמע דמוחזק מלקנות שביתה. ואם כן לא אמר אי נמי הכי דייק אי בעי תרתי דהחזיק וגם אמירה – א"כ לימא הילכתא כרבי יהודה, דבין לרב יוסף ובין לרבה לרבי יהודה בעי תרתי.

תנינא חדא זימנא. דכל ספיקא לר"מ חמר גמל הוא, ומתניתין נמי ספיקא הוא. וקשה: דמהיא היכא הויא שמעינן דהוי הכא ספק לרבי מאיר. ואומר ר"י: דפריך דהוה ליה למיתני כל שיכול וכו' ספק וממילא ידענא דהוי חמר גמל. ומשני: דה"א דהיכא דודאי לא עירב כי הכא – לא הוי חמר גמל. דאפילו אם הוה תנן ספק, הוה מפרשינן: ספק אם חשוב בכך עני כשאר בא בדרך, אם לאו. ולכך לא קנה עירוב, דודאי עני אמרו שמערב ברגליו במקום פלוני, ולא בספק עני ודינו כודאי עשיר, ויהיה כבני עירו – קא משמע לן:

כי תניא ההיא למודד. שאפילו כלה מדתו במערה – לא יכנס אמה אחת יותר. ופ"ה לא נראה. והא דלא קאמר: כי תניא להחשיך אמה חוץ לתחום לא יכנס – דמילתא דפשיטא הוא דאין לו לצאת חוץ לתחומו. אבל בכלה למערה איצטריך לאשמועינן.

הדרן עלך מי שהוציאוהו

ביצד מעברין פגום נכנס. פי' ר"ח: פגום נכנס – בנין העשוי כעין סוכב, כדאמרי' ב"זה בורר" (סנהדרין דף כה:) גבי מפריחי יונים: משישברו את פגמיהם. ומיהו, סוכב ממש אין מתעבר עם העיר, כדאמרינן בגמ'*: וגשרים

תורה אור

כְּמַאן – אכְּרַב יוֹסֵף, וְאַלִּיבָּא דְּר' יוֹסֵי בַּר יְהוּדָה. לָא, כְּרַבָּה וְאַלִּיבָּא דְּר' יְהוּדָה.§ "ר"מ אוֹמֵר: כׇּל שֶׁיָּכוֹל לְעָרֵב כו'".§ הָא תְּנֵינָא חֲדָא זִימְנָא: *סָפֵק, ר"מ וְרַבִּי יְהוּדָה אוֹמְרִים: הֲרֵי זֶה חַמָּר גַּמָּל! אָמַר רַב שֵׁשֶׁת: לָא תֵּימָא טַעְמָא דְּר"מ סָפֵק עֵירֵב סָפֵק לֹא עֵירֵב, הוּא דְּהָוֵי חַמָּר גַּמָּל; אֲבָל וַדַּאי לֹא עֵירֵב – לָא הָוֵי חַמָּר גַּמָּל, אֶלָּא: אֲפִילּוּ וַדַּאי לֹא עֵירֵב – הָוֵי חַמָּר גַּמָּל. דְּהָא הָכָא וַדַּאי לֹא עֵירֵב, וְקָא הָוֵי חַמָּר גַּמָּל.§

מתני' במִי שֶׁיָּצָא חוּץ לַתְּחוּם – אֲפִילּוּ אַמָּה אַחַת לֹא יִכָּנֵס. *ר"א אוֹמֵר: שְׁתַּיִם – יִכָּנֵס, שָׁלֹשׁ – לֹא יִכָּנֵס.§ גמ' א"ר חֲנִינָא: רַגְלוֹ אַחַת בְּתוֹךְ הַתְּחוּם וְרַגְלוֹ אַחַת חוּץ לַתְּחוּם – לֹא יִכָּנֵס, דִּכְתִיב: °"אִם תָּשִׁיב מִשַּׁבָּת רַגְלֶךָ", "רַגְלֶךָ" כְּתִיב. וְהָתַנְיָא: רַגְלוֹ אַחַת בְּתוֹךְ הַתְּחוּם וְרַגְלוֹ אַחַת חוּץ לַתְּחוּם – יִכָּנֵס! הָא מַנִּי – אֲחֵרִים הִיא. דְּתַנְיָא, אֲחֵרִים אוֹמְרִים: לְמָקוֹם שֶׁרוּבּוֹ הוּא *נִזְקָר. אִיכָּא דְּאָמְרִי, אָמַר ר' חֲנִינָא: גרַגְלוֹ אַחַת בְּתוֹךְ הַתְּחוּם וְרַגְלוֹ אַחַת חוּץ לַתְּחוּם – יִכָּנֵס, דִּכְתִיב: °"אִם תָּשִׁיב מִשַּׁבָּת רַגְלֶךָ", "רַגְלֶיךָ" קָרֵינַן. וְהָתַנְיָא: לֹא יִכָּנֵס! הוּא דְּאָמַר כַּאֲחֵרִים, דְּתַנְיָא: לְמָקוֹם שֶׁרוּבּוֹ הוּא נִזְקָר.§ "ר"א אוֹמֵר: שְׁתַּיִם – יִכָּנֵס, שָׁלֹשׁ – לֹא יִכָּנֵס".§ וְהָתַנְיָא, ר"א אוֹמֵר: אַחַת – יִכָּנֵס, שְׁתַּיִם – לֹא יִכָּנֵס! לָא קַשְׁיָא; הָא – דַּעֲקַר חֲדָא וְקָם אַתַּרְתֵּי, הָא – דַּעֲקַר תַּרְתֵּי וְקָם אַתְּלָת. וְהָתַנְיָא, ר"א אוֹמֵר: אֲפִילּוּ אַמָּה אַחַת לֹא יִכָּנֵס! כִּי תַּנְיָא הַהִיא – לְמוֹדֵד. *דִּתְנַן: וּלְמוֹדֵד שֶׁאָמְרוּ נוֹתְנִין לוֹ אַלְפַּיִם אַמָּה – אֲפִילּוּ סוֹף מִדָּתוֹ כָּלָה בִּמְעָרָה.§ מתני' *דמִי שֶׁהֶחְשִׁיךְ חוּץ לַתְּחוּם – אֲפִילּוּ אַמָּה אַחַת לֹא יִכָּנֵס. ר"ש אוֹמֵר: אֲפִילּוּ חֲמֵשׁ עֶשְׂרֵה אַמּוֹת יִכָּנֵס, שֶׁאֵין הַמָּשׁוֹחוֹת מְמַצִּין אֶת הַמִּדּוֹת מִפְּנֵי הַטּוֹעִין.§ גמ' תָּנָא: מִפְּנֵי טוֹעֵי הַמִּדָּה.§

ישעיהו נח

[קדף נה:]

הֲדְרָן עֲלָךְ מִי שֶׁהוֹצִיאוּהוּ

כֵּיצַד המְעַבְּרִין אֶת הֶעָרִים? בַּיִת נִכְנָס בַּיִת יוֹצֵא, פָּגוּם נִכְנָס פָּגוּם יוֹצֵא. הָיוּ שָׁם גְּדוּדִיּוֹת גְּבוֹהוֹת עֲשָׂרָה טְפָחִים, וּגְשָׁרִים

כְּמַאן. בָּעֵינַן הֶחֱזִיק בַּדֶּרֶךְ וְ"לִין פֹּה". וּלְלִישָּׁנָא אַחֲרִינָא הָכִי גָּרְסִינַן: כְּמַאן דְּסַגִּי לֵיהּ בְּהָכִי, וְאַע"ג דְּלָא אָמַר שְׁבִיתָתִי בְּמָקוֹם פְּלוֹנִי – כְּרַב יוֹסֵף אַלִּיבָּא דְּרַבִּי יוֹסֵי בְּר' יְהוּדָה? לָא, כְּרַבָּה וְאַלִּיבָּא דְּרַבִּי (יוֹסֵי בְּרַבִּי) יְהוּדָה. וְה"פ: כְּמַאן הָוֵי – כְּרַב יוֹסֵף וְאַלִּיבָּא דְּרַבִּי יוֹסֵי בְּר' יְהוּדָה, דְּלָא בָּעֵי אֶלָּא לְהַחֲזִיק, וְהַאי נַמִי הֶחֱזִיק וְלָא אָמַר. וּמְשַׁנֵּי: לָא, דְּאָמַר עָסְקִינַן, וּכְרַבָּה אַלִּיבָּא דְּר' יְהוּדָה דְּבָעֵי תַּרְתֵּי. וְהוּא הַדִּין נַמִי לְרַב יוֹסֵף וְאַלִּיבָּא דְּרַבִּי יְהוּדָה, אֶלָּא אַלִּיבָּא דְּרַבָּה עֲדִיפָא לֵיהּ לְאוֹקְמֵי מִשּׁוּם דְּרַבָּה, וְרַב יוֹסֵף הִילְכְתָא כְּרַבָּה, לְבַר מִתְּלָת: שָׂדֶה, עִנְיָן, וּמֶחֱצָה: סָפֵק. בְּפֶרֶק "בַּכֹּל מְעָרְבִין" (לעיל דף לה.): נִתְגַּלְגֵּל חוּץ לַתְּחוּם, נִשְׂרַף, מִבְּעוֹד יוֹם – אֵינוֹ עֵירוּב, מִשֶּׁחֲשֵׁיכָה – הֲרֵי זֶה עֵירוּב. סָפֵק מִבְּעוֹד יוֹם סָפֵק מִשֶּׁחֲשֵׁיכָה, ר' מֵאִיר וְר' יְהוּדָה אוֹמְרִים כו' אַלְמָא: כׇּל סְפֵיקָא חַמָּר גַּמָּל הוּא. וּמַתְנִי' נַמִי סְפֵיקָא הוּא. וּלְלִישָּׁנָא בַּתְרָא הָכִי קַשְׁיָא לֵיהּ: תְּנֵינָא חֲדָא זִימְנָא לְר"מ דְּהֵיכָא דְּעֵירֵב בְּמָקוֹם שֶׁאֵינוֹ עֵירוּב, הֲוָה חַמָּר גַּמָּל: לָא תֵימָא. הָתָם הוּא דְּסָפֵק עֵירֵב וְקָנָה שָׁם שְׁבִיתָה, וְסָפֵק לֹא עֵירֵב וְקָנָה בְּבֵיתוֹ הוּא דְּהָוֵי חַמָּר גַּמָּל. אֲבָל הֵיכָא דְּוַדַּאי לֹא עֵירֵב, כְּגוֹן חוֹזֵר זֶה שֶׁהָיָה לוֹ לְעָרֵב בַּפַּת שֶׁקָּרוֹב לְבֵיתוֹ הָיָה. ל"א: שֶׁהָיָה לוֹ לוֹמַר "שְׁבִיתָתִי בְּמָקוֹם פְּלוֹנִי" לָא הָוֵי חַמָּר גַּמָּל, דְּאֵין כָּאן סָפֵק אֶלָּא לְגַמְרֵי נִתְכַּוֵּון אַבֵּיתוֹ, וִיהֵא כְּאַנְשֵׁי עִירוֹ: אֶלָּא אֲפִילּוּ וַדַּאי לֹא עֵירֵב. שֶׁלֹּא אָמַר שְׁבִיתָתִי לְשָׁם – נַמִי מַחְזְקִינַן לֵיהּ בְּסָפֵק, מִשּׁוּם גַּלּוּיֵי דַּעְתָּא. וּלְלִישָּׁנָא בַּתְרָא דְּפָרְשִׁינַן, דְּרַבִּי מֵאִיר עָשִׁיר מְשַׁוֵּי לֵיהּ, וַאֲפִילּוּ הָכִי הָוֵי חַמָּר גַּמָּל וְלָא כִּבְנֵי עִירוֹ – ש"מ דַּאֲפִילּוּ בְּמָקוֹם שֶׁאֵין סָפֵק, כְּגוֹן נִתְגַּלְגֵּל חוּץ לַתְּחוּם מִבְּעוֹד יוֹם, דְּוַדַּאי לָאו עֵירוּב הוּא – אֲפִילּוּ הָכִי לְרַבִּי מֵאִיר חַמָּר גַּמָּל הוּא, דְּסִילֵּק עַצְמוֹ בְּכַוָּונָתוֹ מֵאַלְפַּיִם שֶׁל צַד שֵׁנִי לְבֵיתוֹ. וְהַהִיא סְתָמָא דְּקָתָנֵי הָתָם מִבְּעוֹד יוֹם אֵינוֹ עֵירוּב, דְּמַשְׁמַע וַהֲרֵי הוּא כִּבְנֵי עִירוֹ – ר' יְהוּדָה הִיא. וְהָא דְּלָא עָרֵיב לְהוּ וְתָנֵי בַּהֲדֵי סֵיפָא, דְּקָתָנֵי "הֲרֵי זֶה חַמָּר גַּמָּל" – מִשּׁוּם דְּר' יְהוּדָה בְּסֵיפָא מוֹדֶה לְר' מֵאִיר, אֲבָל בְּרֵישָׁא – כִּבְנֵי עִירוֹ שָׁוֵי לְהוּ. וְרֵישָׁא ר' יְהוּדָה הִיא: מתני' מִי שֶׁיָּצָא חוּץ לַתְּחוּם. בְּמֵזִיד. וּמִדַּעַת שֶׁלֹּא לְשֵׁם מִצְוָה: שְׁתַּיִם יִכָּנֵס. מִשּׁוּם הַבְלָעַת תְּחוּמִין, כִּדְאָמְרִינַן בְּפִירְקִין (לעיל דף מה.): ר' אֱלִיעֶזֶר לְטַעְמֵיהּ, דְּאָמַר: וְהוּא בְּאֶמְצָעָן: גמ' ה"ג: הָא מַנִּי אֲחֵרִים הִיא: לְמָקוֹם שֶׁרוּבּוֹ שָׁם הוּא נִזְקָר. וְרוּבּוֹ בְּתוֹךְ הַתְּחוּם הוּא: נִזְקָר. כְּלוֹמַר: בָּתַר רוּבּוֹ שָׁדֵינַן לֵיהּ. וְכֵיוָן דְּלָא הָוְיָא אֶלָּא רַגְלוֹ אַחַת חוּץ לַתְּחוּם – עֲדַיִין רוּבּוֹ בְּתוֹךְ הַתְּחוּם, הִילְכָּךְ, יִכָּנֵס: הוּא דְּאָמַר. ר' חֲנִינָא: מַתְנִי' דַּעֲקַר חֲדָא. שֶׁיָּצָא מִן הָאַחַת וְעוֹמֵד בַּשְּׁנִיָּה, וְהָכִי קָאָמַר: אִם בִּשְׁתַּיִם עוֹמֵד – יִכָּנֵס. וּבָרַיְיתָא דְּקָתָנֵי שְׁתַּיִם לֹא יִכָּנֵס – שֶׁיָּצָא מִכׇּל הַשְּׁתַּיִם: לְמוֹדֵד. שֶׁחָשְׁכָה לוֹ, וְאָמַר שְׁבִיתָתִי בִּמְקוֹמִי, וּמוֹדֵד אַלְפַּיִם פְּסִיעוֹת בֵּינוֹנִיּוֹת אוּלַי יִכָּנֵס לִתְחוּם הָעִיר. וְכָלוּ אַלְפַּיִם שֶׁלּוֹ אַמָּה אַחַת חוּץ לַתְּחוּם – לֹא יִכָּנֵס, שֶׁאֲפִילּוּ הָאַלְפַּיִם מוֹלִיכוֹת אוֹתוֹ לְתוֹכוֹ – אֵינוֹ מוּתָּר לָצֵאת מֵאַלְפַּיִם, כִּדְתְנַן: וּלְמוֹדֵד שֶׁאָמְרוּ נוֹתְנִין לוֹ אַלְפַּיִם – אֲפִילּוּ סוֹף מִדָּתוֹ כָּלָה בַּמְּעָרָה לֹא יְהַלֵּךְ לְהַלָּן מֵאַלְפַּיִם, דְּכֵיוָן שֶׁמָּדַד אַלְפַּיִם לְבַד מְקוֹם שְׁבִיתָתוֹ שֶׁהֵן אַרְבַּע – אֵינוֹ יָכוֹל לַעֲבוֹר חוּץ לָאַלְפַּיִם:

מתני' מִי שֶׁהֶחְשִׁיךְ. שֶׁהוּא בָּא בַּדֶּרֶךְ, וְחָשְׁכָה לוֹ חוּץ לַתְּחוּם: אֲפִילּוּ חֲמֵשׁ עֶשְׂרֵה אַמָּה כו'. לָאו דַּוְקָא ט"ו אַמָּה: הַמָּשׁוֹחוֹת. מוֹדְדֵי הַתְּחוּמִין לָעֲיָירוֹת, וְעוֹשִׂין סִימָן לְתוֹךְ הַתְּחוּם: אֵינָן מְמַצִּין אֶת הַמִּדּוֹת. לְהַצִּיב הַסִּימָן בְּסוֹף אַלְפַּיִם, אֶלָּא כּוֹנְסִין אוֹתָן לְתוֹךְ אַלְפַּיִם: מִפְּנֵי הַטּוֹעִין. מִפְּנֵי טוֹעֵי הַמִּדָּה, שֶׁאֵין מַכִּירִין אֶת הַסִּימָן, וּפְעָמִים הוֹלְכִין לְהַלָּן מִמֶּנּוּ וְחוֹזְרִין, וְלָאו אַדַּעְתַּיְיהוּ. ל"א, וְלָא שְׁמַעְתִּיו: דַּוְקָא ט"ו נָקַט, וְטוֹעֵי הַמִּדָּה הֵן הַמָּשׁוֹחוֹת הַקּוֹבְעִין הַתְּחוּמִין, וְאָמְרִינַן לְקַמָּן בְּ"כֵּיצַד מְעַבְּרִין" (דף נז:): אֵין מוֹדְדִין אֶלָּא בְּחֶבֶל שֶׁל חֲמִשִּׁים אַמָּה. אַרְבָּעִים חֲבָלִים יֵשׁ לָאַלְפַּיִם, וְכׇל חֶבֶל וְחֶבֶל מִתְמַעֵט שְׁנֵי אֲחִיזוֹת שֶׁזֶּה תּוֹפֵס מִכָּאן וְזֶה תּוֹפֵס מִכָּאן, וְהָאֲחִיזָה טֶפַח וַחֲצִי אֶצְבַּע – הֲרֵי פ' טְפָחִים וּמ' אֶצְבָּעוֹת, הָעוֹלִין לְיו"ד טְפָחִים, הֲרֵי תִּשְׁעִים טְפָחִים שֶׁהֵן חָמֵשׁ עֶשְׂרֵה אַמּוֹת:

הדרן עלך מי שהוציאוהו

כֵּיצַד מְעַבְּרִין. מְפָרֵשׁ בַּגְּמָרָא לְשׁוֹן אִשָּׁה עוּבָּרָה, דִּתְנַן לְקַמָּן*: הַנּוֹתֵן עֵירוּבוֹ בְּעִיבּוּרָהּ שֶׁל עִיר, אַלְמָא: יֵשׁ עִיבּוּר לָעִיר. וּמְפָרֵשׁ הַשְׁתָּא כֵּיצַד יֵשׁ לָהּ עִיבּוּר: בַּיִת נִכְנָס וּבַיִת יוֹצֵא אוֹ פָּגוּם נִכְנָס וּפָגוּם יוֹצֵא אוֹ הָיוּ גְּדוּדִיּוֹת כו' מוֹצִיאִין הַמִּדָּה כְּנֶגְדּוֹ. כְּלוֹמַר: כְּשֶׁבָּא לְצַיֵּין סִימָן תְּחוּם הָעִיר, וּבָא לִמְדּוֹד אַלְפַּיִם חוּצָה לָהּ, אִם הָיָה מְחִילָּתָהּ שׁוּר אִיגַּר, שֶׁאֵינָהּ חוֹמָה חֲלָקָה אֶלָּא בָּתִּים סְמוּכִין וּמְחוּבָּרִין וְיֵשׁ בַּיִת נִכְנָס לְתוֹךְ הָעִיר, יוֹתֵר מֵחֲבֵירוֹ, וְנִרְאֵית כְּנִיסָתוֹ פְּגוּמָה מִבַּחוּץ, וְיֵשׁ בַּיִת בּוֹלֵט וְיוֹצֵא לַחוּץ יוֹתֵר מֵחֲבֵירוֹ, אוֹ פָּגוּם נִכְנָס אוֹ פָּגוּם יוֹצֵא, שֶׁהָיְתָה עִיר מוּקֶּפֶת חוֹמָה וְיֵשׁ מִגְדָּלִין עֲגוּלִּין בּוֹלְטִין בַּחוֹמָה, פְּעָמִים שֶׁבּוֹלְטִין בִּפְנִים פְּעָמִים שֶׁבּוֹלְטִין בַּחוּץ. אוֹ שֶׁהָיוּ שָׁם לְאַחַת הַקְּרָנוֹת שֶׁל עִיר גְּדוּדִיּוֹת – שִׁבְרֵי חוֹמָה שֶׁל חָרְבוֹת בָּתִּים, וְיֶשְׁנָן בְּתוֹךְ שִׁבְעִים אַמָּה וְשִׁירַיִם לָעִיר, כִּדְמְפָרֵשׁ לְקַמָּן*: אוֹ

[לעיל לה.]

[לעיל מה.]

ס"א נודקר

לקמן סא.

לקמן קה.

[דף ס.]

[לקמן או גשרים כו' הכ"ו רש"ל]